HISTORY IN QUOTATIONS

HISTORY IN QUOTATIONS

M.J. Cohen and John Major

CASSELL

This edition first published in the UK 2004 by
Cassell, Orion Publishing Group,
Orion House, 5 Upper St Martin's Lane, London WC2H 9EA

Reprinted 2004, 2006

British Library Cataloguing in Publishing Data
A catalogue record of this book is available from the
British Library

ISBN 0-304-35387-6

Database and software and typesetting by Librios Publishing
Production by Omnipress Limited, Eastbourne, England
Printed and bound in Germany by
Bercker Graphischer Betrieb GmbH & Co. KG

Contents

Contributors

Many of the following contributed not only to the themes to which their names are attached but far more widely and generously.

Professor M.S. Anderson, formerly London School of Economics and Political Science

Professor K.R. Andrews FBA, formerly University of Hull

M.J. Cohen, editor of Penguin dictionaries of quotations

Professor Mark Elvin, Australian National University, Canberra

David Gwynn, Universities of Auckland and Oxford

Dr Sally Harris, formerly University of Hull

Professor Perween Hasan, University of Dhaka, Bangladesh

Dr John Henry, University of Edinburgh

Annabel Jones, history editor

Dr Matthew Kilburn, *Oxford Dictionary of National Biography*

Dr Roger Lockyer, formerly Royal Holloway College, University of London

Professor Haidee Lorrey, Berklee College of Music, Boston

Dr Henrietta McCall, Department of the Ancient Near East, British Museum, London

Andrew MacLennan, formerly history publisher, Longman

John Major, formerly University of Hull

Rosemary Major

Andrew Marsham, University of Cambridge

Dr Michael E. Martin, University of Birmingham

Richard Milbank, publishing director, Cassell Reference

Brenda Morton, formerly Stroud High School, Gloucestershire

Dr John Mullan, University College, London

Dr Richard Parkinson, Department of Ancient Egypt and Sudan, British Museum, London

Professor Roy Porter, late of the Wellcome Trust Centre for the History of Medicine at University College, London

Dr J.L. Price, University of Hull

Steve Radford

Stephanie Ramamurthy, formerly School of Oriental and African Studies, London University

Dr Marjorie Reeves CBE, FBA, honorary fellow of St Anne's and St Hugh's Colleges, University of Oxford

Richard Rowley, Royal Holloway College, University of London

Dr Philip Tether, University of Lincoln

Professor I.A.A. Thompson, formerly University of Keele

Geoffrey Treasure, formerly Harrow School

Dr Jonathan Tubb, Department of the Ancient Near East, British Museum, London

Elizabeth Warren, formerly Royal High School, Bath

Professor Noel Williams, Daito Bunka University, Tokyo

Dr Yoko Williams, Daito Bunka University, Tokyo

Dr Christine Woodhead, University of Durham

Albert L. Zambone, The Johns Hopkins University, Baltimore and University of Oxford

Foreword by Simon Schama

Sometimes we don't want the whole banquet, soup to nuts. Sometimes, often even, we crave dim sum, tapas, a day filled, stuffed with hors d'oeuvres. And it's then that one needs a good book of quotations to nibble on; a soupçon of 1066; an amuse-bouche of the French Wars of Religion, which were not, to be sure, especially funny.

Oddly enough, for an age said to be plagued by short attention span and even shorter shelf life, we are also a generation of readers that seems to thrive on the doorstopping monumental biography or chronicle; Gibbon or Anthony Beevor on the beach. But, of course, the hunger for 'another damned, thick, square book' is not at all inconsistent with the appetite for those that offer a pleasingly broken texture of many voices, each sounding a particular note in the historical score. *History in Quotations* is one such trove of pleasures; an epic parade of characters and utterances, many of them memorable, all of them worth paying attention to. Though the temptation is to assume that no snippet, a hundred words or much less, could ever have anything serious or evocative or provocative to say about anything that matters historically, that easy assumption is belied time and again by the brilliant choice made by the dauntless editors of the book. Whether it's Orderic Vitalis on the Battle of Hastings or Alexander Herzen describing in painful, poignant detail files of Jewish child recruits to the Imperial Russian Army, plangent, pungent writing takes you right to the heart of the matter.

I sometimes wonder about the self-consciousness of those who seem to have specialized in obiter dicta – the Napoleons and the Marcus Aureliuses – as if grooming themselves for the attention of posterity. Did they, themselves, rehearse the lapidary epigram? Or did they make sure of an inventive amanuensis, the equivalent of an adept presidential scriptwriter, whose assignment was to concoct 'Memorable Sayings' to advertise the significance and gravitas of their employers? There has been, of course, a scant few for whom the economy of wit came truly spontaneously – a Twain or a Wilde (though Whistler accused him of stealing the manner). But for the rest there is the sense of needing to service the perfectly natural human wish to memorialize the memorable in a small, perfect capsule of anecdote.

In any event, there is nothing especially wicked, nor indeed anything trivial about the gulped aperçu. For better or worse it's the way we lead much of our lives; wisdom on the run; and for that matter it was the way in which much of history was experienced too.

So open the pages and take a bite; you'll be coming back for another helping, I guarantee.

[History] hath triumphed over time; which besides it
nothing but eternity hath triumphed over: for it hath carried
our knowledge over the vast and devouring space of many
thousands of yeares, & given so faire and peircing eies to our
minde; that we plainly behold living now (as if we had lived
then) that great world ... as it was then when but new to it
selfe ... And it is not the least debt which we owe unto
History, that it hath made us acquainted with our dead
Ancestoures, and, out of the depth and darknesse of the
earth, delivered us their memory and fame.

Sir Walter Ralegh *The History of the World* (1614) Preface.

Introduction

Throughout the preparation of this book we have frequently asked ourselves, and have frequently been asked by others: 'What are your criteria in choosing quotations for *History in Quotations*? What exactly is a "historical quotation"?'

Our working definition identified it as words that shed light on what are generally accepted to be the important events, ideas, issues and personalities of world history. On this basis, we have sought out quotations that carry a certain compacted freight of historical significance and that capture the essence of time past. As one example, take the celebrated 'Veni, Vidi, Vici', the placarded slogan vaunting Julius Caesar's conquests, in the triumph given him by Rome (75:5). As another, the barely literate cry of anguish from a Kentucky miner in the American depression of the 1930s (765:6). As historical quotations should, both send out powerful reverberations to us, and both strikingly illuminate the history of their day.

Our criteria of what is a 'historical quotation' have been borne in mind by our 37 contributors while they were making their selections for *History in Quotations*. Ultimately, however, their choices have proved to be as varied and individual as they are themselves. As is the case with any substantial collection of quotations, other looser and more personal preferences – whether humour, literary resonance, quirkiness, pathos or even a quality that is no easier to pin down than 'memorability' – inevitably come into play.

History, in the words of the 20th-century British historian S.T. Bindoff, is 'not merely, or even primarily, past politics; it is also past economics, past society, past religion, past civilization, in short, past **everything**'. This is an admirably wide-ranging and inclusive definition, but not even our treasure-chest of 9,000 quotations can be quite as commodious as this. Even so, we can justifiably claim to have produced a work of exceptionally generous scope, both geographical and chronological. We move through 5,000 years, completing the circle from the Iraq of ancient Babylon to the Iraq war of 2003, and taking in the history of Africa, Asia, Europe and the Americas in a grand global sweep. Inevitably, there are some gaps in the coverage: not every important historical episode or historical figure has obligingly supplied a pithy soundbite for posterity.

For our sources we have drawn on a huge historical archive: cuneiform tablets, hieroglyphs, dynastic annals, chronicles, histories, state papers, legal judgements, diaries, letters, memoirs, newspapers, songs, plays, poems and novels: in short, samples of every available written record produced since what we call civilization began are grist to our mill. While this documentation tends to reflect the life and times of the great and the powerful, we have tried wherever possible to register the words of those who enjoyed little power, let alone glory. We have also enriched our choice with perspectives from writers and artists who often give a personal and imaginative insight into the life of their day. And we augment the evidence of contemporary eyewitnesses with verdicts from subsequent commentators and historians, reviewing the past with the advantage (or the distorting mirror) of retrospect.

The 9,000 quotations that make up *History in Quotations* are placed diachronically within 90 thematic chapters, each of which focuses on a key period, theme or movement in world history. The quotations chosen are put to versatile use; they may support an analysis or develop a strong narrative thrust. Whether it be the Byzantine Empire, Islamic Spain, the Black Death, the French Religious Wars, the American Revolution or Britain since 1945, we illustrate each 'episode' graphically as it evolves, sometimes over a great span, sometimes over just a few seminal years. Such an approach has never been taken before in a work of this nature, and in adopting it we do not pretend to be offering a detailed history of the world in quotations. We do, however, believe we have brought out the flavour of the people and the events which have made up that history. In the following pages history speaks to us in a myriad voices, some as personal and emphatic as Genghis Khan, Elizabeth I, George Washington or Mao Zedong, others less celebrated but no less resonant. For quotations have an immediacy that can lead us right into the heart of the perennial dramas of successive ages and, as one of our contributors has put it, ' make you feel you are there'.

History in Quotations is not aimed primarily at students of history (though we believe that they will find much here to excite and stimulate them) but rather at any reader who will be fascinated to hear the babel of thousands of historical voices: monarchs and merchants, crusaders and heretics, explorers and adventurers, rebels and reactionaries, victims and oppressors, dictators and reformers. For us, the quotation sends out a powerful utterance from the past, giving a vivid human (and all too often inhuman) slant on the centuries we have covered. Many quotations speak for themselves, and there are times when a pair placed in sequence can create a sharp and revealing antithesis. Often, however, we have provided 'the story behind the quote' by adding a gloss to clarify its significance for the period or topic in question. This lends what might be called an authorial voice to the subject, not only explaining allusions within the body of the quotation, but, where it seems appropriate, entering judgements of our own.

We have tried throughout to put in those standard quotations with which readers will be familiar, or will half-remember, but we have also striven to venture into less well-known territory: in particular to cite material that evokes an aspect of the life of the times in a more oblique fashion. Examples include a foul-mouthed inscription on an ancient Egyptian tomb warning off grave-robbers, a medieval feminist text and a sardonic flier protesting against the Iraq war of 2003. Wherever possible we have sought to give an exact date and a precise source reference for readers who wish to explore further or to check on authenticity.

In the production of this book we have flown over the changing landscape of five millennia and made the acquaintance of many thousands of the men and women who lived in it. We hope our readers will share the fascination in discovery and rediscovery we have all felt in the process of compilation. To them – and with all due acknowledgement to Cole Porter – we say: 'Brush up your History! Start quoting it now!'

M.J. Cohen and John Major

Acknowledgements

The following are only some of the many people who have been extremely helpful to us in various ways: Nicholas Allen; Susan Appleton; Dr Andrew Ayton; Henry Baynham; Professor John Brewer; Dr Sebastian Brock; Professor Anthony Bryer, Professor Greg Claeys; Lana Cohen; Professor Frank Dikötter; Michael Fitzsimon; Dr Simon Franklin; Peter Furtado; Dimitri Goradetsky; Fr. Bernard Green; Dr Peter Grieder; Karl and Barbara Habermann; Professor Fred Halliday; Professor Kaiser Haq; Michael Heaton; Professor Judith Herrin; Professor Brian Holden Reid; Jerry and Jenny Judge; Professor Hugh Kennedy; Jonathan Leafe; Claire L'Enfant; Dr Brian Levy; Rev. Frank McCarthy; Moira McGregor; Giovanni Magoga; Dr Patrick Major; Deborah Manley; Dr Sharon Messenger; Professor Maxine Molyneux; Dr Philip Morgan; Dr Philip Murphy; Tim and Ilana Nevill; Dr David Omissi; Clifford Owen; Professor David Palliser; Geoffrey Perret; Dr Caterina Pizzigoni; Professor Bernard Porter; Kate Rea; Felicity Redfern; Dr Douglas Reid; Irfon Roberts; Professor Miri Rubin; Professor John Simon; Dr Iain Smith; Teresa Smith; Professor Hew Strachan; Lorri Swanson; Dr Peter Thompson; Dr Anne Walmsley; Sister Benedicta Ward; Professor Donald Cameron Watt; Rev. James Webb; Antony Wood.

We would like to thank the staff of the American Embassy Information Resource Center, London; Beverley Public Library, East Yorkshire; British Library. London; Library of Greenwich, Connecticut; Brynmor Jones Library, University of Hull; Hull Central Library; Library of King's College London; London Library; University of Hull Computer Centre.

Our gratitude to the publishing team: to Richard Milbank, whose idea this book was, who has been everything and more that a publisher should be; to Rosie Anderson for her ever patient role as project manager; to the eagle-eyed editor Lydia Darbyshire, who not only checked our drafts with meticulous care but offered excellent pointers to fresh entries; to Roselle Le Sauteur, who saved us much labour by putting several chapters on to disk. They have all been indispensable to the project.

Note for the Reader

The quotations are arranged chronologically within chapters, which are, themselves, organized in broadly chronological order. The source of each quotation or its speaker is always the first element of the note. The date of the quotation is given wherever possible; when this is impossible, the birth–death dates of the speaker are included. Within individual chapters secondary sources, which follow a semi-colon, are given in full on their first appearance. Thereafter they are given in abbreviated form, with the second name or names of the author or authors and the publication date only. Cross-references in the text are given in the form 334:7, indicating quote 7 on page 334.

ABBREVIATIONS

AD	Anno Domini (after Christ)
Addit.	Additional
Anon.	Anonymous
App.	Appendix
A.S.V.	*Archivio di Stato di Venezia* (Venice State Archives)
attrib.	attributed
BC	Before Christ
Bk	Book
BL	British Library
BM	British Museum
c.	*circa* (about)
Ch./Chs	Chapter/Chapters
Cmd	Command Paper
Co.	County
Col./Cols	Column/Columns
C.S.P.	Calendar of State Papers
d.	died
ed.	editor/edited by
eds	editors
E.H.D.	*English Historical Documents*
edn	edition
f.	folio
ff	following
fl.	flourished

FO	Foreign Office
H.C. Deb.	House of Commons Debates (Hansard)
H.L. Deb.	House of Lords Debates (Hansard)
JM	John Major
Jr	Junior
M.G.H.	*Monumentae Germaniae historica*
MP	Member of Parliament
MS/MSS	manuscript/manuscripts
no./nos.	number/numbers
NS	New Style (dates according to the Gregorian calendar, adopted in Britain in 1752 but not in Russia until 1918; in 'The Russian Revolution, 1914–24' NS dates have been used to avoid confusion and are marked accordingly)
NT	New Testament
OT	Old Testament
p./pp.	page/pages
para.	paragraph
Parl. Deb.	*Parliamentary Debates*
PRO	Public Record Office
Pt	Part
pub.	published
r.	reigned
rep.	reprinted
Sc.	scene
Sect./Sects	Section/Sections
S.I.R.I.O.	Collected Documents of the Russian Historical Association
SJ	Society of Jesus
Sr	Senior
St	Saint
St.	Stanza
trad.	traditional
trans.	translated/translation
v.	versus (in legal cases)
v.	verso
VOC	*Vereenigde Oostindische Compagnie* (Dutch East India Company)
Vol./Vols	Volume/Volumes

Quotations about History

1 Most anthologists of poetry or quotations are like those who eat cherries or oysters, first picking the best and ending by eating everything.
Sébastien-Roch Nicolas Chamfort *Pensées, maximes et anecdotes* (1795).

2 I rarely ever quote; the reason is, I always think.
Thomas Paine; M. Conway (ed.) *The Writings of Thomas Paine* Vol.1 (1904) p.149.

3 I hate quotations. Tell me what you know.
Ralph Waldo Emerson, May 1849; *Journals* Vol.11 (1975) p.110.

4 It is a good thing for an uneducated man to read books of quotations.
Winston Churchill *My Early Life* (1930) Ch.9.

5 The taste for quotations ... is a Surrealist taste.
Susan Sontag *On Photography* (1977) Ch.3.

ANCIENT

6 [I write] in the hope of thereby preserving from decay the remembrance of what men have done.
Herodotus (*c*.485–*c*.425 BC) *The Histories* (1964 trans.) Bk 1.1.

7 With reference to the narrative of events, far from permitting myself to derive it from the first source that came to hand, I did not even trust my own impressions, but it rests partly on what I saw myself, partly on what others saw for me, the accuracy of the reporting being always tried by the most severe and detailed tests possible. My conclusions have cost me some labour from the want of coincidence between accounts of the same occurrences by different eye-witnesses, arising sometimes from imperfect memory, sometimes from undue partiality for one side or the other.
Thucydides *The History of the Peloponnesian War* (*c*.431–*c*.404 BC; 1919 trans.) Bk 1.22.

8 My work is not a piece of writing designed to meet the taste of an immediate public, but was done to last for ever.
Thucydides (*c*.431–*c*.404 BC; 1954 trans.) Bk 1.22.

9 The study of history is in the truest sense an education, and a training for political life.
Polybius (*c*.200–117 BC) *Histories* (1922 trans.) Bk 1.1.

10 History is philosophy teaching by examples.
Dionysius of Halicarnassus (1st century BC) *Ars rhetorica* Ch.11.2.

11 Writing history is a difficult job: in the first place because what you put down has to correspond exactly to the facts; and secondly because if you permit yourself to criticize any wrongdoing, most of your readers will think that you are malevolent, or even envious.
Sallust *The War with Catiline* (44–42 BC; 1931 trans.) Ch.3.

12 The fortunate man, in my opinion, is he to whom the gods have granted the power either to do something which is worth recording or to write what is worth reading; and most fortunate of all is the man who can do both.
Pliny the Younger (*c*.61–113) to Tacitus, *Letters* (1963 trans.) Bk 6.16.

13 *Sine ira et studio.* (Without animus or partiality.)
Tacitus (*c*.56–120) *Annals* (1959 trans.) Bk 1, Ch.1. His personal standard for the writing of history, even better put by Shakespeare, in the words of Othello: 'Nothing extenuate; Nor set down aught in malice' (*Othello* (*c*.1604) Act 5, Sc.2).

14 Everyone who sees mankind reflected through himself and in himself perceives that this world has been disciplined since the creation by alternating periods of good and bad times.
Paulus Orosius *The Seven Books of History against the Pagans* (*c*.418; 1964 trans.) Bk 1, Pt 1.

MEDIEVAL AND EARLY MODERN

15 For if history relates good things of good men, the attentive hearer is inspired to imitate that which is good; or if it mentions evil things of wicked persons, nevertheless the religious and pious hearer or reader ... is the more earnestly inspired to perform those things which he knows to be good and worthy of God.
Bede *Ecclesiastical History* (731; 1990 trans.) Preface.

1 Dwell on the past and you'll lose an eye. Forget the past and you'll lose both eyes.
Old Russian saying; Alexander Solzhenitsyn *The Gulag Archipelago* (1973 trans.) Preface.

2 Whenever one assumes the role of historian, friendship and enmities have to be forgotten; often one has to bestow on adversaries the highest commendation ... often, too, one's nearest relatives, if their pursuits are in error and suggest the desirability of reproach, have to be censured. The historian, therefore, must shirk neither remonstrance with his friends, nor praise of his enemies. For my part, I hope to satisfy both parties ... by appealing to the evidence of the actual events and of eyewitnesses.
The Byzantine princess Anna Comnena *The Alexiad* (c.1148; 1969 trans.) Preface.

3 [An historian's task is] to extol the famous deeds of famous men in order to incite the hearts of mankind to virtue, but to veil in silence the dark deeds of the base or, if they are drawn into the light, by the telling to place them on record to terrify the minds of those same mortals.
Otto of Freising (c.1111–58) *Gesta Friderici imperatoris* (The Deeds of Frederick Barbarossa) (1953 trans.) p.24.

4 The historian and the chronicler have one and the same intention and use the same materials, but their mode of treatment is different and so is their style of writing. Both have the same object in mind because both eagerly pursue truth. The style of treatment is different because the historian marches along with a copious and eloquent diction, while the chronicler steps simply and briefly ... It belongs to the historian to strive for truth, to charm his hearers or readers by his sweet and elegant language, to inform them about the true facts about the actions, character and life of the hero whom he is describing, and to include nothing else but what seems in reason to be appropriate to history.
Gervase of Canterbury (c.1141–c.1210) *The Anglo-Saxon Chronicle* (1953 trans.) p.xviii.

5 The knowledge of past events ... forms a main distinction between brutes and rational creatures, for brutes, whether men or beasts, do not know ... about their origins, their race and the events and happenings in their native lands.
Henry of Huntingdon *Historia Anglorum* (History of the English People) (c.1130; 1996 trans.) pp.4–5.

6 What is all history but the praise of Rome?
The Italian poet Francesco Petrarch (1304–74); Donald R. Kelley *Faces of History* (1998) p.131.

7 I have dwelt single-mindedly on learning about antiquity, among other things because this [present] age has always displeased me, so that ... I have always wished to have been born in any other age whatever, and to forget this one, seeming always to graft myself in my mind on to other ages. I have therefore been charmed by the historians, though I was no less offended by their disagreements.
Francesco Petrarch *Rerum senilium* (Of Things Antique) Bk 18 (1992 trans.) p.1.

8 History is the record of human society, or world civilization; of the changes that take place in the nature of that society ... of revolutions and uprisings by one set of people against another, with the resulting kingdoms and states with their various ranks; of the different activities and occupations of men, whether for gaining their livelihood or in the various sciences and crafts; and, in general, of all the transformations that society undergoes by its very nature.
Ibn Khaldun (1332–1406); Charles Issawi (ed.) *An Arab Philosophy of History* (1950; 1987 edn) pp.26–7.

9 For if old men are considered wise because they have seen more than others, how much more wisdom can history lend us – if it be written correctly. For it contains the deeds of many ages and their reasons, so that one may easily find what to imitate and what to avoid, and be spurred on to great deeds by emulation of outstanding men.
Leonardo Bruni *History of the Florentine People* (from c.1415; 1610).

10 History is more robust than poetry because it is more truthful ... The discourse of historians exhibits more substance, more practical knowledge, more political wisdom ... and more learning of every sort than the precepts of any philosophers ... Without history one remains always a child.
Lorenzo Valla, Italian humanist historian and philosopher (1407–57); *Opera Omnia* (1962 edn) Vol.2, p.6.

11 As for intellectual training, the prince should read history, studying the actions of eminent men to see how they conducted themselves during war and to discover the reasons for their victories or their defeats, so that he can avoid the latter and imitate the former. Above all, he should read history so that he can do what eminent men have done before him: taken as their model some historical figure who has been praised and honoured; and always kept his deeds and actions before them.

Niccolò Machiavelli *The Prince* (1513; 1961 trans.) Ch.14, pp.89–90.

1 In order to manage such affairs as war, peace, treaties, alliances, marriages, the means of increasing one's territories, the loyalty of a people, parties and other business of a kingdom, it seems to me that there is no more useful knowledge than the study of history.

Johann Sleidan (Johannes Philippi), Protestant historian (1506–55); Kelley (1998) pp.167–8.

THE 17TH AND 18TH CENTURIES

2 It is the true office of history to represent the events themselves, together with the counsels, and to leave the observations and conclusions thereupon to the liberty and faculty of every man's judgement.

Francis Bacon *The Advancement of Learning* (1605) Bk 2, Ch.2, Sect.12.

3 Histories make men wise.

Francis Bacon 'Of Studies'; *The Works of Francis Bacon* Vol.1 (1825) p.168.

4 Whosoever, in writing a modern history, shall follow truth too near the heels, it may happily strike out his teeth.

Sir Walter Ralegh *The History of the World* (1614) Preface.

5 Historians desiring to write the actions of men, ought to set down the simple truth and not say anything for love or hatred; also to choose such an opportunity for writing as it may be lawful to think what they will and write what they think, which is a rare happiness of the time.

Sir Walter Ralegh *The Cabinet Council* (pub. posthumously in 1658 by John Milton).

6 The [Aztec] philosophers and wise men had charge of recording all the sciences of which they had knowledge and of which they achieved understanding, and of teaching from memory all the songs that preserved their sources and histories.

The Mexican scholar Fernando de Alva *Obras Históricas* (1600–40; 1775–7 edn) Vol.1, p.527.

7 Who knows whether the best of men be known? Or whether there be not more remarkable persons forgot, than any that stand remembered in the known account of time?

Sir Thomas Browne *Urn Burial* (1658) Ch.5.

8 History and philosophy are the two eyes of wisdom, and if one is missing, then one has only half vision.

Christian Thomasius, German law professor at Halle University (1655–1728); Kelley (1998) p.244.

9 A good historian is timeless and stateless: although he is a patriot, he will never flatter his country in any respect.

François de Salignac de la Mothe Fénelon *Lettre à l'Académie* (1714; 1970 edn) Ch.8.

10 In this dense night of darkness which enshrouds earliest antiquity so distant from us, appears the eternal light, which never sets, of this truth which is beyond any possible doubt: that the civil world has itself been made by men, and that its principles therefore can, because they must, be rediscovered within the modifications of our own human mind.

Giambattista Vico (1688–1744); L. Pompa (ed.) *Selected Writings* (1982) p.198.

11 Thinking to amuse my father once, after his retirement from the ministry, I offered to read a book of history. 'Anything but history,' said he, 'for history must be false.'

Horace Walpole, on his father, Robert; *Walpoliana* Vol.1 (1799) p.60.

12 What are all the records of history but narratives of successive villainies, of treasons and usurpations, massacres and wars?

Dr Samuel Johnson, *The Rambler*, 19 Nov. 1751.

13 The study of antiquity, and the history of former times has ever been esteemed highly commendable and useful, not only to improve the minds of men, but also to incite them to virtuous and noble actions.

Charter of the Society of Antiquaries (1751).

14 To converse with historians is to keep good company: many of them were excellent men, and those who were not such have taken care however to appear such in their writings.

Henry St John, 1st Viscount Bolingbroke *Letters on the Study and Use of History* Vol.1 (1735; pub.1752) Letter 2, p.32.

1 Great abilities are not requisite for an historian; for in historical composition, all the greatest powers of the human mind are quiescent. He has facts ready to his hand; so there is no exercise of invention. Imagination is not required in any degree; only about as much as is used in the lowest kinds of poetry. Some penetration, accuracy, and colouring will fit a man for the task, if he can give the application which is necessary.

Dr Samuel Johnson, 6 July 1763; James Boswell *The Life of Samuel Johnson* (1791).

2 *JOHNSON*: 'We must consider how very little history there is; I mean real authentick history. That certain Kings reigned, and certain battles were fought, we can depend upon as true; but all the colouring, all the philosophy of history is conjecture.'

BOSWELL: 'Then, sir, you would reduce all history to no better than an almanack, a mere chronological series of remarkable events.'

Mr Gibbon, who must at that time have been employed upon his history of which he produced the first volume in the following year, was present; but did not step forth in defence of that species of writing. He probably did not like to *trust* himself with JOHNSON!

James Boswell, 18 April 1775; Boswell (1791) Vol.2, pp.365–6.

3 Happy is the nation without a history.

Cesare Beccaria *Trattato dei delitti e delle pene* (Treatise on Crimes and Punishments) (1764) Introduction.

4 It is a base untruth to say that happy is the nation that has no history. Thrice happy is the nation that has a glorious history.

Theodore Roosevelt, speech, 10 April 1899.

5 All the history of the past, as one of our wits [Fontenelle] used to say, is only an accepted fable.

Voltaire (François-Marie Arouet) *Jeannot et Colin* (1764); *Oeuvres complètes* Vol.21 (1879 edn) p.237.

6 History is nothing more than a tableau of crimes and misfortunes.

Voltaire *L'Ingénu* (1767) Ch.10.

7 History can be well written only in a free country.

Voltaire to Frederick the Great, 27 May 1773.

8 History ... is indeed little more than the register of the crimes, follies and misfortunes of mankind.

Edward Gibbon *The Decline and Fall of the Roman Empire* (1776–88) Vol.1, Ch.3.

9 The history of the world is the world's court of justice.

Friedrich von Schiller 'Resignation' (1786).

10 The histories of mankind that we possess are histories only of the higher class.

Thomas Malthus *An Essay on the Principle of Population as it Affects the Future Improvement of Society* (1798) Ch.1, Sect.2.

THE 19TH CENTURY

11 The historian is a prophet looking backwards.

Friedrich von Schlegel *Dialogue on Poetry and Literary Aphorisms* (1800).

12 History, in general, only informs us what bad government is.

President Thomas Jefferson to John Norvell, 14 June 1807.

13 I like the dreams of the future better than the history of the past.

Thomas Jefferson to John Adams, 1 Aug. 1816; Lester J. Capon (ed.) *The Adams–Jefferson Letters* Vol.2 (1959) p.485.

14 To write history requires a whole life of observation, of inquiry, of labor and correction. Its materials are not to be found among the ruins of a decayed memory.

Thomas Jefferson to Dr J.B. Stuart, 10 May 1817.

15 I value it as a morsel of genuine history, a thing so rare as to be always valuable.

Thomas Jefferson to John Adams, 8 Sept. 1817; Capon Vol.2 (1959) p.520. 'It' was a French pamphlet on the restoration of Louis XVIII.

16 History, real solemn history, I cannot be interested in ... I read it a little as a duty; but it tells me nothing that does not either vex or weary me. The quarrels of popes and kings, with wars or pestilences in every page; the men all so good for nothing, and hardly any women at all.

Jane Austen *Northanger Abbey* (1818) Ch.14.

17 The owl of Minerva spreads its wings only with the falling of the dusk.

Georg Wilhelm Friedrich Hegel *The Philosophy of Right* (1821).

18 What will history say? What will posterity think?

Napoleon; Louis-Antoine Fauvelet de Bourrienne *Mémoires de Napoléon Bonaparte* (1855) Vol.1, p.xxiv.

1 The public history of all countries, and all ages, is but a sort of mask, richly colored. The interior working of the machinery must be foul.
John Quincy Adams, diary entry, 9 Nov. 1822; Allan Nevins (ed.) *The Diary of John Quincy Adams 1794–1845* (1928) p.292.

2 You have reckoned that history ought to judge the past and to instruct the contemporary world as to the future. The present attempt does not yield to that high office. It will merely tell how it really was (*wie es eigentlich gewesen*).
Leopold von Ranke *History of the Romanic and Germanic Peoples* (1824) Preface.

3 No past event has any intrinsic importance. The knowledge of it is valuable only as it leads us to form just calculations with respect to the future. A history which does not serve this purpose, though it may be filled with battles, treaties and commotions, is as useless as the series of turnpike tickets collected by Sir Matthew Mite.
Thomas Babington Macaulay (1800–59) *Works: Essays and Biographies* Vol.1 (1898 edn) pp.212–13.

4 The reading of *histories*, my dear Sir, may dispose a man to satire; but the science of HISTORY – History studied in the light of philosophy, as the great drama of an ever-unfolding Providence has a very different effect. It infuses hope and reverential thoughts of man and his destination.
Samuel Taylor Coleridge *On the Constitution of the Church and State* (1830); J. Colmer (ed.) *The Collected Works of Samuel Taylor Coleridge* Vol.10 (1976) p.32.

5 If men could learn from history, what lessons it might teach us! But passion and party blind our eyes, and the light which experience gives is a lantern on the stern, which shines only on the waves behind us.
Samuel Taylor Coleridge, 18 Dec. 1831; *Table Talk* (1835).

6 The history of man for the nine months preceding his birth would, probably, be far more interesting and contain events of greater moment than all the three-score and ten years that follow it.
Samuel Taylor Coleridge *Miscellanies, Aesthetic and Literary* (1885 edn).

7 The vanishing volatile froth of the present, which any shadow will alter, any thought blow away, any event annihilate, is every moment converted into the Adamantine Record of the past – the fragility of man into the Eternity of God.
Ralph Waldo Emerson, 1832; *Journals* Vol.4 (1964) p.22.

8 Read no history: nothing but biography, for that is life without theory.
Benjamin Disraeli *Contarini Fleming* (1832) Pt 1, Ch.23.

9 History shows you prospects by starlight, or, at best, by the waning moon.
Rufus Choate, speech, 1833; *The Romance of New England History* (1902 edn).

10 What experience and history teach us is this – that peoples and governments have never learned anything from history, or acted on principles deduced from it.
Georg Wilhelm Friedrich Hegel *The Philosophy of History* (1837) Vol.10, Introduction.

11 History is a distillation of rumour.
Thomas Carlyle *The French Revolution* (1837) Pt 1, Bk 7, Ch.5.

12 As I take it, Universal History, the history of what man has accomplished in this world, is at bottom the History of the Great Men who have worked here.
Thomas Carlyle, 5 May 1840; *On Heroes, Hero-Worship and the Heroic in History* (1908 edn) Lecture 1, p.239.

13 Man is explicable by nothing less than all his history.
Ralph Waldo Emerson *Essays, First Series* 'History' (1841).

14 *History* does *nothing*, it possesses *no* immense wealth, it wages *no* battles! It is man, real living man, that does all that, that possesses and fights; 'history' is not a person apart, using man as a means for *its own* particular aims; history is *nothing but* the activity of man pursuing his aims.
Karl Marx and Friedrich Engels *Die heilige Familie* (The Holy Family) (1845).

15 The history of all hitherto existing society is the history of class struggles.
Karl Marx and Friedrich Engels *The Communist Manifesto* (1848) opening sentence.

16 Hegel remarks somewhere that all great world historic facts and personages appear, so to speak, twice. He forgot to add: the first time as tragedy, the second time as farce.
Karl Marx *The Eighteenth Brumaire of Louis Napoleon* (1852) Pt 1.

1 History is nothing but a collection of fables and useless trifles, cluttered up with a mass of unnecessary figures and proper names. The death of Igor, the snake which bit Oleg – what is all this but old wives' tales?
Leo Tolstoy to his friend Nazare'ev, 1852; Isaiah Berlin *The Hedgehog and the Fox* (1953) p.13.

2 History is a picture gallery where there are few originals and many copies.
Alexis de Tocqueville *L'Ancien Régime et la Révolution* (1856; 1951 edn) p.133.

3 Happy the people whose annals are blank in the history books.
Thomas Carlyle *Frederick the Great* (1858) Bk 16, Ch.1.

4 One cannot be a good historian of the outward, visible world without giving some thought to the hidden, private life of ordinary people; and on the other hand cannot be a good historian of this inner life without taking into account outward events where those are relevant.
Victor Hugo *Les Misérables* (1862).

5 The new history is like a deaf man replying to questions which nobody puts to him … The primary question is, what power is it that moves the destinies of peoples? … History seems to presuppose that this power can be taken for granted, and is familiar to everyone, but … anyone who has read a great many historical works cannot help doubting whether this power, which different historians understand in different ways, is in fact so completely familiar to everyone.
Leo Tolstoy *War and Peace* (1863–9) Epilogue, Pt 2, Ch.1; Berlin (1953) p.23.

6 History is fiction which actually happened; fiction is history which could have happened.
Edmond and Jules de Goncourt *Idées et sensations* (Ideas and Feelings) (1866).

7 History is a record of the gradual negation of man's original bestiality by the evolution of his humanity.
Mikhail Bakunin *Dieu et l'état* (God and the State) (1871).

8 The best history is but like the art of Rembrandt; it casts a vivid light on certain selected causes, on those which were best and greatest; it leaves all the rest in shadow and unseen.
Walter Bagehot *Physics and Politics* (1872) Ch.2.

9 Each of the dead leaves behind a small legacy, the remembrance of him, and asks us to cherish it. For the one who has no friends, the guardian must substitute for them … This guardianship is History … It gives life to those dead souls and reanimates them … They live now with us, who feel ourselves to be their relations and their friends. Thus a family is created, a fellowship bringing together the living and the dead.
Jules Michelet *History of the Nineteenth Century* (1872) Vol.2, Preface.

10 History proves to us that the state, government, religion, church, all public institutions, are the only means by which wild and animal man obtains his small share of reason and justice.
Hippolyte Taine to François Guizot, 1873; E. Sparvel-Bayly (ed.) *The Life and Letters of H. Taine* Vol.3 (1908) pp.123–4.

11 That great dust-heap called 'history'.
Augustine Birrell *Obiter Dicta* 'Carlyle' (1884).

12 History is past politics, and politics is present history.
Edward Augustus Freeman *The Methods of Historical Study* (1886) Ch.1.

13 History, that excitable and lying old lady.
Guy de Maupassant *Sur l'eau* (1888).

14 The history of a nation is not in parliaments and battlefields but in what people say to each other on fair days and high days, and in how they farm and quarrel and go on pilgrimage.
W.B. Yeats *Stories from Carleton* (1889) Introduction.

15 Anybody can make history. Only a great man can write it.
Oscar Wilde *The Critic as Artist* (1891) Pt.1.

16 History is about the most cruel of goddesses, and she leads her triumphal car over heaps of corpses, not only in war but also in 'peaceful' economic developments.
Friedrich Engels, 24 Feb. 1893; *Karl Marx and Friedrich Engels: Correspondence 1846–1895* (1934).

17 In history we are too inclined to concentrate above all on the illustrious, striking or ephemeral manifestations of human activity, great events or great men, instead of placing our emphasis on the immense, deliberate movements of institutions, and

of economic and social conditions, which are the really interesting feature of human development, the feature which can be analysed with some certainty and, to a certain degree, be reduced to laws.
Gabriel Monod, founder and editor of *Revue historique*, 1896; M. Réberioux 'Le Débat de 1903: historiens et sociologues' in C.-O. Carbonell and G. Livet (eds) *Au berceau des annales* (At the Cradle of the Annales) (1983) pp.219–20.

1 The very ink in which all history is written is mere fluid prejudice.
Mark Twain *Following the Equator* (1897); Bernard DeVoto (ed.) *The Portable Mark Twain* (1946) p.567.

THE 20TH CENTURY

2 It has been said that though God cannot alter the past, historians can; it is perhaps because they can be useful to Him in this respect that He tolerates their existence.
Samuel Butler *Erewhon Revisited* (1901) Ch.14.

3 I take delight in history, even its most prosaic details, because they become poetical as they recede into the past. The poetry of history lies in the quasi-miraculous fact that once, on this earth, once, on this familiar ground, walked other men and women, as actual as we are today, thinking their own thoughts, swayed by their own passions, but now all gone, one generation vanishing after another, gone as utterly as we ourselves shall shortly be gone, like ghosts at cock-crow.
George Macaulay Trevelyan *Clio, A Muse* (1913).

4 History generally, and the history of revolutions in particular, is always richer in content, more varied, more many-sided, more lively and more 'subtle' than even the best parties and the most class-conscious vanguards of the most advanced classes imagine.
Lenin (Vladimir Ilych Ulyanov) *'Left-Wing' Communism: An Infantile Disorder* (1920) Ch.10.

5 Those who cannot remember the past are condemned to repeat it.
George Santayana *The Life of Reason* (1905–6) Vol.1, Ch.12.

6 Historyans is like doctors. They are always lookin' f'r symptoms. Those iv them that writes about their own times examines th' tongue an' feels th' pulse an' makes a wrong dygnosis. Th' other kind iv histhry is a post-mortem examination. It tells ye what a

counthry died iv. But I'd like to know what it lived iv.
Finley Peter Dunne *Observations by Mr Dooley* (1902); *Mr Dooley on Ivrything and Ivrybody* (1963) p.208.

7 It is impossible to write ancient history because we do not have enough sources, and impossible to write modern history because we have far too many.
Charles Péguy *Clio* (1909–12).

8 History is made out of the failures and heroism of each insignificant moment. If one throws a stone into a river, it produces a succession of ripples. But most men live without being conscious of a responsibility which extends beyond themselves. And that – I think – is at the root of our misery.
Franz Kafka, c.1922; Gustav Janouch *Conversations with Kafka* (1953 trans.) p.131.

9 History: gossip well told.
Elbert Hubbard *The Roycroft Dictionary* (1914).

10 What has history to do with me? Mine is the first and only world! I want to report how I find the world. What others have told me about the world is a very small and incidental part of my experience. I have to judge the world, to measure things.
Ludwig Wittgenstein, 1915; *Notebooks 1914–1916*.

11 'History,' Stephen said, 'is a nightmare from which I am trying to awake.'
James Joyce *Ulysses* (1922) p.34.

12 History is more or less bunk. It's tradition. We don't want tradition. We want to live in the present, and the only history that is worth a tinker's damn is the history we make today.
Henry Ford, *Chicago Daily Tribune*, 25 May 1916.

13 Ignorance is the first requisite of the historian – ignorance, which simplifies and clarifies, which selects and omits, with a placid perfection unattained by the highest art.
Lytton Strachey *Eminent Victorians* (1918) Preface.

14　　After such knowledge, what forgiveness? Think
　　　　now
　　　History has many cunning passages, contrived
　　　　corridors,
　　　And issues.
T.S. Eliot 'Gerontion' (1920).

1 To articulate the past historically does not mean to recognize it 'the way it really was' (Ranke). It means to seize hold of a memory as it flashes up at a moment of danger.
Walter Benjamin (1892–1940) 'Theses on the Philosophy of History' in *Illuminations* (1950) p.257.

2 His face is turned toward the past ... But a storm is blowing from Paradise ... This storm irresistibly propels him into the future to which his back is turned, while the pile of debris before him grows skyward. This storm is what we call progress.
Walter Benjamin, on the angel of history, 'Theses on the Philosophy of History' in *Illuminations* (1950) pp.259–60.

3 Who has fully realized that history is not contained in thick books but lives in our very blood?
Carl Gustav Jung 'Woman in Europe' (1927); *Aspects of the Feminine* (1986 edn) p.72.

4 On the shore where time casts up its stray wreckage, we gather corks and broken planks, whence much indeed may be argued and more guessed; but what the great ship was that has gone down into the deep, that we shall never see.
George Macaulay Trevelyan, inaugural lecture as Regius Professor of Modern History at Cambridge University, 27 Oct. 1927; (1913; 1930 edn).

5 History is the open Bible: we historians are not priests to expound it infallibly: our function is to teach people to read it and to reflect upon it for themselves.
George Macaulay Trevelyan (1913; 1930 edn).

6 History is the most dangerous substance that the chemistry of the intellect has created ... It makes men dream, it intoxicates them, breeds false memories in them, aggravates their responses, takes up their ancient grievances, torments them in their sleep, carries them into the delirium of grandeur or else of persecution, and turns nations bitter, intolerable and vain.
Paul Valéry 'On History' (1928); *Regards sur le monde actuel* (1931) p.45.

7 What we know of the past is mostly not worth knowing. What is worth knowing is mostly uncertain. Events in the past may roughly be divided into those which probably never happened and those which do not matter. This is what makes the trade of the historian so attractive.

W.R. Inge *Assessments and Anticipations* (1929) p.149.

8 Neither the truth nor the character of history depend, in any way, upon its having some lesson to teach us. And if ever we persuade ourselves that the past has taught us something, we may be certain that it is not the historical past which has been our teacher.
Michael Oakeshott *Experience and its Modes* (1933) p.158.

9 It must always show greatness because in greatness, even when it intimidates, the eternal law is visible. Only a conscious awareness of great deeds is the prerequisite for an understanding of the broad context of historical events; the powerless and the insignificant have no history.
German Central Institute of Education, guidelines for the teaching of history in secondary schools, 1938; K.I. Flessau *Dictatorship Schooling* (1982).

10 People think too historically. They are always living half in a cemetery.
Aristide Briand, attrib.

11 All history is the history of thought.
R.G. Collingwood *An Autobiography* (1939) Ch.10.

12 Social history might be defined negatively as the history of a people with the politics left out.
George Macaulay Trevelyan *English Social History* (1942) Introduction.

13 History is written by the winners.
George Orwell, 4 Feb. 1944; *Shooting an Elephant and Other Essays* (1950).

14 History will bear me out, particularly as I shall write that history myself.
Winston Churchill, attrib.

15 Historian – an unsuccessful novelist.
H.L. Mencken *A Mencken Chrestomathy* (1949)

16 Soviet historians must be impassioned, militant Bolshevik propagandists ... Soviet historians must march in the front ranks of the fighters against the bourgeois ideology of Anglo-American imperialism and its reactionary essence, to expose social reformism, which falsifies and adapts history in the interests of its bosses, the imperialists.
Voprosy Istorii (Questions of History) Editorial no.2 (1949) p.13.

1 History must not be written with bias and both sides must be given, even if there is only one side.
John Betjeman 'Love is Dead' in *First and Last Loves* (1952).

2 Study history, study history. In history lie all the secrets of statecraft.
Winston Churchill, 27 May 1953; Martin Gilbert 'Never Despair' (1988) p.835.

3 The past is a foreign country: they do things differently there.
L.P. Hartley *The Go-Between* (1953) Prologue.

4 History speaking.
The egregious Professor Welch answers the telephone in the film of Kingsley Amis's 1954 novel *Lucky Jim*.

5 The historian is like the ogre in the fairy tale. As soon as he scents human flesh, he knows that it is his quarry.
Marc Bloch *Apologie pour l'histoire, ou métier d'historien* (The Historian's Craft) (unfinished on Bloch's death in 1944; 1954 trans.) Ch.1, Sect.2.

6 Misunderstanding of the present is the inevitable consequence of ignorance of the past. But a man may wear himself out just as fruitlessly in seeking to understand the past if he is totally ignorant of the present ... [The] faculty of understanding the living is, in very truth, the master quality of the historian.
Marc Bloch (1954 trans.) Ch.1, Sect.7.

7 History consists of the inside of the outside.
Howard Nemerov *The Homecoming Game* (1957).

8 One would expect people to remember the past and to imagine the future. But in fact ... they imagine [history] in terms of their own experience, and when trying to gauge the future they cite supposed analogies from the past: till, by a double process of repetition, they imagine the past and remember the future.
Lewis Namier *Conflicts* (1942) pp.69–70.

9   Time present and time past
       Are both perhaps present in time future,
       And time future contained in time past.
T.S. Eliot *Four Quartets* 'Burnt Norton' (1943).

10 History is simply man's desperate bid to give substance to his most visionary dreams.
Albert Camus, the Algerian-born French writer, *Actuelles Chroniques* (Running Commentary) Vol.1 (1950).

11 History is, strictly speaking, the study of questions; the study of answers belongs to anthropology and sociology.
W.H. Auden *The Dyer's Hand* (1962) Ch.3.

12 Man is a history-making creature who can neither repeat his past nor leave it behind.
W.H. Auden (1962) Ch.5.

13 So let us today drudge on about our inescapably impossible task of providing every week a first rough draft of a history that will never be completed about a world we can never really understand.
Newspaper publisher Philip L. Graham, on journalism, 29 April 1963.

14 We sometimes speak of the course of history as a 'moving procession'. The metaphor is fair enough, provided it does not tempt the historian to think of himself as an eagle surveying the scene from a lonely crag or as a V.I.P. at the saluting base. Nothing of the kind! The historian is just another dim figure trudging along in another part of the procession.
Edward Hallett Carr *What is History?* (1964 edn) Ch.2, pp.35–6.

15 History, we now know, is not merely, or even primarily, past politics; it is also past economics, past society, past religion, past civilization, in short, past everything.
S.T. Bindoff in H.P.R. Finberg (ed.) *Approaches to History: A Symposium* (1965 edn).

16 Human beings in general can no more ignore their future than they can lose their past. Thus a theme common to all periods of history is that of attitudes towards the future.
Marjorie Reeves *The Influence of Prophecy in the Later Middle Ages* (1969) Preface.

17 One must be careful not to prejudge the past.
William Whitelaw, 25 March 1972; Conor O'Clery (ed.) *Phrases Make History Here* (1987 edn) p.143.

18 Histories do not break off clean, like a glass rod: they fray, stretch, and come undone, like a rope.
Robert Hughes *The Shock of the New* (1980) Ch.8.

19 History is nothing more than a series of script revisions.
The American cartoonist Jules Feiffer, 1982.

20 If the past cannot teach the present and the father cannot teach the son, then history need not have

bothered to go on, and the world has wasted a great deal of time.
Russell Hoban *The Lion of Boaz-Jachin and Jachin-Boaz* (1973) Ch.1.

1 Life is one-tenth here and now, nine-tenths a history lesson.
Graham Swift *Waterland* (1983) Ch.8.

2 There is history that remembers and history that arises from a need to forget.
Christopher Lasch, *Times Higher Education Supplement*, 6 Feb. 1987.

3 What we may be witnessing is not the end of the Cold War but the end of history as such; that is, the end point of man's ideological evolution and the universalization of Western liberal democracy.
Francis Fukuyama *National Interest*, summer 1989.

4 Since my release, I have become more convinced than ever that the real makers of history are the ordinary men and women of our country; their participation in every decision about the future is the only guarantee of true democracy and freedom.
Nelson Mandela *The Struggle is my Life* (1990).

5 *Herstory: A Record of the American Woman's Past*
Title of book (1974) by June Sochen.

6 His 'n' herstory.
John Leo *US News and World Report*, 22 July 1991. A helpful compromise, offered in response to the feminist re-working of the word 'history' as 'herstory' and 'hystery'.

7 Historians are left forever chasing shadows, painfully aware of their inability ever to reconstruct a dead world in its completeness, however thorough or revealing their documentation … We are doomed to be forever hailing someone who has just gone around the corner and out of earshot.
Simon Schama *Dead Certainties* (1991) Afterword.

8 History is a construct, she tells her students. Any point of entry is possible and all choices are arbitrary. Still, there are definitive moments, moments we use as references, because they break our sense of continuity, they change the direction of time. We can look at these events and we can say that after them things were never the same again. They provide beginnings for us, and endings too. Births and deaths, for instance, and marriages. And wars.
Margaret Atwood *The Robber Bride* (1993) p.4.

9 To accept history as a rational process governed by graspable laws is impossible, because it is often too carnivorous. To regard it as an irrational force of incomprehensible purpose and appetite is equally unacceptable, and for the same reason: it acts on our species. A target cannot accept a bullet.
Joseph Brodsky 'Profile of Clio' in *On Grief and Reason* (1995) p.120.

10 [History] is like a nymph glimpsed bathing between leaves: the more you shift perspective, the more is revealed. If you want to see the whole you have to dodge and slip between many different viewpoints.
Felipe Fernandez-Armesto *Truth: A History* (1997).

11 What governs our lives for the most part is the given, the habitual, the sheer inertia of history, circumstance, inheritance. It was a Saul Bellow character who remarked that history was a nightmare during which he was trying to get some sleep.
Terry Eagleton *The Gate Keeper* (2001) p.51. See xxv:11.

HISTORY IN QUOTATIONS

The Tigris and Euphrates, c.3200–c.500 BC

IN THE BEGINNING

1 As for the stars, he set up constellations
corresponding to them.
He designated the year and marked out its
divisions,
Apportioned three stars each to the twelve
months.

The Epic of Creation (1st millennium BC) Tablet 5; Stephanie Dalley *Myths from Mesopotamia* (1989) p.255. The origins of many early civilizations are recorded in myths. Mesopotamia, the name coined by the Greeks for the land that lay between the Tigris and Euphrates, means 'between two rivers'. It was created by the union of Apsu, the god of sweet water, with Tiamat, the goddess of salt water.

2 He made the crescent moon appear, entrusted
night [to it]
And designated it the jewel of the night to mark
out the days.

The Epic of Creation (1st millennium BC) Tablet 5; Dalley (1989) p.256. Shamash, the sun god, was responsible for the cosmic order of the newly created world. The exact date of the epic is not known. Tablets date mostly to the 1st millennium BC, although it doubtless existed in a much earlier oral version. The city-states of Sumer and Akkad in Mesopotamia gave their name to languages. Sumerian is the earliest language written in the cuneiform script, around 2400 BC. Akkadian, written in a simpler form of cuneiform, was the language of scribes in most of the Middle East during the 1st millennium BC. Cuneiform was most usually written on clay tablets using a reed pen or stylus.

CITY AND COUNTRY

3 For seven days and seven nights
The torrent, storm and flood came on.

Atrahasis Tablet 3; Dalley (1989) p.33. The Akkadian myth of Atrahasis describes a flood familiar from the Old Testament, although the myth predates the account in the Bible. The earliest clay tablets we have of the epic can be dated to around 1700 BC, although the story of Atrahasis goes back to the earliest dawn of history. When scholars first deciphered the cuneiform script in the second half of the 19th century the discovery that the story of the Flood in the Book of Genesis could not be literally true caused consternation. Although there is plenty of evidence from silt deposits in sites of the 4th millennium BC for major floods, there is none of a catastrophic flood such as the one described in this myth or the Old Testament (see 16:2 and 25:6).

4 Dismantle your house, build a boat.
Leave possessions, search out living things.
Reject chattels, and save lives!
Put aboard the seed of all living things, into the
boat.

The Epic of Gilgamesh (2nd millennium BC) Tablet 11; Dalley (1989) p.110. Gilgamesh hears the story of the flood from Ut-napishtim, the one who (like his counterpart, Noah) survives the flood.

5 Create Babylon, whose construction you
requested!
Let its mud bricks be moulded, and build high
the shrine!

The Epic of Creation (1st millennium BC) Tablet 5; Dalley (1989) p.262. The creation of Babylon was also part of the establishment of the order of the world. Babylon, the capital city of the Babylonians from the 2nd millennium BC, stood on the banks of the Euphrates, and its patron god was Marduk. The city reached its greatest size under Nebuchadnezzar II (r.605–562 BC), when the outer walls stretched for more than 5 miles. The shrine referred to here was the Temple of Marduk in which every New Year *The Epic of Creation* was recited in front of a statue of the god.

6 You don't speak of that which you have found.
You speak of that which you have lost.

Anon.; Brendt Alster *Proverbs of Ancient Sumer* (1997) p.8. There is a large corpus of proverbs from ancient Sumer, probably inscribed during the first third of the 2nd millennium BC, although much earlier, c.2600 BC, in origin. The written texts doubtless follow a long oral tradition. In an illiterate society proverbs reflected the superiority of the scribal profession and celebrated the experience of wise old people, and they also played a part in the education of children. Most often their imagery is that of daily life, especially agricultural life and animals.

7 To have and insist on more is abominable.
Anon.; Alster (1997) p.11.

8 Although the pea-flour of the household slaves is mixed with honey and fine oil, there is no end to their lamentations.
Anon.; Alster (1997) p.14. Although the household slaves are spoilt, they are always complaining, even though they are given a most superior sort of flour.

9 He brought them the knowledge of letters, sciences and all kinds of techniques. He also taught them to found cities, build temples, promulgate laws and

measure plots of land. Similarly, he revealed to them how to work the land and gather fruits.

Berossos *Babyloniaca* (c.281 BC). Berossos (a priest in the cult of the god Marduk in Babylon) thought that Oannes, a strange half-fish, half-man creature, was responsible for the civilization of the inhabitants of Babylonia. Berossos was writing about Mesopotamia for a Greek audience; although his original work is lost, it was widely used by classical authors, in particular the historian Eusebius of Caesarea (c.260–c.339).

1 When a poor man has bread, he has no salt, and when he has salt he has no bread; if he has some seasoning, he has no meat, and if he has meat, no seasoning.

Sumerian proverb; Jean Bottéro *Everyday Life in Ancient Mesopotamia* (2001) p.67.

2   I will summon brewers and cup-bearers
        To serve us floods of beer and keep it passing
            round!
        What pleasure! What delight!
        Blissfully to take it in,
        To sing jubilantly of this noble liquor,
        Our hearts enchanted and our souls radiant!

Sumerian drinking song; Bottéro (2001) p.71. Clearly life was not always harsh. Although wine was known from earliest times, beer (made from barley) was probably more popular.

3 The ancient city Aqpu, which kings who preceded me had built, had become dilapidated and turned into ruin hills. I rebuilt this city, reconstructed it from top to bottom, completed it, decorated it in a splendid fashion and made it bigger than before. I constructed therein my enormous lordly palace.

King Adad-Nirari II (r.911–891 BC), tablet; A.K. Grayson *The Royal Inscriptions of Assyria: Assyrian Periods* Vol.2 (1976) p.149. The king of Assyria records on a tablet his restoration of Aqpu (Tell Abu Marya in Iraq).

4 Zimri-Lim … king of Mari … builder of an ice-house, something which formerly no king had built on the bank of the Euphrates.

Reign of Zimri-Lim (1779–1751 BC), tablet; D.R. Frayne *The Royal Inscriptions of Mesopotamia* Vol.4 (1990) p.625. Before Zimri-Lim was defeated by Hammurabi of Babylon, he built a unique ice-house in Terqa (Tell Asham in Syria) on the Euphrates and commemorated his achievement.

5 That no assault should reach the wall of Babylon, I did what no earlier king had done … I caused a mighty wall to be built on the east side of Babylon. I dug out its moat, and I built a scarp with bitumen and bricks. Its broad gateways I set within it and fixed in them double doors of cedar wood overlaid

with copper … I surrounded it with mighty floods, as is the land with the wave-tossed sea … The bulwark I fortified cunningly and made the city of Babylon into a fortress.

Nebuchadnezzar II (r.605–562 BC), tablet on his rebuilding of Babylon. According to a 20th-century excavator of Babylon, more than 15 million baked bricks were used. The king also strengthened the defences and surrounded the city with a double set of walls. As crown prince, Nebuchadnezzar II defeated the Egyptians at Carchemish on the Euphrates (in Syria) in 605 BC. In 598 and 587 he besieged Jerusalem and deported its citizens to Babylon, events that are recorded in the Old Testament (see 22:2).

6 It has a solid central tower, one furlong [220 yards] square, with a second erected on top of it and then a third, and so on up to eight. All eight towers can be climbed by a spiral way running round the outside, and about halfway up there are seats for those who make the ascent to rest on. On the summit of the topmost tower stands a great temple.

Herodotus (c.485–c.425 BC) *The Histories* (1910 edn) Bk 1.181. The Greek historian, who was born at Halicarnassus (Bodrum in Turkey), describes the Temple of Bel at Babylon. The first of his nine books on the history of the world as he knew it provides the first history of Mesopotamia. He gives much information about ancient Babylon and its inhabitants, although some of it is open to question.

LIFE, DEATH AND DESTINY

7   Let me show you Gilgamesh, a man of joy and
            woe!
        Look at him, observe his face,
        He is beautiful in manhood, dignified,
        His whole body is charged with seductive
            charm.

The Epic of Gilgamesh (2nd millennium BC) Tablet 1; Dalley (1989) p.57. Gilgamesh tells the story of a semi-historical king of Uruk, a city in southern Mesopotamia where the earliest evidence of writing was discovered in the 4th-millennium BC Temple of Eanna. Gilgamesh sought the secret of eternal life and underwent many trials and had many adventures in the process. In the end he failed in his quest. The oldest copy of the epic dates to the 2nd millennium BC, although it existed in an oral tradition long before that. The epic as we have it today is written on 12 separate clay tablets. Although many Gilgamesh tablets have emerged from different sites in Mesopotamia, there are still gaps in the story that Assyriologists hope one day to fill if further tablets emerge.

8 They shall weep for you, the bear, hyena, leopard, tiger, stag, cheetah, lion, wild bulls, deer, mountain goat, cattle and other wild beasts of the open country.

The Epic of Gilgamesh (2nd millennium BC) Tablet 8; Dalley (1989) p.91. Gilgamesh speaks of the death of his friend and companion, the wild man Enkidu.

1 Nobody sees Death,
   Nobody sees the face of Death,
   Nobody hears the voice of Death.
   Savage Death just cuts mankind down.
   Sometimes we build a house, sometimes we
      make a nest.
   But then brothers divide it upon inheritance.
   Sometimes there is hostility in the land,
   But then the river rises and brings flood-water.
   Dragonflies drift on the river,
   Their faces look upon the face of the Sun,
   But then suddenly there is nothing.
   The sleeping and the dead are just like each
      other,
   Death's picture cannot be drawn.

The Epic of Gilgamesh (2nd millennium BC) Tablet 11; Dalley (1989) p.108. Gilgamesh philosophizes on the meaning of death.

2 They will hold out for you bread of death, so
      you must not eat.
   They will hold out for you water of death, so
      you must not drink.

Adapa, fragmentary tablets found in Egypt (1500–1400 BC) and at Assur on the Tigris (late 2nd millennium BC); *Dalley* (1989) p.187. Adapa, a sage sent by Ea (the god of wisdom) to bring the arts of civilization to mankind, angered Ea and so lost the chance of immortality. When life was somewhat precarious, immortality was a popular theme.

3 He has only to command, and whoever he curses, turns to clay!

Anzu Tablet 1; Dalley (1989) p.209. The myth is about an evil, lion-headed eagle that struggles to possess the Tablet of Destinies, which orders the destiny of mankind, and the attempts of the gods to regain it. There are two versions of the myth: one very fragmentary version dates to the early 2nd millennium BC; the second version, of about 720 lines on three tablets, dates to the 1st millennium BC.

4 If on the first day of the month of *nisan* [April] the sun looks sprinkled with blood and the light is cool: the king will die and there will be mourning in the country.

Babylonian tablet (BM 40085); Wilfred H. van Soldt *Omens of Enuma Anu Enlil* (1995) p.94. The Babylonians were interested in natural phenomena, particularly eclipses. Close observations were made of the movements of the sun and moon and, of course, the stars. This is an omen based on observation of the sun at a certain time of year.

5 If there are yellow cloud banks on all four sides of the sun: at the beginning of the year there will be misfortune and famine in the country.

Babylonian tablet (BM 34709); van Soldt (1995) p.123.

6 If one dog eats another dog – that city will experience hard times.

Anon.; A. Leo Oppenheim (ed.) *Texts from Cuneiform Sources* Vol.4: E. Leichty *The Omen Series: Shumma Izbu* (1970) p.194. Omens were based on the observation of human beings and animals and, in particular, deviations from the normal, such as deformities or unusual behaviour.

7 If a deformed newborn baby has a cropped and inflated right ear – crazed women will seize the land.

Anon.; Leichty (1970) p.194.

8 It must have been a very gaily dressed crowd that assembled in the open mat-lined pit for the royal obsequies, a blaze of colour with the crimson coats, the silver, and the gold; clearly these people were not wretched slaves killed as oxen might be killed, but persons held in honour, wearing their robes of office, and coming, one hopes, voluntarily to a rite which would in their belief be but a passing from one world to another, from the service of a god on earth to that of the same god in another sphere.

Leonard Woolley *Ur of the Chaldees* (1929) p.64. The archaeologist who led the excavations at Ur in 1922–34 describes a royal funeral and the evidence from the finds in the great death-pit, which dated to *c.*2500 BC.

RELATIONSHIPS: HUMAN AND DIVINE

9 Inanna took a bath and rubbed herself with fine
      unguent,
   Put on her splendid royal robe
   And placed a lapis lazuli necklace round her
      neck.
   After which, she waited anxiously …
   Then, Dumuzi opened the door
   And slipped into the house like a moon
      beam …
   Mad with joy, he gazed at her,
   Enfolded her in his arms, kissed her.

Sumerian sacred marriage text; Bottéro (2001) p.109. Inanna, the goddess of love and war, prepares herself for her lover Dumuzi. He comes to the house with gifts of fat, milk and beer and begs to be let in. Inanna, and her Akkadian successor, Ishtar, inspired many myths.

1 Marrying is human. Getting children is divine.
Proverbs, c.2600 BC; Alster (1997). Although a man may marry several wives, having children is in the gift of the gods.

2 If the wife should say to her husband, 'I no longer want you for my husband,' she is to be thrown into the water with her hands and feet tied. On the other hand, if he should say, 'I no longer want you for my wife,' he is to pay her 80 grams of silver.
Marriage contract, c.1700 BC; Bottéro (2001) p.115.

3 When the patient is continually clearing his throat, is often lost for words, is always talking to himself when he is quite alone, and laughing for no reason in the corners of fields ... is habitually depressed, his throat tight, finds no pleasure in eating or drinking, endlessly repeating, with great sighs 'Ah my poor heart!' – he is suffering from lovesickness.
A medical text, c.2600 BC; Bottéro (2001) p.102.

4 Bread is the boat, water is the oar.
Proverb; Alster (1997) p.15.

5 He who eats too much cannot sleep.
Proverb; Alster (1997) p.25. This may be just an injunction not to overdo it before bedtime, but compare Bible, Ecclesiastes 5:12.

6 What has been spoken in secret will be revealed in the women's quarters ...
In my heart you are a human being, but in my eyes you are not a man.
Proverb, c.2600 BC; Alster (1997) pp.20, 22.

7   O my love, dear to my heart,
      The pleasure you give me is sweet as honey!
      You have delighted me! I am all a-tremble
         before you!
      How I wish you had already carried me off to
         your bedroom, my lion!
Akkadian love song, c.2000 BC; Bottéro (2001) p.110.

8 A chattering girl is silenced by her mother. A chattering boy is not silenced by his mother.
Proverb, c.2600 BC; Alster (1997) p.37.

9 Gentlemen's clothes improve year by year. You are the one making my clothes cheaper year by year. By cheapening and scrimping ... you have become rich. While wool was being consumed in our house like bread, you were the one making my clothes cheaper ... an underling of my father has received two new

garments but you keep getting upset over just one garment for me. Whereas you gave birth to me, his mother acquired him by adoption. Whereas his mother loves him, you do not love me.
A son to his mother, c.1500 BC; James B. Pritchard (ed.) *Ancient Near Eastern Texts* (1969) p.629.

POWER AND THE POWERLESS

10 Wealth is far away, poverty is near.
Proverb, c.2600 BC; Alster (1997) p.9. The poor are always with us!

11 If a white partridge is seen on the roof of the palace – a dark day for the king.
Omen; Sally M. Freedman *If a City is Set on a Height* (1998) p.67.

12   Anum and Enlil named me
      To promote the welfare of the people,
      Me, Hammurabi, the devout god-fearing
         prince,
      To cause justice to prevail in the land,
      To destroy the wicked and the evil,
      That the strong might not oppress the weak,
      To rise like the sun over the black-headed
         people,
      And to light up the land.
Babylonian King Hammurabi (r.1792–1750 BC), law code (1969 edn) Prologue, lines 22 ff. This is the earliest complete law code in the world.

13 I am Xerxes, great king, king of kings, the king of all countries which speak all kinds of languages, the king of the entire big far-reaching earth.
King Xerxes I (r.486–465 BC), foundation tablet at Persepolis. With Babylon and Nineveh, Persepolis (near Shiraz) was one of the three major cities of Mesopotamia. The capital city of the Persian empire was begun by Xerxes' father, Darius I (r.521–486 BC). Despite the hyperbole, Xerxes was defeated by the Greeks at the Battle of Salamis (see 55:7).

14 A linen tunic reaching to the feet with a woollen one over it, and a short white cloak on top ... They grow their hair long, wear turbans, and perfume themselves all over; everyone owns a seal and a walking-stick specially made for him.
Herodotus (c.485–c.425 BC) (1910 edn) Bk 1.195. The first evidence for cylinder seals dates to c.3600 BC. They were carved in reverse relief and then rolled over wet clay to leave an impression of the seal's owner.

15 The king with his face covered with white lead and bejewelled like a woman, combing purple wool

in the company of his concubines and sitting among them with knees uplifted, his eyebrows blackened, wearing a woman's dress and having his beard shaved close and his face rubbed with pumice – he was even whiter than milk, and his eyelids were painted.
Athenaios (end of 2nd century) *The Sophists at Dinner* Vol.5 (1933 edn) Bk 12.528. After Herodotus, writers presented ancient Babylon and Nineveh as places of utter depravity. The legendary 7th-century BC King Sardanapalus of Assyria is portrayed by a Greek living in Rome, who also described at some length the funeral pyre on which the king perished, so enormous that it burned for 15 days. At its height, the Assyrian empire stretched from Egypt in the west to the Arabian Gulf in the south and Lake Van (eastern Turkey) in the north.

1 As to Hezekiah the Jew, he did not submit to my yoke. I laid siege to 46 of his strong cities, walled forts and to the countless small villages in their vicinity, and conquered them by means of well-stamped earth-ramps and battering-rams ... I drove out 200,150 people, young and old, male and female, horses, mules, donkeys, camels, big and small cattle beyond counting and considered them booty. Himself I made a prisoner at Jerusalem, his royal residence, like a bird in a cage.
Sennacherib (r.704–681 BC) tells of his siege of Jerusalem; D.D. Luckenbill *The Annals of Sennacherib* (1924 edn) Vol.2, pp.32–3. Sennacherib was one of the great kings of Assyria at the height of its power. This event can also be found (in a somewhat different presentation) in the Bible, I Kings 18 and 19.

2 Taking the lead of my warriors I slithered victoriously with the aggressiveness of a viper the perilous mountain ledges.
Tiglath-Pileser I (r.c.1114–c.1076 BC); Grayson Vol.2 (1976) p.199. The Assyrian king boasts of his prowess as a military leader and his conquest of his enemies, in this case those of the lands of Ishdish and Suru. The exact location of Suru is not known, although it was in Syria, on the Khabur or Middle Euphrates River.

3 I carried off his silver, gold, possessions, property, bronze, iron, tin, bronze casseroles, bronze pans, bronze pails, much bronze property, alabaster, an ornamented dish, his palace women, his daughters, captives of the guilty soldiers together with their property, his gods together with their property, precious stone of the mountain, his harnessed chariot, his teams of horses, the equipment of the horses, the equipment of the troops, garments with multicoloured trim, linen garments, fine oil, cedar, fine aromatic plants, cedar shavings, purple wool, red-purple wool, his wagons, his oxen, his sheep –

his valuable tribute which, like the stars of heaven, had no number.
Ashurnasirpal II (r.883–859 BC); Grayson Vol.2 (1976) p.124. One of the longest and most important Assyrian royal inscriptions describes the siege of the city of Suru and the king's raid on its treasures.

4 I am king, I am lord, I am praiseworthy, I am exalted, I am important, I am magnificent, I am foremost, I am a hero, I am a warrior, I am a lion, and I am virile; Ashurnasirpal, strong king, king of Assyria.
Royal annal of Ashurnasirpal II (r.883–859 BC) at Nimrud; Grayson Vol.2 (1976) pp.195–6.

5 I slew their warriors with the sword, descending upon them like Adad when he makes a rainstorm pour down. In the moat I piled them up, I covered the wide plain with the corpses of their fighting men, I dyed the mountains with their blood like red wool.
Royal annal, 858 BC; Luckenbill (1969 edn) p.277. The Assyrian king Shalmaneser III (r.858–824 BC) on the defeat of an Aramean coalition (see 20:5). The Arameans occupied much of the Levant during the 1st millennium BC, and eventually their script, written alphabetically, replaced the Akkadian language written in cuneiform. Shalmaneser was the son of Ashurnasirpal II. His campaigns may have been as much to control trade routes and protect resources as to establish direct Assyrian rule. He probably also deported Arameans to work on his building projects. The Assyrians traded in cloth, metal, precious stones, stone, timber and wine.

6 Here is a most terrible Example, to all impious and haughty Tyrants ... that if they do not give over in time and leave their Tyranny ... God the Almighty will also come upon them.
Doctor Leonhardt Rauwolff's Travels into the Eastern Counties (1693 trans.). A Dutch traveller and plant collector reflects on the ruins of Babylon in 1575.

OUTSIDERS LOOKING IN

7 [The Assyrians] were clothed in blue, captains and rulers, all of them desirable young men, horsemen riding upon horses.
Bible, OT, Ezekiel 23:6.

8   The Assyrian came down like the wolf on the
          fold,
     And his cohorts were gleaming in purple and gold.
Lord Byron 'The Destruction of Sennacherib' in *Hebrew Melodies* (1815). Byron's poem was written before the archaeological rediscovery of Mesopotamia, which began in

1845. Interpretation of the ancient records brought consternation to many people who thought they challenged what was
recorded in the Bible. Sennacherib had long enjoyed a reputation
as a profligate and licentious ruler, and the Assyrians themselves in the Old Testament were a bloodthirsty and merciless
people. Byron's poem, with his own imaginative additions,
reflected received ideas about the ancient Assyrians.

1   Where, so late,
    Palace, and tower, and temple, battlement,
    And rock-like wall, deemed everlasting, stood,
    Now, yon black waste of smouldering ashes lay!
    So sank, to endless night, that glorious
      Nineveh!

Edwin Atherstone 'The Fall of Nineveh' (1828). A 19th-century
poet broods on the ruins of Nineveh. Before the rediscovery
of ancient Mesopotamia, there was a general disapproval of
the wicked ways of Nineveh and Babylon, sinks of depravity
where anything might happen. When the ancient Mesopotamians
came to light in the middle of the century, they turned out to
be almost as respectable and bureaucratic as the Victorians
had become.

2 I do put forth a claim to originality, as having been
the first to present to the world a literal and, as I
believe, a correct grammatical translation of nearly
200 words of cuneiform writing, a memorial of the
time of Darius Hystaspes, the greater part of which
is in so perfect a state as to afford ample and certain
grounds for a minute orthographical and etymo-
logical analysis.

Henry Creswicke Rawlinson 'The Persian Cuneiform
Inscriptions at Behistun' in *Journal of the Royal Asiatic Society*
Vol.10 (1847). Rawlinson is credited with deciphering the
cuneiform script. The trilingual inscription at Behistun is high
up on cliffs, which had to be scaled by ladder and ropes. A
small boy was set the task of making paper squeezes of the
inscription on which Rawlinson worked.

3 I had ridden to the encampment of Sheikh Abr-ud
Rahman, and was returning to the mound, when I
saw two Arabs of his tribe coming towards me and
urging their mares to the top of their speed. On reaching me they stopped. 'Hasten, O Bey,' exclaimed one
of them – 'hasten to the diggers, for they have found
Nimrud himself. Wallah! It is wonderful but it is true!
We have seen him with our eyes.'

Austen Henry Layard *Nineveh and its Remains* (1849) Vol.1, p.65.
The British archaeologist Layard began to excavate the great
mound of Nimrud in 1845, using a large local workforce. During
the early days of his excavation he described the discovery of
one of the large winged bulls that later found its way to the
British Museum. Before the cuneiform script was deciphered,
Layard believed he was excavating Nineveh, not Nimrud.

4 I am the Bull of Nineveh. I was born in the quarries
beside the river, the great river … As a shapeless
block was my substance borne to its place; there did
the hands of cunning workmen fashion me … the
chisel carved my ear, and I heard; the tool opened
my eyes, and I saw … Beside me was a companion
like myself; we two guarded the threshold … I felt
myself the guardian of the nation's history, the
emblem of its power, and the thought stamped itself
on my features in a smile which has endured till
now.

W.H. Stone 'Fantasy upon a Winged Bull from Nimrud' in
Household Words (1851). This piece may well have been
inspired by the great success of Layard's book *Nineveh and its
Remains* in 1849. At the time there was quite a craze for
ancient Mesopotamia, reflected in the paintings and writing of
the time, as well as in jewellery and ceramics manufactured to
commemorate the rediscovery.

5 Archaeology … deals with a period limited to a
few thousand years and its subject is not the universe,
not even the human race, but modern man. We dig,
and say of these pots and pans, these beads and
weapons, that they date back to 3000 or 4000 BC,
and the onlooker is tempted to exclaim at their age,
and to admire them simply because they are old.
Their real interest lies in the fact that they are new.

Leonard Woolley *Digging up the Past* (1930) p.13. The archaeologist defines his work in the Middle East.

6 Nearly three thousand years old that palace was, it
appeared … I wondered what sort of palaces they
had in those days … But would you believe it, there
was nothing to see but *mud*! Dirty mud walls about
two feet high – and that's all there was to it … I can
tell you it *was* a disappointment! The whole excavation
looked like nothing but mud to me – no marble or
gold or anything handsome – my aunt's house in
Cricklewood would have made a much more
imposing ruin! And those old Assyrians or whatever
they were, called themselves *kings*!

Agatha Christie *Murder in Mesopotamia* (1936) Ch.7. In this
detective story Nurse Leatheran was a newcomer to archaeology and clearly did not find mud brick remains very
interesting, unlike her creator. Agatha Christie first visited the
site of Ur in 1928; on her second visit in 1930 she met a young
archaeologist, Max Mallowan, who became her second
husband. She became fascinated by his work and accompanied
him on every one of his expeditions, learning many of the skills
of archaeology in the process.

Ancient Egypt, c.3000–c.30 BC

THE EGYPTIAN WORLD VIEW

1   I made the four winds that every man might
      breathe in his place.
    This is one deed thereof.
    I made the great inundation, that the wretched
      should have power over it like the great.
    This is one deed thereof.
    I made every man like his fellow;
    I did not ordain them to do evil, (but) it was
      their own hearts which destroyed that which
      I pronounced.
    This is one deed thereof.
    I made that their hearts should refrain from
      ignoring the west,
    for love of making offerings to the gods of the
      provinces.
    This is one deed thereof.

Anon., Coffin Text spell 1130, *c.*1950 BC; R.B. Parkinson *Voices from Ancient Egypt* (1991) p.33. The creator god defends his actions towards humanity in a funerary text.

2   O, but the people are like black ibises,
    and filth is throughout the land.
    At this time, no one at all is clothed in white.

    O, but the land is spinning as does a potter's
      wheel;
    the robber is a lord of riches;
    the [lord of riches] has [become] someone who
      is plundered.

    O, but the river is blood, and they still drink
      from it;
    they push people aside, and still thirst for water.

Anon. 'The Dialogue of Ipuur and the Lord of All' (*c.*1800 BC); R.B. Parkinson *The Tale of Sinuhe and Other Ancient Egyptian Poems* (1997) p.172. In this pessimistic poem the fictional sage Ipuur laments the state of the land, in its mutability and disorder.

3   Do not be proud because you are wise!
    Consult with the ignorant as with the wise!
    The limits of art are unattainable;
    no artist is fully equipped with his mastery.
    Perfect speech is more hidden than malachite,
    yet it is found with the maidservants at the
      millstones.

Anon. 'The Teaching of Ptahhotep' (*c.*1900 BC); Parkinson (1997) p.251. In the first maxim of this poem from the early 12th Dynasty the sage Ptahhotep warns against pride in wisdom.

4   But Truth itself is for eternity.
    To the necropolis in its doer's hand it descends;
    he is entombed, earth joins with him;
    but his name is not effaced on earth.
    He is remembered for his goodness,
    It is the standard of God's word.
    If it is scales, it tilts not;
    if a balance, it is not partial.

Anon. 'The Tale of the Eloquent Peasant' (*c.*1840 BC) speech 8; Parkinson (1997) p.73. This tale includes a series of speeches about 'truth', 'order' (Egyptian *maat*), the central value of Egyptian culture throughout its history.

5   Nileflood, be green, and come!
    Come to Egypt!
    Create its peace, make green the Two Banks!
    Be green and come!
    Nileflood, be green, and come!
    Make mankind and cattle to live,
    with your produce of the meadows!
    Be green and come!
    Nileflood, be green, and come!

Anon. 'The Great Hymn to the Nileflood' (*c.*1500 BC) St.14; M. Lichtheim *Ancient Egyptian Literature: A Book of Readings* Vol.1 (1973) pp.204–9. The annual Nileflood was crucial to the well-being of the country and was celebrated with great festivity. This hymn dates from the early New Kingdom.

6 How are you? How are your people? I'm still alive today, and tomorrow is in the hand of God.

Tjaroy, Late Ramessid letter no.1, *c.*1079 BC; E.F. Wente *Letters from Ancient Egypt* (1990) p.178. This letter, from the scribe Tjaroy, betrays the fatalism often concealed in Egyptian monumental inscriptions.

PHARAOHS

7   The Sun god has placed king N
    in the land of the living
    for eternity and all time;
    for judging mankind, for making the gods
      content,
    for creating Truth, for destroying evil.

He gives offerings to the gods
and funerary offering to the blessed spirits.

Anon. 'The King as Sun Priest' (c.1900 BC); Parkinson (1991)
pp.38–40. The purpose of kingship in Egypt is described in a
liturgical text about the king's role as a priest of the sun god,
which was found carved on the walls of several New Kingdom
temples but possibly dates back to the Middle Kingdom.

1   Unas eats their magic, swallows their spirits:
    Their big ones are for his morning meal,
    Their middle ones for his evening meal,
    Their little ones for his night meal,
    And the oldest males and females for his fuel.
    The Great Ones in the northern sky light him
        fire
    For the kettles' contents with the old ones'
        thighs,
    For the sky-dwellers serve Unas,
    And the pots are scraped for him with their
        women's legs.

Anon. 'The Cannibal Hymn' (c.2400 BC); Lichtheim Vol.1
(1973) p.37. In this funerary spell from the Pyramid Texts
(nos. 273–4), inscribed in royal pyramids of the late Old
Kingdom, King Unas (2356–2323 BC) ascends to heaven and
absorbs the powers of the gods by eating them.

2   Drop everything and bring with you this dwarf
    that you have brought from the land of the
        horizon-dwellers,
    alive, prosperous and healthy,
    for the dances of god, for the entertainment,
    for the delight of the Dual King Neferkare, may
        he live for ever.
    When he goes down with you to the ship
    appoint excellent men to be around him on
        board ship,
    in case he falls into the water!
    When he sleeps in the night,
    appoint excellent men to sleep around him in
        his awning,
    and inspect 10 times at night!
    My Majesty wishes to see this dwarf
    more than all the gifts of the mining region [in
        Sinai] or Punt.

Neferkare Pepy II to Harkhuf, c.2245 BC; Lichtheim (1973)
pp.23–7. The inscription, which was found in the tomb of the
expedition leader, Harkhuf, at Aswan (southern border of
Egypt), includes a letter expressing the king's eagerness to see
a dwarf from the southern land of Punt (perhaps modern
Somaliland).

3   Aggression is bravery;
    Retreat is vile.

He who is driven from his boundary is a true
    back-turner,
since the Nubian only has to hear to fall at a
    word
answering him makes him retreat.
One is aggressive to him and he shows his back;
retreat and he becomes aggressive.
Not people to be respected –
they are wretches, broken-hearted!
My Majesty has seen it – it is not an untruth;

Senwosret III, Semna stela, c.1846 BC; Parkinson (1991) p.45. A
stela erected by Senwosret III on his border at the frontier
fortress of Semna, south of the second cataract, proclaims his
disdain of the black Nubians.

4   Then Avaris was despoiled, and I brought spoil
from there: one man, three women; total, four
persons. His majesty gave them to me as slaves.
    Then Sharuhen was besieged for three years. His
majesty despoiled it and I brought spoil from it: two
women and a hand. Then the gold of valour was given
me, and my captives were given to me as slaves.

Autobiography of Ahmose, son of Ibana (c.1520 BC);
Lichtheim Vol.2 (1974) p.13. The crew commander Ahmose,
son of Ibana, recounts his involvement in King Ahmose's defeat
of the non-Egyptian Hyksos rulers. The text is part of his
autobiography, which is carved in his tomb at el-Kab. Avaris
was the Hyksos' (invaders') capital in the northeastern delta;
Sharuhen was a city in Palestine. These invaders probably came
from Palestine around 1674 BC and ruled Lower and part of
Upper Egypt for 120 years (see 17:1).

5   The donkey that has to carry his wife.

Anon., inscription from the Punt colonnade, c.1463 BC;
K. Sethe Urkunden des 18. Dynastie (1906) p.325. The temple
of Queen Hatshepsut (r.1473–1458 BC) at Deir el-Bahri
includes scenes showing an expedition to the land of Punt. It
includes a depiction of the generously proportioned wife of
the ruler of Punt; close to her is a donkey, with this laconic
caption.

6   [They are too many to record in writing in this
inscription].
    They [are] recorded on a roll of leather in the
temple of Amun to this day.

Tuthmose III (c.1479–1425 BC), annals; Sethe (1906) p.662.
The annals of the warrior pharaoh Tuthmose III are carved
on the walls of the temple of Amun-Re at Karnak (near
Luxor).

7   You, my brother, when I wrote [to you] about
marrying your daughter, in accordance with your
practice of not gi[ving] (a daughter), [wrote to me],
saying, 'From time immemorial no daughter of the

king of Egy[pt] is given to anyone.' Why n[ot]? You are a king; you d[o] as you please. Were you to give (a daughter), who would s[ay] anything? Since I was told of this message, I wrote as follows t[o my brother], saying, '[Someone's] grown daughters, beautiful women, must be available. Send me a beautiful woman as if she were [you]r daughter. Who is going to say, "She is no daughter of the king!"?' But holding to your decision, you have not sent me anyone.

Amarna letter EA 4, c.1360 BC; W.L. Moran (ed.) *The Amarna Letters* (1992) pp.8–9. The king of Babylon, Kadašman-Enlil, writes to his 'brother' Amenhotep III (1390–1352 BC) asking for an Egyptian princess in marriage, The letter is from diplomatic correspondence (in Akkadian), which was found at the royal city of el-Amarna (ancient Akhetaten) in middle Egypt (see 18:8).

1 Gold in your country is dirt; one simply gathers it up. Why are you so sparing of it? I am engaged in building a new palace. Send me as much gold as is needed for its adornment. Why should messengers be made to stay constantly out in the sun and so die in the sun? If staying out in the sun means profit for the kind, then let him stay out and let him die right there in the sun.

Amarna letter EA 16, c.1340 BC; Moran (1992) p.39. Aššuruballit, king of Assyria (see 17:5), writes to his fellow king, Akhenaten, requesting more diplomatic gifts of gold and complaining that the sun-worshipping pharaoh has kept his messengers in the sun during their reception.

2 The time of the enemy of Akhetaten.

Inscription of the scribe Mes, c.1260 BC; K.A. Kitchen *Ramesside Inscriptions* III (1980) p.433. How the reign of Akhenaten was referred to in a text from the tomb of the treasury-scribe of Ptah, Mes, at Saqqara in the reign of Ramses II (c.1279–1213 BC). Akhetaten was the name of the heretic's capital city.

3   Now when his Person appeared as king,
    the temples of the gods and goddesses,
    from Aswan
    to the Delta swamps
    […] had fallen into ruin.
    Their sanctuaries were decayed,
    become as heaps of rubble,
    overgrown with weeds;
    their shrines were like what does not exist;
    their mansions were a footpath.
    The land was in calamity,
    and the gods turned away from this land.
    If an army was sent to Djahy [Palestine]
    to extend the borders of Egypt, no success

    could happen for them.
    If a god was prayed to for advice,
    he did not come at all.

Tutankhamun, restoration stela, 1332 BC; W. Helck *Urkunden der 18. Dynastie* (1957) p.2027. In a stela from the temple of Karnak, King Tutankhamun (r.1332–1322 BC) describes the state of the country under his predecessor, the heretic king, Akhenaten.

4   His majesty spoke: 'What is this, father Amun?
    Is it right for a father to ignore his son?
    Are my deeds a matter for you to ignore?

    I call to you, my father Amun,
    I am among a host of strangers;
    All countries are arrayed against me,
    I am alone, there's none with me!
    My numerous troops have deserted me,
    Not one of my chariotry looks for me;
    I keep on shouting for them,
    But none of them heeds my call.'

Anon. 'The Battle of Qadesh' (1274 BC); Lichtheim Vol.2 (1974) p.65. Ramses II (c.1279–1213 BC) recounts his experiences at the Battle of Qadesh, in which he fought the Hittites, in a text found inscribed on many of his monuments. Here he describes how it was a near disaster, saved only by his own valour and the help of his divine father, Amun-Re.

5   The princes are prostrate saying: 'Shalom!'
    Not one of the Nine Bows lifts his head:
    Tjehenu is vanquished, Khatti at peace,
    Canaan is captive with all woe.
    Ashkelon is conquered, Gezer seized,
    Yanoam made non-existent;
    Israel is wasted, bare of seed,
    Khor is become a widow for Egypt.
    All who roamed have been subdued
    By the King of Upper and Lower Egypt,
        Banere-meramun.
    Son of Re, Merneptah, Content with Maat,
    Given life like Re every day.

Anon., Israel stela, c.1207 BC; Lichtheim Vol.2 (1974) p.77. In this stela from his funerary temple at Thebes (Luxor) King Merneptah recounts his triumph over the Libyans and other foreign peoples. This is the only mention of Israel by name in Ancient Egyptian texts.

6 I've noted all the matters you wrote to me about. As for the mention you made of the affair of these two policemen, saying 'They spoke these charges', join up with Nodjmet and Payshuuben as well, and they shall send word and have these two policemen brought to my house and get to the bottom of their charges straight away. If they find that the charges are true, have them put in two baskets and throw them into the water by night – but don't let anyone in the land find out.

Now, as for Pharaoh, – life prosperity health! – how will he ever get to this land? And as for Pharaoh – life prosperity health!, whose master is he after all?

Piankh, Late Ramessid letter no.21, c.1075 BC; Wente (1990) p.183. The pharaoh's general, Piankh, who was the dominant force in the south of the country, privately expresses his actual opinions about the ruling king, Ramses XI.

1 You [the god Heryshef] protected me in the combat of the Greeks, when you repulsed those of Asia. They slaughtered a million at my sides, and no one raised his arm against me.

Samtouefnakht, Stela 1035 (National Museum, Naples), c.320 BC; O. Perdu 'Le monument de Samtouefnakht à Naples' in Revue d'Égyptologie 36 (1985) p.103. The priest Samtuefnakht alludes to Alexander the Great's battle (332 BC) with the Persian armies occupying Egypt.

RELIGION

2   A crocodile against him in the water!
      A snake against him on the land!
      – him who shall act against this
      (Never did I anything against him)
      It is God who shall judge!

Meni, funerary inscription, c.2200 BC; K. Sethe Urkunden des Alten Reiches (1932) p.23. The steward Meni invokes destruction on anyone who defiles his tomb at Giza and puts his trust in divine judgement.

3 This is an ordinance: Act for the man who acts, to cause him to act.

Anon. 'The Tale of the Eloquent Peasant' (c.1850 BC); Parkinson (1997) p.64. This proverb summarizes the idea of 'truth' (see 7:4) as a principle of reciprocity.

4   I came and went with a steady heart,
      I told no lie to anyone.
      I knew the god who dwells in man,
      Knowing him I knew this from that.
      I did the tasks as they were ordered,
      I did not confuse the report with the reporter,
      I did not speak with low-class words,
      I did not talk to worthless people.
      I was a model of kindliness,
      One praised who came praised from the womb.
      The Mayor of Nekheb, Paheri, the justified.

Paheri, inscription, c.1470 BC; Lichtheim Vol.2 (1974) p.19. The autobiographical inscription from the tomb of the official Paheri at el-Kabab (ancient Nekheb); he is the grandson of Ahmose, son of Ibana (see 8:4). He describes his perfect life and character in quintessentially Egyptian terms.

5   The entire land sets out to work,
      All beasts browse on their herbs;
      Trees, herbs are sprouting,
      Birds fly from their nests,
      Their wings greeting your *ka* [spirit].
      All flocks frisk on their feet,
      All that fly up and alight,
      They live when you dawn for them.
      Ships fare north, fare south as well,
      Roads lie open when you rise;
      The fish in the river dart before you,
      Your rays are in the midst of the sea.

Akhenaten, hymn to the Aten (c.1353–1336 BC); Lichtheim Vol.2 (1974) p.97. This was composed by the 'heretic' king, who replaced the pantheon of Egypt with a single god, the 'Sun disc' (Aten). The hymn shows similarities with Psalm 91.

6   One alone is the hidden God who hides himself
           from them all,
      who conceals himself from gods, whose
           features cannot be known.
      He is farther above than heaven, deeper down
           than the world below
      and no gods at all can know his true nature.

      God is three of all gods
      Amun, Re, Ptah, without any others
      Hidden his name as Amun;
      He is Re in features, his body is Ptah.
      Their cities on earth endure to eternity –
      Thebes, Heliopolis, Memphis, forever.

Anon., hymn (Papyrus Leiden I.350), c.1222 BC; J.L. Foster Hymns, Prayers and Songs: An Anthology of Ancient Egyptian Lyric Poetry (1995) p.77. A hymn to the state god of the New Kingdom, Amun, whose name means 'Hidden one'. Re is the sun god, whose city is Heliopolis, and Ptah is the creator god of Memphis (both near Cairo).

7 I did not know good from bad when I made the transgression against the Peak, and she punished me, I being in her hand night and day. I sat on a brick like a pregnant woman while I called out for breath without its coming to me.

Neferabu, stela, BM EA 589, c.1250 BC; A. McDowell Village Life in Ancient Egypt (1999) p.98. A stela erected by the craftsman Neferabu from Deir el-Medina records how he sinned against the local goddess of the Theban Peak and was punished until he repented. Deir el-Medina was the village of the craftsmen who carved and decorated the royal tombs in the nearby Valley of the Kings.

GLIMPSES OF INDIVIDUAL LIVES

1 'Come here you fucker!'
Tomb of Ti, inner hall, c.2330 BC; P. Montet *Les Scènes de la vie privée dans les tombeaux égyptiens de l'Ancien Empire* (1924) p.3. The tomb at Saqqara (near Cairo) shows scenes from the lives of the tomb-owner's estates; here boatmen swear at each other as they fight.

2 You enchained me! You beat my father! Now I shall be satisfied, for what can you do to escape my hand? My father shall be satisfied!
Reliefs at Saqqara, c.2180 BC; É. Drioton 'Une Mutilation d'image avec motif' in *Archiv Orientalní* 20 (1952) pp.351–5. In the 6th-Dynasty tomb-chapel of the official Niankhpepy, his head has been attacked, and this text is crudely incised nearby, apparently by the man who erased the head.

3 I know the secrets of hieroglyphs, and the manner of conducting festivals; all magic, I am equipped with it, without anything passing me by. Now I am a craftsman excellent of his craft, someone who comes out top through what he knows … I know the movement of a male figure and the coming of a female image, the positions of a caught bird, the crouching posture of someone whom a single man strikes, as an eye glances at its sister, causing the face of the enemy to be fearful, the raising of the arm of someone who strikes a hippopotamus, and the coming of a runner.
Irtisen, stela (Louvre C14), c.1940 BC; W. Barta *Das Selbstzeugnisse eines altägyptischen Künstler* (Autobiography of an Egyptian Artist) in *Münchner ägyptologische Studien* 22 (1970). The overseer of craftsmen and draughtsmen Irtisen describes his ability to represent various figures.

4   I made for him [Heqaib] a shrine in stone,
   its base in stone,
   and I made for him a broad hall as a work of
      eternity
   surrounded with sycamores.
   I brought gifts upon its every side,
   built for it on its four edges,
   with the walls dug as a foundation down to the
      sand.
   I made a room for the priest,
   and a drinking place for Elephantine.

I made for myself a shrine upon the right of this
   noble [Heqaib]
with a statue in it, and a seated figure in it …
As for every mayor, every priest and every
   mortuary priest,
every scribe, every official,
who shall take away (the offerings) from my
   statue,
his strong arm shall be cut off like that of this ox,
and his neck shall be broken like a fowl's,
his position and his son's position shall not
   exist,
his house shall not exist in Southern-land,
his tomb shall not exist in the cemetery,
his god shall not accept his white bread …
I am against him as a crocodile in water,
as a snake on land,
as a ghost in the necropolis.
Sarenput I, Heqaib stela 9, c.1880 BC; D. Franke *Das Heiligtum des Heqaib auf Elephantine: Geschichte eines Provinzheiligtums im Mittleren Reich* (1994) p.157. The local governor of Aswan, Sarenput I, built a temple to a local deified governor, Heqaib, and cursed anyone who might interfere with it.

5 Take great care of Inpu and Sneferu – you die by them and you live by them – take great care! Look there's nothing more important than him in that house with you! Don't ignore this! Now make sure the housemaid Senen is thrown out of the house – take great care – on whatever day Sahathor reaches you with this letter. Look if she spends a day more in my house – watch it! It's you who lets her do evil against my new wife. Look, why must I nag you? What can she do against you, you who hate her?

Also greet my mother Ipy, a 1,000 times, a million times. Also greet Hotepet and the whole household and Nofret. Now what about this evil treatment of my new wife? You go too far. Are you appointed to be my judge? You will stop – how good that would be! Also have an account brought of what is to be collected of the things from PerHaa. Take great care – don't be neglectful.

I came here southward and I fixed rations for you. Now the Nileflood is not very high is it? Look our rations are fixed for us in measure with the Nileflood. Endure this each one of you! I've managed to keep you alive up to today.
Heqanakht, excerpts from letters, c.1900 BC; Wente (1990) pp.58–63. A group of early 12th-Dynasty letters was found at Deir el-Bahri, Thebes. They tell of the extended family of the funerary priest Heqanakht, who writes the passages here.

They formed the basis of Agatha Christie's crime novel *Death Comes as the End* (1945).

1   And then the Majesty of Seth said
to the Majesty of Horus: 'How lovely your
 backside is!'

Anon. 'The Tale of Horus and Seth' (c.1800 BC); Parkinson (1991) p.120. With perhaps the earliest chat-up line known between men, the god Seth attempts to seduce the god Horus in this fictional tale known from a late 12th-Dynasty papyrus from el-Lahun.

2 Year 29, first month of summer, day 13. The gang passed the walls, saying, 'We are hungry!' Sitting at the back of the temple of King Ba-en-Ra Mery-Amen [Merneptah], life, prosperity, health. And they called out to the Mayor of Thebes as he was passing by. He sent Nefer, the gardener of the overseer of cattle, to them, saying, 'Look, I will give you these 30 *khar* [sackfuls] of emmer to be a means of life, which Pharaoh gave you (as) rations.'

Amennakht, Turin Strike Papyrus, c.1158 BC; McDowell (1999) p.236. A papyrus from the regnal year 29 of Ramses III. The scribe Amennakht (see 12:7), records the strike of the craftsmen from Deir el-Medina when their rations repeatedly fell into arrears. Here they leave their village and go to the funerary temple of King Merneptah at Thebes.

3 We took our copper tools and forced a way into the pyramid of this king through his innermost part. We found its underground chambers, and we took lighted candles in our hands and went down. Then we broke through the rubble that we found at the mouth of his recess and found this god lying at the back of his burial-place. And we found the burial-place of Queen Nubkhatats, his queen, situated beside him.

Papyrus Leopold-Amherst, c.1088 BC; J. Capart, A.H. Gardiner and B. van de Walle 'New Light on the Ramesside Tomb-Robberies' in *Journal of Egyptian Archaeology* 22 (1936) p.171. This papyrus contains legal records from the trial of tomb-robbers. One of them confesses and describes how he and his confederates robbed the tomb of King Sobekemsaef (then six centuries old) on the west bank at Thebes.

4 He had sex with the lady Tuy while she was the wife of the workman Qenna; he had sex with the lady Hel while she was with Pendua; he had sex with the lady Hel while she was with Hesysunebef … and when he had had sex with Hel he had sex with Wekhbet her daughter. And Aapehty his son had sex with Wekhbet himself.

Anon., Papyrus Salt 124, c.1195 BC; McDowell (1999) p.47. This legal papyrus records a series of charges against Paneb, the chief workman from Deir el-Medina, who is accused of sexual misdemeanours.

5   Hail to you O Re-Harakhte, father of the gods!
Hail to you o seven hathors! …
Come, make NN born of NN come after me,
like an ox after grass,
like a maid after her children,
like a herdsman after his cattle.
If you do not make her come after me,
I shall set fire to Busiris and burn up Osiris.

Anon., Ostracon Deir el-Medina 1057, ?c.1200 BC; McDowell (1999) pp.32–3. The seven Hathors were goddesses who presided over a person's birth. NN indicates where the beloved's name should be inserted.

6 Write me what you will want since the boy is too muddled to say it. Look, didn't I write you about it: a fine mat of dried grass and also a fine mat of cord?

Anon., Ostracon Deir el-Medina 123, c.1200 BC; McDowell (1999) p.29. A short note from the village of Deir el-Medina.

7   What do they say to themselves
in their hearts every day,
those who are far from Thebes?
They spend the day
dreaming [?] of its name [saying]
'If only its light were ours!'

Ostracon Gardiner 25, c.1170 BC; McDowell (1999) p.158. A poem written by Amennakht, the scribe of Deir el-Medina, praising the nearby metropolis of Thebes.

8   I'm told you've abandoned writings,
And you whirl around in pleasures,
and go from street to street,
stinking of beer …
Beer makes him stop being a man,
And it causes your soul to wander …
you are sitting in the house
and the harlots surround you.

Anon., Papyrus Anastasi IV, no.18, c.1200 BC; R. Caminos *Late Egyptian Miscellanies* (1954) pp.182–8. In this school text the teacher rebukes a student for neglecting his work.

9 I've heard that you are angry and that you have caused me to be maligned through slander on account of that joke which I told the chief taxing master in that letter, although it was Henuttawy who urged me to tell him some jokes in my letter. You are just like the wife blind in one eye who had been living with a man for twenty years, and when he found another woman he said to her 'I shall divorce you because you are said to be blind in one eye'. And she answered, 'Have you just discovered that after the twenty years I've been married to you?' Such am I and such is my joking with you.

Tjaroy, Late Ramessid letter no.46, *c.*1088 BC; McDowell (1999) pp.31–2. The scribe Tjaroy apologizes for an inappropriate joke while telling another.

DEATH AND BURIAL

1   A night vigil will be assigned to you, with holy oils
      and wrappings from the hands of Tayet.
    A funeral procession will be made for you on
         the day of joining the earth,
    with mummy case of gold,
    a mask of lapis lazuli,
    a heaven over you, and you placed in a hearse,
    with oxen dragging you,
    and singers going before you.
    The dance of the Oblivious ones will be done at
         the mouth of your tomb-chamber,
    and the offering-invocation recited for you;
    sacrifices will be made at the mouth of your
         offering-chapel,
    and your pillars will be built of white stone
    in the midst of the royal children's.

Anon. *The Tale of Sinuhe* (*c.*1840 BC); Parkinson (1997) p.36. In this fictional tale the protagonist is urged to return to Egypt with a description of the burial he will receive. Tayet is the goddess of weaving.

2   My soul opened his mouth to me, to answer
         what I said,
    'If you call burial to mind, it is heartbreak;
    it is bringing the gift of tears, causing a man
         misery;
    it is taking a man from his house,
    and throwing him on the high ground.
    You will not come up again to see the sunlight!
    They who built in granite,
    who constructed pavilions in fair pyramids, as
         fair works
    so that the builders should become gods –
    their altar stones have vanished, like the
         oblivious ones'
    who have died on the shore for lack of a
         survivor,
    when the flood has taken its toll,
    and the sunlight likewise,
    To whom only the fish of the water's edge speak.
    Listen to me! Look, it is good to listen to men!
    Follow the happy day! Forget care!'

Death is to me today
    (like) a sick man's recovery,
    like going out after confinement.
Death is to me today
    like the smell of myrrh
    like sitting under a sail on a windy day.
Death is to me today
    like the smell of flowers
    like sitting on the shore of Drunkenness.

Anon. 'The Dialogue of a Man and his Soul' (*c.*1830 BC); Parkinson (1997) pp.156–7, 159–60. Two excerpts from the 12th-Dynasty poem that describes a man discussing the nature of his death with his soul, juxtaposing two very different attitudes to death and burial.

3   I have heard those songs that are in the tombs
         of old,
    What they tell in extolling life on earth,
    In belittling the land of the dead.
    Why is this done to the land of eternity,
    The right and just that has no terrors?

    Those to be born to millions of millions,
    All of them will come to it;
    No one may linger in the land of Egypt,
    There is none who does not arrive in it.
    As to the time of deeds on earth,
    It is the occurrence of a dream;
    One says: 'Welcome safe and sound.'
    To him who reaches the West.

Anon., Neferhotep harpist's song, no.2 (*c.*1300 BC); Lichtheim Vol.2 (1974) pp.115–16. Inscribed on the walls of the tomb-chapel of the priest Neferhotep at Thebes.

4 They did not make themselves pyramids of copper with stelae of iron. They were not able to leave an heir in the form of children [who would] pronounce their names, but they made for themselves an heir of the writings and instructions they had made … A papyrus roll is more useful than a constructed house, than tomb-chapels in the West; better than a constructed mansion, or than a stela in the temple.

    Is there one here like Hordedef? Is there another like Imhotep? There have been none among our relatives like Neferti or Khety, the foremost of them.

Anon., Papyrus Chester Beatty IV, *c.*1170 BC; McDowell (1999) pp.137–8. A papyrus from Deir el-Medina preserves this passage praising the endurance of writing and the fame of ancient writers. Imhotep was a famous sage under King Djoser (*c.*2630–2611 BC), while Hordedef, the son of King Cheops (*c.*2551–2528 BC), was the protagonist of a later work of literature urging wisdom on its readers. Neferti is a fictional sage, supposedly from the reign of King Sneferu (c.2575–2551 BC), while Khety is a 12th-Dynasty author (c.1900 BC).

1 Now after [he] finished speaking [… Then the High Priest of Amun-Re, king of gods] Khonsuemheb sat and wept beside him, with a face [full of tears, and he addressed the] spirit, saying ['How miserable are these spirits] without eating, without drinking, without age, without youth, without the sight of the sun's rays, or the smell of the north wind. Darkness is in [their] eyes every day, and they shall not rise in the morning to depart!'

Anon. 'The Tale of Khonsuemheb and the Ghost' (c.1200 BC); McDowell (1999) p.150. An early tale about a mummy, or rather a ghost, is known from manuscripts from the village of Deir el-Medina. The ghost of a buried official from the early Middle Kingdom appears to a high priest and laments that his tomb has fallen into disrepair. The high priest replies sympathetically.

2 To the excellent spirit Ankhiri:

Now, look you don't let me be happy! I'll be judged with you and wrong will be told from right. Now look, when I was training the officery of the army of Pharaoh, and his chariotry, I made them come and prostrate themselves for you, bring every good thing to lay before you. I didn't conceal anything from you in your day of life. I didn't let you suffer pain, in anything I did with you, in the manner of a lord. You didn't find me disregarding you, in the manner of a farm-labourer who enters another house … And look, I've spent three years to now, dwelling without entering a house, and it isn't right to cause one like me to do this. Now look, I did it because of you. Now look, you can tell good from bad, and you will be judged with me. Now look, the sisters [young women] of the household, I haven't entered one of them!

Anon., Papyrus Leiden I.371, c.1200 BC; Wente (1990) pp.216–17. A husband writes a letter to his dead wife, Ankhiri, asking why she is persecuting him from beyond the grave, despite his good treatment of her when she was alive. The final denials suggest that he may have a bad conscience about sleeping with a servant girl.

3   O my brother, my husband,
        Friend, high priest!
        Weary not of drink and food,
        Of drinking deep and loving!

        Celebrate the holiday,
        Follow your heart day and night,
        Let not care into your heart,
        Value the years spent on earth!

Taimhotep, stela, BM EA 147, 42 BC; Lichtheim Vol.3 (1980) pp.62–3. The funerary stela of Taimhotep, the wife of the high priest of Ptah at Memphis, from their tomb.

EGYPTOLOGY, ANCIENT AND MODERN

4 Here came the scribe Ahmose son of Yptah to see the temple of Djoser, and he found it like heaven in its interior with the Sun god shining in it! Then he said 'Let loaves, oxen and fowl and all good and pure things fall to the spirit of Djoser, true-of-voice: may the sky rain fresh myrrh and drip incense'. Made by the scribe of the Schoolroom Sethemheb and by the young scribe Ahmose.

Graffito, c.1330 BC, Step Pyramid, North Chapel; C.M. Frith et al. Excavations at Saqqara: The Step Pyramid Vol.1 (1935) p.78. It records a tourist's admiration of the complex built at Saqqara, near Cairo, by King Djoser (c.2630–2611 BC).

5 The god Osiris Antinous true of voice – he has become a fair-faced youth, with holiday eyes, whose heart rejoices like a hero since he has received the order of the gods at the moment of his death. One will repeat for him every ritual of the Hours of Osiris, and every ceremony as a mystery.

Anon., obelisk of Monte Pincio, Rome, AD 130; A. Grimm et al. Der Obelisk des Antinoos (1994). The inscription was composed in hieroglyphs for Emperor Hadrian (r.117–138) to commemorate his favourite, Antinous, who drowned in the Nile (see 85:6).

6 Then this most sacred land, home of shrines and temples, will be completely filled with tombs and dead things. O Egypt, Egypt, of your religions only fables will survive, unbelievable to posterity, and only words will survive inscribed on stones that narrate your pious accomplishments.

Anon. Aceplius (c. AD 300) 24; D.M. Parrott (ed.) Nag Hammadi Codices V, 2–5 and VI with Papyrus Berolinensis 8502, 1 and 4 (1979) pp.420–21. This Hellenistic mystical tractate describes, in an apocalyptic section probably written in Egypt, how the glory of Egypt would perish.

7 Feared by time, although everything else in our present world fears time.

Umara al-Yamani, c. AD 1300; H. Schaefer Principles of Egyptian Art (1986) p.24. The Great Pyramid is described by a medieval poet.

8 [It should be inscribed on a stela] of hard stone, in sacred, and native, and Greek characters and set it up in each of the first, and second, [and third rank temples beside the image of the ever-living king].

Anon., Rosetta Stone, 196 BC, hieroglyphic text, last line; R.B. Parkinson *Cracking Codes: The Rosetta Stone and Decipherment* (1999) Frontispiece. This describes how the priestly decree, issued in March, should be carved in three languages and scripts on stelae. These trilingual inscriptions, of which the Rosetta Stone was the first to be discovered, aided Champollion's decipherment.

1 *Je tiens mon affaire!* (I've done it!)
Jean-François Champollion, 14 Sept. 1822; M. Dewachter *Champollion: un scribe pour l'Égypte* (1990) p.45. The words uttered by the decipherer of Egyptian hieroglyphs when he made his breakthrough. He rushed to his brother's office, cried out these words and collapsed in a dead faint, which lasted for five days.

2 Warmth after the day's toil we never felt from December to February, even when sitting closest to the fire which we kindled nightly with unpainted slats of ancient coffins on a hearth of Old Empire bricks. The dead wood, seasoned by four thousand years of drought, threw off an ancient and corpse-like smell, which left its faint savour on the toast which we scorched at the embers.
David G. Hogarth *The Wandering Scholar* (1925) p.248. An early Egyptologist describes life on an expedition to excavate the tombs at Assiut in middle Egypt before the era of scientific archaeology.

3 I was struck dumb with amazement, and when Lord Carnarvon, unable to stand the suspense any longer, inquired anxiously, 'Can you see anything?' it was all I could do to get out the words, 'Yes, wonderful things.' Then widening the hole a little further, so that we both could see, we inserted an electric torch.
Howard Carter and A.C. Mace *The Tomb of Tut-ankh-amen* (1923) Vol.1, p.96. Carter's reaction on first looking into the intact tomb of Tutankhamun through a small hole in 1922.

4 The position of the designer of the first pyramid, who created the earliest stone building on its scale in the world and lived in the only large united state of the time, can never be recovered. Any understanding of ancient Egypt must include an awareness of these and other enormous differences between antiquity and our own times. Yet human beings are in many ways the same everywhere and much of our detailed knowledge of different civilizations will include material as ordinary as anything in our own lives. When approaching an alien civilization we need to know about both the ordinary and the exotic.
John Baines; J. Baines and J. Malek *Cultural Atlas of Ancient Egypt* (2000) p.12.

5 In 1923 Ahmed Kamal proposed that Egyptians be trained to understand, work in, and ultimately administer the archaeology of their own land. The director-general of the Service of Antiquities caustically remarked that with the exception of Ahmed Bey himself, few Egyptians had shown any interest in antiquity. Ahmed Kamal responded: 'Ah, M. Lacau, in the sixty-five years you French have directed the Service, what opportunities have you given us?'
John A. Wilson *Signs & Wonders upon Pharaoh* (1964) pp.192–3.

6 The model reader of any Egyptian writer is not an Egyptologist. The latter, on the other hand, cannot know what the model readers of the ancients were like, since he cannot even know their actual readers, reading by its nature leaving no traces.
Philippe Derchain *Le Dernier Obélisque* (1987) p.1.

The Ancient Levant, c.3000 BC–AD 73

THE LEVANT BEFORE 2000 BC

1 Lord of heaven and earth
    the earth was not, you created it,
    the light of the day was not, you created it,
    the morning light you had not yet made exist.

Anon., prayer, c.2400 BC; G. Pettinato *The Archives of Ebla: An Empire Inscribed in Clay* (1981) p.259. This prayer, inscribed on a clay tablet, was discovered in the royal palace archives of Ebla (Tell Mardikh) north-central Syria. The archives contained a wealth of material, including economic, literary and religious texts, all indicating a prosperous and sophisticated society as early as the 3rd millennium BC. The prayer suggests that, despite the proliferation of gods and goddesses in the Levant, there was the recognition of an overall supreme creator, not unlike the God of the Old Testament.

2 And the Lord said unto Noah, Come thou and all thy house into the ark; for thee have I seen righteous before me in this generation. Of every clean beast thou shall take to thee by sevens, the male and his female; and of beasts that are not clean by two, the male and his female. Of fowls also of the air by sevens, the male and the female; to keep seed alive upon the face of all the earth. For yet seven days, and I will cause it to rain upon the earth forty days and forty nights; and every living substance that I have made will I destroy from off the face of the earth. And Noah did according unto all that the Lord commanded him.

Bible, OT, Genesis 7:1–5. The biblical account of the Flood is strikingly similar to others preserved in ancient Mesopotamian literature, most notably that in the so-called *Atrahasis* epic from Babylonia (see 1:3). In the Babylonian story, Enlil, the god of the earth, having taken offence at the amount of noise made by humankind, decides to destroy it by means of a flood. He gives the hero of the epic, Atrahasis, seven days' warning, during which time he is to build a boat and to load it with provisions, birds and animals. The Babylonian story of the flood was almost certainly based on an earlier Sumerian version, and both clearly belong to the realm of mythology rather than history. The writers of Genesis, living in exile in Babylonia in the 6th century BC, might clearly have drawn on these Mesopotamian traditions when composing their version of the creation and the flood, but equally they might have had knowledge of early Canaanite versions that have not been preserved.

3 If someone lies down with the wife of another man, he will give a piece of multicoloured fabric and a blanket (as penalty). If it concerns a virgin (that is, if one lies down with a virgin), then her behaviour will be examined closely and statements will be heard from both of those charged and he will marry her.

Ebla tablet, c.2400 BC; G. Pettinato *Ebla: A New Look at History* (1986) p.236. This quotation comes from a long document found in the Ebla archives, a treaty between Ebla and Ashur (the later kingdom of Assyria in northern Iraq). It not only shows that social and legal institutions were well developed by the 3rd millennium BC, but it also displays an extraordinary level of tolerance and fairness.

4 You are my brother and I am your brother; to you fellow man, whatever desire comes from your mouth I will grant, just as you will grant the desire that comes from my mouth.

Ebla tablet, c.2400 BC; Pettinato (1986) p.240. The king of Ebla is writing to the king of Hamazi (believed to be a city in northern Iran). The use of the word 'brother' in addressing a fellow ruler of equal status is shown here to have been established by the 3rd millennium BC. The text also demonstrates the surprising scale of diplomatic relations at this period.

5 And Abram journeyed, going on still toward the south. And there was a famine in the land: and Abram went down into Egypt to sojourn there; for the famine was grievous in the land.

Bible, OT, Genesis 12:9–10. Although much of the Hebrew Bible was written hundreds of years after the events depicted and cannot be regarded as accurately historical, many of the individual stories were undoubtedly based on real events, the significance of which was so great that they were preserved in popular tradition. This passage faithfully records the situation at the end of the 3rd millennium BC, when the southern Levant (the countries of the eastern Mediterranean) was plunged into a prolonged period of economic recession, brought about by profound climatic and political changes. Archaeology has shown that many Canaanites entered Egypt at this time, and for the writers of the Bible the remembrance of this catastrophic 'famine' provided the rationale for Abraham's journey into Egypt.

6 The Lord rained upon Sodom and Gomorrah brimstone and fire from the Lord out of heaven; And he overthrew those cities, and all the plain, and all the inhabitants of the cities, and that which grew upon the ground.

Bible, OT, Genesis 19:24–5. The story of the destruction of Sodom and Gomorrah (two of the 'Cities of the Plain'), as recounted in Genesis, almost certainly took as its basis a real catastrophe that occurred towards the middle of the 3rd millennium BC. Archaeology has revealed a number of towns situated above the southeast plain of the Dead Sea that, during the wetter climate that prevailed at that time, were situated on the shore. These towns were exploiting the natural bitumen that rises in great blocks from the floor of the Dead Sea and were processing it for export to Egypt, for building and waterproofing. Around 2600 BC the towns were struck by an earthquake followed by intense conflagration – an event so dramatic as to leave a lasting memory in popular tradition.

THE LEVANT, c.2000–c.1500 BC

1 Haste ye, and go up to my father, and say unto him, Thus saith thy son Joseph, God hath made me lord of all Egypt: come down unto me, tarry not: And thou shalt dwell in the land of Goshen, and thou shalt be near unto me, thou, and thy children, and thy children's children, and thy flocks, and thy herds, and all that thou hast.

Bible, OT, Genesis 45:9–10. These words, spoken by Joseph to his brothers, reflect the situation in the early 2nd millennium BC when Canaanites moved into the Egyptian Delta (land of Goshen) and seized political power. Known as the Hyksos, they established a dynasty that, for a brief period, ruled over the whole of Egypt. Within the context of this 'foreign' dynasty, it is entirely plausible that gifted individuals of non-Egyptian origin might have risen to senior positions within the administration.

2 Now there arose up a new king over Egypt, which knew not Joseph. And he said unto his people, Behold, the people of the children of Israel are more and mightier than we.

Bible, OT, Exodus 1:8–9. The Hyksos were eventually expelled from Egypt by Ahmose, the founder of the native Egyptian 18th dynasty (see 8:4). This expulsion, which occurred c.1560 BC, proved to be one of the major turning points in the history of the Levant, for the Hyksos were not just chased out of Egypt but were pursued deep into Canaan and Syria – a process that led directly to the creation of Egypt's Asiatic empire. It is possible that this event is preserved in the biblical account of 'the exodus' and that this initial statement in the Book of Exodus may be a reference to Ahmose himself.

3 Therefore they did set over them taskmasters to afflict them with their burdens. And they built for Pharaoh treasure cities, Pithom and Raamses.

Bible, OT, Exodus 1:11. Although the literary basis for the story of the exodus most probably reflects events in the 16th century BC, the writer of Exodus chose to set his narrative in the time of Ramses II (c.1279–1213 BC). This powerful ruler initiated many monumental building projects, including the development of two cities in the Delta, Per-Ramses (Raamses above) and Per-Temus (Pithom).

4 And it came to pass, when Pharaoh had let the people go, that God led them not through the way of the land of the Philistines, although that was near; for God said, Lest peradventure the people repent when they see war, and they return to Egypt.

Bible, OT, Exodus 13:17. The biblical story of the exodus must largely be seen as a literary invention but as one that incorporates elements of historical reality, such as Ahmose's expulsion of the Hyksos. Its late writing is revealed by references such as this one to the Philistines, who did not, in fact, appear in the Levant until the 12th century BC, in the time of Ramses III rather than Ramses II.

THE LAND OF CANAAN, c.1400–c.1300 BC

5 Say to the king, my lord, my god, my Sun: Message of Yapahu, your servant, the dirt at your feet. I fall at the feet of the king, my lord, my god, my Sun, seven times and seven times.

Amarna letter EA 297, c.1370 BC; W.L. Moran (ed.) *The Amarna Letters* (1992) p.339. During the period from c.1450 to 1150 BC the land of Canaan came under the direct administrative control of Egypt. Part of this period is documented and illuminated by the so-called 'Amarna letters', which represent the diplomatic correspondence sent by various vassal princes of the Egyptian empire to the pharaohs Amenhotep III (r.1390–1352), Amenhotep IV (Akhenaten) (r.1352–1336), Smenkhkare (r.1335–1332) and Tutankhamun (r.1332–1322). This standard formula begins many of the communications and demonstrates the subservient status of a subject ruler – in this case the king of Gezer in southern Canaan – to the pharaoh (see 9:1).

6 Say to the king of Egypt, my brother: Message of the king of Alasiya, your brother.

Amarna letter EA 39, c.1370 BC; Moran (1992) p.111. The writer of this letter – the king of Alasiya (Cyprus) – considers himself as a ruler of equal status to the pharaoh.

7 Message of Biridaya, the loyal servant of the king … I am indeed guarding Megiddo, the city of the king, my lord, day and night: By day I guard it from the fields with chariots, and by night on the walls of the king, my lord. And as the warring of the Apiru in the land is severe, may the king, my lord, take cognizance of his land.

Amarna letter EA 243, c.1370 BC; Moran (1992) p.297. The king of Megiddo writes to the pharaoh. The Amarna letters make frequent reference to the Apiru, depicted as bands of stateless people, living in the hill country. Composed of dispossessed and disaffected groups who had opted out of an increasingly decadent Egypto-Canaanite society, they posed, through their raids and skirmishes, a major threat to the urban establishment.

1 May the king, my lord, know that since the return to Egypt of the archers, Labayu has waged war against me. We are thus unable to do the plucking [harvesting], and we are unable to go out of the city gate because of Labayu … Look, Labayu has no other purpose. He seeks simply the seizure of Megiddo.

Amarna letter EA 244, c.1370 BC; Moran (1992) p.298. Another letter from the same king of Megiddo appears to implicate Labayu, the ruler of Shechem, in the attack on his city. It seems likely that Labayu and his sons were leaders of the Apiru.

2 Message of Yapahu, the ruler of Gezer, your servant … May the king, my lord, the Sun from the sky, take thought for his land. Since the Apiru are stronger than we, may the king, my lord, give me his help, and may the king, my lord, get me away from the Apiru lest the Apiru destroy us.

Amarna letter EA 299, c.1370 BC; Moran (1992) p.340. An appeal to the pharaoh from the king of Gezer, who is being threatened by the Apiru. The Apiru are almost certainly the Hebrews of the Old Testament, and it is possible that in the Amarna letters we see the origins of historical Israel. The battles and adventures of the Apiru are surely reflected in the conquest stories in the biblical books of Joshua and Judges.

3 And the Lord said unto Joshua, See, I have given into thine hand Jericho, and the king thereof, and the mighty men of valour …

So the people shouted when the priests blew with the trumpets: and it came to pass, when the people heard the sound of the trumpet, and the people shouted with a great shout, that the wall fell down flat, so that the people went up into the city, every man straight before him, and they took the city.

Bible, OT, Joshua 6:2, 20. The story of Joshua's conquest of Canaan must, like the exodus, be seen as a literary invention, composed many centuries after the events that it purports to represent. Biblical chronology would place Joshua's capture of Jericho some time in the late 13th century BC, a time during which archaeology has shown Jericho to have been unoccupied. The writer of the story might well have drawn on popular traditions that associated Jericho with 'tumbling walls'. Excavations have shown that in the 3rd millennium BC the city wall, through intense earthquake activity, collapsed no fewer than 17 times.

4 Come up unto me, and help me, that we may smite Gibeon: for it hath made peace with Joshua and with the children of Israel …

Then spake Joshua to the Lord in the day when the Lord delivered up the Amorites before the children of Israel, and he said in the sight of Israel, Sun, stand thou still upon Gibeon; and thou, Moon, in the valley of Ajalon.

Bible, OT, Joshua 10:4, 12. According to the Bible, Adonizdek, the king of Jerusalem, enlisted the support of four other kings (of Hebron, Yarmuth, Lachish and Eglon) in order to attack Gibeon, a city that had made peace with Joshua. The epic tale in which Joshua came to the aid of Gibeon and commanded the sun to stand still (giving time for all their enemies to be dealt with) is especially reminiscent of the inter-city feuds involving the Apiru described in the Amarna letters.

5 To the king, my lord and my Sun: Thus Labayu, your servant and the dirt on which you tread … The fact is that I am a loyal servant of the king! I am not a rebel and I am not delinquent in duty. I have not held back my payments of tribute.

Amarna letter EA 254, c.1370 BC; Moran (1992) p.307. When he is challenged, Labayu, one of the most interesting characters in the Amarna letters, protests his loyalty to the pharaoh. His role as a leader of the Apiru, however, is clear, and it is surely no coincidence that Labayu was king of Shechem, the city that formed the early focus of Israelite identity.

6 Moreover, when an ant is struck, does it not fight back and bite the hand of the man that struck it?

Amarna letter EA 252, c.1370 BC; Moran (1992) p.305. Having been accused by the pharaoh of failing to guard prisoners of the crown diligently, Labayu offers his excuses.

7 Rib-Hadda says to his lord, king of all countries … Behold, the war of the Apiru against me is severe and, as the gods of your land are alive, our sons and daughters, as well as we ourselves, are gone since they have been sold in the land of Yarimuta for provisions to keep us alive. For lack of a cultivator, my field is like a woman without a husband.

Amarna letter EA 74, c.1370 BC; Moran (1992) p.143. Many of the Amarna letters are from Rib-Hadda, king of Byblos, on the coast of Lebanon, who was also plagued by the Apiru and whose pleas for help from the pharaoh seem to have been as elaborate as they were numerous. In this letter, in order to reinforce his desperate situation, he quotes a contemporary proverb – 'Like a bird in a cage, so am I in Gubla [Byblos]' – to show how Rib-Hadda is cut off without friends or allies.

8 With regard to the girl, my daughter, about whom you wrote to me in view of marriage, she has become a woman; she is nubile. Just send a delegation to fetch her.

Amarna letter EA 3, c.1370 BC; Moran (1992) p.7. Relationships between rulers of equal status were often sealed by diplomatic marriages. Here, the king of Babylon, Kadašman-Enlil I (1364–1350) offers his daughter to the pharaoh, Amenhotep III (see 8:7).

I   I have a word to tell you,
          a story to recount to you:
          the word of the tree and the charm of the stone,
          the whisper of the heavens to the earth,
          of the seas to the stars.
          I understand the lightning which the heavens
              do not know,
          the word which men do not know,
          and earth's masses cannot understand.
          Come, and I will reveal it

Anon., Epic of Baal, c.1350 BC; M.D. Coogan *Stories from Ancient Canaan* (1978) p.92. Dating to the end of the Late Bronze Age (14th–13th centuries BC), the remarkable archives discovered at Ras Shamra, the site of ancient Ugarit, on the Syrian coast, have provided a wealth of pre-biblical literature, documenting the religion, legal institutions, diplomacy and mythology of the Canaanites of the 2nd millennium BC. The striking similarity between many of the texts and passages in the Old Testament makes it quite clear that the biblical stories derive from a much more ancient Canaanite literary heritage. Here we have the words of the Canaanite god, Baal.

2   For seven years let Baal fail,
          eight, the Rider on the Clouds:
          no dew, no showers,
          no surging of the two seas,
          no benefit of Baal's voice

Anon., Story of Aqhat, tablet 3; Coogan (1978) p.41. The curse of Danel (the hero of the epic) following the death of his son, Aqhat. Note the similarity to David's lament over Saul and Jonathan in the biblical Book of Samuel.

3 Ye mountains of Gilboa, let there be no dew, neither let there be rain, upon you, nor fields of offerings.

Bible, OT, 2 Samuel 1:21.

4   Why should I want silver and gleaming gold,
          a controlling share in a mine,
          perpetual slaves, three horses,
          a chariot from the stable, servants?
          Let me have sons,
          let me produce descendants!

Anon., Story of Keret, tablet 1; Coogan (1978) p.59. Keret, a legendary Canaanite king, is talking to the supreme god, El.

THE END OF THE 2ND MILLENNIUM BC

5 The foreign countries made a conspiracy in their islands. All at once the lands were removed and scattered in the fray. No land could stand before their arms, from Hatti, Kode, Carchemish, Arzawa and Alashiya on … They were coming forward toward Egypt, while the flame was prepared before them. Their confederation was the Philistines, Tjeker, Shekelesh, Denyen and Weshesh, lands united.

Inscription from Ramses III's Mortuary Temple at Medinet Habu, c.1175 BC; T. Dothan *The Philistines and their Material Culture* (1982) p.3. At the start of the 12th century BC the Levant, Cyprus and Egypt were subjected to a series of ferocious attacks by people of ultimately Aegean and Anatolian origin, known collectively as the 'Peoples of the Sea'. Some swept across Anatolia and into Syria, where they caused the final downfall of the Hittite empire. Others attacked the Levantine coast and the Egyptian delta directly. Ramses III engaged the Sea Peoples in battle and was able to hold them at bay. He was forced, however, to allow some groups to settle on the Levantine coast, in particular, their best known group, the Philistines, who settled in the south.

6 And Samson went down to Timnath, and saw a woman in Timnath of the daughters of the Philistines. And he came up, and told his father and his mother, and said, I have seen a woman in Timnath of the daughters of the Philistines: now, therefore get her for me to wife.

Bible, OT, Judges 14:1–2. Ramses III's wars with the Peoples of the Sea had crippled the Egyptian economy to such an extent that c.1150 BC the empire was withdrawn from Canaan. The absence of the Egyptians in Canaan and of the Hittites in Syria resulted in a power vacuum that lasted for several centuries. This period of political and social readjustment, which saw the emergence of historical Israel, is depicted in the Book of Judges. The 'Judges' can be thought of as charismatic social leaders who steered the Israelites towards statehood. One of the most colourful was Samson. Timnath (or Timnah), although not one of the principal Philistine cities, was an important town to the east of Ekron.

7 Then the lords of the Philistines gathered them together for to offer a great sacrifice unto Dagon, their god, and to rejoice: for they said, Our god hath delivered Samson our enemy into our hand.

Bible, OT, Judges 16:23. Contrary to later prejudices, the Philistines were a sophisticated and urbane people. Their origins lay in the Aegean, and many of their architectural and artistic traditions can be traced to Mycenaean prototypes (see 37:2). Many Philistine temples have been excavated, and there is good evidence to indicate that their principal god was, indeed, Dagon, as represented in the story of Samson.

8 And these are the golden emerods which the Philistines returned for a trespass offering unto the Lord; for Ashdod one, for Gaza one, for Askelon one, for Gath one, for Ekron one; And the golden mice, according to the number of all the cities of the

Philistines belonging to the five lords, both of fenced cities, and of country villages.

Bible, OT, 1 Samuel 6:17–18. The period following the departure of the Egyptians (c.1150–900 BC) saw the gradual migration of the Hebrews from the hill country to the plains and a corresponding eastward expansion of the Philistines. The conflicts that ensued formed the basis of the marvellous adventure stories captured in the biblical Books of Judges and Samuel (1 and 2). In one such episode, the Philistines, having captured the Ark of the Covenant (the wooden casket containing the tablets of the law) were smitten by haemorrhoids and plagues of mice. In order to appease the God of the Hebrews, they returned the Ark, together with offerings in the form of golden models of haemorrhoids and mice! The text is also of importance as it names the five principal cities of the Philistines, the so-called 'Pentapolis'.

1 And there went out a champion out of the camp of the Philistines, named Goliath, of Gath, whose height was six cubits and a span ... And he stood and cried unto the armies of Israel, and said unto them, Why are ye come out to set your battle in array? Am not I a Philistine, and ye servants to Saul? Choose you a man for you, and let him come down to me. If he be able to fight with me, and to kill me, then will we be your servants: but if I prevail against him, and kill him, then shall ye be our servants, and serve us.

Bible, OT, 1 Samuel 17:4, 8–9. The tale of David and Goliath illustrates another episode in the long-running conflict between the Israelites and the Philistines. This passage is remarkable, however, for the conflict being resolved by the combat of champions. This method of battle, alien to the Land of Canaan, is commonly found in the Homeric legends, and its inclusion in the biblical text emphasizes the Aegean origin of the Philistines. A cubit was roughly the length of a forearm.

2 Then came all the tribes of Israel to David unto Hebron and spake, saying, Behold we are thy bone and thy flesh. Also in time past, when Saul was king over us, thou wast he that leddest out and broughtest in Israel: and the Lord said to thee, Thou shalt feed my people Israel, and thou shalt be a captain over Israel. So all the elders of Israel came to the king to Hebron; and king David made a league with them in Hebron before the Lord: and they anointed David king over Israel.

Bible, OT, 2 Samuel 5:1–3. According to biblical tradition, David, having defeated all of his enemies (including the Philistines), became king of all Israel, and founded what has become known as the 'United Monarchy'. Neither archaeology nor contemporary historical texts have been able to substantiate such a monarchy, and it seems more likely that the 'United Monarchy' was a literary invention of the Judahite writers of the Hebrew Bible in exile, who needed to create a 'Golden Age', an era both earlier and more opulent than

Omri's Israel, the northern kingdom of Israel in the 9th century BC, and based on Jerusalem rather than Samaria. Saul, David and Solomon might well have existed, but they were surely more in the nature of local, Judahite folk heroes than major rulers.

3 Happy are thy men, happy are these thy servants, which stand continually before thee, and that hear thy wisdom. Blessed be the Lord thy God, which delighted in thee, to set thee on the throne of Israel.

Bible, OT, 1 Kings 10:8–9. These words are reported in the Book of Kings to have been said by the Queen of Sheba during her visit to the court of Solomon. As in the case of David, there is considerable doubt about the historicity of Solomon's kingdom. It is likely, however, that the writer of this story drew on the knowledge of a real historical event. It is known that by the 9th century BC there was a flourishing kingdom of Saba (Sheba) in what is now Yemen and that several of its rulers were women. Perhaps the story was based on a real diplomatic trade visit that took place in the 9th century to the court of Omri in Jerusalem or, even later, to the court of Hezekiah in Jerusalem.

THE KINGDOM OF ISRAEL, c.900–c.800 BC

4 I am Mesha, son of Chemosh-yat, king of Moab, the Dibonite. My father was king over Moab for thirty years, and I became king after my father. I built this high place for Chemosh in ... a high place of salvation, because he delivered me from all assaults, and because he let me see my desire upon all my adversaries. Omri, king of Israel, had oppressed Moab many days, for Chemosh was angry with his land. His son succeeded him, and he too said, I will oppress Moab. In my days he said it; but I saw my desire upon him and his house, and Israel perished utterly for ever.

Mesha stele, 9th century BC; J.C.L. Gibson *Textbook of Syrian Semitic Inscriptions: Hebrew and Moabite Inscriptions* Vol.1 (1971) pp.75–6. The kingdom of Israel emerged in the 9th century BC with its capital first at Tirzah and then at Samaria. Under its most famous rulers, Omri and Ahab, it developed into a significant international power, which attempted to expand its territory into neighbouring Transjordan. This passage comes from a stele discovered in 1868 at Dhiban (the biblical Dibon), some 13 miles east of the Dead Sea in Jordan. It commemorates the successful attempt of Mesha, king of Moab, to free his kingdom from Israelite rule.

5 I destroyed, tore down and burned down Karkara, his [Irhuleni of Hamath's] royal residence.

He brought along to help him 1,200 chariots, 1,200 cavalrymen, 20,000 foot soldiers of Hadadezer of Damascus, 700 chariots, 700 cavalrymen, 10,000 foot soldiers of Irhuleni from Hamath, 2,000 chariots, 10,000 foot soldiers of Ahab the Israelite ... 1,000 camel-riders of Gindibu from Arabia ... I slew 14,000 of their soldiers with the sword, descending upon them like Adad when he makes a rainstorm pour down.

Kurkh stele, c.850 BC; J.B. Pritchard (ed.) *The Ancient Near East: An Anthology of Texts and Pictures* (1973 edn) p.190. The 9th century BC saw a series of aggressive military campaigns by the Assyrians, who were intent on extending their empire westward towards the Mediterranean. This text is from the victory stele of the Assyrian king Shalmaneser III (r.c.858–824 BC), who in 853 BC confronted a coalition of western rulers at the city of Karkara (Qarqur) in the Orontes Valley of Syria (see 5:5). The coalition's army included a substantial force from Ahab of Israel. Although Shalmaneser claimed a victory, the truth may have been rather different since the Assyrians were obliged to withdraw for about 12 years before continuing their offensive.

1 The tribute of Jehu, son of Omri; I received from him silver, gold, a golden bowl, a golden vase with pointed bottom, golden tumblers, golden buckets, tin, a staff for a king and wooden hunting spears.

Black obelisk, c.825 BC; Pritchard (1973 edn) p.192. In 841 BC Shalmaneser returned to the west, reaching first Damascus, from where he marched south into Israelite territory. Submission was exacted from the Israelite king, Jehu, who was obliged to pay substantial tribute. The text is taken from the so-called 'black obelisk', a pictorial victory monument carved to adorn the Assyrian monarch's palace in Nimrud in northern Iraq (see 6:3).

2 I killed Jehoram, son of Ahab, king of Israel, and I killed Ahaziahu son of Jehoram, king of the House of David. And I set their towns into ruins and turned their land into desolation.

Tel Dan inscription, late 9th century; I. Finkelstein, I. and N.A. Silberman *The Bible Unearthed: Archaeology's New Vision of Ancient Israel and the Origin of its Sacred Texts* (2001) p.129. The Assyrians were not the only threat to the kingdom of Israel. The words above are those of Hazael, the Aramaean king of Damascus, who, taking advantage of a brief respite in Assyrian aggression, seized territory in Transjordan and Israel. The text comes from a victory stele set up in the city of Dan in the northern part of the kingdom. The text is important as it also acknowledges the nascent state of Judah (Jehoram, king of the House of David).

3 If Matiel deals falsely with Bargayah or his son or his descendants, let his kingdom become as a kingdom of sand, a kingdom of dreams that fade away like fire ... let no grass sprout, nor let anything green be seen, nor let its pasture be seen; let not the sound of the lyre be heard in Arpad and among its people,

but the sound of affliction and confusion and crying and lamentation.

Sefire stele 1, 8th century BC; J.C.L. Gibson *Textbook of Syrian Semitic Inscriptions: Aramaic Inscriptions* Vol.2 (1975) p.29. Israel's neighbours to the north were the powerful Aramaean city-states in Syria. This passage is taken from a stele in Damascus Museum, inscribed in Aramaic. Found near Sefire in Syria, it records a treaty between two kings, Bargayah, king of an unknown city or territory called KTK, and Matiel, ruler of the Aramaean kingdom of Arpad (near Aleppo).

4 In the twelfth year of Ahaz king of Judah began Hoshea the son of Elah to reign in Samaria over Israel nine years ...

Against him came up Shalmaneser king of Assyria; and Hoshea became his servant, and gave him presents ...

In the ninth year of Hoshea the king of Assyria took Samaria, and carried Israel away into Assyria, and placed them in Halah and in Habor by the river of Gozan, and in the cities of the Medes.

Bible, OT, 2 Kings 17:1, 3, 6. The biblical account of the capture of Samaria, and the consequent end of the northern kingdom of Israel, corresponds to the version found in contemporary Assyrian texts.

THE KINGDOM OF JUDAH, c.800–c.600 BC

5 Come, let us make our father drink wine, and we will lie with him, that we may preserve seed of our father ...

Thus were both the daughters of Lot with child by their father. And the firstborn bare a son, and called his name Moab: the same is the father of the Moabites unto this day. And the younger, she also bare a son, and called his name Ben-ammi: the same is the father of the children of Ammon unto this day.

Bible, OT, Genesis 19:32, 36–8. Relations between Judah and her neighbours were generally poor, and there was frequently open conflict with the Iron Age kingdoms of Moab and Edom. This hostility was well known to the writers of Genesis in the 6th century BC, who, in order to demonstrate to their Judahite readers a lower and pejorative status of these neighbouring states, depicted their origins as having arisen from the liaison between Lot and his daughters.

6 This is the tomb of Shebaniah the royal steward. There is no silver or gold here, only his bones and the bones of his maidservant with him. Cursed be the man who opens this.

Shebna inscription, 7th century BC; Gibson Vol.1 (1971) p.24. The southern kingdom of Judah began to flourish following the decline of the northern kingdom of Israel in the late 9th century BC. Its capital, Jerusalem, became a prosperous city. This inscription comes from the lintel of a rock-cut tomb at Silwan, near Jerusalem. The tomb is thought to be that of Shebna (Shebeniah), the steward of King Hezekiah of Judah.

1 Thus saith the Lord God of hosts, Go get thee unto this treasurer, even unto Shebna, which is over the house, and say, What hast thou here? And whom hast thou here, that thou hast hewed thee out a sepulchre here, as he that heweth him out a sepulchre on high, and that graveth an habitation for himself in a rock?

Bible, OT, Isaiah 22:15–16. This text, in which the prophet Isaiah rebukes a treasurer named Shebna for building himself too conspicuous a tomb, almost certainly refers to the same tomb and the same royal steward.

2 In the seventh year, the month of Kislev, the king of Akkad mustered his troops, marched to the Hatti-land, and besieged the city of Judah and on the second day of the month of Adar he seized the city and captured the king. He appointed there a king of his own choice, received its heavy tribute and sent them to Babylon.

Anon. 'Babylonian Chronicle'; R.D. Barnett *Illustrations of Old Testament History* (1968 edn) p.73. This Babylonian account of the capture of Jerusalem (city of Judah) parallels the narrative of the last years of Judah in the biblical books of Chronicles and Jeremiah. In 599 BC the Babylonian king, Nebuchadnezzar II (see 2:5), responding to Judah's failure to pay tribute, launched a punitive military campaign and, after a two-year siege, captured Jerusalem and sent the king, Jehoiakin, and his family into exile. Nebuchadnezzar placed a puppet, Zedekiah, the king's uncle, on the throne, but when Zedekiah rebelled against the Babylonians in 587 BC Nebuchadnezzar acted swiftly and decisively. He invaded Judah again, destroyed Jerusalem, ransacked the Temple and deported the population to Babylonia.

3 To my lord Yaush, Yahweh give my lord to hear peaceable tidings even this day, even this day. What is your servant but a dog that my lord remembers his servant? Let Yahweh send an early sign! There is no other matter which you do not know about.

Lachish letter 2, 587 BC; Gibson Vol.I (1971) p.37. A number of potsherds inscribed in black ink (*ostraca*) were found in the burned ruins of the gatehouse at the city of Lachish in Judah. Known as the Lachish letters, they date to the very last days of the southern kingdom, when the Babylonians under Nebuchadnezzar had invaded Judah and were laying siege to Jerusalem. According to Jeremiah, apart from Jerusalem, only Azekah, about 18 miles southwest of Jerusalem, and Lachish, about 12 miles further on, remained in Judahite hands as the invasion progressed.

4 Yahweh give my lord to hear even this day good tidings. And now – in accordance with all the instructions that my lord has sent – so has your servant acted. I have written on the door in accordance with all the instructions that my lord sent to me …

Let him also know that we are watching for the beacons of Lachish, interpreting them in accordance with all the code-signals that my lord has given; but we do not see Azekah.

Lachish letter 4; Gibson Vol.I (1971) pp.41–2. The implications of this chilling document are clear: Azekah had fallen and only a few days remained before Lachish shared the same fate.

5 For I am to be pitied; I have been seized before my time, the son of a short number of days, a smitten one, an orphan I, the son of a widow.

Eshmunazer, early 5th century BC; J.C.L. Gibson *Textbook of Syrian Semitic Inscriptions: Phoenician Inscriptions* Vol.3 (1982) p.107. Although the kingdom of Judah succumbed to the Babylonians in 587 BC, the coastal cities of the Phoenicians continued to prosper until the conquest of Alexander in 332 BC. This poignant text comes from the sarcophagus of Eshmunazer, king of the Phoenician city of Sidon. He died at the age of 14, having succeeded his father at birth.

6 Now in the first year of Cyrus king of Persia, that the word of the Lord by the word of Jeremiah might be fulfilled, the Lord stirred up the spirit of Cyrus king of Persia, that he made a proclamation throughout all his kingdom, and put it also in writing, saying, Thus saith Cyrus king of Persia, The Lord God of heaven hath given me all the kingdoms of the earth; and he hath charged me to build him an house at Jerusalem, which is in Judah. Who is there among you of all his people? His God be with him, and let him go up to Jerusalem, which is in Judah, and build the house of the Lord God of Israel (he is the God) which is in Jerusalem.

Bible, OT, Ezra 1:1–3. In 539 BC Cyrus II, king of the Medes, marched against the Babylonian king, Nabonidus, entered Babylon without a battle and inherited the vast Babylonian empire, which he united to that of the Medes. According to the biblical account, it was Cyrus who, by instigating a new policy of religious tolerance, allowed the Judahite exiles to return to Judah in order to rebuild the Temple.

7 I returned to these sacred cities on the other side of the Tigris, the sanctuaries of which have been ruins for a long time, the images which used to live therein and established for them permanent sanctuaries. I also gathered all their former inhabitants and returned to them their habitations.

Cyrus II, cylinder, c.539–530 BC; Barnett (1968 edn) p.77. This interesting text comes from a barrel-shaped clay object, which was probably part of the foundation deposit of an important building. In it, Cyrus describes various aspects of his new religious policy, and although it is concerned with cities in Mesopotamia and Iran and does not refer to Judah or Jerusalem, it corroborates the proclamation described in the Book of Ezra.

THE CLASSICAL PERIOD, 333 BC–AD 73

1 And the elders of the Jews builded, and they prospered through the prophesying of Haggai the prophet and Zechariah the son of Iddo. And they builded and finished it, according to the commandment of the God of Israel, and according to the commandment of Cyrus, and Darius, and Artaxerxes king of Persia. And this house was finished on the third day of the month Adar, which was in the sixth year of the reign of Darius the king.

Bible, OT, Ezra 6:14–15. According to biblical tradition, the great Temple of Jerusalem was built by King Solomon. In reality, such a temple is unlikely to have been constructed until Judah became an independent political entity towards the end of the 9th century BC. In any event, this 'First Temple' was destroyed by the Babylonians in 587 BC. According to the biblical record, another temple was built during the Persian period by the exiles (now referred to as Jews rather than as Judahites) following their return from Babylonia. Sometimes known as the Temple of Zerubbabel, it was completely replaced by the somewhat confusingly named 'Second Temple', built by King Herod in the 1st century BC.

2 After Alexander son of Philip, the Macedonian, who came from the land of Kittim, had defeated Darius, king of the Persians and the Medes, he succeeded him as king. (He had previously become king of Greece.)

Bible, Apocrypha, 1 Maccabees 1:1.

3 After this he fell sick and perceived that he was dying. So he summoned his most honoured officers, who had been brought up with him from youth, and divided his kingdom among them while he was still alive.

Bible, Apocrypha, 1 Maccabees 1:5–6. In 333 BC, following the Battle of Issus, the vast empire of the Persians fell into the hands of Alexander the Great (see 64:2). After his death ten years later, the empire was divided between his successor generals. Judah initially came under the control of the Ptolemies

of Egypt, but in 200 BC Ptolemy V was defeated by Antiochus III of the Syrian-based Seleucid dynasty, and Judah was annexed as part of the Seleucid empire. This change in dynasty was perceived by some as an opportunity to proclaim independence for Judah, and there followed a period of turbulence and civil unrest.

4   Israel mourned deeply in every community,
        rulers and elders groaned,
     maidens and young men became faint,
        the beauty of the women faded.
     Every bridegroom took up the lament;
        she who sat in the bridal chamber was
           mourning.
     Even the land shook for its inhabitants,
        and all the house of Jacob was clothed with
           shame.

Bible, Apocrypha, 1 Maccabees 1:25–8. These words convey the sense of outrage felt by the Jews following the attack on Jerusalem in 167 BC by the Seleucid ruler, Antiochus IV. Not only did he sack and loot the Temple of Zerubbabel, but he also issued decrees outlawing Jewish sacrifices, Sabbath observance and circumcision. Instead, he enforced Greek cultic practices and rededicated the Temple of Jerusalem to Zeus.

5   Alas! Why was I born to see this,
        the ruin of my people, the ruin of the holy city,
        and to dwell there when it was given over to the
           enemy,
     the sanctuary given over to aliens!
     Her temple has become like a man without
        honour;
     her glorious vessels have been carried into
        captivity.
     Her babes have been killed in her streets,
        her youths by the sword of the foe.
     What nation has not inherited her palaces
        and has not seized her spoils?
     All her adornment has been taken away;
        no longer free, she has become a slave.

Bible, Apocrypha, 1 Maccabees 2:7–11. These are allegedly the words of Judas ben Mattathias of the House of Hashmon, who, as a direct consequence of Antiochus IV's decree, led the Jews in open revolt against Seleucid rule. Following his death in 166 BC, the nationalistic cause was taken up and developed by his son Judas, known as the Maccabee.

6   How is the mighty fallen,
        the saviour of Israel!

Bible, Apocrypha, 1 Maccabees 9:21. Judas Maccabeus was seen as the hero of the Jewish War of Independence, and his death was much lamented. He and his successors, Jonathan and Simon, through a combination of military action and brilliant political manoeuvring, managed to throw off the Seleucid yoke and to secure a brief period of independence for Judah (c.142–63 BC), the so-called Hamonaean monarchy.

1 A little afterward Pompey came to Damascus, and marched over Coelesyria; at which time there came ambassadors to him from all Syria and Egypt, and out of Judaea also, for Aristobulus had sent him a great present, which was a golden vine, of the value of five hundred talents.

Flavius Josephus (c.37–c.100) *Antiquities of the Jews* (1867 edn) Bk 14, Ch.3, para.1. In 76 BC the situation erupted into civil war between John Hyrcanus II (d.30 BC) and his brother Aristobulus II (d.49 BC). The war was resolved by Rome, which, after many years of conflict, had finally driven the Seleucids out of Syria. In 63 BC Pompey entered Jerusalem, and under the terms of his Eastern Settlement the Hasmonaean kingdom was reduced to the Roman provinces of Judaea and Idumaea. Aristobulus was, in fact, deposed, and Hyrcanus was appointed high priest, but no longer king. Josephus, originally Joseph ben Matthias, took part as a general and, later, historian in the Jewish Revolt against the Romans in AD 66 but then changed sides.

2 Accordingly, in the fifteenth year of his reign, Herod rebuilt the temple, and encompassed a piece of land about it with a wall; which land was twice as large as that before enclosed. The expenses he laid out upon it were vastly large also, and the riches about it were unspeakable.

Flavius Josephus (c.37–c.100) *Wars of the Jews* (1867 edn) Bk 1, Ch.21, para.1. Hyrcanus's chief adviser was Antipater, whose son, Herod, was appointed king of Judaea by the Roman senate in 40 BC. Herod I, known as Herod the Great (r.37–4 BC), was a prolific builder, and one of his most outstanding achievements was the rebuilding of the Temple of Jerusalem. Although few remains of this 'Second Temple' (actually the third) have been preserved, an idea of its splendour is provided by his palatial mountaintop fortresses at Masada and Herodium.

3 And Jesus stood before the governor: and the governor asked him, saying, Art thou the King of the Jews? And Jesus said unto him, Thou sayest.

Bible, NT, Matthew 27:11. Herod died in 4 BC. His son, Herod Archelaus, succeeded him as ethnarch of Judaea, Idumaea and Samaria but proved to be entirely unsatisfactory

as a ruler. He was dismissed and exiled by Augustus in AD 6, and Judaea became a province of the third class, administered by 'procurators'. It was under the fifth of these, Pontius Pilate (AD 27–c.36), that Jesus of Nazareth was put to death.

4 The Jews that dwelt in Caesarea had a synagogue near the place, whose owner was a certain Caesarean Greek: the Jews had endeavoured frequently to have purchased the possession of the place, and had offered many times its value for its price; but as the owner overlooked their offers, so did he raise other buildings upon the place, in way of affront to them, and made working-shops of them, and left them but a narrow passage, and such as was very troublesome for them to go along to their synagogue; whereupon the warmer part of the Jewish youth went hastily to the workmen, and forbade them to build there.

Flavius Josephus (c.37–c.100) *Wars of the Jews* (1867 edn) Bk 2, Ch.14, para.4. This trivial dispute between the Greek and Jewish communities living uneasily side by side in Caesarea illustrates the level of tension and turbulence that ultimately led to the First Jewish Revolt. In AD 66 the Roman prefect of Judaea, Gessius Florus, attempted to rob the Temple treasury. The Zealots, a fundamentalist and nationalist group, immediately instigated a full-scale uprising in Jerusalem. They and another group, the Sicarii, managed to take over all of the Roman strongholds in Jerusalem.

5 Miserable men indeed were they! Whose distress forced them to slay their own wives and children with their own hands, as the lightest of those evils that were before them.

Flavius Josephus (c.37–c.100) *Wars of the Jews* (1867 edn) Bk 7, Ch.9, para.1. The First Jewish Revolt, sometimes known as the Great Revolt, was brutally put down by the Romans, initially under Vespasian (see 81:7), who began the siege of Jerusalem. It was Titus, however, who completed the operation by capturing the city in AD 69. The Temple was looted and utterly destroyed, and the population was subjected to the worst excesses of wholesale slaughter and rape. The Zealots who escaped took refuge at Masada and managed to withstand the Roman siege for three years. When the fortress eventually fell in AD 73 the Roman legionaries discovered that the inhabitants, rather than surrendering, had killed their wives and children and then taken their own lives.

Ancient India, c.2500 BC–c. AD 700

BEGINNINGS, c.2500–c.250 BC

1 The modern inheritors of ancient Egypt and Mesopotamia have completely lost touch with the civilizations that once flourished there thousands of years ago; for them the ancient world is little more than a hidden memory with traditions that are now very distant and very alien. India, however, has preserved its link with the past which remains in ever-present memory.
S. Tammita-Delgoda *A Traveller's History of India* (1994) p.1.

2 There was neither non-existence nor existence then; there was neither the realm of space nor the sky which is beyond. What stirred? Where? In whose protection? Was there water, bottomlessly deep?

There was neither death nor immortality then. There was no distinguishing sign of night or day. That one breathed, windless, by its own impulse. Other than that there was nothing beyond.

Darkness was hidden by darkness in the beginning; with no distinguishing sign, all this was water. The life force that was covered with emptiness, that one arose through the power of heat.
Rig Veda (c.1500–c.1000 BC; 1981 trans.) Hymn 10.129. The *Rig Veda* is the earliest surviving piece of Indo-European literature. It was the first of the four Vedas (books of knowledge), which were composed during the Aryan age (c.1500–c.1000 BC). During the Vedic period semi-nomadic, linguistically related tribes from the steppes of southern Russia and central Asia invaded the north of the Indian subcontinent. Hymns from the *Rig Veda* are still revered, and passages are used at wedding and funeral ceremonies. Many of its more than 1,000 hymns deal with propitiating the gods and conducting sacrifices; others deal with the origin of the world and with appropriate behaviour.

3 When they divided the Man, into how many parts did they apportion him? What do they call his mouth, his two arms and thighs and feet? His mouth became the Brahmin (priest); his arms were made into the Kshatriya (warrior) his thighs the Vaishya (common people), and from his feet the Shudras (servants) were born.

The moon was born from his mind; from his eye the sun was born. Indra and Agni came from his mouth, and from his vital breath the Wind was born.
Rig Veda (c.1500–c.1000 BC; 1981 trans.) Hymn 10.90. This is the first mention of the four classes of society, the *varnas*, which eventually crystallized into what are commonly, though somewhat inaccurately, known as castes. Many hymns are addressed to Indra, the god of war, and Agni, the god of fire.

4 Waters, you are the ones that bring us the life force. Help us to find nourishment so that we may look upon great joy.

For our well-being, let the goddesses be an aid to us, the waters be for us to drink. Let them cause well-being and health to flow over us.
Rig Veda c.1500–c.1000 BC; 1981 trans.) Hymn 10.9. Water has much symbolic, as well as practical, importance in India. Her great rivers are still regarded as sacred and as a source of life.

5 From food are born all creatures, which live upon food and after death return to food. Food is the chief of all things. It is therefore said to be medicine for all diseases of the body. Those who worship food as Brahma gain all material objects. From food are born all things which, being born, grow by food. All beings feed upon food, and, when they die, food feeds upon them.
Taittiriya Upanishad (c.600 BC); Swami Prabhavananda and Frederick Manchester (eds) *The Upanishads: Breath of the Eternal* (1983) pp.82–3. Belief in the sacredness and importance of food is still a significant aspect of Hindu life. A person who prepares food should be in a ritually pure state, and food is offered daily to the gods. Brahma is god seen as spirit, formless, all-pervasive.

6 In a short time, the earth will be submerged in water with all its mountains and trees. This boat has been fashioned out of the assemblage of all the gods in order to protect the assemblage of great living souls, O lord of the earth. Those born of sweat, those born of eggs, or of water, and those living creatures which slough their skins – place them all in this boat and save them, for they have no protector. And when your ship is struck by the winds that blow at the end of the age, fasten the ship to this horn of mine, O king, lord of kings, lord of the earth.
Matsya Purana (c.500–c.1500); W.D. O'Flaherty *Hindu Myths: A Sourcebook Translated from the Sanskrit* (1975) p.183. Matsya, the horned fish, is one of the avatars (incarnations) of the god, Vishnu. In this flood story Manu, progenitor of humankind, is told that the ship carrying all living creatures can be saved if Manu fastens it by a rope to Matsya's horn (see 1:4, 16:2 and 51:6).

1 Ecstatic at the birth of a son, noble-minded Nanda invited Brahmins learned in the Vedas. He performed the lustral bath and adorned himself. Afterwards he requested the Brahmins to proceed with the auspicious recitation preceding the ceremony of the birth ritual, followed by adoration of the gods and the spirits of the ancestors. He gifted to the Brahmins two hundred thousand beautifully ornamented and decorated cows and seven hill-high heaps of sesame seed covered with jewels and gold-embroidered robes.

Bhagavata Purana (c.4th–c.6th century; 1997 edn) Bk 10, Canto 5. This passage about the birth of the god Krishna and the delight of his adoptive father, Nanda, indicates some of the many rituals and ceremonies that followed the birth of a child, at least among the high born. The numbers need not be taken literally!

2 The seniority of Brahmins is from sacred knowledge, that of Kshatriyas from valour, that of Vaishyas from wealth in grain (and other goods), but that of Shudras only from age. A man is not venerable because his head is grey; he who, though young, has studied the Veda, the gods consider to be venerable.

Manusmriti (Laws of Manu) (c.200 BC–c. AD 200; 1886 edn) Ch.2. The book is an attempt to codify precisely the rules relating to each social group and to regulate human behaviour. Although actually a rewriting of earlier law codes, the British, whose influence and rule in India spread during the 18th and 19th centuries, looked on it as *the* original, authoritative, law book for Hindus.

3 The King, Beloved of the Gods, of Loving Regard, when he had been anointed twenty years, came in person and worshipped, because the Buddha Sakyamuni was born here.

He had constructed walls inlaid with stone and had erected [this] stone pillar. Because the Lord was born here the village of Lummini was made exempt from taxation and [subject to payment only] a one eighth share of its produce.

King Ashoka, minor pillar edict, c.248 BC; R. Salomon *Indian Epigraphy* (1998) p.264. Ashoka (r.269–232 BC) issued a series of edicts, inscribed several times over on rocks and pillars scattered throughout India. Some still exist. This edict records Ashoka's visit to the Buddha's birthplace, now known as Rummindei, in Nepal.

4 Sakyamuni (Sage of the Sakyas) Siddhartha Gautama, the Buddha (Enlightened One) was born in Kapilavastu [Nepal] around 563 BC … When he was about thirty, Gautama left his sumptuous life of ease and wandered for the next six years in the woods of Kosala [eastern Gangetic plain] and south through the kingdom of Magadha, before attaining the enlightenment that changed his name and bequeathed to the world one of its great religious philosophies.

Stanley Wolpert *A New History of India* (1982 edn) p.49. The Buddha was born the son of a chief of the Sakya tribe. He died c.480 BC.

5 Mahinda gave the following order to [the learned Buddhist] Sumana: repair to Pataliputra [Patna, northeast India] and address thus the righteous King Ashoka. Your ally, great king, has been converted to the faith of Buddha; grant to him the most excellent relics; he is going to erect a stupa in honour of the teacher [Buddha].

Dipavamsa: An Ancient Buddhist Historical Record (4th century; 1879 edn) p.186. This is the earliest chronicle of Sri Lanka. There is a tradition that King Ashoka sent Mahinda, who was either his son or his younger brother, to Sri Lanka to convert the people to Buddhism. The ally named here is Tissa, the king of Sri Lanka. Sumana asks Ashoka for some Buddhist relics to enshrine in a stupa (a monument covering a sacred relic).

WARS AND LAWS OF THE KINGS, c. 1000 BC–c. AD 700

6 [In northern India] several kingdoms came to be established. In the Kuru-Panchala (Delhi–Meerut–Mathura) region the Kurus ruled from Hastinapur where excavations have revealed settlements belonging to the period 1000–700 BC. They fought a fratricidal war with their collaterals, the Pandavas, in 950 BC at Kurukshetra near Delhi; its magnified version formed the theme of the great epic *Mahabharata*, compiled much later, around the 4th century AD.

D.N. Jha *Ancient India in Historical Outline* (1998) p.57. The *Mahabharata* is one of India's two great epics, the other being the *Ramayana*. It contains an immensely long and largely mythological account of the struggles between the five Pandava brothers and their cousins, the Kauravas, culminating in a terrible battle in which all the Kauravas are killed. It is a source of information about life in India after the Vedic age – that is, from c.1000 BC.

7 On this day tempers had so much worsened that the armies found it impossible to respect the conventions of the war. Both sides discarded the time limit [of fighting only between sunrise and sunset] and fought at night with the help of thousands of torches.

Mahabharata (4th century AD; retold by R.K. Narayan 1978) p.170. The Battle of Kurukshetra lasted 18 bitter days. There are hundreds of versions, translations, editions, abridgements, film and television versions of the *Mahabharata*. The abridgement by the Indian novelist R.K. Narayan is a good introduction for Western readers.

1 When you are about to march on your enemies, do the diplomatic means of persuasion, bribery, alienation and punishment come first and are they well applied? Do you fortify your base before you march out, lord of the people, do you attack to win and having won do you spare them? Is your army with four kinds of troops and eight factors well led by your officers to rout the enemy? Do you attack enemies in battle without disrupting the harvesting and sowing in their country, great king?

Mahabharata (4th century AD; 1978 edn) Vol.2, Bk 2, p.42. The four kinds of troops were 'natives, retainers, allies and forest tribes', and the eight factors were 'chariots, elephants, horses, warriors, footmen, servants, spies and principal inhabitants'. The passage indicates some of the strategies and the preparations a strong ruler of the period would make before embarking on war.

2 The ruler should employ as his security staff only such persons as have noble and proven ancestry and are closely related to him and are well trained and loyal. No foreigners, or anonymous persons, or persons with clouded antecedents are to be employed as security staff for the ruler. In a securely guarded chamber, the chief should supervise the ruler's food arrangements. Special precautions are to be taken against contaminated and poisoned food.

Kautilya *Arthashastra* (Book of Statecraft) (c.320 BC); J. McNeill and J.W. Sedlar (eds) *Classical India* (1969) p.20. Kautilya was a minister of Chandragupta Maurya, who ruled Magadha from c.322 BC. His kingdom was bounded by the River Ganges in the north and by the Vindhya outcrop in the south. The *Arthashastra* is a detailed manual dealing with every aspect of the administration of the state, the system of justice, defence and espionage.

3 A king protects his kingdom only when he is himself protected from persons near him and from enemies, first from his wives and sons … He should guard against princes right from their birth. For, princes devour their begetters, being of the same nature as crabs.

Kautilya (c.320 BC; 1988 trans.) Bk 1, Ch.17.1–5. Some have condemned the *Arthashastra* for its Machiavellian approach, but it was in use at a time when intrigue was rife, and if a ruler was to be successful Kautilya believed he had to guard against treachery, even if this meant killing his own children.

4 Ever since the annexation of the Kalingas, His Majesty has zealously protected the Law of Piety, has been devoted to that law, and has proclaimed its precepts. His Majesty feels remorse on account of the conquest of the Kalingas, because, during the subjugation of a previously unconquered country, slaughter, death and taking away captive of the people necessarily occur, whereat His Majesty feels profound sorrow and regret.

King Ashoka, edict 13, c.256 BC; Vincent A. Smith *Asoka: The Buddhist Emperor of India* (1901) p.130. In this famous edict the king expresses his regret for the slaughter and enslavement of the Kalingas during a bloody war. The Kalinga kingdom bordered the Bay of Bengal. The Law of Piety is a translation of *dharma*, an important concept that signifies an amalgam of religion, law, duty and responsibility. People do not have the same *dharma*, which varies according to status and responsibility.

5 Formerly, in the kitchen of His Sacred Majesty, each day many thousands of living creatures were slain to make curries. But now, when this pious edict is being written, only three living creatures are killed daily for curry … Even these three creatures shall not be slaughtered in future.

King Ashoka, edict 1, c.256 BC; Smith (1901) p.115. After the war with the Kalingas, King Ashoka embraced Buddhism and denounced the taking of life, both human and animal.

6 When Porus was taken prisoner, Alexander asked how he wished to be treated. 'Like a king,' answered Porus. When Alexander further asked if he had anything to request, 'Everything,' rejoined Porus, 'is comprised in the words, like a king.' Alexander then not only reinstated Porus in his kingdom with the title of satrap, but added a large province to it.

Plutarch (c.46–c.127) *Lives* (1896 edn) 'Alexander' Ch.60. In 326 BC the army of Alexander III of Macedon moved through modern-day Afghanistan, across the River Jhelum and into Punjab, where the ruler, King Porus, was defeated. Several accounts by classical writers of historical events in India are extant, and because surviving Indian writings of the period tend to be religious or didactic, the writings of foreigners are a useful record of actual events.

7 No one can stop you if you choose to impose Tamil rule over the whole sea-encircled world. Send your message to the northern countries: 'The great king advances toward the north to bring back a Himalayan stone in which the image of god is to be carved.'

Ilango Adigal (about 3rd century) *Shilappadikaram* (The Ankle Bracelet) (1993 edn) Canto 25. This is a long poem about a faithful wife who avenges her husband's wrongful execution. It includes a romanticized version of some historical episodes. The king of Chera (Kerala, southern India), Shenguttuvan, who was the brother of Ilango Adigal, set out c. AD 90 on a victorious expedition to the Himalayas.

1 When Kanishka was reigning the fear of his name spread to the many regions so far even as to the outlying vassals of China to the west of the Yellow River. One of these vassal states being in fear sent a hostage to the court of King Kanishka, the hostage being apparently a son of the ruler of the state. The king treated the hostage with great kindness and consideration, allowing him a separate residence for each of the three seasons [hot season, cool season and monsoon] and providing him with a guard of four kinds of soldiers.

Thomas Watters *On Hsuan Tsang's Travels in India AD 629–645* (1904 edn) Ch.9, Pt 4. This quotation indicates the extent of the Kushana kingdom in the time of Kanishka (r.c.120–160), the greatest ruler of the Kushana dynasty, which originated in central Asia. His capital, Peshawar (northwest Pakistan), was a centre for art and literature. Hsuan Tsang was a Chinese Buddhist pilgrim, who travelled to India to visit Buddhist sites. His book is an important source of information about 7th-century India and the reign of King Harsha.

2 Kanishka Raja [king] ordered these discourses to be engraved upon sheets of red copper. He enclosed them in a stone receptacle and, having sealed them, he raised over it a stupa with the scriptures in the middle.

Hsuan Tsang *Travels in India 629–645 AD*; M. Edwardes *A History of India* (1961) p.67. The discourses were the records of a great Buddhist council, held in Kashmir, in the far north. King Kanishka is said to have converted to Buddhism, and it was during his time that the Buddha was first represented in human form.

3 The king, whose eyes were closing, recovering consciousness as the sound of the prince's ceaseless weeping fell upon his ear, uttered in faint tones these words: 'You should not be thus, my son. Men of your mould are not infirm of heart. Strength of soul is the people's mainstay, and second to it is royal blood. With you, the vanguard of the stout-hearted, the abode of all pre-eminence, what has weakness to do?'

Bana (7th century) *Harsha-charita* (Deeds of Harsha) (1897 edn) Ch.5. On his deathbed the king appoints his younger son, Harsha, to succeed him. Harsha reluctantly inherited the kingdom of Thanesar, north of Delhi, when he was 16 years old. During his long reign (606–646 or 647) he succeeded in extending his empire over much of northern India. Bana was a Brahmin who served at Harsha's court for many years and left an extensive record of the king's reign.

4 On the very day on which the king's death was rumoured, his majesty Grahavarman was by the wicked lord of Malwa [northwest India] cut off from the living along with his noble deeds. Rajyasri also, the princess, has been confined like a brigand's wife, with a pair of iron fetters kissing her feet, and cast into prison at Kanyakubja [Kanauj, northwest India]. There is moreover a report that the villain, deeming the army leaderless, purposes to invade and seize this country as well.

Bana (7th century) (1897 edn) p.173. Rajyasri was Harsha's sister and Grahavarman was her husband. The events described here occurred at the time Harsha's father died, and led Harsha to invade the king of Malwa's territory.

5 Through him the earth does, indeed, possess a true king. Wonderful is his royalty, surpassing the gods. His liberality cannot find range enough in suppliants, nor his knowledge in doctrines to be learned; his poetical skill finds words fail, as his valour lacks opportunities to exercise it; his energy wants scope and his fame sighs for a wider horizon; his kindly nature seeks in vain more hearts to win, his virtues exhaust the powers of number and all the fine arts are too narrow a field for his genius.

Bana (7th century); R. Mookerji *Harsha* (1926) p.189. Bana's eulogistic description was not entirely unfounded. Harsha began his reign with conquest but, like Ashoka, soon eschewed violence. He was a poet and playwright of note, extraordinarily generous, royal and kindly, and he loved pomp.

THE STATE AND SOCIETY, c. 600 BC–c. AD 650

6 On the banks of the River Sarayu, there was a great and prosperous country named Koshala, inhabited by contented people. In it was the City of Ayodhya. The city's thoroughfares extended for sixty miles; its beauty was enhanced by streets admirably planned, the principal highways being sprinkled with water and strewn with flowers ...

That marvellous city where gold abounded and beautiful women wandered about in groups, rich in jewels of every kind, was adorned with luxurious palaces and mansions. The dwellings of the artisans were so constructed that no space was left between them, and the ground on which they stood was perfectly levelled; all were abundantly stocked with rice and the juice of the sugar cane was employed instead of water.

Valmiki *Ramayana* (c.600 BC; 1962 edn) Bk 1, Ch.5. This is the earlier of India's two great epics, the other being the *Mahabharata* (see 26:6). It tells the mythical story of the god-king Rama and his virtuous wife, Sita. The passage quoted is part of a long description of Ayodhya, the capital of the Koshala kingdom in

Uttar Pradesh, northern India, which, even today, is strongly associated with Rama. It is interesting because it shows women in that age as moving about freely and also describes the life of the common people. Valmiki is said to have been the first to write down the epic, but several well-known, later versions exist.

1 Entering into a treaty is peace. Doing injury is war. Remaining indifferent is staying quiet. Augmenting power is marching. Submitting to another is seeking shelter. Resorting to peace with one and war with another is dual policy. These are the six measures of foreign policy.
Kautilya (c.320 BC; 1988 trans.) Bk 7, Ch.1. This and the following quotations are examples of practical advice to a despotic ruler surrounded by small states ruled by competing despots.

2 A state should always observe such a policy as will help it strengthen its defensive fortifications and life-lines of communications, build plantations, construct villages and exploit the mineral and forest wealth of the country, while at the same time preventing fulfilment of similar programmes in the rival state. Whoever estimates that the rate of growth of the state's potential is higher than that of the enemy can afford to ignore such an enemy.
Kautilya (c.320 BC); McNeill and Sedlar (1969) p.33.

3 A state can indulge in armed invasion only where, by invasion, it can reduce the power of an enemy without in any way reducing its own potential, by making suitable arrangements for protection of its own strategic works.
Kautilya (c.320 BC); McNeill and Sedlar (1969) p.35.

4 If a state is weak in treasury or striking power attention should be directed to strengthen both through stabilization of authority. Irrigation projects are a source of agricultural prosperity. Good highways should be constructed to facilitate movements of armed might and merchandise. Mines should be developed, as they supply ammunition. Forests should be conserved, as they supply material for defence, communication and vehicles. Pasture lands are the source of cattle wealth.
Kautilya (c.320 BC); McNeill and Sedlar (1969) p.36.

5 For cutting the shoots of trees in city parks that bear flowers or fruit or yield shade the fine shall be six *pannas* [copper or silver coins], for cutting small branches twelve *pannas*, for cutting stout branches

twenty-four *pannas*, for destroying trunks the lowest fine for violence, for uprooting the tree the middle fine.
Kautilya (c.320 BC; 1988 trans.) Bk 3, Ch.19.

6 Is there anything that is righteous for those for whom the science of Kautilya, merciless in its precepts, rich in cruelty, is an authority; whose teachers are priests habitually hard-hearted with practice of witchcraft; to whom ministers, always inclined to deceive others, are councillors; whose desire is always for the goddess of wealth that has been cast away by thousands of kings; who are devoted to the application of destructive sciences; and to whom brothers, affectionate with natural cordial love, are fit victims to be murdered?
Bana (7th century); Vincent A. Smith *Oxford History of India* (1958) p.107. Bana, who served the merciful King Harsha, shows his hatred of the cynical principles of the *Arthashastra*.

7 The envoys from Taprobane [Sri Lanka] told us that their people had far more wealth than we had, but that we made greater use of ours. No one had a slave, no one slept beyond daybreak or took a siesta; their buildings were of moderate height; the price of corn never increased; there were no law courts or lawsuits; they worshipped Hercules; the king was elected by the people ... Thirty advisers were assigned to the king by the people and no one could be condemned to death except by a majority vote of these. There was the right of appeal to the people and a jury of seventy was appointed; if they acquitted the accused, the thirty lost their reputation and were held in the deepest disgrace.
Pliny the Elder *Natural History* (c. AD 77; 1991 edn) Bk 5.89–90.

8 To the south of this, the country is called the Middle Kingdom [more or less the land between the Rivers Ganges and Jamuna in northern India]. It has a temperate climate, without frost or snow; and people are prosperous and happy, without registration or official restrictions. Only those who till the king's land have to pay so much on the profit they make. Those who want to go away, may go; those who want to stop, may stop. The king in this administration uses no corporal punishments [*sic*]; criminals are merely fined according to the gravity of their offences.
Fa-Hsien *Travels (399–414 AD), or Record of the Buddhistic Kingdoms* (1923 edn) pp.20–21. Fa-Hsien was the first Chinese Buddhist monk to travel to India and Sri Lanka and to leave an extensive record of his travels.

1 The country of Deccan [a plateau running through much of the southern peninsular] is mountainous and its roads difficult for travellers; even those who know the way, if they wish to travel, should send a present of money to the king who will thereupon depute men to escort them and pass them on from one stage to another, showing them the short cuts.
Fa-Hsien (1923 edn) p.63.

2 Universities flourished [in Hsuan Tsang's time, c.650] and one of the most interesting accounts of [his] travels is a description of the famous seat of learning at Nalanda in Bihar. Discipline was strict ... The curriculum included grammar, mechanics, medicine, logic and metaphysics. Medicine was widely studied and [according to Hsuan Tsang] included 'holding the lancet, in cutting, marking and piercing with it, in extracting darts, in cleaning wounds, in causing them to dry up, the application of ointments and in the administration of emetics, purges and oily enemas'. Astronomy was far advanced and the diameter of the world had been calculated.
M. Edwardes (1961) pp.83–4. Nalanda, a famous university in Bihar, in northeast India, attracted students from many parts of Asia. It derived its wealth from the revenue of 200 villages, granted by the king, and remained in existence until 1199.

TRADE AND COMMERCE

3 Indus civilization, now represented by no fewer than seventy unearthed sites, extended over almost half a million square miles of the Punjab and Sind, from the borderlands of Baluchistan to the desert wastes of Rajasthan, from the Himalayan foothills to the tip of Gujarat ... Thanks to Indus seals found in the Sumerian dig at Ur in 1932, we know that merchants from Harappa and Mohenjo-daro were trading with their Sumerian counterparts between 2300 and 2000 BC. The huge granaries beside the river at Harappa seem to indicate that Indus merchants exported their surplus grain to Sumeria, and possibly elsewhere.
Stanley Wolpert (1982 edn) p.19. The Indus valley civilization lasted from c.2500 to c.1500 BC. The script used on the seals has not yet been deciphered, but archaeological remains have taught us a good deal about the period.

4 By this time (c.2000 BC), the Indus people had begun to spin cotton into yarn and weave it into cloth, a dyed fragment of which has been found at Mohenjo-daro. The use of cotton for clothing is one of India's major gifts to world civilization, and the spinning and weaving of cotton was to remain India's premier industry, with expanding production for both the home market and export.
Stanley Wolpert (1982 edn) p.19.

5 In the same region eastward is a city called Ozene [Ujjain, central India], formerly the capital wherein the king resided. From it there is brought down to Barygaza [Bharuch, northwest India] every commodity for the supply of the country and for export to our own markets – onyx-stones, porcelain, fine muslins, mallow-coloured muslins, and no small quantity of ordinary cottons ... In those days moreover, there were imported, as presents to the king, costly silver vases, instruments of music, handsome young women for concubinage, superior wine, apparel, plain but costly, and the choicest unguents.
Anon., *Periplus of the Erythraean Sea* (c. AD 70; 1879 edn) para.48. The Greek and Roman geographers called the Indian Ocean, including the Red Sea and Persian Gulf, the Erythraean Sea. The *Periplus*, which deals with trade and commerce in the area, was probably written by an Egyptian Greek who had made the voyage between the Red Sea and India. It is recognized as a reliable description of the land, ports and maritime commerce between India and lands of the west.

6 From Comari [Kanyakumari, at the southern tip of India] towards the south the country extends as far as Colchoi [Kolkai, on the southwestern coast], where the fishing for pearls is carried on. Condemned criminals are employed in this service. King Pandion [the Pandya king] is the owner of the fishery.
Anon., *Periplus of the Erythraean Sea* (c. AD 70; 1879 edn) para.59. An interesting sidelight into the Pandyan kingdom of the far south.

7 In return for her exports India wanted little but gold ... The balance of trade was very unfavourable to the West, and resulted in a serious drain of gold from the Roman Empire. This was recognized by Pliny, who, inveighing against the degenerate habits of his day, computed the annual drain to the East as 100 million sesterces [Roman silver coins], 'so dearly do we pay for our luxury and our women'. The drain of gold to the East was an important cause of the financial difficulties in the Roman Empire from the reign of Nero onwards.
A.L. Basham *The Wonder that was India* (1963 edn) p.229. Pliny's comment is in his *Natural History* (c. AD 77) Bk 12.18.

1 We ought not, therefore, to distrust what we are told [by Megasthenes, Greek ambassador to India] regarding the Indus and the Ganges, that they are beyond comparison greater than the Ister [Danube] and the Nile ... Megasthenes has given the names even of other rivers which beyond both the Ganges and the Indus pour their waters into the Eastern Ocean and to the outer basin of the Southern Ocean, so that he asserts that there are eight-and-fifty Indian rivers which are all of them navigable.

Arrian (2nd century AD) *Indica* (1877 edn) Chs 4–5. Arrian, the Greek historian and biographer of Alexander of Macedon (see 61:5), also wrote this book about India.

2 In the broad street of the goldsmiths tiny flags marked the kind of gold sold in each shop ... In the street of the cloth merchants Kovalan made his way through piles of bales, each containing a hundred lengths, woven of cotton, hair or silk. There was a street for grain merchants ... Bags of grain and pepper were to be found there in all seasons. Kovalan also visited the four residential quarters of the four castes. He saw crossings of three or four roads, bazaars, squares, avenues lined with trees, and many smaller streets and lanes.

Ilango Adigal (about 3rd century AD) (1993 edn) Canto 14. This passage illustrates the wealth of the south Indian city of Madurai.

3   (Here are brought)
swift, prancing steeds by sea in ships,
bales of black pepper in carts,
gems and gold born in the Himalayas,
sandal and *akil* wood born in the Western hills,
the pearls of the southern seas
and coral from the eastern ocean,
the yield of Ganges and the crops from Kaviri,
foodstuffs from Ceylon, Burmese ware
and other rare and rich imports.

Katiyalur Uruttirankannanaar *Pattinappalai* (The City and Separation) (*c.*190–*c.*200) lines 185–190; K.V. Zvelebil *Tamil Literature* (1974) p.22. The lines show the extent of trade from Puhar (Kaverippattinam, southeast India) at the time of the greatest Chola king, Karikala (*c.* AD 100). This poem is said to have remained popular at the Chola court for a thousand years.

PEOPLE AND FAMILIES

4 Hitherto it has commonly been supposed that the pre-Aryan peoples of India were on an altogether lower plane of civilization than their Aryan conquerors ... a race so servile and degraded, that they were commonly known as *Dasas* or slaves. Never for a moment was it imagined that five thousand years ago, before ever the Aryans were heard of, the Punjab and Sind, if not other parts of India as well, were enjoying an advanced and singularly uniform civilization of their own, closely akin but in some respects even superior to that of contemporary Mesopotamia and Egypt. Yet this is what the discoveries at Harappa and Mohenjo-daro have now placed beyond question.

John Marshall *Mohenjo Daro and the Indus Civilisation* (1931) Vol.1, Preface. Marshall was responsible for the earliest excavations at Harappa and Mohenjo-daro (southwest Pakistan), when he was in charge of the Archaeological Survey of India in the 1920s. The civilization of the area was already in decline when, *c.*1500 BC, the Aryans spread out to the Indus valley, Afghanistan and Punjab.

5 The man with food who hardens his heart against the poor man who comes to him suffering and searching for nourishment – though in the past he had made use of him – he surely finds no one with sympathy.

The man who is truly generous gives to the beggar who approaches him in search of food. He puts himself at the service of the man who calls to him from the road, and makes him a friend for times to come.

Rig Veda (*c.*1500–*c.*1000 BC; 1981 trans.) Hymn 10.117. An example of Aryan teaching of right behaviour.

6 The avenger has one day's joy; the one who forgives knows joy to the end of the world.

Tiruvalluvar (4th century AD) *Tirukkural* (The Holy Voice) (1969 edn) verse 156. A collection of moral aphorisms expressed in Tamil verse.

7 Into your womb let a foetus come, a male one, like an arrow to a quiver; let a hero be born to you, a ten-months' son. Give birth to a male, a son; then let another male be born. May you be the mother of sons.

Atharva Veda (*c.*900–600 BC) Bk 3, Hymn 23. The last of the four vedas is chiefly a collection of spells and prayers for success in daily life. The importance of bearing a son is stressed in many early writings.

8 The father protects her in infancy; the husband in youth; and sons in old age; a woman does not deserve independence.

Manusmriti (Laws of Manu) (*c.*200 BC–*c.* AD 200; 1886 edn) Ch.9.3. This widely quoted verse has been used to modern times to ensure women's dependence on men. Jha (1998) maintains that this 'has remained the most influential instrument of brahminical [priestly caste] ideology in Indian society' (p.146).

1 A woman well set free! How free I am,
How wonderfully free, from kitchen drudgery.
Free from the harsh grip of hunger,
And from empty cooking pots,
Free too of that unscrupulous man,
The weaver of sunshades.
Calm now, and serene I am,
All lust and hatred purged.
To the shadow of the spreading trees I go
And contemplate my happiness.

Sumangamata *A Woman Well Set Free* (6th century BC);
S. Tharu and K. Lalita *Women Writing in India* Vol.1 (1991)
p.69. This poem from the *Therigata* (Songs of the [Buddhist]
Nuns) shows that not all women longed for marriage, as might
be supposed from other writings.

2 Far sweeter than nectar is the rice in which one's
tiny children have dabbled their hands.

Tiruvalluvar (4th century AD) (1969 edn) verse 64. Many
writers describe the affection and pampering given to children. This easy-going attitude would end at an early age as
children of the wealthy were disciplined by their tutors and
as children of the poor began work.

3 Lucky are fathers whose laps give refuge to the
muddy limbs of adoring little sons, when childish
smiles show budding teeth and jumbled sounds
make charming words.

Kalidasa *Shakuntala* (c. AD 400; 1999 edn) Act 7. In this play
Kalidasa, the greatest Sanskrit poet and playwright, shows
how a king indulges a young child.

4 To bring forth and rear a son is my duty.
To make him noble is the father's.
To make spears for him is the blacksmith's.
To show him good ways is the king's.
And to bear
a bright sword and do battle,
to butcher enemy elephants,
and come back:
that is the young man's duty.

Ponmutiyar *Purananuru* (c. AD 150) poem no.312;
A.K. Ramanujan *Poems of Love and War from ... Classical
Tamil* (1985) p.185. In southern India the Sangam period
(c.100 BC–c. AD 250) saw a great flowering of literature. This
short poem comes from an anthology that includes several by
women and shows them speaking proudly of a son's valour –
even his death – on the battlefield.

5 See how bloodless be our bodies, pierced with how
many wounds, and gashed with how many scars!
Our weapons are now blunt, our armour quite worn
out. We have been driven to assume the Persian garb

since that of our own country cannot be brought up
to supply us. We have degenerated so far as to adopt
a foreign costume. Among how many of us is there
to be found a single coat of mail? Which of us has a
horse? ... We have conquered all the world but are
ourselves destitute of all things.

Quintus Curtius (1st century AD) *History of Alexander* (1896
edn) Ch.3. A Roman historian describes how, after initial
victories in his invasion of India in 326 BC, Alexander the
Great was forced to retreat when his men threatened to
mutiny if he did not send them home. Alexander liked
to adopt the dress of the conquered, but his men saw this
as degenerate (see 64:7).

6 Megasthenes says that those [Indians] who were in
the camp of Sandrakottos [Chandragupta Maurya],
wherein lay 400,000 men, found that the thefts
reported on any one day did not exceed the value of
200 drachmae [Greek coins], and this among a people
who have no written laws, but are ignorant of
writing, and must therefore in all the business of life
trust to memory.

Strabo (c.60 BC–c. AD 24) *Geography* (1901 edn) Bk 15.53.
Megasthenes became the Greek ambassador at Pataliputra
(Patna) c.302 BC. Although most of his writings have been
lost, fragments and quotations in other writings survive,
as here in the pre-eminent Greek geographer. Chandragupta
Maurya founded the great Mauryan dynasty.

7 The pilgrim [Hsuan Tsang] ... was on his way
back to China, and had gone to the great monastery
of Nalanda in Maghada [Bihar, northeast India].
Here he wished to remain for some time continuing
his studies in Buddhist philosophy which he had
begun there some years before. But Bhaskaravarma,
styled Kumara, the king of Kamarupa (Assam), had
heard of him and longed to see him. So he sent messengers to Nalanda to invite and urge the pilgrim to
pay him a visit ... The pilgrim at length yielded,
travelled to that country and was received by the
king with great honour.

Thomas Watters (1904 edn) p.348.

8 With respect to the ordinary people, although they
are naturally light-minded, yet they are upright and
honourable. In money matters they are without craft
and in administering justice they are considerate. They
dread the retribution of another state of existence and
make light of the things of the present world ... With
respect to criminals and rebels, these are few in number
and only occasionally troublesome.

Hsuan Tsang (c. AD 650); Edwardes (1961) p.82.

Archaic China, c.2000 BC–AD 220

BEFORE THE EMPIRE

1   From time's first beginning
    Who can tell us the story?
    Skies and earth still unformed –
    How can they be studied?

    The dark and the light were confused in
       shadow,
    Who can pierce their nature?
    And all things to be – disembodied potential,
    By what means can one know them?

    That day became day and night became night-
       time,
    How did this happen?
    The Bright Force and Dark Force in
       interaction,
    Whence was their source? What their
       transformations?

    The spheres of Heaven, their nine-fold storeys,
    Who planned and who built them?
    Whose this great work?
    Who first gave it being?

Anon. 'Questions of Heaven' (?4th century BC), the enigmatic
opening lines (reordered here following Su Xuelin's controversial
edn); Mark Elvin *Another History* (1996) p.261. The ancient
Chinese were little interested in the question to which other
civilizations responded with a creation myth, and this was
probably as near as they came (compare 1:1 and 7:1).

2   Tian to humankind gave birth,
    Substance bestowed on them, and rules.
    Folk to moral norms hold firm
    For love of that most beauteous virtue.

Anon. *Songs* (late 2nd and early 1st millennium); Elvin (1996)
p.265. The collection of anthems and poems in which these
lines are included became one of the two oldest of the
scriptures of Confucianism. In later times the term 'Tian' more
often meant 'Heaven' or even 'day'. In archaic China, however,
it was a supreme, though not unique, deity with strong human
characteristics. Tian could think, create, decree, act, feel
emotion and send down rewards and punishments. At the
start of the Zhou (Chou) dynasty (just before 1000 BC) Tian was
fused with the concept of Shang Di, the 'Ultimate Ancestor' or
'Lord on High'. Although lacking the transcendence and unique-
ness of the God of the Judaic tradition, Tian thus came close in
many ways to its Western counterpart.

3   Confucius said of the head of the Ji family when he
had eight teams of dancers performing in his courtyard, 'If this man can be endured, who cannot be
endured!'

Confucius *The Analects of Confucius* (late 6th–early 5th century
BC; 1938 trans.) Bk 3.1. The Ji were one of the Three Families
who had usurped most of the powers of the Duke of Lu, ruler
of the small state where Confucius was born and taught. Why
should *eight* teams of dancers have mattered so much to China's
most celebrated sage? In a sense it was the very essence of
Confucius's thinking that lay at the root of his anger in this
instance. The proper functioning of the universe depended on
the perfect interaction of a triad: Heaven (a concept that included
the rotation of the sun and moon and stars and the regularity
and predictability of the weather, as well as being a numinous
force), Earth (the source of the seasonal flourishing and fading
of plants and the comings and goings of animals) and Man.
Human behaviour had to be perfect in its ritual appropriate-
ness, or the regularities of Heaven and Earth became disrupted,
both as symptoms of a human malfunction and as its
punishment. The system was like clockwork in that even the
slightest error could throw out the motions of a whole train
of wheels. Eight was the number of teams of dancers
appropriate to the ducal house (or possibly to the emperor)
but not to an upstart. Hence the disruption was potentially
catastrophic. Ritual was the pre-scribed behaviour and attitudes
not only for what we would think of as ceremonies but also,
ultimately, for every part of life. It was the precondition for
political harmony and economic well-being. Original
Confucianism was a doctrine of ritual equally significant for
the cosmos and daily life.

4   1. Eyes do not see.
    2. An orphan colt has never had a mother.
    3. If a rod one foot in length is cut short every day
by one half of its length, it will still have something
left even after ten thousand generations have passed.
    4. The egg has feathers.
    5. Things die as they are born.
    6. The shadow of a flying bird has never moved.
    7. That which has no thickness nevertheless
covers a thousand square miles.
    8. Killing robbers is not killing people.
    9. A white horse is not a horse.

Typical paradoxes discussed by early Chinese logicians (5th–
3rd centuries BC); Elvin (1996) p.279 (based on A. Graham
Later Mohist Logic (1978) pp.43, 58 and Hu Shih *The Development of the Logical Method in Ancient China* (1922) pp.11, 118–
19). China had a powerful and promising start to logic, above
all in the hands of the Mo-ist school (the followers of Mozi,
who lived ?470–?391 BC). It anticipated aspects of Boolean
logic in arguing that elements can only be true or false, but it

died away during the early imperial age. It must have seemed irrelevant at best amid the grim practical problems of the Warring States (403–221 BC). It was replaced later by a thin line of Buddhist logic that was more imported than native. Tentative explanations (ours, not theirs) follow: (1) The mind does. (2) When the colt had a mother it was not an orphan. (3) By definition, there will always be a half left to cut in half again. (4) In potentiality. (5) Through their transformation from one state to another. The caterpillar perishes to become the chrysalis, and the chrysalis to become the butter-fly. (6) Each successive shadow is a different one, appearing in a sequence. (7) The plane. (8) 'Executing' is not 'murdering'. 'Felons' are not 'people' (that is 'human'). (9) Being a member of a class ('horses') does not prove identity with another member. Some true statements about 'horses' (such as 'Some horses are black') are not true about 'white horses'. These may seem little more than sophisticated entertainments, the last perhaps excepted, but the virtual disappearance of the once-impressive early tradition of logical analysis was one of the underlying differences between Chinese styles of thinking and those in western Europe where – though for long perilously and imperfectly – Greek geometry survived.

1 My Master, oh, my Master! You chop all things to pieces and are not to be accounted moral. You fertilize generation after generation, but are not to be thought of as showing a sensitive concern for others. You come from before the remotest past but are not to be reckoned old. You overarch the heavens and carry the earth on your back, you sculpt the multitude of forms, yet you are not to be regarded as ingenious – It is here that I roam.

Zhuangzi (3rd century BC); Elvin (1996) p.283. China's most extraordinary philosopher and nature mystic is addressing 'the underlying potential that makes the universe work the way it does'. This is the Dao (Way). As far as Zhuangzi was concerned, everything that existed was formed from the same energy-vitality and was constantly being transformed from one pattern or 'thing' into another. All individuals, all good and bad, all truth and falsehood, were equally contingent when seen from the point of view of this whole. He was a brilliant logician, who used logic to undermine any faith in logic. He was also a gifted user of language, whose aim was to lead his listeners away from words and thinking into *action* that was perfectly attuned to its continuously changing environment, a state of being he compared to that of a master craftsman interacting with his materials. Zhuangzi is normally labelled a Daoist but is best thought of as *sui generis*.

2 When the age of decadence arrived, people cut rocks from the mountains, hacking out metals and jades. They extracted the pearls from oysters, and smelted copper and iron ores. After this the multitude of living things multiplied no longer.

They slit open the wombs of wild animals, and butchered their young, after which the unicorn roamed about no more.

They extracted fire with rotating drills, and structured tree trunks into platforms. They hunted by setting the forests ablaze, and fished by draining dry the pools.

People manured the fields and planted cereals. They excavated the ground and drank from wells. They dredged the streams and turned them to advantage. They built walls behind which they could be secure. They seized wild animals and made them into domesticated livestock.

They distinguished between noble status and servile, and differentiated between the virtuous and the unworthy by means of praise and censure, bestowing rewards and inflicting punishments. Following this, offensive weapons and defensive armour abounded, and there were divisive conflicts. The destruction of the people, and their affliction by death at an early age arose from this.

Huainanzi (Book of the Master from South of the Huai River) (late 2nd century BC; 1978 edn) pp.257–61. This was a collective compilation made by the savants attending the elder brother of the founder of the Han dynasty, whose local court was on the south bank of the River Huai, which flows midway between the Yellow River and the Yangzi. Seen from their perspective, economic development and civilization had been an irreversible disaster for mankind. The quest of early Daoism that held to this view was to reverse the catastrophe of progress through deepening spiritual awareness and so restore the lost rapport between human beings and nature. When this happened it was thought that magically auspicious animals, such as the unicorn, would manifest themselves to the universe again. The other details, such as the revolutions that created farming and the working of metals, the invention of stratified societies and cities and the advent of war, are remarkably penetrating.

3 If it happens that the forests of the mountains become exhausted and that only scattered remnants remain of the woods of the piedmont, or that they disappear, and that the thickets and marshes come to the last days of their existence, then the forces of the people will be weakened, the farmlands where cereals and hemp are grown will become uncultivated, and they will lack resources. The superior man should be concerned about this. How could it ever delight him?

Duke Mu of Shan, 524 BC; Mark Elvin 'Three Thousand Years of Unsustainable Growth' in *East Asian History* 6 (Dec. 1993) p.17. What is astonishing about this expression of apprehension over deforestation and the fate of the natural environment is its date. Even at this era there were elements of an environmental crisis in northwest China, the homeland of much of classical Chinese civilization.

1 The way of war is the way of deceit. Thus, if one has a certain capacity, one makes it appear as if one does not. If one has the use of something, one makes it seem to the contrary. If one is nearby, one makes it appear as if one is far away; and if one is far away, as if one is near. One uses the semblance of advantage to lure one's enemy on. One feigns disorder so as to draw him in. One makes a show of solidity to cause him to take precautions, and a display of strength to be able to escape from him. One puts on anger to make him become flustered, a pretence of inferiority to make him overweening, an appearance of laxness in order to incite him to exertions, and a charade of intimacy when one intends to relegate him to one side. One attacks him where he is unprepared. One sallies forth when he is least expecting it. Such are the victories won by experts in warfare, but they cannot be prescribed in advance.

Sun Wu *Sunzi bingfa* (Master Sun's Art of War) (c.345 BC; c.1983 trans.) Ch.1. The half millennium before the unification of the Chinese empire late in the 3rd century BC was one of almost unremitting war. The search for the secrets of success produced several famous military theorists of whom Sun Wu (Sun Tzu), at least nominally the author of the above, was the best known. His main characteristics were practicality (including an acute sense of the high economic cost of war), amorality and an insistence that conflict was, in the last analysis, psychological. The ultimate target was the enemy's mind.

2 The supreme warrior attacks his enemy's strategy, the next best attacks his alliances. The third-best attacks his armed forces, while the most inept attacks his walled cities.

If one knows one's foe and knows oneself, in a hundred battles one is never in danger.

A hundred triumphs in a hundred battles is not the best result of all. The best result of all is to subdue others' armies without fighting.

Sun Wu (c.345 BC; c.1983 trans.) Aphorisms.

3 The battles of the victorious are like the release of water into a valley from a thousand fathoms' height – a matter of position.

Sun Wu (c.345 BC; c.1983 trans.).

4 The positions taken by soldiers should resemble water. Just as the position taken by water avoids the heights and races towards the depths, so the positions taken by soldiers should avoid the foe wherever he is solid and strike wherever he is empty. Water adapts itself to the terrain and so cuts out its

pattern of flow. So should soldiers adapt themselves to the foe, and cut out their pattern of victory.

Sun Wu (c.345 BC; c.1983 trans.).

5 A state that uses good people to govern the wicked will always suffer from disorder until it is destroyed. A state that uses the wicked to govern the good will always enjoy order, and so become strong.

The Book of the Lord of Shang (?early 3rd century BC); Elvin (1996) p.293. Attrib. to Yang of Shang, or Lord of Shang, original name of Gongsun Yang, prime minister of the state of Qin in west-central China, in the 4th century BC. These uncompromising words spell out the creed of the pre-imperial School of Laws (or School of Methods). The welfare of the state and of society as a whole requires values and standards that are diametrically opposed to those customarily regarded as admirable in individuals.

6 What the present age calls 'morality' is instituting what the people like and doing away with what they hate. But if you institute what the people delight in, they will in fact suffer from what they hate. On the other hand, if you institute what they hate, the people will be happy in what they enjoy.

The Book of the Lord of Shang (?early 3rd century BC). Yang did much to build up the economic and military power of Qin. He is said to have believed in the exact and unwavering imposition of rewards for behaving as commanded, and punishments for disobedience, or even for performing too well. In other words, treating people like laboratory rats. This strand of thought was to build up the economic and military power of Qin (221–206 BC) that grew from the state, and has had an influence that has continued to the present day.

THE EARLY CHINESE EMPIRE, 221 BC–AD 220

7   The state established by the Emperor
Is, since all ages past, the foremost.
Descendant of a line of many kings,
He has rooted out rebellion and disorder
With authority effective to the world's four
    bounds,
And exact, undeviating, military justice.

Having climbed up to Mount Yi's summit,
His retinue of officials following his steps,
All think on things far-off now, once long-
    lasting.

They recall the epoch of confused disorder,
The land divided, separate states established

That caused the fissures of strife to open wide,
When battles and assaults arose each day,
And blood flowed forth upon the plains
As since Antiquity it had.

For generations past all count
Down to the time of the Five Emperors
None could forbid it. None could make it stop.

Till now. Till this Our Emperor
Has made the world one family
And weapons of warfare are lifted up no
    longer.

Inscription, after 221 BC; C. Blunden and M. Elvin *Cultural Atlas
of China* (1998 edn) pp.80–81. King Zheng, posthumously
called the first emperor, had these words inscribed on Mount
Yi (probably southern Shandong province) not long after he
had unified the Chinese cultural world following almost 30
years of steady conquest and centuries of interstate warfare.
They evoke an enduring theme that has continued throughout
the rest of Chinese political history: the fear of disorder and
a willingness to endure almost anything to avoid it.

I He makes the rules and measures fair and just.
    He is the regulator of all living beings
    And thus illuminates the affairs of men.
    Father and son he brings together in concord.
    His Sage's wisdom, altruism, and justice

Make clear and bright the principles of the
    Way.

Farming he honours, and puts an end to
    commerce.
It is the black-haired masses whom he enriches.

Vessels and tools have identical proportions,
Documents are written in a single script.
Wherever sun and moon shine down,
Wherever boats and carts proceed,
Everyone lives out his allotted span,
No one there is who attains not his desires.

Inscription, after 221 BC; Blunden and Elvin (1998 edn) p.81.
Another of the first emperor's inscriptions, this time on
Mount Langya (on the northeastern coast), painted a portrait
of the ideal sovereign. The 'black haired masses' was a common
term at this time for the Chinese. The use of the word 'Way'
here should not be taken as indicating that the first emperor
was what we think of as a Daoist. Other inscriptions mention
his deciding on the proper names for things and determining
'the form of the land' by building water-control systems and
removing 'dangerous defiles'. He also had most books burned,
except those dealing with what he regarded as practical
matters, and buried Confucian scholars alive, lest their carping
moralizing diminish his authority. This conception of what the
supreme ruler should be like – a ruthless, sage-like bestower
of unity and uniformity – and a standardized physical and
moral well-being has had a powerful effect on the Chinese
political imagination down to the time of Mao Zedong.

Minoans and Mycenaeans, c.2000–c.1000 BC

1 And Zeus the father made a race of bronze,
　　Sprung from the ash tree, worse than the silver
　　　　race,
　　But strange and full of power. And they loved
　　The groans and violence of war; they ate
　　No bread; but their hearts were flinty-hard;
　　　　they were
　　Terrible men; their strength was great, their
　　　　arms
　　And shoulders and their limbs invincible.
　　Their weapons were of bronze, their houses
　　　　bronze;
　　Their tools were bronze: black iron was not known.

Hesiod (*fl.c.*700 BC) *Works and Days* (1973 trans.) lines 143–51. Hesiod does not literally depict the Bronze Age of archaeology but reflects the relative value of metals and reveals that from time to time people came across prehistoric artefacts and observed that tools and weapons were made of bronze. The poet came from Boeotia in central Greece and composed early in the period of new literacy, although it is not known whether he himself wrote down his poems.

2 Minos, according to tradition, was the first person to organize a navy. He controlled the greater part of what is now called the Hellenic Sea; he ruled over the Cyclades, in most of which he founded the first colonies, putting his sons in as governors.

Thucydides *The Peloponnesian War* (c.431–c.404 BC; 1954 trans.) Bk 1.4. This is thought to refer to the peak of Minoan civilization in the second palace period (c.1600–1420 BC) during the Late Bronze Age, although the description of an organized navy exercising centralized control would now be regarded as anachronistic. Minos was the mythical Bronze Age king of Knossos in Crete, after whom the Minoan civilization was named by Arthur Evans, who began systematic excavation there in 1900. Minoan settlements and local settlements with strong Minoan influence have been excavated on various Greek islands.

3　　Out in the dark blue sea there lies a land called
　　　　Crete, a rich and lovely land,
　　washed by the waves on every side, densely
　　　　peopled and boasting ninety cities.
　　Each of the several races of the isle has its own
　　　　language …
　　One of the ninety towns is a great city called
　　　　Knossos,
　　and there, for nine years, King Minos ruled
　　and enjoyed the friendship of almighty Zeus.

Homer (?8th or 7th century BC) *Odyssey* (1946 trans.) Bk 19, lines 172–9. Homer was a poet and part of a long tradition of orally transmitted poetry. He was not an historian, and any 'historical' information embedded in the poems must be treated with great caution. Some details, however, do appear to be confirmed by archaeology. The Minoan civilization is named after King Minos, known in legend as king of Knossos and, after his death, as a judge in the underworld.

4 And the famous lame god [Hephaestus, god of fire, volcanoes, bronze working] elaborated a dancing-floor on it, like the dancing-floor which once Daedalus built in the broad space of Knossos for lovely-haired Ariadne. On it there were dancing young men and girls whose marriage would win many oxen, holding each other's hands at the wrist … At times they would run round very lightly on their skilful feet … and then they would form lines and run to meet each other. A large crowd stood around enjoying the sight of the lovely dance: and two acrobats among the performers led their dancing, whirling and tumbling at the centre.

Homer (?8th or 7th century BC) *Iliad* (1987 trans.) Bk 18, lines 592–606. Describing the shield of Achilles. The atmosphere seems a convincing reflection of the civilization discernible from the archaeology. Crowds watching a display are depicted on frescoes, and a dancing floor exactly as described was excavated in the town area at Knossos in 1978–9. The *Iliad*, the earliest European epic, recounts an episode in the last year of the Trojan War, the Wrath of Achilles, but it is not possible to establish with any certainty the events, participants or even the fact of the Trojan War. It belongs to the world of poetry and legend.

5 Here is depicted the cruel love of the bull, Pasiphae craftily mated, and the mongrel breed of the Minotaur, half-bull, half-man, record of monstrous love; there the house of toil, a maze inextricable.

Virgil *Aeneid* (c.19 BC; 1916 trans.) Bk 6, lines 2–27. Minos' name is found in the word Minotaur, the story of which seems to show some awareness of the elaborate, maze-like palace at Knossos and the scenes of bull-leaping depicted on the walls and in other art forms. With the *Aeneid* Virgil created an epic for the Romans, linking them to the Trojans and the Homeric world. In the *Iliad* Bk 20 Aeneas is said to be fated to survive and become king of the Trojans elsewhere.

6 Daedalus, an architect famous for his skill, constructed the maze, confusing the usual marks of direction, and leading the eye of the beholder astray by devious paths winding in different directions …

There Minos imprisoned the monster, half-bull, half-man and twice feasted him on Athenian blood … Thanks to the help of the princess Ariadne, Theseus re-wound the thread he had laid, retraced his steps, and found the elusive gateway as none of his predecessors had managed to do. Immediately he set sail for Dia, carrying with him the daughter of Minos; but on the shore of that island he cruelly abandoned his companion.

Ovid *Metamorphoses* (1–8 AD; 1955 trans.) Bk 8, lines 159–76. One of many later versions of the story of Theseus and the labyrinth in which the Minotaur was supposedly kept. A depiction of a labyrinth has been found on a fresco at Knossos, and the labyrinth became the standard symbol on later coins of Knossos. Many myths and legends in Western art and literature derive from the versions in the works of Ovid.

I Thence Theseus retraced his way, unharmed and with much glory, guiding his devious footsteps by the fine thread, lest as he came forth from the mazy windings of the labyrinth the inextricable mystification of the building should bewilder him.

Catullus (c.84–c.54 BC) *Poems* (1913 trans.) 64, lines 112–15. The legend was part of the cultural heritage that the Romans borrowed from the Greeks, but it may have had a particular appeal after Crete was linked to Cyrenaica as a Roman province from 67 BC. It would be interesting to know how much of the Minoan palace was visible. An extensive Roman city grew up on the site of classical Knossos, but the area of the palace itself continued to be avoided. The only known post-Minoan structure on the site of the palace was a sanctuary to the goddess Rhea, mother of Zeus, the foundations of which could still be seen in the 1st century BC, according to Diodorus Siculus (*Library of History* Bk 5.66), in the cypress grove consecrated to her from ancient times.

2 In the 13th year of Nero's reign [AD 66] an earthquake struck at Knossos and laid open the tomb of Dictys in such a way that people as they passed could see a little box … When they opened it they found the linden tablets inscribed with characters unknown to them.

The Chronicles of Dictys of Crete and Dares the Phrygian (?3rd or 4th century; 1966 trans.) Preface. This work, used as a source for the Trojan War by medieval writers, consisted of the supposed diaries of Dictys, companion of the Cretan Idomeneus at Troy, and Dares, priest of Hephaestus, god of fire, at Troy, and was purportedly translated into Latin prose by Lucius Septimius (?4th century). Linear B tablets of Late Bronze Age date were presumably discovered as a result of the earthquake and were taken to the Emperor Nero, who demanded that his Phoenician philologists decipher the writing. Anxious to please the emperor, or afraid to admit their ignorance, the scholars produced a Greek 'translation' of an eyewitness account of the Trojan War.

3 Minos, the king of the Cretans, who was at that time the master of the seas, when he learned that Daedalus had fled to Sicily, decided to make a campaign against that island … He disembarked his troops and sending messengers to King Cocalus he demanded Daedalus of him for punishment. But Cocalus invited Minos to a conference and after promising to meet all his demands he brought him to his home as his guest. And when Minos was bathing Cocalus kept him too long in the hot water and thus slew him … Thereupon the comrades of Minos buried the body of the king with magnificent ceremony, and constructing a tomb of two storeys, they placed the bones in the part of it which was hidden underground, and they made a shrine of Aphrodite in that which lay open to gaze. Here Minos received honours over many generations.

Diodorus Siculus (1st century BC) *Library of History* (1933 trans.) Bk 4.79.1–4. Arthur Evans found a similar tomb (the Temple Tomb) at Knossos (see 38:4).

4 It was impossible to doubt that we had here [the Temple Tomb] hit on the counterpart to the 'secret sepulchre' that, according to the tradition preserved by Diodorus, was constructed beneath the visible shrine of the Goddess … we were clearly approaching the last resting-place of one or more of the Priest-kings of the neighbouring Palace Sanctuary.

Arthur Evans *The Palace of Minos at Knossos* Vol.4 (1935) Pt 2, p.973.

5 In the month of Deukios:

To the Diktaian Zeus:	12 l. oil.
To Daidaleion:	24 l. oil …
To all the gods:	36 l. oil …
To the priestess of the winds:	8 l. oil.

Michael Ventris and John Chadwick *Documents in Mycenaean Greek* (1973 edn) p.306, no.200. This is the only reference to a name derived from Daedalus but, in the context of gods, suggesting a shrine to Daedalus rather than an historical human being. For Linear B tablets see 39:4.

6 Once in the palace make straight for the Queen. Her name is Arete and she comes from the same family as Alcinous the King … Alcinous made her his wife and gave her such homage as no other woman receives who keeps house for her husband in the world today … For she is not only the Queen but a wise woman too, and when her sympathies are enlisted she settles even men's disputes. So if only you can secure her friendly interest, you may well hope to return to your native land, to step under the high roof of your own house and to see your friends once more.

Homer (?8th or 7th century BC) *Odyssey* (1946 trans.) Bk 7, lines 53–77. Athene, goddess of wisdom, gives Odysseus advice. The picture of Arete may reflect the important women, priestesses or rulers, who seem to be depicted in the archaeological record.

1 One of themselves, even a prophet of their own, said, The Cretians are always liars, evil beasts, slow bellies.

Bible, NT, Epistle of Paul to Titus 1:12. The prophet is usually identified as Epimenides (*fl.c.*600 BC), who is thought to have castigated his countrymen thus for continuing to adhere to the worship of 'Minoan' Zeus, a young god who died and whose tomb was shown in the Idaean Cave on Mount Ida in Crete.

2 This island [Thera, or Santorini, in the Cyclades] used to be known as Callista.

Herodotus (*c.*485–*c.*425 BC) *The Histories* (1954 trans.) Bk 4.147. Callista should mean 'very lovely'. This could be a distant memory of the rich Bronze Age site (excavated by Spyridon Marinatos), which flourished before the eruption that blew out the centre of the island. There are close connections with the Minoan civilization, Thera being only 70 miles north of Crete.

3 In those days there was an island opposite the ... Pillars of Hercules, an island larger than Libya and Asia combined ... On this island of Atlantis had arisen a powerful and remarkable dynasty of kings ... This dynasty ... attempted to enslave your country and ours and all the territory within the strait. It was then, Solon, that ... your city ... led an alliance of the Greeks and ... she overcame the invaders and celebrated a victory ... At a later time there were earthquakes and floods of extraordinary violence, and in a single dreadful day and night all your fighting men were swallowed up by the earth, and the island of Atlantis was similarly swallowed up by the sea and vanished ...

That is, in brief, Socrates, the story which Critias told when he was an old man, and which he had from Solon.

Plato *Timaeus* (*c.*347 BC; 1965 trans.) 24–5. This is the famous story of Atlantis, which has given rise to countless theories, including that 'Atlantis' was the island of Thera before the volcanic eruption of Minoan times or even the Minoan civilization itself. In this late work the philosopher Plato was attempting a scientific account of the origin of the universe. In dialogue form, the *Timaeus* begins with a preliminary conversation on the subject of the ideal society.

4 He shrank from killing him – awe of that touched his heart and he could not – but he sent him away to Lycia [southwest Turkey], and sent with him signs of disastrous meaning, many lethal marks that he wrote in a folded tablet, and told him to show them to his father-in-law, to ensure his death.

Homer (?8th or 7th century BC) *Iliad* (1987 trans.) Bk 6, lines 167–70. This is Homer's only definite reference to writing. The Minoans used writing, first a pictographic or hieroglyphic script and later a syllabary, called Linear A. It has not been possible to decipher either of these, but Linear A was adapted by the Mycenaeans for their language, an early form of Greek, probably at Knossos after they had taken control there in the later 15th century BC. This script is known as Linear B and was deciphered by Michael Ventris in 1952 (see 39:6).

5 There are parts of the ring-wall left, including the gate with lions standing on it ... In the ruins of Mycenae is a water-source called Perseia, and the underground chambers of Atreus [king of Mycenae and father of Agamemnon and Menelaus] and his sons where they kept the treasure-houses of their wealth. There is the grave of Atreus and the graves of those who came home from Troy, to be cut down by Aegisthus at his supper party.

Pausanias *Guide to Greece* (AD *c.*150; 1971 trans.) Bk 2.16.4–5. Describing Mycenae, after which the Mycenaean civilization is named. The upper part of the ruins always remained visible. By tradition, it was the city of Agamemnon (who led the Greek forces to Troy) and Clytemnestra (who murdered him on his return). The tholos (beehive) tombs were called the 'treasuries' of Atreus and various members of his family on the basis of Pausanias' description. The portals of the Treasury of Atreus can be seen in the British Museum. The excavations of Heinrich Schliemann in the 19th century established that they were, in fact, tombs, mostly in use in the 15th century BC. Pausanias (*fl.*143–176), traveller and geographer, wrote his description of Greece in ten books.

6 At Metapa: ... women *barley-reapers*. Six women *reapers*, their father a slave and their mother *among the Kytherans* [from the island between Crete and the Peloponnese]; thirteen women *reapers* ... three women *reapers*, their father a slave and their mother a slave *of Diwia*.

Michael Ventris and John Chadwick (1973 edn) p.167, no.28. Surviving examples of Linear B itself – there are thousands of whole or fragmentary unbaked clay tablets – might be expected to provide historical information. Unfortunately, if the script was ever used for such purposes, it was on materials that have not survived. The tablets that have been found were preserved by the chance fact of being baked in the fires that destroyed the archive rooms where they were kept for a single year. They consist of inventories of goods and people that came under the elaborate palace administration.

1   One footstool inlaid with *a* man and *a* horse
and an octopus and a *griffin* in ivory.
One footstool inlaid with ivory lions' heads and
grooves.

Michael Ventris and John Chadwick (1973 edn) p.345, no.246.

2   Two tripod cauldrons of Cretan workmanship,
of ai-ke-u type;
one tripod cauldron with a *single* handle *on* one
foot;
one tripod cauldron of Cretan workmanship,
burnt away at the legs, *useless.*
Three *wine-jars*; one larger-sized *goblet* with
four handles.

Michael Ventris and John Chadwick (1973 edn) p.336, no.236.
This is one of the famous tripod tablets, whose discovery at
Pylos in the southwest Peloponnese, Greece, was published
just after the decipherment, which it triumphantly confirmed.
Attempts to recreate Minoan life from the tablets have not
achieved a consensus, especially as the information does not
always seem entirely consistent with the rest of the archaeological picture. Homer contains reflections of the Mycenaean
world, but we cannot reconstruct history from the *Iliad* and
Odyssey, although there are details that may give us the flavour
of Mycenaean life.

3   In the meantime Polycaste, King Nestor's youngest daughter, had given Telemachus his bath. When
she had bathed him and rubbed him with olive oil,
she gave him a tunic and arranged a fine cloak round
his shoulders, so that he stepped out of the bath
looking like an immortal god.

Homer (?8th or 7th century BC) *Odyssey* (1946 trans.) Bk 3,
lines 464–8.

4   The larnax [bath] is too short to allow a person of
any size to stretch out at length; it was rather a *sitz-
bad* in which the bather sat while water was poured
over him by an attendant. Such was no doubt the
bath in which Telemachus was scrubbed and rubbed
down by Polycaste as recounted in the *Odyssey.*

Carl W. Blegen and Marion Rawson *The Palace of Nestor* Vol. I
(1966) p.188, on the bath found in room 43 at Pylos.

5   But when this race [of bronze] was covered by
the earth,
The son of Kronos [Zeus] made another,
fourth,
Upon the fruitful land, more just and good,
A godlike race of heroes, who are called
The demi-gods – the race before our own.
Foul wars and dreadful battles ruined some;
Some sought the flocks of Oedipus, and died

In Cadmus' land, at seven-gated Thebes;
And some, who crossed the open sea in ships,
For fair-haired Helen's sake, were killed at
Troy.

Hesiod (*fl.c.*700 BC) (1973 trans.) lines 156–65. There was a
rich cycle of legend relating to the Boeotian city of Thebes,
founded by Cadmus, in central Greece, including the story of
Oedipus, who inadvertently killed his father and married his
mother, and his sons who fought over the kingdom. The Trojan
War, caused by the abduction of Helen, wife of Menelaus, king
of Sparta, by Paris, son of Priam, king of Troy, traditionally
dates to the following generation.

6   But it was only – if I may so put it – the day before
yesterday that the Greeks came to know the origin
and form of the various gods, and whether or not all
of them had already existed; for Homer and Hesiod,
the poets who composed our theogonies and described
the gods for us, giving them all their appropriate titles,
offices and powers, lived, as I believe, not more than
four hundred years ago.

Herodotus (c.485–c.425 BC) (1954 trans.) Bk 2.53. Herodotus,
the Father of History, began to make distinctions between
myth and history and to show an awareness of chronology.

7   Ancient estimates of the date of the fall of Troy:

	Years BC
Herodotus (5th century BC)	1250
Parian Chronicle (3rd century BC)	1209
Eratosthenes (3rd century BC)	1183
Ephorus (4th century BC)	1135

John Forsdyke *Greece before Homer* (1957) p.62.

8   I have gazed upon the face of Agamemnon.

Heinrich Schliemann, attrib. Probably apocryphal, the sentence
sums up the sense of telegrams sent to Greek newspapers in
Nov. and Dec. 1876 (and is not in the telegram to the king of
the Hellenes, which is cited in full in his *Mycenae* (1880) and to
which it is usually ascribed), after the discovery of bodies with
gold face masks in the Shaft Graves at Mycenae, beneath one of
which the actual face was preserved. The graves were, in fact,
in use between c.1600 and c.1450 BC, several hundred years
before the supposed date of Agamemnon.

9   Of the third body, which lay at the north end of the
tomb, the round face, with all its flesh, had been
wonderfully preserved under its ponderous golden
mask; there was no vestige of hair, but both eyes
were perfectly visible, also the mouth, which, owing
to the enormous weight that had pressed upon it,
was wide open, and showed thirty-two beautiful
teeth … the man must have died at the early age of
thirty-five.

Heinrich Schliemann *Mycenae* (1880; 1967 edn) p.296.
Archaeology alone cannot give us the history of individual
people, cities and events. The relationship between Homer
(and the other legends of this era) and historical truth remains
highly speculative.

1   Long exile is your lot, a vast stretch of sea must
       you plough;
     and you will come to the land Hesperia [Italy],
     where amid rich fields of men the Tiber flows
       with gentle sweep.
     There in store for you are happy times, a
       kingdom and a royal wife.

Virgil (c.19 BC; 916 trans.) Bk 2, lines 780–4. As Troy falls,
Aeneas' wife foretells how he will found a new kingdom in
Italy for the survivors of Troy – the future Rome. Virgil
developed this legend to take the history of Rome back to the
supposed Trojan War (see 68:1).

2 Kindly tell Pijamaradus either to settle down
peacefully in your country, or to return to my
country. Do not let him use Ahhijawa as a base for
operations against me.

Hittite Emperor Mursilis II (or Muwattallis) to a king of Ahhijawa,
late 14th or early 13th century BC; Denys Page *History and the
Homeric Iliad* (1959) p.12. Attempts have been made to
identify Mycenaeans in the documents of adjacent civilizations,
in particular the Hittites. This, one of about 20 references in
Hittite documents to Ahhijawa, *may* refer to the land of the
Achaeans, Homer's name for the Greeks, but the location of
Ahhijawa varies from the mainland to somewhere on the west
coast of modern Turkey to one of the Greek islands, most
particularly Rhodes.

3 After the Persian Wars [first half of 5th century BC]
… the Athenians consulted the oracle at Delphi and
were instructed by the Pythian [Delphic oracle]
priestess to bring home the bones of Theseus, give
them honourable burial in Athens and guard them as
sacred relics. It was a difficult task to discover the
grave and take away the remains … However, Cimon
[Athenian statesman and general] captured the island
of Scyros [western Aegean] and made it a point of
honour to find the spot where Theseus was buried.
He caught sight of an eagle … pecking at the ground
with its beak and tearing it up with its talons, and by
some divine inspiration he concluded that they
should dig at this place. There they found a coffin of a
man of gigantic size and, lying beside it, a bronze
spear and a sword. When Cimon brought these relics
home on board his trireme, the Athenians were
overjoyed and welcomed them with magnificent
processions and sacrifices, as though the hero himself
were returning to his city. He lies buried in the heart
of Athens.

Plutarch (c.46–c.127) *Lives* (1960 trans.) 'Theseus' 36. The
Athenians were proud of their mythical Bronze Age king,
Theseus, who was supposed to have killed the Minotaur.

4 Pisistratus also inserted into Homer's description of
the underworld the line 'Theseus and Pirithous
[Theseus' companion], illustrious children of the
gods'.

Homer (?8th or 7th century BC) *Odyssey* Bk 11, line 631;
Plutarch (1960 trans.) 'Theseus' 20. Pisistratus, the 6th-century
BC tyrant of Athens, ordered the production of a complete
written edition of the Homeric poems, and Plutarch is
illustrating the ancient belief that the Athenians made
interpolations into Homer to increase the number of references
to themselves (see 53:6).

The Americas before their Conquest, c.1200 BC–AD 1550

1 Columbus did not discover a new world; he established contact between two worlds, both already old.

J.H. Parry *The Spanish Seaborne Empire* (1966) Ch.3.

2 This coastline, too, was swarming with people and it would seem, if we are to judge by those areas so far explored, that the Almighty selected this part of the world as home to the greater part of the human race.

God made all the peoples of this area [the mainland nearest to the Caribbean island of Hispaniola] many and varied as they are, as open and as innocent as can be imagined. The simplest people in the world – unassuming, long-suffering, unassertive and submissive – they are without malice or guilt and are utterly faithful and obedient to their own native lords and to the Spaniards in whose service they now find themselves … Even the common people are no tougher than princes or than other Europeans born with a silver spoon in their mouths and who spend their lives shielded from the rigours of the outside world. They are also among the poorest people on the face of the earth.

Bartolomé de Las Casas *A Short Account of the Destruction of the Indies* (1552; 1992 trans.) Preface. Las Casas left Spain at the age of 18 with the first Conquistadors (see 51:5). He became a priest in the New World and 40 years later wrote his passionate and detailed description of genocide, dedicated and as a warning to King Philip II, on Spanish brutality towards the native inhabitants of the Caribbean and the mainland. Hispaniola, the second largest island of the Caribbean, is now divided between Haiti and the Dominican Republic.

THE OLMECS, c.1200–c.400 BC

3 Whoever the 'Olmec' were, they must have been extremely close to the Maya since they acknowledged the same Era (all Maya started from the beginning of their Era, probably 10 Aug. 3113 BC); also they very probably spoke Mixe-Zoque which is akin to Maya.

Gordon Brotherston *Image of the New World* (1979) p.26. In Nahuatl, the language of the Aztecs, the name Olmec means 'people of the place with rubber (*olli*)'. Scholars regard them as the 'mother culture' of Mesoamerica; their origins can be traced by archaeologists to c.1200 BC.

4 The Olmecs conceived the surface of the earth as a plane defined by four corners and a centre that was the axis of the world. The earth was personified as a mythical being with a V-shaped cut on its head. From this cut emerged a maize plant, a polyvalent symbol of royal power and the cosmic tree that linked the sky with the underworld. The other four points of the plane were similar columns supporting the cosmos.

Alfredo López Austin and Leonardo López Luján *Mexico's Indigenous Past* (1996; 2001 trans.) pp.92–3.

5 Some of the ten monoliths found so far are colossal male heads covered with tight-fitting helmets. Because there are differences in their features they probably are portraits of actual rulers. Other monoliths have been called altars because they have flat tops.

Alfredo López Austin and Leonardo López Luján (1996; 2001 trans.) p.94. The authors continue: 'The fall of the Olmec world … is dated by archaeologists at 400 BC. We do not know with any certainty what happened at that time, but scholars consider that after that date one can no longer speak of the Olmecs as a cultural unit' (p.96).

THE MAYAS, c. AD 250–1000

6 Of the moral effect of the monuments themselves [the Mayan palaces of Copán and Palenque], standing as they do in the depths of a tropical forest, silent and solemn, strange in design, excellent in sculpture, rich in ornament, different from the works of any other people, their uses and purposes and whole history so entirely unknown, with hieroglyphics explaining all but being perfectly unintelligible, I shall not pretend to convey any idea …

There is, then, no resemblance in these remains to those of the Egyptians; and, failing here, we look elsewhere in vain. They are different from the works of any other known people, of a new order, and entirely and absolutely anomalous: they stand alone.

… It is the spectacle of a people skilled in architecture, sculpture and drawing, and, beyond doubt other more perishable arts, and possessing the cultivation and refinement attendant upon these, not derived from the Old World, but originating and growing up here, without models or masters, having a distinct, separate, independent existence; like the plants and fruits of the soil, indigenous.

John Lloyd Stephens *Incidents of Travel in Central America, Chiapas and Yucatán* (1841); Brian M. Fagan (ed.) *Eyewitness to Discovery* (1996) pp.337, 343. Stephens, a New York lawyer, teamed up with a British architect, Frederick Catherwood, to explore the jungle sites of the lost Mayan civilization. Catherwood produced remarkable drawings of what they saw.

1 This is the account of how all was in suspense, all calm, in silence; all motionless, still, and the expanse of sky was empty.

This is the first account, the first narrative. There was neither man, nor animal, birds, fishes, crabs, trees, stones, caves, ravines, grasses, nor forests, there was only the sky.

Anon. *Popol Vuh* (Book of Counsel) (mid-16th century; 1951 trans.) Pt 1, Ch.1. The opening words of the sacred book of the Quiché Maya, explaining their creation myth. The manuscript was found in Guatemala in the 17th century and was translated by a Spanish priest.

2   There was then no sickness;
They had no aching bones;
They had then no fever;
They had then no smallpox;
They had then no burning chest …
They had then no consumption …
At that time the course of humanity was orderly.
The foreigners made it otherwise when they
arrived here.

Anon. *The Book of Chilam Balam of Chumayel* (16th century; 1967 edn); Ronald Wright *Stolen Continents* (1992) p.14. Chilam Balam, the Priest Jaguar, after whom the Yucatán community books are named, foresees the coming of foreigners.

3   See when they come the foreigners bring no
truth.
Yet great secrets are told by the sons of the men
And the women of seven ruined houses
Who is the prophet
Who is the priest who shall read
The word of this book.

Anon. *The Book of Chilam Balam of Chumayel* (16th century; 1933 edn) closing words; Brotherston (1979) p.286.

4 Near here on the road to the city of San Pedro, in the first town within the province of Honduras, called Cópan, are certain ruins and vestiges of a great population and superb edifices, of such skill that it appears they could never have been built by a people as rude as the natives of that province … besides these things, there are many others which prove that here was formerly the seat of a great power, and a great population, civilized and considerably advanced in the arts, as is shown in the various figures and buildings.

Don Diego García de Palacio to Philip II, king of Spain, 1576; Claude Baudez and Sydney Picasso *Lost Cities of the Maya* (1992) p.133. A colonial magistrate is reporting on the site of what later became known as Copán, Honduras. It is interesting that this letter, which showed such respect for Mayan civilization, was not published for a further 300 years.

5 Before the Spaniards had conquered that country, the natives lived together in towns in a very civilized fashion. They kept the land well tilled and free from weeds, and planted very good trees. Their dwelling places were as follows: in the middle of the town were their temples with beautiful plazas … and all around the temples stood the houses of the lords and the priests … and on the outskirts of the town were the houses of the lower class.

Fray Diego de Landa *Relación de las Cosas de Yucatán* (1556; 1941 trans.) p.62. Landa arrived in Yucatán in 1549. Alas, his tolerance later gave way, and he supervised the destruction of Mayan buildings. 'We found a great number of books in these letters (hieroglyphs) of theirs, and because they contained nothing but superstition and the devil's falsehoods, we burnt them all, which upset (the Mayas) most grievously and caused them great pain' (Landa (1556; 1982 edn) pp.104–5).

6 It is well known that the forests of Chiapas and the Péten [in southernmost Mexico] are scattered with ruined monuments (temples, pyramids, stelae) built by the ancient Maya during the Classic period [250–900]. The Lacandon Indians [who live today in these forests] believe these structures to be the work of supernatural beings whom they call *k'uh* (gods). These gods once lived upon the earth, and their houses are still visible there today. The houses of the gods are the same as those of the 'True Men' (the Indians themselves) but instead of palm-leaf roofs, the human eye can see only stone.

Didier Boremanse *Les Vrais Hommes* (1986); Baudez and Picasso (1992) pp.160–61, who note that these Indians 'are the last representatives of a lowland Maya culture … who are at present facing extinction'.

7 The drought that ended this elaborate civilization lasted for more than a century. A farming community that depended on stone tools could not produce enough to support its own fabric. By the time the Spaniards invaded during the 15th century, power resided with the Aztecs, and the Mayans had all but vanished.

Tim Radford, *Guardian*, 18 May 2001, reporting on Professor David Hodell's archaeological research, which suggested that it was a drought that followed a 206-year cycle that destroyed Mayan civilization. There are other theories for their disappearance, such as disease and genocide.

THE TOLTECS, c.1000–c.1200

1 And then these different people went [on]; the Tolteca, the Mexica, the Nahua. All the people, as they sought land, encountered the plains, the deserts, in a valley among the crags, a very dangerous place. And the people wept, they were saddened, they suffered affliction; there was no more to eat; no more to drink.

Fray Bernardino de Sahagún *The Florentine Codex: or the General History of the Things of New Spain* (c.1555; 1950–82 trans.) Bk 10; Nigel Davies *Ancient Kingdoms of Mexico* (1982) p.113.

2 The Toltecs did not in fact lack anything
No one was poor or had a shabby house
And the smaller maize ears they used as fuel.
To heat their steam baths with.

Anon. *Cantares mexicanos*; Sahagún (c.1555; 1950–82 trans.) Bk 3 (*The Origin of the Gods*), Ch.3; Gordon Brotherston *Book of the Fourth World* (1992) p.157. The song is one of nostalgic praise for the Toltec city of Tula, 'the place of rushes' (near Mexico City).

3 Chichen Itzá is most renowned not for its architecture, but for its Sacred Cenote, or Well of Sacrifice, reached by a 900-foot-long causeway leading from the Great Plaza. From Landa comes the following: 'Into this well they have had, and then had, the custom of throwing men alive as sacrifice to the gods, in times of drought, and they believed that they did not die though they never saw them again. They also threw into it a great many other things, like precious stones and things which they prized.'

Michael D. Coe *The Maya* (1966; 1971 edn) p.147. The Toltecs seem to have abandoned their mighty capital of what was later called Chichen Itzá (mouth of the well of the Itzá) in Yucatán around AD 1224.

THE AZTECS IN CENTRAL MEXICO, 1428–1521

4 It is told, it is recounted here how the ancient ones … the people of Aztlan, the Mexicans … came to [found] the great city of Mexico – Tenochtitlán, their place of fame, their place of example, the place where the *tenochtli* cactus stands amid the waters, where the eagle preens … and devours the snake … among the reeds, among the canes.

Hernando de Alvarado Tezozómoc *Crónica Mexicana* (1609; 1975 edn) pp.3–4. Montezuma's grandson recorded the Aztecs' foundation myth.

5 We shall proceed to establish ourselves and settle down, and we shall conquer all people of the universe … and I tell you in truth that I will make you lords and kings of all that is in the world and when you become rulers, you shall have countless and infinite numbers of vassals who will pay tribute to you and shall give you innumerable and most fine precious stones, gold quetzal [multi-hued bird] feathers, emeralds, coral and amethyst.

The supreme god Huitzilopochtli speaks from his cave and conveys a promise through mediums on future conquests for the Aztecs; Tezozómoc (1609; 1944 edn) p.23. The writer announces his credentials at the beginning of his chronicle: 'I who am a grandson of the person who was the great king Montezuma the Younger, and who am descended from his noble daughter, from the body of the princess, my most loved mother, whose husband was Don Diego de Alvarado Huanitzin' (p.7).

6 It is likely that by the mid-1350s, Nahuatl, the language of the Aztecs, was the dominant language in central America.

Michael C. Meyer and William H. Beezley (eds) *Oxford History of Mexico* (2000) p.69.

7 1. The king must never appear in public except when the occasion is extremely important and unavoidable …
  2. Only the king and the prime minister Tlacaelel may wear sandals within the palace …
  7. The commoners will not be allowed to wear cotton clothing, under pain of death …
  8. Only great noblemen and valiant warriors are given licence to build a house with a second storey; for disobeying this law a person receives the death sentence …
  14. There is to be a rigorous law regarding adulterers. They are to be stoned and thrown into rivers or to the buzzards.

Montezuma I, emperor of the Mexican people (r.1440–68), legal code, in Fernando de Alva Ixtlilxochitl *Obras Historicas* (16th century; 1975–7 trans.); Michael E. Smith *The Aztecs* (1996) p.52.

1 The year 1 Rabbit, 1454. In this year of disaster there was widespread death and thirst. And there arrived to stuff themselves in Chalco, frightful packs of boars, poisonous snakes and vultures as well. And the hunger was so great that the imperial Mexicans sold themselves, and others hid away in the forest, where they lived as wood people. In that region there was nothing to eat for all of four years, so that two separate parties of the Mexicans sold themselves into slavery.

Domingo Francisco Chimalpain *Relaciones* (c.1600; 1889 trans.) Ch.7. The historian, an aristocrat from Chalco, Mexico, drew on his knowledge of several languages.

2 In those times these hills and valleys were populated with thousands of souls who lived, following their custom, in many scattered hamlets, a short distance from each other.

Early Spanish observer in Mexico; Juan de la Cruz y Moya *Historia de la Santa y Apostólica Provincia de Santiago* (16th century; 1954–5 edn) Vol.2, p.133.

3 Buying and selling, going forth to all the markets of the land, bartering cloth for jewels, jewels for feathers, feathers for stones, and stones for slaves, always dealing in things of importance, of renown and of high value. These [men] strengthened their social position with their wealth.

Fray Diego Durán *Book of the Gods and Rites and the Ancient Calendar* (1576–8; 1971 edn) p.138. The friar sympathetically explored the Aztecs' history and culture. Here he describes the Aztec merchant class.

4 All the arts: military, religious, mechanical and astrological, which gave them knowledge of the stars. For this they possessed large, beautiful books, painted in hieroglyphics, dealing with all these arts; [and these books] were used for teaching.

Fray Diego Durán (1576–8; 1971 edn) p.293. The *calmecac* was the more exclusive of the two types of Aztec school, which trained the priests, government and military elites.

5 The conquered people gave themselves as vassals, as servants to the Aztecs and they paid tribute in all things created under the sky ... There were such vast quantities of all these things which came to the city of Mexico that not a day passed without the arrival of people from other regions who brought large

amounts of everything, from foodstuffs to luxury items, for the king and the lords.

Fray Diego Durán *The History of the Indies of New Spain* (1581; 1944 trans.) pp.206–7. The dominance of the Aztecs over the other peoples of the region is obvious.

6 The good ruler is a protector; one who carries (his subjects) in his arms, who unites them, who brings them together. He rules, takes responsibilities, assumes burdens. He carries (his subjects) in his cape; he bears them in his arms. He governs; he is obeyed ... (to him) as shelter, as refuge, there is recourse.

Fray Bernardino de Sahagún (c.1555; 1950–82 trans.) Bk 10, Ch.15. The nobles' idea of a good king or head of a city state.

7 The wise men remained not long; soon they went once again. They embarked and carried off the writings, the books, the paintings; they carried away all the crafts, the castings of metals. And when they departed they summoned all those they left behind. They said to them. 'Our lord, the protector of all, the wind, the night, sayeth you shall remain. We go leaving you here. Our lord goeth bequeathing you this land.'

Fray Bernardino de Sahagún (c.1555; 1950–82 trans.) Bk 10. 'He tells a story that can be linked to the fall of Teotihuacán, the first event in Mexican history to which a written source refers' (Davies (1982) p.112). The elders flee from the city in the Valley of Mexico that was destroyed as the centre of the Mayan culture in its classic period c.750. 'In its day probably the largest city in the world,' suggests Brotherston.

8   Proud of itself
        is the city of Mexico – Tenochtitlán.
        Here no one fears to die in war.
        This is our glory.
        This is Your command,
        O Giver of Life!
        Have this in mind, O princes,
        Do not forget it.
        Who could conquer Tenochtitlán?
        Who could shake the foundation of heaven?

Aztec poem; Chimalpain (c.1600; 1889 trans.). 'The city was built to impress visitors, both human and divine. Just as the city awed the first Spaniards who saw it, Tenochtitlán also overwhelmed Aztecs visiting from the provinces' (Smith (1996) p.196).

9 And when he [the priest] had laid him [the captive] upon it [the sacrificial stone on the pyramid's temple], four men stretched him out, [grasping] his arms and legs. And already in the

hand of the fire priest lay the [sacrificial knife] …
and then, when he has split open the breast, he at
once seized his heart. And he whose breast he laid
open was quite alive. and when [the priest] had
seized his heart, he dedicated it to the sun.

Fray Bernardino de Sahagún (c.1555; 1950–82 trans.) Bk 2,
pp.184–5. Sahagún based this account on that of his Nahua
informants. The victims 'were sent rolling down the steps of
the temple, and the steps were bathed in blood' (Durán
(1576–8; 1971 edn) p.81).

1 These wretches played [the ballgame] for stakes of
little value or worth, and since the pauper loses
quickly what he has, they were forced to gamble their
homes, fields, their corn granaries, their maguey plants
[grown for the fibre]. They sold their children in order
to bet and even staked themselves and became slaves.

Fray Diego Durán Book of the Gods and Rites and the Ancient
Calendar (1581; 1971 edn) p.318. The censorious friar on the
dangers of betting. 'The hard rubber ball was struck by knee
or hip (padded) through a carved stone ring. The ball game
was apparently both a competitive sport between cities and a
public religious ceremony' (Smith (1996) p.239).

2 Each tribe had its writers; some wrote annals,
arranging in order the things that came to pass
during each year, together with the day, month and
hour; others had charge of the genealogy of the
descendants of the kings, lords and persons of lineage,
setting down with detailed account those who were
born, and in the same manner striking out the
names of those who died. Some had the care of the
paintings of the boundaries, limits and landmarks of
the lands; whose they were, and to whom they
belonged; others had charge of the books of laws,
rites and ceremonies which they followed.

The hispanified Indian chronicler Fernando de Alva Ixtlilxóchitl
Obras históricas (16th century; 1891–2 edn) Vol.2, Prologue.

3 The philosophers and wise men had charge of
recording all the sciences of which they had knowledge and of which they had achieved understanding,
and of teaching from memory all the songs that
preserved their sciences and histories.

Fernando de Alva Ixtlilxóchitl (16th century; 1975–7 edn)
Vol.1, p.527.

4 The good scribe is honest, circumspect, far
sighted, pensive; a judge of colours, an applier of the
colours, who makes shadows, forms feet, face, hair.
He paints, applies colours, makes shadows, draws
gardens, paints flowers, creates works of art.

Bernardino de Sahagún (c.1555; 1950–82 trans.) Bk 10, p.28.
The skills of the scribe who is, of course, a painter not a
letterer in our sense.

5 Beautiful painted books recorded the possession
of land, as of history, with family trees and maps
supporting the inclination of the ancient Mexicans
to be litigious.

Alonso de Zurita Breve y sumaria relación de los señores … de
la Nueva España (1566–70; 1891 edn) p.107; Victor Wolfgang
von Hagen The Aztec and Maya Papermakers (1943) p.12. Von
Hagen comments: 'Finally paper itself became an important
article of tribute. In one of the most famous of tribute charts
of Montezuma II, the Codex Mendoza (1830–48 edn; Vol.1,
text p.6), we find this sign: Item: 24,000 resmas of (bark) paper
are to be brought yearly to the storehouses of the ruler of
Tenochtitlán. 24,000 resmas is 480,000 sheets by the Aztec
system. Judged by the standards of a primitive civilization this is
an enormous amount of paper, enormous even though the
Spanish word (from which our word ream comes) is only an
expression which fortunately coincided with the Aztec numeral
pilli (20)' (pp.12–13).

6 They have their own skilled doctors who know
how to use many herbs and medicines which suffices
for them. Some of them have so much experience
that they were able to heal Spaniards, who had long
suffered from chronic and serious diseases.

Fray Toribio Motolinía History of the Indians of New Spain
(c.1541; 1971 trans.) p.160.

7 The principal streets are very wide and very
straight. Some of these, and all the smaller streets,
are made as to one half of earth, while the other is a
canal by which the Indians travel in boats, and all
these streets from one end of the town to the other,
are opened in such a way that the water can completely cross them. All these openings – and some
are very wide – are spanned by bridges made of very
solid and well-worked beams, so that across many of
them ten horseman can ride abreast.

Hernán Cortés to Charles V Five Letters to the Emperor (1519–
26; 1908 edn); Jacques Soustelle The Daily Life of the Aztecs on
the Eve of the Spanish Conquest (1955; 1961 trans.) pp.146–7.

8 Montezuma had a palace in the town of such a
kind, and so marvellous, that it seems to me almost
impossible to describe its beauty and magnificence.
I will say no more than that we have nothing like it
in Spain.

Hernán Cortés to Charles V (1519–26; 1908 edn); Soustelle
(1955; 1961 trans.) p.160.

1 You passed through a series of large courts, bigger I think, than the plaza at Salamanca [Spain]. These courts were surrounded by a double masonry wall and paved, like the whole place, with very large smooth white flagstones. Where these stones were absent everything was whitened and polished, indeed the whole place was so clean that there was not a straw or a grain of dust to be found there ... we turned back to the great market and the swarm of people buying and selling. The mere murmur of their voices was loud enough to be heard more than three miles away. Some of our soldiers who had been in many parts of the world, in Constantinople, in Rome and all over Italy, said they had never seen a market so well laid out, so large, so orderly and so full of people.
Bernal Díaz del Castillo *The Conquest of New Spain* (1560s; 1963 trans.) pp.234–5. Díaz wrote about 50 years after serving under Cortés in the conquest of Mexico in 1520.

2 This town [Tenochtitlán] has many squares on which there are always markets, and in which they buy and sell ... But there is another [Tlatelolco] twice the size of the town of Salamanca, completely surrounded by arcades, where every day there are more than sixty thousand souls who buy and sell, and there are all kinds of merchandise from all the provinces, whether it is provisions, victuals or jewels of gold or silver. There is nothing to be found in all the land, which is not sold in these markets ... Each kind of merchandise is sold in its own particular street and no other kind may be sold there: this rule is very well enforced. All is sold by number and measure, but up till now no weighing by balance has been observed. A very fine building in the great square serves as a kind of audience chamber where ten or a dozen persons are always seated, as judges, who deliberate on all cases arising in the market and pass sentence on evil doers ... I have seen them destroy measures which are false.
Hernán Cortés to Charles V (1519–26; 1962 trans.) pp.87–9. Tlatelolco market (twin city to Tenochtitlán) also impressed other writers, including Bernal Díaz and Bernardino de Sahagún.

3 [Governorship of a district devolves] not by inheritance, but at his death, by the election of the most honourable, wise, capable and aged man ... If the dead man had left a son who is fit for the position, he is chosen; it is always a relation who is elected providing that there is one and that he is suited for the post.

Alonso de Zurita (1566–70; 1891 edn) p.96; Soustelle (1955; 1964 trans.) p.68. The nomination rather than election to posts 'in the early days'. Zurita was a Spanish judge of great integrity and experience who compared the miserable state of the Mexican Indian under Spanish rule with an idealized picture of life before the conquest.

4 Some Indians from the village came running to tell all the *caciques* [chiefs] ... that five Mexicans had been seen, the tax-gatherers of Montezuma. On hearing this they went pale, and began to tremble with fear ... they [the tax collectors] wore rich embroidered cloaks, loincloths of the same nature, and their shining hair was raised in a knot on their heads: each had a bunch of flowers in his hand, and he smelt to it.
Bernal Díaz del Castillo sees the effect on the country of the Totonacs of maintaining the Aztec empire, its city, nobles and wars; Soustelle (1955; 1964 trans.) pp.68–9.

5 The *tlatoani* [speaker of supreme council, commander in chief] of Tetzococo took the crown of green stones, all worked in gold, and placed it upon the new ruler's head, and piercing the septum of his nose he inserted a green emerald as thick as a quill pen, and in his ears two round emerald ear-plugs in gold settings, and on his arms from elbow to shoulder two very resplendent gold bracelets, and on his ankles, anklets with dangling gold bells, and the (Tetzcocan) king shod him with jaguar-skin sandals all elegantly gilded and clad him with a precious mantle ... very thin and shining, all gilded and painted with elegant pictures and taking him by the hand he led him to a throne that they called *cuauhicpalli*, meaning eagle-seat, also named jaguar-seat, for it was decorated with eagle feathers and jaguar hides.
Fray Diego Durán *The History of the Indies of New Spain* (1581; 1967 trans.); Richard F. Townsend *The Aztecs* (1992) p.301.

6   Is it true that on earth one lives?
    Not for ever on earth, only a little while.
    Though jade it may be, it breaks;
    Though gold it may be, it is crushed;
    Though it be quetzal plumes, it shall not last.
    Not for ever on earth, only a little while.
Nezahualcoyotl (1418–72), the philosopher king of Texcoco, attrib. in *Cantares Mexicanos* (1975) folio 17, recto 1963, p.72. Of the highly prized quetzal feather mosaics described in the verse only eight examples have survived.

7 From pole to pole through the holes, stretched thin rods strung with numerous human heads pierced through the temple. Each rod held 20 heads. The horizontal rows of skulls filled it from end to end. One of the conquerors assured me they were so numerous that they were impossible to count, so close together that they caused fright and wonder.

Fray Diego Durán (1576–8; 1971 edn) pp.79–80. Durán is describing the *tzompantli* (skull rack); in Nahuatl, literally, 'a row of heads'.

1 Question 14: To whom were they subject when they were heathens; what power did their rulers have over them; what did they pay in tribute; what forms of worship, rites, and good and evil customs did they have?

Reply: They say that in this town, although they recognized Montezuma the Elder and his successors as king, they did not pay tribute beyond participating in his campaigns … They had another local lord whom they obeyed and recognized as king … When the king went out of the house, no one dared look at him except those who accompanied him … for affairs of state, they had two officials like judges who ascertained and verified what had happened when crimes occurred … They had only one idol in the town's public market … to this idol, every 20 days, they sacrificed a child, the offspring of slaves they had captured in war.

Relaciones geográficas (1578–82; 1984–7 edn) Vol.6, pp.201–2. This entry from a multi-volume survey prepared for the Spanish crown refers to the town of Huaxtepec (in the Mexican state of Morelos).

THE INCAS, c.1200–1532

2 In ancient times, they say, the land and provinces of Peru were dark and neither light nor daylight existed. In this time, there lived certain people who had a lord who ruled over them and to whom they were subject … during this time of total night, they say that a lord emerged from a lake in this Land of Peru in the province of Collasuyo [Lake Titicaca region] and that his name was Contiti Viracocha [fundamental god]. They say that he brought with him a certain number of people but they do not remember the number … when he and his people arrived there they say that he suddenly made the sun and the day and ordered the sun to follow the course that it follows. Then, they say, he made the stars and the moon.

Juan de Betanzos *Narrative of the Incas* (1557; 1996 edn) p.7. The Spanish chronicler learned Quechua and drew on the Incas' memories of their origins (see 43:1 and 51:6).

3 The land of Peru, which is the subject of this book, begins at the Equator and extends southward. Its inhabitants below the line have a Jewish cast of feature, speak gutturally and are much given to unnatural vice. For this reason they reject their wives and pay them little respect. The women wear their hair very short and go naked except for a small apron with which they cover their private parts. It is they who sow and grind the corn that is eaten throughout the province and is known in the language of the islands as maize.

Agustín de Zárate *The Discovery and Conquest of Peru* (c.1555; 1968 trans.) p.32.

4 They [the Incas] used to call it Tahuantinsuyu, meaning 'the four quarters of the world'. The name Béru, as has been seen, was the proper name of an Indian and is one used by the Yunca Indians of the plains and seacoast, but not by those of the mountains or in the general language. Peru was a name imposed by the Spaniards, and that it did not occur in the general speech of the Indians, we are given to understand.

Garcilaso de la Vega *Royal Commentaries of the Incas* (1608; 1966 trans.) Bk 1, Ch.5. The illegitimate son of an Inca princess draws on such previous historians as Pedro de Cieza de León and Padre Acosta to substantiate this theory and believes the name Peru was a corruption of an individual Indian's name, misunderstood by the Spanish.

5 The post went from Quito to Cuzco [over 1,000 miles as the crow flies and, given the terrain, half as much again] in eight days. Every half-league, along the road was a small house, where there were always Indians with their wives. One of these ran with the news that had to be transmitted, and before reaching the next house called it out to another runner … Neither mules nor horses could go over such rocky ground in a shorter time.

Pedro de Cieza de León *Travels* (1540s; 1864 edn) p.153. Cieza de León (1518–60) seems to have come out from Seville at the age of 13, served as a soldier and tirelessly travelled the roads of Peru in the 1540s. Although not as committed to the Peruvian view as Garcilaso, he writes repeatedly in admiration of this Inca achievement. In every valley there was a principal station for the Incas, with depots of provisions for the troops. 'Care was taken to keep the road clean, to renew any part of the walls.'

1 Cuzco was grand and stately and must have been founded by a people of great intelligence. It had fine streets, except that they were narrow, and the houses were built of solid stones, beautifully joined … This city was the richest of which we have any knowledge in all the Indies, for great store of treasure was often brought in to increase the grandeur of the nobles; and no gold nor silver might be taken out, on pain of death. The sons of the chiefs in all the provinces came to reside at court with their retinues for a certain time.

Pedro de Cieza de León (1540s; 1864 edn) pp.326–9.

2 I assure you that although they appear rougher they seem to me to have been far more difficult to build than the walls of coursed ashlars. For they are not cut straight but are nevertheless tightly joined to one another. One can imagine the amount of work involved in making them interlock in the way in which we see them … If the top of one stone has a projecting corner there is a corresponding groove or cavity in the stone above to fit it exactly … to make the stones interlock it must have been necessary to remove and replace them repeatedly to test them … and with stones as large as these, it becomes clear how many people and how much suffering must have been involved.

Bernabé Cobo *Historia del Nuevo Mundo* (1653; 1956 edn) Bk 14, Ch.12.

3 The greatest and most splendid building erected to show the power and majesty of the Incas was the fortress of Cuzco, the grandeur of which would be incredible to anyone who had not seen it, and even those who have seen it and considered it with attention, imagine, and even believe, that it was made by enchantment, the handiwork of demons rather than of men.

Garcilaso de la Vega (1608; 1966 trans.) pp.463–4. Born at Cuzco in 1539, Garcilaso describes the former capital in nostalgic detail. It had been looted, besieged, heavily damaged and largely rebuilt in his lifetime; he died in 1616.

4 As regards religion, he [the earliest Inca, *c.*1200] commanded that the Sun should be regarded as supreme god, and that in his temple great sacrifices should be held and thanks should be given, especially for his having sent his son to rule them … promising them, in the name of his father, the Sun, many good things if they observed his rules, and giving them to understand that the Sun himself commanded it.

Fernando Montesinos *Memorias antiguas historiales del Peru* (Ancient Historical Records of Peru) (c.1630; 1920 edn) p.81. Sun worship thus became and remained the basis of Inca religion.

5 He [Inca Roca] honoured the men of the blood royal by permitting them to bore their ears where women do today, but with larger holes … and this was the sign of nobility and of royal caste, and the Spaniards called such men *orejones* on account of the hole in their ears.

Fernando Montesinos (c.1630; 1920 edn) pp.81–2. *Orejón* means 'pull of the ear'.

6 Some of the most learned of the people were chosen to make known the lives of those lords in songs, and the events of their reigns … But these songs could not be recited or made public except in the presence of the lord, and those who were charged with this duty during the reign of the king were not allowed to say anything which referred to him. But after his death they spoke to his successor [saying]: 'Know that the events which occurred in the days of thy fathers are these.'

Pedro de Cieza de León *Second Part of the Chronicle of Peru* (1550; 1883 edn) p.32. The author describes these men as trained and highly honoured ballad singers who passed on their knowledge and skill from one generation to the next, so that 'they can relate what took place 500 years ago as if only ten years had passed … to prevent the great events of the empire from passing into oblivion'. The songs were recited only on important public occasions, when 'those who knew the romances, standing before the Inca, sang with loud voices of the mighty deeds of his ancestors'.

7 The [accounting] system of the Peruvians was by *quipus*. These were long ropes made of knotted cords … On these knots they counted from one to ten, from ten to a hundred and from a hundred to a thousand. On one of the ropes are the units, on another the tens, and so on. Each ruler of a province was provided with accountants called 'quipucamayos' and by these knots they kept account of what tribute was to be paid in the district, with respect to silver, gold, cloth, flocks, down to firewood and other minute details.

Pedro de Cieza de León (1550; 1883 edn) p.33. The *quipus* were made of twisted wool, and each consisted of a large cord with finer threads tied to it by knots. The different colours of the threads, the distance between the knots and variations in the twist itself enabled innumerable meanings to be conveyed.

8 No one, even if he should be the greatest and most powerful among the lords of the empire, could

speak to him [the Inca] or enter into his presence without first removing his shoes ... and placing on his shoulders a burden with which to appear in the presence of the lord.
Pedro de Cieza de León (1550; 1883 edn) p.38.

1 'Mitimaes' is the name of those who are transported from one land to another. The first kind of *mitimaes*, as instituted by the Incas, were those who were moved to other countries after a new province had been conquered ... There they were expected to instruct their neighbours in the ways of peace and civilization ... Among the colonists there were spies – who took note of the conversations and schemes of the natives and supplied the information to the governors, who sent it to Cuzco without delay, to be submitted to the Inca. In this way all was made secure, for the natives feared the *mitimaes*, while the *mitimaes* suspected the natives, and all learned to serve and obey quietly.
Pedro de Cieza de León (1550; 1883 edn) p.68–9. The *mitimaes*, Cieza adds, served according to their skill in many different functions, such as quarrying or sculpting. Others were soldiers garrisoned on the slopes east of the Andes, which were inhabited by wild and warlike tribes. They were, in effect, the essential instruments of a military empire governed by a systematic 'divide and rule' strategy.

2 Throughout Peru the Indians carry this coca in their mouths, and from morning until they lie down to sleep they never take it out. When I asked some of these Indians why they carried these leaves in their mouths (which they do not eat but merely hold between their teeth), they replied that it prevents them from feeling hungry, and gives them great vigour and strength.
Pedro de Cieza de León (1550; 1883 edn) p.352. In the mid-16th century the annual supply of coca to Potosí (see 331:5) alone was reckoned to be worth half a million pesos, and the trade formed a major part of the country's economy.

3 This temple [Curicancha, near Cuzco] was more than four hundred paces in circuit, entirely surrounded by a strong wall ... Within there were four houses ... At the doors of these houses porters were stationed to keep guard over the virgins, many of whom were daughters of great lords, the most beautiful and charming that could be found. They remained in the temple until they became old. If one of them had knowledge of a man, they killed her by burying her alive; and the same penalty was suffered by the man.
Pedro de Cieza de León (1550; 1883 edn) pp.84–5. Curicancha meant 'the place of gold', this being the richest of all the temples in Peru, with doors and doorways of gold, figures adorned with gold and precious stones and 'a vast quantity of treasure'.

4 The health of the city [Cuzco] was promoted by spacious openings and squares, in which a numerous population from the capital and the distant country assembled to celebrate the high festivals of their religion. For Cuzco was the 'Holy City' and the great temple of the sun, to which pilgrims resorted from the furthest borders of the empire, was the most magnificent structure in the New World, and, unsurpassed, probably, in the costliness of its decorations by any building in the old.
William H. Prescott *History of the Conquest of Peru* (1847) Ch.1.

5 Hardly had we left the hut and rounded the promontory than we were confronted with an unexpected sight, a great flight of beautifully constructed stone-faced terraces, perhaps a hundred of them, each hundreds of feet long and ten feet high. They had been recently rescued from the jungle by the Indians ... On top of this particular ledge was a semicircular building ... This might also be a Temple of the Sun ... The flowing lines, the symmetrical arangement of the ashlars, and the gradual gradation of the courses, combined to produce a wonderful effect, softer and more pleasing than that of the marble temples of the Old World. Owing to the absence of mortar, there were no ugly spaces btween the rocks. They might have grown together ... Dimly, I began to realize that this wall and the adjoining semicircular temple over the cave were as fine as the finest stonework in the world.
Hiram Bingham *Lost City of the Incas* (1948); Brian M. Fagan (ed.) *Eyewitness to Discovery* (1996) pp.370–71. The flamboyant American explorer and academic led an expedition in search of Macchu Pichu in 1911.

6 Above all, weaving was developed to a point perhaps unequalled by man in the whole course of human history.
J.H. Parry (1966) Ch.3. On ancient Peru.

7 All their work is organized on an entirely communal basis, there is no social hierarchy or crime, and in the schools the children recite a greeting used in the time of the Incan empire: 'Don't lie, don't steal, don't be lazy.'

Guardian, 5 Jan. 2002, describing the life of the Uros, inhabitants of an island in Lake Titicaca at the end of the 20th century. The paper is reviewing Max Milligan *Realm of the Incas* (2001).

1 Another of these original kingdoms [of the island of Columbus's first landfall, Hispaniola] occupied the northern end of the plain where the royal harbour is today. Known as the Marién, it was a rich region, larger than Portugal, although a good deal more fertile and far better suited to human habitation, crisscrossed as it is by several mighty mountain ranges and seamed with productive gold and copper mines.

Bartolomé de Las Casas (1552; 1992 trans.) 'The Kingdoms of Hispaniola'.

NORTH AMERICA, c.1000–1500

2 The newcomers rowed towards them and stared at them in amazement as they came ashore. They were … dark coloured and evil looking, and their hair was coarse; they had large eyes and broad cheek-bones. They stayed for a while marvelling, and then rode away south round the headland. What the natives wanted most to buy was red cloth; they also wanted to buy swords and spears, but Thorfinni and Snorri forbade that. In exchange for the cloth they traded grey pelts. The natives took a span [about 9 inches] of red cloth for each pelt, and tied the cloth round their heads.

Anon. *The Vinland Sagas* 'The Norse Discovery of America: Eric's Saga' (early 13th century; 1965 trans.) pp.98–9. This often-told story was written down in Iceland (see 163:4). Eric the Red's kinsman Thorfinn, seeking Vinland c.1000, sailed into the river St Lawrence or south to Maine, where he met the native Americans, 500 years before Columbus. He 'found self-sown fields of wheat where the ground was low lying, and vines wherever there was high ground'.

3 There are people on this coast [Newfoundland] whose bodies are fairly well formed but they are wild and savage folk. They wear their hair tied up at the top of their heads like a handful of twisted hay, with a nail or something of the sort passed through the middle and into it they weave a few birds' feathers. They clothe themselves with the fur of animals, both men and women, but the women are wrapped up more closely and snuggly in their furs; they have a belt about their waists. They all paint themselves with certain tan colours.

Jacques Cartier, 12 June 1534; *Voyages* (1924 edn) p.23. The French explorer already had an eye for the furs.

4 It is not known how the Mississippan culture arose; presumably it began locally with ideas and systems derived from the Hopewell culture [c.1000 BC], then … received a strong agricultural base, together with an infusion of new cultural traits that came from the Huastec area of Mexico.

Alvin M. Josephy Jr *The Indian Heritage of America* (1975) p.111.

5 A duke of Twakanah had collected the people from several towns, came out to meet them the people around them, singing, beating their little drums; after danced the ceremony was performed and the band of warriors was invited into the national house.

Iroquois account of Atotarhas VII's embassy of the Five Nations reaching the Mississippi; David Cusick *Sketches of Ancient History of the Six Nations* (1825). This event may have occurred as early as AD 900 or as late as 1680. The League of the Five Nations was an alliance of Iroquois tribes, and the English is the result of translation from Iroquois. Cusick belonged to the Tuscarora, which became the sixth nation.

6 In the beginning before the formation of the earth; the country above the sky was inhabited by Superior Beings, over whom the Great Spirit presided. His daughter having become pregnant by an illicit connection, he pulled up a great tree by the roots, and threw her through the cavity thereby formed; but to prevent her utter destruction, he previously ordered the Great Turtle to get from the bottom of the waters some slime on its back, and to wait on the surface of the water to receive her on it … she began to form the earth, and by the time of her delivery had increased it to the extent of a little island. Her child was a daughter; and as she grew up the earth extended under her arms.

Creation myth, recorded in 1805 in *Journal of Major John Norton* (1816; 1970 edn); Carla Mulford (ed.) *Early American Writings* (2002) p.7. Norton, an anthropologist of Scottish and Cherokee parents, collected accounts such as this from the Nottowegni or Five Nations of the Iroquois. See 43:1 and 48:2.

7   After the flood the Lenape lived close together
            in their houses in Turtle Land;
        Where they live it freezes, it snows, it's windy
            and it's cold.
        Coming out of the northern winter, with
            milder weather, they had many deer and
            buffalo
        And became strong and rich in mind;
        The planters separated [from the hunters].

Anon. *Walam Olum* (17th century) Pt 2; Brotherston (1979) p.193. The Lenape were recording their own history as a nation.

Athens and her Rivals, 766–399 BC

THE EMERGENCE OF THE CITY-STATES, c.800–c.700 BC

1 I begin the real history of Greece with the first recorded Olympiad [a period of four years, from one Olympic games to the next], or 776 BC ... For the truth is, that historical records properly so called, do not begin until after this date ... The times which I thus set apart from the region of history are discernible only through a different atmosphere – that of epic poetry and legend.
George Grote *History of Greece* (1846–56) Preface. This was, and remained for 50 years, the most authoritative work on the subject.

2 Some say that Lycurgus flourished at the same time as Iphitus and joined in the establishment of the Olympic Truce and even Aristotle is among their number. He put forward in evidence the discus at Olympia on which the name of Lycurgus is written down and preserved.
Plutarch (c.46–c.127) *Lives* (1977 trans.) 'Lycurgus' Ch.1. The Olympic Truce did not mean that all wars in Greek lands ceased during the period of the games but that all competitors and others travelling to the games were to be allowed free passage. The games were open to all Greeks and were held every four years until AD 393. The modern Olympic Games were established in 1896. For Lycurgus see 59:7.

3 It appears that the country now called Hellas had no settled population in ancient times; instead there was a series of migrations ... We have no record of any action taken by Hellas as a whole before the Trojan War. Indeed, my view is that at this time the country was not even called 'Hellas' ... Homer ... nowhere uses the name 'Hellenic' for the whole force ... For the rest in his poems he uses the words 'Danaans', 'Argives' and 'Achaeans' ... By 'Hellenic' I mean here both those who took on the name city by city, as a result of a common language, and those who later were all called by the common name.
Thucydides *The History of the Peloponnesian War* (c.431–c.404 BC; 1984 trans.) Bk 1.2–3. Thucydides (c.460–c.400 BC) was an Athenian general in 424 and was exiled after failing to save Amphipolis in northern Greece from the Spartan general Brasidas. He began his history soon after the commencement of hostilities in 431 (see 56:2).

4 Again there is the Greek nation – the common blood, the common language; the temples and religious ritual; the whole way of life we understand and share together.
Herodotus (c.485–c.425 BC) *The Histories* (1954 trans.) Bk 8.144. The 'Father of History' was born in Halicarnassus (Bodrum in Turkey) and travelled widely.

5 The peoples who live in cold climates and in European areas are full of energy, but rather lacking in intelligence and skill; they therefore in general retain their freedom but lack political organization and the ability to control their neighbours. The peoples of Asia on the other hand are better endowed with intellect and skill but lack energy and so remain in political subjection. But the people of Greece occupy a middle geographical position and correspondingly have a share of both characteristics, both energy and intelligence. They therefore retain their freedom and have the best of political institutions; indeed if they could achieve political unity they could control the rest of the world.
Aristotle (384–322 BC) *Politics* (1984 trans.) Bk 7, Ch.7.1327b. Aristotle's wide interests included politics and constitutions as well as biology and moral philosophy.

6 One might reasonably suppose that the city [Athens] lies at the centre of Greece, or rather of the whole inhabited world. For the further we go from her, the more intense is the heat or cold we meet with; and every traveller who would cross from one to the other end of Greece passes Athens as the centre of a circle, whether he goes by water or by road.
Xenophon *Ways and Means* (c.355 BC; 1925 edn) Bk 1.6. Xenophon (c.428–c.354 BC) was a prolific writer, best known for his account in the *Anabasis* (see 57:7) of the march of 10,000 Greek mercenaries to try to put Cyrus on the throne of Persia, in which he played a major part.

7 The Phoenicians ... introduced into Greece ... a number of accomplishments, of which the most important was writing, an art until then, I think, unknown to the Greeks. At first they used the same characters as all the other Phoenicians, but as time went on, and they changed their language, they also changed the shape of their letters.

Herodotus (c.485–c.425 BC) (1954 trans.) Bk 5.58. The Phoenicians were a Semitic people living on the eastern Mediterranean seaboard and trading most famously from Tyre and Sidon (Lebanon). They dominated trade in the area from before 1000 BC, founded Carthage (traditionally in 814 BC) and invented the alphabet by 1000 BC.

1 Pheidon of Argos ... invented weights and measures, and coinage struck from silver and other metals ... Ephorus [a 4th-century BC historian whose works are lost] says that silver was first coined in Aegina, by Pheidon.

Strabo (c.60 BC–AD c.24) *Geography* Vol.6 (1929 trans.) Bk 8, 3.33 and 6.16. The first coins in Greece were struck on the island of Aegina, south of Athens, which was an active trading city in the 7th century, and they date to the last quarter of that century, about 50 years later than the probable date of Pheidon, king of Argos. Strabo was a Greek from the Black Sea. Although he was not a great traveller, his fascinating work covers most of the Roman empire.

LAWGIVERS

2 The Council of the Areopagus had the task of watching over the laws; in fact it controlled the greater and most important part of the life of the community as the only and final authority in regard to the punishment of public offenders and the imposition of fines. It must be observed that the selection of the archons was based on considerations of birth and wealth, and that the Areopagus consisted of former archons.

Aristotle (384–322 BC) *Constitution of Athens* (1950 trans.) 3.6. The Council of the Areopagus lost most of its powers in 462 BC under the democracy.

3 First of all, then, Solon repealed all Draco's laws because of their harshness and the excessively heavy penalties they carried; the only exceptions were the laws relating to homicide. Under the Draconian code almost any offence was liable to the death penalty, so that even those convicted of idleness were executed, and those who stole fruit or vegetables suffered the same punishment as those who committed sacrilege or murder. This is the reason why, in later times, Demades became famous for his remark that Draco's code was written not in ink but in blood. Draco himself, when he was once asked why he had decreed the death penalty for the great majority of offences, replied that he considered the minor ones deserved it, and so for the major ones no heavier punishment was left.

Plutarch (c.46–c.127) (1960 trans.) 'Solon' Ch.17. Draco's laws (c.621 BC) came to be regarded as so severe that the word 'draconian' is used to mean harsh. The codifying of laws was one of the first uses to which the new writing was put. It was an important step on the way to the political constitutions of the 5th century.

4 Croesus [king of Lydia, famous for his wealth] said: 'Well, my Athenian friend, I have heard a great deal about your wisdom, and how widely you have travelled in the pursuit of knowledge. I cannot resist my desire to ask you a question: who is the happiest man you have ever seen?'

'My lord,' replied Solon, '... You are very rich, and you rule a numerous people; but the question you asked me I will not answer, until I know that you have died happily ... Until he is dead, keep the word "happy" in reserve. Till then, he is not happy, but only lucky.'

Herodotus (c.485–c.425 BC) (1954 trans.) Bk 1.30–2.

GREEK TYRANTS

5 The Samians are responsible for three of the greatest building and engineering feats in the Greek world: the first is a tunnel nearly a mile long, eight feet wide and eight feet high, driven clean through the base of a hill nine hundred feet in height. The whole length of it carries a second cutting thirty feet deep and three broad along which water from an abundant source is led through pipes into the town ... Secondly there is the artificial harbour enclosed by a breakwater, which runs out into twenty fathoms [about 120 feet] of water and has a total length of over a quarter of a mile; and lastly the island has the biggest of all known Greek temples.

Herodotus (c.485–c.425 BC) (1954 trans.) Bk 3.60. Work on the tunnel began at both ends and the two teams met within a few feet of an exact join in the middle.

6 Pisistratus [from 561] administered the state moderately, his rule being more like a constitutional government than like a tyranny. For he was benevolent and kind, and readily forgave those who had committed an offence; he even advanced money to the poor so that they could make a living by farming. His purpose was twofold: first, that they might not stay in the city but live scattered all over the country; secondly, that they might be moderately well off but fully occupied with their own affairs so that they would have neither a strong desire nor the leisure to concern themselves with public affairs.

Aristotle (384–322 BC) *Constitution of Athens* (1950 trans.) 16. Solon's constitution was interrupted by a period of 'tyranny', the term used for an unconstitutional ruler or dictator rather than an hereditary king, but not necessarily implying a cruel or arbitrary regime.

1 In the archonship of Telesinus [487/6 BC] they selected, for the first time since the tyranny, the nine archons by lot through the tribes, from among five hundred candidates previously elected …
Previously the archons had all been elected by vote.

Aristotle (384–322 BC) *Constitution of Athens* (1950 trans.) 22. The use of lot, often from a previously selected list, was an important factor in full democracy, because almost anyone could thereby hold high office of state, but because the position was held for only one year, they could not build up a power base. Only the office of general (*strategos*) was never filled by lot, because in war it was essential to have the very best commanders.

2 Cleisthenes enacted new ones [laws] with the aim of winning the people's favour. Among these was the law about ostracism.

Aristotle (384–322 BC) *Constitution of Athens* (1950 trans.) 22. Ostracism involved exiling any citizen who appeared to the people to be too powerful and a potential threat to the constitution. The citizens wrote names on a potsherd (*ostrakon*). Whoever received the greatest number of votes and not fewer than 6,000 had to settle his private affairs within ten days and leave the city for ten years. It did not involve disgrace or loss of property, and during the Persian Wars in the first half of the 5th century those who had been ostracized were recalled to help the city.

3 Athens went from strength to strength, and proved, if proof were needed, how noble a thing freedom is, not in one respect only, but in all; for while they were oppressed under a despotic government, they had no better success in war than any of their neighbours, yet once the yoke was flung off, they proved the finest fighters in the world.

Herodotus (c.485–c.425 BC) (1954 trans.) Bk 5.78. Herodotus reflects the normal ancient view that the main function of the state is military.

THE PERSIAN WARS, c.500–c.450 BC

4 Darius took a bow, set an arrow on the string, and shot it up into the air and cried: 'Grant, O God, that I may punish the Athenians.' Then he commanded one of his servants to repeat to him the words,

'Master, remember the Athenians', three times, whenever he sat down to dinner.

Herodotus (c.485–c.425 BC) (1954 trans.) Bk 5.105. Darius I, the Great, king of Persia (r.522–486 BC), had asked who was responsible for the destruction of Sardes, the political capital of the western province of the Persian empire, in the Ionian revolt of 499–497 BC.

5 Before they left the city, the Athenian generals sent off a message to Sparta. The messenger was an Athenian named Philippides [or Pheidippides] a trained runner … He reached Sparta the day after he left Athens [more than 150 miles]. At once he delivered his message to the Spartan government. 'Men of Sparta, the Athenians ask you to help them, and not to stand by while the most ancient city of Greece is crushed and enslaved by a foreign invader' … The Spartans, though moved by the appeal, and willing to send help to Athens, were unable to send it promptly because they did not wish to break their law. It was the ninth day of the month, and they said they could not take the field until the moon was full. So they waited for the full moon, and meanwhile Hippias, the son of Pisistratus, guided the Persians to Marathon.

Herodotus (c.485–c.425 BC) (1954 trans.) Bk 6.105–6.

6 In the Battle of Marathon some 6,400 Persians were killed; the losses of the Athenians were 192.

Herodotus (c.485–c.425 BC) (1954 trans.) Bk 6.117. These figures are likely to be accurate. The Athenian dead would have been recorded by name on the stelae (tombstones) originally adorning the great mound over the tomb of the fallen warriors still to be seen at Marathon. The moderation of the estimate of Persian dead, who may well have been counted where they lay, makes it trustworthy.

7 Philippides [or Pheidippides] … brought the news of the victory from Marathon and addressed the magistrates in session when they were anxious to know how the battle had ended; 'Rejoice, we've won,' he said and then he died breathing his last breath with those words.

Lucian (c.120–c.180) *A Slip of the Tongue in Greeting* (1904 trans.) Bk 3. This addition to Herodotus' story has given rise to the modern marathon race, the distance from Marathon to Athens being about 25 miles (the marathon distance is 26 miles 385 yards). Lucian has the same man run back to fight at Marathon and then take the good news to Athens. His best known work is *The True Story*, which includes a journey to the moon.

8 This headland was the point to which Xerxes' engineers carried their two bridges from Abydos, a distance of seven furlongs. One was constructed by the Phoenicians using flax cables, the other by the Egyptians with papyrus cables. The work was successfully completed, but a subsequent storm of great violence smashed it up and carried everything away. Xerxes was very angry and gave orders that the Hellespont should receive three hundred lashes and have a pair of fetters thrown into it.

Herodotus (c.485–c.425 BC) (1954 trans.) Bk 7.33–5. Xerxes I (c.519–465 BC) succeeded his father, Darius I, in 486 BC and spent several years preparing his expedition to Greece, including digging a canal across the Athos peninsula (about 1½ miles) and constructing a bridge of boats across the Hellespont (the Dardanelles), which is about 1 mile across, after the first bridges were destroyed.

1 How to deal with the situation Xerxes had no idea; but while he was still wondering what his next move should be, a man from Malis got himself admitted to his presence. This was Ephialtes and he had come, in hope of a rich reward, to tell the king about the track which led over the hills to Thermopylae – and the information he gave was to prove the death of the Greeks who held the pass.

Herodotus (c.485–c.425 BC) (1954 trans.) Bk 7.213.

2 The Greeks, who knew that the enemy were on their way round by the mountain track and that death was inevitable, fought with reckless desperation, exerting every ounce of strength that was in them against the invader. By this time most of their spears were broken, and they were killing Persians with their swords. In the course of that fight Leonidas [Spartan king and overall commander] fell, having fought like a man indeed. Many distinguished Spartans were killed at his side – their names, like the names of all the three hundred ... deserve to be remembered.

Herodotus (c.485–c.425 BC) (1954 trans.) Bk 7.223–4.

3 This is pleasant news ... for if the Persians hide the sun, we shall have our battle in the shade.

Herodotus (c.485–c.425 BC) (1954 trans.) Bk 7.226. The Spartan Dieneces' comment on hearing that there were so many Persian arrows that they hid the sun.

4 The dead were buried where they fell, and with them the men who had been killed before those dismissed by Leonidas left the pass. Over them is this inscription, in honour of the whole force:

> Four thousand here from Pelops' land
> Against three million once did stand.

The Spartans have a special epitaph; it runs:
> Tell them in Sparta, passer-by,
> That here, obedient to their word, we lie.

Simonides, epitaphs, c.480 BC; Herodotus (c.485–c.425 BC) (1954 trans.) Bk 7.228.

5 Zeus the all-seeing grants to Athene's prayer
> That the wooden wall only shall not fail, but
> help you and your children.
> But await not the host of horse and foot coming
> from Asia.

Delphic oracle, 480 BC; Herodotus (1954 trans.) Bk 7.141. This was interpreted by a few older men as the hedge or palisade that originally fenced the Acropolis, but Themistocles, the statesman and naval commander, persuaded the majority that it referred to their ships.

6 This depth of horror Xerxes saw; close to the
> sea
> On a high hill he sat, where he could clearly
> watch
> His whole force both by sea and land. He
> wailed aloud,
> And tore his clothes, weeping; and instantly
> dismissed
> His army, hastening them to a disordered
> flight.

Aeschylus *The Persians* (472 BC; 1961 trans.) lines 65–70. The messenger's description of the Battle of Salamis (480 BC) is the earliest account we have. Because Aeschylus (525–456 BC) either took part in or watched the battle, the play is a serious historical document, even though its prime purpose was to win the drama competition – in which he succeeded – by glorifying the victory of the Athenians.

THE AGE OF PERICLES, c.460–429 BC

7 Nicias once owned a 1,000 slaves in the mines and let them out to Sosias on condition that Sosias paid him an obol per head a day and filled all vacancies as they occurred.

Xenophon (c.355 BC; 1925 edn) Bk 4.14. The wealth of Athens in the 5th century owed much to the silver mines at Laurium, in the southeast of Attica. Individuals such as Nicias could also achieve great personal wealth from mining concessions. An obol was one-sixth of a drachma; jurors were paid a daily allowance of three obols.

8 There were other instances when he would not give way to the Athenians' more reckless impulses. He refused to be swept along with them, when they became intoxicated with their power and good

fortune ... Many people, even as early as this, were obsessed with that extravagant and ill-starred ambition to conquer Sicily, which was afterwards fanned into flame by Alcibiades and other orators.
Plutarch (c.46–c.127) (1960 trans.) 'Pericles' Ch.20. For Alcibiades see 56:3.

1 Phidias the sculptor had been entrusted with the contract for producing the great statue of Athena [for the Parthenon in Athens, 447–438 BC]. His friendship with Pericles ... earned him a number of enemies through pure jealousy ... who persuaded one of the artists working under Phidias to sit in the marketplace as a suppliant and ask for the protection of the state in return for laying information against Phidias ... The charge of embezzlement was not proved because from the very beginning, on Pericles' own advice, the gold used for the statue had been superimposed and laid around it in such a way that it could all be taken off and weighed. This is what Pericles now ordered the prosecution to do.
Plutarch (c.46–c.127) (1960 trans.) 'Pericles' Ch.31.

2 Pericles added to this the money in the other temples which might be used and which came to a considerable sum, and said that, if they were ever reduced to absolute extremities, they could even use the gold on the statue of Athena herself. There was, he informed them, a weight of forty talents of pure gold, all of which was removable.
Thucydides (c.431–c.404 BC; 1954 trans.) Bk 2.13. In 431 BC Pericles made a statement to the assembly on the resources of the Athenian state. Thucydides took part in the early stages of the war but was exiled from Athens in 424 BC. He determined to write its history from 431 BC. He breaks off in 411 BC.

3 When the action took place in which I won my decoration for valour, it was entirely to Socrates that I owed my preservation; he would not leave me when I was wounded, but succeeded in rescuing both me and my arms.
Plato (427–347 BC) Symposium (1951 trans.) 220. Alcibiades, a brilliant young man whose political and military career underwent extreme vicissitudes, both saving and betraying his city (see 57:2 and 57:3), praises Socrates' exploits on military service, here at Potidaea in 432 BC, the siege of which by Athens was one of the immediate causes of the Peloponnesian War.

4 Let us realize that the tyrant city [Athens] that has been established in Greece is there to dominate all alike, with a programme of universal empire. ... Let

us then attack and destroy it and win future security for ourselves and freedom for the Greeks who are now enslaved.
Thucydides (c.431–c.404 BC; 1943 trans.) Bk 1.124. The Corinthians urge the Spartans and their other allies to declare war on Athens.

5 In short, I say that as a city we are the school of Hellas; while I doubt if the world can produce a man, who, where he has only himself to depend upon, is equal to so many emergencies, and graced by so happy a versatility, as the Athenian. ... We have forced every sea and land to be the highway of our daring, and everywhere, for good or ill, we have left imperishable monuments behind us.
Pericles, 430 BC; Thucydides (c.431–c.404 BC; 1984 trans.) Bk 2.41.

6 So these men died as became Athenians ... You must yourselves realize the power of Athens, and feed your eyes upon her from day to day, till you become a lover of her; and then when all her greatness breaks upon you, you must reflect that it was by courage, sense of duty, and a keen feeling of honour in action that men were enabled to win all this ... For heroes have the whole earth for their tomb.
Pericles, 430 BC; Thucydides (c.431–c.404 BC; 1984 trans.) Bk 2.43.

7 The right way to deal with free people is this – not to inflict tremendous punishments on them after they have revolted, but to take tremendous care of them before this point is reached, to prevent them even contemplating the idea of revolt, and, if we do have to use force with them, to hold as few as possible of them responsible.
Thucydides (c.431–c.404 BC; 1954 trans.) Bk 3.46. A certain Diodotus argued for mercy, but the case argued by Cleon for killing the entire population of Mytilene on the island of Lesbos just prevailed.

8 Another trireme was at once despatched in haste, for fear that the first might arrive before it and the city be found destroyed ... the crew made such efforts on the voyage that they took their meals ... while they rowed, and took it in turns to row and sleep. They were lucky to meet no contrary wind, and as the first ship made no haste on its monstrous mission, while the second pressed on as described, the first arrived so little ahead that Pakhes [the commander] had only just had time to read the decree and prepare to carry out its sentence when the second put into harbour and prevented the massacre.

Thucydides (c.431–c.404 BC; 1943 trans.) Bk 3.49. The Athenians rescinded their decision to kill the people of Mytilene and made haste to prevent the initial decision being carried out.

1 About 120 of the prisoners were Spartans … Crazy as Cleon's promise was, he fulfilled it, by bringing the men to Athens within the twenty days as he had pledged himself to do. Nothing in the war surprised Greece as much as this. It was thought that no force or famine could make the Spartans give up their arms, but that they would fight on and die with them in their hands.

Thucydides (c.431–c.404 BC; 1943 trans.) Bk 4.38–40. The Athenians gained a foothold on the southwest Peloponnese in 425 BC, an advantage that eventually led to the Peace of Nicias in 421 BC. The impatience of the Athenians at the length of the blockade of Sphacteria, an island off Pylos where a Spartan unit had landed, led to Cleon, the demagogic leader in the years after Pericles, taking up a challenge from the general Nicias to take a force himself and do better. To the surprise of all he succeeded.

2 At the Olympic games I entered seven chariots for the chariot race (more than any private individual before), took first second and fourth places … It is not a mere useless folly when a man benefits not only himself but his city at his own expense … What I do know is that men of this kind, and all who have attained to any distinction, are unpopular in their lifetime … but that later generations are eager to claim relationship with them … while their country boasts about them.

Alcibiades, 415 BC; Thucydides (c.431–c.404 BC; 1954 trans.) Bk 6.16. Alcibiades seemed uniquely capable of saving the city, even after going over to the Spartans (when the Athenians had condemned him to death). Here he is eager to lead the expedition to Sicily and defends himself against Nicias, who advised the assembly against both the expedition itself and Alcibiades' command. In antiquity, too, sporting success could give huge status.

3 In the midst of these preparations the faces of most of the stone busts of Hermes in the city of Athens – they are the customary square figures, so common in the doorways of private houses and temples – were mutilated one night … Alcibiades was implicated in this charge and it was taken up by those who most disliked him … They accordingly exaggerated the incidents and loudly proclaimed that the parody of the mysteries and the mutilation … were part and parcel of a scheme to overthrow the democracy and that Alcibiades was behind it all.

Thucydides (c.431–c.404 BC; 1943 trans.) Bk 6.27–8. The sacrilege involved was deeply shocking; the Eleusinian mysteries were held in the highest respect, many people from all levels of society being initiates. Despite this setback, the expedition went ahead. Alcibiades was recalled, fled to Sparta and was condemned to death in his absence.

4 This was the greatest action of this war, and, in my opinion, the greatest action that we know of in Greek history – to the victors the most brilliant of successes, to the vanquished the most calamitous of defeats.

Thucydides (c.431–c.404 BC; 1954 trans.) Bk 7.87, on the Athenian defeat at Syracuse in 413 BC.

5 Most of the Athenian prisoners of war perished in the stone quarries from disease and lack of food and water … Some were also saved for their knowledge of Euripides. For it seems that the Sicilians were more devoted to his poetry than any other Greeks living beyond the homeland … Many of the Athenians who reached home in safety greeted Euripides with affectionate gratitude and told him that they had gained their freedom by reciting what they remembered of his works; others had received food and drink as they wandered about after the final battle, in return for singing his choral lyrics.

Plutarch (c.46–c.127) (1915 edn) 'Nicias' Ch.29.

6 Lysander seemed an equivocal and unprincipled character who disguised most of his actions in war with various forms of deceit … He laughed at those who insisted that the descendants of Heracles should not stoop to trickery in warfare and remarked, 'Where the lion's skin [worn by Heracles] will not reach, we must patch it out with the fox's.'

Plutarch (c.46–c.127) (1960 trans.) 'Lysander' Ch.7. The Spartan general finally defeated Athens in 405 BC at the Battle of Aegospotami (Dardanelles), after improving the Peloponnesian navy with financial help from Persia. Athens surrendered in 404 BC.

THE MARCH OF THE 10,000, 401 BC

7 With their generals arrested and the captains and soldiers who had gone with them put to death, the Greeks were in an extremely awkward position … There was an Athenian in the army called Xenophon, who accompanied the expedition neither as a general nor a captain nor an ordinary soldier [but as a friend of one of the generals] … 'If you are willing to take the initiative, I am prepared to follow you. If you appoint me to be your leader I make no excuses about my age …' This was what Xenophon said and after listening to him all the captains urged him to be their leader.

Xenophon *Anabasis* (c.375 BC; 1949 trans.) Bk 3.1. Cyrus, brother of the Persian King Artaxerxes, recruited 10,000 Greek mercenaries to help him seize the throne for himself. He was killed at the battle of Cunaxa, near Babylon, in 401 BC, and the Greek forces had somehow to make their way back to Greece. Xenophon became a general and also recorded the story of the expedition.

1 They came to the mountain on the fifth day, the mountain being called Theches [above Trebizond, Trabzon]. When the men in front reached the summit and caught sight of the sea [Black Sea in eastern Turkey] there was great shouting. Xenophon and the rearguard heard it and thought there were some more enemies attacking in the front … It grew louder and nearer … so Xenophon mounted his horse … and quite soon they heard the soldiers shouting out 'The sea! The sea!' and passing the word down the column. Then they all began to run, rearguard and all with the baggage animals and the horses at full speed; and when they had all got to the top, the soldiers with tears in their eyes embraced each other and the generals and captains. And on a sudden, the soldiers began to bring stones and to build a great cairn.

Xenophon (c.375 BC; 1949 trans.) Bk 4.7. As seafarers, the Greeks believed that once they reached the sea they could always find their way home. But the sea, although visible, was still a hard five days' march away. The cairn was rediscovered in 1996.

THE DEATH OF SOCRATES, 399 BC

2 What is appropriate for a poor man who is a public benefactor and who requires leisure for giving you moral encouragement? Nothing could be more appropriate than free maintenance at the state's expense. He deserves it much more than any victor in the races at Olympia, whether he wins with a single horse or a pair or a team of four. These people give you the semblance of happiness, but I give you the reality; they do not need maintenance, but I do. So if I am to propose a penalty strictly in accordance with justice, I propose free maintenance by the state.

Socrates, 399 BC; Plato (427–347 BC) *Symposium* (1954 trans.) 36. Socrates has the opportunity to ask for a penalty less severe than that called for by the prosecution at his trial – in this case, death.

3 Quite calmly and with no sign of distaste, Socrates drained the cup [of hemlock] in one breath …

The coldness was spreading about as far as his waist when Socrates uncovered his face – for he had covered it up – and said (they were his last words): 'Crito, we ought to offer a cock to Asclepius. See to it and don't forget.'

'No, it shall be done,' said Crito. 'Are you sure that there is nothing else?'

Socrates made no reply, but after a moment he stirred; and when the man uncovered him, his eyes were fixed. When Crito saw this, he closed the mouth and eyes.

Plato (427–347 BC) *Phaedo* (1954 trans.) 117A–118. The death of Socrates in 399 BC. Asclepius was the god of healing. Socrates' request implies that death is the cure for life and so merits a thank offering to the god.

GREEK MEN ON WOMEN

4 If I must say anything on the subject of female excellence to those of you who will now be in widowhood, it will all be comprised in this brief exhortation. Great will be your glory in not falling short of your natural character; and greatest will be hers who is least talked of among the men whether for good or for bad.

Pericles, funeral speech, 430 BC; Thucydides (c.431–c.404 BC; 1984 trans.) Bk 2.45.

5 I think that the wife who is a good partner in the household contributes just as much as her husband to its good; because the incomings are for the most part the result of the husband's exertions, but the outgoings are controlled mostly by the wife.

Socrates (469–399 BC); Xenophon *Oeconomicus* (c.362 BC; 1925 edn) Bk 3.15. Socrates discusses estate management with his friends.

6 Since the marriage of Pericles and his wife was unsatisfactory, with her own consent he parted with her to another man, and himself took Aspasia and loved her with wonderful affection; every day when he left the house or returned from the marketplace, he embraced her with a kiss.

Plutarch (c.46–c.127) (1876 trans.) 'Pericles' Ch.24. Aspasia, an immigrant from Miletus, lived in Athens and belonged to the broad category of women regarded as courtesans (*hetairai*) who could not marry Athenian citizens. Their son was given full Athenian citizenship by decree.

1 The Megarians stole two of Aspasia's girls in retaliation. And that, gentlemen, was the cause of the war that has been raging throughout Greece these six years: it was all on account of three prostitutes. Because Pericles, Olympian Pericles, sent out thunder and lightning and threw all Greece into confusion.
Aristophanes *Acharnians* (425 BC; 1973 trans.) lines 526–31. A satirical view.

2   And, they tell us, we at home
Live free from danger, they go out to battle:
     fools!
I'd rather stand three times in the front line
     than bear
One child.
Euripides *Medea* (431 BC; 1963 trans.) lines 230 ff.

3   I will not allow either boyfriend or husband
To approach me in an erect condition
And I will live at home without any sexual
     activity
Wearing my best make-up and my most
     seductive dresses
To inflame my husband's ardour.
Aristophanes *Lysistrata* (411 BC; 1973 trans.) lines 212–16. The women swear an oath to go on a sex strike until the men end the war.

GREEK SCIENCE

4 We do not feel the heat of the stars because they are so far from the earth … The sun is larger than the Peloponnese. The moon has no light of its own but derives it from the sun … Eclipses of the moon occur when it is screened by the earth, or sometimes by bodies beneath the moon; those of the sun when it is screened by the moon when it is new … The moon is made of earth and has plains and ravines on it.
Anaxagoras (*c*.500–*c*.428 BC); Hippolytus *Refutation of all Heresies* (3rd century AD; 1957 trans.) 1.8.7–10. Scientific inquiry was a hallmark of the 5th century, many thinkers being attracted to Athens under the democracy. Thales was believed to have been the first Greek to predict an eclipse, in 585 BC.

5 I swear by Apollo the physician and Asclepius … that I will fulfil this oath and this written covenant to

the best of my power … The regimen I adopt shall be for the benefit of the patients to the best of my power and judgement, not for their injury or any wrongful purpose. I will not give a deadly drug to any one … and I will not give a woman means to procure an abortion …

I will not abuse my position to indulge in sexual contacts with the bodies of men or women whether slave or free …

Whatever I see or hear, professionally or privately, which ought not to be divulged, I will keep silence on, counting such things to be as religious secrets.
Hippocrates (*c*.460–*c*.377 BC), oath; R.W. Livingstone (ed.) *The Legacy of Greece* (1921), p.213. Hippocrates is now known as the 'Father of Medicine'. Versions of the oath were used in many medical schools until well into the 20th century.

6 Life is short, science is long; opportunity is elusive, experiment is dangerous, judgement is difficult. It is not enough for the physician to do what is necessary, but the patient and the attendants must do their part as well, and circumstances must be favourable.
Hippocrates (*c*.460–*c*.377 BC) *Aphorisms* (1950 trans.) 1.1. The first words are famous in their Latin form: *vita brevis, ars longa*.

SPARTA

7 Lycurgus who gave the Spartans the laws that they obey and to which they owe their prosperity, I regard with wonder; and I believe he achieved the utmost limit of wisdom. For it was not by imitating other states but by devising a system quite different from that of most others that he made his country pre-eminent in prosperity.
Xenophon *Constitution of Sparta* (*c*.388 BC; 1925 edn) Bk 1.2. It is not known when Lycurgus lived (see 52:2), but the constitution that bears his name is generally ascribed to the early 7th century BC.

8 If Sparta were to be depopulated and only the temples and foundations of the buildings left, posterity would never, I think, believe in later ages the reports of her fame … because she has no fully built-up area nor elaborate temples and buildings, but only a group of villages in the old Greek manner … but, if Athens suffered the same fate, men would infer her power had been twice as great as it really has, because of what their eyes could see.
Thucydides (*c*.431–*c*.404 BC; 1943 trans.) Bk 1.10.

1 He [Lycurgus] ordered the maidens to exercise themselves with wrestling, running, throwing the quoit and casting the javelin, to the end that the fruit they conceived might, in strong and healthy bodies, take firmer root and find better growth, and that they might be the more able to undergo the pains of child-bearing.

Plutarch (c.46–c.127) (1876 trans.) 'Lycurgus' Ch.14. A sharp contrast with the secluded life of the wives and daughters of Athenian citizens.

2 Nor was it in the power of the father to dispose of the child as he thought fit … Elders of his tribe … carefully viewed the child, and if they found it stout and well made, they ordered it to be reared and allotted to it one of the nine thousand shares of land … but if they found it puny and ill-shaped, they ordered it to be taken to a sort of chasm under Mount Taygetus.

Plutarch (c.46–c.127) (1876 trans.) 'Lycurgus' Ch.16. The exposure of neonates was not confined to the Spartans.

3 After they were twelve years old, they were no longer allowed to wear any undergarment; they had one coat to serve them a year; their bodies were hard and dry, with but little acquaintance of baths and unguents … They lodged together in little bands upon beds made of the rushes which grew by the banks of the River Eurotas, which they were to break off with their hands without a knife … He set over each band of them for their captain the most temperate and boldest of those they called the *irens*, who were usually twenty years old, two years out of the boys.

Plutarch (c.46–c.127) (1876 trans.) 'Lycurgus' Ch.16. The type of practice that gave rise to the modern use of the word Spartan.

4 So seriously did the Spartan children go about their stealing, that a youth, having stolen a young fox and hidden it under his coat, suffered it to tear out his very bowels with its teeth and claws, and died upon the spot, rather than let it be seen.

Plutarch (c.46–c.127) (1876 trans.) 'Lycurgus' Ch.18.

5 In order that even the kings should eat in public, he assigned to them their own public mess tent and honoured them with a double portion at the meal. This was not so that they might eat enough for two but so that they might have the wherewithal to honour anyone whom they chose.

Xenophon (c.388 BC; 1925 edn) Bk 15.4.

6 In the equipment that he devised for the troops in battle he included a red cloak, because he believed this garment to have least resemblance to women's clothing and to be most suitable for war; and a brass shield because it is soonest polished and tarnishes very slowly. He also permitted men who were past their first youth to wear long hair, believing that it would make them look taller, more dignified and more terrifying.

Xenophon (c.388 BC; 1925 edn) Bk 11.2.

7 The helots [serfs] were invited by proclamation to pick out those among themselves who claimed to have most distinguished themselves against the enemy, in order that they might receive their freedom … As many as two thousand were accordingly selected, who crowned themselves and visited the temples, rejoicing in their new freedom. The Spartans, however, soon afterwards did away with them, and no one ever knew how they died.

Thucydides (c.431–c.404 BC; 1943 trans.) Bk 4.80. Fear of the helots, who vastly outnumbered their Spartan masters, may account for the Spartan way of life and the perceived need to be in a constant state of military readiness. There was a helot revolt in the 460s BC, after an earthquake in 464. The Messenian helots were freed by Thebes in 369 BC, and the city of Messene was founded in the southwestern Peloponnese. The Laconian helots were not freed until the early 2nd century BC.

Alexander and Greece in the 4th Century BC

THE STRUGGLE FOR SUPREMACY IN THE 4TH CENTURY BC

1 'The Thebans are mightier in war,' proclaim the trophies won by victory with the spear at Leuctra.
Inscription, 371 BC; Marcus N. Tod *Inscriptiones Graecae* Vol.2 (1948) 7.2462. This epigram was set up by three Thebans to commemorate the Battle of Leuctra (371 BC), which brought to an end Spartan domination and led to a short period of Theban supremacy under Epaminondas. Thebes is in Boeotia, in central Greece, to the northwest of Attica.

2 Gorgidas of Thebes first formed the Sacred Band of 300 chosen men to whom the State allowed provision and all things necessary for military exercise ... Others say that it was composed of young men attached to one another by personal affection ... for a band cemented by friendship grounded upon love is never to be broken and thereby invincible. Lovers, ashamed to be base in the sight of their beloved as the beloved before their lovers, willingly rush into danger for the relief of one another.
Plutarch (c.46–c.127) *Lives* (1876 trans.) 'Pelopidas' Ch.14. The Sacred Band of 150 pairs of lovers, formed in 378 BC, remained unbeaten until its annihilation at the Battle of Chaeroneia (see 62:1) against Philip of Macedon in 338 BC. Plutarch records that when Philip viewed the dead after the battle and was told who they were, he shed tears and said: 'Perish any man who suspects that these men either did or suffered anything that was base.'

3 Nearly two-fifths of the whole country are held by women: and this is because of the great number of heiresses and the large amount of dowries ... As it now is, a man may give his heiress in marriage to anyone he wishes and, if he dies without leaving directions in the matter, the administrator of his estate may give her to anyone he wishes. As a result, although the country could sustain 1,500 cavalry and 30,000 hoplites [heavily armed infantry], there were fewer than a 1,000 citizens [at the Battle of Leuctra, 371 BC]. Even a single shock was too much for the state; their lack of manpower was fatal.
Aristotle (384–322 BC) *Politics* (1975 trans.) Bk 2, Ch.9.1270a. The philosopher is commenting on the decline of the Spartan population in the 4th century.

4 These descendants of Perdiccas [the Macedonian kings] are, as they themselves claim, of Greek nationality. This was recognized by the managers of the Olympic Games, on the occasion when Alexander wished to compete and his Greek competitors tried to exclude him on the ground that foreigners were not allowed to take part. Alexander, however, proved his Argive descent, and so was accepted as a Greek and allowed to enter for the foot-race. He came in equal first.
Herodotus (c.485–c.425 BC) *The Histories* (1954 trans.) Bk 5.22. Alexander I was king of Macedon from c.495 to c.450 BC.

5 Philip had long ago ordained that the sons of Macedonian notables who had reached adolescence should be attached to the service of the king; and besides general attendance on his person, the duty of guarding them when asleep had been entrusted to them. Again, whenever the king rode out, they received the horses from the grooms and led them up and they mounted the king in Persian fashion and were his companions in the rivalry of the chase.
Arrian (2nd century AD) *The History of Alexander* (1929 trans.) Bk 4.13. Alexander's biographer describes the 'royal pages', who, while occupying a privileged position at court, guaranteed the cooperation of their families. Arrian was a serious historian, trying to use the best sources, although these are, in general, Alexander's own men. He himself was a man of action and governor under Emperor Hadrian of Cappadocia (east central Turkey) in 131–137, where he gained military success.

6 Europe had never produced a statesman like Philip son of Amyntas.
Theopompus (4th century BC), Fragment 27; J.B. Bury *A History of Greece* (1900) p.736. A contemporary view of Philip of Macedon.

7 [Philip was] more reckless in assuming risks than is becoming to a king.
Isocrates *Epistles* (345 BC; 1945 trans.) 2.2.

8 You, Athenians, with larger means than any people – ships, infantry, cavalry and revenue – have never up to this day made proper use of any of them; and your war with Philip differs in no respect from the boxing of barbarians ... So you, if you hear of Philip in the Chersonese [Thrace, in the far north of Greece], vote to send relief there, if at Thermopylae, the same; if anywhere else, you run after his heels up and down and are commanded by him. You have devised no plan for the war, you see no circumstance beforehand … One thing is clear: he will not stop unless someone opposes him.

Demosthenes *First Philippic* (351 BC); James and Janet Maclean Todd *Voices from the Past* (1955) pp.40–3. Demosthenes (384–322 BC), the great orator, warned of the rise of Macedon, urged pre-emptive action against Philip and attacked the appeasers in Athens.

1 More than a thousand Athenians fell in the battle [of Chaeroneia, 338 BC] and no fewer than 2,000 were captured … The story is told that in the drinking after dinner Philip … paraded through the midst of the captives, jeering at the misfortunes of the luckless men. Now Demades, the orator, who was one of the captives, spoke out boldly to curb the king's disgusting exhibition: 'O King, when Fortune has cast you in the rôle of Agamemnon [conqueror of Troy], are you not ashamed to act the part of Thersites?' Stung by this well-aimed rebuke, Philip altered his whole demeanour completely. He … expressed admiration for the man who dared to speak so plainly: he freed him from captivity and … ended by releasing all the Athenian prisoners without ransom and, altogether abandoning the arrogance of victory, sent envoys to the people of Athens and concluded with them a treaty of friendship and alliance.

Diodorus Siculus (1st century BC) *Library of History* (1963 trans.) Bk 16.86–7. Diodorus' 40-volume work was a compilation of earlier sources. Thersites was the abusive commoner who taunted his commander in the *Iliad* and in Shakespeare's *Troilus and Cressida*.

2 At the Battle of Chaeroneia, Alexander is said to have been the first man that charged the Thebans' Sacred Band … His early bravery made Philip [his father] so fond of him that nothing pleased him more than to hear his subjects call himself their general and Alexander their king.

Plutarch (c.46–c.127) (1876 trans.) 'Alexander' Ch.9. For the Sacred Band see 61:2.

3 In this year [336 BC] King Philip opened the war with Persia by sending an advance party into Asia while he himself, wanting to enter upon the war with the gods' approval, asked the Pythia [priestess who transmitted the oracular words of Apollo at Delphi] whether he would conquer the king of the Persians. She gave him the following response: 'Wreathed is the bull. All is done. There is also the one who will smite him.'

Now Philip found this response ambiguous but accepted it in a sense favourable to himself, namely that the Persian would be slaughtered like a sacrificial victim. Actually, however, it was not so, and it meant that Philip himself, in the midst of a festival and holy sacrifice, like the bull, would be stabbed to death while decked with a garland.

Diodorus Siculus (1st century BC) (1963 trans.) Bk 16.91.1–3.

4 Every seat in the theatre was taken when Philip appeared wearing a white cloak, and by his express orders his bodyguard kept away from him and followed only at a distance, since he wanted to show publicly that he was protected by the goodwill of all the Greeks and had no need of a guard of spearmen.

Diodorus Siculus (1st century BC) (1963 trans.) Bk 16.93.1.

5 Pausanias nursed his wrath implacably and … when he saw that the king was left alone, rushed at him, pierced him through his ribs and killed him; then ran for the gates and the horses which he had prepared for his flight … Having a good start he would have mounted his horse before they could catch him had he not caught his foot in a vine and fallen. As he was scrambling to his feet, the rest of the bodyguards caught up with him and killed him with their javelins.

Diodorus Siculus (1st century BC) (1963 trans.) Bk 16.94.3. The murder of Philip in 336 BC, when he was 46 and Alexander was 20 years old, took place in the theatre at the celebration of his daughter's wedding. The assassin, one of Philip's seven high-ranking bodyguards, had a personal grudge, but those who were probably behind the murder were never caught.

6 When he died Olympias [Philip's estranged wife and mother of Alexander] took his baby son, the child of Attalus' niece Cleopatra, and murdered the child and the mother together by dragging them onto a bronze oven filled with fire.

Pausanias *Guide to Greece* (c. AD 150; 1971 trans.) Bk 8.7. This and other stories hostile to Olympias derive from her enemy Cassander, who finally won the struggle for control of Macedonia and Greece after Alexander's death.

7 What was the duty of Athens when she perceived that Philip's purpose was to establish a despotic empire over all Greece? What language, what counsels, were incumbent upon an adviser of the people at Athens … when I was conscious that … our country had ever striven for primacy and honour and renown, and … had expended her treasure and the lives of her sons far more generously than any other Hellenic state fighting only for itself; and knowing as I did that our antagonist,

Philip himself, contending for empire and supremacy, had endured the loss of his eye, the fracture of his collar-bone, the mutilation of his hand and his leg, and was ready to sacrifice to the fortune of war any and every part of his body, if only the life of the shattered remnant should be a life of honour and renown?

Demosthenes *On the Crown* (330 BC; 1926 trans.) 66. The orator and statesman set out to justify his stance against Philip in a case that did not come to court until 330 BC, six years after the death of Philip.

1 In the first place, Philip was the despotic commander of his adherents: and in war that is the most important of all advantages. Secondly they had their weapons constantly in their hands. Then he was well provided with money: he did whatever he chose, without giving notice by publishing decrees, or deliberating in public, without fear of prosecution by informers or indictment for illegal measures. He was responsible to nobody: he was the absolute autocrat, commander and master of everybody and everything. And I, his chosen adversary – it is a fair inquiry – of what was I master? Of nothing at all! Public speaking was my only privilege – and that you permitted to Philip's hired servants on just the same terms as to me.

Demosthenes (330 BC; 1926 trans.) 235–6. The traditional city-state, especially with a democratic constitution, was ill fitted to respond to the ambitions of Philip.

ALEXANDER THE GREAT, 356–323 BC

2 Philip sent for Aristotle, the most learned and celebrated philosopher of his time and rewarded him with great munificence ... For he re-peopled his native city of Stagira, which he had caused to be demolished a little before ... It would appear that Alexander received from him not only his teachings on morals and politics, but also something of the more abstruse and profound theories which the philosophers professed to reserve for oral communication to the initiated ... Doubtless also it was to Aristotle that he owed the inclination he had not only to the theory but also the practice of medicine ... He was naturally a great lover of all kinds of learning and reading ... He constantly laid Homer's *Iliad* ... with his dagger under his pillow, declaring that he esteemed it a perfect portable treasure of all military virtue and knowledge.

Plutarch (c.46–c.127) (1876 trans.) 'Alexander' Ch.7. Aristotle became Alexander's tutor in 343/2 BC.

3 Macedon without Alexander would be like the Cyclops without his eye.

Demades, 4th century BC; N.G.L. Hammond and H.H. Scullard *Oxford Classical Dictionary* (1970 edn) p.323.

4 Eratosthenes [3rd-century BC historical and mathematical scholar] says that Olympias, when she attended Alexander on his way to the army on his first expedition, told him the secret of his birth, and bade him behave himself with the courage appropriate to his divine extraction.

Plutarch (c.46–c.127) (1876 trans.) 'Alexander' Ch.3. Olympias was supposed to have claimed that Alexander was the son of the god Ammon, the Egyptian Amun, whose oracle was at the Siwa oasis in western Egypt (see 10:6) and who was identified by the Greeks with Zeus.

5 As they were leading Bucephalus away as wholly useless and intractable, Alexander said 'What an excellent horse to lose, for lack of skill and boldness in managing him!' ... His father, shedding tears of joy, kissed him as he dismounted, saying, 'O my son, look for a kingdom equal to and worthy of yourself, for Macedonia is too small for you!'

Plutarch (c.46–c.127) (1876 trans.) 'Alexander' Ch.6. Alexander succeeded brilliantly and against all expectations in taming the horse in front of Philip and his company.

6 In the plains [of India] ... Alexander founded cities. [One he called] Bucephala [on the River Jhelum, Pakistan] in memory of his horse Bucephalus which died there, not wounded by anyone, but from exhaustion and age, for he was about thirty years old ... Up to then he had shared Alexander's toils and dangers in plenty, never mounted by any but Alexander himself, since Bucephalus would brook no other rider; in stature he was tall, and in spirit courageous. His mark was an ox-head branded upon him and hence his name Bucephalus; others, however, say that he had a white mark on his head – the rest being black – which was exactly like an ox-head. In Uxia [north of the Persian Gulf] Alexander once lost him, and issued a proclamation throughout that country that he would massacre every Uxian unless they brought him back his horse; immediately after the proclamation Bucephalus was restored to him. Such was Alexander's devotion to him and such was the terror Alexander inspired in the natives.

Arrian (2nd century AD) (1933 trans.) Bk 5.19.

7 Diogenes of Sinope, then living in Corinth, thought so little of him that he never so much as

stirred from where he lived, where Alexander found him lying in the sun. When he saw such a crowd of people, he raised himself a little and condescended to look up at Alexander. When Alexander kindly asked him if he wanted anything, he replied, 'Yes, I would like you to stand out of the sun.' Alexander was so struck at this answer and surprised at the greatness of the man who took so little notice of him, that as he went away he told his followers, who were laughing at the moroseness of the philosopher, that if he were not Alexander, he would choose to be Diogenes.

Plutarch (c.46–c.127) (1876 trans.) 'Alexander' Ch.14. Diogenes (c.400–c.325 BC) founded the Cynic sect of philosophers.

1 It was said of this wagon [in Gordium, northern Turkey] that anyone who untied the knot of the yoke should be lord over Asia. This knot was of cornel bark and no end was visible. Alexander, unable to find how to untie the knot and not wishing to leave it tied … smote it with his sword and cut the knot, saying 'I have loosed it!' So at least some say, but Aristobulus claims that he took out the pole pin, a dowel driven right through the pole, which held the knot together, and so removed the yoke from the pole … At any rate, he and his suite left the wagon with the impression that the oracle about the loosing of the knot had been fulfilled. It is certain that there was that night thunder and lightning, which indicated this, and Alexander in thanksgiving offered sacrifice next day to whatever gods had sent the signs and confirmed the undoing of the knot.

Arrian (2nd century AD) (1929 trans.) Bk 2.3. This is the origin of the expression 'to cut the Gordian knot'.

2 The Great King is there in person with his army, and once the battle is over, nothing remains but to crown our many labours with the sovereignty of Asia.

Arrian (2nd century AD) (1929 trans.) Bk 2.7. Alexander thus rallied his men before the Battle of Issus (on the Mediterranean coast of Turkey) in 333 BC, in which the Persian King Darius III was defeated but escaped to face further defeat at Gaugamela (northern Iraq) in 331 BC.

3 These proposals were made known at a meeting of Alexander's personal advisers, and Parmenio, according to all reports, declared that were he Alexander he would be happy to end the war on such terms and be done with any further adventures. 'That,' replied Alexander, 'is what I should do were I

Parmenio; but since I am Alexander I shall send Darius a different answer.'

Arrian (2nd century AD) (1958 trans.) Bk 2.25.

4 After this an overmastering desire came upon Alexander to pay a visit to Ammon in Libya; partly to consult the oracle, since the oracle of Ammon was reputed to be infallible, and Perseus and Heracles were both said to have consulted it … Besides, Alexander felt a kind of rivalry with Perseus and Heracles, being descended from them both; and he also traced his descent in part from Ammon … At any rate he set out for Ammon with this idea, hoping to learn more accurately about his ancestry, or at least to say he had so learnt.

Arrian (2nd century AD) (1929 trans.) Bk 3.3. In 332/1 BC Alexander made the difficult journey to the oracle of Zeus Ammon in the Siwa oasis (see 66:4). In claiming descent from Heracles, Alexander was asserting his right to rule Greece, and, from Perseus, his right to take over the Persian empire. He also wished to confirm his mother Olympias' claim (see 63:4) that his father was Ammon himself.

5 'The proof of his divine birth will reside in the greatness of his deeds: just as formerly he had been undefeated, so from now he will be unconquerable for all time.' Alexander was delighted with these responses. He honoured the god with rich gifts and returned to Egypt.

Diodorus Siculus (1st century BC) (1963 trans.) Bk 17.51. The response of Zeus Ammon at the oracle.

6 Alexander, as he returned from Ammon, came to the Mareotic Lake, situated not far from the island of Pharos [northwest Nile delta]. Contemplating the nature of the place, he had decided at first to build a city on the island itself; then, as it was apparent that the island was not large enough for a great settlement, he chose for the city the present site of Alexandria, which derives its name from that of its founder. Embracing all the ground between the lake and the sea, he planned a circuit of 80 stadia [about 9 miles] for the walls, and having left men to take charge of the building of the city, he went to Memphis.

Quintus Curtius (1st century AD) History of Alexander (1946 trans.) Bk 4.8. The foundation of Alexandria in Egypt in Jan. 331 BC and of many other new cities throughout his empire showed a fine appreciation of strategic needs and economic potential.

7 Nor do I commend his taking to Median garb instead of the traditional Macedonian dress, especially since he was a descendant of Heracles.

Moreover, he did not blush to exchange the head-gear he had long worn while conquering for the tiara of the conquered Persians.

Arrian (2nd century AD) (1929 trans.) Bk 4.7. Alexander was much criticized for adopting Persian customs. Although his sources are favourable to Alexander, Arrian readily passes judgement on Alexander's behaviour (see 32:5).

1 Alexander sent round a loving cup, a golden one, first to those with whom he had made an arrange-ment about prostration; then the first guest drinking of it rose up, prostrated himself and received a kiss from Alexander; and so they did one by one in order. But when the turn came to Callisthenes, he rose up, drank from the cup and made to kiss Alexander without having prostrated himself ... Alexander there-fore did not permit Callisthenes to kiss him; and Callisthenes remarked, 'I shall go off short of a kiss.'

Arrian (2nd century AD) (1929 trans.) Bk 4.12. Alexander's adoption of oriental practices was not accepted by all. Callisthenes, Aristotle's nephew, wrote a history of Alexander in which he promoted him as the champion of pan-Hellenism and recognized him as son of Zeus Ammon.

2 Alexander could no longer brook the drunken arrogance of Cleitus and leapt up in anger to strike him, but was held back by his boon companions. Still Cleitus did not restrain his insults ... No longer could his friends hold him back. He leapt up and, as some say, snatched a spear from one of his guard and therewith struck and slew Cleitus ... Alexander I pity, since he showed himself the slave of two vices, by neither of which should any self-respecting man be overcome, namely, passion and drunkenness. But for the sequel I commend Alexander, in that he immediately perceived that he had done a foul deed ... He took to his bed and lay there lamenting ... He lay there three days without food or drink and careless of all other bodily needs ... I have high commendation for Alexander, in that he did not brazen out this evil act, nor degrade himself by becoming champion and advocate of his misdeed; but confessed that, being merely human, he had erred.

Arrian (2nd century AD) (1929 trans.) Bk 4.8–9. Cleitus was one of Alexander's oldest associates and had saved his life at the Battle of the Granicus (334 BC). His friendship did not save him from Alexander's anger, however; he was killed by the king at Maracanda in 329 BC after criticizing the king's adoption of oriental ways.

3 Alexander prayed for all sorts of blessings and especially for harmony and fellowship in the empire between Macedonians and Persians.

Arrian (2nd century AD) (1929 trans.) Bk 7.11.

4 I feel that the adoption of Persian equipage was a device, both towards the Persians, so that their king might not appear wholly removed from them, and towards the Macedonians, to mark some turning away from Macedonian abruptness and arrogance.

Arrian (2nd century AD) (1929 trans.) Bk 7.29.

5 Then he came into the country of the Cathaeans, among whom it was the custom for wives to be cremated together with their husbands.

Diodorus Siculus (1st century BC) (1963 trans.) Bk 17.91. Diodorus is describing the Hindu practice of suttee (see 141:6), which Alexander's troops encountered in India.

6 O King Alexander, each man possesses just so much of the earth as this on which we stand; and you being a man like other men, save that you are full of activity and relentless, are roaming all over this earth far from your home, troubled yourself and troubling others. But not so long hence you will die, and you will possess just so much of the earth as suffices for your burial.

Arrian (2nd century AD) (1933 trans.) Bk 7.1. Wise men of India beat their feet on the ground when they saw Alexander and his army. They gave this response to Alexander's request for an explanation.

7 Ecbatana of Media [Hamadan, Iran] contains the palace which is the capital of all Media and store-houses filled with great wealth. Here he refreshed his army for some time and staged a dramatic festival, accompanied by constant drinking parties among his friends. In the course of these, Hephaestion drank very much, fell ill and died. The king was intensely grieved.

Diodorus Siculus (1st century BC) (1963 trans.) Bk 17.110.

8 Alexander threw himself into preparations for the burial of Hephaestion. He showed such zeal over the funeral that it not only surpassed all those previously celebrated on earth but left no possibility for any-thing greater in later ages. He had loved Hephaestion most of all the group of friends who were thought to have been high in his affections, and after his death showed him superlative honour.

Diodorus Siculus (1st century BC) (1963 trans.) Bk 17.114.

9 As for his marriage with Roxane, whose youthful-ness and beauty had charmed him at a drinking entertainment where he first happened to see her taking part in a dance, it was indeed a love affair, yet it seemed at the same time to be conducive to the

subject he had in hand. For it gratified the conquered people to see him choose a wife from among themselves and it made them feel the most lively affection for him to find that in the only passion which he, the most temperate of men, was overcome by, yet he forbore till he could obtain her in a lawful and honourable way.

Plutarch (c.46–c.127) (1876 trans.) 'Alexander' Ch.47. Roxane was a daughter of Oxyartes, ruler of the Sogdian (Uzbekistan).

1 They say that he was already unable to speak when the army filed past; yet he greeted one and all, raising his head, though with difficulty, and signing to them with his eyes … An oracle was given that it was better for him to remain where he was … and shortly afterwards Alexander breathed his last.

Arrian (2nd century AD) (1933 trans.) Bk 7.26. Alexander died in 323 BC of fever after a drinking bout. Stories abounded after his death, including suggestions of poisoning, but it is more likely that he died of natural causes.

2 Alexander lived thirty-two years and eight months; he reigned twelve years and eight months. In body he was very handsome and a great lover of hardships; of much shrewdness, most courageous, most zealous for honour and danger and most careful of religion; most temperate in bodily pleasure, but as for pleasures of the mind, insatiable of glory alone.

Arrian (2nd century AD) (1933 trans.) Bk 7.28. Part of Arrian's summing up on Alexander at the end of his work.

3 Craterus had received written instructions which the king had given him for execution; nevertheless it seemed best to the successors not to carry out these plans … It was proposed to build a thousand warships … for the campaign against the Carthaginians and the others who live along the coast of Libya and Iberia and the adjoining coastal region as far as Sicily; to make a road along the coast of Libya as far as the Pillars of Hercules and, as needed by so great an expedition, to construct ports and shipyards at suitable places.

Diodorus Siculus (1st century BC) (1963 trans.) Bk 18.4. Although Alexander's men had refused to continue further east after overrunning the Punjab, he seems to have hoped that they would be willing to turn west for further conquests had not death brought an end to all ambition.

4 When Arrhidaeus [Alexander's half-brother and joint successor] had spent nearly two years in making ready this work, he brought the body of the king from Babylon to Egypt. Ptolemy, doing honour to Alexander, went to meet it with an army as far as Syria

… He decided for the present not to send it to Ammon [the oracle of Zeus Ammon in the Siwa oasis, Egypt], but to entomb it in the city [Alexandria] that had been founded by Alexander himself … There he prepared a precinct worthy of the glory of Alexander in size and construction.

Diodorus Siculus (1st century BC) (1963 trans.) Bk 18.28. For Alexandria see 64:6.

5 Augustus had the sarcophagus containing Alexander the Great's mummy removed from the Mausoleum at Alexandria and after a look at its features, showed his veneration by crowning the head with a golden diadem and strewing flowers on the trunk. When asked 'Would you like to visit the Mausoleum of the Ptolemies?' he replied: 'I came to see a King, not a row of corpses.'

Suetonius *The Twelve Caesars* (c. AD 120; 1957 trans.) 'Augustus' 18. Suetonius (c.69–c.122) held secretarial posts under the Roman emperors Trajan and Hadrian and had the benefit of the imperial archives when he wrote his biographies of the early emperors.

6 When Alexander surveyed his empire he wept because there was so little left for him still to conquer.

Anon., untraced tribute.

JUDGEMENTS

7 When Julius Caesar was in Spain and had some leisure, he was reading some part of the history of Alexander and, after sitting a long time lost in his own thoughts, burst into tears. His friends were surprised and asked the reason. 'Don't you think that I have something worth being sorry about, when I reflect that at my age Alexander was already king over so many peoples, while I have never yet achieved anything really remarkable?'

Plutarch (c.46–c.127) (1958 trans.) 'Caesar' Ch.11.

8 Caligula wore the uniform of a triumphant general, often embellished with the breastplate which he had stolen from the tomb of Alexander the Great at Alexandria.

Suetonius (c. AD 120; 1957 trans.) 'Gaius Caligula' 52.

9 Beautiful solitary gorgons [mermaids] suddenly surface in the hurly-burly of a Cycladic or Euxine [Black Sea] storm … and ask the captain in ringing tones: 'Where is Alexander the Great?' He must answer at the top of his voice, 'Alexander the Great lives and reigns!' perhaps adding, 'and keeps the world at peace!' At this the gorgon vanishes and the waves subside to a flat calm. If the wrong answer is given, the tempest boils up to a deafening roar, the gorgon tilts the bowsprit towards the sea's bottom and the caique plunges to its destruction with all hands.

Patrick Leigh Fermor *Mani* (1958) p.187. Stories of Alexander are widespread throughout much of the area he conquered, testifying to his enduring fame.

1 Aristotle bequeathed his own library to Theophrastus, to whom he also left his school; and he is the first man, so far as I know, to have collected books and to have taught the kings of Egypt how to arrange a library.

Strabo (*c.*60 BC–*c.* AD 24) *Geography* Vol.6 (1929 trans.) Bk 13.1.54.

2 Owing to the rivalry between King Ptolemy [of Egypt] and King Eumenes [of Pergamum, western Turkey] about their libraries Ptolemy suppressed the export of papyrus; so parchment was invented at Pergamum; and afterwards the use of the material on which the immortality of human beings depends spread indiscriminately.

Pliny the Elder *Natural History* (*c.* AD 77; 1945 trans.) Bk 13.22. After Alexander's death the territory he had conquered was ruled in several separate kingdoms by his generals and their descendants. Greek culture continued to develop throughout Egypt and the Near East.

Rome: The Republic, 753–31 BC

THE FOUNDATION AND THE MONARCHY, 753–510 BC

1 Remember, O Roman, to rule the nations with your command – these shall be your arts – to impose an established order on peace, to spare the defeated and to subdue in war the arrogant.

Virgil *Aeneid* (c.19 BC) Bk 6, lines 851–3. In his great epic poem the poet Virgil traces Roman history back to the legendary war between the Greeks and Trojans. After the fall of Troy Aeneas visits his father, Anchises, in the underworld and is shown the future of Rome. The poet is addressing these words to Augustus in his own time.

2 When the basket in which the infants [Romulus and Remus] had been exposed and was left high and dry by the receding waters, a she-wolf … heard the children crying and made her way to where they were. She offered them her teats to suck and treated them with such gentleness that the king's herdsman, Faustulus, found her licking them with her tongue.

Livy *The History of Rome from its Foundation* (c.26 BC; 1960 trans.) Bk 1.4. Even historians turned to legend for the earliest period of Roman history.

3 As they were twins … they determined to ask the protecting gods of the countryside to declare by augury which of them should govern the new town and give his name to it … Each side promptly saluted their master as king … angry words ensued, followed all too soon by blows and in the course of the affray, Remus was killed. There is a commoner story that Remus, jeering at his brother, jumped over the half-built walls of the new settlement, whereupon Romulus killed him in a fit of rage, adding, 'So perish whoever shall leap over my battlements'.

Livy (c.26 BC; 1960 trans.) Bk 1.6.

4 Rome's greatness seemed destined to be short lived … There were not enough women and no intermarriage with neighbouring communities … Romulus' overtures were nowhere favourably received … Hiding his resentment, he prepared to celebrate a solemn festival in honour of Neptune, and sent notice all over the neighbouring countryside … On the appointed day people flocked to Rome out of sheer curiosity to see the new town … All the Sabines were there too with their wives and children … The show

began and nobody had eyes for anything else … At a given signal all the able-bodied men burst through the crowd and seized the young women.

Livy (c.26 BC; 1960 trans.) Bk 1.9. The story of the rape of the Sabine women explains the fusion of Sabine and Latin elements in early Rome.

5 At this moment, the Sabine women, the original cause of the quarrel, played their decisive part … They parted the angry combatants, beseeching their fathers on one side, their husbands on the other to avoid the curse of shedding kindred blood. 'We are mothers now; our children are your sons – and your grandsons … Or turn your anger against us … We would rather die ourselves than live on either widowed or orphaned.'

Livy (c.26 BC; 1960 trans.) Bk 1.13. The Sabine women bring together the two peoples.

6 One day while Romulus was reviewing his troops on the Campus Martius, a storm broke with violent thunder. A cloud enveloped him, hiding him from everyone's eyes; and from that moment he was never seen again.

Livy (c.26 BC; 1960 trans.) Bk 1.6. Romulus was believed to have been translated into heaven and was subsequently worshipped as Quirinus.

7 How could Romulus have acted with a wisdom more divine, taking all the advantages of the sea while avoiding its disadvantages, than by siting the city on the bank of a never-failing river whose broad stream flows with unvarying current into the sea? Such a river enables the city to use the sea both for importing what it lacks and for exporting what it produces in abundance … Consequently it seems to me that Romulus must at the very beginning have had a divine intimation that the city would one day be the seat and hearthstone of a mighty empire; for scarcely could a city placed upon any other site in Italy have more easily maintained our present widespread domination.

Cicero (106–43 BC) *Republic* (1928 trans.) Bk 2.5.

8 What can be well with a woman who has lost her honour? In your bed, husband, is the impress of another man. My body only has been violated, my heart is innocent and death will be my witness. Give me your solemn promise that the adulterer shall be punished – he is Sextus Tarquinius [the king's son].

Livy (c.26 BC; 1960 trans.) Bk 1.58. With these words Lucretia killed herself. The rape of Lucretia by the son of the seventh king of Rome, Tarquin the Proud, led to the end of the monarchy and the creation of the Republic.

1 Tarquin the Proud reigned for twenty-five years. The whole period of monarchical government, from the founding of Rome [753 BC] to its liberation, was 244 years. Two consuls were elected by popular vote … Lucius Junius Brutus and Lucius Tarquinius Collatinus [Lucretia's husband].

Livy (c.26 BC; 1960 trans.) Bk 1.60.

2   Lars Porsena of Clusium
       By the nine gods he swore
       That the great house of Tarquin
       Should suffer wrong no more …
       Still is the story told,
       How well Horatius kept the bridge
       In the brave days of old.

Thomas Babington, Lord Macaulay *Lays of Ancient Rome* (1842) 'Horatius' St.1–31. Tarquin, the last king of Rome, won the support of the Etruscan king, Lars Porsena, who tried to win back Rome for him. Horatius famously defended the access to the bridge until the Roman troops could destroy it and checked the Etruscan advance. Early Roman history concentrates on improving stories of heroic deeds.

3 Mucius was dragged to where Lars Porsena was sitting … 'I am a Roman … I came here to kill you – my enemy … It is our Roman way to do and to suffer bravely' … Porsena in rage and alarm ordered the prisoner to be burnt alive … whereupon Mucius, crying: 'See how cheap men of honour hold their bodies!' thrust his right hand into the fire … and let it burn there as if he were unconscious of the pain. Porsena was so astonished that he leapt to his feet and ordered his guards to drag him from the altar … The release of Mucius, thenceforward known as Scaevola, or Left-handed, from the loss of his right hand, was swiftly followed by the arrival of envoys from Porsena … with proposals of peace.

Livy (c.26 BC; 1960 trans.) Bk 2.12–3.

THE ETRUSCANS

4 Before the days of Roman domination Etruscan influence, both by land and sea, stretched over a wide area: how great their power was on the upper and lower seas (which make Italy a peninsula) is proved by the names of those seas, one being known by all Italian peoples as the Tuscan and the other as the Adriatic from the Etruscan settlement of Atria.

Livy (c.26 BC; 1960 trans.) Bk 5.33.

5 About signs and omens of public significance the custom had always been to consult only Etruscan soothsayers.

Livy (c.26 BC; 1960 trans.) Bk 1.56. Early Roman history is interwoven with the Etruscans. Numerous aspects of Roman religion and culture have an Etruscan origin, such as the art of the *haruspex* (examiner of the entrails of sacrificed animals and interpreter of signs and portents in general) and gladiatorial shows. There is indirect evidence of written Etruscan history, but nothing survives apart from inscriptions, mostly in tombs, in a language that, though written in Greek letters, is not understood.

6 The Etruscans originated that dignity which surrounds rulers, providing their rulers with lictors and an ivory stool and a toga with a purple band; and in connection with their houses they invented the peristyle [colonnaded courtyard area with rooms opening onto it] … and these things were in general adopted by the Romans. Letters and teaching about Nature and the gods they also improved on, and they elaborated the art of divination by thunder and lightning … Therefore the Romans show honour to these men even today and employ them as interpreters of the omens of Zeus.

Diodorus Siculus (1st century BC) *Library of History* (1963 trans.) Bk 5.40. The lictors were attendants to the chief magistrates; they carried the *fasces* (the origin of the word fascist), a bundle of rods around an axe, as a symbol of authority.

7 Claudius consulted the senate on the question of founding a college of soothsayers, so that the oldest art of Italy should not become extinct through neglect … The Etruscan nobles, voluntarily or at the instance of the Roman senate, had kept up the art and propagated it in certain families.

Tacitus (c.56–120) *Annals* (1937 trans.) Bk 11.15. Apart from recognizing the Etruscan contribution to soothsaying, Roman sources are generally hostile and the Etruscan version of events is almost entirely suppressed. Tacitus records that the Emperor Claudius himself wrote 20 volumes of Etruscan history, but nothing has survived.

ROME: THE CITY-STATE, 510–390 BC

8 There on the Sacred Mount, the commons made themselves a camp … The senatorial spokesman …

is said to have told them the following story. 'Long ago, when the members of the human body did not agree together, but each had its own thoughts and words … the other parts resented the fact that they should have the worry and trouble of providing everything for the belly while it remained idle … So the discontented members plotted together that the hand should carry no food to the mouth … But alas! While they sought to subdue the belly by starvation, they themselves and the whole body wasted away to nothing.' … So successful was his story that their resentment was mollified and negotiations began. Agreement was reached that special magistrates – tribunes of the people – should be appointed to represent the commons, above the law and with the function of protecting the commons against the consuls … This came to be called the 'Secession of the Plebs'.

Livy (c.26 BC; 1960 trans.) Bk 2.32. The patricians long resisted efforts of the plebs to have a role in government. In 494 BC the plebs went on strike, withdrawing to the Sacred Mount.

1 The consul called the troops an army who had betrayed military discipline and deserted its standards. He then asked them individually where their weapons were, or their standards, as the case might be, and gave orders that every soldier who had lost his equipment, every standard-bearer who had lost his standard, every centurion, too, who had abandoned his post, should be first flogged and then beheaded. The remainder were decimated.

Livy (c.26 BC; 1960 trans.) Bk 2.59. This is the earliest (471 BC) recorded example of decimation, the selection by lot of every tenth man for execution. It is probably an instance of the creation of an early precedent for a later practice. It was rarely carried out but was revived at the end of the Republic and used from time to time by emperors (see 78:6).

2 The situation called for a dictator, and, with no dissenting voice, Lucius Quinctius Cincinnatus was named for the post … the one man in whom Rome reposed all her hope of survival, was at that moment working a little three-acre farm west of the Tiber. The mission from the city found him at work – digging a ditch, maybe, or ploughing … The envoys from the city saluted him with congratulations, as dictator, invited him to enter Rome and informed him of the terrible danger to Minucius' army.

Livy (c.26 BC; 1960 trans.) Bk 3.26. The famous call to Quinctius at his plough to save Rome from disaster appears in several versions but was deeply embedded in the Roman view of their simple agrarian past. This story is dated to 458 BC.

3 In Rome a decree was passed inviting Cincinnatus to enter in triumph with his troops. The chariot he rode in was preceded by the enemy commanders and the military standards and followed by his army loaded with its spoils.

Livy (c.26 BC; 1960 trans.) Bk 3.29. The triumph was an early institution, probably Etruscan in origin and dating back to the time of the Tarquins.

4 TABLE VII: Rights concerning Land

The width of a road extends to eight feet where it runs straight ahead, sixteen round a bend …

Persons shall mend roadways. If they do not keep them laid with stone, a person may drive his beasts where he wishes …

Should a tree on a neighbour's farm be bent crooked by a wind and lean over your property, action may be taken for removal of that tree.

It is permitted to gather up fruit falling down on another man's farm.

Law of the Twelve Tables, 449 BC; E.H. Warmington (ed. and trans.) *Remains of Old Latin* (1935) Vol.3, p.471. The codified law, which was set up on bronze plaques in the forum in Rome, was the first landmark in Roman law and was never formally repealed. For the first time the plebeians could appeal to the law in their struggles against the arbitrary power of the patrician magistrates. It reflects the essentially agricultural character of a Roman society of small landowners in the early Republic.

5 The Capitol in Rome passed through a brief period of extreme danger from an attempted surprise … Possibly the Gauls had observed that the rocky ascent near the shrine of Carmenta was easily practicable … It was something of a scramble … But they accomplished the climb so quietly that the Romans on guard never heard a sound, and even the dogs noticed nothing. It was the geese that saved them – Juno's sacred geese, which, in spite of the dearth of provisions, had not been killed. The cackling of the geese and the clapping of their wings awoke Marcus Manlius … and, seizing his sword and giving the alarm, he hurried straight to the point of danger.

Livy (c.26 BC; 1960 trans.) Bk 5.47. The Gauls defeated the Romans at the Battle of Allia on 18 July 390 BC and captured the city of Rome shortly after, but the Capitol itself was strongly defended. The garrison was seriously short of food, but the Gauls were persuaded to abandon their siege after they received a payment of gold. The date of the battle became a 'black day' in the Roman calendar. The event, the one occasion on which Rome itself fell, made a lasting impression and left the Romans with an abiding fear of the Gallic tribes who from time to time penetrated south of the Alps (see 72:7).

1 A thousand pounds of gold was agreed on as the price of a people that was destined presently to rule the world. The transaction itself was a foul disgrace, but insult was added to injury: the weights produced by the Gauls were inaccurate and to the objections of the Romans, the insolent Gaul added his sword to the weight, saying words intolerable to Roman ears – *Vae victis!* [Woe to the conquered!]

Livy (*c*.26 BC; 1960 trans.) Bk 5.48. The story that follows, of the defeat by Camillus of the Gauls as they depart and the withdrawal of the offer of gold, is almost certainly a later, face-saving version, on which Livy further improves.

FOREIGN RELATIONS, 280–16 BC

2 The armies separated; and, it is said, Pyrrhus replied to one who rejoiced with him in his victory, 'If we win one more battle against the Romans, we shall be completely ruined.'

Plutarch (*c*.46–*c*.127) *Lives* (1876 trans.) 'Pyrrhus' Ch.21. The war against Pyrrhus, king of Epirus in northern Greece (280–275 BC), gave rise to the term 'Pyrrhic victory', because Pyrrhus suffered huge losses in the battles, especially at Asculum (southern Italy) in 279 BC, in spite of winning.

3 Pyrrhus admired the Romans even in their defeat and judged them superior to his own soldiers, declaring: 'I should already have mastered the whole inhabited world, if I were king of the Romans.'

Dio Cassius (*c*.155–235) *History of Rome* (1914 trans.) Bk 9.19.

4 At the close of the war [with the Carthaginians] for Sicily, they made another treaty, the clauses of which run: 'The Carthaginians are to evacuate the whole of Sicily and all the islands lying between Italy and Sicily. The allies of both parties are to be secure from attack by the other … The Carthaginians are to pay 1,200 talents within ten years, and a sum of 1,000 talents at once.'

Polybius (*c*.200–117 BC) *Histories* (1922 trans.) Bk 3.27. The First Punic War (264–241 BC) led to the acquisition of Sicily by Rome and made her into a naval power. Excessive demands for reparations were one of the causes of the Second Punic War.

5 Let no love or treaty be between our nations. Arise, unknown avenger, from my ashes to pursue with fire and sword the Trojan settlers … may they have war, they and their children's children!

Virgil (*c*.19 BC; 1916 trans.) Bk 4, lines 624–9. Just before her suicide, Dido, queen of Carthage, abandoned by the Trojan Aeneas, predicts the coming of Hannibal to avenge her. Rome was believed to have been founded by descendants (Romulus and Remus) of the refugees from Troy (see 68:1).

6 It is said that when Hannibal at about nine years of age was entreating his father with every childish wile to take him to Spain, Hamilcar … led the boy up to an altar and made him solemnly swear, with his hand touching the offerings, that as soon as he was old enough he would be the declared enemy of the Roman people.

Livy (*c*.26 BC; 1965 trans.) Bk 21.1. The Roman sources emphasize the supposed traditional hostility of Carthage to Rome, rather than their own seizure of Sardinia and interference in Spain. The formal Roman method of declaring war encouraged the pretence that all its wars were in some sense defensive, even when their acquisition of a vast empire made this inherently improbable.

7 Hannibal began the ascent of the Alps and found himself involved in very great difficulties … [After fending off attacks from the local tribes, with heavy losses on both sides] he joined the cavalry and pack animals and advanced towards the summit of the pass, encountering no massed forces of barbarians, though molested from time to time by those who took advantage of the ground to attack him … In these circumstances the elephants were of the greatest service to him; for the enemy never dared to approach that part of the column in which these animals were, being terrified by the strangeness of their appearance.

Polybius (*c*.200–117 BC) (1922 trans.) Bk 3.50, 53. Hannibal's decision in 218 BC to attack Rome by land from Spain involved an astonishing march with his huge army across the Pyrenees, through southern France and over the Alps. The precise route he took has generated an enormous literature. In Bk 3.60 Polybius estimates that Hannibal lost half his forces from the crossing of the Rhone to the arrival in the Po valley.

8 In the previous year a consul and his army had been lost at Trasimene [lake in central Italy, site of battle], and now there was news not merely of another similar blow, but of a multiple calamity – two consular armies annihilated, both consuls dead, Rome left without a force in the field, without a commander, without a single soldier … nearly the whole of Italy overrun.

Livy (*c*.26 BC; 1965 trans.) Bk 22.54. The defeat at Cannae in 216 BC was Rome's darkest hour, but Hannibal failed to follow up his advantage by marching on the defenceless city.

9 One man by delaying restored the state to us.

Ennius (239–169 BC) *Annals* Bk 12, line 360; Warmington (1935) Vol.1, p.133. The Romans saved the situation by following the advice of Quintus Fabius Maximus, who gained the nickname Cunctator from his delaying tactics. He laid waste the land and harried Hannibal's army, avoiding further pitched battles. Eventually Hannibal was recalled to Carthage and in 202 BC lost the Battle of Zama. Carthage was forced to accept harsh terms.

1 Nothing afflicted Marcellus so much as the death of Archimedes; who was then, as fate would have it, intent upon working out some problem by a diagram, and having fixed his mind along with his eyes upon the subject of his speculation, never noticed the incursion of the Romans, nor that the city was taken … A soldier, on his declining to follow him to Marcellus before he had worked out his problem … drew his sword and ran him through.
Plutarch (c.46–c.127) (1876 trans.) 'Marcellus' Ch.19. In 212 BC, after a siege prolonged by the devices and inventions of Archimedes, the scientist and inventor, the city of Syracuse in Sicily fell to the Romans under their commander Marcellus.

2 *Delenda est Carthago.* (Carthage must be destroyed.)
Cato; Pliny the Elder *Natural History* (c. AD 77; 1945 trans.) Bk 15.74. Cato visited Carthage in 153 BC and was alarmed to see its renewed prosperity. At the end of every speech he made in the senate he argued for the destruction of Carthage, and in 150 BC war was declared. Cato died the following year, but in 146 BC Carthage was defeated, the city was razed to the ground, and the surviving inhabitants were sold into slavery.

3 At first Mummius held back from entering Corinth, even though the gates were open, for fear of an ambush, but two days after the battle he stormed the city and set it on fire. Most of the people who were left there were murdered by the Romans, and Mummius auctioned the women and children … Mummius collected the most marvellous of sacred dedications and works of art.
Pausanias *Guide to Greece* (c. AD 150; 1971 trans.) Bk 7.16. The year 146 BC saw both the defeat of the Achaean League, the foremost power in Greece at the time, and the sack of Corinth. Greece was placed under the governor of Macedonia, which had been made a Roman province two years earlier.

CRISIS IN THE REPUBLIC, 133–63 BC

4 The sword was never carried into the assembly and there was no civil slaughter until Tiberius Gracchus, tribune and lawgiver, was the first to fall to internal commotion … Repeatedly the parties came into open conflict, often carrying daggers, and from time to time in the temples, the assemblies, or the Forum, some tribune, praetor, consul or candidate

for these offices … would be slain. Unseemly violence prevailed almost constantly, together with a shameful contempt for law or justice.
Appian (2nd century AD) *Civil Wars* (1912 trans.) Bk 1, Introduction 2. In 133 BC Tiberius Gracchus was tribune of the people, the third level of state official beneath consuls and praetors. His attempted redistribution of public land marks the beginning of a century of violent upheaval, which finally brought the republic to an end with the victory of Octavian over Antony in 31 BC.

5 Down to the destruction of Carthage, the people and senate shared the government peaceably and with restraint … Fear of its enemies preserved the good morals of the state. But when the people were relieved of this fear, the favourite vices of prosperity – licence and pride – appeared as a natural consequence … The nobles started to use their position, and the people their liberty, to gratify their selfish passions, every man snatching and seizing what he could for himself … One small group of oligarchs had everything in its control alike in peace and war – the treasury, the provinces, all distinctions and triumphs. The people were burdened with military service and poverty, while the spoils of war were snatched by the generals and shared with a handful of friends … Thus the possession of power gave unlimited scope to ruthless greed, which violated and plundered everything … till finally it brought about its own downfall.
Sallust *The Jugurthine War* (c.41–40 BC; 1963 trans.) 41.

6 Only a few held their honour dearer than gold.
Sallust (c.41–40 BC; 1963 trans.) 16. The corruptibility of the Roman upper classes.

7 300,000 armed warriors were on the march and hordes of women and children in much greater numbers were said to be marching with them, all seeking land to support these vast hosts and cities in which to settle, just as, before their time, as they had discovered, the Gauls had seized the best part of Italy from the Etruscans and were still occupying it.
Plutarch (c.46–c.127) (1958 trans.) 'Marius' Ch.11. The Romans retained their fear of northern invaders after the sack of Rome by the Gauls in 390 BC. Northern Italy was known as Cisalpine Gaul (Gaul on this side of the Alps).

8 He enrolled soldiers not from the propertied classes in accordance with tradition, but accepting anyone who volunteered – members of the proletariat for the most part … Indeed if a man is ambitious for power he can have no better supporters than the poor: they are not concerned about their own possessions as they have none, and they consider anything honourable for which they receive pay.

Sallust (c.41–40 BC; 1963 trans.) 86. Marius' acceptance into the army of men without land proved a key element in the civil wars of the late Republic. The loyalty of the soldiers was to the individual commander who raised troops for a particular campaign and not to the senate or state. Awards of money or land to veterans depended on the commander's position in Rome. They were easily persuaded to fight or even to march on Rome on his behalf to secure their own pensions.

1 Soon, however, all envy, hatred and calumny against Marius were done away with and forgotten. Danger threatened Italy from the west. Rome required a great general and Romans sought the best fitted to take the helm in this tempestuous war. At the consular elections no one showed any interest in the candidates from great or rich families and Marius in spite of being absent from Rome was proclaimed consul.

Plutarch (c.46–c.127) (1958 trans.) 'Marius' Ch.11. Marius was elected consul for 107 BC, then annually from 104–100 BC in contravention of the constitution, and again in 86 BC, dying in office. His colleague in that year, Lucius Cornelius Cinna, held the consulship again in the two following years until he was killed in office in 84.

2 Sulla was a man of large ambitions, devoted to pleasure but even more to glory ... He was eloquent, shrewd and an accommodating friend ... His unparalleled good fortune – up to his triumph in the civil war – was well matched by his energy and many people have wondered whether he owed his success more to boldness or to luck. Of his subsequent conduct I could not speak without feelings of shame and disgust.

Sallust (c.41–40 BC; 1963 trans.) 95. Both Marius and Sulla came to prominence through war. For the next 20 years each tried to hold supreme power in Rome, wreaking appalling vengeance on the other side.

3 Pompey told Sulla to bear in mind that more people worshipped the rising than the setting sun, meaning that while his own power was on the increase, that of Sulla was waning.

Plutarch (c.46–c.127) (1958 trans.) 'Pompey' Ch.14.

4 He forthwith proscribed about 40 senators and 1,600 knights ... Some were killed where they were caught, in their houses, in the streets or in the temples ... There was much massacre, banishment

and confiscation too among the Italians ... These accusations were mostly against the rich.

Appian (2nd century AD) (1912 trans.) Bk 1.95–6. Sulla invented the proscriptions (82–81 BC) – the posting of lists of names of those who could be killed with impunity and their goods confiscated.

5 When Spartacus turned on his pursuers, the Romans were entirely routed ... This success turned out to be the undoing of Spartacus since it filled the slaves with over-confidence ... Spartacus, realizing he had no alternative, drew his army up for battle. When his horse was brought to him, he drew his sword and killed it, saying that the enemy had plenty of good horses which would be his if he won, and if he lost he would not need a horse at all.

Plutarch (c.46–c.127) (1958 trans.) 'Crassus' Ch.11. The last major slave revolt was led by Spartacus and his fellow gladiators, who had remarkable success against a number of Roman forces in 73–71 BC. Crassus finally took command and brought the uprising to an end. Pompey managed to gain some credit by slaughtering several thousand fugitives from the final battle, for which he claimed 'to have dug up the war by the roots'.

6 *Civis Romanus sum.* (I am a Roman citizen.)

Cicero (106–43 BC) *Against Verres* 5th speech, sect.147. In 70 BC Cicero won a high-profile case for abuse of power against Verres, who had been governor of Sicily in 73–71 BC. Verres had not even respected the rights of Roman citizens in his depredations of works of art. Lord Palmerston quoted this in Latin in the House of Commons on 25 June 1850 in the Don Pacifico debate (see 680:8).

7 The power of the pirates extended over the whole area of the Mediterranean sea, so that all navigation and all commerce were at a standstill. This caused the Romans, who were already short of provisions and expected a real breakdown in supplies, to send out Pompey with a commission to drive the pirates off the seas. Pompey [tribune of the people in 67 BC] was to be given not only supreme naval command but what amounted in fact to an absolute authority and uncontrolled power over everyone.

Plutarch (c.46–c.127) (1958 trans.) 'Pompey' Ch.25. Pompey's dramatic success against the pirates was an important factor in his powerful unconstitutional position.

8 How long will you abuse our patience, Catiline?

Cicero (106–43 BC) *Against Catiline* 1st speech, sect.1. Among all the political coups and civil wars of the last century of the Roman Republic, one failed attempt is well documented. In his consulship in 63 BC Cicero succeeded in forestalling the Catilinarian conspiracy, for which he was hailed in the senate as *pater patriae* (father of the fatherland). He never let Rome forget but suffered from the phenomenon equally evident today that good news is no news, and he was even banished for a time because of unlawful measures he had taken against the conspirators.

1 *O fortunatam natam me consule Romam!* (O happy Rome, born when I was consul!)

Cicero (106–43 BC); Juvenal *Satires* (c.AD 120) 10, line 122. The poet quotes derisively from Cicero's own poem on his consulship.

2 Among the women who supported Catiline was Sempronia, who had often committed many crimes of masculine daring. In birth and beauty, and also in her husband and children, she was well favoured by fortune; well read in both Greek and Latin literature and able to play the lyre and dance more skilfully than a respectable lady should ... she was a woman of no mean endowments: she could write verses, she was amusing and talked well in language that could be modest or tender or bawdy. In short, she was full of wit and charm.

Sallust *Conspiracy of Catiline* (c.44–42 BC; 1963 trans.) 25. The political and social disturbances of the late Republic saw a number of women, usually of aristocratic background, living lives of considerable emancipation.

JULIUS CAESAR AND HIS AVENGERS, 63–31 BC

3 Julius Caesar was captured by pirates off the island of Pharmacusa [off the coast of Turkey near Miletus]. They kept him prisoner for nearly forty days, to his intense annoyance; he had with him only a physician and two valets, having sent the rest of his staff away to borrow the ransom money. As soon as the stipulated fifty talents arrived and the pirates duly set him ashore, he raised a fleet and went after them. He had often smilingly sworn, while still in their power, that he would soon capture and crucify them; and this is exactly what he did.

Suetonius *The Twelve Caesars* (c. AD 120; 1957 trans.) 'Julius Caesar' 5.

4 I considered that my wife ought not even to be under suspicion.

Plutarch (c.46–c.127) (1958 trans.) 'Caesar' Ch.10. Often rendered as 'Caesar's wife must be above suspicion', the sentence refers to Caesar's divorce of his second wife, Pompeia, because of a scandal caused when, in 62 BC, Clodius (a disaffected aristocrat) donned women's clothing and attended an all-female religious festival (presided over by

Pompeia as the wife of Julius Caesar in his role as head of the State religion).

5 Gaul is a whole divided into three parts.

Julius Caesar (c.100–44 BC) *The Gallic War* (1917 trans.) Bk 1.1. After his consulship of 59 BC Caesar became pro-consul in the existing Gallic provinces in northern Italy and Provence and spent the next ten years conquering the rest of Gaul.

6 Pompey spent all his time with his wife [Julia, daughter of Julius Caesar] ... he had the ability to unbend from his dignity and become really charming in personal relationships – a quality particularly attractive to women ... Later [54 BC] she died in childbirth ... Now there no longer existed the marriage tie which had hitherto cloaked rather than restrained their rival ambitions. Soon, too, the news arrived how Crassus had lost his life in Parthia ... Now fortune had, as it were, removed from the ring the third competitor.

Plutarch (c.46–c.127) (1958 trans.) 'Pompey' Ch.53. The First Triumvirate, a private agreement between Crassus, Pompey and Caesar in 60 BC to help each member advance his own career, was renewed in 56 BC but could not survive the deaths of Julia and then Crassus in the disastrous defeat of his army at Carrhae (southeast Turkey) in 53 BC.

7 Jump down, comrades, unless you wish to betray the eagle to the enemy; I at any rate shall have done my duty to my country and my general.

Julius Caesar (c.100–44 BC) Bk 4.25. Caesar quotes the words of the standard-bearer of the Tenth Legion who led the soldiers off the ships as Caesar's first expeditionary force to Britain arrived offshore in 55 BC.

8 All the Britons dye their bodies with woad, which produces a blue colour, and this gives them a more terrifying appearance in battle.

Julius Caesar (c.100–44 BC) (1951 trans.) Bk 5.14. Caesar made two expeditions to Britain, in 55 and 54 BC, without any very serious intention to conquer it. In Bk 5.12–14 Caesar summarizes what he discovered about Britain and its inhabitants, including the practice of groups of 10 or 12 men, often related, having wives in common.

9 The next day Vercingetorix addressed an assembly. 'I did not undertake the war for private ends, but in the cause of national liberty. And since I must now accept my fate, I place myself at your disposal. Make amends to the Romans by killing me, or surrender me alive as you think best.' A deputation was sent to refer the matter to Caesar, who ordered the arms to be handed over and the tribal chiefs brought out to him. He seated himself at the fortification in front of his camp, and there the chiefs were brought, Vercingetorix was delivered up, and the arms were laid down.

Julius Caesar (c.100–44 BC) (1951 trans.) Bk 7.89. Gallic resistance was effectively at an end after the fall of Alesia (about 160 miles southeast of Paris) to Caesar in 52 BC. Vercingetorix, Gallic chief of the Arverni and leader of the revolt against the Romans, was put to death after Caesar's triumph in 46 BC.

1 *Iacta alea est.* (The die is cast.)

Julius Caesar; Suetonius (AD c.120) 'Julius Caesar' 32. In 49 BC, by crossing with an army the River Rubicon, a stream in northern Italy that marked the frontier between Gaul and Italy proper, Caesar was effectively declaring war on Rome, because his legal military power was restricted to Gaul.

2 [Caesar] arrived at Alexandria just after Pompey's death. When Theodotus came to him with Pompey's head, Caesar refused to look at it, but he took Pompey's signet ring and shed tears as he did so. He offered help and his own friendship to all who had been friends and companions of Pompey … He wrote to his friend in Rome to say that of all the results of his victory, what gave him the most pleasure was that he was so often able to save the lives of those who had fought against him.

Plutarch (c.46–c.127) (1958 trans.) 'Caesar' Ch.48. After being defeated by Caesar in 48 BC at the Battle of Pharsalus (central Greece), Pompey fled to Egypt but was stabbed as he landed.

3 Cleopatra embarked in a small boat and landed at the palace when it was already getting dark. Since there seemed no other way of getting in unobserved, she stretched herself out at full length inside a roll of bedding, and Apollodorus, after tying up the roll, carried it indoors to Caesar. This little trick of Cleopatra's, which showed her provocative impudence, is said to have been the first thing about her to captivate Caesar, and as he grew to know her better he was overcome by her charm.

Plutarch (c.46–c.127) (1958 trans.) 'Caesar' Ch.49. Cleopatra bore Caesar a son, Caesarion, who was killed by Augustus after the defeat of Antony and Cleopatra at Actium in 31 BC.

4 At Alexandria were invaluable libraries, and the unanimous testimony of ancient records declares that 700,000 books, brought together by the unremitting energy of the Ptolemies [kings of Egypt after Alexander the Great], were burned in the Alexandrine wars, when the city was sacked under the dictator Caesar.

Ammianus Marcellinus *The Later Roman Empire* (c.390; 1940 trans.) Bk 22.16. According to Dio Cassius only 'stores of corn and books' were destroyed in Julius Caesar's campaign, but this was later magnified into the entire library. Certainly Strabo found the library intact 23 years later. Antony intended to give Cleopatra 200,000 books from the rival library at Pergamum (western Turkey, see 67:2), presumably in recompense for what had been destroyed, but it is unclear whether they were, in fact, ever sent.

5 *Veni, vidi, vici!* (I came, I saw, I conquered!)

Suetonius (c. AD 120) 'Julius Caesar' 37. The words were written on placards carried in Caesar's quadruple triumph in 46 BC. They relate to the speed of his success in his Pontic (Black Sea, Turkey) campaign in 47 BC culminating in his victory at Zela. Plutarch ('Caesar' Ch.50) says he used the words in a letter to a friend in Rome immediately after the battle.

6 *Soothsayer*: Beware the ides [15th] of March …
   Caesar: The ides of March are come.
   Soothsayer: Ay, Caesar; but not gone.

William Shakespeare *Julius Caesar* (1599) Act 1, Sc.2 and Act 3, Sc.2. Shakespeare based these words directly on Suetonius 'Julius Caesar' 81.

7 *Et tu, Brute?* (You too, Brutus?)

William Shakespeare (1599) Act 3, Sc.1.

8 Caesar was stabbed with twenty-three dagger thrusts and uttered not a word, but only a groan at the first stroke, though some have related that when Marcus Brutus rushed at him, he said in Greek, 'You too, child?'

Suetonius (c. AD 120; 1913 trans.) 'Julius Caesar' 82. The assassination of Julius Caesar on the Ides (15th) of March 44 BC led to another 13 years of civil war before the final victory of Augustus.

9 Friends, Romans, countrymen, lend me your ears;
   I come to bury Caesar, not to praise him.

William Shakespeare *Julius Caesar* (1599) Act 3, Sc.2. Mark Antony's funeral speech and the events surrounding it are based most nearly on Plutarch *Lives* 'Brutus' and 'Antony'.

10 A certain star during all those days appeared in the north towards evening, which some called a comet … while the majority ascribed it to Caesar, interpreting it to mean that he had become immortal, and had been received into the number of the stars. Augustus then took courage and set up in the temple of Venus a bronze statue of him with a star above his head … They put into effect some of

the other decrees passed in honour of Caesar. Thus they called one of the months July after him.
Dio Cassius (c.155–235) (1914 trans.) Bk 45.7. Halley's comet, 44 BC.

1 The Triumvirs joined in making a list of those who were to be put to death – those whom they suspected because of their power, their own personal enemies, and they exchanged their own relatives and friends with each other for death ... They made additions from time to time ... for a grudge merely ... or because of their exceptional wealth, for the triumvirs needed a great deal of money to carry on the war.
Appian (2nd century AD) (1912 trans.) Bk 4.2. In October 43 BC Antony, Augustus and Lepidus formed a triumvirate on the model of the unofficial arrangement between Caesar, Pompey and Crassus 60–49 BC. The Second Triumvirate, unlike the First (see 74:6), was officially ratified in the senate in Nov., giving them power from Jan. 42 BC for five years, and renewed in 37 for a further five years.

2 Cicero ... was proscribed together with his son, his brother, his brother's son and all his household and friends ... The centurion drew his head out of the litter and cut it off, striking it three times ... He also cut off the hand with which Cicero had written the speeches against Antony as tyrant, which he had

entitled Philippics in imitation of Demosthenes ... Antony was delighted beyond measure ... The head and hand of Cicero were suspended for a long time from the Rostra in the Forum where formerly he had made his public speeches ... It is said that even at his meals Antony placed Cicero's head before his table, until he became satiated with the horrible sight.
Appian (2nd century AD) (1912 trans.) Bk 4.4. For Demosthenes' attack on Phillip II of Macedon see 62:7.

3 Now is the time to drink, now to beat the ground with unfettered foot ...
   Wrong it was ere now ... when the queen was plotting wild destruction to our Capitol ...
   ... a woman mad enough to nurse the wildest hopes and drunk with Fortune's favours ... Yet she, seeking to die a nobler death, showed for the dagger's point no woman's fear, nor sought to win with her swift fleet some secret shore;
   ... courageous, too, to handle poisonous asps, that she might draw black venom to her heart ... no craven woman, she!
Horace Odes (c.23 BC; 1914 trans.) Bk 1, no.37. The poet mixes admiration for Cleopatra's courage with joy at the news of her death by suicide after the defeat of Antony at Actium in 31 BC. Shakespeare used the story of the asp in Antony and Cleopatra Act 5, Sc.2.

Rome: The Empire, 31 BC–AD 300

AUGUSTUS ESTABLISHES THE EMPIRE, 31 BC–AD 14

1 A day will come in the passing of the cycles of time when … a Trojan Caesar [Augustus] shall be born, who shall limit his empire with the ocean, his glory with the stars, Julius, inheritor of great Iulus' name [the son of Aeneas] … Then shall wars cease and the rough ages soften. The dread steel-clenched gates of war shall be shut fast.

Virgil *Aeneid* (c.19 BC) Bk 1, lines 283–94. One of several 'prophetic' passages in the *Aeneid* in which Virgil refers to the history of Rome up to and including his own day. The shutting of the gates of war refers to closing the doors of the Temple of Janus (see 77:4).

2 The successes and failures of the early Roman people have been recorded by famous writers and the Age of Augustus did not lack distinguished historians until they were deterred by increasing sycophancy. The reigns of Tiberius, Gaius, Claudius and Nero were recorded falsely during their lifetimes through fear of the consequences, while after their deaths accounts were written when hatreds were still fresh. I intend to say a little about Augustus, especially about the final stages, and to move on to the reign of Tiberius and his successors, without anger or prejudice since in my case the incentives for these are absent.

Tacitus (c.56–120) *Annals* (1956 trans.) Bk 1.1. Writing nearly a century after Augustus' death in AD 14, Tacitus claims to present an objective account of the early empire.

3   It is sweet and glorious to die for one's country.
    Yet death overtakes no less the man who runs,
    Nor spares the limbs and frightened back of
      Coward youth.

Horace *Odes* (c.23 BC) Bk 3, no.2, lines 13–16. *Dulce et decorum est pro patria mori* is in one of the six odes at the beginning of Bk 3 that extol the old Roman virtues that the new emperor, Augustus (r.27 BC–AD 14), wished to promote. See 712:8.

4 The temple of Janus Quirinus, which our ancestors desired to be closed whenever peace with victory was secured by land and sea throughout the entire Roman empire, and which before I was born is recorded to have been closed only twice since the founding of the city, was during my principate three times ordered by the senate to be closed.

Augustus *Res Gestae Divi Augusti* (The Accomplishments of Augustus) (AD 14; 1955 trans.) 13. Augustus' own version of his achievements was inscribed on his instructions on bronze pillars set up at the entrance to his mausoleum, and copies were also sent to cities throughout the empire. It is full of detailed information and reveals how Augustus wished to be appreciated.

5 I declined to become *pontifex maximus* in place of a colleague while he was still alive when the people offered me that priesthood which my father had held. A few years later, when death removed the man who had taken it at a time of civil disturbance [Lepidus, the third member of the Second Triumvirate], I accepted this priesthood and from all Italy there flocked to my election a multitude such as had never previously been recorded at Rome.

Augustus (AD 14; 1955 trans.) 10. Augustus' adoptive father was Julius Caesar.

6 Augustus twice thought of restoring the republic: immediately after the overthrow of Antony … and again when he could not shake off a lingering illness … On further reflection he concluded that entrusting the state to the control of several would jeopardize not only his own life but also national security; so he did not do so.

Suetonius *The Twelve Caesars* (c. AD 120; 1913 trans.) 'Augustus' 28.

7 He seduced the army with bonuses and the citizenry with cheap corn – and everyone with the sweetness of peace. Then he gradually extended his power and took to himself the functions of the senate, the magistrates and the laws. There was no opposition. War or the proscriptions had disposed of all men of spirit. The surviving nobility … had profited from the revolution … and preferred the safety of the present to the dangers of the past.

Tacitus (c.56–120) *Annals* (1956 trans.) Bk 1.2. For proscriptions see 73:4 and 76:1.

8   But nowadays, with no vote to sell, we
      Couldn't care less; once, the people bestowed
        political power,
      Government posts, legions, everything; now
        there are only two things

Left to their anxious concern: bread and
circuses.

Juvenal *Satires* (c.120; 1998 trans.) 10, lines 77–81. The poet
encapsulates the change from republican to imperial governance. Elections for magistrates were transferred from the
people to the senate under Tiberius. In Rome the emperors
took on the provision of public entertainment in the amphitheatre (gladiatorial shows) and Circus Maximus (chariot racing).

1 The system of imperial government as it was
instigated by Augustus and maintained by those
princes who understood their own interest and that
of the people ... may be defined as an absolute monarchy disguised by the forms of a commonwealth.
The masters of the Roman world surrounded their
throne with darkness, concealed their irresistible
strength, and humbly professed themselves the
accountable ministers of the senate, whose supreme
decrees they dictated and obeyed.

Edward Gibbon *The Decline and Fall of the Roman Empire*
(1776–88) Ch.3.

2 Augustus passed laws to tighten the sanctions
against celibacy and to increase revenue. He failed,
however, to make marriage and the raising of children more popular – childlessness was too attractive.

Tacitus (c.56–120) *Annals* (1956 trans.) Bk 3.25. The birth-
rate, particularly of the upper classes, was in decline and family
values had suffered in the civil wars.

3 To keep in touch with provincial affairs Augustus
organized a chariot service, based on posting stations.

Suetonius (c. AD 120; 1957 trans.) 'Augustus' 49.

4 The various modes of worship which prevailed in
the Roman world were all considered by the people
as equally true; by the philosopher as equally false;
and by the magistrate as equally useful. And thus
toleration produced not only mutual indulgence,
but even religious concord.

Edward Gibbon (1776–88) Ch.2.

5 In Germany, three legions were cut to pieces [AD 9]
with their general ... Augustus was so greatly affected
that for several months he left his hair and beard
untrimmed and would sometimes dash his head
against a door, crying: 'Varus, give me back my legions!'

Suetonius (c. AD 120; 1913 trans.) 'Augustus' 23.

6 If a company broke in battle, Augustus ordered
the survivors to draw lots, then executed every tenth
man, and fed the remainder on barley bread instead
of the customary wheat ration.

Suetonius (c. AD 120; 1957 trans.) 'Augustus' 24. For decimation
see 70:1.

7 Augustus so improved the appearance of the city of
Rome that he was justified in his boast: 'I found
Rome a city built of brick and leave her clothed in
marble.'

Suetonius (c. AD 120; 1957 trans.) 'Augustus' 28.

8 In bringing up his daughter and granddaughters he
even had them taught spinning and weaving, and forbade them to say or do anything that could not decently
be recorded in the household day-book ... His satisfaction with the success of this family training was,
however, suddenly shattered. He found out that both
Julias, his daughter and his granddaughter, had been
indulging in every sort of vice and he banished them
... He kept his daughter for five years on the prison
island of Pandateria ... and nothing would persuade
him to forgive her.

Suetonius (c. AD 120; 1957 trans.) 'Augustus' 64–5.

9 At this time [Augustus' death in AD 14] there was
no longer any fighting – except a war against the
Germans, designed less to extend the empire's
frontiers than to avenge the disgrace of the army lost
with Varus. In the capital all was quiet ... The
younger men had been born after the battle of
Actium [31 BC, where Augustus defeated Antony
and Cleopatra] and even most older ones had been
born during the civil wars: how many were left who
had seen truly republican government?

Tacitus (c.56–120) *Annals* (1956 trans.) Bk 1.3. The length of
Augustus' reign, 45 years, made the transfer of power to a
successor much easier. On the other hand, all his efforts to
leave a successor he had chosen came to nothing as one after
another predeceased him. Only Tiberius, the son of his third
wife, Livia (divorced wife of Tiberius Claudius Nero), whom
he had eventually adopted, was left – and he showed considerable reluctance to take on the burden of power. For the
Battle of Actium see 75:3.

10 Augustus advised them [Tiberius and the public]
to be satisfied with their present possessions and
under no circumstances to wish to increase the
empire to any greater dimensions.

Dio Cassius (c.155–235) *History of Rome* (1924 trans.)
Bk 56.33. The Roman politician and writer, who became a
proconsul in Africa c.222, quotes documents that Augustus
left to be read to the senate after his death.

TIBERIUS TO NERO, 14–68

1 Tiberius was faithful to his policy of manipulating foreign affairs by astute diplomacy without resort to warfare.

Tacitus (c.56–120) *Annals* (1956 trans.) Bk 6.32. Tiberius was emperor from AD 14 to 37.

2 There was Agrippina's baby son, Gaius, born in the camp and brought up with the legionaries as his comrades. In their army fashion they nicknamed him Caligula [Little Boots] because as a gesture to win popularity he was often dressed in miniature army boots.

Tacitus (c.56–120) *Annals* (1956 trans.) Bk 1.41. The future emperor Caligula, Augustus' great-grandson through his mother and great-nephew of Tiberius on his father's side, was in the legionary camp on the German frontier when mutiny broke out after the death of Augustus.

3 Sejanus [prefect of the Praetorian Guard] turned his attention to persuading Tiberius to settle in some attractive place far from Rome ... So he increasingly denounced to Tiberius the drudgeries of Rome ... and spoke warmly of peace and solitude, far from vexation and friction.

Tacitus (c.56–120) *Annals* (1956 trans.) Bk 4.41. Sejanus succeeded in persuading Tiberius to move to Capri (an island in the Bay of Naples) in AD 26. He never returned to Rome.

4 The man [Sejanus] whom at dawn they had escorted to the senate house as a superior being, they were now dragging to prison as if no better than the worst ... A little later ... the senate ... condemned him to death. By their order he was executed and his body cast down the stairway, where the rabble abused it for three whole days and afterwards threw it into the river. His children also were put to death by decree, the girl having been first outraged by the public executioner on the principle that it was unlawful for a virgin to be put to death in prison.

Dio Cassius (c.155–235) (1924 trans.) Bk 58.11. In AD 31 Tiberius' eyes were at last opened and he sent a letter of denunciation to the senate. Sejanus had removed several members of the imperial family and was planning to succeed Tiberius himself.

5 Caligula's familiar order [when a victim was being executed] was: 'Make him feel that he is dying' ... He often quoted Accius' line: 'Let them hate me, so long as they fear me.'

Suetonius (c. AD 120; 1957 trans.) 'Gaius Caligula' 30. The Roman Accius (170–c.86 BC) wrote tragedies.

6 To prevent Incitatus, his favourite horse, from growing restive Caligula always sent his soldiers into the neighbourhood on the day before the races to enforce silence. Besides a marble stable, an ivory stall, purple blankets and a collar of precious stones he gave Incitatus a house, a troop of slaves and furniture to provide suitable entertainment for guests invited in the horse's name. It is said that he even planned to award Incitatus a consulship.

Suetonius (c. AD 120; 1957 trans.) 'Gaius Caligula' 55.

7 When the assassins ordered Caligula's courtiers to disperse, pretending that he wished to be alone, Claudius ... slipped away and hid trembling behind the door curtains. A soldier of the Praetorian Guard, wandering vaguely through the palace, noticed a pair of feet beneath the curtain, pulled their owner out for identification and recognized him. Claudius fell to the ground and clasped the soldier's knees, but found himself acclaimed emperor.

Suetonius (c. AD 120; 1957 trans.) 'Gaius Caligula' 10.

8 It doesn't hurt, Paetus.

Pliny the Younger (c.61–113) *Letters* 3.16. Arria plunged a dagger into her own breast, pulled it out with these words and handed it to her husband, Caecina Paetus, when he was condemned in AD 42 for taking part in a conspiracy against Claudius.

9 Claudius' sole campaign was of little importance ... He decided that Britain was the country where a real triumph could be most easily earned ... He crossed the Channel without incident; and was back in Rome six months later. He had fought no battles and suffered no casualties, but reduced a large part of the island to submission. His triumph was a very splendid one.

Suetonius (c. AD 120; 1957 trans.) 'Claudius' 17 (see 82:9).

10 It will seem fantastic that ... on an appointed day and before invited signatories, a consul designate and the emperor's wife [Messalina] should have been joined together in formal marriage ... that the pair should have taken their places at a banquet, embraced and finally spent the night as man and wife ... What I have told and shall tell is the truth.

Tacitus (c.56–120) *Annals* (1956 trans.) Bk 11.27. Messalina's outrageous marriage to Gaius Silius brought about her downfall and led to Claudius' marriage to his niece, Agrippina the Younger.

11 Marriage to a niece, it may be objected, is unfamiliar to us. Yet in other countries it is regular and lawful … Customs change as circumstances change – this innovation too will take root.

Tacitus (c.56–120) *Annals* (1956 trans.) Bk 12.6. Vitellius, a powerful friend of Claudius whose son (also Vitellius) was briefly emperor in AD 68–9, argued for a change in the law so that in AD 49 Claudius could marry Agrippina, great-granddaughter of Augustus and mother of Nero by her first husband.

1 Agrippina had long decided on murder … What was needed was something subtle that would upset the emperor's faculties but produce a deferred fatal effect. An expert in such matters was selected – a woman called Locusta, recently sentenced for poisoning but with a long career of imperial service ahead of her … The poison was sprinkled on a particularly succulent mushroom. But … the effect was not at first apparent … Agrippina was horrified … and she called in a doctor whose complicity she had secured. The story is that, while pretending to help Claudius to vomit, he put a feather dipped in a quick poison down his throat: he was well aware that major crimes, though hazardous to undertake, are profitable to consummate.

Tacitus (c.56–120) *Annals* (1956 trans.) Bk 12.66–7. The murder of Emperor Claudius in AD 54 led to the accession of Nero, Agrippina's son, rather than Claudius' own son, Britannicus.

2 The murderers closed around Agrippina's bed. First the captain hit her on the head with a cudgel. Then as the centurion was drawing his sword to finish her off, she cried, 'Strike here!' – pointing to her womb, and was despatched with repeated wounds … This was the end that Agrippina had anticipated for years – and had treated with contempt. For when she asked astrologers about Nero's destiny, they had answered that he would reign and kill his mother. Her reply was: 'Let him kill me – provided that he becomes emperor!'

Tacitus (c.56–120) *Annals* (1956 trans.) Bk 14.8–9. Nero grew tired of his mother's interference and in AD 59 decided to kill her. When a faked accident failed, the freedman who had suggested the scheme acted openly and sent a detachment of soldiers to despatch her.

3 Disaster followed, whether due to chance or a criminal act of the emperor is uncertain … Now started the most terrible and destructive fire which Rome had ever experienced … A rumour spread that, while the city was burning, Nero had gone to his private stage and, comparing modern calamities with ancient, had sung of the destruction of Troy.

Tacitus (c.56–120) *Annals* (1956 trans.) Bk 15.38, 39, 44. He is describing the great fire of AD 64. To suppress the rumour that the fire had started by order, Nero blamed the Christians (see 89:3).

4 When pressed, the tribune of the Guard, Subrius Flavus admitted his guilt and gloried in it. Asked by Nero why he had forgotten his military oath, he replied: 'Because I hated you. And yet there was not a man in the army truer to you, as long as you deserved to be loved. I began to hate you when you murdered your mother and wife [Octavia] – and turned into a charioteer, an actor and a fire-raiser' … Nothing in this conspiracy fell more shockingly on Nero's ears. For although ready enough to commit crimes, he was unaccustomed to being told about them.

Tacitus (c.56–120) *Annals* (1956 trans.) Bk 15.67. In AD 65 the discovery of the Pisonian conspiracy, named after its leader, Gaius Calpurnius Piso, gave Nero the excuse to get rid of a large number of his enemies as well as genuine conspirators.

5 Soon after the Games, Poppaea died. She was pregnant, and her husband [Nero], in a chance fit of anger, kicked her.

Tacitus (c.56–120) *Annals* (1956 trans.) Bk 16.6.

6 Even his will deviated from the routine deathbed flattery of Nero … Petronius wrote out a list of Nero's sensualities – giving the names of each male and female bedfellow and details of every lubricious novelty – and sent it under seal to Nero. Then Petronius broke the seal so that it could not be used to incriminate others.

Tacitus (c.56–120) *Annals* (1956 trans.) Bk 16.19. Petronius, Nero's arbiter of taste and a former consul, was forced to commit suicide in AD 65 when he fell from favour. He was probably also the author of the *Satyricon*, a picaresque romance.

7 While in Greece he tried to have a canal cut through the Isthmus of Corinth and addressed a gathering of Praetorian Guards, urging them to undertake the task. Nero himself took a mattock and, at a trumpet blast, broke the ground and carried off the first basket of earth on his back.

Suetonius (c. AD 120; 1957 trans.) 'Nero' 19. The canal was opened in 1893.

8 Finally, when his companions unanimously insisted on his trying to escape from the miserable fate threatening him, he ordered them to dig a grave at once … He kept weeping and saying over and over 'What an artist the world is losing with my death!'

Suetonius (c. AD 120; 1957 trans.) 'Nero' 49.

SLAVERY IN THE EARLY EMPIRE, 31 BC–AD 68

1 Certain slave-owners abandoned their sick and worn-out slaves on the island of Asclepius [god of medicine] in the River Tiber since they were loathe to provide them with medical care. Claudius ordered all slaves so abandoned to be granted their freedom, and if they recovered they were not to be returned to the control of their master. Furthermore, he also decreed that any owner who killed a sick slave for the same reason should be charged with murder.

Suetonius (*c.* AD 120; 1914 trans.) 'Claudius' 25.

2 We have a common saying 'You have as many enemies as you have slaves'. More correctly, *we* make them enemies. I will not dwell on our cruel and inhuman treatment of them … Some people say, 'They're just slaves' … But perhaps in spirit he's a free man. 'He's just a slave.' Shall that damn him? Show me someone who isn't a slave. One man is slave to lust, another to greed, another to ambition. And all of us are slaves to hope and fear.

Seneca (c.4 BC–AD 65) *Letters* (1988 trans.) 47. The view of Stoic philosophy towards slavery. Seneca adhered to the Stoic principles of the pursuit of virtue and indifference to the vicissitudes of life. As tutor to Nero, he tried to put his philosophy into practice, with diminishing success, until he himself fell out of favour and died nobly in accordance with his ideals.

3 An ex-consul has been deliberately murdered by a slave in his own home. None of his fellow-slaves prevented or betrayed the murderer, though the senatorial decree threatening the whole household with execution still stands … Exemplary punishment always contains an element of injustice. But individual wrongs are outweighed by the advantage of the community.

Gaius Cassius Longinus; Tacitus (c.56–120) *Annals* (1956 trans.) Bk 14.43–4. When Pedanius Secundus, the city prefect, was murdered by one of his slaves in AD 61 the ancient custom that all household slaves should be executed was challenged by the populace. In a debate in the senate Longinus won the day with his arguments in favour of applying the full rigour of the law. The crowd tried to prevent the execution from being carried out, and detachments of soldiers had to be brought in to ensure that the 400 slaves could be taken to their execution.

4 Larcius Macedo, senator and former praetor [senior magistrate], has been murdered by his own slaves. Admittedly he was a cruel and overbearing master, too ready to forget that his father had been a slave, or perhaps too keenly conscious of it … You see the dangers, outrages and insults to which we are exposed. No master can feel safe because he is kind and considerate; for it is their brutality, not their reasoning capacity, which leads slaves to murder their masters.

Pliny the Younger (c.61–113) (1963 trans.) 3.14. In spite of being a kind master himself as far as we can tell from his letters, Pliny demonstrates the fear that underlay a society dependent on slaves. It was unusual for someone whose father had been a slave to rise to become a senator.

5 That which you would not suffer yourself, seek not to lay upon others. You would not wish to be a slave – look to it that others be not slaves to you.

Epictetus (c.55–c.135) *Fragment* 43. Epictetus was a slave and was allowed to attend philosophy lectures. When he was later freed he became a teacher of Stoicism. His lectures were collected and published and had a strong influence on Emperor Marcus Aurelius (see 85:7). A unique example of anti-slavery?

6 Hail, emperor, those who are about to die greet you.

Suetonius (c.AD 120; 1914 trans.) 'Claudius' 21. The gladiators thus saluted Emperor Claudius before a sham sea-fight on the Fucine Lake in central Italy, which Claudius was about to empty at the conclusion of a major drainage scheme. Most gladiators were slaves or condemned criminals.

THE YEAR OF THE FOUR EMPERORS

7 Now the secret was revealed that an emperor could be made elsewhere than at Rome.

Tacitus (c.56–120) *Histories* Bk 1.4. On the succession to Nero, when armies around the empire proclaimed their man as emperor.

8 Galba seemed greater than just a private citizen as long as he was a private citizen, and everyone agreed that he was capable of being emperor – if he had not become emperor.

Tacitus (c.56–120) *Histories* Bk 1.49. Galba, the first to be declared emperor at the death of Nero (AD 68), was followed in rapid succession by Otho, Vitellius and, finally, the successful Vespasian, so that AD 69 is known as the Year of the Four Emperors.

9 Titus complained of the tax that Vespasian had imposed on the contents of the city urinals (used by the fullers to clean woollens). Vespasian handed him a coin which had been part of the first day's proceeds:

'Does it smell bad, my son?' 'No, Father!' 'That's odd: it comes straight from the urinal!'
Suetonius (*c.* AD 120; 1957 trans.) 'Vespasian' 23. Hence the French word *vespasienne* for a public urinal.

1 When his doctors chided Vespasian for continuing his usual course of actions during his illness and attending to all the duties that belonged to his position, he replied: 'The emperor ought to die on his feet.'
Dio Cassius (*c.*155–235) (1925 trans.) Bk 66.17.

2 As Vespasian's death drew near, he said 'Dear me! I think I am turning into a god.'
Suetonius (*c.* AD 120; 1914 trans.) 'Vespasian' 23. Vespasian was well aware that an emperor who had ruled successfully, as he had, and was dying of natural causes would be deified after his death (AD 79).

3 Titus had such winning ways, perhaps inborn, perhaps cultivated subsequently, or conferred on him by fortune – that he became an object of universal love and adoration.
Suetonius (*c.* AD 120; 1957 trans.) 'Titus' 1. There were high hopes of Vespasian's elder son, Emperor Titus (r.79–81), but he died of a fever on 1 Sept. 81 at the age of 42 after reigning for a little over two years.

4 One evening at dinner, realizing that he had done nobody any favour since the previous night, Titus spoke these memorable words: 'My friends, I have wasted a day.'
Suetonius (*c.* AD 120; 1957 trans.) 'Titus' 8.

5 My uncle perished in a catastrophe which destroyed the loveliest regions of the earth, a fate shared by whole cities and their people … On 24 August, in the early afternoon, my mother drew his attention to a cloud of unusual size and appearance … He changed his plan and what he had begun in a spirit of enquiry he completed as a hero … Ashes were falling, hotter and thicker as the ships drew near, followed by bits of pumice and blackened stones, charred and cracked by the flames … Then the flames and smell of sulphur which gave warning of the approaching fire drove the others to take flight and roused him to stand up. He stood leaning on two slaves and then suddenly collapsed … When daylight returned on the 26th his body was found intact and uninjured, still fully clothed and looking more like sleep than death.
Pliny the Younger (*c.*61–113) (1963 trans.) 6.16. On the eruption of Vesuvius near Naples in AD 79 and the death of his uncle, Pliny the Elder.

6 At the beginning of his reign Domitian would spend hours alone every day catching flies – believe it or not – and stabbing them with a needle-sharp pen. Once, on being asked whether anyone was closeted with the emperor, Vivius Crispus wittily replied: 'No, not even a fly.'
Suetonius (*c.* AD 120; 1957 trans.) 'Domitian' 3. Vespasian's younger son, Domitian, had conspired against his brother before his death. In spite of his competent administration throughout the empire, his relations with the senate deteriorated and he came to be widely feared and loathed.

7 Domitian claimed that all emperors are necessarily wretched, since only their assassination can convince the public that the conspiracies against their lives are real.
Suetonius (*c.* AD 120; 1957 trans.) 'Domitian' 21. The emperor was, in fact, assassinated in AD 96, when friends and freedmen conspired against him with the connivance of his wife, Domitia.

ROMAN BRITAIN, 43–211

8 The various tribes of Britons possessed valour without conduct, and the love of freedom without the spirit of union. They took up arms with savage fierceness, they laid them down, or turned them against each other with wild inconstancy; and while they fought singly, they were successively subdued.
Edward Gibbon (1776–88) Ch.1.

9 The enemy lined the shore in a dense armed mass. Among them were black-robed women with dishevelled hair like Furies, brandishing torches. Close by stood Druids, raising their hands to heaven and screaming dreadful curses. This weird spectacle awed the Roman soldiers into a sort of paralysis. They stood still – and presented themselves as a target. But then they urged each other (and were urged by the general) not to fear a horde of fanatical women. Onward pressed their standards and they bore down their opponents, enveloping them in the flames of their own torches. Suetonius garrisoned the conquered island [Anglesey, north Wales]. The groves devoted to Mona's barbarous superstitions he demolished. For it was their religion to drench their altars in the blood of prisoners and consult their gods by means of human entrails.
Tacitus (*c.*56–120) *Annals* (1956 trans.) Bk 14.30. The Roman occupation of Britain, begun in AD 43 under Claudius (see 79:9), was extended in the following reigns. Suetonius Paulinus became governor of Britain in 58 and had just succeeded in

conquering the island of Anglesey in 61 when he learned of the revolt of the province.

1 Prasutagus, king of the Iceni ... had made the emperor co-heir with his own two daughters, hoping thereby to preserve his kingdom and household from attack ... His widow Boudicca [Boadicea] was flogged and their daughters raped. The Icenian chiefs were deprived of their hereditary estates as if the Romans had been given their whole country [roughly, Norfolk, Suffolk and Cambridgeshire] ... The humiliated Iceni feared still worse ... and so they rebelled.

Tacitus (c.56–120) *Annals* (1956 trans.) Bk 14.31. The immediate cause of the great revolt in Britain in AD 60.

2 [The Britons] particularly hated the Roman former soldiers who had established the colony at Camulodunum [Colchester in Essex] ... It seemed easy to destroy the settlement, for it had no walls ... Meanwhile, for no apparent reason, that statue of Victory at Camulodunum fell down ... At the mouth of the Thames a phantom settlement was seen in ruins and a blood-red colour in the sea and shapes like human corpses left by the ebb tide were interpreted hopefully by the Britons – and with terror by the settlers ... All else was ravaged or burnt and only the temple in which the troops had massed themselves stood a two days' siege and was then taken by storm.

Tacitus (c.56–120) *Annals* (1956 trans.) Bk 14.31–2. The Britons succeeded in taking Camulodunum, massacring the inhabitants. Suetonius Paulinus hurried east. He abandoned Londinium (London), and Verulamium (St Albans) fell too. Tacitus records an estimated 70,000 Roman and allied deaths.

3 Boudicca drove round all the tribes in a chariot with her daughters in front of her. 'We British are used to women commanders in war. I am descended from mighty men! But I am not fighting for my kingdom and wealth now. I am fighting as an ordinary person for my lost freedom, my bruised body and my outraged daughters ... That is what I, a woman, plan to do! – let the men live in slavery if they will.'

Tacitus (c.56–120) *Annals* (1956 trans.) Bk 14.35. Tacitus puts these words in the mouth of Boudicca before the decisive battle in AD 60.

4 The remaining Britons fled with difficulty since their ring of wagons blocked the outlets. The Romans did not spare even the women ... It was a glorious victory, comparable with bygone triumphs. According to one report almost 80,000 Britons fell. Our own

casualties were about 400 dead and a slightly larger number of wounded. Boudicca poisoned herself.

Tacitus (c.56–120) *Annals* (1956 trans.) Bk 14.37. The rebellion petered out after this decisive defeat, and Suetonius Paulinus was soon replaced by a more conciliatory governor.

5 They make a desert and call it peace.

Tacitus (c.56–120) *Agricola* 30. The historian attributes these words to the British leader, Calgacus, before the Battle of Mons Graupius (AD 84) in Caledonia (Scotland).

6 The climate is wretched, with its frequent rains and mists, but there is no extreme cold. Their day is longer than in our part of the world. The nights are light, and in the extreme north so short that evening and morning twilight are scarcely distinguishable ... The soil will produce good crops, except olives, vines and other plants which usually grow in warmer lands.

Tacitus (c.56–120) *Agricola* (1948 trans.) 12. Tacitus' father-in-law, Agricola, was military tribune (AD 61), legionary commander (71–73) and governor (78–84) in Britain.

7 Agricola educated the sons of the chiefs in the liberal arts ... with the result that instead of loathing the Latin language they became eager to speak it effectively. In the same way, Roman dress came into fashion and the toga was everywhere to be seen. And so the population was gradually led into the demoralizing temptations of arcades, baths and sumptuous banquets. The unsuspecting Britons spoke of such novelties as 'civilization', when in fact they were only a feature of their enslavement.

Tacitus (c.56–120) *Agricola* (1948 trans.) 21.

8 When the Empress Julia Augusta [wife of Septimius Severus, emperor AD 193–211] was jesting with a Caledonian [Scottish] lady about the free intercourse of her sex with men in Britain, she replied: 'We fulfil the demands of nature in a much better way than you Roman women do; for we consort openly with the finest men, whereas you let yourselves be debauched in secret by the vilest.'

Dio Cassius (c.155–235) (1927 trans.) Bk 76.16. Dio reports that in northern Britain women were held in common and children were reared communally.

ROME VIEWS THE CELTS

9 The River Ister [Danube] rises among the Celts and the town of Pyrene [at the foot of the Pyrenees] and crosses the whole of Europe. And the Celts are beyond the Pillars of Hercules [Straits of Gibraltar] next to the Cynetes [unknown people], who live furthest west of all the peoples of Europe.

Herodotus (c.485–c.425 BC) *The Histories* (1910 edn) Bk 2.33. The Greek historian specifies the Celts' territory as stretching from the Danube in southern Germany to the Iberian peninsula, an area corroborated by modern archaeology. He may have come across them himself on the shores of the Black Sea.

1 To trade with capital and let it out at interest is unknown, and so it is ignorance rather than legal prohibition that protects them. Land is held by the villages as communities according to the number of cultivators, and is often divided among the freemen according to their rank. The extent of their territories renders this partition easy. They cultivate fresh fields every year and there is still land to spare. They do not plant orchards nor lay off meadow lands, nor irrigate gardens so as to require of the soil more than it would naturally bring forth of its own richness and extent. Grain is the only tribute exacted from their land, whence they do not divide the year into as many seasons as we do.

Tacitus (c.56–120) *Germania* (1900 trans.) Ch.26. Although the Roman historian seems not to have had first-hand experience of Germany, he must have drawn on that of Romans who had and of the slaves who had been captured and brought to Rome.

2 Under this promontory's crest [Brittany in north-western France] the Oestrymnian gulf spreads out and contains the Oestrymnides, islands with broad plains and rich mines of tin and lead. The people here are powerful, proud, energetic and industrious, trading in everything … They do not make hulls of pitch pine, nor do they shape wooden keels in the usual way; but, amazingly, they contrive their ships by stitching skins together [the coracle], and cross the open sea on leather.

It takes a boat two days from there to reach the Sacred Isle, so called by the ancients. This island [Ireland] in the midst of the sea, is very large, mostly inhabited by the Hibernian folk. Nearby, back in the opposite direction, is the island of the Albiones [Britain].

Rufus Festus Avienus (*fl.c.* AD 375) *Ora Maritima* (Maritime Regions) (1887 edn) lines 80 ff. This Latin poet built travellers' tales into his geographical poem.

3 No business, public or private, is transacted except in arms. But it is the rule that no one shall take up his arms until the state has attested that he is likely to

make good. When that time comes, one of the chiefs or the father or a kinsman equips the young warrior with shield and spear in the public council. This with the Germans is the equivalent to our *toga* – the first public distinction of youth.

Tacitus (c.56–120) *Germania* (1948 trans.) Ch.13.

4 On the field of battle it is a disgrace to the chief to be surpassed in valour by his companions, to the companions not to come up to the valour of their chiefs. As for leaving a battle alive after your chief has fallen, *that* means life-long infamy and shame. To defend and protect him, to put down one's own acts of heroism to his credit – that is what they mean by 'allegiance'. The chiefs fight for victory, the companions for their chief.

Tacitus (c.56–120) *Germania* {1948 trans.) Ch.7. Richard Barber (*The Knight and Chivalry* (1970) p.7) considers that Tacitus' picture of the tribal structure remained true until the Carolingian wars with the Saxons in south Germany in the 8th century.

5 [Having reached the Roman forum, the Gauls] found the humbler houses locked and barred but the mansions of the nobility open; the former they were ready enough to break into, but it was a long time before they could bring themselves to enter the latter; something akin to awe held them back at what met their gaze – those figures seated in the open court-yards, the robes and decorations august beyond reckoning, the majesty expressed in those, grave, calm eyes like the majesty of gods. They might have been statues in some holy place, and for a while the Gallic warriors stood entranced; then on an impulse, one of them touched the beard of a certain Marcus Papirius – it was long, as was the fashion of those days – and the Roman struck him on the head with his ivory staff. That was the beginning.

Livy *The History of Rome from its Foundation* (c.26 BC; 1960 trans.) Bk 5.41. The sack of Rome in 390 BC.

6 The chariot drivers gradually withdraw from the battle and position the chariots in such a way that if the fighting men are overwhelmed by enemy numbers they can quickly return to them. They therefore combine the mobility of cavalry with the solidity of infantry in battle, and [the Britons] become so skilled in their use through training and daily practice that they can even control galloping horses on steep and dangerous slopes.

Julius Caesar (c.100–44 BC) *The Gallic War* (1917 trans.) Bk 4.33. Julius Caesar was, of course, writing in the 1st century BC as a Roman commander who had faced these awesome attacks.

1 We must not forget the high regard in which the Gauls hold this plant [mistletoe]. The druids (which is what they call their magicians) consider nothing more sacred than mistletoe and the tree that it grows on, so long as it is an oak … Mistletoe is actually very rare on oak trees, and when it is found, it is gathered with great ceremony. In the first place, the collection must take place on the sixth day of the moon. This day is the beginning of their months, their years and their centuries (the latter last 30 years) … A priest dressed in white climbs the tree, cuts the mistletoe with a golden hook and catches it on a white cloak. Victims are sacrificed with prayers to the god to render this offering propitious to the people who are making it.
Pliny the Elder *Natural History* (c. AD 77; 1945 trans.) Bk 16.95. Like other commentators, the Roman naturalist believed that the Celts practised human sacrifice.

2 The druids take no part in war and do not pay tribute along with the others … they are said to learn large numbers of verses; some remain in training for 20 years. They do not believe it lawful to commit this lore to writing and yet for most public and private purposes and accounts they do use Greek letters. It seems to me that there are two reasons for this practice: one is to prevent their knowledge spreading among common people, the other is to prevent their students losing their memories by relying on writing.
Julius Caesar (c.100–44 BC) (1917 trans.) Bk 6.14.

3 In Gaul there is plenty of native gold that the inhabitants collect without difficulty or mining. As the rivers rush through their winding bends and dash against the foot of mountains they detach lumps of rocks and become full of gold dust. People who do this work collect and break up the dust-bearing rocks, remove the earth by repeated washing and melt the rest in furnaces. In this way they gather a mass of gold that is used for ornaments not only for women but for men as well, for they wear bracelets on their wrists and arms and also solid gold collars round their necks, and fine finger rings and even gold breastplates.
Diodorus Siculus (1st century BC) *Library of History* (1963 trans.) Bk 5.27.

EMPERORS OF THE 2ND AND 3RD CENTURIES

4 If a man were called to fix the period in the history of the world during which the condition of the human race was most happy and prosperous, he would, without hesitation, name that which elapsed from the death of Domitian [AD 96] to the accession of Commodus [AD 180].
Edward Gibbon (1776–88) Ch.3.

5 Trajan [r.98–117] also built libraries. And he set up in his Forum an enormous column, to serve at once as a monument to himself and as a memorial of his work in the Forum.
Dio Cassius (c.155–235) (1927 trans.) Bk 68.16.

6 Antinous was a favourite of the Emperor Hadrian [r.117–138] and died in Egypt. Hadrian honoured Antinous by building a city on the spot where he died and naming it after him; and he set up statues, or rather, sacred images of him, practically all over the world.
Dio Cassius (c.155–235) (1927 trans.) Bk 69.12. Antinoopolis was in Egypt, 200 miles south of Cairo. See 14:5.

7 Our history now [on the death of Marcus Aurelius, r.161–180] descends from a kingdom of gold to one of iron and rust.
Dio Cassius (c.155–235) (1927 trans.) Bk 71.36. Marcus Aurelius' own writings, the *Meditations*, on Stoic philosophy, have survived.

8 Commodus' great simplicity, together with his cowardice, made him the slave of his companions and through them he was led into lustful and cruel habits which soon became second nature … He devoted most of his life to ease and to horses and to combats of wild beasts and men … When he wished to slay both consuls and issue forth in the amphitheatre on New Year's Day both as consul and gladiator … Narcissus, an athlete, was sent in to strangle him while he was taking a bath.
Dio Cassius (c.155–235) (1927 trans.) Bk 72.1, 11, 22. Commodus (r.180–192) ended the dynasty established by Hadrian.

9 Live in harmony, enrich the soldiers and scorn all others.
Dio Cassius (c.155–235) (1927 trans.) Bk 76.15. Purportedly the advice of Septimius Severus (r.193–211) to his sons Geta

(joint emperor 211–212) and Caracalla (r.211–217) just before his death in York. The reliance of the emperor on the army is undisguised, though Severus was generous to the people of Rome as well as to the army. In spite of this and public works, including the triumphal arch in the Roman Forum, he left the finances of the empire in considerable surplus.

1 Caracalla made all the people in his empire Roman citizens; nominally he was honouring them, but his real purpose was to increase his revenues.
Dio Cassius (c.155–235) (1927 trans.) Bk 77.9. Roman citizenship had been extending since the 1st century BC. Caracalla completed the process in AD 212.

2 The emperor is not bound by the laws.
Ulpian, early 3rd century; Justinian *Digest* (c. AD 530) Bk 1.3.31. The power of the emperor became increasingly absolute. Emperor Justinian I (r.527–565) set up a commission to codify Roman law (see 104:6).

3 Twenty-two acknowledged concubines, and a library of sixty-two thousand volumes, attested the variety of his [Emperor Gordian the Younger's] inclinations; and from the productions which he left behind him, it appears that both the one and the other were designed for use rather than for ostentation.
Edward Gibbon (1776–88) Ch.7. A footnote informs the reader that Gordian (briefly emperor in AD 238) left three or four children by each of his concubines, while his literary productions, though less numerous, were by no means contemptible.

4 All these animals Philip [r.244–249] exhibited and slaughtered at the gladiatorial and circus spectacles when he celebrated Rome's thousandth anniversary in his own and his son's consulship [AD 248].
Anon. *Lives of the Three Gordians* (?early 4th century AD); Naphthali Lewis and Meyer Reinhold *Roman Civilization: A Sourcebook* Vol.2 (1955) p.455. In the midst of civil war and anarchy in the troubled 3rd century the thousandth anniversary of the founding of Rome in 753 BC was celebrated, above all with the huge slaughter of exotic animals from around the empire.

5 Gallienus [r.253–268] sprinkled gold dust on his hair and often came into public with the radiate crown [previously the symbol of deified emperors]. At Rome, where previous emperors always wore the toga, he appeared in a purple cloak with jewelled and golden clasps.
Anon. *Lives of the Two Gallieni* (?early 4th century AD); Lewis and Reinhold (1955) p.456. The practices of oriental autocracy became common and were made official under Diocletian (r.284–305).

6 It is our pleasure that the prices listed in the subjoined schedule be held in observance in the whole of our empire.
Diocletian *Edict on Maximum Prices* (296); inscription in Lewis and Reinhold (1955) p.465. Diocletian set about reorganizing the administration of the empire after a long period of military chaos. His tetrarchy, the rule of four men, each with a different area to govern, was short-lived. The edict on prices and wages had equally little success as goods simply disappeared from the markets and inflation continued to be a problem. His reputation was marred in the historical record as a result of his persecution of the Christians (see 90:1).

The Beginnings of Christianity, 30–604

THE FIRST CHRISTIANS, 1–300

1 And Jesus went about all Galilee, teaching in their synagogues, and preaching the gospel of the kingdom, and healing all manner of sickness and all manner of disease among the people. And his fame went throughout all Syria; and they brought unto him all sick people that were taken with divers diseases and torments, and those which were possessed with devils, and those which were lunatick, and those that had the palsy; and he healed them. And there followed him great multitudes of people from Galilee and from Decapolis, and from Jerusalem, and from Judaea, and from beyond Jordan.
Bible, NT, Matthew 4:23–5. The first teachings of Jesus of Nazareth (Jesus Christ), c.28, as described in the Gospel of Matthew, probably written in the late 1st century AD.

2 And he [Jesus] goeth up into a mountain … and he ordained twelve, that they should be with him, and that he might send them forth to preach, and to have power to heal sicknesses, and to cast out devils. And Simon he surnamed Peter; and James the son of Zebedee, and John the brother of James; and he surnamed them Boanerges, which is the sons of thunder; and Andrew, and Philip, and Bartholomew, and Matthew, and Thomas, and James the son of Alphaeus, and Thaddaeus, and Simon the Canaanite, and Judas Iscariot, which also betrayed him.
Bible, NT, Mark 3:13–19. Jesus' appointment of the Twelve Apostles, recorded in the earliest Christian Gospel, the Gospel of Mark.

3 Go ye therefore, and teach all nations, baptizing them in the name of the Father, and of the Son, and of the Holy Ghost: teaching them to observe all things whatsoever I have commanded you.
Bible, NT, Matthew 28:19–20. After his crucifixion (c.30) Jesus appeared again before his disciples and commanded them to spread the Christian faith to the world.

4 The holy apostles and disciples of our Saviour were scattered over the whole world. Thomas, tradition tells us, was chosen for Parthia [Iran–Iraq], Andrew for Scythia [northern Black Sea coast], John for Asia [coastal Asia Minor], where he remained till his death at Ephesus. Peter seems to have preached in Pontus, Galatia and Bithynia, Cappadocia and Asia [southern Black Sea coast, inland Turkey and Asia Minor], to the Jews of the Dispersion. Finally, he came to Rome where he was crucified, head downwards at his own request. What need be said of Paul, who from Jerusalem as far as Illyricum [Hungary and the Balkans] preached in all its fullness the gospel of Christ?
Eusebius of Caesarea *Ecclesiastical History* (c.324; 1965 edn) Bk 3.1. Eusebius (c.260–c.339), the single most important source for the first three centuries of the Christian church, wrote the final version of his history under Constantine, the first Christian Roman emperor (see 90:2). Here he reflects the later Christian understanding of the missionary movements of the apostles after the death of Jesus.

5 Follow, all of you, the bishop, as Jesus Christ followed the Father; and follow the presbyters as the apostles. Moreover, reverence the deacons as the commandment of God. Let no man do anything pertaining to the church apart from the bishop. Let that Eucharist be considered valid which is under the bishop or him to whom he commits it. Wherever the bishop appears, there let the people be, even as wherever Christ Jesus is, there is the Catholic Church.
Ignatius of Antioch *Letter to the Church of Smyrna* (c.107–110; 1919 edn) para.8. Ignatius is the earliest extant Christian writer to refer to 'monarchical' bishops, one bishop to a see, and bears witness to the development by the early 2nd century of a Christian clerical hierarchy of bishops, presbyters and deacons. Smyrna is now Izmir in Turkey.

6 There are 46 presbyters, 7 deacons, 7 sub-deacons, 42 acolytes, 52 exorcists, readers and door-keepers, above 1,500 widows and persons in distress, all of whom are supported by the grace and loving kindness of the Master.
Cornelius of Rome; Eusebius (c.324; 1965 edn) Bk 6, Ch.43. This passage by Cornelius, who was bishop of Rome in 251–253, provides a rare glimpse of the actual size of the early Roman church, just before the outbreak of the first full-scale imperial persecution of Christianity in 251. The numbers of presbyters (the highest rank below the bishop), deacons (who in Rome directly served the bishop) and exorcists (of evil spirits) suggest an overall Christian community of between 30,000 and 50,000.

7 How could one describe those mass meetings, the enormous gatherings in every city, and the remarkable congregations in places of worship? No longer satisfied with the old buildings, they raised from the foundations in all the cities churches spacious in plan.

Eusebius of Caesarea (c.324; 1965 edn) Bk 8.1. Eusebius thus describes a flourishing and numerous church in 300, on the eve of the Great Persecution of Diocletian (see 90:1). Modern assessments of the spread of Christianity at this time vary widely.

CONFLICT IN THE EARLY CHURCH, 31–312

1 Now I beseech you, brethren, by the name of our Lord Jesus Christ, that ye all speak the same thing, and that there be no divisions among you …

For as the body is one, and hath many members, and all the members of that one body, being many are one body: so also is Christ.

Bible, NT, I Corinthians 1:10 and 12:12. Despite the pleas of the Apostle Paul (d.c.65), which themselves suggest that there were conflicts among Christians even in his own lifetime, divisions existed within Christianity from the very beginning, both within individual communities and between different groups.

2 And certain men which came down from Judaea taught the brethren, and said, Except ye be circumcised after the manner of Moses, ye cannot be saved. When therefore Paul and Barnabas had no small dissension and disputation with them, they determined that Paul and Barnabas, and certain other of them, should go up to Jerusalem unto the apostles and elders about this question.

Bible, NT, Acts 15:1–2. The first great division within Christianity, which came to a head c.50, concerning whether Christians should be bound by Jewish customs. The decision to reject the restrictions of the Jewish law was fundamental to the development of Christianity as a universal religion.

3 These are the secret sayings which the living Jesus spoke and which Didymus Judas Thomas wrote down. And he said, 'Whoever finds the interpretation of these sayings will not experience death' … 'Blessed are the solitary and elect, for you will find the Kingdom.'

Gospel of Thomas (1st or 2nd century; 1977 edn). One of the apocryphal works, the Gospel of Thomas was excluded from the eventual canon of Christian scripture but was important to certain branches of Christianity, notably the so-called Gnostics, who believed in the privileged knowledge (gnosis) of a restricted elect.

4 Marcion of Pontus [on the Black Sea] developed his school, advancing the most daring blasphemy against Him who is proclaimed as God by the law and the prophets, declaring Him to be the author of evils, a lover of war, inconstant in judgement, and contrary to Himself. But Jesus being derived from a father who is above the God that made the world … was manifested in the form of a man to those who were in Judaea, abolishing the prophets and the law, and all the works of that God who made the world.

Irenaeus Against Heresies (c.185–190; 1867 edn) Bk 1.25.1. Irenaeus, an eastern Greek who in 177 became a bishop of Lugdunum (Lyons) in Gaul (France), wrote a condemnation of the Gnostics and of Marcion, who was excommunicated in Rome in 144. Marcion taught that the God of the Old Testament could not be the same as the loving Father of Jesus Christ and thus that the New Testament superseded the Old, rather than being its culmination.

5 A recent convert named Montanus, while Gratus was proconsul of Syria [possibly c.172], in the unbridled ambition of his soul for pre-eminence, laid himself open to the adversary, was filled with spiritual excitement and suddenly fell into a kind of trance and unnatural ecstasy. He raved, and began to babble and to utter strange sounds, prophesying contrary to the manner which the church had received from generation to generation by tradition from the beginning … [and] he raised up two women as well, and so filled them with the spurious spirit that they too chattered in a frenzied, inopportune and unnatural fashion, like himself.

Anon.; Eusebius of Caesarea (c.324; 1965 edn) Bk 5, Ch.16. Montanism, the so-called New Prophecy, emphasized spiritual possession and ecstatic prophecy for both men and women – in certain respects it was not unlike more recent charismatic Christianity. It was condemned as a heresy and as a threat to the organized church, even though its adherents included Tertullian (see 89:7), one of the greatest of all Latin theologians.

6 Wisdom and deeds have always from time to time been brought to mankind by the messengers of God. So in one age they have been brought by the messenger called Buddha in India, in another by Zoroaster to Persia, in another by Jesus to the West. Thereupon this revelation has come down, this prophecy in this last age, through me, Mani, messenger of the God of truth to Babylonia.

Mani, fragment from a work written for the king of Persia (1925 edn). Mani (216–c.276) was the founder of Manichaeism, a widespread dualist religion that divided the world between good and evil and that was persecuted by both the pagan Roman empire and by the Christian church. Dualist teachings in various forms had a long history within Christianity, however, attracting even Augustine of Hippo, perhaps the greatest of all Western theologians, and they appeared in various forms in both Byzantium and the medieval West (see 200:4).

PERSECUTION AND TOLERATION, 30–312

1 Render therefore unto Caesar the things which are Caesar's; and unto God the things that are God's.

Bible, NT, Matthew 22:21. The recorded teaching of Jesus, that Christians should not directly oppose the Roman emperor but should distinguish between what was appropriate to the secular and religious spheres.

2 When they heard these things, they were cut to the heart, and they gnashed on him with their teeth. But he, being full of the Holy Ghost, looked up steadfastly into heaven, and saw the glory of God, and Jesus standing on the right hand of God ... Then they cried out with a loud voice, and stopped their ears and ran upon him with one accord. And cast him out of the city, and stoned him; and the witnesses laid down their clothes at a young man's feet, whose name was Saul. And they stoned Stephen, calling upon God, and saying, Lord Jesus, receive my spirit. And he kneeled down, and cried with a loud voice, Lord, lay not this sin to their charge. And when he had said this, he fell asleep.

And Saul was consenting unto his death.

Bible, NT, Acts 7:54–60, 8:1. Stephen was the first martyr of the Christian church, killed c.32 by Jews who were encouraged by the Pharisee Saul, the future Apostle Paul.

3 To get rid of the report [that he had ordered the fire of Rome], Nero fastened the guilt and inflicted the most exquisite tortures on a class hated for their abominations, called Christians by the populace ... An immense multitude was convicted, not so much of the crime of arson, as of hatred of the human race. Mockery of every sort was added to their deaths. Covered with the skins of beasts, they were torn by dogs and perished, or were nailed to crosses, or were doomed to the flames. These served to illuminate the night when daylight failed.

Tacitus (c.56–120) Annals (1942 edn) Bk 15.44. The Roman historian's account, written c.116, of the persecution of Christians after the fire of Rome in 64 demonstrates that by now the Christians were a recognized community in Rome and one widely disliked for their 'hatred of the human race'. But even the hostile Tacitus implies that the Christians were not to blame for the fire (see 80:3).

4 This is the course I have taken with those who were accused before me as Christians. I asked them whether they were Christians, and if they confessed, I asked them a second and third time with threats of punishment. If they kept to it, I ordered them for execution; for I held no question that whatever it was that they admitted, in any case obstinacy and unbending perversity deserve to be punished.

Pliny the Younger Letters (c.112; 1893 edn) 10.96. Pliny was writing as governor of Bithynia, in northern Asia Minor, to Emperor Trajan (r.98–117), concerning his treatment of alleged Christians.

5 They are not to be sought out; but if they are accused and convicted, they must be punished – yet on this condition, that whoso denies himself to be a Christian, and makes the fact plain by his action, that is, by worshipping our gods, he shall obtain pardon.

Trajan's reply; Pliny the Younger (c.112; 1893 edn) Bk 10.97. The exchange of letters between Pliny and Trajan reflects the ambiguity of imperial policy towards Christians in this early period. Christianity was a crime, but Christians were not to be sought out, and open persecution was rare before the mid-3rd century.

6 We worship God only, but in other things we gladly serve you, acknowledging you as emperors and rulers of men and women, and praying that with your imperial power you may also be found to possess sound judgement.

Justin Martyr First Apology (c.151–155; 1997 edn) Ch.17. Justin, who was himself martyred in 165, defends Christianity against the charge of disloyalty and treason. However, while he emphasizes Christian obedience to the emperors, he repeats the Christian rejection of the imperial cult – that is, the worship of the emperor – a characteristic of Christianity that aroused great pagan mistrust and, ultimately, persecution.

7 If the Tiber reaches the walls, if the Nile does not rise to the fields, if the sky does not move or if the earth does, if there is famine, if there is plague, the cry is at once 'The Christians to the lion!' What, all of them to one lion?

Tertullian of Carthage Apology (c.197; 1931 edn) Ch.40.2. For many pagans, as the church father Tertullian here sarcastically observed, the Christian refusal to honour the traditional gods threatened to bring down divine wrath on the empire.

8 The day before we were to fight with the beasts I saw the following vision ... I was standing in the amphitheatre. I looked at the enormous crowd who watched in astonishment. I was surprised that no beasts were let loose on me, for I knew that I was condemned to die by the beasts. Then out came an Egyptian against me, of vicious appearance, together with his seconds, to fight with me. There also came up to me some handsome young men to be my seconds and assistants. My clothes were stripped off, and suddenly I was a man … [and she defeated the Egyptian]. Then I awoke. I realized that it was not with wild animals that I would fight but with the Devil, but I knew that I would win the victory.

Anon. *The Martyrdom of Perpetua* (c.202/3; 1972 edn) para.10. According to tradition, the North African martyr Perpetua kept a diary of her imprisonment, perhaps the only genuine first-person account of the days before a martyrdom.

1 In the nineteenth year of Diocletian's reign [303] … then it was that many rulers of the churches bore up heroically under horrible torments, an object lesson in the endurance of fearful ordeals; while countless others, their souls already numbed with cowardice, promptly succumbed to the first on-slaught. Of the rest, each was subjected to a series of different tortures, one flogged unmercifully with the whip, another racked and scraped beyond endurance.

Eusebius of Caesarea (c.324; 1965 edn) Bk 8, Chs 2–3. Eusebius, an eyewitness to these events, begins his account of the persecution of the church under Emperor Diocletian (r.284–305) (see 87:7).

THE CONVERSION OF CONSTANTINE

2 He [Constantine, r.306–337] began to invoke [his father's God] in prayer, beseeching and imploring him to show him who He was, and to stretch out His right hand to assist him in his plans … About the time of the midday sun, when day was just turning, he said he saw with his own eyes, up in the sky and resting over the sun, a cross-shaped trophy formed from light, and a text attached to it which said 'By This Conquer'.

Eusebius of Caesarea *Life of Constantine* (337–339; 1999 edn) Bk 1, Ch.28. Eusebius here reports, apparently from the emperor's own account, Constantine's famous vision (see 104:1), just before the decisive Battle of the Milvian Bridge (312), which established him as the sole ruler of the Western empire. The exact truth of what Constantine saw will never be known, but from this time onwards he never wavered in his support for the Christian God who, he believed, had given him victory.

3 Our [Emperors Constantine and Licinius] pur-pose is to grant both to the Christians and to all others full authority to follow whatever worship each man has desired; whereby whatsoever divinity dwells in heaven may be benevolent and propitious to us, and to all who are placed under our authority.

Edict of Milan (313); Lactantius *On the Deaths of the Persecutors* (c.315; 1893 edn) Ch.48.2–12. This edict of toleration, while

not explicitly Christian, marked the first official state recognition of Christianity.

4 These persons who devote the services of religion to divine worship, that is, those who are called clerics, shall be exempt from all compulsory public services whatever, lest, through the sacrilegious malice of certain persons, they should be called away from divine worship.

Law of Constantine, Law 2, 313; recorded in the *Theodosian Code* (1952 edn) Bk 16. Perhaps Constantine's greatest impact on Christianity lay in the wealth and privileges that he now pro-vided to the church, of which this law is merely one example.

5 The event [the celebration at Nicaea of Constan-tine's 20th year of rule in 325] was beyond all descrip-tion. Guards and soldiers ringed the entrance to the palace, guarding it with drawn swords, and between these the men of God passed fearlessly, and entered the innermost royal courts. Some then reclined with him, others relaxed nearby on couches on either side. It might have been supposed that it was an imaginary representation of the kingdom of Christ, and that what was happening was a dream, not reality.

Eusebius of Caesarea (337–339; 1999 edn) Bk 3, Ch.15. In the aftermath of persecution, the reaction of the Eastern bishops (including Eusebius himself) who attended the Council of Nicaea (Iznik, Turkey), the first ecumenical (universal) council of the church, which Constantine assembled, is not difficult to understand.

6 In honouring with exceptional distinction the city which bears his name [Constantinople, Istanbul], he embellished it with very many places of worship, very large martyr-shrines, and splendid houses … by these he at the same time honoured the tombs of the martyrs and consecrated the city to the martyrs' God.

Eusebius of Caesarea (337–339; 1999 edn) Bk 3.48. Eusebius' description of the foundation of Constantinople in 330 is somewhat exaggerated, but the 'city of Constantine', on the site of the existing ancient city of Byzantium, was to become the Christian capital of the Roman and later the Byzantine empire (see 104:4).

7 When he [Constantine] became aware that his life was ending, he perceived that this was the time to purify himself from the offences which he had at any time committed … Alone of all the emperors from the beginning of time Constantine was initiated by rebirth in the mysteries of Christ, and exulted in the Spirit … [and] when the due ceremonies were complete he put on bright imperial clothes which

shone like light, and rested on a pure white couch, being unwilling to touch a purple robe again.
Eusebius of Caesarea (337–339; 1999 edn) Bk 4, Chs 61.2–62.5. Like many of his contemporaries, Constantine delayed his baptism until near his death to avoid the danger of further sins following his purification.

CHURCH AND STATE FROM CONSTANTINE TO JUSTINIAN, 306–565

1 You are bishops whose jurisdiction is within the church: I also am a bishop, ordained by God to overlook those outside the church.
Constantine; Eusebius (337–339; 1999 edn) Bk 4, Ch.24. The exact meaning of this statement by Constantine remains uncertain. Although he attended the ecumenical Council of Nicaea and intervened repeatedly in church affairs, Constantine never sought to dictate Christian doctrine himself, nor did he ever either claim to be, or attempt to act as, a member of the ordained clergy.

2 What have Christians to do with kings? Or what have bishops to do with the palace?
Attrib. to the Donatists, a schismatic sect in North Africa that rejected the imperially supported church; Optatus *Against the Donatists* (c.384; 1997 edn) Bk 1.22. Statements rejecting state involvement in the church recur repeatedly in this period, almost always, as in this case, attributed to those whose own attempts to secure state support have recently been rejected.

3 [A silver statue of the Empress Eudoxia was erected in Constantinople, and public games were performed before it in 403.] These John [Chrysostom] regarded as an insult offered to the church, and having regained his ordinary freedom and keenness of tongue [after his first exile], he employed his tongue against those who did these things ... The empress once more applied his expression to herself as indicating marked contempt towards her own person: she therefore endeavoured to procure the convocation of another council of bishops against him. When John became aware of this, he delivered in the church that celebrated oration commencing 'Again Herodias raves; again she is troubled; again she dances; and again she desires to receive John's head on a platter' [the death of John the Baptist, Matthew 14:12].
Socrates Scholasticus *Ecclesiastical History* (440s; 1890 edn) Bk 6, Ch.18. Socrates wrote a continuation of the *Ecclesiastical History* of Eusebius of Caesarea, covering the period from Constantine to the reign of Theodosius II (r.408–450), and, along with his contemporary Sozomen, who wrote another

Ecclesiastical History covering the same period a few years later, is one of the most important sources for this period of church history. John Chrysostom (Goldenmouth), bishop of Constantinople in 398–404, had already been exiled once from his see; this conflict with the empress led to his second and final exile.

4 There are two powers, august emperor, by which this world is ruled from the beginning: the consecrated authority of the bishops, and the royal power. In these matters the priests bear the heavier burden because they will render account, even for rulers of men, at the divine judgement. Besides, most gracious son, you are aware that, although you in your office are the ruler of the human race, nevertheless you devoutly bow your head before those who are leaders in things divine and look to them for the means of your salvation.
Pope Gelasius I to Emperor Anastasius, 494 (1966 trans.). Gelasius, pope in 492–496, lays down the concept of the 'two powers', spiritual and secular, which was extremely influential in the medieval West. See 186:1.

5 Governing under the authority of God our empire which was delivered to us by the Heavenly Majesty, we both conduct wars successfully and render peace honourable, and we uphold the condition of the state. We so lift up our minds towards the help of the omnipotent God that we do not place our trust in weapons or our soldiers or our military leaders or our own talents, but we rest all our hopes in the providence of the Supreme Trinity alone.
Justinian I, ordering the composition of the *Digest* of Roman Law (c.530; 1985 trans.). The *Digest*, part of Justinian's *Corpus juris civilis*, was issued c. 550 (see 104:6).

HERESIES AND CONTROVERSIES, 300–600

6 [Julian] knew that toleration [of the Christians] would intensify their divisions ... experience had taught him that no wild beasts are such dangerous enemies to man as Christians are to one another.
Ammianus Marcellinus *The Later Roman Empire* (c.390; 1986 edn) Bk 22, Ch.5. Julian 'the Apostate', the last pagan emperor of Rome (r.361–363), failed in his attempt to revive state paganism after Constantine, but his assessment of Christian psychology was to prove remarkably accurate in the following centuries.

7 Alexander [bishop of Alexandria] attempted one day [c.320], in the presence of the presbyters and the rest of his clergy, too ambitious a discourse about the unity of the Holy Trinity. Arius, one of the presbyters under his jurisdiction, a man possessed of no inconsiderable logical acumen … said 'If the Father begat the Son, the one that was begotten has a beginning of existence; and from this it is evident, that there was once when the Son was not. It therefore necessarily follows that he had his essence from nothing' … [Alexander] convened a council of many prelates; and excommunicated Arius and the supporters of his heresy.

Socrates Scholasticus (440s; 1890 edn) Bk 1, Chs 5–6. From this initial debate between Alexander and Arius developed the Arian Controversy, centred on the relationship of the Father and the Son, that was to divide the church for the next 60 years.

1 Those citizens of Constantinople who maintained the doctrines of the Nicene Council, conducted Paul to the church. At the same time, those of the opposing multitude seized this occasion and came together in another church … and they ordained Macedonius bishop of Constantinople. This excited frequent seditions in the city which assumed all the appearance of a war, for the people fell upon one another, and many perished … the insurgents entered the house of Hermogenes, set fire to it, killed him, and attaching a cord to his body, dragged it through the city.

Sozomen *Ecclesiastical History* (440s; 1890 edn) Bk 3, Ch.7. The events in Constantinople in 342. Such theologically inspired riots were frequent in the Eastern Roman empire in the 4th and 5th centuries and provide an indication of the degree to which even complex theological debates, in this instance once again the Arian Controversy, could seize the interest of the general public in the 4th-century Christian empire (see 104:4).

2 It [the Arian Controversy] seemed not unlike a contest in the dark; for neither party appeared to understand clearly the grounds on which they abused one another.

Socrates Scholasticus (440s; 1890 edn) Bk 1, Ch.23.

3 Following the holy fathers, we all with one voice confess our Lord Jesus Christ one and the same Son … truly God and truly man … born from the Virgin Mary, the *Theotokos*, as touching the manhood, one and the same Christ, Son, Lord, only-begotten, to be acknowledged in two natures.

Chalcedonian Definition (451; 1886 edn). The fourth ecumenical Council of Chalcedon (Kadiköy), on the Bosphorus, sought to resolve the ongoing debate over how to express the human and divine natures of Christ. However, although the Chalcedonian Definition was accepted in the West and by what would become the Greek Orthodox Church, it was rejected by the majority of Christians in Egypt and Syria, whose churches still remain separate from the modern Protestant, Catholic and Orthodox churches.

CHURCH HIERARCHY AND THE AUTHORITY OF ROME, 300–600

4 In life, as in chess, bishops move obliquely.
Anon.

5 The bishop of Constantinople shall have the primacy of honour after the bishop of Rome, because Constantinople is new Rome.

Council of Constantinople, Canon 3 (381; 1843 edn). The second ecumenical council emphasized the status of the new capital, which led to tension with Alexandria in the east and, above all, with Rome.

6 Make me bishop of Rome, and I will at once be a Christian.

Vettius Agorius Praetextatus; Jerome *Against John of Jerusalem* (398/9; 1892 edn). By the late 4th century the wealth, power and prestige of the Roman see was visible to all, including pagans such as Praetextatus, a pagan senator (d.384), whose remark was heard with horror by Jerome (c.347–c.420), the great Latin translator, exegete and satirist.

7 [June 29, the Feast of Peter and Paul] is to be honoured with special and peculiar exultation in our city, that there may be a predominance of gladness on the day of their martyrdom in the place where the chief of the Apostles met their glorious end … These are they who promoted thee to such glory, that being made a holy nation, a chosen people, a priestly and royal state, and the head of the world through the blessed Peter's holy see thou didst attain a wider sway by the worship of God than by earthly government.

Pope Leo I, Sermon 82.1 (c.440–461; 1984 edn). The concept of 'Roman primacy' developed fully only in the Middle Ages (see 108:5), but even in the 5th century under Leo, bishop of Rome, the popes were beginning to assert their pre-eminence, based above all on the claimed authority of the Apostle Peter. Under Gregory, bishop of Rome 590–604, the conflict for precedence between Rome and Constantinople continued, a conflict that would develop into formal schism in later centuries (see 188:8).

ASCETICS, MISSIONARIES AND LITURGY

8 [Antony] communed with himself and reflected as he walked how the Apostles left all and followed the Saviour; and how they in the Acts sold their possessions and brought and laid them at the Apostles' feet for distribution to the needy, and what and how great a hope was laid up for them in heaven.

Pondering over these things he entered the church, and it happened the Gospel was being read, and he heard the Lord saying to a rich man, 'if thou wouldst be perfect, go and sell that thou hast and give to the poor; and come follow Me and thou shall have treasure in heaven' [Matthew 19:21]. The life of Antony was hugely influential in inspiring later generations of Christian ascetics, including St Augustine and St Jerome.

Athanasius of Alexandria *Life of Antony* (356; 1891 edn) Ch.2. Antony (c.250–356) was the first of the great Christian hermits, renouncing his wealth and retreating alone to a cave on Mount Kolzim in the Egyptian desert, where he defeated demons and performed miracles.

1 It is said that Pachomius at first practised asceticism alone in a cave, but that a holy angel appeared to him, and commanded him to call together some young monks, and live with them for he had succeeded well in pursuing philosophy by himself, and to train them by the laws which were about to be delivered to him, and now he was to possess and benefit many as a leader of communities. A tablet was then given to him, which is still carefully preserved. Upon this tablet were inscribed injunctions by which he was bound to permit everyone to eat, to drink, to work and to fast.

Sozomen (440s; 1890 edn) Bk 3.14. Pachomius (d.346), also an Egyptian, organized the first large monastic communities for monks to live and worship together, establishing a monastic rule from which many later monastic practices derived.

2 I shall try, so far as I can, with the help of God, faithfully to explain only their institutions and the rules of their monasteries, and especially the origin and causes of the principal faults, of which they reckon eight [gluttony, fornication, covetousness, anger, dejection, weariness of heart, vainglory and pride], and the remedies for them according to their traditions ... in accordance with the rule which I have seen followed in the monasteries anciently founded throughout Egypt and Palestine, as I do not believe that a new establishment in the West, in the parts of Gaul, could find anything more reasonable or more perfect than are those customs.

John Cassian *Institutes* (c.419–426; 1895 edn) Preface. Cassian played a vital role in introducing Eastern monastic ideas and practices to the West, and his *Institutes* had a huge influence on the Rule of St Benedict in particular (see 195:3).

3 The blessed Leo [Eastern emperor, 457–474] of pious memory rejoiced in these doings [of the saint

Daniel]; and not long afterwards he visited the place in which the holy man dwelt and asked for the ladder to be set so that he might go up and be blessed. When the ladder was placed, the emperor went up to the servant of God and begged to touch his feet; but on approaching them and seeing their mortified and swollen state he was amazed and marvelled at the just man's endurance. He glorified God and begged the holy man that he might set up a double column and that Daniel would take his stand upon it.

Anon. *Life of St Daniel the Stylite* (c.500; 1948 edn) Ch.44. Daniel (409–493) was a stylite, a hermit who expressed his asceticism by living on a high pillar (*stylos*). This form of radical piety never developed in the West, but there were a number of such saints in the East, usually in the Syrian desert or, in the case of the much-visited Daniel, near Constantinople.

4 Helena, the emperor's mother, being divinely directed by dreams went to Jerusalem [in 326] ... [and] found three crosses in the sepulchre: one of these was that blessed cross on which Christ had hung, the other two were those on which the two thieves that were crucified with him had died. With these was also found the tablet of Pilate, on which he had inscribed in various characters, that the Christ who was crucified was king of the Jews.

Socrates Scholasticus (440s; 1890 edn) Bk 1, Ch.17. The legendary discovery of the most famous of all Christian relics, the True Cross, by Helena, the mother of Constantine, in the Sepulchre of Christ. This myth, although unknown to Eusebius who wrote in Constantine's own lifetime, developed rapidly after Constantine's death, and his mother became known as St Helena.

5 We must now mention in what manner Christianity was spread in [Constantine's] reign: for it was in his time that the nations both of the Indians [Ethiopians] in the interior and of the Iberians [Georgians] first embraced the Christian faith ... A certain woman leading a devout and chaste life was, in the providential ordering of God, taken captive by the Iberians. The woman caused the king of the Iberians to become a preacher of Christ: for having believed in Christ through this devoted woman, he convened all the Iberians who were under his authority ... [and] exhorted them to worship the God of the captive.

Socrates Scholasticus (440s; 1890 edn) Bk 1, Chs 19–20. With imperial support under Constantine came an increase in Christian missionary activity to the peoples living just beyond the Roman empire, in this instance to the inhabitants of modern Ethiopia and Georgia.

1 While the nation of the Angli [Saxons], placed in a corner of the world, remained faithless and worshipping sticks and stones, I determined ... to send to it, God granting it, a monk of my monastery for the purpose of preaching. And he [Augustine], having with my leave been made bishop by the bishops of *Germania*, proceeded with their aid to the aforesaid nation at the end of the world; and already we have received reports of his safety and his work. He and his companions are resplendent with such great miracles in the said nation that they seem to imitate the powers of the apostles in the signs which they display. Moreover, at the festival of the Lord's Nativity this last year, more than ten thousand Angli are reported to have been baptized by our brother and fellow-bishop.

Pope Gregory I to the bishop of Alexandria, Letter 8.30, 598 (1894 edn). Gregory reports the success of the Roman mission to England, which had begun under Augustine (first bishop of Canterbury) in 596 (see 160:3).

2 We believe in One God, the Father, Almighty, Maker of all that is, seen and unseen. And in One Lord Jesus Christ, the Son of God, begotten of the Father, Only-begotten, that is, from the substance of the Father; God from God; Light from Light, True God from True God, begotten not made, consubstantial with the Father, by whom all things were made, both things in heaven and things in earth; who for us and for our salvation came down and was incarnate, was made man, suffered, and rose again on the third day, ascended into heaven, and is coming to judge living and dead. And in the Holy Ghost.

Creed of the Council of Nicaea, 325. The original Nicene Creed, the product of the first ecumenical council, was further refined at the second ecumenical council of Constantinople in 381 and remains the basis of the creed used in every modern church service.

3 You urge me to revise the old Latin version, and, as it were, to sit in judgement on the copies of the Scriptures which are now scattered throughout the whole world; and, since they differ from one another, you would have me decide which of them agree with the Greek original. The labour is one of love, but at the same time both perilous and presumptuous ... is there a man, learned or unlearned, who will not, when he takes the volume into his hands, and perceives that what he reads does not suit his settled tastes, break out immediately into violent language, and call me a forger and a profane person for having the audacity to add anything to the ancient books?

St Jerome *Preface to the Four Gospels* (383; 1892 edn). The *Preface*, addressed to Damasus, bishop of Rome (366–384), marks the beginning of Jerome's great translation of the Bible into Latin, first the Gospels from Greek, then the Old Testament from Hebrew. Jerome thus replaced the existing inaccurate Latin translations with his own 'Vulgate' Bible, which remained the essential Latin Bible until the Reformation.

4   This is he whom seer and sibyl
         Sang in ages long gone by;
     This is he of old revealed
         In the page of prophecy;
     Lo! He comes the promised Saviour,
         Let the world his praises sing.

The Latin poet Aurelius Clemens Prudentius (c.348–410) 'Of the Father's heart begotten', verse 5 (1905 edn).

5   To thee, my leader in battle and defender,
         O *Theotokos*,
     I thy city, delivered from calamity,
     Offer hymns of victory and thanksgiving
     Since thou art invincible in power,
     Set me free from every danger,
     That I may cry to thee: Hail, Bride without
         bridegroom.

Anon. *Akathistos* ('Standing') hymn (c.500–550; 1986 edn). The greatest of Greek hymns to the Virgin Mary, the *Akathistos* was probably composed in the first half of the 6th century and remains integral to the Greek Orthodox Church, particularly during Lent.

THE AGE OF THE CHURCH FATHERS

6 Thanks be to God, the Almighty, the King of the universe, for all His mercies ... Destruction has overtaken the whole brood of God's enemies, and at one stroke has blotted them out from human sight ... and from that time on a day bright and radiant, with no cloud overshadowing it, shone down with shafts of heavenly light on the churches of Christ throughout the world.

Eusebius of Caesarea (c.324; 1965 edn) Bk 10, Ch.1. Thus Eusebius introduces the last book of his *Ecclesiastical History*, celebrating the end of the persecution and the benefits that Constantine brought to the church 312–324.

7 [Many people] now complain of this Christian era, and hold Christ responsible for the disasters which their city [Rome] endured. But they do not make Christ responsible for the benefits they received out of respect for Christ, to which they owed their lives. They attribute their deliverance to their own

destiny; whereas if they had any right judgement
they ought rather to attribute the harsh cruelty they
suffered at the hands of their enemies to the providence
of God. For God's providence constantly uses war to
correct and chasten the corrupt morals of mankind.

St Augustine *The City of God* (413–426; 1972 edn) Bk 1, Ch.1.
Almost a century after Eusebius, Augustine of Hippo (354–
430) wrote his monumental work in part in response to those
who blamed recent disasters, above all the sack of Rome by
Alaric the Visigoth in 410, on the conversion of the empire to
Christianity.

1 The regulations of constitutions formerly promulgated shall suppress any pagans who survive, although
we now believe that there are none.

Theodosius II, law, 423; *Theodosian Code* (1952 edn) Bk 16.10.
By the end of the 4th century Christianity was the official
religion of the Roman empire, and paganism was illegal, although
the declaration of the 'disappearance' of all pagans in this law
of 423 was very much an exaggeration.

2 As the happiness of a future life is the great object
of religion, we may hear, without surprise or scandal,
that the introduction, or at least the abuse, of
Christianity had some influence on the decline and
fall of the Roman empire. The clergy successfully
preached the doctrines of patience and pusillanimity;
the active virtues of spirit were discouraged and the
last remains of military spirit were buried in the
cloister; a large portion of public and private wealth
was consecrated to the specious demands of charity
and devotion; and the soldiers' pay was lavished on
the useless multitudes of both sexes, who could only
plead the merits of abstinence and chastity. Faith,
zeal, curiosity, and the more earthly passions of
malice and ambition kindled the flame of theological
discord; and the church, and even the state, were
distracted by religious factions.

Edward Gibbon *The Decline and Fall of the Roman Empire*
(1776–88), 'General Observations on the Fall of the Roman
Empire in the West' (attached in Ch.38). In the Age of
Enlightenment the attitude of the great English historian to the
rise of Christianity in the Roman empire was very different
from that of the fathers and ecclesiastical historians who
proclaimed the triumph of the church.

China: The Middle Ages and Later Empire, 221–1912

THE CHINESE MIDDLE AGES, 221–1279

1 At that time [4th century AD] the common people were peaceable, having as yet no knowledge of warfare and self-defence. Yu Gun declared: 'Confucius said: "To make the people fight without giving them instruction amounts to abandoning them."'

He therefore called together all the men of some social standing and conferred with them. 'When two or three men of superior quality are placed in a situation of peril,' he told them, 'they will find the means to keep life and honour intact, and to safe-guard their wives and children.'

Jin Fagen *Yongjia luan hou beifang de haozu* (The Great North-ern Families after the Rebellion in the Yongjia Reign Period) (1964) p.27; Mark Elvin *The Pattern of the Chinese Past* (1973) pp.42–3. This was Chinese society *in extremis*. The early empire, after a split that had been briefly healed, had come apart in the 4th century AD, and northern China had been overrun by non-Han peoples or 'barbarians' – that is, those neighbours of the 'mainstream' Chinese who were in varying degrees distinct from them ethnically, linguistically and also culturally, most importantly in this last regard in their kinship practices.

2 The men of old had a saying: 'When a thousand people assemble, but do not choose one of their number to be their leader, they will either scatter or fall into disorder unless they disperse. What shall we do about it?'

They all answered: 'Excellent. Who should be our leader now but you?'

Yu Gun was silent for a while. Then he said to them: 'My friends, in this acute crisis, you have laid ease aside. You have not dared to shirk difficulties. Yet, when men set up a leader, what matters most is that they should obey his orders.'

They thereupon swore an oath to him, saying: 'We shall not take advantage of these troubled times to molest our neighbours or to pillage houses. We shall not burn or carry off the crops that others have grown. We shall not plot immoral acts nor commit injustice. With our united efforts and a singleness of purpose, we shall meet the dangers that face us in a spirit of mutual sympathy.'

Everyone else followed their lead. They at once narrowed the defiles, barricaded the footpaths,

repaired the walls and entrenchment, and set up stockades. They examined each person's achieve-ments, calculated requirements, and shared out work and rest in equitable fashion. They supplied each other's needs. They perfected their military equipment, gauged their strength and trusted to their abilities.

Once everything was in good order, Yu had the large districts select senior persons and the smaller districts select men of worth, and he led them in person. Once social divisions had been made clear, and there was no ambiguity in the structure of command, superiors and inferiors observed the proper etiquette, and young and old the proper ceremonials.

Jin Fagen (1964) p.27; Elvin (1973) pp.42–3. The fortress society set up in the mountains by Yu Gun drew on the Chinese cultural survival kit: cooperation under authority, morality, equity (not equality), and hierarchy, plus vigorous but careful planning in a structured system. It was, and probably remains, an impressively powerful potential that is almost instinctive in times of desperation.

3　　We speak now of Hells, of their hidden
　　　　anguish:
　　Against the sun rises the wood of knives,
　　Ranges of sword-hills, blades piercing the sky,
　　Waves surging upwards from bubbling
　　　　cauldrons,
　　Flames leaping forth from fiery furnaces,
　　And iron-bound battlements that blot out
　　　　daylight,
　　Pillars of bronze red-hot the night through,
　　And all about here – sinners everywhere
　　Glancing around in their torment, lamenting,
　　While ox-browed demons, eyes hate-filled, and
　　　　warders,
　　Cruel-fanged, with pronged forks, pierce
　　　　through their ribs,
　　Pound their livers and hearts,
　　Like fish lying flat on hot-plates of iron,
　　From hell to hell shifting through countless
　　　　kalpas
　　Until such a time as good fortune's repaired,
　　All evil confessed and repentance complete –

Whereat the steaming waters clear, grow calm,
Transformed to flower-filled pools. The fumes
Of furnace coals extend sweet canopies of
   scent.
The fearsome trees of swords become jade
   groves.
The pillars of bronze mutate to dharma flags
That soar aloft in perpetuity.
The iron nets change their shapes. Forthwith
The Pure Land spreads about. Their blades cast
   down,
The devils with oxen's heads again accept
The Triple Refuge: Buddha, Dharma, Sangha
The transients whose heads were lost once
   more
Restore to wholeness their fragmented frames.

Anon. *The Gardens of Dharma and the Pearl-Groves of Doctrine* (7th century); Mark Elvin in *Philosophy East and West* Vol.43.2 (April 1993). As in Europe, there was an age of faith in China in the Middle Ages, but it was a Buddhist (and Daoist) faith, not Christianity. The poem shows a vision of Hell that has both astonishing resemblances to the Christian version and astonishing differences. Although the Buddhist Hell was long-lasting, it was, in the end, temporary – a purgatory – and like everything else made of complex objects, it was *illusory* when seen with the eye of wisdom. Hence the transformation scene that takes place when the sinners' time is up. A *kalpa* was an immensely long period of time; the *dharma* is the Buddhist moral law; and the *sangha* is the Buddhist monastic community.

1 Q: In principle it seems that one should not marry a widow. Is this the case?

A: Yes, it is. One marries to acquire a mate for oneself. If one seeks to acquire a mate for oneself by marrying someone who has lost the virtue proper to her, then one's action has already lost the virtue proper to it. For a wife is someone who follows a single person until her death. For her to remarry is to lose the virtue that is proper to her.

Q: If a widow is alone and impoverished, with no one on whom to depend, may she or may she not remarry?

A: This theory has only arisen in these latter days because people are afraid of dying of hunger and cold. But dying of hunger is a trivial matter. Loss of the virtue that is proper to one is exceedingly serious.

Er Cheng ji (Collected Works of the Two Chengs) (11th century; 1986 edn) Vol.1, p.301. An exchange between Cheng Mingdao and his brother Cheng Yichuan, two of the creators of neo-Confucianism, which vividly conveys the uncompromising tone of this new and essentially non-theistic puritanism. A rather milder version gradually became the dominant ideology of the educated classes in late-imperial times and spread some considerable way down into society, but it always remained at odds with popular customs.

2 Under the Tang dynasty [618–907] the printing of books from wooden blocks was still not fully developed. After Feng Yingwang had first printed the Five Confucian Scriptures in 932, all the canonical works were printed by means of blocks. In 1041–49 a commoner named Bi Sheng also devised movable types. His method was to cut the ideographs in sticky clay to the depth of the edge of a copper coin, each one constituting a separate piece of type. These were then baked to make them hard.

He would previously have prepared an iron plate covered with a mixture of pine resin, wax and paper ash. When he came to print, he would place an iron frame on this plate and in it set up the pieces of ideographic type in a closely packed fashion, so that when the iron frame was full it amounted to a block. He would warm it near a fire so that the composition would melt slightly; and then press a level board on the surface of the type so that they became as flat as a whetstone. This method was too cumbersome for merely printing a few copies, but marvellously quick for printing tens, hundreds or thousands of copies.

Shen Gua *Dream Pool Essays* (1086); Elvin (1973) pp.182–3. This account was written by the celebrated polymath not long after Bi's invention. The problem of casting type, whether in clay, wood or metal, accurately enough to permit solid setting inhibited a wide use of movable types for many centuries, and the simpler method of printing by means of cut wooden blocks remained much commoner. Nonetheless, this passage is eloquent testimony to China's long lead over western Europe in printing (212:3) and long possession of much higher rates of literacy. (Chinese dating by reign-periods has been replaced in the above by Western dates.)

3 On the first day of the first month of the lunar calendar, the prefectural government of Kaifeng permitted three days of purchase by gambling. Scholar-administrators and commoners offered each other the season's greetings from the early hours of the day onward. In the city quarters and blocks of dwellings people would chant out that such goods as foodstuffs, tools, fruits, firewood and coal were available for purchase by gambling. Multi-coloured covered stalls were put up ... Here were spread out on display headgear, combs, pearls, jades, ornaments for the head, clothing, artificial flowers, curios and playthings. Dance-floors were laid out between them and also halls for singers, while carriages and horses chased after each other in criss-crossing fashion. Towards evening the women from families of high social standing enjoyed gambling-purchasing in an uninhibited manner, joined the audiences at entertainments, and drank and feasted in the restaurants in the markets. This had become so customary that no one tittered with surprise at seeing it. Three days of gambling-purchasing were likewise permitted at the Cold Food Festival in the spring and at the winter solstice.

Meng Yuanlao *Dream of the Glories of the Eastern Capital* (c.1148); Lin Dan and Wang Yangzong (eds) *Zhongguo Kexnegeming* (Science and Scientific Revolutions in China) (2002) p.426. Meng describes Kaifeng (capital of the Northern Song) shortly before its government had to flee south under 'barbarian' attack. Purchasing by gambling required the would-be purchaser to give the seller a small sum of money as a stake and then to toss coins, typically three coins ten times. If he obtained a winning combination, commonly no triples of 'heads' or 'tails' in a given number of throws, he got his take back and the goods he wanted. If not, his stake-money was forfeit. Meng paints a vivid picture of the commercialized opulence of Chinese urban life under the later Middle Empire, and shows that the well-known Chinese passion for gambling already had a powerful hold. No stall-keeper would have stayed long in business if he or she had not had at least a roughly accurate knowledge – almost certainly kept a trade secret – of the probabilities of various coin combinations. Under the Southern Song there were no legal limitations on the practice of purchasing by gambling and it became quite common.

1 In the fifth lunar month of 1232 there was a great epidemic in Kaifeng. In the space of fifty days over 900,000 dead were taken out through the gates, those too poor to be buried not being included in this number.

Anon. *History of the Jin Dynasty* (1333–4; 1975 edn) Ch.17, p.14b; Mark Elvin 'Chinese Cities since the Song Dynasty' in P. Abrams and E.A. Wrigley (eds) *Towns in Societies* (1978) p.79.

2 Each day, from each of the twelve gates of the capital, between 1,000 and 2,000 corpses were carried out.

Li Gao, medical doctor; Abrams and Wrigley (1978) p.80. This astonishing death toll occurred when the Jin capital city of Kaifeng was full of refugees just after the Mongols had lifted their first siege of the city; it fell two years later. Li Gao's evidence refers to a period of three months, giving a total of at least 12 × 1,000 × 90, which is just over a million. In spite of recent attempts by some scholars to identify this as plague – that is, caused by the micro-organism *Yersinia pestis* and perhaps linked with the Black Death in Europe, rather more than a century later (see 284:1–290:5) – there is no *positive* evidence that this was so. Equally, there is *no* evidence that it was *not*. What these quotations do confirm is the enormous size of the populations of the largest cities in China at this particular period.

3 There is one driving-belt for wheels both great and small;

When one wheel turns, the others all turn with it.

The rovings are transmitted evenly from the bobbin-rollers.

The threads wind by themselves onto the reeling-frame.

Wang Zhen *Treatise on Agriculture* (1313); Elvin (1973) pp.195–8. The writer is delighting in the water-powered, 32-spindle spinning-machine. It span about 130 pounds of thread in a day and a night and was 'several times cheaper than the women workers it replaces'. It was also, he tells us, 'used in all parts of north China that manufacture hemp'.

4 It takes a spinner many days to spin a hundred catties,

But with water power it may be done with supernatural speed.

Wang Zhen (1313); Elvin (1973) p.198. These machines span loose and roughly twisted hemp cords or 'rovings' into hemp yarn by a process that probably broadly resembled ring-spinning. A related system twisted filaments of freshly reeled silk together. The Italians had water-powered silk-twisting machinery at about the same period in the 'lanterns' used in Bologna and Lucca, but the 13th-century Chinese machinery died out while the Italian continued with some limited modifications over the centuries, notably in Piedmont, until it finally provided some inspiration for the early spinning revolution in 18th-century Britain (see 571:2). The failure in China not only to continue to develop what appears to be an early shift to the mechanization of production but actually its loss in later times is a challenge to our understanding of the economic history of China under the Middle Empire. A cattie was the equivalent of about 21 ounces.

THE MING DYNASTY, 1368–1644

5 The Chinese pottery [porcelain] is manufactured only in the towns of Zaytun and Sin-kalan. It is made of the soil of some mountains in that district, which takes fire like charcoal … They mix this with some stones which they have, burn the whole for three days, then pour water over it. This gives a kind of clay which they cause to ferment. The best quality of [porcelain is made from] clay that has fermented for a complete month … It is exported to India and other countries, even reaching as far as our own lands in the West, and it is the finest of all makes of pottery.

Ibn Battuta (1304–68) *The Travels of Ibn Battuta* (1929 trans.) pp.282–3. The Muslim merchant from Tangier spent 25 years wandering and observing from Constantinople to China.

1 Madame would make her toilette at dawn, seated in her bedroom. Her hundred serfs, young and old, male and female, would all come to report on what they had been doing. Madame would pick out the laziest and have them given a flogging. For those who had toiled diligently she would prepare a goblet of wine with her own hand and mix in marrow to make it ready for drinking. Those who tasted this wine would leave flushed with happiness, and compete with each other to work hard, unmindful of their burdens. Those who had been beaten would blame themselves and say, 'What point is there in not making every effort for her ladyship, and being rewarded with a beaker of wine?' In this way everyone whom Madame employed proved himself capable; her lands supported cattle by the hundred, her streams bred fish and turtles by the picul, and her gardeners tended fruit, melon, mustard, and vegetables by the tens of acres.

Wang Shizhen (16th century); Fu Yiling *Mingdai Jiangnan shimin jingji shitan* (Enquiry into the Economy of the Urban Population of Jiangnan during the Ming Dynasty) (1963) in Elvin (1973) pp.236–7. A not untypical estate owned by a family of the official class in mid-Ming times (1450–1600). 'Madame' was the aunt of Wang Shizhen, a well-known bureaucrat and the author of these lines. He gained the highest degree in the official examinations between 1522 and 1566. According to the law, only official families were allowed to own serfs, but various subterfuges (such as fictive 'adoption') were used to get round this, and it is hard to know how widespread the practice was. A picul was a traditional measure of capacity, about a tenth of a cubic yard.

2 And as for questioning the witnesses in public, besides not confiding the life and honour of one man to the bare oath of another, this is productive of another good, which is that as these audience chambers are always full of people who can hear what the witnesses are saying, only the truth can be written down … But in this country, besides this order observed of them in examinations, they do fear so much their king, and he where he maketh his abode keepeth them so low, that they dare not once stir; in sort that these men are unique in the doing of their justice, more than were the Romans or any other kind of people.

Galeote Pereira *South China in the Sixteenth Century: Being the Narratives of Galeote Pereira, Fr. Gaspar da Cruz, O.P., Fr. Martin de Rada, O.E.S.A.* (pub. 1565); C.R. Boxer (ed.) *South China in the Sixteenth Century* (1953) p.20. A Portuguese soldier and trader, who had himself been a prisoner of the Chinese, is impressed by Chinese justice.

3 Whatsoever person or persons come to any man of quality's house, it is customary to offer him on a fair tray in a porcelain cup … a kind of warm water which they call *cha*, which is somewhat red and very medicinal, which they use to drink, made from a concoction of somewhat bitter herbs.

Gaspar da Cruz (1565); Boxer (1953) p.140. The observant Portuguese Dominican friar visited Canton for a few weeks and here records his introduction to tea.

4   Like the water-chestnut's blossom, cold my
             face in the looking-glass,
         And never, through these last three years, have
             my tears been dried away.
         In the fullness of old age, my parents-in-law
             have departed.
         Once more I taste the frost and snow, the chill
             of the widow's estate.

         But now I, myself, am returning, to that place
             for all time my home.
         You, whom I leave behind me, don't think I'm
             heroic. Not so,
         Under the faith-keeping pines and cedars that
             rise on the Western Slopes,
         Husband and wife, we roam together, where
             delight has bidden us go.

Zeng Rulan; Mark Elvin 'Unseen Lives' in R.T. Ames (ed.) *Self as Image in Asian Theory and Practice* (1998) p.176. Just after she had written this poem, Zeng committed suicide with the utmost composure. Faultlessly dressed, she swallowed a little metal ball. She was a faithful widow, a type of domestic heroine much honoured in late imperial times. The ideology that inspired her was the doctrine of neo-Confucianism, which decreed that a wife should be faithful forever to a single husband (see 97:1). Although such neo-Confucian values crystallized during the Song dynasty, becoming the main creed of the élite, they were only one side of Chinese social behaviour and in perpetual strife with freer, more superstitious and more sensual popular ways. 'The water-chestnut looking-glass' referred to a lady's vanity glass. The Western Slopes were the land where, in the dawn of the Chinese race, the Yellow Emperor married Leizu.

5   Wu folk are excited when they give birth to a
             daughter,
         But it's not because they hope that she'll run a
             family house.
         They wash her young complexion in peach-
             flower water,
         And pray at her young movements men's lust
             will be aroused.
         She's only aged eleven when she puts in rouge
             and powder,

While at twelve she's coaxing tunes from silken
strings.
Her hair, at fourteen years, is tumbling down
her shoulders
And her moth's-antennae eyebrows can
bewitch.

Mama permits herself – a smile of satisfaction.
She'll fetch a thousand – silver – to the ounce,
When the highest class of customers come
seeking her in marriage
And do not spare expense to buy a beauty from
the South …

The client is delighted. He observes to the
mother,
'In no way can one reckon that a thousand is
too much!'
Let tonight become the night that decides a
lifetime's love.
How he piles the golden hairpins and the
bangles up. And up! …

*Off they go, then, unconcerned, with no feelings
for their kin.*
*Once a chick's become a grown-up, well – she
makes her own way.*
*Money is what matters. Flesh and blood mean
nothing.*
*For you, and me, and all of us, the mere thought
of this is hateful.*

Shao Changheng 'Selling a Daughter' (late 17th century); *Qing shiduo* (Qing Bell of Poesy) (1869; 1960 edn) pp.573–4. The sudden shift in tone at the end from prurience to pious Confucian disapproval is a symptom of the tension between the sensual, profit-seeking style of the culture of Wu (the lower Yangzi valley) and the accepted morality. The duality of values evident from the contrast between this poem and the preceding one represents a rift that ran through late-imperial China and has continued, only slightly modified, to the present day. Shao was a child prodigy who gained the first-level degree in the official examinations at the incredibly early age of nine.

THE QING DYNASTY, 1644–1912

1   Miao forts are not fit battlefields for real
military engagements,
And the underground boltholes of *those hardly
human* don't merit consideration.
Not since the world emerged from chaos has
one ever set eyes on the like

Of these forests and thickets of bamboo that
extend beyond the horizon.

We have chiselled through hills, and flattened
highways, drums rumbling to trumpets'
music.
Helmeted on our chargers' backs, parched
grain wrapped for travel food,
Oxcarts carrying those of importance, while
the lesser bore loads on their backs,
Every day, for our Imperial Court, we've
developed new arable lands …

Yesterday victory was proclaimed – our three
outstanding triumphs:
We have lashed their hands behind their backs,
or *swallowed their lands* like Leviathan,
And, with no more than a single blow, they've
been quelled or exterminated,
So these far-off wastelands and tribal domains
yield us menials and serving-girls.

Peng Ermi 'Ballad of Shuixi' (c.1650) in *Guizhou tongzhi* (Comprehensive Gazetteer of Guizhou) (1741; 1968 edn) Ch.45, pp.51b–52b. The Chinese and their rulers under the later empire were vigorous imperialists, seizing the lands of non-Chinese and either settling them with their own people or opening the way for Chinese merchants to extract natural resources. The above lines come from the brush of a gungho conquistador, who was governor of Guizhou (southeastern China). Peng openly proclaims his goals of a colonial environmental and demographic transformation. The Miao people in this southwestern corner of what is today China fought back with determination for a further two centuries, inflicted some savage defeats on their Chinese enemies and were only finally subdued in the 1870s.

2   There had earlier been a major disturbance in
Jizhou in 1644 and 1645. The serfs had risen in
swarms and had been followed by the tenants and
a crowd of mean and worthless fellows. They formed
societies with the ritual slaughter of a bull and a
pig, and engaged in shameless pillaging. In every
village there were hundreds of thousands of them
under rebel leaders. They ripped up pairs of
trousers to serve as flags. They sharpened their hoes
into swords, and took to themselves the title of
'Levelling Kings', declaring that they were levelling
the distinction between masters and serfs, titled
and mean, rich and poor.
   The tenants seized hold of their masters' best
clothes … They tied the masters to pillars and flogged
them with whips and lashes of bamboo. Whenever

they held a drinking bout they would order the masters to kneel and pour out wine for them. They would slap them across the cheeks and say: 'We are all of us equally men. What right had you to call us "serfs"? From now on it is going to be the other way around!'

Anon. scholar, mid-17th century; Fu Yiling *Ming-qing nongcun shehui jingji* (Rural Society and Economy in the Late Ming and Early Qing) (1961) p.109. This is a contemporary account of a serf rising in Jiangxi (southeast China) at the end of the Ming dynasty. The scholar was, of course, on the other side, but even so the justified rage and the passion for equality comes through. In most areas, a major concern of the serfs who rebelled at this time was to seize and burn the written bonds that determined their subordinate status, often derived from past indebtedness but normally hereditary once acquired. Serfdom was already declining during the later Ming. It virtually vanished under the following dynasty, the Qing, leaving a rural society that consisted almost entirely of peasants running fragmented farms as free men who were either tenants or smallholders, or a mixture of the two.

1 The continually increasing population puts merit ceaselessly in competition with merit, and work with work, in a manner that prevents great fortunes.

Anon. *Mémoires concernant l'histoire, les sciences, les arts … des Chinois par les missionaires de Pe-kin* (1776–1814) Vol.4, p.313. Most of the articles in this 17-volume work are not ascribed to a particular author, but the Jesuit fathers who compiled it – J.M. Amiot (1718–93), F. Bourgeois (1723–92), P.M. Cibot (1727–80), A. Kao (1733–80), A. de Poirot (1735–1814) and (posthumously) A. Gaubil (1689–1759) – were in China for most of the 18th century and made many remarks that reveal how society looked to sinologically informed European eyes.

2   The spacious examination hall has opened in
              dignified splendour.
       The provincial candidates, come to do battle,
              are like ants or a fish's scales.
       Facing the south, the Presiding Examiner sits in
              his towering head-gear.
       His assistant officials, forbidden to exit, form
              two lines of black-silk-covered tables.

       The red script of the re-copied papers blurs like
              the red eyes of the covetous,
       And one can imagine these words – written
              with the competitors' blood.

       They sift through the dross of their thoughts
              for gold, but gold is not thus obtained.
       They search for it in their hearts, and in
              darkness silently pray.

But one only hears, once results are up, the
       failed students' resentful anger.

Who spares a thought, at such a time, for the
       sadness that fills the examiners?

Yuan Mei 'Grading Papers' (18th century); *Qing shidou* (Qing Bell of Poesy) (1869; 1960 edn) pp.621–2. The Chinese state examinations, on the basis of which officials had been selected for the imperial service since the end of the first millennium AD, and before that for promotion within the bureaucracy, were ringed about with security measures to prevent cheating and rigged results. In the examinations for the second degree, of which this poem is a description, the candidates' papers had to be copied out in red ink by scribes to prevent their handwriting being recognized. Later in the poem Yuan gives voice to a common view when he writes that 'having one's name among those who are successful is a matter of destiny, literary qualities having no effect'.

3 Since no one here looks for anything in necessities except what is necessary, or for anything in objects of use except what is useful, no one ever pays – or hardly ever – for additional charm. For this reason, fortune never favours the arts of taste, imagination, and fantasy, which is just as the government would wish.

Anon., 1779; *Mémoires* (1776–1814) Vol.4, p.318.

4 In France, the land rests every other year. In many places there are vast expanses of virgin soil. The countryside is broken up by woods, pastures, vineyards, parks, and buildings put up for pleasure. Nothing of all that could exist here.

Anon., 1779; *Mémoires* (1776–1814) Vol.4, p.320.

5 The city of Peking [Beijing] is a novel sight for a European. He will not weary of admiring the manner in which the nearly three million people gathered within its vast enclosure are ruled by the police as schoolchildren by their masters. People coming and going fill streets wider than that which faces the Luxembourg Palace in Paris. The crowd is beyond belief, yet peace reigns everywhere.

Father J.M. Amiot, 1782; *Mémoires* (1776–1814) Vol.8, pp.217–18.

6 I will say nothing of the grandeur of this capital, of the extent of its suburbs, the beauty of its walls, the width of its ramparts, the variety of its public buildings, the alignment of its thoroughfares, the multitude of its palaces, and so forth. One has to see them to appreciate their effect. Architecture here works on a different plan from ours, its magnificence accords with other ideas, and its taste follows different principles, but European prejudices are powerless before the novelties that one beholds.

Father J.M. Amiot, 1782; *Mémoires* (1776–1814) Vol.8, p.219.

1 The little extra efforts and knacks, inventions and discoveries, resources and combinations, which have caused people to exclaim at miracles in gardens, have been transported on a large scale out into the fields and have done marvels.

Anon., 1786; *Mémoires* (1776–1814) Vol.11, p.226. This was the celebrated 'garden-like farming' of late imperial times, with its often extraordinary yields per acre.

2 That which has struck us most forcibly in our observations of the Chinese is that a man who farms one acre instead of three is neither short of time nor overwhelmed with work … It is by these means that heavy toil is kept to a minimum, and the small cares of cultivation become the norm, wherein he is assisted by the women and the children. The lands of peasant proprietors are of an astonishing fertility in contrast with the large estates.

Anon., 1786; *Mémoires* (1776–1814) Vol.11, p.236.

3 My friend Yao Cunpu has praised opium in front of me. He said that it is fragrant and sweet in taste: 'On a miserable rainy day, or when you feel down, light up an opium lamp on a low table, lie face to face, pass the pipe around and inhale. In the beginning you will feel suddenly refreshed, your head and eyes becoming very clear. Soon afterwards, you will experience a sense of quietude and great well-being. After a while, your bones and joints become extremely relaxed and your eyes become sleepy. By then you will slowly fall asleep, detached from all worries, entering a world of dreams and fantasies, completely free like a spirit: what a paradise!'

Yu Jiao (1751–1820) *Mengchang zaji* (Notes from a Dreamy Cabin) (1801; 1988 trans.). This account is one of the earliest descriptions of opium on record. Long known in China as an analgesic, opium became a recreational drug only in the later 18th century. The earliest imports seem to have been brought by the Portuguese, perhaps in 1758.

4 No opium is exposed for sale in the shops, probably because it is a contraband article, but it is used with tobacco in all parts of the empire. The Chinese indeed consider the smoking of opium as one of the greatest luxuries; and if they are temperate in drinking, they are often excessive in the use of this drug. They have more than one method of smoking it: sometimes they envelope a piece of solid gum in tobacco, and smoke it from a pipe with a very small bowl; and sometimes they steep fine tobacco in a strong solution of it … which they smoke in few but deep inhalations.

Clarke Abel *Narrative of a Journey in the Interior of China, and of a Voyage to and from that Country in the Years 1816 and 1817* (1818) pp.214–15. Madak, the mixing of opium with tobacco, which came from the New World, was used in China, at least in any quantity, only in and after the 17th century. This then provided a carrier for the opium and explains the commonest mode of use, namely smoking. It was still smoked for several decades in the 19th century, as the British traveller Clarke Abel noted during the Amherst mission of 1816.

5 Their iron furnaces are seventeen or eighteen feet in height. They are square in shape and solidly constructed of clay, with an opening at the top to allow the smoke to escape. Charcoal is put in at the bottom, and ore in the middle. For every so many hundred catties' weight of ore a certain number of catties' weight of charcoal has to be used, a precise quantity which may not be increased or decreased. At the side more than ten persons will take it in turns to work the bellows. The fire is not put out either by day or by night. The liquid metal and the slag flow out from separate ducts at the bottom of the furnace, the liquid metal turning into iron which is cast in slabs.

Every furnace has an artisan who determines the timing of the fire and who can distinguish the appearance of iron in different stages of completeness. More than ten artisans are hired to serve each furnace … The distances which the ore and charcoal have to be taken vary, but over a hundred men are required for each furnace. Thus six or seven furnaces will give employment to not less than a thousand men.

Once the iron has been cast into slabs it is sometimes manufactured locally into pots and farm tools. A thousand and several hundreds of men are also required locally for this work and for the transport [of the goods]. Thus the larger ironworks in Sichuan and the other provinces regularly have two thousand to three thousand persons, and the smaller ones with but three or four furnaces well over a thousand.

Yan Ruyi, judicial commissioner in Shaanxi province, northwestern China, in the early 19th century; Elvin (1973) pp.285–6. Yan is describing the border country between Sichuan, Shaanxi and Hubei provinces and showing that in the early 19th century, less than a hundred years before the start of her modern age, China already had a large-scale iron-making industry. In the strict sense of 'manufacture' (to make by hand) it could be said that a manufacturing revolution had occurred. The driving force behind developments like this was a mercantile capitalism with large sums to invest and large markets to buy its products.

1 Famed as materials, straight firs, *Castanea* trees,
And pines and cypresses, verdant throughout
the winter,
Are, when collected, useful to meet the people's
needs,
And shipped and traded in both capital cities.

To serve as beams of rafters is only for logs that
are massive.
The destiny of slender lengths is to end in
cookhouse flames.
Merchants, since well-endowed, can provide
investment capital,
And lay plans calmly for returns beyond all
expectations.

The supervision of their accounts is under the
head clerks' direction,
While engineers survey and gauge for the
operations in hand.
The bookkeepers enter the records – of
payments – into their ledgers,
And the labour-contractors organize the sworn
brethren into gangs.

Several fathoms in girth are the multitudinous
trunks,
And once the axes are laid aside, cables are used
to haul them.
Dragged up and down by 'sky-trucks' over the
slopes and summits,
And ferried, along 'sky-bridges', across ravines
and gorges.

Yan Ruyi 'Song of the Timber Yards' (early 19th century);
Mark Elvin *The Retreat of the Elephants: An Environmental History
of China* (2004). These lines about the timber industry in the
southern part of Shaanxi (northwestern China) show that an
essentially capitalist way of organizing production could be
found in late imperial China. The flair for technical innovation
shown by the 'sky trucks' and 'sky bridges' (parts of an early
cable-skidder system) is worth noting. Pressures on the
natural environment were also escalating to a serious degree
before modern times, as was the depletion of natural resources,
both processes propelled by voracious multi-provincial
markets and a swelling population. The poem is an example of
a genre very widely found in late imperial times: sharp and
realistic observation of scenes from the everyday life of
ordinary people, usually with an explicit or implicit comment
of relevance to morality or government policy.

2 At the present time the sea wall is always rebuilt in
the dog days of the summer. The labourers are
boiled and scalded by the scorching heat, suffering
sunstroke in the daytime and exposed to the dews at
night. I do not know how many in all are suddenly
smitten with 'cholera' or heatstroke, and die at the
foot of the wall.

This takes place, moreover, in the midst of the
busy season for farming. Most of them cannot be in
two places at once and come to the work. The wardens
and sea wall constables take advantage of this to cheat
them. Each 'acre' [*mou*] of land incurs three to four
hundred cash, this being known as 'purchasing
leisure'. If any are obdurate and refuse to pay up,
wanting to go and scoop up mud, the constables and
wardens will always find some pretext to make them
melt or dry out in the ferocious sun, vexing them in
many ways until they have no option but to beg for
release.

Anon. Huating county gazetteer for 1875–1907; Morita Akira
Shindai suirishi kenkyû (Researches on the History of Water
Control under the Qing Dynasty) (1974) p.189. Huating is at
the mouth of the Yangzi River. This is one of countless such
grim descriptions. China was in thrall to water to a degree
unimaginable in any Western country, except perhaps the
Netherlands. For more than two millennia water-control
work required forced labour by peasants and also absorbed a
large amount of natural and financial resources and scarce
administrative skills. We can see the human costs of large-
scale operations in close focus. The concentration at the work
site in the warm part of the year of a large number of workers
facilitated the spread of infectious disease. The date is late
enough for the 'cholera' mentioned to have been the classic
cholera, although this is not confirmed. The Chinese acre was
about one-sixth of an English acre.

The Byzantine Empire, 330–1453

CONSTANTINOPLE AND CHRISTIANITY, c.306–527

1 Constantine was advised in a dream to mark the heavenly sign of God on the shields of his soldiers and then engage in battle. He did as he was commanded and by means of a slanted letter X, with the top of its head bent round, he marked Christ on their shields.

Lactantius *On the Deaths of the Persecutors* (c.315; 1984 trans.) p.63. This account of the famous vision differs from that of Eusebius (see 90:2), yet both accounts may be derived from the emperor himself or from sources close to him. The Byzantine empire took its name from the ancient Greek colony of Byzantium, which was re-founded by Emperor Constantine (r.306–337) as Constantinople (Istanbul). Although he embraced Christianity only at the end of his life, Constantine favoured Christianity after the mysterious sign given to him before his victory over his rival Maxentius at the Battle of the Milvian Bridge near Rome (312).

2 The emperor's escort asked, 'How long, our Lord, will you keep going?' The emperor answered, 'I shall keep on until he who walks ahead of me will stop.'

Bishop Philostorgius, 5th century; A.A. Vasiliev *History of the Byzantine Empire* (1964 edn) Vol.1, p.59. When Constantine established his new city in 330 he himself, spear in hand, marked out the boundaries, the extent of which astonished his companions. Yet the Constantinian boundary proved too small, and half a century later Emperor Theodosius I (r.379–395) extended the city limits and built the present splendid walls, a formidable obstacle to barbarian attackers.

3 We are at peace with walls.

The Visigoth chief Fritigern, c.378; A.H.M. Jones *The Later Roman Empire* (1964) Vol.1, p.154. Fritigern was turned back before the wall of Adrianople (Edirne in European Turkey). In the age of the barbarian invasions of Europe the formidable defences of Constantinople were an indispensable asset. The barbarians, it has been remarked, 'bounced off its walls'.

4 The whole city [Constantinople] is full of it, the squares, the market places, the crossroads, the alleyways; old-clothes men, money changers, food sellers: they are all busy arguing. If you ask someone to give you change, he philosophizes about the Begotten and the Unbegotten: if you enquire about the price of a loaf you are told that the Father is greater and the Son inferior; if you ask 'Is my bath ready?' the attendant answers that the Son was made out of nothing.

Bishop Gregory of Nyssa; T. Ware *The Orthodox Church* (1963) pp.43–4. The bishop (c.330–c.395) was remarking on the Byzantine obsession with theology, in this case the Trinity (see 92:1).

5 Standing twixt earth and heaven a man you see
   Who fears no gales that all about him fret;
   Daniel his name. Great Simeon's rival he
   Upon a double column firm his feet are set;
   Ambrosial hunger, bloodless thirst support his
       frame
   And thus the Virgin Mother's Son he doth
       proclaim.

Anon. *Life of Daniel the Stylite* (c.500; 1928 trans.) Ch.36. Early Byzantine society was much influenced by holy men – solitary ascetics reputed to struggle with demons, to perform miracles and sometimes to arbitrate in disputes, 'charismatic ombudsmen' as Peter Brown has called them. Some, following the examples of St Simeon Stylites, lived on top of a column (Greek *stylos*). These verses are reputed to have been inscribed on St Daniel's column (see 93:3).

THE AGE OF JUSTINIAN, 527–565

6 Justice is the constant and perpetual wish to render every one his due … The maxims of law are these: to live honestly, to hurt no one and to give every man his due.

Corpus juris civilis (Civil Laws) (c.550; 1928 edn) Bk 1.1.3. This compilation of legal principles and laws was made by Tribonian under the direction of Justinian I. Justinian was one of the greatest emperors, famous for his laws, his re-conquest of lost provinces and his building programme.

7 A man who borrows anything and uses it for a purpose other than that for which it was lent, commits theft only if he intends to act against the wishes of the owner, and that the owner, if he were aware, would not permit it; for if he really thinks the owner would permit it, he does not commit a crime. For there is no theft without the intention to commit theft.

Corpus juris civilis (c.550; 1928 edn) Bk 2.15.4.7. The law applies the principle that crime is deliberate not inadvertent.

8 It befell Belisarius on that day to win glory such as came neither to his contemporaries nor to men of old. The general kept his men in such good order

that no outrage was committed, nor threat uttered, nor interruption made to the routine of the city … no household was debarred from the wares of the market, clerks drew up their lists as if nothing had happened and the troops bought their breakfast in the market and went quietly about their ways.

Procopius *Wars* (c.550–560; 1961 edn) Vol.3, Bk 21, lines 8–10. The fullest source for the reign of Justinian is by Procopius of Caesarea, in Palestine, who was Belisarius' secretary. He wrote an 'official' history of Justinian's wars and of his buildings. Belisarius (c.505–565), Justinian's great general, took Carthage from the Vandals in 533 and went on to recover much of North Africa and Italy for the empire. Procopius acted as his secretary during these campaigns.

1 So the church has become a spectacle of marvellous beauty overwhelming to those who see it, but to those who know it only by hearsay, incredible. For it soars to a height to match the sky and surging up from among the other buildings, it stands on high … glorying in its own beauty.

Procopius *Buildings* (c.550–560; 1961 edn) Bk 1.1. The greatest architectural achievement of the reign is the Church of the Holy Wisdom (Hagia Sophia, Saint Sophia), built by Justinian in Constantinople in 532–537.

2 Other sovereigns have honoured men whose labour was useless. But our sceptred Justinian honours with a splendid abode the servant of Christ, Sergius … May he in all things guard the rule of the ever-vigilant sovereign and increase the power of the God-crowned Theodora whose mind is bright with piety, whose toil is unsparing efforts to nourish the destitute.

Inscription in the frieze below the dome of the church of the Little Hagia Sophia, also endowed by Justinian; based on A. van Millingen *The Byzantine Churches of Constantinople* (1912) p.73.

3 [Near to the palace in Constantinople] is an immense court very long and wide with colonnades on all sides … excavating this to a great depth, Justinian had a reservoir made to collect for use in the summer the water that otherwise would have been wasted.

Procopius *Buildings* (c.550–560; 1961 edn) Bk 1.11. This was one of many capacious cisterns still visible in Istanbul.

4 [The Emperor Justinian] cared little for sleep and never overindulged in food or drink, but picked at the food with his fingers. He saw these things as a kind of irrelevance necessitated by nature. He often fasted for two days or nights together, or lived on wild herbs and water. He slept for no more than an hour and spent the rest of the night pacing up and down. He made it his business to be always watchful for the sole purpose of bringing a continuous, daily sequence of disasters upon his subjects.

Procopius *Secret History* (c.565; 1966 trans.) Bk 13.32. Procopius's 'secret' history first appeared in print in 1623. It gives a very different picture of the emperor and court from that depicted in his official works.

5 Often in the theatre in full view of all the people she would throw off her clothes and stand naked in their midst, having only a girdle about her private parts … With this minimum covering she would spread herself out and lie face upward on the floor. Servants on whom this task had been imposed would sprinkle barley grains over her private parts, and geese trained for the purpose used to pick them off one by one with their bills and swallow them. Theodora, so far from blushing when she stood up again, actually seemed to be proud of this performance. For she was not only shameless herself, but did more than anyone else to encourage shamelessness.

Procopius (c.565; 1966 trans.) Bk 9.17. The *Secret History* tells many tales of the licentiousness of Empress Theodora, who is depicted with her husband Justinian in the famous mosaics (546–548) of St Vitale in Ravenna, eastern Italy, commissioned by Archbishop Maximian.

6 In every city the people have long belonged either to the Green or the Blue party, according to the places they occupy while watching the games. Without reason they fight with one another, although they know that, even if victorious, they will be taken to prison and tortured and killed. Endless hatred arises [from this rivalry], mitigated neither by marriage, relationship nor friendship.

Procopius *Wars* (c.550–560; 1961 edn) Vol.1, Bk 24, lines 1–4. The hippodrome was, like the Circus in Rome, the scene of chariot races often bitterly contested between the Greens and the Blues, teams that became associated with rival political and religious factions in the empire.

7 [The factions] openly carried weapons at night, while by day they hid two-edged daggers under their cloaks. Collecting in gangs in the evening, they mugged the better-off in the markets and alleyways, taking their cloaks, belts, gold brooches and anything else.

Procopius (c.565; 1966 trans.) Bk 7.19. Some of the factions formed criminal gangs.

8 If you wish, O Emperor, to save yourself yonder is the sea and there are the ships … But I agree with the old saying that the purple is a fair winding sheet.

Empress Theodora, 532; Procopius *De bello Persico* (c.550–560; 1914 edn) Bk 1.35–7. When Justinian contemplated flight at the time of a great revolt in Constantinople in 532, Theodora rallied him with these words. The emperor stayed, and the revolt was repressed; it was said that 30,000 were slaughtered. For the significance of purple see 106:8.

1 Now the Roman [Byzantine] coin had a right good ring, was of bright metal and finely shaped ... but the Persian coin was, to say it in a word, of silver and not to be compared to the gold coin.
Cosmas Indicopleustes *Topographica Christiana* (c.550; 1897 trans.) p.73. An Egyptian monk points out that the Byzantine gold coins were much valued throughout the empire and far beyond. R.S. Lopez called them 'the dollar of the Middle Ages'.

ISLAM AND ICONOCLASM, c.700–900

2 The evil enemies entered the city [Jerusalem] with a rage which resembled that of infuriated beasts and irritated dragons. They gnashed their teeth in fury, bellowed like lions, hissed like serpents. They had no pity in their hearts but raced through the city, tearing with their teeth the flesh of the faithful, respecting neither male nor female, young nor old, priest nor monk ... but slaughtering all.
Antiochus Strategus (7th century) *Chronicle* (1910 trans.) pp.502–17. In 614 occurred the great disaster of the fall of Jerusalem to the Persians under the shah, Chosroes II (r.590–628). The churches were destroyed, the relic of the Holy Cross was taken, and the Christian population was killed or enslaved.

3 Chosroes, the dear friend of the gods, master and king of all the earth, son of the great Hormisdas to our servant the stupid and unspeakable Heraclius. Disobedient to our rule, you claim to be emperor. You steal our wealth and trick our subjects.
Sebeos (7th century) *Heraclius* (1904 trans.) p.79. The contemptuous opening of a letter from the triumphant shah to Emperor Heraclius (r.610–641) preserved in an Armenian chronicle.

4 The Greeks [Byzantines] have been defeated in a neighbouring land. But in a few years they shall themselves gain victory: such being the will of Allah before and after.
Koran *The Greeks* (1956 trans.) sura 30, verse 1. In 630 Heraclius recovered Jerusalem. This verse in the Koran is taken to refer to the Persian successes and their subsequent defeat by Heraclius.

5 The divine nature is completely uncircumscribable and cannot be depicted or represented by artists in any medium whatsoever. The word Christ means both God and Man, and an icon of Christ would therefore have to be an image of God in the

flesh of the Son of God. But this is impossible. The artist would fall either into the heresy which claims that the divine and human natures of Christ are separate or into that which holds that there is only one nature in Christ.
Decree of a council, 754; A. Bryer and J. Herrin *Iconoclasm* (1977) p.183. Between 717 and 843 the Byzantine empire was rent by the iconoclast (image-breaking) controversy, a dispute about whether images (icons) were permissible in Christian worship.

6 Of old, God the incorporeal and uncircumscribed was not depicted at all. But now that God has appeared in the flesh and lived among men, I make an image of the God who can be seen. I do not worship matter but the creator of matter, who for my sake became material and deigned to dwell in matter, who through matter effected my salvation. I will not cease from worshipping the matter through which my salvation has been effected.
John of Damascus (675–749); Bryer and Herrin (1977) p.183. John of Damascus was the ablest defender of the Orthodox, iconodule (image-reverencing) position, which eventually prevailed.

7 The images which impostors once cast down, the pious emperors have restored.
Fragmentary inscription in the mosaic of the Virgin and Child in the apse of Hagia Sophia. The words may belong to the period 787–815, when iconoclasm suffered reverses, or to the later 9th century after the final defeat of iconoclasm, when they were used by the patriarch Photius in a sermon.

THE COURT

8 Cantor: For the sovereigns?
   People: A fair day for victories
   Cantor: And what else for them?
   People: And strengthen them (yes, Lord); save them (yes, Lord); a fair day for victories.
Constantine VII Porphyrogenitus *De ceremoniis aulae Byzantinae* (On the Ceremonies of the Byzantine Court) (early 10th century; 1973 trans.) p.7. This work, a handbook on court ritual, was compiled by the emperor (r.913–959), whose name, Porphyrogenitus, means born in the purple. The acclamations were sung on the birth of a child born in the purple-draped confinement chamber in the imperial palace in Constantinople.

9 Before the emperor's throne stood a tree, made of bronze gilded over, whose branches were filled with birds, also made of gilded bronze, which uttered cries according to its species. The throne itself was so marvellously fashioned that at one moment it seemed a low structure, and at another it rose high into the air. It was guarded by bronze lions who beat the ground with their tails and gave a dreadful roar with open mouth and quivering tongue ... After I had three times made obeisance to the emperor with my face upon the ground, I lifted my head, and behold! The man who just before had been sitting on a moderately elevated seat was now sitting on the level of the ceiling. How it was done I could not imagine, unless perhaps he was lifted by some sort of device as we use for raising the timbers of a wine press.

Liudprand, bishop of Cremona *Antapodosis* (Tit-for-Tat) (*c*.950; 1930 trans.) Bk 6.2. The German Liudprand (*c*.920–*c*.972) was a papal envoy to Constantinople. The Byzantines were fully aware of how ceremony and wealth could be used to impress foreign diplomats.

RULES AND REGULATIONS

1 In this blest city the view of a neighbour shall not be taken away. If for instance he can directly see the sea sitting in his own home, he is not obliged to see it aslant.

... If your wall leans half a foot towards my house, I can compel you to make it upright.

... Persons who live upstairs and throw out water and slops ... shall be restrained.

Ecloga (various dates) Ch.34; E.H. Freshfield *A Manual of Later Roman Law* (1927) pp.179–80.

2 If a farmer neglects to cultivate his own lot ... those who are to pay the land tax shall crop it and when the farmer returns he has no claim against them.

Ecloga (various dates) Ch.35; Freshfield (1927) p.186. Rural life was also controlled.

3 If a crew steal the anchors of another vessel ... by order of the captain and in consequence the ship is lost the captain shall pay for the loss of the ship and those aboard.

If the crew quarrel they must do so verbally and not come to blows. Anyone who causes an injury shall bear the cost of medical treatment and pay his wages during his incapacity.

Rhodian Sea Law Ch.37; Freshfield (1927) p.196.

4 We forbid the making of purple robes except in the permitted widths. We also prohibit the making of robes with rounded bottoms reserved for the emperor. If any is caught making these prohibited garments, his goods shall be confiscated and he shall be made to give up his trade.

Book of the Prefect (10th century; 1929 trans.) pp.605–6. This compilation governs many trades in Constantinople, including lawyers, bankers, soap and candle makers, butchers, bakers and innkeepers. The regulation of silk manufacture and trade, which ran to some 50 clauses, was especially stringent in relation to the imperial near-monopoly of purple silk.

5 'Harlots and showmen have them in Italy,' the Bishop answered, 'for they buy them from Venetian and Amalfitan merchants.'

'They shall do so no longer,' the customs men replied, 'for if they are found they shall be beaten and have their hair clipped.'

Liudprand, bishop of Cremona *Embassy to Constantinople* (*c*.950; 1930 trans.) Ch.55, pp.268–9. The bishop was questioned by customs officials about his possession of purple cloth.

6 [Is bathing permitted on Wednesday and Fridays?] Unlike the Greeks, we do not forbid this. While bathing for pleasure is forbidden on any day, bathing out of necessity is forbidden neither on Wednesday nor Friday.

[Can women who wear trousers be saved?] Whether or not your women wear or do not wear trousers neither impedes salvation nor increases righteousness.

Pope Nicholas I, letter; *Monumenta Germaniae historica* Epistolae VI (1925) no.99, Chs 6, 59. Papal responses to two of 105 queries from Khan Boris I of the Bulgars (r.852–899), a recent convert to Orthodoxy who, fearful of Byzantine domination, made overtures to Rome. Wednesdays and Fridays were penitential days. See 168:1.

MILITARY MATTERS

7 To the Bulgarians the [Byzantine] emperor will appear more formidable if he is at peace with the Pechenegs as the Pechenegs are neighbours to the Bulgarians and if they wish ... to do a favour to the emperor can easily march against them and defeat them.

Constantine VII Porphyrogenitus *De administrando imperio* (On Imperial Administration) (10th century; 1967 trans.) pp.52–3. The emperor composed a manual on diplomacy and other aspects of imperial rule. The Pechenegs lived in the Crimean region.

8 [The Byzantine] commander had towers and siege weapons and flame-throwing tubes which could engulf 12 men at once, so fierce and adherent that none could withstand it.

Ibn al-Athir (1160–1233) *The Perfect History*; A.A. Vasiliev *Byzance et les Arabes* (1935–50) Vol.2, p.150. Greek fire was as effective on land as at sea. The Arab chronicler describes the Byzantine siege (927/8) of the city of Dvin in Armenia, then held by the Arabs.

1 Torsten had this memorial raised after Sven his father and Tore his brother. They had gone out to Greece.

Runic inscription from tombstones in Sweden, 10th–11th century; S.B.F. Jansson *The Runes of Sweden* (1962) pp.23, 27. From the 9th century onwards northern mercenaries (Scandinavians and Anglo-Saxons) came to the empire and formed a military corps, the Varangian guard, the foreign legion of Byzantium. The stone bearing the inscription is in the Ashmolean Museum, Oxford.

2 [Earl Sigurd of Gloucester and his men reached Constantinople] and set the realm of the Greek king free from strife. King Alexius the Tall [Emperor Alexius I Comnenus (r.1081–1118)] offered them to abide there and guard his body as was the wont of the Varangians ... but it seemed to earl Sigurd that it was too small a career to grow old there ... They begged the king for some towns of their own ... [The emperor assigned some unnamed lands in the north, if they could re-conquer them. Some stayed behind and took service in Constantinople] but Sigurd and his men came to this land and had many battles there and they took possession and gave it a name and called it England and they gave names to the towns that were there and called them London and York.

Anon. *Edwardsaga* (13th century; 1894 trans.) pp.427–9. In the 11th century, especially after the Battle of Hastings, Anglo-Saxons also joined the Varangian guard. Place-name evidence in the northeastern Black Sea may support this tale of an English settlement there. For Alexius Comnenus see 109:2.

COURT AND CONFLICT

3 Although she had already passed her seventieth year, there was no wrinkle on her face. Hers was a beauty altogether fresh.

Michael Psellos *Chronographia* (11th century; 1953 trans.) Bk 6.158. On Empress Zoe (980–1050). Zoe, the daughter of Constantine VIII, was a spinster until she was 50 years old, when she took the first of three husbands and embarked on a series of affairs. Her mosaic portrait survives in Hagia Sophia. Next to her stands her first husband, with both the features and caption altered, apparently to adapt the mosaic for her last spouse, Constantine IX (r.1042–55), whom she married in 1042.

4   If perchance you wish to exempt certain pagans
        From punishment, my Christ,

        May you spare for my sake Plato and Plutarch,
        For both were very close to your laws in both
        Teaching and way of life.

Metropolitan John Mauropus, verse prayer, 11th century; D.J. Geanakoplos *Byzantium through Contemporary Eyes* (1984) p.395. An instance of Byzantine reverence for the classics.

5 On Saturday 16 July 1054, just as the afternoon liturgy was about to be sung, Cardinal Humbert and the papal emissaries stalked into the church of Haghia Sophia and laid on the altar a bull excommunicating Michael Cerularius, the patriarch of Constantinople, Leo of Ohrid, the patriarchal chancellor, and all of their followers. Then they strode out of the church, ceremoniously shaking its dust off their feet. A deacon ran out after them and begged them to take back the bull. They refused; and he dropped it in the street.

Steven Runciman *The Eastern Schism* (1955) pp.47–8. This dramatic event is often taken to mark the beginning of the schism. The main theological differences between the churches concerned the wording of the Nicene Creed and the status of the papacy. Moreover, over the centuries many different practices in worship had arisen between Latin West and Greek East (see 188:8).

COMMERCE

6 Great stir and bustle prevails at Constantinople in consequence of the great conflux of merchants who resort thither from all parts of the world, from Babylon, from Medea, from Persia, from Egypt and Palestine as well as from Russia, Hungary, Italy and Spain. In this respect the city is equalled only by Baghdad, the metropolis of the Muslims.

Benjamin of Tudela *Itinerary* (c.1167; 1840 trans.) p.51. A Jewish view of Constantinople.

7 And if you are anxious to know what it contained, my inquisitive friend, as I saw it afterwards when I came down from the hills – well, there was every kind of material woven or spun by men or women, all those that come from Boeotia and the Peloponnese, and all that are brought in trading ships from Italy to Greece. Besides this, Phoenicia furnishes numerous articles, and Egypt, and Spain, and the Pillars of Hercules, where the finest coverlets are manufactured.

Anon. description of the great St Demetrius fair at Thessalonica (northern Greece), c.1160; H. Tozer 'Byzantine Satire' in *Journal of Hellenic Studies* 52 (1881) pp.244–5. Some of the Byzantine provincial cities were also centres of vigorous trade.

EAST AND WEST

1 The Seljuq sultan Alp Arslan ordered a tent to be prepared for the emperor [Romanus IV Diogenes] suitable for his rank and at once invited him to sit beside him at table. This happened twice daily for eight days, the sultan seeking to console him for the ups and downs of life ... When the sultan in the course of these conversations asked the emperor what he would have done had roles been reversed, the emperor replied honestly, 'I should have beaten you black and blue until you died.' 'I shall not follow your savage and cruel ways,' replied the sultan.

Michael Attaleiates (12th century) *Historia* (1853 edn) p.165. In 1071 the Seljuq Turks overwhelmed the Byzantine forces, weakened by treachery, at Manzikert in eastern Turkey and captured Emperor Romanus IV Diogenes. The victory opened Anatolia to the Seljuqs, the first of the Turkish peoples to settle in Byzantine lands. Sultan and emperor made a peace treaty, but in Romanus' absence another emperor had been raised to the throne and Romanus was blinded and died soon afterwards from his injuries.

2 Alexius heard of the approach of innumerable Frankish armies. This he dreaded, for he knew their ferocious aggressiveness, their unstable and inconsistent character and that they were always greedy for money and failed to observe agreements ... These soldiers were, as Homer says, 'as many as the leaves and flowers in the spring' ... I cannot tell the names of the leaders. My tongue is paralysed if I try to mouth these strange unpronounceable names ... [Anna describes how the leaders took an oath of allegiance to Alexius as they passed through his lands] ... after the oath had been taken, a certain reckless nobleman sat down on the emperor's throne. But the emperor said nothing, knowing the Franks' presumption.

Anna Comnena *The Alexiad* (c.1148; 1969 trans.) Bk 10, pp.324–5. The work is a biography and vindication of her father Alexius I Comnenus (r.1081–1118). Tension was high as the armies of the First Crusade assembled in Constantinople in 1096 (see 225:4). This illustrates the Byzantine view of the uncouth Westerners.

3 Also I lay before Thee [Christ] Who loves good, the companions whom in your mercy you call brothers, people drawn from the aged and poor, crushed by poverty and victims of disease. Those ravaged by leprosy will get all the care their condition demands ... wounds will be dressed and they will be solaced by adequate food and clothing. They are petitioners for our sins.

From the *typikon* (foundation charter) of the monastery of the Pantokrator (Christ, ruler of the world) in Constantinople, 1136; P. Gautier 'Le Typikon du Christ Sauveur Pantocrator' in *Révue des études Byzantines* Vol.32 (1974), pp.1–145. The imperial families often founded and endowed monasteries, which were an important element in Byzantine society. Here, Emperor John II Comnenus (r.1118–43) provided for a hospital with 50 beds with the necessary furnishings and utensils for both men and women patients. The staff included a woman doctor, and a hospice provided for 80 old men. The monastic buildings are gone, but the church survives as a mosque.

4 Between us and the Latins [Westerners] has arisen a great gulf. Temperamentally we are utterly different and an immeasurable separation exists. They are obstinate and unbending and it pleases them to mock our polished manners. But we despise their arrogant, proud boasting, as the mucus that keeps their noses in the air.

Nicetas Choniates *Chronicle* (c.1180; 1835 edn) pp.391–2. A Byzantine view of the tensions following the settlement of Italian, especially Venetian, traders.

5 I can assure you that all who had never seen Constantinople before gazed very intently at the city, having never imagined there could be so fine a place in all the world. They noted the high walls and lofty towers, its rich palaces and tall churches of which there were so many ... There was no man so brave that his flesh did not shudder ... Nor was this to be wondered at, for never had so grand an enterprise been carried out by any people since the creation of the world.

Geoffrey de Villehardouin *The Conquest of Constantinople* (c.1208; 1963 trans.) pp.58–9. In May 1203 Villehardouin, a nobleman from Champagne, describes the impression made by the sight of the city on the soldiers of the Fourth Crusade (see 232:3).

6 [The Greek church] has seen in the Westerners nothing but perdition and darkness ... they who should serve Christ and not their own interests have swords dripping with Christian blood. For they spared neither religion, nor age, nor sex ... not content with robbing both rich and poor, they seized the possessions of the church, violating the sanctuaries.

Pope Innocent III, an angry letter; J.P. Migne (ed.) *Patrologia Latina* (1844–64) Vol.215, Col.701. The pope had hoped for reunion with the Orthodox church, but instead Constantinople was sacked.

7 Lord of a quarter and a half of a quarter of the whole empire of Romania.

Title taken by the Venetian *podestà* (consul) in Constantinople in 1205 and later adopted by the Venetian doges. 'Romania' was the common Western name for the Byzantine empire (that is, the land of the Romans, the Byzantines). When the Byzantine lands were partitioned among the crusaders, the Venetians took three-eighths.

THE LAST CENTURIES, 1204–1453

1 Around the lovely Cypress-tree, the ivy gently windeth;
The empress is the Cypress-tree, my Emperor is the ivy.
Here is the world's wide garden ground, he reaches from the centre,
His tendrils softly compassing the plenteous trees and herbage
And holds them flourishing and fair, and crowns them with his glory
The trees he grasps are cities great and lands and peoples many.
Around the lovely Cypress-tree etc.

Nikolaos Eirenikos, verses composed on the marriage of John III Ducas Vatatzes (r.1222–54), emperor in exile in Nicaea, and Constance/Anna, daughter of Frederick II; A. Gardner *The Lascarids of Nicaea* (1922) p.308. After the Fourth Crusade rival Greek families based in Epirus (northwest Greece–Albania), at Trebizond (Trabzon on the Black Sea) and Nicaea (Iznik, near Constantinople) claimed the throne.

2 Eulogia thought that she had better not awaken her brother the emperor at once, fearing a sudden shock might be too much for him – an uncharacteristically sensible precaution in a woman! … so she endeavoured to waken him little by little taking his big toe and squeezing it gently in her fingers.

George Pachymeres *De Michaele et Andronico Palaeologis* (1261–1308; 1835 edn) Vol.1, Bk 2, Ch.29, p.150. In 1261 a detachment of men in the service of Michael VIII Palaeologus, emperor in Nicaea, unexpectedly recaptured Constantinople from the Westerners. A contemporary describes how the good news was brought to Michael by his sister.

3 From dawn to dusk he was entirely absorbed in public affairs, as if indifferent to learning. But in the evening, when he had quit the palace, he gave himself to learning with such devotion that one would have thought him without any other concerns.

Nicephorus Gregoras (1295–1360) *Historia Byzantina* (1829 edn) Vol.1, Bk 20. Of the many scholars who worked in the Byzantine empire, perhaps Theodore Metochites (1270–1332) was one of the greatest. Diplomat, astronomer, poet and statesman, he served as grand logothete (first minister) under Andronicus II before being dismissed and imprisoned by his successor. Metochites rebuilt and decorated the splendid church of St Saviour in Chora, Constantinople.

4 However many celebrities are gathered here
Among the dead, the entombed Tornikes,
Thrice among the greatest or Grand Constable,
Is as a lion, good Sir, to mimicking apes.
As one sprung of royal blood
He lived accordingly, observing his place.

Intricate verse epitaph, mid-14th century, in St Saviour in Chora, of a friend of Metochites, the general Michael Tornikes, who died as a monk.

5 In the name of God the merciful the compassionate. Let God the most high ever lengthen the days of the great emperor, the beneficent, the wise, the lion, the manly, the impetuous in battle, the irresistible, the most learned in his religion, the most just in his lands, the foundation of the faith of the Christians, the unshaken pillar of all the baptized, the support of the dogmas of Christ, the sword of the Macedonians, Samson, the emperor of the Greeks, of the Bulgars, of the Vlaks, of the Rus, of the Alans, the honour of the faith of the Iberians [Georgians] and Syrians, the heir to his empire, the master of the seas and the great rivers and the islands, Angelos Comnenus Palaeologus Cantacuzenus.

Mamluk sultan, al-Malik an-Nasir Hasan to Emperor John VI Cantacuzenus, 30 Oct. 1349 (Greek version of the Arabic original); John Cantacuzenus *Historia* Bk 6 (1828–32 edn).

6 But the crown jewels were made of glass and the banqueting plate was of pewter and clay.

Nicephorus Gregoras (1295–1360) (1829 edn) Bk 15.11, on the coronation of Emperor John VI Cantacuzenus in a chapel of the Palace of Blachernai in Constantinople on 21 May 1347. The grandiose address belied the reality. Following the restoration of 1261 (see 110:2), the emperors were desperately poor. The real crown jewels were in pawn to Venice, and the empress had sold most of the plate to raise money. See also Constantine Cavafy's poem on the subject, 'Of Coloured Glass'.

7 What a grievous thing that this great Christian prince should be driven by unbelievers to visit the distant islands of the west to seek aid against them. What dost thou, ancient glory of Rome?

Adam of Usk (c.1352–1430) *Chronicon* (1904 trans.) p.246. The English chronicler (see 281:5) reflects on the visit of Emperor Manuel II to London in 1400–1 to raise men and money to resist the Turks.

8 We no longer need an emperor but a financial wizard.

Emperor Manuel II, 1422, bewailing his poverty towards the end of his life; G. Sphrantes *Chronicon minus* (c.1478; 1966 edn) Bk 6.15. The visit to England failed to raise adequate resources.

1 The gold coin had already [under the Nicaean emperors (1204–61)] been debased under pressure of events to two-thirds gold [16 carats instead of 24]; under Michael Palaeologus [1261–82] the old inscriptions on the coins were replaced by images of the city and reduced by a further carat. In the next reign there were only fourteen carats and in our day the amounts of gold and alloy are the same.

George Pachymeres (1261–1308; condensed from 1835 edn) Bk 2, pp.493–5.

2 The emperor is not as other rulers and governors; from the beginning the emperors established and confirmed true religion throughout the inhabited world. They it was who convoked the ecumenical councils, confirmed and ordered to be accepted the canons concerning true doctrine and government; they struggled against heresies and fixed the dioceses … The name of the emperor is recited in all places by all patriarchs and bishops wherever men have the name of Christians. If the nations encircle the residence of the emperor, it does not follow that Christians should despise him … if he be reduced to such straits, a worse fate is likely to befall other rulers who have smaller realms … My son you are wrong in saying we have a church but not an emperor: church and empire have a great unity nor is it possible for them to be separated from one another.

Patriarch Antonios IV to Prince Basil I of Moscow, c.1394–7; E. Barker *Social and Political Thought in Byzantium* (1957) pp.194–6. The patriarch rebukes the prince for omitting the name of the emperor from the Russian liturgy. Despite the poverty and encirclement of Constantinople by the Turks, the Byzantines did not lose sight of their universal claims.

3 The mass of the people, who do not pay heed to one another or understand issues easily – partly because of their numbers, and partly because the greater part of them are uneducated – generally give their votes without any rational reflection. On the other hand a body which is reduced to very small numbers tends to consider the private interests of its members, and generally gives bad advice. It is a body composed of moderate numbers, and of men possessing some education, which will provide the best and safest advisers for the whole community.

George Gemisthos Plethon to Emperor Manuel II Palaeologus and his son, Theodore, despot (viceroy) of the Morea (Peloponnese); Barker (1957) p.208. Plethon (c.1353–1452) was the most original philosopher of the Byzantine period.

4 Only one thing I want. Give me Constantinople.

Sultan Mehmed II, early 1453; Steven Runciman *The Fall of Constantinople 1453* (1965) p.74. The 21-year-old Ottoman sultan is determined on the capture of Constantinople.

5 Do not expect me or any of the citizens to surrender the city for we are of one mind in preferring to die first.

Emperor Constantine XI Palaeologus replying to Mehmed's demand for capitulation, 1449–53; (Michael?) Doucas *Historia Byzantina* (c.1462; 1958 edn) Ch.10.

6 Better the Turkish turban than the Latin tiara.

Grand Duke Loukas Notaras, attrib. remark; Doucas (c.1462; 1958 edn) Ch.37. He expresses the deep hostility to the West. After the fall of Constantinople, Loukas and his two sons were put to death.

7 Sometimes [the cannon] demolished a whole section of a tower or turret. No part of the wall was strong enough to resist it … Such was the unbelievable and inconceivable nature of the power of the implement. Such a thing the ancients neither had nor knew about.

Michael Kritovoulos (later 15th century) *History of Mehmed the Conqueror* (1954 trans.) Chs 137–8. In 1452 a Hungarian engineer, Urban, had offered his services to the emperor, who could not afford them. Urban therefore took service under the sultan. He produced many cannon for the siege of Constantinople, the greatest said to be some 25 feet long and projecting balls weighing over 12 hundredweight. Some 60 oxen were needed to move it. Kritovoulos, a Greek of the island of Imbros, accepted Turkish overlordship and became an admirer of the sultan (see 259:3).

8 They placed cradles under the ships and stays to support them. The ships were then dragged by soldiers or by certain machines and capstans. The crews rejoiced, manning the ships as if at sea. Some hoisted the sails with a shout and the breeze bellied them out. Others sat at the benches holding the oars as if rowing. It was a strange spectacle and unbelievable to those who did not actually see it. The Greeks were astounded.

Michael Kritovoulos (later 15th century) (1954 trans.) Chs 173–7. By April 1453 the sultan's naval forces had still not been able to break through the chain or boom that protected the entrance to the Golden Horn from the Bosphorus. The Turkish admiral therefore had a slipway built over the steep land behind the Galata quarter between the Bosphorus and the shore of the Golden Horn. The Turks were able to drag ships overland and expose another section of the sea walls to attack.

9   The spider weaves the curtains in the palace of the Caesars;
   The owl calls the watches in Afrasiab's towers.

Saadi, attrib.; Runciman (1965) p.149. The Persian poet's couplet was said to have been quoted by the sultan when he entered Haghia Sophia after the fall of the city, but it is now thought that the lines may be an extempore exclamation of the sultan. Afrasiab is Samarkand.

1 In the year 1453, June 29, a Friday, there arrived here from Constantinople three ships bringing news that on May 29, a Tuesday, the army of the Turk Celebi [warrior] Mehmed entered Constantinople … And there was great tribulation and lamentation in Crete because of the bad news, for nothing worse than this has ever happened, nor will happen.

Hastily scribbled note on a Greek manuscript, mid-15th century; BL Addit. MS 34060.

2 The tyrant [Mehmed II] ordered cannon to be brought up against that section of the city called Melanoudion [the lower town of Lesbos] and discharging stone balls it was brought crashing to the ground. He did the same to the ramparts and the other towers. The citizens within, therefore seeing …

(Michael?) Doucas (c.1462; 1958 edn) Ch.45. This last page describes the assault on Lesbos in Sept. 1462. Doucas's narrative breaks off at this point. Was he killed in the fighting, murdered afterwards or sold into slavery? No one knows, but the historian's life is not without its dangers.

3   HERE LYETH THE BODY OF
    FERDINANDO PALAEOLOGUS
    DESCENDED FROM YE IMPERIAL
    LYNE OF YE LAST CHRISTIAN
    EMPERORS OF GREECE
    CHURCH WARDEN OF THIS PARISH
    1655   1656
    VESTRYMAN TWENTYE YEARS
    DIED OCTOBER 8 1678

Epitaph from St John's Church, Barbados. After the fall of Constantinople to the Turks in 1453, descendants of the imperial Byzantine families were dispersed throughout the world, even as far as the Caribbean.

JUDGEMENTS

4 There is another history more absurd than the history of Rome after Tacitus: it is the history of Byzantium. This worthless collection contains nothing but declamations and miracles. It is a disgrace to the human mind.

Voltaire (1694–1778); Vasiliev (1964 edn) Vol.1, p.6.

5 [Byzantine history] is a tedious and uniform tale of weakness and misery … The subjects of the empire [of Constantinople] who assume and dishonour the names both of Greek and Roman present a dead uniformity of abject vices which are neither softened by the weakness of humanity nor animated by the vigour of memorable crimes.

Edward Gibbon The Decline and Fall of the Roman Empire (1776–88) Vol.9, Ch.48. Yet Gibbon gave some 20 years to his History, much of which describes what we should call the Byzantine period.

6   I love the church … of the Greeks, and when I
      enter in,
    With smoky fragrance of the incenses,
    Liturgical harmony and cadences,
    The priests and their majestic presences,
    The solemn rhythm of their every movement –
    Arrayed in shining vestments on the
      pavement –
    To the great honours of our race my thoughts
      return,
    The glory of our Byzantine achievement.

Constantine Cavafy 'In Church' (1912; 1951 trans.). Byzantium remained a living tradition to the Greek poet.

7 I had always thought Byzantium the name of a rare and expensive mineral.

Anon. British professor of modern history, on hearing of a substantial grant for Byzantine studies in his university (1980s).

The Barbarian West, 341–751

THE FIRST BARBARIAN KINGDOMS, c.370–533

1 Here in Bordeaux we see the blue-eyed Saxon
Afraid of the land, accustomed as he is to the
  sea …
… Here wanders the Herulian with his blue-
  grey eyes,
Who haunts the uttermost reaches of the
  Ocean
And is almost of one colour with its weedy
  depths.
Here the Burgundian seven-foot high oft
Begs for peace on bended knee …
… From this source the Roman seeks salvation,
And against the hordes of the Scythian clime,
When the Arcadian Bear brings forth
  commotion,
It is your bands, Euric, that are called for,
So that the Garonne, strong in its warlike
  settlers,
May defend the dwindled Tiber.

Sidonius Apollinaris (c.430–487) *Letters and Poems* (1965 trans.) Bk 8, Letter 9. The western Roman empire transformed. In 476, about a century after the first major 'barbarian' migrations into the empire, Sidonius Apollinaris, Gallic aristocrat and bishop of Clermont, arrived in Bordeaux and sent a poem to Lampridius, a poet and teacher of rhetoric at the court of Euric the Visigoth (r.466–484). In 418 the Visigoths had made a treaty with the Romans to establish a kingdom in Aquitaine, southwest France. The Herulians were settled on the lower Rhine. The Burgundian kingdom was based in Lyons. The Arcadian Bear is the northern constellation of the Great Bear. The rivers of the Garonne and Tiber serve as metaphors for the strength of the barbarians in defending a weakened Rome against the 'Scythian' Huns.

2 It is the task of kings – those that have a right to that title – rather than rooting out completely this surfeit of human temperament whenever they restrain the insurgent barbarians, to safeguard and protect them as an integral part of the empire. For this is how things are: he who harries the barbarians to no good purpose sets himself up as king of the Romans alone, while he who shows compassion in his triumph knows himself to be king of all men, especially over those whom he protected and watched over when he had the chance to destroy them utterly.

Themistius *Oratio* (370) no.10; P. Heather and J. Matthews *The Goths in the Fourth Century* (1991) p.39. The philosopher Themistius, a senator, proconsul and ambassador at the imperial court in Constantinople (Istanbul), is urging an inclusive definition of the Roman empire. The Romans had long been concluding federating pacts with barbarian peoples, using them to defend frontier regions in return for land or tax revenue.

3 Now Ablabius the historian relates that in Scythia, where we have said that they were dwelling above an arm of the Pontic Sea, part of them who held the eastern region and whose king was Ostrogotha, were called Ostrogoths, that is, eastern Goths, either from his name or from that place. But the rest were called Visigoths, that is, Goths of the western country.

Jordanes *Gothic History* (c.551; 1915 trans.) Pt 82. Jordanes' work provided the Visigothic people with an origin myth, itself based on the work of historians like Ablabius, who had probably, like Jordanes himself, worked for the Visigothic court. The fixed barbarian identities described by their historians (Visigoths and Ostrogoths, Franks and Vandals) mask far more fluid pre-literate origins. This etymology is completely spurious: they were known as Visigoths and Ostrogoths only from the 5th century.

4 Yet when the report spread widely among the other Gothic peoples, that a race of men hitherto unknown had now arisen from a hidden nook of the earth … and was seizing or destroying everything in its way, the greater part of the people … looked for a home removed from all knowledge of the [Huns]; and after long deliberation [on] what abode to choose they thought that Thrace [parts of Greece and Bulgaria] offered them a convenient refuge, for two reasons: both because it has a very fertile soil, and because it is separated by the mighty flood of the Danube from [the Huns].

Ammianus Marcellinus *History* (390s; 1939 trans.) Bk 31, Pt 3, line 8. The Huns appeared north of the Caspian Sea and encountered the Gothic peoples who were driven westwards. Ammianus Marcellinus was a senior officer in the eastern Roman army and became famous in his own lifetime for his 31-book *History*, which originally covered 96–378 but of which only the period 353–378 survives.

5 The Vandals and Alans entered Gaul by crossing the Rhine on 31 December [406].

Prosper of Aquitaine *Chronicle* (433–455); T. Mommsen *Chronica Minora* Vol.1 (1891) p.465. On the last night of 406 large numbers of barbarians broke through the defences of the Roman empire on the Rhine frontier, taking advantage of the frozen river to do so.

1 I was so stupefied and dismayed that day and night I could think of nothing but the welfare of the Roman community. It seemed to me that I was sharing the captivity of the saints and I could not open my lips until I received some more definite news. All the while, full of anxiety, I wavered between hope and despair, torturing myself with the misfortunes of others. But when I heard that the bright light of all the world was quenched, or rather that the Roman empire had lost its head and that the whole universe had perished in one city: then indeed, 'I became dumb and humbled myself and kept silence from good words.'
St Jerome 'Preface to Ezekiel', 410–414, *Select Letters* (1933 trans.) p.x. On 24 Aug. 410 Alaric, the king of the Visigoths, sacked Rome for three days. Emperor Honorius (r.393–423), secure in Ravenna (east central Italy), had refused to grant a treaty settling Alaric and his followers in Italy. Having left the east and desperate to reward his followers, Alaric needed resources. The Visigoths subsequently abandoned hope of settling in Italy and crossed the Alps into Gaul, where they made a treaty to settle in Aquitaine in southwestern France in 418.

2 In the one thousand one hundred and sixty-fifth year after the founding of the City, the emperor, Honorius, seeing that nothing could be accomplished against the barbarians with so many usurpers opposed to him, ordered that the usurpers themselves be destroyed first. To Constantius, the count, was entrusted the highest command in this war.
Paulus Orosius *The Seven Books of History Against the Pagans* (c.418; 1964 trans.) Bk 7, Pt 42. Orosius describes the problem of civil strife in the western Roman empire, which was a major contributory factor in the loss of the provinces to central imperial control during the 5th century. In 411 Constantius (d.421) was appointed to the senior rank of 'Master of Soldiers' to prosecute a war against the usurper Constantine III (d.411), who had been declared emperor in Britain in 407.

3 [Onegesius' freedman] continued, saying that after a war men amongst the Scythians [Huns] live at ease, each enjoying his own possessions and troubling others or being troubled not at all or very little. But amongst the Romans, since on account of their tyrants not all men carry weapons, they place their hope of safety in others and are thus easily destroyed in war ... In peace misfortunes await one even more painful than the evils of war because of the imposition of heavy taxes and injuries done by criminals.

Priscus of Panium (mid-5th century) *History*; R.C. Blockley (ed.) *The Fragmentary Classicising Historians of the Later Roman Empire* Vol.2 (1983) p.269. In 450 Priscus accompanied the envoy Maximinus on an embassy to Attila, who had achieved an unprecedented unity among the disparate Hunnic nomads of central Asia, leading them after their migration west, into the Roman empire. Here Onegesius' freedman contrasts the security and freedom of the nomadic Huns with the settled, restrictive insecurity of the Romans. Onegesius was a Greek who had been captured by Hunnic raiders. He had bought his freedom and become a senior Hunnic chieftain.

4 The armies met, as we have said, on the Catalaunian Plains. The battlefield was a plain rising by a sharp slope to a ridge, which both armies sought to gain; for advantage of position is a great help. The Huns with their forces seized the right side, the Romans, the Visigoths and their allies the left, and then began a struggle for the as yet untaken crest. Now Theodoric with the Visigoths held the right wing and Aetius with the Romans the left. They placed in the centre Sangiban (who ... was in command of the Alani) ... On the other side ... the battle line of the Huns was so arranged that Attila and his bravest followers were stationed in the centre.
Jordanes (c.551; 1915 trans.) Pt 38.197. In 451 an alliance of Roman troops, Visigoths and other barbarians, led by Aetius (d.454), defeated the Hunnic confederation, under the leadership of Attila, at the Battle of the Catalaunian Plains (near modern Châlons-sur-Marne). Within two years Attila was dead, and the confederacy subsequently collapsed under the competing claims of his sons and the revolt of most of the subject peoples.

5 In the middle of a plain his body was laid out in a silken tent, and a remarkable spectacle was solemnly performed. For in the place where he had been laid out the best horsemen of the whole Hunnic race rode around in a circle, as if at the circus games, and recited his deeds in a funeral chant ... When they had bewailed him with such lamentations, over his tomb they celebrated with great revelry what they call a *strava* and abandoned themselves to a mixture of joy and funereal grief ... They committed his body to the earth in the secrecy of night ... They added the arms of enemies won in combat, trappings gleaming with various precious stones and ornaments of various types, the marks of royal glory. Moreover, in order that such great riches be kept safe from human curiosity, those to whom the task was delegated they rewarded abominably by killing them.
Priscus of Panium (mid-5th century); Blockley Vol.2 (1983) pp.317–19. Attila died in 453 of a massive nosebleed. Priscus

had first-hand experience of the Huns from his embassy to them in 450.

1 Then as the spoil taken from one and another of the neighbouring tribes diminished, the Goths began to lack food and clothing, and peace became distasteful to men for whom war had long furnished the necessities of life. So all the Goths approached their king Theudemir and, with great outcry, begged him to lead forth his army in whatsoever direction he might wish.

Jordanes (c.551; 1915 trans.) Pt 56.283. In about 473, as his followers ran short of supplies, Theudemir, king of the Ostrogoths (r.c.465–c.474), led raids on the Roman empire. A barbarian leader's power and authority depended on his ability to distribute necessities, as well as treasure and precious metal, among his followers. If he failed, they would transfer their allegiance.

2 But the Emperor Zeno, who understood how to settle to his advantage any situation in which he found himself, advised Theodoric to proceed to Italy, attack Odoacer, and win for himself and the Goths western dominion. For it was better for him, he said, especially as he had attained the senatorial dignity, to force out a usurper and be ruler over all the Romans and Italians than to incur the risk of a decisive struggle with the emperor. Now Theodoric was pleased with the suggestion and went to Italy, and he was followed by the Gothic host, who placed in their wagons the women and children and such of their chattels as they were able to take with them.

Procopius *The History of the Wars* (550s; 1914–28 trans.) Bk 5, Pt 1, lines 11–12. Zeno (r.474–491), the Eastern Roman emperor, used Theodoric to overthrow Odoacer in a war that lasted from 489 to 493. Theodoric (r.493–526) was persuaded to replace Odoacer as Zeno's official Roman representative in Italy. Note the reference to the Gothic wagon trains.

3 You [Emperor Anastasius] are the fairest ornament of all realms, you are the healthful defence of the whole world, to which all other rulers rightfully look up with reverence. We [Theodoric] above all, who divine help learned in Your Republic the art of governing Romans with equity ... Our royalty is an imitation of yours, modelled on your good purpose, a copy of the only empire.

Cassiodorus (c.490–c.585) *Variae Epistolae* Bk 1, Letter 1; P. Heather *The Goths* (1996) p.221. Cassiodorus, a Roman administrator who worked for the Ostrogothic kings, was central to maintaining the diplomatic relationship with the Eastern emperor. Theodoric's ambitions were, however, distinctly imperial: in the public expression of his authority in

Italy, still visible at his magnificent tomb in Ravenna, he synthesized Roman and Gothic tradition and maintained a clear notion of his own divine right to rule in the west.

4 King Theodoric to Clovis, king of the Franks:
I take pleasure in my marriage kinship with your courageous spirit, since you have aroused the long idle Frankish race to new wars, and, by your victorious right arm have subdued the Alamannic peoples, who have yielded to a stronger power. But, since crimes should always be avenged on the authors of treachery, and the punishable fault of chieftains should not be rested on the commons, restrain your attack on the exhausted remnants. Those who, as you see, have taken refuge in the protection of your kindred, deserve to escape, by the law of friendship.

Cassiodorus (c.490–c.585) Bk 2, Letter 41, before 507 (1992 trans.). Theodoric intervenes to restrain Clovis, his brother-in-law, from attacking the Alamanni, Germanic neighbours of the Franks. The defeated Alamanni were settled in Italy by Theodoric.

5   Those lofty kings you see seated high on
       thrones,
    Bright in their glowing purple, hedged with
       bristling arms,
    Threatening with visage stern, and grasping in
       the frenzy of their hearts –
    If a man strip from those proud kings the cloak
       of their empty splendour,
    At once he will see these lords within bear
       close-bound chains.

Boethius *Consolations* (c.523; 1918 trans.) Bk 4, Pt 2. Boethius, a Roman aristocrat, became a senior official at Theodoric's court in Ravenna. In 523 he fell foul of court intrigue and was condemned to death. His best known work, *The Consolations of Philosophy*, was written in prison shortly before his execution.

FRANKS, VISIGOTHS AND LOMBARDS, 533–751

6 The Emperor Caesar Flavius Justinian, Conqueror of the Alamanni, the Goths, the Franks, the Germans, the Antes, the Alani, the Vandals and the Africans, Duteous, Fortunate and Renowned, Victorious and Triumphant, Ever Augustus, to the Young, Desirous of Legal Knowledge ... The barbarian races brought under our subjection know our military prowess; and Africa and countless other provinces have after so long a time been restored to Roman obedience through the victories which we, with divine guidance, have achieved and proclaim our empire. But all these peoples are also now governed by the laws which we have made or settled.

Emperor Justinian I *Institutes* (533; 1975 trans.) Preface, p.1. The Eastern emperor's claims to the West at the outset of the war of reconquest that he launched against Africa and Italy (533–561). Africa, Sicily and southern Italy were recaptured for the Roman empire. Northern Italy was held briefly, before the migration of the Lombards in the late 560s. Africa fell to the Arabs in the 7th and 8th centuries, and Sicily in the 9th century.

1 Meanwhile the Gepids and the Lombards were once more moving against each other determined to make war. But the Gepids, fearing the power of the Romans (for they had by no means failed to hear that the Emperor Justinian had made a sworn alliance for offence and defence with the Lombards), were eager to become friends and allies of the Romans. They accordingly straightway sent envoys to Byzantium inviting the Emperor to accept an offensive and defensive alliance with them also. So he without any hesitation gave them the pledges of alliance.

Procopius (550s; 1914–28 trans.) Bk 8, Pt 25, lines 7–8. In the 480s the Gepids and Lombards had migrated into the northern Balkans and upper Danube. In the 540s Emperor Justinian I relied on them to secure his northern frontier, making opportunistic treaties with both groups.

2 Queen Brunhild to a Glorious Lord, and One to be Named with Ineffable Desire, Her Most Beloved Grandson, King Athanagild.

A much desired occasion of great good fortune has come to me, most beloved grandson; by it I am enabled, through the exchange of affectionate letters, to imagine with the eyes of the mind that person whom I often desire to see. In part, my sorrow is relieved, for in you my beloved daughter, whom my sins took from me, is brought back. I have not entirely lost her, if, by God's gift, a descendent is preserved for me … I am communicating certain proposed conditions of agreement to the most merciful emperor by our envoys, to be announced by word of mouth. By them you may recognize if a merciful Christ has ordered those things to be fulfilled which we wish to be arranged.

Queen Brunhild to King Athanagild, late 580s; *Epistolae Austrasiae* (Austrasian Letters) Letter 27. The Frankish Queen Brunhild (d.613) was writing to her grandson, exiled in Constantinople after his father's deposition by Leuvigild (r.568–586) from kingship in Spain.

3 At that time Theuderic, a man of extreme stupidity, ruled with Brunhild, a woman who enthused over the worst vices and was a great friend to the wicked.

King Sisebut of the Visigoths in Spain (r.612–621) *Life and Martyrdom of Saint Desiderius*; A.T. Fear *Lives of the Visigothic Fathers* (1997) pp.4–5. The Frankish King Theuderic II (r.596–613) and Queen Brunhild, his grandmother, were used as models of bad kingship, persecuting the steadfast Desiderius. The negative image struck, and Brunhild became an archetypal manipulative and malicious queen in later historiography.

4 While their king, that is the khagan, was ranging around the walls in full armour with a great company of horsemen to find out from what side he might more easily capture the city, Romilda gazed upon him from the walls, and when she beheld him in the bloom of his youth, the abominable harlot was seized with desire for him and straightway sent word to him by messenger that if he would take her in marriage she would deliver to him the city with all who were in it. The barbarian king, hearing this, promised her with wicked cunning that he would do what she had enjoined and vowed to take her in marriage. She then without delay opened the gates of the fortress of Forum Julii [Cividale, northeast Italy] and let in the enemy to her own ruin and that of all who were there.

Paul the Deacon *Historia Langobardorum* (790s; 1907 trans.) Bk 4, Ch.37. Medieval misogyny and the fall of cities. Romilda, the wife of Gisulf, Duke of Friuli in northern Italy (r.c.590–610), met a suitably ghastly end. The Avars were a group of Central Asian nomads who appeared on the Hungarian Plain in the mid-6th century and raided Europe and Byzantium.

5 Pippin then raised his warbands and set out with speed from Austrasia to do battle with King Theuderic and Berchar. They met near St Quentin at a place called Tertry, and there they fought. Pippin and his Austrasians were the victors: King Theuderic and Berchar were put to flight. The victorious Pippin gave chase and subjugated the region. Shortly afterwards the same Berchar was slain by false and flattering friends at the instigation of his mother-in-law, the lady Anselfledis. Then Pippin secured King Theuderic and his treasure, made all arrangements about the administration of the palace and returned to Austrasia. By his noble and most intelligent wife, Plectrudis, he had two sons, the elder called Drogo and the younger Grimoald.

Anon. *Fredegar Continuatus* (8th century); *The Fourth Book of the Chronicle of Fredegar* (1960 trans.) p.85. By the late 7th century the mayor of the palace was often more powerful than the king. Frankish aristocrats vied for influence in the kingdom through this office. Pippin II (d.714) was the mayor of the palace in Austrasia (north-central France), and Berchar (d.688) in Neustria (northeast France and northwest Germany). The Battle of Tertry (687) did not resolve the conflict between them, but Berchar's assassination did, leaving Pippin in control of Neustria, Austrasia and the king.

1 But let us return to that time when the Saracens entered Spain on the third day before the Ides of November [11 Nov. 714] … The Arabs, after oppressing the region along with the kingdom, killed many with the sword and subjugated the rest to themselves by mollifying them with a covenant of peace. The city of Toledo, victor over all peoples, succumbed, vanquished by the victories of the Ishmaelites; subjected, it served them. They placed prefects throughout all the provinces of Spain and paid tribute to the Babylonian king for many years until they elected their own king and established for themselves a kingdom in the patrician city of Cordoba.

Anon. *The Chronicle of Alfonso III* (880s); K.B. Wolf *Conquerors and Chronicles of Early Medieval Spain* (1990) p.164. An anonymous Christian author composed this chronicle in the 9th century as a continuation of Isidore of Seville's *History of the Kings of Goths*. During the 8th century the Muslim Arabs quickly conquered most of Spain, leaving the small Christian kingdom of Asturias in the northwest (see 152:2). The 'Babylonian kings' are the caliphs in Syria and Iraq (see 136:2).

2 Thereafter Charles summoned his army and marched against Chilperic and Ragamfred. A battle was fought on 21 March [718], a Sunday in Lent, at a place called Vinchy in the Cambrésis; and there were great losses on both sides. Chilperic and Ragamfred were beaten and escaped by flight. Hot in pursuit, Charles hurried to the city of Paris. Then he returned to Cologne and took that city. At this point Plectrudis opened her father's treasure and surrendered it to him, together with control over everything. He himself chose a king, by the name of Chlothar.

Anon. *Fredegar Continuatus* (8th century; 1960 trans.) p.89. The Austrasian aristocrat Charles Martel (c.688–741) fought a series of wars to extend his influence in the Frankish kingdom and to eliminate potential rivals for power. Despite the power of the mayor of the palace, legitimacy still depended on association with a Merovingian king, and he raised Chlothar IV (r.717–718) to the throne.

3 I pray you, O Son of God, that the Catholic order may grow with me, to the benefit of your faithful people; and grant to this temple the same function you assigned to the Temple of Solomon.

King Liutprand, dedicatory inscription on the Church of St Anastasius, Pavia, 729; S. Gasparri 'Kingship Rituals and Ideology in Lombard Italy' in F. Theuws and J. Nelson *Rituals and Power* (2000) p.110. The Lombards are seen as the new Israel. The parallels between the Old Testament Jews and the migrating barbarian peoples were exploited by 7th- and 8th-century kings to legitimize their rule.

4 Prince Charles boldly drew up his battle line against [the Arabs] and the warrior rushed in against them. With Christ's help he overturned their tents, and hastened to battle to grind them small in slaughter. The king Abdirama having been killed, he destroyed [them], driving forth the army, he fought and won. Thus did the victor triumph over his enemies.

Anon. *Fredegar Continuatus* (8th century); P. Fouracre *The Age of Charles Martel* (2000) p.149. Charles Martel is best known for his defeat of the army of the Umayyad emir, Abd al-Rahman I, between Poitiers and Tours (west-central France) in about 733. The battle became famous in the West as the turning point in Arab expansion into Europe.

CONVERSION AND CHRISTIANITY

5 Now the pious band of prisoners, living as they did among the barbarians, converted many of them to the way of piety and persuaded them to adopt the Christian faith instead of the pagan. Among these prisoners were the ancestors of Ulfila … It was this Ulfila who led the exodus of the pious ones, being the first bishop appointed among them.

Bishop Philostorgius *Church History* (5th century); Heather and Matthews (1991) p.143. Sponsored by the Roman empire, Ulfila, a descendant of Christian captives living among the Goths, proselytized among them in the 340s. Conversion was part of the Roman strategy towards the Goths living on their borders.

6 And therefore, in relation to what is contained inside the [Bible], in case it should seem to the reader that in the translated versions one thing is signified in the Greek language and something else in Latin or Gothic, he should take note that if the text displays a discrepancy arising from the rules of the language, it does nevertheless concur in a single meaning.

Codex Brixianus (mid- to late 4th century) Preface; Heather and Matthews (1991), p.171. This was originally a bilingual Latin and Gothic Bible, of which only the Latin survives. The preface, bound into the 6th-century codex, justifies the apparent discrepancies in vernacular translations of the Bible.

7 If anyone steals a consecrated gelded boar (known in the *malberg* as *barcho anomeo chamithetho*), and it can be proven with witnesses that it is consecrated, let him be held liable for 700 *denarii* [silver coins], which make 17½ *solidi* [gold coins], in addition to its value and a fine for the loss of its use.

The Laws of the Salian and Ripuarian Franks (5th or 6th century; 1986 trans.) Salian 2.16. Frankish law was probably recorded in writing after the Franks' conversion to Christianity. However, clauses like this one expose the remnants of Germanic paganism, in which the boar was a very significant animal.

I But, although we rejoice at this, dearly beloved, to see you hasten faithfully to church, we are sad and we grieve because we know that some of you rather frequently go over to the ancient worship of idols like the pagans who have no God or grace of baptism. We have heard that some of you make vows to trees, pray to fountains, and practise diabolical augury … What is worse, there are some unfortunate and miserable people who not only are unwilling to destroy the shrines of pagans but are even not afraid or ashamed to build up those which have been destroyed.

St Caesarius of Arles (c.469–542) Sermons (1956 trans.) Vol.1, Sermon 53. The bishop admonishes the recidivists in his congregation. Pagan practices continued long after the conversion of the ruling elite to Christianity, and many rural areas were too remote from a church to encounter Christianity at all.

2 Bishop Avitus [of Vienne] to Clovis the King:

Let Greece rejoice indeed in having chosen our *princeps*; but now it is not she alone who may deserve a gift showing so great a favour. Its own brilliance shines upon your world too; and light streams out over the western lands in a king whose radiance is no new thing. It is appropriate that the nativity of our Redeemer has begun this illumination; so that, in its turn, the regenerating water of baptism may receive you on that day on which the world received the Lord of heaven as the Son of Redemption.

Bishop Avitus *Epistolae* (c.508) Letter 41. The Frankish king, Clovis, was probably baptized as a Catholic on Christmas Day 508.

3 Bishop Priscus, whom we know to have been a strong opponent of the holy man [Nicetius], gave to a certain deacon the cape which Nicetius had worn … The deacon went everywhere in this garment and thought little about the use to which he had put it … Someone said to him, 'O deacon, if you knew the power of God, and that of him whose garment you wear, you would use it with more care.' He replied, 'I tell you in truth that I wear this cape to cover my

back – and as the hood is too big for me, I shall make socks out of it!' The wretched man did that straight away and fell immediately to the vengeance of divine judgement … the devil seized him and threw him to the ground. He was then alone in the house, and there was no one to help the wretched man. A bloody foam came from his mouth, and his feet were stretched towards the hearth; the fire devoured his feet and the socks as well. This is all I have to say concerning vengeance.

Gregory of Tours *Gregory of Tours: Life of the Fathers* (c.593; 1991 trans.) pp.55–6. Nicetius of Lyons (bishop 552–573) was Gregory's maternal great uncle. He was succeeded in Lyons by Priscus, a rival of Gregory's family, who is made to suffer in Gregory's writings as a consequence. *Rusticitas* ('rural ignorance' in the treatment of relics) was condemned by bishops, whose sacred authority depended in large part on respect for their supernatural power.

4 At this time [*c*.581] there lived near the town of Nice a recluse called Hospicius. He was a man of great abstinence, who had iron chains wrapped round his body, next to the skin, and wore a hairshirt on top. He ate nothing but dry bread and a few dates. In the month of Lent he fed on the roots of Egyptian herbs, which merchants brought home for him. Hermits are greatly addicted to these. First he drank the water in which they were boiled, and then he would eat the herbs themselves. The Lord deigned to perform miracles through the agency of Hospicius. Once the Holy Ghost revealed to him the coming of the Lombards into Gaul. His prophecy went as follows: 'The Lombards,' he said, 'will invade Gaul and they will destroy seven cities, because the wickedness of those cities has grown great in the eyes of the Lord.'

Gregory of Tours *The History of the Franks* (c.593; 1974 trans.) Bk 6, Pt 6. The eremitic holy man was an ambiguous figure in the eyes of the Gallic church hierarchy: at once evidence of God's direct intervention on earth and at the same time an alternative source of authority to bishops and their relics. The name of St Hospice is preserved in the name of a rocky promontory off Cap Ferrat in France.

5 With all the renown he gained by his numerous miracles, the holy man [Benedict] was no less outstanding for the wisdom of his teaching. He wrote a Rule for Monks that is remarkable for its discretion and its clarity of language. Anyone who wishes to know more about his life and character can discover in his Rule exactly what he was like as abbot, for his life could not have differed from his teaching.

Pope Gregory the Great *Dialogues* (590s; 1959 trans.) p.107.
The dialogues were instrumental in promoting the reputation
of St Benedict of Nursia (c.480–c.550). Benedict took his vows
at Lérins and later founded the hilltop monastery of Monte
Cassino southeast of Rome, where he wrote the famous Rule
(see 195:3) for a cenobitic community, based on current
Italian ascetic practice, to which this is the earliest reference.

1 So great then was the rigour of observance in this
monastery that any virgin who entered it renouncing
the world was never again seen outside, except when
she was carried to her tomb, on her last voyage. And
when a mother had a son at the neighbouring
monastery, or a sister had her brother there, neither
of the two knew, at first hand or by hearsay, if the
other was still living, for each of them considered the
other as already buried. It was feared that the sweetness of family memories would break little by little, by
a kind of softening, the bonds of monastic life.

Anon. *Lives of the Fathers of the Jura* (6th century); E. James *The
Origins of France* (1982) p.105. The rigours of the monastic life
as a hoped-for ideal. Family ties gave monks and nuns dual
loyalties: to God and to their kin. For aristocratic families
these ties provided access both to monasteries' spiritual
resources and their landed assets.

2 A great scandal arose in the convent in Poitiers.
Clotild, who used to pretend that she was
Charibert's daughter, gave in to the blandishments
of the Devil. Relying upon the ties which she claimed
with the royal family, she bound the nuns by oath to
bring charges against Leubovera the Abbess, to expel
her from the convent and then to choose herself,
Clotild, as Mother Superior. She walked out of the
convent with 40 or more of the nuns, including her
cousin, Basina, Chilperic's daughter. 'I am going to
my royal relations,' she said, 'to tell them about the
insults which we have to suffer, for we are humiliated
here as if we were the offspring of low-born serving
women, instead of the daughters of kings!'

Gregory of Tours *The History of the Franks* (c.593; 1974 trans.)
Bk 9, Pt 39. In the late 6th century the royal nuns at the
monastery of the Holy Cross in Poitiers rebelled, outraged at
the indignities of the rigorous monastic life. Family connections
with the spiritual and financial power of monasteries were
important, but they depended on the cooperation of the
individuals through whom those connections were made.

3 By the fourteenth year of Theuderic's reign [609],
the reputation of the blessed Columbanus was
increasing everywhere in the cities and provinces of
Gaul and Germany. So generally reputed was he,
and so venerated by all, that King Theuderic used
often to visit him at Luxeuil humbly to beg the

favour of his prayers, and as often the man of God
would rebuke him and ask why he chose to surrender to mistresses rather than to enjoy the blessings of lawful wedlock; for the royal stock should be
seen to issue from an honourable queen, not from
prostitutes.

Jonas of Susa *Life of Columbanus* (640); copied in *The Fourth Book
of the Chronicle of Fredegar* (8th century; 1960 trans.) Pt 36.
Columbanus (d.615) was a missionary from the Irish monastery
of Bangor. He arrived in Francia in about 590 and established
three communities. His criticism of Theuderic II's promiscuity
led to his expulsion from Francia, but Luxeuil was an enormously important monastic centre and the engine of a new wave
of enthusiasm for monasticism among the Frankish elite.

4 To the holy lords and apostolic fathers, bishops,
dukes, counts, regents, servants, lesser officials and
friends, Charles, mayor of the palace, hearty greetings.

Let it be known that the apostolic father Bishop
Boniface has come into our presence and begged us
to take him under our protection. Know then that it
has been our pleasure to do this.

Furthermore, we have seen fit to issue and seal
with our own hand an order that wheresoever he
goes, no matter where it shall be, he shall with our
love and protection remain unmolested and undisturbed, on the understanding that he shall maintain
justice and receive justice in like manner.

Charles Martel, letter of safe-conduct for Boniface (d.754), an
Anglo-Saxon monk from Nursling, near Southampton; C.H.
Talbot *The Anglo-Saxon Missionaries in Germany* (1954), p.75.

5 With the counsel and advice of the latter persons
[near-converts, who abstained from pagan practice],
Boniface in their presence attempted to cut down, at
a place called Geismar, a certain oak of extraordinary
size called by the pagans of olden times the Oak of
Jupiter. Taking his courage in his hands (for a great
crowd of pagans stood by watching and bitterly
cursing in their hearts the enemy of the gods), he cut
the first notch. But when he had made a superficial
cut, suddenly the oak's vast bulk, shaken by a mighty
blast of wind from above, crashed to the ground
shivering its topmost branches into fragments in its
fall. As if by the express will of God (for the brethren
present had done nothing to cause it) the oak burst
asunder into four parts … At the sight of this
extraordinary spectacle the heathens who had been
cursing ceased to revile and began, on the contrary,
to believe and bless the Lord.

Willibald *The Life of Saint Boniface* (754–768); Talbot (1954)
pp.45–6. In the 720s the Anglo-Saxon missionary Boniface
proselytized among the Saxons in northwest Germany.

Missionary conversion worked best where some of the population had already been exposed to Christianity and, as a consequence, were suggestible and open to miracles, such as the destruction of the sacred oak.

LAW AND SOCIETY

1 If anyone is summoned to [undergo] the ordeal of boiling water, and perhaps it is agreed that he who is summoned may redeem his hand and render oath takers; if it is a legitimate dispute [and] it can be proven [that he did what he is accused of doing], he must pay 600 *denarii*, which make 15 *solidi*. And lastly let him redeem his hand with 120 *denarii*, that is, three *solidi*.

The Laws of the Salian and Ripuarian Franks (5th or 6th century; 1986 trans.) Salian 53.1. Trial by ordeal was a universal feature of barbarian law codes. The righteous were supposed to undergo the ordeal fearlessly, the guilty would falter. The Salian law code reflects 5th- or 6th-century Frankish practice. Compare 125:2.

2 1. If a Ripuarian kills a Frankish foreigner, let him be held liable for 200 *solidi* …
   3. If a Ripuarian kills a Roman foreigner, let him be fined twice 50 *solidi* …
   5. If anyone kills a freeborn clerk, let him be held liable for twice 50 *solidi* …
   8. If anyone kills a free-born priest, let him be fined thrice 200 *solidi*.
   9. If anyone kills a bishop, let him be fined thrice 200 *solidi*.
   10. If anyone kills the foetus within a woman or a newborn before he has a name, let him be held liable for twice 50 *solidi*. If he kills the mother along with the foetus, let him be fined 700 *solidi*.

The Laws of the Salian and Ripuarian Franks (5th or 6th century; 1986 trans.) Ripuarian Pt 40. The blood-feud was a feature of barbarian life. All law codes included *wergeld*, a price by which the taking of life could be redeemed without further killing. The social status of the victim affected the price.

3 King Theoderic to the King of the Warni:
   Along with sable furs, and slave-boys who shine with the fair colour of barbarians, your fraternity has sent me swords so sharp that they can cut even through armour, more costly than gold for their steel. Polished splendour glows from them, and reflects in complete clarity the faces of their admirers; their edges converge on the point with such equality that you would think they were cast in a furnace rather than shaped by files. The centre of the blade is hollowed into a beautiful groove wrinkled with serpentine patterns: there such a variety of shadows plays together that you would suppose the gleaming metal to be a tapestry of various tints.

Cassiodorus Bk 5 (c.523–526; 1992 trans.). When Cassiodorus drafted this letter he was probably master of the offices for Theodoric, king of Italy, with special responsibility for receiving envoys. The attention lavished on swords – expensive military technology laden with the symbolism of authority – is a feature of 'barbarian' literature.

4 If anyone pulls a harrow through another's crops after they have germinated, or drives through them with a cart where there is no road, let him be held liable for 120 *denarii*, which make three *solidi*.

The Laws of the Salian and Ripuarian Franks (1986 trans.) Salian 34.3. The economy of western Europe was founded on agriculture, as the overwhelming bulk of 'barbarian' laws indicates.

5 Whoever kills a cattleherd, goatherd or oxherd who is master, shall pay 20 *solidi* as compensation. Moreover, he who kills one of the learners who are following [such a master] shall pay 16 *solidi* as compensation. We speak here of those herders who serve freemen and who have their own houses.

Rothair's Edict (c.568); K.F. Drew *The Lombard Laws* (1973) p.136. The Lombard law code reveals two categories of slaves: those living in their masters' house and those living in some kind of holding of their own. Slavery was widespread throughout the post-Roman world and an important part of the economy. Slaves were one of the most valuable prizes to be gained in war against pagans.

6 I order you to advise the landowner in your province, for the first indiction [537–538], that he must loyally pay his tax money, keeping to the three instalments. Thus no one shall grumble that he has been forced to pay too soon; nor, again, shall anyone claim that he has been passed over by prolonged leniency [leading to arrears]. Let no man exceed the amount of the just weight, and let the scales be altogether just: there will be no end to plundering, should it be permissible to exceed the weight. Furthermore, you are to send my secretariat, in regular form, an accurate four monthly record of the expenses of collection.

Cassiodorus Bk 12 (c.537; 1992 trans.) Bk 12, Letter 16. It is evident that the Ostrogoths maintained the Roman taxation system, dated by 'indiction' and using official scales and weights.

7 Anyone who refuses to go out with the army or with the guard shall pay 20 *solidi* as compensation to the king.

Rothair's Edict (c.568); Drew (1973) pp.56–7. The obligation of military service could be difficult to enforce: many law codes include strictures like these.

1 If anyone should administer a potion to a pregnant woman to produce an abortion, and the child should die in consequence, the woman who took such a potion, if she is a slave, shall receive two hundred lashes, and if she is freeborn, she shall lose her rank, and shall be given as a slave to whomever we [the king] may select.

The Visigothic Code (Forum Judicum) (mid-7th century; 1910 trans.) p.206. As in many cases in 'barbarian' law codes, this law on abortion echoes Roman precedents. The promulgation of written law was a statement of *Romanitas*, or Roman-ness, by the barbarian kings in whose name they were published.

2 Some ask why the art of medicine is not included among the other liberal disciplines. It is because whereas they embrace individual subjects, medicine embraces them all. The physician ought to know literature … rhetoric … arithmetic … geometry … music … [and] astronomy … Hence it is that medicine is called a second philosophy, for each discipline claims the whole of man for itself. Just as by philosophy the soul, so also by medicine the body is cured.

Isidore of Seville *On Medicine* (630s; 1964 trans.) Pt 13, Sect. 1–5. Isidore, bishop of Seville, was a polymath, writing on theology, history, geography and science. Medicine was a purely theoretical discipline for him, part of the classical inheritance of early 7th-century Spain.

Japan, c.450–1863

EMPEROR AND COURT

1   The land of Yamato [Japan]
     Is equal with the heavens.
     It is I that rule it all.
     It is I reign over all.
     Thus I tell my home, my name.

Emperor Yūryaku (r.457–479), opening poem of the *Man'yōshū* (The Collection of Ten Thousand Leaves), a compilation of poems composed between the second quarter of the 7th century and the middle of the 8th century; Geoffrey Bownas and Anthony Thwaite (eds) *The Penguin Book of Japanese Verse* (1964) p.7.

2 He was fond of hunting and of racing dogs and trying horses. He went out and in at all times, taking no care to avoid storms and torrents of rain. Being warmly clad himself, he forgot that the people were starving from cold; eating dainty food, he forgot that the empire was famishing. He gave great encouragement to dwarfs and performers, making them execute riotous music. He prepared strange diversions, and gave licence to lewd vices. Night and day he constantly indulged to excess in sake [rice wine] in the company of the women of the palace. His cushions were of brocade, and many of his garments were of damask and fine silk.

Anon. *Nihon shoki* (Chronicles of Japan) (720; 1972 trans.) Vol.1, p.407. A description of Emperor Buretsu (r.498–506), who is treated by the compilers of the text as a shameless, brutal tyrant who cares little about his people. This blackening of his character followed the Chinese method of discrediting former emperors.

3 The historical texts of the *Kojiki* [Records of Ancient Matters] and *Nihon shoki* [Chronicles of Japan] … [are] the earliest extant Japanese texts we have to gain insight into pre-8th-century political institutions and thought in Japan. Although the two texts were compiled early in the 8th century – the *Kojiki* in 712, and the *Nihon shoki* in 720 – they contain historical episodes and tales derived from a variety of different material whose origins extend backwards to an earlier period of history … We notice that the *Kojiki* completes its story before the calendar system had been introduced into Japan. It does not use the dates of the calendar to record events … The *Nihon shoki*, in contrast, was chronologically compiled using the Chinese dynastic histories as its model. However, due to the fact that Japan did not employ the calendar system until the 6th century, attempts to supply specific dates for the reigns of the emperors prior to the introduction of the calendar system produced much discrepancy in this respect.

Yoko Williams *Tsumi – Offence and Retribution in Early Japan* (2003) pp.5, 14.

4 Harmony is to be valued, and an avoidance of wanton opposition to be honoured …
    In a country there are not two lords; the people have not two masters. The sovereign is the master of the people of the whole country.

Prince Shōtoku, Seventeen Article Constitution, articles 1 and 12, 604; *Nihon shoki* (Chronicles of Japan) (720; 1972 trans.) Vol.2, pp.129, 131.

5 The son of heaven of the land of the rising sun sends greetings to the son of heaven of the land of the setting sun. I trust you are well.

Prince Shōtoku, attrib. letter to the Chinese emperor of the Sui dynasty, 607; *Zuisho Wakokuden* (An Account of Wa [Japan] in the Dynastic History of Sui) (c.636). The letter reveals Prince Shōtoku's ambition to be treated on an equal footing with the great Sui empire, but it angered the Chinese emperor and brought this reply: 'This letter from a barbarian has no courtesy; I do not wish to hear of it again.'

6   I am of this world,
     Unfit to touch a god.

Anon. court lady, poem on the death of Emperor Tenchi, 671; Bownas and Thwaite (1964) p.12.

7 Hereupon the heavenly sovereign commanded saying: 'I hear that the chronicles of the emperors and likewise the original words in the possession of the various families deviate from exact truth, and are mostly amplified by empty falsehoods … So now I desire to have the chronicles of the emperors selected and recorded, and the old words examined and ascertained, falsehoods being erased and the truth determined in order to transmit [the latter] to after ages.'

Ō no Yasumaro *Kojiki* (Records of Ancient Matters) (712) Preface. The oldest extant manuscript of state history offers an explanation of how the imperial family came to rule the land rather than of the origins of the earth and its people.

1 Recently, strange phenomena have appeared in the heavens and the earth shakes often. It is because my teaching did not guide the people well. Thus many people sinned. I alone am to be blamed, and no one else is to be made responsible for this.

In recent years crops fail to harvest, epidemics often spread, shameful and fearful things occur one after another, and I blame myself severely.

Emperor Shōmu, imperial decrees, 734, 741; *Shoku Nihongi* (Chronicles of Japan, Continued) (797). The confessions of an emperor who blamed himself for having brought natural disasters upon his people.

2 On this same night one year ago
I attended the emperor in his palace
And poured out my heart in a poem called Autumn Thoughts.
Here lies the robe that Your Majesty bestowed upon me at that time.
Daily I lift it up and pay homage to its lingering scent.

Sugawara no Michizane, poem (9th century). The poem was written during Sugawara's exile in northern Kyushu, following his banishment from the court by the Fujiwara family. He died in exile in 903, unable to realize his dream of returning to the capital and to the court.

3 When you arise in the morning chant seven times the name of the star for the year. Next look at yourself in a mirror. Next consult the calendar to know the fortune for the day. Next use your toothpick and face west to wash your hands. Next chant the name of the Buddha. At the same time you may also chant the names of those Shinto shrines to which you are affiliated. Next make your diary entry for yesterday. Next eat your rice-gruel (for breakfast). Next set your hair (once every three days, not every day). Next cut your finger and toe nails (cut your finger nails on the day of the ox and your toe nails on the day of the tiger). Then select a day to bathe (once every five days). You must consult the fortune before bathing … Next, if you have to go to your office, put your cap and robe on.

Fujiwara Morosuke, entry in personal diary, *Kyūreki* (Diary of the Lord of Kujō) (c.960); David Lu *Japan: A Documentary History* Vol.1 (1997) pp.73–4. Detailed diaries were kept by many members of the Fujiwara family, which was one of the most politically influential of the traditional families of Japan and which effectively ruled the country for a large part of Japanese history.

4 One evening during the reign of Emperor Murakami, when it had been snowing very heavily and the moon was shining brightly, His Majesty ordered that some snow be heaped on to a platter. Then a branch of plum blossom was stuck into it and the emperor told someone to hand the platter to Hyoe, the lady chamberlain. 'Let us have a poem about this,' he said to her. 'What will you give us?'

'The moon, the snow, the flowers,' she replied, much to His Majesty's delight.

Sei Shōnagon (b.c.965) *Makura no sōshi* (The Pillow Book); Ivan Morris *The Pillow Book of Sei Shōnagon* (1967) p.185.

5 What can compare with an imperial progress? When the emperor passes in his palanquin he is as impressive as a god and I forget that my work in the palace constantly brings me into his presence. Not only His Majesty himself but even people like ladies of the escort, who usually are of no importance, overawe me when I see them in an imperial progress.

Sei Shōnagon (b.c.965) *Makura no sōshi* (The Pillow Book); Morris (1971 edn) p.197. Emperor Murakami (r.946–967) was enthroned when he was very young and was supported by able ministers of the right, such as Fujiwara Morosuke (see 123:3), and the left. The emperor was fond of art and poetry as well as politics, and he held poetry competitions and readings in the court.

6 In the tenth month we moved back to the capital … In due course I was invited to attend court, but Father in his old-fashioned way thought that I would find life there very trying and he persuaded me to remain at home. Several people told him that he was mistaken.

'Nowadays no young woman hesitates to serve at court,' said one of them. 'All sorts of good things happen to people when they have taken service. Really, you should let her go and see what happens.'

So it was that Father reluctantly gave his consent.

My first period of service lasted exactly one night. When I went to the palace, I wore a dark crimson robe of glossed silk over eight thin under-robes of dark red. Having been totally absorbed in Tales, I knew scarcely anyone except the people I used to visit in order to borrow books. Besides, I was so used to staying with my old-fashioned parents at home, gazing hour after hour at the autumn moon or the spring blossoms, that when I arrived at court I was in a sort of daze and hardly knew what I was doing. So at dawn on the following day I returned home.

Lady Sarashina (b.1008) *As I Crossed a Bridge of Dreams* (1975 trans.) pp.75–6. Lady Sarashina (not her real name) was lady-in-waiting at the imperial court. We know little about this work, not even the name of the authoress. Sarashina is the name of a district. Ivan Morris, the translator, notes (p.13) that the name 'is not mentioned a single time in the book; but there is an indirect allusion to the place in one of the author's last poems, and for some reason it was chosen [by scholars] for the title'. The capital here is Kyoto, Japan's capital for a thousand years before its move to Edo (now Tokyo). The 'Tales' were the *Genji Monogatari* (The Tale of Genji), an 11th-century literary masterpiece written by Murasaki Shikibu.

1 Samurai [warriors] who are unused to court cere-monies, wearing the full regalia, including caps and wooden maces, pretentiously participate in the rituals of the imperial palace.

Appointment secretaries at the court who pretend to be wise men, who as the middle men deceive both the court and those who come to the court, but whose falsehood cannot long remain hidden.

Anon. *Kemmu nenkanki* (Records of the Kemmu Era) (?c.1333); Kasahara Kazuo *et al.* (eds) *Seisen Nihonshi shiryōshū* (Selected Documents on Japanese History) (1970 edn) pp.81–2. Such things were in vogue in the capital, Kyoto, in the 14th century in Emperor Godaigo's reign, according to graffiti discovered on the dry bed of the River Nijo in Kyoto.

2 The court's upkeep is at present taken care of by ... the shogun. He devoted the income of the lands around Miyako [the capital] to the court, but since this is insignificant, he annually contributes some-thing from the bowels of his treasury. But this is given so sparingly that the courtiers cannot live on it, or, at least, cannot live as opulently and splendidly as when the mikado [emperor] himself was in control of the empire and the treasury. Consequently, this court exists in splendid poverty: great lords are burdened with great debts because they have to live according to their status, and ordinary servants have to make and sell sandals for people and horses, or items of lesser value, so that they can survive at all.

Engelbert Kaempfer *History of Japan* (1727) Bk 2; Beatrice M. Bodart-Bailey (trans. and ed.) *Kaempfer's Japan: Tokugawa Culture Observed* (1999) p.92. The German physician is observing the Tokugawa-period court on his travels around the country. Under the Tokugawa regime (1603–1867), the shogun ruled from his palace in Edo (now Tokyo); the emperor, bereft of real political power, resided in the ancient capital of Kyoto.

3 And now a great silence fell upon the people. Far as the eye could see on either side, the roadsides were densely packed with the crouching populace in their ordinary position when any official of rank passes by ... As the phoenix car ... with its halo of glittering attendants came on ... the people without order or signal turned their faces to the earth ... no man moved or spoke for a space, and all seemed to hold their breath for very awe, as the mysterious presence, on whom few are privileged to look and live, was passing by.

Japan Times, 26 Nov. 1868. A description of the emperor's first visit to the new capital of Edo from the old capital of Kyoto. With the respectful return of political power by the 15th shogun, Tokugawa Yoshinobu (r.1866–7), to the emperor in 1868, political power was restored to the emperor after a long rule by the military houses.

LAW AND POLITICS

4 Cutting living skin
  cutting the corpse
  white leprosy
  skin excrescences
  violating one's own mother
  violating one's own child
  violating a wife and her child from a former
marriage
  violating a wife and her mother
  transgressions with animals
  calamity from crawling insects
  calamity from the thunder god
  calamity from birds
  the killing of animals through putting a curse
on them
  the occult practice of putting curses on people.

Items of *kunitsutsumi* (earthly offences) found in the *norito* (purification rituals) section of the *Engishiki* (Procedures for Ceremonies of the Engi Period), completed in 922. The offences listed, which probably date from the 3rd and early 4th centuries, were considered to disturb the cosmic order and harm the *kuni* (political unit ruled by one ruler or co-rulers) and its people.

5 Destroying the ridges between rice-fields
  covering up the watercourses in rice-fields
  destroying the water-passage system of rice-fields
  the double planting of seeds
  the erection of rods in rice-fields
  skinning a live animal
  skinning a live animal backwards
  defecation in sacred places.

Items of *amatsutsumi* (heavenly offences), *Engishiki*, 922. These offences interfered with the interests of the early agricultural communities or disturbed sacred rituals. They may be slightly later in origin than the earthly offences (see 124:4). *Kunitsutsumi* and *amatsutsumi*, the earliest types of offence in Japanese history, are recorded in such early historical texts as the *Kojiki* (Records of Ancient Matters) and *Nihon shoki* (Chronicles of Japan).

1 At present things are in a crude and obscure condition, and the people's minds are unsophisticated. Their manners are simply what is customary. Now if a great man were to establish laws, justice could not fail to flourish.

Emperor Jinmu (r.660–585 BC); *Nihon shoki* (Chronicles of Japan) (720; 1972 trans.) Vol.1, p.131. Traditionally believed to have been the first of Japan's great rulers, the emperor notes the need to teach newly conquered peoples in remote areas the standard to be set under his rule. The ascription by the compilers of *Nihon shoki* (Chronicles of Japan) of this promulgation to Jinmu's reign (thereby making him, in effect, the first lawmaker) is open to doubt.

2 Sometimes mud was put into a cauldron and made to boil up. Then the arms were bared, and the boiling mud stirred with them. Sometimes an axe was heated red-hot and placed on the palm of the hand … everyone put on straps of tree-fibre, and coming to the cauldrons, plunged their hands in the boiling water, when those who were true remained naturally uninjured, and all those who were false were harmed.

Anon. *Nihon shoki* (Chronicles of Japan) (720; 1972 trans.) Vol.1, p.317. The text records the trial by the ordeal of boiling water to resolve a dispute between two parties over the issue of family origin during the reign of Emperor Ingyo (r.412–453). Compare 120:1.

3 When [Emperor Buretsu] grew to manhood, he was fond of criminal law and well versed in the statutes. He would remain in court until the sun went down, so that hidden wrong was surely penetrated. In deciding cases he attended to the facts.

Anon. *Nihon shoki* (Chronicles of Japan) (720; 1972 trans.) Vol.1, p.399. Emperor Buretsu (r.498–506) acts as a judge of the facts in criminal cases brought before him.

4 To turn away from that which is private, and to set our faces towards that which is public – this is the path of a minister. Now if a man is influenced by private motives, he will assuredly feel resentments, and if he is influenced by resentful feelings, he will assuredly fail to act harmoniously with others. If he fails to act harmoniously with others, he will assuredly sacrifice the public interests to his private feelings. When resentment arises, it interferes with order and is subversive of law. Therefore in the first clause (of this constitution) it was said that superiors and inferiors should agree together. The purport is the same as this.

Prince Shōtoku, Seventeen Article Constitution, article 15, 604; *Nihon shoki* (Chronicles of Japan) (720; 1972 trans.) Vol.2, p.132. The Constitution expressed, through the employment of Confucian, Buddhist and Legalist ideas, the political ideal of establishing one sovereign as sole ruler of the state. Officers were the vassals of the ruler.

5 Betraying the emperor.

Plotting to damage the emperor's grave or palace.

Plotting to betray the country and obey a false ruler, rebels or foreign countries.

Violence against, and murder of, family members.

Crimes against humanity – e.g., massacre, murder through satanic ritual.

Impolite acts against the emperor – e.g., damaging or stealing from the shrine.

Filial impiety.

Crimes against courtesy and manner – e.g., the murder of a master, the murder of a governor.

Ritsuryō (Laws and Ordinances) (early 8th century); Noel Williams *The Right to Life in Japan* (1997) p.56. These were the *hachigyaku*, the eight most serious or abominable crimes that could be committed and that were considered the most morally detestable deeds.

6 Under the *ritsuryō* system, the discrepancy between the Chinese-originated *ritsuryō* codes and the reality of Japanese society brought with it the practice of customary law. This customary law became the primary law when the warrior class came to attain power … Generally speaking, matters were judged in accordance with customary law, and new laws were made when neither the *ritsuryō* nor the customary law could be applied.

Noel Williams (1997) p.7.

7 Anyone who marries someone from outside the province creates causes for great disturbance, as he may agree to take possession of her estate and send his retainers to serve her family. Therefore such a marriage is strictly forbidden. If anyone disobeys this … a severe reprimand will be administered.

Takeda Shingen, house law, article 4, 1547. Takeda Shingen (1521–73) was a warlord who expelled his father, Nobutora, and took over his position and territory.

8 A lover of honour to the uttermost, very secretive in what he determines, extremely shrewd in the stratagems of war, little if at all subject to the reproof and counsel of his subordinates, feared and revered by all to an extreme degree. Does not drink wine. He is a severe master: treats all the kings and princes of Japan with scorn and speaks to them over his shoulder as though to inferiors, and is completely obeyed by all as their absolute lord. He is a man of good understanding, and clear judgement, despising the [gods] and [Buddha], and all the rest of that breed of idols, and all the heathen superstitions.

Luís Fróis SJ to P. Belchior de Figueiredo SJ, 1 June 1569; C.R. Boxer *The Christian Century in Japan 1549–1650* (1951) p.58. The Jesuit father is describing Oda Nobunaga, who reunified Japan after a long period of fighting between the warlords.

1 Farmers of all provinces are strictly forbidden to have in their possession any swords, short swords, firearms or other types of weapon. If unnecessary implements of war are kept, the collection of annual rent may become more difficult, and without provocation uprisings can be fomented ... Therefore, the heads of provinces, samurai [warriors] who receive a grant of land, and deputies must collect the weapons described above and submit them to Hideyoshi's government.

Toyotomi Hideyoshi, Collection of Swords Edict, article 1, 1588. Limiting the possession of weapons assured the military superiority of the warrior classes over the peasant classes. Toyotomi was appointed *kanpaku* (first minister, chief adviser to the emperor) in 1585.

2 The lords who rule the land have such absolute authority over their vassals that they have no obligation whatever to give any account of it to any man, and the vassals have no way of escape from their authority and no appeal against it, so that the lords can, at will, take away their lives, their families, their honour and their property, and they actually do so, and they need no other cause or reason, merely the desire or will to do it ... And since they depend so much on their lords for everything, they serve them in everything much more than they would if they were their slaves, and the lords impose such obligations and duties on their poor vassals that their position is impossible.

Father Alessandro Valignano, Nagasaki, to Claudio Acquaviva, General of Society of Jesus, 20 Oct. 1600; Jesuit Archives (Japonica Sinica), series no.14 (1), sheet 35 v. Valignano, a Portuguese Jesuit, was sent to Japan in the years prior to the closing of the country to foreigners (1632–1868) as part of the Jesuit mission to convert the Japanese to Christianity, a mission that included the education of the Japanese (see 321:6).

3 Their justice is severely executed without any partiality upon transgressors of the law. They are governed in great civility. I mean, not a land better governed in the world by civil police.

William Adams, letter, 1611; Richard Tames *Encounters with Japan* (1991) pp.66–7. Adams was the British pilot-major of a squadron that arrived in Japan in 1600 to engage in trade with the Japanese. He became an adviser to Tokugawa Ieyasu on matters concerning trade and navigation. Adams eventually became a samurai warrior.

4 Japanese ships are strictly forbidden to leave for foreign countries.

No Japanese is permitted to go abroad. If there is anyone who attempts to do so secretly, he must be executed. The ship so involved must be impounded and its owner arrested, and the matter must be reported to the higher authority.

If any Japanese returns from overseas after residing there, he must be put to death.

Tokugawa Iemitsu (r.1623–51), Edicts 1, 2 and 3, 1635. Legislation dealing with the closing of Japan to all but a few countries. The country was effectively sealed from outside influence for more than 200 years until the American, Commodore Matthew Perry, landed in Japan in 1853.

5 The so-called three fundamental principles [governing human relations] are that the ruler is the lord over his subject, the father is the lord over his son, and the husband is the lord over his wife. The ruler, the father and the husband must be respected equally and served with the same diligence.

There are three followings for women, which are applicable to every woman. Therefore, when the girl is yet to be married, she follows her father. After her marriage, she follows her husband. After the death of her husband, she follows her son. The father is the heaven for the daughter, the husband is the heaven for the wife.

Arai Hakuseki, legal opinion, 1711; *Nihon koten bungaku taikei* Kawaguchi Hisao (ed.) Vol.95 (1969) p.336. Arai (1657–1725) was a Confucian scholar and adviser to two shoguns.

6 The military and warlike strength of the Japanese had long been to Europe like the ghost in a village churchyard, a bugbear and a terror, which it only required some bolder fellow than the rest – like we Yankees – to walk up and discover the ghost to be nothing but moonshine on the gravestones ... Our nation has unclothed the ghost and all the rest of the world will cry 'bah', and take advantage of the discovery.

Member of Commodore Perry's squadron, 1853; Tames (1991) p.21. Commodore Perry landed in Japan in July 1853 to negotiate a treaty with the emperor.

7 Today I am to enter Edo. It will form an important epoch in my life, and a still more important one in the history of Japan.

Townsend Harris, diary entry on meeting the shogun, 1857; Tames (1991) p.23. Harris, the first US consul general in Japan (1855–60), was played by John Wayne in the (historically inaccurate) film *The Barbarian and the Geisha* (1958). The shogun resided in Edo, and Harris describes in his diary the clothes he wore on this occasion: 'My dress was a coat embroidered with gold, blue pantaloons with a broad gold band running down each leg, cocked hat with gold tassels and a pearl dress sword.' His ostentatious dress was one of the main factors leading to a US Congressional resolution prohibiting diplomats from wearing inappropriate dress.

EDUCATION AND LEARNING

1 Request that the vacant post of professor of literature be filled with a person to assist in the various duties. It is my observation that of all the curricula at the university, classics is the greatest. Thus, the positions of professor of classics are never left vacant, and a total of five men are always employed (including the assistant professors and lecturers). Also, there are always two professors in each of the other subjects – mathematics, law, calligraphy and phonetics – even though the students are few.

Literature is, in fact, no less vital a scholarly discipline than classics, but the number of professors is still the same as in calligraphy or mathematics. Not only is the number of professorships small, but one is now vacant. My native ability is limited and the duties of a professor are too great for one man. At present, among able scholars there is a suitable person whom I wish to have appointed to the vacancy so that together we can fulfil the responsibilities of professor of literature.

Sugawara no Michizane, request, 884; *Kanke bunso* (A Collection of the Documents of the Sugawara Family) item 597 in Hisao (1969). The noble Sugawara was a scholar of repute. Appointed to the offices of junior minister of ceremonial and professor of literature (posts he held concurrently), he was accorded the rank of doctor of literature, the supreme accolade in Japan at the time. The classics is a reference to Chinese classical texts. During this period Japanese scholarship was greatly indebted to Chinese scholarship.

2 When children are grown to the point of knowing what is going on around them, they must be taught to read the classics and important books written by the sages of old: this is done in the morning, which is followed by the practice of calligraphy. They may be allowed to play afterwards. They are strictly forbidden to engage in falconry or gambling.

Fujiwara Morosuke, entry in personal diary, c.960; Okubo Toshiaki et al. (eds) *Shiryo ni yoru Nihon no ayumi* (Japanese History Through Documents: Ancient Period) (1960) p.372. The diarist was, of course, referring to the education of the children at court.

3 When my brother, Secretary at the Ministry of Ceremonial, was a young boy learning the Chinese classics, I was in the habit of listening with him and I became unusually proficient at understanding those passages that he found too difficult to grasp and memorize. Father, a most learned man, was always regretting that fact: 'Just my luck!' he would say. 'What a pity she was not born a man!' But then I gradually realized that people were saying 'It's bad enough when a man flaunts his Chinese learning; she will come to no good …'

Her Majesty asked me to read with her here and there from the Collected Works of Po Chü-i, and, because she evinced a desire to know more about such things, to keep it secret we carefully chose times when the other women would not be present, and, from the summer before last, I started giving her informal lessons on the two volumes of 'New Ballads'. I hid this fact from others, as did Her Majesty.

Lady Murasaki Shikibu (c.980–c.1030) *The Diary of Lady Murasaki* (1996 trans.) pp.57–8, Lady Murasaki Shikibu was the author of the masterpiece *The Tale of Genji* (c.1022), the first novel in world literature. The diary recounts her personal recollections of life at the imperial court in Kyoto at a time when it was considered inappropriate for a lady to read the Chinese classics.

4 The pleasantest of all diversions is to sit alone under the lamp, a book spread out before you, and to make friends with people of a distant past you have never known.

People often say that a set of books looks ugly if all volumes are in the same format, but I was impressed to hear the Abbot Koyu say, 'It is typical of the unintelligent man to insist on assembling complete sets of everything. Imperfect sets are better.'

Yoshida Kenkō *Tsurezuregusa* (Essays in Idleness) (1330–33; 1911 trans.) Sect.82. The priest Kenkō notes the Japanese preference for irregularity: 'In everything, no matter what it may be, uniformity is undesirable. Leaving something incomplete makes it interesting, and gives one the feeling that there is room for growth. Someone once told me, "Even when building the imperial palace, they always leave one place unfinished."'

5 Make every effort to rise early in the morning: if you rise late, even your servants will become inattentive and may not obey your command. In this way you cannot attend to your public duties or private needs. As a result your master, the daimyō [lord], may forsake you. Take heed of this [regulation].

In the evening, go to bed before eight. Night thieves without exception come during the hours between midnight and the first crow of the cock. If you engage in lengthy conversation in the evening, and go to bed after midnight, fall sound asleep, and allow the thieves to steal your household goods, what will that do to your reputation? Save on the firewood and lamp oil which you otherwise consume unnecessarily and get up at dawn.

Cleanse yourself, and worship the deities, make yourself presentable, and give orders for the chores to be performed to your wife and retainers, and go to your office before six.

Hōjō Sōun, regulations to vassals, items 1 and 2, c.1495. Hōjō Sōun (1432–1519) was a powerful war lord of the *sengoku* (warring) feudal period.

1 [The Japanese] are very able and of good understanding, and the children are fully capable of taking in all our sciences and disciplines, and they recite and learn to read and write in our language much more easily and more quickly than European children do. And even the lower classes are not so uncouth and ignorant as ours are; indeed for the most part they are of good understanding, well brought up and able.

Father Alessandro Valignano *Sumário de las Cosas de Japon* (1583; 1954 edn) p.5.

2 The king demanded of me, of what land I was, and what moved us to come to his land, being far off. I showed unto him the name of our country, and that our land had long sought out the East Indies, and desired friendship with all kings and potentates in way of merchandise … Then he asked me whether our country had wars? I answered him yea, with the Spaniards and Portugals. He asked me in what did I believe? I said, in God that made heaven and earth. He asked me divers other questions of things of my religion, and many other thing – as what way we came to the country. Having a chart of the whole world I showed him, through the Strait of Magellan. At which he wondered and thought me to lie. Thus, from one thing to another, I abode with him till midnight … In the end, he being ready to depart, I desired that we might have a trade of merchandise, as the Portugals and Spaniards had. To which he made me an answer, but what it was, I did not understand.

William Adams, 1600; Tames (1991) p.9. The shogun in question was Tokugawa Ieyasu, the founder of the Tokugawa dynasty (1600–1868). Here Adams, the first Englishman to visit Japan, describes the first recorded meeting between a Japanese shogun and a representative of the English-speaking world.

3 The study of literature and the practice of the military arts must be pursued side by side.

Tokugawa Ieyasu, Rules for the Military Houses, article 1, 1615; *Kinsei hosei shiryo sosho* (A Compendium of Documents on Early Modern Legal and Institutional History) (1959) Vol.2, p.1. The rules were issued by the shogun to the daimyō (lords).

4 After investigating the size of the world, the multitude of its countries and the smallness of Japan, he was greatly surprised and heartily wished that his land had never been visited by any Christian.

François Caron, 1641; George Sansom *A History of Japan: 1615–1867* (1974) p.43. Caron, head of the Dutch trading station in Japan, was teaching world geography to the third shogun, Tokugawa Iemitsu (r.1623–51).

5 For the children in their sixth [calendar] year: In January when children reach the age of six, teach them numbers one through ten, and the names given to designate 100, 1,000, 10,000 and 100,000. Let them know the four directions, east, west, north and south. Assess their native intelligence and differentiate between quick and slow learners. Teach them the Japanese syllabary from the age of six or seven, and let them learn how to write. From this time on, teach them to respect their elders, and let them know distinctions between the upper and lower classes and between the young and old. Let them learn to use the correct expressions …

From their infancy, truth in word and thought should be made of the first importance. Children should be severely punished for lying or deceit.

A tutor should be a man of upright life. A child should not be put to learn of a disreputable person, no matter how clever he may be.

Books should not be flung about, walked on or used as pillows.

Kaibara Ekken (1630–1714) *Dōjikun* (Instructions for Children); Matsuda, Michio et al. (eds) *Nihon no meicho* (Great Books of Japan) Vol.14 (1969) p.214, and W.G. Aston *A History of Japanese Literature* (1972) pp.238–9. This treatise on education – particularly that of women of the warrior classes – was written by the Confucian scholar when he was in his 80s.

6 A womanly disposition, as shown in modesty and submissiveness.

Womanly language. She should be careful in the choice of words, and avoid lying and unseemly expressions. She should speak when necessary, and be silent at other times. She should not be adverse to listening to others.

Kaibara Ekken, on the two great virtues of women, *Dōjikun*; Aston (1972) p.239.

1 Be respectful and obedient to your parents-in-law.

A woman has no [feudal] lord. She should reverence and obey her husband instead.

Be always circumspect in your behaviour. Get up early. Go to bed at midnight. Do not indulge in a siesta. Attend diligently to the work of the house.

Kaibara Ekken, advice to parents to give their daughters on marriage, *Dōjikun*; Aston (1972) p.240.

2 Most of the time at court is spent studying. There are not only learned aristocrats, or courtiers, but also women who write poetry and books.

Engelbert Kaempfer (1727; 1999 edn) p.92. The German physician Kaempfer made two trips around Japan in 1691 and 1692, and his *History of Japan* served as a source for the libretto of Gilbert and Sullivan's operetta *The Mikado* (1885). The habit of court ladies to be engaged in scholarship continued into Tokugawa Japan (1600–1868).

3 A notable incident in the world's progress, connected with the advancement of our language [English] and of American apparatus for education, deserves to be recorded. It appears that in the public schools of Japan the English language is to be the general basis of study and that American schoolbooks are to be used without any attempt to translate them into the native language.

New York Times, 26 June 1867. To this end, the Japanese commissioners who visited the United States entrusted the business of supplying these books to an American company. No matter how well intentioned, the policy did not prevail.

AESTHETICS

4 I look out from my room at the head of the corridor into the light morning mist. Dew is still on the ground, but His Excellency is already out in the garden ordering his attendants to clear the stream of some obstruction. Plucking a sprig from a large cluster of maiden-flowers that blooms there on the south side of the bridge, he peers in over the top of the curtain frame. The sight of him, so magnificent, makes me conscious of my own dishevelled appearance, and so when he presses me for a poem, I use it as an excuse to move to where my inkstone is kept:

Now I see the colour of this maiden-flower in bloom,
I know how much the dew discriminates against me.

'Quick, aren't we!' says he with a smile and asks for my brush:

It is not the dew that chooses where to fall;
Does not the flower choose the colour that it desires?

Lady Murasaki Shikibu (c.980–c.1030) *The Diary of Lady Muraski* (1996 trans.) p.4.

5 If in this troubled world of ours
I still must linger on,
My only friend shall be the moon,
Which on my sadness shone.
When other friends were gone.

Emperor Sanjō, poem, after 1016; William N. Porter (trans.) *A Hundred Verses from Old Japan* (1979) p.68. After becoming ill, Emperor Sanjō (r.1011–16) saw his palace burn down twice and was made to abdicate the throne by Fujiwara Michinaga, the adviser to Emperor Ichijo (r.986–1011) and his two successors.

6 The winds of spring
Scattered the flowers
As I dreamt my dream.
Now I awaken,
My heart is disturbed.

Saigyō, poem, *Sankashū*, late 12th century); Bownas and Thwaite (1964) p.101. The poet-priest Saigyō (1118–90) entered the priesthood at the age of 23 after serving as a military attendant to the former Emperor Gotoba.

7 Overcome with pity for this world,
My tears obscure my sight;
I wonder, can it be the moon
Whose melancholy light
Has saddened me tonight?

Saigyō, poem, *Sankashū*, late 12th century; Porter (1979) p.86.

8 The current of a running stream flows on unceasingly, but the water is not the same: the foam floating on the pool where it lingers, now vanishes and now forms again, but is never lasting. Such are mankind and their habitations.

The dew may fall, leaving the flower behind; but even so, the flower fades with the morning sun. Again the flower may wither, while the dew remains; but even so, it cannot last until evening.

When I hear the copper pheasant with his cry of 'horo, horo' I wonder whether it is my father or my mother? When the stag from the mountain approaches without shyness, I realize how far I am separated from the world.

Kamo no Chōmei *Hōjōoki* (Notes from a Hermit Cell) (1212); Aston (1972) pp.146–7, 155. The poet-priest was a member of the Kamo family, who were the guardians of the Kamo shrine in Kyoto. He forsook the world when he was in his 50s.

1   We come and we see
The capital of old.
Desolate as a swamp
Unkempt with wild reeds.
The light of the moon
Streams in unshaded:
The wind of autumn
Pierces my bones.

Anon. *Heike monogatari* (The Tale of the Heike) (mid-13th-century); Bownas and Thwaite (1964) p.92. This war tale, which tells of the rise and fall of the Heike clan, was originally recited to a lute accompaniment, played by a blind priest. A chamberlain sings this song three times to the empress and her ladies-in-waiting until they are reduced to tears. The occasion was the viewing of the moon.

2   It is not displeasing,
When composing verse,
To hear sounds of the pounding
Of a fine tea.
With interest aroused,
One longs also to hear
The elegant plucking of a lute.

Emperor Saga, poem, 814; Ono no Minemori *et al. Ryourishu Gunsho ruiju* (A Collection of Japanese Classical Manuscripts) Vol.6 (1899) p.476.

3 The gate was extremely small, and one had to bend one's body to enter. Set back deep in the property was a building where everything was made of fine wood. There were ink landscape paintings on all four walls … The room was decorated with important objects, and tea from Uji was prepared.

Anon. *Hekizan nichiroku* (The Blue Cliff Record) (1462); *Kaitei shiseki shuran* Vol.25 (1984) p.256. The record was kept by a Zen priest at Tōfukuji temple, Kyoto. Uji in Kyoto is famous for its tea plantations.

4 The tea ceremony of the small tea room is first of all a Buddhist spiritual practice for attaining the way. To be concerned about the quality of the dwelling in which you serve tea or the flavour of the food served

with it is to emphasize the mundane. It is sufficient if the dwelling one uses does not leak water and the food served suffices to stave off hunger. This is in accordance with the teachings of the Buddha and is the essence of the tea ceremony. First, we fetch water and gather firewood. Then we boil the water and prepare tea. After offering some to the Buddha, we serve our guests. Finally, we serve ourselves.

Sen no Rikyū (1522–91) attrib. *Nanpōroku* (Notes by Nanpō); Sen Soshitsu (ed.) *Chado koten zenshū* (1956) Vol.4, p.3. These words by the great Zen master illustrate the importance of the spirit in the tea ceremony of his day.

5 Entering the room from the veranda, one should bow to the host. Then one should move slightly toward the alcove and appreciate ever so quietly whatever is hung there … Flowers may be arranged in a bamboo boat suspended from the ceiling or arranged in a vase hung on the pillar of the alcove, and these should be admired quietly too.

Anon., 1566; Soshitsu (1956) Vol.3, p.128. The proper way for guests to enter the room for the tea ceremony.

6 That which creates seed and blossom of the full range of *nō* is the mind playing through [the actor's] whole person. Just as the emptiness of crystal gives forth fire and water … the accomplished master creates all the colours and forms of his art out of the intention of his mind. Many are the adornments of this noble art; many are the natural beauties that grace it. The mind that gives forth all things, even to the four seasons' flowers and leaves, snows and moon, mountains and seas – yes, even to all beings, sentient and insentient – that mind is heaven and earth.

Zeami Motokiyo *Kadensho* (1440–42); Royall Tyler *Japanese Nō Dramas* (1992) p.19. Zeami (1363–1443), the great writer and actor of the *nō* theatre, comments on the need for constant self-improvement: 'A man's life has an end, but there is no end to the pursuit of the *nō*. For him music is the soul of the *nō*.' The essence of the *nō* form of theatre, he believed, was imitation: 'In principle, the aim is to imitate all objects, whatever they may be.'

7   Isles of blest Japan!
Should your Yamato spirit
Strangers seek to scan,
Say – scenting morn's sunlit air,
Blows the cherry wild and fair!

Motoori Norinaga, (1730–1801) poem; Nitobe Inazo *Bushido: The Soul of Japan* (1900; 1998 edn) p.259.

Islam, c.610–1055

BELIEFS

1 And many a warrior, baring his teeth, who
   leads a compact host,
   … Whose body I pierced with my lance,
   whereupon he swayed,
   As a bough bends down, cut from a supple
   jujube tree.
   And many a fragrant wine, like scattered musk,
   … Have I quaffed in the early morning before
   dawn …
   … And many a maid, like a gazelle of al-Jaww,
   tender and soft,
   Her saliva tastes as if mixed with wine,
   Have I dallied with half the night, and she with
   me …
   … Youth is gone and has sworn never to return
   again,
   And hoariness has settled firmly on my head.
   Hoariness is a shame to the man in whose court
   it dwells.
   How wonderful were my black locks, now
   forever gone!

Abid Ibn al-Abras (early 6th century) 'Self-Praise and Remembrance of Youth'; S. Sperl and C. Shackle (eds) *Qasida Poetry in
Islamic Asia and Africa* (1996) Vol.2, p.67. Poetry was the
prestige cultural product of pre-Islamic Arabian society, and
poets had great authority, acting as the spokesmen of their
tribes. Youth and its passing had a more than personal
significance: as in many pagan societies, fate and the inevitability
of mortality were central ideas in their worldview.

2 This is the tribe which took its origin and had its
name from Ishmael, the son of Abraham, and the
ancients called them Ishmaelites after their progenitor
… Such being their origin, they practise circumcision
like the Jews, refrain from the use of pork, and observe
many other Jewish rites and customs. If, indeed, they
deviate in any respect from the observances of that
nation, it must be ascribed to the lapse of time, and
to their intercourse with the neighbouring nations.

Sozomen *Ecclesiastical History* (440s; 1891 trans.) p.375. The
Arabs were widely believed to be the descendants of Ishmael,
Abraham's son by his concubine, Hagar, as opposed to the
Jews, who were descended from Isaac and Sarah. This Greek
history suggests that a version of Judaic monotheism was
practised in the Arabian peninsula in the 5th century. For
Sozomen see 91:3.

3 In the Name of God, the Compassionate, the
Merciful.
   Recite in the name of your Lord who created –
created man from clots of blood.
   Recite! Your Lord is the Most Bountiful One, who
by the pen taught man what he did not know.

Koran *Clots of Blood* (1956 trans.) sura 96, verses 1–5. When he
was about 40 years old Muhammad (c.570–632), a merchant
from Mecca, in northwest Arabia, took to spiritual retreat on
a mountain near the town. It was there that he saw the angel
Gabriel, through whom he received the revelation of the Koran
from God. These verses are usually believed to have been the
first revelation. He continued to receive revelations during
the rest of his life, and they were memorized by his followers
and are traditionally held to have been collected in writing as
a unified corpus within a generation of his death.

4 Khadija believed in him and accepted as true what
he brought from God, and helped him in his work.
She was the first to believe in God and His Messenger,
and in the truth of his message. By her God lightened
the burden of His prophet. He never met with contradiction and charges of falsehood, which saddened
him, but that God comforted him by her when he
went home. She strengthened him, lightened his burden, proclaimed his truth, and belittled men's opposition. May God Almighty have mercy upon her!

Ibn Ishaq (c.704–767) *The Life of Muhammad* (in the recension of
Ibn Hisham; d.833) (1955 trans.) p.111. Muhammad's first wife,
Khadija (d.619), a widow and wealthy trader, was his first
follower and remained steadfast even when his message
provoked conflict in Mecca, where it disrupted traditional
power structures.

5 When the Quraysh became distressed by the trouble
caused by the enmity between them and the Messenger
and those of their people who accepted his teaching,
they stirred up against him foolish men who called
him a liar, insulted him, and accused him of being a
poet, a sorcerer, a diviner, and of being possessed.
However, the Messenger continued to proclaim what
God had ordered him to proclaim, concealing nothing,
and exciting their dislike by contemning their religion,
forsaking their idols, and leaving them to their
unbelief.

Ibn Ishaq (c.704–767) (1955 trans.) p.130. The Quraysh were
the wealthy tribe of merchants who had dominated Mecca since
at least the 6th century. Muhammad's message threatened their
authority and provoked their persecution of him. He was exiled
in 622 but returned to conquer Mecca in 630.

1 A'isha said: The messenger of God, may God bless him and peace be upon him, died in my house, between dawn and daylight. Gabriel had called to him with a summons when he became ill. I went to him when I was called to him. He raised his eyes to the heavens, and spoke to the heavenly companion [Gabriel]. She said: Abd al-Rahman Ibn Abu Bakr came in, with a fresh date-palm branch in his hand. He looked at it, and I thought that he had need of it. She said: I chewed its head, cleaned it, made it palatable and gave it to him. He cleaned his teeth with it, as well as I had seen him clean his teeth. Then he made to chew it, but it fell from his hand, or his hand dropped it. God joined my saliva and his in the last hour of this world and the first day of the next.

Ibn Sa'd (c.784–845) *Kitab al-Tabaqat al-kabir* (The Large Book of Categories) (1905 edn) Vol.2, p.50. Most traditions about the death of the Prophet place it in May or June 632. Abd al-Rahman was the Prophet's brother-in-law through A'isha, widely supposed to have been his favourite wife.

2 When Abu Bakr was proclaimed caliph, certain Arab tribes apostatized from Islam and withheld the alms-tax. Some of them, however, said, 'We shall observe prayer but not pay the alms-tax.' In reference to that Abu Bakr said, 'If they refuse me a one-year alms-tax, I shall surely fight against them.' According to other reports, he said, 'If they refuse me a two-year alms-tax.'

Al-Baladhuri (d.892) *The Origins of the Islamic State* (1916 trans.) p.143. The death of Muhammad almost resulted in the disintegration of the new community. The first leader of the Muslim community in Medina after Muhammad, Abu Bakr (r.632–634), is credited with re-uniting the wider federation of Muslim tribes. The Muslims' leader came to be known as a 'caliph' – that is, 'deputy' (either of God or of his Prophet).

3 [Muhammad] said, 'He of whom I am the *mawla* [patron], Ali is his *mawla*. O God, be the friend of him who is his friend and be the enemy of his enemy.'

Ibn Hanbal (780–855) *Musnad* (Collection) (1895–6 edn) Vol.4, p.370. This became the proof text for the Shi'a claim that Ali, the Prophet's cousin and son-in-law, was the Prophet's rightful successor, usurped by Abu Bakr, who had become the first caliph after the Prophet's death in 632. The meaning of *mawla* here is obscure: it probably implies the role of patron, lord or protector; it is certainly clear that Muhammad is giving Ali parity with himself in this function, and Ali eventually became the fourth caliph (r.656–660). The claims of his descendants were the foundation of Shi'ism, the roots of which lay in these earliest conflicts about the leadership of the Islamic community.

4 [Ibn Abi Waqqas] met al-Husayn in a place on the Euphrates known as Karbala. Al-Husayn was leading 62 (or 72) men from his family and his companions; Amr ibn Sa'd was leading 4,000. They prevented [Husayn] from getting to water and surrounded him, cutting him off from the Euphrates. He adjured them by God but they refused unless he fought them or surrendered … [Husayn] was standing motionless on his horse … with a son who had been born to him that day … An arrow came, struck the throat of the child and killed him. Al-Husayn pulled the arrow from [the child's] throat and was spattered with his blood … Then he came to them and killed a great number of them but an arrow struck him and hit him between the neck and the chest and exited through the nape of his neck. He fell, and the people rushed in, chopped off his head and sent it to Ubayd Allah Ibn Ziyad.

Al-Ya'qubi (d.897) *Ta'rikh* (History) (1883 edn) Vol.2, pp.289–91. The martyrdom of Husayn Ibn Ali is commemorated annually by Shi'i Muslims. He refused allegiance to the Umayyad caliph, Yazid Ibn Mu'awiya (r.680–683), and Yazid's governor, Ubayd Allah, and was killed with his family at Karbala (Iraq) on 10 Muharram 680 (Day of Atonement). Rebellion in the name of the descendants of Ali was common: Shi'is, Zaydis and Isma'ilis came to recognize different individuals from Ali's descendants as God's rightful representatives on earth.

5 The Commander of the Faithful has seen fit, out of thanks to God for his blessings, to give them pardon, forgive their sins, to encompass all of them in his justice, by which he restrains the ignorant from ignorance, the misguided from error. He makes it known that his station is from God, and asks for His power and assistance, for he is the God-fearing representative [caliph] of God, and the imam who unifies.

Caliph Hisham Ibn Abd al-Malik (r.724–743) to defeated rebels; I. Abbas *'Abd al-Hamid ibn Yahya al-Katib wa-ma tabqa min rasa'ilihi wa-rasa'il Salim Abi al-'Ala'* (Abd al-Hamid ibn Yahya, The Secretary, and what Remains from his Letters and the Letters of Salim Abu al-Ala) (1988) p.318. This letter was sent from the Umayyad caliph, Hisham, to defeated rebels who had supported a rebellion in 739. The rhetoric is that of Umayyad legitimacy: unrelated by blood to the Prophet, they have been chosen by God, and their victories over their enemies testify to their right to the caliphate.

6 Right [to rule] has come back to where it originated, among the people of the house of your Prophet, people of compassion and mercy for you and sympathy toward you. O people! By God we did not rebel seeking this authority to grow rich in silver and gold; nor to dig a canal or build a castle. What made us rebel was the shame of their taking away our rights, our anger for our cousins, our grief for your affairs

and the burden that oppressed us for your sakes ...
Woe, woe to the Banu Harb Ibn Umayya and the
Banu Marwan!

Dawud Ibn Ali, excerpt from sermon on behalf of the first
Abbasid caliph, Abu al-Abbas al-Saffah (r.750–754); al-Tabari
(c.839–923) *The History of al-Tabari* Vol.27 (1985 trans.)
pp.154–5. In 749 a revolution against the ruling Umayyad family
took place. This speech focuses on the resentment of the Iraqi
Muslims against the Syrian domination of the Umayyads. The
new Abbasid dynasty claimed the right to rule on the basis of
their relationship to Muhammad via his uncle, Abbas. They, in
turn, faced opposition from Alids (later, Shi'is), who claimed
that only descendants of Muhammad's daughter, Fatima, could
become caliphs.

1 I went to Abu Hanifa and asked him about some
questions. I went away for some twenty years, then
went back to him, and lo, he had gone back on those
questions. I had given them to people as my juridical
opinions. I told him of this. He said, 'We see one view,
the next day we see another and take it back.'

Abu Hamza al-Sukkari (d.c.784); C. Melchert *The Formation of
the Sunni Schools of Law, 9th–10th Centuries* (1997) p.11. In the
late 8th and early 9th centuries lawyers in the Islamic world
were divided according to whether they were adherents of
tradition or of individual interpretation. By the mid-9th century
the traditionalists had won the struggle: individual reasoning
was not to function without reference to the Hadith reports
attributed to the Prophet and his closest companions.

2 Glory to the Him who made His servant go by
night from the Sacred Temple to the farther Temple
whose surroundings We have blessed, that We might
show him some of Our signs. He alone hears all and
observes all.

Koran *The Night Journey* (1956 trans.) sura 17, verse 1. Sufism
is the ascetic and mystical branch of Islam. It derives its name
from the woollen garments of ascetics and mystics. In the
Mi'raj (Ascent or Night Journey) Muhammad was taken by
Gabriel from Mecca to the Temple Mount in Jerusalem, and
from there up to the seven heavens and the throne of God. It
became a paradigmatic text for Sufis' own mystical journeys.

3 God is light of the heavens and the earth. His light
may be compared to a niche that enshrines a lamp,
the lamp within a crystal of star-like brilliance. It is
lit from a blessed olive tree neither eastern nor western.
Its very oil would almost shine forth, though no fire
touched it. Light upon light; God guides to His light
whom He will. God speaks in metaphors to men.
God has knowledge of all things.

Koran *Light* (1956 trans.) sura 24, verse 35. Koran verses are
incorporated into most Islamic public buildings. The beautiful
brick-patterned, Seljuq-era minaret at Damghan in northern
Iran, which is decorated with blue-glazed tiles and was built
(1031–5) for a congregational mosque, carries the 'lamp verse'.

CALIPHATES AND SULTANATES

4 The Messenger wrote a document concerning the
emigrants [Muhajirun] and the helpers [Ansar] in
which he made a friendly agreement with the Jews
and established them in their religion and their
property, and stated the reciprocal obligations, as
follows: In the name of God, the Compassionate, the
Merciful. This is a document from Muhammad the
Prophet [governing relations] between the believers
and Muslims of Quraysh and Yathrib [Medina] ...
They are one community [*umma*] to the exclusion
of all men ... Each must help the other against anyone who attacks the people of this document.

Constitution of Medina; Ibn Ishaq (c.704–767) (1955 trans.)
pp.231–3. In 622 Muhammad fled from Mecca and set up the
first Muslim community in the nearby town of Yathrib (later
Medina). The so-called 'Constitution of Medina' was a collection
of treaties drawn up between Muhammad, those who had left
Mecca with him (the Muhajirun) and the Ansar (the inhabitants
of Yathrib). Its unusual definition of the community tends
to suggest that it is indeed a very early text, from the years
after 622.

5 When Abu Bakr was done with the case of those
who apostatized, he saw fit to direct his troops against
Syria. To this effect he wrote to the people of Mecca,
al-Ta'if, al-Yaman, and all the Arabs in Najd and the
Hijaz [northeast and west of Medina in Saudi Arabia]
calling them for *jihad* and arousing their desire for it
and for the booty obtainable from the Romans.
Accordingly, people, including those motivated by
greed as well as those motivated by the hope of divine
remuneration, hastened to Abu Bakr from all quarters
and flocked to Medina.

Al-Baladhuri (d.892) (1916 trans.) Vol.1 p.165. The Muslims
had begun to raid outside the Hijaz during the lifetime of
Muhammad. However, the conquest of much of the Roman
empire and all of the Persian empire occurred under the first
caliphs, Abu Bakr (r.632–634) and Umar I (r.634–644). By the
740s the caliphate stretched from the south of France in the
west to western China and northern India in the east.

6 The people of Tustar opposed them fiercely, but
the Basrans and Kufans drove them back until they
reached the gates of Tustar ... Then one of the
Persians asked for safety in exchange for guiding
them to the polytheists' weak spot. He became a
Muslim, stipulating that a stipend be given to his son
and himself ... Abu Musa [the Muslim commander]
... sent with him a man of Shayban named Ashras
Ibn Awf. Together they waded the Tigris on a row of
stones. When they had entered the city in this way,

he pointed out al-Hurmuzan [the commander in Tustar] to Ashras, who sent him back to the camp. Abu Musa sent ahead 40 men with Majza Ibn Thawr and had 200 follow them up. This took place in the night ... They killed the guards and shouted 'God is Great' upon the ramparts of the city.

Al-Baladhuri (d.892) (1916 trans.) Vol.2, p.117. Tustar was a city in Fars (southwest Iran). Besieged by the Muslims of the two newly founded garrison cities of Basra and Kufa (Iraq), it was a well-garrisoned walled city, which could be taken only by betrayal. It fell in the mid-7th century. Persian nobles retained independence on the margins of Iran decades after the fall of the Sasanian king in 658.

I In July of the same year [659–660] the emirs and many Arabs gathered and proffered their right hand to Mu'awiya. Then an order went out that he should be proclaimed king in all the villages and cities of his dominion and that they should make acclamations and invocations to him. He also minted gold and silver, but it was not accepted, because it had no cross on it. Furthermore, Mu'awiya did not wear a crown like other kings in the world. He placed his throne in Damascus and refused to go to Muhammad's throne.

The Anonymous Maronite Chronicle (between 664 and 727); A. Palmer, S. Brock and R. Hoyland *The Seventh Century in the West-Syrian Chronicles* (1993) p.31. Although his father had been an opponent of Muhammad, Mu'awiya I (r.661–680) rose to prominence in the early Muslim community and became caliph after a long civil war. Here, an anonymous Christian, writing in Syriac, recorded his accession. As the first caliph to rule from (post-Roman) Syria, Mu'awiya had appropriated many of the attributes of a Roman emperor.

2 And whosoever is now engaged in warfare [against the Muslims] let him be summoned to Islam before he is engaged in battle; if he accepts Islam, he shall enjoy the privileges of the Muslims and be subject to the duties laid upon them, and he shall retain what he had of family property when he accepted Islam. And if he be of the People of the Book and pay the *jizya* [poll tax] and withhold his hands [from injury to the Muslims], we accept that from him.

Fiscal rescript of Umar II (r.717–720); Ibn Abd al-Hakim (d.829) *Sirat Umar Ibn Abd al-Aziz* (The Life of Umar Ibn Abd al-Aziz) (1959 trans.) p.3. Defeated non-Muslims who were Jewish, Christian or Zoroastrian were allowed to retain their religious beliefs in return for status as 'protected people', who paid more tax.

3 The time for your affair has come, so prepare and make ready. When the year 130 [747–748] comes in, make your summons to the cause public, dye your clothes black, sharpen your weapons. Do not proceed

precipitously to open action before that, unless the situation forces you; then act in defence of yourselves.

Abu Salama (d.750) to the partisans of the Abbasids in Jurjan (northwest Iran); Anon. *Akhbar al-Dawlat al-'Abbasiyya* (Accounts of the Abbasid Revolution) (9th century; 1971 edn) p.267. The Abbasid revolution of 749 was the culmination of decades of clandestine conspiracy against the Umayyads. Hostility to the ruling Syrian regime of the Umayyads was strongest in the east (modern Iraq and Iran). Black was chosen as the colour of the revolutionaries: white and green had been favoured by the Umayyads.

4 The Palace contained, among other things, farms and farmers, private livestock and four hundred baths for its inhabitants and retinues. During the reign of al-Muktafi bi'llah, may the blessings of God be upon him, it had 20,000 household servant-boys and 10,000 servants – blacks and Slavs. It is generally believed that in the days of al-Muqtadir bi'llah, may the blessings of God be upon him, the Palace contained 11,000 servants – 7,000 blacks and 4,000 white Slavs – 4,000 free and slave girls and thousands of chamber servants. Each of the shifts in charge of guarding the Palace consisted of 5,000 bodyguards, 400 sentries and 800 attendants. The city police under Nazuk, the amir in charge of security, consisted of 14,000 horsemen and footmen.

Hilal al-Sabi (969–1056) *The Rules and Regulations of the Abbasid Court* (1977 trans.) pp.13–14. In the 9th century the Abbasid caliphs moved their capital from Baghdad (on the Tigris in modern Iraq) to Samarra (upstream of Baghdad). The huge number of personal slaves and attendants described here, purchased from and captured in Africa and eastern Europe, is no great exaggeration.

5 It has been the tradition for the caliph to sit on an elevated seat on a throne covered with pure Armenian silk, or with silk and wool ... The caliph wears a long-sleeved garment, dyed black; the outer garment is either plain or embroidered with white silk or wool ... He wears a tall, black Persian hat on his head, and adorns himself with the sword of the Prophet, may God bless him. He also keeps another sword on his left between the two cushions of the throne. On his feet he wears red boots; and in front of him he has the Koran of Uthman ... On his shoulders he wears the garment of the Prophet, may God bless him; and in his hand he holds the Prophet's staff. The household servant-boys ... stand, wearing swords, behind and in front of the throne, and in their hands they carry battle-axes and clubs. Slavic servants stand behind the throne and on its sides, chasing flies with gold and silver capped fly-whisks. A brocade curtain is hung in front of the caliph. When the people are admitted to his presence the curtain is lifted; and when he wants to dismiss them the curtain is lowered. Hilal al-Sabi (969–1056) (1977 trans.) pp.73–4. The Abbasid caliph was set apart from his subjects by an elaborate ceremonial in which the vast wealth of the caliphate was displayed. The Koran of Uthman (r.644–656) provided a link with the early caliphs. Likewise, his sword, staff and cloak were said to have belonged to Muhammad himself and so emphasized the Abbasid's claims to be the legitimate rulers of Muhammad's community.

1 The Turks are likewise owners of tent-poles, residents of deserts, and masters of flocks. They are the Bedouins of the non-Arabs … They are not preoccupied by crafts and business, medicine, agriculture, or architecture, nor by planting, building, river irrigation, or collecting crop revenues. They are concerned solely with raid and foray, hunting riding horses, duelling heroes, the search for booty, and subduing countries … That became their craft and their commerce, their pleasure and their pride, their daytime conversation and their evening's entertainment. Al-Jahiz (c.776–c.869) *The Virtues of the Turks* (1988 trans.) p.208. In the 9th century the Abbasids began to recruit Turks from Central Asia into their personal army. They were bought as slaves when they were boys, to ensure complete loyalty.

2   My congratulations, O generous prince, for
          your arrival upon which our epoch smiles
     You have established your camp in a noble
          land, prepared for you by glorious angels.
     The sanctuary and its environs, its lofty shrines
          are exalted
     And in the West is an exalted residence where
          prayer and fasting are accepted:
     It is al-Mahdiyya, sacred and protected, as the
          sacred city is in Tihama.
     Your footsteps make the ground wherever you
          tread like the Maqam Ibrahim
     Just as the pilgrim kissed the [sacred] corner, so
          do we kiss the walls of your palace.
Anon. North African poet, 10th century; P. Sanders *Ritual, Politics and the City in Fatimid Cairo* (1994) p.40. The Fatimid caliphs traced their origins to Ali, the Prophet's cousin, and his wife, Fatima, the Prophet's daughter, and drew their support from a revolutionary mystic movement, the Isma'ilis. In 910 the first Fatimid caliph, Ubayd Allah (r.910–934), was acclaimed caliph in opposition to the Abbasids. This poem commemorates the establishment of his capital, al-Mahdiyya (in modern Tunisia), in 920. The mystic character of Fatimid rule is reflected in the comparison of his palace to the Ka'ba in Mecca.

3 The Buyid family, when … power passed into their hands, imitated the example of the caliphs; nay,

they made it still worse, and their title-giving was nothing but one great lie, when they called their viziers, for example, 'The Most Able of the Able', 'The Single Able One', 'The Only One Amongst the Able'.
     The family of Saman, the rulers of Khurasan, had no desire for such titles, contenting themselves with their agnomens (such as Abu Nasr, Abu al-Hasan, Abu Salih, Abu al-Kasim and Abu al-Harith). Al-Biruni (973–1048) *The Chronology of the Ancient Nations* (1879 trans.) p.131. The mathematician al-Biruni laments the inflated titles handed out by the caliphs and their Buyid sultans. In 945 Ahmad Ibn Buwayh had seized power in Baghdad, leaving the caliph to rule in name only. The caliph also ceded control of the eastern frontier to the Samanids, a noble Persian family, who ruled from 900 to 999.

4   For ever flourishing be Shah Mahmud,
     His head still green, his heart with joy imbued.
     I have so lauded him that publicly
     And privily my words will never die.
Firdawsi *The Shahnama of Firdausi* (1010; 1906 trans.) Vol.9, p.122. In the 11th century the Ghaznavids, a Turkic people from southeastern Afghanistan, eclipsed the Samanids, who had dominated the caliphate in the 10th century. Firdawsi finished his epic poem after the victories of the Ghaznavids and dedicated it to Mahmud of Ghazna (r.998–1030). His use of Persian reflects the Persian renaissance that occurred under the Ghaznavids in the 10th and 11th centuries.

5 The wife of the king of the Turks used to make her husband fear the amir Seljuq ibn Tuqaq and prevented him from trusting him or being at ease with him … One day she said to her husband … 'You will not savour the wine of kingship unless Seljuq is killed' … Thereupon the amir Sejuq went with his horses and soldiers to the land of Islam and was vouchsafed the bliss of the true religion. Choosing the neighbourhood of Jand, he drove out the infidel rulers and established himself there. Amir Seljuq lived for a hundred years. One night in a dream he saw himself ejaculate a fire, the sparks of which reached to the East and to the West. He asked an interpreter of dreams, who said, 'From your seed kings will be born who will rule the farthest ends of the world.' Al-Husayni (fl.c.1180–c.1225) *Akhbar al-dawla al-Saljuqiyya* (Accounts of the Seljuq State); B. Lewis *Islam from the Prophet Muhammad to the Capture of Constantinople* (1974) Vol.1, p.69. The imagery of Seljuq's dream recalls Turkic beliefs in their divine right to rule the whole world. The Seljuq Turks migrated from Central Asia into the Islamic world from the end of the 10th century. Within a few decades they had overwhelmed the caliphate and in 1055 replaced the Buyids as its protectors.

SOCIAL, ECONOMIC AND INTELLECTUAL LIFE

1 'This is the site on which I shall build. Goods can come here via the Tigris, the Euphrates, and various canals. Only a place like this can support both the army and the populace.' He marked the boundaries of the city and calculated the extent of its construction. With his own hand he set the first brick in place while saying the words, 'In the name of God' and 'Praise God' and the 'The earth belongs to God who makes heirs of it those of His servants whom he wishes, and the outcome is to the upright' [Koran 7.128]. He concluded with the statement 'Build, then with God's blessing'.
Al-Tabari (c.839–923) Vol.28 (1995 trans.) p.241. Al-Mansur founded Madinat al-Salam in 762. The name Baghdad belonged to a nearby village. It was a round city with a congregational mosque and the caliph's palace at its centre, surrounded by administrative buildings and the garrisons of the caliph's guards. The area outside the ramparts grew rapidly, becoming a vast, bustling, cosmopolitan city.

2 Know that Baghdad was great in the past but is now falling in ruins. It is full of troubles, and its glory is gone. I neither approve it nor admire it, and if I praise it, it is mere convention. Fustat [part of Cairo] of Egypt is today what Baghdad was in the past, and I do not know of any greater city in all Islam.
Al-Muqaddassi (mid- to late 10th century) Ahsan al-taqalim fi ma'rifat al-aqalim (The Best Divisions for Knowledge of the Regions); Lewis (1974) Vol.2, pp.80–1. Civil wars took their toll on the city of Baghdad. In 969 Cairo became the capital of the rival Fatimid caliphate, but its location between Africa and the Mediterranean had already ensured that it had become a large, thriving, commercial centre.

3 A new school had arisen among these foreign clients of the Arabs, a new group of upstarts emerged, who claim that the foreign convert, by virtue of his clientage, has become an Arab, since the Prophet, may God bless him and grant him peace, said, 'The client of a tribe belongs to it' … We know that when the Kingdom and the Prophethood belonged to non-Arabs, they were nobler than the Arabs. When God transferred these to the Arabs, they in turn became nobler than the non-Arabs … What can be more galling than that your slave should claim to be nobler than you are, while admitting that he became noble because you freed him?
Al-Jahiz (c.776–c.869) Rasa'il (Letters); Lewis (1974) Vol.2., pp.199–201. The tensions provoked by conversion into Islam of non-Arabs in the 8th and 9th centuries are reflected in this epistle on the subject by the thinker al-Jahiz, a champion of the racial superiority of Arabs.

4 Today … they cold-shoulder a free woman [who remarries] after she has already been married to one husband, and attach social disgrace to the man who espouses her as well, and include both him and her in the blame and shame of such conduct. Yet men will take as concubine a slave who has been in the hands of innumerable masters. Who, however, can [reasonably] approve of this in a slave and object to it in a free woman? They are not jealous over slaves (who may become mothers of their children or favourites of monarchs), and yet are jealous over free women!
Al-Jahiz (c.776–c.869) The Epistle on Singing-Girls of Jahiz (1980 trans.) p.22. Most wealthy Muslims owned slaves and concubines. Al-Jahiz satirizes inconsistencies in attitudes to sexual relations with free women and concubines.

5 Ibn Hanbal was a traditionist of the first class, and composed a *masnad* or collection of authenticated traditions more copious than those any other person had till then been able to form; it is said that he knew by heart one million of these traditions … al-Shafi in speaking of him said, 'I went forth from Baghdad and left not behind me a more pious man or a better jurisconsult than Ibn Hanbal.' In the year 220 [835], some time between the 20th and 30th Ramadan, he was required to declare that the Koran was created, but would not, and although beaten and imprisoned, persisted in his refusal.
Ibn Khallikan (1211–82) The Biographical Dictionary of Ibn Khallikan (1842 trans.) Vol.1, p.44. Islamic law was based on traditions about the conduct of Muhammad, collected and organized by men like Ibn Hanbal (780–855), one of the founders of Islamic law. He was imprisoned during the *mihna* (inquisition) of 833–852, but refused to change his beliefs and was instrumental in the Abbasid caliphs' failure to control Islamic orthodoxy.

6 The best of physicians is he who occupies himself and reads and studies constantly in the books of the ancient physicians and especially the books of the Prince of Physicians, Galen, who speaks at great length and deals most thoroughly with the treatment of illnesses … One should therefore busy oneself with the experience of the ancients in the course of millennia, which in the generosity of their hearts and their pity for us they wrote down, preserving their experience for us.
Isaac Israeli (c.855–c.955) Sefer Musar Rof'im; Lewis (1974) Vol.2, pp.183. Many doctors were Jews or Christians. Isaac was the Jewish doctor of the first Fatimid caliph, Ubayd Allah al-Mahdi (r.910–934). Galen (c.129–c.199) was the most important classical influence on Islamic medicine.

1 How beautiful is that which [Aristotle] said in this matter! We ought not to be ashamed of appreciating the truth and of acquiring it wherever it comes from, even if it comes from races distant and nations different from us. For the seeker of truth nothing takes precedence over the truth; and there is no disparagement of the truth, nor belittling of him who utters it or of him who conveys it. [The status of] no one is diminished by the truth; rather does the truth ennoble all.

Al-Kindi (d.c.870) *On First Philosophy*; A.L. Ivry *Al-Kindi's 'On First Philosophy' and Aristotle's 'Metaphysics'* (1975) p.20. Al-Kindi came to be regarded as theologically suspect by other Muslim thinkers because of his excessive respect for 'pagan' philosophy as a route to truth.

2 I read the *Metaphysics* [of Aristotle], but I could not comprehend its contents ... even when I had gone back and re-read it forty times and had got to the point where I had memorized it ... But one day in the afternoon when I was at the booksellers' quarter a salesman approached with a book ... He offered it to me, but I refused with disgust, believing that there was no merit in this science. But he said, 'Buy it, because its owner needs the money and so it is cheap. I will sell it to you for three dirhams [silver coins].' So I bought it and, lo and behold, it was Abu Nasr al-Farabi's book on the objects of the *Metaphysics*. I returned home and was quick to read it, and in no time the objects of that book became clear to me ... I rejoiced at this and the next day gave much alms to the poor in gratitude to God, who is exalted.

Al-Juzjani (11th century) *The Life of Ibn Sina* (1974 trans.) pp.33–5. Ibn Sina (980–1037), the prolific philosopher, scientist and physician, recalls the day when he began to understand Aristotelian metaphysics through the exegesis of al-Farabi (c.878–c.950).

ENCOUNTERS WITH OTHER CULTURES

3 This, therefore, is the whole world, inhabited regions and uncultivated ones. It is divided according to the empires. The pillars of the empires of the world are four. The most prosperous of them, the most plentiful in good things, the best of them in the ordering of its politics, the management of its territories and the abundance of its taxation, is the empire of Iranshahr, of which the centre is the region of Babil, being the empire of Fars [Persia]. The frontiers of this empire were well defined in the time of the Persians, but after the coming of Islam, this empire took from others portions of their territories: from the Roman empire it annexed Syria, Egypt, North Africa and Spain; from the empire of China it took Transoxiana. Subsequently, these important regions made up part of the empire of Iranshahr.

Ibn Hawqal (mid- to late 10th century) *Kitab Surat al-ard* (The Book of the Depiction of the Earth) (1938 edn) Vol.9, p.9. Ibn Hawqal was a merchant, geographer and, perhaps, Isma'ili missionary. Here he describes the world of his own day, looking back to the Arab conquests of the 7th and 8th centuries and beyond into ancient history. The Persian term Iranshahr implies 'the Ancient Persian Empire' (or 'Fars' in Arabic), which included the regions that became the Islamic provinces of Iraq and Iran (roughly modern Iraq and Iran). 'Babil' is the ancient city of Babylon, on the Euphrates in Iraq. It was in ruins in Ibn Hawqal's time but was remembered as the most ancient city in Iraq.

4 There is no god but God alone/and Muhammad OFFA is the Messenger THE KING of God.

Obverse and reverse field inscriptions on a copy of an Islamic coin, minted in England in the name of the Christian Mercian king, Offa (r.757–796; see 161:4), now in the British Museum. OFFA REX (king) is inscribed upside-down in relation to the Arabic script, the English die-engraver who copied it being completely ignorant of the significance of the Arabic. It was copied because of the enormous prestige of Arabic coins in northern Europe, which had arrived there in huge quantities by way of trade with Scandinavia.

5 During the Yung-hui reign period (650–656) of the Great T'ang, the Arabs sent an embassy to the court to present tribute. It is said that their country is west of Persia. Some [also] say that in the beginning there was a Persian who supposedly had the help of a spirit in obtaining edged weapons [with which] he killed people, subsequently calling for all the Persians to become his followers ... After this the masses gradually gave their allegiance, and subsequently Persia was extinguished and Byzantium was crushed, as also were Indian cities; [the Arabs] were everywhere invincible.

Tu Yu *T'ung tien* (768–801); R. Hoyland *Seeing Islam as Others Saw It* (1997) p.245. The Chinese official, Tu Yu, presented his encyclopedic administrative tract, *T'ung tien*, to the throne. It was based on earlier Chinese works.

6 As regards the people of the northern quadrant ... such as the Slavs, the Franks, and those nations that are their neighbours. The power of the sun is weak among them ... cold and damp prevail in the regions, and snow and ice follow one another in endless succession. The warm humour is lacking among them; their bodies are large, their natures gross, their manners harsh, their understanding dull, and their tongues heavy. Their colour is so excessively white that it passes from white to blue; their skin is thin and their flesh thick. Their eyes are also blue, matching the character of their colouring; their hair is lank and reddish because of the prevalence of damp mists. Their religious beliefs lack solidity, and this is because of the nature of cold and the lack of warmth.

Al-Mas'udi (c.896–c.956) *Kitab al-Tanbih wa'l-ishraf* (The Book of Information and Overviews); Lewis (1974) Vol.2, p.122. The Slavs were known to the Arabs as one of the races from which they derived their slaves. The Franks were little known to them before the crusades, although many of the slaves had been captured by the Franks and then sold on, through intermediaries, to the Muslim world.

1 Let the Commander of the Armies – may God help him – give him victory and provide him with assistance, and all the governors of the provinces take good care of the two communities of the Jews who live under the protection of Islam and are encompassed by the rule of justice in the provinces of this kingdom, in such a manner as to turn them away from riots and keep them safely away from undesirable actions ... Let them also give orders to protect them and care for them, and to keep harm and oppression from them ... Written on Wednesday, this eleventh day of Jumada, in the year four-hundred and fifteen [1024].

Decree by the Fatimid caliph al-Zahir (r.1021–36) concerning the Karaite and Rabbinate Jews; from the archives of the Karaite community in the Cairo Geniza (a store of redundant texts) in G. Stern *Fatimid Decrees* (1964 trans.) pp.27–8.

2 Then came one who was nearest related to the dead man. He took a piece of wood and fired it. Then he went backwards towards the ship with his face towards the people and held the torch in one hand ... He was naked. Thus the wood which lay under the ship was fired after they had laid the slave woman whom they had killed by the side of her master. Then people came ... everyone had a piece of burning wood ... The fire took hold of the pyre, then of the ship, then of the tent and of the man and of the girl and of all that was in the ship ... By the side of me stood a man who was of the Rus tribe and I heard him talk with the interpreter who was with him. I asked him what he had said ... 'You Arabs are stupid.' 'Why?' I asked and he answered: 'Well, because you take those who you love and honour the most and put them in the earth and the worms and the earth devour

them. We burn them in the blinking of an eyelid so that he goes to paradise at that very moment.'

Ibn Fadlan (fl. early 10th century); P. Foote and D. Wilson *The Viking Achievement* (1970) p.410–11. Ibn Fadlan wrote a travel narrative about his embassy of 921–922 from the Abbasid caliph al-Muqtadir (r.908–932) to the king of the Bulgars, a recent convert to Islam. This is an excerpt from his extensive description of the funerary rites accorded to a chieftain of the Rus of the Volga basin.

3 In that famous place where once stood the magnificently constructed Temple, near the eastern wall, the Saracens now frequent a rectangular house of prayer which they have built in a crude manner, constructing it from raised planks and large beams over some remains of ruins. This house can, as it is said, accommodate at least 3,000 people.

Arculf in Adomnan *De Locis Sanctis* (Of the Holy Places) (680s); Hoyland (1997) p.221. The Gallic bishop, Arculf, probably made his pilgrimage to the Holy Land in the 670s. He described the mosque on the Temple Mount in Jerusalem, now known as al-Aqsa, which was probably built by the caliph Umar I (r.634–644), who conquered the city.

4   O God, bless your messenger and servant, Jesus son of Mary.
Peace be upon him the day he was born, the day he dies, and the day he is raised again.
Say only the truth about Jesus over whom you dispute: he is the son of Mary!
It is not fitting that God should beget or father a child.
Glory be unto God!

Part of the inscription of the inner arcade of the Dome of the Rock, Jerusalem, 692; S. Nuseibeh and O. Grabar *The Dome of the Rock* (1996) p.108. This inscription indicates that the message of the Dome of the Rock (built on the Temple Mount in Jerusalem) was also aimed at Christians (or at Muslims who needed arguments against Christians), whom the Koran indicated had misunderstood Jesus to be the son of God.

5 We do not say three Gods ... but we say that God and His Word and His Spirit are one God and One Creator ... We do not say that God begat His Word as any man begets – God forbid! Rather we say that the Father begat His Word as the sun begets rays, as the mind begets speech and as the fire begets heat.

Anon. *Fi tathlith Allah al-wahid* (On the Triune Nature of God) (c.788); Hoyland (1997) p.502. This is the earliest Christian apologetic in Arabic to have survived. It is concerned with the most fundamental Muslim objection to Christianity, which appears in the Koran – namely, that God is not three and 'God does not beget and was not begotten'.

1 But the Apostle and the men who shared his faith fought with their goods and with their persons. These shall be rewarded with good things. These shall surely prosper. God has prepared for them Gardens underneath watered by running streams, in which they abide for ever. That is the supreme triumph.

Koran *Repentance* (1956 trans.) sura 9, verses 88–9. *Repentance* is the only sura in the Koran that does not open with the phrase 'In the name of God, the Beneficent, the Merciful'. Verses 88–89 describe the rewards of Paradise for those who wage *jihad* against idolaters.

2 I advise you ten things: do not kill women, children or an aged or infirm person; do not cut down fruit-bearing trees; do not destroy an inhabited place; do not slaughter sheep or camels except for food; do not burn bees and do not scatter them; do not steal from the booty; and do not be cowardly.

Abu Bakr (r.632634) to his commander, Yazid Ibn Abi Sufyan; Malik Ibn Anas (d.796) *Al-Muwatta* (The Prepared Way) (1989 trans.) Ch.21.3.10. This Hadith, attributed not to the Prophet but to the first caliph, became an important tradition in the Islamic law of armed conflict.

3 In the year 283 [896] the presents sent by Amr Ibn al-Laith al-Saffar arrived in Baghdad. Noteworthy among them were a hundred Mehri camels from Khurasan, a great number of dromedaries, many chests of precious materials and 4,000,000 dirhams.

There was also a brass idol representing a woman. She had four arms and was wearing two silver belts embellished with red and white stones. In front of this idol there were other smaller ones, whose arms and faces were decorated with gold and jewels. The idol was placed on a wagon specially fitted out for them, drawn by dromedaries.

All the presents were first taken to Mu'tadid's palace. The brass statue was then sent to the police station in the eastern quarter to be exhibited in public for three days, after which it was taken back to Mu'tadid's palace – this happened on Thursday, 4 Rabi' al-thani of the same year.

The people nicknamed the idol Shugl – 'A Hard Day's Work' – because everyone stopped what they were doing to go and see it during the days it was on view.

Al-Mas'udi (c.896–c.956) *The Meadows of Gold: The Abbasids* (1989 trans.) p.335. The increasingly independent governors of the provinces expressed their loyalty to the caliph by sending gifts from their campaigns back to the capital. In this case it included booty from a 'pagan' shrine.

1,000 Years of Muslim India, c.700–1757

EARLY MUSLIMS IN INDIA, c.700–c.1200

1 The king of the Isle of Rubies [Sri Lanka] sent as a present to Hajjaj certain Muhammadan girls who had been born in his country, the orphan daughters of merchants who had died there. The king hoped by this measure to ingratiate himself with Hajjaj; but the ship in which he had embarked these girls was attacked and taken by some [pirates] … [Hajjaj] then sent an ambassador to Dahir to demand their release, but Dahir [ruler of Sind] replied, 'They are pirates … over them I have no authority.' Afterwards, Hajjaj … appointed Muhammad, son of Kasim, to command on the Sindian frontier.

Al Baladhuri (d.892) *Futuhu-l Buldan* (Conquests of Countries); H.M. Elliot and J. Dowson *The History of India as Told by its own Historians* (1867–77; 2001 edn) Vol.1, pp.118–19. Baladhuri wrote in Baghdad, at the court of al Mutawakkil (r.847–861), a caliph of the Abbasids (749–1258), the second dynasty of Islam (see 132:6). Hajjaj was one of the governors of Iraq during the rule of the early Umayyads (661–750), the Muslim dynasty that ruled from Damascus. Even before the Arab conquest of Sind (the southern province of Pakistan) in 711–713, Arab Muslim traders had settled along the coast of southern India and in Sri Lanka (Ceylon).

2 Be it known to your bright wisdom that, after traversing deserts and making dangerous marches, I arrived in the territory of Sind, on the banks of the … Mihran [River Indus, which flows through Pakistan]. That part of the territory which is opposite the fort of Baghrur [Nirun] on the Mihran is taken … Some of the people have been taken prisoners, and the rest through fear have fled away … It is hoped that with the divine assistance, the royal favour and the good fortune of the exalted prince, the strongest forts of the infidels will be conquered, the cities taken, and our treasuries replenished.

Muhammad Kasim to his cousin, Hajjaj, in Ali Kufi *Chach-nama* (History of Chach) (1216, Persian trans. of anon. Arabic original); Elliot and Dowson (1867–77; 2001 edn) Vol.1, pp.163–4. Little is known of Ali Kufi except that he probably came from Kufa (in Iraq) and settled in Uch (in Sind, Pakistan) in the early 13th century. The *Chach-nama* is the earliest written record of the Muslims in the subcontinent and the best and most detailed account of the early 8th century. Chach was the father of Raja Dahir.

3 When the plunder and the prisoners-of-war were brought before Kasim … it was found that Ladi, the wife of Dahir, was in the fort with two daughters of his by his other wives … Veils were put on their faces, and they were delivered to a servant to keep them apart. One-fifth of all the prisoners were chosen and set aside; they were counted as amounting to twenty thousand in number, and the rest were given to the soldiers.

Ali Kufi (1216); Elliot and Dowson (1867–77; 2001 edn) Vol.1, p.181. The women were considered booty earned in war. Some were sent to the caliph to be sold or granted as rewards.

4 Protection was given to the artificers, the merchants and the common people, and those who had been seized from those classes were all liberated. But he [Kasim] sat on the seat of cruelty, and put all those who had fought to the sword.

Ali Kufi (1216); Elliot and Dowson (1867–77; 2001 edn) Vol.1, p.181. Soldiers who had fought against Kasim, Arab conqueror of Sind, were killed, but all others spared.

5 Muhammad Kasim fixed a tax upon all the subjects, according to the laws of the Prophet. Those who embraced the Muhammadan faith were exempted from slavery, the tribute and the poll tax; and from those who did not change their creed a tax was exacted according to three grades. The first grade was of great men, and each of these has to pay silver, equal to forty-eight *dirams* [silver coins] weight, the second grade twenty-four *dirams*, and the lowest grade twelve *dirams*.

Ali Kufi (1216); Elliot and Dowson (1867–77; 2001 edn) Vol.1, p.182.

6 As they have made submission, and have agreed to pay taxes to the Khalifa [Umayyad caliph al-Walid; r.705–715] nothing more can be properly required from them. They have been taken under our protection, and we cannot in any way stretch out our hands upon their lives or property. Permission is given them to worship their gods. Nobody must be forbidden or prevented from following his own religion. They may live in their houses in whatever manner they like.

Hajjaj to Muhammad Kasim in Ali Kufi (1216); Elliot and Dowson (1867–77; 2001 edn) Vol.1, pp.185–6. Hajjaj is giving instructions about the treatment of inhabitants of Brahmanabad, the capital of southern Sind.

1 All people, the merchants, artists and agriculturists were divided separately into their respective classes … Muhammad Kasim then ordered twelve *dirams* weight of silver to be assigned to each man, because all their property had been plundered … He ordered all the Brahmins [the priestly or highest caste among the Hindus] to be brought before him, and reminded them that they had held great offices in the time of Dahir … As he had entire confidence in their honesty and virtue, he had entrusted them with these offices, and all the affairs of the country would be placed under their charge. These offices were granted to them and their descendants, and would never be resumed or transferred.

Ali Kufi (1216); Elliot and Dowson (1867–77; 2001 edn) Vol.1, p.183.

2 All their [Hindus'] fanaticism is directed against those who do not belong to them – against all foreigners. They call them *mlechha*, i.e., impure, and forbid having any connection with them, be it by intermarriage or any other kind of relationship, or by sitting, eating and drinking with them, because thereby, they think, they would be polluted … By the bye, we must confess, in order to be just, that a similar depreciation of foreigners not only prevails among us and the Hindus, but is common to all nations towards each other.

Alberuni *Kitab-al-Hind* (Book on India) (1030); Edward C. Sachau (trans.) *Alberuni's India* (1888; 2002 edn), p.3. Alberuni, born in the town of Khiva, Uzbekistan, travelled in India in 1017–30. He earned fame as the first Muslim sociologist because of his study of Hindu society.

3 Yamin-addaula Mahmud marched into India … God be merciful to both father and son! – Mahmud utterly ruined the prosperity of the country, and performed there wonderful exploits, by which the Hindus became like atoms of dust scattered in all directions, and like a tale of old in the mouth of the people. Their scattered remains cherish, of course, the most inveterate aversion towards all Muslims. This is the reason, too, why Hindu sciences [such as astronomy, astrology and medicine] have retired far away from those parts of the country conquered by us, and have fled to places where our hand cannot yet reach, to Kashmir [state in northern India], Benares [Varanasi, holiest city of the Hindus in Uttar Pradesh] and other places.

Alberuni (1030; 2002 edn) p.6. Mahmud, son of Sabuktigin and ruler of Ghazni in Afghanistan, made several raids into India. His entourage included Alberuni.

4 According to their [Hindus'] belief, there is no country on earth but theirs, no other race of man but theirs, and no created beings beside them have any knowledge or science whatsoever. Their haughtiness is such that, if you tell them of any science or scholar in Khorasan or Persis [provinces in Iran], they will think you to be both an ignoramus and a liar. If they travelled and mixed with other nations, they would soon change their mind, for their ancestors were not as narrow-minded as the present generation is.

Alberuni (1030; 2002 edn) p.6.

5 This is what educated people [among Hindus] believe about God. They call him *isvara*, i.e. self-sufficing, beneficent, who gives without receiving. They consider the unity of God as absolute, but that everything beside God which may appear as a unity is really a plurality of things … If we now pass to those [ideas] of the common people, we must first state that they present a great variety. Some of them are simply abominable, but similar errors also occur in other religions … Nay, even in Islam we must decidedly disapprove, e.g. of … the prohibition of the discussion of religious topics, and such like.

Alberuni (1030; 2002 edn) p.15.

6 If a wife loses her husband by death, she cannot marry another man. She has only to choose between two things – either to remain a widow as long as she lives or to burn herself; and the latter eventuality is considered the preferable, because as a widow she is ill-treated as long as she lives. As regards the wives of kings, they [Hindus] are in the habit of burning them, whether they wish it or not, by which they desire to prevent any of them by chance committing something unworthy of the illustrious husband. They make an exception only for women of advanced years and for those who have children; for the son is the responsible protector of his mother.

Alberuni (1030; 2002 edn) p.563. The practice of suttee.

EARLY MUSLIM RULE: THE DELHI SULTANATE, 1206–1526

7 [Iltutmish's] brothers began to grow envious … They therefore brought him away from his mother and father and they sold him to certain merchants; the merchants brought him towards Bukhara [in Uzbekistan] and sold him to one of the kinsmen of the [chief ecclesiastic] of Bukhara … From that priestly and saintly family a merchant purchased [him].

Subsequently, another merchant purchased him and brought him to the city of Ghazni [in Afghanistan] … Malik Kutb-ud din [Sultan Aibak; r.1206–10] purchased [him] and … discerning within him proofs of rectitude and integrity advanced him from one position to another …

When Sultan Aibak died, [the commander of troops] besought [Iltutmish to come and assume authority] … Having come, he ascended the throne of the kingdom of Delhi.

Minhaj us Siraj *Tabaqat-i-Nasiri* (History of the Muslim Dynasties of Asia Dedicated to Sultan Nasiruddin Mahmud) (1260; 1995 edn) Vol.I pp.599–606. Minhaj came from Ghor to Sind, where he held high ecclesiastical and judicial offices. His history, which was not published until 1881, is the most important source for the early slave period in India. This is an account of how Iltutmish (d.c.1236) rose from slave to sultan. Minhaj's patron and dedicatee, Nasiruddin Mahmud (r.1246–66), was one of Iltutmish's sons and successors.

1 Sultan Raziyyat [Raziya] … was a great sovereign … and was endowed with all the admirable attributes and qualifications necessary for kings; but as she did not attain the destiny, in her creation, of being computed among men, of what advantage were all these excellent qualities to her?

… [On becoming sultan she] laid aside the female dress and issued from [her] seclusion, and donned the tunic, and assumed the head-dress of a man, and appeared among the people; and, when she rode out on an elephant … all people used, openly, to see her.

Minhaj us Siraj (1260; 1995 edn) Vol.I, pp.637–8, 643. Raziya, the daughter of Iltutmish, was the only woman ruler in the history of Muslim India. Her reign (1236–40) was brought to an end by violent factionalism among the nobles.

2 The desire for overthrowing infidels and knocking down idolaters and polytheists does not fill the hearts of the Muslim kings [of India]. On the other hand, out of consideration for the fact that infidels and polytheists are payers of tribute and protected persons [*zimmis*], these infidels are honoured, distinguished, favoured and made eminent; the kings bestow drums, banners, ornaments, cloaks of brocade and caparisoned horses upon them, and appoint them to governorships, high posts and offices.

Zia-ud-Din Barani (1282–1358) *Fatwa i-Jahandari* (Advice on Governance); Samina Rahman (ed.) *Pre-Mughal India: A Book of Readings from Contemporary Sources* (1987) pp.159–60. Barani belonged to a distinguished immigrant family of high officials. From his criticism of tolerant Muslim kings, it is evident that,

for reasons of statecraft, Hindus were allowed freedom to worship and much more: freedoms Barani thoroughly disapproved of.

3 The *jizya*, or poll tax, had never been levied from Brahmins; they had all been excused in former reigns. The sultan convened a meeting of the learned men and suggested to them that an error had been made in holding Brahmins exempt from the tax. The learned lawyers gave it as their opinion that the Brahmins ought to be taxed. They [Brahmins] were determined to burn themselves rather than pay the tax. The Hindus told the Brahmins that it was not right to kill themselves on account of the *jizya*, and that they would undertake to pay it for them.

Shams-i-Siraj Afif *Tarikh i-Firoz Shahi* (History of the Reign of Firoz Shah) (c.1400); Elliott and Dowson (1867–77; 2001 edn) Vol.3, pp.355–6. Afif was a courtier in the reign of Sultan Firoz Shah Tughluq (r.1351–88). The Brahmins got preferential treatment compared with the rest of the Hindus and enjoyed a privileged position within the Hindu community. The dissension ends with a compromise: the sultan relents and agrees that of the three rates of tax that were levied in Delhi, the Brahmins would have to pay only a fraction above the lowest.

4 The inhabitants of the Maldives [islands southwest of Sri Lanka] are all Muslims, pious and upright … their bodies are weak, they are unused to fighting, and their armour is prayer … They are very cleanly and avoid filth … Their garments are simply aprons; one they tie around their waists in place of trousers, and on their backs they place other cloths … Most of [their womenfolk] wear only an apron from their waists to the ground, the rest of their bodies being uncovered. When I held the *qadi*-ship [*qadi* = judge] there, I tried to put an end to this practice and ordered them to wear clothes, but I met with no success.

Ibn Battuta (1304–68) *The Travels of Ibn Battuta* (1929 trans.) pp.242–4. Muhammad Ibn Battuta was a Moroccan Muslim theologian, who set out for India to seek his fortune, and his accounts of his travels are one of the best sources of 14th-century history. In Delhi the sultan first gave him a judicial appointment and in 1342 appointed him as the head of a mission to the imperial court in China, where he served for 18 months, again as a *qadi*.

5 I set out again, and we spent 43 nights at sea, arriving eventually at the land of Bangala [Bengal]. This is a vast country, abounding in rice, and nowhere in the world have I seen any land where prices are lower than there; on the other hand it is a gloomy place, and the people of Khorasan [province in Iran] call it 'A hell full of good things'.

Ibn Battuta (1304–68) (1929 trans.) p.267. After reaching the Maldives Ibn Battuta decided to sail for China in earnest, but on the way he went to Bengal to visit a *shaykh* (Islamic mystic) in Assam, northeast Bengal. The Khorasanian pronouncement about Bengal still holds good!

THE EARLY MUGHAL RULERS: BABUR AND HUMAYUN, 1526–55

1 Up to the time that I conquered Hindustan [India, in 1526], five Muslim *padishahs* [kings] and two infidels had ruled there. Although the mountains and jungles are held by many petty *rays* and *rajahs* [Hindu kings], the important and independent rulers were the following five:

… the Afghans, who took the capital Delhi, and held … Bhera [in Punjab, Pakistan] to Bihar [in eastern India]. The second was Sultan Muzaffar in Gujarat [western India] … Third were the Bahmanids in the Deccan [southern India] … Fourth was Sultan Mahmud in the province of Malwa [in central India]. Fifth was Nusrat Shah in Bengal.

Babur *The Babur-nama, Memoirs of Babur, Prince and Emperor* (1508–29; 1996 trans.) pp.330–31. Descended from Genghis Khan and Timur (see 257:1) and ruler of Fergana in Uzbekistan. Babur was the founder of the Mughal dynasty in India (1526–1858).

2 Hindustan is a place of little charm. There is no beauty in its people, no graceful social intercourse, no poetic talent or understanding, no etiquette, nobility or manliness. The arts and crafts have no harmony or symmetry. There are no good horses, meat, grapes, melons or other fruit. There is no ice, cold water, good food or bread in the markets. There are no baths and no madrasas [Islamic schools]. There are no candles, torches or candlesticks … The one nice aspect of Hindustan is that it is a large country with lots of gold and money … Another nice thing is the unlimited numbers of craftsmen and practitioners of every trade.

Babur (1508–29; 1996 trans.) pp.350–51.

3 I gave reality to the inner calling to refrain from wine … and totally renounced the drinking of intoxicants … Upon the completion of this intention … a decree obeyed by all the world was issued to the effect that within the protected realm absolutely no creature would commit the sin of imbibing intoxicants or endeavour to acquire, produce, sell, purchase, possess or transport the same.

Babur (1508–29; 1996 trans.) pp.375–6. Drinking wine or any alcohol is prohibited by Islam. The decree was issued in 1526–7 and was effective over much of northern India, stretching from Kabul (in Afghanistan) in the west to Bihar (in eastern India).

4 His majesty [Emperor Humayun] had a certain servant, a water-carrier. As he [the emperor] had been parted from his horse in the river at Chausa [Bihar] and this servant betook himself to his help and got him safe and sound out of the current, his majesty now seated him on the throne … and ordered all the emirs [high officials] to make obeisance to him. The servant gave everyone what he wished and made appointments. For as much as two days the emperor gave royal power to that menial.

Gulbadan Begum *Humayun-nama* (The History of Humayun) (from c.1587; 1989 edn) p.140. Humayun, son of Babur, reigned 1530–40 and again 1555–6. Gulbadan, his sister, wrote this history at the request of Emperor Akbar (r.1556–1605), his successor.

5 For forty days the begum [lady] resisted and discussed and disagreed. At last her highness my mother … advised her, saying: 'After all you will marry someone. Better than a king who is there?' The begum said: 'Oh yes, I shall marry someone; but he shall be a man whose collar my hand can touch, and not one whose skirt it does not reach.' Then my mother again gave her much advice.

At last after forty days' (discussion), at midday … (September, 1541), his majesty took the astrolabe into his own blessed hand and, having chosen a propitious hour summoned (an officer) to make fast the marriage bond.

Gulbadan Begum (from c.1587; 1989 edn) p.151. The story relates Humayun's wooing of Hamida Banu, Emperor Akbar's mother. She is said to have been 14 years old at the time; he was 33 and already had a number of other wives.

6 They were all night in the snow, and (at first) there was neither wood for fire nor food to eat. They grew very hungry and feeble. The Emperor gave orders to kill a horse. There was no cooking pot, so they boiled some of the flesh in a helmet, and some they roasted. They made fires on all four sides, and with his own blessed hand the Emperor roasted some meat which he ate.

Gulbadan Begum (from c.1587; 1989 edn) pp.166–7. Emperor Humayun fled from India to Persia, pursued by his brothers and Sher Shah Afghan, all contenders for the throne.

THE GREAT MUGHALS:
AKBAR, 1556–1605

1 Himun ... was sounding the trumpet of pride in Delhi, and had given himself the title of Raja Bikramajit [Invincible King] ...

In the early morning of Friday [5 Nov. 1556] the news of his approach was received from the scouts; and the powerful *amirs* [commanders] put the troops in line of battle, and devoted their energy to the destruction of the enemy ... Himun, with his elephants, repeatedly threw himself on the imperial army ... By chance an arrow struck Himun in the eye, and passed through the back of his head. ... The next day, the victorious standards started from Panipat [north of Delhi]; and did not halt anywhere between that place and Delhi. Crowds of the great and common people ... of [Delhi] hastened to welcome them; and carried out the ceremonies of making offerings and sacrifices.

Khwaja Nizamuddin Ahmad *The Tabaqat-i-Akbari* (A History of India from the Early Musalman Invasions to the Thirty-eighth Year of the Reign of Akbar) (1593–4; 1996 edn) Vol.2, pp.217–21. The author of this important source book was an experienced Mughal administrator. The Battle of Panipat and the defeat of Himun (also spelled Himu, Hemu) during the first year of Akbar's reign is described here. From humble beginnings Himun (a Hindu) had risen to become the chief minister of Adil Shah, one of the Afghan claimants to the throne of Delhi, and later set himself up independently. He occupied Delhi when Akbar, who had just been crowned king, was still in the Punjab. At Akbar's death the whole of north India, from Kabul to Bengal and parts of the Deccan, had been brought under Mughal rule.

2 His majesty [Akbar] forms matrimonial alliances with princes of Hindustan and of other countries; and secures by these ties of harmony the peace of the world.

Abul Fazl *Ain-i-Akbari* (Regulations of Akbar) (c.1590; 1993 edn) Vol.1, p.45. Abul Fazl was Akbar's court historian. Although earlier Muslim rulers had married Hindus, Akbar made alliances for reconciliation and allowed his wives to practise Hindu rites in the harem.

3 In the course of twenty-four hours his Majesty eats but once and leaves off before he is fully satisfied; neither is there any fixed time for his meal, but the servants have always things so far ready, that in the space of an hour, after the order has been given, a hundred dishes are served up.

Abul Fazl (c.1590; 1993 edn) Vol.1, p.59. Abul Fazl then relates how the emperor cared very little for meat.

4 His Majesty looks upon fruits as one of the greatest gifts of the Creator, and pays much attention to them. The horticulturists of Iran and Turan [Transoxiana, Central Asia] have, therefore, settled there, and the cultivation of trees is in a flourishing state. Melons and grapes have become very plentiful and excellent; and water-melons, peaches, almonds, pistachios, pomegranates etc. are everywhere to be found.

Abul Fazl (c.1590; 1993 edn) Vol.1, p.68.

5 Bigoted followers of the letter of the law are hostile to the art of painting; but their eyes now see the truth. One day, his majesty ... remarked: 'There are many that hate painting; but such men I dislike ... a painter had quite peculiar means of recognizing God ... in sketching anything that has life ... [he] must come to feel that he cannot bestow individuality upon his work and is thus forced to think of God, the giver of life, and will thus increase in knowledge.'

Abul Fazl (c.1590; 1993 edn) Vol.1, p.115. The Muslim aversion to figural painting originates in the Islamic tradition forbidding figural art, which is regarded as an act that challenges the creative power of God and is, therefore, blasphemous.

6 His majesty plans splendid edifices ... Thus mighty fortresses have been raised, which protect the timid, frighten the rebellious and please the obedient ... They afford excellent protection against cold and rain, provide for the comforts of the princesses of the harem and are conducive to that dignity which is so necessary for worldly power.

Abul Fazl (c.1590; 1993 edn) Vol.1, p.232.

7 From reasons of auspiciousness, and as an opportunity of bestowing presents upon the poor, his majesty is weighed twice a year. Various articles are put into the scales.

Abul Fazl (c.1590; 1993 edn) Vol.1, p.276. The weighing was against precious articles, such as gold and silver as well as grains, which were used to balance the scales and later distributed to the poor. An old Hindu custom, this ceremony was introduced to the Mughals by Akbar.

8 The Shahinshah's [emperor's] court became the home of the inquirers of the seven climes, and the assemblage of the wise of every religion and sect ... The bigoted Ulama [religious scholars in Islam] and the routine lawyers, who reckoned themselves among the chiefs of philosophies and leaders of enlightenment, found their position difficult. The veil was removed from the face of many of them.

Abul Fazl *The Akbar-nama* (History of Akbar) (c.1590; 1989 edn) Vol.3, p.366. Discussions on different religions were held every Thursday night in the Ibadat-Khana (House of Prayer) in Akbar's new capital of Fatehpur Sikri (near Delhi).

1 Every year, a number of men of enlightened minds from Hindustan ... received provisions and the expenses for the journey, from the public treasury, and went with the Mir Haj [superintendent of pilgrims to the annual Haj in Mecca] ... and reached the sacred land. Up to the time of the rising of the sun of this sovereign, no other monarch had attained to such an honour and grandeur that he should send a caravan from Hindustan to Mecca the revered, and should remove the custom of need from the poor of that honoured place.

Khwaja Nizamuddin Ahmad *The Tabaqat-i-Akbari* (A History of India from the Early Musalman Invasions to the Thirty-eighth Year of the Reign of Akbar) (1593–4; 1996 edn) Vol.2, p.472.

2 Although he [Akbar] was illiterate, he had sat so much with sages and learned men in discussions that no one could guess from his appearance that he was illiterate. He comprehended the subtleties of prose and poetry so well that it is impossible to imagine any better.

Jahangir *The Jahangir-nama, Memoirs of Jahangir, Emperor of India* (1605–24; 1999 trans.) p.36. Emperor Jahangir is here describing his late father.

THE GREAT MUGHALS: JAHANGIR, 1605–24

3 Sultan Khurram [later Emperor Shahjahan] was born of Jagat Gosain, the daughter of Mota Raja [Raja Udai Singh Rathor of Marwar], in [1592] the thirty-sixth year of the royal accession of my father [Emperor Akbar] ... in Lahore ... As his years progressed real potential was noticed of him. He served my exalted father more and better than any of my sons, and my father was very pleased with him and his service.

Jahangir (1605–24; 1999 trans.) p.30.

4 One year before becoming emperor I had decided that on Friday [the Muslim sabbath] eves I would not commit the sin of drinking wine. I hope that as long as I live the divine court will grant me constancy in this decision.

Jahangir (1605–24; 1999 trans.) p.30. Drinking was a passion for the emperor and took its toll on his health.

5 Towards the end of my exalted father's reign ... because of the corruption of mischief-makers, [his] mind was quite turned against me, and it was certain that if [Abul Fazl, the author of *Akbar-nama*] succeeded in reaching him he would create more discord. It was therefore absolutely necessary that he be prevented from reaching him.

Jahangir (1605–24; 1999 trans.) p.32. Jahangir had Abul Fazl ambushed and killed, and he admits that although this caused distress to his father, gradually the bad blood subsided between them. Abul Fazl was one of Akbar's favourite courtiers and a successful general. He was known to be hostile to Prince Salim (Jahangir), the emperor's eldest son and the second most powerful man in the empire, whom he considered to be debauched and unreliable.

6 It has long been the custom among the ... people to make eunuchs of some of their sons and give them in lieu of taxes to the rulers ... Every year many children are ruined and castrated as the custom has gained great currency ... I ordered that henceforth no one was to do this hideous thing and that the buying and selling of eunuchs of tender years should be completely abolished.

Jahangir (1605–24; 1999 trans.) p.98.

7 I set out with the ladies of the harem to hunt [lions]. When the lions came into view, Nurjahan Begum [the queen] ... hit two of them with one shot each and the other two with two shots, and in the twinkling of an eye the four lions were deprived of life with six shots. Until now such marksmanship had not been seen – from atop an elephant and from inside a howdah she had fired six shots, not one of which missed. As a reward for such marksmanship I scattered a thousand *ashrafis* [gold coins] over her head, and gave her a pair of pearls and a diamond worth a *lac* [100,000] of rupees.

Jahangir (1605–24; 1999 trans.) p.219. A very accomplished woman, Nurjahan wielded enormous power during her husband's reign. The gold coins would be given away as charity to the poor.

8 I [Emperor Jahangir] derive such enjoyment from painting and have such expertise in judging it, that even without the artist's name being mentioned ... I ... instantly recognize who did it. If in a single painting different persons have done the eyes and eyebrows, I can determine who drew the face and who made the eyes and eyebrows.

Jahangir (1605–24; 1999 trans.) p.268. The era was known for the great development of painting.

1 [Inayat Khan] was one of my closest servants and subjects. He became obsessed with wine ... and was afflicted with diarrhoea ... He looked incredibly weak and thin ... Even his bones had begun to disintegrate ... It was so strange I ordered the artists to draw his likeness ... I gave him a thousand rupees for travelling expenses and gave him leave to depart [for Agra, southeast of Delhi]. He died the second day.

Jahangir (1605–24; 1999 trans.) pp.280–81. The painting *The Dying Inayat Khan* is in the Museum of Fine Arts, Boston (no.14.679).

2 I was shown a wild ass. It was extremely strange, for it was for all the world exactly like a tiger. Tigers have black and yellow stripes, but this one was black and white ... It was so strange some thought it might have been painted, but after inspection it was clear that that was how God had made it.

Jahangir (1605–24; 1999 trans.) p.360. The animal described is a zebra, and the artist Mansur was commissioned to paint a picture of it. It is now in the Victoria and Albert Museum, London (IM 23–1925). Jahangir was almost a naturalist in his keen observations of life.

THE GREAT MUGHALS: SHAHJAHAN, 1628–57

3 [In] 1631 died Nawab Aliya Begum [known as Mumtaz Mahal, Shahjahan's queen over whose grave the emperor built the Taj Mahal, Agra], in the fortieth year of her age, to the great grief of her husband the emperor. She had borne him eight sons and six daughters.

Abdul Hamid Lahori (d.1654) *Badshah-nama* (History of Kings); Elliot and Dowson (1867–77; 2001 edn) Vol.7, p.27. Little is known of the author of this chronicle except that he was summoned from Patna (in Bihar) and recommended to Shahjahan who was looking for an author to write the memoirs of his reign in the style of Abul Fazl's *Akbar-nama* (History of Akbar). The *Badshah-nama*, a history of the first 20 years of the reign of Shahjahan, is considered one of the best authorities of his reign. Mumtaz, who died in childbirth, was the mother of Aurangzeb, the next emperor.

4 Under the rule of the Bengalis a party of Frank merchants came trading to Satganw [Satgaon, a port

in southwest Bengal]. One *kos* [about 2¼ miles] above that place, they occupied some ground on the bank of the estuary ... through the ignorance and negligence of the rulers of Bengal, these Europeans increased in number and erected large substantial buildings, which they fortified with cannons, muskets and other implements of war ... A considerable place grew up ... known [as] the Port of Hugli ... Some of the inhabitants by force, and more by hopes of gain, they infected with their Nazarene teaching, and sent them off in ships to Europe.

Abdul Hamid Lahori (d.1654); Elliot and Dowson (1867–77; 2001 edn) Vol.7, pp.31–2. This is the background to the events of 1632, when Emperor Shahjahan instructed the governor of Bengal to take possession of Hugli and crush the Portuguese power there.

5 There was to be given to [Be-Badal Khan, the superintendent of the goldsmith's department] ... one *lac* of *tolas* [about 2,900lb] of pure gold. The throne was to be three *gaz* [about 3 yards] in length, two and a half in breadth and five in height ... The outside of the canopy was to be of enamel work with occasional gems, the inside was to be thickly set with rubies, garnets and other jewels, and it was to be supported by twelve emerald columns ... This throne was completed in the course of seven years at a cost of 100 *lacs* of rupees.

Abdul Hamid Lahori (d.1654); Elliot and Dowson (1867–77; 2001 edn) Vol.7, pp.45–6. The peacock throne, created for Shahjahan, was carried away to Iran by Nadir Shah in 1739.

6 As such a valuable diamond as this [of 100 *ratis* i.e., 60 carats, from Golconda] had never been brought to the [royal] threshold since his accession to the throne ... the pious monarch ... made a vow to send it to the pure sepulchre of the last of the Prophets.

Abdul Hamid Lahori (d.1654); Elliot and Dowson (1867–77; 2001 edn) Vol.7, p.84. Sending gifts to the Prophet Muhammad's tomb in Medina (in Saudi Arabia) was regarded as a pious act.

7 The means employed by the king [Shahjahan] in these happy times to protect and nourish his people ... his administration of the country, and calling for and examining annual statements of revenue ... all these contributed in a great measure to advance the prosperity of his empire. The *pargana* [district], the income of which was three *lacs* of rupees in the reign of Akbar, yielded in this happy reign, a revenue of ten *lacs*.

Rai Bhara Mal *Lubbu-t Tawirikh-I Hind* (Best of Indian Histories) (c.1690); Elliot and Dowson (1867–77; 2001 edn) Vol.7, p.171. The author was a revenue officer of Prince Dara Shukoh, son of Shahjahan.

THE GREAT MUGHALS: AURANGZEB, 1658–1707

1 The emperor … is remarkable for his rigid attachment to religion … From his great piety, he passes whole nights in the mosque which is in his palace, and keeps company with men of devotion. In privacy he never sits on a throne … He has learnt the Koran [the holiest book in Islam, believed to be divinely revealed to the Prophet Muhammad] by heart. He has written two copies of the holy book with his own hand … and sent them to the holy cities of Mecca and Medina.

Bakhtawar Khan (d.1684) *Mirat-i Alam* (Universal History); Elliot and Dowson (1867–77; 2001 edn) Vol.7, pp.157, 162. The author was a favourite officer of Emperor Aurangzeb, and his work is considered a useful and comprehensive account of his reign. Aurangzeb ascended the throne after a fierce struggle with his brothers and the imprisonment of his father, the old emperor.

2 Id-ul-fitr [Muslim day of celebration after the month-long fasting of Ramadan] … [1674] … Promotions and gifts bestowed on [princes and peers] … Prince Muhammad Mu'azzam [Aurangzeb's son] was given a robe, a pearl necklace … A special robe, a jewelled dagger and a gracious *farman* [letter] were sent to Rana Raj Singh and a special robe to Maharaja Jaswant.

Saqi Must'ad Khan *Maasir-i-Alamgiri* (A History of the Emperor Aurangzeb-Alamgir) (1710; 1990 edn) p.86. Gifts were bestowed on all who were loyal, regardless of whether they were Muslim or, as in the case of the last two mentioned, Hindu. The author, another high official in the imperial service, was a ward of Bakhtawar Khan, whom he assisted in the composition of *Mirat-i Alam*.

3 The residence of the [Mughal] governor [of Bengal, residing in Dhaka, now Bangladesh] is an enclosure of high walls, in the middle of which is a poor house merely built of wood. He ordinarily resides under tents, which he pitches in a large court in this enclosure. The Dutch … have built a very fine house, and the English have also got one which is fairly good. The church of the Rev. Augustin Fathers is all of brick, and the workmanship of it is rather beautiful.

Jean-Baptiste Tavernier *Travels in India* (1676; 1989 edn) Vol.1, p.104. Tavernier was a French traveller and trader in jewels. He describes a visit to Bengal in Jan. 1666, by which time the Europeans already seem to be well established.

4 The princesses, whether they are the emperor's [Aurangzeb's] wives, his daughters or his sisters, never leave the palace except when they go to the country for a few days' change of air and scene. Some of them go, but rarely, to visit the ladies of the nobles … [They] generally go out at nine o'clock in the morning, and have only three or four eunuchs to accompany them, and ten or twelve female slaves who act as ladies of honour. The princesses are carried in pallankeens [palanquins] followed by a small carriage … When the princesses arrive at the houses … [the men who carry the] pallankeens are allowed to go only to the first gate; the princesses then change into the carriages, and are drawn by the ladies of honour to the women's apartments.

Jean-Baptiste Tavernier (1676; 1989 edn) Vol.1, pp.312–13. The visitor describes the segregated lives led by the royal women.

5 Aurangzeb … ordered that all Christians, excepting physicians and surgeons, should leave the city and remove to … beyond the suburbs at one league's distance from the city. There they had leave to prepare and drink spirits on condition they did not sell them.

After the issue of this order he directed the *kotwal* [chief of police] to search Mahomedans and Hindus who sold spirits, everyone of whom was to lose one hand and one foot … and during the period of strictness the nobles, who found it hard to live without spirits, distilled in their houses, there being few who do not drink secretly.

Niccolao Manucci *Storia do Mogor or Mogul India* (1705; 1981 edn) Vol.2, p.3. Manucci was a Venetian who reached India in 1639, when he was 16 years old, and who died in Madras in 1717. Aurangzeb tried to enforce the Islamic prohibition on wine. Christian physicians and surgeons were allowed to remain in the city because their professional services were valued.

6 [The Portuguese] soldiers [in Goa] were the perpetrators of much oppression. When I was present at the house of the lord archbishop, there came a woman there and cried aloud for help, because a soldier had carried off from her house a maiden daughter … The archbishop, sent word for the woman to go to a public scribe and reduce her petition to writing … On perusing this, he would dispose of the case. The woman went home weeping. I was amazed to see such inattention, and I was revolted.

Niccolao Manucci (1705; 1981 edn) Vol.3, p.156. Goa, on the western coast of India, was a Portuguese possession (see 318:1).

1 The great age of the emperor, who is more than eighty-six years old, and the ambition to gain the throne continuously displayed by his sons and grandsons, give rise to the apprehension of some catastrophe quite as tragic as that supervening at the close of Shahjahan's reign.

Niccolao Manucci (1705; 1981 edn) Vol.3, p.237. See 146:3.

2 The power of the Mahrattas [Marathas] increased day by day. They penetrated into the old territories of the imperial throne [of the Mughals], plundering and destroying wherever they went. Their daring went beyond all bounds. They divided all the districts among themselves, and following the practice of the imperial rule, they appointed their provincial governors, revenue collectors and toll collectors.

Muhammad Hashim Khafi Khan *Muntakhab-ul Lubab* (Selections of the Best) (c.1732); Elliot and Dowson (1867–77; 2001 edn) Vol.7, p.374. Khafi Khan, who was in Aurangzeb's service, wrote during the period of confusion following the emperor's death in 1707, through the short reigns of nine of his successors and until the 14th year of the reign of Muhammad Shah (r.1719–48), the first emperor after Aurangzeb to rule for any appreciable length of time. This passage refers to how the ageing Emperor Aurangzeb was fast losing control over his vast territories. After him the empire began to disintegrate. The Marathas consisted of the many Hindu clans in the Deccan, the triangular plateau in southern India that had withstood many invaders.

THE BREAK-UP OF THE MUGHAL EMPIRE, 1719–57

3 The rumour of the instability of the royal house of Hind, having reached the lords and commons of all quarters of the globe, Nadir [Shah] of Isfahan [capital of Persia] invaded it with his troops resembling the waves of the sea, and put all the natives of the provinces of Kabul [in Afghanistan], the Punjab [the Indus Valley] and Delhi at once to the sword.

Muhammad Muhsin Sadiki *Jauhar-I Samsam* (Jewel of Samsam) (c.1739); Elliot and Dowson (1867–77; 2001 edn) Vol.8, p.74. The work is named after Samsamu-d daula, commander-in-chief of the emperor, Muhammad Shah, and this excerpt refers to the invasion of India in 1738 by Nadir Shah, ruler of Iran. Nadir's haul from India was so big that all taxes in Persia were remitted for the next three years.

4 (15 April, 1748) the Emperor breathed his last. Those who were present … were of [the] opinion that the wisest course to pursue would be to conceal from the public the news of the emperor's death till the arrival of the Prince [the future emperor, Ahmad Shah] … [They] then put the corpse into the wooden case of a European clock, which was very long … and for a shroud they procured a cloth from the *darogha* [superintendent] of the kitchen, pretending it was required for the dinner table. They buried him in the garden.

Anon. *Tarikh-I Ahmad Shah* (History of Ahmad Shah) (c.1754); Elliot and Dowson (1867–77; 2001 edn) Vol.8, p.111. Muhammad Shah's death was kept secret to avoid confusion. It is ironic that the great Mughal emperor had a tablecloth shroud and a clock-box coffin.

5 At this time, in consequence of the weakness of … Muhammad Shah, and the want of unanimity among his nobles, the armies of the Mahrattas [Marathas] of the south had spread themselves over Bengal … The city of Calcutta [in the present state of West Bengal, India] … inhabited by a tribe of English who have settled there, is … extensive and thickly populated … All the different tribes of Europeans have got different names, such as Fransis [French], Angrez [English], Walandiz [Dutch] and Partagis [Portuguese] … Many tradesmen and professors of different arts have come from Europe and taken up their abode here … carrying on their trade as they do in their own land. A great many of the Bengalis have become skilful and expert from being with them as apprentices.

Khwaja Abdul Karim Khan *Bayan-I Waki* (Truthful Commentary of Khwaja) (c.1750); Elliot and Dowson (1867–77; 2001 edn) Vol.8, p.127. The author came from Kashmir and had travelled to Bengal, and his account covering the reigns of Muhammad Shah and Ahmad Shah (r.1719–54) tells us how the Europeans had made themselves at home in Bengal.

6 Ahmad Shah Abdali in … (1757–8) came from the country of Kandahar [in Afghanistan] to Hindustan and … had an interview with the emperor at the palace at Shah Jahanabad [in Delhi]; he exercised all kinds of severity and oppression on the inhabitants of that city.

Nawab Ibrahim Khan Bahadur *Tarikh-I Ibrahim Khan* (History of Ibrahim Khan) (1786); Elliot and Dowson (1867–77; 2001 edn) Vol.8, p.264. Ahmad Shah Abdali, a lieutenant of Nadir Shah, later proclaimed Afghanistan independent of Persia. This was the fourth invasion by the Afghans since 1748, and Delhi was plundered and pillaged.

1 At Madras was Colonel Clive, an officer of the army, and a servant of the king of England, who had command over the factories in the Dakhin [Deccan, south]. In those days he had fought against the French and had taken from them some of their possessions in the [south]. After consultation, Colonel Clive and the gentlemen from Calcutta embarked in ships … and sailed to recover Calcutta.

Muhammad Ali Khan *Tarikh-I Muzaffari* (History of Muzaffar) (c.1800); Elliot and Dowson (1867–77; 2001 edn) Vol.8, p.325. The work was composed in honour of Muzaffar Jang, the title of Nawab Muhammad Riza Khan. In 1756 Calcutta was lost by the English to Nawab Siraj-ud Daula, the ruler of Bengal (1756–7). Robert Clive had joined the East India Company (see 404:1) in 1743.

2 On [23 June 1757] fire was opened on every side [on the battlefield of Plassey, West Bengal], and the engagement became warm. Europeans are very skilful in the art of war and in the use of artillery, and they kept up such an incessant fire that the hearers were deafened, and the beholders blinded. Many were killed and many [wounded] … On learning the condition of his army, Siraju-d daula was filled with dismay; he feared his enemies in front, and his hostile servants around him, and fled towards Murshidabad [the provincial capital].

Muhammad Ali Khan (c.1800); Elliot and Dowson (1867–77; 2001 edn) Vol.8, pp.329–30. With the fall of the nawab, Muslim rule in Bengal ended, and soon the remnants of the Mughal empire crumbled.

3 At this time [1765] the emperor of Delhi [Shah Alam II] made an alliance with the British, and the district of Allahabad was assigned to him for his residence. He agreed to grant the [East India] Company possession of the Bengal province, in return for which he was to receive annually twenty-five *lacs* of rupees.

Murtaza Husain *Hadikatu-I Akalim* (The Surrounding Regions) (c.1789); Elliot and Dowson (1867–77; 2001 edn) Vol.8, p.182. After working for the nobility from different parts of India, the author was appointed as Persian reader and writer to Warren Hastings in 1776. The East India Company (see 400:5), chartered in 1600, had, by 1700, important trading posts in India, such as Madras, Bombay and Calcutta, and by the middle of the century it was locked in rivalry with the French East India Company. The Mughal emperor had to give up his residence in Delhi and live in much diminished imperial style in Allahabad. The Company was still an official 'servant' of the Mughals, but the façade was fast collapsing.

4 The salaries of the *mansabdars* [commanders, a rank in the Mughal administrative system] were in our terms enormous but … they included the upkeep of their prescribed military contingents. Thus a commander of 5,000 [the highest rank in the earlier days] had a salary equivalent to 24,000 [pounds] of Elizabethan or Stuart purchasing power, at a time when the total revenue of England was something less than a million pounds. Two hundred years later the Governor General's salary was 25,000 [pounds] a year.

Percival Spear *A History of India* (1965; 1977 edn) Vol.2, p.46. Spear was an Englishman who travelled to India in 1924 and spent several years there teaching history. He also taught South Asian history in Cambridge University and wrote several books on India.

Islamic Spain, 711–1498

RELIGIONS COEXIST, 711–1050

1 People say that in ancient times it was called Iberia, taking its name from the River Ebro. Later it was known as Bética, from the River Betis, which runs through Cordova. Later still it was called Hispania after a man named Hispan who had once ruled there. Some people say that its true name is Hesperica, which is derived from Hesperus, the evening star in the west. Nowadays we call it al-Andalus after the Andalusians who settled it.

The Islamic geographer al-Bakri (d.1094) *Al-Masālik wa'l mamālik* (French trans. *Description de l'Afrique septentrionale* (Description of North Africa) 1913); Richard Fletcher *Moorish Spain* (1992) p.9.

2 In 711, which was the fourth year of the rule of Justinian II [of Byzantium] and when al-Walid I (r.705–715) was in the fifth year of his reign as caliph, Roderick violently usurped the crown with the support of leading members of the nobility. He reigned for one year. He gathered the full strength of his army to face the Arabs together with the Moors sent by Musa ibn Nusayr [governor of the Maghrib, the North African Islamic states], that is Tariq ibn Ziyad [governor of Tangier] and the others who had for long been raiding the province assigned to him and despoiling many cities ... Roderick met and joined battle with them ... and was killed in the fight [Battle of Rio Barbate] together with the whole Gothic army as it fled, those who had supported him when he treacherously sought to win the crown. In this way Roderick lost both the crown and his realm in the general destruction caused by wicked rivalries, al-Walid being the agent of it.

Anon. *Continuatio Isidoriana Hispana* (754) Sect.68 in *Monumenta Germaniae historica* (from 1826) Vol.2 *Chronica minora* p.352; Colin Smith *Christians and Moors in Spain: 711–1150* Vol.1 (1988) p.10. This first surviving chronicle account of the Islamic invasion was written by a priest, who gives a strongly Christian view of the event. The take-over was probably not, in fact, as destructive as this, since the Muslims were taught to respect both Jews and Christians as 'peoples of the Book'. A large Christian population lived on for centuries in al-Andalus, the Muslim part of Spain, enjoying both legal and religious freedoms.

3 When al-Andalus was conquered, someone came to Musa ibn Nusayr and said to him, 'Send someone with me and I will show you a (buried) treasure.'

Musa sent people with him and the man said 'dig here'. They did so and emeralds and rubies such as they had never seen before poured out over them. When they saw it they were overawed and said, 'Musa ibn Nusayr will never believe us.' They sent someone to get him and he saw it for himself. (The same sources) relate that when Musa ibn Nusayr conquered Andalus he wrote to (the caliph) Abd al Malik: 'It's not a conquest so much as the Day of Judgement.'

Ibn Abd al-Hakam *Chronicle* (late 9th century; 1947 edn) p.99. An account by a writer in Egypt (from where the conquest of North Africa was masterminded) of the Muslim conquest of Spain in 711. This is the earliest surviving account from the conquerors' viewpoint.

4 The whole realm was empty of inhabitants, full of blood, bathed in tears and loud with war-cries; a host to foreigners, alienated from its natives, abandoned by its inhabitants, widowed and bereft of its children, plunged into confusion by the barbarians, weakened by wounds, lacking all sinew and strength, comfortless and without the support of its own people ... The Moors dashed babies at the breast against the walls, wounded the older boys and put young men to the sword, the older men died in the battles, and all were destroyed by war; the cruelty of the Moors put to shame those who deserved honour at the end of their days.

Anon. *Estoria de Espagna* or *Primera Crónica general* (from 1270) Ch.559, p.19. The official history, starting from Spain's mythical foundation, was commissioned by King Alfonso X of Castile-Léon. This chapter is a lament for the Spain that has gone.

5 He [an early Arab governor in Spain, in 734] found it, even after all that it had been through, to be abundant with every good thing and, even after all its suffering, to be filled with beauty so that you could say that it was like an August pomegranate.

Anon. *Continuatio Isidoriana Hispana* (754); Fletcher (1992) p.171.

6 There are uncultivated lands, but the greater part of the country is cultivated and densely settled ... plenty and content govern every aspect of life. Possession of goods and the means of acquiring wealth are common to all classes of the population.

These benefits even extend to artisans and workmen, thanks to the light taxes, the good state of the country and the wealth of its ruler – for he has no need to impose heavy levies and taxes.

Ibn Hawqal *Description of the World* (c.990; 1939 edn); Richard Fletcher *The Quest for El Cid* (1989) p.17. This geographical handbook was composed by an Arab traveller who was impressed by the prosperity of al-Andalus in 948.

1 The whole of the Christian north of Spain is flat and most of the land is covered in sand. Their food-stuffs are mainly millet and sorghum and their normal drinks are apple cider and bushka, which is a drink made with flour(meal). The inhabitants are a treacherous people of depraved morals, who do not keep themselves clean and only wash once or twice a year in cold water. They do not wash their clothes once they have put them on until they fall to pieces on them, and assert that the filth that covers them thanks to their sweat is good for their bodies and keeps them healthy. Their clothes are very tight-fitting and have wide openings, through which most of their bodies show.

Ibrahim al-Turtushi (probably 960s); al-Bakri (late 11th century; 1968 edn) pp.71–3. The Muslim writer of al-Andalus is quoting an earlier Jewish traveller.

2   Carlon the king, our emperor Charlemagne,
Full seven long years has been abroad in Spain,
He's won the highlands as far as to the main;
No castle more can stand before his face,
City nor wall is left for him to break,
Save Zaragoza in its high mountain place;
Marsilion holds it, the king who hates God's name,
Mahound [Muhammad] he serves, and to Apollyon [the devil] he prays;
He'll not escape the ruin that awaits.

Anon. *The Song of Roland* (last quarter of 11th century; 1957 trans.) St.1. This greatest of the *chansons de geste* (songs of the deeds) mythologizes the disastrous French incursion into Spain in 778 and turns it into a crusade against the infidel, the Saracens of Spain. In fact, the action of 300 years earlier arose when a number of Spanish Islamic princes asked for Charlemagne's help against rival Islamic princes. The crusades to the Holy Land exerted a strong influence on the epic narrative: 'Paynims are wrong, Christians are in the right!' (St.79).

3 Lesson 5. Then St Charlemagne divided his forces into two: he ordered one to go through the Coll de Panissas, where he built a church dedicated to St Martin, while he sent the other through a trackless area of the mountains. The Saracens realizing he had divided his forces and fearing they might be caught in a pincer movement, began to withdraw towards the city of Gerona …

Lesson 9. It happened that one Friday, by divine aid, at the hour of compline [the canonical hour before bedtime] the sky being full of brightness, there appeared over the mosque of Gerona [where the cathedral now stands] a huge disc surrounded by a red glow. It remained there four hours visible to everyone; drops of blood could be seen falling throughout.

Special liturgy celebrating Charlemagne, containing a prayer and nine lessons, 786. It was to be read in Gerona on the feast-day of the emperor, who was canonized in 1165 by the antipope Paschal III to commemorate the Franks taking this important town on the border between France and Catalonia in northeastern Spain. Antipopes were rival pontiffs, set up in opposition to those canonically elected, especially from 1378 to 1417, during the Great Schism. In all, 39 antipopes resided in Avignon, southern France (see 192:3). In fact, Charlemagne was not present, but he was widely credited with this gain from the Moors.

4 The biggest city in Spain is Cordova, which has no equal in the Maghrib and hardly in Egypt, Syria or Mesopotamia, for the size of its population, its extent, the space occupied by its markets, the cleanliness of its streets, the architecture of its mosques, the number of its baths and caravanserais. Natives of Cordova who have travelled to Mesopotamia say that it is about the same size as one of the divisions of Baghdad.

Ibn Hawqal (c.990; 1939 edn); Fletcher (1992) p.65. The writer, a traveller from the eastern Islamic world, was scathing about the Andalusians' fighting abilities and horsemanship. Fletcher comments that putting a figure to Cordova's population is very difficult: 'Something in the region of 100,000 is a widely favoured figure [which would make it] roughly equivalent in size to Constantinople, the other great city of the Mediterranean world and several times bigger than even the largest towns of western Europe in the 10th century.'

5 Do not talk of the Court of Baghdad and its magnificence, do not praise Persia or China and their manifold advantages; for there is no spot on earth like Cordova.

Anon. Arabic historian; Sir John Glubb *The Course of Empire* (1965) p.80.

6 Another of the wonders of az-Zahra was the Hall of the Caliphs, the roof of which was of gold and solid but transparent blocks of marble of various colours, the walls being likewise of the same materials

... There was in the centre of the room a large basin filled with quicksilver; on each side of it eight doors fixed on arches of ivory and ebony, ornamented with gold and precious stones of various kinds, resting upon pillars of variegated marble and transparent crystal. When the sun penetrated through these doors into the hall, so strong was the action of its rays upon the roof and walls that the reflection only was sufficient to deprive beholders of sight. And when the caliph wished to frighten any of the courtiers that sat with him, he had only to make a sign to one of his slaves to set the quicksilver in motion, and the whole room would look in a instant as if it were traversed by flashes of lightning; and the company would begin to tremble, thinking that the room was moving away.

Al-Maqqari (d.1041) *History of the Mohammedan Dynasties in Spain* (1840–43 trans.); Fletcher (1989) p.23. A description of the new palace at Madinat az-Zahra (northwest of Cordova) begun by Abd al-Rahman III in 936.

1 It is our duty to record what happened to the land of Galicia [northwestern Spain] after Charlemagne's death. It remained at peace for a long time after this, but then, by the devil's prompting, there arose in Cordova a certain Saracen, al-Mansur, who proclaimed that he would conquer for himself all the lands of Galicia and Spain which Charlemagne had long ago taken from his predecessors. He gathered all his numerous army, pillaging the lands far and wide until he reached Compostela and pillaged all he found there. He also ransacked the whole church of Santiago, stealing from it manuscripts and silver tables and bells and other ornaments. The Saracens lodged themselves and their horses in the church and these vile people consumed their food before the altar itself. In divine retribution, some of them suffered looseness of the bowels and excreted whatever they had been eating. Others lost their sight.

Anon. *Liber Sancti Jacobi* (Book of St James) (c.1140; 1944 edn) Bk 4, 'Turpin's History', p.395. This work's purpose is to promote St James and his enormously popular shrine of Compostela in northwestern Spain, which attracted pilgrims from throughout Europe (see 202:1). The miracle of the dysentery reappears in other Spanish chronicles. The fourth book purports to be by Archbishop Turpin of Rheims (d.794), who, in another mythologizing account, *The Song of Roland* (see 151:2), is identified with one of the 12 peers of Charlemagne, also called Turpin, who is killed in the Battle of Roncesvalles.

2 An embassy from the Christians of the north of Spain arrived for negotiations with the caliph, who wished to overawe them with the magnificence of his court. He therefore had mats unrolled from the gates of Cordova to the entrance of Madinat al-Zahra' [his palace about three miles outside the city], and stationed a double row of soldiers along the route, their naked swords, both broad and long, meeting at the tips like the rafters of a roof. On the caliph's orders the ambassadors processed between the ranks as though in a roofed passage. The fear that this inspired was indescribable ... At regular intervals he placed dignitaries whom they took for kings, for they were seated on splendid chairs and dressed in brocade and silk ... each time the ambassadors saw one of these dignitaries they prostrated themselves before him, imagining him to be the caliph, whereupon they were told 'Raise your heads! This is only a slave of his slaves!'

At last they reached a courtyard strewn with sand. At the centre was the caliph. His clothes were coarse and short ... He was seated on the ground, with head bowed; before him was a Koran, a sword and a fire. 'Behold the ruler.'

Muhyi'l-din Ibn-al-Arabi, describing the ritual of Cordova's court, 10th century; Jan Read *The Moors in Spain and Portugal* (1974) p.75. The strong theatrical sense of the caliph, al-Nasir, is evident.

3 Fig trees are grafted in the manner called *tari*'; the winter corn grows up; and most of the fruit trees break into leaf. It is now that the falcons of Valencia lay eggs on the islands of the river and incubate for a month. Sugar cane is planted ... The first roses and lilies appear. In kitchen gardens, the beans begin to shoot.

Recemundo (Rabi 'b. Zayd) *Calendar for the Month of March* (961). The writer was a Mozarab (someone who was allowed to practise as a Christian on condition that he paid allegiance to the Moorish ruler) who had been sent in 956 to establish diplomatic relations with the German emperor, Otto I (r.936–973). Otto had earlier approached al-Nasir for help in suppressing the Muslim pirates who were harrying the coast of southern France.

4 Despite his humble antecedents and the fact that he was not of the royal house – for he had no right to inherit the kingdom from his ancestors – and since he was not all that powerful, al-Mansur achieved great things thanks only to his shrewdness and courting of the common people ... Had he not proclaimed allegiance to the caliph, had he not appeared to submit to him in all his actions and obey him and meet all his needs ... had he not reduced to obscurity the men who had been prominent in the

caliphate of al-Hakam and had he not ruthlessly eliminated them … al-Mansur would not have achieved what he aspired to, nor would he have reached in all this the highest goal.

Abd Allah b. Buluggin (d.1090) *Al-Tibyan* (Memoirs)(1986 trans.) p.44; Hugh Kennedy *Muslim Spain and Portugal* (1996) p.110. The writer is analysing the political strategy of the ablest general, who took Islamic power to its highest point.

1 The peasantry of al-Andalus were unequal to such a task [of fighting off the Christians] and complained to him [al-Mansur] of their inability to fight and that expeditions would prevent them from farming the land. Moreover, they were not a warlike people. Al-Mansur therefore conceded to them the right to concentrate on the cultivation of their lands, while in turn they willingly agreed to make annual contributions to support the troops to act in their stead.

Abd Allah b. Buluggin (d.1090) (1986 trans.) pp.44–5; Kennedy (1996) p.110. The general's army consisted of Berbers, recruited from North Africa, not the Amirids from the region. The writer was himself a Berber.

2
Black slave	160	*mithquals*
Slave	28	
House at Cordova	160	
Ditto	280	
Garden in Cordova	240	
Horse	24	
Mule	60	*dinars*

Ibn Sahl, table of al-Andalus prices, 1065–7; Read (1974) p.36. A *mithqal* seems to have been worth ¹⁵/₁₆ of a *dinar*.

3 Then negotiations began and envoys plied back and forth … He then demanded 50,000 gold pieces. I pointed out to him, however, that the country's resources were meagre, that I could not possibly afford to pay that amount and that it would make me easy prey for Ibn Abbad [ruler of Seville] … Alfonso accepted my plea after much effort on my part and I finally agreed to pay him 25,000 pieces, half the amount he had demanded. Then, as presents for him, I gathered a large number of carpets, garments and vessels and placed all these in a large tent. I then invited him to the tent. But when he saw the presents he said they were not enough. So it was agreed that I should increase the amount by 5,000 pieces, bringing it to a total of 30,000.

Abd Allah of Granada, describing his negotiations with Alfonso VI of Castile-Léon, c.1075; Fletcher (1992) p.100. On the collapse of the Amirid dynasty after 1008, the Muslim empire had fractured into *taifas*, rival small states, which would enrol the expensive help of the Christian king in their internecine warfare.

4   O people of al-Andalus, return what you have
        borrowed; it is not customary to borrow
        without giving back.
    Do you not see the pawn of the unbelievers has
        become a queen, while our king is
        checkmated on the last square?

Anon. poem (c.1085); Charles Melville and Ahmad Ubaydli *Christians and Moors in Spain: Arabic Sources, 711–1501* Vol.3 (1992) p.91. An Islamic poet is reacting to the fall of Toledo and the victory of the Christians. The irony is that the word checkmate comes from the Arabic.

5   Weep for the splendour of Cordova, for
        disaster has overtaken her;
    Fortune made her a creditor and demanded
        payment for the debt.
    She was at the height of her beauty; life was
        gracious and sweet.
    Until all was overthrown and today no two
        people are happy in her streets.
    Then bid her good-bye, and let her go in peace
        since depart she must.

Ibn Idhari, lament in *Al-Bayan al mughrib* (Maghrib Declaration) (after 1031; 1901–4 edn); Robert Hillenbrand in Salma Khadira Jayyusi (ed.) *The Legacy of Medieval Spain* (1992) p.27. Control in Cordova, the cultural centre of Spanish Islam, passed to the Almoravid dynasty of Seville in 1091.

6 I would rather be a camel herd among the Almoravids than a pig-swain among the Christians.

Al-Mu'tamid of Seville (end of 11th century); Melville and Ubaydli Vol.3 (1992) p.92. Al-Mu'tamid (d.1095), who was the last Abbasid ruler of Seville, which he controlled in 1069–90, is expressing the long (250 years') quandary of the Muslim rulers of Spain who were squeezed between the militant Islamic dynasty of North Africa in the south and the Christian powers to the north.

EL CID, c.1043–99

7 Furthermore, King Alfonso gave him [El Cid] this concession and privilege in his kingdom, written and confirmed under seal, by which all the land or castles which he himself might acquire from the Saracens in the land of the Saracens should be absolutely his in full ownership, not only his but also his sons' and daughters' and all his descendants.

Anon. *Historia Roderici* (2nd half of 12th century); Fletcher (1989) p.153. The biographer of Rodrigo Díaz de Vivar – better known as El Cid (The Lord) or El Campeador (The Champion or Warrior) – on the deal that a successful commander could strike with his king, Alfonso VI, in his campaign against the Almoravids in al-Andalus. El Cid is the hero of many Spanish legends and ballads.

1   Great is the rejoicing
      in that place
      When my Cid took Valencia
      and entered the city.
      Those who had gone on foot
      became knights on horses;
      and who could count the gold and silver?
      All were rich
      as many as were there.
      My Cid Don Rodrigo
      sent for his fifth of the spoils,
      In coined money alone
      thirty thousand marks fell to him,
      And the other riches,
      who could count them?
      My Cid rejoiced
      and all who were with him,
      When his flag flew from the top
      of the Moorish palace.

Anon. *Poema de mio Cid* (12th century; 1959 trans.) Canto 74. The author of this great epic poem is not writing history but evoking the triumphant and lucrative sack of Valencia on 15 June 1094.

2 I am a man who never ruled, and none of my ancestors was a ruler either. From the day I entered this city [Valencia], I was delighted by it and wanted it for myself and prayed to our Lord to give it to me. You can see how powerful God is from the fact that the day I began the siege of Cebolla I had no more than a few crusts of bread but now God had given me Valencia and I rule it. If I conduct myself justly here and bring order to the city, God will allow me to continue in possession; but if I commit wrong here through injustice or pride, I know well enough he will take it from me. From today, let everyone go to his estate and repossess it. If he finds that it has been worked he should compensate the occupier for what he has spent, and resume ownership as Moorish law dictates. Furthermore I order the city's tax collectors to take no more than the tithe [tenth] as your law lays down.

El Cid, addressing the leaders of the Moorish city he entered after a siege of 10 months, 1094; Smith Vol.1 (1988) p.115. El Cid had been a mercenary in Muslim Zaragoza for many years after 1081 and was, therefore, fully aware of Islamic laws

and anxious to preserve the status quo. Smith believes that he is also likely to have made his speech in Arabic.

3 When Valencia was organized to the liking of the Campeador [El Cid] – may God curse him! – he laid hold of its Islamic judge, Ibn Jahhaf, his family and relations, and arrested them all. They were subjected to an inquisition ... He continued to extract what they had, until he had confiscated all their property and left them destitute ... When he had taken everything, he ordered a fire to be lit ... In the end he gave in to the appeals of the citizens, and let the women and children go. A hole was dug for the judge, who was lowered in up to his waist. The ground was flattened round him and he was encircled by fire. When it got near him and lit up his face he cried, 'In the name of God, the Compassionate, the Merciful,' and pulled the burning material towards him and was burnt to death, may God have mercy on him!

Ibn Idhari (after 1031; 1967 edn) Vol.4, pp.33–8; Melville and Ubaydli Vol.3 (1992) p.103. El Cid, a hero to the Christians, becomes the villain to the Muslim chronicler, while Ibn Jahhaf is the martyr.

4 After a period of nearly 450 years had elapsed since this disaster [the Muslim invasion of Spain] the most merciful Father deigned to take pity on his people and raised up the ever-victorious leader Rodrigo the Campeador [El Cid] as avenger of the shame of his servants and as champion of the Christian religion; and he, after many famous victories which he won by divine aid, with a thirst for riches and a great number of men, took the immensely rich city of Valencia. This was after defeating a vast number of Almoravids and the barbarians of all Spain, and in shorter time than anyone could believe possible, without loss to his men. He dedicated the mosque ... to God as a church with the following endowment from his own resources to the worthy priest Hieronymus, consecrated as bishop.

Later version of the original charter of 1098; Menéndez Pidal (ed.) *La España del Cid* (1929) pp.867. The Almoravids, a fundamentalist Islamic dynasty, had expanded from northern Africa into Spain around 1086.

EMBATTLED COEXISTENCE, 1100–1500

5 [The] king of the Moroccans commanded the Almoravids and on this side of the sea the Spanish Moors, and many others far and wide, and the islands and the nations of the sea, like a snake

thirsting in the heat of summer raised his head, as though he would triumph over our great king [Alfonso VI] after his death, called together all the princes and commanders and soldiers of the Almoravids together with a great army of Arab mercenaries, and many thousands of horsemen and slingers and great companies of foot soldiers, as many as the sands on the shore of the sea.

Anon. *Chronica Adefonsi Imperatoris* (1147; 1950 edn) Sect.96. The chronicle's author, who may have been Bishop Arnault, is describing the massed attack on Toledo, the centre of power for the Christian kingdom, which took place in 1109.

1 The Spanish are being continually worn down by such a succession of disasters and by so many deaths of the sons of God as a result of the oppression of the pagans [Moors] we believe that not one of you will lie low … We concede to all fighting firmly in this expedition the same remission of sins which we have given to the defenders of the Eastern Church. But if those who have put the sign of the cross on their clothes for this purpose have not made an effort to fulfil their vows between this Easter and the next, we banish them thereafter from the bosom of Holy Church until they make satisfaction.

Pope Calixtus II, proclaiming a crusade in Spain and encouraging the faithful, 2 April 1123; L. and J. Riley-Smith *The Crusades: Idea and Reality* (1981) Pt 2, Doc.12.

2 I therefore approached specialists in the Arabic language, from which comes the deadly poison which has infected half the world, and I persuaded them – by pleas and by offering payment – to translate from Arabic into Latin the origin, life and laws of that damned soul [Muhammad] which is called the Koran … in order that the translation should be completely accurate, and in order that no detail should escape us through deceit, I added a Saracen to the team of Christian translators.

Peter the Venerable, 1142; J.P. Migne (ed.) *Patrologia Latina* (1844–64) Vol.189, Col.671. The abbot of the great abbey of Cluny in Burgundy (1122–56) visited Cluniac monasteries in Spain and took drastic action to draw the poison.

3 When the whole army had set up camp near Seville, every day raiding parties rode out, pillaging the territories around Seville, Cordova and Carmona, burning all the land, the towns and fortresses. Often these were empty as the inhabitants had fled. They carried off innumerable captives, male and female, quantities of horses and mares, camels and donkeys, cattle, sheep and goats. They bore back to camp vast amounts of grain, oil and wine. They razed to the ground every mosque they found and killed the holy men and doctors of law that they met. They burned, too, any books of their faith that they found in the mosques.

Anon. *Chronica Adefonsi Imperatoris* (1147; 1950 edn) Sect.36. King Alfonso VII's blitzkrieg of al-Andalus in 1133 shows that a new violence had replaced earlier tolerance between Christians and Muslims. This change coincided with the aftermath of the First Crusade in the Holy Land, the appointment of French Cluniac monks to influential positions in the Spanish church and the fierce fundamentalism of the Almoravid dynasty.

4 He [the Italian scholar, Gerard of Cremona] was trained from childhood at centres of philosophical study and had come to a knowledge of all of this that was known to the Latins; but for love of the *Almagest*, which he could not find among the Latins, he went to Toledo. There, seeing the abundance of books in Arabic on every subject and regretting the poverty of the Latins in these things, he learned Arabic in order to be able to translate. In this way he passed on the Arabic literature in the manner of the wise man who, wandering through a green field, threads together a crown of flowers, made up not from just any, but from the prettiest.

Obituary at the death of Gerard of Cremona, 1187; Fletcher (1992) p.151. The scholar had spent 47 years in Spain, devoting himself to translating into Latin the texts in the immensely rich Graeco-Arabian tradition which had been unknown in the West. The *Almagest* was the Arabic name for Ptolemy's *Syntaxis mathematica* (mid-2nd century), the classic text of geocentric astronomy.

5 You should know that it has come to our notice that when a public ceremony of baptism is celebrated in your church, and many Saracens gather for it eagerly seeking baptism, their owners, whether Jews or even Christians, fearing to lose a worldly profit, presume to forbid them.

Pope Innocent III to the canons of Barcelona Cathedral, 1206; Fletcher (1992) p.140. The pope's missionary zeal was hampered by the slave-owners' self-interest. A Muslim slave could earn manumission by converting to Christianity, so his or her master had a powerful interest in forbidding it.

6 On their side there fell in the battle 100,000 men, perhaps more, according to the estimates of Saracens we captured later. Of the army of the lord – a fact not to be mentioned without the most fervent thanksgiving, and one scarcely to be believed, unless it be thought a miracle – only some twenty or thirty Christians in our whole host fell.

In order to show how immense were the numbers of the enemy, when our army rested after the battle for two days in the enemy camp, for all the fires which were needed to cook food and bread and other things, no other wood was needed than that of the enemy arrows and spears which were lying around, and even then we burned scarcely half of them.

Alfonso VIII of Castile and Toledo to Pope Innocent III, July 1212; Julio González *Alfonso VIII* (1960) Vol.3, pp.566–7. The king is reporting on the victory at Las Navas de Tolosa (between Madrid and Cordova). The pope had proclaimed a crusade, and St Dominic (the Spanish founder of the Dominican order; see 203:2) read the papal bull in Spain in 1206. The pope wrote to every bishop in France to encourage crusaders to come to the aid of Castile in its battles against the Almohads. The casualty figures are as unbelievable as Alfonso says. However, Colin Smith suggests that he was only counting the loss of the knights in his army, not of common soldiers (*Christians and Moors in Spain: 1195–1614* Vol.2 (1989) p.15).

I The main reason for this defeat [at Las Navas] was the divisions in the hearts of the Almohads. In the time of Abu Yusuf Ya'qub they drew their pay every four months without fail. But in the time of this Abu 'Abd-Allah, and especially during this particular campaign, their payment was in arrears. They attributed this to the viziers, and rebelled in disgust. I have heard from several of them that they did not draw their swords nor train their spears, nor did they take any part in the preparations for battle. With this in mind, they fled at the first assault of the Franks.

Al-Marrakushi *al-Mu'jib* (1224); Melville and Ubaydli Vol.3 (1992) p.141. The writer was probably in Baghdad. The term Franks was used for all Spanish Christians, just as it was used for the European crusaders. The other side labelled as Moors all the Muslims in Spain and north Africa. Such industrial action in battle could obviously prove highly dangerous to the demotivated soldier.

2　　Ask Valencia what has become of Murcia,
　　　And where is Játiva or where is Jaén?
　　　Where is Cordova, the seat of great learning,
　　　And how many scholars of high repute remain
　　　　there?
　　　And where is Seville, the home of mirthful
　　　　gatherings
　　　On its great river, cooling and brimful of water?
　　　These cities were pillars of the country.

Al-Rundi, elegy on the fall of Seville, mid-13th century; Fletcher (1992) p.129. The poet is looking back. After a prolonged siege, the city was taken in Dec. 1248 by the king of Castile, Ferdinand III, and all the Muslim inhabitants were forcibly ejected, leaving a ghost city to be resettled by the Christians.

3 Furthermore, my son, you should not consider a Moorish woman as a woman at all, but rather as a beast, for she keeps no law other than that of her master Muhammad; he gave them that evil faith in which they live, in order to plunge them deeper into those things which our law considers sinful and bad, but which for them counts towards salvation, while what we consider good for our salvation is to them a sin. The Moors have no belief other than that which can best free their flesh for the enjoyment of worldly pleasures, and that is what they most prize.

Sancho IV of Castile-Léon *Castigos e documentos* (Advice and Documents) (1293; 1952 edn) p.128. The king is supposedly addressing his son and successor. This convention recurs and is called 'the mirror of princes'. Its sententious tone on sexual matters is typical and probably reflects the fact that such guidance actually came not from father to son, but from a team of clerics.

4 1. It is agreed that each ruler should be an ally of the allies of the other, and an enemy to his enemies against all the rulers of the Islamic world.

2. Item, that Sultan Abu'l-Rabi shall pay 2,000 *doblas* for each galley with its full crew and supplied for four months …

4. Item, Sultan Abu'l-Rabi shall pay the wages of 1,000 horsemen on a war footing until he has carried out his plan with regard to Ceuta …

6. Item, when Ceuta is captured, all the movable spoils shall go to the king of Aragon, while all persons and the place itself shall remain the property of Sultan Abu'l-Rabi.

Treaty between James II of Aragon and Sultan Abu'l-Rabi of Morocco, Barcelona, 3 May 1309; M.L. de Mas Latrie *Traités de paix et de commerce* (1866) Documents pp.297–9. The treaty was against the king of Granada, who had snatched the Moroccan fortified city of Ceuta in 1306 (see 315:1). The king of Aragon offers to hire galleys and cavalry in support of one Islamic ruler in outflanking another. The deal looks cast iron for the Christian king, but in the event Granada and Morocco did a deal themselves.

5 The situation of the place, its seaport and two mighty castles made Malaga an exceptionally strong city. However, the king of Spain besieged it for six whole months [in fact, four months] by sea and by land, preventing the entry of supplies, and reducing the inhabitants to such starvation that the watchmen on the walls received only two ounces of bread a day and the poor and others were forced to make bread from wood and the upper parts of palm trees, which they softened and ground up … Finally Malaga surrendered unconditionally to the king [Ferdinand] who sold 5,000 of its people one by one as slaves at 30 ducats each, but allowing anyone able to purchase his freedom to do so for the same sum … The king of Spain, knowing that 700 years before the Moors had ordered all the Christians of Malaga to be killed, down to the last person, swore to do the same to them; but in his clemency and humanity he sold them into slavery instead.

Hieronymus Münzer *Itinerarium* (c.1494–5); Smith Vol.2 (1989) p.153. Münzer was a sympathetic and observant Austrian traveller and doctor who visited Spain.

1 It [the Alhambra] was the royal abode of the Moorish kings, where, surrounded by the splendours and refinements of Asiatic luxury, they held dominion over what they vaunted as a terrestrial paradise and made their last stand for empire in Spain. The royal palace forms but a part of a fortress, the walls of which, studded with towers, stretch irregularly around the whole crest of a hill, as spur of the Sierra Nevada or Snowy Mountains, and overlook the city … in the time of the Moors the fortress was capable of containing within its outward precincts an army of forty thousand men, and served occasionally as a stronghold of the sovereigns against their rebellious subjects.

Washington Irving *The Alhambra* (1832; 1991 edn) p.752.

2 At the foot of the mountains, on a good plain, Granada has, for almost a mile many orchards and leafy spots irrigable by water channels; orchards, I repeat, full of houses and towers, occupied during the summer, which, seen together from afar, you would take to be a populous and fantastic city … The Saracens like orchards very much, they are very ingenious in planting and irrigating them to a degree that nothing surpasses.

Hieronymus Münzer *Viaje por España y Portugal* (c.1494–5; 1987 edn) p.46.

3 Since the common people of the city of [Granada] were suffering so badly, they gathered in groups to cry out to the king [Boabdil, Mohammad XI] that he should come to an agreement with the Christians; and if he did not, they would, since they were in desperate straits. And this reached the king's ears, and he was deeply saddened by it. In addition to this, the king was advised by many old Moors who had a great deal of military experience to reach an accommodation with their majesties [King Ferdinand and Queen Isabella] and they reminded him of many things that prompted him to take this course.

Alonso de Santa Cruz *Crónica de los reyes Católicos* (Chronicle of the Catholic Kings) (1550; 1951 edn) Vol.1, p.39. A Spanish Christian account of the last days of the Nasrid dynasty, which ruled in Granada from 1238 to 1492.

4 Our enemy has gained power over us because
   of our sinfulness; the lions and leopards of
   the enemy have wreaked havoc on us.
   Yes, they have pillaged our homelands, our
   lives and our possessions; its abundance has
   been allowed them as legitimate spoils;
   They have ravished her without providing a
   bride price; no spears have been whetted for
   them, nor have her menfolk fought them for
   her;
   The Franks have howled down at us from every
   hilltop and their vows to the cross have been
   completely achieved.

Anon. lament on the fall of Granada in 1492; Melville and Ubaydli Vol.3 (1992) p.185. The poet saw the loss as divine retribution for the sins of the Nasrid dynasty.

5 The royal procession advanced to the principal mosque, which had been consecrated as a cathedral. Here the sovereigns offered up prayers and thanksgivings, and the choir of the royal chapel chanted a triumphant anthem, in which they were joined by all the courtiers and cavaliers. Nothing (says Fray Antonio Agapida) could exceed the thankfulness to God of the pious King Ferdinand, for having enabled him to eradicate from Spain the empire and name of that heathen race, and for the elevation of the cross in that city wherein the impious doctrines of Mahomet had so long been cherished.

Washington Irving *The Conquest of Granada* (1829; 1910 edn) Ch.100. The 19th-century American writer pretended that his avowedly romantic account of the *reconquista* was based on a chronicler (Antonio Agapida) whom he invented. In the revised edition (1850) he owned up to the invention, but in fact here Irving is echoing a real Jesuit father, Mariana (p.437 footnote).

6 When the Christian king saw that the people had ceased to emigrate and decided to remain as subject people, wishing to stay in their native homeland, he began to default on the conditions which they had first made with him, and he continued to default on one after another, until he had gone back on the whole thing. Respect for Islam ceased and he treated the Muslims with scorn and contempt. The Christians became overbearing towards them, imposed various injunctions and heavy fines on them, and stopped the call to prayer from the minarets …

After that, he summoned them to become Christians and compelled them to do so. This was in 1498; they entered his faith under duress, and the whole of al-Andalus became Christian.

Islamic account of the aftermath of the fall of Granada, 1498; Melville and Ubaydli Vol.3 (1992) p.189. King Ferdinand is seen as treacherous in reneging on the terms of the truce.

JUDGEMENTS

1 The misguided Spanish knew not what they were doing. The exile of the Moors delighted them; nothing more picturesque and romantic had occurred for some time ... they did not understand that they had killed their golden goose. For centuries Spain had been the centre of civilization, the seat of arts and sciences, of learning and every form of refined enlightenment ... The Moors were banished; for a while Christian Spain shone like the moon, with a borrowed light; then came the eclipse, and in that darkness Spain has grovelled ever since.

Stanley Lane-Poole *The Moors in Spain* (1890) p.279. A passionate requiem from the standard account of the late 19th century.

2 The *reconquista*, by becoming the most important and durable enterprise of the entire nation, accustomed too many men – to quote an expression from the *Cantar del Cid* – to 'obtain their bread by taking it from others'. What is more, this unending war did not lead to the fusion of the conquerors with the conquered, but opened deep rifts where originally there was no insurmountable cleavage.

Robert S. Lopez *The Birth of Europe* (1962; 1967 trans.) p.249.

3 In the end, it is probably impossible to tell how far these various factors, demography, military technology, and military and political structures, led to the demise of al-Andalus. But it remains a central and intriguing question why the self-confident and dominant Muslim society of the year 1000 should have divided, shrunk and, eventually, half a millennium later, disappeared from Iberian soil completely.

Hugh Kennedy (1996) p.308, final words.

Saxons and Vikings, c.410–1066

THE DEPARTURE OF THE ROMANS, c.410

1 The island of Britain lies virtually at the end of the world, towards the west and northwest ... It is ornamented with twenty-eight cities and a number of castles, and well equipped with fortifications – walls, castellated towers, gates and houses, whose sturdily built roofs reared menacingly skyward.

Gildas *The Ruin of Britain* (c.540; 1978 trans.) Ch.3.1. During the Roman occupation Britain certainly flourished, although the cities were Roman fortified administrative centres and the castles were not those of modern romantic perception. Gildas, a monk, was educated in Wales and wrote this work when he was 46 years old, before moving on to Ireland and, finally, to Brittany.

2 Ireland is far more favoured than Britain by latitude, and by its mild and healthy climate ... There are no reptiles, and no snake can exist there; for although often brought over from Britain, as soon as the ship nears land, they breathe the scent of its air, and die.

The island abounds in milk and honey.

Bede *Ecclesiastical History* (731; 1955 trans.) Bk 1.1. The snakes were reputed to have been driven from Ireland by St Patrick in the 5th century. Bede, known as the Venerable, spent his life at the monasteries at Wearmouth and Jarrow in the north of England, where he died in 735. He was a prolific writer, becoming known throughout Europe for his biblical commentaries and for his history.

3 The Romans therefore informed our country that they could not go on being bothered with such troublesome expeditions ... Rather, the British should stand alone, get used to arms, fight bravely, and defend with all their powers ... their life and liberty.

Gildas (c.540; 1978 trans.) Ch.18.1. Gildas includes no dates in his history, but the last of the Roman army left c.410, and the Romano-British, with no army of their own, appear to have dwindled gradually in strength and presence.

4 As the Romans went back home, there eagerly emerged from the coracles that had carried them across the sea-valleys the foul hordes of Scots and Picts ... They were to some extent different in their customs, but they were in perfect accord in their greed for bloodshed: and they were readier to cover their villainous faces with hair than their private

parts and neighbouring regions with clothes ... there was no respite from the barbed spears flung by their naked opponents, which tore our wretched countrymen from the walls and dashed them to the ground.

Gildas (c.540; 1978 trans.) Ch.19.1. After the departure of the Romans, the Picts (from Scotland) and the Scots (from Ireland) ravaged the now undefended land, prompting, c.449, Vortigern, a king of the British, to plead for help from the first of the incursive Saxons, Hengest and Horsa. There were almost certainly peaceful Saxons already settled in the southeast, along what the Romans called the Saxon Shore.

5 Odin died in his bed in Sweden. But when he felt death approaching he had himself marked with the point of a spear, and he declared as his own all men who fell in battle. He said he was about to depart to the abode of the gods and would there welcome his friends. He would live forever ... at the old Asgarth.

Snorri Sturluson 'The Saga of the Ynglings' in *Heimskringla* (c.1220; 1964 trans.) Ch.9. Snorri Sturluson was lawspeaker (president) of the Icelandic high court, and he wrote down many of the traditional Scandinavian sagas. Warriors who fell in battle found their way to Valhalla, the home of Odin at Asgarth, the Germanic counterpart of Mount Olympus. Odin, as Woden, was the god from whom all the Angle and Saxon royal houses, as well as the Scandinavians, traced their claimed lineage. As such, he is the only pagan god mentioned in the early writings and has survived to modern times in Woden's day or Wednesday. The names of other Norse gods – Tiw (Tuesday), Thor (Thursday) and Freyr (Friday) – have also survived in, literally, everyday usage.

THE COMING OF THE ANGLES AND SAXONS, c.449

6 All the major towns were laid low by the repeated battering of enemy rams; laid low, too, all the inhabitants ... in the middle of the squares the foundation stones of high walls and towers that had been torn from their lofty base, holy altars, fragments of corpses, covered (as it were) with a purple crust of congealed blood, looked as though they had been mixed up in some dreadful wine-press. There was no burial to be had.

Gildas (c.540; 1978 trans.) Ch.24.3. The Angles and Saxons carried all before them but were routed by the British at the Battle of Mount Badon, probably c.495. Gildas, writing about 50 years later and within the memory of men still living, attributes the leadership of the British at the battle to

Ambrosius Aurelianus, claimed to be a descendant of the Roman emperors. He appears to have not known of a King Arthur, the heroic leader of later legends (see 160:4).

1 They are accustomed on the eve of departure to kill one in ten of their prisoners by drowning or crucifixion, performing a rite … they think it a religious duty to exact torture rather than ransom from a prisoner.

Sidonius Apollinaris *The Letters* (c.480; 1915 trans.) Bk 4, p.150. Sidonius, a bishop at Clermont in France, wrote this letter to his friend Namatius, deploring the Saxon practice of human sacrifice.

2 When [Columba] … was for a number of days in the land of the Picts, he had to cross the River Ness. The monster … lurked in the depth of the river. Feeling the water above disturbed … it suddenly swam up to the surface and with gaping mouth and with great roaring rushed towards the man swimming in the middle of the stream.

Adamnan *Life of Columba* (c.690; 1991 trans.) Ch.2.27. An early (c.575) sighting of the Loch Ness monster. Columba, an Irish prince, founded and became abbot of a monastery on the island of Iona (off southwestern Scotland), from where he intended to carry Christianity to Scotland.

3 One day some merchants who had recently arrived in Rome displayed their many wares in the marketplace. Among the crowd who thronged to buy was Gregory, who saw among other merchandise some boys exposed for sale. These had fair complexions, fine-cut features and beautiful hair. Looking at them with interest, he enquired from what country and what part of the world they came. 'They come from the island of Britain,' he was told … 'What is the name of this race?' 'They are called Angles,' he was told. 'That is appropriate,' he said, 'for they have angelic faces … And what is the name of the province from which they have been brought?' 'Deira,' was the answer.

Bede (731; 1955 trans.) Bk 2.1. The story of the slave boys would have particularly interested Bede, as Deira was the southern part of his native Northumbria and the boys would have been children of his own countrymen. Shortly after this, in 590, Gregory was elected pope, and sent Augustine to England, earning himself the sobriquet Apostle of the English (see 94:1).

4   He charged before three hundred of the finest
      He cut down both centre and wing
      He fed black ravens on the ramparts of a
         fortress

Though he was no Arthur.
      Among the powerful ones in battle,
      In the front rank Gwawrddur was a palisade.

Aneirin (c.600) *Y Gododdin* (1988 trans.) lines 967–72. The Gododdin were a tribe that emigrated from Berwickshire in southeastern Scotland to mid-Wales in the 6th century. This is probably the earliest mention of an heroic chieftain called Arthur. The hero of this verse, Gwawrddur, is obscure.

5 Then Arthur, with the kings of Britain, fought against them, though he was the commander in battle … The twelfth battle was fought at Mount Badon, where in one day there fell nine hundred and sixty men to the assault of Arthur; and none fell except by his hand alone.

Nennius *Historia Brittonum* (c.800; 2002 trans.) Ch.56. Arthur is not described as a king in this narrative, although Nennius develops the legend.

6 This Arthur is the hero of many wild tales among the Britons even in our own day, but assuredly deserves to be the object of reliable history rather than of false and dreaming fable.

William of Malmesbury *Gesta Regum Anglorum* (Deeds of the Kings of England) (c.1125; 1998 trans.) Bk I.8. Although William was certainly striving for reliable history, the legend of King Arthur was turned into a mostly fictional bestseller by Geoffrey of Monmouth over the following decade. Sir Thomas Malory completed the romanticizing of the legend, in English, with *Le Morte D'Arthur* (c.1470).

7 It is better for a man to avenge his friend than to mourn him long. We must all expect an end to life in this world; let him who can win fame before death, because that is a dead man's best memorial.

Anon. *Beowulf* (probably 8th century; 1957 trans.) p.37. The heroic code encompassed fame, loyalty to one's lord and the defence of one's kin. If the historical characters in the poem are those we can identify, then Beowulf, the hero of this great epic poem in Old English, would probably have lived in the mid-6th century.

8   He was the man most gracious and
         fair-minded,
      Kindest to his people and keenest to win fame.

Anon. *Beowulf* (probably 8th century; 1999 trans.) The hero's epitaph and the last lines of the poem.

9 First banish afar the foul worship of idols, on their profane altars let the blood of animals smoke no more, nor the soothsayer look for omens in warm entrails, nor the meaningless augur attend to the song of birds: let all the images of the gods be smashed to the ground.

Alcuin *The Bishops, Kings and Saints of York* (c.780; 1982 trans.) lines 158–62. Bishop Paulinus explains the first step of conversion to Edwin, king of Northumbria (r.616–633). The king's pagan high priest, Coifi, promptly mounted a stallion and rode off to desecrate his pagan altars. Because all records were kept by men of the Christian church, this is one of few references to the survival of the old gods and to pagan customs. Alcuin, head of the cathedral school at York, moved c.782 to the court of Charlemagne, king of the Franks and, from 800, Holy Roman Emperor (see 187:1).

1 So peaceful was it in those parts of Britain under King Edwin's jurisdiction that the proverb still runs that a woman could carry her newborn babe across the island from sea to sea without any fear of harm.

Bede (731; 1955 trans.) Bk 2.16. King Edwin's Northumbria was peaceful in 630, but after his death in 633 the fighting started again, and Mercia, the centre of England, became the dominant kingdom.

2 George was in heathen days a rich noble under the cruel emperor, who was called Datian, in the province Cappadocia …

Datian, with devilish anger commanded that George be hung up on a gibbet, and his limbs be torn with iron claws, and torches be kindled on both sides of him; after that to be led out of the city, to be tortured with scourges, and rubbed with salt; but George remained unhurt.

Then the magician Athanasius took a cup with a death-bearing drink … and gave it to George to drink; but the fiendish liquor harmed him not a whit …

Thereupon Datian endited this decree, 'Take this guilty one … and drag him prone with his face to the earth through all the streets and stony ways.'

Aelfric *Lives of the Saints* (c.1000; 1881 trans.) Ch.14. George survived being drawn through the streets, but was then summarily decapitated, as was the unsuccessful magician Athanasius. Emperor Datian did not survive either, being struck by lightning on the way home. George came from Cappadocia, eastern Turkey, and lived, probably, in the early 4th century. He was known in England by the 8th century, and his life was written by Aelfric, with no reference to a dragon, c.1000. He was not adopted as the patron saint of England until c.1348.

THE COMING OF THE VIKINGS, 793

3 York, with its high walls and lofty towers, was first built by Roman hands … as a haven for ocean-going ships from farthest ports … To York from divers peoples and kingdoms all over the world, they come in hope of gain, seeking wealth from the rich land, a home, a fortune, and a hearth-stone for themselves.

Alcuin (c.780; 1982 trans.) lines 19–37. York had in early years a population that included many peaceful Scandinavian settlers, becoming in the 9th century the hub of the Viking half of England.

4 There was in Mercia … a certain vigorous king called Offa, who terrified all the neighbouring kings and provinces around him, and who had a great dyke built between Wales and Mercia from sea to sea.

Asser *Life of King Alfred* (c.893; 1983 trans.) Ch.14. Offa's Dyke was for many years the boundary between Wales and England. In places it was 60 feet high, with a ditch 13 feet deep, and it stretched for 170 miles between the rivers Dee and Severn. Much of it is still visible today.

5 You have written to us also about merchants, and by our mandate we allow that they shall have protection and support in our kingdom, lawfully, according to the ancient custom of trading. And if in any place they are afflicted by wrongful oppression, they may appeal to us or our judges … Similarly our men, if they suffer any injustice in your dominion, are to appeal to your equity.

Charlemagne to King Offa of Mercia, 796; D. Whitelock (ed.) *English Historical Documents* Vol.1 (1955) p.781. Possibly the first recorded trade agreement in northern Europe. The great Charlemagne, king of the Franks, did not consider King Offa his equal, however, and he did not refer to Mercia as a kingdom.

6 [In 896 the aged King Charles the Simple of France decided that] it was advisable to make a show of royal munificence as he was unable to contain the Vikings. Accordingly it was decided by treaty that Rollo should be baptized, and then hold the north of the country of the king as his lord.

The inbred and untameable ferocity of the man may well be imagined; for, on receiving this gift, as the bystanders suggested that he ought to kiss the foot of his benefactor, disdaining to kneel down, Rollo seized the king's foot and hoisted it to his mouth as he stood erect. The king fell flat on his back, and the Norsemen laughed.

William of Malmesbury (c.1125; 1854 trans.) p.111. After ravaging in the north of England, Rollo – who was 'of such great size that no horse could bear him, so he always journeyed on foot' – became the first Duke of Normandy in 911. His great-great-great-grandson was William the Conqueror (see 215:2).

THE AGE OF ALFRED THE GREAT, 871–900

1 One day, when his mother was showing him and his brothers a book of English poetry … she said 'I shall give this book to whichever one of you can learn it the fastest' … Spurred on by these words and attracted by the beauty of the initial letter in the book, Alfred … immediately took the book from her hand, went to his teacher and learnt it, took it back to his mother and recited it.

Asser (c.893; 1983 trans.) p.75. Alfred was sent to Rome when he was five years old, possibly to be consecrated, and he grew from precocious childhood into a most unusual combination: a warrior and king who was literate and who is credited with several extensive translations from Latin into the vernacular.

2 [King Alfred, c.876] noticing the cottage of a certain unknown swineherd, directed his path towards it and sought a peaceful retreat; he was given refuge, and he stayed there for a number of days, impoverished, subdued and content with the bare necessities. Now it happened by chance one day, when the swineherd was leading his flock to their usual pastures, that the king remained at home with the swineherd's wife. The wife, concerned for her husband's return, had entrusted some kneaded flour to the oven. As is the custom among country-women, she was intent on other domestic occupa-tions, until, when she sought the bread from the oven, she saw it burning from the other side of the room. She immediately grew angry and said to the king (unknown to her as such), 'Look here, man, you hesitate to turn the loaves which you see burning, yet you're quite happy to eat them when they come warm from the oven.' The king … sub-mitting to the woman's scolding, not only turned the bread but even attended to it as she brought out the loaves when they were ready.

Anon. *Vita St Neoti* (c.1150); Asser (c.893; 1983 trans.) App.I. The story was almost certainly invented and written into the Life of St Neot to extend the tenuous connection between Alfred and Neot. It was taken up by many later writers, who elaborated the story, colouring in the character of the swine-herd's wife and changing the bread to cakes.

3 This is the peace which King Alfred and King Guthrum and the councillors of all the English race and all the people who are in East Anglia have all agreed on …

First concerning our boundaries: up the Thames, and then up the Lea, and along the Lea to its source, then in a straight line to Bedford, then up the Ouse to the Watling Street.

Treaty, 889; E.H.D. Vol.I (1955) p.380. Every battle, win or lose, meant that the Danish King Guthrum had fewer men under his command, and they could not be easily replaced. He was a politician, however, and after he had lost a battle against King Alfred at Edington, he decided to be converted to Christianity, was baptized and became the godson of Alfred. Their treaty left London in the area controlled by Alfred and divided England diagonally, creating what became known as the Danelaw, where Danish customary law prevailed in the local courts, rather than the English law of the Mercians or West Saxons.

4 So completely had learning decayed in England that there were very few men on this side of the Humber who could apprehend their services in English or even translate a letter from Latin into English … there were so few of them that I cannot even recollect a single one south of the Thames when I succeeded to the kingdom.

King Alfred, translation of Pope Gregory's *Pastoral Care* (c.890) Preface; E.H.D. Vol.I (1955) p.818. The preface was a letter attached to the copy of the translation that was sent to each of the king's bishops.

5 [We must] bring it to pass … if we have the peace, that all the youth now in England, born of free men who have the means that they can apply to it, may be devoted to learning … until such time as they can read well what is written in England.

King Alfred (c.890) Preface; E.H.D. Vol.I (1955) p.819. The king outlines his programme to restore learning to his kingdom.

6 (896) Then King Alfred had long ships built to oppose the Danish warships. They were almost twice as long as the others. Some had 60 oars, some more. They were both swifter and less flexible and also higher than the others. They were built neither on the Frisian nor the Danish pattern.

The Anglo-Saxon Chronicle, (1961 trans.). The annal for 896 tells of the English navy getting some teeth and beginning to hold its own against the Vikings.

7 No man grows wise without he have his share of winters.

Anon. *The Wanderer*, (possibly written down c.900); M. Alexander (ed.) *Early English Poems* (1966) p.72.

8 He [King Edgar] commanded Hywel, king of the Welsh, to pay him a yearly tribute of 300 wolves, and this he performed for three years, before declaring that he could find no more wolves.

William of Malmesbury *Vita Swythuni* (c.1125; 1854 trans.). Nothing changes – the government in trouble with endangering a rare species as long ago as 960.

AETHELRED THE UNREADY, 978–1016

1 When the saintly King Edward had reigned for five years, he was killed by the faithless treachery of his people, toward the evening at the gap of Corfe [in Dorset] … It is said that his stepmother, that is the mother of King Aethelred, stabbed him with a dagger while stretching out a cup to him.

Henry of Huntingdon *Historia Anglorum* (History of the English People) (c.1130; 1996 trans.) Bk 1.27. The accusation that Aelfthryth, third wife of King Edgar, arranged the murder in 979 of her stepson to put her own son in the throne, created more bad press for King Aethelred. His nickname 'unraede', a pun on his name Aethelred, translates more nearly to 'ill-advised' than to 'unready', the label he received in later centuries.

2 It is right that reeves work diligently and always provide for their lords aright. But now it has happened all too greatly that since Edgar died … there are more robbers than righteous men.

Wulfstan *The Institutes of Polity* (c.1010); M. Swanton (ed.) *Anglo-Saxon Prose* (1975) p.130. The peaceful time of King Edgar (r.959–975) was longed for but never attained during the reign of his son Aethelred. The reeves, originally retainers and administrators of their lord, developed into royal and government officials, such as the town reeve and port reeve and the shire reeve, who became sheriff.

3 Leofsunu lifted up his voice and raised his shield, his buckler … This I avow, that I will not flee a foot-space hence, but will press on and avenge my liege-lord in the fight. About Sturmer the steadfast heroes will have no need to reproach me now that my lord has fallen, that I made my way home and turned from the battle, a lordless man. Rather shall weapon, spear-point and iron blade, be my end.

Anon. *The Battle of Maldon* (c.1000) line 244; E.H.D. Vol.1 (1955) p.296. After their lord, Ealdorman Brihtnoth, had been killed in the battle in Essex in 991, as the heroic code demanded, his men fought on to the death.

4 The king named this dragon-ship the Long Serpent. It had 34 benches, each for two oars. The head and the coils of the dragon's tail were all ornamented in gold. The Long Serpent was the finest ship built in Norway, and the most costly.

Anon. *The Saga of Olaf Tryggvason* (c.1250; 1895 trans.) Ch.223. The Vikings fought battles at sea by coming alongside

their enemy and fighting hand to hand across the decks. This formidable ship carried more warriors than the more normal ships of some 30 or 36 oars and towered over them in battle.

5 Rime-crusted and ready to sail, a royal vessel with curved prow lay in harbour. They set down their dear king amidships, close by the mast. A mass of treasure was brought there … No ship was ever so well equipped with swords, corselets, weapons and armour. On the king's breast rested a heap of jewels which were to go with him far out into the keeping of the sea.

High overhead they set his golden standard; then, surrendering him to the sea, they sadly allowed it to bear him off. And no one can truly say who received that cargo.

Anon. *Beowulf* (probably 8th century; 1957 trans.) p.27. The funeral of King Scyld described at the start of the tale of Beowulf, although a king was more often buried in an earth barrow. Sometimes a ship was itself buried, as at Sutton Hoo, Suffolk, and at Gokstad, Norway, where an almost complete ship was excavated in 1880.

6 Ashore they [the Vikings] found self-sown fields of wheat where the ground was low lying, and vines wherever there was high ground … [the natives] were dark, ugly men who wore their hair in an unpleasant fashion. They had big eyes and were broad in the cheek …

They said that kings ruled over them, and that one of them was called Avaldamon and the other Avaldidida. There were no houses there, they said; the people lived in caves or holes. A country lay on the other side, they said, opposite their own land, where lived men who dressed in white clothes and carried poles, and were festooned with streamers, and whooped loudly.

Anon. *The Saga of Eric the Red* (early 13th century; 1961 trans.) pp.151, 156. This story, told and re-told over the years, was finally written down in Iceland. Eric the Red had left there and settled in the south of Greenland. His son, Leif Ericson, sailed on to Newfoundland, while his kinsman, Thorfinn, seeking Vinland, the land where the wine berries grow, sailed much further c.1000, either into the river St Lawrence or south to Maine, where he encountered the native Americans, 500 years before Columbus. Historians at Yale University unearthed a medieval map that identifies Vinland, but it is of doubtful authenticity.

7 [King Olaf] … had all the most prominent men taken. And they all were compelled to become Christians or else suffer death or flee abroad if they were able. And they who let themselves be baptized surrendered to the king their sons as hostages for their good faith.

Snorri Sturluson 'Saga of Olaf the Saint' in *Heimskringla* (c.1220; 1964 trans.) Ch.111. Olaf became king of Norway in 1014 and was made a saint after he converted his people to Christianity. His methods were somewhat fearsome.

1 (991) It was determined that tribute should first be paid to the Danish men because of the great terror they were causing along the coast. The first payment was 10,000 pounds. Archbishop Sigeric first advised that course.

(994) ... and the whole army came then to Southampton and took winter quarters there; and they were provisioned throughout all the West Saxon kingdom, and they were paid 16,000 pounds in money ...

(1012) Ealdorman Eadric and all the chief councillors of England ... came to London before Easter ... and they stayed there until the tribute, namely 48,000 pounds, was all paid after Easter.

(1018) In this year the tribute was paid over all England, namely 72,000 pounds in all, apart from what the citizens of London paid, namely ten and a half thousand pounds.

The Anglo-Saxon Chronicle (1961 trans.). In the manner of extortioners, the Vikings always went away after they had been paid off and always came back for more. By the time of the last payment, Cnut (Canute, Knut) was king, and the money was probably used to pay off his army. The payments, for increasingly vast sums, are difficult to relate to modern amounts.

2 There was present no slave, no man freed from slavery, no low-born man, no man weakened by age; for all were noble, all strong with the might of mature age, all sufficiently fit for any type of fighting, all of such fleetness that they scorned the speed of horsemen.

Anon. *Encomium Emmae Regina* (c.1020; 1949 trans.) Bk 2.4. A description of the traditional crews of Viking boats, in this case in the fleet commanded by King Cnut. No space was wasted, and any rowing needed was done by the warriors. The *Encomium* was written to laud Emma, the queen of both Aethelred and Cnut.

3 83. And he who violates these laws which the king has now given to all men, whether he be Danish or English, is to forfeit his wergild to the king.

83.1. And if he violates it again, he is to pay his wergild twice.

83.2. And if he then is so presumptuous that he violates it a third time, he is to forfeit all that he owns.

Laws of Cnut; E.H.D. Vol.1 (1955) p.430. Three strikes and you're out. For hundreds of years the rating of the wergild, or blood price, of an ealdorman, a thegn or a ceorl governed the amount of his fine. In the time of King Cnut a persistent offender with any property would have had to be very careful.

4 Cnut was lord of three kingdoms [Denmark, England and Norway]; he found few who dared to disobey him. And nevertheless he was disobeyed, and his command despised. He was in London on the Thames; the tide was flowing near the church which is called Westminster ... Cnut held his sceptre in his hand, and he said to the tide, 'Return back; flee from me, lest I strike thee.' The sea did not retire for him, more and more the tide rose; the king remained, and struck the water with his sceptre. The river retired not for that, so it reached the king and wetted him.

Geoffrey Gaimar *Estoire des Engleis* (History of the English) (c.1140; 1854 trans.) p.786. Cnut was a Viking, and this famous story was propaganda to show his Christian humility.

5 I tell thee also, brother Edward, that you do wrong in abandoning the English practices which your fathers followed, and in loving the practices of heathen men who begrudge you life, and in so doing show by such evil habits that you despise your race and your ancestors, since in insult to them you dress in Danish fashion with bared neck and blinded eyes.

Anon., letter, probably c.1010; E.H.D. Vol.1 (1955) p.825. A personal letter that develops into a more general admonition against collaborating with the enemy.

6 Earl Godwine ... took him [Alfred, son of King Aethelred] under his protection ... and led him into the town called Guildford, and lodged his soldiers there. But when it was morning the innocent men were led out ... and some were sold for money, some were beheaded, some were blinded, some were mutilated, some were scalped shamefully. Then they took Alfred, slung him naked across a horse and brought him to Ely. There they put out his eyes.

Geoffrey Gaimar (c.1140; 1854 trans.) p.788. Alfred, brother of Edward the Confessor, who posed a threat to the authority of both Godwine, Earl of Wessex, and the new king, Harold I, was then murdered by disembowelling.

7 The Danes kept them [the English] in a very degraded position, and often did them dishonour. If a hundred English met one Dane, evil arose if they did not bow themselves to him; and if they came upon a bridge they were required to wait; it was a crime if they moved before the Dane passed. In passing every one inclined himself; whoever did not, if he were taken, was shamefully beaten. In such vileness were the English, so did the Danes vilify them.

Geoffrey Gaimar (c.1140; 1854 trans.) p.787. A hundred years later Gaimar, a Norman, showed surprising sympathy for the oppressed English, possibly because it was the pagan Viking yoke under which they had suffered rather than the civilized and Christian Normans of his time.

EDWARD THE CONFESSOR, 1042–66

1 He was a very proper figure of a man – of outstanding height, and distinguished by his milky white hair and beard, full face and rosy cheeks, thin white hands, and long translucent fingers; in all the rest of his body he was an unblemished royal person.

Anon. *Vita Edwardi Regis* (c.1067; 1992 trans.) Bk 1.1. The familiar portrait of the last of the long line of English kings, Edward the Confessor.

2 Siward, the valiant earl of the Northumbrians … went to Scotland with an army of cavalry and a powerful fleet, and fought a battle with Macbeth, king of Scots; and having slain many Scottish soldiers … he routed Macbeth, and as the king [Edward the Confessor] directed, appointed Malcolm, son of the king of the Cumbrians, king.

Simeon of Durham *History of the Kings* (c.1110; 1855 trans.) p.538. Macbeth had made a pilgrimage to Rome four years earlier, in 1050, and was, for 17 years, the strong ruler of a prospering Scotland. His reputation, coloured by Shakespeare, is hardly justified. This is a very rare mention of the English having used cavalry; their leaders normally rode to battle on horseback, dismounted and then fought on foot.

3 The countess Godiva who … longed to free the town of Coventry from a heavy tax, often besought her husband [Earl Leofric of Mercia] that … he would free the town from that service … [the earl said] 'Mount your horse and ride naked, before all the people, through the market of the town … and on your return you shall have your request.'

Whereupon the countess … loosed her hair and let down her tresses, which covered the whole of her body like a veil, and then mounting her horse and attended by two knights, she rode through the marketplace, without being seen, except her fair legs.

Roger of Wendover *Flores Historiarum* (Flowers of History) (c.1220; 1849 trans.) 1057, p.314. Retold here, 160 years after

the event, by the monk Roger of Wendover, this story still holds people's imagination. Earl Leofric kept his word and removed the tax.

4 The elder, Harold, was the taller, well practised in endless fatigue and doing without sleep and food, and endowed with mildness of temper and a more ready understanding. He could bear contradiction well, not readily … retaliating on a fellow citizen or compatriot … The fault of rashness or levity is not one that anybody could charge against him or Tostig …

Tostig was endowed with very great and prudent restraint – although occasionally he was a little overzealous in attacking evil – and with bold and inflexible constancy of mind … sometimes he was so cautiously active that his action seemed to come before his planning, and this, often enough, was advantageous to him in the theatre of the world.

Both persevered with what they had done; but Tostig vigorously, Harold prudently; the one in action aimed at success, the other also at happiness.

Anon. *Vita Edwardi Regis* (c.1067; 1992 trans.) Bk 1.5. The brothers Harold and Tostig were the two most prominent earls, one of whom, although it remained unspoken, was likely to succeed Edward the Confessor as king. Tostig's thegns rebelled against him, almost certainly on the prompting of Harold, and he had to appear before the king to defend himself.

5 But this distinguished earl [Tostig] had in his time so reduced the number of robbers and cleared the country of them by mutilating or killing them, and by sparing no one, however noble, who was caught in this crime …

Not a few charged that glorious earl with being too cruel, and with punishing disturbers more for desire of their property which would be confiscated than for love of justice … It was also said that they had undertaken this madness against their earl at the artful persuasion of his brother, Earl Harold (which heaven forbid). But I dare not and would not believe that such a prince was guilty of this detestable wickedness against his brother. Earl Tostig himself, however, publicly testifying before the king and his assembled courtiers, charged him with this; but Harold, rather too generous with oaths (alas), cleared this charge too with oaths.

Anon. *Vita Edwardi Regis* (c.1067; 1992 trans.) Bk 1.7. The anonymous monk who wrote this account of the life of King Edward was probably a chaplain of Queen Edith, sister of Harold and Tostig, and appears to have slightly favoured the younger brother, Tostig. The acid mention of Harold's generosity with oaths is often thought to refer to an oath that the Normans claimed to have been made by Harold – that he would support William, Duke of Normandy as the successor to King Edward (see 215:5). The king was reluctantly forced to exile his friend Tostig, which left the field clear for Harold. Within weeks the king died, and Harold usurped the throne.

1 Tostig quitted the king's court in a rage and came to Hereford, where his brother Harold had prepared a great feast for the king. He cut off the limbs of all the servants, and put an arm, or some other member, in each of the vessels of wine, mead, ale or pickle. He then sent a message to the king that there was prepared food seasoned to his mind, and that he should take care to take some of the delicacies away with him.

Roger of Wendover (c.1220; 1849 trans.) 1065, p.322. This was a colourful, though possibly fictional, accusation, with English lack of civilization being emphasized by a Norman.

2 Since those who have climbed to the highest offices in the kingdom of England, the earls, bishops and abbots, and all those in holy orders, are not what they seem to be, but on the contrary, are servants of the devil, within a year and a day after the day of your death God has delivered all this kingdom, cursed by him, into the hands of the enemy, and the devils shall come through all this land with fire and sword and the havoc of war.

Anon. *Vita Edwardi Regis* (c.1067; 1992 trans.) Bk 2.11. On his deathbed Edward the Confessor had a vision in which was predicted the invasion of the Normans less than a year later.

3 Unexpectedly there now came a true report from England that the land was bereft of her king Edward, and his crown was worn by Harold. This insane Englishman was not a choice of the people, but on that sorrowful day when the best of kings was buried and the whole nation mourned his passing, he seized the royal throne with the acclaim of certain iniquitous confederates and thereby perjured himself. He was made king by the unholy consecration of Stigand, who had been deprived of his ministry by the justified fervour of papal anathema.

William of Poitiers *Gesta Willelmi ducis Normannorum et regis Anglorum* (Deeds of Duke William) (c.1071–4; 1997 trans.)

Ch.60. This was the Norman version of the taking of the throne in 1066, and those with Harold at the bedside of the dying king certainly had been his supporters, chief among whom were his sister, Queen Edith, and the excommunicated archbishop of Canterbury, Stigand.

4 Harald for many years took part in the campaign in Saracen Land and in Sicily. It is said that in all these campaigns he fought eighteen great battles.

Snorri Sturluson 'The Saga of Harald Sigurtharson' in *Heimskringla* (c.1220; 1964 trans.). Nephew of St Olaf, Harald Sigurtharson, known as Hardrada, commanded a force of mercenaries in the service of Empress Zoe, who ruled the Greek empire from Byzantium (see 108:3). The most experienced general of his time, he became king of Norway in 1047 and, with Tostig, invaded England in 1066.

5 A single Norwegian, worthy of eternal fame, resisted on the bridge, and felling more than forty Englishmen with his trusty axe, he alone held up the entire English army until three o'clock in the afternoon. At length someone came up in a boat and through the openings of the bridge struck him in the private parts with a spear.

Henry of Huntingdon (c.1130; 1996 trans.) Bk 6.27. A narrow plank bridge over the River Derwent divided the armies at the Battle of Stamford Bridge, in Yorkshire, in which King Harold II defeated his brother Tostig and King Harald Hardrada of Norway in late Sept. 1066, just three weeks before the disastrous battle at Hastings.

6 Far and wide the ground was covered with the flower of English nobility and youth, soiled by their own blood. The two brothers of the king were found lying beside him. He himself, all dignity lost, was recognized not by his face but by certain indications and was carried to the camp of the duke, where his burial was entrusted to William surnamed Malet, and not to his mother, who offered for her beloved son his weight in gold.

William of Poitiers (c.1071–4; 1997 trans.) Ch.78. Of the sons of Godwine, Earl of Wessex, Swegn died in exile, Tostig was killed by his brother at Stamford Bridge, and Harold, Gyrth and Leofwine were killed in the battle at Hastings (see 216:2). The youngest, Wulfnoth, survived as a hostage in Normandy where he had been since 1051. Their mother, Gytha, with her grandsons, continued to fight against William.

Rus and Muscovy, 839–1613

RUS, 839–1275

1 There also came envoys from the Greeks sent by the Emperor Theophilus ... The emperor [Charlemagne] received them with due ceremony on 18 May 839 at Ingelheim [in Germany]. The purpose of their mission was to confirm the treaty of peace and perpetual friendship between the two emperors [of the Eastern and Western Roman empires] and their subjects. He also sent with the ... envoys some men who said they – meaning their whole people – were called the people of Rus and had been sent to him by their king whose name was the Khagan [Khan] for the sake of friendship, so they claimed. Theophilus requested in his letter that the emperor in his goodness might grant them safe conducts to travel through his empire ... for the route by which they had reached Constantinople had taken them through primitive tribes that were very fierce and savage ... When the emperor investigated more closely the reason for their coming here, he discovered that they belonged to the people of the Swedes. He suspected that they had really been sent as spies to this kingdom of ours rather than seekers of friendship, so he decided to keep them with him until he could find out for certain whether they came in good faith or not.
Anon. *The Annals of St-Bertin* (847) Vol.I (1991 edn) p.44. Swedes had visited Charlemagne's court from 829, but this is the first record of the name Rus to identify Scandinavians from lands east of the Baltic.

2 [In the year 882] Oleg set himself up as a prince in Kiev and declared: 'May this be the mother of Russian cities.'
Anon., mid-960s, *Primary Chronicle* (Laurentian text) (1953 trans.) p.61.

3 Russia is an island around which is a lake, and the island in which they dwell is a three days' journey through forests and swamps covered with trees and it is a damp morass such that when a man puts his foot on the ground it quakes owing to the moisture ...

When a child is born to any man among them, he takes a drawn sword to the newborn child and places it between his hands and says to him: 'I shall bequeath to thee no wealth and thou will have naught except what thou doest gain for thyself with this sword of thine.'

They have no landed property nor villages, nor cultivated land; their only occupation is trading in sables and grey squirrel and other furs, and in these they trade and they take as the price in gold and silver.
Ibn Rusta *Kitab al-A'lakal-nafisa* (Book of Precious Jewels) (?903–913); Carlile A. Macartney *The Magyars in the 9th Century* (1930) pp.213–14. The Arab scholar is describing a nomadic people.

4 The story of this achievement begins on 18 June 860, when a fleet of two hundred Viking ships, coming from the Black Sea, sailed into the Bosphorus and turned against Constantinople. The city's position was serious indeed: the Byzantine fleet was probably in the Mediterranean, fighting the Arabs, the army and the emperor were campaigning in Asia Minor. The suburbs and the coastline were powerless against the savage depredations of the barbarians ... The violent emergence of these Vikings – known to the Byzantines as Rus ... on the horizon of East Rome was the outcome of a century-long process of expansion which led the Scandinavians, mostly Swedes ... to sail up the Baltic rivers over the great watershed of the eastern European plain.
Dimitri Obolensky *Byzantium and the Slavs: Collected Studies* (1994) Vol.2, p.494.

5 Moving light as a leopard, making many wars, he did not take wagons on his travels, nor kettles, neither did he have his meat boiled. But he would cut off a strip of horseflesh, game or beef, roast it on the coals and eat. There was no tent for him, he just laid him out a sweat-cloth, with a saddle at his head.
Anon., mid-960s, *Primary Chronicle* (1950 edn) Vol.I, p.46; Simon Franklin and Jonathan Shepard *The Emergence of Rus 750–1200* (1996) p.143. The chronicle in the version that has come down to us represents the major source of information on the period. It was compiled by monks, and its description of the young Sviatoslav of Kiev (d.972) is clearly still of a nomadic leader. 'The *Primary Chronicle* in its present form owes most of all to one of these monks, who about 1113 carried out a thorough revision of his predecessors' work, and by incorporating much new material, particularly of Byzantine origin, greatly enhanced the chronicle's scope' (Dimitri Obolensky *The Byzantine Commonwealth* (1971) pp.332–3). It was Sviatoslav's son, Vladimir, who was to establish himself as lord of Kiev.

1 The Bulgars bow down and sit, and look further and hither and thither like men possessed; there is no joy among them but only sorrow and a dreadful stench. Their religion is not good. Then we went to the Germans and we saw them celebrating many services in their churches, but we saw no beauty there. Then we went to the Greeks [to Constantinople] and they led us to the place where they worship their God, and we knew not whether we were in heaven or on earth: for on earth there is no such vision nor beauty, and we do not know how to describe it; we know only that there God dwells among men. We cannot forget that beauty.

Anon., 986, *Primary Chronicle* (1953 trans.) p.11. The returning delegation enthusiastically recommends the Eastern Church to Prince Vladimir (r.980–1015). Earlier he had received delegations promulgating Islam, Judaism and Christianity. He had opted for Christianity and now the choice is further narrowed.

2 They went into the water and stood there, some up to the neck, others up to the chest, the young nearest the bank up to their chests, some held children and the adults walked about, and the priests stood still, saying prayers. And heaven and earth could be seen to rejoice at the salvation of so many souls.

Anon., 988, *Primary Chronicle* (1950 edn) Vol.1, p.81. Following the conversion and baptism of Prince Vladimir, the Bright Sun, the inhabitants of Kiev are baptized in the River Dnieper.

3 Thus his father, Vladimir, ploughed and softened the earth, that is, enlightened the land with baptism; while he sowed the hearts of believing peoples with the words of books, and we harvest, accepting the teaching of books ... For we acquire wisdom and temperance from the words of books: for they are rivers satisfying the thirst of the universe, they are sources of wisdom; in books there is immeasurable depth, we are consoled by them in sorrow, they are a bridle of temperance.

Anon., mid-960s, *Primary Chronicle* (1950 edn) Vol.1 p.102. The chronicler is praising Yaroslav (r.1019–54) for continuing the work of Vladimir, who had first installed Christianity in Rus, some 50 years before. Yaroslav built the Cathedral of St Sophia in Kiev and encouraged the translation of the scriptures into the vernacular.

4 And in the month of June they move off down the River Dnieper ... and there they gather over two or three days; and when all the dug-out canoes are collected together, then they set out and come down the said River Dnieper ... and first they come to the first rapid called Essoupi, which means in the Rus

and Slavonic languages 'do not sleep' .... In the middle of it are rooted high rocks which stand out like islands ... Taking up the goods which they have on board the boats, [they] conduct the slaves in their chains past by land, six miles until they are through the barrage.

Emperor Constantine VII Porphyrogenitus *De administrando imperio* (early 10th century; 1967 trans.) pp.59–63. Porphyrogenitus means 'born in the purple', the title given to all children born to a reigning sovereign in Byzantium (see 106:8). The emperor (r.913–59) left his son and successor an instructional manual on how to rule. Here he is describing the fierce journey of the Scandinavian-Rus warrior-traders and their voyage to Constantinople. This involved the use of rollers to drag their boats overland, and they even dismantled and reassembled them as they encountered a succession of rapids.

5 I conceive it is always greatly to the advantage of the emperor of the Romans [Byzantium] to be minded to keep peace with the nation of the Pechenegs [of the southern Russian steppes] and to conclude conventions and treaties of friendship with them and to send every year to them from our side a diplomatic agent with presents suitable and fitting to that nation.

Emperor Constantine VII Porphyrogenitus (early 10th century; 1967 trans.) p.48.

6 If someone rapes a boyar's [member of the old aristocracy's] daughter or a boyar's wife [then he is to pay] 5 grivnas [coins] of gold for the dishonour, and 5 grivnas of gold to the bishop; and if she be [a daughter or a wife] of lesser boyars 1 grivna of gold, and 1 grivna of gold to the bishop ... [if she be a daughter or wife] of common people, 15 grivnas [of fur] to her and 15 grivnas [of fur] to the bishop.

Yaroslav the Wise, Statute, article 3, mid-11th century; V.L. Ianin *Zakonodatel'stvo Drevnei Rusii* (Laws of Ancient Russia) (1984) p.189. The prince's laws specify the crime and the fine or prison sentence. He also introduced fixed penalties in the ecclesiastical courts.

7 Sviatopolk's retainers began the discussion and remarked: 'It is not advisable to go to war in the spring, for we will ruin the peasants and their ploughing.' And Vladimir [Monomakh] replied, 'I am surprised, comrades, that you are so concerned about the beasts the peasant uses to plough. Why do you not bear in mind that if the peasant starts to plough, a Polovtsian may come and shoot him down with his bow, ride on into his village and carry off his wife, his children and all his possessions? Are you

concerned for the horse but not for the peasant himself?' And Sviatopolk's supporters had no answer. And Sviatopolk said, 'I am ready now.'

Anon., 1103, *Primary Chronicle* (1953 trans.) p.200. It was the prince's duty and in his interests to protect his peasants, whose tribute provided his income.

1 The soul sits in the head, having within it the mind like a bright eye filling the whole body with its power. Just as you, prince sitting here in your land act throughout all the land by means of your commanders and servants while you yourself are the lord and prince, so the soul acts throughout all the body by means of its five servants, that is by means of the five senses.

Nikifor I; Albrecht Dölker *Der Fastenbrief* (Lenten Letters) (1985) pp.38–40. The Byzantine metropolitan of Kiev (1104–21) preaches a sermon at Lent to Prince Vladimir Monomakh on his role. Coincidentally, Monomakh himself wrote an 'Instruction' to his sons on how to fulfil a prince's duties. His attitude to power and delegation is very different from Nikifor's.

2 Be not lazy in your household but oversee everything yourself; do not look to your steward ... when going to war, be not lazy nor look to your commanders ... Set the guards yourself ... Whatever my *otrok* [lad] was to do, I have done myself, in war and in the hunt, night and day, in the heat and in winter, not giving myself rest.

Anon., mid-960s, *Primary Chronicle* (1950 edn) Vol.1, p.157. The contrast between Nikifor and Monomakh is made in Franklin and Shepard (1996) p.313.

3 Hear, you princes, who oppose your elder brethren and stir up war and incite the pagans against your brethren – lest God should reprove you at the Last Judgement – how saints Boris and Gleb endured from their brother not only the taking away of their domains but also the taking away of their lives. Yet you cannot endure even one word from your brother, and for the merest slight you stir up mortal enmity and receive aid from the pagans against your brethren.

Anon. *Homily on Princes* (c.1200); *Pamiatniki literatury drevnei Rusii* (Literary Relics of Ancient Russia) Vol.12, Ch.5, p.338. The story of the martyrdom of the princes, killed by their elder brother Sviatopolk, is typical of saints' lives and full of echoes of Christ's sacrifice. It is retold as an exemplar for succeeding generations and culminates in a hymn of intercession. The problem of inheritance among warring younger brothers was a chronic one.

4 I tell you truly that I would straightway set at naught all the honour and glory if only I could be one of the stakes in the fence before the monastery gates, or if I could lie as a bit of dirt in the Monastery of the Caves, so that men would trample upon me, or if I could become one of the poor, begging at its gates.

Anon. *Das Paterikon* (1220s) p.99; Obolensky (1971) p.300. The prestige of the Kiev monastery was unrivalled, and a prelate feels intense nostalgia for his alma mater.

5 They returned from the River Dnieper and we know not whence they came and whither they went. Only God knows whence they came against us for their sins.

Anon., 1223; *Novgorod Chronicle* (1914 trans.) p.63. A laconic report on the first Tatars, which did not seem an ominous beginning of the Mongol invasions, just another incursion from the steppe.

6 The prince [of the important town of Ryazan] with his mother, wife and sons, the boyars and inhabitants, without regard to age or sex, were slaughtered with the savage cruelty of Mongol revenge ... Priests were roasted alive, and nuns and maidens were ravished in the churches before their relatives. No eye remained open to weep for the dead.

Anon. chronicler, 2nd half of 13th century; N.M. Karamzin *History of the Russian State* (1842–3 edn) Vol.3, Cols 167–8. The Mongol advance of 1236–7 begins.

7 At that time the [attacks of the] people of Lithuania were multiplied, and they began to lay waste the lands of Alexander. But he went out and slaughtered them. On one occasion he sallied forth and defeated seven armies in one sortie, and he killed a multitude of their princes and others he took prisoner. His service men, mocking them, bound them to the tails of their horses. And from then on they began to hold his name in awe.

Anon. *Second Pskov Chronicle* (2nd half of 13th century) p.14; J.L.I. Fennell *The Crisis of Medieval Russia 1200–1304* (1983) p.103. In this anonymous life of Alexander (given the sobriquet Nevsky after his victory over the Swedes on the River Neva in 1240), the hero and saint is ascribed mythical feats at his legendary victory on the ice of Lake Peypus against the Teutonic Knights in 1242. It figured in Sergei Eisenstein's film (1938) and Sergei Prokofiev's accompanying score.

8 My children, know you that the sun of the land of Suzdal [the principality near Rostov, east of

Moscow] has now set! For nevermore shall such a prince be found in the land.

Anon. *Life of Alexander* (2nd half of 13th century) p.193; Fennell (1983) p.120. The metropolitan's funeral oration on the death of Alexander Nevsky in 1263 in his capital Vladimir (near and to the northeast of Moscow), where there are still buildings dating from Nevsky's time and earlier.

1 They [the Mongols] attacked Russia, where they made great havoc, destroying cities and fortresses and killing men; and they laid siege to Kiev, the capital of Russia; after they had besieged the city for a long time, they took it and put the inhabitants to death. When we were journeying through that land we came across countless skulls and bones of dead men lying on the ground. Kiev had been a very large and thickly populated town but now it has been reduced almost to nothing, for there are at the present time space two hundred houses there and the inhabitants are kept in complete slavery. Going on from there, fighting as they went, the Tatars destroyed the whole of Russia.

John of Plano Carpini *History of the Mongols* (c.1246–7); Christopher Dawson (ed.) *The Mongol Mission* (1955) p.29. The French Franciscan friar (see 248:3) was sent by Pope Innocent IV to the Mongol Khan in Karakorum to persuade him to convert to Christianity. He is giving an eyewitness account of a visit to Kiev in Feb. 1246, about six years after the Mongols had sacked it.

2 To the north of this province lies Russia, which is everywhere covered with forests and extends from Poland and Hungary to the River Don, and it was all ravaged by the Tatars, and still being ravaged every day. For the Tatars prefer the Saracens to the Ruthenians, who are Christians, and when the latter can give no more gold nor silver, they are driven off to the wilds, them and their little ones, like flocks of sheep there to herd their cattle.

William of Rubruck *Journey to the Far Eastern Parts of the World* (1253–5; 1900 edn) p.93. Another intrepid friar (see 248:4) was sent by the French king, Louis IX, as a missionary.

3 The khan received him [Yaroslav] with honour, gave him his armour and ordered that he be instructed in the ceremony [of appointing him] to the grand principality. He ordered Vladimir of Ryazan and Ivan of Starodub, who were in the Horde at the time, to lead his horse. And in August he let him go and sent him with his envoy.

Jani Beg, 1264; V.N. Tatishchev *Istoriya Rossiyskaya* (1962–8) Vol.5, p.44. This description makes clear that the second of Nevsky's brothers, Yaroslav (d.1271), in becoming the grand

prince of Sarai, capital of the western Mongols or Golden Horde (see 249:6), was dependent on the Tatars who were responsible not only for the ceremony but also for the patent under which he would govern the principality. Nevsky himself had also paid his dues to the Tatar overlords.

4 In that year the Tatars and the Russians marched against Lithuania and having achieved nothing returned. But the Tatars did much wrong and much violence to the Christians [the Russian population] as they marched to Lithuania, and on their way back they did still more evil things … they plundered houses, took away horses, cattle and possessions, and whenever they met anyone, they robbed him and sent him away naked … This I have written so that people will remember and learn from it.

Anon., 1275; *Trinity Chronicle* (15th century; 1950 edn) pp.332–3. The Tatars were clearly not kept under control by their Russian commanders. According to Fennell (1983; p.140), this passage was probably by a contemporary.

MUSCOVY, 1330–1633

5 Article 117 and if anyone tears another's beard and there is a witness, that witness shall take the oath and go to the duel against the defendant, and if the witness wins, the amend fine for the tearing of the beard is five roubles and there is the princely fine besides. And only one witness is admitted.

Article 118 and if anyone buys a cow at a price agreed upon, and after the purchase (the cow gives birth to a calf), the seller may not sue the buyer for that calf; (on the other hand) if the cow discharges bloody urine, it may be returned and the money is to be refunded.

Article 119 and a duel may be ordered between two women but neither may have a substitute.

Charter of the city of Pskov (northwest Russia), 1397, based on laws dating from 1330s onwards; G. Vernadsky (ed.) *Medieval Russian Laws* (1947 edn) p.82.

6 When Grand Prince Ivan Danilovich sat on the grand princely throne of all Russia, there was great peace for forty years; the pagans ceased to fight against the Russian land and kill Christians; the Christians found rest and relief from great oppression, the many burdens and from Tatar violence and there was great peace in all the land.

Anon. *Trinity Chronicle* (15th century; 1950 edn) p.359. The chronicler looks back through rose-tinted spectacles at the reign of Ivan I, the 'Moneybag' of Moscow (r.1331–40). In the less idealistic judgement of Robert O. Crummey: 'His actions reveal him as a crafty and ruthless opportunist, and ambitious and grasping land-owner and tax-collector. In his career, we see little of the visionary and absolutely no signs of a chivalrous crusader' (*The Formation of Muscovy 1304–1613* (1987) p.40).

1 Am I then, the Grand Prince, not free to dispose of my sons and my throne? I shall give it to whom I please.

Ivan III to the Pskovian envoy on his right to disgrace his grandson, 1497; R. Auty and D. Obolensky (eds) *An Introduction to Russian History* (1976) p.96. Until that time the division of territory on the death of a grand prince had been according to appanage (grants made to the younger members of the royal family), but thenceforward a system of the supreme ruler with precedence over his brothers etc. became the norm.

2 [The tsar] is on earth the sole emperor of the Christians, the leader of the Apostolic church which stands no longer in Rome or Constantinople, but in the blessed city of Moscow. She alone shines in the whole world brighter than the sun … Two Romes have fallen, but the third stands and a fourth there will not be.

Philotheus of Pskov to Tsar Basil III, 1510; N.H. Baynes and H. St L.B. Moss *Byzantium* (1948) p.385. The monk expresses the view that Moscow is the heir to Constantinople. The fall of Constantinople in 1453 (see 112:1) left the Orthodox churches without a centre, just at the time when Moscow, linked by cultural and diplomatic ties to Byzantium, was emerging from Tatar domination.

3 Russia is very plentiful both of land and people and also wealth of such commodities as they have. They be great fishers for salmons and small cods: they have much oil which we call train oil … to the north part of that country are the places where they have there furs, as sables, martens, beavers, foxes white, black and red, minks, ermines, miniver [white fur] and harts … The Dutch merchants have a staple house there. There is also great store of hides, and at a place called Plesco: and thereabouts is great store of flax, hemp, wax, honey.

  Moscow is from Yaroslav two hundred miles. The country betwixt them is very well replenished with small villages which are so well filled with people that it is a wonder to see them: the ground is so well stored with corn which they carry to the city of Moscow in such abundance that it is wonder to see it. You shall meet in a morning seven or eight hundred sleds coming or going thither, that carry corn and some carry fish.

Captain Richard Chancellor to his uncle, 1553; E.D. Morgan and C.H. Coote (eds) *Early Voyages and Travels in Russia and*

Persia (1886) pp.290–92. Chancellor was part of a three-ship expedition to find the northeast passage to the fabled wealth of Cathay. He escaped the fate of the other two ships, whose crews froze to death, by sailing his ship into the White Sea. He was well received by Ivan IV (the Terrible), and through this visit he inaugurated trade and diplomatic relations between the two countries.

4 We with Christian belief and faithfulness … are furthermore willing that you send unto us your ships and vessels, when and as often as they may have passage, with good assurance on our part to see them harmless and if you send one of your Majesty's counsel to treat with us whereby your country merchants may with all kinds of wares, and where they will make their market in our dominions, they shall have their free mart with all free liberties through my whole dominions with all kinds of wares to come and go at their pleasure, without any let, damage or impediment.

Ivan IV to Edward VI of England, Feb. 1554; Samuel Purchas (ed.) *Hakluytus Posthumus or Purchas his Pilgrimes* (1625; 1906 edn) Vol.2, pp.621–3. This letter, following Chancellor's visit (see 171:3), was, in fact, received by Mary I after Edward's death.

5 The twentieth of September I came unto Vologda [northern Russia], which is a great city and the river passeth through the same. The houses are builded with wood of fir trees, joined one with another, and round without; the houses are four-square without any iron or stone work, covered with birch barks, and wood over the same. Their churches are all of wood, two for every parish, one to be heated for winter and the other for summer. On the tops of their houses they lay much earth, for fear of burning: for they are sore plagued with fire.

Anthony Jenkinson, 1557; Purchas (1625; 1906 edn) Vol.2, pp.628–30. An English merchant escorting Ivan IV's ambassador from London back to Moscow gives his first impressions of Russia.

6 They have many sorts of meats and drinks when they banquet, and delight in eating of gross meats and stinking fish. Before they drink they used to blow in the cup: their greatest friendship is in drinking: they are great talkers and liars, without any faith or trust in their words, flatterers and dissemblers. The women be there very obedient to their husbands, and are kept straightly from going abroad, but at some seasons.

Anthony Jenkinson, 1557; Purchas (1625; 1906 edn) Vol.2 p.634.

1 Josaf, by the grace of God archbishop of Constantinople, the new Rome, and ecumenical patriarch. Our beatitude has truly learnt and determined through the tales of many men worthy of credence, but also through writings, and through the accounts of chroniclers that the present reigning tsar of Moscow and Novgorod, Astrakhan, Kazan, Nagai and all great Russia, the lord Ivan is descended in lineage and royal blood from that ever memorable tsaritsa and sovereign, lady Anna, sister of the autocrat and tsar Monomachus, of the lineage of the pious tsar Constantine (the Great) and born to the purple.
Josaf, patriarch of Constantinople, charter, 1561; *Russkaya istoricheskaya biblioteka* (Russian Historical Library) (1872–1927) Vol.22, Col.68. Josaf's recognition of Ivan IV's right to the title of tsar is based on the legendary crowning of Vladimir Monomakh. This link back to the Byzantine emperors and church remained of central importance to both sides.

2 By command of the pious tsar and grand prince of all Russia Ivan [IV] Vasil'evich and with the blessing of his eminence Metropolitan [of Moscow] Makarii, they began to study the art of printing books in the year 1553, and they began at first to print these sacred books, the Acts of the Apostles, and the general epistles … on April 19 1563.
Ivan Fedorov, printer's afterword to the first edn of the Acts of the Apostles and Epistles (1564). Printing took several years to be properly established, and in Moscow it subsequently became a state monopoly.

3 We had thought you had been ruler over your land … but now we perceive that there be other men that do rule, and not men but bowers [peasants] and merchants … and you flow in your maidenly estate like a maid.
Ivan IV, the Terrible, to Elizabeth I of England, 24 Oct. 1570; G. Tolstoy *The First 40 Years of Intercourse between England and Russia, 1553–1593* (1875) p.114.

4 We know and feel for a surety, the Muscovite, enemy to all liberty under the heavens, daily to grow mightier … while not only wares but also weapons heretofore unknown to him, and artificers and arts be brought unto him: by means whereof he maketh himself strong to vanquish all others … therefore we know that know best, and border upon him, do admonish other Christian princes in time, that they do not betray their dignity, liberty and life of them and subjects to a most barbarous and cruel enemy.
Sigismund II of Poland to Elizabeth I of England, protesting about English trade with Moscow; Tolstoy (1875) pp.30 ff.

5 You have written that I am 'corrupt in understanding to a degree unparalleled even among the (godless) peoples'. And yet I will again place you as judge over my self; are you corrupt or am I, in that I wished to rule you and you did not wish to be under my power, and that for this I inflicted disgrace upon you? … How many evils I received from you, how many insults, how many injuries and rebukes! And for what? What was my guilt before you in the first place? Whom did I offend (and) in what?
Ivan IV to Prince A.M. Kurbsky 1577; J.L.I. Fennell (ed. and trans.) *The Correspondence between Prince A.M. Kurbsky and Tsar Ivan IV of Russia, 1664–79* (1955) p.189. In this extraordinary exchange of letters the tsar, Ivan the Terrible (r.1533–84), justifies himself to the prince who had been a favourite but had deserted to Poland.

6 But as for what he used to do when he came of age, at about twelve or later, I will be silent on most things; however this I will relate. At first he began to spill the blood of dumb animals, hurling them from the top storeys of houses and to do many other unbefitting things as well, betraying in himself the future merciless will … But while the tutors flattered him by allowing this and praising him, they taught the child to their own detriment. And when he came to his fifteenth year he began to harm people.
Prince Andrey Mikhaylovich Kurbsky *History of Ivan IV* (c.1573; 1965 trans.) p.11. The prince's biography is not unnaturally a hatchet job on Ivan. The tsar had been outraged by the desertion of a boyar whom he had trusted and promoted, and he regarded Kurbsky's betrayal as symptomatic of the disloyalty of the boyars.

7 The great and awesome Ishmaelite race [Muslims, specifically the Tatars] before which the whole universe trembled – not only did the universe tremble, but it was even laid waste by them … during a few years the boundaries of our Christian land were expanded not only to the extent of the devastation which the Russian land had suffered from them, but to a far greater degree; for where previously in the devastated Russian districts there had been Tatar winter-quarters, there fortresses and towns were built.
Prince Andrey Mikhaylovich Kurbsky (c.1573; 1965 trans.) p.25. The prince reflects a Russian pride and confidence in no longer suffering the Tatar yoke.

8 The great sovereign tsar and grand prince has ordered [me] to tell this to you, his beloved sister, Elizabeth the queen: We have questioned Dr Roman who came from your land, whether in your land there is a royal daughter, or a royal widow, or any woman or maiden of royal descent, and Doctor Roman has told us ... that (Lord) Huntington has a daughter, Mary Hastings, who is your niece, Elizabeth the queen. And you, our beloved sister Elizabeth the queen, should order that your niece be shown to our envoy Fedor and should have her portrait made and sent to us on canvas and frame, so that (we can see) whether she is suitable for our royal rank.

Ivan IV, instructions to his envoy, Fedor Pisemskii, 1582; G. Vernadsky and R.T. Fisher (eds) *A Source Book of Russian History* Vol.1. (1972) p.151. At the time Ivan had been married at least five times. He explains that none of the consorts was of sufficiently high rank and that he would 'put his wife away' so as to wed Elizabeth I's niece. The queen replied that Mary Hastings 'is fallen into such an indisposition of health that there is small hope she ever will recover such strength as is requisite' and urged her envoy to 'use all the best persuasions you can to dissuade him from that purpose'. Ivan also sought political ties with England, although Elizabeth was interested only in trade. He requested political asylum, should he have to flee Muscovy, and the queen acceded to this. An instruction from Ivan was closer to an ultimatum. He issued deadlines to 'his beloved sister', but kept her envoy waiting four months for an audience!

1 We, Boris Phedorowick [Boris Godunov], created lord emperor and great duke of all Russia and of many other dominions, seated in our kingdom, anointed and crowned in the same according to former princely rites and ceremonies, do desire of you, our loving sister Queen Elizabeth, continuance of the same intercourse of love and friendship which passed betwixt the late emperor ... And those your merchants which have recourse into any of our countries shall have the full fruition of the like privilege for your sake, our loving sister, as heretofore they have enjoyed ... For proof whereof we have, immediately after our enthronement, caused a new privilege to be given to your merchants to trade freely into all our kingdoms and dominions without paying any manner of toll or custom.

Boris Godunov to Elizabeth I, 23 March 1598; *Egerton Papers* pp.290–91. The sea route to Russia had been opened up by Richard Chancellor in 1553 (see 171:3). Two years later the Muscovy Company was founded to promote trade with the tsar's dominions. Boris Godunov (r.1598–1605), who had just seized the Russian throne, confirms the privileges granted to English merchants by his predecessors.

2 Your Don Cossacks harry the town of Azov; your same Cossacks from the Don and Samara have come by stealth to the Ovechii waters to our camp and they steal cattle. The sultan has written to me that he has lost money, that he took the town of Derbent but now his people have no route from Azov to Derbent: Russian Cossacks who live on the Terek at the portages and narrow places attack them; the sultan cannot suffer this to happen and with a great army he wants to take the town and make war on Moscow.

Khan Islam Girei to Boris Godunov, c.1587; S.M. Solovyev *History of Russia from Earliest Times* (1959–66) Vol.4, p.262. A somewhat petulant Tatar khan, whose two nephews have found political asylum in Muscovy, complains to the tsar. The khan was by this time also dependent on Turkish support. Cossack (*kazak*) is a Russian term borrowed from an Arabic and Turkic word, which can mean 'adventurer', 'nomad soldier' or 'free and independent person'.

3 You wish to honour and to adorn the great land and holy church [of Russia] ... with the lofty throne of the patriarchate, and with that great deed to glorify and enhance all the more the reigning city, Moscow, and all your great Russian tsardom ... for the ancient city of Rome has fallen through the Apollinarian heresy. The second Rome, which is Constantinople, is held by the Ishmaelites – the godless Turks. And the third Rome – your great Russian tsardom, O pious tsar – has surpassed them all in piety, and all pious people have been united in your tsardom. And you alone on earth are called a Christian tsar everywhere and among all Christians.

Patriarch Jeremiah, addressing Tsar Fyodor I Ivanovich before taking the important step of establishing a patriarchate in Moscow, 1589; *Kormchaya kniga Nomocanon* (Collection of Canons) (1787) Pt I, p.15.

4 The manner of their government is much after the Turkish fashion: which they seem to imitate ...

The state and form of their government is plain tyrannical, as applying all to the behoof of the prince, and that after a most open and barbarous manner ... farther then it giveth the nobility a kind of injust and unmeasured liberty; to command and exact upon the commons and baser sort of people in all parts of the realm come, specially in the place where their lands lie, or where they are appointed by the emperor to govern under him.

Dr Giles Fletcher *Of the Russe Commonwealth* (1591); Lloyd E. Berry (ed.) *The English Works of Giles Fletcher the Elder* (1964) p.200. Fletcher, an English diplomat, was sent to Russia by Queen Elizabeth I to negotiate a trade agreement with Tsar Fyodor I Ivanovich. He also recorded: 'Likewise of ickary or cavery [caviar] a great quantity is made upon the river of Volga, out of the fish called bellougina, the sturgeon.'

1 They have certain hermits (whom they call holy men) ... They used to go stark naked, save a clout about their middle, with their hair hanging long and wildly about their shoulders, and many of them with a iron collar or chain about their necks, or mids, even in the extremity of winter. These they take as prophets and men of great holiness and give them a liberty to speak what they list, without any control-ment, though it be of the very highest himself ...

Of this kind there are not many, because it is a very hard and cold profession, to go naked in Russia, especially in winter.

Dr Giles Fletcher (1591; 1964 edn) p.274.

2 Father, great patriarch Iov! May God be my witness that there will not be a poor man in my tsardom! ... And even to my last shirt I will share with all.

Boris Godunov, at his coronation, 1 Sept. 1598; Ian Grey *Boris Godunov* (1973) p.140. He tore the collar theatrically from his gown to demonstrate his sincerity. The oath of loyalty that all were required to swear to the new tsar forbids the handling of 'poisonous herbs and roots' to do him harm; nor must they 'invoke witches or witchcraft to harm in any way the sovereign' (S.F. Platonov *Boris Godunov* (1921) p.138).

3 When the ploughland is ready (for cultivation) you shall distribute it to the peasants and to the volunteer post riders, find suitable places around the forts; but you shall not give the Tatar ploughland, whatever land is ploughed by the Tatars for us and for themselves in accordance with local conditions, so that our treasury should derive the greatest pos-sible profit and the peasants should plough as much land as they need to feed themselves; and you shall distribute grain for seeds to the peasants and volun-teer post riders from our grain stores.

Boris Godunov, instructions to the commander of Turinsk, 30 Aug. 1601. Careful plans are laid for the colonization of the frontier in the opening up of Siberia.

4 He [the pretender, or False Dimitri who was threatening to overthrow Boris Godunov] is a young man of good presence, brown of complexion, with a large birthmark on his nose by his right eye, with long white hands, so shaped as to indicate noble extraction. He is spirited in speech and in his behaviour and manner of treating others he has true grandeur.

Papal ambassador Rangoni to Pope Clement VIII, 1604; Philip Barbour *Dimitry: Called the Pretender* (1967) p.34. The young man was, in fact, Grigori Otrepiev, a runaway monk, who pretended to be the dead Prince Dimitri. He enlisted the help of the Catholic king of Poland, Sigismund III (r.1587–1632), and secretly became a Catholic himself. The pope saw his claim as a chance to weaken the Orthodox Church and establish the Roman Church in Russia.

5 The most holy father Pope Paul V sends peace and his apostolic blessing to his most beloved son Dimitri [the pretender now installed a s tsar on Godunov's death] ... Now, with God's help you reign in tranquillity; your power rests on a firm foundation ... you have a vast field in which you can plant, sow and reap; in which you can instil every-where the virtues of Christian godliness; in which you can erect edifices whose roofs will touch the heavens.

Jan Wielewicki, 10 April 1606; Vernadsky and Fisher Vol.1 (1972) p.184. The Polish Jesuit father went to Moscow with the Polish delegation that year, but papal hopes of establishing Catholicism in Muscovy were dashed. The new tsar was murdered a month later.

6 Each began to elevate himself above his station; the slaves desiring to be masters and the bondmen escaping to freedom. They disregarded reasonable men altogether, and no one dared to say a word against them. With the tsar they played as with a big child, and each wanted a greater recompense than was his due.

Abraham Palitsyn *Skazanie Abravamiya Palitsyna* (The Tale of Abraham Palitsyn) (early 17th century; 1955 edn) p.117. Palitsyn was a government servant who was forced to become a monk during the regency of Boris Godunov, the common form of punishment for political crimes. He is describing the chaotic period known as the 'Time of the Troubles' (c.1600–13).

7 Thus the Muscovite capital was burned down, with great bloodshed and incalculable damage. This city which covered a vast area had been affluent and wealthy; those who have travelled in foreign lands report that neither Rome nor Paris nor Lisbon equals this city in its circumference. The Kremlin remained intact, but Kitaigorod was looted and plundered by the mob and the teamsters during the confusion; not even the churches were spared.

Stanislas Zolkiewski, 1611; *Expedition to Moscow* (1959 edn) p.125. The author was an experienced diplomat, the repre-sentative of the Polish king, Sigismund III, and responsible for the occupation of Moscow.

8 The Russians can endure extreme heat. In the bathhouse they stretch out on benches and let themselves be beaten and rubbed with bunches of birch twigs and wisps of bast (which I could not stand); and when they are hot and red all over and so exhausted that they can bear it no longer in the bathhouse, men and women rush outside naked and pour cold water over their bodies; in winter they even wallow in the snow and rub their skin with it as if it were soap; then they go back into the hot bathhouse.

Adam Olearius *The Travels of Olearius in Seventeenth-century Russia* (1633–9; 1967 trans.). Olearius went on three missions to Muscovy as secretary to a north German delegation. His travels were widely translated, though not into Russian, and were influential in the forming of European opinion. He vividly describes the sauna, but he makes it clear he is not tempted to take part.

JUDGEMENT

I These people did, indeed, found kingdoms and sustain vigorous conflicts with the various nations that came across their path. Sometimes, as an advanced guard – an intermediate nationality – they took part in the struggle between Christian Europe and unchristian Asia. The Poles even liberated beleaguered Vienna from the Turks; and Slavs have to some extent been drawn within the sphere of Occidental Reason. Yet this entire body of peoples remains excluded from our consideration because hitherto it has not appeared as an independent element in the series of phases that reason has assumed in the world.

G.W.F. Hegel *Lectures on the Philosophy of History* (1872 edn) p.363. Hegel was not able to 'find room for the Slavs' in his historical conspectus (G. Vernadsky *Kievan Russia* (1959) p.10).

The Jews, c.890–1790

JEWISH COMMUNITIES

1 These merchants speak Arabic, Persian, Roman [Greek and possibly also Latin], Frankish, Spanish, and Slavonic. They travel from the East to the West and from the West to the East by land as well as by sea. They bring from the West eunuchs, slave girls, boys, brocade, beaver skins, marten furs and other varieties of fur, and swords. They embark in the land of the Franks in the Western Sea and they sail toward al-Farama [in the Nile delta, Egypt] … On their return from China they load musk, aloe wood, camphor, cinnamon and other products of the eastern countries … Sometimes the Jewish merchants embarking in the land of the Franks on the Western sea, sail toward Antioch. From there they proceed by land to al-Jabiya [possibly Jubba on the River Euphrates, Iraq], where they arrive after three days' journey. There they take a boat on the Euphrates and they reach Baghdad, from where they go down the Tigris to al-Ubullah [a suburb of Basra on the northern shore of the Persian Gulf]. From al-Ubullah they sail for, successively, Oman, Sind, Hind, and China.
Ibn Khurradadhbah (846–886) *The Book of the Routes and the Kingdoms* (1889 trans.) p.114. The Arab writer is describing the routes taken by Jewish merchants. They were more widely travelled in the Middle Ages than their Christian counterparts, and we have material evidence and historical records from as early as Anglo-Saxon England detailing connections with the Middle and Far East through Jewish merchants. The normal routes for merchants from Europe were either through France, leaving by ship from Marseilles, or overland to Venice for the journey to ports in the Middle East.

2 I always ask the ambassadors of these monarchs who bring gifts about our brethren the Israelites, the remnant of the captivity, whether they have heard anything concerning the deliverance of those who have languished in bondage and have found no rest. At length mercantile emissaries of Khorasan [Iran] told me that there is a kingdom of Jews which is called al-Chazar. But I did not believe these words for I thought that they told me such things to procure my goodwill and favour. I was therefore wondering, till the ambassadors of Constantinople came [between 944 and 949] with presents and a letter from their king to our king, and I interrogated them concerning this matter. They answered me: 'It is

quite true, and the name of that kingdom is al-Chazar. It is a fifteen days' journey by sea from Constantinople, but by land many nations intervene between us; the name of the king now reigning is Joseph; ships sometimes come from their country to ours bringing fish, skins and wares of every kind.'
Rabbi Hasdai Ibn Shaprut, letter, c.960; Jacob Rader Marcus *The Jew in the Medieval World: A Sourcebook, 315–1791* (1938) pp.227–32. The Khazars, a powerful Turkish tribe occupying the steppes of southern Russia, reportedly became converts to Judaism around the year 740. More than two centuries later the news of the existence of this Jewish kingdom aroused the curiosity of Hasdai Ibn Shaprut (c.915–c.970). He was the personal physician of Abd al-Rahman III (r.929–961) and his son, Hakam II (r.961–976), caliphs in Muslim Spain. He also held the post of inspector-general of customs and served as an adviser. Hasdai wrote to the ruler of the Khazars around 960 and some time later received an answer. In response to the letter, Joseph, the reigning king, reportedly wrote down the historical details of the group's conversion to Judaism and described their lives and beliefs.

3 As the judge of the city [Speyer, Germany] hears cases between citizens, so the chief rabbi shall hear cases which arise between the Jews or against them. But if by chance he is unable to decide any of them they shall go to the bishop or his chamberlain. They shall maintain watches, guards and fortifications about their district, the guards in common with our vassals. They may lawfully employ nurses and servants from among our people. Slaughtered meat which they may not eat according to their law they may lawfully sell to Christians, and Christians may lawfully buy it. Finally, to round out these concessions, I have granted that they may enjoy the same privileges as the Jews in any other city of Germany. Lest any of my successors diminish this gift and concession, or constrain them to pay greater taxes, alleging that they have usurped these privileges, and have no episcopal warrant for them, I have left this charter as a suitable testimony of the said grant.
Rudiger Huozmann, bishop of Speyer, charter, 1084; Roy C. Cave and Herbert H. Coulson (eds) *A Source Book for Medieval Economic History* (1936; 1965 edn) pp.101–2. This document on the rights and privileges given to the Jews of the city of Speyer was drafted by the city's bishop. Huozmann actually created a ghetto outside the city limits for the Jews: 'Lest they should be too easily disturbed by the insolence of the citizens, I surrounded them with a wall.' He stipulated that an annual tax of three and a half pounds in the money of the

time be paid by the Jews of Speyer and granted them the right to use the harbour, to lend money and to engage in commerce, and he made a grant of church land to the community for use as a cemetery. This was not the first ghetto created in medieval Europe. There is legislation detailing the construction of a 'Jewry' as early as the 700s in various places, but certain details are common: the Jews are housed in a separate (sometimes walled) area, and they have various restrictions placed upon them as well as specific privileges in exchange for a special tax.

1 No Jews live in the city [Abydos, on the Hellespont], for they have been placed behind an inlet of the sea. An arm of the Sea of Marmara [Turkey] shuts them in on the one side, and they are unable to go out except by way of the sea, when they want to do business with the inhabitants ... No Jew there is allowed to ride on horseback. The one exception is R. Solomon Hamitsri, who is the king's physician, and through whom the Jews enjoy considerable alleviation of their oppression.

Benjamin of Tudela *Itinerary* (c.1167); Elkan Nathan Adler (ed. and trans.) *Jewish Travellers of the Middle Ages* (1987) p.41. Rabbi Benjamin ben Jonah of Tudela in Spain was the most famous Jewish traveller of the Middle Ages (see 108:6). Through Palestine and Persia, he reached the borders of China and returned by way of Egypt and Sicily. The first European to describe the Far East, he also provided one of the best eye-witness accounts of Jewish life in continental Europe, Asia Minor and the Mediterranean area.

2 If sometimes those to whom they entrusted their money at interest produce Christian witnesses to the fact of repayment, more credence is placed in the document which the indiscreet debtor has left with his creditor through negligence or carelessness than in the witnesses he produces. Nay, in such a matter witnesses are not permitted against the Jews, so that their insolence has gone so far that – we refer to it with shame – the Jews of Sens built next to a certain old church a new synagogue, not a little higher than the church, in which place they celebrate their services in the Jewish rite. This they do, not as was the case before they were ejected from the kingdom, i.e., in a low tone, but with a great clamour, not scrupling to avoid disturbing the more holy celebrations in the church [of the Christians].

Anon. protest to Philip II (Philip Augustus) of France, 1204; Cave and Coulson (1936; 1965 edn) p.178. The issue of French Jews lending money was a bone of contention between Philip Augustus and Pope Innocent III. They differed over the practice of charging interest and the regulation of the Jewish monetary trade. The pope complained about the protection granted by the French king to the Jews and their usurious practices. Although obliged to accept the church's ruling on usury, the king later found a way to make money on his own account. He would banish the Jews on charges of usury and

fraud and then agree to rescind the order if the Jewish communities paid him a fine. The king, who went on the Third Crusade, needed to finance the expedition, and this method of raising money was common.

3 Inasmuch as we desire that men of all classes dwelling in our land should share our favour and good will, we do therefore decree that these laws, devised for all Jews found in the land of Austria, shall be observed by them without violation ... Likewise, a Jew is allowed to receive all things as pledges which may be pawned with him – no matter what they are called – without making any investigation about them, except bloody and wet clothes, which he shall under no circumstances accept.

Emperor Frederick II, privilege granted to the Jews of his duchy of Austria, July 1244; Julius Aronius (ed.) *Commission for the History of the Jews in Germany*, 1887–1902 Regesten no.403. This important document was soon adopted, with some changes, by most East European countries to which the masses of Jews finally drifted: Hungary, Bohemia, Poland, Silesia and Lithuania. The law expressly permitted Jews to take any article as a pledge, without inquiring into the right of possession of the borrower, except bloody or wet garments, when robbery or even murder might reasonably be suspected.

4 We can see ... with disrespectful sons, and in those who to their benefactors return evil for good, that which is foul for that which is sweet ... 'Thy destroyers and they that made thee waste shall go forth of thee.'

Berachya ha-Natronai *Parabolae Vulpium/Mischle Shu'alim* (Fox Fables) (mid-12th century; 1648 Latin/Hebrew edn) no.42 'The Ironsmith and the Bush'. *Fox Fables*, a prototype of the medieval tales of Reynard the Fox, echo the form of Aesop's Fables. This one contains the only explicit reference to Jewish conversion to Christianity. It is a story of those who do bad deeds in return for good. Berachya is quoting Isaiah 49:17, which was often interpreted as referring to those who left the Jewish community.

5 What is it that lies behind anger and shame? The cause of the fault [sin] is resentment [rage] that has become overly hot. The way of pride is abominable and detestable, and an even more abominable poison to the soul is arrogance. The proud heart tears asunder all our safety, where in time passion and effrontery bring us into conflict and break us apart.

Joseph Hyssopeus *Paropsis argentea, cum Latina interpretatione* (Sweets from the Silver Age, with Latin Commentary) (12th century; 1559–61 edn) p.30. This sermon by a Spanish rabbi was a commentary on a predecessor, Saadia Gaon, one of the foremost philosophers of 11th-century Jewish scholarship. Both Hyssopeus's commentary and Saadia's text record one of the greatest problems that the Jewish communities faced in the Middle Ages. As well as external pressures from Christian society, they were subject to internal strife, fragmentation and dissolution. It was difficult enough, many Jews felt, to maintain good relations with Gentiles in bad times, without having to be on guard against one's co-religionists as well. Rabbi Hyssopeus considers that pride and envy – often of material goods – were at the root of internal dissent in a community.

1 Whereupon Aaron the Jew, who held us in his debt, coming to the house of St Alban in great pride and boasting ... kept on boasting that it was he who made the window for our St Alban, and that with his money he had prepared for the saint a home when he was without one.

Anon. *Gesta Abbatum Monasterii Sancti Albani* (Deeds of St Albans Abbey) (late 12th century; 1867 edn) Vol.1, pp.193–4. Aaron of Lincoln (d.c.1186), possibly the most celebrated financier and usurer of his time, was no stranger to insults and grudges from both Jews and Gentiles. He made no secret of either his prosperity or his pride in the material success he had worked to achieve. A financial giant and real-estate magnate, he had apparently boasted on many occasions about his extensive financial support of the large monastery of St Albans, north of London. When he died he was possibly the wealthiest person in England, and his investments and holdings were so vast that it was necessary to create a special branch of the Exchequer, the *Scaccarium Aaronis*, to sort out his estate. The task took almost five years.

2 The Jews of Cambridge owe half a mark of gold for having an agreement among themselves; Benedict the Jew owes three marks to have respite in the plea between him and Moyses the Jew; Josce Salvage renders count of ten marks for a respite of the pleas between the Jews of Lincoln on the surety of Aaron the Jew ... Judas, Jew of Bristol, owes two ounces of gold for an inquisition made in a chapter of the Jews as to whether a Jew ought to take usury from a Jew.

Calendar of Pipe Rolls (1235; 1847 edn) Vol.1, p.93. Aaron appears again in this financial record detailing transactions between several members of the Jewish communities of Cambridge, Lincoln and Bristol. Two issues emerge: first, the way transactions were handled between Jews within their own community; second, the larger issue raised at the end of the record, whether it was appropriate or even acceptable to charge a fellow Jew interest on a loan. Many Jewish rabbis had suggested that the question of interest, or the excessive interest designated as usury, belonged in the category of actions that were *Hillul ha Shem* (a desecration of the name of God), which included any action that caused wilful harm to others.

3   Let not profit,
Envy, pollution and decay
Bring the day of misfortune,

For what does it profit a man if he gains the world?

Meir ben Elijah of Norwich, liturgical poem (c.1270); A.M. Habermann (ed.) *Hebrew Poems of Meir of Norwich* (1875) in V.I. Lipman *The Jews of Medieval Norwich* (1967) App.2. Habermann's original edition was of only 25 copies, all of which have disappeared.

4 It was witnessed by the entire community of the Jews that if any Jew were by anyone asked of what law he was, and he did not forthwith answer that he was a Jew, he would thenceforth no more be held by them as a Jew. Therefore Josce Bundy is no Jew, nor of any Law.

Calendar of the Plea Rolls of the Exchequer of the Jews (1277; 1929 edn) Vol.3, pp.95–6. This case, which took place in Oxford, set a precedent in legally defining a person's identity as a Jew. Josce Bundy, a man who was already notorious for various criminal activities in his own community, was on trial for counterfeiting the king's coin. A jury of Jews stated that he was not an observant Jew and had no right to be tried as one. Josce Bundy, when asked directly by the court if he was a Jew or not, asked if he could have a few days to consider his answer.

5 Whereas Swetcota is not a Christian and was never baptized, certain of her enemies, maliciously feigning that she had been baptized between the two battles of Lewes and Evesham, have defamed her concerning this, to the damage and grievance of her and Moses: the king orders the justices to enquire the said truth in this matter by Christians and Jews, according to custom, and if they find that Swetcota was not baptized, to cause Moses and her to have peace in this matter.

Calendar of Close Rolls of the Reign of Edward I (1900–8) Vol.1, p.99. This legal case, reported on 10 Feb. 1288, involved identity. Moses de Horndon and his wife, Swetcota, went before the king's justices to prove that Swetcota, contrary to unfounded rumour, was not an apostate from Judaism. Notwithstanding the bad name that she would have in the Jewish community, if she *had* converted to Christianity her property would be confiscated by the crown and the king could dispose of it as he pleased.

6 A Jew may take usury by a Christian hand, and if it seem unjust to his opponent, let him go before the Masters of his Law in Chapter, and implead him there, because matters of this sort touching his Law ought not to be corrected elsewhere.

Abraham ben Joce of York, 1272; J.M. Rigg (ed.) *Select Pleas, Starrs and other Records from the Rolls of the Exchequer of the Jews, 1220–1284* (1902) p.65. This statement by the rabbi and legalist gives the other side of the question about usury that many Jews – moneylenders and rabbis alike – were debating at the time. This assertion placed the question of usury charged to a Christian client squarely in the hands of the Gentile courts, not the Jewish ones, whereas issues concerning debts between Jews were handled exclusively in the Jewish arena. The Hebrew word *shetar* (contract) passed into legal Latin as *starrum* or *starra* and was Anglicized as 'star' or 'starr'.

1 Two people came to argue their case before Rabbi Solomon. The wife complained that her husband had divorced her but had not treated her in accordance with Jewish custom.

The following decision was given by the rabbi in this dispute: 'This fellow, though a member of the household of our Father in heaven, has acted cruelly toward the wife of his youth as God himself can testify. According to the law of right it is incumbent upon him to treat her as custom prescribes for all Jewish women; and if he does not care to receive her back in kindness and in respect, then he must divorce her and pay her the entire amount stipulated in her marriage contract.'
Rabbi Rashi (Shlomo Yitzhaqi) of Troyes, northern France, ruling, before 1105; Marcus (1938) pp.301–3. This is a famous judgement of Rashi (1040–1105), who was one of the best known medieval Jewish legalists. His scholarship and fame made northern France a great centre of rabbinic scholarship in the 12th and 13th centuries.

2 The Jew shall stand on a sow's skin and the five books of Master Moses shall lie before him, and his right hand up to the wrist shall lie on the book and he shall repeat after him who administers the oath of the Jews: 'Regarding such property of which the man accuses you, you know nothing of it nor do you have it. You never had it in your possession, you do not have it in any of your chests, you have not buried it in the earth, nor locked it with locks, so help you God who created heaven and earth, valley and hill, woods, trees, and grass, and so help you the law which God himself created and wrote with His own hand and gave Moses on Sinai's mount. And so help you the five books of Moses that you may nevermore enjoy a bite without soiling yourself all over as did the King of Babylon.'
Oath taken by Jews in Frankfurt am Main, Germany, c.1392; Marcus (1938) pp.49–50. Oaths that had to be ratified by the civil authorities in the medieval and early modern era did not employ the same standards for Christians, Muslims and Jews. If the state was Christian or Muslim, no Jew could or would swear after the Christian or Muslim manner, which would usually entail swearing on the New Testament or on the Koran, or, in Muslim lands, invoking faith in Allah. In a Christian land such an oath would have meant recognition of Jesus or the Trinity and would not have been binding on Jews. For their

convenience, therefore, an oath 'according to the Jewish custom' was instituted. One of the oldest surviving authentic oaths of this type was promulgated by Emperor Constantine VII (r.913–959), but the one above may be even older. The Byzantine formula, which is probably based on a Hebrew or Aramaic original, was employed, with considerable variations, in most of Europe in the Middle Ages.

3 No woman except those unmarried or a bride in the first year of her marriage shall wear costly dresses of gold cloth, or olive-coloured material or fine linen or silk, or of fine wool. Neither shall they wear on their dresses trimmings of velvet or brocade or olive-coloured cloth. Nor shall they wear a golden brooch nor one of pearls, nor a string of pearls on the forehead, nor dresses with trails on the ground more than one third of a *vara* [about a yard] in measure, nor fringed Moorish garments, nor coats with high collars, nor cloth of a high reddish colour, nor a skirt of *bermeia* thread, except as for the skirt and stockings, nor shall they make wide sleeves on the Moorish garments of more than two palms in width, but they may wear silver brooches and silver belts provided that there is not more than four ounces of silver on any of them. No son of Israel of the age of fifteen or more shall wear any cloak of gold thread, olive-coloured material or silk or any cloak trimmed with gold or olive-coloured material or silk, nor a cloak with rich trimmings nor with trimmings of olive-coloured or gold cloth.
Synod of Castilian Jews, ruling at Valladolid, 1432; Louis Finkelstein *Jewish Self-government in the Middle Ages* (1924) p.375. The Synod of the kingdom of Castile (the largest of the Spanish kingdoms), summoned by Don Abraham Benveniste, its chief rabbi, is ruling on matters relating to community life.

RELATIONS WITH OTHER FAITHS

4 The Jews are for us the living words of Scripture, for they remind us of what our Lord suffered. They are dispersed all over the world so that by expiating their crime they may be everywhere the living witnesses of our redemption ... Under Christian princes they endure a hard captivity, but 'they only wait for the time of their deliverance'. Finally, we are told by the Apostle that when the time is ripe all Israel shall be saved.
St Bernard of Clairvaux to Archbishop Henry of Mainz; *The Letters of Bernard of Clairvaux* (1953 edn) pp.462–3. St Bernard (see 196:4), although known at times for making statements opposing the violent actions taken against Jews, trod the

'official' line regarding the place of the Jew in the medieval world in church theology: Jews were dispersed throughout the world as a punishment for their role in Christ's crucifixion, an interpretation that was gaining power in 12th-century Europe, and was supported in the minds of many by folktales such as the story of the Wandering Jew.

1 It is surprising that in the land of the Isle [England] they [Jews] are lenient in the matter of drinking strong drinks of the Gentiles and along with them. For the Law is distinctly according to those Doctors who forbid it on the ground that it leads to inter-marriage. But perhaps, as there would be great ill feeling if they were to refrain from this, one should not be severe upon them.

Rabbi Tosafoth Elchanan Halberstamm; MS f.48b in Joseph Jacobs (ed.) *The Jews of Angevin England: Documents and Records* (1893) p.269. There were strong proscriptions from both Jewish and Christian authorities on Judeo–Christian social interactions. One such objection was the fear many medieval rabbis expressed about community members consuming non-kosher food or drink at mixed social gatherings. Another was common to both Jewish and Christian authorities: the fear that too much social contact would promote conversions on either side.

2 And so too that well-known saying of Henry of London was heard by many. For there were one day in the Church of St Paul at London many bishops and abbots taking cognizance of certain ecclesiastical cases by order of our lord the Pope, and with them a great multitude of clergy, citizens, soldiers and others. There chanced to enter certain Jews of London, who mixed with these and others in seeking their debtors if they might see them. And among them came a certain Bishop of the Jews. And to him Henry said in joke: 'Welcome, Bishop of the Jews! Receive him among ye, for there are scarcely any of the Bishops of England that have not betrayed their lord the Archbishop of Canterbury, except this one. In this Israelite Bishop there is no guile.'

Anon., ?1168; J.C. Robertson *Materials for the History of Thomas Becket* (1875–85) Vol.4, p.151. The fact that English Jews and Christians were not segregated – there were no formal ghettos in medieval England – and that the two groups often mingled is reflected in this anecdote. 'Bishop' was a term applied in England to each of the three judges who constituted the Beth Din (ecclesiastical tribunal) that decided cases between Jews.

3 The eternal providence has appointed me to watch over the life and health of Thy creatures. May the love for my art actuate me at all time; may neither avarice nor miserliness, nor thirst for glory nor for a great reputation engage my mind; for the enemies of truth and philanthropy could easily deceive me and make me forgetful of my lofty aim of doing good to Thy children. May I never see in the patient anything but a fellow creature in pain. Grant me the strength, time and opportunity always to correct what I have acquired, always to extend its domain; for knowledge is immense and the spirit of man can extend indefinitely to enrich itself daily with new require-ments ... Oh, God, Thou has appointed me to watch over the life and death of Thy creatures; here am I ready for my vocation and now I turn unto my calling.

Moses Maimonides (1135–1204) 'Oath of Maimonides' (pub. 1793); *Bulletin of the Johns Hopkins Hospital* (1917) no.28, pp.260–61. The Oath, which encapsulates his beliefs not only as a physician but also as a Jew, is still used by physicians. It reflects the spirit of *convivencia* (living together peacefully). Maimonides, also a rabbi and philosopher, moved from Cordova in Islamic Spain to Cairo (c.1165) and became physician to Saladin (see 230:2). His greatest work, *The Guide to the Perplexed* (1190), attempted to reconcile Greek philosophy and Judaism.

4 Suppose a monk or priest approaches a Jewish Pietist ... to debate about the Torah [the Pentateuch] ... Even if you are more learned than he, do not permit a less learned person to overhear your debates. The other person might be persuaded, since he does not understand [which position is] the true one.

Joseph Kimhi, 1240s; Robert Chazan 'Joseph Kimhi's *Sefer ha-Berit* [Book of the Rite]: Path-breaking Medieval Jewish Apologetics' in *Harvard Theological Review* no.85 (1992) p.424. One of medieval Germany's most notable rabbinical scholars expresses an idea about intellectual debate and exchange between Jews and Christians that was common to both sides. Just as Christians were aware that the existence of Jews posed a challenge to their own beliefs, Jews were also conscious that Christianity held the same challenge for them. The Pentateuch, the first five books of the Old Testament, was ascribed to Moses.

5 It is necessary to understand that when we met the first time to talk matters over, this Jew and I agreed to debate against each other without fighting or shouting, without any desire to defeat the other, but in peace and in tranquillity, with neither of us interrupting the other and, should one of us raise a problem, the other would hear him out quietly until he had finished his argument.

Peter of Cornwall *Liber disputationum contra Symonem Judaeum* (1222) (MS Eton College 130, f.92r); R.W. Hunt 'The Dispu-tation of Peter of Cornwall against Symon the Jew' in *Studies in Medieval History Presented to F.M. Powicke* (1948) p.153. Peter of Cornwall's disputation encapsulates a utopian view of Judeo-Christian theological disputations in the 12th and 13th centuries. The theological dialogue was (in theory) to be a gentlemanly and philosophical give-and-take of ideas. This was not, however, often the case.

1 Palermo is the chief town of Sicily, and contains about 850 Jewish families, all living in one street, which is situated in the best part of the town. They are artisans, such as copper-smiths and iron-smiths, porters and peasants, and are despised by the Christians because they wear tattered garments. As a mark of distinction they are obliged to wear a piece of red cloth, about the size of a gold coin, fastened on the breast. The royal tax falls heavily on them, for they are obliged to work for the king at any employ-ment that is given them; they have to draw ships to the shore, to construct dykes and so on. They are also employed in administering corporal punish-ment and in carrying out the sentence of death.
Obadiah Jaré da Bertinoro *Letters* (1487–90); Adler (1987) p.210. Obadiah of Bertinoro (*c.*1450–*c.*1516) was one of the most respected Italian rabbis of his day. As well as the letters describing his travels and his contacts with Jews of other lands, he was the author of a commentary on the Mishnah (a collection of commentaries on written Hebrew law) known as the 'Bertinoro', which remains a standard rabbinical text. Obadiah emigrated to Palestine in 1487, reorganized and revitalized the demoralized Jewish community there and probably stayed as their rabbi until his death.

2 And in every city we entered Marranos came, men and women, great and small, and kissed my hand, and the Christians were jealous of me, and said to them: 'Show him great honour, but do not kiss his hand but only the hand of the King of Portugal alone.' Some were of stout heart, because they believed in me with a perfect faith, as Israel believed in our Master, Moses, on whom be peace!
David Reubeni, diary entry from 1522–5; Adler (1987) p.288. The diary of this colourful, Renaissance, Jewish figure (possibly from Ethiopia) allows us a look at Jewish life throughout the Mediterranean world from his extensive travels. His account also documents the condition of the Marranos or Conversos (converts to Christianity) living in Spain and Portugal under the shadow of the Spanish Inquisition, who often continued to practise Judaism in secret. From records that go beyond Reubeni's own journal, we know something of his further experiences in Spain, Flanders and Italy and that he even acted as a negotiator in a diplomatic exchange with Emperor Charles V when trying to raise support for a joint Christian–Jewish crusade in 1532.

3 I had made up my mind to write no more either about the Jews or against them. But since I learned

that these miserable and accursed people do not cease to lure to themselves even us, that is, the Christians, I have published this little book, so that I might be found among those who opposed such poisonous activities of the Jews who warned the Christians to be on their guard against them. I would not have believed that a Christian could be duped by the Jews into taking their exile and wretchedness upon himself.
Martin Luther *On the Jews and Their Lies* (1543); *Works* (1971) Vol.47 in *The Christian in Society* Vol.4, p.268. Luther's anti-Semitic treatise sparked a massive series of attacks against the Jews of Germany and elsewhere in Europe. The document was used extensively as the basis for many early modern anti-Semitic laws and treatises.

4 What do you say, O scholars of Islam, shining luminaries who dispel the darkness (may God lengthen your days!)? What do you say of the innovations introduced by the cursed unbelievers [Jewish and Christian] into Cairo, into the city of al-Muizz [founder of Cairo, 969] which by its splen-dour in legal and philosophic studies sparkles in the first rank of Muslim cities?
Anon. Muslim scholar, 1772; Marcus (1938) p.15. A Muslim scholar in Cairo was asked how Jews and Christians should be treated. This question, and its corresponding answer did not become the basis for legal treatment but did express the opinion of a conservative Muslim at the time.

STEREOTYPES AND ACCUSATIONS

5 The Provost then did judgement on the men
      Who did the murder, and he did them serve
      A shameful death in torment there and then
      On all those guilty Jews; he did not swerve
      'Evils shall meet the evils they deserve.'
      And he condemned them to be drawn apart
      By horses. Then he hanged them from a cart.
Geoffrey Chaucer *The Canterbury Tales* (*c.*1387; 1951 edn) 'The Prioress's Tale' lines 141–7. This is a direct allusion to the accusation, trial and execution of 18 innocent Jews and the backlash against the Jewish communities of England in the investigation into what, or who, killed young Hugh of Lincoln in 1255. As Chaucer added: 'O Hugh of Lincoln, likewise murdered so/By cursed Jews, as is notorious/(For it was but a little time ago).' The disappearances of Christian children in the Middle Ages were often quickly followed by allegations that a 'ritual murder' had been committed by Jews. This practice, an invention arising from medieval stereotypes about Jews, popular preaching and superstition, suggested that Jews kidnapped Christian children at Passover to use their blood – the 'blood libel'. By 1255 this extremely dangerous belief had

been invoked in England to explain the death of young Hugh of Lincoln, and it led Henry III to execute the Jews for the imaginary crime.

1 They [rulers] would do better to compel the Jews to work for their living, as is done in parts of Italy … In the same way, and for the very same reason, princes would suffer loss of revenue if they were to allow their subjects to enrich themselves by fraud and piracy.

St Thomas Aquinas *De regimine Judaeorum* (On the Governance of Jews) (1271; 1948 edn) p.88. Some medieval theologians commented on why stereotypes or the 'Jewish image' had developed in particular ways. Thomas Aquinas noted that many professions were closed or barely open to Jews. In some areas money-lending or banking was the only profession in which a Jew could legally engage. Furthermore, because charging interest on a loan was expressly forbidden by church law, Jews were not only forced to charge interest in order to survive but also encouraged to do so by the laws of the lands in which they lived.

2 Among the Jews of the East, every man lives by the work of his hands, for the kings of Ishmael [Arabs, believed to be the descendants of Abraham's son Ishmael by his handmaiden Hagar], however sinful and evil they are, have enough judgement to levy a fixed annual tax on them … It is different in our countries; for as far as our kings and princes are concerned, they have no thought but to harass us and strip us entirely of our gold and silver … what sort of a life have we, what is our strength and our power? We must thank God for having multiplied our wealth, because this enables us to protect our lives and those of our children, and to halt the schemes of our persecutors. What then is our crime and what do they want of us?

Jacob ben Elie to Pablo Christiani, c.1270; S. Grayzel *The Church and the Jews* App.A, p.340. Jacob ben Elie, a well-known scholar in French rabbinical circles, wrote this letter to a former Jew who had become a papal inquisitor, discussing the problem pointed out by Thomas Aquinas.

3 Benedict is no Christian but the Devil's man instead!

Baldwin of Exeter, archbishop of Canterbury (1184–91); Roger of Howden *Chronicles* (c.1189; 1868–71 edn) Vol.1, p.12. Benedict of York was one of the most prominent Jewish financial magnates of 12th-century England, who launched himself into public memory by being one of the few Jews to survive the York massacre (his daughter Belaset was another). Benedict accepted conversion to Christianity at the hands of an angry mob to save his life (as did his daughter), but afterwards told the archbishop of Canterbury that he was 'a Christian in fact, but by way of life, completely opposed to it'.

The archbishop was so infuriated with Benedict's suit to rescind his forced conversion that he is recorded by several chroniclers as having shouted this line during the hearing.

PERSECUTION

4 The famous Joce cuts the throat of Anna, his dear wife, with a sharp knife, and did not spare his own sons. And when this was done by the other men, that wretched elder [Rabbi Yomtob of Joigny] cut Joce's throat, so that he might be more honoured than the rest.

William of Newburgh *Historia rerum Anglicarum* (History of English Affairs) (1190s; 1885–90 edn) Vol.1, p.318. The chronicle was written at most ten years after the massacre by the canon of a Yorkshire priory. One of the major motifs of Jewish persecution that stretched back long before the Middle Ages was the concept of *Kiddush-ha-Shem* (martyrdom to prove one's faithfulness as a Jew). This could often take the form of suicide or mass suicide. The most famous incident of this in Jewish history comes from the battle of the Jews against the Roman general Flavius Silva at the fortress of Masada in Israel in AD 70 (see 24:5) rather than suffer at the hands of a violent mob or be subjected to torture or forced conversion. Community members in these circumstances would draw lots to see who would act as executioners. Sometimes the elders of the community or the members who were *shochets* (men trained in the kosher regulations of animal slaughtering) were designated to assure the most painless and quickest death.

5 The martyrs endured the extreme penalty normally inflicted only upon one guilty of murder. Yet, it must be stated with certainty that God is a righteous judge, and we are to blame. Then the evil waters prevailed.

Solomon bar Simson, attrib., c.1140; Solomon Eidelberg *The Jews and the Crusaders* (1977) p.25. 'Evil waters' is a medieval Jewish term for baptism.

6 [Nicholas Donin] was a rebel against the words of the Wise Men [the elder rabbis of France], and believed only what was written in the Torah of Moses, without interpretation. Therefore have we separated him and excommunicated him. From that time until now he has been planning evil against us, to destroy everything.

Rabbi Yehiel of Paris, statement for the defence in the Paris disputation, 1240; S. Grayzel (ed.) *The Church and the Jews, Collected Documents 300–1300* (1989) p.339. Yehiel was the rabbinical opponent to the inquisitor Nicholas Donin in a battle to save the Talmud (books of Judaic legal commentary and interpretation on the Torah) from public condemnation by the Christian religious authorities in France. Donin, born a Jew himself, had converted to Christianity in 1225 and had spent 15 years harassing his former Jewish community in Rouen before becoming part of the effort to suppress the

Jewish communities of France. He was seeking to shake the very foundations of medieval Jewish thought and the communities it supported.

1 Whereas by our letters patent we have granted to our dearest mother Eleanor, Queen of England, that no Jew shall dwell in or abide in any of the towns which, by assignment of our father, King Henry [III], and Ourself, she, our mother, has for her dower within our realm … and for this cause we have provided that the Jews of Marlborough be deported to our town of Devizes, the Jews of Gloucester to our town of Bristol, the Jews of Worcester to our town of Hereford, and the Jews of Cambridge to our city of Norwich, with their Chirograph Chests and all their goods, and that they henceforth dwell and abide in the said towns and cities among our other Jews of those places.

Calendar of Patent Rolls of Edward I (1275) p.76; Rigg (1902) p.85. This edict of Edward I was a precursor to the Expulsion Edict of 1290, by which all Jews residing in England had their possessions forfeit to the crown, and were formally denied permission to live within the boundaries of Edward I's realm. The letter above details the circumstances in 1275 when Edward I moved any Jews living in cities that belonged to his mother, Eleanor of Provence, as part of her dowry to others within England, noting that they were to bring with them their 'Chirograph Chests' (the chests in which the deeds and starrs of financial transactions and debts were kept). Furthermore, the instruction that the transplanted Jews were to live among the Jews already in those places shows another development in pre-expulsion England: Jewish residences, businesses and synagogues were becoming increasingly confined to the 'Jewry', an area where the Jewish population was already concentrated within a city or town.

2 Afterwards, in the year 4551 [1190] the Wanders [*sic*] came upon the people of the Lord in the city of Evoric [York] in England, on the Great Sabbath [before Passover] and the season of the miracle was changed to disaster and punishment. All fled to the house of prayer. Here Rabbi Yom-Tob stood and slaughtered sixty souls, and others also slaughtered. Some there were who commanded that they should slaughter their only sons, whose foot could not tread upon the ground from their delicacy and tender breeding. Some, moreover, were burned for the Unity of their Creator. The number of those slain and burned was one hundred and fifty souls, men and women, all holy bodies.

Ephraim of Bon, account of the York massacre, 1190; Joseph ha-Cohen Emek ha-Bakha (Valley of Tears) (16th century) in Cecil Roth A History of the Jews in England (1941) Ch.2. The York massacre was one of the most widely documented

episodes of persecution in medieval England, with records in both Jewish and non-Jewish sources of the Middle Ages. On the night of Friday, 16 March 1190, crusaders, preparing to leave for the Holy Land, and a group of disgruntled nobles, most of whom owed huge sums of money to the Jewish moneylenders of York, incited a mob to attack the Jewish community and to threaten them with conversion or death. Some 150 Jews and Jewesses sought protection in Clifford's Tower from the mob (led by Richard Malebys, one of the wealthiest and most indebted nobles of York) and chose to die at each other's hand rather than be forcibly converted to Christianity.

3 In the matter of this plague the Jews throughout the world were reviled and accused in all lands of having caused it through the poison which they are said to have put into the water and the wells – that is what they were accused of – and for this reason the Jews were burnt all the way from the Mediterranean into Germany, but not in Avignon, for the pope protected them there.

Jacob Marcus (1938) p.48. The episode referred to as the Cremation of Strasbourg took place in the Jewry on 14 Feb. 1349, when the community of Jews living in the city of Strasbourg was massacred. City officials who attempted to save the Jews were overthrown by a mob led by the butchers' and tanners' guilds and by the nobles. The people of Strasbourg, who had thus far escaped the Black Death sweeping Europe in that year (see 286:4) and who thought that by killing off the Jews they would protect themselves against it in the future, were doomed to disappointment, for the plague came to the city and, it is said, took 16,000 lives.

4 And in the year 5252 [1492], in the days of King Ferdinand, the Lord visited the remnant of his people a second time [the first Spanish visitation was in 1391] and exiled them. After the King had captured the city of Granada from the Moors, and it had surrendered to him on the 7th of January of the year just mentioned, he ordered the expulsion of all the Jews in all parts of his kingdom – in the kingdoms of Castile, Catalonia, Aragon, Galicia, Majorca, Minorca, the Basque provinces, the islands of Sardinia and Sicily, and the kingdom of Valencia. Even before that the Queen had expelled them from the kingdom of Andalusia [1483]. The King gave them three months in which to leave … About their number there is no agreement, but, after many inquiries, I found that the most generally accepted estimate is 50,000 families, or, as others say, 53,000.

Anon. Italian Jew, April/May 1495; Marcus (1938) pp.51–2. In the spring of 1492, after the Battle of Granada and on the eve of Christopher Columbus's historic voyage to the New World, Ferdinand and Isabella of Spain expelled all the Jews from their lands (see 335:2). The official reason circulated in

Spain was that Jews encouraged Marranos to persist in their Jewishness and would not allow them to become Christians.

1 They journeyed with great suffering and misfortune ... There was hardly a Christian who did not feel sorry for them, and wherever they went the Jews were invited to be baptized. Some converted and stayed behind, but very few. Instead, the rabbis went among them, urging them on and making the women and boys sing and play drums and tambourines to raise their spirits. Thus they left Castile.

Anon., 1492; Richard L. Kagan in Jay A. Levenson (ed.) *Circa 1492: Art in the Age of Exploration*, Catalog of National Gallery of Washington, D.C. (1992).

THE OLD WORLD AND THE NEW, 1615–1790

2 One is permitted to wear only two rings on weekdays, four on the Sabbath, and six on holidays. Both men and women are absolutely forbidden to wear precious stones. An exception is made in the case of a pregnant woman who is permitted to wear a ring with diamonds because of its curative powers. Otherwise no exception will be made, under penalty of three ducats.

Sumptuary law of Cracow, Poland, 1615–16; Marcus (1938) p.195. Such laws were self-imposed and policed by the Jewish community, anxious to avoid ostentation and the anti-Semitism it might arouse. It is a reaction typical of the insecurity of the Ashkenazi Jews of eastern and central Europe. The Sephardic Jews were of Spanish or Portuguese descent.

3 Even in 1616 Rabbi Uziel was able to report to a correspondent, 'At present, [our] people live peaceably in Amsterdam. The inhabitants of this city, mindful of the increase in population make laws and ordinances whereby the freedom of religions may be upheld. Each may follow his own belief but may not openly show that he is of a different faith from the inhabitants of the city.' At a time when the murderous riots were being unloosed against Jews in Frankfurt, this relative liberty represented a miraculous asylum.

Simon Schama *The Embarrassment of Riches* (1987) p.589. Frankfurt, like many cities and towns in Europe, changed its perspective on religious tolerance with the onset of the Thirty Years War (1618–48; see 458:7). The Jewish populations of many towns in Germany, Moravia and France were expelled, but after the war all three countries began to encourage immigration (including Jews) to rebuild their economies.

4 The events of this week are all concerned with the affair of the Jews and their earnest request to be admitted to domicile in these realms. A Jew came from Antwerp and ... when introduced to his highness [i.e., Oliver Cromwell] he began not only to kiss but to press his hands and touch ... his whole body with the most exact care. When asked why he behaved so, he replied that he had come from Antwerp solely to see if his highness was of flesh and blood, since his superhuman deeds indicated that he was more than a man ... The Protector ordered [i.e., set up] a congregation of divines, who discussed in the presence of himself and his council whether a Christian country could receive the Jews. Opinions were very divided. Some thought they might be received under various restrictions and very strict obligations. Others, including some of the leading ministers of the laws, maintained that under no circumstances and in no manner could they receive the Jewish sect in a Christian kingdom without very grave sin. After long disputes and late at night the meeting dissolved without any conclusion.

Giovanni Sagredo, Venetian ambassador in England, to the doge and senate, 31 Dec. 1655; Calendar of State Papers (C.S.P.) Venetian Vol.30 (1930) pp.160–61. After the Expulsion Edict of 1290 (see 424:4) Jews did not begin to return to Britain until the 17th century. With the rise of the Puritans, a more favourable image of Jews began to be presented to the public because of their connection with the Bible. Cromwell, like most Puritans, was an avid reader of the Old Testament and was familiar with Jewish history. Because the Puritans were a 'godly' minority in the country as a whole, he had sympathy with similar minorities. He hoped for a consensus on legislation to permit the Jews to settle in England once again. When this was not forthcoming, he allowed them to do so in an informal manner and in 1656 agreed to their re-admittance, which marked the beginning of the official resettlement.

5 The members of the Portuguese nation [Sephardic Jewish community] residing in this city [Amsterdam] respectfully remonstrate to your honours that it has come to their knowledge that your honours raise obstacles to the giving of permits or passports to the Portuguese [Sephardic] to travel and go to reside in New Netherland, which if persisted in will result to the great disadvantage of the Jewish nation. It can be of no advantage to the general company.

Petition of the Jewish Nation to the Honourable Directors of the Chartered Dutch West India Company, Chamber of the City of Amsterdam, Jan. 1655; Jacob Rader Marcus (ed.) *The Jew in the American World* (1966) p.30. The elders intercede on behalf of would-be colonists to what became New York. These were refugees from the Spanish Inquisition and from the fall of Pernambuco (Recife). This stronghold of Dutch Brazil had been recaptured by the Portuguese in 1654. In fact, the first 23 Jews, probably refugees from Brazil, arrived in New Amsterdam in 1654. Peter Stuyvesant, the governor (see 433:2), wished to expel them 'as they (with their customary usury and deceitful trading with the Christians) were very repugnant to the inferior magistrates' (Marcus (1996) p.29).

1 We would have liked to effectuate and fulfil your wishes and requests that the new territories should no more be allowed to be infected by people of the Jewish nation, for we see therefrom the same difficulties which you fear. But after having weighed and considered the matter, we observe that this would be somewhat unreasonable and unfair, especially because of the considerable loss sustained by this nation [the Jewish community] with others in the [Portuguese re-] taking of Brazil, as also because of the large amount of capital which they still have invested in this company.
Directors of Dutch West India Company to Peter Stuyvesant, 26 April 1655; Marcus (1966) p.32.

2 For the purposes of obtaining this favour they [the Jews] applied to the celebrated de Witson, burgomaster of Amsterdam, the Dutchman whom Peter [the Great] honoured with the greatest share of familiarity and begged him to endeavour to prevail on his Czarian Majesty to permit the Jews, as other foreigners, to settle in Russia to trade and establish manufactories ... and they offered to present the monarch with the sum of one hundred thousand florins as the first mark of their gratitude ... He [Peter] answered with a smile, 'Myhnheer Witson, you know the Jews, and the spirit of my people; I am acquainted with both; it is not yet time to open a passage for the Jews into my country. You will, therefore, tell them from me, that I thank them for their offers, but that if they settled in my dominions at present, I would not be able to repress my pity; though they are reported to have the secret of deceiving all the world, I fear that my Russians would make them dupes in their turn.'
Jacob von Staehlin-Storcksburg, 1716; *Original Anecdotes of Peter the Great* (1785; 1788 edn) pp.42–4. Between 1700 and 1721 Peter I, the Great (see 444:6), fought against (and eventually defeated) Charles XII of Sweden and Stanislaus I Leszczynski, the pretender of Poland. Jews living in areas controlled by both sides were forced to pay heavy taxes, especially in the cities occupied by Swedish forces. After Charles XII's defeat at Poltava (see 445:3), a special fine was imposed on the Jewish communities and mobility was curtailed as a punishment for not supporting the Russians during the Great Northern War. Peter's response to the petition reflects the level of anti-Semitism in Russia at this time.

3 The means of making the Jews happy and useful? Here it is: stop making them unhappy and unuseful. Accord them, or rather return to them, the right of citizens, which you have denied them against all divine and human laws and against your own interests, like a man who thoughtlessly cripples himself.
Zalkind Hourwitz (1738–1812), a Polish Jew; Lynn Hunt (ed. and trans.) *The French Revolution and Human Rights: A Brief Documentary History* (1996) pp.48–50. In 1787–8 the Royal Society of Arts and Sciences of Metz held a competition on the question, 'Are there means for making the Jews happier and more useful in France?' Metz had the largest Jewish population in the West. Among the winners declared in 1788 was Hourwitz, whose essay earned him a reputation in reformist circles. Here he represents an assimilationist position: that granting rights to the Jews would make them more like the rest of the French.

4 The Jews must be refused everything as a separate nation, and be granted everything as individuals.
Marquis de Clermont-Tonnerre, debate at Convention, Paris, 27 Sept. 1791; Norman Davies *Europe, A History* (1997) p.483. In 1789 40,000 Jews lived in France, most of them in the eastern provinces of Alsace and Lorraine, and in some respects they were better treated than Calvinists. Under the law before the Revolution Jews could legally practise their religion, though their other activities were severely restricted. They had no civil or political rights, except the right to be judged by their own courts, and they faced local prejudice.

5 If they are good workmen, they may be of Assia [*sic*], Africa, or Europe. They may be Mahometans [Muslims], Jews, or Christian or any Sect – or they may be Atheists.
George Washington to his aide, Tench Tilghman, 24 March 1784; *Writings* (1997 edn) pp.555–6. Washington clearly set no religious requirements for his employees and did not see Jews, atheists or Muslims as dangerous elements in early American society. Three years later he took this attitude to the Constitutional Convention and maintained his stance for unilateral tolerance in the language of the US Constitution.

6 All possess alike liberty of conscience and immunities of citizenship. It is now no more that toleration is spoken of, as if it was by the indulgence of one class of people that another enjoyed the exercise of their inherent natural rights. For happily the Government of the United States, which gives to bigotry no sanction, to persecution no assistance requires only that they who live under its protection should demean themselves as good citizens, in giving it on all occasions their effectual support.
George Washington to a Jewish congregation in Newport, Rhode Island, 18 Aug. 1790; *Writings* (1997 edn) p.767. Washington is demonstrating the religious tolerance that he upheld throughout his term of office as first President of the USA.

Popes and Princes, c.800–1500

PROLOGUE, 4TH–8TH CENTURIES

1 As a matter of fact, the republic is not included in the church, but the church is included in the republic, that is, in the Roman empire; for above the emperor there is no one except God.

Optatus, an African bishop (4th century), on the relationship of church and state; Robert S. Lopez *The Birth of Europe* (1962; 1967 trans.) p.17.

2 It is one thing to worship a picture, it is another by means of pictures thoroughly to learn too the story that should be venerated. For what writing makes present to those reading, the same picturing makes present to the uneducated, to those perceiving visually, because in it the ignorant see what they ought to follow, in it they read who do not know letters. Wherefore, and especially for the common people, picturing is the equivalent of reading.

Pope Gregory I, the Great, to Bishop Serenus of Marseilles, 600, Letters XI.10; Mary Carruthers *The Book of Memory* (1990) Ch.7, p.223. There was an ongoing controversy about whether images were idolatrous or helpful to the illiterate (see 106:5).

3 On the first day after my reception of ... Holy Baptism and the cure of my body from the filthiness of leprosy, I understood that there is no other God but the Father, the Son and the Holy Spirit whom most blessed Sylvester the pope preaches ... and the same venerable father told us clearly how great power in heaven and earth our Saviour gave to the apostle, blessed Peter ... and when I learned these things ... we – together with all the Roman people which is subject to the glory of our rule – considered that, since he is seen to be set up as the vicar of God's Son on earth, the pontiffs who act on behalf of that prince of the apostles should receive from us and our empire a greater power of government than the earthly clemency of our imperial serenity is seen to have conceded to them ... and inasmuch as our imperial power is earthly, we have decreed that it shall venerate and honour his most holy Roman Church and the sacred see of blessed Peter shall be gloriously exalted above our empire and earthly throne.

Donation of Constantine (8th century) from 'The Forged Decretals'; H. Bettenson (ed.) *Documents of the Christian Church* (1950) pp.135–8. The authenticity of this document, supposedly written by the Emperor Constantine, the first Christian emperor and founder of Constantinople in 330 (see 90:2), was not really questioned until the 15th century.

4 We must resist the temptation to treat the 'Donation' as a forgery; its very language, which is certainly anachronistic, betrays the uncouthness of Roman culture in the 8th century, yet its authenticity was not seriously questioned before the Renaissance. Forgery presupposes an intention to deceive; but clerks who drew up the 'Donation' to fill what they felt to be a lacuna in the archives were no doubt convinced that the facts had been much as they described them. Since God had willed that the pope should have the West in his tutelage and Pepin the Frankish monarchy in his power, it was an act of faith to provide an incontestable legal basis for them.

Robert S. Lopez (1962; 1967 trans.) p.85.

5 The Franks, so the elders among them say, have not held a synod for more than eighty years, nor had archbishops, nor have the churches conferred canonical rights on anyone in the churches, nor removed them. But for the most part the episcopal sees in the cities have been given over to greedy laymen, adulterous clerks, fornicators and publicans, and used for worldly enjoyment.

St Boniface to Pope Zacharias, 742, on the decadence of the church in Germany. St Boniface was one of two great English missionaries to the Friesians and Saxons in the 8th century (the other was St Willibrord). Boniface, a staunch champion of papal authority, opposed pagan customs, even destroying the sacred Donar oak at Geismar, central Germany (see 119:5).

CHARLEMAGNE, KING OF THE FRANKS AND EMPEROR IN THE WEST, 747–814

6 1. We wish that our estates, which we have set up to serve our needs, shall work entirely for our benefit and not for that of other men.

2. That the people on our estates should be properly taken care of and that no one reduces them to poverty.

3. That the stewards do not dare to enlist our people in their own service. They should not force them to carry out agricultural work, cut wood or do other tasks for them. Nor should the stewards accept

any presents from them, whether a horse or an ox, a cow or pig, sheep or piglet, lamb or anything else except bottles of wine, garden produce, fruit, chickens and eggs.

4. If any of our people commit robbery or any other crime against our interests let him make good the damage, and further let him be punished by whipping in fulfilment of the law.

Capitulary *De Villis* (Concerning Estates) in *Capitularia regum Francorum*, probably issued by Charlemagne himself, late 8th century; P.D. King *Charlemagne: Translated Sources* (1987) p.83. Capitularies were ordinances made by the Frankish kings in consultation with their chief councillors to deal with the management of the royal estates and public order. 'His manors were his true wealth' (J.M. Wallace-Hadrill *The Barbarian West* (1957) p.118).

1 In the eternal reign of our lord Jesus Christ, I Charles, by the grace of God and the gift of his mercy, king and rector of the kingdom of the Franks and devout defender and humble adjutant of the holy church, to all the ranks of ecclesiastical piety and dignitaries of secular power ...

18. To priests: Further in the same council that people are not to be allowed to become sorcerers, magicians, enchanters or enchantresses ...

40. To all: In the council of Africa: that virgins consecrated to God to be watched over with diligent vigilance by persons of graver character ...

43. To all: Further in the same that a wife cast aside by her husband is not to take another during her husband's lifetime nor the husband another wife during his first wife's lifetime ...

62. Let peace, concord and unanimity reign among all Christian people ... for without peace we cannot please God ...

72. Let them [the clergy] join and associate to themselves not only children of servile condition, but also sons of freemen. And let schools be established in which boys may learn to read. Correct carefully the Psalms, the written symbols, the songs, the calendar, the grammar, in each monastery or bishopric, and the Catholic books; because often men desire to pray to God properly, but they pray badly because of incorrect [inaccurate] texts. And do not let mere boys corrupt them in reading or writing. If the gospel, psalter and missal have to be copied let men of mature age do the copying, with the greatest care.

Charlemagne *The Admonitio* (789); King (1987) p.211. 'The *Admonitio* ... envisages a Christian society living at peace with itself, united under its king and fearing nothing but injustice. The force of this inspiration must not be minimized. It lighted

the handful of men who somehow saved barbarian Europe from itself' (Wallace-Hadrill (1957) p.104).

2 He [Charlemagne] cultivated the liberal arts most assiduously ... In the study of grammar he sat under Peter of Pisa ... In other studies his master was Alcuin ... a Saxon of Britain by birth and the most learned man of his day ... He tried also to learn to write and usually placed tablets and sheets of parchment under his pillows so that he could practise forming letters at odd moments. But he made little advance in this strange task, because he started too late in life ... At Aix [-la-Chapelle, Aachen, his capital on the western border of Germany] he built a church of extraordinary beauty ... where he could attend services morning and evening ... He gave much attention to correct reading and psalm-singing ... for he was an expert ... he sang only in unison or to himself.

Einhard *Life of Charlemagne* (c.815; 1922 edn) pp.41–2. Alcuin was the great stimulus behind the Carolingian renaissance – that is, the enthusiastic collection of books and scholars at Charlemagne's court. Many books came from England. 'England transported [to the continent] that rarest of commodities, learning, when it was most needed' (Wallace-Hadrill (1957) p.106). A century later King Alfred emulated Charlemagne in attempting to be a scholar-king (see 162:5).

3 With Aaron [Harun al-Rashid] king of the Persians, who ruled over all the east, with the exception of India, he entertained so harmonious a friendship that the Persian king valued his favour before the friendship of all the kings and princes in the world ... and forwarded immense presents to Charles – robes and spices, and the other rich products of the east – and a few years earlier he had sent him at his request an elephant, which was then the only one he had.

Einhard (c.815; 1922 edn) pp.28–9. The fifth Abbasid caliph indeed ruled from Baghdad in Iraq an empire that stretched from North Africa to Central Asia. He was a great patron of the arts. He also waged war with enthusiasm against the Byzantine empire, so when Einhard emphasizes that he valued Charlemagne's friendship above all other rulers, it is an oblique reference to his rival emperor in the East.

4 He was so careful in the bringing up of his sons and daughters that when at home he never dined without them, and they always accompanied him on journeys, his sons riding by his side, and his daughters following close behind.

Einhard (c.815; 1877 edn) pp.70–71. Einhard's biography of Charlemagne, based on the classical model of Suetonius, is famous as an early medieval biography of a secular ruler.

Einhard was intimate with Charlemagne and his family, and he wrote the life just after Charlemagne's death in 814.

1 He took constant exercise in riding and hunting, which is natural to a Frank, since scarcely any nation can be found to equal them in these pursuits. He also delighted in the natural warm baths, frequently exercising himself by swimming, in which he was very skilful, no one being able to outstrip him. It was on account of the warm baths there that he built the palace at Aachen.
Einhard (c.815; 1922 edn) p.38.

2 Until now there have been three men of the highest rank in the world. The first is the supreme apostle governing from the throne of the blessed St Peter, prince of the apostles, as his vicar; what has been done to him who sat on that throne [Leo III] you have in kindness advised me. The second is the imperial dignity and imperial power of the other Rome [Constantinople]; it is rumoured far and wide how the ruler of that empire [Constantine VI] has been impiously deposed not by strangers but by his own people and fellow citizens. The third is the royal dignity which by the dispensation of our Lord Jesus Christ is conferred on you as governor of the Christian people; and this is more excellent than the other dignities in power, more shining in wisdom, more sublime in rank.
Alcuin to Charlemagne, June 799; *Monumenta Germaniae historica Epistolarium* Vol.4 (1895 edn) p.288. Alcuin here gives a judicious judgement on the 'hot potato' of the relationship between papal, imperial and royal authority in the crucial months before Charlemagne's Christmas coronation. It is notable that he rates highest, not the imperial nor the papal title, but the royal Frankish kingship, which derived from pagan origins. Charlemagne was already at odds with Empress Irene, regent for Constantine VI.

3 It was at the time he received the title of emperor and Augustus, to which at first he was so averse that he remarked that had he known the intention of the pope, he would not have entered the church on that day, great festival though it was.
Einhard (c.815; 1877 edn) pp.82–3. Of the coronation in Rome on Christmas Day 800. Why was Charlemagne reluctant? Was it because of delicate relationships with the eastern emperors? Or was it because he had intended to crown himself? The eastern ritual on solemn feast-days was that the pope crowned the king *and then adored him.* This remains one of the great unanswerable questions of the Middle Ages.

4 Under this tomb is placed the body of Charles, the great and orthodox emperor, who gloriously

enlarged the realm of the Franks, and successfully reigned for forty-seven years.

He died in the seventy-third year of his age.

Jany XXVIII Anno Domini DCCXIV indiction vii.
Inscription in the great chapel at Aachen; Einhard (c.815; 1877 edn) p.86.

CHARLEMAGNE: THE LEGEND

5 White are his locks and silver is his beard,
His body noble, his countenance severe.
Anon. *Chanson de gestes* (11th–12th centuries). Charlemagne became one of a series of medieval legends in which a saviour figure rises from the dead to save his country in time of great crisis. Other legendary saviours were King Arthur, Emperor Frederick I and King Sebastian of Portugal.

6 Durendal, fair, hallowed and devote;
What store of relics lie in thy hilt of gold!
St Peter's tooth, St Basil's blood, it holds,
Hair of my lord St Denis, there enclosed,
Likewise a piece of Blessed Mary's robe;
To Paynim hands 'twere sin to let you go;
You should be served by Christian men alone,
Ne'er may you fall to any coward soul!
Many wide lands I conquered by your strokes
For Charles [Charlemagne] to keep whose
        beard is white as snow,
Whereby right rich and mighty is his throne.
Anon. *The Song of Roland* (last quarter of 11th century; 1957 trans.) St.173. The dying knight is addressing his sword, Durendal. According to Charlemagne's biographer Einhard, Basques ambushed the rearguard of the Frankish army in 778 at Roncesvalles in the Pyrenees (see 152:1). The legend of Roland and Oliver stems from this incident.

7 Here the lord pope shall give the sceptre of empire and say: 'Receive the sceptre, the emblem of royal power, the straight wand of kingship, the wand of virtue by which you shall well govern yourself and with royal courage defend from evil men the holy church and the Christian people entrusted to you by God.'
Imperial coronation order C, first used in 1014 at the coronation of Henry II; P. Fabre and L. Duchesne (eds) *Liber Censuum* (Book of Censuses) (1901) Bk 1.6.

THE RISING POWER OF THE POPES, 1000–c.1250

8 You are said to have publicly condemned the Apostolic and Latin church, without either a hearing or a conviction. And the chief reason for this condemnation, which displays an unexampled presumption and an unbelievable effrontery, is that the Latin church dares to celebrate the commemoration of the Lord's passion with unleavened bread. What an unguarded accusation is this of yours, what an evil piece of arrogance! You place your mouth in heaven, while your tongue 'going through the world', strives with human arguments and conjectures to undermine and subvert the ancient faith.

Pope Leo IX to the Byzantine emperor, Michael Cerularius, Sept. 1053; Bettenson (1950) p.134. The letter *In terra pax hominibus* from Rome triggered the final schism between the Eastern and Western churches in 1054 (see 92:7).

1 Everything is in fact done in a perverted order, in rejection of the holy canons and in utter contempt of the whole of Christian religion, and the first things come last and the last first. For the lay authority comes first in electing and confirming, and then, willy-nilly, the consent of the laity, people and clergy follows, and the metropolitan's decision comes last of all.

Cardinal Humbert of Silva Candida *Libri III adversus simoniacos* (c.1058); Pullan (1966) Pt 3, Ch.2. Simony, the sin of buying or selling spiritual offices, derived from the biblical story of Simon Magus (Acts of the Apostles 8:18–20).

2 That the Roman church was founded by God alone.

That only the bishop of Rome is by law called universal …

That the pope is the only man whose feet shall be kissed by all princes …

That he may depose emperors …

That he must not be judged by anyone …

That the Roman church has never erred, nor, as witness Scripture, will ever do so.

Pope Gregory VII, Decree *Dictatus Papae*, 1075; Pullan (1966) Pt 3, Ch.2. Gregory also issued decrees against clerical marriage and simony.

3 You have decided that they [other clergy] all know nothing and you alone know everything, and have sought to use your knowledge not to build but to destroy so that on these grounds we may believe that St Gregory, whose name you have claimed for yourself, was prophesying when he said: 'The mind of the prelate is often exalted by the abundance of his subjects and he thinks he knows more than anybody else when he sees that he has more power than they!'

Henry IV to Gregory VII, Jan. 1076; Pullan (1966) Pt 3, Ch.2.

4 In the name of God almighty, the Father, the Son and the Holy Ghost, through thy power and authority, I withdraw the government of the whole kingdom of the Germans and of Italy from Henry the king, son of Henry the emperor. For he has risen up against thy church with unheard of arrogance. And I absolve all Christians from the bond of the oath that they have made to him or shall make. And I forbid anyone to serve him as king.

Gregory VII, deposition of Henry IV, Feb. 1076; Bettenson (1950) p.144. The power of the church caused the defection of many of Henry's chief vassals to the papal cause.

5 On the morning of 25 January 1077 … Henry IV standing barefoot in the snow and clothed in the woollen robe of the penitent knocked at the fortress door. There he remained until evening, moaning, weeping and craving pardon. On the two following days a like scene was enacted. In the evening of the third day, he betook himself to a tiny chapel dedicated to St Nicholas, where he found the Countess Matilda and the Abbot of Cluny at prayer. He redoubled his entreaties and at length the Countess Matilda (in whose castle the pope was lodged at Canossa), and afterwards also St Hugh consented to approach the pope. Gregory himself was won over and promised to restore the king to communion with the faithful on the morrow, subject to the following conditions: first that Henry should appear before a diet composed of the princes of the empire and there answer whatever accusations were lodged against him; and secondly, that until judgement had been pronounced he was to take no part whatever with the government of the kingdom and should make whatever satisfaction was demanded of him.

Fernand Mourret *Histoire générale de l'église*, Vol.4 (1916) p.196; Fernand Haynard *History of the Popes* (1931) p.160. See 190:1.

6 What fruits are produced by the transformations and annihilations of kingdoms is a problem which must be left to God, from whom nothing useless can proceed. Nevertheless, there is no lack of people to maintain that God wished to humble the kingdom in order to exalt the church. In fact, nobody doubts that the church, exalted and enriched by the strength of the kingdom and the beneficence of the kings … has been able to humiliate the kingdom to such a point … that it is destroyed not only by the spiritual sword but by its own material sword.

Otto of Freising *Chronicle 'The Two Cities'* (1143–6), on the interaction of church and state. He was both a Cistercian monk (see 196:2–196:7) and half-brother of Conrad III, king of Germany (r.1138–52), so he saw both sides of the argument. The Cistercians were very pro-papacy.

1 At daybreak the attendants of the lord pope hastened to the church of St Mark the evangelist [in Venice] and closed the central doors of the great portal in front of the church, and thither they brought much timber and deal planks and ladders and so raised up a lofty and splendid throne … Thither the pope arrived before the first hour of the day [6 a.m.] and soon after ascended to the highest part of his throne to await the arrival of the emperor … When he [Frederick I] reached it, he threw off the red cloak he was wearing and prostrated himself before the pope, and kissed first his feet and then his knees. But the pope rose, and taking the head of the emperor in both his hands he embraced him and kissed him, and made him sit at his right hand and at last spoke the words, 'Son of the church, be welcome' … And when the ceremony was over, they both left the church together. The pope mounted his horse and the emperor held his stirrup and then returned to the doges' palace.

Anon. *De Pace Veneta Relatio*, 23 July 1177; J.J. Norwich *A History of Venice* (1982) p.113. The writer was probably a German churchman and eyewitness to the reconciliation between Pope Alexander III and Frederick I at Chioggia, thus establishing the Peace of Venice.

2 Assuredly there is nothing that is not laudable in the desire to understand the Scriptures, but to meet in secret, to usurp the ministry of preaching, to dispense with the ministry of the priest to the extent of scorning it, there lies the evil … If when endeavouring to penetrate the depth of meaning in the scriptures learned men recognize themselves as being insufficient, you will be more so in that you are simple and illiterate … common people may not presume by their intellect to attain to the sublime height as of revelation nor preach it to others … There remains for you but one thing to do, to obey.

Pope Innocent III to the faithful at Metz, 1199; J.P. Migne (ed.) *Patrologia Latina* (1844–64) Vol.214, Cols 695–9. The following quotation shows Innocent's continuing efforts to keep lay groups within the church.

3 Since in the vineyard of the heavenly Father, weeds often flourish among the vines, so, just as the prudent vine-dresser seeks a remedy which in destroying the weeds does not destroy the vines, so the pastors of the church must take care lest, in their solicitude,

to destroy the wickedness of heresy they condemn the innocent … We understand that … the clergy of Verona have proceeded without discretion … and have excommunicated some who, although called Humiliati by the people … are the orthodox faith and seek to live in humility of heart and body … we enjoin you to summon such before you … If you find nothing of heretical depravity in them, declare them to be Catholic.

Pope Innocent III to the bishop of Verona, c.1198; Migne (1844–64) Vol.204, Cols 788–9. The church claimed to control the belief and practice of every man, but the pope tried to keep religious experimenters within the fold. He gave the Humiliati of Lombardy in northern Italy a Rule in 1201 (see 199:4).

4 The perverseness of heresy, which has corrupted men throughout the ages, is constantly on the increase in the region of Toulouse. We admonish your royal serenity most carefully and we encourage you in the Lord and enjoin you for the omission of sins to arm yourself strongly and powerfully to root out such degenerate shoots … you must eliminate such harmful filth, so that the purity of your faith, which as a Catholic prince you hold as an ideal, may be revealed in deeds by vigorous action and also so that perfidious heretical sectaries, worn out by the force of your power, may be brought back amid the sufferings of the war at least to a knowledge of the truth.

Pope Innocent III to Philip II, king of France, 17 Nov. 1207; Migne (1844–64) Vol.215, Cols 1246–7. Indulgences were granted by the papacy to those who fought against heretics, whether in the Holy Land or, as here, against the Albigensians (see 200:1), in Europe.

5 You must not fail to bring to bear on him [Count Raymond VI of Toulouse, whose servant had murdered the papal legate, Peter of Castelnau, on 14 Jan. 1208] the full weight of persuasion so that he may make satisfaction to us and to the Church, but most important of all to God, by expelling him and his followers from the castles under his lordship and taking their lands where, after the heretics have been banished, Catholic inhabitants must be put in their place, who, according to the teaching of your orthodox faith, must serve in holiness and justice before God.

Pope Innocent III to the ecclesiastical provinces of Narbonne, Arles, Embrun, Aix and Vienne in southern France, 10 Mar. 1208; Peter of Vaux-de-Cernay *Historia Albigensis* Vol.1, p.65. The chronicle recounts how local lords who harboured heretics, such as the Albigensians (Cathars), were fiercely condemned by the papacy.

1 An ecumenical council was for a medieval pope, the equivalent of a plenary assembly of feudal vassals for a king ... The Fourth Lateran Council, 1215 proposed to regenerate humanity. Nothing less! ... It would be the great instrument for social progress.

A. Luchaire *Innocent III, le Concile de Latran et la réforme de l'église* (1908) pp.3–5. The Fourth Lateran Council represented the papacy at the height of its power. No aspect of social life was beyond its control, and its legislation sought to regulate the conduct of the laity, parish priests, bishops, monks, craftsmen and merchants. Papal authority reached throughout every part of medieval society, from prohibiting the foundation of new orders, passing decrees on usury and instituting the annual confession of all the faithful to defining the roles of bishops, priests and teachers. Lateran councils were universal, as distinct from regional, church councils. Every part of the western Latin church was represented.

2 Behold the beast that comes up from the sea.

Pope Gregory IX, letter, 1239, opening words (from Revelation 13:1–2). The pope is calling on the faithful to withdraw allegiance from the rebellious emperor, Frederick II (r.1212–50). 'A prime example of the peculiar force that apocalypticism could give to current events by placing them within the sphere of history at its most universal and critical moment' (B. McGinn *Visions of the End* (1979) p.172). For Frederick II's propaganda see 199:3.

3 Since thou Bethlehem of the Marches, are not the least among our princes for out of thee has come a leader [*dux*], the prince of the Roman empire, who will rule and protect his people.

Frederick II to his birthplace, Jesi (eastern Italy), 1239; J. Huillard-Bréholles *Historia Diplomatica Frederici Secundi* (1857) Vol.I, p.375. In propaganda replying to the papal accusation that he was the Antichrist, the Hohenstaufen emperor assumes the messianic role concerning Bethlehem (Micah 5:2), traditionally applied to Christ.

4 Greatest of the princes of the world, Frederick [II] who bewildered the world and brought extraordinary change.

Matthew Paris *Principum mundi maximus Frethericus stupor quoque mundi et immutator mirabilis*; John Larner *Italy in the Age of Dante and Petrarch 1216–1380* (1980) p.21. Though not meant as praise, Frederick retained the sobriquet 'Stupor Mundi' for subsequent generations, and J.C. Burckhardt calls him 'the first man of a modern type who sat on a throne' (*The Civilization of the Renaissance in Italy* (1860; 1944 edn) p.2).

5 We thought it right to charge you to preach the cross in the kingdom of Hungary against Frederick, called emperor, the son of perdition, and since several people in that kingdom have received the sign of the cross to aid the Holy Land ... [we] concede to your devotion by the authority of the present letter the unrestricted power to commute effectively the vows of these crusaders to the defence of the cross against the same Frederick, if they agree to it, and to grant that indulgence which was given in the general council to those going to the aid of the Holy Land to them, and to any others who redeem their vows, provided that you forward for this defence of the money which they would have spent going to the Holy Land, staying there and returning from there and which they assign into your hands.

Pope Gregory IX to his legate in Hungary, 14 Feb. 1241, authorizing crusaders to commute their vows against Frederick II, who had advanced on Rome; A. Theiner *Vetera monumenta historica Hungariam sacram illustrantia* (Ancient Historical Documents Illustrative of the Hungarian Church) (1859) in L. and J. Riley-Smith *The Crusades: Idea and Reality* (1981) Pt 2, Doc.16.

6 Method, art and processes to employ for the interrogation of heretics, believers (followers of heretics) and their accomplices.

Bernard Gui *The Inquisitor's Handbook* (c.1332; 1956 edn) Title to Pt 5. Episcopal attempts to deal with heresy proved inefficient, so Gregory IX gave special powers to inquisitors, from which the papal Inquisition evolved. Gui's famous manual represents a high point in inquisitorial professionalism. He was careful and fair in his inquisitions in the area around Toulouse from c.1307 to 1324, unlike Umberto Eco's portrait of him in his novel *The Name of the Rose* (1980; 1983 trans.).

THE PAPACY: DECLINE AND EXILE, 1265–1378

7 Seek a loan. Seek it from the king, from his brother, from prelates, from monks, from bourgeois, from usurers, from everybody, even if you've already had ten refusals.

Pope Clement IV to his legate in France, 1265; Larner (1980) p.43. The pope is seeking to raise money for his imminent campaign in 1266 against the Hohenstaufen Manfred, king of Sicily and Naples and natural son of Frederick II. Pope Urban IV (Clement's predecessor), who wanted to replace the German emperors with French Angevins, had offered Manfred's kingdom to Charles, Count of Anjou.

8 The trustworthy tradition of our ancestors affirms that great remissions and indulgences for sins are granted to those who visit this city [Rome], the venerable basilicas of the Prince of the Apostles ... wherefore we ... in the plenitude of apostolic authority, grant to all who being truly penitent, visit these basilicas in this present year and in each succeeding hundredth year, not only a full and copious, but the most full pardon of all their sins.

Pope Boniface VIII *Registres* (1300; 1907–39 edn) no.3875. The announcement of the great jubilee year was a triumphant expression of papal power. One chronicler (no doubt exaggerating) put the figure of those who streamed in from all over western Europe at two million. Architects and artists gathered under papal patronage for the adornment of Rome. Dante himself was a pilgrim there. It was a 'fair beginning' of a reign that ended in papal ruin.

1 We learn from ... the gospel that in the church and in her power are two swords, the spiritual and the temporal ... (both are in the power of the church, the spiritual sword and the material) ... But the latter is used for the church, the former by her ... The one sword, then, should be under the other and the temporal authority subject to the spiritual ... Furthermore we declare ... that it is altogether necessary for salvation for every human creature to be subject to the Roman pontiff.

Pope Boniface VIII *Unam sanctam* (bull), 1302; A. Freemantle (ed.) *Papal Encyclicals in their Historical Context* (1956) pp.73–4. Boniface's unconditional declaration marks the high point of papal monarchy in theory, but he had already clashed fiercely with the secular monarchies of France and England over clerical taxation in the bull *Clericis laicos* (1296), and the French king, Philip IV, had responded by seizing the pope at Anagni (southeast of Rome).

2   I see the fleur-de-lys enter Alogna (Anagni),
and, in his vicar, Christ made captive,
a second time I see him mocked.

Dante Alighieri *The Divine Comedy* 'Purgatory' (c.1308–21) Canto 20, lines 85–8. On 7 Sept. 1303 Sciarra Colonna, with other malcontents and a contingent of soldiers, seized Boniface VIII in the name of Philip IV of France. The pope, who was about 86 years old, was soon released by an Italian mob but died on 12 Oct. Dante, who had castigated Boniface in his person, regarded this outrage against the sacred office as a second passion of Christ. Many shared this view, combining anger against power-hungry popes with 'reverence for the holder of the keys'. Sciarra Colonna belonged to one of the two chief feuding Roman families (the other was the Orsinis). The Colonnas were powerful patrons, including of the poet Petrarch.

3 In the fourteenth century it was not possible even for an essentially spiritual power to dominate the world except by basing its means of action on territorial and fiscal resources ... Giovanni Villani in his *Istorie Fiorentine* [Florentine Histories; 1330s and 1340s] recounts how John XXII left more than 18 million gold florins.

G. Mollat *Les Papes d'Avignon* (1949) p.44. Intimidation from the French monarchy led to the election of a French pope,

Clement V, in 1305 and the removal of the papacy to Avignon (next to, but not part of, the French realm). Thus began the 'Babylonish captivity' of the church, which lasted till 1378. During this period the administration of the church was centralized effectively, but politically the papacy was crippled. The days of *Unam sanctam* were gone. The chronicler quoted died in the Black Death in 1348 (see 286:2).

4 Avignon is indeed the mother of fornication and lust and drunkenness, full of abomination and all filthiness and seated upon the rushing waters of the Rhone, the Durance and the Sorgue. And her prelates are indeed like the scarlet woman, clothed in purple and gold and silver and precious stones, and drunk with the blood of the martyrs and Christ.

Benvenuto da Imola (c.1331–c.1380); P. Toynbee 'Benvenuto da Imola and his Commentary on the *Divine Comedy*' in *An English Miscellany Presented to Dr Furnival* (1901) p.440. The Italian was the author of one of the earliest and most valuable commentaries on the *Divine Comedy*. He shows bitterness over the pope's desertion of Rome and hatred of the French and Angevin royal houses.

5 The ship of Peter is shaken by the waves, the fisherman's net is broken, the serenity of peace turns to clouds, the disaster of wars devastates the lands of the Roman church and nearby provinces ... There is no doubt that in the see of Peter you will reside more securely, will shine more brightly, in his land you will live with more tranquillity and, distant from kings, princes and peoples, your position will be more admirable.

J.D. Mansi *Sacrorum Conciliorum Nova et Amplissima Collectio* Vol.25 (1782) Col.125. The cardinals in Rome announce his election to Clement V in 1305 and appeal to him to come back to Rome from Avignon.

6   Foul Babylon has overstepped the mark,
and crammed itself with scandalous misdeeds
Almost to bursting, having made its gods
of Venus and Bacchus and the like.

Francesco Petrarch *Canzoniere*, poem 137 (c.1343; 2000 trans.). The great Italian poet and scholar (see 267:2) of the generation following Dante does not mince his words.

7 In place of apostles who went bare-foot, one sees today 'satraps' on horses covered in gold, like kings of Persia or Parthia that demand adoration and must not be approached empty-handed. Poor old men. You have taken so much trouble – for whom? You have tilled the fields of the Lord – for whom? You have spilled so much blood – for whom?

Francesco Petrarch, Epistle 16, 1343; Abbé J.F.A. de Sade *Mémoires pour la vie de François Pétrarque* (1764) p.95.

1 These papal collections gathered together many gifts and purchased acquisitions: precious stones, ecclesiastical copes and chasubles embroidered in gold and other rich decorations, vessels of gold and silver etc.

Anon. contemporary source; Yves Renouard *La Papauté à Avignon* (1954) p.113. The luxury that popes displayed in their palace at Avignon, particularly the greed of John XXII (r.1316–34), became a by-word for corruption.

2 Peter preached, of course, but today's pope fights.
The one seeks souls, the other greedily seeks riches.
The first was killed for God's law, the second kills,
And yet God maintains no such law as that.
The one arouses faith through his innocence, not by force;
The other rouses armies on parade.

John Gower *Vox Clamantis* (1382–4) Bk 3, lines 631–6; John Barnie *War in Medieval Society* (1974) p.123. The English poet inveighs against the pope's worldliness, greed and involvement in the 100 Years War.

THE CONCILIAR MOVEMENT AND BEYOND, 1409–60

3 It is impossible for the General Council to be held … without the authority of the pope. But to convene such a council in the present case the authority of the pope cannot step in because no single person is universally recognized as pope.

Conrad of Gelnhausen *Epistolae Concordiae* (1379); E.F. Jacob *Essays in the Conciliar Epoch* (1943) p.9. The antipope was a rival or usurping pope set up in opposition to the one canonically elected. Of the 39 antipopes, those residing in Avignon during the Great Schism (1378–1417) are the best known, but the last of the antipopes was Felix V (r.1439–49). More than 30 years of two popes (a *monstrum biceps*, two-headed monster, one elected in Rome and one in France) had brought western Christendom – rulers, churchmen, lawyers and academics – to the point of instigating a desperate search for a formula to break the impasse.

4 The church, or the general council representing her, is the rule laid down by the Holy Spirit … so that everyone of whatever estate, even papal, is bound to obey her … The general council, though it cannot take away the plenitude of papal power … can yet limit its use under certain rules … and this is the stable foundation of all ecclesiastical reform.

Jean Gerson *Opera* (c.1415) Vol.11, p.205; Jacob (1943) p.12. Two French scholars, Peter d'Ailly and Jean Gerson, led the debate that, based on theological and legal arguments, declared the power of the church resided at its fullest in the general council, which represented all its parts.

5 The pope, once the wonder of the world, has fallen … Now is the reign of Simon Magus … the papal court turns God's houses into a market … golden was the first age of the papal court; then came the baser age of silver; next the iron age long set its yoke on the stubborn age. Then came the age of clay. Could ought be worse? Aye, dung, and in dung sits the papal court.

Dietrich Uric (c.1420; 1897 trans.) Vol.1, p.300. Uric, a German poet, attended the Council of Constance (1414–18). The scandal of papal corruption was felt particularly in Germany, and pressure, notably from the king, Sigismund (later emperor; r.1433–7), finally led to the convening of a second general council, which was deliberately located in imperial territory, far removed from Roman influence.

6 The holy synod of Constance … declares that, being lawfully assembled in the Holy Spirit … and representing the Catholic Church, it derives its power directly from Christ, and to it everyone of whatever rank … including the pope.

Canon *Sacrosancta*, 1415; Denys Hay (ed.) *De Gestis consilii Basiliensis Commentariorum Libri II* (1967) pp.xiii–xiv. Following the declaration and after intricate negotiations, the backers of the papal claimants were persuaded to withdraw their support. The way was cleared for the ending of the schism and the election of Pope Martin V in 1417.

7 General councils shall meet frequently in the future. The next will be held in five years' time, the second seven years after that, and thereafter they will be celebrated every ten years.

Summary of the key provisions in the Decree *Frequens* (Oct. 1417); Hay (1967) p.xv. This decree theoretically tied the papacy to the superior authority of the general council. In practice, 15th-century popes ignored the decree and from Martin V onwards became mainly secular Italian princes.

8 On a solemn day the pope, with all the court of Rome, the emperor of the Greeks and all the bishops and prelates clergy assembled in Santa Maria del Fiore [Florence cathedral] … On the one side sat the pope with the cardinals and prelates of the Roman Church; on the other side, the emperor … with all the Greeks … the pope wore full pontifical vestments; all the cardinals wore their copes … the Greeks in their robes of silk … had a more goodly and dignified appearance than the Latins … The

Greeks promised never more to be in discord with the Roman Church, as in the past ... All Florence was there to witness this noble function.

Vespasiano da Bisticci *The Vespasiano Memoirs* (1439; 1926 trans.) p.25. A Florentine bookseller gives an eyewitness account of the union between the Latin and Greek churches at the culmination of the Council of Florence (1439). The prescribed general council had duly met at Basle in southern Germany in reforming mood, but Pope Eugenius (Eugene) IV skilfully drew support away and trumped the Basle assembly (which he declared schismatic) by the Council of Florence. This achieved a symbolic triumph for the papacy in giving Rome supremacy of the Greek church. But it was a hollow victory, quickly repudiated by the Greek church.

1 The council is superior to the pope ... since the representation of the church in the general council is surer and more infallible than the pope alone.

Nicholas of Cusa *De concordantia catholica* (1433); Jacob (1943) p.17. This late work by a leading 15th-century theologian accepted the plenitude of papal power but argued that the general council was a surer judge of doctrinal difficulties because it was more representative of the church's rich variety. In the 15th century, however, popes set their sights on absolute papal monarchy. The last attempts at conciliar action were killed off by the bull *Execrabilis* (1460), in which Pius II condemned any appeal to a future council as an 'execrable abuse, unheard of in former times'.

2 Be baptized and no prince in the world will be your equal in glory and power. We will call you emperor of the Greeks and of the Orient, and what you now possess by force and injury, you will hold by right. All Christians will venerate you and make you the judge of their disputes ... the see of Rome will love you like any Christian king and so much the more as your position will be greater than theirs.

Pope Pius II to Mehmed II, *c*.1460 (but never sent); *Letters* (1953 edn) pp.113–14. Pope Pius had a great sense of theatre. After Constantinople fell to the Ottomans in 1453 he made an offer the sultan could refuse.

JUDGEMENTS

3 The papacy is not other than the ghost of the deceased Roman empire, sitting crowned upon the grave thereof.

Thomas Hobbes *Leviathan* (1651) Ch.47.

4 This agglomeration which was called and still calls itself the Holy Roman Empire was neither holy, nor Roman, nor an empire in any way.

Voltaire (François-Marie Arouet) *Essai sur le mœurs et l'esprit des nations* (1756) Ch.70.

The Medieval Church, 1000–1500

AROUND THE FIRST MILLENNIUM

1 When I was a boy I heard a sermon in Paris prophesying that as soon as a thousand years was completed the advent of Antichrist would take place and not long after the time of universal judgement would follow.

Abbot Cibbo of Fleury, 998; J.P. Migne (ed.) *Patrologia Latina* (1844–64) Vol.139, Col.471. The abbot is recalling rumours about the end of the world in 1000.

2 The great crowds in Jerusalem expected the infamous Antichrist and the end of the times.

Ralph Glaber *Historiarium sui temporis libri quinque* (1028–33) Bk 5; E. Pognou (ed.) *L'An mille* (The Millennium) (1947) p.81. The Burgundian chronicler is describing the pilgrimage of Odalric, bishop of Orleans, to Jerusalem in 1028. The official attitude of the church over the crucial period seems to have been to play down all emotional outbursts.

THE BLACK MONKS

3 Whenever matters of importance have to be decided ... let the abbot summon the whole congregation ... after hearing the advice of the brethren let him ... do what he judges most advantageous ... Seven times a day do I praise thee ... this will be fulfilled by us in seven services [i.e., in the chapel]. A monk should own nothing at all: neither a book, tablets nor a pen ... The brothers shall wait on each other in turn; no one should be excused from the kitchen work unless he be sick ... We think it sufficient for the daily meal that there should be two cooked dishes ... all must abstain from the flesh of four-footed beasts, except the delicate and sick ... At fixed times the brethren ought to be occupied in manual labour, and again at fixed times in sacred reading ... for bedding a mattress or woollen blanket, a woollen under-blanket and a pillow shall suffice.

St Benedict *A Very Little Rule for Beginners* (6th century). The Rule formed the basis of all succeeding monastic orders. It is notable for its moderation and common sense in contrast to the excesses of some preceding hermits.

4 Hear, my son, the precepts of the master. Whoever thou art, renounce thy will, gird on the mighty and resplendent arms of obedience, and go to war under the true king, Christ the Lord.

St Benedict, call to the monastic life from Monte Cassino (southeast of Rome), which he established c.529; R.S. Lopez *The Birth of Europe* (1962; 1967 trans.) p.39.

5 And so, oh God of glory ... you inspired my father Odeler to give me up and surrender me wholly to you. Weeping, he gave a weeping child to Reginald the monk, and sent me into exile for your love – nor ever after saw me. A small boy did not presume to contradict his father, but I obeyed him in all things, since he promised me that I should possess paradise with the innocent ... I left my country, my parents, all my kindred and all my friends ... At ten years old I crossed the Channel, and came, an exile to Normandy, knowing no one, known to none. Like Joseph in Egypt I heard a tongue I knew not. Yet by your grace I found among strangers every kindness and friendship. I was received to the monastic life in the monastery at St Evroul by the venerable Mainer [the abbot] on [Sunday, 21 Sept. 1085]. I was given in place of my English name, which seemed ugly to the Normans, the name Vitalis, a name borrowed from one of the companions of St Maurice the martyr, whose martyrdom was then being celebrated.

Orderic Vitalis *Ecclesiastical History* (c.1114–43; 1969–80 edn) Bk 13. The Anglo-Norman historian, who was born near Shrewsbury, Shropshire, on 16 Feb. 1075, poignantly remembers the abrupt end of his childhood in England, when his father consigned him, at the age of ten, to monastic life in Normandy. The presentation of child oblates (children offered as future monks by their parents) was a common practice.

6 The ideal for which Cluny stood ... was the regular, tireless, all but ceaseless liturgical service ... using every means of chant, of ceremony and of ornament available to render that service more solemn and more splendid. Peter Damian [a visiting monk in 1063] said that even in the longest days the monks had hardly half an hour's free time in the day.

David Knowles *The Monastic Order in England* (1950) pp.149–50. Cluny was founded in Burgundy, eastern-central France, in 910. Its 'daughters' spread widely, including throughout the British Isles. Eight services, called offices, were chanted around the clock in the monastic church.

1 Whoever thou art, if thou seekest to extol the glory of these doors,
Marvel not at the gold and the expense but at the craftsmanship of the work.
Bright is the noble work; but, being nobly bright, the work
Should brighten the minds so that they may travel, through the true lights,
To the True Light where Christ is the true door.

Abbot Suger c.1081–1151; Gerda Panofsky-Soergel (ed.) *Abbot Suger on the Abbey Church of St Denis and its Art Treasures* (1979) pp.47, 49. Suger justifies in verse the gilded doors to the resplendent church of Saint-Denis, near Paris. The abbot believed: 'The holy martyrs themselves tell us with their own lips: "We want the very best that can be had."' 'St Bernard [of Clairvaux] had launched a scarifying attack on the luxury and ornamentation of the Cluniac churches' (William Anderson *The Rise of the Gothic* (1985) p.31).

THE WHITE MONKS

2 There were amongst them men of middle age, who had shone in the councils of princes, and who had hitherto worn nothing less than the furred mantle or the steel hauberk, which they now came to exchange for the poor cowl of St Benedict; but the greater part were men of noble features and deportment, and well might they be, for they were of the noblest houses of Burgundy. The whole troop was led by one young man of about twenty-three years of age and of exceeding beauty.

Anon. Cistercian monk *A Concise History of the Cistercian Order* (1852) p.96. The author is describing the arrival at the abbey of Cîteaux in 1113 of the future St Bernard and his 29 friends, asking to be admitted as novices.

3 To talk of the 12th century without mentioning St Bernard would be like talking about the 16th century without mentioning Luther.

Gordon Leff *Medieval Thought* (1958) pp.134.

4 What do the apostles teach us? Not to read Plato ... or Aristotle ... they have taught me how to live.

St Bernard (1090–1153); Migne (1844–64) Vol.183, Col.647. St Bernard exercised tremendous political influence in the 12th century, but he believed that the highest knowledge was mystical, and he opposed scholasticism, accusing Abelard of allowing human reason to usurp the role of faith (see 197:6). He had great charisma and could carry contemporaries with him.

5 Ailred was a favourite with King David [of Scotland] ... but the king saw how ... sometimes he would stand in a dream, sharing out food among others but eating none himself ... one day [in 1134] he rode south to York where he heard about the white monks [Cistercians] ... how they had settled by a lonely stream like a flock of white seagulls ... on the way home he came to the edge of a hill where he looked down on the rough huts of the monks at Rievaulx. He said to his servant: 'Shall we go down and see this holy place?' The reply was 'Yes!' The monks flocked to meet them and they stayed.

Walter Daniel *Life of Ailred of Rievaulx* (2nd half of 12th century; 1922 edn) Ch.2. Ailred (Aethelred; 1109–67) became a famous abbot of the Yorkshire abbey, the first Cistercian house in England, from where the order spread throughout the country. Daniel says that on feast-days the church was packed with monks 'as closely as a hive with bees'.

6 That brother is a kindly man, affable ... and bountiful ... a literate man and eloquent, a very proper man ... Nay, it would be an onus rather than an honour to have such a man for he is over-nice about his food ... knows how to spend much and gain little, snores when others keep vigil ... a man that loves and cherishes flatterers ... From such a ruler may the lord deliver us!

Jocelyn of Brakelond *Cronica* (12th century; 1949 trans.) pp.12–13. Two monks at Bury St Edmunds, Suffolk, in eastern England, discuss candidates for the position of abbot.

7 As an illustration of this spiritual building I shall give you Noe's ark ... you shall see colours, shapes and figures which please the eye but know that they are set there to teach you wisdom, understanding and virtue ... The ark signifies the church and the church is Christ's body, so I have drawn the whole person of Christ, head and members [limbs] in visible shape, to picture it for you clearly.

Hugh of St Victor *De arca Noe morali* (The Moral of Noah's Ark) Bk 1.3.629; B. Smalley *The Study of the Bible in the Middle Ages* (1941) p.71. Hugh, a canon of the Augustinian abbey of St Victor, Paris, is teaching a monastic audience how to study the scriptures allegorically. The sacred text of the Bible was studied in four 'senses': literal, allegorical, moral and analogical (that is, pointing to heavenly things).

UNIVERSITIES

8 Thierry of Chartres [chancellor of that school in northern France from 1142] describes in his *Heptateuchon* the undergraduate course in the seven liberal arts: grammar, logic and rhetoric (the

trivium) and arithmetic, geometry, astronomy and music (the *quadrivium*).

Gordon Leff *Paris and Oxford Universities in the 13th and 14th Centuries* (1968) pp.118–19. These subjects were taught first in cathedral schools and then in universities such as Paris and Oxford. The higher stages of learning were doctorates in law, medicine and theology ('the queen of sciences'). Leff also points out that the division into seven liberal arts 'had underlain the educational reforms of Alcuin and his associates under Charlemagne and had been carried down into the revival of learning in the 11th and 12th centuries' (Leff (1968) p.118). For Charlemagne see 186:6–188:7.

1 Proposition: that the non-existence of God is inconceivable … So true is it that there exists something than which a greater is inconceivable, that its non-existence is inconceivable: and this thing art Thou, O Lord our God.

St Anselm (1033–1109) *Proslogion* Ch.3. His 'ontological argument for the existence of God' uses logic in the service of theology. Anselm anticipates the new scholasticism, a methodology of asking questions and analysing arguments.

2 Some of your pupils are spreading far and wide – and rightly – the praise of your keen insight and wisdom … They say that you have perfectly and fully resolved the key mysteries of the Holy Trinity … I have written all this to you, not presuming to teach you who is pre-eminent in Holy Scripture but desiring to know whether you acknowledge that your knowledge of God is imperfect.

Walter of Mortaigne to Peter Abelard, c.1138; R.W. Southern *Scholastic Humanism and the Unification of Europe* Vol.2 (2001) pp.104, 106. In Paris Abelard was breaking new ground in applying logic to theology. Excited students flocked to him, but this letter contains an implied rebuke for his arrogance.

3 Relying on the abilities with which I have been richly endowed by the will of the giver of all knowledge, I am confident that I have made contributions to the peripatetic [so-called wandering scholars] literature which are neither fewer nor less important than those made by the writers held in the highest regard by Latin scholars.

Peter Abelard *Dialectica* (c.1140); Southern (2001) p.109. In spite of the final condemnation of his *De unitate et trinitate divina* (Of the Divine Unity and Trinity), brought about by St Bernard in 1140, in this work, written near the end of his life, Abelard shows that he still believed in the power of dialectical reasoning to solve the mysteries of theology.

4 For there was in this city of Paris a certain young girl, by the name of Héloïse. She was the niece of a certain canon, Fulbert by name, who because he loved her so much, was so much the more zealous in advancing her in all knowledge of letters, as far as he could. She, while not the meanest in her countenance, was the highest woman by virtue of her wealth of learning. For since this good (I mean a knowledge of letters) is rarely found in women, so much the more did it distinguish the girl and made her famous in the entire kingdom.

Peter Abelard *History of My Misfortunes* (c.1132; 1977 edn) Ch.6. The great scholastic teacher looks back with self-censure on his seduction of Héloïse. At the same time, he gives a sense of the excitement the new learning generated in Paris in the early 12th century.

5 Bernard of Chartres used to say [c.1130] that we are like dwarfs on the shoulders of giants, so that we can see more than they and at a greater distance, not by virtue of any sharpness of sight on our part … but because we are carried high.

John of Salisbury *Metalogicon* (1159; 1848 edn) Bk 3, Ch.4. Reverence for ancient authorities counterbalanced the forward drive of scholastic reasoning. The same metaphor was used of his scientific discoveries by Isaac Newton in 1676 (see 365:2) and by Samuel Taylor Coleridge in 1818.

6 Afterward one of these went to Bologna and unlearned what he had taught, so that on his return he also untaught it.

John of Salisbury (1159); R.L. Poole (ed.) *Illustrations of the History of Medieval Thought* (1920) pp.203 ff. The same author sees the other side of academic thought. John was a student from 1136 to 1147, chiefly in Paris and Chartres, studying dialectic under, first, Abelard and then two other teachers. After 12 years he returned to Paris as a bishop, finding his old companions: 'As before and where they were before; nor did they appear to have reached the goal in unravelling the old questions, nor had they added one jot of a proposition. The aims that once inspired them, inspired them still: they had progressed in one point only: they had unlearnt moderation, they knew not modesty; in such wise that one might despair of their recovery. And thus experience taught me a manifest conclusion, that whereas dialectic furthers other studies, so if it remain by itself it lies bloodless and barren, nor does it quicken the soul to yield fruit of philosophy, except the same conceive from elsewhere' (Poole (1920) p.212).

7 The word *universitas* has nothing whatever to do with the supposed ideal of universal knowledge. It was one of the ordinary words in classical Latin for a guild or corporation of any kind. Its two synonyms in the Middle Ages were *studium* and *studium generale* … Bologna and Paris grew up gradually and, so far as can be seen, simultaneously towards the beginning of the twelfth century. Bologna was a guild of students and Paris a guild of masters.

G.G. Coulton *Medieval Panorama* (1938; 1949 edn) p.394.

1 I made a detour through Paris. When I saw the wealth of goods, the cheerfulness of its population, the regard the clerks enjoy, the majesty and glory of the church, the various occupations of its philosophers, full of admiration I thought I saw angels ascending and descending Jacob's ladder which was touching the sky.

John of Salisbury to Thomas Becket, 1164. The writer, a close friend of Becket (see 237:6), became bishop of Chartres, near Paris, in 1176.

2 One only passes from the darkness of ignorance to the enlightenment of science if one re-reads with ever increasing love the works of the ancients. Let the dogs bark, let the pigs grunt! I will nonetheless be a disciple of the ancients. All my care will be for them and each day the dawn will see me studying them.

Peter of Blois (c.1135–c.1212); J. Le Goff *Les Intellectuels au moyen age* (1957) p.14. Peter of Blois was a pupil of John of Salisbury and studied civil law and theology at Paris. He lamented the tendency to neglect the classics for professional studies.

3 They [university students] wrangled and disputed about the various sects or about some discussions, but the differences between the countries also caused dissensions, hatreds and virulent animosities among them, and they impudently uttered all kinds of affronts and insults against each other. They affirmed that the English were drunkards and had tails, the sons of France proud, effeminate and carefully adorned like women. They said the Germans were furious and obscene at their feasts; the Normans vain and boastful.

Jacques de Vitry, c.1220; D.C. Munro *The Medieval Student* (1899) p.9. The French chronicler became bishop of Acre in 1216 and cardinal bishop of Tusculum in 1228 (see 233:3).

4 For this branch of Perspective thoroughly known shows us how to make things very far off seem very close at hand and how to make large objects which are near seem tiny and how to make distant objects appear as large as we choose, so that it is possible for us to read the smallest letters at an incredible distance or to count sand, or grain or grass, or any other minute objects.

Robert Grosseteste *De Luce* (c.1253); L. Thorndike *A History of Magic and Experimental Science* (1923) Vol.2, p.441. Bishop of Lincoln from 1235, first chancellor of Oxford University, classicist and scientist, Grosseteste is suggesting the use of lenses to magnify. The invention of spectacles for nearsightedness dates from Italy in the 1280s.

5 Wonder was the motive that led people to philosophy ... wonder is a kind of desire in knowledge. It is the cause of delight because it carries with it the hope of discovery.

St Thomas Aquinas *Summa Theologiae* (1266–73) I–II, Q.32.a.8. Aquinas embraced enthusiastically Aristotle's investigations of the natural world. He wrote commentaries on ten of Aristotle's works, redressing the balance against the otherworldliness of much medieval theology. Aquinas, who preferred Aristotle to Plato, was the master of the analytical method applied to theology, as in his *Summa Theologiae*, but he was also the 'angelic doctor', a mystic who found God in the whole of creation.

6 If it happen that anyone strikes a student except in self defence ... all laymen who see [the act] shall in good faith seize the malefactor or malefactors and deliver them to our judge ... neither our provost nor our judges shall lay hands on a student for any offence ... unless such a crime has been committed by the student, that he ought to be arrested. And in that case, our judge shall arrest him on the spot, without striking him at all, unless he resists, and shall hand him over to the ecclesiastical judge.

Philip II, king of France, charter for the University of Paris, 1200; *Translations and Reprints from the Original Sources of European History* Vol.2, no.3 (1910) pp.7–11. The protection and control of university teachers and students was important to both papal and royal powers, partly because they supplied governments with learned clerks and partly to preserve law and order.

7 The holiday in the summer is not to be longer than one month ... We forbid the students to carry weapons in the city and we forbid the university to protect trouble-makers among the students. Those who call themselves students but do not go to lectures or belong to a Master are not to have the privileges of students.

Pope Gregory IX, charter to the University of Paris, 1231.

8 To our very dear and respected parents, M Martre, knight and M his wife, M and S your sons send you greetings and filial obedience. This is to tell you that by divine mercy we are living in good health in the city of Orleans and are giving all our time to study ... so that we have enough of the things we need to go on studying, we beg you to send us money to buy parchment, ink, a desk and some other things we need, so that we can finish our studies and do you credit when we come home.

Student begging letter, 12th century; C.H. Haskins *The Rise of the Universities* (1979) p.80. The letter was a blueprint for students to copy out, since many such begging letters from impoverished students have survived.

1   When the hour is nigh me,
Let me in the tavern die
With a tankard by me.
While the angels looking down,
Joyously sing o'er me,
Deus sit propitius
Huic potatori!
(May God be merciful to this drinker!)

The Archpoet *His Confession* (12th century); Helen Waddell *Medieval Latin Lyrics* (1952 edn) p.189. Wandering scholars, such as this anonymous poet, moved from one university to another, and by no means all were serious students. Some of these lyrics are collected in the *Carmina burana* (1937), set to music by Carl Orff. Their disruptive behaviour was a source of trouble to the ecclesiastical authorities.

2   The thread upon his overcoat was bare ...
He preferred having twenty books in red
And black, of Aristotle's philosophy,
Than costly clothes, fiddle or psalter.
Though a philosopher, as I have told,
He had not found the stone for making gold
Whatever money from his friends he took
A tone of moral virtue filled his speech
And gladly would he learn and gladly teach.

Geoffrey Chaucer *The Canterbury Tales* (c.1387; 1951 edn) Prologue, lines 285–308. Among the portraits of the diverse pilgrims who prepared to ride from Southwark to Canterbury is Chaucer's unworldly 'clerke' at Oxenforde. A 'perpetual student' as well as a cleric, he was avid for the learning he prized above worldly goods.

LAY RELIGIOUS MOVEMENTS AND HERETICS

3 *Raymond of Deventer*: This – oh Waldo – is the principle cause of complaint against you. You are in a state of rebellion against the church of Rome! You no longer obey her priests or bishops. You violate the principles of scripture which says; 'Obey your rulers.'

Peter Waldo: If bishops and priests disobey the Word of God, we must choose to obey God rather than Man.

Raymond: Having disobeyed the church you now usurp the sacred office of preaching, both men and women. This is scandalous because this office does not become the laity.

Bernard of Fontis Callidi *Liber adversus sectam Waldensium* (c.1190); Migne (1844–64) Vol.204, Prologue, pp.793 ff. From

a disputation that took place c.1170 at Narbonne, southern France, between Raymond of Deventer ('a god-fearing noble by birth') and Peter Waldo, a rich merchant of Lyons, southern France, who heard the scriptures and was struck to the heart by the words 'Go sell all thou hast and give to the poor'. This early clash shows that initially the Waldensians incurred the opposition of the church not for theological reasons but for lay aspirations that infringed clerical control.

4 A congregation of men and women in Italy, and particularly in Lombardy [in the north] following a regular rule, who call themselves Humiliati, who clothe themselves in poverty and austerity, are grave and sober in their ways and words and show great humility in their works. They live in common for the most part from the labour of their own hands. They do not have many goods or possessions. They say all the canonical hours by day and night [times of prayer appointed in the breviary]. Nearly all are literate ... Reading, prayer and work occupy their time. These brothers, both clergy and literate lay people, are authorized by the pope who confirmed their rule, to preach not only in their own congregations, but in market places and parish churches with the priests' consent. They convert many nobles and powerful citizens ... They preach against heretics and publicly confound them from the Scriptures.

Jacques de Vitry *Historia Occidentalis* (History of the West) (c.1200; 1597 edn) p.338. Some of these fraternities were accused of heresy, but in 1201 Innocent III gave the Lombardy Humiliati a licence to preach, except on articles of faith or the sacraments (see 190:3).

5 In this year [1260] almost in the whole of Italy there was a miracle. For in Perugia men began to go through the city naked, beating themselves hard with rods and clamouring 'Sacred Maria, receive the sinners' ... and this clamour reverberated (from city to city).

Anon. *Annals of Genoa* (1260); *Monumenta Germaniae historica Scriptores* Vol.18, p.24. The grim movement of the Flagellants arose spontaneously in Italian towns when bands of half-naked men marched from city to city flagellating themselves in expectation of the Last Judgement. Similar outbreaks occurred at intervals in western Europe.

6   Day of anger, day of terror [literally, that day]
All shall crumble into ashes
Witness David and the Sibyl.
What a terror will be present
When the Judge shall come to judgement
Shattering all at once asunder!

Thomas of Celano (c.1190–c.1260), opening verses (freely trans.) of *Dies Irae* (Day of Wrath). The author was a follower of St Francis of Assisi, whose biography he wrote. The hymn, now part of the Requiem Mass, was probably sung by the Flagellants. A sibyl was an ancient Greek or Roman prophetess.

1 Satan possessed the greater part of southern France.
William of Puylaurens *Chronique sur la guerre des Albigeois* (mid-12th century). The author of a primary source on the Albigensians is referring to the heretical sect, which was named after the city of Albi in southern France.

2 The sect acknowledges two Gods ... a good God and a bad God. They believe that the creation of things visible and material is not the work of a good God, Father ... but the devil, that is Satan, the bad god, the God of this age and the prince of this world ... All the sacraments of the Roman Church ... the Eucharist, baptism by water, extreme unction, penitence and marriage ... are vain and useless ... They deny the resurrection of the body.
Bernard Gui *The Inquisitor's Handbook* (c.1332; 1926 edn) Pt I, p.11. Bishop Gui's famous manual (see 191:6) represents a high point in inquisitorial professionalism. He was careful and fair in his inquisitions. Here he is describing part of the belief of the Albigensians (Cathars). Gui himself convicted 930 heretics in all, of whom 42 died at the stake and 307 went to prison; the others had to wear the legally prescribed badge of infamy.

3 That the devil with his angels ascended in to heaven and having made war with the Archangel Michael and the good angels, captured a third of the angelic beings and imprisoned them in human and animal bodies.
 That the devil was the author of the Old Testament (with the exception of certain books).
 That Abraham (and all the patriarchs) were ... ministers of the devil.
 That this material world will have no end.
 That carnal marriage is a mortal sin.
 That to eat flesh, eggs or *caseum* [cheese] is a mortal sin because they are the product of carnal intercourse.
Raynier Sacchoni *Summa* (c.1250). The author, a former Albigensian (Cathar), converted to Catholicism and became an inquisitor. There were two ranks among the Albigensians: the perfect (leaders) and believers (followers). The rank of perfect was attained through a ceremony of laying on of hands (*consolamentum*) and entailed an extremely rigorous way of life. Believers generally postponed this until they were on their deathbeds.

4 I believe that God created the physical things which are good for human beings to use, such as men themselves and animals ... that are useful to

man ... and all edible fruits of the earth and trees. On the other hand I do not believe that God made wolves, flies, lizards and other creatures harmful to men; nor do I believe that he made the Devil.
A peasant girl's beliefs, in a version of dualism, c.1320; E. Ladurie *Montaillou: Cathars and Catholics in a French Village 1294–1324* (1978) p.290.

5 Let the Church of England now approve the true and whole translation of simple men.
John Purvey Lollard Bible (c.1388) General Prologue; M. Deanesley *The Lollard Bible* (1920) p.304. Archbishop Sharpe describes the Lollard aim as 'to pick out sharp sentences ... of holy scriptures ... to maintain their sect and lore against ... holy church' (Deanesley (1920) p.228). Late in the 14th century the Oxford scholar John Wycliffe inspired a group of followers, lay and clerical, who became known as Lollards. They campaigned for simpler ritual in the church and especially for their Lollard Bible, a vernacular translation made in 1380–84. The sect was condemned in 1401, but the unauthorized translation became the inspiration of 16th-century translations.

6 Henry Hoiges of Bodmin of the county of Cornwall, gentleman [certifies] how John Harvey of the said town of Bodmin, priest ... of his malice and evil will, imagining by subtle crafts of enchantment, witchcraft and sorcery ... broke my leg ... through which I was in despair of my life ... and moreover in open place he said that by the same subtle craft of enchantment, witchcraft and sorcery he would make me break my neck.
Calendar of Proceedings in Chancery (1430–39) Introduction. This rare case of medieval witchcraft appears in an appeal for help to the lord chancellor. Although resort to superstitious magic was probably widespread (as in the case of the old woman who saved the consecrated wafer from mass to guard her cabbages from caterpillars), few cases of actual witchcraft are reported until the 16th and 17th centuries when persecution of witches was common in England and also in New England (see 432:4).

7 It has indeed lately come to our ears, not without afflicting us with bitter sorrow that ... many persons of both sexes, unmindful of their own salvation and straying from the Catholic faith, have abandoned themselves to devils, incubi and succubi, and by their incantations, spells, conjurations, and accursed charms and crafts, enormities and horrid offences, have slain infants yet in the mother's womb ... Our dear sons Henry Kramer and James Sprenger, Professors of Theology, of the Order of Friars Preachers, have been by letters Apostolic appointed as Inquisitors of these heretical pravities.

Pope Innocent VIII, *Summis desiderantes* (bull), 1484. The pope opens the war against witchcraft in introducing the work *Malleus Maleficarum* (The Hammer of Witchcraft) (1484), which was largely the work of Sprenger, who 'claimed to have gathered disinterested statements from eyewitnesses, confessions of witches maintained even to the stake. He revels in the preposterous and even more in the sensual. Altogether the *Malleus Maleficarum* is one of the wickedest and most obscene books ever written' (Geoffrey Parrinder *Witchcraft* (1958) p.23).

PILGRIMAGES

1 The praiseworthy magnificence of the pope [Calixtus II; r.1119–24] in increasing good went further, to restrain the unbridled and congenital greed of the Romans. At this time there were no ambushes for travellers around Rome, no injuries to those entering the city. The offerings of St Peter's, which the powerful had seized out of impudence and greed, abusing with disgraceful insults previous popes even for murmuring, Calixtus recalled to their proper use, that is the public purposes of the ruler of the holy see ... He therefore urged English pilgrims to go to St David's [in southwest Wales] rather than to Rome, because of the length of the journey [saying that] those who went to that place twice would gain the same amount of blessing as they would have if they went once to Rome.

William of Malmesbury *Gesta Regum Anglorum* (The Deeds of the Kings of England) (1125; 1887–9 edn) Vol.2, pp.507–8. The chronicler reveals that pilgrimages were big business for Roman citizens and the papacy, the route dangerous and exploitation common.

2 Elizabeth de Burgh, lady of Clare, petitions the pope that she may choose a confessor to 'transmute' the vow she made in her husband's lifetime to visit the Holy Land and Santiago, 'which, being forty, she cannot hope to fulfil'.

Calendars of Entries in the Papal Registries Relating to Great Britain and Ireland (1343) Petitions pp.22–3. It was common practice for those who were rich enough to commission someone else to fulfil their vow to make the pilgrimage on their behalf, or even to include instructions in their wills.

3 And then she remained in Bristol by the bidding of God, awaiting shipping for six weeks, inasmuch as there were no English ships that might sail thither [to the shrine of St James of Compostela, northwestern Spain], for they were arrested and taken up for the king.

Margery Kempe *The Book of Margery Kempe* (c.1432–6; 1936 edn) pp.138–40. This remarkable book 'whilst it no doubt follows precedent in being written from a wish to improve people's morals ... is our first extant prose narrative in English on a large scale' (R.W. Chambers (1936 edn) Introduction). Margery, who referred to herself in the third person or as 'this creature', set out from what was then one of England's leading towns, King's Lynn, Norfolk. Ch.15 of her book is headed 'Our Lord orders her to go to Rome, the Holy Land and St James and to wear white clothing', an instruction she followed faithfully.

4 When divers men and women will go after their own wills finding out on pilgrimage, they will ordain to have with them both men and women that can sing wanton songs. And some pilgrims will have with them bagpipes ... so that every town they come through, what with the noise of their singing and with the sound of their piping, and with the jangling of their Canterbury bells, and with the barking of dogs after them, they make more noise than if the king came there with all his clarion and many other minstrels.

Anon. Lollard, 1407. The follower of John Wycliffe (see 200:5) is complaining in Archbishop Arundel's court about the levity and noisiness of the pilgrims.

5 It is right well done that pilgrims have with them both singers and also pipers; that when one of them that goeth barefoot striketh his toe against a stone and hurteth him sore, and maketh him to bleed, it is well done that he or his fellow begin then a song or else take out of his bosom a bagpipe for to drive away with such mirth the hurt of his fellow; for with such solace the travail and weariness of pilgrims is lightly and merrily borne.

Desiderius Erasmus *Pilgrimages to St Mary of Walsingham and St Thomas of Canterbury* (1875 edn) pp.xxi–vi. Archbishop Arundel (who was, in any case, anti-Lollard) adroitly overlooks the complaint that the songs were 'wanton'. And of course such religious tourism was very good for his church at Canterbury, site of the richest and most celebrated shrine in England.

6   A worthy woman all her life, what's more
   She'd had five husbands, all at the church door,
   Apart from other company in youth;
   No need just now to speak of that, forsooth.
   And she had thrice been to Jerusalem,
   Seen many strange rivers and passed over them;
   She'd been to Rome and also to Boulogne,
   St James of Compostela and Cologne
   And she was skilled in wandering by the way.

Geoffrey Chaucer (c.1387; 1951 edn) Prologue, lines 459–67. Chaucer's Wife of Bath was both an inveterate marrier and an inveterate pilgrim. The journey to Jerusalem was long and hazardous for a woman, no matter how 'skilled in wandering by the way', to undertake once, let alone three times, and she had also visited shrines in Italy, Germany and northwest Spain.

1 When we from France desire to enter the apostle's basilica [church in Compostela] we go to the north side. Outside the door is the hospice of the poor pilgrims of St James and here too … is a forecourt or paradise, to which nine steps lead down. In the forecourt … are sold the shells which are the badges of St James and also wineskins, shoes, purses … and much else. In this venerable basilica … the revered body of the blessed James rests under the magnificent altar … The church was begun in 1078 … [Since then] the church has been celebrated for the miracles performed by the blessed James: here health is given to the sick … the fetters of sins are cast off, the sky opens to those who knock … and hosts of people from all parts of the world (come) to bring the Lord their gifts and their praise.

Anon. *Liber Sancti Jacobi* (Book of St James) (c.1140); Amery Picard 'The Pilgrim's Guide to St James' in A.A. Layton *The Way of St James* (1976) p.212. The popularity of the shrine of St James at Compostela, which was second only to the Holy Land in attracting pilgrims, rested on the 9th-century legend that the apostle had travelled to Spain and was buried there. Travel guides such as this were written to help pilgrims find their way. Pilgrimages were social events; pilgrim songs enlivened travellers on the recognized routes from northern Europe. Songs sung by pilgrims as they travelled to Compostela have survived.

2 When you come to Venice you should buy a bed by St Mark's church. You should have a feather bed, a mattress and two pillows, two pairs of sheets and a quilt and you should pay three ducats and when you come again bring the same bed back to the man and you shall have a ducat and a half again, though it be broken and worn … You shall often have need of your victuals, bread, cheese, eggs, fruit and baking (bread), wine and others to make your collation … buy you a cage for half a dozen hens or chickens to have with you in the galley … Half a bushel of millet seed of Venice for them must not be forgotten.

William Wey *Itineraries* (c.1462; 1857 edn) pp.5–6. The author, a fellow of Eton College, made pilgrimages to Compostela in 1456 and to Jerusalem in 1458 and 1462 and then wrote a guidebook for fellow pilgrims. It is full of practical details, including Arabic phrases for making conversation. The journey to the Holy Land was the greatest pilgrimage, not to be undertaken lightly. Five galleys a year left from Venice on a voyage that could take up to six weeks.

3 A pilgrim to the Holy Land ought to be on his guard, not only against becoming sinful in his mind … but also against carelessness lest he receive hurt to his body and life.

In general physicians advise pilgrims to beware of fruit, of drinking water, of sea air and of fish … [they give] much more advice … Yet I confess that this is what I myself have seen: I have known pilgrims who were so careful and exact in following the advice of their physicians that they dare not swallow anything unless recommended … and nevertheless became sick … and some of whom died. On the other hand I have seen men who ate, drank and did what they pleased … yet never took to their beds and were cheerful and happy.

Felix Fabri *The Wanderings of B. Felix Fabri* (1480–83 and 1494; 1892 trans.) Vol.1, pp.158–9. Fabri was a Dominican friar and pilgrim from Ulm, in southern Germany.

THE RISE OF THE FRIAR ORDERS

4 Hear, all of you and understand: – Until now have I called Peter Bernardone my father, but for that I purpose to serve the Lord, I give back to him the money over which he was vexed and all the clothes that I have had from him.

Anon. *The Legend of St Francis by the Three Companions* (1246) Ch.6.20. St Francis's father had beaten and imprisoned him to prevent him following a life of poverty, but in 1205, in front of the bishop and a large crowd, he stripped off all his rich clothes and stood naked in front of them.

5 By the inspiration of the divine Spirit … a vision … was shown unto him (Innocent III) from heaven … for in a dream he saw … the Lateran Basilica about to fall, when a little poor man of mean stature and humble aspect propped it up with his own back and thus saved it from falling. 'Verily,' saith he, 'he it is that by his work and teaching shall sustain the church of Christ.'

St Bonaventure *The Great Legend* (1260–63) Ch.3. Giotto (c.1267–1337), the great Florentine painter, pictured St Francis's dream in the Franciscan church at Assisi but with a young, vigorous Francis. The Lateran church was one of the principal churches in Rome. The pope gave his verbal approval to the little group that would become the friars at this juncture, but the full rule of what was by then the order of Minorites did not receive formal papal approval until 1221. In 1257 Bonaventure, author of the biography of St Francis, himself became head of the Franciscans.

1 Another time, when he was walking with a certain brother … he chanced on a great host of birds … singing among the bushes … he said to his companion: 'Our sisters, the birds, are praising their Creator; let us too go among them and sing unto the Lord' … When they had gone into their midst, the birds stirred not from the spot … the holy man turned to the birds, saying: 'My sisters, cease from singing while we render our due praises unto the Lord.' Then the birds forthwith held their peace … until having rendered his praises, the holy man of god again gave them leave to sing. Then they once more took up their song.
St Bonaventure (1260–63) Ch.8. The Minorites grew amazingly as recruits flooded into Assisi from all over Europe.

2 He [Dominic] forbade the brethren to concern themselves with temporal things with the exception of those of them who had charge of such matters. As to the others, he wished them to apply themselves unremittingly to study, prayer or preaching. And if he knew that one particular friar preached with success, he forbade any other office whatever to be given to him.
Father Rodolfo *Proces Bon* (1210) no.32; George Holmes *Florence, Rome and the Origins of the Renaissance* (1986) p.153. The procurator of the convent of Bologna in eastern Italy gives an eyewitness account of St Dominic's attitude.

3 In these latest days at the end of the age our two orders have arisen … drawing to themselves not a few men … These are (to God be the glory, not ourselves) two great lights which shining in the gloom and shadow of death, illuminate all lands … These are the two cherubim, full of knowledge, whose wings extend over the people … These are the two bright stars shining in this last age.
Encyclical letter from the two heads of the Franciscans and Dominicans, 1255; L. Wadding *Annales Minorum* (Annals of the Minorites) (1731) Vol.3, p.380. The two orders, dedicated to the service of the papacy, believed that they were called to a special prophetic mission as the world approached its end. Infiltrating all parts of society, they exercised tremendous influence. The Franciscans called themselves the Minor Order (OM); the Dominicans, the Preachers (OP).

4 Those who are merely under suspicion of heresy shall be smitten with the sword of anathema and shunned by everyone until they make suitable amends, unless they prove their own innocence by clearing themselves properly (the nature of the suspicion and also their personal character being taken into

account). If they have persisted in their excommunication for one year, they shall be condemned as heretics.
Fourth Lateran Council (1215) Canon III; B. Pullan *Sources for the History of Medieval Europe* (1966) Pt 2, Ch.17. Inefficiency of episcopal investigations leads, first, to the appointment of special commissioners by the pope and eventually to the establishment of the papal Inquisition in 1273. The Dominicans supplied a number of inquisitors.

PROPHECY AND APOCALYPTICISM

5 A king of the Greeks will go forth against them [the barbarians] in great wrath … and there will be peace on earth the like of which had never existed before: it will be the last peace of the perfection of the world. There will be joy from the whole earth … Priests and men will rest from labour … and torture … men will sit down in repose: they will eat, drink and take wives … They will build edifices and plant vineyards … [with] no thought of wickedness and no fear … Then the Son of Perdition [Antichrist] will arrive. The king of the Greeks will place his diadem on the Holy Cross, stretch out his two hands to heaven and hand over the kingship to God the Father.
Pseudo-Methodius *Apocalypse* (c.690); P.J. Alexander *The Byzantine Apocalyptic Tradition* (1978) pp.48–50. Written in Syrian and translated into Greek and Latin shortly after, this prophecy of a 'Last World Emperor' who would rule the world immediately before the coming of Antichrist became a medieval bestseller. It was first printed in 1498.

6 'There are seven kings [heads] of the dragon: five have been, one is, and one has yet to come. The five which were are Herod, Nero, Constantine the Arian, Mahomet [and] Melsemutus [Arab king]. Saladin is the one who is. The one yet to come is Antichrist.'
  'Where will Antichrist be born ?'
  'Antichrist is already born in the city of Rome.'
  'Then he is Pope Clement!'
Roger Howden *Chronicles* (winter 1190–91; 1868–71 edn) Vol.2, pp.151–5. A conversation (recorded by Howden who was present) at Messina, Sicily, between Richard I, *en route* for the Third Crusade, and Abbot Joachim of Fiore. Richard had asked to meet the Abbot Joachim, who had expounded the meaning of the Dragon (Book of Revelation 13:2). The question of the Antichrist is typical of medieval preoccupations. Joachim always associated the true pope with Jerusalem. If, therefore, an Antichrist was to be born in Rome, this would be a secular regime and involve an Antipope in wicked coalition with an infidel. This was, of course, relevant to Richard I, on his way to try to regain Jerusalem from the infidel Saladin (see 230:5).

1 The inventor of the new prophetic system, who was to be the most influential one known to Europe until the appearance of Marxism, was Joachim of Fiore (1145–1202).

Norman Cohn *The Pursuit of The Millennium* (1970 edn) p.108.

2 From the north spreads all evil.

The imperial office of the Germans has always been to us hard, terrible and extraordinary (*durum, dirum et mirum*).

Anon. slogans, often repeated, 1240s; Anon. Joachite (follower of Joachim) *On Jeremiah*. In the Italian apocalyptic scenario the German empire had become Antichrist.

3 For some forty years it has been prophesied that in these days there will be a pope who will purge canon law and the church from … lawyers, frauds, and give universal justice. And by the good news and truth of this pope the Greeks will be brought back to the Roman obedience, most of the Tatars will be converted, the Saracens destroyed and there will be one flock and shepherd.

Roger Bacon *The Third Book* (1267–8); *Opera Inedita* (Unedited Works) (1909 edn) p.86. This English Franciscan at Oxford makes one of the earliest references to an 'Angelic Pope' based on Joachim's expectation of a reformed papacy in the third age.

4 The king of France by divine election will be crowned [emperor] by the holy pope [Angelic Pope] … resisting the golden imperial crown, the emperor will ask for a crown of thorns out of reverence for the King of Kings.

Telesphorus of Cosenza *De Magnis Tribulationibus* (Concerning Great Tribulations) (1516) f.21v. In 1356–90 this hermit from southern Italy collected all the prophecies about a great schism, battles between good and evil emperors and popes, and the final triumph of the divinely ordained emperor and pope. His work became a powerful text for the French monarchy and a bestseller in the 15th and 16th centuries.

Medieval Society, 1000–1500

CULTIVATING THE LAND

1 With an ox plough you shall till rather than with a horse plough if the land be not stony so that the ox cannot help himself with his feet ... and when the horse is old and worn out then hath he nothing but his skin. But when the ox is old with 10d of grass he will be made fat to kill or to sell for as much as he cost you.

Walter of Henley, 13th century; Dorothea Oschinsky (ed.) *Walter of Henley: Husbandry and Other Treatises on Estate Management and Accounting* (1971) p.319. The English Dominican friar and agronomist denies the advantage of speed that the introduction of the horse could bring to the farmer.

2 The good shepherd should be watchful and kindly, so that the sheep are not tormented by his wrath but crop their pasture in peace and joyfulness. It is a token of the shepherd's kindliness if the sheep be not scattered abroad but browse round him in a company. Let him have a good barkable dog and lie nightly with his flock.

Walter of Henley *Husbandrie* (13th century; 1890 edn) 'How you Must Keep Your Sheep'.

3 Sir steward, the parker [park-keeper] John complaineth of Geoffrey of the moor that ... this Geoffrey and John his huntsman came [to the lord's park] with two greyhounds and they went up hill and down dale spying what they would have ... (The parker fetches some witnesses.) They saw the said Geoffrey and John chasing with their dogs a buck which Geoffrey shot right through the flanks ... they skinned it and hid it ... Outside the parker said: 'Fair friend Geoffrey, seemingly peradventure thou hast done it more than once,' and he answered neither this nor that.

13th-century case, summarized in *The Court Baron* (1890) Vol.5, p.34. The lord's park was his hunting ground – forest and scrub – and unless he gave special privileges to tenants, he had exclusive rights to all the animals, timber and grazing in the park. The fine imposed – £10 – was a large one for that period.

4 [The lessee promises to] prune, hoe, harrow, plough for a second time, to prepare well all posts, poles, withers all at the expense of the labourer, and to stake out and plant each and every part of the

vineyards and to drain ... and he promises each year to bring and to bear to the city of Arezzo [Tuscany, central Italy] at the house of the aforesaid lessor or where he should wish, one half of the grapes, figs, nuts, pears and each and every fruit in the same vineyard, at the total expense and risk of that labourer.

Anon. *Scripta anecdota glossatorum* (c.1240; 1901 edn) Vol.3, p.305. In Italy the leasehold contract took over from feudal obligations.

5 There are neither wolves, bears nor lions in England; the sheep lie out at nights without their shepherds, penned up in folds, and the lands are improving at the same time; whence it comes to pass that the inhabitants are seldom fatigued with hard labour, and they lead a life more spiritual and refined: so did the patriarchs of old who chose rather to keep flocks and herds, than to disturb their peace of mind with more laborious employments of tillage and the like.

Sir John Fortescue, lord chancellor to Henry VI, *The Laws of England* (c.1470); Lord Clermont *Sir John Fortescue and his Descendants* (1869) Vol.1, p.413. A sanguine vision of John of Gaunt's 'blessed plot', but Fortescue was an eminent lawyer, describing trial by jury, who is here straying into agricultural utopianism.

THE LOCAL LORD AND HIS RIGHTS AND DUTIES

6 Juliana, daughter of Richard de Hilleleye gives the lord 22s. for a licence to marry.

The unmarried daughters of Richard Gervayse take possession of their father's lands and give the lord 5s.

Ralph de Attewood has five daughters. The third, Alice, is married without the lord's licence, for which he is fined 2s. If this happens again his goods and chattels are to be confiscated.

Court Rolls of the Manor of Hales, Worcestershire (English Midlands), 1270–1307, ed. by John Amphlett, Sidney Graves Hamilton and R.A. Wilson. Manorial lords zealously guarded their rights over their tenants' marriages.

7 In the beginning, every man in the world was free, and the law is so favourable to liberty that he who is once found free and of free estate in a court of

record, shall be holden free for ever, unless it be that some later act of his makes him villein.

Justice Herle *Eynsham Cartulary* (1309) Vol.2, pp.26–7. The great medieval lawyer shows how difficult it could be for a lord to recover one of his serfs if he had fled. The lord had only four days to use his own powers, after which he had to turn to the courts.

1 There was a usage in England and in several other countries for the nobles to have strong powers over their men and to hold them in serfdom; that is, that by right and custom they have to till the lands of the gentry, reap the corn and bring it to the big house, put it in the barn, thresh and winnow it, mow the hay and carry it to the house, cut logs and bring them up, and all such forced tasks; all this the men must do by way of serfage to their masters. In England there is a much greater number than elsewhere of such men who are obliged to serve the prelates and the nobles. And in the counties of Kent, Essex, Sussex and Bedford in particular, there are more than in the whole of the rest of England.

Jean Froissart *Chronicles* (from 1373; 1968 edn) Bk 2.381. He is describing the background to the Peasants' Revolt of 1381 (see 279:1–280:4).

COURTLY CULTURE AND CHIVALRY

2 King Arthur held his yuletide festivities at London and the nobles and their sons and womenfolk came from far and near. There was much envy, for one accounted himself high, the other much higher. Arthur sat down at the tables and beside him Guinevere, his queen, and then the earls, barons and knights in order. They were served with meat according to their rank. Presently there were angry blows ... then 'it saith in the tale' that he [Arthur] went to Cornwall and caused a marvellous table to be made by a carpenter, which had three remarkable properties: it could seat sixteen hundred; it was arranged that the high should be even with the low; it could be carried with Arthur wherever he wished to ride. The result was that all were satisfied.

Layamon *Brut* (after 1204); *Arthurian Romances* (1912 edn) p.209. Maurice Keen comments: 'The trinity of tables – that at which the last supper was eaten, the Grail table that Joseph set up in the desert, and the Round Table – symbolizes the connections ... The whole story encapsulates the outline of an explanation of chivalry's independent origin and standing as a Christian order' (*Chivalry* (1984) p.118).

3 Yet some men say in many parts ... King Arthur is not dead but had by the will of our Lord Jesu into another place; and men say he shall come again and win the Holy Cross. Yet I will not say that it shall be so; but rather I would say; here in this world he changed his life. And many men say that there is written on his tomb this verse:

Hic jacet Arthurus, Rex Quondam Rexque Futurus

(Here lies Arthur: the once and future king.)

Sir Thomas Malory *Le Morte D'Arthur* (c.1470; 1954 edn) Bk 21, Ch.7 (see 160:6).

4 'You are a good knight, so fine a man, so feared, so loved and so wise, that you are thought to be one of the first knights in the world. I say to you in all loyalty that you must be chosen.'

He [William the Marshal] asserts that when he [accepted the care of the young Henry III] he said: 'I will carry him on my shoulders, one leg on each side, from isle to isle, from land to land, and I will not fail him, even if I were forced to beg my bread.' The author adds, 'May God help those who do good and act loyally!'

Anon. *Guillaume le Maréchal* (History of William the Marshal) (after 1219; 1891–1901 edn) lines 15692–8; Antonia Gransden *Historical Writing in England c.550 to c.1307* (1974) p.351. When he was 72 years old William Marshal (c.1147–1219) reluctantly agreed to become regent for nine-year-old Henry III after the death of his father, King John. The poem emphasizes that William had been loyal and trustworthy to a succession of kings and that these characteristics were a reflection of the knightly ideal.

5 In the world you have had more honour than any other knight for prowess, wisdom and loyalty. When God granted you his grace to this extent, you may be sure he wished to have you at the end. You depart from the age with honour. You have been a gentleman and you die one.

Aimery de St Maur, master of the Temple in England, at William Marshal's deathbed, *Guillaume le Maréchal* (after 1219); Sidney Painter *William Marshal* (1933) p.284.

6 Folcon was in the battle lines, with a hauberk [coat of mail], seated on an excellently trained horse, swift and fiery and crested. And he was most graciously armed ... and when the king saw him he stopped and went to join the Count of Auvergne, and said to the French: Lord look at the best knight that you have ever seen ... he is brave and courtly and skilful, and noble and of good lineage and eloquent, handsomely experienced in hunting and falconry; he knows how to play chess and backgammon, gaming and dicing. And his wealth was never denied to any, but each has as much as he wants … and he has never been slow to perform honourable deeds. He dearly loves God and the Trinity. And since the day was born he has never entered a court of law where any wrong was done or discussed without grieving if he could do nothing about it … And he always loved a good knight; he has honoured the poor and lowly; and he judges each according to his worth.

Anon. *Girart* (mid-12th century); L. Paterson 'Knights and the Concept of Knighthood in the 12th-century Occitan Epic' in *Forum for Modern Languages Studies* 17 (1981). The author of a Provençal epic describes the ideal knight.

1 In his youth a man should use without laziness or delay his prowess, his valour, and the strength of his body for the honour and profit of himself and his dependants; for he who passes his youth without exploit may have cause for great shame and grief. The young nobleman, knight or man-at-arms could work to acquire honour, to be renowned for bravery, and to have temporal possessions, riches and heritages on which he can live honourably.

Philippe de Navarre *Les Quatres âges de l'homme* pp.38–9; Painter (1933) p.30. This represents one aspect of the idealized portrait of the 'good knight'. It was also his duty to build up his estates for his family – William Marshal, for example, took care to marry a rich feudal heiress.

2 The good man took the sword, girded him with it and kissed him, telling him that with the sword he had given him the highest order that God had created and ordained, the order of knighthood, which ought to be blameless.

Chrétien de Troyes *Le Roman de Perceval ou le conte del Graal* (c.1180; 1956 edn) Bk 2, lines 1632–7. The religious element in the ceremony of knighthood was vital both to the church and to knightly ideals. If not knighted on the battlefield, the knight would often prepare for the ceremony by a vigil before a church altar. The legend of the Grail was another of the myths that was popular in France and that became linked to Arthur.

3 Through their error, present-day knights and squires (some who go to war, some who stay in their halls, the covetous and proud) are one and all doing harm, for which reason all the rest of society is embroiled in folly.

John Gower *Mirour de l'omme* (1376–8; 1899 edn) line 24,169; John Barnie *War in Medieval Society* (1974) p.122. The poet takes a hostile view of the role of the knight in the Hundred Years War. The superior power of foot soldiers was already becoming apparent.

4   Truly to take and truly to fight,
    Is the profession and the pure order that
        belongs to knights;
    Whoever passeth that point betrays
        knighthood.
    For they should not fast …
    But faithfully defend and fight for truth,
    And never leve for love in hope to lack silver.

William Langland *Piers Plowman* (c.1377; 1896 edn) B-text, lines 190 ff. A late 14th-century view of knighthood. Chivalric practices were maintained by Edward III (see 278:2 for the origins of the Knights of the Garter), but the English longbow would soon render warfare by mounted knights anachronistic.

5 When your lord is ready for dinner pour out water and hold the towel till he has finished. Stand by your lord till he tells you to sit. Cut your bread, don't break it. Don't lean on the table or dirty the cloth, or hang your head over the dish or eat with your mouth full. Don't dip your bread in the salt cellar or put your knife in your mouth or eat noisily. When the meal is over clean your knives and put them in their places, smile, without laughing and joking and go to your lord's table and stand there till grace is said.

Anon., instructions to young pages; Marjorie Reeves *The Medieval Feast* (1962) p.51. The inhabitants of a castle often included boys from other families being trained as pages – the first step in knighthood. Their etiquette and manners were carefully supervised.

TOWNS AND THEIR GUILDS

6 *Communia est tumor plebis, timor regni, tepor sacerdotii.*

Richard of Devizes *Chronicon de rebus gestis Ricardi Primi* (c.1189–92); Susan Reynolds *An Introduction to the History of English Medieval Towns* (1977) p.104. The Benedictine monk's words have been freely trans. by Denys Hay as 'a bloated swelling of the people, a terror of the kingdom, a wet blanket on the church' (*The Medieval Centuries* (1953; 1964 edn) p.111). The chronicler is referring to the grant of a *communia* (commune or sworn association of townspeople) to Londoners by King John, standing in for his absent brother Richard I, the Lionheart. Although such indications of urban aspiration were not common in England at the time, the chronicler neatly expresses the reactions of the powers that be.

7 The Lord King [Henry III] ordered it to be officially announced … throughout the whole city of London and elsewhere by public crier that he had instituted a new fair to be held at Westminster to continue for a full fortnight … and he also absolutely forbade on penalty of weighty forfeiture and fine all markets usually held in England for such a period … (and) all trade normally carried out in London … a vast crowd … flocked there and so [the Feast of St Edward] was amazingly venerated by the people assembled there … but they suffered great inconvenience because of the lack of roofs apart from canvas awnings, for the variable gusts of wind, usual at that time of year … The bishop of Ely, because of the loss of his fair … which the royal edict had suspended, made a very serious complaint … But he gained nothing except empty words.

Matthew Paris, 13 Oct. 1248; *Chronica Majora* (Greater Chronicle) (c.1235–59; 1993 edn). This grant of a fair reveals clearly the power of the English crown to create a monopoly that affected the economics of all English towns, and it was highly unpopular. Matthew Paris, Benedictine chronicler of St Albans, continued the great chronicle begun by Roger of Wendover. His chronicle is a major source until 1259, although he has been called a 'crusty old gossip'.

1 Henry by the grace of God King of England, Lord of Ireland, Duke of Normandy and Aquitaine, Earl of Anjou. To his archbishops … abbots, earls, barons, justices, sheriffs … and to his bailiffs and faithful people who shall inspect the present charter, Greeting. Know that we … have quitclaimed to our citizens of Worcester and to their heirs for ever … the 'farm' of the city (in return for thirty pounds [of silver]) … Also we have granted to the same citizens that no one of our sheriffs shall … introit [intrude] himself upon them concerning any plea … Saving [except] the pleas of our crown … also we have granted [them] that they shall have a guild merchant [with a monopoly on the making of merchandise] … if any bondman [villein] shall remain in the aforesaid city … for one year and one day … he shall remain in the said city free. Moreover we have granted to the said citizens … that they shall have soc and sac, thol and theam and infangentheof [be free of various tolls and customs] throughout our dominions.

Henry III, charter to the city of Worcester, 1227; *Calendar of Charter Rolls 1226–57* p.23. In return for an increased payment, Worcester, a pre-Conquest city already enjoying privileges, is given the 'farm of the city' – that is, the right to collect its own taxes. The monopoly of the guild merchant is an important right over trade, while the grant of freedom to serfs encouraged run-away villeins to settle, thereby increasing the city's population. The concluding list of strange rights granted jurisdiction over criminals and exemption from the payment of various tolls. The royal power to overrule the rights of local sheriffs and lords is clearly demonstrated.

2 If it is the [French] king's pleasure that they may hold four fairs in said Lyons, just as they used from antiquity to hold them there – and that those of Geneva may similarly hold four others, provided that the subjects of the king should be permitted to attend only two of the said fairs in Geneva, this would contribute to the maintenance and advantage of the said city of Lyons and to the profit and commerce of the king and the kingdom.

Report on negotiations for a calendar of international fairs, April 1467; F. Borel *Les Foires de Genève au quinzième siècle* (1892) p.161. These international fairs were of immense importance to the trade of Europe.

3 The population increases every day, and the city [Milan] spreads out with new buildings … The fertility of the area and the abundance of all goods useful for human consumption are evident … any man, if he is healthy and not a good-for-nothing, can earn his living with the dignity appropriate to his position. On feast-days, when one looks at the merry crowds of dignified men, both of the nobility and of the people, as well as the bustling throngs of children forever scurrying about, and the comely groups, the bevies of handsome ladies and girls strolling up and down or standing on their doorsteps, with all the dignity of royalty who would say that he has ever met such a wonderful show of people on either side of the sea.

Fra Buonvicino della Riva *On the Marvels of the City of Milan* (1288); Robert S. Lopez *The Birth of Europe* (1962; 1967 trans.) p.258. Contemporary statistics confirm that Milan had 200,000 inhabitants at the time, more than 40,000 citizens capable of bearing arms, 12,500 houses with one or more rooms, more than 1,000 shops, 120 doctors of law, almost 2,000 doctors or surgeons and 25 hospitals. In general, Italian towns developed earlier and into much larger, self-governing communes than English towns.

4 The brethren of the said guild (of the glorious martyr, St George) and their successors shall yearly choose the mayor of the said city [Norwich] at that time being a brother of the said guild for all the year next following after his discharge of his office of mayoralty.

Charter, 1324; Charles Haskins *Ancient Trade Guilds and Companies of Salisbury* (1912) p.28. This type of guild, which represented all the chief merchants and craftsmen, controlled the politics of the town.

1 If it so befall that any of the brotherhood fall into poverty through old age that he cannot help himself, or through … fire or water, thieves or sickness, or any other hap, so it be not through his own fault, then he shall have in the week 14d from the common box.

Charles Haskins (1912); Marjorie Reeves *The Medieval Town* (1953) p.55. One of the purposes of the guilds was to help members through old age or bad times. Equally important were regulations on hours of work and fixing prices. Every guildsman paid a yearly contribution to the common box to cover the expenses of helping poor brethren, paying for the funerals of the poor and providing for festivals.

2 No member [of the tailors' guild] was to engage a stranger or alien as an apprentice under a penalty of 20s. No apprentice should be taken on for less than seven years … No master stranger should be received into the guild unless he paid 40s into the common box.

Charles Haskins (1912) p.122. As a rule, guilds guarded their monopoly fiercely and were suspicious of strangers.

3 Ye shall pray for the souls of all the brethren and sisters, being quick [alive] and dead, and in special for the souls of those which were good doers in their lives.

Anon. prayer, *The Taylors' Book* (1479); Reeves (1953) p.61. From the Tailors' Guild service at St Thomas's Church, Salisbury. The annual festival was held at midsummer. First, there was a great feast for three days. Then, on midsummer's eve, all the guilds processed through the town, with the tailors in front with their mascot, a giant figure and his little page, Hobnob. Finally, they all went to church, which was decorated with red roses.

4 If any butcher rub any suet on any flesh to make it seem fat or otherwise he shall forfeit the moitie [half] thereof and further be punished at the discretion of the mayor and bailiffs for the deceit used to the subjects.

That no person nor persons shall buy any flesh or fish coming to the market to sell again at a dearer price upon pain of forfeiture of the same to be punished as a forestaller.

Anon. *The Dormont Book* 'Constitutions, Orders, Provisions, Articles and Rules to be Observed in the Maintenance of the Commonwealth', articles 116 and 117 (renewed in 1561); R.S. Ferguson and W. Nanson *Some Municipal Records of the City of Carlisle* (1887) p.73. In all, there were 300 pages of by-laws.

TRADE AND INDUSTRY

5 He it was who induced the merchants of England to grant the king forty shillings for each sack of wool

… and because he sinned against the wool mongers he was drowned in a ship laden with wool.

Anon. chronicle of Dunstable priory (early 14th century); Eileen Power *Medieval People* (1924) p.79. The chronicler records (with relish) the death of the great wool merchant Laurence Ludlow, who had negotiated the grant for the king, Edward I, in 1294–7. The monk did not forgive Ludlow easily for agreeing to this tax because the priory, in Bedfordshire, was heavily dependent on selling wool.

6 I thank God and ever shall
It is the sheep hath paid for all.

Anon. motto, 1480s; Power (1924) p.134. The words appear in the stained-glass window of the new house built near Newark in Nottinghamshire by a rich English wool merchant, John Barton of Holme.

7 By your letter you avise me for to buy wool in Cotswold, for which I shall have of John Cely his gathering 30 sack, and of Will Midwinter of North-leach 40 sack. I am avised to buy no more; wool in Cotswold is at great price, 13.4d a tod [about 28lb], and great riding for wool in Cotswold as was any year this seven year.

Thomas Betson, wool merchant of the Staple (wool market), letter, 1480; *Cely Papers, Selected from the Correspondence of the Cely Family, Merchants of the Staple 1475–88* (1900) pp.31–2. In another letter (29 Oct. 1480) Betson explains the increase in the cost: 'Nor have I not bought this year a lock of wool for the wool of Cotswolds is bought by Lombards [from northern Italy], wherefore I have the less haste for to pack my wool at London' (p.48).

8 The bill of lading, for instance, of a ship arriving in Genoa from Roumania on 21 May 1396 listed '37 bales of pilgrims' robes, 191 pieces of lead and 80 slaves'. Another ship, sailing from Syracuse to Majorca, carried 1547 leather hides and 10 slaves, and one sailing from Venice to Ibiza '128 sacks of woad, 55 bales of brass, 15 sacks of raw cotton, 5 sacks of cotton yarn, 4 bales of paper, 3 barrels of gall-nuts [to eat?] and nine Turkish heads'. The '9 heads' were then forwarded to Valencia to be sold, with a letter stating that one of them was a woman who could 'sew and do everything', and who was therefore, in the writer's opinion, 'too good for the people of Ibiza – for they are like dogs'. 'Your money,' he added, 'will be well placed in her.'

Francesco di Marco Datini, May 1396; Iris Origo *The Merchant of Prato* (1963) p.100. The papers of the Tuscan merchant (c.1335–1410) are a rich source of information on Mediterranean trading in the late 14th century. The first page of his ledger is inscribed: 'In the name of God and of profit.' One of the effects of the deaths of many labourers from the plague 50 years earlier (see 288:5) was to increase the demand for slaves.

1 As for the nation of the Angles and Saxons, they have come and were wont to come with their merchandise and wares … [Formerly] when they saw their trunks and sacks being emptied at the gates, they grew angry and started rows with the employees of the treasury. The parties were wont to hurl abusive words and in addition very often inflicted wounds upon one another. But in order to cut short such great evils … the king of the Angles and Saxons and the king of the Lombards agreed together as follows: the nation of the Angles and Saxons is no longer to be subject to the *decima* [10% tax]. And in return for this the king of the Angles and Saxons and their nation are bound and obligated to send to the palace in Pavia [northern Italy] and to the king's treasury, every third year, fifty pounds of refined silver, two large, handsome greyhounds, hairy or furred, in chains, with collars covered with gilded plates sealed or enamelled with the arms of the king, two excellent embossed shields, two excellent lances, and two excellent swords wrought and tested. And to the master of the treasury they are obligated to give two large coats of miniver [white fur] and two pounds of refined silver. And they are to receive a safe-conduct from the master of the treasury that they may not suffer any annoyance as they come and go.

Regulations of the royal court at Pavia, c.1010–c.1020 (based on 10th-century sources); A. Solmi *L'amministrazione finanzaria del regno italico* (1932) pp.21–4. A trade agreement designed to prevent violence.

2 Remember well what I have to tell you. Take the leaves of red colewort and of avens. Take also an herb called tansy and some hempseed (now known as cannabis [?]). Crush these four herbs together in equal quantities. Take of the madder twice as much as each of the others and crush it. Then put these five herbs in pot, infusing them in white wine, the best you can procure and taking care that the mixture is not too thick to drink. Do not drink too much at a time, an eggshell will contain enough for a dose provided it be full.

Villard de Honnecourt (c.1225–50) *The Sketchbook* (1959 edn) p.238. A recipe to cure wounds. De Honnecourt considered that it was not enough to be the greatest architect and engineer of his age but that one should also be proficient in medicine.

3 Entering the abbey [Clairvaux] under the boundary wall, which like a janitor allows it to pass, the stream first hurls itself impetuously at the mill where in a welter of movement it strains itself, first to crush the wheat beneath the weight of the millstones, then to shake the fine sieve which separates the flour from bran. Already it has reached the next building; it replenishes the vats and surrenders itself to the flames which heat it up to prepare beer for the monks, their drink when the vines reward the wine-grower's toil with a barren crop. The stream does not yet consider itself discharged. The fullers established near the mill beckon to it. In the mill it had been occupied in preparing food for the brethren; it is therefore only right that it should now look to their clothing … It enters the tannery, where in preparing leather for the shoes of the monks it exercises as much exertion as diligence … [in] cooking, turning, grinding, watering or washing, never refusing its assistance in any task. At last, in case it receives any reward for work which it has not done, it carries away the waste and leaves everywhere spotless.

Report on a Cistercian monastery, 12th century; D. Luckhurst 'Monastic Watermills' in *Society for the Protection of Ancient Buildings* no.8. Jean Gimpel points out that 'this great hymn to technology could have been written 742 times over; for that was the number of Cistercian monasteries in the 12th century, and the report would have held true for practically all of them' (*The Medieval Machine, The Industrial Revolution of the Middle Ages* (1988 edn) p.5). At abbeys in Britain, such as at Rievaulx in Yorkshire, the change from producing (and exporting) raw wool to cloth-making was largely due to the use of waterpower.

4 Grievous complaint [was made] that mochel people of the same town [Colchester, Essex] brewing their ale and maken their meat with water of the river of the said town, the which said river there ben certain persons dwelling upon, as Barbers [tanners] and White Tawyers [leather workers], that layen many divers hides … [to the] impairing and corruption of the river beforesaid, and in destruction of the fish therein [and] to great harming and noissaunce of the said people.

Colchester records, 1425; W. Page and J.H. Round (eds) *The Victoria History of The County of Essex* Vol.2 (1907) p.459. Tanners and leather workers had a particularly bad reputation as polluters of rivers. Attempts to regulate their activities were only partially successful.

5 As the king learns from the complaints of prelates and magnates of his realm, who frequently come to London for the benefit of the Commonwealth by his order, and ... of his citizens and all his people dwelling there ... that the workmen [in kilns] ... now burn them and construct them of sea-coal instead of brush wood or charcoal, from the use of which sea-coal an intolerable smell diffuses itself throughout the neighbouring places and the air is greatly affected to the annoyance of the magnates, citizens and others there dwelling and to the injury of their bodily health.

Royal proclamation addressing the pollution from industry, 1307; F.R.S. Smith *Sea Coal for London* (1961) p.3. Despite fines on the first offence and the threat of demolishing the furnaces on a second, London was already – as it remained – a polluted town. By this time London might rival some European cities in size, but not in independence: it was still the king's city.

METALS AND MINING

1 We have granted likewise, that the chief warden of the stannaries and his bailiffs through him, have over the aforesaid tinners, plenary power to do them justice and to hold them to the law.

King John, charter, c.1200; G.R. Lewis *The Stannaries, A Study of the English Tin Miner* (1924) p.36. The charter freed the tin miners from the jurisdiction of the local magistrate and made them answerable only to the wardens and bailiffs of the newly founded mine law courts. Gimpel (1988 edn; p.98) points out that production soon rose, increasing the tax yield to the royal treasury, which held an option on all tin mined in Devon and Cornwall.

2 Where a gallery or mine has been discovered or worked then shall a man have possession of 4½ *lehen* [a *lehen* was equal to 7 fathoms, or about 42 feet] of the roof and 1 *lehen* of the floor, height and depth in equal measure.

For the man who discovers a new mine shall be measured 7 *lehen*, and on both sides 1 *lehen* for the lord king and 1 for the citizens.

The discoverers of the mine shall give to those who have measured the mine 7 short shillings.

Statutes of the Mines and Mountains, mid-13th century; A. Zycha *Das Böhmische Bergrecht des Mittelalters* (Bohemian Mining Rights of the Middle Ages) Vol.2 (1900) p.39. These regulations for German mining underline the advanced state and political importance of mining in the area in the late Middle Ages. The abbey of Clairvaux was situated at the centre of one of the great iron-ore areas of France and gradually took over a large number of the mines.

3 Use of iron is more needful to men in many things than use of gold. Though covetous men have more gold than iron, without iron the commonalty be not sure against enemies, without dread of iron the common right is not governed; with iron innocent men are defended; and foolhardiness of wicked men is chastened with dread of iron. And well nigh no handiwork is wrought without iron, neither tilling craft used nor building builded without iron.

Bartholomew, an English Franciscan friar and encyclopedist, 1260; T.A. Rickard *Man and Metals* Vol.2 (1932) p.879. The introduction of iron tools, such as the ploughshare, represented a silent revolution as the vast woodlands of early times were gradually consumed.

LITERACY AND THE VERNACULAR

4 The earliest attempt to endow a commercial school seems to have been made by Simon Eyre [mayor], citizen and draper of London, who died in 1459 and left his vast fortune to establish a college and school at the Leadenhall and 'Also one master, with an usher, for grammar, one master for writing, and the third for song, with housing there newly built for them for ever; the master to have for his salary ten pounds, and every other priest eight pounds, every other clerk five pounds, six shillings and eight pence, and every other chorister five marks'.

Nicholas Orme *English Schools in the Middle Ages* (1973) pp.78 ff. Orme, quoting John Stow (*A Survey of London* (1598; 1912 edn) p.139), notes that writing in this context 'probably meant drafting and scriveners' work rather than the simple ability to write which was learnt in the grammar course'.

5 In all the grammar schools of England children leave French and construe in English.

Ranulf Higden *Polychronicon* (1340s; c.1387 trans. by John of Trevisa) Vol.1 (1969 edn) p.196. The change from French as the *lingua franca* to vernacular English was rapid. In the 1360s the lord chancellor began to open Parliament in English, and in 1362 a petition urged that pleading in the law courts should be in English because French was too little known.

6 Following appeareth, parcelly, divers and sundry manner of writings, which I, William Ebesham, have written for my good and worshipful master, Sir John Paston, and what money I have received, and what is unpaid.

First, I did write to his mastership a little book of physic, for which I had paid by Sir Thomas Lewis, in Westminster ... 20d ...

First, for writing of the Coronation; and other treatises of Knighthood, in that quire which containeth 13 leaves, after 2d a leaf ... 2s 2d.

Item, De Regimine Principum (A Treatise

Concerning the Government of Princes), which containeth 45 leaves, after 1 penny a leaf, which it is right well worth … 3s 9d.

Item, for rubrishing [rubricking] of all the book … 3s 4d.

The Paston Letters no. 264. (c.1469; 1924 edn) Vol.2, pp.38–40. The editors of the 1924 edition, John Fenn and Mrs Archer-Hind, comment: 'We are furnished with a curious account of the expenses attending the transcribing of books previous to the noble art of printing. At this time the common wages of a mechanic were, with diet, 4d, and without diet 5½d or 6d a day; we here see that a writer received 2d for writing a folio leaf, three of which he could with ease finish in a day, and I should think that many quick writers at that time could fill four, five or even six in a day: if so, the pay of these greatly exceeded that of common handicraft men.' Rubricking means either ornamenting the whole text with red capital letters or writing the heads of several treatises or chapters in red letters, the origin (red letter) of the word rubric.

1 Now the world runneth upon another wheel. For now at 5 o'clock by the moonlight I must go to my book and let sleep and sloth alone, and if our master happens to awake us, he bringeth a rod 'stead of a candle. Now I leave pleasures that I had sometime; here is nought else preferred but admonishing and stripes. Breakfasts that were sometime brought at my bidding are driven out of country and never shall come again.

William Nelson (ed.) *A Fifteenth Century School Book* (1956) p.1. This is the first 'Passage for Translation into Latin', entitled 'Morning', from 400 exercises set by an Oxford teacher to a schoolboy in the 1490s. A rueful description of the pains of education.

2 In Florence, around the year 1336, with an annual birth-rate of 5,500–6,000 live births, it is calculated that there were between 8,000 and 10,000 school-boys learning to read, more than 1,000 studying mathematics [it was, of course, a major financial centre] and 550–600 grappling with literature and philosophy.

Robert S. Lopez (1962; 1967 trans.) p.261. Note the high rate of literacy in 14th-century Florence. Dante's writings in Tuscan vernacular as well as Latin were in circulation, as were Boccaccio's. Curiously Florence did not develop its own university to rival those of Padua and Bologna.

3 His [Caxton's] services to literature in general, and particularly to English literature, as a translator and publisher, would have made him a commanding figure if he had never printed a single page. In the history of English printing he would be a commanding figure if he had never translated or published a single book. He was a great Englishman, and among his many activities, was a printer. But he was not, from a technical point of view, a great printer.

Daniel B. Updike *Printing Types: Their History, Forms and Use: A Study in Survivals* (1952 edn); S.H. Steinberg *Five Hundred Years of Printing* (1955) p.70. William Caxton learned the art of printing in Cologne, Germany, set up his own press in 1473 in Bruges, Belgium (see 306:6), and then returned to England in 1476 to set up as its first printer. In Nov. 1477 *Dictes or Sayings of the Philosophers* was the first book to be published on English soil. Of the more than 90 books he produced by his death in 1491, 74 were in English, a considerable number of them translated by Caxton himself.

FAMILIES

4 An archdeacon in Genoa, northern Italy, orders a certain Pietro di Ortoxeto: to take back Druda [his wife] in the house of his father and treat her with marital affection, that is to say to lie with her in the same bed, to pay there his conjugal debt and to eat with her at table from one trencher … Item, he orders that he shall not hold any concubine publicly in the place where he is living, nor lead any concubine into his father's house, and that he shall treat the said Druda, his wife, in all those ways in which a good husband ought to treat his good wife.

Court order, 1222; L.T. Belgrano *Della Civitata dei Genovesi* (1875) p.319. Although the man's position is dominant, both religious and civil government tried to protect the woman from sexual abuse.

5 After all, what the devil are we women fit for in our old age except to sit around the fire and stare at the ashes? … When we're old neither our husbands nor any other man can bear the sight of us, and they bundle us off into the kitchen to tell stories and count the pots and pans.

Giovanni Boccaccio *The Decameron* (1349–51; 1972 edn) p.46. Emilia takes a jaundiced view of the woman's position in an Italian bourgeois family.

6 To make bread, clean capons, sift, cook, launder, make bread, weave French purses … embroider in silk, cut wool and linen clothes, put new feet into socks, and so forth, so that when you marry her off, she won't seem a fool, freshly arrived from the wilds. And they will not curse you who brought her up.

Paolo di Messer Pace da Certaldo *Libro di buoni costumi* (Book of Good Manners) (1945 edn) p.128; J. O'Faolain and L. Martines *Not in God's Image* (1973) p.169. Advice to a father on the premarital education of his daughter. He did not consider it necessary that a daughter should learn to read 'unless she is going to be a nun'.

1 He says he has a female slave and a horse and two donkeys and three-fifths of an ox. Let us put them down at 70 florins.

Francesco di Marco Datini, 1392; Origo (1963) p.199. The slave is considered as an object rather than a person, and her value is calculated with that of domestic animals.

2 Know, dear sister [wife], that if you wish to follow my advice you will take great care and regard for what you and I can afford to do, according to our estate. Have a care you be honestly clad, without new devices and without too much or too little frippery ... When you go to town or to church go suitably accompanied by honourable women according to your estate and flee suspicious company ... and as you go bear your head upright and your eyelids low and without fluttering, and look straight in front of you about four rods ahead, without looking round at any man or woman to the right or to the left, nor looking up, nor glancing from place to place, nor stopping to speak to anyone on the road.

Anon. *ménagier* of Paris *Treatise on Morals and Domestic Economy* (1392–4) Vol.1, pp.13–15; Power (1924; 1941 edn) p.98. This book was written by the *ménagier* (householder) to instruct his young wife after their marriage. He calls his new wife 'sister' affectionately throughout his work.

3 I could hardly find a book on morals where, even before I had read it in its entirety, I did not find several chapters or certain sections attacking women, no matter who the author was. This reason alone, in short, made me conclude that, although my intellect did not perceive my own great faults and, likewise, those of other women because of its simpleness and ignorance, it was however truly fitting that such was the case ... and I finally decided that God formed a vile creature when He made woman, and I wondered how such a worthy artisan could have deigned to make such an abominable work, from what they say is the vessel as well as the refuge and abode of every evil and vice.

Christine de Pisan *The Book of the City of Ladies* (1405; 1983 edn) p.5. This extraordinary allegory by a remarkable woman is, among other things, a medieval feminist text that employs a fine irony.

WAR

4 Every year on the day called Shrove Tuesday, boys from the schools bring fighting cocks to their master, and the whole morning is given to boyish sport; for they have a holiday in the schools that they may watch their cocks do battle.

William FitzStephen (d.c.1190); Nicholas Orme *Medieval Children* (2001) p.185. The chronicler gives a famous and vivid description of London life in the 12th century. Orme comments: 'But in 1365 Edward III complained that people followed "dishonest and useless" games like stone-casting, ball games and cock-fighting, and ordered the male population to practise on feast-days with bows and arrows or bolts ... In 1512 men with boys between seven to seventeen in their houses were ordered to provide them with a bow and two arrows'.

5 The crossbow is a weapon of the barbarians [western crusaders], absolutely unknown to the Greeks. In order to stretch it, one does not pull the string with the right hand while pushing the bow with the left away from the body; this instrument of war ... fires weapons to an enormous distance ... Arrows of all kinds are fired. They are very short, but extremely thick with a heavy iron tip ... [the arrows] transfix a shield, cut through a heavy iron breast-plate and resume their flight on the far side, so irresistible and violent is the discharge. An arrow of this type has been known to make its way right through a bronze statue ... Such is the crossbow, a truly diabolic machine. The unfortunate man who is struck by it dies without feeling the blow; however strong the impact he knows nothing of it.

Anna Comnena *The Alexiad* (c.1148; 1969 trans.) Bk 10, pp.316–17, footnote 36. The author, writing some 40 years after the crusade, recalls the horrible effectiveness of the western crossbow, seen by her at the start of the First Crusade. 'The crossbow had been initially banned by the church (in 1139), at least in wars between Christians, on the grounds of its frightfulness. By the 1280s, however, it was becoming increasingly common. It was less accurate than the longbow, had a slower rate of fire (one shaft to the longbow's six a minute) and was much more expensive' (John Larner *Italy in the Age of Dante and Petrarch 1216–1380* (1980) p.216).

6 The king [Henry V] therefore ordered that every archer, throughout the army, was to prepare for himself a stake or staff, either square or round, but six feet long, of sufficient thickness and sharpened at both ends. And he commanded that whenever the French approached to give battle and break their ranks with such bodies of horsemen, all the archers were to drive their stakes in front of them in a line ... so that the cavalry when the charge had brought them close in sight of the stakes, would either withdraw in great fear or, reckless of their safety, run the risk of having both horses and riders impaled.

Anon. *Gesta Henrici Quinti* (The Feats of Henry V) (c.1416; 1975 trans.) pp.68–71; slightly adapted in Anne Curry and

Michael Hughes *Arms, Armies and Fortification in the 100 Years War* (1994) p.16. The official chronicler (a royal chaplain) describes the tactics employed at the Battle of Agincourt (1415), which exemplified the English use of the longbow as a lethal weapon against the French cavalry (see 278:5).

1 These instruments [cannons] which discharge balls of metal with most tremendous noise and flashes of fire … were a few years ago very rare and were viewed with greatest astonishment and admiration. But now they have become as common and familiar as any kind of arms. So quick and ingenious are the minds of men in learning the most pernicious arts.

Francesco Petrarch *De Remedius* (1350s) Bk 1, dialogue 99, p.22. An early forecast of the revolution in warfare brought about by guns.

2 He [Charles VII, setting out for Normandy] had the greatest number and variety of battering cannon and bombards, veuglaires, serpentines, crapaudines, culverines and ribaudequins that had ever been collected in the memory of man.

Enguerrand de Monstrelet (c.1390–1453) *Chronique* (1840 trans.) Vol.2, p.158; Richard Barber *The Knight and Chivalry* (1970) Ch 12. Barber suggests that the variety of this armoury was necessary because the giant cannon or bombard was not very efficient, but this great number was obviously a record. Guns were beginning to bring about a revolution by the mid-15th century, but it was the expedition of Charles VII's grandson, Charles VIII, the Affable (r.1483–98), that finally brought the devastating Italian wars to an end, demonstrating the much greater destruction of lives and property wreaked by the guns. Yet Henry VIII of England and Francis I of France could still play at chivalry in single combat at the Field of the Cloth of Gold near Calais, northern France, in 1520.

3 War is not an evil thing, but good and virtuous; for war, by its very nature, seeks nothing other than to set wrong right and turn dissension to peace, in accordance with scripture. And if in war many evil things are done, they never come from the nature of war, but from false usage.

Honoré Bonet *Tree of Battles* (1390s; 1949 trans.) p.125. A very untypical judgement on war by the prior of Salon in Provence.

The Normans, 1066–1154

1066 AND ALL THAT

1 [The Danes] were from the first a cruel and war-like people and were governed by powerful kings; but they rejected the faith of Christ for a very long time. The mighty leader Rollo, with the Normans, was of this race; they first conquered Neustria, which is now called Normandy after the Normans. For in the English language … Norman means 'man of the north', and his bold roughness had proved as deadly to his softer neighbours as the bitter wind to young flowers.

Orderic Vitalis *Ecclesiastical History* (c.1114–41; 1969–80 edn) Bk 9.3. The English-born Norman chronicler (see 195:5) records the origins of the Normans, who were proud of their Norse heritage but a bit vague on specifics. Indeed, Normandy was not racially monolithic, and its name reflects the broad origins of its ruling elite not those of the population at large.

2 And so, in the 912th year from the incarnation of Our Lord Jesus Christ, archbishop Franco baptized Rollo, after he had been instructed in the Catholic faith of the Holy Trinity … And [Rollo] had his counts and knights and the whole complement of his army baptized and instructed in the observances of the Christian faith by teaching.

Dudo of Saint-Quentin *The Manners and Deeds of the First Dukes of Normandy* (c.1015–26) Bk 2.30. In 911, by the so-called Treaty of St-Clair-sur-Epte (on the Norman/French border), Rollo, the founder of the Norman ducal line, was granted full possession of what would become Normandy and also extensive rights in Brittany by Charles the Simple, king of the Franks. Conversion was part of the deal. As elsewhere, the Christianization of the Scandinavian settlers was a top-down and political process, not a matter of individual conscience.

3 In the agreement which was made between the Franks and the Normans in the time of Count Richard I … it was ordained that the count of the Normans should not perform service to the king of the Franks for the land of the Normans, nor do him any other service, unless the king of the Franks should give him a fief [another territory outside Normandy] in France from which service would be owed. Wherefore the count of the Normans should, concerning Normandy, do homage and fealty to the king of the Franks only to the extent of [protecting] his life and earthly honour.

Robert de Torigny *Chronicle* (c.1149; 1890 edn); W.L. Warren *Henry II* (1973) p.226. Robert records the tradition, dating back to Duke Richard I – in fact, Count of Rouen but by convention the third Norman duke (r.942–996) and great-grandfather of the Conqueror – that, while the dukes of Normandy acknowledged the king of France as their overlord, this was a personal allegiance and did not mean that Normandy itself was a fief (a territory held in return for the performance of military or other service) of the French crown.

4 The English at that time [1066] wore short garments, reaching to the mid-knee; they had their hair cropped, their beards shaven, their arms laden with golden bracelets, their skin adorned with punctured designs; they were wont to eat until they became surfeited and to drink until they were sick. These later qualities they imparted to their conquerors; as to the rest, they adopted their [Norman] manners.

William of Malmesbury *Gesta Regum Anglorum* (Deeds of the Kings of England) (c.1125); David C. Douglas and George W. Greenaway (eds) *English Historical Documents* Vol.2 (1953) p.291.

5 In a council [probably 1064] assembled at Bonneville-sur-Touques [near Deauville on the Norman coast] Harold took an oath of fealty to William in a religious ceremony; and, according to the testimony of truthful and distinguished men of high repute who were present, Harold, in the final stages of his oath, of his own free will made these distinct promises: that he would be William's proxy in the court of his lord, King Edward [the Confessor], as long as the king lived; that after Edward's death he would use all his influence and resources to secure the English throne for William; and that in the meantime he would deliver the town of Dover to the custody of William's men and fortify it at his own pains and cost.

William of Poitiers *Gesta Willelmi ducis Normannorum et regis Anglorum* (Deeds of Duke William) (c.1071–4; 1952 edn) p.100. On a brief French visit that went wrong, Harold (by now head of the powerful Godwin clan and shortly to become the Confessor's designated successor) is supposed to have been rescued by Duke William from arrest by the neighbouring lord of Ponthieu, and pressurized into making this celebrated oath (which appears prominently on the Bayeux Tapestry). However, Norman assertions about the event need to be read with caution, since Harold's subsequent breaking of the oath, if it was given, provided moral validation for the invasion of 1066. For Edward the Confessor see 165:1.

1 On the journey [to Normandy] Harold incurred the danger of being taken prisoner, from which, using diplomacy and force, I rescued him. Through his own hands he made himself my vassal, and with his own hand he gave me a firm pledge concerning the kingdom of England.

William, Duke of Normandy, attrib.; William of Poitiers (c.1071–4; 1952 edn) p.176. These words, supposedly uttered on the eve of Hastings, emphasize the idea of the invasion of England as a just war because of Harold's supposed betrayal of his oath.

2 Then Earl William came from Normandy into Pevensey [on the Sussex coast], on the eve of the Feast of St Michael, and as soon as they were fit made a castle at Hastings market-town. Then this became known to King Harold and he gathered a great raiding army, and came against him at the grey apple tree. And William came upon him by surprise before his people were marshalled. Nevertheless the king fought very hard against him with those men who wanted to support him, and there was a great slaughter on either side. There were killed King Harold, and Earl Leofwine his brother, and Earl Gyrth his brother, and many good men. And the French had possession of the place of slaughter; just as God granted them because of the people's sins.

The Anglo-Saxon Chronicle, (Worcester Manuscript, 1066; 1996 trans.). Harold set out from London on 11 Oct., and his tired and depleted forces joined battle with Duke William, 8 miles north of Hastings, on 14 Oct. This is the only contemporary written description in English of the battle to survive.

3 Then began the death-bearing clouds of arrows. There followed the thunder of blows. The clash of helmets and swords produced dancing sparks … Duke William instructed the archers not to shoot their arrows directly at the enemy, but rather into the air, so that the arrows might blind the enemy squadron. This caused great losses amongst the English.

Henry of Huntingdon Historia Anglorum (History of the English People) (c.1130; 1996 trans.) Bk 2.30. The Battle of Hastings at its height.

4 *Hic Harold rex interfectus est et fuga verterunt Angli.* (Here King Harold has been killed and the English have turned to flight.)

Bayeux Tapestry, before 1082. The Tapestry – in fact, a commemorative embroidery some 230 feet long and 20 inches wide – provides an incomparably vivid, and all but contemporary, account of the Norman invasion of England in some 70 scenes, with brief explanatory 'captions'. This is the last of them, depicting the close of the Battle of Hastings. The origins of the tapestry are uncertain, but it may have been made (probably in England) for the Conqueror's half-brother, Odo, bishop of Bayeux, who was himself present at the battle and features prominently in the work.

5 How many thousands of the human race have fallen upon evil days! The sons of kings and dukes and nobles and the proud ones of the land are fettered with manacles and irons, are in prison and in gaol. How many have lost their limbs by the sword or disease, have been deprived of their eyes, so that when released from prison the common light of the world is a prison for them! They are the living dead for whom the sun – mankind's greatest pleasure – has now set.

Goscelin of Saint-Bertin Liber confortatorius (c.1081; 1955 edn) p.77. A Flemish monk, long resident in England, laments the fallen greatness of the English aristocracy and other losers in the years after the Norman Conquest.

WILLIAM I, 1066–87

6 William the king greets William, bishop of London, and Gosfrith the Portreeve [principal magistrate, mayor], and all the burgesses of London with friendship. I give you to know that I will that you be worthy of all the laws you were worthy of in the time of King Edward [the Confessor]. And I will that every child shall be his father's heir after his father's day. And I will not suffer any man to do you wrong. God preserve you.

William I, charter to London, before 1075. The charter was written in English, not Latin.

7 [King William] rode to all the remote parts of his kingdom and fortified strategic sites against enemy attack. For the fortifications called castles by the Normans were scarcely known in the English provinces, and so the English – in spite of their courage and love of fighting – could put up only a weak resistance to their enemies.

Orderic Vitalis (c.1114–41; 1969–80 edn) Bk 4.184. The castle was to become a major instrument in Norman hands for the domination first of England and later of Wales and Ireland.

8 My narrative has frequently had occasion to praise William, but for this act which condemned the innocent and guilty alike to die by slow starvation I cannot commend him. For when I think of helpless children, young men in the prime of life, and hoary greybeards perishing alike of hunger I am so moved to pity that I would rather lament the griefs and sufferings of the wretched people than make a vain attempt to flatter the perpetrator of such infamy. Moreover, I declare that assuredly such brutal slaughter cannot remain unpunished. For the almighty Judge watches over high and low alike ... as the eternal law makes clear to all men.

Orderic Vitalis (c.1114–41; 1969–80 edn) Bk 4.2.196. In the campaigns known as the Harrying of the North (1069–70) William brutally but decisively crushed rebellion in northern England. His savagery offended contemporary opinion; but it was effective.

1 When the renowned conqueror of England, King William ... had subjugated the farthest limits of the island ... he ordained that the people subject to him should submit to written laws and customs. Accordingly, the laws of the English having been set before him in their triple form – that is Mercian law, Danish law, and the laws of the West Saxons – some he rejected while others he approved, adding to them also those laws of Neustria [Normandy] which seemed likely to be most effective in preserving the peace of the realm.

Richard FitzNigel, attrib., *Dialogus de Scaccario* (Dialogue of the Exchequer) c.1178–9, Bk 1.16; E.H.D. Vol.2 (1953) pp.529–30.

2 He wore his royal crown three times each year, as often as he was in England. At Easter he wore it in Winchester, at Pentecost in Westminster, at midwinter in Gloucester; and there were then with him all the powerful men over all England: archbishops and diocesan bishops, abbots and earls, thegns [freemen holding land in return for military service] and knights.

The Anglo-Saxon Chronicle (Peterborough Manuscript, 1086/1087; 1996 trans.).

3 Your legate ... has admonished me to profess allegiance to you and your successors, and to think better regarding the money which my predecessors were wont to send to the church of Rome. I have consented to the one but not to the other. I have not consented to pay fealty, nor will I do so, because I never promised it, nor do I find that my predecessors ever did it to your predecessors.

William I to Pope Gregory VII, c.1080; E.H.D. Vol.2 (1953) p.647. William agrees to pay money to the pope but firmly repudiates papal claims to allegiance in respect of his English kingdom.

4 I entreat you to pray the divine mercy that long life may be granted to my lord the king of England, and peace from all his enemies ... For while he lives, we have peace of a kind; but after his death we expect to have neither peace nor any other benefits.

Lanfranc, archbishop of Canterbury to Pope Alexander II, c.1070, *Lanfranci Epistolae* 1; Margaret Gibson *Lanfranc of Bec* (1978) p.151. A voice of exceptional authority confirms William's achievement in the eyes of his contemporaries: no matter what the rigours of his rule, it was effective – and, in the circumstances of 11th-century Europe, that was not to be taken for granted.

5 You might see churches rise in every village, and, in the towns and cities, monasteries built after a style unknown before; you could watch the country flourishing with renewed religious observance; each wealthy man counted the day lost in which he had neglected to perform some outstanding benefaction.

William of Malmesbury (c.1125); E.H.D. Vol.2 (1953) p.291. The urban and rural landscape of England was thus transformed after the Conquest. It is not just the extent of the new building, both ecclesiastical and lay, that is so astonishing, but also its scale: Winchester Cathedral, for example, substantially a Norman building of 1079–93, is, at 560 feet, the longest of all Europe's medieval cathedrals. One should not underestimate the genuine piety that underlay this phenomenal aristocratic activity, but more worldly considerations of display, status and emulation must clearly have played their part.

6 We poor wretches destroy the works of our forefathers only to get praise to ourselves. The happy age of holy men knew not how to build stately churches: under any roof they offered themselves as living temples to God. But we neglect the care of souls, and labour to heap up stones.

Wulfstan, bishop of Worcester (c.1095); Ralph Arnold *A Social History of England 55 BC–AD 1215* (1967) p.311. St Wulfstan, by 1080 the last remaining Anglo-Saxon bishop, contemplates the rebuilding of his own cathedral.

7 Verily, [William I] was a very great prince: full of hope to undertake great enterprises, full of courage to achieve them: in most of his actions commendable, and excusable in all. And this was not the least piece of his Honour, that the kings of England which succeeded, did account their order only from him: not in regard of his victory in England, but generally in respect of his virtue and valour.

John Hayward *The Lives of the Three Normans, Kings of England* (1613) p.122. One practical proof of the Conqueror's impact: even today it remains the case that the kings of England are conventionally listed, and numbered, from William the Conqueror, and not from any of his great Anglo-Saxon or

Danish predecessors, such as Alfred (see 162:1), Edgar (see 162:8) and Cnut (see 164:4).

DOMESDAY BOOK FROM 1085

1 [After Christmas 1085] the king had great thought and very deep conversation with his council about this land, how it was occupied, or with which men. Then he sent his men all over England into every shire, and had them ascertain how many hundreds of hides [about 120 acres] there were in the shire, or what land and livestock the king himself had in the land, or what dues he ought to have in 12 months from the shire. Also he had it recorded how much land his archbishops had, and his diocesan bishops, and his abbots, and his earls, and ... what or how much each man had who was occupying land here in England, in land or in livestock, and how much money it was worth. He had it investigated so very narrowly that there was not one single hide, not one yard of land, not even (it is shameful to tell – but it seemed no shame to him to do it) one ox, not one cow, not one pig was left out, that was not set down in his record. And all the records were brought to him afterwards.

The Anglo-Saxon Chronicle (Peterborough Manuscript, 1085; 1996 trans.). The immediate trigger of the Domesday Survey was the threat in 1085 of a Norse invasion, which did not, in fact, materialize. William decided to establish exactly who held what in England, and from whom, and what they owed on it. The main task was completed within two years – a tribute not only to the formidable drive of the Conqueror but also to the administrative mechanisms of the Anglo-Saxon state he inherited. Nothing equivalent was seen again in Europe for centuries.

2 Ralph holds Langelei [Langley] from the Count. It answers for 1½ hides. Land for 16 ploughs. In lordship, none, but 2 possible. 1 Frenchman with 4 villagers and 5 smallholders have 2 ploughs; 12 ploughs possible. 2 mills at 16s; 2 slaves; meadow for 3 ploughs; pasture for the livestock; woodland; 240 pigs. Total value 40s; when acquired £4; before 1066 £8. Thorir and Seric, two of earl Leofwine's men, held this manor.

Domesday Book (1086; 1999 edn) p.134. The entry for Kings Langley in Hertfordshire (1086). The tenant-in-chief – the 'Count' – from whom Ralph held the manor of Kings Langley, was Count Robert of Mortain (d.1091), half-brother of William the Conqueror. Before the Conquest the place had been held by two men (note the Anglo-Danish names) in the service of Earl Leofwine of Kent (a younger brother of King

Harold). It can be seen that Kings Langley had not prospered since the Conquest: it may have been devastated in the post-Hastings campaign, since it was near here that William I and his army received the submission of London in the autumn of 1066.

3 When the king went on expedition by land, 10 Burgesses of Warwick went for all the others; whoever was notified but did not go paid a fine of 100s to the king. But if the king went against his enemies by sea they sent him either 4 boatmen or £4 of pence.

Domesday Book (1086; 1999 edn) p.24. Towns, like individuals holding land under feudal tenure, owed obligations to the king. Here the royal clerks list the contribution – in properly equipped men – required of Warwick (many miles inland) when the king went to war by land or sea and the penalties for failing to comply.

4 In this manor [at Thetford] there used to be a market on Saturdays. But William Malet made his castle at Eye, and he made another market in his castle on Saturdays, and thereby the Bishop's market has been so far spoilt that it was of little value.

Little Domesday Book, entry for Thetford, Norfolk, 1086; T. Hinde (ed.) *The Domesday Book: England's Heritage, Then and Now* (1999 edn) p.26. Markets held at regular intervals were the *raison d'être* of many small towns and were very valuable – and hotly competitive – assets to the lords who fostered them. Here, the bishop's market at Thetford has been upstaged by the Conqueror's chamberlain, a great East Anglian landholder, at Eye, some 20-odd miles away.

5 This book is called by the English 'Doomsday', that is, by metaphor, the day of judgement. For just as the sentence of that strict and terrible Last Judgement cannot be evaded by any art or subterfuge, so, when a dispute arises in this realm concerning facts which are there written down, and an appeal is made to the book itself, the evidence it gives cannot be set at naught or evaded with impunity.

Richard FitzNigel (c.1178–9) Bk 1.16; E.H.D. Vol.2 (1953) p.530.

WILLIAM II, 1087–1100

6 By the holy face of Lucca.

William II's favourite oath, alluding to the miracle-working wooden statue of Christ, still displayed in the cathedral of Lucca in Tuscany, northwestern Italy, as reported by Eadmer, William of Malmesbury and others.

7 The plough is the church. In England two oxen, superior to all the rest, I mean the king and the archbishop of Canterbury, drag the plough, that is to say rule the church, the former by means of secular justice and authority, the latter by divine learning and instruction. One of these oxen, Lanfranc [archbishop of Canterbury] has died, and the other [William Rufus], who is still young and has the ferocity of an unbroken bull, rushes on with the plough; and in the place of the dead man, you want to join me [St Anselm], an old and feeble sheep, to the untameable bull.

Eadmer *Historia Novorum in Anglia* (History of Modern Times in England) (c.1095–1123; 1884 edn) p.36. St Anselm endeavours to evade his fate, but in vain. He succeeded Lanfranc as archbishop of Canterbury in 1093, after a four-year vacancy. His troubled tenure, at odds with both William II and Henry I over the liberties of the church, involved two exiles, but he was eventually reconciled with Henry in 1107.

1 'What business is it of yours?' retorted the king. 'Aren't they my abbeys?' 'You do what you like with your manors, and shall not I do as I like with my abbeys?' Anselm replied: 'They are yours to defend and guard as their patron; but not yours to assault or lay waste.'

Eadmer (c.1095–1123; 1884 edn) pp.49–50. Rufus exclaimed to Anselm that: 'Your predecessor [Lanfranc] would never have dared talk in this way to my father!' and declared that the archbishop had forfeited his love. To which Anselm replied: 'I would rather have you angry with me than have God angry with you.'

2 Our ancestors used to wear decent clothes, well-adapted to the shape of their bodies; they were skilled horsemen and swift runners, ready for all seemly undertakings. But in these days the old customs have almost wholly given way to new fads. Our wanton youth is sunk in effeminacy, and courtiers, fawning, seek the favours of women with every kind of lewdness. They add excrescences like serpents' tails to the tips of their toes where the body ends, and gaze with admiration on these scorpion-like shapes. They sweep the dusty ground with the unnecessary trains of their robes and mantles; their long, wide sleeves cover their hands whatever they do; impeded by these frivolities they are almost incapable of walking quickly or doing any kind of useful work ... They curl their hair with hot irons and cover their heads with a fillet or a cap.

Orderic Vitalis (c.1114–41; 1969–80 edn) Bk 8.10. Orderic throws up his hands at the degeneracy of the trendy young people at the court of William Rufus. His grumpy protestations have a timeless ring.

3 After dinner [Rufus] went into the forest with a very small number of attendants. Among these the most intimate with the king was Walter, surnamed Tirel, who had come from France attracted by the liberality of the king. This man alone remained with him, while the others were widely scattered in the chase. The sun was now setting, and the king drawing his bow let fly an arrow which slightly wounded a stag which passed before him. He ran in pursuit, keeping his gaze rigidly fixed on the quarry, and holding up his hand to shield his eyes from the sun's rays. At this instant Walter ... tried to transfix another stag, which by chance came near him while the king's attention was otherwise occupied. And thus it was that unknowingly, and without power to prevent it (oh gracious God!) he pierced the king's breast with a fatal arrow.

William of Malmesbury (c.1125); E.H.D. Vol.2 (1953) p.293. William II is killed while hunting in the New Forest in Hampshire on 2 Aug. 1100. It seems to have been a genuine accident. Contemporary chroniclers, disapproving of the king's worldly lifestyle, saw it as divine judgement, and it was left to modern historians to suspect conspiracy and intent.

HENRY I, 1100–35

4 When Henry was a child he had been put to the study of letters by his parents, and he was well instructed in both natural philosophy and knowledge of doctrine. When he attained manhood Lanfranc, archbishop of Canterbury, presented him for knighthood for the defence of the kingdom ... in the name of the Lord, as a king's son born in the purple.

Orderic Vitalis (c.1114–41; 1969–80 edn) Bk 8.1. Henry was the youngest of William I's sons and the only one to be born after his father's accession to the English throne – hence 'born in the purple' (see 106:8). His education earned him the later sobriquet of Henry Beauclerk, although disaffected Norman contemporaries, mocking Henry's marriage to the Anglo-Saxon princess, Edith (re-named Matilda, which sounded less uncouth), referred contemptuously to the royal couple as 'Godric' and 'Godiva'.

5 Throughout his life he was wholly free from carnal desires, for as we have learned from those who are well informed, his intercourse with women was undertaken not for the satisfaction of his lusts, but from his desire for children ... Thus he did not condescend to carnal intercourse unless it might produce that effect. Wherefore he was the master of

his passions rather than their slave ... He was plain in his diet, seeking rather to justify his hunger than to sate himself with a multitude of delicacies. He drank simply to allay his thirst, and he deplored the least lapse into drunkenness both in himself and others. His sleep was heavy, and marked with much snoring.

William of Malmesbury (c.1125); E.H.D. Vol.2 (1953) p.296. Since Henry I, with over 20, had more known bastards than any other English king, this tribute to his chaste mind and devotion to policy rings rather hollow to the modern ear. He did not marry until 1100, when he was 32 years old – exceptionally late by medieval standards – and his illegitimate children were to prove significant political assets in his later years. His failure to father more legitimate ones proved a disaster after his death, given that his only male heir, William, died before him.

1 And the king said to [Gilbert]: 'You were always pestering me for a portion of Wales. Now I will give you the land of Cadwgan ap Bleddyn [King of Powys, in mid-Wales]. Go and take possession of it.' And he gladly accepted it from the king. And then, gathering a host, along with his comrades he came to Ceredigion [Cardigan]. And he took possession of it, and built two castles there.

Anon. *Brut y Tywysogyon* (Chronicle of the Princes) (late 12th century but based on earlier materials; 1955 edn) p.24. Henry I gives (1110) royal patronage, but no royal resources, to Gilbert FitzRichard of Clare in extending Norman power and influence into Wales. William I and Henry I were keen to see strong subordinates establish themselves – by way of intrusion, castle-building and the founding of new towns around them – along and across the borders of Wales, pressing ever further westward. The marcher lordships thus created had a significant degree of independence and steadily drew large parts of Wales towards and within the Norman/ Angevin polity.

2 'By the death of Christ,' for that was his favourite oath, '... It is we who hold the power, and so are free to commit acts of violence and injustice against these people [the Welsh]; and yet we know full well that it is they who are the rightful heirs to the land.'

Henry I; Gerald of Wales *The Journey through Wales* (c.1188; 1978 trans.) Bk 1, Ch.2. An unexpected insight, given that Henry was not the most tender-hearted of kings in pursuing his interests.

3 On 25 November [1120] the king gave orders for his return to England, and set sail from Barfleur on the evening of that day. But [Prince William] who was just over seventeen and himself a king in all but name, commanded that another vessel should be prepared for himself, and all the young nobility,

being his boon companions, gathered round him. The sailors, too, who had drunk overmuch, cried out with true seaman's hilarity that they must overtake the ship that had already set out since their own ship was of the best construction and newly equipped. Wherefore these rash youths, who were flown with wine, launched their vessel from the shore though it was now dark.

William of Malmesbury (c.1125); E.H.D. Vol.2 (1953) p.297. The White Ship sets sail. Its wreck, and the drowning of Henry I's heir, Prince William (and with him a sister and many of the sons of the Norman aristocracy), precipitated the civil wars after Henry's death, between his nephew and successor, Stephen, and his daughter, the Empress Matilda. The chronicler continues: 'No ship ever brought so much misery to England; none was ever so notorious in the history of the world.'

4 He had been hunting, and when he came back [to Lyons-la-Forêt, Normandy], he ate the flesh of lampreys, which always made him ill, though he always loved them. When a doctor forbade him to eat the dish, the king did not take this salutary advice. As it is said, 'We always strive for what is forbidden and long for what is refused.' So this meal brought on a most destructive humour ... and a sudden and extreme convulsion ... When all power of resistance failed, the great king departed on the first day of December [1135].

Henry of Huntingdon (c.1130; 1992 edn) Bk 3.43. As the most effective of the Conqueror's successors, it seems unjust that Henry I is popularly remembered principally for succumbing (at the then advanced age of 67) to a 'surfeit of lampreys' (an eel-like, parasitic freshwater fish). His entrails and brain were buried in Rouen, the Norman capital, but the rest of his body was brought back to England.

5 Here lies the late King Henry, one to be respected for his intellect, his riches, his condition toward the injured, and his decent severity towards the oppressor; he was excellent, wealthy and easy of access. He was the peace and glory of the earth.

Robert de Torigny (c.1149; 1890 edn) p.26. Said to be the epitaph of Henry I. The king was buried in the chancel of Reading Abbey, his own foundation, of which only fragments now remain.

6 After thorough study of past histories, I confidently assert that no king in the English realm was ever more richly or powerfully equipped than Henry in everything that contributes to worldly glory.

Orderic Vitalis (c.1114–41; 1969–80 edn) Bk 11.23.

STEPHEN AND MATILDA, 1135–54

1 The Empress Matilda [daughter of Henry I] returned to her native land after her husband's [Emperor Henry V's] death [1125] although she was greatly loved abroad. The king of England, her father, gave her in marriage [1127] to Geoffrey, Count of Anjou, and in the year of our Lord 1133 she bore him a son called Henry, to whom many people look as their future lord, if almighty God, in whose hands all things are, shall so ordain.

Orderic Vitalis (c.1114–41; 1969–80 edn) Bk 10.1. Henry, the son of Geoffrey Plantagenet and Matilda, would become Henry II, the first of the Plantagenet kings of England. The name is traditionally believed to derive from the Latin for broom (*Planta genista*), which the Angevin count (Angevin = 'of Anjou') used as a badge or wore in his cap.

2 [Stephen] was a man of less judgement than energy; an active soldier, of remarkable spirit in difficult undertakings, lenient to his enemies and easily placated, courteous to all. Though you admired his kindness in making promises, you doubted the truth of his words and the reliability of what he promised. This was why after a short time he put aside the counsel of his brother [Henry of Blois, bishop of Winchester], by whose aid, as I have said, he had pushed aside his adversaries and ascended the throne.

William of Malmesbury *Historia Novella* (c.1140–43; 1955 edn) p.16. A contemporary verdict on Stephen, perhaps the most sympathetic personally, but undoubtedly the least effective politically, of the Norman kings. The son of Adela of Louvain, the Conqueror's formidable daughter, he was the nephew of Henry I, and thrived under his uncle's patronage. On Henry's death he swiftly had himself crowned king of England despite the oath he had taken, in 1127, to respect the claim of Matilda (now Countess of Anjou) to the throne.

3 She at once put on an extremely arrogant demeanour instead of the modest gait and bearing proper to the gentle sex, began to walk and speak and do all things more stiffly and more haughtily than she had been wont, to such a point that soon, in the capital of the land subject to her, she actually made herself queen of all England and gloried in being so called.

Anon. *Gesta Stephani* (Deeds of King Stephen) (from 1148; 1976 edn) pp.10–11. Civil war ensued when Matilda arrived in person (1139) to retrieve her inheritance. The formidable empress seems to have been imperious by nature as well as by calling; but the author of the *Gesta Stephani* may also be showing contemporary clerical prejudice about dynamic women in a man's world.

(In fact, through all the ups and downs of the civil war, Matilda never managed to get herself crowned queen.)

4 For every man built himself castles and held them against the king; and they filled the whole land with these castles. They sorely burdened the unhappy people of the country with forced labour on the castles; and when the castles were built they filled them with devils and wicked men. By night and by day they seized those whom they believed to have any wealth, whether they were men or women; and in order to get their gold and silver, they put them into prison and tortured them with unspeakable tortures … [The ravagers] plundered and burnt all the villages, so that you could easily go a day's journey without ever finding a village inhabited or a field cultivated … If two or three men came riding towards a village, all the villagers fled before them, believing that they were robbers. The bishops and clergy were forever cursing them [the plunderers], but that was nothing to them, for they were all excommunicated and forsworn and lost.

The *Anglo-Saxon Chronicle* (Peterborough Manuscript, 1137; 1996 trans.). This famous description of the so-called Anarchy has been immensely influential, but how far such conditions were real, general or sustained is much debated. It concludes memorably: 'Wherever the ground was tilled the earth bore no corn, for the land was ruined by such doings; and men said openly that Christ and his saints slept.'

5 In the assembly of bishops, earls and other magnates, the king [Stephen] first recognized the hereditary right which Duke Henry held in the kingdom of England; and the duke graciously conceded that the king should hold the kingdom all his life, if he wished, provided that the king himself, the bishops and other magnates should declare on oath that, after the death of the king, the duke should have the kingdom, if he survived him, peacefully and without contradiction.

Robert de Torigny (c.1149; 1890 edn) Bk 4.177. On 6 Nov. 1153 Stephen and Henry were reconciled at Winchester. The sudden death of Stephen's own heir, Eustace, on 17 Aug. had eased the situation. Stephen appointed Henry as his successor, and, obligingly, himself died within a year (on 25 Oct. 1154). Robert provides an interesting further detail of the agreement: 'Also concerning those castles which had come into being since the death of [Henry I]; their number was said to be more than 1115 and they were to be destroyed.'

1 Great by birth, greater by marriage, greatest in
her offspring,
Here lies the daughter, wife and mother of
Henry.

Epitaph of the Empress Matilda, on her tomb in the Norman
abbey church of Bec-Hellouin. Matilda lived on in Normandy
until 1167, based in Rouen, and often acting as deputy for her
son in his absences. Her successive Henries were her father,
King Henry I of England; her first husband, Emperor Henry V
(king of Germany from 1106, Holy Roman Emperor from
1111); and her son, King Henry II of England.

THE NORMANS IN THE MEDITERRANEAN WORLD, 1016–1189

2 There [the Norman pilgrims] saw a man clad in
the Greek manner, called Melus. They were amazed
at the peculiar costume of the stranger, one which
they had never seen before, with his head tied up in
a bonnet wrapped around it. On seeing him they
asked who he was and where he came from. He
replied that he was a Lombard, a citizen of noble
birth from Bari, and that he had been forced to flee
from his native land by the cruelty of the Greeks.
When the Gauls sympathized with his fate he said, 'If
I had the help of some of your people, it would be
easy for me to return, provided you are willing'...

So after [the Normans] had returned to their
native land, they immediately started to encourage
their relatives to come with them to Italy. They
talked of the fertility of Apulia (the heel of Italy), and
of the cowardice of those who lived here ... By such
means they persuaded many to go, some because
they possessed little or no wealth, others because they
wished to make the great fortune they had greater
still. All of them greedy for gain.

William of Apulia *La Geste de Robert Guiscard* (The Deeds of
Robert Guiscard) (c.1095–99; 1961 edn) Bk 1, lines 11–79.
The fateful chance meeting in 1016 at the shrine of St Michael
on Monte Gargano, southeastern Italy, of a group of Norman
pilgrims with Melus, a Lombard expelled from the southern
Italian city of Bari for fomenting rebellion against Byzantine
Greek rule, marks – according to a very early tradition – the
start of the systematic Norman involvement with southern
Italy and Sicily.

3 They saw that their own neighbourhood would
not be big enough for them, and that when their
patrimony was divided not only would their heirs
argue among themselves about the share-out, but
the individual shares would simply not be big
enough. So, to prevent the same thing happening in

future as had happened to them, they discussed the
matter among themselves. They decided that, since
the elders were at that time stronger than those
younger to them, they should be the first to leave
their homeland and go to other places seeking their
fortunes through arms, and finally God led them to
the Italian province of Apulia.

Geoffrey Malaterra *Deeds of Count Roger and his Brother Robert
Guiscard* (c.1100) Bk 1.5. The door once opened to them, the
Normans kept on coming. Ambitions, unrealizable in Normandy, sent many younger sons adventuring abroad (and
particularly in southern Italy), none with more spectacular
success than these, the sons of Tancred de Hauteville, a
Norman lord of modest means. Four of them – William,
Drogo, Humphrey and Robert Guiscard – were to become
successive rulers of Apulia (the 'heel' of Italy), and the
youngest, Roger, Great Count of Sicily.

4 This Robert was a Norman by birth, of obscure
origin, with an overbearing character and a
thoroughly villainous mind; he was a brave fighter,
very cunning in his assaults on the wealth and power
of great men; in achieving his ends absolutely
inexorable, diverting criticism by incontrovertible
argument. He was a man of immense stature ... he
had a ruddy complexion, fair hair, broad shoulders,
eyes that all but shot out sparks of fire ... in him all
was admirably proportioned and elegant ... he was
no man's slave, owing obedience to nobody in the
world.

Anna Comnena *The Alexiad* (c.1148; 1969 trans.) Bk 1, p.54.
Robert Guiscard, 'the Wily', seen through the hostile eyes of
the daughter of the Byzantine emperor, Alexius I (*The Alexiad*
is her celebratory life of her father). Anna had good reason to
resent Robert, whose Italian fortunes were built to a large
extent at the expense of the Greeks. Relations between
Greeks and Franks were further poisoned by the irruption
into Byzantine territory of the First Crusade, of which
Guiscard's son, Bohemond, was one of the leaders.

5 Here lies Guiscard, terror of the world ...

William of Malmesbury (c.1125); G.A. Loud *The Age of Robert
Guiscard* (2000) p.4. The opening of Robert Guiscard's epitaph
at the abbey church of Venosa, near Melfi, in southern Italy.
The quintessential Norman adventurer, he died as Duke of
Apulia in 1085.

6 The sight of him inspired admiration, the mention
of his name terror ... There was a certain charm
about him, but it was somewhat dimmed by the
alarm his person as a whole inspired; there was a
hard, savage quality in his whole aspect, due, I
suppose, to his great stature and his eyes; even his
laugh sounded like a threat to others. Such was his

constitution, mental and physical, that in him both courage and love were armed, both ready for combat … His words were carefully phrased and the replies he gave were regularly ambiguous.

Anna Comnena *The Alexiad* (c.1148; 1969 trans.) Bk 13, pp.422–3. Robert Guiscard's eldest son, Bohemond, who established himself as prince of Antioch (in former Byzantine territory) after its capture in 1098 during the First Crusade. Anna's attraction to the 'barbarian' (in the classical sense of a non-Greek-speaking outsider) is as clear as her hostility.

1   The right hand of God gave me courage.
      The right hand of God raised me up.

Motto inscribed on the sword of Roger 'the Great Count', after his victory over the Muslims at Cerami (1063). The younger brother of Robert Guiscard, he helped Robert conquer Calabria (the 'toe' of Italy), before, in 1061, moving against the Muslim domination of Sicily. After the capital, Palermo, was captured in 1071 Roger became first Count of Sicily and founder of what would emerge as its royal line.

2 The Normans of Apulia were seated on the verge of the two empires, and, according to the policy of the hour, they accepted the investiture of their lands from the sovereigns of Germany [Holy Roman Emperors] or Constantinople [Byzantine emperors]. But the firmest title of these adventurers was the right of conquest: they neither loved nor trusted; they were neither trusted nor beloved.

Edward Gibbon *The Decline and Fall of the Roman Empire* (1776–88) Ch.56.

3 They are a most astute people, eager to avenge injuries, looking rather to enrich themselves from others than from their native fields. They are eager and greedy for profit and power, hypocritical and deceitful about almost everything, but between generosity and avarice they take a middle course. Their leaders are, however, very generous since they wish to achieve a great reputation … Unless they are held in thrall by the yoke of justice, they are a most unbridled people. When circumstances require they are prepared to put up with hard work, hunger and cold; they are much addicted to hunting and hawking, and they delight in fancy clothes and fancy trappings for their horses and decorations on their other weapons.

Geoffrey Malaterra (c.1100) Bk 1, Ch.3. The Normans, characterized by a contemporary chronicler in southern Italy, himself of Norman origin.

4 We grant and give you and sanction to you and to your heirs the crown of the kingdom of Sicily, and

Calabria and Apulia, and of all the lands which we and our predecessors have granted to your predecessors, the dukes of Apulia, namely Robert Guiscard and [Roger the Great Count] his son. This kingdom is to be held by you in perpetuity and ruled by you always with all regal honours and all royal rights. We appoint Sicily as the head of your kingdom. Further we sanction and grant that you and your heirs shall be anointed and crowned as kings by the hands of archbishops of your own kingdom and of your own choice and in the presence of such bishops as you may wish. And we give and sanction to you and your heirs the principality of Capua – and the honour of Naples – and the support of the men of Benevento.

Antipope Anacletus II, bull conferring on Roger II (son of Roger, the Great Count) the title of king of Sicily, 27 Sept. 1130. The antipopes recurred as rival pontiffs to the officially elected ones, especially between 1378 and 1417, during the Great Schism at Avignon (see 193:3).

5 He adopted the customs of Muslim kings with regard to the officers he appointed to his court. Here he departed from the usual practice of the Franks who did not comprehend the functions of such officials. Roger, moreover, always treated Muslims with great honour. He was familiar with many of them, and favoured them even against the Franks.

Ibn al-Athir (1160–1233) *The Perfect History*; M. Amari (ed.) *Bibliotheca Arabo-Sicula* (1880) Vol.1, p.433. A Muslim historian writing of Roger II of Sicily (r.1130–54), only 30 years or so after Roger's death. Under Roger, who himself spoke both Greek and Arabic, Sicily's Arab-Norman culture reached its apogee.

6 The earth is round like a sphere, and the waters adhere to it and are maintained on it through natural equilibrium which suffers no variation.

Al-Edrisi *The Book of Roger* (1154) p.1; J.J. Norwich *The Kingdom in the Sun* (1970) p.102. One of Norman Sicily's most enduring contributions to Christendom was as a channel by which Arab (and, through the Arabs, classical Greek) scientific, geographic, astronomic and medical knowledge was conveyed to the West. Roger II actively fostered this interest in learning. The Arab scholar al-Edrisi dedicated his major geographical treatise to Roger, his patron and friend. It offers a wealth of topographical information, much of it strikingly accurate.

7 If they [the king's pages, who were said to be all Muslims] find themselves in the presence of their master at the [Islamic] time of prayer, they go out of the king's chamber, one after the other, in order to recite their prayers – which they often do in some place within view of the King, but Allah (may he be exalted!) casts a veil over them.

Ibn Jubayr *The Travels of Ibn Jubayr* (1952 edn); R.H.C. Davis *The Normans and Their Myth* (1976) p.74. A Spanish Muslim visitor to Palermo in 1184 comments on the tolerance at the court of William II, the last of the direct line of the Norman rulers of Sicily, who died on 18 Nov. 1189. But his frequently cited admiration contrasts with other remarks he makes, which show that the status and security of the Arab community in Norman Sicily was deteriorating from what it had been in the cosmopolitan world of the two Rogers.

THE NORMANS: LOOKING BACK

1 Always the Norman lords, when they have crushed their enemies, since they cannot avoid acting brutally, crush their own men also in wars. This is increasingly apparent in the lands that God has made subject to them, that is, in Normandy and England, Apulia, Calabria, Sicily [Italy] and Antioch [Antakiyah, Turkey].

Henry of Huntingdon (c.1130; 1992 edn) Bk 2.38. The English chronicler comments wryly on the Norman character as reflected across the formidable range of Norman conquests. However, his contemporary, the chronicler William of Malmesbury, while not denying their love of violence saw also their powers of adaptation and assimilation.

2 [The Normans] are a race inured to war and can hardly live without it ... they envy their equals; they wish to vie with their superiors; and they plunder their subjects, though they defend them from others. They are faithful to their lords unless a slight offence gives them an excuse for treachery ... They are the most polite of people, they consider strangers to deserve the courtesy they show one another, and they intermarry with their subjects.

William of Malmesbury (c.1125); E.H.D. Vol.2, p.291.

3 The Norman Conquest was a Good Thing, as from this time onwards England stopped being conquered and thus was able to become top nation.

W.C. Sellar and R.J. Yeatman *1066 and All That* (1930) Ch.11. This cheery and enduring satire casts a shrewd eye on the way English history was perceived, and taught, in late Imperial Britain.

The Crusades, 1096–1291

BEFORE THE CRUSADES

1 By March 1047 I was in Jerusalem. The people of Syria call Jerusalem the Holy City. Anyone of that province who cannot perform the pilgrimage to Mecca visits Jerusalem, and carries out the statutory rites and offers the customary feast-day sacrifice there. Some years more than 20,000 people come. They bring children to be circumcised, too. Christians and Jews come in large numbers from Constantinople and other regions to worship at the church and synagogue here.

Nasir-i-Khosrau *Journey through Syria and Palestine* (1893 trans.); Elizabeth Hallam (ed.) *Chronicles of the Crusades* (1989; 1997 edn) p.29. As far as this Persian Muslim was concerned, Jerusalem was a highly important point in his pilgrimage, since it was from there that Muhammad ascended into heaven. But he is clear that it is also sacred to other religions.

2 In this way the hoped-for pilgrimage was launched. Abbot Richard [of Saint-Vannes, Verdun, France], that man of God, led seven hundred pilgrims and adequately catered for their sustenance from his own resources. They came to the land of the Saracens, and when Abbot Richard entered their cities he preached Jesus Christ to all. He trusted in his Lord God because there was no guile in his personality.

Hugh of Flavigny *Chronicon* (1026); *Monumenta Germaniae historica* (M.G.H.) Scriptores Vol.7 in Hallam (1989; 1997 edn) p.27. Before the era of the crusades, Christian pilgrims to Jerusalem were protected and supported by the caliphs.

THE FIRST CRUSADE AND ITS AFTERMATH, 1096–9

3 Ambassadors from the emperor of Constantinople came to the synod [at Piacenza, Italy, Feb. 1095] and humbly implored the lord pope and all faithful Christians to send him help to defend the Holy Church against the pagans. For these pagans were then ravaging those parts, and had conquered almost all the territory up to the walls of Constantinople.

Bernold of Constance *Chronicon* (1099); (M.G.H.) Scriptores (from 1826) Vol.5, p.461.

4 There was a great stirring of hearts throughout all the Frankish lands, so that if any man, with all his heart and all his mind, really wanted to follow God and faithfully to bear the cross after him, he could make no delay in taking the road to the Holy Sepulchre as quickly as possible. For even the pope set out across the Alps as soon as he could, with his archbishops, bishops, abbots and priests, and he began to deliver eloquent sermons and to preach.

Anon. *Gesta Francorum* (The Feats of the Franks) (1100/01; 1962 trans.) Bk 1, Ch.1. This contemporary account was written by an anonymous follower of Bohemond I of Antioch.

5 A grave report has come from the lands of around Jerusalem and from the city of Constantinople we have heard it very often already – that a people from the kingdom of the Persians, a foreign race, a race absolutely alien to God, a generation, that is, that set not their heart aright: and whose spirit was not faithful to God, has invaded the land of those Christians, has reduced the people with sword, rapine and flame and carried off some as captives to its own land, has cut down others by pitiable murder and has either completely razed the houses of God to the ground or enslaved them to the practice of its own rites.

Pope Urban II, sermon at the Council of Clermont, France, 27 Nov. 1095; Robert of Rheims *Historia Hierosolymitana* (The History of Jerusalem) (before 1107) Vol.1, pp.727–9. The author of this popular account of the First Crusade was present at the council, and his version (one of the five from contemporary chroniclers) cries up the role of the French. He wrote before 1107, but looking back at a crusade that had been successfully accomplished.

6 Let those who were brigands become soldiers of Christ; let those who have been fighting against their own brothers and relations now rightfully fight barbarians; let those who recently were hired for a few pieces of silver, win their eternal reward! Let those who have wearied themselves to the destruction of body and soul now work for the honour of both!

Pope Urban II, at Clermont, 1095; Fulcher of Chartres *Chronicle of the First Crusade* (1100–27; 1941 trans.) Bk 1, Ch.3. The pope dons the hat of the recruiting sergeant.

7 In this land you [the French] can scarcely feed the inhabitants. That is why you use up its goods and excite endless wars among yourselves.

Pope Urban II, at Clermont, 1095; Robert of Rheims (before 1107) Vol.1, pp.727 ff. Land-hunger drove both peasants and lords to join the crusade and seek new lands to settle.

1 Bishops should also be careful not to allow their parishioners to go without the advice and fore-knowledge of the clergy. You must also see to it that young married men do not rashly set out on such a long journey without the agreement of their wives.
Pope Urban II, at Clermont, 1095; H. Hagenmeyer *Die Kreuzzugsbriefe* (Letters of the Crusades) (1901) p.137.

2 Frequently he burned with anxiety because the warfare he engaged in as a knight seemed to be contrary to the Lord's commands. The Lord, in fact, ordered him to offer the cheek that had been struck together with his other cheek to the striker, but secular knighthood did not spare the blood of relatives. The Lord urged him to give his tunic and his cloak as well to the man who would take them away; the needs of war impelled him to take from a man, already despoiled of both, whatever remained to him.
Radulph of Caen *Gesta Tancredi Principis in Expeditione Hierosolymitana* (c.1113); Terry Jones and Alan Ereira *Crusades* (1994) p.18. Tancred's 'official' biographer, who arrived in the Holy Land himself in 1108, describes the spiritual dilemma of the youthful Norman knight (or indeed of any Christian knight) in 1096. But the pope's call to take arms against the infidel removed such doubts.

3 He [the author's father, the Byzantine Emperor Alexius Comnenus] heard a rumour that countless Frankish armies were approaching. He dreaded their arrival, knowing as he did their uncontrollable methods of attack, with their inevitable consequences; their greed for money, for example, which always led them, it seemed, to break their own agreements without scruple for any chance reason.
Anna Comnena *The Alexiad* (c.1148; 1928 trans.) Bk 10, p.308. The biography of her father was written some 40 years after the First Crusade.

4 Full of enthusiasm and ardour they thronged every highway, and with these warriors came a host of civilians, outnumbering the sand of the seashore or the stars of heaven, carrying palms and bearing crosses on their shoulders.
Anna Comnena (c.1148; 1928 trans.) Bk 10, p.309. A request from Anna's father, the Byzantine emperor, for help against the Turks had borne unexpected fruit in this first influx of an unofficial raggle-taggle army led by Peter the Hermit. The so-called People's Crusade ended disastrously in Anatolia (Asian Turkey).

5 In five weeks time we shall be at Jerusalem, unless we are held up at Antioch.

Stephen of Blois, writing optimistically to his wife from Dorylaeum in Anatolia, June 1097; Hallam (1989; 1997 edn) p.72. Stephen was married to William the Conqueror's daughter, Adela of Louvain, to whom he wrote regularly. The army was still 700 miles short of Jerusalem. The crusaders were not to take Antioch until a year later and Jerusalem two years later.

6 The city of Antioch fell on the third day of June [1098], but it had been under attack from around 22 October of the preceding year. Our troops refrained from attacking the citadel while they examined and took inventory of the spoils; and further oblivious to God, the bestower of so many favours, they gourmandized sumptuously and splendidly as they gave heed to dancing girls.
Raymond d'Aguilers *History of the Franks who Took Jerusalem* (1098/9; 1968 trans.) Ch.6. This chronicler was chaplain to Raymond of Toulouse.

7 After taking Antioch the Franks camped there for twelve days without food. The wealthy ate their horses and the poor ate carrion and leaves from the trees. Their leaders, faced with this situation, wrote to Kerbuqa [the Turkish emir of Mosul] to ask for safe conduct through his territory, but he refused, saying: 'You will have to fight your way out.'
Ibn al-Athir (1160–1233) *The Perfect History* (1851–76 edn) Vol.10, p.188; Amin Maalouf *The Crusades Through Arab Eyes* (1983; 1984 trans.) p.34. This monumental Islamic history gives the view from the other side. Ibn al-Athir was an eyewitness to Saladin's role in the crusades.

8 On the top of Solomon's Temple, to which they had climbed in fleeing, many were shot to death with arrows and cast down headlong from the roof. Within this Temple about 10,000 were beheaded. If you had been there, your feet would have been stained up to the ankles with the blood of the slain. What more shall I tell? Not one of them was allowed to live. They did not spare the women and children.
Fulcher of Chartres (1100–27; 1941 trans.) Bk 1, Ch.27. The capture of Jerusalem on 15 July 1099. Albert of Aachen, writing after c.1100, says that 300 were beheaded. L. and J. Riley-Smith comment: 'The most important narratives were those written by learned churchmen in the West ... who never left their churches and monasteries but had the intellect and command of language to place crusading convincingly in a theological and scriptural context' (*The Crusades: Idea and Reality* (1981) p.16).

9 More than forty silver candelabra, each of them weighing 3,600 drams, and a great silver lamp weighing forty-four Syrian pounds, as well as a hundred and fifty smaller silver candelabra and more than twenty gold ones, and a great deal more booty.

Ibn al-Athir (1160–1233) (1851–76 edn); Francesco Gabrieli *Arab Historians of the Crusades* (1969 trans.) p.11. The Syrian historian describes the pillage of the Dome of the Rock, Jerusalem, on 15 July 1099 by the young Norman knight Tancred and his followers. The Foundation Stone, a bare rock in the Dome, is a holy place for Judaism, Christianity and Islam.

1 Consider … how in our time God turned the West into the East; for we who were Westerners are now Orientals; he who was a Roman or a Frank has in this land become a Galilean or a Palestinian, he who was from Rheims or Chartres has been made into a Tyrian or Antiochene … We have already forgotten the places of our birth … He who was born an alien has become a native.

Fulcher of Chartres (1100–27; 1969 trans.) Bk 2, Ch.3. Fulcher, who had settled in Jerusalem after the First Crusade, and was successively bishop of Tyre and patriarch of Jerusalem, describes how the 'colonists' feel a generation later, c.1125.

2 Before he [Imad ed-din Zengi] came to power the absence of strong rulers to impose justice, and the presence of the Franks close at hand, had made the country a wilderness, but he made it flower again.

Ibn al-Athir (1160–1233) (1851–76 edn) Vol.2, pp.72–4; Gabrieli (1969 trans.) p.54. The historian from Aleppo, along with other chroniclers, records Zengi's leadership, the discipline of his soldiers and the protection of civilians. Islam had found a champion.

THE SECOND CRUSADE, 1147–9, AND ITS AFTERMATH TO 1187

3 We enjoin it for the remission of sins, that … the more powerful and the nobles, should vigorously gird themselves to oppose the multitude of the infidels who are now rejoicing in the victory they have gained over us … by so much spilling of your father's blood.

Pope Eugenius III, *Quantum praedecessores* (bull), 1 Dec. 1145, addressed to Louis VII of France, proclaiming the Second Crusade; P. Rassow *Der Text der Kreuzzugsbulle Eugens III* (Text of the Bull on the Crusades) (1924) pp.302 ff. On Christmas Eve 1144 Zengi had broken into the city of Edessa and massacred the Frankish inhabitants.

4 Are you a shrewd business man, said St Bernard, a man quick to see he profits of this world? If you are, I can offer you a splendid bargain. Do not miss this opportunity. Take the sign of the cross. At once you will have indulgence for all sins which you confess with a contrite heart. It does not cost you much to buy and if you bear it with humility you will find that it is worth the kingdom of heaven.

St Bernard of Clairvaux exhorts the English to join the Second Crusade, 1145; H.E. Mayer *The Crusades* (1972 trans.) p.37. The saint is being shrewd in his appeal, for the church promised to protect the crusader's family and property if he took the cross, and he would also avoid his creditors and the law by responding to the call to arms. Bernard's influence was felt throughout western Europe.

5 I opened my mouth, I spoke; and at once the crusaders have multiplied to infinity. Villages and towns are now deserted. You will scarcely find one man to every seven women. Everywhere you see widows whose husbands are still alive.

St Bernard to Pope Eugenius III, 1146; J.P. Migne (ed.) *Patrologia Latina* (1844–64) Vol.182. Bernard is describing the effect of his sermons on the Germans. The king himself, Conrad III (r.1138–52), was supposed to have burst into tears on hearing the appeal and to have taken the cross on the spot.

6 It was common talk, and probably quite true, that these perilous wanderings [of the Western armies in Asia Minor on the Second Crusade] were devised with the knowledge and at the command of the Greek emperor, who has always envied the successful advance of the Christians. For it is well known that the Greeks have always looked with distrust on all increase of power by the Western nations (as they still do), especially by that of the Teutonic nation, as rivals of the empire. They take it ill that the king of the Teutons [Conrad III] calls himself the emperor of the Romans.

William of Tyre *Historia Rerum in Partibus Transmarinis Gestarum* (A History of Deeds Done Beyond the Sea) (1170; 1844 edn) Bk 16, Ch.21.

7 Reports kept coming in – from Constantinople; from the territory of the Franj [Franks or Westerners more generally], and from nearby lands too that the kings of the Franj were on their way from their countries to attack the land of Islam. They had emptied their own provinces, leaving them devoid of defenders, and had brought with them riches, treasures and immeasurable matériel. They numbered, it was said, as many as a million foot-soldiers and cavalry, perhaps even more.

Ibn al-Qalanisi *Appendix to the History of Damascus* (1149); Maalouf (1983; 1984 trans.) p.146. Although he is, of course, dramatically inflating the tens of thousands of Frankish and

German crusaders already on their way, the earliest Arab historian wrote with objectivity and first-hand experience of both the First and Second Crusades.

1 When they met eye to eye, the infidels made their famous charge upon the Muslims, but the Muslims split up into detachments which attacked them from various directions and swarmed over them … When the haze was dispersed, God, to whom be praise and thanks, had bestowed upon the Muslims the victory over the polytheists [Christians] and they lay upon the ground prostrate and dust-befouled, bereft of the fruits of their warfare … The accursed prince, their leader [Raymond of Antioch] was found stretched out amongst his guard and his knights; he was recognized and his head cut off and carried to Nur ed-Din, who awarded the bearer of it with a handsome gift.

Ibn al-Qalanisi *Appendix to the History of Damascus* (1149; 1932 trans.). The siege of Damascus took place in 1148. Nur ed-Din was Zengi's second son and successor.

2 The Lord, apparently provoked by our sins, has seemed to some extent to have judged the world before time, rightly of course, but forgetful of his mercy. He has not spared his people, not even his own name. Surely they are saying among the nations, Where is their God? No wonder. The sons of the church and those who are counted as Christians have been overthrown in the desert, slain by the sword or consumed by hunger.

St Bernard *De consideratione* (1148–9) explains that the failure of the Second Crusade must be accepted as God's judgement; L. and J. Riley-Smith (1981) Pt 2, Doc.7.

3 I have read the lives of the kings of old and after the right-guided caliphs … I have not found one more upright nor a sterner advocate of justice … among his virtues were austerity, piety and a knowledge of theology.

Ibn al-Athir (1160–1233) (1851–76 edn) Vol.11, pp.264–7; Gabrieli (1969 trans.) p.70. The historian is praising Nur ed-Din. William of Tyre, writing from the opposite viewpoint, corroborates his opinion: 'A wise and prudent man, and, according to the superstitious traditions of his people, one who feared God' ((1170; 1844 edn) Vol.2, p.146).

4 The opposing lines were drawn up at a place called Hattin, in the hills behind Tiberias on the Sea of Galilee. At the precise instant that the fighting began, Raymond III, Count of Tripoli, left the spot, feigning flight. The story is that he did this by pre-

arrangement, so that our troops would scatter, apparently stricken by terror at the desertion of the one who should have been their support, while the spirits of the enemy were raised. So the Lord 'gave his people over also unto the sword' [Psalm 78:62], embroiled in conflict, consigning his inheritance to slaughter and pillage, as the sins of mankind demanded. What more is there to say?

Anon. *Itinerarium regis Ricardi* (1864 edn); Hallam (1989; 1997 edn) p.7. The anonymous chronicler bewails the decisive defeat of the Crusaders by Saladin on 4 July 1187.

5 The prisoners were sent to Damascus, where the barons were lodged in comfort and the poorer folk were sold in the slave-market. So many were there that the price of a single prisoner fell to three dinars, and you could buy a whole healthy family, a man, his wife, his three sons and his two daughters, for eighty dinars the lot. One Muslim even thought it a good bargain to exchange a prisoner for a pair of sandals.

Steven Runciman *A History of the Crusades* Vol.2 (1952) Bk 5, Ch.2. Saladin's rout of the crusaders in 1187 at the Horns of Hattin, near the Sea of Galilee, led to his recapture of Jerusalem and the Third Crusade.

6 The anger of heaven too did not fail to punish these arrogant and impure men; on several occasions, so it is said, an unseasonable deluge of rain removed more of our army than was consumed by enemy swords. So by far the greater part of two huge armies was overthrown by different misfortunes and disasters; with the remainder those two great princes [Conrad III of Germany and Louis VII of France] and barely escaped destruction, reached Jerusalem. They then returned ingloriously, having achieved nothing of note.

William of Newburgh *The History of English Affairs* (1190s; 1988 trans.) Bk 1, Ch.20. How the débâcle of the Second Crusade seemed to an English contemporary chronicler from an Augustinian priory in the north of England.

THE MILITARY ORDERS

7 A new order of knights lately sprung up is heard of on earth, and in that region which formerly the Light of the World [Christ] visibly came from on high in fleshly form. A new order of knights, I say, and an order inexperienced in worldly matters – an order which untiringly engageth in a twofold conflict, warring both against flesh and blood and against spiritual wickedness in high places ... For how often thou who engagest in warfare in a spirit of worldliness, dost thou fear lest thou either kill an adversary in the body, but thyself in the soul, or lest thou perchance be slain by him both in body and in soul? ... But the knights of Christ fight safely the battles of their lord, in no wise bearing either sin from slaying enemies, or the danger of their own destruction.

St Bernard *De laude novae militiae* (In Praise of the New Knighthood) (1119; 1963 edn) Vol.3. The much respected abbot of Clairvaux supports the newly founded Order of the Temple (the Templars). He contrasts the condition of the ordinary soldier with that of the new order. The Templars followed a rule with 73 clauses, of which about 30 were based on those of St Benedict (see 195:3), so they were both monks and soldiers of Christ.

1 In the same year, certain noble men of knightly rank, devoted to God, religious and God-fearing, professed to wish to live in chastity, obedience and without property in perpetuity, binding themselves in the hands of the lord patriarch to the service of Christ in the manner of regular canons ... since they did not have a church, nor a settled place to live, the king conceded a temporary dwelling to them in his palace, which he had below the Temple of the Lord [in Jerusalem] ... Moreover, the lord king [Baldwin II] with his nobles, as well as the lord patriarch with his prelates, gave to them certain benefices from their own demesnes, some in perpetuity, some on a temporary basis, from which they could be fed and clothed. The first element of their profession, enjoined on them for the remission of their sins by the lord patriarch and other bishops, was 'that they should protect the roads and routes to the utmost of their ability against the ambushes of thieves and attackers, especially in regard to the safety of pilgrims'.

William of Tyre (1170; 1844 edn) Bk 12, Ch.7. Founded in 1118, the order received its rule in 1128. Its initial aim was to protect pilgrims travelling the roads of the Holy Land. William, archbishop of Tyre, is describing their modest beginnings, but he was in fact no champion of the Templars.

2 The brothers of the military orders are ordained to defend Christ's church with the material sword, especially against those who are outside it.

Jacques de Vitry *Historia Hierosolimitana* (early 13th century); J. Riley-Smith *What were the Crusades?* (1977; 1992 edn) Ch.4. The bishop of Acre and French chronicler (see 198:3) defends the Templars about 80 years after St Bernard's championship of them. The bishop was rare in aiming to proselytize the Muslims in his diocese.

3 They [the Mamluks] caused the Franks terrible losses and played the major part in the victory. They fought furiously: it was they who flung themselves into the pursuit of the enemy: they were Islam's Templars.

Ibn Wasil *The Dissipator of Anxieties Concerning the History of the Ayyubids* (2nd half of 13th century) f.3691; Gabrieli (1969 trans.) p.299. The Mamluk dynasty took power in Egypt in 1250. 'Mamluk' means someone who is owned – that is, a slave. These slave soldiers were an important part of Islamic armies. They formed the bodyguard of Sultan as-Salih (r.1240–49) and on his death took power. They ruled Egypt until 1517. The contemporary Arabic chronicler can find no higher praise for the Egyptian fighters at Damietta (in the Nile Delta, Egypt) in the Fifth Crusade.

4 It is not easy for anyone to gain an idea of the power and wealth of the Templars – for they and the Hospitallers have taken possession of almost all the cities and villages with which Judaea was once enriched ... and have built castles everywhere and filled them with garrisons, besides the very many, and indeed numberless, estates which they are known to possess in other lands.

Theoderich's Description of the Holy Places (c.1172; 1891 edn) pp.30–32. A pilgrim visiting Jerusalem comments on the growth of the Templars' property 50 years after their inception. The two orders were constant rivals. The Knights Hospitallers of St John of Jerusalem founded c.1070, with Muslim permission, a hospital for sick pilgrims in Jerusalem and were made a formal order in 1099, when the city fell to the First Crusade.

5 [The military orders] have such a great quantity of rents and crops and possessions on this side of the Mediterranean Sea, which for a long time now have made insufficient contribution to the Holy Land. Since on occasions of great necessity these orders have many times been divided among themselves, and on this account in confusion, and therefore with very great scandal exposed to mockery, it is expedient and necessary, if the cause of the Holy Land is to go forward, to unite them in administration, habit, status and goods, as will seem expedient to a holy council. Those members living in the holy land should subsist from their property there and in Cyprus.

Pierre Dubois *Concerning the Recovery of the Holy Land* (c.1306; 1891 edn) p.13; Malcolm Barber *The Trial of the Templars* (1978) p.16. Dubois, a Norman lawyer and propagandist for the policies of the French monarchy, advocates a merger between the two great military orders. But by the end of his treatise he seems to have decided that: 'It will be expedient to destroy the order of Templars completely, and for the needs of justice to annihilate it totally.'

THE THIRD CRUSADE, 1189–92

1 Taking advantage of the dissension which the malice of men at the suggestion of the devil had recently roused in the land of the Lord, Saladin came upon those regions with a host of armed men … There advanced against him the king, the bishops, the Templars, the Hospitallers and the barons with the knights and the people of the land and the relic of the Lord's cross, which used to afford a sire safeguard and desired defence against the invasion of the pagans … They were attacked and, when our side had been overpowered, the Lord's cross was taken … The bishops, moreover and the Templars and Hospitallers were beheaded in Saladin's sight.
Newly elected Pope Gregory VIII to the Germans, describing the Horns of Hattin (see 228:4) and proclaiming a Third Crusade, 3 Nov. 1187; Anon. *Historia de Expeditione Friderici imperatoris* (1928 edn).

2 He [Conrad, Marquis of Montferrat, saviour of Tyre and moving spirit of the Third Crusade] had a picture of Jerusalem painted showing the Church of the Resurrection, the object of pilgrimage and deepest veneration to them; according to them the Messiah's tomb is there, in which he was buried after his crucifixion … Above the tomb the marquis had a horse painted, and mounted on it a Muslim knight who was trampling the tomb, over which his horse was urinating. This picture was sent abroad to the markets and meeting places; priests carried it about, clothed in their habits, their heads covered, groaning: 'O the shame!' In this way they raised a huge army, God alone knows how many, among them the king of Germany with his troops.
Baha ad-Din (1145–1234) *Sultanly Anecdotes and Josephly Virtues*; *Recueil des historiens des croisades orientaux* (1841–96) Vol.3. The biographer and eyewitness of the crusade was a member of Saladin's household, and his is the most complete portrait of the Muslim leader there is. The title refers to Saladin's personal name, Yusuf (Joseph). Baha ad-Din remained in the service of Saladin from before the Battle of Hattin until the sultan's death.

3　I saw Saladin, aloof, alone.
　　　Higher I raised my brows and further scanned,
　　And saw the master of the men who know
　　　Seated amid the philosophic band.
Dante Alighieri *The Divine Comedy* 'Purgatory' (c.1308–21) Canto 4, lines 129 ff. Dante places Saladin in the first circle of hell, next to Aristotle and among those whose crime was that they did not really have the opportunity to embrace Christianity.

4 From there they [the German army] advanced towards Antioch, but found a river in their path, beside which they camped. The king [Frederick I, Barbarossa] went down to the river to wash himself, and was drowned at a place where the water was not even up to his waist. Thus God liberated us from the evil of such a man.
Ibn al-AthirI (160–1233) (1851–76 edn) Vol.12, p.32. The death of Barbarossa in June 1190 at the age of 67 spelled disaster to the Germans' crusade and was a great relief from the Muslim standpoint. The chronicler added: 'Thus did God spare us the maleficence of the Germans.' Disease struck the army at Antioch, and Frederick's son, soon to die before Acre, was not able to command such unity as his legendary father.

5 Each person will give this year in alms for the aid of the land of Jerusalem a tenth of his income and movable goods, except for his arms, horses and clothes in the case of a knight; likewise except for his horses, books, clothes, vestments and any sort of furniture in the case of a cleric; and except for precious stones belonging to both clergy and laity … but clerics and knights who have taken the cross will give nothing of that tenth, except what they give for their personal property and for their demesne lands; and whatever their men have owed must be collected for the crusaders' enterprise.
Saladin Tithe, 1188; W. Stubbs *Select Charters* (1913 edn). A tax was levied in England towards financing Richard I's participation in the Third Crusade.

6 The king of England was courageous, energetic, and daring in combat. Although of lower rank than the king of France [Philip II], he was richer and more renowned as a warrior. On his way east he had seized Cyprus, and when he appeared before Acre, accompanied by 25 galleys loaded with men and equipment for war, the Franj let out cries of joy and lit great fires to celebrate his arrival. As for the Muslims, their hearts were filled with fear and apprehension.
Baha ad-Din (1145–1234) *The Rare and Excellent History of Saladin*; Maalouf (1983; 1984 trans.) Ch.11.

7 When the English king [Richard I] saw that Saladin delayed in carrying out the terms of the treaty [for the surrender of Acre] … they brought up the Muslim prisoners … more than three thousand men in chains. They fell on them as one man and slaughtered them in cold blood, with sword and lance.
Baha ad-Din (1145–1234) *The Rare and Excellent History of Saladin*; Gabrieli (1969 trans.) p.239. Elsewhere the figure is

given as 2,700 survivors of the city's garrison, who were killed in sight of Saladin's army in July 1191. The contrast with Saladin's clemency to his prisoners after the victory at the Horns of Hattin (see 228:4) is striking.

1 I am to salute you, and tell you that the Muslims and Franks are bleeding to death, the country is utterly ruined and goods and lives have been sacrificed on both sides. The time has come to stop this. The points at issue are Jerusalem, the cross and the land. Jerusalem is for us an object of worship that we could not give up even if there were only one of left. The land from here to beyond the Jordan must be consigned to us. The cross, which for you is simply a piece of wood with no value, is for us of enormous importance. If the sultan [Saladin] will deign to return it to us, we shall be able to make peace and to rest from this endless labour.

Richard I to Saladin, 1191; Baha ad-Din (1145–1234) *The Rare and Excellent History of Saladin* in Gabrieli (1969 trans.) p.226.

2 Jerusalem is ours as much as yours; indeed it is even more sacred to us than to you for it is the place where our Prophet made his journey through the night [Muhammad's ascension] and the city where our people will be gathered [on the Day of Judgement]. Do not imagine that we can surrender to you or compromise on this. The land belonged to us from the beginning, while you have only just arrived, and have taken it over only because of the weakness of the Muslims living there at the time. God will not allow to be rebuilt a single stone as long as the war lasts. As for the cross, its ownership is a high card in our hands and it cannot be surrendered except in exchange for something of priceless benefit to all Islam.

Saladin's reply to Richard I, 1191; Baha ad-Din *The Rare and Excellent History of Saladin* in Gabrieli (1969 trans.) p.226. The peace negotiations took over a year of diplomacy.

3 The king was a very giant in the battle [of Jaffa, 1192] and was everywhere in the field – now here, now there, wherever the attacks of the Turks raged the hottest. He slew numbers with his sword which shone like lightning; some of them were cleft in two from their helmets to their teeth, whilst others lost their heads, arms and other limbs, which were lopped off at a single blow.

Ambroise d'Evreux (*fl.c.*1190) *L'Estoire de la guerre sainte* (The Crusade of Richard the Lionheart) (1897; 1941 trans.) p.153; Hallam (1989; 1997 edn) p.153. With relish the chronicler cries up the bravery of Richard I. But although Richard came within sight of Jerusalem, he did not reconquer it and had to

be satisfied with negotiating for a three-year truce with Saladin before turning for home. Richard, canon of the Holy Trinity Augustinian priory in London, based the early books of his *Itinerarium regis Ricardi* (early 13th century) on Ambroise's account.

4 Look at the state of the country, ruined and trampled under foot, at your subjects, beaten down and confused, at your armies, exhausted and sick, at your horses, neglected and ruined. There is little forage, food is short, supply bases are far away, the necessities of life are dear.

Saladin to his emirs before the truce, 1192; John Gillingham *Richard the Lionheart* (1978) Ch.10.

5 He [Saladin, who died only five months after Richard had left Acre] was a man wise in counsel, valiant in war and generous beyond measure … for this very reason, he was distrusted by our nobles who had keener foresight … there is no better means by which princes can win the hearts of their subjects … than by showing lavish bounty towards them.

William of Tyre (1170; 1844 edn) Vol.2, p.405. His open-handedness was seen by William as a powerful factor in his success.

6 The only crusade to be a complete success was the first, in which no crowned head had taken part. A crusade of barons, more or less homogeneous in race, would avoid the royal and national rivalries that had so greatly damaged the second and third crusades.

Steven Runciman *A History of the Crusades* Vol.3 (1954) Bk 2, Ch.1 on the thinking of Pope Innocent III in 1199.

THE FOURTH CRUSADE, 1202–4

7 We order that an empty trunk be placed in each church, locked with three keys; the first to be put in the charge of the bishop, the second in the charge of the priest of the church and the third in the charge of some devout layman. All the faithful should be advised to put their alms in it for the remission of their sins – the amount will depend on what the Lord inspires them to give – and this ought to be publicly and repeatedly announced once a week at mass in all the churches.

Pope Innocent III, *Graves orientalis terrae*, 31 Dec. 1199. The pope preaches a new crusade, urging nobles and priests throughout France and northern Italy to take the cross. He also announced a tax on the clergy themselves to finance the crusade.

1 We will build transports to carry 4,500 horses and 9,000 squires, and other ships to accommodate 4,500 knights and 20,000 foot sergeants. We will also include in our contract a nine months' supply of rations for all these men and fodder for all the horses. This is what we will do for you, and no less, on condition you pay us five marks per horse and two marks per man ...

We will provide, for the love of God, fifty additional armed galleys, on condition that so long as our association lasts we shall have one half, and you the other half, of everything we win, either by land or sea.

Enrico Dandolo, doge of Venice in 1192–1205; Geoffrey de Villehardouin *The Conquest of Constantinople* (c.1208; 1963 trans.) Ch.2. The French chronicler Villehardouin was one of the six delegates sent to negotiate with Venice in April 1201, and he records that he had been ordered to kneel to the Venetians and not to rise until they had 'agreed to take pity on the Holy Land over the sea'.

2 Sirs ... you are associated with the best and bravest people in the world in the highest enterprise anyone has ever undertaken. Now I am an old man, weak and in need of rest, and my health is failing. All the same I realize no one can control and guide you like myself, who am your lord. If you will consent to my taking the cross ... then I shall go to live or die with you and with the pilgrims.

Enrico Dandolo, Sept, 1201; Villehardouin (c.1208; 1963 trans.) Ch.4. The doge addressed the congregation in San Marco, and the Venetians responded: 'We beg you in God's name to take the cross and go with us.'

3 Let me tell you here of an outstanding deed of valour. The doge of Venice, although an old man and completely blind, stood at the bow of his galley with the banner of St Mark unfurled before him. He ordered his men to drive the ship ashore. And so they did, and the men leaped down and planted the banner before him in the ground. As soon as the others saw the standard of St Mark and the doge's galley beached, they were ashamed and followed him ashore.

Geoffrey de Villehardouin (c.1208; 1963) Ch.9. Villehardouin describes the events that took place under the walls of Constantinople on July 1203.

4 Nor do I think that in the 40 richest cities of the world there had been so much wealth as was found in Constantinople. For the Greeks say that two thirds of the wealth of this world is in Constantinople.

Robert of Clari (d.c.1216) *The Conquest of Constantinople* (1936 trans.) 'The Taking of the City'. The French knight and chronicler was an eyewitness of the siege.

5 They smashed the holy images and hurled the sacred relics of the martyrs into places I am ashamed to mention, scattering everywhere the body and blood of the Saviour ... As for their profanation of the Great [St Sophia], they destroyed the high altar and shared out the pieces among themselves ... and they brought horses and mules into the church, the better to carry off the holy vessels, and the pulpit, and the doors, and the furniture wherever it was to be found; and when some of these beasts slipped and fell, they ran them through with their swords, fouling the church with their blood and ordure ...

A common harlot was installed in the patriarch's chair, to hurl insults at Jesus Christ; and she sang bawdy songs, and danced immodestly in the holy place ... nor was there mercy shown to virtuous matrons, innocent maids or even virgins consecrated to God.

Nicetas Choniates *Historia* (early 13th century; 1975 edn); John Julius Norwich *A Short History of Byzantium* (1997) Ch.22. The Greek chronicler's eyewitness view of the rape of the city.

THE CHILDREN'S CRUSADE, 1212

6 In 1212 a rather remarkable expedition took place: children from many different areas took part. The first to reach Paris came from the region of the Vendôme, then about 30,000 of them journeyed to Marseilles to take ship for Saracen lands ... The men who betrayed the children are said to have been Hugh Ferreus and William Porcus, merchants of Marseilles. As captains of the ships they ought to have conveyed the children across the sea at no cost as they had promised before God. They had filled seven large ships with them and when they were two days out – at the island of St Peter [off Sardinia] at the rock called Recluse – a storm blew up and two ships were lost. All the children from these two ships were drowned ... Those double-crossing sea-captains sailed the five remaining ships to Bougie and Alexandria [Egypt] and there sold all the children to Saracen noblemen and merchants.

Aubrey of Trois-Fontaines, early 13th century; Hallam (1989; 1997 edn) p.244. A contemporary chronicle on the tragic fate of the French children. Thousands of German children also made a fruitless journey to Rome. 'Research has suggested that the crusaders were not children so much as young

persons on the margins of society – persons of no importance. The Children's Crusade reflected the prevalent idea that
simplicity and poverty might remedy all the church's ills ... the
cult of the Holy Innocents begins at this time' (Jane Sayer
Innocent III (1994) p.176).

THE FIFTH CRUSADE, 1214–21

1 If anyone of those setting out to that place are
strictly held by oath to repay usuries, we order with
same strictness that their creditors be compelled by
a similar censure to restore them. And we command
Jews to be compelled by means of the secular power
to remit usuries ... and we excommunicate and
anathematize those false and impious Christians
who carry weapons, iron and wood for building
galleys to the Saracens, against the interests of Christ
himself and the Christian people.
Pope Innocent III, at the Fourth Lateran Council, 30 Nov.
1215. The pope legislates for the Fifth Crusade and, to finance
it, imposes a tax of 5% on clerical salaries for three years. For
the Fourth Lateran Council see 191:1.

2 But to those declining to take part, if indeed there
be by chance such men ungrateful to the Lord our
God, we firmly state on behalf of the apostle that
they should know that they will have to reply to us
on this matter in the presence of the Dreadful Judge
on the Last Day of Severe Judgement.
Pope Innocent III, *Ad Liberandum* (bull), from the Fourth
Lateran Council, 1215; Riley-Smith (1977; 1992 edn) Ch.3.

3 Many of our men died because of the severe winter
and the dreadful cold, besides the usual river floods
and the high tides caused by the swollen sea, many
more by far than died at the hands of the Saracens ...
We prepared petraries [type of large catapult],
trebuchets, ladders and other instruments of war
and we also dug mines to bring down the towers on
the walls or to enter the city through underground
passages. We trust that the Lord will soon deliver the
city into the hands of the Christians, for few have
remained in it and are suffering very much from a
shortage of food.
Jacques de Vitry (early 13th century) to Pope Honorius III,
describing the failing siege of Damietta in the Nile delta, Egypt,
Aug. 1218–Sept. 1219. This was an attempt to launch a
crusade through Egypt. The crusading bishop of Acre describes the collapse of Innocent III's dream to his successor.

4 Our disastrous situation was exacerbated by the
fact that the men were mostly drunk that night with

wine which could not be taken away on account of
its quantity, and had therefore been offered free of
charge and guzzled heedlessly; they [the crusaders]
were now left behind asleep in the camp or lay in the
road and could not be roused, and were for the most
part slaughtered or captured and so lost to us ... The
Templars led the rearguard, in the greatest peril,
keeping well together with their weapons held in
readiness to protect those who were marching ahead
of them. But the men in front headed off in different
directions and wandered through the dark night like
stray sheep.
Oliver of Paderborn (early 13th century; 1894 edn); Hallam
(1989; 1997 edn) p.255. The writer was bishop of Paderborn
in 1224–5. Having preached the Fifth Crusade in Germany for
Innocent III with great success, he became one of its leaders
and subsequently wrote its history. He was secretary to
Cardinal Pelagius, who was the legate appointed by Pope
Honorius III to head the crusade. After the Venetian high-
jacking of the Fourth Crusade, the papacy wanted to control
the Fifth Crusade through its own clerical leaders.

5 Because of the legate [the Spanish cardinal
Pelagius] who governed and led the Christians,
everyone says in truth, we lost that city through folly
and sin ... Greatly should Rome be humiliated for
the loss of Damietta.
Guillaume le Clerc *Le Besant de Dieu* (1226–7; 1869 edn);
Palmer A. Throop *Criticism of the Crusade: A Study of Public
Opinion and Crusade Propaganda* (1977) p.32. The Norman
cleric had strong feelings against the religious actually fighting.
A five-year truce was magnanimously offered to the crusaders
by Sultan al-Kamil, Saladin's nephew.

THE SIXTH CRUSADE, 1228–9

6 He [Frederick II] was an adroit man, cunning,
greedy, wanton malicious, bad-tempered, but at
times when he wished to reveal his good and courtly
qualities, consoling, witty, delightful, hard working.
Salimbene di Adam *Chronicle* (1282–90); M.G.H. Scriptores
(from 1862) Vol.32, pp.348–9. The Italian Franciscan
chronicler was extremely hostile to Frederick and included a
good deal of scandal in his chronicle. A Joachite (see 204:1),
he identified the emperor with Antichrist.

7 I am your friend. It was you who urged me to make
this trip. The pope and all the kings of the West now
know of my mission. If I return empty-handed I will
lose much prestige. For pity's sake give me Jerusalem, that I may hold my head high.
Frederick II to Sultan al-Kamil, 1229; Maalouf (1983; 1984
trans.) p.228. The sultan had appealed to him to come to

the Holy Land where he wanted support against his brother and rival.

1 I must also take opinion into account. If I deliver Jerusalem to you it could lead not only to a condemnation of my actions by the caliph, but also to a religious insurrection that would threaten my throne.

Sultan al-Kamil's reply to the appeal from Frederick; Maalouf (1983; 1984 trans.) p.228. Frederick, 'the wonder of the world' to his admirers but the Antichrist (see 191:4) to his enemies, king of Sicily since 1198, spoke Arabic and had far more understanding of Islam than other crusading monarchs. He used diplomacy to regain Jerusalem, Bethlehem and Nazareth and to establish a truce for ten years. The hand-over of Jerusalem on 18 Feb. 1229 was a diplomatic arrangement between two secular monarchs whose primary concern was the preservation of their own imperial position. No blood was shed. Frederick II was execrated by Pope Gregory IX and became the object of a holy war himself.

THE ASSASSINS

2 One of the points laid down by Ali [Muhammad's son-in-law] is that if a man is killed while obeying his lord's orders his soul goes into a more pleasing body than before. That is why the Assassins are not in any way averse to being killed as and when their lord [known as the Old Man of the Mountain] orders, because they believe they will be happier after death than when they were alive.

Jean de Joinville (early 14th century; 1963 trans.) Pt 2, Ch.12. Joinville is describing the Old Man of the Mountain, who was visiting his master, Louis IX, at Acre in 1250–51.

3 I shall now relate things about this elder which appear ridiculous but which are attested by the evidence of reliable witnesses, this Old Man has by his witchcraft so bemused the men of his country, that they neither worship nor believe in any god but himself. Likewise he entices them in a strange manner with such hopes and such promises of such pleasures with eternal enjoyment that they prefer to die rather than to live ... The most blessed, so he affirms, are those who shed the blood of men and in revenge for such deeds suffer death. When therefore any of them have chosen to die in this way ... He himself hands them knives which are so to speak consecrated to this affair, and then intoxicates them with such a potion that they are plunged into ecstasy and oblivion ... and promises them eternal possession of these things in reward.

Arnold of Lübeck *Chronicon Slavorum* (1192; 1907 edn) Bk 4.16, pp.178–9. The German chronicler, writing at the

time of the Third Crusade, describes the power of the Assassins. The radical Islamic group deliberately targeted both Muslims and Christians, in that respect contrasting with early 21st-century terrorists. Their daggers had already struck down a number of Muslim princes and in 1192 found their first crusader victim in Conrad of Montferrat, king of the Latin Kingdom of Jerusalem.

4 Now no man was allowed to enter the garden save those whom he [the Old Man of the Mountain] chose to be his ashishin. There was a fortress at the entrance to the garden, and there was no other way to get in. He kept at his court a number of the youths of the country, from 12–20 years of age, such as had a taste for soldiering and to these he used to tell tales about paradise, just as Muhammad had been wont to do, and they believed him just as the Saracens believe in Muhammad.

Then he would introduce them into his garden ... having first made them drink a certain potion which cast them into a deep sleep ... So when they awoke and found themselves in a place so charming, they deemed that it was paradise in very truth.

So when the Old Man would have a prince slain, he would say to such a youth: 'Go thou and slay so-and-so; and when thou returnest, my angels will bear thee into paradise. And shouldst thou die, nevertheless even so will I send my angels to carry thee back into paradise.'

Marco Polo *The Travels of Marco Polo* (1298; 1903 trans.) pp.139–143. 'In one respect the Assassins are without precedent – in the planned, systematic and long-term use of terror as a political weapon they may well be the first terrorists' (Bernard Lewis *The Assassins: A Radical Sect in Islam* (1967) p.129).

THE SEVENTH CRUSADE AND BEYOND, 1248–91

5 Although I had less than a thousand livres a year from my land I had undertaken, when I went overseas, to bear, in addition to my own expenses, the cost of keeping nine knights and two knights-banneret. It so happened that by the time I arrived in Cyprus, I had in hand, after my ship had been paid for, no more than 240 *livres tournois*. On that account some of my knights told me that unless I provided myself with funds they would leave me.

Jean de Joinville *The Life of St Louis* (early 14th century; 1963 trans.) Pt 2, Ch.3. The author, a noble from Champagne, accompanied his king on the crusade and wrote his biography in his old age, after Louis's death in 1270 and the fall of Acre in 1291, which marked the end of the Christian rule in Outremer, the Latin kingdom of Jerusalem.

1 Apart from the Christians I have already mentioned, as also men of another religion, there are among the Tatars [Mongols] a great number of people who belong to the Greek Church. Whenever the Tatars want to make war on the Saracens they send these Christians to fight them, while on the other hand using the Saracens in any war against Christians ...

The envoys returned from the king of the Tatars bringing a letter to our king [Louis IX] stating: 'Peace is a good thing; for when a country is at peace, they that go on four feet may graze in the fields undisturbed, while those who go on two can also till the soil – which brings forth all good things – in perfect tranquillity. We are telling you this by way of warning, for you cannot have peace unless you are at peace with us.'

Jean de Joinville (early 14th century; 1963 trans.) Pt 2, Ch.13. The Mongols are confident in their powerful position (see 248:4). Louis IX had sent William of Rubruck to the Mongol court (1253–5).

2 Emir Husam ad-Din described a conversation he had had with King Louis IX. 'The king of France,' he said, 'was an unusually wise and intelligent man. During one of our conversations I asked him: "How did a man of your majesty's character, wisdom and good sense ever conceive the idea of embarking on a ship, riding the waves of the sea and journeying to a land so full of Muslims and warriors, assuming that you could conquer it and become its king?" Louis laughed, but said nothing. "In our land," I continued, "when a man voyages on the sea, exposes himself and his worldly goods to such risks, his witness is not accepted as evidence in any court of law." "Why not?" asked King Louis. "Because such behaviour implies to us that he is lacking in sense, and such a man is unfit to give evidence." Louis laughed and declared: "By God, whoever said that was right; who ever ruled thus was not in error."'

Ibn Wasil (2nd half of 13th century; 1702 edn); Hallam (1989; 1997 edn) p.273. The Arab chronicler served the Mamluk sultan Baibars I (r.1260–77). Here he describes the impression that Louis IX made during the month of captivity, April 1250, while he awaited the colossal ransom demanded of the crusaders. The price came down to 800,000 bezants and the surrender of Damietta! But Louis remained in the east a further four years, waiting until the other crusaders captured at the Battle of Mansourah were at last released in 1254.

3 The sultan's standards entered the city [Damietta] on Friday 3 May 1250 and were raised on the walls, proclaiming once again the rule of Islam. The king of France St Louis was set free and went, with the remains of his army, over to the western shore. The next day, Saturday, he went abroad and set sail for Acre. He stayed some time in Palestine and then returned home. So God purified Egypt of them, and this victory was many times greater than the first because of the large number of the enemy killed and captured; so many that the prisons of Cairo were full of Franks. The joyful news spread to all the other countries, and public manifestations of joy and happiness were seen.

Ibn Wasil (2nd half of 13th century); MS Paris Archives 1702, f.372. St Louis' departure is seen by the Arab chronicler as purifying Egypt. One church's saint was another's devil.

4 Our purpose here is to give you news of what we have just done, to inform you of the utter catastrophe that has befallen you ... While we were taking up our position in front of the city [Antioch] your troops rode out to measure themselves in combat against us. They were defeated ... we took the city by storm bringing despair to all those you had chosen to garrison and defend it. Not one of them but has certain wealth, and now there is not one of us but owns one of them and his money. You would have seen your knights prostrate beneath the horses' hooves, your houses stormed by pillagers, and ransacked by looters, your wealth weighed by the quintal [100lb], your women sold four at a time and bought for a dinar of your own money.

Sultan Baibars I to Bohemond VI, 1268; Ibn Abd Az-Zahir (1233–93), MS Paris Archives 1707, f.105. This famous and gloating victory letter was dictated to Ibn Abd Az-Zahir, secretary and biographer to the Mamluk sultans, Baibars and Qalawun; and his manuscript of material about both survived. Baibars gave information the recipient had not yet heard from his own sources. It meant the capitulation of the crusader states after 200 years.

5 All must know that I am in the company of my lord Edward, the eldest son of the king of England, in order to go with him to the Holy Land with four knights besides myself. I will remain in his service for a whole year, beginning at the time of the next crossing to the East in September. And in return for undertaking this, he has given me 600 marks in money and transport to cover everything, that is to say the rental of the ship and water for as many persons and horses as befit knights.

Service contract between Lord Edward (later Edward I) of England and Adam of Jesmond, 20 July 1270; H.G. Richardson and G.O. Sayles *The Governance of Medieval England* (1963) p.465. Edward's crusade was short lived. He was wounded by a spy he employed, who turned out to be a double agent.

1 If a Frankish king sets out from the West, to attack the lands of the sultan or of his son, the regent of the kingdom and the grand masters of Acre shall be obligated to inform the sultan of their action, two months before their arrival … If an enemy comes from among the Mongols, or elsewhere, whichever of the two parties first learns of it must alert the other. If – may God forbid! – Such an enemy marches against Syria and the troops of the sultan withdraw before him, then the leaders of Acre shall have the right to enter into talks with this enemy with the aim of saving their subjects and territories.

Truce, 1283. The truce, between Baibar's successor Sultan Qalawun of Egypt (r.1280–90) and the Kingdom of Acre, was to last for 10 years, 10 months, 10 days and 10 hours.

2 Then on Friday 18 May 1291, before daybreak, there came the loud and terrible sound of the kettledrum … the Saracens assaulted the city of Acre on every side. The place where they got in was through this damned tower which they had taken.

They came in countless numbers, all on foot; in front came men with great tall shields, after them men throwing Greek fire and then men who shot bolts and feathered arrows so thickly that they seemed like rain falling from the sky.

When Henry of Lusignan, King of Jerusalem and Cyprus, witnessed this disaster, he went to the master of the Hospitallers; they saw clearly that no advice or help could do any good, so they fled and went aboard the galleys.

Anon. *Chronicle of the Templar of Tyre* in Philip of Novara *Les Gestes des Chiprois* (Acts of the Cypriots) (1887 edn); Hallam (1989; 1987 edn) pp.280–81. The anonymous Templar gives his eyewitness account of the death throes of the Crusader kingdoms, with the abandonment of Acre in May 1291.

3 With these conquests, all their lands of the coast were fully returned to the Muslims, a result undreamed of. Thus were the Franj, who had once nearly conquered Damascus, Egypt and many other lands, expelled from all of Syria and the coastal zones. God grant that they never set foot there again!

Abu al-Fida *Historical Compendium*; *Recueil des historiens des croisades orientaux* (1872–1906) Vol.1 in Maalouf (1983; 1984 trans.) Ch.14. The chronicler's triumph and relief are prompted by the sultan, al-Ashraf Khalil, taking Acre. The *coup de grâce* after almost 200 years of Frankish intervention in the Orient.

THE LAST WORD

4 Crusades – superior piracy, that is all.

Friedrich Nietzsche *Nietzsche in Outline and Aphorism* (1911) 'Definitions'.

The Earlier Plantagenets, 1154–1327

HENRY II, 1154–89

1 I have heard that his mother's [the Empress Matilda's] teaching was to this effect, that he should spin out the affairs of everyone, hold long in his own hand all posts that fell in, take the revenues of them, and keep the aspirants to them hanging on in hope; and she supported this advice by an unkind analogy: the untamed hawk, when raw meat is frequently offered to it and then snatched away or hidden from it, becomes keener and more prone to obey and attend.

Empress Matilda instructs her son, the future Henry II, in *realpolitik*; Walter Map *Of Courtiers' Trifles* (1181–92; 1983 edn) p.479. Map's book is a collection of court gossip and pointed anecdotes, the work of a satirist rather than a historian. He didn't approve of the empress's influence, adding: 'But I confidently impute to her teaching all [Henry's] unattractive qualities.'

2 I have married a monk, not a king!

Eleanor of Aquitaine attrib. The queen, a glamorous, as well as powerful, figure on the European stage, voices her exasperation, reported by William of Newburgh and others, after 15 years of childless marriage to Louis VII of France. The marriage was annulled. Barely eight weeks later, on 18 May 1152 and to Louis's fury, Eleanor married the young Henry Plantagenet, Duke of Normandy. Since Eleanor was Duchess of Aquitaine in her own right, this meant the transfer of direct control of almost half of France from Louis to his most powerful vassal.

3 Know that I have granted to my citizens of Winchester all the liberties which they had in the time of King Henry [I], my grandfather. And I order that they have and hold all their purchases and pledges and their tenements according to the custom of the city as freely, quietly and honourably as ever they did in the time of King Henry. And if other customs have unjustly grown up in the war, let them be suppressed.

Henry II, charter to the citizens of Winchester, summer 1155; David C. Douglas and George W. Greenaway (eds) *English Historical Documents* Vol.2 (1953) p.974. Having succeeded to the throne of England on the death of Stephen (see 221:5), the new king acts to restore order – explicitly returning to the position under Henry I.

4 When our courtiers had gone ahead almost the whole day's ride, the king would turn aside to some other place ... with accommodation for himself and no one else. I hardly dare say it, but I believe that in truth he took a delight in seeing what a fix he put us in. After wandering some three or four miles in an unknown wood, and often in the dark. we thought ourselves lucky if we stumbled upon some filthy hovel. There was often a sharp and bitter argument about a mere hut, and swords were drawn for possession of lodgings a pig would have shunned.

Peter of Blois to the archbishop of Palermo, Sicily, c.1177; J.P. Migne (ed.) *Patrologia Latina* (1844–64) Vol.207, Letter 14. The adult king was famous for his restless energy – and his lack of consideration.

5 We, therefore, supporting with due fervour your pious and praiseworthy desire, and granting our generous assent to your petition, are well pleased to agree that, for the extension of the boundaries of the Church, for the restraint of vice, for the correction of morals and for the implanting of virtues, and for the increase of the Christian religion, you may enter that island [Ireland] and perform therein the things that have regard to the honour of God and the salvation of that land.

Pope Adrian IV, *Laudabiliter* (bull), 155; W.L. Warren *Henry II* (1973) p.196. The pope sanctions the young Henry II's as yet unformed plans for the subjection of Ireland. Henry's securing of papal approval was precautionary; in practice he didn't move until 1171, when the success of freelance Anglo-Norman adventurers there necessitated his own intervention. Ironically for future Anglo-Irish relations, Adrian IV was the only English pope – Nicholas Breakspear, born at Langley, near St Albans.

6 One day [the king and Becket] were riding together through the streets of London. It was a hard winter and the king noticed an old man coming towards them, poor and clad in a thin and ragged coat. 'Do you see that man?' said the king. 'Yes, I see him,' replied the chancellor. 'How poor he is, how frail and how scantily clad!' said the king. 'Would it not be an act of charity to give him a thick, warm cloak?' 'It would indeed; and right that you should attend to it, my king.' ... Said the king to the chancellor, 'You shall have the credit for this act of charity,' and, laying hands on the chancellor's hood tried to pull off his cape, a new and very good one of scarlet and grey, which he was loth to part with.

William FitzStephen *Life of St Thomas* (c.1174); J.C. Robertson *Materials for the History of Thomas Becket* (1875–85) Vol.3, pp.24–5. Thomas Becket, a London merchant's son, so impressed Henry with his abilities that he appointed him chancellor in 1155. This famous anecdote, with its edgy, aggressive horseplay, tells us much about the character of both men and their intimate but destructive relationship. Becket was eventually forced to part with his cloak. 'The king then explained what had happened to his attendants. They all laughed loudly.'

1 'You are indeed my liege lord, but [God] is lord of both of us, and to ignore His will in order to obey yours would benefit neither you nor me … Submission should be made to temporal lords, but not against God, for as St Peter says, "We ought to obey God rather than men".' To this the king replied, 'I don't want a sermon from you: are you not the son of one of my villeins?' 'It is true,' said the archbishop, 'that I am not of royal lineage; but, then, neither was St Peter.'

Roger of Pontigny *Life of St Thomas* (c.1176); Robertson (1875–85) Vol.4, pp.27–9. In forcing Becket's appointment to the vacant archbishopric of Canterbury (he was invested on 3 June 1162), Henry sought greater influence over the English church. However, once archbishop, Becket went out of his way to challenge the king on a wide range of ecclesiastical and lay matters.

2 If a dispute shall arise between laymen, or between clerks [clerics] and laymen, or between clerks, concerning advowson [the right of patronage of ecclesiastical benefices] and presentation to churches, let it be dealt with and settled in the court of the lord king.

Constitutions of Clarendon, Jan. 1164; E.H.D. Vol.2 (1953) p.719. The first of the 16 articles of the Constitutions through which Henry attempted, by codifying the supposed customs governing the relations of church and state in the time of Henry I, to limit clerical and papal authority in England and to assert the power of the royal (lay) courts.

3 Know that Thomas who was archbishop of Canterbury has been judged publicly in my court by full counsel of the barons of my realm to be a wicked and perjured traitor to me … Help me to avenge my dishonour on my great enemy.

Henry II, proclamation against Becket, 1164; Robertson (1875–85) Vol.5, p.134. At the Council of Northampton (Oct. 1164) Henry attempted to dispossess Becket of his archbishopric on the grounds that he had proved himself a disobedient vassal. But Becket had already fled, remaining in exile abroad until 1170.

4 Will no one rid me of this turbulent priest?

Henry II, attrib. The traditional words of the exasperated king, away in Normandy in Dec. 1170, which precipitated Becket's

murder by four of the king's knights, three of whom had been vassals of Becket when he was chancellor. Eager to win the king's favour, they secretly left for England the same evening, and by the time the king realized what was happening it was too late to recall them.

5 The third knight inflicted a terrible wound as he lay prostrate, at which blow the sword struck the stone paving, and the crown of the head, which was large, was separated from the rest, so that the blood, whitened by the brains, and the brains, reddened with the blood, stained the floor of the cathedral with the white of the lily and the red of the rose, the colours of the Virgin Mother of the church and of the life and death of the confessor and martyr.

Edward Grim *Life of St Thomas* (1172); Robertson (1875–85) Vol.2, p.438. Becket died in Canterbury Cathedral on 29 Dec. 1170. Grim was present at the scene and was wounded in the arm when attempting to shield the archbishop.

6 Approaching Canterbury, he got down from his horse, and setting aside all royal insignia, with bare feet, and in the guise of a penitent and pilgrim, came to the cathedral … Meanwhile, the bishop of London was ordered by the king to make plain, in a sermon given to the populace, that he had not commanded, nor wanted, nor by any contrivance sought, the death of the martyr, which had been taken place because his murderers had misinterpreted the king's words, spoken in haste. For which reason he asked for absolution from the bishops present, and, having bared his back, received between three and five lashes from each of the many ecclesiastics who were gathered there.

Roger of Wendover *Flores Historiarum* (1230s; 1890 edn). Henry II does public penance at Becket's shrine on 12 July 1174. Becket had been canonized by Pope Alexander III the previous year.

7 Nowadays [late 12th century] when English and Normans live close together and marry and give in marriage to each other, the nations are so mixed that it can scarcely be decided (I mean in the case of the freemen) who is of English birth and who of Norman.

Richard FitzNigel, attrib., *Dialogus de Scaccario* (Dialogue of the Exchequer) (c.1178–9; 1950 trans.) p.53.

8 His pedigree was longer than his purse.

Gerald of Wales *The Conquest of Ireland* (after 1186) Bk 1, Ch.12, on Richard de Clare (Strongbow). Strongbow was the most famous of the Anglo-Normans who went to Ireland to make (or, in his case, mend) their fortunes. After Henry II confiscated his earldom of Pembroke, he joined up with the Irish king of Leinster in 1170, marrying his daughter. His rise spurred Henry's own Irish expedition in 1171. By a timely submission, Strongbow both secured his gains and retrieved his earldom.

1 Crossing the deep sea, he [Henry II] visited Ireland with a fleet [1171] and gloriously subdued it; Scotland also he vanquished, capturing its king, William [the Lion; 1174] … He remarkably extended the kingdom's limits and boundaries [until they reached] from the ocean on the south to the Orkney islands in the north. With his powerful grasp he included the whole island of Britain in one monarchy, even as it is enclosed by the sea.

Gerald of Wales *Liber de Prinicipis Instructione* (after 1216; 1861–91) p.156. Gerald, by no means an uncritical admirer, salutes Henry II's ascendancy. However, even Henry – the most active and assiduous of the Norman/Plantagenet kings in such interventions – was not aiming at military conquest of the outlying regions of Britain, but rather asserting an unprecedented overlordship of the entire British Isles.

2 Pious Queen, most illustrious queen, we all of us deplore, and are united in our sorrow, that you, a prudent wife if ever there was one, should have parted from your husband. Once separated from the head, the limb no longer serves it. Still more terrible is the fact that you should have made the fruits of your union with our Lord King rise up against their father. For we know that unless you return to your husband, you will be the cause of general ruin.

Rotrou, archbishop of Rouen, to Queen Eleanor, 1173; Alison Weir *Eleanor of Aquitaine* (1999) p.208. The marriage of Eleanor and Henry – from the outset a political partnership of two autocratic temperaments – produced eight children, but by 1173 the king and queen were estranged. Urged to return to her husband, Eleanor was amenable neither to persuasions nor threats of excommunication; instead, later this same year, she became involved in the revolt of her son, Henry the Young King, against his father, and was captured and then imprisoned for the rest of the reign.

3 From the Devil they came, and to the Devil they will return.

St Bernard of Clairvaux, attrib.; Gerald of Wales (after 1216; 1861–91 edn) p.309. The allusion is to the legendary descent of the counts of Anjou (hence Angevins) from a she-demon, Melusine – a tale of which, characteristically, the Plantagenets themselves were cheerfully proud. For St Bernard see 196:2.

4 Now your king, that is the king of England, lacks nothing, and possesses everything, men, horses, gold, silk, jewels, fruits, and wild beasts. And we in France have nothing except bread and wine and gaiety.

Louis VII, king of France; Map (1181–92; 1923 edn) p.249. Walter Map made a special note of this remark 'for it was merrily said, and truly'. The kings of France were indeed at a disadvantage beside other European rulers, given their often purely nominal control of their mighty vassals – and nowhere more so than in the vast swathe of French territories now in the hands of the English king. But Louis's son, Philip Augustus (who succeeded to the throne as Philip II in 1180) would change all that, and for good, adroitly playing the Angevins off against each other.

5 [Henry, the Young King] made chivalry live again, for she was dead, or nearly so. He was the door by which she entered. He was her standard bearer. In those days the great did nothing for young men. He set an example and kept men of worth by his side. And when men of high degree saw how he brought together all men of worth they were amazed at his wisdom and followed his lead.

Anon. *Guillaume le Maréchal* (History of William the Marshal) (after 1219; 1891–1901 edn) Vol.3, lines 37–8. The grace of Henry II's eldest surviving son had a natural appeal for William Marshal, himself a great chivalric exemplar (see 206:4), especially in comparison with the Young King's father, who was down-to-earth and unromantic. He was crowned in his father's lifetime (on the death in 1156 of his older brother William), hence the sobriquet, but died in revolt against him in 1183.

6 My other sons are the bastards; this one alone has shown himself my true and legitimate son.

Gerald of Wales; John P. Appleby *England without Richard 1189–99* (1965) p.8. Henry II on his illegitimate son Geoffrey, later archbishop of York, who alone of his sons remained loyal to him at the end.

7 Shame, shame on a conquered king.

Henry II; Gerald of Wales (after 1216; 1861–91 edn) p.296. Reputedly the last words of the old king, dying at Chinon in the Loire Valley on 6 July 1189, outmanoeuvred by his rebellious sons, his last days darkened by the news that John had joined Richard in league against him with Philip II, king of France.

RICHARD I, 1189–99

8 Richard Yea and Nay.

The troubadour Bertrand de Born (d.c.1202–12). Richard I's contemporary nickname – Coeur de Lion (Lionheart) was a posthumous accolade – reflected his reputation for self-confidence and decisiveness: as it were, 'Black and White'.

9 Henry was a shield but Richard was a hammer.

Gerald of Wales; Weir (1999) p.199, comparing Richard with his elder, and less forceful, brother, Henry, the Young King.

1 'You have three daughters,' [Fulk] said, 'and as long as they remain with you, you will never receive the grace of God. Their names are Superbia, Luxuria and Cupiditas.' For a while the king did not know what to answer. Then he replied: 'I have already given these daughters away in marriage. Pride I gave to the Templars, Lechery I gave to the Benedictines, and Covetousness to the Cistercians.'

Gerald of Wales *The Journey through Wales* (c.1188; 1978 trans.) Bk 1, Ch.3. Richard was nobody's fool. In turning the tables on the preacher, Fulk of Neuilly, he takes a swipe at the overmighty clerical institutions of the time.

2 I would have sold London itself if I could have found a buyer.

Richard I, attrib. Richard's notorious reflection on his campaign (1189) to fund his contribution to the Third Crusade (see 230:5). The king spent only some six months of his ten-year reign in England – partly because of the Third Crusade and his subsequent imprisonment in Germany, partly because it was the most stable of his vast dominions, and partly because, clearly, his sympathies and interests lay elsewhere. In his absence, the country was run by his delegates.

3   O Richard! O my king, the universe forsakes thee!
   On earth there is none but I who cares for thy welfare.

Blondel attrib. lament for the imprisoned Richard; Thomas Carlyle *The French Revolution* (1837) Pt 1, Bk 7, Ch.2. On his way home from the Third Crusade Richard I was captured by his fellow crusader, Leopold of Austria, and held to ransom by Leopold's lord, Emperor Henry VI. According to later tradition, the troubador Blondel was supposed to have discovered the king's whereabouts by singing his favourite song outside likely castles until eventually, at Durnstein on the Danube, he heard Richard joining in. Carlyle tells us that it was sung by Louis XVI and Marie-Antoinette at dinner at Versailles on 1 Oct. 1789 – four days before the royal couple were hauled back to Paris by the revolutionary mob.

4 Look to yourself, for the devil is loosed.

Philip II; Roger of Howden *Chronicle* (before 1202) in W.L. Warren *King John* (1961) p.45. The king of France warns Prince John, with whom he had been conspiring (each for his own advantage), that Richard has been released from his captivity and will soon be back.

5 Think no more of it, John; you are only a child who has had evil counsellors.

Richard I, May 1194; Roger of Howden (before 1202; 1868–89 edn) Vol.3, p.252. On Richard's return from crusade and prison (March 1194), Prince John, having nowhere to hide, threw himself on his brother's mercy at Lisieux in Normandy. Richard's response must have been a relief but hardly flattered the 27-year-old prince.

6 With wondrous art he [St Hugh of Lincoln] built the fabric of the cathedral; whereunto he supplied not only his own wealth, and the labours of his servants, but even the sweat of his own brow; for he oftentimes bore the hod-load of hewn stone or of binding lime. In this structure, the art equals the precious materials; for the vaults may be compared to a bird stretching out her broad wings to fly; planted on its firm columns it soars to the clouds.

Anon. *Metrical Life of St Hugh* (after 1220); C.G. Coulton *Social Life in Britain from the Conquest to the Reformation* (1918) p.472. St Hugh was bishop of Lincoln from 1186 to 1200, and his rebuilding would make the cathedral one of Europe's most splendid embodiments of the new 'Early English' Gothic style.

7   I can [know] noughte perfitly my pater-noster
      as the prest it syngeth,
   But I can rhymes of Robyn Hood.

William Langland *Piers Plowman* (c.1377), B-text, Passus 5, lines 400–3. This passage – spoken by Sloth, personifying Langland's idea of negligent churchmen – is the earliest surviving reference so far found to Robin Hood, the most enduring yet elusive of all Richard I's contemporaries.

JOHN, 1199–1216

8 And thus, within a short space of time, haughty Normandy and Anjou and the whole of Brittany and Maine, along with the Touraine [virtually all the north French territories held or dominated by King John], were subjected to the lordship of King Philip … From Duke William, who conquered the kingdom of the English, down to King John, who lost the duchy and many other lands across the sea in the fifth year of his reign, the kings of England had always been dukes of Normandy, holding the duchy and kingdom together for 139 years.

Ralph of Coggeshall *English Chronicle* (1187 onwards; 1875 edn) p.146. The fall of Rouen to the French under their king Philip II in June 1204 confirmed the loss of Normandy from the kings of England to the kings of France and the end of the Angevin empire, although the struggle went on, and Normandy, Anjou and Poitou were not formally and finally surrendered to the French king until the Treaty of Paris (1259), long after John's death.

9 Inspired by the Holy Spirit – not induced by force or compelled by fear, but of our own free and spontaneous will, and by the common counsel of our barons – we offer and freely yield to God, and His holy apostles Peter and Paul, and to the Holy Roman Church our mother, and to the lord Pope

Innocent and his catholic successors, the whole kingdom of England and the whole kingdom of Ireland, with all their rights and appurtenances, for the remission of our sins and the sins of our whole family, both living and dead; so that from henceforth we hold them from him and the Roman Church as a vassal.

King John, Charter, 15 May 1213; Warren (1961) p.208. Here, with his territories crumbling around him, John submits to the pope by making England and Ireland feudal fiefs of the apostolic see. His action secured his immediate aims of ending a papal interdict and his own excommunication (1209) and of prompting papal intervention on behalf of England in his ongoing struggle against the French king, Philip II.

1 In this year [1215] a great discord arose between the king of England and the barons … for in the time of his father and more especially in his own time [the free customs and liberties conceded by previous kings] had been corrupted and diminished. For some [barons] he had disinherited without judgement of their peers; some he had condemned to a cruel death; of others he had violated their wives and daughters; and so, instead of law, there was tyrannical will.

Anon. *The Waverley Annals*; *Annales Monastici* (1864–9 edn) Vol.2, p.282. The Great Charter or Magna Carta, originally so-called from its exceptional length and complexity, rather than its constitutional significance, was extorted from the reluctant king in the summer of 1215.

2 No freeman shall be arrested, or detained in prison, or disseised [deprived of his freehold], or outlawed, or exiled, or in any way molested, neither will we set forth against him or send against him, except by the lawful judgement of his peers and by the law of the land.

To no one will we sell, to no one will we deny or delay, right or justice.

Magna Carta, Clauses 39 and 40, 1215. There were 63 clauses in the final charter, covering a great variety of matters, from widows' rights to the clearing of fish traps, but it was on clauses such as these that the charter's future constitution, and symbolic, role would be built.

3 Wherefore we wish and firmly enjoin that the English church shall be free, and that the men in our kingdom shall have and hold all the aforesaid liberties, rights and concessions well and peacefully, freely and quietly, fully and completely for themselves and their heirs from us and our heirs, in all matters and in all places for ever, as is aforesaid. An oath, moreover, has been taken, as well on our part

as on the part of the barons, that all these things aforesaid shall be observed in good faith and without evil disposition. Given by our hand in the meadow which is called Runnymede between Windsor and Staines on the fifteenth day of June, in the seventeenth year of our reign.

Magna Carta, closing words, 1215. After John's death the charter was reissued in 1216, 1217 and 1225, the last version being consolidated into English statute law – the earliest statute on the English statute book.

4 He lost all his carts, wagons and sumpter horses, his treasure, his precious plate and everything he valued most, for the ground opened in the midst of the waters, and whirlpools sucked in everything, men and horses.

Roger of Wendover (1230s; 1886–9 edn) Vol.2, pp.195–6. King John, already ill with the dysentery that would kill him within the week, lost his baggage train and treasure, including the coronation regalia, when crossing the treacherous sands along the shore of the Wash on the east coast of England on 12 Oct. 1216.

5   This England never did, nor never shall,
Lie at the proud foot of a conqueror
But when it first did help to wound itself.
Now these her princes are come home again,
Come the three corners of the world in arms,
And we shall shock them. Naught shall make
      us rue
If England to itself do rest but true.

William Shakespeare *King John* (c.1598) Act 5, Sc.7. The closing words of the play, spoken after the death of John by Faulconbridge (supposedly the bastard son of Richard I), reveal its strong patriotic feeling. For the Elizabethans John is a champion of English unity against both the pope and the French.

HENRY III, 1216–72

6 The young prince's governor [carried] him in his arms. The child, who was well bred, greeted the Marshal and said to him, 'Sire, greetings. I entrust myself to God and to you. May God grant you look after us well.' The Marshal replied, 'Sire upon my soul, I shall neglect nothing to serve you faithfully so long as I have strength to do so.' All burst into tears, the Marshal like the rest … When it became known that the Marshal had charge of the king and the kingdom, there was universal rejoicing. 'God protect us,' people said, for there is no one in England who would be capable of acquitting himself as well of this charge.'

Anon. *Guillaume le Maréchal* (History of William the Marshal) (after 1219); Harry Rothwell (ed.) *English Historical Documents* Vol.3 (1975) pp.82, 84. Henry III was only nine at John's death (18 Oct. 1216). The country was in turmoil, with an invading French army loose on English soil. William Marshal, already almost 70 years old and the loyal servant of all the Angevin rulers in succession – no mean achievement, given their mutual antagonisms – became regent (see 206:4). Defeating the French at Lincoln, he negotiated their final departure in 1217. At his own death (14 May 1219) the country was at peace once more.

1 At this time the king daily, and not just slowly, lost the affection of his natural subjects. For like his father he openly attracted to his side whatever foreigners he could, and enriched them, introducing aliens and scorning and despoiling Englishmen.

Matthew Paris *Chronica Majora* (Greater Chronicle) (c.1235–59; 1872–83 edn) Vol.5, p.229. Henry III declared himself of age in 1227. With Normandy lost and a growing sense of Englishness among the baronage at home, the king was widely criticized for the favour he showed to 'aliens', particularly the relatives and hangers-on of his wife, Eleanor of Provence, whom he had married in 1236.

2 On the morrow [the king] summoned one after another into his private room, like a priest calling his penitents to confession. He tried to do with them singly what he could not do with them in the mass … He would say, 'See, this abbot has given me so much, and that so much,' and would hold out a roll on which the sums promised were written, although as a matter of fact no promises had been made. By this means he carefully caught many in his net.

Matthew Paris (c.1235–59; 1872–83) Vol.4, p.182. Henry's constant need for money and his unscrupulous ways of getting it – as here, in 1242, squeezing it out of monastic grandees – fomented the general resentment, fostering the baronial revolt under the king's brother-in-law, Simon de Montfort, which broke out in 1258.

3 In the beginning of May [1258], the barons appeared at court, in full armour … Henry [III] was startled by their warlike appearance. 'What is this, my lords? Am I taken captive by you?' Earl Roger Bigod spoke for all the barons and outlined their scheme: 'No, my lord king, no. But the intolerable Poitevins and all aliens should flee from your presence and ours … Swear total observance to our counsels … Swear, touching Holy Gospel, you and your son and heir Edward that you will not act without the advice of twenty-four good men of

England, namely, the elected bishops, earls and barons.'

Anon. *Annales Monastici: Tewkesbury* (1864–9 edn) Vol.1, p.164. Under baronial pressure, Henry agrees to the principle of a council and to convene Parliament in Oxford on 9 June 1258. The French-born Simon de Montfort, Earl of Leicester, was already a leading figure among the disaffected barons. (Poitevins are specifically men from Poitou in France, but is here a catch-all term for foreigners.)

4 When parliament opened [in Oxford], the proposal and unalterable intention of the magnates was adopted, most firmly demanding that the king should faithfully keep and observe the charter of liberties of England [i.e., Magna Carta], which his father, King John, had made and granted to the English and sworn to keep; and which he, King Henry the Third, had many times granted and sworn to keep … And they insisted that the king should frequently and regularly consult them, and conform to their counsel and necessary provisions.

Matthew Paris (c.1235–59); E.H.D. Vol.3 (1975) p.123. Henry and his son (later Edward I) reluctantly accepted – and, as soon as circumstances allowed, repudiated – the Provisions of Oxford, which established the new governing council (in fact of 15, rather than 24; see 242:3), which was required to meet at three specified times a year. Magna Carta is already assuming its symbolic role as the guarantor of the rule of law in England.

5 When the earl [Simon de Montfort knew of the king's arrival, he went joyfully and serenely to meet him, and, greeting him reverently, as was fitting, and, by way of comforting him, said, 'What is it you fear? The storm has now passed over.' To which the king replied, not jestingly but seriously and with a severe look, 'I fear thunder and lightning beyond measure; but, by God's head, I fear you more than all the thunder and lightning in the world.'

Matthew Paris (c.1235–59); E.H.D. Vol.3 (1975) p.299. In July 1258, a month after the Provisions of Oxford, Henry III, while dining on the Thames, was forced by a violent storm to seek refuge in the bishop of Durham's riverside palace, where de Montfort was staying.

6 Being aware of the desolation, destruction, and irreparable loss which threaten the whole land, so that it cannot be avoided in any way by any other, after God, except you alone, may it please you to take up this burden.

Baronial document, 1261, addressed to Louis IX of France; Margaret Wade Labarge *Simon de Montfort* (1962) p.196. St Louis (himself Henry III's brother-in-law) is invited to arbitrate in the increasingly bitter struggle between the English king and his recalcitrant magnates. Eventually, on

23 Jan. 1264 at Amiens in northern France, Louis gave judgement – against the Provisions of Oxford. Outright warfare ensued.

1 To what purpose does free law wish kings to be bound? That they may not be stained by an adulterine [false] law. And this constraining is not of slavery, but is the enlarging of kingly virtue … Let [the king] know that the people is not his own but God's … The commonalty comes first, law rules the royal dignity, for law is light and rules the world.

Anon. *The Song of Lewes*; F.M. Powicke *King Henry III and the Lord Edward* (1947; 1966 edn) p.471. The Battle of Lewes (14 May 1264) was a conclusive victory for De Montfort. Written shortly after the battle, perhaps by a Franciscan in the entourage of the bishop of Chichester, *The Song of Lewes* urges the restraint of royal power by law and its operation with consent. It asserts: 'The faith and fidelity of Simon alone is become the security of the peace of all England.'

2 All things were ordered by him [Simon de Montfort] … all the castles of the king were committed to his control. Now even the king himself, who was already in the fiftieth year of his reign, had nothing but the shadow of a name.

Roger of Wendover (d.1236)) *Flores Historiarum* (1890 edn) Vol.2, pp.504–5. With both Henry III and Prince Edward in his keeping, de Montfort became, *de facto*, ruler of England, and summoned the Parliament of 1265 on which his later constitutional reputation rests because of the exceptionally wide representation from the shires and towns. This was political expediency rather than principle, as he sought to neutralize a few key magnates; but the precedent was to hold.

3 Let us commend our souls to God, because our bodies are theirs [i.e., our enemies'].

Simon de Montfort at the Battle of Evesham, 4 Aug. 1265; William de Rishanger (13th century) *Chronicle of the Barons' War* (1840 edn) p.45. By the summer of 1265 Prince Edward had escaped and been able to mobilize growing opposition to de Montfort. Here, de Montfort refuses to flee as the battle turns against him. He was killed, with many of his supporters, and his body mutilated.

4 As regard the origins of the matter it seems to me, with due respect for wiser opinion, that a reform of the laws in England was essential. The king was misled by evil counsels when, as his father had done before another unhappy law [i.e., King John and the baronial unrest that resulted in Magna Carta], he presumed to annul the pact to which he was solemnly pledged with his subjects.

Anon. MS (MS 385, Corpus Christi College, Cambridge), late 13th century; Powicke (1947; 1966 edn) p.470. This view (probably from a Cistercian monk) suggests how events were

seen by much of the country. It was not a wasted struggle: despite the final royalist victory, important precedents had been set and lessons learned. Edward I (a far shrewder and tougher man than his father) would rule by law.

5   Further along, the centaur checked his pace
     Beside a second gang, who seemed to start
     Far as the throat from the stream's boiling race.
     He showed one shade, set by itself apart,
     Saying 'There stands the man who dared to smite,
     Even in the very bosom of God, the heart
     They venerate still on Thames.'

Dante Alighieri *Divine Comedy* 'Inferno' (c.1308–21; 1949 trans.) Canto 12, lines 115–21. There was a bitter postscript. On 13 March 1271 Prince Henry of Cornwall, the king's nephew, was murdered at mass in San Silvestro, Viterbo, north of Rome, by de Montfort's sons, Guy and Simon, to avenge their father's death at the Battle of Evesham and the desecration of his body. The blasphemy shocked Europe. Guy, the main perpetrator, achieved literary immortality for his action as a damned soul in the Seventh Circle of Hell. Ironically, Prince Henry, Prince Edward (the victor at Evesham) and the two de Montforts were all first cousins.

EDWARD I (1272–1307) AND EDWARD II (1307–27)

6 They say, however, that at that time his wife, a Spaniard and the sister of the king of Castile, showed her husband great faithfulness; for with her tongue she licked his open wounds all the day, and sucked out the humour, and thus by her virtue drew out all the poisonous material; whereby, when the scars of his wound were formed, he felt himself fully cured.

Bartolomeo Fiadoni *Historia Ecclesiatica* (1320s); John Carmi Parsons *Eleanor of Castile* (1995) p.30. After the tensions of the de Montfort period Prince Edward went on crusade to the Holy Land (1270–72), with his wife, Eleanor of Castile (the daughter of Ferdinand III, king of Castile). An attempt was made on his life at Acre (17 June 1272) with a poisoned dagger (see 235:5). Eleanor's celebrated intervention first appears – explicitly as 'they say' – some 50 years later in the work of this Italian Dominican. On their way home Edward learned of the death of his father, Henry III (16 Nov. 1272).

7 The best lance in the world.

Anon. troubadour about Edward I, 1272; Powicke (1947; 1966 edn) p.688. Edward was a man of action, a formidable exponent of knightly skills, whose pleasures when not fighting were hawking and hunting.

8 It is likewise commanded that the highways from market towns to other market towns be widened where there are woods or hedges or ditches, so that there may be no ditch, underwood or bushes where one could hide with evil intent within two hundred feet of the road on one side or the other, provided that this statute extends not to oaks or to large trees so long as it is clear underneath. And if by the default of a lord, who will not fill up a ditch or level underwood or bushes in the manner aforesaid, robberies are committed, the lord shall be answerable.

Statutes of Winchester, clause, 1285; E.H.D. Vol.3 (1975) p.461. The massive Statutes of Westminster (beginning in 1275) were inaugurated immediately after his coronation by Edward I's first London Parliament, and they covered a vast range of practical matters. The king's aim was to bring clarity, efficiency and system to the existing law, not the imposition of revolutionary new principles. On them is largely founded his later reputation as 'the English Justinian'.

1 Divine providence, which is unerring in its dispositions, among other gifts of its dispensation with which it has deigned to honour us and our kingdom of England has now, of its grace, wholly and entirely converted the land of Wales, previously subject to us by feudal right with its inhabitants, into a dominion of our ownership, every obstacle being overcome, and has annexed and united it to the crown of the said kingdom as a constituent part of it.

Statute of Wales, Preamble, 1284; E.H.D. Vol.3 (1975) p.422. In two campaigns (1276–7 and 1282–3) Edward I achieved mastery over Wales. In this landmark statute, issued at Rhuddlan in North Wales on 12 March 1284, the king makes clear that his previous overlordship of Wales has now become direct rule. His parallel campaigns in Scotland (see 245:5–247:8) would not have such permanent results.

2 Here is a prince who will be acceptable to you, since he was born in Wales and speaks no English.

Edward I, attrib. On 25 April 1284 Eleanor of Castile gave birth, in Caernarvon, to the future Edward II. The king is traditionally said (since at least the time of John Stow in the 1580s) to have presented the baby to the Welsh leaders with some variant of the above quip.

3 In case you should wonder where so much money could go in a week, we would have you know that we have needed – and shall continue to need – 400 masons, both cutters and layers, together with 2,000 minor workmen, 100 carts, 60 waggons, and 30 boats bringing stone and sea-coal; 200 quarrymen; 30 smiths; and carpenters for putting in the joists and floorboards and other necessary jobs. All this takes no account of the garrison mentioned above,

nor of purchases of materials, of which there will have to be a great quantity.

Report to Edward I, 27 Feb. 1296; A.J Taylor *The King's Works in Wales 1277–1330* (1974) p.399. A key aspect of Edwardian government in Wales was the construction of a ring of royal castles, many associated with the foundation of new towns. Here, James of St George (Edward's Master Mason, a Savoyard) gives a progress report on the new castle at Beaumaris (Anglesey, north Wales), which was started the previous year. Anticipating the short-tempered king's tetchiness over the cost, he gives an insight into the sheer scale of such an operation – itself only one of many going ahead at the time.

4 And the request was repeated and the Earl Marshal asked to go, and he said, 'With you I will gladly go, O king, in front of you in the first line of battle as belongs to me by hereditary right.' And the king replied, 'You will go without me, too, with the others.' But he, 'I am not bound, neither is it my will, O king, to march without you.' Enraged, the king burst out, 'By God, O Earl, you will either go or hang.' And he, 'By the same oath, O king, I will neither go nor hang.' And, without leave, he went away.

William of Guisborough *Chronicle* (covering 1296/7); E.H.D. Vol.3 (1975) p.226. This tense scene (triggered when Edward required 'certain of the magnates to cross over to Gascony' to fight for him while he himself was in Flanders) brings home the limitations of royal power: the Earl Marshal's obligations to the king were personal, not professional; he would go with him but had no intention of going instead of him.

5 We send you a big trotting palfrey which can hardly carry its own weight, and some of our bandy-legged terriers from Wales, which can well catch a hare if they find it asleep, and some of our running dogs, which go at a gentle pace; for we well know that you take delight in lazy dogs. And, dear cousin, if you want anything from our land of Wales, we can send you plenty of wild men if you like, who will know well how to teach breeding to young heirs or heiresses of great lords.

The future Edward II to Louis of Evreux, 1305; Michael Prestwich *Edward I* (1988), p. 227. The young Prince Edward (created Prince of Wales in 1301) was very different from his formidable father, as this engagingly frivolous letter suggests.

6 You baseborn whoreson, do you want to give away lands now, you who never gained any? As the Lord lives, if it were not for fear of breaking up the kingdom you should never enjoy your inheritance.

Edward I to his son, the future Edward II; William of Guisborough in Harold F. Hutchinson *Edward II* (1971) p.49. The ageing king turns on the Prince of Wales when the infatuated prince sought the earldom of Cornwall for his Gascon favourite, Piers Gaveston. Gaveston was promptly banished (26 Feb. 1307). Within five months the king was dead and Gaveston was back.

1 [Gaveston] himself, confident that he had been confirmed for life in his earldom, albeit he was an alien and had been preferred to so great dignity solely by the king's favour, had now grown so insolent as to despise all the nobles of the land; among whom he called the Earl of Warwick (a man of equal wisdom and integrity) 'the Black Dog of Arden'. When this was reported to the earl, he is said to have replied with calmness: 'If he call me a dog, be sure that I will bite him, so soon as I shall perceive my opportunity.'

Anon. *The Chronicle of Lanercost 1272–1346* (1913 trans.). The chronicler was a Franciscan in the (English) Augustinian priory of Lanercost on the Anglo-Scottish borderland. Edward II was soon at odds with his barons, not least over Gaveston. In 1312 Warwick (Guy de Beauchamp) was as good as his word, seizing Gaveston from a safe conduct that had been agreed by his fellow lords and precipitating his execution (on 19 June 1312) for treason. In many respects this can be seen as the start of the long tit-for-tat cycle of aristocratic carnage that would climax in the Wars of the Roses.

2 We have seen, by your letters lately written to us, that you well remember the charges we enjoined you on your departure from Dover, and you have not transgressed our commands in any point that was in your power to avoid. But to us it appears that you have not humbly obeyed our commands as a good son ought his father, since you have not returned to us, to be under our government ... but have notoriously held companionship, and your mother also, with Mortimer, your traitor and mortal enemy ... for truly he is neither a meet companion for your mother nor for you, and we hold that much evil to the country will come of it.

Edward II to Prince Edward (later Edward III), March 1326; *The Letters of the Kings of England* Vol.1, p.35. By 1326 Edward's French queen, Isabella, had retreated to France with her lover, Roger Mortimer. They now had control of the 12-year-old prince (sent by Edward to do homage to the king of France for Edward's French territories), in whose name the pair invaded England in Sept. the same year. There was little support for the unpopular and discredited king: on 16 Nov. he was captured by his pursuers.

3 There [in Westminster Hall on 13 Jan. 1327], by the common consent of all, it was solemnly declared by the archbishop of Canterbury how the good king Edward [I] when he died had left the lands of England, Ireland, Wales, Gascony and Scotland

quite at peace, and how the son had as good as lost the lands of Gascony and Scotland through bad counsel and bad custody, and how likewise through bad counsel he had caused to be slain a great part of the noble blood of the land, to the dishonour and loss of himself, his realm and the whole people, and had done many other astonishing things. Therefore it was agreed by absolutely all the aforesaid that he ought no longer to reign but that his eldest son, the duke of Guyenne [Edward III] should reign and wear the crown in his stead.

The Pipewell Chronicle; E.H.D. Vol.3 (1975) p.287. The Westminster Parliament of early Jan. 1327, summoned in the king's name by Isabella and Mortimer, effectively deposes Edward II in his absence.

4 Edward sometime king was brought from Kenilworth to the castle of Berkeley, where he was slain with a hot spit put thro the secret place posterial. Wherefore many people say that he died a martyr and did many miracles; nevertheless being kept in prison, vile suffering and an opprobrious death cause not a martyr, but [only] if the holiness of the life before be correspondent ... But women longing to go on pilgrimage increase much the rumour of such veneration.

Ranulf Higden *Polychronicon* (1340s; c.1387 trans. by John of Trevisa) (1982 edn) p.313. Edward II's final humiliation is to be best remembered for his (supposedly) lurid end in Berkeley Castle, Gloucestershire, with the connivance of Mortimer, and, almost certainly, the knowledge of Isabella. His death was announced on 21 Sept. 1327; but the method of execution is speculation, although the rumours started early. A miracle-working cult promptly grew up around the murdered king's tomb in Gloucester Cathedral – indeed, proceeds from pilgrims were sufficient to pay for remodelling the cathedral's south transept (1331–7), the first major building in the new 'Perpendicular' Gothic style.

THE SCOTTISH WARS OF INDEPENDENCE, 1286–1388

5 He [John Balliol] came to our parliaments at our command, and was present in them as our subject, like others of our realm.

Edward I; Davies (1990) p.124. The unexpected death in 1286 of Alexander III, king of Scotland, inaugurated 40 years of struggle for independence. There were 13 contestants (known as 'the Competitors') with a feasible claim to the Scottish throne, and they agreed to accept the arbitration of Edward I, who decided in favour of John Balliol, who was duly crowned (Nov. 1292). Edward, however, treated him thereafter as 'a subject, like others of our realm', clearly intending Scotland to submit to his overlordship. The Scots were soon in revolt.

1   Ah, freedom is a noble thing
        Freedom makes man to have liking [his
            pleasure, his will].
        Freedom all solace to man gives,
        He lives at ease that freely lives.

John Barbour *The Bruce* (1370s) Bk 1, lines 225–37. Barbour reflects on the downside of Scottish thraldom under Edward I. The archdeacon of Aberdeen wrote his vast biographical epic, the first substantial work of literature in Scots, around the twin figures of Robert Bruce and his companion-in-arms James Douglas.

2 He was a tall man with the body of a giant, cheerful in appearance with agreeable features ... but with a wild look ... a most spirited fighting man, with all his limbs very strong and firm. He was most liberal in all his gifts, very fair in his judgements, most compassionate in comforting the sad, a most skilful counsellor, very patient when suffering, a distinguished speaker, who above all hunted down falsehood and deceit and hated treachery.

Walter Bower *Scotichronicon* (1440s) Vol.6 (1991 edn) p.83. Given his significance, both to his own time and to posterity, William Wallace, a younger son of a minor landowning family, remains a frustratingly shadowy figure, and this vivid description is not, alas, contemporary though it may embody valid traditions.

3 William Wallace, knight, Guardian of the kingdom of Scotland and commander of its armies, in the name of the famous prince the Lord John, by God's grace illustrious king of Scotland, by consent of the community of that realm.

William Wallace, May 1297; formal style on one of the four recorded writs and charters issued in his own name or in association with his ally, Andrew Murray. They show that Wallace, in his brief period of ascendancy, saw himself as acting for the absent king – John Balliol was now a prisoner of Edward I in the Tower of London – and with the authority of the nation at large. Even the English at his trial did not accuse him of aiming at a personal dictatorship.

4 In the same year [1297], the Scots rose against the king of England, having as leader of their army William Wallace who had previously been outlawed and was supported secretly by the magnates of Scotland ... But when the English crossed the bridge of Stirling on the Wednesday next before the feast of the Exaltation of the Holy Cross, before the English were drawn up for battle, the Scots, with their line of battle drawn up ready, fell upon the English.

Bartholomew Cotton *English History*; E.H.D. Vol.3 (1975) p.218. At the Battle of Stirling Bridge (11 Sept. 1297) the rebel Scots, led by Wallace and Andrew Murray, defeated a larger English force. Murray later died of wounds received there.

5 I have brought you to the ring, hop [dance] if you can.

William Wallace, July 1298, addressing his soldiers before the Battle of Falkirk; Lord Hailes *Annals of Scotland* Vol.1 (1776; 1816 edn) p.315.

6   The vilest doom is fittest for thy crimes
        Justice demands that thou shouldst die three times
        Thou pillager of many a sacred shrine
        Butcher of thousands, threefold death be thine!
        So shall the English from thee gain relief,
        Scotland! be wise, and choose a nobler chief.

Anon. *The Chronicle of Lanercost 1272–1346* (1913 trans.); Graeme Morton *William Wallace: Man and Myth* (2001) p.27. Wallace was eventually betrayed to the English in 1305 and tried, and then hanged, drawn and quartered at Smithfield, London. Sir John de Segrave, who had brought Wallace in chains to London, took back his dismembered corpse to Scotland and northern England for public display. Perth, Stirling, Berwick and Newcastle each received a quarter; Segrave got 15 shillings; and Wallace's head was set on London Bridge.

7   Now are the islanders all joined together,
        And Albany [Scotland] united to the regalities
        Of which King Edward is proclaimed lord.
        Cornwall and Wales are in his power
        And Ireland the great at his will.
        There is neither king nor prince of all the
            countries
        Except King Edward, who has thus united them.

Peter Langtoft (d.c.1307) *The Chronicle of Peter Langtoft*; T. Wright (ed.) *Rolls Series, 1866–8* Vol.2, pp.264–7. In 1305 Edward I's triumph seemed complete – English royal power was dominant across the British Isles, and to contemporaries a single kingship seemed imminent. But it was not to be.

8 'I doubt I've slain the Red Comyn.' 'Doubt ye? I'll mak siccar [sure].'

Trad. words of Robert Bruce and his associate Roger Kirkpatrick, 10 Feb. 1306, spoken during Bruce's attack on his rival for the Scottish throne, John Comyn (the 'Red Comyn', a nephew of John Balliol), in Greyfriars Church, Dumfries. Six weeks later Bruce had himself crowned king of Scotland at Scone.

9   He misdid [sinned] there greatly for sure
        That gave no respect to the altar.
        Therefore such hard mischief him fell [befell]
        That I heard never a romance tell
        Of a man so hard fraught [beset] as was he
        That after came to such bounty.

John Barbour (1370s) Bk 2, lines 43–8 (slightly modernized).
The murder, in church, by Bruce of the Red Comyn has
presented a problem to posterity in affirming Scotland's
national hero. Barbour here rather neatly both confronts and
sidesteps the issue.

1 I hear that Bruce never had the good will of his
own followers or of the people generally so much
with him as now. It appears God is with him, for he
has destroyed King Edward [I]'s power both among
English and Scots … [Bruce] will find the people all
ready at his will more entirely than ever, unless King
Edward can send more troops; for there are many
people living loyally in his peace so long as the
English are in power. May it please God to prolong
King Edward's life, for men say openly that when he
is gone the victory will go to Bruce.

Alexander Abernethy, attrib., letter, 15 May 1307;
G.W.S. Barrow *Robert Bruce* (1976 edn) p.245. One of the
Scottish lords on the English side registers the growing
impetus of Bruce's campaign in Scotland and the fragility of the
English administration. Edward I died on 7 July, leaving a host
of problems on both sides of the border for his unlucky
successor, Edward II.

2 *Edvardus Primus Scotorum malleus hic est, 1308.
Pactum Serva.*

Edward I was buried at Westminster Abbey on 27 Oct. The
famous inscription on his tomb – 'This is Edward I, the
Hammer of the Scots. Keep your troth' – is thought to be a
later addition, probably of the 17th century.

3 In all this fighting the Scots were so divided that
often a father was with the Scots and his son with the
English, or one brother was with the Scots and
another with the English, or even one individual was
first on one side and then on the other. But all this
or most of those Scots who were with the English
were with them insincerely or to save their lands in
England; for their hearts if not their bodies were
always with their home people.

Anon. *The Chronicle of Lanercost 1272–1346*; Barrow (1976
edn) p.271. The chronicler shows the tensions for the southern Scottish population in 1311–12 as, under Edward II, English
domination began to unravel and Bruce's strength increased.

4 For eight years or more I have struggled with
much labour for my right to the kingdom and for
honourable liberty. I have lost brothers, friends and
kinsmen. Your own kinsmen have been made
captive, and bishops and priests are locked in prison.
Our country's nobility has poured forth its blood in
war. Those barons you see before you, clad in mail,
are bent upon destroying me and obliterating my

kingdom, nay our whole nation … For us, the name
of the Lord must our hope of victory in battle.

Robert Bruce, 23/24 June 1314, addressing his followers
before the Battle of Bannockburn; Bower (1440s) Bk 2,
pp.249–50. The battle was a disaster for the English forces
under Edward II.

5   And Bannockburn between the braes [banks]
       With men and horse so charged was
       That upon drowned horse and men
       Men might pass dry across it then.

John Barbour (1370s) Bk 13, lines 337–40. There was a
massive slaughter. Bruce, King Robert I of Scotland, was at last
to be master of his kingdom. The Scots had reason to exult.

6 To him [Bruce], as the man through whom
salvation has been wrought in our people, we are
bound both by right and as what he deserves for
preserving our freedom, and to him we will in all
things adhere … For, as long as a hundred men are
left, we will never submit in the slightest to the
dominion of the English. It is not for glory, riches or
honour we fight, but only for liberty, which no good
man loses but with his life.

Declaration of Arbroath, 6 April 1320; E.H.D. Vol.3
(1975) p.541. The epoch-marking letter was addressed to
Pope John XXII.

7 We will and concede for us and all our heirs and
successors, by the common counsel, assent and
consent of the prelates, magnates, earls and barons
and communities of our realm in our parliament
that the kingdom of Scotland shall remain forever
separate in all respects from the kingdom of
England, in its entirety, free and in peace, without
any kind of subjection.

Edward III, Feb. 1328, recognizing the independence of
Scotland; Barrow (1976 edn) p.363.

8 I therefore had my information from both sides,
and they agreed that this battle [of Otterburn, 1388]
was as stubborn and hard fought as any battle in
history. This I easily believe, for both English and
Scots are excellent fighters, and they do not spare
each other when they meet. As long as they have
lances, axes, swords or daggers, and the breath to
wield them, they fight on.

Jean Froissart *Chronicles* (from 1373; 1967 edn) Bk 3.126.
Bannockburn was a turning point but not a terminus: the
Anglo-Scottish wars went on, degenerating into endemic
border raiding, and living on today in the Border Ballads of
which this, the Battle of Otterburn (5 Aug. 1388) in
Northumberland, gave rise to two of the greatest, *The Battle
of Otterbourne* and *The Ballad of Chevy Chase*.

The Mongols, 1200–1500

VIEWS OF THE MONGOLS

1 The Mongol empire of the 13th and 14th centuries was the largest continuous land empire that has so far existed. At its greatest extent it stretched from Korea to Hungary, including, except for India and the southeast of the continent, most of Asia, as well as a good deal of eastern Europe. As a whole it lasted for well over a century, and parts of it survived for very much longer. It was merely one, albeit by far the most extensive, of a series of great steppe empires; and it should be seen in the context provided by its predecessors. The major difference between the Mongols and previous conquerors is that no other nomad empire had succeeded in holding both the Inner Asian steppe and the neighbouring sedentary lands simultaneously.
David Morgan *The Mongols* (1986) p.5.

2 The home of the Tatars [Mongols], and their origin and birthplace, is an immense valley, whose area is a journey of seven or eight months both in length and breadth. In the east it marches with the land of the Khitai [Cathay, northern China] in the west with the country of the Uighur [Xinjiang, northern China], in the north with the Qirqiz [Kirghiz Turks, in the upper reaches of the Yenisei River, Siberia] and the River Selengei [Mongolia] and in the south with the Tangut [of northwest China] and the Tibetans.
Ala-ad-Din Juvaini *Ghenghis Khan: The History of the World Conqueror* (c.1260; 1997 edn) pp.21–2. Juvaini was a Persian who spent years in the service of the Mongols. He was the Mongol governor of Baghdad and Iraq and travelled twice to Mongolia.

3 In appearance the Tatars [Mongols] are quite different from all other men, for they are broader than other people between the eyes and across the cheekbones. Their cheeks also are rather prominent above their jaws; they have a flat and small nose, their eyes are little and their eyelids raised up to the eyebrows. For the most part, but with a few exceptions, they are slender about the waist; almost all are of medium height.
John of Plano Carpini *History of the Mongols* (c.1246–7); Christopher Dawson (ed.) *The Mongol Mission* (1955) p.6. Carpini was a Western monk who, after the Mongol invasions

of Europe in 1241–2, travelled to the court of the Great Khan with messages from the pope.

4 The men shave a square on the top of their heads and from the front corners of this they continue the shaving in strips along the sides of the head as far as the temples. They also shave their temples and neck … and their forehead in front to the top of the frontal bone, where they leave a tuft of hair which hangs down as far as the eyebrows. At the sides and the back of the head they leave the hair, which they make into plaits, and these they braid round the head to the ears.
William of Rubruck *Journey to the Far Eastern Parts of the World* (1253–5); Dawson (1955) pp.101–2. Carpini and other missionaries had told of the Nestorian Christians at the Mongol court. The Nestorians were followers of a 5th-century patriarch of Constantinople, whose doctrines were condemned as heretical by Pope Celestine I in 430. These missionaries' accounts inspired William of Rubruck, a devout Flemish monk in the service of Louis IX of France, to embark on his own unofficial mission to the Mongol court. His purpose was to preach the gospel, carrying with him only a letter of introduction from the French king (see 170:2), who was reluctant to provide more support lest the Mongol khan should think Louis had submitted to him.

5 The costume of the girls is no different from that of the men except that it is somewhat longer. But on the day after she is married a woman shaves from the middle of her head to her forehead, and she has a tunic as wide as a nun's cowl, and in every respect wider and longer, and open in front, and this they tie on the right side.
William of Rubruck (1253–5); Dawson (1955) p.102.

6 After leaving Soldaia [in the Crimea] we came across the Tatars; and when I came among them it seemed indeed to me as if I were stepping into some other world.
William of Rubruck (1253–5); Dawson (1955) p.93. When Rubruck reached the steppe near the River Don the solitude seemed to him to resemble a great sea.

LIFE ON THE STEPPE

7 In some parts the country is extremely mountainous, in others it is flat, but practically the whole of it is composed of very sandy gravel. In some districts there are small woods, but otherwise it is completely bare of trees … Not one hundredth part of the land is fertile, nor can it bear fruit unless it be irrigated by running water, and brooks and streams are few there, and rivers very rare. And so there are no towns or cities there with the exception of one which is said to be quite big and is called Karakorum.

John of Plano Carpini (c.1246–7); Dawson (1955) p.5.

1 As for the city of Karakorum I can tell you that, not counting the Khan's palace, it is not as large as the village of Saint-Denis, and the monastery of Saint-Denis is worth ten times more than that palace. There are two districts there: the Saracens' quarter where the markets are, and many merchants flock thither on account of the court which is always near it and on account of the number of envoys. The other district is that of the Cathayans who are all craftsmen. Apart from these districts there are the large palaces of the court scribes. There are twelve pagan temples belonging to the different nations, two mosques in which the law of Muhammad is proclaimed, and one church for the Christians at the far end of the town. The town is surrounded by a mud wall and has four gates.

William of Rubruck (1253–5); Dawson (1955) p.183. Genghis Khan chose the site for his capital in the mountainous region of northern Mongolia near the Orkhon River. The site was probably Karakorum, or somewhere near it. Genghis Khan's son, Ogedei (r.1229–41), made Karakorum his capital when he surrounded it with a defensive wall. Rubruck, visiting in 1254, met the Great Khan Mongke (r.1251–9), Ogedei's nephew, who also made it his capital. Kara-kum means 'black sand'. Nothing of that city remains today; the Chinese destroyed it in 1388. For Saint-Denis see 196:1.

2 In the winter they always make at least two fur garments, one with the fur against the body, the other with the fur outside to the wind and snow, and these are usually of the skins of wolves or foxes or monkeys, and when they are sitting in their dwelling they have another softer one. The poor make their outer ones of dog and goat.

They also make trousers out of skins. Moreover the rich line their garments with silk stuffing which is extraordinarily soft and light and warm. The poor line their clothes with cotton material and with the softer wool which they are able to pick out from the coarser. With the coarse they make felt to cover their dwellings and coffers and also for making bedding. Also with wool mixed with a third part of horse-hair they make their ropes. From felt they make saddle pads, saddle cloths and rain cloaks, which means they use a great deal of wool.

William of Rubruck (1253–5); Dawson (1955) p.101. The friar came from Flanders, the heart of the European trade, and hence his eye for wool.

3 The Tatars never remain fixed, but as the winter approaches remove to the plains of a warmer region, in order to find sufficient pasture for their cattle; and in summer they frequent cold situations in the mountains, where there is water and verdure, and their cattle are free from the annoyance of horse-flies and other biting insects. During two or three months they progressively ascend higher ground, and seek fresh pasture, the grass not being adequate in any one place to feed the multitudes of which their herds and flocks consist.

Marco Polo *The Travels of Marco Polo* (1298; 1908 edn) p.123. Marco Polo spent 20 years at the court of Kublai Khan, returning to Venice in 1295. He saw far more of the Mongol empire than previous travellers, but it is for his authoritative and vivid account of the Mongols' period in China that his evidence is most valuable (see 255:6).

4 Their huts or tents are formed of rods covered with felt, and being exactly round, and nicely put together, they can gather them into one bundle, and make them up as packages, which they carry along with them in their migrations, upon a sort of car with four wheels. When they have occasion to set them up again, they always make the entrance front to the south.

Marco Polo (1298; 1908 edn) pp.123–4.

5 They subsist entirely upon flesh and milk, eating the produce of their sport, and … eat flesh of every description, horses, camels, and even dogs, provided they are fat. They drink mares' milk, which they prepare in such a manner that it has the qualities and flavour of white wine. They term it in their language *kumis*.

Marco Polo (1298; 1908 edn) p.125.

6 We saw a vast town on the move with all its inhabitants, containing mosques and bazaars, the smoke from the kitchens rising in the air (for they cook while on the march) and horse-drawn wagons transporting them. On reaching the encampment, they took the tents off the wagons and set them upon the ground, for they were very light, and they did the same with the mosques and shops.

Ibn Battuta (1304–68) *The Travels of Ibn Battuta* (1929 trans.) p.147. In 1334 Ibn Battuta, a Muslim merchant from Tangier,

North Africa, and inveterate traveller (see 98:5 and 142:5), was in the northern approaches to the Caucasus in the land of the Golden Horde, the western khanate of the Mongol empire ruled by Batu Khan, Genghis Khan's grandson (see 170:3 and 252:3).

1 Each man has as many wives as he can keep, one a hundred, another fifty, another ten ... It is the general custom for them to marry any of their relations, with the exception of their mother, daughter and sister by the same mother ... a younger brother may marry his brother's wife after his death; or another younger relation is expected to take her. All other women they take as wives without any distinction and they buy them at a very high price from their parents.
John of Plano Carpini (c.1246–7); Dawson (1955) p.7.

2 The men do not make anything at all, with the exception of arrows, and they also sometimes tend the flocks, but they hunt and practise archery, for they are all, big and little, excellent archers, and their children begin as soon as they are two or three years old to ride and manage horses and to gallop on them ...

Young girls and women ride and gallop on horseback with agility like the men. We even saw them carrying bows and arrows. Both the men and the women are able to endure long stretches of riding. They have very short stirrups; they look after their horses very well, indeed they take the very greatest care of all their possessions. Their women make everything, leather garments, tunics, shoes, leggings and everything made of leather; they also drive the carts and repair them, they load the camels, and in all their tasks they are very swift and energetic. All the women wear breeches and shoot like the men.
John of Plano Carpini (c.1246–7); Dawson (1955) p.18.

3 These men, that is to say the Tatars, are more obedient to their masters than any other men in the world, be they religious or seculars ... Fights, brawls, wounding, murder are never met with among them. Nor are robbers and thieves who steal on a large scale found there; consequently their dwellings and the carts in which they keep their valuables are not secured by bolts and bars.

They show considerable respect to each other and are very friendly together, and they willingly share their food with each other, although there is little enough of it. They are also long-suffering ... On

horseback they endure great cold and they also put up with excessive heat.
John of Plano Carpini (c.1246–7); Dawson (1955) p.15.

4 They are most arrogant to other people and look down on all, indeed they consider them as nought, be they of high rank or low born ... They are quickly roused to anger with other people and are of an impatient nature; they also tell lies to others and practically no truth is to be found in them. At first indeed they are smooth-tongued, but in the end they sting like a scorpion ... They consider the slaughter of other people as nothing.
John of Plano Carpini (c.1246–7); Dawson (1955) p.16.

5 They pay great attention to divinations, auguries, soothsayings, sorceries and incantations, and when they receive an answer from the demons they believe that a god is speaking to them. This god they call Itoga ... and they have a wondrous fear and reverence for him and offer him many oblations and the first portion of their food and drink, and they do everything according to the answers he gives. When the moon is new, or at full moon, they embark on anything fresh they wish to do, and so they call the moon the great Emperor and bend the knee and pray to it ... They also say that the sun is the mother of the moon because it receives its light from the sun. They believe, to put it shortly, that everything is purified by fire.
John of Plano Carpini (c.1246–7); Dawson (1955) p.12.

GENGHIS KHAN, c.1162–1227

6 Before the appearance of Genghis Khan they had no chief or ruler. Each tribe or two tribes lived separately; they were not united with one another, and there was constant fighting and hostility between them. Some of them regarded robbery and violence, immorality and debauchery as deeds of manliness and excellence ...

And they continued in this indigence, privation and misfortune until the banner of Genghis Khan's fortune was raised and they issued forth from the straits of hardship into the amplitude of well-being.
Ala-ad-Din Juvaini (c.1260; 1997 edn) pp.21–2. By 1206 Temuchin had conquered and unified the Mongolian tribes. He was acclaimed Great Khan at a ceremony in 1206 and given the title Genghis Khan.

1 The sentry who is inattentive will be killed.

The arrow-messenger who gets drunk will be killed.

Anyone who harbours a fugitive will be killed.

The warrior who unlawfully appropriates booty for himself will be killed.

The leader who is incompetent will be killed.

Laws, late 12th and early 13th centuries; Michael Hoang *Genghis Khan* (1988; 1990 trans.) p.153. Dictated to Uighur scribes, the original manuscripts for these laws are lost but have been reconstructed later by others. Although he could neither read nor write, Genghis Khan realized that if the tribes were to remain united new laws were needed that had to be written down so that all the conquered tribes could understand them. Custom governed life on the steppe and formed the basis for his laws.

2 In accordance and agreement with his own mind he established a rule for every occasion and a regulation for every circumstance; while for every crime he fixed a penalty. And since the Tatar peoples had no script of their own, he gave orders that Mongol children should learn writing from the Uighur; and these yasas and ordinances should be written down on rolls. These rolls are called the *Great Book of Yasas* and are kept in the treasury of the chief princes. Wherever a khan ascends the throne, or a great army is mobilized, ... they produce these rolls and model their actions thereon; and proceed with the disposition of armies or the destruction of provinces and cities in the manner therein prescribed.

Ala-ad-Din Juvaini (c.1260; 1997 edn) p.25.

3 What army in the whole world can equal the Mongol army? ... They have divided all the people into companies of ten, appointing one of the ten to be the commander of the nine others; while from among each ten commanders one has been given the title of 'commander of the hundred' all the hundred having been placed under his command ... And so it is with each thousand men and so also with each ten thousand.

Ala-ad-Din Juvaini (c.1260; 1997 edn) pp.31–2.

4 Now, by Eternal Heaven and by Heaven and Earth, my might has been so increased that the whole nation has been united under my rule. Choose therefore sentries from within the units of a thousand men and enter them in my service. Take more night-guards and quiver-bearers into my service too, to a total of ten thousand men ... Let the sons of the commanders of one thousand men and of a hundred men enter my service as guards. And let the sons of ordinary people – those who are skilful, strong, handsome and fit to serve at our side – also enter our service. The sons of the commanders of a thousand men shall bring ten companions with them, and each companion shall bring a younger brother to take his pace if necessary.

Anon. *The Secret History of the Mongols* (1228 or 1240); trans. and adapted as *The Golden History of the Mongols* (1993) pp.116–17. *The Secret History* is the only Mongol account of Ghengis Khan's life we have. The original manuscript, probably written in the Mongolian language (but not the Uighur script chosen by Genghis Khan), does not survive but was transcribed into Chinese during the 14th century. It is the only source for the Mongols not written by their enemies or those whom they had conquered.

5 He [Genghis Khan] paid great attention to the chase and used to say that the hunting of wild beasts was a proper occupation for the commanders of armies; and that instruction and training therein was incumbent on warriors and men-at-arms, [who should learn] how the huntsmen come up with the quarry, how they hunt it, in what manner they array themselves and after what fashion they surround it according as the party is great or small. For when the Mongols wish to go a-hunting, they first send out scouts to ascertain what kinds of game are available and whether it is scarce or abundant. And when they are not engaged in warfare, they are ever eager for the chase and encourage their armies thus to occupy themselves; not for the sake of the game alone, but also in order that they may become accustomed and inured to hunting and familiarized with the handling of the bow and the endurance of hardships.

Ala-ad-Din Juvaini (c.1260; 1997 edn) pp.23–34.

6 Being the adherent of no religion and the follower of no creed he eschewed bigotry, and the preference of one faith to another, and the placing of some above others; rather he honoured and respected the learned and pious of every sect, recognising such conduct as the way to the Court of God. And as he viewed the Muslims with the eye of respect, so also did he hold the Christians and idolaters in high esteem.

Ala-ad-Din Juvaini (c.1260; 1997 edn) p.26.

7 They believe in one God, and they believe that He is the maker of all things visible, and invisible; and that it is He who is the giver of the good things of this world as well as the hardships; they do not, however, worship Him with prayers or praises or any kind of ceremony. Their belief in God does not prevent them from having idols of felt made in the image of man, and these they place on each side of the door of the dwelling; below them they put a felt model of an udder, and they believe that these are the guardians of the cattle and grant them the benefit of milk and foals; yet others they make out of silken materials and to these they pay great honour.

John of Plano Carpini (c.1245–7); Dawson (1955) p.9. The Mongols did not appear to outsiders to have strong religious beliefs, but their toleration for other religions was often a cause for comment. Their own beliefs were based on the worship of Tengri, or Heaven, and the cult of sacred mountains, usually referred to as shamanism.

1 An international team of geneticists has made the astonishing discovery that more than 16 million men in Central Asia have the same male Y chromosome as the great Mongol leader.

It is a striking finding: a huge chunk of modern humanity can trace its origins to Genghis Khan's vigorous policy of claiming the most beautiful women captured during his merciless conquest.

Robin McKie, *Observer*, 2 March 2003.

THE EMPIRE SPREADS AND DIVIDES

2 [Genghis Khan] made many laws and statutes, which are observed inviolably by the Tatars. We will give only two of these. One is that if anyone, puffed up by pride, wishes to be Emperor on his own authority without an election by the princes, he shall be put to death without any mercy … Another is that they are to bring the whole world into subjection to them, nor are they to make peace with any nation unless they first submit to them, until the time for their own slaughter shall come.

John of Plano Carpini (c.1246–7); Dawson (1955) p.25.

3 Genghis had in his lifetime indicated that his third son Ogedei should succeed him as Great Khan, and the *quriltai* [election] that was held in 1229 confirmed this … Ghenghis's eldest son, Jochi, had died just before his father, but Jochi's son Batu inherited his allotment of territory, which was the land to the west as far as the hoof of Mongol horse had trodden. The traditional Steppe practice of granting grazing

lands furthest away from the home camp to the eldest son was thus upheld … Batu was not in fact Jochi's eldest son. This was Orda, the founder of a Mongol khanate to the east of Batu's future Golden Horde and known as the White Horde. Very little indeed is known about its history. Genghis's second son Chaghatai received territory in Central Asia, roughly the former lands of the Qara-Khitai to which Transoxiana was added during Ogedei's reign. The youngest son Tolui, received the original Mongol home in Mongolia, the 'hearthlands', birthright of a nomad chief's youngest son.

David Morgan (1986) pp.112–13. Batu's lands extended from the north of the Caspian Sea to the Volga River in the west and the Irgiz River in the east.

4 Who would find it easy to describe the ruin of Islam … [my] report comprises the story of a … tremendous disaster such as had never happened before, and which struck all the world … it may well be that the world from now until its end … will not experience the like of it again, apart perhaps from Gog and Magog.

Ibn al-Athir (1160–1233) *The Perfect History* (1851–76 edn) Vol.12, pp.233 ff. The Arab historian was writing soon after the first Middle Eastern campaigns of Genghis Khan. He also left us an eyewitness account of the Third Crusade (see 230:4). Gog and Magog were mythical giants (and symbols of evil), which had terrorized Europe before being defeated by Alexander the Great.

5 Now … to report how the evil spread everywhere. It moved across the lands like a cloud before the wind. A people set out from China, overran those fair lands of Turkestan, Kashgar and Balasaghun [west of the Altai Mountains], and advancing into Transoxiana [across the Syr'darya River] toward Samarkand and Bukhara [Uzbekistan], took them and pushed toward Rayy [to the east of modern Tehran, Iran], Hamadan, into the [Zagros] mountains and on to the threshold of Iraq. Then they turned to Azerbaijan and Arran, devastated these … In less than one year things happened the like of which [until then] had never been heard.

Ibn al-Athir (1160–1233) (1851–76 edn) Vol.12, pp.233–5. The historian was describing the Middle Eastern conquests of Genghis Khan in 1218–24.

6 Transoxiana comprises many countries, regions, districts and townships, but the kernel and cream thereof are Bukhara and Samarkand [Uzbekistan] … Bukhara's environs are adorned with the brightness of the light of doctors and jurists and its surroundings embellished with the rarest of high attainments. Since ancient times it has in every age been the place of assembly of the great savants of every religion.

Now one man had escaped from Bukhara after its capture and had come to Khorasan. He was questioned about the fate of that city and replied: 'They came, they sapped, they burnt, they slew, they plundered and they departed' …

In that moment the Emir … who was the chief and leader of the *sayyids* of Transoxiana and was famous for his piety and asceticism, turned to the learned Imam Rukn-ad-Din Imamzada, who was one of the most excellent savants in the world … and said: '*Maulana*, what state is this? That which I see do I see it in wakefulness or in my sleep, O Lord?'

Maulana Imamzada answered: 'Be silent: it is the wind of God's omnipotence that bloweth, and we have no power to speak.'

Ala-ad-Din Juvaini (c.1260; 1997 edn) pp.97 ff. The writer is describing the fate of Bukhara at the hands of the Mongols in March 1220. Transoxiana was the land between the River Oxus (the Amu'darya, Turkmenistan/Uzbekistan) and the River Jaxartes (the Syr'darya, Uzbekistan).

1 Ogedei Khan said: 'Here I sit upon my father's great throne, and the deeds I have accomplished since my father's death are these: for my first deed, I finished off his campaign against the Jaqut people [the Chin of northern China]. For my second, I established post-stations so that our messengers could gallop swiftly on their way and our necessary goods be easily transported. For my third, I had wells dug in places where there was no water, so that water could be brought forth. For my fourth, I placed scouts and garrison commanders among the peoples of the outlying cities in all directions, and I have allowed the people of my nation to rest their feet upon the earth, their hands upon the ground. I have let them live again.'

Anon. The Golden History of the Mongols (1993) p.166. Genghis Khan died on 18 Aug. 1227, having largely subdued northern China. Although there were other possible candidates, he was eventually succeeded as Great Khan by his son, Ogedei (r.1229–41).

2 By the time we got there a large pavilion had already been put up made of white velvet, and in my opinion it was so big that more than two thousand men could have got into it. Around it had been erected a wooden palisade, on which various designs were painted … all the chiefs were assembled and each one was riding with his followers among the hills and over the plains round about.

On the first day they were all clothed in white velvet, on the second in red – that day that Guyuk came to the tent – on the third day they were all in blue velvet and on the fourth in finest brocade.

John of Plano Carpini (c.1246–7); Dawson (1955) p.61. After Ogedei's death there were rivals for the succession. His widow became regent, and eventually his son Guyuk (r.1246–8) was elected. This is Carpini's description of his coronation.

3 Sarai [probably New Sarai, about 225 miles above Astrakhan between the Volga and Ural rivers in Russia] is one of the finest of towns, of immense extent and crammed with inhabitants, with fine bazaars and wide streets … One day we walked across the breadth of the town, and the double journey, going and returning, took half a day, this too through a continuous line of houses, with no ruins and no orchards. It has thirteen cathedrals [mosques] … The inhabitants belong to divers nations; among them are Mongols, who are the inhabitants and rulers in this country and are in part Muslims … the Russians and the Greeks who are all Christians. Each group lives in a separate quarter with its own bazaars. Merchants and strangers from Iraq, Egypt and Syria, and elsewhere, live in a quarter surrounded by a wall, in order to protect their property.

Ibn Battuta (1304–68) (1929 trans.) pp.165–6. In his account of his journey to Central Asia the Arab traveller included a description of Sarai, the capital of the Golden Horde, the western empire of the Mongols, just before the final disintegration of the khanate (see 170:3).

SWARMING LIKE LOCUSTS OVER THE FACE OF THE EARTH

4 In this night of misery we lay siege to the ears of your Holinesses, crying with our hearts and mouths at the same time until the moaning of those in shackles reaches your merciful hearing to induce you to take revenge on the blood of the servants of God shed, … We also waited for the help of our Mother Church so as to be able to withstand the enemies of the name of Christ at the fords of the Danube but there came no help. Finally as the Danube froze the way was free for them everywhere

and they were able to cross the Danube. On coming over they ranged over the land full of wicked intentions to fulfil the wickedness they planned.
Letter from Hungarian churchmen, requesting help from the pope in the face of the Mongol invasions, 2 Feb. 1242.

1 Swarming like locusts over the face of the earth, they have brought terrible devastation to the eastern parts [of Europe], laying it waste with fire and carnage. After having passed through the land of the Saracens, they have razed cities, cut down forests, overthrown fortresses, pulled up vines, destroyed gardens, killed townspeople and peasants. If perchance they have spared any suppliants, they have forced them, reduced to the lowest condition of slavery, to fight in the foremost ranks against their own neighbours ... they are without human laws, know no comforts, are more ferocious than lions or bears, have boats made of ox-hides, which ten or twelve of them own in common; they are able to swim or to manage a boat, so that they can cross the largest and swiftest rivers without let or hindrance, drinking turbid or muddy water when blood fails them (as beverage). They have one-edged swords and daggers, are wonderful archers, spare neither age, nor sex, nor condition.
Matthew Paris *Chronica Majora* (Greater Chronicle) (c.1235–59; 1852–4 edn) Bk 3, p.488. The Mongol invasions of Europe in 1241–2 were so terrifying that for many in the church they were seen as the herald of Armageddon. The greatest English chronicler of the 13th century gathered what information he could about the Mongols, to convey the terror that their invasions of Europe had inspired.

2 Hejnal, which derives from the Hungarian word for the dawn and, by extension for reveille, has passed into the Polish language as a term for the trumpet-call which sounds the alarm on the enemy's approach.

Today, the *hejnal mariacki* or 'trumpet call of St Mary's' is one of the many curiosities of old Cracow. It is sounded from the top of the tower of the ancient church which overlooks the city square. It is sounded on the hour, every hour of the day and night, winter and summer; and each time it is repeated four times: to north, south, east and west ... It commemorates the trumpeter who, whilst raising the alarm in 1241, or perhaps in 1259, was shot through the throat by a Mongol arrow. His call, though interrupted, enabled the burghers to flee. The survivors undertook to endow a town trumpeter in perpetuity.

Norman Davies *Europe, A History* (1996) p.365. In 1241 the Mongols, led by their general Baidar, reached the gates of Cracow, Poland. They sacked the city, only to return in 1259.

3 The eternal God has slain and annihilated these lands and peoples, because they have neither adhered to Genghis Khan, nor to the Khagan [supreme ruler] nor to the command of God ... From the rising of the sun to its setting, all the lands have been made subject to me. Who could do this contrary to the command of God?

Now you should say with a sincere heart: 'I will submit and serve you.' Thou thyself, at the head of the all the Princes, come at once to serve and wait upon us! At that time I shall recognize your submission.

If you do not observe God's command, and if you ignore my command, I shall know you as my enemy. Likewise I shall make you understand. If you do otherwise, God knows what I know.
Guyuk Khan to Pope Innocent IV, Nov. 1246 in John of Plano Carpini (c.1246–7); Dawson (1955) pp.85–6. After the Mongol invasions of Europe in 1241–2, following the news of the death of Ogedei (Dec. 1241) it was thought that the invaders would return. The new pope, Innocent IV (r.1243–54), wanting to find out more about them, sent several missions by different routes into Mongol territory, to complain of their invasions of Europe. The first to leave was the corpulent, 60-year-old French Franciscan friar, John of Plano Carpini (see 248:3), chosen for his diplomatic experience. After two years, having reached the court of the Mongol khan, Carpini returned with this reply: a demand for the submission of Europe to the Mongol court.

KUBLAI KHAN, 1260–94

4 When Kublai's khanate had reached the apogee of its power, at the moment when the sun stood at its noblest point, he extended this city [Beijing] as a residence, and built a four-walled city ... He commanded that artists and craftsmen should be brought from all directions to this city. Because of the number of its inhabitants and the milling crowds, this city in a short time became a place of assembly resplendent and ornamented overall. On one side of this city he built the ... throne of rule ... It was built from wood and planks, and was also square with each of its four sides four hundred paces long. This elysian structure was endowed with a cupola and windows, putting to shame the pinnacles of the celestial tabernacle, with solid pillars richly decorated and embellished with ornament. The floor was inlaid with jasper. Statues were set up and pictures painted, with both art and wit, radiating talismanic art ... the grilles in front of the windows were made of gold and silver, and above the pinnacles of the canopy the moon in its three stations ... trembles with jealousy ...

In this way, the business of the empire and the foundations of prosperity were organized; the opinions and thoughts of both the nobles and the common people were turned toward obedience and devotion.

Wassaf *History* (end of 13th century; 1856 trans.) p.45; Berthold Spuler *History of the Mongols* (1972) pp.169–70. Kublai Khan was the second son of Genghis Khan's fourth son, Tolui. He and his elder brother, the Great Khan Mongke, embarked on the conquest of Song China in 1252. In 1259 Mongke died, to be succeeded as Great Khan by Kublai, although his conquest of southern China was not complete until 1279.

1 He [Nayan, a rebel Mongol prince] was wrapped very tightly and bound in a carpet and there was dragged so much hither and thither and tossed up and down so rigorously that he died; & then they left him inside it; so that Nayan ended his life in this way. And for this reason he made him die in such a way. For the Tatar [Kublai Khan] said that he did not wish the blood of the lineage of the emperor be spilt on the ground.

Paul Pelliot (ed.) *Marco Polo: The Description of the World* (1938) p.199. The Mongols believed that the soul resided in the blood. Those of noble birth were put to death without their blood being shed.

2 He [Kublai Khan] wrote to the nobles in the various countries ... How can it be reasonable to give a thousand *balish* [gold coins] to one man while another hangs himself in despair and who can approve of this? Whoever provides against all expectation more than is required, is bound to lack what is required in the event of real need ...

With this in mind he laid down a rule which sums up the general principles of monarchical justice, which encompasses the universal order and governs the existence of the sons of men, which is approved and justified by reason as well as by tradition and adorns the latter as the light of the eye adorns the eyeball.

Wassaf (end of 13th century; 1856 trans.) Vol.1, pp.37–9. The historian Wassaf was a member of the Persian bureaucracy under Mongol rule.

3 It is moreover the custom in making presents to the grand khan, for those who have it in their power to furnish nine times nine of the article of which the present consists. Thus, for instance, if a province sends a present of horses, there are nine times nine, or eighty-one head in the drove; so also of gold or cloth, nine times nine pieces. By such means his majesty receives at this festival no fewer than a hundred thousand horses.

Marco Polo (1298; 1908 edn) pp.189–90.

4 Upon being asked the motive for this conduct [of observing different religious festivals], he [Kublai Khan] said, 'There are four great Prophets who are reverenced and worshipped by the different classes of mankind. The Christians regard Jesus Christ as their divinity; the Saracens, Mahomet; the Jews, Moses; and the idolaters, Sogomombar-kan, [probably Buddha] the most eminent amongst their idols. I do honour and show respect to all the four, and invoke to my aid whichever amongst them is in truth supreme in heaven.'

Marco Polo (1298; 1908 edn) p.159. Kublai Khan's policy was to be fairly even-handed in his treatment of different religions, but he recognized the importance of the Confucian tradition to his Chinese advisers, and although he favoured Buddhism, it was in its Lamaistic, Tantric form from Tibet.

5 From the city of Kanbalu [Beijing] there are many roads leading to the different provinces, and upon each of these, that is to say, upon every great road, at the distance of twenty-five or thirty miles, accordingly as the towns happen to be situated, there are stations, with houses of accommodation for travellers, called *yamb* or posthouses. These are large and handsome buildings, having several well-furnished apartments, hung with silk, and provided with everything suitable to persons of rank ... At each station four hundred good horses are kept in constant readiness, in order that all messengers going and coming upon the business of the grand khan and all ambassadors may have relays, and leaving their jaded horses, be supplied with fresh ones.

Marco Polo (1298; 1908 edn) pp.207–8. Genghis Khan had set up a sophisticated courier system throughout his empire, and when Marco Polo visited the court of Kublai, his grandson, this network impressed him greatly.

6 The noble and handsome city of Zaitun [Qhanzhou opposite Taiwan] ... has a port on the sea-coast celebrated for the resort of shipping, loaded with merchandise, that is afterwards

distributed through every part of the province of Manji [Fukien]. The quantity of pepper imported there is so considerable, that what is carried to Alexandria [Egypt, through which most of the Eastern trade passed] to supply the demand of the western parts of the world, is trifling in comparison, perhaps not more than the hundredth part. It is indeed impossible to convey an idea of the con-course of merchants and the accumulation of goods, in this, which is held to be one of the largest and most commodious ports in the world.
Marco Polo (1298; 1908 edn) pp.317–18.

1   In Xanadu did Kubla Khan
    A stately pleasure-dome decree:
    Where Alph, the sacred river, ran
    Through caverns measureless to man
    Down to a sunless sea.
    So twice five miles of fertile ground
    With walls and towers were girdled round:
    And there were gardens bright with sinuous
        rills
    Where blossom'd many an incense-bearing
        tree.
Samuel Taylor Coleridge 'Kubla Khan or a Vision in a Dream' (1816). The vast size of the Mongol empire described in reports from Western explorers and travellers helped to contribute to a fantastical vision of the rulers of the empire, perhaps exemplified by Coleridge's opium-inspired vision of Xanadu, the summer capital, Shang-tu, where Kublai was declared Great Khan in 1260. The poet noted that he fell asleep reading in the travel book *Purchas's Pilgrimage* by Samuel Purchas: 'Here the Khan Kubla commanded a palace to be built, and a stately garden thereunto; and thus ten miles of fertile ground were enclosed with a wall.'

TIMUR AND SAMARKAND, 1370–1405

2 He ranged over the Middle East like a roaring lion, seeking whom he might devour. He conquered from the Levant and Hellespont to the borders of China; in the north he dominated at least for a time southern Russia and parts of Siberia and southwards he carried his banners to victory over northern India. From his victories he brought back to Samarkand the loot of many cities and not a few men of learning, artists and craftsmen.
J.H. Sanders in Ahmed Ibn Arabshah (1388–1450) *Tamerlane or Timur the Great Amir* (1936 trans.) Introduction. Timur (Tamerlane) was born in 1336 at Kesh in Transoxiana, about 50 miles south of Samarkand. Often referred to as Timur the Lame or Tamerlane, he was the great-grandson of the

commander-in-chief to Jagatai, Genghis Khan's second son, who had inherited Khorasan (in Central Asia) as part of his portion of Genghis's empire. By 1360 Timur had conquered Khorasan and ascended the throne. His cruelty became legendary as he went on to become one of the world's great conquerors. Among those compelled to return with him to Samarkand after the conquest of Damascus in 1401 was Ibn Arabshah, aged 12, who later became secretary to Sultan Ahmed of Baghdad, and wrote a life of Timur that, though biased against him, is an important source for historians.

3 Then Timur returned to Khorasan with a fixed purpose of taking revenge on [the city of] Seistan whose inhabitants went out to him asking for peace and agreement, which he granted them on condition that they should hand over their arms to him, of which they produced the whole equipment which they had, hoping in this way to escape from their extremity; and he put them on oath and ordered them to swear plainly that no further weapons were left in the city.
    And as soon as they had given this guarantee, he drew the sword against them and billeted upon them all the armies of death. Then he laid the city waste, leaving in it not a tree or a wall and destroyed it utterly, no mark or trace remaining.
Ahmed Ibn Arabshah (1388–1450; 1936 trans.) p.23.

4 Timur was tall and of lofty stature as though he belonged to the remnants of the Amalekites, big in brow and head, mighty in strength and courage, wonderful in nature, white in colour, mixed with red, but not dark, stout of limb, with broad shoulders, thick fingers, long legs, perfect build, long beard, dry hands, lame on the right side, with eyes like candles, without brilliance, powerful in voice; he did not fear death; and though he was near his eightieth [in fact, seventieth] year, yet he was firm in mind, strong and robust in body, brave and fearless, like a hard rock.
Ahmed Ibn Arabshah (1388–1450; 1936 trans.) p.295.

5 We set out from Samarkand and reached Tirmidh [Termez, Uzbekistan], a large town with fine buildings and bazaars and traversed by canals. It abounds in grapes and quinces of an exquisite flavour, as well as in flesh-meats and milk. The inhabitants wash their heads in the bath with milk instead of fuller's earth; the proprietor of every bath-house has large jars filled with milk, and each man as he enters takes a cupful to wash his head. It makes the hair fresh and glossy.
Ibn Battuta (1304–68) (1929 trans.) p.174.

1 In the whole habitable world there are few cities so pleasantly situated as Samarkand … There are many palaces and gardens that belonged to Timur both in Samarkand and the suburbs. Timur built in the citadel of Samarkand, a stately palace, four storeys high, which is famous by the name of Gok-serai … To the east of Samarkand there are two gardens. The one which is the more distant is called the Perfect Garden; the nearer, the Heart-delighting Garden. From the first there is a public avenue, planted on each side with pine-trees. In the other there has also been built a large palace, in which is a series of paintings, representing the wars of Timur in Hindustan.

Babur *The Babur-nama, Memoirs of Babur, Prince and Emperor* (1508–29; 1909 edn) p.30. Babur (d.1530), the founder of the Mughal dynasty in India (see 143:1), was descended from both Timur and Genghis Khan.

2 The hyacinth was brought to him from Balkhshan and the turquoise from Nisabur, Kazarun and the mines of Khorasan and the ruby from India, and from India and Sind the diamond and the pearl from Hormuz and silk and down and agate and musk and other things from Cathay and from other countries refined silver and pure gold.

Ahmed Ibn Arabshah (1388–1450; 1936 trans.) p.309.

3 The city of Samarkand is also very rich in merchandise which comes from all parts. Russia and Turkey send linen and hides. China sends silks, which are the best in the world, and musk which is not found anywhere else in the world, also rubies and diamonds, pearls, rhubarb and many other things. The merchandise which comes from China is the best and most valuable which arrives in this city, and it could be said that the Chinese are the most skilful craftsmen in the world. They themselves say that they have two eyes, whereas the French have only one and the Moors are blind, so that they are superior to all other countries. From India come spices such as nutmeg, clove, mace, cinnamon, ginger and many others that do not reach Alexandria.

Ruy Gonzales de Clavijo, Castilian envoy to the court of Tamerlane, 1403–6; Jean-Pierre Drège and Emil M. Buhrer *The Silk Road Saga* (1989 edn) p.202. The Spanish diplomat Clavijo (d.1412) left an important neutral account of Timur's court and stories of his campaigns.

4   Nature, that fram'd us of four elements
     Warring within our breasts for regiment,
     Doth teach us all to have aspiring minds:
     Our souls, whose faculties can comprehend
     The wondrous architecture of the world,
     And measure every wandering planet's course,
     Still climbing after knowledge infinite,
     And always moving as the restless spheres,
     Will us to wear ourselves, and never rest,
     Until we reach the ripest fruit of all,
     That perfect bliss and sole felicity,
     The sweet fruition of an earthly crown.

Christopher Marlowe *Tamburlaine the Great* (before 1587) Pt 1, Act 2, Sc.7. Marlowe was a contemporary of Shakespeare. His fascination with Timur lay in the way in which the ruler embodied aspects of the Renaissance man – the achievement of power and magnificence by creative men who have the energy to realize their ambitions. However, to achieve all he desires, cruelty, treachery and brutality are required as well as the strength, military genius and vision.

The Ottoman Empire, 1300–1760

BUILDING AN EMPIRE, c.1300–1520

1 [While staying in the house of a certain holy man, Osman] dreamt that a moon rose out of the holy man's breast and came and entered his own. As soon as it did so, a tree sprouted from his navel and its shade covered the whole world. Beneath its shade were mountains, each with streams flowing from its foot. Some people drank from those streams, some watered orchards, some set up fountains. He immediately told the holy man his dream. 'Osman, my son,' said the holy man, 'I congratulate you for the sovereignty which will be given to you and your descendants. My daughter Malhun Hatun shall be your wife.'

Ashikpashazade *History* (2nd half 15th century; 1970 edn) p.6. The prophetic dream of Osman I, the first Ottoman sultan (r.c.1300–26), the principal Ottoman foundation myth, as told by an Ottoman soldier and historian. The English word Ottoman is derived from 'Othomano', the Italian form of Osman's name, from the original Arabic 'Uthman.

2 The tree of the Ottoman state was planted by Osman Shah Gazi [c.1300–26] and nourished by the endeavours of his successors until it reached the limit of mature perfection in the time of Kanuni Sultan Suleyman Khan [1520–66]. Thereafter, it experienced variously both autumnal decay and distress and spring restoration and rejuvenation, but eventually suffered such misfortunes that it was reduced to a miserable condition. Then by the skill and enterprise of Sultan Mahmud Khan II [1808–39] it was restored.

Ahmed Jevdet Pasha *History* (1891) Vol.1, p.36. An Ottoman government minister and historian surveys the course of Ottoman history to his day. The epithet *gazi* (warrior for the faith) was adopted, possibly in the later 14th century, as one of the titles of the Ottoman sultans and remained so into the 20th century. The first president of the Turkish republic on its foundation in 1923 was often referred to officially as Gazi Mustafa Kemal Atatürk.

3 [When Osman Gazi died c.1326 his sons] Orhan Gazi and Alaeddin Pasha met with other prominent men to see what [property] Osman had left and to decide what the brothers should inherit. There was only the land he had conquered. There was no money, no gold. He left a fairly new saddle cloth, some armour, a container for salt and one for spoons, and a pair of strong boots. He also had some good horses and several flocks of sheep ... a few mares and several pairs of oxen. Osman had no other possessions.

Ashikpashazade (2nd half 15th century; 1970 edn) p.36. The historian stresses that Osman I was a genuine leader, not someone who sought riches for himself.

4 The city of Bursa [is] a great and important city with fine bazaars and wide streets, surrounded on all sides by gardens and running springs. In its outskirts there is a river of exceedingly hot water which flows into a large pond; beside this have been built two [bath] houses, one for men, one for women. Sick persons seek a cure in this hot pool and come to it from the most distant parts of the country.

Ibn Battuta *Travels in Asia and Africa 1325–1355*; H.A.R. Gibb (ed. and trans.) *The Travels of Ibn Battuta* (1962) Vol.2, pp.449–50. The famous Arab traveller Ibn Battuta (1304–68) visited the first Ottoman capital, Bursa in northwest Turkey, in 1331.

5 [The sultan of Bursa is Orhan Bey], son of the sultan Osman ... This sultan is the greatest of the kings of the Turkmen and the richest in wealth, lands and military forces. Of fortresses he possesses nearly a hundred, and for most of his time he is continually engaged in making the round of them, staying in each fortress for some days to put it into good order and examine its condition. It is said that he has never stayed for a whole month in any one town. He also fights with the infidels continually and keeps them under siege.

Ibn Battuta; Gibb (1962) Vol.2, pp.451–2. Orhan Bey (r.1326–60) was the second ruler of the Ottoman empire.

6 Covered in blood and longing for martyrdom, Sultan Yildirim Bayezid Khan spurred his horse on into the thick of the battle, aiming for Timur [Tamburlaine] himself. He personally felled several Tatar and Mongol soldiers, sending their heads rolling in the dust. No one could withstand him. Fearlessly, heedlessly, alone, single-handed, he reached the place where Timur stood and came face to face with his guards ... Realizing that this was Yildirim Khan himself, Timur ordered him to be captured and bound with ropes ... His men set upon Yildirim from all sides, pulled him from his horse and ... eventually, by sheer force of numbers took him prisoner.

Solakzade (d.c.1658) *History* (1876 edn) pp.77–8. Bayezid I (r.1389–1402), nicknamed Yildirim (Thunderbolt) because of his swift, decisive campaigns, was defeated by Timur (see 256:2) at the Battle of Ankara (1402). Bayezid I died in captivity shortly after the battle, the Ottoman possessions were divided among his sons and their previous rulers, and the empire was restored under single rule only in 1413.

1 By the time Bayezid I ascended the throne, the Ottoman state ... had been securely established in the Balkans and Anatolia. The fact that this political structure, which Bayezid had strengthened and doubled in size, withstood two great tests like the battles of Nicopolis (1396) and Ankara (1402), one of which ended in a brilliant victory and the other in the capture of the sultan, shows how unshakeable were its foundations.

M.F. Koprulu *The Origins of the Ottoman Empire* (1935; 1992 trans.) p.111. At the Battle of Nicopolis on the Danube, Bayezid I easily defeated a Christian crusading army led by Sigismund, king of Hungary.

2 The hour was already advanced, the day was declining and near evening, and the sun was at the Ottomans' backs but shining in the faces of their enemies. This was just as the sultan had wished; accordingly he gave the order first for the trumpets to sound the battle-signal, and the other instruments, the pipes and flutes and cymbals too, as loud as they could. All the trumpets of the other divisions, with the other instruments in turn, sounded all together, a great and fearsome sound. Everything shook and quivered at the noise.

Michael Kritovoulos *History of Mehmed the Conqueror* (later 15th century; 1954 trans.) pp.66–7. The Greek historian describes the Ottoman siege of Constantinople in 1453 (see 112:2). Kritovoulos's chronicle of Mehmed II's reign to 1467 is based mainly on events that he himself witnessed (although he was not present at the siege of Constantinople) and seeks to provide a favourable image of the sultan.

3 Sultan Mehmed, when he had carefully viewed the City [of Constantinople] and all its contents, went back to the camp and divided the spoils. First he took the customary toll of the spoils for himself. Then also, as prizes from all the rest, he chose out beautiful virgins and those of the best families, and the handsomest boys, some of whom he even bought from the soldiers ... [Later] he settled all the [other] captives whom he had taken as his portion, together with their wives and children, along the shores of the city harbour ... He gave them houses and freed them from taxes for a specified time.

Michael Kritovoulos (later 15th century; 1954 trans.) pp.82–3.

4 When [Mehmed II] conquered Istanbul ... he sent messengers to all the provinces promising houses, gardens, orchards and property to [people who would be important] and would come to the city. He gave such things to those who came and the city began to flourish. Then he ordered his commanders and judges in the provinces to send rich and poor families, which they did in abundance, and to these also houses were given and the city prospered.

Ashikpashazade (2nd half 15th century; 1970 edn) p.132. Mehmed II, who had personally supervised the assault on Constantinople, took care to repopulate and revitalize the city as his imperial capital.

5 It is proper for whichever of my sons is favoured by God with the sultanate to execute his brothers for the good order of society. Most doctors of the religious law have declared this permissible.

Law of Fratricide from Book of Laws of Mehmed II, late 15th century; Leslie Peirce *The Imperial Harem: Women and Sovereignty in the Ottoman Empire* (1993) p.44. Contemporary Western observers frequently commented on this attitude, which led either to immediate civil war among the surviving male heirs of a deceased sultan or to the death by strangulation of a new sultan's brothers by order of the latter immediately he ascended the throne. For various reasons, this practice ceased after the deaths of 19 princes (mainly children) on the accession of Mehmed III in 1595 and was replaced by a system of succession by seniority among the male members of the Ottoman dynasty. Daughters, who had no claim whatsoever to the Ottoman sultanate, were usually given in marriage to important viziers to maintain a network of loyal dynastic supporters.

6 All those [pages] who are in the service of the Grand Turk, who are about 340 in number, all alike are sons of Christians in part taken in military expeditions into foreign countries and in part drawn from his own subjects ... the greater part of the lords, captains and great men who are in the service of the Great Turk receive their education in the royal palace.

Giovanni Maria Angiolello; Barnette Miller *The Palace School of Muhammad the Conqueror* (1941) pp.38–9. Angiolello, himself an Italian captive, spent more than a decade as a page in Ottoman service in the 1470s and 1480s. He refers to the infamous *devshirme* (child levy) system by which many high Ottoman officials were recruited and which supplemented the number of slaves taken as captives in war.

7 The whole Turkish Kingdom is governed by one ruler, the others all being his servants; and his Kingdom is divided into sanjaks [provinces], to which he sends various administrators, whom he changes and moves as he pleases. But the King of France is placed amidst a great number of hereditary lords, recognized in that state by their own subjects, who are devoted to them. They have their own hereditary privileges, which the King disallows only at his peril … It is difficult to overcome a state of the Turkish type but, if it has been conquered, very easy to hold it. On the other hand, in some respects it is easier to conquer a state like France, but it is very difficult to hold it.

Niccolò Machiavelli *The Prince* (1513; 1998 trans.) Ch.15.

SULEYMAN THE MAGNIFICENT, 1520–66

1 Once the winter was over and the campaign season had arrived, [Oruj and Hayreddin] fitted out two ships and sailed from [Tunis in north Africa]. They came upon a ship from Genoa laden with grain and seized it on the spot. Then they saw a fortress-like galleon, a merchant ship laden with cloth, and took that without any difficulty. Returning to Tunis, they handed over the fifth of booty [due to the ruler of Tunis], divided the rest, and set out again with three ships for the infidel coasts [of Spain and Italy].

Katib Chelebi (Hajji Khalifa) (1609–57) *History of the Maritime Wars of the Turks* (1910 edn) p.32 The Ottoman historian describes a typical episode, c.1518, in the early career of the North African corsair leader Hayreddin Barbaros Pasha, who became grand admiral to Suleyman the Magnificent in the 1530s. It illustrates the importance of the continuous 'little war' of piracy in the Mediterranean as a crucial aspect of Ottoman–European relations.

2 The emperor stood beneath the banner of the Prophet and raised his hands in prayer. 'Oh God, yours is the power and the strength, yours the bestowing of aid in battle; yours is the grace and the favour, yours the kindness, yours the protection. Turn not away from this powerless body of Muslims. Take not the part of the strong-armed enemy.' The soldiers of Islam witnessed the tears falling from the sultan's eyes as he prayed. To a man they gave out a wondrous moan and weeping, which all took for a sign of divine favour. As the autumn leaves fall from the trees, they fell from their horses and pressed their faces to the black earth. In that moment they cried out with broken-hearted humility and all committed themselves to eternal life.

Solakzade (d.c.1658) (1876 edn) pp.77–8. The public prayer of Sultan Suleyman I before the Battle of Mohács in Hungary (1526), one of the most celebrated Ottoman victories in south-central Europe. The battle led to the establishment of the Ottoman province of Hungary in 1541 within only a few days' march of Vienna, capital city of Ferdinand, Habsburg king of northeastern Hungary and brother of the Holy Roman Emperor, Charles V.

3 The day of judgement is at hand, and will destroy Gog the Turk and Magog the Pope, the one the political and the other the ecclesiastical enemy of Christ.

Martin Luther, Nov. 1529; K.M. Setton *Europe and the Levant in the Middle Ages and the Renaissance* (1974) p.153. After the unsuccessful Ottoman siege of Vienna, the Protestant reformer draws parallels between the Muslim and papal threats to Reformation Europe. Gog and Magog symbolize the enemies of the Kingdom of God (Revelation 20:8). For Luther see 355:3–358:3.

4 While it is true that not every war against the Turks is just and pious, it is also the case that non-resistance to the Turks is nothing other than betraying Christianity to its most savage foes, and abandoning our brothers to a servitude which they do not deserve.

Desiderius Erasmus *Consultatio de bello Turcis inferendo* (1530); N. Housley (ed.) *Documents on the Later Crusades, 1274–1580* (1996) p.178. Published one year after the Ottoman siege of Vienna, Erasmus' view encapsulates the humanist dilemma regarding the Muslim threat to Christian Europe and the policies of its Catholic leader, Charles V. For Erasmus see 275:4 and 355:1.

5 There should be no personal ambition in a grand vizier. All his actions should be for God, in the path of God, for the sake of God, for there is no higher service which he could attain.

Lutfi Pasha (d.1568) *Asafname* (1910 edn) pp.6–7. In 1539–41 Lutfi Pasha was grand vizier – that is, the sultan's deputy to whom he delegated all routine administrative business – to Suleyman the Magnificent. His book of advice for grand viziers was written after the fall of Suleyman's favourite, the over-mighty Ibrahim Pasha, and (probably) during the vizierate of Rustem Pasha, who was suspected of bribery and intrigue.

6 The king's greatest treasure is a wise vizier.

Ta'likizade *Ta'likizade's Sehname-i humayun: A History of the Ottoman Campaign into Hungary 1593–4* (c.1596; 1983 edn) p.194.

7 Sultan Suleyman Khan campaigned in both east and west, capturing personally a total of 360 fortresses. He promoted all branches of knowledge and learning, he regulated the learned professions and laid down sound ordinances for financial and other matters. He expanded the numbers both of household troops and of the revenue-holding provincial soldiers, regulating and improving the *kanun* [administrative law] and other regulations under which they operated.

Ahmed Jevdet Pasha (1891) Vol.1, pp.40–41. An assessment of the achievements of Suleyman, known in Turkish as Kanuni (the Lawgiver) but to awe-struck Europeans as 'the Magnificent' on account of his wealth and power.

1 I who am the sultan of sultans, the sovereign of sovereigns, the shadow of God on earth, sultan and emperor of the White Sea [Mediterranean] and the Black Sea;

of the lands of the Greeks [Greece and the Balkans];

of Anatolia, Karamania and the land of Rum [all parts of Turkey] …

of Egypt, Damascus, Aleppo, Jerusalem and all the Arab lands;

of Baghdad, Basra, Aden and Yemen;

of the Tatars and the steppelands [in southern Russia];

of the throne of Hungary and its tributaries,

and of many other countries which we have conquered by the sword –

I who am Sultan Suleyman Shah, son of Sultan Selim Shah Khan, to you Charles, king of the land of Spain.

Suleyman I to the Holy Roman Emperor, Charles V, June 1547; A.C. Schaendlinger (ed.) *Die Schreiben Suleymans des Prachtigen an Karl V, Ferdinand I und Maximilian II* (Writings of Suleyman the Magnificent to Charles V, Ferdinand I and Maximilian II) (1983) p.12. Such a rhetorical catalogue of Ottoman territories was a standard salutation in letters to rulers considered inferior in status. The Ottomans were well aware that Charles V was more than just king of Spain!

2 The European foot soldiers of [Suleyman's] era were a mere rabble ignorant of the art of war, the cavalry were an ill-disciplined mass drawn from the followers of nobles who were always challenging [the power of] their rulers. The imperial [Ottoman] state, on the other hand, possessed a highly organized and, for that time, well-trained infantry and cavalry – the reputation and force of which made all corners of the earth quake in fear.

Ahmed Jevdet Pasha (1891) Vol.1, p.40.

3 The glory and magnificence of but an hour earlier were in an instant changed to grief and despair. Not only for prince Mustafa's own men but for the whole Ottoman army it was as if the final day of reckoning had come. No sooner had the prince fallen victim to the sultan's wrath than the sultan's treasurer went to his camp and seized his treasury and all his tents,

horses and slaves for the imperial treasury; his household troops were [dispersed] and given military livings in the provinces. All held Rustem Pasha responsible. Poets composed chronograms and elegies of longing and sadness, openly blaming Rustem Pasha.

Ibrahim Pechevi (d.c.1640) *History* (1861 edn) Vol.1, p.303. On the sudden execution on Suleyman's orders of his eldest son, Mustafa, in 1553 as the unsuspecting prince entered his father's tent near Amasya. Suleyman was apparently persuaded by the grand vizier that Mustafa was threatening to rebel against him. The affair resulted in implicit criticism of Suleyman himself.

4 [Suleyman's] dignity of demeanour and his general physical appearance are worthy of the ruler of so vast an empire. He has always been frugal and temperate, and … even in his earlier years did not indulge in wine or in those unnatural vices to which the Turks are often addicted … He is a strict guardian of his religion and its ceremonies, being not less desirous of upholding his faith than of extending his dominions.

Ogier Ghiselin de Busbecq *Turkish Letters* (c.1555; 1968 edn) p.65. The writer was Charles V's ambassador to Suleyman the Magnificent.

5 The Mufti is the principal head of the Muhammadan Religion or Oracle of all doubtful questions in the Law and is a person … famous for his Learning in the Law, and eminent for his virtues and strictness of life … His power is not compulsory, but only resolving and persuasive in matters both Civil and Criminal, and of State: his manner of resolves is by writing; the question being first stated in Paper briefly and succinctly, he underneath subscribes his sentence by Yes, or No, or in some other short determination called a Fetva … In matters of State the Sultan demands his opinion, whether it be in condemnation of any great man to death, or in making War or Peace, or other important affairs of the Empire; either to appear the more just and religious, or to include the people more willingly to obedience.

Paul Rycaut *The Present State of the Ottoman Empire* (1668) pp.105–6. Rycaut spent 17 years in the Ottoman empire, first as secretary to the English embassy in Istanbul (1661–7) and then as English consul in Izmir (1667–78). His authoritative treatise immediately became a major source of European information on the Ottomans.

6 Question: If one of the sons of a just sultan ceases to obey him, occupies several fortresses, extorts money from the people, amasses troops and begins to kill people when he cannot take things by other means, is it lawful to kill him and his troops until they disperse [and are no longer a threat]?

Answer: It is lawful, as proved by a verse in the Koran.

Ebussu'ud (d.1574); M.E. Duzdag (ed.) *Seyhulislam Ebussuud Efendi fetvalari* (The Legal Opinions of the Chief Jurisconsult) (1983) p.191. The writer was Suleyman I's chief legal authority. The *fetva* (legal opinion) given by him sanctioned the sultan's action against another of his sons, Bayezid, who rebelled against the sultan in the late 1550s and was executed in 1562.

1 In terms of power and authority, of the territorial extent of the empire and its wealth, the highest attainment was achieved in the reign of Sultan Suleyman Khan. Yet even in his time there appeared signs of the future disruption of the realm.

Kochu Beg *Kochu Beg risalesi* (The Treatise of Kochu Beg) (c.1630; 1885 edn) p.93. Kochu Beg (d.c.1650) was an Ottoman bureaucrat and composer of a significant reform treatise on the seeds of Ottoman 'decline'.

2 Slaves constitute the main source of gain to the Turkish soldier. If he brings back with him from a campaign nothing but one or two slaves, he has done well and is amply rewarded for his toil; for an ordinary slave is valued at forty or fifty crowns, while, if the slave has the additional recommendation of youth or beauty or skill in craftsmanship, he is worth twice as much.

Ogier Ghiselin de Busbecq (c.1555; 1968 edn) p.102. The ambassador describes the attractions of slavery.

3 I went to see the Turks' market, which they call a bazaar and which is where the poor Christians captured on Sicily, Malta and Gozo are sold to the highest bidders. In accordance with ancient oriental custom, slave dealers are allowed to parade their captives quite naked to show that they have no physical defects, and to have their eyes and teeth inspected as if they were horses.

Nicolas de Nicolay, c.1551; M.-Ch. Gomez-Geraud and S. Yerasimos (eds) *Dans l'empire de Soliman le Magnifique* (1989) p.83. The slave market in Tripoli, North Africa.

4 This militia [the janissary corps] considers the Grand Signor's grandeur their own; and though for the most part renegade Christians, they profess greater hatred of the Christians than do the others, and all of them are firmly convinced that if they die in combat against a Christian, they will go straight to Paradise.

Bernardo Navagero, 1553; Lucette Valensi *Venice and the Sublime Porte: the Birth of the Despot* (1987) p.24. As retiring Venetian ambassador to Istanbul, Navagero was reporting to the doge and senate on the sultan's elite infantry bodyguard, which was feared throughout Europe.

SULEYMAN'S SUCCESSORS, 1571–1760

5 The fleet destroyed, by order of God.

In 1571 the land commander Pertev Pasha and the chief admiral Ali Pasha were sent out with 250 galleys to raid infidel lands. The admiral had little knowledge of naval affairs, and Pertev Pasha neglected military matters. They came face to face with a Venetian fleet of 300 galleys off the Greek coast, gave battle and the Ottoman fleet was heavily defeated. The admiral Ali Pasha was killed, Pertev Pasha took flight, some galleys were scattered but the majority sank to the bottom of the sea. Only the governor of Algiers, Kilij Ali Pasha, escaped and returned to Istanbul with 30 or 40 ships. This naval campaign is known simply as 'the rout of the fleet'.

Solakzade (d.c.1658) (1876 edn) p.593. The matter-of-fact description of the Battle of Lepanto (see 296:1) reveals Ottoman annoyance and distress at its 'mismanagement'.

6 In the midst of all this joy [for the Christian victory at Lepanto] … one of the chief prisoners of the Turks, hearing it compared with the [Venetian] loss of Cyprus (for that Selim had at Lepanto lost his fleet, his best men of war, with great store of ordnance) by a fit comparison showed it not to be so saying, That the battle lost, was unto Selim as if a man should shave his beard, which would ere long grow again; but that the loss of Cyprus [in 1570] was unto the Venetians, as the loss of an arm, which once cut off, could never be again recovered. Declaring thereby the great inequality of the loss.

Richard Knolles *The Generall Historie of the Turkes* (1603; 1610 edn) p.885. Knolles, headmaster of a boys' grammar school in Kent, wrote the first major and the best known early English history of the Ottomans. The sultan referred to is Suleyman I's son, Selim II (r.1566–74).

7 [Having been ordered to build 150 new galleys over the winter of 1571–2 to replace those lost at Lepanto] the chief admiral Kilij Ali Pasha complained to the grand vizier: 'Building the hulls is easy, but how are we to find the 500 or 600 anchors, the sails and all the other equipment necessary for these ships?' Mehmed

Pasha replied: 'The power and wealth of the state are such that if the sultan commanded all the anchors in the fleet to be made of silver, the ropes of silk and the sails of satin, it could be done. For whatever is lacking from any ship, ask me.'
Katib Chelebi (1609–57) *History of the Maritime Wars of the Turks* (1910 edn) p.95.

1 It truly merits serious consideration that the wealth, the power, the government, in short, that the entire state of the Ottoman Empire is founded on and entrusted to people who were all born into the Christian faith and who, by various means, were enslaved and borne off into the Muhammadan sect.
Marcantonio Barbaro, 1573, Venetian ambassador to Istanbul, reporting to the doge and senate; Valensi (1987) p.24.

2 No sultans or previous dynasties have conquered and dominated both land and sea as have the Ottomans. The infidel Frankish rulers are as [agile as] frogs in sea battles but they suffer ignominy on land.
Ta'likizade *Shema'ilname* (The Book of Distinguishing Qualities [of the Ottoman Sultans]) (c.1593); unpublished MS, Topkapi Sarayi Library, Istanbul, folio 102b. He is reflecting on Ottoman control of the eastern Mediterranean 20 years after Lepanto.

3 King and subjects, especially army leaders and statesmen, all constitute one organism, serving in various ways, at times [the king's] seeing eyes, his grasping hands, as his battle-ready shield, at times as his wing and pinion ready to fly, at times as his speaking tongue or his walking foot [but always] being bold enough to set aside fear and awe and to speak out the word of truth.
Mustafa Ali *Mustafa Ali's Counsel for Sultans of 1581* (1581; 1979 edn) Pt 1, p.25. A prominent and critical Ottoman historian, Ali had strong views on the ideal relationship between sultan and servants, particularly viziers.

4 [The sultans of] this praiseworthy dynasty ... reside all by themselves in a palace like unique jewels in the depth of the oyster-shell, and totally sever all relations with relatives and dependants. The slave girls and slave pages that have access to their honoured private quarters, who are evidently at least three to four thousand individuals, are all strangers and the person of the monarch is like a single gem in their midst ... [they are] so much attached to him with complete submission and affection.
Mustafa Ali (1581; 1979 edn) p.38. The imperial remoteness and splendour of the harem-based sultan Murad III (r.1574–95) is contrasted with the lives of earlier warrior sultans.

5 There are nine kitchens in this Seraglio [Topkapi Palace] ... the butchers are obliged to send every day one hundred sheep, the poulterers eight hundred chickens and pullets, and the hunters usually two hundred birds ... The (number of mouths) that are regularly [fed] in the Seraglio is 13,400, including more than eight hundred women and about the same number of eunuchs.
Domenico Hierosolimitano *Domenico's Istanbul* (c.1620; 2001 trans.) p.23. A Jewish rabbi and physician to Murad III for several years, Domenico had detailed knowledge of the Ottoman palace. His account was probably written in Italy shortly before his death.

6 The principal thing of beauty in Constantinople is the Arsenal, which makes a stupendous sight on the shore, having 180 gates, into each of which a galley enters, but each one is so large that two or three galleys can stand there under cover. [There are] moreover the great workshops which are inside, and there is the prison (*bagnio*) of the slaves, that is the place where they are kept locked up at night. There were never fewer than 4000 of these (slaves) ... in the time of Murad [III], the number of slaves exceeded 32,000.
Domenico Hierosolimitano (c.1620; 2001 trans.) pp.23–4. For the Venice arsenal see 294:5.

7 [Murad III] loved Musick, but had not the patience to attend the tuning of instruments, so as the Venetians sending him a Consort which he desyred to heare, they could not be so ready after they had long expected him, but that upon his sodeine Coming they were forced to spend a little tyme in tuning their instruments, whereat he grew so impatient, as he went away in anger, and would never come again to heare them.

He was by nature carried to extremes, seldom holding the mean, and easily believed the first information without due examination thereof, but he was said to be more courteous and merciful, and to have gathered more treasure than any of his Ancestors.
Fynes Moryson *Shakespeare's Europe: Unpublished Chapters of Fynes Moryson's Itinerary* (c.1600; 1903 edn) pp.44–5. A gentleman traveller in Istanbul c.1597, Moryson gained much information and opinion from the resident English ambassador there, Edward Barton (see 293:6). The contrariness of Murad III is also commented upon, although less obviously, by Ottoman historians.

8 Sultan Murad Khan left 27 surviving daughters and seven pregnant concubines. On his death all of these, with the mothers of the sultan's children, other concubines who had shared his bed, their nurses and eunuchs, together with all their goods and chattels, immediately brought down from [the saddlery at] Sarrach-hane large bags, chests and baskets. Several hundred porters took up their loads, carts were filled and, moaning and lamenting, they transferred to the Old Palace.

Mustafa Selaniki (d.1600) *Tarih-i Selaniki* (Selaniki's History) (1989 edn) Vol.2, p.436. Selaniki is reporting the custom whereby on the accession of a new sultan his household promptly replaced that of his predecessor.

1 Touching foreign Princes, England was so far removed from Turkey as from the forces thereof the Turks could expect neither good nor ill, and when the [Turkish] Emperor beheld England in a Map, he wondered that the king of Spain did not dig it with mattocks, and cast it into the Sea. But the heroic virtues of Queen Elizabeth, her great actions in Christendom, and especially her prevailing against the Pope and the king of Spain, her professed enemies, made her much admired of the Emperor, of his mother, and of all the great men of that Court.

Fynes Moryson (c.1600; 1903 edn) p.31.

2 The greatest terror of the world.

Richard Knolles (1603; 1610 edn) Introduction. Knolles summarizes his view of the Ottomans.

3 There is no kingdom in which Christian and Jewish communities are so numerous and flourishing as in this firmly established state.

Ta'likizade (c.1596; 1983 edn) p.122. The author is commenting on Ottoman religious toleration and contrasting it to that of Catholic Spain in particular.

4 Our Ambassador told me that the Turkish Emperor gives daily stipend to some 180,000 persons, and that as well in peace, as in War. The number seemed incredible to me … But no doubt his Army is maintained as well in peace as war, so as it seems War is little more chargeable unto him than peace, yea more profitable by the gaining of Towns and Territories, save that it consumes his Subjects … Men of experience in Turkish affairs agree that the Emperor cannot gather all his forces into one Army, no Country being able to feed them, besides that the Christian Subjects living under great tyranny might have means to rebel by such remote absence of the soldiers.

Fynes Moryson (c.1600; 1903) p.40. Western observers were always impressed with the extent of the Ottoman standing army (which also served as a kind of provincial police force) and the ease by which it could be called up at very little notice. This contrasted with the widespread use of far less reliable mercenary armies by debt-ridden European monarchs.

5 Their [military] discipline is singular in duly giving rewards, and punishment. Whosoever disobeys his Commander or neglects his charge, may himself go to the gallows, for he shall never escape it, and he that fights or performs his charge bravely, may of a poor tribute child become the chief Vizier of that Empire. They keep Wonderful silence in the Army, speaking with becks, and signs, so as they will rather let a Captive escape by flight, than they will make the least noise to stop him.

Fynes Moryson (c.1600; 1903) pp.43–4. Such favourable comments on Ottoman military discipline and promotion by merit were frequently made by western writers against their own societies' failings.

6 Above all the great Potentates of the world, the King of Persia was most feared and esteemed by the Turk, not only by reason of his great force, and that the borders of his Dominions run a long space on the confines of the Turks; but because it is almost impossible, by reason of the vast Deserts, and uninhabited places, to carry the War into his Country … The nearness of their Faith, though derived from the same Founder, but afterwards receiving some difference by the interpretation of Ali, is … a ground and matter of their fear and jealousy, lest at any time waging a War against the Persian, that Heresy should begin to be set on foot amongst the [Ottoman] people, which … may breed those intestine civil distractions, which may prove of more danger and ruin than the former War.

Paul Rycaut (1668) p.94. The Ottomans saw Iran as a greater threat than any country in Christian Europe. For the divisions between Sunnis and Shi'ites see 132:3.

7 Article 2: that in imperial Ottoman letters the [Holy] Roman Emperor should no longer be addressed [merely] as 'king'.

Mustafa Na'ima (d.1718) *Tarih* (History) (1862 edn) Vol.1, p.455. Na'ima is summarizing the article in the Treaty of Zsitva-Torok (1606) that confirmed Ottoman recognition of Habsburg diplomatic equality and that ended a 13-year Ottoman–Habsburg war in Hungary. It was taken as a significant turning point in Ottoman–European relations and enabled the Habsburgs to stop paying an annual tribute of 30,000 ducats.

1 In Constantinople there have happened many fearful fires ... lately in the year 1607, October 14, there were burned above 3,000 houses, of which I saw a number of ruins as yet unrepaired. It is subject also to divers earthquakes ... especially in the year 1509 ... in which time more than 13,000 persons were all smothered and dead and laid up in heaps unburied.

William Lithgow (d. after 1630) *The Rare Adventures and Painful Peregrinations of William Lithgow* (1974 edn) pp.87–8. An unscrupulous Scot who insisted on travelling the Mediterranean alone and on foot, Lithgow (see 300:3) is constantly aware of dangers and oddities. However, his worst experience, being a Protestant, was not at the hands of the Ottomans but in the torture chamber of the Spanish Inquisition in Spain.

2 This year in October [1613], the Turks observing their feasts of Bayram ... a Turk having drunk wine too freely (the drinking whereof is forbidden amongst them, although they love it well, and drink in private) was apprehended, and carried before the Grand Vizier: who seeing the fact verified, inflicted this punishment upon him, to have boiling lead poured into his mouth and ears, the which was speedily executed.

Richard Knolles (continued by Edward Grimston) (1603; 1621 edn) p.1332.

3 One of the greatest Monarchs in the world was first affronted by mutinied troops; his own slaves, almost unarmed, and few in number, no man taking up a sword to defend him: and they who began this madness, not meaning to hurt him, by the increase of their own fury, which had no bounds, deposed him against their own purpose, and at last exposed his life, against their will, to the counsels of other men whom they equally hated. And now they mourned for their dead King as freshly, as they raged unreasonably; knowing they had stained their honour, being the first of their Emperors they ever betrayed.

Richard Knolles (1603; 1631 edn) p.1408. This report on the deposition and assassination of Osman II (r.1618–22) was added to Knolles' text with other material from the despatches of Sir Thomas Roe, English ambassador in Istanbul in 1621–8.

4 Until 1574, grand viziers had complete independence of action. No one was able to interfere in the affairs of the grand vizierate. Control and authority, dismissal and appointment were in their hands. No one was privy to their interviews with the sultan and no one had any power to interfere in any matter. [However], since that time, the companions and other close associates of the sultan have found position and rank, and have interfered in the affairs of the sultanate.

Kochu Beg (c.1630; 1885 edn) pp.30–31. The bureaucrat criticizes the undermining of the grand vizier's authority and, hence, the proper running of the state as he saw it in the early 17th century.

5 The natural life of man is reckoned in three parts: the age of growth, the age of attainment and maturity, the age of decline ... Similarly, societies, of which states consist, also have three ages of growth, maturity and decline, which can be distinguished from each other. History shows that some states have declined soon after the age of growth; some have been cut off in their prime by a disaster of fate; and some, like this illustrious Ottoman state, have enjoyed a long period of maturity because they are built on firm foundations and good principles. However, in both individuals and in societies the signs of the third age are [eventually] discernible.

Katib Chelebi (1609–57) *Dusturu-l-amel* (Guiding Principles) (1979 edn) pp.122–3. The historian, polymath and government official Katib Chelebi was invited by Mehmed IV (r.1648–87) to make a realistic assessment of the strength of the Ottoman empire.

6 It is certainly a good maxim for an ambassador in this country not to be over-studious in procuring a familiar friendship with Turks; a fair comportment towards all in a moderate way is cheap and secure; for a Turk is not capable of real friendship towards a Christian; and to have him called only, and thought a friend who is in power, is an expense without profit.

Paul Rycaut (1668) pp.90–91.

7 From [tobacco's] first appearance in Turkey, which was about the year 1601 ... various preachers have spoken against it individually, and many of the Ulema [doctors of the law] have written tracts concerning it ... the eminent surgeon Ibrahim Efendi devoted much care and attention to the matter, conducting great debates in ... [Istanbul], giving warning talks at special public meetings in the mosque of Sultan Mehmed, and sticking copies of fetwas onto walls. He troubled himself to no purpose. The more he spoke, the more people persisted in smoking ... Sultan Murad IV [r.1623–40] towards the end of his reign, closed down the coffee-houses in order to shut the gate of iniquity, and also

banned smoking, in consequence of certain outbreaks of fire. [But] people being undeterred … His
Majesty's severity in suppression increased, and so
did people's desire to smoke.

Katib Chelebi (1609–57) *The Balance of Truth* (1957 trans.)
p.51.

1 We lodged in a very large and handsome kane
[caravanserai], far exceeding what is usually seen in
this sort of buildings. It was founded by the second
Koprulu [Ottoman grand vizier, d.1676], and
endowed with a competent revenue, for supplying
every traveller that takes up his quarters in it, with a
competent portion of bread, and broth, and flesh,
which is always ready for those that demand it, as
very few people of the country fail to do. The kane
we found crowded with a great number of Turkish
hadjis, or pilgrims, bound for Mecca. But nevertheless we met with a peaceable reception amongst
them, tho' our faces were set to a different place.

Henry Maundrell *A Journey from Aleppo to Jerusalem in 1697*
(c.1698; 1963 edn) pp.6–7.

2 The Gr. Sigr [sultan] hath good sums of money in
his Treasury; But all the Pashas and Provinces are
exceedingly poor, so that in case of a war they will
come very weak into the field. Neither hath the Gr.
Sigr any Pashas of Experience in War, nor old
Officers, except a few among the Janissaries and the
Troops will be almost all composed of raw men.

Sir Robert Sutton *The Despatches of Sir Robert Sutton,
Ambassador in Constantinople 1710–1714* (1953 edn) p.27.
Sutton's assessment of Ottoman strength on the eve of the
campaign of 1711 against Muscovy contrasts well with the
observations of Moryson and Lithgow just a century
previously.

3 The government here is entirely in the hands of
the army; and the Grand Signior, with all his
absolute power, as much a slave as any of his subjects,
and trembles at a janissary's frown … it is hard to

judge whether the prince, people, or ministers, are
most miserable.

Lady Mary Wortley Montagu *Letters* (c.1717; 1906 edn) p.111.
As wife of the English ambassador to Istanbul (1716–18), Lady
Mary had ample opportunity to report on Ottoman affairs
through her contacts with important Ottoman women.

4 'Tis very easy to see [Turkish women] have more
liberty than we have. No woman, of what rank so
ever, being permitted to go into the streets without
two muslins; one that covers her face all but her eyes,
and another that hides the whole dress of her head,
and hangs halfway down her back, and their shapes
are wholly concealed by a thing they call a *ferigee* …
this has straight sleeves, that reach to their finger-
ends, and it laps all round them, not unlike a riding-
hood … there is no distinguishing the great lady
from her slave … and no man dare either touch or
follow a woman in the street.

Lady Mary Wortley Montagu (c.1717; 1906 edn) pp.115–16.

5 In Muhammadan empires the peoples derive from
religion a part of the astonishing respect they have
for their prince.

It is religion that slightly corrects the Turkish
constitution. Those subjects who are not attached to
the glory and greatness of the state by honour are
attached to it by force and by religious principle.

Charles, Baron de Montesquieu *The Spirit of the Laws* (1748;
1989 trans.) p.61.

6 It is constantly said that justice should be rendered
everywhere as it is in Turkey. Can it be that the most
ignorant of all peoples have seen clearly the one
thing in the world that it is most important for men
to know? … In Turkey, where one pays very little
attention to the fortune, life or honour of the
subjects, all disputes are speedily concluded in one
way or another. The manner of ending them is not
important, provided that they are ended.

Charles, Baron de Montesquieu (1748; 1989 trans.) pp.74–5.

The Renaissance, 1300–1600

HUMANISTS: LOOKING BOTH WAYS

1 In the year 1294 died in Florence a splendid citizen who had the name of Ser Brunetto Latini who was a great philosopher and high master of rhetoric, both spoken and written. It was he who expounded Cicero's *Rhetoric* and made the good and useful book called the *Tesoro* … Here was a worldly man but we mention him because he began the process of civilizing the Florentines and making them expert in speaking well and knowing how to guide and govern our republic according to political science.

Giovanni Villani *Chronicle* (1363) Bk 8, Ch.10. The Florentine chronicler interestingly connects the classical theory of rhetoric with the practice of good government. Villani's chronicle covered the history of Florence to 1363.

2 After the darkness has been dispelled, our grandsons will be able to walk back into the pure radiance of the past.

Francesco Petrarch (1304–74); Denys Hay (ed.) *The Age of the Renaissance* (1986) Ch.4, p.102. The great Italian poet and scholar, who was born in Arezzo, central Italy, anticipates the Renaissance.

3 There are fools who seek to understand the secrets of nature and the far more difficult secrets of God, with supercilious pride, instead of accepting them in humble faith. They cannot approach them, let alone reach them.

Francesco Petrarch *De sui ipsius et multorum ignorantia liber* (The Book of His Own Ignorance and of that of Many Others) (mid-14th century; 1968 trans.); A. Bullock *The Humanist Tradition in the West* (1985) Ch.1.

4 If we are too frightened to follow in the footsteps of men, for shame! It is women who hold first place in this honour. A woman was the inventor of the letters that we use. Let us not be influenced by that trite, vulgar saying that there is nothing new, or nothing new to be said, since Solomon and Terence wrote this, how much lustre has accrued to philosophy, how much improvement to poetry, how much light to history!

Francesco Petrarch to Francesco Bruni, 9 April 1363; *Letters of Old Age* (1992 trans.) Bk 2, no.3. The poet was writing to the secretary of Pope Urban V and seemingly ascribes the creation of letters to the goddess Minerva, 'inventor of the various arts'.

5 All the learned men of the world flocked to Rome of their own free will … the pope searched for Latin and Greek books in places where they ought to be found, never regarding the price. He collected many of the best scribes and gave them continuous employment … It was the desire of Pope Nicholas to found a library at St Peter's … and this would have been a wonderful work but, forestalled by death, he left it unfinished … Pope Nicholas was the ornament and light of literature and of learned men.

Bisticci Vespasiano *Memoirs* (1455; 1926 trans.) pp.46–9. A Florentine bookseller on Pope Nicholas V (r.1447–55).

6 If the authority of the Holy See were visibly displayed in majestic buildings, imperishable memorials and testimonials seemingly planted by the hand of God himself, belief would grow and strengthen from one generation to another, and all the world would accept and revere it.

Pope Nicholas V, on his deathbed, 1455, attrib. by his biographer, Grannozzo Manetti; P. Partner *Renaissance Rome 1500–1559* (1976) p.16. He is accentuating the sacred function of the new architecture and pointing the way to the great architectural works of the near future.

7 The splendour of the entertainment reached its height in a grand banquet. There was a representation in viands of Atalanta's race, of Perseus, of Andromeda and the dragon. There was a concert and masques. Famous lovers of antiquity … Jason and Medea, Theseus and Phaedra danced in triumph … Next day was given to a representation of the miracles of Corpus Christi; the day following, the life of John the Baptist.

Bernardino Corio *Storia di Milano* (1473) Bk 6; summarized in M. Creighton *A History of the Papacy from the Great Schism to the Sack of Rome* (1897; 1901 edn) Vol.4, pp.74–5. Corio is describing the festivities that were given by Pope Sixtus IV to honour the visit of Leonora, Duchess d'Este, recently married to Ercole, in which Christian and classical themes alternated. (It took four pages to carry one of the silver dishes at that banquet.) Francesco di Savona, a reforming Franciscan theologian, became pope in 1471 and quickly became renowned for lavish display and nepotism.

8 Illustrious master, today after supper Don Geraldo Saraceni and I betook ourselves to the illustrious Madonna Lucrezia [Borgia] to pay our respects in the name of your Excellency and his majesty, Don Alfonso ... she is very beautiful but her charm of manner is still more striking. In short, her character is such that it is impossible to suspect anything, but on the contrary we look for only the best.

Rome, December 23 1501, the sixth hour of the night.

Your Excellency's servant, Johannes Lucas.

Gianlucca Pozzi, Ferrarese ambassador, 23 Dec. 1501; Ferdinand Gregorovius *Lucrezia Borgia: A Chapter from the Morals of the Italian Renaissance* (1901; 1948 edn) p.137. Pozzi is reporting on Lucrezia to his master, Duke Ercole d'Este of Ferrara, as a potential daughter-in-law. Her reputation was hardly unblemished. According to Francesco Guicciardini, she was the daughter of Pope Alexander VI (*History of Italy* (1538; 1969 trans.) p.124). 'There was a report that not only did the two brothers commit incest with their sister Lucrezia, but even the father himself lay with her also; and who, when raised to the pontificate, took her forcibly away from her first husband not thinking him good enough for her and so married her to Giovanni Sforza, Lord of Pesaro; but even then, not being able to bear that this other husband should be a kind of rival to him, he accordingly annulled the said marriage' (Alexander Gordon *Life of Pope Alexander VI* (1729) p.273).

1 We have spoken of the golden age. We have spoken of your felicity ... therefore now act, most blessed father. See how God calls you by so many voices, so many prophecies, so many deeds well done.

Cardinal Egidio da Viterbo, celebratory sermon to Pope Julius II, 1506; published as a pamphlet entitled 'Concerning the Golden Age'.

2 It is assuredly very difficult to be at the same time a secular prince and a priest, for the two things have nothing in common ... the popes, although calling themselves Vicars of Christ, have introduced a new religion which has nothing of Christ in it but the name ... Christ commanded humility and they desire to rule the world.

Francesco Vettori (1474–1539) *A Contemporary Judges Pope Julius II*; Ferdinand Gregorovius *History of the City of Rome in the Middle Ages* (1859–72; 1902 trans.) Vol.8, pp.116–17.

3 Duke Federico [Montefeltro of Urbino] of glorious memory in his day was the light of Italy. Nor are there lacking today any number of reliable witnesses to his prudence, humanity, justice, generosity and unconquerable spirit, and to his military skill, which was brilliantly attested by many victories ... so we can fairly compare him with many famous men of the ancient world. Among his other commendable enterprises, Duke Federico built on the rugged site of Urbino a palace which many believe to be the most beautiful in all Italy ... At great cost he collected a large number of the finest and rarest books, in Greek, Latin and Hebrew, all of which he adorned with gold and silver, believing that they were the crowning glory of his great palace.

Baldassare Castiglione *The Courtier* (1528; 1967 edn) Bk 1. Castiglione holds up the duke as a model ruler. As military commander, builder and book collector, he epitomizes what Castiglione saw as the Renaissance qualities.

4 I wish then that this courtier of ours should be nobly born ... endowed not only with talent and beauty of person and feature, but with a certain grace ... The principal and true profession of the courtier ought to be that of arms ... I would have him ... know all bodily exercises ... whereof I think the first should be to handle every kind of weapon well on foot and on horse ... I would have our courtier a prefect horseman ... And as we read of Alcibiades ... so I would have this courtier excel all others and each in that which is most their profession ... [The count] will teach the courtier how to speak and write well ... whether in the Tuscan or any other dialect ... I am not content with our courtier unless he be also a musician to have acquaintance with divers instruments ... to know how to draw and to have acquaintance with the very art of painting.

Baldassare Castiglione (1528; 1967 edn) Bk 1. A composite picture of the perfect courtier, drawn from the discussion at Urbino that went on all night. Alcibiades was a famous Athenian citizen of the 5th century BC (see 57:2). Castiglione was writing nostalgically of the Duke Federico di Montefeltro's court at Urbino.

5 What you must do ... is to obey your lord in everything that redounds to his profit and honour, but not as regards things which bring him loss and shame. Therefore, if he were to order you to commit some treacherous deed not only are you not obliged to do it, but you are obliged not to do it, both for your own sake and to avoid ministering to your master's shame.

Baldassare Castiglione (1528; 1967 edn) Bk 2.

6 I suppose that nowhere else in the whole world, whether in ancient or modern times, would it be easy to find so many distinguished men of genius as there are now in the glorious court of Urbino [central Italy]. Here for instance you have Pietro Bembo, a man justly famous for his great knowledge ... whom we may truly call the father ... of the modern Italian tongue. Then there are the two brothers Fregoso ... both of them illustrious for their noble character and for virtue and learning ... as well as Baldassare Castiglione and Cesare Gonzaga ... celebrated alike for their valour in arms and for their achievements in arts and letters ... This city is indeed the ... home of the Muses today, famous for learning and holiness.

Jacopo Sadoleto (1477–1547), the brilliant humanist, cardinal and secretary to Pope Leo X; J. Cartwright *The Perfect Courtier* (1908) Vol.1, p.205. The concept of the perfect humanist is one of all-round achievement and 'virtue'.

ARTS AND SCIENCES

1 The test set by the Board of Works was that everyone should do a scene for the doors [of the baptistery] ... To me was conceded the palm of victory by all the experts and by my fellow competitors ... They [the judges] were very expert men, including painters and sculptors in gold and silver and marble. There were thirty-four judges, counting those from the city and the surrounding area.

Lorenzo Ghiberti *Commentaries* (c.1450; 1949 trans.); Alison Brown *The Renaissance* (1988) 'Documents'. The sculptor is describing the famous commission (Nov. 1403) to design the bronze doors of the Baptistery of Florence Cathedral. The artist undertook to deliver at least three panels a year. The work lasted for the next 50 years, almost until his death in 1455.

2 We judge those men worthy of honour and commendation who are distinguished by intelligence and outstanding skill, and most of all with that expertise which has always been prized among both the ancients and the moderns, that of architecture, founded as it is on the arts of arithmetic and geometry, which are the chief among the liberal arts because they are nearest to the demonstrable truth of things and have that scientific and intellectual element which we greatly value and esteem.

Contract of Luciano Laurana to work on Duke Federico's palace in Urbino, 1468; John Hale *The Civilization of Europe in the Renaissance* (1993) p.402. Hale points out how closely involved the duke was in the building and underlines the status of architecture as a liberal rather than a mechanical art.

3 From almost the earliest years of my boyhood I strove with all my might, main, effort and concentration to assemble as many books as I could on every sort of subject. Not only did I copy many in my own hand when I was a boy or youth, but I spent on

books anything I could spare from my small savings ... Since then, I have concentrated all my efforts and my time, all my powers on seeking out Greek books. For I feared – indeed I was consumed with terror – lest all these wonderful books, the fruit of so much toil and study by the greatest human minds, those very beacons to the world, should suddenly be in danger of destruction ... I came to understand that I could not select a place more suitable and convenient for men like me, of Greek background. Though nations from almost all over the earth flock in vast numbers to your city, the Greeks are most numerous of all: as they sail from their own region they make their first landfall in Venice, and have such a tie with you that when they put into your city they feel they are entering another Byzantium ... So I have give and granted all my books, both in Latin and Greek, to the most holy shrine of the Blessed Mark in your glorious city, sure in the knowledge that this is a duty owed to your generosity, to my gratitude, and to the country which you wanted me to share.

Cardinal Bessarion, letter accompanying his deed of donation, which formed the basis for the library of St Mark's, Venice, 1468; Ludwig Mohler *Kardinal Bessarion als Theologe, Humanist und Staatsman* (1942) Vol.3, pp.541–3. Bessarion came to Italy as a delegate to the Council of Florence (1438; see 193:8) and stayed. A Greek Roman Catholic dedicated to uniting the Eastern and Western Christian churches, he chose to give his magnificent library of books and manuscripts to Venice rather than to Florence.

4 The painter is lord of all types of people and of all things. If the painter wishes to see beauties that charm him it lies in his power to create them, and if he wishes to see monstrosities that are frightful, buffoonish or ridiculous, or pitiable, he can be lord and god thereof ... In fact whatever exists in the universe, in essence ... the painter has first in his mind and then in his hand ... He who despises painting loves neither philosophy nor nature.

Leonardo da Vinci *Notebooks* (1952 edn) pp.194–5.

5 I have perused and studied the works of all those who call themselves inventors of the machinery of war, and I find that their inventions are in no way different from the ones generally in use already. Accordingly, I dare to address myself to your excellency, and to offer to show you the following:

I am able to build very light, sturdy and portable bridges, to pursue and, when necessary, rout the enemy. I can build others which are more solid, which are fire- and attack-resistant, and easy to raise and take down. And I can equally burn and destroy those of the enemy ... Where cannon cannot be used, I can build catapults, and other marvellously efficient, little-known machines ... In times of peace I believe I can give perfect satisfaction to the equal of any other in architecture and the construction of buildings both public and private, and in guiding water from one place to another. I can carry out sculpture in marble, bronze and clay.

Leonardo da Vinci, setting out his credentials in successfully seeking the patronage of Ludovico Sforza, Duke of Milan, 1482; Lisa Jardine *Worldly Goods* (1996) p.239.

1 When I reflect that men are endowed with the same nature, born under the same skies, brought up under the same stars, I am compelled to think that they have always been afflicted by the same diseases ... for if the laws of nature are examined, they have existed unchanged on countless occasions since the beginning of the world. Wherefore I am prepared to show that a similar disease has arisen from similar causes also in past ages.

Niccolò Leoniceno, 1497; W.P.D. Wightman *Science and the Renaissance* (1962) Vol.1, p.272. The distinguished professor of medicine at the University of Padua attacks the popular view that syphilis was a completely new disease (later to be attributed to Columbus's sailors bringing it back from the New World). His position sounds eminently rational and scientific, yet he goes on to blame the rise in the level of Italy's rivers (particularly the Tiber), which disturbed the humours, traditionally seen as the chief bodily fluids: blood, phlegm, yellow bile and black bile.

2 Rather may Your Holiness, always keeping alive the imitation of the antique, equal it and surpass it, as you in fact do with great buildings.

The great Italian artist Raphael to Pope Leo X, 1519; André Chastel *The Renaissance: Essays in Interpretation* (1982) 'The Arts during the Renaissance'.

3   The greatest artist does not have any concept
          Which a single piece of marble does not itself
               contain
          Within its excess, though only
          A hand that obeys the intellect can discover it.

Michelangelo Buonarroti 'Sonnet for Vittoria Colonna', no.151 (1538–41/4) in *The Poems* (1996 trans.).

4   But God, in his graciousness, does not show
               himself
          More fully elsewhere to me than in some lovely
               mortal veil;

          And I love that solely because in it He is
               reflected.

Michelangelo Buonarroti 'Sonnet for Tommaso Cavalieri', no.106 (1536–42, revised 1546; 1996 trans.).

5 Although the arts of sculpture and painting continued to be practised until the death of the last of the twelve Caesars, they failed to maintain their previous excellence. Then in 1013 the reconstruction of the beautiful church of San Miniato sul Monte [Florence] showed that architecture had regained some of its earlier vigour ... From these beginnings art and design began slowly to revive and flourish in Tuscany ... Having seen how the art was developed from small beginnings to reach the heights and then from such a noble position crashed to their ruin, like other arts resembling human bodies in being born, growing, ageing and dying, the process by which their rebirth came about can be understood more easily.

Giorgio Vasari *Lives of the Artists* (1568 edn; 1965 trans.) Preface.

6 We can surely say that he was sent by heaven to renew the art of architecture. For hundreds of years, men had neglected this art and had squandered their wealth on buildings without order, badly executed and poorly designed.

Giorgio Vasari (1568 edn; 1965 trans.) p.133. Of Filippo Brunelleschi, particularly famous for the construction of the dome of Florence Cathedral.

7 Apart from 600 others, there are two things in particular which interrupt my work. First, the frequent letters of learned men which come to me from every part of the world and which would cost me whole days and nights if I were to reply. Then there are the visitors who come, partly to greet me, partly to see what new work is in hand, but mostly because they have nothing better to do. 'All right,' they say, 'let's drop in on Aldus!' ... I say nothing of those who come to recite a poem to me or a piece of prose, usually rough and unpolished, which they want me to publish for them.

Aldus Manutius' Introduction to Pseudo-Cicero in *Rhetorica ad Herennium* (1514; 1976 edn) p.129. The Venetian printer and publisher, writing in one of his bestsellers, rues the success of his small-format editions of the classics.

8 In 1498 the five volumes [of Aristotle's works] were offered in Aldus' sales catalogue at a total cost of 11 ducats. Set against the annual salary of a

well-paid humanities professor who might earn as much as 150 ducats a year, this price was high.
Lisa Jardine (1996) p.135.

1 It seems to me that, as far as I have been able to find out in our own days, authors seldom receive money from their books, for they are usually given to the printers, the authors receiving some copies when they are printed.
Abraham Ortelius, 1586; Jardine (1996) p.178. The much-published cartographer shares with his nephew the fruits of his experience.

2 Men like Benvenuto [Cellini], unique in their profession, stand above the law.
Pope Paul III on the privileged position of the artist; J.H. Plumb (ed.) *The Horizon Book of the Renaissance* (1961) p.343. The artist took him at his word.

3 Messer Jacopo Guidi, his Excellency's secretary, called me and, talking through his twisted mouth, said in a haughty voice: 'the Duke [Cosimo de' Medici] says that you are to let him know what you want for your [statue of] Perseus' … this way of behaving – which was completely unexpected – made me furiously angry, above by the way the message was delivered by such a venomous toad. I said that even if the Duke were to give ten thousand crowns, it would not be enough …

The following day, when I came to the court to pay my respects, his excellency beckoned me across and when I approached, said angrily, 'cities and great palaces are built with tens of thousands of ducats.'

I immediately replied that his Excellency would find any number of men who knew how to build cities and palaces, but as for making statues like my Perseus, I doubted whether he would find a single one in the whole world.
Benvenuto Cellini *Autobiography* (1558–62; 1956 trans.) pp.312 ff, 370 ff. The artist appears totally certain of his own worth and attuned to arrogance, though perhaps not his own.

4 Early Renaissance works of art which today we admire for their sheer representational virtuosity were part of a vigorously developing worldwide market in luxury commodities. They were at once sources of aesthetic delight and properties in commercial transactions between purchasers, seeking ostentatiously to advertise their power and wealth, and skilled craftsmen with the expertise to guarantee that the object so acquired would make an impact.
Lisa Jardine (1996) Prologue.

THE VIEW FROM FLORENCE

5 Our city of Florence, daughter and creation of Rome, is rising and destined to achieve great things.
Giovanni Villani (1363); Hay (1986) Ch.1. Villani did not live to see his prophecy fulfilled; he died in 1348 in the Black Death (see 286:2).

6 Since we have spoken about the income and expenditure of the commune of Florence in this period [1336–8], I think it is fitting to mention this and other great features of our city, so that our descendants in days to come may be aware of any rise, stability, and decline in condition and power that our city may undergo, and also that, through the wise and able citizens who at the time shall be in charge of its government, (our descendants) may try to advance it in condition and power, seeing our record and example in this chronicle. We find after careful investigation that in this period there were in Florence about 25,000 men from the ages of fifteen to seventy fit to bear arms, all citizens. Among them were 1,500 noble and powerful citizens who as magnates gave security [i.e., put up bail] to the Commune …

The banks of money-changers were about eighty. The gold coins which were struck amounted to some 350,000 gold florins and at times 400,000 a year.
Giovanni Villani (1363; 1832 edn) Vol.6, p.183. The chronicler provides detailed statistics for posterity of the numbers, from judges (the same figure as money-changers) to melons entering the city and distributed in the month of July – 4,000.

7 The hope of winning public honours is the same for all, provided they possess industry and natural gifts, and lead a serious-minded and respected way of life … it is marvellous to see how powerful this access to public office, once it is offered to a free people, proves to be in awakening the talents of the citizen. For when men are given hope of attaining honour in the state, they take courage and raise themselves to a higher plane; when they are deprived of that hope, they grow idle and lose their strength.
Colluccio Salutati (1331–1406); A. Murray *Reason and Society* (1978) pp.20–21. The learned Salutati, chancellor of Florence (1375–1406), idealizes republics.

8 The Florentine republic is neither completely aristocratic nor completely popular but is a combination of the two forms. This is demonstrated by the fact that the nobility, who dominate in numbers and in power, are not allowed to hold office in the city, and this contradicts aristocratic government. On the other hand those who carry out the menial jobs, the lowest level of worker, are not entitled to administer the republic, and this seems undemocratic. Thus, avoiding both extremes, this city embraces men of the middle class or rather; it favours the well born and richer as long as they don't become too powerful.

Leonardo Bruni *History of the Florentine People* (c.1415; 1610); E. Cochrane and J. Kirshner (eds) *The Renaissance* (1986) p.140. A view of the republic from a later chancellor of Florence (1427–44), who began writing his history c.1415.

1 Equal liberty exists for all – the hope of gaining high office and to rise is the same for all.

Leonardo Bruni, funeral oration for Nanni Strozzi, 1428. Strozzi was a member of one of Florence's most powerful families.

2 Florence harbours the greatest minds: whatever they undertake, they easily surpass all other men, whether they apply themselves to military or political affairs, to study or philosophy or to merchandise.

Leonardo Bruni *Panegyric on the City of Florence* (1403–4); Hay (1986) Ch.1.

3 First of all, Florence is more beautiful than your city of Venice, and more ancient by 540 years. Furthermore we spring from three honourable ancestries: Roman, French and Fiesolan. Just compare your own descent, also from three stems: Slavs, Paduans ... and fishermen from Malamocco and Chioggia. We are the disciples of St John [the Baptist], not of your St Mark, and there is the same difference as between French wool and the wool stuffed into rough mattresses ... We have two guilds, greater and worthier than four of yours put together, namely the wool and cloth guilds ... they export more than the cities of Venice, Genoa and Lucca put together.

Benedetto Dei (c.1472; 1952 edn) pp.103 ff; David Chambers and Brian Pullan (eds) *Venice: A Documentary History 1450–1630* (1992) p.68. A thoroughly biased and inaccurate diatribe from a Florentine merchant and secret agent.

4 The French historian [and diplomat], Philippe de Commines, described the bank not merely as the most profitable organization in Europe but as the greatest commercial house that there had ever been anywhere. 'The Medici name gave their servants and agents so much credit ... that what I have seen in Flanders and England almost passes belief.'

Christopher Hibbert *The Rise and Fall of the House of Medici* (1974) p.89. In the 1470s the Medici Bank provided the family with an immense fortune. It had, for instance, in 1466 gained

the right to exploit the alum mines in the Papal States. Alum, vital to the dying process, had been imported into Europe until these vast deposits were found.

5 If we are to call any age golden, it must surely be ours, which has produced a wealth of golden intellects. We have only to look at the innovations of today. For this century, like a golden age, has brought back to light the liberal arts that were well nigh dead: grammar, poetry, oratory, painting sculpture, architecture, music ... and all this in Florence. The two gifts revered in antiquity but almost forgotten since then, have been reunited in our own age.

Marsilio Ficino to Paul of Middleburg, 1492; *Opera* (1576) Vol.1, p.944. The leading humanist praises Paul for reviving Platonic studies.

6 Italy had never enjoyed such prosperity or known so favourable a situation as that in which it found itself so securely at rest in the year of our Christian salvation, 1490, and the years immediately before and after. The greatest peace and tranquillity reigned everywhere; the land under cultivation no less in the most mountainous and arid regions than in the most fertile plains and areas; dominated by no power other than her own, not only did Italy abound in inhabitants, merchandise and riches, but she was also highly renowned for the magnificence of many princes, for the splendour of so many most noble and beautiful cities ... Many factors kept her in that state of felicity ... but it was most commonly agreed that, among these, no small praise should be attributed to the industry and skill of Lorenzo de' Medici, so eminent among the ordinary rank of citizens in the city that the affairs of that republic were governed according to his counsels.

Francesco Guicciardini *History of Italy* (1561; 1969 trans.) p.4. The Florentine statesman and historian started writing his account at the end of his life, with nostalgia for the golden past of 40 years before.

7 Tyrants are incorrigible because they are proud, because they love flattery, and will not restore ill-gotten gains ... The tyrant is wont to occupy the people with shows and festivals, in order that they may think of their own pastimes and not of his designs, and growing used to the conduct of the commonwealth, may leave the reins of government in his hands.

Girolamo Savonarola, sermon against tyrants, directed at Lorenzo de' Medici, 1491; J.A. Symons *The Renaissance in Italy: Italian Literature* (1883) Vol.1, p.386. The Dominican friar was called to Florence in 1489 and became its virtual ruler from 1494 to 1496. He wished to depose Pope Alexander VI, whom he accused of profligacy and corruption, but was himself forbidden to preach, excommunicated for heresy and burned in Florence's Piazza della Signoria in 1498.

1 The first city to be renewed will be Florence ... as God elected the people of Israel to be led by Moses through tribulation to felicity ... so now the people of Florence have been called to a similar role led by a prophetic man, their new Moses [Savonarola himself] ... In the Sabbath Age men will rejoice in the Chiesa Nuovata [New Church] and there will be one flock and one shepherd.

Girolamo Savonarola, sermon on the New Age, 1490s; summarized in M. Reeves *The Influence of Prophecy* (1969; 1999 edn) p.436. Florentine citizens were moved to cast their ornaments and jewellery into Savonarola's 'bonfire of the vanities' (a phrase adopted by Tom Wolfe as the title of his 1987 novel).

2 You [God the Father is addressing mankind], constrained by no limits, in accordance with your own free will, in whose hand I have placed you, shall ordain for yourself the limits of your nature. I have set you at the world's centre so you may more easily observe the world from there. I have made you neither of heaven nor of earth, neither mortal nor immortal, so that with freedom of choice and with honour, as though the maker and moulder of yourself, you may fashion yourself in whatever shape you prefer.

Giovanni Pico della Mirandola *Oration on the Dignity of Man* (1496); E. Cassirer, P.O. Kristeller and J.H. Randall (eds) *The Renaissance Philosophy of Man* (1948) p.224. In Pico della Mirandola two worlds meet: he is the ardent humanist glorifying the status of man but he becomes one of the ardent disciples of Savonarola, known as *piagnoni* (penitents).

3 Sandro painted this picture at the end of the year 1500 in the troubles of Italy ... according to the XIth chapter of St John in the second woe of the Apocalypse in the loosing of the devil for three and a half years. Then he will be chained in the XIIth chapter and we shall see him trodden down as in this picture.

Sandro Botticelli, inscription on his painting *The Mystic Nativity* (1500), which is about the future rather than the past. In the foreground angels embrace men and the devil slinks away. The Florentine painter was also Savonarola's disciple, sharing an apocalyptic vision of the new age.

4 Look at the habits of Florence, how the women of Florence have married off their daughters. They put them on show and doll them up so they look like nymphs, and first thing they take them to the Cathedral. These are your idols, whom you have put in my temple ... You would do well to obliterate these figures that are painted so unchastely. You make the Virgin Mary seem dressed like a whore.

Girolamo Savonarola *Sermons on Amos* (1496; 1971 edn) Vol.1, p.309. The friar is castigating painters for their treatment of holy subjects.

5 The husband and wife must have separate bedrooms, not only to insure that the husband is not disturbed by his wife, when she is about to give birth or is ill, but to allow them, even in summer, an uninterrupted night's sleep whenever they wish. Each room should have its own door, and a shared side door as well, so that they can seek each other's company unnoticed. There should be a dressing room off the wife's bedroom, and off the husband's a library.

Leon Battista Alberti *On the Art of Building* (1452; 1988 trans.) p.149. The architect, student of the arts, physics and mathematics, humanist, painter and writer acknowledged that, as prosperity grew, there was a need for greater domestic space. Alberti, who believed that 'men can do all things if they will', was cited by Jacob Burckhardt as the greatest example of *l'uomo universale* (all-sided man) in his universality (*The Civilization of the Renaissance in Italy* (1860; 1944 edn) p.87).

6 Every day they [fathers] should look very carefully at their children's behaviour to see what their most persistent and recurrent characteristics are, what they like doing most and what least. This will reveal clearly what they are really like ... and so by watching his children every day a careful father will learn to interpret their slightest words and gestures.

Leon Battista Alberti *On the family* (1434–43); *The Family in Renaissance Florence* (1969 edn) p.68. Alberti's views on the family were echoed by many later thinkers.

7 We are all well and studying. Giovanni is able to spell. You can see for yourself how my writing is getting on. As for Greek, I work at it with Martino's help but do not get very far ... Lucrezia sews, sings and reads, Lugia can talk quite a lot ... nothing is wanting to us but to have you here.

Piero de' Medici to his father, Lorenzo, 1479; C. Ady *Lorenzo de' Medici* (1955) p.105. Piero (1471–1503) wrote to his father in Latin; his tutor was Martino da' Comedia. At this time Lorenzo's wife and family were in a country villa for safety.

POLITICS AND WAR

1 The majority of Italians who lived in the 13th and 14th centuries never heard the word 'Italy'. It was a country in which only the literate lived. Consciousness of its meaning arose from three sources: the classics, xenophobia and exile.

John Larner *Italy in the Age of Dante and Petrarch 1216–1380* (1980) p.1.

2 Before this year 1494, wars were protracted, the days were not bloody, and the ways of taking land by storm were slow and difficult; and although artillery was already in use, it was managed with such lack of skill that it did little harm ... but the French infused our wars with such liveliness that up to the year 1521 [when the new design of fortifications proved effective] whenever the terrain was lost, the state was lost with it.

Francesco Guicciardini *History of Florence* (1538; 1966 trans.) p.124.

3   Charles the eighth of the name
          Son of the very illustrious *fleur de lis*
          ... Will fight such great battles
          That he will subdue the Italians
          The Spaniards and the Aragonese ...
          He will enter the city of Rome
          And obtain the double crown
          Being named king of the Romans
          Against the will of the Germans ...
          He will possess in his life
          The high lordship of this universal earth.

Guilloche the Breton (*fl.c.*1494); trans. from text pub. by Marquis de la Grange (1869). This versification of the second Charlemagne prophecy was presented to Charles VIII of France and it, and other prophecies, inspired the French king's invasion of Italy in 1494, which, ironically, triggered the ruthless power struggle of the Italian wars.

4 When evening comes, I return home [from the local tavern] and go into my study. On the threshold I strip off my muddy, sweaty working clothes, and put on the robes of court and palace, and in this graver dress I enter the courts of the ancients and am welcomed by them ... and there I make bold to speak to them and ask the motives of their actions, and they, in their humanity, reply to me. And for the space of four hours I forget the world, remember no vexation, fear poverty no more, tremble no more at death; I pass into their world.

Niccolò Machiavelli to a friend, 10 Dec. 1513; *Literary Works of Machiavelli* (1961 trans.) p.139. In 1512 the Florentine Republic exiled their secretary, Machiavelli, who here describes his rapport with the classical authors and the inspiration for writing *Discourses* and *The Prince*. During his exile he simultaneously wrote the *Discourses on Livy*, in which he poured out all his admiration for the Roman republic as a model, and *The Prince*, in which, as a sharp political realist, he propounded a drastic, short-term remedy for the corruption of Italian politics.

5 Mercenary and auxiliary troops are both useless and dangerous; if any prince bases his state upon mercenaries, he will never succeed in making it stable or secure ... a point which should require little emphasis, since the present ruin of Italy is the result of having for many years now put her trust in mercenary armies – to the point where they have led her into slavery and ignominy.

Niccolò Machiavelli *The Prince* (1513) Ch.12.

6 Still, a prince should make himself feared in such a way that if he does not win love, he at least avoids hatred. For fear and the absence of hatred may well go together. In fact, it is always possible, if the ruler who refrains from appropriating the property of his citizens and subjects, or their women ... Above all, he must refrain from taking property, for men forget the death of their father more readily than the loss of their patrimony.

Niccolò Machiavelli (1513) Ch 17. Machiavelli dedicated *The Prince* to Lorenzo de' Medici, Duke of Urbino, the grandson of Lorenzo the Magnificent.

7 Everyone knows how admirable it is in a prince to keep faith and live by integrity, not by deceit. Nevertheless the experience of our age shows that the princes who have done remarkable things are the ones who have paid little heed to keeping faith and who have had the adroitness to confuse minds. In the end they have overcome those who relied on loyalty.

Niccolò Machiavelli (1513) Ch.18.

8 This opportunity must not therefore be allowed to pass, for letting Italy at length see her liberator. I cannot express the love with which he would be received in all those provinces which have suffered under these foreign invasions, with what thirst for vengeance, with what steadfast faith, with what love, with what grateful tears ... What Italian would rebel against him? This barbarous domination stinks in the nostrils of everyone. May your illustrious house

therefore assume this task with that courage and those hopes which are inspired by a just cause, so that under its banner our fatherland may be raised up.
Niccolò Machiavelli (1513) Ch.26. In the book's final paragraph Machiavelli appeals to Lorenzo de' Medici, the dedicatee, to save Italy from disintegration – the only short-term remedy for her woes. His attitude to foreign intervention has become hostile, although he had welcomed it initially.

1 With regard to prudence and stability, I say a people is more prudent, more stable and more just than a prince.
Niccolò Machiavelli *Discourses on Livy* (c.1513; 1813 edn) Bk I, Ch.58. This judgement reveals Machiavelli's real allegiance to republicanism.

2 It had reached such a point that not only the monks from pulpits but even the ordinary Romans went around the public squares proclaiming in loud threatening tones, not only the ruination of Italy but the end of the world. And there were people who, convinced that the present situation could not get worse, said that Pope Clement [VII] was the Antichrist.
Benedetto Varchi *Storia fiorentina* (1858 edn) Bk 10, Ch.8. The contemporary Florentine historian, whose work covered the period 1527–38, describes the panic just prior to the sack of Rome by German troops in 1527.

3 All political power is rooted in violence.
Francesco Guicciardini (1538; 1969 trans.); Brown (1988) p.118.

THE SPREAD NORTHWARDS

4 You ask how England pleases me ... I have found there ... so much human learning, not of the outworn, commonplace sort, but the profound, accurate ancient Greek and Latin learning, that I now scarcely miss Italy ... When I listen to my friend Colet ... I seem to hear Plato himself. Who would not marvel at the perfection of encyclopaedic learning in Grocyn? What would be keener ... than Linacre's judgement? What has nature ever fashioned gentler ... than the character of Thomas More? ... It is marvellous how thick upon the ground the harvest of ancient literature is here everywhere flowering.
Desiderius Erasmus to Robert Fisher in Italy (1499); P.S. Allen (ed.) *Selections from Erasmus* (1918). Erasmus (c.1466–1536), a 'citizen of Europe', travelled continuously in Europe, communicating everywhere in Latin with his humanist friends. John Colet (c.1466–1519) was dean of St Paul's and founded St Paul's school, London, in 1509. Thomas Linacre (c.1460–1524) founded the Royal College of Physicians in 1518.

5 Of course sacred Scripture is the authority in everything; yet I sometimes run across ancient sayings or pagan writings – even the poets' – so purely and reverentially expressed, and so inspired, that I can't help believing that their authors' hearts were moved by some divine power. And perhaps the spirit of Christ is more widespread than we understand, and the company of saints includes many not in our calendar.
Desiderius Erasmus *The Godly Feast* (1957 trans.) p.155. A wonderful expression of the humanist's response to classical authors.

6 They paint in Flanders only to deceive the external eye ... Their painting is of stuff [material things], bricks and mortar, the grass of the fields, the shadows of trees, and bridges and rivers, which they call landscapes, and little figures here and there, and all this ... is certainly done without reasoning or art, without symmetry or perspective, without care in selecting and rejecting.
Michelangelo Buonarroti, dismissing the art of the north; Denys Hay and John Law *Italy in the Age of the Renaissance 1380–1530* (1989) p.312. Italian patrons were more appreciative.

7 Here I am a gentleman, at home I am a parasite.
Albrecht Dürer, letter from Venice, 1506; Erwin Panofsky *Albrecht Dürer* Vol.1, p.244. The German painter notes the difference between the position of the artist in Germany and in Italy.

8 Just imagine me in France, at a secret meeting of the cabinet. The king himself is in the chair and round the table sit all his expert advisers, earnestly discussing ways and means of solving the following problems: how can His Majesty keep a grip on Milan and get Naples back into his clutches? How can he conquer Venice, and complete the subjection of Italy? How can he then establish control over Flanders, Brabant and finally, the whole of Burgundy.
Thomas More *Utopia* (1516; 1965 edn) p.57. A practical politician himself and chancellor to Henry VIII (see 345:7), More is fantasizing on the mechanisms of diplomacy. But earlier one of his characters notes: 'Most kings are more interested in the science of war ... than in useful peacetime techniques. They're far more anxious, by hook or by crook, to acquire new kingdoms than to govern their existing ones properly' (p.42).

9 No one could ever pay me to paint a picture again with so much labour ... Herr Georg Tausy himself wanted me to paint him a Madonna in a landscape with the same care and in the same size as this

picture, and he would have given me 400 florins for it … But very careful nicety does not pay. Therefore I shall stick to my engraving, and if I had done so before I should be richer today by 1,000 florins.
Albrecht Dürer, 1520s; Jardine (1996) p.227. The artist considers the commercial advantage to be gained from the reproduction of his engravings.

1 The times when I was a student were not as fit and favourable to learning as they are today … indeed the times were still dark … but thanks be to God, learning has been restored in my age to its former dignity and enlightenment … Why, the very women and girls aspire to the glory and reach out to the celestial manna of sound learning.
François Rabelais *Gargantua and Pantagruel* (1532 onwards; 1955 trans.) pp.194–5. The great French comic writer mocks the growth of education: 'I find robbers, hangmen, freebooters, and grooms nowadays more learned than the doctors and preachers were in my time.'

2 Although I too am a Behaim of Nuremberg, my family and coat of arms have been no help *to me*. I tell you this so that you will not presume on the same, for people truly attach no importance to such things. Today it is no different in Nuremberg than elsewhere in the world: one who has money advances, while one who has nothing gets little in addition. People observe that one has nothing; they do not ask who one is.
Michael Behaim to his cousin, 1534; Steven Ozment *Three Behaim Boys: Growing up in Early Modern Germany* (1990) p.90. The well-born merchant warns that only money speaks.

3 I have only printed 1,000 copies. My intention was to have printed double that number in a single run, which would greatly have enhanced my profit, but the job would have been in press that much longer to the dissatisfaction of those who were daily awaiting its publication.
Christophe Plantin, the French printer, of his breviary (1569); Jardine (1996) p.161. Printing was capital intensive. For instance, William Caxton, the father of English printing (see 212:3), invested money he had made as a mercer (cloth-dealer). Bestsellers, such as Plantin's Hebrew Bible of 1566, had a run of 3,000–4,000 copies.

4 Those whom nature hath made to keep home and to nourish their family and children, and not to meddle with affairs abroad.
Sir Thomas Smith, on the position of women, *The Common Wealth of England* (1589); Hale (1993) p.270.

5 What in former days even the experts could not master, can in our time be understood by plain, ordinary, and scarcely half-learned men. There will come a time when none of the secrets of nature will be out of the reach of the human mind.
Matthias Quadt, 1599; Gerald Strauss *Sixteenth Century Germany: Its Topography and Topographers* (1959) p.147. A German scholar reflects the optimism of the age.

JUDGEMENTS

6 The Renaissance of the fifteenth century was, in many things, great rather by what it designed than by what it achieved. Much which it aspired to do, and did but imperfectly or mistakenly, was accomplished in what is called the *éclaircissement* of the eighteenth century, or in our own generation; and what really belongs to the revival of the fifteenth century is but the leading instinct, the curiosity, the initiatory idea.
Walter Pater *The Renaissance* (1873) 'Pico della Mirandola'.

7 The Renaissance world aspired towards a society that was to have the leisure to enjoy the life of the spirit, not only in science but in all the arts – the arts that offered visions and models we were to strive to realize.
Bernard Berenson, diary entry, 26 Mar. 1952.

8 In its efforts to rediscover antiquity it created something quite different.
André Chastel *The Renaissance: Essays in Interpretation* (1982) 'The Arts during the Renaissance'.

9 So much glamour has accrued to the term [Renaissance], with its implication that mankind can heave itself free from the dragging weight of centuries and make a fresh, born-again start, and so great is its convenience in directing attention to the dovetail connecting one phase of a particular country's experience to the next, that to reject it is artificial. As long, that is, as it is accepted that its use is also artificial; it implies that the achievement of a few men of genius can represent the circumstances of the many; it would be hazardous to put the formative agents of cultural change, as contributors or patrons, at more than a thousandth part of the population of Europe … It becomes a medal used to congratulate the acceptance of an Italian flavour within another country's culture.
John Hale (1993) p.322.

The Hundred Years War, 1337–1453

THE FIRST PHASE: EDWARD III AND THE BLACK PRINCE, 1327–77

1 Now showeth the history that this Philip le Beau [Philip IV, the Fair], King of France, had three sons and a fair daughter named Isabel, married into England to King Edward the Second. And these three sons [Louis X, Philip V, Charles IV] … were all kings of France after their father's decease by right succession each after other, without having any male issue of their bodies lawfully begotten. So that after the death of Charles, last king of the three, the twelve peers and all the barons of France would not give the realm to Isabel, the sister, who was Queen of England, because they said and maintained, and yet do, that the realm of France is so noble that it ought not to go to a woman, and so consequently to Isabel, nor to the King of England, her eldest son: for they determined the son of the woman to have no right or succession by his mother, since they declared the mother to have no right.

Jean Froissart *Chronicles* (from 1373; 1963 edn) Bk 1.3. Froissart sets the scene for what we call the Hundred Years War (in fact, a series of intermittent wars separated by long truces), which began in 1337 and ran on to 1453. Froissart, the incomparably vivid chronicler of the times, knew both France and England at first hand. The text is a modern edition of the splendid translation (1523–5) commissioned by Henry VIII from Lord Berners (John Bourchier).

2 Wherefore we benignly wish that all and each of the natives of the kingdom who will subject themselves willingly to us, as the true King of France according to wise counsel, before next Easter … should be admitted to our peace and grace and to our special protection and defence.

Edward III assumes the title of king of France, 8 Feb. 1340; A.R. Myers (ed.) *English Historical Documents* Vol.4 (1969) p.67. Edward was the grandson of Philip IV of France; the new king, Philip VI, was merely his nephew.

3 After nine o'clock when he had the wind and sun at this back and the flow of the tide with him, with his ships divided into three columns, [Edward III] gave his enemies the challenge they wished for. A terrifying shout rose to the heavens above the wooden horses; an iron shower of quarrels from crossbows and arrows from the longbows brought death to thousands of people; all those who wished or dared to do so fought hand in hand with spears, battle axes and swords; stones hurled from the turrets of masts dashed out the brains of many; to sum up, there was joined without any doubt a great and terrible naval battle.

Geoffrey le Baker *Chronicle* (mid-14th century; 1889 edn); E.H.D. Vol.4 (1969) p.69. At the Battle of Sluys, 24 July 1340, on the Flanders coast Edward III destroyed most of the French fleet, which had been harassing the English Channel ports. This is the first sea battle in British history of which real details are available; as was usual at the time, it was fought essentially as a land battle, albeit on boats.

4 Why are the English less brave than the French? Because they wouldn't jump into the sea in full armour, like our gallant knights.

Jester of Philip VI of France on the defeat at Sluys; Robin Neillands *The Hundred Years War* (2001) p.84. Courtiers were reluctant to tell the king of the disaster, and eventually his jester was said to have broken the news with this riddle.

5 When they saw that their crossbowmen were not harming the English at all, the French men-at-arms, mounted on young warhorses and agile coursers, rode down the crossbowmen, standing to the number of 7,000 between them and the English, crushing them under the feet of their horses, rushing impetuously forward to show the English how brave they were … The English in contrast, invoking the mother of Christ, having sanctified that day of Saturday with fasting, hastily dug many holes in the ground in front of their lines, one foot in depth and the same dimension in breadth, so that [if] they were too hard pressed by the French cavalry, the horses would stumble in the holes.

Geoffrey le Baker (mid-14th century; 1889 edn) describes the Battle of Crécy, 26 Aug. 1346; E.H.D. Vol.4 (1969) p.80. The traditional invincibility of heavy cavalry was challenged by such tactics – and, above all, by the devastating firepower of the massed English archers with their longbows, which could shoot faster, further and more penetratingly than the crossbow.

6 Then the king said, 'Is my son dead or hurt, or on the earth felled?' 'No, sir,' quoth the knight, 'but he is hardly matched [hard pressed], wherefore he hath need of your aid.' 'Well,' said the king, 'return to him, and to them that sent you hither, and say to them that they send no more to me, as long as my son is alive. And also say to them that they suffer him this day to win his spurs; for if God be pleased, I will this journey [day] be his and the hour thereof, and to them that be about him.'

Jean Froissart (from 1373; 1963 edn) Bk 1.130. Edward III and the Black Prince at Crécy. Prince Edward (the familiar nickname is not contemporary) was 16 years old and in the van of battle. The leaders of the prince's battalion sent Sir Thomas Norwich to the king, 'who had taken up a position on a little hill, by a windmill', to seek reinforcements. The king's refusal, according to Froissart, 'greatly encouraged them', and the ultimate victory secured the young prince's military reputation.

1 *Ich dien* (I serve)

The German motto *Ich dien* was said to be that of the blind King John of Bohemia, an ally of the French king, who fought and died at Crécy. The Black Prince then adopted it, partly as a tribute to a brave man, partly to emphasize that it was his father who had commanded at Crécy. It has been the badge of the Princes of Wales ever since.

2 In this season [1344] the King of England [Edward III] took pleasure to new re-edify the castle of Windsor, the which was begun by King Arthur; and there first began the Table Round, whereby sprang the fame of so many noble knights throughout all the world. Then [*c*.1348] King Edward determined to make an order and a brotherhood of a certain number of knights, and to be called Knights of the Blue Garter, and a feast to be kept yearly at Windsor on Saint George's Day.

Jean Froissart (from 1373; 1963 edn) Bk 1.100. Windsor had no traditional connection with King Arthur, but legend by now was of immense symbolic importance to the world of chivalry (see 207:4), and the association was glamorous. The first of the secular orders of chivalry (which were to loom so large in the late Middle Ages) seems to have been the Order of the Band, founded by Alfonso XI of Castile *c*.1330. The Order of the Garter was next in what would prove to be a very long line. Its impact is a tribute to Edward's prestige on the European stage.

3 *Honi soit qui mal y pense.* (Evil [shame] to him who thinks evil.)

The motto of the Most Noble Order of the Garter, traditionally because, after the Countess of Salisbury lost a garter at a court festival, it was picked up by Edward III, who reproved the tittering onlookers by binding it around his own knee with this chivalrous remark.

4 The queen, being great with child, knelt down and sore weeping said: 'Ah, gentle sir, since I passed the sea in great peril, I have desired nothing of you; therefore I now humbly require you, in the honour

of the Son of the Blessed Mary and for the love of me, that ye will take mercy of these six burgesses!'

Jean Froissart (from 1373; 1963 edn) Bk 1.146. Philippa of Hainault, wife of Edward III, protects the burgesses of Calais in Aug. 1347 from her husband's wrath when they surrendered the town after an 11-month siege. The story could be true, but it is not described in any other contemporary record. It would bear impressive fruit in Rodin's noble bronze group *Les Bourgeois de Calais* (1884–6), which was set up in Calais in 1895, with a replica being erected outside the Houses of Parliament, London, in 1915. Calais remained an English enclave until it was lost in Jan. 1558 by Mary Tudor (see 350:3).

5 Then the battle began on all parts, and the battles [battalions] of the marshals of France approached, and they set forth that were appointed to break the array of archers. They entered a-horseback into the way where the great hedges were on both sides. As soon as the men of arms entered, the archers began to shoot on both sides and did slay and hurt horses and knights, so that the horses when they felt the sharp arrows they would in no wise go forward, but drew aback and flung and took so fiercely, that many of them fell on their masters, so that for press they could not rise again.

Jean Froissart (from 1373; 1963 edn) Bk 1.162. Even though the French were forewarned, the longbow proved as decisive at the Battle of Poitiers on 19 Sept. 1356 as it had at Crécy.

6 Whenever the French wanted to buy anything, they were charged a steep price, and there was a danger of serious riots breaking out on this score. The Scots accused the French of doing them more harm than the English, and when asked to explain said: 'You have trampled on all our crops – wheat, barley and oats – on your way through the country, and you will not deign to keep to the roads.' The Scots demanded compensation before the French left, or the latter would find neither ship nor sailor to take them home again.

Jean Froissart (from 1373; 1963 edn) Bk 1.173. Like Flanders, the Anglo-Scottish border was a regular theatre of conflict in the Hundred Years War, with the Franco-Scottish allies harrying the English. But allies could be as much trouble as the enemy – as here, in 1384, when a French expeditionary force under Jean de Vienne ravaged the borderland.

7 Without doubt this king had been among all the kings and princes of the world renowned, beneficent, merciful, and august; given the epithet 'the Favoured One' on account of the remarkable favour through which he distinguished himself.

Thomas Walsingham *English History* (after 1392; 1863–4 edn) Vol.1, pp.327–8. When Edward III died (21 June 1377) the

Black Prince was already dead, and the first great phase of English victories in France was long past. This late 14th-century tribute to the king is not just a conventional gesture. It is surprising that he does not loom larger in the national folk-memory – perhaps he needed a Shakespeare to inject him permanently into the national bloodstream.

THE PEASANTS' REVOLT, 1381

1 Wherefore in the parliament by the assent of the prelates, earls, barons, and those of the commonalty assembled there, in order to refrain the malice of the servants, there are ordained and established the underwritten articles:

First, that carters, ploughmen, drivers of the plough, shepherds, swineherds, daymen, and all other servants, shall take the liveries and wages accustomed in the twentieth year, or four years before.

Statute of Labourers, provision 1, 1351; E.H.D. Vol.4 (1969) p.993. In the aftermath of the Black Death, with the costs of labour soaring, Edward III and the land-owning community of the realm try to put back the clock to the wage levels that obtained in 1347 (the 20th anniversary of the king's accession in 1327), before the plague struck.

2 In the first place the lords and commons are agreed that, for ['various needs which were shown to them as well as for the safety of the realm and for the keeping of the sea'], contribution should be made by every lay person in the realm, both in franchises and outside, males and females alike, of whatever estate or condition, who has passed the age of fifteen years, of the sum of three groats [1 shilling], except for true beggars, who shall be charged nothing.

Rotuli Parliamentorum III, 90; E.H.D. Vol.4 (1969) p.127. Parliament's declaration of the poll tax in Nov. 1380, the third such tax since Richard II's accession in 1377, sparked the Peasants' Revolt the following year. Its main centres were Kent, Essex and London itself.

3 And there they made their chief a certain Wat Tyler of Maidstone to maintain them and be their counsellor. And on the next Monday after the feast of the Holy Trinity they came to Canterbury before the hour of noon, and 4,000 of them entered into the minster church of St Thomas and, kneeling down, they cried with one voice to elect a monk to be arch-bishop of Canterbury, 'for he who is now archbishop is a traitor, and will be beheaded for his iniquity'. And so he was five days afterwards!

Anonimalle Chronicle (covers 1333–81); E.H.D. Vol.4 (1969) p.130. The Kentish rebels, led by Wat Tyler, seized Canter-bury on 10 June 1380. This anonymous chronicle was probably compiled at St Mary's Abbey, York.

4 And so that he might infect the more with his doctrines, at Blackheath where 20,000 of the commons were gathered together, he began a sermon in this manner:

> When Adam delved and Eve span,
> Who was then the gentleman?

And continuing the sermon thus begun, he strove … to prove that from the beginning all men were created equal by nature, and that servitude had been introduced by the unjust oppression of wicked men, against God's will; because, if it had pleased him to create serfs, surely in the beginning of the world he would have decreed who was to be a serf and who a lord.

Thomas Walsingham (after 1392; 1863–4 edn) Vol.2, p.32; E.H.D. Vol.4 (1969) p.141. On 11 June the rebels began their march on London. John Ball, the other leader of the Kentish revolt, standing on high ground at Blackheath, looking down on London, preaches to the crowd. Walsingham adds: 'He taught, moreover, the perverse doctrines of the perfidious John Wycliffe' (see 200:5). Ball may have been a follower of Wycliffe, but Wycliffe himself condemned the Peasants' Revolt.

5 Let us go to the King. He is young, and we will show him our miserable slavery, we will tell him it must be changed, or else we will provide the remedy ourselves.

John Ball, address at Blackheath, 1381; Froissart (from 1373; 1967 edn) Bk 2.73. The rebels remained committedly loyal to the 14-year-old king, whom they did not hold responsible for the actions of his council.

6 [Wat Tyler and the peasants] required that no man should be a serf, nor do homage or any manner of service to any lord, but should give fourpence rent for an acre of land, and that no one should serve any man but at his own will, and on terms of regular covenant. And at this time the king caused the commons to arrange themselves in two lines, and caused a proclamation to be made before them that he would confirm and grant them their freedom and all their wishes generally, and that they should go through the realm of England and catch all traitors and bring them to him in safety and that he would deal with them as the law required.

Anonimalle Chronicle (covers 1333–81); E.H.D. Vol.4 (1969) p.135. The boy king meets the rebels at Mile End, outside the gates of London, on 14 June, and concedes the main demands – that is, legal recognition of what was, in any case, becoming increasingly the social reality: an end to serfdom and the realistic regulation of a wage-earning economy.

1 We must judge them by their works; for they slew the father of the whole clergy, the head of the English Church, the archbishop of Canterbury [Simon of Sudbury]. See, too, what they did against the faith; how they compelled masters of grammar schools to swear that they would never again teach grammar to children! And what more? They strove to burn all ancient muniments, and slew all such as could be found capable of commemorating to posterity either ancient records or modern events; it was perilous to be recognized as a clerk, and far more perilous if any were caught bearing an inkhorn at his side.

Thomas Walsingham *Historia Brevis* (1381); G.G. Coulton *Social Life in Britain from the Conquest to the Reformation* (1918) p.56. In an increasingly regulated society even illiterate peasants recognized how far their lives had come to be penetrated and dominated by the written word – and reacted accordingly. Captured by the rebels in the Tower of London and executed on 14 June, Simon of Sudbury, chancellor as well as archbishop and therefore held responsible for the hated poll tax, was the most prominent victim of the Revolt.

2 And when [Wat Tyler] had dismounted, he half bent his knee, and took the king by the hand, and shook his arm forcibly and roughly, saying to him, 'Brother, be of good comfort and joyful for you shall have within the next fortnight 40,000 more of the commons than you have now, and we shall be good companions.' And the king said to Wat, 'Why, will you not go back to your own country?' And the other replied with a great oath that neither he nor his fellows would depart until they had their charter.

Anonimalle Chronicle (covers 1333–81); E.H.D. Vol.4 (1969) p.136. At a further meeting between the king and the rebels, at Smithfield on 15 June, Tyler behaved with both familiarity and insolence to Richard – he toyed with his dagger and 'called for a flagon of water to rinse his mouth because he was in such a heat, and when it was brought he rinsed his mouth in a very rude and disgusting manner before the king'. Matters turned ugly. Tyler was killed while resisting arrest by London's Lord Mayor, Sir William Walworth.

3 Sirs, will you shoot your king? I am your captain, follow me.

Anonimalle Chronicle (covers 1333–81); E.H.D. Vol.4 (1969) p.136. The young Richard II saves the situation, spurring his horse forward and confronting the angry but frightened and bewildered peasants. Essentially, this was the end of the Peasants' Revolt. The mass of rebels dispersed, content with the royal promises; the king, sanctioned by his council, promptly

rescinded them; and the rebel leaders were duly hunted down and executed.

4 Villeins [serfs] you are, and villeins you shall remain.

Richard II, according to Walsingham (after 1392; 1863–4 edn); Nigel Saul *Richard II* (1997) p.74. The king's response to a demand from the Essex rebels (on 22 June, when the crisis point had passed) for the ratification of the royal promises forced out of him at Mile End. But, while nothing was outwardly gained by the insurgents, villeins they did *not* remain.

THE FALL OF RICHARD II, 1389–99

5 'Well! Know that I have for long been ruled by tutors; and it was not possible for me to act at all, or almost at all, without them. Now henceforth I will remove those from my council, and, as heir of lawful age, I will appoint whom I will to my council, and conduct my own affairs. And I order that in the first place the chancellor should resign to me his seal.' The archbishop of York delivering it, the king put it in his bosom and went forth.

Thomas Walsingham (after 1392; 1863–4 edn) Vol.2, p.181; E.H.D. Vol.4 (1969) p.164. Richard II's uncle, John of Gaunt, had some success in moderating the young king's autocratic tendencies and lack of judgement, but when Gaunt left England in 1386 to pursue his Spanish interests, Richard's authority was soon challenged by a baronial faction led by his uncle, Thomas of Woodstock. Here, on 3 May 1389, the 22-year-old king finally takes control of his government once more. Richard, who neither forgot nor forgave, was hungry for revenge.

6 Sire, you ought first to hazard your life in capturing a city from your enemies, by feat of arms or force, before you think of giving up or selling any city which your ancestors, the kings of England, have gained or conquered.

Anon. *Chronique de la traison et mort de Richard Deux Roy Dengleterre* (1846 trans.) pp.118–21. Thomas of Woodstock, Duke of Gloucester (the king's hated uncle and a leader of the opposition to him), exasperated by Richard's surrender of Brest to the French in June 1397, insults him at a banquet in Westminster. The king was sensitive to the reproach that, unlike his bellicose father and grandfather, he had never been in the thick of a real siege or battle. On 10 July Gloucester was arrested on a charge of treason, dying in prison in Calais in dubious circumstances soon after.

7 After this, the king of solemn days and great feasts, in which he wore his crown and went in his royal attire, ordered and had made in his chamber a throne, wherein he was wont to sit from after supper until evensong time, speaking to no man, but over-looking all men; and if [the king] looked on any man, whatever the estate or degree that he were of, he must kneel.

Anon. *An English Chronicle* (1856 edn) p.12. By 1397 the difficult and autocratic king was increasingly estranged from nobility and commons alike and seems to have gone out of his way to antagonize them. He depended on his personal bodyguard of Cheshire archers, to whom, by contemporary standards, he allowed an equally unacceptable degree of familiarity. Indeed, one is recorded as saying to him, 'Dick, sleep safely while we remain awake, and fear not while we live, seest thou' (*Kenilworth Chronicle* in Mary Louise Bruce *The Usurper King* (1986) p.155).

1 He [John of Gaunt] was a man advised and wary in his passage of life, liking safe courses with reason than happy by chance; of his own glory, he was neither negligent, nor ambitiously careful; towards the king he carried himself in terms honourable enough for a moderate prince, and yet not so plausible as a vain man would desire; whereby there never happened to him any extraordinary matter, either in prejudice or in performance.

Sir John Hayward *The First Part of the Life and Reign of King Henry IV* (1599). Despite the unpopularity and suspicion that his immense wealth and power earned him among the commons (especially Londoners), Gaunt served his nephew well and was a restraining influence on him.

2 The Earl of Derby [Henry of Bolingbroke, son of John of Gaunt and the future Henry IV] said the following words, in all good faith, and not thinking that they would ever be repeated – not that in fact there was anything wicked or treacherous about them: 'Holy Mary, dear cousin, what is our cousin the king up to? Will he drive all the nobles out of England? There'll soon be nobody left. He shows quite clearly that he does not want to advance the fortunes of the kingdom.'

Henry of Bolingbroke to Thomas Mowbray, Duke of Norfolk; Froissart (from 1373; 1967 edn) Bk 4.94. In the overheated atmosphere of the time, Mowbray then accused Henry before the king of treason, provoking a major (and avoidable) crisis, of which the king – who hated and feared them both – took full advantage.

3 [Henry Bolingbroke] was quickly horsed, and closed his visor, and cast his spear into the rest, and when the trumpet sounded set forward courageously towards his enemy six or seven paces. The Duke of Norfolk was not fully set forward when the king cast down his warder [baton] and the heralds cried 'Ho, ho!' Then the king caused their spears to be taken

from them, and commanded them to repair again to the chairs, where they remained two long hours, while the king and his council deliberately consulted what order was best to be laid in so weighty a cause.

Raphael Holinshed *Chronicles of England, Scotland and Ireland* (1577 and 1587; 1927 edn) Vol.3, p.605. The quarrel of Mowbray and Bolingbroke was to be resolved by an elaborately staged duel outside the walls of Coventry on 16 Sept. 1398. But at the climactic moment the king stopped proceedings and banished them both. There was uproar, with the king outraging all parties. Within the year Bolingbroke (now the rightful Duke of Lancaster, on the death of John of Gaunt) returned to claim his inheritance – and took the throne.

4   This royal throne of kings, this scept'red isle,
    This earth of majesty, this seat of Mars,
    This other Eden, demi-paradise;
    This fortress, built by Nature for herself
    Against infection, and the hand of war.

William Shakespeare *Richard II* (c.1595) Act 2, Sc.1. The speech that Shakespeare gives John of Gaunt is itself an important historical document in the development of English nationalism. Shakespeare's audience would have been aware that the Lancastrian side of Elizabeth I's descent came directly from Gaunt (via the Beauforts), while no blood of the childless Richard II or of Henry IV flowed in her veins (see 205:5).

5 On Saint Matthew's day [21 September] … I, the writer of this history, was in the Tower, wherein King Richard was a prisoner … And there and then the king discoursed sorrowfully in these words: 'My God! A wonderful land is this, and a fickle; which has exiled, slain, destroyed, or ruined so many kings, rulers, and great men, and is ever tainted and toileth with strife and variance and envy.'

Adam of Usk *Chronicle* (covers 1377–1404); E.H.D. Vol.4 (1969) p.180. Imprisoned in the Tower of London, the king awaits his deposition. This, from an eyewitness, is the Richard that Shakespeare immortalized in *Richard II* (Act 3, Sc.2).

6 In the name of God, Amen! I Richard by the grace of God king of England and of France and lord of Ireland … resign all my kingly majesty, dignity and crown … And with deed and word I leave off and resign them and go from them for evermore, for I know, acknowledge and deem myself to be, and have been, insufficient, unable and unprofitable, and for my deserts not unworthily to be put down.

Richard II, abdication document, read aloud by the archbishop of York to Parliament in Westminster Hall, 30 Sept. 1399; C.L. Kingsford *Chronicles of London* (1905) p.21. The reign of Henry IV had begun. Richard himself died (almost certainly murdered) in prison at Pontefract early in the new year.

THE WAR RENEWED:
HENRY V AND JOAN OF ARC, 1413–53

1 For these Frenchmen, puffed up with pride and lacking in foresight, hurling mocking words at the ambassadors of the King of England, said foolishly to them that as Henry was but a young man, they would send him little tennis-balls to play with … When the king heard these words he [responded] to those standing about him: 'If God wills, and if my life shall be prolonged with health, in a few months I shall play with such balls in the Frenchmen's courtyards that they will lose the game eventually, and for their game win but grief.'

John Strecche *Chronicle for the Reign of Henry V* (shortly after Henry V's death in 1422); E.H.D. Vol.4 (1969) p.208. Henry V came to the throne in 1413. The contemptuous response of the French dauphin (the future Charles VII) to the new king's embassy to France in the spring of 1414 was both ill judged and ill timed: the following year Henry embarked with his army from Southampton. The next phase of the Hundred Years War was under way.

2 War without fire is like sausages without mustard.

Henry V, attrib.; John Gillingham *The Wars of the Roses* (1981) p.24.

3 Sire. There are enough to kill, enough to capture, and enough to run away.

Dafyd Gam, 24 Oct. 1415; Neillands (2001) p.214. After taking Harfleur, Henry's successful, but by now weary, forces were intercepted on their way back to Calais by a massive French army. Gam, from Brecon in Wales, was one of Henry V's squires. Asked by the king for his guess of the number of the approaching French army, this – according to contemporary tradition – was his laconic reply.

4 The King daily and nightly in his own person visited and searched the watches, orders and stations of every part of his host, and whom he found diligent he praised and thanked, and the negligent he corrected and chastized.

Anon. *First English Life of Henry V* (1513–14; 1911 edn). The eve of Agincourt. This is early evidence of what Shakespeare was to call 'a little touch of Harry in the night'.

5   Upon Saint Crispin's day
        Fought was this noble fray,
        Which fame did not delay
        To England to carry.
        Oh, when shall English men
        With such acts fill a pen,

        Or England breed again
        Such a King Harry?

Michael Drayton 'The Ballad of Agincourt' (1606). Henry V's conclusive victory at Agincourt (25 Oct. 1415) established him as a national hero, both for his own time and in subsequent popular tradition.

6 It was agreed between our said father of France and us, that … after the death of our said father, and from thence forward, the crown and realm of France, with all their rights and appurtenances, shall remain and abide and belong to us and our heirs for evermore.

Treaty of Troyes, 1420; E.H.D. Vol.4 (1969) p.225. The treaty established the terms of peace with France: Henry V was to marry Catherine, daughter of the mad Charles VI (hence 'our father of France'), and was formally accepted as the next French king when Charles should die. However, against all expectation, Henry died first, on 31 Aug. 1422, leaving an heir, Henry VI, only nine months old (see 308:5).

7 In that year [1429] … while Orléans was besieged, there came to King Charles [VII] of France, at Chinon where he was then staying, a young girl who described herself as a maid of twenty years of age or thereabouts named Joan, who was clothed and habited in guise of a man, born in the parts between Burgundy and Lorraine at a town named Domrémy very near Vaucoulleurs … [She] asserted that she was a maid inspired by divine providence, and sent to King Charles to restore him and bring him back into the possession of all his kingdom generally, from which he was, as she said, wrongfully driven away and put out.

Jean Waurin *Recueil des chroniques de la Grande Bretagne* (1891 trans.) Vol.3, p.261. On 12 Oct. 1428 the English laid siege to Orléans. Joan of Arc arrived to inspire and energize the French royalist cause. Everyone was nonplussed by her appearance. A French aristocrat, the Lord of Gamaches, called her 'a girl who came from no one knows where and has been God knows what' (Elizabeth Hallam (ed.) *The Chronicles of the Wars of the Roses* (1988) p.175).

8 You, the English captains, must withdraw from the kingdom of France and restore it to the King of Heaven and his deputy, the King of France, while the Duke of Burgundy should return at once to his true allegiance. Take yourself off to your own land, for I have been sent by God and his angels, and I shall drive you from our land of France. If you will not believe the message from God, know that wherever you happen to be, we shall make such a great Hahaye as has not been made in France these thousand years.

Joan of Arc's challenge to the English leaders in France, March 1329; Neillands (2001) p.259. At that point they were unimpressed; but the Maid managed to enter the besieged city of Orléans on 30 April with the vanguard of the relieving army and went into action. On 8 May the English lifted the siege and withdrew.

1 And at the hour the king was consecrated and also when they had placed the crown on his head, every man cried out 'Noel!' And the trumpets sounded so that it seemed as though the walls of the church should have crumbled. During the aforesaid mystery, the Maid was always at the king's side, holding his standard in her hand. It was fine to see the elegant manners not only of the king but also of the Maid, and God knows that you would have wished them well.

Report of the coronation of Charles VII by 'three gentlemen from Anjou'; R. Pernoud and M.V. Clin *Joan of Arc* (2000 edn) p.66. On 18 June 1429 Charles VII was crowned in Rheims Cathedral – the traditional venue for French coronations – seven years after his accession and with Joan beside him.

2 She mounted her horse armed as would a man, adorned with a doublet of rich cloth-of-gold over her breastplate; she rode a very handsome, very proud grey courser, and displayed herself in her armour and her bearing as a captain would have done … and in that array, with her standard raised high and fluttering in the wind, and well-accompanied by many noble men, she sallied forth from the city, about four hours past midday.

Georges Chastellain *Chronique des ducs de Bourgogne* (c.1455; 1863–6 edn); Pernoud and Clin (2000 edn) p.86. A last view of Joan in splendour, riding out from Compiègne before her capture by the Burgundians on 23 May 1430.

3 In this battle [May 1430] the witch of France [Joan of Arc], known as 'la Pucelle' [the Maid], was also captured, dressed in full armour. Her followers, and all the French, were confident that her cunning sorcery would overcome the English army. But God was lord and master of our victory and her downfall, so she was taken and held captive by the king and his council for ever, at his will.

The (English) continuation of *The Brut* (to c.1437); Hallam (1988) p.173. The Burgundians, who were masters of playing off the English against the French to their own political and financial advantage, eventually sold Joan to the English for 10,000 *livres tournois*. Joan was taken in chains to Rouen to await trial for witchcraft and heresy.

4 Close to the village of Domrémy, there is a tree called the Tree of the Ladies; others call it the Tree of the Fairies … Sometimes I used to walk around there with the other girls, and from that tree I made garlands for the image of Our Lady in Domrémy … I don't know if I danced round that tree after the age of reason; I might have danced with the children, but I sang more than I danced.

Joan of Arc, at her trial, Feb.–May 1431; Pernoud and Clin (2000 edn) p.112. Pressed about the origin of her voices and visions, Joan talks of her upbringing in Domrémy (in Lorraine) – and provides a touchingly vivid picture of medieval childhood.

5 They bound her to a stake on the platform, which was made of plaster, and lit the fire under her. She died quickly, and her clothes were burned away; then they raked back the fire and showed her naked body to all the people so that they could see the secret parts that a woman should have, and there were no doubts left in their minds … Many people there and elsewhere said that she had died a martyr for her own true lord. Others said this was not so, and that the men who had supported her for so long had done wrong. That is how people talked, but whatever good or ill she had done, she was burned that day.

Anon. *Journal d'un bourgeois de Paris*; Hallam (1988) p.174. Duly condemned, Joan of Arc was burned in the marketplace of Rouen on 30 May 1431.

6 [The English] asked for favourable terms. The king [of France] agreed to this for two reasons: first, he was ready to surrender good for evil; secondly, he took account of the great mortality in his camp … The town and city of Bordeaux was to be restored and given up to the King of France, and all the inhabitants … to recognize and affirm that the King of France was their sovereign lord. The English had permission to leave by means of their ships either for England or Calais, as should seem best to them. This agreement was made on 17th October in the year 1453.

J. Chartier *Chronique de Charles VII* (1858 edn) Vol.3.7; E.H.D. Vol.4 (1969) p.271. After the disastrous Battle of Castillon (17 July 1453) the English abandoned their hopes of reclaiming Gascony. They negotiated their withdrawal from its chief town, Bordeaux, and were left with nothing in France apart from their enclave at Calais.

The Black Death and Later Plagues

1 The name, Black Death, was never used in the Middle Ages. Apparently the first to coin the term were Danish and Swedish chroniclers of the 16th century. 'Black' here connoted not a symptom or a colour, but 'terrible', 'dreadful'. The name was slow to achieve currency in the other north European languages, German and English.

David Herlihy *The Black Death and the Transformation of the West* (1997) Ch.1.

THE EASTERN MEDITERRANEAN

2 The plague attacked almost all the sea-coasts of the world and killed most of their people. For it swept not only through Pontus, Thrace and Macedonia, but even Greece, Italy and all the islands, Egypt, Libya, Judaea, Syria, and spread throughout almost the entire world.

John VI Cantacuzenus, c.1348; C.S. Bartsocas 'Two 14th Century Greek Descriptions of the Black Death' in *Journal of History of Medicine* Vol.21, no.4 (1966) p.395. The author abdicated as Byzantine emperor in 1355 to write a history of that empire. He considered that the plague originated in the steppes of Scythia (southern Russia) and that it was transmitted westwards by the Mongols of the Golden Horde (see 249:6).

3 I asked him the reason for this, and he informed me that he had vowed during the epidemic that, if it relented and a day passed without having to pray for any dead, he would arrange a feast. He then said to me: 'Yesterday I did not pray for any dead, so I will give the promised feast.' I found that those whom I had known among the sheikhs of Jerusalem had almost all ascended to God the almighty.

Ibn Battuta *Travels in Asia and Africa 1325–1355* (1853–8 French edn) Vol.4, pp.319–21. The celebrated Arab traveller and geographer reports from Jerusalem, where he met a preacher who invited him to the feast. This suggests that by mid-1348 the plague was already subsiding in that city.

4 The deaths had increased until it had emptied the streets ... I only saw lamps burning in a few of the shops along the street. I didn't find merchandise because of the scarcity of people who bring the merchandise to the shops. The cost of one pomegranate reached half a *dinar* [gold coin]. Flour from an *irdabb* of wheat reached the price of a florin. The horror of this is too long to recount, but this is indicative of the calamity.

Ibn al-Furat *History*; Michael W. Dols *The Black Death in the Middle East* (1977) p.277. This volume of al-Furat's original history is lost, but the eyewitness account of Cairo in 1347 was preserved by Ibn Hajar in his contemporary treatise on the plague.

5 Civilization both in the East and the West was visited by a destructive plague which devastated nations and caused populations to vanish. It swallowed up many of the good things of civilization and wiped them out ... Civilization decreased with the decrease of mankind. Cities and buildings were laid waste, roads and way signs were obliterated, settlements and mansions emptied, dynasties and tribes grew weak. The entire inhabited world changed. The East, it seems, was similarly visited, though in accordance with and in proportion to the East's more affluent civilization.

Ibn Khaldun (1332–1406) *The Muqaddimah: An Introduction to History* Vol.1 (1967 edn) p.46. The Great Arab historian and philosopher expresses his belief that 'growth in numbers, with a corresponding progress in civilization, finally culminates in the highest form of sedentary culture man is able to achieve; it declines from this peak when the number of cooperating people decreases' (Franz Rosenthal, the modern editor of *The Muqaddimah*, Vol.1, Introduction).

6 The country was not far from being ruined. The piercing [of the plague] also occurred to cats, dogs and wild animals. One found in the desert the bodies of savage animals with the buboes under their arms. It was the same with horses, camels, asses and all the beasts in general, including birds, even the ostriches.

Ibn Iyas *Chronicle* Vol.1 (1453–8; 1960 Arabic edn) p.191; Dols (1977) p.156. The Arab chronicler is writing 100 years later of the prevalence of inflamed nodes among the animals.

ITALY IN THE GRIP

7 Three galleys put in at Genoa driven by a fierce wind from the east, horribly infected and laden with a variety of spices and other valuable goods. When the inhabitants of Genoa learnt this, and saw how suddenly and irremediably they infected other people, they were driven forth from that port by burning arrows and divers engines of war; for no man dared touch them; nor was any man able to trade with them, for if he did he would be sure to die forthwith. Thus they were scattered from port to port.

Anon. Flemish chronicler, *Breve Chronicon clerici anonymi*, Jan. 1348; De Smet *Receuil des chroniques de Flandres* (1956) Vol.3, pp.14–15 in Philip Ziegler *The Black Death* (1969) p.17. The three major centres for the dissemination of the pandemic in southern Europe were Sicily and the north Italian ports of Genoa and Venice.

1 The years of the beatific incarnation of the Son of God had reached the tale of one thousand three hundred and forty-eight, when in the illustrious city of Florence, the fairest of all the cities of Italy, there made its appearance that deadly pestilence, which, whether disseminated by the celestial bodies, or sent upon us mortals by God in His just wrath by way of retribution for our iniquities, had had its origin some years before in the East, whence, after destroying an innumerable multitude of living beings, it had propagated itself without respite from place to place, and so, calamitously, had spread into the West.

Giovanni Boccaccio *The Decameron* (1349–51; 1930 trans.) 'First Day' p.4. The Florentine writer's collection of stories opens with a description of the plague. He then introduces a group who have fled from the city and tell each other stories over ten days to while away their terrified exile. A similar device was used by Geoffrey Chaucer for his pilgrims in *The Canterbury Tales* (c.1387).

2 In this extremity of our city's suffering and tribulation the revered authority of laws, human and divine, was abased and all but totally dissolved, for lack of those who should have administered and enforced them, most of whom, like the rest of the citizens, were either dead or sick, or so hard pressed for servants that they were unable to execute any office; whereby every man was free to do what was right in his own eyes.

Giovanni Boccaccio (1349–51; 1930 trans.) 'First Day' p.7.

3 Nor was it once or twice only that one and the same bier carried two or three corpses at once; but quite a considerable number of such cases occurred, one bier sufficing for husband and wife, two or three brothers, father and son, and so forth.

Giovanni Boccaccio (1349–51; 1930 trans.) 'First Day' p.10.

4 Such and so grievous was the harshness of heaven, and perhaps in some degree of man, that, what with the fury of the pestilence, the panic of

those whom it spared, and their consequent neglect or desertion of not a few of the stricken in their need, it is believed without any manner of doubt, that between March and the ensuing July upwards of a hundred thousand human beings lost their lives within the walls of the city of Florence, which before the deadly visitation would not have been supposed to contain so many people!

Giovanni Boccaccio (1349–51; 1930 trans.) 'First Day' p.11.

5 Laura, illustrious by her virtues, and long celebrated in my songs, first greeted my eyes in the days of my youth, 6 April 1327, at Avignon; and in the same city, at the same hour of the same 6 April, but in the year 1348, withdrew from life, whilst I was at Verona, unconscious of my loss. The melancholy truth was made known to me by letter, which I received at Parma on 19 May ... To write these lines in bitter memory of this event, and in the place where they will most often meet my eyes, has in it something of a cruel sweetness, but I forget that nothing more ought in this life to please me, which by the grace of God need not be difficult to one who thinks strenuously and manfully on the idle cares, the empty hopes, and the unexpected end of the years that are gone.

Francesco Petrarch, note written on MS of his copy of Virgil, 1348; George Deaux *The Black Death* (1969) Ch.4. Petrarch records the plague very differently from his contemporary and friend Boccaccio as he mourns the loss of his beloved Laura. Petrarch was then a canon of Parma cathedral, and that city and the nearby Reggio tried to keep infection spreading from Venice, Florence, Genoa and Pisa. But by June 1348, they had failed and lost around 40,000 of their inhabitants over the next six months.

6 And no bells tolled and nobody wept no matter what his loss because almost everyone expected death ... and people said and believed, 'This is the end of the world.'

Agnolo di Tura, chronicler of Siena in central Italy, 1348; Ferdinand Schevill *Siena* (1909) p.211.

7 It was a plague that touched people of every condition, age and sex. They began to spit blood and then they died – some immediately, some in two or three days, and some in a longer time. And it happened that whoever cared for the sick caught the disease from them, or, infected by the corrupt air, became rapidly ill and died in the same way. Most had swellings in the groin, and many had them in the left and right armpits and in other places; one could almost always find an unusual swelling somewhere on the victim's body.

Giovanni Villani *Chronicle* (1363; 1825 edn) Bk 1, Ch.2. This contemporary Florentine chronicler traces the origins of the plague to the maritime parts of China and India.

1 It was expected that, given the lack of people, there would be a superfluity of all things which the earth produces. On the contrary, through men's ingratitude an unprecedented scarcity affected everything, and this lasted a long time. Certain countries, as we shall tell, suffered from severe and unprecedented famines. And again it was thought that there ought to be a wealth and abundance of clothing, and of all the other things that the human body needs ... but the opposite happened ... most things cost twice or more what they cost before the epidemic.

Giovanni Villani (1363; 1825 edn) Bk 1, Ch.5.

2 Serving girls and unskilled women with no experience in service and stable boys want at least 12 florins a year, and the most arrogant among them 18 or 24 florins, and nurses too and minor artisans and hand-workers expect around three times their usual pay, while farm workers all demand oxen and seed, and want to work the most fertile lands and abandon all the rest.

Giovanni Villani (1363; 1825 edn) Bk 1, Ch.93. Villani's chronicle stops in mid-sentence – 'In the midst of this pestilence there came to an end ...' – as he himself succumbed to the plague at the age of 68 (see 271:5).

3 It was thought that the people, whom God by his grace had preserved, having seen the destruction of their neighbours and of all the nations of the world ... would become better, virtuous and catholic, avoiding iniquities and sins and overflowing with love and charity for one another. But the opposite happened.

Giovanni Villani (1363; 1825 edn) Bk 1, Ch.4; Herlihy (1997) Ch.3.

THE PLAGUE MOVES NORTH

4 How contemptible the Church has grown, especially in its most important representatives, who lead a bad life and have sunk even deeper than the others. For the shepherds of the Church feed themselves instead of their flocks, these they shear or rather fleece; their conduct is not that of the shepherd but of the wolf! All beauty has vanished from the Church of God; from head to toe there is not a sound spot in it. Simony has become so prevalent among the clergy that all secular and regular clerics, whether of high, middle or low rank, shamelessly buy and sell ecclesiastical livings without blame from anyone and much less with punishment.

Minor Friar Johannes of Winterthur, Switzerland, and Dominican Heinrich of Herford from Westphalia, Germany, bear witness to the after-effects of the plague, 1348 and 1349; Johannes Nohl *The Black Death: Chronicle of the Plague* (1926) Ch.7. Its horror was seen as the fruits of sin and the work of the devil: 'These pestilences were for pure sin' (William Langland *Piers Plowman* (c.1377) B-text, Passus 5, line 13).

5 Precious knowledge which the mad rage of pestilential death has stifled throughout the wide realms of the world.

Emperor Charles IV, 1348; Anna Campbell *The Black Death and Men of Learning* (1931) p.150. The Holy Roman Emperor is reacting to the catastrophic effect of the Black Death on learning. To ensure its survival he founded the university of Prague in 1348 and gave his imperial accreditation to five other universities over the next five years. In Cambridge, England, three new colleges were founded over the same period.

6 Balavignus, a Jewish physician, inhabitant of Thonon, was arrested at Chillon, since he had been found in the neighbourhood. He was put on the rack for a short time, and when taken down confessed after much hesitation that about ten weeks before Rabbi Jacob of Toledo ... sent him by a Jewish boy ... a powder sewn into a thin leather pouch accompanied by a letter, commanding him, on pain of excommunication, and by requiring his obedience to the law, to throw this poison into the larger and more frequented wells of the town of Thonon.

Confession, 15 Sept. 1348, in the Castle of Chillon, Savoy, southeast France, by Jews arrested in Neustadt; Deaux (1969) Ch.7. The blame for the plague was thus attached to the Jews, and Balavignus was one of ten who confessed 'his design of destroying and extirpating all Christians'. Later centuries would use the word pogrom for just such violent outbreaks of anti-Semitism and 'the walls of the ghetto, though not yet physical, had risen' (Barbara W. Tuchman *A Distant Mirror* (1978) Ch.5).

7 Faces became pale, and the doom which threatened the people was marked upon their foreheads. It was only necessary to look into men's and women's faces to read there recorded the blow which was about to fall; a marked pallor announced the approach of the enemy, and before the fatal day the sentence

was written unmistakably on the victim's face. No climate seemed to have any effect on the strange disease. Neither heat nor cold seemed to halt it. High and healthy places suffered as much as low and damp ones. It spread in the cold of winter as rapidly as in the heat of summer.

Simon of Covino *Concerning the Judgement of the Sun at the Banquet* (1350); *Bibliothèque de l'école des chartes* (1840–41) Series 1, Vol.9, pp.206 ff. The writer, a doctor, astrologer and poet in Paris, was recording in verse his memory of the plague in Montpellier in southern France.

1 To put the matter shortly, one half, or more than a half of the people of Avignon are already dead. Within the walls of the city there are now more than 7000 houses shut up; in these no one is living, and all who have inhabited them have left; the suburbs hardly contain any people at all. A field near 'Our Lady of Miracles' has been bought by the Pope [the papacy was operating out of Avignon] and consecrated. In this from 13 March 11,000 corpses have been buried. This number does not include those interred in the cemetery of St Anthony's hospital, in cemeteries belonging to the religious bodies, and in the many others which exist in Avignon.

Anon. canon to friends in Bruges, Belgium, 27 April 1348; Deaux (1969) Ch.5.

2 As many as 2,000 people come from the neighbouring districts [near Avignon]; amongst them many of both sexes are barefoot, some are in sackcloth, some with ashes, walking in tears and tearing their hair, and whipping themselves, sufficient to draw blood. The Pope was personally present at some of these processions, but then they were within the precincts of his own palace. What will be the end or from whence all this has started, God alone knows … Some wretched men have been caught carrying a certain dust … and whether justly or unjustly God only knows, they are accused of poisoning the water, and people are afraid to drink from wells; for this many have been burnt and are still every day.

Anon. canon, 27 April 1348; Deaux (1969) Ch.5.

3 The multitude of people who died in the years 1348 and 1349 was so large that nothing like it was ever heard, read of or witnessed in past ages. And the said death and sickness often sprung from the imagination, or from the society and contagion of another, for a healthy man visiting one sick hardly ever escaped death. So in many towns, small and

great, priests retired through fear, leaving the administration of the sacraments to religious who were more bold. Briefly, in many places, there did not remain two alive out of every twenty.

Guillaume de Nangis *Chronicle* (c.1368); Deaux (1969) Ch.5. The Parisian chronicler is describing the situation in his city and seems to be suggesting people could die through expecting to.

4   For many have certainly
      Heard it commonly said
      How in one thousand three hundred and forty-nine
      Out of one hundred there remained but nine.
      Thus it happened that for lack of people
      Many a splendid farm was left untilled,
      No one ploughed the fields,
      Bound the corn and gathered the grapes,
      Some offered triple wages
      But twenty-fold would not suffice
      Since so many were dead.

Guillaume de Machaut *Jugement du roi de Navarre* (c.1350); Monique Lucenet *Les Grandes Pestes* (The Major Plagues) (1985) p.45. A contemporary courtly musician and poet describes the plague's effect on the economy of rural France.

5 Relatives were cared for as though they were dogs. They threw food and drink to them in bed and then fled the house. When they finally died, strong peasants came from the mountains of Provence [southern France], miserable, poor and foultempered … at least for a high price they carried the dead to burial. No relatives or friends cared what was happening. No priest came to hear the confession of the dying, or to administer the last sacraments to them. People cared only for their own health (and that of their families).

Louis Sanctus de Beeringen, letter, 1348; De Smet (1956) Vol.3, p.17. The situation in Avignon in southern France.

6 About Michaelmas 1349 over six hundred men came to London from Flanders, mostly of Zeeland and Holland origin. Sometimes at St Paul's and sometimes at other points in the city they made two daily public appearances wearing cloths from the thighs to the ankles, but otherwise stripped bare. Each wore a cap marked with a red cross in front and behind. Each had in his right hand a scourge with three tails. Each tail had a knot and through the middle of it sometimes sharp nails were fixed. They marched naked in single file and with these scourges whipped their naked and bleeding bodies. Four of

them would chant in their native language and another four in response like a litany.

An eyewitness describes Flagellants in London; W.O. Hassall *They Saw it Happen* (1973) p.156. This self-scourging was one of the reactions to the plague.

1 Already Flagellants under pretence of piety have spilt the blood of Jews, which Christian charity preserves and protects, and frequently also the blood of Christians, and when opportunity offered, they have stolen the property of the clergy and the laity.

Pope Clement VI, bull, 26 Sept. 1349, against the Flagellants for killing both Jews and Christians, stealing property and taking upon themselves the authority of their superiors; J.D. Mansi (ed.) *Annales ecclesiastiques* (1750) Vol.6, p.476.

2 The continuing pestilence of the present day, which is spreading far and wide, has left many parish churches and other livings in our diocese without parson or priest to care for their parishioners. Since no priests can be found who are willing, either out of zeal and devotion or for a stipend, to take on the pastoral care of these places … all men, in particular those who are sick or should fall sick in the future … if they are on the point of death and cannot secure the services of a priest, then they should make confession to each other, as is permitted in the teaching of the apostles, whether to a layman or, if no man is present, even to a woman.

Ralph of Shrewsbury, Jan. 1349; D. Wilkins *Concilia Magnae Brittaniae et Hibernia* (1737) Vol.2, pp.735–6. The bishop of Bath and Wells in southwest England reacting to the staffing situation in his diocese. It has been estimated that as much as 47.6% of the beneficed clergy in the diocese succumbed to the plague.

3   Parsons and parish priests pleaded with the
        bishop,
     Their parishes being poor since the time of the
        Plague,
     To have licence to leave and live in London,
     And sing Simoniac mass there (for silver is
        sweet).

William Langland (c.1377; 1981 edn) B-text, Prologue.

4 We see death coming into our midst like black smoke, a plague which cuts off the young, a rootless phantom which has no mercy for the fair countenance. Woe is me of the shilling in the arm-pit; it is seething terrible, wherever it may come, a head that gives pain and causes a loud cry, a burden carried under the arms, a painful angry knob, a white lump.

It is in the form of an apple, like the head of an onion, a small boil that spares no one.

Jeuan Gethin, March/April 1349; W. Rees 'The Black Death in England and Wales' in *Proceedings of the Royal Society of Medicine* Vol.16, Pt 2, p.34. A Welsh poet describes the symptoms in vivid horror.

5 This year [1349] was wonderful and full of prodigies in many ways: still it was fertile and abundant, although sickly and productive of great mortality. In the convent of the Minorites of Drogheda 25 and in that of Dublin 23, friars died before Christmas …

And I, brother John Clyn, of the order of the Friars Minor and the convent of Kilkenny, have written these noteworthy things, which have happened in my time and which I have learnt as worthy of belief … and that the writing may not perish with the scribe, and the work fail with the labourer, I add parchment to continue it, if by chance anyone may be left in the future and any child of Adam may escape this pestilence and continue the work thus commenced.

Friar John Clyn, Friars Minor of Kilkenny, Ireland, 1349; Deaux (1969) Ch.5. The friar did not survive but his message did.

6 In the year 1350 there was, in the kingdom of Scotland, so great a pestilence and plague among men … as from the beginning of the world even unto modern times, had never been heard of by man … for to such a pitch did that plague wreak its cruel spite, that nearly a third of mankind were thereby made to pay the debt of nature.

John of Fordun *Chronicle of the Scottish Nation* (c.1350; 1872 edn); Ziegler (1969) p.206. His international figure is echoed by his contemporary Andrew of Wyntoun.

7   In Scotland, the first pestilence
     Begot, of so great violence
     That it was said, of lywand men
     The third part it destroyéd then
     Efftyr than in till Scotland.

John of Fordun (c.1350; 1872 edn) Vol.2, p.482.

8 A third of the world died.

Jean Froissart *Chronicles* (from 1373); Tuchman (1978) Ch.5. Tuchman estimates that Froissart's 'casual words' imply a total of 20 million deaths but points out that the figure was drawn from the mortality by plague in the Book of Revelation in the Bible, 'the favourite guide to human affairs in the Middle Ages'.

PRECAUTIONS AND REMEDIES

1 Three things by which each simple man
From plague escape and sickness can,
Start soon, flee far from town or land
On which the plague has laid its hand,
Return but late to such a place
Where pestilence has stayed its pace.

Rhazes (Razi) (c.865–c.935); Nohl (1926) Ch.4. This recommended remedy against the plague originated in a work by a Persian doctor, circulated in various forms when epidemics struck. In Paris an ointment called 'Blanc de Razès' was on sale at apothecaries and was said to be effective against almost any ailment.

2 Equal parts of black pepper, and red and white sandal, two parts of roses, half a part of camphor, add four parts of bol armeniac. All but the camphor are to be ground very fine, sifted and shaken, pounded for a week with rosewater, then mix in the camphor, then the camphor mixed with them, and the apples made with a paste of gum Arabic and rosewater.

Arab physician Yuhanna Ibn Masawayh, prescription against the plague, 9th century; Campbell (1931) p.68.

3 Everyone sick of the plague is to be brought out of town to the fields, there to die or recover. Those who have nursed plague patients are to remain secluded for ten days before having intercourse with anyone. The clergy are to examine the sick and report to the authorities on pain of being burnt at the stake and confiscation of their possessions. Those who introduce the plague shall forfeit all their goods to the state. Finally, with the exception of those set apart for the purpose, no one shall administer to those sick of the plague on pain of death and forfeiture of their possessions.

Visconte Bernabo, plague regulation issued at Reggio, Italy, 17 Jan. 1374; Nohl (1926) Ch.5. These fierce rules were issued at a later outbreak, but it is difficult to envisage them being successfully implemented.

4 Because the killing of great beasts, from whose putrid blood running down the streets and the bowels cast into the Thames, the air in the city is very much corrupted and infected, whence abominable and most filthy stench proceeds, sickness and many other evils have happened to such as abode in the said city, or have resorted to it; and great dangers are feared to fall out for the time to come, unless remedy be presently made against it; we, willing to prevent

such dangers, ordain, by consent of the present parliament, that all bulls, oxen, hogs, and other gross creatures be killed at either Stratford or Knightsbridge [to the east and west of the city respectively].

Royal proclamation to the mayor and sheriffs of London, 1361; Dreux (1969) Ch.6. The plague had arrived in late 1348, but 13 years later insanitary conditions had clearly not improved and a Sanitation Act was not passed until 1388. Another school of medical thought believed that 'attendants who take care of latrines and those who serve in hospitals and other malodorous places are nearly all to be considered immune' (John Colle in Ziegler (1969) p.75).

AFTER-EFFECTS AND RECURRENCE

5 The world goeth fast from bad to worse, when shepherd and cowherd for their part demand more of their labour than the master-bailiff was wont to take in days gone by. Labour is now at so high a price that he who will order his business aright, must pay five or six shillings now for what cost two in the past … The poor and small folk … demand to be better fed than their masters. Moreover they bedeck themselves in fine colours and fine clothes, whereas (were it not for their pride and their privy conspiracies [and] personal ambitions) they would be clad in sack cloth in the old days.

John Gower, 1375; G.G. Coulton *Social Life in Britain from the Conquest to the Reformation* (1918) p.353. The English poet is describing the inflationary aftermath of the plague and the social pattern that had changed through the resulting shortage of labour.

6 Meanwhile the king [Richard II] sent into each shire a message that reapers and other labourers should not take more than they had been wont to do under threat of penalties defined in the statute. The workmen were, however, so arrogant and obstinate that they did not heed the king's mandate, but if anyone wanted to have them he had to give them what they asked, so he either had to satisfy the greedy and arrogant wishes of the workers or lost his crop. When the king was told that they were not observing his order, and had given higher wages to their workmen, he levied heavy fines on abbots, priors, knights of greater and lesser consequence and others, both great and small, throughout the countryside, taking 100 shillings from some, 40 or 20 from others, according to their ability to pay … Then the king had many labourers arrested, and sent them to prison, and many of them escaped and fled to the forests and woods for a time, and those who were captured were severely punished. And most of such labourers swore that they would not take daily wages in excess of those allowed in ancient custom, and so they were set free from prison.

Henry Knighton *Chronicle* (late 14th century); A.R. Myers (ed.) *English Historical Documents* Vol.4 (1969) p.90. Knighton, a canon of Leicester Abbey, wrote some time after the Black Death, of which he had been an eyewitness. Clearly he considered that the royal intervention had won over supply and demand, where Gower did not.

1 A pontiff should make his subjects happy.

Pope Clement VI, issuing a bull in 1343; Tuchman (1978) Ch.5. The pope was announcing that 1350 would be a Jubilee Year. Boniface VIII had established this highly successful fund-raiser in 1300, and a free indulgence was offered to all those (reputedly two million) repentant sinners who made the pilgrimage to Rome in that year. The original papal intention was that such jubilees should be repeated every 100 years, but in the aftermath of the plague Rome requested a repeat after 50 years. The city had suffered also from the removal of the popes to Avignon (see 192:3).

2 From London it was reported that scarcely every tenth man survived. The number of deaths is said to be underestimated at 100,000. At Bristol hardly one tenth of the population remained. At Norwich out of a population of 70,000 there died 57,374. In England of the clergy alone there died 25,000. From the town of Smolensk in Russia in 1386 there remained only five persons alive. The islands of Cyprus and Iceland are said to have been depopulated to the last inhabitant.

Johannes Nohl (1926) Ch.1. These figures can hardly be accurate but were among a range of contemporary estimates.

3 Next day, towards dinner time, I felt very tired, as if I had been walking for miles, and when I tried to eat I was attacked by a fierce headache. At the same time I discovered some swellings on my left arm, and a carbuncle on the outside of my left wrist.

Everyone in the house was terrified: my friend, the fat cow, and the little one, all ran away and I was left alone with a wretched shopboy who refused to leave me. I felt stifled round my heart and I knew for certain I was as good as dead.

Benvenuto Cellini *Autobiography* (1728; 1956 trans.) p.56. The Italian artist is describing a scare in Rome in 1523. He believed partying was the way to combat the disease. He died in 1571.

4 Follow me still further: there is another trench [in Vienna in 1679] and in it lie many thousand persons like pickled game in a barrel, with the sole difference that quick-lime is used, not salt. Behold there her whose ruddy lips were sweeter to you than sugar-candy – now the quick-lime has consumed this delicacy, and now the teeth grin like those of a snarling dog on its chain.

Abraham à Santa-Clara, account of the plague of 1679; Deaux (1969) Ch.7.

JUDGEMENT

5 The end of an age of submission came in sight. To that extent the Black Death may have been the unrecognized beginnings of modern society.

Barbara W. Tuchman (1978) Ch.5.

Venice: Maritime Power, 1350–1600

OCEAN'S CHILD

1 'Tis said that when the Huns overran Italy some mean fishermen and others left the mainland and fled for shelter to these despicable and muddy islands, which in process of time, by industry, are to the greatness of one of the most considerable states, considered as a republic, and having now subsisted longer than any of the four ancient monarchies, flourishing in great state, wealth and glory, by the conquest of great territories in Italy, Dacia, Greece, Candy [Crete], Rhodes and Slavonia, and at present challenging the empire of all the Adriatic sea, which they yearly espouse by casting a gold ring into it with great pomp and ceremony on Ascension Day; the desire of seeing this was one of the reasons that hastened us from Rome.

John Evelyn, 1645; *Diary* (1890 edn) p.159.

2 According to another legend, patricians of the mainland, fleeing from barbaric invaders, were supposed to have established themselves on the lagoon on 25 March 421. Although this was much earlier than the invasions of the Huns and the Lombards, which may well have caused a mass exodus to the lagoon, it was not long after Alaric's entrance into Rome and may have been meant to imply a providential replacement of the one city by the other. 25 March was the recognized anniversary of the Annunciation of the Virgin Mary.

D.S. Chambers *The Imperial Age of Venice 1380–1580* (1970) p.13. The idea of the Venetians as 'new Romans' was also a claim that competed with Constantinople, that other 'New Rome' (see 104:1). The identification was widely expressed in the 15th and 16th centuries. Rome was sacked by the Visigoths in 410. For the Huns and Lombards see 113:1–117:4.

3 It is not to be expected that they should attain to the perfection and grandeur of the ancient Romans, for their bodies are not so able to bear the fatigues of war, neither are they of such a martial genius; for they never make war on the continent in their own persons, as the Romans did; but they send their *provveditori* [directors] and other officers, with their general, to furnish his army with provisions and to assist him in his councils of war. But their naval expeditions are wholly managed by their own

people; their fleet, both galleys and ships, being manned by their own subjects, and commanded by their own nobility. Another great advantage they have in not fighting their land wars in person, is that there is no man among them bold and ambitious enough to make any attempt to seize power … They have no tribunes of the people, as they had in Rome (and those tribunes were in part the cause of its destruction); the people among them are of no authority, are consulted in no affair of state, and are unable to hold any office; for all their officers except the secretaries, are chosen from the gentry; and thus the majority of the population have no share in government.

Philippe de Commines *Mémoires* (1524; 1901 trans.) Vol.2, p.172. A French ambassador to Venice compares and contrasts.

4 *Veneziani, poi Christiani!* (Venetians first, afterwards Christians!)

Anon. slogan; William H. McNeill *Venice: the Hinge of Europe 1081–1797* (1974) p.6. McNeill comments that this 'accurately sums up the city's relationship to Latin Christendom'.

5 The men were brave and skilled in naval warfare. They were sent forth at the imperial behest, by densely peopled Venice, a land rich in wealth and in men, where the farthermost gulf of the Adriatic lies under the northern stars. The sea surrounded the walls of this nation and its people cannot visit each other's house unless they travel by boat. For they dwell ever among the waters, and no nation is more valiant than they at fighting at sea, or steering their craft over the waters.

William of Apulia (11th century); John Julius Norwich *A History of Venice* (1982) p.65. The Norman chronicler characterizes the Venetians.

6 Our forefathers were always attentive to maritime affairs, knowing them to be the cause of the growth of our state and, above all, the means of holding it secure.

Venetian senate, 1400; C. Manfroni 'La Battiglia de Gallipoli' in *Ateneo Veneto* Vol.25 (1902).

7 The coiffure which Venetian women have recently taken to wearing could not be more indecent in the eye of God and men, since by means of this coiffure women conceal their sex and strive to please men by pretending to be men, which is a form of sodomy.

Council of Ten, decree, 1480; Lord Orford *Legge e memorie venete* (1870–72) p.233. The Council of Ten was effectively 17 since it was augmented by the signoria and the doge. It was the signoria (the 'cabinet') that by the 15th century adopted the name *La Serenissima* – the most serene. This superlative, probably borrowed from a title of German princes, later spread to become a title for the Venetian republic itself.

THE GREAT TRADING CAPITAL

1 At that time [*c*.1275] the emperor [Michael VIII Palaeologus of Constantinople] decided to humble the Genoese, who were full of impudence. In fact, the Venetians and their community [probably those in Constantinople itself] formerly greatly surpassed them in wealth, in arms and in all kinds of materials because they made greater use of the narrow waters [straits] than did the Genoese and because they sailed across the open sea with galleys, and they succeeded in gaining more profit than the Genoese in transporting merchandise.

George Pachymeres *De Michaele et Andronico Palaeologis* (1261– 1308; 1835 edn) Bk 5.30; R.S. Lopez and I.W. Raymond *Trade in the Mediterranean World* (1955) p.127. The Byzantine historian points up the rivalry between the Italian cities over the lucrative Black Sea trade. See III:1.

2 Whereas our (fellow citizens) frequenting Cyprus [a Venetian colony] have of late engaged in the formation of rings and conspiracies in the trade of transporting cotton to Venice, entering into mutual obligations and pacts to prevent the transport of more than a certain amount; and whereas this is against the interest of the Commune, which loses its customs duty on what should be imported, as in the past, over and above the said amount; and it is also against the best interests of the city because cotton needed in the west is transported to Ancona [its fiercest rival, down the Adriatic coast] and elsewhere while it should be transported to Venice. And [thus the cartel is] building up foreign countries while ruining ours; and it is also against the good of the community and of individuals because the profit which used to be spread among the whole community is monopolized by three or four [people].

Motion passed in the Venetian senate, 28 April 1358; Venice State Archives (A.S.V.) Senato misti 28, f.44v. Notice that the argument is posited on the good of the community, a sound Venetian concept.

3 This great city, in which I have lately taken refuge from the storms of the world, owes its remarkable growth to navigation, next after justice … I got up and climbed to the top floor of my house which overlooks the harbour … one vessel was perhaps bound for the River Don, for that is the limit of navigation in the Black Sea; but some of its passengers will there disembark and will not halt until they have crossed the Ganges, and the Caucasus, and have come to the farthest Indies and have reached the eastern ocean. Whence comes this fierce, insatiable thirst for possessions that rides the minds of men?

Francesco Petrarch to Francesco Bruni, newly appointed papal secretary, 9 April 1363; Morris Bishop (ed.) *Letters from Petrarch* (1966) pp.230–31.

4 [Philip Gross of Nuremberg, a German merchant] is wont to transport and to have transported large quantities of wool to the territory of Lombardy … for these he obtains by way of barter Lombard cloth which he transports to Venice … and this would result in great profit to our commune and to the advantage of our merchant citizens and of Philip himself if only he were assisted by this special privilege … he be permitted to remove that cloth from the *fondaco* [the trading post at which foreign traders were controlled] and to put it in store in Rialto, which has a window, with the purpose of exhibiting the cloth and of selling it as best he can, paying our commune the tolls established for the said cloth.

Appeal to lift the restrictions usually placed on foreign merchants in Venice, 19 June 1383; H. Simonsfeld *Der Fondaco dei Tedeschi in Venedig* (The German Trade Warehouse in Venice) (1887) Vol.I, p.113.

5 Know that today also three ships arrived from Syria, from whose crew we are reliably informed that our Venetians have bought large amounts of spices, above all, pepper and ginger … as a result of this news we all feel that there will be adequate supplies of spices on offer this year in Venice, as far as we can tell. It is not, however, possible to fix the conditions of sale in writing yet.

Venetian merchant Francesco Amadi to his Nuremberg trading agent, 1392; Lisa Jardine *Worldly Goods* (1996) p.53.

6 It is our wish that all other mercers' wares made in Venice or outside it, be subject to our craft, i.e. combs of ivory, felt caps of all kinds and felts for making caps, cotton and silk veils, spools, weaver's paste, handkerchiefs (whether worked in silk or not) fans, veils, coifs, vestments, gold from Cologne, pewter which comes with the Flanders galleys, or into the German exchange house, cushions made of chequered cloth and of tapestry and pouches. Be it understood that all the aforesaid items, whether mentioned specifically or not, being articles which mercers have been accustomed to stock, shall all be subject to our rule book.

Item 1446, from the rule book of the mercers' guild (1471–1787) f.10r.–f.14r.; David Chambers and Brian Pullan (eds) *Venice: A Documentary History 1450–1630* (1992) p.281.

1 As you know, I have loaded according to your order, 3 casks of malmsey of the usual sort, of 12 *quarte* each, in your galley for London. They are marked by an iron seal impressed in the front and also marked by your iron seal. These wines are regarded as very good, clean and pure. Please sell them in England for the best price you can get, using them as if they were your own …

Also I have delivered to you a small bundle of pure silk handkerchiefs … since the silk is sheer, as I have said, I am sure you will sell it as Malaga silk. And as it is a small quantity and you will not be calling at Malaga [southern Spain], as I presume, because of the war with the king of Castile, I am sure you will be able to get a good price …

From the proceeds from these wines and silk, then, I should like you first of all to get for me three curtains of fine fast-dyed satin, by the yard – the kind and amount illustrated on the sheet of paper I gave you, where the lengths and widths are specified … Also I want you to get some fine pewter bought for me in London.

Alvise da Cadamosto *Le navigazione atlantiche* (c.1475; 1929 edn) pp.347–8. The Venetian merchant (see 316:5) empowers the captain of the galley to act as his agent.

2 A contemporary estimate of the income of the various governments in the 1470s gave Venice 1,000,000 ducats a year, Milan and Naples 600,000, Florence 300,000, Savoy 100,000, Mantua, Bologna and Siena 60,000 each. The pope with some 400,000 was only just better off than Florence and had, of course, a much less coherent territory to manage.

Denys Hay *Europe in the 14th and 15th Centuries* (1966 edn) p.186.

3 To the city of St Mark the loss of the spice trade would be like the loss of milk to an infant.

Girolamo Priuli, July 1501; *Diaries* (1494–1512; 1911 edn) in Heinrich Kretschmayr *Geschichte von Venedig* (History of Venice) (from 1905). The diarist laments the expected effects on Venice of the Portuguese opening up the route to India round the Cape.

4 Now that this new route is found, the king of Portugal will bring all the spices to Lisbon. And there is no doubt that the Hungarians, Germans, Flemish and French, who formerly came to Venice to spend their money on spices, will all turn towards Lisbon, for it is nearer to them, and easier to reach.

Girolamo Priuli foresees the new pattern of trading, 1501; Jardine (1996) p.290. It may surprise us that he considered it easier for Hungarians *et al.* to get to Lisbon than to Venice.

5 Yearly figures for pepper imports before Portuguese interference was felt … about 1,150,000lb English.

Yearly average, 1560–64 inclusive, 1,310,454lb.

Frederic C. Lane 'The Mediterranean Spice Trade: Further Evidence of its Revival in the Sixteenth Century' in *American Historical Review* Vol.45 (1940). Lane comments: 'The Portuguese did not reduce the Levantine spice trade to permanent insignificance. Although the flow of spices through the traditional routes of the Levant was severely checked during the first decades of the 16th century, it later found its way through the obstacles raised by the Portuguese. Even pepper came through the Red Sea in approximately the volume of the years before the Portuguese opened this new route to India.'

6 I observed English ships going forth from Venice with Italian ships to have sailed to Syria and returned to Venice twice, before the Italian ships made one return, whereof two reasons may be given, one that the Italians pay their mariners by the day, how long soever the voyage lasteth, which makes them upon the least storm, put into harbours, whence only few winds can bring them out, whereas the English are paid by the voyage, and so beat out storms at sea, and are ready to make the first wind anything favourable unto them. The other that Italian ships are heavy in sailing, and great of burden, and the governors and mariners not very expert, nor bold.

Fynes Moryson *Itinerary Containing his Ten Years Travel* (1590s; 1903 edn) p.135. There is perhaps some national pride in this comparison. Moryson was one of two brothers visiting Venice on his way to the Holy Land (see 263:7).

7 The queen [Elizabeth of England] had, by imposts insupportable to foreigners, virtually shut the Venetians out of England, and the English had become most expert and powerful on the seas from

here to the Atlantic and, indeed, in every place, and to a large extent they were depriving the Venetians of trade in western merchandise; and, a thing still more hateful, they had entered these seas in the guise of brigands, although they brought merchandise too; and they treated every ship they met as an enemy, without distinguishing whether it belonged to friend or foe. This evil was accentuated by the Dutch acting in the same way; they were now bringing up their ships, had penetrated within the Straits of Gibraltar, were even coming to Venice and had learnt how to sail the Adriatic as well as any native of the country.

Nicolò Contarini, c.1603, *Historie* Vol.2, Bk 6 in A.S.V. Miscellanea Codia no.80, f.31v.; Alberto Tenenti *Piracy and the Decline of Venice* (1967 trans.) p.58. The official historian of Venice sees the competition as anything but healthy, since the English combined legitimate trade with piracy.

1 The trade of Syria can match the trade of any European city, as many nations from divers parts bring hither a vast array of very rich commodities, spices, silk, indigo, cotton, cloth made of wool, silk and gold, and infinite other things … Of all the nations here in Aleppo the Venetians are the greatest in sheer numbers, reputation and the volume of their transactions; their annual trade is over two millions in gold.

G. Berchet, Venetian consul, writing from Aleppo, 1597; *Le relazione dei consoli veneti nella Siria* (Reports of the Venetian Consuls to Syria) (1896) pp.79–80.

2 The rich cargoes of spices, moreover, had returned to Venice both as a result of Portuguese failure to keep the Atlantic route open, and of the revival of the traditional caravan routes in the Levant.

Domenico Sella; Brian Pullan (ed.) *Crisis and Change in the Venetian Economy in the 16th and 17th Centuries* (1968) p.89.

3 A great deal of fine Spanish wool is wrought into cloth in foreign states and notably in Como and other towns in the State of Milan, where cloth is being produced in increasing quantities in perfect imitation of our own fabrics, but with great advantages as regards wages and other things pertaining to production; those foreign fabrics are then shipped to the Levant by way of Ferrara and Ancona, and are vented more cheaply than ours.

A.S.V. Mr. riposte, reg. 139, 5 Dec. 1597; Pullan (1968) p.116.

4 Foreigners and strangers from remote countries have become masters of all the shipping; the English

in particular, after driving our men from the Western voyage at present sail the Levantine waters, voyage to the islands and harbours in our own dominion … and have even secure permission to lade in this very city goods for the Levant.

A.S.V. Mr. reg. 141, 15 July 1602. The Venetians were horrified at the inroads in their trade caused by English shipping.

WAR FOR THE MEDITERRANEAN

5 For as at Venice, in the Arsenal in winter-time,
    they boil the gummy pitch
To caulk such ships as need an overhaul.
Now that they cannot sail – instead of which
One builds him a new boat, one toils to plug
Seams strained by many a voyage, others stitch
Canvas to patch a tattered jib or lug,
Hammer at the prow, hammer at the stern, or
    twine
Ropes, or shave oars, refit and make all snug.

Dante Alighieri *The Divine Comedy* 'Inferno' (c.1308–21) Canto 21. The arsenal was built in 1104. Medieval Venice had one of Europe's biggest shipyards and was already a naval power by Dante's time, although by 1495 the incoming French ambassador, Philippe de Commines, was suggesting that their supremacy is less sure and that the Turkish fleet rivalled them (*Mémoires* (1524; 1901 trans.) Vol.2, p.171). For the Constantinople arsenal see 263:6.

6 Indeed, the efficiency and predictability associated with modern factory assembly lines were, to some extent, realized by the Venetian arsenal. In its heyday, the arsenal was capable of assembling a completely equipped galley in less than an hour. This feat was performed for Henry III of France during his visit to Venice in 1574.

William H. McNeill (1974) p.6.

7 The most illustrious *provveditori* [directors] and *patroni all'Arsenal* with the approval of our government have reached agreement with the governors of the hospital of Santi Giovanni and Paolo to have made up to a good standard of workmanship:

Mainsails, reefs and foresails to equip the 100 light galleys, at the prices quoted below, on the understanding that the material will be delivered ready cut …

Mainsails 45 lire each.

Anon. estimate, 1584; A.S.V. (1958 edn) Instituti di ricovero e di educazione (Educational Institutes and Hospitals).

1 I, as commander, vigorously attacked the first galley [of the Turks] who put up a stout defence being excellently manned by courageous Turks who fought like dragons. With God's help I overcame her, and cut most of the said Turks to pieces ... The battle lasted from early morning till past two o'clock; we took six of their galleys, with their crews, and nine galleots. And the Turks that were on them were all put to the sword, including the admiral and all his nephews and many other captains ... Aboard the captured vessels we found Genoese, Catalans, Sicilians, Provençals and Cretans, of whom those who had not perished in the battle I myself ordered to be cut to pieces and hanged – together with all pilots and navigators, so the Turks have no more of those at present ... a warning to any Christians base enough to take service with the infidel henceforth ... We can now say that the power of the Turk in this region has been utterly destroyed, and will remain so for a long time to come. I have eleven hundred prisoners.

Admiral Pietro Loredan, report to the doge and Signoria (his six counsellors), 2 June 1416; John Julius Norwich *A History of Venice: The Greatness and the Fall* (1981) p.36. Until this battle at Gallipoli, Venice and Turkey had managed to co-exist peacefully and had even signed a treaty three years before, despite their trade rivalry.

2 At first I estimated it at 300 sail; now I would put it at 400. The whole sea appeared like a forest ... I swear that from the first ships to the last the fleet is over six miles long. To confront so mighty a force, I consider that we shall need at least a hundred good galleys, even then I would not be sure of the outcome ...

Now must our Signory show its strength. Setting aside all else, it must send at once all the ships, men, provisions and money it can raise. Otherwise Negropont [the Greek island of Euboea] is in grave danger; and if Negropont falls, all our Eastern Empire, even including our neighbour Istria, will fall with it. For next year the Turk will be half as strong again, and emboldened by this year's success.

Geronimo Longoto to his brothers, June 1470; D. Malipiero *Annali Veneti 1457–1500* pp.49–52 in Archivio storico italiano Vol.7 (1843). The Venetian galley commander makes a desperate appeal for reinforcements against the threat of the Turkish fleet. Euboea, the Venetians' part of the share-out after the Fourth Crusade, was an important strategic and trade port. As Norwich (1981) comments: 'Europe still refused to lift a finger. Venice with her empire stood alone against the ever encroaching power.' Constantinople had fallen to the Ottomans in 1453.

3 Venice routinely kept 40,000 soldiers under arms, plus up to as many as 100 galleys [about 20,000 men] at sea. Such forces made Venice a great naval power by the standards of the day.

Marc Antonio Bragadin *Repubbliche Italiane sul Mare* (1951) p.146.

4   Nor even that against the avid claws
    Of the wing-bearing Lion he will stand
    Firm and unwavering, nor yet because,
    When the French torch sets all the lovely land
    Of Italy ablaze, she'll have no cause
    To fear, alone exempt from the demand
    For tribute.

Ludovico Ariosto *Orlando Furioso* (1516, 1975 trans.) Canto 3, verse 50. The poet is describing the resistance of Ercole I d'Este, of the house of Ferrara. Venice, 'the wing-bearing lion' and dominating neighbour, declared war on Ferrara in 1492, although Ercole had led the Venetian forces himself 25 years earlier. The French torch had been lit by Charles VIII, who invaded Italy in 1494, in alliance with the papacy, notably the warrior-pope, Julius II.

5 Tell the Signoria that they have done with wedding the sea [the ceremony of 28 Feb.], it is our turn now.

Turkish vezir to Alvise Manenti, the Venetian ambassador, 1500; Norwich (1981) p.127. In the 20 preceding years, with a non-militant sultan in Bajazet II, the Venetian empire had grown, as Norwich describes: 'Rovigo and the Po delta had come to her in 1484, Cyprus in 1488; after Charles VIII's withdrawal from Naples, she had acquired three valuable ports on the Apulian coast – Brindisi, Trani and Otranto; and on 10 September 1499 her troops had entered Cremona.'

6 To put an end to the losses, the injuries, the violations, the damages which Venetians have inflicted, not only on the Apostolic see but on the Holy Roman Empire, on the house of Austria, on the dukes of Milan, on the kings of Naples and on divers other princes, occupying and tyrannically usurping their goods, their possessions, their cities and castles, as if they had deliberately conspired to do ill to all around them ...

Thus we have found it not only well advised and honourable, but even necessary to summon all people to take their just revenge and so to extinguish, like a great fire, the insatiable rapacity of the Venetians and their thirst for power.

League of Cambrai, 10 Dec. 1508, Preamble; Norwich (1981) p.139. Norwich hears the papal voice even though Julius II did not formally join the league at the start.

7 Selim, Ottoman sultan, emperor of the Turks, lord of lords, king of kings, shadow of God, lord of the earthly paradise and of Jerusalem, to the signory of Venice:

We demand of you Cyprus, which you shall give us willingly or perforce … and do not awake our horrible sword, for we shall wage most cruel war against you everywhere, neither put your trust in your treasure for we shall cause it suddenly to run from you like a torrent.

Beware therefore lest you arouse our wrath …
Selim II, 1567; Norwich (1981) p.205.

1 Since the Majesty of the Lord God has granted to all Christendom and especially to this republic the favour of so fortunate and glorious a victory over the Turk by the disruption of his fleet, it is appropriate to show some sign of gratitude towards Jesus Christ our blessed defender and protector by making a demonstration against those who are enemies of his holy faith, as are the Jews.
1571; A.S.V. Senato, Terra row 58; Chambers and Pullan (1992) p.537. After the victory at the Battle of Lepanto (Oct. 1571) a resolution is passed to expel the Jews from the city of Venice, in gratitude and revenge. The Venetians' attitude had been always ambivalent, and they invoked their forefathers' anti-Semitic order of 1527 to strengthen their position.

2 They have taught us by their example that the Turks are not insuperable, as we had previously believed them to be … Thus it can be said that as the beginning of this war was for us a time of sunset, leaving us in perpetual night, now the courage of these men, like a true life-giving sun, has bestowed upon us the most joyful day that this city, in all her history, has ever seen.
Paola Paruta, funeral oration on the victims of the Battle of Lepanto, 1571. Paruta preceded Nicolò Contarini in writing the official history of Venice.

3 War, the begetter of all things, the creature of all things, the river with a thousand sources, the sea without a shore: begetter of all things except peace, so ardently longed for, so rarely attained. Every age constructs its own war, its own types of war. In the Mediterranean, official hostilities were over after Lepanto. Major war had now moved north and west to the Atlantic coasts – and was to stay there for centuries to come, where its true place was, where the heart of the world now beat. This shift, better than any argument, indicates and underlines the withdrawal of the Mediterranean from the centre of the stage.
Fernand Braudel The Mediterranean and the Mediterranean World in the Age of Philip II (1966 edn; 1973 trans.) Vol.2, p.891. The great French historian resonantly describes the battle as a turning point in European history. See 262:5.

4 They [the Uskoks] think the damage that they inflict on possessions and subjects of Your Serenity to be fully justified, because Venice prevents them from going to plunder the Turks, and they hold this belief because it is taught and preached to them by their friars and priests, who are ignorant and iniquitous knaves.
Vittore Barbaro, early 17th century, A.S.V. Relatione (Reports); Tenenti (1967 trans.) p.12. Barbaro is making his official report to the Venetian doge on the continuing threats from the Uskoks, notorious for their piracy from around the 1540s, who operated out of the eastern Adriatic, opposite Venice, in what is now Croatia. But these pirates had their uses: 'Concerning the galley crews which the pope [Sixtus V] desired, I have been informed from Rome that in the last few days his holiness gave instructions to the chiefs of Segna and Fiume to make him in those regions some 2,000 slaves of persons subject to the Turk … so that he can use them as crews for his galleys. When they bring them to Ancona, they should have their money' (report from Venice, March 1588; Florence State Archives Del Principato Mediceo (The Medici Principality) cover 3084, f.598).

5 The opinion of many is that this state cannot long continue according to the rule of preserving by the same skills as of getting, because they here change their manners, they are grown factious, vindictive, loose and unthrifty. Their former course of life was merchandising: which is now quite left and they look to landward, buying house and land, furnishing themselves with coach and horses, and giving themselves the good time with more show and gallantry than was wont … In matter of trade the decay is so manifest that men conclude within 20 years' space here is not one part left of three. The wonted course of bringing Indian merchandise to Alexandria, from thence hither, and from hence transporting it to other parts was the cause of the greatness of trade. These merchandises now being brought about by sea into our [English] parts have so changed the case that whereas pepper and other spice was wont to be brought here by our men, it is now brought from our ports and here sold.
Sir Dudley Carleton, the English ambassador, notes for a report, probably spring 1612; PRO SP99, file 8, f.341.

THE VENETIAN STATE

6 Those who are for a time doges I would warn to study the image this sets before their eyes, that they may see as in a mirror, that they are leaders, not

lords, nay not even leaders, but honoured servants of the state.

Francesco Petrarch, after the execution of Doge Marino Falier, 1355; Frederic C. Lane *Venice: A Maritime Republic* (1973) p.181.

1 Venice – rich in gold but richer in fame; mighty in her resources, but mightier in virtue; solidly built on marble, but standing more solid on a foundation of civil concord; ringed with salt water but more secure with the salt of good counsel.

Francesco Petrarch to Pietro da Muglio of Bologna, from Venice, 10 Aug. 1364; Bishop (1966) p.234. The poet was a valued visitor to Venice and a friend of Doge Andrea Dandolo (r.1343–54). Petrarch goes on to describe the celebrations following the Venetian victory in Crete (see 297:2).

2 The size of the multitude is hard to reckon and hard to believe ... The doge himself with a great band of the leading men occupied the loggia above the church vestibule [of St Mark's]; at their feet, below this marble tribune, the crowd was massed. This is where the four gilded bronze horses stand, the work of some ancient unknown but illustrious sculptor. On their high place they look almost alive, whinnying and stamping. To avoid the heat and dazzle of the descending summer sun, the loggia was everywhere protected with varicoloured awnings ...

On the right a great wooden grandstand had been hastily erected for this purpose only. There sat four hundred young women of the flower of nobility, very beautiful and splendidly dressed ... Nor should I overlook the presence of certain high noblemen from Britain, kinsmen of the king, who had journeyed here by sea to celebrate our victory, and who were reposing after the hardships of ship life.

Francesco Petrarch to Pietro da Muglio of Bologna, 10 Aug. 1364; Bishop (1966) pp.237–8. The poet is describing Venice as it celebrates successfully putting down a rebellion in its chief colony, Crete. The splendid horses that decorate St Mark's façade were part of the booty from the sack of Constantinople in 1204.

3 The special traits of a Venetian governor are a sense of humanity and clemency, to make yourself loved where other lords rule cities from the heights of their citadels.

Zaccaria Trevisan to his successor as *capitano* (governor) of Padua, 1407; Chambers (1970) p.98. Trevisan, himself 'a shining example of Latin prudence and Greek amiability', took Greek lessons when he was governor of Candia (Crete) in 1403–4.

4 The doge's assertion that ten million ducats were invested annually [in the spice trade] and produced a profit of 4,000,000 ducats (however he may have calculated profit) cannot be too far from the truth.

William H. McNeill (1974) p.32. McNeill is referring to Doge Tomaso Mocenigo who, in 1423, made public the state's stake in the trade (Jules Sottas *Les Messageries maritimes de Venise au XIVième et XVième siècles* (Venetian Sea Freight in the 14th and 15th Centuries) (1938) p.50).

5 During that time [the nine years since he became doge in 1414] we have reduced our national debt, arising out of the wars of Padua, Vicenza and Verona, from 10 million ducats to six ... and now our foreign trade runs at another 10 millions, yielding an interest of not less than two millions. Venice now possesses 3,000 smaller transports, carrying 17,000 seamen, and 300 large ones, carrying 8,000 ... Among our citizens we number 3,000 silk workers and 16,000 manufacturers of coarser cloth. Our rent roll amounts to 7,050,000 ducats ...

If you continue in this wise, your prosperity will increase still further and all the gold of Christendom will be yours. But refrain, as you would from a fire, from taking what belongs to others or making unjust wars, for in such errors God will not support princes. Your battles with the Turk have made your valour and seamanship renowned; you have six admirals, with able commanders and trained crews enough for a hundred galleys; you have ambassadors, and administrators in quantity, doctors in diverse sciences, especially that of law, to whom foreigners flock for consultations and judgements. Every year the mint strikes a million gold ducats, and 200,000 in silver.

Tomaso Mocenigo, doge from 1414, issues this remarkable bulletin from his deathbed, 1423; Norwich (1981) p.42.

6 Beware, then, lest the city decline. Take care over the choice of my successor, for much good or much evil can result from your decision ... Many, however, incline towards Messer Francesco Foscari, not knowing him for a vainglorious braggart ... If he becomes doge you will find yourselves constantly at war; he who now has 10,000 ducats will be reduced to 1,000; he who possesses two houses will no longer have one; you will waste, with your gold and your silver, your honour and your reputation. Where now you are masters, you will become the slaves of your men at arms and their captains.

Tomaso Mocenigo, 1423; Norwich (1981) p.42. Despite this warning, Foscari, the next doge, held the post for 34 years.

1 Citizens, whether laymen or clerics, should conduct themselves with honour so that they can live in peace with the *contadini* [countrymen], the *contadini* with them, because for good or ill, things are so conjoined that citizens cannot live without *contadini* and vice versa.
Venetian republic to the subject city of Verona, 1442; Hay and Law (1989) p.59.

2 This city of Venice is a free city, a common home to all men, and it has never been subjugated by anyone, as have been all other cities. It was built by Christians, not voluntarily but out of fear, not by deliberate decision but out of necessity. Moreover it was founded not by shepherds as Rome was, but by powerful and rich people, such as have ever been since that time, with their faith in Christ, an obstacle to barbarians and attackers … This city, amidst the billowing waves of the sea, stands on the crest of the main, almost like a queen restraining its force … Every day the tide rises and falls, but the city remains dry … as another writer has said, its name has achieved such dignity and renown that it is fair to say Venice merits the title 'Pillars of Italy', deservedly it may be called the bosom of all Christendom.
Marino Sanudo *Laus urbis Venetiae* (In Praise of the City of Venice) (1493; 1880 edn) p.28; Chambers and Pullan (1992) p.4.

3 This holy republic is governed with such order that it is a marvellous thing. She has neither popular sedition nor discord among patricians, but all unite in promoting her greatness; and therefore, as wise men say, she will last for ever.
Marino Sanudo *Diaries* (1496–1533). Sanudo (1466–1536) wrote 58 volumes of his diary as well as a *Chronachetta* (Chronicle). These were intended as material for a history of his own time. His eulogy of the republic was not, unsurprisingly, echoed by Galeazzo Sforza of the ducal family of Milan. See 299:5.

4 On 23 June [1482] Pope Sixtus [IV] decreed in consistory that the divine offices should be suspended in Venice itself and throughout the Venetian state, unless the siege of Ferrara was abandoned within 15 days.

The words of the interdict were as follows: If within fifteen days the lords of Venice fail to raise the siege of Ferrara, they themselves and their subjects, supporters, advisers and followers, together with other specified cities, lands and places subject to their rule, not to mention all persons, both lay and clerical dwelling therein, shall, if they fail to obey the prescribed admonitions, orders and commandments, be accursed and excommunicated in their persons, while their possessions shall be laid open to plunder by all nations.
Domenico Malpiero *Venetian Annals* (1843 edn) p.281. The pope's hostility was fuelled by Venetian imperial ambitions in the territory close to the papal states and Venice's attitude to ecclesiastical property.

5 I am of opinion that their affairs are managed with more prudence and discretion at this day [1493] than the affairs of any other princes or states in the world.
Philippe de Commines (1524; 1901 trans.) Vol.2, p.118.

6 These were not the true reasons for the animosity to the house of Aragon; the real occasion was, because the father and son restrained them and kept them from extending their conquests both in Italy and Greece; for their eyes were upon them on every side, and yet, without any title or pretence, they had lately subdued the kingdom of Cyprus. Upon these considerations the Venetians thought it would be highly to their advantage if a war started between our king [Charles VIII of France] and the house of Aragon; hoping it would not be brought to a conclusion as quickly as it was and that it would only weaken the power of their enemies and not destroy them.
Philippe de Commines, 1493; (1524; 1901 trans.) Vol.2, p.121. He is describing the Venetian reaction to the alliance of 1478 made against the republic by the Turkish sultan, Mehmed II, the conqueror of Constantinople in 1453 (see 259:2), Ferdinand of Aragon and the king of Hungary. Venice had become the guardian of the kingdom of Cyprus in 1473 but was detested by the Cypriots. In 1489, in an act of ruthless *realpolitik*, Venice took control of the island, which held a strategic position between the city and the Levant.

7 In losing their shipping and their overseas empire, the Venetians will also lose their reputation and renown and gradually, but within a very few years, will be consumed altogether.
Girolamo Priuli (1494–1512; 1911 edn); Norwich (1981) p.130. In 1499 the Venetian banker saw the eclipse of the republic in the loss of its overseas influence.

8 O great and famous Romans, O Marcus Curtius and infinite other Roman nobles, who exposed their lives for the least danger to their country, how deservedly their glory and fame will last for ever, and the Venetian senators are not to be compared at all to these holy Romans, as I choose to call them for the glorious experiences they saw and the deeds they did. And the Venetian fathers are not worthy to govern such a republic on their present showing. Girolamo Priuli, 1509; Chambers (1970) p.66. The Venetian patrician bewails the failure of the state to withstand attack from the papal forces after a French victory in May 1509. Priuli, a private banker, was ruined by the collapse of the republic and despaired at the prospect of the king of France camping on the shores of the Venetian lagoon.

1 The whole manner of the commonwealth's government belongeth to the senate. That which the senate determineth is held to be ratified and inviolable. By their authority and advice is peace confirmed and war denounced. The whole rents and receipts of the commonwealth are at their appointment collected and gathered in, and likewise out again and defrayed. If there be any new taxations or subsidies to be laid upon the citizens, they are imposed and likewise levied by the senate's decree ... Besides, the senate by a perpetual prerogative hath authority to choose such ambassadors as are to be sent to foreign princes, and likewise to create the college of those whose office is to assemble the senate and to report unto them. Gasparo Contarini *De magistratibus et republica Venetorum libri quinque* (1543; 1599 trans. as *The Commonwealth and Government of Venice*) p.66. Gasparo Contarini (1483–1543) was an active patrician, cardinal and devout reformer. The *collegio* or college was, in effect, a cabinet of *savi* (sages), which held office for periods of six months. In 1512 of the senate's 200 members, 39 were surnamed Contarini.

2 Thus on these occasions the body, which the prince accompanies as head, consists of a variety of persons and magistrates. And they go in order, thus: first the 80 banners which were presented by the pope, then the silver trumpets borne on the shoulders of children, and two by two the heralds ... the latter are always dressed in blue except for those of the proprio [personal to the doge], with long gowns, wearing on their heads a red biretta with a small gold medal on one side with the emblem of St Mark ... Behind these come the pipers and trumpeters, wearing red, all playing harmoniously. Francesco Sansovino *Venezia: città nobilissima e singolare* (1581) p.194.

3 The habit, manner of speech, gesture etc. of the gentlemen of Venice all alike (sic).

Betwixt the old families and the new a perpetual faction. The new are formost in number, the old in wealth and dignity; the new by this means carry away all principal offices in the government as the duke [doge] is ever of late chosen amongst them but the old have the love of the people. The opinion of many is that this will one day be the ruin of their commonwealth. Sir Dudley Carleton, 1612; PRO SP99, file 8, f.340. There were 24 old families, including such famous names as Contarini, Dandolo, Loredan and the diarist/historian Sanudo. Among the 16 new families were Mocenigo and that other diarist/historian, Priuli.

4 The remarkably long life of the Venetian empire rose from a judicious blend of centralized bureaucratic administrative and institutional forms that encouraged local communities of Venetians resident overseas to participate in public affairs. William H. McNeill (1974) p.34.

VENICE AS OTHERS SAW HER

5 You Venetians, it is certain, are very wrong to disturb the peace of other states rather than to rest content with the most splendid state of Italy, which you already possess. If you knew how you are universally hated, your hair would stand on end ... do you believe that these powers in Italy, now in league together, are truly friends among themselves? Of course they are not, it is only necessity, and the fear which they feel of you and your power, that has bound them in this way ... You are alone, with all the world against you, not only in Italy but beyond the Alps too. Know then that your enemies do not sleep. Take good counsel, for, by God, you need Galeazzo Sforza. Galeazzo Sforza, Duke of Milan, to Giovanni Gonnella, secretary of the Venetian republic, 1467; Norwich (1981) p.103.

6 Most of their people are foreigners. Philippe de Commines (1524; 1901 trans.); Chambers and Pullan (1992) p.325.

7 Venice makes both herself and me the slaves of everyone – she to preserve, myself to win back. Otherwise, working together, we might have found some way of freeing Italy from the tyranny of foreigners. Pope Julius II to Antonio Giustinian, July 1504; *Dispacci* (1876 edn) in Norwich (1981) p.136. The 'warrior pope' writes to the Venetian ambassador to Rome (1502–5).

1 As we sailed further on, we found before our eyes the famous, great, wealthy and noble city of Venice, the mistress of the Mediterranean, standing in wondrous fashion in the midst of the waters with lofty towers, great churches, splendid houses and palaces. We were astonished to see such weighty and such tall structures with their foundations in the water. Presently we sailed in to the city, and went along the Grand Canal as far as the Rialto where on each side of us we saw buildings of wonderful height and beauty.

Felix Fabri *The Wanderings of B. Felix Fabri* (1480–83 and 1494; 1892 trans.) Vol.1, p.35. The friar from Ulm in southern Germany approaches Venice from the Adriatic in 1483, to re-embark there on a pilgrim galley to the Holy Land.

2 They all walked two by two, as I said, after the doge in perfect order. This is very different from the practices I have witnessed in other courts, both ecclesiastical and secular, where the moment the prince has passed all go pell-mell (as we say in our tongue *a rubo*) and without any order. In Venice both before and behind the doge, everyone goes in the best order imaginable.

Canon Pietro Casolo *Pilgrimage to Jerusalem in the Year 1494* (1907 trans.) p.338. A Milanese pilgrim returning from the Holy Land describes the impressive ceremony of the All Saints' Day procession.

3 The Venetians, howsoever of old, they have been great warriors; they are now more desirous to keep, than to enlarge their dominions, and by presents and money rather than by the sword or by true valour, so whatever they lose to battle it is observed they recover again by treaties.

William Lithgow *The Total Discourse, of the Rare Adventures, and Painful Peregrinations of Long Nineteen Years Travels, from Scotland to the Most Famous Kingdoms in Europe, Asia and Africa* (1632) pp.39–40. A 17th-century traveller's reactions. See 265:1.

4 Yesterday was the Feast of Corpus Christi, celebrated by express commandment of the state (which goeth farther than devotion) with the most sumptuous procession that ever had been seen here, wherein the very basins and ewers were valued in common judgement at 200,000 pound sterling, besides many costly and curious pageants, adorned with sentences of scripture fit for the present. The reasons for this extraordinary solemnity were two as I conceive it.

First to contain the people in good order with superstition, the foolish band of obedience. Secondly, to let the pope know (who wanteth not intelligencers) that notwithstanding his interdict, they had friars enough and other clergymen to furnish out the day.

Sir Henry Wotton, 1606; Logan Pearsall Smith (ed.) *The Life and Letters of Sir Henry Wotton* (1907) Vol.1, p.350. The English ambassador reports on the conspicuous ceremony and the political propaganda behind it – as the pope was in dispute with Venice at the time.

5 There never happened unto any other common-wealth, so undisturbed and constant tranquillity and peace in herself, as is that of Venice, wherefore this must proceed from some other cause than Chance. And we see that as she is of all others the most quiet, so the most equal, commonwealth. Her body consists of one order, and her senate is like a rolling stone (as was said) which never did, nor, while it continued upon that rotation, ever shall gather the moss of a divided or ambitious interest.

James Harrington *The Commonwealth of Oceana* (1656); Norwich (1981) p.21. Harrington had visited and been inspired by Venice 20 years before, and he saw the republic as a utopia, promoting both stability and liberty. He influenced many political theorists and practitioners in Britain and America, including William Penn (see 433:3).

6   Once did she hold the gorgeous east in fee;
     Once was the safeguard of the west; the worth
     Of Venice did not fall below her birth,
     Venice the eldest child of Liberty.
     She was a maiden City, bright and free;
     No guile seduced, no force could violate;
     And when she took unto herself a Mate,
     She must espouse the everlasting Sea.
     And what if she had seen those glories fade,
     Those titles vanish and that strength decay:
     Yet shall some tribute of regret be paid.

William Wordsworth 'On the Extinction of the Venetian Republic' (1807).

7   Sun-girt city, thou hast been
     Ocean's child, and then his queen;
     Now is come a darker day,
     And thou soon must be his prey.

Percy Bysshe Shelley 'Lines Written among the Euganean Hills' (1818) lines 115–18.

Ducal Burgundy, 1363–1477

PHILIP THE BOLD, 1363–1404

1 Where did you learn to serve the King of England before the King of France when they are at the same table?

Philip the Bold, attrib.; Barbara W. Tuchman *A Distant Mirror* (1978) p.191. When he was 14 years old, Philip, youngest son of John II of France, fought alongside his father against the English at Poitiers (1356) and shared his subsequent captivity in England. According to Froissart (see 277:1), at a banquet given for his prisoners by the victorious Edward III the young prince indignantly struck the butler for serving his master before the French king. 'Verily, cousin,' said the amused King Edward, 'you are Philip the Bold.' And the nickname stuck, although some say that he earned the sobriquet by his very presence at Poitiers. He would become the founder of the late-medieval Burgundian 'state' and the first of its four celebrated dukes.

2 On Trinity Sunday 1364, Charles, the eldest son of the late King John of France, was crowned and consecrated King Charles V by the archbishop of Rheims in the great church of Our Lady at Rheims … When King Charles returned to Paris he gave the Duchy of Burgundy to his younger brother, Philip, who then left Paris, accompanied by a great retinue, to take possession of his duchy and to receive homage from its barons, knights, cities, castles and towns.

Jean Froissart *Chronicles* (from 1373; 1967 edn) Bk 1.223. On succeeding to the French throne, Charles V confirms in public his father's private grant of the duchy to Philip the Bold the previous year. Bringing this important region of eastern France under the direct control of the immediate royal (Valois) family was intended to stabilize their hold on their fragmented and war-torn land. It was not to work out that way.

3 Negotiations for the marriage had been going on for seven years without arriving at any conclusion … Finally, Madame Margaret [mother of the Count of Flanders], angered by the lack of control she had over her son, went to see him … and, revealing her breast, said with passion: 'Since you refuse to obey the wishes of your king and your mother, I intend, in order to shame you, to cut off this breast which fed you and throw it to the dogs. I would have you know that I hereby disinherit you, and you will never have my county of Artois.' The count, deeply moved and alarmed, threw himself at his mother's feet and promised to give the heiress of Flanders to the Duke of Burgundy.

Amable de Barante *Histoire des ducs de Bourgogne de la Maison de Valois* (1824–8; 1860 edn) Vol.1, p.81. On 19 June 1269 Philip the Bold married Margaret of Male, his predecessor's widow and the daughter and sole heiress of the Count of Flanders, whose lands, in addition to great swathes of the Low Countries, included the County of Burgundy, to the east of, but separate from, the French-controlled duchy. Because of this vast inheritance Margaret was beset by royal suitors from both France and England, putting the count in a political dilemma, which was resolved in the French interest by Margaret's grandmother, herself a French princess. These lands, to which the couple succeeded in 1384, vastly increased the scale, wealth and strategic importance of the ducal domain, not least by extending them far beyond the borders of France itself.

4 In Flanders once there was a company
 Of youngsters haunting vice and ribaldry,
 Riot and gambling, stews and public-houses
 Where each with harp, guitar or lute carouses,
 Dancing and dicing day and night, and bold
 To eat and drink far more than they can hold.

Geoffrey Chaucer *The Canterbury Tales* (c.1387; 1951 edn) 'The Pardoner's Tale' lines 1–6. The County of Flanders stretched along the North Sea coast from Dunkirk and Lille to Antwerp, but the word Flanders was used more widely to mean the Low Countries generally – that is, modern Belgium, Luxembourg and the Netherlands – as well as stretches of northern France. Dominated by its great industrial and trading cities, it had – in the predominantly rural world of northern Europe – a distinctly urban reputation, as Chaucer's Pardoner disapprovingly attests. *The Canterbury Tales* is exactly contemporary with Philip the Bold's rule there.

5 And though Flanders is a little land, it is full plenteous of many profitable things, and of richness of pasture, of beasts, of merchandise, of rivers, of harbours by the sea and of good towns. The men of Flanders are fair, strong and rich; and bring forth many children; and are peaceable to their neighbours, true to strangers, noble craftsmen and great makers of cloth that they sendeth about well nigh all of Europe.

Ranulf Higden *Polychronicon* (1340s; c.1387 trans. by John of Trevisa) Vol.1 (1969 edn) p.289. The wealth of the Flemish cities was built largely on the cloth trade, for which they were internationally famous, and much of its raw material was imported English wool.

6 For of wool, that they have out of England, they make cloth of divers colours, and send it into other provinces and lands as Flanders does. For, though

England has wool of the best, it has not so great plenty of good water for divers colours and hues [the dyeing process] as Flanders hath and Brabant.

Ranulf Higden (1340s) Vol.1 (1969 edn) p.289. Higden describes neighbouring Brabant.

1   In making cloth she showed so great a bent
   She bettered those of Ypres and of Ghent.

Geoffrey Chaucer (c.1387; 1951 edn) Prologue, lines 447–8. Chaucer introduces the Wife of Bath, a highly successful provincial businesswoman, who had made her money in cloth-weaving. For her, as for her times, professional standards were set by Flanders, where both Ypres and Ghent were situated.

2 The Duke of Burgundy was riding on the flank when, startled by the cries of the pages and the pounding of the horses' hooves, he looked across and saw the king [Charles VI] chasing his brother [Louis of Orleans] with the naked sword. He was horror-struck and called out: 'Ho! Disaster has overtaken us! The king has gone out of his mind! After him, in God's name! Catch him!' And then: 'Fly, nephew, fly! The king means to kill you!'

Jean Froissart (from 1373; 1967 edn) p.395. Philip the Bold witnesses Charles VI's collapse into insanity in Aug. 1392. For all his lands beyond France, Philip remained intimately connected with, and attendant on, French royal politics, and he was present when his nephew, Charles VI, went mad while riding out near Le Mans in Normandy, murderously attacking his own retinue until he was overpowered. The king's two uncles, Burgundy and John, Duke of Berry, who had acted as regents during his minority, resumed their joint role during his incapacity. Philip was to maintain his hold on power in France until his death in 1404.

3 I observed, when I was a young man, that you were called Philip Lackland; now God has generously bestowed on you a great name, and placed you alongside the mighty ones of the earth.

Honoré Bonet, prior of Salon, Provence, *Somnum materia schismatio*; Joseph Calmette *The Golden Age of Burgundy* (1962) p.56. Bonet, a fashionable author active in the 1390s in Paris where he enjoyed the duke's patronage, testifies to the impact that the rise of Philip the Bold had on his contemporaries.

JOHN THE FEARLESS, 1404–19

4 At the humble request of the burgomasters ... and good people of our town of Bruges [we grant] to the craft guilds of our town of Bruges authority to have banners to be used reasonably according to the conditions, restrictions and obligations hereinafter declared. That is to say, if in future the members of the craft guilds or any one of them or their successors make – which God forbid – any disturbance or armed riot, popular revolt or alliance of any kind against us or our heirs and successors ... then the person or persons charged and convicted with these misdeeds ... shall be decapitated in the marketplace at Bruges and their goods confiscated to the profit of us and our heirs and successors.

John the Fearless to the magistrates of Bruges, 25 April 1407; V.L. Gillodts van Severen *Inventaire des archives de la ville de Bruges, 13e–16e siècle* (1871–8) Vol.4, pp.14–16. The new duke, who succeeded his father, Philip, in 1404, apparently granting a gracious concession to the guilds of Bruges, in practice puts them under ruthless restraint. The powerful cities of the Low Countries had a long tradition of self-assertion, and there was constant tension between them and their rulers, frequently breaking out into actual revolt.

5 Bailiff, accomplish what I have written to you about or, if not, I shall show you how displeased I am.

John the Fearless to the bailiff of Bruges, 9 Sept. 1408; Richard Vaughan *John the Fearless* (1966) p.55. The letter instructing the bailiff urgently to find money to pay a contingent of Scottish soldiers who were serving in an action against the city of Liège ends with this postscript, written by the duke personally – his only surviving autograph, apart from signatures, and very characteristic, too.

6 Dear and well-beloved, we have received the parrot you sent us which arrived in good fettle, and we are grateful for the trouble you have taken. But we pray you earnestly, as soon as you've seen these letters, to purchase at Bruges or elsewhere ... the smallest monkey you can find and send it to us as soon as possible, letting us know what it cost so that we can refund you. God keep you.

Margaret of Bavaria, Duchess of Burgundy, to Robert de Capples, bailiff of Bruges, Ghent, 4 Nov. 1407; Archives générales du royaume, Brussels, Trésor de Flandres (1) 2514. A friendlier approach to the Bruges officials from Margaret, wife of John the Fearless. The Burgundian dukes were necessarily peripatetic; their duchesses tended to stay in Flanders and act as regent, and their huge households and luxurious lifestyle were significant factors in the wealth for which the region was known throughout Europe.

7 For these festivities and weddings, which very much concern the well-being and honour of us and our subjects, considerable expenditure both in provisions and household expenses and in purchase of jewellery, as well as otherwise in various ways, will be necessary. We cannot accomplish these things without a large sum of money which, at the moment, we cannot obtain from our revenues for this present year. Yet nevertheless we must have it.

John the Fearless, letter, 12 June 1406; Vaughan (1966) p.114. The elaborate ceremonies for which the Burgundian court was famous had political as well as cultural purpose – and they came at a political cost. The duke puts the screws on various nobles, who were compelled to stand surety for his mounting debts.

1 The nobleman [seen by Jaquette] was bareheaded and was playing with a glove or a muffle and, it seemed to her, singing. After she had watched for a moment she left the window to put her child to bed. But almost at once she heard someone say: 'Kill him! Kill him!' She returned hurriedly to the window, still holding her child, and saw the nobleman on his knees in the middle of the street … with seven or eight masked men around him who were armed with swords and axes. These men were striking the nobleman, whom she saw once or twice ward off a blow with his arm, exclaiming: 'What's this? Who does it come from?' To which nobody replied. Then she saw him fall, all stretched out in the middle of the street, while the men continued to lay about him with all their might … as if they were beating a mattress. She yelled: 'Murder!' as loud as she could; on which one of the men in the street … called out: 'Shut up, you damned woman! Shut up!'

Jaquette Griffart, wife of Jehan, a shoemaker, testifying to the murder, on 23 Nov. 1407, of Louis, Duke of Orleans, in a Paris street by agents of John the Fearless; Vaughan (1966) pp.45–6. This vivid eyewitness account was given on oath before the provost of Paris the next day. The frequent bouts of madness of the unfortunate Charles VI of France led to a struggle for control of the royal government between the king's younger brother, Orleans, and their cousin, John the Fearless, which John solved in his own way. The duke would pay dearly for the crime 12 years later.

2 The deed that has been done was perpetrated, as I shall now proceed to explain, for the safety of the king's person and that of his children, and for the general good of the realm … My thesis is the following syllogism:

The major: It is permissible and meritorious to kill a tyrant.

The minor: The Duke of Orleans was a tyrant.

The conclusion: Therefore the Duke of Burgundy did well to kill him.

John the Fearless; Enguerrand de Monstrelet (c.1390–1453) *Chronique* (1857–62 edn) Vol.1, p.177. The duke's brazen defence of his assassination of Louis of Orleans was given verbally to the French royal court on 8 March 1408 and then circulated in Europe in written form. He now controlled French affairs as well as Burgundy; but his ascendancy over the French royal government was not to last.

3 The young prince was already in the wooden enclosure [especially built for the conference] in the middle of the bridge. The duke advanced, leaving his men a little behind him. The crowd pressing around the barriers at the entrance to the bridge saw him raise his cap of black velvet, then go down on one knee on the ground before the dauphin. Hardly had he risen, when the shout was heard, 'To arms! To arms! Kill! Kill!', and the dauphin's men were seen hacking at the duke with their axes and their swords.

Amable de Barante (1824–8; 1835 edn) Vol.3. p.293. On 10 Sept. 1419 John the Fearless was assassinated during a parley with the dauphin, the future Charles VII, on the bridge at Montereau, southeast of Paris. It seems to have been a premeditated killing, Charles at a stroke both wiping out his most formidable rival for the control of French affairs and avenging the murder of his uncle, Louis of Orleans (see 303:2). The great 19th-century historian of ducal Burgundy reconstructed the scene at Montereau from contemporary sources.

4 This is the hole through which the English made their way into France.

Trad. words of the prior of the Charterhouse at Dijon, showing the damaged skull of John the Fearless to King Francis I of France, a century after Montereau. In the vacuum left by the duke's murder Henry V of England – victor at Agincourt five years earlier – moved centre-stage, married the French king's daughter and was proclaimed Charles VI's heir, dispossessing the dauphin for his pains (see 282:6).

PHILIP THE GOOD, 1419–67

5 He walked solemnly, carrying himself well and with nobility. He sat but little, stood for long periods, dressed smartly but in rich array and was always changing his clothes … He was skilful on horseback, liked the bow and shot very well, and was excellent at tennis. Outside, his chief pastime was hunting, and he spared no expense over it. He lingered over his meals. Though the best-served man alive, he was a modest eater.

Georges Chastellain *Declaration of the Noble Deeds and Glorious Adventures of Duke Philip of Burgundy* (before 1475; 1863–6 edn) Vol.7, p.221. Philip the Good is described by his official chronicler, who adds (significantly, since a crown was the one earthly accolade the Burgundian dukes never finally achieved): 'Such looks, and such a figure, seemed more befitting an emperor or a king than an ordinary man … and he deserved a crown on the strength of his physical appearance alone.'

6 It is noteworthy that the duke heard mass every day between two and three in the afternoon. This was invariably his habit, for he stayed up at night almost till dawn, turning night into day to watch dances, entertainments, and other amusements all night long. He maintained this way of life until death, which amazed some good people, not without reason.

Jehan Maupoint, Sept. 1461; *Journal parisien* (1877 edn) pp.47–8. The contemporary Parisian chronicler comments on (the by then elderly) Philip the Good's luxuriant lifestyle during the duke's visit to Paris.

1 Duke Philip loved and very much honoured women and could not hear evil about them. He used to say that by being nice to women he was inevitably making himself popular with their menfolk, because women were normally dominant and there was scarcely a single household in forty where the woman was not mistress.

Philippe Wielant, early 15th-century Flemish lawyer, on Philip the Good; Richard Vaughan *Charles the Bold* (1973) p.158.

2 My Lord Sharp-Wits … Since I wrote to you I have no further news. I beg you, tell me about the fair lady, all that can be put into writing, and about your doings, if such is your pleasure, fine sir. The citizens of Ghent still have as much love for me as for the Devil, and are as amiable as they are wont to be. Farewell, turd, you shall have no more, for I am going to see if I can puff myself up after your fashion, you know how, or whether I have lost the knack! Heigh-ho!

Philip the Good to his nephew, John, Duke of Cleves, in (probably) 1452; Richard Vaughan *Philip the Good* (1970) p.131. The duke reveals high, unbuttoned good humour (despite the usual friction with the burghers of Ghent), writing informally and in autograph.

3 We wish to arrange for certain important works, which he is to occupy himself with, and we could find no other artist to our liking who is so accomplished in his art and science.

Philip the Good to his accounting office in Lille, 13 March 1435; Elisabeth Dhanens *Van Eyck* (1980) p.43. The Burgundian territories were a vibrant meeting place for the various cultural schools of northern Europe. The duke orders his officials to make good overdue payments on the pension he had awarded to his 'well-beloved chamberlain and painter, Jan van Eyck' in case he left his service. The artist, the dominant figure among the founders of the Early Netherlandish school of painting, was a trusted servant of the duke and undertook various confidential missions for him as well as artistic commissions.

4 As a result, Giovanni [da Bruggia, Jan van Eyck] … began to ponder a means of producing a kind of varnish which would dry in the shade without putting his paintings in the sun. And after he had experimented with many materials … he finally discovered that linseed and walnut oil dried faster than all the other oils he had tested. Thus, by boiling these oils with some other mixtures he made, he produced the varnish that he – or, rather, all of the painters in the world – had long desired. After testing many other materials, he realized that mixing his colours with these kinds of oils gave them a very strong consistency, and that when they dried, not only were they waterproof, but the colours gleamed so brightly that they possessed lustre by themselves without the need for varnish, and, what seemed even more amazing to him, they could be blended even better than tempera.

Giorgio Vasari *The Lives of the Artists* (1550–68; 1991 edn) p.186. Tradition, particularly as transmitted through Vasari's immensely influential work, credited van Eyck (frustrated by the cracking of a painted panel after it had been set in the sun to dry) with having 'invented' the technique of oil painting. Certainly it was from Flanders, via the agency of the Italian painter Antonello da Messina (who, Vasari asserts, travelled in person to Bruges for the purpose), that oil painting was transmitted to Italy.

5 Paid to Colard le Voleur, valet de chambre and painter of my lord the duke, the sum of £1,000 … for the following work that he has carried out at Hesdin castle … For making or refurbishing the three figures which can be made to squirt water at people and wet them, a contrivance at the entrance to the said gallery for wetting the ladies as they walk over it, and a distorting mirror; and for constructing a device over the entrance to the gallery which, when a ring is pulled, showers soot or flour in the face of anyone below. Also … another contrivance, at the exit from the gallery, which buffets anyone who passes well and truly on the head and shoulders.

Account book for work carried out at the ducal castle of Hesdin in Artois, northern France, 1433; Vaughan (1970) p.138. Not all artistic commissions were as exalted as Jan van Eyck's major works. Philip the Good paid to update the mechanical contrivances for the practical jokes that enlivened the feasts for which Burgundy was famous.

6 The fair which is held here is the largest in the whole world, and anyone desiring to see all Christendom, or the greater part of it, assembled in one place can do so here. For here come many and divers people, the Germans, who are near neighbours, likewise the English. The French attend also in great numbers, for they take much away and bring much. Hungarians and Prussians enrich the fair with their horses. The Italians are here also, [with] ships and galleys from Venice, Florence and Genoa. As for the Spaniards, they are as numerous, or more numerous, at Antwerp than anywhere else … Indeed, there is nothing one could desire which is not found here in abundance.

Pero Tafur *Travels and Adventures* (c.1450; 1926 edn) p.203. The fair at Antwerp was described by a Castilian who travelled through Flanders in 1438. He adds: 'The duke of Burgundy comes always to the fair, which is the reason so much splendour is to be seen at his court.'

1 This city of Bruges is a large and very wealthy city … It is said that two cities compete with each other for commercial supremacy, Bruges in Flanders in the west, and Venice in the east. It seems to me, however, and many agree with my opinion, that there is much more commercial activity in Bruges than in Venice. The reason is as follows. In the whole of the west there is no other great mercantile centre except Bruges, although England does some trade, and thither repair all the nations of the world, and they say that at times the number of ships sailing from the harbour of Bruges exceeds 700 a day. In Venice, on the contrary, however rich it may be, the only persons engaged in trade are the inhabitants.

Pero Tafur (c.1450; 1926 edn) p.198. The great commercial entrepôt of Bruges was described by Tafur on his visit to Flanders in 1438.

2 [Arras] is a pleasant place, and very rich, especially by reason of its woven cloths and all kinds of tapestries, and although they are made in other places, yet it well appears that those which are made in Arras have the preference.

Pero Tafur (c.1450; 1926) pp.201–2. The cloth trade had various specialisms. Tafur went from Bruges to Arras (in nearby Artois), which was internationally famous for its pictorial woven hangings – so famous, in fact, that the word 'arras' came to mean a wall-hanging or tapestry in English.

3 For the reverence of God and the maintenance of our Christian faith, and to honour and exalt the noble order of knighthood; and also for the following three reasons: first, to do honour to old knights, who for their high and noble deeds are worthy of being recommended; second, so that those who are at present still capable and strong of body, and do each day deeds appropriate to chivalry, shall have cause to continue from good to better; and third, so

that those knights and gentlemen who shall see [this order worn] … should be encouraged to employ themselves in noble deeds … and deserve in their time to be chosen to bear the said order.

Jean le Fèvre *Chronicle* (c.1430); D'A.J.D. Boulton *The Knights of the Crown* (1987) p.361. The aims of Philip the Good's new foundation, the Order of the Golden Fleece, are described by Jean le Fèvre, lord of St-Rémy, the order's first King of Arms. Philip founded the order on 10 Jan. 1430 on the occasion of his marriage to Isabella of Portugal, closely modelling it on Edward III's hugely influential Order of the Garter (see 278:2). Politically, it provided a much-needed unifying element to secure aristocratic loyalty in the diverse territories of the Burgundian dukes.

4 It was at your urgent request that I took part in your French war. For my part I have so far accomplished everything that I agreed to … It is also true, most redoubted lord, that, according to the agreement drawn up on your part with my people, you ought to have paid me the sum of 19,500 francs of royal money each month for the expenses of my troops before Compiègne, as well as the cost of the artillery … My most redoubted lord, I cannot continue these [military operations] without adequate provision in future from you … and without payment of what is due to me, both on account of the two months above-mentioned and for the artillery. Thus, most redoubted lord, I ask and entreat you most humbly to see that the said sums are paid over at once to my people at Calais, who have been waiting there or this purpose for some time.

Philip the Good to Henry VI of England, from Arras, 4 Nov. 1430; Vaughan (1970) pp.24–5. In the latter stages of the Hundred Years War the dukes of Burgundy successfully played the French and English off against each other, often holding the balance of power as military fortunes came and went (see 311:5). But their regular changes of side in the Anglo-French struggle cannot be put down wholly to strategic vision: much was also due to the sheer unreliability of their ally of the moment, since France and England were equally hard pressed and divided. Here the duke presses the English king for overdue subsidies.

CHARLES THE BOLD, 1467–77

5 He was hot-blooded active and irritable and, as a child, wanted his own way and resented correction. Nevertheless, he had such good sense and understanding that he resisted his natural tendencies and, as a young man, there was no one more polite and even-tempered … More than anything, he had a

natural love of the sea and the ships. His pastime was falconry with merlins, and he hunted most willingly whenever he had time. He played chess better than anyone. He drew the bow more powerfully than any of those who were brought up with him. He played at quarterstaffs in the Picard fashion.

Olivier De la Marche *Mémoires* (after 1477, 1882–8 edn) Vol.2, p.217. Charles, the last of the four Valois dukes of Burgundy, succeeded when his father, Philip the Good (from whom he had long been estranged), died on 15 June 1467. He is described by a Burgundian courtier and chronicler who was brought up with him and knew him well.

1 Even though he is in camp, every evening he has something new sung in his quarters, and sometimes his lordship sings, though he does not have a good voice. But he is skilled in music.

Johanne Petro Panigarola, Milanese ambassador at the Burgundian court, reporting back on Charles the Bold; Vaughan (1973) p.162. The Burgundian lands were a centre of international importance for the development of music as well as of the visual arts. Charles the Bold was a notable patron and had musicians around him, even on campaign, as in 1474–5 at the siege of Neuss (see 307:2).

2 He who cannot dissimulate cannot rule.

Louis XI of France, attrib. saying; Giovanni Botero *The Reason of State* (1589) Bk 5, Ch.5. Louis (the son of Charles VII of France, with whom his relations were even more tense than those between the last two Burgundian dukes) was the mortal enemy of Charles the Bold. Known as 'the universal spider', the French king was suspicious, treacherous and adroit – a consummate Machiavellian 50 years before Machiavelli (see 274:4).

3 My Lady Margaret was married on Sunday last part [3 July 1468] at a town that is called The Damme, three miles out of Bruges, at 5 of the clock in the morning. And she was brought the same day to Bruges to her dinner, and there she was received as worshipfully as all the world could devise, as with procession with ladies and lords best beseen of any people that ever I saw ... And as for the duke's court, as of lords, ladies and gentlewomen, knights, squires and gentlemen, I heard never of none like it save King Arthur's court.

John Paston III to Margaret Paston, 8 July 1468; *The Paston Letters* (1963 edn) pp.164–5. Charles the Bold married, as his third wife, Margaret of York, sister of Edward IV and Richard III, to cement an alliance with England against Louis XI. Paston was in the retinue of the Duchess of Norfolk, the princess's chief lady attendant.

4 To help people whose cases had been pending before the judges without being brought to a conclusion, and to receive all sorts of complaints

from poor people, he held audience three times a week, Monday, Wednesday and Friday after dinner, with all the courtiers seated on benches in order of rank, no one daring to absent himself ... He had the petitions read to him and then decided according to his pleasure. There he remained, for up to two or three hours according to the number of petitions, often to the great annoyance of those present.

Georges Chastellain (before 1475; 1863–6 edn) Vol.5, p.370. Charles the Bold began centralizing and systematizing the administration of his varied territories to turn them into something approaching a unified state. But his efforts – infringing local jurisdictions and antagonizing local power structures – helped to undermine his position in the final crises of his reign.

5 Among us Portuguese [Charles's mother was Isabel of Portugal] there is a custom that, whenever anyone we have reckoned among our friends makes friends with our enemies, we commend them to all the hundred thousand devils in Hell.

Charles the Bold to the French ambassadors, 15 July 1470; Chastellain (before 1475; 1863–6 edn) Vol.5, pp.450–53. Charles's furious outburst against Louis XI (who was protecting Warwick the Kingmaker in the latter's struggle with Edward IV, the duke's brother-in-law; see 311:1) was widely reported throughout Europe.

6 When she [Margaret of York, Duchess of Burgundy] had seen them soon she found a fault in my English which she commanded me to amend, and moreover commanded me straightly to continue and make an end of the remainder then not translated, whose dreadful commandment I durst not disobey because I am servant unto her said grace, and receive her yearly fee and many other good and great benefices.

William Caxton *Recuyell of the Historyes of Troye* (1475) Prologue. Not the least of the Burgundian state's contributions to European culture was the duchess's patronage of Caxton, who was in her service in Bruges, where he published this volume (a translation from the French by Raoul Lefevre, a chaplain to Philip the Good) – the first book ever printed in English. The formidable duchess seems to have acted as editor as well as patron, perhaps necessarily, as Caxton himself acknowledged in the Prologue: 'My simpleness and unperfectness that I had in both languages, that is to wit in French and in English, for in France I was never, and was born and learned my English in Kent in the Weald where I doubt not is spoken as broad and rude English as is in any place of England.' See 212:3.

7 At one end of the hall stood a treasury, ten stages high, on which stood firstly, thirty-three gold and silver vessels of many kinds. Also, seventy jugs, large and small. Also, a hundred dishes and cups decorated with pearls and precious stones. Also, six large silver ladles and twelve gold and silver basins for washing hands. Also, six unicorns' horns, two of which were the length of an arm. Also, six silver jugs, each of twelve quarts. Also, a large silver basket, to hold the reliquaries on the princes' table … [The hall] was hung with rich cloth of gold tapestries with the history of Gideon the regent of Israel, and many precious and costly stones were sewn into them, which stood out and twinkled like stars.

Anon. *Libellus de magnificentia ducis Burgundiae* (1470s); *Basler Chroniken* (1887 edn) Vol.3, pp.361–4. The description of a feast given by Charles the Bold for the Emperor Frederick III at St Maximin (near Trier in Germany) on 7 Oct. 1473 suggests that the duke was wealthier and more powerful than any of the crowned heads of his time. Charles brought the Burgundian state to its zenith and is here revealed at the height of his splendour. He was hoping to get the emperor to revive the old Kingdom of Burgundy (within the Holy Roman Empire) and thereby gain a long-sought crown.

1 From your earliest years, indeed, because of your fecklessness and vanity of character you have had an inordinate desire to conquer Germany, to lay claim to the Roman empire, and to break the bonds of human society, never being content with your own territories. You lead armies, ravage the lands of others, and either massacre or subjugate free peoples … And since we find you proud, arrogant and rebellious against us and the King of France, and claiming to be free of the fief you hold from us, behaviour which least befits a vassal, we proclaim our intention of wiping you out with might and main, both in Upper Germany and in the coastal areas of the Channel, and of there wreaking your ruin and downfall.

Emperor Frederick III, manifesto against Charles the Bold, issued in Frankfurt, 3 Dec. 1474; Vaughan (1973) pp.337–9. Charles and the emperor were soon at loggerheads, and by the end of 1474 the duke's territorial ambitions had succeeded in getting both his feudal suzerains – Louis XI of France and the emperor – at his throat simultaneously. At this point his armies were deep in the heart of the Rhineland, besieging the town of Neuss, northwest of Cologne.

2 On one side I hear the cheery cry 'A right royal drink!'; on the other, 'Jesus', to encourage those who are in the last agony of death. There are whores in some rooms; in others the cross which leads the lifeless body to the grave. To God alone who knows the cause of these diversities these and other things must be referred.

Philippe de Croy, Count of Chimay, 1474–5; Vaughan (1973) p.328. De Croy, one of Charles's captains, describes life at the siege of Neuss. He was lodged in a local abbey, which was having to double up as military quarters. De Croy's bafflement would intensify as the increasingly reckless Charles's luck ran out: the siege had to be raised, the English and the French came to terms behind his back, and when he took on the Swiss he started to suffer a series of major defeats (1476).

3 After the battle [5 Jan. 1477], in the evening at about midnight … several great lords passed by the Pont des Morts at the city of Metz in great disorder. And the next day, which was Epiphany, and even eight days afterwards, Burgundians returning to their own country were continually passing through and near the said city. Among the first arrivals there was not a man who could say where my lord of Burgundy was.

Anon. *Chroniques de la ville de Metz* (1470s; 1837 edn) p.424. The aftermath of the Battle of Nancy (south of Metz, in Lorraine, northeast France). Charles the Bold was defeated and killed by an alliance of Swiss and other anti-Burgundian forces in his increasingly desperate struggle to defend his acquisitions. It took two days of searching the battlefield to find and identify his body, which had been stripped and mutilated and the face partially eaten by wolves or dogs.

4 Now you see the deaths of so many great men in so short a time, men who have worked so hard to become great and win glory, and have thereby suffered so much from passions and cares and shortened their lives; and perchance their souls will pay for it … To speak plainly, might it not have been better for these men … to have undertaken fewer enterprises, felt a livelier fear of God and persecuting people … and to have contented themselves with taking their ease and honest pleasure? Their lives would thereby have been longer, illness would have come later, their passing would have been more widely regretted and less desired, and they would have had less reason to dread death.

Philippe de Commines *Mémoires* (1524; 1924–5 edn) Vol.2, pp.8, 340–41. Commines, a servant of the Burgundians until 1472, when he transferred his allegiance to Louis XI, comments ruefully on the upheavals of his time. Charles the Bold would certainly have been one of the great men he had in mind. After Charles's death his territory was divided: ducal Burgundy went back to France, and – through the marriage of his daughter and heiress, Mary of Burgundy, to Maximilian of Austria, the son of Frederick III – the Low Countries became part of the Habsburg lands. The Valois Burgundian state, as well as its ruler, was slain outside the walls of Nancy.

The Wars of the Roses, 1455–85

THE LANCASTRIAN INHERITANCE

1 Having knowledge that the prince his son had taken [the crown] away, [the king] caused him to come before his presence, requiring of him what he meant so to misuse himself. The prince with a good audacity answered: 'Sir, to mine and all men's judgement you seemed dead in this world; wherefore I, as your next heir apparent, took that as mine own, and not as yours.' 'Well, fair son' (said the king with a great sigh), 'what right I had to it, God knoweth.' 'Well' (said the prince), 'if you die king, I will have the garland and trust to keep it with the sword against all mine enemies, as you have done.' Then said the king, 'I commit all to God, and remember you to do well.'

Raphael Holinshed *Chronicles of England, Scotland and Ireland* (1577 and 1587; 1927 edn) p.68. The relations of the confident, ambitious Prince of Wales and his by now invalid father were tense at the close of Henry IV's reign. Here Holinshed relates the version of their traditional reconciliation that Shakespeare would immortalize (*Henry IV Pt 2* Act 4, Sc.5).

2 Then said the king: 'Lauds be to the father of heaven, for now I know that I shall die here in this chamber; according to the prophecy of me declared, that I should depart this life in Jerusalem.'

Raphael Holinshed (1577 and 1587; 1927 edn) p.69. The ailing Henry IV's plan to seek forgiveness for his usurpation through a crusade was not to be. Now reconciled with the Prince of Wales, he died on 20 March 1413 in the Jerusalem chamber at Westminster.

3   Turn again, Whittington,
   For thou in time shalt grow
   Lord Mayor of London

Trad. rhyme. London's Bow Bells recall Dick Whittington back to the city, where he would become three times mayor (1395, 1406, 1419), leaving his great wealth to charitable purposes. His celebrated cat is thought to be an allusion to the trading ships ('cattes') by which he made his money.

4   Now gracious God may save our king,
   His people and all his well willing.
   Give him good life and good ending,
   That we with mirth may safely sing
   Deo gratias, Deo gratias, Anglia
   Redde pro victoria.

Anon. 'Agincourt Carol', last stanza. Henry V's achievements in France (see 282:5) turned him into a popular hero at home – temporarily binding the political wounds of the Lancastrian succession. (The Latin refrain translates as: 'To God your thanks, England, render for the victory.')

5 A majesty was he that both lived and died a pattern in princehood, a lode-star in honour, and mirror of magnificence; the more highly exalted in his life, the more deeply lamented at his death, and famous to the world always.

Raphael Holinshed (1577 and 1587; 1927 edn) p.89. Henry V died in 1422, aged about 35, leaving a nine-month-old baby to succeed.

6 It happened once that, at Christmas time, a certain great lord brought before him a dance or show of young ladies with bared bosoms, who were to dance in that mode before the king, perhaps to prove him or to entice his youthful mind. But the king was not blind to it, nor unaware of the devilish wile … and very angrily averted his eyes, turned his back upon them, and went out to his chamber, saying 'Fy, fy, for shame, forsooth ye be to blame'.

John Blacman *Memoir* (1919 edn) pp.29–30, 30–36. Blacman knew Henry VI personally. The young king grew up pious, unworldly and without military experience or ambition – personally virtuous but politically disastrous for a society that depended on strong central government, especially at a time when others had presentable claims to the English crown.

7 We ordain … that each and every student to be chosen for our royal college of Cambridge for the years of probation shall be poor and indigent scholar clerks, who have received the first tonsure, adorned with good manners and birth, sufficiently grounded in grammar, honest in conversation, able and apt for study, desiring to proceed further in study, not already graduates, and not bound to any other college, except our royal college of Eton.

Statutes of King's College, Cambridge, 1443. The college was founded by Henry VI in 1441, a year after Eton.

8 [In 1450] the men of Kent arose and chose themselves a captain, a ribald, an Irishman, called John [Jack] Cade, who at the beginning took upon him the name of a gentleman … he also called himself John Amend-All, since then and long before the realm of England had been ruled by untrue counsel, as a result of which the common people, oppressed with taxes and tallages [feudal levies], could not live by their handiwork and husbandry, and so complained bitterly against those who had governance of the land.

Anon. *An English Chronicle* (soon after 1461); A.R. Myers (ed.) *English Historical Documents* Vol.4 (1969) p.265. Cade's Revolt was in part a protest at the humiliations, as well as the expense, of the war in France.

1 [Henry VI] was his mother's stupid offspring, not his father's, a son greatly degenerated from his father, who did not cultivate the art of war … a mild-spoken, pious king, but half-witted in affairs of state.

Whethamsted's Register (1452–65); Keith Dockray *Henry VI, Margaret of Anjou and the Wars of the Roses* (2000) p.6. The king suffered a complete mental collapse in August 1453. John Whethamsted, abbot of St Albans, Hertfordshire, lays the genetic responsibility for the king's illness at the door of Henry's French mother, Catherine, daughter of the mad king, Charles VI (see 282:6).

2 Item, the Queen hath made a bill of five articles, desiring those articles to be granted; whereof the first is she desireth to have the whole rule of this land.

John Stodeley, report from London to the Duke of Norfolk, 19 Jan. 1454; *The Paston Letters* (c.1469; 1924 edn). Henry's French wife, Margaret of Anjou, seeks the regency during the king's incapacity. She was to be thwarted: Richard, Duke of York (Henry VI's closest adult relative) was himself made Protector by Parliament on 16 April 1454.

3 Blessed be God, the king is well amended, and hath been since Christmas Day … And on the Monday afternoon the queen came to him and brought my lord prince with her; and then he asked what the prince's name was, and the queen told him Edward; and then he held up his hands and thanked God thereof. And he said he never knew him till that time, nor understood not what was said to him, nor knew not where he had been whilst he hath been sick until now. And he asked who were the Godfathers, and the queen told him, and he was well pleased.

Edmund Clere to John Paston from Greenwich, 9 Jan. 1455; *The Paston Letters* (c.1469; 1924 edn). Clere writes with news of the king's sudden return to his senses. Poignant as the scene is from a personal point of view (Prince Edward was now 14 months old), the king's recovery was a disaster for the political order of the realm. York lost the Protectorship, and animosities soon led to warfare.

WAR BEGINS: HENRY VI, 1453–61

4   And here I prophesy: this brawl today
Grown to this faction in the Temple Garden
Shall send, between the Red Rose and the White
A thousand souls to death and deadly night.

William Shakespeare *Henry VI Pt I* Act 2, Sc.4. Shakespeare's History Plays have had a crucial role in giving posterity a Tudor view of the Wars of the Roses. This famous scene of the polarization of the Yorkist and Lancastrian factions as they pluck white and red roses respectively in the Temple Garden at London is doubly misleading: it is not only an invention, but the programme and personnel of the combatants were not then defined and consistent. Aims and alliances were of the moment, and only very slowly would a larger coherence emerge.

5 The battle started at 10 o'clock, but because the place was small few combatants could fight there; and matters became so critical that four of those who were of the king's bodyguard were killed in his presence by arrows, and even the king was wounded in the shoulder by an arrow, but it only grazed the skin. At last, when they had fought for three hours, the king's party saw that they had the worst and broke away on one side and began to flee.

Anon. report on the first Battle of St Albans, sent to the Duke of Burgundy and preserved in the archives at Dijon; E.H.D. Vol.4 (1969) p.277. The king, with the Duke of Somerset, set out to intercept the Duke of York, and the two forces met, almost accidentally, at St Albans, northwest of London, on 22 May 1455. This opening battle of the Wars of the Roses was a small-scale affair, but it was a decisive victory for York: the king was taken and Somerset was killed.

6 The queen was defamed and denounced, that he who was called prince was not her son but a bastard conceived in adultery; wherefore she, dreading that he should not succeed his father in the crown of England, sought the alliance of all the knights and squires of Cheshire, to have their goodwill and hold open household amongst them.

Anon. *English Chronicle* (soon after 1461); E.H.D. Vol.4 (1969) p.282. By 1459 the queen, Margaret of Anjou, was in the ascendant, with the king – nominally in charge once more – safely under her control. This (biased) source sounds a new and ominous note, for the divisions in the country were beginning to cast a shadow over the crown itself rather than just over the current royal advisers.

7 And when [the Duke of York] arrived there [the parliament chamber at Westminster] he advanced with determined step until he reached the royal throne … And while he stood there, looking down at the people and awaiting their applause, Master Thomas Bourchier, the archbishop of Canterbury, came up and, after a suitable greeting, asked him whether he wished to come and see the lord king. At this request the duke seemed to be irritated, and replied curtly in this way: 'I know of no person in this realm whom it does not behove to come to me and see my person, rather than that I should go and visit him.'

Whethamsted's Register (1452–65); E.H.D. Vol.4 (1969) pp.283–4. Following the change in Yorkist fortunes after the Battle of Northampton, the Duke of York entered London and went to Westminster on 10 Oct. 1460, clearly intending to take the throne for himself, but, at this climactic moment, he could not ignore the lack of a spontaneous parliamentary endorsement for the deposition of the hapless Henry.

1 The duke and his sons, Edward Earl of March [later Edward IV] and Edmund Earl of Rutland, who had both reached the age of discretion, were to swear fealty to the king and to recognize him as their king for as long as he might live – this much having been already decreed in Parliament – but it was added, with the king's own consent, that immediately upon the king's death the duke and his heirs be sanctioned to … take possession of the crown of England.

Crowland Chronicle, Second Continuation (begins 1459); Dockray (2000) p.97. This compromise, reached on 31 Oct. saved Henry's crown but put the Duke of York's ambitions on hold and disinherited the Prince of Wales. The duke then 'withdrew from the palace of Westminster to his London house, leaving the king and his men in peace'.

2 'I have often broken their [the English] battle line. I have mowed down ranks far more stubborn than theirs are now. You who once followed a peasant girl [Joan of Arc] now follow a queen … I will either conquer or be conquered with you.' All marvelled at such boldness in a woman, at a man's courage in a woman's breast, and at her reasonable arguments. They said that the spirit of the Maid, who had raised Charles [VII of France] to the throne, was renewed in the queen.

Report of an address by Margaret of Anjou to her captains from the *Commentaries* of Pope Pius II (r.1458–64); Dockray (2000) p.16. Although no doubt anecdotal – unlike Joan of Arc, she did not fight in person – it testifies to the queen's contemporary reputation: she, and not Henry, was the engine of the Lancastrian cause.

3 They stood him on a little anthill and placed on his head, as if a crown, a vile garland made of reeds, just as the Jews did to the Lord, and bent the knee to him saying in jest: 'Hail King, without rule. Hail King, without ancestry. Hail leader and prince, with almost no subjects or possessions.' And, having said this and various other shameful and dishonourable things to him, at last they cut off his head.

Whethamsted's Register (1452–65); Dockray (2000) p.100. The death of Richard, Duke of York, after the Battle of Wakefield. York and his son the Earl of Rutland went north to put down Lancastrian resistance, but met disaster at Wakefield on 30 Dec. 1460. Rutland was killed in the battle; York was butchered after it. His head, wearing a paper crown, would be displayed on the walls of York.

4 And in that conflict Owen Tudor was taken and brought to [Hereford], and he was beheaded at the market place, and his head was set at the highest pinnacle of the market cross, and a mad woman combed his hair, and washed the blood off his face and got candles, and set about him, burning, more than a hundred. This Owen Tudor was father to the Earl of Pembroke and had wedded Queen Catherine, mother to King Henry VI … He said, 'That head shall lie on the stock that was wont to lie on Queen Catherine's lap,' and put his heart and mind wholly on God, and very meekly took his death.

Gregory's Chronicle (covers 1450–69; 1876 edn); E.H.D. Vol.4 (1969) p.285. Owen Tudor, a young Welshman of no particular prospects, had won the heart of Henry V's widow, Catherine of Valois, and secretly married her. He was the grandfather of Henry VII and progenitor of the Tudor royal line (see 281:4).

5 And upon the Thursday following the earls of March and the Earl of Warwick with a great power of men, but few of name, entered into the City of London, the which was of the citizens joyously received, and upon the Sunday following the said earl caused to be mustered his people in St John's Field, where unto that host were proclaimed and showed certain articles and points that King Henry VI had offended in, whereupon it was demanded of the said people whether the said Henry were worthy to reign as king any longer or no. Whereupon the people cried hugely and said, 'Nay! Nay!' And after it was asked of them whether they would have the Earl of March for their king, and they cried with one voice, 'Yea! Yea!'

Great Chronicle of London; J.R. Lander *The Wars of the Roses* (1990) p.90. After Wakefield, the Lancastrians failed to secure their triumph by taking possession of a hostile London. The Yorkists took the capital instead. Less than five months after the Duke of York failed to depose Henry VI in London (see

309:3), York's son – some six weeks short of his 19th birthday – succeeds: the reign of Edward IV had begun (March 1461).

1 Just now, although matters in England have undergone several fluctuations, yet in the end my lord of Warwick has come of the best and made a new king of the son of the Duke of York.

Francesco Coppini, the papal legate, report to Francesco Sforza, Duke of Milan, on the latest developments in England, March 1461; Lander (1990) p.91. Richard Neville, Earl of Warwick (at this point Edward IV's champion and would-be manipulator) begins his career as Kingmaker.

2 [The Lancastrian] ranks being now broken and scattered in flight, the king's army eagerly pursued them, and cutting down the fugitives with their swords, just like so many sheep for the slaughter, made immense havoc among them for a distance of ten miles, as far as the city of York … the blood of the slain, mingling with the snow which at this time covered the whole surface of the earth, afterwards ran down in the furrows and ditches along with the melted snow, in a most shocking manner, for a distance of two or three miles.

Crowland Chronicle, First Continuation (begins 1459); Keith Dockray *Edward IV* (1999) p.22. The new king, Edward IV, immediately set out in pursuit of the retreating but undefeated Lancastrians, resulting in the biggest and bloodiest of all the battles of the Wars of the Roses, at Towton in West Yorkshire, on 28/29 March 1461, fought in the snow. The result was a disaster for the Lancastrians: Henry, Margaret and the Prince of Wales escaped, but their supporters were cut down in great numbers.

3 If any conflict breaks out in England, one or other of the rivals is master within ten days or less. Our affairs are not conducted in this fashion … out of all the countries which I have personally known, England is the one where public affairs are best conducted and regulated with the least violence to the people. There neither the countryside nor the people are destroyed, nor are buildings burnt or demolished. Disaster and misfortune fall only on those who make war, the soldiers and the nobles.

Philippe de Commines *Mémoires* (1524); Gillingham (1981) p.28. There was (relatively) little dislocation in England at large during the Wars of the Roses, especially when compared with the devastation of much of France in the Hundred Years War. No cities were sacked, no regions were systematically despoiled, and the vast part of the population was neither personally involved in the political and factional struggles nor (unless in the immediate locality of an army on the march) much affected by them.

WAR CONTINUES: HENRY VI AND EDWARD IV, 1461–71

4 Edward was of a gentle nature and cheerful aspect: nevertheless, should he assume an angry countenance he could be very terrible to beholders. He was easy of access to his friends and to others, even the least notable … He was so genial in his greeting that, if he saw a newcomer bewildered at his appearance and royal magnificence, he would give him courage to speak by laying a kindly hand on his shoulder.

Dominic Mancini *The Usurpation of Richard III*; Lander (1990) p.168. Mancini was an Italian cleric who visited England on papal business in 1482. His portrait of the new king, Edward IV, also commented on licentiousness – which makes it the more curious that Edward was to bring immense trouble on himself in 1464 by marrying an unsuitable commoner, for love.

5 She [Margaret of Anjou] arrived there poor and alone, destitute of goods and all desolate; [she] had neither credence, nor money, nor goods, nor jewels to pledge. [She] had her son, no royal robes nor estate; and her person without adornment fitting a queen. Her body was clad in one single robe, with no change of clothing. She had no more than seven women for her retinue … It was a thing piteous to see, truly, this high princess so cast down and laid low in such great danger, dying of hunger and hardship.

Georges Chastellain (c.1405–75); Lander (1990) p.108. The fugitive Margaret of Anjou attempted to rally the Scots, the French and the Burgundians to restore her fortunes. Here the Duke of Burgundy's official historiographer (see 303:5) records her arrival in 1463 at the Burgundian court to plead (unsuccessfully) with her old enemy. She retired, for the time being, to exile in France.

6 [When the king's marriage became known] the nobility truly chaffed and made open speeches that the king had not done according to his dignity; they found much fault with him in that marriage, and imputed the same to his dishonour, [that] he was led by blind affection and not by rule of reason.

Polydore Vergil *Anglicae historiae libri XXVI* (26 Books of English History) (1534; 1844 edn) pp.116–17; Dockray (1999) p.49. Edward secretly married Elizabeth Woodville – a commoner, the widow (with two children) of a Lancastrian killed at the Second Battle of St Albans – in May 1464, 'in which marriage men more commended the maiden's fortune than the master's wisdom,' as Sir Thomas More commented in his *History of King Richard III*. The news enraged Warwick, for whom the young king was not proving a pliable puppet, and he soon began to plot with the king's younger brother, George, Duke of Clarence. Vergil travelled to England as a papal tax collector in 1502 and found favour with Henry VII, who encouraged him to write the *English History* (see 343:1).

1 [A man] in good favour of the king's grace ... came into the king's chamber clad in a short coat, a pair of boots upon his legs as long as they might [reach his thighs], and in his hand a long marsh pike [i.e. a punting pole]. When the king had beholden his apparel he asked him what was the cause of his long boots and of his long staff. 'Upon my faith, sir,' said he, 'I have passed through many counties of your realm, and in places that I have passed the Rivers have been so high that I could scarcely scrape through them [unless I searched] the depth with this long staff.' The king knew that he meant by it the great rule which the Lord Rivers and his blood bare that time within his realm, and made thereof a disport. But this was an ill prognostication.

Great Chronicle of London (1938 edn) p.208. A barbed – and risky – jest, at court in early 1469, at the expense of the queen's relatives. The rapaciousness of the Woodvilles had become a major issue. (Elizabeth's father was Earl Rivers; her brother, Anthony, had now inherited the title.)

2 This boy [Edward, son of Henry VI], though only thirteen years of age, already talks of nothing but cutting off heads or making war, as if he had everything in his hands or was the god of battle or the peaceful occupant of the [English] throne.

The Milanese ambassador to France, at Bourges, 14 Feb. 1467; Dockray (2000) p.128. The Prince of Wales, away in French exile with his mother, grew up in her aggressive image rather than his father's.

3 Angers, 24th July 1470: The Queen of England [Margaret of Anjou] and the Prince of Wales, her son, arrived here the day before yesterday, and on the same day the Earl of Warwick also arrived. The same evening the king [of France, Louis XI] presented him to the queen. With great reverence Warwick went on his knees and asked her pardon for the injuries and wrongs done to her in the past. She graciously forgave him and he afterwards did homage and fealty there, swearing to be a faithful and loyal subject of the king, queen and prince as his liege lords unto death. They have not yet spoken of the marriage alliance, though it is considered as good as accomplished.

The Milanese ambassador to France to his master, the Duke of Milan; E.H.D. Vol.4 (1969) p.304. The old enemies, Warwick and Queen Margaret, now both exiles in France, make up their differences (at Angers, on the Loire) under the watchful eye of the astute Louis XI, happy to be fomenting trouble for

an English king (see 306:5). The queen did not trust the earl but was prepared for her son to marry his daughter, Anne Neville, to commit them both. An invasion was planned. Warwick set sail for England on 9 Sept.

4 [On 15 Oct. 1470] the Duke of Clarence, accompanied by the Earl of Warwick and ... many other noble men, rode to the Tower and fetched thence King Henry, and conveyed him through the streets of the city, riding in a long gown of blue velvet to St Paul's.

Great Chronicle of London 1512; Dockray (1999) p.73. Invading England and driving Edward IV into exile, Warwick and Clarence (Edward's younger brother) entered London in triumph, and collected the poor bedraggled Henry VI (still not quite 49 years old) from the Tower, where he had been held by Edward since 1465, and reinstated him on the throne. But not for long.

5 My lord and brother [Edward IV] offered him his hand, but King Henry came and embraced him, saying: 'My cousin, you are very welcome, I know that my life will be in no danger in your hands,' and my lord and brother replied that he should have no worries and should be of good cheer.

Margaret of York, Edward's sister and Duchess of Burgundy, letter; Christine Weightman *Margaret of York, Duchess of Burgundy 1446–1503* (1989) p.96. On 14 March 1471 Edward IV landed in Yorkshire with a modest army. Marching south, he was able to enter London unopposed and met his fellow king. Henry was wrong: within six weeks, when Edward was secure, he had him killed.

6 There they fought, from 4 o'clock in the morning unto 10 o'clock of the forenoon. And at various times the Earl of Warwick's [Lancastrian] party had the victory, and supposed that they had won the field. But it happened so that the Earl of Oxford's men had upon them their lord's livery, both in front and behind, which was a star with stream, which was much like King Edward's livery, a sun with streams. And the mist was so thick that a man might not properly judge one thing from another; so the Earl of Warwick's men shot and fought against the Earl of Oxford's men. And at once the Earl of Oxford and his men cried 'Treason! Treason!' and fled away from the field.

John Warkworth *Chronicle* (c.1478–83); E.H.D. Vol.4 (1969) p.309. Edward and Warwick finally confronted one another at the climactic Battle of Barnet, north of London (14 April 1471). Whether or not the confusion over the (Lancastrian) Earl of Oxford's livery was a factor, Edward won a decisive victory. Warwick was killed. Ironically, only a few hours later the second Lancastrian invasion force, with Queen Margaret and Prince Edward, landed at Weymouth.

1 This same earl was a wise man and a courageous warrior, and of such strength, what with his lands, his allies and favour with all the people, that he made kings and put down kings almost at his pleasure – and it were not impossible for him to have attained [the throne] himself if he had not reckoned it a greater thing to make a king than to be a king.
Thomas More *The History of King Richard III* (1543; 1931 edn). More's famous verdict on Richard Neville, Earl of Warwick, seems now both generous and misguided.

2 The king assembled his people and drew towards his enemies and finally met them at a place or village called Tewkesbury, where after a short fight he sub–dued his enemies and took Queen Margaret and her son alive.
Great Chronicle of London, 1512; E.H.D. Vol.4 (1969) p.315. Both Tewkesbury and its battle (4 May 1471), where Edward roundly defeated the Lancastrians, were more substantial than this late and laconic account suggests. Prince Edward was promptly executed (though according to some reports he was killed in the battle), and the Yorkists triumphed. After Tewkesbury they had only themselves to fear.

3 Edward has not chosen to have the custody of king Henry any longer, although he was in some sense innocent, and there was no great fear about his proceedings, the prince his son and the earl of Warwick being dead as well as all those who were for him and had any vigour, as he has caused King Henry to be secretly assassinated in the Tower where he was a prisoner … He has, in short, chosen to crush the seed.
The Milanese ambassador reports home from France, 17 June 1471; Dockray (2000) pp.130–31. Throughout his long captivity there had been no point in eliminating Henry VI merely to empower his more dynamic and charismatic son; but with Prince Edward dead, Edward IV wasted no time. The very night of his return to London after Tewkesbury he had Henry killed (21 May 1471). The official announcement was that Henry had died 'of pure displeasure and melancholy' at the news of the Lancastrian defeat.

THE FINAL PHASE: EDWARD IV AND RICHARD III, 1471–85

4 I send you 5s to buy with sugar and dates for me. I would have 3 or 4lb of sugar … and send them to me as hastily as ye may. And send me word what price a pound of pepper, cloves, maces, ginger, cinnamon, almonds, rice, raisins of currants, galingale, saffron, grains and comfits – of each of these send me word what a pound is worth, and if it be better cheap at London than it is here I shall send you money to buy such stuff as I will have.
Margaret Paston to her son, John Paston III, 5 Nov. 1471; *The Paston Letters* (1983 edn) p.203. The Wars of the Roses were both spasmodic and limited, and a succession of gory quotes seriously misrepresents their role in the everyday life of the buoyant, confident, prospering England of the later 15th century. Here, briefly to represent that normal world, is Margaret Paston in Norfolk writing to her son in London, with more immediate concerns than whose hand is on the sceptre this week.

5 [Edward IV] suddenly fell into a fact most horrible, commanding rashly and suddenly the apprehension of his brother George, Duke of Clarence, and his putting to death, who was drowned, as they say, in a butt of malmsey. As touching the cause of his death, although I have enquired of many … yet I have no certainty … A report was even then spread amongst the common people that the king was afraid by reason of a soothsayer's prophecy, and so became incensed against his brother George, which prophecy was that, after King Edward, should reign someone the first letter of whose name should be G.
Polydore Vergil (1534); Dockray (1999) p.98. The major internal challenge in Edward IV's 'second reign' was from the ever-duplicitous Clarence (who had deserted him for Warwick in 1469 and then deserted Warwick for Edward in 1471). Vergil was obviously suspicious of the malmsey story, but it was a contemporary rumour and, unlikely as it seems, may have been true.

6 He was little of stature, deformed of body, the one shoulder being higher than the other, a short and sour countenance, which seemed to savour of mischief, and utter evidently craft and deceit. The while he was thinking of any matter, he did contin-ually bite his nether lip, as though that cruel nature of his did so raise itself in that little carcass. Also he was wont to be ever with his right hand pulling out of the sheath to the middest, and putting in again, the dagger which he did always wear.
Polydore Vergil (1534); E.H.D. Vol.4 (1969) p.346. Richard, Duke of Gloucester (Richard III to be) may not, in fact, have been misshapen, outside the realms of Tudor propaganda, although he was small, especially next to his hefty brothers (Edward IV's skeleton proved to be over 6 feet 3 inches when it was examined in the 18th century).

1 The queen herself sat alone, alow on the rushes, all desolate and dismayed – whom the archbishop comforted in the best manner he could, showing her the matter was nothing so sore as she took it for, and that he was put in good hope and out of fear by the message [that Gloucester 'assureth you that all shall be well'] sent him from the Lord Chamberlain. 'Ah, woe worth him!' quoth she, 'for he is one of them that laboureth to destroy me and my blood.' 'Madam,' quoth he, 'be ye of good cheer. For I assure you if they crown any other king than your son, whom they now have with them, we shall on the morrow crown his brother, whom you have here with you.'

Thomas More (1543; 1931 edn) Vol.1, p.410. After Edward IV died unexpectedly (9 April 1483) Richard seized the new child-king, Edward V, causing Queen Elizabeth to flee for sanctuary to Westminster Abbey, with the young king's only full brother, Richard, Duke of York. She was eventually per-suaded – she had little choice – to surrender the boy to the aged archbishop of Canterbury, who turned him over to Richard. She was not to see either child again.

2 Word sprang quickly of a gentleman being in the parts of Brittany named Henry, and son to the Earl of Richmond, that made speedy provision to come into England to claim the crown as his right, consi-ering the death of King Edward's children, of whom as then men feared not openly to say that they were rid out of this world. But of their death were many opinions, for some said that they were murdered between two feather beds, some said they were drowned in malmsey, and some said that they were pierced with a venomous poison. But howsoever they were put to death, certain it was that before that day they were departed from this world.

Dominic Mancini (1969 edn) p.93. Mancini, an Italian briefly resident in London at the time (see 311:4), wrote his account before the fall of Richard III in 1485. The princes were held in the Tower of London, but by the autumn of 1483 they had disappeared from view and rumours abounded. The future Henry VII, in exile in Brittany, became the focus of Lancastrian and anti-Richard aspirations.

3 For Sir James Tyrrell [on the instructions of Richard III] devised that they should be murdered in their beds … Then, all the others being removed from them, this Miles Forrest and John Dighton, about midnight (the silly [innocent] children lying in their beds) came into the chamber and suddenly lapped them up among the clothes, so bewrapped them and entangled them, keeping down by force the feather bed and pillows hard unto their mouths,

that within a while, smothered and stifled … they laid their bodies naked out upon the bed, and fetched Sir James to see them.

Thomas More (1543; 1976 edn) p.86. More's version (written c.1513) of the death of the princes in the Tower is the one that has established itself in popular consciousness. He himself acknowledged that it was speculative: 'Not after every way that I have heard, but after that way that I have so heard by such men and such means as me thinketh it were hard but it should be true.'

4 His countenance and aspect was cheerful and courageous, his hair yellow like the burnished gold, his eyes grey, shining and quick: prompt and ready in answering, but of such sobriety that it could never be judged whether he were more dull than quick in speaking (such was his temperance).

Raphael Holinshed (1577 and 1587; 1927 edn) p.176. Henry Tudor, Earl of Richmond – the obscure, but now leading, claimant of the Lancastrian line – was descended from both the kings of England (his mother, Margaret Beaufort, was the great-granddaughter of John of Gaunt) and/or France (through Owen Tudor's marriage to Queen Catherine, the widow of Henry V); moreover, on Christmas Day 1483, with the consent of the now-sonless Queen Elizabeth, he was betrothed to Elizabeth of York, daughter and now heiress of Edward IV. He thus could unite the Lancastrians and the increasing number of Yorkists who were loyal to the late Edward IV but disaffected from Richard III.

5 A horse! A horse! My kingdom for a horse!

William Shakespeare *Richard III* (c.1593) Act 5, Sc.4. The last words – at least according to Shakespeare – of Richard at the Battle of Bosworth Field (22 Aug. 1485).

6 What misery, what murder and what execrable plagues this famous region hath suffered by the division and dissension of the renowned houses of Lancaster and York, my wit cannot comprehend nor my tongue declare. But the old divided controversy … by the union celebrated and consummated between the high and mighty Prince King Henry the seventh and the lady Elizabeth his most worthy queen … was suspended, and appalled in the person of their most noble, puissant and mighty heir, King Henry the eight, and by him clearly buried and perpetually extinct.

Edward Hall *The Union of the Two Noble and Illustre Families of Lancaster and York* (1548) Introduction; Charles Ross *Richard III* (1981) p.xlv. Hall was Shakespeare's principal source.

Portugal, Africa and the East, 1415–1583

ROUND THE CAPE, 1375–1550

1 Through this place pass the merchants who travel to the land of the Negroes of Guinea, which place they call the valley of Dra'a.

Abraham Cresques *Catalan Atlas* (1375); John Vogt *Portuguese Rule on the Gold Coast 1469–1682* (1979) p.1. This famous atlas included a map of North Africa indicating the pass in the Atlas Mountains through which the Arabs conducted their trade across the Sahara between the Mediterranean and the commercial centres of Guinea, notably Timbuktu. The Iberians, although excluded from this trade, showed a lively interest in it, even before Henry the Navigator of Portugal took the city of Ceuta on the southern side of the Straits of Gibraltar in 1415.

2 And as to the profit of our world from this achievement [the capture of the city of Ceuta] east and west alike are good witnesses thereof, since their peoples can now exchange their goods without any great peril of merchandise, for of a surety no one can deny that Ceuta is the key of all the Mediterranean sea.

Gomes Eannes de Azurara *The Chronicle of the Discovery and Conquest of Guinea* (1453; 1896 trans. and edn) Vol.1, p.16. The first step in Portuguese oceanic expansion down the African coast to India and beyond. To the Portuguese, led by Henry the Navigator, Ceuta seemed the key to the Mediterranean, particularly to the northern shore of Africa, where their enemies, the Moors, were entrenched.

3 For, said the mariners, this much is clear, that beyond this cape [Bojador on the coast of west Africa] there is no race of men nor place of inhabitants; nor is the land less sandy than the deserts of Libya, where there is no water, no tree, no green herb, and the sea so shallow that a whole league from land it is only a fathom deep, while the currents are so terrible that no ship having once passed the cape will ever be able to return.

Gomes Eannes de Azurara (1453; 1896 trans. and edn) Vol.1, p.31. Prince Henry dispatched successive expeditions for 12 years down that coast before finally, in 1433, Captain Gil Eannes doubled the promontory and so opened the way down and eventually round the coast of Africa.

4 Of a surety I doubt, if since the great power of Alexander and Caesar there has ever been any prince in the world that had set up the marks of his conquest so far from his land.

Gomes Eannes de Azurara (1453; 1896 trans. and edn); K.N. Panikkar *Asia and Western Dominance* (1953) p.29.

Azurara is glorifying Henry the Navigator's search for the eastern route.

5 But what heart could be so hard as not to be pierced with piteous feeling to see that company [of African prisoners]? For some kept their heads low and their faces bathed in tears, looking upon one another; others stood groaning ... But to increase their suffering still more there now arrived those who had charge of the division of the captives, who began to separate one from another, in order to make an equal partition of the fifths; and then it was needful to part fathers from sons, husbands from wives, brothers from brothers.

Gomes Eannes de Azurara (1453; 1896 trans. and edn) Vol.1, pp.81–2. The expedition of 1445 that brought back these 235 captives was the first to be privately promoted. Its aim was to return a profit by plunder and slave-raiding, the crown (in the person of Prince Henry) being entitled to one-fifth of the proceeds. Azurara and the crowd felt shock and sympathy at what was then a novel spectacle. A decade later such scenes would be taken for granted. Such was the beginning of the Portuguese trade in African slaves, which until this time had been an Arab monopoly.

6 Our joy is immense to know that our dear son, Henry, Prince of Portugal, following in the footsteps of his father of illustrious memory, King John, inspired with a zeal for souls like an intrepid soldier, has carried into the most distant and unknown countries the name of God and has brought into the Catholic fold the perfidious enemies of God and of Christ, such as the Saracens and the Infidels.

Pope Nicholas V, bull, 1454; Panikkar (1953) p.30. The pope confers on Henry the Navigator the right to all discoveries made *en route* to India.

7 There are in this country wild men who live in the mountains and forests, whom the Negroes of Beny [Benin, western Nigeria] call Oosaa. They are very strong and covered with bristles like pigs. They have all the characteristics of ... human beings, except that they shout instead of talking; I have heard their shouts at night, and possess the skin of one of these wild creatures.

Duarte Pacheco Pereira *Esmeraldo de Situ Orbis* (c.1505–8; 1937 edn) p.127. The meaning of 'Esmeraldo' remains unknown, but the title probably means 'Guide to Geography'. The author is presumably referring to chimpanzees, knowing well enough that they were not human but hoping perhaps to arouse interest by claiming possession of such a skin.

1 Ten leagues [about 30 miles] beyond the Areaees [places consisting of nothing but sand] is a point called Cape Cross, which has a stone pillar with an inscription in three languages, Latin, Arabic and Portuguese ... giving the date ... when King John II of Portugal ordered the discovery of this coast by Diogo Cão.

Duarte Pacheco Pereira (c.1505–8; 1937 edn) p.149. This *padrão* remained *in situ* until 1893, when it was carried off to Kiel by the captain of a German ship. Cão continued only a short distance before he died at sea – a fitting end for one of the greatest Portuguese explorers.

2 The River Nile rises in the Mountains of the Moon beyond the equator towards the Antarctic Pole. These mountains, according to the description of Ptolemy, and the place of the Nile's rising, 35° south of the equator, must be the rocky mountains of Cabo de Boa Esperança [Cape of Good Hope]. And flowing from its springs it forthwith forms two great lakes and thence flows through the land of the Ethiopians.

Duarte Pacheco Pereira (c.1505–8; 1937 edn) p.16. Pacheco pictured the Nile as rising in the deep south, near the Cape, although he also shared the then common view that another branch of the Nile flowed from west Africa eastwards. His record of coastal west Africa was, considering its date, extraordinarily accurate.

3 In this year 1493 the king [John II of Portugal] ... commanded that all who were minors, youths and girls were to be taken captive from among those Castilian Jews in his kingdom ... After commanding all of them to turn Christian, he sent them to the said island [São Tomé, in the Gulf of Guinea] ... and the result was that the island came to be more densely populated, on account of which it began to thrive exceedingly.

Ruy de Pina *Chronica del Rey Dom João II* (Chronicle of King John II) (c.1500); J.W. Blake (ed.) *Europeans in West Africa 1450–1560* Vol.1 (1942) pp.86–7. São Tomé quickly became a major producer of sugar and a key entrepôt in the trans-atlantic slave trade.

4 The chief industry of the people [of São Tomé] is to make sugar, which they sell to the ships which come each year bringing flour, Spanish wines, oil, cheese and all kinds of leather for shoes, swords, glass vessels, rosaries and shells, which in Italy are called *porcelettte* [porcelains] – little white ones – which we call *buzios*, and which are used for money in Ethiopia.

Anon. Portuguese pilot, c.1540; Blake Vol.1 (1942) p.157. *Buzios* were the cowrie shells that constituted the coinage of western Africa at that time, when the term 'Ethiopia' was used vaguely to indicate the greater part of central and southern Africa. The Italian word *porcellana* (little pig) was given to these shells because of their hog-backed shape.

5 Having reached these waters [the upper Niger] with the salt, they proceed in this fashion: all those who have the salt pile it in rows, each marking his own. Having made these piles, the whole caravan retires half a day's journey. Then there come another race of Blacks who do not wish to be seen or to speak ... they place a quantity of gold opposite each pile and then turn back, leaving salt and gold. When they have gone the Negroes who own the salt return: if they are satisfied with the quantity of gold, they leave the salt and retire with the gold. Then the Blacks of the gold return and remove those piles which are without gold. By the other piles of salt they place more gold, if it pleases them, or else leave the salt. In this way, by long and ancient custom, they carry on their trade without seeing or speaking to each other.

Alvise da Cadamosto *The Voyages of Cadamosto* (1507; 1937 edn) pp.22–3. This 'silent trade' had persisted since ancient times, having first been described by Herodotus (see 52:4). The salt came from the huge deposits at Taghaza in the Sahara and elsewhere, and the gold from the rich mining areas of the kingdom of Mali (west Africa). Cadamosto, a Venetian gentleman, led two voyages from Portugal (in 1455 and 1456) down the coast of west Africa to Cape Verde and beyond (see 293:1).

6 Horses are highly prized in this country of the Blacks ... A horse with its trappings is sold for from nine to fourteen Negro slaves, according to the condition and breeding of the horse.

Alvise da Cadamosto (1507; 1937 edn) pp.49–50.

7 I had a quadrant when I went to these parts, and I wrote on the table of the quadrant the altitude of the Arctic pole and I found it better than the chart. It is true that the course of sailing is seen on the chart, but when once you get it wrong, you do not recover your true position.

Portuguese navigator Diogo Gomes, on his voyage of 1457; Alvise da Cadamosto (1507; 1937 edn) pp.101–2. This is the earliest known reference to the use of the quadrant for purposes of navigation. The quadrant was a refinement for nautical purposes of the astrolabe, used formerly in astrology.

8 Here [in Timbuktu] are great store of doctors, judges, priests and other learned men, that are bountifully maintained at the king's cost and charges. And hither are brought divers manuscripts or written books out of Barbary, which are sold for more money than any other merchandise.

Leo Africanus *History and Description of Africa* (1550; 1896 trans.) Vol.1, p.825. Born in Granada, southern Spain, of Moorish parents, the writer's family emigrated to Fez in Morocco to evade persecution, his name then being al-Hassan Ibn Muhammad al-Wazzani. He was captured at sea by Christian corsairs in 1518, and his talent and learning were so impressive that his captors took him to Rome and presented him to Pope Leo X, who adopted him and called him after himself. Timbuktu had great natural advantages as a commercial and cultural centre, lying as it does on the River Niger between the Sahara to the north, savannah grasslands to the south and Senegal to the west. It was then at the height of its wealth and fame as a focus of the gold trade.

THE INVASION OF THE EAST, 1487–1515

1 Late on Saturday [18 Nov. 1497] we beheld the Cape [of Good Hope]. On that same day we again stood out to sea, returning to the land in the course of the night. On Sunday morning [19 Nov.] we once more made for the Cape, but were unable to round it … At last on Wednesday [22 Nov.] at noon, having the wind astern, we succeeded in doubling the Cape and then ran along the coast.

Anon. *Journal of the First Voyage of Vasco da Gama* (early 16th century; 1898 edn) p.9. Bartolomeu Dias probably coined the name the Cape of Good Hope in 1488 but did not round it. This journal circulated as a 'rutter' (mariner's guide).

2 At night [off Mombasa, main port of Kenya] the captain-major questioned two Moors whom we had on board by dropping boiling oil upon their skin, so that they might confess any treachery intended against us. They said that orders had been given to capture us as soon as we entered the port, and thus to avenge what we had done at Mozambique. And when this torture was being applied a second time, one of the Moors, though his hands were tied, threw himself into the sea, whilst the other did so during the morning watch.

Anon. *Journal* (early 16th century; 1898 edn) p.37. This incident typifies the violent temper and insensate cruelty that Vasco da Gama exhibited throughout his known career in his treatment not only of enemies but also of any others who crossed his path.

3 We were much pleased with the Christian pilot whom the king [of Malindi, north of Mombasa on the coast of Kenya] had sent us.

Anon. *Journal* (early 16th century; 1898 edn) p.46. In fact, this pilot was no Christian but an Arab, whose services the Portuguese were fortunate to obtain. Ahmad Ibn Majid was a sailing-master with unrivalled experience of the Indian Ocean, and by guiding da Gama's fleet safely to India he demonstrated what they could not otherwise have known – the art of navigating those particular waters.

4 The captain-major sent one of the convicts [João Nunez, a 'New Christian', i.e., a converted Jew, who spoke Arabic] to Calicut [southwest India] and those with whom he went took him to two Moors from Tunis who could speak Castilian and Genoese. The first greeting he received was: 'May the devil take thee. What brought you hither?' They asked him what he sought so far away from home, and he told them that we came in search of Christians and spices.

Anon. *Journal* (early 16th century; 1898 edn) p.48. One of the Moors accompanied Nunez back to the ships offshore and is reported as exclaiming: 'A lucky venture. Plenty of rubies, plenty of emeralds. You owe great thanks to God for having brought you to a country holding such riches.'

5 On Wednesday [29 Aug. 1497] the captain-major and the other captains agreed that inasmuch as we had discovered the country we had come in search of, as also spices and precious stones, and it appeared impossible to establish cordial relations with the people, it would be as well to take our departure. And it was resolved that we should take with us the men whom we detained, as on our return to Calicut they might be useful to us in establishing friendly relations.

Anon. *Journal* (early 16th century; 1898 edn) p.76.

6 To establish his estate the more safely and to preserve the friendship of the king of Portugal and also to keep the great profit which accrued to him from this commerce, he [the king of Cochin] put aside all the hinderers and was pleased to grant a site for the building of the fortress, where it now stands: and this was the first which was made in India.

Afonso de Albuquerque *The Commentaries of the Great Afonso Dalbuquerque* (1503–15; 1875–84 edn) Vol.1, p.6. These 'commentaries' consist of the dispatches sent by Albuquerque from the east to Manuel I of Portugal. Cochin, lying about 90 miles south of Calicut, had been the main centre for Portuguese trade since da Gama established it in 1502. The chief 'hinderers' in Cochin were, of course, Muslim merchants.

7 The more fortresses your Majesty might possess, the more your power will be divided: all your forces should be on the sea … insofar as you are powerful on the sea, all India will be yours, but if you do not possess this kind of power on the sea, fortresses ashore will do you precious little good.

Francisco de Almeida to Manuel I of Portugal, 1508; B.W. Diffie and G.D. Winius *Foundations of the Portuguese Empire, 1415–1580* (1977) p.229. In 1505 Almeida was appointed viceroy for three years to command Portuguese forces and possessions in the east. He handed over power to Albuquerque in 1509, after heavily defeating a combined force of Egyptians, Gujarati and Calicutians off Diu, in effect securing the Portuguese eastern empire for the next century or so.

1 Sire, I captured Goa because your Highness ordered me to do so … But when once Goa was conquered, everything else was at our command without any further trouble, and when Goa was taken, that one victory alone did more for the advance of your Highness' prestige than all the fleets that have come to India during the last 15 years.

Afonso de Albuquerque to Manuel I, 1510; Albuquerque (1503–15; 1875–84 edn) Vol.3, pp.258–9. Albuquerque stresses that 'a dominion founded on a navy alone cannot last', referring expressly to those who advocated 'placing all your power and strength in your marine only'. As he pointed out, the conquest of Goa, formerly ridiculed as impossible by Almeida and his friends, was already bringing the princes of western India to pay their respects to the Portuguese conquerors.

2 Singapura, whence this city [Singapore] takes its name, is a channel through which all the shipping for those parts passes, and signifies in the Malay language 'treacherous delay'; and this designation suits the place very well, for sometimes it happens that when ships are there waiting for a monsoon there comes so fierce a storm that they are lost.

Afonso de Albuquerque (1503–15; 1875–84 edn) Vol.3, p.73. Singapore, at the southern end of the Malaysian peninsula, was much more exposed to wind and weather than Malacca, which lay further north, well within, and protected by, the strait of that name. Both were great centres of commerce at the time.

3 The king [sultan of Malacca] and his son, who were mounted upon their elephants, seeing they were pursued by our men, turned back again with 2,000 men … The Portuguese captains awaited their coming at the head of a street, and with great effort and brave determination fell upon the elephants with their lances, as they were coming on in the vanguard … and whereas elephants will not bear being wounded, they turned tail and charged the Moors behind them and put them to rout. The elephant on which the king was riding, maddened by the mortal wound it had received, seized with its trunk the black man who was leading it; and roaring loudly dashed him to pieces, and the king, being

already wounded in the hand, sprang out of the castle, but escaped because he was not recognized.

Afonso de Albuquerque (1503–15; 1875–84 edn) Vol.3, p.106. Albuquerque attacked and took Malacca in 1511 with a force much smaller than that commanded by the sultan. This was the boldest and strategically most valuable of his victories, establishing Portuguese control of the gateway between the Indian and Pacific oceans.

4 It is true that there does exist a common right to all to navigate the seas and in Europe we recognize the rights which others hold against us; but the right does not exist beyond Europe and therefore the Portuguese as Lords of the sea are justified in confiscating the goods of all those who navigate the seas without their permission.

João de Barros *Décadas da Asia* (1552–63) 1st decade; Panikkar (1953) p.42. Only the first three decades, dealing with Asia, were published in Barros's lifetime; he died in 1570. The whole work was to cover Africa and Brazil.

IN SEARCH OF PRESTER JOHN, 1520–40

5 They pray or chant very loud, without art in singing, and they do not recite verses, but all sing straight on. Their prayers are psalms and on feast days besides psalms they recite prose – according as the feast is, so is the prose. They always stand in the churches; at matins they say only one single lesson: this is said by a priest or a monk, rather shouted than intoned (in the way that, in representing the passion of our Lord, we speak the words of the Jews); and besides, their voices being so harsh, they say it as quickly as a man's tongue can.

Francisco Alvares *A True Relation of the Lands of the Prester John* (1540; 1961 edn) pp.76–7. Alvares was a member of the Portuguese mission sent to Ethiopia in 1520 to make contact with its ruler, identified in Europe as the legendary Prester John, who would, it was hoped, prove a powerful ally in the struggle against Islam. The then king of Ethiopia, Lebna Dengel, was indeed a Christian ruling a Christian kingdom.

6 When they make these marriages they enter into contracts as for instance: if you leave me or I you, whichever causes the separation shall pay such and such a penalty … If either of them separate, that one immediately seeks a cause of separation for such and such reasons, so that few incur the penalty, and so they separate when they please, both the husbands and the wives. If there are any that observe the marriage rule they are the priests who can never separate, and cultivators who have an affection for their wives because they help them to bring up their beasts and sons.

Francisco Alvares (1540; 1961 edn) p.101.

1 Circumcision is done by anybody without any ceremony, only they say that so they find it in the books, that God commanded circumcision. And let not the reader of this be amazed – they also circumcise the females as well as the males, which was not in the Old Law.

Francisco Alvares (1540; 1961 edn) p.109. The 'Old Law' is presumably an allusion to God's command to Abraham in the Bible (Genesis 17:10) or, possibly, Mosaic law (Leviticus 12:3), both of which refer to males only.

2 They take a clove of garlic, large and moist, and place it on the corner of the eye (or wherever else they want to make the mark); with a sharp knife they cut round the garlic, and then with the fingers widen the cut, and put upon it a little paste of wax, and over the wax another paste of dough, and bandage it for one night with a cloth, and there remains for ever a mark which appears like a burn, because their colour is dark.

Francisco Alvares (1540; 1961 edn) pp.110–11. He describes this operation as part of the ceremony of baptism in Ethiopia. The cutting of babies' skins (scarification) was common throughout Africa and had various magical connotations.

3 The above mentioned valley reaches to the very high mountain where they put all the sons of Prester John. These are like banished men; as it was revealed to King Abraham [Yemrehana, an early king of the region] ... that all his sons should be shut up on a mountain, and that none should remain except the first born, the heir, and that this should be done for ever to all the sons of the Prester of the country and his successors: because if this were not so done there would be much trouble.

Francisco Alvares (1540; 1961 edn) p.237, referring to the 'Princes Mountain' of Amba Gesen, lying to the west of the party's route south. The Portuguese were forbidden to go anywhere near the cliff upon which it stood but were shown a door that led, allegedly, to an ascent. Anyone foolish enough to pass that door would have his eyes put out and his feet and hands cut off.

4 They brought down from the church four large and very splendid umbrellas ... [The Prester] then ordered that they should plant the umbrellas on the ground in the sun like a tent, and tell me that when he travelled and wished to rest, either he or the queen his wife, they set up one of these and rested under their shade, or ate and slept if they so desired ... These umbrellas were so big round that ten men could very well be under the shade of each of them, all covered with silk.

Francisco Alvares (1540; 1961 edn) pp.334–5. The processional umbrella, some nine feet high, was important in Ethiopian ritual, being used to cover and protect the *tabot* (ark).

5 In the tank stood the old priest, the Prester's chaplain, who was with me on Christmas night, and he was naked as when his mother bore him, and quite dead with cold, because there was a very sharp frost, standing in the water up to his shoulders or nearly so, for so deep was the tank that those who were to be baptized entered by the steps naked, with their backs to the Prester, and when they came out again they showed him their fronts, the women as well as the men.

Francisco Alvares (1540; 1961 edn) p.346, describing the yearly ceremony of baptism practised in Ethiopia at Epiphany (6 January). This was one of the most important festivals of the Ethiopian church, celebrated by mass baptisms in which kings, clergy and people took part.

6 When he saw that we wanted to leave, a passionate desire to return to his country came upon him. He went to ask leave of the Prester and we went with him and urged it with great insistence and begged it of him. Yet no order for it was ever given. This Pero da Covilhã is a man of great wit and intelligence, and there is no one else like him at court; he is one who knows all the languages that can be spoken, both of Christians, Moors, Abyssinians and heathens, and who got to know all the things for which he was sent; he gives an account of them as though he had them present before him. For this reason he is much liked by the Prester and all the court.

Francisco Alvares (1540; 1961 edn) pp.375–6. Covilhã had been sent by King John II of Portugal in 1487 to explore the Levant and the adjoining regions of Asia and Africa to find the sources of spices and to make contact with the Prester John (John the Priest). After extensive travels in the east, he reached Ethiopia and was much honoured there, being presented with a rich wife, lands and titles, but he was never permitted to leave the country.

THE PORTUGUESE AND CHINA, 1512–87

7 Cambay stretches out two arms, with her right hand she reaches towards Aden and with the other towards Malacca, as the most important places to sail to.

Armando Cortesão *The Suma Oriental of Tomé Pires* (1550; 1944 edn) Bk 1, p.42. Pires, the Portuguese crown factor in Malacca (1512–15), describes the strategic importance of the port of Gujarat.

1 One of our ships of 400 tons could depopulate Canton, and this depopulation would bring great loss to China ... With ten ships the governor of India who took Malacca [Albuquerque] could take the whole of China along the sea coast.

Armando Cortesão (1550; 1944 edn) Bk 1, p.123. Tomé Pires expresses the arrogance (and ignorance) of the Portuguese at that time. For Albuquerque see 318:1.

2 The custom with ambassadors in Piquim [Peking; Beijing] is to place them in certain houses with large enclosures, and there they are shut in on the first day of the moon; and on the 15th day of the moon they go to the king's [emperor's] palace ... and proceed to measure their length five times before a wall of the king's palace all in order with both knees on the ground and head and face flat on the earth.

Cristovão Vieira, letter from prison in Canton, 1524; D. Ferguson 'Letters from Portuguese Captives in Canton, Written in 1534 and 1536' in *Indian Antiquary* Vol.31 (1902) p.11.

3 I heard one of my fellows say that he told in one bridge forty arches ... The arches are not made after our fashion, vaulted with sundry stones set together; but paved, as it were, whole stones reaching from one pillar to another, in such wise that they lie both for the arches' heads and gallantly serve also for the highway. I have been stunned to behold the hugeness of these aforesaid stones; some of them are twelve paces long and upward.

Galeote Pereira *South China in the Sixteenth Century: Being the Narratives of Galeote Pereira, Fr. Gaspar da Cruz, O.P., Fr. Martin de Rada, O.E.S.A.* (pub. 1565) in Richard Willis *History of Travayle in the West and East Indies* (1577); C.R. Boxer (ed.) *South China in the Sixteenth Century* (1953) pp.7–8. While he was engaged in smuggling off the coast of Fukien in south-eastern China in 1549, the Portuguese trader Pereira was captured by a Chinese patrol and taken great distances overland before he managed to escape in 1553 (see 99:2). Here he describes the famous Loyang bridge, some 6 miles northeast of Ch'uan-chou in Fukien, one of many such bridges in that province.

4 There is also in Canton, along the wall on the outside, a street of victualling houses, in all of which they sell dogs cut in quarters, roasted, boiled and raw, with the heads pulled, and with their ears, for they scald them all like pigs. It is a meat which the base people do eat, and they sell them alive about the city in cages.

Gaspar da Cruz *Treatise in which the Things of China are Related at Great Length* (1569–70); Boxer (1953) p.134 (Boxer based his translation on that of Samuel Purchas Vol.3 (1625) pp.166–98). Although da Cruz, a Dominican friar, relied heavily on Pereira and others and his personal knowledge of China was based on only a few weeks' stay in Canton in 1556, his was the first book specifically about China to be published in Europe, and he made a substantial contribution to contemporary European knowledge of that country.

5 With 5,000 Spaniards at the most the conquest of this country might be made, or at least of the maritime provinces ... With half a dozen galleons and as many galleys one would be master of all the maritime provinces of China, as well as of all that sea and the archipelago which extends from China to the Moluccas.

Gerónimo Román, observations accompanying a letter from Matteo Ricci, 1584; Juán González de Mendoza *History of the Great and Mighty Kingdom of China* (1587; 1854 edn) Vol.1, p.lxxvi. Ricci spent 18 years in China (1582–1600) and became an outstanding authority on its culture, government and the like. Román, factor in the Philippines, reflects the attitude of the Spaniards from Manila, which was by no means shared by the Jesuit Ricci.

6 They say that the men hath induced them unto this custom, for to bind their feet so hard, that almost they do lose the form of them, and remain half lame, so that their going is very ill, and with great travail: which is the occasion that they go but little abroad, and few times do rise up from their work that they do; and was invented only for the same intent.

Juán González de Mendoza (1587; 1854 edn) p.31. The actual origin of foot-binding remains a mystery.

7 They have amongst them many coaches and wagons that go with sails, and made with such industry and policy that they do govern them with great ease: this is credibly informed by many that have seen it: besides that, there be many in the Indies and in Portugal that have seen them painted upon clothes [cloths] and on their earthen vessel that is brought from thence to be sold: so that it is a sign that their painting hath some foundation.

Juán González de Mendoza (1587; 1854 edn) p.31. Such sailing carriages had been used for centuries in China.

THE PORTUGUESE AND JAPAN, 1548–83

1 They [the Japanese] read and write in the same manner as do the Chinese; their language is similar to German.

García de Escalante Alvarado, 1548; 'A Contribution to the History of the Discovery of Japan' in Transactions and Proceedings of the Japan Society Vol.11 (1912–13) p.245. The notion that China (and by extension Japan) was 'the end of Almayne' (Germany) recurs in Iberian reports around this time, reflecting the prevailing ignorance of Russia, Siberia and the east in general.

2 The people whom we have met so far are the best who have yet been discovered, and it seems to me that we shall never find among heathens another race to equal the Japanese. It is a people of very good manners, good in general and not malicious; they are men of honour to a marvel, and prize honour above all else in the world.

Francis Xavier SJ, from Kagoshima (southern tip of Japan), 5 Nov. 1549 to the Jesuits at Goa (western India); C.R. Boxer *The Christian Century in Japan 1549–1650* (1951) p.401. Xavier's ecstatic first impression had little basis in fact because, as he sadly admitted, neither he nor his Jesuit companions understood Japanese. When he left Japan two years later, however, there remained a Christian community of a thousand souls, which grew many times over in the ensuing years.

3 On the evening of this day of All Souls [15 August 1561] many people go outside the city to receive the souls of their ancestors, and reaching a place where they imagine they can meet [them] they begin to converse with them ... saying unto them, 'Come and welcome! We have not met for a long time; you must be tired, pray be seated and eat a little,' and such like words ... On the evening of the second day many people roam through the hills and fields with torches and lights, saying they are showing the souls the way back.

Father Gaspar Vilela, letter from Sakai (Osaka), Honshu Island, Japan, 17 Aug. 1561; Boxer (1951) pp.51–2. Vilela is describing the Buddhist festival of *O-Bon*. He spent 17 years in Japan, acquiring the language and a knowledge of its culture, including Buddhism, but he remained one of the least tolerant of Jesuits.

4 When the Portugales go from Macao in China to Japan, they carry much white Silk, Gold, Musk, and Porcelains; and they bring from thence nothing but Silver. They have a great carrack which goeth thither every year, and she bringeth from thence every year above six hundred thousand *crusadoes* [ducats]; and

all this silver of Japan, and two hundred thousand *crusadoes* more in Silver which they bring out of India, they employ to their great advantage in China; and they bring from thence Gold, Musk, Silk, Copper, Porcelains, and many other things very costly, and gilded.

Ralph Fitch *The Voyage of M. Ralph Fitch ... 1583–1591*; Richard Hakluyt *The Principal Navigations, Voyages and Discoveries of the English Nation* (1589, rev. 1598–1600; 1903–5 edn) Vol.5 p.498. 'Christianity in Japan depended first, last and all the time on the Great Ship from Macao' (Boxer (1951) p.104). The sale of its cargoes largely financed the Jesuit mission as well as persuading local lords to welcome the missionaries to their estates, since they likewise profited from the trade, incidentally allowing the visitors to spread the gospel among their tenants. Fitch, a London merchant, travelled widely in the east in 1583–91 and made this most valuable report to Elizabeth I's government.

5 They [the Japanese] are the most false and treacherous people of any known in the world, for from childhood they are taught never to reveal their hearts, and they regard this as prudence and the contrary as folly, to such a degree that those who lightly reveal their mind are looked upon as nitwits, and are contemptuously termed single-hearted men ... Finally, since this people is the best and most civilized of all the east, with the exception of the Chinese, so it is likewise the most apt to be taught and to adopt our holy law.

Father Alessandro Valignano *Sumario de las Cosas de Japon* (1583); Boxer (1951) pp.75–6. This Italian visited the Jesuit missions in the East in 1574–1606. Here he gives the first of many reports – some contradictory – on missions in Japan (see 126:2).

6 It sometimes happens that the Portuguese go with their ships to the fiefs of heathen lords who bitterly persecute the padres and Christianity, wrecking churches and burning images, which causes great scandal and contempt of the Christian religion. Since we cannot now force the captain-majors [of the Great Ship] to go into the ports that we wish, it seems both necessary and expedient that we should obtain a brief from his Holiness forbidding the Portuguese, on pain of excommunication, to enter the ports of lords who persecute Christianity, or who are reluctant to allow their vassals to be converted.

Father Alessandro Valignano (1583); Boxer (1951) p.97. The prospects for Christianity in Japan (see 128:4). For the Great Ship see 321:4.

1 It will be wise at the court of His Majesty in Portugal, and in Rome and in the majority of the cities through which they journey, that they be shown all extraordinary and great things, such as buildings, churches, palaces, gardens and similar places, as well as silver objects, rich sacristies and other things which will contribute to their edification, but without having them see or know about other things which would give them a contrary conception.

Father Alessandro Valignano (1583); D.F. Lach *Asia in the Making of Europe* (1965) Vol.1, p.691. The Italian missionary is giving instructions for the trip to Europe in 1583 of a group of Japanese youths. The boys were to be chaperoned by a priest and friar at all times and to have no unsupervised contacts with outsiders. This was a carefully organized brainwashing operation.

2 Thus the pope, while labouring with all his might for the restoration of the Catholic religion in those neighbouring countries which have been shaken by error, has seen the faith take root and grow in far distant countries as well. This consoling fact, which hitherto has been known to him only by report, he can now touch with his own hand and make known to all the world.

Gaspar Gonçalves, Latin address, 1583; L. Pastor *The History of the Popes* (1930) Vol.20, pp.462, 583. A Portuguese Jesuit speaks at the papal reception in Rome of the Japanese youths (see 322:1). Evidently the Japanese visit was intended to benefit Europe as well as Japan and, indeed, the rest of mankind.

3 For the padres [fathers] to come to Japan and convert people to their creed, destroying Shinto and Buddhist temples to this end, is a hitherto unseen and unheard-of thing ... To stir up the *canaille* to commit outrages of this sort is something deserving of severe punishment ... I am resolved that the padres should not stay on Japanese soil. I therefore order that having settled their affairs within twenty days they must return to their own country ... As the Great Ship comes to trade, and this is something quite different, the Portuguese can carry on their commerce unmolested.

Toyotomi Hideyoshi, decree, 25 July 1587; Boxer (1951) p.148. Hideyoshi, the soldier who had continued the unification of Japan, had favoured the Jesuits since his accession but turned abruptly and violently against them with this proclamation.

4 The Portuguese cannot enter the Philippines, nor can the Spaniards trade at Malacca and Macao, which last place is where the Portuguese live at 18 leagues [about 54 miles] distance from the great city of Canton. And it often happens that through a storm or chance event some Spanish ships are wrecked or forced into Portuguese ports, where they immediately have the cargoes confiscated and their men imprisoned and very badly treated ... Forasmuch as throughout all the kingdom of China there is an enormous quantity of fine gold of more than 22 carats touch; if this were brought to New Spain [Mexico] or to Castile a profit of 75 or 80 per cent would be made.

Pedro de Baeza, report, c.1609; Boxer (1951) p.425. A Spaniard refers to the Far East in the 1590s and argues for the right of his compatriots from the Philippines to share the China–Japan trade with the Portuguese, who then monopolized it. Both were, after all, subjects of the king of Spain, to whom this plea was addressed.

5 He [Toyotomi Hideyoshi] originally ordered all the padres to be killed, but he subsequently stated that he only wished to punish the Castilian friars from the Philippines and their converts. He finally ordered the crucifixion of six friars and three Japanese brothers of the Company [of Jesus, the Jesuits] along with them, besides another 17 Japanese Christians ... When I sailed for China, all those crucified were still on their crosses.

Commander of the Great Ship, expedition of 1596–7, dispatch from Macao, Nov. 1597; Boxer (1951) p.417. The Spanish crown had expressly endorsed the Jesuits' monopoly of the China–Japan trade, but the Franciscans refused to accept exclusion, persisting in their trade from Manila and in their militant religious campaigning, despite repeated and emphatic orders from Madrid to withdraw. The conflict between Jesuits and Franciscans was not merely financial, but national (Portuguese and Spanish) and even, according to some on either side, religious.

6 These stoves are found in very large rooms, and there is a house with more than 170 of them in various rooms which open onto each other, where more than a thousand people roast the *cha*: there are others with fewer people. This town would have 15 or 20 principal houses making *cha* and employing more than 5,000 or 6,000 people.

João Rodrigues's Account of Sixteenth-Century Japan (16th century; 2001 edn) p.274. The original Portuguese no longer exists, this text being a translation of the 1740s copy of the *Historia da Igreja do Japão* (History of the Church in Japan). The town described was Uji, a few miles south of Miyako (Kyoto), which for centuries had been the centre of production of the finest *cha* (tea).

JUDGEMENTS

1   No more, Muse, no more, my lyre
    Is out of tune and my throat hoarse,
    Not from singing but from wasting song
    On a deaf and coarsened people.
    Those rewards which encourage genius
    My country ignores, being given over
    To avarice and philistinism,
    Heartlessness and degrading pessimism.
    I do not know by what twist of fate
    It has lost that pride, that zest for life,
    Which lifts the spirits unfailingly
    And welcomes duty with a smiling face.
    In this regard, my King, whom Divine
    Will has set up on the royal throne,
    Take note of other nations, and applaud
    The excellence of those who call you lord.

Luis Vaz de Camões *The Lusiads* (1572; 1997 trans.) Canto 10, verses 145–6. Camões, the author of Portugal's great Renaissance poem, spent 17 years in the Portuguese east. He died in poverty in 1580, depressed by the disastrous defeat of the Portuguese army by their old enemies, the Arabs, at the Battle of Alcazarquivir, in Morocco in 1578. The poem is an epic of knowledge and its extension rather than of commerce. Although Vasco da Gama and his associates figure and speak in the poem, its hero is really not any individual but Portugal itself.

2 Portugal and Spain held the keys of the treasure house of the east and the west. But it was neither Portugal with her tiny population, and her empire that was little more than a line of forts and factories 10,000 miles long, nor Spain, for centuries an army on the march and now staggering beneath the responsibilities of her vast and scattered empire, devout to fanaticism, and with an incapacity for economic affairs which seemed almost inspired, which reaped the material harvest of the empires into which they had stepped, the one by patient toil, the other by luck. Gathering spoils which they could not retain, and amassing wealth which slipped through their fingers, they were little more than the political agents of minds more astute and characters better versed in the arts of peace … The economic capital of the new civilization was Antwerp … its typical figure, the paymaster of princes, was the international financier.

R.H. Tawney *Religion and the Rise of Capitalism* (1926; 1937 edn) p.78. Tawney sees in the early European invasions only the hand of the grasping merchants of Antwerp.

Explorers and Conquistadors, 1492–1542

CHRISTOPHER COLUMBUS, 1492–1563

1 From the city of Lisbon westward in a straight line to the very noble city of Quinsay [Hangchow] 26 spaces are indicated on the chart, each of which covers 250 miles … But from the island of Antilia known to you, to the far-famed island of Cipangu [Japan] there are ten spaces … So there is no great space to be traversed over unknown waters.

Paolo Toscanelli to Fernão Martins in Portugal, 1474; S.E. Morison *Journals and Other Documents on the Life and Voyages of Christopher Columbus* (1963) pp.13–14. A Florentine physician is advocating a western voyage to the Far East. Columbus acquired a copy of this letter, wrote to Toscanelli about it and received in return a chart illustrating the concept. Academic authority, right or wrong, was just what Columbus needed. Antilia was the mythical 'Island of the Seven Cities' usually supposed to lie somewhere in the Atlantic.

2 So, after having expelled all the Jews from your kingdoms and dominions, in the same month of January Your Highnesses commanded me to go with a suitable fleet to the said regions of India. And for that you granted me great favours and ennobled me so that thenceforth I might call myself Don and be Grand Admiral of the Ocean Sea and viceroy and perpetual governor of all the islands and lands I might discover.

Bartolomé de Las Casas *Diary* (1530s; 1989 edn) p.2. Las Casas based his diary on Columbus's lost journal. He sometimes quotes and sometimes summarizes it. Las Casas's copy of the journal then also disappeared, not to be rediscovered until about 1790. Las Casas, 'the apostle of the Indies', was remarkably erratic and opinionated, but this text is still the chief source of information on the 1492 voyage. 'Your Highnesses' were Ferdinand and Isabella, king and queen of the Spanish kingdoms of Aragon and Castile (see 334:2).

3 Sunday 9 Sept. [1492]. He made 15 leagues [about 45 miles] that day and decided to report less than those actually travelled so that in case the voyage proved long the men would not be frightened and lose courage.

Bartolomé de Las Casas (1530s; 1989 edn) p.29. In the true reckoning he kept for his own use Columbus greatly overestimated his speed and consequently the distance covered, so that the supposedly false reckoning was, in fact, more nearly correct than the one he thought true. On the return voyage, however, 'he pretended to have gone a greater distance to confuse the pilots and sailors who were charting

their course so that he would remain the master of the route to the Indies' (p.375).

4 Thursday 11 Oct. [1492]. A sailor named Rodrigo de Triana saw this land first, although the admiral at the tenth hour of the night, while on the sterncastle, saw a light … It was like a small wax candle which rose and lifted up … The admiral was certain they were near land, on account of which, when they recited the *Salve*, which sailors are accustomed to sing, all being present, the admiral exhorted them to keep a good lookout … At two hours after midnight the land appeared.

Bartolomé de Las Casas (1530s; 1989 edn) p.59. Approaching the island of San Salvador (for a time Watlings Island) in the Bahamas.

5 They are credulous and aware that there is a god in heaven and convinced that we come from there. And they repeat very quickly any prayer we tell them and make the sign of the cross. So your Highnesses should resolve to make them Christians, for I believe that if you begin you will soon convert to our holy faith a multitude of people, acquiring large dominions and great riches for Spain. Because without doubt there is in these lands a very great quantity of gold.

Bartolomé de Las Casas (1530s; 1989 edn) p.145. Columbus is writing in Oct. 1492 to his royal patrons of the tractability of the indigenous Taino Indians.

6 It is certain, says the admiral, that this is the mainland, and that I am off Zayton and Quinsay [Shanghai and Hangchow, both Chinese ports] 100 leagues [about 300 miles] distant more or less from the one and the other, and this is shown by the sea, which looks different from what it has been until now.

Bartolomé de Las Casas (1530s; 1989 edn) pp.128–9. Thus on 1 Nov. 1492, coasting Cuba, he decided he was off the Chinese mainland.

7 Thereupon it was … covenanted and agreed that a boundary or straight line be determined and drawn north and south from pole to pole on the said ocean sea, from the arctic to the antarctic pole … at a distance of 370 leagues [about 1,110 miles] west of the Cape Verde Islands [off the coast of Senegal, west Africa] … And all lands, both islands and mainlands, found and discovered already or to be found and discovered hereafter by the said king of Portugal and by his vassals on this side of the said line ... shall belong to and remain in possession of and pertain forever to the said king of Portugal and his successors. And all other lands, both islands and mainlands, found or to be found hereafter, which have been or shall be discovered by the said king and queen of Castile, Aragon, etc. and by their vessels on the western side of the said bound ... shall belong to and remain in the possession of and pertain forever to the said king and queen of Castile, Léon, etc. and to their successors.

Treaty of Tordesillas between Spain and Portugal, 1494; F.G. Davenport *European Treaties Bearing on the History of the United States* (1917) p.95. Ferdinand and Isabella obtained this grant from Pope Alexander VI in 1493, but John II, king of Portugal, objected, and relations were severely strained until this agreement. Thus Portugal later successfully claimed Brazil.

1 He was informed that the natives suffered from such a severe famine that more than 50,000 men had already perished and that people continued to die daily as cattle do in time of pest. This calamity was the consequence of their own folly, for when they saw that the Spaniards wished to settle in their island, they thought they might expel them by creating a scarcity of food.

Peter Martyr d'Anghiera *De Orbe Novo* (Concerning the New World) (early 16th century; 1912 edn) Vol.I, p.108. Peter Martyr (1457–1526), an Italian at the Spanish court, was the first person to recognize the importance of Columbus's discovery. From the admiral and other explorers he collected information about this 'New World' (a term he probably coined), and in his famous letters to friends and important contacts, published serially in the early years of the 16th century, described it in detail. In 1493 Columbus is already reporting the decline of the Indian population, which continued at a catastrophic rate.

2 Entering the city of Santo Domingo [capital of Hispaniola] ... he found all at sixes and sevens, for all the families of the island were infected with a disorderly and rebellious spirit. Some of the people he had left were dead and of the survivors more than 160 were sick with the French sickness.

Ferdinand Columbus *The Life of the Admiral Christopher Columbus by his Son Ferdinand* (1571; 1960 edn) p.192. The original biography in Spanish is lost. Modern versions derive from the Italian edition. Ferdinand is referring to his father's third voyage and to syphilis, which about this time became rampant in Europe. Thus many came to believe – rightly or wrongly – that the disease came from the New World to Europe, brought by returning colonists.

3 He [Columbus] had been placed in chains in the sovereigns' name, he said, and would wear them until the sovereigns ordered them removed, for he was resolved to keep those chains as a memorial of how well he had been rewarded for his many services. And this he did, for I always saw them in his bedroom, and he wanted them buried with his bones.

Ferdinand Columbus (1571; 1960 edn) p.219. Francisco de Bobadilla, sent out to Hispaniola as royal commissioner with unlimited powers in 1500, sent Columbus home in chains to be charged with various misdeeds.

4 Now that these regions are truly and amply explored and another fourth part has been discovered by Amerigo Vespucci I do not see why anyone can prohibit its being given the name of its discoverer, Amerigo, wise man of genius.

Martin Waldseemüller *Cosmographiae Introductio* (1507). Vespucci (1451–1512), a Florentine merchant, writer and self-advertising adventurer, claimed to have discovered America in a voyage of 1497. No such voyage occurred, but that did not prevent Vespucci writing a lively account of it. He did, however, sail to the New World more than once later and wrote interestingly about his experience (see 326:2). A rival, less likely source for the name has been advanced in the person of Richard Ameryk, sheriff of Bristol, who financed John Cabot's voyage to America in 1497, five years after Columbus. Cabot is said to have applied his patron's name to the new land, either in gratitude or as part of the financial negotiation.

THE EXPLORATION OF BRAZIL, 1500–63

5 On this day [22 April 1500] at the vesper hours we caught sight of land, that is, first of a large mountain ... To this high mountain the captain [Cabral] gave the name of *Monte Pascoal* [Easter Mountain], and to the land, *Terra de Vera Cruz* [Land of the True Cross].

Pedro Vaz de Caminha, from the coast of Brazil, to King Manuel of Portugal, 1 May 1500; W.B. Greenlee (ed.) *The Voyage of Pedro Álvarez Cabral to Brazil and India* (1938) pp.6–7. Whether the discovery of Brazil was accidental has been much debated. The main purpose of the expedition was to reach India via the Cape of Good Hope, so why did Cabral sail so far westward? He must have chosen the course deliberately. This country came to be called Brazil a little later, when the trade in the red dye-wood known as brazilwood began to boom – that is, the country was called after the wood, not vice versa.

6 In appearance they are dark, somewhat reddish, with good faces and good noses, well shaped. They go naked, without any covering; neither do they pay more attention to concealing or exposing their shame than they do to showing their faces, and in this respect they are very innocent. Both [captives] had their lower lips bored and in them were placed pieces of white bone … They put them through the inner part of the lip, and that part which remains between the lip and the teeth is shaped like a rook in chess.

Pedro Vaz de Caminha, 1 May 1500; Greenlee (1938) pp.10–11. The Tupinamba Indians here described occupied the whole coast of Brazil from the mouth of the Amazon River southward to the Rio Grande do Sul, sharing the same language and customs.

1 While we were taking on the wood two carpenters made a large cross from one piece of wood which was cut for this yesterday. Many of them came there to be with the carpenters; and I believe they did so more to see the iron tools with which they were making it than to see the cross, because they have nothing of iron. They cut their wood and boards with wedge-shaped stones fixed into pieces of wood.

Pedro Vaz de Caminha, 1 May 1500; Greenlee (1938) p.26.

2 They have no laws or faith, and live according to nature. They do not recognize the immortality of the soul, they have among them no private property, because everything is common; they have no boundaries of kingdoms and provinces, and no king. They obey nobody, each is a lord unto himself; no justice, no gratitude, which to them is unnecessary.

Amerigo Vespucci to Pierfrancesco de' Medici, 1502; S.E. Morison *The European Discovery of America: The Southern Voyages 1492–1616* (1974) p.285. Known as the Bartolozzi letter, after the man who discovered the original manuscript in 1789, this famous and highly imaginative report was based on Vespucci's brief experience as a subordinate in the Portuguese voyage of 1501–2 led by Gonzalo Coelho. Vespucci did not invent the myth of the noble savage (see 483:3), but he made a lasting contribution by associating it especially with the natives of Brazil. His book, *Mundus Novus* (New World), was a bestseller and earned him fame as the greatest of the discoverers.

3 For although all of them confess human flesh to be wonderfully good and delicate, nonetheless it is more out of vengeance than for the taste (except for what I said specifically concerning the old women, who find it such a delicacy); their chief intention is that by pursuing the dead and gnawing them right down to the bone, they will strike fear and terror into the hearts of the living.

Jean de Léry *History of a Voyage to the Land of Brazil* (1578; 1990 edn) p.127. Léry spent two years (1556–8) with the Tupi tribes of eastern Brazil (near Rio de Janeiro). While cannibalism was generally used to justify European enslavement and

execution, witnesses like Léry did their best to understand and explain it. Indeed Léry, a devout Huguenot, expressly refers to the massacres of his fellow Protestants on St Bartholomew's Day 1572 in France (see 377:2) when, he claims, parts of the victims' bodies were publicly sold and eaten in Lyons.

4 These people are wild in the same way as we say that fruits are wild, when nature has produced them by herself and in her ordinary way; whereas in fact it is those that we have artificially modified and removed from the common order that we ought to call wild. In the former the true, most useful and natural virtues and properties are alive and vigorous; in the latter we have bastardized them and adapted them only to the gratification of our corrupt taste.

Michel de Montaigne *Essays* (1580 edn; 1958 trans.) 'On Cannibals' p.109. Montaigne met these Brazilians in 1562 at Rouen, west of Paris, some two years after the destruction of the French colony in Brazil by the Portuguese. The French philosopher was actually less interested in the 'savages' than in the 'civilized' people for whom he wrote and the evils of *their* civilization.

5 The first awareness that these savages have of what surpasses the earth is of one whom they call Monan, to whom they attribute the same perfection as we do to God. They say he is without end or beginning, being of all time, and that it was he who created the sky, the earth and the birds and animals that are in them. They do not, however, mention the sea, born of Aman Atoupave, which means 'showers of water' in their language. They say the sea was caused by an accident that happened on earth, which was previously united and flat with no mountains whatsoever.

André Thevet *La Cosmographie universelle* (1575); Suzanne Lussagnet (ed.) *Les Français en Amérique pendant la deuxième moitié du XVIe siècle: Le Brésil et les Brésiliens* (1953) p.38. Thevet, a Franciscan friar, was at Guanabara, near Río de Janeiro, in 1555–6. For other creation myths see 1:1 and 16:1.

6 He [Cabeza de Vaca] caused certain passages of the royal charter to be read aloud, in which special mention was made of the treatment of the Indians. He further enjoined the monks, clergy and other ecclesiastics to take the Indians under their particular care and to protect them from ill-treatment and to inform him of anything done contrary to these orders, promising to supply all things necessary for this holy cause and for the celebration of the sacraments in the churches and monasteries.

Pero Hernández *The Commentaries of Alvar Núñez Cabeza de Vaca* (1555); L.L. Dominguez (ed.) *The Conquest of the River Plate 1535–1555* (1891) pp.128–9. Cabeza de Vaca, having survived his eight-year ordeal in the wilds of Texas (see 332:6), returned to Spain but then set off again in 1540 to explore. He delivered this address at Asunción, far in the interior of Paraguay, in 1542.

1 We now think that the gates are open for the conversion of the heathen in this captaincy, if Our Lord God would arrange that they be placed under the yoke. For these people there is no better preaching than by the sword and iron rod. Here more than anywhere it is necessary to adopt the policy of compelling them to come in.

José de Anchieta, 1563; John Hemming Red Gold: *The Conquest of the American Indians* (1978) p.106. The faithful secretary to Manoel da Nóbrega who led the first Jesuit mission to Brazil in 1549 and later helped in the expulsion of French Protestants from Brazil. Brazil had the world's largest Catholic community at the beginning of the 21st century.

CORTÉS AND THE CONQUEST OF MEXICO, 1518–27

2 As soon as Diégo Velásquez was in bed … he [Hernán Cortés] went in the profound silence of the night in the utmost haste to awaken the rest of his friends telling them it was advisable to embark at once. Taking with him a company sufficient to defend his person, he immediately went off to the slaughterhouse and although it troubled the contractor who had to supply the whole town with meat, he took it all away without leaving a single cow, pig or sheep and had it carried to the ships.

Bartolomé de Las Casas *History of the Indies* (c.1560; 1951 edn) Vol.3, pp.224–5. Las Casas (1474–1566) wrote this, his most comprehensive work, late in life. Velásquez, governor of Cuba, had authorized this expedition to the newly discovered coast of Mexico, but Cortés, whom he nominated to lead it, became a law unto himself, in Nov. 1518 engaging ships, men and money as he saw fit.

3 As Doña Marina proved herself such an excellent woman and good interpreter throughout the wars in New Spain, Tlascala and Mexico … Cortés always took her with him, and during that expedition she was married to a gentleman named Juan Jaramillo … Doña Marina … was a person of the greatest importance and was obeyed without question by the Indians throughout New Spain.

Bernal Díaz del Castillo *The Conquest of New Spain* (1560s) Vol.1 (1908 edn) p.133. The writer (1492–c.1581), who served Cortés loyally as a soldier in the conquest of Mexico, wrote his account of it when he was in his seventies. The book was eventually published in 1632. Brought up in Tabasco,

Mexico, Doña Marina converted to Christianity when the Spaniards captured that town. She became Cortés's mistress and bore him a son, Don Martín Cortés, one of Hernán's numerous bastards.

4 We arrived at a broad causeway and continued our march … and when we saw so many cities and villages built in the water and other great towns on dry land and that straight and level causeway going towards Mexico, we were amazed and said that it was like the enchantments they tell of … the great towers and temples and buildings rising from the water, all built of masonry. And some of our soldiers even asked whether the things we saw were not a dream.

Bernal Díaz del Castillo (1560s) Vol.1 (1908 edn) p.133. The city of Mexico was on an island at the heart of a lake some 50 miles long and 20 miles wide. Until after its conquest and destruction the city was known by its Aztec name, Tenochtitlán. The Spaniards entered the city on 8 Nov. 1519.

5 Besides these four chieftains there were four other great *caciques* [chiefs], who supported the canopy over their heads, and many other lords who walked before the great Montezuma, sweeping the ground where he would tread and spreading cloths on it, so that he should not tread on the earth. Not one of these chieftains dared even to think of looking him in the face, but kept their eyes lowered with great reverence, except those four relations, his nephews, who supported him with their arms.

Bernal Díaz del Castillo (1560s) Vol.2 (1910 edn) p.41. Montezuma comes to meet Cortés at the entrance to the city of Tenochtitlán. Montezuma II (r. 1502–20) succeeded on the death of his uncle. Once elected, however, he had attained a semi-divine authority as high priest, head of state and commander of the army.

6 When they sacrifice a wretched Indian they saw open the chest with stone knives and hasten to tear out the palpitating heart and blood and offer it to their idols in whose name the sacrifice is made. Then they cut off the thighs, arms and head and eat the former at feasts and banquets, and the head they hang up on some beams; the body of the man is not eaten but given to their fierce animals.

Bernal Díaz del Castillo (1560s) Vol.2 (1910 edn) pp.66–7.

7 The greatest of these idols and those in which they placed most faith and trust I ordered to be dragged from their places and flung down the stairs, which done I had the temples which they occupy cleansed, for they were full of the blood of human victims who had been sacrificed, and placed in them the image of Our Lady and other saints.

Hernán Cortés to Charles V Five Letters to the Emperor (1519–26; 1962 trans.) pp.90–91. He describes the idols as 'many times greater than the body of a large man' and claimed that the largest of the many temples was enclosed by a wall within which 'one could set a town of 15,000 inhabitants'.

1 Let us go on and speak of the skilled workmen he [Montezuma] employed in every craft that was practised among them. We will begin with lapidaries and workers in gold and silver and all the hollow work, which even the great goldsmiths in Spain were forced to admire, and of these there were a great number in a town named Atzcapotzalco, a league [about 3 miles] from Mexico. Then for working precious stones and chalchihuites, which are like emeralds, there were other great artists. Let us go on to the great craftsmen in feather work, and painters and sculptors who were most refined.

Bernal Díaz del Castillo (1560s) Vol.2 (1910 edn) p.67.

2 He [Montezuma] told them to consider how for many years past they had known for certain, through the traditions of their ancestors which they had noted down in their books of records, that men would come from the direction of the sunrise to rule these lands, and that then the lordship and kingdom of the Mexicans would come to an end. Now he believed from what his gods had told him that we were these men, and the priests had consulted Huichilobos about it and offered up sacrifices, but their gods would no longer answer them.

Bernal Díaz del Castillo (1560s) Vol.2 (1910 edn) pp.124–5. Huichilobos was the Mexican god of war. Later legends of the Aztecs made much of alleged omens warning Montezuma of the advent of white, bearded men mounted on strange beasts (horses were unknown to the Aztecs). The idea that the conquest was predestined, influenced not only the Aztecs but also the Spaniards, who were inclined to perceive the hand of God in these events.

3 With my men he [Montezuma] sent his own, ordering them to visit the rulers of those cities [throughout his empire] and to require of each one of them in my name a certain measure of gold. And so it came about that each one of those lords to whom he sent gave very freely when he was asked, whether jewels, small bars and plates of gold and silver or other valuables.

Hernán Cortés to Charles V (1519–26; 1962 trans.) p.84. Cortés describes the loot in some detail, particularly 'the fifth due to your Majesty' worth 2,400 pesos of gold, apart from

some 100,000 ducats' worth of precious stones and ornaments set aside for his Majesty, 'so marvellous on account of their novelty and strangeness as to be almost without price'. Since his invasion of Mexico was unauthorized and illegal, Cortés was careful to insure his winnings with enormous bribes – 'freely' acquired, of course.

4 At this moment in the fiesta, when the dance was loveliest and when song was linked to song, the Spaniards were seized with an urge to kill the celebrants. They all ran forward, armed as if for battle. They closed the entrances and passageways, all the gates of the patio ... They posted guards so that no one could escape, and then they rushed into the sacred patio to slaughter the celebrants.

Fray Bernardino de Sahagún The Florentine Codex: or the General History of the Things of New Spain (c.1555; 1950–82 trans.); Miguel León Portilla (ed.) The Broken Spears: The Aztec Account of the Conquest of Mexico (1992) pp.74–6. Sahagún (1499–1590), a Franciscan missionary, immersed himself in the life, culture and history of the Aztecs. The three-volume Codex, written in two columns, one in Nahuatl and the other in Spanish, provides an illustrated encyclopedia of Mexican civilization. This action was the immediate cause of the revolt that drove the Spaniards out of the city.

5 At this time New Spain was extremely full of people, and when the smallpox began to attack the Indians it became so great a pestilence among them throughout the land that in most provinces more than half the population died ... They died in heaps, like bedbugs. Many others died of starvation.

Fray Toribio Motolinía History of the Indians of New Spain (c.1541; 1950 edn) p.38. The friar was one of the first group to arrive in Mexico in 1524.

6 Montezuma was placed by a battlement on the roof with many of us soldiers guarding him and he began to speak to them [his people] with very affectionate expressions telling them to desist from the war, and that we would leave Mexico ... Suddenly such a shower of stones and darts was discharged ... that he was hit by three stones, one on the head, another on the arm and another on the leg, and although they begged him to have the wounds dressed and to take food, and spoke kind words to him about it, he would not. Indeed when we least expected it they came to say he was dead. Cortés wept for him, and all of us captains and soldiers.

Bernal Díaz del Castillo (1632) Vol.2 (1910 edn) pp.237–8. Cortés treated Montezuma like a child, mingling affection with pity and contempt.

1 There was no way to cross the remaining five or six canals, which were a good twelve feet wide and full of deep water, except that our Lord provided us with Indian men and women who carried our baggage. As these entered the first canal they drowned, and the heap made a bridge for those on horseback to pass over. In this way we kept pushing the loaded bearers ahead of us, reaching the other side over the bodies of the drowned, until we had crossed the rest of the canals. And in the confusion of drowning Indians some Spaniards also were lost.

Francisco de Aguilar, 1520s; Patricia de Fuentes *The Conquistadors* (1963) p.157. Aguilar, a common soldier repenting his past, entered the Dominican order in 1529, when he was 50 years old. He is describing the long-lamented *noche triste* (sad night) in which Cortés and his men were driven out of Tenochtitlán. Francisco López de Gómara, in another account, states that during the night of 1 July 1520 '450 Spaniards died, 4,000 Indian friends, 46 horses and, I believe, all the prisoners' (*Cortés: The Life of the Conqueror by his Secretary* (1552; 1966 trans.) pp.221–2).

MAGELLAN AND THE CIRCUMNAVIGATION OF THE WORLD, 1519–21

2 Speaking with Magellan, I asked him what route he intended to follow and he replied that he was going by way of Cape Santa Maria, which we now call Río de la Plata [between Uruguay and Argentina], and that from there, following the coast, he expected to run into the strait. Then I asked, 'What if you do not find the strait through which to pass to the other sea?' He replied that if he did not find it he would go by the route the Portuguese followed.

Bartolomé de Las Casas (c.1560; 1951 edn) Vol.3, p.175. Las Casas is recalling an encounter with Ferdinand Magellan in 1518 at Valladolid. Magellan thus contemplated sailing east to the Moluccas if he failed to find a strait into the Pacific. The tiny but very rich Spice Islands (Indonesia) were still independent but much coveted by the Portuguese. Magellan's revolutionary proposal to reach them by sailing west was scornfully rejected by the king of Portugal. Magellan therefore transferred his allegiance to King Charles I of Spain, who handsomely backed the project, hoping to establish a Spanish presence in the Far East.

3 Suddenly one day we noticed a naked man of giant proportions on the harbour shore, dancing, singing and throwing sand on his head … When this giant came into the captain-general's presence he began to be astonished and frightened, raising one finger on high, believing we had come from the sky … When

we showed him his likeness in a steel mirror he was greatly terrified and jumped back, throwing three or four of our men to the ground.

Antonio Pigafetta *Journal* (1525; 1963 trans.) pp.101–2. An Italian gentleman, Pigafetta went along as a supernumerary and produced what is by far the most interesting account of the voyage. The fleet wintered in the bay of San Julián, Argentina, from April to Aug. 1520. This was the first of many such tales about these people, who became known to Europe as Patagonians, possibly because their hide-wrapped feet reminded Magellan of a dog's paw (*pata de cano*).

4 The crew began to murmur about the eternal hatred between the Portuguese and the Spaniards and about Magellan's being Portuguese. He, they suggested, might best win glory in his own country by contriving to wreck this fleet.

Maximilian of Transylvania to Cardinal Lang of Salzburg, 23 Oct. 1522; Lord Stanley (ed. and trans.) *The First Voyage Round the World by Magellan* (1874) pp.193–4. Such talk led to open mutiny on 2 April 1520 at Port San Julián. Magellan put down the mutiny, executed its leaders and so restored discipline, but this episode starkly revealed his unfortunate situation. As a Portuguese he was disliked and mistrusted by his leading officers, who, like many of the crew, were Spanish, but was also regarded as a traitor by Portuguese at home and abroad.

5 The men returned within three days and reported that they had seen the cape and the open sea. The captain-general wept for joy and called that cape Cape Deseado, for we had been desiring it a long time.

Antonio Pigafetta (1525; 1963 trans.) p.117. Having entered the strait at Cape Virgins on 21 Oct. 1520, Magellan and his men reached its western exit, and, Pigafetta continued, 'debouched from that strait, engulfing ourselves in the Pacific Sea'. Núñez de Balboa had already (1513) discovered this ocean (see 332:2) and named it the South Sea (*Mar del Sur*), a name that later voyagers often preferred, knowing its anything but pacific nature.

6 We were three months and twenty days without getting any kind of fresh food. We ate biscuit which was no longer biscuit but its powder; swarming with worms, for they had eaten what was good. It stank strongly of rats' urine. We drank yellow water already putrid for many days … Rats were sold for half a ducat apiece … The gums of both the lower and upper teeth of some of our men swelled, so that they could not eat under any circumstances and therefore died.

Antonio Pigafetta (1525; 1963 trans.) pp.122–3. Thus 19 men died of scurvy, and another 25 or 30 fell sick. The crossing from the strait to Guam, in the South Pacific and their next landfall, took 14 weeks.

1 The captain told them to burn their idols and to believe in Christ, and that if the sick man were baptized he would quickly recover; and if that did not happen they could behead him then and there. Thereupon the king replied that he would do it, for he truly believed in Christ. So we walked in procession from the square to the house of the sick man with as much pomp as possible. There we found him in such a condition that he could neither speak nor move. We baptized him and his two wives and ten girls. Then the captain asked him how he felt. He spoke immediately and said that by the grace of our Lord he felt very well. That was a most manifest miracle.

Antonio Pigafetta (1525; 1963 trans.) p.163. Pigafetta thus depicts the climax of an extraordinary surge of religious mania that appears to have overtaken not only himself and Magellan but the entire population of the Philippine island of Cebu, reached on 7 April 1521.

2 They rushed upon him with iron and bamboo spears and with their cutlasses until they killed our mirror, our light, our comfort and our true guide. When they wounded him he turned back many times to see whether we were all in the boats, which were already pulling off … I hope that the fame of so noble a captain will not be eclipsed in our time. Among the other virtues which he possessed, he was more constant than anyone else in the greatest adversity.

Antonio Pigafetta (1525; 1963 trans.) pp.171–2. Magellan was killed on 27 April 1521 in a quite unnecessary attack on the tiny island of Mactan in the Philippines.

3 It would be performing the best service to your Highness if I commanded their heads to be cut off … I detained them in the Moluccas because it is an unhealthy place, to see if the climate would kill them: I did not venture to order them killed because I did not know your Highness's will.

Portuguese commander of Ternate (in the Moluccas) to the king of Portugal concerning Gómez de Espinosa, one of the survivors among Magellan's officers, and his crew; José Ramos-Coelho (ed.) *Alguns Documentos do Archivo Nacional* (1892) pp.473–4. The crew had reached Tidore half-dead from starvation and disease in Nov. 1522, only to find both islands in Portuguese hands. Espinosa got back to Seville after serving years of hard labour in the Portuguese East and was then imprisoned by the Spanish authorities for seven months. Another officer, Sebastián del Cano, sailed the *Victoria* back to Spain, completing the first circumnavigation on 6 Sept. 1522.

PIZARRO, PERU AND GOLD, 1527–61

4 Those who remained with Don Francisco Pizarro on Gallo island [off the coast of Colombia] had sent him [the governor of Panama] a secret message, begging him to allow no more men to go to their death in this dangerous and profitless mission, in which many men had already died, and that they should themselves be recalled. Pedro de los Ríos therefore sent a lieutenant with orders that all who wished should be free to return to Panama, and no one forced to remain. On hearing this proclaimed [in 1527], Pizarro's men immediately embarked with great joy, as if fleeing from the land of the Moors.

Agustín de Zárate *The Discovery and Conquest of Peru* (c.1555; 1981 trans.) p.31. In fact, 13 men were honoured by the queen of Spain for having opted to stay with their leader. In *Royal Commentaries of the Incas* (1608) Garcilaso de la Vega describes him tracing a line in the sand with his sword, challenging his men either to depart or stay with him and win eternal glory. Garcilaso, not born until 1539, was an incurable romantic, and his version was popularly accepted. The 'land of the Moors' was a reference to the Moorish occupation of southern Spain until 1492.

5 He [Atahualpa] was seated on a low chair … He had a cord tied round his head and a red fillet on his forehead. He did not spit on the floor; if he hawked or spat a woman held out her hand and he spat into it. And any hairs that fell from his head on to his clothes were picked up by the women and eaten. The reason of these customs is known: the spitting was out of majesty; the hairs because he was afraid of being bewitched.

Agustín de Zárate (c.1555; 1981 trans.) pp.91–2. Having defeated his half-brother, the rightful heir to the throne of the enormous empire of Peru, Atahualpa had slaughtered almost all the imperial family and massacred the tribes who had chosen the wrong side. The scarlet fringe or fillet symbolized supreme and divine authority.

6 The governor asked him how much he would give and how soon. Atahualpa said he would give a room full of gold. The room measured 22 feet long by 17 feet wide and [was to be] filled to a white line half way up its height … He would also give the entire hut filled twice over with silver.

Francisco de Xerez, Pizarro's secretary's, report, 1534; C.R. Markham (ed.) *Reports on the Discovery of Peru* (1872) p.65. Atahualpa made this offer initially to save his own life, because he feared the Spaniards would kill him, and Pizarro was delighted to accept it, promising to restore the Inca his liberty. The bargain was kept by one side only.

1 They brought Atahualpa out to execution, and when they carried him into the square he said he wished to become a Christian. The governor was immediately informed and said he must be baptized. He was baptized. The governor then ordered that he should not be burned but tied to a post in the square and strangled. This was done and the body was left there till the next morning, when the friars, the governor and other Spaniards carried him to be most solemnly buried in church, with all possible honours. Such was the end of this man who had been so cruel.
Agustín de Zárate (c.1555; 1981 trans.) p.124. This passage draws on the narrative by Pedro Pizarro, who, at the age of 15, joined his cousin Francisco to fight in Peru and in 1572 published an account of the events he had witnessed.

2 Both sides shouted 'Long live the King' and for battle-cry 'Almagro' or 'Pizarro'. When the two lines were near they charged against each other, and the [watching] Indians gave a great shout.
Pedro de Cieza de León *The War of Las Salinas* (1550s; 1923 edn) p.200. This, the fourth part of Cieza de León's chronicle about the civil wars in Peru, was unpublished until the 20th century. The ferocious Battle of Las Salinas (the salt pits), 1½ miles outside Cuzco, took place in April 1538 and resulted in the defeat of the Almagrists by the Pizarrists, led by Hernando Pizarro. Diego de Almagro, known as the *Adelantado* (governor), was Pizarro's partner on this brutal and fruitless expedition. Pizarro had him garrotted in prison in 1538.

3 At length, after having received many wounds, without a sign of weakness or abatement of his brave spirit, the Marquis [Francisco Pizarro] fell dead upon the ground. His death occurred at eleven in the morning on 26 June 1541.
Pedro de Cieza de León *The War of Chupas* (1550s; 1918 edn) p.109. Thus was Francisco Pizarro murdered by followers of Diego de Almagro, son of the *Adelantado*, who thereby avenged his father.

4 In this game, just as my father was raising the quoit to throw, they all rushed upon him with knives, daggers and some swords. My father, feeling himself wounded, strove to make some defence, but he was one and unarmed, while they were seven, fully armed. He fell to the ground covered with wounds and they left him for dead ... The Spaniards, seeing that my father had ceased to breathe, went out of the gate in high spirits saying, 'Now that we have killed the Inca we have nothing to fear.'
Pedro de Cieza de León *The War of Quito* (1550s; 1913 edn) p.165. Manco Inca's son here describes the murder of his father (the last Inca ruler) by a group of Almagrists at Viticos, some 80 miles westnorthwest of Cuzco in 1545.

5 Some four years ago, to complete the perdition of this land, there was discovered a mouth of hell, into which a great mass of people enter every year and are sacrificed by the greed of the Spaniards to their 'god'. This is your silver mine called Potosí [Bolivia].
Domingo de Santo, dispatch, 1 July 1550; R. Vargas Ugarte *Historia del Perú Virreinato 1551–1600* (History of the Viceroyalty of Peru) (1949). This Dominican missionary says the Indians were conscripted by force and treated like slaves. But Cieza de León reports that 'these Indians got silver every day ... so that people assembled from all parts with provisions and other necessaries for their support' (*Travels* (1550s; 1864 edn) p.391). Potosí had a population of 160,000 in 1611.

6 Instead of bringing the food he [Francisco de Orellana] went down the river [Napo, leading to the Marañón, later named the Amazon] ... displaying towards the whole expeditionary force the greatest cruelty that ever faithless men have shown ... Because they [those left in the lurch] had eaten in this wild country more than one thousand dogs and more than one hundred horses without any other kind of food whatsoever.
Fray Gaspar de Carvajal *Discovery of the Amazon River* (1894; 1934 trans.) pp.56–7. Gonzalo Pizarro, the younger brother of the conqueror of Peru, led the 1541 expedition in search of the fabled King El Dorado (the Golden Man) who was supposed to powder himself with gold-dust afresh each morning. Pizarro sued Orellana for desertion. Carvajal was the expedition's chronicler.

7 Although we did wish to go back up the river, that was not possible on account of the heavy current, [while] to attempt to go by land was out of the question as we were in great danger of death because of the great hunger we endured; and so ... it was decided that we should choose of two evils the one which to the captain and to all should appear to be the lesser, which was to go forward and follow the river.
Fray Gaspar de Carvajal (1894; 1934 trans.) p.171. Having left Pizarro nine days before, Orellana reckoned he was 600 miles down river when his crew persuaded him, against his will, not to try to return. Fearing rightly that they would be charged with desertion, they all, including Carvajal, signed a document excusing this decision, and in the end their story was officially accepted, Pizarro's case being rejected. Orellana reached the Atlantic eight months after parting company with his commander.

1 We ourselves saw these women, who were there fighting in front of all the Indian men as women captains … so courageously that the Indian men did not dare turn their backs, and anyone who did they killed with clubs right there before us … These women are very white and tall and have hair very long and braided and they are very robust and go about naked [but] with their privy parts covered.

Fray Gaspar de Carvajal (1894; 1934 trans.) p.214. Carvajal dubbed these ladies 'Amazons', thereby earning for himself some derision and for the great river a name that stuck.

NORTH AND WEST FROM THE CARIBBEAN, 1517–62

2 He [Balboa] commanded a halt, and went alone to scale the peak, being the first to reach its top. Kneeling upon the ground, he raised his hands to heaven and saluted the South Sea; according to his account he gave thanks to God and to all the saints for having reserved this glory for him, an ordinary man.

Peter Martyr d'Anghiera (early 16th century; 1912 edn) Vol.1, p.286. Vasco Núñez de Balboa (c.1475–1519), noted for his humane conduct towards the American Indians, became a chief's blood-brother and married his daughter, although he was as obsessed with gold as any of the conquistadors. Several versions of this scene describe Balboa wading into the sea, sword in hand, to annex for Spain the entire ocean and all lands therein.

3   Then felt I like some watcher of the skies
     When a new planet swims into his ken;
     Or like stout Cortés when with eagle eyes
     He star'd at the Pacific – and all his men
     Looked at each other with a wild surmise –
     Silent, upon a peak in Darien.

John Keats 'On First Looking into Chapman's Homer' (1816). Keats drew on his schooldays' reading of William Robertson's *History of America* (1777). He is using poetic licence generously in merging Balboa's first sight of the Pacific with Cortés's first sight of the city of Mexico.

4 It is certain that John Ponce de León, besides the main Design of making new Discoveries, as all the Spaniards then aspired to do, was intent upon finding out the Spring of Bimini and a River in Florida, the Indians of Cuba and Hispaniola affirming that old People bathing themselves in them became young again.

John Stevens *The History of America* (1740) Vol.2, pp.37–8. Juan Ponce de León set out from the Caribbean island of Puerto

Rico in 1513 and sailed northwest in search of the so-called 'fountain of youth', inspired by an old European legend. He discovered a land that he named Florida after its profusion of flowers.

5 The entire land is covered by thick bush and is so stony there is not a single square foot of soil. No gold has been discovered, nor is there anything else of value. The people are the most abandoned and treacherous in all the lands discovered to this time, who never yet killed a Christian except by foul means … Not once have I questioned them on any matter when they have not answered 'yes' so as to get rid of me and send me somewhere else.

Francisco de Montejo, letter to the crown from Campeche, Yucatán, Mexico, 10 Aug. 1534; Robert S. Chamberlain *The Conquest and Colonization of Yucatán 1517–1550* (1948) p.164. Yucatán was first discovered by Spaniards in 1517 in a disastrous expedition that not only lost many Spanish lives but also caused a smallpox epidemic. This reduced the indigenous Maya population to about 250,000, a third of its former level.

6 Their custom is to bury the dead, unless it be those among them who have been physicians. These they burn. While the fire kindles they are all dancing and making high festivity until the bones become powder. After the lapse of a year the funeral honours are celebrated, everyone taking part in them, when that dust is presented in water for the relatives to drink.

Alvar Núñez Cabeza de Vaca *Relation* (1542; 1871 edn) p.76. The Spanish explorer is describing the people of Malhado (Bad Luck) Island, possibly the modern Galveston Island, Texas, where he and some 80 companions were wrecked in 1528. By the following May most of these had died of cold and starvation, and Cabeza de Vaca survived only by getting himself adopted as a medicine-man to one of the mainland tribes, with whom he travelled as a sort of slave until 1533, when he finally escaped and set out westwards for Mexico.

7 Thence it may at once be seen that to bring all these people to be Christians and to the obedience of the Imperial Majesty, they must be won by kindness, which is a way certain, and no other is.

Alvar Núñez Cabeza de Vaca (1542; 1871 edn) p.175. Cabeza de Vaca's hard – indeed often harsh – experience with the Indians, far from turning him against them, won them his respect. He became a champion of their rights and a strong critic of the cruelty that he had observed among their Christian conquerors.

8 On that day [18 Oct. 1540 at Mavilla, Alabama] the Indians killed more than 20 of our men and upwards of 250 were wounded; we received more than 660 arrow shots. During the night we dressed the wounds of our men with the fat of dead Indians. No other medicine remained for our use, all that we possessed having been burned in the affray.

Luís Hernández de Biedma *A Relation of What Took Place during the Expedition of Captain Soto,* presented to King Charles I of Spain, 1544; Appendix to Richard Hakluyt *The Discovery and Conquest of Terra Florida by 'a gentleman of Elvas'* (1611 trans.; 1851 edn). The account states that 2,500 Indians were killed on this occasion and that Hernando de Soto refrained from sending news for fear that 'no man would seek to go thither, when he should have need of people'. Biedma, as factor, represented the king on the expedition, and his report was official.

1 We quitted the village [Quizquiz] and proceeded to encamp upon the bank of the river [the Mississippi, here called the Great River] in order to see how we could pass it. We perceived a number of Indians with a great many canoes, on the opposite side, ready to dispute our passage. We resolved upon making four large pirogues [barges], each capable of containing 60 or 70 men and five or six horses … We crossed the river with much order; it was about a league broad and the depth from 19 to 20 fathoms.

Luís Hernández de Biedma (1540s; 1851 edn) pp.189–90. In the event, the Indians offered no resistance to the crossing in 1541.

2 They spent three days on this bank looking for a passage down to the river, which looked from above as if the water was six feet across, though the Indians said it was half a league wide. Three men attempted the descent but returned after a day's effort, reporting that they had been down about a third of the way and that the river seemed very large.

Pedro de Castañeda *Account of the Expedition to Cibola* (1550s); G.P. Winship (ed. and trans.) *The Journey of Coronado 1540–42* (1904) pp.35–6. In Aug. 1540 the party discovered the Grand Canyon on the Río Colorado. They called the river the Tisón, meaning 'Firebrand'. Unable to reach it, approaching it from the south via Tusayán, they had to turn back southwards, but this was the most memorable achievement of an otherwise frustrating venture.

The Rise and Decline of Spain, 1492–1700

A MESSIANIC EMPIRE

1 God's destiny set up on Spanish soil the empire which the great power of the Goths tore from the empire of Rome, which the barbarian invader from Africa defeated and oppressed, which Ferdinand the Catholic re-conquered, which his grandson re-established, and the two Philips extended over the entirety of this terrestrial globe, passing it on to our King Philip IV.

Gonzalo de Cespedes y Meneses *Historia de Don Felipe IV* (1634); Otis H. Green *Spain and the Western Tradition* Vol.4 (1968) p.8.

2 Events almost identical in every stage of time and the remarkable way that God has elected and directed the Spanish nation show that we are his chosen people in the New Dispensation, just as the Hebrews were in the time of the written Law.

Fray Juan de Salazar *Política Española* (1619); Green Vol.4 (1968) p.5, note 7. The foundations of Spain's greatness were laid by the Catholic monarchs, Ferdinand II of Aragon (r.1479–1516) and Isabella of Castile (r.1474–1504), whose marriage in 1469 brought their two kingdoms together. Their reigns saw domestic order restored, Granada re-conquered and Spanish power in Italy consolidated, as well as the discovery of the Americas, the establishment of the Inquisition and the expulsion of the Jews.

3 Ferdinand of Aragon, the present king of Spain, can almost be called a new prince, for from the weak king that he was, he has become in fame and glory the foremost king in Christendom; and if you consider his deeds you will find all of them great, and some of them extraordinary.

Niccolò Machiavelli *The Prince* (1513; 1949 trans.) Ch.21.

4 We owe everything to this man.

Philip II, king of Spain (r.1556–98), before a portrait of Ferdinand, according to Baltasar Gracián *El político Don Fernando el Católico* (1640); Roger Highfield (ed.) *Spain in the Fifteenth Century 1369–1516* (1972) p.415.

5 That was a golden time indeed, and a time of justice.

Gonzalo Fernández de Oviedo (1478–1557); Highfield (1972) p.399. Like many Spaniards, the chronicler looked back to the time of the Catholic kings, before involvement with the Habsburgs and their European wars, as Spain's true Golden Age.

GOLD, STEEL AND FAITH: THE BASES OF SPANISH POWER

6 This Monarchy's true basis lies in the favour of divine law; its growth in man's good government of arms and letters; and its substance in mines and trade. In these this Monarchy abounds more than any other ever has, stretching as it does from pole to pole, and by sea and land reaching to the confines of the entire universe. But being divided by the sea, without command of the sea it will be endangered.

Paper to the council of state, c.1610; *Colección de documentos inéditos* (1842–95) Vol.106, pp.482–5.

7 In peace time, His Majesty [Philip II] has an annual income from all his possessions of five million in gold ... On the other hand his expenses amount to over six million. He makes up the difference with special taxes which he imposes at will. You might think he would have great trouble finding the money for military operations, since he uses all the revenues from his kingdoms for ordinary needs. But this present king in recent years has found the means to maintain so many armies ... that someone estimated the total cost at more than ten million in gold. This example shows that even when their expenses exceed their incomes, powerful rulers can usually find large sums of money in emergencies. This is especially true of the king of Spain, and not so much because of his mines in Spain and the Indies, which the Spaniards, who are very boastful, are always talking about. More important than those are his many lands and vassals, almost all of them rich. They supply him with many grants of money, not because they are forced to, but because the subjects see that both the state and they as individuals stand to gain.

Michele Suriano, Venetian ambassador to the court of Philip II, 1559; James C. Davis (ed.) *Pursuit of Power. Venetian Ambassadors' Reports on Turkey, France and Spain in the Age of Philip II, 1560–1600* (1970) pp.57–8.

8 The great Secret of the Power of Spain: which Power, well sought into, will be found rather to consist in a Veteran Army ... than in the strength of the Dominions and Provinces.

Francis Bacon, 1624; John X. Evans (ed.) *The Works of Sir Roger Williams* (1972) p.141.

1 The chief instrument of empire is language … With this squadron of graduates, who are for the most part religious or secular clergy … they reinforce their empire and monarchy no less than with garrisons and regiments of soldiers.

Fray Juan de Salazar (1619: 1945 edn) pp.151–2.

2 With this aim, the kings of Spain put all their efforts into the unity of the Catholic religion so that their peoples, realms and estates should love each other, not allowing to live amongst them Jew, Moor, or any heretic who might impede or contribute to the undoing of this bond and union.

Fray Juan de Salazar (1619; 1945 edn) p.151.

3 Had there been no Inquisition, there would have been many more heretics, and the country would be in a lamentable state, like others where there is no Inquisition as we have in Spain.

Philip II, 1569; Henry Kamen *Philip of Spain* (1997) p.235. The Inquisition was established in Spain in 1480 to suppress heresy and maintain orthodoxy.

4 Bodily death is so good that one may even say that it benefits the wicked, putting a stop to the sins in which they are involved and preventing them from committing the others they would commit if they lived longer, on account of which sins, if death did not stop them, they would suffer more grievously in perpetual punishment.

Alejo Venegas *Agonía del tránsito de la muerte* (1537); Green Vol.4 (1968) p.152, note 44.

5 From now on none of our subjects and countrymen may leave these kingdoms in order to go to study, teach, learn, attend or reside at any university, institute or college outside these kingdoms. Those at present attending and residing in such universities, institutes and colleges are to leave them within four months of the date of this edict, and not remain any longer in them.

This law of 1559 aimed to prevent the influx of contagious heterodoxies from abroad; Ricardo García Cárcel *La Leyenda Negra* (1998) p.51. The Black Legend was an hispano-phobic view that portrayed Spain in the worst light.

6 [The Inquisition in Spain] is more feared than the flames … day by day the Inquisition is becoming so hateful to the Spaniards, particularly in Aragon and Catalonia, that it is impossible that it will not give rise to great disturbances and seditions.

French ambassador Raymond Fourquevaux, 12 Nov. 1571; C. Douais (ed.) *Dépêches de M. de Fourquevaux ambassadeur du Roi Charles IX en Espagne 1565–1572* (1896–1904) Vol.2, p.394, no.296.

7 To hear a familiar [a local, lay executive of the Inquisition] utter the words 'In the name of the Holy Inquisition' is to be instantly abandoned by father, mother, relatives, and friends. For no one would dare to take up his defence, or still less to intercede for a man about whom these words had been spoken, for fear of himself becoming suspect in matters of the faith.

Juan Alvarez de Colmenar, author of *An Annal of Spain and Portugal*, 1741; Jean Defourneaux *Daily Life in Spain in the Golden Age* (1970) p.127.

8 You are right: our country is a land of envy and pride. You might add: of barbarism … If anyone possesses a certain amount of learning, he is found to be full of heresies, errors, traces of Judaism. Thus they have imposed silence on men of letters; those who pursued learning have come to feel, as you say, a great terror.

Don Rodrigo Manrique, son of the Inquisitor General, to Luis Vives, 1533; Green Vol.4 (1968) p.157.

SOCIETY AND GOVERNMENT

9 There is no nation which boasts more of being noble, nor which puts more value on being honoured than the Spaniards.

Bernabé Moreno de Vargas *Discursos de la nobleza de España* (1622).

10 I would never have believed that universally every Spaniard would have affected this ridiculous concern for his honour. It comes, sir, from that pride which is so natural to him and which makes them believe that all the other nations are as nothing in comparison with theirs. Indeed, you cannot see the meanest tramp who does not wear a sword. They imagine that to be Spanish is to be noble, so long as one does not descend from a moor, a jew, or a heretic.

Jean Muret, a cleric in the company of the French ambassador, 1666; J. García Mercadal (ed.) *Viajes de extranjeros por España y Portugal* Vol.2 (1959) p.717.

11 There are two kinds of nobility in Spain, a greater, which is *hidalguía*, and a lesser, which is *limpieza*, by which we mean 'Old Christian'. And although to have the former, *hidalguía*, is more honourable, it is more shameful to be without the latter, because in Spain we hold in more esteem a commoner who is pure of blood [*limpio*] than an *hidalgo* who is not.

Anon., early 17th century; Antonio Domínguez Ortiz *La clase social de los conversos en Castilla en la Edad Moderna* (1955) p.229.

1 We declare that the so-called *conversos*, offspring of perverse Jewish ancestors, must be held by law to be infamous and ignominious, unfit and unworthy to hold any public office or benefice within the city of Toledo or its jurisdiction, or to be commissioners for oaths or notaries, or to have any authority over the true Christians of the Holy Catholic Church.

Toledo city statute, 1449; Defourneaux (1970) p.36. From the mid-15th century increasing numbers of local statutes restricted the membership of governing bodies, guilds, military and religious orders, chapters and university colleges to the 'pure of blood'. The Marranos or Conversos were Moors or Jews who accepted baptism to avoid death (see 181:2).

2 The lackey carries in his breast his own deed of honour, which is his certificate of baptism, and he is as good as the master he serves, even though he be a grandee of Spain.

Francisco Santos *El no importa de España* (1667; 1973 edn) p.lxii. One effect of *limpieza* (see 335:11) was to democratize honour.

3 Certain it is, as the Spaniard in all things standeth mainly upon his Reputation ... so he vaunteth not a little of his antiquity, deriving his pedigree from Tubal, the Nephew of Noah. But (especially as they draw it) how often hath the Line of Tubal, been bastarded, degenerated, and quite expelled, by invasions of Phoenicians, oppressions of the Greeks, incursions of the Carthaginians, the conquest and planting of Provinces, and Colonies of the Romans, the general deluge of the Goths, Huns, and Vandals: and lastly, by the long and intolerable Tyranny of the Moors, whose slavish yoke and bondage in 800 years, he could scarcely shake off; his own Histories bear sufficient Testimony and Record. Then it is manifest, that this mixture of Nations, must of necessity make a compounded Nature, such as having affinity with many, have no perfection in any one.

William Lithgow *The Rare Adventures and Painefull Peregrinations* (1632; 1906 edn) p.188. *Limpieza* was in part a reaction to the negative foreign image of Spain's national identity created by the legacy of her multi-cultural past.

4 We should refrain completely from calling power 'absolute'. What the prince is permitted to do by natural, divine and human law, even if it is the derogation of human laws, is his ordinary power ... for the law allows nothing absolute to anyone, however powerful a prince he may be.

Diego de Covarrubias y Leiva, president of the royal council (1572–7), *Textos jurídico-políticos* (1957 edn) p.169.

5 Truly, for the common good private individuals may, and must, suffer, even guiltlessly.

Dr Alvaro de Villegas, justice in the royal council, 23 May 1621; Angel González Palencia (ed.) *La Junta de Reformación* (1932) p.86.

6 '*Todos somos reyes* [We are all kings],' say the Spaniards, but this has not prevented Philip from being the most absolute monarch in the world.

The Swiss writer Thomas Platter *Journal of a Younger Brother* (1599; 1963 edn) p.226.

7 Here it is not the style to claw and compliment with the King, or idolize him by *Sacred Sovereign*, and *Most Excellent Majesty*; but the Spaniard when he petitions to his King, gives him no other character but *Sir*, and so relating his business, at the end doth ask and demand justice of him.

James Howell to Captain Nic. Leat, 5 Jan. 1622; *Epistolae Ho-elianae: The Familiar Letters of James Howell* (1645–55; 1890 edn) p.156. Howell spent 1622–4 in Spain on business.

8 What is surprising in Spain is that, although their government is absolute, their kings do nothing without the councils, they sign nothing without them, and even the most minor questions of public policy they do not resolve alone.

Jacob Sobieski, 1611; García Mercadal Vol.2 (1959) p.332. The father of John III of Poland reports on his study tour of western Europe.

9 The King here took to himself Authority Royal only, and submitted all Jurisdiction Spiritual to the Pope, whom under Penalty of Excommunication he was bound to obey.

Sir Ralph Winwood *Memorials of Affairs of State* (1725 edn) Vol.2, p.69. The English diplomat Winwood (c.1563–1617) was among those urging Sir Walter Ralegh to pillage Spanish settlements in South America (see 382:4).

10 Sire, no town councillor in Spain, no constable, no notary, no lord, no grandee, no squire, nobody who owns the sales tax of a village, nobody who has a *juro* [government bond] on it, nobody who has

any property, nor any man of influence in the place where he lives, pays taxes, and in this context nobody means nobody, without exception.

Gaspar de Guzmán, Count-duke of Olivares, chief minister of Philip IV, 1638; John H. Elliott and José F. de la Peña *Memoriales y cartas del Conde Duque de Olivares* (1978) Vol.2, p.171.

1 The government has come to be, and continues to be, more like a Republic than a Monarchy.

Lorenzo Cenami, ambassador of the Italian city of Lucca, 1674; A. Pellegrini *Relazioni inedite di ambasciatori lucchesi alla corte di Madrid* (1903) p.90.

2 Though this be a great monarchy, yet it has at present much aristocracy in it, where every Grandee is a sort of prince.

Alexander Stanhope, English ambassador in Madrid, 1691; Lord Mahon *Spain under Charles the Second* (1844) p.18.

3 All these provinces are different in law, constitution, customs and usages, and while some think this is a reason for discord, others regard such variety as a force for stability.

Juan Alfonso de Lancina *Comentarios Políticos* (1687); S. Magariños *Alabanza de España* (In Praise of Spain) (1950) p.115.

4 We, who are worth as much as you, make you our King and Lord provided that you guard for us our *fueros* [constitutions] and liberties, and if not, not.

The legendary oath of Sobrarbe, supposedly taken by the Aragonese Cortes at the accession of the king; Ralph A. Giesey *If Not, Not* (1968) p.6.

5 Nowhere is of value to Your Majesty except only the kingdom of Castile, for Aragon, Valencia, Catalonia and Navarre contribute nothing for these purposes, nor can Your Majesty employ your states in Italy for these needs ... yet it cannot be sound policy to use up and exhaust the substance of these kingdoms of Castile, which are the root and heart of this monarchy.

Conde de Salazar, president of finance, 23 Oct. 1620; Archivo General de Simancas, Guerra Antigua 1305.

6 The greater a prince's power, the less the freedom of the dominant nation, and the greater its burdens to sustain his conquests.

Diego de Saavedra Fajardo *Locuras de Europa* (1640).

A COLOSSUS STUFFED WITH CLOUTS?

7 A great colossus outwards, but inwardly stuffed with clouts; a man subject to melancholy and meeting in these years with disgraces, deadly and mortal passions follow. One that keeps all his own reckonings to cover his bare estate from others; and this is the scarecrow of the world that her Majesty hath to contend with.

William Herlle, English agent in Rome, to Lord Burghley, 17 July 1585; Calendar of State Papers (C.S.P.) Domestic Vol.2 (1581–90) p.252.

8 I may therefore conclude this matter with comparing the Spaniards unto a drone, or an empty vessel, which when smitten upon yieldeth a great sound and that afar off; but come near and look into them, there is nothing in them: or rather like the ass which wrapped himself in a lion's skin and marched far off to strike terror into the hearts of the other beasts, but when the fox drew near he perceived his long ears and made him a jest unto all the beasts of the forest.

Richard Hakluyt *The Principal Navigations, Voyages and Discoveries of the English Nation* (1589, rev. 1598–1600; 1927 edn); W.S. Maltby *The Black Legend in England* (1971) p.64.

9 The French in a slighting way compare his Monarchy to a beggar's cloak made up of patches. They are patches indeed, but such as he hath not the like; the East Indies is a patch embroider'd with pearls, rubies and diamonds; Peru is a patch embroider'd with massy gold, Mexico with silver; Naples and Milan are patches of cloth of tissue; and if these Patches were in one piece what would become of his Cloak embroidered with Flower-de-luces?

James Howell, from Madrid, to Viscount Colchester, 18 Feb. 1623; Howell (1645–55; 1890 edn) p.204.

10 They are extremely proud, and the silliest of them pretend to a great portion of wisdom, which they would seem to express in a kind of reserved state and silent gravity, when perhaps their wit will scarce serve them to speak sense. But if once their mouths be got to open, they esteem their breath too precious to be spent upon any other subject but their own glorious actions. They are the most unjust neglectors of other Nations and impudent, vain flatterers of themselves. Superstitious beyond any other people: which indeed commonly attends those which affect to be accounted religious, rather than to be so. For how can a hearty devotion stand with cruelty, lechery, proud Idolatry, and those other Gothish, Moorish, Jewish, Heathenish, conditions of which they still saviour.

John Speed 'The Description of Spain' in *A Prospect of the Most Famous Parts of the World* (1631). This was published just after the death in 1629 of the great English cartographer and historian.

1 From the high opinion these people have of themselves and the disparagement with which they look down on others derives, I will not say the hate, but the justifiable disdain which they, with good reason, bring down upon themselves from foreigners … I would say as well that the more hated they are, the more they hate everyone else.

Barthelemy Joly, counsellor accompanying the French visitor of the Cistercian Order in Spain, 1604; García Mercadal Vol.2 (1959) p.124.

2 Among themselves the Spaniards are at daggers drawn, each extolling his own province over that of his companions, and out of an exaggerated desire for singularity, creating far greater differences between their nationalities than we have in France. The Aragonese, the Valencians, the Catalans, the Basques, the Galicians, the Portuguese bait each other, throwing in each others' faces the vices and failings of their provinces; but should a Castilian appear among them, then see how at one they are in launching themselves upon him all together, as bulldogs upon a wolf.

Barthelemy Joly, 1604; Garcia Mercadal Vol.2 (1959) p.125.

3 These Italians, although they are not Indians, have to be treated as such, so that they will understand that we are in charge of them and not they in charge of us.

Comment on letter of Marquis of Ayamonte, governor-general of Milan, to Philip II, 2 Feb. 1570; H.G. Koenigsberger *The Government of Sicily under Philip II of Spain* (1951) p.48.

SPAIN AND ITS ENEMIES

4 The principal end and desire held by His Majesty [King Ferdinand] was general peace among Christians and war against the infidel … and he desired both those holy purposes like the salvation of his soul.

Secretary Pedro de Quintana, 1516; Highfield (1972) p.413.

5 God has entrusted to Your Majesty principally the remedying not only of resistance to the Turk, capital enemy of the Christian, but also of all the errors and evils that for our sins have occurred in our time in the greater part of Europe.

Loyal response to the address from the throne in the Cortes, 1566; *Actas de las Cortes de Castilla* (1877–2001) Vol.2, p.32.

6 You can assure His Holiness that, rather than suffer the least damage to religion and the service of God, I would lose all my states and a hundred lives, if I had them; for I neither desire, nor intend, to be a ruler of heretics.

Philip II to Don Luis de Requesens, his ambassador in Rome, 12 Aug. 1566; H.G. Koenigsberger, 'The Statecraft of Philip II' in *European Studies Review* Vol.1, no.1, Jan. 1971, p.11. The king was referring to the Netherlands, where revolt had broken out (see 381:1). The religious issue and the situation in the Netherlands seriously damaged the historic community of interests between Spain and England, as expressed in the famous apothegm of the Duke of Alba: 'War with the whole world, but peace with England' (C.S.P. Venetian Vol.8 (1581–91) p.296).

7 Those Low Countries were one of the two stones of Scandal, that this Monarchy gives to all other Nations.

Sir Charles Cornwallis, English ambassador in Madrid, to Robert Cecil, Earl of Salisbury, 16 Nov. 1607; BL Addit. MS 39853 f.121. The other stone was the Inquisition.

8 Sir, if the Pope must fall, then the Pillars or Main Supporters upon which his power standeth must first be removed: And if so, then Spain must first be aimed at, who is his Right Hand; for he, and only he, viz. the Spaniard, maintains that bloody Inquisition, that crimson Gulf in which thousands of poor souls are (on all occasions) secretly swallowed up and sent to their Beds of Darkness.

Anon. *Dialogue* (c.1655); Maltby (1971) p.121.

9 It can be presumed to be true, as it is, that England has been and remains the source of all the ills of the Crown of Spain, from the very beginning of her great pre-eminence.

Probably by the Scottish Colonel William Semple 'Discourse of War and State' (c.1625); Museo Naval, Navarrete, Vol.9, f.11.

10 We are in an excellent land, but among the worst people in the world. These English are very unfriendly to the Spanish nation.

Ruy Gómez, in London, 1554; Kamen (1997) p.58. Under Elizabeth I, English incursions into the Indies, threats to the

Treasure fleets, attacks against the Spanish mainland and intervention in the Netherlands finally brought Philip II to retaliate.

I He taketh not Arms against us by any pretence of title to the Crown of this Realm, nor led altogether with an ambitious desire to command our Country, but with hatred towards our whole Nation and Religion.

Captain Antony Winkfield, 1589; Hakluyt (1589; 1927 edn) Vol.4, p.350. The English tended to see the Armada as principally a Catholic enterprise.

2 The Church of Rome, that pretended apostolic see, is become but a donative Cell of the king of Spain. The Vicar of Christ is become the king of Spain's Chaplain.

Francis Bacon 'Discourse in the Praise of Queen Elizabeth', probably Nov. 1592; Gustav Ungerer *A Spaniard in Elizabethan England* (1975) Vol.1, p.48, no.26. However, a successful invasion of England by Philip II was not unequivocally to be desired by the pope or by any other ruler.

3 As for the enterprise against England … neither the Pope nor any other prince can consent to such an aggrandizement of the Spanish. For, although the king of Spain is very restrained and declares that he has no desire for what belongs to others, still the opportunity and the natural thirst for dominion, common to all, may quite soon produce such complications that the remedy will be beyond the power of any to apply, should he some day desire to make himself sole Monarch of Christendom.

Vincenzo Gradenigo, Venetian ambassador in Madrid, 22 Feb. 1586; C.S.P. Venetian Vol.8 (1581–91) p.141.

4 Some made but little account of the Spanish force by sea; but I do warrant you, all the world never saw such a force as theirs was.

Lord Howard of Effingham to Sir Francis Walsingham, 8 Aug. 1588; Navy Records Society Vol.2, p.59.

5 [The loss of the Armada was an event] worthy to be wept over for ever … because it lost us respect and the good reputation among warlike people which we used to have. The feeling it caused in all of Spain was extraordinary … Almost the entire country went into mourning. People talked about nothing else.

Fray Jerónimo de Sepúlveda, chronicler of San Lorenzo de El Escorial, 1605; Colin Martin and Geoffrey Parker *The Spanish Armada* (1988) p.260. The disaster of 1588 generated an intense debate within Spain regarding the state of the nation and the responsibilities of empire.

6 His Majesty should, if possible, withdraw the armies he has in Flanders and France, and that in itself will be an appropriate and condign punishment for the rebels who do not choose to follow the Holy Faith, for since they choose to be damned, let them be damned.

Francisco de Monzón, proctor for Madrid in the Cortes, 19 May 1593; *Actas de las Cortes de Castilla* (1877–2001) Vol.12, p.473.

THE SUNSET OF THE GOLDEN AGE, 1598–1700

7 The Church is more under siege than ever from heretics and enemies, and your kingdoms not merely insecure but defenceless, invested and invaded; the waters of the Mediterranean and the Atlantic virtually commanded by your enemies; and the Spanish nation, which always regarded itself as invincible, now cowed and frightened, feeling put upon and distressed. Your Majesty has a Crown in which justice lies prostrate and lost, your royal patrimony consumed, reputation and credit finished. The result is that Your Majesty finds everyone, of all sorts, the great, the middling and the lowest, disconsolate and discontented.

Discurso addressed to Philip III, on his accession in Sept. 1598; Museo Naval, Navarrete Vol.8, f.260–76 at f.260v.

8 The whole Kingdom, but especially Castile is exceedingly overburthen with charges and impositions … Thus is this miserable country daily drawn into increase of penury and wretchedness, under which they pitifully groan but are desperate of all means to lighten their shoulders.

Sir Charles Cornwallis 'Discourse' (1607); BL Addit. MS 39853, f.153v., 102.

9 We also note that today with a population only half of what it used to be, there are twice as many monks, clerics and students, for they can find no other way of earning the bare necessities of life.

Petition of the merchant guild of Toledo, 1618; Defourneaux (1970) p.91.

10 Formerly our commerce and industry were the best in the world, since not only did we make the goods of which Spain had need, but we also produced merchandise for the whole of Europe and the Indies. Today it is these foreigners who bring their

merchandise, especially their cloths, to Spain, and in exchange take away a full measure of hard cash.
Petition of the merchant guild of Toledo, 1618; Defourneaux (1970) p.91.

1 The best kind of war is to let them ruin themselves with their bad government … with good government [this king] would be master of the world.
Simon Contarini, Venetian ambassador, 1605; Green Vol.4 (1968) p.11.

2 The Court was in confusion. The king did not rule, neither was he ruled … the benevolence of Philip III and the insatiability of his ministers had reduced the body of this Monarchy to a cadaver.
Virgilio Malvezzi *Historia de los primeros años del reinado de Felipe IV* (1968 edn). Philip IV's chief minister, the Count-duke of Olivares, came to power in 1621 determined to reverse the failings of the previous reign and to remedy the political divisions and economic inadequacies of the monarchy.

3 Your Majesty should have as the most important objective of your Monarchy to make yourself King of Spain. By that I mean, sire, that you should not be content with being king of Portugal, of Aragon, of Valencia, count of Barcelona, but that you should work and contrive by secret and careful planning to reduce these kingdoms of which Spain is composed to the laws and practices of Castile, so that there should be no differences … damaging to government or demeaning to royal authority … and if Your Majesty succeeds, you will be the most powerful prince in the world.
Gaspar de Guzmán, Count-duke of Olivares 'Gran Memorial' (1624); Elliott and de la Peña (1978) Vol.1, p.96.

4 I confess that as long as I have been serving the king … I have wanted to find some way of securing that the kingdoms of His Majesty should be each for each, one for all and all for one.
Gaspar de Guzmán, Count-duke of Olivares to Don Fernando de Borja, 2 Dec. 1625; Elliott and de la Peña (1978) Vol.1, p.173.

5 Sire, Your Majesty finds yourself in a situation in which no part of any of your dominions is not under attack from your enemies, in league and conspiracy so extensive that one can without any exaggeration say that the whole of the rest of the world is turned against Your Majesty alone, in Asia, Africa and Europe.
Gaspar de Guzmán, Count-duke of Olivares to Philip IV, 26 July 1625; BL Egerton MS 2053, f.227. The costs of war undermined the early expectations of the regime.

6 Not in a hundred reigns before
Has Spain been taxed as much as yours,
And the suffering people in desperation,
Now fear you'll tax them for respiration.
Francisco de Quevedo (1580–1645); R.L. Kagan and G. Parker (eds) *Spain, Europe and the Atlantic World* (1995) p.142 (note). Quevedo, the great Spanish poet, was a brilliant satirist, supporter first, then critic of the regime of Olivares.

7 Your Majesty is not king, you are someone whom the Count [Olivares] wants to preserve so that he can use the office of King.
Court manifesto, June 1629.

8 King Philip, you are great – as is a hole; the greater it is, the less there is in it.
Francisco de Quevedo (1580–1645); Green Vol.4 (1968) p.57.

9 Your Majesty will return victorious, because God is the enemy of the great and the friend of the poor, and in Spain now there are neither great, nor small, nor rich.
Pasquinade, circulating in Madrid, mid-1642; *Memorial Histórico Español* Vol.16 (1862) pp.377–8. The lampoon ironically predicted the success of Philip IV's visit to the front in Aragon to lend his personal inspiration to the war against the French and the Catalans.

10 Olivares has left this Monarchy totally exhausted, the rules of justice, war, politics and economics subverted, the navy and the Indies fleets destroyed, the armies in Catalonia and Aragon such that they cannot muster 1,200 horse and 2,000 infantry.
Ambassador Grana to Emperor Ferdinand III, 30 Jan. 1643; Haus-Hof-und-Staats Archiv Vienna, Spanien Korrespondenz, bundle 29, f.88v. Olivares fell from power in Jan. 1643.

11 It is true that we are approaching our end, but in other hands we would have perished faster.
Don Antonio Hurtado de Mendoza, 1629; J.H. Elliott *The Count-Duke of Olivares* (1986) p.419. Hurtado de Mendoza was a poet, royal secretary and part of Olivares's propaganda machine.

12 This country is in a most miserable condition, no head to govern, and every man in office does what he pleases, without fear of being called to account.
Alexander Stanhope, 1694; Mahon (1844) p.68.

13 You live in such dishonour that you neither reign nor endeavour to reign … You are a contemptible phantom.
Street placard about Charles II, 1699; Green Vol.4 (1968) p.12.

1 An easy Man ... but of mean capacity, and not at all active; which makes the Spaniards often cry out, when shall we have a King of our own complexion; they speak very slightingly of him, as of an Innocent, but yet are very loyal, laying all the miscarriages in the Government on the Ministers, who are changed often enough.

Mme d'Aulnoy on Charles II, 1691, *Letters of the Lady's Travels into Spain* (1706) p.286. The French countess recapitulated what James Howell had written (5 Jan. 1623) about Philip IV's brother, Don Carlos, who was so different from the king, 'for he is black-haired and of a Spanish hue' and 'he is the better belov'd of his People for his complexion; for one shall hear the Spaniard sigh and lament, saying, "O when shall we have a King again of our own Colour!"' (Howell (1645–55; 1890 edn) p.155).

2 It is beyond understanding how this monarchy survives, and it is certain that in its present condition it would not be able to continue or to have lasted had the rules laid down at the beginning by its founders not established a basis strong enough to make possible this miracle.

Giovanni Cornaro, Venetian ambassador, 1683; N. Barozzi and G. Berchet *Relazioni degli Stati Europei dagli Ambasciatori Veneti* (1860) Serie I – Spagna, Vol.2, p.489.

3 If one looks closely at the government of this monarchy, one will find in it an excessive disorder, but given the state it is in, it is scarcely possible to bring about change without exposing it to dangers more to be feared than the evil itself. A total revolution would be necessary before perfect order could be established in this state.

Comte de Rébénac, the French envoy, 1689; Charles Weiss *L'Espagne depuis le règne de Philippe II jusqu à l'avènement des Bourbons* (1844) Vol.2, p.55.

DECLINE: INTERPRETATIONS AND JUDGEMENTS

4 Spain is, in many places, not to say most, very thin of people, and almost desolate. The causes are. 1. A bad religion. 2. The tyrannical inquisition. 3. The multitude of whores. 4. The barrenness of the soil. 5. The wretched laziness of the people, very like the Welsh and Irish, walking slowly, and always cumber'd with a great cloak and long sword. 6. The expulsion of the Jews and Moors, the first of which were planted here by the Emperor Adrian, and the latter by the Caliphs after the conquest of Spain. 7. Wars and plantations.

Francis Willughby 'Relation of a Voyage Made through a Great Part of Spain' (1664); John Ray *Travels through the Low Countries* (1738 edn) Vol.1, p.423.

5 If the departure of so many Spaniards to so many countries to preach the Catholic faith is contributing to the depopulation of Spain, then happy she and happy the ruler of such workers. If France, Germany and Italy are more populous because their inhabitants do not engage in such ministries ... let them envy our depopulation, since we are in this imitating the work of the Apostles.

Fray Benito de Peñalosa *Libro de las Cinco Excelencias del Español* (1629); M. Herrero García *Ideas de los españoles del siglo XVII* (1966) p.45.

6 What has most diverted us from the proper activity so necessary for this country is having accorded so much honour and esteem to the avoidance of labour, and valued so little those occupied in agriculture, trade, commerce or any kind of manufacturing, contrary to all good statecraft, such that it would seem to be nothing other than a desire to reduce these kingdoms to a country of enchanted beings living outside the order of nature.

Martín González de Cellorigo *Memorial de la política necesaria y útil restauración a la república de España* (1600; 1991 edn) p.79.

7 Of their fantastical and ridiculous pride, and that too in the extremest poverty, all the world rings. If there be any employment that you would set them about which they think themselves too good for, they presently say, 'Send for a Frenchman'. Indeed, the French do almost all the work in Spain. All the best shops are kept by Frenchmen, the best workmen in every kind are French, and I believe near one fourth or one fifth part of the people in Spain are of that nation. I have heard some travellers say that, should the King of France recall all his subjects out of Spain, the Spaniards would hazard to be all starved to death.

Francis Willughby (1664; 1738 edn) Vol.1, p.426.

8 What has most harmed these kingdoms is that the very riches they have received have impoverished them ... and that has been because wealth has been riding upon the wind in the form of papers and contracts, mortgages and bills of exchange, money and silver and gold, instead of in goods that fructify and by their value attract riches from abroad, thus sustaining our people at home. We see, then, that the reason why there is no money, gold or silver in

Spain is because there is too much, and Spain is poor because she is rich.
Martín González de Cellorigo (1600; 1991 edn) p.89.

1 Poor, we conquered the riches of others; rich, those riches conquer us.
Francisco de Quevedo (1580–1645); J.J. Linz 'Intellectual Roles in 16th- and 17th-century Spain' in *Daedalus* Summer 1972, p.96.

2 When the mines begin to be exhausted, or close down, you will see the Monarchy come to an end and Spain return to her ancient state. In truth, arms and letters never flourished there except when she had silver, which is what sustained the armies of the Emperor and the wars in Flanders and other monstrous expenditures.
Tomé Pinheiro da Veiga *Fastiginia* (1605; 1973 edn) p.137.

3 Spain is no more than the channel by which the Gold of the Indies passes to discharge itself in the vast Ocean of other countries.
Antoine Brunel, 1655; Henry Kamen *Crisis and Change in Early Modern Spain* (1993) p.43, note 82. See 328:3.

4 The ridiculous Latin, ignorant and ungrammatical, which is used in all their colleges, and the little skill the people reveal in all the mechanical arts they practise, are evidence of the limited talent they have in theology, in jurisprudence, in administration, in languages, in medicine, in surgery, in astrology, mathematics, architecture, sculpture, painting, in short in any of the sciences, in creativity, or in the practice of any of the arts and manual crafts.
Barthelemy Joly, 1604; García Mercadal Vol.2 (1959) p.121.

5 In the city [of Valencia] is an university. I heard a professor read logic. The scholars are sufficiently insolent and very disputatious ... None of them understood anything of the new philosophy, or had so much as heard of it; none of the new books to be found in any of their booksellers shops; in a word, the university of Valence is just where our universities were 100 years ago.
Francis Willughby (1664; 1738 edn) Vol.1, p.406.

6 Castile, initially a country of soldiers, became a country of students, jurists, clerics, theologians, writers, artists, as happens in any society when the increase of national wealth enables it to guarantee enough of its members a long period of study and leisure.

The historian Pierre Vilar, 1965; Janine Fayard *Les membres du Conseil de Castille a l'époque moderne* (1979) p.218.

7 Monarchies maintain themselves with the customs on which they were built. They have always been acquired by captains always corrupted by scholars ... armies, not universities, gain them and defend them.
Francisco de Quevedo (1540–1645); Linz (1972) p.96.

8 He told me that ... that work was a perfect paradox, being the best and worst romance that ever was wrote. For, says he, though it must infallibly please every man that has any taste of wit, yet has it had such a fatal effect upon the spirits of my countrymen, that every man of wit must ever resent it; for, continued he, before the appearance in the world of that labour of Cervantes, it was next to an impossibility for a man to walk the streets with any delight, or without danger. There were seen so many cavalieros prancing and curvetting before the windows of their mistresses, that a stranger would have imagined the whole nation to have been nothing less than a race of knight errants. But after the world became acquainted with that notable history, the man that was seen in that once celebrated drapery, was pointed at as a Don Quixote, and found himself the jest of high and low. And I verily believe, added he, that to this, and this only, we owe that dampness and poverty of spirit, which has run through all our councils for a century past, so little agreeable to those nobler actions of our famous ancestors.
Captain George Carleton, prisoner-of-war in Spain in 1710, *Military Memoirs (1672–1713)* (1929 edn) p.207. He records a conversation with Don Felix Pacheco, a gentleman of San Clemente de la Mancha, the homeland of Cervantes' great literary creation, *Don Quixote*.

9 Many talented pens have been worn out describing the root of our ills. Some say the cause is the union with the Habsburgs and with the Netherlands, that graveyard of Spaniards and ruin of their treasure; others claim it is the conquest of America, which has taken our sons and wearied our bodies in extracting its riches; others identify it with the expulsion of the Moriscos, who supported our agriculture, that producer of soldiers and population ... But the principal reason for our lament is the innate hostility with which all foreigners have always regarded Spain.
Respuesta de un amigo (A Friend's Reply), 1714; Kamen (1993) p.40.

The Tudors, 1485–1603

HENRY VII, 1485–1509

1 His body was slender but well built and strong; his height above the average. His appearance was remarkably attractive and his face was cheerful, especially when speaking; his eyes were small and blue, his teeth few, poor and blackish; his hair was thin and white; his complexion sallow … He had a most pertinacious memory. Withal he was not devoid of scholarship. In government he was shrewd and prudent, so that no one dared to get the better of him through deceit or guile … But all these virtues were obscured latterly only by avarice, from which … he suffered.

Polydore Vergil *Anglicae historiae libri XXVI* (26 Books of English History) (1534; 1950 trans.) pp.145–7. Vergil, a native of Urbino, with an international reputation as an author, came to England in 1502 and in 1505 was commissioned by Henry VII to write its history (see 311:6).

2 There were taken prisoners, amongst others, the counterfeit Plantagenet, now Lambert Simnel again … The king would not take his life, both out of magnanimity (taking him but as an image of wax that others had tempered and moulded), and likewise out of wisdom; thinking that if he suffered death he would be forgotten too soon; but being kept alive he would be a continual spectacle, and a kind of remedy against the like enchantments of people in time to come.

Francis Bacon *History of Henry VII* (1622); *Works* Vol.5 (1826 edn) p.35. Lambert Simnel, the 12-year-old son of an Oxford organ-maker, was put forward by the Yorkists in 1486 as the Earl of Warwick, nephew of Edward IV, and therefore the rightful heir to the throne. Although Bacon, in his pioneering historical biography, was writing more than a century after Henry's death, he had access to oral memories and to documents that have since disappeared.

3 Upon the Saturday following … was drawn from the Tower [of London] unto Tyburn Perkin or Peter Warbeck … at which place of execution was ordained a small scaffold, whereupon the said Perkin, standing, showed to the people there in great multitude being present that he was a stranger born, according unto his former confession, and took it upon his death that he was never the person that he was named for – that is to say, the second son of

King Edward IV … After which confession he took his death meekly, and was there upon the gallows hanged.

Anon. 'Vitellius Chronicle' (c.1503); C.L. Kingsford *Chronicles of London* (1905) p.227. Perkin Warbeck (c.1474–99), the son of a Tournai customs officer, was put forward by the dissident Yorkists in 1491 as Richard, Duke of York, one of the two children of Edward IV, the 'princes in the Tower' (see 314:2 and 314:3). He became a serious threat to Henry VII but was captured in 1497.

4 At present, all the beauty of this island is confined to London … Although this city has no buildings in the Italian style, but of timber or brick like the French, the Londoners live comfortably, and it appears to me that there are not fewer inhabitants than at Florence or Rome … In one single street, named the Strand … there are fifty-two goldsmiths' shops, so rich and full of silver vessels, great and small, that in all the shops in Milan, Rome, Venice and Florence put together I do not think there would be found so many of the magnificence that are to be seen in London.

Anon. Venetian noble *A Relation … of the Island of England* (c.1500; 1847 trans.) pp.41–3. At this time London was far and away the biggest town in Britain, with a population of about 60,000. During the 16th century it increased rapidly in size and by 1600 contained some 225,000 inhabitants.

5 Christopher Columbus, fearing lest, if the King of Castile … should not condescend unto his enterprise, he should be enforced to offer the same again to some other prince … sent into England a certain brother of his … who … began to deal with King Henry the seventh … unto whom he presented a map of the world … After [Henry] had seen the map, and that which my father Christopher Columbus offered unto him, he accepted the offer with joyful countenance and sent to call him into England. But because God had reserved the said offer for Castile, Columbus was gone.

Ferdinand Columbus *The Life of the Admiral Christopher Columbus by his son Ferdinand* (1571); Richard Hakluyt *The Principal Navigations, Voyages and Discoveries of the English Nation* (1589, rev. 1598–1600; 1903–5 edn) Vol.4, pp.135–8. Bartolomeo Columbus arrived in England in 1489 with the aim of securing Henry's financial support for his brother's projected westward voyage to 'Asia' (see 324:1). Henry is reported to have set up a committee to examine the proposal, but its conclusions were presumably negative, since Bartholomeo left England empty-handed.

1 The Venetian, our countryman, who went with a ship from Bristol in quest of new islands, is returned, and says that 700 leagues [2100 miles] hence he discovered land ... The king has promised that in the spring our countryman shall have ten ships, armed to his order ... The king has also given him money wherewith to amuse himself till then, and he is now at Bristol ... His name is [John] Cabot and he is styled 'the great admiral' ... The discoverer of these places planted on his new-found land a large cross, with one flag of England and another of St Mark, by reason of his being a Venetian.

Lorenzo Pasqualigo to his brothers, 23 Aug. 1497; Calendar of State Papers (C.S.P.) Venetian Vol.1 1202–1509 (1864) p.262. John Cabot was a merchant from either Genoa or Venice who settled in Bristol towards the end of the 15th century. He shared Columbus's ambition to reach Asia by sailing west. In 1497 he made landfall, probably in Newfoundland.

2 This year [1502] were brought unto the king three men taken in the new-found islands by Sebastian Cabato [Cabot] ... These men were clothed in beasts' skins, and ate raw flesh, but spake such a language as no man could understand them. Of which three men, two of them were seen in the king's court at Westminster two years after[wards], clothed like Englishmen, and could not be discerned from Englishmen.

Raphael Holinshed Chronicles of England, Scotland and Ireland (1577 and 1587; 1808 edn) Vol.3, p.528. Holinshed provided much of the material for Shakespeare's history plays.

3 Howbeit I am a sinful creature, in sin conceived and in sin have lived, knowing perfectly that of my merits I cannot attain to the life everlasting, but only by the merits of thy blessed passion and of thy infinite mercy and grace; nevertheless, my most merciful redeemer, maker and saviour ... We give and bequeath to the altar within ... our said tomb our great piece of the holy cross ... and also the precious relic of one of the legs of Saint George ... the which piece of the holy cross and leg of Saint George we will [i.e., command] be set upon the said altar for the garnishing of the same upon all principal and solemn feasts.

Henry VII, will, 31 March 1509; Thomas Astle (ed.) The Will of King Henry VII (1775) pp.2, 33–4. Henry was buried in the chapel at Westminster Abbey that bears his name.

HENRY VIII, 1509-47

4 King Henry was 29 years old and much handsomer than any other sovereign in Christendom – a great deal handsomer than the king of France [Francis I] ... Hearing that King Francis wore a beard, he allowed his own to grow, and as it was reddish he had then got a beard which looked like gold. He was very accomplished and a good musician; composed well; was a capital horseman and a fine jouster; spoke good French, Latin and Spanish; was very religious, heard three masses daily when he hunted and sometimes five on other days.

Sebastian Giustiani, report to the doge and senate, 10 Sept. 1519; C.S.P. Venetian Vol.2 1509–1519 (1867) p.559. The Venetian ambassador to England on his return to Venice.

5 Truth it is, Cardinal Wolsey, sometime archbishop of York, was an honest poor man's son, born in Ipswich within the county of Suffolk. And being but a child, [he] was very apt to learning; by means whereof his parents, or his good friends and masters, conveyed him to the university of Oxford, where he prospered so in learning that, as he told me [in] his own person, he was called the boy-bachelor, forasmuch as he was made bachelor of arts at fifteen years of age, which was a rare thing and seldom seen.

George Cavendish Life of Cardinal Wolsey (1558; 1827 edn) p.66. Cavendish entered Wolsey's service in the 1520s and held the office of gentleman-usher until the cardinal's fall from power in 1529.

6 Mine own good cardinal, I recommend me unto you with all my heart, and thank you for the great pain and labour that you do daily take in my business and matters, desiring you ... when you have well established them, to take some pastime and comfort, to the intent you may the longer endure to serve us ... Surely you have so substantially ordered our matters both of this side the sea and beyond that in mine opinion little or nothing can be added ... Written with the hand of your loving master, Henry R.

Henry VIII to Cardinal Wolsey, 1518; Archaeologia Vol.17 (1814). Henry VIII, who was only 17 years old when he became king, had little interest in the details of government and was only too happy to leave routine administration in Wolsey's capable hands.

7 If I had served God as diligently as I have done the king, He would not have given me over in my grey hairs. Howbeit, this is the just reward that I must

receive for my worldly diligence and [the] pains that
I have had to do the king service, only to satisfy his
vain pleasure, not regarding my godly duty.
George Cavendish (1558; 1827 edn) pp.387–8. Although a
cardinal and archbishop, Wolsey's position and wealth
depended on royal favour, and when this was withdrawn, he
had nothing to fall back on.

1   Farewell? A long farewell to all my greatness!
     … O how wretched
     Is that poor man that hangs on princes'
        favours!
     There is, betwixt that smile we would aspire to,
     That sweet aspect of princes, and their ruin,
     More pangs and fears than wars or women
        have;
     And when he falls, he falls like Lucifer,
     Never to hope again.
William Shakespeare Henry VIII (1613) Act 3, Sc.2.

2 By turning over in my thoughts the contents of
your last letters, I have put myself into a great agony,
not knowing how to understand them – whether to
my disadvantage, as I understood some others, or
not. I beseech you now, with the greatest earnestness, to let me know your whole intention as to
the love between us two … I beg you to give an entire
answer to this my rude [i.e., unpolished] letter, that
I may know on what and how far I can depend.
Henry VIII to Anne Boleyn, 1527; The Harleian Miscellany Vol.3
(1809) pp.54–5. Anne, who had Protestant leanings, was
actively involved in the plotting that brought about Wolsey's
overthrow.

3 His majesty has so diligently studied this matter
[the validity of his marriage to Catherine of Aragon]
that I believe in this case he knows more than a great
theologian and jurist. He told me plainly that he
wanted nothing else than a declaration whether the
marriage is valid or not – he himself always
presupposing its invalidity; and I believe that an
angel descending from heaven would be unable to
persuade him otherwise. We then discussed the
proposal to persuade the queen to agree to enter
some approved religious house. And this solution
was extremely pleasing to him.
Cardinal Lorenzo Campeggio to J.B. Sanga, Oct. 1528; Letters
and Papers of the Reign of Henry VIII Vol.4, Pt 2 (1872) p.2101.
Sanga was the pope's special envoy in England, and Campeggio
was the cardinal whom the pope had sent as his legate to
preside over the court, sitting in London, that would give a
decision on Henry's 'great matter' – the annulment of his
marriage to Catherine of Aragon. If Catherine agreed to enter

a convent, she would, in effect, be withdrawing from the
world, thereby making it much easier for the pope to annul
Henry's marriage.

4   Alas, sir!
     In what have I offended you? What cause
     Hath my behaviour given to your displeasure,
     That thus you should proceed to put me off,
     And take your good grace from me? Heaven
        witness,
     I have been to you a true and humble wife.
     At all times to your will conformable.
William Shakespeare (1613) Act 2, Sc.4. Catherine of Aragon's
speech before the legatine court in June 1529 is based on
her actual words.

5 By divers sundry old authentic histories and
chronicles it is manifestly declared and expressed
that this realm of England is an empire, and so hath
been accepted in the world, governed by one
supreme head and king having the dignity and royal
estate of the imperial crown of the same, unto whom
a body politic, compact of all sorts and degrees of
people divided in terms and by names of spiritualty
and temporalty, be bounden and owe to bear, next
to God, a natural and humble obedience.
Act of Appeals, 1533; Statutes of the Realm Vol.3 (1817) p.427.
This act, by claiming an imperial authority for the king,
affirmed that Henry VIII was subject only to God and not to
any human institution. This was one step in a strategy,
probably worked out by Thomas Cromwell, whereby Henry
used parliamentary statute to free himself from papal jurisdiction. The Act of Appeals was designed to ensure that the
final decision on the king's marital problems would be taken
in England, not Rome.

6 Albeit the king's majesty justly and rightfully is
and ought to be the supreme head of the Church of
England, and so is recognized by the clergy of this
realm … yet nevertheless, for corroboration and
confirmation thereof … be it enacted by authority of
this present Parliament that the king our sovereign
lord, his heirs and successors, kings of this realm,
shall be taken, accepted and reputed the only
supreme head on earth of the Church of England.
Act of Supremacy, 1534; Statutes of the Realm Vol.3 (1817)
p.492. The act confirmed Henry's claim that his sovereignty
over his realm extended to the church as well as the state.

7 I, rejoicing, told Sir Thomas More how happy he
was whom the king had so familiarly entertained …
'I thank our Lord, son,' quoth he, 'I find his grace
my very good lord indeed, and I do believe he doth

as singularly favour me as any subject within this realm. Howbeit, son Roper, I may tell thee I have no cause to be proud thereof, for if my head would win him a castle in France (for then there was wars between us) it should not fail to go.'

William Roper *The Life of Sir Thomas More* (c.1536; 1879 edn) pp.14–15. Roper became very close to his father-in-law and, after More's execution, wrote an account of his life. More was a distinguished scholar and lawyer, whom Henry appointed lord chancellor in 1529. He was also a devout Catholic, whose conscience would not permit him to take the oath prescribed by the Succession Act of 1534, confirming that Henry's marriage with Catherine of Aragon was invalid and that Anne Boleyn was rightful queen.

1 Your sheep that were wont to be so meek and tame, and so small eaters, now ... be become so great devourers, and so wild, that they eat up and swallow down the very men themselves. They consume, destroy and devour whole fields, houses and cities. For look in what parts of the realm doth grow the finest, and therefore dearest, wool; there noblemen and gentlemen (yea, and certain abbots, holy men no doubt) ... leave no ground for tillage. They enclose all into pastures; they throw down houses; they pluck down towns and leave nothing standing but only the church, to be made a sheep-house ... The husbandmen [i.e., labourers] be thrust out of their own ... [and] must needs depart away ... men, women, husbands, wives, fatherless children ... All their household stuff, which is very little worth, though it might well abide the sale, yet being suddenly thrust out they be constrained to sell it for a thing of naught. And when they have wandered abroad till that be spent, what can they then else do but steal, and then justly ... be hanged ... or else go about a-begging?

Sir Thomas More *Utopia* (1516; 1879 edn) pp.32–3. In this, his most famous work, More gave a new word to the English language. *Utopia* is, outwardly, the description of an imaginary society, but More's account of it throws much light on the social and economic problems of his own day.

2 So was he brought by Mr Lieutenant out of the Tower and from thence led towards the place of execution, where, going up the scaffold, which was so weak that it was ready to fall, he said to Mr Lieutenant ... 'See me safe up; and for my coming down let me shift for myself.' Then desired he all the people thereabouts to pray for him and to bear witness with him that he should then suffer death in and for the faith of the holy Catholic Church; which

done, he kneeled down, and after his prayers said, he turned to the executioner and with a cheerful countenance spake unto him: 'Pluck up thy spirits, man, and be not afraid to do thine office. My neck is very short.'

William Roper (c.1536; 1879 edn) p.55. Henry had assured More that his reservations about the king's marital problems would not harm him. In the event, however, Henry determined to crush all opposition, and More was executed on 6 July 1535. He was canonized 400 years later.

3 I never have read, heard nor known that princes' counsellors and prelates should be appointed by rude and ignorant common people; nor that they were persons meet [i.e., suitable] or of ability to discern and choose meet and sufficient counsellors for a prince. How presumptuous then are ye, the rude commons of one shire – and that one of the most brute and beastly of the whole realm – and of least experience, to find fault with your prince for the electing [i.e., choosing] of his counsellors and prelates, and to take upon you, contrary to God's law and man's law, to rule your prince, whom ye are bound by all laws to obey and serve with both your lives, lands and goods, and for no worldly cause to withstand: the contrary whereof you, like traitors and rebels, have attempted, and not like true subjects, as ye name yourselves.

Henry VIII's *Answer to the Petitions of the Traitors and Rebels in Lincolnshire*, Oct. 1536; M.H. and R. Dodds *The Pilgrimage of Grace* (1915) Vol.1, p.136. A conservative rebellion against the religious changes imposed by Henry VIII and Cromwell broke out in Lincolnshire in Oct. 1536. Henry's stinging response to the rebels' demands reflects his anger at their challenge to his authority and his conviction that his actions were fully justified.

4 Ye shall not enter into this our Pilgrimage of Grace for the commonwealth, but only for the love that ye do bear unto Almighty God His faith, and to the Holy Church militant and the maintenance thereof; to the preservation of the king's person and his issue; to the purifying of the nobility; and to expulse all villein blood and evil counsellors against the commonwealth from his grace and his privy council ... [And] ye shall not enter into our said Pilgrimage for no particular profit to yourself, nor to do any displeasure to any private person ... nor slay nor murder for no envy. But in your hearts put away all fear and dread, and take afore you the cross of Christ, and in your hearts his faith, the restitution of the Church [and] the suppression of these heretics and their opinions.

The Oath of the Pilgrims Oct. 1536; Dodds (1915) Vol.1, p.182. Although the Lincolnshire rising was short lived, a major rebellion, known as the Pilgrimage of Grace, broke in Yorkshire, where it was organized by a charismatic lawyer called Robert Aske, who drew up this oath.

1 Ye shall provide … one book of the whole bible of the largest volume in English, and the same set up in some convenient place within the said church that ye have cure of, where … your parishioners may most commodiously resort to the same and read it … Ye shall discourage no man … from the reading or hearing of the said bible, but shall expressly provoke, stir and exhort every person to read the same, as that which is the very lively word of God, that every Christian man is bound to embrace, believe and follow, if he look to be saved; admonishing them, nevertheless, to avoid all contention [and] altercation therein, but to use an honest sobriety in the inquisition of the true sense of the same, and [to] refer the explication of obscure places to men of higher judgement in scripture.

Thomas Cromwell, Injunctions to the Clergy, Sept. 1538; Gilbert Burnet *The History of the Reformation of the Church of England* (1679) Vol.4 (1865 edn) p.342. Cromwell, the son of a Putney cloth-worker, had been Wolsey's right-hand man and took his place as the king's chief minister. Cromwell commissioned Miles Coverdale to produce an authorized version of the Scriptures in English. This, the Great Bible, was published in 1539 with a preface by Thomas Cranmer.

2 Upon the defacing of the late monastery of Boxley [Kent] and plucking down of the images of the same, I found in the image of the rood, called 'The Rood of Grace' – the which heretofore hath been had in great veneration of people – certain engines and old wire, with old rotten sticks in the back of the same, that did cause the eyes of the same to move and stir in the head thereof, like unto a lively thing; and also the nether lip in like wise to move, as though it should speak … [I] did convey the said image unto Maidstone … and in the chief of the market time did show it openly unto all the people there being present, to see the false, crafty and subtle handling thereof, to the dishonour of God and illusion of the said people.

Geoffrey Chamber to Thomas Cromwell, 1538?; Sir Henry Ellis (ed.) *Original Letters Illustrative of English History* 3rd series, Vol.3 (1846) pp.168–9. A rood was a figure of Christ on the cross. It was often placed above an ornate rood screen, which divided the nave of a church from the choir. The Boxley Rood was one of the most famous icons of the pre-Reformation Church in England, and pilgrims flocked to see the wooden figure apparently come to life. The reformers were delighted when this particular example of monkish chicanery was exposed.

3 Whereas certain … religious houses have lately made free and voluntary surrenders into his grace's hands, his grace's highness hath commanded me … to advertise you that unless there had been overtures made by the said houses that have resigned, his grace would never have received the same, and that his majesty intendeth not in any wise to trouble you, or to devise for the suppression of any religious house that standeth, except they shall either desire of themselves, with one whole consent, to … forsake the same, or else misuse themselves, contrary to their allegiance – in which case they shall deserve the loss of much more than their houses and possessions: that is, the loss also of their lives.

Thomas Cromwell, draft letter to the heads of religious houses, March 1538; R.B. Merriman (ed.) *Life and Letters of Thomas Cromwell* (1902) Vol.2, p.132. After the defeat of the Pilgrimage of Grace, Cromwell set about dissolving the remaining monasteries. This was done by so-called 'voluntary' surrenders, but the iron hand was clearly visible within the velvet glove. The abbot of Woburn was hanged outside his own monastery, supposedly for denying the royal supremacy over the church, and the heads of three other large monasteries were also executed.

4 The king's grace's pleasure is that, with convenient speed, ye repairing to the monasteries of St Osyth and Colchester shall, for certain reformation and other considerations which his grace intendeth as well there as in other places, dissolve and take the same to his use. And be your discretions, considering the age, qualities, conditions and towardness [i.e., cooperativeness] of the persons there, shall assign unto them their annual pensions.

Thomas Cromwell to his agents, Dr Thomas Legh and William Cavendish, 6 Nov. 1538; Merriman (1902) Vol.2, p.159. Cromwell's agents were at work in 1538, as they had been in 1535–6, carrying out visitations of the remaining monasteries, but this time their task was to arrange 'voluntary' surrenders. Heads of houses who were cooperative were well treated. Some thirty or so eventually became bishops, and all were rewarded with generous pensions. The monks also were given pensions, though these were barely more than adequate.

5 Where divers and sundry abbots, priors, abbesses, prioresses and other ecclesiastical governors and governesses of divers monasteries, abbacies, priories, nunneries … and other religious and ecclesiastical houses … within this our sovereign lord the king's realm of England and Wales, of their own free and voluntary minds, good wills and assents, without constraint … or compulsion of any manner of person … [have granted their houses and all their possessions] to our said sovereign lord, his heirs and successors … Be it therefore enacted … that the king our sovereign lord shall have, hold, possess and enjoy to him, his heirs and successors forever, all and singular such late monasteries, abbacies [etc.].

Act dissolving the monasteries, 1539; *Statutes of the Realm* Vol.3 (1817) p.733. The purpose of this legislation was to give statutory confirmation to the surrenders that had already taken place. It marked the formal end of centuries of English monasticism.

1   Level, level with the ground
     The towers do lie,
     Which with their golden glittering tops
     Pierced once to the sky …
     Sin is where Our Lady sat,
     Heaven turned is to hell
     Satan sits where Our Lord did sway.
     Walsingham, O farewell.

Eamon Duffy 'The Stripping of the Altars' (1992) pp.377–8. A lament for the dissolved abbey of Walsingham in Norfolk.

2 Whereas you send unto me, willing me to confess a truth, and so to obtain your favour … let not your grace ever imagine that your poor wife will ever be brought to acknowledge a fault where not so much as a thought ever proceeded. And to speak a truth, never prince had wife more loyal in all duty and in all true affection than you have ever found in Ann Bullen – with which name and place I could willingly have contented myself, if God and your grace's pleasure had so been pleased.

Anne Boleyn to Henry VIII 'from my doleful prison in the Tower, this sixth of May, 1536'; *Scrinia Sacra: Mysteries of State and Government in Letters of Illustrious Persons* (1691) p.1. Anne was brought before a special court made up of peers and presided over by her uncle, the Duke of Norfolk, acting as lord high steward. It gave a unanimous verdict against her, and she was found guilty of incest and adultery.

3 What love and charity is amongst you when the one calleth the other 'heretic' and 'anabaptist', and he calleth him again 'papist', 'hypocrite' and 'pharisee'? Be these tokens of charity amongst you? Are these the signs of fraternal love between you? …

I am very sorry to know and hear how unreverently that most precious jewel, the word of God, is disputed, rhymed, sung and jangled in every alehouse and tavern, contrary to the true meaning and doctrine of the same. And yet I am even as much sorry that the readers of the same follow it, in doing, so faintly and coldly. For of this I am sure, that charity was never so faint amongst you, and virtuous and godly living was never less used, nor God himself, amongst Christians, was never less reverenced.

Henry VIII, last speech to Parliament, 24 Dec. 1545; John Foxe *Acts and Monuments* (1563; 1838 edn) Vol.5, p.535.

EDWARD VI, 1547–53

4 After having considered, my dear and well-beloved uncle, how much they displease God who waste all their time on the follies and vanities of this world – spending it in trifling sports and diversions, from whence comes no profit or benefit to themselves or mankind – I have determined to employ myself about the doing something which will be, as I hope, profitable to myself and acceptable unto you. Having then considered that we see many papists not only curse us but call and name us heretics, because we have forsaken their antichrist and its traditions and followed the light which God hath been pleased to afford us, we are inclined to write something to defend us against their contumelies, and lay them, as it is just, upon their own backs. For they call us heretics, but alas, they are so themselves whilst they forsake the pure voice of the gospel and follow their own imaginations.

Edward VI to Duke of Somerset, 31 Aug. 1549 (trans. from the French); *Writings of Edward VI* (1831) p.25. Edward was not yet ten years old when he came to the throne in Jan. 1547, and his uncle, Edward Seymour, whom he created Duke of Somerset, carried on the government as lord protector. Edward's mother, Jane Seymour, had died shortly after his birth, and he had a lonely upbringing. He took life seriously, was deeply interested in religion, and, unlike his father, was a convinced Protestant. Edward completed his self-appointed task in this instance by writing *A Small Treatise against the Primacy of the Pope*.

5 Where of long time there hath been had in this realm of England and Wales divers forms of common prayer … His highness … hath appointed the archbishop of Canterbury and certain of the most learned and discreet bishops and other learned men of this realm to … draw [up] and make one convenient and meet [i.e., suitable] order, rite and fashion of common and open prayer and administration of the sacraments ... The which ... is of them concluded, set forth and delivered to his highness, to his great comfort and quietness of mind, in a book entitled *The Book of the Common Prayer and Administration of the Sacraments and other Rites and Ceremonies of the Church ... of England.*

First Act of Uniformity, 1549; *Statutes of the Realm* Vol.4 (1819) p.37. The Book of Common Prayer, which was authorized by this act, was largely the work of Thomas Cranmer, and it demonstrates his mastery of English prose as well as his deep theological learning. It was relatively moderate, since both Cranmer and Protector Somerset hoped to make it acceptable to as wide a range of opinion as possible.

1 My father was a yeoman and had no lands of his own. Only he had a farm of £3 or £4 by year at the uttermost, and hereupon he tilled so much as kept half a dozen men. He had walk for a hundred sheep, and my mother milked thirty kine [i.e., cows] ...
He kept me to school, or else I had not been able to have preached before the king's majesty now.
He married my sisters with £5 ... apiece, so that he brought them up in godliness and fear of God.
He kept hospitality for his poor neighbours, and some alms he gave to the poor.

Bishop Hugh Latimer, sermon, 1549; *The Sermons of ... Hugh Latimer* (1824) Vol.1, p.93. Latimer, a committed Protestant and one of the most famous preachers of his day, was acutely aware of the changes taking place in English society, mainly as a result of rapid inflation.

2 Item ... In September [1547] began the king's visitation at [St] Paul's, and all images pulled down; and the 9th day of the same month the said visitation was at St Bride's, and after that in divers other parish churches; and so all images pulled down through[out] all England at that time, and all churches new whitelimed, with the [ten] commandments written on the walls ... Item, the 16th day of the same month [Nov.], at night, was pulled down the rood in St Paul's, with Mary and John, with all the images in that church ... Also at that same time was pulled down through all the king's dominions in every church all roods with all images, and every preacher preached in their sermons against all images ... And at this time was much preaching against the mass, and the sacrament of the altar pulled down in divers places through the realm.

Anon. *Chronicle of the Grey Friars of London* (mid-16th century; 1852 edn) pp.54–5. This chronicle was written by one of the last of the Franciscan monks in London. The first year of

Edward VI's reign saw their home, the Grey Friars, turned into a parish church. As England became officially Protestant, there was a sustained assault on images, stained-glass windows, roods, rood screens and other symbols of 'idolatry'. Church walls were covered with lime wash, on which the Ten Commandments were prominently displayed. The rood at St Paul's Cathedral, in common with many other churches, was flanked by images, in this case of the Virgin Mary and St John, before its destruction.

3 Where there hath been a very godly order set forth by authority of Parliament for common prayer and the administration of the sacraments, to be used in the mother tongue within the Church of England, agreeable to the word of God and the primitive Church ... be it enacted ... that from and after the feast of All Saints [1 November] next coming, all and every person and persons inhabiting within this realm ... shall diligently and faithfully ... resort to their parish church or chapel accustomed ... upon every Sunday and other days ordained and used to be kept as holy days, and then and there to abide orderly and soberly during the time of the common prayer, preachings or other service of God there to be used and ministered, upon pain of punishment by the censures of the church.

Second Act of Uniformity, 1552; *Statutes of the Realm* Vol.4 (1819?) p.130. In late 1549 Somerset was toppled from power by his rival, Warwick, and subsequently executed. Under Warwick, who now became Duke of Northumberland, the pace of religious change accelerated, and the Prayer Book of 1549 was replaced by a new one, also the work of Cranmer.

MARY I, 1553–8

4 [Queen Mary] is of low stature, with a red and white complexion, and very thin. Her eyes are white and large and her hair reddish. Her face is round, with a nose rather low and wide, and were not her age on the decline she might be called handsome rather than the contrary. She is not of a strong constitution, and of late she suffers from headache and serious affection of the heart, so that she is often obliged to take medicine and also to be blooded. She is of very spare diet and never eats until 1 or 2 p.m., although she rises at daybreak, when, after saying her prayers and hearing mass in private, she transacts business incessantly until after midnight, when she retires to rest.

Giacomo Soranzo, former ambassador to England, report to the doge and senate, 18 Aug. 1554 (trans. from the Italian); C.S.P. Venetian Vol.5 1534–1554 (1873) pp.532–3.

1 The high mass being done, which was celebrated and said by my lord bishop of Winchester … the king of heralds openly, in presence of both their majesties and the whole audience, solemnly proclaimed this their new style and title … Philip and Mary, by the grace of God King and Queen of England, France, Naples, Jerusalem and Ireland, Defenders of the Faith, Princes of Spain and Sicily, Archdukes of Austria, Dukes of Milan, Burgundy and Brabant, Counties of Habsburg, Flanders and Tyrol. This style and title being thus proclaimed, the king and queen departed, hand in hand.

Anon. *The Chronicle of Queen Jane and of Two Years of Queen Mary* (c.1555; 1850 edn) p.142. The marriage of Philip and Mary took place in Winchester Cathedral on 25 July 1554. The Spanish empire over which Philip II ruled included, apart from Spain itself, Sicily, southern Italy and the Netherlands in Europe, as well as Mexico, Peru and other areas of central and South America (see 334:7). He had a hereditary claim to the long-extinct crusader Kingdom of Jerusalem through the Lusignan dynasty. Mary likewise had a hereditary claim to France deriving from Edward III.

2 They brought a faggot, kindled with fire, and laid the same down at Dr Ridley's feet. To whom Master Latimer spake in this manner: 'Be of good comfort, Master Ridley, and play the man. We shall this day light such a candle, by God's grace, in England as I trust shall never be put out.' And so, the fire being given unto them, when Dr Ridley saw the fire flaming up towards him, he cried with a wonderful loud voice, 'In manus tuas, Domine, commendo spiritum meum. Domine recipe spiritum meum [Into thy hands, O Lord, I commend my spirit. Receive my spirit, O Lord]', and after[wards] repeated this latter part often in English, 'Lord, Lord, receive my spirit' – Master Latimer crying as vehemently on the other side, 'O father of heaven, receive my soul', who received the flame as it were embracing of it. After that he had stroked his face with his hands, and, as it were, bathed them a little in the fire, he soon died, as it appeareth with very little pain or none.

The Execution of Ridley and Latimer, 16 Oct. 1555, in John Foxe (1563; 1838 edn) Vol.7, p.550. 'Foxe's Book of Martyrs' became one of the basic texts of the Church of England, almost as widely known and read as the Bible itself. Nicholas Ridley, bishop of London, and Hugh Latimer, former bishop of Worcester, were two of the most prominent figures in the Protestant Church set up by Edward VI, and they refused to accept the Catholicism re-imposed by Mary. They were executed at Oxford.

3 When I am dead and opened you shall find 'Calais' lying in my heart.

Mary I, attrib.; Holinshed (1577 and 1587; 1808 edn) Vol.4, p.137. Calais was the last relic of the empire in France built up by Edward III and Henry V, and the queen, along with most of her subjects, felt bitter at its capture in 1558 by the French.

ELIZABETH I, 1558–1603

4 [Queen Elizabeth] was a lady upon whom nature had bestowed, and well placed, many of her fairest favours. Of stature mean, slender, straight and amiably composed; of such state in her carriage as every motion of her seemed to bear majesty; her hair was inclined to pale yellow, her forehead large and fair, a seeming set for princely grace; her eyes lively and sweet, but short-sighted; her nose somewhat rising in the midst; the whole compass of her countenance somewhat long, but yet of admirable beauty; not so much in that which is termed the flower of youth as in a most delightful composition of majesty and modesty in equal mixture.

Sir John Hayward *Annals of the … Reign of Queen Elizabeth* (1630; 1840 edn) p.7. Hayward, born c.1564, was a historian who got into trouble with the queen for dedicating his first work, a life of Henry IV, to the Earl of Essex, just before the fallen favourite attempted a coup d'état against Elizabeth's government. Hayward was committed to prison as the author of a seditious pamphlet and stayed there until the accession of James I in 1603.

5 When [Elizabeth] smiled, it was pure sunshine, that everyone did choose to bask in, if they could. But anon came a storm from a sudden gathering of clouds, and the thunder fell in wondrous manner on all alike.

Sir John Harington *Nugae Antiquae* (1769; 1804 edn) Vol.1, p.362. Harington (c.1561–1612) was Queen Elizabeth's godson and became a noted wit and writer. He is said to be the inventor of the water-closet. A collection of his letters and miscellaneous writings, under the title *Nugae Antiquae* (literally 'old trivia') was published in 1769.

6 Point forth some of the best given gentlemen of this court, and all they together show not so much good will, spend not so much time, bestow not so many hours daily, orderly and constantly, for the increase of learning and knowledge, as doth the Queen's majesty herself. Yea, I believe that beside her perfect readiness in Latin, Italian, French and Spanish, she readeth here now at Windsor more Greek every day than some prebendary of this

church doth read Latin in a whole week. And that which is most praiseworthy of all, within the walls of her privy chamber she hath obtained that excellency of learning, to understand, speak and write, both wittily with head and fair with hand, as scarce one or two rare wits in both the universities have in many years reached unto.

Roger Ascham *The Scholemaster* (1570; 1863 edn) p.63. Ascham had been Elizabeth's tutor and therefore spoke from his own knowledge.

1 To promote a woman to bear rule, superiority, dominion or empire above any realm, nation or city is repugnant to nature, contumely to God, a thing most contrarious to His revealed will and approved ordinance. And finally it is the subversion of good order, of all equity and justice ... For who can deny but it ... repugneth to nature that the blind shall be appointed to lead and conduct such as shall see? That the weak, the sick and impotent persons shall nourish and keep the whole and strong? And finally that the foolish, mad and frenetic shall govern the discreet and give counsel to such as be sober of mind? And such be all women compared unto man in bearing of authority. For their sight in civil regiment [i.e., rule] is but blindness, their strength weakness, their counsel foolishness, and judgement frenzy, if it be rightly considered.

John Knox *A First Blast of the Trumpet against the Monstrous Regiment of Women* (1558); *Works* (1846–8) Vol.5 (1895 edn) pp.373–4. John Knox, one of the most outspoken of the Scottish Presbyterians, wrote this tract while he was in exile in Geneva (see 360:4). He had in mind a number of female rulers who had displayed their 'unfitness' for government by opposing the Protestant Reformation, particularly Mary I, who died in the year of publication and was succeeded by the Protestant Elizabeth. It is hardly surprising that the new queen developed a strong aversion to Presbyterianism.

2 I give you this charge, that you shall be on my privy council and content yourself to take pains for me and my realm. This judgement I have of you: that you will not be corrupted with any manner of gift, and that you will be faithful to the state, and that, without respect of my private will, you will give me that counsel that you think best. And if you shall know anything necessary to be declared unto me of secrecy, you shall show it to myself only, and assure yourself I will not fail to keep taciturnity therein. And therefore herewith I charge you.

Elizabeth I to William Cecil, 20 Nov. 1558; Harington (1769; 1804 edn) Vol.1, pp.68–9. Elizabeth gave this charge to Cecil when she appointed him her personal secretary and also principal secretary of state. She never had cause to regret her choice, for Cecil served her faithfully until his death in 1598.

3 The principal note of her reign will be, that she ruled much by faction and parties, which she herself both made, upheld and weakened as her own great judgement advised. For I disassent from the common opinion that my lord of Leicester was absolute and alone in her favour and grace ... For proof whereof ... I will relate both a story and a known truth, and it was thus: Bowyer, the gentleman of the black rod, being charged by her express command to look precisely to all admissions into the privy chamber, one day stayed a very gay captain (and a follower of my lord of Leicester) from entrance, for he was neither well known nor a sworn servant to the queen ... Leicester, coming to the contestation, said ... that he [i.e., Bowyer] was a knave, and should not continue long in his office; and so, turning about to go to the queen, Bowyer ... stepped before him and fell at her majesty's feet, relates the story and humbly ... [enquires] whether my Lord of Leicester was king or her majesty queen? Whereunto she replied, with her wonted [i.e., accustomed] oath *God's Death*, 'My lord, I have wished you well, but my favour is not so locked up for you that others shall not participate thereof ... And if you think to rule here, I will take a course to see you forth coming. I will have here but one mistress and no master.'

Fragmenta Regalia p.9. Robert Dudley, Earl of Leicester, was Elizabeth's favourite from her accession onwards and remained so until his death in 1588. His influence acted as a counterweight to that of William Cecil, but although the two men had their disagreements over policy, they also worked together in government. Elizabeth was not averse to playing off one individual or interest group against another in order to preserve her freedom of action, but the secret of her success as a ruler consisted in her personality, her intelligence and her innate capacity for rule. Bowyer's authority as an officer of the queen's household was symbolized by the black rod he carried. Great officers of state, such as the lord treasurer, carried a white staff.

4 They were married with all the solemnities of the popish time, saving that he heard not the mass ... All honour that may be attributed to any man by a wife, he hath it wholly and fully ... All dignities that she can endue him with are already given and granted. No man pleaseth her that contenteth not him. And what may I say more, she hath given over unto him her whole will, to be ruled and guided as himself best liketh ... Upon Saturday ... at 9 hours at night, by four heralds at sound of the trumpet, he was

proclaimed king. This was the night before the marriage. This day, Monday, at 12 of the clock, the lords – all that were in this town – were present at the proclaiming of him again; when no man said so much as 'Amen', saving his father, that cried out aloud 'God save his grace.'

Thomas Randolph to Earl of Leicester, Edinburgh, 31 July 1565; Ellis 1st series, Vol.2 (1825) pp.201–2. Randolph was describing the marriage of Mary, queen of Scots, and Lord Darnley. By marrying Darnley – who, like her, was directly descended from Henry VII's daughter, Margaret – Mary strengthened her claim to be acknowledged as Elizabeth's successor. Although it led to the birth of a child, the future James VI of Scotland and I of England, the marriage was not a happy one, and Mary was probably an accessory to Darnley's murder in Feb. 1567.

1 We do, out of the fullness of our apostolic power, declare the foresaid Elizabeth to be a heretic and favourer of heretics, and her adherents … to have incurred the sentence of excommunication and to be cut off from the unity of the body of Christ. And moreover [we declare] her to be deprived of her pretended title to the aforesaid crown and of all lordship, dignity and privilege whatsoever.

Pope Pius V, *Regnans in Excelsis* (bull of deposition), 1570; G.R. Elton (ed.) *The Tudor Constitution* (1982 edn) p.427. The papacy had been alarmed by the reluctance of English Catholics to stand up for their faith and oppose the policies of Elizabeth and her ministers. It was in order to make their duty plain that the pope issued this bull.

2 Then … one of the executioners holding of her slightly with one of his hands, she endured two strokes of the other executioner with an axe, she making very small noise or none at all, and not stirring any part of her from the place where she lay … Her lips stirred up and down a quarter of an hour after her head was cut off … Then one of the executioners, pulling off her garters, espied her little dog which was crept under her clothes, which could not be gotten forth but by force, yet afterward would not depart from the dead corpse but came and lay between her head and her shoulders.

Execution of Mary, queen of Scots, 8 Feb. 1587; Ellis 2nd series, Vol.3 (1827) pp.113–18. After the papal bull of deposition (see 352:1) Mary became a potential danger to Elizabeth, since she was, in Catholic eyes, the rightful ruler of England.

3 [One of the Spanish defenders] brake the bone of Sir Philip's thigh with a musket shot. The horse he rode upon was rather furiously choleric than bravely proud, and so forced him to forsake the field, but

not his back, as the noblest and fittest bier to carry a martial commander to his grave. In which sad progress, passing along by the rest of the army … and being thirsty with excess of bleeding, he called for drink, which was presently brought him. But as he was putting the bottle to his mouth, he saw a poor soldier carried along, who had eaten his last at the same feast, ghastly casting up his eyes at the bottle. Which Sir Philip perceiving, [he] took it from his head before he drank and delivered it to the poor man with these words: 'Thy necessity is yet greater than mine.'

Sir Fulke Greville *Life of Sir Philip Sidney* (1652; 1907 edn) pp.128–9. Sidney, a much loved and admired figure and a notable poet, went to the Netherlands to support the Dutch struggle for independence from Spain. He was fatally wounded at Zutphen at the age of only 31.

4 [Walter Ralegh] was born at Budleigh in this county [Devonshire], of an ancient family but decayed in estate. He was bred in Oriel College in Oxford, and thence coming to court found some hopes of the queen's favours reflecting upon him. This made him write in a glass window, obvious to the queen's eye, 'Fain would I climb, yet fear I to fall.' Her majesty, either espying or being shown it, did under-write, 'If thy heart fails thee, climb not at all.'

Thomas Fuller *The History of the Worthies of England* (1662; 1811 edn) Vol.1, p.287. Although Fuller wrote his account well after Sir Walter's death, he had access to those who had known him personally. Sir Walter Ralegh was one of the brightest stars at Elizabeth's court, until he offended the queen by having an affair with one of her maids of honour, whom he subsequently married.

5 This country our general [Francis Drake] named Albion, and that for two causes: the one in respect of the white banks and cliffs which lie towards the sea; the other, that it might have some affinity, even in name also, with our own country, which was sometime so called.

Sir Francis Drake *The World Encompassed by Sir Francis Drake* (1628; 1854 edn) p.132. Francis Drake claims 'New Albion' (California) for Queen Elizabeth in July 1579, described in an account of his voyage of circumnavigation compiled by his nephew (also called Sir Francis Drake) from the notes of Francis Fletcher, Drake's chaplain. Drake had already made his name as a seaman by preying on Spanish treasure and shipping in the Caribbean when he set out to circumnavigate the world in 1577.

6 The wind commands me away. Our ship is under sail. God grant we may live so in His fear as the enemy may have cause to say that God doth fight for her majesty as well abroad as at home, and give her long and happy life and ever victory against God's enemies and her majesty's.

Sir Francis Drake to Secretary Walsingham from Plymouth, 2 April 1587; John Barrow *The Life, Voyages and Exploits of Admiral Sir Francis Drake, Knight* (1843) p.221. As evidence mounted that Philip II of Spain (see 339:3) was preparing a great army and fleet to attack England, Drake was sent off on an expedition to destroy Spanish shipping and supplies in the port of Cadiz. The operation – popularly known as 'singeing the king of Spain's beard' – was highly successful and delayed the dispatch of the Armada until 1588.

1 In our last fight with the enemy [the Spanish Armada] … we sunk three of their ships and made some … so leaky as they were not able to live at sea. After that fight, notwithstanding that our powder and shot was well near all spent, we set on a brag [i.e., bold] countenance and gave them chase as though we had wanted [i.e., lacked] nothing, until we had cleared our own coast and some part of Scotland of them. And then, as well to refresh our ships with victuals – whereof most stood in wonderful need – as also in respect of our want of powder and shot, we made for the Firth [of Forth] and sent certain pinnaces to dog the fleet until they should be past the Isles of Scotland … We are persuaded that they either are passed about Ireland, and so do what they can to recover their own course, unless that they are gone for some part of Denmark.

Lord Howard of Effingham, commander of the English fleet, to Secretary Walsingham, 7 Aug. 1588; Barrow (1843) pp.306–7. In 1588 Philip II finally dispatched his Armada. It consisted of some 140 vessels, manned by 7,000 sailors and carrying 17,000 soldiers. Elizabeth had at her disposal 34 warships and 170 or so armed merchantmen.

2 I know I have the body but of a weak and feeble woman; but I have the heart and stomach of a king, and of a King of England too, and think foul scorn that Parma or Spain or any prince of Europe should dare to invade the borders of my realm; to which, rather than any dishonour shall grow by me, I myself will take up arms, I myself will be your general, judge, and rewarder of every one of your virtues in the field.

Elizabeth I, address to the troops gathered at Tilbury to resist a possible Spanish invasion, Aug. 1588; *Somers Tracts* (1748) Vol.I (1809 edn) p.430. Alessandro Farnese, Duke of Parma, was governor of the Spanish Netherlands (and Belgium) and commanded the army that was supposed to cross from there into England.

3   Drake he's in his hammock and a thousand
            mile away
         (Captain, art thou sleeping there below?)
         Slung atween the roundshot in Nombre Dios
            Bay
         And dreaming all the time of Plymouth Hoe …
         'Take my drum to England, hang it by the
            shore,
         Strike it when your powder's running low.
         If the Dons sight Devon, I'll quit the port of
            heaven
         And drum them up the Channel as we
            drummed them long ago.'

Sir Henry Newbolt 'Drake's Drum' (1897). Drake became a legend in his own lifetime, and the news of his death in Jan. 1596 was a profound shock. He had been leading yet another plundering expedition in the West Indies, but this time without success.

4 Whereas I have proposed in all this treatise to confine myself within the bounds of this isle of Britain, it cannot be impertinent, at the very entrance, to say somewhat of Britain, which is the only subject of all that is to be said, and well known to be the most flourishing and excellent, most renowned and famous isle of the whole world. So rich in commodities, so beautiful in situation, so resplendent in all glory, that if the Most Omnipotent had fashioned the world round, like a ring, it might have been most worthily the only gem therein.

William Camden *Remains concerning Britain* (1605; 1870 reprint of the 1674 edn) p.1. Camden was the most distinguished antiquary and historian of Elizabethan and early Stuart England.

5   This precious stone set in a silver sea,
         Which serves it in the office of a wall,
         Or as a moat defensive to a house,
         Against the envy of less happier lands.
         This blessed plot, this earth, this realm, this
            England.

William Shakespeare *Richard II* (c.1595) Act 2, Sc.1. John of Gaunt's speech is the finest and most famous expression of Elizabethan Englishmen's pride in, and love for, their country (see 281:4).

6 Forasmuch as we find by daily experience the great inconvenience that groweth to this city and the government thereof by the said plays, I have emboldened myself to be an humble suitor to your good lordship to be a means for us rather to suppress all such places built for that kind of exercise than to erect any more of the same sort. I am not ignorant, my very good lord, what is alleged by some for defence of these plays – that the people must have some kind of recreation, and that policy requireth to divert idle heads and other ill disposed from other worse practice by this kind of exercise.

Lord Mayor of London to the Lord Treasurer, William Cecil, Lord Burghley, 3 Nov. 1594; Malone Society Collections Vol.1 (1907–11) pp.75–6. While Shakespeare and his fellow playwrights and actors are now regarded as among the finest products of the Elizabethan age, this would not have been the view of the majority of their contemporaries.

1 What shall be the conclusion of this war? ... The end, I assure me, will be very short ... Although there should none of them fall by the sword, nor be slain by the soldier, yet ... they would quickly consume themselves and devour one another. The proof whereof I saw sufficiently ensampled in those late wars in Munster. For notwithstanding that the same was a most rich and plentiful country, full of corn and cattle, that you would have thought that they would have been able to stand long, yet ere one year and a half they were brought to such wretchedness as that any stony heart would have rued the same.

Edmund Spenser A View of the Present State of Ireland 1596; A.B. Grosart (ed.) The Complete Works ... of Edmund Spenser (1882–4) Vol.9, pp.161–2. Direct English rule in Ireland had been confined to an area known as the Pale, which stretched north from Dublin for some 50 miles and extended 20 miles inland. Outside this enclave the land was occupied by Gaelic-speaking clans under their traditional chieftains. In the 1560s Elizabeth's government took a decision to extend English rule to the whole country, but this provoked a revolt in Munster, southern Ireland, which was not suppressed until 1583. The poet Spenser saw at first hand the terrible consequences of the war for the Irish peasantry.

2 [Queen Elizabeth's] mind was oft time like the gentle air that cometh from the westerly point in a summer's morn; 'twas sweet and refreshing to all around her. Her speech did win all affections, and her subjects did try to show all love to her commands, for she would say her state did require her to command what she knew her people would willingly do from their own love to her ... Surely she did play well her tables to gain obedience thus without constraint: again, she could put forth such alterations when obedience was lacking as left no doubtings whose daughter she was.

Sir John Harington (1769; 1804 edn) Vol.1, pp.355–6.

3 Although God hath raised me high, yet this I esteem the most glory of my crown, that I have reigned with your loves ... To be a king and wear a crown is a thing more glorious to them that see it than it is pleasant to them that bear it ... And for my part, wer't not for conscience' sake – to discharge the duty which God hath laid upon me, and to maintain His glory and your safety – in my own disposition I should willingly resign the place I hold to another, and glad to be free from the glory with the labour. For it is not my desire to live nor reign longer than my life and reign shall be your good. And though you have had, and may have, many mightier and wiser princes sitting in this seat, yet you never had, nor shall have, any that will love you better.

Elizabeth I, speech to Parliament, 30 Nov. 1601; T.E. Hartley (ed.) Proceedings in the Parliaments of Elizabeth I Vol.3 (1995) pp.295–7. Elizabeth was a natural orator and consciously used her gift to win the hearts of her people. This speech shows that even in old age she still knew how to charm them.

Reformation and Counter-Reformation, 1500–1700

ERASMUS AND LUTHER, 1503–46

1 I shall try to cause certain malicious critics, who think it the height of piety to be ignorant of sound learning, to realize that, when in my youth I embraced the finer literature of the ancients and acquired, not without much midnight labour, a reasonable knowledge of the Greek as well as the Latin language, I did not aim at vainglory or childish self-gratification, but had long ago determined to adorn the Lord's temple, badly desecrated as it has been by the ignorance and barbarism of some, with treasures from other realms, as far as in me lay; treasures that could, moreover, inspire even men of superior intellect to love the Scriptures.

Desiderius Erasmus *Enchiridion Militis Christiani* (The Handbook of the Christian Knight) (1503); *Collected Works of Erasmus* Vol.66 (1988) p.127. Erasmus, one of the greatest scholars of his age, fused the Renaissance (275:4) with the Reformation by using his classical knowledge to produce new and more accurate editions of the Bible and other basic Christian texts.

2 I strongly disagree with the people who do not want the Bible, after it has been translated into everyday language, to be read by the uneducated. Did Christ teach such complex doctrines that only a handful of theologians can understand them? Is Christianity strong in proportion to how ignorant men are of it? Royal secrets may well be best concealed, but Christ wants his mysteries told to as many as possible. I want the lowliest woman to read the gospels and Paul's letters ... I would like to hear a farmer sing scripture as he ploughs, a weaver to keep time to his moving shuttle by humming the Bible, the traveller to make his journey better by such stories.

Desiderius Erasmus *Novum Instrumentum* (1516); W.G. Naphy (ed.) *Documents on the Continental Reformation* (1996) p.5.

3 As a monk I led an irreproachable life. Nevertheless, I felt that I was a sinner before God. My conscience was restless, and I could not depend on God being propitiated by my satisfactions. Not only did I not love, but I actually hated the righteous God who punishes sinners ... Then finally God had mercy on me, and I began to understand that the righteousness of God is that gift of God by which a righteous man lives – namely faith – and that ... the merciful God justifies us by faith, as it is written: 'The righteous shall live by faith.' Now I felt as though I had been reborn altogether and had entered Paradise.

Martin Luther; H.J. Hillerbrand (ed.) *The Reformation in its Own Words* (1964) p.24. Luther, born in Saxony (Germany) in 1483, became an Augustinian friar in 1505, but despite observing all the rigours of the monastic life he found no peace of mind until the revelation he describes here.

4 It is incredible what this ignorant and impudent friar [Tetzel] gave out. He said that if a Christian had slept with his mother, and placed the sum of money in the pope's indulgence chest, the pope had power in heaven and earth to forgive the sin, and if he forgave it, God must do so also ... Item, so soon as the coin rang in the chest, the soul for whom the money was paid would go straightway to heaven. The indulgence was so highly prized that when the commissary entered a city the Bull was borne on a satin or gold-embroidered cushion, and all the priests and monks, the town council, schoolmasters, scholars, men, women, maidens and children went out to meet him with banners and tapers, with songs and procession ... In short, God himself could not have been welcomed and entertained with greater honour.

Anon. contemporary description; B.J. Kidd (ed.) *Documents Illustrative of the Continental Reformation* (1911) pp.19–20. Indulgences were papal grants that were supposed to free souls from purgatory. Pope Leo X had authorized the sale of indulgences to finance the rebuilding of St Peter's basilica at Rome, and Johann Tetzel was one of the agents employed for this purpose in 1517.

5 21. Those preachers of indulgences err who say that a papal pardon frees a man from all penalty and assures his salvation ...

28. It is certain that avarice is fostered by the money clinking in the chest, but to answer the prayers of the church is in the power of God alone ...

31. Those who believe themselves made sure of salvation by papal letters will be eternally damned, along with their teachers ...

50. Christians are to be taught that if the pope knew the exactions of the preachers of indulgences he would rather have St Peter's church in ashes than have it built with the flesh and bones of his sheep.
Martin Luther, theses, 31 Oct. 1517; Preserved Smith *The Life and Letters of Martin Luther* (1911) pp.41–2. Luther, who believed that salvation depended solely on faith in God, was appalled by indulgences, which encouraged people to think they could buy a short cut to heaven. He made his own views plain in 95 theses, which he posted on the church door at Wittenberg, Saxony.

1 I have heard a very evil report of myself, Most Blessed Father ... saying that I have tried to diminish the ... authority of the Supreme Pontiff, and therefore accusing me of being a heretic, an apostate and a traitor, besides branding me with an hundred other calumnious epithets ... Most Blessed Father, I cast myself and all my possessions at your feet. Raise me up or slay me, summon me hither or thither, approve me or reprove me as you please. I shall recognize your words as the words of Christ speaking in you.
Martin Luther to Pope Leo X, from Wittenberg, May 1518; Smith (1911) pp.44–5. Luther had intended his theses to provide the basis for a formal, academic disputation on the subject of indulgences, not to challenge papal authority. They were, however, quickly printed, both in the original Latin and in a German translation, and created a ferment of excitement.

2 My die is cast. I despise the fury and favour of Rome. I will never be reconciled to them nor commune with them. Let them condemn and burn my books. On my side, unless all the fire goes out, I will condemn and publicly burn the whole papal law, that slough of heresies. The humility I have hitherto shown – all in vain – shall have an end, lest it still further puff up the enemies of the Gospel.
Martin Luther to G.B. Spalatin, chaplain to Elector Frederick of Saxony, 10 July 1520; Smith (1911) p.75. In a disputation with John Eck, a distinguished German theologian, at Leipzig in July 1519 Luther asserted that the authority of the church and pope was inferior to that of the Bible as interpreted by informed private judgement. Leo X responded by issuing a bull condemning Luther as a heretic.

3 Now that I have learned ... that my name is known to you on account of my little treatise on indulgences, and as I also learn from your preface to the new edition of your *Handbook of the Christian Knight* that my ideas are not only known to you but approved by you, I am compelled to acknowledge my debt to you as the enricher of my mind, even if I should have to do so in a barbarous style.

Martin Luther to Erasmus, 28 March 1519; Smith (1911) pp.200–1. Luther, who was professor of divinity at the University of Wittenberg, bought a copy of Erasmus's edition of the Greek New Testament in 1516 and used it as a key element in his regular lectures on the Bible.

4 I laid an egg. Luther hatched a bird of a quite different species.
Desiderius Erasmus, attrib. Although he had a great deal of sympathy for Luther's desire to cleanse the church of its impurities, Erasmus was increasingly mistrustful of Luther's abrasive style and his relish for public confrontation.

5 At present all Germany is in commotion. Nine out of every ten cry 'Luther', and the tenth, if he do not care for what Luther says, at least cries 'Death to the court of Rome!' and every one demands and shrieks 'Council! Council!' and will have it in Germany.
Cardinal Aleander, papal legate in Germany, report, 8 Feb. 1521; Kidd (1911) p.82. Aleander was charged with promulgating the papal bull excommunicating Luther, which Leo X issued in Jan. 1521. His reports show the extent to which Luther had become a popular hero, appealing on nationalist as well as on religious grounds.

6 Luther is piling on both liberal studies and myself a massive load of unpopularity. Everyone knew that the church was burdened with tyranny and ceremonies and laws invented by men for their own profit. Many were already hoping for some remedy and even planning something; but other remedies unskilfully applied make matters worse, and the result is that those who try, and fail, to shake off the yoke are dragged back into slavery more bitter than before. Oh, if that man had either left things alone, or made his attempt more cautiously and in moderation! Luther means nothing to me. It is Christ's glory that I have at heart; for I see some people girding themselves for the fray to such a tune that, if they win, there will be nothing left but to write the obituary of Gospel teaching.
Desiderius Erasmus, letter, Feb. 1521; *Collected Works* Vol.8 (1988) p.155. Erasmus had hoped and believed that reform of the church could be brought about gradually, by peaceful means, but he came to regard Luther as a dangerous bull let loose in a china shop and in 1524 openly broke with him.

7 When, therefore, your Majesty and your lordships ask for a straightforward answer, I will give you one ... Unless I am persuaded by the testimony of Scripture or by plain reason – for I believe neither in popes nor in councils alone, since it is known that they have often erred and contradicted themselves –

then I remain committed to the passages I have cited from Scripture and my conscience is captive to the Word of God. I cannot and I will not recant anything, for to act against the dictates of conscience is neither right nor safe. *Hier stehe ich. Ich kann nicht anders. Gott helfe mir* [Here I stand. I can do nothing else. God help me]. Amen.

Martin Luther, speech at the Diet of Worms, 18 April 1521; Kidd (1911) p.85. The diet, or parliament, was summoned by the newly elected Holy Roman Emperor, Charles V, who sent Luther a safe-conduct in the hope that he could be persuaded to recant. The final words (in German) of Luther's speech are probably a later interpolation.

1 My predecessors ... were until death the truest sons of the Catholic Church, defending and extending their belief to the glory of God, the propagation of the faith, the salvation of their souls. They have left behind them the holy Catholic rites that I should live and die therein, and so until now with God's aid I have lived, as becomes a Christian emperor. What my forefathers established ... it is my privilege to uphold. A single monk, led astray by private judgement, has set himself against the faith held by all Christians for a thousand years and more, and impudently concludes that all Christians up till now have erred. I have therefore resolved to stake upon this cause all my dominions, my friends, my body and my blood, my life and soul.

Charles V, declaration at the Diet of Worms, 19 April 1521; Kidd (1911) pp.85–6.

2 If we lose this man, who has written more clearly than any one who has lived for one hundred and forty years, may God grant his spirit to another ... His books are to be held in great honour, and not burned, as the emperor commands, but rather the books of his enemies. O God! If Luther is dead, who will henceforth expound to us the gospel? What might he not have written for us in the next ten or twenty years?

Albrecht Dürer, diary entry, 17 May 1521; Smith (1911) p.120. Dürer, the great German artist, had been so impressed by Luther's theses that he sent him a present of his own woodcuts. Dürer was implicitly comparing Luther to the Bohemian reformer John Hus (c.1372–1415), who attacked indulgences and other abuses. The ecclesiastical Council of Constance condemned him to death, and he was burned at the stake even though he had been given a safe-conduct by the emperor.

3 By the allegiance which I owe you, I deem it my duty to urge you not to allow the sale of Luther's books within the realm, nor give his pupils shelter or encouragement of any kind, till the coming council of the church shall pass its judgement ... I know not how your grace can better win the love of God, as well as of all Christian kings and princes, than by restoring the Church of Christ to the state of harmony that it has enjoyed in ages past.

John Brask, bishop of Linköping (north Sweden) to King Gustav I Vasa, 21 May 1524.

4 Regarding your request that we forbid the sale of Luther's writings, we know not by what right it could be done, for we are told his teachings have not yet been found by impartial judges to be false. Moreover, since writings opposed to Luther have been circulated throughout the land, it seems but right that his too should be kept public, that you and other scholars may detect their fallacies and show them to the people. Then the books of Luther may be condemned.

Gustav I Vasa to John Brask, 8 June 1524; Kidd (1911) p.153. The spread of Luther's reform movement would have been far less rapid had it not been for the support of lay rulers, including his own protector, Frederick the Wise, Elector of Saxony. Luther's awareness of this helps to explain the violence of his reaction to challenges to the existing social order, such as that posed by the rebellious peasants in the following year.

5 Wherefore, my lords, free, save, help and pity the poor people. Stab, smite and slay, all ye that can. If you die in battle you could never have a more blessed end, for you die obedient to God's Word in Romans 13, and in the service of love to free your neighbour from the bands of hell and the devil. I implore every one who can to avoid the peasants as he would the devil himself. I pray God will enlighten them and turn their hearts. But if they do not turn, I wish them no happiness for evermore ... Let none think this is too hard who consider how intolerable is rebellion.

Martin Luther *Against the Thievish, Murderous Hordes of Peasants*, May 1525; Smith (1911) p.163. Luther's rejection of papal and imperial authority encouraged the downtrodden peasants of Germany to throw off their chains. Luther, however, insisted that the spiritual freedom that he advocated was quite different from secular freedom. Lutheranism's survival depended, in his view, on cooperation with the existing social order rather than disruption of it.

6 Our great and urgent needs require us openly to protest against the said resolution [to put an end to innovation in religion] ... as being ... null and void, and, so far as we ourselves and our people, one and all, are concerned, not binding ... In matters which concern God's honour and the salvation and eternal life of our souls, everyone must stand and give account before God for himself, and no one can excuse himself by the action or decision of another.

'Protest' made at the Diet of Speyer, April 1529; Kidd (1911) pp.244–5. The majority of members of the diet accepted the emperor's demand that there should be no more religious innovations in Germany, but a minority registered a formal protest against this decision. They and their supporters therefore became known as Protestants.

1 I would not change my Katie for France and Venice, because God has given her to me, and other women have much worse faults, and she is true to me and a good mother to my children. If a husband always kept such things in mind he would easily conquer the temptation to discord which Satan sows between married people. The greatest happiness is to have a wife to whom you can trust your business and who is a good mother to your children. Katie, you have a husband who loves you. Many an empress is not so well off. I am rich; God has given me my nun and three children. What care I if I am in debt? Katie pays the bills.

Martin Luther, table talk; Smith (1911) p.179. Luther married a former nun, Catharine von Bora, in June 1525.

2 I doubt not that there are many seeds of virtue in a mind touched by music, and I consider those not affected by it as stocks and stones. We know that music is hateful and intolerable to devils. I really believe, nor am I ashamed to assert, that next to theology there is no art equal to music, for it is the only one, except theology, which can give a quiet and happy mind, a manifest proof that the devil, the author of racking care and perturbation, flees from the sound of music.

Martin Luther, Oct. 1530; Smith (1911) pp.346–7. One of Luther's reforms was the use of the vernacular instead of Latin in church services. He also wrote more than 40 hymns in German, of which the most famous is *Ein' feste Burg ist unser Gott* ('A safe stronghold our God is still').

3 The Philistine of genius in religion – Luther.

The Victorian poet and critic Matthew Arnold *Mixed Essays* (1879) 'Lord Falkland'.

ZWINGLI, THE ANABAPTISTS AND CALVIN, 1519–64

4 After the usual words of thanks and good wishes well and truly spoken [Zwingli] went on to say that

he had resolved, with God's help, to preach the gospel according to Saint Matthew in full and in consecutive order and not divided into the prescribed extracts. He would expound it from the Bible and not according to other men's commentaries, and all this to the honour of God and His only son our Lord Jesus Christ, for the true salvation of men's souls and for the instruction of simple pious people … To this end he would do his utmost to treat things in so Christian a fashion that no one well affected to evangelical truth would have any reasonable cause of complaint. On Saturday, New Year's Day 1519, he preached his first sermon at Zürich.

Heinrich Bullinger *Reformationsgeschichte* (History of the Reformation) (1564); G.R. Potter *Huldrych Zwingli* (1978) pp.14–15. Huldrych or Ulrich Zwingli (1484–1531) was elected people's priest in Zürich in late 1518 and set in train a reformation similar to, but independent of, Luther's. His belief in the supreme importance of the Bible derived from Erasmus. Bullinger, the author of this extract, succeeded Zwingli at Zürich.

5 On Wednesday in Holy Week [12 April 1525] the last Mass was celebrated in Zürich, and … all altars which were still in the churches were stripped bare, and all the week was no more singing nor reading, but all the books were taken out of the choir and destroyed. Yet what pleased one man well did not please his neighbour.

Anon. contemporary account; Kidd (1911) p.443. Under sustained pressure from Zwingli the ruling council of the city decided, by a narrow majority, to abolish the Mass and replace it by a simple communion service.

6 We take our stand on the Word of God. The Word says, in the first place, that Christ has a body – this I believe. This body has ascended to heaven and sits at the father's right hand – this too I believe. The Word then says: This body is in the Lord's Supper and is given us to eat – I also believe this, because my Lord Jesus Christ can easily do that if he so wills. And the fact that he wills to be present he affirms in his Word. In this I will firmly trust until he himself, through his own Word, says something to the contrary.

Martin Luther at the Marburg Colloquy, Oct. 1529; Heinrich Bornkamm *Luther in Mid-career 1521–1530* (1983) p.642. The Marburg Colloquy was summoned by Landgrave Philip, ruler of Hesse, with the aim of producing unity among the leaders of the evangelical reform movements in Germany and Switzerland. Luther rejected the Catholic doctrine that, after priestly consecration in the Mass, the elements of bread and wine were 'transubstantiated' into the body and blood of Christ, but he nevertheless believed that Christ was in some sense corporeally present. After making his affirmation he threw back the tablecloth to reveal the words *Hoc est Corpus Meum* (Here is my Body), which he had earlier chalked on the table. Zwingli, by contrast, insisted that Christ was present in a spiritual sense only and that the communion service was simply a commemoration of the Last Supper.

1 Three times Zwingli was thrown to the ground by the advancing forces, but in each case he stood up again. On the fourth occasion a spear reached his chin and he fell to his knees, saying, 'They can destroy the body but not the soul.' And after these words he fell asleep in the Lord. After the battle, when our forces had withdrawn to a stronger position, the enemy had time to look for Zwingli's body, both his presence and his death having been quickly reported. He was found, judgement passed on him, his body was quartered and burnt to ashes. Three days after the foes had gone away Zwingli's friends came to see if any trace of him was left, and what a miracle! In the midst of the ashes lay his heart, whole and undamaged.
Oswald Myconius (Oswald Geishüsler) *Ulrich Zwingli* (1532); Potter (1978) p.146. The Swiss were divided between Catholic and Protestant cantons, and the outcome was civil war. Zwingli's death occurred at the Battle of Kappel (Oct. 1531).

2 We believe ... that infant baptism is a silly, blasphemous outrage, contrary to all Scripture.
Conrad Grebel, Sept. 1524; Kidd (1911) p.452. Grebel, a native of Zürich, wanted a far more radical reformation than anything contemplated by Zwingli. He acknowledged no authority other than the Bible and believed that baptism should be carried out only after a process of spiritual regeneration. He and his followers were called Anabaptists.

3 If anyone here shall baptize another, he will be ... drowned without mercy. Wherefore everyone knows how to order himself and to take care that he bring not his own death upon himself.
Zürich city council, mandate, 7 March 1526; Kidd (1911) p.455. The lay rulers of Zürich were alarmed by the spread of Anabaptism, which acknowledged no secular authority. Hence their savage reaction.

4 As he came down ... to the fish-market and was led through the shambles to the boat he praised God that he was about to die for His truth. For Anabaptism was right and founded on the Word of God ... On the way his mother and brother came to him and exhorted him to be steadfast, and he persevered in his folly even to the end. When he was bound

upon the hurdle and was about to be thrown into the stream by the executioner, he sang with a loud voice: *In manus tuas, Domine, commendo spiritum meum*, 'Into thine hands, O Lord, I commend my spirit'. And herewith was he drawn into the water by the executioner, and drowned.
Heinrich Bullinger (1564); T.J. van Braght *A Martyrology* (1850) Vol.1, p.16. Felix Mantz, whose death on 5 Jan. 1527 is here recorded, was a leader of the Zürich Anabaptists and the first to suffer the punishment of drowning.

5 John of Leyden betakes him to his sleep and continues in a dream three days together. Being awaked, he ... propounds certain doctrines unto the ministers and requires them to confute them by testimonies of Scripture, if they were able; if not, he would relate them unto the people and enact them for laws. The doctrines were these: 'That no man was bound to one only wife, and that every man may take as many as he pleaseth' ... It was in vain for them to resist, and therefore they yielded and for three days together discourse unto the people of the lawfulness of polygamy. The issue was that Leyden first takes three wives ... Many other follow his example, so that at length he was thought most praiseworthy that had most wives.
Anon. 'A Warning for England' (1642); *The Harleian Miscellany* Vol.7 (1811) pp.385–6. Religious radicals from the Netherlands gained control of the German city of Münster in Feb. 1534 and expelled all inhabitants who were not in favour of Anabaptism. The Dutchman Jan van Leyden (Jan Bokelson) seized control of the community, declared himself king and introduced communism and polygamy.

6 I began in the name of the Lord to preach publicly from the pulpit the word of true repentance, to point the people to the narrow path, and in the power of the scripture openly to reprove all sin and wickedness, all idolatry and false worship, and to present the true worship; also the true baptism and the Lord's Supper, according to the doctrine of Christ, to the extent that I had at that time received from God the grace. I also faithfully warned everyone against the abominations of Münster, condemning king, polygamy, kingdom, sword, etc. After about nine months or so, the gracious Lord granted me His fatherly spirit, help and hand.
Menno Simons *Reply to Gellius Faber* (1554); Hillerbrand (1964) p.270. Menno Simons, a Dutchman and former Catholic priest, led a movement of renewal among Anabaptists, which took them away from violence and other excesses associated with Münster, thereby enabling the movement, the Mennonites, to survive.

1 When I was yet a very little boy, my father had destined me for the study of theology. But afterwards, when he considered that the legal profession commonly raised those who followed it to wealth, this prospect induced him suddenly to change his purpose. Thus it came to pass that I was withdrawn from the study of philosophy and was put to the study of law. To this pursuit I endeavoured faithfully to apply myself, in obedience to the will of my father, but God, by the secret guidance of his providence, at length gave a different direction to my course.

John Calvin *Commentary on the Book of Psalms* (1557; 1845 trans.) Vol.I, p.xl. Calvin (1509–64) was born at Noyon, near to Paris. His father was a lawyer; his mother at that time a devout Catholic.

2 Since I was too obstinately devoted to the superstitions of popery to be easily extricated from so profound an abyss of mire, God, by a sudden conversion, subdued and brought my mind to a teachable frame, which was more hardened in such matters than might have been expected from one at my early period of life. Having thus received some taste and knowledge of true godliness, I was immediately inflamed with so intense a desire to make progress therein that although I did not altogether leave off other studies I yet pursued them with less ardour.

John Calvin (1557; 1845 trans.) Vol.I, pp.xl–xli. Calvin's spiritual conversion probably took place in 1532.

3 Calvin left Italy – which he was wont to say he had only entered that he might be free to leave it – and returned to France. After settling his affairs … his purpose was to return to Basel or Strasbourg. Owing to the war [between the emperor and the French], the other roads were shut up, and he was obliged to proceed through Switzerland. In this way he came to Geneva … A short time before, the gospel of Christ had been introduced in a wonderful manner into that city by the exertions of … Guillaume Farel … [who] strongly urged [Calvin], instead of proceeding farther, to stay and labour with him at Geneva. When Calvin could not be induced to consent, Farel thus addressed him: 'You are following only your own wishes, and I declare, in the name of God almighty, that if you do not assist us in this work of the Lord, the Lord will punish you for seeking your own interest rather than his.' Calvin, struck with this fearful denunciation, submitted to the wishes of the … magistrates, by whose suffrage, the people

consenting, he was not only chosen preacher (this he had at first refused) but was also appointed Professor of Sacred Literature – the only office he was willing to accept. This took place in August 1536.

Theodore Beza *Life of Calvin* (1575; 1864 edn) pp.27–9. Opponents of Farel and Calvin were elected into office at Geneva in 1538, and the two reformers were expelled. Meanwhile, religious and political affairs within Geneva fell into confusion, and in Sept. 1541 Calvin returned to the city, where he lived until his death. His place was taken by Beza, his principal disciple.

4 There are four sorts of offices that our Lord instituted for the government of his church – that is to say, first pastors, then teachers, after which elders, and, in the fourth place, deacons. With respect to the pastors … it is their duty to proclaim the word of God so as to indoctrinate, admonish, exhort and reprimand both publicly and privately; to administer the sacraments and exercise fraternal discipline with the elders … The proper duty of teachers is to instruct the faithful in sound doctrine, in order that the purity of the gospel may not be corrupted either by ignorance or evil opinions … Next, the third order, which is that of elders … Their office is to keep watch over the lives of everyone, to admonish in love those whom they see erring and leading disorderly lives, and, whenever necessary, to report them to the body which will be designated to make fraternal corrections … The fourth order [is that of] the deacons. There were always two orders of deacons in the ancient church, the one being charged with receiving, distributing and guarding the goods of the poor … the other, to take watch and ward of the sick, and administer the pittance for the poor. And this custom we have preserved to the present.

Ecclesiastical ordinances of the city of Geneva, 1541; Hillerbrand (1964) pp.189–92. Calvin's Presbyterian system became a model for the organization of Protestant churches in many places, including France, Scotland and parts of Germany as well as in Switzerland.

5 Unless it otherwise pleases the Almighty, religious affairs will soon be in an evil case in France, because there is not one single province uncontaminated. Indeed, in some … three-fourths of the kingdom, congregations and meetings, which they call assemblies, are held [in which] they read and preach according to the rites and uses of Geneva, without respect either for the ministers of the king or the commandments of the king himself. This

contagion has penetrated so deeply that it affects every class of persons, and ... even bishops and many of the principal prelates.

Report of the Venetian ambassador to France, 1561; Calendar of State Papers (C.S.P.) Venetian Vol.7 (1890) p.322. It seemed only a matter of time before the French Calvinists, the Huguenots, would come to dominate the religious life of the country. Civil war broke out in 1562 and lasted until the promulgation of the Edict of Nantes in 1598, which gave the Huguenots limited freedom of worship (see 380:3).

1 [Calvin] lived 54 years, 10 months, 17 days, the half of which he spent in the ministry. He was of moderate stature, of a pale and dark complexion, with eyes that sparkled to the moment of his death and bespoke of his great intellect. In dress he was neither over-careful nor mean, but such as became his singular modesty ... When, in the course of dictating, he happened to be interrupted for several hours, as soon as he returned he commenced at once to dictate where he had left off ... In the doctrine which he delivered at the first, he persisted steadily to the last, scarcely making any change: of few theologians within our recollection can the same thing be affirmed.

Theodore Beza (1575; 1864 edn) Vol.1, pp.97-8.

2 Our God is divided into three parts. This means that we are, in effect, without God – that is to say, we are atheists ... And not only the Mohammedans and the Jews but the beasts in the field would make fun of us if they heard tell of our preposterous belief.

Miguel Servetus *De Trinitatis Erroribus* (1531); E. Doumergue *Jean Calvin* (1926) Vol.6, p.228. Servetus, a Spaniard by birth and an anti-trinitarian by conviction, had to flee from his native country to escape the Inquisition, which was pursuing him on grounds of heresy.

3 [Servetus], in an evil hour, came to this place, when, at my instigation, one of the syndics ordered him to be conducted to prison. For I do not disguise it, that I considered it my duty to put a check, so far as I could, upon this most obstinate and ungovernable man, that his contagion might not spread farther.

John Calvin, letter, Sept. 1553; Hillerbrand (1964) pp.287-8.

4 It appears to us that you, Servetus, have for a long time propagated false and plainly heretical doctrine ... even writing and publishing books against God the Father, Son and Holy Ghost ... Moreover, you have not shrunk from setting yourself up against the

majesty of God and the Holy Trinity, and have gone out of your way to infect the world with your stinking heretical poison ... For these and other just reasons ... we condemn you, Michael Servetus, to be bound and taken to the place called Champel and there attached to a stake and burned alive – along with your books, both manuscript and printed – until your body is reduced to ashes.

Judgement of the syndics of Geneva, 26 Oct. 1553; Doumergue Vol.6 (1926) p.358. Servetus was executed the following day.

THE COUNTER-REFORMATION, 1521-63

5 The attack had gone on for some considerable time when a cannon ball struck one of his legs and shattered it completely; at the same time, in passing between his legs, wounding the other gravely ... So they began anew that butchery, during which, as in all those he had suffered so far and was still to suffer, he never spoke a word nor showed any signs of pain, except by tightly clenching his fists. In spite of everything, his condition worsened. He lost the power of taking nourishment, and the other symptoms which herald the approach of death appeared.

Ignatius Loyola *Confessions* (1538); James Brodrick SJ *Saint Ignatius Loyola* (1956) p.60. Loyola, who was born in northern Spain in 1491, pursued a military career until he was wounded in the leg in 1521. Unexpectedly, he survived the operation, and during his long convalescence he underwent a spiritual conversion that convinced him he must commit himself to God's service. He was canonized in 1622.

6 They went about with a burning desire in their hearts to serve God. And they were comforted and quickened in their good purpose by the vow of poverty, by familiar intercourse day by day with one another, by sweet peace, by concord, love and the sharing of what they had, and by the communion of the saints. And they imitated the usage of the ancient holy fathers and invited one another to dinner, according to their means, and took advantage of the occasion to talk of the spirit and urge one another to a contempt of this world and a desire for things divine.

Pedro de Ribadeneira *Vida del P. Ignacio de Loyola, fundador de la Compañia de Jesús* (Life of Ignatius Loyola, Founder of the Society of Jesus) (1572; 1880 edn) p.123. In Spain, and also in Paris where he went to study, Loyola gathered around him a close band of friends and disciples. Ribadeneira was St Ignatius's secretary as well as his biographer.

1 In order that you may know how great a benefit God has conferred on me by making me acquainted with Master Iñigo [Loyola], I give you my word that never in all my life shall I be able to pay my debt to him. Over and over again, both with his purse and his friends, he has succoured my necessities, and thanks to him I have withdrawn from bad company which, owing to my lack of experience, I did not recognize … Believe everything he says. He is so God-fearing and of such high character that you will derive great benefit from his conversation and counsels.

Francis Xavier to his elder brother, Juan, from Paris, 25 March 1535; Sedgwick (1923) pp.157–8. Xavier, one of Loyola's earliest disciples, was canonized in 1622.

2 Let him who would fight for God under the banner of the cross and serve the Lord alone and his vicar on earth [the pope] in our Society, which we desire to be distinguished by the name of Jesus, bear in mind that after a solemn vow of perpetual chastity he is part of a community founded primarily for the task of advancing souls in Christian life and doctrine and of propagating the faith by the ministry of the word, by spiritual exercises, by works of charity, and expressly by the instruction of children and unlettered persons in Christian principles.

Proposals drawn up by Loyola and his companions, June 1539; James Brodrick SJ The Origin of the Jesuits (1940) pp.72–3. In Sept. 1540 Pope Paul III issued the bull Regimini militantis Ecclesiae granting permission for the formation of the Society of Jesus.

3 By this name of *Spiritual Exercises* is understood any method of examining one's conscience, meditating, contemplating, praying vocally and mentally, and other spiritual operations … Because, as walking, going and running are bodily exercises, in like manner all methods of preparing and disposing the soul to remove from herself all disorderly attachments, and, after their removal, to seek and find the divine will in the laying-out of one's life to the salvation of one's soul, are called *Spiritual Exercises* … For the following exercises there are allotted four weeks, corresponding to the four parts into which the *Exercises* are divided – that is to say, the first is the consideration and contemplation of sins. The second is the life of Christ our Lord as far as Palm Sunday inclusive. The third is the passion of Christ our Lord. The fourth is his resurrection and ascension.

Ignatius Loyola Spiritual Exercises (1548); J. Rickaby The Spiritual Exercises of St Ignatius Loyola (1959) pp.3–4. Loyola originally

devised his Spiritual Exercises, approved by Pope Paul III in 1548, in order to assist his fellow students and disciples who wished to practise meditation. They subsequently became the foundation of Jesuit training.

4 We have nothing more to write to you from here except that we are ready to sail. We conclude with the request that our Lord Christ may give us the favour of seeing each other and of being physically united with each other again in the other life; for I do not know if we shall ever see each other again in this life, not only because of the great distance from Rome to India, but also because of the great harvest which waits for us there without our having to go elsewhere to look for it. Whoever goes first to the other life, and does not find his brother there whom he loves in the Lord, should ask Christ our Lord to unite us all there in his glory.

Francis Xavier to Loyola and the Jesuit fathers, Lisbon, 18 March 1541; G. Schurhammer Francis Xavier, His Life and Times (1973) Vol.1, p.719. Loyola had envisaged his new Society as a missionary order, with the whole world as its province. Xavier led the Jesuit campaign in India and southeast Asia (see 321:2).

5 In this region of Travancore [southwestern India] where I now am … I made Christians of more than ten thousand. This is the method I have followed. As soon as I arrived in any heathen village where they had sent for me to give baptisms, I gave orders for all men, women and children to be collected in one place. Then, beginning with the first elements of the Christian faith, I taught them there is one God – father, son and holy ghost – and at the same time … I made them each make three times the sign of the cross. Then, putting on a surplice, I began to recite in a loud voice and in their own language the form of a general confession, the apostles' creed, the ten commandments [and] the Lord's prayer … Where the people appeared to me sufficiently instructed to receive baptism, I ordered them all to ask God's pardon publicly for the sins of their past life, and to do this with a loud voice and in the presence of their neighbours still hostile to the Christian religion … Then at last I baptize them in due form and I give to each his name written on a ticket. After their baptism, the new Christians go back to their houses and bring me their wives and families for baptism. When all are baptized, I order all the temples of their false gods to be destroyed and all the idols to be broken in pieces. I can give you no idea of the joy I find in seeing this done.

St Francis Xavier to the Jesuit fathers at Rome from Cochin, India, 27 Jan. 1545; H.J. Coleridge *The Life and Letters of St Francis Xavier* (1886) Vol.1, pp.280–81.

1 We have chosen the city of Trent as that wherein an ecumenical council is to be held ... fixing upon that place as a convenient one whereat the bishops and prelates can assemble very easily indeed from Germany and from the other nations bordering on Germany, and without difficulty from France, Spain and the other remoter provinces. And in fixing the day for the council, we have had regard that there should be time both for publishing this our decree throughout the Christian nations and for allowing all prelates an opportunity of repairing to Trent.

Pope Paul III *Initio Nostri*, 22 May 1542; J. Waterworth *The Canons and Decrees of the ... Council of Trent* (1848) pp.8–9. The summoning of a general council of the church, to meet at the northern Italian town of Trent (Trento), was a significant stage in the papacy's counter-offensive against the Protestant reformers.

2 Canon 1. If anyone denieth that in the sacrament of the most holy eucharist are contained truly, really and substantially, the body and blood, together with the soul and divinity, of our Lord Jesus Christ ... but saith that he is only therein as in a sign ... Let him be anathema.

Canon 2. If anyone saith that in the sacred and holy sacrament of the eucharist the substance of the bread and wine remains conjointly with the body and blood of our Lord Jesus Christ, and denieth that wonderful and singular conversion of the whole substance of the bread into the body, and of the whole substance of the wine into the blood ... which conversion indeed the Catholic Church most aptly calls transubstantiation – Let him be anathema.

Decrees of the Council of Trent, 11 Oct. 1551; Waterworth (1848) p.82. Canon 1 was a rejection of the Zwinglian position on the sacrament, and Canon 2 of the Lutheran. Over its many sessions the council gave detailed definition to all the doctrines of the Catholic Church and also tightened up its discipline. Bishops, for instance, were instructed to live simply and be resident in their sees, and all priests were commanded to preach regularly and instruct their flocks in the principles of the faith.

3 Why should you be planning for the publication of any new work at a time when nearly all the books which have thus far appeared are being taken away from us? It seems to me that, at least for some years to come, no one among us will dare to write anything but letters. There has just been published an Index of the books which, under penalty of excommunication, we are no longer permitted to possess. The number of those prohibited (particularly of works originating in Germany) is so great that there will remain but few ... I shall begin tomorrow going over my own collection, so that nothing may be found in it which is not authorised. Should I describe the process as a shipwreck or a holocaust of literature?

Latinus Latinius, a scholar, to Andrea Masius, Rome, Jan. 1559; G.H. Putnam *The Censorship of the Church of Rome* (1906) Vol.1, p.176. The Index of prohibited books issued by Pope Pius IV in Jan. 1559 was another weapon in the armoury that the papacy was assembling to combat Protestantism. Luther and his fellow reformers had made unprecedented use of the printing press to propagate their ideas, but Catholics were now banned from reading their books.

4 Don Juan Ponce was turned over to them [the Spanish Inquisition] so that his confession could be heard and he brought back to the Catholic faith ... He had been involved in great error and heresy – for example, that there was no purgatory, that the inquisitors were anti-Christian, that one should not believe or obey the pope ... This Don Juan was sentenced to die at the stake ... But our Lord, in His immeasurable goodness, caused him to see his error and led him back to the holy Catholic faith. He died with many tears of remorse over his sins. Indeed, still at the stake he endeavoured to persuade the others to desist from their errors and to convert themselves to the holy Catholic faith and to the Roman Church.

An account of an *auto-da-fé* (act of faith), at Seville, southern Spain, 24 Sept. 1559; Hillerbrand (1964) pp.468–9. The Spanish Inquisition, designed to weed out heretics and suppress their unorthodox beliefs, had been set up, with papal approval, in the late 15th century and was very effective in preventing the spread of Protestantism into the Iberian peninsula. In 1542 Pope Paul III established the Holy Office at Rome with inquisitorial powers over all Catholics.

The Scientific Revolution, 1500–1700

ANCIENTS AND MODERNS

1 I can say that there are in the Indies a thousand different kinds of birds and animals of the mountains that have never been known by name or shape, and of which there is no memory among the Latins or the Greeks, nor any other nations of the world.

José de Acosta *Historia natural y moral de las Indias* (1590) Bk 4, Ch.36. A Jesuit theologian, Acosta was appointed (1576) provincial of the vast territories in Spanish Central and South America, known then as the Indies. By describing many natural phenomena and creatures not recorded in the ancient authorities, Acosta helped to encourage a more empiricist approach to nature.

2 Contemporary anatomists are so firmly dependent upon I-know-not-what quality in the writing of their leader [Galen] that ... they have shamefully reduced Galen's writings into brief compendia and never depart from him ... by the breadth of a nail ... So completely have all yielded to him that there is no physician who would declare that even the slightest error had ever been found, much less can now be found, in Galen's anatomical books, although it is now clear to me from the reborn art of dissection ... that he never dissected a human body.

Andreas Vesalius *De Humani Corporis Fabrica* (On the Fabric of the Human Body) (1543) Preface. Professor of surgery at Padua, Vesalius discovered numerous errors in the anatomical writings of the ancient Greek medical authority, Galen (c.130–201). These errors had previously remained undiscovered owing to deference to ancient authority, and refusal by university-trained physicians to dissect bodies (see 368:4).

3 I began to be annoyed that the movements of the world machine, created for our sake by the best and most systematic Artisan of all, were not understood with greater certainty by the philosophers ... For this reason I undertook the task of rereading the works of all the philosophers, which I could obtain to learn whether anyone had ever proposed other motions of the universe's spheres than those expounded by the teachers of astronomy in the schools. And in fact first I found in Cicero that Hicetas supposed the Earth to move. Later I also discovered in Plutarch that certain others were of this opinion ... Therefore ... I too began to consider the mobility of the Earth.

Nicolaus Copernicus *On the Revolutions of the Heavenly Spheres* (1543; 1978 edn) Dedicatory Epistle, pp.4–5. Believing that the ancients knew more than the moderns, Copernicus, a Polish cleric and self-taught astronomer, looks for (and finds) evidence of heliocentric astronomy in the past.

4 Above all, if a man could succeed, not in striking out some particular invention, however useful, but in kindling a light in nature – a light which should in its very rising touch and illuminate all the border-regions that confine upon the circle of our present knowledge; and so, spreading further and further should presently disclose and bring into sight all that is most hidden and secret in the world – that man (I thought) would be the benefactor indeed of the human race – the propagator of man's empire over the universe, the champion of liberty, the conqueror and subduer of necessities.

Francis Bacon *De Interpretatione Naturae* (Of the Interpretation of Nature) (1603) Proemium; James Spedding, Robert Ellis and Douglas Heath (eds) *The Works of Francis Bacon* (1887–1901 edn) Vol.3, p.518. Believing the moderns are capable of superseding the ancients, Bacon, a civil servant who later became lord chancellor of England and one of the founders of modern science, forges his own modernizing ambitions.

5 It ought not to go for nothing that through the long voyages and travels which are the mark of our age many things in nature have been revealed which might throw new light on natural philosophy. Nay it would be a disgrace for mankind if the expanse of the material globe, the lands, the seas, the stars, was opened up and brought to light, while, in contrast with this enormous expansion, the bounds of the intellectual globe should be restricted to what was known to the ancients.

Francis Bacon *Cogitata et Visa* (Thoughts and Conclusions) (1607); Benjamin Farrington *Philosophy of Francis Bacon* (1964) p.94. Bacon was one of many whose desire to reform natural philosophy was largely inspired by new findings in natural history resulting from Renaissance voyages of discovery.

6 For these three have changed the whole face and state of things throughout the world; the first in learning, the second in warfare, the third in navigation; whence have followed innumerable changes; insomuch that no empire, no sect, no star seems to have exerted greater power and influence in human affairs than these mechanical discoveries.

Francis Bacon *Novum Organum* (1620) Bk 1, Aphorism 129; Spedding, Ellis and Heath (1887–1901 edn) Vol.4, p.114. Referring to the recent invention of printing, gunpowder and the magnetic compass, which Bacon saw as proof that the moderns had superseded the ancients. Compare 486:6.

1 Simplicio is confused and perplexed, and I seem to hear him say, 'Who would there be to settle our controversies if Aristotle were to be deposed? What other authors would we follow in our schools, academies, universities? What philosopher has written the whole of natural philosophy, so well arranged, without omitting a single conclusion? ... Should we destroy that haven, that Prytaneum where so many scholars have taken refuge so comfortably; where without exposing themselves to the inclemencies of the air, they can acquire a complete knowledge of the universe by merely turning over a few pages?'

Galileo Galilei *Dialogue Concerning the Two Chief World Systems* (1632; 1953 edn) p.56. A great prose stylist, the Italian physicist Galileo chose to deliver his scientific theories in dialogues between interested parties. Here one of the characters (Sagredo) ridicules the contemporary slavish adherence to Aristotelianism, as represented by the character Simplicio.

2 If I have seen further it is by standing on the shoulders of giants.

Isaac Newton to Robert Hooke, 5 Feb. 1675/6; H.W. Turnbull (ed.) *The Correspondence of Isaac Newton* (1959–77) Vol.1, p.416. A rare display of modesty from the greatest English mathematician and natural philosopher, Newton. Perhaps adapted from Robert Burton's *The Anatomy of Melancholy* (1621) – 'Pigmies placed on the shoulders of giants see more than the giants themselves' (which Newton knew) – this trope has been traced back to Bernard of Chartres in the early 12th century (see 197:5) and was echoed by Samuel Taylor Coleridge in 1818.

3 The commonwealth of Learning, is not at this time without Master-Builders, whose mighty Designs, in advancing the Sciences, will leave lasting Monuments to the Admiration of Posterity; But every one must not hope to be a Boyle, or a Sydenham; and in an Age that produces such Masters, as the great Huygenius, and the incomparable Mr Newton, with some other of that Strain; 'tis Ambition enough to be employed as an Under-Labourer in clearing Ground a little, and removing some of the Rubbish, that lies in the way to Knowledge.

John Locke *Essay Concerning Human Understanding* (1690; 1961 edn) Epistle to the Reader, p.xxxv. Arguably the founding father of modern philosophy, modestly suggesting that his analysis of how we come to know things and how our understanding works is merely a supplement to the discoveries of recent natural philosophers (or scientists, as we would say).

4 An ordinary Sea-man or Traveller, that had the opportunity with Columbus to sail along the several Coasts of it [the New World], and pass up and down through the Country, was able at his return to Inform Men of an hundred things, that they should never have learn'd by Aristotle's philosophy or Ptolemy's Geography ... one, that had a candid and knowing Friend intimate with Columbus, might better rely on His Informations about many particulars of the Natural History of those Parts, than on those of an hundred School-Philosophers, that knew what they learned from Aristotle, Pliny, Aelian, and the like ancient Naturalists.

Robert Boyle *The Christian Virtuoso* (1690); M. Hunter and E.B. Davis (eds) *The Works of Robert Boyle* (2000) Vol.11, p.314. A leading English natural philosopher of the day rejects ancient authority and shows the continuing inspiration of Renaissance voyages of discovery. Boyle (1627–91) was one of the founder members of the Royal Society (see 372:3).

5 By what proportion gravity decreases by receding from the Planets the ancients have not sufficiently explained. Yet they appear to have adumbrated it by the harmony of the celestial spheres, designating the Sun and the remaining six planets ... by means of Apollo with the Lyre of seven strings, and measuring the intervals of the spheres by the intervals of the tones ... But by this symbol they indicated that the Sun ... acts upon the planets in that harmonic ratio of distances by which the force of tension acts upon strings of different lengths, that is reciprocally in the duplicate ratio of the distances.

Isaac Newton, MS draft for addition to proposed 2nd edn of *Principia Mathematica* (c.1694); J.E. McGuire and P.M. Rattansi 'Newton and the "Pipes of Pan"' in *Notes and Records of the Royal Society of London* 21 (1966) pp.108–43, 116. Believing, like Copernicus (see 364:3), that supreme wisdom was to be found among the ancients, Newton suggests that the Pythagorean notion of the harmony of the spheres was a cryptic way of alluding to the universal principle of gravitation (see 482:3).

EXPERIENCE AND EXPERIMENT

6 He who wishes to explore nature must tread her books with his feet. Writing is learnt from letters, Nature, however, [by travelling] from land to land ... Thus is the *Codex Naturae*, thus must its leaves be turned.

Paracelsus (Theophrast Bombast von Hohenheim) *Defensiones und Verantwortungen* (Defences and Justifications) (1537–41); *Sämtliche Werke* (1928–33 edn) Vol.11, pp.145–6. Drawing on the familiar trope of the book of nature, the itinerant alchemist and healer Paracelsus makes an early plea for the importance of observation and experience.

1 Human knowledge and human power meet in one.

Francis Bacon *Novum Organum* (1620) Bk I, Aphorism 3; Spedding, Ellis and Heath (1887–1901 edn) Vol.4, p.47. One of numerous statements in which Bacon insists that knowledge of the natural world should be put to use for the practical benefit of mankind.

2 Those who have handled sciences have been either men of experiment or men of dogmas. The men of experiment are like the ant; they only collect and use; the reasoners resemble spiders who make cobwebs out of their own substance. But the bee takes a middle course; it gathers its material from the flowers of the garden and of the field, but transforms and digests it by a power of its own. Not unlike this is the true business of philosophy; for it neither relies solely or chiefly on the powers of the mind, nor does it take the matter which it gathers from natural history and mechanical experiments and lay it up in the memory whole, as it finds it; but lays it up in the understanding altered and digested.

Francis Bacon *Novum Organum* (1620) Bk I, Aphorism 95; Spedding, Ellis and Heath (1887–1901 edn) Vol.4, pp.92–3. Bacon extols the importance of a combination of rational analysis and empirical knowledge in attempts to understand the world, as opposed to a purely rationalist or purely empiricist approach.

3 For like as a man's disposition is never well known or proved till he be crossed, nor Proteus ever changed shapes till he was straitened and held fast, so nature exhibits herself more clearly under the trials and vexations of art than when left to herself.

Francis Bacon *De Augmentis Scientiarum* (1623) Bk 2, Ch.2; Spedding, Ellis and Heath (1887–1901 edn) Vol.4, p.298. A justification of the use of artificially set up experimental procedures for understanding the natural world against contemporaries who believed that such procedures would inevitably lead to unnatural results.

4 As in Mathematics, so in Natural Philosophy, the Investigation of difficult Things by the Method of Analysis, ought ever to precede the Method of Composition. This Analysis consists in making Experiments and Observations, and in drawing general Conclusions from them by Induction, and by admitting of no Objections against the Conclusions, but such as are taken from Experiments, or other certain Truths.

Isaac Newton *Opticks* (1704; 1730 edn) p.404. Induction from experimental data, as opposed to deduction from presupposed axioms, was a characteristic feature of Baconian natural philosophy, and Newton not only endorses that view

but also tries to suggest his 'mathematical principles' are equally firmly based on natural phenomena.

MATHEMATIZATION OF THE WORLD PICTURE

5 The author of this work has done nothing blameworthy. For it is the duty of an astronomer to compose the history of the celestial motions through careful and expert study. Then he must conceive and devise the causes of these motions or hypotheses about them. Since he cannot in any way attain to the true causes, he will adopt whatever suppositions enable the motions to be computed correctly from the principles of geometry for the future as well as for the past. The present author has performed both these duties excellently … For this art, it is quite clear, is completely and absolutely ignorant of the causes of the apparent non-uniform motions. And if any causes are devised by the imagination, as indeed very many are, they are not put forward to convince anyone that they are true, but merely to provide a reliable basis for computation …

So far as hypotheses are concerned, let no one expect anything certain from astronomy, which cannot furnish it, lest he accept as the truth ideas conceived for another purpose, and depart from the study a greater fool than when he entered it.

Andreas Osiander 'Concerning the Hypotheses of this Work', unsigned preface added to Copernicus (1543; 1978 edn) p.xx. Interpolated at the beginning of Copernicus's book without permission, Osiander, a cleric entrusted by Copernicus's friends to supervise the publication, seeks to defend Copernicus from intellectual and religious censure by drawing on a standard assumption that mathematics was entirely instrumental and could tell us nothing about the way things really are.

6 I was impelled to consider a different system of deducing the motions of the universe's spheres for no other reason than the realization that astronomers do not agree among themselves in their investigations … On the contrary, their experience was just like some one taking from various places hands, feet, a head, and other pieces, very well depicted, it may be, but not for the representation of a single person; since these fragments would not belong to one another at all, a monster rather than a man would be put together from them.

Nicolaus Copernicus (1543; 1978 edn) Dedicatory Epistle, p.4. Copernicus acknowledges that mathematical astronomy is incompatible with learned assumptions about what the world system is really like. He presents this as one of the reasons he felt compelled to develop his heliocentric system.

1 It seems to me that your Reverence and Signor Galileo act prudently when you content yourselves with speaking hypothetically and not absolutely, as I have always understood that Copernicus spoke. To say that on the supposition of the Earth's movement and the Sun's quiescence all the celestial appearances are explained better than by the theory of eccentrics and epicycles is to speak with excellent good sense and to run no risk whatsoever. Such a manner of speaking is enough for a mathematician. But to want to affirm that the Sun in very truth is at the centre of the universe … is a very dangerous attitude and one calculated not only to arouse all Scholastic philosophers and theologians but also to injure our holy faith by contradicting the Scriptures.

Roberto Bellarmino, Cardinal Inquisitor of the Holy Office, to Paolo Antonio Foscarini, defender of Copernicus, 12 April, 1615; Georgio de Santillana *The Crime of Galileo* (1955) p.99. The cardinal (unwittingly following Osiander) believes that Copernicus did not claim that his mathematics revealed physical truth and warns Foscarini and Galileo against assuming otherwise. Bellarmino summarizes the church's view, which was based not simply on scriptural fundamentalism but also on the common belief about the inadequacy of mathematics for establishing physical truths.

2 Philosophy is written in this grand book, the universe, which stands continually open to our gaze. But the book cannot be understood unless one first learns to comprehend the language and read the letters in which it is composed. It is written in the language of mathematics, and its characters are triangles, circles, and other geometric figures without which it is humanly impossible to understand a single word of it; without these one wanders about in a dark labyrinth.

Galileo Galilei *The Assayer* (1623); Stillman Drake (ed.) *Discoveries and Opinions of Galileo* (1957) pp.237–8. Galileo makes the radical claim that natural philosophy can be understood only through mathematics. The usual view at this time was that mathematics could give a special description of physical events but could do nothing to *explain* them and was not, therefore, strictly relevant to natural philosophy.

3 Those long chains of reasonings, quite simple and easy, which geometers are accustomed to using to teach their most difficult demonstrations, had given me cause to imagine that everything which can be accompanied by man's knowledge is linked in the same way, and that, provided only that one abstains

from accepting any for true which is not true, and that one always keeps the right order for one thing to be deduced from that which precedes it, there can be nothing so distant that one does not reach it eventually, or so hidden that one cannot discover it.

René Descartes *Discourse on Method* (1637; 1968 edn) p.41. The French mathematician and natural philosopher sets up the certainty of geometrical proofs in support of his rationalistic natural philosophy.

4 I do not accept or desire in Physics any other principles than in Geometry or abstract Mathematics; because all the phenomena of nature are explained thereby, and certain demonstrations concerning them can be given.

René Descartes *Principles of Philosophy* (1644; 1983 edn) Pt 2, Sect.64, p.76. Descartes now feels the battle has been won (see 369:7 and 370:7) and routinely invokes not only the certainty of mathematics but also its explanatory power.

MATTER IN MOTION

5 I am much occupied with the investigation of physical causes. My aim in this is to show that the celestial machine is not similar to a divine animated being, but similar to a clock.

Johannes Kepler to Hewart von Hohenburg, Bavarian chancellor and patron, 10 Feb. 1605; *Gesammelte Werke* (1945–59) Vol.15, p.146. An early illustration by the greatest mathematical astronomer before Newton of the tendency to see the world system in terms of a complex machinery.

6 And there are absolutely no judgements in Mechanics which do not also pertain to Physics, of which Mechanics is a part or type: and it is as natural for a clock, composed of wheels of a certain kind, to indicate the hours, as for a tree, grown from a certain kind of seed, to produce the corresponding fruit. Accordingly, just as when those who are accustomed to considering automata know the use of some machine and see some of its parts, they easily conjecture from this how the other parts which they do not see are made: so, from the perceptible effects and parts of natural bodies, I have attempted to investigate the nature of their causes and of their imperceptible parts.

René Descartes (1644; 1983 edn) Pt 4, Sect.203, pp.285–6. A classic statement of the principal assumptions of mechanical philosophy.

7 For the basic problem of philosophy seems to be to discover the forces of nature from the phenomena of motions and then to demonstrate the other phenomena from these forces ... If only we could derive the other phenomena of nature from mechanical principles by the same kind of reasoning! For many things lead me to have a suspicion that all phenomena may depend upon certain forces by which the particles of bodies, by causes not yet known, either are impelled toward one another and cohere in regular figures, or are repelled from one another and recede. Since these forces are unknown, philosophers have hitherto made trial of nature in vain.

Isaac Newton *Principia Mathematica* (1687; 1999 trans.) Preface, p.383. Recognizing the inadequacy of Cartesian principles, Newton, much to the chagrin of mechanical philosophers, introduced non-mechanical attractive and repulsive forces into his natural philosophy.

1 For truly in nature there are many operations that are far more than merely mechanical. Nature is not simply an organized body like a clock, which has no vital principle of motion in it; but is a living body which has life and perception, which are much more exalted than a mere mechanism or a mechanical motion.

Anne, Lady Conway *Principles of the Most Ancient and Modern Philosophy* (1692; 1996 edn) p.64. An autodidact, Lady Conway's anonymously published book was assumed to have been written by a man. It contributed to the debate about the inadequacy of the mechanical philosophy for explaining all phenomena.

2 I have not as yet been able to deduce from phenomena the reason for these properties of gravity, and I do not feign hypotheses. For whatever is not deduced from the phenomena must be called a hypothesis; and hypotheses, whether metaphysical or physical, or based on occult qualities, or mechanical, have no place in experimental philosophy. In this experimental philosophy, propositions are deduced from the phenomena and are made general by induction. The impenetrability, mobility and impetus of bodies, and the laws of motion and the law of gravity have been found by this method. And it is enough that gravity really exists and acts according to the laws that we have set forth.

Isaac Newton, General Scholium (added at end of 2nd edn of *Principia Mathematica* 1713; 1999 trans.) p.943. A famous defence of his non-mechanical philosophy against Continental mechanical philosophers, rejecting the need to imagine unconfirmed (and usually unconfirmable) mechanisms by which gravity or other phenomena might take place (see 482:3).

ANATOMY AND PHYSIOLOGY

3 The anatomy of the Italians, is the anatomy of corpses.

Paracelsus *Von den natürlichen Wassern* (On Natural Waters) (1525–6); *Sämtliche Werke* (1928–33 edn) Vol.2, p.325.

4 Especially after the devastation of the Goths, when all the sciences, formerly so flourishing and fittingly practised, had decayed, the more fashionable physicians, first in Italy in imitation of the old Romans, despising the use of the hands, began to relegate to their slaves those things which had to be done manually for their patients and to stand over them like architects ... And so in the course of time the art of treatment has been so miserably distorted that certain doctors assuming the name of physicians have arrogated to themselves the prescription of drugs and diet for obscure diseases, and have relegated the rest of medicine to those whom they call surgeons, but consider scarcely as slaves. They have shamefully rid themselves of what is the chief and most venerable branch of medicine, that which based itself principally upon the investigation of nature.

Andreas Vesalius (1543) Preface. The great Belgian anatomist blames lack of progress in medical knowledge on the rejection by elite physicians of the supposedly banausic enterprise of surgery, which was relegated to socially inferior barber-surgeons.

5 And sooth to say, when I surveyed my mass of evidence, whether derived from vivisections, and my various reflections on them, or from the ventricles of the heart and the vessels that enter into and issue from them ... I frequently and seriously bethought me, and long revolved in my mind, what might be the quantity of blood which was transmitted, in how short a time its passage might be effected, and the like; and not finding it possible that this could be supplied by the juices of the ingested aliment ... unless the blood should somehow find its way from the arteries into the veins ... I began to think whether there might not be A MOTION, AS IT WERE, IN A CIRCLE.

William Harvey *Exercitatio Anatomica de Motu Cordis et Sanguinis in Animalibus* (On the Motion of the Heart and Blood) (1628) Ch.8; Robert Willis (ed.) *Works of William Harvey* (1847) pp.45–6. The English anatomist and royal physician announces his discovery of the circulation of blood.

6 The heart, consequently, is the beginning of life; the sun of the microcosm, even as the sun in his turn

might be designated the heart of the world … it is the household divinity which, discharging its function, nourishes, cherishes, quickens the whole body, and is indeed the foundation of life, the source of all action.
William Harvey (1628); Willis (1847) Ch.8, p.47. Drawing on traditional beliefs about the conformity of the microcosm and the macrocosm, Harvey did not simply see the heart as a pump.

1 I suppose the body to be just a statue or a machine made of earth.
René Descartes *Treatise on Man* (1633); Stephen Gaukroger (ed.) *The World and other Writings* (1998) p.99. True to his mechanical philosophy, Descartes believed there was no distinction between living systems and non-living: all were merely machines.

2 The flesh of the heart contains in its pores one of those fires without light of which I have spoken about earlier and which makes it so fiery and hot that … it is promptly inflated and dilated. Similarly, it can be demonstrated experimentally that the blood or milk of some animal will be dilated if you pour it a drop at a time into a very hot flask. And the fire in the heart of this machine that I am describing to you has as its sole purpose to expand, warm, and refine the blood.
René Descartes (1633); Gaukroger (1998) p.101. The heart described not so much as a pump, as an internal combustion engine, driven by a fire continually burning, and replenished, in its ventricles.

3 Now I also affirm the same of innate heat and of blood, namely that they are not fire nor do they take their origin from fire, but partake of a different and more divine body than fire, and therefore do not act by any faculty of the elements.
William Harvey *Disputations touching the Generation of Animals* (1651; 1981 edn) Ch.71, p.377. Harvey rejects the so-called Cartesian fire (see 369:2) and the mechanistic interpretation of the body.

4 This is all very fine, but it won't do – anatomy, botany. Nonsense, Sir! I know an old woman in Covent Garden who understands botany better, and as for anatomy, my butcher can dissect a joint full as well. No, young man, all this is stuff: you must go to the bedside, it is there alone you can learn disease.
Thomas Sydenham, responding to Hans Sloane's letter of introduction, c.1685; William Wadd *Mems, Maxims and Memoirs* (1827) p.231. Always a strictly empiricist physician, Sydenham believed bedside experience was more useful to a physician than theoretical science.

5 A physician may as well do without a scrupulous enquiry into the anatomy of the parts, as a gardener may by his art and observation, be able to ripen, meliorate and preserve his fruit without examining what kinds of juices, fibres, pores etc. are to be found in the roots, bark or body of the tree.
Thomas Sydenham 'Anatomie' (1668); K. Dewhurst *Dr Thomas Sydenham* (1966) p.86. Like Paracelsus, Sydenham prefers to focus on understanding disease rather than the anatomy of corpses.

THE SENSES AND THE UNDERSTANDING

6 Hence I think that tastes, odours, colours and so on are no more than mere names so far as the object in which we place them is concerned, and that they reside only in our consciousness.
Galileo Galilei (1623); Drake (1957) p.274. Galileo begins the process, which culminates with Locke (see 370:2), of separating our immediate experiences from our understanding of what causes those experiences.

7 In putting forward an account of light, the first thing that I want to draw to your attention is that it is possible for there to be a difference between the sensation that we have of it … and what it is in the objects that produces the sensation in us, that is, what it is in the flame or in the Sun that we term 'light'. For although everyone is commonly convinced that the ideas that we have in our thought are completely like the objects from which they proceed, I know of no compelling argument for this.
René Descartes *The World* (1632; 1998 edn) p.3. Descartes believed that light was a pulse rapidly transmitted through the invisibly small particles that filled the world and was conscious of the counterintuitive nature of his theory.

8 The next care to be taken, in respect of the Senses, is a supplying of their infirmities with Instruments, and, as it were, the adding of artificial Organs to the natural; this in one of them has been of late years accomplished with prodigious benefit to all sorts of useful knowledge, by the invention of Optical Glasses. By the means of Telescopes, there is nothing so far distant but may be represented to our view; and by the help of Microscopes, there is nothing so small, as to escape our enquiry; hence there is a new visible World discovered to the understanding. By this means the Heavens are open'd, and … in every little particle of … matter, we now behold almost as great a variety of Creatures, as we were able before to reckon up in the whole Universe it self.

Robert Hooke *Micrographia* (1665) Preface, sig.A2v. Hooke expresses the general optimism about the potential for discovery by using newly invented scientific instruments.

1 As if (for instance) it be demanded how Snow comes to dazzle the Eyes, they will answer, that 'tis by a Quality of Whiteness that is in It which makes all very white Bodies produce the same Effect; And if You ask what this Whiteness is, They will tell you no more in substance, then that 'tis a real entity which denominates the Parcel of Matter to which it is Joyn'd, White.

Robert Boyle *Origine of Formes and Qualities* (1666); Hunter and Davis Vol.5 (1999) pp.12–13. A representative dismissal of standard Aristotelian view of the qualities of bodies, this critique is more widely known from Molière's satire *Le Malade imaginaire* (1674), in which a doctor explains the ability of opium to put one to sleep in terms of its dormitive property.

2 Besides those … primary qualities in bodies, viz. bulk, figure, extension, number and motion of their solid Parts; all the rest, whereby we take notice of bodies, and distinguish them one from another, are nothing else, but several powers in them, depending on those primary qualities, whereby they are fitted … to produce several different Ideas in us.

John Locke (1690; 1961 edn) Bk 2, viii, 26. A famous distinction between primary qualities, those of the shape, size and motion of the invisible particles, which were held by mechanical philosophers to constitute all bodies, and secondary qualities, such as colour, odour, taste and the like, which were merely the result of the actions of the particles on our senses.

GOD AND NATURE

3 But I do not feel obliged to believe that that same God who has endowed us with senses, reason and intellect has intended to forgo their use and by some other means to give us knowledge which we can attain by them.

Galileo Galilei 'Letter to the Grand Duchess Christina' (1615); Drake (1957) p.183. Seeking to defend Copernican theory against charges that it contradicts Scripture, Galileo tries to separate natural knowledge from knowledge based on authority.

4 I would say here something that was heard from an ecclesiastic of the most eminent degree: 'That the intention of the Holy Ghost is to teach us how one goes to heaven, not how heaven goes.'

Galileo Galilei, 1615; Drake (1957) p.186. Galileo says in a note that it was Cardinal Cesare Baronius (1538–1607), a leading church historian, who made this remark. Again, Galileo is trying to separate the teachings of science from the teachings of Scripture.

5 God forbid that we should give out a dream of our own imagination for a pattern of the world: rather may He graciously grant to us to write an *apocalypse* or true vision of the footsteps of the Creator imprinted on his creatures … Wherefore if we labour in thy works with the sweat of our brows thou wilt make us partakers of thy vision and thy Sabbath.

Francis Bacon *The Great Instauration* (1620) 'The Plan of the Work'; Spedding, Ellis and Heath (1887–1901 edn) Vol.4, p.33. Bacon's concern for the pragmatic value of scientific knowledge was not simply dictated by his concerns as a minister of state but also by his millenarian beliefs. He believed that scientific advance would usher in the ultimate Sabbath, the Day of Judgement.

6 *Eppur si muove!* (Yet it does move!)

Galileo Galilei, attrib., 1632; Stillman Drake *Galileo at Work* (1978) pp.356–7. Referring to the motion of the Earth and supposedly spoken as Galileo arose from his knees in the Inquisition, immediately after formally abjuring his belief in Copernican theory. There is no evidence for this and it is extremely unlikely. Even so, a painting by the Spanish painter Murillo, dated 1643 and depicting Galileo pointing to these words on the wall of his cell, shows that it is an early tradition.

7 As far as the general and first cause is concerned, it seems obvious to me that this is none other than God Himself, who, being all-powerful, in the beginning created matter with both movement and rest; and now maintains in the sum total of matter, by His normal participation, the same quantity of motion and rest as He placed in it at that time.

René Descartes (1644; 1983 edn) Pt 2, Sect.36, p.58. Descartes' natural philosophy, in which all is explained in terms of entirely inert particles of matter colliding to combine with or rebound from one another, would have been extremely austere if it were not for the fact that God was invoked as a supreme overseer.

8 The heart of a pismire is more magisterial than the Escurial, the proboscis of a flea more evident of industry in its construction than Roman Aqueducts or the Arsenal at Venice … the meanest piece of nature throws disparagement and contempt upon the greatest masterpiece of Art.

Walter Charleton *The Darkness of Atheism Dispelled by the Light of Nature* (1652) pp.66–7. An early statement by one of the first promoters of the mechanical philosophy in England of the argument for the existence of God based on the seeming design in the natural world. This argument was to become the basis of the major tradition of natural theology in Britain until after Darwin.

1 *Le silence éternel de ces espaces infinis m'effraie.* (The silence of these infinite spaces terrifies me.)

Blaise Pascal *Pensées* (1669) Sect.3, no.206. The French mathematician later rejected natural philosophy in favour of a fideistic religion. Heaven was usually held to be beyond the outermost sphere of the geocentric universe (the sphere of the fixed stars), but the Copernican world picture had stars scattered throughout an infinite space, leaving no place for God, the angels and the blessed.

2 There is incomparably more Art expressed in the structure of a Dog's foot, than in that of the famous Clock at Strasbourg.

Robert Boyle *Disquisition about the Final Causes of Natural Things* (1688); Hunter and Davis (2000) Vol.11, p.98. Another famous statement of the argument from design. The cathedral clock at Strasbourg was known for the ingenious complexity of its mechanical displays.

3 When I wrote my treatise about our System, I had an Eye upon such Principles as might work with considering men, for the belief of a Deity, & nothing can rejoice me more than to find it useful for that purpose.

Isaac Newton to Rev. Dr Richard Bentley, 10 Dec. 1692; Turnbull (1959–77) Vol.3, p.233. Bentley, an ambitious Anglican churchman, was appointed to deliver a series of lectures to combat atheism and chose to do so by developing a Newtonian version of the argument from design. He wrote to Newton for his approval and assistance, and this was Newton's reply.

4 To make this system therefore with all its motions, required a Cause which understood, & compared together, the quantities of matter in the several bodies of the Sun & Planets & the gravitating powers resulting from thence, the several distances ... from ... & the velocities with which these Planets could revolve ... about those quantities of matter in the central bodies. And to compare and adjust all these things together ... argues that cause to be not blind & fortuitous, but very well skilled in Mechanics & Geometry.

Isaac Newton to Rev. Dr Richard Bentley, 10 Dec. 1692; Turnbull (1959–77) Vol.3, p.235. A classic statement of the argument from design.

5 According to their doctrine, God Almighty wants to wind up his watch from time to time: otherwise it would cease to move ... Nay, the machine of God's making, is so imperfect, according to these gentlemen;

that he is obliged ... to mend it, as a clockmaker mends his work.

Gottfried Wilhelm Leibniz to Caroline, Princess of Wales, Nov. 1715; H.G. Alexander (ed.) *The Leibniz–Clarke Correspondence* (1956) p.11. The German mathematician was amazed by these aspects of Newton's theology, which he took to denigrate God's omnipotence.

6 The notion of the world's being a great machine, going on without the interposition of God, as a clock continues to go without the assistance of a clockmaker; is the notion of materialism and fate, and tends ... to exclude providence and God's government in reality out of the world.

Samuel Clarke to G.W. Leibniz (transmitted by Caroline, Princess of Wales), 26 Nov. 1715; Alexander (1956) p.14. An Anglican clergyman and Newton's friend and follower, Clarke reveals why Newton took the line that so outraged Leibniz. Newton believed that only a world in which God's intervention could be shown to be periodically required could thwart atheistic attempts to appropriate natural philosophy.

7 I do not know what I may seem to the world, but as to myself, I seem to have been only like a boy playing on the sea-shore and diverting myself in now and then finding a smoother pebble or a prettier shell than ordinary, whilst the great ocean of truth lay all undiscovered before me.

Isaac Newton to Andrew Michael Ramsay, 1727, attrib. by Joseph Spence in *Anecdotes, Observations and Characters, of Books and Men* (1820; 1966 edn) Sect.1259, Vol.1, p.462. Perhaps too poetic to be authentically Newton's words, but they surely illustrate Newton's feeling (manifested in the important 'Queries' at the end of his *Opticks*) that he raised more questions than he managed to answer.

INSTITUTIONS OF SCIENCE

8 Further, it will not be amiss to distinguish the three kinds and as it were grades of ambition in mankind. The first is of those who desire to extend their own power in their own native country, which kind is vulgar and degenerate. The second is of those who labour to extend the power of their country and its dominion among men. This certainly has more dignity, though not less covetousness. But if a man endeavour to establish and extend the power and domination of the human race itself over the universe, his ambition (if ambition it can be called) is without doubt both a more wholesome thing and more noble than the other two.

Francis Bacon *Novum Organum* (1620) Bk I, Aphorism 139; Spedding, Ellis and Heath (1887–1901 edn) Vol.4, p.114. A sentiment repeated often in Bacon's writings, suggesting that he was not simply motivated by his role as a minister of state.

1 A collection of history natural and experimental, such as I conceive it and as it ought to be, is a great, I may say a royal work, and of much labour and expense.

Francis Bacon *Novum Organum* (1620) Bk 1, Aphorism 111; Spedding, Ellis and Heath (1887–1901 edn) Vol.4, p.101. Bacon hoped to interest the crown in his schemes to reform natural philosophy and make it more pragmatically useful, but he never succeeded.

2 The End of our Foundation is the knowledge of Causes, and secret motions of things; and the enlarging of the bounds of Human Empire, to the effecting of all things possible.

Francis Bacon *New Atlantis* (1627); Spedding, Ellis and Heath (1887–1901 edn) Vol.3, p.156. A summary of the aims of Salomon's House, a scientific research institute imagined in detail by Bacon in his utopian *New Atlantis*.

3 The Rules YOU have prescrib'd YOUR selves in YOUR Philosophical Progress do seem the best that have ever yet been practised. And particularly that of avoiding Dogmatizing, and the espousal of any Hypothesis not sufficiently grounded and confirmed by Experiments. This way seems the most excellent, and may preserve both Philosophy and Natural History from its former Corruptions.

Robert Hooke (1665) Dedication to the Royal Society, sig.A2v. One of the leading natural philosophers in England praising the Royal Society, a scientific institution, founded in 1660 and granted its royal charter in 1662. It deliberately avoided the scholasticism of the universities.

4 As for what belongs to the Members themselves, that are to constitute the Society: It is to be noted that they have freely admitted Men of different Religions, Countries, and Professions of Life. This they were obliged to do, or else they would come far short of the largeness of their own Declarations. For they openly profess, not to lay the Foundation of an English, Scottish, Irish, Popish, or Protestant Philosophy; but a Philosophy of Mankind.

Thomas Sprat *The History of the Royal Society of London* (1667) Pt 2, Sect.6, p.63. Commissioned as a promising young writer, Sprat describes, in what is more a manifesto than a history, a scientific institution that claims to be free from ideological bias and to offer only objective knowledge.

GENDER AND SCIENCE

5 I am come in very truth leading to you Nature with all her children to bind her to your service and make her your slave.

Francis Bacon *Temporis Partus Masculus* (Masculine Birth of Time) (1603) Ch.1; Farrington (1964) p.62. Claimed by feminist writers as representative of early modern attitudes to nature which were aggressive, exploitative and, in a word, masculine.

6 Nature cannot be conquered but by obeying her.

Francis Bacon (1607); Farrington (1964) p.93. Arguably a more typical expression of Bacon's attitude to nature.

7 The careless neglects and despisements of the masculine sex to the effeminate, think … it impossible we should have either learning or understanding, wit or judgement, as if we had not rational souls as well as men. And we out of custom of dejectednesse think so too, which makes us quit all industry towards profitable knowledge.

Margaret Cavendish, Duchess of Newcastle *Philosophical and Physical Opinions* (1655) sig.B2v. A perceptive indication of the social difficulties encountered by women from one of the very few female natural philosophers of the period.

8 For though the Muses, Graces and Sciences are all of the female gender, yet they were more esteemed in former ages, than they are now; nay, could it be done handsomely, they would turn them all from Females into Males; so great is grown the self conceit of the Masculine, and the disregard of the Female Sex.

Margaret Cavendish, Duchess of Newcastle *Observations upon Experimental Philosophy* (1666) 2. An indication of the possible masculinization of the rhetoric of intellectual life.

9   Philosophy, I say, and call it, He,
        For whatsoe'r the Painter's Fancy be,
        It a Male Virtue seems to me.

Abraham Cowley 'To the Royal Society' St.1; Sprat (1667) sig.B. The apparent confirmation of Cavendish's observation by a leading Restoration poet who was inspired by the new philosophy.

The French Religious Wars, 1562–98

BEFORE THE WARS: COUNTRY AND FAITH

1 Heroism of action, heroism of creativity … The 16th century is a hero.

Jules Michelet *Histoire de France* (1833–67) Vol.7. The great 19th-century historian contrasts the Renaissance spirit with that of the 'bizarre, monstrous and prodigiously artificial period we call the Middle Ages'.

2 The vast majority of French people were able to put a name on every face they met. They met in church … at weddings and at *charivari*. A network of marriages, kinships, friendships and feuds enclosed these villages.

Jacques Dupâquier *La Population rurale du bassin parisien à l'époque de Louis XIV* (1979) p.204. In 1568 the Venetian ambassador estimated France's population to be 'around 15–16 million souls'. That is broadly accepted by historians. Any increase in the next 150 years would come mainly from the acquisition of new lands.

3 France is not a synchronized country: it is like a horse whose four legs move in different time.

Sanche de Gramont *Les Français* (1970) p.454. In the 16th century provinces such as Brittany and Languedoc were less like English shires than separate countries, such as Ireland or Scotland.

4 God will change the world and you will be there to witness it.

The humanist theologian and reformer Jacques Lefèvre d'Étaples to Guillaume Farel, 1512; A. Renaudot 'Paris from 1494 to 1517' in W.L. Gundersheimer (ed.) *French Humanism, 1479–1600* (1969) p.89. For Guillaume Farel see 360:3.

5 Sir, we are a nation given to tragedies.

Anon.; Alexandre de Tilly *Mémoires* (1801–16; 1965 edn) p.224. The comte de Tilly, former page of Marie-Antoinette, noted roué, now émigré, in nostalgic post-Revolution mood had good reason to remember this remark of an elderly courtier.

6 I hold it to be the principal cause of preservation of this monarchy that only with difficulty might they [subjects] come to dissension and discord.

Claude de Seyssel *La Grande Monarchie de France* (1541 edn) Vol.1, Ch.8. To the experienced jurist, writing from the relative security of the reign of Francis I, checks on royal power consisted of the obligation to obey the fundamental laws of the state, to submit to the legal obligation to respect the privileges of provinces, towns and social classes, and to give heed to *parlements*, the guardians of law.

7 When it is a question of the country, the citizen should take into account neither justice nor injustice, neither pity, cruelty, honour nor shame, but, leaving aside every preoccupation, should ensure that the country is saved, be it with honour or with shame.

Niccolò Machiavelli *Discourse on the First Ten Books of Titus Livy* (1515–19) Vol.2, Ch.41. Such precepts, reflecting Machiavelli's own experience of the foreign invasions of Italy, would have some appeal to the house of Valois in France. In bad times it may have seemed that what was necessary must be right, but they would be aware of the need to retain the goodwill and respect of the people – at least, of the more important people, the 'political nation'.

8 There are two main pillars upon which are based the security of the king's estate: the integrity of religion and the benevolence of the people. If they are strong it is not necessary to fear that obedience be lost.

Charles de Marillac, archbishop of Vienne, at the Council of Fontainebleau, 1560; Russell Major *From Renaissance Monarchy to Absolute Monarchy* (1994) pp.49–50.

9 I brought this state of mind to the administration of affairs, being of the opinion of the Ancients, that one's country is a second divinity, that laws come from God and that those who violate them are sacrilegious parricides.

Jacques-Auguste de Thou, *c.*1610; Marie-Madeleine Martin *The Making of France* (1948; 1951 trans.) p.140. Expressing the idealism and civic sense of the *parlementaire*, steeped in Roman law, the old chancellor recalls the patriotism that was part of his *parlementaire* youth.

10 The kings of France were so pleasing unto God that he chose them to become his lieutenants on earth.

André Duchêsne *Antiquités et recherches de la grandeur et de la majesté des rois de France* (1609); Martin (1948; 1951 trans.) p.170. It would need the chastening experience of civil war to prepare Frenchmen for the extension of this idea to that of the divine right of kings as a sanction for absolutism.

11 The developing theory and practice of the Valois monarchy in the first half of the 16th century had already made it an object of hostility and disillusion amongst important sectors of the French ruling class.

Quentin Skinner *Foundations of Modern Political Theory* (1976) Vol.1, p.255. Ostentatious display, building great *châteaux*, the practice of selling offices and royal ordinances applicable to the whole kingdom, supported by constitutional theories stressing royal power, all played a part.

1 The French king protecting Italian liberty is just like a highwayman protecting a pretty woman on the road from another robber. He defends her until he is ready to rob her.

Alfred de Musset *Lorenzaccio* (1834; 1978 edn) Act 5, Sc.4. Successive French kings pursued Italian claims. When the Treaty of Cateau-Cambrésis (1559) brought an end to the 1546–59 phase of Habsburg–Valois rivalry, noble warriors, accustomed to the challenges and rewards of Italy and without another calling, were all too ready to take up arms in civil war.

2 Whether *pays* [land] or *patrie* [homeland] was used, it was principally the idea of France that was making progress, the idea of the cohesion of a kingdom and a people ... having the same material and spiritual inheritance which became as real as a living person.

Marie-Madeleine Martin (1948; 1951 trans.) p.123. In the religious wars the tension between the idea of unity and the reality of local interests and family feuds was seen as tragic by some who held office; by others, however, it was regarded as something to exploit.

3 There is no such thing as French history; only European history.

Marc Bloch *The Historian's Craft* (1949; 1954 trans.) p.89. For Philip II of Spain and Elizabeth I of England France would be but one theatre among several in the European war (see 379:3). At stake were the survival of the United Provinces (the Netherlands, at war with Spain since the revolt of 1572; see 381:1) and the crowns of England and France. Theological issues transcended state borders. After 1589 both Spanish and English forces campaigned on French soil.

4 Early Protestantism in France was so wide and open that you could enter it without believing that you had left Catholicism.

H. Lemonnier 'Aux origines de la réforme Cévenole' in *Annales* no.39 (1984) p.242. The view helps to account for the wide spread of Protestantism during the reigns of Francis I and Henry II. In 1560 the Huguenot leader, Coligny, estimated that there were 2,150 Protestant churches and communities in the country. Numbers declined during the civil wars, then settled, by the end, at around 1.25 million. In 1598 there were 800 pastors serving 694 churches and the 257 chapels the nobles were allowed to retain.

5 I know that it is hard to leave the country of one's birth, especially for a woman of position and of advanced years like yourself ... But we must reject all thought of difficulties for a higher consideration: namely that we should prefer to our own country any part of the world where God is adored in purity ... and that we should desire no better rest for our old age than to dwell in His Church.

Protestant John Calvin to Mme de Cany, about to emigrate to Geneva, 1540; Martin (1948; 1951 trans.) p.135. In the same spirit, for younger Protestants, the duty was to stay, resist and, if necessary, fight. For Calvin see 360:1–360:4.

6 More than a thousand students have been marauding through Paris for a fortnight, wrecking orchards and vineyards, killing or wounding those who dared to oppose them.

The *avocât-général* (senior crown lawyer) testifies before *parlement*, Sept. 1554. A restless society was fertile ground for religious radicalism. Huguenotism was early identified (by its enemies) with tumult, armed revolt, 'vandalism, pillage and murder' and, in Paris, with students.

7 To maintain the Catholic religion and further it without tolerating any other.

The traditional coronation oath of the kings of France.

8 I swear that if I can settle my disputes abroad I will make the streets run with the blood and the heads of the vile Lutheran dogs.

Henry II at the Treaty of Cateau-Cambrésis, April 1559; Martin (1948; 1951 trans.) p.145. Even in 1559 the king's threat to Lutherans was an empty one. Calvinist heresy was becoming so widespread, entrenched and formalized that the crown would have to move from inquisition and coercion towards licensed co-existence.

9 I denounce the persecution of those whose only crime is the dauntlessness of their faith. They compare favourably with those who commit grave offences against religion and go unpunished.

Anne du Bourg, June 1559; J.H. Shennan *The Parlement of Paris* (1968) p.207. Du Bourg speaks in *parlement*, before Henry II, who has required magistrates to say how they would deal with heresy. One offence mentioned by this brave man was adultery, a reference that Henry chose to take personally. Du Bourg went to the Bastille and was executed.

10 Outwardly correct and well-regulated, his [Henry II's] court was the most elegant in Europe, the centre of refinement and good taste, of courtesy and knightly chivalry. But the elegance ... was little more than a veneer glossing over a turbulence which frequently burst out in fits of anger and acts of violence.

N.M. Sutherland *The French Secretaries of State in the Age of Catherine de Medici* (1962) p.53. Henry II's death in July 1559, after a wound received in the jousting held to celebrate the Treaty of Cateau-Cambrésis, altered the course of French history. It released uncontrollable tensions. Like England before the Wars of the Roses, France was bankrupt and divided. The heir to the throne was Francis II, a delicate boy of 15. In theory, Francis was of an age to rule; in practice, informal regency (to end with Francis's death in December 1560) lay with the duc de Guise, the uncle of Francis II's wife, Mary, and a celebrated soldier. After Francis's death the Guise faction could not be reconciled to its loss of power. Their pretensions were opposed by Montmorency and Antony of Navarre, nearest blood relation, and pushed forward by his ambitious brother, Louis, Prince de Condé.

1 It is sufficient to say that she [Henry II's wife, Catherine de' Medici] is a woman, and Florentine to boot, born of a simple house, altogether beneath the dignity of the kingdom of France.

A foreign ambassador, 1547; J.E. Neale *Catherine de Medici* (1943) p.103. This does seem to have been the attitude of the typical French nobleman. Yet she was charming and vivacious and was respected by those who served her for her bravery and understanding of the needs and methods of government. The early years of her marriage were a test of character. For seven years she had no children; she then had ten, before being left a young widow. Unsurprisingly, she proved to be a possessive mother.

2 The wisest philosophers have for long taught that it is impossible to avoid sedition in a kingdom if persons of worth see themselves rejected and lose hope of achieving the dignities they think they have merited by their birth and virtue.

Pomponne de Bellièvre, chancellor 1599–1607; J.H.M. Salmon *Society in Crisis: France in the Sixteenth Century* (1975) p.318. The favour shown to one individual – to Guise under Francis II or to Coligny under Charles IX – was bound to offend another. Each had the means and influence to raise armies.

3 Not only most noble but also possessed of the highest virtue together with extraordinary gentleness and humanity.

Giovanni Ricasoli, Florentine ambassador, lauds the cardinal of Lorraine, 1559; A. Desjardins *Négotiations diplomatiques de la France avec la Toscane* (1859–75) Vol.3, p.215. The cardinal was able, but he came to be feared and hated. In the partnership of brothers he was the politician, unscrupulous in pursuit of power. François of Guise was the man of action, an excellent soldier, inspiring devotion. He was held responsible for the massacre of a Huguenot congregation at Vassy (March 1562) and was himself assassinated in Feb. 1563.

4 Almost everyone was committed in advance, whether through fealty and patronage, religion, ambition, greed, passion or, more likely, a confusion of motives and an inability to resist the force of circumstances.

N.M. Sutherland (1962) p.109.

5 For all the bloody tragedies which have since been played on this pitiful French state, arose and proceeded from these first quarrels, and not from differences of religion, as simpletons and idiots have been made to believe.

Anon.; *Satire Menippée* (pamphlets, by several hands), 1593.

THE EARLY CIVIL WARS, 1562–72

6 After fifty years' service for the several kings my masters and latterly His Majesty's lieutenant in the provinces of Tuscany [garrisoned by the French after Francis I's invasion in 1525] and Guienne, and Marshal of France, finding myself maimed in almost all my limbs with arquebus shots, cuts and thrusts with pikes and swords ... without strength even to be cured of that great arquebus shot in my face ... I thought fit to employ the remains of my life in a description of the several combats that I had the honour to command.

Blaise de Monluc *Commentaires* (1592; 1971 trans.) p.31. The veteran's account was boastful and callous, but it offers a valuable picture of 16th-century warfare and the religious wars in particular.

7 I called for a pair of breeches of crimson velvet which I had brought from Alba, laid over with gold lace ... I put on a doublet of the same under which I had a shirt finely wrought with crimson silk and gold twist. I took a buff collar, over which I put on the gorget of my arms. I wore grey at that time in honour of a fair lady ... I therefore put on a hat of grey silk of the German fashion with a grand silver hatband and a plume of heron's feathers, thick set with silver spangles.

Blaise de Monluc (1592; 1971 trans.) pp.149–50. The marshal recalls cutting a dash in Siena, where he was deputy governor and garrison commander, after the city's revolt against imperialist rule in 1554. Famous for his stout defence, he returned to France a hero.

8 Nobody knows how to fight but the *noblesse* ... Our nation cannot suffer long ... yet it is not the fault in the air of France or in the nature of the people, but in the leader.

Blaise de Monluc (1592; 1971 trans.) p.80. Are noble virtues, courage and *élan* offset by a casual approach to command, reluctance to train and indifference to the welfare of ordinary soldiers?

1 The mentality of the old nobility scorned these [parvenu] virtues, strict economy and precise administration of seigneuries but preferred to dwell on their birth, their alliances, their privileges and their horses.

P. Goubert *Beauvais et le Beauvaisis de 1600 à 1730* (1960) p.220. An alternative route to betterment was barred since *dérogeance* (loss of noble status) followed participation in trade or manufactures.

2 Their [his sons'] desire is rather to gain goods and honours, and in the winning of them to hazard their persons, and even to serve the Turk rather than remain idle. If they did otherwise I should not look on them as mine.

Blaise de Monluc (1592; 1971 trans.) p.21.

3 Monsieur my brother, I do not know how to tell you of the pleasure that it is for me to hear your news and I am very sorry that you have been wounded by a pike ... You ask me to return the gloves that you have lost, but I have not seen them. I thank you for the ring you sent me ... You will see that I have sent you an ensign which I hope you will carry ... I beg you to believe that everything I have in the world is yours.

Edmée d'Anjou to her brother, Nicolas, fighting in Italy, probably 1557; K.B. Neuschel 'Noblewomen and War' in E. Wolfe (ed.) *Changing Identities in Early Modern France* (1996) p.130. Unless they are in positions of power, women tend to be invisible to historians of early modern Europe. How much did noble warriors depend on the approval and urging of their womenfolk?

4 So wicked and disastrous that the thought of them [Amboise conspirators] terrifies me. It is something unheard of in this kingdom ... God grant that this fire may not spread for it is highly dangerous and of great consequence in this kingdom, which begins to be strongly tainted by the [new] religion.

Claude de Laubespine, seigneur de Chateauneuf, to Anne, 1st duc de Montmorency, March 1560; Sutherland (1962) p.103. The plan, which was backed by many Huguenots but which miscarried, was to seize Francis II at Amboise in March 1560 and free him from Guise control.

5 They were all vagabonds, thieves and murderers ... These slaughtermen were the flotsam of war, riddled with the pox and fit for the gibbet. Dying of hunger, they took to roads and fields to pillage, assault and ruin the people of the towns and villages, who fell into their clutches in the places where they lodged.

Claude Haton *Mémoires* (1578; 1857 edn). A soldier-priest of Brie, Haton is a reliable witness to *les misères de guerre*. Between 1560 and 1598 some 130 separate engagements, with 13 major battles, have been recorded. Yet villagers would note less the formal end of one of the nine wars and start of another and more the recurring menace of local brigands. Haton's account explains the yearning for strong rule, which Henry IV would exploit.

6 We are kings now. That man [Charles IX] is a little lump of shit.

Anon.; Monluc (1592; 1971 trans.) p.207. The peasants of Saint-Mézard (Gascony) were up in arms in 1562, and Monluc quelled their rising with some hangings. Charles IX (r.1560–74) was the second son of Henry II and Catherine de' Medici.

7 Each one then stood firm, thinking in his heart that the men he saw coming towards him were not Spanish, English or Italian, but Frenchmen, and of the bravest, among whom were some of his own companions, kinsmen or friends; which gave some horror to the deed but did not diminish the courage.

François de la Noue, describing the Battle of Dreux, Dec. 1562; Fernand Braudel *The Identity of France* (1986; 1988 trans.) p.122. The familiar tale of civil wars: divided families and loyalties (here between Catholics and Huguenots) and the courage of conviction – or desperation. At the end of his life, doughty Huguenot captain, de la Noue, would come to argue for the conversion of his leader, Henry of Navarre (who became Henry IV in 1589).

8 It is sweet to incur danger for God and one's country.

The motto of Louis de Bourbon, Prince of Condé; Martin (1948; 1951 trans.) p.139. Condé was murdered after the Battle of Jarnac in March 1569. The duc de Guise had been assassinated in 1563 (an act of Huguenot revenge for the massacre of Vassy), and it is surprising that Condé should have lasted so long.

9 This morning we created thirty-two knights of the Order [St Michael] because there was nothing else to give them.

Catherine de' Medici, 1563; Major (1994) p.109. The order, founded by Louis XI, was of potential value to the crown in attracting nobles to royal service. The story of the last Valois reigns is of the progressive devaluation of honours and the power of patronage, along with the waste of the crown's material resources.

10 I was told that they [the Huguenots] imposed taxes upon the people, made captains and listed soldiers, keeping their assemblies in the houses of several lords ... of this new religion ... I met also with the strange names of elders, deacons, consistories, synods and colloquies, having never before breakfasted on such viands.

Blaise de Monluc (1592; 1971 trans.) p.200. As *gentilhomme*, Monluc was concerned about the threat to property; as royal commander in Guienne (Bordeaux area in southwestern France), he was affronted by the Huguenot claim that they had the right to enlist troops.

1 We fought the first war like angels, the second like men, and the third like devils.

Anon. Huguenot leader on the Third Religious War (1568–70); Neale (1943) p.71.

ST BARTHOLOMEW'S EVE, 1572

2 What more could a poor woman with a handful of children do?

Henry IV, Aug. 1572; Neale (1943) p.102. Apparently posed apropos the St Bartholomew's massacre (1572), the question remains easier to ask than to answer. On St Bartholomew's Eve, 23 Aug., Charles IX sanctioned the execution of Huguenot leaders, but what Catherine de' Medici had intended to be a selective cull became a bloodbath. It was too great a task for the Guise and royal guards to accomplish on their own. The city militia was brought out, and others joined in the hunt, with consequences that appalled the king but for which Catherine would take credit in her correspondence with Catholic rulers. At least 3,000 people were killed in Paris and 10,000 in other parts of France.

3 Of such value and prudence and of such service, glory and honour to God and universal benefit to all Christendom that to hear of it [the massacre] was for me the best and most cheerful news which could come to me.

Philip II of Spain, Aug. 1572; Neale (1943) p.80.

4 I was awakened about three hours after midnight by the sound of all the bells and the confused cries of the populace. Upon entering the street I was seized with horror at the sight of the furies, who rushed from all parts, and burst open the house, bawling out, 'Slaughter, slaughter, massacre the Huguenots' … I would, if it were possible, bury for ever the memory of a day for which the divine vengeance punished France by six and twenty years of disasters, carnage and horror.

Maximilien de Béthune, duc de Sully, Aug. 1572; *Mémoires* (1812 trans.) Vol.1, p.31. The young Huguenot Béthune, later Henry IV's superintendent of royal finances, escaped, wearing a scholar's gown and with a Catholic breviary under his arm, to the Collège de Bourgogne, where he lay hidden for two days. His two tutors were killed.

5 With this 'catechism' our king has converted more souls to Christ than all the preachers and catechists together in the past twenty years.

Anon. Jesuit, Aug. 1572; A.L. Martin, 'Jesuits and the Massacre of St Bartholomew's Day' in *Archivum Historicum Societatis Jesu* 43 (1974) p.113.

6 It is more a divine thing than a human one.

Ortiz de Valderram, Catholic priest, Aug. 1572; P. Benedict *Rouen during the Wars of Religion* (1981) p.131. Around 500 Huguenots were killed in Rouen. Following the loss of so many leaders, some Huguenots were also inclined to accept that misfortune could be a divine message. While the Huguenot position in the south and southwest was consolidated, Protestantism virtually disappeared from eastern France.

HENRY III, 1574–89:
THE LAST OF THE VALOIS

7 A young fool with little experience of affairs.

Nicholas de Neufville, seigneur de Villeroy, 1568; Sutherland (1962) p.165. The then duc d'Anjou (the future Henry III) would preside over the disintegration of the country. He did not, however, lack ability, as Villeroy (who was secretary of state for 21 years) would soon realize. Even a steadier personality might have found it impossible to prevent the drift to anarchy.

8 The times we live in engender nothing but monsters.

Nicholas de Neufville, seigneur de Villeroy, Feb. 1584; E. Cabié *Guerres de religion dans le Sud-ouest de la France* (1906) p.343.

9 Everyone has conspired to ruin her [France] … There are judgements of God that no man can either comprehend or evade.

Nicholas de Neufville, seigneur de Villeroy, 29 Aug. 1585; Bibliothèque nationale MSS Fr.16092, f.411.

10 The Leaguers ask for everything
The king gives them everything
The Guisard [Guise family] deprives him of
    everything
The soldier ravages everything
The poor people bear everything
The queen mother arranges everything
The chancellor seals everything
The *parlement* approves everything
The duc d'Épernon spoils everything
Religion covers everything
The Pope pardons everything
And the devil in the end will take the lot.

Popular doggerel, Dec. 1586; P. L'Estoile *Journal du règne d'Henri III* (1574–89; 1943 edn) p.478.

1 The king [Henry III at Lyons] goes every night to balls and does nothing but dance. During four whole days he was dressed in mulberry satin with stockings, doublet and hose to match. The cloak was very much slashed in the body and had all its folds set with buttons and adorned with ribbons, white and scarlet and mulberry, and he wore bracelets of coral on his arm.

P. L'Estoile (1574–89; 1943 edn) July 1576, p.122.

2 Their heads sat on their ruffs like the head of John the Baptist on a platter.

P. L'Estoile (1574–89; 1943 edn); Neale (1943) p.89. Henry III enjoyed the company of *mignons* (young men), but there was a serious political purpose behind the lavish patronage: he needed devoted, reliable men around him.

3 Never do bad subjects lack a pretext to take up arms against their rulers; and equally, never do rulers lack right on their side in their dealings with such subjects. God, who created kings, God who has placed them above peoples, takes their cause in His hand, and is Himself wounded through insults to their persons.

Rémonstrances à la France sur la protestation des chefs de la Ligue faite à l'an 1585: mémoires de messire Philippe de Mornay (1624) p.431. The Holy League was formed in 1584, after the death of Henry III's younger brother and heir, Alençon. Tied to Spain by secret treaty and subsidy, its objects were the extirpation of heresy in the Netherlands and France and the exclusion of Henry of Navarre (later Henry IV) from the throne.

4 The artisan dropped his tools; the merchant left his counting house, the university its books, the *procureurs* their briefs, the *avocats* their bonnets; and the very *présidents* and judges themselves took hold of halberds. One heard nothing but fearful shouts, murmurs and seditious words to excite and alarm the people.

P. L'Estoile (1574–89; 1943 edn) p.552. The Day of the Barricades, 12 May 1588, saw the king lose control of his capital and the open ascendancy of the Guise family and the Holy League. Henry III was now king in name only, his nervous suspicion bordering on paranoia.

5 You can cut but you cannot sew.

Catherine de' Medici on hearing of Henry III's coup at Blois. Attrib. but apocryphal.

6 Monsieur Duplessis, the ice is broken, but not without a number of warnings that, if I went to meet him [Henry III] I should be dead … The people shouted *Vivent les rois*. Send up my baggage. Advance the troops.

Henry IV; *Lettres intimes d'Henri IV* (1876) p.116. In April 1589 Henry of Navarre joined Henry III. The other 'king' had been Henry of Guise, assassinated the previous year. Henry III was himself assassinated in Aug. 1589.

7 Provided he undertakes this act not from any motive of private or public vengeance but solely from his zeal for God's honour and for his religion, for his country's welfare and general peace, he need have no fear of doing violence to his conscience. He will on the contrary earn great merit and God will take pleasure in the deed.

A Dominican friar to Jacques Clément June 1989; R. Mousnier *The Assassination of Henry IV* (1964; 1973 trans.) p.214. Clément, a zealous Jacobin monk, was seeking advice on how to counsel a penitent. He went on to assassinate Henry III himself (Aug. 1589). The doctrine of lawful tyrannicide was widely taught on both sides of the religious divide, on the Catholic side, most notoriously, by John Mariana in *De Rege et Regis Institutio* (Concerning Kings and Kingship) (1598). The book ran to several editions and was used by the Jesuits.

8 Jacques Clément was regarded by many compatriots as one of the everlasting glories of France. He was God's instrument sustained and fortified physically and mentally by a strength superior to his own.

John Mariana (1598) Bk 1, Ch.6.

HENRY IV, 1589–1610, AND THE END OF CIVIL WAR, 1598

9 Vested in red soutane, with a cuirass over it and a hat of the same colour with long ribbons. He had in his hand a cup of blood from which he seemed to want to drink and from his mouth came a scroll bearing these words: keep your helmet on, polish your lances and put on your breastplates.

Pierre Pithou *Satire Menippée: 'Harangue de M. d'Aubray'* (1593). This portrait of the cardinal de Guise captures the fanatical spirit of the 1590s – and the *politiques'* revulsion from it. They argued for the interest of the state against that of religious party. The satire was written by various hands, of whom one is identifiable as the jurist and historian Pithou.

10 Kill, massacre and boldly burn everything. The papal legate will forgive all … I will be father confessor to you and to France as well if she is wise enough to die as a good Catholic and to make the Lorrainers and the Spaniards her heirs.

Pierre Pithou (1593). Typical *politique* satire makes effective propaganda.

1 The *plat pays* has been completely ruined by a vast horde of bandits. The poor farmers … have been reduced to famine. Their wives and daughters have been raped and their livestock stolen. They have had to leave their lands untilled … while great numbers languish in prison for failure to meet the enormous *tailles* [direct taxes] and subsidies both parties have levied upon them.
Circular distributed in Périgord, March 1594: Salmon (1975) p.284. Faced with disturbances like this peasant revolt in southwestern France, the propertied classes would eventually put aside their factional interests and struggles to acknowledge Henry IV.

2 The king's [Henry IV's] cause is more just than the League's, I am better than you [Villars] and my mistress [Queen Elizabeth] is more beautiful.
Robert Devereux, Earl of Essex, Nov. 1591; G. Valdory *Discours du siège de la ville de Rouen in 1591* (1871) p.16. Essex besieged the city but failed. Rouen was under the control of the League until March 1594.

3 Neighbouring nations would be in happier case when France should be subject, not to one sceptre but to twenty petty kings.
Elizabeth I, 1592; W. Camden *The History of the Most Renowned and Victorious Princess, Elizabeth, Late Queen of England* (1688) p.444. Should she then join with Spain – or at least withhold support for Henry IV? She did neither – but was surely tempted, at a time when England had the chance, seemingly, of recovering its ancient rights in France.

4 It was reported that he was a man of no beliefs, who laughed at his Huguenot ministers even when they were in the pulpit, and had been known to bombard them with cherry stones even as they preached.
Ambassador M.N. Tommase (ed.) *Relations des ambassadeurs vénetiens sur les affaires de France* Vol.2 (1838) p.637. It was easy to question Henry IV's sincerity. Having sought and been granted papal absolution from his earlier errors in 1572, Henry had afterwards reverted to Calvinist doctrines.

5 For no kingdom would I exchange the religion which I have, so to speak, drunk with my mother's milk … except for that which will be proposed to me by an ecclesiastical council.
Henry IV, Aug. 1589; Jacques-Auguste de Thou *Histoire universelle depuis 1543 jusqu'en 1607* Vol.9 (1734) p.13. The king is looking at the possibility of a conversion that will look sincere, not motivated solely by political considerations, no matter how pressing.

6 Never … did any city equal the heroism of Paris in 1590. All the inhabitants took up arms, all wished to be soldiers. The suffering endured defies all description … At the most modest reckoning 30,000 died of famine.
A. Franklin (ed.) *Journal du siège de Paris en 1590* (1876) Introduction. The resistance of Paris under the radical rule of the *Seize* (the governing council) to the besieging royal army was a harsh lesson to Henry IV: to win his capital he must win its Catholic heart.

7 Munching meat and drinking wine he [Henry IV] would discuss affairs of state amidst a babble of *primero*-playing soldiers, or greet early morning visitors all untrussed and what he had been doing God knoweth.
T. Coningsby *Journal of the Siege of Rouen* (1591; 1847 edn) p.45. Henry's casual manners were to become part of the legend: novel – but it worked. It served to stress the majesty of kingship, the institution, through the palpable humanity of the king, the person.

8 Either live continuously in the saddle, helmet on head and pistol in hand … or take the other way, to accommodate yourself, in your religion, to the desire of the greatest number of your subjects; you would not then have so many enemies and troubles.
Maximilien de Béthune, duc de Sully, 1593; Martin (1948; 1951 trans.) p.138. Characteristic advice to Henry IV from the man who was to be his chief minister.

9 What prevents us from driving out these unwelcome guests, these pitiful fellows, insolent animals who devour our substance and our goods like grasshoppers? … Come Sir Legate, return to Rome … Come agents and ambassadors of Spain, we are tired of killing each other in order to afford you pleasure.
Pierre Pithou (1593) expresses the yearning for peace.

10 Wife, let us live in the old fashion.
Michel de Montaigne, 1592; Martin (1948; 1951 trans.) p.137. The philosopher and moralist announces his separation from the Huguenot cause.

11 Paris is worth a mass.
Henry IV, attrib.; also attrib. to the duc de Sully in conversation with Henry. Does it represent the spirit of Henry IV's decision to convert? He attended mass at Saint-Denis in July 1593. Leaguers were not convinced – and fought on.

12 I call on you Frenchmen. I espouse no man's passions … I am not blind. I wish members of the Faith to live in peace in my kingdom … We are all French and fellow-citizens of the same country.
Henry IV, Aug. 1593; Martin (1948; 1951 trans.) p.145. The appeal followed his conversion.

1 If I had not been born to inherit the crown I would have been a yokel myself.
Henry IV, after the 1594 rising; L'Estoile (1574–89; 1943 edn) p.420.

2 Sire, as by God's will I was born a true *François* ... when in the dead season of my autumn I saw her [France] ... in extreme affliction imploring the help of her children, in my compassion for her plight I could do no less than offer her all the help that every well-born child naturally owes to her mother.
Gérard François *De la maladie du grand corps de la France* (1595). Henry IV's doctor offers a loyal pun.

3 You see me here in my study ... not in royal attire, like my predecessors, nor with cloak and sword, nor as a prince who has come to speak with foreign ambassadors, but dressed like the father of a family, in a doublet, to speak freely to his children. ... but [later in *parlement*] I shall nip in the bud all factions and all attempts at seditious preaching. I have leapt onto the walls of towns; surely I can leap over barricades which are not so high.
Henry IV, Jan. 1599; L'Estoile (1574–89; 1943 edn) pp.364–5. After an informal meeting, Henry addresses *parlement* and requests the registration of the Edict of Nantes (1598). It ended the civil war.

4 It is high time that all of us, drunk with war, sobered up.
Henry IV to deputies from Toulouse, Nov. 1599; D. Buisseret *Henry IV* (1968) p.73.

5 People like you are all scoundrels. I do not mind if a hundred have hanged themselves.
Henry IV, 1610; Mousnier (1964; 1973 trans.) p.198. The king harshly rebuffs a petitioner, brother of a woman who has hanged herself and six young children, after being made destitute by the *taille* and forced to sell her cow.

6 The king does not care to deal justly with us but I feel certain that God in heaven will soon do so, and very soon.
The petitioner replies, 1610; Mousnier (1964; 1973 trans.) p.199. Henry IV was murdered the next day, 13 May 1610, by François Ravaillac.

7 His carriage had been forced to stop because the street is much hemmed in by shops which have been built against the wall of the cemetery of the Holy Innocents.
P. de l'Estoile *Registraux-journaux* Vol.1 (1878) p.578. This was the scene of Henry IV's assassination, where Henry II had ordered the shops' demolition in 1554.

8 The knife was merely Ravaillac's instrument but Ravaillac was the tool of others who drove him to this crime, placing the weapon in his hand and the idea of parricide in his mind ... The guilt lies solely with the Jesuits and their disciples.
R. Mousnier (1964; 1973 trans.) p.24.

9 What we saw at court beggars description. The whole court shocked and stunned with grief, stood silent and motionless as statues, sighing deeply from time to time.
Rélation Gillot Vol.30; Bibliothèque Nationale MS Dupuy 90. The dawn of another royal minority, another uncertain age. Louis XIII, eldest son of Henry IV and Marie de' Medici, was nine years old.

10 France is gifted not so much for battle as for civil war.
Marco Ferro *La Grande Guerre 1914–18* (1969) p.24. Writing about 'the first long and truly patriotic war', a French historian finds elements of civil war in previous conflicts: none was more ferocious and embittered than the sequence of civil wars from 1562 to 1598.

The Rise of the Dutch Republic, 1567–1795

THE DUTCH REVOLT, 1567–1609

1 In order to prevent the ruin and desolation of these lands, which are being assaulted by the Spaniards, whose steady purpose it is only to bring them and hold them in intolerable slavery, sorrow, and misery under their government, despite the contracts, leagues and privileges which they violate every day, upon which the prosperity of this country is wholly dependent and which His Majesty has affirmed, confirmed and sworn by solemn oath.

William I of Orange, commission to Louis of Nassau, 1568; Herbert H. Rowen (ed.) *The Low Countries in Early Modern Times* (1972) p.38. Acting as a sovereign prince, William authorizes his brother to take military action against the Spanish in the Netherlands (roughly modern Belgium and the Netherlands, at the time ruled by Philip II of Spain), marking the effective start of the Eighty Years War for independence between the Dutch and Spain.

2 Having decided to find my grave there [Holland].

William I of Orange on departing for Holland, autumn 1572; J.I. Israel *The Dutch Republic: Its Rise, Greatness and Fall, 1477–1806* (1995) p.178. At this point the revolt had been defeated in the south of the Netherlands, and William departed for Holland with every reason to believe that the same fate awaited the north. In the event, the revolt here held out to become the core of a new state – the Dutch Republic.

3 If he [Requesens] were to die at this juncture it would be the ruin and confusion of the country: for everyone would want to be master, and the Estates would control the government and many evil-minded people would rush in to create a mess.

Maximilien Morillon, vicar-general of the archbishopric of Mechelen, to Cardinal Granvelle, 18 Dec. 1575; E. Poulet and C. Piot (eds) *Correspondance de Cardinal Granvelle* (1878–96) Vol.5, p.436. Don Luis de Requesens was Philip II of Spain's governor-general of the Netherlands, and when he did indeed die in the following year serious mutinies broke out in the Spanish army of Flanders, and the Spanish position in the region was so weakened that the rebels of Holland and Zeeland (southwestern Holland) were able to unite with the rest of the Netherlands in the Pacification of Ghent (Nov. 1576).

4 Orange is the pilot who steers the ship of state and on whom it depends whether it sinks or reaches a safe haven.

Don Juan of Austria to Philip II, 16 March 1677; K.W. Swart *Willem van Oranje en de Nederlandse Opstand, 1572–1584* (William of Orange and the Revolt of the Netherlands) (1994)

p.107. The importance of William I of Orange to the revolt as seen by Philip II's governor-general in the Netherlands.

5 Firstly, the aforesaid provinces will form an alliance, confederation and union among themselves, as they do hereby form an alliance, confederation and union, in order to remain joined together for all time, in every form and manner, as if they constituted only a single province, and they may not hereafter divide or permit their division or separation by testament, codicils, donations, cessions, exchanges, sales, treaties of peace or marriage, or for any other reason whatsoever.

Union of Utrecht, 1579; Rowen (1972) p.70. The Union of Utrecht was more an alliance between the northern provinces of the Netherlands for the better prosecution of the war with Spain than the constitution of a new state, but it was the only founding document the Dutch Republic ever had, and its contents were subsequently interpreted as constitutional provisions.

6 Let him be a king in Castile, in Aragon, at Naples, amongst the Indians, and in every place where he commandeth at his pleasure: yea let him be a king if he will, in Jerusalem, and a peaceable governor in Asia and Africa, yet for all that I will not acknowledge him in this country, for any more than a duke and a count, whose power is limited according to our privileges, which he swore to observe, at his gladsome entrance.

William I of Orange *Apology* (1581); Martin Van Gelderen 'From Domingo de Soto to Hugo Grotius' in Graham Darby (ed.) *The Origins and Development of the Dutch Revolt* (2001) p.154. This is an assertion of the core doctrine of the political justification of the revolt against Philip II, namely that it was the king not the rebels who had violated the ancient constitution.

7 But we may still in truth say that the state of Holland and Zeeland was never conquered by the sword or brought into subjugation as a result of foreign or domestic wars during the period of eight hundred years; we do not know if this can be said now of any other country, except perhaps the Republic of Venice. No other reason can be given for this except that there was always good union, love and understanding between the princes and the States of this country, because the princes (who possessed no power in their own right) could do nothing whatever without the nobles and cities of the country.

François Vranck *Korte verthooninghe* (Brief Illustration) (1587); Rowen (1972) p.107. Vranck's work was a classic assertion of the political rights of provincial states, nobles and towns against the central government, published during the Earl of Leicester's period as governor-general (after the alliance between the Dutch and England in 1585) when he came into conflict with the States of Holland. Leicester lost the struggle and returned to England.

1 This siege [of the port of Ostend] was like an academy, or university for all sorts of soldiers, as well as officers and engineers.

H. Hondius, 1624; Frans Westra *Nederlandse ingenieurs en de fortificatiewerken in het eerste tijdperk van de Tachtigjarige Oorlog, 1573–1604* (Dutch Engineers and Fortifications in the First Period of the Eighty Years War) (1992) p.71. The siege of Ostend (Belgium) lasted from 1601 to 1604, becoming a showcase for the best military and engineering techniques of the time, before the town finally fell to the Spanish.

2 According to the judgement of all knowledgeable people it is considered certain that the war in this land will neither cease nor be ended as long as the king of Spain remains peaceably in possession of the kingdom of Portugal and that kingdom's East Indian dependencies; and of the West Indies, which have made him powerful and rich such that he can afford to continue the war here in the Netherlands.

Anon. pamphlet (early 17th century); Benjamin Schmidt *Innocence Abroad: The Dutch Imagination and the New World, 1570–1670* (2001) p.172. Spain's colonies were regarded as the root of Spanish wealth and power. Silver from Spanish America in particular was seen as the fuel of the Spanish military effort. So the Dutch East and West India Companies (especially the latter) were seen as having a vital role to play in the struggle against Spain (see 401:3).

3 His Excellency [Maurice] represented to the States the opposition, arising out of his concern for the condition of the country, which he had always maintained against entering into these negotiations, because in these the sole intention of the enemy is to deceive us.

Count Maurice of Nassau, addressing the assembly of the States-General, Oct. 1607; H.H.P. Rijperman (ed.) *Resolutiën der Staten-Generaal, 1576–1609* Deel 14 (1607–9) (1970) p.85. Maurice (son of William I of Orange) was governor (*stadhouder*) of a number of provinces and commander of the Dutch army. He was a fierce opponent of the peace negotiations with Spain, which were taking place at that time, and of the Twelve Years Truce (1609), which was their outcome.

4 The success of the business doth depend upon the resolution of Holland, the gentry of which province

doth profess for the truce, and of the 18 which have voice all declare themselves (in favour) except Amsterdam and Delft which yet make difficulty by reason that administration of the India company do fear the freedom of commerce into Spain which as a consequent of this truce, will in short time divert all the merchants and mariners from that tedious and dangerous navigation.

Sir Ralph Winwood and Sir Richard Spencer to Sir Robert Cecil, chief minister of King James I of England, 17 Nov. 1608; J.I. Israel *The Dutch Republic and the Hispanic World 1606–1661* (1982) p.40. The 'business' is the peace negotiations with Spain. The Dutch East India Company, founded in 1602, had been granted a monopoly by the States General on trade with the East. For Winwood see 336:9.

5 [The Battle of Nieuwpoort was very risky] for not only was the life of his Excellency [Maurice of Nassau], his lordship his brother, all the chiefs, their lordships, the States and the whole army in the utmost danger: but the fate of the whole country and the church of God in these lands consequently was hanging on a silk thread.

Johannes Uyttenbogaert, court preacher to Maurice, 1600; Leen Dorsman *1600: Slag bij Nieuwpoort* (2000) p.68. This was one of the very few major battles fought during the Eighty Years War, which was mainly a war of sieges. Dutch victory averted disaster, but brought them little or no advantage.

6 His final immutable resolution, 'Only to do this service so pleasant to Our Lord will I consent to cede the sovereignty of the said provinces [the Netherlands] that belong to me ... so that the inhabitants and subjects might enjoy it and be free – if they would concede [to the public practice of the Catholic religion].'

Philip III to Albert, archduke of Austria, 31 Oct. 1608; Antonio Rodriguez Villa *Ambrosio Spinola* (1905) pp.230–31. Archduke Albert was the nominal ruler of the Spanish Netherlands (1598–1621), but his policy with regard to the war with the North was effectively still controlled by Spain. The Dutch refused to give way on the issue of Catholic worship and the Treaty of Antwerp (1609) consequently brought a truce for 12 years rather than a final peace between the Dutch and Spain, with Philip III refusing to give full recognition to Dutch independence.

THE DUTCH REPUBLIC, 1609–1795

7 It cannot properly be styled a Commonwealth, but is rather a Confederacy of Seven Sovereign Provinces united together for their common and mutual defence, without any dependence one upon the other.

Sir William Temple *Works* (1673; 1972 edn) Vol.1, p.52. A well-informed English statesman's comment on the Dutch system of government.

1 Scarce any subject occurs more frequent in the discourses of ingenious men than that of the marvellous progress of this little state which, in the space of about a hundred years ... hath grown to a height, not only infinitely transcending all the ancient republics of Greece, but not much inferior in some respects even to the greatest monarchies of these latter ages.

William Aglionby *The Present State of the United Provinces of the Low Countries* (1669) p.A4.

2 For since they have cast off the yoke of Spanish slavery, how wonderfully are they improved in all humane policy? What great means have they obtained to defend their liberty against the power of so great an Enemy? And is not all this performed by their continual industry in the trade of Merchandise? Are not their Provinces the Magazines and Store-houses of wares for most places of Christendom, whereby their Wealth, Shipping, Mariners, Arts, People, and thereby the publique Revenues and Excizes are grown to a wonderful height?

Thomas Mun *England's Treasure by Forraign Trade* (1664) pp.73–4.

3 Holland is a country where the demon gold is seated on a throne of cheese, and crowned with tobacco.

Claude de Saumaise (Claudius Salmasius); Simon Schama *The Embarrassment of Riches* (1987) p.188. The author was a French Protestant exile teaching at the university of Leiden and author of a controversial work on the legitimacy of usury (see 182:1).

4 So as Prince Henry [Frederick Henry] was used to answer some that would have flattered him into the designs of a more arbitrary power, that he had as much as any wise Prince would desire in this State; since he had all indeed, besides that of Punishing men. And raising Money; whereas he had rather the envy of the first should lye upon the Forms of the Government; and he knew the other could never be supported without the consent of the people.

Sir William Temple (1673; 1972 edn) p.73. Frederick Henry, as *stadhouder* and captain-general of the army, was the effective political leader of the Republic from 1624 to 1647, but he was not formally the ruler of the country.

5 That the Lords States-General of the United Provinces, and the respective Provinces thereof, with all their associated Territories, Towns and dependent Lands, are free and sovereign States, Provinces and Lands, unto which, as unto their aforesaid associated Territories, Towns and Lands, he the Lord King makes no pretension, nor shall his heirs and successors for themselves, either now or hereafter, evermore make any pretension thereunto.

Treaty of Münster, article 1, 1648; P. Geyl *The Netherlands in the Seventeenth Century* (1961) Pt 1, p.155. The formal recognition by Spain of Dutch independence.

6   The prince deceased,
     My gift's increased,
     No news pleased more,
     In years four score.

Anon.; Charles Wilson *Profit and Power: A Study of England and the Dutch Wars* (1957) p.49. A verse said to have been placed, evidently by a republican opponent of the prince, in the collection box of an Amsterdam church after the death of the *stadhouder*, William II of Orange, in Nov. 1650. Earlier in the same year the prince had attempted a coup by arresting six leading regents of Holland and sending troops to capture Amsterdam. This attack failed, and a dangerous political deadlock between William and Holland was resolved only by his death.

7 A man of unwearied Industry, inflexible Constance, sound, clear and deep Understanding, and untainted Integrity; so that whenever he was blinded, it was by the passion he had for that which he esteemed the good and interest of his State.

Sir William Temple (1673; 1972 edn) p.95. Praise for Johan de Witt from the former English ambassador to the Republic.

8 For the Pensioner De Witt, who had the great influence in the Government, the whole train and expense of his Domestic went very equal with other common Deputies or Ministers of the State; His Habit grave, and plain, and popular; His Table what only serv'd turn for his Family, or a Friend; His Train (besides Commissaries and Clerks kept for him in an Office adjoining to his House, at the public charge) was only one man, who performed all the Menial service of his house at home; ... He was seen usually in the streets on foot and alone, like the commonest Burger of the Town.

Sir William Temple (1673; 1972 edn) p.71.

9 He replied that he liked better the condition of Stadhouder which they had given him and that he

believed himself obliged in conscience and honour not to prefer his interest before his obligation.
William III of Orange to the English ambassadors, June 1672; S.B. Baxter *William III* (1968) p.88. The French army were on the borders of the province of Holland, and Dutch defeat seemed inevitable. The English ambassadors offered to make the young prince the ruler of a rump Dutch state after the French and English had taken what they wanted.

1 If it is the case now in our country, that one is not allowed to speak the truth, then we are in a very bad way; nevertheless I shall speak it as long as my eyes are still open.
Michiel de Ruyter, lieutenant-admiral of Holland, report to the States General, 1673; Ronald Prud'homme van Reine *Rechterhand van Nederland: Biografie van Michiel Adriaenszon de Ruyter* (The Netherlands's Right Hand: A Biography of Michiel de Ruyter) (1996) p.248. De Ruyter had been a supporter as well as a colleague of Johan de Witt (who was assassinated in 1672) and refused to bow to pressure to play down the pensionary's great services to the Dutch navy.

2   Behold the hero, the right hand of the States,
    The rescuer of the fallen fatherland
    Who forced two great kingdoms
    Three time to haul down the proud flag,
    The rudder of the fleet, the arm of God,
    Through him return peace and freedom.
Gerard Brandt on de Ruyter, 1673; van Reine (1996) p.280. The ability of the Dutch navy, led by de Ruyter to hold the combined English and French fleets at bay in 1672 and 1673 was a vital contribution to the survival of the Dutch state.

3 Firstly, it is very painful for men of honour and property to see the rabble, who have nothing to lose, take possession of their offices and dispose of their property, for, to take the example of Rotterdam alone, it is certain that, of those who have come into the government there, there are only two individuals who have any property, while those who have left it have together more than three million.
Pieter de Groot to Abraham de Wiquefort, 30 Jan. 1673; F.J.L. Krämer (ed.) *Lettres de Pierre de Groot à Abraham de Wiquefort* (1894) pp.92–3. When William III came to power in the summer of 1672 he purged the town governments of Holland of supporters of Johan de Witt. De Groot, pensionary and member of the council in Rotterdam, lost his offices and was forced to flee into exile.

4 The prince answered, that, if he was invited by some men of the best interest, and the most valued in the nation, who should both in their own name, and in the name of others who trusted them, invite him to come and rescue the nation and the religion,

he believed he could be ready by the end of September to come over.
William III of Orange, attrib., April 1688; Baxter (1968) p.225. This sums up very neatly the formal justification for the prince's armed intervention in England later the same year, which led to the Glorious Revolution (see 428:7).

5 An absolute conquest is intended under the specious and ordinary pretences of religion, liberty, property and a free Parliament, and a religious, exact, observation of the laws, this ... they make account, will be but a work of a month's time.
Marquis d'Albeville, Oct. 1688; Israel (1995) p.849. An assessment of Dutch intentions towards England by James II's ambassador to the Republic.

6 I fail to see what advantage there is for us always to take the Romans as our model. I very much prefer a Republic, contented with its possessions, only seeking to preserve them, and securing for its inhabitants a peaceful and tranquil life ... if good sense reclaiming its rights makes us lose those ancient prejudices, which give honour only to the art of killing ones neighbours and depopulating the earth.
Elie Luzac (1766); W.R.E. Velema *Enlightenment and Conservatism in the Dutch Republic* (1993) p.70. An 18th-century supporter of the House of Orange writing in praise of republics.

7 The painting of the repentant Judas returning to the high priest the pieces of silver ... can withstand comparison with anything ever made in Italy, or for that matter with everything beautiful and admirable that has been preserved since the earliest antiquity.
Constantijn Huygens on Rembrandt, c.1629–30; Gary Schwartz *Rembrandt* (1985) p.74. An early contemporary recognition of the greatness of Rembrandt van Rijn (1609–69). Huygens was a leading poet and also secretary to Frederick Henry, Prince of Orange.

8   O, Rembrandt, paint Cornelis's voice
    The visible part is the least of him:
    The invisible is perceived through the ears
        alone.
    He who would see Anslo must hear him.
Joost van den Vondel, 1644; Seymour Slive *Dutch Painting 1600–1800* (1995) p.74. A comment by the poet and dramatist Vondel on a portrait by Rembrandt of Cornelis Anslo, a preacher of the Dutch Protestant Mennonite sect (see 359:6).

THE ECONOMIC BOOM OF THE 17TH CENTURY

1 For never any country traded so much and consumed so little: They buy infinitely, but 'tis to sell again, either upon improvement of the Commodity, or at a better Market. They are the great Masters of the Indian Spices, and of the Persian Silks; but wear plain Woollen, and feed upon their own Fish and Roots. Nay, they sell the finest of their own Cloth to France, and buy coarse out of England for their own wear. They send abroad the best of their own Butter into all parts, and buy the cheapest out of Ireland, or the North of England, for their own use. In short, they furnish infinite Luxury, which they never practise, and traffic in Pleasures which they never Taste.
Sir William Temple (1673; 1972 edn) p.119.

2 [The Baltic trade] can be said to be the soul of all our commerce, on which all other trades and commerce depend.
Anon. *Nootwendig vertoog over den Oosterschen handel* (Necessary Discourse on the Baltic Trade) (1646); Jan de Vries and Ad van der Woude *Nederland 1500–1815* (1995) p.439. The Baltic grain trade was known to contemporaries as the 'mother trade' and was regarded as the foundation of Dutch commercial success in the 17th century.

3 'Tis evident to those who have read the most, and travelled farthest, that no country can be found either in this present Age, or upon Record of any Story, Where so vast a Trade has been managed, as in the narrow compass of the Four Maritime Provinces of this Commonwealth: Nay it is generally esteemed, that they have more Shipping belongs to them, than there does to all the rest of Europe.
Sir William Temple (1673; 1972 edn) p.108. Temple was looking back from the vantage point of 1672.

4 It is a great advantage for the Traffick of Holland, that Mony may be taken up by Merchants at 3½ per cent for a year without Pawn or Pledge; whereas in other countries there is much more given, and yet real Estates bound for the same: So that it appears, that the Hollanders may buy and lay out their ready Money a whole Season before the Goods they purchase are in being, and manufactured, and sell them again on Trust (which cannot be done by any other trading Nation, considering their high Interest of Money) and therefore is one of the greatest means whereby the Hollanders have gotten most of the Trade from other Nations.

Pieter de la Court *Interest van Holland* (1662); Violet Barbour *Capitalism in Amsterdam in the 17th Century* (1950) p.85. De la Court was an influential political and economic theorist. A fervent republican, his book has come to be regarded as the classic text of Dutch mercantile republicanism.

5 Above all things war, and chiefly by sea, is most prejudicial (and peace very beneficial) for Holland.
Pieter de la Court, 1660s; C.R. Boxer *The Dutch Seaborne Empire* (1965) p.84. Despite such sentiments, the Dutch Republic was, in fact, at war for over half of the 17th century.

6 [Amsterdam] is now the chief magazine of Europe, as Lisbon is of the Indies; but truly this town may claim this title as much as the other, for whatsoever the Old or New World produces may here be found … The arms of Amsterdam have been formerly a little ship called a kogge, wherein did stand two Holland counts. Now their arms are crowned with an imperial crown, bestowed on them by Maximilian, king of the Romans, and are supported by lions.
William, Lord Fitzwilliam, 1663; Kees van Strien *Touring the Low Countries. Accounts of British Travellers, 1660–1720* (1998) p.29.

7 They fish up in nets the slime and soil which lies at the bottom of these bogs, and then spread it about a foot thick upon a little neck of land, which every turf-digger's cottage is furnished withal, and there they let it lie till it begins to harden by the weather, and then they cut it out with an iron instrument into the shape and size of large bricks. And after letting them continue in that state some time, they pile them up hollow … where after having remained a year they become saleable and serviceable.
John Leake, 1712; Van Strien (1998) p.172. Peat was an important fuel for the Dutch for both industrial and domestic purposes.

8 The Dutch are the most expert Founders in the World, and furnish most Countries with Ordnance. The German, Spanish, Italian, African and Turkish Troops have their arms principally from Amsterdam; as also their Cannon, Mortars, Powder and Lead. What is more, during the last two general Wars, Louis XIV, who thought to carry every Art and Manufacture to its highest Perfection, and particularly all that appertained to the Art Military, was however obliged to the Gunsmiths and Founders of Amsterdam, the Metropolis of an Enemy, for Arms and Ammunition for his Troops.
Anon. *A Description of Holland* (1743); Barbour (1950) pp.41–2.

RELIGIOUS TOLERATION

1 In my opinion I cannot see that anyone should be subject to compulsion in matters of conscience, but that everyone should enjoy complete freedom in this respect.

C.P. Hooft; H.A. Enno van Gelder *De levensbeschouwing van Cornelis Pieterszoon Hooft* (1918) p.112. Hooft was a prominent figure in Amsterdam politics from 1584 until his death in 1626.

2 Of all other Religions, every man enjoys the free exercise in his own Chamber, or his own House, unquestioned and unespied; And if the followers of any Sect grow so numerous in any place, that they affect a public Congregation, and are content to purchase a place of Assembly, to bear the charge of a Pastor or Teacher, and to pay for this Liberty to the Public, They go and propose their desire to the Magistrates … Who inform themselves of their Opinions, and manners of Worship, and if they find nothing in either, destructive to Civil Society … They easily allow it.

Sir William Temple (1673; 1972 edn) p.104.

3 Now, seeing that we have the rare happiness of living in a republic, where everyone's judgement is free and unshackled, where each may worship God as his conscience dictates, and where freedom is esteemed before all things dear and precious, I have believed that I should be undertaking no ungrateful or unprofitable task, in demonstrating that not only can such freedom be granted without prejudice to the public peace, but also, that without such freedom, piety cannot flourish nor the public peace be secure.

Baruch Spinoza, 1670; *The Chief Works of Spinoza* Vol.1 (1951 edn) p.6. Spinoza, born into the Jewish community in Amsterdam in 1632, was perhaps the greatest philosopher of his time, and this passage involves both praise of Dutch freedom and a challenge to the conventional thinking that regarded an imposed orthodoxy as essential to both piety and public order.

4　Hence *Amsterdam, Turk-Christian-Pagan-Jew*,
　　Staple of Sects and Mint of Schism grew;
　　That *Bank of Conscience*, where not one so
　　　strange
　　Opinion but finds Credit, and Exchange.
　　In vain for *Catholicks* our selves we bear;
　　The *universal Church* is onely there.

Andrew Marvell 'The Character of Holland' (1653); *The Poems and Letters of Andrew Marvell* (1971 edn) Vol.1, pp.101–2.

Anti-Dutch propaganda written during the First Anglo-Dutch War but also a witty expression of the contemporary distrust of religious toleration.

THE TRUCE CRISIS, 1609–21

5　Whether the Death of Christ is Intended for
　　Everyone:
　　For whom it is intended, to those it is applied.
　　But it is not applied to all.
　　Therefore it is not intended for all.

William Ames (1618); Keith L. Sprunger *The Learned Doctor William Ames* (1972) p.58. A syllogism by an English Calvinist, exiled in the Dutch Republic and supporting the strict predestinarian doctrine of the Counter-Remonstrants, who were struggling for control of the Dutch Reformed Church against the rather more flexible beliefs of the Remonstrants. The controversy helped to bring down the Advocate of Holland, Johan van Oldenbarnevelt (see 386:8), and seemed at one point to threaten civil war in the Dutch state in the first decades of the 17th century.

6 The Churchmen bear the name (as I am persuaded not without cause) of this great distraction here amongst these people; but they that see further into the matter then such as I am can doe, say: it is neyther Religion nor Predestination, but playne contention for the souvrainty (though per indirectum) that keeps them all at variance.

Sir John Ogle, Utrecht, 28 April 1617; *Papers of William Trumbull the Elder, Sept. 1616–Dec. 1618* (1995) p.169. A comment on the growing crisis in the Dutch Republic by an English officer in the Dutch army. He was sympathetic to Oldenbarnevelt and the Remonstrants.

7 Of Sir John Ogle I will not write you anything, for the carriage of him self in this business in his government of Utrecht is not answerable to the expectation that generally heretofore hathe been received of him. A strong Arminian [Remonstrant] he professeth to be, I fear he is worse.

Sir John Throckmorton, 1617; *Papers of William Trumbull* (1995) p.316. Another English resident in the Republic is clearly a partisan of the Counter-Remonstrants.

8 That he did not wish to accuse the judges, but that he had now come to a period, when other political principles prevailed, than those of his time and that he therefore should not be judged according to them.

Johan van Oldenbarnevelt, at his trial, 1619; H. Gerlach *Het Proces tegen Oldenbarnevelt en de 'Maximen in den Staet'* (The Trial of Oldenbarnevelt and the 'Maxims in the State')

(1965) p.1. Oldenbarnevelt had dominated Dutch politics for the best part of 40 years and can be seen as the effective founder of the Dutch state. His condemnation in a special court was indeed an act of policy rather than justice.

1 Men, believe not that I am a traitor. I have borne myself uprightly and honourably, as a good patriot, and the same I shall die.

Johan van Oldenbarnevelt, declaration on the scaffold just before his execution, 1619; Geyl (1961) Pt 1, p.63.

2 Grandfather, this has to be done at this time. The need and the service of the country demand it.

Maurice of Nassau, 1618; J.J. Poelhekke *Frederik Hendrik* (1978) p.108. Comment addressed to the eminent (and ageing) Amsterdam regent, C.P. Hooft, on the occasion of Maurice's purging of the Amsterdam town government of supporters of Oldenbarnevelt as part of his assumption of power.

3 William the Silent said that there were two reasons for the Revolt: safeguarding the constitution and liberty of conscience. The constitution was never so openly violated by the Spaniards as by Calvin's followers in 1618, at the instigation of the ministers … Liberty of conscience was safeguarded not only by the writings of Prince William, but by the Pacification of Ghent … and later by the Union of Utrecht … all true Calvinists are professed enemies to such liberty, as is shown by what happened to Servetus at Calvin's hands.

Hugo Grotius, 1640s; Richard Tuck *Philosophy and Government, 1572–1651* (1993) p.201. Grotius was a close associate of Oldenbarnevelt and was also arrested in 1618 but escaped from prison, although he had to spend the rest of his life in exile. He is regarded as the father of international law.

4 It is hardly to be imagined how all the violence and sharpness, which accompanies the differences of Religion in other countries, seems to be appeased or softened here, by the general freedom which all men enjoy, either by allowance or connivance; Nor how Faction and Ambition are thereby disabled to colour their Interested and Seditious Designs, with the pretences of Religion, Which has cost the Christian World so much blood for these last Hundred and fifty years.

Sir William Temple (1673; 1972 edn) p.106. Temple was writing in 1672, more than 50 years after the religious disputes of the early 17th century.

THE ANGLO-DUTCH WARS, 1653–74

5 The English are about to attack a mountain of gold; we are about to attack a mountain of iron.

Adriaan Pauw, grand pensionary of Holland, 1653; Boxer (1965) p.85.

6 I have run my course. Have good courage.

Maarten Harpertsz Tromp, attrib., 1653; Roger Hainsworth and Christine Churches *The Anglo-Dutch Naval Wars 1652–1674* (1998) p.86. Reportedly the last words of the Dutch admiral after being mortally wounded in battle with the English fleet off Terheijde (near Scheveningen).

7 A state half popular, where every one doth pretend to be a great politician, and few are so in effect.

Pierre Chanut, 1655; Herbert H. Rowen *John de Witt, Grand Pensionary of Holland, 1625–1672* (1978) p.134. The French diplomat Chanut was voicing the disdain of a servant of a monarchy for a republican system of government.

8 In Holland itself (however Mr De Witt carries it) there is nothing of inclination to breake with England, to say no more, they love themselves and their trade too well and know they have more reason to thinke of ways, and good husbandry, of paying that infinite debt which yet lies upon them than to contract more.

Sir George Downing, English ambassador to the Dutch Republic, 1662; Israel (1995) p.756. In fact, the Dutch proved all too ready to fight to protect their interests, and the Second Anglo-Dutch War (1665–7) was the result.

9 'Tis not to be imagined how infinitely high all sorts of people are, as if they have victory in their laps; and the commanders of their fleet say that they will not make any long business with their great guns, but clap board on board and conquer or be conquered.

Sir George Downing, 1665; Wilson (1957) p.131. By the beginning of the Second Anglo-Dutch War the English ambassador had changed his mind about Dutch readiness to fight.

10 But it was pretty news came the other day so fast, of the Dutch fleets being in so many places, that Sir W. Batten at table cried, 'By God!' says he, 'I think the Devil shits Dutchmen.'

Samuel Pepys, 19 July 1667; *The Diary of Samuel Pepys* Vol.8 (1974) p.345. In the last few months of the Second Anglo-Dutch War Dutch naval superiority in general and the notorious raid on Chatham in particular shocked the English, who had been led to expect an easy victory. The great English diarist Pepys was a prominent naval administrator in 1684–9.

1 But since the time of Queen Elizabeth there had been only a continual fluctuation in the conduct of England, with which one could not concert measures for two years at a time.

Johan de Witt, 1668; Temple (1673; 1972 edn) Vol.1, p.333. This all-too-prophetic remark was made to Temple during negotiations with De Witt (grand pensionary of Holland and effectively political leader of the Republic) that led to the Triple Alliance of 1668 between the Dutch, England and Sweden. Within two years Charles II had indeed changed sides and formed an alliance, the Treaty of Dover (1670), with France against the Dutch (see 427:1).

THE DUTCH SEABORNE EMPIRE IN THE 17TH CENTURY

2 My intention is to demonstrate briefly and clearly that the Dutch – that is to say, the subjects of the United Netherlands – have the right to sail to the East Indies, as they are now doing, and to engage in trade with the people there. I shall base my argument on the following most specific and unimpeachable axiom of the Law of Nations, called a primary rule or first principle, the spirit of which is self-evident and immutable, to wit: Every nation is free to travel to every other nation, and to trade with it.

Hugo Grotius *Mare liberum* (1609); Rowen (1972) p.150. This is the classic exposition of the principle of free trade based on the principles of natural law; specifically it asserted the Dutch East India Company's right to trade with the East Indies despite Spanish and Portuguese opposition.

3 After various private merchants joined with others in the 1590s and after the turn of the century to form companies, first in Amsterdam and then in other cities of [the provinces of] Holland and Zeeland to open up and undertake travel and trade with the East Indies ... the States General came to the conclusion that it would be more useful and profitable not only for the country as a whole but also for its inhabitants individually ... that these companies should be combined and this navigation and trade be placed and maintained on a firm footing, with order and political guidance.

Pieter van Dam *Beschryvinge van de Oostindische Compagnie* (Description of the East India Company) (1701); Rowen (1972) p.147. The Dutch East India Company was a chartered company granted a monopoly of trade to the East Indies by the States General in 1602, one year later than the founding of the English East India Company (see 400:5).

4 So that it is no wonder that so few admirable, and so many ignorant, lazy, prodigal and vicious men sail to the Indies in the service of those companies. But it is twice as astonishing that we find any intelligent, thrifty, industrious and virtuous men, especially Hollanders, who are prepared to enlist in such a slavish service unless in the greatest need.

Pieter de la Court (1662); Boxer (1979) p.6. De la Court opposed on economic grounds the trading monopolies of both the Dutch East and West India Companies.

5 Your honours must fully realize that nobody comes out to Asia except with the idea of making some money and then in due course returning to live in the fatherland, as daily experience has shown us all too well. We are therefore of the opinion that Netherlanders will never be able to form a stable colony in Asia, or that the Company will gain any financial relief thereby.

Governor-general and council of the Indies to the Heren XVII (General Council), 1649; Boxer (1979) p.36. Low pay and restrictive conditions of service were blamed for the poor quality of the personnel of the East India Company.

6 There is hardly a single Hollander of any consideration in Java [Indonesia], who does not have a concubine – a way of life that is deplorable, and which can give very little inducement to the natives to become converts to our religion.

Rev. François Valentijn, 1706; Boxer (1979) p.67. Valentijn was a minister of the Reformed Church, but such criticisms of the moral degeneration of the Dutch in the East were commonplace by this time.

7 Of all the wonderful things that have been done in our age by these United Provinces ... I have found the most remarkable to be the foundation of the West India Company. For the Company has implemented its plans and executed its programmes so successfully, and with so few forces and so little burden to the Commonwealth, and with the combined resources of so few subjects of this land, that the whole world has marvelled at its success; and the pride of the Spanish has been made to yield.

Johannes de Laet, 1644; Schmidt (2001) p.185. Written at the height of the company's success, notably in Brazil. The situation looked very different only a few years later.

8 As to the natives of this country, I find them entirely savage and wild, strangers to all decency, yea, uncivil and stupid as garden stakes, proficient in all wickedness and ungodliness, devilish men who

serve nobody but the Devil … They have so much witchcraft, divination, sorcery and wicked acts, that they can hardly be held in by any bands or locks. They are as thievish and treacherous as they are tall, and in cruelty they are altogether inhuman, more than barbarous.

Jonas Michaëlius, one of the first letters from Manhattan; Schmidt (2001) p.214. Michaëlius was the first minister of the Dutch Reformed Church in the New Netherlands (later New York state) (see 433:1).

9 In fertility, moderation, suitability for trade, harbours, waters, fisheries, weather and wind, as other valuable conditions … so like the Netherlands … or to be closer to the truth, overall outdoes it, so there are good reasons for it to be called New Netherlands, being as much as to say another or new Netherlands.

Adriaen van der Donck *Beschryinge van Nieuw-Nederlant* (Description of the New Netherlands) (1655); Jaap Jacobs *Een zegerijk gewest. Nieuw-Nederland in de zeventiende eeuw* (A Triumphant Province: New Netherlands in the 17th Century) (1999) p.33.

Commerce and Slavery in the Atlantic, 1600–1800

TRADE RELATIONS, 1604–1782

1 All our creeks seek to one river, all our rivers run to one port, all our ports join in one town, all our towns make but one city, all our cities and suburbs to one vast unwieldy and disorderly Babel of buildings which the world calls London.
Thomas Milles, customs official at Sandwich, Kent, bemoans the capital's power, 1604; Denys Hay (ed.) *The Age of the Renaissance* (1986) Ch.6.

2 Coming into contact with barbarian peoples you have nothing more to fear than touching the left horn of a snail. The only things one should be really anxious about are the means of mastery of the waves of the sea – and, worst of all dangers, the minds of those avid for profit and greedy of gain.
Zhang Xie *Zong Xiyang kao* (Advice to Traders) (1618); J. Needham *Science and Civilization in China* Vol.6 (1963) in Basil Davidson *The African Past: Chronicles from Antiquity to Modern Times* (1964) p.115. From the mid-18th century on there are frequent allusions among Chinese writers to *yin qiao*, which translates as 'the obscene or excessive ingenuity' of the West.

3 There were in England three such acts [British Navigation Acts, but other countries had similar laws]; that of 1647, which attempted to ensure that no plantation should allow its products to be shipped save in English ships; that of 1650, which provided that all foreign ships trading with plantations had to be licensed; and that of 1651, the Navigation Act proper which provided that no goods from Asia, Africa, or America could be imported into any English territory, colonies included, except in English-built ships directed by an English master, and manned by a crew at least three-quarters English in origin. Between 1660 and 1672, further laws provided that most colonial produce had to be sent to England, and, on the English ships which carried the goods, three-quarters of the crew had to be English.
Hugh Thomas *The Slave Trade* (1997) p.189.

4 *Power*, which according to the old Maxim, was used to follow *Land*, is now gone over to *Money*.
Jonathan Swift *The Examiner etc.* (1710–11; 1940 edn) p.5.

5 SOME GENERAL MAXIMS OF TRADE:
An Importation of Commodities, brought partly for Money and partly for goods, may be of National Advantage; if the greatest part of the Commodities thus imported are again exported, as in the case of East-India Goods: and generally all Imports of goods which are re-exported, are beneficial to a Nation.
That the Importation of such Goods as hinder the consumption of our own, or check the progress of any of our Manufactures, is a visible Disadvantage, and necessarily tends to the Ruin of multitudes of People.
The British Merchant: A Collection of Papers relating to the Trade and Commerce of Great Britain and Ireland (1743 edn) pp.1–5. Largely written by Daniel Defoe, the author of *Robinson Crusoe* (1719), the papers first appeared in 1713 and were regarded as an authority on trade during the early part of the century.

6 When either by the deficiency of a sufficient quantity of our own product to be exported, and given in Exchange to other nations, or (which is sometimes the Case) when by a greater share of Industry we are outdone by Foreign States, in the Improvement of the same Manufactures and Merchandises, whereby the Balance of Trade is turned against us, and our artificers and labouring people thereby driven from us to seek for employment elsewhere; then the wisdom of the State has sometimes thought fit to send such of their People as can be spared, to settle themselves in various Climates, where some new Species of Product might be raised, and sent home to revive Commerce, and to assist the Public by restoring to it again the lost Balance of National Trade.
Sir William Keith *History of the British Plantations in America* (1738) p.10. The governor of Pennsylvania is expressing a mercantilist relationship between the mother country and its colonies.

7 With such high duties and such restrictive freights and other notable hindrances, it may be said that we have shut the door of the Indies upon the manufacturers of Spain, and invited all other nations to supply those goods to the Spanish dominions, since every port in fourteen thousand leagues of coast is open to them, and those provinces must be supplied from somewhere.

José Campillo y Cosío *Nuevo sistema de gobierno económico para la América* (1789). The words were attrib. to Campillo, Spanish finance minister and economist, who died in 1743, 'before he had time to put into effect the proposals made in the book' (J.H. Parry *Trade and Dominion* (1971; 2000 edn) p.342). The smugglers seem to have had the upper hand.

1 The weakness of the Spaniards is, properly speaking, the weakness of their government. There wants not people, there wants not a capacity of defence, if a government and royal officers were not so wanting in their duty ... so it seems to be a thing out of dispute, that it is not so much the weakness of the Spaniards, as the weakness of their councils, which have occasioned their losses in those parts.

The Spanish Empire in America by an English merchant (1747); Parry (1971; 2000 edn) p.28. This was, in fact, written by John Campbell, whom Parry describes as the 'much admired mercantile economist, historian and political commentator'. Parry points out that Campbell may not be impartial but that the Spanish empire was judged by its rivals to be overextended and heavily bureaucratic.

2 The colonies being established solely for the use of the metropolis, it follows that:

1. They should be immediately dependent upon it and consequently protected by it;

2. That they should trade exclusively with the founders.

L'Encyclopédie (1751–68). The great French encyclopedia, epitomizing the Enlightenment (see 479:2), supports protectionism unequivocally; D.K. Fieldhouse *The Colonial Empires* (1966) p.43.

3 The maintenance of this monopoly has hitherto been the principal, or more properly the sole, end and purpose of the dominion which Great Britain assumes over her colonies ... The expense of the ordinary peace establishment of the colonies amounted, before the commencement of the present disturbances [American War of Independence] to the pay of twenty regiments of foot ... to the expense of a very considerable naval force which was constantly kept up, in order to guard, from the smuggling vessels of other nations, the immense coast of North America, and that of the West Indian islands ... The whole expense of this peace establishment was a charge upon the revenue of Great Britain, and was, at the same time, the smallest part of what the dominion of the colonies has cost the mother country ... We must add to it, in particular, the

whole expense of the late war ... The late war [Seven Years War] was altogether a colony quarrel, and the whole expense of it, in whatever part of the world it had been laid out, whether in Germany or the East Indies, ought justly to be stated to the account of the colonies. It amounted to more than ninety million pounds sterling ... The Spanish war which began in 1739, was principally a colony quarrel ... the whole expense is, in reality, a bounty which has been given in order to support a monopoly ... under the present system of management, therefore, Great Britain derives nothing but loss from the dominion which she assumes over her colonies.

Adam Smith *The Wealth of Nations* (1776) Bk 4, Ch.7. For Adam Smith see 481:8; for the Seven Years War see 471:5; for the American War of Independence see 500:1–513:2. The Spanish War, the War of Jenkins' Ear, lasted from 1739 to 1741, becoming part of the wider War of the Austrian Succession (1740–48).

4 We prefer trade to dominion.

Earl Shelburne, 1782; Parry (1971; 2000 edn) p.273. As prime minister (1782–3), Shelburne began negotiations for the Peace of Paris, ending the War of American Independence (see 509:6).

BUCCANEERS AND PRIVATEERS

5 The term 'privateer' was not in fact used till the seventeenth century, when it came to denote a ship sailing to take plunder from the enemy in compensation for goods lost by its owner through that enemy's depredations. The privateer was distinguished from other pirates by the fact he was, in theory, acting by licence under some recognized authority.

Angus Calder *Revolutionary Empire* (1981) p.98.

6 A good cheese for the whole voyage; three pounds of biscuit, half a pound of butter, and a quatern [quarter pint?] of vinegar per week; about a pint of fresh water per diem; every Sunday three-quarters of a pound of flesh; six ounces of salted cod every Monday and Wednesday; a quarter of a pound of stock-fish for every Tuesday and Saturday; grey pease and three-quarters of a pound of bacon, for Thursday and Friday: Besides this, as much oatmeal boiled in water as they could eat.

Buccaneers' rations on the Dutch group of ships captained by Hendrick Brouwer of Amsterdam, 1643; Peter T. Bradley *The Lure of Peru: Maritime Intrusion into the South Sea, 1598–1701*

(1989) p.76. This diet suggests that the buccaneers fared better than their fellow sailors.

1 When the provisions are on board and the ship is ready to sail the buccaneers resolve by common vote where they shall cruise. They also draw up an agreement or *chasse partie*, in which it is specified what the captain will have for himself and for the use of his vessel. Usually they agree on the following terms. Providing they capture a prize, first of all these amounts would be deducted from the whole capital. The hunters' pay would generally be 200 pieces of eight. The carpenter, for his work in repairing and fitting out the ship, would be paid 100 or 150 pieces of eight. The surgeon would receive 200 or 250 pieces of eight for his medical supplies, according to the size of the ship. Then came the agreed awards for the wounded, who might have lost a limb or suffered other injuries. They would be compensated as follows: for the loss of a right arm 600 pieces of eight or six slaves; for a left arm 500 pieces of eight or five slaves.
A.O. Exquemelin *The Buccaneers of America* (1678; 1969 trans.) p.71. This eyewitness account of English, French and Dutch sea-rovers was published in Holland and became an instant bestseller. It is written from inside and gives a vivid portrait of Henry Morgan, the notorious, brutal (and, from this distance, charismatic) Welsh pirate. The buccaneers took their name from the method of smoke-drying beef, which became their stock in trade. The meat was cured over a wooden frame, and the Carib word *boucan* was applied to both the griddle and the process. The buccaneers were sometimes Protestant drop-outs, committed to plundering Catholic Spain. They developed their own community code of conduct: the Custom of the Coast.

2 Yet even this man had not suffered all the torments which the buccaneers inflicted on the Spanish to make them divulge their hidden wealth. Some they hung up by their genitals, till the weight of their bodies tore them loose. Then they would give the wretches three or four stabs through the body with a cutlass and leave them lying in that condition until God released them from their miserable plight by death. Some poor creatures lingered on for four or five days. Others they crucified, with burning fuses between their fingers and toes. Others they bound, smeared their feet with grease and stuck them in the fire.
A.O. Exquemelin (1678; 1969 trans.) p.151. Henry Morgan, whose torture techniques are here described, was arrested and transported to London as a sop to the Spanish in 1672. But when war broke out again between the two countries he was knighted. He died in 1688, a wealthy planter and deputy governor of Jamaica.

SLAVES AND SUGAR, 1518–1802

3 Indeed there is an urgent need for Negro slaves, as I have written to inform his Highness (and in as much as Your Lordship will see that part of my letter to His Highness) … Ships sail from these islands [he is writing from Hispaniola in the Caribbean] for Seville to purchase essential goods such as cloth of various colours as well as other merchandise, which is used as ransom for Cape Verde whither the goods are carried with the permission of the King of Portugal. By virtue of the said ransom, let ships go there and bring away as many male and female Negroes as possible, newly imported and between the ages of fifteen to eighteen or twenty years. They will be made to adopt our customs in this island and be settled in villages and married to their women folk. The burden of work of the Indians will be eased and unlimited amounts of gold will be mined. This is the best land in the world for Negroes, women and old men, and it is very rarely that one of these people die.
Judge Alonso de Zuazo to Cardinal Ximénes de Cisneros, regent of Spain, 22 Jan. 1518; José Antonio Saco *Historia de la Esclavitud en el Nuevo Mundo* (1875–93) Vol.1, pp.143–4. Saco was a Cuban historian and politician, exiled from his own country. Hispaniola was Columbus' first landfall (see 325:2) and the main Spanish island in the Caribbean.

4 It is public opinion and knowledge that no end of deception is practised and a thousand acts of robbery and violence are committed in the course of bartering and carrying off Negroes from their country and bringing them to the Indies and to Spain … since the Portuguese and Spaniards pay so much for a Negro, they go out to hunt one another without the pretext of a war, as if they were deer. They embark four and five hundred of them in a boat, which sometimes, is not a cargo boat. The very stench is enough to kill most of them, and, indeed, very many die. The wonder is that 20 per cent of them are not lost.
Fray Tomas de Mercado *Suma de tratos y contratos* (written 1569; 1587) Bk 2, Ch.20. The Spanish Dominican friar did not question the institution of slavery although he deplored the way it worked. He had himself observed the horrifying conditions under which the slaves were transported.

5 There are no [free] men who cultivate the ground, nor men who work by the day, nor anyone who is willing to work for a wage; only slaves labour and serve. Men who are powerful have a great number of slaves whom they have captured in war or whom they have purchased. They conduct business through these slaves by sending them to markets where they buy and sell according to the master's orders.

Anon. report, end of 16th century; Paul E. Lovejoy *Transformations in Slavery* (1983; 2000 edn) p.42. The report is describing the position around São Salvador in the Congo and the indigenous roots of slavery.

1 The reason for slavery is non-belief and the Sudanese non-believers are like other kafir, whether they are Christians, Jews, Persians, Berbers, or any others who stick to non-belief and do not embrace Islam … This means there is no difference between all the kafir in this respect. Whoever is captured in a condition of non-belief, it is legal to own him, whosoever he may be, but not he who converted to Islam voluntarily, from the start, to whatever nation he belongs … These are free Muslims, whose enslavement is not allowed in any way.

Ahmad Baba, legal interpretation, c.1614; Bernard Barbour and Michelle Jacobs 'The Mir'aj: A Legal Treatise on Slavery' in J.R. Willis (ed.) *Slaves and Slavery in Muslim Africa* (1985) Vol.1. Baba was an Islamic scholar from Timbuktu who held strong opinions on freeing Muslims wrongly enslaved.

2 All the male children that proceed from these Marybuckes [Marabouts, Muslim holy men] are taught to write and read, and in regard they have no paper amongst them, but we or others bring them in the way of Trade; and therefore is of esteem, they have for their books a small smooth board, fit to hold in their hands, in which the children's lessons are written, with a kind of black ink they make, and the pen is in manner of a pencil. The Characters they use being much like the Hebrew, which in regard I understood not.

Richard Jobson *The Golden Trade* (1623); C. Howard *West African Explorers* (1951) p.38. Although Jobson's main function was to advance the gold trade on the coast round the estuary of the River Gambia, he observed the culture of the peoples he described as Mandingos (of Senegal) or Ethiopians. Here he is obviously impressed by Islamic education.

3 [A slave named 'Sambo' asked Ligon to help him become a Christian.] But when Ligon enquired of his master [Sir Thomas Modyford], the latter replied that under the laws of England, a Christian could not be made a slave. Why not though, asked Ligon, make a slave a Christian? His answer was, That it was true, there was a great difference in that: But, being

once a Christian he could no more account him a Slave, and so [they would] lose the hold they had of them as Slaves, by making them Christians; and by that means should open such a gap, as all the Planters in the Island would curse him. So I was struck mute, and poor *Sambo* kept out of the Church; as ingenious, honest, and as good a natured poor soul, as ever wore black, or eat green.

Richard Ligon *A True and Exact History of the Island of Barbados* … (1657; 1673 edn); Calder (1981) p.327. Ligon was a Cavalier (Royalist) who worked in Barbados in 1647–50 for Colonel Thomas Modyford. Modyford was son of the mayor of Exeter and an astute and successful example of the sugar gentry. He was in turn governor of both Barbados and Jamaica and was reckoned to have made over £100,000 through his sugar plantations (Richard S. Dunn *Sugar and Slaves: The Rise of the Planter Class in the English West Indies 1624–1713*, (1973) p.81).

4 Although the planters find more profit in the production of sugar than in that of cotton or indigo, it is necessary to maintain the cultivation of the latter, inasmuch as there is reason to expect that the islands, in proportion as their lands are cleared and put in cultivation, will produce too large a quantity of sugar. Variety in cultivation is more conducive to their welfare.

Jean-Baptiste Colbert to his representative in the French islands, 1664; Eric Williams *From Columbus to Castro: The History of the Caribbean 1492–1969* (1970; 1983 edn) p.117. Louis XIV's shrewd controller general of finances (see 459:7) was of course thinking of the metropolitan interests of France rather than those of her Caribbean possessions when he warned of the danger of monoculture. In fact, the French plantations were far more productive than those of the British West Indies. When the British occupied the French island of Guadeloupe for three years during the Seven Years War (1756–63), they introduced 40,000 Negroes – a huge increase on the previous rate. A century after Colbert, at the end of that war, Britain returned the islands it had captured: Cuba to Spain and Guadeloupe to France. In return it acquired Florida and Canada. 'What does a few hats signify,' asked the shrewd anonymous writer of the pamphlet *Letter from a Gentleman in Guadeloupe to his Friend in London* in 1763, 'compared with that article of luxury, sugar?' Canada's furs did not rate in the scales with King Sugar. The same writer went on to point out that the way to keep North America dependent was to leave the French in Canada (Eric Williams *Capitalism and Slavery* (1944; 1964 edn) p.114).

5 This increase [in the population of the islands in the French West Indies] … results in the increase of the consumption of the goods of Old France, and in the cultivation of the land, which results in the increase of the products which it brings forth, and these two things should produce wealth and benefits for the company.

Jean-Baptiste Colbert to directors of the French West India Company who were being sent to the Americas, 1670; C.W. Cole *Colbert and a Century of French Mercantilism* (1939) Vol.2, p.42.

1 The three *European* forts have but little authority over the *Blacks,* and serve only to secure the trade, the *Blacks* here being of a temper not to suffer anything to be imposed on them by *Europeans*; which, if they should but attempt, it would prove their own ruin.

John Barbot *A Description of the Coasts of North and South Guinea and of ... Angola* (c.1680); A. and J. Churchill (eds) *A Collection of Voyages and Travels* (1732) p.181. Barbot is writing of Accra, on the Gold Coast (Ghana), but this situation was general, even where forts existed, because they could control only a few corners of West Africa.

2 Old, feeble and sick slaves were to be fed and cared for by their masters. The minimum food for slaves was fixed, and on a fairly liberal basis, for it was provided that each slave was to be given each week 2½ measures of manioc flour or three cassavas weighing 2½ pounds each, or the equivalent, or three pounds of fish or the equivalent. A slave freed in the West Indies was to become a French citizen without need of any naturalization proceedings ... The *Code noir* reflected the growing piety of Louis XIV. It excluded Jews from the islands (reversing Colbert's policy), thus confirming the provisions of an ordinance of 3 September 1683 issued shortly after that minister's death. It further forbade all religions save the Catholic, insisted that all slaves must be baptized, and required the observance of Sundays.

Summary of part of the *Code noir,* issued in March 1685; C.W. Cole *French Mercantilism 1683–1700* (1943) p.83. Compare the buccaneers' diet 391:6.

3 An infinite quantity of Iron Wares ready wrought ... all sorts of Tin-Ware, Earthen-ware and Wooden-ware – hoes and hinges, soap and rope, cloth, hats, shoes – 'How many Spinners, Knitters and Weavers are kept at work here in England, to make all the Stockings we wear?' – saddles and bridles, locks and muskets, flour and beer, cheese and butter and candles. And also every year, 'thousands of Barrels of Irish Beef'.

Anon. Barbadian pamphleteer 1689; Calder (1981) p.320. The author is cataloguing the wares that the Caribbean island bought from Britain.

4 By a kind of magnetic force England draws to it all that is good in the plantations. It is the centre to which all things tend. Nothing but England can we relish or fancy: our hearts are here, wherever our bodies be ... all that we can rap and rend is brought to England.

Anon. Barbadian agent, 1689; Williams (1944; 1964 edn) pp.85–6. Eric Williams was prime minister of Trinidad and Tobago for 30 years and took his country into independence in 1962 with the slogan 'Discipline, Production and Tolerance'. His book propounded the theory that the Atlantic slave trade generated the capital that financed the industrial revolution, a radical interpretation that stimulated much debate and controversy.

5 The Kingdom's Pleasure, Glory and Grandeur ... are all more advanced by that [sugar] than by any other Commodity we deal in or produce, Wool not excepted.

Sir Dalby Thomas *An Historical Account of the Rise and Growth of the West Indies Colonies ... 1690; Harleian Miscellany* Vol.2 (1744) p.349. The writer was agent general of the Royal African Society at Cape Coast (Ghana) 'a would-be Cortès or Clive in the wrong place at the wrong time' (Calder (1981) p.353), since his power over the local African kingdoms supplying slaves was very limited. Sir Dalby Thomas went further – every person employed on the sugar plantations was 130 times more valuable to England than one at home (Calder (1981) p.347).

6 Nor can I imagine why they [the slaves] should be despised for their colour, being what they cannot help ... I can't think there is any intrinsic value in one colour more than another, that white is better than black, only we think it so, because we are so, and are prone to judge favourably in our own case.

Captain Thomas Phillips *A Journal of a Voyage in the* Hannibal, *1694* (1746) p.233. A remarkable and sanguine statement from a London slave captain. He also describes the practice of branding: 'We marked the slaves we had bought on the breast or shoulder with a hot iron, having the ship's name on it, the place being before anointed with a little palm oil, which caused but little pain, the mark being usually well in four or five days' (Thomas (1997) p.394).

7 I hope you will slave your ship easy and what shall remain over as above slaving your ship lay out in teeth [ivory] which are there [Africa] reasonable ... [The captain was then to proceed to the West Indies and load up with] sugar, cotton, ginger if to be had ... We leave the whole management of the concern to you and hope the Lord will direct you for the best ... endeavour to keep all your men sober for intemperance in the hot country may destroy your men and so ruin your voyage … We commit you to the care and protection of the Almighty.

Instructions from the Liverpool family firm of Norris to the captain of the slaver *The Blessing*, Oct. 1700; Calder (1981) p.357. The captain was to pick up provisions from Kinsale in Ireland at the start of this typical triangular voyage. The Norrises were lords of the manor of Speke Hall and also dominating merchants in the city: Thomas Norris was sheriff of Lancashire and MP for Liverpool; Sir William was ambassador to the Great Moghul in India; Richard was Lord Mayor of Liverpool in the year this ship set sail.

1 To live in perpetual Noise and Hurry and the only way to render a Person angry, and Tyrannical too; since the Climate is so hot, and the labour so constant, that the Servants night and day stand in great Boiling houses, where there are Six or Seven large Coppers or Furnaces kept perpetually boiling; and from which with heavy Ladles and Scummers they skim off the excrementatious parts of the Canes; till it comes to its perfection and cleanness, while others as Stokers, Broil as it were alive, in managing the Fires; and one part is constantly at the Mill, to supply it with Canes, night and day.

Thomas Tryon, c.1700; Carl Bridenbaugh *Myths and Realities of the Colonial South* (1952) p.303. Tryon is actually pitying his master and the tyranny of service to 'King Sugar'. According to Calder (1981; p.255) 'The sugar mill prefigured the later cotton factory' as a parallel of production and labour (see 571:2).

2   Others seek out to Afric's torrid zone,
         And search the burning shores of Serra Lone
           [*sic*];
         There in insufferable heats they fry,
         And run vast risks to see the gold and die:
         The harmless natives basely they trepan,
         And barter baubles for the souls of men:
         The wretches they to Christian climes bring
           o'er,
         To serve worse heathens than they did before.
         The cruelties they suffer there are such,
         Amboyna's nothing , they've outdone the
           Dutch.

Daniel Defoe *Reformation of Manners* (1702). Defoe was his usual clear-sighted self in pillorying the practices of the slave trade. For his parallel with Anglo-Dutch relations in the Dutch East Indies see 390:5.

3 Foreign commerce should scarcely be permitted save for goods necessary to life, dress, medicine and certain industries, for which the materials are not found at home, unless one does as the Dutch, who

go to seek useless things abroad only to sell them elsewhere. It should be forgiven when, for goods which have to do only with luxury and fashion, it causes more money to flow out of the kingdom than it brings in; but that which can bring us new money cannot be sought after too zealously.

Sébastien Vauban, 1707; C.W. Cole *French Mercantilism 1683–1700* (1943) pp.234–5. Vauban was the greatest military engineer of his time, and his frontier fortifications (33 constructed and 300 renewed) enabled Louis XIV to wage war on his neighbours. In retirement he alienated his king by publishing his theories on equitable taxation (see 461:4) and here attacks mercantilism.

4   Barbados Isle inhabited by slaves
         And for one honest man ten thousand knaves
         Religion to thee's Romantic story;
         Barbarity and ill got wealth thy glory
         All Sodom's Sins are Centred in thy heart
         Death is thy look and Death in every part
         Oh! Glorious Isle in Villainy Excel
         Sin to the Height – thy fate is Hell.

T. Walduck to James Petiver, 12 Nov. 1710; *Journal of Barbados Museum and Historical Society* 15 (1957–8) p.50. Walduck was a Barbadian who wrote to a London friend describing the colony. Looking back on nearly a century of settlement he contrasted 'the industry and integrity of the first planters who had brought it to such a flourishing state in the 1660s and roundly condemned the debauched people who now managed the place' (Dunn (1973) p.340).

5 A treaty could scarce have been contrived of so little benefit to the nation.

M. Postlethwayt *Great Britain's Commercial Interest Explained and Improved* (1759) Vol.2, p.479. In 1713 the Treaty of Utrecht (see 466:10) secured for Britain the much coveted and abused *asiento* 'from the French, who had acquired it in their turn in 1702, the licence to supply 4,800 slaves per annum to the Spanish colonies, with the right to send an annual ship to trade at the Portobelo [Puerto Belo, Panama] fair' (Patrick Richardson *Empire and Slavery* (1968) p.49). Hailed as a diplomatic triumph, because payment for the slaves and manufactured goods was made in Spanish bullion, it was advantageous to British slave traders but not to British planters, since it encouraged competitors by supplying them with slave labour.

6   To thee belongs the rural reign;
         Thy cities shall with commerce shine;
         All thine shall be the subject main,
         And every shore it circles thine.
         'Rule, Britannia, rule the waves;
         Britons never will be slaves.'

James Thomson *Alfred: a Masque* (1740) Act 2. The Scottish poet provided what has become Britain's second national anthem.

1 The most approved Judges of the Commercial Interests of these Kingdoms have been of the opinion that our West-India and African Trades are the most nationally beneficial of any we carry on. It is also allowed on all Hands that the Trade to Africa is the Branch which renders our American Colonies and Plantations so advantageous to Great Britain: that Traffic only affording our Planters a constant Supply of Negro servants for the Culture of their Lands in the Produce of Sugars, Tobacco, Rice, Rum, Cotton, Fustick [yellow dye], Pimento and all our other Plantation Produce: so that the extensive Employment of our Shipping, in, to, and from America, the great Brood of Seamen consequent thereupon, and the daily Bread of the most considerable of our British Manufactures, are owing primarily to the Labour of Negroes; who, as they were the first happy Instruments of raising our Plantations, so their Labour only can support and preserve them, and render them still more profitable to their mother Kingdom. The Negro-Trade therefore, and the natural consequences resulting from it, may be justly esteemed an inexhaustible fund of Wealth and Naval Power to this Nation.

Anon. pamphlet (1749); Richardson (1968) p.125. Of the slave traders listed in 1755, 237 belong to Bristol, 147 to London and 89 to Liverpool. According to J. Latimer (*Annals of Bristol in the Eighteenth Century* (1893) p.271), the Royal Africa Company had lost its monopoly in 1698, and with free trade the numbers of slaves increased enormously. Bristol alone shipped 160,950 Negroes to the sugar plantations in the nine years following the opening of the trade (Latimer (1893) p.272).

2 The labours of the people settled in these islands are the sole bases of the African trade; they extend the fisheries and culture of North America, afford a good market for the manufactures of Asia, and double, perhaps treble, the activity of all Europe. They may now be considered the principal cause of the rapid motion which now agitates the universe. This ferment must increase, in proportion as cultures, that are so capable of being extended shall approach nearer to their higher degree of perfection.

Abbé Guillaume Raynal, 1750s; G.S. Callender *Selections from the Economic History of the United States 1765–1860* (1909) pp.78–9. The Abbé Raynal considered that slavery was contrary to nature and so universally wrong. His fierce book, *Histoire philosophique et politique des Indes* (1770) (on which Denis Diderot, among others, collaborated), was highly influential and 'much read by slave captains'. For Diderot see 482:8.

3 Many of the Boers [the Dutch farmers living outside Cape Town] possess 200 or 300 oxen, 100, 150 or more cows, 2,000 to 3,000 sheep, 40 or 50 horses, 20, 30 or more bond slaves, and a large estate. Many an African Boer, therefore, would think twice about changing places with a German nobleman.

F. Mentzel *Life at the Cape in the mid-18th Century* (1919) p.129. The Boers nearest the Cape came to town to sell their meat to provision the passing ships on which the whole economy depended.

4 Some gentlemen may, indeed, object to the slave trade as inhuman and impious; let us consider that if our colonies are to be maintained and cultivated, which can only be done by African Negroes, it is surely better to supply ourselves with those labourers in British bottoms, than purchase them through the medium of French, Dutch or Danish factors.

Temple Luttrell, speech in House of Commons, 23 May 1777; *Parliamentary History* Vol.19, p.305. The MP was the grandson of the governor of Jamaica.

5 The general power which a master exercises ... over his slaves is rather by implication (from slaves being bought as chattels in the same way as horses or other beasts) than by any positive law defining what the power of a master shall be in this island.

Sir Philip Yorke, attorney general, at inquiry in the House of Commons into the condition of slavery in Barbados, 1788; Reports and Papers: British Parliamentary series Vol.67, pp.308, 316 in Thomas (1997) p.472. Asked the further question, 'What is the protection granted by the law to slaves in Barbados?' Yorke's reply was 'Effectually none'. The French had a *Code noir* explaining how slaves were to be treated (see 394:2).

6 I can assure you I was shocked at the first appearance of human flesh exposed to sale. But surely God ordained 'em for the use and benefit of us. Otherwise, his divine Will would have made itself manifest by some particular or token.

John Pinney, late 1770s; R. Pares *A West India Fortune* (1950) p.121. The writer was a young sugar planter from a Bristol family with plantations in the Caribbean island of Nevis.

7 There remains only to tell you that gold commands the trade. There is no buying a slave without one ounce of gold at least on it ...

Formerly, owners of ships used to send out double cargoes of goods, one for [buying] slaves and the other for [buying] gold. If slaves happened to be dearer than usual, the cargo for [buying] gold was thrown into the slave cargo in order to fill the ship.

On the other hand, if slaves were reasonable the gold cargo was disposed of for gold and ivory at a profit of thirty, forty, or fifty per cent … how strangely things are reversed now … [when] we scarcely see a ship go off with her complement of slaves, notwithstanding her cargo [is arranged to allow for payment of] eighteen or twenty pounds sterling [per slave] on average.

English buying agent, report from the Gold Coast (Ghana) to his London directors,1771; Basil Davidson *Africa in History* (1968) pp.183–4. Portuguese traders were bringing gold from Brazil to pay for the slaves, whose value had increased as their numbers decreased. Hence the changing trade pattern. The mortality rate on the voyage west was lower on the Portuguese ships because they were less overcrowded.

1 The real or supposed necessity of treating the Negroes with rigour gradually brings a numbness upon the heart and renders those who are engaged in it too indifferent to the sufferings of their fellow *creatures*.

Rev. John Newton 'Thoughts on the African Slave Trade' in *Letters and Sermons* (1780) pp.103 ff; Thomas (1997) p.308. Newton, the slave captain of the Liverpool ship the *Duke of Argyll*, later entered the church. He admitted that he knew 'no method of getting money not even that of robbing for it upon the highway, which has so direct a tendency to efface the moral sense'. He read prayers twice a day to his slave crews and wrote while still a captain the popular hymn 'How Sweet the Name of Jesus Sounds'. His chief sense of guilt was over lust for the African women he was transporting rather than over his part in the slave trade. He later became an abolitionist.

2 During the time I was engaged in the slave trade I never had the least scruple as to its lawfulness. It is indeed accounted a genteel employment, and is usually very profitable. I considered myself a sort of gaoler or turnkey.

Rev. John Newton (1780); Jack Beeching *An Open Path: Christian Missionaries 1515–1914* (1979) p.80. Beeching calls Newton's epitaph 'a sad prevarication':

JOHN NEWTON
CLERK
Once an Infidel and Libertine
A Servant of slaves in Africa

3   Negroes for Sale
A cargo of very fine stout Men and Women
in good order and fit for immediate service, just
imported from the windward Coast of Africa, in the
Ship Two Brothers
Conditions are one half Cash or Produce, the
other half payable the first of January next, giving
bond and Security if required.

The sale to be opened at 10 o'clock each Day, in
Mr Bourdeaux's Yard, at No. 8 on the Bay.
May 19, 1784 John Mitchell.

American advertisement for the sale of slaves, 1784; Davidson (1968) p.88.

4 When I looked round the ship and saw a large … copper boiling … I no longer doubted my fate … I fell motionless on the deck and fainted. When I recovered, I found some black people about me who, I believed, were some of those who had brought me on board, and had been receiving their pay; they talked in order to cheer me, but all in vain. I asked them if we were not to be eaten by those white men, with horrible looks, red faces and loose hair. They told me I was not, and one of the crew brought me a small portion of spirituous liquor in a wine glass.

Olaudah Equiano *Equiano's Travels* (1789; 1967 edn) p.76. The eloquent former slave describes his kidnapping in Gambia in a raid by a rival tribe. He was sold eventually to the English, transported to Barbados in the horrifying Middle Passage from West Africa to the Caribbean. He was taught to read and write by a kindly ship's captain and eventually freed. He lectured in England on the evils of slavery and his book was widely read and influential in the campaign for abolition.

5 The stench of the hold while we were on the coast was so intolerably loathsome that it was dangerous to remain there for any time, and some of us had been permitted to stay on the deck for the fresh air; but now that the whole ship's cargo were confined together, it became absolutely pestilential. The closeness of the place and the heat of the climate, added to the number in the ship, which was so crowded that each had scarcely room to turn himself, most suffocated us. This produced constant perspirations, so that the air soon became unfit for respiration … and brought on a sickness among the slaves, of which many died, thus falling victims to the unprovident avarice, as I may call it, of the purchasers. This wretched situation was again aggravated by the galling of the chains, now become insupportable; and the filth of the tubs, into which the children often fell, and were almost suffocated. The shrieks of the women, and the groans of the dying, rendered a scene of horror almost inconceivable.

Olaudah Equiano (1789; 1967 edn) p.78. The slave Equiano is describing in horrific vividness the first stage of his journey to the Caribbean. The space allotted to each slave on the Atlantic crossing measured 5½ feet in length and 16 inches in breadth (Williams 1944; 1964 edn) p.35).

1 [I was sold in Barbados] after the usual manner, which is this: on a signal given [as the beat of a drum], the buyers rush at once into the yard, where the slaves are confined, and make choice of that parcel they like best. The noise and clamour with which this is attended, and the eagerness visible in the countenance of the buyers serve not a little to increase the apprehensions of the terrified Africans … in this manner, without scruple, are relations and friends separated, most of them never to see one another again.

Olaudah Equiano (1789; 1967 edn) p.63.

2 The Moors, who inhabit the countries on the north of the River Senegal, are particularly infamous for their predatory Wars … The French, to encourage them in it, make annual presents to the Moorish kings. These are given under certain conditions, first that their subjects shall not carry any of their gum to the English at Portendic; and, secondly, that they shall be ready on all occasions, to furnish slaves. To enable them to fulfil this last article, they never fail to supply them with ammunition, guns, and other instruments of War …

The Wars which the inhabitants of the interior parts of the country, beyond Senegal, Gambia, and Sierra Leona [sic] carry on with each other, are chiefly of a predatory nature, and owe their origin to the yearly number of slaves, which the Mandingos, or the inland traders suppose will be wanted by the vessels that will arrive on the coast. Indeed these predatory incursions depend so much on the demands for slaves, that if in any one year there be a greater concourse of European ships than usual, it is observed that a much greater number of captives from the interior is brought to market the next.

C.B. Wadström Observations on The Slave Trade (1789) p.1. The chief director of the Swedish assay office had come 'to make discoveries in botany, mineralogy and other branches of science', but is immediately struck by the economics of the slave trade.

3 The method at Liverpool [to obtain sailors for the slave ships] is by the merchants' clerks going from public house to public house, giving them liquors to get them into a state of intoxication and, by that, getting them very often on board [this was called 'crimping']. Another method is to get them in debt and then, if they don't choose to go aboard of such guinea men then ready for sea, they are sent away to gaol by the publicans they may be indebted to.

James Towne, carpenter in the navy to House of Commons committee on the Slave Trade, 1790; Reports and Papers: British Parliamentary series Vol.82, p.27.

4   Hear, oh, BRITANNIA! Potent Queen of ideas,
On whom fair Art, and meek Religion smiles,
How AFRIC's coasts thy craftier sons invade
With murder, rapine, theft, – and call it Trade!
– The SLAVE, in chains on supplicating knee,
Spreads his wide arms and lifts his eyes to Thee;
With hunger pale, with wounds and toil
     oppressed,
'ARE WE NOT BRETHREN?' sorrow chokes
     the rest; –
AIR! bear to heaven upon thy azure flood
Their innocent cries! – Earth! Cover not their
     blood.

Erasmus Darwin The Botanic Garden (1789–91) Pt 2. Leading figures of the Enlightenment 'joined a swelling chorus of castigation'. 'Slavery is a crime against the human species that all who practise it deserve to be extirpated from the earth,' cried Thomas Day, who had written an anti-slavery poem, 'The Dying Negro', in 1773. In 1791 the potter Josiah Wedgwood, a third member of the Birmingham Lunar Society (see 486:5), manufactured thousands of cameos of a kneeling slave, with manacled hands raised in supplication. They bore the motto: 'Am I not a man and a brother?' The Lunar Society grew out of this group of friends who met once a month in Birmingham at the full moon and 'the very hub of the modern technological world'.

5 [These 35 slaves] are commonly secured, by putting the right leg of one, and the left leg of another, into the same pair of fetters. By supporting the fetters with a string, they can walk, though very slowly. Every four slaves are likewise fastened together by the necks, with a strong rope of twisted thongs; and in the night, an additional pair of fetters is put on their hands, and sometimes a light iron chain passed round their necks.

Mungo Park Travels in the Interior Districts of Africa in the Years 1795–97 (1799; 1971 edn) p.318. Some of these slaves seemed to have awaited sale for three years in this captivity, according to the slave merchant with whom Park travelled up the Gambia River in West Africa. The great Scottish explorer, surgeon and naturalist travelled with two Africans. He suffered terrible hardships and was imprisoned by Arabs, but he was drawn irresistibly back from life as a doctor in Scotland to the Niger in 1805, and there met his death.

6 There is a great difference between the treatment of these slaves and [that] meted out to those who are yearly shipped to America from the Congo and Angola. At the Cape they are, in the majority of cases

at least, looked upon as permanent family servants
… The abundance of the necessaries of life and the
comparatively easy work of fetching and carrying
wood, herding cattle, tilling the fields, labouring in
the vineyards [and] attending to the daily
housework makes their lot in life quite tolerable.
J.A. de Mist *Memorandum of a Commissary* (1920) p.252;
Lovejoy (1983, 2000 edn) p.136. Commissary general
J.A. de Mist is recalling being sent to the Cape in 1802.

JUDGEMENTS

1 Commerce, which has enriched English citizens,
has helped to make them free, and this freedom in its
turn has extended commerce, and that has made the
greatness of the nation. Commerce has gradually
established the naval forces thanks to which the
English are masters of the seas. At the present time
they have nearly two hundred ships of the line.
Posterity will perhaps learn with surprise that a small
island which has no resources of its own except a
little lead, some tin, some fuller's earth and coarse
wool has through its commerce become powerful
enough to send, in 1723, at one and the same time,
three fleets to three extremities of the world, one
before Gibraltar, conquered and held by its forces,
another to Porto Belo [Puerto Belo, Panama] to cut
off the treasures of the Indies from the King of
Spain, and the third into the Baltic to prevent the
Northern Powers from fighting.
Voltaire *Letters on England* (1733; 1980 trans.) p.51. Voltaire
apparently fled to England in May 1726 after falling foul of a
French aristocrat, the Chevalier de Rohan, to escape
punishment. He stayed almost three years.

2 The discovery of America, and that of a passage to
the East Indies by the Cape of Good Hope , are the
two greatest and most important events in the history of mankind … what benefits or what misfortunes to mankind may hereafter result from those
great events, no human wisdom can foresee … By
uniting, in some measure, the most distant parts of
the world, by enabling them to relieve one another's
wants, to increase one another's enjoyments, and to
encourage one another's industry, their general
tendency would seem to be beneficial … To the
natives, however, both of the East and West Indies,
all the commercial benefits which can have resulted
from those events have been sunk and lost in the
dreadful misfortunes which they have occasioned.
Adam Smith *The Wealth of Nations* (1776; 1904 edn) Vol.2,
p.125.

3 The very idea of distant possessions will be even
ridiculed. The East and West Indies, and everything
without ourselves will be disregarded, and wholly
excluded from all European systems; and only those
divisions of men, and of territory, will take place
which the common convenience requires, and not
such as the mad and insatiable ambition of princes
demands. No part of America, Africa, or Asia, will be
held in subjection to any part of Europe, and all the
intercourse that will be kept up among them will be
for their mutual advantage.
Joseph Priestley *Lectures to the Right Honourable Edmund Burke*
(1791). Inspired by the American and French Revolutions, the
radical disciple of the Enlightenment saw the end of European
colonialism. Priestley, another member of the Birmingham
Lunar Society, was far-sighted and far from typical.

4 The discovery of America, the rounding of the
Cape opened up fresh ground for the rising bourgeoisie. The East Indian and Chinese markets, the
colonization of America, trade with the colonies, the
increase in the means of exchange and in commodities generally gave to commerce, to navigation,
to industry an impulse never before known, and
thereby, to the revolutionary element in the tottering feudal society, a rapid development.
Karl Marx and Friedrich Engels *Manifesto of the Communist
Party* (1848: 1955 edn) p.53.

Trade and Dominion: Europe and the East, 1600–1800

PRELUDE, 1574–1599

1 It is an astounding thing to see the facility and frequency with which the Portuguese embark for India ... Each year four or five carracks leave Lisbon full of them; and many embark as if they were going no further than a league from Lisbon, taking with them only a shirt and two loaves in the hand, and carrying a cheese and a jar of marmalade, without any other kind of provision.
Father Alessandro Valignano, 1574; C.R. Boxer *The Portuguese Seaborne Empire 1415–1825* (1969) p.218. The Italian Jesuit was himself making the outward journey. He was the great organizer of the Jesuit missions in Asia in the last quarter of the 16th century.

2 Two years ago the English opened up the trade, which they still continue, to the Levant, which is extremely profitable to them, as they take great quantities of tin and lead thither, which the Turk buys from them almost for its weight in gold, the tin being vital for casting guns and the lead for the purpose of war. It is of double importance to the Turks now, as a consequence of the excommunication pronounced *ipso facto* by the Pope on anybody who provides or sells to infidels materials such as these.
Bernardino de Mendoza, Spanish ambassador in London, warning Philip II of Spain of the commercial advantage to the English of their quarrel with the church of Rome, May 1582; Lisa Jardine *Worldly Goods* (1996) p.376.

3 If another year they come not, then without fail it will be performed and the great and rich people [of the East Indies] be left greedily gaping for any nation to trade that will bring the like commodities, which I dare undertake the merchants of London shall do if her Majesty [Queen Elizabeth] shall stay the carracks from going thither.
Earl of Cumberland, 1598; G.C. Williamson *George, Third Earl of Cumberland* (1920) p.221. The earl is over-estimating the depredations of his privateering expedition to the East Indies on the Portuguese. 'The essential difference between the privateering venture and the semi-official expedition is that whereas the former was wholly financed and directed by private individuals, the latter was a national undertaking in which the queen's interest predominated' (Kenneth R. Andrews *Elizabethan Privateering* (1964) pp.5–6). At this period privateering was a way of waging war.

4 Let the Spaniards show any just and lawful reasons ... why they should bar her Majesty [Queen Elizabeth] and all other Christian princes and states, of the use of the vast, wide and infinitely open ocean, and of access to the territories and dominions of so many free princes, kings and potentates in the East ... for [the Spaniards] have no more sovereign command or authority, than we, or any Christians whatsoever.
Appeal by London merchants, 1599, fiercely disputing the Treaty of Tordesillas; Giles Milton *Nathaniel's Nutmeg* (1999) Ch.3. Under the treaty, the pope had divided the world of future discoveries between the Spanish and Portuguese (see 324:7). Since England was in delicate negotiation with Spain, the Privy Council prevaricated, despite the queen's backing for the merchants.

THE EAST INDIA COMPANIES, 1600–1795

5 An assembly of the persons hereunder named, holden the 24 of September 1599. [There follows a list of 57 names.] Whereas the several persons above-named, together with divers others whose names are registered in the beginning of this book, by the sufferance of Almighty God, after royal assent of our sovereign lady the queen's most excellent majesty first thereunto had and obtained, do intend, for the honour of our native country and for the advancement of trade of merchandise within this realm of England ... to set forth a voyage this present year to the East Indies and other of the islands and countries thereabouts, and there to make trade by the sale of such commodities as upon further deliberation shall be resolved to be provided for those parts, or otherwise by buying or bartering of such goods, wares, jewels or merchandise as those islands or countries may yield or afford ... It is agreed, ordained and resolved ... that all shipping to be employed in this voyage shall be bought and provided by such as shall be thereto appointed, for ready money only ... [Also] that all goods, wares and other things shall be bought and prepared by such as shall be thereunto appointed as committees and directors of the said voyage, for the buying and providing of shipping and merchandise.

Court minutes of the East India Company, 1599; R.H. Tawney and E. Power (eds) *Tudor Economic Documents* (1924) Vol.2, pp.83–5. The English were slow to join in the race to the Far East, since the Portuguese and the Dutch had got there first. However, on the last day of 1600 Elizabeth I issued a charter to the East India Company and set it off on a career that was to lead to domination of the Indian subcontinent. Unlike earlier companies, which were made up of independent merchants trading on their own individual accounts, the East India Company insisted on a joint stock, with control of policy in the hands of elected directors.

1 And the reason why the general's men stood in better health than the men of other ships was this; he [James Lancaster, the commander of the East India Company's first fleet] brought to sea with him certain bottles of the juice of lemons, which he gave to each one, as long as it would last, three spoonfuls every morning, fasting; not suffering them to eat anything after it till noon ... by this means the general cured many of his men and preserved the rest.

Anon. diarist aboard the *Red Dragon*, the flagship of this first company voyage to the Spice Islands, explaining the diet not shared by the other ships, 1602; Milton (1999) p.79. This effective cure for scurvy seems to have been forgotten until Captain Cook rediscovered it 170 years later.

2 For He [God] hath not only supplied my necessity to lade these ships I have, but hath given me as much as will lade as many more ships if I had them to lade. So that now my care is not for money but rather where I shall leave these goods ... in safety till the return of ships out of England.

James Lancaster reports back to his London directors from Aceh, northwest Sumatra, 1602; John Keay *The Honourable Company: A History of the English East India Company* (1991) p.18. Although the voyage to the East Indies was for pepper, Lancaster had acquired great quantities of Indian cottons. With the connivance of the sultan of Aceh, Ala-uddin Shah, to whom he had promised 'a fair Portugal maiden' in gratitude, he had trapped and overpowered a huge Portuguese carrack. It took his men six days to unload, but it doubled the value of the trading stock he was carrying.

3 [The founding of the VOC] was not a popular move and was bitterly opposed by the Amsterdam merchants, but on the evening of 20 March 1602, an agreement was struck and the Dutch East India Company came into being. Known as the VOC [Vereenigde Oostindische Compagnie] or more colloquially as the Seventeen [Heren XVII] after its 17-strong council, it was given a total monopoly over the spice trade for 21 years. It was to prove a formidable rival to its English counterpart.

Giles Milton (1999) Ch.5. The VOC was really an instrument of the Dutch government, whereas the East India Company was politically independent and remained under the control of London merchants.

4 That they [the Dutch] are not only to lend us their experience but give every assistance to our merchants trading in the East and West Indies, leaving them free to trade on whatever coasts they choose in full security and liberty and to associate with them [French merchants] in their navigation to the said countries.

Cardinal Richelieu, 1627, *Mémoires* Vol.18; Henry Weber *La Compagnie française des Indes, 1604–1875* (1904) p.70. The Cardinal sets out his conditions for helping the Dutch in the war to establish their independence from Spain (see 381:1–382:6).

5 The good return of our East Indian ships hath put such life into that trade that our merchants mean to go roundly to work, and in less than a fortnight have underwritten for £400,000 to be employed in that voyage in four years, by equal portions; by which means, if they and the Hollanders can agree, they are like enough to engross the whole trade of those parts ... Our East India Company are in a great bravery, having closed up their books for underwriters the last of January, and find adventurers of £1,400,000 for these four years following, which in truth is a very great sum and a great deal more than was expected, but divers have underwritten for ten, twelve and fourteen thousand pound apiece.

John Chamberlain to Sir Dudley Carleton, 25 Nov. 1613 and 8 Feb. 1616; John Chamberlain *Letters* Vol.1, p.488 and Vol.2, p.53. The East India Company was to become one of the richest and greatest of all the trading companies.

6 We do all of us make an agreement that the commodities in the two foresaid islands [Ai and Run], namely mace and nutmegs, we cannot nor will sell to any other nation, but only to the King of England his subjects ... and whereas all the orankayas [leaders] of the foresaid islands have made this agreement, let it be credited that it was not made in madness or loosely as the breathing of the wind, but because it was concluded upon in their hearts, they cannot revolt from or swerve from the same again.

Agreement between the Banda Islands and the British Crown, 1616; Milton (1999) p.273. This made James I, king of England, France, Scotland and Ireland also 'King by the mercy of God King of Pooloway [Ai] and Poolaroone [Run]' and confirmed England's short-lived victory in breaking the Dutch spice monopoly. The Dutch were ruthlessly subjugating the population and preserving their monopoly of the enormously lucrative trade in nutmeg, mace, cloves and other spices, against the English. Jan Pieterszoon Coen, governor-general of the Dutch East Indies, threatened his masters in Amsterdam: 'You can be assured that if you do not send a large capital at the earliest opportunity … the whole Indies trade is liable to come to nothing.'

1 If you mean the [East India] Company to have any trade with these islands [the Bandas], or the Moluccas [Spice Islands], it must not be deferred any longer, but to send such forces the next westerly monsoon that we have, or else all is gone, and not to be expected hereafter any more trade this way … Our wants are extreme; neither have we any victuals or drink, but only rice and water, which had not God sent in four or five junks to have relieved us with rice I must have been fain to have given up our King and Company's right for want of relief, which relief is weak.

Nathaniel Courthope to his employers, 1618; Milton (1999) pp.290–92. As the company's representative, with only 38 men, Courthope was remote and vulnerable, besieged by far stronger Dutch forces. Here he is echoing his Dutch counterpart's plea (see 401:6).

2 At home men are famous for doing nothing; here they are infamous for their honest endeavours. At home is respect and reward; abroad disrespect and heart-breaking. At home is augmentation of wages; abroad nothing so much as grief, cares and displeasure. At home is safety; abroad is bondage. And in a word at home all things are as a man might wish, and here nothing answerable to merit.

George Ball, 1618; Keay (1991) p.121. The company's president in Bantam (northwestern Java) contrasts his life on the edge of the known world with that of his London masters.

3 Your Honours should know by experience that trade in Asia must be driven and maintained under the protection and favour of your honours' own weapons, and that the weapons must be paid for by the profits from the trade; so that we cannot carry on trade without war nor war without trade.

Jan Pieterszoon Coen, founder of Batavia (Jakarta), Java, to Heren XVII, 1614; C.R. Boxer *The Dutch Seaborne Empire 1600–1800* (1965) Ch.4. Coen (1587–1629) was writing to the 17 directors who ruled the Dutch East India Company (VOC) under the direction of the States General.

4 We ourselves bring insufficient supplies of merchandise to the Moluccas and prevent others from bringing enough. The inhabitants cannot pick any cloves, because the high cost of importing foodstuffs

forces them to grow food crops instead. They themselves now have to get the sago, which used to be brought by the Javanese, from further afield at five times the old price. The Indian textiles [which are often low quality] have to be bought from us [Dutch East India Company] at such high prices it does not make it worth their while to go and pick the cloves [which is difficult and dangerous work]. Besides we are so greedily set on our revenue and profits that we don't permit anyone to make a penny from us.

Dr Laurens Reael, VOC governor general in the Dutch East Indies before Coen, to Heren XVII, criticizing the Dutch monopoly on spice, 20 April 1618; Boxer (1965) Ch.5.

5 The people that we call Red-hairs or Red Barbarians are identical with the Hollanders and they live in the Western ocean. They are covetous and cunning, are very knowledgeable concerning valuable merchandise, and are very clever in the pursuit of gain. They will risk their lives in search of profit, and no place is too remote for them to frequent. Their ships are very large, strong and well-built, and they are called in China double-planked ships.

Anon. Chinese 17th-century chronicler on the Europeans; Boxer (1965) Ch.8. The Dutch carried out piratical raids on Chinese junks and kidnapped Chinese to populate Batavia (Jakarta), so this attitude was understandable. The Dutch sank 80 Chinese junks in 1622 for infringing their trade monopolies in the spice trade.

6 A true Relation of the Unjust, Cruel and Barbarous Proceedings against the English at Amboina.

Title of pamphlet, 1624. The violent Anglo-Dutch rivalry came to a head in the massacre of Amboyna in 1623, when ten Englishmen and ten Japanese men were executed by the Dutch, who believed they were plotting to overthrow the Dutch authorities. The island was important for both strategic reasons and as a producer of cloves. Anglo-Dutch enmity engendered three wars in the second half of the century and was resolved only in 1674 with the Treaty of Westminster, which renewed the terms of the Treaty of Breda (see 403:4).

7 In this great town [Amsterdam], where apart from myself there lives no one who is not engaged in trade, everyone is so much out for his own advantage that I should be able to live my whole life here without ever meeting a mortal being.

René Descartes, c.1649; Boxer (1965) Ch.6. The great French philosopher (see 367:3) who lived in Holland for several years and married there, is being less than generous about Dutch materialism. Among those living in the city at the time were the painter Rembrandt van Rijn (1606–69) and the poet and dramatist Joost van den Vondel (1587–1679).

1 Wherever they once come, there they mean to settle for the rest of their lives, and they never think of returning to Portugal again. But a Hollander, when he arrives in Asia, thinks 'When my six years are up, then I will go home to Europe again.'

Johann Saar, a Dutch corporal in Ceylon (Sri Lanka), gives *his* view of the difference in the attitude between the two countries, c.1662; Boxer (1969) p.120.

2 Trade is the cause of a perpetual combat in war and in peace between the nations of Europe.

Jean-Baptiste Colbert to Louis XIV, c.1664; Glyndwr Williams *The Expansion of Europe in the Eighteenth Century* (1966). The Compagnie française des Indes orientales was founded by Colbert, Louis XIV's finance minister (see 459:7) in 1664. It remained under-capitalized and precarious for 50 years, until it was incorporated into the comprehensive Compagnie des Indes in 1719. This went bankrupt and was re-established in 1723 as a financial organization that was also given a monopoly of the eastern trade. Colbert was the most systematic exponent of mercantilist principles.

3 Any Dutch captain has full powers and plenty of money to utilize on any occasion and he is authorized to spend regardless when necessary. With us we have to obtain permission from superior authority for the smallest thing, and such permission often arrives too late, moreover, as we are all ill-provided, we are always compelled to beg our way wherever we go, which in turn makes it impossible for us to accomplish anything, since nothing can be done without money, above all with the natives of India.

Anon. Portuguese commander on the Malabar coast to the viceroy, 1664; Boxer (1969) p.115. Another view of the contrast between these two countries.

4 Both parties shall keep and possess hereafter, with plenary right of sovereignty, propriety and possession, all such lands, islands, cities, forts, places and colonies … [as] they have by force of arms, or any other way whatsoever, gotten and detained from the other party.

Treaty of Breda, 1667, under which the English accepted the loss of their possessions in the Dutch East Indies in exchange for the Dutch relinquishing New Netherlands, which the English had occupied in 1664. New Amsterdam was renamed New York after the Duke of York, Charles II's brother and the future James II.

5 [Cloves] were [formerly] used by the [Dutch East India] Company for annual dividend payments in place of money, and they have therefore dropped to a low price, but consumption has thereby increased and their use spread throughout Europe.

Court of Directors of the VOC to Batavia, 1673; Boxer (1965) Ch.7. Boxer comments: 'The company succeeded in maintaining an effective monopoly of the Moluccan spices down to the eve of its dissolution. When the warehouses in the Netherlands became full to overflowing, 1,250,000lb of surplus nutmegs were destroyed in 1735.'

6 The aims: To establish such a polity of military and civil power, and create and secure such a large revenue to maintain both … as may be the foundation of a large well-grounded, sure English dominion in India for all time to come.

Sir Josiah Child, governor of the East India Company, 1687; H.H. Dodwell (ed.) *Cambridge History of India* Vol.5 (1929) p.102.

7 Vote passed for the New East India Company, subscribing 2 millions, which was generally looked upon as a great hardship to the old and to the ruin of many adventurers who had put their whole stock into [the] old company.

John Evelyn, 21 June 1698; *The Diary of John Evelyn* (1955 edn) Vol.5. p.291.

8 The town [the factory at Pulicat in southern India near Madras] itself is not unattractive. There are many streets inhabited only by the Dutch, including several whose houses are all built in the special Dutch style, with three rows of trees at the front; and you can enjoy a pleasant stroll either in the day or evening.

David Havart *Op-en ondergang van Coromandel* (Rise and Fall of Coromandel) (1693); Boxer (1965) Ch.7. Havart served with the VOC from 1672 to 1685 on the coast of Coromandel, southeast India.

9 Its use has become so common in our country that unless the maids and seamstresses have their coffee every morning, the thread will not go through the eye of the needle.

Rev. François Valentijn, grumbling about the power of coffee or elevenses, 1724; G.H. Betz *Het Haagsche Leven in de tweede helft der Zeventiende eeuw* (1900) in Boxer (1965) Ch.6.

10 At this day, for two or three millions of guilders in specie, which the Dutch company sends to the East Indies, they bring home 15 or 16 millions in goods, of which a twelfth or fourteenth part is consumed amongst themselves; the rest is re-exported to the other countries of Europe, for which they are paid in money.

Anon. *A Description of Holland* (1743). These figures are a reminder of how important the trade with other countries of Europe was to the Dutch.

1 The company fears any increase in its domaine. Its object is not to gain territorial power, our role should be one of complete neutrality.

Directors of the Compagnie française des Indes to Dupleix, governor-general in Pondicherry (the French company's headquarters), 1752; Weber (1904) p.394. Joseph-François, Marquis Dupleix was Robert Clive's great rival in the struggle between the French and British East India companies for commercial and political control in India.

2 As the Armenians are likewise educated in all servilities of Asia, and understanding how to accommodate themselves to indignities which a free nation will hardly submit to, they are in some measure the better qualified to carry on a commerce through foreign dominions.

Jonas Walden Hanway An Historical Account of British Trade over the Caspian Sea (1754); Philip Curtin Cross-Cultural Trade in World History (1984) p.204. Curtin continues: 'As one English competitor put it, with a combination of envy and cultural arrogance.'

3 But so large a sovereignty may possibly be an object too extensive for a mercantile company; and it is to be feared that they [the directors of the East India Company, behind whose backs he was writing] are not themselves able, without the nation's assistance, to maintain so wide a dominion. I have therefore presumed, sir, to represent this matter to you [William Pitt, the Elder], and to submit to your consideration, whether the execution of a design that may hereafter be still carried to greater lengths ['perhaps of giving a king to Hindustan', as he explained to his father] be worthy of the government's taking in hand.

Robert Clive to William Pitt, Jan. 1759; Keay (1991) p.326. The company's governor and president in Bengal wrote this clandestine letter to the grandson of Thomas Pitt, the company's governor in Madras in 1697–1709. Thomas Pitt was known as Diamond Pitt from the priceless stone he acquired from an Indian merchant in 1701 and that is still part of the French state jewels.

4 Look around … observe the magnificence of our metropolis – the extent of our empire – the immensity of our commerce and the opulence of our people.

Charles James Fox, speech in House of Commons, 1763; Parliamentary History Vol.17, p.147 in Linda Colley Britons: Forging the Nation 1707–1837 (1972; 1994 edn) p.108. Colley describes Fox as still young and conventionally chauvinistic.

5 Not only are the Europeans very able navigators, but they endeavour continuously to increase their competency. The new skills and knowledge they acquire are simplified and systematized, so that they are easily taught to novices. This they do not only in the case of navigational science but of other branches of learning as well. This trait is peculiar to Europeans. Their courage and industry have made them the most powerful race on earth.

Mirza Sheikh I'tesamuddin The Wonders of Vilayet, Being the Memoir, originally in Persian, of a Visit to France and Britain in 1765 (2002 trans.) p.34. The Bengali official, employed by the East India Company, travelled to Britain to seek royal protection for the Mogul emperor. He was the first Indian to visit and record, with great vividness, the long sea journey and his impressions of Vilayet (Europe) and Britain in particular.

6 Most of the principal towns are sadly decayed, and instead of finding every mortal employed, you meet with multitudes of poor creatures who are starving in idleness. Utrecht is remarkably ruined. There are whole lanes of wretches who have no other subsistence than potatoes, gin and stuff which they call tea and coffee; and what is worst of all, I believe they are so habituated to this life that they would not take work if it should be offered to them.

James Boswell, 1764; F.A. Pottle (ed.) Boswell in Holland 1763–1764 (1952) pp.280–81. Boxer (1965) thinks that Boswell may be somewhat exaggerating the contrast between Holland in the 17th century and its decay in the 18th century or 'Periwig Period'.

7 The riches of Asia have been poured in upon us, and brought with them not only Asiatic luxury, but, I fear, Asiatic principles of government. Without connections, without any natural interest in the soil, the importers of foreign gold have forced their way into Parliament, by such a torrent of private corruption, as no private hereditary fortune could resist.

William Pitt, speech in the House of Lords quoted by the Marquis of Rockingham to the Countess of Chatham, Jan. 1770, when commiserating over Pitt's bout of illness (gout); The Correspondence of William Pitt, Earl of Chatham Vol.3 (1839) p.405.

8 An European that remains here [in Deshima] is in a manner dead and buried in an obscure corner of the globe. He hears no news of any kind; nothing relative to war, or other misfortunes and evils that plague and infest mankind; and neither the rumours of inland or foreign concerns delight or molest his ear … The European way of living is in other respects the same as in other parts of India [i.e., Asia], luxurious and irregular.

The Swedish botanist and explorer Carl Peter Thunberg, Nov. 1775; *Travels in Europe, Africa and Asia, 1770–1779* (1795) Vol.3, pp.63–4. His version of life in the trading stations. The Dutch were the only Europeans allowed a trading station in Japan, which they had moved to Deshima in 1641.

1 The pride which some of the weaker-minded officers in the Dutch service very imprudently exhibit to the Japanese, by ill-timed contradiction, contemptuous behaviour, scornful looks and laughter, which occasion the Japanese in their turn to hate and despise them; a hatred which is greatly increased upon observing in how unfriendly and unmannerly a style they usually behave to each other, and the brutal treatment which the sailors under their command frequently experience from them.

C.P. Thunberg (1795) Vol.3, p.29. The Swedish traveller is describing the reaction of the Japanese. He had been taught botany by Carl Linnaeus himself, and on his journeys to South Africa, Japan and Java he collected and described 3,000 plants, many of them new to science.

2 He enumerated several of the instances in which the despotism of Mr Hastings' government appeared to him most notorious, extraordinary, and inexcusable. This plan of carrying on a system of extortion among those poor defenceless natives was equally shocking and detestable. He tyrannized over the countries which he was bound only to govern for the good of the company, and that of the individuals governed.

Edmund Burke, speech on the charge against Warren Hastings for launching a war against the Rohillas (a warlike Afghan tribe) without the authority of councillors from Britain, 1 June 1786; *The Writings and Speeches of Edmund Burke* Vol.6 (1991) p.109. Warren Hastings was governor of Bengal from 1772 to 1785. He there expanded the authority of the East India Company's administration over those of local rulers. On his return from Bengal he was accused of corruption, and in 1787 a lengthy impeachment procedure began, managed for the prosecution by Edmund Burke. The case explored the anxieties of the British ruling class about their government in India. Hastings was acquitted in 1795.

THE SECOND AGE OF DISCOVERY, 1688–1788

3 The inhabitants of this country are the miserablest people in the world. The Hotmadods [Hottentots, the Nama people of Namibia] of Monomatapa, though a nasty people, yet for wealth are gentlemen to these; who have no houses, skin garments, sheep, poultry, ostrich eggs, and fruits of the earth as the Hotmadods have … Their only food is a small sort of fish, which they get by making weirs of stone across little coves or branches of the sea … at their places of abode the old people and infants await their return; and what providence has bestowed on them they presently broil on the coals and eat it in common. Whether it be much or little every one has his share … they must attend the weirs or else they must fast, for the earth affords them no food at all. There is neither herb, root, pulse, nor any sort of grain for them to eat, that we saw, nor any bird or beast that they can catch, having no instruments wherewith to do so.

William Dampier, 1688; *A New Voyage Around the World* (1697; 1931 edn) pp.142–4. The former buccaneer, who became a captain in the Royal Navy, compares the Aborigines of New Holland, Australia's west coast, unfavourably with the Nama of Namibia. Dampier's experiences and achievements were extraordinary, and his ability to describe them made his the most widely read English travel book since Sir John Mandeville's invented adventures of the 14th century.

4 What comparison can be made between the execution of a project such as this, and the conquest of some little ravaged province – of two or three cannon-shattered fortresses, acquired by massacre, ruin, desolation, bought at the expense a hundred times greater than that needed for the whole of the discovery proposed?

Charles de Brosses *Histoire des navigations aux terres australes* (1756); Williams (1966) p.159. The scholarly and persuasive president of the *parlement* in Dijon in Burgundy advances the case for further exploration of a southern continent. His book was intended to divert French energies away from hugely costly and destructive European wars and into colonizing and developing trade in a southern continent. The book was published in the very year that the ruinous Seven Years War started.

5 You are to proceed to the southward in order to make discovery of the continent abovementioned [the so-called southern continent] until you arrive in the latitude of 40°, unless you sooner fall in with it. But not having discovered it or any evident signs of it in that run, you are to proceed in search of it to the westward between the latitude before mentioned and the latitude of 35° until you discover it or fall in with the eastern side of the land discovered by Tasman and now called New Zealand.

Instructions issued by the Lords of the Admiralty to Captain James Cook in July 1768, prior to his first expedition; J.C. Beaglehole *The Life of Captain James Cook* (1974) pp.148–9. Before proceeding as directed, Cook was to visit the island of Tahiti in the Pacific to observe and record the expected 'transit of Venus', the passage of that planet between the earth and the sun, an astronomical event of major significance for navigation.

1 Thank heaven I have a sufficiency and I do not know why I may not keep him as a curiosity as well as some of my neighbours do lions and tigers at a larger expense than he will probably ever put me to; the amusement I shall have in his future conversation and the benefit he will be of to this ship, as well as what he may be if another should be sent into these seas, will I think fully repay me.
Sir Joseph Banks, July 1769; J.C. Beaglehole (ed.) *The Endeavour Journal of Joseph Banks 1768–1778* (1962) Vol.2, pp.312–13. Banks, a wealthy gentleman and collector who sailed with a number of personal servants in Cook's first expedition, refers here to the Tahitian priest Tupaia, who sailed from Tahiti with Cook and provided him with valuable information about the geography of the islands. Banks was the President of the Royal Society (see 372:3) for 41 years, founded the African Association and helped settlement in New South Wales. As a botanist he transferred the breadfruit from Tahiti to the West Indies and the mango from Bengal. His name is commemorated in *Banksia*, a genus of some 50 species of trees and shrubs from Australia.

2 I can by no means justify my conduct in attacking the people in the boat, who had given me no just provocation and were wholly ignorant of my design.
Captain James Cook, at Poverty Bay, New Zealand, 10 Oct. 1769; Beaglehole (1974) p.200. When Cook's landing was resisted by a party of the native Maori, he responded with gunfire, killing two or three. Cook agonized at length about this incident, as did Banks, who was the first to shoot, recording in his journal: 'The most disagreeable day my life has yet seen, black be the mark for it and heaven send that such may never return to embitter future reflection.' The attitude thus exhibited by both men was so different from the prevailing callousness in such matters that it seems to strike a new note in the literature of discovery.

3 The old people said 'Yes, it is so: these people are goblins; their eyes are at the back of their heads; they pull on shore with their backs to the land to which they are going.'
J.C. Beaglehole *The Discovery of New Zealand* (1961) p.89. This memory of the Maori peoples' first sight of the English oarsmen at Coromandel on the North Island of New Zealand in 1852, also recalls how Cook got the Maori aboard to sketch in charcoal on the deck a chart of their land, which he then copied onto paper. This remarkable communication had taken place in Nov. 1769.

4 These [Maori] are the only people who kill their fellow creatures purely for the meat, which we are well assured they do by laying in wait for one another as a sportsman would for his game … carrying in their ears the thumbs of those unhappy sufferers.
Journal of the young officer Richard Pickersgill, Jan. 1770; J.C. Beaglehole (ed.) *The Journals of Captain James Cook: The Voyage of the Endeavour 1768–1771* (1955) p.236. Cook and others confirmed this statement with plenty of gruesome evidence collected in Queen Charlotte's Sound at the northern end of the southern island of New Zealand.

5 The country, though in general well enough clothed, appeared in some places bare; it resembled in my imagination the back of a lean cow, covered in general with long hair, but nevertheless where her scraggy hip bones have stuck out farther than they ought, accidental rubs and knocks have entirely bared them of their share of covering.
Sir Joseph Banks; Beaglehole (1962) Vol.2, p.51. Banks is describing the country around Jervis Bay on the coast of what became New South Wales, Australia. Keeping well out to sea and sailing northwards, Cook passed this place on 25 April 1770.

6 Some malicious person or persons in the ship took advantage of his being drunk and cut all the clothes from off his back; not being satisfied with this, they some time after went into his cabin and cut off part of both his ears as he lay asleep in his bed.
Captain James Cook; Beaglehole (1974) p.232. The victim was Richard Orton, Cook's clerk, and this event occurred on 22 May 1770 at Bustard Bay on the New South Wales coast. Cook suspected one of the midshipmen called Magra, but could not be sure of either the culprit or the motive. This incident, though not untypical of shipboard violence in those cruel times, worried Cook as an insult to his authority.

7 The eastern coast from the latitude of 38°S down to this place I am confident was never seen or visited by any European before us.
Captain James Cook, 21 Aug. 1770; Beaglehole (1974) p.249. He therefore went on to declare that entire coast annexed to the dominions of King George III, naming it New South Wales.

8 I concur that it is difficult to conceive of such a large number of low-lying islands and land almost submerged, without supposing that there must be a continent nearby. But Geography is a science of facts.
Louis-Antoine de Bougainville *Voyage autour du monde* (1771) pp.183–4. The great French explorer had in 1668 discovered Samoa and spent ten days in Tahiti. He remains sceptical of a great southern continent, *Terra Australis*. Captain Cook's second voyage took place in 1772, a year after the first

publication of Bougainville's book. The French admiral gave his name to one of the Solomon Islands and to the tropical plant, bougainvillea.

1 To make new discoveries the navigator must traverse or circumnavigate the globe in a higher parallel than has hitherto been done … by an easterly course on account of the prevailing westerly winds in all high latitudes … It is humbly proposed that the ships may not leave the Cape of Good Hope before the latter end of September … when having the whole summer before them they may safely steer to the southward and make their way to New Zealand – between the parallels of 45° and 60°.

Captain James Cook, memorandum to the Earl of Sandwich, first lord of the Admiralty, 6 Feb. 1772, outlining the plan for his second expedition; Beaglehole (1974) p.286.

2 It has ever been a maxim with me to punish the least crimes any of my people have committed against these uncivilized nations; their robbing us with impunity is by no means a sufficient reason why we should treat them in the same manner … The best method in my opinion to preserve a good understanding with such people is first to show them the use of firearms and to convince them of the superiority they give you over them, and to be always upon your guard.

Captain James Cook, Nov. 1773; Beaglehole (1974) p.358. Cook had few illusions about the Maori, whom he called, in the normal parlance of those times, savages, nor about the savagery of his own crewmen, but he was far ahead of his time in learning to understand and forgive the former while refusing to condone the latter. Remarkable is the humane intelligence that enabled him to think this through for himself despite the prevailing climate of opinion.

3 Captain Vancouver used to say that he had been nearer the South Pole than any other man, for when the immortal Cook in latitude 72 was stopped in his progress by impenetrable mountains of ice and was prepared to tack about, he went to the very end of the bowsprit and, waving his hat, exclaimed 'Ne plus ultra' [thus far and no farther].

The Naval Chronicle Vol.1 (1799) p.125; Beaglehole (1974) p.365. Cook himself wrote on 30 Jan. 1774: 'I, whose ambition leads me not only farther than any other man has been before me, but as far as I think it possible for man to go, was not sorry at meeting with this interruption [innumerable mountains of ice] being at that time in the latitude of 71° 10'S, longitude 106° 54'W.' George Vancouver sailed on Captain Cook's second and third voyages. As a captain himself, he later (1792–4) surveyed the North American Pacific coast, sailing around Vancouver Island off Canada's west coast.

4 The gigantic statues so often mentioned are in my opinion not looked upon as idols by the present inhabitants … They are built or rather faced with hewn stones of a very large size and the workmanship is not inferior to the best plain piece of masonry we have in England … We could hardly conceive how a nation like these, wholly unacquainted with any mechanical power, could raise such stupendous figures and afterwards place the large cylindric stones … upon their heads.

Captain James Cook; J.C. Beaglehole (ed.) The Voyage of the Resolution and Adventure, 1772–1775 (1961) pp.357–8. Cook, honest and modest as ever, did not attempt to conceal his bafflement by the mysteries of Easter Island.

5 On Saturday the 29th [July 1775] we made the land near Plymouth and the next morning anchored at Spithead. Having been absent from England three years and eighteen days, in which time I lost but four men and only one of them by sickness.

Captain James Cook; Beaglehole The Voyage of the Resolution and Adventure, 1772–1775 (1961) p.682. In matters of health Cook was a pragmatist, having apparently scant knowledge even of what passed for medical science in his day. Perhaps this accounts for his remarkable success in this respect.

6 Upon your arrival on the coast of New Albion, you are … to proceed northward along the coast as far as the latitude of 65° [and then] carefully to search for and to explore such rivers or inlets as may appear to be of considerable extent and pointing towards Hudson's or Baffin's Bays.

Lords of the Admiralty, secret instructions to Captain Cook concerning his third voyage, 1776; Beaglehole The Voyage of the Resolution and Discovery, 1772–1775 (1967) Pt 1, pp.ccxxi–ccxxii. They state that the object of the voyage was 'to find out a northern passage by sea from the Pacific to the Atlantic Ocean'. 'New Albion' was the name given by Sir Francis Drake to the northwest coast of America, which he visited in 1579 in the course of his circumnavigation of the world.

7 As there were some venereal complaints on board both the ships, in order to prevent its being communicated to these people [of Hawaii], I gave orders that no women on any account whatever were to be admitted on board the ships … [But] the opportunities and inducements to an intercourse between the sex[es] are there too many to be guarded against.

Captain James Cook ; Beaglehole (1967) Pt 1, pp.265–6. Some of Cook's men had contracted venereal disease at the Society Islands. Hawaiian historians and American missionaries later unjustly blamed Cook, whose officers found it impossible to prevent their men bringing women aboard, sometimes dressed up as men. Cook had reached the Hawaiian Islands in Jan. 1778.

1 They were clothed in skins made into a dress like a shirt, or rather more like a waggoner's frock; it reached nearly as low as the knee and there was no slit either behind or before.

Captain James Cook; Beaglehole (1967) Pt 1, p.344. Cook thus described his first contact with the people of the southern coast of Alaska, whom he compared to (but did not identify as) 'Eskimo', now called 'Inuit'. Cook remained in this neighbourhood from mid-May until the beginning of July 1778, vividly depicting the inhabitants: 'Some, both men and women, have the underlip slit quite through horizontally, and so large as to admit the tongue, which I have seen them thrust through [as] was first discovered by one of the seamen, who called out there was a man with two mouths' (Beaglehole (1967) p.350).

2 This point of land, which I named Cape Prince of Wales, is the more remarkable by being the western extremity of all America hitherto known.

Captain James Cook; Beaglehole (1967) Pt 1, p.409. Reaching this point on 9 Aug. 1778, Cook thus passed into the Bering Strait and then pushed northward through it to explore the neighbouring Arctic waters as far as the polar ice, seeking still a passage eastward according to his instructions. Failing inevitably in this endeavour, he returned south through the strait early in Sept.

3 After we became acquainted with these Russians some of our gentlemen at times visited their settlement, where they always met with a hearty welcome. Such of the natives [of Unalaska] as belong to the Russians were all males and are taken, perhaps purchased, from their parents when young and brought up by the Russians.

Captain James Cook; Beaglehole (1967 Pt 1, pp.451–8. Cook met these Russian fur-traders on Unalaska, the southern

peninsula of Alaska, in Oct. 1778. With them also were people from Kamchatka, the peninsula of Asiatic Russia lying to the west, opposite Unalaska. Cook evidently liked the Russians and particularly admired their severe subjection of the natives, whom he, in typically English style, called 'Indians'.

4 The captain called to them to cease firing and to come in with the boats, intending to embark as fast as possible; this humanity perhaps proved fatal to him: the natives on the firing of the boats had fallen back a little, but seeing it cease pressed on again in great numbers … [Cook and those with him tried to reach their boats, and] had got close down to the sea side when a chief gave him a stab in the neck or shoulder with an iron spike, by which he fell, with his face in the water. The Indians set up a great shout and hundreds surrounded the body to dispatch him with daggers and clubs.

Lieutenant James King, journal entry; Beaglehole (1967) Pt 1, pp.556–7. Although this became the classic version of Cook's demise, it was not an eyewitness account, nor did Lieutenant Molesworth Phillips, the other chief informant, though directly involved in the fight, actually see his commander struck down. Cook was killed on 14 Feb. 1779 at Kealakekua Bay, Hawaii, while attempting to recover a large cutter stolen by locals during the preceding night.

5 What could you learn, sir? What can savages tell, but what they themselves have seen? Of the past, or the invisible, they can tell nothing. The inhabitants of Otaheité and New Zealand are not in a state of pure nature; for it is plain they broke off from some other people. Had they grown out of the ground, you might have judged of a state of pure nature.

Samuel Johnson, 29 April 1776; James Boswell *The Life of Johnson* (1791; 1953 edn) p.751. Dr Samuel Johnson gives his celebrated put-down to Boswell's wish to spend time among the peoples of the South Pacific to indulge in a quest for a Rousseau-like noble savage.

The Two Cardinals: Richelieu and Mazarin

RICHELIEU'S RISE TO POWER, 1602–24

1 God's will be done! I shall accept everything for the good of the church and the glory of our name.

Armand-Jean du Plessis de Richelieu, 1602; L. Lacroix *Richelieu à Luçon: sa jeunesse, son épiscopat* (1890) p.35. Richelieu, who had first trained for a military career, accepts the bishopric of Luçon (western France), in the family gift, after his elder brother, Alphonse, had turned it down to become a Carthusian monk.

2 The bishop has been an excellent administrator, and the bishop has trained the minister.

L. Lacroix (1890) p.319. Richelieu was a model bishop in Counter-Reformation style. In particular, being near to La Rochelle, he learned at first hand about the problem of the Huguenots (French Protestants). He soon began to use his diocese as a base for political campaigning and assumed the mantle of leader of the *dévôt* (ultramontane and pro-Spanish) party among the bishops.

3 Being of your disposition, that is a bit vainglorious, I should much like, it being more comfortable, to make a better appearance. It is a great pity – impoverished nobility.

Richelieu to his eldest brother Henri, 1610; D.L.M. Avenel (ed.) *Lettres et instructions diplomatiques et papiers d'état du Cardinal de Richelieu* (1853–77) Vol.1, p.55. Aged 25, the young bishop is planning to visit Paris, where he had studied, first at the Collège de Navarre and then at Pluvinel's military academy. The sudden death in 1590 of his father, who had been Grand Provost at the court of Henry III, left his mother Suzanne a widow with more debts than resources. The relative poverty of the family affords clues to his brothers' determined pursuit of family interests, and Richelieu's own ambition 'to be considerable'.

4 What is now happening is simply a pact guaranteeing that the rebels will get millions and lordships and fortresses whenever they want.

Maximilien de Béthune, duc de Sully, after the 'peace' of St Ménéhould, 1614; G.R.R. Treasure *Cardinal Richelieu* (1972) p.51. After his careful management of finances as *surintendant* (finance minister) under Henry IV, Sully had a special concern about the weakness of government under Henry's widow, the regent, Marie de' Medici.

5 I have lived 49 years in this house where I have seen the armies come through, but I have never heard talk of people such as this nor of such destruction as they bring ... Never before has any been lodged in

what belongs to me. If they had only lived honestly one would scarcely have complained of them but each one ransoms his host and they want to take women by force.

Suzanne du Plessis, Richelieu's mother, Nov. 1615; *Archives de la famille* XIV, f.12 in Elizabeth Marvick *The Young Richelieu* (1983) p.59. She is complaining about the conduct of the troops of Condé (one of the great families) in Poitou. Richelieu's views about order and stability in the state were influenced by his experience of these years, recalling the anarchic conditions that obtained during the Religious Wars (see 376:5).

6 Action is worth more than contemplation; it is worth much more to love God than incessantly to consider whether or not one loves him.

Richelieu *Traité de conversion* (1629); Marvick (1983) p.107. He understood that the meritorious life for a Christian was a perpetual will to action.

7 The grandeur of his house has been his greatest folly.

Gédéon Tallemant de Réaux *Historiettes* (1657–9; 1862 edn) Vol.1, p.460. Although generally regarded as an untrustworthy source, Tallemant, a counsel to *parlement* until c.1657, here represents the view of many contemporaries as they saw rise the Palais Cardinal in Paris and the magnificent château and new town of Richelieu. Richelieu's land purchases were concentrated in western France, where his personal domination was assured by governorships and through clients. His large fortune, estimated at his death at 22 million *livres*, was by far the largest of any subject to date. While he loved what wealth could buy, his acquisitions, like his accumulation of church benefices, were strategic – in state, as in church – to enable him to exercise control and to influence policy.

8 Grief at the loss of my brother, who died a few days ago, holds me so much in its grip that it is impossible for me to speak or to write to my friends.

Richelieu, July 1619; Avenel (1853–77) Vol.1, p.603. The death in a duel of his eldest brother, Henri, came at a time when Richelieu was making a good impression in court and army circles. His grief was compounded by the sense of loss for the family enterprise. It undoubtedly sharpened his sense of responsibility for the family and his appetite for power.

9 He had so great a command of his passions that even in the most extreme adversity they were at his beck and call.

Gabriel du Grés *Jean-Armand du Plessis, Duke of Richelieu and Peer of France* (1643 trans.) p.54.

1 To be *proviseur* [president] of the Sorbonne gives me more pleasure than to be a cardinal.

Richelieu, 1622; L. Batiffol *Autour de Richelieu* (1937) p.110. A few days after his appointment he was made cardinal by Pope Gregory V, as he expected. His interest in the Sorbonne (where he would eventually be buried) and the appeal of scholarship were beyond doubt. Like his creation of the Académie française (see 414:6), it should also be viewed in the context of his political design to control opinion through teaching and writing.

RICHELIEU IN POWER, 1624–42

2 As soon as Your Majesty was pleased to admit me into the management of your affairs I resolved to use my utmost endeavours to facilitate your great designs, as useful to this state as glorious to your person.

Richelieu *Testament politique* (1643; 1995 edn) p.41. The cardinal was effectively *premier ministre* from 1624 to 1642, and he began as he meant to go on, deferring to the king, Louis XIII, and treating him as if he were always the prime mover in policy.

3 He [Richelieu] wrote lucidly and powerfully, not only with a polish that betrays a deliberate and studied artistry, but also with a penetration and force that tells us that what he wrote was distilled from experience. His *Testament* and *Maximes* are struggle recollected in tranquillity.

G.R.R. Treasure (1972) p.246. The *Testament* may have been dictated to, and probably compiled by, secretaries, but it is the cardinal's voice and his political philosophy, enlarging upon the memoranda he regularly composed for Louis XIII.

4 It was the minister's habit, during habitual bouts of early morning wakefulness, to use the time thus abstracted from sleep for work with a secretary ... He often awakened around 2 a.m. and worked until about 5 p.m.

Elizabeth Marvick (1983) p.122. The chronic insomniac also suffered from migraines. They were rarer after his confirmation in office in 1630. Before that date 'my headache is killing me' is a frequent refrain in his letters.

5 The most royal task which Your Majesty can undertake is to restore order where it has been destroyed, to regulate the mechanical arts which are in monstrous confusion, to re-establish trade and commerce which have been troubled and interrupted for so long.

Antoine de Montchrétien *Traité d'économie politique* (1615; 1889 edn). The decline in the flow of silver from Spain into France and the tightening hold of the newly independent Dutch on colonial and European trade reinforced the arguments of those, like Montchrétien, later to be called 'mercantilist' (see 459:7). They were to have a strong influence on Richelieu's thinking and the policies about commerce, colonies and the navy that he outlined at the meeting of the Notables in 1626.

6 It has till now been a great shame that the king, who is the eldest son of the church, should be inferior in his maritime power to the smallest prince in Christendom. His Majesty is resolved ... to make himself as powerful at sea as he is on land ... These miseries will now cease, His Majesty having decided to maintain 30 good warships with which to guard the coasts, keep his subjects in their obedience, and teach his neighbours the respect due to so great a nation.

Richelieu, memorandum for use at the meeting of Notables, Nov. 1626; R.J. Knecht *Richelieu* (1991) p.153. By buying out the offices of Admiral of France and, as Surintendant-général de la navigation et commerce de France, securing for himself overall control, Richelieu strengthened royal control and created a navy. By 1642 there were some 60 ships. Under Colbert (see 460:5), Louis XIV would virtually make a fresh start after the navy had decayed during Mazarin's period, but the vision and the groundwork were Richelieu's. The personal elevation, which upset his enemies, and the extension of the power of the state were, for Richelieu, parts of the same essential process.

7 The establishment of the reign of God and conformity to the principles of reason are, according to the *Testament politique* the two ends of political action ... God is at the very heart of the political machine whose successes are seen as indication of divine favour.

François Hildesheimer 'Au Coeur Réligieux du Ministeriat' in *Revue d'histoire de l'Église de France* no.84, 1998, pp.21–37. A corrective, from the editor of the *Testament*, to the view that the zealous bishop of Luçon became a cynical, and in his critics' view 'Machiavellian', minister. Reasons of state did not preclude spiritual vision and purpose.

8 Such grandeur in his designs; such boldness in executing them.

Duc de la Rochefoucauld *Mémoires* (1665; 1831 edn) p.390. The future rebel expresses an aristocrat's view of Richelieu: this rebel was bound to oppose, but likely to admire.

9 You will make of this realm not a Republic of Plato, where all consisted of nothing but ideas, but an animated body which will act by its own springs and where all things will be seen infallibly to occur as will have been resolved that they should under your authority.

Mathieu de Morgues *Restauration de l'Etat* (1617) p.30. This pamphlet, which Richelieu may have written himself, exemplifies the hyperbole and wishful thinking of propaganda and the gap between the self-sustaining world of ideas and the situation on the ground.

1 We may compare them [the common people] to mules who, being accustomed to the burden suffer more from long rest than from work. But just as such work should be moderated so that the load be proportionate to their strength, so it should be for the taxes for the people.

Richelieu (1643; 1995 edn) p.180. Richelieu is surely here in sententious mood, rather than expressing the callous humour that is often noted when only the first part of his observation is quoted.

LOUIS XIII, 1601–43

2 This child belongs to everyone.

His father, Henry IV, 27 Sept. 1601. To the alarm of the midwife, the king displayed the few hours-old Louis to the assembled court. It was a public start to a public life. France, in a sense, would belong to Louis XIII; Louis would also belong to France.

3 What a remarkable thing that under a prince who exercised neither authority himself nor full freedom, royal power was more firmly established than it had been under the monarchs who were least dependent on their ministers and most adept in the art of governing.

Pierre Bayle *Dictionnaire historique* (1734 edn) Vol.3, p.796. Remarkable indeed. Bayle's acceptance of the conventional prejudice of his time against minister-favourites leads him to a misjudgement that has been echoed in accounts of Louis XIII until recent years.

4 I owe justice to my subjects and in this instance I prefer justice to mercy.

Louis XIII, 1617; L. Batiffol *Le Roi Louis XIII à vingt ans* (1910) p.177. Louis 'The Just', as he was to be called, aged 16, having already been on the throne for some five years, gives an early indication of the way he would see his royal duty. Resisting the wife's plea, he refuses mercy to baron de Guémadeuc, who was charged with murder, and sets the tone of his reign: the maintenance of public order in the face of any threat to his authority.

5 The late king did not lack sense; but his mind bent towards back-biting. He had difficulty in speaking and, being timid, that caused him to act ever less on his own. At times he reasoned passably well in a council meeting, and even appeared to have the

advantage over the cardinal. Perhaps the latter was shrewdly giving him this little satisfaction.

Gédéon Tallemant de Réaux (1657–9; 1862 edn) Vol.2, p.77.

6 Our customs are our true civil laws.

G. Coquille *Institution du droit des français* (The Institution of the Rights of the French) (1639) p.39. High claims were made for royal authority, God-given and absolute. In reality it was limited by the requirement that it be exercised in accordance with divine and natural justice, in particular to preserve the customary rights and liberties of subjects. It rested on a mass of contractual relationships with the 'orders', estates, provinces, municipalities and *corps* of a country that would not, until the Revolution, be a unitary state with citizens equal under the law.

THE HUGUENOT CHALLENGE, 1625–9

7 Everything now conspires to humble the pride of Spain … There has never been such a splendid opportunity for the king to increase his power and clip the wings of his enemies.

Richelieu, 1625; P. Grillon (ed.) *Papiers de Richelieu* (1975–86) Vol.1, p.181. Richelieu's promised intervention to cut the Spanish lines of communication in the Val Telline (the Alpine valley that was a vital link for the Habsburgs between Milan, Germany and Flanders) was aborted because of the Huguenot rising in Feb. led by the dukes of Rohan and Soubise. Everything – his own religious conviction, the advantage that it would appeal to the *dévôts* and the paramount need to secure his home base before sending troops abroad – came together to convince him that the time was ripe for the destruction of the Huguenot port and principal stronghold, La Rochelle. The siege of a fortress with access to the sea was generally held to be most hazardous.

8 Huguenots shared the state with you, the grandees behaved as if they had not been your subjects, and the most powerful governors of provinces as if they had been sovereigns in their offices.

Richelieu (1643; 1995 edn) p.41. Richelieu recollects identifying for his king the most serious challenges to his authority.

9 I promised Your Majesty that I would use my utmost endeavours and all the authority you were pleased to give me to ruin the Huguenot party, to abate the pride of the grandees and to raise your name again in foreign nations to the degree it ought to be … So long as the Huguenot party subsists in France the king will not be absolute in his kingdom and he will not be able to establish the order and rule to which his conscience obliges him and which the necessity of his people requires.

Anon. (but certainly Richelieu), Nov. 1625; Grillon (1975–86) Vol.1, p.226.

1 The army of His Majesty in such beautiful order around their finely positioned stronghold, well defended on one side by the marshes and on the other by the sea ... this town encircled and blockaded by many well-constructed forts, by such well-regulated lines of communication, by a dyke so firmly established, by ships so well positioned ... could a man, on seeing these works in such great symmetry have said anything other than Spinola [Spanish general] has said – that our king was a living God who commanded these works of Archimedes, these miracles?

Anon. *Discours d'état sur les importants succès des affaires jusqu'à la prise de La Rochelle* (1629) p.21. The triumphalist appeal of this royalist pamphlet to Roman discipline and values conveys a potent message: an ordered community pulls itself together to combat the forces of anarchy; monarchy as part of the universal order is a vital element in the chain of being that links the highest and lowest forms of existence. In the philosophy as in the practice of politics, the capture of La Rochelle marked a crucial stage in the evolution of absolutism.

2 Your cardinal is the first man in the world.

George Villiers, Duke of Buckingham, to his prisoner, Beaulieu-Persac, Nov. 1627, after his failure to relieve La Rochelle (see 420:4); Treasure (1972) p.102.

3 The roots of heresy, rebellion, disorder and civil war, which have exhausted France for so long, are dried up. Now all your subjects will compete with each other in rendering the obedience which is due to you.

Richelieu to Louis XIII, June 1629; P. Benedict 'La Population réformée française de 1600 à 1685' in *Annales* 42 (1987).

4 It is certain that the end of La Rochelle is the end of the miseries of France and the beginning of her happiness.

Richelieu, 1629; Avenel (1853–77) Vol.3, p.161. Richelieu's confidence was soon to be shaken by a political and personal crisis. In addition, the fall of La Rochelle freed troops for aggressive operations over the Alps.

WAR AND DIPLOMACY, 1628–43

5 It is said that we are starting an interminable war in the midst of necessities of state and the people's misery, and that under the pretext of relieving Casale we wish to enter Milanese territory.

Cardinal Bérulle to Richelieu, Feb. 1629; Grillon (1975–86) Vol.5, p.111. A leading *dévôt* and Richelieu's former mentor, the cardinal is anxious that by becoming involved in the succession of Mantua (northern Italy) the state will inevitably have to levy higher taxes.

6 If the king resolves on war it will be necessary to give up all thoughts of repose, economy and reform inside the kingdom. If ... he wants peace it will be necessary to give up thoughts of Italy in the future.

Richelieu, April 1630; Grillon (1975–86) Vol.5, p.208. The cardinal faces the king with what he already realized would be a crucial decision and one that would determine the future course of the reign. Pinerolo, on the edge of Piedmont, had been seized by French troops in March 1630. By deciding to hold it as a base from which to challenge Spanish power in north Italy, Louis XIII committed himself to the policy that would eventually lead to open war and to the personal direction that he enjoyed. As Richelieu would also say: 'Great undertakings are not without difficulty and one can do little good in them if one is not on the spot.'

7 Each person believed the cardinal ruined. The king ordered him to follow him to Versailles; and His Majesty, with a visage revealing indignation, also ordered M. the Keeper of the Seals [Michel de Marillac] to follow.

R. Arnauld d'Andilly *Journal inédit* Vol.10 (covers 1630–32) (1888–1909 edn) p.122. War or peace? It will depend on the outcome of the domestic crisis, the power struggle between the king and his mother, Marie de' Medici. There is no entirely reliable account of this tense period, which culminated in the Day of Dupes, 11 Nov. 1630, so called because the cardinal's enemies believed that Richelieu had been dismissed when in reality the king had resolved to confirm him in office.

8 I order you absolutely to remain and to continue directing my affairs; that is my irrevocable decision.

Louis XIII to Richelieu, Nov. 12, 1630; Knecht (1991) p.39. The gist of the king's words as relayed by Richelieu to a friend. Louis had escaped finally from the tutelage of his mother. He would never see her again. The next day Michel de Marillac was dismissed.

9 I wish for your glory more than any servant has ever wished it for his master ... The singular demonstration yesterday ... of your goodwill pierced my heart ... For my part I shall never be content except in making it known to Your Majesty that I am the most faithful creature, the most committed subject, and most zealous servant that any king and master has in the world. I will live and die in this position,

being a hundred times more Your Majesty's servant than I am my own.
Richelieu to Louis XIII, 12 Nov. 1630; Grillon (1975–86) Vol.5, p.644. Nervous prostration, high emotion and sheer relief may be read into these fervent words. The cardinal would be as good as his word, and the odd but effective partnership would continue to his death.

1 A republic [the French army], whose cantons are made up of the forces of the corps commanders.
Michel le Tellier, 1650; Knecht (1991) p.118. As war minister since 1643, Le Tellier was well placed to judge the central weakness of the army and that it was not under central control nor truly a royal army.

2 I ask you to tell Renaudot [editor of the *Gazette*] not to print anything about this action until I send him the account. I have seen one that is unsatisfactory and hurts all our galley captains.
Richelieu to secretary of state Chavigny, 15 Sept. 1635; Avenel (1853–77) Vol.7, p.180. A few days later Richelieu sent in *his* account. Théophraste Renaudot, who like Richelieu and Chavigny came from Poitiers (southwestern France), founded the *Gazette* in 1634. He was given the monopoly of publishing news. This weekly publication gave Richelieu scope for trumpeting good news, putting a favourable gloss on bad and promoting adulatory views of the regime.

3 I swear the devil must be in this friar's body … He penetrates my most secret thoughts, knows things that I have communicated only to a few people of tried discretion.
Duc de Bouillon; Treasure (1972) p.232. It was not only foreign princes who had reason to fear Richelieu's intelligence service, here personalized in the shape of Father Joseph, Richelieu's *éminence grise* and his close ally and trusted diplomatic agent.

4 Great negotiations ought to be carried forward without a moment's pause. One must pursue what one undertakes with a steady and consistent purpose; so that one acts only in accordance with reason and without any slackening of purpose, whether from indifference about things, vacillation in thinking or contrariness.
Richelieu (1643; 1995 edn) p.269. Under the direction of the cardinals Richelieu and his protégé Mazarin (see 414:7–417:2) French diplomats earned a reputation for skill and tenacity in negotiation. They could demand only what military success could justify. The negotiations at Munster and Osnabrück (Germany), which eventually led to the Peace of Westphalia (1648), lasted for four years. Throughout, taking their instructions from Mazarin, the French envoys were faithful to the precepts and purpose of Richelieu.

DOMESTIC ISSUES, 1624–43

5 The Cardinal de Richelieu, to diminish the authority of the princes and the greater men which are governors of provinces, hath begun another work of great importance which the provincial governors did usually practise … to call the Assemblies of the States, either for the levying of monies in the countries for the king's service, or to consult of other occasions.
Sir Thomas Edmondes, English ambassador, Sept. 1629; J. Russell Major *Representative Government in Early Modern France* (1980) p.254. Following court gossip, Edmondes may have exaggerated the absolutist tendency of the cardinal, a pragmatist in such matters.

6 I can hardly believe my own eyes and impressions when I consider the present and recall the past. It is no longer the old France that until recently was torn apart, ill and decrepit. No longer are the French the enemies of their country … Behind their face I see other men and in the same realm another state. The form remains but the interior has been renewed.
Guez de Balzac *Le Prince* (1631); W.F. Church *Richelieu and Reason of State* (1972) p.221. Balzac's work centres on Louis XIII but is effusively eulogistic towards Richelieu. He sees the renovation of the French state after the chaos of the Religious Wars as the king's greatest achievement, but that is not a view that would find favour with noble enemies, certainly not with the king's brother, Gaston of Orléans, inveterate plotter and rebel.

7 For a long time Cardinal de Richelieu has had a well-formed plan to make himself ruler of the land under the title of First Minister. For a while he is prepared to allow you to retain the crown. However he seeks to make you dependent on him and having rid himself of both you and me, he plans to gain supreme power … The last third [of the peasantry] are not only reduced to begging but languish in such conditions that some actually die of starvation while the rest live like wild beasts surviving only on acorns, plants and such things. The least pitiful of this last group are those who eat only the husk of the grain dipped in the blood they collect from the gutters by butchers' shops.
Gaston of Orléans to Louis XIII, May 1631; G. Mongrédien *Novembre 1630. La Journée des dupes* (1961) pp.215–17. The force of this alarming indictment is somewhat reduced by the fact that Gaston was currently in exile, actively plotting against the cardinal. Gaston went on to describe the way in which Richelieu has gained complete control of administration, armed forces and finance; then he describes the destitution of the people.

1 Harshness towards individuals who flout the laws and commands of the state is for the public good. No greater crime against the public interest is possible than to show leniency to those who violate it.

Richelieu (1643; 1995 edn) p.212. In 1632 the marquis de Cinq-Mars, who had been a favoured friend of the king, was another who paid the supreme penalty for conspiracy or rebellion. Richelieu could rely on Louis to stand firm in face of the arguments of class or sentiment and the pleas of relations and friends.

2 The principal difficulty before us is whether we should make prisoners of all the tax collectors … if we put pressure on them, then most would go bankrupt.

Claude de Bouthillier and fellow *surintendant* Claude de Bullion to Richelieu, Feb. 1636; R. Bonney *Society and Government in France under Richelieu and Mazarin, 1624–61* (1988) pp.44–5. The *surintendants* had the unenviable task of finding the money to finance the war. This is one of innumerable references to the parlous state of the royal finances – and this at the start of a war that was to go on until 1659. The weary and cynical tone is characteristic of ministers in this period, who were having to make the best of a bad job. To reinforce – in some cases actually to take over from – the local tax officials, the crown appointed *intendants* (commissioners) and gave them draconian powers. So the twin emergencies of war and finance stimulated the development of the state.

3 You are here only to judge master Peter and master John, and I mean to keep you in your place. If you continue your machinations I will cut your nails to the quick.

Louis XIII to a deputation of magistrates of *parlement*, Jan. 1632; Mathieu Molé *Mémoires* (1855–7 edn) Vol.2, pp.143–4. A good example of the king's brisk, not to say brutal, style in dealing with what he held to be unreasonable opposition.

4 They protest that they are good Frenchmen who would rather die than continue under the tyranny of the Parisians and financiers who have reduced them to the despair and extreme poverty under which their province labours as a result of new and heavy taxes invented during the course of this reign. These burdens have forced many to give up their landholdings in order to beg for bread, leaving the land uncultivated, the draught animals unable to live off the saffron crop, abandoning clothes and farm implements to be seized by the bailiffs.

Anon., 1636; W.M. Bercé *Histoire des Croquants* (1974) Vol.2. pp.736–7. This account of a rising of the peasants of Saintonge and Angoumois, in southwest France, illustrates the two main aspects of provincial outrage throughout the reign: the oppression and extortion of 'Parisians', essentially foreigners; and the novelty, as well as the weight, of the impositions.

5 Your Majesty's financial officials are thieves greedy to fill their own purses … They are ravenous … eating the poor ploughmen right down to the bone.

A typical extract from a *Croquant* document from Périgord, southwestern France, May 1637; W.M. Bercé *History of Peasant Revolts* (1986; 1990 trans.) p.120. The extraordinary scale of the fiscal demands and the fierce methods employed by tax collectors provoked numerous risings in town and country. The most serious were those of the peasant bands, Croquants, that spread through the southwest in 1636–7.

6 There [at the Academy] assemble a great many poor zealots who learn to compose frauds and to disguise ugly acts and make ointments to soothe the wounds of the public and the cardinal. He promises some advancement and gives small favours to this rabble who combat truth for bread.

Mathieu de Morgues; Church (1972) p.348. He was at first a confidant, then, from exile in Brussels, a bitter critic of the cardinal. Richelieu founded the Académie française in 1635 to enhance artistic and artistic activity and prestige, but it was widely seen as an instrument of propaganda.

MAZARIN, 1602–61

7 To a gentleman [*galantuomo*] any country is his homeland.

Guilio Mazarini to Walter Montagu, Sept. 1637; G. Dethan *Mazarin* (1981) p.114. The Roman diplomat (b.1602) has already served Richelieu in important negotiations. Now he is beginning to see himself as a Frenchman, 'by gratitude and temperament', and was looking forward to entering royal service. He was formally invited to come to France in 1639. Thereafter he was Jules Mazarin, Frenchman by adoption, although to his French critics he would always be a foreigner.

8 Colmardo must remember that powers [the king's] greater than his [Richelieu's] take notice only of performance and scorn those who have more capacity for airy proposals and empty discourse than for useful actions.

Richelieu to Mazarin, Nov. 1640; Avenel (1853–77) Vol.7, p.830. Mazarin (Colmardo was one of Richelieu's teasing nicknames for him) wanted to go to a projected congress to prepare for a German peace. Instead Richelieu sent him to Savoy, to settle affairs in the aftermath of a failed Spanish invasion – and test him for 'the greatest and most important negotiations for which you are destined'. His proven diplomatic capacity commended him to Richelieu and, crucially, to Louis XIII, and led them to think of him as a future minister.

9 Tall, of good appearance, a handsome man, with chestnut hair, lively and amused eyes, and a great sweetness in his face.

Olivier d'Ormesson, 1641; Dethan (1981) p.157. A year younger than Anne of Austria, Mazarin, with his courtesy and willingness to talk her native language, made a strong impression on the queen.

1 I am persuaded that Mazarin is my servant ... I wish to avail myself of a person who is not in any way dependent on Monsieur [Gaston of Orléans] or the prince de Condé.

Anne of Austria, April 1643; Henri Loménie de Brienne *Mémoires* (1838–41 edn) p.76. Anne realizes that Louis XIII is about to die and that she will become regent. She thinks that the experienced Italian will serve single-mindedly, without the client obligations and factious spirit of a French grandee. Her dependence on Mazarin will be as much political as emotional.

2 Monsieur the Cardinal de Richelieu, having died on 4 Dec. 1642, and the king on 14 May 1643, everybody believed that the change of government would bring about some transformation of affairs ... This did not happen because M. the Cardinal Mazarin was called to the ministry and openly and loudly protected the family and the remnants of M. the Cardinal of Richelieu, to whose memory he was obliged because of his Cardinal's hat.

Omer Talon *Mémoires* (1648; 1839 edn) p.299. Talon, advocate general in *parlement*, was expected to be authoritative on matters of law. As the reader of royal messages to *parlement*, and thus interpreter of the crown to *parlement* and of *parlement* to the crown, his was a delicate position, which he would take most seriously. He was, therefore, a pivotal figure in the civil wars of 1648–52, known as the Fronde. Mazarin's status as cardinal (since 1641) entitled him to preside at meetings of council.

3 Monsieur the Cardinal de Richelieu entered the ministry and surmounted all the obstacles placed before him. He elevated his fortune on the ruins of those who attacked him. He maintained himself principally by the profusion of royal finances, with which he corrupted the great nobles and those who were necessary to him both within the kingdom and abroad. In order to do this he suffered that those who were in the administration of the king's finances did what they wanted at a time when the kingdom was rich and abundant in wealth.

Omer Talon (1648; 1839 edn) p.270. A fair summary of *parlementaire* opinion at the outset of Mazarin's ministry. It gives an idea of what was expected of the new regime.

4 Mazarin was greatly disliked as a foreigner. He was accused of having refused to sign peace [at Westphalia, in 1648, with Spain; war continued

until 1659]. He was accused of having transported the wealth of the kingdom to Italy. He made no friends because in all the gifts there was something that diminished their value. He did not understand the conduct of domestic policy ... In the *parlement* of Paris he was despised; among the populace he was hated.

Omer Talon (1648; 1839 edn); J.-F. Michaud and J.-J.F. Poujoulart *Nouvelles collections des mémoires pour servir à l'histoire de France* (1839) p.272. Looking back from the outbreak of the Fronde, Talon summarizes the main charges against Mazarin's ministry from 1643 to 1648.

5 No new taxes are to be imposed except as a result of edicts verified in the sovereign courts which have cognizance and the implementation of the edicts and declaration shall be reserved to the courts.

Omer Talon, proposals of the deputies of the sovereign courts in the Chambre St Louis, 3 July 1648; Michaud and Poujoulart (1839) p.241. The Chambre St Louis became in name, as in its novel proceedings, the focal point of constitutional conflict at the outset of the Fronde. The old issue of arbitrary taxation and a new constitutional claim of *parlement* come together in this demand. To accept it would be to so limit the powers of monarchy as to reverse the absolutist trend and achievement of Richelieu.

6 I know that a soul as delicate as yours, and as jealous of his glory, would scarcely allow himself to be tarnished by those terrible names, rebel, conspirator, traitor. However these phantoms of infamy that public opinion has conjured up to alarm vulgar souls cause no shame to those who know them for brilliant actions, when their outcome is happy. Scruples and grandeur have always been incompatible and these feeble maxims of common prudence owe more to the school of the people than to that of great lords ... The crime of usurping a crown is so illustrious that it can pass for a virtue.

Paul de Gondi *La Conjuration de Fiesque* (1639) p.33. Gondi (later Cardinal de Retz and author of famous memoirs) uses an episode of Italian history to express his own values. The style and ideas convey much of the spirit of the noble Fronde, its cult of heroic individualism and its flavour of adventure. They show why he was suspected by Richelieu and, as agitator and mob-master, was so dangerous to Mazarin. Although he may have exaggerated his role in the popular rising and erection of barricades that precipitated the Fronde in Aug. 1648, he was certainly seen by the court as their most dangerous enemy.

7 He [Gondi] has a talent for mixing gunpowder with his oils.

Mathieu Molé, attrib., *Premier président* (senior judge), Jan. 1649, at the ceremony of registration of the Peace of Rueil;

G.R.R. Treasure *Mazarin* (1995) p.153. Gondi derived political influence from his ecclesiastical position as aide and presumed successor to the archbishop of Paris and enjoyed support from Paris priests, despite his dishonesty and blatant sexual affairs.

1 At 4 in the morning the king left Paris. The queen left at six … Monsieur the duc d'Orléans … and chief members of the royal court left at the same time for Saint-Germain-en-Laye in about 20 carriages. There was consternation in Paris at the news. All the people, great and small, were excited.

Omer Talon, 6 Jan. 1649; (1648; 1839 edn) p.318. A bold and risky bid. The ensuing siege of Paris led to the Peace of Rueil (April 1649) and the end of the first, *parlementaire*, phase of the Fronde. But it also ensured that when the nobles renewed the challenge they would have much support in Paris.

2 The insolence and tyranny with which he [Cardinal Mazarin] carries on, after having perverted all the good rules of a legitimate and reasonable government by his extreme ignorance and malice, and made enormous thefts from the treasure of the realm, and carried off scandalously and perilously the sacred person of the king and Monsieur his brother, seduced the other princes of the blood and impudently and falsely accused members of this august body of *parlement* of correspondence with enemies of the state, because of which, having by solemn *arrêt* [decree] declared him a perturbator of public peace and enemy of the king and his state, he will be pursued ceaselessly until he is secured within the hands of justice to be publicly and exemplarily executed.

Contrat de mariage du parlement avec la ville de Paris, Feb. 1649; Hubert Carrier (ed.) *La presse de la Fronde; Mazarinades* (1989) Vol.1, p.7. *Parlement*'s programme for action followed a recital of grievances. The challenge to leaders of the Fronde, *parlementaire* and noble alike, was to achieve unity and convey that impression to the court.

3 This foreign rogue, juggler, comedian, famous robber, low Italian fellow fit only to be hanged.

Guy Patin, Jan. 1649; Treasure (1995) p.143. Patin, a well-known Parisian doctor, seems to have had his finger on the pulse of popular opinion at a time when his very name became a term of abuse and Paris coachmen would urge on their horses with the phrase 'or Mazarin will get you'.

4 The design of the Cardinal de Mazarin has no other purpose than to oppress, destroy the *parlement* and city of Paris and to subject the other provinces to a common oppression. He seeks to establish his tyranny to such an extent that he would be absolute master of all that is most considerable in

the state … Acting together … we will secure the state by preventing a civil war which would have no other cause but the ambition of a foreigner.

Parlement of Paris to other *parlements*, 18 Jan. 1649; R. Mousnier (ed.) *Lettres et mémoires adressées au chancelier Séguier* Vol.2, pp.901–2. *Parlement* appeals for help to resist impending attack. Paris is levying troops. Armand de Bourbon, Prince de Conti and other nobles will command them.

5 We, the undersigned, recognize from experience the prejudice which the king and the state receive from the detention of Messieurs the princes of Condé and Conti and the duc de Longueville. [We should] unite in order to halt, by all legitimate means possible, the oppression of these three princes who have been arrested and held prisoner against the law of the kingdom … Cardinal Mazarin is notoriously the author of their detention and cause of the disorders which have preceded and followed it.

Union of the Frondes, 30 Jan. 1651. A. Feillet *et al. Oeuvres de Retz* (1870–96) Vol.3, pp.549–50.

6 Ah Madame! What have you done. These are children of the royal house.

Mathieu Molé, attrib., Jan. 1650; Claude Joly *Mémoires* Series 3, Vol.2 (1838) p.161. Molé, first president of the *parlement* in 1641–53, is shocked by the arrest of the princes, ordered by Mazarin. His concern was justified by subsequent events: the so-called War of the Princesses, the release (Feb. 1651) of the princes and the first exile of Mazarin.

7 The passion that I have for you furnishes reasons to excuse you for everything you do, even to my prejudice, for surrounded by villains combining to deceive you … how can you protect yourself? I reply that the remedy is to get out of Paris.

Mazarin to Anne of Austria, 7 July 1651; J.A.D. Ravenel *Lettres du Cardinal Mazarin à la reine* (1836) p.169. Impatient to be recalled, trying to control events from his exile in Germany, Mazarin writes as a lover. The verdict of those best informed at the time, and of modern scholarship, is that they were not lovers but friends and allies, bound by mutual need and respect.

8 The king and queen, by an authentic act, have declared me a public thief, incompetent and an enemy to the peace of Christendom.

Mazarin, 26 Sept. 1651; Ravenel (1836) p.292. He writes from exile, after he has heard that *parlement* had registered the edict of banishment. Meanwhile Louis XIV, who is now aged 13, has been declared of age. Mazarin fears for his future and resolves to return.

9 I have created the College of the Four Nations so that the children of the new provinces should come to learn in Paris the advantage of being subjects of so great a king … so that in the end all our provinces will become French of their own free will, just as they now are through the domination of His Majesty.

Mazarin, will (written in 1658); Treasure (1995) p.310. Mazarin left a prodigious fortune, the largest of any French subject of the *ancien régime*. Avarice is a justifiable charge. Yet his will shows a grander vision. Among his legacies to his adopted country were a solid peace, a king well-schooled in the arts of rule and a well-trained team of devoted ministers, notably Michel le Tellier and Colbert.

1 He was French and Italian, soldier and doctor of law, layman and cardinal, foreigner and royal servant, exile and plenipotentiary, subject and friend of the king, a most notable victim, a phoenix; a Phoebus after the clouds have rolled away; the arbiter of great peoples and nations.

Père Léon of Mazarin, March 1661; Treasure (1995) pp.309–10. The Carmelite friar, who was preaching at Rome, struck appropriate notes of paradox in depicting the 'lights and shades' in his subject's career and the 'mysterious enigma of the whole'.

2 It is good that France should always be the victor.

Pierre Corneille *Toison d'Or* (Golden Fleece) (1659) Prologue. The great French dramatist is referring to the Treaty of the Pyrenees. The reward for costly years of war and patient diplomacy, it secured for France Artois, Cerdagne and Roussillon (regions in north, central and southern France) and set out the terms for the marriage of Louis XIV to Maria Teresa, infanta of Spain. The Spanish Succession would be the major diplomatic issue of Louis XIV's reign (see 465:6).

The Stuarts and the English Revolution, 1603–88

JAMES I, 1603–25

1 Whereas it was the expectation of many who wished not well unto our Sion [i.e., land] that upon the setting of that bright occidental star, Queen Elizabeth of most happy memory, some thick and palpable clouds of darkness would so have overshadowed this land that men should have been in doubt which way they were to walk ... the appearance of your majesty, as of the sun in his strength, instantly dispelled those supposed and surmised mists.

Authorized Version of the Bible ('The King James Bible') (1611) Preface. Although the transition from Elizabeth to James I was accomplished peacefully, this extract suggests the relief at James's unchallenged accession and that he had heirs to succeed him. See 419:3.

2 [Mayerne says that] King James' legs were slender, scarcely strong enough to carry his body ... that his skin was soft and delicate, but irritable, and that when he vomited it was with so great an effort that his face would be sprinkled with red spots for a day or two; that he never ate bread, always fed on roast meat, and seldom or never ate of boiled, unless it was beef; that he was very clumsy in his riding and hunting, and frequently met with accidents ... that he was very often thirsty, drank frequently and mixed his liquors, being very promiscuous in his use of wines.

Sir Theodore Mayerne, Memorandum of his professional attendance upon King James; Sir Henry Ellis (ed.) Original Letters Illustrative of English History 2nd series, Vol.3 (1827) pp.198–9. Mayerne was principal physician to James I from 1611 to 1625 and subsequently served Charles I.

3 Our blessed queen ... was more than a man, and (in troth) sometime less than a woman. I wish I waited now in her presence-chamber, with ease at my food and rest in my bed. I am pushed from the shore of comfort, and know not where the winds and waves of a court will bear me ... My father had much wisdom in directing the state, and I wish I could bear my part as discreetly as he did.

Sir Robert Cecil to Sir John Harington, 23 May 1603; Sir John Harington Nugae Antiquae (1769; 1804 edn) Vol.1, p.345. Cecil was the second son of William Cecil, Lord Burghley,

Elizabeth's right-hand man. He was appointed principal secretary of state in 1596 and, in the last years of the queen's reign, began a secret correspondence with James VI of Scotland, which ensured the latter's peaceful accession in 1603. He dealt with the multifarious problems that the change of ruler brought with it. Hence the tone of regret for more settled days.

4 A custom loathsome to the eye, hateful to the nose, harmful to the brain, dangerous to the lungs, and in the black stinking fume thereof nearest resembling the horrible Stygian smoke of the pit that is bottomless.

James I A Counterblast to Tobacco (1604; 1900 edn) p.54. Tobacco was first brought from the New World into France about 1560. Some years later Sir John Hawkins introduced it into England. James's Counterblast was published anonymously shortly after he ascended the English throne. Only in 1616 did he openly acknowledge his authorship (see 430:3).

5 We have thought good to discontinue the divided names of England and Scotland out of our regal style, and do intend and resolve to take and assume unto us ... the name and style of King of Great Britain, including therein, according to the truth, the whole island ... And to the end the same may be the sooner and more universally divulged both at home and abroad, our will and pleasure is that the style be from henceforth used upon all inscriptions upon our current moneys and coins of gold and silver hereafter to be minted.

James I, proclamation, 20 Oct. 1604; Thomas Rymer Foedera (1704–35) Vol.7, Pt 2, p.126. James, who had been king of Scotland before ascending the English throne, felt that his God-given task was to unify the two kingdoms. A statutory union had to wait until 1707. James had to be content to be king of Great Britain by royal proclamation.

6 With all humble and due respect to your majesty, our sovereign lord ... we most truly avouch

First, that our privileges and liberties are our right and due inheritance, no less than our very lands and goods.

Secondly, that they cannot be withheld from us, denied or impaired, but with apparent wrong to the whole state of the realm.

Thirdly ... that our making of request in the entrance of Parliament to enjoy our privilege is an act only of manners.

Form of Apology and Satisfaction, June 1604; J.R. Tanner (ed.) *Constitutional Documents of the Reign of James I* (1930) p.221. At the beginning of every Parliament the Speaker of the Commons asked the king to confirm the House's privileges. James took this as evidence that all such privileges derived from him and that, by implication, they could be withheld. The Commons' rejection of this view is contained in the 'Form of Apology,' even though it was never formally adopted by the House.

1 On the 5th of November we began our Parliament, when the king should have come in person, but he refrained through a practice [i.e., plot] but that morning discovered. The plot was to have blown up the king at such time as he should have been set in his royal throne, accompanied with his children, nobility and commoners, and assisted with all the bishops, judges and doctors, at one instant – a blast to have ruined the whole state and kingdom of England. And for the effecting of this there was placed under the Parliament House, where the king should sit, some thirty barrels of powder, with good store of wood, faggots, pieces and bars of iron. How this came forth [was revealed] is sundry ways delivered. Some say by a letter sent to the Lord Monteagle, wherein he was warned not to come to the Parliament the first day … Others otherwise. But howsoever, certain it is that upon a search lately made on Monday night, in the vault under the Parliament chamber before spoken of, one Johnson was found with one of those close lanterns, preparing the train [i.e., fuse] against the next morrow.

Sir Edward Hoby to Sir Thomas Edmondes, British ambassador at the court of Brussels, 19 Nov. 1605; T. Birch (ed.) *The Court and Times of James the First* (1848) Vol.1, p.36. The 'Johnson' found in the vaults preparing the slow fuse was in fact Guido, or Guy, Fawkes, a Catholic convert who had served with the Spanish army in the Netherlands and was experienced in handling gunpowder.

2 Kings are justly called gods for that they exercise a manner or resemblance of divine power upon earth. For if you will consider the attributes of God, you shall see how they agree in the person of a king. God hath power to create or destroy; make or unmake at his pleasure; to give life or send death; to judge all and to be judged nor accountable to none; to raise low things and to make high things low at his pleasure. And the like power have kings.

James I, speech to Parliament, 21 March 1610; Tanner (1930) p.15. James's belief in the divine right of kings was common currency not only among rulers of this period but also their subjects. James was unusual in that he took a philosophical interest in analysing the nature of divine right and making known his conclusions.

3 When your highness had once, out of deep judgement, apprehended how convenient it was that … there should be one more exact translation of the holy scriptures into the English tongue, your majesty did never desist to urge and to excite those to whom it was commended that the work might be hastened and that the business might be expedited in so decent a manner as a matter of such importance might justly require.

Authorized Version of the Bible (1611) Preface. The American title for the Authorized Version, namely 'The King James Bible', accurately reflects the major part played by the king in securing a new translation of the scriptures, which has become one of the pillars of the Anglican Church and one of the glories of English literature.

4 Be your holiness persuaded that I am, and ever shall be, of such moderation as to keep aloof, as far as possible, from every undertaking which may testify any hatred towards the Roman Catholic religion. Nay, rather I will seize all opportunities, by a gentle and generous mode of conduct, to remove all sinister suspicions entirely; so that, as we all confess one undivided Trinity and one Christ crucified, we may be banded together unanimously into one faith.

Prince Charles to Pope Gregory XV, 20 April 1623; Sir Charles Petrie (ed.) *The Letters … of King Charles I* (1935) p.16. The pope took a keen interest in the negotiations for a marriage between Prince Charles (the future Charles I) and the sister of Philip IV of Spain since he hoped it might lead to the re-conversion of England to Roman Catholicism.

5 My sweet boys, Your letter … hath strukken me dead. I fear it shall very much shorten my days … But as for my advice and directions that ye crave in case they will not alter their decree, it is, in a word, to come speedily away if ye can get leave, and give over all treaty [i.e., negotiations] … except ye never look to see your old dad again, whom I fear ye shall never see if ye see him not before winter. Alas, I now repent me sore that ever I suffered you to go away. I care for [the Spanish] match nor nothing so I may once have you in my arms again. God grant it! God grant it! God grant it!

James I to Prince Charles and George Villiers, Duke of Buckingham, James's favourite, in Madrid, 14 June 1623; BL Harleian MSS 6987, f.100. James had hoped that the marriage negotiations would be swiftly concluded once his son was in the Spanish capital, but they dragged on. Charles therefore announced his intention to return to England, but it was made plain, politely but firmly, that he would not be permitted to do so until agreement had been reached. Charles reported this to James and asked him to summon him home at once. James's reply speaks for itself.

1 For the maintenance of that war that may here-upon ensue, and more particularly for the defence of this your realm of England, the securing of your kingdom of Ireland, the assistance of your neighbours the states of the United Provinces [i.e. the Dutch] and other your majesty's friends and allies, and for the setting forth of your royal navy ... [we] have resolved to give ... the greatest aid which ever was granted in Parliament to be levied in so short a time.

Subsidy Act, 1624; *Statutes of the Realm* Vol.4 (1819) p.1247. Prince Charles and Buckingham, working in alliance with the unofficial leaders of the Commons, persuaded the House to offer, and James to accept, a grant worth some £350,000.

CHARLES I AND THE ENGLISH CIVIL WARS, 1625–49

2 The face of the court was much changed in the change of the king, for King Charles was temperate, chaste and serious; so that the fools and bawds, mimics and catamites of the former court grew out of fashion, and the nobility and courtiers, who did not quite abandon their debaucheries, had yet that reverence to the king to retire into corners to prac-tise them. Men of learning and ingenuity in all arts were in esteem and received encouragement from the king, who was a most excellent judge and a great lover of paintings, carvings, [en]gravings, and many other ingenuities, less offensive than the bawdry and profane abusive wit which was the only exercise of the other court.

Lucy Hutchinson *Memoirs of the Life of Colonel Hutchinson* (written 1664–71; 1906 edn) p.69.

3 [The Lords and Commons] do therefore humbly pray your most excellent majesty that no man hereafter be compelled to make or yield any gift, loan, benevolence, tax or such like charge without common consent by act of Parliament, and that none be ... confined or otherwise molested or dis-quieted concerning the same or for refusal thereof. And that no freeman in any such manner as is before mentioned be imprisoned or detained. And that your majesty would be pleased to remove the said soldiers and mariners, and that your people may not be so burdened in time to come.

Petition of Right, 1628; *Statutes of the Realm* Vol.5 (1819) p.24. In view of the arbitrary actions taken by the crown in 1627, Parliament determined to clarify the law in regard to subjects' liberties. Charles refused to accept any statutory limitation on

his prerogative, but Sir Edward Coke, drawing on his encyclo-pedic knowledge of the law, proposed a Petition of Right, which would have much the same effect. Charles eventually accepted the Petition, which thereupon became law.

4 They talk of an expedition of ships and infantry ... to be commanded by the Duke in person ... They will be put on thirty ships at Portsmouth forthwith ... I gather on good authority that these troops and ships are bound for La Rochelle.

Alvise Contarini, Venetian ambassador in England, to the doge and senate, 26 March 1627; *Calendar of State Papers* (C.S.P.) Venetian Vol.20 (1914) pp.159–60. Relations between Britain and France deteriorated as Louis XIII and his chief minister Cardinal Richelieu attempted to curtail the rights of the Huguenots, the French Protestants, and, in particular, to subdue the Huguenot stronghold of La Rochelle (see 411:7). Charles I had promised to defend the Rochellois, and he and Buckingham were now planning an expedition to the Île de Ré, which guarded the approaches to the port.

5 On Saturday, being the 23rd of August [1628], the Isle of Ré soldiers went to the Duke of Buckingham to kiss his hand and to take their leaves; of which one Felton (whom the duke had disappointed of two Lieutenants' places, and bid him, if he knew not how to live, to hang himself) being the last, stabbed the duke in the left pap, who, drawing out his sword for revenge and saying 'Traitor, thou hast killed me!' fell into his surgeon's arms and died. This Felton, who was before a great melancholist, had now nothing less in him than sorrow, saying that he thought it better for one man to die than that all England should go to ruin.

'A passage concerning the Duke of Buckingham's death'; R.F. Williams (ed.) *Court and Times of Charles I* (1848) Vol.1, pp.389–90. John Felton, who had served under Buckingham in the Île de Ré expedition, had been persuaded by the remon-strance drawn up against the favourite at the end of the 1628 Parliament that 'the excessive power of the Duke of Bucking-ham, and the abuse of that power, are the chief cause of these evils and dangers to the king and kingdom'. It therefore became a duty, as he saw it, to remove the duke from the scene.

6 Ye need not make very great haste, though I would have you come before winter; my meaning being that my commands at this time should not discommode your particular affairs, yet be assured that come when you will, ye shall be welcome to your assured friend, Charles R.

Charles I to Wentworth from Berwick-upon-Tweed, 23 and 27 July 1639; W. Knowler (ed.) *The Earl of Strafford's Letters and Dispatches* (1740) Vol.2, pp.372, 374. Sir Thomas Wentworth began as a critic of the king's policies in the House of Commons, but in 1631 he accepted office as lord deputy, or viceroy, of

Ireland and was so effective in imposing the king's will that he became feared and hated in both Ireland and England. He was just the sort of man that Charles needed in a crisis, and the king not only summoned him back but showed his approval by creating him Earl of Strafford.

1 Here are before me the things most valued, most feared by mortal men – life and death. To say, sir, there hath not been a strife in me were to make me less man than, God knoweth, my infirmities make me … But with much sadness, I am come to a resolution of that … which is most principal in itself, which, doubtless, is the prosperity of your sacred person and the commonwealth – things infinitely before any private man's interest. And therefore … I do most humbly beseech your majesty, for prevention of evils which may happen by your refusal, to pass this bill.

Earl of Strafford to Charles I, 4 May 1641; John Rushworth *Historical Collections of Private Passages of State, 1618–48* Vol.4 (1692) p.251. No sooner did the Long Parliament meet than Strafford was accused of treason and the two Houses passed a bill of attainder, condemning him to death. All that was now needed was the king's signature, but Charles had promised Strafford that no harm would come to him. The deadlock was broken when Strafford urged the king to put reasons of state above personal considerations. He was beheaded on Tower Hill on 12 May 1641.

2 The duty which we owe to your majesty and our country cannot but make us very sensible and apprehensive that the multiplicity, sharpness and malignity of those evils under which we have now many years suffered, are fomented and cherished by a corrupt and ill-affected party who, amongst other their mischievous devices for the alteration of religion and government, have sought by many false scandals and imputations, cunningly insinuated and dispersed amongst the people, to … get themselves a party and faction amongst your subjects for the better strengthening themselves in their wicked courses, and hindering those provisions and remedies which might, by the wisdom of your majesty and consel of your Parliament, be opposed against them. For preventing whereof, and the better information of your majesty, your peers and all other your loyal subjects, we have been necessitated to make a declaration of the state of the kingdom … which we do humbly present to your majesty, without the least intention to lay any blemish upon your royal person, but only to represent how your royal authority and trust have been abused, to the great prejudice and danger of your majesty and of all your good subjects.

Grand Remonstrance, presented to Charles I, 1 Dec. 1641; Rushworth Vol.4 (1692) p.437. The Remonstrance, with more than 200 clauses listing all the offences of commission and omission with which the royal government was charged, was largely the work of the radical John Pym. It was a massive exercise in propaganda, designed to swing public opinion, both at Westminster and in the country, behind those who felt that Charles could not be trusted and that it was essential to impose even more binding restrictions upon him.

3 His majesty made this speech … 'I must declare unto you here that albeit no king that ever was in England shall be more careful of your privileges, to maintain them to the uttermost of his power, than I shall be, yet you must know that in cases of treason no person hath a privilege … Well, since I see all the birds are flown I do expect from you that you shall send them unto me as soon as they return hither' … When the king was looking about the House, the Speaker standing by the chair, his majesty asked him whether he saw any of them? … To which the Speaker, falling on his knee, thus answered: 'May it please your majesty, I have neither eyes to see, nor tongue to speak in this place, but as the House is pleased to direct me, whose servant I am here.'

John Rushworth Vol.4 (1692) pp.477–8, reporting the attempted arrest of the five Members, 4 Jan 1642. As the political crisis deepened in 1641, Charles I became convinced that a kernel of radical members in the Commons and Lords was planning to strip him of his authority.

4 Monday, being the 22nd of August [1642] … his majesty … rode to Nottingham, where was great preparation for the setting up of the standard that day, as was formerly appointed … It was conducted to the field in great state, his majesty, the prince, and Prince Rupert (whom his majesty had lately made Knight of the Garter) going along with it, with … a great company of horse and foot, in all to the number of about 2000 … A herald-at-arms made ready to publish a proclamation declaring the ground and cause of his majesty's setting up of his standard – namely, to suppress the rebellion of the Earl of Essex in raising forces against him, to which he required the aid and assistance of all his loving subjects … After the reading whereof, the whole multitude threw up their hats and cried 'God save the king'.

John Rushworth Vol.4 (1692) pp.783–4. Prince Rupert was Charles's nephew, the son of his sister Elizabeth and her husband, the Elector Palatine, the 'Winter King and Queen' (see 452:9). The Earl of Essex, son of Elizabeth I's favourite, had been appointed by Parliament to command the forces it was raising. The setting up of the royal standard was a symbolic declaration of war against the king's enemies. As it happened, the standard so proudly erected was later blown down by the wind.

1 With the ascension of Charles I to the throne we come at last to the Central Period of English History (not to be confused with the Middle Ages, of course), consisting in the *utterly memorable Struggle between the Cavaliers (Wrong but Wromantic) and the Roundheads (Right but Repulsive)*. Charles I was a Cavalier King and therefore had a small pointed beard, long flowing curls, a large, flat, flowing hat, and *gay attire*. The Roundheads, on the other hand, were clean-shaven and wore tall, conical hats, white ties and *sombre garments*. Under these circumstances a Civil War was inevitable.

W.C. Sellar and R.J. Yeatman *1066 and All That* (1930) p.63. This irreverent but perceptive analysis of the causes of the Civil War comes from the classic work described by its authors as *A Memorable History of England, comprising all the parts you can remember, including 103 Good Things, 5 Bad Kings and 2 Genuine Dates.*

2 Oh Lord! Thou knowest how busy I must be this day: if I forget thee, do not thou forget me.

Sir Jacob Astley, the royalist commander's prayer before the Battle of Edgehill, 23 Oct. 1643, at which he was described as being 'hurt'; Sir Philip Warwick *Memoirs* (1701) p.229. Astley (1609–83) was a steadfast royalist. Warwick, politician and historian, was a member of the Long Parliament and another loyal supporter, much trusted by Charles I, to whom he acted as secretary. Both sides claimed victory in this first battle of the Civil War, fought on a ridge in southern Warwickshire.

3 I would rather have a plain russet-coated captain that knows what he fights for, and loves what he knows, than that which you call a 'gentleman' and is nothing else.

Oliver Cromwell to Sir William Spring and Maurice Barrow, Sept. 1643; Thomas Carlyle (ed.) *Oliver Cromwell's Letters and Speeches* (1845; 1897 edn) Vol.1, p.167. Cromwell's willingness to employ and advance people of no matter what social rank on grounds of merit alone contributed to the ultimate success of Parliament's forces, but at the same time it made the army a hotbed of radicalism, since traditional attitudes of respect and deference were constantly called into question.

4 When I saw the enemy draw up and march in gallant order towards us, and we a company of poor ignorant men, to seek how to order our battle – the General [Fairfax] having commanded me to order all the horse – I could not (riding alone about my

business) but smile out to God in praises in assurance of victory, because He would, by things that are not, bring to naught things that are. Of which I had a great assurance – and God did it.

Oliver Cromwell after his victory at the Battle of Naseby, 14 June 1644; Wilbur Corke Abbott *Writings and Speeches of Oliver Cromwell* (1937) Vol.1, p.365.

5 Truly, England and the Church of God hath had a great favour from the Lord in this great victory given unto us, such as the like never was since this war began. It had all the evidences of an absolute victory obtained by the Lord's blessing upon the godly party principally. We never charged but we routed the enemy. The left wing which I commanded, being our own horse ... beat all the prince's [i.e. Prince Rupert's] horse. God made them as stubble to our swords. We charged their regiments of foot with our horse and routed all we charged. The particulars I cannot relate now, but I believe of twenty thousand the prince hath not four thousand left. Give glory, all the glory, to God.

Oliver Cromwell to Colonel Valentine Walton, 5 July 1644; Thomas Carlyle *Oliver Cromwell's Letters and Speeches* (1897 edn) Vol.1, p.188. The Battle of Marston Moor, just outside York, which Cromwell is here reporting, took place on 2 July 1644. Prince Rupert had some 18,000 men; the parliamentary forces half as many again. It was a major defeat for the king and deprived him of any further influence in northern England. The royalists lost 4,000 dead, as well as 1,500 prisoners; their opponents a mere 300.

6 I think that the poorest he that is in England hath a life to live as the greatest he; and therefore ... I think it's clear that every man that is to live under a government ought first, by his own consent, to put himself under that government; and I do think that the poorest man in England is not at all bound in a strict sense to that government that he hath not had a voice to put himself under.

Colonel Thomas Rainborough, speaking in the Putney Debates, 28 Oct. 1647; A.S.P. Woodhouse (ed.) *Puritanism and Liberty* (1986 edn) p.53. After the Battle of Naseby (June 1645) the civil war was virtually over. The New Model Army, which Parliament had brought into being, was a forcing house for radical political ideas, and the council of the army met in Putney parish church to discuss how England should be governed in future. Rainborough was the Leveller spokesman. (The Levellers were committed to religious freedom and a much greater degree of equality, based on the rights of man.) Such radicalism found little favour with the majority of the officers, who shared the more conservative views of Cromwell.

1 I go from a corruptible to an incorruptible Crown, where no disturbance can be, no disturbance in the world.

Charles I, last words from the scaffold, 30 Jan. 1649; C.V. Wedgwood *The Trial of Charles I* (1964) p.152.

2   He nothing common did or mean
    Upon that memorable scene,
    But with his keener eye
    The axe's edge did try;
    Nor called the gods with vulgar spite
    To vindicate his helpless right,
    But bowed his comely head
    Down as upon a bed.

Andrew Marvell 'An Horatian Ode upon Cromwell's Return from Ireland' (1650). Charles I was executed on a scaffold built outside Inigo Jones's Banqueting House in Whitehall on 30 Jan. 1649. Throughout the trial, and again on the scaffold, Charles behaved with great dignity, as even his opponents acknowledged.

COMMONWEALTH AND PROTECTORATE, 1649–60

3 Whereas it is and hath been found by experience that the office of a king in this nation and Ireland, and to have the power thereof in any single person, is unnecessary, burdensome and dangerous to the liberty, safety and public interest of the people ... be it therefore enacted and ordained by this present Parliament, and by authority of the same, that the office of a king in this nation shall not henceforth reside in or be exercised by any one single person.

Act for abolishing the kingly office in England and Ireland, 17 March 1649; C.H. Firth and R.S. Rait (eds) *Acts and Ordinances of the Interregnum* (1911) Vol.2, p.19.

4 Be it declared and enacted by this present Parliament, and by the authority of the same, that the people of England ... are and shall be, and are hereby constituted, made, established and confirmed to be a Commonwealth and Free State, and shall from henceforth be governed as a Commonwealth and Free State by the supreme authority of this nation, the representatives of the people in Parliament, and by such as they shall appoint and constitute as officers and ministers under them for the good of the people. And that without any king or House of Lords.

Act declaring England to be a Commonwealth, 19 May 1649; Firth and Rait (1911) Vol.2, p.122.

5 About five o'clock in the evening, we began the storm [of Drogheda, in eastern Ireland] ... Divers of the enemy retreated into the Mill-Mount, a place very strong and of difficult access ... The governor ... and divers considerable officers being there, our men getting up to them were ordered by me to put them all to the sword. And indeed, being in the heat of action, I forbade them to spare any that were in arms in the town, and I think that night they put to the sword about 2,000 men ... I am persuaded that this is a righteous judgement of God upon these barbarous wretches who have imbrued their hands in so much innocent blood, and that it will tend to prevent the effusion of blood for the future.

Oliver Cromwell to Speaker Lenthall, Dublin, 17 Sept. 1649; Carlyle (1845; 1897 edn) Vol.2, pp.59–60. The collapse of royal power in Ireland as well as in England and Scotland encouraged the native Catholic population to throw off the British yoke. Their rebellion began in Oct. 1641 and led to the massacre of large numbers of Protestants. Cromwell regarded it as his mission not simply to return Ireland to obedience but to punish the Catholic population for its connivance in the massacres. In military terms his operation was highly successful, but he left behind him a legacy of bitterness.

6 I beseech you in the bowels of Christ, think it possible you are mistaken.

Oliver Cromwell, letter from Musselburgh, near Edinburgh, to the General Assembly of the Church of Scotland, 3 Aug. 1650; Carlyle (1850 edn) Vol.3, p.25. Cromwell was vainly attempting to persuade the elders of the Scottish church to avoid the bloodshed his invasion of their country was bound to entail.

7 Cromwell ... makes haste to the House, where he sat down and heard the debate for some time. Then ... suddenly standing up, [he] made a speech wherein he loaded the Parliament with the vilest reproaches, charging them not to have a heart to do anything for the public good ... [and] accusing them of an intention to perpetuate themselves in power ... [Then] he stepped into the midst of the House, where, continuing his distracted language, he said 'Come, come. I will put an end to your prating.' Then, walking up and down the House like a madman and kicking the ground with his feet, he cried out 'You are no Parliament. I say you are no Parliament. I will put an end to your sitting. Call them in! Call them in!' Whereupon the serjeant attending the Parliament opened the doors, and Lieutenant-Colonel Worsley with two files of musketeers entered the House ... Then Cromwell ... commanded the mace to be taken away, saying

'What shall we do with this bauble? Here, take it away!'

Oliver Cromwell, forcibly dissolving the Rump Parliament, 20 April 1653; Edmund Ludlow *Memoirs* (1698–99; 1720–22 edn) Vol.2, pp.455–7. Ludlow, a committed republican, refused to acknowledge the legitimacy of Cromwell's Protectorate. He avoided execution after the Restoration by fleeing to the continent and spent his long years in exile composing his *Memoirs*.

1 You have sat here too long for any good you have been doing. Depart, I say, and let us have done with you. In the name of God, go.

Oliver Cromwell, speech expelling the Rump Parliament, 20 April 1653; Bulstrode Whitelocke *Memorials of the English Affairs* (1732 edn) p.529. The Rump Parliament was the remnant of the Long Parliament. It had ordered the execution of Charles I, abolished both the monarchy and the House of Lords and established the Commonwealth. It was highly unpopular. It was recalled six years later to mark the end of the Protectorate and dissolved itself in 1660 to prepare for the Restoration (see 425:2). The swingeing words Cromwell used in his furious expulsion of its members vary slightly among the three contemporary accounts (including that of Ludlow; see 423:7) that have come down to us. Whitelocke, the keeper of the great seal, was an eyewitness.

2 The supreme legislative authority of the Commonwealth of England, Scotland and Ireland ... shall be and reside in one person and the people assembled in Parliament. The style of which person shall be 'The Lord Protector of the Commonwealth' ... The exercise of the chief magistracy and the administration of the government over the said countries and dominions, and the people thereof, shall be in the Lord Protector, assisted with a council ... The office of Lord Protector over these nations shall be elective and not hereditary, and upon the death of the Lord Protector another fit person shall be forthwith elected to succeed him.

Instrument of Government 1653; S.R. Gardiner *The Constitutional Documents of the Puritan Revolution, 1625–60* (1889; 1936 edn) pp.405–15. After trying various constitutional experiments in order to return the country to civilian rule, none of which was successful, Cromwell now accepted a written constitution, closer to the traditional model. The Instrument of Government retained a unicameral Parliament, but this was to be held in check by a Lord Protector – Cromwell himself – wielding quasi-monarchical powers.

3 Mr Lely, I desire you would use all your skill to paint my picture truly like me, and not flatter me at all, but remark all these roughnesses, pimples, warts and everything as you see me. Otherwise I never will pay a farthing for it.

Oliver Cromwell, to the painter, Peter Lely, c.1650; Horace Walpole *Anecdotes of Painting in England* (1762–71; 1828 edn) Vol.3, pp.31–2. Although Cromwell lived in considerable state as Lord Protector, he was not a man who valued ostentation and ceremonial for their own sakes. His down-to-earth honesty, epitomized in this exchange with Lely, was one of his most appealing characteristics. The portrait is now in the Art Gallery, Birmingham.

4 Is there not yet upon the spirits of men a strange itch? Nothing will satisfy them unless they can press their finger upon their brethren's consciences, to pinch them there. To do this was no part of the contest we had with the common adversary. For indeed, religion was not the thing at first contested for at all. But God brought it to that issue at last ... and at last it proved to be that which was most dear to us. And wherein consisted this more than in obtaining that liberty from the tyranny of the bishops to all species of Protestants to worship God according to their own light and consciences? ... What greater hypocrisy than for those who were oppressed by the bishops to become the greatest oppressors themselves so soon as their yoke was removed?

Oliver Cromwell, speech to Parliament, 22 Jan. 1655; Carlyle (1845; 1987 edn) Vol.3, pp.103–5. In social matters Cromwell was relatively conservative, but he favoured a wide degree of religious toleration. He would not extend this to Roman Catholics, whom he regarded as followers of the Antichrist, nor to Anglicans so long as they remained unreconciled to his rule, but he invited the Jews to re-settle in Britain (see 184:4).

5 His highness [Cromwell] would not hearken to the title 'king', because it was not pleasing to his army and was matter of scandal to the people of God ... His highness returned answer presently [i.e., immediately] to this effect ... That for his part he loved the title, a feather in a hat, as little as they did ... That it is time to come to a settlement and lay aside arbitrary proceedings, so unacceptable to the nation. And by the proceedings of this Parliament you see they stand in need of a check or balancing power (meaning the House of Lords, or a House so constituted).

Thomas Burton, diary entry, 7 March 1657; R.T. Rutt (ed.) *Diary* (1828) pp.382–4.

6 I was moved to write to Oliver Cromwell, and laid before him the suffering of Friends in the nation and in Ireland, and was moved to go again to Oliver Cromwell, and told him that they which would put him on an earthly crown would take away his life.

And he asked me, 'What say you?' and I repeated the same words over to him again. And he thanked me, after I had warned him of many dangers and how he would bring shame and a ruin upon himself and posterity. And after this I met him riding into Hampton Court park ... and I saw and felt a waft of death go forth against him, that he looked like a dead man.

George Fox *The Journal of George Fox* (1694; 1911 edn) Vol.1, p.327. Fox was the founder of the Society of Friends, popularly known as Quakers. This meeting took place when Cromwell was considering whether to take the crown.

1 [Cromwell] returned again to Whitehall, when his physicians began to think him in danger, though the preachers who prayed always about him ... declared, as from God, that he should recover. And he himself did not think he should die, till even the time that his spirits failed him; and then declared to them that he did appoint his son to succeed him, his eldest son, Richard. And so [he] expired upon the third day of September – a day he thought always very propitious to him, and on which he had triumphed for several victories – 1658; a day very memorable for the greatest storm of wind that had ever been known, for some hours before and after his death, which overthrew trees, houses, and made great wrecks at sea.

Edward, Earl of Clarendon *History of the Rebellion and Civil Wars in England* (1702; 1888 edn) Vol.6, pp.90–91. Using the authority given him by the written constitution, Cromwell nominated his eldest son, Richard, as his successor.

2 To Westminster Hall, where I heard how the Parliament had this day dissolved themselves and did pass very cheerfully through the Hall, and the Speaker without his mace. The whole Hall was joyful thereat, as well as themselves, and now they begin to talk loud of the king. Tonight I am told that yesterday, about 5 a-clock in the afternoon, one came with a ladder to the great Exchange and wiped with a brush the inscription that was upon King Charles, and that there was a great bonfire made in the Exchange, and people cried out 'God bless King Charles the Second'.

Samuel Pepys, 16 March 1660; *The Diary of Samuel Pepys* (1970 edn) Vol.1, p.89. The Long Parliament first met in Nov. 1640 and had been in nominal existence for all but 20 years when it at last dissolved itself. A niche in the Royal Exchange in London had contained a statue of Charles I, which had been taken down in 1650 and the space covered with the inscription *Exit tyrannus, ultimus rex* (Out goes the tyrant, the last king).

Pepys recorded his impressions in the shorthand diary that he had already started and kept up for nine years.

CHARLES II, 1660–85

3 Let all our subjects, how faulty soever, rely upon the word of a king, solemnly given by this present declaration, that no crime whatsoever, committed against us or our royal father before the publication of this, shall ever rise in judgement or be brought in question against any of them ... we desiring and ordaining that henceforth all notes of discord, separation and difference of parties be utterly abolished among all our subjects, whom we invite and conjure to a perfect union among themselves, under our protection, for the re-settlement of our just rights and theirs in a free Parliament, by which, upon the word of a king, we will be advised.

Charles II, Declaration of Breda, 4 April 1660; *The Parliamentary History of England* Vol.22 (1763 edn) pp.239–40. The declaration was designed to reassure the English people that the restored monarchy would work in close harmony with Parliament and that past offences would be cast into oblivion.

4 This day came in his majesty Charles the 2d to London after a sad and long exile and calamitous suffering both of the king and Church, being 17 years. This was also his birthday, and with a triumph of above 20,000 horse and foot brandishing their swords and shouting with inexpressible joy. The ways strowed with flowers, the bells ringing, the streets hung with tapestry, fountains running with wine ... The windows and balconies all set with ladies; trumpets, music, and myriads of people flocking the streets, and was as far as Rochester, so as they were 7 hours in passing the city, even from 2 in the afternoon till nine at night. I stood in the Strand and beheld it and blessed God. And all this without one drop of blood, and by that very army which rebelled against him.

John Evelyn, 29 May 1660; *The Diary of John Evelyn* (1955 edn) Vol.3, p.246. Evelyn, whose family had made a fortune out of the manufacture of gunpowder, is the second great diarist of the late 17th century (Pepys being the first).

5 The king is a suitor to you ... that you will join with him in restoring the whole nation to its primitive temper and integrity, to its old good manners, its old good humour and its old good nature ... If the old reproaches of 'cavalier' and 'roundhead' and 'malignant' be committed to the grave, let us not find more significant and better words to signify worse things … Let not piety and godliness be measured by a morosity in manners … Very merry men have been very godly men, and if a good conscience be a continual feast, there is no reason but men may be very merry at it.

Earl of Clarendon, speech at the adjournment of the Convention Parliament, about 12 Sept. 1660; *The Parliamentary History of England* Vol.22 (1763 edn) pp.489–91. Edward Hyde followed the future Charles II into exile, acting as his close adviser. Shortly after the Restoration Charles created Hyde Earl of Clarendon and relied on him, as lord chancellor, to carry on the government. Clarendon and Charles were largely responsible for the fact that the Restoration was accomplished with the minimum of blood-letting.

1 The king's most excellent majesty, taking into his gracious and serious consideration the long and great troubles, discords and wars that have for many years past been in this kingdom, and … out of a hearty and pious desire to put an end to all suits and controversies that by occasion of the late distractions have arisen and may arise between all his subjects, and to the intent that no crime whatsoever committed against his majesty or his royal father shall hereafter rise in judgement or be brought in question against any of them … is pleased that it may be enacted … that all and all manner of … offences, crimes, contempts and misdemeanours counselled, commanded, acted or done [from 1 Jan. 1638 to 24 June 1660] by virtue or colour of any command … from his late majesty King Charles or his majesty that now is … from both Houses or either House of Parliament … be pardoned, released, indemnified, discharged and put in utter oblivion.

An 'Act of free and general pardon', indemnity and oblivion, 1660; *Statutes of the Realm* Vol.5 (1819) p.226. This act marks the acceptance by Parliament of Clarendon's belief that the events of the previous twenty years should be consigned to oblivion. But Parliament exempted from the general pardon all those who had been directly involved in the execution of Charles I.

2 This day, much against my will, I did in Drury Lane see two or three houses marked with a red cross upon the doors, and 'Lord have mercy upon us' writ there – which was a sad sight to me, being the first of that kind that to my remembrance I ever saw.

Samuel Pepys, 7 June 1665; (1970 edn) Vol.6, p.120.

3 I went forth and walked toward Moorfields to see (God forgive my presumption) whether I could see

any dead corpse going to the grave, but as God would have it, did not. But Lord, how everybody's looks and discourse in the street is of death and nothing else, and few people going up and down, that the town is like a place distressed and forsaken.

Samuel Pepys, 30 Aug. 1665; (1970 edn) Vol.6, p.207. Bubonic plague had been endemic in England ever since its dramatic arrival from Europe in 1348, when it caused the Black Death (see 284:7). The great plague of 1666, which killed some 56,000 people, marked the end of this dreadful scourge.

4 To Whitehall, and there up to the king's closet in the chapel, where people come about me and I did give them an account dismayed them all. And word was carried in to the king, so I was called for and did tell the king and Duke of York what I saw, and that unless his majesty did command houses to be pulled down, nothing could stop the fire. They seemed much troubled, and the king commanded me to go to my Lord Mayor from him and command him to spare no houses but to pull down before the fire every way … At last met my Lord Mayor in Canning Street, like a man spent, with a hankercher about his neck. To the king's message he cried, like a fainting woman, 'Lord, what can I do? I am spent. People will not obey me. I have been pulling down houses, but the fire overtakes us faster than we can do it.'

Samuel Pepys, 2 Sept. 1666; (1970 edn) Vol.7, p.269. The great fire of London broke out in a baker's shop in Pudding Lane and rapidly engulfed the whole city. The Tower of London survived, but St Paul's Cathedral, the Royal Exchange and many livery company halls and parish churches were destroyed. The Monument, which was erected to mark the site of the outbreak, still stands there.

5 Guin [Gwyn], the indiscreetest and wildest creature that ever was in a court, continued to the end of the king's life in great favour, and was maintained at vast expense … She acted all persons in so lively a manner, and was such a diversion to the king, that even a new mistress could not drive her away. But, after all, he never treated her with the decencies of a mistress, but rather with the lewdness of a prostitute – as she had been, indeed, to a great many. And therefore she called the king her Charles the Third, since she had been formerly kept by two of that name.

Gilbert Burnet *History of My Own Time* Vol.1 (1723; 1833 edn) pp.483–4. The actress Eleanor Gwyn, known as Nell or Nelly, began her professional career as an orange-seller at the Theatre Royal in Drury Lane. She first appeared on stage there in 1665, and became a favourite with London audiences – Pepys called her 'pretty witty Nell'. She made the king's acquaintance in 1669 and a year later bore him a son, whom Charles created Duke of St Albans.

1 The court of France ... well understood how much the establishment of an arbitrary power in the [English] crown would contribute to weaken that force which had been so formidable under a free government, [and] had instructed the Duchess of Orleans not only to offer money to her brother in case the usual way of supplying his luxury by parliamentary aids should fail, but also to give him assurances of whatever number of forces he should judge requisite to render the monarchy absolute and uncontrolled. To those, she herself had added another argument to be proposed, no less prevalent where it was to be applied than the former. For she had in her train one Mrs Queroualle ... who ... had passed in France for a great beauty.

Edmund Ludlow (1698–9; 1720–22 edn) Vol.3, p.227. Charles II had considerable admiration for Louis XIV, the greatest monarch in Europe, and in the Treaty of Dover (May 1670) he agreed to support Louis in his projected war against the Dutch in return for subsidies. However, the secret clauses of the treaty stated that these subsidies would be paid only after Charles had declared his adhesion to the Roman Catholic Church, and that Louis would provide 6,000 troops to put down any rebellion. Charles's motives, and sincerity, in committing himself to this treaty remain obscure. He was doubtless influenced by his sister, the Duchess of Orleans, who came to England specially to persuade him. The young beauty she brought with her was Louise de Quérouaille, who soon replaced Barbara Castlemaine as Charles's principal mistress.

2 Whereas we have been informed that a portion of the imposition laid upon coals, which by an act of Parliament is appointed and set apart for the rebuilding of the cathedral church of St Paul's in our capital city of London, doth at present amount to a considerable sum ... and whereas, amongst divers designs which have been represented to us, we have particularly pitched upon one ... we do therefore, by these presents, signify our royal approbation of the said design ... and do will and require you forthwith to proceed ... beginning with the east end or choir.

Charles II to the Commissioners for the Rebuilding of St Paul's Cathedral, 14 May 1675; PRO State Papers Domestic 44/27, f.68. Sir Christopher Wren, the king's surveyor-general, produced a master-plan for the rebuilding of London after the fire, but the vested interest of property-owners prevented this from being fully implemented. Wren did, however, design a large number of new churches, to take the place of those which had been ravaged or destroyed by the fire. Instead of rebuilding the Gothic cathedral of St Paul's, he replaced it by the baroque masterpiece that still stands at the heart of the city.

3 Here lies a great and mighty king
Whose promise none relies on.
He never said a foolish thing,
Nor ever did a wise one.
This is very true, for my words are my own and
my actions are my ministers'.

There is no definite source for these quotations. Thomas Hearne (1678–1735), the Oxford antiquary, records the poet John Wilmot, Earl of Rochester, as writing 'We have a pretty witty king, And whose word no man relies on' (*Reliquiae Hearnianae* (1857) p.114), but he does not give Charles's supposed reply. Nevertheless, both the mock epitaph and Charles's response ring true. Rochester was one of the 'court wits' in whose company Charles delighted.

4 At this time was the marriage agreed on between the Prince of Orange and the lady Mary, first daughter to his royal highness, which gave great content to the nation and abated the fears of popery that she was married to a Protestant prince. My lord Danby, lord treasurer, believed to be the adviser of this match, got a good reputation by it.

Sir John Reresby *The Memoirs of Sir John Reresby* (1734; 1875 edn) p.124. William III of Orange, who held a quasi-monarchical position in Holland and was renowned for his military campaigns against the Catholic Louis XIV of France, married Mary, the daughter of James, Duke of York, on 4 Nov. 1677. Since James had no male children, the Protestant Mary was heir presumptive to the throne after James himself. Reresby, born into a royalist family in Yorkshire, became actively involved in politics after the Restoration.

5 The discovery of this [Popish] Plot put the whole kingdom into a new fermentation, and filled people universally with unspeakable terror ... Not so much as a house was at that time to be met with but what was provided with arms; nor did any go to rest at night without apprehensions of somewhat that was very tragical that might happen before morning. And this was the case not for a few weeks or months only, but for a great while together.

Edmund Calamy (1671–1732) *An Historical Account of My Own Life* Vol.1 (1830 edn) pp.82–4. In Sept. 1678 a renegade Jesuit called Titus Oates 'revealed' the existence of a Popish Plot to kill the king and replace him with his brother, the Catholic James. England was swept by a wave of hysteria, and Charles had to manoeuvre skilfully in order to preserve his throne.

6 The diversions the king followed at Newmarket were these: – Walking in the morning till ten o'clock. Then he went to the cockpit till dinner time. About three he went to the horse races. At six to the cockpit for an hour. Then to the play, though the comedians were very indifferent. So to supper. Next to the duchess of Portsmouth's till bedtime, and then to his own apartment to bed.

Sir John Reresby, 22 March 1684; (1734; 1875 edn) pp.299–300. The cockpit was the place where cockfights took place. The Duchess of Portsmouth was Charles's mistress.

1 The king, who seemed all the while to be in great confusion, fell down all of a sudden in a fit like apoplexy: he looked black, and his eyes turned in his head … The duke immediately ordered Huddlestone, the priest that had a great hand in saving the king at Worcester fight … to be brought … [He] made the king go through some acts of contrition and … gave him extreme unction … The king went through the agonies of death with a calm and a constancy that amazed all who were about him and knew how he had lived … He recommended Lady Portsmouth over and over again to [the duke]. He said he had always loved her, and he loved her now to the last, and besought the duke, in as melting words as he could fetch out, to be very kind to her and to her son. He recommended his other children to him, and concluded 'Let not poor Nelly starve'.

Gilbert Burnet Vol.2 (1723; 1833 edn) pp.466–73. Charles II died on 6 Feb. 1685. He had long been a Catholic at heart, and on his deathbed he welcomed the suggestion that a Catholic priest should be sent for. Father John Huddlestone (who had helped the young Charles escape after his defeat by Cromwell in the Battle of Worcester on 3 Sept. 1651) was quickly summoned, and he formally received Charles into the Roman Catholic Church. Lady Portsmouth, Louise de Quérouaille, was popularly known as 'the French whore' to distinguish her from Nell Gwyn ('poor Nelly'), the English one.

JAMES II, 1685–9

2 The duke (now K. James the 2d) went immediately to his council and before entering into any business, passionately declaring his sorrow, told their lordships that since the succession had fallen to him, he would endeavour to follow the example of his predecessor in his clemency and tenderness to his people; that however he had been misrepresented as affecting arbitrary power, they should find the contrary.

John Evelyn, 6 Feb. 1685; (1955 edn) Vol.4, p.411. Sir John Reresby comments that James's declaration 'in a great measure did quiet the minds and apprehensions of people'.

3 The Duke of Buckingham gave me once a short but severe character of the two brothers [Charles II and James, Duke of York, later James II]. It was the

more severe because it was true. The king, he said, could see things if he would, and the duke would see things if he could. He had no true judgement, and was soon determined by those whom he trusted, but he was obstinate against all other advices.

Gilbert Burnet Vol.1 (1723; 1833 edn) p.304.

4 To London, at which time the D[uke] of Monmouth invaded this nation, landing with but 150 men at Lyme in Dorsetshire, which wonderfully alarmed the whole kingdom, fearing the joining of disaffected people, many of the trained bands [i.e., the county militias] flocking to him. He had at his landing published a declaration charging his majesty with usurpation and several horrid crimes, upon pretence of his own title and the calling of a free Parliament. This declaration was condemned to be burnt by the hangman, the duke proclaimed a traitor, [and] a reward of £5,000 to him that should kill him.

John Evelyn, 17 June 1685; (1955 edn) Vol.4, p.449. James Scott, Duke of Monmouth, the oldest of Charles II's illegitimate children, was living in Holland at the time of the king's death. He claimed that Charles had secretly married his mother and that he was, therefore, the rightful ruler of Britain.

5 The duke of Monmouth, from the beginning of this, his desperate attempt, had shown the conduct of a great captain, insomuch as the king said himself he had not made one false step. And thus this great storm, which began from a little cloud (for the number of men which he brought ashore was not above 150) was fortunately dispersed; for had he got the day, it was to be feared the disaffected were so numerous that they would have risen in several parts of England, to the very hazard of the crown. The number of the slain on the enemy's side was computed about 1,200; on our side near 300 killed and wounded. We took about 600 prisoners …

To complete the king's good fortune came the news of the duke of Monmouth's being taken in a wood, disguised, by a company of country fellows hunting after him … When the duke was taken he was almost spent, having not been in bed of three weeks. He had no arms, nor made any defence. Only he carried a watch in his pocket and £300 in gold, which was the only money he had left.

Sir John Reresby, 7–9 July 1685; (1734; 1875 edn) pp.339–40. Monmouth, condemned of treason by act of attainder, was beheaded on 15 July 1685.

6 [Judge Jeffreys] was sent [on] the western circuit to try the prisoners. His behaviour was beyond anything that was ever heard of in a civilized nation. He was perpetually either drunk or in a rage, liker a fury than the zeal of a judge. He required the prisoners to plead guilty, and in that case he gave them some hope of favour if they gave him no trouble. Otherwise, he told them, he would execute the letter of the law upon them in its utmost severity. This made many plead guilty who had a great defence in law. But he showed no mercy … He hanged, in several places, about six hundred persons.

Gilbert Burnet Vol.3 (1723; 1833 edn) pp.59–60. James sent Judge Jeffreys on what became known as the 'Bloody Assize' with instructions to pass judgement on all those who had fought for Monmouth. He carried out his orders in so brutal a manner that it harmed James's reputation. Nevertheless, the king remained firm in his support for Jeffreys, whom he appointed lord chancellor.

1 We cannot but heartily wish … that all the people of our dominions were members of the Catholic Church, yet we humbly thank Almighty God it is and hath of long time been our constant sense and opinion … that conscience ought not to be constrained nor people forced in matters of mere religion.

Declaration of Indulgence, 4 April 1687; Edward Cardwell (ed.) *Documentary Annals of the Reformed Church of England* Vol.2 (1844) pp.359–61. The Declaration applied to both Catholics and Protestant dissenters, but James's real concern was with the former.

2 The king had renewed his proclamation for liberty of conscience, with an order to the bishops to have it read in all the churches of their respective dioceses. The Archbishop of Canterbury and [six other bishops] … petitioned the king and set forth thereby that they could not obey his majesty therein … The king, upon their refusal, gave a very angry answer, and they were … committed to the Tower … The bishops [were] tried in the [court of] King's Bench for framing and publishing a seditious libel (meaning the paper which they presented to the king …), [but] the jury would not find them guilty … Westminster Hall and the Palace Yard, with the streets near them,

were so full of people, and their huzzas and shouts for joy of their lordships' delivery so great, that it looked like a little rebellion in noise, though not in fact.

Sir John Reresby, 26 May–29 June 1688, pp.394–97. The indictment of the seven bishops was a major error on James's part, since it turned Anglican opinion definitively against him.

3 Being Trinity Sunday, about four minutes before ten in the morning, was born the Prince of Wales, to the great joy of the court.

Sir John Reresby, 10 June 1688; (1734; 1875 edn) p.396. The birth of an heir to James transformed the political situation, because James's subjects could no longer console themselves with the knowledge that he would be succeeded, in due course, by his Protestant daughter, Mary, Princess of Orange. The baby prince, christened James Edward, is known to history as the Old Pretender (see 489:3).

4 We have great reason to believe we shall be every day in a worse condition than we are, and less able to defend ourselves … Your highness may be assured there are nineteen parts of twenty of the people throughout the kingdom who are desirous of a change, and who, we believe, would willingly contribute to it if they had such a protection to countenance their rising as would secure them from being destroyed before they could get to be in a posture able to defend themselves.

Invitation to William III of Orange, 30 June 1688; Sir John Dalrymple *Memoirs of Great Britain and Ireland* Vol.2 (1790) pp.107–10. Faced with the prospect of an indefinite Catholic monarchy in England, a small group of key figures decided to take the extremely risky step of inviting William of Orange to come over with his army in order to save England from popery. They salved their consciences by asserting that the newborn son was not the queen's but had been smuggled into her bed in a warming-pan.

5 The Liberties of England and the Protestant religion I will maintain.

William III of Orange; words embroidered on his flag and flown on his ship, *The Brill*, when he landed at Brixham, Devon, on 5 Nov. 1688. To this day, this is the motto of Brixham.

Colonial North America, 1612–1763

THE FIRST SETTLEMENTS: VIRGINIA, 1612–60

1 Whereas at the suit of divers and sundry of our loving subjects, as well adventurers as planters of the first colony in Virginia, and for the propagation of Christian religion, and reclaiming of people barbarous to civility and humanity, we have, by our letters patent … given and granted unto them, that they … should be one body politic, incorporated by the name of the Treasurer and Company of Adventurers and Planters of the City of London for the first Colony in Virginia.

Third charter of the Virginia Company, 12 March 1612; Merrill Jensen (ed.) *English Historical Documents* Vol.9 (1955) p.65. Virginia was named after Elizabeth I, the 'Virgin Queen', and the hope was that a colony so positioned would be able to prey on the Spanish treasure fleets on their way home. However, the first foundations were abortive, and it was not until 1607 that Jamestown, named after Elizabeth's successor, James I, became the first permanent English settlement in North America. The third charter was a normal trading arrangement, with the Crown giving up any direct control. Virginia's territory at this time was more extensive than that of the present state, even before it lost West Virginia in 1863.

2 They [the natives] are inconstant in every thing, but what fear constrains them to keep. Crafty, timorous, quick of apprehension and very ingenious. Some are of disposition fearful, some bold, most cautious, all Savage. Generally covetous of copper, beads and such like trash. They are soon moved to anger, and so malicious that they seldom forget an injury: they seldom steal from one another, lest their conjurers should reveal it, and so they be pursued and punished. That they are thus feared is certain, but that any can reveal their offences by conjuration I am doubtful.

Captain John Smith *A Map of Virginia with a Description of the Country, the Commodities, People, Government and Religion* (1612) pp.19 ff. Smith set out with the Virginia colonists and became head of the colony in 1608.

3 At [Smith's] entrance before the king [Powhatan], all the people gave a great shout. The Queen of Appamatuc was appointed to bring him water to wash his hands, and another brought him a bunch of feathers, instead of a towel to dry them: having feasted him after their best barbarous manner they could, a long consultation was held, but the conclusion was, two great stones were brought before Powhatan: then as many as could laid hands on him, dragged him to them, and thereon laid his head, and being ready with their clubs, to beat out his brains. Pocahontas the king's dearest daughter, when no entreaty could prevail, got his head in her arms, and laid her own upon his to save him from death.

Captain John Smith *The General History of Virginia, New England, and the Summer Isles* (1624); *The Complete Works of John Smith* Vol.2 (1986) pp.150–51. Pocahontas saves John Smith; it was possibly an initiation ceremony rather than an execution. In 1614 Pocahontas, who had become a Christian, married the colonist John Rolfe, and they travelled to England in 1616. She died of smallpox in 1617 as her ship left the Thames on its return to the New World. Rolfe had discovered a method of curing tobacco, which had been introduced into cultivation in Virginia from the West Indies in 1611, and it quickly became the basis of the colony's trade and prosperity. There was already an anti-smoking lobby, and by the beginning of the 17th century some even blamed it for London's fog (actually caused by coal-burning fires, a problem at least 300 years old; see 210:5). It even aroused the fury of James I himself who published (anonymously) *A Counterblast to Tobacco* in 1604 (see 418:4).

4 All our riches for the present do consist in Tobacco, wherein one man by his own labour hath in one year raised to himself to the value of 200£ sterling; and another by the means of six servants hath cleared one crop a thousand pound English. These are true, yet indeed rare examples, yet possible to be done by others. Our principal wealth (I should have said) consists in servants: But they are chargeable to be furnished with arms, apparel, and bedding and for their transportation and casual [dress] both at sea, and for their first year commonly at land also: But if they escape [death] they prove very hardy, and sound able men.

John Pory to Sir Dudley Carleton, Virginia, 30 Sept. 1619; Lyon Gardiner Tyler (ed.) *Narratives of Early Virginia, 1606–1625* (1907) pp.284–5. Pory was a traveller and geographer; Carleton was a diplomat, who served in, among other places, Venice (see 299:3) and the Hague, and left a voluminous correspondence.

5 I have nothing at all, no not a shirt to my back, but two Rags nor no Clothes but one poor suit, nor but one pair of shoes, but one pair of stockings, but one Cap, but two bands, my Cloak is stolen by one of my own fellows, and to his dying howl would not tell me what he did with it ... but I am not half a quarter so strong as I was in England, and all is for want of victuals, for I do protest unto you, that I have eaten more in a day at home than I have allowed me here for a Week ...

O that you did see my daily and hourly sighs, groans, and tears, and thumps that I afford my own breast, and rue and Curse the time ... I thought no head had been able to hold so much water as hath and doth daily flow from mine eyes.

Richard Frethorne to his parents, 20 March, 2 and 3 April 1623; Susan Myra Kingsbury (ed.) *The Records of the Virginia Company of London* (1906–35) Vol.4, pp.58–9, 62. 'A basic fact in the peopling of the colonies was that the majority of the people ... came at the expense of others. This was made possible by the system of indentured servitude which lasted down into the 19th century. An immigrant signed a contract to work, usually from four to seven years, in payment for his passage ... The system was begun by the Virginia Company ... Its importance is indicated by a Virginia census of 1624–5, which showed that 487 out of a total population of 1,227 were indentured servants' (E.H.D. Vol.9 (1955) p.481).

1 Thus I have given a succinct account of the Indians; happy, I think, in their simple State of Nature, and in their enjoyment of Plenty, without the Curse of Labour. They have on several accounts reason to lament the arrival of the Europeans, by whose means they seem to have lost their Felicity, as well as their Innocence. The English have taken away great part of their Country, and consequently made every thing less plenty amongst them. They have introduced Drunkenness and Luxury amongst them, which have multiplied their Wants, and put them upon desiring a thousand things, they never dreamt of before.

Robert Beverley *The History and Present State of Virginia* (1705; 1947 edn) pp.232–3. Beverley held various official posts and was a member of the Virginia House of Burgesses.

2 I purpose to go up to the Lake [at the head of the Delaware River], from whence I hope to find a way that leads into that Mediterranean Sea, and from the Lake, I judge that it cannot be less than 150 or 200 leagues [450–600 miles] to the North Ocean, and from thence I purpose to discover the mouths thereof, which discharge themselves both into the North and South Seas.

Captain Thomas from the falls of the Delaware River, 20 Oct. 1634; C.A. Weslager *The English on the Delaware: 1610–1682* (1967) pp.48–9. Even as late as 1634 explorers could still believe that a passage to the Pacific Ocean was just around the

next bend of the river. Delaware, the first US state to be founded, lies on the Atlantic coast between New Jersey and Maryland. It was named after Thomas West, 3rd or 12th Baron de la Warr (1577–1618), the soldier and first governor of Virginia.

3 The soil appears particularly fertile, and strawberries, vines, sassafras, hickory nuts, and walnuts, we tread upon everywhere, in the thickest woods. The soil is dark and soft, a foot in thickness, and rests upon a rich and red clay. Everywhere there are very high trees, except where the ground is tilled by a scanty population. An abundance of springs afford water. No animals are seen except deer, the beaver, and squirrels, which are as large as the hares of Europe. There is an infinite number of birds of various colours, as eagles, herons, swans, geese, and partridges. From which you may infer that there is not wanting to the region whatever may serve for commerce or pleasure.

Father Andrew White *A Report of the Colony of the Lord of Baltimore in Maryland, near Virginia* (1633; 1847 edn) p.24. One of the two Jesuit missionaries who went with the first fleet of colonists to settle in Maryland describes its natural wonders to the head of his order in Rome. Although not specifically written as a promotional pamphlet for the new Catholic plantation, it appeals to those who were escaping persecution.

AS A CITY ON A HILL: NEW ENGLAND, 1620–1700

4 In the Name of God, Amen. We, whose names are underwritten ... Having undertaken for the Glory of God, and Advancement of the Christian Faith, and the Honour of our King and Country, a Voyage to plant the first colony in the northern Parts of Virginia; Do by these Presents, solemnly and mutually in the Presence of God and one another, covenant and combine ourselves together into a civil Body Politick, for our better Ordering and Preservation, and Furtherance of the Ends aforesaid; And by Virtue hereof do enact, constitute, and frame, such just and equal Laws, Ordinances, Acts, Constitutions, and Offices, from time to time, as shall be thought most meet and convenient for the general Good of the Colony; unto which we promise all due Submission and Obedience.

Mayflower Compact, 11 Nov. 1620, in William Bradford *Of Plymouth Plantation 1620–1647* (c.1651; 1952 edn); Henry Steele Commager (ed.) *Documents of American History* (1968) pp.15–16. Yorkshire-born Bradford (1590–1656) emigrated to Amsterdam in 1607 before joining the group that sailed from Devon in Aug. 1620 to found New Plymouth, Massachusetts: 'They began to incline to this conclusion: of removal to some other place. Not out of any newfangledness or such like giddy humour … but for sundry and solid reasons.' The Compact was made while they were still on board the *Mayflower*. In fact, only a minority of them were Puritans (the groups who sought to purify and reform English Protestantism). They landed at Cape Cod in Nov. and decided to make their settlement there. In 1621 Bradford became the second governor of the Plymouth Colony.

1 But that which was most sad and lamentable was, that in two or three months' time, half of their company died, especially in January and February, being the depth of winter and wanting houses and other comforts; being infected with the scurvy and other diseases, which this long voyage and their inaccommodate condition had brought upon them.
William Bradford (*c.*1651; 1952 edn) pp.75 ff. In his old age, Bradford remembers the colony's inauspicious start.

2 Divers objections which have been made against this plantation, with their answers and resolutions.
Objection 1: We have no warrant to enter upon that land which hath been so long possessed by others.
Answer 1: That which lies common and hath never been replenished or subdued is free to any that will possess and improve it, for God hath given to the sons of men a double right to the earth: there is a natural right and a civil right: the first right was natural when they held the earth in common, every man sowing and feeding where he pleased, and then as men and the cattle increased, they appropriated certain parcels of ground by enclosing and peculiar manurance [cultivation], and this in time gave them a civil right … The natives in New England, they enclose no land neither have they any settled habitation nor any tame cattle to improve the land by, and so have no other but a natural right to those countries. So if we leave them sufficient for their use we may lawfully take the rest, there being more than enough for them and us.
John Winthrop *Reasons to be Considered for … the Intended Plantation in New England* (1629); Alan Heimert and Andrew Delbanco *The Puritans in America: A Narrative Anthology* (1985) p.73. A legalistic rationale for the expropriation of the Indians' land. Winthrop, a farmer from Suffolk, gives a systematic response to the objections that might be raised against the Massachusetts Bay enterprise by his Puritan brethren. He himself embarked next year.

3 We shall find that the God of Israel is among us, when ten of us shall be able to resist a thousand of our enemies; when He shall make us a praise and glory that men shall say of succeeding plantations, 'may the Lord make it like that of New England'. For we must consider that we shall be as a city upon a hill. The eyes of all people are upon us. So that if we shall deal falsely with our God in this work we have undertaken, and so cause Him to withdraw His present help from us, we shall be made a story and a by-word through the world. We shall open the mouths of enemies to speak evil of the ways of God, and all professors for God's sake.
John Winthrop *A Model of Christian Charity* (1630); David Hollinger and Charles Capper *The American Intellectual Tradition* Vol.1 (2001) p.15. The remarkable lay sermon delivered on the flagship *Arbella* as the first fleet of Puritan settlers sailed towards Massachusetts Bay. Compare President Ronald Reagan (914:1).

4 After several questions propounded and negative answers Returned, she at last acknowledged that Goody Johnson made her a witch, And sometime last summer she made a red mark in the devil's book with the forefinger of her Left hand, And the Devil would have her hurt Martha Sprague, Rose Foster and Abigail Martin which she did upon Saturday and Sabbath Day last, she said she was not above a quarter of an hour in coming down from Andover to Salem [about 16 miles]: to afflict, she says she afflicted the above three persons by squeezing her hands.
Testimony of a Salem 'witch', from the 'Examination of Mary Barker Before Maj'r Gidney, Mr Hauthorn and Mr Cor, 1st Paper', 29 Aug. 1692; William E. Woodward *Records of Salem Witchcraft* (1864) Vol.1. The trials were the basis of Arthur Miller's play *The Crucible* (1953), which drew parallels with McCarthyism in the United States in the 1950s (see 902:10–903:3).

5 We have been advised by some credible Christians yet alive, that a malefactor, accused of witchcraft as well as murder, and executed in this place more than forty years ago, did then give notice of an horrible plot against the country by witchcraft, and a foundation of witchcraft then laid, which if it were not seasonably discovered, would probably blow up, and pull down all the churches in the country. And we have now with horror seen the discovery of such a witchcraft! An army of devils is horribly broke in upon the place which is the centre, and after a sort, the firstborn of our English settlements: and the houses of the good people there are filled with doleful shrieks of their children and servants, tormented by invisible hands, with tortures altogether preternatural.

Rev. Cotton Mather *The Wonders of the Invisible World* (1692); Heimert and Delbanco (1985) p.340. The Boston minister and scholar 'was the most active and forward of any minister in the country in these matters', according to a former follower, but his reputation suffered through his rabid witch-hunting in the Salem trials of 1692. Mather was a scientist as well as a minister and the author of 382 works. He was also an early and powerful advocate of inoculation against smallpox, one example of his fearless attempts at social improvement in the face of public anger.

NEW NETHERLANDS AND PENNSYLVANIA, 1609–1708

1 The land is the finest for cultivation that I ever in my life set foot upon, and it also abounds in trees of every description. The natives are very good people, for when they saw that I would not remain they supposed that I was afraid of their bows, and taking the arrows, they broke them in pieces and threw them into the fire.

Henry Hudson, fragment of his lost journal, as transcribed by a Dutch merchant, 1609; Giles Milton *Nathaniel's Nutmeg* (1999) pp.182–3. The English explorer, who was employed by the Dutch, had arrived at the island of Manhattan. 'That side of the river [named the Hudson River after him] that is called Manna-hata' – the island that became New York. Hudson had been commissioned to open a northern route to the Spice Islands (Dutch East Indies) via the Northwest Passage, of whose existence he, like many mariners, was convinced. He was, therefore, about 4,000 miles from where he was supposed to be.

2   Sift not that sand, for their lies Stuyvesant
    Who once was overlord of all New Netherland
    Against his will, this land he handed to the foe;
    If rue and aggravation trouble hearts, his heart
    A thousand deaths did die, suffering
        insufferable smart.
    At first too high and rich; at last too poor and
        low.

Henricus Selyns 'Epitaph for Peter Stuyvesant, Late Governor of New Netherland' (1672); Mulford (2002) p.719. The Dutch administrator Stuyvesant (c.1610–72), the last governor of New Amsterdam, was forced by an English fleet to surrender. In 1667 the colony was exchanged for Britain's interests in the Spice Islands under the Treaty of Breda (see 403:4) and renamed New York, after the Duke of York, Charles II's brother and later James II.

3 Colonies then are the seeds of nations begun and nourished by the care of wise and populous countries; as conceiving them best for the increase of human stock, and beneficial for commerce.

Some of the wisest men in history have taken their fame from this design and service … Nor did any of these ever dream it was the way of decreasing their people or wealth … With justice therefore I deny the vulgar opinion against plantations, that they weaken England; they have manifestly enriched and strengthened her …

Let it be considered that the plantations employ many hundreds of shipping and many thousands of seamen, which must be in divers respects an advantage to England, being an island and fitted for navigation above any country in Europe.

William Penn *Some Account of the Province of Pennsylvania* (1681); E.H.D. Vol.9 (1955) p.122. Penn, the founder of the colony of Pennsylvania, named in memory of his father, Admiral Sir William Penn (1621–70), justifies the creation of colonies as a means of strengthening the mother country. Pennsylvania was also intended to be a refuge for his fellow Quakers, members of the Society of Friends, a Christian sect that prized the equality of all persons before God at the expense of traditional social and religious hierarchies – a belief that led to their persecution in Britain. Freedom of conscience was a notable feature of the Quaker faith and thus of the Quaker colony.

4 What I have here written, is not a Fiction, Flam, Whim, or any sinister Design, either to impose upon the Ignorant, or Credulous, or to curry Favour with the Rich and Mighty, but in mere Pity and pure Compassion to the Numbers of Poor Labouring Men, Women, and Children in England, half starved, visible in their meagre looks, that are continually wandering up and down looking for Employment without finding any, who here need not lie idle a moment, nor want due Encouragement or Reward for their Work, much less Vagabond or Drone it about. Here are no Beggars to be seen (it is a Shame and Disgrace to the State that there are so many in England) nor indeed have any here the least Occasion or Temptation to take up that Scandalous Lazy Life.

Gabriel Thomas *An Historical Description of the Province and Country of West-New-Jersey in America* (1698); Albert Bushnell Hart (ed.) *American History Told by Contemporaries* (1898) Vol.1, p.575. Each colony – here Pennsylvania – claimed to be the best 'poor man's country'.

5 O Pennsylvania what hast thou cost me? Above thirty thousand pounds more than I ever got by it, two hazardous and mostly fatiguing journeys, and my son's soul almost.

William Penn, while in the Fleet Prison for debtors, ?1708; Edwin Danson *Drawing the Line: How Mason and Dixon Surveyed* the *Most Famous Border in America* (2001) p.21. Penn's journeys were from England to the fledgling colony. His son William had become an alcoholic while in Pennsylvania. Penn also insisted that lands should scrupulously be purchased from their Indian owners; compare Winthrop (432:2).

I [Pennsylvania] possesses great liberties above all other English colonies, inasmuch as all religious sects are tolerated there. We find there Lutherans, Reformed, Catholics, Quakers, Mennonists or Ana-baptists, Herrnhuters or Moravian Brethren, Pietists, Seventh Day Adventists, Dunkers, Presbyterians, Newborn, Freemasons, Separatists, Freethinkers, Jews, Mohammedans, Pagans, Negroes and Indians. The Evangelicals and Reformed, however, are in the majority. But there are many hundred unbaptized souls there that do not even wish to be baptized. Many pray neither in the morning nor in the evening, neither before nor after meals. No devotional book, not so speak of a Bible, will be found with such people. In one house and one family, four, five and even six sects may be found.

Gottlieb Mittelberger *Journey to Pennsylvania* (c.1750) pp.54–5; E.H.D. Vol.9 (1955) p.547. A German pastor remarks on the huge religious diversity and tolerance of Pennsylvania.

CRIME AND PUNISHMENT

2 The blasphemous words whereof Arabella was found guilty were spoken in great passion occasioned by the spilling of some scalding pitch upon one of his feet.

By an act passed in Maryland, 30 Oct. 1704, to punish Blasphemy, for the first offence the offender is to be bored through his tongue and fined 20 pounds sterling to H.M. [Queen Anne] towards defraying the County charge where such offence was committed, or if ye party hath not an estate sufficient to answer that sum, then to suffer six months imprisonment … the said Charles Arabella in having been bored through the tongue and lain in prison six months (and more) has thereby fully suffered ye penalty of the Law for such his offence … The premises considered, if H.M. shall judge him a fit object of her royal compassion and shall be graciously pleased to order that he be released out of prison.

Council of Trade and Plantations to Lord Dartmouth, secretary of state, Whitehall, 19 Dec. 1710; Colonial Office Series 5, Vol.717, no.19.

3 My name is Captain Kidd, who has sail'd, who
    has sail'd
My name is Captain Kidd, who has sail'd;
My name is Captain Kidd.
What the laws did still forbid
Unluckily I did while I sail'd, while I sail'd.

Anon. ballad, 1700, popular on both sides of the Atlantic; John Franklin Jameson *Privateering and Piracy in the Colonial Period: Illustrative Documents* (1923) p.254. In 1695 Kidd, a Scottish merchant, was hired by the British colonial service to combat piracy in the Indian Ocean, but he turned pirate and began to attack merchant ships. In 1699 he gave himself up in Boston on promise of a pardon, but he was imprisoned and dispatched to London, where he was convicted and hanged in 1701. Piracy filled the new reading public with avid horror and fascination (see 392:1).

4 Whereas the great number of convicts of late years imported into this province have not only committed several murders, burglaries and other felonies, but debauched the minds and principles of several of the ignorant and formerly innocent inhabitants thereof, so far as to induce them to commit several of the like crimes … that every inhabitant of this province that hereafter shall buy any convict servant, shall be and is by this act obliged, within twenty days … to give and enter into recognizance, in the sum of thirty pounds current money of Maryland.

Law, 1723; Bernard C. Steiner (ed.) *Archives of Maryland* Vol.38 (1918) p.320. A British law passed in 1718 authorized the transportation of convicts to the colonies. The dumping ground survived until 1783, when transportation was switched to Australia.

ENLIGHTENMENT, 1640–1740

5 After God had carried us safe to New England, and we had built our houses, provided necessaries for our livelihood, reared convenient places for God's worship, and led the civil government, one of the next things we longed for and looked after was to advance learning and perpetuate it to posterity; dreading to leave an illiterate ministry to the churches, when our present ministers shall lie in the dust. And as we were thinking and consulting how to effect this great work, it pleased God to stir up the heart of one Mr Harvard (a godly gentleman and a lover of learning, there living among us) to give the one-half of his estate (it being in all about £700) toward the founding of a college, and all his library.

Anon. *New England's First Fruits … of the Progress of Learning in the College of Cambridge in Massachusetts Bay* (1643). Rev. John Harvard left London for Massachusetts in 1637. He bequeathed over 300 books and £779 to the founding of the university, which bears his name since he was its largest benefactor.

1 It being one chief project of ye old deluder, Satan, to keep men from the knowledge of ye Scriptures, as in former times by keeping them in an unknown tongue, so in these latter times by persuading from ye use of tongues, that so at least ye true sense & meaning of the original might be clouded by false glosses of saint seeming deceivers … It is therefore ordered, that every township in this jurisdiction, after ye Lord hath increased their number to 50 householders, shall then forthwith appoint one within their town to teach all such children as shall resort to him to write & read, whose wages shall be paid either by ye parents or masters of such children, or by ye inhabitants in general.

Massachusetts School Law, 1647; Commager (1968) p.29. This was the first state to demand the education of an entire populace.

2 For my Part, I must be of Opinion, as I hinted before, that there is but one way of Converting these poor Infidels, and reclaiming them from Barbarity, and that is, Charitably to intermarry with them, according to the Modern Policy of the most Christian King in Canada and Louisiana [Louis XIV].

William Byrd II 'The History of the Dividing Line' (1728; pub. 1841); Mulford (2002) p.529. An exceptionally tolerant perspective on relations of the English and the indigenous population of Virginia. Byrd, a Fellow of the Royal Society and eloquent spokesman of Virginian planters, inherited over 26,000 acres and owned 180,000 acres by his death in 1744.

3 Temperance: Eat not to Dulness. Drink not to Elevation.

Silence: Speak not but what may benefit others or your self. Avoiding trifling conversation.

Order: let all your Things have their Places. Let each Part of your Business have its Time.

Resolution: Resolve to perform what you ought. Perform without fail what you resolve.

Industry: Lose no Time. Be always employ'd in something useful. Cut off all unnecessary Actions.

Benjamin Franklin, the first 5 of 13 rules for his personal conduct, c.1730; *Autobiography* (1868; 1986 edn) pp.67–8. The most famous of Philadelphia's citizens was a statesman, diplomat, printer, publisher, inventor and scientist. He certainly set himself extraordinary standards when he was in his twenties – and became famously lecherous.

4 Nothing certainly can be more improving to a Searcher into Nature, than Objections judiciously made to his Opinions, taken up perhaps too hastily: for such Objections oblige him to restudy the Point, consider every Circumstance carefully, compare Facts, make Experiments, weigh Arguments, and be slow in drawing Conclusions. And hence a sure Advantage results; for he either confirms a Truth, before too slightly supported; or discovers an Error and receives Instruction from the Objector.

Benjamin Franklin to John Perkins, Philadelphia, 4 Feb. 1753; *Writings* (1987 edn) p.454. That Franklin was not merely a moralizer but also a thoughtful experimental scientist can be seen from his ideas on experimentation and scientific interchange.

5 It has pleased God in his Goodness to Mankind, at length to discover to them the Means of securing their Habitations and other Buildings from Mischief by Thunder and Lightning. The Method is this: Provide a small Iron Rod (it may be made of the rod-iron used by the Nailers) but of such a Length, that one End being three or four Feet in the moist Ground, the other may be six or eight Feet above the highest Part of the Building. To the upper End of the Rod fasten about a Foot of Brass Wire, the Size of a common Knitting-needle, sharpened to a fine Point; the Rod may be secured to the House by a few small Staples. If the House or Barn be long, there may be a Rod and Point at each end, and a middling Wire along the Ridge from one to the other.

Benjamin Franklin *How to secure Houses, &c. from LIGHTNING* (1751–2); *Writings* (1987 edn) p.1278. This, of all Franklin's proposals, gave him the highest measure of fame among his contemporaries, not only in America but throughout the entire Western world (see 512:1).

6 It is further the design of this college to instruct and perfect the youth in the learned languages and in the arts of reasoning exactly, of writing correctly and speaking eloquently; and in the arts of numbering and measuring, of surveying and navigation, of geography and history, of husbandry, commerce and government; and in the knowledge of all nature in the heavens above us, and in the air, water, and earth around us, and the various kinds of meteors, stones, mines and minerals, plants and animals, and of every thing useful for the comfort, the convenience, and elegance of life in the chief manufactures relating to any of these things. And finally, to lead them from the study of nature to the knowledge of themselves and of the God of nature and their duty to Him, themselves, and one another, and everything that can contribute to their true happiness both here and hereafter.

Samuel Johnson of New York, advertises for students to attend the new King's College, 31 May 1754; E.H.D. Vol.9 (1955) p.572. Note the emphasis on practical and useful disciplines, which set it apart from the more classically directed colleges of Oxford and Cambridge. Johnson became first president of King's College, later Columbia University.

SOCIAL RELATIONS AND DIVISIONS

1 If once reason obtains the advantage over their old customs, with the example of the French, which they esteem and respect, inciting them to work, it seems that they will set themselves straight, withdrawing from a life so full of poverty and affliction, that they will take their place beside the Frenchmen and Christian Savages.

Anon. *Véritables motifs de Messieurs et Dames de la société de Notre-Dame de Montréal* (1643) p.106. The pious hopes of the founders of Montreal.

2 It was believed for a very long time that domiciling the savages near our habitations was a very great means of teaching theses peoples to live like us and become instructed in our religion. I notice, Monseigneur, that the very opposite has taken place, because instead of familiarizing them with our laws, I assure you, that they communicate very much to us all they have that is the very worst, and take on likewise all that is bad and vicious in us.

Governor Denonville to the French ministry, 13 Nov. 1685; Public Archives of Canada, Series CIIA, Vol.7, pp.46–7. Denonville is referring particularly to the traffic in brandy.

3 The observation concerning the Importation of *Germans* in too great Numbers into Pennsylvania is, I believe, a very just one. This will in a few years become a German Colony; Instead of their Learning our Language, we must learn theirs, or live as in a foreign Country. Already the English begin to quit particular Neighbourhoods surrounded by Dutch [Deutsch or Germans] … the Dutch under-live, and are thereby enabled to under-work and under-sell the English; who are thereby extremely incommoded, and consequently disgusted, so that there can be no cordial affection or Unity between the two Nations. How good subjects they may make, and how faithful to the British interest, is a Question worth considering.

Benjamin Franklin to James Parker, Philadelphia, 20 March, 1750; Leonard W. Larabee (ed.) *The Papers of Benjamin Franklin* Vol.4 (1961) pp.120–21.

4 His administration, if small things may be compared with great ones, was for Louisiana, with regard to splendour, luxury and military display, and expenses of every kind, what the reign of Louis XIV had been for France.

Charles Gayarré *History of Louisiana* (1750) Vol.2, p.66. Pierre de Rigaud de Cavagnal, Marquis de Vaudreuil, governor of Louisiana, holds court in the parish of New Orleans, which numbered about 600 families.

TRADE AND AGRICULTURE

5 They also fatten bears which they keep two or three years for the purpose of their banquets. I observed that if this people [the Huron] had domestic animals they would be interested in them and care for them very well. I showed them the way to keep them, which would be an easy thing for them, since they have good grazing grounds in their country … yet with all their drawbacks they seem to me to be happy.

Samuel de Champlain *Voyages and Discoveries in New France, 1615–18* (1619; 1882 trans.); Mulford (2002) p.117. The French traveller describes the purpose of navigation: 'We attract and bring to our own land all kinds of riches; by it the idolatry of paganism is overthrown and Christianity proclaimed throughout the regions of the earth.'

6 We may likewise diminish our importations, if we would soberly refrain from excessive consumption of foreign wares in our diet and raiment …

The value of our exportations likewise may be much advanced when we perform it ourselves in our own Ships, for then we get not only the price of our wares as they are worth here, but also the Merchants' gains, the charges of insurance, and freight to carry them.

Thomas Mun *England's Treasure by Foreign Trade* (1664; 1903 edn); David Brion Davis and Steven Mintz (eds) *The Boisterous Sea of Liberty: A Documentary History of America from Discovery Through the Civil War* (1998) p.88.

7 The Farmers deem it better for their profit to put away their cattle and corn for clothing, than to set upon making of cloth.

Edward Johnson *Johnson's Wonder-Working Providence of Sion's Saviour in New England* (c.1650; 1910 edn) p.211; John J. McCusker and Russell R. Menard *The Economy of British America: 1607–1789* (1985) p.97. Johnson first visited New England in 1630 as a trader and returned there with his family in 1636.

He is explaining the failure of the cloth industry in New England, but all manufacturing was affected. Although the colonies were expanding, they did not meet the growing local market themselves but imported better quality goods from England.

1 Souls! Damn your souls! Make tobacco!

Sir Edward Seymour, a lord of the Treasury, attrib., early 1660s; G.A. Macon *Damned Souls in a Tobacco Colony: Religion in Seventeenth-Century Virginia* (2000) p.vii. An English official is unequivocal: Virginians' function was to nurture the soil not the soul.

2 Last Saturday night [9 Oct. 1669] came in the Nonsuch ketch from the North West Passage. Since I have endeavoured to find the proceeds of their voyage, and understand they were environed with ice about six months first hauling their ketch on shore, and building them a house. They carried provisions on shore and brewed Ale and beer and provided against the cold which was their work. They report the natives to be civil and say that Beaver is Very plenty. Those that carried out no Venture brought home 10 li or 12 li worth of beaver.

Report on the return of the *Nonsuch* to England when, in June 1669, the ship was released from the ice; state papers of Charles II. Jean-Baptiste Groseilliers, the veteran French fur trader, had sought this opportunity for 14 years. 'Here were Indians unspoilt by competitive trading with European fur seekers. The tariff was absurdly low, and as the winter passed, with the *Nonsuch* crew huddling close to the fires, Groseilliers baled up beaver skins bought in exchange for tools and trinkets, laying the basis of centuries of Hudson's Bay Company trade … On 2 May 1670, Charles II signed the charter granting sweeping imperial powers to the company of Adventurers of England trading into Hudson's Bay' (Douglas Mackay *The Honourable Company: A History of the Hudson's Bay Company* (1937) p.29).

3 No goods or merchandises whatsoever shall be imported into, or exported out of, any colony or plantation to his Majesty, in Asia, Africa, or America, belonging, or in his possession … or shall be laden or carried from any one port or place in the said colonies or plantations to any other port or place in the same, the kingdom of England, dominion of Wales, or town of Berwick-upon-Tweed, in any ship or bottom, but what is or shall be of the built of England, or of the built of Ireland, or the said colonies or plantations, and wholly owned by the people thereof, or any of them, and navigated with the masters and three fourths of the mariners of the said places only.

Navigation Act, 1696; Commager (1968) p.38. The act was the essential expression of mercantilism, the idea that an empire could be an enclosed economic community for the

exclusive benefit of the 'mother' country (see 393:5). As a contemporary commentator put it: 'The same respect is due from them [the colonies] as from a tenant to his landlord.'

4 It seems therefore a severity without a precedent, that a people who have the misfortune of being a thousand leagues distant from their sovereign, a misfortune great in itself, should unsummoned, unheard, in one day be deprived of all their privileges which they and their fathers have enjoyed for near an hundred years.

Jeremiah Dummer *A Defence of New England Charters* (1715); Heimert and Delbanco (1985) p.369. The lawyer Dummer lived most of his life in England, yet was nonetheless vociferous in defending New England's constitutional rights.

5 You will please to observe that the whole trade to and in America, belonging to his Majesty's British and American subjects … amounts yearly to £9,478,000. This includes the value of the whole navigation, the annual supplies from Great Britain and Ireland, the natural and improved produce remitted to Europe from the plantations and colonies, as well as the supplies given each other by their traffic and commerce from one colony or plantation to another …

I believe there is no less than 100,000 Negroes in the Colonies on the main of America …

Upon the foregoing observations and calculations, I believe, you will think that the British Empire of America is of inestimable value to the nation of Great Britain.

Robert Dinwiddie, report to the Board of Trade on the trade of the colonies, April 1740; E.H.D. Vol.9 (1955) pp.369–70. Dinwiddie was the surveyor-general of customs for the Southern District (from Maryland to the West Indies) from 1738 until 1751. A shrewd administrator, he was later made lieutenant-governor of Virginia. Note the figure he puts on the slave population.

6 The illicit trade which appears to have been carried on in this province and some of the neighbouring colonies … must be highly destructive of the interests of Great Britain, by lessening the vent of her woollen and other manufactures and commodities in her own plantations, making her cease to be a staple of the European commodities for supplying them, letting foreigners into the profits of the plantation trade, and finally weakening the dependence which the British northern colonies ought to have upon their mother country.

Governor William Shirley, Boston, New England, report to the Board of Trade on illegal trade in the colonies, 26 Feb.

1743; E.H.D. Vol.9 (1955) p.371. Shirley was a British appointee, who had been in Massachusetts for 12 years.

1 That the Sales are pitifully low, needs no words to demonstrate … Can it be otherwise than a little mortifying then to find, that we, who raise none but Sweet scented Tobacco, and endeavour I may add, to be careful in the management of it, however we fail in the execution, & who by a close and fixed correspondence with you, contribute so largely to the dispatch of your Ships in this Country should meet with such unprofitable returns? Surely I must answer No!

George Washington to his British agents, Robert Cary & Company, from Mount Vernon, 20 Sept. 1765; George Washington *Writings* (1997 edn) p.113. How much profit a Virginia planter made on his tobacco crop was a mark of his skill as a farmer; to make no profit was a public humiliation. These humiliations led Washington, like many others, to plant wheat – and thereby make his fortune.

CHRISTIAN REVIVAL: THE GREAT AWAKENING

2 The soul does not merely perceive and view things, but is some way inclined with respect to the things it views or considers; either is inclined to 'em, or is disinclined, and averse from 'em; or is the faculty by which the soul does not behold things, as an indifferent unaffected spectator, but either as liking or disliking, pleased or displeased, approving or rejecting. This faculty is called by various names: it is sometimes called the *inclination*: and, as it has respect to the actions that are determined and governed by it, is called the *will*: and the *mind*, with regard to the exercises of this faculty, is often called the *heart*.

Jonathan Edwards *A Treatise Concerning Religious Affections* (1746); *Works* Vol.2 (1959 edn) pp.95 ff. Edwards was both a revivalist preacher and one of the greatest American philosophers and theologians. He is trying to give a philosophical framework to the outpouring of religious emotion that contemporaries called the 'Great Awakening'.

3 'See there!' said he, pointing to the lightning, which played on the corner of the pulpit – 'Tis a glance from the angry eye of Jehovah! Hark!' continued he, raising his finger in a listening attitude, as the distant thunder grew louder and louder, and broke in one tremendous crash over the building. 'It was the voice of the Almighty as he passed by in his anger!' As the sound died away, he covered his face

with his hands, and knelt beside his pulpit, apparently lost in inward and intense prayer. The storm passed rapidly away, and the sun bursting forth in his might, threw across the heavens a magnificent arch of peace. Rising and pointing to the beautiful object, he exclaimed: 'Look upon the rainbow, and praise him that made it. Very beautiful it is in the brightness thereof. It compasses the heavens about with glory; and the hands of the Most High have bended it.'

John Gillies *Memoirs of the Rev. George Whitefield* (1834) pp.267–8. Whitefield's early biographer is describing the Methodist revivalist of the Great Awakening. The evangelist was known as the 'Divine Dramatist'; it is easy to see why.

SLAVERY, 1662–1757

4 Whereas some doubts have arisen whether children got by any Englishman upon a Negro woman shall be slave or free, *be it therefore enacted and declared by this present Grand Assembly*, that all children born in this country shall be held bond or free only according to the condition of the mother; and that if any Christian shall commit fornication with a Negro man or woman, he or she so offending shall pay double the fines imposed by the former act.

Virginia Slave Law, Dec. 1662; Davis and Mintz (1998) p.58.

5 My employer, having a Negro woman, sold her and directed me to write a bill of sale, the man being waiting who bought her. The thing was sudden, and though the thoughts of writing an instrument of slavery for one of my fellow creatures felt uneasy, yet I remembered I was hired by the year, that it was my master who directed me to do it, and that it was an elderly man, a member of our society, who bought her; so through weakness I gave way and wrote it, but at the executing it, I was so afflicted in my mind that I said before my master and Friend that I believed slave keeping to be a practice inconsistent with the Christian religion.

John Woolman 'He Decides Against Slavery' in *Journal*, c.1740; Mulford (2002) p.542. The Quaker preacher Woolman was the first prominent American abolitionist, and he persuaded his fellow members of the Society of Friends to free all the slaves they owned. His *Journal* was first published in 1774.

6 [It is shocking] to human nature that any race of mankind … should be sentenced to perpetual slavery; nor in justice can we think otherwise of it, than they are thrown amongst us to be our scourge one day or another for our sins; and as freedom to them must be as dear as to us, what a scene of horror must it bring about.

Scottish colonists in Darien, Georgia, 1743; Thomas Clarkson *The History of the Rise, Progress of the Accomplishment of the Abolition of the African Slave Trade* (1808) Vol.1, p.184. Their fear was justified – there had been slave revolts in the city of New York in 1712 and 1733. Georgia, named after King George II, was founded in 1733 to give asylum to debtors, though only six debtors are known to have gone there (John R. Alden *Pioneer America* (1966) p.45). It did not allow the importation of slaves. The lobbyists argued however: 'But if it plainly appears that Georgia, as a colony, cannot barely exist without them, surely an admission of them under limitations, suitable to the present situation of affairs, is absolutely necessary to its support' (*A Brief Account of the Causes that have Retarded the Progress of the Colony of Georgia in America* (1743) pp.93–4). Slaves were introduced!

1 Like Adam we are all apt to shift off the blame from ourselves and lay it upon others ... The Negroes are enslaved by the Negroes themselves before they are purchased by the masters of the ships who bring them here. It is to be sure our choice whether we buy them or not, so this then is our crime, folly or whatever you please to call it ... to live in Virginia without slaves is morally impossible. Before our troubles, you could not hire a servant or slave for love or money, so that unless robust enough ... you must starve, or board in some family where they both fleece and half starve you ... This of course draws us all into the original sin and curse of the country of purchasing slaves, and this is the reason we have no merchants, traders or artificers of any sort but what become planters in a short time.

Peter Fontaine, a French Protestant minister of Westover, Virginia, defends slavery to his brother, Moses, 30 March 1757; Ann Maury (ed.) *Memoirs of a Huguenot Family* (1853) pp.351–2.

2 [I] find that She esteems [slaves'] value at no higher rate than I do. We both concluded ... that if in Mr Carter's, or in any Gentleman's Estate, all the Negroes should be sold, & the Money put to Interest in safe hands, and let the lands which these Negroes now work lie wholly uncultivated, the bare Interest of the Price of the Negroes would be a much greater yearly income than what is now received from their working the Lands, making no allowance at all for the trouble & Risk of the Master as to the Crops, & Negroes.

Anne Tasker Carter, letter; Hunter Dickinson Farish (ed.) *Journal and Letters of Philip Vickers Fithian, 1773–1774: A Plantation Tutor of the Old Dominion* (1943) p.123. The extraordinarily frank and dismissive view of slavery. The writer's

husband, Robert Carter III, would later free his slaves in the largest manumission to occur in Virginia before the Civil War.

WAR AND CONFLICT, 1637–1763

3 Those that escaped the Fire were slain with the Sword ... so as they were quickly dispatched, and very few escaped: the Number they thus destroyed, was conceived to be above four hundred [a large proportion of whom were women and children]. At this time is [*sic*] was a fearful sight to see them thus frying in the Fire, and the Streams of Blood quenching the same; and horrible was the stink and scent thereof; but the victory seemed a sweet Sacrifice, and they [the English] gave the praise thereof to God, who had wrought so wonderfully for them, thus to enclose their Enemies in their hands, and give them so speedy a Victory over so proud, insulting and blasphemous an enemy.

Nathaniel Morton *New England's Memorial* (1937 edn) p.101; Douglas Edward Leach *Arms for Empire: A Military History of the British Colonies in North America, 1607–1763* (1973) p.46. The Puritan chronicler is describing an attack on 25 May 1637 on a village on the Mystic River, Narragansett Bay, in the Pequot War. The Pequots, pushed into an area on Long Island Sound by the Iroquois, alienated the British by trading exclusively with the Dutch. Leach appends the sinister addition that follows.

4 We had sufficient light from the word of God for our proceedings.

John Underhill *News from America: A New and Experimental Discovery of New England*; Charles Orr (ed.) *History of the Pequot War* (1897) p.81. Underhill was a participant in the settlers' attack on the Pequot town on the Mystic River.

5 *The Redeemed Captive Returning to Zion: A Faithful history of Remarkable Occurrences in the Captivity and Deliverance of Mr John Williams, Minister of the Gospel, in Deerfield, Who, in the Desolation, which befell that Plantation, by an Incursion of the French and Indians, was by Them carried away, with his Family and his Neighborhood Unto Canada.*

Title of the short account (1707) by Rev. John Williams of the destruction and massacre in the New England town of which he was pastor, his capture by Indians, forced march to Quebec and eventual release by Philippe de Rigaud, Marquis de Vaudreuil, the governor of New France (Canada). Vaudreuil was the father of Pierre (see 436:4), who moved from Louisiana to become the last governor of New France in 1755. The book went through six editions in the 18th century and five editions in the 19th century. During the French and

Indian Wars, the spasmodic struggles that grew out of European conflict from 1689 embroiled the Native Americans in New York, New England and the province of Quebec and culminated in the Seven Years War (1756–63). See 471:5 and 493:2.

1 Two or three independent Highland Companies … they are hardy, intrepid, accustomed to a rough country, and no great mischief if they fall.

James Wolfe to a friend serving in Nova Scotia, 1751; Angus Calder *Revolutionary Empire* (1981) p.607. Wolfe, the hero of Quebec (see 440:6), had been present at the Battle of Culloden in 1745. He is advocating the use of Scottish troops in the remote frontier province.

2 I had scarcely 40 men under my Command, and about 10, or a doz. Indians, nevertheless we obtained a most signal Victory … We had but one man killed, 2 or 3 wounded and a great many more within an Inch of being shot …

I fortunately escaped without a wound, though the right Wing where I stood was exposed to & received all the Enemy's fire and was the part where the man was killed & the rest wounded. I can with truth assure you, I heard the Bullets whistle and believe me there was something charming in the sound.

Major George Washington to John Augustine Washington, 31 May 1754; *Writings* (1997 edn) p.48. The young major gives his younger brother, Jack, an account of the fight with French troops under Ensign Jumonville. The colonial skirmishing between England and France, of which this is an instance, contributed to the outbreak of the Seven Years War.

3 He would not say so if he had been used to hear many.

George II, the last British monarch to lead his troops into battle, comments on Washington's letter to his brother, after it was printed in the *Gentleman's Magazine*; Douglas Southall Freeman *George Washington, A Biography* Vol.1 (1948) p.423.

4 Of about 12 or 13 hundred which were in this action 8 or 9 hundred were either killed or wounded; among who a large proportion of brave and valuable

Officers were included. The folly and consequence of opposing compact bodies to the sparse manner of Indian fighting, in woods, which had in a manner been predicted, was now so clearly verified that from hence forward another mode obtained in all future operations.

George Washington describes Braddock's massacre, 9 July 1755; 'Comments on David Humphrey's Biography' in *Writings* (1997 edn) p.616. He is analysing an unsuccessful attempt to seize the site of the future Pittsburgh (Fort Duquesne) from the French army. General Edward Braddock was killed; Washington conducted an orderly retreat.

5 Mad, is he? Then I hope he will *bite* some of my other generals.

George II to the Duke of Newcastle, who complained that General Wolfe was mad; Henry Beckles Willson *Life and Letters of James Wolfe* (1909) Ch.17. Compare Abraham Lincoln on General Grant's drinking (591:11).

6 The General [James Wolfe] suddenly broke off and said with a good deal of animation, 'I can only say, Gentlemen, that if the choice were mine, I would rather be the author of these verses [Gray's *Elegy*] than win the battle which we are to fight tomorrow morning.'

John Robinson, an earwitness; Christopher Hibbert *Wolfe at Quebec* (1959) p.130. Wolfe admired and had memorized Thomas Gray's *Elegy Written in a Country Churchyard*. On the eve of the Battle of the Plains of Abraham, in which the British captured Quebec from the French on 13 Sept. 1759, both he and his opponent, Marquis de Montcalm, the French commander in Canada, were killed.

7 Our superiority in this war [Seven Years War] rendered our regard to this people [Native Americans] still less, which had always been too little … Decorums, which are as necessary at least in dealing with barbarous as with civilized nations, were neglected.

The Annual Register, or a view of the History, Politics, and Literature. For the Year 1763 (1765 edn) p.22. An admission at the end of the war of the atrocities that had been inflicted upon the Native Americans unwittingly caught up in the rivalry of the European powers.

Russia of the Early Romanovs, 1613–1796

FOUNDING THE DYNASTY, 1613–82

1 The Russian state had been torn asunder by innumerable parties owing to the ambition of Godunov, for the Poles had seized Moscow and the Swedes Novgorod the Great. Yet, after such calamities, the Russians cleared their country of these two powerful enemies and restored their monarchy ... In less than fifty years they took back all the provinces they had had to sacrifice, except Ingria [on the Baltic] and part of Karelia [adjoining Finland] ... All this they accomplished under the rule of sovereigns who were not noted for special bravery or for intellectual acumen, and, who, moreover, came from such a new family that their first tsar, Michael, would certainly not have been able to prove his rights in a German court.

Johann Vockerodt, memorandum, 1737; E. Herrmann (ed.) *Russia under Peter the Great* (1872) p.2. Vockerodt spent many years in Russia as secretary to the Prussian legation. Although he was not a member of the old ruling family, Michael Romanov's great aunt had been the first wife of Ivan IV, and he was elected tsar by a council of representatives of townsmen and local militias. No one could have anticipated that his dynasty would rule Russia for 300 years. It was removed only by the 1917 Revolution. For Boris Godunov see 173:1.

2 The sovereign, tsar and grand prince of all Russia Mikhail Fedorovich [Romanov] decreed and the boyars [land-owning nobles] resolved that [fugitive peasants] of the sovereign, tsar and grand prince of all Russia [who have fled] during the past ten years are to be brought back into his sovereign crown villages and into the *volosti* [parishes] inhabited by state peasants, upon trial and investigation and according to the title deeds.

Michael Romanov, decree on runaways, 1641; *Collected Acts of Imperial Russia* (1830–1916) Vol.3, p.396. This decree is 'commonly considered to be one of the important steps in the development of serfdom' (G. Vernadsky and R.T. Fisher (eds) *A Source Book of Russian History* Vol.1 (1972) p.244).

3 As opinions are divided we shall first take the view of those learned in the canon law, who assert that the tsar's authority must be subordinate to episcopal authority, to which Almighty God has entrusted the keys of the kingdom of heaven and given, on earth, the power to bind and to loose; moreover episcopal power is spiritual, while that given to the tsar is of

this world ... The clergy is a more honoured and higher authority than the state itself.

Patriarch Nikon *A Refutation or Demolishment* (c.1663); W. Palmer *The Patriarch and the Tsar* Vol.1 (1871) in George Vernadsky and R.T. Fisher *A Source Book of Russian History* Vol.1 (1972) p.256. Patriarch Nikon led the movement to reform the Russian Orthodox Church in the 17th century, particularly in the use of uncorrupted texts. A long struggle ensued between the reformers and the so-called Old Believers, who would not accept the new versions. Michael Romanov (r.1613–45) and his son Alexis I (r.1645–76) both relied heavily on the church for support and combined their royal status with a priestly role.

4 He [Stenka Razin] had with him a Persian princess whom he had taken, together with her brother. He gave the brother to the governor of Astrakhan but kept the sister for his concubine. Being now in the height of his cups ... he suddenly broke out into these extravagant terms speaking of the River Volga:

Well, said he, thou art a noble river and out of thee I have had so much gold, silver and many things of value. Thou art the sole mother and father of my fortune and advancement: but, unthankful man that I am, I have never offered thee anything: well, now I am resolved to manifest my gratitude. With these words he took her into his arms and threw her into the Volga with all her rich habit and ornaments ... the lady was of an angelic countenance, amiable, of a stately carriage and body and always pleasing in her demeanour towards him yet at last became the instance of his cruelty.

John Struys *The Voyages and Travels of John Struys* (1669; 1684 trans.) pp.186–7. The writer, a Dutchman in the tsar's service, tells the story of the legendary Stepan Razin. The rebel's name became familiarly Stenka Razin and the basis of a famous Russian ballad.

5 Clause 63. It shall be strictly forbidden for a foreigner to trade or sell or exchange any goods with [another] foreigner, since in the custom houses the great sovereign suffers great loss in collecting [taxes] for his treasury, while Russian men suffer difficulties and impoverishment in their trade, and if foreigners should begin to trade among themselves, and this is discovered for certain, these goods will be taken for the great sovereign.

Alexis I, new trade statute, 22 April 1667. The number of foreign traders in Russia was obviously increasing, and there was constant tension between them and their Russian counter-parts. The tsars wanted to encourage foreigners to come to the country, but Alexis (and later Peter I) found it a difficult balancing act.

1 Courtiers are forbidden to adopt foreign, German and other customs, to cut the hair on their heads and to wear robes, tunics and hats of foreign design, and they are to forbid their servants to do so.

Alexis I, decree, 6 Aug. 1675. Although Alexis was eager to use foreigners to help modernize Russia, he was reluctant to allow his subjects to adopt their customs.

PETER I, 1682–1725

2 The whole Russian race is rather in a state of slavery than freedom … The people are rude of letters … devoid of honest education, they esteem deceit to be the height of wisdom … They despise liberal arts, prohibit philosophy and consider astronomy magic. The tsar is endeavouring to frame a better state of things in his kingdom.

J.G. Korb *Diary of an Austrian Secretary of Legation at the Court of Peter the Great* (1700/1; 1863 edn) Vol.1, p.154.

3 I am represented as a cruel tyrant: this is the opinion foreign nations have formed of me; but how can they judge! They do not know the circumstances I was in at the beginning of my reign; how many people opposed my designs, counteracted my most useful projects and obliged me to be severe: but I never treated anyone cruelly, nor ever gave proofs of tyranny.

Peter I, c.1715; Jacob von Staehlin-Storcksburg *Original Anecdotes of Peter the Great* (1785; 1788 edn) pp.292–3. There were, in fact, many occasions when he acted with great cruelty. Staehlin, a member of the Imperial Academy at St Petersburg, collected his anecdotes from people who had known Peter well.

4 I know that the favour I am obliged to grant them [the foreigners] publicly does not please all my subjects … Let them reflect a little what we were before I had acquired knowledge in foreign countries and had invited well-informed men to my dominions: let them consider how I should have succeeded in my enterprises, and made head against the powerful enemies I have had to encounter, without their assistance!

Peter I, c.1720; Staehlin-Storcksburg (1785; 1788 edn) pp.74–5. This hit at the very heart of the belief that stressed continuity rather than change and the superiority of all things Russian.

5 The products or manufactures of Russia … are potash, weed ash, leather, furs, linen, flax, hemp, seal skins, train oil [whale oil extracted by boiling blubber] rosin, pit ash, tar, caviar, tallow, honey, wax, isinglass [a sort of gelatine made from the sturgeon's air bladder] – one type of which is used for windows for ships and one for glue – as also masts, timber, plank and fir.

John Perry, c.1712; *The State of Russia under the Present Tsar* (1716) p.245. Perry, an English civil engineer, travelled to Russia in 1698 to work on canals and waterways.

6 Primitive methods of agriculture impoverish the country and many families run away when they find themselves insolvent and hide in the forests. Then their neighbours are forced to make up the full sum of the tsar's taxes as if there was no deficiency in the number of inhabitants. It follows of course that at length being ruined themselves … they follow the example of their brethren and fly to the forests.

Friedrich Christian Weber, c.1714–19; *The Present State of Russia* (1722–3) Vol.1, p.70.

THE GREAT EMBASSY, 1697–8

7 Most commonly when he [Peter] came to a sea port he went about in a Dutch skipper's habit, that he might go among the shipping and be less taken notice of.

He chose to take a small house on the East India Wharf … here he lived for some months … He wrought one part of the day with the carpenter's broad axe among the Dutchmen: at other times diverted himself with sailing and rowing upon the water.

John Perry (1716) p.265. Perry describes the tsar's stay in Zaandam, Holland, while he was studying ship-building during his visit to western Europe. Generally known as 'the great embassy', its aim was to gain technical expertise from the West and recruit shipwrights, sailors and artisans. Peter's great interest in ships and sailing had started when he was a boy. Historians have often commented that his truly original contribution to Russia was building the fleet.

8 The tsar emperor of Muscovy, having a mind to see the building of ships, hired my house at Sayes Court, and made it his court and palace, lying and remaining in it, new furnished for him by the king.

John Evelyn, 6 Feb. 1698; *The Diary of John Evelyn* (1955 edn) Vol.5, p.284. Evelyn's house was at Deptford by the River Thames, to the southeast of London.

1 I went to Deptford to view how miserably the tsar of Muscovy had left my house after 3 months making it his court, having gotten Sir Christopher Wren his majesty's surveyor and Mr London his gardener to go down and make an estimate of the repairs, for which they allowed 150 pounds in their report to the Lord of the Treasury.

John Evelyn, 9 June 1698; (1955 edn) Vol.5, p.291. The sum of money allocated to Evelyn was high. A footnote on this page mentions Evelyn's story of Peter letting his servants push him through the holly hedge in a wheelbarrow.

2 Henceforth, in accordance with this, His Majesty's decree, all court attendants ... provincial service men, government officials of all ranks, military men, all the members of the wholesale merchants' guild and members of the guilds purveying for our household must shave their beards and moustaches.

Peter I, decree, 16 Jan. 1705; Collected Acts of Imperial Russia (1830–1916) Vol.4, pp.282–3. There was an opportunity to remain unshaven and pay a fine, but most men complied. The decree about shaving brought Peter into conflict with the Orthodox Church, which taught that men should regard their facial hair as a special gift from God and not violate it. Other observers described how the tsar had himself cut the beards of some of the court officials when he returned from western Europe.

3 Either our decrees are not accurately observed, or there are few people who wish to go into the business of manufacturing ... Our people are like children who never want to begin the alphabet unless they are compelled by their teacher ... So ... we must act and even compel them to become good economists.

Peter I, decree on the development of factories, 5 Nov. 1723; Collected Acts of Imperial Russia (1830–1916) Vol.7, pp.150–51.

4 I thank God that the Russian nation in such a short time with such a small number of foreigners has studied and learned with the results that I can run great works, factories and mines with them ... But without increasing the number of good foreign masters it will be impossible to prosper.

Wilhelm Henning to Peter I, 30 Aug. 1724; Letters and Documents of Peter the Great (1948–64) Vol.10, p.107. Henning, a German citizen, was an adviser to the tsar.

5 There are some people [landlords] who wantonly despoil their own villages and ... impose all types of unbearable burdens on the peasants, beat and torment them, which makes them run away, thus depopulating the countryside. Therefore the [local governors] should be on the watch not to allow such ruinous practices.

Peter I, instruction to local governors, Jan. 1719; Collected Acts of Imperial Russia (1830–1916) Vol.5, pp.728–9. The tsar's instructions seem to show more concern for rural depopulation, which could lead to lower tax revenues, than for the enslaved peasants. However, a second instruction (April 1721) tried to stop the practice of selling serfs separately from their families.

6 His Tsarist Majesty, our most gracious sovereign, following the example of other Christian countries, has conceived a most gracious intention to set up the following state colleges ... to wit: foreign affairs, revenues, justice, accounting, commerce, disbursements, mining and manufactures. In these colleges he has decided to appoint presidents, vice-presidents, as well as other necessary members and office personnel.

Peter I, general statute for the colleges, 28 Feb. 1720; Collected Acts of Imperial Russia (1830–1916) Vol.6, p.141. From 1713 Peter began to experiment with colleges (a system of administration by committees, widespread in Scandinavia and Germany) on the advice of Gottfried Wilhelm Leibniz, the German philosopher, whom he had met in 1711.

7 [His subjects] beg His Majesty, in the name of the whole Russian people, to accept from them, following the example of other rulers, the title of 'Father of the Fatherland, Emperor of All Russia, Peter the Great'.

Proclamation of the Empire of All Russia, 22 Oct. 1721; Collected Acts of Imperial Russia (1830–1916) Vol.6, pp.444–8. A decree of 11 Nov. 1721 gave the tsar's new style and title – 'We, Peter I, by the grace of God emperor and autocrat of all Russia' – and went on to name all the provinces over which he reigned. This title was to be used in all correspondence with foreign courts.

8 In all the provinces the children of nobles and of state officials between the ages of 10 and 15 shall be taught arithmetic and some geometry ... students from the mathematical schools shall be sent to ... teach. While they are teaching they shall receive 10 kopecks a day ... and they must not accept anything from their pupils, but when the pupils have thoroughly mastered the subjects the teachers shall issue them with a certificate signed by them. Without these certificates the students are forbidden to marry.

Peter I, decree on compulsory education for the sons of nobles, 28 Feb. 1714; Collected Acts of Imperial Russia (1830–1916) Vol.5, p.86. Few Russians could afford to send their sons abroad to be educated, and this decree aimed to give young Russian nobles some rudimentary education to fit them for military service.

1 They were a sham patriarch and a complete set of clergy dedicated to Bacchus … He that bore the assumed honours of the patriarch was conspicuous in the vestments proper to a bishop … Cupid and Venus were the insignia on his crosier, lest there should be any mistake about what flock he was pastor of. The remaining rout of Bacchanalians came after him, some carrying great bowls of wine, others mead, others again beer and brandy, that last joy of heated Bacchus.

J.G. Korb (1700/1; 1863 edn) Vol.1, p.225. Korb describes a session of Peter's notorious drinking club, the Most Drunken Synod. He and his followers mocked the rituals of the Orthodox Church in their ceremonies, a practice that most people found shocking.

2 Having looked into the situation of the clerical estate, we found it full of disorder and quite lacking in direction, and our conscience was troubled … Therefore … we can see no better means than to set up a conciliar authority. For a single person is seldom unbiased and … he often takes poor care of his office.

A government college is nothing but a governing council where certain appropriate matters are administered not by one person but by several suitable persons appointed by the supreme power.

Peter I, statute of the Holy Synod, 25 Jan. 1721; *Collected Acts of Imperial Russia* (1830–1916) Vol.6, pp.315–18. The tsar first set out his reasons for establishing the Holy Synod, which was to be just like a department of state but with responsibility for ecclesiastical affairs. The Russian patriarchate was abolished and replaced by a collegiate system.

3 When I think of my successor … when I see you, my heir, unfit for the management of state affairs … you have no wish to hear anything about military affairs [and] it is one of the two activities necessary to government; order and defence … Lacking knowledge how can you direct affairs … I am a man and subject to death. To whom shall I leave all this sowing? … Better a stranger who is able than someone of one's own blood who is useless.

Peter I to the Tsarevich Alexis, 17 Oct. 1715; N.G. Ustrialov *Istorya tsarstvovaniya Petra Velikovo* (History of Tsar Peter the Great) (1858–63) Vol.6, p.346. Peter had a difficult relationship with his son, whom he regarded as weak. Alexis became a focus of discontent and made no secret of the fact that, when his father died, he would undo all his changes. Peter, however, hesitated to remove him from the succession. In 1716 Alexis fled to Vienna, making Peter fear that any rebellion would have the support of the Austrian emperor.

4 My Son, Your disobedience and the contempt you have shown for my orders are known to all the world. Neither my words nor my corrections have been able to bring you to follow my instructions and, last of all, having deceived me when I bade you farewell and in defiance of the oaths you have made, you have carried your disobedience to the highest pitch by your flight and by putting yourself like a traitor under foreign protection …

If you submit to my will by obeying and if you return, I will love you better than ever. But if you refuse, then I as your father, by virtue of the power I have received from God, give you my everlasting curse; and as your sovereign, I declare you traitor and I assure you I will find the means to use you as such.

Peter I to Tsarevich Alexis, 10 July 1717; Ustrialov (1858–63) Vol.6, p.389. By this time Alexis was in Naples, but the promise of safe conduct persuaded him to return to Russia, where he was promptly tried and condemned for treason.

5 The tsarevich has made himself unworthy of the clemency and pardon which was promised to him by his lord and father …

[He] contemplated a horrible double parricide against his lord: first against the father of his country and second against his own natural father … who tried to educate the son for government, and to instruct him carefully in the important military arts, in order to make him capable and worthy of succession to such a great empire.

It is with an afflicted heart and tearful eyes that we, as servants and subjects, pronounce this sentence.

Court sentence on Tsarevich Alexis, 3 July 1718; L.J. Oliva *Peter the Great* (1970) pp.64–5. Four days after this sentence was announced, Alexis died mysteriously in the Peter and Paul fortress in St Petersburg.

6 More rumours of the king of Spain's [Charles II's] death and of the tsar of Muscovy coming to invade Sweden: the weather mild.

John Evelyn, 13 Oct. 1700; (1955 edn) Vol.5, p.429. Peter made an alliance with Denmark and Saxony to attack Sweden, hoping to take advantage of the inexperience of the young Swedish king, Charles XII (r.1697–1718). Thus began the Great Northern War, which lasted until 1721 and in which, at first, Sweden was overwhelmingly successful.

7 The infantry are armed with bad muskets and do not know how to use them. They fight with their side arms, with lances and halberds and even these are blunt. For every foreigner killed there are three, four and even more Russians killed. As for our cavalry, we are ashamed to look at them ourselves, let alone show them to the foreigner. They consist of sickly, ancient horses, blunt sabres, puny badly dressed men who do not know how to wield their weapons.

Ivan Pososhkov, memorandum on military conduct, 1701; *Russian History Texts* Vol.8 (1911) p.120. Pososhkov, a shrewd observer of conditions in Russia, submitted this report on the infantry on his own initiative to the government after the Battle of Narva (1700).

1 We have received your letter of 26 December in which you write that recruits are fleeing to the forests. Therefore it is necessary to hold them fast by making them stand surety for each other in groups of twenty men or more and making them responsible for each other.

Peter I to Automon Ivanovich Ivanov, 13 Jan. 1709; *Letters and Documents of Peter the Great* (1948–64) Vol.9, p.23. By trial and error the government eventually came up with the idea of conscripting one recruit from every 20 peasant households. In this way between 30,000 and 35,000 recruits were raised in each levy.

2 Poltava was a very considerable and unexpected victory – in a word, the whole army has met with Phaeton's destiny. Now the final stone has been laid of the foundation of St Petersburg.

Peter I to his ministers from the battlefield, 27 June 1709; L.K. Beskrovnyi and B.B. Kafengauz (eds) *Readings in Russian History* (1963) Vol.18, p.5. The improvements in the Russian army, which Charles XII refused to acknowledge, combined with the fact that the Swedes had advanced far into Russia, thereby overextending their lines of communication, led to a remarkable Russian victory at the Battle of Poltava in southern Russia, a humiliating defeat for the Swedish army. Peter compared their fate to that of Phaeton, who, in Greek mythology, asked if he might drive the sun god's chariot across the sky. He could not control the horses and perished when he drove too close to the sun. Swedish prisoners of war were used to build St Petersburg, but the tsar probably also meant that the new capital would now be safe from future Swedish attacks.

3 The Swedes have had an entire defeat at Poltava; 14,000 yielded themselves prisoners … The strange reverse of fortune has wholly changed the face of affairs in these parts.

James Jefferyes to the secretary of state in London, 13 July 1709; *Captain James Jefferyes's Letters from the Swedish Army 1707–9* (1953 edn) pp.76–7. The Englishman Jefferyes, who had been born in Sweden, was a volunteer with the Swedish army in Russia. He sent dispatches to London throughout the campaign and from Jan. to Oct. 1719 was British ambassador in Russia. The Battle of Poltava (1709) did not end the war with Sweden, but it changed the balance of power in the Baltic.

Sweden was finished as a great military power, but the West was understandably worried about Russia's intentions, some contemporaries even referring to Peter as the 'Turk of the North'.

4 After noon I set off for the Admiralty wharf to be present at the raising of the stem of a 50-gun ship … The tsar as the chief shipwright (a post for which he receives a salary), supervised everything, took part in the work along with the others, and, where necessary, swung an axe, which he wields more skilfully than all the other carpenters there.

Just Juel, 10 Dec. 1709; E.V. Anisimov *The Reforms of Peter the Great* (1989) p.21. Juel, the Danish envoy at the Russian court from 1709 to 1711, shared an interest in ships with the tsar. In 1710 he described how Peter hurried to find him in the dark and rain to offer his sympathy for storm damage to the Danish fleet. The tsar used his experience during the Great Embassy (see 442:7) to create a fleet. He was overjoyed when this fleet won a great victory over the Swedes at the Battle of Cape Hango in 1714.

ST PETERSBURG: WINDOW ON THE WEST

5 Accordingly, in the beginning of 1703, many thousands of workmen raised from all corners of the vast Russian empire, some of them coming journeys of 200 to 300 German miles, made a beginning on the works of the new fortress.

Friedrich Christian Weber (1722–3) Vol.1, pp.299–300. Weber was the ambassador of Hanover (a principality in north Germany) in 1714–19. The building of St Petersburg was an important part of the tsar's policy. It gave Russia a new city with access to the Baltic Sea (even though the Neva – the river on which the new city stood – was navigable for only 218 days a year) and all the trading possibilities that this implied. The site was a difficult one, which was frequently flooded and was little more than a swampy waste. Forced labourers were used in vast numbers to develop it, and the work was by no means finished at Peter's death in 1725.

6 On this place the tsar has fixed his point of view to raise a town for the residence of merchants, which in a few years is to be the equal to Amsterdam in its wealth and beauty, and to be the Venice of the north, in which the trade of all Russia is to centre.

Charles Whitworth to the secretary of state in London, 17 June 1712; *Collected Documents of the Russian Historical Association* (S.I.R.I.O.) Vol.61 (1888). Whitworth was the British ambassador. The Admiralty shipyard, begun in 1704, was built first and was working by 1705. The city grew quickly, and there were 40,000 permanent residents by 1725. Peter encouraged commerce by giving the city the monopoly of the export of tar, caviar, potash and some types of leather.

1 The tsar obliges the nobility against their will to come and live at Petersburg, where they are obliged to build new houses for themselves.

John Perry (1716) pp.275–6. Perry says that food cost three or four times more in St Petersburg than Moscow and that forage for horses is as much as eight times dearer. It was a considerable achievement not only to build the city but to get people to live there.

2　　From this spot we shall smite the Swede; a city
　　　　shall be founded here
　　To chasten our ambitious neighbour;
　　Here we are pre-ordained by nature
　　To hew a window into Europe,
　　And stand with firm foot by the sea;
　　Here, upon waters new to them, the flags of
　　　　every state shall sail
　　And we shall banquet on the main.

Alexander Pushkin *The Bronze Horseman* (1833; 1963 trans. by Antony Wood) Prologue. The famous equestrian statue of Peter by Étienne-Maurice Falconet in the city is given a voice by the great Russian poet.

JUDGEMENTS ON PETER I

3 What is this? O, Russians, what have we lived to witness? What do we see? What are we doing? We are burying Peter the Great! Is it not a dream, an apparition? Alas our sorrow is real, our misfortune certain! Contrary to everybody's wishes and hopes he has come to life's end, he who has been the cause of our innumerable good fortunes …

What manner of man did we lose? He was your Samson [the strong man] Russia … he was your Japhet [builder of the Ark/fleet] … your Moses [the law-giver] … your Solomon [the wise king] … your David [warrior] … Most distinguished man! Can a short oration encompass his immeasurable glory?

Feofan Prokopovich, funeral oration for Peter the Great, 8 March 1725; *Works of Feofan Prokopovich* (1961 edn) pp.126–9. Prokopovich, archbishop of Novgorod, was one of Peter's closest collaborators in ecclesiastical matters and was responsible for the thinking behind the Ecclesiastical College. He was a keen propagandist for the tsar's policies. Peter was only 53 when he died, but he had not spared himself. By the summer of 1724 he was seriously ill with a bladder infection. He improved enough to go sailing in Oct., but in Nov. he caught a chill as a result of helping to rescue sailors whose ship had gone aground. Although this story, related by Staehlin-Storcksburg (1785; 1788 edn, pp.360–63), is typical of Peter's impetuousness, it was not the cause of his death, because he lingered until 28 Jan. 1725.

4 This monarch brought our fatherland to a level with others; he taught us to recognize that we are people; in a word, whatever you look at in Russia, all has its beginnings with him and whatever is done henceforth will also derive its source from that beginning.

Ivan Ivanovich Nepliuev *Memoirs* (1893 edn) p.122. Nepliuev was one of those young Russians sent to study abroad at the beginning of Peter's reign. He was personally examined by the tsar and passed the tests to become superintendent of the St Petersburg docks. In this position he came into almost daily contact with Peter, and in later life recorded his memories.

5 We became citizens of the world but ceased in certain respects to be citizens of Russia. The fault is Peter's.

Nikolai Karamzin *Memoir on Ancient and Modern Russia* (1810; 1959 edn) p.124. Karamzin (1766–1826) lived during the reigns of Catherine II, her son Paul I and her grandson Alexander. He was unable to publish his memoir during his own lifetime. He believed that Peter's achievement was to speed up the pace of change in Russia. Without him, Karamzin believed, Russia would have needed 600 years to catch up with the West.

CATHERINE II, 1762–96

6 I watched princess Sophia grow up and witnessed the progress she made in her studies … From her early youth, I merely observed in her a cold, calculating and serious disposition, but also one that was as far from being outstanding or brilliant as it was from lightness and extravagance. In short, I formed the opinion that she would turn out a very ordinary woman.

Baroness von Prinzen, report on Princess Sophia, 1743; V.A. Bilbasov, *History of Catherine the Great* (1900) p.64. The baroness was lady-in-waiting to the Duchess of Anhalt-Zerbst (the area around Stettin in northern Germany). Sophia and her mother were summoned to Russia in 1744 by the Empress Elizabeth (daughter of Peter the Great) who had seized the throne herself in 1740. Elizabeth had no children and had made her nephew her heir, creating him Grand Duke Peter. She was now looking for a wife for him and chose this rather obscure 14-year-old German princess.

7 April 21, 1744, my birthday, I was fifteen years old. The empress and the Grand Duke wished to have the Bishop of Pskov visit me and speak with me about the dogmas of the Greek Church. The Grand Duke thought that he would convince me of what I had been firmly convinced since my first entrance in the empire – that the heavenly crown could not be separated from the earthly crown ... I had been instructed in the Lutheran religion by a churchman ... who had often told me that every Christian up to the day of his first communion might choose the religion that seemed most convincing to him. I had not yet been to communion, and so I found him right in every respect ... He had no trouble converting me.

Catherine II *Memoirs* (1907; 1927 trans.) p.45. Throughout her life Catherine wrote a great deal on a variety of subjects, and when she died she left a package of writings addressed to her son, Paul. These were copied and read by a few trusted people, but her grandson, Alexander I, suppressed them. They were not published in Russian until 1907. In common with all converts to the Orthodox religion, Sophia took a new name; her choice was Catherine.

1 Since I tried on principle to please the people with whom I had to live, I adopted their habits and customs, I wished to be Russian in order to be liked by the Russians.

Catherine II (1907; 1927 trans.) pp.58–60. Catherine found it hard to please her husband but seems to have succeeded with her other two aims. She was fascinated by all things Russian. She learned the language, adopted the religion, and tried to learn everything about her new homeland, unlike her husband who preferred all things German.

2 Our entry into the city beggared all description. Countless people thronged the streets shouting and screaming, invoking blessings upon us and giving vent to their joy in a thousand ways, while the old and the sick were held at open windows by their children to enable them to see with their own eyes the triumph that shone on everyone's face.

Princess Dashkova *Memoirs* (1859; 1958 trans.) p.89. Princess Dashkova, lady-in-waiting to Catherine, described the scene as Catherine entered St Petersburg to be proclaimed empress in place of her husband (Peter III) in 1762.

3 It has become obvious to all true sons of the Russian fatherland what great danger has been facing the whole Russian state. First the foundations of our Greek Orthodox religion were shaken and its traditions destroyed ... Second, the glory of Russia, brought to a high pitch by her victorious arms at the expense of much blood, has now been trampled underfoot by the conclusion of peace with her most villainous enemy.

Manifesto of the accession of Catherine II to the throne, 28 June 1762; *Collected Acts of Imperial Russia* (1830–1916) Vol.16, p.3. Catherine used two arguments to justify her usurpation: first, she suggested that Peter III would not follow the

Orthodox religion, and, second, she acknowledged the unpopularity of his pro-Prussian foreign policy.

4 This princess seems to combine every kind of ambition in her person. Everything that may add lustre to her reign will have some attraction to her. Science and the arts will be encouraged to flourish in the empire; projects useful to the domestic economy will be undertaken. She will endeavour to reform the administration of justice and to invigorate the laws; but her policies will be based on Machiavellianism.

Laurent Bérenger, report to Louis XV of France, 3 Sept. 1762; S.I.R.I.O. (1867–1916) Vol.140, pp.646–8. The French diplomat's comments are remarkably prescient. He realized that Catherine was an intelligent politician.

5 [Tsar Peter III] died of colic, his unexpected death being 'evidence of God's divine intent which had prepared Catherine's way to the throne'.

Catherine II, manifesto, 7 July 1762; S.M. Solovyev *Istoriya Rosii v drevneyshik vremyon* (History of Russia in Ancient Times) (1863; 1959–66 edn) Vol.13, pp.14–15. Peter died in mysterious circumstances on 5 July 1762. The announcement was made two days later. There was a cover-up, and none of those involved in his death were ever punished – in fact, 454 people who helped Catherine seize the throne were rewarded with money, serfs, decorations and estates. The extent of her personal involvement was the subject of intense speculation.

6 It must be confessed that the empress of Russia understands the proper manner of governing her subjects much better than could have been expected from a foreign princess. She is well acquainted with their genius and character, and she makes so good a use of this knowledge that their happiness seems to the nation in general to depend on the duration of her reign.

Henry Shirley, British chargé d'affaires in St Petersburg, 20 July 1768; I. de Madariaga *Russia in the Age of Catherine the Great* (1981) p.573. A later ambassador, Lord Cathcart, reported that she rose at 5 a.m. to start work and paid close attention to detail.

7 Russia is a European power ...

The sovereign is absolute ...

It is better to obey the law under one master than to please several.

The purpose of autocracy is not to deprive people of their natural freedom, but to guide their actions so as to attain the maximum good ...

The use of torture is repugnant ...

Laws ought to be written in the common tongue.

It would be improper suddenly or by means of a

general law to liberate a large number [of slaves or serfs].

Catherine II , Instruction, 6 Feb. 1767; Nikolai Chechulin Catherine II's Instruction for the Delegates to the Legal Commission *(1907). The Instruction contained more than 500 points, which were detailed, comprehensive and quite liberal, based on Catherine's reading of writers of the French Enlightenment. The deliberations of the commission led to few useful suggestions, but in general merely confirmed the traditional stratified views of Russian society. The commission was disbanded in 1768.*

1 [In the villages] each house contains one or at most two rooms … beds are by no means usual … the family generally slept upon benches on the ground or over the stove … The number of persons crowded into a small space, which sometimes amounted to twenty, added to the heat of the stove, rendered the room intolerably warm, and produced a suffocating smell, which nothing but use enabled us to support.

The peasants are well clothed … and seem to enjoy plenty of wholesome food. They render the rye bread more palatable by stuffing it with onions and groats, carrots or green corn, and seasoning it with sweet oil.

The backwardness of the peasants in all the mechanical arts, when compared with those of the other nations of Europe is visible to the most superficial observer.

William Coxe, c.1778–9; Travels into Poland, Russia, Sweden and Denmark *(1784–90) Vol.1, pp.435, 441–2. Coxe was a historian and writer and an archdeacon in the Anglican church. He spent seven months travelling as tutor to George Herbert, later Earl of Pembroke.*

2 The governing Senate … has deemed it necessary to make known that the serfs and peasants owe their landlords proper submission and absolute obedience in all matters … all persons who dare to incite serfs and peasants to disobey their landlords shall be arrested and punished. (And if any serfs) should make bold to submit unlawful petitions complaining of their landlords … they shall be punished with the knout [i.e., whip] and deported to Nerchinsk [in Siberia] to penal servitude for life.

Decree prohibiting complaints by serfs, 22 Aug. 1767; Collected Acts of Imperial Russia *(1830–1916) Vol.17, p.10. This decree was published by the senate at the very time that Catherine was collecting opinions from the country and setting up an international essay competition on serfdom, which asked: what is more useful in society, that the peasant should own land or only moveable property, and how far should his rights over the one or the other extend? The competition*

winner, Béarde de l'Abbaye, wrote that there could be no question of a peasant owning property when the peasant himself was not free.

3 In the capital city of each province there shall be one upper level public school.

One of the subjects for study shall be a book on the duties of a man and a citizen.

The fourth grade shall review Russian geography, Russian history, world geography, geometry, mechanics, physics, natural history and civil architecture.

Instruction shall be given in the fundamentals of Latin … and whatever foreign language shall be useful for social intercourse.

Lower schools are to instruct in their native languages.

The director of the public schools shall be selected by the governor. He must be a lover of scholarship, order and virtue who is well disposed towards the young and knows the value of education.

Catherine II, statute concerning public education, 5 Aug. 1786; Collected Acts of Imperial Russia *(1830–1916) Vol.22, pp.646–8. This statute was largely the work of Theodore Iankovich de Mirievo (1741–1814), who had helped to reorganize schools in Austria and who came to Russia as a member of the commission on education. The statute was detailed and extensive but encountered difficulties because the curriculum was too ambitious.*

PUGACHEV AND POTEMKIN, 1773–91

4 From the autocratic emperor, our great sovereign Peter Feodorovich of all Russia.

Through this my sovereign decree, be it expressed to the Iaik [Ural] Cossacks, just as you my friends, and your grandfathers and fathers served former tsars to the last drop of blood, now you should serve me the great sovereign and emperor for the good of the fatherland.

Emilian Pugachev, decree, 17 Sept. 1773; Russian Central Archive at the Time of Pugachev (1926–9) Vol.1, p.25. Pugachev, a Don Cossack and former soldier in the Russian army, pretended to be Catherine's dead husband, Tsar Peter III. He appealed to several discontented groups in Russia, repeating the old complaints about foreign customs, shaving beards and attacks on the Orthodox Church . Most of his support came from the Cossacks. The revolt was finally put down by Potemkin, Catherine's lover.

5 The Crimea by its position, creates a breach in our borders … The present Khan [ruler of the Crimea]

does not please the Turks because he will not let them enter through the Crimea into our very heart. Now just imagine that the Crimea is yours and no longer a thorn in your side: suddenly our frontier situation becomes splendid … the Turks adjoin us directly and therefore have to deal with us themselves and not use others as cover … Just as the annexation will bring you glory, so will posterity shame and reproach you if continued disturbances lead it to say, 'She had the power to act but would not or let the moment slip by'.

Prince Gregory Potemkin, note to Catherine II, c.1776–80; Solovyev (1863; 1959–66 edn) Vol.13, pp.102–3. The Pugachev rising raised the question of the safety of the southern borders of Russia. Potemkin had become Catherine's lover in 1774, and they were probably married in secret later that year. He lived like a royal consort, and his fortune was estimated at several million roubles. A capable statesman and soldier, he realized the advantages of annexing the Crimea.

1 We have decided to take under our dominion the Crimean peninsula … we make a sacred and unshakeable promise [to the inhabitants of these regions] on behalf of ourselves and our successors … to maintain them on the basis of equality with our hereditary subjects.

Catherine II, manifesto on the annexation of the Crimea, 8 April 1783; Collected Acts of Imperial Russia (1830–1916) Vol.21, pp.897–8. Russian armies under Potemkin invaded the area and took it over. Potemkin was then appointed governor of the Crimea, or New Russia as it was called. This beautiful and fertile area, with its warm climate and sea coast, was a great prize for Russia. Catherine and Potemkin had grandiose plans to capture Constantinople and eventually to install her grandson, Constantine, as emperor in that city.

2 Kherson [Ukraine] is not eight years old, and it can claim to be one of the finest military as well as commercial towns of the empire. All the houses are of hewn stone … the efforts of prince Potemkin have transformed the town and this region.

Catherine II to Baron Friedrich Melchior von Grimm, 15 May 1787; S.I.R.I.O. (1867–1916) Vol.23, p.116. Grimm, a German literary critic who lived in France, was one of Catherine's strongest supporters in the world of letters. She wrote to him over at least 20 years to put over her point of view and show herself in the best possible light as an academic and liberal thinker. Catherine wanted other countries to see her as an enlightened ruler and to know what Potemkin had achieved.

3 Prince Potemkin caused to be transplanted into a really magical English garden exotic trees as big as himself …

I forgot to tell you that the King of Poland

[Stanislaus Poniatowski, a former lover of Catherine] awaited us at Kanev on the Dnieper.

Prince de Ligne to Mme de Coigny, 1787; Katherine Wormeley (ed.) Prince de Ligne: His Memoirs, Letters and Miscellaneous Papers Vol.2 (1899 edn) p.15. Potemkin wanted to show off to Catherine what he had achieved in the new province. New towns had been started, everything with great magnificence. One of the party, the Saxon envoy in Russia, Georg von Helbig, started the myth of 'Potemkin villages' that has persisted to modern times. He claimed that façades of houses were specially created along the roads where the empress was to pass rather like a film set. Modern research suggests that Potemkin achieved far more than he was given credit for in his lifetime or after his death.

4 One cannot discern how far the empress and Prince Potemkin act together, or differ in their views.

Georg von Helbig, dispatch, 7 March 1791; E. Herrmann Diplomatic Correspondence (1791–7) p.102. Helbig did not succumb to Potemkin's charms and was critical of him. In the last years of his life Potemkin, who died in Oct. 1791, was often away from court, commanding the army in the Russo-Turkish Wars (1768–74, 1787–92) or as governor of the Crimea, but he was in daily communication with Catherine. The stormy, passionate relationship between the two continued after their physical affair had ended, even though both took younger lovers.

5 In order to put an end to various inconveniences resulting from the free and unrestrained printing of books, we have deemed it necessary to issue the following orders:

Censorship boards … shall be established in both our capital cities … (and other important cities).

No books written within our state may be printed … without examination by one of the censorship boards.

The … censorship boards shall observe the same rules with regard to books brought from foreign countries.

Printing houses operated by private persons … shall be abolished.

Catherine II, decree on censorship, 16 Sept. 1796; Collected Acts of Imperial Russia (1830–1916) Vol.23, pp.933–4. The influence of the French Revolution led to increased numbers of subversive pamphlets being published in Russia.

6 The 18th century which once prided itself on being the gentlest, the most enlightened, of ages, has generated the most wicked of beings in the midst of the most famous of cities. Fie upon the abominable creatures.

Catherine II to Baron Friedrich Melchior von Grimm, 13 April 1793; S.I.R.I.O. (1867–1916) Vol.23, pp.581–2. Catherine was horrified by the French Revolution and especially by the execution of Louis XVI in Jan. 1793. All her liberal and enlightened sympathies vanished, and she re-imposed censorship and clamped down on freedom.

JUDGEMENTS ON CATHERINE II

1 Should we compare all the known epochs of Russian history, virtually all would agree that Catherine's epoch was the happiest for Russian citizens.

Nikolai Karamzin (1810; 1959 edn) p.134. It is hard to imagine the serfs or the conquered peoples who lost their traditional freedoms agreeing with Karamzin's assessment. As a Ukrainian song puts it: 'Katerina, devil's mother, what have you done!/ To the wide steppe and the gay land you have brought destruction' (de Madariaga (1981) p.579).

2 With all her inconsistencies, her overweening confidence in her powers, her certainty that she was nearly always right, Catherine rendered signal service to Russia … Imperfect as many of her enactments were, they were carefully elaborated and she was rarely arbitrary in their implementation … A hundred years later, and with a lighter touch, as befits a woman, Catherine did for Russia what Louis XIV had done for France … Those who remembered her rule looked back on it as a time when despotism had been turned into monarchy, when men obeyed through honour, not through fear.

Isabella de Madariaga (1981) p.588. Catherine achieved much as ruler. She extended the boundaries of the country, encouraged culture and developed contacts with the West. She had read widely and wished to be regarded as an enlightened ruler, but she ended her reign as a typical Russian monarch, determined to preserve traditional Russian society and its institutions.

The Thirty Years War, 1618–48

BEFORE THE WAR

1 I am very much afraid that the states of the empire, quarrelling fiercely among themselves, may start a fatal conflagration embracing not only themselves … but also those countries that are in one way or another connected with Germany. All this will undoubtedly produce the most dangerous consequences, bringing about the total collapse and unavoidable alteration in the present state of Germany. And it may also perhaps affect some other states.

Maurice, Landgrave of Hesse-Kassel, Germany, to Louis XIII of France, 23 March 1615; Geoffrey Parker *The Thirty Years War* (1984) p.12.

2 In the year 1517 a Lutheran celebration was held by Dr Martin Luther, the highly esteemed and valued prophet of Germany, the shining light that brought forth the word of God. To commemorate this all Lutheran churches held a feast of joy and all the children in the territory of Ulm [south Germany] were given a special half batzen [worth two kreuzer] coin to mark the occasion … The celebration was held on St Martin's Day 11 November 1617. It was the start of the war as one can read in all the Catholic accounts since this celebration was to them a very sore wound.

Hans Heberle (1618–72) *Chronicle* (1975 edn) pp.92–3. In his chronicle Heberle, a cobbler, ascribes the war to Catholic reaction to Protestants marking the centenary of Luther's 95 theses (see 355:5).

3 It has been noted that, in the 57 marriages contracted by the members of the dynasty [the Habsburgs] between *c*.1450 and *c*.1650, 51 spouses came from the same seven families, and 24 came from just three. Philip IV of Spain had only four great-grandparents, instead of eight! Perhaps the repeated incest (in effect) of the House of Habsburg explains the infertility of its members during this period.

P.S. Fichtner 'Dynastic Marriage in 16th-century Habsburg Diplomacy and Statecraft: an Interdisciplinary Approach' in *American Historical Review* LXXXI (1976). It was the way in which the Habsburg princes worked together, after 1618, in pursuit of common goals that made them so threatening, not only to Protestant princes but also to Catholic France, for whom the overriding concern was security.

4 Whatever the king does in acts belonging to his kingly office should be considered in the same light as if the state did them.

Hugo Grotius *The Law of War and Peace* (1625; 1925 edn) p.138. The great Dutch authority on international law was himself involved in the Dutch revolt of 1567–1609 (see 387:3).

5 Then truly in May great troubles will not be avoided in those places and in those affairs, where everything is ready ahead of time and especially where the community otherwise has great freedom, unless there is a wakeful eye on them.

Johannes Kepler; Max Caspar *Kepler* (1959 trans.) p.300. The astronomer's famous prediction proved correct. A 'great difficulty' did indeed occur in Bohemia, starting on 23 May 1618, with the defenestration by Protestant dissidents of the two Catholic regents, Jaroslav Martinitz and Count William Slavata, from the Hrádcin Palace in Prague. They were held responsible for the intolerant policy of King Ferdinand (soon to become Emperor Ferdinand II).

6 It seems necessary for Your Majesty to consider which will be of greater service to you, the loss of these provinces [of Bohemia] or the dispatch of an army of fifteen or twenty thousand men to settle the matter.

Count Õnate, Spanish ambassador to the Holy Roman Empire, to his king, Philip III, May 1618, on the defenestration of Prague. Throwing the regents out of the window triggered the third revolt in Bohemia in a decade and the war that followed. Supposedly, one of the rebels shouted, 'We shall see if your Mary can help you!' A second later, as Martinitz was seen to move, the rebel exclaimed, 'By God, his Mary has helped!' They had landed in a midden.

7 For the most part, national feelings could be exploited by the sovereign with whose rule they were connected, and the dynasty was, with few exceptions, more important in European diplomacy than the nation. Royal marriages were the rivets of international policy and the personal will of the sovereign or the interests of his family its motive forces … For all practical purposes France and Spain are misleading terms for the dynasties of Bourbon and Habsburg.

C.V. Wedgwood *The Thirty Years War* (1938; 1944 edn) pp.14–15.

8 Germany's disaster was in the first place one of geography, in the second place one of tradition.

From remote times she had been a highway rather than an enclosure, the marching ground of tribes and armies, and when at last the tides of movement ceased, the traders of Europe continued the ancient custom.
C.V. Wedgwood (1938; 1957 edn) p.33.

WAR IN EUROPE, 1618

1 Everything that belonged to the use and commodity of man was and is there … Nature seemed to make the country [Bohemia] her storehouse or granary.
Anton Gindely *Geschichte des dreissigjähren Krieg* (1869; 1885 trans.) Vol.1, p.156; Wedgwood (1938; 1957 edn) p.66.

2 If it is true … the Bohemians are about to depose Ferdinand [Emperor Ferdinand II, a hard-line Catholic] and elect another king, let everyone prepare at once for war lasting twenty, thirty or forty years. The Spaniards and the House of Austria will deploy all their worldly goods to recover Bohemia; indeed the Spaniards would rather lose the Netherlands than allow their House to lose control of Bohemia so disgracefully and so outrageously.
Count Solms, the Palatinate ambassador at Frankfurt, July 1619; G. Parker *Europe in Crisis 1598–1648* (1979) p.163. The count is anticipating the duration of the Thirty Years War.

3 The wars of mankind today are not limited to a trial of natural strength, like a bull-fight, nor even mere battles. Rather they depend on losing or gaining friends and allies, and it is to this end that good statesmen must turn all their attention and energy.
Count Gondomar, ambassador to London, to Philip III of Spain, 28 March 1619. He is anticipating the politicization of the conflict that was to come.

4 This business is like to put all Christendom in combustion.
Dudley Carleton to John Chamberlain, 18 Sept. 1619; M. Lee (ed.) *Dudley Carleton to John Chamberlain 1603–1624* (1972). The English ambassador in The Hague went on to note that the Dutch leaders' reaction was that 'since the revolution of the world is like to carry us out of this changing time, it is better to begin the change with advantage than disadvantage'. He saw the Habsburg reaction: 'God knows, being pushed on by the Jesuits and commanded by a new emperor, who flatters himself with prophecies of extirpating the reformed religion and restoring the Roman Church to the ancient greatness.'

5 To convince ourselves that we can conquer the Dutch is to seek the impossible, to delude ourselves

… To those who put all blame for our troubles on the truce, and foresee great benefits from breaking it, we can say for certain that whether we end it or not we shall always be at a disadvantage.
Don Baltasar de Zúñiga, chief minister of Spain, on the military position in April 1619; Parker (1984) p.57. The Twelve Year Truce (1609–21) ended the fighting that had lasted since 1572 and accorded provisional independence to the United Provinces (see 383:5). Zúñiga's pessimism did not deter the Spanish crown from renewing hostilities on the expiry of the truce, however.

6 Almost all the kings and princes of Europe are jealous of your greatness. You are the main support and defence of the Catholic religion. For this reason you have renewed the war against the Dutch and with the other enemies of the church who are their allies; and your principal obligation is to defend yourself and to attack them.
Gaspar de Guzmán, Count-duke of Olivares, Nov. 1621, to his new king, Philip IV, whose chief minister he was until 1643; J. Lynch *Spain under the Habsburgs* Vol.2 (1969) p.68. In Spanish eyes neither aggressive nor expansionist, Spanish policy aroused hostility because of the range of her possessions. To preserve communications between them her troops had to cut across foreign lands and spheres of interest.

7 It is quite possible that the house of Austria may be turned out of Germany bag and baggage. If the Protestants succeed in doing this they will then join the Dutch in an attack upon these provinces [Flanders], not only in return for the help they are getting from them, because they will imagine that whilst your Majesty's forces are here, they will not be left undisturbed in the enjoyment of their new possessions. If all the German and Dutch Protestants were to unite in attacking us after a victory in Germany it would be hopeless for us to attempt to resist them.
General Ambrosia de Spinola, 1619; D. Maland *Europe at War 1600–50* (1980) p.68. The Italian-born general advises Philip III of Spain of the interdependence of defeating the Bohemian rebels and of conquering the Dutch.

8 You are king only by permission of the nobles – their temporary permission that is.
Contemporary Bohemian lampoon on their new king, the Elector Frederick; G. Pagés *The Thirty Years War* (1939; 1970 trans.) p.69. Frederick V, who became king of Bohemia in 1619, found that it was one thing to accept the crown of Bohemia, another to win the confidence of the Bohemian nobles.

9   Oh! Poor winter king, what have you done?
How could you steal the emperor's crown

By pursuing your rebellion? Now you do well
   to flee
Your Electoral lands and Bohemia.
You will pay for your mistake with grief
And suffer mockery and shame.
Oh! Pious emperor Ferdinand grant him
   pardon!

Anon. There is irony and pity in this popular song, circulating
after the Battle of the White Mountain near Prague (Nov.
1620) and the expulsion of the Elector; Pagés (1939; 1970
trans.) p.73. The Elector Frederick V, king of Bohemia, and his
wife, Elizabeth (the daughter of James I of England), were
known as the Winter King and Queen, from their brief
sojourn in the city of Prague, where they had enjoyed but one
winter (see 421:4).

1 In the year 1621 the haggling started and everyone
wanted to get rich overnight. Some ran this way and
some that way until they had exported all the good
coin in return for bringing into our territory
debased, loose change which was nothing more than
copper and brass. All the territories were ruined by
it and prices shot up especially in 1622–4, creating
chaotic conditions, the likes of which have never
been seen since the beginning of the world.

Hans Heberle (1618–72) (1975 edn) pp.96–102. The
chronicler describes the appalling inflation that hit food and
clothes and made the populace destitute in 1621–4.

2 It is certain that if the [German Protestant] side is
completely ruined the brunt of the House of Austria
might will fall on France … The worst advice that
France can take is to act in such a way that she is left
alone to maintain the struggle against the emperor
and Spain.

Cardinal Richelieu, memorandum to Louis XIII, written after
the defeat of the Swedes at the Battle of Nördlingen (Sept.
1634). France could no longer rely on allies to neutralize Habsburg power in Germany.

3 If Germany is lost, France cannot survive.

Cardinal Richelieu, 1621; Wedgwood (1938; 1957 edn) p.139.

4 God is Spanish and fights for our nation these
days.

Gaspar de Guzmán, Count-duke of Olivares, first minister of
Spain, to Count Gondomar, 1625, the year of several major
Spanish victories; Jonathan Brown and J.H. Elliott *A Palace for
a King* (1980) p.190. 'There must have been moments in 1625,
that *annus mirabilis* for Spanish arms, when even Spain's
enemies may grudgingly have conceded that the Count-duke of
Olivares was not entirely unjustified in his confident assessment of the divinity's national affiliation for Spanish arms'
(Parker (1984) p.103).

5 I will capture it though it be attached by chains to
heaven.

Albrecht Wenzel Eusebius von Wallenstein, attrib.;
Wedgwood (1938; 1957 edn) p.209. The capture of a Baltic
port – Stralsund on the coast of Pomerania – was the prime
objective of Habsburg strategy after the defeat of the
Protestant princes in 1626.

6 France suffers from four evils: The unbridled
ambition of Spain, the excessive licence of the
nobility, the lack of soldiers and the absence of any
reserve of saving for the prosecution of the war.

Cardinal Richelieu, 1628; *Mémoires* (1907–31) Vol.8, p.114.
The cardinal could have added the challenge of the
Huguenots, for he was still engaged in the siege of La Rochelle
(see 411:7). He was not yet ready to commit French troops,
but unless some new ally could be found, the Habsburgs
would retain the upper hand.

7 I mean to make use of all religions to encompass
my ends.

James I, 1621; Calendar of State Papers (C.S.P.) Domestic
1623–5 p.195. The king successfully resisted Protestant
pressure and the urging of George Abbot, archbishop of
Canterbury, to become engaged on behalf of his son-in-law,
Frederick V, the Winter King of Bohemia.

8 We, Ferdinand, by the grace of God, Holy Roman
Empire etc are determined for the realization both
of the religious and profane peace to dispatch our
imperial commissioners into the empire; to reclaim
all the bishoprics, prelacies, monasteries, hospitals
and endowments which the Catholics had possessed
at the time of the Treaty of Passau [1552] and of
which they have been illegally deprived; and to put
into all these Catholic foundations qualified persons
so that each may get his proper due.

Edict of Restitution, 1629; Benecke (1978) p.14. The edict
denied any legitimate existence to the Calvinists and denied
the right of a Protestant to buy land. It also denied the
validity of any previous legal judgements on church land, making
the emperor's power paramount. Military action to enforce the
edict and recover secularized bishoprics, notably the siege and
sack of Magdeburg in 1631, prompted the intervention of
Gustavus Adolphus of Sweden (r.1611–32) and the further
widening of the war.

9 The edict must stand firm, whatever evil might
finally come from it. It matters little that the
emperor, because of it, lose not only Austria but all
his kingdoms … provided he save his soul, which he
cannot do without the implementation of the edict.

Father Guillaume Lamormaini SJ, c.1629; R. Bireley SJ *Religion
and Politics in the Age of the Counter Revolution* (1981) p.125.
Lamormaini, confessor to Ferdinand II, was fiercely

intransigent about giving any concessions to the Protestants, as the emperor was inclined to do.

THE DISMAL COURSE OF THE CONFLICT

1 Things are come to this pass, that all the wars that waged in Europe are commingled and become one, as is shown by the action of the Papists in Germany … as well as by sundry consultations holden at the emperor's court where … it was resolved to press on, by the occupation of these Scandinavian lands, to that tyranny over body and soul which they lust after.

Gustavus Adolphus to Axel Oxenstierna, April 1628; Michael Roberts *Gustavus Adolphus: A History of Sweden 1611–1632* (1958) Vol.2, p.363.

2 The count is so powerful that one must be grateful to him for contenting himself with a land like Mecklenburg … The emperor in his goodness, in spite of all warning, has given the count such power that one cannot fail to be anxious.

The Spanish ambassador on Wallenstein's power; Gindely (1869) Vol.1, p.368.

3 Since the Duke of Friedland [Wallenstein] has up to now disgusted and offended to the utmost nearly every territorial ruler in the empire; and although the present situation has moved him to be more cautious, he has not given up his plans to keep hold of Mecklenburg by virtue of his imperial command.

Anselm Casimir von Wambold, Dec. 1629; Parker (1984) p.101. At a meeting of the Catholic League the new Elector of Mainz demands that the emperor sack his entrepreneurial general.

4 On 7 September [1631] by the grace of God, the king of Sweden won a noble victory over Tilly and thereafter he occupied Königshofen on 29 September. Once the Swedish army had entered Franconia in full force the popish priests lost no time in disguising themselves, and with their cooks and housekeepers they ran away.

Batholomäus Dietwar; Benecke (1978) p.46. A Protestant priest records the decisive defeat of the army of the Catholic League, under the generalship of Count Tilly, at the First Battle of Breitenfeld near Leipzig in 1631.

5 I seek not my own advantage in this war, nor any gain save the security of my own kingdom [Sweden]; I can look for nothing but expense, hard work, trouble and danger to life and limb. I have found

reason enough for my coming in that Prussia has twice sent aid to my enemies and attempted to overthrow me; thereafter they tried to seize the east port, which made it plain what designs they had against me.

Gustavus Adolphus to the Elector of Brandenburg, July 1630; Peter Limm *The Thirty Years War* (1984) 'Documents'. The Swedish king is writing to his brother-in-law to complain about the unenthusiastic reaction of the German princes to his invasion.

6 God be my witness, you yourselves are the destroyers, wasters and spoilers of your fatherland … my heart sickens when I look upon one of you.

Gustavus Adolphus, Sept. 1632; Jacob Wagner *Chronik über die schwedischen Okkupation in Augsburg* (1902) pp.20–21. The king blames his German officers who had been stealing cattle.

7 'If we were all as cold as you,' the king [Gustavus Adolphus] berated him, 'we should freeze.' 'If we were all as hot as Your Majesty,' replied Oxenstierna, 'we should burn.'

Baron F.C. Moser (ed.) *Patriotisches Archiv* (1792–4) Vol.5, p.8; Wedgwood (1938; 1957 edn) p.241.

8 What they could do with round here is a good war. What else can you expect with peace running wild all over the place? You know what the trouble with peace is? No organization. And when do you get organization? In a war.

Bertolt Brecht *Mother Courage and her Children* (1949; 1955 trans.) Sc.1. The speaker is the sergeant recruiting for the army of the Swedish commander, Count Oxenstierna, in Poland in 1624.

9 The Alsatian town of Hagenau three times occupied in eighteen months lamented: 'We have had blue-coats and red-coats and now come the yellow-coats. God have pity on us.'

Hanauer Geschichtverein (Hanau History Association) Vol.1 (1948) p.175; Wedgwood (1938; 1957 edn) p.292. Each occupying army appropriated all available food and ravaged everything.

10   God help the day!
'Tis the peasant's hide for their sport must pay.
Eight months in our beds and stalls have they
Been swarming here, until far around
Not a bird or a beast is longer found,
And the peasant to quiet his craving maw,
Has nothing now left but his bones to gnaw.
Ne'er were we crushed with a heavier hand,

When the Saxon was lauding it o'er the land:
And these are the emperor's troops, they say!

Friedrich von Schiller *Wallenstein's Camp* (1798; 1823 trans.)
Sc.1.

1   The emperor was
My austere master only, not my friend.
There was already war 'twixt him and me
When he delivered the commander's staff
Into my hands; for there's a natural
Unceasing war 'twixt cunning and suspicion;
Peace exists only betwixt confidence
And faith.

Friedrich von Schiller *The Death of Wallenstein* (1799; trans.
that year by Samuel Taylor Coleridge) Act 3, Sc.18. Wallenstein, the hero of Schiller's dramatic trilogy, is speaking, and it
is clear that (in Schiller's view at least) he is a victim not a
monster.

2 And now they began to unscrew the flints from
their pistols and to jam the peasants' thumbs into
them, and to torture the poor lads as if they were
witches. Indeed, one of the victims had already been
pushed into the bread oven and a fire lit under him,
though he had confessed nothing. They put a noose
around the head of another, twisting it tight with a
piece of wood until the blood spurted from his
mouth, ears and nose. In short, each soldier had his
personal way of torturing the peasants and each
torture got his personal treatment.

Johann J.C. von Grimmelshausen *Der abenteuerliche
Simplicissimus* (The Adventures of a Simpleton) (1669; 1962
trans.) Bk 1, Ch.4. This powerful picaresque novel reflected
all too accurately its author's experience and the savagery
of the war. But Wedgwood (p.228) points out the scene is
also a set piece, strikingly parallel to a picture (1633) by
Jacques Callot on the horrors of war.

3 I thought less about my food and survival than
about the enmity which existed between soldiers
and peasants ... I could only come to the conclusion
that there must be two species of human being in the
world, not both descended from Adam; one tame
and one wild, like the beasts of the field, since they
pursued each other so relentlessly.

Johann J.C. von Grimmelshausen (1669; 1962 trans.) Bk 1,
Ch.13.

4 If peace is made with the Protestants ... his
Holiness will withdraw his aid, the more so because,
since the eruption of mount Vesuvius, the collection
of tithes has become more difficult.

Francesco Barberini, papal secretary of state, to Rocci, nuncio
in Germany, 27 Dec. 1631; Parker (1984) p.130. Parker
reckons this brilliant excuse for not subsidizing the church
was not very strong, because, although the destruction was
heavy, few papal subjects were affected. Urban VIII (Maffeo
Barberini), pope in 1623–44, was able to spend 30 million
thalers (five times the annual papal revenue) on his three
nephews by the end of his pontificate.

5 I expect of him, under the article 'virtue', that
he shall be of good life and conversation, diligent
in ordering, laborious in performance, valorous
in danger, various in his capacities, and swift in
execution.

Gustavus Adolphus, requirement of his soldiers, c.1621;
Roberts (1958) Vol.2, p.238. Regular training, new tactical
units, uniforms, strict moral discipline and regular prayers and
sermons contributed to a formidable discipline – as long as
Gustavus Adolphus lived to command. Genius and character
combined to make him a great soldier, one of seven whom
Napoleon claimed to respect.

6 Between their most serene majesties the kings of
Sweden and France there shall be an alliance for the
defence of the friends of each and both of them, for
the safeguarding of the Baltic and Oceanic Seas, the
liberty of commerce; and the restitution of the
oppressed States of the Roman empire; and also to
ensure that the fortresses and defence-works which
have been constructed, in the ports and on the
shores ... be demolished and reduced to the state in
which they were immediately before the present
German war.

Treaty of Bärwalde, 13 Jan. 1631; Michael Roberts (ed.)
Sweden as a Great Power 1611–97 (1968) p.136.

7 He should have as security an imperial pledge on
an Austrian hereditary territory as recompense for
his regular expenses ...
    As recompense for his extraordinary expenses,
he should be allowed to exercise the highest
jurisdiction in the empire over the territories that
he occupies ...
    As in confiscation of lands so also in granting
pardons, he, the Duke of Friedland [Wallenstein],
shall be allowed to act as he pleases.

Contract between Wallenstein and the emperor, Ferdinand II,
Göllersdorf (Austria), 1632; H. Schulz (ed.) *Der dreissigjährige
Krieg* (The Thirty Years War) (1917) Vol.1, pp.124–6.

8 The day before yesterday a great battle occurred
between His Grace, the Duke of Mecklenburg
[Wallenstein] and the king from Sweden. The battle
ran from 10 o'clock in the morning until well into

the dark night. On both sides well up to 15,000 men remained [were left] lying on the field, the king is also dead ... the enemy took five or six of our standards, but we took about 30 of theirs.

Imperialists' press release on the Battle of Lützen, 18 Nov. 1632; G. Droysen (ed.) *Gedruckte Relationionen über die Schlacht bei Lützen* (Sad Stories of the Battle of Lützen) (1903) p.4.

1 A fourth blow is given when Wallenstein is already stretched out, and as his guts spill out Colonel Butler (who has already thrust a pike into him three times) says: 'Ugh, the rebellious scoundrel has been taking too much tobacco today: that's why he stinks so.'

Anon., Niedersächsisches Staatsarchiv (Lower Saxony State Archive), 1634; Benecke (1978) p.92. A dramatic version of Wallenstein's assassination by Irish and Scottish officers in his retinue.

2 The man of flesh and blood, with the sombre groundwork of his soul, his harshness and greed, his secretiveness and his copious candour, his dreams and his sufferings ... After all, not every leader of his day was execrated, exalted and interminably discussed in this way. That was his fate, not that of his rivals. He provoked it without always being true to his aura.

Golo Mann *Wallenstein: His Life Narrated* (1976) p.400. A modern historian's view.

3 The house of Austria wishes to subjugate all Germany, extirpating liberty and the Reformed religion. So in this extremity we must look to France.

William, Landgrave of Hesse-Kassel, Nov. 1634; Ruth Altmann *Landgraf Wilhelm von Hessen-Kassel* (1938) Vol.5, p.84. Hesse-Kassel was Sweden's oldest ally among the Protestant German states. Count Axel Oxenstierna, chancellor of Sweden, withdrew his country from the Protestant League in Dec. 1634, and William saw Catholic France as the only salvation for the Protestant states.

4 We must let this German business be left to the Germans, who will be the only people to get any good of it (if there is any), and therefore not spend any more men or money here, but rather try by all means to wriggle out of it.

Axel Oxenstierna to the Swedish council of state, 7 Jan. 1635; Parker (1984) p.156.

5 Although the peasant has been plagued with almost unbearable amounts of war tax, it has helped little since we are still in great danger because of the war situation. Our liberties are under very serious attack ...

The war from outside is dangerous to us, yet the war within even more so.

Heinrich Grote, a nobleman and politician of the Lippe estates, to Levin von Donop, 18 Nov. 1635; Staatsarchiv Detmold, Archive L.0, Titel 1, no.7. He is trying to persuade Donop to return to the country.

6 Saxony has made his peace but that will have no effect on us save to make us renew our efforts to keep all in train.

Cardinal Richelieu, memorandum, May 1635; D.L.M. Avenel (ed.) *Lettres, instructions diplomatiques et papiers d'état du Cardinal de Richelieu* (1853–73) Vol.5, pp.82–3. The Peace of Prague (1635), which abandoned the Edict of Restitution (see 453:8), appeared generous to the German Protestant party but did not end the war. Because France now entered the war openly and renewed its alliance with Sweden, the Electors of Saxony and Brandenburg found themselves committed to the emperor for a further period of war – and suffered accordingly at the hands of the Swedes.

7 Just in the last 5 years [since the great victory of Ferdinand at Nördlingen in 1634] out of the 1,046 communicants in our churches in 1630, only 338 remain. 518 have been killed by various misfortunes.

Superintendent Valentin Andrea of the Lutheran churches in Calw near Württemberg (Swabia) on the desolation of war, c.1645; P. Antony and H. Christmann *Andreä: ein Schwäbischer Pfarrer im dreissigjährigen Krieg* (Andrea: A Schwabian Pastor in the Thirty Years War) (1970) p.128. Andrea goes on to note losing among these 5 close and 33 other friends, 20 relatives and 41 fellow clerics: 'I weep for them because I remain here so impotent and alone. Out of my whole life I am left with scarcely 15 persons alive with whom I can claim some trace of friendship.'

8 On November 24th [1638] one of Bernard's soldiers, a prisoner, died in the castle; before the body could be taken away for burial his comrades had torn it to pieces and devoured the flesh. In the weeks that followed six other prisoners died and were eaten. On a single morning 10 bodies were found in the town's main square of citizens who had dropped dead from hunger, and by December it was being whispered that poor and orphaned children were disappearing.

Alemannia Vol.42 (1638) p.55; Wedgwood (1938; 1957 edn) p.371. The siege of Breisach. Bernard of Saxe-Weimar was one of the princely mercenaries whose ambitions and greed – in this case for Alsace and the French subsidies – helped to keep the war going.

9 Spain is like a canker, which devours the whole body to which it is attached.

Cardinal Richelieu, 1639; Wedgwood (1938; 1957 edn) p.377. The balance of Habsburg power was changing. From 1618 to

1634 Spain had provided much of the support for the emperor. After 1634 and the defeat of the Swedes at Nördlingen, in Bavaria, Spanish resources went mainly, and unsuccessfully, to the defence of their position in the Netherlands (see 382:7–383:2). In 1640 the suppression of a revolt in Catalonia and Portugal was given precedence over the imperial cause in Germany.

1 I did not expect to find the kingdom of Bohemia so lean, wasted and spoiled, for between Prague and Vienna everything has been razed to the ground and hardly a living soul can be seen on the land.
Swedish General Johan Baner to Chancellor Axel Oxenstierna, 1639; Wedgwood (1938; 1957 edn) p.391. Compare the description of the country as a bread basket (see 452:1).

2 One should not easily and without great advantage accept battle, even if the enemy presents himself. Unless one is compelled to do so by the lack of supplies and money for the continuance of the war; for not to be beaten is itself a great victory.
Count John of Nassau; Hajo Holborn *A History of Modern Germany: The Reformation* (1959) p.345. The campaigns of the later years of the war were determined as much by the need to find supplies to keep the armies (and their generals' authority) in being as by strategic considerations.

3 Although in the year 1632 the whole country, as the said little town of Ummerstadt, near Coburg was very populous, so that it alone contained ... up to 800 souls, yet from the ever-continuing war troubles and the constant quartering of troops, the people became in such-wise weakened, that from great and incessant fear, a pestilence sent upon us by the all-powerful and righteous God, carried off as many as 500 men in the years 1635 and 1636 ... Those whose lives were still prolonged by almighty God, have from hunger, the dearness of the times and the scarcity of precious bread, eaten and lived upon bran, oil-cakes and linseed husks, and many have also died of it; many also have been dispersed over all countries, most of whom have never again seen their dear fatherland. In the year 1640 ... the population became quite thin, and there were not more than 100 souls forthcoming.
Anon., chronicle, 17th century; G. Freytag *Pictures of German Life* Vol.2 (1862) pp.86 ff. The 19th-century editorial commentary mentions that in 1850 Ummerstadt had 893 inhabitants, suggesting that there had been a slow return to its earlier population.

4 It is agreed by the unanimous consent of His Imperial Majesty and all the states of the empire that whatever rights and benefits are conferred upon the

states and subjects attached to the Catholic and Augsburg faiths ... shall also apply to those who are called Reformed ... Beyond the religions mentioned above, none shall be received or tolerated in the Holy Empire.
Peace of Westphalia, section B, signed 24 Oct. 1648, after negotiations at Osnabrück (Westphalia) between Sweden, the emperor and the Protestant German princes.

5 The empire wins universal respect for its size and for the number of virtues of its peoples; its constitution, which takes from conquerors the means and will to conquer, is of benefit to all and makes it a perilous reef to the invader. Despite its imperfections, this imperial constitution will certainly, while it lasts, maintain the balance in Europe; no prince need fear lest another dethrone him. The Peace of Westphalia may well remain the foundation of our political system for ever.
Jean-Jacques Rousseau 'Extrait du projet de paix perpétuelle de Monsieur l'Abbé de St Pierre' (1761); *Oeuvres complètes* Vol.3. (1964 edn) p.572. A romantically optimistic view from the French philosopher.

6 The Treaty of Westphalia was like most peace treaties, a rearrangement of the European map ready for the next war.
C.V. Wedgwood (1938; 1957 edn) p.459. Note the year this judgement was first published.

7 Future patterns can be seen emerging from Westphalia; the potential of Brandenburg to set against the heavy German presence of Sweden; the weight of Holland in the world's markets; indications of the future collapse of Poland; the accelerating decline of Spain; the beginnings of re-orientation of Austrian policy as emperors faced the renewed Ottoman challenge and focused more narrowly on the hereditary lands; correspondingly the predominance of France.
G.R.R. Treasure *Mazarin* (1995) p.248.

8 It might have been more useful for achieving a general peace if the war could have been pursued a little longer in Germany, instead of our haste to find an accommodation as we have done. Yet this would have implied we were in a position to prolong negotiations when instead there was the threat that Sweden might have betrayed us and acted on her own urgent desire to conclude hostilities.
Cardinal Mazarin to Abel Servien, French envoy at the negotiations on the Peace of Westphalia, Oct. 1648; Benecke (1978)

p.18. Mazarin's hand had already been weakened by the Dutch withdrawal from the war in Jan. 1648. The advantage of a German peace now was that France could concentrate on its war with Spain.

1 I was born in war. I have no home, no country and no friends, war is all my wealth and now where can I go?

Camp-follower at Olmütz, Moravia, where the Swedish army had been quartered for eight years, 1649; *Chronik des Minoriten Guardians* (c.1649) p.600.

2 The Swedes alone were accused of destroying nearly 2,000 castles, 18,000 villages and over 1,500 towns. Bavaria claimed to have lost 80,000 families and 900 villages, Bohemia five-sixths of its villages and three-quarters of its population.

Beda Dudik *Die Schweden in Böhmen und Mauren* (The Swedes in Bohemia and Moravia) (1879) p.37; Wedgwood (1938; 1957 edn) p.447. Claims were often exaggerated as princes and towns vied for compensation. The reality was grim enough.

3 Population losses are estimated at one-third of the city population and two-fifths of the rural population ... The population of about 20 million having dropped to between 12 and 13 million.

Hajo Holborn *A History of Modern Germany: 1648–1840* (1964) pp.22–3.

JUDGEMENTS

4 The war solved no problem. Its effects, both immediate and indirect, were either negative or disastrous. Morally subversive, economically destructive, socially degrading, confused in its causes, devious in its course, futile in its result, it is the outstanding example in European history of meaningless conflict ... They wanted peace and they fought for thirty years to be sure of it. They did not learn then, and have not since, that war breeds only war.

C.V. Wedgwood (1938; 1957 edn) p.460.

5 This [Wedgwood's judgement] is both untrue and unfair. The war in fact settled the affairs of Germany in such a way that neither religion nor Habsburg imperialism ever produced another major conflict there.

Geoffrey Parker (1984) p.217.

6 All the carnage and destruction of the Thirty Years War had not changed the old dilemma of German history. Ever since the breakdown of the might of the medieval emperors particularist forces had been able to thwart the rebuilding of a central German authority.

Hajo Holborn (1964) p.3

7 On the face of it the Thirty Years War may indeed have taken religion out of politics, and it may indeed have established an international *ad hoc* European balance of power, yet it was not a total war of the sort we know from the twentieth century. It produced no immediate drastic social changes and no major, revolutionary, democratic or technological advances. What it did produce was bureaucratic and fiscal proliferation of state power, grinding down all the more harshly any independent estates' and peasant-artisan development in politics, law, local government and labour relations, in the interest of absolutism and its expert manipulators – officialdom.

Gerhard Benecke (1978) pp.59–60.

The Age of Louis XIV, 1643–1715

1 *Louis le Dieu donné* (Louis, the gift of God)

Title given to Louis XIV at his birth, 1638. His parents, Louis XIII and Anne of Austria, had been childless for 23 years.

2 *Le Roi Soleil* (The Sun King)

Title adopted by Louis XIV, 1651. Between 1651 and 1659 the king appeared in nine court masques as Apollo, the sun god. He used the sun motif as a badge throughout his reign.

TAKING THE REINS, 1655–61

3 Everyone knows how much trouble your meetings have caused my state … I have learned that you intend to continue discussing the edicts which were recently published. I forbid you to do this.

Louis XIV to *parlement*, 13 April 1655; Ragnhild Hatton *Louis XIV and his World* (1972) p.25. Louis, then aged 17, used this occasion to tell the Paris *parlement* that he would brook no interference in his method of government. The Paris *parlement*, which was not elected and in no way represented the people, often tried to extend its powers by criticizing the content of edicts placed before it. Louis was taking control. Cardinal Mazarin (see 414:7–417:2) had ruled on his behalf since he acceded to the throne at the age of five in 1648.

4 *L'état c'est moi.* (I am the state.)

Louis XIV, attrib., 13 April 1655; J.-A. Dulaure *Histoire de Paris* (1834). Even if he did not use these words, which were possibly invented by the 18th-century French philosopher Voltaire in *Le Siècle de Louis XIV* (1751), his meaning is clear. Bishop Jacques-Bénigne Bossuet, the most eloquent exponent of the theory of divine right (that royal power came directly from God) wrote of Louis, 'all the state is in him' (1709), while a Huguenot (French Protestant) pamphlet of 1689 said 'the king has taken the place of the state'.

5 Monsieur, I have called you, together with my secretaries and ministers of state, to tell you that up to this moment I have been pleased to entrust the government of my affairs to the late cardinal [Mazarin]. It is now time that I govern them myself. You will assist me with your counsels when I ask for them … And you, messieurs, my secretaries of state, I order you not to sign anything, not even a passport, without my command, to render account to me personally each day and to favour no one.

Louis XIV to the chancellor, Pierre Séguier, and the secretaries of state, 10 March 1661, the day after the death of Cardinal Mazarin; J.B. Wolf *Louis XIV* (1968) p.133. Louis became his own first minister.

6 Nothing is so dangerous as weakness … to command others one must rise above them.

When one has the state in view one is working for oneself. The welfare of the one enhances the glory of the other.

Louis XIV *Mémoires* (1806; 1970 trans.); Victor Mallia-Milanes *Louis XIV and France* (1986) p.12. Some writers have suggested that the second sentence could have been the origin of the phrase *l'état c'est moi*. From the time Louis took personal control of government he kept notes of his ideas and opinions, and royal secretaries transcribed the text during the late 1660s. Further notes were intended as a manual of statecraft for his eldest son.

DOMESTIC POLICIES

7 I realized that I should give serious attention to financial recovery … For ever since I took control of my affairs I had daily uncovered new evidence of … wastefulness.

Louis XIV (1806; 1970 trans.); David W. Smith *Louis XIV* (1972) pp.25–6. Soon after Louis assumed the reins of power he removed the arrogant Nicolas Fouquet from his office as controller general of finances and replaced him with Jean-Baptiste Colbert. Colbert reduced expenditure and augmented revenues in the early years until the high cost of war undermined his system. He followed mercantilist doctrines: that is, he held that there was a more or less fixed volume of commerce, money and economic activity while supply and demand were fairly inelastic and that the government should, therefore, control economic as well as political affairs.

8 I have given orders for purchasing in Brittany 1,000 tons of grain and for transporting them to Paris in order to remedy the famine.

Louis XIV to Maréchal de la Meilleraye, 18 Feb. 1662; Louis XIV (1806; 1970 trans.). Colbert, finance minister from 1661 until his death in 1683, did not help agriculture in the same way as he tried to control industry. In fact, he seemed almost unaware that agriculture was France's main industry. Agricultural prices were far too low and this led to under-production and frequent famines.

9 I believe that it is only the abundance of money in a state which makes a difference to its greatness and its power. It is certain that by means of manufactures, a million people who languish in idleness will gain their livelihood.

Jean-Baptiste Colbert *Memoir on Commerce, A Document Presented to the King*, 3 Aug. 1664; Smith (1972) p.32.

1 Trade involves a constant struggle in peace and war between the countries of Europe as to who carries off the greatest amount. The Dutch, the English and the French are the main combatants in this struggle.

Jean-Baptiste Colbert memoir to the king, 1669; Pierre Clément (ed.) *Lettres, instructions et mémoires de Colbert* Vol.2 (1863) p.266. Colbert explains his belief that control of trade is the main cause of international rivalry.

2 The royal inspectors are to find out if the industry of the given city is organized in guild form. If so, they are to see whether the masters are registered at the town hall. If not, this is to be done and no one not so registered is to work as a craftsman.

Jean-Baptiste Colbert, instruction concerning the implementation of general regulations for manufactures, 13 Aug. 1669; C.W. Cole *Colbert and a Century of French Mercantilism* (1939) Vol.2, p.419. Colbert's regulations were so detailed that they prevented freedom of action by entrepreneurs, which sometimes hindered commercial development.

3 All Spanish style cloths, white, grey or mixed, shall be made one and one-half ells wide including the selvage, and the aforesaid selvages are not to be more than two inches wide. The piece is to be 21 ells long.

Royal ordinance regulating the production of cloth, Aug. 1669; Cole (1939) Vol.2, p.383. Another example of Colbert's minute regulations, which were intended to standardize production and control quality in the textile industry. An ell was 44¼ inches.

4 Your Majesty knows that his finances were reduced to 23 million livres in 1661 ... [but] within two years increased to 58 and then 70 million livres. During those nine years of abundance, administration and expenditure were based on this ... This year I find that abundance has disappeared because of the increased expenditure and problems in getting money out of the provinces ...

Your Majesty thinks of war ten times more than he thinks of his finances ... [but if war occurs] it will oblige us to begin using the revenues of coming years.

Jean-Baptiste Colbert, memorandum to the king, 1670; Clément Vol.7 (1870) pp.233 ff. Between 1661 and 1670, despite being involved in several wars, France enjoyed a period of prosperity, but Colbert, like any prudent finance minister, realized the extent to which further wars would deplete the treasury. The king was not pleased with this advice.

5 I was master enough of myself yesterday to conceal from you the sorrow I felt at hearing a man whom I

have overwhelmed with benefits, as I have you, talk to me in the manner that you did. I have been very friendly toward you [and this] has appeared in what I have done, I still have such a feeling now, and I believe I am giving you real proof of it by telling you that for a single moment I restrained myself for your sake.

Louis XIV to Colbert, 23 April 1671; Cole (1939) Vol.1 pp.289–90. Colbert did not always have his own way in policy. There was a constant struggle between him and the Marquis de Louvois, the war minister. Wars required heavy expenditure and necessitated additional methods of raising money, which often led to discontent and occasionally open rebellion.

6 Because commerce is the source of public wealth and the fortunes of individuals, we have for several years taken great care to make it flourish in our kingdom. This was why we created several trading companies, by means of which our subjects can now draw from distant lands those goods which previously they could acquire only through the intervention of other nations.

Commercial ordinance, March 1673; F.A. Isambert *Recueil des lois* (Collection of Laws) (1822–33) Vol.19. The French East and West India trading companies had been set up in 1664 (see 393:5 and 403:2).

THE PEOPLE'S SUFFERINGS AND RESISTANCE

7 There are four branches of revenue in France, customs duties, a tax on wine sold in taverns, tobacco, tin and other goods, a tax on salt, and a land tax ...

In Tours, May 1677, they gave the king 45,000 livres to be excused providing winter quarters (for troops), one tenth of the rent of their houses in addition to the usual taxes.

John Locke *Travels in France, 1675–9* (1953 edn) p.146. The British philosopher and author of *Essay Concerning Human Understanding* (1690) (see 365:3) was also an economist. He lived in various parts of France in 1675–9 and observed both rich and poor. In some areas people preferred to pay a large sum of money rather than have troops quartered on them in winter, when fighting was not taking place.

8 It is forbidden to give shelter to the salt tax collector ... The tax on a hogshead of wine shall be no more than 100 sous ... and stamped paper shall be burned.

Anon. *The Peasant Code* (July 1675). The pamphlet was published by rebels in Brittany who objected to new taxes on wine and legal documents and signed themselves 'The Skull Breaker and the People'.

1 The day before yesterday, a good for nothing, who had started the violence and looting over the stamped duty, was broken on the wheel. He was drawn and quartered and the body divided among the four quarters of the town [Rennes, Normandy].
Mme de Sévigné to her daughter, Mme de Grignan, 30 Oct. 1675; *Lettres de Mme de Sévigné* (1725). Mme de Sévigné was a member of the court circle, but reduced economic circumstances forced her daughter to live in the south of France.

2 I cannot find words, Monsieur, to describe the destruction caused by the troops on the march. The queen's battalion, leaving Rennes to go to Saint-Brieuc, has pillaged every house within four leagues [about 12 miles] of its path between the two towns.
Duc de Chaulnes to the Marquis de Louvois, minister for war, 9 Feb. 1676. To deal with the tax rebellion in the previous year the governor of Brittany had been forced to use troops, a fairly common occurrence in the days before a civilian police force. The duke was pointing out to Louvois that the conduct of troops on the march made the situation more difficult.

3 We order that there shall be freely received into this poorhouse of our good city of Paris the poor children and the aged of either sex ... all able-bodied persons of either sex, aged sixteen years or above, who have the necessary strength to gain their own livelihood, and who are found begging in the city and suburbs ... shall be employed on the harshest work which their bodies will stand.
Regulations for the administration of the Paris poorhouse, 23 March 1680. The regulations show that it was not only the impoverished outlying areas of France that were suffering hardship. People often came to the capital hoping to find work, thereby increasing the problems.

4 Near a tenth part of the people are actually reduced to beggary, but of the other nine parts not five of them are in a condition to give alms to that tenth by reason of the miserable condition they are reduced to and the small pittance that is left to them.
Sébastien Vauban *A Project for a Royal Tithe or General Tax* (1708). Vauban, the outstanding military engineer of the 17th century, built great fortifications at most of the strategic places on France's northern and eastern frontiers, many of which can still be seen. When he retired from active service, he was struck by the plight of the ordinary people and drew up a plan for more equitable taxation. His suggestions made him unpopular at court.

5 It is necessary only to consider a contrast on the one hand the 24 million paid for the chateau, the gardens and the waters of Versailles, or the Maintenon Aqueduct, where 30,000 men worked for 3 years to carry water 16 French leagues from a river to the reservoirs of the same Versailles, [and] on the other hand, the misery of the poor people and the folk of the countryside, exhausted by the land tax, by the billeting of soldiers and by the salt tax.
Ezechiel Spanheim *Relations de la cour de France* (1690; 1882 edn); H.G. Judge *Louis XIV* (1965) p.13. From 1680 to 1689 Spanheim was a diplomat from Brandenburg (an independent principality in north Germany) to the French court.

6 Must peace be awaited before it is possible to save the lives of at least 2 or 3,000 creatures who perish every year from poverty, especially in childhood.
Pierre le Pesant, Lord of Boisguillebert *A Detailed Account of France 1697* (1843 edn) pp.240–42. Boisguillebert, deputy governor of the area around Rouen (Brittany), saw that, despite all the achievements of the reign, the cost of war, building projects and general extravagance had produced a looming financial crisis. Like Vauban, he realized that the main problem was the inequitable system of taxation, which put the heaviest burdens on those least able to pay. The situation was modified only by the 1789 revolution.

JANSENISTS AND HUGUENOTS, 1673–1713

7 The right of the *régale* which we have in all churches of this kingdom is one of the oldest royal prerogatives ... nevertheless, the archbishops, bishops and clergy in several provinces declare themselves exempt from it ... We wish our right to be universally recognized.
Royal edict concerning the *régale*, 10 Feb. 1673; L.E. Dupin *Histoire de l'église française* (1714) Vol.3. The *régale* was the king's right to receive and administer all revenues of French dioceses when a vacancy occurred and until a new bishop was appointed. During the 17th century several new provinces were added to France, and some bishops claimed that the practice had not previously existed in their dioceses and that the king was claiming a new right. They appealed to the pope.

8 We have already told your majesty clearly and repeatedly that your declaration of 1673 extending the *régale* to dioceses never before subject to it is harmful to the liberties of the church.
Pope Innocent XI to Louis XIV, 29 Dec. 1679; Dupin (1714) Vol.3. The pope's unequivocal reply over the *régale* and later attempt to enforce his view led to a stand-off with the king. A majority of the clergy felt that the independence of the French church was threatened and petitioned the king to call a general assembly of the clergy.

1 Kings and princes are not subjected by the ordinance of God to any ecclesiastical authority in temporal affairs ...

Full authority in spiritual matters is, however, inherent in the Apostolic See [the papacy] ...

Hence the exercise of the Apostolic authority should be moderated by the canons established by the Holy Spirit ... In questions of faith, the leading role is to be that of the pope; and his decrees apply to all churches in general and to each of them in particular. But his judgement is not immutable, unless it receives the consent of the church.

Four Gallican Articles, 19 March 1682. Drawn up by Bishop Bossuet and agreed by the general assembly of French clergy, the articles made a clear division between the king's and the pope's powers in France. Bossuet, the chief exponent of the divine basis of royal authority, had been tutor to Louis' eldest son. Louis issued an edict requiring the articles to be taught throughout France. The pope was furious and refused to promote any members of the clergy who had taken part in the church assembly. In turn, Louis refused to support any clergy who had not taken part. By 1688 there were 35 sees in France without a bishop, and the pope excommunicated Louis, who retaliated by seizing the papal city of Avignon in southern France. Innocent XI died in Aug. 1689, and a compromise was reached.

2 I paid a visit to one of the ablest [Jesuits] in company with my trusty Jansenist ... being anxious to learn something of a dispute which they have with the Jansenists about what they call actual grace ... Actual grace according to their definition, is an inspiration of God, whereby He makes us to know His will and excites within us a desire to perform it.

Blaise Pascal *The Provincial Letters* no. 4, 25 Feb. 1656. Pascal, the eminent mathematician, scientist and moralist, had close links with the Jansenists and lived for some years at the convent at Port-Royal near Paris where his sister was a nun. Jansenists followed the teaching of Cornelius Jansen (1585–1638), set out in his book *Augustinus*, which was published after his death in 1640. Jansen, formerly bishop of Ypres (1635–8), argued that man was saved by God's grace alone, a view that contrasted with the Jesuit teaching that salvation depended on man's free will working in conjunction with the will of God. By the 17th century the Jesuits (see 362:2) were in powerful positions both as teachers and as confessors to most of the Catholic kings of Europe, including Louis XIV.

3 We hereby declare that the bull [*Vineam Domini*] of our Holy Father the pope be received and published throughout our kingdom so that it may be enforced and observed to the letter.

Royal edict confirming the papal bull (against Jansenism) 31 Aug. 1705; Dupin (1714) Vol.4. The Jansenists, however, continued to be a source of irritation to the king.

4 Eight days ago ... the chief of police for Paris presented himself at the gates of Port-Royal des Champs in the king's name ... when the king's wishes were made known to the Mother Prioress she assembled the chapter to tell them the news ... the only thing to do was to leave with nothing but a staff and a breviary [service book]. Troops have been left in the convent to guard it.

Marquise d'Huxelles to Marquis de la Garde, 5 Nov. 1709; Philippe de Courçillon, Marquis de Dangeau *Journal de la cour de Louis XIV* (1854–9 edn). The nuns at Port-Royal had refused to accept the bull in 1709, and the convent was closed and the congregation dispersed. A year later the building was demolished; even the cemetery was dug up and the nuns' bones scattered.

5 We cannot applaud enough the zeal of our most dear son in Jesus Christ, Louis, the Most Christian King of France ... for the defence and preservation of the purity of the Catholic faith and for the extirpation of heresy.

Pope Clement XI, *Unigenitus* (bull), 8 Sept. 1713. This bull finally marked the end of Jansenism as a force in France, but Louis had to seek papal help to achieve his purpose.

6 I believed that the best way to reduce gradually the number of Huguenots [French Protestants] in my kingdom was not to oppress them at all by any new rigour against them, but to implement what they had obtained during previous reigns.

Louis XIV, 1661 (1806; 1970 trans.). By the Edict of Nantes (1598) Louis XIV's grandfather, Henry IV, had granted freedom of worship to the Huguenots (in those areas where they were already established), the right to fortify certain towns, establish schools and have their own courts (see 380:3). There is a marked difference between the liberal sentiments expressed here and the ruthless implementation of the revocation.

7 All temples of the ... so-called reformed religion should be demolished forthwith.

We forbid our subjects of the so-called reformed religion to assemble any more for public worship.

We ... forbid all lords to carry out heretical services.

We order all ministers of the so-called reformed religion who do not wish to be converted ... to depart ... within 15 days ... on pain of the galleys [being chained to the oars of ships].

We prohibit private schools for the instruction of children of the so-called reformed religion.

Revocation of the Edict of Nantes, Oct. 1685.

8 *Ludovicus magnus Rex Christianissimus* (Louis the Great, the Most Christian King)

Extincta Haeresis Edictum Octobris MDCLXXXV
(Heresy extinguished, the Edict of Oct. 1685).
Legend on the medal struck to commemorate the revocation.

1 The French persecution of the Protestants raging
with utmost barbarity, exceeding what the very
heathens used. The most cruel and violent persecution that there ever was in France.
John Evelyn, 3 Nov. 1685; *The Diary of John Evelyn* (1959 edn)
pp.832–3. Most foreign observers were highly critical of the
methods used to implement the revocation, but most of them
were, like the English diarist Evelyn, Protestant (see 425:4).

2 Four [dragoons] were sent to our house where
they began in the shop. They threw all the books on
to the ground, brought their horses into the shop
and used the books as litter. Then they went through
the rooms and threw everything into the street ...
The commander of the dragoons shouted at my
mother; 'You bitch, you still have not changed your
religion, and neither has your whore of a daughter.
You bugger of a bitch you really are for it now!'
Thomas Bureau, a Huguenot bookseller at Niort, west-central
France, 1685; Richard Wilkinson *Louis XIV, France and Europe*
(1998) p.39. Huguenots were forced to convert to Catholicism
or face severe penalties. Their children were taken away
and placed with Catholic families.

3 The old trollop and Father la Chaise persuaded the
king that all the sins he had committed with the
Montespan would be forgiven if he persecuted and
expelled the Huguenots and by doing this he would
get to heaven. The poor king believed every word for
never in his life had he read one word of the Bible,
and this was the origin of the persecution which we
had seen ... the king thought that religion consisted
in the fulfilment of his confessors' instructions.
They made him believe that it was forbidden to
reason on religious questions and that in order to be
saved he had to keep reason captive.
Duchess of Orléans, letter, 21 Oct. 1719; *Complete Letters of
the Duchess of Orléans* (1843 edn) p.171. Elizabeth-Charlotte
(Liselotte), a German princess from the Rhineland, became
the second wife of Louis' younger brother in 1671. The 'old
trollop' was Mme de Maintenon, who was Louis' mistress
after Mme de Montespan and became his second wife.

KING AND COURT

4 Louis XIV was made for a brilliant court. In
the midst of other men, his figure, his courage, his
grace, his beauty, his grand mien, even the tone of

his voice and the majestic and natural charm of
his person distinguished him till his death as the
king bee.
Duc de Saint-Simon *Memoirs* (1690–1723; 1964 trans.) p.129.
From 1692 Saint-Simon was a member of Louis XIV's court,
which had moved to Versailles, 20 miles outside Paris, in 1682.
He was a shrewd, if somewhat waspish observer and keenly
aware of court intrigues.

5 Another of his contrivances was the ceremony of
the candlestick, which he allowed some courtier to
hold at his *coucher*. He always chose from the most
distinguished persons present and called his name
aloud as he went out from prayers.
Duc de Saint-Simon (1690–1723; 1964 trans.) p.224. The
nobles were made subservient by their need to be noticed. If
a nobleman did not come to court the king would say that he
did not know him, which resulted in social death. The *coucher*
was the ceremony of the king's retiring to bed.

6 Although he is not brilliant or very penetrating in
his judgement ... he has taste and discrimination
and sufficient shrewdness not to let himself be taken
by surprise.
Ezechiel Spanheim (1690; 1882 edn) pp.4, 9.

7 The royal apartments at Versailles are the last
word in inconvenience, with back views over the
privies and other dark and evil smelling places.
Duc de Saint-Simon (1690–1723; 1964 trans.) p.145.

8 I have just come back from Versailles, I saw these
beautiful apartments and I was charmed by it. If I
had read it in a novel, it would have been a castle in
the air. It was magical ... everything was big,
magnificent, the music and the dancing were
perfection. But what pleased above all was the time
spent with the king – it was enough to please the
whole kingdom which passionately wanted to see its
master.
Mme de Sévigné to her daughter, Mme de Grignan, 12 Feb.
1683; John Lough *Introduction to 17th-century France* (1960)
p.172.

9 Madame de Montespan was covered with
diamonds the other day, such a brilliant divinity that
one's eyes dazzled. The attachment [to the king]
seems stronger than it has ever been; they're at the
stage when people can't stop looking at each other.
There can never have been another example on this
earth of love starting again like theirs.
Mme de Sévigné to her daughter, Mme Grignan, 1677; Nancy
Mitford *The Sun King* (1966) p.77. Relations between the king

and his mistress had been strained, and the reconciliation did not last long.

1 The king did not care for me for quite a long time, he even had an aversion towards me. He feared me for my wit, imagining that I was a difficult person who only cared for sublime things.

Mme de Maintenon, 1685; Prince Michael of Greece *Louis XIV: The Other Side of the Sun* (1979; 1983 trans.) p.167. When Louis was having problems with Mme de Montespan, who was often difficult and bad tempered, he would confide in Mme de Maintenon. Her good advice led him to trust her more and more, and eventually he came to love her. She replaced Mme de Montespan as his mistress, and after the death of Queen Marie-Thérèse he married her in secret, probably in 1683.

2 You are going down Madame? I am going up.

Mme de Maintenon to Mme de Montespan, attrib., when they met on the staircase at Versailles; Mitford (1966) p.113. Each of Louis' long-term mistresses was introduced to him by her predecessor.

3 We must now pass on to another kind of love affair, which astounded foreign nations no less than earlier ones had shocked them. This time it was a love which the king carried with him to the grave. From these words everyone will recognize the famous Françoise d'Aubigné, Marquise de Maintenon.

She was an exceedingly able woman, who had acquired polish and a knowledge of the world from the high society where she was at first tolerated and later cherished.

Duc de Saint-Simon (1690–1723; 1964 trans.) p.241. The duke was a snob and keenly aware of rank, and he felt that Mme de Maintenon had caught Louis at a vulnerable time after the death of the queen. Her religious scruples would not allow her to remain a mistress for long. There has been much discussion among historians about her influence over the king, particularly in religious matters.

4 We live under a king who is the enemy of fraud: a king who can read the heart, and whom all the arts of impostors cannot deceive … On men of worth he bestows immortal glory; but he dispenses his favour without blindness and his love for the truly great does not prevent him from the horror which the vicious must inspire … Merit with him is never lost and he remembers good better than evil.

Molière (Jean Baptiste Poquelin) *Tartuffe* (1664) Act 5, Sc.7. In the penultimate scene of his play Molière, the great comic dramatist, brings the king's officer on stage to arrest the villainous Tartuffe.

5 I understand that in describing the favourable gifts which Persée has received from the gods and the

astonishing enterprises which he has achieved so gloriously, I am tracing a portrait of the heroic qualities and the wonderful deeds of your Majesty.

Jean-Baptiste Lully *Persée* (Perseus) (1682) Preface. Glorification of the sun king was a major function of the arts in the period, and from the mid-1680s there was a whole industry dedicated to enhancing the king's image. The opera *Persée* was written by Lully, the favourite court composer.

6 I would have praised you more if you had praised me less.

Louis XIV in conversation with Jean Racine; Wilkinson (1998) p.87. Racine, the great tragic dramatist of the age, considered language itself 'a precious instrument to praise the glory of our august protector'. Despite the flattery, or maybe because of it, Louis appointed Racine his official historian.

INTERNATIONAL RELATIONS

7 It is, as you know, not enough for companies to be fully manned, and if possible they must be made up of men fitted to serve by their age, dress and arms … a determined effort must be made to purge the infantry of the so-called malingerers … we must not tolerate … that the soldiers should be ill-shod or badly clothed, nor that their arms should be unserviceable because of either the calibre or the quality of their muskets.

Marquis de Louvois, minister for war, to Jean Martinet, inspector general of the infantry, 20 Dec. 1668; Camille Rousset *Histoire de Louvois et de son administration politique et militaire* (1862–3) Vol.3, pp.207–9. Martinet enforced discipline and standards within the army, including seemingly obvious things like getting the troops to march in step and wear uniform. He was killed by 'friendly fire' in 1672 at the siege of Duisburg. His name became an eponym for a strict disciplinarian.

8 It is neither the ambition of possessing new states nor the desire of winning glory which inspires the most Christian king with the design of maintaining the right of the queen his wife.

French manifesto to Spain at the start of the War of Devolution (1667–8). The Treaty of the Pyrenees (1659) ended the wars between France and Spain that had been going on since 1635. As part of the treaty Louis married the Spanish infanta, Maria Teresa, who became Queen Marie-Thérèse and who renounced her claim to the Spanish throne in return for a dowry (see 417:2). The dowry was never paid. In 1665 her father, Philip IV, died, and the name War of Devolution was coined to show that the land that Louis then claimed for France was the French queen's devolved inheritance.

9 The United Netherlands [Dutch] carried the commerce of the Indies where it almost destroyed the power of Portugal, it treated as an equal with England ... whose vessels it burned in the Thames ... Blinded by prosperity it failed to recognize the hand that so many times had strengthened and supported it ... The king tired of these insolences, resolved to punish them. He declared war on the Dutch [in 1672].

Jean Racine *The Official History of the Campaigns of Louis the Great* (1678); Wolf (1968) p.633. The dramatist Racine was employed by Louis to write the official history of his wars in 1667. The king wanted to put the best possible gloss on his actions.

1 Its [the Dutch War's] only cause was a desire for glory and vengeance [on the Dutch for perceived ingratitude] ... It is useless to say that these were necessary to your state, the property of another is never necessary to us ... The allies prefer waging a losing war to concluding peace with you.

François de Salignac de la Mothe Fénelon to Louis XIV, 1694; *Works of Fénelon* (1861) pp.425–8. Fénelon, archbishop of Cambrai in northern France, was tutor to Louis' grandson, the Duke of Burgundy, but he quarrelled with the king and was banished to his archdiocese from where he became a critic of royal policy. This was an open letter, but it is unlikely that the king ever saw it.

2 The king was at this time at the height of his greatness. Victorious since he had begun to reign ... for six years the terror of Europe and at last her arbitrator and peace maker, he now added Franche Comté, Dunkirk [on the northern frontier with the Spanish Netherlands] and half Flanders to his possessions.

Voltaire (François-Marie Arouet) (1751; 1926 trans.) p.126. Voltaire, the great 18th-century French writer, produced an influential history of Louis XIV's reign. He describes the Peace of Nijmegen, which ended the Dutch war in 1679. France's neighbours had to accept territorial losses or prepare for an inevitable resumption of hostilities by making alliances. William III of Orange, the Dutch protestant ruler, was already an implacable enemy. In 1677 he married the English princess, Mary, and became king of England when the Catholic king, James II, was removed by the Glorious Revolution of 1688 (see 488:1).

NINE YEARS WAR, 1688–97

3 His Majesty commanded me to inform you that he wishes you to burn twenty villages as close as possible to Charleroi ... take the necessary steps in carrying this out so that not a single house in these twenty villages remains standing.

Marquis de Louvois, 18 Feb. 1684; Rousset (1862–3) Vol.3, p.209. The Spanish could do nothing to prevent these attacks on their territory, and the emperor, Leopold I, was unable to take action against France. Instead, he made a truce with Louis, which allowed France to keep all the lands he had acquired since 1681. Encouraged by this appeasement, France invaded the Rhineland when its new ruler proved unsympathetic to France.

4 The state of the king of Spain's [Charles II's] health gives grounds for fearing that he does not have long to live ... It is essential to make plans in the event of his death because the opening of the succession question would inevitably cause another war.

First Partition Treaty, 11 Oct. 1698; Arsène Legrelle *L'Acceptation du testament de Charles II* (1892) Vol.2. Charles II of Spain was an invalid, who had not been expected to reach adulthood. He had no children. His three half-sisters were his heirs. One had married Louis XIV, one the emperor and one the ruler of Bavaria. Their descendants stood to inherit the Spanish empire, which included large areas of Europe (in addition to Spain itself) and possessions across the world.

5 It has been concluded and agreed that should the king of Spain die without children ... the Dauphin [eldest son of Louis XIV] will have for his share Naples and Sicily, parts of Tuscany and the lands of the Duke of Lorraine.

The Crown of Spain (and its colonies) shall be given to the Archduke Charles, second son of the emperor.

Second Partition Treaty, 13–25 March 1700. This treaty appeared to give the emperor's son the lion's share of Spanish possessions. The colonies, especially in South America, were an immensely rich source of trade, and silver from the mines in Peru supported the ailing Spanish economy. However, Charles II of Spain was furious when he realized that his empire was being carved up without his consent, and in the last months of his life he made his own will.

WAR OF THE SPANISH SUCCESSION, 1702–13

6 I declare my successor to be ... the Duke of Anjou, second son of the Dauphin.

Article 13 of the will of Charles II of Spain, 2 Oct. 1700. Louis XIV's second grandson became Philip V of Spain and ruled from 1700 to 1746. The choice of Louis' second grandson as king of Spain was *meant* to prevent a possible future union between France and Spain under the same ruler.

7 The Pyrenees are no more.

Castel de Rios, *Mercure Gallant*, Nov. 1700. The reaction of the Spanish ambassador to France on hearing of Charles II's will. Voltaire, however, claims the line for Louis himself (1751; 1926 trans. Ch.26). The implication was that Philip V would be influenced by his grandfather in the short term and that his descendants might even rule both countries.

1 Gentlemen, here is the King of Spain.

Louis XIV to the French court, Nov. 1700; Dangeau (1854–9). The king was introducing his grandson (later Philip V) to the court and acknowledging at the same time that he accepted Charles II's will, which contradicted the terms of the Second Partition Treaty of March 1700.

2 The war is a struggle for the commerce and riches of the Indies (the Spanish empire).

Louis XIV, 1701 (1806; 1970 trans.).

3 The emperor, the king [William III] of Great Britain and the United Provinces [Netherlands] have sought a strict conjunction and alliance between themselves necessary for repelling the greatness of the common danger.

Grand Alliance, 7 Sept. 1701. William himself died soon after making this alliance, and the war was fought during the reign of Queen Anne. The English armies were commanded by John Churchill, usually known by his later title, Duke of Marlborough, and most of the fighting took place in Flanders (Belgium), Germany and Spain.

4 At our age, maréchal, one is not lucky.

Louis XIV, aged 68, to François Villeroi, the French marshal defeated by Marlborough at the Battle of Ramillies (Belgium), 1706. This battle prevented the French from overrunning Belgium. Louis was usually sympathetic to defeated generals, and Villeroi was a life-long friend.

5 Had there been one more hour of daylight the battle would have ended the war.

John Churchill, Duke of Marlborough, to Queen Anne, of the Battle of Oudenarde (Belgium), 11 July 1708; David Green Queen Anne (1970) p.19.

6 Has God then forgotten what I have done for him?

Louis XIV, attrib., after the defeat at Malplaquet, Sept. 1709.

7 It is very easy to govern a kingdom from an office with a decree: but when one has to defy half of Europe after the loss of five great battles and the atrocious winter of 1709, it is not so simple.

Louis XIV, 1709; Wilkinson (1998) p.126. The five great battles were Blenheim, Ramillies, Oudenarde, Lille and Malplaquet.

8 You are quite wrong if you think that no complaints are heard here – nothing else is heard of night and day … The king is so firmly resolved to continue the war that yesterday he substituted the earthenware table service for the gold; he has sent the gold to the mint to be made into coins.

Duchess of Orléans, letter from Versailles, 8 June 1709; (1843 edn) Vol.1, p.367.

9 Our father who art at Versailles, thy name is no longer hallowed, thy realm is no longer great, thy will is no longer done on earth or at sea. Give us today our daily bread which we totally lack. Forgive our enemies who have defeated us, and our generals who have allowed them to do this. And deliver us from the Maintenon. Amen.

Anon. blasphemous parody of the Lord's Prayer; Wilkinson (1998) p.138. In the last years of the war tragedy struck the royal family. Louis was predeceased by his son (the Dauphin), his brother (the Duke of Orléans), two of his grandsons and even his elder great-grandson. With only one great-grandson left to succeed him (apart from his grandson, Philip V of Spain), Louis declared that should the legitimate succession fail his bastard sons would be eligible to inherit.

10 Since I must go on fighting I would rather it were against my enemies than my grandchildren.

Louis XIV, 12 June 1709; Mitford (1966) p.224. One of the allies' peace terms was that French troops should be used to expel Louis' grandson, Philip V, from the Spanish throne. Not surprisingly, the French refused. The emperor, Joseph I, died in 1711, and the Austrian candidate, whom the allies had been supporting, succeeded him as Charles VI. This left the French candidate, Philip V, unopposed as king of Spain. Under the Treaties of Utrecht (1713) and Rastadt (1714) Philip V kept Spain and its American colonies. France retained Strasbourg, Lille and Béthune but lost other frontier towns. The emperor gained the former Spanish Netherlands, Naples, Sardinia and Milan. England gained the *asiento* (the right to supply slaves to the Spanish empire), Gibraltar, Minorca and various other overseas possessions that laid the foundations of the British empire.

DEATH AND JUDGEMENTS

11 Ambition and glory are always pardonable in a prince … I have loved war too much.

Why do you weep? Did you think that I was immortal?

I depart, France remains.

My child [to his five-year-old great-grandson who was to succeed him], you are about to become a great king. Do not imitate my love of building nor my liking for war.

The little one will have a lot to go through. I was a king at five years of age and I well remember the troubled times that came my way.

Some of Louis XIV's famous 'last words'; Saint-Simon (1690–1723; 1964 trans.) pp.210–16. Louis was terminally ill from mid-Aug. 1715. His dying was as public as his life and his words and actions fully recorded.

1 Louis XIV, King of France ... died on September 1 of this year 1715, scarcely regretted by his whole kingdom on account of the exorbitant sums and heavy taxes he levied on all his subjects ... During his life, he was so absolute that he passed above all the laws to do his will. The priests and nobility were oppressed, the *parlements* had no more power. The clergy were shamefully servile in doing the king's will.

Parish priest of St Sulpice, near Blois (northern France); Robin Briggs *Early Modern France* (1977) pp.164–5. After a reign of 72 years few people mourned Louis' death. 'People drank, sang and laughed,' according to Voltaire, and called out insults as the hearse passed by.

2 It seems to me that one can hardly view all his works and efforts without some sense of gratitude, nor without being stirred by the love for the public weal which inspired them ... Louis XIV did more good for his country than 20 of his predecessors together.

Voltaire (1751; 1926 trans.) p.338.

3 France of the present day is still in many respects what the wars of Louis XIV have made it. The provinces which he conquered ... remain yet incorporated within France.

François Guizot *Louis XIV Builder of France* (1828–30) p.209. Guizot was both an historian and a politician.

4 He carried the principle of monarchy to its utmost limit and abused it – to the point of excess.

Albert Sorel (1842–1906) 'Louis XIV Arbitrary Despot' in William F. Church (ed.) *The Greatness of Louis XIV: Myth or Reality* (1959) p.63.

5 With Louis XIV royalty reached its zenith.

Jules Michelet (1798–1874) *Précis de l'histoire moderne* (A Concise Modern History) (1893 edn) p.187. Michelet, another outstanding 19th-century French historian, worked with Guizot at the Sorbonne in Paris. He refused to swear loyalty to Louis-Napoleon when he seized power by a coup d'état in 1851 and was forced out of his posts. He had to retire to Brittany, where he died.

Frederick the Great and Prussia, 1712–86

FATHER AND SON

1 The mind of Frederick William was so ill regulated, that all his inclinations became passions, and all his passions partook of the character of moral and intellectual disease. His parsimony degenerated into sordid avarice. His taste for military pomp and order became a mania, like that of a Dutch burgomaster for tulips.

Lord Macaulay 'Frederick the Great' (1842); *Critical and Historical Essays* (1903 edn) Vol.3, p.181. Macaulay's fierce judgement on Frederick the Great's father, Frederick William I.

2 [Of his inability to understand] what went on in that little head; I know that he does not think as I do and that there are people who teach him different views and encourage him to question everything; they are scoundrels.

Frederick William I of his son, Frederick, then aged 11, March 1724; Theodor Schieder *Frederick the Great* (1983; 2000 trans.) p.18.

3 I now, therefore trust confidently that my dear Papa will think over all this and be again gracious to me, while I assure him that still I shall not willingly transgress; and regardless of his disfavour am, with the most submissive and filial respect, my dear Papa's most faithful and obedient servant and son, Frederick.

Frederick to Frederick William, Sept. 1728; Edith Simon *The Making of Frederick the Great* (1963) pp.60–61.

4 His obstinate wicked heart, which does not love his father, for when one does do everything [that is, everything required of one], particularly loving one's father, then one does what [that father] wishes, not only when [the father] is there to see it, but also when he is not there. Further he knows full well that I cannot abide an effeminate fellow, who has no inclinations worthy to be called human, who disgraces himself, being able neither to sit his horse properly, nor hit his target, and who is withal offensive in his person, dresses his hair like a fool and will not get it cut.

Frederick William I, 11 Sept. 1728; Simon (1963) pp.60–61. Frederick William's reply to his son was couched in the third person singular, the form used towards strangers of inferior

class. The authoritarian king's difficulty in comprehending his son increased. It led to Frederick's attempting to escape and then his capture, court martial and house arrest. He was reconciled ultimately and agreed to the king's choice of a wife for him, Elisabeth Christina, daughter of Ferdinand Albert II, Duke of Brunswick.

5 You think his passion is music, I wish to God it were so! But he has a stronger inclination: he wants to write verse and become a poet. While he hasn't a clue whether his ancestors won Magdeburg in a game of cards or whatever, he can count out Aristotle's poetic rules on his fingers, and for the last two days has been torturing himself to render into French some German verses.

Christoph Werner Hille to Count Grumbkow, 18 Dec. 1730; J.G. Droysen et al. (eds) *Politische Correspondenz Friedrichs des Grossen* (1879–1939) Vol.1, pp.13–14 . Hille was tutor to Crown Prince Frederick.

6 A king of Prussia must take great care to maintain good relations with all his neighbours, and since his lands cross Europe diagonally, cutting it in two, it follows that he must develop understanding with all kings, since he can be attacked from different directions. In this situation he would be deficient in imagination simply to let matters rest there. If one does not advance one retreats.

Frederick to a 'Gentleman of his Household', Karl von Natzmer, Oct. 1732; David Fraser *Frederick the Great* (2000) p.43. The 19-year old crown prince had no illusions about the vulnerability of the kingdom he was to inherit in 1740.

7 I think there are on this earth no two men quite like them, father and son.

Field Marshal Count Friedrich Wilhelm von Grumbkow to his paymaster, Field Marshal Graf Ludwig Heinrich von Seckendorff, 4 Nov. 1742; Droysen (1879–1939) Vol.1, p.59. Both were diplomats who played crucial roles in the Prussian court and the relations between father and son.

8 Only his care, his untiring work, his scrupulously just policies, his great and admirable thriftiness and the strict discipline which he introduced into the army which he himself had created, made possible the achievements I have so far accomplished.

Frederick of his father; W. Hubatsch *Frederick the Great of Prussia: Absolutism and Administration* (1975 trans.) p.125.

THE WARRIOR KING

1 The army must be well rooted in the population – Frederick William instituted a cantonal system for recruitment, so that each of his regiments had its recruiting district (the districts varied widely in size) and its responsibilities for registration, maintaining lists of young men, organizing the periodic enrol-ments, recording the extensive rolls of exemption for skilled artisans and so forth. Only half of any registration were actually called up and after initial training the 'cantonist' served two months in the year with the colours, and went home for the balance, always liable to recall in an emergency. For much of a peacetime year, therefore, the cost of a man's subsistence did not fall to the state ... 'Who will seem the most brave,' Frederick wrote in 1768, 'Friends and relations who fight together don't lightly let each other down.'
David Fraser (2000) pp.9–10.

2 His approach to military matters was that of a drill sergeant rather than a commander-in-chief.
David Fraser (2000) p.11.

3 Mirabeau is deemed to have coined the *bon mot* that Prussia was not a state, but simply the territory on which the Prussian army subsisted.
Theodor Schieder (1983; 2000 trans.) p.43. Comte de Mirabeau, the French revolutionary politician (see 477:4), went on a secret mission to visit the court of Frederick II in Jan. 1786. The dying king was put off by Mirabeau's extra-ordinary clothes and bad manners. For his part Mirabeau responded with a spiteful book, *Histoire secrète de la Cour de Berlin*, relaying scandal about the royal family. His later, monu-mental, four-volume *Sur la monarchie Prussienne sous Frédéric le Grand* (1787), however, was partly compiled by a Prussian co-author, Jakob Mauvillon (1743–94), who also translated it into German.

4 My dear Voltaire,
   The most unexpected event in the world prevents me from chatting as I would like to. The emperor [Charles VI, Frederick's overlord] is dead. My pacifism is shaken ... My affair with Liège wound up [the treaty with the bishop of Liège, Belgium] but the new situation is of far greater consequence for Europe; the old political system is in the melting pot; Nebuchadnezzar's rock is about to crush the statue of the four metals and destroy everything. I am getting rid of my fever [he had been ill] because I need my machine to take advantage of these

circumstances ... Adieu, dear friend, never forget me and be sure of the tender esteem with which I am your faithful friend ... Frederic.
Frederick II to Voltaire (François–Marie Arouet), 26 Oct. 1740; Droysen (1879–1939) Vol.1, p.7. Frederick is envisaging the demise of the Habsburgs after 300 years of imperial power. Though the Holy Roman Emperor, Charles VI, had, under the Pragmatic Sanction, left his hereditary thrones to his daughter, Maria Theresa, under Salic law a woman was not entitled to the succession. The War of the Austrian Succession followed and lasted from 1740 to 1748, although Prussia ceased fighting in 1745.

5 'When the ministers discuss negotiations,' he reminded the Foreign Office shortly after his accession, 'they know their business, but when they talk about war it is like an Iroquois discoursing on astronomy.'
G.P. Gooch *Frederick the Great* (1947; 1990 edn) p.3.

6 Silesia is the portion of the Imperial heritage to which we have the strongest claim and which is most suitable for the house of Brandenburg. It is con-sonant with justice to maintain one's rights and to seize the opportunity of the emperor's [Charles VI's] death to take possession. The superiority of our troops, the promptitude with which we can set them in motion, in a word the clear advantage we have over our neighbours, gives us in unexpected emergency an infinite superiority over all other powers of Europe. If we wait till Saxony and Bavaria start hostilities we could not prevent the aggrandize-ment of the former which is wholly contrary to our interests. If we act at once, we keep her in subjection and by cutting off the supply of horses prevent her from moving ... England and France are foes. If France meddles in the affairs of the empire England could not allow it, so I can always make a good alliance with one or the other. England could not be jealous of my getting Silesia, which would do her no harm, and she needs allies. Holland will not care, all the more since the loans of the Amsterdam business world secured on Silesia will be guaranteed.
Frederick II, memorandum, 1740; Gooch (1947; 1990 edn) p.4. The young king gives his immensely shrewd appraisal of the military and diplomatic situation on the eve of the Prussian annexation of Silesia. He described it as 'a rich, fertile country, well populated and buzzing with trade'. Giles MacDonagh adds that it 'paid half the tax bill for Austria and Bohemia, or a quarter of the total for all the Habsburg lands' (*Frederick the Great* (1999) p.153).

1 Unless heaven frowns on us we shall have the finest game in the world. I intend to strike my blow on December 8 and to launch the boldest and biggest enterprise that any prince of my house has ever undertaken. Adieu, my heart promises me good luck and my troops victory.

Frederick II to his foreign minister Heinrich von Podewils, Dec. 1740.

2 I have crossed the Rubicon with flapping flags and beating drums; my troops are full of goodwill, and the officers ambition; and our generals are thirsty for glory, and will go according to plan ... I shall not return to Berlin until I have made myself worthy of my blood.

Frederick II to Podewils, 16 Dec. 1740; Samuel Formey *Choix des mémoires et abrégé de l'histoire de l'académie de Berlin* (1767) Vol.I, pp.10–11. The secretary of the academy quotes the letter that reflects Frederick's grasping the opportunity offered by the death of the Holy Roman Emperor to launch his invasion of the long-disputed region of Silesia. By New Year's Eve he was camped outside its capital, Breslau.

3 The gates will be opened and we will encounter too little resistance to make any claims to true glory ... if the mountains of Moravia don't stop us, we will soon be before Vienna.

Frederick II to his sister, Wilhelmina, 23 Dec. 1740; *Letters of Baron Bielfeld* (1768–70 trans.) Vol.I, pp.161–6. Bielfeld had first met Frederick in Aug. 1738, when Prince Frederick was received into the Freemasons.

4 There are no laurels for the lazy ... If by bad luck I am ever captured I command you – and you will answer for it with your head – that in my absence you will disregard my orders, that you will advise my brother, and that the state will stoop to no unworthy act to achieve my liberation. On the contrary, in such an event I order that even greater energy shall be displayed. I am king only when I am free. If I am killed I wish my body to be burned in the Roman way, the ashes to be placed in an urn at Rheinsberg [the palace where Frederick and his wife, Elisabeth Christina, established their court].

Frederick II to Podewils, 7 March 1741. He had been king for less than a year, but the letter shows his powerful sense of destiny and history.

5 The king of Prussia returned to Berlin to enjoy the fruits of his victory. He was received under triumphal arches. All the people tossed him laurel wreaths crying: 'Es lebe Friedrich der Grosse.' Others shouted, 'Vivat Friedericus Magnus' or 'Vivat, vivat Friedricus rex, victor, augustus, magnus, felix, pater patriae!' Whatever the language, the feeling was much the same. The people were overjoyed to see their victorious king: Frederick the Great.

Voltaire *Histoire de la guerre de 1741* (1749; 1971 edn) p.174; MacDonogh (1999) p.177.

6 In this way all the affairs of state could be expedited in an hour ... It was rare that ministers or secretaries of state met him. There were some who never spoke to him. His father, the king, had put finances in such good order, everything was executed with military precision, [and] obedience was so blind, that a land four hundred leagues long [about 1,200 miles] was administered like an abbey.

Voltaire *Mémoires ... suivis de lettres à Fréderic II* (circulated 1774, after Voltaire's death; 1988 edn) p.44. Voltaire is impressed by Frederick's habit of making decisions by scribbling a few words in a document's margin, but he is exaggerating for effect here. There were important administrative differences – provincial diets and the like – among different parts of the Prussian kingdom. MacDonogh (1999; p.180) suggests that Voltaire's opinion is to overestimate Frederick's omniscience, but adds: 'Frederick's Berlin-based General Directory numbered 73 persons in 1747–8, including six ministers. On top of these there were five private secretaries and fifteen more lowly clerks. Three years later the number of civil servants in all was still around 3,000. That was very small.'

7 The king of Prussia is an extremely contradictory character. He loves greatness, glory and almost everything that improves his fame abroad. Despite this he is the shyest and most indecisive person, without a spark of courage or nerve. He always sees events in the blackest light and suffers from the greatest fear ... The king is distrustful by nature and generally thinks that mankind is beyond redemption.

Richard Talbot, Lord Tyrconnell, report to the French foreign minister, 1742; Hans Jessen *Friedrich der Grosse und Maria Theresa in Augenzeugenberichte* (Eyewitness Accounts of Frederick the Great and Maria Theresa) (1965) pp.254–5. The diplomat gives a rather different picture of the king as soldier and decision-maker.

8 For every state, from the smallest to the greatest, the principle of enlargement is the fundamental law of life.

Frederick II *History of My Own Time* (1743); Simon (1963) pp.60–61, epigraph.

9 I have the honour and sup with him almost every day. He has more wit than I have wit to tell you;

speaks solidly and knowingly of all kinds of subjects; and I am much mistaken, with the experience of four campaigns, if he is not the best officer in his army. He has several persons with whom he has almost the familiarity of a friend, but no favourite; and he has a natural politeness for everyone who is about him.

James Keith to his brother, George; Edith Cuthell *The Scottish Friend of Frederick the Great: The Last Earl Marischal* (1915) Vol.1, p.231. This Scottish Jacobite lord, who had taken up arms against George I, entered Frederick's service in 1747 (see 472:3). 'Created next day a field marshal, with a quarter's pay of two thousand thalers and journey money in advance and invited to Potsdam' (Cuthell (1915) p.230). He thereupon wrote to his brother with flattering enthusiasm for his new master to encourage George to join him in Prussia. James Keith had previously served as a general to the Russian tsar.

1 Politics consists more in profiting from favourable circumstances than preparing them in advance.

Frederick II *Testament politique* (1752); Fraser (2000) p.276.

2 In Prussia one need not fear political factionalism and rebellion; it is necessary only that the ruler govern with moderation, and beware of a few debt-ridden or disgruntled nobles, or some titled prebendaries or monks in Silesia. But even these are not outright enemies … strictness is needed only on a few occasions.

Frederick II (1752); Gerhard Ritter *Frederick the Great: An Historical Profile* (1968) p.162. This contrasts with Frederick William, his father, who in his political testament of 1722 emphasized the need to 'destroy the authority of the Junkers [young noblemen] and establish the king's sovereignty like a rock of bronze'.

3 This acquisition will make the Poles scream a lot, who ship their corn through Danzig, and who rightly fear they will become dependent on Prussia through the taxes it would impose on all those goods which the Poles sell in other countries and for which they use the Vistula or its estuary.

Frederick II (1752) p.335. He anticipated in his *Testament politique* the economic implications of his gradually conquering parts of Poland. Here he is explaining to his successor his intention of linking up East Prussia and Pomerania with a land bridge, which would incorporate Danzig.

4 I am innocent of this war [against an Austro-Russian alliance] … I have done what I could to avoid it. However great may be the love of peace, one may never sacrifice honour and security … now we must think only of the means of carrying out this war which removes the pleasure our enemies derive from disrupting the peace.

A self-justifying Frederick II to his brother, William, 26 Aug. 1755; Frederick II *Oeuvres* (1846–57 edn) Vol.26, p.116.

5 At the same time he was resolved to win as much territory as he could in that first campaign in order better to protect the states of the [Prussian] king and push the war as far away as possible, and finally, to establish the conflict in Bohemia if that was at all possible.

Frederick II *Histoire de la guerre de sept ans* (1764); *Oeuvres* (1846–57 edn) Vol.4, pp.39 ff. Writing in the third person, as Julius Caesar had done before him, distances the king from the aggressive annexation, as he puts his gloss on the beginning of the Seven Years War (1756–63).

6 I read the writings of the king of Prussia with the same avidity as those of Voltaire. You will think that I am making up to you, if I tell you today that I am a profound admirer of His Prussian Majesty.

Catherine II of Russia to Charles Hanbury-Williams, the British ambassador to Berlin, 20 Nov. 1756; Earl of Ilchester and Mrs Langford-Brooke *The Life of Sir Charles Hanbury-Williams: Poet, Wit and Diplomatist* (1928) pp.235. Catherine, the German-born wife of the Russian tsar Peter III, was later Catherine the Great (see 446:6–450:2). Frederick advised: 'All future rulers of Prussia must cultivate the friendship of these barbarians' (Gooch (1947; 1990 edn) p.330).

7 Rascals, do you want to live for ever?

Frederick II, attrib., to the hesitant guards at the Battle of Kolin on 18 June 1757; MacDonogh (1999) p.255. One fleeing grenadier reputedly replied: 'Fritz, for eight pence, we've had enough for today!'

8   And our great king Frederick comes,
     and slaps his woollen breeches.
     Off sprints the Kaiser's army then,
     E'en faster than the Frenchies.

Anon. popular rhyme after the victory of Rossbach, 5 Nov. 1757; MacDonogh (1999) p.264. The battle has often been called the Agincourt of the German nation. After a march of 170 miles in two weeks, the Prussians, with 21,000 men, beat a French army of around twice that number.

9 I must take this step or all will be lost, we must beat the enemy or bury ourselves before his guns … think of yourselves as Prussians for all that, you will certainly not show indignity in this advantage; if there is any one of you who is frightened to share these dangers with me, he can take his leave today without suffering the slightest reproach.

(The officers fell into rapt silence which was

broken by Major von Billerbeck shouting, 'Imagine any cur wanting to do that!' The king continued) I already knew that none of you would desert me … now farewell, gentlemen, in a short while we shall have beaten the enemy or we shall never meet again.

Frederick II, Parchwitz Declaration, 3 Dec. 1747, as described by Prince Ferdinand; *Oeuvres* (1846–57 edn) Vol.27, Pt 2, p.262. It was rare that Frederick expressed himself in German rather than French. Two days later he won what he considered 'the greatest victory of the generation, and perhaps of the century' at the Battle of Leuthen, near Breslau, to regain Silesia, which the Austrians had partially overrun.

1 Then those rulers of the empire who were already wavering and indecisive would have begged him [Frederick] to grant them neutrality. French operations in Germany would have been disrupted and perhaps even halted. Sweden would have become more pacific and cautious, and even the court at St Petersburg would have considered its steps more carefully. The King could then easily have strengthened his forces in East Prussia and perhaps sent reinforcements to the Duke of Cumberland as well.

Frederick II *Histoire de la guerre de sept ans* (1764). The king is the historian looking back on 1757.

2 If fortune continues to treat me so pitilessly no doubt I shall succumb; she alone can deliver me from my present position.

Frederick II to Marquis d'Argens, Jan. 1762; *Oeuvres* (1846–57 edn) Vol.19, p.283. Prussia's fortunes were at their lowest ebb. Prussia's resources were much more limited than those of its opponents, the king had lost many of his trained soldiers, and the provincial diets baulked at the weight of taxes he had to levy.

3 I beheld the king. It was a glorious sight. He was dressed in a suit of plain blue, with a star and a plain hat with a white feather. He had in his hand a cane. The sun shone bright. He stood before his palace, with an air of iron confidence that could not be opposed. As a lodestone moves needles, or a storm bows the lofty oaks, did Frederick the Great make the Prussian officers submissive bend as he walked majestic in the midst of them … I beheld the king who had astonished Europe by his warlike ideas. I beheld (pleasant conceit!) the great defender of the Protestant cause, who was prayed for in all the Scots kirks. I beheld the *philosophe* de Sanssouci.

James Boswell, July 1764; Frederick Pottle (ed.) *Boswell on the Grand Tour: Germany and Switzerland 1764* (1953) pp.17–18. The author of *The Life of Samuel Johnson* had an introduction

to his fellow Scot, George Keith, the Earl Marischal, who had served Frederick so well as a general (see 470:9).

4 The mere contributions levied by the invaders amounted, it was said, to more than a hundred million dollars; and the value of what they extorted was probably much less than the value of what they destroyed. The fields lay uncultivated. The very seed-corn had been devoured in the madness of hunger … Famine, and contagious maladies produced by famine, had swept away the herds and flocks; and there was reason to fear that a great pestilence among the human race was likely to follow in the train of that tremendous war. Near fifteen thousand houses had been burnt to the ground. The population of the kingdom had in seven years decreased to the frightful extent of ten per cent. A sixth of the males capable of bearing arms had actually perished on the field of battle.

Lord Macaulay (1903 edn) Vol.3, p.253. The English historian is describing Frederick's kingdom at the end of the Seven Years War (1756–63). He points out, however, that there was no debt outstanding – 'no arrear was left to embarrass the finances in time of peace' – which is not how Frederick himself saw it (see 473:1).

5 The memoirs … which I have just finished, convince me more and more that to write history is to compile the follies of man and the blows of fate. Everything runs on these two lines, and so the world has gone on for eternity.

Frederick II to his Scottish general, George Keith, Earl Marischal, on completing his *Histoire de la guerre de sept ans* (1764).

6 Politics of state:

The politics reduce themselves to three principles.

The first to govern and aggrandize oneself according to circumstances.

The second to ally oneself only if an advantage is got.

The third to make oneself feared and respected even in the most untoward circumstance …

See now my dear nephew, how I have carried out these three principles.

Frederick II Second *Testament politique* (1768), addressed to his nephew and successor, later Frederick William II; Sir J. William Whittall (ed. and trans.) *Frederick the Great on Kingship* (1901) pp.39, 59.

7 War is like the other arts: helpful when used well and pernicious when abused; the prince who goes to war because he is worried, frivolous, disorganized

or ambitious is as damnable as a judge who uses the sword of justice to stab an innocent.
Frederick II (1768) p.160; MacDonogh (1999) p.346.

1 But what afflicts me is the state of affairs in my kingdom … since '56 I have lost under arms more than 300,000 men. The population is by a good third less numerous than it was. The race of horses and other animals has diminished by more than half. The treasures of my father have been eaten up, and my coinage I debased by one tenth. All the provinces pay twice as much as in '56, owing to the interest on the sums they have been forced to borrow in order to pay the contributions, which it is impossible for me to repay to them. I no longer have any but internal commerce, because my currency loses too much in exchange with foreign countries, and the bankruptcy of M. de Donenville has lost me all my credit. Most of my warehouses are empty, my artillery is very bad, and I have but few munitions of war.
Frederick II (1768); Whittall (1901) p.59.

2 The acquisition of 76,000 square miles of territory, over a third of the Prussian state as it was in 1780. The population of this expanding state rose in the course of the century, in spite of slow natural growth, from 2.2 million to 5 million. The new territory was acquired by conquest in the case of Silesia, or by inheritance in the case of East Friesland, or by diplomatic negotiations, reinforced by Prussia's evident military strength, in the case of West Prussia – Prussia's gain from the unsavoury first Partition of Poland [1772].
Olwen H. Hufton *Europe: Privilege and Protest 1730–1789* (1980) p.91. The historian is analysing what has been described 'as the miracle of the house of Brandenburg, the expansion of Prussia'.

3 Has he [Frederick] a single friend? Is he not compelled to distrust the whole world? What a life when there is no humanity! No matter how great your talents, you cannot know everything. Beware of falling into spiteful ways. Your heart is not yet evil, but it will become so.
Maria Theresa to her son, Emperor Joseph II, c.1772; Edward Crankshaw *Maria Theresa* (1969) p.297. The queen mother is castigating the emperor by analogy to Frederick, whom he greatly admired. Frederick and Maria Theresa suffered, admired and detested each other in their lifelong rivalry.

4 That acquisition was one of the most important we could have made because it attached Pomerania to East Prussia, and because in making us masters of the Vistula, we gained the double advantage of being able to defend our kingdom and charge large tolls on the Vistula, because all Polish commerce uses that river.
Frederick II *Mémoires depuis le paix de Hubertsbourg jusqu'à la paix de Teschen*; *Oeuvres* (1846–57 edn) Vol.6, p.7. Frederick, on the strategic value of what two centuries later became known as the Polish corridor and once more writing history as well as making it, is shrewd and direct about his acquisition. Danzig and the Vistula were the keys. Frederick compared them to the last leaves of the artichoke, to be consumed after the rest.

THE PHILOSOPHER AND THE KING

5 There is a prince in this world who thinks like a man, a philosophic prince who will make men happy … be assured that one day, if the whirlwind of events and the evilness of man don't alter so divine a character, you will be adored by your people and cherished by the entire world. Philosophers worthy of the name will flock to your lands; and, as famous craftsmen arrive *en masse* in a country where they know their work to be appreciated, thinking men will arrive to surround your throne.
Voltaire to Frederick, 1736; *Oeuvres* (1846–57 edn) Vol.21, pp.9–10. The flattering beginning of a (sometimes) beautiful 42-year relationship between the future king and the great French philosopher. They admired each other from a distance, but were sourer in proximity.

6 Hate me if you must. I would not deny you the pleasure that this primitive feeling would give you. But be not indifferent to me, I beg you, as I could not tolerate it. Ridicule my scientific studies and my translations from the classics of antiquity, if it gives you pleasure to treat me with contempt, but do not ignore me … do not look upon me as a mere appendage … I am in my own right a whole person, responsible to myself alone for all that I am, all that I say, all that I do. It may be there are metaphysicians and philosophers whose learning is greater than mine, although I have not met them. Yet, they are but frail humans, too, and have their faults; so, when I add the sum total of my graces, I confess that I am inferior to no one.
Émilie du Châtelet to Frederick, 1730s; Samuel Edwards *The Divine Mistress* (1970) p.1. The misogynist Crown Prince Frederick, the future king, had snubbed this brilliant woman, although he also wrote fulsomely to her and of her to her lover, Voltaire. The latter described her as 'more to me than

a father, brother, or a son!' (Gooch (1947; 1990 edn) p.158). The Marquise du Châtelet was extremely jealous of Frederick's hold over Voltaire. She was not only an experimental scientist but had translated Newton's seminal *Principia* into French (see 365:5) and wrote a physics textbook herself, *Institutions de physique* (1740) – of which Frederick was highly critical.

1 There may be greater kings but there are few more amiable men. What a miracle that the son of a crowned ogre, brought up with the beasts of the field, should understand the graces and subtleties of Paris. He is made for society.

Voltaire, letter to Paris, 1740; Nancy Mitford *Frederick the Great* (1970) p.93. The philosopher called Frederick's court the modern Athens, but he is patronizing in his praise, for 'made for society' of course means 'made for French society'.

2 Men are not made for truth. I see them as a troop of stags in a great lord's park, they have no other function than to stock and restock the enclosure … Deceit, bad faith and falsehood are sadly the dominant characteristics of most of the men who govern nations and who should be examples to their people. The study of the human heart is a truly humiliating subject.

Frederick II to Voltaire, 1741; *Oeuvres* (1846–57 edn) Vol.22, p.80. He remains insistently caustic, despite the philosopher's reproving him for his cynicism.

3 Had Frederick been a religious man, his Protestant faith would have lent his self-abandon a certain impetus and made his actions more palatable to his subjects … But he was far removed from this and stood alone in his belief that he could expect no help from any quarter, not even Heaven. It was part of his stoical approach to life, summoning all his energies to confront imminent danger while always being prepared for the possibility of defeat. He feared nothing and hoped for nothing; he lived only for the need to fulfil his duty.

The great 19th-century German historian Leopold von Ranke describes Frederick's position in the spring of 1745; Schieder (1983; 2000 trans.) p.242.

4 It is always a mistake to look for the motives behind men's actions, beyond the human heart and human passions … A prince is the first servant and first magistrate of the state; it is he who decides to what use taxes should be put; he levies them in order to be able to defend the state by means of the troops he maintains, in order to uphold the dignity with which he is invested, to reward service and merit, to establish some sort of balance between rich and poor, to relieve the unfortunate in every walk of life, in order to breed magnificence in every limb of the body of the state in general. If the sovereign has an enlightened mind and an honest heart, he will direct all expenditure for the commonweal and to the greatest advantage of his subjects.

Frederick II *Mémoire pour servir à l'histoire de la maison de Brandebourg* (1746 but constantly revised); *Oeuvres* (1846–57 edn) Vol.1, p.123. This famous and idealistic declaration of the role of the enlightened monarch was written just before he returned to war.

5 It is a great pity that such a cowardly soul should be joined to such a great genius. He has all the lovableness and maliciousness of a monkey … I am not going to make a fuss because I need him for the study of French elocution. You may learn pretty things from a Scoundrel. I want to know his French; how important is the moral issue? The man has found the means to combine opposites. You admire his mind at the same time as despising his character.

Frederick II to Count Francesco Agarotti, 12 Sept. 1749; *Oeuvres* (1846–57 edn) Vol.28, pp.65–6. He is complaining to his trusted friend about Voltaire, whose much-needed visit is delayed by the pregnancy at the age of 43 of his mistress, Émilie du Châtelet. Frederick had been pouring out poetry with which he was dissatisfied, and he needed Voltaire's critical faculties. Émilie died in childbirth, just as this letter was being written.

6 Damocles' supper; after which I left with a promise to return and with the firm intention never to see him again for the rest of my life … My friend means 'my slave'; 'my dear friend' means 'you mean less than nothing to me'; you must understand by 'I will make you happy', 'I will put up with you until I no longer have a need of you'; 'come to dinner' means 'I feel like making fun of you'.

Voltaire, 1752; *Mémoires* (circulated from 1784, after Voltaire's death; 1988 edn) pp.60, 153. Voltaire is describing a dinner Fredrick gave for him, but recollected in anything but tranquillity and in Voltaire's dramatic voice.

7 With age I feel more and more incredulous when it comes to histories, theology and physicians. There are few known truths in the world, we look for them, and while we do so we satisfy ourselves with the fables that are created for us, and the eloquence of charlatans.

Frederick II *Oeuvres* (1846–57 edn) Vol.18, p.89.

8 The completest tyrant that God sent for to scourge an offending people. I had rather been a post-horse with Sir J. Hynde-Cotton on my back than his first minister; or his brother, or his wife … There is nothing here but an absolute prince and a people, all equally miserable, all equally trembling before him, and all equally detesting his iron government.

The thing His Prussian Majesty has in greatest abhorrence is matrimony. No man, however great a favourite, must think of it. If he does, he is certain never to be preferred.

The British ambassador, Sir Charles Hanbury-Williams, c.1748; Ilchester and Langford-Brooke (1928) pp.211, 215–17. Hynde-Cotton was a Jacobite MP who was 'evidently a very fat or cruel baronet', explains MacDonogh (1999; p.242). The king's coterie at the Palace of Sanssouci near Potsdam was all male, and the queen – who had bored him from the start of their marriage – lived separately.

1 The most determined flatterer will readily agree that war always drags plague and famine in its train if he has glimpsed the hospitals of the armies in Germany and has been in certain villages in which some great warlike exploit has been performed. It is certainly a very fine art that desolates the countryside, destroys dwellings, and brings death to 40,000 out of 100,000 men in an average year.

Voltaire *Philosophical Dictionary* (1764; 1972 trans.) 'War' p.231. The dictionary had been suggested by Frederick and started while Voltaire was at his court, but the falling-out between them is reflected in the entry for 'War'. Voltaire's mathematics were obviously confused in publication, as the attrition rate would be impossible. Theodore Besterman, the great Voltaire scholar and translator, suggests that the philosopher meant that between 40,000 and 100,000 men could die in an average year.

2 I have studied all systems of philosophy and I have adopted that which seemed to me the least unreasonable, and I have observed well, that to be happy you must have morality, enlightenment, occupation, and live moderately without making too much of a business of life … (there is) humanity in certain cases and barbarism in others, that is how the world lies, for better or for worse, you must accept it for what it is.

Heinrich de Catt, 1758; Reinhold Koser (ed.) *Unterhaltungen mit Friedrich den Grossen* (Conversations with Frederick the Great) (1884) p.44. In 1752 Catt was on his way back to his native Switzerland when he met Frederick on the boat from Utrecht (where he had been studying) to Amsterdam. Frederick was travelling incognito, and Catt did not recognize him. Six years later he got a letter inviting him to enter Frederick's service.

3 I am ashamed of humanity; I blush for the age. Let us admit the truth; philosophy and the arts are only diffused among a few; the great mass, the people and the vulgar nobles, remain as nature made them, that is, malevolent animals.

Frederick II to Voltaire, 11 April 1759; *Letters of Voltaire and Frederick the Great* (1927 trans.) p.249.

4 [Your reserves of wisdom] are distorted by the passions inseparable from a great imagination; a little by moodiness; and by thorny situations which inject a little bile into your soul; and finally by the malicious pleasure you have in wanting to humiliate other men, in wanting to say and write cutting things … It is a pleasure which is unworthy of you, all the more so because you are on a higher level than them, by virtue of your blood and your unique talents.

Voltaire to Frederick II; *Oeuvres* (1846–57 edn) Vol.23, p.77. Frederick replied: 'I know very well that I have great faults. I assure you that I don't treat myself with kid gloves. I forgive nothing when I speak to myself' (MacDonogh (1999) p.292).

5 Human intelligence is feeble; more than three-quarters of mankind is made for slavery or the most absurd fanaticism … In every man is a wild beast; most of them don't know how to hold it back and the majority give it full reign when they are not restrained by terror of the law.

Frederick II to Voltaire (pub. 1759–68). The letter was prompted by Voltaire's suggestion that the king should read his book on Peter the Great. Frederick fought a fierce battle with the Russians at Zorndorf in August 1758, and an even worse one at Kunersdorf in 1759.

6 Everyone must fulfil his destiny and submit to the fatality which holds events in check and forces man to suffer what he may not avoid. I don't know whether there is predestination or not. I can hardly believe that Providence takes an interest in our miseries, but I know for certain from experience, that circumstances force men into taking certain positions, that they don't influence the future at all [but] they lay schemes which are tossed about in the wind and often the very opposite happens to what they imagined and determined.

Frederick II to his French chamberlain Jean Baptiste, Marquis d'Argens, during the 1761 campaign; *Oeuvres* (1846–57 edn) Vol.18, pp.226–7. He is echoing his childhood and his father's belief in pre-determinism.

7 There is no more extravagant idea than wanting to destroy superstition. Prejudice is the treason of the people, and does this imbecile people deserve enlightenment? Don't we see that superstition is one of the ingredients that nature has put into man's nature? How should we fight nature, how should we go about destroying an instinct which is so universal? Everyone is entitled to his opinion if he respects those of others. This is the only way of living in peace during the little pilgrimage that we make on this earth, and peace, Madame, is possibly the only piece of happiness which has any effect on us.

Frederick II to Countess Sophie Caroline Camas, about Oct. 1759; *Oeuvres* (1846–57 edn) Vol.18, p.215. The recipient was the wife of one of his officers and one of his female friends. He felt great affection for her and called her 'chère Maman'.

1 In the 1760s the total number of book titles published annually in Germany – about 1,500 – was no greater than it had been in 1610; and it was only at the end of the seventeenth century that Latin was replaced by German as the country's main literary language … its growth was further retarded by the immense cultural prestige of France.

M.S. Anderson *Europe in the 18th Century* (1987 edn) p.285. Frederick's voluminous writing – around 30,000 letters as well as volumes of poetry and prose – was in French.

2 You would be enchanted by the clarity of his judgement, his good taste and actually by the way he talks about his enemies. He apologizes for their mistakes and seeks to find a way of attributing their black judgements to respectable motives. Last night we walked up and down his picture gallery. We spent nearly two hours there and it seemed to me that he spoke as well about painting as he does about war and politics.

Jean le Rond d'Alembert to his mistress, 1768; Droysen (1879–1939) Vol.3, pp.132–3. The French *encyclopédiste* (see 479:2), resident at the Palace of Sanssouci, is clearly deeply impressed by the king where his predecessor, Voltaire, was equivocal.

3 We know the crimes which religious fanaticism has engendered. Let us take care to keep philosophy free of fanaticism; it should be characterized by moderation. In society tolerance should allow everyone the liberty to believe in what he wants; but tolerance would not be extended to authorizing outrageous behaviour or licensing young scatter-brains to rudely insult the things that others revere. These are my views, which suit the maintenance of liberty and public security, which is the first object behind all legislation.

Frederick II; *Oeuvres* (1846–57 edn) Vol.23, pp.103–4. Frederick was frightened that the *philosophes* would turn against the tolerance that he held so dear. MacDonogh (1999; p.341) points out that Frederick's fears were, alas, justified. The French Revolution broke out only three years after his death. The philosopher and mathematician Condorcet (one of his correspondents) would be its victim in 1794 (see 514:9).

4 The concert began by a German flute concerto, in which His Majesty executed the solo parts with great precision; his *embouchure* was clear and even, finger brilliant and his taste pure and simple … his Majesty played three long and difficult concertos successively and all with equal perfection.

Charles Burney, Oct. 1772; Percy Scholes *The Great Dr Burney* (1958) Vol.1, p.233. Burney, the musicologist and father of Fanny (author of *Evelina*), had, like Boswell (see 472:3), an introduction to the Lord Marischal, who arranged for him to hear the king play.

5 We had to tell stories of Frederick II, and their interest in the great king was so great that we kept quiet about his death, so as not to incur the hatred of our hosts as the harbingers of bad tidings.

Johann Wolfgang von Goethe *Italian Journey* (1816–29; 1976 edn) p.366. The greatest figure in German literature recalls a dinner in Sicily that took place eight months after the king's death in 1768 and reflects on his compatriot's fame throughout Europe.

6 Gradually even the masses began to feel that he was fighting for Germany. Of all his victories Rossbach [1757, defeating the French] most powerfully influenced our national life. The monarchy had now completely outgrown the narrow-mindedness of territorial life and attracted all the healthy energies of the Empire. Prussia was now the one really living state among the German peoples.

Johann Wolfgang von Goethe; Gooch (1947; 1990 edn) p.356.

JUDGEMENTS

7 He was born with a first-class intelligence which pushes him towards great designs; he is full of fire; he has a keen and penetrating sense of what men are like, quick to pounce on and take advantage of their foibles; never asks advice and indeed could not do so safely since he is surrounded by people in the pay of Austria. He has no heart whatever.

Charles Fouquet, Comte de Belle-Isle, the French diplomat and commander, to Cardinal Fleury, 1740; Mitford (1970) p.103.

1 A man who gives battle as readily as he writes an opera; who takes advantage of all the hours other kings waste following a dog chasing after a stag; he has written more books than any of his contemporary princes has sired bastards; he has won more victories than he has written books.
Voltaire, 1772; *Oeuvres* (1846–57 edn) Vol.23, p.447.

2   In their turn every land has reigned over this
      world,
      By laws, through the arts, and above all by the
      sword.
      The Prussian century has finally arrived.
Voltaire, lines adapted from his play *Mahomet* (1741) and sent to Frederick at the end of his life; *Oeuvres* (1846–57 edn) Vol.23, p.326. MacDonogh (1999; p.386) comments that the best epitaphs on Frederick were written before his death.

3 He was, during half his reign, the god of war; we shall see him, during the other half, the god of peace …
   This prodigious man was much more his own work than that of nature.
Comte Jacques Antoine de Guibert *Éloge du roi de Prusse* (In Praise of the King of Prussia) (1787) pp.240, 291. The French author of a famous book on tactics visited the king in 1773. 'Frederick thought receiving a book on tactics from a philosopher was like getting a work on tolerance from the pope' (MacDonogh (1999) p.333).

4 Everyone is gloomy, no one sad. Not a face but indicates relief and hope; no regrets, not a sigh, no praise. So that is the end of all his victories and glory, a reign of half a century filled with great events. Everyone wished for the end and welcomed it when it came.
Comte de Mirabeau at Frederick's death, 1786; Gooch (1947; 1990 edn) p.108. He nonetheless described him as the greatest man of his century.

5 When Napoleon stood beside the coffin in the Garnison Kirche at Potsdam after the battle of Jena, he observed to his generals: 'If he were alive we would not be here.'
G.P. Gooch (1947; 1990 edn) p.110. Bonaparte in 1806 testifies to the enduring military reputation of Frederick, as he visits the king's tomb 20 years after his death, having just won his victory over the Prussian army (see 534:9).

6 Then I also was a Prussian in my views, or, to speak more correctly, a Fritzian; since what cared we for Prussia? It was the personal character of the great king that worked upon all hearts … On the

situation in 1757, in spite of all vicissitudes, the image of Frederick, his name and glory, soon hovered again above all. The enthusiasm of his worshippers grew always stronger and more animated; the hatred of his enemies more bitter.
Johann Wolfgang von Goethe *Dichtung und Wahrheit* (Poetry and Truth) Vol.I (1811; 1971 translated as *Autobiography*) pp.43, 71.

7 Attentive reading of the works of the king of Prussia is eminently suitable to the formation of great characters.
C. Paganel *Histoire de Frédéric le Grand* (1830) Vol.2, p.414.

8 The greatest king that has, in modern times, succeeded by right of birth to a throne … His own exertions were such as were hardly to be expected from a human body or a human mind … In spite of his many attractive qualities, under this fair exterior he was a tyrant, suspicious, disdainful and malevolent.
Lord Macaulay (1842; 1883 edn) pp.791, 805, 810.

9 In Frederick we behold a character of the greatest grandeur and force, though not purged of all alloy of baser matter, yet genuine and massive …
   In finance, and his whole internal administration, Frederick followed in the footsteps of his father.
Leopold von Ranke *Memoirs of the House of Brandenburg in the Seventeenth and Eighteenth Centuries* (1849) Vol.2, pp.416, 460.

10 This was a man of infinite mark to his contemporaries; who had witnessed surprising feats from him in the world; very questionable notions and ways, which he had contrived to maintain against the world and its criticisms as an original man has always to do; much more an original ruler of men. The world, in fact, had tried hard to put him down, as it does, unconsciously or consciously with all such.
Thomas Carlyle *The History of Frederick II of Prussia called Frederick the Great* (1858–65) Vol.I, Bk I, Ch.I.

11 I define him to myself as hitherto the last of the Kings; when the next will be, is a very long question!
Thomas Carlyle (1858–65) Vol.8. Bk 21, Ch.9, final paragraph. Carlyle's epitaph, so to speak, at the end of his monumental biography.

12 The central characteristic of this powerful nature was his pitiless and cruel German realism. Frederick presents himself as he is and sees things as they are …

Before this time to be a Prussian had been an arduous duty, but it now became an honour …

The solemn earnestness of his life utterly consecrated to duty is separated by the heaven's breadth from the loose and fragile morality of the Parisian Enlightenment … The French are his welcome guests for the pleasant hours of supper; but his respect is given to the Germans.

Heinrich von Treitschke *History of Germany in the Nineteenth Century* Vol.1 (1876; 1915 trans.) pp.57, 71, 95–6. 'The German Macaulay' succeeded von Ranke as Prussian historiographer in 1886. He believed in a strong, militaristic and imperial Prussia.

1 All the barbarous German squabbles started by Frederick had only one common significance for all Germans, namely, that they weakened Germany and secured her defeat in the struggle for the lost provinces [i.e., essentially Alsace] and for a 'place in the sun' at the very moment when these might have been secured.

W. Hegemann *Frederick the Great* (1925; 1929 trans.) p.317.

2 Nature had combined in him, in a unique mixture, a kingly will with the spirit of a reasoning philosopher and also a heart which was warm and easily moved.

W. Dilthey *Gesammelte Schriften* (Collected Writings) Vol.3 (1937) p.105. An encomium rather than an appraisal, shortly before Germany prepared to fight in World War II.

3 This personality of Frederick's was a symbol of strength for Germany's future, right up to the present day, and indeed into a far more distant one. Frederick shaped millions of German souls … He stood for the power of the State and for justice. He formed a special Prussian consciousness of State.

Constance Lily Morris *Maria Theresa, the Last Conservative* (1937) p.336.

The Enlightenment, 1697–1800

SELF-IMAGES OF AN AGE

1 Necessity has so violently agitated the Wits of men at this time, that it seems not at all improper, by way of distinction, to call it, *The Projecting Age*.

Daniel Defoe *An Essay upon Projects* (1697) Introduction. 'Projects' were schemes for improvement: technological, economic, even political. Defoe's *Essay* proposes modern improvements, including state pensions, better roads and a proper education for women. Although now best known as a novelist, the author of *Robinson Crusoe* (1719) spent much of his career writing widely on economics, politics and society. A self-consciously 'modern' man, he often expressed enthusiasm for social and intellectual, as well as technological, progress (see 390:5).

2 Our century is supremely the century of philosophy.

Jean le Rond d'Alembert *Éléments de philosophie* (1759); *Oeuvres complètes* (1821–2 edn) Vol.1, p.122. D'Alembert, a mathematician and philosopher, was the principal editor (with Diderot) of the collaborative *magnum opus* of French intellectuals in the 18th century, the *Encyclopédie*. It appeared in 35 volumes between 1751 and 1776 and included Montesquieu, Rousseau and Voltaire among its contributors. As this quotation suggests, d'Alembert was a prophet of intellectual progress; the *Encyclopédie* was to be the textbook of a new age.

3 How blind we are in the midst of so much enlightenment.

Jean-Jacques Rousseau *Letter to D'Alembert* (1758); John Hope Mason (ed.) *The Indispensable Rousseau* (1979) p.311. Rousseau wrote this work in response to d'Alembert's article on Geneva in Vol.7 (1757) of the *Encyclopédie*, itself the textbook of the French Enlightenment. D'Alembert had suggested that the Genevans lacked only a theatre, and Rousseau wrote this open 'letter' to argue the corrupting influences of public theatres. The work as a whole, like this aphorism, displays Rousseau's scepticism about the assumptions of many Enlightenment intellectuals.

4 *Enlightenment is man's emergence from his self-incurred immaturity. Immaturity is* the inability to use one's own understanding without the guidance of another. This immaturity is *self-incurred* if its cause is not lack of understanding, but lack of resolution and courage to use it without the guidance of another. The motto of enlightenment is therefore: *Sapere aude!* Have courage to use your *own* understanding!

Immanuel Kant 'An Answer to the Question: What is Enlightenment?' (1784); Hans Reiss (ed.) *Kant: Political Writings* (1970 trans.) p.54. Despite leading a sequestered academic life at the University of Königsberg, where he taught logic and metaphysics, Kant came to exert a huge influence. *Sapere aude* (dare to know), a tag from the Roman poet Horace, was often cited in the 18th century. Kant's brief essay declares the creed of a self-conscious intellectual movement.

5 There is no effectual way of improving the institutions of any people but by enlightening their understandings.

William Godwin *An Enquiry Concerning Political Justice* (1793; 1946 edn) Vol.2, p.184. Godwin made a connection between intellectual progress, on the one hand, and radical social and political change, on the other. He believed that he was taking to its logical conclusions the work of Enlightenment predecessors. Social improvement would come through the spreading of truth, revealed by reason. (Political movements and associations, on the contrary, dangerously appealed to men's passions.)

BEING REASONABLE

6 There is nothing that I know, hath done so much mischief to Christianity, as the disparagement of Reason, under pretence of respect, and favour to Religion; since hereby the very foundations of the Christian faith have been undermined, and the world prepared for atheism.

Joseph Glanvill *A Seasonable Recommendation and Defence of Reason* (1670) Ch.1. Glanvill was one of many who attempted to show that reason and religion were not in dispute with each other. A Fellow of the Royal Society, he was an advocate of the empirical pursuit of knowledge and an opponent of religious dogmatism. He was also much preoccupied with witchcraft, in whose existence he firmly believed and about which he wrote extensively.

7   Reason, an *ignis fatuus* in the mind,
        Which, leaving light of nature, sense, behind,
        Pathless and dangerous wandering ways it takes
        Through error's fenny bogs and thorny brakes;
        Whilst the misguided follower climbs with pain
        Mountains of whimseys, heaped in his own brain.

John Wilmot, 2nd Earl of Rochester 'A Satire against Reason and Mankind' (c.1675) lines 12–17. Rochester (1647–80) was a courtier and wit, whose notorious libertinism encompassed both his sexual conduct and his 'free thinking'. He was much influenced by the materialism of the Roman poet Lucretius and the 17th-century philosopher Thomas Hobbes. In his poetry, written for private circulation, scepticism sometimes amounts to nihilism.

I　Dim, as the borrowed beams of moon and stars
　　To lonely, weary, wand'ring travellers,
　　Is Reason to the soul: and as on high
　　Those rolling fires discover but the sky,
　　Not light us here; so Reason's glimmering ray,
　　Was lent, not to assure our doubtful way,
　　But guide us upward to a better day.

John Dryden *Religio Laici; or A Layman's Faith* (1682) opening lines. Dryden's poem was occasioned by the translation into English of Père Richard Simon's *Critical History of the Old Testament* (1678), a work that controversially treated the Bible as a historical document and that might have been seen as undermining Christian faith. Dryden here voices the argument that would continue to be important for Christians: that reason need not corrode religious belief.

2 Reason therefore here, as contra-distinguished to Faith, I take to be the discovery of the Certainty, or Probability, of such Propositions, or Truths, which the Mind arrives at, by Deduction made from such Ideas, which it has got by the use of its natural Faculties, viz by Sensation, or Reflection.

John Locke *Essay Concerning Human Understanding* (1690) Bk 4, Ch.18. Locke's *Essay* was a founding work of empiricism, in which all knowledge derives from experience. Humans have no innate ideas but must use reason to learn from the observation of external objects ('Sensation') or the operation of the mind ('Reflection'). Controversial when it was first published, it became in England a standard textbook early in the 18th century (see 365:3).

3　Know then thyself, presume not God to scan;
　　The proper study of Mankind is Man.
　　Placed on this isthmus of a middle state,
　　A being darkly wise, and rudely great:
　　With too much knowledge for the Sceptic side,
　　With too much weakness for the Stoic's pride,
　　He hangs between; in doubt to act, or rest;
　　In doubt to deem himself a God, or Beast;
　　In doubt his Mind or Body to prefer,
　　Born but to die, and reas'ning but to err.

Alexander Pope *An Essay on Man* Epistle 2 (1733) lines 1–10. Pope's poem is dedicated to the limitations of human knowledge and the weakness of human reason. Its confident couplets, however, made it seem to many to be an assertion of the powers of reason. Although Pope was a Roman Catholic, to his dismay, some took his poem to vindicate Deism, the belief that true religion required reason but not biblical revelation.

4 To consider the matter aright, reason is nothing but a wonderful and unintelligible instinct in our souls, which carries us along a certain train of ideas, and endows them with particular qualities, according to their particular situations and relations. This instinct, 'tis true, arises from past observation and experience; but can any one give the ultimate reason, why past experience and observation produces such an effect, any more than why nature alone should produce it?

David Hume *A Treatise of Human Nature* (1739) Bk 1, Pt 3, Sect.15. Hume became the representative of what is usually called the 'Scottish Enlightenment', of which other leading figures were his close friend Adam Smith, Francis Hutcheson and James Watt. This, Hume's earliest major work, sought to explain human understanding and conduct by 'experimental' reasoning (and without any reference to religion). Even our certainties about causes and effects have only the authority of experience and the solidity of mere habit.

5 Reason is, and ought only to be, the slave of the passions, and can never pretend to any other office than to serve and obey them.

David Hume (1739) Bk 2, Pt 3, Sect.3. With a great display of elegant reasoning, Hume demonstrated the small powers of reason. Men and women, he argued, were actuated by their passions. Reason might show only how they could be gratified.

6 It is an old and true Distinction, that Things may be above our Reason without being contrary to it. Of this Kind are the Power, the Nature, and the universal Presence of God, with innumerable other Points.

Jonathan Swift, sermon 'On the Trinity' (1744); Herbert Davis (ed.) *The Prose Writings: Irish Tracts 1720–1730 and Sermons* Vol.9 (1948) p.164. As a public spokesman for his Anglican faith (he was dean of St Patrick's Cathedral, Dublin), Swift is attempting to preserve a respect for 'mysteries' in the face of attacks by rationalists. The sermon was published posthumously and might have been composed at almost any time over the previous 30 years.

7 *Voilà mes philosophes.* (Here are my philosophers.)

Julien Offray de La Mettrie *Histoire naturelle de l'âme* (A Treatise on the Soul) (1745) Vol.1, p.54. The French materialist La Mettrie used to say this of the senses, asserting that physical experience was to be his only guide. He claimed to have reached this insight during a fever, when he realized that his intellect was entirely subject to his body. The work in which this assertion appears attempts to turn philosophy into medicine or physiology.

8 Barbarism lasts for centuries; it seems that it is our natural element; reason and good taste are only passing.

Jean le Rond d'Alembert *Preliminary Discourse* (1751; 1972 trans.) p.103. This sentence is taken from d'Alembert's provocative introduction to the *Encyclopédie*, of which he and Diderot were chief editors. It treated natural religion (as opposed to Christianity) with respect, talked of the empirical basis of knowledge and broached the relationship between intellectual and political progress.

1 Since everything that comes into human understanding enters through the senses, man's first reason is a sensitive reason. It is this that serves as a foundation for intellectual reason; our first teachers in natural philosophy are our feet, hands and eyes. To substitute books for them does not teach us reason, it teaches us to use the reason of others rather than our own.

Jean-Jacques Rousseau *Émile* (1762; 1992 trans.) Bk 2. *Émile*, a treatise on education written in the form of a fictional narrative, attempts to show how a child might be allowed to grow according to his natural impulses. Though he might not have developed 'intellectual reason', he already has 'sensitive reason'. He should be encouraged to follow this and not treated as a being to be curbed and civilized.

2 In their writings and conversation the philosophers of antiquity asserted the independent dignity of reason; but they resigned their actions to the commands of law and of custom.

Edward Gibbon *The Decline and Fall of the Roman Empire* (1776–88) Vol.1, Ch.2. A *magnum opus* of Enlightenment learning, Gibbon's *Decline and Fall* coolly analysed the powers of superstition and fanaticism in human history. After a youth of different religious enthusiasms, Gibbon became a sceptic and a lover of ancient learning.

3   I must Create a System, or be enslaved by
          another Man's;
       I will not Reason and Compare: my business is
          to Create.

William Blake *Jerusalem* (1804–20) f.10, lines 20–21. The poet, painter and engraver was little known in his own lifetime, his work collected by a handful of patrons. Long after his death, however, he began to be more widely admired. His antagonism to the Enlightenment gave force to some of his visionary work. He denounced empiricism, which, he believed, denied the creative powers of human beings. One of the grim deities of his poetry is even called Urizen ('your reason').

HOW TO LIVE, WHAT TO DO

4 If Philosophy be, as we take it, *the Study of Happiness*; must not Every-one, in some manner or other, either skilfully or unskilfully *philosophize*?

Anthony Ashley Cooper, 3rd Earl of Shaftesbury *The Moralists. A Rhapsody* (1709) Pt 3, Sect.52. Though groomed for public life – his grandfather had been a Whig grandee, his tutor was the philosopher John Locke – Shaftesbury lived in retirement on his Dorset estate because of ill health. *The Moralists*

is a Socratic dialogue, which celebrates the order and harmony of the universe and likens moral judgement to aesthetic appreciation.

5 The nearer we search into human Nature, the more we shall be convinced, that the Moral Virtues are the Political Offspring which Flattery begot upon Pride.

Bernard Mandeville *The Fable of the Bees* 'An Enquiry into the Origin of Moral Virtue' (1714; 1924 edn) Vol.1, p.51. Mandeville's satirical and deliberately shocking work proposed that society would be wrecked – and the economy ruined – if human beings did truly believe in what was commonly called 'virtue'. In fact, he suggested, 'virtue' was a useful fiction for rulers to foist upon the ruled.

6 What is toleration? It is the prerogative of humanity. We are all steeped in weakness and errors; let us forgive one another's follies, it is the first law of nature.

Voltaire *Philosophical Dictionary* (1764; 1972 trans.) 'Toleration' p.387. Voltaire is famed for a quotation about toleration that cannot be certainly attributed to him: 'I disapprove of what you say, but I will defend to the death your right to say it.' He did, however, advocate toleration, without supposing that it was a virtue easily accepted by governments.

7 Oh virtue! Sublime science of simple souls, are so many difficulties and preparations needed to know you? Are not your principles engraved in all hearts, and is it not enough in order to learn your Laws to return into oneself and listen to the voice of one's conscience in the silence of the passions? That is true philosophy.

Jean-Jacques Rousseau *Discourse on the Sciences and Arts* (1751) Pt 2; Roger D. Masters and Christopher Kelly (eds) *The Collected Writings* Vol.2 (1992) p.22. This passage, which is taken from Rousseau's earliest significant work, amounted to an attack on the idea of progress and the value of civilization. Knowledge and culture might not produce virtue. Rousseau argued that the sophistication of a commercial society and its inequalities made the achievement of virtue ever more difficult. This marks him out as an Enlightenment writer opposed to some of the main tenets of the Enlightenment.

8 It is not from the benevolence of the butcher, the brewer or the baker, that we expect our dinner, but from their regard to their own interest. We address ourselves, not to their humanity but to their self-love, and never talk to them of our own necessities but of their advantages.

Adam Smith *The Wealth of Nations* (1776) Bk 1, Ch.2 'Of the Principle Which Gives Occasion to the Division of Labour'. After his friend David Hume, Smith was the leading thinker of the Scottish Enlightenment (see 480:4). A moral philosopher, he here calmly separated the field of political economy from that of morals. He made intellectually unavoidable the proposition that had seemed diabolical when framed by Mandeville at the beginning of the 18th century: that economic progress and prosperity proceeded from the unleashing of man's self-interest (see 485:8).

1 There is, therefore only a single categorical imperative and it is this: *act only in accordance with that maxim through which you can at the same time will that it become a universal law.*

Immanuel Kant *Groundwork of the Metaphysics of Morals* (1785); *The Cambridge Edition of the Works of Immanuel Kant: Practical Philosophy* (1996) p.73. Kant set out to establish, from the most fundamental principles, a base on which dependable knowledge could be built (thus the apparently awkward title of the work from which this quotation is taken). Here he proposes a universal principle of moral judgement.

2 Nature has placed mankind under the governance of two sovereign masters, *pain* and *pleasure*. It is for them alone to point out what we ought to do, as well as to determine what we shall do.

Jeremy Bentham *An Introduction to the Principles of Morals and Legislation* (1789) Ch.1, Sect.1. This is from the opening chapter, Of the Principle of Utility, of Bentham's earliest outline of Utilitarianism (see 602:7). Bentham argued that people should maximize utility and that this meant maximizing pleasure and minimizing pain. Bentham spent a lifetime drawing up schemes according to these principles for states, laws, prisons, currency systems and more. Almost all were unpublished at his death.

NATURE AND THE UNIVERSE

3 All the diversity of created things, each in its place and time, could only have arisen from the ideas and the will of a necessarily existing being.

Isaac Newton *Principia Mathematica*, General Scholium (1713) p.942. Newton's *Principia* appeared in 1687 (see 365:5); the brief General Scholium was introduced to the second edition of 1713. In it Newton asserts that his mechanical philosophy is compatible with belief in God, although he gives an austere version of a very distant God.

4 All nature is but art, unknown to thee;
    All chance, direction, which thou canst no see;
    All discord, harmony, not understood;
    All partial evil, universal good:
    And, spite of pride, in erring reason's spit,
    One truth is clear, 'Whatever is, is RIGHT'.

Alexander Pope *An Essay on Man* Epistle 1 (1733) lines 289–94.

5 But the life of a man is of no greater importance to the universe than that of an oyster.

David Hume 'Of Suicide' (1755); S. Copley and A. Edgar (eds) *Selected Essays* (1993) p.319. Hume became notorious for his sceptical attitude to Christianity (his enemies called him an 'atheist'). In this deliberately shocking aphorism he undermines the common 18th-century belief that 'Man' is the noblest work of nature. This essay, which argues against the idea that suicide is 'wrong', was not published in the volume for which it was intended, being judged too provocative for many readers.

6 A world thus furnished with advantages on the one side and inconveniences on the other, is the proper abode of reason, is the fittest to exercise the industry of a free and thinking creature.

Oliver Goldsmith *An History of the Earth and Animated Nature* (1774) Vol.1, p.400. Goldsmith was certainly no naturalist, and this work, published posthumously, was composed from secondary reading. However, its very existence is a testimony to the appetites of a genteel readership, especially when we know that Goldsmith received the relatively huge advance of 800 guineas for its composition.

7 Look round this universe. What an immense profusion of beings, animated and organized, sensible and active! You admire this prodigious variety and fecundity. But inspect a little more narrowly these living existences, the only beings worth regarding. How hostile and destructive to each other! How insufficient all of them for their own happiness! How contemptible or odious to the spectator! The whole presents nothing but the idea of a blind nature, impregnated by a great vivifying principle, and pouring forth from her lap, without discernment or parental care, her maimed and abortive children.

David Hume *Dialogues Concerning Natural Religion* (1779; 1976 edn) Pt 11, p.241. Hume's *Dialogues*, too controversial to be published in his lifetime, consider the argument from design for the existence of God – that is, the very arrangement of the universe as evidence of a benevolent deity. These sentiments are voiced by Philo, the most sceptical of the three major personae (and the one who is usually taken to speak for Hume).

8 When we compare the infinite multiplicity of natural phenomena with the limitations of our understanding and the weakness of our organs and when we consider how slowly our work progresses, forever hampered by long and frequent interruptions and by the scarcity of creative geniuses, can we ever expect anything from it but a few broken and isolated fragments of the great chain that links all things together?

Denis Diderot *Pensées sur l'interprétation de la nature* (1754) Sect.6; John Hope Mason (ed.) *The Irresistible Diderot* (1982) p.62. This is taken from Diderot's numbered sequence of ideas and conjectures concerning the scientific study of nature. Here he reflects on the fact that scientific discovery relies on something more than the capacity of ordinary men to collect facts. Something more like creative genius is required to perceive the threads of connection that others cannot see.

1 Two things fill the mind with ever new and increasing admiration and awe, the oftener and more steadily we reflect on them: the starry heavens above me and the moral law within me.

Immanuel Kant *A Critique of Practical Reason* (1788; 1956 trans.) Conclusion, p.166.

2 In nature there is wisdom, system and consistency. For having, in the natural history of this earth, seen a succession of worlds, we may from this conclude that there is a system in nature; in like manner as, from seeing revolutions in the planets, it is concluded, that there is a system by which they are intended to continue those revolutions. But if the succession of worlds is established in the system of nature, it is in vain to look for any thing higher in the origin of the earth. The result, therefore, of our present enquiry is, that we find no vestige of a beginning – no prospect of an end.

James Hutton 'Theory of the Earth' in *Transactions of the Royal Society of Edinburgh* (1788) p.304. Hutton was a physician and geologist who argued that mountains decomposed to produce material that became the basis of new strata. The earth was providentially self-sustaining.

NATURAL MAN

3 I am as free as Nature first made man
'Ere the base Laws of Servitude began
When wild in woods the noble Savage ran.

John Dryden *The Conquest of Granada Pt I* (1672) Act I, Sc.I, lines 207–9. This is the first recorded appearance in English of the phrase 'the noble savage'. The lines are spoken by the virtuous Almanzor, who has just been sentenced to death by Boabdelin, king of Granada, whose absolute authority he challenges. The phrase later became associated with Rousseau, who, although undoubtedly a critic of the corruptions of 'civilization', did not specifically associate virtue with an uncivilized state.

4 Pity is not natural to man. Children are always cruel. Savages are always cruel. Pity is acquired and improved by the cultivation of reason.

Samuel Johnson, Wednesday, 20 July 1763; James Boswell *The Life of Johnson* (1791). Johnson was a staunch opponent of

primitivism and frequently denounced Rousseau (whom Boswell had met and admired).

5 If we are asked therefore, Where the state of nature is to be found? We may answer, It is here; and it matters not whether we are understood to speak in the island of Great Britain, at the Cape of Good Hope, or the Straits of Magellan. While this active being is in the train of employing his talents, and of operating on the subjects around him, all situations are equally natural.

Adam Ferguson *An Essay on the History of Civil Society* (1767) Pt I, Sect.I. Ferguson, a leading figure of the so-called Scottish Enlightenment (see 480:4), is often regarded as the father of modern sociology. His *Essay* corrects the assumptions of those (notably Rousseau) whose views of society are based on a view of human nature in its 'original', pre-social condition. Inasmuch as there is a 'state of nature', he argues, we live as much in it now as in previous ages.

6 I would willingly believe the most primitive people on earth, a Tahitian, who has kept scrupulously to the laws of nature, nearer to a good code of laws than any civilized people.

Denis Diderot *Supplément au voyage de Bougainville* (1772); Mason (1982) p.314. The occasion for this work was the account published by Louis-Antoine de Bougainville, a French sailor and man of letters (he was secretary to Louis XV in 1772), who voyaged around the world in the 1760s. Bougainville visited Tahiti and indeed returned to France with a Tahitian (see 406:8). On his return he discussed admiringly the sexual freedom of the Tahitians, and this is a central topic in Diderot's *Supplément*.

7 I here throw down my gauntlet, and deny the existence of sexual virtues, not excepting modesty. For man and woman, truth, if I understand the meaning of the word, must be the same.

Mary Wollstonecraft *A Vindication of the Rights of Woman* (1792; 1993 edn) Ch.3, p.119. As its title suggests, Wollstonecraft's daring work was a polemical supplement to Thomas Paine's *The Rights of Man* (see 518:4). Much of her book is given over to analysing and repudiating supposedly feminine qualities, 'modesty' being the most fundamental of these. Wollstonecraft, who married William Godwin in 1797, denies that there are inherently female traits of human character.

RELIGIOUS BELIEF

8 As a man is, so is his God.

Baruch Spinoza *Tractatus Theologico-politicus* (1670) Ch.2. Spinoza says this in his treatment of biblical prophecies, noting that the image of God changes with the different character of each of God's prophets.

1 God acts like the greatest geometer, who prefers the best constructions of problems.

Gottfried Wilhelm Leibniz *A Specimen of Discoveries about Marvellous Secrets of Nature in General* (c.1686); G.H.R. Parkinson (ed.) *Philosophical Writings* (1973) p.76. Leibniz became known, even notorious, for the proposition that God creates the best possible world (a proposition memorably mocked in Voltaire's *Candide*; see 486:7). Here Leibniz argues that the mathematical order of the universe is the very pattern of God's original creative activity.

2 Since you are pleased to enquire what are my thoughts about the mutual toleration of Christians in their different professions of religion, I must needs answer you freely, that I esteem that toleration to be the chief characteristical mark of the true church.

John Locke *A Letter Concerning Toleration* (1689). Locke's argument for toleration by the state of different Christian denominations was, in its day, deeply controversial. This is the work's opening sentence.

3 The system of the Gospel, after the fate of other systems, is generally antiquated and exploded, and the mass or body of the common people, among whom it seems to have had its latest credit, are now grown as much ashamed of it as their betters; opinions, like fashions, always descending from those of quality to the middle sort, and thence to the vulgar, where at length they are dropped and vanish.

Jonathan Swift *An Argument against Abolishing Christianity in England* (1708). Dean Swift's bleakly ironical (and anonymous) pamphlet purports to address a nation in which Christianity is on the brink of legal extinction. It argues for its continuance, but for a series of merely pragmatic and unprincipled reasons.

4 Survey most nations and most ages. Examine the religious principles which have, in fact, prevailed in the world. You will scarcely be persuaded that they are anything but sick men's dreams.

David Hume *The Natural History of Religion* (1757) Sect.1.

5 *Oui, je le soutiens, la superstition est plus injurieuse à Dieu que l'atheisme.* (Yes, I maintain that superstition is more offensive to God than atheism.)

Denis Diderot *Pensées philosophiques* (1746) Sect.12; *Oeuvres* Vol.1 (1994 edn) 'Philosophie' p.21. In this work, published anonymously, Diderot provocatively tested his sometimes contradictory views of religion. Their tendency was towards deism, a 'natural religion' independent of the doctrines or practices of Christianity.

6 *Si Dieu n'existait pas, il faudrait l'inventer.* (If God did not exist, it would be necessary to invent him.)

Voltaire *Épitres*, 96, 'À l'auteur du livre des trois imposteurs' (1769). Once Voltaire had coined this line, he liked to quote it in his letters. Yet Voltaire, despite his antagonism to Christianity, was not himself an atheist.

7 Ignorance and fear are the two hinges of all religion. The uncertainty in which man finds himself in relation to his God, is precisely the motive that attaches him to his religion.

Baron Paul-Henri d'Holbach *Good Sense, or Natural Ideas vs Supernatural Ideas* (1772) 'Refutation of Arguments for the Existence of God' Sect.10. The German-born Paul Henri Thiry, Baron d'Holbach lived in Paris, was a patron of intellectuals and was a contributor to the *Encyclopédie*. He was a materialist and the most outspoken atheist of his age. Hume, visiting Paris, thought him a kind of dogmatist in his very atheism. D'Holbach believed that men would be free only when they were free of religious delusion.

8 The legitimate powers of government extend to such acts only as are injurious to others. But it does me no injury for my neighbour to say there are twenty gods, or no god. It neither picks my pocket nor breaks my leg.

Thomas Jefferson *Notes on Virginia* (1787) Query 17; Joyce Appleby and Terence Ball (eds) *Jefferson: Political Writings* (1999) p.394. In his youth the third president of the United States had believed in some of the pagan virtues of the ancient writers and had regarded Christianity with scepticism or distaste. Later he was to return to Christianity, but always of the most liberal kind. Here he articulates the belief that the state should play no part in determining an individual's religious profession of faith.

9 All national institutions of churches – whether Jewish, Christian or Turkish – appear to me no other than human inventions set up to terrify and enslave mankind and monopolize power and profit.

Thomas Paine *The Age of Reason* Pt 1 (1794) p.2. Paine's anti-religious work provoked a flurry of antagonistic pamphlets. Paine argued that the ruling classes of all ages and all civilizations used religion to mystify those they subjugated.

KINDS OF SOCIETY

10 The great and chief end, therefore, of men's uniting into commonwealths, and putting themselves under government, is the preservation of their property.

John Locke *The Second Treatise of Government* Ch.9. Locke's great work of political philosophy was composed during the 1680s but published only after the Glorious Revolution of 1688 (see 488:1). It seemed to justify that event: the expulsion of an absolutist monarch (James II) by parliamentary representatives. It argued that states and governments, including monarchical ones, were not divinely ordained but the artificial arrangements of consenting individuals.

1 The English nation is the only one on earth which has succeeded in controlling the power of kings by resisting them, which by effort after effort has at last established this wise system of government, in which the Prince, all-powerful for doing good, has his hands tied for doing evil, in which the aristocrats are great without arrogance and vassals, and in which the people share in the government without confusion.

Voltaire *Letters on England* (1733; 1980 trans.) Letter 8 'On Parliament'. Voltaire visited England in 1726 to avoid imprisonment in France and stayed three years. Britain seemed thoroughly modern compared with France, and he admired the country's religious tolerance and political freedom. When his reflections on his stay were published in Paris, they were promptly banned.

2 In England, philosophers are honoured, respected; they rise to public offices, they are buried with the kings … In France warrants are issued against them, they are persecuted, pelted with pastoral letters: Do we see that England is any the worse for it?

Denis Diderot; J. Assézat (ed.) *Diderot: Oeuvres complètes* (1875–7) Vol.2, p.80.

3 *L'homme est né libre, et partout il est dans les fers.* (Man was born free and everywhere he is in chains.)

Jean-Jacques Rousseau *Du contrat social* (The Social Contract) (1762) Bk 1, Ch.1. This is the memorable first sentence of a work in which Rousseau sets out to establish the essential principles for the constitution of any just state (see 514:3).

4 Society is produced by our wants, and government by our wickedness; the former promotes our happiness positively by uniting our affections, the latter negatively by restraining our vices.

Thomas Paine *Common Sense* (1776) 'Of the origin and design of government in general. With concise remarks on the English constitution'. This sentence comes from the first paragraph of Paine's pamphlet, published anonymously in Philadelphia in the year of the American Declaration of Independence.

5 Our first concern, as lovers of our country must be to enlighten it.

Richard Price *A Discourse on the Love of Our Country* (1790) pp.11–12. Price was a dissenting preacher, and this discourse began as an oration at the Presbyterian chapel in London's Old Jewry. It was delivered to the Society for Commemorating the Revolution in Great Britain, a group that celebrated the heritage of the Glorious Revolution of 1688 (see 517:3).

As well as being a mathematician and moral philosopher, Price was a supporter of the American Revolution and the revolutionaries in France. This discourse provoked Edmund Burke to reply with his *Reflections on the Revolution in France* (1790) (see 526:9).

EDUCATION AND LEARNING

6   By education most have been misled,
      So they believe, because they so were bred.
      The Priest continues what the nurse began,
      And thus the child imposes on the man.

John Dryden *The Hind and the Panther* Bk 3, lines 389–92. Dryden had a Puritan religious upbringing, turned to moderate Anglicanism and finally converted to Catholicism. The poem was written to announce and justify this conversion. As in these lines, Dryden frequently expresses scepticism about the means by which any person discovers certainty in his or her particular brand of religious faith. But, as with others of his age, Dryden's doubt drove him to faith.

7 Of all the men we meet with, nine parts of ten are what they are, good or evil, useful or not, by their education. It is that which makes the great difference in mankind.

John Locke *Some Thoughts Concerning Education* (1693) no.1. As a philosopher who argued that humans have no innate ideas – that all ideas derive from experience and our reasoning upon experience – Locke naturally argued for the high importance of education. The characteristics of individuals were fashioned, not pre-ordained. His liberal educational treatise, which condemned both bribery and 'slavish and corporal punishments', was much respected and frequently cited through the 18th century.

8 We were originally made to be learned; we have become so perhaps by a sort of abuse of our organic faculties, and at the expense of the State which nourishes a host of sluggards whom vanity had adorned with the name of philosophers.

Bernard Mandeville (1714; 1924 edn). Mandeville became notorious for his attack on all theories of natural human benevolence (see 481:5). His verse satire 'The Grumbling Hive' (1705), which was included in *The Fable of the Bees* (1714), affirmed that men were self-interested and that their pursuit of their own interests was beneficial for society as a whole. In later editions, his verses acquired lengthy prose notes, from one of which this is taken.

9   We ply the Memory, we load the brain,
      Blind rebel Wit, and double chain on chain,
      Confine the thought, to exercise the breath;
      And keep them in the pale of Words till death.

Whate'er the talents, or howe'er design'd,
We hang one jingling padlock on the mind.

Alexander Pope *The Dunciad* (1742 version) Bk 4, lines 157–62. *The Dunciad* is an elaborate mock-epic poem detailing the stupidity of authors and the corruption of learning. Its fourth and last Book features scholars, scientists and pedagogues. These lines are spoken by the ghost of Dr Busby, a famous headmaster of Westminster School and a representative of traditional education.

1 Today we receive three different or opposing educations: that of our fathers, that of our schoolmasters and that of the world. What we are told by the last upsets all the ideas of the first two.

Charles, Baron de Montesquieu *The Spirit of the Laws* (1748; 1989 trans.) Pt 1, Ch.4 'The difference in the effect of education among the ancients and among ourselves'. Montesquieu was a minor nobleman and lawyer whose work of social theory championed a constitutional monarchy much like that of Britain (where he had lived in 1729–31). Here he contrasts what the young learn by tradition (which is shaped by religion) and what they learn by empirical observation.

2 When we run over libraries, persuaded of these principles, what havoc must we make? if we take in our hand any volume; of divinity or school metaphysics, for instance; let us ask, *Does it contain any abstract reasoning concerning quantity or number?* No. *Does it contain any experimental reasoning concerning matter of fact and existence?* No. Commit it then to the flames: for it can contain nothing but sophistry and illusion.

David Hume *An Enquiry Concerning Human Understanding* (1746) Ch.12 'Of the academical or sceptical philosophy'. In this work Hume reframed the arguments of the first book of his *Treatise of Human Nature* in order to make them more accessible to his prospective readers. Here, with some rhetorical exaggeration, he suggests the standards by which theology and much traditional philosophy fails to measure up as any kind of knowledge.

3 God makes all things good; man meddles with them and they become evil. He forces one soil to yield the products of another. One tree to bear another's fruit.

Jean-Jacques Rousseau *Émile* (1762; 1992 trans.) Bk 1, Sect.5. Rousseau's hugely influential account of a child's 'natural' upbringing was a passionate critique of the educational assumptions of his age. In Rousseau's version, education should involve not instruction so much as the encouragement of the child's inherent virtues. Rousseau was also one of the first to argue for universal education by the state.

4 What education is to the individual man, revelation is to the whole human race.

Gotthold Ephraim Lessing *Die Erziehung des Menschengeschlechts* (The Education of the Human Race) (1777); Henry Chadwick (ed.) *Lessing's Theological Writings* (1956) p.82. Lessing, the son of a Lutheran minister, is best known for his poetry and plays, as well as for his literary and dramatic criticism. He entered the University of Leipzig to study theology and never lost his interest in religious studies. Enlightenment thinking in Germany rarely acquired the anti-Christian flavour that predominated in France, and here Lessing suggests that Christianity is a valuable stage in educational development.

5 He that undertakes the education of a child undertakes the most important duty of society.

Thomas Day; James Kerr (ed.) *An Account of the Life and Writings of Thomas Day* (1791) p.104. Day, a follower of Rousseau, was a member of the Birmingham Lunar Society, along with Erasmus Darwin and Joseph Priestley (see 398:4). He was known for *The History of Sandford and Merton* (3 vols, 1783–9), which contrasts the upbringing of the privileged but obnoxious Merton with that of the humble but virtuous Sandford.

THE POSSIBILITY OF IMPROVEMENT

6 The greatest Inventions were produced in Times of Ignorance; as the use of the *Compass, Gunpowder* and *Printing*; and by the dullest Nation, as the *Germans*.

Jonathan Swift 'Thoughts on Various Subjects'; Davis Vol.1 (1939). This was found in a collection of such 'thoughts' dated 1706 and was written some time in the ten years before this. Such sardonic reflections might have been prompted by Swift's admiration for the *Maximes* of La Rochefoucauld.

7 *Cela est bien dit, répondit Candide, mais il faut cultiver notre jardin.* ('That is well said,' Candide replied, 'but we must cultivate our garden.')

Voltaire *Candide* (1759) Ch.30. The meaning of this, the famous last sentence of Voltaire's satire, has been much discussed. It is usually taken to imply the modesty of man's proper ambitions or the preference for practical over speculative activities.

8 All the arts, the sciences, law and government, wisdom and even virtue itself tend all to this one thing, the providing meat, drink, raiment and lodging for men, which are commonly reckoned the meanest of employments and fit for the pursuit of none but the meanest and lowest of people.

Adam Smith *Lectures on Jurisprudence*, 28 March 1763 (1978 edn) p.338. Smith's lectures are recorded only in the notes of some of those who attended. Here his clear-eyed interest in the economic means by which men and women survive and perhaps prosper is in evidence. This sets the tone for the later *Wealth of Nations* (see 481:8).

1 When a language begins to teem with books, it is tending to refinement; as those who undertake to teach each other must have undergone some labour in improving themselves, they set a proportionate value on their own thoughts, and wish to enforce them by efficacious expressions; speech becomes embodied and permanent; different modes and phrases are compared, and the best obtains an establishment.

Samuel Johnson *A Journey to the Western Islands of Scotland* (1775) 'Ostig in Sky'. Although Johnson was dismissive of contemporaries who were leaders of Enlightenment thought, notably Hume and Rousseau, he himself was responsible for one of the great Enlightenment textbooks: his *Dictionary of the English Language* (1755). In this passage, reflecting on the Gaelic language, which he calls 'the rude speech of a barbarous people', he expresses the belief that only writing and printing make improvement possible.

2 The Gothic idea that we are to look backwards instead of forwards for the improvement of the human mind, and to recur to the annals of our ancestors for what is most perfect in government, in religion & in learning, is worthy of those bigots in religion & government, by whom it is recommended, & whose purpose it would answer. But it is not an idea which this country [America] will endure.

Thomas Jefferson to Joseph Priestley, 27 Jan. 1800; Appleby and Ball (1999) p.264. Jefferson was an intellectual leader of the revolution against British rule in America, and in this letter to his British friend and sympathizer Priestley, he attacked the idea that 'the improvement of the human mind' would be achieved by looking 'backwards instead of forwards'.

3 I have lived to see a diffusion of knowledge, which has undermined superstition and error – I have lived to see the rights of men better understood than ever; and nations panting for liberty, which seemed to have lost the idea of it.

Richard Price (1790); Marilyn Butler (ed.) *Burke, Paine, Godwin and the Revolution Controversy* (1984) p.31. Price was speaking in the first glow of sympathy for the revolutionaries in France, supposing that their insurrection against an absolutist monarch would follow that of the bloodless Glorious Revolution of 1688 in England (see 517:3).

4 In the groves of *their* academy, at the end of every vista, you see nothing but the gallows.

Edmund Burke *Reflections on the Revolution in France* (1790; 1968 edn) p.171. Burke, once a supporter of the revolutionaries in America, wrote his *Reflections* before the Revolution in France turned to violence. It seemed prescient as a result. Here he predicts the eventual end of the innovations of the French Revolution. 'They' are the intellectuals who have supplied the revolutionaries with their justification.

5 There is no science that is not capable of additions; there is no art that may not be carried to a still higher perfection. If this be true of all other sciences, why not of morals? If this be true of all other arts, why not of social institutions?

William Godwin (1793; 1946 edn) Vol.1, p.119. When he wrote the *Enquiry*, which was hugely influential during the 1790s, Godwin believed that human history was necessarily a history of improvement, an improvement based on the growth and dissemination of knowledge.

6 Are we not arrived at the point when there is no longer anything to fear, either from new errors, or the return of old ones; when no corrupt institution can be introduced by hypocrisy, and adopted by ignorance or enthusiasm, when no vicious combination can affect the infelicity of a great people?

Marquis de Condorcet *Sketch for a Historical Picture of the Human Mind* (1794) Introduction. Condorcet believed that human institutions and faculties were developing towards perfection and that the 'the era of one of the grand revolutions of the human race' had now been reached.

7 The more I see of the world, the more I am convinced that civilization is a blessing not sufficiently estimated by those who have not traced its progress, for it not only refines our enjoyments, but produces a variety which enables us to retain the primitive delicacy of our sensations.

Mary Wollstonecraft *Letters Written during a Short Residence in Sweden, Norway, and Denmark* (1796) Letter 2. Wollstonecraft's travel book is indirectly a meditation on the failed ideals of the French Revolution, whose turn to violence and terror the author had herself witnessed. Its faith in civilization opposes it to the beliefs of Rousseau and his followers.

LOOKING BACK

8 In the most general sense of progressive thought, the Enlightenment has always aimed at liberating men from fear and establishing their sovereignty. Yet the fully enlightened earth radiates disaster triumphant.

Theodor Adorno and Max Horkheimer *Dialectic of Enlightenment* (1944; 1972 trans.) p.3.

9 The age of enlightenment, was also an age of fanaticisms.

Ronald Knox *Enthusiasm* (1950) p.288.

Britain: The Long 18th Century

WILLIAM III AND MARY II, 1689–1702

1 That King James the Second, having endeavoured to subvert the constitution of the kingdom, by breaking the Original Contract between king and people, and by the advice of Jesuits, and other wicked persons, having violated the fundamental laws, and having withdrawn himself out of this kingdom, has abdicated the government, and that the throne is thereby become vacant.

Resolution of the Commons in the Convention, 28 Jan. 1689; W. Cobbett *Parliamentary History* Vol.5 (1802) Col.50. Following William of Orange's successful invasion of England, James II fled London on 11 Dec. 1688, destroying the Great Seal of England and burning the writs ordering elections to a new parliament. James was captured by some fishermen at Rochester and returned to Whitehall, but he had no interest in staying as William's puppet, nor did William intend to rule through his father-in-law. James was allowed to leave for France on 23 Dec. William called a Convention, effectively an unofficial parliament, made up of the House of Lords and a Commons largely drawn from the last parliament of Charles II. The resolution declaring the crown vacant aimed to satisfy as many elements in the English political nations as possible. It attempted to invoke the contract between king and people without wholly embracing it and so emphasized the unauthorized departure of James II from the kingdom instead. However, the implication that by leaving his country without the consent of his subjects a king had abdicated was an innovation in European law.

2 King James the Seventh, being a professed Papist, did assume the Regal power, and acted as king, without ever taking the oath required by law, and hath by the advice of evil and wicked counsellors, invaded the fundamental constitution of the kingdom, and altered it from a legal limited monarchy, to an arbitrary despotic power … whereby he hath forefaulted the right to the crown, and the throne is become vacant.

Claim of Right, 11 April 1689; G. Donaldson (ed.) *Scottish Historical Documents* (1997 edn) p.255. In Scotland, where James II had ruled as James VII, the act of removing the king from the throne was made explicit in the Claim of Right, whereas it was not part of the Bill of Rights in England. The Scottish parliament decided that James had lost the crown because of his conduct as king.

3 Though some wished to make him a doge of Venice, he would, since he had been called to the throne by God, maintain the authority reposed in him.

William III, speaking at the Earl of Shrewsbury's, 5 Jan. 1690; H. Horwitz *Parliament, Policy and Politics in the Reign of William III* (1977) p.42. The Convention placed William III of Orange and his wife, James II's daughter Mary, on the English throne as William III and Mary II; Scotland followed suit. Executive authority was vested in William alone, who was determined to exercise it fully despite the intentions of some parliamentarians. The doge of Venice, the elected ruler of that Italian city, was widely regarded as the passive tool of an oligarchy. William intended to be the real as well as the titular ruler of England. Nonetheless, the House of Commons did gain a greater say over expenditure and could not be prorogued indefinitely.

4 You are hereby ordered to fall upon the rebels, the MacDonalds of Glencoe, and to put all to the sword under seventy. You are to have a special care that the old fox and his sons do upon no account escape your hands. You are to secure all the avenues that no man escape. This you are to put in execution at five of the clock precisely; and by that time, or very shortly after it, I'll strive to be at you with a stronger party. If I do not come to you at five, you are not to tarry for me, but to fall on. This is by the King's special command, for the good and safety of the country, that these miscreants be cut off root and branch.

Major Robert Duncanson of Fassokie to Captain Robert Campbell of Glenlyon, 12 Feb. 1692; John Prebble *Glencoe* (1968 edn) p.203. The Scottish administration under John Drummond, Master of Stair, wanted the MacDonalds of Glencoe, who challenged the power of Stair's allies, the Campbells, in the west of Scotland, removed. Unwilling to know of the MacDonalds' belated agreement to swear allegiance to William III and Mary II, the government, with the approval of the king, ordered that the clan be massacred on 13 Feb. 1692.

5 The smallpox increasing and exceedingly mortal: Queen Mary died thereof, full of spots … What this unexpected accident may produce as to the present government, many are the discourse, and a little time may show. The King seemed mightily afflicted, as indeed it behoved him.

John Evelyn, 29 Dec. 1694; *The Diary of John Evelyn* (1955 edn) Vol.5, p.200. Mary II died on 28 Dec. 1694. William III was genuinely inconsolable and refused to consider remarriage to secure the Protestant succession. Mary's death appeared to threaten the security of William's rule, but attempts by the supporters of James II, the Jacobites, to restore the deposed king proved unsuccessful.

1 The people are now in much better humour and relish the peace more than they will do a year hence, when they shall find taxes in a good measure continued, troops lying heavier upon them as being in greater numbers dispersed about the country, and that there will not be so quick a consumption for their goods nor their corn and cattle bear so high a price as in time of war.

James Vernon to Charles Talbot, Duke of Shrewsbury, 30 Sept. 1697; Horwitz (1977) p.218. William III had reconstructed the English state's finances so that it could fund the Nine Years War against France, leading to an increased burden of taxation and the need to finance the new national debt.

2 He delivered his own country from the dangers and pressures they laboured under and afterwards when our rights and liberties and religion were invaded by his father in law King James the Second, he made a descent into England and rescued us: he forced France to terms of peace and was now engaged to win the quarrel of Europe ... He was the supporter of the Protestant religion, of the liberty of Europe, and an enemy to France, the only obstacle ... that hindered [Louis XIV] from being universal monarch.

Sir Richard Cocks on the death of William III, 8 March 1702; *The Parliamentary Diary of Sir Richard Cocks, 1698–1702* (1996 edn) p.238.

QUEEN ANNE, 1702–14

3 I know my own heart to be entirely English.

Queen Anne to Parliament, 11 March 1702; E. Gregg *Queen Anne* (1980) p.152. Anne's accession speech evoked memories of the revered Elizabeth I. She contrasted herself with the Dutch William III and her French-reared Catholic half-brother and rival for the throne, James Edward Stuart, known as the Old Pretender.

4 I believe nobody was ever so used by a friend as I have been by her ever since my coming to the Crown. I desire nothing but that she will leave off teasing and tormenting me, and behave herself with the decency she ought both to her friend and Queen, and this I hope you will make her do.

Queen Anne to John Churchill, 1st Duke of Marlborough, 25 Oct. 1709; F. Harris *A Passion for Government: The Life of Sarah, Duchess of Marlborough* (1992) p.160.

5 I have not time to say more, but to beg you will give my duty to the Queen, and let her know her army has had a glorious victory. Monsieur Tallard

and two other generals are in my coach, and I am following the rest. The bearer, my aide de camp Colonel Parkes, will give her an account of what has passed. I shall do it in a day or two by another more at large.

John Churchill, Duke of Marlborough to the Duchess of Marlborough, 13 Aug. 1704; H.L. Snyder (ed.) *Marlborough–Godolphin Correspondence* (1975) Vol.1, p.349. Anne came to the throne with her main political advisers already in place – John Churchill, 1st Duke of Marlborough (1650–1722); his wife Sarah (1660–1744) and Sidney Godolphin, 1st Earl of Godolphin (1645–1712). The relationship between Anne and the duchess became strained after Anne's accession, partly because Anne would not follow Sarah's political advice, and from 1703 Sarah spent less and less time at court, although the women managed to hide the deterioration in their friendship for several years. Meanwhile Marlborough was established as captain-general of the armed forces and in Aug. 1704 won the spectacular and bloody victory at Blenheim (Blindheim) in Bavaria over the French during the War of the Spanish Succession (1702–13) (see 466:5). He was rewarded with the royal manor of Woodstock and a new house to be built on the site, known as Blenheim Palace, Oxfordshire, designed by John Vanbrugh and mainly built between 1706 and 1719.

6 1. That the two kingdoms of England and Scotland shall upon the First day of May which shall be in the year One thousand seven hundred and seven, and for ever after, be united into one kingdom by the name of Great Britain ...

4. That all the Subjects of the United Kingdom of Great Britain shall, from and after the Union, have full Freedom and Intercourse of Trade and Navigation to and from any port and place within the said United Kingdom, and the Dominions and Plantations thereunto belonging ...

19. That the Court of Session, or College of Justice, do after the Union, and notwithstanding thereof, remain in all time coming within Scotland, as it is now constituted by the Laws of that Kingdom, and with the same authority and privileges.

Some of the articles of the Act of Union, 1707; Donaldson (1997 edn) pp.268–75.

7 And so the Union commenced on the first of May 1707, a day never to be forgot by Scotland. A day on which the Scots were stripped of what their predecessors had gallantly maintained for many hundred years – I mean the independency and sovereignty of the kingdom. Both which the Earl of Seafield so little valued that when he, as Chancellor, signed the engrossed exemplification of the Act of

Union, he returned it to the clerk, in the face of Parliament with this despising and contemning remark: 'now there's ane end of ane old song.'

George Lockhart of Carnwath, 1707; 'Scotland's Ruine', Lockhart of Carnwath's Memoirs of the Union (1995 edn) p.204. The union of England and Scotland into the new kingdom of Great Britain gave Scotland access to England's commercial markets and ensured that the crowns of the two countries would not be separated on Anne's death. A separate act ensured that the presbyterian government of the Church of Scotland would be preserved, in contrast to the episcopalian structure of the Church of England (see 360:4).

1 He could not with any decency press the Queen too much against her nature, because it would be like running upon the rock where his predecessors had split.

Jonathan Swift on Robert Harley, 1st Earl of Oxford, 9 Aug. 1714; Prose Works Vol.8, pp.103–4; G. Holmes, British Politics in the Age of Anne (1987 edn), p.208. In 1710 Harley formed an administration that was heavily reliant on Tory support in the House of Commons. The Tories were generally sympathetic to the queen's prerogative, and Harley's power depended on his respect for the queen's right to exercise executive authority. He was regarded with hostility by his former allies in the Whig Party, who were associated with toleration for nonconformist Protestant denominations, which was disliked by the Tories. The Whigs saw the Treaty of Utrecht with France (1713), by which Britain withdrew from the War of the Spanish Succession (see 466:10), as a betrayal of their European allies and, potentially, as the beginning of a realignment that could see James II's son, the Old Pretender, a Catholic, placed on the throne by Jacobite supporters among the Tories.

2 Not dead? She is as dead as Julius Caesar.

William Delaune, president of St John's College, Oxford, 1 Aug. 1714; Gregg (1980) p.395. Delaune, a supporter of the Hanoverian succession in a college dominated by Tories and Jacobites, was remarking on the drastic change in the political world occasioned by the queen's death. Her successor, George I, who, as Elector of Hanover, had been one of the allies abandoned by the Treaty of Utrecht, was expected to return the Whigs to power, which he did. The impact of Anne's death was remembered much later by the saying 'Queen Anne's dead', originated by the playwright George Colman the Younger in his play Heir-at-Law (1797) to mock archaic opinions and habits.

3 The Parliament met, and the Lords and Commons took the oaths. Thank God everything is quiet.

Viscountess Dupplin to Abigail Harley, 3 Aug. 1714; The Manuscripts of His Grace the Duke of Portland (1891–1931 edn) Vol.5 p.482. Jacobites were expected to stir up substantial civil unrest on the accession of George I, but in the event it did not take place.

GEORGE I, 1714–27

4 Sad pleadings: some sons drawn in by their fathers, and Mr Shafto by his son, who forced him to take arms.

Mary, Countess Cowper, 19 Feb. 1716; Diary of Mary, Countess Cowper (1865 edn) p.78. The countess is commenting on the trials of the Jacobite rebels at Preston following the rising of 1715. The Shaftos were one of the Northumberland Jacobite families involved in the rising; many were reluctant to commit themselves to either side and were not ardent Jacobites.

5 Our bumpkins in the country are very waggish and very insolent. Some honest justices met to keep the Coronation day at Wattleton, and towards the evening when their worships were mellow they would have a bonfire. Some bumpkins upon this got a huge turnip and stuck three candles just over Chetwynd's house ... They came and told their worships that to honour King George's Coronation day a blazing star appeared above Mr Chetwynd's house. Their worships were wise enough to take horse and go and see this wonder, and found, to their no little disappointment, their star to end in a turnip.

Rev. William Stratford, 1718; E.P. Thompson Customs in Common (1991) p.75. George I, the great-grandson of James I, succeeded to the throne of Great Britain and Ireland in 1714. He was already the Elector of Hanover, the German state, and hence became the first of the Hanoverians. A turnip was a sign of cuckoldry. Opponents of George I never missed an opportunity to mock him for his wife Sophia Dorothea's affair with Count Philip Königsmarck in the 1690s, which had led to Königsmarck's disappearance and to George divorcing and imprisoning Sophia Dorothea for life in 1694.

6 Hence (for in his peculiar reign were laid
   Schemes, that produced the sure increase
     of trade)
Shall generations, yet unborn, be told,
Who gifted them with silver mines and gold;
Who gave them all the commerce of the Main,
And made South Seas send home the wealth
     of Spain.

L. Eusden 'Poem in Honour of the Birthday of His Majesty King George' (1720); J. Carswell The South Sea Bubble (1993 edn) p.127. The transfer of much of the burden of the national debt to the South Sea Company was somehow meant to enrich its bondholders as well as enable Britain to overtake Spain's Pacific trade. The scheme was flawed and made worse by the artificial inflation of the price of stock, much of which was given away to influential people, including the king's mistress, Melusine von der Schulenburg, Duchess of Kendal. The bursting of the 'South Sea Bubble' that resulted from the exposure of the practice ruined several investors and embarrassed the government.

1 La Schulenburg: 'Good people, why do you plague us so? We have come for your own goods.'

Mob: 'Yes, and for our chattels too'.

Anon: R. Hatton *George I: Elector and King* (1978) p.131.

2 He [George] would not wait upon Duchess of Kendal till things were far advanced; that now he intended it, and that her interest did everything; that she was, in effect as much queen of England as ever any was; that he did everything by her.

Robert Walpole, 23 April 1720; Cowper (1865 edn) p.132. George I's Hanoverian courtiers, led by his mistress, the Duchess of Kendal, were popularly regarded as rapacious parasites living off the British public purse. However, the Duchess of Kendal's influence with George I was appreciated by ambitious politicians such as Robert Walpole, who became first lord of the treasury in 1721. His effective management of the Commons and his success in eclipsing his rivals has led him to be regarded as the first 'prime minister'.

GEORGE II, 1727–60

3 Her predominant passion was pride, and the darling pleasure of her soul was power; but she was forced to gratify the one and gain the other, as some people do health, by a strict and painful régime, which few besides herself could have patience to support, or resolution to adhere to.

John, Lord Hervey, writing after 1733; R. Sedgwick (ed.) *Lord Hervey's Memoirs* (1931) Vol.1, pp.253–4. John Hervey, Baron Hervey of Ickworth (1696–1743), vice-chamberlain to the king in 1730–40, adored George II's queen, Caroline of Brandenburg-Ansbach, and fostered the image of Caroline as a highly intelligent woman married to a dull husband. His diaries, though partial, are one of the best and most entertaining sources for the early part of the reign of George II.

4 A minister sometimes must swim with the tide against his inclination, and that the current was too strong at present against this proposal of the Dissenters for any judicious minister to think of stemming it.

Robert Walpole, 1732; Sedgwick (1931) Vol.1, pp.128–9. Walpole's argument to the Dissenters (Protestants dissenting from the established church). They were pressing for a repeal of the Test and Corporation Acts, which denied office to anyone who was not a member of the Church of England. A general election was approaching, and Walpole was suggesting that they try again after the election to avoid stirring up Anglican resentment. Walpole was effective in playing off his disparate supporters against each other to maintain power.

5 They liked your Grace very well, but were very much dissatisfied with what had lately happened; for that he and his neighbours had heard, that bread and meat would have been taxed if it had not been for a petition from Bristol.

William Hay to the Duke of Newcastle, 14 Aug. 1733; BL Addit. MS 32688, f.98. The Excise Crisis proved the worst threat to Walpole's hold on power. He miscalculated that the extension of the excise to tobacco would prove more popular than the existing land tax it was meant to offset. Rumour begat rumour and ordinary people feared that the government meant to tax the most basic goods.

6 *Ch*: … Your Ministers, Sir, are only your instruments of government.

K: (smiles) Ministers are the kings in this country.

Ch: If one person is permitted to engross the ear of the Crown, and invest himself with all its power, he will become so in effect; but that is far from being the case now, and I know no one now in Your Majesty's service who aims at it.

Discussion between Philip Yorke, 1st Earl of Hardwicke, lord chancellor (Ch) and George II (K), 5 Jan. 1745; L. Namier *England during the Age of the American Revolution* (1961) p.46. George II often wished to remove the government of Henry Pelham, who came to power in 1743, but he was unable to find an alternative ministry that could lead in the Commons. Despite the king's limited freedom of manoeuvre, Hardwicke spoke the truth when he said that there was no sole minister. All the cabinet, including its leading figures, were dependent on the king's support, without which the government could not function; however, political managers, such as Walpole and Pelham, were sufficiently talented to demand and receive that support.

7 A little after seven he went into the water-closet – the German valet-de-chambre heard a noise, louder than royal wind, listened, heard something like a groan, ran in and found the hero of Oudenarde and Dettingen on the floor, with a gash on his right temple by falling against the corner of a bureau – he tried to speak, could not and expired.

Horace Walpole to George Montagu, 25 Oct. 1760; W.S. Lewis et al. (eds) *Horace Walpole's Correspondence* (1937–83 edn) Vol.9, p.311. The death of George II had been long awaited by the political world, and the indignity of his death was more memorable than the sincerity or duration of the mourning.

THE JACOBITE REBELLION, 1745

8 I am come home.

Prince Charles Edward Stuart, on being told by Alexander MacDonald of Boisdale on 31 July 1745 that he should go home to France from Scotland; F. McLynn *Charles Edward Stuart* (1991) p.129. This began the rising of 1745, which seemed for a short time to presage a Jacobite restoration. Charles Edward was the son of James, the Old Pretender, and was therefore known as the Young Pretender.

1 The men I have defeated were your Majesty's enemies, it is true, but they might have become your friends and dutiful subjects when they had got their eyes opened to see the true interest of their country which I am come to save, not to destroy.

Charles Edward Stuart to his father, James, after victory over government forces at the Battle of Gladesmuir, 21 Sept. 1745; Robert Forbes *The Lyon in Mourning* (1895) Vol.1, pp.211–12.

2 We have beat the rebels, beat 'em in a set battle, and I assure you *de la bonne manière*, losing very few of our own and destroying a good number of those vermin.

Colonel Henry Seymour Conway to Horace Walpole, 18 April 1746, the day of the Battle of Culloden; Lewis *et al.* (1937–83 edn) Vol.37, p.238.

3 For several days they killed man, wife and child many miles from the field of battle. At five miles distance an honest poor woman on the day of battle who was brought to bed Sunday before, flying with her infant, was attacked by 4 dragoons, who gave her seven wounds in the head through one plaid which was eight fold and one in the arm. The one of them took the infant by the thigh, threw it about his hand and at last to the ground.

Rev. James Hay, account of barbarities after Culloden; Forbes (1895) Vol.2, p.307. A false letter had been circulated, leading government soldiers to believe they would be slaughtered if the Jacobites won. The government forces were commanded by William, Duke of Cumberland, third son of George II, whose brutality earned him the sobriquet Butcher Cumberland.

4 She had not that happiness before, she did not look for it now, but that a sight of him would make her happy, though he was on a hill and she was on another.

Flora MacDonald (of herself) to Colonel Felix O'Neil, 20 June 1746, immediately before being told of her intended role in Charles Edward's escape from pursuit by Hanoverian forces; H. Douglas, *Flora MacDonald, The Most Loyal Rebel* (1999) p.26. In defeat, Charles Edward Stuart, 'Bonnie Prince Charlie', became a more romantic figure than ever before, and the focus of a nostalgia for a Highland Scots way of life that was disappearing under economic pressures, as crofts were cleared for sheep and landlords encouraged their tenants to emigrate to North America.

5 As the intercourse between this part of Great Britain and the capital daily increases, both on account of business and amusement, and must still go on increasing, gentlemen educated in Scotland have long been sensible of the disadvantages under which they labour, from their imperfect knowledge of the English tongue, and the impropriety with which they speak it.

Regulations of the Select Society, 1761; *Scots Magazine*, Vol.23 (1761) p.389.

6 If our agriculture and manufactures were improved and carried on to the height they could bear, we might be near as easy and convenient in our circumstances, as even the people of our sister kingdom of England; seeing neither our soil nor our climate is unfriendly, and since we enjoy the same privileges of trade with them … if we are far behind, we ought to follow further.

Secretary of the Society of Improvers in the Knowledge of Agriculture, c.1760; N.T. Phillipson 'Public Opinion and the Union' in N.T. Phillipson and R. Mitchison (eds) *Scotland in the Age of Improvement* (1970) p.143. The 1745 rebellion had confirmed many English prejudices about Scotland as a barbaric, untrustworthy region. In the second half of the 18th century many Scottish thinkers, mainly in Edinburgh and the Lowlands (see 480:4), consciously sought to reinvent Scotland as a commercial nation and an effective partner for England in the British Empire.

GEORGE III, THE EARLY YEARS, 1760–89

7 The interest of my country ever shall be my first care, my own inclinations shall ever submit to it. I am born for the happiness or misery of a great nation, and consequently must often act contrary to my passions.

George III to Lord Bute, Nov. 1759; J. Brooke *King George III* (1972) p.72. The king was writing to his mentor acknowledging that he could not marry a commoner, but also expressing his wider sense of obligation.

8 The only difference of conduct I adopted was to put an end to those unhappy distinctions of party called Whigs and Tories, by declaring that I would countenance every man that supported my administration and concurred in that form of government which had been so wisely established by the Revolution.

George III's ambitions on his accession, as remembered later in his reign; Brooke (1972) p.90.

1 That she has no title to praises due to a fine form or face, every one agrees, but that she has every requisite to adorn an amiable mind is as generally allowed; and does she not then deserve to be Queen of England?

Caroline Powys, describing the coronation of George III and Queen Charlotte, 25 Sept. 1761; *Passages from the Diaries of Mrs Philip Lybbe Powys* (1899) p.90. Princess Charlotte of Mecklenburg-Strelitz arrived in London on 8 Sept. 1761 and, although she had not met him before, married George III the same day.

2 Every friend of his country must lament that a prince of so many great and amiable qualities, whom England truly reveres, can be brought to give the sanction of his sacred name to the most odious measures, and to the most unjustifiable public declarations, from a throne ever renowned for truth, honour, and unsullied virtue.

John Wilkes, *North Briton* no.45, 23 April 1763; P.D.G. Thomas *John Wilkes, A Friend to Liberty* (1996) pp.27–8. The politician John Wilkes founded a newspaper, the *North Briton*, to attack the ministry of Lord Bute, popularly seen in London as effecting a Scottish take-over of England. He is condemning the Treaty of Paris, which ended the Seven Years War and which was negotiated by Bute's government. Wilkes was subsequently arrested, beginning a lengthy legal procedure that confirmed his status as a folk hero to the London mob and a focus of the general suspicion of George III's ministers.

3 An English gentleman … has no rank above his fellow citizens – but what his manners, his affability, his knowledge, his justice, the popular use of his fortune give him – The people will look up to, and confide in the laborious, the vigilant the active – but they have little hope in a court.

Edmund Burke, speech on the Middlesex election, 15 April 1769; P. Langford (ed.) *The Writings and Speeches of Edmund Burke* Vol.2 (1981) p.230. Burke justifies the rule of an aristocratic oligarchy over Britain but warns that if gentlemen did not earn their place at the head of society power would seep back to the crown. The Middlesex election controversy concerned the election of Wilkes to the Commons for Middlesex in 1768. The government expelled him from the Commons in Feb. 1769 on the grounds that he had been convicted for libel in the *North Briton* case and for obscenity in his *Essay on Woman*, but he won at three successive by-elections.

4 The farmer grown familiar asked the gentleman, as he thought, if he had seen the King; and being answered in the affirmative, the farmer said 'Our neighbours say, he's a good sort of man, but dresses very plain'. 'Aye,' said his Majesty, 'as plain as you see me now,' and rode on.

An oft-told story about George III; L. Colley *Britons* (1992) p.233.

5 The influence of the crown has increased, is increasing and ought to be diminished.

John Dunning, resolution proposed in the House of Commons, 6 April 1780; Cobbett Vol.21 (1814) Col.90. Dunning was a supporter of political and financial reform in government; his motion passed the Commons, against the wishes of Lord North's ministry, by 233 votes to 215. Several government offices were abolished under the second administration of the Marquess of Rockingham in 1782.

6 Blue banners had been waved from tops of houses at Whitehall as signals to the people, while the coaches passed, whom they should applaud or abuse. Sir Geo. Savile's and Ch. Turner's coaches were demolished. Ellis, whom they took for a popish gentleman, they carried prisoner to the Guildhall in Westminster, and he escaped by a ladder out of a window. Lord Mahon harangued the people from the balcony of a coffee-house and begged them to retire – but at past ten a new scene opened … The mob forced the Sardinian minister's chapel in Lincoln's Inn Fields, and gutted it. He saved nothing but two chalices; lost the silver lamps, etc., and the benches being tossed into the street, were food for a bonfire, with the blazing brands of which they set fire to the inside of the chapel, nor, till the Guards arrived, would suffer the engines to play.

Horace Walpole, giving an account of the Gordon riots to the Countess of Upper Ossory, 3 June 1780; Lewis *et al.* (1937–83 edn) Vol.33, pp.177–8. The Gordon riots in London, instigated by Lord George Gordon, exploited popular distrust of Roman Catholics following the Catholic Relief Act of 1778.

7 Genius is an indefinite term. I never think a man really an able man, unless I see that he has attained the object of his pursuits, whatever they may be. I try Charles Fox by that test. He has had three favourite pursuits – gaming, politics, women. He addicted himself to play and thought himself a skilful player, but lost an immense fortune almost before he was of age. Power was his grand object, yet he has never been able to keep possession of it, scarcely for a twelvemonth. He was desirous of shining as a man of gallantry, and he married a whore.

George Selwyn to Lord Mansfield and Sir Walter Farquhar, c.1793; F. Bickley (ed.) *The Diaries of Sylvester Douglas* (1928) Vol.2, p.320. Charles James Fox was the leading Whig spokesman in the Commons from the 1770s onwards. He held office briefly in 1782, 1783 and 1806, but spent most of his career in opposition. He was infamous for his dissolute lifestyle, spent drinking and gambling at clubs such as Brook's, but was hugely respected for his political acumen by his followers. He married the courtesan Elizabeth Armitstead in 1795.

1 Depend upon it … it will be a mincepie administration.

Frances, Lady Crewe, on the prospects for the new administration led by William Pitt, the Younger, Dec. 1783; J. Ehrman *The Younger Pitt: The Years of Acclaim* (1969) p.133. Lady Crewe and other supporters of Fox thought the ministry would not survive Christmas. In the event Pitt remained in office until Feb. 1801.

2 Think not, Maria, my beloved wife, that I have deceived them or mean to deceive them in the least by what I have said. No, I have looked upon myself as married for above this year and half, ever since I made to thee and thou madest to me in the face of heaven, a vow mutually to regard one another as man and wife … I have principles which I glory in, principles of honour and justice, from which I can at no time deviate; on the contrary, to which I must ever most steadfastly adhere, especially when they are strengthened by love and the consciousness of acting right.

George, Prince of Wales to Maria Fitzherbert, 3 Nov. 1785; A. Aspinall (ed.) *The Correspondence of George, Prince of Wales* Vol.1 (1963) p.196. On 14 Dec. 1785 the Prince of Wales (later George IV) underwent a ceremony of marriage with Mrs Fitzherbert, who was twice widowed and a Roman Catholic. Marriage to a Catholic would have barred the Prince of Wales from succession to the British throne by the Act of Settlement of 1701 and the Act of Union of 1707; however, as the marriage did not have the consent of the prince's father, George III, it was invalid under the terms of the Royal Marriages Act of 1772. The government used the marriage as a lever on the prince; if he renounced Mrs Fitzherbert and stopped supporting the opposition they would pay his debts and find him a more suitable royal bride.

3 In order… to obviate every minute cause through which the public may be imposed on by the agents of other prints, as that a paper, ever devoted to their information and amusement on every subject, useful or interesting, may stand distinguished by a title, at once more laconic, and comprehensive of its design, and less apt to be mistaken for another; the public are respectfully informed, that on and after the 1st of January next [the *Daily Universal Register*] will be published under the title of *The Times*.

John Walter, advertising leaflet, Dec. 1787. Walter (1739–1812), a bankrupt coal merchant, took up printing in 1782 and founded the *Daily Universal Register* in 1785. He changed the name to *The Times* in 1788, as a shorter name was more

distinctive. *The Times* was not particularly distinguished in Walter's lifetime, but was built up into a leading opinion-forming newspaper by Walter's son John Walter II (1776–1847), who managed the paper from 1803. The Walter family continued to own the paper until 1908 and remained major shareholders until 1967.

4 The King lives, Glory to God in the highest, on Earth Peace, Goodwill towards men; G. IIId. R. glories in the name of Britons; Britons glory in the name of G. IIId. R.

London Chronicle, 31 March 1789. Slogans displayed by Mr Silvester of Cannon Street, Manchester, to celebrate the recovery of George III from his first serious attack of 'madness', probably brought on by the physiological condition porphyria.

CRIME

5 I know that if one would be agreeable to men of dignity one must study to imitate them, and I know which way they get money and places. I cannot wonder that the talents requisite for a great statesman are so scarce in the world since so many of those who possess them are every month cut off in the prime of their age at the Old Bailey.

John Gay, 1723; *Letters* (1966 edn) p.45. Gay's cynical comparison of politicians and criminals was further explored in his satire *The Beggar's Opera*, which opened at Lincoln's Inn Fields theatre on 29 Jan. 1728.

6 A superstitious reverence of the vulgar for a corpse, even of a malefactor, and the strong aversion they have against dissecting them, are prejudicial to the public; for as health and sound limbs are the most desirable of all temporal blessings, so we ought to encourage the improvements of physick and surgery.

Bernard Mandeville *An Enquiry into the Causes of the Frequent Executions at Tyburn* (1725) pp.23–4. A frequent sight following an execution was the battle between the family and friends of the executed criminal and surgeons who wanted the corpse for dissection. In the wake of the Gordon riots in London in June 1780 executions at Tyburn ended in 1783, but crowds continued to gather outside Newgate yard where 'private' executions were held.

7 Highway robberies prevail in England more than in any other nation of Europe. Are not the persons who commit them frequently such as are unwilling to make their distress public, and, finding themselves sunk in spite of industry, grow desperate and run the risk of an ignominious death to satisfy these voracious harpies that occasion all their misery.

Royal Archives, Stuart Papers 123/59, 1728; F. McLynn *Crime and Punishment in 18th-century England* (1989) p.57. Highway robbery remained the offence most likely to be punished by the death penalty.

1 It was a damned scandalous villainous thing, and the most dangerous that was ever known, for them to offer to come to search a Gentleman's house, for to take away such a small sample of liquor; that should they attempt to carry it away, he would not be in their clothes for ever so much; that it would not be possible for them to carry it two miles; that he wondered that anybody dared to come to Waltham on such an account.

William Cooley and Robert Turvin, Customs House officers in Southampton, report to the Treasury, 6 Sept. 1748; PRO T/1331. The activities of customs and excise officers against smuggling were considered infringements of the rights of a free people by many in England.

2 Nearly exhausted they lay for some time, till the savages of the adjacent places rushed down upon the devoted victims. The lady was just able to lift a handkerchief up to her head, when her husband was torn from her side. They cut his buckles from his shoes, and deprived him of every covering. Happy to escape with his life, he hastened to the beach in search of his wife, when horrible to tell! her half-naked and plundered corpse presented itself to his view.

Annual Register (1774) pp.113–14. The practice of 'wrecking' was defended by coastal inhabitants as lawful claim on goods in public domain. This incident followed the wreck of the *Charming Jenny* off Anglesey in 1774. An act of Parliament in 1753 failed to stem wrecking or the belief that the practice was legitimate.

SOCIAL LIFE

3 It is very natural for a man, who is not turned for mirthful meetings of men, or assemblies of the fair sex, to delight in the sort of conversation which we find in coffee-houses. Here a man, of my temper, is in his element; for, if he cannot talk, he can still be more agreeable to his company, as well as pleased in himself, in being only a hearer.

Richard Steele, *The Spectator* no.49, 26 April 1711. The coffee-house was an institution of early 18th-century London. Many were taverns that had come to specialize in the newly available and fashionable drink of coffee. Some became

meeting-places for specialist groups, such as Lloyd's, where marine insurers met; others eventually evolved into exclusive gentlemen's clubs, such as White's or Brook's.

4 I went to bed last night it was Wedn Sept. 2, and the first thing I cast my eye upon this morning at the top of yr paper was Thursday Sept. 14 ... have I slept away 11 days in 7 hours, or how is it? For my part I don't find I am more refreshed than after a common night's sleep.

Letter in the *Gentleman's Magazine*, Sept. 1752. The Julian calendar (ascribed to Julius Caesar in 46 BC and in general use in western Europe) was modified by Pope Gregory XIII in 1582 in keeping with greater astronomical accuracy. Also known as the New Style, the revised calendar suppressed ten days. Gradually adopted by the rest of western Europe, it was not adopted by England and Scotland until 1752.

5 Give us back our eleven days!

Election campaign slogan, 1754.

6   In seventeen hundred and fifty-three
        The style it was changed to Popery.

Anon.; David Duncan Ewing *The Calendar* (1998) Ch.14. The change was painted as a Catholic plot.

7 The schools of Oxford and Cambridge were founded in a dark age of false and barbarous science; and they are still tainted with the vices of their origin. Their primitive discipline was adapted to the education of priests and monks; and the government still remains in the hands of the Clergy, an order of men, whose manners are remote from the present World, and whose eyes are dazzled by the light of Philosophy. The legal incorporation of these societies by the charters of Popes and Kings had given them a monopoly of the public instruction; and the spirit of monopolists is narrow, lazy and oppressive.

Edward Gibbon *Memoirs of my Life* (1796; 1966 edn) p.49. Gibbon spent only one academic year at Oxford University (1752–3) but found the experience so alienating that he was driven by it to convert, briefly, to Roman Catholicism. The scholarship that led him to write *The Decline and Fall of the Roman Empire* (1776–88) owed more to independent study and in Switzerland under a Reformed Church minister, Mr Pavilliard, than to the period spent at Oxford, then largely devoted to the education of Church of England clergy and the 'finishing' of gentlemen.

8 Everybody here can choose the society he prefers, as, contrary to the custom which generally prevails in England, no distinction is made between the several classes; so that you never know, unless you actually come across them, whether the Duke of York (who is seldom absent), or any other member of the royal family, is present or not; and you are not expected to take off your hat to them.

F. Kielmansegge *Diary of a Journey to England in the Years 1761–1762* (1902) p.24. Among the centres of entertainment in 18th-century London were the pleasure gardens, where different social classes could mingle on an evening, provided they could afford the entry price, and enjoy musical performances, food and drink or make public or clandestine meetings. The most prominent were Vauxhall, south of the Thames, and Ranelagh, in Chelsea; Kielmansegge was visiting the latter.

RELIGION

1 Nothing can be more disserviceable to probity and religion, than the management of the stage. It cherishes those passions, and rewards those vices, which 'tis the business of reason to discountenance. It strikes at the root of principle, draws off the inclinations from virtue, and spoils good education: 'tis the most effectual means to baffle the force of discipline, to emasculate people's spirits, and debauch their manners.

Jeremy Collier *A Short View of the Immorality and Profaneness of the English Stage* (1698) p.287. Collier (1650–1725), a non-juror (a clergyman who refused to swear allegiance to William III and Mary II on the grounds that James II could not be lawfully deposed), became famous as an opponent of the theatre on the grounds that the portrayal of ill-conduct on stage promoted the breakdown of the social and religious order. His views were widely shared and contributed towards the foundation of the Society for the Promotion of Christian Knowledge (SPCK) in 1698 in an attempt to reform England's 'manners'.

2 Surely, Sir, I am not to look upon every man as my enemy who differs from me in opinion upon any point of religion. This would be a most unchristian way of thinking, therefore I must think, that the Jews are in much the same case with the other dissenters from the Church of England: we ought not to look on them as enemies to our ecclesiastical establishment, but as men whose conscience will not allow them to conform to it; therefore we may, in charity we ought to, indulge them so far as not to endanger thereby our ecclesiastical establishment; and from them we have less danger to fear than from any other sort of dissenters, because they never attempt to make converts, and because it would be more difficult for them to succeed in any such attempt.

Henry Pelham, speech defending the Jewish naturalization bill, 17 April 1753; Cobbett Vol.14 (1813) Col.1414. The Jewish

naturalization bill, which allowed Jews to become British subjects without having to receive communion in the Church of England, became the focus of great opposition inside and outside Parliament. Pelham eventually abandoned it. Although religion was cited as the main reason for opposing the measure, behind it lay anxieties about foreign ownership of property and an eagerness on the part of Pelham's opponents to find a reason to embarrass the government before the general election due in 1754.

3 In the evening I went very unwillingly to a society in Aldersgate Street, where one was reading Luther's preface to the Epistle to the Romans. About a quarter before nine, while he was describing the change which God works in the heart through faith in Christ, Christ alone, for salvation; and an assurance was given me, that he had taken away my sins, even mine, and saved me from the law of sin and death.

John Wesley, account of his conversion, 24 May 1738; W. Gibson (ed.) *Religion and Society in England and Wales 1689–1800* (1998) p.110.

4 Those who had been members of the Church had none either to administer the Lord's Supper or to baptize their children. They applied in England over and over, but it was to no purpose. Judging this to be a case of real necessity I took a step which for peace and quietness I had refrained from taking for many years: I exercised that power which I am fully persuaded the Great Shepherd and Bishop of the Church has given me. I appointed three of our labourers to go and help them, by not only preaching the word of God, but likewise administering the Lord's Supper and baptizing their children.

John Wesley, Minutes of the Methodist Conference, 1786; Gibson (1998) p.133. Wesley was not the first extra-parochial preacher emphasizing 'new birth' as the foundation of a revived Christian life – Howell Harris and George Whitefield had gone before him – but his energies led Wesleyan Methodism to become its mainstream movement in England, if not across the British world as a whole. In 1786 he ordained three ministers despite not being a bishop, effectively separating from the Church of England; the split was formalized after his death.

IRELAND, 1689–1789

5 I still think the slaughter on the place was not 1,000 men of the enemy, nor half as many as ours, but the consequence has been of great extent.

Sir Robert Southwell, William III's secretary of state for Ireland, 4 July 1690, on the Battle of the Boyne; P. Wauchope

Patrick Sarsfield and the Williamite War (1992) p.113. Following his departure from England in Dec. 1688, James II travelled to Ireland in March 1689. He aimed to secure it against William III with French help and use it as a springboard for his restoration in England and Scotland. William arrived in June 1689, beginning a two-year war. The Battle of the Boyne, 1 July 1690, lost James II Dublin and confined effective Irish and Jacobite control of Ireland to the west and south of the country. Although it was not the decisive battle of the conflict, it was mythologized by Ulster Protestants, and the anniversary of the Boyne would later become the focus of the 'marching season' of the summer months and an enduring symbol of the perpetuation of ethnic and religious tension in Ulster.

1 It was of the Catholic aristocracy that the battle had taken its heaviest toll. There was scarce a noble family, whether Gaelic or Anglo-Norman, that did not mourn a son … Aughrim was more fatal to the old aristocracy of Ireland than Flodden had been to the knighthood of Scotland, or Agincourt to the chivalry of France … The Catholic aristocracy disappeared from the Irish scene, and the political leadership of the Irish people passed into other hands.

Diarmuid Murtagh on the Battle of Aughrim, 1691; Tony Geraghty *The Irish War* (1998) p.254. The Battle of Aughrim was fought on 12 July 1691 at Aughrim Hill, Co. Galway, between the Jacobite and Irish forces led by a French nobleman, Charles Chalmont, Marquis de St Ruth, and the mainly English army of William III, led by a Dutch nobleman, Godard van Reede-Ginckel. Ginckel's army was losing until a cannonball decapitated St Ruth; the Irish Jacobite commander Patrick Sarsfield, who had been left in an auxiliary role, ended up covering the retreat while Ginckel was victorious. Aughrim was the most decisive battle of the war between the Jacobites and William's forces and threw the emphasis of Irish resistance to William's invasion on to Limerick.

2 As low as we are now, change kings with us and we will willingly try our luck with you again.

Jacobite commander Patrick Sarsfield, 1st Earl of Lucan, to English officers after the surrender of Limerick, 1691, which marked the end of Irish military resistance to English rule; Geraghty (1998) p.256. The defeated Jacobite troops were given a choice of permanent exile in France or swearing an oath of allegiance to William. The vast majority, around 12,000 troops, threw in their lot with Sarsfield and chose exile. They would become the 'Wild Geese', a military diaspora that would fight in the armies of Spain, Naples, France and Habsburg Austria. The terms of the Treaty of Limerick, 3 Oct. 1691, negotiated between Sarsfield and William's commander, Godard van Reede-Ginckel, were later overridden and a new colonization scheme implemented, entailing confiscation from the native Irish of huge swathes of land. By the end of the 17th century more than 80% of Irish land was owned by non-Irish.

3 Have not multitudes of acts of parliament both in England and Ireland declared Ireland a complete kingdom? Is not Ireland styled in them all the kingdom or realm of Ireland? Do these names agree to a colony? Have we not a parliament and courts of judiciature? Do these things agree with a colony?

William Molyneux *The Case of Ireland* (1698) pp.115–16; S.J. Conolly *Religion, Law and Power* (1992) p.105. Molyneux helped set the agenda for Irish Protestant political claims in the 18th century: that although they lived in a subordinate kingdom they had the same rights as the king of England's Protestant subjects in Great Britain. Irish politicians who pressed this claim became known as 'patriots'.

4 The pride of England in this case, is the pride of wrong, and the pride of usurpation. The pride of Ireland is the pride of right, the pride of justice, the pride of constitution. I will not ask you, after that, which ought to give way.

Henry Flood to the Irish House of Commons, 10 June 1782; *Parliamentary Register (Ireland)* Vol.1, pp.406–7. Flood, an Irish politician of 17th-century English descent, supported the demands of many moderate patriot politicians in the Irish Commons for the repeal of British laws restricting Irish commerce, but went further in demanding that Britain repeal the Declaratory Act (1719), which asserted the right of the British Parliament to legislate for Ireland. Flood competed with Henry Grattan for the leadership of the patriot parliamentary movement. Britain assented to Irish legislative independence in 1783, but economic equality with Britain was not won, nor were many Protestant politicians interested in enfranchising the Roman Catholic majority.

5 Among them are militia regiments without a Roman Catholic officer; Roman Catholic chapels without steeples, while the board of first-fruits is erecting those marks of distinction on all churches for the established religion; and country gentlemen, to use their own expression, making 'pets' of Protestant yeomen, or in common language giving them the preference in every occurrence of life.

Edward Wakefield *Account of Ireland, Statistical and Political* (1812) Vol.2, pp.589–90. The Act of Union (1800) had been intended to incorporate Ireland into a new United Kingdom, the Irish Catholics being compensated with Catholic emancipation and the abolition of a separate Irish administration. In practice, emancipation was not immediately forthcoming, the Protestant-dominated Irish administration survived in Dublin and little was done in post-Union Ireland to meet Catholic grievances.

ECONOMIC CONDITIONS

6 Trade is the game of the Politick Public, who screen its industrious arts from the idle Nobility and Gentry by glaring, dazzling notions and starve 'em even in Lace and Grandeur, and make them administer to their Riches and plenty and are only gilded Blocks to mount them and their Families upon.

George Bowes, 1728; E. Hughes *North Country Life in the Eighteenth Century: The North East* Vol.1 (1952) p.68.

1 I think it very necessary (if not absolutely so) to have a Confederacy formed to save the coal trade from destruction and the neighbourhood of the River of Tyne from oppression.

William Cotesworth to Colonel Liddell, 1722; Hughes (1952) p.233. Cotesworth's letter led to the Grand Alliance between the major coal owners of Northumberland and Durham, first brokered in 1726 and renewed several times later into the 19th century. They agreed not to hinder each others' businesses nor help third parties to do the same, operating as a cartel to keep the price of coal high.

2 Cardiganshire … is the richest county I ever knew, and the one which contains the fewest clever or ingenious people … They have raised at Darren Vawr Hill, near Aberystwyth, for some years, 200 tons every quarter of a year, which is 800 ton per ann. The ore contains 50 to 60 ounces silver … there is a clear profit of £12,000 a year; and all within the compass of 200 yards.

Lewis Morris to William Morris, 11 Feb. 1742; H. Owen (ed.) 'Additional Letters of the Morrises of Anglesey' in *Y Cymmrodor*, Vol.49, Pt 1 (1947) p.113. Morris, a major literary figure of North Wales, was complaining that despite the abundant natural resources of Cardiganshire, the people there stuck to traditional methods and were not maximizing their resources. This tension was met several times in the early period of industrialization by those whose innovations challenged established ways of living.

3 I am obliged here to call begging an employment, since it's plain if there is more work than hands to perform it, no man that hath his limbs and his senses needs to beg and those that have not ought to be put in a condition not to want it.

Daniel Defoe *Giving Alms no Charity* (1704) pp.11–12; D. Marshall *The English Poor in the Eighteenth Century* (1926) p.232.

4 Great numbers of sturdy beggars, loose and vagrant Persons, infest the Nation, but no place more than the City of London and parts adjacent. If any person is born with any defect or deformity, or maimed by fire or other casualty, or any inveterate distemper, which renders them miserable objects, their way is open to London, where they have free liberty of showing their nauseous sights to terrify people, and force them to give money to get rid of them; and those vagrants have for many years past

moved out of several parts of the three kingdoms, and taken their station in this metropolis, to the interruption of conversation and business.

Joshua Gee *The Trade and Navigation of Great Britain Considered* (1729) p.41; Marshall (1926) p.232.

5 To provide a comfortable subsistence for the poor, is most certainly a duty highly obligatory upon every person in whom the traces of moral virtue are not quite obliterated; the performance of which is equally required by policy and religion … by employing the poor in parish workhouses, will very much promote the commerce, wealth and peace of this kingdom. These houses will also become proper schools to train up the children of the poor to religious sobriety and industry, who would otherwise be brought up in sloth, ignorance and vice. They will likewise be nurseries for spinners, weavers and other artificers, in the woollen, linen and cloth manufacture, and give occasion to the exercise of many other trades and useful employments.

William Bailey *A Treatise on the Utility of Workhouses* (1758) p.1; Marshall (1926) p.20. Throughout the 18th century complaints were aired about the inefficiency of the Poor Law of 1601, which placed the burden for supporting the unemployed on the unfortunate individual's home parish. The two acts of parliament, authored by the poor law campaigner and MP Thomas Gilbert (1720–98) and passed in 1782, attempted to distinguish between the deserving and undeserving poor and encouraged the creation of parish unions that would administer workhouses for the sick and aged and create work and shelter for the able-bodied; the administrative structures barely existed to support such a system and more lasting reform had to wait until the 1830s.

6 It was a rare thing in my memory to see any gold or silver lace on the clothes of a domestic servant in livery: lace of wool, cotton or with a mixture of silk contented us. Now we behold rich vestments, besilvered and begilded like the servants of sovereign princes.

Jonas Walden Hanway *Letters on the Importance of the Rising Generation of the Labouring Part of our Fellow Subjects* (1767) Vol.2, p.173. Hanway's complaint about the cult of luxury in the 18th century threatening social hierarchy was frequently and widely shared by other commentators.

GEORGE III, GEORGE IV AND WILLIAM IV, 1789–1837

7 Harris, I am not well; pray get me a glass of brandy.

George, Prince of Wales to James Harris (later 1st Earl of Malmesbury), 5 April 1795, on the arrival of the prince's fiancée, Princess Caroline of Brunswick-Wolfenbüttel; S. Parissien *George IV: The Grand Entertainment* (2001) p.75. The marriage took place on 8 April, but the groom and his bride were not suited. George, obsessive about self-presentation, reacted badly to the untidy and unhygienic Caroline. George had abandoned Maria Fitzherbert (see 494:2) but had then taken the Countess of Jersey as a new mistress and neglected his new wife for his gambling cronies. George and Caroline lived as man and wife for only two or three weeks, long enough, however, for Caroline to conceive a daughter, Charlotte Augusta (1796–1817).

1 None of your damned Scotch metaphysics, Mr Dundas!

George III to Henry Dundas, 28 Jan. 1801; M. Fry *The Dundas Despotism* (1992) p.238. Henry Dundas followed William Pitt, the Younger in arguing that a measure of Catholic emancipation should follow the Act of Union of 1800 that united the king-doms of Great Britain and Ireland. The king feared that a measure on the scale Pitt proposed would violate his corona-tion oath; when Dundas argued that the oath bound the king only in his executive and not his legislative capacity, the king denounced the distinction.

2 Oh, my country! How I leave my country!

The last words of William Pitt, the Younger, 23 Jan. 1806, as recorded by James Stanhope; John Ehrman *The Younger Pitt: The Consuming Struggle* (1996) p.829. Ehrman, author of a comprehensive three-part biography of Pitt, prefers this to the many other variations on Pitt's last words. Others include: 'Oh, my country! How I love my country' (a misreading of Stanhope); 'I am sorry to leave the country in such a situation' (George Canning, on the authority of Pitt's friend George Pretyman Tomline, bishop of Lincoln); and, most notoriously, 'I think I could eat one of Bellamy's pork pies' (possibly an invention of Benjamin Disraeli, who claimed he had been told the story by an old House of Commons doorkeeper).

3 That Mahomet's Paradise, Carlton House. I do not know whether *we* all looked like *Houris*, but I for one was certainly in the seventy-seventh heaven ... The sight and sound were both animating, the kettledrums and cymbals, the glitter of spangles and finery, of dress and furniture that burst upon you were quite *éblouissant*.

Lady Elizabeth Feilding to her sister, 10 Feb. 1813; E.A. Smith *George IV* (1999) p.135. While he was Prince of Wales and prince regent, George IV was renowned for his lavish entertainments, many of which were held at his seaside palace, Brighton Pavilion. His London base was Carlton House, on the north side of The Mall, which he rebuilt at the staggering cost for the day of over £300,000 in the 1780s and 1790s. The alterations were largely cosmetic and never confronted the structural problems of the house, which George demolished in 1827.

4 He only wishes to be powerful in order to exercise the most puerile caprices, gratify ridiculous resentments, indulge vulgar prejudices, and amass or squander money; not one great object connected with national glory or prosperity ever enters his brain.

Charles Greville, courtier and diarist, 1829; Smith (1999) p.268. In his later years George IV was blind and increasingly confused. He was also reactionary in his politics. As a recluse who no longer held social gatherings, his selfishness became more obvious to those around him and to the country. When he died in 1830 the obituaries were unprecedentedly hostile.

5 Why, damn it all, such a position was never held by any Greek or Roman: and if it only lasts three months, it will be worth while to have been Prime Minister of England.

Tom Young, private secretary to William Lamb, 2nd Viscount Melbourne, when Melbourne was contemplating rejecting William IV's invitation to become prime minister, July 1834, attrib.; David Cecil *Lord M* (1954) p.111.

The American Revolution, 1761–91

PRELIMINARIES TO DIVORCE, 1761–75

1 An extensive empire must be supported by a refined system of policy and oppression: in the centre, an absolute power, prompt in action and rich in resources; a swift and easy communication with the extreme parts; fortifications to check the first effort of rebellion; a regular administration to protect and punish; and a well-disciplined army to inspire fear, without provoking discontent and despair.

The historian Edward Gibbon *The Decline and Fall of the Roman Empire* Vol.5 (1788) Ch.49. Gibbon was writing of the Carolingian empire (see 186:6) but may well have had in mind the experience of the British empire in North America. He is said to have met Benjamin Franklin in France in 1777, the year after the publication of the first volumes of *Decline and Fall*, when Franklin was reported to have asked him if he were contemplating a work on the decline and fall of the British empire. The story, perhaps apocryphal, is related in William Cobbett *Works* (Vol.7, p.244).

2   Westward the course of empire takes its way;
      The first four acts already past,
      A fifth shall close the drama of the day:
      Time's noblest offspring is the last.

Bishop George Berkeley *On the Prospect of Planting Arts and Learning in America* (1729). The Irish philosopher Berkeley was living in the colony of Rhode Island at the time. This is a remarkable augury of the imperialism that Americans themselves came to express, in, for instance, the paraphrase by John Quincy Adams in his Plymouth Oration of 22 Dec. 1802: 'Westward the star of empire takes its way.'

3 Indeed, my lord, I don't know whether the neighbourhood of the French [in Canada] to our North American colonies was not the greatest security for their dependence on the mother country, which I feel will be slighted by them when their apprehension of the French is removed.

Duke of Bedford to Duke of Newcastle, 9 May 1761. Bedford was in charge of the negotiations with France to end the war that began in 1756, the global conflict known in Britain as the Seven Years War and in the United States as the French and Indian War.

4 We do hereby strictly forbid, on pain of our displeasure, all our loving subjects from making any purchases or settlements whatever, or taking possession of any of the lands above reserved, without our special leave and license for that purpose first obtained.

George III, proclamation, 7 Oct. 1763; Henry Steele Commager (ed.) *Documents of American History* (1973 edn) p.49. The king was referring to lands reserved to the Indians west of the Appalachian mountains, thus barring colonial settlement in the area and presenting the colonists with a serious grievance against Britain.

5 The several changes in interests and territories which have taken place in the colonies of the European world in the Event of Peace, have created a general impression of some new state of things arising … some general idea of some revolution of events, beyond the ordinary course of things.

Thomas Pownall *The Administration of the Colonies* (1764) p.1. Pownall, a former governor of Massachusetts, utters a remarkable premonition.

6 This country cannot be long subject to Great Britain, nor indeed to any distant power; its extent is so great, the daily increase of its inhabitants so considerable, and having everything within themselves for (more than) their own defence, that no nation whatsoever seems better calculated for independency.

A French traveller in America, 1765; H. Aptheker *The American Revolution 1763–1783* (1960) p.32. The population of the American colonies at this time was approaching 3 million, roughly half the size of the English population.

7 Caesar had his Brutus – Charles the First, his Cromwell; and George the Third ('Treason!' cried the Speaker …) – *may profit by their example*. If *this* be treason, make the most of it!

Patrick Henry in the Virginia legislature, 29 May 1765; Richard Beeman *Patrick Henry* (1974) pp.37–8. The quick-witted Henry was protesting against the Stamp Act of 23 March 1765, whereby the British Parliament levied excise duties on the 13 American colonies towards the cost of their defence. 'Treason' because Marcus Junius Brutus took part in the assassination of Julius Caesar in 44 BC (see 75:8) and because Oliver Cromwell ordained the execution of Charles I on 30 Jan. 1649 (see 423:2). Notes by a French observer of the speech, discovered in 1921, suggest that Henry in fact apologized after the Speaker's intervention, although Henry's biographer, William Wirt, is said to have checked the wording with the former president, Thomas Jefferson, who was also present in the House of Burgesses in 1765.

1 They always had their Geniuses, who (by the *Mob Whistle*, as horrid as the *Iroquois Yell* ...) could fabricate the Structure of Rebellion from a single Straw ... As for the People in general, they were like the Mobility of all Countries, perfect Machines wound up by any Hand who might first take the Winch.

Peter Oliver, chief justice of Massachusetts, commenting on the 1764 pamphlet by the dissident James Otis of Massachusetts, *Right of the British Colonies Asserted and Proved*; Douglas Adair and John A. Schutz (eds) *Peter Oliver's Origins and Progress of the American Revolution: A Tory View* (1967) pp.65, 74–5. The Iroquois Yell was the war-whoop of the Indian tribe based in what is now upstate New York.

2 It may be called silly and mad, but mad people, or persons who have entertained silly and mad ideas, have led the people to rebellion, and over-turned empires.

Lord Chief Justice Mansfield in the House of Lords, 24 Feb. 1766, taking Otis's broadside more seriously; William Cobbett (ed.) *Parliamentary History* Vol.13 (1813) Col.172.

3 The said colonies and plantations in *America* have been, are, and of right ought to be, subordinate unto, and dependent upon the imperial crown and parliament of *Great Britain*.

Declaratory Act, 18 March 1766; Commager (1973 edn) pp.60–61. The act was passed soon after the repeal of the Stamp Act, a practical concession followed immediately by a full-blooded assertion in principle of British supremacy.

4 I am fully persuaded with you, that a *Consolidating Union*, by a fair and equal representation of all the parts of this empire in Parliament, is the only firm basis on which its political grandeur and prosperity can be founded.

Benjamin Franklin to Lord Kames, 11 April 1767; Esmond Wright (ed.) *Benjamin Franklin* (1989) p.156. Franklin, then agent of the Pennsylvania Assembly in London, was proposing a conciliatory solution to the Anglo-American quarrel.

5 If Great Britain can order us to come to her for necessaries we want and can order us to pay what taxes she pleases before we take them away, or when we land them here, we are as abject as France and Poland can show in wooden shoes and with uncombed hair.

John Dickinson *The Farmer's Letters* no.2, 7 Dec. 1767. Dickinson was commenting on the Townshend Revenue Act of 29 June 1767, by which Britain imposed customs duties on certain imports into the American colonies.

6 Quash this spirit at a Blow without too much regard to Expence and it will prove economy in the End. If the Principles of Moderation and Forbearance are again adopted ... there will be an End to these Provinces as British Colonies.

General Thomas Gage to the secretary at war, Lord Barrington, 28 June 1768; John Shy *A People Numerous and Armed* (1976) p.90. Gage (1721–87) was commander of British forces in North America.

7 They left their native land in search of freedom, and found it in a desert. Divided as they are into a thousand forms of policy and religion, there is one point in which they all agree:- they equally detest the pageantry of a king, and the supercilious hypocrisy of a bishop.

The anon. pamphleteer 'Junius', 19 Dec. 1769; John Cannon (ed.) *The Letters of JUNIUS* (1978) p.167. The identity of 'Junius', here holding the king responsible for the rift with America, as well as his ministers in Parliament, has never been established, although several candidates, including Sir Philip Francis, have been put forward.

8 I immediately dressed myself in the costume of an Indian ... having painted my face and hands with coal dust in the shop of a blacksmith ... We then were ordered by our commander to open the hatches and take out all the chests of tea and throw them overboard ... first cutting and splitting the chests with our tomahawks, so as thoroughly to expose them to the effects of the water.

George Hewes, a participant in the 'Boston Tea Party' of 16 Dec. 1773, a spectacular protest against the Revenue Act of 1767; Alfred F. Young 'George Hewes' in *William and Mary Quarterly* (1981) pp.591–2. Hewes, then aged 91, was interviewed by the writer James Hawkes in 1833. His disguise, though crude, was necessary to avoid identification.

9 I would rather [they] were led up to the altar, on to the Liberty Tree, there to be exalted and rewarded according to their merit or demerit than that Britain should disgrace herself by receding from her just authority.

The reaction of the British prime minister, Lord North, to the news of the Boston Tea Party, Jan. 1774; Hugh Brogan *Longman History of the United States of America* (1985 edn) p.165. The Liberty Tree was a large elm in Boston, dedicated in Sept. 1765 as a focus for protests against the Stamp Act. North clearly saw it as a gallows for traitors.

10 I believe England will be conquered some day or other in New England or Bengal.

Horace Walpole to Sir Horace Mann, 2 Feb. 1774; *The Letters of Horace Walpole* (1904 edn) Vol.8, p.419. Bengal had to wait until 1947 (see 864:6).

1 Like a young phoenix she will arise full plumed and glorious from her mother's ashes.

Arthur Lee to Samuel Adams, 24 Dec. 1772; *The Life of Arthur Lee* Vol.1 (1829) p.225. Lee was looking forward to an America loosed from Britain's apron-strings.

2 If we neither can govern the Americans nor be governed by them; if we can neither unite with them, nor ought to subdue them; what remains, but to part with them on as friendly terms as we can?

Josiah Tucker *The True Interest of Great-Britain Set Forth with Regard to the Colonies* (1774). Tucker was dean of Gloucester Cathedral and a rare advocate of American independence.

3 The inhabitants of the English colonies in North America, by the immutable laws of Nature, the principles of the English constitution, and the several charters or compacts, have the following right ... They are entitled to life, liberty and property, and they have never ceded to any sovereign power whatever a right to dispose of either without their consent.

Declaration of Rights of the First Continental Congress, 14 Oct. 1774; National Archives and Records Service *The Formation of the Union* (1970) p.8.

4 I think I can announce it as a fact, that it is not the wish or interest of that government, or any other upon the continent, separately or collectively, to set up for independency. I am as well satisfied as I can be of my existence that no such thing is desired by any thinking man in all North America.

George Washington to Captain Robert Mackenzie, 9 Oct. 1774; *The Writings of George Washington* Vol.3 (1931) pp.244 ff. The future commanding general of the Revolution was no hot-headed radical.

5 If I must be enslaved, let it be by a KING at least, and not by a parcel of upstart lawless Committee-men. If I must be devoured, let me be devoured by the jaws of a lion, and not *gnawed* to death by rats and vermin.

Samuel Seabury *Free Thoughts on the Proceedings of the Congress*, 16 Nov. 1774; William Nelson *The American Tory* (1961) p.76. Seabury, together with a third of the population of the colonies, was a devoted loyalist.

6 I am not sorry that the line of conduct seems now chalked out ... The New England Governments are in a state of rebellion, blows must decide whether they are to be a subject to this country or independent ... The people are ripe for mischief ... We must either master them or totally leave them to themselves and treat them as aliens.

George III to Lord North, 18 and 19 Nov. 1774; Esmond Wright (ed.) *The Fire of Liberty* (1983) p.18.

7 The next Augustan age will dawn on the other side of the Atlantic. There will, perhaps, be a Thucydides at Boston, a Xenophon at New York.

Horace Walpole to Sir Horace Mann, 24 Nov. 1774; *The Letters of Horace Walpole* Vol.10 (1904 edn) p.100. A pro-American view from the son of Britain's first prime minister. The reign of the first Roman emperor, Augustus, was seen as the pinnacle of the Roman imperial achievement. For Thucydides and Xenophon see 52:3 and 52:6.

8 Our disputes with North America have not at present the foundation of Interest, for the contest will cost us more than we can ever gain by our success.

Lord Barrington to Lord Dartmouth, 24 Dec. 1774; Shy (1976) p.288, n.30. Dartmouth, the American secretary at the Foreign Office, was, like the king, a hard-liner.

9 This I know, a successful resistance is a *revolution*, not a *rebellion*. Who knows whether in a few years the *independent* Americans may not celebrate the glorious era of the revolution of 1775 as we do that of 1688?

Lord Mayor of London, John Wilkes, in the House of Commons, 2 Feb. 1775; *Parliamentary History* Vol.18 (1813) Col.238.

10 To conquer a great continent of 1,800 miles, containing three millions of people, all indissolubly united on the great Whig bottom of liberty and justice, seems an undertaking not to be rashly engaged in ... It is obvious, my lords, that you cannot furnish armies, or treasure, competent to the mighty purpose of subduing America [and] whether France and Spain will be tame, inactive spectators of your efforts and distractions, is well worthy the consideration of your lordships.

Lord Camden in the House of Lords, 16 March 1775; *Parliamentary History* Vol.18 (1813) Cols 441–3. A prophetic utterance on both counts.

11 Is life so dear, or peace so sweet, as to be purchased at the price of chains and slavery? Forbid it, Almighty God! I know not what course others may take, but as for me, give me liberty or give me death!

Patrick Henry to the Virginia Convention, 23 March 1775; William Wirt *Sketches of the Life and Character of Patrick Henry* (1817). There is some doubt as to whether Henry spoke these much-quoted words. Like Henry's speech of 29 May 1765 (see 500:7), it may have been reconstructed by Wirt.

1 We won't be their Negroes. I say we are as handsome as old English folks, and so should be as free.

John Adams, *Boston Gazette*, 1774; Niall Ferguson *Empire* (2003) p.93. The future president of the United States equates British colonialism with American enslavement.

2 If slavery thus be fatally contagious, how is it that we hear the loudest yelps for liberty among the drivers of Negroes?

Samuel Johnson *Taxation No Tyranny*, a pamphlet written at the British government's request and completed in early March 1775; *The Works of Samuel Johnson* Vol.10 (1977) p.454.

3 Magnanimity in politics is not seldom the truest wisdom; and a great empire and little minds go ill together.

The Irish politician Edmund Burke in the House of Commons, 22 March 1775; *Parliamentary History* Vol.18 (1813) Cols 535–6.

OUTBREAK OF WAR, 1775–6

4   And yet, through the gloom and the light,
        The fate of a nation was riding that night;
        And the spark struck out by that steed in his
            flight
        Kindled the land into flame with its heat.

Henry Wadsworth Longfellow 'Paul Revere's Ride'. The poem was completed on 19 April 1860, almost 85 years to the day in 1775 when Revere rode out to warn of a British army force marching to seize a cache of weapons stored by the American militia at Concord, Massachusetts. Revere was intercepted before he reached Concord. One of his two fellow riders did get through, but Revere was given all the glory.

5 Stand your guard. Don't fire unless fired upon, but if they mean to have a war, let it begin here.

Captain John Parker, commander of the militiamen on the green at Lexington, Massachusetts, where the first Americans were killed by British troops in the early hours of 19 April 1775; attrib.

6   By the rude bridge that arched the flood,
        Their flag to April's breeze unfurled,
        Here once the embattled farmers stood,
        And fired the shot heard round the world.

Ralph Waldo Emerson 'Concord Hymn' (4 July 1837), written in celebration of the clash at Concord, Massachusetts, 19 April 1775, shortly after the engagement at Lexington.

7 Even women had firelocks. One was seen to fire a blunderbuss between her father and her husband from their windows. There they three, with an infant child, soon suffered the fury of the day.

Anon. British observer of the British withdrawal from Concord on 19 April 1775; Wright (1983) pp.26–7. The British army wreaked vengeance on roadside houses for the losses they suffered from American snipers as they marched back to Boston.

8   They came three thousand miles, and died,
            To keep the Past upon its throne;
        · Unheard, beyond the ocean tide,
            Their English mother made her moan.

James Russell Lowell 'Graves of Two English Soldiers on Concord Battleground' (1849).

9 Don't one of you fire until you see the whites of their eyes!

Colonel William Prescott, commander of the American militia on Breed's Hill, Boston, 17 June 1775; attrib. This is the engagement known as the Battle of Bunker Hill, when American militiamen fortified the heights overlooking Boston harbour, forcing the British to take them in a murderous uphill struggle. Also credited to Israel Putnam, although he probably transmitted Prescott's order to the militiamen.

10 I did not leave the entrenchment until the enemy got in. I then retreated ten or fifteen rods [55 to 80 yards]; then I received a wound to my rite arm, the bawl going through a little below my elbow, breaking the little shel bone. Another bawl struck my back, taking a piece of skin about as big as a penny. But I got to Cambridge that night.

Amos Farnsworth, a fighter on Breed's Hill; Wright (1983) p.35. Cambridge is 8 miles from the hill.

11 It was a dear bought victory; another such would have ruined us.

General Sir Henry Clinton MP; Wright (1983) p.37. Clinton was speaking after the seizure of Breed's Hill in which the British assault force lost some 40% of its officers and men killed and wounded.

12 The trials we have had show that the rebels are not the despicable rabble too many have supposed them to be, and I find it owing to a military spirit encouraged among them for a few years past, joined with an uncommon degree of zeal and enthusiasm, that they are otherwise.

General Gage to Lord Dartmouth, 25 June 1775; K.G. Davies (ed.) *Documents of the American Revolution* Vol.9 (1975) p.199. Gage was doubtless referring to such grandees as Earl of Sandwich, who in the House of Lords on 16 March 1775 had said: 'Suppose the colonies do abound in men, what does that signify? They are raw, undisciplined, cowardly men'

(*Parliamentary History* Vol.18 (1813) Col.446). Gage was replaced by General Sir William Howe in Oct. 1775.

1 Respect, and control, and subordination of government … depend in a great measure upon the idea that trained troops are invincible against any numbers or any position of undisciplined rabble; and this idea was a little in suspense since the 19th April.

General John Burgoyne to the colonial secretary, Lord George Germain, 20 August 1775; Shy (1976) p.103. Burgoyne was explaining the decision to mount a frontal assault on Breed's Hill in order to wipe out the notion, current since Lexington and Concord on 19 April, that the Americans were a serious fighting force.

2 If America and Britain should come to a hostile rupture I am afraid an insurrection among the slaves may and will be promoted … It is prudent such attempts should be concealed as well as suppressed.

The future president, James Madison, Nov. 1774; Jeremy Black *The War for America* (1998 edn) p.33.

3 I do hereby … declare all indented servants, Negroes or others (appertaining to Rebels) free, that are able and willing to bear arms, they joining His Majesty's Troops as soon as may be, for the more speedily reducing this Colony to a proper sense of their duty to His Majesty's crown and dignity.

Lord Dunmore, governor of Virginia, proclamation, 7 Nov. 1775; P.L. Force (ed.) *American Archives* 4th Series, Vol.3, p.1385.

4 If my Dear Sir that Man is not crushed before Spring, he will become the most formidable Enemy America has – his strength will increase as a Snow ball by Rolling; and faster, if some expedient cannot be hit upon to convince the Slaves and Servants of the Impotency of His designs.

General George Washington to Richard Henry Lee, 26 Dec. 1775, on Dunmore's proclamation; *Writings of George Washington* Vol.2, p.611. Washington himself was, of course, a slave-owner.

5 Every Argument which can be urged in Favor of our own Liberties will certainly operate with equal Force in Favor of that of the Negroes: nor can we with any Propriety contend for the one while we withhold the other.

Ebeneezer Hazard, 1777; Duncan MacLeod *Slavery, Race and the American Revolution* (1974) pp.17–18.

6 There is something absurd, in supposing a Continent to be perpetually governed by an island.

In no instance hath nature made the satellite larger than its primary planet; and as England and America, with respect to each other, reverse the common order of nature, it is evident that they belong to different systems. England to Europe; America to itself … Every spot of the old world is overrun with oppression. Freedom hath been hunted round the Globe. Asia and Africa have long expelled her. Europe regards her like a stranger, and England hath given her warning to depart. O! receive the fugitive and prepare in time an asylum for mankind.

Tom Paine *Common Sense* 10 Jan. 1776; M.D. Conway (ed.) *The Writings of Thomas Paine* (1894 edn) Vol.1, pp.92, 100–1. The English radical Paine, a devotee of revolution, first in America, then in France (see 518:4), served in the American army.

7 What a poor, ignorant, malicious, short-sighted, crapulous mass, is Tom Paine's *Common Sense*.

John Adams to Thomas Jefferson, 22 June 1819; *Adams–Jefferson Letters* Vol.2 (1959) p.542.

8 If any of the provinces of the British empire cannot be made to contribute towards the support of the whole empire, it is surely time that Great Britain should free herself from the expence of defending these provinces in time of war, and of supporting any part of their civil or military establishments in time of peace, and endeavour to accommodate her future views and designs to the real mediocrity of her circumstances.

Adam Smith *An Inquiry into the Nature and Causes of the Wealth of Nations* (1776) Bk 5, Ch.3. The celebrated Scots economist was one of the first to support the idea of American independence.

INDEPENDENCE PROCLAIMED, 1776

9 I long to hear that you have declared an independency – and by the way in the new Code of Laws I suppose it will be necessary for you to make I desire you would Remember the Ladies, and be more generous and favourable to them than your ancestors. Do not put such unlimited power in the hands of the Husbands. Remember all Men would be tyrants if they could. If perticular care is not paid to the Ladies we are determined to foment a Rebellion, and will not hold ourselves bound by any laws in which we have no voice, or Representation.

Abigail Adams to her husband, John, 31 March 1776; Richard D. Brown (ed.) *Major Problems in the Era of the American Revolution* (1992) pp.302–5.

1 That these colonies are, and of right ought to be, free and independent States, that they are absolved from all allegiance to the British Crown, and that all political connection between them and the State of Great Britain is, and ought to be, totally dissolved.

Resolution by Richard Henry Lee, adopted by the second Continental Congress on 2 July 1776; Commager (1973 edn) p.100.

2 The Second Day of July 1776 ... ought to be commemorated, as the Day of Deliverance by solemn Acts of Devotion to God Almighty. It ought to be solemnized with Pomp and Parade, with Shews, Games, Sports, Guns, Bells, Bonfires and Illuminations from one End of this Continent to the other from this Time forward forever more.

John Adams to his wife, Abigail, 3 July 1776; *Adams Family Correspondence* Vol.2 (1963) p.30. The day of jubilee was, of course, to be 4 July, when American independence was more elaborately declared in Jefferson's deathless proclamation.

3 We hold these Truths to be self-evident, that all Men are created equal, that they are endowed by their Creator with certain unalienable Rights, that among these are Life, Liberty and the Pursuit of Happiness – That to secure these Rights, Governments are instituted among Men, deriving their just Powers from the Consent of the Governed, that whenever any Form of Government becomes destructive of these Ends, it is the Right of the People to alter or to abolish it and to institute new Government, laying its Foundation on such Principles and organizing its Powers in such Form, as to them shall seem most likely to effect their Safety and Happiness.

Thomas Jefferson, Declaration of Independence, 4 July 1776; National Archives and Records Service *The Formation of the Union* (1970) p.26.

4 He has waged cruel war against human Nature itself, violating it's most sacred rights of Life and Liberty in the persons of a distant People, who never offended him, captivating and carrying them into Slavery in another Hemisphere, or to incur miserable Death in their Transportation thither.

This clause in Jefferson's Declaration, indicting George III for the slave trade, was deleted at the insistence of the delegates from South Carolina and Georgia; J.R. Pole (ed.) *The Revolution*

in America 1754–1788 (1970) Pt 1. Jefferson was himself a slave-owner.

5 The *Thing* is in its nature so good, that no Cookery can spoil the Dish for the palates of Freemen.

Richard Henry Lee, consoling an anguished Jefferson after the revision of his draft Declaration; Saul Padover *Jefferson* (1942) p.63.

6 The Declaration of Independence I always considered as a theatrical show. Jefferson ran away with all the stage effect of that ... and all the glory of it.

The famously acidulous John Adams to the physician Dr Benjamin Rush, 21 June 1811.

7 Glittering generalities! They are blazing ubiquities!

Ralph Waldo Emerson to Rufus Choate, 1856, after Choate had spoken of 'the glittering and sounding generalities of natural right which make up the Declaration of Independence'.

8 The Declaration of Independence was a piece of literature, a salad of illusions. Admiration for the noble savage, for the ancient Romans (whose republic was founded on slavery and war), mixed with the quietistic maxims of the Sermon on the Mount, may inspire a Rousseau but it cannot guide a government.

George Santayana *The Middle Span* (1945) Ch.8.

9 [It] gave liberty not alone to the people of this country, but hope to all the world, for all future time ... I would rather be assassinated on the spot than surrender it.

President Abraham Lincoln, 22 Feb. 1861; J.G. Nicolay and John Hay (eds) *Abraham Lincoln: Complete Works* (1920 edn) Vol.1, p.691. Lincoln died from an assassin's bullet on 15 April 1865.

10 Long did I endeavour, with unfeigned and unwearied zeal, to preserve from breaking that fine and noble china vase, the British Empire for I knew that, once being broken, the separate parts could not retain even their shares of the strength and value that existed in the whole, and that a perfect reunion of those parts could scarce ever be hoped for.

Benjamin Franklin to Admiral Lord Howe, commander of the British fleet, 20 July 1776; Wright (1983) p.217.

11 There, I guess King George will be able to read that.

John Hancock, president of the Continental Congress, after appending a huge signature to the Declaration of Independence at the signing ceremony on 2 Aug. 1776; attrib.

'John Hancock' subsequently became common American parlance for 'signature'.

1 Gentlemen, we must now all hang together or we shall most assuredly hang separately.

Benjamin Franklin, after the signing of the Declaration, 2 Aug. 1776; attrib.

2 *E Pluribus Unum* (One out of Many)

Motto for the Great Seal of the United States, proposed by Adams, Franklin and Jefferson on 10 Aug. 1776 and adopted on 20 June 1782. Ironically, also the motto of *The Gentleman's Magazine* (see 506:3), a compilation of reprinted newspaper articles.

3 We hold, they say, these truths to be self-evident: That all men are created equal. In what are they created equal? Is it in size, strength, understanding, figure, moral or civil accomplishments, or situation of life? All men, it is true, are equally created, but what is this to the purpose? Every plough-man knows that they are not created equal in any of these. It is certainly no reason why the Americans should turn rebels, because the people of Great-Britain are their fellow creatures, *i.e.* are created as well as themselves.

The Gentleman's Magazine, Sept. 1776, pp.403–4.

4 An Influenza more wonderful and at the same time more general than that of the Witchcraft in the Province of Massachuset's Bay in the last Century! The Annals of no Country can produce an Instance of so virulent a Rebellion, of such implacable madness and Fury, originating from such trivial Causes, as those alledged by these unhappy People.

Ambrose Serle, under secretary for the colonies, 1776; *The American Journal of Ambrose Serle* (1940) pp.46–7. The witch-craft reference is to the trial at Salem, Massachusetts, in 1692, after which 20 people (mostly women) were hanged (see 432:4). The episode was dramatized by Arthur Miller in his 1953 play *The Crucible*, a barely disguised indictment of McCarthyism (see 902:10).

STRUGGLE FOR MASTERY, 1776–9

5 I only regret that I have but one life to lose for my country.

Nathan Hale, before being hanged by the British as a spy, 22 Sept. 1776; George Dudley Seymour *Captain Nathan Hale* (1933) p.39. Hale may well have been quoting from Joseph Addison's *Cato* (1713), a favourite inspiration for Americans who were fond of comparing the United States with the

Roman Republic. In Act 4, Sc.4 come the lines: 'What pity is it/That we can die but once to serve our country!'

6 To place any dependence upon Militia, is, assuredly, resting upon a broken staff. Men just dragged from the tender Scenes of domestick life, unaccustomed to the din of Arms; totally unacquainted with every kind of Military Skill, which being followed by a want of confidence in themselves, when opposed to Troops regularly trained, disciplined, and appointed, superior in knowledge and superior in Arms, makes them timid and ready to fly from their own shadows.

General George Washington to John Hancock, 24 Sept. 1776; *Writings of George Washington* Vol.6, pp.106–15.

7 These are the times that try men's souls. The summer soldier and the sunshine patriot will, in this crisis, shrink from the service of their country; but he that stands it *now*, deserves the love and thanks of man and woman. Tyranny, like hell, is not easily conquered; yet we have this consolation with us, that the harder the conflict the more glorious the triumph.

Tom Paine 'The American Crisis' no.1, 19 Dec. 1776; *The Works of Thomas Paine* (1894 edn) p.170. Written after a sharp setback for the Americans, Washington's retreat from New Jersey to Philadelphia, Paine's pamphlet was read out to the army on 23 Dec. and helped to galvanize it into a new attack across the River Delaware, launched on Christmas Night.

8 As the rascals are skulking about the whole country, it is impossible to move with any degree of safety without a pretty large escort, and even then you are exposed to a dirty kind of *tiraillerie* [sniper-fire].

James Murray, a British officer, to his sister, 25 Feb. 1777; Eric Robson (ed.) *Letters from America 1773–1780* (1951) p.38.

9 The regaining their affection is an idle idea, it must be the convincing them that it is in their interest to submit, and then they will dread further broils.

George III, criticizing the relative leniency of General Howe and his brother Admiral Lord Howe, spring 1777; Piers Mackesy *The War for America 1775–1783* (1964) p.150. General Howe was replaced by General Sir Henry Clinton the following year.

10 We beat them tonight or Molly Stark's a widow!

The American Colonel John Stark before the Battle of Bennington, 16 Aug. 1777. Stark survived, as he had survived Breed's Hill; he lived to be 93.

1 Cannons Roaring muskets Cracking Drums Beating Bumbs Flying all Round. Men a dying woundeds Horred Grones which would Greave the Heardist Hearts to See Such a Dollful Sight as this to see our Fellow Creators Slain in Such a manner.
Elisha Stevens, an American soldier at the Battle of Brandywine Creek, 11 Sept. 1777, an American defeat; Charles Royster *A Revolutionary People at War* (1979) p.225.

2 *BURGOYNE:* Jobbery and snobbery, incompetence and Red Tape. I have just learnt, sir, that General Howe is still in New York … He has received no orders, sir. Some gentleman in London forgot to despatch them. He was leaving for his holiday, I believe. To avoid upsetting his arrangements, England will lose her American colonies.
George Bernard Shaw *The Devil's Disciple* Act 3 (1896). Shaw, the inveterate Irish gadfly of the English ruling-class, repeats the myth that Lord George Germain did not order Howe to advance north to meet Burgoyne marching south from Canada and so brought about Burgoyne's surrender at Saratoga on 17 Oct.; for the reality, see Mackesy (1964) pp.117–18. Germain left it to his secretary to draft the order on his behalf; the secretary sent it, but did not keep a copy.

3 The voice of fame, ere this reaches you, will tell how greatly fortunate we have been in this department. Burgoyne and his whole army have laid down their arms, and surrendered themselves to me and my Yankees … If Old England is not by this lesson taught humility, then she is an obstinate old slut, bent upon her ruin.
General Thomas Gates to his wife, 20 Oct. 1777; Wright (1983) p.108.

4 It ought to be engraven on the tombs of the 800 who fell in the late action, 'Passenger, go tell in England that we died for having violated her holy constitution.'
John Wilkes in the House of Commons, 10 Dec. 1777; *Parliamentary History* Vol.19 (1814) Cols 567–8. Wilkes was adapting the inscription on the memorial to the Spartans who died at Thermopylae: 'Go tell the Spartans, you who pass us by, that here, obedient to their laws, we lie' (see 55:5).

5 [I hope] they will not think of sending more troops; for I suppose they may as well think of subduing the moon as America by force of arms.
Duke of Marlborough's reaction to the news of the surrender at Saratoga; Charles Ritcheson *British Politics and the American Revolution* (1954) p.234.

6 Poor food – hard lodging – cold weather – fatigue – nasty clothes – vomit half my time – soaked out of my senses – the Devil's in it – I can't endure it – why are we sent here to starve and freeze?
Albigence Waldo at Valley Forge, 14 Dec. 1777; Wright (1983) pp.16–17. Despite Saratoga, this was a low point in American morale.

7 You cannot, I venture to say, *you cannot conquer America.* If I were an American, as I am an Englishman, while a foreign troop was landed in my country, I never would lay down my arms, never – never – never!
Earl Chatham, 18 Nov. 1777, on the British use of Hessian mercenaries; *Parliamentary History* Vol.19 (1814) Col.363.

8 The contest now was not whether America should be dependent on the British Parliament, but whether Great Britain or America should be independent. Both could not be so, for such would be the power of that vast continent across the Atlantic that was her independence, this island must expect to be made a dependent province.
Earl Nugent in the House of Lords, 21 Nov. 1777; *Parliamentary History* Vol.19 (1814) Col.442. A prophecy that was to be realized in the 20th century.

9 By Heavens! If our rulers had any modesty, they would blush at the idea of calling in foreign aid! It is really abominable, that we should send to France for soldiers, when there are so many sons of America idle.
Major Samuel Shaw on hearing the news of the Franco-American alliance of 6 Feb. 1778; Wright (1983) pp.121–2. The alliance was dedicated to American 'liberty, sovereignty and independence absolute and unlimited'.

10 The sun of Great-Britain is set, and we shall no longer be a powerful or respectable people, the moment that the independency of America is agreed to by our government!
Earl Shelburne, 5 March 1778, reacting to the news of the Franco-American alliance; *Parliamentary History* Vol.19 (1814) Cols 850–51. As prime minister in 1782 Shelburne began negotiations for a peace treaty based on American independence.

11 I would cement the two countries together by a mutual naturalization, in all rights and franchises to the fullest extent. We are derived from the same stock, the same temper, the same love of liberty and of independence; and if we must be seemingly divided, let there be at least an union in that partition.
David Hartley MP, 9 April 1778; *Parliamentary History* Vol.19 (1814) Cols 1077–8. Hartley's project of an Anglo-American partnership was based on the desire to nullify the

Franco-American alliance, which faced Britain with a war on two fronts.

1 I am willing to love all mankind, *except an American*.
Samuel Johnson, 15 April 1778; James Boswell *The Life of Samuel Johnson* (1791).

2 The enemy killed, scalp't, and most barbarously murdered thirty-two women and children … burnt twenty-four houses with all the grain [and] committed the most inhuman barbarities on most of the dead.
Survivor's account of an Indian attack led by the British on Cherry Valley, New York, Nov. 1778; Wright (1983) p.146.

3 We had driven out the brat in his infancy and exposed him in an uncultivated forest to the mercy of wild beasts and savages without any further inquiry after him, 'till we imagined he might be brought to render us some essential services. We then took him again under our parental protection; provided him with a strait waistcoat, and whenever he wriggled or winched, drew it up a hole tighter, and behaved so like a step-mother to our son, now grown a very tall boy, that he determined to strip off his waistcoat, and put on the togs at once, and is now actually *carrying fire and water through the whole empire* wherever he pleases.
Josiah Wedgwood to Thomas Bentley, 9 May 1779; *Selected Letters of Josiah Wedgwood* (1965) pp.232–3.

4 Should America succeed … the West Indies must follow them … Ireland would soon follow the same plan and be a separate state. Then this island would be a poor island indeed.
George III to Lord North, 11 June 1779; Sir John Fortescue *The Correspondence of King George the Third* (1967 edn) Vol.4, p.351. The British West Indies did not, in fact, begin to achieve independence until the 1960s. Ireland was granted its own parliament in 1780, and after a failed rebellion in 1798 lost it through the Act of Union in 1800.

5 I have not yet begun to fight!
John Paul Jones, American captain of the *Bonhomme Richard* at the outset of his victorious engagement with HMS *Serapis* off Flamborough Head, Yorkshire, on 23 Sept. 1779; attrib.

6 An English aunt sent word that if the report was true she hoped he would have an arm or a leg shot off in his first battle. She had her wish, as he lost one [leg] on 9th October [1779 at the Battle of Savannah]. After the war, he placed the leg bone in an elephant mahogany case, to which he affixed the date of the loss. This [Samuel] Warren sent to his aunt with a note to the effect that, while her wish had been fulfilled, he would rather be a rebel with one leg than a royalist with two.
William B. Stevens; A.L. Lawrence *Storm over Savannah* (1951). The aunt may have had the satisfaction of knowing that the American attack on Savannah was a complete disaster.

7 The demand for quarter, seldom refused to a vanquished foe, was at once found to be in vain. Not a man was spared, and it was the concurrent testimony of all the survivors that for fifteen minutes after every man was prostrate, they went over the ground, plunging their bayonets into everyone that exhibited any signs of life.
The American surgeon, Dr Robert Brownfield, on the massacre of several hundred Virginia troops by the men of the Tory Colonel Banastre Tarleton in mid-May 1780 after the Battle of Waxhaw Creek, after they had raised a flag of surrender; Wright (1983) pp.186–7. The American film *The Patriot* (2000) portrays the British and their Tory collaborators as a merciless partnership, but atrocities were committed by both sides in the war.

8 Our countrymen have all the folly of the ass and all the passiveness of the sheep in their composition. They are determined not to be free … If we are saved, France and Spain must save us.
Alexander Hamilton to John Laurens, 30 June 1780; *The Papers of Alexander Hamilton* Vol.2 (1961) pp.347–8. Hamilton was to be one of the key figures in the early years of the Republic. His gloom was not borne out, though French intervention made it impossible for Britain to bring all its military and naval power to bear on America and so made a critical contribution to the American cause.

FROM WAR TO PEACE, 1780–83

9 The first gun which was fired I could distinctly hear pass through the town … I could hear the ball strike from house to house, and I was afterward informed that it went through the one where many of the officers were at dinner, and over the tables, discomposing the dishes, and either killed or wounded the one at the head of the table. And I also heard that the gun was fired by the Commander-in-Chief [Washington] who was designedly present in the battery for the express purpose of putting the first match.
Colonel Philip van Cortlandt, recalling the opening of the bombardment of Yorktown, the decisive battle of the Revolutionary War, on 9 Oct. 1781; Wright (1983) p.233.

1 The British officers in general behaved like boys who had been whipped at school. Some bit their lips, some pouted, others cried. Their round, broad-brimmed hats were well adapted to the occasion, hiding those faces they were ashamed to show. The foreign regiments made a more military appearance, and the conduct of their officers was far more becoming men of fortitude.

An American officer witnessing the British surrender at Yorktown on 19 Oct. 1781, which effectively ended the war; Wright (1983) p.236. The British redcoats are said to have marched out to the tune of 'The World Turned Upside Down'.

2 He opened his arms, exclaiming wildly, as he paced up and down the apartment during a few minutes, 'O God! It is all over!' – words which he repeated many times under emotions of the deepest consternation and distress.

Lord George Germain, witnessing the reaction of the prime minister, Lord North, to the news of the Yorktown capitulation; N. Wraxall *Historical Memoirs of my own Time* (1815) p.398.

3 My dying eyes have seen the Romans flee.

The veteran French statesman Count Jean Frédéric de Maurepas, on hearing the news of Yorktown; *The Letters of Horace Walpole* (1904 edn) Vol.12, p.109. Maurepas on his deathbed was quoting Racine's *Mithridates* (1666) Act 5, Sc.5.

4 A German officer, who has served in America of high rank, has assured the King that if the coast of America, ten miles from the sea was burnt, and reduced to desert, a thing entirely practicable, the war would soon be over.

London *Morning Herald* 10 Aug. 1782.

5 I cannot conclude without mentioning how sensibly I feel the dismemberment of America from this empire ... Did I not also know that knavery seems to be so much the striking feature of its inhabitants that it may not in the end be an evil that they will become aliens to this kingdom.

George III to the prime minister, Shelburne, 10 Nov. 1782; Wright (1983) p.241.

6 In my opinion, *there never was a good war or a bad peace.*

Benjamin Franklin to the eminent botanist Sir Joseph Banks, 27 July 1783; Wright (1983) p.251. The Peace of Paris was signed on 3 Sept. 1783, acknowledging the 13 United States to be 'free, sovereign and independent States'.

7 *America*, I have proved beyond the Possibility of a Confutation, ever was a Millstone hanging about the Neck of this Country, to weigh it down: And as we ourselves had not the wisdom to cut the Rope, and to let the Burthen fall off, the Americans have kindly done it for us.

Dean Josiah Tucker of Gloucester *Four Letters on Important National Subjects* (1783).

8 It will not be believed, that such a force as Great Britain has employed for eight years in this country could be baffled in their plan of subjugating it, by numbers infinitely less, composed of men often-times half starved, always in rags, without pay, and experiencing every species of distress, which human nature is capable of undergoing.

George Washington to Nathanael Greene, 1783; Aptheker (1960) p.111.

9 To future ages it will appear to be an incredible thing ... that these kingdoms should maintain (as they have done) a glorious but unequal conflict for several years with the most formidable and unprovoked confederacy that should be formed against them.

Rector of Hanbury, Staffordshire, 1 Jan. 1779; Linda Colley *Britons: Forging the Nation 1707–1837* (1996 edn) pp.152–3.

FRAMING A CONSTITUTION, 1777–93

10 Each State retains its sovereignty, freedom and independence, and every Power, Jurisdiction and right, which is not by this confederation expressly delegated to the United States in Congress assembled.

Articles of Confederation, article 2, agreed 15 Nov. 1777; Commager (1973 edn) p.111. The formula proved a recipe for anarchy.

11 I am lost in amazement when I behold what intrigue, the interested views of desperate characters, ignorance, and jealousy of the minor part, are capable of effecting, as a scourge on the major part of our fellow citizens of the Union ... Let the reins of government then be braced and held with a steady hand, and every violation of the Constitution be reprehended. If defective, let it be amended, but not suffered to be trampled on whilst it has an existence.

George Washington to Henry Lee, 31 Oct. 1786; Samuel Eliot Morison *Sources and Documents Illustrating the American Revolution and the Formation of the Federal Constitution* (1923).

1 No sooner were the State Governments formed than their jealousy and ambition began to display themselves. Each endeavoured to cut a slice from the common loaf, to add to its own morsel, till at length the confederation became frittered down to the impotent condition in which it now stands.

James Wilson of Pennsylvania to the Constitutional Convention, 8 June 1787: Max Farrand (ed.) *Records of the Federal Convention of 1787* Vol.1, pp.166–7.

2 [We planned to] march directly to Boston, plunder it, and then … *to destroy the nest of devils who by their influence, made the Court enact what they please*, burn it and lay the town of Boston in ashes.

The insurgent farmer Daniel Shays, interviewed in the *Massachusetts Sentinel*, 20 Jan. 1787. Shays's rebellion reinforced the feeling that the United States were on the verge of disintegration. Egalitarianism had already been evident in Boston during the revolutionary war, as the British MP James Harris noted in 1779: 'The liberal, levelling spirit went so far that even their own (mock) Governor durst not keep a valet de chambre, but went regularly to the barber's shop to be shaved, and that, the rule being that the *first* should be *first* served, the Governor, if he found a cobbler before him, was obliged to wait until that worthy cobbler had been shaved first' (Black (1998 edn) p.248).

3 God forbid that we should ever be 20 years without such a rebellion … If they [the people] remain quiet under such misconceptions it is a lethargy, the forerunner of death to the public liberty … The tree of liberty must be refreshed from time to time with the blood of patriots & tyrants. It is it's natural manure.

Thomas Jefferson to William Stephens Smith, 13 Nov. 1787; *The Papers of Thomas Jefferson* Vol.12 (1955) p.365.

4 I believe the British government forms the best model the world ever produced … All communities divide themselves into the few and the many. The first are the rich and well born, the other the mass of the people … The people are turbulent and changing; they seldom judge and determine right. Give therefore to the first class a distinct, permanent share in the government. They will check the unsteadiness of the second … Nothing but a permanent body can check the impudence of democracy.

Alexander Hamilton to the Constitutional Convention, 11 June 1787; Morison (1923) p.259. Supreme irony, given the American accusations since 1763 of British denial of their constitutional freedoms. The Convention met in Philadelphia from 14 May to 17 Sept. to draft a constitution to replace the Articles of Confederation. It is worth noting that the

Convention's presiding officer, General Washington, shared Hamilton's aversion to democracy wholeheartedly, and under the new constitution future presidents were to be elected not by popular vote but by an electoral college of the country's elite.

5 In the government of this commonwealth, the legislative department shall never exercise the executive and judicial powers, or either of them: the executive shall never exercise the legislative and judicial powers, or either of them: the judicial shall never exercise the legislative and executive powers or either of them: to the end it may a government of laws and not of men.

John Adams, Massachusetts Bill of Rights, article 30, 1780; Commager (1973 edn) p.110. This was the essential political philosophy underlying the new Constitution of 1787. In *The Commonwealth of Oceana* (1656) James Harrington spoke of 'the empire of laws and not of men'.

6 We the People of the United States, in Order to form a more perfect Union, establish Justice, insure domestic Tranquility, provide for the common defence, promote the general Welfare, and secure the Blessings of Liberty to ourselves and our Posterity, do ordain and establish this Constitution for the United States of America.

Preamble to the new Constitution, 17 Sept. 1787; Commager (1973 edn) p.139.

7 Well, Doctor, what have we got – a republic or a monarchy?

A republic, madam, if you can keep it.

Benjamin Franklin's reported response to a question asked as he left the Convention, from notes taken by a Maryland delegate, Dr James McHenry; *American Historical Review* Vol.11 (1906) p.618.

8 As the British Constitution is the most subtile organism which has proceeded from the womb and the long gestation of progressive history, so the American Constitution is, so far as I can see, the most wonderful work ever struck off by the brain and purpose of man.

William Ewart Gladstone, the once and future British prime minister, writing in *The North American Review* (Sept. 1878) p.185.

9 Every project has been found to be no better than committing the lamb to the custody of the wolf, except that one which is called a balance of power.

John Adams on the US Constitution, 1789.

1 Ambition must be made to counteract ambition … It may be a reflection on human nature that such devices should be necessary to control the abuses of government … In framing a government which is to be administered by men over men, the great difficulty lies in this: You must first enable the government to control the governed; and in the next place, oblige it to control itself.

James Madison of Virginia in *The Federalist* no.51, early 1788; Max Beloff (ed.) *The Federalist* (1948) p.265. Madison was the author of the compromise of 16 July 1787, which produced the final text of the Constitution. In *The Federalist* arguments in favour of the Constitution were rehearsed to influence the process of ratification by the 13 states by which alone it could be endorsed. The three anonymous contributors were Madison, Hamilton and John Jay, then secretary of state.

2 Among other deformities, it has an awful squinting. It squints towards monarchy … Your President may easily become King … Where are your checks in this government? I would rather infinitely … have a King, Lords and Commons, than a government so replete with such insupportable evils.

Patrick Henry to the Virginia Ratifying Convention, 5 June 1788; Morison (1923) pp.330, 331. An odd preference from the man who had sailed so close to urging the assassination of George III in 1765. Virginia endorsed the Constitution, however, as did every other state, and it came into force on 21 June 1788.

3 A tribute which I owe … as a Missionary of Liberty to its Patriarch.

Marquis de Lafayette to President George Washington, on sending Washington one of the keys to the Bastille; Wright (1983) p.7. The seizure of the royal fortress-prison in Paris on 14 July 1789 marked the starting point of the French Revolution (see 516:3). Lafayette had fought alongside Washington as a French ally after 1778 and following the capture of the Bastille was appointed commander of the French National Guard. His draft of the Declaration of Rights (see 502:3) was framed in collaboration with Thomas Jefferson and strongly influenced by Jefferson's Declaration of Independence (see 505:3). The key still hangs in Washington's Virginia mansion, Mount Vernon.

4 Our new Constitution is now established, and has an appearance that promises permanency, but in this world nothing can be said to be certain, except death and taxes.

Benjamin Franklin to Jean-Baptiste Leroy, 13 Nov. 1789; *Works* (1817) Ch.6.

5 A *national language* is a band of *national union*. Every engine should be employed to render the people of this country *national*; to call their attachments home to their own country; and to inspire them with the pride of national character … *NOW* is the time, and *this* the country, in which we may expect success, in attempting changes favorable to language, science and government … Let us then seize the present moment, and establish a *national language*, as well as a national government.

Noah Webster *Dissertations on the English Language* (1789) pp.397, 406. The eminent lexicographer Webster was also a super-patriot, and his appeal for a cultural as well as a political revolution led to the adoption of a distinctive American mode of spelling.

6 I hope the French Revolution will issue happily. I feel that the permanence of our own leans in some degree on that, and that a failure there would be a powerful argument to prove there must be a failure here.

Thomas Jefferson to Edward Rutledge, 25 Aug. 1791; *The Papers of Thomas Jefferson* (1982) p.75.

7 Article 1. Congress shall make no law respecting an establishment of religion, or prohibiting the free exercise thereof; or abridging the freedom of speech, or of the press; or the right of the people peaceably to assemble, and to petition the Government for redress of grievances.

Article 2. A well regulated Militia, being necessary to the security of a free State, the right of the people to keep and bear arms, shall not be infringed …

Article 5. No person … shall be compelled in any criminal case to be a witness against himself, nor be deprived of life, liberty, or property without due process of law.

Three of the ten articles of the Bill of Rights, each an amendment to the Constitution, in force on 3 Nov. 1791; Commager (1973 edn) p.146.

8 All the old spirit of 1776 is rekindling.

Thomas Jefferson to James Monroe, 5 May 1793; *The Papers of Thomas Jefferson* Vol.25 (1992) p.661. Jefferson wrote as France and Britain were once again at war, but although the United States was still on paper the ally of France, there was no question of intervention against Britain, as France had intervened in 1778. The phrase is most usually rendered as 'the spirit of '76', the title of the celebrated painting by Archibald Willard executed for the 1876 Centennial of the Declaration of Independence.

CONCLUSIONS

9   The glorious fourth – again appears
    A Day of Days – and year of years.
    The sum of sad disasters,

Where all the mighty gains we see
With all their Boasted liberty,
Is only Change of Masters.

Hannah Griffitts, 1785, on what she saw as no more than a palace revolution; Linda K. Kerber *Women of the Republic* (1980) p.84.

1 The history of our Revolution will be one continued lie from one end to the other. The essence will be that Dr. Franklin's electrical rod smote the earth and out sprang General Washington. That Franklin electrified him with his rod – and thenceforward these two conducted all the policy, negotiations, legislatures, and war.

John Adams to Benjamin Rush, 4 April 1790. Franklin invented the lightning conductor in the early 1750s. Adams wrote shortly before Franklin's death on 17 April: no doubt his watchword was: 'Never speak well of the living.' Compare the tribute paid in 1778 by Franklin's admirer the French economist Baron Anne-Robert-Jacques Turgot: 'He snatched the thunderbolt from heaven and the sceptre from tyrants' (*Eripuit coelo fulmen, sceptrumque tyrannis*).

2 The Americans ... restricted themselves to establishing new powers and substituting them for the powers which the British nation had hitherto exercised over them. None of these innovations reached the mass of the people. Nothing changed the relations which had developed between individuals. In France, by contrast, the Revolution had to embrace the entire social structure, change all social relationships, and penetrate the last links of the political chain.

Marquis de Condorcet *Esquisse du Progrès de l'Esprit Humain* (Sketch of the Progress of the Human Spirit) (1793) 9th Epoch. Condorcet, one of the leading intellectual progenitors of the French Revolution, evidently felt it had surpassed its American forerunner. But revolution French-style cost him his life. Arrested during the Terror in May 1794, he died in jail, perhaps by his own hand (see 514:9).

3 What do We Mean by the Revolution? The War? That was no part of the Revolution; it was only an Effect and the Consequence of it. The Revolution was in the Minds of the People, and this was effected from 1760 to 1775, before a drop of blood was shed at Lexington.

John Adams to Thomas Jefferson, 24 Aug. 1815; L.J. Cappon (ed.) *The Adams-Jefferson Correspondence* (1959) p.455.

4 In America a new people had risen up without a king, or princes, or nobles, knowing nothing of tithes and little of landlords, the plough being for the most part in the hands of the free holders of the soil.

They were more sincerely religious, better educated, and of purer morals than the men of any former republic. By calm meditation and friendly councils they had prepared a constitution which in the union of freedom with strength and order, excelled ever one known before, and which secured itself against violence and revolution by providing a peaceful method for every needed reform.

George Bancroft *History of the Formation of the Constitution of the United States of America* (1884 edn) p.367. In his day Bancroft was considered to be America's leading historian. His glowing tribute to the Revolution is extraordinary given that it was first published on the eve of the Civil War.

5 The story of the revolted colonies impresses us first and most directly as the supreme manifestation of the law of resistance, as the abstract revolution in its purest and most perfect shape ... On this principle they erected their commonwealth, and by its virtue lifted the world out of its orbit and assigned a new course to history. Here or nowhere we have the broken chain, the rejected past, precedent and statute superseded by unwritten law, sons wiser than their fathers, ideas rooted in the future, reason cutting as clean as Atropos.

Lord Acton, 1889, reviewing James Bryce's *The American Commonwealth* (1888). Atropos was one of the three Fates of ancient Greek mythology, with the power to change the course of human life by scissoring the thread of existence.

6 It cannot be said ... that the members of the Convention were 'disinterested'. On the contrary, we are forced to accept the profoundly significant conclusion that ... as practical men they were able to build the new government upon the only foundations which could be stable: fundamental economic interests. The concept of the Constitution as a piece of abstract legislation, reflecting no group interests, recognizing no economic antagonisms, is entirely false. It was an economic document drawn with superb skill by men whose property interests were immediately at stake.

Charles Beard *An Economic Interpretation of the Constitution of the United States* (1913) Chs 5 and 6.

7 The Americans were much more conservative than the French. But their political and social systems ... were too intimately connected to permit that one should remain unchanged while the other was radically altered. The stream of revolution, once started, could not be confined within narrow banks, but spread abroad upon the land. Many economic desires, many social aspirations were set free by the political struggle, many aspects of colonial society profoundly altered by the forces let loose.

J. Franklin Jameson *The American Revolution Considered as a Social Movement* (1926) pp.10–11.

1 The most obvious peculiarity of our American Revolution is that, in the modern European sense of the word, it was hardly a revolution at all ... The United States was born in a *colonial* rebellion ... The more familiar type of colonial rebellion – like that which recently occurred in India – is one in which a subject people vindicates its local culture against foreign rulers. But the American Revolution had very little of this character. On the contrary, ours was one of the few conservative colonial rebellions of modern times. [The Americans] were fighting not so much to establish new rights as to preserve old ones ... The ablest defender of the Revolution ... was also the great theorist of British Conservatism, Edmund Burke.

Daniel Boorstin *The Genius of American Politics* (1953) pp.68–75.

2 The Constitution ... crowned the American Revolution ... It strongly resembled the old order ... but it had eliminated from that order all those features which seemed obsolete or unjust in the New World ... Liberty and law were its two guiding lights; as understood by the Founding Fathers they have served America pretty well ... The astonishing fact [is] that so wise and effective a settlement emerged from thirty years of revolution ... No other revolution, worthy of the name, has ended so happily.

Hugh Brogan (1985 edn) pp.221, 222. The Founding Fathers were the men who made the Revolution and the Constitution. The phrase was coined by President Warren Harding (see 763:9).

The French Revolution, 1789–95

SIGNS AND PORTENTS, 1762–88

1 *Après nous le déluge.* (When the world is washed away, *we'll* be safely out of reach.)
Attrib. by their enemies to both Louis XV, who died in 1774, and his mistress Mme de Pompadour, who died in 1764, much as 'Let them eat cake' was put in the mouth of Queen Marie-Antoinette (see 517:1). It was, in fact, a common saying.

2 Whoever did not live in the years before 1789 does not know what pleasure life can give.
Charles-Maurice, duc de Talleyrand-Périgord (1754–1838); François Guizot *Memoirs* (1858) Vol.1, Ch.6.

3 Each of us comes together to place his person and all his power under the supreme direction of the general will, and we in a body admit each member as an indivisible part of the whole. This act of association produces a moral and collective entity ... As for the associates, they all take on the name of the *people* when they participate in the sovereign authority, and call themselves specifically *citizens* and *subjects* when they are placed under the laws of the State.
Jean-Jacques Rousseau *Du contrat social* (The Social Contract) (1762) Bk I, Ch.6. Rousseau was the intellectual progenitor of the Revolution's severe authoritarianism (see 485:3).

4 All that is wrong. I am certainly not prepared to hand myself over to my fellow citizens unreservedly. I am not going to give them the power to kill me and rob me by majority vote. I undertake to help them and be helped; to do justice and obtain it. No other arrangement.
Voltaire (François-Marie Arouet), libertarian critic of Rousseau's vision; R. Grimsley (ed.) *Du contrat social* (1972) p.115.

5 *Ecrasez l'Infâme!* (Crush the Abomination!)
Voltaire *Le Sermon des cinquante* (The Sermon of the Fifty) (1762), written in 1752 for the private amusement of the king of Prussia, Frederick the Great. In the *Sermon* a dining-club of 50 members meet annually to listen to a sacrilegious homily preached by their chairman. Voltaire's onslaught on the church foreshadowed a key element in the Revolution's policy. It so consumed him that he took to signing his letters with an abbreviated version of the slogan, 'Ecrlinf'. After reading one of Voltaire's missives, a censor is said to have remarked: 'That M. Ecrlinf doesn't write badly!' (Peter Gay *Voltaire's Politics* (1972) p.239).

6 I never go to Versailles without coming away with a feeling of silent indignation at seeing us subjected to the caprices of valets ... Their so-called superiority over the people who are ransomed to support them inspire strong republican sentiments in me.
Abbé de Véri *Journal 1774–80* (1928) Vol.2, p.147; John Hardman (ed.) *The French Revolution Sourcebook* (1999) p.13. Evidently not all French clerics were abominable.

7 I called the Tax-Collector; and, yielding to my generous compassion, I nobly paid forty-six livres, for which five persons were to be reduced to straw and despair. After such a simple action you cannot imagine what a chorus of benedictions echoed around me from the spectators! ... I was watching this spectacle when [a] younger peasant, leading a woman and two children, rushed towards me, saying to them: 'Let us all fall at the feet of this Image of God.'
Choderlos de Laclos *Les Liaisons dangereuses* (1782) Letter 21, Viscount de Valmont to Marchioness de Merteuil. Cynical self-congratulation on an act of charity to the local tenantry, neatly illustrating the power of the aristocracy in pre-revolutionary France.

8 You think you're a great genius because you're a great lord! ... Title, wealth, rank, office, that's what makes you so high and mighty! What have you done to deserve so much? You gave yourself the trouble to be born, and nothing else. Otherwise, you're a pretty ordinary fellow, whereas, my God, me! I'm lost in the faceless crowd. I've had to use my head more, play more tricks, just to scrape along, than it would have taken to run the Spanish Empire for a century.
Pierre-Augustin de Beaumarchais *Le Mariage de Figaro* (1784) Act 5, Sc.3. The servant Figaro soliloquizes about his master, the Spanish Count Almaviva. It took three years to have the text passed by the French royal censors, not surprisingly in view of its sharp commentary on the injustices of the France of the *ancien régime*.

9 America has given us this example. The act which declared its independence is a simple and sublime expression of these rights so sacred and so long forgotten ... The spectacle of a great people where the rights of man are respected is useful to all others, despite differences of climate, of customs, and of constitutions.

Marquis de Condorcet *L'Influence de la révolution en Amérique sur l'Europe* (1786). Condorcet was arrested and died in captivity in the spring of 1794.

1 To the king alone belongs sovereign power in his kingdom. He is accountable to God alone for the exercise of supreme power. The bond which unites the king and the nation is indissoluble by its very nature.

Chrétien-François de Lamoignon, minister of Louis XVI, to the *Parlement* (high court) of Paris, 19 Nov. 1787; J.M. Roberts (ed.) *French Revolution Documents* Vol.1 (1966) p.18.

2 The will of the king is not a law unto itself; the mere expression of this will is not part of our national practice ... Such is the French constitution, which is as old as the monarchy.

Remonstrance of the *Parlement* of Paris, 11 April 1788; Roberts (1966) pp.24–5. The *Parlement* had a long-standing right to criticize royal authority and had periodically clashed with the crown.

3 As a Frenchman I want the Estates-General; as a minister I am bound to tell you that they may destroy your authority.

Charles de la Croix Castries to Queen Marie-Antoinette, Aug. 1787; Hardman (1999) p.15. After the failure of the 1787 Assembly of Notables to deal with the country's financial crisis, the Estates-General (a body representing nobility, clergy and the bourgeois Third Estate) was summoned to meet at the Palace of Versailles; it had last convened in 1614!

4 Experience teaches that the most dangerous moment for a bad government is usually when it begins to reform itself. Only great genius can save a ruler who takes on the task of improving the lot of his subjects after long oppression. The evil which was borne patiently as inevitable seems unendurable as soon as the idea of escaping from it is conceived. All the abuses then removed seem to throw into greater relief those that remain, so that their irritation is more acute.

Alexis de Tocqueville *L'Ancien Régime et la Révolution* (1856) Bk 3, Ch.4. An oft-quoted warning to belatedly reformist tyrannies.

5 One opinion pervaded the whole company, that they are on the eve of some great revolution in the government. [A] great ferment amongst all ranks of men ... and a strong leaven of liberty, increasing every hour since the American revolution, altogether form a combination of circumstances that promise ere long to ferment into motion if some master hand of

very superior talents, and inflexible courage is not found at the helm to guide events instead of being driven by them.

Arthur Young, Paris, 17 Oct. 1787; J.M. Thompson (ed.) *English Witnesses of the French Revolution* (1938) pp.20–21.

6 Sire, the State is in danger ... a revolution in the principles of government is being prepared ... Let the Third Estate foresee what could be ... the outcome of infringing on the rights of the Clergy and the Nobility ... The French monarchy must decline into despotism or become a democracy – two opposite kinds of revolution, but both calamitous.

Princes of the Blood (the immediate relatives of the king), memorandum to Louis XVI, 12 Dec. 1788; Roberts (1966) pp.45–6, 48.

1789: THE TRIUMPH OF THE THIRD ESTATE

7 The division between the three orders [nobility, clergy and Third Estate], each with its rights, objectives and conflicting interests, is a great misfortune for the nation and a great obstacle to the general good ... If the rights were equal, all would have the same will.

The *cahier* of Les Arcs, Provence, early 1789; Hardman (1999) p.83. The *cahiers de doléances* (schedules of grievances) were drawn up nationwide to be presented to the Estates-General when they met at Versailles on 1 May 1789.

8 We have three questions to put to ourselves:
  1. What is the Third Estate? Everything.
  2. What has it so far been in the political hierarchy? Nothing.
  3. What does it demand? To be Something.
  Who would dare to say that the Third Estate does not possess within itself everything needed to embody a nation? It is a strong, robust man with one arm in chains. Remove the structure of privilege and the nation would be not less, but more.

Abbé Emmanuel-Joseph Sieyès, the opening of *Qu'est-ce que c'est que le Tiers État?* (What is the Third Estate?), Jan. 1789.

9 Are not the Third Estate also my children – and a more numerous progeny? And even when the nobility lose a portion of their privileges and the clergy a few scraps of their income, shall I be any less their king?

Louis XVI, May 1789; Countess d'Adhémar *Souvenirs* (1836) Vol.3, p.157 in Hardman (1999) p.94.

1 To it, and it alone, belongs the right to interpret and express the general will of the nation. Between the throne and this Assembly there can exist no veto, no power of negation.

Declaration of the self-styled National Assembly (formed by an overwhelming majority of the Third Estate), 17 June 1789; Roberts (1966) p.107.

2 We swear never to break away from the National Assembly, and to meet wherever circumstances demand, until the constitution of the kingdom is established and confirmed on solid foundations.

Tennis Court Oath, Versailles, 20 June 1789; Roberts (1966) p.110. Representatives of the Third Estate took the oath in the real tennis court of the Palace of Versailles because the Third Estate's meeting-place in the palace was closed for a royal session of the whole Estates-General on 23 June, and the secessionists believed that they had been deliberately locked out.

3 In the keep I found a Swiss soldier crouching with his back to me; I aimed at him, shouting: drop your weapons; he turned round startled and laid down his arms, saying: 'Comrade, don't kill me! I'm for the Third Estate and I'll defend you to the last drop of my blood; you know I've got my orders; but I haven't fired.'

Jean-Baptiste Humbert, watchmaker and participant in the assault on the Bastille, the royal fortress-prison in Paris, 14 July 1789; Jacques Godechot *The Taking of the Bastille* (1970) p.374. The Swiss Guard were troops of the royal household.

4 *Rien.* (Nothing.)

Entry in Louis XVI's journal for 14 July 1789. The reference is not to an uneventful political day but to the fact that he had scored no kills in the hunting field; Simon Schama *Citizens: A Chronicle of the French Revolution* (1989) p.419.

5 *Louis XVI*: So what is it, a riot?

Duke de la Rochefoucauld-Liancourt: No, Sire, it is a revolution.

Question and answer at Versailles after the fall of the Bastille; attrib.

6 The greatest Revolution that we know anything of has been effected with, comparatively speaking, if the magnitude of the event is considered, the loss of very few lives: from this moment we may consider France as a free country; the King a very limited Monarch, and the Nobility as reduced to a level with the rest of the Nation.

Lord Dorset, British ambassador to France, 16 July 1789; O. Browning (ed.) *Despatches from Paris, 1784–1790* Vol.2 (1910) p.242.

7 How much the greatest event it is that ever happened in the world! And how much the best!

The Whig statesman Charles James Fox on the taking of the Bastille, 30 July 1789; Lord John Russell *The Life and Times of Charles James Fox* Vol.2 (1859) p.361.

8 What, then, is their blood so pure?

Antoine Barnave on the lynching of two royal officials on 22 July 1789; Schama (1989) p.406. Barnave, the spokesman for the French slave-owners of the Caribbean, was guillotined in Nov. 1793.

9 On 29 July 1789 a party of two hundred brigands from another area ... came to my château near Argentan, and after forcing the locks of the chests which held my title-deeds, took out a great many of them along with the registers ... and carried them off or burned them in the woods ... I am all the more devastated by this loss because I have never set the hateful burden of antiquated feudalism on the backs of my tenants.

Count de Germiny to the National Assembly, 20 Aug. 1789; Roberts (1966) pp.140–41. De Germiny was complaining of his treatment during the so-called Great Fear, which swept across France between 20 July and 6 August.

10 1. The National Assembly abolishes the feudal system in its entirety ...

11. All citizens, regardless of birth, may be admitted to all ecclesiastical, civil and military functions and dignities, and no useful profession shall entail loss of status ...

17. The National Assembly solemnly proclaims King Louis XVI Restorer of French Liberty.

Decree on the abolition of feudalism, 4 Aug. 1789; Roberts (1966) pp.151, 153.

11 1. Men are born and remain free and equal in their rights. Social distinctions can be based only on the common interest.

2. The object of every political association is the maintenance of the natural and inalienable rights of man. These rights are liberty, property, security and resistance to oppression.

3. The fundamental source of all sovereignty lies in the Nation. No institution, no individual may wield authority which does not stem explicitly from it ...

6. The law is the expression of the general will.

Declaration of the Rights of Man and the Citizen, 26 Aug. 1789; Roberts (1966) pp.171–2. The Declaration was drafted largely by the Marquis de Lafayette with not a little help from the United States minister to France, Thomas Jefferson, principal author of the American Declaration of Independence of 1776 (see 505:3).

1 Let them eat cake! (*Qu'ils mangent de la brioche!*)
Queen Marie-Antoinette, attrib. The words appear in Rousseau's *Confessions*, written between 1765 and 1767, and were probably commonly ascribed to the heartless rich. The queen may have been tagged with them at the time of the march on Versailles on 5 Oct. 1789, a popular protest against the supposed 'famine plot', which ended in the royal family being taken to Paris. Earlier in the year one of the king's officials, François Joseph Foulon, was alleged to have said 'Let them eat hay'. He had been decapitated by a mob on 22 July and his lifeless mouth stuffed with hay (Schama (1989) pp.405–6, 446).

2 To forbear running from one extreme to another is no easy matter, and should this be the case, rocks and shelves, not visible at present, may wreck the vessel, and give a higher-toned despotism than the one which existed before.
President George Washington to Gouverneur Morris, Jefferson's successor as US envoy to France, 13 Oct. 1789; Richard Cobb *The French Revolution: Voices from a Momentous Epoch* (1988) p.94.

3 After sharing in the benefits of one Revolution, I have been spared to be a witness to two other Revolutions, both glorious … Be encouraged all ye friends of freedom, and writers in its defence! … Behold, the light you have struck out, after setting AMERICA free, reflected to FRANCE, and there kindled into a blaze that lays despotism in ashes, and warms and illuminates EUROPE!
Richard Price to the Society for Commemorating the Revolution in Great Britain (the 1688 Revolution), 4 Nov. 1789; Alfred Cobban (ed.) *The Debate on the French Revolution 1789–1800* (1950) Pt 1, p.64. For Price see 485:5.

1790: THE DAWN OF LIBERTY

4 After breakfast, walk in the gardens of the Thuilleries [*sic*], where there is the most extraordinary sight … The king, walking with six grenadiers of the *milice bourgeoise*, with an officer or two of his household, and a page … [The Queen] also was attended so closely by the *gardes bourgeoises* that she could not speak, but in a low voice, without being heard by them. A mob followed her, talking very loud, and paying no other apparent respect than that of taking off their hats wherever she passed, which was indeed more than I expected.
Arthur Young, Paris, 4 Jan. 1790; *Travels in France* (1792; 1924 edn) p.288.

5 The purpose of the book is clear on every page: its author, infected and full of the French madness, is trying in every possible way to break down respect for authority and for the authorities, to stir up in the people indignation against their superiors and against the government.
Catherine the Great, empress of Russia, May 1790, notes on Alexander Radishchev's *A Journey from St Petersburg to Moscow*. Catherine had Radishchev arrested on 11 July; he was first sentenced to death, then given 10 years' banishment for this publication.

6 Several reigns of absolute government would not have done as much for royal authority as a single year of liberty.
Count de Mirabeau to the queen, 3 July 1790; Hardman (1999) p.112. Mirabeau, the darling of the Third Estate, was conducting a secret correspondence with the court, and its disclosure after his death destroyed his reputation. His judgement is in glaring contrast with Young's testimony (see 517:4).

7 If this country ceases to be a monarchy it will be entirely the fault of Louis XVI. Blunder upon blunder, inconsequence upon inconsequence, a total want of energy of mind accompanied with personal cowardice, have been the destruction of his reign.
Lord Gower, British ambassador to France, July 1790; Oscar Browning (ed.) *The Despatches of Earl Gower* (1885).

8 How frantically the French have acted and how rationally the Americans! But Franklin and Washington were great men. None have yet appeared in France.
Horace Walpole, 1 July 1790; *The Letters of Horace Walpole* (1904 edn) Vol.14, p.256.

9   Bliss was it in that dawn to be alive,
          But to be young was very heaven! O times,
          In which the meagre, stale, forbidding ways
          Of custom, law, and statute, took at once
          The attraction of a country in romance!
William Wordsworth *The Prelude* Bk 11, lines 108–12. Wordsworth, a Cambridge undergraduate, spent the long vacation of 1790 in France on a walking tour. A very different *joie de vivre* from Talleyrand's (see 514:2).

1 *Ça ira, ça ira, ça ira!*
La liberté s'établira.
Malgré les tyrans, tout réussira.
(It'll be all right, all right, all right!/Liberty will stand firm./In spite of the tyrants, all will be well.)

The *Ça ira* revolutionary anthem originated by workers preparing the Champ de Mars for the first anniversary celebration of the seizure of the Bastille. Words attrib. to the American envoy to France, Benjamin Franklin, when asked about the prospects for the American Revolution a decade earlier; *Le Chronique de Paris*, 9 July 1790 and 4 May 1792.

2 *LIBERTÉ, ÉGALITÉ, FRATERNITÉ* (Liberty, Equality, Fraternity)

Watchwords of the Revolution, said to have been coined by Benjamin Franklin.

3 Little did I dream that I should have lived to see such disasters fallen upon her in a nation of gallant men, in a nation of men of honour and cavaliers. I thought ten thousand swords must have leaped from their scabbards to avenge even a look that threatened her with insult. But the age of chivalry is gone. That of sophisters, economists and calculators has succeeded, and the glory of Europe is extinguished for ever.

Edmund Burke *Reflections on the Revolution in France* (1790). Burke's paean to Marie-Antoinette.

4 [Burke] is not affected by the reality of distress touching his heart, but by the showy resemblance of it striking his imagination. He pities the plumage, but forgets the dying bird … His hero or his heroine must be a tragedy victim, expiring in show, and not the real prisoner of misery, sliding into death in the silence of a dungeon.

Tom Paine *The Rights of Man* Pt I (1791; 1945 edn) p.260. This famous passage by a leading English admirer of the Revolution bears a curious resemblance to another attack on Burke by the Scot Sir James Mackintosh in his *Vindiciae Gallicae*, completed in Sept. 1791. It reads (from the Introduction): '[He] agonizes at the slenderest pang which assails the heart of sottishness or prostitution, if they are placed by fortune on a throne.' This depiction of Louis XVI and Marie-Antoinette was to be echoed by Mackintosh's fellow countryman, Robert Burns, in 1795 (see 524:7).

5 They will swear … to be loyal to the nation, the law and the king, and to uphold with all their power the Constitution decreed by the National Assembly and accepted by the king.

Oath required of the clergy by the Assembly decree of 27 Nov. 1790 complementing the Civil Constitution of the Clergy of 19 July 1790; Roberts (1966) p.232. A drastic expression of

the Revolution's anti-clericalism; refusal to take the oath could cost a priest his life.

6 The State, it seems to me, is not made for religion, but religion made for the State.

Abbé Guillaume Raynal, a pronouncement of 1780; Schama (1989) p.484.

1791: CONSTITUTIONAL MOMENT

7 1. Woman is born free, and remains equal to Man in rights …
4. The exercise of Woman's natural rights has no limit other than the tyranny of Man's opposing them …
17. Property is shared or divided equally by both sexes.

Olympe de Gouges *Les Droits de la femme et du citoyen* (The Rights of Woman and the Citizen) (1791); Norman Davies *Europe, A History* (1996) p.716. This feminist revolutionary was guillotined in Nov. 1793. The Revolution did not include women in political society, and French women were not enfranchised until 1946.

8 He is a stern man, rigid in his principles, plain, unaffected in his manners, no foppery in his dress, certainly above corruption, despising wealth, and with nothing of the volatility of a Frenchman in his character … When I … said he would be the man of sway in a short time, and govern the million, I was laughed at.

The political journalist William A. Miles on Maximilien Robespierre, 1 March 1791; Thompson (1938) p.106.

9 *AUX GRANDS HOMMES LA PATRIE RECONNAISSANTE* (The Thankful Country to its Great Men)

Inscription on the portico of the Panthéon in Paris, the church of Ste Geneviève rededicated as a national shrine. Its first dead hero was Mirabeau, interred with great ceremony on 4 April 1791 and, after his exposure as a double-dealer, unceremoniously removed in 1793.

10 1. The abolition of every kind of corporate body for citizens of the same trade or profession is one of the fundamental bases of the French constitution …
4. All gatherings composed of artisans, workers, journeymen or day-labourers, or agitated by them, shall be deemed seditious assemblies, and, as such, will be dispersed by the agencies of public order.

Le Chapelier law, 14 June 1791; Eric Cahm (ed.) *Politics and Society in Contemporary France, 1789–1871* (1972) p.40. The law was passed as part of the Revolution's huge reinforcement of the powers of the state over any potentially competing bodies.

1 All is lost, my dear father, and I am in despair. The king was stopped at Varennes, 16 leagues [about 48 miles] from the frontier. Imagine my distress and pity me.

The Swedish count, Axel Fersen, 23 June 1791; Cobb (1988) p.118. Fersen was coachman to the royal family in their abortive bid to leave the country and escape from the Revolution.

2 When the last king is hanged with the bowels of the last priest, the human race can hope for happiness.

The journal *La Bouche de Fer* (The Iron Mouth), 11 July 1791. Credit for this grisly expectation has been given to the renegade priest Jean Meslier, in his *Testament*, published in the 1720s, though Voltaire uses a similar turn of phrase in a letter of 5 May 1761, as does Denis Diderot in a poem written in 1772. A variant appeared as graffiti in the Paris student upsurge of May 1968: 'When the last sociologist has been strangled with the guts of the last bureaucrat, shall we still have problems?'

3 His Majesty the Emperor [of Austria] and His Majesty the King of Prussia ... declare jointly that they regard the present situation of the King of France as a subject of common interest to all the sovereigns of Europe ... They will not refuse to employ ... the most effective means relative to their strength to assist the King of France ... Their said Majesties ... are resolved to act promptly in mutual accord, with the force necessary, to bring about the proposed common aim.

Declaration of Pillnitz, 27 Aug. 1791; Clive Parry (ed.) *The Consolidated Treaty Series* Vol.51 (1969) p.235. A blank salvo against the Revolution since Austro-Prussian action was made to depend on the agreement of all the European powers by the insertion of the phrase 'then and in that case'. 'Then and in that case is with me the law and the prophets,' wrote the Emperor Leopold II to Prince von Kaunitz. 'If England fails us, the case is non-existent' (T.C.W. Blanning *The French Revolutionary Wars 1787–1802* (1996) pp.58–9).

4 There is no longer any nobility nor peerage nor hereditary distinctions of orders nor feudal regime nor patrimonial justice nor any title, denomination or prerogative ... There is no longer venality nor heredity in any public office and neither for any section of the nation nor for any individual can there be any exemption from the common law of the French.

Preamble to the Constitution of 14 Sept. 1791; Schama (1989) p.574. The brave new world adumbrated.

5 We can never govern a people against its inclinations. This maxim is as true at Constantinople as in a republic; the present inclinations of this nation are for the Rights of Man, however senseless they are.

Louis XVI to his two brothers in exile, 25 Sept. 1791; Hardman (1999) p.138.

6 I have just written to the Emperor, the Empress of Russia [and] to the Kings of Spain and Sweden, and have laid before them the idea of a congress of the great powers of Europe, supported by an armed force, as the best means of putting a stop to the factions here, or furnishing the resources to establish a more desirable state of affairs, and of preventing the evil that torments us from engulfing the other states of Europe.

Louis XVI to Frederick William II, king of Prussia, 3 Dec. 1791; J.H. Stewart (ed.) *A Documentary Survey of the French Revolution* (1951) Ch.4, p.279.

7 The Americans ... were taught by nature and habit to support liberty with moderation, decency, and dignity. The French were born slaves ... and the sudden possession of this invaluable treasure seems to have render[ed] them incapable of supporting their happy reverse of fortune with tolerable temperance.

Edward Church, US consul-designate at Bilbao, to Thomas Jefferson, 16 Dec. 1791; *The Papers of Thomas Jefferson* Vol.22 (1982) pp.413–14.

1792: REVOLUTION EMBATTLED

8 It will be a crusade for universal liberty. Each soldier will say to his enemy: brother, I am not going to cut your throat, I am going to free you from the yoke which burdens you; I am going to show you the road to happiness. Like you, I was once a slave; I took up arms, and the tyrant vanished; look at me now that I am free; you can be so too; here is my arm in support.

Jacques-Pierre Brissot de Warville, leader of the 'Brissotin' war party, in the Jacobin Club, early 1792; Blanning (1986) p.111. Brissot was guillotined on 30 Oct. 1793.

9 Unquestionably there never was a time in the history of this country, when, for the situation in

Europe, we might more reasonably expect fifteen years of peace than at the present moment.

British prime minister, William Pitt, 17 Feb. 1792; *Parliamentary History* Vol.29 (1816). Within a year Britain was at war with France, a war that, with two short intermissions, went on for over 22 years.

1 The French nation, true to the principles enshrined in the Constitution, of not entering on any war in order to make conquests and never to use its forces against the freedom of any people, takes up arms only to preserve its liberty and independence. The war it is forced to wage is not a war of nation against nation, but the just defence of a free people against the unjust aggression of a king.

Legislative Assembly declaration of revolutionary war on Austria, 20 April 1792; Roberts (1966) p.451.

2   *Allons, enfants de la patrie*
    Le jour de gloire est arrivé.
    Contre nous de la tyrannie
    L'étendard sanglant est levé ...
    Aux armes, citoyens!
    Formez vos bataillons!
    Marchez! Marchez!
    Q'un sang impur
    Abreuve nos sillons!

(Forward, children of the fatherland!/The day of glory has come./The bloody standard of tyranny is raised against us .../To arms, citizens!/Form up in battle order!/March! March on!/And let their tainted blood drench our furrows!)

Claude-Joseph Rouget de Lisle 'La Marseillaise', composed on 16 April 1792; Cobb (1988) p.149.

3 Yesterday, at half-past three, there was used for the first time the machine destined to cut off the heads of criminals condemned to death ... This machine was rightfully preferred to other forms of execution; It in no way soils the hands of the man who murders his fellow man, and the promptness with which it strikes the condemned is more in the spirit of the law, which may often be stern, but must never be cruel.

Le Chronique de Paris, 26 April 1792, hailing the advent of the guillotine, named after Dr Joseph-Ignace Guillotin, advocate of humane capital punishment.

4   Madame Veto had promised
    To have all Paris slaughtered.
    But her plot misfired
    Thanks to our gunners.

Let's dance the Carmagnole!
Long live the boom! Long live the boom!
Let's dance the Carmagnole!
Long live the cannon's boom!

A version of 'La Carmagnole', one of the Revolution's leading theme-tunes; Cobb (1988) p.191. It relates to the mass demonstration at the Tuileries Palace on 20 June 1792, backed up by cannon deployed by the revolutionary militia of Paris, the National Guard. The confrontation was prompted by Louis XVI's use of the suspensive veto on Assembly legislation, with Marie-Antoinette allegedly its greatest enthusiast, looking forward to a counter-revolutionary coup. The song was named after the town of Carmagnola in northern Italy.

5 Since the internal and external security of the State are threatened and since the Legislative Body has judged it necessary to take emergency measures, it proclaims ... Citizens, the country is in danger.

Legislative Assembly, decree, 5 July 1792; Roberts (1966) pp.487-8.

6 If the least violence, the least outrage, is done to their majesties King Louis XVI, Queen Marie-Antoinette and the royal family ... They will exact exemplary and eternally memorable revenge, handing over the city of Paris to military execution and total overthrow, and handing over the insurgents guilty of the attacks to be punished as they deserve.

Brunswick Manifesto, issued in the names of Austria and Prussia, 25 July 1792; Cobb (1988) p.150.

7 I suggest that all the Protestant powers embrace the Greek religion to save themselves from this immoral, anarchic, wicked and diabolical plague, which is against God and the throne ... You would only need to seize two or three hovels in France, and all the rest would collapse by themselves ... Twenty thousand Cossacks would be too many to make a green carpet from Strasbourg to Paris.

Catherine the Great, empress of Russia, 1792; Henri Troyat *Catherine the Great* (1977) Ch.25. As the quotation suggests, Catherine left it to Austria and Prussia to deal with France, since she preferred to intervene against an uprising in Poland. The Greek religion was the Orthodox Christianity practised in Russia, to which Catherine, daughter of a Protestant German princeling, had converted as wife of Tsar Peter III.

8 During this time the inhabitants of all the Fauxbourgs [*sic*] were repairing to the Palace [the Tuileries] ... calling out for the dethronement of the King ... The first resistance was from the top of the grand staircase, where the Swiss made a very firm stand, but the mob, unawed, and encouraged by the cry of Liberty, Victory or Death, soon made their way up the staircase, when the Swiss gave way, and a general massacre ensued.

The Times, 16 Aug. 1792, on the events of 10 Aug., a watershed in the Revolution since it marked the final collapse of the monarchy and the prelude to a republic. The Swiss Guard formed the royal bodyguard; the *faubourgs* were the working-class districts on the outskirts of the capital.

1 The Revolution before the 10th of August, was as different from the Revolution after that day as light from darkness; as clearly distinct in principle and practice as liberty and slavery.

Arthur Young *The Example of France ... A Warning to Britain* (1793) pp.3–4.

2 The tocsin that rings out will resound throughout all France. It is no alarm bell; it is the clarion call to fall on the enemies of the fatherland! To defeat them, gentlemen, we need daring, more daring, forever daring, and France will be saved!

Georges-Jacques Danton in the Legislative Assembly, 2 Sept. 1792; *Archives parlementaires* Vol.49, p.209. The enemies within were dealt with in the 'September Massacres', the slaughter of prisoners held in Paris jails.

3 Let me beg you not to mix with the shallow herd who throw an odium on immutable principles, because some of the mere instruments of the revolution were too sharp. – Children of any growth will do mischief when they meddle with edged tools.

Mary Wollstonecraft to William Roscoe on the September Massacres; Claire Tomalin *The Life and Death of Mary Wollstonecraft* (1974) pp.119–20. An observation at once complacent and patronizing from the radical feminist enthusiast for the nascent French Republic.

4 This is the beginning of a new era in history, and you can claim to have witnessed it.

The German writer Johann Wolfgang von Goethe, to Prussian troops after the defeat of their invasion by the French at Valmy on 20 September; L. Blumenthal and W. Loos (eds) *Goethe's Works* (1981) p.235.

5 How can we understand Greece without Salamis, Rome without the legions, Christianity without the sword, Islam without the scimitar, our own Revolution without Valmy?

Colonel Charles de Gaulle *Le Fil de l'épée* (The Edge of the Sword) (1932). The Athenian fleet defeated the Persian fleet at the Battle of Salamis in 480 BC (see 55:7). De Gaulle later became president of the Fifth Republic. Conservative Catholics of his background had long been hostile to the Revolution. Now it was an icon of patriotism, and Valmy had

become as much of an emblem of national resistance to foreign attack as the Battle of the Marne, which had saved Paris from the Germans in Sept. 1914.

6 The National Convention declares, in the name of the French nation, that it will grant fraternity and aid to all peoples who wish to regain their freedom, and instructs the Executive Power to give generals the necessary orders to bring help to these peoples.

Decree, transforming the war into a crusade for the liberation of Europe, 17 Nov. 1792; John Hardman (ed.) *French Revolution Documents* Vol.2 (1973) p.389. The National Convention, the legislature of the Republic, opened on 20 Sept. 1792.

7 Let us suppose that a people emerged in Europe who added to austere virtues and a national militia a set plan of expansion, and who did not lose sight of this objective – understanding how to wage war thriftily and to subsist on the back of its victories ... We would see this people conquer their neighbours and overturn our feeble structure of government as the north wind bows frail reeds.

Count de Guibert *Essai général de tactique* (General Essay on Tactics) (1774); a famous prophecy, although the count could not have known how soon it was to be borne out.

8 Certainly none of us will ever suggest that France should keep its disastrous race of kings; we know too well that all dynasties are nothing but rapacious cannibals ... Those who love freedom may rest assured: this talisman will be destroyed, its magical properties will dazzle men no longer. I therefore demand that by solemn law you order the abolition of royalty.

Abbé Henri Grégoire to the National Convention, 21 Sept. 1792; Cobb (1988) p.164. The motion was passed and the First Republic established.

9 No one can be a king and not do harm. (*On ne peut point régner innocement.*)

Louis Antoine Léon de Saint-Just, calling for the execution of Louis XVI, 13 Nov. 1792. (The full text of the speech may be found in Michael Walzer (ed.) *Regicide and Revolution* (1974) p.124.) Saint-Just was making a philosophical point about the nature of power, but as he was to prove so amply when he himself was in power shortly afterwards, the capacity to do harm was by no means limited to kings.

10 I demanded the abolition of the death penalty in the Assembly ... But Louis must die that the country may live.

Maximilien Robespierre to the National Convention, 3 Dec. 1792; Hardman (1999) pp.160, 161. A heroic victory of expediency over principle.

1 *Reformers* pronounce coolly, *that no revolution can be brought about without some blood being shed …* the French philosophic anti-legislators … pretend to discover equality and the rights of mankind in sluicing the veins of their countrymen and of any nation they can reach.

Horace Walpole to Rev. Robert Nares, 14 Dec. 1792; *The Letters of Horace Walpole* (1904 edn) Vol.15.

1793: REPUBLICAN JUSTICE

2 The liberty of the whole earth was depending on the issue of the contest, and was ever such prize won with so little blood? My own affections have been deeply wounded by some of the martyrs to this cause, but rather than that it should have failed, I would have seen half the earth desolated. Were there but an Adam and an Eve in every country, and left free, it would be better than as it now is.

Thomas Jefferson to William Short, 3 Jan. 1793; *The Papers of Thomas Jefferson* Vol.25 (1986) p.14. A classic example of Jefferson's anarchic liberalism.

3   Fame, let thy trumpet sound …
    Tell all the world around –
    How Capet fell.
    And when great George's poll
    Shall in the basket roll,
    Let mercy then control
    The Guillotine.

The American camp-follower of revolution, Joel Barlow, on the execution of Louis XVI on 21 Jan. 1793; Tomalin (1974) p.133. Capet was the king, a scion of the Capet dynasty; Great George was King George III. This doggerel was meant to be sung to the tune of 'God Save the King'; it was composed by an opponent of capital punishment!

4 The tree of liberty does not flourish unless moistened with the blood of kings. I vote for death.

The Robespierrist lawyer Bertrand Barère, voting in the Convention on the fate of Louis XVI, *The Times*, 23 Jan. 1793.

5 All potentates owe it to their individual honour, but still more to the happiness of their people collectively, to crush these savage regicides in their dens, who aim at the ruin of all nations and the destruction of all Governments … Armed with fire and sword we must penetrate into the recesses of this land of blood and carnage.

The Times, editorial, 25 Jan. 1793, on the execution of Louis XVI on 21 Jan.

6 It must be feared that the Revolution, like Saturn, will devour its children one after the other.

Pierre Vergniaud, before the Convention, 13 March 1793; Alphonse de Lamartine *Histoire des Girondins* (1847) Bk 18, Ch.20. Vergniaud was guillotined on 31 Oct. 1793 as part of a purge within the revolutionary leadership in which the relatively moderate Girondins (named after the Gironde region of southwest France) were eliminated by the Jacobins, whose original headquarters was the Jacobin convent in Paris.

7 Brave *sans-culottes*, your enemies only get away with it because you keep your arms folded; wake up for fuck's sake; stand up and you'll soon see them grovel. Disarm all the buggers who piss cold water on us patriots, the ones who don't want anything to do with the Revolution. The poison of moderation kills quicker than Austrian steel. Once you're winners the whole country'll think you're great; but whatever you do, strike while the iron's hot. If you drop off even for a few seconds, you can expect to wake up slaves, fuck it …

The extreme Jacobin journal *Le Père Duchesne* attacks the Girondins, May 1793, no.239; Cobb (1988) p.184. *Culottes* (breeches) were the garb of the ruling class; workers (*sans-culottes*) wore trousers. The description was first used as a term of ridicule early in 1791 before it acquired its political flavour.

8 1. The French Republic is one and indivisible …
    4. [Citizenship belongs to] every man born and domiciled in France over 21 years of age …
    122. This constitution guarantees all Frenchmen equality, liberty, security, the rights of property … freedom of worship, a common education, public assistance, unlimited freedom of the press, the right to assemble in popular societies and the enjoyment of all the rights of man.

Constitution, 25 June 1793; Hardman (1999) pp.174, 176–7. A charter of political and social democracy (for men, if not women), which was never put into effect.

9 Liberty is but a vain phantom when one class of men can starve the other with impunity. Equality is but a vain phantom when the rich exercise the power of life and death over their fellows through monopolies.

The *sans-culotte* Jacques Roux, an early critic of capitalism, speaking in the Convention, 25 June 1793; Hardman (1999) p.179.

10 Our Father, which art in Heaven, whence you protect so admirably the French Republic and the Sans-Culottes, its most ardent defenders; may your name be sanctified and blest by us, as it has always been. May your constant Will to make a man live free, equal and happy, be respected on Earth as it is in Heaven. Give us this day our daily bread in spite of the vain efforts of the Pitts, the Coburgs and all the Coalition Tyrants to starve us. Forgive us the faults we have committed by supporting for so long the Tyrants we have purged from France, as we forgive the Slave Nations, when they did as we did. Do not allow them to delay any longer in breaking the chains that bind them and which they have striven to throw off, but may they deliver themselves, as we have, from Nobles, Priests and Kings. Amen.

A *sans-culotte* parody of the Lord's Prayer; Hardman (1973) p.367. The British prime minister, William Pitt, waged a twofold war on France, forging a coalition of European allies fighting on land and mounting a sea blockade by the Royal Navy to strangle the Republic economically. Coburg was the Duke of Saxe-Coburg, commander of the coalition's largest army.

1 And so we stand here and write into the declaration of the rights of man the holy right of property. And now we find where that leads … Every man his own millionaire. Man against man, group against group in happy mutual robbery.

Jean-Paul Marat, the arch-publicist of the *sans-culottes*, as imagined by Peter Weiss in his play *The Persecution and Assassination of Marat as Performed by the Inmates of the Asylum of Charenton under the Direction of the Marquis de Sade* (1964) Act 1, Sc.15.

2 O heart of Marat, *sacré coeur* … can the works and benevolence of the son of Mary be compared with those of the Friend of the People and his apostles to the Jacobins of our holy Mountain? … Their Jesus was but a false prophet but Marat is a god.

Eulogy at the funeral of Marat, 16 July 1793; Schama (1989) p.744. He had been assassinated by Charlotte Corday three days earlier, stabbed with a kitchen knife as he lay in his bath trying to cool his severe psoriasis. Marat's tabloid was *L'Ami du peuple* (The Friend of the People); the Mountain signifies the Jacobins, so called because they sat on the highest benches in the legislative chamber.

3 All French citizens are subject to permanent requisition to serve in the armed forces. Young men will be sent on active service; married men will make weapons and transport supplies. Women will make tents and uniforms and work in the hospitals. Children will tear up old linen for bandages. Old people will be taken to public places to stir up

the courage of the combatants, hatred for kings, and republican unity.

Decree for mass conscription (the *levée en masse*), 23 Aug. 1793; Cobb (1988) p.194.

4 Let us attack perfidious Albion on her coasts.

The Paris newspaper *Le Calendrier républicain*, 5 Oct. 1793. A century earlier Jacques Bénigne Bossuet, the high priest of Gallicanism (the religious version of French nationalism), spoke of 'perfidious England'.

5 Lyons made war on freedom. Lyons no longer exists.

Decree for an inscription on a column to be erected in the ruins of the defeated royalist city of Lyons, 9 Oct. 1793; Cobb (1988) p.200.

6 There is no hope of prosperity so long as the last enemy of liberty has a breath left in his body. You must punish not only the traitors but the ones who do not take sides, whoever is a passenger in the Republic and does nothing for her, because since the French people proclaimed their will, whoever opposes it excludes himself from the sovereign power, and whoever does that is our enemy.

Louis Antoine Léon de Saint-Just in the National Convention, 10 Oct. 1793; Hardman (1973) p.155.

7 Oh, Liberty! How many crimes are committed in thy name!

The Girondin Manon Roland, last words before her execution on 8 Nov. 1793, as she passed the plaster statue of Liberty by the artist Jacques-Louis David, erected next to the scaffold; Sébastien Mercier *Nouveaux tableaux de Paris* (1799). Mme Roland had earlier maintained that 'Blood is necessary to cement revolution.' The BBC war correspondent Wynford Vaughan Thomas recalled the muttered expostulation of a French general in 1944 as he drank a glass of fine vintage wine warmed by a US army doctor over a spirit stove: 'Liberation, Liberation, what crimes have been committed in thy name!' (*How I Liberated Burgundy* (1985) p.158).

8 Imagine beings without morals, without ideas, honesty, religion, probity – in a word, with no regard for the laws of society … These girls are rarely amenable; they are born, they die, they live their lives in Paris … with no more thoughts in their heads than if they had been born Hottentots … The only politics they know is at the Grève; it's only there they see an act of public authority.

Restif de la Bretonne, chronicler of the Parisian lower depths; Richard Cobb *Reactions to the French Revolution* (1972) Ch.4. The Place de Grève was the traditional site of public executions, where the guillotine was first set up.

1 Along the Paris streets, the death-carts rumble, hollow and harsh. Six tumbrils carry the day's wine to La Guillotine ... In front of it, seated in chairs, as if in a garden of public diversion, are a number of women, busily knitting ... Crash! – a head is held up, and the knitting-women who scarcely lifted their eyes to look at it a moment ago when it could think and speak, count One.
Charles Dickens *A Tale of Two Cities* (1859) Ch.15. A classic Dickensian image that helped to reinforce the mid-Victorian aversion to the politics of the Continent.

2 The bloody knives and the tumbrils rolling to and fro create in his mind a special and sinister vision which he has succeeded in passing on to generations of readers. Thanks to Dickens, the very word 'tumbril' has a murderous sound; one forgets that a tumbril is only a sort of farm-cart. To this day, to the average Englishman, the French Revolution means no more than a pyramid of severed heads.
George Orwell *Inside the Whale* 'Charles Dickens' (1939).

3 The inn previously called The Orleans Arms will now be re-named The Sans-Culottes' Rendezvous. The tavern that used to be known as the St Louis will now be The Equality. The hostelry that was formerly The Golden Cross will be The Revolutionary Army.
Decree of the township of Pierrefonds (Oise), 14 Nov. 1793; Hardman (1973) pp.168–9.

4 We know the true wish of France, it is our own, namely to recover and preserve our holy, apostolic and Roman Catholic religion. It is to have a King who will serve as father within and protector without ... You have introduced atheism in the place of laws, men who are tyrants in the place of the King who was our father.
Abbé Bernier, 'Address to the French', late May 1793; Schama (1989) p.705. Bernier was a leader of the conservative insurgency in the Vendée, on the Atlantic coast south of Brittany. It broke out shortly after the execution of Louis XVI in Jan. 1793.

5 I have crushed the children under the hooves of the horses, massacred the women ... who ... will breed no more brigands ... I have wiped out all ... The roads are strewn with corpses ... We take no prisoners; it would be necessary to feed them with the bread of Liberty.
General François-Joseph Westermann's answer to the Vendeé rebels, Dec. 1793; Hoffman Nickerson *The Armed Horde, 1793–1939* (1940) p.91. Westermann was guillotined in April 1794.

6 Having seen what was done in the name of fraternity, if I had a brother, I would call him cousin.
The Austrian Prince Clemens Metternich, subsequent orchestrator of European counter-revolution; Denis Brogan, *The Price of Revolution* (1951) Ch.1, p.11. The wit Sébastien Chamfort turned the revolutionary slogan 'Fraternity or Death!' into 'Be my brother or I will kill you!' He was arrested in April 1794 and died not long after a failed suicide attempt.

1794: CLIMAX OF TERROR

7 What is there in the delivering over a perjured Blockhead & an unprincipled Prostitute to the hands of the hangman?
Robert Burns, 12 Jan. 1795, on the execution of Louis XVI and Marie-Antoinette, who was guillotined on 16 Oct. 1793; *The Letters of Robert Burns* Vol.2 (1985) p.334. By the time of his death in 1796 Burns, the Revolution's sympathizer, had become an ardent supporter of the war to destroy it.

8 Happiness is a new idea in Europe.
Louis Antoine Léon de Saint-Just, 3 March 1794, in his *Report on the Means of Implementing the Decree against the Enemies of the Revolution*. A bizarre pronouncement coming from a man who sent so many to their deaths in the name of the Revolution. Ten days later he defined his notion of happiness as 'a plough, a field, a cottage free of the tax office, a family out of reach of the lust of a brigand', something, perhaps, akin to the 'pursuit of happiness' proclaimed in the American Declaration of Independence.

9 I am not a flatterer, a conciliator, an orator, a protector of the people; I myself am the people.
Maximilien Robespierre to the Assembly, 27 April 1792; G. Laurent (ed.) *Le Défenseur de la Constitution* (1939) p.39. Compare *L'état c'est moi*, attrib. to Louis XIV (see 459:4).

10 The impulse behind the people's revolutionary government is virtue and terror: virtue without which terror is pernicious; terror without which virtue is impotent ... The government of the Revolution is the despotism of liberty over tyranny.
Maximilien Robespierre to the Convention, 7 Feb. 1794.

11 O thou seagreen Incorruptible!
Thomas Carlyle *The French Revolution* (1837) Pt 3, Bk 1, Ch.6. 'Seagreen' is Carlyle's idea of the colour of Robespierre's complexion.

12 *Robespierre*: We killed tyranny, don't forget that.
Camille Desmoulins: We didn't kill it! Where's the difference between the arbitrary rule of Royal ministers and that of a handful of men whom we've made more powerful than ever they were?

Jean Anouilh *Poor Bitos* (1964) Act 2. Bitos (prick) is Robespierre. Desmoulins, his revolutionary colleague, went to the guillotine on 5 April 1794.

1 In September I fed the cubs of the Revolution with the butchered collops of the aristos. My voice forged weapons from the gold of the Nobility and the riches of the People. My voice was the gale that buried the lackeys of despotism beneath a wave of bayonets.
Danton at his trial, April 1794, according to Georg Büchner *Dantons Tod* (Danton's Death) (1834) Act 3, Sc.4. He recalls the days of the September Massacres and the victory at Valmy, where the invading Prussian army was turned back.

2 If I left my balls to Robespierre and my legs to Couthon, that would help the Committee of Public Safety for a while.
Georges-Jacques Danton, overheard in the Luxembourg Palace while awaiting execution; Cobb (1988) p.218. Robespierre was allegedly impotent, Georges Couthon, his revolutionary coadjutor, was a cripple.

3 At least they can't stop our heads from kissing in the basket.
Georges-Jacques Danton to his fellow victim, Hérault de Séchelles, after a guard had stopped them giving each other a last embrace on the scaffold, 5 April 1794; Antoine-Vincent Arnault *Souvenirs d'un sexagénaire* (1833).

4 Don't forget to show my head to the people. It's a pretty sight.
Georges-Jacques Danton to the executioner, Charles-Henri Sanson, 5 April 1794; Arnault (1833). Danton was an outstandingly ugly man, and such self-mockery, just seconds before his death, is breathtaking.

5 [The Republic] shall hold festivals every ten days, as follows: To the Supreme Being and Nature; to the human race; to the French people; to the benefactors of humanity; to the martyrs who died for liberty; to Liberty and Equality; to the Republic; to the freedom of the world; to love of country; to the hatred of tyrants and traitors; to truth; to justice; to modesty; to glory and immortality; to friendship; to frugality; to courage; to good faith; to heroism; to unselfishness; to love; to conjugal fidelity; to fatherly love; to mother love; to filial piety; to childhood; to youth; to manhood; to old age; to adversity; to farming; to industry; to our ancestors; to posterity; to happiness.
Decree founding the Cult of the Supreme Being, 7 May 1794; Hardman (1973) pp.244–5.

6 The operation of the Terror has blunted the sense of crime, as strong liquors blunt the palate.

Louis Antoine Léon de Saint-Just, summer 1794; Hardman (1999) p.219. By this time Saint-Just and Robespierre were wading in the blood of their supposed enemies.

7 The Terror isolated and stupefied the deputies just as it did ordinary citizens. On entering the Assembly each member, full of distrust, watched his words and actions, lest a crime be made out of them. And indeed everything mattered: where you sat, a gesture, a look, a murmur or a smile.
Antoine-Claire Thibaudeau on the Terror of 1793–4; Hardman (1999) p.170. This evokes a chilling comparison with the fear engendered in political assemblies in Stalin's Soviet Union.

8 *Police report*: A clerk of the former Parlement has said: 'the present order of things cannot last.'
Robespierre's directive: Find the address of the delinquent and have him arrested.
Robespierre's police state in action, 11 June 1794; Hardman (1999) p.228.

9　　Great God of battles, here lies a wretched poet
　　Alone, a prisoner, close to death …
　　I beg you, let me live, and may that tainted
　　　horde
　　Feel my javelins run them through.
The poet and one-time revolutionary sympathizer André Chénier, waiting for the guillotine, summer 1794. He was executed on 25 July, three days before the Terror came to an end; Francis Scaife *André Chénier* (1965) pp.337–8.

10 People are ceaselessly telling the judges: take care to protect the innocent; and I say to them, in the name of the *patrie*: tremble to save the guilty.
Claude-François Payan, 8 July 1794; Hardman (1999) p.229.

11 He that would make his own liberty secure, must guard even his enemy from oppression, for if he violates this duty, he establishes a precedent that will reach to himself.
Tom Paine 'Dissertation on First Principles of Government' (1795); *The Writings of Thomas Paine* Vol.3 (1895 edn) p.277.

12 If one day it be asked why the National Convention organized a plan of surveillance demanding more officials than the literate population of Europe, Frenchmen will reply: 'this plan was wise and necessary: our enemies were so great in number and so widely disseminated … that every citizen had to consider himself a sentinel at his post.'
The quartermaster general of the army Robert Lindet, 20 Sept. 1794, shortly after the end of the Terror, with the execution of 100 Jacobin leaders, including Robespierre, Saint-

Just and Couthon, between 28 and 30 July in the coup d'état of Thermidor. Thermidor (the time of heat) was the 11th month in the Republic's calendar, running from 19 July to 17 Aug.

1 *J'ai vécu.* (I survived.)

Abbé Emmanuel-Joseph Sieyès, who famously staked out the claims of the Third Estate in 1789, when asked about his experiences in the Revolution. He also survived under Napoleon and died a natural death in 1836.

1795: STASIS

2 Who will dare lay hands on one who has organized victory in the French armies?

Jean Denis, Count de Lanjuinais, in the Convention, 29 May 1795, speaking of the 'organizer of victory', Lazare Carnot. Carnot had masterminded French military success since 1792 but now came close to being purged in the aftermath of Robespierre's liquidation; he, too, survived, however, dying in 1827.

3 What is the French Revolution? A war declared between patricians and plebeians, between rich and poor ... In all the Declarations of Rights, except that of 1795, the preamble exalted that first, most important maxim of eternal justice: the purpose of society is the general welfare. We took great steps, we made much rapid progress towards this end up to the present time. Since then we have marched away from that social purpose, away from the goal of the Revolution, towards communal ruin and towards the welfare of a small minority. Let us be bold enough to say that the Revolution, in spite of all the obstacles and the opposition it faced, advanced up to the 9th of Thermidor [the day of Robespierre's arrest, 27 July 1794], and that it has retreated ever since.

Gracchus Babeuf, *La Tribune du peuple*, 6 Nov. 1795. Babeuf, seen by some as the first Communist, was executed in 1797 for plotting against the Republic.

4 At least half the windows of fine old painted glass, 'richly dight', were broken; all the monuments torn down, and the bones of the dead exposed to view, and commingled with the ruins of their tombs, the names and armorial devices being utterly defaced, and the coffins taken away and converted into bullets ... The figures with which the altar had been adorned, were carefully separated from it, and triumphantly guillotined in the middle of the great square of the town.

Major Trench, Royal Marines, Quimper Cathedral, Brittany, 2 March 1795; Thompson (1938) p.258. Trench was taken prisoner after a sea battle in the autumn of 1794 and landed at Brest.

5 Impiety and revolt have been the cause of all the torments you experience ... You must return to that holy religion which showered down upon France the blessings of Heaven ... You must restore the government which for fourteen centuries constituted the glory of France and the delight of her inhabitants.

Louis XVIII, Declaration of Verona, 24 June 1795, after the death in captivity on 8 June of his nephew, the small son of Louis XVI, technically considered to have been Louis XVII; Cobb (1988) p.240.

6 The courtiers who surround him have forgotten nothing and learned nothing.

General Charles François du Périer Dumouriez on Louis XVIII, Sept. 1795; *Examen impartial d'un document intitré Declaration par Louis XVIII*, p.40. Also attrib. to Talleyrand, in the form 'They have learned nothing and forgotten nothing', at the time of the restoration of Louis XVIII in the spring of 1814.

7 The enemies attacked us at the Tuileries. We killed a good many of them; they killed thirty of our men and wounded sixty. We have disarmed the sections and all is quiet. As usual, I was not wounded.

General Napoleon Bonaparte to his brother Joseph, 6 Oct. 1795, after smashing the attempted royalist coup of Vendémiaire; J.E. Howard (ed.) *Letters and Documents of Napoleon* Vol.1 (1961) p.61.

8 Six years ago, this Whiff of Grapeshot was promised; but it could not be given then; could not have profited then. Now, however, the time is come for it, and the man; and behold, you have it; and the thing we specifically call *French Revolution* is blown into space by it, and become a thing that was!

Thomas Carlyle *The French Revolution* (1837) Pt 3, Bk 7, Ch.7. Carlyle's oft-quoted comment on Napoleon's suppression of the royalist rising in Paris; his judgement on its impact on the Revolution does not stand up.

9 [Anarchy will prevail] until some popular general ... shall draw the eyes of all men upon himself ... But the moment in which that event will happen, the person who really commands the army is your master; the master ... of your king, the master of your assembly, the master of your whole republic.

Edmund Burke *Reflections on the Revolution in France* (1790). Burke's prediction of a military coup was also voiced by none other than Robespierre (see 530:3).

VERDICTS

1 The whole history of the French Revolution presents us with nothing but a regular progress in robbery and murder. The first Assembly, for instance, wheedling their king out of his title and his power; they then set him at defiance, proscribe or put to death his friends, and then shut him up in his palace, as a wild beast in his cage. The second Assembly send a gang of ruffians to insult and revile him, and they then hurl him from his throne. The third Assembly cut his throat. What is there in all this but a regular and natural progression from bad to worse, and so with the rest of their abominable action.
William Cobbett *Democratic Principles Illustrated* (1798) p.48.

2 The interest of the bourgeoisie in the 1789 Revolution, far from having been a 'failure', 'won' everything ... That interest was so powerful that it vanquished the pen of Marat, the guillotine of the Terror, and the sword of Napoleon as well as the crucifix and the blue blood of the Bourbons. The Revolution was a 'failure' only for the mass.
Karl Marx and Friedrich Engels *Der heilige Familie* (The Holy Family) (1845). In the Marxian scheme of things the French Revolution was merely the intermediate bourgeois phase between feudalism and socialism.

3 The people generally counted for much more than its leaders ... These brilliant, powerful orators who voiced the thinking of the masses, are wrongly taken for the prime movers ... The prime mover is the people ... I have had to reduce to their true proportion the ambitious marionettes whose strings it pulled.
Jules Michelet *Histoire de la Révolution française* (1847) Preface. The romantic, populist view, influenced, perhaps, as much by the Revolution of 1830 as by the Revolution of 1789.

4 The Revolution had two very distinct phases – the *first*, in which the French seemed to want to abolish everything from the past; the *second* when they wanted to regain part of what they had jettisoned. There were in the *ancien régime*, a great many laws and political customs which disappeared at a stroke in 1789 and which reappeared some years later, just as certain rivers submerge beneath the earth's surface to re-emerge a little farther on ... Absolute government found huge scope for its rebirth [in]

that man who was to be both the consummator and the nemesis of the Revolution.
Alexis de Tocqueville *L'Ancien Régime et la Révolution* (1856) Preface and Bk 3, Ch.8. De Tocqueville, an aristocrat, saw basic affinities in the pre- and post-revolutionary experience, as the title of his book indicates.

5 The murderous dictatorship ... of the porter's lodge, the clerk, the concierge, the servant, of all the jealousy and spite of the lower orders.
The writer Edmond de Goncourt, 21 Dec. 1866, on the consequences for him of the French Revolution; *Journal* Vol.7 (1956) pp.228–9.

6 Out of the peasant, the worker and the bourgeois – all softened and tamed by the age-old process of civilization – there suddenly surges the barbarian, worse still, the primitive animal, the grimacing ape, blood-crazed and bestial, who kills while he smirks and frolics over the ruins he has created. Such is the nature of the government to which France was handed over.
Hippolyte Taine *La Révolution* Vol.2 (1884). Taine expresses the deep conservative alarm that the revolutionary violence of French politics in the century after 1789 had bred in the French Right.

7 The whole development of French society appears in a different light if we recognize that the revolution was a triumph for the conservative, propertied, land-owning classes, large and small ... It was a revolution not for, but against, capitalism ... The bourgeois ... of the French Revolution were landowners, *rentiers* and officials ... who all knew ... that without the pervasive influence of the social hierarchy and the maintenance of individual and family property rights against any interference by the state, their way of life, confined, unchanging, conservative, repetitive, would come to an end. The revolution was theirs, and for them at least it was a wholly successful revolution.
Alfred Cobban *The Social Interpretation of the French Revolution* (1964) pp.172–3. Doctrinaire Marxism exploded.

8 As a classic bourgeois revolution, it marks ... the beginning of capitalist and liberal democracy in the French experience. As a revolution of peasants and people ... it transcends its bourgeois limits ... Here lies the meaning of the thrill the world felt and the impact the French Revolution has had on the consciousness of the men of our century. This awareness in its own right is revolutionary: it exalts us still.

Albert Soboul *La Révolution française* (1967) Conclusion. Soboul's nationalism here exceeds his Marxism in his insistence on the continuing relevance of the French Revolution in the 50th anniversary year of the Russian Revolution.

1 The Revolution put into circulation ideas and values which fascinated, first Europe, then the world at large ... Yet one can wonder whether the catastrophes which have fallen on the West do not stem from it as well ... People's heads have been filled with the idea that society is the product of abstract thought when in fact it is formed by habits and customs, and in grinding them between the millstones of reason, ways of life based on long tradition are pulverized, and individuals are reduced to the state of interchangeable, anonymous atoms.

Claude Lévi-Strauss *De près et loin* (From Near and Far) (1988).

2 It's too soon to tell.

The Chinese prime minister, Zhou Enlai (Chou En-lai), on the historical significance of the French Revolution; Schama (1989) Preface.

Napoleon and the Struggle for Europe, 1796–1815

RISING STAR, 1791–9

1 Ambition, which overturns states ... which fattens on blood and crime, ambition which inspired Charles V, Philip II, Louis XIV, is like all unbridled passions, a violent, irrational delirium which only ceases with life; just as a fire, fanned by a relentless blast, only dies out when there is nothing left to burn.

Napoleon *Le Discours de Lyon* (The Lyons Treatise) (1791). An early meditation on power: the junior artillery officer reveals his paragons, Charles V and Philip II of Spain and Louis XIV of France.

2 I believe that in a free society he is a dangerous man; he seems to me to have the attributes of a tyrant, and I believe he would be one, if he were king, and that his would be a name of horror to posterity and to the sensitive patriot.

Lucien Bonaparte, Napoleon's brother, June 1792; Correlli Barnett *Bonaparte* (1978) p.28.

3 Soldiers, you are naked, ill-fed; though the Government owes you much, it can give you nothing ... I want to lead you into the most fertile plain in the world. Rich provinces, great cities will lie in your power; you will find there honour, glory and riches.

Napoleon to the army of Italy, spring 1796 (in fact, composed on the remote South Atlantic island of St Helena where he was exiled in 1815 – a classic example of Napoleon's capacity to rewrite history). During the campaigns of 1796 and 1797 Napoleon brought the whole of northern Italy under French control.

4 There can be no question of republicanizing Italy. The people are not at all inclined to accept liberty, neither are they worthy of this boon. In view of their degradation, all we can hope for is the silence born of cowardice and the respect born of fear; they execrate our principles as contrary to their passions and their prejudices.

Consul Fourcade to the Directory, May 1796; T.C.P. Blanning *The French Revolutionary Wars 1787–1802* (1996) p.173. An expression of French revolutionary disdain for an Italian populace seen as the slaves of clericalism and absolutism.

5 We are still too young to think of liberty. Let us think of being soldiers, and when we have a hundred thousand bayonets, then we can talk.

Ermelao Federigo, officer in Napoleon's Grande Armée; Stuart Woolf *A History of Italy 1700–1860* (1979) p.205. Italy did achieve independence in 1861 but, unlike Germany, not through its own military resources; French intervention made all the difference.

6   Poland has not perished yet,
        So long as we still live.
        That which alien force has seized
        We at sword point will retrieve.
        March, march, Dabrowski!
        From Italy to Poland!
        Let us now rejoin the nation
        Under thy command.

Josef Wybicki 'Marching Song of the Polish Legion'; Norman Davies *God's Playground: A History of Poland* (1981) Vol.2, p.16. The Legion was raised in France in 1797, placing its hopes in France for the restoration of the Polish state, which had been partitioned among Austria, Russia and Prussia between 1772 and 1795. Instead, Napoleon created the Grand Duchy of Warsaw as a French satellite in 1807. The song later became the Polish national anthem. Jan Henryk Dabrowski fought for France throughout the Napoleonic Wars.

7   Once did she hold the gorgeous East in fee;
        And was the safeguard of the West: the worth
        Of Venice did not fall below her birth,
        Venice, the eldest child of Liberty.

William Wordsworth 'On the Extinction of the Venetian Republic' (1802). Venice, once the mightiest sea power in the eastern Mediterranean, was now a mere pawn in international politics, consigned to Austria by France in 1797 as a result of Napoleon's conquests in Lombardy and Venetia.

8 It remains for me only to return to the crowd, to return, like Cincinnatus, to the plough, and to give an example of respect for the magistrates and of hatred of military rule, which has destroyed so many republics.

Napoleon to the Directory, 10 Oct. 1797; *Letters and Documents of Napoleon* Vol.1 (1961) p.206. The hero of Roman antiquity, Cincinnatus was chosen as dictator of the Republic in 458 BC when its survival was in doubt. He accomplished his rescue mission and then, after only 16 days, resigned power to return to his farm. Napoleon here is being utterly disingenuous, as the item below shows.

9 I have seen kings at my feet, I could have had fifty million in my coffers, I could have laid claim to many other things; but I am a French citizen, I am the senior general of the *Grande Nation*; I know that posterity will do me justice.

Napoleon, 17 Nov. 1797; Jean Tulard *Napoléon* (1977; 1984 trans.) p.84. Napoleon proclaims the grandeur of France to his troops before returning home from Italy to command the army assembled for the invasion of Britain. The phrase *Grande Nation* became a synonym for France in the era of Bonaparte's epic achievement.

1 Soldiers! Think how from the tops of these pyramids forty centuries look down upon you!

Napoleon in Egypt, before the Battle of the Pyramids, 21 July 1798; Gaspard Gourgaud *Mémoires* Vol.2 (1823) p.239. In May a French military expedition sailed for the eastern Mediterranean to deny the Levant to Britain and so threaten the overland route to British India. In this battle Napoleon defeated the Islamic Mameluk dynasty and momentarily seized control of Egypt and Syria, although Nelson's victory at the Battle of the Nile on 1 Aug. (see 532:7) cut off his seaborne route back to Europe.

2 If ever I have the luck to set foot in France again, the reign of hot air is over.

Napoleon, Cairo, 11 Aug. 1799; R.M. Johnston *The Corsican* (1910). Napoleon indicates his contempt for parliamentarianism before returning overland to France to mount his coup d'état against the regime of the Directory, in power since the fall of Robespierre in 1794.

FIRST CITIZEN, 1799–1804

3 Frenchmen, be wary, even of your generals' glory … Take care that a citizen does not emerge in France so dangerous as to make himself your master. He will either hand you over to the court and rule in its name, or usurp both people and crown to erect on the ruins of them both, a legal dictatorship, the worst of all tyrannies.

Maximilien Robespierre *Le Défenseur de la constitution* (The Defender of the Constitution) May 1792. Robespierre, like Burke (see 526:9), prophesies the dénouement that came on 9 Nov. 1799 with the coup of 18 Brumaire (revolutionary calendar).

4 Gentleman, we have a master: this young man does everything, can do everything and will do everything.

Emmanuel Sieyès to the legislature, 11 Nov. 1799. Sieyès, a leading figure in the events of 1789 (see 515:8), was a minister in the Directory and, together with the 30-year-old Napoleon, engineered its destruction.

5 His proclamations, in which he speaks only of himself and says that his return has given rise to the hope that he will put an end to France's troubles, have convinced me more than ever that in everything he does he sees only his own advancement.

The writer and liberal oppositionist Benjamin Constant to Sieyès, 11 Nov. 1799; Tulard (1977; 1984 trans.) p.17.

6 Citizens, the Revolution is established upon its original principles: it is consummated.

Bonaparte, Emmanuel Sieyès and Roger Ducos, proclamation, 15 Dec. 1799; J.M. Thompson *Napoleon Bonaparte* (1953) p.143. This inaugurated the new regime, the Consulate, with Napoleon as First Consul for a term of ten years. It was an attempt to give the coup the imprimatur of the Revolution but also to draw a line under a revolutionary process that, to critics such as Napoleon, threatened to dissolve into anarchy. The Consulate can be said to have come close to achieving this difficult balancing act.

7 For the sake of rest and order, the nation throws itself into the arms of a man who is believed sufficiently strong to arrest the Revolution and sufficiently generous to consolidate its gains.

Alexis de Tocqueville, unpublished sketch for a sequel to *L'Ancien Régime et la Révolution*; John Lukacs (ed.) 'The European Revolution' and Correspondence with Gobineau (1959) p.147.

8 I am the bookmark that shows the page where the Revolution has been stopped; but when I die it will turn the page and resume its course.

Napoleon, attrib.

9 I wish to throw blocks of granite on to the soil of France.

Napoleon on his restructuring on the French legal system under the Civil Code (renamed the Code Napoleon in 1807), one of his most enduring achievements; Thierry Lentz *Napoleon* (1998) p.64. Napoleon believed that the Revolution had dissolved French society into 'grains of sand'; the Code was an act of consolidation, to bring back the social coherence and stability supposedly lost in the turmoil of the 1790s.

10 The belief that a sheet of paper can be of any value unless it is supported by force has been one of the cardinal mistakes of the Revolution … A constitution ought to be made so that it does not impede the action of government.

Napoleon; D.G.M. Sutherland *France 1789–1815* (1985) p.360.

11 You see me master of France; well, I would not undertake to govern her for three months with liberty of the press.

Napoleon to Prince Metternich; Louis-Antoine Fauvelet de Bourrienne *Mémoires de Napoléon Bonaparte* (1855) Vol.1. This calls to mind the old East European joke: Xerxes, Alexander and Napoleon are watching the May Day parade in Red Square. Napoleon, reading *Pravda*, the Communist Party newspaper, exclaims: 'With a paper like this, no one would have heard of Waterloo!'

1 Doubtless the government of Buonaparte is the best that can be contrived for Frenchmen. Monkeys must be chained, though it may cost them some grimaces. If you have read the last senatus consultum, you will find that not an atom of liberty is left.
Walter Savage Landor to his brother, 16 Aug. 1802; Malcolm Elwin *Savage Landor* (1958). Landor uses the Italianate spelling of Napoleon's surname, which Napoleon himself had dropped by this stage. The 'senatus consultum', modelled on Roman practice, was a decree of the unelected senate, reflecting the authoritarian nature of the new regime. Landor was an implacable opponent of Napoleon, to the extent that he spent a considerable sum of his own money to equip volunteers to fight in Spain after the French invasion of 1808.

2 You are free to hold your own opinion; nevertheless, I must warn you that the first man not to vote for the Consulate for life will be shot in front of the regiment.
Stanislas de Girardin, prefect of Seine Inférieure, quoting a general advising his troops how to vote in the referendum on whether Napoleon should be made Consul for life; Tulard (1977; 1984 trans.) p.120.

3 I defy you to show me a republic, ancient or modern, which did not have an honours system. You call them baubles? So be it, men are led by baubles!
Napoleon to his chief of staff, Alexandre Berthier, on the projected Légion d'Honneur, 14 May 1802; Johnston (1910). The Légion d'Honneur, created on 19 May, established a new elite (numbering some 35,000 by 1815), owing their distinction entirely to Napoleon, whose profile was at the centre of the order's red-ribboned medal. It remains one of Napoleon's permanent legacies.

4 When a divisional chief replied to Napoleon's questioning satisfactorily, fluently and without hesitation, he returned from the Tuileries with the ribbon of the Légion d'Honneur, or with the dignity of a councillor of state. This was one of the compensations for an iron rule: when a man was talented ... Napoleon with his Herculean arm, would seize him by the hair and place him on a pedestal, saying: 'Behold my creature!'
Ymbert *Moeurs administratives* (1826).

5 I see in the physical situation and composition of the power of Bonaparte, a physical necessity for him to go on in this barter with his subjects and to promise to make them masters of the world if they consent to be his slaves.
Richard Brinsley Sheridan, Dec. 1802; Arthur Bryant *The Years of Victory* (1944) p.39.

6 My power proceeds from my reputation, and my reputation from the victories I have won. My power would fall if I were not to support it with more glory and more victories. Conquest has made me what I am; only conquest can maintain me.
Napoleon, 30 Dec. 1802; Johnston (1910).

EMPEROR, 1804–14

7 So he too is nothing but a man. Now he also will trample all human rights underfoot, and only pander to his own ambition; he will place himself above everyone else and become a tyrant.
The German composer Ludwig van Beethoven, on hearing that Napoleon had declared himself emperor, May 1804; Ferdinand Ries *Biographical Notes on Ludwig van Beethoven* (1838). Ries was Beethoven's pupil and witnessed Beethoven tear the title-page of his third symphony in two; now known as the Eroica, it had been dedicated to Napoleon.

8 When a work displeased him, he threw it into the fire ... If the author was not among his favorites, or if he spoke too well of a foreign country, that was sufficient to condemn the volume to the flames. On this account I saw his Majesty throw into the fire a volume of the works of Madame de Staël, on Germany.
Constant Wairy, first valet to Napoleon; Proctor Jones (ed.) *Napoleon* (1992) p.142. Napoleon, and the liberal woman of letters Mme de Staël were sworn political enemies, and her book *On Germany* had to be published in London.

9 'Look up there,' he told him. 'Do you see anything?' 'No,' answered Fesch, 'I see nothing.' 'Very well, in that case, know when to shut up,' replied the emperor. 'Myself, I see my star; it is that which guides me. Don't pit your feeble and incomplete faculties against my superior organism.'
Auguste Marmont *Mémoires* Vol.3 (1857) pp.339–40. Cardinal Joseph Fesch was the half-brother of Napoleon's mother, Marmont one of his illustrious marshals.

10 I have come too late; men are too enlightened; there is nothing great left to do ... Look at

Alexander; after he had conquered Asia and been proclaimed to the peoples as the son of Jupiter, the whole of the East believed it … with the exception of Aristotle and some Athenian pedants. Well, as for me, if I declared myself today the son of the eternal Father, there is no fishwife who would not hiss at me as I passed by.

Napoleon to Admiral Decrès, 3 Dec. 1804, the day after he had crowned himself emperor in the cathedral of Notre Dame.

1 As soon as I had power, I immediately re-established religion. I made it the groundwork and foundation upon which I built. I considered it as the support of sound principles and good morality, both in doctrine and in practice. Besides, such is the rest-lessness of man, that his mind requires that some-thing undefined and marvellous which religion offers; and it is better for him to find it there, than to seek it of Cagliostro, of Mademoiselle Lenormand, or of the fortune-tellers and impostors.

Napoleon, 1 June 1816; Emmanuel-Augustin Las Cases *La Vie, exil et conversations de Napoléon Bonaparte* Vol.2 (1823). The Italian Count Cagliostro, necromancer and freemason, died in 1795 after a long career of charlatanry. Mlle Marianne Lenormand was a fashionable fortune-teller, reading the cards for Parisian high society.

2 For the pope's purposes I am Charlemagne … I therefore expect the pope to accommodate his conduct to my requirements. If he behaves well I shall make no outward changes; if not, I shall reduce him to the status of bishop of Rome.

Napoleon to Cardinal Fesch, 7 Jan. 1806; Thompson (1953) p.136. In July 1809, after Pope Pius VII had excommunicated him, Napoleon had the pope arrested and imprisoned (he did not return to the Vatican until 1815). Charlemagne was crowned Holy Roman Emperor by the pope in 800 (see 188:7) and immediately asserted the religious supremacy of the empire over the papacy, in line with the practice of all Roman emperors since Constantine.

3 Q: What are our duties towards Napoleon Bonaparte, our Emperor?

A: We owe … love, respect, obedience, loyalty, military service and the taxes ordered for the preservation and defence of the empire and his throne. We also owe him fervent prayers for his safety and for the spiritual and temporal prosperity of the state.

Q: Why are we bound in all these duties towards our Emperor?

A: Because God … has made him the agent of His power on earth. Thus it is that to honour and serve our Emperor is to honour and serve God Himself.

Imperial Catechism; E.E.Y. Hales *Revolution and Papacy* (1960) pp.88–9. The Catechism, drilled into all French children approaching their first communion, enshrined the veneration expected by the new emperor. It was ordained that 16 Aug. be kept as St Napoleon's Day, presumably to eclipse the Feast of the Assumption of the Virgin on 15 Aug.

4 Never was a scene more beautiful; what opportunities it offers to the genius of painting. It is the precursor of the immortal battle that signalled the coronation anniversary of His Majesty. Thus will an astonished posterity cry when it observes this picture: 'What men and what an emperor!'

The dedicated admirer of Bonaparte, the painter Jacques-Louis David, 19 June 1806, on his canvas *The Distribution of the Eagles*; Warren Roberts *Jacques-Louis David* (1989) p.164. The battle in question was Austerlitz, fought on 2 Dec. 1805, exactly one year after Napoleon's coronation, a crushing defeat of Austria, which gave the French empire complete ascendancy over central Europe.

5 It is not enough to give power to those whom the people reject ; it must be forced to choose them. It is not enough to forbid press freedom; one needs newspapers that parody it. It is not enough to silence a representative assembly; one must maintain a false pretence of opposition, tolerated when it is futile and dispersed when it overshadows. It is not enough to dispense with the national will; the minority must offer support in the name of the majority.

Benjamin Constant *Principes de Politique*, completed in 1806 after his expulsion by Napoleon from the Tribunat (the upper house of the legislature) and not published in full until 1980; Jack Hayward *After the French Revolution* (1991) p.118.

NELSON AND THE WAR AT SEA, 1797–1805

6 Before this time tomorrow, I shall have gained a peerage, or Westminster Abbey.

Horatio Nelson, 1 Aug. 1798, on the eve of the Battle of the Nile, where he annihilated Napoleon's Mediterranean fleet; Roger Hudson (ed.) *Nelson and Emma* (1994) pp.128–9. Also credited to Nelson before Cape St Vincent on 14 Feb. 1797. By the end of the 18th century Westminster Abbey had become the burial ground of British national heroes; Nelson, however, was entombed in St Paul's Cathedral, as was Wellington.

7 I had the happiness to command a band of brothers.

Horatio Nelson to Admiral Lord Howe after the Battle of the Nile, Aug. 1798. Was this a self-conscious echo of Shakespeare's *Henry V*: 'We few, we happy few, we band of brothers' (Act 4, Sc.3)?

1 You know, Foley, I have only one eye – I have a right to be blind sometimes … I really do not see the signal.

Horatio Nelson at the Battle of Copenhagen, 2 April 1801; Carola Oman *Nelson* (1947) Ch.14, from the eyewitness Colonel William Stewart. He had lost the sight of his right eye at the siege of Calvi, Corsica, on 12 July 1794; here he famously uses his impairment to justify disregarding an order to break off action against the Danish fleet. Captain Thomas Foley commanded Nelson's flagship HMS *Elephant*. The action was taken to force Denmark to leave a grouping that included Russia, Prussia and Sweden, banding the four Baltic states together in protest against British interference with their maritime trade. It succeeded, and the Baltic conglomerate was dissolved in June.

2 Those far-distant, storm-beaten ships, upon which the Grand Army never looked, stood between it and the dominion of the world.

Captain Alfred Thayer Mahan USN *The Influence of Sea Power upon History* Vol.2 (1892). Mahan refers to the blockade of continental Europe imposed by the Royal Navy to strangle the Napoleonic empire economically and to contain French forces to the European shoreline.

3 I do not say they cannot come. I only say they cannot come by sea.

Admiral Earl St Vincent, First Lord of the Admiralty, 1801. As long as the Royal Navy held the English Channel, 'they' – the French – could not cross it to make a seaborne invasion of Britain.

4 We will form a more complete coastal system and England will weep for the war she undertakes, with tears of blood.

Napoleon to the Council of State, 1 May 1803, on the resumption of hostilities with Britain after the brief interlude of the Peace of Amiens; Miot de Melito *Memoirs*. His rejoinder to the blockade was the Continental System, the economic consolidation of French-occupied Europe.

5 He could not know who I was, but he entered at once into conversation with me, if I can call it conversation, for it was almost all on his side and all about himself, and in, really, a style so vain and silly as to surprise and almost disgust me.

Sir Arthur Wellesley (later Duke of Wellington) on his one and only meeting with Nelson on 12 Sept. 1805; Oman (1947) p.522. Once Nelson discovered who Wellesley was, his demeanour changed completely.

6 When I came to explain to them the '*Nelson touch*', it was like an electric shock. Some shed tears, all approved – 'It was new – it was singular – it was simple!'

Horatio Nelson to Emma, Lady Hamilton, 1 Oct. 1805; Hudson (1994) p.213. The 'Nelson touch' was Nelson's battle-plan to cut through the Franco-Spanish fleet at two points and destroy it piecemeal.

7 In case signals can neither be seen nor perfectly understood, no captain can do very wrong if he places his ship alongside that of the enemy.

Horatio Nelson, 9 Oct. 1805.

8 England expects that every man will do his duty.

Horatio Nelson, signal to the British Fleet from his flagship HMS *Victory* before the Battle of Trafalgar, 21 Oct. 1805, as remembered by Captain Henry Blackwood RN, an eyewitness; Hudson (1994) p.222.

9 Engage the enemy more closely.

Horatio Nelson, last signal to the fleet during the Battle of Trafalgar; literally 'Close Action', no.16 in the Signal Book.

10 'Kiss me, Hardy,' said he. The Captain now knelt down and kissed his cheek, when his Lordship said: 'Now I am satisfied; thank God, I have done my duty.'

Sir William Beatty *Authentic Narrative of the Death of Lord Nelson* (1807). Nelson's last words to his flag-captain, Thomas Hardy, after being mortally wounded by an enemy sharp-shooter at the height of the battle. Beatty was chief surgeon in *Victory* and an eyewitness of Nelson's dying moments.

11 When the game began, I wished myself at Warnborough with my plough again; but when they had given us one duster, and I found myself snug and tight, I set to in good earnest, and thought no more about being killed than if I were at Murrell Green Fair, and I was presently as busy and as black as a collier. How my fingers got knocked overboard I don't know, but off they were, and I never missed them till I wanted them. We have taken a rare parcel of ships, but the wind is so rough we cannot bring them home, else I should roll in money, so we are busy smashing 'em, and blowing 'em up wholesale.

A seaman from *Royal Sovereign*, writing home after the Battle of Trafalgar; Hudson (1994) pp.237–8.

12 England has saved herself by her exertions, and will, I trust, save Europe by her example.

British prime minister William Pitt, 9 Nov. 1805; R. Coupland *War Speeches of William Pitt* (1915) p.35. The news of the victory at Trafalgar reached London on 6 Nov. This is from Pitt's speech at the Lord Mayor's banquet.

THE SPANISH ULCER: WELLINGTON AND THE PENINSULAR WAR, 1808–13

1 *¡Guerra a cuchillo!* (War to the Knife!)
José de Palafox, governor of Saragossa, to the French invading forces, 4 Aug. 1808. French troops entered Spain on 16 Feb. to supplant the unreliable Spanish Bourbon dynasty and make Spain part of Napoleon's Europe-wide dominion. Joseph Bonaparte, Napoleon's brother, was declared king on 9 May.

2 Women, or rather furies let loose, threw themselves with horrible shrieks upon the wounded, and disputed who should kill them by the most cruel tortures; they stabbed their eyes with knives and scissors, and seemed to exult with ferocious joy at the sight of their blood.
M. de Rocca *Memoirs of the War of the French in Spain* (1816) p.255.

3   Not a drum was heard, not a funeral note,
   As his corse to the rampart we hurried,
   Not a soldier discharged his farewell shot
   O'er the grave where our hero we buried.
Charles Wolfe 'The Burial of Sir John Moore after Corunna' (1817). General Moore was killed on 16 Jan. 1809 in a rearguard action covering the evacuation of his forces to the Spanish port of La Coruña. Moore became legendary as an heroic loser, in a well-established English tradition.

4 I construe that perforce it must be one of the alternative duties, as given below … 1. To train an army of uniformed British clerks for the benefit of the accountants and copy-boys in London, or perchance, 2. To see to it that the forces of Napoleon are driven out of Spain.
An exasperated Sir Arthur Wellesley (later Duke of Wellington) responding to the bureaucratic demands of the War Office in London; Peter G. Tsouras *Warriors' Words* (1992) p.97.

5 I don't know what effect these men will have upon the enemy, but, by God, they frighten me!
Sir Arthur Wellesley from Portugal on the men under his command, 1809.

6 I have seen many persons hanging in the trees by the sides of the road, executed for no reason that I could learn, excepting that they had not been friendly to the French invasion … the route of their

column on their retreat could be traced by the smoke of the villages to which they set fire.
Sir Arthur Wellesley to the war minister, Lord Castlereagh, 18 May 1809; *Despatches* Vol.4, pp.317, 318. Reminiscent of a scene from Goya's etchings *The Disasters of War*, recording the atrocities committed by the French occupation forces.

7 Soon after daylight the bugle sounded for two hours' plunder … One of our officers saw a man go among a number of women and force off all their ear-rings. Those that would not give way [he] broke off a bit of their ear … I passed many wounded … 8 or 10 shot through the face, their heads one mass of clotted blood, many with limbs shattered, some shot in the body & groaning most piteously and, oh shame to the British soldiers, the fatigued officers could not get the men moved all day from their plunder and intoxication.
George Hennell, 94th Foot, 9 April 1812, on the aftermath of the capture of Badajoz on 7 April; Michael Glover (ed.) *A Gentleman Volunteer* (1979) pp.17, 18.

8 It is quite impossible for me or any other man to command a British army under the existing system. We have in the service the scum of the earth as common soldiers.
Viscount Wellington, 2 July 1813; *Despatches* Vol.10, pp.473, 495–6. Wellington was elevated to the peerage in Sept. 1809.

GERMANY: GENESIS OF A NATION, 1806–10

9 I saw the emperor – that world spirit – riding on parade through the city. It is indeed a wonderful sensation to see such an individual here on horseback, who begirds the world and rules it.
The philosopher and Napoleonophile, Georg Wilhelm Friedrich Hegel, on the emperor's entry into Jena, Oct. 1806; Karl Löwith *From Hegel to Nietzsche* (1965) p.215. Prussia was comprehensively defeated in the Battle of Jena on 14 Oct., and Hegel had a poor reward for his devotion. The University of Jena was closed by the French, and Hegel lost his position as professor of philosophy.

10 I see that God has given [Napoleon] dominion over the world; never has that been clearer to me than in this war.
The Swiss historian and royal historiographer in the Prussian capital, Berlin, Johannes von Müller, soon after the overwhelming Prussian defeat at Jena; Paul Sweet *Friedrich von Gentz* (1941) p.134. Müller's idolatry paid off better than Hegel's, when Napoleon made him secretary of state for Westphalia in 1807.

1 Though … the bones of our national unity … may have bleached and dried in the storms and rains and burning suns of several centuries, yet the reanimating breath of the spirit world has not ceased to inspire. It will yet raise the dead bones of our national body and join them bone to bone so that they shall stand forth grandly with a new life … No man, no god, nothing in the realm of possibility can help us, but we alone must help ourselves, as long as we deserve it.

Johann Gottlieb Fichte *Addresses to the German Nation* (1807); G.S. Ford *Stein and the Era of Reform in Prussia* (1965) p.111. Fichte the philosopher became the arch-exponent of German nationalism with the publication of this mystical call to arms.

2 The events in Spain have made a distinct impression and are a visible proof of what we should long ago have perceived. It would be very helpful if in discreet ways the news about them could be spread, since they show to what lengths cunning and the desire to dominate may go, as well as what a nation may do when it has the strength and courage.

Baron vom Stein to Prince Wittgenstein, 15 Aug. 1808; Ford (1965) p.153. Stein, one of the architects of reform in Prussia after the humiliation of Jena, was dismissed as a senior minister when Napoleon discovered the contents of this letter. It was written not long after Madrid had risen against the French on 2 May, a high inspiration to Stein, a dangerous precedent to Bonaparte.

3 Germania, sacred fatherland,
      A German's passion and his hope!
      Thou land supreme! Thou glorious land!
      We swear to thee anew;
      Forbidden ground to knaves and slavish serfs;
      They'll feed the crow and raven!
      While we march on to Hermann's field,
      And we will have our vengeance!

Ernst Moritz Arndt *Hymne an der Vaterland* (1808). Hermann (Arminius), the German tribal chief, destroyed the Roman army led by Varus in the Thuringian forest in the year AD 9. The victory was a huge inspiration to German nationalists, including the dramatist Heinrich von Kleist, in his play *The Battle of Arminius*, also written to celebrate the 1800th anniversary of the battle. During the final days of World War II an SS detachment is said to have made a last stand in the forest around the statue of Hermann.

4 Clasp your spear to your faithful breast,
      It clears the way to freedom.
      Now cleanse the earth
      Of German land
      With thy pure German blood!

The poet Karl Theodor Körner, mortally wounded in battle against the French on 26 Aug. 1813.

5 Let the nation learn to trace itself to its source, delve into its roots: it will find in its innermost being a fathomless well-spring which rises from subterranean treasure; many minds have already been enriched by drawing on the hoard of the Niebelungen; and still it lies there inexhaustible, in the depths of its lair.

The writer Josef Görres, 1810; *Collected Writings* (1854) Vol.1, pp.125 ff. The Niebelungen were a mythical community of dwarfs living deep under the earth, guardians of a fabulous hoard of gold.

6 *Q*: What is your opinion of Napoleon, the Corsican, the great emperor of the French?
  A: I see him as a detestable man, as the fount of all evil and the death of everything good, as a criminal there are not enough words to indict; the very angels will run out of breath when they try to list his offences on judgement day.
  Q: How do you picture him?
  A: As a spirit of destruction, who rises from hell, glides through the temple of nature and makes its columns tremble.

The German playwright Heinrich von Kleist *Katechismus für Deutsche* (1809); *Works* Vol.4. Compare the Imperial Catechism (see 532:3).

RETREAT FROM MOSCOW, 1812

7 For ever I see him high on horseback, the eternal eyes set in the marble of that imperial visage, looking on with the calm of destiny at his Guards as they march past. He was sending them to Russia, and the old grenadiers glanced up at him with so awesome a devotion, so sympathetic an earnestness, with the pride of death: *Te, Caesar, morituri salutant* [Caesar, they who are about to die salute you].

The German poet Heinrich Heine *Englische Fragmente* (English Jottings). Heine was 15 years old when Napoleon invaded Russia in 1812. He never quite outgrew his adolescent crush on the great man.

8 [They imagined] that they knew what they were doing and did it of their own free will, but they were all involuntary tools of history, carrying on a work concealed from them but comprehensible to us. Such is the inevitable fate of men of action, and the higher they stand in the social hierarchy the less they are free … Providence compelled these men, striving to attain personal aims, to further the accomplishment of a stupendous result no one of them at all expected – neither Napoleon nor [Tsar] Alexander, and still less any of those who did the actual fighting.

Leo Tolstoy *War and Peace* (1868/9) Vol.2, Bk 3, Ch.1. The famous determinist view of the Franco-Russian collision.

1 This long road is the road to India. Alexander left from as far away as Moscow to reach the Ganges.

Napoleon to Count Louis-Marie de Narbonne, his envoy in Vienna, 1811; attrib.

2 The emperor is mad, completely mad, and he will turn us all, such as we are, arse over heels, and the whole thing will end in an appalling catastrophe.

Anon. minister to Marshal Marmont, 1809; Tulard (1977; 1984 trans.) p.297.

3 If the Emperor Napoleon sent his army into the Russian interior, it would be annihilated like Charles XII's at Poltava, or forced to make a hasty retreat.

The French Captain Leclerc, Jan. 1812; Tulard (1977; 1984 trans.) p.300. Charles XII of Sweden was routed by Tsar Peter the Great at Poltava in 1709 (see 445:2).

4 There is the sun of Austerlitz.

Napoleon before the Battle of Borodino, west of Moscow, 7 Sept. 1812; Thompson (1953) p.332. On the morning of Austerlitz, 2 Dec. 1805, the sun broke through the mist to reveal the battlefield and pave the way for the French triumph that followed. The French also won at Borodino, but unlike Austerlitz it was a pyrrhic victory – Napoleon losing a quarter of his army, dead and wounded – and did not end the war.

5 This is a war of extermination, a terrible strategy which has no precedent in the history of civilization … To burn down their cities! A demon has got into them! What ferocious determination1 What a people! What a people!

Napoleon's reaction to the burning of Moscow after his entry into the city on 14 Sept. 1812; E.V. Tarle *1812* (1959) p.585.

6 The flames of Moscow were the aurora of the liberty of the world.

The liberal writer Benjamin Constant *The Spirit of Conquest* (1813) Preface.

7 The leaders, pushed on by those who came behind them, pushed back by the guards or the bridge-engineers, or held up by the river, were crushed, trampled under foot or hurled into the drifting ice of the Beresina. There arose from this immense and

horrifying throng, sometimes a deafening hum, sometimes a huge clamour mixed with wailing and dreadful curses.

Philippe Paul Ségur *Histoire de Napoléon et la Grande Armée pendant l'année 1812* (1824) Ch.8. Ségur was himself involved in the disastrous retreat from Moscow after 18 Oct.; here we have his nightmare recollection of the crossing of the River Beresina on 26–28 Nov.

8 The dull monotonous thud of our footsteps, the crackle of the frozen snow and the feeble moans of the dying, were the only things to break that vast and doleful silence … Even the most determined of our men lost heart. Sometimes the snow opened up under their feet; more often the glassy surface gave them no support. They slid at every step and stumbled continually as they marched on … Soon they fell on their hands and knees … finally their heads dropped into the snow, reddening it with a livid bloodstain, and their torment was over.

Philippe Paul Ségur (1824) Ch.9.

9 It's a long way to Carcassonne.

Words attrib. to a dying French soldier on the retreat from Moscow. Carcassonne, in southwest France, is indeed many, many days' march from Moscow.

IMPERIAL COLLAPSE, IMPERIAL REVIVAL, 1813–15

10 In order to have good soldiers, a nation must always be at war.

Napoleon in conversation with one of his mythologists, Barry O'Meara, on St Helena, 26 Oct. 1816; B. O'Meara *A Voice from St Helena* (1822).

11 You can't stop me! I spend thirty thousand men a month.

Napoleon, speaking to the Austrian foreign minister, Prince Metternich, 1810.

12 Conscription is the vitality of a nation, the purification of its morality, and the real foundation of its habits.

Napoleon *Political Aphorisms*.

13 Then, only one man seemed to be alive in Europe; everyone else tried to fill their lungs with the air he had breathed. Each year France made this man a present of 300,000 of her youth; it was the tribute paid to Caesar, and if he had not had that flock of sacrificial lambs behind him, he could not have

followed his star. It was the escort he needed to propel him across the world and finally to dwindle away in a little valley on a lonely island, under a weeping willow.

Alfred de Vigny *Confession d'un enfant du siècle* (Confession of a Child of the Century) (1836) Ch.2. The poet de Vigny served in the Royal Guards throughout most of the Bourbon Restoration after Napoleon's downfall.

1 Some have produced sores on their arms and legs by blistering themselves, and to make these sores, so to speak, incurable, they dressed them with water and arsenic. Many have given themselves hernias and some apply violent acids to their genitals.

Prefect Stanislas de Girardin on resistance to conscription in 1813; Tulard (1977; 1984 trans.) p.319.

2   I have served, commanded, conquered forty
          years.
      I have seen the destiny of the world in my
          hands,
      And I have always known that at every turn
      The fate of States hinges on a single moment.

Napoleon, 31 Aug. 1813, quoting from Voltaire's 1736 drama *La Mort de César* (The Death of Caesar) Act 1, Sc.1, at the point when his grip on central Europe began to weaken.

3 My star was growing paler; I felt the reins slipping from my fingers; and I could do nothing. Only a thunderstroke could save us. I had, therefore, to fight it out; and day by day, by this or that piece of ill-fortune, our chances were becoming more slender.

Napoleon, 19 Oct. 1813, after his defeat at the Battle of Leipzig; Johnston (1910). The battle was known as the 'Battle of the Nations' because Napoleon faced a multinational force, supposedly fused by a common resistance to his imperialism.

4 To kill myself would be a gambler's death. I am condemned to live. Besides, only the dead do not return.

Napoleon, 11 April 1814; *Correspondence* Vol.31, pp.485–6. He spoke after abdicating as emperor and before going into exile on the Mediterranean island of Elba, off the northwest coast of Italy.

5 The young people, and above all the military, are not satisfied by the change of government. The former because a career of glory and fortune is closed to them; the latter because they have to leave these things behind!

François Espinasse to William Lorrain, Le Havre, June 1814; *A Border Schoolmaster: The Written Effects of William Lorrain* (2000) p.146. The French naval lieutenant Espinasse was taken prisoner in 1809 and became a good friend of the Scots schoolmaster William Lorrain. He returned briefly to France after Napoleon's abdication before settling in Scotland. His letter gives one good reason why the emperor was to make his comeback in 1815.

6 Victory will advance at the charge. The eagle, with the national colours, will fly from steeple to steeple all the way to the towers of Notre Dame.

Napoleon, proclamation of 9 March 1815, issued at Grenoble after his escape from Elba; David Hamilton-Williams *Waterloo: New Perspectives* (1999 edn) p.57.

7 [Marshal Ney] said, among other things, that he would bring Napoleon in a cage: to which the King [Louis XVIII] replied – *'Je n'aimerais pas un tel oiseau dans ma chambre!'* [I shouldn't fancy a bird like that in my room!']

The Hon. H.G. Bennet in conversation with the confidant of the great, Thomas Creevey, 3 April 1815; John Gore (ed.) *The Creevey Papers* (1963) p.129. Louis XVIII had been placed on the French throne after Napoleon's abdication in 1814. Ney, who had served Napoleon, went over to Louis at the Restoration but defected to Napoleon and fought with him at Waterloo. He was later shot for high treason.

8   The Tiger has broken out of his den.
      The Ogre has been three days at sea.
      The Wretch has landed at Fréjus.
      The Buzzard has reached Antibes.
      The Invader has arrived in Grenoble.
      The General has entered Lyons.
      Napoleon slept at Fontainebleau last night.
      The emperor will proceed to the Tuileries
          today.
      His Imperial Majesty will address his loyal
          subjects tomorrow.

Paris broadsheet, issued late March 1815, charting the changing national mood on Napoleon's northward march from Provence, thence up the Rhône valley to Paris.

9 You are weakening and chaining me ... France is asking what has become of the emperor's strong right arm, the arm she needs to master Europe. Why speak to me of goodness, abstract justice, and natural law? The foremost law is necessity, the foremost justice is national security.

Napoleon to the Council of State, April 1815, in response to its call for a degree of constitutionalism; John Holland Rose *The Life of Napoleon I* (1902) p.451.

10 This man – I mean Napoleon – has been cured of nothing and returns as much of a despot, as eager for conquests, in fact, as mad as ever ... The whole of

Europe will fall on him; it is impossible for him to hold out and all will be finished within four months.
Joseph Fouché to Etienne Pasquier (political survivors both), April 1815; Tulard (1977; 1984 trans.) p.334. An accurate prediction by a man who had been a ruthlessly efficient minister of police for the emperor but who now saw the way the wind was blowing and stood ready to pave the way for a second Bourbon restoration (see 543:3).

WATERLOO, 18 JUNE 1815

1 There, it all depends upon that article whether we do the business or not. Give me enough of it, and I am sure.
Duke of Wellington to Thomas Creevey, Brussels, late May–early June 1815; Gore (1963) p.142. The target of the duke's comment was a British infantry private who was sightseeing in the city centre; Creevey, the well-connected diarist, was always, apparently, in the right place at the right time.

2 Suddenly a dark mass of cavalry appeared for an instant on the main ridge, and then came sweeping down the slope in swarms, reminding me of an enormous surf bursting over the prostrate hull of a stranded vessel, and then running, hissing and foaming, up the beach.
Cavalié Mercer *Journal of the Waterloo Campaign* (1927 edn) p.168. A British horse-artilleryman gives an unforgettable picture of a French cavalry charge at Waterloo on 18 June.

3 Just as it is difficult, if not impossible, for the best cavalry to break into infantry who are formed into squares and who defend themselves with coolness and daring, so it is true that once the ranks have been penetrated, then resistance is useless and nothing remains for the cavalry to do but to slaughter at almost no risk to themselves.
The French Captain Duthilt *Mémoires* (1909 edn) p.42. Wellington could be said to have won at Waterloo not least because his British infantry squares – static formations walled by artillery, musket and bayonet – held firm in the face of multiple French cavalry onslaughts.

4 Then we got among the guns … Such slaughtering! I can hear the Frenchmen yet crying *Diable* when I struck at them, and the long-drawn hiss through their teeth as my sword went home … The artillery drivers sat on their horses weeping aloud as we went among them; they were mere boys.
Corporal Dickson of the Union Brigade: John Keegan *The Face of Battle* (1976) p.201.

5 By God! I've lost my leg!
  Have you, by God?
Exchange between the stricken Lord Uxbridge and the Duke of Wellington, late in the day at Waterloo; Marquis of Anglesey *One-Leg* (1961) p.149.

6 *La Garde recule!* (The Guard is falling back!)
At about 7.30 p.m., when the outcome was still in doubt, Napoleon sent in the experienced veterans of his Old Guard. Their repulse marked the decisive turning point of the battle, and the French were soon routed; Elizabeth Longford *Wellington: The Years of the Sword* (1969) p.481.

7 *Merde, je ne me rends pas!* (Shit, I'm not surrendering!)
General Pierre de Cambronne, commander of the Guard, when called on to surrender; Longford (1969) p.481. 'Merde' subsequently passed into legend as 'le mot de Cambronne', and the response is often bowdlerized as 'The Guard dies, but it does not surrender!'

8 Just close up to within a yard or two of a small ragged hedge which was our own line, the French lay as if they had been mowed down in a row without any interval. It was a distressing sight, no doubt, to see every now and then a man alive amongst them, and calling out to Lord Arthur [Hill]] to give them something to drink.
Thomas Creevey on the field of Waterloo two days after the battle; Gore (1963) p.152. Hill was Wellington's second-in-command.

9 It has been a damned nice thing – the closest run thing you ever saw in your life.
Duke of Wellington to Thomas Creevey, 19 June 1815; Gore (1963) p.150.

10 It was the most desperate business I ever was in. I never took so much trouble about any Battle, & never was so near being beat.
Duke of Wellington to his brother, 19 June 1815; *Camden Miscellany* (1948) Vol.18.

11 Never did I see such a pounding match. Both were what the boxers call gluttons. Napoleon did not manoeuvre at all. He just moved forward in the old style, in columns, and was driven off in the old style.
Duke of Wellington to General Beresford, 2 July 1815; *Despatches* Vol.12, p.529.

12 I am wretched even at the moment of victory, and I always say that next to a battle lost, the greatest misery is a battle gained.

Duke of Wellington, July 1815; *The Diary of Frances, Lady Shelley* Vol.1 (1912) p.102. In his despatch on Waterloo, Wellington wrote: 'Nothing except a battle lost can be half so melancholy as a battle won' (*The Times*, 22 June 1815).

1 On one side, precision, foresight, geometry, prudence, retreat assured, reserves economized, obstinate composure, imperturbable method ... war directed, watch in hand, nothing left voluntarily to intuition...; on the other, flashing glance, a mysterious something which gazes like the eagle and strikes like the thunderbolt, prodigious art in disdainful impetuosity, all the mysteries of a deep soul, intimacy with Destiny ... Waterloo is a battle of the first rank won by a captain of the second.
Victor Hugo *Les Misérables* (1862) Cosette, Ch.16.

2 They planned their campaigns just as you might make a splendid piece of harness. It looks very well; and answers very well; until it gets broken, and then you are done for. I made my campaigns of ropes. If anything went wrong, I tied a knot; and went on.
Duke of Wellington; Sir W. Fraser *Words on Wellington* (1899) p.37.

3 I come, as Themistocles did, to seat myself at the hearth of the British people. I put myself under the protection of its laws, a protection which I claim from Your Royal Highness as the strongest, the most resolute, and the most generous of my enemies.
Napoleon to the Prince Regent, 13 July 1815; J.M. Thompson (ed.) *Napoleon's Letters* (1934). Themistocles, architect of the victory of Athens over Persia in 480 BC, was expelled from Athens ten years later and found a welcome in Persia, where he subsequently died. Napoleon I – unlike Napoleon III – was not given asylum in Britain.

4 Wherever wood can swim, there I am sure to find this flag of England.
Napoleon, embarking for exile on the far-off island of St Helena, July 1815, paying tribute to the omnipresence of British sea-power.

VERDICTS

5 Napoleon was a man! His life was the stride of a demi-god.
The German writer Johann Wolfgang von Goethe *Gespräche mit Eckermann* (Conversations with Eckermann) (1828). Goethe met Napoleon at Erfurt on 2 Oct. 1808.

6 Napoleon's jealousy of Davout had so completely lodged in the minds of the other generals the idea that the emperor wished to see no trace in them of talent superior to his, that they considered it wise to act always like pure automatons rather than let themselves be guided by their own intelligence, even when unforeseen circumstances seemed to demand personal initiative. How different was the thinking in 1796 during the immortal Italian campaign, when they all burned with republican fervour, obeying with zeal but, if no orders reached them from the commanding general, daring to be self-reliant.
The French novelist Stendhal (Henri Beyle), who had served Napoleon loyally but not uncritically; *The London Magazine* (Feb. 1825). Davout was one of Napoleon's most brilliant (and ruthless) marshals.

7 He put his foot upon the neck of kings, who would have put their yoke upon the necks of the people: he scattered before him with fiery execution, millions of hired slaves, who came at the bidding of their masters to deny the right of others to be free. The monument of greatness and glory he erected, was raised on ground forfeited again and again to humanity – it reared its majestic front on the ruins and the shattered hopes and broken faith of the common enemies of mankind. If he could not secure the freedom, peace, and happiness of his country, he made her a terror to those who by sowing civil dissension and exciting foreign wars, would not let her enjoy those blessings.
William Hazlitt *Political Essays* (1819) Preface. The writer Hazlitt fell into deep melancholy after Waterloo (see 541:3).

8 O lank-haired Corsican! How lovely was your France
Beneath the mighty sun of Messidor!
She was a wild and rebel thoroughbred
With no steel bit nor reins of gold to hold in check;
An untamed mare, her rustic rump still reeking of the blood of kings,
But proud, her great hoof pounds the ancient earth,
Free for the first time in her life ...
With withered hocks, she's at last gasp and spent,
And staggering at every step,
She begged for mercy from her alien cavalier;
But executioner, you paid no heed!
Weary at last of journeys without end,
Of moving on but never reaching home,

Of making all creation new,
And scattering the human race like dust.

Auguste Barbier *The Idol* (1831) Sect.3. Messidor, the tenth month of the revolutionary calendar, ran from 19/20 June to 19/20 July.

1 The truth is that he loved it [France] as a rider loves his horse … [forcing] it on over ever wider ditches and ever higher fences – come up, now, one more ditch, just another fence … But after what seemed like the last hurdle, there are always new barriers to jump, and in any case the horse must inevitably remain what it always was – a mount, and an overburdened one.

Hippolyte Taine *Les Origines de la France contemporaine: Régime moderne* (The Origins of Present-day France: The Modern Era) Vol.1 (1891) p.129.

2 It is quite something to be all at once a national glory, a revolutionary guarantee, and a principle of authority.

The French statesman and historian François Guizot, 1840; Tulard (1977; 1984 trans.) p.347.

3 It is possible to lead astray an entire generation, to strike it blind, to drive it insane, to direct it towards a false goal. Napoleon proves this.

The Russian liberal revolutionary Alexander Herzen, c.1855; R.V. Sampson *Tolstoy* (1973) p.61.

4 He left France smaller than he found it, true; but you can't measure a nation like that. As far as France is concerned, he had to happen. It's rather like Versailles: it just had to be built. Don't let us haggle over greatness.

President Charles de Gaulle in conversation with his minister of culture André Malraux, 1969; André Malraux *Les Chênes qu'on abat* (The Oaks We Fell) (1971). The huge baroque Palace of Versailles, outside Paris, was built for Louis XIV as the emblem of royal grandeur, and just as it symbolized the glory of France, so too did Napoleon. No doubt de Gaulle himself felt that for France he, also, 'had to happen'.

Revolution and Counter-Revolution in Europe, 1815–48

ACTION AND REACTION ON THE CONTINENT, 1815–21

1 The world's great age begins anew,
The golden years return.
The earth doth like a snake renew
Her winter weeds outworn:
Heaven smiles and empires gleam,
Like wrecks of a dissolving dream.

The British poet Percy Bysshe Shelley 'Hellas' (1821) Canto I, lines 1060 ff. A vision engendered by the Greek revolt against Ottoman Turkey.

2 The French are not conquered … They have been fighting for freedom … You cannot kill all the French. You cannot knock their foreteeth out. You cannot keep the sun from shining in France.

The polemical journalist William Cobbett to the British foreign secretary, Viscount Castlereagh; *Weekly Political Register* Vol.38, pp.40–41. Castlereagh was returning to the Congress of Vienna, where the fate of France was to be determined after the second abdication of Napoleon.

3 You would tear out this mighty heart of a nation, and lay it bare and bleeding at the foot of despotism: you would slay the mind of a country to fill up the dreary aching void with the old, obscene, drivelling prejudices of superstition and tyranny: you would tread out the eye of Liberty (the light of nations) like 'a vile jelly', that mankind may be led about darkling to its endless drudgery, like the Hebrew Sampson [*sic*](shorn of his strength and blind), by his insulting taskmasters.

The essayist William Hazlitt 'What is the People?', 7 March 1818; *Complete Works* Vol.7 (1932 edn) pp.259. For Samson see 19:6.

4 It is not to be believed how the destruction of Napoleon affected him; he seemed prostrated in mind and body, he walked about, unwashed, unshaved, hardly sober by day, and always intoxicated by night, literally, without exaggeration, for weeks.

Hazlitt's friend, the painter Benjamin Robert Haydon, writing about Hazlitt's reaction to Waterloo, June 1815; A.C. Grayling *The Quarrel of the Age: The Life and Times of William Hazlitt* (2000) p.193.

5 Before ten years have passed, all Europe will be Cossack or Republican.

Napoleon in conversation with his resident historian Emmanuel-Augustin Las Cases on St Helena, 3 April 1816; *Mémorial de Ste Hélène* (1823; 1842 edn) Vol.1, p.454. Las Cases accompanied Napoleon and recorded their conversations. A later version reads (presumably after neither prediction had come to pass in 1826): 'In fifty years, Europe will be Republican or Cossack.' But even in 1866 Switzerland remained the only republic in Europe, and Russia had not moved west.

6 A new Prometheus, I am chained to a rock to be gnawed by a vulture. Yes, I have stolen the fire of Heaven and made a gift of it to France. The fire has returned to its source and I am here.

Napoleon, note found after his death on 5 May 1821; Christopher Herold (ed.) *The Mind of Napoleon* (1955).

7 Conformably to the word of the Holy Scriptures … the three contracting Monarchs will remain united by the bonds of a true and indissoluble fraternity, and considering each other as fellow countrymen, they will on all occasions, and in all places lend each other aid and assistance; and regarding themselves towards their subjects and armies as fathers of families, they will lead them, in the same spirit of fraternity with which they are animated to protect religion, peace and justice.

Declaration by the Holy Alliance, formed on 26 Sept. 1815 by Austria, Russia and Prussia to contain any future spread of revolution in continental Europe; Clive Parry (ed.) *The Consolidated Treaty Series* Vol.65, pp.201–2.

8 [The Allied Powers] desire nothing but to maintain peace, to free Europe from the scourge of revolution and to prevent, or to lessen, as far as in their power, the evil which arises from the violation of all the principles of order and morality. On these conditions they think themselves entitled, as the reward of their cares and exertions, to the unanimous approbation of the world.

Protocol addressed to the chancelleries of Europe by Austria, Russia and Prussia, 8 Dec. 1820. Issued from the Congress of Troppau, convened to prepare counter-measures against the liberal revolutions in Naples, Spain and Portugal and continued at Laibach in 1821 (see 542:7).

AUSTRIA: THE METTERNICH SYSTEM, 1815–32

1 Austria is Europe's House of Lords: so long as it is not dissolved, it will keep the Commons in check.

Charles-Maurice de Talleyrand-Périgord, attrib. Talleyrand was briefly Louis XVIII's prime minister after his second restoration in 1815, having served Napoleon until he deserted him in 1814.

2 You see in me the chief Minister of Police in Europe. I keep an eye on everything. My contacts are such that nothing escapes me.

Prince Clemens Metternich to Carl von Dalberg, Grand Duke of Frankfurt, 1817; G. de Bertier de Sauvigny *Metternich and his Times* (1962) p.105. Metternich was Austrian foreign minister from 1809 and head of government in Austria from 1815 to 1848. As such, he masterminded counter-revolutionary forces throughout the 36 member states of the Germanic Confederation, which he created and which Austria dominated.

3 They are recruited from the lower classes of the merchants, of domestic servants, of workers, nay even of prostitutes, and they form a coalition which traverses the entire Viennese society as the red silk thread runs through the rope of the English navy. You can scarcely pronounce a word at Vienna which would escape them.

The American commentator Charles Sealsfield on Metternich's secret police informers; Andrew Milne *Metternich* (1975) p.111.

4 The precedence of the positive sciences over the philosophical and critical must be vindicated. Herein lies one of the best means of bringing back the preponderance of authority over false freedom; for anyone can philosophize and criticize (and mystify and poetize) as he pleases; but positive sciences have to be *learned*; and if the younger generation decides again for real learning, it will again become capable of an intellectual subordination without which the entire academic life is only a prelude to the wild anarchy in which all political life today is revolving.

Friedrich von Gentz to Adam Muller, June 1819; Paul R. Sweet *Friedrich Gentz* (1941) pp.222–3. Gentz was Metternich's publicist, writing here as the Carlsbad Decrees were being framed. Through the decrees the universities of the Germanic Confederation were placed under strict supervision after the assassination of the reactionary dramatist August von Kotzebue by a German student, Karl Sand. Gentz is clearly trying to steer German undergraduates away from speculative and imaginative studies that to him could only produce a subversive cast of mind. He no doubt wanted to forget that as a young man he had been a supporter of the French Revolution in its constitutionalist phase (see his *Letters* (1909) Vol.1, p.178).

5 Exaggerated, because the criminal doctrines of certain scholars, the extravagances of a number of young men can be coped with – even justified! – by the existing authorities, and do not require the scandalous setting up of an extraordinary tribunal of inquisition; and perfidious, because Ministers enamoured of arbitrary rule and fearing for their positions have intimidated their monarchs by the phantom of revolution.

Baron vom Stein to the Greek Count Capodistrias, 29 Dec. 1820; H.G. Schenk *The Aftermath of the Napoleonic Wars* (1947) p.99. Stein's attack on the Carlsbad Decrees stemmed from his reformism (see 535:2) and from his Prussian dislike of Austrian hegemony over the German states.

6 My life has coincided with a wretched epoch. I came into the world too soon or too late; today I know I can do nothing. Earlier I should have enjoyed the pleasures of my age; later I should have helped in reconstruction. Now I spend my life in propping up buildings mouldering in decay. I ought to have been born in 1900 and to have had the twentieth century before me.

Prince Clemens Metternich, 6 Oct. 1820; Alan Palmer *Metternich* (1972) p.193.

7 Revolution must be fought with flesh and blood. Moral weapons are manifestly powerless … With cannon and Cossacks on the one side, and fire-brands and volunteers on the other, both systems must in the end fight a life-and-death struggle, and to him who remains standing belongs the world.

Friedrich von Gentz to the Laibach Congress of the Holy Alliance, Feb. 1821; Sweet (1941) p.233. The congress sanctioned the use of Austrian troops to suppress a revolution in the Kingdom of Naples. Laibach, then in Austria, is now Ljubljana, capital of the state of Slovenia, which broke away from Yugoslavia in 1991.

8 Regicides and *sans-culottes* do not suddenly appear. In France there were first Encyclopedists, then Constitutionalists, next Republicans, and finally regicides and high traitors. In order not to have the last type one must prevent Encyclopedists and Constitutionalists from becoming established.

Campz, Austrian minister to Prussia, 5 March 1824; Gentz (1909) Vol.3, p.272. The Encyclopedists were the intellectual precursors of the French Revolution, prominently Diderot and d'Alembert; the Constitutionalists were the leading figures of the Revolution in its early phase, such as Lafayette and Mirabeau.

1 You have my authority to tell His Majesty that the implementation of this plan would bring about England's ruin.

Prince Clemens Metternich to the Austrian ambassador to Britain, 1825; Bertier de Sauvigny (1962). Metternich was referring to the proposal to found University College, London, the 'Godless institution in Gower Street', so called because it was to be a non-religious seat of learning, with no chapel. The riposte of the Church of England was to promote King's College, like its contemporary, Durham University, suitably High Anglican.

2 Change nothing in the foundations of the structure of the state; govern and change nothing … Bestow on Prince Metternich my most faithful servant and friend, the trust which I have reposed in him during so many years. Take no decision on public affairs, or respecting persons, without hearing him.

Extract from the will of Francis II, Austrian emperor, 1832, supposedly drafted by Metternich.

FRANCE: RESTORATION, 1815–30

3 Suddenly the door opened; and silently there entered vice leaning on the arm of crime, M. de Talleyrand supported by Fouché … the trusty regicide, kneeling, put the hand which had made Louis XVI's head roll, in the hands of the martyred king's brother; the apostate bishop stood surety for the oath.

The writer Viscount de Chateaubriand *Mémoires d'outre-tombe* (Memoirs from beyond the Grave) (after 1830) Vol.4, Bk 6, Ch.20. Two ruthless survivors swear fealty to the twice-restored Louis XVIII after Waterloo, July 1815; a famous vignette.

4 Waterloo … is intentionally a counter-revolutionary victory. It is Europe against France … it is the *status quo* against the forces of movement; it is the 14th of June, 1789, attacked by the 20th March 1815; it is the monarchies clearing the decks for action against indomitable French upsurge. The final extinction of this vast people, for twenty-six years in eruption, such was the dream. [But] the age which Waterloo would have checked, has marched on and pursued its course. This inauspicious victory has been conquered by liberty.

Victor Hugo *Les Misérables* (1862) Cosette, Ch.17.

5 We remain the martyrs of an everlasting cause! … Millions of men weep for us, the homeland sighs, and glory is in mourning! … we struggle here against the oppression of the Gods and the wishes of the nations are for us.

Napoleon on St Helena, preparing posterity for his posthumous triumph; Las Cases (1823) Vol.1, Pt 1, p.407.

6 I entertain no doubt how this contest will end. The descendants of Louis XV will not reign in France, and I must say, and always will say, that it is the fault of Monsieur and his adherents … I wish Monsieur would read the histories of our Restoration and subsequent Revolution, or that he would recollect what passed under his own view, probably at his own instigation, in the Revolution.

Duke of Wellington to T.C. Villiers, 11 Jan. 1818; *Supplementary Despatches* Vol.12, p.213. A prescient comment in view of what was to come in July 1830. 'Monsieur' was the title given to the heir-apparent in France, that is, Louis XVIII's brother Charles, Count of Artois, later Charles X. The parallel Wellington draws is with the English Charles II's brother, James II, who succeeded him in 1685 and was forced into exile in 1688 through his refusal to accept the Restoration Settlement that had placed Charles II on the throne in 1660. Artois likewise was adamantly opposed to the limited monarchy brought in by the constitutional Charter of 1814, which his brother was wise enough to swallow.

7 This cannot go on! It will never last! Can you believe that the King dines at seven o' clock, and that the bodyguard wear white trousers? Hitherto, all Kings have dined at one o' clock, and their bodyguards have worn scarlet trousers. Mark my words, sir, there will be another Revolution!

François Poumiès de la Siboutie *Souvenirs d'un Parisien* (1863) pp.147–8. An ultra-royalist deplores the compromises of Louis XVIII.

8 All grandeur, all power, all subordination rests on the executioner: he is the horror and the bond of human association. Remove this incomprehensible agent from the world, and at that moment order gives way to chaos, thrones topple, and society disappears. God, who is the author of sovereignty, is the author also of punishment.

Count Joseph de Maistre *The St Petersburg Dialogues* (1965 edn) p.192. De Maistre, a leading Ultra (extreme counter-revolutionary), was the envoy of Sardinia to Russia from 1803 to 1817.

9 When children talked of glory, they said to them: 'Become a priest'; when they spoke of ambition:

'Become a priest'; of hope, love, influence, life: 'Become a priest.'

Alfred de Musset *Confession d'un enfant du siècle* (1835) Ch.2. With the fall of Napoleon, the army was no longer the road to advancement, and with the religious revival that accompanied the Bourbon restoration the church took its place.

1 'Me, a poor peasant from the Jura,' he muttered to himself repeatedly. 'Me, condemned to wear this dismal outfit for life! Just my luck! Twenty years ago I'd have worn uniform, like them! In those days, a man like me was either killed or *a general at thirty-six* … It's true, though, with this black soutane, by the time you're forty you can have a hundred thousand francs a year and be decorated, like my lord bishop of Beauvais. Alright,' he said to himself, 'I'm brighter than them; I know how to choose the rig of the day.'

Stendhal (Henri Beyle) *Le Rouge et le Noir* (Scarlet and Black) (1830) Pt 2, Ch.13. Scarlet for the tunic of the army, black for the garb of the church.

2 The profanation of the sacred utensils, and of the consecrated hosts, is the crime of sacrilege … The profanation of the sacred utensils shall be punished with death. The profanation of the sacred wafers shall be punished in the name of parricide.

Legislation passed soon after the accession of Charles X, a hyper-zealous Catholic; *Annual Register* for 1825, p.139. The crime of parricide was justified by the doctrine of transubstantiation, whereby the wafer given to communicants at the Eucharist had become the body of Christ, son of God the father.

3 Today … who does not see the danger of granting anyone and everyone … the terrible liberty to indoctrinate, in religion and in politics, a public which everywhere is made up largely of mistaken, ignorant, and violent men? … There is no true liberty of the press … except under the guarantee of censorship to prevent licence of thought. There is no civil liberty without laws to prevent actions that create disorder.

Louis, Viscount de Bonald *On Opposition to the Government and the Liberty of the Press* (1827) pp.60–66.

FRANCE: JULY REVOLUTION, 1830

4 The King reigns but does not govern.

Adolphe Thiers, *Le National*, 4 Feb. 1830. Thiers was a prominent figure in the constitutionalist opposition to Charles X, writing in the journal that had become the main organ of opposition thinking.

5 The people are on their way.
They are the high tide,
Rising unstoppably,
Drawn onwards by their star.

Victor Hugo 'Musings of a passer-by about a king', 18 May 1830. Hugo not so long before had been an ardent royalist; now he entered his populist phase.

6 There is nothing to be feared from the mob of the capital. It is noteworthy that their stature has shrunk in the past fifty years; the people of the Paris faubourgs [suburbs] are smaller than before the Revolution. They are not dangerous. In a word, they are scum.

Jules-Jean Baptiste Anglès, prefect of police in Paris, report, 1819, quoted by Victor Hugo in *Les Misérables* (1862). Anglès could not have been more wrong. When revolution came in July 1830, after Charles X tried to tear up the restoration settlement, the people of Paris were its enthusiastic rank-and-file.

7 I remember very well what happened then [in 1789]. The first concession made by my brother [Louis XVI] was the signal for his destruction … He yielded and lost everything … Rather than be conducted to the scaffold, we will fight and they will have to kill us on our horses.

Charles X, reacting to the news of the revolutionary outbreak in Paris, July 1830; Vincent Beach *Charles X of France* (1971) p.346.

8 This century of 1830, distanced by only three days from that other century of 1829.

Jules Janin; J. Miège *Jules Janin* (1933) p.161. The three days of revolution – 27, 28 and 29 July 1830 – known in France as *Les Trois Glorieuses*.

9 We struck up the Marseillaise … The great crowd roared out its '*Aux armes, citoyens!*' with the power and precision of a trained choir … Remember … that most of them, men, women and children, were hot from the barricades, their pulses still throbbing with the excitement of the recent struggle, and then try to imagine the effect of that stupendous refrain. I literally sank to the floor.

The composer Hector Berlioz *Memoirs* (1987 edn) p.90. The joyous aftermath of the July Revolution, celebrated by an open-air performance of the revolutionary hymn.

10 We are moving to a general revolution. If the transformation under way follows its course and meets no obstacle, if popular understanding continues to develop progressively, if the education of the lower classes suffers no interruption, nations will be levelled to an equality in liberty. If that transformation is halted, nations will be levelled to an equality in despotism.

Viscount de Chateaubriand (after 1830) Vol.5, p.338.

1 The most recent French revolution and the outbreaks bursting forth shortly thereafter at so many points make indubitable the truth previously suspected, which for years was evident to any thinking person, that the revolutionary movements of all lands arise from one focus and that this centre is in Paris ... In Austria these wicked sects found a tougher task because His Majesty's just and powerful administration and the continual watchfulness of his officials did not let intrigues or propaganda take root. If this watchfulness was previously salutary, it is now an indispensable duty.

Prince Clemens Metternich, 11 Oct. 1830; Donald Emerson *Metternich and the Political Police* (1968) pp.134, 135.

2 There has been no revolution. There has only been a change in the person of the king.

Casimir-Pierre Périer, 1830; S. Charlety *La Monarchie de Juillet* (1921). Périer, a high conservative, tries to reassure the world that nothing revolutionary has happened as a result of the July Days.

SPAIN: END OF EMPIRE, 1814–30

3 All the freedoms of the ancient monarchical constitution have been overturned, while all the revolutionary and democratic principles of the French Constitution of 1791 have been copied ... Thus are promulgated not the fundamental laws of a limited monarchy, but those of a popular government presided over by a chief or magistrate, who is only a clerk, not a king ... I declare their constitution and their decrees null and void now and forever.

Ferdinand VII of Spain, 4 May 1814; J.H. Robinson and C.A. Beard *Readings in Modern European History* Vol.2 (1909) pp.23, 25. One of Ferdinand's first acts was to annul the liberal constitution of 1812, following his restoration after the French expulsion from Spain.

4 Success will crown our efforts, because the destiny of America has been irrevocably settled. The tie that bound her to Spain has been severed ... The hatred that the Peninsula has inspired in us is greater than the ocean that separates us. It would be less difficult to unite the two continents than to reconcile the spirits of the two countries ... there is nothing we have not suffered at the hands of that unnatural stepmother – Spain. The veil has been torn asunder. Now we have seen the light; yet they want to plunge us back into darkness. Our chains have been broken and we have been freed; yet our enemies seek to enslave us anew. For this reason America fights desperately, and seldom has desperation failed to win victory.

Simón Bolívar to Henry Cullen, 6 Sept. 1815; Vicente Lecuna (ed.) *Letters of the Liberator* (1929) Vol.1, pp.183–4. Bolívar was a Creole, or man of Spanish blood born in the Americas, a class denied power by the Peninsulares – that is, Spaniards from Spain who came out to the Americas to govern but not to settle. The revolt of the Creoles was sparked by Napoleon's invasion of Spain and Portugal in 1808 and heightened by Ferdinand's scrapping of the 1812 constitution. Bolívar, already a leading figure in the insurgency, was at this time waiting his next opportunity in Jamaica. By 'America' it should be understood that he is referring not to the United States, but to Latin America (see 546:3).

5 And there ... what do you think I saw? Why, the most excellent Protector of half of the New World, seated on a bullock's skull, at a fire kindled on the mud floor of his hut, eating beef off a spit, and drinking gin out of a cow-horn! He was surrounded by a dozen officers in weather-beaten attire, in similar positions, and similarly occupied with their chief. All were smoking, all gabbling.

A Scots visitor to the rustic dictator José Artigas at his Uruguay headquarters, c.1815; William Spence Robertson *Rise of the Spanish American Republics* (1918) p.173.

6 I have listened to your wishes, and, as a tender father, have consented to that which my children think conducive to their happiness. I have sworn to that constitution for which you were sighing, and I will ever be its firmest supporter ... Spaniards ... trust to your king, then, who addresses you ... with a deep sense of the exalted duties imposed on him by Providence.

Ferdinand VII, 10 March 1820, restoring the 1812 constitution at the behest of a military junta headed by Major Rafael de Riego. *Trágala, perro!* (Swallow it, dog!) chanted the crowds, jubilant at Ferdinand's humiliation. The change lasted a mere three years, and in 1823 Spanish absolutism was back in place thanks to the intervention of the Holy Alliance spearheaded by the French army of Louis XVIII. De Riego was executed on 7 Nov. 1823.

7 The revolution in Spain is of the same nature as our own revolution; both of these revolutions were

caused by oppression: the object of both revolutions is to ensure liberty to the people. But Spanish America can view the liberal constitution of Spain only as a fraudulent attempt to conserve a colonial system which can no longer be maintained by force.
José de San Martín, address to the people of Lima, Peru, Sept. 1820; Robertson (1918) pp.195–6. San Martín was second only to Simón Bolívar as the liberator of Hispanic America from Spain.

I All these concessions are insults we suffer, not only on account of the rights of our mothers who were Indians, but also by reason of the pacts of our fathers, the conquistadors, who gained everything at their own cost and risk, with the kings of Spain … America is ours because our fathers took it, thus creating a right; because it was of our mothers; and because we were born in it … God has separated us from Europe by an immense sea and our interests are distinct. Spain never had any right here.
The Mexican Dominican friar Servando Teresa de Mier *Memorial* (1821) p.124; D.A. Brading *The First America* (1995) p.595. De Mier had been an activist for independence since 1795, when he was exiled to Spain for ten years; here he introduces a new dimension into the movement – seeing independence as the birthright not only of the Creoles (native-born whites) but of the entire population: Creole, Indian and mestizo (half-breeds).

2 Contemplating Spain, such as her ancestors had known her, I resolved that if France had Spain, it should not be Spain 'with the Indies'. I called the New World into existence, to redress the balance of the Old.
The British foreign secretary, George Canning, 12 Dec. 1826; *Parl. Deb.* Vol.16 (1827) Col.397. The claim was largely bogus. Although Britain supported the Spanish American liberation struggle, independence was mainly achieved from within the subcontinent. Britain, however, was the only external power able to sustain it.

3 There is no good faith in America, neither among men, nor among nations. Their treaties are scraps of paper, their constitutions mere books, their elections open combat; liberty is anarchy, and life itself is a torment.
Simón Bolívar, speech at Quito, Ecuador, 1829; *Works* (1964 edn) Vol.3, p.501. 'America' here denotes Latin America.

4 America is ungovernable to us. He who serves the revolution ploughs the sea … This country will inexorably fall into the hands of uncontrollable multitudes, thereafter to pass under … tyrants of all colours and races.

Simón Bolívar, after the assassination of his right-hand man, General José Antonio de Sucre, 1839; *Works* (1964 edn) Vol.3, pp.844–6. Again, by 'America', Bolívar understands Latin America.

5 I have not yet seen and do not now see any prospect that they will establish free or liberal institutions of government … They have not the first elements of good or free government. Arbitrary power, military or ecclesiastical, is stamped upon their education, upon their habits, and upon all their institutions.
Secretary of state John Quincy Adams to Henry Clay, March 1821; Samuel Flagg Bemis *John Quincy Adams and the Foundations of American Foreign Policy* (1949) p.354. Adams speaks of the Spanish Americans, the very people whose independence the United States was pledged to uphold through the Monroe Doctrine of 1823 (see 614:7).

GREECE: A SECOND HELLAS? 1821–4

6   The mountains look on Marathon –
        And Marathon looks on the sea;
        And musing there an hour,
        I dreamed that Greece might still be free.
The poet Lord Byron *Don Juan* (1819–24) Canto 3, St.86. In 1809 Byron visited the battlefield of Marathon, where the Greeks defeated the Persians in 490 BC (see 54:6). He saw it as an inspiration for a Greek rising against the Ottoman Turkish empire, which had occupied Greece since the capture of Constantinople in 1453.

7 This day, the festival of the Greek St Constantine, has cost the lives of 16 Greeks shot in the Bazaar, so very fanatic are these deluded people. They [saw it] as the day appointed by heaven to liberate them from the Ottoman yoke and to restore their Race of Princes to the throne and possession of Constantinople. The Turks, who entered on their fast of Ramazan yesterday, heard this, and began their fast in the evening with human sacrifice.
The English traveller Francis Werry, Smyrna, 2 June 1821; Richard Clogg 'Aspects of the Movement for Greek Independence' in *The Struggle for Greek Independence* (1973) p.23. The Greek revolt against the Turks began in the spring of 1821.

8 [The Turks] were taken out of the town, and above 12,000 men, women and children, were put to death by their inhuman conquerors. Some were hanged, others impaled, many roasted alive by large fires; the women outraged in the first instance, and then ripped open (many of them far advanced in pregnancy) and dogs' heads put into them; upwards of 200 Jews who were inhabitants of the city, were put to death, some of them by crucifixion.

Consul P.J. Green, I Nov. 1821, on the surrender of Tripolitsa on 5 Oct.; *Sketches of the War in Greece* (1827) p.69.

1 Over and over again [Voutier] has been struck with admiration for the Greek soldiers whom he has seen overcoming their enemies and trampling them underfoot, shouting *Zito Eleutheria*! (Long Live Liberty!). During the siege of Athens, when the Greeks carried their attack to within pistol-shot of the city walls, he was so much impressed by the magnificent head of a Turk who appeared on the battlements that he prevented a soldier from shooting at him.

The painter Eugène Delacroix, 12 Jan. 1824; *The Journal of Eugène Delacroix* (1951) p.20. This entry was written on the day Delacroix began work on his picture 'The Massacre of Chios', portraying a huge Turkish atrocity on the island of Chios. In 1823 the French Colonel Voutier had published an account of his experiences in Greece.

2 When the limbs of the Greeks are a little less stiff from the shackles of four centuries – they will not march so much 'as if they had gyves on the legs' – At present the chains are broken indeed – but the links are still clanking – and the Saturnalia is still too recent to have converted the slave into a sober citizen.

Lord Byron, 28 Sept. 1823; Leslie A. Marchand (ed.) *Byron's Letters and Journals* Vol.11 (1981) pp.32–3. Byron had gone out to Greece to aid the rebels, only to become heavily disillusioned; he died of fever at Missolonghi on 19 April 1824.

3 We are all Greeks. Our laws, our literature, our religion, our arts have their roots in Greece. But for Greece ... we might still have been savages and idolaters ... The modern Greek is the descendant of those glorious beings whom the imagination almost refuses to figure to itself as belonging to our kind, and he inherits much of their sensibility, their rapidity of conception, their enthusiasm, and their courage.

Percy Bysshe Shelley 'Hellas' (1822) Preface. The classic expression of Hellenophilia.

4 About the fate of the Greeks one is permitted to reason, just as of the fate of my brothers the Negroes – one may wish both groups freedom from unendurable slavery. But it is unforgivable puerility that all enlightened European peoples should be raving about Greece. The Jesuits have talked our heads off about Themistocles and Pericles, and we have come to imagine that a nasty people, made up of bandits and shopkeepers, are their legitimate descendants.

The Russian poet Alexander Pushkin to Peter Vyazemsky, 24/25 June 1824; *The Letters of Alexander Pushkin* (1967) p.161. Themistocles and Pericles were heroes of the Athenian struggle against Persia in the 5th century BC (see 55:6 and 56:2).

ITALY: DIVERGENT ROADS TO FREEDOM, 1820–47

5 But the Russians, Spaniards, Americans, how far have they not flown in a few years, not to say in a few months? Italy! Would you ever dare believe yourself worthy of taking a seat – I will not say alongside Russia, Spain, the great peoples of America – but merely alongside the nation of Haiti? Oh, most unhappy Italy! The Russian, the Spaniard can with reason call you superstitious, ignorant, savage and base ... Yes, yes; they, they have the right to call you the last nation of Europe.

The central Italian broadsheet *The Romagnol Collector*, 30 March 1820, lamenting the backwardness of Italy, even as compared with the black Caribbean republic of Haiti. The reference to the progress of Russia is mystifying.

6 Property boundaries shall be erased, all possessions shall be reduced to communal wealth, and the one and only patria, most gentle of mothers, shall furnish food, education and work to the whole body of her beloved and free children. This is the redemption invoked by the wise. This is the true re-creation of Jerusalem. This is the manifest and inevitable decision of the Supreme Being.

Oath sworn by members of the highest grade of the Carbonari sect as organized by Filippo Buonarotti, 1818; A. Saitta *Filippo Buonarotti* (1950) Vol.1, pp.91–2. Buonarotti was a disciple of the French revolutionary Gracchus Babeuf, executed in 1797, and was the pre-eminent figure in Italian nationalist circles in the 1820s.

7 Italy is strong enough to free herself without external help ... Nationality ... can never be created by any revolution, however triumphant, if achieved by foreign arms ... The one thing wanting to twenty millions of Italians, desirous of emancipating themselves, is not power, but *faith*.

Giuseppe Mazzini, the declaration of Young Italy, 1831; *The Life and Writings of Giuseppe Mazzini* (1891 edn) Vol.1, pp.96–113. Mazzini took over from Buonarotti as the leader of extreme nationalism in the 1830s.

1   Oh my country so fair and wretched!
Oh remembrance of joy and of woe!
Golden harps of the Prophets, oh tell me!
Why so silent ye hang from the willow?
Once again sing the songs of our homeland.
Sing again of the days that are past.
We have drunk from the cup of affliction,
And have shed bitter tears of repentance.
Oh inspire us Jehovah with courage
So that we may endure to the last.

Temistocle Serala, librettist to Giuseppe Verdi; the Hebrew slaves' chorus from Act 3 of the opera *Nabucco* (Nebuchadnezzar), which was performed for the first time at La Scala, Milan, in 1842. The sufferings of the Jews in the Babylonian captivity were clearly understood by Italian audiences as a metaphor for the tribulations of Italy under foreign occupation, particularly by the Austrians in the north and the Spanish Bourbons in the south.

2 Rest assured that when the opportunity arises, *my life, my children's lives, my arms, my treasure, my army, all shall be given in the cause of Italy*.

Count Massimo d'Azeglio reporting the pledge of King Charles Albert of the northern kingdom of Piedmont-Sardinia, given to him in Oct. 1845; *Things I Remember* (1966 edn) pp.338–42. In 1821, as Regent of Piedmont, Charles Albert had crushed a nationalist revolt; hence d'Azeglio's comment: 'These are his words: God alone knows his inner thoughts.' In 1848 the king did support the nationalist movement but was forced into abdication after military defeat by Austria, the power in control of neighbouring Lombardy and Venetia, and retired to a monastery in Portugal.

3 The papacy is supremely ours and our nation's because it created the nation and has been rooted here for eighteen centuries ... That the pope is naturally and should be effectively, the civil head of Italy is a truth forecast in the nature of things ... Nor, to achieve this confederation, is there any need for the pope to receive or take over any new power, but only to revive an ancient and inalienable right that has merely been interrupted ... namely, that of bringing the Italian states together in union.

Vincenzo Gioberti *On the Moral and Civil Primacy of the Italians* (1843). Gioberti's faith in the pope was misplaced: both as a secular ruler across the central belt of the peninsula and as a dedicated opponent of the liberalism that accompanied the nationalist urge, the Pontifex Maximus was no friend of such a proposal.

4 Why should not a new Rome, the Rome of the Italian people ... arise to create a third and still

vaster Unity: to link together and harmonize earth and heaven, right and duty, and utter, not to individuals, but to peoples, the great word association – to make known to free men and equal their mission here below?

Giuseppe Mazzini, thoughts conceived in prison in Savona after a failed rising in 1830, a vision radically different from Gioberti's; *Life and Writings of Joseph Mazzini* (1864 edn) Vol.1, pp.1–40.

5 Communications, which promote the movement of people in every direction, and which will force people into contact with those they do not know, should be a powerful assistance in destroying petty municipal passions born of ignorance and of prejudice ... The building of the railways will help to consolidate mutual confidence between governments and people, and this is the basis of our hopes for the future.

Count Camillo Cavour, *La Revue Nouvelle*, 1 May 1846. The Piedmontese Cavour, who became the first prime minister of a united Italy, was a pragmatist and a gradualist in his nationalism.

6 The word 'Italy' is a geographical expression, a description which is useful shorthand, but has none of the political significance the efforts of the revolutionary ideologues try to put on it, and which is full of dangers for the very existence of the states which make up the peninsula.

Prince Clemens Metternich to the Austrian ambassador in France, 12 April 1847; Richard Metternich-Winneburg (ed.) *From Metternich's Surviving Papers* (1883) Vol.7, p.388.

THE PAPACY: CHURCH INTRANSIGENT, 1814–46

7 There is no public morality or national character without religion, no European religion without Christianity, no Christianity without Catholicism, no Catholicism without the pope, no pope without his supremacy.

Count Joseph de Maistre to Count de Blacas, 1814; Fernand Baldensperger *The Movement of Ideas in the French Emigration, 1789–1815* (1924) Vol.2, p.244. For de Maistre see 543:8.

8 His role, his mission is to prepare and hasten the final convulsions which must precede the regeneration of society; that is why God has delivered him into the hands of the basest kind of men; ambitious, greedy, corrupt, frenzied idiots who call upon the

Tatars to re-establish in Europe what they call *order*, and who adore the saviour of the church in the Nero of Poland, in the crowned Robespierre who is carrying through, at this very moment, his imperial '93.

Félicité de Lamennais to Countess de Senfft, 10 Feb. 1832; Emile Forgues *Correspondence de Lamennais* (1863) Vol.2, p.235. Father Lamennais was the high priest of Liberal Catholicism; he here condemns the deeply illiberal papacy. 'The Tatars' are the Russians, 'the Nero of Poland' and 'the crowned Robespierre' Tsar Nicholas I. 'His imperial '93' was the equivalent of the Terror in the French Revolution, as Russia ruthlessly put down the Polish rising.

I Everything which disturbs the tranquillity of a state she firmly forbids to the ministers of God, who is the author of peace and who came to bring peace to the earth. Bishops should, therefore, with Saint Paul, preach obedience and submission, and above all be on their guard against conduct which would be unseemly in the holy ministry and make it odious.

Pope Gregory XVI to the bishops of Poland, 9 June 1832; E.E.Y. Hales *Revolution and Papacy* (1960) p.267. The pope here admonishes those Polish bishops who supported the revolt of 1830–31 against Russia. 'She' is Mother Church.

2 When the sacred bonds of religion are once contemptuously cast aside ... all legitimate power is menaced by an ever-approaching abyss of bottom-less miseries ... in which heresies and sects have so to speak vomited as into a sewer all that their bosom holds of license, sacrilege and blasphemy.

Pope Gregory XVI, *Mirari Vos* (encyclical), 15 Aug. 1832; Anne Fremantle (ed.) *The Papal Encyclicals in their Historical Context* (1963) p.128. A condemnation of Lamennais' doctrine, following Lamennais' audience with Gregory in Rome.

3 A priest who abuses the sacred books in order to corrupt the world, who pretends to be inspired and who dispenses what he himself must know to be poison, is an abject being ... The practice of burning heretics and their works has been abandoned: that is a matter for regret in the present instance.

Prince Clemens Metternich to the Austrian envoy in Rome, 16 May 1834, on the subject of Lamennais; Charles Boutard *Lamennais* (1913) Vol.3, p.76. Metternich is believed to have inspired the encyclical *Singulari Vos*, an outright anathema on Lamennais, which followed on 24 June.

4 Religion is the sigh of the oppressed being, the essence of a heartless world, just as it is the embodi-ment of social conditions from which the intellect is banned. It is the opium of the people.

Karl Marx *Critique of Hegel's Philosophy of Law* (1843–44) Introduction.

5 God is stupidity and cowardice; God is hypocrisy and falsehood; God is tyranny and poverty; God is evil. For as long as men bow before altars, mankind will remain damned, the slave of kings and priests.

Pierre-Joseph Proudhon *Economic Contradictions* (1846) Vol.1, p.384. Proudhon the anarchist saw any form of authority as baneful, and for Proudhon the atheist God was at the root of the cancer.

6 The execrable doctrine called communism ... is wholly contrary to natural law itself; nor could it establish itself without turning upside-down all rights, all interests, the essence of property, and society itself.

Pope Pius IX, *Qui Pluribus* (encyclical), 9 Nov. 1846; Claudia Carlen (ed.) *The Papal Encyclicals 1740–1878* (1981) pp.277 ff. The first pronouncement on communism by Rome. The word 'communism' first entered the European political vocabulary in 1840, according to *Le Petit Robert* (1993; p.417).

GERMANY: ROMANTIC REVOLT, 1817–47

7 At seven the students, some six hundred of them, each with a torch, marched up the hill to the triumphal bonfire ... On the hill-top songs were sung, and another speech delivered by a student. Afterwards trial by fire was held over the following articles, which were first displayed high in the air on a pitch-fork to the assembled multitude, and then with curses hurled into the flames. The articles burnt were these: a bagwig, a guardsman's cuirass, a corporal's cane.

Lorenz Oken, an eyewitness of the student festival on the Wartburg Mountain, 19 Oct. 1817; J.G. Legge *Rhyme and Revolution in Germany* (1918) pp.22–5. The festival was held to celebrate the tercentenary of the Lutheran Reformation and the fourth anniversary of Napoleon's defeat at the Battle of Leipzig. The items thrown on to the fire symbolized the oppression of the *ancien régime* in Germany, that is, the obsolete authoritarianism of the monarchies back in place after the collapse of Napoleonic France.

8 The Gallic cock has crowed a second time, and the dawn is rising in Germany too.

The German poet Heinrich Heine, writing from Paris soon after the July 1830 Revolution in France.

9 The day will come ... when sublime Germania shall stand on the bronze pedestal of liberty and justice, bearing in one hand the torch of enlightenment, which shall throw the beam of civilization into the remotest corners of the earth, and in the other the scales of justice. People will beg her to settle their disputes; those very people who now force us to believe that might is right, and stamp on us with scornful contempt.

The journalist Siebenpfeiffer, one of the organizers of the nationalist Hambach Festival, 27 May 1832; Legge (1918) p.107. Germania, the female embodiment of the nation, like Britannia, Columbia and Marianne for the United Kingdom, the United States and France, respectively.

1 Just go to Darmstadt and see how the high and mighty make merry at your expense, and then tell your hungry wives and children that their bread has been snatched from them to fill the bellies of lordly strangers; tell the wearers of fine clothes they are dyed by the sweat of the poor, and tell the ladies with their fancy ribbons they are cut out by their calloused hands; tell those who live in grand houses they are built on the bones of the people. Then crawl into your smoky hovels and bend over your stony fields so that one day your children may trudge over them too.

Georg Büchner *The Hessian Country Courier* (1834). Büchner, the author of *Dantons Tod* (see 525:1), wrote this pamphlet to provoke the peasantry to rebellion; most handed their copies to the police.

2 When once that restraining talisman, the cross, is broken, then the smouldering ferocity of those ancient warriors will blaze up again; then again will be heard the deadly clang of that frantic Berserker wrath of which the Norse poets say and sing so much … A drama will be enacted in Germany in comparison with which the French Revolution will seem a harmless episode … You have more to fear from a liberated Germany than from the entire Holy Alliance, with all its Croats and Cossacks.

Heinrich Heine *History of Religion and Philosophy in Germany* (1834) Conclusion. A warning to France from a German Francophile of the consequences likely to follow the unleashing of German nationalism in the wake of a breakdown of Christian standards of behaviour.

3 Germany needs a war of her own to feel her power: she needs a feud with Frenchdom to develop her national life in all its fullness. This occasion will not fail to come.

Ludwig Jahn, veteran Francophobe nationalist of the Napoleonic era; Carl Euler *Father Ludwig Jahn* (1881) pp.440–41.

4   *Deutschland, Deutschland, über Alles,*
         Über Alles in der Welt.
(Germany, Germany, above everything,/Above everything in the World.)

A.H. Hoffmann von Fallensleben *German Hymn* (1841), set to music by Haydn, the same tune as for the hymn 'Glorious things of thee are spoken'.

5 Let us put our trust in the eternal spirit which destroys and annihilates only because it is the unsearchable and eternally creative source of all life. The passion for destruction is also a creative passion.

Mikhail Bakunin 'Reaction in Germany' in *German Yearbook*, Oct. 1842. Having fled to Germany, the Russian anarchist Bakunin hoped that the Germans would take up his version of revolution where the Russians had failed. He was also to say of the Germans, however: 'They will never rise. They would sooner die than rebel … perhaps even a German, when he has been driven to absolute despair, will cease to argue, but it needs a colossal amount of unspeakable oppression, insult, injustice and suffering to reduce him to that state.'

6 The philosophers have only *interpreted* the world in various ways; the point, however, is to *change* it.

Karl Marx *Theses on Feuerbach* (1845).

7 The old year ended in scarcity, the new one with starvation. Misery, spiritual and physical, traverses Europe in ghastly shapes – the one without God, the other without bread. Woe if they join hands!

Count Galen, 20 Jan. 1847; L.B. Namier *1848: The Revolution of the Intellectuals* (1944) p.5.

RUSSIA: IMPERIAL GENDARME, 1822–47

8 There is evidently nothing in Europe capable of making head against such a power as this. Not all Europe combined in opposition will be able to resist its progress, wherever this vast machinery is seriously brought to bear upon the independence of other nations by an able and ambitious emperor … we may see at last the two-headed eagle extend his wings and unfurl his charts triumphantly over the Tower of London itself.

A.H. Everett *Europe: or a General Survey of the Present Situation of the Principal Powers* (1822) pp.319–20, 360. The double-headed eagle was the symbol of Imperial Russia.

9 The people have conceived a sacred truth – that they do not exist for governments, but that government must be organized for them. This is the cause of struggle in all countries; peoples, after tasting the sweetness of enlightenment and freedom, strive toward them; and governments, surrounded by millions of bayonets, make efforts to repel these peoples back into the darkness of ignorance ... We are unable to live like our ancestors, like barbarians or slaves.

The Decembrist Peter Kakhovsky to General Levashev, 8 March 1826. On 26 Dec. 1825, less than a month after the death of Tsar Alexander I, Russia experienced a short-lived liberal rebellion by aristocratic army officers. It was soon suppressed and five of its leaders executed, including Kakhovsky.

1 Persecuted six years in a row, stained by expulsion from the service, exiled to an out-of-the-way village for two lines in an intercepted letter, I of course could not bear good will towards the late tsar, although I gave full justice to his true merits. But I never preached rebellion or revolution.

The poet Alexander Pushkin to Vasily Zhukovsky, late Jan. 1826; *The Letters of Alexander Pushkin* (1967) p.303. In the spring of 1824 Pushkin had been dismissed as a civil servant and exiled to his mother's estate after his letter fell into the hands of the tsarist authorities. Here, he is clearly in fear of his life as a suspected accomplice to the Decembrist coup.

2 If we ask what will become of Europe as a result of the unleashing of thirty million serfs and an army of 300,000 men, the revolutionaries ask themselves the same question, and they see in the prospect life and triumph of their cause, whereas we, and all the enlightened leaders of Europe, can only see death.

Prince Clemens Metternich on the Decembrists, 27 Jan. 1826; Bertier de Sauvigny (1962) p.201.

3 It is Our duty to think of our security. When I say *Ours*, I mean the tranquillity of Europe.

Tsar Nicholas I to his brother, 18 Aug. 1830; W. Bruce Lincoln *Nicholas I* (1978) p.132.

4 We can only pity the Poles. We are too powerful to hate them; the war which is about to begin will be a war of extermination – or at least so it ought to be.

Alexander Pushkin to Elizaveta Khitovo, 9 Dec. 1830; *The Letters of Alexander Pushkin* (1967) p.447. A full-scale insurrection in Poland against Russian domination had begun in late Nov. 1830.

5 The suburbs are destroyed, burned ... Moscow rules the world! O God, do You exist? You're there and You don't avenge it. How many more Russian crimes do You want – or – are You a Russian too!!? ... Sometimes I can only groan, and suffer, and pour out my despair at the piano! God, shake the earth,

let it swallow up the men of this age, let the heaviest punishment fall on France, that would not come to help us.

The Polish composer Frédéric Chopin, Sept. 1831; Ates Orga *Chopin* (1976) pp.52–3. Chopin is writing in torment about the Russian suppression of Warsaw at the close of the Polish rising.

6 Warsaw is surrounded, it is under fire; Warsaw surrenders ... and now, it is said, order reigns in Warsaw.

Deputy Mauguin in the French Chamber of Deputies, 19 Sept. 1831, commenting on the statement on 16 Sept. by the foreign minister, Sébastiani, that 'tranquillity reigns in Warsaw' after the city's capitulation to Russian forces on 8 Sept.

7 All revolutionary objects, such as the sword and sash of Kósciuszko, should be confiscated and sent here to the Cathedral of the Transfiguration ... In a word, gradually remove everything that has historical or national value, and deliver it here.

Tsar Nicholas I, instructions after the suppression of the Polish rising; Norman Davies *God's Playground: A History of Poland* (1981) Vol.2, p.332. The Polish patriot Tadeusz Kósciuszko led an unsuccessful insurrection against Russia in 1794.

8   Hail, O Christ, Thou Lord of Men!
    Poland, in Thy footsteps treading,
    Like Thee suffers, at Thy bidding;
    Like Thee too, shall rise again!

Kasimierz Brodzinski, 1831; Davies (1981) p.9.

9 Poland will arise and free nations of Europe from bondage. *Ibi patria, ubi male*; wherever in Europe liberty is suppressed and is fought for, there is the battle for your country.

Adam Mickiewicz *The Books of the Polish Nation and of the Polish Pilgrims* (1832) p.81. Mickiewicz (1798–1855), the great Romantic poet, became the leader of the Poles in exile, dedicated to fight for nationalism throughout Europe as legionaries against the Holy Alliance.

10 That sad inheritance of triumphant wrong.

The British foreign secretary, Lord Palmerston, on Poland, attrib. A fine phrase, but Britain was incapable of righting the wrong by military intervention, either then or in 1939, when Hitler and Stalin divided Poland between them. As Palmerston said to the exiled head of the insurrectionary regime, Prince Adam Czartoryski: 'We cannot send an army to Poland, and the burning of the Russian fleet would be about as effectual as the burning of Moscow' (Czartoryski's *Memoirs* (1888) Vol.2, p.329).

1 Our common duty is to see to it that, in accordance with the supreme intention of our August Monarch, the education of the people is carried out in the united spirit of Orthodoxy, Autocracy and Nationality.

S.S. Uvarov, Russian minister of education, 21 March 1833; Lincoln (1978) p.241. Uvarov's watchwords became the Holy Trinity of Russian traditionalists in the 19th century.

2 I had made up my mind to collect all the evil things I knew, and then to make fun of them – this is the origin of 'The Inspector General'. This was the first work I planned in order to produce a good influence on society.

Nikolai Gogol to the poet V.A. Zhukovsky on his ribald satire on tsarist bureaucracy, given its première on 1 May 1836 in the presence of the tsar, who enjoyed it enormously.

3 Isolated in the world, we have given nothing to the world and we have learned nothing from the world. We have not added a single idea to the totality of human thought. We have contributed nothing to the progress of the human spirit, and everything transmitted to us from that progress we have disfigured.

Peter Chaadeyev 'A Philosophical Letter' in the review Teleskop, 1836. Chaadeyev, a passionate believer in the need for Russia to adopt Western models of thought and practice, was declared insane by the tsar; compare the treatment of dissidents in Brezhnev's Soviet Union in the 1970s.

4 I am your master, and my master is the emperor. The emperor can issue his commands to me and I must obey him; but he issues no commands to you. I am the emperor on my estate; I am your God in this world and I have to answer for you to the God above.

A Russian landlord to his serfs in the 1840s; Baron von Haxthausen-Abbenberg The Russian Empire (1856) Vol.1, p.335.

5 Stern and severe – with fixed principles of *duty* which *nothing* on earth will make him change; very *clever* I do *not* think him, and his mind is an uncivilized one.

Queen Victoria on Tsar Nicholas I, 11 June 1844; Letters of Queen Victoria Vol.2 (1911) p.223.

6 A State without an absolute monarch is an orchestra without its conductor … The more deeply one looks into the workings of our administration, the more one admires the wisdom of its founders; one feels that God Himself, unseen by us, built it

through the hands of the sovereigns. Everything is perfect, everything is sufficient unto itself. I cannot conceive what use could be found for even one more official.

Nikolai Gogol Selected Passages from My Correspondence with My Friends (1847) Chs 10, 28. A decade on from The Inspector General, the satirist of the tsarist regime had become its panegyrist.

7 Russia sees her salvation not in mysticism, nor asceticism, nor pietism, but in the progress of civilization, enlightenment and human values. What she needs is not sermons (she has had enough of them!) or prayers (she has mouthed them too often!) but the awakening of human dignity, which for so many centuries has been buried in mud and filth.

Vissarion Belinsky, 15 July 1847, in reply to Gogol's declaration of faith in the tsarist system.

FRANCE: BOURGEOIS MONARCHY, 1830–48

8 I want to secure the political preponderance of the middle classes in France, the final and complete organization of the great victory that the middle classes have won over privilege and absolute power from 1789 to 1830.

François Guizot, the politician at the centre of the July Monarchy; Pierre Rosanvallon Le Moment Guizot (1985) p.171.

9 We seek to hold to the *juste milieu* [golden mean], equally distant from the excesses of popular power and the abuses of royal authority.

King Louis-Philippe, speech from the throne, Jan. 1831. The July Monarchy aimed to steer a central course between radicalism and reaction.

10 Each manufacturer lives in his factory like the colonial planters surrounded by slaves, one against a hundred, and the sedition at Lyons is a kind of rising at Santo Domingo … The middle class should realize its position: it has beneath it a population of proletarians who agitate and tremble without knowing where they are going … From there can emerge the Barbarians which will destroy it.

The deputy Saint-Marc Girardin, 1831; Jean-Paul Sartre Les Temps Modernes (1966) pp.1924–5. The subject was the violent upsurge of the silk weavers of Lyons, ruthlessly suppressed by the government, and seen as a token of the volcanic forces lying beneath the complacent surface of the new regime, comparable to the tensions generated by slavery in the French and Spanish West Indies.

1 In our Charter there are rights … there are no tax exemptions, anyone is eligible for government posts, we have free labour, religious toleration, freedom of the press, individual liberty! … Given all these things, what need would there be to bring in this absurd political equality, this blind application of political rights to everyone?

François Guizot in the Chamber of Deputies, 1837; *Mémoires* Vol.4, pp.270–71.

2 *Enrichissez-vous!* (Enrich yourselves!)

Guizot to the Chamber, 1 March 1843. The full version reads: 'Support your government, consolidate your institutions, enlighten yourselves, enrich yourselves, improve the moral and material condition of our France.' Later the same year he urged his constituents in Lisieux to 'enrich yourselves by work, thrift and integrity'. The phrase *enrichessez-vous* is usually taken as an exhortation to make money as an end in itself and was interpreted by the regime's enemies as a token of its gross materialism.

3   Like a crow perched on a spindly cypress,
    Hunched night and day with his beak in his
        chest,
    On a barren tree he calls his doctrine.

The poet Alfred de Vigny on Guizot; *Journal* (1867) p.90.

4 Master of everything as no aristocracy had ever been or perhaps will never be, the middle class, which one has to call the governing class, having entrenched itself in power and soon afterwards in its self-interest, seemed like a private industry. Each of its members scarcely gave a thought to public affairs except to make them function to profit his own private business, and had no difficulty in forgetting the lower orders in his little cocoon of affluence. Posterity … will possibly never realize how far the government of the day had in the end taken on the appearance of an industrial company, where all operations are carried out with a view to the benefit the shareholders can draw from them.

Alexis de Tocqueville on the Guizot administration of the 1840s; *Recollections* p.31.

5 These people are walking coffins which contain a Frenchman of another age; he sometimes gives a start and thumps on the walls of his capsule, but ambition holds him down and he lets himself be suffocated.

The novelist Honoré de Balzac *La Cousine Bette* (1846), on the *bon bourgeois* of the July Monarchy.

6   Gross, fat and stupid,
    His hand turns into a spade,
    His head turns into a pear,
    His belly into a barrel.

Altaroche, editor of *Le Charivari*, on Louis-Philippe; H.A.C. Collingham *The July Monarchy* (1988) pp.139–40. The caricature of the king's head as an evolving pear was a favourite of the satirists of the Paris press.

7 The French love the dead Napoleon more than the living Lafayette. To the French Napoleon is a magic word that electrifies and dazzles them. A thousand cannon sleep within that name as they do in the Vendôme Column, and the Tuileries will tremble if one day those cannon awake.

Heinrich Heine, 1832. Lafayette helped manage the transition from one version of monarchy to another in July 1830, avoiding both a republic and a Bonapartist revival. The Column, topped by a statue of the emperor, stood in the Place Vendôme in Paris as a towering reminder of the Napoleonic achievement. The Tuileries Palace, not far away on the Rue de Rivoli (named after Napoleon's victory over Austria in 1797) was the residence of the king.

8 I wish my ashes to rest on the banks of the Seine, in the midst of the French people I have loved so well.

Napoleon, codicil to his will, 16 April 1821, unconsciously expressing his sense of distance from France. Corsica, his birthplace, had become French territory only a year before he was born in 1769. In an effort to draw on the emperor's enduring prestige, the July Monarchy had Napoleon's remains brought back from St Helena and interred in the Hôtel des Invalides on 15 Dec. 1840. Louis-Philippe also sought to borrow lustre from Louis XIV through his refurbishment of the Palace of Versailles, reopened on 10 June 1837, and prominently inscribed with the motto 'TO ALL THE GLORIES OF FRANCE'.

9 *La France s'ennuie.* (France is bored.)

The Romantic poet and politician Alphonse de Lamartine in the Chamber, 10 Jan. 1839, and to his Mâcon constituents on 18 July 1847. A famous phrase, hitting at the complacency of the regime of Louis-Philippe. The full version of the 1839 speech reads: 'The generations coming of age after us are not tired: they want to act before they grow tired in their turn. What proof of action have you given them? France is a nation that is bored! And beware: the boredom of peoples easily leads to upheaval and ruin.'

10 If I had to reply to the following question: *What is slavery?* and in only one word I would reply: *It is murder*, my thinking would immediately be understood. I would not need to make a long argument to show that the power to take away from a man thought, will, personality, is a power of life and death, and that to enslave a man is to kill him. Why then to this other question: *What is property?* may I not answer equally: *It is theft!*

Pierre-Joseph Proudhon *What is Property?* (1840). This tract made the anarchist socialist Proudhon one of the key *bêtes noires* of the administration, threatening as it did everything it stood for.

■ We had been accustomed to connect the word 'Paris' with memories of the great events, the great masses, the great men of 1789 and 1793, memories of a colossal struggle for an idea, for rights, for human dignity … The name of Paris was closely bound up with all the noblest enthusiasms of contemporary humanity. I entered it with reverence, as men used to enter Jerusalem and Rome.

The Russian liberal revolutionary, Alexander Herzen, on reaching Paris from Russia in March 1847; E.H. Carr *The Romantic Exiles* (1933) Ch.2. Herzen evokes the enduring aura of Paris as the hub of progressive politics, something the July Monarchy had done its best to make France and Europe forget, but which was now once again beginning to exert its power and produce a further revolution.

The 1848 Revolutions

'THE SPRINGTIME OF THE PEOPLES'

1 Minds were in such a state that if someone had arrived and said, 'The good Lord has just been chased out of heaven; the Republic has been proclaimed there!', then everyone would have believed him and no one would have been amazed.

The aristocratic Russian anarchist Mikhail Bakunin on the outbreak of the 1848 revolutions, Aug. 1851; Lawrence D. Orton (ed.) *The Confession of Mikhail Bakunin* (1977) p.57. Bakunin wrote his confession for Tsar Nicholas I during his imprisonment in the aftermath of the 1848 upheaval.

2 There will be no wars on questions of partition, domination, nationality and influence. No more weak and strong, oppressed and oppressors. Every country, free to enjoy its liberties and to live its own life, will hasten to enjoy the life and liberty of all.

Etienne Garnier-Pagès *Histoire de la Révolution de 1848* (1866) Vol.7, p.177.

3 Soon, perhaps, in less than a year, the monstrous Austrian empire will be destroyed. The liberated Italians will proclaim an Italian republic. The Germans, united into a single great nation, will proclaim a German republic. The Polish democrats after seventeen years in exile will return to their homes. The revolutionary movement will stop only when Europe, the whole of Europe, *not excluding Russia*, is turned into a federal democratic republic.

Mikhail Bakunin in the journal *La Réforme*, 13 March 1848. How this recalls the heady days of 1989–91, when the Soviet empire in eastern Europe collapsed and the USSR itself was thought capable of metamorphosing into 16 liberal democracies.

4 We are living in a time which seems to break with the past; the battle will be prolonged if the break is only partial, if all the debris of the collapse is not removed ... It will not only be a matter of political change; a social revolution will inevitably follow on its heels ... It is terrible how we are situated on the storm side of history, between the death of the past and the hour of birth for the future – but this moment had to come.

The German Fanny Lewald, journal entry, Paris, 22 March 1848; Hanna Ballin Lewis (ed.) *A Year of Revolutions* (1997) p.81.

5 A spectre is haunting Europe – the spectre of Communism ... The history of all previous society is the history of class struggles ... All society is increasingly splitting up into two great hostile classes: the bourgeoisie and the proletariat ... Modern bourgeois society which has conjured up such gigantic means of production and exchange ... has also produced the modern workers, the PROLETARIANS ... its own grave-diggers. Its downfall and the victory of the proletariat are equally inevitable ... The Communists ... openly declare that their ends can only be attained by the forcible overthrow of existing social conditions. Let the ruling class tremble at a Communist revolution. The proletarians have nothing to lose but their chains. They have a world to win. WORKERS OF ALL LANDS, UNITE!

Karl Marx and Friedrich Engels *The Communist Manifesto* (Jan. 1848). A celebrated proclamation, written in late 1847 and published on the eve of the revolutionary outbreak in Paris. The founding fathers of Marxist Socialism had high hopes, not to be fulfilled in their lifetimes.

FRANCE: UPSURGE AND RECOIL, JANUARY–SEPTEMBER 1848

6 Look at what is going on among the working classes ... Do you not see that little by little opinions and ideas are spreading in their midst which are not aimed simply at overturning this or that law or ministry or government, but society itself, shaking it to the very foundations on which it rests ... I believe that at this moment we are sleeping on a volcano.

The historian and politician Alexis de Tocqueville in the Chamber of Deputies, 27 Jan. 1848; *The Recollections of Alexis de Tocqueville* (1959) pp.12–13.

7 What is the producer? Nothing! What should he be? Everything!

Pierre-Joseph Proudhon, banner heading of his broadsheet *The Representative of the People*, 7 Feb. 1848. Proudhon seeks to move the revolution from the political into the social phase, echoing Sieyès's celebrated *Qu'est-ce que c'est que le Tiers État?* (What is the Third Estate?) of 1789 (see 515:8). He wrote more than two weeks before the roof fell in on the July Monarchy (see 553:7).

8 They drove the bloody corpses of those that had fallen at Guizot's ministry on wagons through the streets. Men with burning torches illuminating the gaping wounds with their fiery light surrounded these wagons and the cry, 'To arms! They are murdering us' rang through the night air, drowning out the drumbeats and the sound of the alarm bells. Barricades arose as if by magic and spread through the whole city.

Fanny Lewald on the aftermath of the mass shooting of demonstrators outside the Foreign Ministry on 23 Feb., which triggered the 1848 revolution in Paris; Lewis (1997) p.48. Street barricades had been a leading feature of the successful Paris upsurge of July 1830.

1 In 1830 we were barged out of the way; now in 1848 we are compelled to start again.

Adolphe Crémieux, a moderate Republican, in the Chamber of Deputies, 24 Feb. 1848, looking for republicanism to seize its second chance.

2 The July Revolution was carried out by the people, but the middle class which had touched it off and led it, was its chief beneficiary. The February Revolution, on the other hand, seemed to have been the work of forces completely outside the framework of the bourgeoisie and directed against it.

Alexis de Tocqueville (1959) pp.91–2.

3 One cannot believe that a great nation like this can really submit to the dictation of a few low demagogues, none of them, except Lamartine, of any personal following, but hoisted into power by base desertion of duty on the part of all the armed forces, and at the pleasure of the very scum of the earth.

Marquis of Normanby, 24 Feb. 1848; *Journal of a Year of Revolution* (1857) Vol.1, p.96. The marquis was British ambassador to France; Lamartine was president of the brand-new Second Republic, proclaimed that day.

4 They are a crowd of lawyers and writers, each more ignorant than the next, who will fight for a share of power. I will have nothing to do with them.

The French anarchist Pierre-Joseph Proudhon, diary entry, 24 Feb. 1848; *Mélanges* (1868) Vol.2, pp.6–8. His subject-matter is the members of the provisional government of the republic.

5 The red flag has only been paraded round the Champ de Mars, dragged through the blood of the people. The tricolour has girdled the world with the reputation, the glory and the liberty of the country.

Alphonse de Lamartine, 25 Feb. 1848. The new president fends off the bid to make the flag of the workers the national banner, replacing the red, white and blue flag of France first

flown in 1792. His rejection demonstrated the conflict from the outset between moderate and extreme republicans.

6 Keep the tricolour if you want to as the symbol of our nationality. But remember that the red flag represents the final revolution … The red flag is the federal standard of humanity!

Pierre-Joseph Proudhon, March 1848; *La Solution du problème social* (1848). Proudhon implies the need to spread the revolution beyond the borders of France.

7 The Provisional Government of the French Republic undertakes to guarantee the livelihood by work of the workers; it undertakes to guarantee work for all citizens; it recognizes that workers must combine in order to enjoy the legitimate benefits of their labour.

Decree on the right to work, 25 Feb. 1848; J.A.R. Marriott *The French Revolution of 1848 in its Economic Aspects* (1913) Vol.2, p.19. The decree led to the establishment of the national workshops to provide work for the unemployed. The most controversial act of the new regime, it was drafted by the radical revolutionary Louis Blanc.

8 The proclamation of the French Republic is not an act of aggression against any form of government … War is not now the principle of the French republic, as it was the fatal and glorious necessity of the republic of 1792 … The French republic, therefore, will not commence war against any state … It will not pursue secret or incendiary propagandism among neighbouring states. It is aware that there is no real liberty for nations except that which springs from themselves and takes its birth from their own soil.

Alphonse de Lamartine, Manifesto to Europe, 6 March 1848; *A History of the French Revolution of 1848* (1905 edn) pp.278–85. Lamartine intended the manifesto as a reassurance that France was not about to embark on a revolutionary crusade, as it had done in the 1790s.

9 Some regiments are handing in their weapons. Others are dismissing their officers. There are even soldiers who refuse to do duty in the guardroom. What a mess! And what a state for an army to be in!

Marshal de Castellane, diary entry, 16 March 1848.

10 They must concern themselves with one thing only, namely with choosing as their representatives men of recognized integrity who are frankly resolved to set up a Republic in France that respects the sacred rights of religion, liberty, property and the family.

Bishop of Rennes to his parish clergy on the eve of the general election of April 1848, instructing them to mobilize the electorate to vote the right way; Roger Price (ed.) *1848 in France* (1975) p.92.

1 I found myself behind three *Blouses* [labourers in coarse shirts] evidently belonging to the *Ateliers Nationaux* [national workshops] ... One of them was saying to the other two: 'They're awarding themselves 25 francs a day. They're giving us 30 sous [one-eightieth as much], and they call that equality.'

British ambassador Lord Normanby; (1857) Vol.1, p.391. Normanby was overhearing the grievances of the Parisian working-class against the members of the newly elected parliament, 15 May 1848, the day of a failed coup by extreme revolutionaries.

2 Unmarried workers aged between 18 and 25 years will be invited to enlist under the flag of the republic in order to make up the numbers of the various regiments of the army. Those who refuse voluntary enlistment will be taken off the nominal rolls of the National Workshops.

The first section of the order dissolving the national work-shops, drafted on 24 May and published on 20 June, sparking the protests that led to the 'June Days', in which an attempt by the militant left to mount a second insurrection was mercilessly suppressed; Marriott (1913) Vol.2, pp.271–4.

3 *Du Pain ou du Plomb!* (Bread or Lead!)

Slogan on banners carried by working-class demonstrators in Paris, 23 June 1848. In other words: 'If you don't give us a livelihood, there'll be civil war.'

4 The crowds who took possession of the Pantheon were either shot through the windows and as they came out, or were driven into the vaults beneath, where they will be compelled by hunger to surrender at discretion. A company of guards hemmed in between two barricades were completely annihilated. Parties were forbidden on pain of death to open a window; I ventured to open mine in the morning, but a party of guards noticed me and made signs for me to withdraw immediately; a few moments of hesitation would probably have exposed me to a shower of bullets.

An Englishman in Paris, Sir Edward Frankland, 24 June 1848; *Sketches from the Life of Sir Edward Frankland* (1902).

5 The wretched men piled into the attics, under the roof leads, suffocating, gasping for air, were putting their heads through a narrow skylight so they could breathe ... Every head that showed served as a target

for the National Guards stationed below and was greeted by a musket ball ... The bourgeoisie was capable of the September massacres [of 1792], and yet ... the men of September killed people they believed were the enemies of France: grocers will kill people they think are the enemies of their shops.

The writer Ernest Renan, then a student, 10 July 1848, on the sequel to the June Days; *Complete Works* (1885) Vol.9, p.1097.

6 Paris is burying her dead. The pavements used for the barricades have been replaced – to be torn up again, perhaps, tomorrow ... A hateful scene of destruction; even the Spirit of Liberty on top of the Bastille column has a bullet through her body.

The composer Hector Berlioz, 16 July 1848; *Memoirs* (1987 edn) p.16. The column commemorating the fall of the Bastille stood in the working-class quarter at the east end of the city, and the statue of Liberty was clearly the target of a vengeful counter-revolutionary.

7 The Republic is lucky; it can fire on the people.

Louis-Philippe in exile, attrib. Not to say that his regime had not done its share of coercion.

8 Family, institutions, liberty, fatherland, all were stricken in the heart, and, under the blows of these new barbarians, the civilization of the nineteenth century was threatened with destruction. But no! ... This we swear by all of France, which rejects with horror those savage doctrines in which the family is only a name and property is only theft.

National Assembly resolution, 28 June 1848; F.A. de Luna *The French Republic under Cavaignac 1848* (1969) p.152. Note the explicit reference to Proudhon's dictum, 'Property is Theft' (see 553:10).

9 If the people impose duties on me, I know how to fulfil them: but I reject all those who would credit me with ambitious intentions I do not possess. My name is a symbol of order, national feeling and glory, and it would be with the deepest sorrow that I would see it used to compound the difficulties and the rifts within the country. To avoid such a misfortune I would rather stay in exile.

Louis-Napoleon, nephew of Napoleon, statement issued from London, 14 June 1848; Normanby (1857) Vol.1, p.475. Louis Napoleon headed the Bonapartist cause and had been jailed for several years after a failed coup in 1840. Now elected to the National Assembly, he disclaims any further bid for power. In December 1848 he was elected president of the Republic.

10 In the midst of all this, lost in a clutter of mediocrity, one could have noticed one canvas that was simple, serious and unpretentious. A seated woman supports two children at her breasts; at her feet two children read. The Republic nourishes her children and instructs them ... On that day I cried, *Long live the Republic!* For the Republic had made a painter: DAUMIER.

Jules Champfleury *Revue des Arts et des Ateliers*, 6 Aug. 1848. The radical artist and caricaturist Honoré Daumier had been a committed Republican throughout the July Monarchy. His painting was meant as a tribute to the victory of republicanism, but it went on exhibition just as the regime's political enemies began to take over.

1 When I heard the rally call I went out with my musket. They gave me some drinks and led me to the barricade blocking the way. There they said to me 'Look, are you going to shoot?' 'Hell,' I said, 'who at?' ... I only fired twice ... A man like me is easily led astray.

Testimony of a railway labourer at his court martial, as reported in the newspaper *Le National*, 7 Sept. 1848. His fate is unknown, but it was almost certainly execution or transportation to the newly acquired colony of Algeria.

2 What is *the* problem today? It is the problem of creating respect for property in people who do not own any ... You have to make them believe in God ... the God who dictated the ten commandments and who gives robbers their everlasting punishment.

Charles de Montalembert in the National Assembly, 20 Sept. 1848. Montalembert, a distinguished liberal Catholic, here suffers a momentary attack of fundamentalism, brought on by his short-lived support for Louis-Napoleon.

AUSTRIA: THE FALL OF METTERNICH, MARCH–JUNE 1848

3 When France has a cold, all Europe sneezes.

Prince Clemens Metternich, attrib.

4 Everyone tells me that something must happen. That is entirely right. But what? Our monarchy is an old house. We cannot break through the walls, open new windows and undertake great internal changes without danger.

Prince Clemens Metternich, 29 Feb. 1848, after the news of the French Republic reached Vienna, as recorded in the diary of Baron von Hübner.

5 To see Metternich weak, deaf, reduced to a shadow, senile, is to make one sense that he will not have the strength to weather the storm. I saw the Emperor recently at a court ball: I would never have believed him in such a terrible condition. The Empress spends all her time with her confessor, but she will not pray away the trouble.

The Prussian Count Karl Witzhum, 29 Feb. 1848; Istvan Déak *The Lawful Revolution* (1979) p.60. Could there be a touch of *Schadenfreude* here, coming from Austria's rival for mastery in central Europe?

6 That fury which alone makes a revolution, that holy rapture of enthusiasm which overthrows in a moment what centuries of evil have built up and which all at once tears away and washes away the rocks of the old like a cloudburst – they had made their appearance!

The Viennese student August Silberstein, 13 March 1848, the day of the demonstration that brought down Metternich; *Geschichte der Aula* (History of the University) pp.18–19.

7 Who can judge how far a wildly excited and uneducated mob can be led by the Utopia of the abolition of property, of the common ownership of goods, and the like? In short, anarchy stood clearly before my eyes.

Eduard Bauernfeld on speeches made on 15 March 1848; *Memories of Old Vienna* (1923) p.274.

8 Metternich plays the violin very well. There is an old one ... in the tower. He keeps playing the Marseillaise on it and whistles a spasmodic accompaniment in the moonlight.

Justinus Kerner, c.2 April 1848; *Correspondence with his Friends* Vol.2. Metternich was given refuge in Kerner's country house *en route* to exile in Britain. Can it really be true that the impresario of European reaction performed the battle-hymn of the revolution that had just deposed him?

9 The wonder is not that the accumulated pressure should at last have broken the barrier and have deluged the country, but that his artificial impediments should have produced stagnation so long.

Lord Palmerston on Metternich, letter to Leopold I of the Belgians, 15 June 1848; E. Ashley *The Life of Henry Temple, Viscount Palmerston* (1876) Vol.1, p.104.

10 Error has never come into my mind.

Prince Clemens Metternich to his fellow exile, the French ex-prime minister, François Guizot, on the steps of the British Museum, summer 1848; Alan Palmer *Metternich* (1972) p.317.

HUNGARY: THE MAGYAR CHALLENGE

11 From the charnel house of the Vienna System a noxious stench wafts towards us, paralysing our nerves and denying our national feeling ... We are the people who can save the dynasty, link its future to the commonwealth of the different ethnic groups in Austria, and substitute the firm cement of a free constitution for the evil binding force of bayonets and bureaucratic oppression.

The Hungarian nationalist leader Lajos Kossuth, 3 March 1848; J.G. Legge *Rhyme and Revolution in Germany* (1918) pp.261–2. Kossuth seizes the opportunity to go on to the attack in the wake of the news of the revolution in Paris. The Vienna System was the repression imposed on Austria and the states of Germany by Metternich since 1815. The dynasty was the Habsburgs, the ruling house of the Austrian empire.

1 All measures proposed as aids to our constitutional progress … can only attain real value when a national government shall exist independent of foreign influence … and which … shall be responsible to the nation, the voice of which it will duly represent.

Proclamation by the Hungarian diet, 14 March 1848; E. Szabad *Hungary Past and Present* (1854) p.279.

2 The prerequisites for the unity of the state are one political nationality and one state language. This language can only be that of the race which has conquered the fatherland by blood … Our citizens of other languages must therefore become Magyars when they are in contact with public institutions.

The nationalist paper *Pesti Hirlap*, 6 April 1848. Magyars constituted some 40% of Hungary's population; the remainder, mostly Slavs, were clearly due to be brought into line with the new ruling class.

3 Do not deceive yourselves, citizens! The Magyars stand alone in the world against the conspiracy of the sovereigns and nations which surround them; the Emperor of Russia besets us … In Vienna the courtiers and statesmen are calculating the advent of the day when they shall be able again to rivet the chains of their old slaves the Magyars, an undisciplined and rebellious race. Oh, my citizens, it is thus that tyrants have ever designated free men. You are alone, I repeat. Are you ready and willing to fight?

Lajos Kossuth to the Hungarian diet, 11 July 1848; *Annual Register*, 1848, p.412. This nightmare of encirclement was no exaggeration, as 1849 was to prove.

4   Let us colour our flags black and red
      Because mourning and blood
      Will be the fate of the Hungarian nation.

The Magyar nationalist poet Sandor Petöfi, summer 1848; L. Deme *The Radical Left in the Hungarian Revolution of 1848* (1976) p.91. An all-too-accurate prophecy.

5   You Serbs, Croats, Germans, Slovaks, Romanians,
      Why do you all ravage the Hungarian? …
      There shall be no peace until the last drop of blood
      Flows from your evil hearts.

Sandor Petöfi *'Life or Death'*, Sept. 1849; Deme (1976) pp.72–3. By the time this poem was written the Hungarian revolution had been crushed by the intervention of the Russian army, invited in by Metternich's successor, Schwarzenberg, and enthusiastically aided by Austria's loyal Croats under Count Josef Jellacic.

THE SLAV PREDICAMENT

6 If the Austrian empire did not exist, in the interest of Europe, nay of humanity, it would be necessary to make haste to create it.

Frantisek Palacky, 11 April 1848; Stanley J. Pech *The Czech Revolution of 1848* (1969) pp.81–2. The Czech nationalist was declining an invitation to sit in the forthcoming German parliament in Frankfurt and adapting Voltaire in the process ('If God did not exist, it would be necessary to invent Him').

7 The chief champion of the Tschechian nationality, Professor Palacky, is himself but a learned German run mad, who cannot even now speak the Tschechian language correctly and without foreign accent.

Friedrich Engels; Pech (1969) p.337. 'Tschechian' was the original spelling for what is now rendered as 'Czech'.

8 Austria is clearly beginning to decompose, but the Slavs particularly feel the necessity of combining so as not to be swallowed up either by Russia or Germany.

Frantisek Zach to the Polish prince, Adam Czartoryski, 9 June 1848, as the Slav Congress foregathered in Prague; L.D. Orton *The Prague Slav Congress of 1848* (1978) p.30. Like the Hungarians, the Slavs (principally Poles, Czechs and Slovaks) were caught in a Mitteleuropean pincer, as they were again between 1938 and 1989.

9 Under the guise of sympathy for the Slavic tribes supposedly oppressed in other states, there is hidden the criminal thought of a union of these tribes, in spite of the fact that they are subjects of neighbouring and in part allied states. And they expected to attain this goal not through the will of God, but by means of rebellious outbreaks to the detriment and destruction of Russia herself … And if, indeed, a combination of circumstances produce such a union, this will mean the ruin of Russia.

Tsar Nicholas I, marginalia on the deposition of the imprisoned Pan-Slav propagandist Ivan Aksakov, 1849; Orton (1978) p.55. The tsar had had Aksakov arrested as a potential subversive.

1 Austria had sense and meaning only as a German power; the destiny was to elevate the primitive Slav peoples to the level of German civilization, and to offer them as a dowry to Germany. From the moment when the Austrian government, through weakness or lack of self-confidence, is no longer able to fulfil this calling, Austria [will] collapse and deserves to disintegrate. Then only one power can take over the mission which Austria has let fall from its hands: it is the German empire which is being forged in Frankfurt.

Ignaz Kuranda, *Die Grenzboten*, May 1848; Orton (1978) p.43. A German, or more particularly, a Prussian challenge to Austrian hegemony in central Europe at a moment of critical Austrian weakness.

2 No less sacred to us than man in the enjoyment of his natural rights is the *nation*, with its sum total of spiritual needs and interests. Even if history has attributed a more complete human development to certain nations than to others, it has none the less always been seen that the capacity of those other nations for development is in no way limited ... We Slavs ... extend a brotherly hand to all neighbouring nations, irrespective of their political power or size.

Frantisek Palacky, declaration of the Slav Congress, 12 June 1848; *Slavonic and East European Review* Vol.26, pp.310, 311. An over-optimistic declaration: three days later the Congress had been dispersed by Austrian military power when the forces of Windischgrätz took Prague, and both Polish and Czechoslovak nationalism had to wait 70 years to come to fruition.

ITALY: DIVIDE AND RULE

3 Every time you use the word 'faction', we will thrice repeat that we are a Nation, a Nation, a Nation.

Count Massimo d'Azeglio, attrib. D'Azeglio came from Piedmont, the launch-pad of the Italian bid for a full national identity.

4   Three colours, three colours,
     Sings the Italian as he marches on.

Luigi Mercantini, 'Hymn of War', 1848, invoking the Italian flag of red, white and green, first adopted by Italian proto-nationalists during Napoleon's Lombardy campaign in 1797.

5 The character of this people has been altered as if by magic, and fanaticism has taken hold of every age group, every class, and both sexes ... It is the most frightful decision of my life, but I can no longer hold Milan. The whole country is in revolt.

The Austrian Marshal Radetzky to von Ficquelmont, 21 and 22 March 1848, under attack by the invading Piedmontese army; *Archiv für österreichische Geschichte* (Archive for Austrian History)(1906) Vol.95, pp.156, 159. The Austrian composer, Johann Strauss the Elder, was to write the famous Radetzky March to celebrate the marshal's reconquest of Lombardy, which came in July and Aug.

6 We will support your just desires, confident as we are in the help of that God who is manifestly on our side; of the God who has given Pius IX to Italy; of God whose helpful hand has wonderfully enabled Italy to rely on her own strength (*fare da sé*).

Charles Albert, king of Sardinia-Piedmont, 23 March 1848; C. Casati *Nuove relazioni su I fatti di Milano nel 1847–1848* (New Accounts of the Events in Milan in 1847–8) (1885) Vol.2, p.203. *L'Italia farà da sé* (Italy will be self-reliant) was to become one of the classic watchwords of Italian nationalism. Pope Pius IX was not, in fact, in any way a supporter of the Italian *Risorgimento* (Resurrection), and 1848 showed that Italy could not go it alone to achieve nationhood.

7 It is vital that the Italian states, in their composition and extension, should be based upon historical tradition. Peoples who have different origins and customs should not be forced together, therefore, otherwise civil war will follow the war of independence. Finally, no state should be refused the republican form of government if it feels better suited to it than to the transitional stage of a constitutional monarchy.

The Venetian Daniele Manin, 7 June 1848; P. Ginsborg *Daniele Manin and the Venetian Revolution of 1848–49* (1979) p.226. Manin wanted to restore the Venetian Republic destroyed by Napoleon; he did not want Venice to be absorbed into a united Italy.

8 We cannot refrain from repudiating, before the face of all nations, the treacherous advice ... of those who would have the Roman Pontiff to be the head and to preside over some form of novel republic of the whole Italian people ... We do urgently warn and exhort the said Italian people ... to abide in close attachment to their respective sovereigns, of whose good will they have already had experience, so as never to let themselves be torn away from the obedience they owe them.

Statement by Pope Pius IX, 29 April 1848; L.C. Farini *The Roman State 1815–1850* (1854) p.111. So much for the hopes of a papal commitment to Italian unification.

9 Article 1. The temporal government of the papacy in Rome is now at an end, in fact and in law.
   Article 2. The Roman pontiff will have every

guarantee needed for the independent exercise of his spiritual power.

Article 3. The form of government at Rome shall be that of pure democracy, and it will take the glorious name of the Roman Republic.

Article 4. The Roman Republic will enter into such relations with the rest of Italy as our common nationality demands.

Declaration of the Constituent Assembly of Rome, 9 Feb. 1849; G. Spada *Storia della Rivoluzione di Roma* (1870) Vol.3, pp.201–2. The Roman Republic was the creation of Giuseppe Mazzini, and the last revolutionary area of the peninsula to hold out until suppressed by the intervention of France in June–July 1849. France, by now an extremely conservative republic under the presidency of Louis-Napoleon, came in to prove its counter-revolutionary credentials.

1 Nothing but a rope's end will serve to persuade us Italians to pull together ... If we wish to pass for lions, instead of, as hitherto, rabbits – to overawe our insolent neighbours – we want the whole nation armed: that is, two millions of soldiers – and the clergy honestly employed in draining the Pontine Marshes.

Giuseppe Garibaldi *Autobiography* (1889) Vol.2, pp.140–42. Garibaldi had tried and failed to hold Rome against the French but played a decisive part in bringing the southern kingdom of Naples and Sicily into a united Italy in 1860 and mounted an unsuccessful expedition to incorporate Rome in 1862. The Pontine Marshes, the swamplands close to Rome, were eventually drained by Mussolini's fascist regime in the 1920s.

GERMANY: THE ABORTIVE REICH

2 At the head of the procession Professor Kinkel bore the tricolour, black, red and gold, which so long had been prohibited as the revolutionary flag. Arrived in the market square, he ... spoke with a wonderful eloquence ... as he depicted a resurrection of German unity and greatness and new liberties and rights of the German people which now must be conceded by the princes or won by force by the people.

The university student Carl Schurz, Bonn, 18 March 1848; *Reminiscences* (1907). Schurz, like many other German insurgents, eventually went into exile in the United States, where he became a significant political figure. In 1850 he rescued Kinkel from prison in Berlin; the professor had been jailed after trying to engineer a revolutionary coup in Baden on 2 May 1849.

3 The Crown itself has thrown the earth upon its coffin.

Prince Bismarck on the king of Prussia, Frederick William IV, March 1848; A.J. Butler *Bismarck, the Man and Statesman* (1898) Vol.2, p.335. When the revolutionary ferment reached the Prussian capital, Berlin, demonstrators were shot down by royal troops on 18 March. Next day, the king stood to salute the bodies of the dead insurrectionists. The ultra-royalist Bismarck was appalled.

4 The dear Austrians! They are now pondering how they can unite themselves with Germany without uniting themselves with Germany! That will be hard to do – just as hard as if two people who wanted to kiss each other simultaneously wanted to turn their backs on one another.

The dramatist Friedrich Hebbel, 18 April 1848; *Diaries* Vol.2, p.299. The problem for Austria was this: how could its multinational empire be fused with a purely German empire? The non-German territories of Austria could not be brought into a German Reich, and if the German territories alone entered it, Austria as the entity it had been for over three centuries would cease to exist.

5 Liberalism is a disease ... Black is called white, darkness light, and the victims (convicts, galley-slaves, Sodomites, etc.) ... succumb to a sinful, God-damned frenzy ... I know only one medicine for it: 'The Sign of the Cross on Breast and Forehead.'

Frederick William IV to Count Christian von Bunsen, 13 May 1848; Legge (1918) pp.354–5.

6 From its rising to its setting the sun shall look upon a beautiful, free Germany, and on the borders of the daughter-lands, as on the frontiers of their mother, no downtrodden, unfree people shall dwell; the rays of German freedom and German gentleness shall light and warm the French and Cossacks, the Bushman and Chinese.

The German composer Richard Wagner, speech to the Dresden branch of the Fatherland Society, 14 June 1848; *Art and Politics* (1895). An interesting declamation, considering what Germany did to France in 1870–71, 1914–18 and 1940–45; to Russia in 1914–18 and 1941–5; to the tribes in its colony of Southwest Africa in the 1900s; and, as the self-proclaimed successors of Attila, in its Chinese concession of Shandong between 1898 and 1914.

7 It is universal anarchy, the world turned upside-down, divine madness made visible. The Old One must be shut away if this continues. This is the fault of the atheists who so greatly enraged Him.

Heinrich Heine to Campe, 3 July 1848; *Letters* Vol.22, p.287. A curious outburst from the long-time devotee of revolution. 'The Old One': God; Joachim Heinrich Campe was Heine's Hamburg publisher.

1 Let Russia, France or England try to interfere in our just cause! We will answer them with a million and a half armed men … They will not dare … because they know that … this would generate a German national upsurge the like of which world history has not yet seen … which could at the same time start an avalanche liable to destroy the thirty-four crowned heads of Germany and a great deal else that lies in its path.

Heinrich Simon in the Frankfurt parliament, 5 Sept. 1848; Franz Wizard (ed.) *Stenographic Record of the German Constituent Assembly* (1848) Vol.3, p.1884. Simon was opposing the armistice ending the war between Prussia and Denmark over Schleswig-Holstein. The parliament met on 18 May to draft a constitution for a new German empire.

2 All the royal buildings are filled to the roof with soldiers. There are four to five hundred men in the Bank and in the Admiralty. In the halls, women hawkers are selling bread, brandy, sausages, and tobacco. In the evenings, the soldiers lounge around on the stair steps, so that you almost have to climb over them when you walk through the smoke-filled rooms. Even the Museum has been turned into a barracks.

Fanny Lewald, Berlin, 18 Nov. 1848; Lewis (1997) p.148. This massive show of military strength ended the revolution in Prussia.

3 *Gegen Demokraten, helfen nur Soldaten.* (Only soldiers are any use against democrats.)

Wilhelm von Merkel, last line of a counter-revolutionary ballad, *Die fünfte Zunft* (The Fifth Tribe), distributed in broadsheet form in 1848.

4 The crown which the Ottonians, the Hohenstaufen and the Habsburgs have worn, a Hohenstaufen can of course wear; it honours him superabundantly with the glitter of a thousand years. THE one, however, which you unfortunately mean, dishonours superabundantly with its carrion reek of the 1848 revolution, the most absurd, the most stupid and the worst, if not, God be praised, also the most evil thing of this century … Should the thousand-year-old crown of the German nation, which has been in abeyance for 42 years, be given away again, then I am HE and my EQUALS, WHO WILL GIVE IT AWAY. Woe to him who usurps that to which he has no right.

Friedrich Wilhelm IV to Count von Bunsen, 13 Dec. 1848; Hagen Schulze *The Course of German Nationalism* (1991) p.140. The king, confident now that the revolution in Prussia had been smashed by his forces, formally refused the crown of the German empire (formerly known as the Holy Roman Empire) when it was offered to him by the Frankfurt parliament on 3 April 1849. This was partly through deference to Austria,

but mainly because it was tainted, coming from a body born of the revolution. The Ottonian dynasty were emperors from 962; the Hohenstaufen (later rulers of Prussia) held the title from 1138; the Habsburgs (the ruling house of Austria) took it in 1273 and kept it until 1806.

RUSSIA: DAMAGE CONTROL

5 Gentlemen, saddle your horses! A republic has been declared in France!

Tsar Nicholas I, 5 March 1848; W. Bruce Lincoln *Nicholas I* (1978) p.281. Almost certainly apocryphal. On 6 March the tsar told the commanders of the Imperial Guards regiments: 'I give you my word that not one drop of Russian blood will be spilt on account of these worthless Frenchmen' (Lincoln (1978) pp.280–81). Compare the reaction of Catherine the Great to the French Revolution in 1792 (see 520:7).

6 Louis-Philippe loses his usurped throne … Thus the hand of God is clearly seen.

Tsar Nicholas I to Friedrich Wilhelm IV of Prussia, 7 March 1848; L.B. Namier *1848: The Revolution of the Intellectuals* (1944) p.38. Compare his reported comment on the burning down of the British Houses of Parliament in 1834: 'God's judgement on the Reform Bill.'

7 In France there is a *Republic* [under] a National Assembly and a council [including] *Albert*, a WORKER … This is what we have come to! A repetition of the terrible events at the end of the last century.

Grand Duke Konstantin, diary entry, 5 March 1848; Lincoln (1978) p.279. In other words, a second French Revolution.

8 After a blessed peace of many years, the western part of Europe suddenly has been disturbed by the present troubles, threatening the overthrow of legitimate powers and the entire social order. At this very moment, this insolence, knowing no limits, threatens with its madness even Our Russia, entrusted to Us by God. But it will not succeed! Following the example of Our Orthodox ancestors, and invoking the help of Almighty God, We are ready to meet our enemies [and] We shall, in indissoluble union with Our Holy Russia, defend the honour of the Russian name and the inviolability of our frontiers.

Tsar Nicholas I, 26 March 1848; Lincoln (1978) p.287.

9 The soldiers will mutiny, orators will arouse the people to carnage, the rabble will pull down taverns, rape women, torture nobles … The Caucasus will boil up like a cauldron … and the Mongols … will burst out of the steppes of Central Asia to the Volga and beyond.

The would-be revolutionary Alexander Balasoglo; J.P. Seddon *The Petrashevsty* (1965) p.208. An apocalyptic vision, no doubt shared, from the opposite perspective, by the tsar himself.

1 Awaken from your slumber, O Russian people! Your brothers: Germans, French, Italians, Austrians … have already blazed the trail for you … We are free: follow us!

Leaflet printed in Germany and distributed in Kiev, March 1848; Lincoln (1978) p.289.

2 Our main defence against a mass revolution lies in the fact that among us are neither the elements nor the instruments for it … because freedom of the press, popular representation, national guards, and things of that nature, are complete nonsense to nine-tenths of the Russian population.

The Russian Baron Korf; Lincoln (1978) p.271.

3 What remains standing in Europe? Great Britain and Russia! Would it not be natural to conclude from that that our close union is perhaps called on to save the world?

Tsar Nicholas I to Queen Victoria, 3 April 1848; *The Letters of Queen Victoria* Vol.2 (1911) p.166.

4 Russia and the Revolution are the only two forces in Europe. The survival of the one will mean the extinction of the other. The political and religious future of mankind depends … on the result of the struggle … the greatest conflict that the world has ever seen. Russia is Christian and the Revolution is anti-Christian to the core … Russia alone can defeat the Revolution, and not only will she defeat it, but she will benefit by it, for she will emancipate and unite under the tsar's sceptre all the Slav peoples whom the Revolution frees from the Austrian and Hungarian yoke. That is Russia's undoubted mission.

The poet (and imperial censor) Feodor Tyutchev to the tsar, July 1848; Lincoln (1978) p.251. Russia did act to smash the Hungarian rising in 1849, but Tyutchev's dream of a Pan-Slav crusade in central Europe was not to the liking of the tsar (see 559:9).

5 The sentence of death was read to us, we were all made to kiss the cross … and we were told to don our white execution shirts. Then three of us were tied to the stakes in order to be shot … Then an order from His Imperial Majesty was read which granted us our lives.

Feodor Dostoevsky, 22 Dec. 1849; Lincoln (1978) p.310. The writer Dostoevsky was one of a revolutionary circle arrested and personally interrogated by the tsar.

AFTERMATH

6 1848 was the turning point at which modern history failed to turn.

George Macaulay Trevelyan *British History in the Nineteenth Century* (1922) Ch.19.

7 A curse upon you, year of blood and madness, year of the triumph of meanness, beastliness, stupidity! … What did you do, revolutionaries frightened of revolution, political tricksters, buffoons of liberty? … Democracy can create nothing positive … and therefore it has no future … Socialism left a victor on the field of battle will inevitably be deformed into a commonplace bourgeois philistinism. Then a cry of denial will be wrung from the titanic breast of the revolutionary minority and the deadly battle will begin again … We have wasted our spirit in the regions of the abstract and general, just as the monks let it wither in the world of prayer and contemplation.

Alexander Herzen *From the Other Shore* (1849).

8 If the revolutions of 1848 have clearly brought out any fact, it is the utter failure of newspaper states-men. Everywhere they have been tried: everywhere they have shown great talents for intrigue, eloquence and agitation – how rarely have they shown even fair aptitude for ordinary administration.

The political commentator Walter Bagehot; Norman St John Stevas (ed.) *The Collected Works of Walter Bagehot* Vol.4 (1968) p.75. By 'newspaper statesmen' he meant academic theorists, out of their depth in the real world of politics.

9 From humanity via nationalism to inhumanity.

The Austrian poet, Franz Grillparzer, 1849.

10 *Plus ça change, plus c'est la même chose.* (The more things change, the more they stay the same.)

Alfonse Karr *Les Guêpes* (The Wasps), Jan. 1849, p.305.

The Birth of Industrial Society in Britain, 1776–1851

NEW ORDER, 1776–1848

1 It is a complete revolution; it is the 1789 of trade and industry.

Alphonse de Lamartine in the French Chamber of Deputies, 14 April 1836; *Archives parlementaires* p.48. The notion of industrialization as a revolution first took shape in France in the early 19th century, linked, of course, as here, to the French experience, even though France was half a century behind Britain as an industrial state.

2   I stood among my valleys of the south
And saw a flame of fire, even as a Wheel
Of fire surrounding all the heavens: it went
From west to east, against the current of
Creation, and devour'd all things with loud
Fury and thundering course round heaven and
         earth.

William Blake *Jerusalem: The Emanation of the Giant Albion* (1804–20) Ch.4, Preface, lines 1–6. Blake's apocalyptic vision of industrialism.

3 Every individual … intends only his own gain, and he is in this, as in many other cases, led by an invisible hand to promote an end which was no part of his intention. By pursuing his own interest he frequently promotes that of the society more effectively than when he really intends to promote it. I have never known much good done by those who affected to trade for the public good.

Adam Smith *The Wealth of Nations* (1776) Bk 4, Ch.2. Smith's book soon became the bible of the apostles of capitalist development according to the principles of laissez-faire – minimal government interference with individual entrepreneurship. The mystical concept of the invisible hand was to justify liberal economic thinking for a century and a half until the Great Depression of the 1930s.

4 The progressive state is in reality the cheerful and the hearty state to all the orders of society; the stationary state is dull; the declining melancholy.

Adam Smith (1776). 'Progressive' here means moving forward, in the material rather than the political sense; active, not inert. Used as the epigraph to his book *The Coal Question* (1865) by the economist William Stanley Jevons, with the gloss *Non progredi est regredi* (Not to advance is to retreat), a telling indication of the power of Smith's influence on 19th-century economic thought.

5 I cannot … regard the stationary state of capital and wealth with the unaffected aversion so generally manifested towards it by the political economists of the old school … I confess I am not charmed with the ideal of life held out by those who think that the normal state of human beings is that of struggling to get on; that the trampling, crushing, elbowing, and treading on each other's heels which form the existing type of social life, are the most desirable lot of human kind, or anything but the disagreeable symptoms of one of the phases of industrial progress.

John Stuart Mill *Principles of Political Economy* (1848) Vol.2, p.328, unconvinced by the Smithian maxim.

6 Adam Smith's book is … a tedious and hardhearted book [which] considers man as a manufacturing animal; it estimates his importance, not by the sum of goodness and of knowledge which he possesses … not by his immortal destinies for which he is created; but by the gain which can be extracted from him.

Robert Southey 'On the State of the Poor' (1812); *Essays* Vol.1, p.112.

7 Were we required to characterize this age of ours by any single epithet, we should be tempted to call it the Mechanical Age … There is no end to machinery … We remove mountains, and make seas our smooth highway; nothing can resist us. We war with rude Nature; and, by our resistless engines, come off always victorious, and loaded with spoils.

Thomas Carlyle *Signs of the Times* (1829). A classic expression of the high confidence of the early industrial era.

8 The productions of Nature, varied and numerous as they are, may each, in some future day, become the basis of extensive manufactures, and give life, employment and wealth to millions of human beings. But the crude treasures perpetually exposed before our eyes contain within them other and more valuable principles. All these, in their innumerable combinations, which Ages of labour can never exhaust, may be destined to furnish, in perpetual succession, the source of our wealth and happiness.

Charles Babbage *On the Economy of Machinery and Manufactures* (1832). Another believer in the certainty of infinite progress.

1 Many land animals and birds are disappearing before the advance of civilization. Draining, cultivation, cutting down of forests, and even the introduction of new plants and animals, destroy some of the old and alter the relations between those that remain. The inaccessible cliffs of the Himalayas and Andes will afford a refuge to the eagle and condor, but the time will come when the mighty forests of Bhutan, of the Amazon and Orinoco, will disappear with the myriads of their joyous inhabitants.

Mary Somerville *Physical Geography* (1848; 1877 edn) p.504. An apprehension unusual for the times.

MARKET FORCES, 1770–1807

2 Agriculture is the grand product that supports the people ... Both public and private wealth can arise from only three sources, *agriculture, manufactures, and commerce* ... Agriculture exceeds both the others; it is even the foundation of their principal branches ... None but a fool can imagine that the landlords of this great empire of above fourscore millions of acres are to yield to the transitory sons of trade and manufacture.

Arthur Young *A Six Months' Tour through the North of England* (1770) Vol.4, p.525 and *The Farmer's Tour through the East of England* (1771) Vol.4, p.362. On the eve of the take-off into industrial growth, farming was still, as it always previously had been, the bedrock of the economy.

3 To found a great empire for the sole purpose of raising up a people of customers, may at first sight appear a project fit only for a nation of shopkeepers.

Adam Smith (1776) Bk 4, Ch.7, Pt 1. 'Nation of shopkeepers' is also attributed to Napoleon on St Helena (Barry O'Meara *Napoleon in Exile* (1822) Vol.2, p.81).

4 The desire of food is limited in every man by the narrow capacity of the human stomach, but the desire of the conveniences and ornaments of building, dress, equipage, and household furniture, seems to have no limit or certain boundary.

Adam Smith (1776) Bk 1, Ch.11, Pt 2.

5 The Great People have had these Vases in their Palaces long enough for them to be seen and admired by the *Middling Class* of People, which Class we know are vastly, I had almost said, infinitely superior, in number to the Great, and though a *great price* was, I believe, at first necessary to make the Vases

esteemed *Ornaments for Palaces*, that reason no longer exists. Their character is established, and the middling People would probably buy quantitys of them at a reduced price.

Josiah Wedgwood to Thomas Bentley, 23 Aug. 1772; *The Selected Letters of Josiah Wedgwood* (1965) p.131. Wedgwood, the great potter, was one of the founding fathers of the consumer society, by opening up a wider market for items hitherto seen as luxuries, affordable only by the aristocracy and gentry.

6 You cannot spend in luxury without doing good to the poor.

Samuel Johnson; Peter Mathias *The Transformation of England* (1980) p.302. One of the earliest assertions of the 'trickle-down effect', the debatable notion that conspicuous consumption by the upper classes percolates to the lowest strata of society and so benefits the entire community.

7   The world is too much with us; late and soon,
    Getting and spending, we lay waste our powers.

William Wordsworth 'The world is too much with us' (1807). The poet was a devotee of plain living and high thinking and highly resistant to the consequences of industrialization, for example in his opposition to a railway penetrating his beloved Lake District.

8 All the country girls and women are without shoes or stockings; and the ploughmen at their work have neither sabots nor feet to their stockings. This is a poverty that strikes at the root of national prosperity; a large consumption among the poor being of more consequence than among the rich: the wealth of a nation lies in its circulation and consumption; and the case of poor people abstaining from the use of manufactures of leather and wool ought to be considered as an evil of the first magnitude.

Arthur Young *Travels in France* (1792) Vol.1, p.38. Twenty years on from his paean to agriculture, Young could begin to see the dividends from trade and industry.

SCIENCE ON THE MARGIN, 1775–1842

9 It was an ill policy in Leo the Tenth to patronize polite literature. He was cherishing an enemy in disguise. And the English hierarchy (if there be anything unsound in its constitution) has equal reason to tremble even at an air pump or an electrical machine.

Joseph Priestley *Experiments and Observations on Different Kinds of Air* (1775–86). Priestley, the scientist and political radical, saw science as the force destined to break open the old status quo. Leo X (Giovanni de' Medici) was pope from 1513 to 1521, at the height of the Renaissance.

1 That a country, eminently distinguished for its mechanical and manufacturing ingenuity, should be indifferent to the progress of inquiries which form the highest departments of that knowledge on whose more elementary truths its wealth and rank depend, is a fact well deserving the attention of those who shall inquire into the causes that influence the progress of nations.

Charles Babbage *Reflections on the Decline of Science and Some of its Causes* (1830) p.1. An appeal for Britain to move beyond the inventiveness that had made it the foremost industrial power and probe the fundamentals of the material world.

2 The first idea which I remember of the possibility of calculating tables by machinery occurred either in 1820 or 1821 ... We had decided on the proper formulae and had put them in the hands of two computers [mathematicians] for the purpose of calculation. We met one evening for the purpose of comparing the calculated results, and finding many discordancies, I expressed to my friend the wish, that we could calculate by steam, to which he assented as to a thing within the bounds of possibility.

Charles Babbage *History of the Invention of Calculating Engines* (1834) p.10. Babbage was the progenitor of the information technology that eventually came to birth in the 1940s, a long gestation.

3 What shall we do to get rid of Babbage's calculating machine ... worthless to science in my view. If it would now calculate the amount and the quantum of benefit to be derived to science it would render the only service I ever expect to derive from it.

Sir Robert Peel, the prime minister, late 1842; Anthony Hyman *Charles Babbage: Pioneer of the Computer* (1982) p.191. The Conservative belies the hopes of the Visionary.

COUNTRY AND CITY, 1798–1846

4 The following propositions are intended to be proved:

Population is necessarily limited by means of subsistence.

Population invariably increases where the means of subsistence increase, unless prevented by some very powerful and obvious checks.

These checks, and the checks which repress the superior power of population, and keep its effects on

a level with the means of subsistence, are all resolvable into moral restraints, vice, and misery.

Thomas Malthus *An Essay on the Principle of Population* (1798). In spite of this grim prognosis, population in the industrializing world grew at a phenomenal rate in the next half century.

5 The law of nature bids a man *not starve* in a land of plenty, and forbids his being punished for taking food wherever he can find it. Your law of nature is sitting at Westminster, to make the labourer pay taxes, to make him fight for the safety of the land, to bind him in allegiance, and when he is poor and hungry, to cast him off to starve, or to hang himself if he takes food to save his life!

The radical journalist William Cobbett *Open Letter to Malthus*, 8 May 1819. To Cobbett, the misery of the poor was man-made, contrary to natural law and inflicted by a heartless legislature sitting in the Westminster Parliament.

6 He acknowledges that he has frequently been 'hard put to it'. He has sometimes barely had *bread* for his children: not a morsel for himself! having often made a dinner of *raw hog peas*: saying, that he has taken a handful of peas, and ate them with as much satisfaction as he had eaten better dinners, adding, that they agreed with him very well, and that he was able to work upon them as upon other food.

William Marshall, interview with a farm labourer, in his *The Rural Economy of the Midland Counties* (1796) Vol.2, pp.197–8.

7 Gave poor Roberts one of my old Shirts to put on in the small-Pox – His, poor Fellow, being so extremely coarse and rough, that his having the small-Pox so very full, his coarse Shirt makes it very painful to him. I sent his family a Basket of Apples and some black currant Robb.

Rev. James Woodforde, 8 March 1791, in *The Diary of a Country Parson* (1992 edn) p.314. Robb was a fruit conserve.

8 A boy by the name of Phipps was inoculated in the arm from a pustule on the hand of a young woman who was infected by her master's cows ... The boy has since been inoculated for the small pox, which, as I ventured to predict, produced no effect.

Edward Jenner to Edward Gardner, 19 July 1796, on his successful injection against smallpox on 14 May 1796; John Baron *The Life of Edward Jenner, M.D.* (1827) pp.137–8.

9 I am persuaded that mischief frequently arises, from a practice common in many back streets, of leaving the vaults of the privies open. I have often observed, that fevers prevail most in houses exposed to the effluvia of dunghills in such situations. In a house in Bootle Street, most of the inhabitants are paralytic, in consequence of their situation in a blind alley, which excludes them from light and air. Consumption, distortion, and idiocy, are common in such recesses.

Dr John Ferriar, on the new industrial town of Manchester, Jan. 1792; Dr John Aikin *A Description of the Country from Thirty Miles round Manchester* (1795) p.192.

1   Here a huge town, continuous and compact,
  Hiding the face of earth for leagues – and there,
  Where not a habitation stood before,
  The abodes of men irregularly massed
  Like trees in forests, – spread through spacious
    tracts …
  And, whereso'er the traveller turns his step,
  He sees the barren wilderness erased,
  Or disappearing.

William Wordsworth *The Excursion* (1814).

2 How different is this from Paris! There vastness and filth, here simplicity and astonishing cleanliness; there wealth and poverty in continued contrast, here a general appearance of sufficiency; there palaces out of which crawls poverty, here tiny brick cottages out of which health and contentment walk with an air of dignity and tranquillity – lord and artisan almost indistinguishable in their immaculate dress.

Nikolai A. Karamzin *Letters of a Russian Traveller 1789–90* (1957 edn) pp.265–7. London as seen by an impressionable Anglophile.

3 In London this smoke is found to blight or destroy all vegetation … Other phenomena are produced by its union with fogs, rendering them nearly opaque, and shutting out the light of the sun; it blackens the mud of the streets by its deposit of tar, while the unctuous mixture renders the foot-pavement slippery … It must in a future age be … difficult to believe that the Londoners could have resided in the dense atmosphere of coal-smoke above described.

Sir Richard Phillips *A Morning's Walk from London to Kew* (1817). London as seen by a long-time resident.

4 A sort of black smoke covers the city. The sun seen through it is a disc without rays. Under this half-daylight 300,000 human beings are ceaselessly at work … From this foul drain the greatest stream of human industry flows out to fertilize the whole world. From this filthy sewer pure gold flows. Here humanity attains its most complete development

and its most brutish; here civilization makes its miracles, and civilized man is turned back almost into a savage.

Alexis de Tocqueville, on Manchester, *Journeys to England and Ireland* (1835). Clearly no civic improvement had taken place since Aikin's survey in the 1790s.

5 Such is the absence of civic economy in some of our towns that their condition in respect to cleanliness is almost as bad as that of an encamped horde, or an undisciplined soldiery … whilst the houses, courts, lanes and streams are polluted and rendered pestilential. The civic officers have generally contented themselves with the most barbarous expedients, or sit still amidst the pollution, with the resignation of Turkish fatalists, under the supposed destiny of their prevalent ignorance, sloth, and filth.

Edwin Chadwick *The Sanitary Condition of the Labouring Population* (1842) Vol.26, p.43. It was Chadwick who finally got to grips with the problem of public health in the industrial towns, notably by the installation of an efficient sewerage system.

6 It is an aggregate of masses … portentous and fearful … as of the slow rising and gradual swelling of an ocean which must, at some future and no distant time, bear all the elements of society aloft upon its bosom, and float them Heaven knows whither. There are mighty energies slumbering in these masses.

W. Cooke Taylor *Notes of a Tour in the Manufacturing Districts of Lancashire* (1842) pp.4–6.

7 It's surpriseing to see the number of servants that are walking about the streets out of place [unemployed] … Servants are so plentifull that gentlefolk will only have those that are tall, upright, respectable-looking young people and must bare the very best character, and mechanics are so very numerous that most tradespeople send their sons and daughters out to service rather than put them to a trade. By that reason, London and every other tound is over run with servants.

William Tayler *Diary of William Tayler, Footman* (1837) p.33.

8 I dare say you need not be told how sensual vice abounds in rural districts. Here it is flagrant beyond anything I ever could have looked for: and here while every justice of the peace is filled with disgust and every clergyman with (almost) despair at the drunkenness, quarrelling and extreme licentiousness with women – here is dear good old

Wordsworth for ever talking of rural innocence and deprecating any intercourse with towns, lest the purity of his neighbours should be corrupted.

Harriet Martineau writing from the Lake District (Wordsworth country) in 1846 to Elizabeth Barrett; R.K. Webb *Harriet Martineau* (1960) pp.260–61.

CANALS, ROADS, RAILWAYS, 1768–1835

1 Every improvement of the means of locomotion benefits mankind morally and intellectually as well as materially.

Thomas Babington Macaulay *The History of England* (1849) Vol.1, Ch.3.

2 I was astonished at the vastness of the plan, & the greatness of Stile in the execution. The Walls of the Locks are truly admirable, both for their strength and beauty of workmanship … In short, to behold ten of these locks, all at one view, with their Gates, Aqueducts, Cisterns, sluices, bridges, &c &c, the whole seems to be the work of Titans rather than a production of our Pigmy race of beings.

The master-potter Josiah Wedgwood, Jan. 1773, on the Runcorn locks, which completed the Duke of Bridgewater's canal linking Manchester and Liverpool. Canals were to be the main artery of heavy goods traffic in Britain until the advent of the railway in the late 1820s.

3 They may piss, but they've stood.

Duke of Bridgewater, comment on the locks of his canal. Its designer, James Brindley, disagreed with the duke's insistence on locks with walls of brick ribbed with stone, on the grounds that they would leak and collapse. This was the ducal response.

4 Of all the cursed roads that ever disgraced this kingdom in the very ages of barbarism, none ever equalled that from Billericay to the *King's Head* at Tilbury. It is for near 12 miles so narrow that a mouse cannot pass by any carriage; I saw a fellow creep under his waggon to assist me to lift, if possible, my chaise over a hedge. The ruts are of an incredible depth.

Arthur Young *A Six Weeks' Tour through the Southern Counties of England and Wales* (1768) p.27. Young was famously critical of mid-18th-century British roads, for very good reason.

5 The Plan upon which he proceeds in road-making is this: first to level and drain, then, like the Romans, to lay a solid pavement of large stones … This road is as nearly as perfect as possible. After

the foundation has been laid, the workmen are charged to throw out every stone which is bigger than a hen's egg.

Robert Southey on the road engineer Thomas Telford, who revived construction techniques lost for over a thousand years; *Journal of a Tour of Scotland in 1819* (1929 edn) p.54.

6 We are credibly informed that there is a Steam Engine now preparing to run against any mare, horse or gelding that may now be produced at the next October meeting at Newmarket.

The Times, 8 July 1808, on the railway engine built by Richard Trevithick, an inexhaustible iron horse.

7 I will send them the Locomotive to be the great Missionary among them.

The railway engineer George Stephenson, attrib. Stephenson constructed his first locomotive in 1814.

8 I see no reason to suppose that these machines will force themselves into general use.

Duke of Wellington on railway engines, 1827; J.A. Gere and John Sparrow (eds) *Geoffrey Madan's Notebooks* (1981) p.117. Wellington's view was doubtless confirmed when he witnessed the death of the former cabinet minister William Huskisson, fatally injured by Stephenson's *Rocket* at the opening of the Liverpool to Manchester railway on 15 Sept. 1830.

9 The quickest motion is to me *frightful*; it is really flying, and it is impossible to divest yourself of the notion of instant death to all upon the least accident happening. It gave me a headache which has not left me yet.

Thomas Creevey, 14 Nov. 1829, on travelling by railway at 23 miles an hour; John Gore (ed.) *The Creevey Papers* (1970 edn) p.301.

10 You cannot conceive what that sensation of cutting the air was; the motion is as smooth as possible, too. I could have either read or written; as it was, I stood up, and with my bonnet off 'drank the air before me'. The wind, which was strong, or perhaps the force of our thrusting against it, absolutely weighed my eyelids down. When I closed my eyes this sensation of flying was quite delightful, and strange beyond description.

The actress Fanny Kemble, travelling on a trial run of the *Rocket*, 26 Aug. 1830; *Records of a Girlhood* (1878).

11 To whirl through the confused darkness, on those steam wings, was one of the strangest things I have experienced … the likest thing to a Faust's flight on the Devil's mantle; or as if some huge steam night-bird had flung you on its back, and was sweeping through unknown space with you.

Thomas Carlyle describes his first train ride in 1839; James Anthony Froude *Thomas Carlyle: A History of his Life in London* (1885) Vol.1, p.144.

1 If ever I go mad, I shall have the ghost of the opening of the railway walking before me … and when it steps forward, a little swarm of devils in the shape of leaky pickle-tanks, uncut timber, half-finished station houses, sinking embankments, broken screws, absent guard plates, unfinished drawings and sketches, will, quietly … lift up my ghost and put him a little further off than before.

The greatest of Victorian railway engineers, Isambard Kingdom Brunel, on his first triumph, the Great Western Railway, in a letter to Charles Saunders, 3 Dec. 1837; L.T.C. Rolt *Isambard Kingdom Brunel* (1957) p.114. Brunel made sure his nightmare never became a reality, unlike Railtrack, made responsible for the maintenance of the decaying British railway network at the end of the 20th century.

2 Why not make it longer, and have a steamboat go from Bristol to New York and call it the *Great Western*?

Isambard Kingdom Brunel, Oct. 1835, on his project for a transatlantic passenger vessel, as a logical extension of the London to Bristol railway; Rolt (1957) p.191. *Great Western* was built and made the crossing to New York in 15 days, arriving on 23 April 1838, soon after the much smaller *Sirius*, which had a slight start.

INDUSTRY, 1765–1848

3 I came into Mr Watt's parlour without ceremony, and found him sitting before the fire, having lying on his knee a little tin cistern, which he was looking at … At last he looked at me, and said briskly, 'You need not *fash* yourself any more about that, man; I have now got an engine that shall not waste a particle of steam. It shall be all boiling hot; – aye, and hot water injected if I please.

Professor John Robison *A Narrative of Mr Watt's Invention of the Improved Engine* (1796). Robison dated the encounter at 1765, when Watt began to perfect his steam engine.

4 I wish Johnson had been with us … The vastness and the contrivance of some of the machinery would have 'matched his mighty mind'. I shall never forget Mr Bolton's expression to me: 'I sell here, Sir, what all the world desires to have, – POWER.'

James Boswell, 22 March 1776; *The Life of Samuel Johnson* (1791). Boswell had been on a visit to the Birmingham engine works of James Watt's partner, Matthew Boulton (not, as Boswell has it, Bolton).

5 Colebrook Dale itself is a very romantic spot … Indeed … too beautiful to be much in unison with that variety of horrors art has spread at the bottom: the noise of the forges, mills, & c., with all their vast machinery, the flames bursting from the furnaces with the burning of the coal and the smoak of the lime kilns, are altogether sublime.

Arthur Young at the birthplace of the industrial revolution in Shropshire, 13 June 1776; *Tours in England and Wales* (1791).

6 Manufactures … prosper most where the mind is least consulted, and where the workshop may, without any great effort of imagination, be considered as an engine, the parts of which are men.

Adam Ferguson *An Essay on the History of Civil Society* (1767). Compare the objective of Josiah Wedgwood in a letter to Thomas Bentley of 9 Oct. 1769: 'to make such *Machines* of the *Men* as cannot err.'

7 On Tuesday morning we heard their drum at about two miles distance from Bolton, a little before we left the place, and their professed design was to take Bolton, Manchester and Stockport on their way to Crumford, and to destroy all the engines, not only in these places, but throughout all England.

Josiah Wedgwood to Thomas Bentley, 9 Oct. 1779; *Selected Letters of Josiah Wedgwood* (1965) p.242. Wedgwood was writing about an early outbreak of machine-breaking, in part, perhaps, brought on by the regimentation Wedgwood sought to instil in the industrial workforce. Cromford was the site of the cotton mill of Sir Richard Arkwright, set up in 1771 (see 569:9).

8 If you Don't Pull them Down in a Forght Nights Time Wee will pull them Down for you Wee will you Damd infernold Dog. And Bee four Almighty God wee will pull down all the Mills.

Anon. note from an early machine-breaker to a Gloucestershire cloth manufacturer, c.1786; Anthony Burton *Remains of a Revolution* (1975) p.199.

9 I well know that a peasantry maintain'd by their own ground or by the cultivation of others' ground must abide, but a fear strikes me that this (our over-stretch'd) commerce may meet a shock, and then what becomes of our rabble of artisans!! The bold rock opposite this house is now disfigur'd by a row of new houses built under it, and the vales are every way block'd up by mills … These cotton mills, seven storeys high and fill'd with inhabitants, remind me of a first-rate man of war and, when they are lighted up on a dark night, look most luminously beautiful.

Colonel John Byng, 18 June 1790, on the Arkwright mill at Cromford; Donald Adamson (ed.) *Rides Round Britain* (1996) pp.187, 188.

1 So dreadfully deleterious are the fumes of arsenic impregnating the air of these places, and so profuse is the perspiration occasioned by the heat of the furnaces, that those who have been employed at them but a few months become most emaciated figures, and in the course of a few years are generally laid in their graves.

W.G. Morton on the smelting-houses of Hayle, Cornwall, in a tour made in the mid-1790s; Burton (1975) p.187.

2 They all become old men in the prime of man-hood. So do the Rope-makers who yet only work from 7 till noon. A pin machine has been lately introduced, after a rebellion among the men and but for the same deplorable Delusion 2 thirds of that Labour might be done by machines, which now eats up the Rope men like Giant in a fairy tale.

Samuel Taylor Coleridge to Robert Southey, 24 March 1804; *Letters of Coleridge* (1956). Coleridge was describing the naval dockyard at Portsmouth.

3 Information has just been given that you are a holder of those detestable Shearing Frames and I ... give you fair Warning to pull them down ... If they are not taken down by the end of next week, I will detach one of my Lieutenants with at least 300 men to destroy them [and burn] your Buildings down to Ashes and if you have the Impudence to fire upon any of my Men, they have orders to murder you, & burn all your Housing.

Luddite warning to a Huddersfield manufacturer, 10 March 1812; W.B. Crump *The Leeds Woollen Industry 1780–1820* (1931) p.229. The Luddites, named after Ned Ludd, were the most organized band of machine-breakers yet seen in Britain, but they stood no chance of reversing the inexorable march of industrial technology. Ludd himself has been described as 'a Leicestershire idiot', who destroyed stocking frames c.1782.

4 By machines mankind are able to do that which their own bodily powers would never effect to the same extent. Machines are the produce of the *mind* of man; and their existence distinguishes the civilized man from the savage.

William Cobbett, 'A Letter to the Luddites', 30 Nov. 1816; *Political Register* Vol.31.

5 These unhappy wretches scarce ever see the light of the sun; they are buried in the bowels of the earth; there they work at a severe and dismal task, without the least prospect of being delivered from it; they subsist upon the coarsest and worst sort of fare; they have their health miserably impaired, and their lives cut short, by being perpetually confined in the close vapour of those malignant minerals.

Edmund Burke *A Vindication of Natural Society* (1753), on the coal miners who fuelled the industrial revolution.

6 A slight trembling, as from an earthquake, was felt for half a mile around the workings; and the noise of the explosion, though dull, was heard to three or four miles distance, and much resembled an unsteady fire of infantry.

Rev. John Hodgson *Funeral Sermon of the Felling Colliery Sufferers* (1813). The Felling mine explosion in County Durham killed nearly 100 men and boys on 25 May 1812.

7 In plunging a light surrounded by a cylinder of fine wire-gauze on to an explosive mixture I saw the whole cylinder become quietly and gradually filled with flame; the upper part of it soon appeared red-hot, yet *no* explosion occurred.

Humphry Davy, late 1815; Anne Treneer *The Mercurial Chemist* (1963) p.167. Davy's work on safety lamps for mines was stimulated by the Felling disaster.

8 It is impossible to contemplate the progress of manufactures in Great Britain within the last thirty years without wonder and astonishment. Its rapidity, particularly since the French revolutionary war, exceeds all credibility. The improvement of the steam engines, but above all the facilities afforded to the great branches of the woollen and cotton manufactories by ingenious machinery, invigorated by capital and skill, are beyond all calculation.

Patrick Colquhoun *A Treatise on the Wealth, Power and Resources of the British Empire* (1815) p.68.

9 I was one day through the iron and coal works of this neighbourhood, – a half-frightful scene! A space ... covered over with furnaces, rolling-mills, steam-engines and sooty men. A dense cloud of pestilential smoke hangs over it for ever, blackening even the grain that grows upon it; and at night the whole region burns like a volcano spitting fire from a thousand tubes of bricks ... It is in a spot like this that one sees the sources of British power.

Thomas Carlyle to Alexander Carlyle, 11 Aug. 1824, describing a visit to the Black Country, the British Midlands heartland of pottery manufacture; *Letters of Thomas Carlyle* (1886).

1 The demoralizing effects of the system are as bad, I know it, as the demoralizing effects of slavery in the West Indies. I know that there are instances and scenes of the grossest prostitution amongst the poor creatures who are the victims of the system, and in some cases are the objects of the cruelty and rapacity and sensuality of their masters. These things I never dared to publish, but the cruelties which are inflicted personally upon the little children, not to mention the immensely long hours which they are subject to work, are such as I am very sure would disgrace a West Indian plantation.

Richard Oastler, the advocate of a 10-hour working day, on factory conditions in the wool-town of Bradford; *Parliamentary Papers* 1831–2, Vol.15, pp.445–55.

2 The dull routine of a ceaseless drudgery, in which the same mechanical process is incessantly repeated, resembles the torment of Sisphysus – the toil, like the rock, recoils perpetually on the wearied operative. The mind gathers neither stores nor strength from the constant extension and retraction of the same muscles. The intellect slumbers in supine inertness; but the grosser parts of nature attain a rank development. To condemn man to such severity of toil is, in some measure, to cultivate in him the habits of an animal.

Dr James Phillips Kay *The Moral and Physical Condition of the Working Classes Employed in the Cotton Manufacture in Manchester* (1832) pp.6–11.

3 Each workman performing, or rather superintending as much work as could have been done by *two or three hundred men* sixty years ago ... When it is remembered that all these inventions have been made within the last seventy years it must be acknowledged that the cotton mill presents the most striking example of the dominion obtained by human science over the powers of nature, of which modern times can boast.

Edward Baines *History of the Cotton Manufactures of Great Britain* (1835); Burton (1975) p.215.

4 We might with some plausibility maintain that the people live longer because they are better fed, better lodged, better clothed and better attended in sickness, and that these improvements are owing to that increase in national wealth which the manufacturing system has produced.

Thomas Babington Macaulay *Edinburgh Review* (1830). But see 572:9.

5 In the factory, every member of the loom is so adjusted that the driving force leaves the attendant nearly nothing to do, certainly no muscular fatigue to sustain, while it procures for him good, unfailing wages, besides a healthy workshop gratis: whereas the non-factory weaver, having everything to execute by muscular exertion, finds the labour irksome ... while he loses his health by poor diet and the dampness of his hovel.

Andrew Ure *The Philosophy of Manufactures* (1835). A notorious paean of praise to the factory.

6 For several years after I began to work in the mill, the hours of labour at our works did not exceed *ten* in the day, winter and summer, and even with the labour of those hours, I shall never forget the fatigue I often felt before the day ended, and the anxiety of us all to be relieved from the unvarying and irksome toil we had gone through ... A Dr URE is, it seems, ... trying, not to get the manufacturers down to *ten* hours' labour a day, but to lengthen the period to *fifteen* or *sixteen* hours a day, by telling us that some of our competitors work that long time.

John Fielden *The Curse of the Factory System* (1836), a stinging riposte to Ure.

7 A race whose wisdom consists in that cunning which enables them to devise the cheapest possible means for getting out of the youngest possible workers the greatest possible amount of labour, in the shortest possible amount of time, for the least possible amount of wages.

Parson Bull of Bierley in the *Manchester and Salford Advertiser*, 29 Nov. 1835, on the industrialists of his day.

8 Here he builds furnaces and there chimney stacks ... And the next day the peasants hear a loud rhythmical noise coming from the factory – like the breathing of some enormous monster who, once he has begun to work, will never stop ... Government officials ... do not realize that this silent man who seldom puts pen to paper is far more likely to turn their old world upside down than many a revolutionary who has his pockets stuffed with political programmes and manifestos.

A contemporary on the impact on Belgium of the Lancashire entrepreneur John Cockerill, 1835; W.O. Henderson *Britain and Industrial Europe 1750–1870* (1954) p.130. In 1817 Cockerill and his brother built the first locomotive to run on the European mainland in their ironworks at Seraing, near Liège. Belgium was the first Continental country to industrialize, largely under British auspices.

1 He conceived it to be a delusion to suppose that ... the continent would suffer England to be the workshop for the world.
Benjamin Disraeli, 14 March 1838; *Parl. Deb.* Vol.41, Col.940.

2 Rose before six to prayer and meditation. Ah, blessed God, how many in the mills and factories have risen at four, on this day even, to toil and suffering.
The reformer Lord Shaftesbury, Christmas Day 1843; Edwin Hodder *The Life and Work of the Seventh Earl of Shaftesbury* (1888).

3 I am a trapper in the Gawber pit. It does not tire me, but I have to trap without a light, and I'm scared. Sometimes I sing when I have a light, but not in the dark; I dare not sing then. I don't like being in the pit.
Sarah Gooder, aged eight; *Parliamentary Papers* 1842, Vol.16, p.252. This child from the West Riding of Yorkshire operated the trap door through which waggons passed to and from the coal face.

4 If the children were excluded from the factories and workshops it is not very clear what would become of them. At home they could not remain even if they were disposed to do so; there is no legal provision for compelling them to attend schools – their only resource would be the street, with all its perils and temptations ... We would rather see boys and girls earning the means of support in the mill than starving by the road-side, shivering on the pavement, or even conveyed in an omnibus to Bridewell.
W. Cooke Taylor *Factories and the Factory System* (1844) pp.23–4. Bridewell was a house of correction in London, and the word became a general term for prison.

5 A factory labourer can be very easily known as he is going along the streets; some of his joints are almost sure to be wrong. Either the knees are in, the ankles swelled, one shoulder lower than the other, or he is round-shouldered, pigeon-breasted, or in some other way deformed.
W. Dodd *The Factory System Illustrated* (1842) pp.112–13.

6 Even those who leave this work at an early age retain permanently injured health, a broken constitution; and, when married, bring feeble and

sickly children into the world. All the medical men interrogated by the commissioner agreed that no method of life could be invented better calculated to destroy health and induce early death.
Karl Marx's collaborator Friedrich Engels *The Condition of the Working Class in England* (1845). Engels was the radical son of a German cotton manufacturer and so owed his fortune to industrial capitalism. He lived mostly in England from 1842 on.

7 The slave owner is seldom as depraved in the management of his gangs of purchased workmen as are the owners of our British Collieries in the case of their free labourers; nor did we ever hear of the lash of the slave driver being more cruelly applied than by the overseers of these bands of wretched children. It has turned me quite sick, it is dreadful.
Elizabeth Grant, 11 May 1842; *The Highland Lady in Ireland: Journals 1840–1850* (1991 edn).

8   With fingers weary and worn,
       With eyelids heavy and red,
       A Woman sat, in unwomanly rags,
       Plying her needle and thread –
       Stitch! stitch! stitch!
       In poverty, hunger, and dirt,
       And still with a voice of dolorous pitch
       She sang the 'Song of the Shirt'!
Thomas Hood *The Song of the Shirt* (1843) St.1.

9 Hitherto it is questionable if all the mechanical inventions yet made have brightened the day's toil of any human being. They have enabled a great population to live the same life of drudgery and imprisonment, and an increased number of manufacturers and others to make fortunes. They have increased the comforts of the middle classes. But they have not yet begun to effect those great changes in human destiny, which it is in their nature and in their futurity to accomplish.
John Stuart Mill *Principles of Political Economy* (1848). A striking contrast with Macaulay (see 571:4).

THE GREAT EXHIBITION OF 1851

10 Mr Paxton, in his speech at Derby ... let fall a sentence, that in letters of coloured glass, should appear over the doors of the great crystal palace.
Douglas Jerrold in *Punch*, 2 Nov. 1850, Vol.19, p.1831. Joseph Paxton was the architect of the huge glass exhibition hall in Hyde Park that housed the display of the arts and manufactures

of the world in 1851, designed to celebrate the achievements of industrialization. It was *Punch* that gave the building its name.

1 [I] would advise persons residing near the park to keep a sharp look-out for their silver forks and spoons and servant maids ... An exhibition of the industry of all nations, forsooth! An exhibition of the trumpery and trash of foreign countries, to the detriment of our own already too much oppressed manufacturers.

Colonel Charles Sibthorpe MP, an unsparing critic of the Exhibition, not to say everything to do with the modern world; *Parl. Deb.* 4 July 1850, Col.903, and 26 July 1850, Col.353.

2 I made my way into the building; a most gorgeous sight; graceful; beyond the dreams of the Arabian romances. I cannot think that the Caesars ever exhibited a more splendid spectacle. I was quite dazzled, and I felt as I did on entering St Peter's.

Thomas Babington Macaulay, diary entry, 1 May 1851, the opening day of the Exhibition; G.O. Trevelyan *The Life and Letters of Lord Macaulay* (1876).

3 Went to the machinery part, where we remained 2 hours, and which is excessively interesting and instructive ... What used to be done by hand and used to take months doing is now accomplished in a few instants by the most beautiful machinery ... We next saw models of locomotion, amongst which one of a most ingenious contrivance for transferring mail bags on railways, going at full speed.

Queen Victoria at the Exhibition, 7 and 24 June 1851; C.R. Fay *Palace of Industry, 1851* (1951) pp.57, 61.

4 Crowds went to admire it, but they might collect crowds in any square to look at a dead cat ... Would those who had already made £300,000 by it [the Crystal Palace] ... keep up this palace of tomfoolery at their own expense?

Colonel Sibthorpe again, distinctly underwhelmed; *Parl. Deb.* 22 May 1851, Col.1309, and 29 July 1851, Col.1727.

5 Passing a great 48 cannon, cast in copper at Seville ... I startled a sparrow in the maw of the Spanish monster. 'Poor survivor of the massacre of the innocents, fear not, I shan't denounce you. On the

contrary – here!' And, taking from my pocket a biscuit which the master of ceremonies had pressed on me at St Paul's the day before, I crumbled it on to the ground.

The French composer Hector Berlioz at the Exhibition, 9 June 1851; David Cairns *Berlioz* (1999) Vol.2, p.463. Sparrows inside the Crystal Palace presented an obvious problem. When asked by the queen what could be done about them, the Duke of Wellington had advised: 'Try sparrow-hawks, Ma'am.'

6 We shall by that means [the Exhibition] break down the barriers that have separated the people of different nations, and witness the universal republic; the year 1851 will be a memorable one, indeed: it will witness a triumph of industry instead of a triumph of arms.

The Liberal free trader Richard Cobden, taking a highly optimistic view of the Exhibition's impact; Jeffrey Auerbach *The Great Exhibition of 1851: A Nation on Display* (1999) p.163.

7 Do not let us nourish our national vanity by fondly congratulating ourselves that, as we were successful, we had little to fear ... It is a grave matter of reflection, whether the exhibition did not show very clearly and distinctly that the rate of industrial advance of many European nations, even of those who were obviously in our rear, was greater than our own.

The scientist Lyon Playfair, rightly fearful of the long-term importance of the Exhibition for Britain's industrial leadership; *Tallis's History and Description of the Crystal Palace, and the Exhibition of the World's Industry in 1851* (1852) Vol.2, p.195.

8 You feel that something significant has been achieved here, some victory or triumph. It's even as if you begin to fear something ... Mustn't one really accept all this as ultimate truth, and fall silent once and for all? It's all so triumphant, victorious and proud that it begins to take your breath away ... You sense that it would require a great deal of eternal spiritual fortitude and denial not to yield to the impression ... and not to worship Baal, that is, not to accept the world that exists as one's own ideal.

The Russian writer Feodor Dostoevsky *Winter Notes on Summer Impressions* (1863) Ch.5. A religious reactionary mistrusts the power of materialism on display in the Exhibition.

Democracy in America, 1791–1861

LIBERTY AND UNION, 1795–1860

1 The President ... errs as other men do, but errs with integrity.

Thomas Jefferson to William Giles, 31 Dec.1795, on President George Washington; *The Papers of Thomas Jefferson* Vol.28 (2000) p.565.

2 You could as soon scrub the blackamore white, as to change the principles of a profest Democrat ... he will leave nothing unattempted to overturn the Government of this Country.

George Washington to the secretary of war, James McHenry, 30 Sept. 1798; *Writings of George Washington* Vol.37, p.474. Washington was writing soon after the passage of the Alien and Sedition Acts, aimed by the federalist administration of President John Adams not only at French revolutionary sub-version but at Adams's supposedly pro-French Republican opponents, notably Jefferson. The conservative Washington was deeply hostile to Jefferson's democratic sympathies.

3 No connection, no friendship, no consideration whatever should screen the man, to whom the smallest suspicion is attached ... 'PURGE YOUR COUNTRY, but especially all its Public Offices, BEFORE IT IS TOO LATE, OF DOMESTIC TRAITORS.'

The lexicographer Noah Webster, *Commercial Advertiser*, 4 June 1799. A foreshadowing of the Red Scare of 1919 and the McCarthyist rampage of the early 1950s (see 902:10).

4 [We should] sever ourselves from that Union we so much value, rather than give up the rights of self government which we have reserved, and in which alone we see liberty, safety & happiness.

Thomas Jefferson to James Madison, 23 Aug. 1799. Jefferson and Madison respectively wrote the Kentucky and Virginia Resolutions condemning the Alien and Sedition Acts. Their case was based on the superiority of states' rights over federal laws, such as the Alien and Sedition legislation, and here Jefferson took it to the point of threatening secession. He was persuaded to drop the threat, but the line he took was close to the nullification argument propounded by Calhoun in the early 1830s (see 575:7).

5 We are all Republicans – we are all Federalists. If there be any among us who would wish to dissolve this Union or to change its republican form, let them stand undisturbed as monuments to the safety with which error of opinion may be tolerated where reason is left free to combat.

President Thomas Jefferson at his first inauguration, 4 March 1801; Albert Fried (ed.) *The Essential Jefferson* (1963) p.403. Jefferson makes a virtue of necessity, pouring oil on the troubled waters whipped up by the crisis of 1798–9.

6 Laws and institutions must go hand in hand with the progress of the human mind ... We might as well require a man to wear still the coat which fitted him when a boy as civilized society to remain ever under the regimen of their barbarous ancestors.

Thomas Jefferson to Samuel Kercheval, 12 July 1816; Dumas Malone *The Sage of Monticello* (1981) p.346.

7 The power to tax involves the power to destroy ... The States have no power, by taxation or other wise, to retard, impede, burden, or in any manner con-trol, the operations of the constitutional laws enacted by Congress to carry into execution the powers invested in the general government.

John Marshall, Chief Justice of the US Supreme Court, 6 March 1819 in the case of McCulloch v. Maryland; Henry Steele Commager (ed.) *Documents of American History* (1973 edn) pp.219, 220. By declaring as unconstitutional the claim by Maryland to tax the Bank of the United States, Marshall struck a powerful blow for the federal government in the developing battle between it and the component states of the Union, which stood on the confederal doctrine of states' rights.

8 The judiciary of the United States is the subtle corps of sappers and miners constantly working under ground to undermine the foundations of our confederated fabric ... A judiciary independent of a king or executive alone, is a good thing; but independence of the will of the nation is a solecism, at least in a republican government.

Thomas Jefferson to Thomas Ritchie, 25 Dec. 1820; P.L. Ford (ed.) *The Writings of Thomas Jefferson* Vol.10 (1899) pp.170–71. Despite his earlier call for constitutional flexibility, as a staunch champion of states' rights Jefferson was deeply mis-trustful of the central authority upheld by the Supreme Court.

9 The apprehended danger from the experiment of universal suffrage applied to the whole legislative department is no dream of the imagination. It is too mighty an experiment for the moral constitution of men to endure. The tendency of universal suffrage is to jeopardize the rights of property, and the principles of liberty.

Chancellor James Kent, New York State Constitutional Convention, 1821; Commager (1973 edn) p.233. When the

Constitution of 1787 was drawn up, the vote was confined to white men of property and education. By the 1820s the movement was gathering pace to extend the vote to all white adult males, regardless of qualification: in short, to make the United States a democracy. Supporters of the status quo, such as Kent, saw this as a disaster, but they were on the losing side.

1 The ricketty and scrofulous little wretch who first sees the light in a work-house, or in a brothel, and who feels the effects of alcohol before the effects of vital air, is not equal in any respect to the ruddy offspring of the honest yeoman.

Senator John Randolph of Virginia, 2 March 1826; *Register of Debates* Vol.2, Col.126. As it was to his fellow Virginian, Jefferson, Randolph's Republic was an agrarian polity, but democracy was to go hand in hand with urbanization from the 1820s on.

2 Cut glass and china to the amount of several thousand dollars had been broken in the struggle to get the refreshments. Punch and other articles had been carried out in tubs and buckets, but had it been in hogsheads it would have been insufficient … Ladies fainted, men were seen with bloody noses, and such a scene of confusion took place as is impossible to describe – those who got in could not get out by the door again but had to scramble out of windows … The noisy and disorderly rabble in the President's house brought to my mind descriptions I have read of the mobs in the Tuileries and at Versailles. I expect to hear the carpets and furniture are ruined; the streets were muddy, and these guests all went thither on foot.

Mrs Samuel Harrison Smith *The First Forty Years of Washington Society* (1829). Mrs Smith, a leading Washington hostess, describes the chaos in the White House on the day of President Andrew Jackson's first inauguration, 4 March 1829. To women of her background it was an unnerving reminder of the French Revolution's *journées*, 6 Oct. 1789 and 10 Aug. 1792, when the Paris mob dispossessed the royal family of their palaces.

3 When my eyes shall be turned to behold for the last time the sun in heaven, may I not see him shining on the broken and dishonored fragments of a once glorious Union; on States dissevered, discordant, belligerent; on a land rent with civil feuds, or drenched, it may be, in fraternal blood! … Liberty *and* Union, now and forever, one and inseparable!

Senator Daniel Webster of Massachusetts, 26 Jan. 1830; *Register of Debates* p.80. A typically magniloquent peroration from Webster, prompted by a crisis between the North and the South over the issue of the tariff. His speech ominously foreshadowed the Civil War, which broke out in 1861.

4 Our Federal Union! It must and shall be preserved!

President Andrew Jackson, toast at a dinner on the anniversary of Jefferson's birthday, 13 April 1830; Marquis James *Andrew Jackson* (1937) p.235. The pointed reply from the arch-apologist of states' rights, Senator John C. Calhoun of South Carolina, was: 'The Union, next to our liberty, most dear.'

5   My country, 'tis of thee,
        Sweet land of liberty,
        Of thee I sing.
        Land where my fathers died,
        Land of the Pilgrims' pride,
        From every mountain side
        Let freedom ring!

Samuel Francis Smith 'America' (4 July 1831). A hymn composed for the Boston Sabbath School Union, which endures as a powerful expression of American patriotism (although it is sung to the tune of the British national anthem).

6 There it is – Old Glory!

Captain William Driver, saluting his new national flag, Dec. 1831. During the Civil War Driver, a supporter of the Union, although living in the Confederate state of Tennessee, hid the flag for the duration and brought it out to be flown after the capture of Nashville by Union forces in Dec. 1864.

7 The right of interposition … be it called what it may – State-right, veto, nullification, or by any other name – I conceive to be the fundamental principle of our system, resting on facts as historically certain as our revolution itself … Stripped of all its covering, the naked question is, whether ours is a federal or a consolidated government; a constitutional or an absolute one; a government resting ultimately on the solid basis of the sovereignty of the States, or on the unrestrained will of a majority.

Senator John C. Calhoun of South Carolina, 26 July 1831; Ross M. Lence *Union and Liberty: The Political Philosophy of John C. Calhoun* (1992) pp.371, 383.

8 The claim was asserted of a right by a State to annul the laws of the Union, and even to secede from it at pleasure … If it be the will of Heaven that the recurrence of its primeval curse for the shedding of a brother's blood should fall upon our land, that it be not called down by any offensive act on the part of the United States.

President Andrew Jackson, proclamation to the people of South Carolina, 10 Dec. 1832; James D. Richardson (ed.) *Messages and Papers of the Presidents of the United States* Vol.2 (1896) pp.640 ff. South Carolina had issued an Ordinance of Nullification on 24 Nov., claiming the right to void whatever federal legislation it disapproved. Jackson was prepared to use force to bring the state into line, but at this stage the conflict did not come to a military showdown.

1 His hot-headed democracy has done a fearful injury to his country. Hollow and unsound as his doctrines are, they are but too palatable to a people, each individual of whom would rather derive his importance from believing that none are above him, than from consciousness that in his station he makes part of a whole noble.

Frances Trollope *Domestic Manners of the Americans* (1832) Ch.29. The English writer Mrs Trollope lived in the United States from 1827 to 1831, hated a good deal of it and published her bilious observations soon after her return to Britain. It goes without saying that they made her deeply unpopular in the USA.

2 They boldly *preach* what they *practice*. When they are contending for *victory*, they avow their intention of enjoying the fruits of it. If they are successful, they claim, as a matter of right, the advantages of success. They see nothing wrong in the rule that to the VICTOR belong the spoils of the ENEMY.

Senator William Marcy of New York on democratic politics in the Empire State, 25 Jan. 1832; *Niles Register*, 1 Sept. 1832.

3 It is to be regretted that the rich and powerful too often bend the acts of government to their selfish purposes ... But when the laws undertake ... to make the rich richer and the powerful more potent, the humble members of society – the farmers, mechanics and laborers – who have neither the time nor the means of securing like favors to themselves, have a right to complain of the injustice of their government.

President Andrew Jackson, 10 July 1832; Richardson Vol.2 (1896) pp.589–90. Jackson was waging political war on the Bank of the United States as an agency of privilege.

4 It has all the fury of a chained panther biting the bars of his cage. It is really a manifesto of anarchy – such as Marat or Robespierre might have issued to the Faubourg St Antoine: and my hope is that it will contribute to relieve the country of the dominion of these miserable people.

Nicholas Biddle to Senator Henry Clay, 1 Aug. 1832; Arthur Schlesinger Jr *The Age of Jackson* (1945) p.91. Biddle, head of the Bank of the United States, comments on Jackson's attack on the bank, to him all too evocative of the French Revolution.

5 America ... is the land of the future, where, in the ages that lie before us, the burden of the world's

history shall reveal itself. It is a land of desire for all those who are weary of the historical lumber-room of Europe.

The German philosopher Georg Wilhelm Friedrich Hegel *The Philosophy of History* (1832). Or, as Hegel's fellow countryman Goethe put it, *Amerika, du hast es besser* (America, you have it better).

6 In the United States, as in every country where the people rules, it is the majority which governs in the name of the people ... If ever liberty dies in America, we shall have to blame it on the omnipotence of the majority which will have reduced the minorities to despair and compelled them to make an appeal to physical force. We shall then see anarchy, but it will come as the consequence of despotism.

The French historian Alexis de Tocqueville *Democracy in America* (1835) Bk 1, Pt 2, Chs 1, 7. A pessimistic view from the most celebrated 19th-century foreign commentator on the American political system.

7 When the day of election approaches, visit your constituents far and wide. Treat liberally, and drink freely, in order to rise in their estimation, though you fall in your own. True, you may be called a drunken dog by some of the clean-shirt and silk-stocking gentry, but the real roughnecks will style you a jovial fellow. Their votes are certain, and frequently count double.

David Crockett *Exploits and Adventures in Texas* (1836) pp.56–9. Crockett, 'king of the wild frontier' and martyr of the Alamo (see 615:3), was also an accomplished democratic politico. This view of the democratic process is echoed in Ch.13 of Charles Dickens's *Pickwick Papers* (1837), describing the Eatanswill election.

8 I believe the heaviest blow ever dealt at Liberty's Head, will be dealt by this nation in the ultimate failure of its example to the Earth. See what is passing now – Look at the exhausted Treasury; the paralyzed government; the unworthy representatives of a free people; the desperate contest between the North and the South; the iron curb and brazen muzzle fastened upon every man who speaks his mind ... the intrusion of the most pitiful, mean, malicious, creeping, crawling, sneaking party spirit into all transactions of life – even into the appointment of physicians to pauper madhouses – the silly, drivelling, slanderous, wicked, monstrous Party Press.

The English novelist Charles Dickens to W.C. Macready, 1 April 1842; *The Letters of Charles Dickens* Vol.3 (1974) pp.175–6. It is not surprising that Dickens swiftly outranked

Mrs Trollope as an Americanophobe (see 576:1). His hostility was soon to be amplified in his novel *Martin Chuzzlewit*, published in 1844.

1 We are the depositories of the *democratic principle*, and a stern and jealous principle it is, which will admit of no divided empire. It claims for itself this continent, as a rallying ground, from which to move the world; and it will not tolerate the existence of any other political principle in its neighborhood, for the simple reason that, should it do so, it would aid in its own destruction.
The Western Review, April 1846, p.186. American democracy militant, facing Hispanic despotism on the eve of the war with Mexico.

2 In the prosecution of my favorite study of history, I have thought that I discerned two great events, towards which the movement of society and the arrangements of Providence have converged, in the ancient and modern worlds respectively: – the introduction of Christianity and the birth of American democracy.
James D. Nourse *Remarks on the Past and its Legacy to American Society* (1847) p.v.

3 We hold these truths to be self-evident: that all men and women are created equal … The history of mankind is a history of repeated injuries and usurpations on the part of man toward woman, having in direct object the establishment of an absolute tyranny over her … Because women do feel themselves aggrieved, oppressed, and fraudulently deprived of their most sacred rights, we insist that they have immediate admission to all the rights and privileges which belong to them as citizens of the United States.
Elizabeth Cady Stanton *Declaration of Sentiment* at the Seneca Falls Women's Rights Convention, 19 July 1848; *History of Woman Suffrage* Vol.1 (1881). Women did not achieve the vote in the United States until 1920.

4 If the first woman God ever made was strong enough to turn the world upside down all alone, these women ought to be able to turn it back, and get it right side up again! And now they is going to do it, the men better let them.
The black woman emancipationist, Sojourner Truth (Isabella Van Wagener), at the Ohio Women's Convention, 1851; *The Narrative of Sojourner Truth* (1878).

5 Thou too, sail on, O Ship of State!
Sail on, O Union strong and great!
Humanity with all its fears,

With all the hopes of future years,
Is hanging breathless on thy fate!
Henry Wadsworth Longfellow 'The Building of the Ship' (1849). A reflection of the vulnerability of the republic in the face of the growing antagonism of North and South.

6 I know no South, no North, no East, no West to which I owe my allegiance. I owe allegiance to two sovereignties and only two … My allegiance is to the American Union and to my own State.
Senator Henry Clay of Kentucky, 14 Feb. 1850; *Congressional Globe* Vol.19, p.368. Clay had put together a package of resolutions as a compromise between North and South over the issues of slavery and states' rights, which was designed to stave off civil war. Note his priorities, the reverse of those proclaimed by Calhoun in 1830 (see 575:7).

7 I had rather be right than be President.
Senator Henry Clay, 14 Feb.1850; *Congressional Record*. Clay had several times tried and failed to run for the presidency, and here he tries to give his failure moral force. When in 1890 Representative William M. Springer invoked the by then classic words of Clay, he was told by the Speaker of the House, Thomas Brackett Reed: 'Well, the gentleman need not be disturbed. He will never be either.'

8 Either some Caesar or Napoleon will seize the reins of government with a strong hand, or your republic will be as fearfully plundered and laid waste by barbarians in the twentieth century as the Roman Empire was in the fifth; with this difference, that the Huns and Vandals who ravaged the Roman Empire came from without and that your Huns and Vandals will have been engendered within your own country by your own institutions … Your constitution is all sail and no anchor.
Thomas Babington Macaulay to Henry Stephens Randall, 23 May 1857; Thomas Pinney (ed.) *The Letters of Thomas Babington Macaulay* (1981) Vol.6, p.96.

9 Vote early and vote often.
Representative W.P. Miles of South Carolina, 31 March 1858; *Congressional Record*. Also attributed to John Van Buren, son of President Martin Van Buren.

10 An honest politician is one who, when he's bought, stays bought.
Simon Cameron, Republican political boss of Pennsylvania, 1860, attrib. Lincoln reluctantly made Cameron his secretary of war in 1861, and Cameron soon made the war department a byword for corruption. He was removed in Jan. 1862 and sent as minister to Russia to get him out of Washington. In April 1862 his conduct as secretary of war was censured by the House of Representatives.

THE WEST, 1805–61

1 This little fleet although not so respectable as those of Columbus or Captain Cook were still viewed by us with as much pleasure as those deservedly famed adventurers ever beheld theirs ... we were now about to penetrate a country at least two thousand miles in width, on which the foot of civilized man had never trodden; the good or evil it had in store for us was for experiment yet to determine.

Meriwether Lewis, 7 April 1805; *Journal* Vol.1, p.285. In 1803 President Thomas Jefferson bought the huge tract of Louisiana from France, doubling the size of the United States. The following year he commissioned Meriwether Lewis and William Clark to explore a passage through the territory and beyond it to the Pacific. The central purpose was to discover 'a North American route to India' for the trade of the United States. The expedition set off in the spring of 1804 and reached the Pacific coast on 7 Nov. 1805.

2 The whole continent of North America appears to be destined by Divine Providence to be peopled by one *nation*, speaking one language, professing one general system of religious and political principles, and accustomed to one general tenor of social usages and customs.

John Quincy Adams to his father John Adams, 31 Aug. 1811; *Writings of John Quincy Adams* Vol.4, p.204.

3 The pioneers are a people peculiar to our country; they live of choice in the forest, and they are unwilling to submit to the restraints of society ... They are brave, patient of fatigue, and capable of enduring wonderful hardships ... They are honest and very generous. Crimes of magnitude seldom occur among them.

American Quarterly Review, June 1829, p.356. Westerners as they themselves liked to be seen.

4 [On the Plains] may spring up new mongrel races, like new formations in geology, the amalgamation of the 'debris' and 'abrasions' of former races, civilized and savage; the remains of broken and almost extinguished tribes; the descendants of wandering hunters and trappers; of fugitives from the Spanish and American frontiers; of adventurers and desperadoes of every class and country yearly ejected from the bosom of society into the wilderness.

The writer Washington Irving *Astoria* (1836) Vol.1, p.232. 'The Wild West' as seen by an Easterner.

5 The time must come when the powerful elastic spring of our rapidly increasing numbers shall fill up our wide spread territory with a dense population – when the great safety valve of the west will be closed against us – when millions shall be crowded into our manufactories and commercial cities – then will come the great and fearful pressure upon the engine.

Thomas R. Dew *Southern Literary Messenger*, March 1836, p.277. The West as a release from the pressures of industrialization and urbanization.

6 The gorgeous scenery of some of our western and southern districts – of the vast valley of Louisiana, for example – a realization of the wildest dreams of paradise ... the real Edens of the land lie far away from the track of our most deliberate tourist.

The writer Edgar Allan Poe 'The Elk' (1844); *Works of Edgar Allan Poe* Vol.2 (1914) pp.77–8.

7 we went over a great hye mountain as strait as stair steps in snow up to our knees ... the Bears took the provision the men had cashed and we had but very little to eat ... Some of the compana was eating them that died ... 3 died and the rest eat them. Thay was 11 day without any thing to eat but the Dead ... O Mary I have not rote you half of the truble we have had but I have rote you anuf to let you now that you don't now what truble is but thank god we have all got throw and the only family that did not eat human flesh.

Virginia Reed, aged 12, to Mary Keyes, 16 May 1847; George R. Street *Ordeal by Hunger* (1960 edn) pp.360–61. The child describes the ordeal of the Donner Party in its westward crossing of the Rocky Mountains between Nov. 1846 and April 1847.

8 Beautiful for situation, and the ultimate joy of the whole earth, is the Stake of Zion established in the mountains ... The notes of millennial jubilee reverberate from the mountain heights of Zion. Let all that can, gather up their effects, and set their faces as a flint to go Zionward.

The Mormon *Millennial Star* (published in Liverpool), 1 Feb.1848, pp.40–41. The Church of Jesus Christ of Latter-Day Saints under its leader Brigham Young settled in the Utah Territory in 1848, consciously modelling themselves on the biblical Israelites marching out of bondage in Egypt into the land of Canaan.

9 A frenzy seized my soul ... Piles of gold rose up before me ... castles of marble, thousands of slaves ... myriads of fair virgins contending with each other for my love – were among the fancies of my fevered imagination. The Rothschilds, Girards, and

Astors appeared to be but poor people; in short, I had a very violent attack of gold fever.

Hubert Howe Bancroft, 1849; Geoffrey C. Ward *The West* (1996) p.123. The Rothschilds were European bankers of legendary wealth. The American financiers Stephen Girard (1750–1831) and John Jacob Astor (1763–1848) made their initial fortunes in trade. On 24 Jan. 1848 gold was found in California, triggering a gold rush that drew tens of thousands of prospectors into the state.

1 Go west, young man, go west!

John B.L. Soule, editor of the *Terre Haute Express*, Indiana, 1851. Usually attributed, wrongly, to Horace Greeley.

2 Eastward I go only by force; but westward I go free … I must walk toward Oregon, and not toward Europe … We go eastward to realize history and study the works of art and literature, retracing the steps of the race; we go westward as into the future, with a spirit of enterprise and adventure.

Henry David Thoreau 'Walking' in *Atlantic Monthly* (1862). High admiration of the West by a son of the East coast, but see 579:3.

3 The whole enterprise of this nation which is not an upward, but a westward one, toward Oregon, California, Japan etc., is totally devoid of interest to me, whether performed on foot or by a Pacific railroad … It is perfectly heathenish, – a filibustering *toward* heaven by the great western route. No; they may go their way to their manifest destiny, which I trust is not mine.

Henry David Thoreau to Harison Blake, 27 Feb. 1853; *Writings of Henry David Thoreau* Vol.6, p.210.

4 The *Land of Promise*, and the *Canaan* of our time, is the region which, commencing on the slope of the Alleghenies, broadens grandly over the vast prairies and mighty rivers, over queenly lakes and lofty mountains, until the ebb and flow of the Pacific kisses the golden shores of the El Dorado.

Charles Dana *The Garden of the World, or the Great West* (1856) p.13. A rhapsodic picture, bringing together the allure of the West as a religious haven, a land of opportunity and a world of unspoilt nature. The Allegheny mountains, running south from Pennsylvania to North Carolina, form the watershed between the Atlantic and the Mississippi.

5 Imagine a vast waveless ocean stricken dead and turned to ashes. Imagine this solemn waste tufted with ash-dusted sage brushes; imagine the lifeless silence and solitude that belong to such a place; imagine a coach creeping like a bug through the midst of this shoreless level, and sending up tumbled volumes of dust as if it were a bug that went by steam.

Mark Twain (Samuel Langhorne Clemens), July 1861; Ward (1996) p.183. To Twain, *en route* to Nevada to avoid the Civil War, the West's only attraction was as a bolt-hole.

NATIVE AMERICANS, 1803–64

6 In truth, the ultimate point of rest and truth for them is to let our settlements and theirs meet and blend together, to intermix, and become one people. Incorporating themselves with us as citizens of the United States, this is what the natural progress of things will bring on, and it will be better to promote than to retard it.

President Thomas Jefferson, to Colonel Benjamin Hawkins, 1803; Richard Drinnon *Facing West: The Metaphysics of Indian-Hating and Empire-Building* (1980) p.83.

7 We are powerful and they are weak … The poor children of the forest have been driven by the great wave which has flowed in from the Atlantic Ocean to almost the base of the Rocky Mountains, and, overwhelming them in its terrible progress, has left no other remains of hundreds of tribes, now extinct, than those which indicate the remote existence of their former companion, the mammoth of the New World.

Representative Henry Clay, 20 Jan. 1819; *Annals of Congress* (1819) p.639.

8 Such is their condition, at present, that they must be civilized or exterminated; no other alternative exists. He must be worse than a savage, who can view, with cold indifference, an exterminating policy. All desire their prosperity, and wish to see them brought into the pale of civilization.

Report of Committee on Indian Affairs, 23 March 1824; *Niles Weekly Register*, 10 April 1824, p.93.

9 I am on the hilltop, and must go down into the valley; and when Uncas follows in my footsteps, there will no longer be any of the blood of the Sagamores, for my boy is the last of the Mohicans.

James Fenimore Cooper *The Last of the Mohicans* (1826). The speaker is the Mohican chief, Chingachgook, and in his words Cooper captures the sense of doom already gathering around the Indian peoples.

10 You and my white children are too near to each other to live in harmony and peace … Beyond the great river Mississippi, where a part of your nation has gone, your father has provided a country large enough for all of you, and he advises you to remove to it. There your white brothers will not trouble you; they will have no claim to the land, and you can live upon it, you and all your children, as long as the grass grows or the water runs, in peace and plenty. It will be yours forever.

President Andrew Jackson to the Creek Nation, 23 March 1829; *Niles Weekly Register*, 13 June 1829, p.258. In 1813–14 Jackson made his military reputation campaigning in Alabama against the Creeks, allies of the British in the War of 1812 (Second Anglo-American War).

1 Philanthropy could not wish to see this continent restored to the condition in which it was found by our forefathers. What good man would prefer a country covered with forests and ranged by a few thousand savages to our extensive Republic, studded with cities, towns, and prosperous farms, embellished with all the improvements which art can devise or industry execute, occupied by more than 12,000,000 happy people, and filled with all the blessings of liberty, civilization, and religion?

President Andrew Jackson, Message to Congress, 1830; Richardson Vol.2 (1896) p.521. In 1832 Jackson defied a judgement of the US Supreme Court to begin the process of removing the Cherokee Indians from their homeland in Georgia halfway across the continent to the Oklahoma Territory, along the notorious 'Trail of Tears'.

2 [The Indians] listened to our professions of friendship. We called them brothers and they believed us. They yielded millions of acres to our demands and yet we crave more. We have crowded the tribes upon a few miserable acres of our southern frontier: it is all that is left to them of their once boundless forests; and still, like the horse-leech, our insatiated cupidity cries, give! give! give!.

Senator Theodore Frelinghuysen, 1830; Ward (1996) p.81.

3 Expedients by which ignorant, intractable, and savage people were induced without bloodshed to yield up what civilized people had a right to possess by … command of the Creator.

A western governor's view of treaties with the Indians; David Burner *et al. America: A Portrait in History* (1978) p.169.

4 [These regions] might in future be seen (by some great protecting policy of government) preserved in their pristine beauty and wildness, in a magnificent park, where the world could see for ages to come, the native Indian in his classic attire, galloping his wild horse … amid the fleeting herds of elks and buffaloes. What a beautiful and thrilling specimen for America to preserve.

George Catlin, letter to the New York *Daily Commercial Advertiser*, 1833. From 1824 on the painter and writer Catlin worked to give posterity images of the Indians of the Great Plains before their culture was wiped out by the encroachment of white settlers.

5 Think of your wives, children, brothers, sisters, friends, and in fact all that you hold dear. All are dead or dying, with their faces all rotten, caused by those dogs the whites. Think of all that, my friends, and rise together and leave not one of them alive.

The Four Bears, Mandan chief, dying of smallpox contracted from settlers, 1837; Ward (1996) p.74.

6 What is America, and who are Americans? The fashionable answer in these times is 'the natives of this continent, to be sure!' But let us ask again, in that case, whether our old friends Uncas and Chingachgook … are to be considered Americans par excellence? Alas, no! for they, poor fellows! are all trudging towards the setting sun, and soon their red and dusky figures will have faded in the darker shadows of the night!

Putnam's Monthly, May 1855, p.533.

7 The former wild prairie, now a cultivated farm; the floating palaces on the bosom of the river which but a little while ago rolled on undisturbed in its lovely beauty; the churches and school-houses that now stand where stood a few summers since the Indian's wigwam; the steam-cars that fly across the land swifter than the light-footed Chippewa, the arrow from his bow, or the deer that he hunted.

N.H. Parker *The Minnesota Handbook for 1856–57*, a brochure to attract new incomers to a tamed wilderness.

8 I heard of one instance of a child a few months old being thrown in the feedbox of a wagon, and after being carried some distance left on the ground to perish; I also heard of numerous instances in which men had cut out the private parts of females and stretched them over the saddle-bows and wore them over their hats while riding.

US army lieutenant testifying about the Sand Creek, Colorado, massacre of 29 Nov. 1864; Ward (1996) p.204.

IMMIGRANTS, 1783–1859

1 The bosom of America is open to receive not only the Opulent and respectable Stranger, but the oppressed and persecuted of all Nations and Religions; whom we shall wellcome to a participation of all our rights and privileges if, by decency and propriety of conduct, they appear to merit the enjoyment.
George Washington, Dec. 1783; Maldwyn Jones *American Immigration* (1960) p.79.

2 To these [American constitutional principles] nothing can be more opposed than the maxims of absolute monarchies. Yet from such we are to expect the greatest number of emigrants. They will bring with them the principles of the governments they leave, imbibed in their early youth; or, if able to throw them off, it will be in exchange for an unbounded licentiousness, passing, as is usual, from one extreme to another. It would be a miracle were they to stop precisely at the point of temperate liberty. The principles, with their language, they will transmit to their children. In proportion to their numbers, they will share with us the legislation. They will infuse it with their spirit, warp and bias its directions, and render it a heterogeneous, incoherent, distracted mass.
Thomas Jefferson, c.1792; *Works of Thomas Jefferson* Vol.3 (1904) pp.486–9.

3 John brings home as many apples as he can carry when he comes home from school; also cherries, grapes, and peaches. We get as much bread as we can all eat in a day ... Dear mother, I wish you were all as well off as we now are ... We have a gallon of spirits every week; and I have a bottle of porter per day myself ... I live like an Indian Queen.
Alice Barlow, 13 Aug. 1818, writing home from the land of plenty.

4 If they cannot accommodate themselves to the character, moral, political, and physical, of this country, the Atlantic is always open to them to return to the land of their nativity and their fathers. To one thing they must make up their minds; or, they be disappointed in every expectation of happiness as Americans. They must cast off the European skin, never to resume it. They must look forward to their posterity rather than backward to their ancestors.
Secretary of state John Quincy Adams, on German immigrants, 4 June 1819.

5 Let foreigners find in this country an asylum of rest, an escape from oppression. Here let them buy, and build, and plant; let them spread and flourish, pursuing interest and happiness in every mode of life which enterprise can suggest, or reason justify; but let them be exonerated from the toils of government. We do not need their hands to steady the ark.
Samuel Whelpley *A Compendium of History from the Earliest Times* Vol.2 (1825) pp.204–5. In other words, no vote for the foreign-born.

6 *Then* our accessions by immigration were real accessions of strength from the ranks of the learned and the good, from the enlightened mechanic and artisan, and intelligent husbandman. *Now* immigration is an accession of weakness, from the ignorant and the vicious, or the priest-ridden slaves of Ireland and Germany, or the outcast tenants of the poorhouses and prisons of Europe ... They are transported in thousands, nay, in *hundreds of thousands*, to our shores, to our loss and Europe's gain.
Samuel Morse *Imminent Dangers to the Free Institutions of the United States through Foreign Immigration* (1835) pp.23–9. The inventor of the electric telegraph was indefatigably hostile to immigrants, particularly after moving to the main entry-port of the influx, New York City, in 1823. He contrasts current circumstances with the fancied good old days of Jefferson, whose wariness (see 581:2) he more than shared.

7 The Irish are the most inclined to linger about the cities by which they have been first received, and into the vices and follies of which they are most liable to be betrayed by the ardor of their temperament and the recklessness of their habits. The Germans, the Swiss, and other natives of the continent would seem to be inclined to seek a more remote settlement in the West ... and while they subsist in a friendly connexion with the community, for a long time resist an entire integration with it ... It is the Englishman chiefly who passes, by an easy transition, into the bosom of American society, and repelled by no inaptitude or prejudice, readily adapts himself to the pursuits of American industry, securing, at the same time, his own permanent attachment to the country.
A.H. Everett *North American Review* (1835) pp.460 ff.

1 The only true policy for a government like ours was, to throw open the doors to immigration … They came here from choice, prompted by an innate love of liberty; and our free institutions can never be in danger from men who have abandoned so much, and periled so much, to enjoy the blessings they bestow. The sooner they are made citizens after becoming acquainted with our institutions, the better for us, the better for them.

Representative J.B. Bowlin of Missouri, Dec. 1845; *Congressional Globe.* The South was anxious to attract European immigrants, but few came, largely because they had more chance of acquiring land in the north and west.

2 For what are we not indebted to foreign emigration, since we are all Europeans or their descendants? We cannot travel on one of our steamboats without remembering that Robert Fulton was the son of an Irishman. We cannot walk by St Paul's churchyard without seeing the monuments which admiration and gratitude have erected to Emmet and Montgomery. Who of the thousands who every summer pass up and down our great thoroughfare, the North River, fails to catch at least a passing glimpse of the column erected to the memory of Kosciusko? I cannot forget that only last night a portion of our citizens celebrated with joyous festivities the birthday of the son of Irish emigrants, I mean the Hero of New Orleans!

Thomas L. Nichols *Lecture on Immigration and Right of Naturalization* (1845) pp.24 ff. Fulton put his first steamboat on the Hudson in 1807. Emmet and Montgomery were Irish patriots; Kosciusko, the Polish nationalist, fought for the United States in the War of Independence. The Hero of New Orleans, Andrew Jackson, had defeated the British at New Orleans on 8 Jan. 1815.

3 Settled by the people of all nations, all nations may claim her for their own. You cannot spill a drop of American blood without spilling the blood of the whole world … We are not a nation, so much as a world.

The writer Herman Melville *Redburn: His First Voyage* (1849).

4 Large numbers in a short time, a few months or weeks, after getting into the country, and very many before they have remained the full time of probation, fall into the hands of demagogues and unscrupulous managers of elections, and by the commission of perjury and other crimes are made to usurp against law a portion of the political sovereignty of the country.

Garrett Davis, 15 Dec. 1849; *Speeches of the Hon. Garrett Davis* (1855) p.7.

5 Everybody should know that we have for our mission to convert the world – including the inhabitants of the United States – the people of the cities, and the people of the country, the officers of the navy and the marines, commanders of the army, the Legislatures, the Senate, the Cabinet, the President, and all!

The Roman Catholic archbishop of New York John Hughes; *Freeman's Journal,* 23 Nov. 1850. Hughes had entered the United States as an immigrant from Ireland in 1817 and here provides generous quantities of ammunition for the enemies of the Irish community.

6 It is not indiscriminate masses of Europe that are shipped hitherward, but the Atlantic is a sieve through which only or chiefly the liberal, sensitive, *America-loving* part of each city, clan, family are brought. It is the light complexion, the blue eyes of Europe that come: the black eyes, the black drop, the Europe of Europe, is left … The energy of the Germans, Swedes, Poles, and Cossacks, and all the European tribes … will construct a new race, a new religion, a new state, a new literature, which will be as vigorous as the new Europe which came out of the smelting-pot of the Dark Ages.

Ralph Waldo Emerson, 1851, *Journals* Vol.8, p.226; Maldwyn Jones *American Immigration* (1960) pp.160–61. Zangwill's 'melting-pot' anticipated (see 640:1).

7 The worst part of the refuse class which is … thrown upon our shores, here clan together and remain in the city nor can they be persuaded to leave it. These mostly consist of imbecile and thriftless parish paupers and dependants, the former inmates of poor-houses and even of prisons, who being unwilling or unable to gain an honest subsistence anywhere, have been sent here, in order to rid the country from which they came of their support, and who become a burden and a nuisance from the moment of their arrival. Many of them are afflicted with pestilential diseases, more or less developed, which, as they wander about in search of shelter, are disseminated through the city to the manifest detriment of public health, and to the destruction of life.

Annual Report, New York Association for Improving the Condition of the Poor (1852) pp.32–3.

8 To be overrun by the diverse races of Europe is doubtless evil enough, but whether Celt, Teutonic or

Anglo-Saxon, confraternity, if impossible, is at least approachable. But even the Dutchman and the Irishman would join in the national horror with which the prospective inundation of oriental barbarism threatens our country.

The leading nativist Humphrey Marshall, 1854; Thomas J. Curran *Xenophobia and Immigration, 1820–1930* (1975) p.80. In the 1850s Chinese coolie labour began entering the United States in significant numbers, mostly to work on railway construction.

1 No Alexander or Caesar in the height of their conquests, ever made such acquisitions of power as immigration brings to us … Those who are against the cause of their country … contend that immigrations brings with it destitution, poverty and crime. Trace these bands of strong-limbed but poor foreigners until they plant themselves upon the hitherto useless land of the West, and see how wealth is evolved by their very contact with the soil. They were poor, and the fertile land was valueless, but combine these two kinds of poverty and the wealth which alchemists dreamed of, is the magical result.

Horatio Seymour, governor of New York State, 1855; Rush Welter *The Mind of America 1820–1860* (1975) p.324.

2 She left our free and happy shores unwilling and reluctant … constrained by force of the civil authorities of the State … The offence of this poor woman, for which she was thus violently and ignominiously expelled from Massachusetts, was the fact that she was born in Ireland and is called a pauper.

Boston Daily Advertiser, 16 May 1855. Immigrants could be deported if they were considered to be a burden on the resources of the local government, and the ruling class of New England had a strong antipathy to the Irish.

3 As a nation we began by declaring that '*all men are created equal*.' We now practically read it 'all men are created equal *except negroes*.' When the Know-Nothings get control, it will read 'all men are created equal, *except negroes, and foreigners, and Catholics*.' When it comes to this I should prefer emigrating to some country where they make no pretense of loving liberty – to Russia, for instance, where despotism can be taken pure, and without the base alloy of hypocrisy.

Abraham Lincoln, 24 Aug. 1855; *The Essential Lincoln* (1962) p.181 The Know-Nothings, a political party calling for the tightest possible restrictions on immigration, reached its peak

in 1855, electing six state governors, but in the presidential election of 1856 its candidate, Millard Fillmore, carried only one state.

4 You are welcomed by a figure in a blue flannel shirt and pendant beard, quoting Tacitus, having in one hand a long pipe, in the other a butcher's knife; Madonnas upon log walls; coffee in tin cups upon Dresden saucers; barrels for seats, to hear a Beethoven's symphony on the grand piano … a book-case half-filled with classics, half sweet potatoes.

Frederick Law Olmsted *A Journey Through Texas* (1857) p.430. Olmsted, the creator of Central Park in New York City, on a visit to a German immigrant's house in Texas.

5 We see the vigorous elements of all nations, we see the Anglo-Saxon … with his spirit of independence, of daring enterprise and of indomitable persever-ance; the German, the original leader in the move-ment of ideas, with his spirit of inquiry and his quiet and thoughtful application; the Celt with the impulsive vivacity of his race; the Frenchman, the Scandinavian, the Scot, the Hollander, the Spaniard and the Italian – all these peaceably congregating together on virgin soil, where the backwoodsman's hatchet is the only battle-axe of civilization – undertaking to found a new cosmopolitan nation with-out marching over the dead bodies of slain millions.

The German immigrant Carl Schurz, 18 April 1859; *Speeches, Correspondence and Political Papers of Carl Schurz* (1913). The heterogeneity of the USA contrasted with the Europe he left behind in 1852. A rose-tinted picture if one considers the slaughter that took place in the Indian Wars, the recent war with Mexico and the Civil War, which was just two years ahead.

6 The German and Irish millions, like the Negro, have a great deal of guano in their destiny. They are ferried over the Atlantic, and carted over America, to ditch and to drudge, to make corn cheap, and to lie down prematurely to make a spot of green grass on the prairie.

Ralph Waldo Emerson *The Conduct of Life* (1860) Ch.1.

SLAVERY AND THE SOUTH, 1784–1861

7 I tremble for my country when I reflect that God is just: that his justice cannot sleep forever.

Thomas Jefferson *Notes on Virginia* (1784). A fearful thought on slavery, following on from Jefferson's unsuccessful attempt to have a condemnation of the slave trade written into his Declaration of Independence in 1776 (see 505:4).

1 There were a number of very respectable Gentlemen at Mrs Greene's who all agreed that if a machine could be invented which could clean the cotton with expedition, it would be a great thing both to the Country and to the inventor ... I made one before I came away which required the labor of one man to turn it and with which one man will clean ten times as much cotton as he can in any other way before known, and also cleanse it much better than in the usual mode.

Eli Whitney to his father, 11 Sept. 1793; *American Historical Review* Vol.3 (1898) pp.99–101. Whitney was the inventor of the cotton gin, which revived the dwindling cotton industry and made it the basis of the economy of the South, giving slavery a new lease of life.

2 We have the wolf by the ear, and we can neither hold him, nor safely let him go. Justice is in one scale, and self-preservation in the other.

Thomas Jefferson to John Holmes, 22 April 1820; *The Writings of Thomas Jefferson* Vol.10, p.157. The son of the Enlightenment admits the inhumanity of slavery, while the Southerner in him dreads the consequences of black emancipation.

3 This momentous question, like a fire bell in the night, awakened me and filled me with terror. I considered it at once as the knell of the Union. It is hushed, indeed, for the moment. But this is a reprieve only, not a final sentence. A geographical line, coinciding with a marked principle, moral and political, once conceded and held up to the angry passions of men, will never be obliterated, and every new irritation will mark it deeper and deeper.

Thomas Jefferson to John Holmes, 22 April 1820; *The Writings of Thomas Jefferson* Vol.10, p.157. Jefferson is writing of the Missouri Compromise, whereby Missouri was admitted to the Union as a slave-owning state and Maine as a non-slave-owning state. The remainder of the Louisiana Territory acquired in 1803 was to be free of slavery west of Missouri and north to the Canadian border. The Compromise reflected the fierce tensions between North and South, which Jefferson feared would one day tear it apart, as they did in 1861.

4 When Israel was in Egypt's land,
　　Let my people go;
　　Oppressed so hard they could not stand,
　　Let my people go.

Anon. 'Go Down Moses', early-19th-century Negro spiritual. The biblical parallel of the suffering of the Jews in pharaonic Egypt and their exodus to Canaan was an inspiration to American slaves, as it was to Italian nationalists (see 548:1).

5 I am aware that many object to the severity of my language; but is there not just cause for severity? I

will be as harsh as truth and as uncompromising as justice. On this subject I do not wish to think, or speak, or write, with moderation. No! Tell a man whose house is on fire to give a moderate alarm; tell him to moderately rescue his wife from the hands of the ravisher; tell the mother to gradually extricate her babe from the fire in which it has fallen – but urge me not to use moderation in a cause like the present. I am in earnest – and I will not equivocate – I will not excuse – I will not retreat a single inch – AND I WILL BE HEARD!

The abolitionist William Lloyd Garrison in the first issue of his publication *The Liberator*, 1 Jan. 1831; *William Lloyd Garrison* Vol.1 (1885) p.225. The final sentence is inscribed on his monument in Boston.

6 Armed with a hatchet, and accompanied by Will, I entered my master's chamber; it being dark, I could not give him a death-blow, the hatchet glanced from his head, he sprang from the bed and called his wife, it was his last word. Will laid him dead with a blow of his axe, and Mrs Travis shared the same fate, as she lay in bed. The murder of his family, five in number, was the work of a moment, not one of them awoke, there was a little infant sleeping in a cradle, that was forgotten, until we had left the house and gone some distance, when Henry and Will returned and killed it. It was my object to carry terror and destruction where-ever we went.

Nat Turner *The Confessions of Nat Turner* (1832). Turner led the bloodiest slave insurrection in American history, beginning on 21 Aug. 1831, and put down with the utmost ferocity.

7 Slavery, set against democratic liberty and the progressive thinking of our age, is an institution which cannot endure. It will be ended either by the action of the slave or the master. In both cases, great tribulations must be accepted. If freedom is denied to the blacks of the South, the result will be their violent seizure of it; if it is granted to them, they will not be slow to abuse it.

Alexis de Tocqueville *Democracy in America* (1835) Bk 1, Pt 2, Ch.10.

8 Direct slavery is just as much the pivot of bourgeois industry as machinery, credits, etc. Without slavery you have no cotton; without cotton you have no modern industry. It is slavery that gave the colonies their value; it is the colonies that created world trade, and it is world trade that is the precondition of large-scale industry. Without slavery, North America, the most progressive of countries,

would be transformed into a patriarchal country. Wipe North America off the map of the world, and you would have anarchy – the complete decay of modern commerce and civilization. Cause slavery to disappear and you will have wiped America off the map of nations.
Karl Marx *The Poverty of Philosophy* (1847) pp.111–12.

1 A peculiar institution.
The *New York Tribune*'s definition of slavery, 19 Oct. 1854.

2 Never before has the black race of Central Africa attained a condition so civilized and so improved, not only physically but morally and intellectually. It came among us in a low, degraded, and savage condition, and in the course of a few generations, it has grown up under the fostering care of our institutions … to its present comparatively civilized condition.
Senator John C. Calhoun, 6 Feb. 1837; *Works of John C. Calhoun* Vol.2 (1856).

3 Ranaway, a negro woman and two children; a few days before she went off, *I burnt her with a hot iron*, on the left side of her face, I tried to make the letter M.
The North Carolina *Raleigh Standard*, 18 July 1839, advertisement by Micajah Ricks; Theodore Dwight Weld *American Slavery As It Is: Testimony of a Thousand Witnesses* (1839) p.77.

4 The dark stout MULATTO GIRL, 'SARAH', Aged about twenty years, general house servant, valued at *nine hundred dollars*, and guaranteed … Will be Raffled for At 4 o' clock P.M., February first.
Sale notice; David Burner *et al. America: A Portrait in History* (1978) p.269.

5 The manners of an overseer to negroes should be kind. Kindness, and even gentleness, is not inconsistent with firmness and inexorable discipline. If they require whipping, whip them, and be done with it.
De Bow's Review, 1856.

6 When the Constitution of the United States was framed and adopted … [negroes] had for more than a century before been regarded as beings … altogether unfit to associate with the white race, either in social or political relations; and so far inferior that they had no rights which the white man was bound to respect; and that the negro might justly and lawfully be reduced to slavery for his benefit … The right of property in a slave is distinctly and expressly affirmed in the Constitution … It is the opinion of the court that the Act of Congress which prohibited

a citizen from holding and owning property of this kind in the territory of the United States north of the line therein mentioned, is not warranted by the Constitution, and is therefore void.
Chief Justice Roger B. Taney of the US Supreme Court, decision in the Dred Scott case, 7 March 1857. This momentous judgement annulled the Missouri Compromise of 1820, whereby slavery was barred north of latitude 36 degrees 30 minutes, and widened the gulf between North and South.

7 In all social systems there must be a class to do the menial duties, to perform the drudgery of life. Such a class you must have, or you would not have that other class which leads to progress, civilization, and refinement … It constitutes the very mudsills of society and of political government … Fortunately for the South, she found a race adapted to that purpose to her hand … No sir, you dare not make war on cotton. No power on earth dares make war upon it. Cotton is King!
Senator James H. Hammond, 4 March 1858; *Congressional Record.*

8 God forgive us, but ours is a *monstrous* system, and wrong and iniquity! … Like the patriarchs of old our men live all in one house with their wives and their concubines, and the mulattoes one sees in every family exactly resemble the white children – and every lady tells you who is the father of all the mulatto children in everybody's household, but those in her own. These, she seems to think, drop from the clouds, or pretends so to think.
Mary Chesnut of South Carolina, diary entry for 18 March 1861; *Mary Chesnut's Civil War* (1981) p.29.

9 An Abolitionist is any man who does not love slavery for its own sake, as a divine institution; who does not worship it as the corner stone of civil liberty; who does not adore it as the only possible social condition on which a permanent Republican government can be erected; and who does not, in his innermost soul, desire to see it extended and perpetuated over the whole earth, as a means of human reformation second in dignity, importance and sacredness, alone to the Christian religion.
Southern Literary Messenger, March 1861 Vol.32, p.344.

SLAVERY AND THE NORTH, 1837–59

10 I was frequently told of the 'endearing relations' subsisting between masters and slaves; but, at the best, it appeared to me the same 'endearing relation' which subsists between a man and his horse, between a lady and her dog. As long as the slave remains ignorant, docile, and contented, he is taken good care of, humoured, and spoken of with a contemptuous, compassionate kindness. But, from the moment he exhibits the attributes of a rational human being, – from the moment his intellect seems to come into the most distant competition with that of whites, the most deadly hatred springs up, – not in the black but in his oppressors. It is a very old truth that we hate those whom we have injured.

Harriet Martineau *Society in America* (1837). The English social reformer Miss Martineau spent two years in the United States between 1834 and 1836.

1 Resolved: That the compact between the North and the South is a covenant with death and an agreement with hell, involving both parties in atrocious criminality, and should be immediately annulled.

William Lloyd Garrison, Resolution adopted by the Massachusetts Anti-Slavery Society, 27 Jan. 1843; Archibald H. Grimke *William Lloyd Garrison* (1891) Ch.16. Garrison became the most aggressive spokesman for the abolition of slavery.

2 There is a civilization possible having negro slavery for its foundation, and a cultivation not wanting in many elements of moral and intellectual beauty; but it is a civilization and a society of the Middle Ages with the lighter circumstances of the 19th century – a feudal castle with modern furniture. Such is the society south of Mason and Dixon's line. The north, on the contrary, is the creature of the day, never behind the march of nations, but a pioneer.

N.S. Shaler *The Autobiography of Nathaniel Southgate Shaler* (1909) p.216. Charles Mason and Jeremiah Dixon were surveyors who delimited a boundary line between the colonies of Pennsylvania and Virginia in the 1760s. It later came to be seen as the dividing line between the free-soil states of the North and the slave-owning states of the South.

3 This is an age of the world when nations are trembling and convulsed. A mighty influence is abroad, surging and heaving the world, as with an earthquake. And is America safe? Every nation that carries in its bosom great and unredressed injustice has in it the elements of this last convulsion.

Harriet Beecher Stowe *Uncle Tom's Cabin* (1852) Ch.45. This novel was a hugely influential indictment of slavery. The author's reference is undoubtedly to the 1848 revolutions in Europe, and the premonition of civil war in the United States is clear.

4 I was the conductor of the Underground for eight years, and I can say what most conductors can't say – I never ran my train off the track and I never lost a passenger.

Harriet Tubman; Lyde Cullen Sizer *Divided Houses* (1992) Ch.7. During the 1850s Harriet Tubman, born a slave, assisted more than 300 runaway slaves in the South to escape to the North along a route known as the Underground Railroad.

5 COLORED PEOPLE OF BOSTON, ONE & ALL, You are hereby respectfully CAUTIONED and advised, to avoid conversing with the Watchmen and Police Officers of Boston ... If you value your LIBERTY, and the *Welfare of the Fugitives* among you, *Shun* them in every possible manner, as so many HOUNDS on the track of the most unfortunate of your race.

Poster, 24 April 1851. By the Fugitive Slave Act of 18 Sept. 1850 authorities in the North were required to send back to the South black runaways from the plantations.

6 To him, your celebration is a sham; your boasted liberty, an unholy license; your national greatness, swelling vanity; your sounds of rejoicing are empty and heartless; your denunciation of tyrants, brass-fronted impudence; your shouts of liberty and equality, hollow mockery; your prayers and hymns, your sermons and thanksgivings, with all your religious parade and solemnity, are, to Him, mere bombast, fraud, deception, impiety, and hypocrisy – a thin veil to cover up crimes which would disgrace a nation of savages.

Frederick Douglass, 5 July 1852; *The Life and Writings of Frederick Douglass* Vol.2, p.192. Douglass, the leading black protagonist of anti-slavery, speaks about the meaninglessness of Independence Day celebrations for his community.

7 With the South, the preservation of slavery is placed above all other things – above party success, denominational unity, pecuniary interest, legal integrity and constitutional obligation. With the North, the preservation of the Union is placed above all other things – above honor, justice, freedom, integrity of soul, the Decalogue and the Golden Rule – the infinite God himself.

William Lloyd Garrison, 4 July 1854; Grimke (1891). By the Decalogue he meant the Ten Commandments; the Golden Rule is 'Do as you would be done by'. Garrison went on to burn copies of the Fugitive Slave Act and the American Constitution before his church congregation.

8 'A house divided against itself cannot stand.' I believe this government cannot endure permanently

half *slave* and half *free*. I do not expect the Union to be *dissolved*; I do not expect the house to *fall*; but I *do* expect it will cease to be divided. It will become *all* one thing, or *all* the other.

Abraham Lincoln, 16 June 1858; *The Collected Works of Abraham Lincoln* Vol.3 (1953) pp.1–2. Lincoln quotes St Mark's Gospel 3:25. He had earlier used the phrase 'half slave, half free' in a letter to George Robertson on 15 Aug. 1855.

1 I will say then that I am not, nor ever have been in favor of bringing about in any way the social and political equality of the white and black races … There is a physical difference between [them] which I believe will forever forbid the two races living together on terms of social and political equality.

Abraham Lincoln, 18 Sept. 1858; Vol.3 (1953) pp.145–6. Lincoln was speaking in the fourth of seven debates with his opponent for the Senate seat in Illinois, Stephen Douglas. In 1854 Douglas had put through the Kansas–Nebraska Act, whereby the issue of whether a territory was to be slave-owning or not was decided by popular election within the territory. This made Douglas deeply unpopular in the North, but he bore the hostility with stoicism, saying: 'I could travel from Boston to Chicago by the light of my own effigies.'

2 It is an irrepressible conflict between opposing and enduring forces, and it means that the United States must and will, sooner or later, become entirely a slaveholding nation, or entirely a free-labor nation.

Senator William Henry Seward, 25 Oct. 1858. Seward, an abolitionist senator from New York, here coins the classic definition of the looming clash between North and South.

3 I John Brown am now quite *certain* that the crimes of this *guilty* land: will never be purged *away*; but with Blood.

The militant abolitionist John Brown, on the day of his execution, 2 Dec. 1859; *A John Brown Reader* (1959) p.159. On 16 Oct. 1859 Brown and his followers seized the federal arsenal at Harper's Ferry, Virginia, retaken two days later by US troops commanded by Colonel Robert E. Lee, later commanding general of the Confederacy. Brown was found guilty of murder, promoting a slave insurrection and treason against Virginia, and his execution made him a martyr for many in the North. The song 'John Brown's Body' became the anthem of the Union forces in the Civil War. The words 'Guilty Land' were to be used as the title of Patrick van Rensburg's book attacking the apartheid policy of South Africa, published in 1962.

4 The death of Brown is more than Cain killing Abel; it is Washington slaying Spartacus.

Victor Hugo, 2 Dec. 1859. Cain, the evil son of Adam and Eve, killed his virtuous younger brother Abel (Genesis 4:8). Spartacus was leader of a slave revolt in the Roman Republic; he was executed in 71 BC.

The American Civil War, 1861–5

1861: SCHISM

1 Match the two broken pieces of the Union, and you will find the fissure that separates them zig-zagging itself half across the continent like an iso-thermal line, shooting its splintery projections, and opening its re-entering angles, not merely according to the limitations of particular States, but as a county or other limited section of ground belongs to freedom or to slavery.
Oliver Wendell Holmes Sr *The Complete Writings of Oliver Wendell Holmes* Vol.8 (1892) pp.87–8.

2 The bird of our country is a debilitated chicken, disguised in eagle feathers. We have never been a nation; we are only an aggregate of communities, ready to fall apart at the first serious shock.
George Templeton Strong, 1861; Geoffrey C. Ward *The Civil War* (1995) p.33. Strong, an eminent New York lawyer, kept a diary throughout the Civil War.

3 A Union that can only be maintained by swords and bayonets, and in which strife and civil war are to take the place of brotherly love and kindness, has no charm for me.
Robert E. Lee to his son, 23 Jan. 1861; J. William Jones *Personal Reminiscences, Anecdotes and Letters of General Robert E. Lee* (1874) p.137. Lee was to become the general-in-chief of the armies of the secessionist Confederate States of America.

4 Some of the manufacturing States think a fight would be awful. Without a little blood-letting, this Union will not, in my estimation, be worth a rush.
Senator Zachariah Chandler of Michigan to Governor Austin Blair, 11 Feb. 1861; *Congressional Globe*, p.1247.

5 Say to the seceded States, 'Wayward sisters, depart in peace!'
General Winfield Scott to the incoming secretary of state, William Henry Seward, 3 March 1861. Scott was commanding general of the US army but also a son of the secessionist state Virginia. By this time seven states had seceded from the Union; they were shortly to be joined by four more.

6 The streets of Charleston present some such aspect as those of Paris in the last revolution [1848]. Crowds of armed men singing and promenading the streets, the battle blood running through their veins – that hot oxygen which is called 'the flush of victory' on the cheek … Sumter has set them distraught; never such a victory. It is a bloodless Waterloo.
William Howard Russell, correspondent of the London *Times*, April 1861. The first shot of the war was fired across the harbour of Charleston, South Carolina, at the Union island bastion of Fort Sumter, on 12 April. The US army garrison surrendered after a 34-hour bombardment.

7 It will require the exercise of the full powers of the Federal Government to restrain the fury of the noncombatants.
General Winfield Scott after hearing the news of the loss of Fort Sumter on 13 April 1861; Peter G. Tsouras (ed.) *Military Quotations from the Civil War* (1998) p.128.

8   John Brown's body lies a-moldering in the grave;
      His soul is marching on!
Rev. William Patton 'John Brown's body' (April 1861). One of the most famous marching songs of the Union Army, celebrating the abolitionist Brown, executed in Dec. 1859 (see 587:3).

9   For Dixie's land we'll took our stand,
      To lib an' die in Dixie!
Daniel Decatur Emmett 'Dixie' (April 1859). This song became virtually the national anthem of the Southern Confederacy, although Emmett, a white star of minstrel shows, was from Ohio, Northern and Unionist.

10   Avenge the patriotic gore
     That flecked the streets of Baltimore,
     And be the battle-queen of yore,
     Maryland! My Maryland!
James R. Randall 'Maryland, My Maryland!' (1861). Randall, a journalist and song-writer, composed this after Union troops fired on a crowd in Baltimore protesting against the Federal government on 19 April. Maryland, its sympathies sharply divided, did not secede from the Union.

11 I look upon secession as anarchy. If I owned the four millions of slaves in the South, I would sacrifice all for the Union – but how can I draw my sword upon Virginia?
The Virginian General Robert E. Lee, April 1861; Jones (1874).

12 We are organizing. We will be compelled to shoot, burn & hang, but the thing will soon be over.
Senator David Atchison of Missouri to the Confederate President Jefferson Davis; Ward (1995) p.21.

1 They do not know what they say. If it comes to a conflict of arms, the war will last at least four years. Northern politicians do not appreciate the determination and pluck of the South, and Southern politicians do not appreciate the numbers, resources, and patient perseverance of the North. Both sides forget that we are all Americans, and that it must be a terrible struggle if it comes to war.
General Robert E. Lee, May 1861; J. William Jones *The Life and Letters of Robert Edward Lee* (1906). The war was to last precisely four years.

2 You might as well attempt to put out the flames of a burning house with a squirt-gun. I think this is to be a long war – very long – much longer than any politician thinks.
Colonel William Tecumseh Sherman, 1861; Ward (1995) p.81. Sherman was to become one of the most formidable generals of the Union armies (see 591:4).

3 I was a soldier two weeks once in the beginning of the war, and was hunted like a rat the whole time. Familiar? My splendid Kipling himself hasn't a more burnt-in, hard-baked and unforgettable familiarity with that death-in-the-pale-horse-with-hell-following-after which is a raw soldier's first fortnight in the field – and which without any doubt, is the most tremendous fortnight and vividest he is ever going to see.
Mark Twain (Samuel Langhorne Clemens) recalling in 1890 his brief experience in the Confederate army before making off for Nevada with his brother; Daniel Aaron *The Unwritten War* (1973) p.133.

4 Look, there is Jackson with his Virginians, standing like a stone wall!
General Barnard E. Bee at Bull Run, 21 July 1861; Ward (1995) p.67. The Confederate General Thomas Jonathan Jackson checked the Union forces at the Battle of Bull Run. (Manassas) and so earned the nickname of 'Stonewall'.

5 I perceived several waggons coming from the direction of the battlefield, the drivers of which were endeavouring to force their horses past the ammunition carts going in the contrary direction ... drivers and men cried out with the most vehement gestures, 'Turn back! Turn back! We are whipped!'
William Howard Russell, *Times* correspondent at Bull Run; *William Russell, Special Correspondent of* The Times (1995) p.211. Russell's candid reporting of the Union defeat made him comprehensively *persona non grata* with the Federal government, and he returned to Britain in April 1862.

6 All quiet along the Potomac.
General George McClellan, commander of the Union Army of the Potomac (the river flowing through Washington, D.C.), late summer 1861. A despatch designed to steady the nerves of Washingtonians after Bull Run.

7 War is not a question of valor, but a question of money. It is not regulated by the laws of honor, but by the laws of trade. I understand the practical problem to be solved in crushing the rebellion of despotism against representative government is who can throw the most projectiles. Who can afford the most iron or lead?
Representative Roscoe Conkling of New York, 1 Aug. 1861; Ward (1995) p.127. Conkling was right to see the war as a conflict of economic forces, and the defeat of the agrarian South by the industrial North was only a matter of time as long as the North held its ground.

8 The workmen in a mood of grim humor had put little flags upon his great head and arms and the monster seemed to be alive with patriotism. The sight was most suggestive and encouraging. I could have cried for joy or sung hallelujahs to the Lord of Hosts for all was clear then. There, and everywhere through the loyal States, was that same mighty force working for us – the Providential arm of the 19th century.
Samuel Osgood *Harper's New Monthly Magazine*, 1867. A eulogy to the steam engine, the symbol of the North's overwhelming industrial power.

9 I will hold McClellan's horse if he will only bring us success.
President Abraham Lincoln to John Hay, 13 Nov. 1861. General McClellan had just snubbed the President and Hay, his secretary, believed he should be dismissed. Shortly afterwards, however, Lincoln appointed McClellan to succeed the elderly General Scott as general-in-chief.

10 The President is nothing more than a well-meaning baboon ... 'the original gorilla'.
General George McClellan to his wife, late 1861; Ward (1995) p.75.

11 Mine eyes have seen the glory of the coming of the Lord:
He is trampling out the vintage where the grapes of wrath are stored;
He hath loosed the fateful lightning of his terrible swift sword:
His truth is marching on ...
He has sounded forth the trumpet that shall never call retreat;

He is sifting out the hearts of men before his
    judgment seat:
Oh! Be swift my soul to answer Him! Be
    jubilant, my feet!
Our God is marching on ...
In the beauty of the lilies Christ was born across
    the sea,
With a glory in his bosom that transfigures you
    and me:
As He died to make men holy, let us die to
    make men free,
While God is marching on.

Julia Ward Howe 'Battle Hymn of the Republic', set to the
tune of 'John Brown's Body', which Howe heard Union
troops singing at a review on 17 Nov. 1861. She wrote it in a
creative frenzy in the early hours of the following morning,
and it was published in the *Atlantic Monthly* in Feb. 1862.

1 It is looked upon as one of the disasters of the war,
although it cannot be shown that it had any connection with the war. When Eternal Justice decrees the
punishment of a people, it sends not War alone, but
also its sister terrors, Famine, Pestilence, and Fire.

John T. Trowbridge on the fire that devastated Charleston on
13 Dec. 1861; *The South* (1866) p.514.

1862: EMANCIPATION

2 No terms except an unconditional and immediate
surrender can be accepted. I propose to move
immediately upon your works.

General Ulysses S. Grant to the Confederate General Simon
Bolivar Buckner, 16 Feb. 1862; Geoffrey Perret *Ulysses S.
Grant* (1997) p.173. Buckner's surrender of Fort Donelson,
Tennessee, meant the loss of Kentucky and Tennessee to the
Confederacy and made Grant the most successful Union
commander to date. On unconditional surrender in World
War II see 852:1.

3 If General McClellan does not want to use the
Army, I would like to *borrow* it for a time, provided
I could see how it could be made to do something.

President Abraham Lincoln, exasperated with McClellan's
inaction, relieved him as general-in-chief on 11 March 1862;
Ward (1995) p.90.

4 Get there first with the most men.

Confederate cavalry commander General Nathan Bedford
Forrest, attrib. Usually rendered as 'Git thar fustest with the
mostest men', though this is more likely to have been said by
Al Capp's General Jubilation T. Cornpone than by Forrest.

5 I will receive 200 able-bodied men if they will
present themselves at my headquarters by the first of
June with a good horse and gun. I wish none but
those who desire to be actively engaged ... Come on,
boys, if you want a heap of fun and to kill some
Yankees.

General Nathan Bedford Forrest, April 1862; *Henry 'First with
the Most' Forrest* (1944) p.82.

6 Neither confiscation of property, political
execution of persons, territorial organization of
States, or forcible abolition of slavery, should be
contemplated for a moment ... Military power
should not be allowed to interfere with the relations
of servitude either by supporting or impairing the
authority of the master, except for repressing
disorder.

General George McClellan to President Lincoln, 7 July 1862.
In spite of his demotion to a field command, McClellan still
believed he knew better than his commander-in-chief – here
over the issue of slave emancipation. He was dismissed as
commanding general of the Army of the Potomac in Nov.
1862 and stood against Lincoln in the presidential election
of 1864.

7 My paramount object in this struggle *is* to save the
Union, and is *not* either to save or destroy Slavery. If
I could save the Union without freeing *any* slave, I
would do it; and if I could save it by freeing *all* the
slaves I would do it; and if I could do it by freeing
some and leaving others alone, I would also do that.

President Abraham Lincoln to the editor of the New York
Tribune, Horace Greeley, 22 Aug. 1862; F. Moore (ed.) *The
Rebellion Record* Vol.12, pp.480 ff.

8 It was no longer a question of the Union as it was
that was to be re-established. It was the Union as it
should be – that is to say, washed clean from its
original sin ... We were no longer merely the soldiers
of a political controversy ... we were now the
missionaries of a great work of redemption, the
armed liberators of millions ... The war was
ennobled; the object was higher.

General Régis de Trobriand, soon after the Emancipation
Proclamation of 22 Sept. 1862; Ward (1995) p.166. The
Proclamation was, in fact, less far-reaching than de Trobriand
supposed. Only slaves in states unoccupied by Union forces
were liberated; those in slave-owning states now held by the
Union remained in slavery. As secretary of state Seward
reportedly put it, the government freed slaves 'where we
cannot reach them' and kept them 'in bondage where we can
set them free'.

1 'Shoot, if you must, this old gray head,
  But spare your country's flag,' she said.

John Greenleaf Whittier 'Barbara Frietchie' (1863). On 13 Sept. 1862 Confederate troops seized the town of Frederick, Maryland, where the nonagenarian Barbara Frietchie supposedly waved the Union flag at them. Stonewall Jackson, in charge of the detachment, reputedly threatened the execution of any man who touched her.

2 There is no doubt that Jefferson Davis and other leaders of the South have made an army; they are making, it appears, a navy; and they have made what is more than either: they have made a nation.

William Ewart Gladstone, speech on 7 Oct. 1862; Peter J. Parish 'Gladstone and America' in Peter J. Jagger (ed.) *Gladstone* (1998) p.97. Coming from a senior British cabinet minister, this was taken as a signal that Britain was poised to give the South diplomatic recognition, although in the event recognition was not given.

3 I've pretty much made up my mind that the South have achieved their independence & I am almost ready to hope spring will see an end … Believe me, we never shall lick 'em … I think before long the majority will say that we are vainly working to effect what never happens – the subjugation (for that is it) of a great civilized nation. We shan't do it – at least the Army can't.

Oliver Wendell Holmes Jr, 19 Nov. 1862; *Touched with Fire: Civil War Letters and Diary of Oliver Wendell Holmes* (1946) p.73. The 21-year-old Holmes had almost been killed at the Battle of Antietam on 15 Sept., and his letter reflects the sense of despondency that had overcome the North at this stage of the war.

4 Thousands will perish by the bullet or sickness; but war must go on – it can't be stopped. The North must rule or submit to degradation and insult forevermore.

General William Tecumseh Sherman to his brother Senator John Sherman, 24 Nov. 1862.

5 Out of that silence … rose new sounds more appalling still … a strange ventriloquism, of which you could not locate the source, a smothered moan … as if a thousand discords were flowing together into a key-note weird, unearthly, terrible to hear and bear, yet startling with its nearness.

Colonel Joshua Chamberlain, 13 Dec. 1862, on the aftermath of the Battle of Fredericksburg; Ward (1995) p.172.

6 At times he regarded the wounded soldiers in an envious way. He conceived persons with torn bodies to be peculiarly happy. He wished that he, too, had a wound, a red badge of courage.

Stephen Crane *The Red Badge of Courage* (1895). Crane was too young to have known the war, but his insight into it in this novel was extraordinary.

7 In *giving* freedom to the *slave*, we *assure* freedom to the *free* – honorable alike in what we give, and what we preserve. We shall nobly save or meanly lose the last, best hope of earth.

President Abraham Lincoln, annual message to Congress, 1 Dec. 1862; *The Collected Works of Abraham Lincoln* Vol.5 (1953) p.537.

1863: ATTRITION

8 It is exhaustion of men and money that finally terminates all modern wars.

Quartermaster-General Montgomery Meigs, 1863; Peter J. Parish *The American Civil War* (1975) p.159.

9 Yes, we'll rally round the flag, boys, we'll rally
  once again,
  Shouting the battle-cry of Freedom.

George F. Root 'The Battle-Cry of Freedom' (1863).

10 I have heard … of your recently saying that both the Army and the Government needed a dictator … Only those generals who gain success can set up dictators. What I now ask of you is military success, and I will risk the dictatorship.

President Abraham Lincoln to General Joseph Hooker, 26 Jan. 1863; Ward (1995) p.202. After the Battle of Fredericksburg Hooker had told a newspaper correspondent that the country should place itself under a dictator. Lincoln nonetheless appointed him commander of the Army of the Potomac.

11 Let me know what brand of whiskey Grant uses. For if it makes fighting generals like Grant, I should like to get some of it for distribution.

President Abraham Lincoln to a Congressional delegation, 1863, attrib. Grant had a reputation for hard drinking, and his enemies in Congress told Lincoln he was not fit for high command.

12 The Government seems determined to apply the guillotine to all unsuccessful generals. It seems rather hard to do this where a general is not in fault, but perhaps with us now, as in the French Revolution, some harsh measures are required.

General Henry Halleck, general-in-chief since July 1862; *War of the Rebellion* Vol.16.

1 Captain, my religious belief teaches me to feel as safe in battle as in bed. God has fixed the time for my death.

General Stonewall Jackson to General John Imboden, 1862; *Battles and Leaders* Vol.1 (1887).

2 Let us cross over the river and rest under the trees.

General Stonewall Jackson, last words, 10 May 1863; Douglas Southall Freeman *Lee's Lieutenants* Vol.2 (1944) p.36. Jackson had been accidentally shot by his own men during the Battle of Chancellorsville on 2 May. In 1950 Ernest Hemingway was to publish a novel entitled *Across the River and into the Trees*.

3 He could order men to their death as a matter of course. Napoleon's French conscription could not have kept him in awe. He used up his command so rapidly. Hence, *while he was alive*, there was much fudge in the talk of his soldiers' love for him.

General Alexander Lawton, one of Jackson's officers, on his commander, 5 Dec. 1863; *Mary Chesnut's Civil War* (1981) p.499. Mary Chesnut of South Carolina recorded this observation in her diary.

4 Must I shoot a simple-minded soldier boy who deserts, while I must not touch a hair of the wily agitator who induces him to desert?

President Abraham Lincoln to Erasmus Corning, 12 June 1863; Tsouras (1998) p.67. The South had its sympathizers in the North, who, like Representative Clement Vallandigham of Ohio, publicly called on Union soldiers to desert. These were the so-called Copperheads, named after a species of poisonous snake.

5 Although we are now engaged in a great war between one another, we are not, as a race, so much disposed to fight and kill one another as our red brethren.

President Abraham Lincoln to the Plains Indians, spring 1863; Geoffrey C. Ward *The West* (1996) p.197.

6 Thair is a great controversy out hear about the nigger Question … If thay go to Sending them out hear to fight they will get Enough of it for it Will raise a rebellion in the army that all the abolitionist this side of Hell could not stop. The Southern Peopel are rebels to government but they are White and God never intended a nigger to put White People down.

Sergeant Enoch T. Baker, US army, 1863; Ward (1995) p.189.

7 Once let the black man get upon his person the brass letters, 'U.S.', let him get an eagle on his buttons and a musket on his shoulder and bullets in his pocket, and there is no power on earth which can deny that he has earned the right to citizenship in the United States.

Frederick Douglass, 1863; Ward (1995) p.246. Douglass, born a slave, was one of the most prominent spokesmen for the black community of the United States.

8   Two months after marching through Boston
        half the regiment was dead;
        at the dedication,
        William James could almost hear the bronze
            Negroes breathe.

Robert Lowell 'For the Union Dead' (1964). On 18 July 1863 the all-black 54th Massachusetts, commanded by the white Colonel Robert Gould Shaw, lost half its men, including Shaw, assaulting Fort Wagner, South Carolina. On 1 May 1897 a memorial to them was unveiled in Boston, on the edge of the Common, close to the Old State House. William James, psychologist and philosopher, was the elder brother of the novelist Henry James. Lowell's 19th-century kinsman, James Russell Lowell, also wrote a tribute in verse to Shaw.

9 One of the grand results of this war is to be the assimilation of all American blood … their fighting side by side with the descendants of those who laid the foundation of the Republic, will do more to Americanize them and their children than could be effected in a whole generation of peaceful living … The blood that mixes in the battlefield, in one common sacrifice, will be a cement of American Nationality nothing else could supply.

New York Times, 4 June 1863.

10 My pen is heavy … O, you dead, who died at Gettysburgh have baptized with your blood the second birth of freedom in America, how you are to be envied! I rise from a grave whose wet clay I have passionately kissed, and I look up to see Christ spanning this battlefield.

Samuel Wilkeson, *New York Times*, 6 July 1863. Wilkeson, the *Times*'s correspondent, had just lost his son at Gettysburg.

11 A rich man's war and a poor man's fight.

Slogan of the protesters against conscription in New York, 13 July 1863. The phrase originated in the South in 1861. $300 bought exemption from the draft, introduced by Lincoln in the summer to replenish the Union Army.

12 And, by way of pastime, chasing every stray police officer, or solitary soldier, or inoffensive Negro, who crossed the line of their vision; these three objects – the badge of a defender of the law, – the uniform of the Union army, – the skin of a helpless and outraged race – acted upon these madmen as water acts upon a rabid dog.

Anna Dickinson on the New York draft riots of 13 July 1863; *What Answer?* (1868) p.249. The Irish community of the city took the lead in the disturbances.

1 No wonder St Patrick drove all the venomous vermin out of Ireland! Its biped mammalia supply that island its full average share of creatures that crawl and eat dirt and poison every community they infest. Vipers were superfluous. But my own theory is that St Patrick's campaign against the snakes is a Popish delusion. They perished of biting the Irish people.

George Templeton Strong, diary entry, 19 July 1863; Allan Nevins (ed.) *Diary of the Civil War 1860–1865* (1962) pp.342, 343.

2 You may take fieldworks in which there are small garrisons by assault, but when you have to attack a whole army, well intrenched, you will suffer terribly in getting to them.

General Andrew A. Humphreys; Isaac R. Pennypacker *General Meade* (1901). Humphreys was chief of staff to General George Meade, commander of the Army of the Potomac from 28 June 1863. Here he underlines the capacity of riflemen in trench emplacements to inflict slaughter on an attacking force, a lesson lost on European armies throughout World War I.

3 Like a witches' prayer – a saintly orison read backwards, the phenomenon of modern warfare presents a horrible parody of the doctrine of compensation. More men can be killed, and they can hold out before they *are* killed. Soldiers are fain to become earth-clads, as, on the ocean, sailors trust in iron-clads. Analogically, the difference is very slight between plating the sides of your ship and burrowing in the earth like a mole.

George Augustus Sala *My Diary in America in the Midst of War* (1865) Vol.1, p.391. Sala was war correspondent of the London *Daily Telegraph*.

4 It is ordered that for every soldier of the United States killed in violation of the laws of war, a rebel soldier shall be executed.

President Abraham Lincoln, proclamation of 30 July 1863, made in response to massacres of black US army troops by Confederate forces.

5 The Father of Waters again goes unvexed to the sea.

President Abraham Lincoln to James C. Conkling, 26 Aug. 1863; *The Essential Lincoln* (1962) p.436. The fall of Vicksburg on 4 July placed the entire length of the Mississippi in Union

hands and cut the Confederacy in two. For the next 80 years Vicksburg refused to celebrate Independence Day, coinciding as it did with the city's surrender.

6 They are the most dangerous set of men that this war has turned loose upon the world. They are splendid riders, first-rate shots, and utterly reckless … These men must all be killed or employed by us before we can hope for peace.

General William Tecumseh Sherman to General Halleck on the young bloods of the South, 17 Sept. 1863; Edmund Wilson *Patriotic Gore* (1962) p.195.

7 Fourscore and seven years ago our fathers brought forth on this continent, a new nation, conceived in Liberty, and dedicated to the proposition that all men are created equal.

Now we are engaged in a great civil war, testing whether that nation or any nation so conceived and so dedicated can long endure. We are met on a great battlefield of that war. We have come to dedicate a portion of that field, as a final resting place for those who gave their lives that that nation might live. It is altogether fitting and proper that we should do this.

But, in a larger sense, we can not dedicate – we cannot consecrate – we can not hallow – this ground. The brave men, living and dead, who struggled here, have consecrated it far above our poor power to add or detract. The world will little note nor long remember what we say here, but it can never forget what they did here. It is for us, the living, rather to be dedicated here to the unfinished work which they who fought here have thus far so nobly advanced. It is rather for us to be here dedicated to the great task remaining before us – that from these honored dead we take increased devotion to that cause for which they gave the last full measure of devotion; that we here highly resolve that these dead shall not have died in vain; that this nation, under God, shall have a new birth of freedom; and that government of the people, by the people, for the people, shall not perish from the earth.

President Abraham Lincoln, the Gettysburg Address, 19 Nov. 1863; *Bartlett's Familiar Quotations* (1980 edn). At Gettysburg, Pennsylvania, on 1, 2 and 3 July 1863 one of the bloodiest battles of the war was fought. On 19 Nov. at a ceremony to make part of the terrain a national cemetery, the eminent Greek scholar Edward Everett spoke at very great length. Lincoln's contribution, which followed, was so brief as to go virtually unnoticed, but the next day Everett wrote to him: 'I should be glad if I could flatter myself that I came as near the central idea of the occasion in two hours as you did in two minutes.' The final words echoed those of Theodore

Parker at the Anti-Slavery Convention on 29 Sept. 1850: 'A government of all the people, by all the people, for all the people.'

1864: ENDGAME

1 We propose … that we immediately commence training a large reserve of the most courageous of our slaves, and further that we guarantee freedom within a reasonable time to every slave in the South who shall remain true to the Confederacy in this war.

General Patrick Cleburne, 2 Jan. 1864; Tsouras (1998) p.160. A token of the growing desperation of the South, the proposal was vetoed by President Jefferson Davis, who by the end of 1864 had, however, changed his mind.

2 Father Hamilton said that at one time the prisoners died at the rate of a hundred and fifty a day, and he saw some of them die on the ground without a rag to lie on or a garment to cover them … It is dreadful. My heart aches for the poor wretches, Yankees though they are, and I am afraid God will suffer some terrible retribution to fall upon us for letting such things happen.

Eliza Andrews on the Confederate prisoner-of-war camp for Union soldiers at Andersonville, Georgia; *The War-Time Journal of a Georgia Girl* (1908) pp.78–9. The commandant of the camp, Henry Wirz, was executed on 10 Nov. 1865. Conditions in Northern POW camps were often no better.

3 Gentlemen, suppose all the property you were worth was in gold, and you had put it in the hands of Blondin to carry across the Niagara River on a rope, would you shake the cable or keep shouting out to him – 'Blondin, stand up a little straighter – Blondin, stoop a little more – go a little faster – lean a little more to the North – lean a little more to the South'?

President Abraham Lincoln, 1864; Francis Carpenter *The Life and Public Services of Abraham Lincoln* (1865) p.752. The French tightrope walker, Charles Blondin, crossed over the Niagara Falls in 1859.

4 I do the very best I know how – the very best I can; and I mean to keep doing so until the end. If the end brings me out all right, what is said against me won't amount to anything. If the end brings me out wrong, ten angels swearing I was right would make no difference.

President Abraham Lincoln, 1864; Francis Carpenter *Six Months at the White House with Abraham Lincoln* (1866).

Carpenter was an artist commissioned to paint scenes at the White House during the first half of 1864.

5 I could as easily bail out the Potomac River with a teaspoon as attend to all the details of the army.

President Abraham Lincoln, 1864; Allen Thorndike Rice *Reminiscences of Abraham Lincoln* (1886).

6 I claim not to have controlled events, but confess plainly that events have controlled me.

President Abraham Lincoln to Colonel Albert G. Hodges of Kentucky, 4 April 1864; *The Essential Lincoln* (1962) p.452. Hodges was one of a deputation protesting against the enrolment of slaves in the Union army.

7 In God We Trust.

Although the United States was founded as a secular state, this religious motto was ordered to be put on US currency by Lincoln's secretary of the treasury, Salmon P. Chase, and first appeared in 1864. This at the prompting of a clergyman who felt that the defeats the Union had suffered stemmed from 'our national shame in disowning God'. The inscription remains to this day.

8   Just before the battle, mother,
    I am thinking most of you;
    While upon the field we are watching,
    With the enemy in view.

George F. Root 'Just before the Battle, Mother' (1864).

9 Don't duck! They couldn't hit an elephant at this dis …

General John Sedgwick, last words before being shot by a Confederate sniper at the Battle of Spotsylvania, 9 May 1864; Jonathon Green *Famous Last Words* (1979) p.27.

10 I propose to fight it out on this line if it takes all summer.

General Ulysses S. Grant to General Halleck, 11 May 1864; Perret (1997) p.318. Grant originally wrote 'if it takes me all summer' but struck out 'me' as it sounded too egocentric.

11 He is a scientific Goth, resembling Alaric, destroying the country as he goes and delivering the people over to starvation. Nor does he bury his dead, but leaves them to rot on the battlefield.

John Tyler on General Grant, 7 June 1864. After a costly failure at the Battle of Cold Harbor on 2 June, Grant was familiarly known as 'Butcher Grant'.

12   In glades they meet skull after skull
    Where pine cones lay – the rusted gun,
    Green shoes full of bones, the moldering coat
    And cuddled-up skeleton;
    And scores of such. Some start as in dreams,

And comrades lost bemoan:
By the edge of these wilds Stonewall had
        charged –
But the year and the Man were gone.

The writer Herman Melville on the macabre debris of civil war battle; Ward (1995) p.288.

1 For thirty days now it has been one funeral procession past me, and it is too much.

General Gouverneur K. Warren, June 1864. Warren was the Union Army's chief engineer.

2 Damn the torpedoes! Full speed ahead!

The veteran US navy admiral David Farragut at the Battle of Mobile Bay, 5 Aug. 1864. The Union victory in this engagement secured the coast of Alabama. Torpedo was the contemporary name for a floating mine.

3 Eat out Virginia clear and clean, so far as they go crows flying over it will have to carry their provender with them.

General Ulysses S. Grant to General Halleck, transmitting orders for the Army of the Shenandoah to lay waste to the Shenandoah Valley, Aug. 1864; Perret (1997) p.346.

4 The main thing in true strategy is simply this: first deal as hard a blow at the enemy's soldiers as possible, and then cause so much suffering to the inhabitants of a country that they will long for peace and press their Government to make it. Nothing should be left to the people but eyes to lament the war.

General Philip Sheridan, on the scorched-earth policy now brought into play, 1864; Tsouras (1998) p.235.

5 Until we can repopulate Georgia, it is useless for us to occupy it; but the utter destruction of its roads, houses and people will cripple their military resources. I can make this march, and make Georgia howl.

General William Tecumseh Sherman to General Grant, 9 Sept. 1864, before beginning his devastating march 'from Atlanta to the sea'.

6 You cannot qualify war in harsher terms than I will. War is cruelty, and you cannot refine it.

General William Tecumseh Sherman to the mayor of Atlanta, 12 Sept. 1864; *Memoirs of General William Tecumseh Sherman* (1887) Vol.2, pp.125–7.

7 I have had the question put to me often: 'Is not a negro as good as a white man to stop a bullet?' Yes, and a sand-bag is better; but can a negro do our skirmishing and picket duty? Can they improvise

roads, bridges, sorties, flank movements & c, like the white man? I say no ... Negroes are not equal to this.

General William Tecumseh Sherman to General Halleck, 14 Sept. 1864; *War of the Rebellion* Series 1, Vol.38.

8 Good, now we shall have news from Hell before breakfast.

General William Tecumseh Sherman, on hearing that three war correspondents had been killed by artillery fire.

9   'Hurrah! Hurrah! We bring the jubilee!
      Hurrah! Hurrah! The flag that makes you free!'
   So we sang the chorus from Atlanta to the sea,
   While we were marching through Georgia.

Henry Clay Work 'Marching through Georgia' (Dec. 1864), portraying Sherman as a liberator of Georgia's blacks. The port of Savannah fell to the Union on 21 Dec. 1864.

1865: REUNION

10 With malice toward none; with charity for all; with firmness in the right, as God gives us to see the right, let us strive on to finish the work we are in; to bind up the nation's wounds; to care for him who shall have borne the battle, and for his widow, and his orphan – to do all which may achieve and cherish a just, and a lasting peace, among ourselves, and with all nations.

President Abraham Lincoln, second inaugural address, 4 March 1865; *The Collected Works of Abraham Lincoln* Vol.8 (1953) p.333.

11 They will never shoulder a musket in anger again. And if Grant is wise he will leave them their guns to shoot crows with, and their horses to plow with. It would do no harm.

President Abraham Lincoln on the defeated Confederate Army, 5 April 1865; Tsouras (1998) p.195. General Lee surrendered to General Grant at Appomattox Court House, Virginia, on 9 April 1865, and Grant followed Lincoln's line.

12 General Lee had not been conquered in battle, but surrendered because he had no longer an army with which to give battle. What he surrendered was the skeleton, the mere ghost of the Army of Northern Virginia, which had been gradually worn down by the combined agencies of numbers, steampower, railroads, mechanism, and all the resources of physical science.

General Jubal A. Early, 19 Jan. 1872; Jones (1874).

1 He was a Caesar without his ambition; Frederick without his tyranny; Napoleon without his selfishness; and Washington without his reward.
Benjamin Hill on Lee, 18 Feb. 1874; *Senator Benjamin Hill of Georgia: His Life, Speeches and Writings* (1893) p.406.

2 I think that Lee should have been hanged. It was all the worse that he was a good man and a fine character and acted conscientiously … It's always the good men who do the most harm in the world.
The Bostonian Henry Adams; Ward (1995) p.284.

3 Could he have been persuaded that he was to be tried for treason, and pursued as a traitor, the surrender never would have taken place. Gen. Lee would this day be at large and a great part of the late rebel Armies would be scattered over the South, with arms in their hands, causing infinite trouble.
General Ulysses S. Grant to the secretary of war, Edwin M. Stanton, 20 June 1865; Tsouras (1998) p.197. Grant crossed out these lines from his despatch reviewing the course of the war.

4   When Johnny comes marching home again,
     Hurrah! Hurrah!
   We'll give him a hearty welcome then,
     Hurrah! Hurrah!
   The men will cheer, the boys will shout,
   The ladies they will all turn out,
   And we'll all feel gay
   When Johnny comes marching home.
Patrick Sarsfield Gilmore 'When Johnny Comes Marching Home' (1863). Close on 600,000 combatants did not come marching home in 1865. The death toll of North and South totalled more than US deaths in World Wars I and II combined (some 520,000).

5 Assassination is not an American practice or habit, and one so vicious and so desperate cannot be engrafted into our political system. This conviction of mine has steadily gained strength since the civil war [began]. Every day's experience confirms it.
Secretary of state William Henry Seward, 1864; Ward (1995) p.362.

6 *Sic Semper Tyrannis!* (Thus Always To Tyrants!)
The motto of Virginia, shouted by the assassin of Lincoln, John Wilkes Booth, as he jumped down on to the stage of Ford's Theatre, Washington, D.C., on 14 April 1865, after mortally wounding President Lincoln.

7   When Abraham Lincoln was murdered,
    The one thing that interested Matthew Arnold
    Was that the assassin
    Shouted in Latin
    As he leapt on the stage.
    This convinced Matthew
    There was still hope for America.
Christopher Morley (1890–1957) *Point of View.*

8 Now he belongs to the ages.
Secretary of war Edwin M. Stanton, 15 April 1865, immediately after the death of Lincoln.

9 Fellow citizens! God reigns, and the Government at Washington still lives!
Representative James Garfield, speaking in New York, 16 April 1865; Allan Peskin *Garfield* (1978) p.250. Garfield himself became the next US president to suffer assassination, dying on 19 Sept. 1881.

10   When lilacs last in the dooryard bloom'd
    And the great star drooped in the western sky
     in the night,
    I mourn'd, and yet shall mourn with ever-
     returning spring.
Walt Whitman 'When Lilacs Last in the Dooryard Bloom'd' (1865–6).

11   O Captain! My Captain! Our fearful trip is
     done,
    The ship has weathered every wrack, the prize
     we sought is won.
    The port is near, the bells I hear, the people all
     exulting,
    While follow eyes the steady keel, the vessel
     grim and daring;
    But O heart! heart!
    O the bleeding drops of red,
    Where on the deck my Captain lies,
    Fallen cold and dead.
Walt Whitman 'O Captain! My Captain!' (1865). Lincoln had a recurrent dream of sailing on board ship to an unknown destination.

12 The catastrophe of Lincoln, though it was a great shock, does not cloud the prospect. How could one have wished him a happier death? He died almost unconsciously in the fullness of success, and martyrdom in so great a cause consecrates his name through all history. Such a death is the crown of a noble life.
John Stuart Mill to Max Kyllman, 30 May 1865; *Collected Works of John Stuart Mill* Vol.16 (1972) p.1063.

1 For an enemy so relentless in the war for our subjugation, we could not be expected to mourn; yet, in view of its political consequences, it could not be regarded otherwise than as a great misfortune for the South. He had power over the Northern people, and was without personal malignity toward the people of the South.

Jefferson Davis *The Rise and Fall of the Confederate Government* (1881) Vol.2, p.683. Magnanimity towards Lincoln from the president of the defeated Confederacy.

2 He is not a cheap Judas. I do not think he would have sold the Savior for thirty shillings; but for the successorship to Pontius Pilate he would have betrayed Christ and the apostles and the whole Christian Church.

General Winfield Scott on Jefferson Davis. Scott and Davis had been at daggers drawn long before the Civil War, from the time when Davis served as secretary of war in the Pierce administration of 1853–7.

3 He was preeminently the white man's President … ready and willing at any time to deny, postpone, and sacrifice the rights of humanity in the colored people to promote the welfare of the white people of this country … You are the children of Abraham Lincoln. We are at best his step-children; children by adoption, children by force of circumstances and necessity.

The one-time slave, Frederick Douglass, 14 April 1876, speaking to a white audience at the unveiling of the freedmen's monument to Lincoln in Washington, D.C.; *Life and Writings of Frederick Douglass* Vol.4, p.312.

RETROSPECT

4 Our land is the dearer for our sacrifices. The blood of our martyrs sanctifies and enriches it. Their spirit passes into thousands of hearts. How costly is the progress of the race. It is only by the giving of life that we can have life.

Rev. E.J. Young *Monthly Religious Magazine*, May 1865.

5 The war has purified and elevated our natures … War … makes men live, labor and fight for each other; and continually seeing and feeling their mutual inter-dependence, it begets brotherly love.

The Southerner George Fitzhugh, 1866; Edmund Wilson *Patriotic Gore* (1962) p.362.

6 Some hundreds of thousands of men killed and hurt: some hundreds of thousands of widows and orphans: some billions of money destroyed by being created: some millions of characters male and female demoralized: some hundreds of thousands of boys doomed to ignorance by their inability to study on account of the noise of the shells: some billions of property burned by the intense heat: and a miscellaneous mass of poverty, starvation, disease and dirt precipitated upon the people: so suddenly that many were buried underneath those vast fragments beyond hope of extrication save by that Good Samaritan – Death, who may pull some out.

Sidney Lanier of Georgia; *The Centennial Edition of the Works of Sidney Lanier* (1945) Vol.5, p.204.

7 Light it with every lurid passion, the wolf's, the lion's lapping thirst for blood – the passionate, boiling volcanoes of human revenge for comrades, brothers slain – with the light of burning farms, and heaps of smutting, smoldering black embers – and in the human heart everywhere black, worse embers – and you have an inkling of this war.

Walt Whitman *Collected Writings* Vol.7 (1963) p.81.

8   In seeds of laurel in the earth
        The blossom of your fame is blown,
        And, somewhere, waiting for its birth,
        The shaft is in the stone.

The Southern poet Henry Timrod, tribute to the Confederate dead in Magnolia Cemetery, Charleston, South Carolina.

9 We have shared the incommunicable experience of war. We have felt, we still feel, the passion of life to its top … In our youth, our hearts were touched with fire.

Oliver Wendell Holmes Jr, the young Union soldier who later became a venerable Supreme Court Justice, speech on Memorial Day, 1884; *Touched with Fire* (1946). Memorial Day, the last Monday in May, was America's day of remembrance for the dead of the Civil War.

10 Future years will never know the seething hell … of the Secession War; and it is best they should not – the real war will never get in the books … It was not a quadrille in a ball-room. Its interior history will not only never be written – its practicality, minutiae of deeds and passions will never even be suggested.

Walt Whitman Vol.7 (1963) pp.116, 117.

Reform in Britain, 1776–1865

GREEN SHOOTS, 1776–83

1 Some share ... in the power of making those laws, which deeply interest them, and to which they are expected to pay obedience, should be reserved even to this inferior, but most useful set of men in the community ... We ought always to remember ... that all government is instituted for the mass of the people to be governed.

John Wilkes, in the House of Commons, 1776; *Parliamentary Register* Vol.3, Cols 432–41. Wilkes had made his name as a highly controversial figure in the 1760s, and in 1774 he was elected Lord Mayor of London. It was from this eminence that he made his call for male suffrage, revolutionary to a legislature chosen on an extremely restricted franchise.

2 Personality is the sole foundation of the right of being represented; and ... property has, in reality, nothing to do with the case. The property of any one, be it more or be it less, is totally involved in the man. As belonging to him and to his peace, it is a very fit object of the attention of his representatives and parliament, but it contributes nothing to his right of having that representation.

John Cartwright *Take Your Choice!* (1776) p.22. Cartwright, the so-called Father of Reform, embraced every conceivable radical measure, campaigning for them all until his death in 1824.

3 If the nation ... will submit to be led by Scotch fanatics, and to the tune of the bagpipe – set Newgate loose, and burn London ... such a nation *cannot* be saved.

Duke of Richmond to Marquis of Rockingham, 12 June 1780; Alison Gilbert Olson *The Radical Duke* (1961) p.56. The duke refers to the Gordon riots of the previous week, led by Lord George Gordon, scion of a noble Scottish family, and directed against any move towards the emancipation of British Catholics from their many legal disabilities. Newgate was the prison in the City of London from which condemned criminals set off on their journey to the scaffold. As Lord Mayor, the ultra-liberal Wilkes had to play a significant part in the suppression of the mayhem, and to compound the irony Richmond had, on 3 June, introduced a bill for universal male suffrage!

4 Societies are justifiable which eject from the full enjoyment of the rights of citizens persons to whom those rights could not be continued without danger to the public. [The franchise might be granted] to every class of men, who, from the possession of property to some small amount may be thought likely to exercise their franchise freely, and for the public good.

Rev. Christopher Wyvill, 15 Aug. 1783; Ian Christie *Wilkes, Wyvill and Reform* (1962) p.169. Wyvill, who began an electoral reform movement in Yorkshire in the 1780s, stopped well short of democracy.

BLIGHT, 1791–1801

5 Sovereignty, as a matter of right, appertains to the Nation only, and nothing individual; and a Nation has at all times an inherent indefeasible right to abolish any government it finds inconvenient, and establish such as accords with its interest, disposition, and happiness ... What we now see in the world, from the Revolutions of America and France, are a renovation of the natural order of things, a system of principles as universal as truth and the existence of man, and combining moral with political happiness and national prosperity.

Thomas Paine *The Rights of Man* Pt 1 (1791) pp.157–8. Paine, the devotee of revolution in the United States (see 504:6) and then in France (see 518:4), issued this clarion call for Britain to follow in those nations' footsteps on 13 March 1791. It caused an uproar.

6 He seems cocksure of bringing about a revolution in Great Britain and I think it quite likely he will be promoted to the pillory.

The American Gouverneur Morris, diary entry, 16 Feb. 1792; John Keane *Tom Paine* (1995) p.328. Morris wrote on the day of the publication of Pt 2 of Paine's *The Rights of Man*. A deep-dyed conservative, Morris had been Paine's political enemy ever since they had crossed swords during the American Revolution in the 1770s.

7 If Mr Paine should be able to rouze up the lower classes, their interference will probably be marked by wild work and all we now possess, whether in private property or public liberty, will be at the mercy of a lawless and furious rabble.

Rev. Christopher Wyvill to James Martin, 28 April 1792; *Political Papers* Vol.5 (1800) p.23.

8 At length came a cart ... on the flake of which behind, was placed the figure of a man, which I thought was a real living being. A rabble which followed the cart, kept throwing stones at the figure,

and shouting – 'Tum Pain a Jacobin' – 'Tum Paine a thief' … whilst others with guns and pistols kept discharging them at the figure. They took care to stop when they came to the residence of a reformer.
Samuel Bamford *Early Days* (1849) p.44. Recollections of an anti-Paine demonstration seen as a boy in 1793.

1 We live in times of violence and extremes, and all those who are for creating or even for retaining checks upon power are considered as enemies to order … Good God! That a man should be sent to Botany Bay for advising another to read Paine's book.
Charles James Fox to Lord Holland, Dec. 1793; *Memorials and Correspondence of Charles James Fox* Vol.3 (1854) p.62.

2 The Government of this free country! & free people! – long reeling indeed from the right line of rectitude & *freedom* had readily found pretexts & pretences for bending it to aside, that it might be the more easily broken when the fit opportunity presented itself … It was calculated upon as a certainty that this weight added to the already powerful confederacy would soon put a stop to the march of intellects, & if found necessary, put an extinguisher upon the rights of man.
Thomas Bewick *A Memoir* (1862 edn) Ch.15. In this autobiography, written in 1822, the famous engraver reflects on the political consequences of Britain's entry into the war with revolutionary France in coalition with the counter-revolutionary monarchies of Europe.

3 Let not men … in the pride of power, use the same argument that tyrannic kings and venal ministers have used, and fallaciously assert that woman ought to be subjected because she has always been so … Women ought to have representatives, instead of being arbitrarily governed without having any direct share allowed them.
Mary Wollstonecraft *A Vindication of the Rights of Woman* (1792) Chs 3, 9. A celebrated early call for women's suffrage by an ardent admirer of the French Revolution (which did not introduce it).

4 That hyena in petticoats, Mrs Woolstonecroft [*sic*] who to this day discharges her ink and gall on Marie Antoinette.
Horace Walpole to Hannah More, 26 Jan. 1795; *Letters* Vol.31 (1961) p.397. Walpole in misogynistic mode to a noted literary lady and philanthropist. Marie-Antoinette, the queen of France, was executed on 16 Oct. 1793 (see 524:7).

5 The principle of our constitution is the representation of property, imperfectly in theory, but efficiently in practice … The great mass of property, both landed, monied and commercial, finds itself represented; and that the evils of such representation are trivial, will appear from the ease, happiness and security of all the lower classes, hence possibly virtual representation takes place even where the real seems most remote.
Arthur Young *The Example of France … A Warning to Britain* (1794) p.106. Retraction from reform by a first-hand witness of the course it had taken across the Channel (see 515:5). 'Virtual representation' was the doctrine that the interests of those without the vote were cared for by those who possessed it, a most ingenious paradox.

6 I affirm that *every* man, and *every* woman, and *every* child, ought to obtain something more, in the general distribution of the fruits of labour, than food, and rags, and a wretched hammock with a poor rug to cover it; and that, without working twelve or fourteen hours a day … from six to sixty.
John Thelwall *The Rights of Nature* (1796) Letter 1. A demand for social justice, going beyond the narrower bounds of political reform.

7 When engaged with the enemy off Brest, March 9th 1797, they even beat us at our quarters though on the verge of eternity and said I'll beat you until I make you jump overboard, damn you, you rascal, etc. Jump overboard or be God damd. I will not send a boat after you.
Ship's company of HMS *Nymphe*, 19 April 1797; G.E. Manwaring and B. Dobrée *The Floating Republic* (1935) pp.59–60. From Feb. to June 1797 the Royal Navy was hit by mutinies at Spithead and the Nore, highly troubling to a British ruling class fighting a war against a country based on revolutionary principles, when its first line of defence was the fleet.

8 I cannot help fearing the evil is … deeply rooted in the influence of Jacobin Emissaries and the Corresponding Society.
Thomas Grenville, 9 May 1797; *Buckingham Memoirs* p.380. A government inquiry ordered by the prime minister, William Pitt, found no evidence of Gallic subversion. Corresponding societies were working-class political organizations and, as such, equally suspect.

9 I have snapped my squeaking baby-trumpet of sedition, and the fragments lie scattered in the lumber-room of penitence. I wish to be a good man and a Christian, but I am no Whig, no Reformist, no Republican.
The writer Samuel Taylor Coleridge to Rev. George Coleridge, April 1798; *Letters of Samuel Taylor Coleridge* Vol.1 (1895) p.243. Coleridge, like his fellow poet, William

Wordsworth, had been an enthusiast for the early French Revolution but now (also like Wordsworth) had cooled off markedly, particularly as pro-revolutionary partisanship could be positively dangerous.

1   Mock on, mock on, Voltaire, Rousseau;
     Mock on, mock on: 'tis all in vain!
     You throw sand against the wind,
     And the wind blows it back again.

William Blake 'Mock on' (1801). The poem, a world away from the heady idealism of 'Jerusalem', is again symptomatic of the revulsion against what the French Revolution had led to.

SWELL OF DISCONTENT, 1812–30

2 I Ham going to inform you that there is Six Thousand men coming to you in Apral and then We Will go and blow Parlement house up and Blow up all afour hus. Labring Peple Cant Stand it No Longer. Dam all Such Roges as England governes but Never mind Ned lud when general nody and his harmey Comes We Will soon bring about the great Revolution then all these great mens heads gose of.

Anon. Luddite letter found in Chesterfield, about May 1812; Edward Thompson *The Making of the English Working Class* (1991 edn) p.784. The Luddite movement was an artisans' protest at the unemployment brought about by the machinery introduced in farming and the textile industry, and machine-breaking was its answer to the problem. The upsurge also had a political dimension, as this threatening letter shows.

3 If an Aristocrat happen to meet a Weaver in the street, and the latter does not choose to *off with his hat*, the man of consequence cannot harm him. Hence arises that contempt for assuming greatness and petty despotism which we may observe in all manufacturing towns. And from this contempt proceeds ... that downright rooted hatred, that we may observe when we hear an Aristocratical-minded man speak of those parts of the country wherein manufactures and political influence have flourished.

Sherwin's Political Register, 24 May 1817. The coming breach between landed and industrial wealth foreshadowed.

4 Mr Owen's conduct appears to me to cover the face of the country with workhouses, to rear up a city of slaves, and consequently to render the labouring part of the People absolutely dependent upon the men of property.

Sherwin's Political Register, 20 Sept. 1817. The textile magnate Robert Owen made his reputation as an early socialist, building model townships for his operatives at New Lanark in

Scotland and New Harmony in Indiana. His efforts were clearly not appreciated by those who saw these communities as company towns where workers were bound hand and foot to their master, off duty as well as on.

5 The Negro slave in the West Indies, if he works under a scorching sun, has possibly a little breeze of air sometimes to fan him: he has a space of ground and time allowed to cultivate it. The English spinner slave has no enjoyment of the open atmosphere and breezes of heaven. Locked up in factories eight storeys high, he has no relaxation till the ponderous engine stops.

Black Dwarf, 30 Sept. 1818. A frequent comparison between wage slavery and chattel slavery, drawn here by a radical journal.

6 I distrust your calculation as to the improving state of Man in society. In proportion as knowledge is diffused among the lower orders, the fears and vigilance of the government will increase ... and if they will not be kept down, we shall burst out into Revolution.

Charles Bage to William Strutt, 25 Feb. 1818; Arnold Pacey *The Maze of Ingenuity* (1974) p.245. An unmistakable blow at such working-class organizations as the Society for the Diffusion of Useful Knowledge.

7 The circumstances of the workmen do not in the least depend on the prosperity or profits of the masters, but on the power of the workmen to *command* – nay, to extort a high price for their labours.

The Gorgon, 21 Nov. 1818. 'Trickle-down' denied by the voice of incipient unionism.

8 The cavalry ... evidently could not, with all the weight of men and horse, penetrate that compact mass of human beings; and their sabres were plied to hew a way through naked held-up hands and defence-less heads; and then chopped limbs and wound-gaping skulls were seen; and groans and cries were mingled with the din of that horrid confusion.

Samuel Bamford on the 'Peterloo Massacre' of 16 Aug. 1819; *Passages in the Life of a Radical* (1844) p.207. A landmark episode in the post-war struggle for reform, when mounted yeomanry rode into a huge political demonstration in St Peter's Fields, Manchester, killing up to 15 people and wounding hundreds of others.

9 It is very clear to me that they won't be quiet till a large number of them 'bite the dust', as the French say, or till some of their leaders are hanged, which would be the most fortunate result.

Duke of Wellington to one of the *grandes dames* of London society, Mrs Harriet Arbuthnot, 27 Aug. 1819; Elizabeth Longford *Wellington: Pillar of State* (1972) p.62. The High Tory duke was no friend of radicals.

1   If you have acted *once* a generous part,
     The World, not the World's masters will
       decide,
     And I shall be delighted to learn who,
     Save you and yours, have gained by Waterloo?

The poet Lord Byron *Don Juan* (1819–24) Canto 9. Written in the aftermath of Peterloo.

2   I met Murder on the way –
     He had a mask like Castlereagh. …
     Rise like Lions after Slumber
     In unvanquishable number,
     Shake your chains to earth like dew
     Which in sleep had fallen on you, –
     Ye are many, they are few.

Byron's fellow radical, the poet Percy Bysshe Shelley *The Masque of Anarchy* (1819). Shelley's target was the British foreign secretary, Viscount Castlereagh, whom he held responsible for Peterloo, along with his cabinet colleagues Eldon and Sidmouth.

3 Just so at the beginning of the French Revolution: the first work of the Reformers was to loosen every established political relation, every legal holding of man to man, to destroy every corporation, every subsisting class of society, and to reduce the nation into individuals, in order, afterwards, to congregate them into mobs.

Blackwood's Magazine Vol.7 (Jan. 1820) p.13.

4 Just as if women were made for nothing but to cook oat-meal and to sweep a room! Just as if women had no minds! Just as if Hannah More and the Tract Gentry had reduced the women of England to a level with the Negresses of Africa! Just as if England had never had a queen!

The radical journalist William Cobbett, *Weekly Political Register*, 29 Dec. 1819. An early bid to associate women with reformism. 'Hannah More and the Tract Gentry' was a reference to the intensely conservative High Anglicans, who concentrated their energies on saving souls rather than committing themselves to political change.

5 The manufacturers … are transferred to great towns [and] they have now seen the danger of suffering a great population to be … entirely separated from the influence of their employers, and given over to the management of their own societies,

in which the cleverest and most important fellows always get the management of the others, and become bell-wethers in every sort of mischief.

The novelist Sir Walter Scott *Familiar Letters* Vol.2 (1820) p.78. In this context, the bellwether, the leading sheep in a flock, with a bell tied round its neck, was a dangerous ringleader.

6 As education has increased amidst the people, infidelity, vice and crime have increased. At this moment the people are far more vicious and criminal, in proportion to their numbers, than they were when they were comparatively uneducated. The majority of criminals consist of those who have been 'educated'.

Blackwood's Magazine Vol.22 (Oct. 1827) p.427.

7 The rising hope of the stern and unbending Tories who follow, reluctantly and mutinously, a leader whose experience and eloquence are indispensable to them, but whose cautious temper and moderate opinions they abhor.

Thomas Babington Macaulay, *Edinburgh Review*, April 1829, p.231. The subject is the future Liberal prime minister, William Ewart Gladstone, then highly illiberal on the question of Catholic emancipation. The removal of the various disabilities inflicted on English Catholics since the Elizabethan era was put through by the Tory government of Wellington and Peel and became law on 13 April 1829.

8 Depend upon it, the working people never will, as they never have, obtain anything by such appeals. The struggle is a struggle of strength and 'the weakest must go to the wall'. Whatever the people either gain or even retain, is gained or retained, and must always be gained or retained, by power.

Francis Place to John Doherty, April 1829; Anthony Burton *Remains of a Revolution* (1975) p.226. Place was one of the leading figures in the movement for reform; he refers here to a pamphlet appealing against the reduction of wages.

9 Three poor fellows digging stone for the roads … told me that they never had anything but bread to eat, and water to wash it down. One of them was a widower with three children; and his pay was eighteen pence a day, that is to say, about three pounds of bread a day each, for six days in the week: nothing for Sunday, and nothing for lodging, washing, clothing, candlelight, or fuel. Just such was the state of things in France at the eve of the Revolution. Precisely such; and such were the causes.

William Cobbett, spring 1830; *Rural Rides* Vol.2 (1830) pp.253–4. *Rural Rides* reprinted articles from Cobbett's *Weekly Political Register*, which he founded in 1802.

1 We tasted of fear ... Oh, the horror of those fires – breaking forth night after night, sudden, yet expected, always seeming nearer than they actually were, and always said to have been more mischievous to life and property than they actually had been!

Mary Mitford *Our Village* Vol.5 (1832) p.6. A witness of the rural arson that broke out across the English countryside in 1830.

2 I induced the magistrates to put themselves on horseback, each at the head of his own servants and retainers, grooms, huntsmen, game-keepers, armed with horsewhips, pistols, fowling-pieces and what they could get, and to attack in concert, if necessary, those mobs, disperse them, and take and put in confinement those who could not escape. This was done in a spirited manner, in many instances, and it is astonishing how soon the country was tranquillized, and that in the best way, by the activity and spirit of the gentlemen.

Duke of Wellington; David Williams *John Frost* (1939) pp.59–60. The national hero's response to agrarian incendiarism.

3 This is to inform you what you have to undergo gentelmen if providing you don't pull down your messhenes and rise the poor mens wages ... we will burn down your barns and you in them this is the last notis.

Anon. threatening letter to farmers during the 'Captain Swing' revolt of agricultural labourers, Aug. 1830-Aug. 1831; Eric Hobsbawm and George Rudé *Captain Swing: A Social History of the Great English Agricultural Uprising* (1968) p.208.

4 High above the grim and grimy crowd of scowling faces a loom had been erected, at which sat a tattered, starved-looking weaver, evidently set there as a *representative man*, to protest against this triumph of machinery, and the gain and glory which the wealthy Liverpool and Manchester men were likely to derive from it.

The actress Fanny Kemble, 15 Sept. 1830; *Records of a Girlhood* (1878). Kemble was a passenger on the train that officially opened the Liverpool and Manchester Railway, here recalling a dramatic tableau as it entered the terminus in Manchester.

REFORM ENACTED, 1830–32

5 The whole scheme of our Government is essentially corrupt, and no corrupt system ever reformed itself. Our system could not reform itself if it would. Take away corruption and nothing remains.

Francis Place, 1830; Graham Wallas *The Life of Francis Place* (1898) p.256.

6 They [opponents of reform] want to keep the bees from buzzing and stinging, in order that they may rob the hive in peace.

The celebrated ecclesiastical wit, Rev. Sydney Smith *The Works of the Rev. Sydney Smith* (1850 edn) p.570. Smith stood as a reform candidate for Taunton in the 1831 election.

7 The greatest happiness of the greatest number is the foundation of morals and legislation.

Jeremy Bentham, progenitor of the doctrine of Utilitarianism, encapsulated in this oft-quoted dictum; *Works* Vol.10, p.142 (see 482:2). The original coiner of the phrase may well have been the Scottish moral philosopher Francis Hutcheson in *Inquiry into the Original of Our Ideas of Beauty and Virtue* (1722); the Italian economist and jurist Cesare Beccaria, in his *Trattato dei delitti e delle pene* (Treatise on Crimes and Punishments) (1764), also has a claim on it.

8 Any plan must be objectionable which, by keeping the Franchise very high and exclusive, fails to give satisfaction to the middle and respectable ranks of society, and drives them to a union, founded on dissatisfaction, with the lower orders. It is of the utmost importance to associate the middle with the higher orders in the love and support of the institutions of the country.

Francis Jeffrey, c.1830; H. Cockburn *Letters on the Affairs of Scotland* (1874) p.258. The Scots judge Jeffrey, co-founder of the *Edinburgh Review*, preaches the alliance of the bourgeoisie and the aristocracy in order to prevent a revolutionary misalliance between the middle classes and the workers.

9 We are not of that number of those who inculcate patient submission to undeserved oppression. A favourite toast of Dr Johnson was, 'Success to an insurrection of the Blacks!' Shall we say – 'Success to the rising of the WHITES!'? We should at once answer yes, did we not think some measures would be speedily adopted to mitigate the bitter privations and avert the further degradations of the labouring classes.

John Wade *The Extraordinary Black Book* (1831); Burton (1975) p.225.

10 Not only do I think Parliamentary Reform unnecessary but that it would be so injurious as that Society, as now established in the Empire, could not exist under the system which must be its Consequence.

Duke of Wellington to Sir James Shaw, 12 Oct. 1830; Longford (1972) p.224. Wellington was prime minister but resigned on 15 Nov., to be followed by the Whig Earl Grey.

1 A Head of a House, a clergyman also, gravely declared that the rotten boroughs should instantly be abolished without compensation to their owners; that slavery should be destroyed with like disregard of the *claims* (for rights he would allow none) of the proprietors, and a multitude of extravagances of the same sort.

The poet William Wordsworth, Nov. 1830; *Prose Works* Vol.3, p.309. The one-time admirer of the early French Revolution had long since moved far across to the political right. The 'rotten boroughs' were those parliamentary constituencies that were, literally, the property of the grandees who bought them, nominated their candidates and controlled an electorate who had to vote in public under the eye of the local patron.

2 Is the House of Commons to be reconstructed on the principle of a representation of interests, or of a delegation of men? If on the former, we may, perhaps, see our way; if on the latter, you can never, in reason, stop short of universal suffrage; and in that case, I am sure that women have as good a right to vote as men.

Samuel Taylor Coleridge, 21 Nov. 1830; *Table Talk* (1835). Like Wordsworth, Coleridge had foresworn liberalism (see 599:9), and this exercise in logic was designed to demonstrate the absurdity of the argument for universal suffrage, not to support votes for women.

3 The country is in a terrible state, thanks to all the people who have been lauding the French revolution to the skies and dinning in the ears of the people that, if they choose to rise, nothing can resist them.

Mrs Arbuthnot, 29 Nov. 1830; F. Banford and Duke of Wellington (eds) *The Journal of Mrs Arbuthnot 1820–1832* (1950). The French revolution in question is that of July 1830, which brought in the Orleanist monarchy (see 544:4). This event greatly excited the hopes and fears of English radicals and conservatives, respectively, but the hopes were doomed to disappointment and the fears were groundless.

4 I dinna pretend to be a profit, but I naw this, and lots of ma marrers [mates] na's te, that wer not tret as we owt to be, and a great filosopher says, to get noledge is to naw yer ignorant. But weve just begun to find that oot, and ye masters and owners may luk oot, for yor not gan to get se much o yor way, wer gan to hey some o wors now.

Anon. letter from a County Durham miner to the colliery manager after a riot in 1831; Duncan Steen and Nicholas Soames *The Essential Englishman* (1989) p.109.

5 What ... would be his surprise ... to be taken to a stone wall, with three niches in it, and told that those three niches sent two Members to Parliament? ... But his surprise would increase to astonishment if he were carried into the North of England, where he could see large flourishing towns, full of trade and activity, containing vast magazines of wealth and manufactures. And were told that these places had no Representatives in the Assembly.

Lord John Russell, introducing the Reform Bill in the House of Commons, 1 March 1831; *Parl. Deb.* Vol.2, Cols 1061 ff. Russell speaks of mere geographical place-names such as Gatton in Cornwall and Dunwich in Suffolk, which had no inhabitants but which counted as parliamentary constituencies, unlike populous industrial centres, such as Manchester and Birmingham, which were not on the electoral map.

6 All history is full of revolutions, produced by causes similar to those which are now operating in England. A portion of the community which had been of no account expands and becomes strong. It demands a place in the system, suited, not to its former weakness, but to its present power ... Such ... is the struggle which the middle classes in England are maintaining against an aristocracy the principle of which is to invest a hundred drunken potwallopers in one place or the owner of a ruined hovel in another, with powers which are withheld from cities renowned to the farthest ends of the earth for the marvels of their wealth and of their industry.

Thomas Babington Macaulay, 2 March 1831; *Parl. Deb.* Vol.2, Cols 1355–6. The Whigs forge their nexus with the middle class. 'Potwallopers' were kitchen-boys, bribed with drink to vote the right way; see Charles Dickens's famous account of the uproarious Eatanswill election in Ch.13 of *Pickwick Papers* (1837).

7 It may be asked, Will a reform of the Parliament give the labouring man a cow or a pig; will it put bread and cheese into his satchell instead of infernal cold potatoes; will it give him a bottle of beer to carry to the field instead of making him lie down upon his belly to drink out of the brook; will it put on his back a Sunday coat and send him to church, instead of leaving him to stand hanging about shivering with an unshaven face and a carcass half covered with a ragged smock-frock, with a filthy cotton shirt beneath it as yellow as a kite's foot? ... The enemies of reform jeeringly ask us, whether reform would do these things for us; and I answer distinctly, that IT WOULD DO THEM ALL!

William Cobbett, 2 April 1831; *Weekly Political Register* Vol.72, No.1, pp.4–5.

1 There is no one more decided against annual parliaments, universal suffrage, and the ballot, than I am. My object is not to favour, but to put an end to such hopes and projects.
Earl Grey, Nov. 1831; Thompson (1991 edn) p.892. A candid avowal that he was no democrat.

2 TO STOP THE DUKE, GO FOR GOLD.
Francis Place, 12 May 1832; Wallas (1898) p.308. The king had forced Grey's resignation on 9 May, and Wellington was asked to form an administration. Fearing that the duke would wreck the Reform Bill, Place advised a run on the Bank of England. In the event Grey returned within the week, and the Bill became law on 7 June.

3 The revolution is made, that is to say, that power is transferred from one class of society, the gentlemen of England, professing the faith of the Church of England, to another class of society, the shopkeepers, being Dissenters from the Church, many of them Socinians, others atheists.
Duke of Wellington to the Irish Tory, John Wilson Croker, 6 March 1833; L.L. Jennings (ed.) The Correspondence and Diaries of John Wilson Croker Vol.2 (1884) pp.205–6. Dissenters were Protestants who refused to become members of the Church of England and were persecuted for their refusal. Socinians were members of a sect that denied the divinity of Christ.

4 The great peculiarity causing a difference between the Political Unions and the Unions of the working classes was, that the first desired the Reform Bill to prevent a revolution, the last desired its destruction as the means of producing a revolution.
Francis Place; Wallas (1898) pp.290–91. The political unions were agencies of the middle classes.

5 Mark my words, within two years you will find that we have become unpopular for having brought forward the most aristocratic measure that ever was proposed in parliament.
Earl Grey to the ultra-reactionary Tory, Viscount Sidmouth, after the passage of the Reform Act in 1832. Grey spoke no less than the truth: the Act consolidated the grip of the aristocracy on the House of Commons in the coming generation.

THE END OF SLAVERY, 1772–1833

6 Every man who comes to England is entitled to the protection of the English law, whatever oppression he may heretofore have suffered, and whatever may be the colour of his skin, whether it is black or whether it is white.

Earl Mansfield, decision in the Somersett habeas corpus case, May 1772; State Trials Vol.20, p.1. This judgement made slavery in England illegal and gave a sharp stimulus to the embryonic campaign to abolish the British slave trade, operating between Africa and the British colonies in America and the West Indies.

7 O Thou God of love ... have compassion upon those outcasts of men, who are trodden down as dung upon the earth! Arise, and help those who have no helper, whose blood is spilt upon the ground like water! ... O burst Thou all their chains in sunder; more especially the chains of their sins!
The Methodist John Wesley 'Thoughts Upon Slavery' (1774); Works of John Wesley (1872 edn) Vol.11, Ch.6.

8 The African Slave-Trade has been publicly supported and encouraged by the *Legislature of this Kingdom* for near a century last past; so that the *monstrous destruction of the Human Species*, which is *annually* occasioned thereby, may be certainly esteemed a *National Crime* of the most aggravating kind, which (according to the usual course of God's Providence in the World) will probably draw down some exemplary vengeance upon the unrepenting Inhabitants of this Island! ... The burthen not only of the *much-injured African Strangers*, but also of *our Country's Ruin, must rest on the heads of those who withhold their* Testimony against the CRYING SIN OF TOLERATED SLAVERY!
Granville Sharp The Law of Retribution (1776) Opening and Conclusion. In 1787 Sharp became chairman of the Committee for the Abolition of the Slave Trade.

9 To abolish a *status*, which in all ages God has sanctioned, and man has continued, would not only be *robbery* to an innumerable class of our fellow-subjects, but it would be extreme cruelty to the African savages, a portion of whom it saves from massacre, or intolerable bondage in their own country, and introduces into a much happier state of life; especially now when their passage to the West Indies and their treatment there is humanely regulated. To abolish that trade would be to 'shut the gates of mercy on mankind'.
James Boswell, 23 Sept. 1777; The Life of Samuel Johnson (1791). Johnson himself was a passionate abolitionist.

10   Fleecy locks and black complexion
      Cannot forfeit nature's claim;
      Skins may differ, but affection
      Dwells in black and white the same.
William Cowper 'The Negro's Complaint' (1788).

1 Their lodging rooms below the deck ... are sometimes more than five feet high, and sometimes less; and this height is divided towards the middle, for the Slaves lie in two rows, one above the other, on each side of the ship, close to each other, like books upon a shelf ... They are kept down, by the weather, to breathe a hot and corrupted air, sometimes for a week; this, added to the galling of their irons, and the despondency which seizes their spirits, soon becomes fatal.

Rev. John Newton *Thoughts Upon the African Slave Trade* (1788).

2 ABSCONDED from John Munro's wharf ... a NEGRO SAILORMAN, of the Coromantee nation; he is about 5 feet 5 inches high, his face furrowed by the small pox marks, he has no brand mark, his back has got several lumps which in some manner resemble a bunch of grapes ... He is artful ... A suitable reward will be given to any person who will lodge him in any gaol or workhouse in this island, or conduct him to this wharf.

Kingston, Jamaica, *Daily Advertiser*, 7 June 1790.

3 Am I Not A Man And A Brother?

Motto of the Committee for the Abolition of the Slave Trade, set on a cameo by Josiah Wedgwood, 1790.

4 They are not my men and brethren, these strange people ... Sambo is not my man and my brother.

The writer William Makepeace Thackeray; G.N. Ray *Thackeray* (1955) p.216.

5 I would rather be on friendly terms with a man who had strangled my infant son than support an administration guilty of slackness in suppressing the Slave Trade.

James Stephen, c.1790; Rupert Furneaux *William Wilberforce* (1974) p.85. A lifelong campaigner against slavery after personally witnessing it in the West Indies.

6   Thou hast left behind
    Powers that will work for thee; air, earth and
        skies;
    There's not a breathing of the common mind
    That will forget thee: thou hast great allies;
    Thy friends are exultations, agonies,
    And love, and man's unconquerable mind.

William Wordsworth 'Toussaint L'Ouverture' (1802). The Haitian Toussaint L'Ouverture (1746–1803), born a slave, led a movement for independence from France. The Revolution had ordered the abolition of slavery, but Napoleon reintroduced it, and Toussaint died in France after his capture.

7 The mass of owners have, practically at least, gone upon the system of working out their Slaves in a few years, and recruiting their gangs with imported Africans. The abolition would give the death blow to this system [but] it would be the grossest violation and the merest mockery of justice and humanity, to emancipate them at once, in their present unhappy condition ... The stoppage of all further importations from Africa ... is the very shortest and safest path by which the Slaves can travel to the enjoyment of their true liberty.

William Wilberforce *A Letter on the Abolition of the Slave Trade* (1807). The name of Wilberforce, more than any other, is associated with the anti-slavery movement. Here, he urges the ending of the trade before emancipation, that is, the abolition of the institution of slavery itself.

8   Go, W– with narrow skull,
    Go home and preach away at Hull.
    No longer in the Senate cackle
    In strains that suit the tabernacle;
    I hate your little wittling sneer,
    Your pert and self-sufficient leer.
    Mischief to trade sits on your lip,
    Insects will gnaw the noblest ship.
    Go, W–, begone, for shame,
    Thou dwarf with big resounding name.

James Boswell on Wilberforce, 1807; Furneaux (1974) p.283.

9 How much more pure and perfect felicity must he enjoy in the consciousness of having preserved so many millions of his fellow-creatures, than the man with whom he had compared him, on the throne to which he had waded through slaughter and oppression.

The lawyer and reformer Sir Samuel Romilly in his encomium to Wilberforce, 23 Feb. 1807; *Parl. Deb.* Vol.8, Cols 978–9. The comparison was between Wilberforce and Napoleon, made in the House of Commons debate on the abolition of the slave trade, which became law on 16 March 1807.

10 Every man has an inborn indefeasible right to the free use of his own bodily strength and exertion; it follows that no man can be kept one moment in a state of bondage, without the guilt of ROBBERY; therefore, the West Indian negroes should be set free.

Henry, Lord Brougham, *Edinburgh Review*, 1824. Brougham wrote a year after a motion for the abolition of slavery was put to the House of Commons.

11 Shooting is too honourable death for men whose conduct has occasioned so much bloodshed, and the loss of so much property. There are five hanging woods in St James and Trelawnay, and we do sincerely hope, that the bodies of all Methodist preachers who may be convicted of sedition, may diversify the scene.

Jamaica *Courant*, 6 Jan. 1832. A protest on behalf of the plantation-owners against the Methodists alleged to have promoted a recent slave revolt, inspired by the imminent prospect of abolition.

1 Thank God that I should have lived to witness a day in which England is willing to give twenty millions sterling for the Abolition of Slavery.

William Wilberforce, 27 July 1833, on hearing the news that the abolition of slavery in the British empire was guaranteed after the passage of the second reading of the bill for abolition in the Commons. He died two days later. The £20 million was the compensation paid to the planters for the loss of their human property.

BOURGEOIS MONARCHY, 1834–48

2 If the spirit of the Reform Bill implies merely, a careful review of institutions, civil and ecclesiastical, undertaken in a friendly temper, combining, with the firm maintenance of established rights, the correction of proved abuses, and the redress of real grievances, – in that case, I can for myself and colleagues undertake to act in such a spirit and with such intentions.

Sir Robert Peel, Tamworth Manifesto, 18 Dec. 1834; *Memoirs* Vol.2 (1857) pp.58–67. This declaration marked the metamorphosis of the Tory Party into the Conservative Party, stating, as it did, a guarded acceptance of the consequences of the Reform Act (1832). Disraeli, then an unregenerate Tory, described it as 'an attempt to construct a party without principles' (Robert Blake *Disraeli* (1966) p.179).

3 Every penny bestowed that tends to render the condition of the pauper more eligible than that of the independent labourer is a bounty on indolence and vice.

Report of the Poor Law Commissioners, 1834, Para.206B. One of the earliest products of the 'Age of Reform' that followed the 1832 Act was the Whigs' Poor Law Act of 1834, which dealt with the widespread problem of poverty by imposing an extremely harsh workhouse regime on the country.

4 As regards the able-bodied labourers who apply for relief, giving them hard work at low wages by the piece, and exacting more work at a lower price than is paid for any other labour in the parish. In

short … to let the labourer find that the parish is the hardest taskmaster and the worst paymaster he can find, and thus induce him to make his application to the parish his last and not his first resort.

Principle of Poor Law administration adopted by the parish of Cookham, Berkshire; *Parliamentary Papers* for 1834 Vol.27, p.128.

5 Some two millions, it is now counted, sit in Workhouses, Poor-law prisons; or have 'outdoor relief' flung over the wall to them … their hopes, outlooks, share of this fair world, shut-in by narrow walls. They sit there, pent up, as in a kind of horrid enchantment; glad to be imprisoned and enchanted, that they may not perish starved.

Thomas Carlyle, *Past and Present*, Jan. 1843.

6 Since the steam engine has concentrated men into particular localities – has drawn together the population into dense masses – and since an imperfect education has enlarged and to some degree distorted their views, union is become easy and from being so closely packed, simultaneous action is readily excited. The organization of these working-class societies is now so complete that they form an empire within an empire of the most obnoxious description. Labour and capital are coming into collision – the operative and the master are at issue, and the peace and well being of the kingdom are at stake.

Peter Gaskell *The Manufacturing Population of England* (1833) p.6. Class war prophesied as a product of the industrial revolution.

7 Trade unions are for botching up the old system; Chartists are for a new one. Trade unions are for making the best of a bad bargain; Chartists are for a fresh one; and everyone must admit that trade unions partake of the tampering spirit of monopoly.

Bricklayer at a trade union conference, 1839; E.R. Wickham *Church and People in an Industrial City* (1957) p.102. A harsh verdict on the unions, which had suffered a body-blow with the transportation of the 'Tolpuddle martyrs', leaders of an agricultural union, in 1834. The recently founded Chartist movement demanded universal male suffrage, the secret ballot, annual parliaments and the payment of Members of Parliament, all in an attempt to move beyond the moderate compromise of the Reform Act of 1832.

8 [Christianity] renders the inequalities of the social scale less galling to the lower orders, whom she also instructs, in their turn, to be diligent, humble, patient; reminding them that their more lowly path has been allotted to them by the hand of God; that it is their part faithfully to discharge its duties, and contentedly to bear its inconveniences; that the present state of things is very short; that the objects about which worldly men conflict so eagerly are not worth the contest; that the peace of mind which religion offers indiscriminately to all ranks, affords more true satisfaction than all the expensive pleasures which are beyond the poor man's reach.

William Wilberforce *A Practical View* (1834) pp.301–2. Though radical on slavery, Wilberforce was deeply conservative on other issues, so much so that Francis Place could describe him as 'an ugly epitome of the devil' (Furneaux (1974) p.283).

1 They preached Christ and a crust, passive obedience and non-resistance. Let the people keep from those churches and chapels. Let them go to those men who preached Christ and a full belly, Christ and a well-clothed back – Christ and a good house to live in – Christ and universal suffrage.

Methodist local preacher at a Chartist meeting; the *Halifax Guardian*, 25 May 1839. The preacher was expelled from the Methodist Church for making this speech.

2 On one side we have an ill-used people suffering want, and thinking, justly, that if they had their rights the want would be relieved … On the other hand, what do the Whigs and Tories do? Madly refuse the people's rights, thereby convincing them that the democrats speak truly, and that aristocracy will yield nothing; that the people are lost if they trust to anything but arms. Madness on both sides.

Sir Charles Napier, 25 May 1839; Sir W. Napier *The Life and Opinions of General Sir Charles Napier* (1857).

3 I have great faith in the poor; to the best of my ability I always endeavour to present them in a favourable light to the rich; and I shall never cease, I hope, until I die, to advocate their being made as happy and as wise as the circumstances of their condition, in its utmost improvement, will admit of their becoming.

Charles Dickens to J.V. Staples, 3 April 1844; *The Letters of Charles Dickens* Vol.4 (1977) p.95.

4 We warn Wellington and Peel, we warn Toryism in general, against this young writer. If they had at their disposal the Bastilles and *lettres-de-cachet* of another day, we would advise their prompt application … There is that in them [Dickens's writings] all which is calculated to hasten on the great crisis of the English Revolution (speed the

hour!) far more effectively than any of the open assaults of Radicalism or Chartism.

United States Magazine and Democratic Review, April 1842. *Lettres-de-cachet* were royal orders for summary imprisonment or exile in the France of the old regime.

5 The Right Honourable gentleman caught the Whigs bathing and walked away with their clothes.

Benjamin Disraeli on Robert Peel, 28 Feb. 1845; *Parl. Deb.* Vol.48, Cols 154–5. Disraeli had broken with Peel, especially on the issue of abandoning the policy of protection. The agricultural interests of Tory landowners had been protected by tariffs on imported wheat imposed by the Corn Laws. The industrial middle class was now campaigning for the repeal of the Corn Laws in favour of free trade, and Peel was to bring about repeal, which many members of his party saw as an outright betrayal.

6 A Conservative government is an organized hypocrisy.

Benjamin Disraeli, 17 March 1845; *Parl. Deb.* Vol.78, Col.1028. A further barb aimed at Peel.

7 His smile was like the silver plate on a coffin.

The Irish political leader Daniel O'Connell on Peel; attrib. Peel, unlike Disraeli, was a stranger to charm.

8 I was told that the Privileged and the People formed Two Nations, governed by different laws, influenced by different manners, with no thoughts or sympathies in common; with an innate inability of mutual comprehension.

Benjamin Disraeli *Sybil* (1845) Bk 4, Ch.8. His novel was a manifesto for what became known as 'One-Nation' Toryism, or Tory Democracy, the political alliance of the upper and lower classes against the middle classes who formed the solid core of the future Liberal Party.

9 A bread-taxing oligarchy, a handful of swindlers, rapacious harpies, labour-plunderers, monsters of impiety, putrid and sensual *banditti*, titled felons, rich robbers, and blood-sucking vampires.

The robust political invective of the Anti-Corn Law League on the landed aristocracy; N. McCord *The Anti-Corn Law League* (1958) p.56.

10 I shall leave a name execrated by every monopolist … but it may be … sometimes remembered with expressions of goodwill in the abodes of those whose lot it is to labour and to earn their daily bread in the sweat of their brow.

Sir Robert Peel, 29 June 1846; *Parl. Deb.* Vol.87, Col.1055. Peel spoke after the passage of the act repealing the Corn Laws, which also destroyed his political career.

1 'We cannot regulate the demands for labour. No man or set of men can do it. It depends on events which God alone can control. When there is no market for our goods, we suffer just as much as you can do.' 'Not as much I'm sure, sir, though I'm not given to Political Economy; but I can use my eyes. I never see the masters getting thin and haggard for want of food.'

Elizabeth Gaskell *Mary Barton* (1847) Ch.37. Dialogue between a mill-owner and a worker on the realities of life in the 'Hungry Forties', as the decade of the 1840s in Britain was known. Mrs Gaskell's radical attitude towards the propertied class in this novel of industrial Manchester raised a storm of criticism among its reviewers.

2 Never was so grand and glorious Demonstration of loyalty of feeling. All ranks from the Duke to the artificer were associated together in this imposing Band of Special Constables. No French fraternity here. At no period in our history have the upper and middle classes been more united. Why have we been so wonderfully preserved while Europe has been convulsed to the centre? By the comparative sound-ness of our social system.

The politician W.S. Dugdale, diary entry, 11 April 1848. On 10 April the Chartists organized a huge protest meeting in London, but it turned out to be a damp squib, thanks largely to massive government countermeasures. Among the special constables recruited for the occasion was Prince Louis-Napoleon, future president of the French Second Republic and then emperor in the French Second Empire. 'No French fraternity here' alluded to a flat rejection of the revolutionary fervour that had gripped France since the revolution of February 1848 (see 557:3).

3 Anything is better than allowing such an evil as this to go on increasing. But if these multitudes of discontented men can be daunted into submission, fearful considerations remain behind. We have an enormous overgrown population, a vast proportion of which are in undeniable misery, and are soured and exasperated by their sufferings. To expect such beings to be reasonable, and still more to be logical, is to expect a moral impossibility.

Charles Greville on the aftermath of the Chartist demon-stration of 10 April; Christopher Hibbert (ed.) *Greville's England* (1981) p.218.

4 I thinks them Chartists are a weak-minded set; they was too much a-frightened at nothink, – a hundred o' them would run away from one blue-coat [policeman], and that wasn't like men. I was often at Chartist meetings, and if they'd do all they said there was a plenty to stick to them, for there's somethink wants to be done very bad, for everythink is a-getting worser and worser every day.

Henry Mayhew 'The Master Sweepers' in *London Labour and the London Poor* (1851); Peter Quennell *Mayhew's Characters* (1949) p.171.

5 We have shown the example of a nation, in which every class of society accepts with cheerfulness the lot which Providence assigned to it, while at the same time every individual of each class is constantly striving to raise himself in the social scale – not by injustice and wrong, not by violence and illegality, but by persevering good conduct, and by the steady and energetic execution of the moral and intellectual faculties with which his Creator has endowed him.

Lord Palmerston, 25 June 1850; *Parl. Deb.* Vol.112, Cols 443–4. Complacency, but justified complacency, on the collapse of Chartism.

6 We had obtained concessions of inestimable value, not by beating the drum, not by ringing the tocsin, not by tearing up the pavement, not by running to the gunsmith's shops to search for arms, but by the mere force of reason and public opinion.

Thomas Babington Macaulay, 2 Nov. 1852; *The Complete Writings of Lord Macaulay* Vol.18 (1900) p.171. The English 1848 in retrospect by the Whig of Whigs.

7 England, the country that turns whole nations into its proletarians ... seems to be the rock against which the revolutionary waves break, the country where the new society is stifled even in the womb ... Only a *world* war can overthrow the old England, as only this can provide the Chartists, the party of the organized English workers, with the conditions for a successful rising against their gigantic oppressors.

Karl Marx, *Neue Rheinische Zeitung*, 1 Jan. 1849.

THE IRISH QUESTION, 1780–1848

8 What has posterity done for us?

The Irish politician Sir Boyle Roche, 1780; attrib. Sir Boyle was speaking at a time when Ireland was demanding its own parlia-ment, in the wake of the revolt of the American colonies.

9 [Ireland has asserted] her liberty according to the form of the British Constitution, her inheritance to be enjoyed in perpetual connection with the British Empire ... Connected by freedom as well as by allegiance, the two nations, Great Britain and Ireland, form a constitutional confederation as well as an Empire ... The people of this kingdom have never expressed a desire to share the freedom of England without declaring a determination to share her fate likewise, standing or falling with the British nation.

Henry Grattan's Irish Declaration of Independence, 1782; William Lecky *History of Ireland in the Eighteenth Century* Vol.2 (1892) pp.300–1. As the quotation demonstrates, Grattan did not demand full independence but was content with the legislative autonomy that Britain conceded in 1782 when 'Grattan's Parliament' was established in Dublin.

1 What is Ireland but a secondary kingdom? An inferior member of a great empire without any movement or orbit of its own ... Where are our ambassadors? What treaties do we enter into? With what nation do we make peace or war? Are we not a mere cipher in all these, and are not these what give a nation consequence and fame? All these are sacrificed to the connection with England ... A suburb to England, we are sunk in her shade.

Sir Lawrence Parsons, 1790; Lecky Vol.3 (1892) p.7.

2 We have no National Government. We are ruled by Englishmen and the servants of Englishmen whose object is the interest of another country, whose instrument is corruption, whose strength is the weakness of Ireland.

The Irish patriot James Napper Tandy, 9 Nov. 1791, at the foundation of the Dublin Society of United Irishmen; Robert Kee *The Green Flag* (1972) p.53. A Belfast Society had been founded the previous month. The unity, short-lived, was between Protestant and Catholic Irishmen.

3 From Reflection, Interest, Prejudice, the spirit of Change, the misery of the great bulk of the nation and above all the hatred of the English name resulting from the Tyranny of near seven centurys, there seems little doubt but that an Invasion would be supported by the People.

Wolfe Tone, 1794; *Trial of the Rev. William Jackson* (1795) p.81. Jackson was a French agent sent to Ireland to explore the possibility of a French invasion. Arrested and condemned to death for high treason, he committed suicide in the dock on 30 April 1795. Tone took part in an abortive French invasion in 1798 and also committed suicide after his capture, on 19 Nov., to become one of the martyrs of Irish nationalism.

4   Oh, I met with Napper Tandy and he took me
          by the hand,
     And he says, how's poor oul' Ireland and how
          now does she stand?
     'Tis the most distressful country that ever yet
          was seen,

     For they're hanging men and women for the
          wearing of the green.

Song to commemorate the 1798 rebellion, which was mercilessly surpressed by the British; Kee (1972) p.47. In the wake of the rebellion, the Dublin parliament was abolished and the Act of Union passed in 1800, compelling Irish MPs to sit in the Parliament of Westminster.

5 The moment the very name of Ireland is mentioned, the English seem to bid adieu to common feeling, common prudence, and common sense, and to act with the barbarity of tyrants, and the fatuity of idiots.

Rev. Sydney Smith 'Peter Plymley's Letters' no.2; *The Works of the Rev. Sydney Smith* (1850 edn) p.492.

6 Let no man write my epitaph; for as no man who knows my motives dare now vindicate them, let not prejudice or ignorance asperse them. Let them rest in obscurity and peace, my memory left in oblivion and my tomb remain uninscribed, until other times and other men can do justice to my character. When my country takes her place among the nations of the earth, then and not till then let my epitaph be written.

Robert Emmet, 19 Sept. 1803; Raymond Postgate (ed.) *Revolution* (1931) p.305. Emmet led a rising in the summer of 1803 and was rapidly tried and executed. This is the famous conclusion of his speech after sentencing.

7 The voice of the nation must decide whether Protestantism or Popery shall prevail ... whether these kingdoms shall be at once the cradle and the citadel of Protestantism and real liberty, or the hotbed of Popery, with its scarlet train of mental and political despotism.

Duke of Newcastle, *Morning Post*, 18 Sept. 1828. The duke was reacting to the campaign for Catholic emancipation in the United Kingdom, which would have (to him) the dangerous effect of giving Irish Catholics the vote.

8 I would not ... 'fling British connexion to the winds'; I desire to retain it. I am sure that separation will not happen in my time; but I am equally sure that the connexion cannot continue if you maintain the Union on its present basis ... We only want a House of Commons, which you could place upon the same basis as your reformed parliament ... I call upon you to do my country justice. I call upon you to restore her national independence.

The Irish political leader Daniel O'Connell, 22 April 1834; *Parl. Deb.* Vol.22, Cols 1157, 1158. After achieving Catholic emancipation, O'Connell worked for the repeal of the Union of 1800 by constitutional means.

1 I feel and know that the Repeal [of the Union] must lead to the dismemberment of this great empire; must make Great Britain a fourth-rate power in Europe, and Ireland a savage wilderness.

Sir Robert Peel, April 1834; *Parl. Deb.* Vol.23, Col.70.

2 We are arrived at a stage of society, in which the peaceable combination of a people can easily render its wishes omnipotent.

Daniel O'Connell, 1840; T.W. Moody and F.X. Martin *The Course of Irish History* (1967) p.258. O'Connell continued to persist in the grossly optimistic belief that Britain would change its Irish policy in the face of political pressure rather than violence.

3   To do at once what is to do
       And trust OURSELVES ALONE.

The Irish nationalist journal *The Nation*, 3 Dec. 1842. 'Ourselves Alone' in Irish is *Sinn Féin*. The militant rejection of the moderate view that Ireland should cooperate with Britain in the quest for independence.

4 That dense population in extreme distress inhabits an island where there is an established Church which is not their Church and a territorial aristocracy the richest of whom live in distant capitals. Thus you have a starving population, an absentee aristocracy, and an alien Church, and in addition the weakest executive in the world. That is the Irish question.

Benjamin Disraeli, 1844; *Parl. Deb.* Vol.72, Col.1016.

5 Ireland! Ireland! That cloud in the west, that coming storm, the minister of God's retribution upon cruel and inveterate and but half-atoned injustice.

William Ewart Gladstone to his wife, Catherine, 12 Oct. 1845; Richard Shannon *Gladstone* Vol.1 (1982) p.183.

6 Their habitations are wretched hovels, several of a family sleep together upon straw or upon the bare ground ... Their food commonly consists of dry potatoes, and with these they are ... obliged to stint themselves to one spare meal in the day.

Report of the Commissioners for Inquiry into the Condition of the Poorer Classes in Ireland (1836) p.3. In Sept. 1845 blight caused a partial failure of the potato crop, and a second and worse failure followed in 1846, bringing a devastating famine to the country.

7 The only way to prevent the people from becoming habitually dependent on Government is to bring the operations to a close. The uncertainty about the new crop only makes it more necessary ... Whatever may be done hereafter, these things should be stopped now, or you run the risk of paralysing all private enterprise and having this country on you for an indefinite number of years.

Charles Trevelyan, assistant secretary of the Treasury, to Sir Randolph Routh, commissary general in Ireland, 17 and 21 July 1846. Trevelyan, with his eye on the budget, recommends the closure of relief agencies at a time when famine was taking hold with a vengeance.

8 Six famished and ghastly skeletons, to all appearances dead, were huddled in a corner on some filthy straw, their sole covering what seemed a ragged horsecloth, their wretched legs hanging about, naked above the knees. I approached with horror, and found by a low moaning they were alive – they were in fever, four children, a woman and what had once been a man.

Nicholas Cummins, *The Times*, 24 Dec. 1846, on his visit to the village of Skibbereen on 15 Dec.

9 I hold it to be a more hideous national calamity for ten men to be cast out to die of hunger, like dogs in ditches, than for ten thousand to be hewn to pieces, fighting like men and Christians in defence of their rights.

John Mitchel, *The United Irishman*, 12 Feb. 1848.

10 If the peasants do take to arms they'll be faced by England's disciplined soldiery and end as corpses on their native fields, or, if they did manage to have a local success, on the gibbet ... But even if that were not so, where are your peasantry? – sicklied, hungry, wasted, exiled or in their graves. If you want to arm – I tell you your best chance – go to Skibbereen, re-animate the corpses that are huddled there and bid them arm.

Michael Doheny, *The Nation*, 5 Feb. 1848. Doheny became a founder-member in 1858 of the Irish Republican Brotherhood (the Fenians).

11 If we are no slaves and braggarts, unworthy of liberty, Ireland will be free before the coming summer fades into winter ... All over the world – from the frozen swamps of Canada to the rich corn-fields of Sicily – in Italy, in Denmark, in Prussia and in glorious France, men are up for their rights.

Gavan Duffy, *The Nation*, 4 March 1848. The Irish struggle seen as at one with the universal upsurge in the 'year of revolutions', but famine-stricken Ireland was in no condition to enter the revolutionary fray.

STALEMATE, 1850–65

1 If this or any Free Trade Government *then* acquire a majority, the game is up; and I firmly believe we shall be in a rapid progress towards a republic in name as well as in reality ... We are falling into the fatal sleep which precedes mortification and death.
Lord Derby to John Wilson Croker, 1850; O.F. Christie *The Transition from Aristocracy 1832–1867* (1927) p.60.

2 The Queen leads the Nation, and landlords in a similar manner lead their tenants ... I expect of my tenants that they shall not engage their votes before they have communicated with me and come to know my wishes.
Sir Charles Monck, 1852; R.J. Olney *Lincolnshire Politics 1832–1885* (1973) p.35.

3 I say that for men who are charged with the high and important duty of choosing the best man to represent the country in Parliament, to go sneaking to the ballot-box and, poking in a piece of paper, looking around to see that no one could read it, is a course which is unconstitutional and unworthy of the character of a straightforward and honest Englishman.
Lord Palmerston, July 1852; Jasper Ridley *Lord Palmerston* (1970) p.404.

4 The poor have come out of leading strings, and cannot any longer be governed or treated like children ... Whatever advice, exhortation, or guidance is held out to the labouring classes, must henceforth be tendered to them as equals, and accepted by them with their eyes open. The prospect of the future depends on the degree in which they can be made rational beings ... It will sooner or later become insupportable to the employing classes to live in close and hourly contact with persons whose interests and feelings are in hostility to them.
John Stuart Mill *The Principles of Political Economy* (1852).

5 Mostly unused to arms, utterly untrained and undisciplined, without sufficient dependence on themselves or one another, the working-classes of this country are in every way unfit for rebellion.

They are equally unfit for the passive resistance which might answer as well as action.
The Northern Tribune, Jan. 1854, p.38.

6 As for Parliamentary Reform I hold that we might as well call out for the millennium.
Richard Cobden to George Wilson, 23 Sept. 1856; D.G. Wright *Democracy and Reform 1815–1885* (1970) p.127.

7 I have not the smallest doubt that if we had a purely democratic government here ... either the poor would plunder the rich, and civilization would perish; or order and property would be saved by a strong military government, and liberty would perish.
Thomas Babington, Lord Macaulay to the American Henry Stephens Randall, 23 May 1857; Thomas Pinney (ed.) *The Letters of Thomas Babington Macaulay* Vol.6 (1981) pp.94–5.

8 Of course we cannot certainly *know* what the lowest classes of England would do if they were placed in power, for we have not tried. The experiment, unfortunately, is a nervous one to make, for if it fails it cannot be retraced. Political power that has descended from a higher class in a society to a lower, is never yielded back except to a despot.
Lord Robert Cecil 'The Theories of Parliamentary Reform' in *Oxford Essays* (1858). The ultra-conservative Cecil was to become prime minister as Lord Salisbury.

9 It is every day becoming more clearly understood, that the function of Government is negative and restrictive, rather than positive and active; being resolvable principally into protection – protection of life, liberty, and property ... Indeed all experience serves to prove that all the worth and strength of a State depends far less upon the form of its institutions than upon the character of its men ... The healthy spirit of self-help created amongst working people would more than any other measure serve to raise them as a class, and this, not by pulling down others, but by levelling them up to a higher and still advancing standard of religion, intelligence, and virtue.
Samuel Smiles *Self-Help* (1859). This book became the bible of mid-Victorian liberalism with its doctrine of minimalist action on the part of the state and reliance on individualism to bring about improvement.

10 I am for peace, retrenchment, and for reform – thirty years ago the great watchwords of the great Liberal Party.
The veteran radical, John Bright, 28 April 1859. The phrase was first used by William IV, on opening parliament on

17 Nov. 1830, when the Whig administration of Earl Grey took office.

1 I say, all these fancy franchises are absurd … proposed and intended to make it appear that you are giving something, when they really spring from the fear you have lest you should give something.
John Bright, 28 Feb. 1859; *Parl. Deb.* Vol.152, Col.1025. Bright was criticizing a Conservative reform bill that had been introduced that day, including a complex variety of franchises that widened the electorate but fell well short of universal suffrage. It was defeated in the Commons and the 1832 Act remained in force.

2 He is not frivolous enough for me; if he were soaked in boiling water … I do not suppose a single drop of fun would ooze out.
Emily Eden to Lord Clarendon, 1860, on Gladstone; Herbert Maxwell *Life of the Fourth Earl of Clarendon* Vol.2 (1913) p.224. A worthy successor to Peel? See 607:7.

3 I venture to say that every man who is not presumably incapacitated by some consideration of personal unfitness or of political danger is morally entitled to come within the pale of the Constitution.
William Ewart Gladstone on universal suffrage, 11 May 1864; *Parl. Deb.* Vol.175, Col.324. This speech was taken – wrongly – as a statement that Gladstone was committed to democracy.

4 No doubt many working men are as fit to vote as many of the Ten Pounders, but if we open the Door to the Class, the Number who may come in may be excessive and may swamp the Classes above them.
Lord Palmerston to Gladstone, 11 May 1864; Philip Guedalla *Gladstone and Palmerston* (1928) p.280. 'Ten pounders' were householders owning property with a rateable value of at least £10 a year, a provision set up in 1832.

5 He is a dangerous man; keep him in Oxford, and he is partially muzzled; but send him elsewhere, and he will run wild.
Lord Palmerston on Gladstone; Shannon (1982) p.544. Gladstone was MP for Oxford University, a bastion of traditional politics.

6 At last, my friends, I am come amongst you. And I am come … 'unmuzzled'.
William Ewart Gladstone to the electors of South Lancashire, 18 July 1865; Shannon (1982) p.546. Gladstone had lost his Oxford seat in the 1865 election and moved to South Lancashire. This speech, too, was taken as a sign that Gladstone was in favour of one man, one vote, but a close reading does not bear this out. With Palmerston's death the following October, however, the way was open for Gladstone to become leader of the Liberal Party and a new political era began.

America and the World, 1783–1914

EAGLE ASCENDING, 1816–1910

1 In Latin America dominance, in the Far East cooperation, in Europe abstention.
Captain Alfred Thayer Mahan's prescription for US world policy at the end of the 19th century. An accurate reflection of the status of the United States vis-à-vis other states in each region: in Latin America, a colossus; in the Far East, an equal; in Europe, a spectator.

2 Our country! In her intercourse with foreign nations, may she always be in the right; but our country, right or wrong.
Commodore Stephen Decatur, US navy, toasting the company at a dinner in his honour, April 1816; A.S. Mackenzie *Life of Stephen Decatur* (1848) p.295. Decatur had recently completed a successful campaign against the Barbary pirates of North Africa.

3 There are today two great peoples on the earth who, setting off from different points of departure, seem to be advancing towards the same goal: they are the Russians and the Anglo-Americans … Each of them seems to be summoned by a secret plan of Providence one day to hold in its hands the destinies of half the world.
Alexis de Tocqueville *Democracy in America* (1835) Bk 1, Pt 2, Ch.10. A famous early prediction of Russo-American ascendancy.

4 There is not a nation upon earth which, in fifty years, can by all possible reformation place itself in circumstances so favorable as our own for the free, unembarrassed applications of physical effort and pecuniary and moral power to evangelize the world.
Lyman Beecher *A Plea for the West* (1835) p.10.

5 All the armies of Europe, Asia and Africa combined, with all the treasure of the earth (our own excepted) in their military chest; with a Buonaparte for a commander, could not by force take a drink from the Ohio or make a track on the Blue Ridge in a trial of a thousand years.
Abraham Lincoln, 21 Jan. 1838; *The Collected Works of Abraham Lincoln* Vol.1 (1953) p.109.

6 We have at length reached the condition of one of the great Powers of the earth, and yet we are but in the infancy of our career … The man is still living,

who will live to see one hundred and fifty millions of people, free, prosperous, and intelligent, swaying the destinies of this country, and exerting a mighty influence upon those of the world.
Senator Lewis Cass, 10 Feb. 1852; *Congressional Globe*, App.162c.

7 That the United States are bound finally to absorb all the world and the rest of mankind, every well-regulated American mind is prepared to admit.
San Francisco *Alta California*, 3 Feb. 1869.

8 By 1980 the world Anglo-Saxon race should number at least 713,000,000. Since North America is much bigger than the little English isle, it will be the seat of Anglo-Saxondom … If the consummation of human progress is not to be looked for here, if there is yet to flower a higher civilization, where is the soil that is to produce it?
Rev. Josiah Strong *Our Country* (1885) p.168. The Congregationalist minister Strong was in his day the leading American spokesman of Social Darwinism, the doctrine of 'the survival of the fittest'. Because of its 20th-century embrace of contraception, his forecast of the global tally of Anglo-Saxondom proved a serious overestimate.

9 The great nations are rapidly absorbing for their future expansion and their present defense, all the waste places of the earth. It is a movement which makes for civilization and the advancement of the race. As one of the great nations of the world the United States must not fall out of the line of march.
Senator Henry Cabot Lodge, *Forum*, March 1895, pp.8–17. The Boston Brahmin Lodge emerged as an arch-nationalist in the generation that saw the United States become a world power.

10 We are penetrating into Europe, and Great Britain especially is gradually assuming the position of a dependency … The United States will outweigh any single empire, if not all empires combined. The whole world will pay her tribute. Commerce will flow to her from east and west, and the order which has existed from the dawn of time will be reversed.
Brooks Adams *The New Empire* (1902).

11 There is nothing even remotely resembling 'imperialism' or 'militarism' involved in the present development of that policy of expansion which has

been part of the history of America from the day when she became a nation.
President Theodore Roosevelt, 1901; Christopher Thorne *Allies of a Kind* (1979 edn) pp.21–2.

1 The old nations of the earth creep on at a snail's pace; the Republic thunders past with the rush of the express. The United States, the growth of a single century, has already reached the foremost rank among nations, and is destined soon to outdistance all others in the race.
Andrew Carnegie *Triumphant Democracy* (1902) p.1. An immigrant from Scotland, Carnegie rose to be one of the most powerful industrialists in the USA, making a huge fortune in steel, much of which he later disbursed through various philanthropies.

2 In fact, we ourselves are becoming, owing to our strength and geographical situation, more and more the balance of power of the whole world.
Former president Theodore Roosevelt to Hermann von Eckardstein, 1910; Beale (1954) p.447.

SOUTH OF THE BORDER, 1786–1914

3 Our confederacy must be viewed as the nest from which All America, North and South, is to be peopled. We should take care too not to think it for the interest of that great continent to press too soon on the Spaniards. Those countries cannot be in better hands. My fear is that they are too feeble to hold them till our population can be sufficiently advanced to gain it from them piece by piece.
Thomas Jefferson to Archibald Stuart, 25 Jan. 1786; *Papers of Thomas Jefferson* Vol.9 (1954) p.218. Jefferson, then US minister to France, feared that Britain would move in first as patron of the successor-states of the Spanish empire.

4 I do not hesitate to say that the moment we acknowledge them, they will adopt every feature of our government and constitution, and such is the idea which they have of the justice, wisdom, and disinterestedness of our country, that they will be guided by our advice in everything.
Henry Brackenridge to Henry Clay, 3 March 1816; *Papers of Henry Clay* Vol.2, p.446. Brackenridge, successively church-man, judge and nationalistic writer, was corresponding with Clay, Speaker of the House of Representatives, later senator for Kentucky and would-be presidential nominee (see 624:5).

5 The day is not distant when we may formally require a meridian of partition thro' the ocean which separates the two hemispheres, on the hither side of which no European gun shall ever be heard, nor an American on the other, and when during the eternal wars of Europe, the lion and the lamb within our regions shall lie down together in peace.
Thomas Jefferson to William Short, 4 Aug. 1820; *Writings of Thomas Jefferson* Vol.15, p.263. The Monroe Doctrine adumbrated (see 614:7 and 618:8).

6 It is scarcely possible to resist the conviction that the annexation of Cuba to our federal republic will be indispensable to the continuance and integrity of the Union itself. It is obvious … that for this event we are not yet prepared … but there are laws of political, as well as physical gravitation, and if an apple, severed by the tempest from its native tree, cannot but choose but fall to the ground, Cuba, forcibly disjoined from its own unnatural connec-tion with Spain, and incapable of self-support, can gravitate only toward the North American Union, which, by the same law of nature, cannot cast her off from its bosom.
Secretary of state John Quincy Adams to Hugh Nelson, 28 April 1823; *Instructions to United States Ministers* Vol.9, pp.183 ff. Nelson was US minister to Spain. Jefferson had seen Cuba as 'the most interesting addition that would ever be made to our system' and in 1808 made overtures to Spain to buy it.

7 We owe it … to candor and to the amicable relations existing between the United States and those [European] Powers to declare that we should consider any attempt on their part to extend their system to any portion of this hemisphere, as dangerous to our peace and safety. With the existing colonies or dependencies of any European Power we have not interfered and shall not interfere. But with the Governments who have declared their indepen-dence and maintained it, and whose independence we have, on great consideration and on just prin-ciples, acknowledged, we could not view any inter-position for the purpose of oppressing them or controlling in any other manner their destiny, by any European Power in any other light than as the manifestation of an unfriendly disposition toward the United States.
President James Monroe, message to Congress, 2 Dec. 1823; James D. Richardson (ed.) *Messages and Papers of the Presidents* Vol.2 (1896) pp.209 ff. This famous declaration later became known as the Monroe Doctrine and constituted the basis of US Latin American policy throughout and beyond this period.

1 The United States appear to be destined by Providence to plague America with misery in the name of liberty.

Simón Bolívar, attrib. The greatest of the founding fathers of Spanish American independence, Bolívar wished the new republics to develop without reference to the United States. 'America' to him is '*América*', that is, Hispanic America (see 545:4).

2 The more the American population is increased, the more readily will the Mexican Government give it up. A gentle breeze shakes off a ripe peach. Can it be supposed that the violent political convulsions of Mexico will not shake off Texas so soon as it is ripe to fall?

Stephen Austin, promoter of the secession of Texas from Mexico in 1836 and its adherence to the United States in 1845, speaking in the early 1830s; Geoffrey C. Ward *The West* (1996) p.68.

3 FELLOW-CITIZENS, I am besieged by a thousand or more Mexicans, under Santa Anna … The enemy have demanded a surrender at discretion, otherwise the garrison is to be put to the sword, if the fort is taken. I have answered the demand with a cannon shot, and our flag still waves proudly from the walls. *I shall never surrender nor retreat …* VICTORY OR DEATH.

Lieutenant Colonel W. Barrett Travis, 24 Feb. 1836. Travis was commander of the small band of secessionist Texans and their sympathizers in the Alamo fortress, which was taken by the Mexicans under their general Santa Anna, on 6 March 1836, when the entire garrison was wiped out after an epic last stand.

4 Remember the Alamo!

Battle-cry of the Texan leader Sam Houston at San Jacinto, 21 April 1836, when the Texans defeated and slaughtered Mexican troops as comprehensively as the Mexicans had annihilated the defenders of the Alamo the previous month.

5 Other nations have undertaken to intrude themselves … for the avowed object of thwarting our policy and hampering our power, limiting our greatness and checking the fulfilment of our manifest destiny to overspread the continent allotted by Providence for the free development of our yearly multiplying millions … Whatsoever may hold the balance, though they should cast into the opposite scale all the bayonets and cannon, not only of France and England, but of Europe entire, how would it kick the beam against the simple solid weight of the two hundred and fifty or three hundred millions –

and American millions – destined to gather beneath the flutter of the stripes and stars, in the fast hastening year of the Lord 1945?

John O'Sullivan, *United States Magazine and Democratic Review*, July-Aug. 1845. A famous pronouncement, 'Manifest Destiny' became the rallying-cry of US Latin American policy in the imminent war with Mexico and again half a century later come the war with Spain.

6 The Mexicans are in the condition of those whom God seeks to destroy having first made mad. They are doing their best to compel us to conquer them, It is now impossible that it should be otherwise. Mark my words – our people will never surrender an inch of soil they have won. They are too certainly of the Anglo-Norman breed for that.

The Southern writer William Gilmore Simms to Senator James H. Hammond, 1847; Edmund Wilson *Patriotic Gore* (1962) p.xv. The United States declared war on Mexico on 12 May 1846 after an attack on US forces by Mexican troops, depicted by the US government as an act of aggression.

7 The race is perfectly accustomed to being conquered, and the only lesson we shall teach is that our victories will give liberty, safety, and prosperity to the vanquished, if they know enough to profit by the appearance of our stars. To *liberate* and *ennoble* – not to *enslave* and *debase* – is our mission.

Moses Y. Beach, *New York Sun*, 22 Oct. 1847. Beach owned the *Sun*.

8 If I were a Mexican I would tell you, 'Have you not enough room in your own country to bury your dead men? If you come into mine, I will greet you with bloody hands and welcome you to hospitable graves.'

Senator Thomas Cousin, 11 Feb. 1846.

9 Such a war of conquest … must be regarded as a war against freedom, against humanity, against justice, against the Union, against the Constitution, and against the Free States … All good citizens [should aid] the country to retreat from the disgraceful position of aggression which it now occupies towards a weak, distracted neighbor and sister republic.

Charles Sumner's resolution put to the Massachusetts legislature in 1847. Sumner, a leading campaigner for the abolition of slavery, saw the war partly as a bid to extend slavery into the territory taken from Mexico; so it proved.

10 Under our government it would speedily be *Americanized*, as Louisiana has been … Cuba, justly appreciating the advantages of an annexation, is now ready to rush into our arms. Once admitted, she would be entirely dependent for her prosperity, and even existence, upon her connexion with the Union.

Secretary of state James Buchanan to Romulus M. Saunders, minister to Spain, 17 June 1848; Ruhl J. Bartlett *The Record of American Diplomacy* (1964 edn) p.236. This dispatch was sent almost immediately after ratification of the treaty ending the war with Mexico, whereby the United States acquired half the territory of Mexico, comprising the future states of New Mexico, Arizona, Nevada, Utah and California. Buchanan was proposing the purchase of Cuba from Spain for $100 million, a huge sum compared with previous payments (Mexico was given $15 million for the territory it lost; Louisiana was bought for $15 million). Spain rejected the offer outright.

1 The other nations of America consider themselves subjected to this species of protectorate which they have not asked for, and which must not be imposed on them by force. Such guardianship is highly injurious to the rights of those nations whose inherent sovereignty and independence are conceded.

The Latin American Minister Irissari to the secretary of state, William March, 19 May 1856; Philip S. Foner *A History of Cuba* Vol.2 (1963) pp.110–11.

2 All these evils became negligible with the swollen torrents of shysters who came from Missouri and other states of the Union ... These legal thieves, clothed in the robes of the law, took from us our lands and our houses, and without the least scruple enthroned themselves in our houses like so many powerful kings. For them existed no law but their own will and caprice that recognized its right by that of force.

Californian Mariano Guadalupe Vallejo, whose estate under American rule in the 1850s was reduced from a quarter of a million acres to fewer than 300 acres; Ward (1996) p.152.

3 Napoleon has no right to Mexico. Mexico may deserve a licking. That is possible enough. Most people do. But nobody has any right to lick Mexico except the United States. We have a right, I flatter myself, to lick the entire continent, including ourselves, any time we want to.

'Artemus Ward' *Artemus Ward among the Mormons* (1865). Ward (real name Charles Farrar Browne) was a humorist; here, he was not being funny. Taking advantage of the US Civil War, the French emperor, Napoleon III, launched an intervention in Mexico to install the Austrian Archduke Maximilian as head of state. The expedition was a disaster, and Maximilian died before a Mexican firing squad on 19 June 1867.

4 Poor Mexico! So far from God, so close to the United States!

Porfirio Díaz, president of Mexico from 1877; attrib.

5 I look to Porfirio Díaz, the president of Mexico, as one of the great men to be held up to the hero worship of mankind.

Elihu Root, Theodore Roosevelt's secretary of state from 1905 to 1909; Lesley Bird Simpson *Many Mexicos* (1967) p.292. A florid tribute to a leader who, despite whatever his private feelings may have been, normally upheld the interests of the United States in Mexico during his long tenure of office, ended only by his deposition in 1911, after the outbreak of the Mexican Revolution, when he was 80 years old.

6 To control at the Isthmus we must have a very large Navy – and we must begin to build as soon as the first spadeful of earth is turned at Panama. That this will be done I don't for a moment hope, but unless it is we may as well shut up about the Monroe Doctrine at once.

Captain Alfred Thayer Mahan to Samuel Ashe, 12 March 1880; Robert Seager III *Alfred Thayer Mahan* (1977) p.122. In 1879 the French builder of the Suez Canal, Ferdinand de Lesseps, bought a concession to construct a canal through the Isthmus of Panama. Mahan, an ultra-nationalist, saw this as a direct challenge to the Monroe Doctrine's denial of further European penetration in the Americas, but the naval expansion he sought did not begin until the late 1890s.

7 During any war in which the United States of America or the United States of Colombia might be a party, the passage of armed vessels of a hostile nation through the canal at Panama would be no more admissible than would the passage of the armed forces of a hostile nation over the railway lines joining the Atlantic and Pacific shores of the United States or of Colombia ... The United States seeks only to use for the defense of its own coasts the same forecast and prevision which Her Majesty's Government so energetically employs in the defense of the British Empire [through] the mastery of the Mediterranean [and] a controlling interest in the Suez Canal.

James G. Blaine to James R. Lowell, US minister in London, 24 June 1881 and 19 Nov. 1881; *Papers Relating to the Foreign Relations of the United States* (1882) pp.538–9, 555. Blaine, the secretary of state, was protesting at Britain's refusal to give up the right it shared with the United States to control an isthmian canal under the Clayton-Bulwer Treaty of 1850, when since 1875 it had effectively held a monopoly over the Suez Canal. Colombia, by a treaty of 1846, was the ally of the United States, which guaranteed its sovereignty.

1 It surely needs no prophetic eye to see the civilization of the *United States* is to be the civilization of America, and that the future of the continent is ours.
Rev. Josiah Strong *Our Country* (1885) p.167. Strong, like Bolívar (see 546:3), means by 'America', the Americas. A Congregationalist minister, he was one of the most celebrated ultra-nationalists of his day.

2 From the tyranny of Spain Spanish America knew how to free itself; and now the hour for Spanish America to declare its second independence has arrived … Only a unanimous and strong reply … can liberate the Spanish American peoples from … the … policy of a powerful and ambitious neighbour, which has never wished to further their interests, nor turned to them except to hinder their extension, as in Panama, or to take possession of their territory, as in Mexico, Nicaragua, Santo Domingo, Haiti and Cuba, or to cut off their dealings with the rest of the Universe, as in Colombia, or to oblige them, as at the present time, to buy what they cannot sell and to confederate for its domination.
José Martí , 2 Nov. 1889; *Collected Works* Vol.2, pp.129–39. Martí, a Cuban nationalist, was writing soon after the opening of the first International Conference of American States in Washington. Here, Blaine proposed a permanent organization of all the states of the hemisphere, which Martí saw as an attempt to institutionalize US hegemony over Latin America, as already exemplified in the various instances he cites. The organization came into being, with its headquarters in the US capital, so located, according to some observers, that the shadow of the nearby Washington Monument passed across it every day!

3 Today the United States is practically sovereign on this continent, and its fiat is law upon subjects to which it confines its interposition. Why? It is not because of the pure friendship or good will felt for it. It is not simply by reason of its high character as a civilized state, nor because wisdom and justice and equity are the invariable characteristics of the dealings of the United States. It is because, in addition to all other grounds, its infinite resources combined with its isolated position render it master of the situation and practically invulnerable as against any or all other powers.
Richard Olney to the US ambassador in London, Thomas F. Bayard, 18 May 1895; Bartlett (1964 edn) pp.344–5. Olney, the secretary of state, was categorically (not to say brutally) asserting the right of the United States to determine the boundary between Venezuela and the colony of British Guiana, a right denied in principle by Britain, which was, however, in practice powerless to resist it.

4 I have lived in the bowels of the beast and I know it from the inside.
José Martí to Manuel Mercado, 18 May 1895. Martí was in Cuba to begin a revolt against Spain, but here he refers to the United States, where he had lived, mostly in New York, for over a decade, in an accurate foreboding that the American government would move in to wrest Cuba from Spain itself. This was his last, unfinished letter; he was killed in a Spanish ambush the next day.

5 PLEASE REMAIN. YOU FURNISH PICTURES. I WILL FURNISH WAR.
William Randolph Hearst, owner of the *New York Journal*, telegram to the artist Frederic Remington, March 1898; L. Snyder and R. Morris (eds) *A Treasury of Great Reporting* (1962) p.236. Perhaps apocryphal, but Hearst, if not instigating war with Spain, certainly looked forward to it, not least for its impact on the circulation of the *Journal*. The quotation features in Orson Welles's film *Citizen Kane* (1941), a diaphanously veiled portrait of Hearst.

6 Stout hearts, my laddies! If the row comes, REMEMBER THE MAINE, and show the world how American sailors fight.
Clifford Berryman, caption underneath cartoon in the *Washington Post*, 3 April 1898. The US navy battleship *Maine* blew up in the harbour of Havana, Cuba, on 15 Feb. 1898, and the United States used the incident as a reason for declaring war on Spain on 25 April.

7 The United States hereby disclaims any disposition or intention to exercise sovereignty, jurisdiction, or control over said Island except for the pacification thereof, and asserts its determination, when that is accomplished, to leave the government and control of the Island to its people.
Teller Amendment on Cuba, 16 April 1898; *Congressional Record*, 16 April 1898, pp.3988–9. This self-denying ordinance, proposed by Senator Henry Moore Teller, was to be superseded by the blank cheque of the Platt Amendment of 2 March 1901 (see 618:1).

8 Don't cheer, boys – the poor devils are dying.
John W. Philip USN, speaking of the crew of a crippled Spanish cruiser in the Battle of Santiago, 3 July 1898, the decisive naval engagement that effectively ended the war.

9 It has been a splendid little war, begun with the highest motives, carried on with magnificent intelligence and spirit, favored by that Fortune which loves the brave.
Secretary of state John Hay to Theodore Roosevelt, 27 July 1898; William Roscoe Thayer *The Life and Letters of John Hay* Vol.2 (1915) p.337.

1 The government of Cuba consents that the United States may exercise the right to intervene for the preservation of Cuban independence [and] the maintenance of a government adequate for the protection of life, property, and individual liberty.
Third provision of the so-called Platt Amendment of 2 March 1901, written by secretary of war Elihu Root, introduced by Senator Orville Platt and subsequently written into the Cuban Constitution of 1903; Bartlett (1964 edn) p.536. In force until its abrogation in 1934.

2 We had found a baby on our doorstep and the spirit of fatherhood required that we should put it asleep o' nights and provide for its maintenance.
Representative Joseph Cannon, Speaker of the House of Representatives, opining on Cuba during a Congressional junket thereto in March 1907; J. Hampton Moore *With Speaker Cannon through the Tropics* (1907) p.305.

3 I have always been fond of the West African proverb: 'Speak softly and carry a big stick; you will go far.'
Governor of New York Theodore Roosevelt, 1899; G. Wallace Chessman *Theodore Roosevelt and the Politics of Power* (1969) p.70.

4 The Republic of Panama grants to the United States the rights, power and authority within the zone … which the United States would possess and exercise if it were the sovereign of the territory … to the entire exclusion of the exercise by the Republic of Panama of any such sovereign rights, power or authority.
Article 3 of the Canal Convention between the United States and Panama, 18 November 1903. The article was drafted by the Frenchman Philippe Bunau-Varilla, who had been an engineer on the de Lesseps project in the 1880s. The convention was signed barely a fortnight after Panama had seceded from Colombia with the connivance of the United States, which in 1846 had agreed by treaty to guarantee Colombia's national sovereignty. The zone referred to was a 10-mile-wide strip of land centred on the line of the future Panama Canal. When the Panamanian treaty negotiators arrived to find that their heartland had been alienated in their absence one of them swooned on the spot.

5 The crisis came at a period when I could act unhampered. Accordingly I took the Isthmus, started the canal, and then left Congress – not to debate the canal, but to debate me.
Former President Theodore Roosevelt, speech at the Berkeley campus of the University of California, 23 March 1911; John Major *Prize Possession: The United States and the Panama Canal 1903–1979* (1993) p.63. Most often misquoted as 'I took the Canal'.

6 We stole it fair and square.
The eminent philologist Professor Samuel Hayakawa, playing dextrously with words during his successful campaign to become a senator for California in 1976.

7 The inevitable effect of our building the canal must be to require us to police the surrounding premises … In that region … the United States must exercise a dominant influence. It is there that the true justification and necessity of the Monroe Doctrine is to be found.
Secretary of state Elihu Root; Philip Jessup *Elihu Root* Vol.1 (1938) p.471.

8 Chronic wrongdoing, or an impotence which results in a general loosening of the ties of civilized society, may in America, as elsewhere, ultimately require intervention by some civilized nation, and in the Western Hemisphere the adherence of the United States to the Monroe Doctrine may force the United States, however reluctantly, in flagrant cases of such wrongdoing or impotence, to the exercise of an international police power.
President Theodore Roosevelt, annual message to Congress, 6 Dec. 1904, known as the Roosevelt Corollary to the Monroe Doctrine; Bartlett (1964 edn) p.539. This assertion was prompted by Anglo-German action against Venezuela in 1903 on behalf of creditors on whose loans Venezuela had defaulted. Intended to block any further European interference in the hemisphere, it was subsequently used as the justification for several US interventions against financially unsound regimes in Central America.

9 Some time soon I shall have to spank some little brigand of a South American republic.
President Theodore Roosevelt to Douglas Robinson, 31 Aug. 1905; Elting Morison (ed.) *The Letters of Theodore Roosevelt* Vol. 4 (1951).

10 Dollar Diplomacy.
This famous phrase first appeared in *Harper's Weekly*, 23 April 1910; its exegesis follows.

11 When an American republic is on the brink of bankruptcy, no friendlier or politically wiser action could be taken by the United States than to seek, through the instrumentalities of American capital, by one stroke to remove all question of European intervention, and at the same time to start the country concerned upon the road to progress, peace and prosperity.
Editorial in the *Washington Post*, Jan. 1911.

12 If you hear of my being stood up against a Mexican stone wall and shot to rags, please know that I think that a pretty good way to depart this life. It beats old age, disease or falling down the cellar stairs. To be a Gringo in Mexico – ah, that is euthanasia.

Ambrose Bierce to his niece, 1913. The writer Bierce, then aged 71, went to Mexico to join the revolution which broke out in 1910 and may have been killed in a battle in Jan. 1914.

1 This government would have on its hands what in reality would be a war of conquest of a people animated by the most intense hatred for the conquering race. History has a sufficient number of instances of this kind of conflict to demonstrate that such work is not child's play.

James Reuben Clark of the State Department, 26 Feb. 1912, on the inadvisability of intervening in the Mexican Revolution; P. Edward Haley *Revolution and Intervention* (1970) p.41.

2 It must be a cause of grief that what is probably the most dramatic story in which an American diplomatic officer has ever been involved should be a story of sympathy with treason, perfidy and assassination in an assault on constitutional government.

William B. Hale, 28 June 1913; Haley (1970) p.95. The journalist Hale was President Woodrow Wilson's personal representative in Mexico, investigating the role of the US ambassador, Henry Lane Wilson, in the assassination of the Mexican president, Francisco Madero, on 22 Feb. 1913. Lane Wilson was dismissed by the president for his implication in the murder.

3 The future ... is going to be very different for this hemisphere from the past ... We must show ourselves friends [to the Latin American states] by comprehending their interest whether it squares with our own interest or not.

President Woodrow Wilson, speech of 27 Oct. 1913; *The Papers of Woodrow Wilson* Vol.28 (1978) pp.448, 450. In practice, Wilson was more interventionist than any president since Polk, the victor of Mexico in the war of 1846.

4 I am going to teach the South American republics to elect good men.

President Woodrow Wilson, 1913; Harley Notter *The Origins of the Foreign Policy of Woodrow Wilson* (1937) p.274.

5 My ideal is an orderly and righteous government in Mexico; but my passion is for the submerged 85 per cent of the people of that republic who are now struggling toward liberty.

President Woodrow Wilson, 27 April 1914, in an interview published in the *Saturday Evening Post* on 23 May 1914. Wilson intervened militarily in Mexico on 21 April 1914 by having US forces seize the port of Veracruz.

ACROSS THE PACIFIC, 1783–1912

6 Navigation will carry the American flag around the globe itself; and display the Thirteen Stripes and New Constellation at Bengal and Canton ... and with commerce will import the wisdom and literature of the east ... A time will come when six hundred millions of the human race shall be ready to drop their idolatry ... should American missionaries be blessed to succeed in the work of Christianizing the heathen, in which the Romanists and foreign Protestants have very much failed, it would be an unexpected wonder, and a great honor, to the *United States.*

Ezra Stiles, president of Yale University, May 1783; Richard Van Alstyne *The Genesis of American Nationalism* (1970) p.59.

7 The American road to India will also become the European track to that region. The European merchant, as well as the American, will fly across our continent on a straight line to China. The rich commerce of Asia will flow through our center ... In no instance has it [the Asiatic trade] failed to carry the nation, or the people who possessed it, to the highest pinnacle of wealth and power, and with it the highest attainments of letters, arts, and sciences.

Senator Thomas Hart Benton, 7 Feb. 1849; *Congressional Globe.* In commissioning the expedition of Lewis and Clark (see 578:1), President Jefferson had seen it as opening up a vital trade route, 'a North American road to India'. That had not happened, but with the acquisition of California in 1848, the United States stood on the Pacific littoral and in 1850 began to build a railway across the isthmus of Panama, which was regarded as the prelude to an isthmian canal. This was destined as a short-cut between the eastern manufacturing states of the USA and the supposedly limitless market of China, recently broken into by Britain's defeat of the Chinese empire in the war of 1839–42, soon after which Washington signed a commercial treaty with Beijing.

8 The gates of the Chinese empire must be thrown by the men from the Sacramento and the Oregon, and the haughty Japanese tramplers upon the cross be enlightened by the doctrines of republicanism and the ballot box. The eagle of the republic shall poise itself over the field of Waterloo, after tracing its flight among the gorges of the Himalaya or the Ural mountains, and a successor of Washington ascend the chair of universal empire! ... The people stand ready to hail tomorrow ... a collision with the proudest and the mightiest empire upon earth.

J.D.B. DeBow in his very own *DeBow's Review*, 1850. The Southern publicist DeBow was based in New Orleans, and his journal was the voice of the South in the decade before the Civil War.

1 To demand as a right, and not to solicit as a favor, those acts of courtesy which are due from one civilized nation to another; to allow none of those petty measures which have been unsparingly visited upon those who had preceded me, and to disregard the acts as well as the threats of the authorities, if they in the least conflicted with my own sense of what was due to the dignity of the American flag.

Commodore Matthew Perry USN to the secretary of the navy, John P. Kennedy, 3 Aug. 1853, summarizing the objectives of his forthcoming mission to the hermit empire of Japan; Bartlett (1964 edn) p.270. Perry secured a treaty with Japan on 31 March 1854, opening it decisively to the outside world.

2 I belong to the great American Navy – that glorious institution which scatters civilization with every broadside and illuminates the dark places of the earth with the light of its rockets and bombshells.

Bayard Taylor, who sailed with the Perry expedition; Arthur Walworth Black Ships off Japan (1946) p.36.

3 The military and warlike strength of the Japanese had long been to Europe like the ghost in a village churchyard, a bugbear and a terror which it only required some bolder fellow than the rest – like we Yankees – to walk up and discover the ghost to be nothing but moonshine on the gravestones, or a poor old white horse. Our nation has unclothed the ghost and all the rest of the world will cry 'bah' and take advantage of the discovery.

Unknown seaman on Perry's flagship, 28 June 1854; G.H. Preble The Opening of Japan (1962 edn). Preble, too, sailed with Perry.

4 I have a full conviction that the seclusion policy of the nations of Eastern Asia is not according to God's plan of mercy to these peoples, and their governments must change through fear of force, that the people may be free.

Perry's interpreter, the Protestant missionary Rev. S. Wells Williams; Walworth (1946) p.39.

5 China is like a lamb before the shearers, as easy a conquest as were the provinces of India ... It is my opinion that the highest interests of the United States are involved in sustaining China – maintaining order here, and gradually engrafting on this worn-out stock the healthy principles which give life and health to government, rather than to see China

become the theater of a widespread anarchy, and ultimately the prey of European ambition.

Humphrey Marshall to the secretary of state, William Marcy, 10 July 1853; P.H. Clyde United States Policy Toward China (1940) Ch.5.

6 Consider: if you incorporate these tropical countries with the Republic of the United States, you will have to incorporate their people too.

Senator Carl Schurz, 11 Jan. 1871; Congressional Globe Vol.43, p.26. Schurz was anti-imperialist, not least on the grounds that peoples of non-European origin were unfitted for democratic citizenship (see 583:5). People in incorporated territories such as Alaska were granted all the privileges of the US Constitution; Schurz doubts whether they deserved that status.

7 Hawaii ... is the key to the maritime dominion of the Pacific states, as Cuba is the key to the Gulf trade. The material possession of Hawaii is not desired by the United States any more than was that of Cuba. But under no circumstances can the United States permit any change in the territorial control of either which would cut it adrift from the American system, whereto they both indispensably belong.

Secretary of state James G. Blaine to James M. Comly, US minister in Hawaii, 1 Dec. 1881; Papers Relating to the Foreign Relations of the United States 1881 (1882) p.638. Hawaii was annexed to the United States on 12 Aug. 1898.

8 I am of the earnest conviction that the policy of the United States in China, and toward the Chinese in America, should be with us as it is with them – purely selfish – coming, as it ought to, under the universal law of right and justice, but by no means governed by the fallacious idea of international friendship, or even the broader ground of a common brotherhood.

Commodore Robert W. Shufeldt USN to Senator Sargent, 1 Jan. 1882; Clyde (1940) Ch.23. Shufeldt, who signed a treaty opening Korea to American trade in May 1882, came close to dismissal from the navy when this letter was published.

9 Let me say to the businessmen of America, look to the land of the setting sun, look to the Pacific! There are teeming millions there who will ere long want to be and clothed the same as we are. There is the great market that the continental powers are today struggling for.

Representative William Sulzer, 1898; Congressional Record Vol.31, Pt 6, p.5906. The concept of Asia as a huge market for American exports was a myth as long as the Asian masses were too poor to do more than live at subsistence level, and US trade and investment in the area remained minuscule as compared with its economic stake in Europe and Latin America.

I The mission of the United States is one of bene-volent assimilation, substituting the mild sway of justice and right for arbitrary rule.
President William McKinley to General Harrison Gray Otis, 21 Dec. 1898. McKinley was writing shortly after Spain ceded the Philippines following its defeat in the war of 1898. Otis had served as a commander of volunteers before resuming his career as owner and editor of the highly conservative *Los Angeles Times*. Filipino nationalists took the view that the replacement of Spanish 'arbitrary rule' by American colonialism was a poor substitute for their own independence.

2 What I hope you will do, is to have a healthy despotism governing these tropical semi-savages and even Spanish creoles. No talk of suffrage or any such constitutional privileges for them, but steady government by the firmest, most honest men you can find, and no interference if possible by Congress.
James Bryce to Theodore Roosevelt, 12 Sept. 1898; Joseph Bucklin Bishop *Theodore Roosevelt and His Times* (1920) Vol.1, pp.106–7. The English academic Bryce, author of *The American Commonwealth* (1888), later became British ambassador to the United States.

3 We assume that what we like and practice, and what we think better, must come as a welcome blessing to Spanish-Americans and Filipinos. This is grossly and obviously untrue. They hate our ways. They are hostile to our ideas. Our religion, language, institutions and manners offend them … The most important thing which we shall inherit from the Spaniards will be the task of suppressing rebellions … My patriotism is of the kind which is outraged by the notion that the United States never was a great nation until in a petty three months' campaign it knocked to pieces a poor, decrepit, bankrupt old state like Spain.
William Graham Sumner, 1898; *War and Other Essays* (1911) pp.303–5, 334. As a fervent advocate of the survival of the fittest, Sumner might have been expected to be a full-blooded imperialist, but he took his belief in laissez-faire to its logical conclusion in arguing that Cuba and the Philippines should be left to their own devices. His prophecy of rebellion was soon fulfilled, when Filipino nationalists under Emilio Aguinaldo launched an insurgency against their new American masters, put down with maximum force.

4   Underneath the starry flag,
    Civilize 'em with a Krag.
US army song about the Filipino insurrectionists. The Krag was the American soldier's rifle.

5 The little brown brother.
William Howard Taft, US commissioner in the Philippines, giving his view of the Filipinos as junior members of the

American family. It was not shared by at least one US citizen living in the colony: 'He may be a brother of Big Bill Taft,' wrote Robert F. Morrison in the *Manila Sunday Times*, 'but he ain't no brother of mine.' Compare Thackeray 605:4.

6 The power that rules the Pacific … is the power that rules the world. And with the Philippines, that power is and will forever be the American Republic … God has not been preparing the English-speaking and Teutonic peoples for a thousand years for nothing but vain and idle self-contemplation and self-admiration. No! He has made us the master organizers of the world to establish system where chaos reigns … And of all our race He has marked the American people as His chosen nation to finally lead in the regeneration of the world. This is the divine mission of America.
Senator Albert Beveridge, 9 Jan. 1900; *Congressional Record* pp.385, 387–8.

7 Our geographical position, our wealth, and our energy preëminently fit us to enter upon the development of Eastern Asia and to reduce it to part of our own economic system.
Brooks Adams *America's Economic Supremacy* (1900) p.51.

8 I argued that the idea of supporting the independence and integrity of China would accord with the sentiments of our people; that it was this principle of helping other nations to maintain their independence and integrity that had made the Monroe Doctrine so popular amongst them.
Secretary of state John Hay to John Bassett Moore, 1 July 1900. Hay was writing two days before the issue of the second 'Open Door' note to the states involved in the suppression of the Chinese Boxer Rising, aimed at the imperialist powers in China. The first note, issued on 6 Sept. 1899, had called for equal economic access to China by all foreign countries; the second also pledged the United States to work for 'Chinese territorial and administrative entity'. In 1823 President Monroe had likewise declared the intention to defend Latin America against a potential revival of European imperialism, but by the end of the century his Doctrine had burgeoned into an assertion of US mastery and few Latin Americans thought of it as anything else. Hay, however, seems to have believed his own propaganda.

9 I was apprehensive lest she [Russia] at the very outset whipped Japan on the sea she might assume a position well-nigh intolerable toward us … I was thoroughly well pleased with the Japanese victory, for Japan is playing our game.
President Theodore Roosevelt to his son, Theodore Jr, 10 Feb. 1904; Morison Vol. 4 (1951) p.724. Roosevelt was

hailing the Japanese sinking of the Russian Pacific fleet in a surprise attack on 8 Feb.

1 Japan has a paramount interest in what surrounds the Yellow Sea, just as the United States has a paramount interest in what surrounds the Caribbean; but with … no more desire for conquest of the weak than we had shown ourselves to have in the case of Cuba.

President Theodore Roosevelt to Cecil Spring Rice, 13 June 1904; Morison Vol.4 (1951) p.830. An interesting comparison, although the parallel does not hold up on the score of motivation. Spring Rice was an English friend of Roosevelt and became British ambassador to Washington in 1913.

2 Our vital interest is to keep the Japanese out of our country, and at the same time to preserve the goodwill of Japan … Our interests in Manchuria are really unimportant, and not such that the American people would be content to run the slightest risk of collision about them.

Theodore Roosevelt to President Taft, 22 Dec. 1910; Morison Vol.7 (1954) pp.189–92. Since the 1880s the United States had been anxious to minimize Asiatic settlement on its Pacific coast; Chinese had been excluded absolutely and an agreement negotiated with Japan. Under Taft after 1909 the government had mounted an energetic bid to elbow out Russian and Japanese interests in the Chinese province of Manchuria; to Roosevelt this was a pointless and dangerous exercise, even given America's self-appointed role as China's protector under the Open Door policy.

3 In the midst of Dr Wang's speech, someone started, 'My Country 'Tis Of Thee'. How the great anthem bellowed and surged throughout the auditorium. The first republic and the last joined hearts and voices in a mighty burst of patriotic fervor as the audience rose to its feet as only Methodists can sing, 'Sweet Land of Liberty'.

Bishop William Bashford to secretary of state Philander Chase Knox, 15 May 1912; Paul Varg *The Making of a Myth* (1968) p.170. The bishop voices the emotionalism underlying the idea of a special American relationship with China in this account of the harmony of American Methodists and their Chinese converts in the wake of the foundation of the Chinese Republic three months earlier. To Americans such as this, the Chinese revolution of 1911 was the prelude to an ever-closer Sino-American union.

THE OLD WORLD, 1789–1909

4 Judging upon probable grounds, the Mississippi was never designed as the western boundary of the American empire. The God of nature never

intended that some of the best part of his earth should be inhabited by the subjects of a monarch 4,000 miles from them. And may we not venture to predict that, when the rights of mankind shall be more fully known, and the knowledge of them is fast increasing both in Europe and America, the power of European potentates will be confined to Europe, and their present American dominance become like the United States, free, sovereign, and independent empires.

Jedediah Morse *The American Geography* (1789) p.469. The Congregationalist divine and 'Father of American Geography', Morse was an uncompromising conservative and an appropriate father for the xenophobic Samuel Morse (see 581:6).

5 Let Americans disdain to be the instruments of European greatness! Let the thirteen States, bound together by strict and indissoluble union, concur in erecting one great American system, superior to the controul of all transatlantic force or influence, and able to dictate the terms of the connection between the old and the new world.

Alexander Hamilton *The Federalist* (1787); *Papers of Alexander Hamilton* Vol.4, p.345.

6 If I had not controuled the Fury of his Vanity, instead of relieving this country from Confusion as Bonaparte did France, he would have involved it in all the Bloodshed and distractions of foreign and civil war at once.

Former president John Adams on Hamilton, 1804. In the war between Britain and revolutionary France that broke out in 1793, the conservative Hamilton leaned emphatically towards Britain, although the United States remained neutral. In 1800 he prevented the re-election of Adams as president, and here Adams writes a vindictive obituary after Hamilton's death following a duel, on 12 July 1804. For him, it was, perhaps, *De mortuis nil nisi malum.*

7 The great rule of conduct for us in regard to foreign nations is, in extending our commercial relations to have with them as little *political* connection as possible … Why quit our own to stand upon foreign ground? Why, by intertwining our destiny with that of any part of Europe, entangle our peace and prosperity in the toils of European ambition, rivalship, interest, humor or caprice? … Against the insidious wiles of foreign influence … the jealousy of a free people ought to be constantly awake … Taking care to keep ourselves by suitable establishments on a respectable defensive posture, we may safely trust to temporary alliances for extraordinary emergencies.

President George Washington, farewell address, 17 Sept. 1796; Richardson Vol.1 (1896) pp.213–24. This famous pronouncement formed the basis of the US policy of isolation vis-à-vis Europe up to 1917. First drafted in 1792, as Washington did not then wish a second term in office, it was written, among others, by Alexander Hamilton.

1 Peace, commerce, & honest friendship with all nations – entangling alliances with none.

President Thomas Jefferson, inaugural address, 4 March 1801; Saul K. Padover *Jefferson* (1942) p.293. Jefferson steered a difficult neutral course in the war between the British and Napoleonic empires, although coming close to war with Britain in 1807 over its interference with American shipping.

2 The acquisition of Canada this year as far as the neighborhood of Quebec, will be a mere matter of marching … Perhaps they will burn New York or Boston. If they do, we must burn the city of London, not by expensive fleets … but by employing a hundred or two Jack-the-painters, whom madness, famine, desperation and hardened vice, will abundantly furnish from among themselves.

Thomas Jefferson to William Duane, 4 Aug. 1812; P.L. Ford (ed.) *The Writings of Thomas Jefferson* Vol.9, p.366. The United States had gone to war with Britain on 19 June after the British naval blockade's infringement of US neutral rights had become intolerable. Jefferson, an ardent expansionist, wanted to use the war as a means of seizing Canada, but the American invasion came to nothing.

3 The year 1812 will, I hope, be immortal in the history of the world for having given the first check to the overgrown power and tyranny of Britain and France. Russia and the United States may now be hailed as the deliverers of the human race.

The physician Benjamin Rush to John Adams, 10 April 1813. The reference to Russia is to the repulse of Napoleon's invasion (see 536:8).

4 Tell the men to fire faster and not to give up the ship; fight her till she sinks.

Captain James Lawrence USN, commander of USS *Chesapeake* in the engagement with HMS *Shannon* on 1 June 1813; usually rendered as 'Don't give up the ship!' Lawrence had been mortally wounded and soon afterwards *Chesapeake* struck her colours.

5 When the detachment sent to destroy Mr Madison's house entered his dining parlour, they found a dinner-table spread, and covers laid for forty guests … They sat down to it … and having satisfied their appetites … and partaken pretty freely of the wines, they finished by setting fire to the house which had so liberally entertained them.

British troops took the US capital, Washington, D.C., on 24 Aug. 1814 and burned many of the public buildings, including the White House; *A Narrative of the Campaigns of the British Army at Washington, Baltimore and New Orleans* (1821) pp.134–5.

6   Oh, say, can you see by the dawn's early light
What so proudly we hailed at the twilight's last
  gleaming?
Whose broad stripes and bright stars, through
  the perilous fight,
O'er the ramparts we watched were so gallantly
  streaming?
And the rockets' red glare, the bombs bursting
  in air,
Gave proof through the night that our flag was
  still there.
Oh, say, does that star-spangled banner still
  wave
O'er the land of the free and the home of the
  brave?

Francis Scott Key 'The Star-Spangled Banner', written on 14 Sept. 1814 after the British bombardment of Baltimore harbour the previous night; adopted as the US national anthem in 1931.

7 We are considered not merely as an active and enterprising, but as a grasping and ambitious people … The universal feeling of Europe in witnessing the gigantic growth of our population and power is that we shall, if united, become a very dangerous member of the society of nations.

Secretary of state John Quincy Adams to Richard Rush, 20 May 1818; *Writings of John Quincy Adams* Vol.6, pp.319–27. Although seriously damaged in the war with Britain, the United States won the final Battle of New Orleans and after 1815 was beginning to be recognized as a potentially formidable proposition.

8 Wherever the standard of freedom and independence … shall be unfurled, there will her heart, her benedictions and her prayers be. But she does not go abroad in search of monsters to destroy … She well knows that by once enlisting under other banners than her own, were they even the banners of foreign independence, she would involve herself, beyond the power of extrication, in all the wars of interest and intrigue, of individual avarice, envy and ambition, which assume the colours and usurp the standard of freedom.

Secretary of state John Quincy Adams, 4 July 1821; Walter LaFeber (ed.) *John Quincy Adams and Continental Empire* (1965) p.45. Adams here resists the temptation to join a crusade against the counter-revolutionary monarchies of Europe.

1 Fifty-Four Forty or Fight!

Senator William Allen, 1844. War-cry of Americans who wanted the entire Oregon Territory in the Pacific Northwest, disputed between the United States and Britain. Its notional northern boundary was latitude 54 degrees 40 minutes north, but in 1846 the US accepted the compromise boundary of the 49th parallel, already established as the frontier between the United States and Canada by an Anglo-American treaty of 1818.

2 That mighty Nation, whose veins are filled with our blood, whose minds are nourished by our literature, and upon whom is entailed the rich inheritance of our civilization, our freedom, and our glory.

Thomas Babington Macaulay (1800–59), an early apostle of Anglo-American 'hands across the sea'.

3 If it be their united destiny ... that they shall be called upon in the cause of humanity, and in the cause of freedom, to stand against a world in arms, they are of a race and of a blood to meet that crisis without shrinking from danger, and without quailing in the presence of earthly power.

Secretary of state Daniel Webster, 23 Feb. 1852. Webster was a champion of the European liberal nationalist movements of 1848, Hungary in particular, and this pledge was made during the visit to the USA by the exiled Magyar leader Lajos Kossuth. But it was a simple declaration of principle, not a summons to a crusade which Webster well knew the American public would not support.

4 That policy which caused us to stand still and look with indifference upon the exciting conflicts of interest and ambition, of tyranny and of liberty, which grew out of the first French Revolution, has accomplished more during the last ten years for the real progress of free institutions than will ever be attained by *filibustering interveners* and locomotive politicians.

Senator Jacob Miller, 26 Feb. 1852; *Congressional Globe*. The authentic voice of isolationism in reply to Webster's florid rhetoric. Intervention *did* come during the decade in question, but against Mexico, not in Europe, and American filibusters (annexationist adventurers) operated in the Caribbean, not across the Atlantic.

5 Far better it is for ourselves, for Hungary, and for the course of liberty that ... we should keep our lamp burning brightly on this western shore as a light to all nations, than to hazard its utter extinction amid the ruins of fallen or falling republics in Europe.

Senator Henry Clay, 1852; Cushing Strout *The American Image of the Old World* (1963) p.54. This was Clay's last important speech; he died soon afterwards.

6 'We send ambassadors,' the Americans said, 'not to kings but to peoples.' Hence arose the idea of giving a diplomatic dinner to the enemies of all existing governments ... [a] *red* dinner, given by the defenders of *black* slavery. [After the meal] Sanders wanted to compensate himself there for the absence at dinner of vehement toasts to the future universal (white) republic [and] proposed a ceremonial singing of the Marseillaise in chorus. It proved that only Worcell knew the tune properly ... the American Mrs Sanders had to be summoned, and she played the Marseillaise on the guitar.

The Russian liberal-in-exile Alexander Herzen *My Past and Thoughts* (1974 edn) pp.478–81, on the extraordinary banquet given to himself, Mazzini, Garibaldi, Orsini, Ledru-Rollin, Kossuth and other outcast European luminaries in London on 21 Feb. 1854. Worcell was an exiled Polish aristocrat, George N. Sanders the US consul in London and a fervent admirer of European republicanism.

7 The great but quiet migration of peoples has now closed into a circle around the earth. From hospitable shores, Americans and Russians are looking at each other across the ocean as neighbours. The Slavs, who for three centuries were fated to press against the sun, now stand with their immeasurable realm in front of the United States ... which at the same time and in a like manner has irrepressibly pressed on with the sun to the west.

Alexander von Middendorf *Travels in Eastern Siberia* (1860) Vol.1, p.137.

8 Russian-America was declared to be a 'barren, worthless, God-forsaken region', whose only products were 'icebergs and polar bears'. The ground was 'frozen six feet deep', and the 'streams were glaciers'. 'Walrussia' was suggested as a fitting name for it, if it deserved to have any. Vegetation was 'confined to mosses', and 'no useful animals could live there'. There might be some few 'wretched fish', only fit for 'wretched Esquimaux' to eat. But nothing could be raised or dug there. Seven millions of good money was going to be wasted in buying it. Many millions more would have to be spent in holding and defending it, for it was 'remote, inhospitable and inaccessible'.

Frederick W. Seward *The Autobiography of William H. Seward* (1891) Vol.3, p.367. In 1867 tsarist Russia sold Alaska to the United States for $7.2 million as part of the expansionist policy of secretary of state Seward. Sections of the American press (quoted here) deplored the purchase at the time; Russia came to regret the transaction later, for both strategic and economic reasons.

1 Amidst the calamities which war has brought on our country, this one benefit has accrued – that our eyes are withdrawn from England, withdrawn from France, and look homeward.

Ralph Waldo Emerson *Letters and Social Aims* (1876). After the trauma of the Civil War of 1861–5, many Americans, like Emerson, took comfort in a focus on internal rehabilitation.

2 The genius of our institutions, the needs of our people in their home life, and the attention which is demanded for the settlement and development of the resources of our vast territory dictate the scrupulous avoidance of any departure from that foreign policy commended by the history, the traditions, and the prosperity of our Republic. It is the policy of independence, favored by our position and defended by our known love of justice and by our power. It is the policy of peace suitable to our interests. It is the policy of neutrality, rejecting any share in foreign broils and ambitions upon other continents and repelling their intrusion here. It is the policy of Monroe and of Washington and Jefferson.

President Grover Cleveland, inaugural address, 4 March 1885; Richardson Vol.8 (1898).

3 As the New England characteristics are gradually superseded by those of other races, other forms of belief, and other associations, the time may come when a New Englander will feel more as if he were among his own people in London than in one of our seaboard cities.

Oliver Wendell Holmes Sr *One Hundred Days in Europe* (1888) pp.310–13. Holmes, the grand old man of American letters, then almost 80, reflects the unease of his generation at the rising tide of immigration, which was beginning to challenge the supremacy of America's east-coast elite and reinforce its tendency to look to what some Bostonians still call 'the old country'.

4 No State, in the European sense of the word, and indeed barely a specific national name. No sovereign, no court, no personal loyalty, no aristocracy, no church, no clergy, no diplomatic service, no country gentlemen, no palaces, no castles, nor manors, nor old country houses, nor parsonages, nor thatched cottages nor ivied ruins; no cathedrals, nor abbeys, nor little Norman churches; no great Universities nor public schools – No Oxford, nor Eton, nor Harrow, no literature, no novels, no museums, no pictures, no political society – no Epsom nor Ascot!

The American man of letters Henry James, on everything lacking in the United States and abundantly on offer in England, where he spent the last forty years of his life; Richard Kenin *Return to Albion* (1979) p.111. From this lament one can see why Theodore Roosevelt termed James 'a miserable little snob'.

5 The United States will doubtless be led, by undeniable interests and aroused national sympathies, to play a part, to cast aside the policy of isolation which befitted her infancy, and to recognize that, whereas once to avoid European entanglement was essential to the development of her individuality, now to take her share of the travail of Europe is but to assume an inevitable task, an appointed lot in the work of upholding the common interests of civilization.

Captain Alfred Thayer Mahan USN *North American Review* Vol.159 (1894) p.558.

6 If the Kaiser were a Frederick the Great or a Gustavus Adolphus, if he were a Cromwell, a Pitt, or like Andrew Jackson, had the 'instinct for the jugular', he would recognize his real foe and strike savagely at the point where danger threatens.

Theodore Roosevelt to Cecil Spring Rice, 13 Aug. 1897; Morison Vol.1 (1951) p.645. The German emperor had just adopted the Tirpitz programme of naval expansion, directed against Britain; for the pro-British (and anti-Russian) Roosevelt, tsarist Russia posed the main threat to Germany, though German military planners were well aware of that. Roosevelt was mistaken about Jackson. Rufus Choate said of John Quincy Adams, not Jackson: 'He has ... an instinct for the jugular and the carotid artery, as unerring as that of any carnivorous animal.' Compare the jibe against James R. Schlesinger, US secretary of defense 1973–5: 'He has an instinct for the capillaries.'

7 England is sad to me – very sad. Like you I hope she may revive, but I admit my hope is faint. The current is flowing away from her. I do not apprehend any sudden or violent change, but I fancy England will grow gradually more and more sluggish, until, at length, after our day, she will drop out of the strenuous competition of the new world which is forming.

Brooks Adams to Senator Henry Cabot Lodge, 14 Oct. 1900.

1 I think the twentieth century will be the century of the men who speak English.

Vice-President Theodore Roosevelt to Cecil Spring Rice, 16 March 1901; Morison Vol. 2 (1951).

2 The world will break its damned neck within five and twenty years; and a good riddance. This country cannot possibly run it ... I incline to let the machine smash, and see what pieces are worth saving after-wards ... I incline to let England sink; to let Germany and Russia try to run the machinery, and to stand on our own internal resources alone.

Henry Adams to Brooks Adams, 7 Feb. 1901; Harold Cater *Henry Adams and his Friends* (1947) p.504. The historian Henry Adams was brother to Brooks.

3 We have got to support France against Germany, and fortify an Atlantic system beyond attack; for if Germany breaks down England or France, she becomes the center of a military world, and we are lost.

Henry Adams to Elizabeth Cameron, 27 Aug. 1905; *The Letters of Henry Adams* (1938) p.461.

4 The isolation which has meant so much to the United States, and still means so much, cannot persist in its present form ... Hitherto, the American preference and desire for peace has constituted the chief justification for its isolation. At some future time the same purpose ... may demand intervention ... If [the United States] wants peace, it must be spiritually and physically prepared to fight for it ... The power of the United States might well be sufficient when thrown into the balance, to tip the scale in favor of a comparatively pacific settlement of international complications. Under such conditions a policy of neutrality would be a policy of irresponsibility and unwisdom.

Herbert Croly *The Promise of American Life* (1909) pp.311, 312. Croly, like all pro-interventionists before him, realized, however, that American public opinion was still adamantly hostile to involvement in Europe.

Anti-Semitism and Zionism, 1835–1914

RUSSIA, 1835–1913

1 The children were led to the exercise yard and had to line up in rows of four. It was the most heart-breaking scene I have ever seen … poor, poor kids! … Pale, exhausted, in their rough military great-coats, they cast frightened glances at the brutal soldiers who drilled them. Their white lips and the circles under their eyes showed their fatigue and their fever. These sick children, deprived of care and affection, exposed to the icy wind of the Far North, were heading towards their graves.

The Russian liberal Alexander Herzen *Recollections and Reflections* Vol.1 (1861) pp.308–9. Herzen encountered these Jewish children on his way to exile in northern Russia in 1835. The Statute of Conscription and Military Service of 1827 demanded that Jews had to provide recruits aged between 12 and 25 for the army.

2 How can the Army slander the Jew, when tens of thousands of Jews are serving in the ranks and performing honestly and faithfully their duty to the Tsar and the Fatherland? Were not the ramparts of Fort Sebastopol coloured with the blood of Jewish, as well as Russian soldiers, of Jewish soldiers who fought in the many battles for that stronghold even against their co-religionists in the enemy ranks? Let us be worthy of our century, let us denounce the unfortunate custom in our literature to mock and disdain the Jew.

Peter S. Lebedev, *Russkii Invalid* (The Russian Veteran), 1858. Lebedev, as editor of this army journal, refers to the Crimean War of 1853–6 (see 695:4).

3 The time for making attacks on the Jews has passed, and passed for ever. Rather let us defend ourselves against their justified attacks, and through our actions nullify the truth of Shylock's famous words: 'The villainy you teach me, I will execute'.

Russkii Vestnik (The Russian Messenger), editorial, no.18, Nov. 1858, p.126. During the reign of Alexander II a more liberal attitude was displayed towards the Jews, manifested in the abolition of juvenile conscription and a lifting of restrictions on the Jewish community.

4 They are at the root of the revolutionary socialist movement and of regicide, they own the periodical press, they have in their hands the financial markets; the people as a whole fall into financial slavery to them; they even control the principles of contemporary science and strive to place it outside of Christianity.

The arch-reactionary Constantin Pobedonostev to the writer Feodor Dostoevsky, 1879; Robert F. Byrnes *Pobedonostev: His Life and Thought* (1968) p.205.

5 Having adopted strict measures to suppress the earlier disturbances and mob rule and to protect Jews against violence, the government feels justified in pursuing speedily an equally energetic course in order to remove the existing abnormal relations between the original inhabitants and the Jews. It must protect the Russian people against the Jews' injurious activities which, according to local reports, were responsible for the disorders.

Count Nikolai P. Ignatiev, memorandum to Tsar Alexander III, 22 Aug. 1881; Salo W. Baron *The Russian Jew Under Tsars and Soviets* (1964) p.55. The Russian minister of the interior was responding to events following the assassination of Tsar Alexander II in March 1881, for which the Jews in Russia were blamed. The Secret League of Nobles (*Sviaschennaia Druzhina*) engaged in widespread anti-Jewish propaganda, aimed at inciting violence against the Jewish community by the peasantry.

6 The Jews in the Pale of Settlement constitute a 'state within a state', with its own administrative and judicial organs, and with a national government – a state whose centre lies outside Russia, abroad, whose highest authority is the 'Universal Jewish Alliance' in Paris.

Ivan Aksakov, in the journal *Rus*, 10 Oct. 1881. The Pale consisted of the western regions of European Russia where Jews were legally compelled to live. Paris was still seen (in Russia at least) as the capital of European revolution, though Berlin had by then taken its place.

7 We are your brethren, we are Jews just as you are. We repent of the fact that we regarded ourselves as Russians and not as Jews. The events of the last years have shown us that we were sadly mistaken.

Aleinikov, a Jewish student, addressing a service in a synagogue in Kiev, 1880s; Louis Greenberg *The Jews in Russia: The Struggle for Emancipation* Vol.2 (1965) p.161. Jewish students were among the first to organize self-defence groups in Russia following the pogroms in 1881 and to reject assimilation into Russian society.

1 We have on the one hand 5,000,000 Jews, Russian subjects, clamoring to be freed from all special restraints, and we have on the other, 85,000,000 Russian subjects clamoring to have the 5,000,000 expelled from the Empire. What is to be done in such a case?

Count Nikolai P. Ignatiev, Russian minister of the interior, to Wickham Hofman, US chargé d'affaires, April 1882; *Papers Relating to the Foreign Relations of the United States* (1882) p.452. Ignatev's bid to justify the Russian government's persecution of the Jewish community was in direct response to an official communiqué from the US articulating its concern at the 1881 pogroms.

2 Under Yourkoffsky's personal supervision, the whole quarter was ransacked, apartments forced open, doors smashed, every bedroom without exception searched, and every living soul, men, women, and children routed out for examination as to their passports. The indignities which the women, young and old alike, underwent at the hands of the Cossacks may not be described ... As a result, over 700 men, women and children were dragged at dead of night through the streets to the *outchastoks* or police stations ... Of these unhappy people ... some were afterward marched away ... chained together with criminals and forced along the roads by Cossacks ... The rest were summarily shipped to the Pale.

Harold Frederic, *The Times*, 30 March 1891. The Edict of Expulsion of 29 March 1891 ordered the removal of 30,000 Jews from Moscow.

3 This Government has found occasion to express ... to the Government of the Czar its serious concern because of the harsh measures now being enforced against the Hebrews in Russia ... It is estimated that over 1,000,000 will be forced from Russia within a few years ... A decree to leave one country is in the nature of things an order to enter another – some other. This consideration, as well as the suggestion of humanity, furnishes ample ground for the remonstrances which we have presented to Russia.

US President Benjamin Harrison, 9 Dec. 1891: Baron (1964) p.59. Harrison was evidently concerned not only about the inhuman treatment of Jews in Russia but also about the addition to an already huge influx of Jewish immigrants into the United States.

4   We are small.
    We shall not rise up against you,
    To cleave pregnant women with axes
    (As you do); nor shall we set fire

To your roofs over your heads, and with iron
    bars
We shall not shatter the skulls of babes!
Not until with your brute hand you have
    uprooted,
Not until with your contaminated palms you
    have erased altogether
The image of God stamped upon us,
The tokens of ancient nobility of spirit,
And descent from princely generations.

Saul Tchernichovski 'This Be Our Revenge' in *Shirim* (1892) p.317. Tchernichovski (1875–1943) was a major Russian Jewish poet of the late-19th-century Hebrew renaissance. He visited the USA in 1928–9 and later settled in Tel Aviv.

5 [Russian Jews] never seem for an instant to lose the consciousness that they are a race apart. It is in their walk, in their sidelong glance, in the carriage of their sloping shoulders, in the curious gesture of the uplifted palm.

Harold Frederic *The New Exodus: Israel in Russia* (1892) pp.79–80.

6 According to the records of secret Jewish Zionism, Solomon and other learned Jewish men already, in 929 BC, thought out a scheme in theory for a peaceful conquest of the whole universe by Zionism ... As history developed, this scheme was worked out ... with the slyness of the symbolic serpent ... As this serpent penetrated into the hearts of the nations which it encountered, it got under and devoured the non-Jewish power of these states.

Protocols of the Elders of Zion, Epilogue; Norman Cohn *Warrant for Genocide* (1967) App.3, p.285. This forgery by the tsarist secret police was first published in the anti-Semitic Russian daily *Znamya* in Aug.–Sept. 1903 and partly based on a work by the French writer Maurice Joly, published in 1864.

7 The cry of 'down with autocracy!' comes from the blood-suckers who are commonly known as Jews, Armenians and Poles. Beware of the Jews! They are the root of all evil, the sole cause of our misfortunes.

Propaganda of the League of the Russian People (popularly known as the Black Hundreds) at the time of the 1905 Revolution (see 677:6); H. Valentin *Anti-Semitism Historically and Critically Examined* (1936) p.86. The Jews were seen as responsible both for the Revolution and for Russia's defeat by Japan in the war of 1904–5 (see 688:3).

8 Never has ... a trial in Russia ... attracted, to so great a degree, the attention of the broad masses ... The Beilis affair has pushed aside all other internal and foreign affairs ... [The Russian people understand that] the Jewish question is not only a Jewish question but a Russian question; that the untruth and corruption uncovered at the Beilis trial is an all-Russian untruth and corruption.

The Liberal journalist Vladimir Korolenko, 1913; Albert S. Lindemann *The Jew Accused* (1991) p.183. The Beilis case concerned the discovery on 19 March 1911 of the body of a 13-year-old boy in a cave near Kiev. This was popularly believed to be a Jewish ritual murder. Mendel Beilis, manager of a local brick factory, was charged with the crime on the flimsiest of evidence, even though the identity of the real killers was known. His trial took place in the summer of 1913, and he was acquitted.

GERMANY AND AUSTRIA, 1848–1906

1 What is the secular cult of the Jew? *Haggling*. What is his secular god? *Money*. Well then! Emancipation from *haggling* and *money*, from practical, real Judaism would be the self-emancipation of our time … Money is the jealous God of Israel, beside which no other God may stand.

Karl Marx *On the Jewish Question* (1848); Quentin Hoare (ed.) *Early Writings* (1978) pp.236, 239. Marx, himself a Jew, expresses the loathing felt by many assimilated Jews towards the unassimilated Orthodox.

2 Our whole European art and civilization, how-ever, have remained to the Jew a foreign tongue; for, just as he has taken no part in the evolution of the one, so has he taken none in that of the other; but as a homeless person has been a cold, nay more, a hostile onlooker.

Richard Wagner, 1850; *Richard Wagner's Prose Works* Vol.3 (1929) pp.429 ff. Wagner, currently feuding with the popular Jewish composer Giacomo Meyerbeer, voices the customary anti-Semitism of his time. Because one of his most prominent admirers was Hitler, performances of his music are officially banned in Israel.

3 You know that Heine is dead, but did you know that Ludwig Simon of Trier had pissed on his grave – I meant to say, passed water – in the New York *New Times* … The poet or troubadour of the Jew-broad high-shit, high-ash, or high-lime of Frankfurt-on-Main discovers, of course, that Heine was no poet. He had 'no soul', he was 'full of meanness', and he did not only insult … but also Börne's lady friend, the great Börne's mouse, or muse or cunt, Mrs Strauss.

Karl Marx to Friedrich Engels, 10 April, 1856. *Works* Vol.29, pp.38–9. A crude assault on the writers Heinrich Heine

(1797–1856) and Ludwig Börne (1786–1837), Jewish liberal writers and journalists, who, because they had been baptized as Christians, were accepted by neither Jews nor Christians and were attacked by both.

4 The blindness of the masses, their propensity to yield themselves to oratory as empty as it is sonorous, makes them an easy prey … We must as much as possible sustain the proletariat and bring it within the reach of those who have money at their disposal. By this means we shall be able to use the masses whenever we please, to lead them into upheavals and revolutions. Each of these catastrophes will advance by a long stride our own racial interests and will rapidly bring us nearer to our own great end – that of reigning over all the earth as it has been promised to us by our father Abraham.

Hermann Goedsche *Biarritz* Vol.1 (1868) pp.130 ff. Goedsche acted as a spy for the Prussian secret police. This fabrication of his formed one basis of the so-called *Protocols of the Elders of Zion* (see 628:6).

5 I do not like the Jews at all, I even detest them in general. I see in them nothing but the very much degenerated sons of a great but vanished past. As a result of centuries of slavery, these people have acquired servile characteristics, and that is why I am so unfavourably disposed to them. Besides, I have no contact with them. There is scarcely a single Jew among my friends and in the society which surrounds me [in Berlin].

Ferdinand Lassalle *Une Page d'amour de Ferdinand Lassalle* (1878) pp.47–50. Lassalle, a Jew, was one of the founding fathers of the Social Democrat movement in Germany, who died after a duel in 1864. He was hotly opposed to Marx but, like him, deeply contemptuous of Judaic orthodoxy (see 629:1).

6 If by some miracle all our 1,400,000 Jews were to be taken from us, it would help us very little, for we ourselves have been infected with the Jewish spirit.

Baron von Vogelsang, in his journal *Das Vaterland* (The Fatherland), 10 Oct. 1875. Von Vogelsang, a leading Austrian Catholic, was passionately hostile to liberalism and capitalism, which he saw as the twin progeny of the assimilated Jews of Europe.

7 It is a rather generally accepted error to speak of the Jews as Germans, Hungarians or Frenchmen, who happen to have a different confession than most of the other inhabitants of Germany, Hungary or France. One often forgets that the Jews are a distinctively delineated nation and that a Jew can no more become a German any more than a Persian, or Frenchman, or New Zealander, or African.

Theodor Billroth *Über das Lehren und Lernen der medicinischen Wissenschaften an den Universitäten der deutschen Nation* (On the Teaching and Learning of the Medical Sciences in the Universities of the German Nation) (1876) pp.146–54.

1 We Germans completed in the year 1848 our abdication in favour of the Jews … Life and the future belong to Judaism, death and the past to Germandom.

Wilhelm Marr *Der Sieg des Judentums über das Germanentum* (The Victory of Jewry over the German Spirit) (1879 edn) pp.27, 44. Marr, the son of a baptized Jew, is generally believed to have invented the expression 'anti-Semitism'. In this darkly pessimistic work he asserts that the Germans have lost the economic battle with the Jews by allowing them to take over the financial institutions of the country.

2 Every son of a Jewish mother, every human being with Jewish blood in its veins, is born without honour and must therefore lack in every decent human feeling. Such a person cannot differentiate between what is pure and what is dirty. Ethically he is the lowest of the low. It follows from this that contact with a Jew dishonours; hence any contact with a Jew must be avoided.

Waidhofer Resolution of the Austrian student fraternities, 1882; Arthur Schnitzler (1862–1931) *My Youth in Vienna.*

3 I decide who is a Jew.

Karl Lüger, mayor of Vienna, 1891; Peter G.J. Pulzer *The Rise of Political Anti-Semitism in Germany and Austria* (1964) p.204. The utilitarian racism of a political boss, reminiscent of the South African Nationalist government's decision in the 1960s to classify Japanese as white because of the economic value of trade with Japan.

4 The Jew is our misfortune.

The historian Heinrich von Treitschke, who lent his illustrious name to the wave of hostility towards the Jews of Germany that swept the country in the 1890s. Under Hitler, from 1933 on, Germany was to prove the Jews' greatest-ever misfortune.

5 The development of modern means of communication will probably within the course of the twentieth century make the Jewish question a world problem which will finally be solved by other nations through the complete segregation and, if required by the needs of self-defence, the eventual annihilation of the Jewish people.

German anti-Semitic programme of 1899, anticipating the Final Solution; Hans Rogger and Eugen Weber *The European Right: A Historical Profile* (1965) p.291.

6 I have not kept my anti-Semitic views, and consciously not kept them, because a great people must be capable of assimilating elements of foreign nations, be they Jews or Poles, and to incorporate them into its history, instead of adopting a closed-shop point of view towards such elements.

Friedrich Naumann, Protestant pastor, 1903; T. Heuss *Friedrich Naumann: Der Mann, das Werk, die Zeit* (The Man, The Work, The Era) (1949 edn) p.312. Naumann had been a founder of the anti-Semitic *Verein deutscher Studenten* (German Students' Union) in the 1880s, but by the mid-1890s he had parted company with it.

7 I assert that the attitude of educated Germans towards Judaism has become totally different from what it was only a few years ago … The Jewish Question is today no longer a question of 'whether?' but only one of 'how?'

Friedrich Lange *Reines Deutschtum* (Pure German Essence) (1905) pp.90–91. In 1894 Lange founded the right-wing *Deutschbund* (German League), which was permeated by a doctrine of racial purity and uncompromising anti-Semitism. By 1905 he was confident that Jewish influence in Germany would soon be eradicated.

8 I came as a seventeen-year-old boy to Vienna … I left Vienna as a 100 per cent anti-Semite, a deadly enemy of the whole Marxist movement, and a Pan-German in my political outlook.

Adolf Hitler to the court in Munich after his failed *Putsch* of 9 Nov. 1923 (see 752:7), describing himself as he was in 1906; *Der Hitler-Prozess* (The Trial of Hitler) (1924) p.262.

FRANCE, 1869–1904

9 The Jew is a lord crushed and degraded by deprivation. He demeaned himself repeatedly, made a mask of his filth. But he feels the nobility of his blood and the slightest breeze uplifts him. You see him then reclaim the rights of his nobility with as much ease and nonchalance as the man who, on an icy night, wrapped himself in a disgusting blanket at an inn, washed his body at dawn, and put on the previous day's clothes.

Chevalier Gougenot des Mousseaux *Le Juif, le judaïsme et la judaïsation des peuples chrétiens* (The Jew, Judaism and the Jew-ification of Christian Peoples) (1869) p.386. One of the earliest anti-Semitic works by a notable Catholic in France, this received the support of Pope Pius IX.

10 Do not hope, O Jews, to be able to escape the calamity that once more threatens you … The future belongs to us. Lucifer and his emissaries will be forced to haul down their Masonic flag; Satan and the evil spirits who tour the world for the purpose of ruining souls will be cast back into Hell, from which they have audaciously climbed to assault the City of God.

L. Meurin *La Franc-Maçonnerie, Synagogue de Satan* (1893) pp.466–8. Meurin, archbishop of Port-Louis, Mauritius, was convinced that human history had to be understood in terms of a Judeo-Masonic conspiracy, which was on the verge of achieving its goal.

1 At the end of this work, what do you see? I see just one figure and it is the only one I wanted to show you: the figure of Christ, humiliated, insulted, lacerated by thorns, crucified. Nothing has changed in 1800 years … He is everywhere, hanging in cheap shop windows, abused by caricaturists and writers in this Paris full of Jews, as obstinate in their deicide as in the time of Caiaphas.

Edouard Drumont *La France Juive* (Jewish France) (1885) pp.568–9. Drumont produced this vicious work in response to the so-called Panama Scandal, in which a French attempt to construct a canal across the isthmus of Panama collapsed in a welter of corruption. The project had been headed by a Jew, Ferdinand de Lesseps, the architect of the Suez Canal, and several Jewish financiers were implicated. Drumont seized on the affair to mount a hate campaign against French Jewry in general.

2 I was only an artillery officer, whom a tragic error prevented from pursuing his normal career. Dreyfus the symbol … is not me.

Alfred Dreyfus, 1906; Stephen Wilson *Ideology and Experience: Anti-Semitism in France at the Time of the Dreyfus Affair* (1982) p.1. Dreyfus, an officer in the French army and an assimilated Jew, was wrongfully charged in 1894 with passing military secrets to Germany. He was sentenced to life imprisonment in Devil's Island penal colony off the coast of French Guiana, and eventually exonerated 11 years later after the continual efforts of his supporters to prove his innocence. His case split the country sharply in two.

3 Why are the snob, the German, the Italian, the half-breed for Dreyfus? Why is it that whoever is anti-French, or has a blemish, a sore, an intellectual deformity, a moral infection, sides with Dreyfus? Why is it that anybody who has sold out, been bribed, besmirched, contaminated, corrupted, is for Dreyfus?

Edouard Drumont, 1894; Jacques Kayser *L'Affaire Dreyfus* (1946) p.143. Drumont, in his inimitably leprous style, was quick to champion the witch-hunt against Dreyfus.

4 We seem to discern the pressure of so-called public opinion, or rather of the populace, the rabble, that is often misdirected. It mindlessly howls 'death' against this Jew because he is Jewish and because today anti-Semitism pulls the strings, just as it howled 'the aristocrats to the lamp-post' a hundred years ago.

Louis Lyautey, 1894; R. Lyautey *Dreyfusards!* (1965) pp.46–7. The future marshal of France was at this time a member of the French expeditionary force to Indo-China. To be pro-Dreyfus as an army officer was extremely unusual.

5 The [Dreyfus] Affair opened the eyes of the French and even they will one day realize that the Jew has no Fatherland and therefore knows no Fatherland.

Karl Lüger, *Deutsches Volksblatt* (German People's Paper), 15 Jan. 1895. Lüger, soon to be mayor of Vienna, was addressing an electoral meeting.

6 Just as Satan is the ape of God, so we can say that the Masons are the third estate of Jewry. The Jew, the leper and bloodsucker of the people, is going to arise arrogantly like a gigantic boa whose constricting coils are tied around a dying world, squeezing and crushing it.

Monsignor Ernest Jouin, 1898; Leon Poliakov *History of Anti-Semitism from Voltaire to Wagner* Vol.3 (1985) p.362.

7 When it comes down to it, you no longer have republican blood in your veins … It's a general you want in your bed … France, if you're not careful, you're on the road to dictatorship. And do you know where else you're going, France? You're on the way to the Church, you're going back to the past, that past of intolerance and theocracy, which your children fought, which they thought they'd killed, by sacrificing their body and their spirit.

Émile Zola *Letter to France*, 6 Jan. 1898; Roderick Kedward *The Dreyfus Affair* (1965) pp.81–2. A week later Zola published his famous letter to President Felix Fauré, 'J'accuse'. In this he named the men who had brought Dreyfus down (see Kedward (1965) pp.18–20). Zola died in 1902 of asphyxiation caused by fumes from a blocked chimney – blocked, perhaps, deliberately by his political enemies.

8 They come to France to make money, but the moment a fight is on, they hide behind the first tree. There are so many in the army because the Jew likes to parade around in fancy uniforms. Every country chases them out, there is a reason for that, and we must never allow them to occupy such a position in France.

The painter Pierre-Auguste Renoir, 15 Jan. 1898; quoted by his fellow artist Édouard Manet in his *Journal* p.148.

1 What predominates in Busk, besides the ducks and the geese, are greasy Jews … hook noses, clawlike hands gripping vague objects and relinquishing them only in exchange for solid cash.

Georges Clemenceau *Au Pied du Sinaï* (At the Foot of Sinai) (1898) pp.125–6. Clemenceau here describes the Jews of central Europe during a stay in Carlsbad. A key supporter of Dreyfus, and a friend of the Jews, Clemenceau is nevertheless unable to avoid racial stereotyping.

2 I believe that the Jews are a race, even more, a species … I truly believe that the Jew is born of a special anthropoid like the black race, the yellow race, the red skin … Today they are too dangerous to tolerate.

Maurice Barrès to Jules Soury at the second Dreyfus trial, Rennes, 1899; R. Soucy *Fascism in France: the Case of Maurice Barrès* (1972) p.141. Barrès played a central role in formulating the ideals of the generation of conservatives that came to the fore under the Nazi occupation of France from 1940 to 1944.

3 The Affair was like a sore which broke out suddenly on a sick body, on an organism in which the blood, weakened and polluted by disease, was decomposing. What was serious was the deep organic sickness of which the sore was the visible and definite sign.

Henri de Saint-Poli (Abbé Brugerette) *L'Affaire Dreyfus et la mentalité catholique en France* (1904) p.107. A penetrating anatomy of the French body politic from that rarity, a pro-Dreyfus Catholic.

BRITAIN, 1884–1913

4 Foreign Jews … either do not know how to use the latrine, water and other sanitary accommodation provided, or prefer their own semi-barbarous habits and use the floor of their rooms and passages to deposit their filth. Even in places where caretakers see that yards and closets are cleared away every morning, dirt and destruction follow the same day.

Eastern Post and City Chronicle, editorial, 22 Nov. 1884; Colin Holmes *Anti-Semitism in British Society 1876–1939* (1979) p.17. There was a widespread feeling in the East End of London during the 1880s that Jewish immigration was contributing to the pauperization of the indigenous population.

5 Some of the newspapers which opposed Nelson's commemoration were owned and inspired by people who had not a drop of English blood in their veins … This manipulation of the Press by a handful of philosophic Semites who have no more

predilection for England than for France, and who regard political questions from a pecuniary and cosmopolitan, and not from a British, standpoint, is an evil which exists, is growing and must be abated.

Arnold White, *Pall Mall Gazette*, 3 Nov. 1897. White is referring to Trafalgar Day (21 Oct.), co-equal with Waterloo Day (18 June) as sacrosanct anniversaries in the British patriotic calendar, now slurred by alien forces. A writer and journalist, he was concerned to make the British public stop and think about what was happening to its society as a consequence of alleged Jewish penetration.

6 In the heart of the crowd is a figure of a man furious at being jostled by a well clad Jew. The eyes are squinting rage, and an execration foams on his lips. The object of his rage is a rich man, with the horrible cast of countenance so common among the sweaters of modern Israel.

The Irish writer James Joyce, 'Royal Hibernian Academy "Ecce Homo"', 1899; Ellsworth Mason and Richard Ellmann (eds) *James Joyce: Critical Writings* (1989) p.37. Joyce's essay was on Mihály von Munkácsy's 1896 painting, 'Ecce Homo', depicting the moment when the Roman governor of Palestine, Pontius Pilate, consigns Christ to the Jews for execution (John 19:6). 'Sweaters' were the owners of sweatshops, whose employees worked for starvation wages.

7 In Brighton, at the Sassoons … we were forced to attend a long, hot and pompous dinner, crowded with innumerable Sassoon young ladies. Although I have no prejudices against the race (far from it) I began to understand the point of view of those who are opposed to foreign immigration!

The Conservative cabinet minister Arthur Balfour to Lady Elcho, 1900; Kenneth Young *Arthur Balfour* (1963) p.139. Although a public supporter of Zionism and later the architect of the Balfour Declaration (see 786:1), Balfour nevertheless reveals his prejudice in private. The Sassoons were extremely rich Jewish members of London high society.

8 The Jews are par excellence the international financiers … They fastened on the Rand … as they are prepared to fasten upon any other part of the globe … Primarily they are financial speculators, taking their gains not out of the genuine fruits of industry, even the industry of others, but out of the construction, promotion and financial manipulation of companies.

J.A. Hobson *The War in South Africa* (1900 edn) pp.189, 195, 197. Hobson, the radical economist, viewed the Jewish involvement in southern Africa as financially parasitic and part of a 'Jew-Imperial' strategy. The Rand was the site of the gold-mining industry in the Transvaal Republic, where Jewish financiers undoubtedly played a key role, but alongside many Gentile counterparts, such as Cecil Rhodes.

1 One particularly deplorable result of the popularity of scrofula among our imports is the extraordinary extent to which the native element is becoming infected. Many a young Englishman accustomed to travel on the railways in London is as bald as a billiard ball from letting his head rest against a cushion that had been touched by the favus-afflicted scalp of a Jew.

Joseph Bannister *England Under the Jews* (1907 edn) p.64. Bannister's rantings against Jewish immigrants in London focused on their alleged propensity to contaminate the poor in the East End. The 1905 Aliens Act stipulated that no alien be admitted to Britain if suffering from diseases such as favus, a scalp infection.

2 The best man by far in sheer intellect was a Balliol man of Polish-Jewish origin and I did my best for him, but the Warden and majority of Fellows shied at his race, and eventually we elected the two next best.

A.F. Pollard, letter to his parents, 1911; J. Namier *Lewis Namier* (1971) p.101. Pollard refers to the rejection of the application of Lewis Namier the historian for a fellowship at All Souls, Oxford, in 1911 on the grounds of his Jewish background.

3 The Jew Kings were come, but the Parliament of England was gone. I was pointed out a Jew King of opium and a Jew King of railways, and a Jew King of petrol, and a Jew King of silver, a Jew King of soap, and a Jew King of salt and soda and nickel; while lesser Princes and Powers of the Oriental immigration showed their swarthy profiles in equal distribution of patronage among the subjugated natives.

F. Hugh O'Donnell, *New Witness*, 6 Feb. 1913, p.425. O'Donnell, a former Irish Nationalist MP, describes the members of the Westminster Parliament.

ZIONISM, 1860–1914

4 No member of the Jewish race can renounce the incontestable and fundamental right of his people to its ancestral land without thereby denying his past and ancestors ... What European power would today oppose the plan that the Jews, united through a Congress, should buy back their ancient fatherland? Who would object if the Jews flung a handful of gold to decrepit old Turkey and said to her: 'Give me back my home and use this money to consolidate the other parts of your Ottoman empire'?

E. Laharanne *La Nouvelle Question d'Orient: Réconstitution de la Nation Juive* (1860). Laharanne was Napoleon III's private secretary. He was one of the first to focus on Turkish-occupied Palestine as the haven for Jewish nationalists, with Jerusalem (Zion) as its capital.

5 What we have to do at present for the regeneration of the Jewish nation is, first to keep alive the hope of the political rebirth of our people, and, next, to reawaken that hope where it slumbers. When political conditions in the Orient shape themselves so as to permit the organization of a beginning of the restoration of a Jewish state, this beginning will express itself in the founding of Jewish colonies in the land of their ancestors, to which enterprise France will undoubtedly lend a hand. France, beloved friend, is the saviour who will restore our people to its place in universal history.

Moses Hess *Rome and Jerusalem* (1862); Arthur Hertzberg *The Zionist Idea* (1959) p.133. Hess, born in Bonn in 1812, was part of the first generation of German Jews to grow up under the influence of German culture, but he became a pioneer of the movement to re-establish a Jewish presence in Palestine. His faith in an enlightened France was sadly misplaced (see 630:9).

6 Judeophobia is a form of demonopathy, with the difference that the Jewish ghost has become known to the whole race of mankind, not only to some peoples, and that it is not disembodied like other ghosts. As a being of flesh and blood, it suffers the most excruciating pain from the wounds inflicted upon it by a timorous mob who imagine themselves threatened by it. Judeophobia is a psychic disorder. As such it is hereditary and, as a disease transmitted for two thousand years, it is incurable.

Leo Pinsker *Auto-Emancipation* (1882) p.2. Pinsker, a distinguished Russian Jewish physician, lived outside the Pale of Settlement. He was the leader of a group who believed that the only option for the Jews following the devastating experience of the pogroms was to return to their Old Testament homeland. In other words, assimilation was a lost cause.

7 Next year in Jerusalem.

Slogan of the early Zionist movement.

8 I have no sympathy with the currently fashionable idea, with the movement to make the Jewish people a pure secular nationality in place of the combination of religion with nationality that has enabled us to survive to this day. Whatever merit there may be to this theory, it is to be found only in its possible value as applied to the assimilated Jews, that is, to those de-Judaized individuals who have remained members of the Jewish faith in name only and are ready to drop out of the Jewish community.

Yehiel Pines *Emet me-Erez* (1895) Vol.3, pp.23–5. Pines, born in Russian Poland, voices the disquiet of the Orthodox at the secular values of Zionism.

1 We are one people – our enemies have made us one whether we will or not, as has repeatedly happened in history. Affliction binds us together, and thus united, we suddenly discover our strength. Yes, we are strong enough to form a State, and, indeed, a model State. We possess all the requisite human and material resources.

Theodor Herzl *Der Judenstaat* (The Jewish State) (1896) p.76. Herzl, son of a rich Jewish merchant and a citizen of the Austro-Hungarian empire, became Paris correspondent of the Vienna *Neue Freie Press*. His experience in Paris during the Dreyfus affair converted him to the Zionist cause in the belief that assimilation could never be the answer to the Jewish predicament. In 1897 he promoted the first Zionist Congress in Basle. His programme was highly ambitious and, in the circumstances of the time, exceedingly optimistic.

2 It was this gigantic outpouring of grief from the depths of millions of souls that made me realize for the first time how much passion and hope this lone and lonesome man had borne into the world through the power of a single thought ... By his prophetic instinct he had foreseen the entire tragedy of his race at a time when it had not appeared to be an inevitable fate.

Stefan Zweig *The World of Yesterday: An Autobiography* (1943) pp.102, 109. A sombre reflection on Herzl's early death in 1904 from the perspective of the Nazi Holocaust (see 836:5–844:1).

3 Palestine is a country without a people; the Jews are a people without a country. The regeneration of the soil would bring the regeneration of the people.

Israel Zangwill, *New Liberal Review* Vol.2 (Dec. 1901) p.627. The classic expression of the Zionist blindness to the existence of the immensely more numerous Arab population of Palestine. Zangwill also proclaims the early Zionist belief in the virtues of agrarian democracy, via the *kibbutz*, the farming community that would rescue Jews from the urban tradition that had supposedly corrupted them. It is ironic that in 1908 Zangwill wrote a play, *The Melting Pot*, which was hailed as a call for American Jews to be absorbed into the culture of the United States, the very antithesis of Zionist particularism (see 640:1).

4 The idea of a Jewish nationality runs counter to the interests of the Jewish proletariat, for it fosters among them, directly or indirectly, a spirit hostile to assimilation, the spirit of the 'ghetto'.

Lenin (Vladimir Ilyich Ulyanov), *Iskra* (The Spark), 22 Oct. 1903. As a Marxist Socialist, Lenin was committed to internationalism and an enemy of nationalism in whatever form. His comment carries weight even so. The ghetto, or segregated quarter, was forced on Jews by Gentile authority, but for Orthodox Jews it was preferable to assimilation, since it gave them a community in which their values alone could prevail. A Zionist enclave in Palestine would have the same purpose.

5 Mankind awaits the founder of a new religion, and the struggle of its decisive round is approaching, as in the year one of our era. Once again, humanity has a choice between Judaism and Christianity, between trade and culture, between woman and man, between the species and the individual, between emptiness and value, between nothingness and divinity. There is no third kingdom.

Otto Weininger *Sex and Character* (1903) p.500. Weininger, who committed suicide at the age of 24, a few months after his book was published, foretells an apocalypse. Hitler was to say of him that 'he was the only Jew who deserved to live'.

6 The reawakening of the Arab nation, and the growing Jewish efforts at rebuilding the ancient monarchy of Israel on a very large scale – these two movements are destined to fight each other continually, until one of them triumphs over the other.

Neguib Azoury *Le Réveil de la nation arabe* (1905); Martin Gilbert *The Dent Atlas of the Arab-Israeli Conflict* (1993) p.4. The Arab writer Azoury warns presciently of the looming conflict between Arabs and Jews as Jewish settlement in Palestine gains momentum and as the Arab struggle for emancipation from the Ottoman Turks gathers strength.

7 We Jews have been living for more than two thousand years among cultured peoples and we cannot and must not descend once more to the cultural level of semi-savages. Indeed our hope that one day we shall be masters of the country is not based on the sword or on the fist but on our cultural advantage over the Arabs and Turks which will gradually increase our influence.

Yosef Klausner *Ha-Shiloah* (1907); Yosef Gorny *Zionism and the Arabs 1882–1948* (1987) p.49. It was, however, military, not cultural, superiority that created the state of Israel in 1948 and kept it in being thereafter.

8 Our Government has always shown friendship and hospitality towards your people, whenever they came to settle here. Your skill and knowledge are very beneficial to the country and its development. Our Government is aware that the Jews are not concerned with 'politics' but desire to live and work in peace ... Like that of all other good Ottoman citizens, your work is appreciated, but you must become true sons of the Fatherland, and not stepsons and nationals of foreign countries.

Mahdi Bey, Turkish governor of Palestine, address to Jewish settlers, 1912; Moshe Smilansky *Prakim B'Toledoth Ha-Yishuv* (Chapters in the History of Jewish Settlement in Palestine). The Young Turks who took power in 1908 realized the advantages of Jewish settlement in their colony, but to see the Zionists as non-political was a serious misreading of their programme.

I While gathering our strength, reinforcing our armies, and getting ready to return to Palestine – let us show to the whole world that we are as fit as any people to live as an independent political community. Maybe England will chance upon an empty piece of land in need of a white population, and perhaps the Jews will happen to be those whites – three cheers for the new match! ... We cannot take Palestine yet, even if it were given to us.

Chaim Weizmann *Zionism Needs a Living Content* (1914); Paul Goodman (ed.) *Chaim Weizmann* (1945) pp.153–5. Weizmann, Herzl's effective successor and later first president of Israel, shows his readiness (like Herzl) to accept a Zionist alternative to Palestine pending the acquisition of a Palestinian homeland.

Democracy in America, 1865–1917

THE WEST, 1866–93

1 Don't forget: the Western is not only the history of this country; it is what the Saga of the Nibelungen is for the Europeans.

Film director Fritz Lang; Peter Bogdanovich *Fritz Lang in America* (1967). The Norse Nibelung Saga, recounting the legendary exploits of a mythical kingdom, was poetically embellished in medieval Germany and became the basis of Richard Wagner's four operas in *Der Ring des Nibelungen* cycle.

2 All dead bodies stripped naked, crushed skulls, with war clubs, ears, nose and legs had been cut off, scalps torn away and the bodies pierced with bullets and arrows, wrists, feet and ankles leaving each attached by a tendon … We walked on the internals and did not know it in the high grass.

Private John Guthrie after the massacre of a US army detachment by Sioux Indians at Sand Creek, Wyoming Territory, Dec. 1866; Geoffrey C. Ward *The West* (1996) p.232.

3 We must act with vindictive earnestness against the Sioux, even to their extermination, men, women, and children. Nothing less will ever reach the root of the case.

General William Tecumseh Sherman to General Ulysses S. Grant, 1867, after the Sand Creek massacre; Ward (1996) p.235. The warrior tribe, the Sioux, were concentrated in the Dakota Territories.

4 The only good Indians I ever saw were dead.

General Philip Sheridan, allegedly said to the Comanche chief Toch-a-way, Jan. 1869, but denied by Sheridan. On 28 May 1868 Congressman J.M. Cavanaugh of Montana told the House of Representatives: 'I have never in my life seen a good Indian (and I have seen thousands) except when I have seen a dead Indian.'

5 I don't go so far as to think that the only good Indians are dead Indians, but I believe nine out of ten are, and I shouldn't inquire too closely into the cause of the tenth. The most vicious cowboy has more moral principle than the average Indian.

Theodore Roosevelt to his friend Owen Wister, 1885. Outside the Museum of Natural History in New York stands a statue of Roosevelt on horseback, with his bridle held by a faithful Indian.

6 If I were an Indian, I would certainly prefer to cast my lot … to the free open plains rather than submit to the confined limits of a reservation, there to be the recipient of the blessed benefits of civilization with its vices thrown in.

General George Armstrong Custer, 1874; Samuel Eliot Morison *The Oxford History of the American People* (1965).

7   I see over my own continent the Pacific
        Railroad surmounting every barrier,
    I see continual trains of cars winding along the
        Platte carrying freight and passengers,
    I hear the locomotives rushing and roaring,
        and the shrill steam-whistle,
    I hear the echoes reverberate throughout the
        grandest scenery in the world.

Walt Whitman *Passage to India* (1870). The railroad ran from coast to coast after the Central Pacific and Union Pacific lines joined each other at Promontory Point, Utah, on 10 May 1869. The Platte is one of the main river systems west of the Mississippi.

8 I have been on a train when the black, moving mass of buffaloes before us looked as if it stretched down to the horizon … [It] was the greatest wonder that more people were not killed, as the wild rush for the windows, and the reckless discharge of rifles and pistols, put every passenger's life in jeopardy.

Mrs Elizabeth Custer; Ward (1996) p.261. The vast herds of buffalo, on which the Plains Indians relied for their food and clothing, were virtually wiped out for sport by white incomers, many – as here – shooting them down from passing trains.

9 Mammoth Lager Beer Saloon, in the basement, corner Main and Virginia Streets, Austin, Nevada. Choice liquors, wines, lager beer and cigars, served by pretty girls, who understand their business and attend to it. Votaries of Bacchus, Gambrinus, Venus or Cupid can spend an evening agreeably at the Mammoth Saloon.

Advertisement in the Austin daily paper; Samuel Bowles *Our New West* (1869) p.279. A wide-open frontier town, catering for all appetites.

10 J.B. Hickok … shot one Mulrey at Hays Tuesday. Mulrey died yesterday morning. Bill has been elected sheriff of Ellis County.

Leavenworth, Kansas, *Times and Conservative*, 26 Aug. 1869; Ward (1996) p.279. The flamboyant gunslinger 'Wild Bill' Hickok claimed to have killed more than a hundred men (in fact, probably fewer than ten). He was shot in the back in Deadwood City, Dakota Territory, on 2 Aug. 1876, as he played poker, holding the fateful 'dead man's hand' (two pairs, aces and eights).

1 Dodge City is a wicked little town … Here those nomads in regions remote from the restraints of moral, civil, social and law-enforcing life, the Texas cattle-drovers … the embodiment of waywardness and wantonness, end the journey with their herds, and here they loiter and dispute, sometimes for months, and share the boughten dalliances of fallen women.
Washington Evening Star, 1 Jan. 1878. Ranchers drove their steers north from Texas to cowtowns such as Dodge City, Kansas, to be shipped by rail to the stockyards in Chicago. Their cowboys' reputation for wild living was legendary but, after weeks on the trail, understandable.

2   O bury me not on the lone prairie,
    Where the wild coyotes will howl o'er me,
    Where the rattlesnakes hiss and the crows fly
       free.
    O bury me not on the lone prairie.
Cowboy song of the period.

3 The women … pushed the point of an awl into each of his ears, into his head. This was done to improve his hearing, as it seemed he had not heard what our chiefs in the south had said when he smoked the pipe with them. They told him then that if ever afterward he should break that peace promise and should fight the Cheyennes, the Everywhere Spirit surely would cause him to be killed.
The Indian Kate Big Head on the treatment of General Custer's body after he and all his men were killed in the Battle of the Little Big Horn, Montana Territory, 4 July 1876; Ward (1996) pp.302–3. The Cheyenne, like the Sioux, were Indians of the Northern Plains.

4 I have carried a heavy load on my back ever since I was a boy. I learned then that we were but few while the white men were many, and that we could not hold our own with them. We were like deer. They were like grizzly bears.
Chief Joseph of the Nez Percé tribe; *North American Review*, 1879.

5 There is no actor in the company, except Buffalo Bill, who says nothing, shoots badly, and is pretty much kept in the background … The animals are cribbed, confined, and have to be whipped into a display of a little animation. We hope that Buffalo Bill, the Indians, the cowboys and the bisons will be let loose in the open again.
New York *World*, Thanksgiving Day 1886, on William Cody's Wild West Show. After a varied career, including time as a buffalo hunter and US army scout, Cody toured the United States and Europe with his circus version of life on the frontier, itself a sure sign that the West was wild no more.

6   Across the plains where once there roamed the
       Indian and the Scout,
    The Swede with alcoholic breath sets rows of
       cabbages out.
A lament for the passing of the untamed West, now the domain of bibulous, though industrious, Scandinavian settlers; D.W. Brogan *The American Problem* (1944) p.36.

7 We *made* this country … and made a safe range out of this. Some of us died doing it. And then people moved in, fenced off my range, and fenced me off from water. Some of 'em like you plow ditches and take out irrigation water, and so the crick runs dry sometimes. I've got to move my stock because of it. And you say we have no right to the range.
The rancher Rufus Riker to the farmer Joe Starrett, in Jack Schaefer's novel *Shane* (1949), set in the year 1889. The subject is the conflict between cattlemen and sodbusters, ultimately decided in the latters' favour.

8 The West is the most American part of America … What Europe is to Asia, what England is to the rest of Europe, what America is to England, that the Western States and Territories are to the Atlantic States, the heat and pressure and hurry of life always growing as we follow the path of the sun.
The British political commentator James Bryce *The American Commonwealth* (1888) Pt 6, Ch.12.

9   In summer the wild buckwheat
    Shone like fox fur and quill work,
    And dusk guttered on the creek.
    Now in serene attitudes
    Of dance, the dead in glossy
    Death are drawn in ancient light.
'Wounded Knee Creek'; Ward (1996) p.380. On 29 Dec. 1890 most of a Sioux encampment of some 350 were massacred by the US army 7th Cavalry, bringing a bloody end to the Indian wars of the past three centuries.

10 Up to and including 1880 the country had a frontier of settlement, but at the present the

unsettled area has been so broken up by isolated bodies of settlement that there can hardly be said to be a frontier line. In the discussion of its extent, its westward movement, etc., it cannot, therefore, any longer have a place in the census reports.
Superintendent of the 1890 census *Bulletin* (1891).

1 What the Mediterranean Sea was to the Greeks, breaking the bond of custom, offering new experiences, calling out new institutions and activities, that, and more, the ever-retreating frontier has been to the United States directly, and to the nations of Europe more remotely. And now, four centuries from the discovery of America, at the end of a hundred years of life under the Constitution, the frontier has gone, and with its going has closed the first period of American history.
Frederick Jackson Turner 'The Significance of the Frontier in American History', paper given to the American Historical Association, 12 July 1893; *The Frontier in American History* (1920) p.38. The 'Turner Thesis' was an immensely influential piece of historical writing, drawing a line under America's westward expansion as indicated by the 1890 census. The West now passed definitively into myth and legend.

HUDDLED MASSES, 1869–1916

2 The 60,000 or 100,000 Mongolians on our Western Coast are the thin end of the wedge which has for its base the 500,000,000 of Eastern Asia. [Failing a check on Chinese immigration] the youngest home of the nations must in its early manhood follow the path and meet the doom of Babylon, Nineveh and Rome ... Here, plain to the eye of him who chooses to see, are dragon's teeth [from which will] spring up armed men marshalled for civil war.
Henry George, *New York Tribune*, 1 May 1869. Later, in the 1880s, George was to make something of a reputation as a socialist, but he maintained his prejudices to the full in his book, significantly entitled *Social Problems* (1884).

3 It has pleased Almighty God to bring to the shores of America and to bestow upon us as a free gift, the passion of the French, the calm logic of the Teutons, the Scotchman's perseverance, the fiery eloquence and sturdy sinews of the Irishman, the Englishman's great head and purse, the Negro cheerfully toiling under the torrid sun, the patient industry of the Chinese, the Spaniard's gravity, and the indomitable spirit of the Indian warrior – the excellencies of all

the families of the earth combined in our American nationality.
Robert Patterson 'Our Indian Policy' in *Overland Monthly*, Sept. 1873, pp.213–14. A fervid tribute to the American ethnic mix.

4 We have taken into our body politic the refuse of the Paris Commune, incendiaries from Berlin and from Tipperary, some hundreds of thousands of European agitators, who are always at war with every form of government thus far known among civilized nations.
New York Tribune, 25 July 1877. Immigrants could often be branded as subversives, in this instance seen as the force behind the great railway strike currently being staged.

5 Numerous complaints have been made in regard to the Hebrew immigrants who lounge about Battery Park [public gardens, south Manhattan], obstructing the walks and sitting on the chains. Their filthy condition has caused many of the people who are accustomed to go to the park to seek a little recreation and fresh air to give up this practice.
New York Tribune, 13 June 1882. Jewish immigrants from tsarist Russia began to flood into the United States after the pogroms that followed the assassination of Alexander II in March 1881 (see 677:1).

6   'Keep, ancient lands, your storied pomp!' cries she
With silent lips. 'Give me your tired, your poor,
Your huddled masses yearning to breathe free,
The wretched refuse of your teeming shore.
Send these, the homeless, tempest-tost to me.
I lift my lamp beside the golden door!'
Emma Lazarus 'The New Colossus' (1883). Written to celebrate the forthcoming Statue of Liberty, erected in New York harbour and unveiled on 4 July 1886.

7 The immigrant, however illiterate or ignorant he may be, always learns too soon.
Henry Frick, the industrial magnate; Alistair Cooke *Alistair Cooke's America* (1973) p.293. Frick used new immigrants as strike-breakers, but they all too quickly began to unionize.

8 I have stood near Castle Garden and seen races of far greater peril to us than the Irish. I have seen the Hungarians and the Italians and the Poles. I have seen these poor wretches trooping out, wretches physically, wretches morally, and stood there almost trembling for my country, and said, what shall we do if this keeps on?
Rev. E.J. Johnson *Baptist Congress Proceedings* (1888) pp.83–4. Castle Garden, on Ellis Island in New York harbour, served as

America's immigration depot from 1855 to 1890, when it was superseded by the Ellis Island reception centre, in business until 1954.

1 The knife with which he cuts his bread he also uses to lop off another 'dago's' finger or ear … He is quite as familiar with the sight of human blood as with the sight of the food he eats.

Appleton Morgan *Popular Science Monthly* Vol.38 (1890) p.177.

2 There is a disposition in the United States to use the immigrants, and especially the Irish, much as the cat is used in the kitchen to account for broken plates and food which disappears.

The British analyst of Americana, James Bryce; M.R. Werner *Tammany Hall* (1928) p.62.

3 Beaten men from beaten races, representing the worst failures in the struggle for existence. They have none of the ideas and aptitudes which … belong to those who are descended from the tribes that met under the oak trees of old Germany to make laws and choose chieftains.

Francis A. Walker *Publications of the American Economic Association* Vol.6, p.37.

4 I pledge allegiance to my flag and to the republic for which it stands: one nation indivisible, with liberty and justice for all.

Francis M. Bellamy 'Pledge to the Flag' in *Youth's Companion*, 18 Sept. 1892. The pledge was part of a concerted effort to inculcate a new national loyalty into the immigrant communities, especially their children. It was first sworn at the inaugural celebration of Columbus Day on 21 Oct. 1892, and the ceremony is repeated each morning in every school in the USA. Two important changes were later made: the words 'my flag' were replaced by 'the flag of the United States of America'; and in 1945 Congress inserted the words 'under God' after 'one nation', a controversial move in a country whose constitution (in the First Amendment) forbade laws 'respecting an establishment of religion'.

5   America! America!
       God shed his grace on thee
       And crown thy good with brotherhood
       From sea to shining sea.

Katharine Lee Bates 'America the Beautiful' (1893). A further hymn to American nationhood, reinforcing the drive to assimilation.

6 The exclusion of immigrants unable to read or write, as proposed by this bill, will operate against the most undesirable and harmful part of our present immigration and shut out elements which

no thoughtful or patriotic man can wish to see multiplied among the people of the United States.

Senator Henry Cabot Lodge of Massachusetts, 16 March 1896; *Congressional Record*. Lodge campaigned energetically for a literacy test to restrict the inflow of immigrants. Legislation was repeatedly vetoed by successive presidents until it eventually came into force in Feb. 1917.

7 It was their skill, their intelligence, their hardy power of labor, their knack at succeeding and driving duller rivals out, rather than their alien habits, that made them feared and hated … The unlikely fellows who came in at the eastern ports were tolerated because they usurped no place but the very lowest in the scale of labor.

Future president Woodrow Wilson *A History of the American People* Vol.5 (1902) pp.213–14. This excerpt was used against Wilson in the 1912 election, when he narrowly lost California but won the presidency.

8 It is unwise to depart from the old American tradition and to discriminate for or against any man who desires to come here as a citizen, save on the grounds of that man's fitness for citizenship … We cannot afford to consider whether he is a Catholic or a Protestant, Jew or Gentile; whether he is English-man or Irishman, Frenchman or German, Japanese, Italian, Scandinavian, Slav, or Magyar.

President Theodore Roosevelt, message to Congress, 5 Dec. 1905; *The Works of Theodore Roosevelt* Vol.15 (1926) pp.319, 320. In his message of 3 Dec. 1901 Roosevelt had asked for a tightening of immigration restrictions, and he consistently approved a continuing ban on Chinese immigrants.

9 Our confidence in the American race of the future is due to the commingling on this continent of the blood and the characteristics of many people quite as much as to the unhampering environment of a new land.

Magazine *Outlook*, editorial, Vol.79 (1905) p.219.

10 Bringing with them slavery, concubinage, prostitution, the opium vice, the disease of leprosy, the offensive and defensive organization of clans and guilds, the lowest standard of living known, and a detestation of the people with whom they live and with whom they will not even leave their bones when dead, they form a community within a city and there live the Chinese life.

Senator George C. Perkins of California, 1906; Harvey Wish *Society and Thought in Modern America* (1962 edn) p.233. Chinese immigration had been reduced to virtually nil by legislation passed in 1882, but the West Coast states, where most Asian immigrants settled, were deeply hostile to them.

1 America is God's crucible, the great Melting-Pot where all the races of Europe are melting and re-forming! God is making the American.

Israel Zangwill *The Melting-Pot* (1908) Act I. A famous phrase, paying full homage to assimilation, though it is perhaps significant that Zangwill, an English Jew, does not include non-Europeans in the process.

2 I am responsible to the mothers and fathers of Sacramento County who have their little daughters sitting side by side in the school rooms with matured Japs, with their base minds, their lascivious thoughts, multiplied by their race and strengthened by their mode of life ... I have seen Japanese twenty-five years old sitting in the seats next to the pure maids of California ... I shudder to think of such a condition.

Grove Johnson, 1909; Franklin Hichborn *The Story of the Session of the California Legislature of 1909* (1909) p.207. Japanese immigration was curtailed by a diplomatic agreement between Washington and Tokyo.

3 I would quarantine this Nation against people of any government in Europe incapable of self-government for any reason, as I would against the bubonic plague.

Representative Martin Dies Sr of Texas; *Hearings Relative to the Further Restriction of Immigration* (1912) pp.49–50. How appropriate that Congressman Dies's son should follow in his father's footsteps to become chairman of the House Un-American Activities Committee.

4 Hirsute, low-browed, big-faced persons of obvious low mentality. Not that they suggest evil. They simply look out of place in black clothes and stiff collar, since clearly they belong in skins, in wattled huts at the close of the Great Ice Age.

Edward A. Ross *The Old World in the New* (1914) pp.285–6.

5 From all over the world, the Children of Israel are flocking to this country, and plans are on foot to move them from Europe *en masse* ... to empty upon our shores the very scum and dross of the *Parasite Race*.

Tom Watson *Watson's Magazine* Vol.21 (1915) p.296.

6 The refusal of the native American to work with his hands when he can hire or import serfs to do manual labor for him is the prelude to his extinction and the immigrant laborers are now breeding out

their masters and killing by filth and by crowding as effectively as by the sword.

Madison Grant *The Passing of the Great Race* (1916) Ch.1.

THE LEGACY OF SLAVERY, 1865–1916

7 They have a rope ready for this or that Union man when the Yankee bayonets are gone. They will show the Northern interlopers that have settled down here to live on their substance the way home. They will deal largely in tar and feathers. They have been in the country and visited this or that place where a fine business is done in the way of killing Negroes. They will let the Negro know what freedom is, only let the Yankee soldiers be withdrawn.

Carl Schurz, 31 July 1865; *Georgia History Quarterly* Vol.35, p.244. Schurz reported to President Andrew Johnson on conditions in the South immediately after the close of the Civil War; here he describes the situation in Savannah, Georgia.

8 These gentlemen of the south mean to win. They meant it in 1861 when they opened fire on Sumter. They meant it in 1865 when they sent a bullet through the brain of Abraham Lincoln. They mean it now. The moment we remove the iron hand from the Rebels' throats they will rise and attempt the mastery.

Horace Greeley in the newspaper he founded, *New York Tribune*, 15 Nov. 1865.

9 Persons of color constitute no part of the militia of the State, and no one of them shall, without permission in writing from the District Judge or Magistrate, be allowed to keep a fire arm, sword, or other military weapon; except that one of them, who is the owner of a farm, may keep a shot gun or a rifle, such as is ordinarily used in hunting, but not a pistol, musket or other fire arm or weapon appropriate for purposes of war.

Article 13 of the South Carolina 'Black Code', enacted Dec. 1865; *Major Crises in American History* Vol.2 (1962) p.23. The defeated Southern states were determined to preserve a monopoly of fire power in white hands in case of black insurrection.

10 If I had the power, I would arm every wolf, panther, catamount [mountain lion] and bear in the mountains of America, every crocodile in the swamps of Florida, every negro in the south, every devil in Hell, clothe him in the uniform of the Federal army, and then turn them loose on the rebels of the south and exterminate every man, woman and child south of the Mason and Dixon's line.

William Gannaway Brownlow, governor of Tennessee, 1866. Brownlow, a fire-eating Methodist popularly known as 'the Fighting Parson', was that curiosity, a Southern Unionist. Charles Mason and Jeremiah Dixon were surveyors employed in 1763 to delimit the boundary between the colonies of Pennsylvania and Maryland. The line they established became thought of as the divide between North and South, and hence between free states and slave states.

1 All persons born, or naturalized in the United States, and subject to the jurisdiction thereof, are citizens of the United States and of the State wherein they reside. No State shall make or enforce any law which shall abridge the privileges and immunities of citizens of the United States, nor shall any State deprive any person of life, liberty, or property, without due process of law; nor deny to any person within its jurisdiction the equal protection of the laws.

Section 1 of the Fourteenth Amendment to the Constitution, ratified on 28 July 1868. This amendment was designed to give political substance to Abraham Lincoln's Emancipation Proclamation (see 590:8) and endow the blacks of the South with full rights of citizenship. In the event, it was to be flouted with impunity after the withdrawal of Northern troops in 1877 and soon became used instead to protect business corporations against government interference (see 642:8).

2 The right of citizens of the United States to vote shall not be denied or abridged by the United States or by any State on account of race, color, or previous condition of servitude.

Section 1 of the Fifteenth Amendment to the Constitution, ratified on 30 March 1870. This amendment, too, was framed to give the blacks of the South a critical part of their citizenship rights, but it also was disembowelled by Southern legislation after 1877, and Southern blacks did not begin to achieve their due until the passage of the laws put through by President Lyndon Johnson in the mid-1960s (see 905:8).

3 If any Senator now, in looking over the record of crime of all ages, can tell me of an association, a conspiracy, or a band of men who combined in their acts and in their purposes more that is diabolical than this Ku Klux Klan I should like to know where it is. They are secret, oath-bound; they murder, rob, plunder, whip, and scourge; and they commit these crimes, not upon the high and lofty, but upon the lowly, upon the poor, upon feeble men and women who are utterly defenseless.

Senator John Sherman of Ohio, 18 March 1871; *Congressional Record*. Sherman was castigating the self-styled 'Invisible

Empire' of the Ku Klux Klan, a secret society founded in May 1866 to defend white interests by force. The name was a bastardization of the Greek word *kuklos* (circle). Headed by a Grand Wizard (the former Confederate General Nathan Bedford Forrest), its members wore white hoods to protect their anonymity and burned fiery crosses in front of their black victims' houses. The Klan was formally disbanded in 1869 but its values persisted throughout the South.

4 In the South, the war is what A.D. is elsewhere; they date from it.

Mark Twain (Samuel Langhorne Clemens) *Life on the Mississippi* (1883).

5 The Old South rested everything on slavery and agriculture, unconscious that these could neither give nor maintain healthy growth. The New South presents a perfect democracy … and a diversified industry that meets the complex needs of this complex age.

Henry W. Grady, editor of the Atlanta *Constitution*, speech to the New England Club, New York, 1886; William J. Cooper Jr and Thomas E. Terrill *The American South* (1990) p.452. Grady followed General Sherman, terminator of the South in the final year of the Civil War. Their speeches set the seal on the reconciliation of North and South that followed the withdrawal of Northern occupation forces in 1877. The 'New South' was, of course, still akin to the 'Old South' in that it had its blacks under firm control, thanks to the acquiescence of the North, and it was far from the 'perfect democracy' claimed by Grady.

6 I recognize the Republican party as the sheet anchor of the colored man's political hopes and the ark of his safety.

The black leader Frederick Douglass, 15 Aug. 1888; Douglass Papers, Library of Congress. The party of Lincoln in fact did very little for the blacks of the South in the closing years of the century, but they had no other political home.

7 The wisest among my race understand that the agitation of questions of social equality is the extremest folly and that progress of all the privileges that will come to us must be the result of severe and constant struggle rather than of artificial forcing. No race that has anything to contribute to the markets of the world is long in any degree ostracized.

The black spokesman Booker T. Washington, 18 Sept. 1895; Wish (1962 edn) p.52. Washington stood for cautious moderation on the part of blacks, and it is not surprising that this speech was warmly applauded by his white audience in Atlanta, Georgia. To his supporters he was a realist, to his critics a servile 'Uncle Tom'.

8   I know why the caged bird sings, ah me,
      When his wing is bruised and his bosom sore,

When he beats his bars and he would be free;
It is not a carol of joy or glee,
But a prayer that he sends from his heart's deep
core.

Paul Laurence Dunbar 'Sympathy' (1895). A metaphor of the
plight of the blacks of the South.

1   Southern trees bear strange fruit,
Blood on the leaves and blood at the root.
Black bodies swinging
In the southern breeze,
Strange fruit hanging
From the poplar trees.

Lewis Allan 'Strange Fruit' (1939). The 1890s were disfigured
by a severe outburst of lynching of blacks by whites, more
than in any other decade.

2 We consider the underlying fallacy of the
plaintiff's argument to consist in the assumption
that the enforced separation of the two races stamps
the colored race with a badge of inferiority. If this be
so, it is not by reason of anything found in the act,
but solely because the colored race chooses to put
that construction upon it.

Supreme Court Justice Henry Brown, stating the majority
opinion in the case of Plessy v. Ferguson, 1896; H.S. Commager
(ed.) Documents of American History (1973 edn) p.629. The
court pronounced on the constitutionality of an 1890 act by
the Louisiana state legislature providing for 'equal but
separate' railway carriages for whites and non-whites. The
facilities in question were certainly separate but by no means
equal, yet the judgement prevailed for nearly 60 years (see
904:5).

3 What can more certainly arouse race hate ... than
state enactments which in fact proceed on the
ground that colored citizens are so inferior and
degraded that they cannot be allowed to sit in public
coaches occupied by white citizens? ... Our Constitution is color-blind, and neither knows nor
tolerates classes among citizens ... In respect of civil
rights, all citizens are equal before the law. The
humblest is the peer of the most powerful.

Supreme Court Justice John Harlan, dissenting in the case of
Plessy v. Ferguson, 1896; Commager (1973 edn) p.630.

4 The problem of the twentieth century is the
problem of the color line.

The black activist W.E.B. DuBois To the Nations of the World
(1900).

5 He would not Africanize America, for America has
too much to teach the world and Africa. He would

not bleach his Negro soul in a flood of white
Americanism, for he knows that Negro blood has a
message for the world. He simply wishes to make it
possible for a man to be a Negro and an American,
without being cursed and spit upon by his fellows,
without having the doors of Opportunity closed
roughly in his face.

W.E.B. DuBois, 1901; Cooper and Terrill (1990) p.552.

6 I fought beside the colored troops at Santiago, and
I hold that if a man is good enough to be put up and
shot at, then he is good enough for me to do what
I can to get him a square deal,

President Theodore Roosevelt, 27 May 1903; Edmund Morris
Theodore Rex (2001) p.233. The phrase 'square deal' became
the hallmark of Roosevelt's presidency. On 16 Oct. 1901,
shortly after becoming president, Roosevelt had Booker T.
Washington to dinner in the White House, the first black man
to be entertained there. Roosevelt could do little, however,
to improve the plight of blacks in general during his time in
office. The president had, as head of his volunteer cavalry
squadron of 'Rough Riders', taken part in the Battle of
Santiago in the Spanish-American war of 1898.

7 [Mississippi] disfranchised not only the ignorant
and vicious black, but the ignorant and vicious
white as well, and the electorate in Mississippi is now
confined to those, and to those alone, who are
qualified by intelligence and character for the proper
and patriotic exercise of this great franchise.

Representative Eaton J. Bowers of Mississippi, 1904; Morris
(2001) p.540. A justification for what was, in effect, the denial
of the vote to blacks.

8 Our legislature was composed of a majority of
Negroes, most of whom could neither read nor
write. They were the easy dupes and tools of as dirty
a band of vampires and robbers as ever preyed upon
a prostrate people ... Life ceased to be worth having
on the terms under which we were living, and in
desperation we determined to take the government
away from the Negroes ... [This] we regard as a
second declaration of independence by the Caucasian
[ethnically white] from African barbarism.

Senator Ben Tillman of South Carolina, 21 Jan. 1907;
Congressional Record. Tillman looks back to the days of
Reconstruction, in the decade after the Civil War, when
assemblies with black majorities were imposed on the beaten
South. The answer, when Reconstruction ended in 1877, was
to eliminate the blacks from the political life of the South by
every piece of chicanery known to white law-makers.

9 The native American has always found and finds
now in the black man willing followers who ask only

to obey and to further the ideals and wishes of the master race, without trying to inject into the body politic their own views, whether racial, religious, or social. Negroes are never socialists or labor unionists and as long as the dominant imposes its will on the servient race and as long as they remain in the same relation to the whites as in the past, the Negroes will be a valuable element in the community, but once raised to social equality their influence will be destructive to themselves and to the whites.
Madison Grant (1916) Ch.7.

GILDED AGE POLITICS, 1865–83

1 If colored men get their rights, and not colored women theirs, you see the colored men will be masters over the women, and it will be just as bad as before.
The black woman activist Sojourner Truth (Isabella Van Wagener), to the American Equal Rights Association, 1867; Miriam Schnier *Feminism: The Essential Historical Writings* (1972) Pt 3.

2 I urge a sixteenth amendment because 'manhood suffrage', or a man's government, is civil, religious and social disorganization. The male element is a destructive force, stern, selfish, aggrandizing, loving war, violence, conquest, acquisition, breeding in the moral and material world alike discord, disorder, disease and death.
Elizabeth Cady Stanton, 1868, at the Washington Women Suffrage Convention. A constitutional amendment giving women the vote was to be enacted, but not until 1920.

3 It was we, the people; not we, the white male citizens; nor yet we, the male citizens: but we, the whole people, who formed the Union. And we formed it, not to give the blessings of liberty, but to secure them; not to the half of ourselves and the half of our posterity, but to the whole people – women as well as men.
Susan B. Anthony, 17 June 1873; Ida Husted Harper *The Life and Work of Susan B. Anthony* (1898) Ch.25. Spoken in court after her conviction for trying to vote in the presidential election of 5 Nov. 1872. Susan Anthony was eventually given her due when a dollar coin was struck in her honour in 1979.

4 Perhaps the fact that I am not a Radical or a believer in the all-powerful ballot for woman to right her wrongs and that I do not scorn womanly duties, but claim it as a privilege to clean up and sort

of supervise the room and sew things, etc., is winning me stronger allies than anything else.
Ellen Henrietta Swallow Richards, 11 Feb. 1871; Caroline L. Hunt *The Life of Ellen H. Richards* (1912) Ch.5.

5 The system of corporate life and corporate power, as applied to industrial development, is yet in its infancy ... It, perhaps, only remains for the coming man ... to put Caesarism at once in control of the corporation and of the proletariat, to bring our vaunted institutions within the rule of all historic precedent.
Charles Francis Adams Jr and Henry Brooks Adams 'A Chapter of Erie' in *North American Review*, July 1869. The Adams brothers, scions of the famous Boston family that had given the United States two presidents, found post-Civil War industrial capitalism grossly distasteful and combined to write a devastating exposé of the manifold corrupt practices of the burgeoning railway network.

6 Let Us Prey.
Caption to *Harper's Weekly* cartoon of the Tweed Ring by the illustrator Thomas Nast, c.1871. William Marcy Tweed was a deeply corrupt New York politician, here attacked by Nast in the most graphic possible way. The cartoon shows Tweed and his confederates gloating over the bones of Law, Justice and Liberty.

7 I placed it where it would do the most good.
Representative Oakes Ames of Massachusetts, 1872. Ames sold Crédit Mobilier stock at a fraction of its real value to a number of leading political figures in an attempt to forestall an inquiry into his dubious dealings in the Union Pacific Railroad. He was formally censured by Congress in 1873 and died soon afterwards.

8 I think I can say, and say with pride, that we have some legislatures that bring higher prices than any in the world.
Mark Twain *Sketches, New and Old* (1875). Perhaps the origin of the phrase 'The finest Congress money can buy'.

9 Turn the rascals out!
Charles A. Dana, *New York Sun*, 1872. A slogan coined for the Democratic and Liberal Republican candidate for the presidency, Horace Greeley, who failed to deny Ulysses S. Grant a second term and died a few weeks after his overwhelming defeat.

10 Their real object is office and power. When Doctor Johnson defined patriotism as the last refuge of a scoundrel, he was unconscious of the then undeveloped possibilities of the word 'reform'.
Senator Roscoe Conkling of New York on the reformers of the 1870s; D.W. Brogan *The American Political System* (1933) p.189.

1 The robber baron, the medieval merchant, the despotic tax-gatherer, reappear in merchant princes, 'protected' manufacturers, 'national' bankers, and railway 'magnates'.
Willard C. Flagg, president of the Illinois State Farmers' Association, quoted by E.L. Godkin, editor of *The Nation*, 28 Jan. 1875. Matthew Josephson's bestselling book *The Robber Barons* was published in 1934.

2 There is fast forming in this country an aristocracy of wealth, the worst form of aristocracy that can curse the prosperity of any country.
Peter Cooper, c.1875; Peter Lyon 'The Honest Man' in *American Heritage*, Feb. 1959. The inventor and philanthropist Cooper was no uncritical admirer of the capitalism that made him a considerable fortune.

3 If you have to pay money to have the right thing done, it is only just and fair to do it … If a man has the power to do great evil and won't do right unless he is bribed to do it, I think the time spent will be gained when it is a man's duty to go up and bribe the judge.
Collis P. Huntington, 1877; Josephson (1934) p.354.

4 The great mass of the people are interested in only three things – food, clothing, and shelter. A politician in a district such as mine sees to it that his people get these things. If he does, then he doesn't have to worry about their loyalty and support.
Martin Lomasney, ward boss of Boston's Ward Eight; Leslie Ainley *Boston Mahatma: Martin Lomasney* (1949).

5 It was said that $1 a day was not enough to support a wife and six children. It was not enough if a man smoked, if he drank beer and if he and his family wanted superior clothing, food and shelter. But is not $1 a day enough to buy bread? And water costs nothing; and a man that can't live on bread is not fit to live.
Rev. Henry Ward Beecher, *New York Herald*, 23 July 1877. Sermon preached during the national rail strike.

6 Mrs W.H. Vanderbilt herself personated a Venetian princess … and on her head was a Venetian cap covered with magnificent jewels, among them a peacock in many-colored gems … Mr W.H. Vanderbilt appeared as the Duke de Guise; Mr Cornelius Vanderbilt as Louis XVI; Mrs Cornelius Vanderbilt as the Electric Light, in white satin trimmed with diamonds, and with a superb diamond head-dress.
Description of a New York society ball held on 26 March 1883; William A. Croffurt *The Vanderbilts and the Story of Their Fortune* (1886) pp.196–7. The Vanderbilt family owed the beginnings of their stupendous fortune to Cornelius Vanderbilt Sr, father of William Henry and grandfather of Cornelius Jr. Now railway magnates and financiers, they were proud to display their wealth by extravaganzas of this kind, aping the European aristocracy on the grandest scale, though it is doubtful whether the Venetian Republic ever boasted a princess of its own.

7 The public be damned! I'm working for my stockholders.
William H. Vanderbilt, 1883; attrib.

8 Cornelius Vanderbilt was the greatest and most useful communist of his day … as the exponent of a small class of men who have achieved enormous fortunes in a single life, and yet have done more than any other men to bring an ample subsistence within the easy reach of all at a less and less cost.
Edward Atkinson *Century Magazine* Vol.33 (1888) p.241.

9 The forgotten man works and votes – generally he prays – and his chief business in life is to pay.
William Graham Sumner *The Forgotten Man* (1883). The words 'forgotten man' were to be used to great effect 50 years later by Franklin D. Roosevelt (see 766:8).

REVOLT OF THE MASSES, 1885–1900

10 When class antipathies are deepened; when socialistic organizations, armed and drilled, are in every city, and the ignorant and vicious power of crowded populations has fully found itself; when the corruption of city government is grown apace … with idle workmen gathered, sullen and desperate, in the saloons; with unprotected wealth at hand; with the tremendous forces of chemistry within easy reach … THEN will come the real test of our institutions.
Josiah Strong *Our Country: Its Possible Future and its Present Crisis* (1885) pp.143–4.

11 [The bombing of 1886] had brought to the fore, once and for all, as by a flash of lightning, the whole problem of mass against class … It changed, quite as an eruption might, the whole face of the commercial landscape.
Theodore Dreiser *The Titan* (1914). The reference is to the killing of seven policemen by bomb-throwing anarchists in Haymarket Square, Chicago, on 4 May 1886.

1 The 'dead line' has been definitely fixed between the forces of disorder and anarchy and those of order. Bomb-throwing means swift death to the thrower. Rioters assembling in numbers and marching to pillage will be remorselessly shot down.
Andrew Carnegie *Forum* Aug. 1886. The generalissimo of the American steel industry issues his declaration of war on industrial dissidence.

2 I can hire one half of the working class to kill the other half.
Jay Gould, attrib. The railroad financier Gould was the very prototype of a ruthless capitalist, well capable of a pronouncement like this.

3 The table glittered with plate and costly china. The ladies were sumptuously dressed and wore the jewels of queens. The scene was of costly elegance and lavish luxury ... I sat in silence until Edith began to rally me on my sombre looks, What ailed me? ... 'I have been in Golgotha,' at last I answered. 'I have seen humanity hanging on a cross! ... Do you not know that close to your doors a great multitude of men and women, flesh of your flesh, live lives that are agony from birth to death?'
Edward Bellamy in his utopian novel *Looking Backward 2000–1887* (1888) Ch.28. The novel looks to a United States in the year 2000, in which there is nationalization of industry and equal distribution of wealth, in contrast with the capitalist jungle of the late 1880s.

4 Conspicuous consumption of valuable goods is a means of reputability to the gentleman of leisure. As wealth accumulates on his hands, his own unaided effort will not avail to sufficiently put his opulence in evidence by this method. The aid of friends and competitors is therefore brought in by resorting to the giving of valuable presents and expensive feasts and entertainments.
Thorstein Veblen *The Theory of the Leisure Class* (1899) Ch.4.

5 The day is not far distant when the man who dies leaving behind him millions of available wealth ... will pass away 'unwept, unhonoured, and unsung' ... Of such as those the public verdict will be: 'The man who dies rich dies disgraced.' Such, in my opinion, is the true gospel concerning wealth, obedience to which is destined some day to solve the problem of the rich and poor, and to bring 'Peace on earth, among men good will.'
Andrew Carnegie 'Wealth' in *North American Review*, June 1889. The British Liberal leader W.E. Gladstone, after he had

met Carnegie, noted in his diary for 13 July 1887: 'He said he should consider it disgraceful to die a rich man.' The steel magnate Carnegie left huge bequests in his will, notably for public libraries and for his Endowment for International Peace.

6 Money is power. Every good man and woman ought to strive for power, to do good with it when obtained. Tens of thousands of men and women get rich honestly. But they are often accused by an envious, lazy crowd of unsuccessful persons of being dishonest and oppressive. I say, Get rich! But get money honestly, or it will be a withering curse.
Baptist minister Russell H. Conwell *Acres of Diamonds* (1890) p.19.

7 The purification of politics is an iridescent dream. Government is force ... The Decalogue [Ten Commandments] and the Golden Rule ['Do as you would be done by'] have no place in a political campaign ... The commander who lost the battle through the activity of his moral nature would be the derision and jest of history.
John J. Ingalls, *New York World*, 1890.

8 The fruits of the toil of millions are boldly stolen to build up colossal fortunes for a few, unprecedented in the history of mankind; and the possessors of these, in turn, despise the republic and endanger liberty. From the same prolific womb of governmental injustice we breed the two great classes – tramps and millionaires.
Ignatius Donnelly, Platform of the People's Party of America, 1892, Preamble; Louis M. Hacker (ed.) *The Shaping of the American Tradition* Vol.2 (1947) p.835. The People's Party (or Populists) was formed to contest the presidency, largely in the name of the farmers of the Middle West. The Populists marked the last throw of Jefferson's agrarian democracy, now superseded by the industrial capitalism of the urban east.

9 The lessons of paternalism ought to be unlearned and the better lesson taught that while the people should patriotically and cheerfully support their government, its functions do not include the support of the people.
President Grover Cleveland, inaugural address, 4 March 1893. The winner of the 1892 election emphatically rejects the Populists' call for an interventionist White House.

10 God has bestowed upon us certain powers and gifts which no one is at liberty to take from us or to interfere with. All attempts to deprive us of them is theft. Under the same head may be placed all purposes to deprive us of the right to earn property or to use it as we see fit.

James McCosh *Our Moral Nature* (1892) p.40. No Proudhonist he (see 549:5)!

1 By the Fourteenth Amendment it is provided that no State shall deprive any person of property without due process of law nor deny to any person within its jurisdiction the equal protection of the laws. That corporations are persons within the meaning of this Amendment is now settled.

US Supreme Court Justice John Harlan, voicing majority opinion in the case of Smyth v. Ames, 1897. The Fourteenth Amendment of 1868 was designed to safeguard the rights of American blacks, but in the 1880s, notably in the case of Santa Clara County v. Southern Pacific Railroad (1886), it was argued that industrial corporations were to be regarded as 'persons' and given legal protection against any encroachment on their rights.

2 Every child should be taught that useful work is worship and that intelligent labor is the highest form of prayer.

Robert G. Ingersoll *How to Reform Mankind* (1896).

3 Like the ogres in fairy-tales, the cholera sucks out the lives of the children. A boa would not leave them like the summer in New York leaves the children of the poor – corroded, deprived, emptied-out and skinny. Their eyes appear cavernous, their skulls the bald heads of old men, their hands, bundles of dried twigs.

José Martí, early 1890s; *Complete Works* Vol.39 (1941) p.189. The Cuban nationalist Martí spent some years in New York before meeting his death in the insurrection against Spain in 1895.

4 There are those who believe that if only you will legislate to make the well-to-do prosperous, their prosperity will leak through on those below. The Democratic idea, however, has been that if you make the masses prosperous, their prosperity will find its way up through every class which rests above them.

The Democratic candidate for the presidency, William Jennings Bryan, accepting the party's nomination, 8 July 1896; Commager (1973 edn) p.628. An early reference to the 'trickle-down effect'.

5 You shall not press down upon the brow of labor this crown of thorns. You shall not crucify mankind upon a cross of gold.

William Jennings Bryan, 8 July 1896; Commager (1973 edn) p.628. A famous piece of political rhetoric, which Bryan had

already foreshadowed in a speech in the House of Representatives on 22 Dec. 1894.

6 A half-baked glib little briefless jack-leg lawyer ... grasping with anxiety to collar that $50,000 salary, promising the millennium to everybody with a hole in his pants and destruction to everybody with a clean shirt.

John Hay on Bryan, 1896; Paolo Coletta *William Jennings Bryan* (1964) pp.194–5.

PROGRESSIVE ERA, 1901–17

7 Now look, that damned cowboy is President of the United States.

Senator Mark Hanna of Ohio on Theodore Roosevelt, 16 Sept. 1901; Morris (2001) p.30. Vice-President Roosevelt succeeded President William McKinley on the latter's death eight days after an assassination attempt on 6 Sept. Hanna, a highly conservative Republican, was rightly apprehensive about the attitude Roosevelt would take towards business interests.

8 If we have done anything wrong, send your man to my man and they can fix it up.

John Pierpont Morgan to President Roosevelt, Feb. 1902; Frederick Lewis Allen *The Great Pierpont Morgan* (1950) p.220. The stupendously rich financier Morgan clearly equated himself with the head of the American state and government after Roosevelt had determined to prosecute Morgan's Northern Securities Company for breach of the Sherman Anti-Trust Act of 1890. As Roosevelt put it: 'Mr Morgan could not help regarding me as a big rival operator, who either intended to ruin all his interests, or else could be induced to come to an agreement to ruin none' (Allen (1950) p.221).

9 The rights and interest of the laboring man will be protected and cared for – not by the labor agitators but by the Christian men to whom God in His infinite wisdom has given the control of the property interests of the country, and upon the successful management of which so much depends.

George F. Baer, Pennsylvania mine-owner, to a striker, 17 July 1902; *Literary Digest*, 30 Aug. 1902, p.258.

10 It will be a great mistake for the community to shoot the millionaires, for they are the bees that make the honey, and contribute most to the hive even after they have gorged themselves full.

Andrew Carnegie *The Empire of Business* (1902) p.132.

11 The leader and his captains have their hold because they take care of their own. They speak pleasant words, smile friendly smiles, notice the baby, give picnics up the River or the Sound, or a slap on the back; find jobs, mostly at the city's expense, but they have also news-stands, peddling privileges, railroads and other business places to dispense; they permit violations of the law, and if a man has broken the law without permission, see him through the court.

Lincoln Steffens, *McClure's Magazine*, Nov. 1903. The investigative journalist Steffens depicts the political machine of the American city.

1 I don't own a dishonest dollar. If my worst enemy was given the job of writin' my epitaph when I'm gone, he couldn't do more than write: George W. Plunkitt. He Seen His Opportunities and He Took 'Em.

George Washington Plunkitt, the legendary boss of Tammany Hall, New York, expounds the philosophy of 'honest graft'; William L. Riordan *Plunkitt of Tammany Hall* (1905) p.8.

2 The overthrow of capitalism is the object of the Socialist Party. It will not fuse with any other party and it would rather die than compromise. The Socialist Party comprehends the magnitude of its task and has the patience of preliminary defeat and the faith of ultimate victory.

The socialist leader Eugene V. Debs, 1 Sept. 1904; Hacker Vol.2 (1947) p.965. A century on, socialism in America still awaits its ultimate victory.

3 The United States is the one country in which the ... Marxist theory of evolution has been most minutely fulfilled; in the accumulation of capital it has reached the stage ... immediately preceding the Götterdämmerung of the capitalist world. [But the American worker] is not in any way antagonistic to the capitalistic economic system as such ... Indeed ... he enters into it with all his heart. I believe he loves it.

The German economist Werner Sombart, 1906; Robert W. Smuts *European Impressions of the American Worker* (1953) p.13.

4 I believe the power to make money is a gift of God ... to be developed and used to the best of our ability for the good of mankind. Having been endowed with the gift I possess, I believe it is my duty to make money and still more money, and to use the money I make for the good of my fellow men according to the dictates of my conscience.

John D. Rockefeller, the oil billionaire; Josephson (1934) p.325. Rockefeller, one of the richest men in the world, taught in a Sunday School. His benefactions during his lifetime

totalled more than $500 million, notably to the Rockefeller Institute for Medicine, later Rockefeller University.

5 The liberty of the citizen to do as he likes so long as he does not interfere with the liberty of others to do the same, which has been a shibboleth for some well-known writers, is interfered with by school laws, by the Post Office, by every state or municipal institution which takes his money for purposes thought desirable, whether he likes it or not. The Fourteenth Amendment does not enact Mr Herbert Spencer's *Social Statics*.

Supreme Court Justice Oliver Wendell Holmes Jr, 1905, in the case of Lochner v. New York; Commager (1973 edn) p.41. A celebrated assault on the doctrine of laissez-faire, as taken to its extreme in the propagandist work of the political philosopher Spencer, published in 1851.

6 Taxes are what we pay for civilized society.

Oliver Wendell Holmes Jr, in the case of Compañía General de Tabacos de Filipinas v. Collector of Internal Revenue, 1904. Engraved high on a Federal government building in the 'Hoover Mile' in Washington, D.C.

7 We saw a hog that had just been killed, cleaned, washed, and started on its way to the cooking room, fall from the sliding rail to a dirty wooden floor and slide part way into a filthy men's privy. It was picked up by two employees, placed upon a truck, carried to the cooling room and hung up with other carcasses, no effort being made to clean it.

Upton Sinclair, author of *The Jungle* (1906), prompted this Congressional Report of 4 June 1906. Sinclair, like Steffens, was a crusading journalist, working to expose the dark underside of American capitalism.

8 The men with the muckrakes are often indispensable to the well-being of society, but only if they know when to stop raking the muck, and to look upward to the celestial crown above them ... If they gradually grow to feel that the whole world is nothing but muck, their power of usefulness is gone.

President Theodore Roosevelt, 14 April 1906; *Works* Vol.16 (1926) p.418. Writers like Sinclair were given the nickname of 'muckrakers'. Roosevelt here cautions them not to go too far, citing John Bunyan's *The Pilgrim's Progress* Pt 2 (1684).

9 The moral flabbiness born of the exclusive worship of the bitch-goddess SUCCESS. That – with the squalid cash interpretation put on the word 'success' – is our national disease.

The philosopher William James to the British writer H.G. Wells, 11 Sept. 1906; Henry James (ed.) *The Letters of William James* Vol.2 (1920) p.260.

1 We are under a Constitution, but the Constitution is what the judges say it is, and the judiciary is the safeguard of our liberty and of our property under the Constitution.

Charles Evans Hughes, governor of New York, 3 May 1907; *Addresses and Papers of Charles Evans Hughes, Governor of New York, 1906–1908* (1908) p.139. Hughes later became Chief Justice of the US Supreme Court, which remained a bastion of the status quo until 1937 (see 768:7).

2 It may well be that the determination of the government (in which, gentlemen, it will not waver) to punish certain malefactors of great wealth, has been responsible for some of the trouble [on the stock market] ... I regard this contest as one to determine who shall rule this free country – the people through their governmental agents, or a few ruthless and domineering men whose wealth makes them peculiarly formidable because they hide behind the breastworks of corporate organization.

President Theodore Roosevelt, 20 Aug. 1907; *Works* Vol.16 (1926) p.84.

3 I am reminded of the drunk who, when he had been thrown down the stairs of a club for the third time, gathered himself up, and said, 'I am on to those people. They don't want me in there.'

Admirable good humour from three-time loser William Jennings Bryan, 1908, after his final defeat as Democratic candidate for the presidency.

4   Hallelujah, I'm a bum!
   Hallelujah, bum again!
   Hallelujah, give us a handout
   To revive us again.

Industrial Workers of the World Songbook (1908). The IWW (or 'Wobblies'), founded in 1905, formed the extreme left wing of the American trade union movement.

5   It is we who plowed the prairies;
   Built the cities where they trade;
   Dug the mines and built the workshops;
   Endless miles of railroad laid;
   Now we stand outcast and starving,
   'Mid the wonders we have made;
   But the Union makes us strong.

Ralph Chaplin 'Solidarity Forever!' (1908). Sung to the tune of 'John Brown's Body'.

6   You will eat, bye and bye,
   In that glorious land above the sky;
   Work and pray, live on hay.
   You'll get pie in the sky when you die.

Lyric by the radical labour organizer and song-writer Joe Hill, 1910. Hill was a leading figure in the IWW (see 649:7).

7 No organization of men, not excepting the Ku Klux Klan, the Mafia, or the Black Hand Society, has ever produced such a record of barbarism as this so-called organized labor society, which through mis-directed sympathy, apathy, and indifference, has been permitted to grow up to cripple our industries and to trample in the dust the national and consti-tutional rights of our citizens.

John Kirby Jr, president of the National Association of Manufacturers, 11 Jan. 1910; Francis X. Sutton *et al. The American Business Creed* (1956) p.389. Big business gives its verdict on the IWW. The Mafia, the Sicilian secret society, was then busily extending its criminal operations into the United States. The Black Hand was a Serbian terrorist organization.

8 Other nations have been rich and powerful, but the United States has believed that it had an original contribution to make to the history of society by the production of a self-determining, self-restrained, intelligent democracy. It is in the Middle West that society has formed on lines least like Europe. It is here, if anywhere, that American democracy will make its stand against the tendency to adjust to a European type.

Frederick Jackson Turner, 1910; *The Frontier in American History* (1920) pp.281–2. The voice of Middle America, political as well as geographical.

9 Combinations in industry are the result of an imperative economic law which cannot be repealed by political legislation ... The way out lies, not in attempting to prevent such combinations, but in completely controlling them in the interest of public welfare.

Theodore Roosevelt, 31 Aug. 1910; *The New Nationalism* (1961 edn) p.27. Roosevelt accepted the fact of big business; others did not.

10 Is there not a causal connection between the development of these huge, indomitable trusts and the horrible crimes now under investigation? Is it not irony to speak of equality of opportunity in a country cursed with bigness?

Louis D. Brandeis *Survey*, 30 Dec. 1911. Brandeis, later a Supreme Court Justice, became one of the chief spokesmen for a campaign against business monopolies.

11 When all the combinations are combined ... then there is something that even the government of the nation itself might come to fear – something for the law to pull apart, and gently, but firmly and persistently, dissect.

Woodrow Wilson, 1912; *The New Freedom* (1913) p.188. Wilson, soon to be president, campaigned for the presidency on a policy of fragmenting business monopolies, but once in office he did little in practice to follow through. His rhetoric, however, was to inspire one wing of the New Deal in the 1930s (see 768:7).

1 It matters not one iota what political party is in power, or what president holds the reins of office. We are not politicians or public thinkers: we are the rich; we own America; we got it, God knows how; but we intend to keep it.

Frederick T. Marten *The Passing of the Idle Rich* (1911).

2 We stand at Armageddon, and we battle for the Lord.

Theodore Roosevelt, 17 June 1912, on the eve of the Republican National Convention; William Roscoe Thayer *Theodore Roosevelt* (1919) p.364. Ex-President Roosevelt once again sought the Republican presidential nomination, which went to President William Howard Taft. He then formed the Progressive Party to contest the 1912 election, lost the election, but made certain that Taft lost it too – to Woodrow Wilson.

3 This party comes from the grass roots. It has grown from the soil of the people's hard necessities.

Former senator Albert Beveridge at the Progressive Party Convention, 5 Aug. 1912; Claude G. Bowers *Beveridge and the Progressive Era* (1932) p.426.

4 The extreme complexity of the administrative problems presented by modern industrial civilization is beyond the compass of the capitalistic mind. If this be so, American society, as at present organized, with capitalists for the dominant class,

can concentrate no further, and, as nothing in the universe is at rest, if it does not concentrate, it must, probably, begin to disintegrate.

The congenitally pessimistic historian Brooks Adams *The Theory of Social Revolutions* (1913) Conclusion.

5 We are all of us immigrants in the industrial world, and we have no authority to lean upon … Is it a wild mistake to say that the absence of central authority has disorganized our souls, that our souls are like Peer Gynt's onion, in that they lack a kernel?

Walter Lippmann *Drift and Mastery* (1914) Pt 2, Ch.10. Agonized soul-searching from a man who was to be one of the most influential newspaper columnists of the century. Peer Gynt was the protagonist of the epic poem (1867) by the Norwegian Henrik Ibsen.

6 There is a steadily growing disposition to shift responsibility for personal progress and welfare to outside agencies. What can be the result of this tendency but the softening of the moral fiber of the people? When there is unwillingness to accept responsibility for one's own life and for making the most of it there is a loss of strong, red-blooded, rugged independence and will power to grapple with the wrongs of the world and to establish justice through the volition of those concerned.

Samuel Gompers, *American Federationist*, Feb. 1915. Gompers, writing in the organ of the American Federation of Labor, which he headed, was an ultra-conservative trade unionist, here voicing the pure liberalism of the past century.

7 Don't waste any time in mourning. Organize!

Joe Hill to William 'Big Bill' Haywood, 18 Nov. 1915. Hill was executed by firing squad next day for allegedly killing two policemen in Salt Lake City. His followers claimed that the execution was political murder and that he had been convicted on false evidence.

Democracy in Britain, 1865–1914

LIBERAL DEMOCRACY, 1866–1911

1 We cannot look, and we hope no man will look, upon it as some Trojan horse approaching the walls of the sacred city, and filled with armed men, bent upon ruin, plunder, and conflagration.
William Ewart Gladstone, 12 March 1866; *Parl. Deb.* Vol.182, Cols 59–60. Gladstone on democracy, as he introduced the Liberal bill for an extension of the franchise to some sections of the male working class.

2 If you want venality, if you want ignorance, if you want drunkenness, and facility for being intimidated; or if, on the other hand, you want impulsive, unreflecting, and violent people, where do you look for them in the constituencies? Do you go to the top or to the bottom? … As long as we have not passed this Bill we are masters of the situation. Let us pass this Bill, and in what position are we? That of the Gibeonites – hewers of wood and drawers of water.
Robert Lowe, 13 March and 26 April 1866; *Parl. Deb.* Vol.182, Cols 147–9, Lowe was leader of the Liberal opposition to widening the vote. Gibeonites, the citizens of Gibeon, were enslaved by the Israelites (Joshua 9:27).

3 I believe it will be absolutely necessary that you should prevail on our future masters to learn their letters.
Robert Lowe, 15 July 1867; *Parl. Deb.* Vol.188, Col.1540. Lowe's celebrated comment on the franchise bill introduced by the Conservatives is usually rendered as 'We must educate our masters.'

4 The lower classes ought to be educated to discharge the duties cast upon them. They should also be educated that they may appreciate and defer to higher cultivation when they meet it; and the higher classes ought to be educated in a very different manner, in order that they may exhibit to the lower classes that higher education to which, if it were shown to them, they would bow down and defer.
Robert Lowe, letter to *The Times*, 4 Nov. 1867. On deference see 654:2.

5 If you can show me a fair chance that a republic here will be free from the political corruption which hangs about the monarchy, I say, for my part – and I believe that the middle classes in general will say – let it come.

Sir Charles Dilke, 6 Nov. 1871; Roy Jenkins *Sir Charles Dilke* (1958) p.70. Dilke's republicanism was prompted by the reclusive behaviour of Queen Victoria after the death in 1861 of her husband, Prince Albert.

6 You behold a range of exhausted volcanoes. Not a flame flickers on a single pallid crest. But the situation is still dangerous. There are occasional earthquakes, and ever and anon the dark rumbling of the sea.
Benjamin Disraeli, 3 April 1872; T.E. Kebbel (ed.) *Selected Speeches of the Late Earl of Beaconsfield* Vol.2 (1882) p.516. Gladstone's reforming government of 1868 had put through a huge programme of legislation, and Disraeli, as leader of the Opposition, here mocks the apparently played-out Liberal front bench.

7 So vy arrogant, tyrannical and obstinate with no knowledge of the World or human nature [and] a fanatic in religion. All this and much want of *égard* towards my feelings … make him a vy dangerous & unsatisfactory Premier.
Queen Victoria to her eldest daughter, Crown Princess Victoria of Prussia, 24 Feb. 1874, on the subject of Gladstone.

8 He speaks to me as if I was a public meeting.
Queen Victoria on Gladstone; G.W.E. Russell *Collections and Recollections* (1898) Ch.14.

9 He has not a single redeeming defect.
Benjamin Disraeli on Gladstone, attrib.

10 A sophistical rhetorician, inebriated with the exuberance of his own verbosity, and gifted with an egotistical imagination, that can at all times command an interminable and inconsistent series of arguments to malign his opponents and glorify himself.
Benjamin Disraeli on Gladstone, July 1878; Robert Blake *Disraeli* (1966) p.650.

11 Posterity will do justice to that unprincipled maniac Gladstone – an extraordinary mixture of envy, vindictiveness, hypocrisy and superstition; and with one commanding characteristic – whether prime minister or leader of Opposition, whether preaching, praying, speechifying or scribbling – never a gentleman.
Benjamin Disraeli on Gladstone; Blake (1966) p.606.

1 He did not object to the old man always having a card up his sleeve, but he did object to his insinuating that the Almighty had put it there.

Liberal MP Henry Labouchère on Gladstone; Earl Curzon *Modern Parliamentary Eloquence* (1913) p.25. Gladstone frequently appealed to 'a higher power' to justify his policies. *Dictionary of National Biography 1912–1921* gives a slightly different rendering of this quote.

2 The Grand Old Man.

Description of Gladstone, said to have been coined by the Liberal MP, Henry Labouchère, April 1881; Richard Shannon *Gladstone* (1999) p.253. Often abbreviated to GOM.

3 Since the beginning of the century … it is certain that Britain has, in the intervals of her blindness, had some inspiring visions of the kingdom of justice one day to be established among men and it is not to be denied that, taken broadly, the Liberal Party has striven to follow the fiery pillar of conscience into this promised land.

The Nonconformist, 1 Jan. 1880. Nonconformity saw itself as the mainstay of the Liberal Party in Gladstone's day, here speaking in appropriately biblical language (Exodus 13:21).

4 Lord Salisbury constitutes himself the spokesman of a class – a class to which he himself belongs, who 'toil not neither do they spin'.

Joseph Chamberlain, 30 March 1883. The then ardent Radical attacks the House of Lords, again in biblical terms (Matthew 6:28). The House of Lords, with a built-in Conservative majority, possessed a veto on legislation passed by the House of Commons, which Liberals believed would be used to wreck any measures of which the Conservative Party disapproved.

5 Mend Them or End Them.

Liberal Party slogan on the House of Lords, 1884, said to have been coined by John Morley.

6 'They have no work,' you say. Say rather that they either refuse work or quickly turn themselves out of it. They are simply good-for-nothings, who in one way or another live on the good-for-somethings – vagrants and sots, criminals and those on the way to crime, youth who are burdens on hard-worked parents, men who appropriate the wages of their wives, fellows who share the gains of prostitutes; and then, less visible and less numerous, there is a corresponding class of women.

Herbert Spencer 'The Coming Slavery' in *Contemporary Review* Vol.45 (1884) pp.461–2. The apostle of late 19th-century liberalism on the undeserving poor. A recurrent comment on this Victorian underclass was, 'They'll neither work nor want',

which JM sometimes used to hear from his maternal grandmother, a lifelong Liberal, born in 1865.

7 The great problem of our civilization is still unsolved. We have to account for and grapple with the mass of misery and destitution in our midst, co-existent as it is with the evidence of abundant wealth and teeming prosperity. It is a problem which some men would put aside by reference to the eternal laws of supply and demand, to the necessity of freedom of contract, and to the sanctity of every private right of property … Our object is the elevation of the poor, of the masses of the people – a levelling up of them by which we shall do something to remove the excessive inequality in social life.

Joseph Chamberlain, 8 Sept. 1885; Denis Judd *Radical Joe* (1977) p.122. In the autumn of 1885 Chamberlain published his unauthorized 'Radical Programme', designed to move the Liberal Party sharply away from the absolute dedication to laissez-faire that had been its dominant creed for the past 40 years.

8 The 'pet idea' is what they call construction … taking into the hands of the state the business of the individual man. Both this Liberalism and Tory Democracy have done much to estrange me, and have had for many, many years.

William Ewart Gladstone to Lord Acton, 1885; John Morley *Life of W.E. Gladstone* Vol.3 (1903) p.173. Gladstone, a politician of an earlier vintage than Chamberlain, recoiled from his radicalism.

9 All the world over I will back the masses against the classes.

William Ewart Gladstone, election speech, 28 June 1886; Shannon (1999) p.445. In public, when exalted by contact with a mass audience, Gladstone could deserve his nickname of the 'People's William'.

10 Our modern legislation … with reference to labour, and education, and health, invoking as it does manifold interference with freedom of contract, is justified on the ground that it is the business of the state, not indeed directly to promote moral goodness, for that, from the very nature of moral goodness, it cannot do, but to maintain the conditions without which a free exercise of the human faculties is impossible.

T.H. Green 'Liberal Legislation and Freedom of Contract'; *The Works of Thomas Hill Green* Vol.3 (1889) p.374. The philosopher Green was hailed in the 1880s as the father of the so-called New Liberalism, which accepted a measure of state intervention in socio-economic affairs, as opposed to the unadulterated individualism of the mid-century.

1 There is no doubt that the New Liberalism rejects the heartless conclusions of doctrinaire Political Economy … The old dread of state action has passed away now that there is some guarantee that the resources of the government will be used not to create or buttress the privilege of the few but to promote the well-being of the entire community.

Rev. Hugh Price Hughes, *Methodist Times*, 4 Nov. 1886. Nonconformity begins to move away from pure laissez-faire.

2 We are all socialists now.

The future Liberal leader Sir William Harcourt, 1888. A throwaway remark, not to be taken too literally, even as far as the nascent Labour movement itself was concerned.

3 We live at a time when there is a disposition to think that the government ought to do this and that, and that the government ought to do everything … If the government takes into its hands that which the man ought to do for himself, it will inflict upon him greater mischiefs than all the benefits he will have received or all the advantages that will accrue from them.

William Ewart Gladstone, 26 Oct. 1889; *The Speeches of W.E. Gladstone* Vol.10 (1892) p.132. Gladstone holds true to individualism.

4 As in Africa, it is all trees, trees, trees, with no other world conceivable; so it is here – it is all vice and poverty and crime. To many the world is all slum, with the Workhouse as an intermediate purgatory before the grave … Who can hope to make headway against the innumerable adverse conditions which doom the dweller in Darkest England to eternal and immutable misery?

William Booth and W.T. Stead *In Darkest England and the Way Out* (1890). Booth, the founder of the Salvation Army, and Stead, the crusading journalist, sought in this book to prod Gladstone into dealing with the problem of poverty in Britain's cities, but Gladstone remained focused on Ireland until his retirement in 1894.

5 The present mongrel political combination of teetotallers, Irish revolutionists, Welsh demagogues, Small Englanders, English separatists and general uprooters of all that is national and good.

Conservative Party leaflet, July 1895, on the Liberals, who were branded as puritanical abstainers from drink, partisans for the Irish enemy and vilifiers of the empire, which the Conservatives had elevated into a national necessity.

6 All doors open, some flowers, fearful mess in street, bread, meat, paper, vegetables, old tins.

Heavy rain but street full of children, bare heads and bare feet. Most windows broken and blocked with boards, stuff or brown paper … Drunk and rough, wife beating, assaults, 'but not criminal, no thieves, housebreakers or prostitutes, maybe a few van draggers'. DARK BLUE-barred as map.

George Duckworth, 22 June 1899, of Hollington Street, Kennington; *The Streets of London. The Booth Notebooks. South East* (1997) p.65. The Liberal Charles Booth published *Life and Labour of the People in London* between 1899 and 1903, based on reports such as this by a team of investigators. The streets were colour-coded, and Dark Blue signified 'Very Poor, Casual, Chronic Want'.

7 A family living upon the scale allowed for in this estimate [£1.08 a week] must never spend a penny on railway fare or omnibus … They cannot save, nor can they join a sick club or Trade Union because they cannot pay the necessary subscriptions. The children must have no pocket money for dolls, marbles or sweets. The father must smoke no tobacco and must drink no beer. The mother must never buy any pretty clothes for herself or for her children … Should a child fall ill, it must not be attended by the parish doctor: should it die, it must be buried by the parish. Finally, the wage earner must never be absent from his work for a single day.

Another Liberal researcher into the working-class standard of living, Seebohm Rowntree *Poverty: A Study of Town Life* (1901) pp.133–4. This was an investigation of conditions in York during 1899.

8 My watchword if I were in office at this moment would be summed up in one single word – the word 'efficiency'. If we have not learned from this war that we have greatly lagged behind in efficiency, we have learned nothing, and our treasure and our lives are thrown away unless we learn the lessons which the war has given us.

The former Liberal leader Lord Rosebery, 15 Dec. 1901; E.T. Raymond *The Life of Lord Rosebery* (1923) pp.194–5. Rosebery was speaking of the South African War, which broke out in 1899 and which revealed an alarmingly poor state of health in working-class volunteers for the army. Rosebery's model of efficiency was imperial Germany, and his thinking provided much of the basis for the reforms introduced by the Liberal government that came into office in Dec. 1905.

9 I do not want to impair the vigour of competition, but we can do much to mitigate the causes of failure. We want to draw a line below which we will not allow persons to live and labour, yet above which they may compete with all the strength of their manhood. We do not want to pull down the structure of science and civilization – but to spread a net above the abyss.

Winston Churchill, Jan. 1906; Randolph Churchill *Winston S. Churchill* Vol.2 (1967) p.277. Churchill was then a junior member of the Liberal government that had just won the general election with an overwhelming majority. Its victory was probably a victory for Gladstonian values, but it went ahead to put through large-scale reforms, which laid the foundations of what became the British welfare state. Here Churchill summarizes its philosophy.

1 Campbell-Bannerman is a mere cork, dancing on a torrent which he cannot control, and what is going on here is a faint echo of the same movement which has produced massacres in St Petersburg, riots in Vienna, and socialist processions in Berlin.

Arthur Balfour, Jan. 1906; John Ramsden *The Age of Balfour and Baldwin 1902–1940* (1978) p.23. Balfour, the former Conservative prime minister, equates the new Liberal administration with the Russian Revolution of 1905 and other such continental upheavals. For once, the coolly rational Balfour had lost his grip on political reality.

2 A fully equipped duke costs as much to keep up as two Dreadnoughts – and they are just as great a terror – and they last longer … Let them realize what they are doing. They are forcing a revolution, and they will get it … The question will be asked whether five hundred men, ordinary men chosen accidentally from among the unemployed, should override the judgement – the deliberate judgement – of millions of people who are engaged in the industry which makes the wealth of the country.

David Lloyd George, Liberal chancellor of the exchequer, 9 Oct. 1909; John Grigg *Lloyd George: The People's Champion* (1978) pp.223, 224–5. The House of Lords was poised to reject the budget Lloyd George had introduced in April 1909, triggering a massive constitutional crisis. It forced two elections in 1910, followed by the Parliament Act of 1911, abolishing the Lords' veto on Commons legislation. The all-big-gun battleship HMS *Dreadnought*, launched in 1906, immediately made obsolete every other battleship in the world.

3 It is, indeed, implied that the state is vested with a certain overlordship over property in general and a supervisory power over industry in general, and this principle of economic sovereignty may be set side by side with that of economic justice as a no less fundamental conception of economic liberalism. For here, as elsewhere, liberty implies control.

L.T. Hobhouse *Liberalism* (1911) Ch.8. The doctrine of interventionist liberalism spelled out by its most influential contemporary spokesman.

TORY DEMOCRACY, 1867–1909

4 We do not … live – and I trust it will never be the fate of this country to live – under a democracy. The propositions which I am going to make tonight certainly have no tendency in that direction … We are of opinion that numbers, thoughts and feelings have since [1832] been created which it is desirable should be admitted within the circle of the Constitution. We wish that admission to take place in the spirit of our existing institutions, and with due deference to the traditions of an ancient state … Why should we conceal from ourselves that this country is a country of classes, and a country of classes it will ever remain? What we desire to do is to give everyone who is worthy of it a fair share in the government … but we are equally anxious … to prevent a preponderance of any class.

Benjamin Disraeli, 18 March 1867; *Parl. Deb.* Vol.186, Cols 6–13, 25. Disraeli was introducing a Conservative reform bill going well beyond the Reform Act of 1832 and bringing in a measure of democracy, although, as he makes clear, a strictly limited measure.

5 No doubt we are making a great experiment and 'taking a leap in the dark', but I … entertain a strong hope that the extended franchise … will be the means of placing the institutions of this country on a firmer basis.

Conservative leader Lord Derby, 6 Aug. 1867; *Parl. Deb.* Vol.189, Col.952.

6 'The equality of men', any man equal to any other; Quashee Nigger [West African tribesman] to Socrates or Shakespeare; Judas Iscariot to Jesus Christ; – and Bedlam and Gehenna to the New Jerusalem, shall we say?

Thomas Carlyle 'Shooting Niagara: and After?' in *Macmillan's Magazine*, Aug. 1867. A characteristically hyperbolic comment on the 1867 Reform Act by one of the most celebrated writers of his day. Gehenna was a valley near Jerusalem used for the worship of the pagan god Moloch, then by the Jews for the deposit of refuse and the corpses of animals and criminals (2 Kings 23:10).

7   The year of the great crime,
     When the false English Nobles, and their Jew,
     By God demented, slew
     The Trust they stood twice pledged to keep
          from wrong.

The poet Coventry Patmore '1867' in *The Unknown Eros* (1877). Patmore's target is Disraeli.

1 I trust ... that we shall not be like Frankenstein, & have raised a spirit that we cannot control! – it is a dangerous power to give them, but they are so determined to have it, and all we can do is to keep them on the right road.

Major Charles Keith-Falconer to Lord Nevill, 1 Sept. 1867; Richard Shannon *The Age of Disraeli* (1992) p.19. The reference is to Mary Shelley's novel *Frankenstein* (1818), in which a Genevan student creates a monster from dead tissue. Keith-Falconer was to be secretary of Conservative Central Office, the party's headquarters.

2 A deferential community ... is more suited to political excellence. The highest classes can rule in it; and the highest classes must, as such, have more political ability than the lower classes ... In communities where the masses are ignorant, but respectful, if you once permit the ignorant class to begin to rule, you may bid farewell to deference for ever.

Walter Bagehot *The English Constitution* (1867); Norman St John Stevas (ed.) *The Collected Works of Walter Bagehot* Vol.5 (1974) pp.380, 381–2. The section in question was first published in the *Fortnightly Review*, 15 June 1865.

3 I have climbed to the top of the greasy pole.

Benjamin Disraeli, on becoming prime minister on 27 Feb. 1868; William Fraser *Disraeli and his Day* (1891) p.52. The greasy pole was a fairground sideshow. Whoever could climb it to the top was given a prize; few succeeded.

4 Mr Disraeli ... has always behaved extremely well to me, and has all the right feelings for a minister towards the sovereign ... He is full of poetry, romance and chivalry. When he knelt down to kiss my hand, which he took in both of his, he said 'in loving loyalty and faith'.

Queen Victoria to her daughter Crown Princess Victoria of Prussia, 4 March 1868; Roger Fulford (ed.) *Your Dear Letter* (1971) p.176.

5 Murmurings of children in a dream. The royal project of gracious interposition with our rival is a mere phantom. It pleases the vanity of a court deprived of substantial power.

Benjamin Disraeli to Lord Derby, 21 Oct. 1866; Blake (1966) p.452. His comment on the queen's offer to mediate with the Liberals over electoral reform. A very different Disraeli from the oleaginous flatterer of the Widow of Windsor.

6 He can forward Radical changes in a way that no other minister could do – because he alone can silence & paralyze the forces of Conservatism. And in an age of singularly reckless statesmen, he is, I think, beyond question the one who is least restrained by fear and scruple.

Lord Salisbury to a Mr Gaussen, 11 May 1868, on Disraeli; Blake (1966) p.500. Salisbury had bitterly opposed Disraeli's Reform Act, but he was to become his foreign secretary in the 1870s.

7 Everywhere the proletariat are the tag, rag and bobtail of the official parties, and if any party has gained additional strength from the new voters it is the Tories.

Friedrich Engels to Karl Marx, 18 Nov. 1868; *Correspondence* (1936) p.254.

8 A vague idea that the poorer men are the more easily they are influenced by the rich; a notion that those whose vocation it was to bargain and battle with the middle class must on that account love the gentry; an impression – for it could be no more – that the underclass of minds would be more sensitive to traditional emotions; and an indistinct application to English politics of Napoleon's (then) supposed success in taming revolution by universal suffrage.

Lord Salisbury, *Quarterly Review*, Oct. 1869, pp.541–2. How wrong he was!

9 [Liberals] are ... suspicious and afraid of Disraeli: they think him the enemy of the capitalist class, and remember his writings of 30 years ago, of which one leading idea seemed to them to be the union of the aristocracy and peasantry in an attack on manufacturers and merchants.

J. Pender, Liberal MP for Wick, to Lord Derby, in Derby's diary for 18 Sept. 1873; Shannon (1992) p.150. A judgement much closer to the mark.

10 By the Conservative cause, I mean the splendour of the Crown, the lustre of the peerage, the privileges of the Commons, the rights of the Poor. I mean that harmonious union, that magnificent concord of all interests, of all classes, on which our national greatness depends.

Benjamin Disraeli, 24 June 1872; R. Mackenzie *Angels in Marble* (1968) pp.35–6. 'Angels in marble' was the phrase coined by *The Times* for Disraeli's working-class following.

11 The dangerously naïve tripartite optimism that the human race collectively has before it splendid destinies and that the road to them is to be found in the removal of all restraints on human conduct, in the recognition of a substantial equality ... and in fraternity or general love ... Such ... is the religion of which I take 'Liberty, Equality, Fraternity' to be the creed. I do not believe it.

Sir James Fitzjames Stephen *Liberty, Equality, Fraternity* (1873) p.53.

1 With savages, the weak in body or mind are soon eliminated; and those that survive commonly exhibit a vigorous state of health. We civilized men, on the other hand, do our utmost to check the process of elimination; we build asylums for the imbecile, the maimed, and the sick; we institute poor-laws; and our medical men exert their utmost skill to save the life of every one to the last moment … No one who has attended to the breeding of domestic animals will doubt that this must be highly injurious to the race of man … excepting in the case of man himself, hardly any one is so ignorant as to allow his worst animals to breed.

Charles Darwin *The Descent of Man* (1874 edn) pp.205, 206.

2 As the progress of democracy is the result of general social development, an advanced society, while commanding a greater share of political power, will, at the same time, protect the state from democratic excesses. If the latter should anywhere prevail, for a time, they will be promptly repressed.

Sir Thomas Erskine May *Democracy in Europe* Vol.I (1877) p.lxxi. The eminent authority on parliamentary government was a rock-ribbed anti-democrat.

3 As he lived, so he died – all display, without reality or genuineness.

William Ewart Gladstone on Disraeli, after his death on 19 April 1881; Blake (1966) p.753.

4 When we think of them as a body, we think … of the dwellings in which the lower half of them reside, of those endless streets and squares of three-storied houses stretching over countless acres of this metropolis, all of the same uniform height and shape and of all the same dull whitey-brown colour, which looks as if the sun never shone upon it.

T.E. Kebbel *National Review* (1883) p.687. The compiler of Disraeli's speeches casts a snooty eye over the suburban housing of the London Tory heartland.

5 You ask me to tell you in two words what it is. That is a question I am always in a fright lest someone should put it to me publicly. To tell the truth I don't know myself what Tory Democracy is, but I believe it is principally opportunism. Say you are a Tory Democrat and that will do.

Lord Randolph Churchill to Wilfrid Scawen Blunt, 14 April 1885; W.S. Blunt *Nineteenth Century* (1906) p.407. Blunt, later a highly radical Liberal, was momentarily attracted to joining the Conservative Lord Randolph's 'Fourth Party', disciples of Disraeli's 'One Nation' politics.

6 You, who are ambitious, and rightly ambitious, of being the guardians of the British Constitution, trust the people, and they will trust you – and they will follow you and join you in the defence of that Constitution against any and every foe.

Lord Randolph Churchill, 16 April 1884; R.J. White (ed.) *The Conservative Tradition* (1950) p.232.

7 If for four centuries there had been a very widely extended franchise and a very large electoral body in this country, there would have been no reformation of religion, no change of dynasty, no toleration of Dissent, not even an accurate Calendar. The threshing-machine, the power-loom, the spinning-jenny, and possibly the steam engine, would have been prohibited.

Sir Henry Maine *Popular Government* (1885); George Feaver *From Status to Contract* (1969) p.224.

8 Toryism in other days had two legs to stand upon: a sound leg and a lame leg. Its sound leg was reverence: its lame leg was class interest. Reverence it has almost forgotten. It no longer leans upon that leg. It leans now upon its lame leg, the leg of class interest, more, much more; and to mend the matter, as it stumps along, it calls out progress.

William Ewart Gladstone, 10 Dec. 1885; *Prime Minister's Papers* Vol.4, p.104.

9 We have a narrow path to tread. On the one hand, we must avoid that dangerous apathy which attempts to cure the suffering of the people by simply ignoring it; on the other, we must shun that far more dangerous wandering into economic error, which would plunge the whole country into economic disaster.

Lord Salisbury, *The Times*, 26 Nov. 1891. In other words, effective neutrality on the social issues of the day.

10 I see little glory in an empire which can rule the waves and is unable to flush its sewers.

Winston Churchill, Dec. 1901; Randolph Churchill Vol.2 (1967) p.276.

11 [Social legislation] raised the cost of production; and what can be more illogical than to raise the cost of production in the country and then to allow the products of other countries which are not surrounded by any similar legislation, which are free from any similar cost and expenditure – freely to enter our country in competition with our own goods … If these foreign goods come in cheaper, one of two things must follow … either you will take lower wages or you will lose your work.

Joseph Chamberlain, 6 Oct. 1903; Alan Sykes *Tariff Reform in British Politics 1903–1913* (1979) p.56. Chamberlain's campaign to abandon free trade, the cornerstone of British commercial policy since 1846, helped cost the Conservative Party the 1906 election. Yet he was right: Britain had long since lost its virtual monopoly of world trade in industrial goods, and when other countries placed tariffs on its exports, it too had to adopt protectionism. But free trade died hard. Protection was to deny Baldwin victory in the election of 1923, and it was not adopted until 1932.

1 Oliver Cromwell invented a little House of Lords on his own for the express purpose – as he put it – of protecting the people of England against 'an omnipotent House of Commons – the horridest arbitrariness that ever existed in the world'. In all seriousness, my lords, we have a right to ask where this kind of thing is going to stop.

Lord Lansdowne, 22 Nov. 1909; *Parl. Deb.* Vol.4, Col.375. Lansdowne, leader of the Conservative Party in the House of Lords, was speaking of the constitutional crisis provoked by the Lords' intention to reject the Liberal government's budget. They did so on 30 Nov. and in 1911 lost their power of veto through the Parliament Act.

2 I shouldn't call him v clever. He was – I don't quite know how to put it – better than competent … Lansdowne had the mentality of the great Whigs … I was always fond of him. I was his fag at Eton.

Arthur Balfour on Lord Lansdowne; Blanche Dugdale *Balfour* Vol.1 (1936) pp.335–6. Balfour was deposed as leader of the Conservative Party after it lost both the elections of 1910, called in an attempt to resolve the dispute between Lords and Commons.

SOCIAL DEMOCRACY, 1867–1912

3 A political combination of the lower classes as such and for their own objects, is an evil of the first magnitude; … a permanent combination of them would make them (now that so many of them have the suffrage) supreme in the country; and their supremacy, in the state they now are, means the supremacy of ignorance over instruction and of numbers over knowledge.

Walter Bagehot (1867) pp.5 ff.

4 According to [the Communists]: 'From everyone according to his abilities: to everyone according to his needs.' In other words, no man is to profit by his own strength, abilities or industry; but is to minister to the wants of the weak, the stupid and the idle.

Sir Thomas Erskine May Vol.1 (1877) pp.lxv–lxvi. Erskine May quotes from Marx's 1875 'Critique of the Gotha Programme' (see 665:8).

5 I ran for 250 miles. In that time I was never allowed to leave the engine. I took my meals and everything on the engine. I never left the engine. I complained to my fireman and told him that I found difficulty in keeping my eyes open.

Driver's testimony to the Royal Commission on Railway Accidents, 1877; N. McKillop *The Lighted Flame* (1950).

6 In England prolonged prosperity has demoralized the workers … The ultimate aim of this most bourgeois of lands would seem to be the establishment of a bourgeois aristocracy and a bourgeois proletariat side by side with the bourgeoisie … The revolutionary energy of the British workers has oozed away … It will take long before they can shake off their bourgeois infection … They totally lack the mettle of the old Chartists.

Karl Marx, c.1880; Isaiah Berlin *Karl Marx* (1963) p.275. A bitter conclusion for Marx to draw as his life's work came to a close, but no less true for that.

7 It is a very difficult country to move, Mr Hyndman, a very difficult country indeed, and one in which there is more disappointment to be looked for than success.

Benjamin Disraeli to Henry Hyndman, March 1881; Blake (1966) p.764. Hyndman was leader of the Social Democratic Federation, Britain's first Marxist socialist party. Disraeli, also at the end of his career, was, like Marx, bleak on the subject of a British revolution, though from the opposite end of the political spectrum.

8 We, perhaps, alone among the peoples can carry out with peace and order, and contentment, those changes which continental revolutionists have sought through anarchy and bloodshed.

Henry Hyndman *England for All* (1881) p.194. Optimism undimmed.

9 My belief is that the old order can only be overthrown by force; and for that reason it is all the more important that the revolution should not be an ignorant, but an educated revolution. What I should like to have now would be a body of able, high-minded competent men who should act as instructors of the masses and as their leaders.

William Morris, interview with the *Daily News*, about Dec. 1884; Ian Bradley *William Morris and His World* (1978) p.84. Morris, the quintessentially English socialist, sounds here remarkably like Lenin (see 678:6).

1 A party informed at all points by men of gentle habits and trained reasoning may achieve a complete revolution without a single act of violence. A mob of desperate sufferers abandoned by the leadership of exasperated sentimentalists and fanatic theorists may, at vast cost of bloodshed and misery, succeed in removing no single evil, except, perhaps, the extinction of the human race.

George Bernard Shaw, on the socialism of Morris and Hyndman, 1886; Michael Holroyd *Bernard Shaw* Vol.1 (1988) p.175. Shaw was one of the key figures in the Fabian Society, which was dedicated to evolutionary, not revolutionary, socialism. He reacts here in horror at the violent disturbances that followed a meeting staged by Hyndman in Trafalgar Square on 7 Feb. 1886.

2 For the right moment you must wait, as Fabius did most patiently when warring against Hannibal, though many censured his delays; but when the time comes you must strike hard, as Fabius did, or your waiting will be in vain and fruitless.

Frank Podmore, motto of the Fabian Society, 1884. The Roman general Fabius (d.203 BC) won battles by delaying tactics. The Fabian Society believed that a similar policy of 'permeation' could bring about socialism by slow degrees.

3   England, arise! The long, long night is over.
     Faint in the East I see the dawn appear.
     Out of your evil dream of toil and sorrow
     Arise, O England, for the day is here!

Edward Carpenter 'England, Arise!' (1886); C. Tsuzuki *Edward Carpenter* (1980) p.70. Hymn for the workers by a middle-class writer.

4 This struggling mass fought desperately and tigerishly, using the last remnants of their strength to get work for an hour or half-an-hour ... For what? The possession of a ticket which at best would afford four hours' labour. And the men, old and young, fought for these few shillings as men fight for life. Coats, flesh, even ears, were torn off. Men were crushed to death in the struggle.

Ben Tillett *The Docker's Bitter Cry* (1887). Tillett, the dockers' trade union leader in the East End of London, here describes the scramble for work outside the dock gates at the start of the working day.

5 No rent paid in the East End till the docker gets his tanner.

The Star, 26 Aug. 1889. The London dockers were on strike for a wage of 6d (a tanner, 2½p) an hour.

6   The people's flag is deepest red;
     It shrouded oft our martyred dead,
     And ere their limbs grew stiff and cold,
     Their heart's blood dyed its every fold.
     Then raise the scarlet standard high!
     Within its shade we'll live or die.
     Tho' cowards flinch and traitors sneer,
     We'll keep the red flag flying here.

The Irishman James M. Connell 'The Red Flag' (1889). This became the anthem of the British labour movement for the next century.

7 A great number of them looked like respectable city gentlemen; wore very good coats, large watch-chains and high hats ... Among the 'new' delegates not a single one wore a tall hat. They looked like workmen. They were workmen.

John Burns *The Liverpool Congress* (1890) p.6. The labour activist Burns describes the Trades Union Congress of 1890. The TUC, hitherto the exclusive preserve of the skilled workers, now admitted representatives from the 'new unionism' of the unskilled labour force, which had had its baptism of fire in the dock strike of 1889.

8 The individualist town councillor will walk along the municipal pavement, lit by municipal gas, and cleaned by municipal brooms with municipal water ... 'Socialism, Sir,' he will say, 'don't waste the time of a practical man by your fantastic absurdities. Self-help, Sir, individual self-help, that's what made our city what it is.'

Sidney Webb *Socialism in England* (1890) pp.116–17. The Fabian Webb preached the gospel of 'municipal socialism', whereby socialism secured a bridgehead at local authority level before making its bid for national power.

9 Socialism itself will be of value simply because it will lead to Individualism ... With the abolition of private property ... we shall have true, beautiful, healthy Individualism. Nobody will waste his time in accumulating things, and the symbols for things. One will live. To live is the rarest thing in the world. Most people exist, that is all.

The playwright Oscar Wilde *The Soul of Man under Socialism* (1891); *Plays, Prose Writings and Poems* (1991 edn) pp.258, 263. The aesthete Wilde, surely one of the oddest socialists of the period, indulges his taste for paradox in this political tract for the times.

1 If there were fifty red revolutionary parties in Germany, he would rather have the solid, progressive, matter-of-fact fighting trade unionist of England, and for that reason he desired that they should keep away from their name any term of socialism … He had become thoroughly sick of people who bore on their foreheads 'socialism' and who were no more socialists than Bismarck.

Ben Tillett, as reported in *The Times*, 14 Nov. 1893, at the foundation conference of the Independent Labour Party (ILP), one more component in the genesis of socialist politics in Britain. Bismarck had been chancellor of imperial Germany until 1890.

2 The life of one Welsh miner is of greater commercial and moral value to the British nation than the whole Royal Crowd put together, from the Royal Great Grand-mama down to this puling Royal Great Grand-child.

Keir Hardie, *Labour Leader*, 1894; Ian McLean *Keir Hardie* (1975) p.168. Hardie, a founder-member of the ILP, on a Welsh mining disaster that left 250 men dead. The great-grandmother was Queen Victoria; the great-grandchild was the future Edward VIII, born on 23 June 1894.

3 At last there is a United Labour Party, or perhaps it would be safer to say, a little cloud no bigger than a man's hand, which may grow into a United Labour Party.

R.B. Suthers, correspondent of *The Clarion*, 10 March 1900. The Labour Representation Committee, the precursor of the Labour Party, was founded in Feb. 1900 as a confederation of the Trades Union Congress, the Independent Labour Party, the Fabian Society and the Social Democratic Federation. The reference to the cloud is taken from 1 Kings 18:44.

4 The crying need of the nation is not for better morals, cheaper bread, temperance, liberty, culture, redemption of fallen sisters and erring brothers, nor the grace, love and fellowship of the Trinity, but simply for enough money. And the evil to be attacked is not sin, suffering, greed, kingcraft, demagogy, monopoly, ignorance, drink, war, pestilence, nor any other of the scapegoats which reformers sacrifice, but simply poverty.

George Bernard Shaw, Preface to his play, *Major Barbara* (1905).

5 Socialism … is not a system of economics. It is life for the dying people.

Keir Hardie; Godfrey Elton *England, Arise!* (1931) p.174.

6 We want to apply the remedy which was used by a Scotch farmer to a mad dog. He was told the way to cure its madness was to cut off part of its tail. He carried out that advice and when subsequently asked about what he had done, he explained that he had cut off the tail from behind the ears. That is our plan for dealing with the House of Lords.

Keir Hardie, about Feb. 1910; McLean (1975) p.140. In the event, the Lords had only their tail docked. In other words, they lost their power to veto Commons legislation but escaped abolition.

7 As a general instruction the soldiers had been warned that if obliged to use their bayonets they should only be applied to that portion of the body traditionally held by trainers of youth to be reserved for punishment.

General Sir Nevil Macready on the South Wales Miners' Strike, Nov. 1910. The general was in command of troops sent in to suppress the rioting that accompanied the strike when the local police failed to do so. The home secretary, Winston Churchill, came in for lasting criticism for using the army, though no lives were lost.

8 When WE go on strike to better our lot … YOU are called on by your officers to MURDER US. DON'T DO IT! … Your fight is Our fight … Think things out and refuse any longer to MURDER YOUR KINDRED. Help US to win back BRITAIN for the BRITISH, and the WORLD for the WORKERS.

Open letter to British soldiers, *Sheldrake's Gazette*, 1 March 1912. In the national coal strike of 1912 the trade union leader Tom Mann was sentenced to six months in jail for incitement to mutiny by reprinting this letter in the union paper *The Syndicalist*. The Syndicalist movement aimed to use strikes as a political weapon against the government of the day, following the continental model developed by Georges Sorel (see 672:7).

9 The class war is the most brutal of wars and the most pitiless. The lesson is that, in future strikes, the striker must protect against the use of arms, with arms; protest against shooting, with shooting; protest against violence, with violence … The other lesson is that Parliament is a farce and a sham, the rich man's Duma [Russian parliament], the employer's Tammany, the Thieves' Kitchen, and the working man's despot.

Ben Tillett on the London dock strike of 1912. The years immediately before World War I saw an upsurge of strikes, climaxing in a movement towards a general strike. The Labour Party was dedicated to the parliamentary road to socialism, but because the Liberals and Conservatives were evenly balanced in the Commons after 1910, it had no choice but to hope for the best from the Liberals. Militants such as Tillett saw no future in this approach and went for direct action instead. For Tammany, the corrupt New York political machine (see 647:1).

VOTES FOR WOMEN, 1866–1914

1 I have always been of the opinion that if there is to be universal suffrage, women have as much right to vote as men.

Benjamin Disraeli, 27 April 1866; *Parl. Deb.* Vol.183, Col.99. Disraeli was speaking in the debate on the Liberal suffrage bill. When he put through the Conservative bill a year later there was no mention of a vote for women.

2 People will be much more willing to listen to the assertion that single women and widows of property have been unjustly overlooked, and left out from the privileges to which their property entitles them, than to the much more startling general proposition that sex is not a proper ground of distinction in political rights.

Helen Taylor to Barbara Bodichon, 9 May 1866; Harold L. Smith *The British Women's Suffrage Campaign 1866–1928* (1998) p.85. In the Reform Act of 1832 ownership of property had been the sole criterion for giving men the vote, but propertied women were to be denied the franchise in the Reform Acts of both 1867 and 1884.

3 The true virtue of human beings is fitness to live together as equals; claiming nothing for themselves but what they as freely concede to everyone else.

John Stuart Mill *The Subjection of Women* (1869) Ch.2. When Mill spoke in the House of Commons on 20 May 1867 in favour of women's suffrage, the Liberal MP Samuel Laing said that it would reduce the country to the primitivism of the West African territory of Dahomey.

4 John Stuart Mill cannot help claiming the suffrage for the Negro – and the woman. Such conclusions are the inevitable results of the premises whence he started ... [and their] *reductio ad absurdum*.

Editorial in the *Anthropological Review* Vol.4 (1866) p.115.

5 While the shrieking sisterhood remains to the front, the world will stop its ears.

Eliza Lynn Linton, *The Saturday Review* Vol.28 (1869).

6 The Queen is most anxious to enlist everyone who can speak or write or join in checking this mad, wicked folly of 'Woman's Rights' with all its attendant horrors, on which her poor feeble sex is bent, forgetting every sense of womanly feeling and propriety. Lady Amberley ought to get a *good whipping*.

Queen Victoria to Theodore Martin, about March 1870; Roger Fulford *Votes for Women* (1958) p.65. Lady Amberley was a vocal feminist.

7 I am inclined to say that the personal attendance and intervention of women in election proceedings ... would be a practical evil not only of the gravest but even of an intolerable character.

William Ewart Gladstone, 3 May 1871; *Parl. Deb.* Vol.206, Col.91.

8 While it is generally admitted that with woman the powers of intuition, of rapid perception, and perhaps of imitation, are more strongly marked than in man ... some, at least, of these faculties are characteristic of the lower races, and therefore of a past and lower state of civilization.

Charles Darwin Vol.2 (1874 edn) p.858. The towering evolutionist adds his considerable weight to the opposition to women's rights.

9 The real fact is that man in the beginning was ordained to rule over the woman, and this is an eternal decree which we have no right and no power to alter.

Lord Percy (later Duke of Northumberland), 1873; Fulford (1958) p.77.

10 All these risks and all this great change we are asked to make – for what? To arm the women of this country against the men of this country. To arm them, that they may defend themselves against their fathers, their husbands, their brothers, and their sons. To me the idea has something in it strange and monstrous.

The radical Liberal John Bright, 26 April 1876.

11 No woman who loves her husband would wish to usurp his province. It is only those whose instincts are inverted, or whose anti-sexual vanity is insatiable, who would take the political reins from the strong hands which have always held them to give them to others – weaker, less capable, and wholly unaccustomed.

Eliza Lynn Linton 'The Wild Women as Politicians' in *The Nineteenth Century* Vol.30 (1891) p.82.

12 What new forces were they prepared to bring against the anarchy, socialism and revolution which were arrayed against them? The granting of women's suffrage would be against the disintegrating power of the other side, as women were everywhere anti-revolutionary forces.

Millicent Garrett Fawcett reported in *The Times*, 25 Nov. 1891. Mrs Fawcett was speaking to the National Union of Conservative Associations to urge them to support votes for women as a force for conservatism. The Liberal Party was hostile to women's suffrage for precisely that reason, and it is odd that British Conservatives should have been so slow to grasp the truth of this argument.

1 I ... was amazed and disgusted to learn that I was classed among criminals, infants and lunatics – in fact, that my status as a woman was worse than any of these.

Hanna Sheehy Skeffington, 1900; Rosemary Cullen Owens *Smashing Times* (1984) p.39. In British electoral law convicts, males under the age of 21 and the insane were all denied the vote – together with members of the House of Lords.

2 I believe in Emmeline Pankhurst – Founder of the Women's Social and Political Union. And in Christabel Pankhurst, her eldest daughter, our Lady, who was inspired by the Passion for Liberty – born to be a leader of women. Suffered under Liberal Government, was arrested, tried and sentenced. She descended into prison; the seventh day she returned again to the world. She was entertained to breakfast, and sat on the right hand of her mother, our glorious Leader, from thence she went forth to judge both the government and the Antis [opponents of women's suffrage]. I believe in Votes for Women on the same terms as men, the policy of the Women's Social and Political Union, the equality of the sexes, Representation for Taxation, the necessity for militant tactics, and Freedom Everlasting. Amen!

Creed of the Women's Social and Political Union (WSPU), parody of the Apostles' Creed, 1908; Antonia Raeburn *The Militant Suffragettes* (1973) p.63. The WSPU was founded by Emmeline Pankhurst in 1903 to campaign for women's suffrage. It is odd to see no mention of Mrs Pankhurst's second daughter, Sylvia, an equally vigorous activist.

3 If I were a woman I'd simply refuse to speak to any man or do anything for men until I'd got the vote. I'd make my husband's life a burden and everybody miserable generally. Women should have a revolution. They should shoot, kill, maim, destroy until they are given the vote.

George Bernard Shaw, March 1909; Raeburn (1973) p.16.

4 As the nozzle turned at the end of my nose to enter my gullet it seemed as if my left eye was being wrenched out of its socket. Then the food, a mixture of cocoa, Bovril, medicines and a drug to keep me from vomiting when the tube was drawn out, was poured into the funnel and down into my aching, bruised, quivering body.

Mary Richardson *Laugh a Defiance* (1953) p.84. Some women, after being jailed for causing criminal damage as part of their campaign, went on hunger strike. They were then forcibly fed; the first such feeding took place on 25 Sept. 1909.

5 Personally I am dead against Forcible Feeding which always ends in the release of the prisoner long before her time. I want to keep these ladies under lock and key for five years and I am willing to feed them with Priests' Champagne and Michaelmas Geese all the time, if it can be done but ... these wretched hags ... are obstinate to the point of death.

Augustine Birrell, Liberal chief secretary of Ireland, to John Dillon, 15 Aug. 1912; Cullen Owens (1984) p.64. In April 1913 the so-called Cat and Mouse Act was passed, avoiding the practice of forcible feeding by having convicted women released from jail before they embarked on hunger strike and then pulling them in again at the government's convenience.

6 The mob played a sort of Rugby football with us. Seizing a woman they pushed her into the arms of another group who in their turn passed her on ... Eventually, with a number of men escorting us, we managed to board a tramcar, the last of the hooligans speeding our departure with a fusillade of cabbages.

Hannah Mitchell *The Hard Way Up* (1968) pp.150–51.

7 The argument of the broken pane of glass is the most valuable argument in modern politics.

Emmeline Pankhurst, *Votes for Women*, 23 Feb. 1912. Windows were broken as an act of protest, the first on 30 June 1908. Mrs Pankhurst's suffragettes were willing to use violence; the moderate suffragists were not.

8 Shout! Shout! – up with your song,
Cry with the wind that the dawn is breaking;
March! March! Sing you along,
Wide blows our banner and hope is waking!

The composer Dr Ethel Smyth 'The March of the Women', song written for the protest day of 1 March 1912, when shop windows were smashed all over London's West End.

9 If ever Parliament concedes the vote to woman in England, it will be accepted by the militant suffragist ... as a victory which she will value only for better carrying on of her fight *à outrance* against the oppression and injustice of man. A conciliation with hysterical revolt is neither an act of peace; nor will it bring peace ... Peace will return ... when woman ...

comes to recognize that she can, without sacrifice of dignity, give a willing subordination to the husband or father, who, when all is said and done, earns and lays up money for her.
Sir Almroth E. Wright, letter to *The Times*, 28 March 1912; *The Unexpurgated Case Against Woman Suffrage* (1913) p.86. Wright, an eminent physiologist, believed that the root of feminism was hormonal.

1 There is something that governments care far more for than human life, and that is the security of property, and so it is through property that we shall strike the enemy ... Those of you who can break windows – break them! ... I incite this meeting to rebellion!
Emmeline Pankhurst, 17 Oct. 1912; Miriam Schnier *Feminism: The Essential Historical Writings* (1972) Pt 5. The meeting was in the Albert Hall, London, and it marked a schism in the suffrage movement between the militants and the moderates. On 4 June 1913 the militants' campaign produced its first martyr when Emily Wilding Davison died after throwing herself under the king's horse during the Derby. 'Deeds not words' was the epitaph inscribed on her gravestone.

2 This demand for Votes for Women means a revolt against wrongs of many kinds – against social injustice and political mismanagement ... But more than all that it is a revolt against the evil system under which women are regarded as subhuman and as the sex-slaves of men.
Christabel Pankhurst *The Great Scourge and How to End It* (1913).

3 Is the pure-minded Christabel aware that a brothel is a temptation to youth provided by her own sex? Yet the inmates may be preferable to the ice-bound, callous creature called a suffragette.
Male rejoinder by the anon. 'Robert le Diable'; Fulford (1958) p.256.

4 I have tried to destroy the picture of the most beautiful woman in mythological history as a protest against the government for destroying Mrs. Pankhurst who is the most beautiful character in modern history.
Mary Richardson, 10 March 1914; Midge Mackenzie *Shoulder to Shoulder* (1988 edn) p.261. That day Miss Richardson attempted to vandalize Velázquez' painting *The Rokeby Venus* in the National Gallery. This picture was chosen because it depicted its sitter entirely as a sex object.

5 I can never feel that setting fire to houses and churches and letter-boxes and destroying valuable pictures helps to convince people that women ought to be enfranchised.

Dame Millicent Fawcett, 1914; Fulford (1958) p.175. Dame Millicent was leader of the moderate suffragists. Neither her moderation nor the Pankhursts' guerrilla warfare had succeeded in gaining the vote for women by the time war broke out in Aug. 1914. Only the experience of that war produced the concession (see 711:8).

IRELAND

6 My mission is to pacify Ireland.
William Ewart Gladstone, 2 Dec. 1868; Shannon (1999) p.57. Gladstone had just been told that he had won the general election. For the next 25 years Ireland was to be his main political preoccupation.

7 Yes, I believe in all things for the liberation of Ireland. If dynamite is necessary to the redemption of Ireland, then dynamite is a blessed agent and should be availed of by the Irish people in their holy war ... Every creature of God is good and nothing is to be rejected when it can be made to subserve a good cause; speaking in all soberness, I do not know how dynamite could be put to better use than in blowing up the British Empire.
Patrick Ford, owner and editor of the New York *Irish World*, early 1870s; Tom Corfe *The Phoenix Park Murders* (1968) p.60.

8 None of us, whether we be in America or in Ireland, or wherever we may be, will be satisfied until we have destroyed the last link which keeps Ireland bound to England.
Charles Stewart Parnell, speaking in Cincinnati, 20 Feb. 1880; R.B. O'Brien *The Life of Charles Stewart Parnell* Vol.1 (1899) pp.201–3. The Protestant Parnell was the leader of a largely Catholic Irish nationalist party. This was rhetoric for an Irish-American audience, since Parnell sought the restoration of the Dublin parliament lost in 1800, not outright Irish independence.

9 When a man takes a farm from which another has been evicted ... by leaving him severely alone, by putting him into a sort of moral Coventry, by isolating him from the rest of his kind as if he were a leper of old, you must show him your detestation of the crime he has committed.
Charles Stewart Parnell, 19 Sept. 1880; F.S.L. Lyons *Charles Stewart Parnell* (1977) p.134. Irish farmers who could not keep up their rent were evicted by their landlords. This was Parnell's response, applied most famously to Captain Charles Boycott, land agent for Lord Ernle of County Mayo; hence the term 'boycott', which now passed into the language.

10 Force is not a remedy.
John Bright, 16 Nov. 1880; G.M. Trevelyan *The Life of John Bright* (1913) p.429. Evictions were countered by murder,

most notably the murder of Lord Mountmorres in Galway. In response, Gladstone's government then applied coercion and jailed Parnell.

1 For every Irishman murdered we will take the life of a British minister. For every hundred Irishmen murdered we will sacrifice the lives of the entire British ministry. For every two hundred Irishmen murdered we will make England a smouldering ruin of ashes and blood.

John Devoy, New York, Jan. 1881; Lyons (1977) p.154. Devoy led the American Fenians, the most militant wing of the nationalist movement.

2 Tenant Right is Landlord Wrong.

Slogan coined in opposition to Gladstone's Land Act of Aug. 1881, aiming to establish 'the three Fs' – that is, fair rents, freedom of sale and fixity of tenure. This law, marking as it did an extraordinary intervention by government in the private contractual relationship between landlord and tenant, demonstrates just how much Gladstone – a dedicated supporter of laissez-faire – was determined to cut out the economic roots of Irish disaffection. Landlords saw it as a capitulation to agrarian disorder.

3 Though I regret the accident of Lord Cavendish's death I cannot refuse to admit that Burke got no more than his deserts.

Richard Piggott, letter forged in Parnell's name, dated 15 May 1882 and published in *The Times*, 18 April 1887. On 6 May 1882 Gladstone's son-in-law, Lord Frederick Cavendish, the newly appointed chief secretary of Ireland, and his under-secretary, Thomas Burke, were slashed to death in Phoenix Park, Dublin. This supposed letter from Parnell was designed to discredit him irreparably, but the plan misfired when it was exposed as a forgery.

4 The possession of an Ireland is our peculiar punishment, our unique affliction, among a family of nations. What crime have we committed, with what peculiar vice is our national character chargeable, that this chastisement should have befallen us?

Lord Salisbury, *Quarterly Review* Vol.156 (Oct. 1883).

5 No man has a right to fix a boundary to the march of a nation ... We have never attempted to fix the *ne plus ultra* of Ireland's nationhood, and we never shall.

Charles Stewart Parnell, *Freeman's Journal*, 21 Jan. 1885; Lyons (1977) pp.260–61. Words inscribed on Parnell's tomb.

6 I decided that if the GOM [Gladstone] went for Home Rule, the Orange card would be the one to play. Please God it may turn out to be the ace of trumps and not the two.

Lord Randolph Churchill to Lord Justice Fitzgibbon, 16 Feb. 1886; Winston Churchill *Lord Randolph Churchill* Vol.2 (1906) p.59. Gladstone introduced his bill to give Ireland Home Rule (political autonomy) on 8 April 1886. The 'Orange card' was the overwhelmingly Protestant Ulster, which refused to be part of a devolved Ireland, then and since. It proved a decisive stumbling block to both of Gladstone's attempts (1886 and 1893) to put through Home Rule.

7 I am convinced that the moving spring in this new agitation in Ireland is identical with that in Italy, that is, the spirit of the revolution so loudly and so authoritatively condemned by the Holy See ... We all know what the Revolution has done in Rome and in France ... France was once as Catholic as Ireland, but the Revolution undermined her faith.

Cardinal Paul Cullen (d.1878), quoted in *The Tablet*, 27 March 1886. The Irish Catholic hierarchy, if not the Irish priesthood, was deeply antagonistic to Home Rule.

8 Home Rule, not Rome Rule.

Protestant slogan in opposition to Gladstone's policy, regardless of the proclaimed opinion of Cardinal Cullen.

9 I do not believe that local patriotism is an evil. I believe it is stronger in Ireland even than in England. The Irishman is profoundly Irish, but it does not follow that because his local patriotism is keen he is incapable of Imperial patriotism.

William Ewart Gladstone, 8 April 1886; *Parl. Deb.* Vol.304, Col.1082. From his speech introducing the Home Rule bill.

10 Ulster at the proper moment will resort to the supreme arbitrament of force: Ulster will fight; Ulster will be right; Ulster will emerge from the struggle victorious.

Lord Randolph Churchill, 26 April 1886; Winston Churchill Vol.2 (1906) p.65.

11 An old man in a hurry.

Lord Randolph Churchill on Gladstone, June 1886; Winston Churchill Vol.2 (1906) App.5. Gladstone was then aged 76. Churchill's jibe claimed that Gladstone was desperate to secure Home Rule for Ireland before he died. The Home Rule bill, however, was defeated in the Commons on 8 June thanks to the defection of 93 Liberals, many of whom, including Joseph Chamberlain, crossed the floor to join the Conservatives as Liberal Unionists.

12 *Tennyson*: Couldn't they blow up that horrible island and carry it off in pieces – a long way off?
Allingham: Why did the English go there?
Tennyson: Why did the Normans come to England? The Normans came over here and seized the country, and in a hundred years the English had

forgotten all about it, and they were living with them on good terms … The Irish, with their damned unreasonableness are raging and foaming to this hour! … The stupid clumsy Englishman – knock him down, kick him under the tail, kick him under the chin, do anything to him, he gets on his legs and goes on; the Kelt rages and shrieks and tears everything to pieces.
Dialogue between the poet laureate, Alfred, Lord Tennyson, and William Allingham; recorded by Allingham in *A Diary* (1907) pp.297–8.

1 We do not hesitate to say that if the Irish race deliberately selected as their recognized representative an adulterer of Mr Parnell's type they are as incapable of self-government as their bitterest enemies have asserted. So obscene a race as in those circumstances they would prove themselves to be would obviously be unfit for anything except a military despotism.
Rev. Hugh Price Hughes, *Methodist Times*, 20 Nov. 1890. Parnell had just been publicly exposed as the lover of Mrs Katharine O'Shea, the wife of a fellow Irish MP, Captain William O'Shea. The scandal dealt a body-blow to the cause of Home Rule.

2 It was odd that the man who was a rock to all the world was like a bit of wax in the hands of a woman.
William Ewart Gladstone on Parnell, 27 Nov. 1890; James Carty *Ireland 1851–1921* (1951) p.62.

3 Will you give him up to the Saxon wolves who howl for his destruction? Or will you rally round him as your fathers rallied round the men of '98 [1798], and shout with a thousand voices, 'No surrender!'?
Irish Daily News, 18 Dec. 1890. After nearly a year of struggle, Parnell died on 6 Oct. 1891. 'No surrender!' was to become the clarion call of Ulster.

4 *Hysterica passio* dragged their quarry down. None shared our guilt; nor did we play a part Upon a painted stage when we devoured his heart.
W.B. Yeats 'Parnell's Funeral' (1891).

5 I believe it is our Gaelic past which … is really at the bottom of the Irish heart. What we must endeavour to never forget is this, that the Ireland of today is the descendant of the Ireland of the seventh century; then the school of Europe and the torch of learning. We must teach ourselves not to be ashamed of ourselves, because the Gaelic people can never produce its best before the world as long as it remains tied to the apron-strings of another race and another island.
Douglas Hyde, 25 Nov. 1892; *The Revival of Irish Literature and Other Addresses* (1894) pp.126–7. The 'Celtic revival' marked a move away from politics towards Irish cultural reassertion, and it was strengthened by the defeat of Gladstone's second Home Rule bill in the House of Lords on 9 Sept. 1893.

6 His romantic theme was the enduring revelation of the Primitive Pastoral Pagans of Ancient Ireland who sat watching Golden Sunsets on Primeval Evenings, communing with Nature in a seerlike trance of inspiration.
The nationalist journal *United Ireland*, Dec. 1897, commenting sarcastically on a talk by Yeats on the Celtic movement; R.F. Foster *W.B. Yeats* (1997) p.187.

7 [The government] would, of course, be very glad if they were able by kindness to kill Home Rule.
Conservative Irish secretary Gerald Balfour, reported in *The Times*, 17 Oct. 1895. The British government itself tried to take Ireland out of politics by making substantial economic concessions to the Irish farming community.

8 If an attempt were made to deprive these men of their birthright – as part of a corrupt parliamentary bargain – they would be justified in resisting such an attempt by all means in their power, including force … I can imagine no length of resistance to which Ulster can go in which I would not be prepared to support them.
Conservative and Unionist Party leader Andrew Bonar Law, 27 July 1912; F.S.L. Lyons *Ireland since the Famine* (1982) p.303. A public declaration in favour of civil war if need be, in defiance of a third Home Rule bill brought in by the Liberals.

9 Civil war is an awful thing, not to be lightly encountered, but it is not the greatest evil which confronts us if the coercion of Ulster is tried … If officers throw up their commissions and troops refuse to fire, Home Rule is dead, but a great deal else is dead too. I won't dwell on the dangers of foreign complications, real though they may be, but how will you meet another general strike on the railways or in the mines? It is not civil war that is the greatest peril, but anarchy.
Conservative politician Austen Chamberlain to Lord Willoughby de Broke, 23 Nov. 1913; Ramsden (1978) p.83.

10 We may make mistakes in the beginning and shoot the wrong people; but bloodshed is a cleansing and a sanctifying thing, and the nation which regards it as the final horror has lost its manhood.

There are many things more horrible than bloodshed; and slavery is one of them.

Padraic Pearse *The Coming Revolution* (1913); *Padraic Pearse: Political Writings and Speeches* (1952) pp.98–9. In 1916 Pearse went on to mount the Easter Rising in Dublin (see 794:8).

1 The people of Ulster have behind them the Unionist Party; behind them is the Lord God of Battle; in His name and in your name I say to the prime minister [Asquith]: 'Let your armies and batteries fire. Fire if you dare; fire and be damned!'

Conservative Sir William Joynson-Hicks, 6 Dec. 1913, as quoted back at him by the Labour politician Philip Snowden in the House of Commons on 23 June 1927.

2 Should a German army land in Ireland tomorrow, we should be perfectly justified in joining it.

Irish republican and labour leader James Connolly, 1 Aug. 1914. In Jan. 1911 the Ulster Protestant MP Captain James Craig had said (as reported by the *Morning Post*, 9 Jan. 1911): 'Germany and the German Emperor would be preferred to the rule of John Redmond, Patrick Ford and the Molly Maguires.' Redmond was leader of the Irish Nationalists; Ford was editor of the American *Irish World* (see 661:7); the Molly Maguires were a secret society of Irish terrorists. Extremists on both sides did have something in common.

Right and Left in Europe, 1850–1914

MARX AND ENGELS, 1850–83

1 M. Marx is by origin a Jew. He unites in himself all the qualities and defects of that gifted race. Nervous, some say, to the point of cowardice, he is immensely malicious, vain, quarrelsome, as intolerant and autocratic as Jehovah, the God of his fathers, and like Him, insanely vindictive.

The Russian anarchist Mikhail Bakunin on Karl Marx; Isaiah Berlin *Karl Marx* (1963) pp.109–10.

2 While the democratic petty bourgeois wish to bring the revolution to a conclusion as quickly as possible … it is our intention and our task to make the revolution permanent, until all more or less possessing classes have been forced out of their position of dominance, until the proletariat has conquered state power.

Karl Marx and his partner Friedrich Engels, Address to the Central Committee of the Communist League, March 1850; *Selected Works* Vol.I (1951) p.110.

3 The class struggle necessarily leads to the *dictatorship of the proletariat* … this dictatorship itself only constitutes the transition to the *abolition of all classes* and to a *classless society*.

Karl Marx to Josef Wedemeyer, 5 March 1852; *Karl Marx and Friedrich Engels, Selected Correspondence* (1965 edn) p.69.

4 Darwin's book is very important and serves me as a basis in natural science for the class struggle in history.

Karl Marx to Ferdinand Lassalle, 16 Jan. 1861; *Karl Marx and Friedrich Engels, Selected Correspondence* (1965 edn) p.123. Lassalle was leader of one wing of the German Social Democrat Party. Marx's reference is to Charles Darwin's *The Origin of Species*, published in 1859, which portrayed the natural world as engaged in an endless struggle for existence in which only the fittest survived.

5 While there is a progressive diminution in the number of capitalist magnates, there is of course a corresponding increase in the mass of poverty, enslavement, degradation and exploitation, but at the same time there is a steady intensification of the revolt of the working class – a class which grows ever more numerous, and is disciplined, unified and organized by the very mechanism of the capitalist method of production … The centralization of the means of production and the socialization of labour reach a point where they prove incompatible with their capitalist husk. This bursts asunder. The knell of private property sounds. The expropriators are expropriated.

Karl Marx *Capital* Vol.I (1867) Ch.22. The apparently unassailable formula for the emergence of socialism from capitalism in Marx's *magnum opus*.

6 From Blanqui's assumption, that any revolution may be made by the outbreak of a small revolutionary minority, follows of itself the necessity of a dictatorship after the success of the venture. This is, of course, a dictatorship, not of the entire revolutionary class, the proletariat, but of a small minority that has made the revolution.

Friedrich Engels, *Der Volkstaat* (The People's State), 26 June 1874. The Frenchman Louis Blanqui preferred a short cut to revolution via a coup d'état rather than wait for inexorable economic forces to work themselves out. He had tried and failed to make such a revolution in Paris in 1839. Engels here attacks Blanqui's elitism, although Lenin was to preach and practise revolution on the basis of just such an exclusive leadership.

7 The difference between … revolutionary dictatorship and the modern state is only one of external trappings. In substance both are a tyranny of the minority over the majority in the name of the people – in the name of the stupidity of the many and the superior wisdom of the few – and so they are equally reactionary, devising to secure political and economic privilege to the ruling minority, and the … enslavement of the masses, to destroy the present order, only to erect their own rigid dictatorship on its ruins.

Mikhail Bakunin on the Marxist version of socialism; Berlin (1963) p.233. As a proponent of anarchist socialism, Bakunin was utterly opposed to Marxism, which accepted the power of the state as a necessity for the achievement of socialist revolution.

8 [Only] in a higher phase of communist society … can the narrow horizon of bourgeois right be crossed in all its entirety and society inscribe on its banners: From each according to his ability, to each according to his needs.

Karl Marx 'Critique of the Gotha Programme' (1875); *Karl Marx and Friedrich Engels, Collected Works* Vol.24 (1989) p.87.

In 1875 the two warring factions of the German Social Democrat Party came together in the town of Gotha to unite on an agreed programme. It was sent to Marx for his comments, which came in the form of a blistering attack on what he considered a betrayal of the revolutionary cause.

1 Just as Darwin discovered the law of evolution in organic nature, so Marx discovered the law of evolution in human history; he discovered the simple fact ... that ... the production of the immediate material means of subsistence and consequently the degree of economic development ... form the foundation upon which the state institutions, the legal conceptions, the art and even the religious ideas of the people concerned have been evolved.

Friedrich Engels, oration at Marx's funeral, March 1883; W.O. Henderson *The Life of Friedrich Engels* (1976) p.569.

2 The philosophers have only interpreted the world in various ways; the point, however, is to change it.

Inscription below the bust of Marx, next to his tomb in Highgate cemetery, London; a quotation from his work *The German Ideology* (1846).

RELIGION AND IRRELIGION, 1850–1904

3 The church and the army alone preserve intact the high feeling of the inviolability of authority, of the holiness of obedience, and the divinity of self-sacrifice; they are now the only representatives of European civilization ... What would become of the world, of civilization, were there neither priests nor soldiers?

The reactionaries' reactionary, the Spanish Count Maria Donoso Cortés 'The General Condition of Europe' 30 Jan. 1850. A hard-line reassertion of traditionalism after the earthquake of 1848–9.

4 I want by this means to make the influence of the clergy all-powerful; I demand that the influence of the priest should be forceful, much more so than it is now, because I rely a great deal on him to spread that sound philosophy which teaches that man is here to suffer, and not that other philosophy which says to man on the contrary: enjoy yourself.

Louis-Adolphe Thiers on the Loi Falloux of 1850; J. and M. Lough *An Introduction to Nineteenth-century France* (1978) p.113. Thiers, the pillar of the July Monarchy, was, with the Count de Falloux, one of the principal architects of the law giving the Roman Catholic Church in France extensive power over the French education system, an act aimed against the spread of socialist ideas.

5 *My* God is the God of Socrates, Franklin, Voltaire and Béranger! I'm for the Savoyard curé's statement of faith and the immortal principles of '89! And I don't believe in the kind of God who strolls round his garden with his walking-stick, plants his friends in the belly of a whale, cries out when he dies and comes back to life after three days: this sort of thing is absurd in itself and what's more completely contrary to all the laws of physics.

The atheist M. Homais in Gustave Flaubert's novel *Madame Bovary* Pt 2, Ch.1 (1856). A paean to rationalism from a devotee of the Revolution. Socrates, the Athenian philosopher of the 5th century BC, the American Benjamin Franklin (see 501:4), Voltaire, the maestro of the French Enlightenment (see 484:6), the Bonapartist versifier Pierre-Jean de Béranger, and Jean-Jacques Rousseau, the Savoyard curé and the intellectual precursor of the Revolution (see 514:3), formed a pantheon of religious sceptics.

6 A free church in a free state.

The Italian Count Camillo Cavour, attrib. Supposedly said to his confessor on his deathbed, June 1861. The watchword of Italian liberalism, which intensely mistrusted the influence of the papacy in Rome and which had achieved national unity at the papacy's expense.

7 39. The state, being the origin and source of all rights, is endowed with a unique right not circumscribed by any limits ...

55. The church ought to be separated from the state, and the state from the church ...

76. The abolition of the temporal power belonging to the Apostolic See would contribute in the highest degree to the liberty and prosperity of the church.

77. In the present day it is no longer acceptable that the Catholic religion should be maintained as the one and only religion of the state to the exclusion of all other forms of worship ...

79. It is untrue that the civil liberty of every single form of worship, and the complete freedom, given to all, of overtly and publicly expressing any opinions whatsoever ... tend more easily to corrupt the morals and minds of the people, and to spread the plague of indifferentism.

80. The Roman Pontiff can, and should, reconcile himself, and come to terms with progress, liberalism and modern civilization.

Pope Pius IX *Syllabus errorum* (The Syllabus of Errors), 8 Dec. 1864; Anne Fremantle (ed.) *The Papal Encyclicals in their Historical Context* (1963) pp.147, 149, 152. Pius IX had lost most of the papal territory in central Italy to the liberal Italian kingdom founded in 1861, and the papacy and the Italian state were to be enemies for generations to come. The Syllabus was promulgated to demonstrate the evil of liberal thinking and to assert the axioms of Catholic doctrine.

1 When the Sovereign Pontiff has proclaimed a pastoral decision, no one has the right to add or to suppress the smallest vowel ... Whatever he affirms, that is true forever.

The French Ultramontane Catholic Louis Veuillot *The Liberal Illusion* (1866) pp.76–7. The Ultramontanists (literally 'across the Alps') believed in papal supremacy over the church within their cisalpine states.

2 If [Spain] has the misfortune to throw herself into the fleshless arms of religious liberty, on that day the Spain of memories, the Spain of ancient glories is dead ... On that day – may God forbid it! – this poor nation will become a charnel-house; the exterminating angel will have collected its cold ashes [and] will have heaped them on the foul tomb of oblivion.

The Spanish priest Manterola, 1869; J. Salwyn Schapiro *Anticlericalism* (1967) p.180. Words uttered the year after the Spanish monarchy was replaced by a republic in which anti-clerical forces were well to the fore.

3 The Roman Pontiff, when ... he defines a doctrine regarding faith or morals to be held by the universal church is, by the divine assistance promised to him in Blessed Peter, possessed of that infallibility with which the divine Redeemer [Christ] wills that His church should be endowed.

Dogma of papal infallibility, issued by the Vatican Council in Rome, 13 July 1870; Fremantle (1963) p.27. This asseveration of absolute papal authority in the theological realm was published on the eve of the Franco-Prussian war, when the French garrison, which had been in Rome since 1849, was withdrawn, and Rome fell to the forces of the Italian monarchy. After this point the temporal power of the pope was restricted to the Vatican City, in glaring contrast with the papal claim to doctrinal paramountcy.

4 *Nach Canossa gehen wir nicht.* (We are not going to Canossa.)

Otto von Bismarck to the German Reichstag, 14 May 1872; Golo Mann *The History of Germany since 1789* (1974) p.296. Bismarck spoke at the time of the *Kulturkampf*, the struggle for influence between the papacy and the German Reich, dominated by Protestant Prussia, which mirrored the enmity in Italy between church and state. The 1070s witnessed an epic battle for supremacy between the German Holy Roman Emperor, Henry IV, and Pope Gregory VII. In Jan.1077 the emperor was constrained to travel to Canossa in northern Italy to do humiliating penance before the pope. The episode (see 189:5) left an enduring bitterness in German historical memory.

5 It is at bottom ... the contest, which, under the name of the conflict between the German kings and the popes, filled the history of the Middle Ages until the dissolution of the German empire ... It is really a question of protecting the state ... of fixing the boundary between priesthood and kingship, and this line of demarcation must be so placed that the state can maintain its existence. For in the kingdom of this world the state must have precedence and command.

Otto von Bismarck on the significance of the *Kulturkampf*; H. Hahn *Geschichte des Kulturkampfes in Preussen* (1881) pp.118 ff.

6 We are confronting only one enemy, but it is a well-organized, well-disciplined enemy. Its first weapon is passive obedience and it subverts through the money it extracts from the stupid and the superstitious. Its method of approach overthrows all obstacles, because it has no scruples, and it hates modern society, not just in France but throughout the whole world. That's your enemy!

Léon Gambetta, 2 Oct. 1872; René Rémond *Anti-Clericalism in France* (1976) p.177. Gambetta returned to the charge in a speech of 4 May 1877. Both declarations were steeped in the conviction that the Catholic church was the implacable adversary of the Third Republic, as indeed it was. The basilica of the Sacré Coeur was built on the hill of Montmartre to remind Paris that it must expiate its sins, above all the sin of the Commune of 1871 (see 671:5). The anti-clericals retaliated by erecting close by a statue of the Chevalier de la Barre, the martyr of the *ancien régime*, exalted by their patron saint Voltaire.

7 We speak of that sect of men ... called socialists, communists or nihilists ... They assail the right of property sanctioned by natural law; they strive to seize and hold in common whatever has been acquired either by title or by lawful inheritance, or by labour of brain and hands, or by thrift in one's mode of life ... The boldness of these evil men ... day by day more and more threatens civil society and strikes the souls of all with anxiety and fear.

Pope Leo XIII, 28 Dec. 1878; Claudia Carlen (ed.) *The Papal Encyclicals 1878–1903* (1981) pp.11–12.

8   Onward, sons of the Republic,
        Voting day is here!
        The hateful banner of the black gang is raised
            against us.
        Do you hear all those demons cawing their
            stupid chants?

They'd want once more, the devils, to foul our
    children and our wives!
To the polls, citizens, against the priests!
Let's vote, let's vote, and let our ballots scatter
    their flock.

Léo Taxil (Gabriel-Antoine Jogand-Pagès) 'The Anti-Clerical
Marseillaise' (1881). 'La Marseillaise' had just been adopted as
the French national anthem (see 520:2).

1 Working men's associations should be so organized
and governed as to ... help each individual member to
better his condition to the utmost in body, mind and
property. It is clear that they must pay special and
chief attention to the duties of religion and morality
... otherwise they would wholly lose their special
character, and end by becoming little better than
those societies which take no account whatever of
religion.

Pope Leo XIII *Rerum Novarum* (encyclical), 15 May 1891;
Fremantle (1963) p.192. An attempt to meet socialism on its
own ground by forming Catholic trade unions.

2 If today on the soil of the Republic there are
thousands of schools where millions of children are
raised in the light of naturalistic morality, science
and reason – we owe it to the spirit of the Revolution.

Jean Jaurès, 3 March 1904; Harvey Goldberg *The Life of Jean
Jaurès* (1962) p.89. The battle between church and state in
France – particularly over education – resulted in their formal
separation in 1905, annulling Napoleon's Concordat of 1801.

FRANCE: A SECOND NAPOLEON, 1851–70

3 A dwarf on the crest of a wave can reach the height
of a cliff.

Alexis de Tocqueville to Beaumont, 29 Jan. 1851; *Works*
Vol.8/2, p.369. Acid comment on Louis-Napoleon, then
president of the Second Republic.

4 Now you come along to ... grasp in your tiny fist
the sceptre of Titans, the sword of giants. And for
what purpose? What, after Augustus but Augustulus?
What now? Because we have had the Great
Napoleon, must we now have the Little Napoleon?

Victor Hugo, 17 July 1851; *Napoléon le Petit* (1852) p.133. Few
believed that Louis-Napoleon could begin to match the
achievement of his imperial uncle. After this sally in the
Chamber of Deputies, Hugo was a marked man and went into
exile in the Channel Islands in 1852, not returning to Paris
until after Napoleon's fall in Sept. 1870.

5 The year 1852 is close at hand ... The masses want
blood, wine and pillage ... There is no woman

brought to bed in our day who was not brought to
bed by a socialist ... When the crisis comes in a few
months a great man will establish an absolute
dictatorship ... After a short and bloody struggle, a
strong power will open the new authoritarian era.

The die-hard rightist Auguste Romieu *The Red Spectre of 1852*
(1851).

6 Paris looked like a woman raped by four brigands,
with a knife to her throat, who, unable to move,
closes her eyes and accepts her fate.

The anarchist socialist Pierre-Joseph Proudhon, diary entry,
3 Dec. 1851; Pierre Haubtmann *Pierre-Joseph Proudhon: Sa vie
et sa pensée* (1988) p.138. On 2 Dec. 1851, the anniversary
of the Battle of Austerlitz (see 532:4), Louis-Napoleon staged a
coup d'état in Paris, whereby he became president for life. A
year later he proclaimed himself Emperor Napoleon III
(in deference to Napoleon I's son, who never succeeded
his father).

7 This Bonaparte, who constitutes himself *chief of
the lumpenproletariat* ... who recognizes in the
scum, offal, refuse of all classes the only class upon
which he can base himself unconditionally, is the
real Bonaparte ... Liberty, Equality, Fraternity ...
when what this republic really means is Infantry,
Cavalry, Artillery.

Karl Marx *The Eighteenth Brumaire of Louis Bonaparte* (1852);
Karl Marx and Friedrich Engels, Selected Works Vol.1 (1962)
p.295. Marx compares the coup of Louis-Napoleon with his
uncle's *Putsch* in the autumn of 1799 (see 530:6).

8 Most of them chose him, not for his ability, but for
his supposed mediocrity. They thought he would be
a tool they could use at will and break whenever it
suited them ... In this they were grossly deluded.

Alexis de Tocqueville on Louis-Napoleon, *Souvenirs* (1851)
Pt 3, Ch.2; *Works* Vol.12 (1964). The same was true of the
conservatives who installed Hitler as chancellor in 1933
(see 753:9).

9 If this man's reign is destined to continue, even for
a brief duration, the world will witness the most
heterogeneous jumble of despotism and demagogy,
of socialism and corruption that history has ever
chronicled.

'An Englishman', letter to *The Times*, 20 Dec. 1851.

10 For me, as a landowner, as an industrialist, as
a lawyer, who knows the peasants and the people
thoroughly, Napoleon was at once the guarantee
of order and the promise of welfare within well-
defined limits.

Riché-Tirman to the Duke de Morny, minister of the interior, 26 Jan. 1852; Theodore Zeldin *The Political System of Napoleon III* (1958) Ch.4. Morny masterminded the coup of 2 Dec. 1851. An echo here of the slogan of the father of positivism, Auguste Comte: 'Order and Progress' (later adopted as the motto of Brazil).

1 I saw the tinsmith opposite climb quickly up a ladder and hammer off his sign the words 'to the King' which followed the word 'tinsmith' … When I next went down the Rue des Capucines I saw on the sign 'to the Emperor' in place of 'to the King'.

Edmond de Goncourt, 24 Feb. 1868, recalling the change of regime from July Monarchy to Second Empire; *Journal* Vol.8 (1956) p.89.

2 The Empire is peace.

Louis-Napoleon, 15 Oct. 1852, anticipating the proclamation of the Second Empire on 2 Dec. 1852. Under the empire French troops were to fight in the Crimea, Italy, China, Vietnam, Mexico and, finally, on their own territory against Prussia in 1870.

3   No more anarchic streets, running free, rough
      and ready …
Alignment! That's the watchword of today.
Paris, which you the duellist ran through,
Takes the thrust of fifteen, twenty new
      diagonals
Conveniently leading out from barracks!
Boulevard and square proclaim your name,
And the whole production anticipates a
      cannonade.

Victor Hugo, 1869; Robert L. Herbert *Impressionism* (1988) p.307. The town-planner Baron Haussmann transformed the centre of Paris by cutting wide boulevards and avenues through the warren of streets in the old quarters. Besides giving a big stimulus to housing and shopping development, they made it much more difficult for dissidents to erect barricades, which had made revolutionary street fighting possible in 1830 and 1848, and gave an excellent field of fire to government artillery.

4 From the duchess to the drab, the shop-keeper to the dandy, all have their brokers; increase of luxury, larger need of cash, in a word, 'pecuniary considerations', have done more to strangle incipient revolution than the army.

The American Henry Tuckerman *Papers about Paris* (1867) pp.15–17. The Second Empire's formula for smothering revolution by affluence.

5 Each morning upon awakening the Minister of the Interior rings a telegraphic doorbell from the privacy of his office and gathers all the Prefects intangibly around him to give them the orders of the day.

Eugène Pelleton *Les Droits de l'homme* (1867) pp.291–2. Traditional French centralism is reinforced by the latest technology.

6 This office, witness to so many fearful sights … is (can one believe it?) crammed with glowing erotic pictures: naked sluts, provocative young girls with pretty faces, which not only cover the walls (papered in frightful Empire-style with golden bees all over) but which are scattered on the chairs, the desk and the rest of the furniture, stacked everywhere!

Edmond de Goncourt, 29 June 1863, in the inner sanctum of the Paris prefect of police; *Journal* Vol.6 (1956) p.88.

7 How could you expect the empire to function smoothly? The Empress is a Legitimist; my half-brother Morny is an Orleanist; my cousin Jerome is a Republican; and I am said to be a socialist. Among us, only Persigny is a Bonapartist, and he is insane.

Napoleon III, attrib. An emperor with a sense of humour. Legitimists were adherents of the Bourbon pretender, 'Henri V', grandson of Charles X, ousted in 1830 (see 544:7). Orleanists supported the Bourgeois monarchy, which collapsed in 1848. The Duke of Persigny was a loyalist of Louis-Napoleon from as early as the 1830s and had his reward, first as minister of the interior and then as ambassador to Britain.

8 To preach liberty, sword in hand, to the whole world … and to make us live under the institutions of the First Empire and of the early part of it too, without even the corrective of the Additional Act, this had become an intolerable contrast and almost ludicrous.

Louis-Adolphe Thiers to Louis Buffet, 1 Dec. 1860; Zeldin (1958) Ch.7. On 24 Nov. 1860 Napoleon had made some concessions to liberalism and slackened the tight autocracy of the past decade. The Additional Act of April 1815 sought to liberalize the First Empire after Napoleon's return from Elba.

9 I tried to be above the left as well as above the right, and to form a new mean in which both could meet. To speak the language of Proudhon, I was no more on the side of the *thesis* than on that of the *antithesis*. I tried to construct a *synthesis* … The truth in politics as in all else is at the centre.

Émile Ollivier to Henri-Alexandre Wallon, 16 March 1872; Theodore Zeldin *Émile Ollivier* (1963) p.195. Ollivier was appointed Napoleon's prime minister in Jan. 1870, with the task of making the empire a parliamentary regime. Here he offers a retrospective justification of his short-lived experiment, ended by the overthrow of Napoleon after the Battle of Sedan in Sept. 1870.

1 And around this grotesque and hideous mask of death, the hair, the gorgeous hair, retained its glory and flowed in a golden stream. Venus was decomposing. It seemed as if the infection she had picked up in the gutters, from the indulgence of a putrefied society, the poisonous disease she had passed on to everyone she touched, was climbing up into her face and rotting it away. The room was empty. A great frenzied wave of sound rose from the boulevard and flared the curtain. 'To Berlin! To Berlin! To Berlin!'
Émile Zola *Nana* (1880) last words. The life and death (in July 1870) of Nana, the *poule de luxe* (expensive courtesan), symbolizes the decadence of the empire soon to be destroyed in the war with Prussia.

2 A bastard monarchy, despised by the enlightened classes, hostile to liberty, governed by intriguers, adventurers and valets … It will certainly die in war but its death will cost us dear.
Alexis de Tocqueville *Souvenirs* and letter, 9 Jan. 1852; *Works* Vol.12 pp.224–5 and Vol.6, p.133.

FRANCE: PARIS COMMUNE, 1871

3 I am in heaven. Paris is a true paradise; no police, no nonsense, no oppression of any kind, no disputes. Paris runs itself as if on wheels. It should always be like this. In short, it is sheer bliss.
The painter Gustave Courbet, March 1871; Roger Williams *The World of Napoleon III* (1957) p.231. In March 1871, immediately after the end of the war with Prussia, left-wing militants proclaimed the Paris Commune and took control of the city. For the revolutionary artist Courbet the millennium had arrived.

4 Here is what we want and nothing else. A united and indivisible Republic; the separation of church and state; free and compulsory education by lay teachers; the abolition of all standing armies and every citizen to bear arms in his own district, that is, the National Guard; the abolition of … all the police, including the gendarmes.
Letter from a young Parisian Communard to his family, 9 March 1871; J. Rougerie *Procès des Communards* (1964) pp.176–7.

5 Workers, make no mistake – this is all-out war, a war between parasites and workers, exploiters and producers. If you are tired of vegetating in ignorance

and poverty; if you want your children to grow up to enjoy the fruits of their labour rather than be some sort of animal reared for the factory or the battlefield … if you want justice to reign, workers, use your intelligence, arise! Let your strong hands crush the forces of reaction!
Proclamation by the central committee of the National Guard, 5 April 1871; *Journal Officiel*, 7 April 1871. Issued after the first attack on the Commune by the right-wing republican government on 2 April.

6 Suddenly, there it is, like the flap of a gigantic bird's wing, a huge zigzag through the air! Ah, I shall never forget that colossal shadow falling across my eyes! Flop! A cloud of smoke. All is over. The column lies on the ground, split open, its stony entrails exposed to the wind. Caesar is lying prostrate and headless. The laurel-wreathed head has rolled like a pumpkin into the gutter.
M. Vuillaume *Mes cahiers rouges au temps de la Commune* Vol.5 (1914) p.178. The column in the Place Vendôme, topped by a statue of Napoleon I, was pulled down in an operation supervised by Courbet.

7 Scorn – to be scorned by France – is perhaps required punishment for the arrant cowardice with which the Parisians submitted to riot and to the desperadoes who led it. It's a sequel to the desperadoes of the Empire. Different felons, same cowardice.
The writer George Sand to Gustave Flaubert, 28 April 1871; Francis Steegmuller (ed.) *The Letters of Gustave Flaubert 1857–1880* (1982) p.174.

8 If tomorrow we executed a hundred of those who are refusing to fight – which is not a lot – and exhibited their bodies on the boulevards with placards showing the crimes they had committed, you can be sure that the day after tomorrow crowds of people would come forward to serve the Commune.
Elderly speaker at a women's club, 12 May 1871; P. Fontoulieu *Les Églises de Paris sous la Commune* (1873) pp.271–5. A war to the death on both sides.

9 A friend of mine saw a house in the Boulevard Malesherbes visited by a squad of soldiers. They asked the concierge if there were any Communards concealed there. She answered that there were none. They searched the house, and found one. They took him out and shot him, and then shot her.
The American W. Hoffman *Camp, Court and Siege* (1877) pp.278–83.

1 I've just set the fucking Tuileries on fire. Now a king can come; he'll find his palace in ashes.

Florence Wandeval; Edith Thomas *The Women Incendiaries* (1967) p.157. Wandeval was one of the *pétroleuses* (arsonists) who set central Paris ablaze as the Commune went down, including the royal palace of the Tuileries and the Hôtel de Ville, the seat of municipal government in Paris.

2 As we stood there, silent and still (history seemed to unfold before our eyes) watching the fire sweep across the city until the break of day; the Athenians leaving their city to be burned and sacked by the Persians rather than let themselves be captured … Saragossa defending itself inch by inch, burning its houses at the approach of the invader; Moscow in flames offering itself in sublime sacrifice to Russia!

P.-O. Lissagary *Les Huit Journées de mai* (1871) pp.102–4. Athens was abandoned to the forces of the Persian ruler Xerxes in 480 BC (see 55:6). Saragossa was taken in the Peninsular War in 1809, and Moscow was burned during Napoleon's invasion of Russia in 1812.

3 When I consent to be a Republican, *I do evil, knowing that's what I do* … I say *Long live Revolution!* as I would say *Long live Destruction! Long live Expiation! Long live Punishment! Long live Death!*

Charles Baudelaire, 1866; *Complete Works* p.1456. Baudelaire died in 1867 and so did not live to see the Commune, but this hymn to nihilism is perfectly in tune with the orgy of vengeance engaged in by all those involved.

4 Cavalry rode into view, threatening, sabre in hand, surrounding a batch of prisoners … These men had an extraordinary pallor and I shall never forget the distant look on their faces … A stolid bourgeois who had counted them said to the man standing next to him: 'They're going to be shot.' Almost the same instant … a volley, with something of the mechanical precision of a machine-gun about it … Then, like a collection of drunks, the firing squad came out of the gate, some of them with blood on the tips of their bayonets.

Edmond de Goncourt, 28 May 1871; *Journal* Vol.10 (1956) p.15. Retribution on captured Communards, on a scale not seen since the June Days of 1848 (see 557:5).

5 The ground is strewn with corpses. This dreadful sight shall serve as a lesson.

Louis-Adolphe Thiers, May 1871, attrib. Thiers directed the liquidation of the Commune, in which some 20,000 insurgents died. It was the last chapter in the French revolutionary upsurge that had begun in 1789.

6 Stand up! soul of the proletarian.
Let us work and form our ranks at last.
Stand up! the wretched of the earth!
Stand up! the slaves of hunger,
To conquer poverty and obscurity.
Servile crowd, stand up! stand up!
We are in the right, we are in the majority.
We who were nothing, shall be everything.
This is the final struggle.
Let us come together and tomorrow
The International will be the human race.
There are no supreme redeemers,
No god, no Caesar, no tribune.
Workers, let us make our own salvation,
Let us work for the good of all
To make the robbers disgorge,
To rescue our spirit from the scaffold.
Let us fire our mighty forge!
And strike the iron while it's hot!

Eugène Pottier 'L'Internationale' (June 1871). Composed in the immediate aftermath of the annihilation of the Commune, this became the anthem of European socialism for a century to come. The International was the International Working Men's Association, founded in 1864 and dissolved in 1876. The Second International, launched in 1889, collapsed with the outbreak of World War I in 1914.

FRANCE: THIRD REPUBLIC, 1871–1914

7 I shall not permit the standard of Henri IV, of François I and of Jeanne d'Arc, to be snatched from my hands … I received it as a sacred trust from the old king, my grandfather, when he died in exile … It floated over my cradle; may it overshadow my grave.

Comte de Chambord ('Henri V'), the Bourbon pretender to the French throne, 5 July 1871; Comte de Falloux *Mémoires d'un Royaliste* Vol.3 (1925) p.238. The republic proclaimed in Sept. 1870 was willing to return to monarchy, but the pretender refused to accept the tricolour as his banner. Ironically, the flag bequeathed by his grandfather, Charles X, was not the flag of Henry IV, Francis I or Joan of Arc: that was blue; his banner was white.

8 The Republic will be a peasant republic or it will not exist at all.

Jules Ferry, 16 April 1875, attrib. The Constitution of Jan. 1875 established a Third Republic on extremely conservative foundations. France was then – and remained for years to come – a basically agrarian society, dominated by the interests of a distinctly non-revolutionary class. The politician Ferry later became prime minister.

1 There are three things I call for ... to instil deeply into all Frenchmen the patriotic spirit which makes them adore their country passionately; the military spirit which teaches them to serve enduringly and willingly; the national spirit which educates them to know the nation's needs and interests.

Paul Déroulède, 18 May 1882; Peter Rutkoff *Revanche and Revision* (1981) p.32. Déroulède founded the League of Patriots, a right-wing organization that aimed to mould the republic in its image.

2 The Boulangist movement is in reality a two-fold character: it is at once patriotic and anti-parliamentary ... Experience has proved beyond question the utter powerlessness of the parliament-ary system of government as it exists today in France. The present regime is, properly speaking, nothing more or less than a hunt for portfolios unrestrained by any close season. The guiding principle of all our politicians is the simple one, 'Move over, I'm taking your place!' Owing to the adoption of this principle no ministry is stable. A cabinet is at the mercy of any hostile coalition.

Henri Rochefort *Fortnightly Review* Vol.2 (1888) pp.11 ff. General Georges Boulanger enjoyed a brief vogue in the late 1880s as the figurehead of anti-democratic political forces, and his movement revealed a deep scepticism about parliamentarianism that was to endure in France throughout the Third Republic. Prosecuted by the government, Boulanger fled the country and shot himself on his mistress's grave in 1891.

3 I pledge myself to fight against every republican regime. The Republic of France is the regime of the foreigner. The republican spirit disorganizes national defence and favours religious influences hostile to traditional Catholicism. A regime which is French should be restored to France.

Action française, membership oath, 15 Nov. 1899. Like the League of Patriots, this group rejected parliamentary democracy and eventually came into its own under the Vichy government formed in 1940.

4   *Dansons la Ravachole!*
    Vive le son! Vive le son!
    Dansons la Ravachole!
    Vive le son
    De l'explosion!

(Let's dance the Ravachol!/Long live the sound! Long live the sound!/Let's dance the Ravachol!/Long live the sound/Of the explosion!)

Parody of the Carmagnole (see 520:4) sung after the guillotining of the anarchist Ravachol, 1892; James Joll *The*

Anarchists (1964) p.136. Anarchism, which flourished most in the backward extremities of Europe – Spain, Italy and Russia – also had its enthusiasts in France, like Ravachol, committing political murder ('the insurrectionary deed') in the name of freedom.

5 I sha'n't kill an innocent, killing the first bourgeois to pass by.

Léon Jules Léauthier, 1894; Joll (1964) p.169.

6 I brought to the struggle a profound hatred, intensified every day by the revolting spectacle of society where all is base, all is cowardly ... I wanted to show the bourgeoisie that ... their golden calf would tremble violently on its pedestal until the final shock would cast it down in mud and blood.

Émile Henry, 1894; Jean Maitron *Histoire du Mouvement anarchiste en France* (1951) pp.529 ff.

7 Men who are participating in a great social movement always picture their coming action as a battle in which their cause is certain to triumph. These visions ... I propose to call myths; the syndicalist general strike and Marx's catastrophic revolution are such myths [which] lead men to prepare themselves for a combat which will destroy the status quo.

Georges Sorel to Daniel Halévy, 15 July 1907; *Reflections on Violence* (1907) Introduction. Sorel's attack on the bourgeois French state took the form of the general strike, in which workers would bring the economy to a standstill and so, he believed, produce the revolution that individual acts of anarchist terror could never achieve.

8 Everything starts as mystique and ends as politics [but] a mystique should not be devoured by the politics to which it has given birth ... When one sees what clerical politics have made of the Christian mystique, how can one be surprised by what Radical politics have made of the Republican mystique?

Charles Péguy *Notre Jeunesse* (Our Youth) (1910); *Complete Works* (1916) pp.460–61. Disillusion with the manoeuvrings of French politicians by a once-fervent believer in a socialist future. Péguy was to transfer his idealism entirely to the cause of Catholicism before his death in World War I.

9 I reject the omnipotence of the secular state because I see it as a tyranny: others reject it because it is not their tyranny ... We made the French Revolution. Our fathers thought it was to free themselves. Not at all; it seems it was only to change masters ... We have guillotined the King: long live the state-King! ... We have dethroned the Pope: long live the state-Pope ... I know the state. It has a long history, full of murder and blood … The state is by its nature implacable: it has no soul, no entrails, it is deaf to pity.

The radical Georges Clemenceau, 17 Nov. 1903; David Watson *Georges Clemenceau* (1974) p.158. A thoroughgoing liberal profession of faith from a politician who was perfectly ready to use the power of the French state to break a strike movement by invoking conscription and calling up the strikers into the armed forces. Clemenceau's definition of the state calls to mind Nietzsche's description: 'A state is the coldest of all cold monsters. It lies coldly too; and this lie creeps from its mouth: "I the state am the people" ' (*Also sprach Zarathustra* (1883) Ch.11).

1 Precisely because it is a party of revolution, precisely because it has not paused in its continuous campaign against capitalism and bourgeois property, it is the most active party of reform … the only party which can turn into the starting point for more far-reaching, more extensive conquests … The proletariat, as a final recourse, may appeal to insurrection; but it doesn't confuse those vast collective movements … with futile skirmishes against the full power of the bourgeois state.

Jean Jaurès, introducing the manifesto of the Socialist Party, Oct. 1908; Goldberg (1962) p.403. Constitutional socialism, with the *ultima ratio* of workers' power held in reserve.

2 There is less difference between two legislators, one of whom is a revolutionary and the other is not, than between two revolutionaries, one of whom is a legislator and the other is not.

Robert de Jouvenel *La République des camarades* (The Republic of Cronies) (1914) Pt 1, Ch.1. A celebrated *jeu d'esprit*, which – like the title of de Jouvenel's book – cuts to the quick of democratic politics in pre-1914 France. Sorel, however, has a prior claim on it: 'All the deputies agree that there is very little difference between a bourgeois representative and a representative of the proletariat' (letter to Daniel Halévy, 15 July 1907; *Reflections on Violence* (1907) Introduction).

GERMANY AND BISMARCK, 1852–90

3 The noble ideals of political morality, legality, civic virtue, freedom and equality, the rose-coloured dreams of the eighteenth century for which our ancestors so heroically faced death, and in which we, no less eager for martyrdom, copied them – there they lie at our feet, shattered, destroyed, like shards of porcelain.

The poet Heinrich Heine to Gustav Kolb, 13 Feb. 1852; *Briefe* (Letters) Vol.23, p.181. The bitter aftermath, for a liberal, of 1848.

4 Money will subvert marriage and school, the family and the Sabbath, state and church … the pillars and the fundamentals of our fatherland, and finally the army and the throne.

Ludwig von Gerlach, 1851; Hans Rogger and Eugen Weber (eds) *The European Right* (1965) p.278. A high conservative's fears of enduring liberal influence in Prussia. Von Gerlach wrote in the *Kreuzzeitung*, a right-wing paper, so called from the Iron Cross on its heading.

5 Our political and religious attitude are inseparable; it is impossible to be conservative in the state and destructive in the church, impossible to be both for the order that comes from God and against the faith that comes from God. Despite all gradations there are only two possible attitudes: one is to support the throne and altar undivided, the other to support revolution.

Friedrich Julius Stahl, von Gerlach's comrade-in-arms; Mann (1974) p.228.

6 No parliamentary regime and no ministerial responsibility; personal kingship by the grace of God and not that of a constitution; clerical marriage, Christian school, Christian authority … no promotion and no exclusive domination of finance capital.

Programme of the reactionary Prussian *Volksverein* (People's Union), 1861.

7 Out of the mud-bath of a new revolution Prussia can emerge with new strength; in the sewer of doctrinaire liberalism she will rot without redemption … An efficient army is [her] only feasible protection.

General Albrecht von Roon, Prussian minister of war, June 1861; Michael Howard (ed.) *Soldiers and Governments* (1957) p.80.

8 I told the King that I had told him four years ago that we were living in a period of revolution. The question was whether he wanted to follow Charles I and Louis XVI in allowing power to be wrested from his hands even before open battle had been entered. He still had the power and had the army today; if he yielded at the expense of the army … all he would achieve would be to undermine the army's faith in his steadfastness.

General Edwin von Manteuffel to the king of Prussia, April 1862; Gerhard Ritter *The Sword and the Sceptre* Vol.1 (1972) p.141. The issue was whether the Prussian parliament should have a voice in the affairs of the army. Charles I and Louis XVI had each been executed by a republican government (see 423:1 and 522:3).

1 The Prussian monarchy has not yet completed its mission; it is not yet ready to become a purely ornamental decoration of your constitutional Parliament; not yet ready to be manipulated as a piece of lifeless machinery of parliamentary government.

Otto von Bismarck, 27 Jan. 1863; Grant Robertson *Bismarck* (1918) p.124. Bismarck had been appointed prime minister of Prussia in Sept. 1862 in order to put a stop to the increasing influence of liberalism, which had made huge gains in the 1861 elections.

2 The oppressors of yesterday are the saviours of today; right has become wrong and wrong right. Blood appears, indeed, to be a special elixir, for the angel of darkness has become the angel of light before whom the people lie in the dust and adore. The stigma of violation of the constitution has been washed from his brow, and in its place the halo of glory rings his laurelled head.

Wilhelm Liebknecht, the German socialist leader, 5 Aug. 1866. Liebknecht was speaking soon after the stunning Prussian victory over Austria in the war of 1866, a triumph that made the Prussian conservatives unassailable by their political opponents.

3 The French need a sound thrashing. If the Prussians win ... the weight of German power will transfer the centre of gravity of the labour movement in Western Europe from France to Germany.

Karl Marx, 20 July 1870; *Marx and Engels, Selected Correspondence* (1956) p.301. Another Prussian victory was in the offing, and it did shift the headquarters of European revolution from Paris to Berlin.

4 What a paradise this land is! What clean clothes, what good faces, what tranquil contentment, what prosperity, what genuine freedom, what superb government!

Mark Twain (Samuel Langhorne Clemens) to William Dean Howells, 4 May 1878; *Twain–Howells Letters* Vol.1 (1960) p.227.

5 Give the working man a right to work as long as he is healthy, assure him care when he is sick, assure him maintenance when he is old. If you do that and do not fear the sacrifice, or cry out at state socialism – if the state will show a little more Christian solicitude for the working man, then I believe that the gentlemen of the social-democratic programme will sound their bird-call in vain.

Otto von Bismarck, 9 May 1884; Robertson (1918) p.382. The introduction of Bismarck's welfare state in the 1880s made Germany a model of progressive social legislation as well as undercutting the appeal of socialism.

6 What we have suffered under this regime!!! How utterly corrupting his influence has been ... on the political life of Germany! It has made Berlin almost intolerable to live in, if one is not his abject slave! His party, his followers and admirers are fifty times worse than he is! One feels as if one would like to send up one great cry for deliverance and that if it were answered, one great deep sigh of relief would be given. Alas, all the mischief wrought would take years to repair!!

Crown Princess Victoria of Germany to her mother, Queen Victoria, 8 Jan. 1888; *The Letters of the Empress Frederick* (1928) p.220. The young Victoria writes of Bismarck. On 9 March her equally liberal husband became Emperor Friedrich III, but died of throat cancer three months later. He was succeeded by his son, Wilhelm II, who dismissed Bismarck on 20 March 1890. Wilhelm did this not out of any sympathy for liberalism, however; he was to prove an immensely wilful autocrat.

GERMANY: WILHELMINE EMPIRE, 1890–1914

7 You have sworn loyalty to me. You have only one enemy and that is my enemy. In the present social confusion it may come about that I order you to shoot your relatives, brothers or parents, but even then you must follow my orders without a murmur.

Wilhelm II, Nov. 1891; Tyler Whittle *The Last Kaiser* (1977) p.150. Not for nothing was Wilhelm thought to be more than slightly unhinged – 'not all there', as Lord Salisbury put it.

8 I am convinced that the Guiding Hand of Providence lies behind this elemental and natural drive of the Kaiser's to direct the affairs of the Kingdom in person. Whether it will ruin us or save us I cannot say. But I find it difficult to believe in the decline of Prussia's star.

Philipp Eulenburg to Friedrich von Holstein, 2 Dec. 1894; John Röhl *The Kaiser and his Court* (1994) p.47. Eulenburg was the Kaiser's confidant.

9 The masses will always remain the masses. There can be no culture without its servants. It is self-evident that if there were no men to perform the menial tasks of life, it would be impossible for the higher culture to exist. We come then to realize that millions toil at the plough, the forge, and the carpenter's bench in order that a few thousands may be students or painters or poets. This sounds brutal but it is true, and it will remain true for all time.

Heinrich von Treitschke *Die Politik* (Politics) Vol.I (1897) pp.50–52; H.W.C. Davis *The Political Thought of Heinrich von Treitschke* (1914) p.137.

1 One can envisage that the old society could peacefully grow into the new one ... in democratic republics such as France and America, or in monarchies like England. But in Germany, where the Government is almost omnipotent and the Reichstag and other representative bodies for all practical purposes powerless, to proclaim anything like this in Germany would be to remove the fig leaf from absolutism and use it to conceal one's own nakedness.

Friedrich Engels, 1891; *Die Neue Zeit* (The New Age) Vol.20/I (1901–2) pp.5–13 (an article not published for ten years). Engels was criticizing the Erfurt Programme of the Social Democrats, which assumed that Germany could evolve into a parliamentary democracy. In 1913 the Social Democrats formed the largest party in the Reichstag, but since the chancellor was appointed by the emperor, there was no possibility that he could emerge from the mechanism of the parliamentary system. Only a fundamental change in the German constitution could bring that about, and the German ruling class was not prepared to put that through.

2 Nobody has any idea of destroying bourgeois society as a civilized, orderly social system. On the contrary, social democracy does not wish to dissolve this society and to make proletarians of all its members. Rather, it labours incessantly at lifting the worker from the social position of a proletarian to that of a 'bourgeois' and thus to make 'bourgeoisie' – or citizenship – universal.

Eduard Bernstein *The Pre-Conditions of Socialism and the Tasks of Social Democracy* (1899) p.181. Bernstein aimed to revise Marxism, arguing that the workers' state would come by a process of evolution, not by revolution, as Marx had prophesied. Rising standards of living, coupled with the achievement of a socialist majority in parliament, would bring this about without any need for a violent upsurge. His book caused a furore in the socialist movement, with orthodox Marxists denouncing it as apostasy.

3 I do not believe that they will allow social democracy to develop indefinitely along legal lines. The more it increases its political power, the more certain it is that its adversaries will overthrow the constitution and replace it with a regime in which the workers are violently oppressed, their organizations are broken up by force – a regime based on

brute force which will require the most vigorous counter-measures.

The leading German socialist Karl Kautsky in his paper *Die Neue Zeit* (The New Age), 1904.

4 The first measures which must be taken, at the same time as the state of siege is declared, are the suppression of all papers which follow the revolutionary line, and the arrest of their editors, along with all persons known to be leaders and agitators, without taking any notice of the immunity of the Reichstag members ... There can be only one condition – unconditional surrender. All ringleaders or whoever is caught with a weapon in his possession are to be executed.

General Freiherr von Bissing, order to the VII Army Corps, 30 April 1907; Martin Kitchen *The German Officer Corps 1890–1914* (1968) p.165.

5 *Voigt*: Luck is the first requirement of a commander, Mein Herr, in the words of Napoleon the Great. Of course, I had something else on my side.

Chief of Police: What?

Voigt: Well, we do dearly love a uniform, don't we? I almost think the uniform could have done it on its own.

Carl Zuckmayer *The Captain from Köpenick* (1931) Act 2, Sc.7. Zuckmayer's play was based on a true incident in Oct. 1906. Wilhelm Voigt, an ex-convict, dressed himself in a second-hand army officer's uniform, took over the town hall in the Köpenick district of Berlin, arrested the mayor and seized the contents of the municipal treasury before any action was taken against him.

RUSSIA: TSAR LIBERATOR, 1855–81

6 It is only now beginning to become evident how terrible the past twenty-nine years were for Russia. Administration is in chaos; moral feeling has been trampled on; intellectual development has been stopped ... All this is fruit of a scorn for the truth and a blind and barbarous faith in material force alone.

The imperial censor A.V. Nikitenko, diary entry, 1855; W. Bruce Lincoln *Nicholas I* (1978) p.324. Tsar Alexander II succeeded his father Nicholas I in March 1855.

7 Serfdom is a shackle which we drag around with us, and which holds us back when other peoples are racing ahead unimpeded. Without the abolition of serfdom none of our problems, political, administrative or social, can be solved.

The liberal Russian historian Boris Chicherin, 1856.

1 I did more for the Russian serf in giving him land as well as personal liberty, than America did for the negro slave set free by the proclamation of President Lincoln.

Alexander II, interviewed on 17 Aug. 1879. The Russian serfs were landless peasants in bondage to their masters for life. They were freed by the 'Tsar Liberator', Alexander II, in 1861, the year before Lincoln's Emancipation Proclamation (see 590:8).

2 The Liberals are afraid of losing their liberty – we have none … A man who lives in furnished rooms finds it far easier to move than one who has acquired a house of his own. Europe is sinking because it cannot rid itself of its cargo … In our case, all this is artificial ballast; out with it and overboard, and then full sail into the open sea!

The Russian liberal Alexander Herzen Letters from France and Italy 1847–1851 (1995 edn) Introduction.

3 Enemy of mysticism and absolutism, you mystically bow down before the Russian sheepskin coat and see in it the great abundance, innovation and originality of future social forms … You raise your altar to this new unknown god. But … your god loves madly what you hate and hates what you love. Your god accepts precisely what you reject on his behalf.

The novelist Ivan Turgenev to Alexander Herzen, 8 Nov. 1862; A.V. Knowles (ed.) Turgenev's Letters (1983) pp.109, 110. Herzen was attracted by the idea that the Russian peasantry could be the basis of a movement towards democracy in Russia; Turgenev sought to disabuse him.

4 The dynasty of the Romanovs and the Petersburg bureaucracy must perish … What is dead and rotten must of itself fall into the grave. All we have to do is to give a last push and cover their stinking corpses with earth.

D. Pisarev Select Philosophical, Social and Political Essays (1958) p.147.

5 With faith in ourselves and our strength, in the people's sympathy with us, in the glorious future of Russia, to whose lot it has fallen to be the first country to achieve the glorious work of socialism, we will utter a single cry: 'Seize your axes!'

P.G. Zaichnevsky Young Russia (1861); Geoffrey Hosking Russia: People and Empire (1997) p.347. An over-optimistic prognosis: Russia was not to have an undisputed socialist government for 60 years.

6 Aristocracy, liberalism, progress, principles – think of it, what a lot of foreign and useless words! To a Russian they're not worth a straw … In these days the most useful thing we can do is to repudiate – and so we repudiate … And that is called nihilism.

Ivan Turgenev in his novel Fathers and Sons (1862) Ch.10. The speaker is a nihilist, that is, a revolutionary dedicated to the violent destruction of existing society before building on its ruins.

7 The revolutionary is a lost man; he has no interest of his own, no cause of his own, no feelings, no habits, no belongings; he does not even have a name … He will be an implacable enemy of this world, and if he continues to live in this world, that will only be so as to destroy it the more effectively.

Sergei Nechaev Catechism of the Revolutionary (1869); Hosking (1997) pp.347–8. A chilling creed, written, most probably, in collaboration with Mikhail Bakunin.

8 I am not a Communist because Communism, by concentrating all property in the state, necessarily leads to the concentration of all the power of society in the state. I want to abolish the state; my aim is the complete destruction of the very principle of state authority which up to now has meant the enslavement, suppression, exploitation and humiliation of mankind.

Mikhail Bakunin; Julius Braunthal History of the International 1864–1914 (1966) p.139. The anarchist socialist Bakunin was the ideological enemy of Karl Marx, whose philosophy he attacks here. Marx succeeded in having him expelled from the First International in 1872.

9 Go to the people and tell it the whole truth to the very last word. Tell it that man must live according to the law of nature. According to this law all men are equal; all men are born naked; all men are born equally small and weak.

Vasily Bervy-Flerovsky, 1873; Franco Venturi Roots of Revolution (1952) p.498. Manifesto of the Populists, who believed, like Herzen, in the revolutionary potential of the peasantry. When the Populists went on missions to the countryside, however, the peasants tended to hand them over to the police, a reaction similar to the one experienced by Büchner in Germany (see 550:1).

10 You are representatives of authority; we are opponents of any enslavement of man by man, therefore you are our enemies and there can be no reconciliation between us. You must be destroyed and you will be destroyed! … While you keep the present savage lawlessness in existence, our dark

court will permanently hang over you like the sword of Damocles, and death will be the answer to each of your attacks against us.

S.M. Kravchinsky to the agents of tsarist government, 1878; Martin McCauley and P. Waldron (eds) *The Emergence of the Modern Russian State 1855–1881* (1988). Kravchinsky had just assassinated the chief of the tsarist secret police; he escaped to London.

1 It is too early to thank God!

Words shouted to Alexander II by his assassin, the Polish student Hriniewicki, 13 March 1881; Peter Ustinov *My Russia* (1983) p.108. The tsar was ambushed by revolutionaries the same day he had signed a decree giving a measure of liberalization. After a first bomb was thrown without harming him, he got out of his carriage and thanked God for his deliverance. This was the reply.

RUSSIA: PATH TO REVOLUTION, 1881–1905

2 Russia has been strong thanks to autocracy, thanks to the limitless mutual trust and the close tie between the people and the tsar ... We suffer quite enough from talking-shops, which, under the influence of worthless journals, simply stoke up popular passions.

Constantin P. Pobedonostev, procurator of the Holy Synod, to Tsar Alexander III after the assassination of his father in 1881; Hosking (1997) p.338. After the murder of Alexander II Russia entered a period of intense repression, embodied by this close adviser to the new tsar.

3 If ever Blanquism – the phantasy of overturning an entire society through the action of a small conspiracy – had a certain justification for its existence, that is certainly in Petersburg.

Friedrich Engels to Vera Zasulich, 1885; *Karl Marx and Friedrich Engels, Correspondence 1846–1885* (1934) p.437. Zasulich had shot and wounded the chief of police in the Russian capital, St Petersburg, in Jan. 1878 and was sensationally acquitted at her trial in April. With precious little sign of an industrial proletariat on the horizon, the veteran revolutionary changes his mind on Blanqui (see 665:6) and looks to an insurrectionary coup as the only way forward – as Lenin also did in 1917 (see 724:8).

4 The main supports of crime are idleness, law and authority; laws about property, laws about government, laws about penalties and misdemeanours; and authority, which takes upon itself to manufacture those laws and to apply them. No more laws! No more judges! Liberty, equality, and practical human

sympathy are the only effective barriers we can oppose to the anti-social instincts of certain among us.

Prince Peter Kropotkin *Law and Authority* (1886). The prince was one of the most celebrated Russian anarchists of the 19th century.

5 If Russia chooses to develop purely on her own line and to resist the growth of liberalism, then she may put off the day of reckoning; but she cannot ultimately avert it, and ... she will sometime experience a real terror which will make the French Revolution pale.

The future American President Theodore Roosevelt to Cecil Spring Rice, 13 Aug. 1897; Elting Morison (ed.) *The Letters of Theodore Roosevelt* Vol.1 (1951) p.647.

6 We are being pushed further and further into the depths of poverty, injustice, and ignorance; we are being so stifled by despotism and arbitrary rule that we cannot breathe. Fire, we have no more strength! Our endurance is at an end. We have reached that awful moment when death is preferable to the continuation of intolerable suffering.

Petition of workers and residents of St Petersburg for submission to the tsar, 22 Jan. 1905; Sidney Harcave *First Blood* (1964) p.285. In 1904 Russia had gone to war with Japan and suffered a humiliating defeat. This exposure of the blatant weakness of the tsarist system produced a revolutionary upsurge in 1905, beginning with a procession to petition the tsar. It was met with overwhelming force on 'Bloody Sunday', 22 Jan., and many hundreds were killed.

7 There is no God any longer. There is no Tsar!

The Orthodox priest Father Gapon, leader of the protest on 'Bloody Sunday', as Cossacks cut down the protesters; Walter Sablinsky *The Road to Bloody Sunday* (1976) p.243. It has been said that Gapon (who survived) was acting as an agent provocateur, but this seems unlikely.

8 There were only two ways open; to find an energetic soldier and crush the rebellion by force ... That would mean rivers of blood, and in the end we should be where we had started ... The other way out would be to give the people their civil rights, freedom of speech and press, also to have laws confirmed by a state Duma [Parliament] – that, of course, would be a constitution.

Nicholas II to his mother, the dowager empress, 24 Jan. 1905; *The Secret Letters of Tsar Nicholas II* (1938). To an autocrat such as Nicholas, a constitutional monarchy was tantamount to abdication.

1 Men of Odessa! Before you lies the body of Grigory Vakulintchuk, a sailor savagely killed by the senior officer of the ironclad *Prince Potemkin* for saying 'The soup is not good.' Let us make the sign of the cross and say, 'Peace to his ashes.' Let us avenge ourselves on the bloodthirsty vampires! Death to the oppressors! Death to the bloodsuckers! And hurrah for freedom!

Constantine Feldman, June 1905; *The Revolt of the Potemkin* (1908). In June 1905 the ship's company of the Black Sea warship *Potemkin* mutinied and killed the officers. In 1925 the episode was made into one of the greatest silent films of the 20th century by the director Sergei Eisenstein.

2 1. [We] grant the people the unshakeable foundations of civic freedom on the basis of genuine personal inviolability, freedom of conscience, speech, assembly, and association.

2. [We] admit immediately to participation in the state Duma ... those classes of the population that are now completely deprived of electoral rights.

3. [We] establish as an inviolable rule that no law may go into force without the consent of the state Duma.

Nicholas II, the October Manifesto, 30 Oct. 1905; Harcave (1964) p.196. A huge series of concessions, which appeared to transform Russia into a constitutional state.

3 Freedom of assembly is granted, but the assemblies are surrounded by the military. Freedom of speech is granted, but censorship exists as before. Freedom of knowledge is granted, but the universities are occupied by troops. Inviolability of the person is granted, but the prisons are overflowing.

Leon Trotsky, commenting on the October Manifesto of 1905; Harcave (1964) p.244. At the time, Trotsky was a Menshevik (see 728:1).

4 The people are sending you, not to exchange compliments, but to obtain land and freedom, and to impose on the authorities the curb of the people's supervision.

Instructions to an elected deputy to the first Duma, April 1906; Hosking (1997) p.428. 'Land' and 'freedom' had been the watchwords of the opponents of tsarism since the 1860s. Russia seemed to have achieved democracy, but the years ahead showed that the regime's conversion was more apparent than real.

LENIN AND BOLSHEVISM, 1901–1904

5 Terror is at the moment being promoted not as a *modus operandi* for an army in the field, one that is closely connected with and integrated into the whole system of struggle, but as an independent and occasional attack that is unrelated to any army ... It is our duty to warn with all our energy against a passion for terror, against accepting it as the principal and basic method of struggle ... At best it can serve as only one of the methods employed in the decisive storming action.

Lenin *Where to Begin?*, published in the Marxist journal *Iskra* (The Spark), May 1901; *Selected Works* Vol.2 (1934) p.17. Lenin (the revolutionary pseudonym of Vladimir Ilyich Ulyanov) dismissed terrorism as an infantile strategy, which could destroy leading figures in the tsarist apparatus but which could never supplant tsarism itself.

6 The history of all countries shows that the working class, exclusively by its own efforts, is able to develop only trade-union consciousness, i.e., the conviction that it is necessary to combine in unions, fight the employers, and strive to compel the government to pass necessary labour legislation, etc. The theory of socialism, however, grew out of the philosophical, historical and economic theories elaborated by educated representatives of the propertied classes, by intellectuals. By their social status, the founders of modern scientific socialism, Marx and Engels, themselves belonged to the bourgeois intelligentsia.

Lenin *What is to be Done?* (Feb. 1902); *Collected Works* Vol.5 (1960) p.375. Lenin rejected trade unionism as an inadequate response to capitalism, since it merely made the status quo more palatable to the proletariat, while leaving it fundamentally intact. Educated leaders (such as himself) could teach the workers to know better.

7 In an autocratic state the more we *confine* the membership of such an organization [the Marxist political party] to people who are professionally engaged in revolutionary activity and who have been professionally trained in the art of combating the political police, the more difficult it will be to wipe out such an organization.

Lenin *What is to be Done?* (1902); *Collected Works* Vol.5 (1960). Lenin attacks the proposition that a Marxist party in the repressive circumstances of tsarist Russia could function in the open, contending that it must be an underground movement with strictly limited membership, operating in the closest secrecy.

8 We must take sides on the question of armed insurrection. Those who are opposed to it, those who do not prepare for it, must be ruthlessly dismissed from the ranks of the supporters of the revolution, sent packing to its enemies, to the traitors or the cowards.

Lenin *Selected Works* Vol.1 (1946) pp.447–8. Revolution by coup d'état was seen by most Marxists as a deviation from the schema set out by Marx and Engels, whereby capitalism would fall as a result of the inexorable process of historical development, when the time was ripe for the advent of socialism. Lenin was to mount just such a coup in 1917.

1 Lenin desires unity as a man desires unity with a piece of bread: he swallows it.

Georgi Plekhanov, 1903; Bertram D. Wolfe *Three who Made a Revolution* (1948) p.611. Plekhanov, the doyen of Russian Marxism, correctly identified Lenin's voracious determination to dominate its theory and practice. In 1903, when the Social Democrat Party met at its second congress, Lenin forced a split between his own faction, the Bolsheviks (Majority), and the Mensheviks (Minority), who opposed his party line.

2 *One Step Forward, Two Steps Back.*

Lenin, 6 May 1904; the title of a vitriolic broadside against the Mensheviks, attacking what to Lenin was their retrograde approach to Marxist revolution.

3 The party organization is substituted for the party, the Central Committee is substituted for the party organization, and finally a 'dictator' is substituted for the Central Committee ... A proletariat capable of dictatorship over society will not tolerate dictatorship over itself.

Leon Trotsky (revolutionary pseudonym of Lev Davidovich Bronstein) *Our Political Tasks* (1904); Robert V. Daniels (ed.) *A Documentary History of Communism* (1987) pp.21, 22. A famous rejoinder to Lenin's polemic from a man who in 1904 was a Menshevik but who went over to Lenin in 1917.

4 The ultra-centralism advocated by Lenin ... appears to us as something which, in its whole essence, is not informed with the positive and creative spirit, but with the sterile spirit of the night-watchman ... Social Democratic centralization cannot be based on a blind obedience, on mechanical subordination of the party fighters to their central authority ... and on a sharp separation of the organized nucleus of the party from the surrounding revolutionary milieu.

Rosa Luxemburg *Leninism or Marxism?* (1904). The Polish Marxist Luxemburg likewise stood out against Lenin in 1904, but tried to emulate his 1917 seizure of power by mounting a Marxist *Putsch* in Berlin in Jan. 1919. She failed and, together with her fellow revolutionary Karl Liebknecht, was executed by the right-wing forces of the German *Freikorps*.

Imperialism, 1830–1914

DEVOTEES AND REJECTIONISTS

1 From the moment of the Declaration of Independence [1776] it mattered little whether England counted for less or more with the nations around her. She was no longer a mere European power, no longer a mere rival of Germany or Russia or France. She was from that hour a mother of nations ... Her work was to be colonization.

J.R. Green *A Short History of the English People* (1874) p.762.

2 [French assimilation] is not that of which England and Rome have dreamt in their egotistic and materialistic policies. It is the assimilation of intellects, the conquest of wills.

The historian Jules Michelet *Introduction à l'histoire universelle* (1831). The French brand of imperialism went far beyond political control in aiming at the metamorphosis of local elites into Frenchmen and so depriving them of any original cultural identity. The radical democrat Michelet clearly assumed that this was for the best.

3 Too often, their territory has been usurped; their property seized; their numbers diminished; their character debased; the spread of religion impeded. European vices and diseases have been introduced amongst them, and they have been familiarized with the use of our most potent instruments for the subtle or the violent destruction of human life, viz. Brandy and gunpowder.

Thomas Fowell Buxton, 1837, on the British empire's treatment of its subjects; *Parliamentary Papers* (1837) Vol.7. The anti-slavery campaigner Buxton turned to attack colonialism after the abolition of slavery in the empire in 1833.

4 Wherever the European has trod, death seems to pursue the aboriginal. We may look to the wide extent of the Americas, Polynesia, the Cape of Good Hope and Australia, and we find the same result.

Charles Darwin, 12 Jan. 1836; *The Voyage of the Beagle* (1839) Ch.19. Darwin, perhaps the greatest natural scientist of the 19th century, was able to make personal observations in all these regions during his voyage in HMS *Beagle* from Dec. 1831 to Oct. 1836, evidently studying anthropology as well as fulfilling his brief to research the plant and animal worlds.

5 Our little Isle is grown too narrow for us; but the world is wide enough yet for another Six Thousand Years ... What a future; wide as the world, if we have the heart and heroism for it – which, by Heaven's blessing, we shall.

Thomas Carlyle in the journal *Horoscope*, 1849.

6 Moscow, Peter's city [St Petersburg], and Constantine's city [Constantinople] – these are the sacred capitals of the Russian Empire. But where are its limits? Where its boundaries? ... From the Nile to the Neva, from the Elbe to China, from the Volga to the Euphrates, from the Ganges to the Danube, behold the Russian realm, and never will it end, as the Spirit foresaw and Daniel foretold.

Feodor Tyutchev 'Russian Geography' (1849); Hans Kohn *Pan-Slavism* (1960 edn) p.157. The Russian poet Tyutchev was one of the most ardent propagandists of Pan-Slavism, the concept of a Russian-led empire of all Slavonic peoples.

7 It is a noble work to plant the foot of England and extend her sceptre by the banks of streams unnamed, and over regions yet unknown – and to conquer, not by the tyrannous subjugation of inferior races, but by the victories of mind over brute matter and blind mechanical obstacles. A yet nobler work is to diffuse over a new created world the laws of Alfred, the language of Shakespeare and the Christian religion, the last great heritage of man.

Edinburgh Review (1850) Vol.41, p.61.

8 As the Roman, in days of old, held himself free from indignity, when he could say *Civis Romanus sum* [I am a Roman citizen]; so also a British subject, in whatever land he may be, shall feel confident that the watchful eye and the strong arm of England will protect him against injustice and wrong.

British foreign secretary Lord Palmerston, in the House of Commons, 25 June 1850; *Parl. Deb.* Vol.112, Col.444. See 73:6.

9 What then, Sir, was a Roman citizen? He was the member of a privileged caste: he belonged to a conquering race, to a nation that held all others bound down by the strong arm of power. For him there was to be an exceptional system of law; for him principles were to be asserted, and by him rights were to be enjoyed, that were denied to the rest of the world. Is such, then, the view of the noble lord, as to the relation that is to subsist between England and other countries?

William Ewart Gladstone's riposte to Palmerston, 27 June 1850; *Parl. Deb.* Vol.112, Col.586.

1 Human history is like an immense tapestry ... The two most inferior varieties of the human species, the black and yellow races, are the crude foundation, the cotton and the wool, which the secondary families of the white race make supple by adding their silk; while the Aryan group, circling its finer threads through the noble generation, designs on its surface a dazzling masterpiece of arabesques in silver and gold.

Count Arthur de Gobineau *Essay on the Inequality of the Human Races* (1855) Conclusion. The French aristocrat was the intellectual father of 19th-century racism. Aryan, from the Sanskrit word for 'noble', denoted the whites, destined, in Gobineau's view, to have absolute supremacy over the other two main racial groups in the world.

2 I believe that much of the power and influence of this Country depends upon its having large Colonial possessions in different parts of the world.

Earl Grey, 1853; P.J. Marshall (ed.) *The Cambridge Illustrated History of the British Empire* (1996) p.30.

3 I call him a savage ... a howling, whistling, clucking, stamping, jumping, tearing savage ... cruel, false, thievish, murderous; addicted more or less to grease, entrails, and beastly customs; a wild animal with the questionable gift of boasting; a conceited, tiresome, bloodthirsty, monotonous humbug.

Charles Dickens 'The Noble Savage' in *Household Words*, 11 July 1853, Vol.7, p.337. Intemperate as only he could be, the novelist wanted nothing to do with the civilizing mission of empire.

4 The idea of defending, as integral parts of our Empire, countries 10,000 miles off, like Australia, which neither pay a shilling to our revenue ... nor afford us any exclusive trade ... is about as quixotic a specimen of national folly as was ever exhibited.

Richard Cobden, note to Edward Ellice, 1856; John Bright and James E. Thorold Rogers (eds) *Speeches on Questions of Public Policy by Richard Cobden M.P.* (1878) p.248.

5   Her pirate flag is flying
      Where the East and the West are one.
      And her drums when the day is dying
      Salute the rising sun.

The Irish-American versifier John Jeffrey Roche (1847–1908), broadside against the British empire. A hostile variation on the theme proudly trumpeted by John Wilson (Christopher North): 'His Majesty's dominions, on which the sun never sets' (*Noctes Ambrosianae*, April 1829).

6 We stand with [the Poles] because we are firmly convinced that the absurdity of an empire stretching from Sweden to the Pacific, from the White Sea to China, cannot bring any good to the peoples which Petersburg leads on a chain. The universal empire of the Chingizes and Tamerlanes belong to the most primitive and savage periods of development, to those times when the entire glory of the state was made up of military strength and vast territories. They could exist only with inescapable slavery at the bottom and unlimited tyranny at the top ... We are against the empire because we are for its people!

The Russian liberal Alexander Herzen applauding the Polish rising of 1863; Mark Bassin *Imperial Visions* (1999) p.271. By Chingizes Herzen meant Genghis Khan, the Mongol conqueror of the late 12th and early 13th centuries (see 250:6). Tamerlanes was Tamerlane (Timur), the Tatar lord of central Asia in the late 14th century (see 256:2).

7 It cannot but happen ... that those will survive whose functions happen to be most nearly in equilibrium with the modified aggregate of external forces ... This survival of the fittest implies multiplication of the fittest.

Herbert Spencer *Principles of Biology* (1865) Pt 3, p.164. Spencer the sociologist applied to politics the evolutionary principles set out by Charles Darwin in his seminal work *On the Origin of Species*, published in 1859, and became a potent influence on racialist and imperialist thinking in the pre-1914 generation. See 665:4.

8 They are beardless children whose life is a task and whose chief virtue consists in unquestioning obedience.

Anthropological Review Vol.4 (1866) p.120; on the underclass of the world due to be colonized by their racial superiors.

9 This is what [England] must either do or perish: she must found colonies as fast and as far as she is able, formed of her most energetic and worthiest men; – seizing every piece of fruitful waste ground she can set her foot on, and there teaching these her colonists that ... their first aim is to be to advance the power of England by land and sea.

John Ruskin, inaugural lecture at Oxford University, 8 Feb. 1870; *The Works of John Ruskin* Vol.20 (1905) p.42. A rousing summons to action, highly uncharacteristic of a man whose reputation is as an art historian and environmentalist.

10   His daring foot is on land and sea everywhere
      He colonizes the Pacific, the archipelagos,
      With the steamship, the electric telegraph.
      The newspaper, the wholesale engines of war,

With these and the world-spreading factories
He interlinks all geography, all lands.

The American poet Walt Whitman 'Years of the Modern' in *Leaves of Grass* (1860). The poet exults in the technical prowess of the masters of the universe.

1 If you look to the history of this country since the advent of Liberalism – forty years ago – you will find there has been no effort so continuous, so subtle, supported by so much energy, and carried on with so much ability and acumen, as the efforts of Liberalism to effect the disintegration of the Empire of England.

From Benjamin Disraeli's famous Crystal Palace Speech, 24 June 1872; John S. Galbraith 'Myths of the "Little England" Era' in *American Historical Review* Vol.67 (1961–2) p.35. In reinforcing the myth of mid-Victorian, anti-imperialist Liberalism, Disraeli is indulging in effective party propaganda.

2 What does Imperialism mean? It means the assertion of absolute force over others … If we can, by abating somewhat of our extreme right, or even by larger concessions, avert the calamities of war, that is utterly repugnant to Imperialism … It does not follow that the strongest party is always in the wrong, but the triumph of Imperialism is most complete when power is most clearly manifested; and of course the victory is doubled when the victory is not only over weakness but over right.

Robert Lowe, *Fortnightly Review*, 1 Oct. 1878, pp.458–9. Lowe was not, as this quotation might suggest, a raging Radical, but an anti-Disraeli Conservative, at a time when Disraeli was glorying in Britain's imperial power.

3 The extension of British rule throughout the world … the colonization by British subjects of all the lands where the means of livelihood are attainable by energy, labour and enterprise, and especially the occupation by British settlers of the entire Continent of Africa, the Holy Land, the Valley of the Euphrates, the islands of Cyprus and Candia [Crete], the whole of South America, the islands of the Pacific not heretofore possessed by Great Britain, the whole of the Malay Archipelago, the seaboard of China and Japan, the ultimate recovery of the United States of America as an integral part of the British Empire.

The megalomaniac objectives of the 22-year-old Cecil Rhodes as expressed in his first will, 1875; Sir Lewis Michell *The Life of the Rt. Hon. Cecil Rhodes* Vol.1 (1910) p.68.

4 When the German Reich centuries ago stood at the pinnacle of the states of Europe, it was the foremost trade and sea power. If the new Germany wants to protect its newly-won position of power for a long time, it must heed its *Kultur*-mission and, above all, delay no longer in the task of renewing the call for colonies.

Friedrich Fabri *Does Germany Need Colonies?* (1879) p.112. The German chancellor, Bismarck, was deeply resistant to the clamour for an overseas empire, but Kaiser Wilhelm II took it up enthusiastically after his accession in 1888.

5 We seem, as it were, to have conquered and peopled half the world in a fit of absence of mind.

Sir John Seeley *The Expansion of England* (1883) Lecture 1. Seeley is expressing his bewilderment at the general British indifference to the phenomenon of empire.

6 Those who are weak must perish; the earth is to the strong, and the fruits thereof. For every tree that grows a score shall wither, that the strong one may take their share. We run to place and power over the dead bodies of those who fail and fall; nay, we win the food we eat out of the mouths of starving babes. It is the scheme of things.

Henry Rider Haggard *She* (1887) p.215. Proclaiming this hyper-imperialist doctrine is Ayesha, the 2,000-year-old priestess.

7 It was the mission of the Anglo-Saxon race to penetrate into every part of the world, and to help in the great work of civilization. Wherever its representatives went, the national conscience should go … Native races were like children; they must be protected against the superior brain power of the races which had reached maturity.

Thomas Hodgkin *The Aborigines' Friend*, July 1896.

8 I believe in this race, the greatest governing race the world has ever seen; in this Anglo-Saxon race, so proud, tenacious, self-confident and determined, this race which neither climate nor change can degenerate, which will infallibly be the predominant force of future history and universal civilization.

Joseph Chamberlain, British colonial secretary, *The Times*, 12 Nov. 1895. The idea of an Anglo-Saxon brotherhood, consisting of Britain, the United States, Germany, Canada, Australia, New Zealand and South Africa, was at the heart of racist-imperialist doctrine and provided the rationale for the Rhodes Scholarships to Oxford University, founded after Cecil Rhodes's death in 1902. Scholars were chosen only from these countries on the assumption that they represented the cream of the world's intellect.

9 As the great champion of freedom and national independence, he conquers and annexes half the world, and calls it Colonization … He does everything on principle. He fights you on patriotic principles; he robs you on business principles; he enslaves you on imperial principles.

George Bernard Shaw *The Man of Destiny* (1895); *Plays Pleasant and Unpleasant* Vol.2 (1898) p.20. In his play Shaw puts these words into the mouth of Napoleon. Shaw himself believed in a British empire based on enlightened Fabian socialist principles (see 683:4).

1   God of our fathers, known of old,
    Lord of our far-flung battle-line,
    Beneath whose awful Hand we hold
    Dominion over palm and pine –
    Lord God of Hosts, be with us yet,
    Lest we forget – lest we forget!

Rudyard Kipling 'Recessional' (1897). Written for Queen Victoria's Diamond Jubilee, this was curiously elegiac verse coming from the arch-poet of empire.

2   Onward, Christian soldiers!
    On to heathen lands!
    Prayer-books in your pockets!
    Rifles in your hands!
    Take the glorious tidings
    Where trade can be won.
    Spread the peaceful gospel –
    With a Maxim gun.

Henry Labouchère 'Pioneers' Hymn'. The Liberal MP Labouchère here parodies the well-known hymn set to music by Sir Arthur Sullivan. For the Maxim gun see 693:8.

3 We show, in fact, a well-deserved enthusiasm for all expeditions which aim at extending our colonial domain; we register with a jealous care all our conquests; we bring a certain vanity to the act of planting our flag on every shore; but when it is necessary to develop, to put to use the incomparable colonial domain which we possess, this enthusiasm cools off singularly.

Henri Lecomte *Bulletin de la Société de géographie commerciale de Paris* (1899) pp.17–32. The underdevelopment to which the French botanist Lecomte refers arose out of an unwillingness by Frenchmen to settle or to invest in the territories acquired in Southeast Asia and Africa. Moreover, the areas taken by the French, though vast, lacked population and natural resources compared with the British and Dutch possessions.

4 You seem to suggest … it is important for the Transvaal and the world in general that a paternal Imperialism should direct its industrial development … The imperialist-militarist movement has *not* been a movement having for its aim the welfare of the native races, still less the regulation of capitalism in the interest of wage earners … That is to say [you] condone the fundamental absurdity of asserting that the British have a right to the whole earth and a duty of annexing as much of it as they can lay hands on – in order that they … may hold up holy hands and talk about all the good we shall do with it. We shall not do good.

The Fabian Sydney Olivier to George Bernard Shaw, 1899; Shaw Papers Addit. MSS 50543. Olivier was reacting to Shaw's pro-imperialist tract 'Fabianism and the Empire'. The reference to the Transvaal is to the conflict between Britain and the Boer republics for control of the gold fields of Johannesburg, which led to the South African War of 1899–1902 (see 692:7). Olivier was a member of the Colonial Service and secretary for India in the 1924 Labour government.

5 The path of progress is strewn with the wreck of nations; traces are everywhere to be seen on the hecatombs of inferior races, and of victims who found not the narrow way to the greater perfection. Yet these dead people are, in very truth, the stepping-stones on which mankind has arisen to the higher intellectual and deeper emotional life of today.

Karl Pearson *National Life from the Standpoint of Science* (1900) p.64. Not surprisingly, Pearson was a professor of eugenics, the science of breeding.

6 The old century is very nearly out, and leaves the world in a pretty pass, and the British Empire is playing the devil in it as never an empire before on so large a scale. We may live to see its fall. All the nations of Europe are making the same hell upon earth in China, massacring and pillaging and raping in the captured cities as outrageously as in the Middle Ages. The Emperor of Germany gives the word for slaughter and the Pope looks on and approves. In South Africa our troops are burning farms under Kitchener's command, and the Queen and the two Houses of Parliament, and the bench of bishops, thank God publicly and vote money for the work. The Americans are spending fifty millions a year on slaughtering the Filipinos; the King of the Belgians has invested his whole fortune on the Congo, where he is brutalizing the Negroes to fill his pockets. The French and Italians for the moment are playing a less prominent part in the slaughter, but their inactivity grieves them. The whole white race is revelling openly in violence, as though it had never pretended to be Christian. God's curse be on them

all! So ends the famous nineteenth century in which we were so proud to have been born!

Wilfrid Scawen Blunt, diary entry, 22 Dec. 1900; *My Diaries* (1932 edn) pp.375–6.

1 Land of hope and glory,
  Mother of the free.
  How shall we extol thee,
  Who are born of thee? …
  Wider and still and wider
  Shall thy bounds be set!
  God, who made thee mighty,
  Make thee mightier yet!

A.C. Benson 'Land of Hope and Glory' (1902). Benson's 'Coronation Ode' was set to music by Edward Elgar. In Aug. 1914, soon after the outbreak of war, Elgar – a sensitive imperialist – altered the words of the last four lines cited on the grounds that they were 'liable to [be] misunderstood' (Bernard Porter 'Edward Elgar and Empire' in *Journal of Imperial and Commonwealth History* (Jan. 2001) p.13).

2 In spite of the fact that we do not have the fleet we should have, we have conquered for ourselves a place in the sun. It will now be my task to see to it that this place in the sun remains our undisputed possession … for our future lies upon the water.

Wilhelm II, June 1901; C. Gauss *The Kaiser as Shown in his Public Utterances* (1915) p.18. A recognition that it was sea power that created and held the British empire; so, too, it would be for imperial Germany with the High Seas Fleet then under construction.

3 Analysis of Imperialism, with its natural supports, militarism, oligarchy, bureaucracy, protection, concentration of capital and violent trade fluctuations, has marked it out as the supreme danger of modern national States. The power of the imperialist forces within the nation to use the national resources for their private gain, by operating the instrument of the State, can only be overthrown by the establishment of a genuine democracy, the direction of public policy by the people for the people through representatives over whom they exercise a real control.

J.A. Hobson *Imperialism: A Study* (1902) Ch.7. This book was written under the impact of the South African War and became hugely influential, not least on Lenin when he came to write his own treatise on the subject. Its thesis that British trade and investment were dominated by imperial interests was misplaced, however. Most went to areas outside the formal empire – that is, to the USA, Latin America and Europe.

4 It was just robbery with violence, aggravated murder on a great scale, and men going at it blind – as is very proper for those who tackle a darkness. The

conquest of the earth, which mostly means the taking it away from those who have a different complexion or slightly flatter noses than ourselves, is not a pretty thing when you look at it too much. What redeems it is the idea only.

Joseph Conrad *Heart of Darkness* (1902) p.10.

5 [Imperialism] is a matter of extending overseas to regions only yesterday barbarian the principles of a civilization of which one of the oldest nations in the world has a right to be proud.

Gabriel Hanotaux, French historian and politician, *L'Energie française* (1902) p.365. The voice of the *mission civilisatrice* (the civilizing mission), the high-minded rationale of colonization, even though it left untouched the great mass of the populace in what the French liked to think of as *la France d'outre-mer* (France overseas).

6 Your fathers worked hard, fought hard and died hard to make this Empire for you. Don't let them look down from heaven, and see you loafing about with hands in your pockets doing nothing to keep it up.

General Robert Baden-Powell *Scouting for Boys* (1908) p.267. Baden-Powell, a national hero after his successful defence of Mafeking against the Boers between Oct. 1899 and May 1900 in the South African War of 1899–1902, went on to found the Boy Scouts Association.

7 He was never tired of impressing upon me that the fact of being an Englishman was the greatest prize in the lottery of life.

Colonel Sir Alexander Weston Jarvis *Jottings from an Active Life* (1928), on the wise counsel given him by Cecil Rhodes. Quoted in slightly different form by Peter Ustinov in his autobiography *Dear Me* (1977) Ch.4.

THE FAR EAST AND CENTRAL ASIA, 1840–1905

8 [The British flag] has always been associated with the cause of justice, with the opposition to oppression, with respect for national rights, with honourable commercial enterprise, but now, under the auspices of the noble lord, that flag is hoisted to protect an infamous contraband trade.

William Ewart Gladstone, condemning Palmerston's espousal of the so-called Opium War on China, 7 April 1840; *Parl. Deb.* Vol.53, Col.816. In 1839 the Chinese government began a determined attempt to stamp out the trade in opium, so profitable to the British East India Company. Britain went to war with China, partly to secure the trade and partly to open up the Chinese empire as a whole to its commerce. The immediate gain in 1842 was the colony of Hong Kong, the entering wedge for subsequent large-scale foreign penetration of China.

1 We note that you English barbarians have formed the habits and developed the nature of wolves, plundering and seizing things by force … In trade relations, you come to our country merely to covet profit … Your seeking profit resembles the animal's greed for food … You have killed and injured our common people … and you disastrously damaged the Buddhist statues in several monasteries … If we do not completely exterminate you pigs and dogs, we will not be manly Chinese.

Placard of the patriotic people of Kwangtung, denouncing the English barbarians, 1841; Ssu-yu Teng and John K. Fairbank (eds) *China's Response to the West* (1965) p.35. Fighting words from the citizens of Guangdon (Canton) province, but not enough to prevent a military humiliation.

2 Never was the military spirit half so rampant in this country since 1815 as at the present time. Look at the news from Rangoon … This makes 5400 persons killed by our ships in the East during the last five years, without our having lost one man by the butcheries. Now give me Free Trade as the recognized policy of all parties in this country, and I will find the best possible argument against these marauding atrocities.

Richard Cobden 'How Wars are got up in India', 1853; *The Political Writings of Richard Cobden* (1903 edn) pp.457–8. Cobden, one of the leading Manchester Free Traders, decrying the evils of British imperialism in Burma.

3 We have raised a righteous army to inflict the vengeance of God above on those who have deceived Heaven and to relieve the suffering of the Chinese people below. We urgently hope all Manchus will be wiped out. We hope to enjoy together the happiness of great peace. He who obeys Heaven will be amply rewarded; and he who disobeys Heaven will be killed openly.

Proclamation by the high command of the Taiping Rebellion, c.1851; Ssu-yu Teng *The Taiping Rebellion and the Western Powers* (1971) p.83. The Taiping Rebellion lasted from 1850 to 1864 and cost the lives of up to 20 million Chinese. Its ideology was a bastardized form of Christianity, and its leader named himself the younger brother of Christ. Its main objectives were the destruction of the Manchu dynasty, which had ruled China since 1644, and its replacement by the Heavenly Kingdom of Great Peace (*Taiping tianguo*).

4 The Time is fast coming when we shall be obliged to strike another Blow in China … These half-

civilized governments … all require a Dressing every eight or Ten years to keep them in order … They care little for words and they must not only see the Stick but actually feel it on their Shoulders before they yield.

Lord Palmerston, 29 Sept. 1850, following China's defeat in the Opium War (1839–42); W.C. Costin *Great Britain and China 1833–1860* (1937) pp.149–50. Beijing found itself in the ensuing years signatory to a series of 'unequal' treaties with Western nations, which seriously compromised China's sovereignty. When the 1842 treaty came up for revision in 1854 the Chinese refused to agree to London's demand to open the country further to its trade, a refusal Palmerston found intolerable.

5 Half of Asia – China, Japan, Tibet, Bukhara, Khiva, Persia – belongs to us if we want … Lay new roads into Asia or search out old ones, if only in the tracks indicated by Alexander the Great and Napoleon, set up caravans, girdle Asiatic Russia with railroads, send steamships along all of its rivers and lakes, connect it with European Russia … You will increase happiness and abundance across the entire globe.

The Russian Mikhail Pogodin, 1854; Bassin (1999) pp.67, 68. Bukhara and Khiva were central Asian khanates east of the Caspian Sea. Russia was currently absorbing Central Asia and stood poised to detach much of northeastern China, while China was preoccupied with an Anglo-French assault in 1857–60.

6 The whole of Manchuria is as necessary to the undisturbed commerce of the Amoor as Louisiana was to our use of the Mississippi; consequently, in my opinion, nothing short of the Wall of China will be a sufficient boundary on the south, and that is not so remote to Russia here at this day as the Rocky Mountains in Jefferson's day were to us … Twenty thousand Cossacks would overrun and hold the country as easily as our little army moved on to Santa Fe and conquered New Mexico.

The American Perry McDonough Collins *Siberian Journey down the Amoor to the Pacific 1856–1957* (1962 edn) pp.95–6. Advice to an ambitious imperialist power from one with considerable expansion behind it. The River Amur (Amoor) runs through northeast China, and the Great Wall was built across northern China to keep out invaders. The American references are to the Louisiana Purchase in 1803 (see 578:1) and the Mexican War of 1846 (see 615:6).

7 At her earliest opportunity Japan should occupy Kamchatka with an army and place the Sea of Okhotsk under her sole control. Liu Chiu should be instructed to make her kind come in person to pay homage to Japan … Japan should upbraid Korea for her long negligence in the observation of her duty to Japan and have her send tribute-bearing envoys … In the north Manchuria should be sliced off.

Shoin Yoshida, late 1850s; Delmer Brown *Nationalism in Japan* (1955) p.121. The Japanese nationalist sketches out his programme for Japan's expansion beyond the home islands; he was executed for conspiring against the government in 1860. Kamchatka lies to the north of Japan, east of the Sea of Okhotsk. The Liu Chiu island chain links Japan with the Chinese island of Taiwan (Formosa), which was also listed by Yoshida for take-over. Korea, a Chinese satellite, was Japan's bridge to the Asian mainland, and Manchuria, the homeland of the ruling Chinese dynasty, borders Korea. Tribute missions were the traditional Asian expression of homage to a suzerain.

1 I understand … that Europe cannot reason against the force which is thrusting it beyond itself and against the activity which is driving it afar, and indeed, that societies do what they must do, even though their deeds often work completely inversely to their true interests. I therefore limit myself to stating this fact – that Asia is a most alluring dish, but one which poisons those who eat it.

Count Arthur de Gobineau *Trois ans en Asie* (1859) p.482. See 681:1.

2 We accordingly went out, and after pillaging it, burned the whole place, destroying, in a Vandal-like manner, most valuable property, which could not be replaced for four millions … The people are civil, but I think the grandees hate us, as they must after what we did to the Palace. You would scarcely imagine the beauty and magnificence of the places we burnt … Quantities of gold ornaments were burned, considered as brass. It was wretchedly demoralizing work for an army. Everybody was wild for plunder.

Captain Charles George Gordon, Royal Engineers, Oct. 1860, on the destruction of the Chinese imperial Summer Palace; Demetrius C. Boulger *The Life of Gordon* Vol.1 (1896) p.46. The imperial Summer Palace was sacked in reprisal for the Chinese execution of several British and French prisoners taken in the war of 1857–60. 'Chinese' Gordon went on to serve Beijing as a leader of the 'Ever-victorious Army', recruited to help suppress the Taiping Rebellion (1850–64) (see 685:3).

3 The existence of the present dynasty in China hangs upon the patience of foreign governments, who have too great a stake in the country to sink the ship so long as there is a hope of her floating.

A.B. Freeman-Mitford, counsellor of the British legation in China in 1865–6; *The Attaché at Peking* (1900) pp.240–41. This diplomat was writing in the aftermath of the Second Opium War (1856–60), even more disastrous for China than the first. China had also faced the calamity of the Taiping Rebellion (see 685:3), which brought swathes of destruction and the deaths of millions. Together, these two events had brought the empire to the verge of annihilation, but the foreign powers had not recognized the Taipings as an alternative regime, preferring a weak empire with just enough stability to guarantee their interests.

4 The flavour and delicacy of opium excite as much attention in the East, as those qualities in the wines of France and Spain in Europe … It is only opium of the best quality which is fit for the China market. Opium of a good season and vintage of 20 or 25 years old commands a fabulous price, and is only to be had in the houses of the rich.

H.D. Daly *Report on the Administration of the Territories within the Central India Agency for the Year 1873–74* (1874). Good to know that far from making money out of drug addiction, Britain was dealing in nothing that was not in the best possible taste.

5 We will work on the mandarins, and if the fruit does not fall by itself we will shake the tree; let us know how to be patient. My intention is to maintain the treaty of 1862 up to the point where circumstances give us the right to tear it up by way of reprisal.

Admiral La Grandière, governor of Cochin-China, to Maudrut Dupleix, 17 Jan. 1865; Archives d'Outre-Mer Indochine A-30 (6). Although the 1862 treaty between France and Vietnam had given France half the provinces of Cochin-China, the others remained in Vietnamese hands, but France was determined to acquire them and did so in 1885.

6 Are not the Javanese poor? But yes. And why? They are pagans. Thus, the more the Dutch work among the Javanese the more our wealth prospers and their poverty increases. It's predestined.

Max Havelaar *Multatuli* (1878) p.105. A cynical comment made by the preacher, Caquet, in this novel depicting the worst excesses of the Dutch colonial system in the East Indies, which included the widespread exploitation and ill-treatment of the Javanese and rampant corruption by colonial officials.

7 All that is our work, and the chief cause of it is our obsession for proselytizing, our mania for assimilation. Traditional Annamite society, so well organized to satisfy the needs of the people, has in the final analysis been destroyed by us.

Anon. French observer, pamphlet, 1905; Anon. *La Politique indigène en Cochinchine* (1905). Annam (meaning 'pacified south') was the Chinese term for Vietnam after its conquest in the late 9th century AD.

1 I hold it as a principle that in Asia the duration of peace is in direct proportion to the slaughter you inflict upon the enemy. The harder you hit them the longer they will be quiet afterwards. My system is this. To strike hard, and keep on hitting until resistance is completely over; then at once to form ranks, cease slaughter, and be kind and humane to the prostrate enemy.

General Mikhail Skobelev, Russian conqueror of Turkmenistan; quoted approvingly by the future viceroy of India, George Curzon, in his *Russia in Central Asia* (1889) pp.85–6. On 24 Jan. 1881 Skobelev's troops massacred 8,000 people after the fall of the fortress of Tekke.

2 In Europe we were hangers-on and slaves, but in Asia we are masters. In Europe we were Tatars, but in Asia we too are Europeans. The mission, our civilizing mission in Asia, will give us spirit and draw us out there, if only we could get on with it! Build just two railroads for a start – one into Siberia and the other into Central Asia – and you will see the results immediately.

Feodor Dostoevsky 'Geok Teppe' (1881), written soon after Skobelev's conquest of Turkmenistan. The name Tatars (or Tartars) was applied to the Mongol hordes of Genghis Khan, which swept into Europe from central Asia in the late 12th and early 13th centuries (see 252:2). The Trans-Siberian Railway, linking European Russia with the Pacific outpost of Vladivostok, was built in the 1890s.

3   What need we yield
    To ancient glories?
    The time is near
    When again we shall build
    A mound of ears.

The Japanese poet Yosano Hirashi, celebrating the declaration of war on China in 1894. In a 16th-century war with China, Japan had raised a heap of ears, sliced from the defeated Chinese.

4 The faces of the people look human but their customs and spirit are like those of apes. If you showed them in Japan, you could charge an admission fee.

The Japanese army private Watanabe Keiji on the Chinese, 5 April 1895; Stewart Lone *Japan's First Modern War* (1994) p.64. Japan fought a victorious war against China in 1894–5, which gave it the island of Taiwan (Formosa) and laid the foundations of an Asian mainland empire in Manchuria (1905) and Korea (1910).

5 The more inert countries of Asia will fall prey to the powerful invaders and will be divided up between them ... The problem of each country concerned is to obtain as large a share as possible of the Chinese Colossus. Russia, both geographically and historically, has the undisputed right to the lion's share of the expected prey ... The absorption by Russia of a considerable portion of the Chinese Empire is only a matter of time.

Count Sergei Witte, Russian finance minister, c.1896; David Dallin *The Rise of Russia in Asia* (1949) p.35. At this very moment China made an alliance with Russia to protect itself against Japan!

6 The various powers cast upon us looks of tiger-like voracity, hustling each other in their endeavours to be the first to seize upon our innermost territories. They think that China, having neither money nor troops, would never venture to go war with them. They fail to understand.

Cixi (Tz'u-hsi), empress dowager of China, 11 Nov. 1899; Marina Warner *The Dragon Empress* (1972) p.175. At this point the 'scramble for China' – that is, the rush by Britain, Russia, Japan, Germany and France for more concessions – was well underway. The dowager's faith in China's powers of resistance to this onslaught was a sad delusion.

7 After this notice is issued to instruct you villagers ... if there are any Christian converts, you ought to get rid of them quickly. The churches which belong to them should be unreservedly burned down. Everyone who intends to spare someone, or to disobey our order by concealing Christian converts, will be punished according to the regulation ... and he will be burned to death to prevent his impeding our programme.

Boxer poster, 1900; Chester Tan *The Boxer Catastrophe* (1967) p.95. The Boxers, a militant secret society, swore to defend the ruling Qing (Ch'ing) dynasty and to rid China of 'foreign devils'. They besieged the foreign legation compound in Beijing from May to Aug. 1900 but were crushed by an international expeditionary force. China was then compelled to make a huge financial indemnity, mortgaging its future for years to come.

8 Just as the Huns under their King Etzel [Attila] created for themselves a thousand years ago a name which men still respect, you should give the name of German such cause to be remembered in China that no Chinaman, no matter whether his eyes be slit or not, will dare look a German in the face.

Wilhelm II, 1900; Michael Balfour *The Kaiser and his Times* (1964) p.226. The Kaiser addresses troops leaving for China to join the international expedition to crush the Boxer Rising. The Huns were the nomad invaders of southeast Europe in the late 4th century AD (see 113:4).

1 Twenty millions or more of Boxers, armed, drilled, disciplined and animated by patriotic – if mistaken – motives, will make residence in China impossible for foreigners ... and will carry the Chinese flag and Chinese arms into many a place that even fancy will not suggest today, thus preparing for the future upheavals and disasters never even dreamt of. In fifty years' time there will be millions of Boxers in serried ranks and war's panoply at the call of the Chinese Government: there is not the slightest doubt of that.

Sir Robert Hart *These from the Land of Sinim* (1901) pp.54–5. As inspector-general of the imperial maritime customs service from 1861 to 1908, Hart was the most influential foreigner in China. In 1951, 50 years on, the Chinese communist army had driven American forces out of North Korea (see 880:1).

2 What is the way that will save us from danger and destruction, and enable us to pursue progress? I say that we must smash to fragments – that we must pound to powder – the tyrannical and confused structure that we have had for the last few thousand years, so that the hordes of officials and clerks who resemble tigers or wolves – or locusts, or venom-spitting toads, or maggots – lose the means to brow-beat others, and this will enable us to clean out our [social] digestive system and so mount up the path of progress.

Liang Qichao (Liang Ch'i-ch'ao) *Theory of a New Citizenry* (1902); Mark Elvin *Another History* (1996) p.379. The reformer Liang, writing in the aftermath of the Boxer Rising, looked to a democratic China as the replacement for the humiliated Manchu dynasty. It was a compelling but unattainable vision.

3 Lord Curzon and his friends pushed for a Japanese alliance and paved the way for the present war; it may well be that one day they will live to regret having helped Japan to success ... as Japan may become too powerful a neighbour for her allies, and, for the aspirations of native nationalism, too encouraging an example.

René Pinon *Revue des deux mondes*, 1 June 1905. The French commentator was writing at the close of the Russo-Japanese War, which resulted in a conclusive victory for Japan, Britain's ally since 1902. Asian nationalism *was* immediately inspired by the outcome, and by the 1930s Japan had become a deadly threat to European imperialism in Asia (see 793:2).

THE ARAB WORLD, 1833–1908

4 Mehemed-Ali's real design is to establish an Arabian kingdom including all the countries in which Arabic is the language ... as it would imply the dismemberment of Turkey, we could not agree to it. Besides Turkey is as good an occupier of the road to India as an active Arabian sovereign would be.

Lord Palmerston to the British minister at Naples, 21 March 1833; Sir Henry Bulwer *Life of Henry John Temple, Viscount Palmerston* Vol.2 (1871). Mehemed-Ali, Egypt's Albanian military ruler, was determined to build an Arab empire out of the sultan's dominions. His growing power and reach threatened Britain's access to the overland route to India, while the dismemberment of Turkey prompted fear of Russian hegemony over Constantinople.

5 The economic calculations ... belittled the value of colonies. The old nations must have outlets in order to alleviate the demographic pressures exerted on big cities ... To open new sources of production is, in effect, the surest means of neutralizing this concentration without upsetting the social order ... It is the surest way of preventing the seeds of hostility that are being sown among the working classes, not only against the government but also against society and against property.

Conclusions of the French *Commission d'Afrique*, set up in 1833; Mahfoud Bennoune *The Making of Contemporary Algeria 1830–1987* (1988) p.35. The commission was sent to Algeria to report on the possible colonization of the territory, which, after its final conquest in 1848, was made an integral part of metropolitan France.

6 It is certain that the shortest path [towards European civilization] is terror; without violating the laws of morality, or international jurisprudence, we can fight our African enemies with powder and fire, joined by famine, internal division, war between Arabs and Kabyles [Berbers], between the tribes of the Tell and those of the Sahara, by brandy, corruption and disorganization. That is the easiest thing in the world to do.

French justification for the colonization of Algeria, c.1840; Bennoune (1988) p.40. In 1841 Alexis de Tocqueville remarked that 'we are making war in a manner more barbaric than the Arabs themselves' (p.41).

7 'Egypt for the Egyptians' is the sentiment to which I would wish to give scope; and could it prevail it would I think be the best, the only good solution of the 'Egyptian Question'.

British prime minister William Ewart Gladstone to his foreign secretary Earl Granville, 4 Jan. 1882; Richard Shannon *Gladstone: Heroic Minister 1865–1898* (1999) p.293. In Sept. 1881 an Arab rising in Egypt against Turkish and European domination produced a huge international crisis. Despite his liberal instincts, Gladstone was to be drawn into the occupation of Egypt six months later.

1 As regards the Suez Canal, England has a double interest; it has a predominant commercial interest, because 82 per cent of the trade passing through the Canal is British trade, and it has a predominant political interest caused by the fact that the Canal is the principal highway to India, Ceylon, the Straits, and British Burmah ... and also to China, where we have vast interests [and] to our Colonial Empire in Australia and New Zealand.

Sir Charles Dilke, 25 July 1882; *Parl. Deb.* Vol.272, Col.1720. Justification for the intervention in Egypt, which began two weeks earlier, and for a British military presence there, which was to last until 1956.

2 Everywhere I came upon the same abiding universal sentiment: hatred of the Turks. The notion of concerted action to throw off the detested yoke is gradually shaping itself ... An Arab movement, newly risen, is looming in the distance; and a hitherto downtrodden race will presently claim its due place in the destinies of Islam.

D. de Rivoyre *Les Vrais Arabes et leurs pays* (1884) pp.294–5. The burgeoning Arab discontent against the Turks was far too weak unaided to overthrow the authority of the sultan-caliph at Constantinople.

3 On Sunday, P.M. July 26 ... the whole empire burst forth in universal rejoicing ... Public meetings were held, cities and towns decorated; Moslems were seen embracing Christians and Jews, and inviting one another to receptions and feasts ... The universal voice of the Moslems was [that] we shall henceforth know each other only as Ottomans ... Long live the Sultan!

Anon., 1908; Henry Harris Jessup *Fifty-Three Years in Syria* Vol.2 (1910) pp.785–7. From an eyewitness account of the reaction in Syria when the restoration of the Midhat Constitution of 1876 was announced following a bloodless revolution in 1908 by the Young Turks, the new rulers of the Ottoman empire.

INDIA

4 Life in India is really nothing but one long fever, and India itself but a large sickroom.

Sir John William Kaye *Peregrine Pultney* Vol.2 (1844) p.293. For Britons living in India, with its severe climate and poor physical conditions, sudden death was an ever-present hazard. During the course of this story, a Calcutta party hostess urges

a guest not to miss the fun by visiting a dying friend because it could well turn out to be a waste of time.

5 The burning of widows is your custom. Prepare the funeral pile. But my nation also has a custom. When men burn women alive, we hang them and confiscate all their property. My carpenters shall therefore erect gibbets on which to hang all concerned when the widow is consumed. Let us all act according to national customs.

Sir Charles Napier, c.1844: Sir William Napier *History of General Sir Charles Napier's Administration of Scinde* (1851) p.35. The conqueror of Sindh reacts to the Hindu practice of suttee, whereby a man's widow was expected to throw herself on to her late husband's funeral pyre.

6 The truth is, that it is too much our way to kick a man, and then to complain that he is not grateful. This is the way we treat the Hindoos.

Sir John William Kaye *Long Engagements* (1846) p.124.

7 The evil is a money-getting earthly mind, that dares to view a large portion of God's world, and many millions of God's creatures, as a more or less profitable investment, as a good return for money laid out upon them, as a providential asylum for younger sons.

William Delafield Arnold *Oakfield; or, Fellowship in the East* (1853) Vol.2, pp.222–3. Arnold was not alone in viewing British standards in India as being dictated predominantly by greed.

8 'Quick, brothers! Rouse the guard! Close the gates!' ... It was a cry to heal all strife within those rose-red walls, for the dearest wish of every faction was to close them against civilization; against those prying western eyes and sniffing western noses, detecting drains and sinks of iniquity. So the clamour grew.

Flora Annie Steel *On the Face of the Waters* (1896) p.194. Romantic novels about the Indian Mutiny of 1857 featured regularly in British fiction of this period. In this novel the mutineers, on reaching Delhi, make the famous Red Fort a bastion against the West.

9 The rise and fall of empires are not affairs of greased cartridges.

Benjamin Disraeli, 27 July 1857: *Parl. Deb.* Vol.147, Col.475. The immediate cause of the Indian Mutiny of 1857–8 was the issue to Indian troops of cartridges greased with a mixture of cow and pig fat. Cows were sacred to Hindus, and pigs were unclean to Muslims. For Disraeli the motivation for the Mutiny ran deeper. As a Conservative, he blamed the upsurge on the Whig reformists' disregard of Indian traditions, although his critics believed that his Jewish ancestry gave him a natural affinity with the non-whites of the subcontinent.

1 'How many natives have you under your orders?'

'Well Sir, about 500 of 'em altogether.'

'Do you speak their language?'

'No Sir, I don't'.

'Well then how do you manage to let these natives understand what they are to do?'

'Oh Sir I'll tell you, I tell these chaps three times in good plain English, and if they don't understand that, I take the *lukri* [stick] and we get on very well.'

English foreman involved in the construction of the Indian railway at Bhore Gat, in conversation with Sir Bartle Frere, chief commissioner of Sind, 1858; *John Brunton's Book; Being the Memories of John Brunton, Engineer, from a Manuscript in his own Hand Written for his Grandchildren and now First Printed* (1939) p.107.

2 That force is the basis of our rule I have no doubt … The grave, unhappy doubt which settles on my mind is, whether India is the better for our rule, so far as regards the social condition of the great mass of the people. We have put down widow-burning, we have sought to check infanticide; but I have travelled hundreds of miles through a country peopled with beggars and covered with wigwam villages.

William Russell, 13 Feb. 1858; Roger Hudson (ed.) *William Russell, Special Correspondent of 'The Times'* (1995) p.108. Russell was in India during the last stage of the Mutiny. 'Widow-burning' refers to the practice of suttee, whereby a widow was expected to throw herself on to her dead husband's funeral pyre (see 689:5). Infanticide, in the absence of contraception, was the chief means of birth control. Both were anathema to a reformist British Raj.

3 Education has no doubt spread to a considerable extent in the country. But what sort of education is it? It is calculated to prepare clerks and writers, that is, men only fit to serve … The English Government is perhaps the most partial government India ever had. In short, no rulers who have ever ruled India have injured this country as it has been injured by the English rulers.

Maharashtra Mitra, 17 June 1875; Ram Gopal *How India Struggled for Freedom* (1967) p.41. Reform had its limits.

4 A vast bridge over which an enormous multitude of human beings are passing … from a dreary land.

Sir James Stephen on the force for good of British power in India, *The Times*, 4 Jan. 1878.

5 India … is of all countries that which is least capable of evolving out of itself a stable government.

The historian Sir John Seeley *The Expansion of England* (1883) p.196. The 1857 Mutiny confirmed a belief in many Britons that India was reactionary and barbaric and would never become a civilized state. Such a notion furnished the Raj with a plausible rationale, but it was disputed by the Indian Congress Party, which emerged in 1885 as a pressure group for self-government.

6 Their notion of governing India is by pure force, and because they do not see that the only mode of making widespread education and a free press safe in a country like this is to afford some legitimate outlet for the aspirations and feelings which we have called into existence.

Lord Ripon, viceroy of India, to W.E. Forster, 6 March 1883; Anthony Denholm *Lord Ripon* (1982) p.157. The British community in India loathed Ripon's liberal attitude to the Indians. When a statue to him was erected in 1915, Indians were the only subscribers to the fund.

7 Little did I dream … that I should ever become the proud reble [*sic*] and Patriot that I am this day against the government of your Illustrious Mother: but the injustice, the cruel opposition, and the humiliation which have been inflicted upon me by England have opened my eyes as to what that Power really is, though professing a high Code of Christian Morality. I am convinced in my own mind that, if there be a God in the Universe, the British Empire of India which is founded upon swindle and fraud will come to an ignominious end eventually.

Duleep Singh to Crown Princess Victoria of Prussia, 25 Aug. 1887; Michael Alexander and Sushila Anand *Queen Victoria's Maharajah* (2001 edn) p.265. Duleep Singh was deposed as maharajah of the Punjab in 1849, and his most prized possession, the legendary Koh-i-noor (Mountain of Light) diamond, was surrendered to Queen Victoria. He wrote from Russia, where he had tried unsuccessfully to enlist the tsar as his ally against Britain.

8 The statement has been made in the course of this debate that the Indians before the advent of the English were a pack of barbarians or semi-barbarians … Let me remind this House that they come – the Hindus of India … from a great and ancient stock; that at a time when the ancestors of the most enlightened European nations were roaming in their native woods and forests, our fathers had founded great empires.

Surendranath Banerjea, principal Indian speaker in a debate at the Oxford Union, April 1890; Ram Gopal *How India Struggled for Freedom* (1967) p.68. A mission from the British committee of the Indian National Congress visited Britain in 1890 to propagate knowledge of Indian (or, at least, Hindu) culture.

1 1127. οὗτος – 'ho there', *heus tu*. The expression could only be used by a superior to his inferior, the barbarian Polymester being as inferior to Agamemnon as an Indian rajah to the Viceroy of India.
Rev. John Bond and Rev. Arthur Sumner Walpole (eds) *The Hecuba of Euripides* (1897) p.114. Notes to a Greek text, giving a revealing glimpse into late-Victorian imperialist assumptions. In principle, the Indian rajahs were partners of the British in their principalities; in practice, they were their subordinates.

2 My mother used to talk about Queen Victoria as the mother of the country … I remember when I was in school, every day we were made to sing 'Britannia Rule the Waves, Britons never, never, never shall be slaves' … I didn't know what I was singing until it was pointed out to me later by my father: 'Baby, you know, you mustn't sing that song, it's not necessary. You're trying to say that Britons shall never be slaves, but why should anyone be a slave?' So I ceased to sing that song.
Harindranath Chattopadhyaya, Indian poet, discussing his schooling at the end of the 19th century; Zareer Masani *Indian Tales of the Raj* (1987) p.82.

3 It is only when you get to see and realize what India really is – that she is the strength and greatness of England – it is only then that you feel that every nerve a man may strain, every energy he may put forward, cannot be devoted to a nobler purpose than keeping tight the cords that hold India to ourselves.
Lord Curzon, viceroy of India 1899–1905; Charles Allen (ed.) *Plain Tales from the Raj* (1976 edn) p.243.

4 Keep the natives in their place, my boy. They will think all the more of you for it. And never trust any of them further than you can help.
Edmund Candler *The General Plan* (1911) p.18. The novel includes this advice from an old India hand to a young man about to join the Indian civil service, an elite of administrators akin to the mandarins of imperial China.

5 The term Satyagraha … means holding on to truth … In politics, its use is based upon the immutable maxim that Government of the people is possible only so long as they consent either consciously or unconsciously to be governed. And therefore the struggle on behalf of the people mostly consists in opposing error in the shape of unjust laws. When you have failed … the only remedies open to you … [are] Civil Disobedience or Civil Resistance.
Mohandas Gandhi's call for non-violent resistance, 1914; Richard M. Brace (ed.) *The Imperialism Reader* (1962) pp.417–18. Before 1914 Gandhi lived in South Africa where he developed his ideas of Satyagraha as a response to the discrimination against the Indians who had been brought into the English-speaking province of Natal. He began to apply them to India after his arrival there in 1914.

AFRICA SOUTH OF THE SAHARA, 1840–1909

6   Shine, the leader of applauding nations,
To scatter happiness and peace around her,
To bid the prostrate captive rise and live,
To see new cities tower at her command,
And blasted nations flourish in her smile.
Thomas Fowell Buxton, June 1840; Geoffrey Moorhouse *The Missionaries* (1975) p.31. Following his crusade to end slavery in the British empire, the evangelical Buxton urged British Christians to help regenerate Africa, on the basis that all human beings were of equal value in the sight of God.

7 There is no more Christian affection between most if not all the brethren and me than between my riding-ox & his grandmother.
David Livingstone, letter, 1850; I. Schapera *David Livingstone: South African Papers 1849–1853* (1974). The Scottish missionary Livingstone had little respect for any of his co-religionists in South Africa.

8 There is a time to leave the Dark Continent and that is when the *idée fixe* begins to develop itself. Madness comes from Africa.
Sir Richard Burton *Camoens* (1881) Vol.2, pp.514–17. The explorer spent several years in East and West Africa from 1856 to 1862, beginning with a quest for the source of the Nile.

9 There is a group of the most respectful Arabs, and as I come nearer I see the white face of an old man among them … I am shaking hands with him. We raise our hats, and I say:
   'Dr Livingstone, I presume?'
   And he says, 'Yes'.
The journalist Henry Morton Stanley, on finding David Livingstone in Central Africa, 10 Nov. 1871; *New York Herald*, 10 Aug. 1872. The *Herald* had commissioned Stanley to locate Livingstone who had not been seen for several years.

10 I do not want to miss a good chance of getting us a slice of this magnificent African cake.
Leopold II of the Belgians to Henri Solvyns, Belgian ambassador to London, 1876; A. Roeykins *Les Débuts de l'oeuvre africaine de Léopold II* (1955). In 1885 Leopold was granted the immense territory of the Congo Free State as his personal estate. He exploited it abominably.

11 Dearest Madam,
   We your servants have *join* together and thoughts

its better to write you a nice loving letter ... We *wish* to have your laws in our towns. We want to have every fashion altered, also we will be according to your Consul's word ... We never have answer from you, so we wish to write to you *ourselves*.

Petition for a British protectorate, sent to Queen Victoria by a number of chiefs in the Cameroun, 1880; Thomas Pakenham *The Scramble for Africa 1876–1912* (1992) pp.182–3. The territory was soon to be made over to Germany.

1 I agree with you that there is something absurd in the sudden Scramble for colonies, and I am as little disposed to join in as you can be; but there is a difference between wanting new acquisitions and keeping what we have; and both Natal and Cape Colony would be endangered, as well as inconvenienced, if any foreign power chose to claim possession of the coast between the two, which is virtually ours now, but not ours by any formal ties that other nations are bound to recognize.

Lord Derby to Lord Granville, 28 Dec. 1884; PRO 30/29/120. Written just after the Berlin Conference, which arranged the partition of Africa among the European powers. Derby's aversion to colonialism clearly had its limitations.

2 Does this House think that it is right that men in a state of pure barbarism should have the franchise and the vote ... Treat the natives as a subject people ... be the lords over them ... the native is to be treated as a child and denied the franchise ... If I cannot keep my position in the country as an Englishman on the European vote, I wish to be cleared out, for I am not going to the native vote for support ... We must adopt a system of despotism such as works so well in India, in our relations with the barbarians of South Africa.

Cecil Rhodes, debate on the Voters' Registration Act in the Cape Colony House of Assembly, June 1887; Vindex (Rev. F. Verschoyles) *Cecil Rhodes: His Political Life and Speeches* (1900) p.150. Blacks in the Cape were not given the vote, but the Cape Coloureds (men of mixed blood) were already enfranchised until the Afrikaner Nationalist government of South Africa took away their voting rights in 1956.

3 I knew that Africa was the last uncivilized portion of the Empire of the world, and that it must be civilized; and that those who lived at the healthy base [Southern Africa], with the energy that they possess, would be the right and proper individuals to undertake the civilization of the back country.

Cecil Rhodes, 6 Jan. 1894; Vindex (1900) pp.339–40.

4   The sand of the desert is sodden red, –
     Red with the wreck of a square that broke; –
     The Gatling's jammed and the Colonel dead,
     And the regiment blind with dust and smoke.
     The river of death has brimmed his banks,
     And England's far and Honour a name,
     But the voice of a schoolboy rallies the ranks:
     'Play up! Play up! And play the game!'

Sir Henry John Newbolt 'Vitaï Lampada' in *Admirals All and Other Verses* (1897). At the Battle of Abu Klea in Jan. 1885, during the expedition to relieve General Gordon, besieged in Khartum, the Sudanese Dervishes broke into the British infantry square and Colonel Frederick Burnaby was speared to death. The Gatling, an early machine-gun, was named after its inventor, Dr R.J. Gatling.

5 Then came forward the pipers and wailed a dirge, and the Sudanese played 'Abide with Me'. Perhaps lips did twitch a little to see the ebony heathens fervently blowing out Gordon's favourite hymn, but the most irresistible incongruity could hardly have made us laugh at that moment.

G.W. Steevens *With Kitchener to Khartum* (1898) pp.310–15. Gordon had been killed by the forces of the Sudanese religious leader, the Mahdi, during the siege of Khartum, in 1885. The journalist Steevens gives an account of his funeral after the British recapture of Khartum in 1898, the climax of the British expedition to re-take the Sudan.

6 I have no intention of being an indifferent looker-on if the distant Powers have the idea of dividing up Africa, for Ethiopia has been for more than fourteen centuries an island of Christians in the middle of the sea of pagans.

Emperor Menelik of Ethiopia, address to the European powers, 10 April 1891; Pakenham (1992) p.470. On 1 March 1896 an Italian invasion of Ethiopia was repelled by Ethiopian forces at the Battle of Adowa, and many Italian troops were horribly mutilated. In Oct. 1935 the Italians again invaded and annexed the country (see 788:8).

7 British influence is not exercised to impose an uncongenial foreign system upon a reluctant people. It is a force making for the triumph of the simplest ideas of honesty, humanity and justice.

Sir Alfred Milner, British high commissioner for South Africa, on the South African War, which broke out between Britain and the Boer republics of the Transvaal and the Orange Free State, Oct. 1899; Edward Crankshaw *The Forsaken Idea* (1952) p.37. To the Boers, this was the diametric opposite of the truth.

8 A phrase often used is that 'war is war'. But when one comes to ask about it, one is told that no war is going on – that it is not war. When is war not a war? When it is carried on by methods of barbarism in South Africa.

Henry Campbell-Bannerman, leader of the Liberal Party, *The Times*, 15 June 1901. Campbell-Bannerman was responding to the revelation by Emily Hobhouse of the inhumane British treatment of Boer civilians. To break Boer resistance the British destroyed their farms and moved the women and children into concentration camps (in imitation of Spanish policy in the war with Cuba, 1895–8). Many died there from disease, and the episode left an enduring legacy of bitterness among the Afrikaner population.

1 They want to sweep the English into the sea, to lick their own nigger and to govern South Africa with a gun instead of a ballot box. It is only the little Englanders in London who say that the Transvaal is merely fighting for its independence; but here both sides realize it is a question of which race is to run the country.

Rudyard Kipling to D.J. Conland, 20 Feb. 1901; Charles Carrington *Rudyard Kipling: His Life and Work* (1955) p.317.

2 The white man must rule, because he is elevated by many, many steps above the black man; steps which it will take the latter centuries to climb, and which it is quite possible that the vast bulk of the black population may never be able to climb at all.

Alfred, Viscount Milner, 18 March 1903; *The Milner Papers: South Africa* Vol.2 (1933) p.467. Milner is writing a year after Britain's victory in the South African War, a war most emphatically not fought to liberate the blacks of the Boer republics from their Afrikaner masters. In 1910 South Africa became independent on the basis of white minority rule, by agreement between Britain and those Boers who were prepared to reach an accommodation with British power.

3 A Western civilization cannot be imposed on an Eastern or a Temperate upon a Tropical, people. We can no more send our civilization to central Africa than we can send our climate there.

Independent Labour Party pamphlet, *Imperialism: Its Meaning and Its Tendency*, May 1900, p.7. Anti-imperialism on a racial basis.

4 The missionary says that we are the children of God like our white brothers ... But just look at us. Dogs, slaves, worse than baboons on the rocks – that is how you treat us.

Herrero tribesman in German Southwest Africa to a German settler, Jan. 1904; Pakenham (1992) p.602. In 1904–5 a rebellion by the tribes against German rule was ruthlessly suppressed.

5 Wild beasts – the leopards – killed some of us while we were working away in the forest and others got lost or died from exposure or starvation and we begged the white men to leave us alone, saying we could get no more rubber, but the white men and their soldiers said: 'Go. You are only beasts yourselves. You are only Nyama [meat]' ... Many [of us] were shot, some had their ears cut off; others were tied up with ropes round their necks and bodies and taken away.

Roger Casement, 'Congo Report' to the British foreign secretary, Marquess of Lansdowne, 11 Dec. 1903; Peter Singleton-Gates and Maurice Girodia *The Black Diaries of Roger Casement* (1959) pp.108, 112, 114, 118. The Irishman Casement is citing Congolese victims of Belgian atrocities under the forced labour system practised in King Leopold's domain.

6 I think that your advocacy of the black man's interest can be made more helpful to the black man if while fighting with all your power against brutal & inhuman & inconsiderate treatment for the black man you do not build a halo round the black man & convert him into a kind of being which it will take a hundred years of intercourse with the white man to become.

Sir William Lever to E.D. Morel, 18 April 1911; Bernard Porter *Critics of Empire* (1968) p.283. Lever was a millionaire soap manufacturer; Morel was the colleague of Casement in the campaign for reform of the Belgian Congo.

7 It was necessary to create near Dakar a large segregation camp to which we could send, after isolation and disinfection, the native population of Dakar. There is a danger and mutual annoyance in letting two groups cohabit which have completely distinct views on their way of life. Let us allow them, if need be let us make them, have two different installations conforming to their tastes: on the one side the European town with all the requirements of modern hygiene, on the other the native town with all the freedom to build out of wood or straw, to play the tom-toms all night, and to pound millet from four in the morning on.

Lieutenant governor of the French West African colony of Senegal to the municipal council, Oct. 1905, in response to a second outbreak of yellow fever in Dakar; Bruno Salléras *La Politque sanitaire de la France à Dakar de 1900 à 1920* (1980) p.92.

8   Whatever happens, we have got
    The Maxim gun, and they have not.

Hilaire Belloc 'The Modern Traveller' (1909). A succinct verdict by the British writer on the balance of power between imperialism and its subjects in the closing decade of this period. The Maxim gun was the machine-gun invented by the American arms manufacturer Hiram Maxim in 1883.

War and Peace, 1853–1914

MISE EN SCÈNE

1 The means of destruction are approaching perfection with frightening rapidity. The Congreve rockets … the Shrapnel howitzers … the Perkins steam-guns which vomit forth as many bullets as a battalion, will multiply the possibilities of devastation as though the hecatombs of Eylau, Borodino, Leipzig and Waterloo were not enough to decimate the peoples of Europe.

Antoine Henri de Jomini *Summary of the Art of War* (1836). One of the two 19th-century grand masters of strategic doctrine looks back on the battles of the Napoleonic era as a mere foretaste of what was to come, though even this prediction was to prove a huge underestimate. Congreve rockets were missiles developed by Colonel Sir William Congreve and first used against Boulogne in 1806. Lieutenant Henry Shrapnel devised the eponymous shell in 1784. The mighty Perkins steam-gun dated from the mid-1820s.

2 If a bloody slaughter is a horrible sight, then that is ground for paying more respect to War, but not for making the sword we wear blunter and blunter by degrees from feelings of humanity, until someone steps in with one that is sharp and lops off the arm from our body.

Karl von Clausewitz *Vom Kriege* (On War) (1833) Bk 4, Ch.11. The other towering theorist of battle shows his contempt for the champions of restraint in warfare, who were to lose out decisively in the generations ahead.

THE CONTAINMENT OF RUSSIA: THE CRIMEA AND THE BALKANS, 1853–78

3 We have a very sick man on our hands, and it would be a great misfortune if he should escape us, especially before all the necessary dispositions had been taken.

Nicholas I to the British ambassador, Sir George Hamilton Seymour, 9 Jan. 1853; R.W. Seton-Watson *Britain in Europe 1789–1914* (1945) p.305. H.W.V. Temperley (*England and the Near East: The Crimea* (1936) p.272) renders 'sick man' as 'the dying bear'. 'You may give him musk,' says the tsar, 'but even musk will not long keep him alive.' The 'sick man' was Turkey, which controlled the exit from the Black Sea to the Mediterranean. Russia aimed to take over that position and become a power in the Levant. Britain, which needed the area in friendly hands because of its importance as a stage on the existing route to India, was equally determined to prevent this from

happening. By the end of the century, however, Britain was pro-Turkish no longer (see 703:10).

4 Russia has two generals whom she can trust: General Janvier and General Février.

Nicholas I, attrib., remembered gleefully in the satirical journal *Punch*, 10 March 1855. The reference is to the Russian winter, which had helped destroy Napoleon's invasion in 1812 (see 536:8). Tsar Nicholas died on 2 March 1855, from a cold caught in Feb.

5 The ground flew beneath their horses' feet; gathering speed at every stride, they dashed on towards that thin red streak tipped with a line of steel.

The Times correspondent William Howard Russell on the Russian cavalry charge against the Highland Brigade at Balaclava on 25 Oct. 1854; Roger Hudson (ed.) *William Russell: Special Correspondent of* The Times (1995) p.29. Britain and France had gone to war with Russia on behalf of Turkey in 1854, with their main theatre of operations in the Crimean peninsula in the Black Sea, The 'thin red streak' later metamorphosed into 'the thin red line'.

6   Theirs not to make reply,
        Theirs not to reason why,
        Theirs but to do and die.
        Into the Valley of Death
        Rode the six hundred.

Alfred, Lord Tennyson 'The Charge of the Light Brigade', 2 Dec. 1854. On 25 Oct. British cavalry were wrongly ordered to make a frontal assault on heavy Russian guns; few survived. Tennyson wrote the poem after reading the account of the engagement in *The Times* on 14 Nov.

7 *C'est magnifique, mais ce n'est pas la guerre.* (It is magnificent, but it is not war.)

General Pierre Bosquet, witnessing the charge of the Light Brigade, 25 Oct. 1854.

8 *J'y suis, j'y reste.* (Here I am, and here I stay.)

General Marie de MacMahon, after the seizure of the Malakoff fortress on 8 Sept. 1855, attrib. Elected president of the Third Republic in 1873, he repeated the slogan but was forced to resign on 30 Jan. 1879.

9 In the midst of this appalling horror (we are steeped up to our necks in blood) – there is good. As I went my night rounds among the newly wounded that first night, there was not one murmur, not one groan, the strictest discipline, the most absolute silence and quiet prevailed, only the step of the sentry. The poor fellows bear pain and mutilation with unshrinking heroism, and die or are cut up without complaint.

Florence Nightingale, in Scutari hospital after the Battle of Inkerman on 5 Nov. 1854; Sue Goldie (ed.) 'I Have Done My Duty': The Selected Letters of Florence Nightingale (1987). The nurse Florence Nightingale became a national heroine for her role in tending British army wounded in the Crimea.

1   A Lady with a Lamp shall stand
  In the great history of the land,
  A noble type of good,
  Heroic womanhood.

The American poet Henry Wadsworth Longfellow 'Santa Filomena' (1858). Florence Nightingale carried a lantern with her as she walked the wards at Scutari.

2 He described him to us ... walking through his palace in the middle of the night, with that stony tread of his, the tread of the statue of the Commendatore. He went up to a sentinel, snatched his musket from him and shouted 'On your knees!', himself falling to his knees opposite the man and saying 'Let us pray for victory'.

The French Goncourt brothers on the description by the Russian Alexander Herzen on 8 Feb. 1856 of the behaviour of the tsar after a Russian defeat in the Crimea, Journal (1956 edn) Vol.7, p.50. In the last act of Mozart's opera Don Giovanni the statue of the Commendatore comes to life and consigns the Don to Hell.

3 A company of marines almost mutinied because they were about to be relieved from a battery where they'd withstood bombardment for 30 days. Soldiers extract the fuses from bombs. Women carry water to the bastions for the soldiers. Many are killed and wounded. Priests with crosses go to the bastions and read prayers under fire ... It's a wonderful time ... It's beautiful in Sevastopol now.

The Russian writer Count Leo Tolstoy, 20 Nov. 1854, serving in the besieged city of Sebastopol; R.F. Christian (ed.) Tolstoy's Letters Vol.1 (1978) p.44. The fall of Sebastopol on 11 Sept. 1855 marked the effective end of the war.

4 Sebastopol is not Moscow, the Crimea is not Russia. Two years after we set fire to Moscow, our troops marched in the streets of Paris. We are still the same Russians, and God is still with us.

Alexander II after the fall of Sebastopol, 1855; Paul Kerr et al. The Crimean War (1997) p.173. Nicholas I's successor strives to keep his spirits up with this reference to 1812 (see 536:6).

5 For Valour

Wording on the Victoria Cross, the highest British military decoration, instituted in 1856 and fashioned from the metal of Russian guns captured in the Crimea. Churchill quoted it as the inscription on his wreath to George VI at the king's funeral in Feb. 1952.

6 Nothing has changed in Russia's policy ... Her methods, her tactics, her manoeuvres may change, but the pole star – world domination – is immutable.

Karl Marx, 22 Jan. 1867; Saul K. Padover (ed.) On the First International (1972) p.84.

7 Russia is cramped in the Black Sea and she should, directly or indirectly, own the exit, that is, the Straits, as much to protect the security and welfare of the south of Russia as for political and economic reasons. Russia must become the master in Constantinople ... If we lived in friendship with the Sultan and were in charge of his ministers, we would be able to prepare the Orthodox Christians for autonomy and to make Turkey harmless to us.

N.P. Ignatiev, Russian envoy to Turkey, 1864–77; Martin McCauley and Peter Waldron (eds) The Emergence of the Modern Russian State 1855–81 (1988) p.171. The Straits are the narrows linking the Black Sea with the Mediterranean. Constantinople (Istanbul) was the capital of the Turkish empire, of which the sultan was head. Most Christians living in the Turkish empire subscribed to Orthodox Christianity, as did Christians in Russia. Russia counted for support on its partners in the Three Emperors' League of 1873, Austria and Germany, but both were disinclined to give it.

8 Let the Turks now carry away their abuses in the only possible manner, namely by carrying off themselves ... One and all, bag and baggage, shall, I hope, clear out from the province they have desolated and profaned.

William Ewart Gladstone, 5 Sept. 1876, in his pamphlet The Bulgarian Horrors and the Question of the East. The Turks had recently massacred many thousands of Orthodox Christians in their Balkan province of Bulgaria, and Gladstone's moral fervour overrode the strategic necessity to support Turkey against Russian encroachment. He had resigned as leader of the Liberal Party in Jan. 1875 but not as a major force in British politics.

9   We don't want to fight, but by jingo if we do,
  We've got the ships, we've got the men, we've
    got the money too.
  We've fought the Bear before, and while we're
    Britons true,
  The Russians shall not have Constantinople.

G.W. Hunt 'By Jingo' (1877). A rousing music-hall summons to action, highly popular in a traditionally Russophobe Britain.

1 Oh if the Queen were a man, she would like to go and give those horrid Russians, whose word one cannot trust, such a beating.

Queen Victoria to her prime minister, Benjamin Disraeli, Jan. 1878; Robert Blake *Disraeli* (1966) p.637. A remark made at a moment when the Russians were advancing on Constantinople. Britain did not, in fact, go to war, as it had in the Crimea, but exerted pressure on Russia via the Royal Navy and a partial military mobilization.

2 Russians, in the name of Christian love, began to kill their fellow-men. It was impossible not to think about this, and not to see that killing is an evil repugnant to the first principles of any faith. Yet prayers were said in the churches for the success of our arms.

Leo Tolstoy *A Confession* (1879). Russia had intervened in the Balkans in April 1877, ostensibly on behalf of the Orthodox Christians persecuted by the Turks but actually to gain access to the Mediterranean and to establish a protectorate over any breakaway Balkan states. Note Tolstoy's change in attitude since the Crimea (see 695:3).

3 If we are to negotiate peace … I imagine a more modest role … more that of an honest broker, who really intends to do business.

Otto von Bismarck, 19 Feb. 1878; *Complete Works* Vol.11, p.526. The German Chancellor, Bismarck, with no stake in the Balkan crisis, convened a peace conference in Berlin, which met on 13 June 1878.

4 Lord Salisbury and myself have brought you back peace – but a peace, I hope, with honour.

Benjamin Disraeli, 16 July 1878 (see 825:9). Disraeli returned from Berlin having signed a treaty that detached some of the Balkans from Turkey but kept Russia out of Constantinople.

5 If ever there is another war in Europe, it will come out of some damned silly thing in the Balkans.

Otto von Bismarck, attrib. How true! Part of the Treaty of Berlin gave Austria-Hungary a protectorate over the Balkan territory of Bosnia-Herzegovina. When Austria annexed the area in 1908, it generated one of the causes of World War I (see 704:7).

WARS FOR NATIONHOOD, 1860–71

6 Italy and Victor Emmanuel.

Giuseppe Garibaldi, 15 March 1860. In alliance with France, the north Italian king of Savoy, Victor Emmanuel, had gone to war with Austria in 1859 and detached Lombardy from the Austrian empire. In March 1860 plebiscites in various other northern territories voted for union with the new Italian

kingdom. The republican nationalist Garibaldi wished to go beyond this and invade southern Italy to complete the unification process, although as a republican he was making a big concession to monarchy in adopting this battle-cry. The king and his prime minister, Count Camillo Cavour, adamantly opposed such a campaign, but Garibaldi went ahead and landed in Sicily on 11 May.

7 *Camicia rossa, camicia ardente.* (Red shirt, flaming shirt.)

Rocco Traversa, marching song of the troops of Garibaldi, who wore red tunics, redolent of socialism to Italian conservatives.

8 *Mon Dieu,* of course it would be a great misfortune, but if the Neapolitan cruisers were to capture and hang my poor Garibaldi he would have brought this sad fate upon himself. It would simplify things a good deal. What a fine monument we should get erected to him.

Victor Emmanuel, June 1860; H. De Ideville *Journal d'un diplomate en Italie* Vol.1 (1872) pp.53–61. The Neapolitan cruisers were the warships of the Kingdom of Naples and Sicily, which Garibaldi had just attacked.

9 To the *lazzaroni* [riffraff of the impoverished Italian south] Garibaldi was a saint sent by God to deliver them … Neapolitans think he is invulnerable, that he has only to shake his red shirt and bullets will fall harmless at his feet. Perhaps this superstition saved him from assassination. Don't forget, he arrived in Naples alone, when there still apparently six thousand Bourbon soldiers there.

Marc Monnier *Garibaldi* (1861) pp.301–3. Garibaldi reached Naples on 10 Sept. 1860. Bourbon soldiers were troops of the Neapolitan kingdom, which was ruled by the Bourbon dynasty.

10 Rome or Death!

Slogan adopted by Garibaldi on 19 July 1862 for his campaign to march on Rome and incorporate it, too, into the Italian kingdom. He was halted by the Italian army at the Battle of Aspromonte on 29 Aug. The papal territory of Rome had been held by French troops since 1849, and the French empress, Eugénie, is said to have commented, 'Death, yes; Rome, never!' (see Denis Mack Smith *Garibaldi* (1974) pp.534, 538–41).

11 Because of the policy of Vienna, Germany is clearly too small for us both … Austria will remain the only state to whom we can permanently lose or from whom we can permanently gain … In the not too distant future we shall have to fight for our existence against Austria.

Otto von Bismarck *Prachtbericht* (State Paper) (1856). At this time the Austrophobe Bismarck was Prussian representative at the Austrian-dominated diet in Frankfurt.

1 Prussia's frontiers, as laid down by the Vienna treaties [of 1815], are not conducive to a healthy national life; it is not by means of speeches and majority resolutions that the great issues of the day will be decided – that was the great mistake of 1848 and 1849 – but by iron and blood.

Otto von Bismarck to the Prussian Landtag, 29 Sept. 1862; Lothar Gall *Bismarck: The White Revolutionary* (1986) p.204. A much-quoted statement of Prussian ambition.

2 You know how passionately I love Prussia; but when I hear a shallow *Junker* like Bismarck boast about the 'iron and blood' with which he hopes to subjugate Germany it seems to me even more ridiculous than vulgar.

Heinrich von Treitschke to Wilhelm Nokk, 29 Sept. 1862; W.M. Simon *Germany in the Age of Bismarck* (1969) p.118. Apprehension of the Prussian-dominated Germany that was to come.

3 There are only three men who have ever understood it: one was Prince Albert, and he is dead; the second was a German professor and he went mad; I am the third and I have forgotten all about it.

The British prime minister, Lord Palmerston, on the Schleswig-Holstein question, 1863. In 1864 Prussia and Austria went to war with Denmark over the disputed territories of Schleswig-Holstein on Denmark's southern border. After Denmark's defeat they divided the area between them, but in the war of 1866 Prussia seized Austria's share of the booty.

4 I would call out the police to arrest them.

Otto von Bismarck, attrib., when asked what he would do if the British landed on the Baltic coast to intervene in the Schleswig-Holstein dispute. In the event Britain could do no more than watch the war unfold.

5 Be as rude as you like about this army of lawyers and oculists, but it will get to Vienna just as soon as it likes.

François Certain Canrobert, 1866; Germain Bapst *Le Maréchal Canrobert* Vol.4 (1898) p.34. Canrobert's comment on the highly trained conscripts of the Prussian army, which went to war with Austria in 1866.

6 All the issues from which an empire had summoned its might and the Kaiser and his people to the field were being decided, and … the toil of generations of emperors, warriors, and statesmen were about being lost for ever. The genius of the Prussians was in the ascendant … When Austria marched from the wreck of Königgrätz, she found that the sceptre of the German Caesars had been stricken from her hand.

William Howard Russell, *The Times*, 11 July 1866. The Prussians defeated the Austrians on 3 July 1866, and the war was over in six weeks.

7 Now, forty million Frenchmen, concentrated in our territory, are hardly enough to equal the fifty-one million Germans which Prussia may bring together on our frontier; not to speak of the expanding population of Russia in a slightly more distant future.

Lucien Prévost-Paradol *La France Nouvelle* (1869) pp.413–14.

8 Nobody wants this terrible collision; there are screams and hasty gestures; the gears are put into reverse; the brakes squeal and are destroyed. The effort is futile because the momentum comes from too far away.

Lucien Prévost-Paradol on the looming clash between France and Prussia; Pierre Guiral *Prévost-Paradol* (1955) pp.503–4. He committed suicide immediately after the outbreak of the Franco-Prussian War.

9 *Allez trouver son Excellence et priez-le de venir baiser mon c-l.* (Go and find his Excellency and ask him to come and kiss my arse.)

Wilhelm I of Prussia, 13 July 1870; Wilfrid Scawen Blunt *My Diaries* (1920) pp.389–90. Reply relayed to the French ambassador, Count Benedetti, in the gardens at the spa town of Ems, when asked to renounce in perpetuity the candidature of a member of the Prussian royal house for the vacant throne of Spain. This was to be the *casus belli*, put in more diplomatic language by Bismarck in the celebrated Ems telegram.

10 If the war were to last a year, we would not need to buy a single gaiter button.

The French minister of war, Marshal Edmond Leboeuf, 15 July 1870. Hyper-confidence, soon to be shattered.

11 I accept it with a light heart.

The French prime minister, Émile Ollivier, 15 July 1870; Michael Howard *The Franco-Prussian War* (1961) p.56. This acceptance of the entry into war was immediately qualified as, 'I mean with a heart not weighed down with remorse, a *confident* heart', but the phrase was to haunt Ollivier for the rest of his life.

12 Have arrived in Belfort. Have not found my brigade, have not found my divisional commander.

What should I do? Do not know where my regiments are.
General Michel to the French war department, 21 July 1870.

1 *Nous sommes dans un pot de chambre, et nous y serons emmerdés.* (We are in a chamber-pot, and we are going to be shat on.)
General Auguste Ducrot, 31 Aug. 1870, on the eve of the catastrophic French defeat at Sedan; Howard (1961) p.208.

2 The toils were closing around the prey. Indeed, it occurred to me over and over again that I was looking at some of those spectacles familiar to Indian sportsmen, where a circle of beaters closes gradually in on a wild beast marked in his lair. The angry despairing rushes of the French here and there – the convulsive struggles at one point – the hasty and tumultuous flight from others – gave one an idea of the supreme efforts of the surrounded tiger.
William Howard Russell at Sedan, 1 Sept. 1870; Hudson (1995) p.312.

3 *Welch' eine Wendung durch Gottes Führung!* (What an outcome through God's guidance!)
Wilhelm I, king of Prussia, Berlin, 3 Sept. 1870, greeting the news from Sedan; *Questions on German History* (1989) p.198. The war was not over, however, as the new republican government refused to ask for peace terms.

4 What breaks my heart is (1) human ferocity; (2) the conviction that we are about the enter an era of stupidity. We'll be utilitarian, militaristic, American, and Catholic. Very Catholic! You'll see. The war with Prussia concludes and destroys the French Revolution.
French novelist Gustave Flaubert to the writer George Sand; Francis Steegmuller (ed.) *The Letters of Gustave Flaubert 1857–1880* (1982) p.164.

5 A merry Christmas … Hospitals crowded with the dying; heaps of dead on our surrounding heights; hardly a family which is not in mourning … starvation staring us in the face; fuel burnt out; meat a recollection, and vegetables a passing dream.
Felix Whitehurst, 25 Dec. 1870; *My Private Diary during the Siege of Paris* (1875). After Sedan Paris was surrounded by German forces, holding out against hopeless odds.

6 We shall prolong the struggle to extermination, we shall ensure that there cannot be found in France a man or an Assembly to adhere to the victory of force, and we shall thus strike with impotence conquest and occupation.

Prime minister Léon Gambetta to Jules Favre, Jan. 1871; Howard (1961) p.373. Brave words, but the Third Republic was compelled to accept a punishing peace treaty on 1 March 1871. It made the new German empire, proclaimed in the Palace of Versailles on 18 Jan., the foremost military power in continental Europe.

7 What would have been the result of French victory: the re-establishment of the divisions and impotence of Germany from which every European war for the last three centuries has come, and a new lease of Napoleonism, *i.e.* the establishment thenceforth on a tolerable firm basis by Napoléon le Petit of the ideas of Napoléon le Grand.
The British diplomat Sir Robert Morier to Lady Derby, 5 Jan. 1871; Rosslyn Wemyss (ed.) *Memoirs and Letters of the Rt. Hon. Sir Robert Morier* Vol.2 (1911) p.219.

8 This war represents the German Revolution, a greater political event than the French Revolution of last century … What has really come to pass in Europe? The balance of power has been entirely destroyed, and the country which suffers most, and feels the effects of this great change most, is England.
Benjamin Disraeli, 9 Feb. 1871; *Parl. Deb.* Vol.204, Cols 81 ff.

THE SHAPE OF BATTLE, 1862–1913

9 Almost a week ago [the British] discovered that their whole wooden navy was useless … These are great times … Man has mounted science, and is now run away with … Before many centuries more … science may have the existence of mankind in its power, and the human race commit suicide by blowing up the world.
The American Henry Adams, London, March 1862; *Collected Works* p.102. Wooden men-of-war were made obsolete by the advent of the ironclad battleship, first the French *La Gloire*, then the British HMS *Warrior*.

10 If to the most spirited dash one opposes a quiet steadiness, it is fire effect, nowadays so powerful, which will determine the issue … Little success can be expected from a mere frontal attack, but very likely a great deal of loss.
The victor of Sedan, Field Marshal Helmuth von Moltke *Instructions for Commanders of Large Formations* (1869); J.F.C. Fuller *The Conduct of War 1789–1961* (1961) pp.117–18.

11 Put a man in a hole, and a good battery on a hill behind him, and he will beat off three times his number, even if he is not a very good soldier.

The American Theodore Lyman, 1869, drawing on the bloody experience of the US Civil War.

1 The art of war is subject to many modifications by industrial and scientific progress. But one thing does not change, the heart of man. In the last analysis success in battle is a matter of morale. In all matters which pertain to an army, organization, discipline and tactics, the human heart in the supreme moment of battle is the basic factor.
Colonel Charles Ardent du Picq *Études sur le combat* (1880).

2 In 1882 I was in Vienna, where I met an American Jew whom I had known in the States. He said: 'Hang your chemistry and electricity! If you want to make a pile of money, invent something that will enable those Europeans to cut each other's throats with greater facility.'
The American Hiram Maxim, *The Times*, 11 July 1915. Maxim went on to perfect the machine-gun in 1883, the 'queen of battles' in subsequent colonial wars and, above all, in the trench warfare of 1914–18.

3 Combat has for its end to break by force the will of the enemy and to impose on him our own. Only the offensive permits the obtaining of decisive results. The passive defence is doomed to certain defeat; it is to be rejected absolutely ... At a signal from the Colonel the drums beat, the bugles sound the advance and the entire line charges forward with cries of *en avant, à la baionette!* ['forward, with bayonets fixed!']
French Army Field Service Regulations, 1895; Hew Strachan *European Armies and the Conduct of War* (1983) pp.105, 116.

4 Every body of men appointed for defence ... must immediately entrench itself ... Sheltered behind such works, and in a position to devote all their energy to fire against the enemy, the defenders will sustain losses comparatively slight ... while the attacking bodies will be exposed to the uninterrupted fire of the defenders, and deprived almost of all possibility of replying to their fire ... The attacking army will have to deal with auxiliary obstacles ... obstructions formed of beams, networks of wire, and pitfalls. To overcome these obstacles great sacrifices must be made.
I.S. Bloch *Is War Now Impossible?* (1898) p.11.

5 Blindness to moral forces and worship of material forces inevitably lead in war to destruction ... All that trash written by M. Bloch before 1904 about

zones of fire across which no living being could pass, heralded nothing but disaster. War is essentially a triumph, not of a chassepot over a needle-gun, not of a line of men entrenched behind wire entanglements and fire-swept zones over men exposing themselves in the open, but of one will over another weaker will.
Sir Ian Hamilton *Compulsory Service* (1910) pp.121–2. General Hamilton was commander of the British and Australian–New Zealand (Anzac) assault on entrenched Turkish positions at Gallipoli in 1915, an operation that proved a prolonged disaster (see 713:6). The chassepot, the French breech-loading rifle, was adopted in 1866 and was superior to the Prussian equivalent, the needle-gun.

6 The consideration of what fire one may oneself receive ... becomes a secondary matter; the troops are on the move and must arrive ... To march and march quickly, preceded by a hail of bullets ... Such is the fundamental formula to be adopted.
General Ferdinand Foch *Des Principes de la guerre* (1913). General Foch rose to be generalissimo of the Allied armies on the Western Front in March 1918. The doctrine of the outright offensive was to cost millions of lives on both sides.

HAWKS, 1877–1914

7 War ... must be recognized as an instinct of humanity, of divine origin, not to be replaced, as idealists hope, by any human device like tribunals of arbitration or submissive trust in the generosity of competitors.
O.H. Ernst 'War' in *Johnson's New Universal Cyclopaedia* (1877 edn). The movement for the arbitration of international disputes had in 1872 resulted in the settlement of a wrangle between Britain and the United States over British responsibility for building the Confederate cruiser *Alabama*, which had preyed on Union shipping during the Civil War. Arbitration, however, proved an unappealing alternative to war.

8 Perpetual peace is a dream – and not even a beautiful dream – and war is an integral part of God's ordering of the universe. In war, man's noblest virtues come into play: courage and renunciation, fidelity to duty and a readiness for sacrifice that does not stop at giving up life itself. Without war the world would be swamped in materialism.
Field Marshal Helmuth von Moltke to the Swiss international lawyer Johann Kaspar Bluntschli, 11 Dec. 1880; Arnold Toynbee *A Study of History* Vol.4 (1939) p.643.

1 You shall love peace as a means to new wars – and the short peace more than the long … You say it is the good cause that hallows even war? I say unto you: it is the good war which hallows every cause.
Friedrich Nietzsche *Also sprach Zarathustra* (Thus Spake Zarathustra) (1884) Ch.10.

2 Power, force, is a faculty of national life; one of the talents committed to nations by God … The ability to put forth the nation's power … is one of the clear duties involved in the Christian word 'watchfulness' … and, where evil is mighty and defiant, the obligation to use force – that is, war – arises.
Captain Alfred Thayer Mahan USN 'The Peace Conference and the Moral Aspects of War' in *North American Review*, Oct. 1899, pp.444, 445. Mahan was a US representative at the Hague Peace Conference of 1899.

3 The necessary foundation of a State is a cemetery.
Maurice Barrès *Scènes et doctrines du nationalisme* (1902). The ultra-nationalist Barrès recorded this aphorism after visiting the cemetery at Chambières, near Metz, burial ground of French troops killed in the Franco-Prussian War of 1870–71.

4 An army, in fact, tries to *work together* in a battle or a large manoeuvre in much the same way as a football team *plays together* in a match … The army *fights* for the good of its country as the team *plays* for the honour of the school … Exceptionally gallant *charges* and heroic *defences* correspond to brilliant *runs* and fine *tackling*.
Captain F. Gruggisberg *Modern Warfare, or How Our Soldiers Fight* (1903) p.94.

5 It is necessary to make it clear to ourselves and to the children growing up around us, whom we have to train, that a time of rest has not yet come, that the prediction of a final struggle for the existence and greatness of Germany is not a mere fancy of ambitious fools, but that it will come one day, inevitably, with full fury.
Field Marshal Colmar von der Goltz *The Nation in Arms* (1906) p.475.

6 We will glorify war – the world's only hygiene – militarism, patriotism, the destructive acts of the anarchists, beautiful ideas worth dying for, and contempt for women.
Manifesto of the Italian Futurists, *Le Figaro*, 20 Feb. 1909; R.W. Flint (ed.) *Marinetti: Selected Writings* (1972) pp.41–2.

7 Militarism is the great preserver of our ideals of hardihood, and human life with no use for hardihood

would be contemptible … So long as anti-militarists propose no substitute for war's disciplinary function, no *moral equivalent* of war … so long they fail to realize the full inwardness of the situation.
William James 'The Moral Equivalent of War' in *International Conciliation*, Feb. 1910, pp.13 ff.

8 War is a biological necessity of the first importance, a regulative element in the life of mankind which cannot be dispensed with … But it is not only a biological law but a moral obligation, and, as such, an indispensable factor in civilization.
Friedrich von Bernhardi *Germany and the Next War* (1912) Ch.1. Ch.3 was entitled 'World Power or Decline'.

9 It will be more beautiful and wonderful to live for ever among the heroes on war memorials in a church than to die an empty death in bed, nameless … Let that be heaven for young Germany. Thus we wish to knock at our God's door.
Anon. German writer, Jan. 1913; Martin Kitchen *The German Officer Corps 1890–1914* (1968) pp.139–41.

10 The Army is the great protector
Which baptizes us all as Frenchmen.
Paul Déroulède; Raoul Girardet *Le Nationalisme français 1871–1914* (1970) p.23.

DOVES, 1862–1907

11 What was needed here was not only weak and ignorant women, but, with them and beside them, kindly and experienced men, capable, firm, already organized, and in sufficient numbers to get to work at once in an orderly fashion. In that case many of the complications and fevers which so terribly aggravated wounds originally slight, but very soon mortal, might have been avoided.
Henry Dunant *A Memoir of Solferino* (1862). The Swiss Dunant was the founder of the Red Cross, whose flag was the flag of Switzerland with its colours inverted. He was present at the Battle of Solferino on 24 June 1859 between the Austrians and the forces of France and Savoy and witnessed the efforts of the women of the village of Castiglione to minister to the many wounded.

12 What, gentlemen, is the essence of all our work? To reduce, to mitigate the sufferings of war by works of charity … To humanize war – if that is not a contradiction in terms – that is our mandate. Let us proclaim our deep regret, our sorrow that we cannot do more; let us protest against the great collective iniquity called war … but after this unequivocal protest, taking war for what it is, let us unite our efforts to relieve its distress.

Louis Appia *Secours aux blessés* (Aid for the Wounded) (1864). Appia had served as a doctor behind Prussian lines in the war with Denmark. Here he shows his awareness of the criticism levelled against the work of organizations such as the Red Cross by outright pacifists, namely, that it only made war more palatable by reducing its afflictions.

1 Considering the progress of civilization should have the effect of alleviating, as much as possible, the calamities of war; that the only legitimate object which States should endeavour to accomplish is to weaken the military force of the enemy; that for this purpose, it is sufficient to disable the greatest number of men; that this object would be exceeded by the employment of arms which unnecessarily aggravate the sufferings of disabled men, or render their death inevitable; that the employment of such arms would therefore be contrary to the laws of humanity.

St Petersburg Declaration, Dec. 1868; Leon Friedman (ed.) *The Law of War: A Documentary History* (1972) p.192.

2 I have long since reached the sad conclusion that, in spite of the undeniable reality of modern progress, we have not yet escaped the shadow of the great crimes and misfortunes which our century flattered itself it had done.

John Stuart Mill to Gustave d'Eichthal, 28 Aug. 1870; *The Letters of John Stuart Mill* Vol.2 (1910) p.270 (trans. from the original French). Writing soon after the outbreak of the Franco-Prussian War, Mill expresses the loss of his faith in international peace. In 1848 he had written: 'It is commerce which is rapidly rendering war obsolete [as] the principal guarantee of the peace of the world' (*Principles of Political Economy* (1848) Bk 3, Ch.17, Sect.5).

3 There is many a boy here today who looks on war as all glory, but, boys, it is all hell. You can hear this warning voice to generations yet to come. I look upon war with horror.

General Tecumseh Sherman, 11 Aug. 1880, speaking to the Convention of the Grand Army of the Republic. The ruthless terminator of the Confederacy in the American Civil War spoke from personal experience (see 591:4). The warning is usually abbreviated to the phrase 'war is hell'.

4 Still better would it be if the science of artillery could progress to such a point that any army could fire a shot which would smash the whole army of the enemy at one blow. Then, perhaps, all waging of war would be entirely given up.

Bertha von Suttner *Die Waffen Nieder!* (Lay Down Your Arms!) (1892) pp.351–2. The Austrian Baroness von Suttner was at the forefront of the European pacifist movement in the pre-1914 generation. The ultimate weapon did emerge with the atomic bomb in 1945, but armies could make do with a large variety of penultimate weapons, and war went on.

5 The prize would be awarded to the man or the woman who had done most to advance the idea of general peace in Europe … What I have in view is that we should soon achieve the result … that all states should bind themselves absolutely to take action against the first aggressor. Wars will then become impossible.

Alfred Nobel to Bertha von Suttner, Jan. 1893; H. Schick and R. Sohlman *The Life of Alfred Nobel* (1929) pp.203–4. The Swedish inventor Nobel discovered dynamite in 1867 and devoted most of the resultant vast fortune to funding annual prizes in the fields of physics, chemistry, medicine, literature and peace. Von Süttner was awarded the peace prize in 1905.

6 If you have to ravage the country which you attack, – to destroy for a score of future years, its roads, its woods, its cities, and its harbours; – and if, finally, having brought masses of men, counted by hundreds of thousands, face to face, you tear those masses to pieces with jagged shots, and leave the fragments of living creatures countlessly beyond all help of surgery, to starve and parch, through days of torture, down into clots of clay – what book of accounts shall record the cost of your work; – What book of judgement sentence the guilt of it?

John Ruskin *The Crown of Wild Olives* (1895) pp.112–13.

7 Your violent and chaotic society, even when it calls for peace, when it seems to be in a state of calm, still carries war within itself just as the slumbering thunder-cloud contains the storm.

The French socialist Jean Jaurès to the Chamber of Deputies, 7 March 1895; Gilles Candas (ed.) *Jean Jaurès* (1984) p.104. A dramatic expression of the classic Marxist thesis that capitalism equalled war.

8 The economic crises, due in great part to the system of armaments *à l'outrance*, and the continual danger which lies in this massing of war material, are transforming the armed peace of our days into a crushing burden, which the peoples have more and more difficulty in bearing. It appears evident, then, that if this state of things were prolonged, it would inevitably lead to the very cataclysm which it is desired to avert, and the horrors of which make every thinking man shudder in advance.

Nicholas II, rescript of 24 Aug. 1898; Sardi E. Cooper *Patriotic Pacifism* (1991) p.222. From this document sprang the Hague International Conference of 1899. Cynics alleged that it was motivated less by a principled concern for world peace than by Russia's inability to afford an expensive arms race with other powers.

1 Could we ... a monarch holding personal command of his army, dissolve his regiments sacred with a hundred years of history and relegate their glorious colours to the walls of armouries and museums (and hand over his towns to anarchists and Democracy)?

Wilhelm II to Nicholas II, 29 Aug. 1898; *Die Grosse Politik* Vol.5, pp.151–2. A flat refusal to contemplate the disarmament the tsar appeared to have in mind.

2 It is well understood that all questions concerning the political relations of states and the order of things established by treaties, as generally all questions which do not directly fall within the programme adopted by the cabinets, must be absolutely excluded from the deliberations of the Conference.

Russian government circular, Jan. 1899; *Parliamentary Papers* Vol.110 (1899) pp.101–2. A Russian climb-down, which effectively nullified in advance the utility of the Hague Conference.

3 The signatory powers agree to prohibit: (1) the discharge of projectiles and explosives from balloons or in other analogous new ways; (2) the use of projectiles the sole object of which is the diffusion of asphyxiating or deleterious gases; (3) to abstain from the use of bullets which expand or flatten easily in the human body.

Declarations of the Hague Conference of 1899; *Proceedings* (1920) pp.220–22, 225–6, 227–8. These bans on aerial bombardment, poison gas warfare and dumdum bullets were subject to ratification by the signatory states, and this proved difficult, if not impossible, to achieve.

4 Never before has war received so much homage at the lips of men, and reigned with less disputed sway in their minds ... It has perverted the intelligence of men, women and children, and has made the speeches of Emperors, Kings, Presidents and Ministers monotonous with ardent protestations of fidelity to peace. Indeed, war has made peace altogether in its own image: a martial, over-bearing, war-lord sort of peace.

Joseph Conrad 'Autocracy and War' (1905); *Notes on Life and Letters* (1921) pp.143–6.

5 The submarine may be the cause of bringing conflict to a halt altogether, for fleets will become useless, and as other war matériel continues to improve, war will become impossible.

The French writer Jules Verne 'The Future of the Submarine', 1904. In his 1869 science-fiction novel *Vingt Mille lieues sous le mers* (Twenty Thousand Leagues under the Sea) Verne's dark hero, Captain Nemo, undertook a one-man peace mission in his giant submarine *Nautilus*, destroying warships at will wherever he considered them a threat to international security.

6 As a peace machine, [its] value to the world will be beyond computation. Would a declaration of war between Russia and Japan be made, if within an hour thereafter, a swiftly gliding aeroplane might take its flight from St Petersburg and drop half a ton of dynamite above the [Japanese] war offices? Could any nation afford to war upon any other with such hazards in view?

The American John Brisben Walker, owner of the magazine *Cosmopolitan*, March 1904. A remarkable view considering that the Wright brothers had made their first powered flight only three months earlier. War between Russia and China had broken out on 4 Feb. 1904 with the Japanese surprise attack on Port Arthur, the Russian naval base in Manchuria.

7 The battlefield as a place of settlement of disputes is gradually yielding to arbitral courts of justice.

US President William Howard Taft *The Dawn of World Peace* (1911). As a lawyer, Taft placed great faith in judicial settlements.

8 The fate of humanity has never been as precarious, as wretched, as threatened as it has been since the corruption of the modern era began. It is clear that in the 18th century ... barbarism was pushed back farther from the borders of culture than it is today. Everywhere today we see wars, massacres, folly – even in the world of rationalism. Barbarism is resurfacing. Everywhere the flood of barbarism is rising.

The French writer Charles Péguy 'Par ce demi-clair matin', Nov. 1905. This grim vision was not published until July 1939, when it appeared in the *Nouvelle Revue française*, weeks before the outbreak of a second world war in which France was to suffer its worst-ever defeat (see 848:2).

9 If a war threatens to break out, it is the duty of the working classes and their parliamentary representatives ... to exert every effort in order to prevent the outbreak of war by the means they consider most effective ... In case war should break out anyway, it is their duty to intervene in favour of its speedy termination, and with all their powers to utilize the economic and political crisis created by the war to rouse the masses and thereby to hasten the downfall of capitalist class rule.

Resolution of the 7th International Socialist Congress at Stuttgart, 24 Aug. 1907; Julius Braunthal *History of the International 1864–1914* (1966) p.363. The resolution was drafted by the Marxist trio of Lenin, Rosa Luxemburg and Julius Martov. It neither prevented the outbreak of World War I nor put a serious curb on its early momentum.

SEEDS OF WAR, 1871–1908

I   Land of pity, sweet land of France,
     The honour I render, the love I owe
     Inspire nothing more in me than hatred and
         vengeance:
     A dream of bloodshed fills my mind in your
         glades.

Victor Laprade 'To the Land of France' (1873).

2 Let us not speak of our lost territory, but let it be understood that we think of it all the time.

Léon Gambetta, 16 Nov. 1871. Gambetta was speaking of the provinces of Alsace and Lorraine, surrendered to Germany by the treaty that ended the Franco-Prussian War. Their statues in the Place de la Concorde were draped in black as a token of national mourning.

3 Germany is in reality a great camp ready to break up for any war at a week's notice with a million of men.

Odo Russell, British ambassador in Berlin, March 1873; Lord Newton *Lord Lyons* Vol.2 (1913) p.41.

4 If the United States and Russia hold together for another half century, they will at the end of that time, completely dwarf such old European states as France and Germany, and depress them into a second class. They will do the same to England, if at the end of that time England still thinks of herself as simply a European state.

Sir John Seeley *The Expansion of England* (1883) Lecture 4. For Seeley the British empire was the indispensable basis of Britain's claim to be a power of the first rank. Involvement in European politics to him necessarily implied a reduced status.

5 The great powers of our time are like travellers, unknown to one another, whom chance has brought together in a carriage. They watch each other, and when one of them puts his hand into his pocket, his neighbour gets ready his own revolver in order to be able to fire the first shot.

Otto von Bismarck, 1879; Carlton J. Hayes *A Generation of Materialism 1871–1900* (1963) p.18.

6 All politics reduces itself to this formula: try to be one of three, as long as the world is governed by the unstable equilibrium of five great powers.

Otto von Bismarck; C.J. Bartlett *Peace, War and the European Powers 1814–1914* (1996) p.93. Bismarck had achieved this objective by 1882, with the Triple Alliance of Germany, Austria-Hungary and Italy. This left the other two, France and Russia, in isolation until they came together in the alliance of 1894. Bismarck seems to have ignored the sixth power, Britain (see 704:5).

7 The soil of Germany, the German fatherland, belongs to the masses as much and more than to the others ... If Russia, the champion of terror and barbarism went to attack Germany to break and destroy it ... we are as much concerned as those who stand at the head of Germany.

August Bebel *Verhandlungen* (Discussions) (1891) p.285. The Marxist leader of the Social Democratic Party foreshadows the nationalism that rallied the party to the Reich in 1914.

8 We hold Europe between the jaws of a vice. At the first insult we shall turn the screw ... On the day when the Cossacks gallop through the streets of Old Stamboul [Constantinople, Istanbul], a French battalion will be presenting arms in front of the Kléber statue in Strasbourg.

François Coppée *Avant la grande guerre* (1918). The French writer was glorying in the Franco-Russian alliance of 1894, which, so he thought, locked in Germany and its partners from both east and west. Jean-Baptiste Kléber, a French general of the revolutionary era, was born in Strasbourg in 1753 and assassinated in Cairo in 1800.

9 We have stood alone in that which is called isolation – our splendid isolation, as one of our Colonial friends was good enough to call it.

Edward Goschen, 26 Feb. 1896. At this time Britain stood outside any alliance system. The 'Colonial friend' was the Canadian Sir George Eulas Foster, who used the phrase on 16 Jan. 1896.

10 The parting of the ways was in 1853, when the Emperor Nicholas's proposals were rejected. Many members of this House will keenly feel the nature of the mistake that was made when I say that we put all our money upon the wrong horse.

Lord Salisbury, 19 Jan. 1897; *Parl. Deb.* Vol.45, Col.29. Salisbury signals an end to a century of British backing for

Turkey against Russia. His patience had run out with an Ottoman regime that continually failed to put through the reforms Britain demanded as the price of its support. For Tsar Nicolas I in 1853 see 694:3.

1 Germany, from this point of view, is a powder magazine. All her neighbours are in terror for fear she will explode, and sooner or later, explode she must.

The American historian Henry Adams, writing from St Petersburg in 1901; Golo Mann *The History of Germany since 1789* (1974) p.404.

2 This seems a golden opportunity for fighting the Germans in alliance with the French … We could have the German Fleet, the Kiel Canal, and Schleswig-Holstein within a fortnight.

The First Sea Lord, Admiral Sir John Fisher, to the foreign secretary, Lord Lansdowne, 22 April 1905; Ruddock Mackay *Fisher of Kilverstone* (1973) p.327. The over-confident Fisher wrote at the time of the first crisis over Morocco, engineered by Germany to break the 1904 entente between Britain and France, Britain's first commitment to intervention in Europe. The Admiralty had identified Germany as Britain's foremost potential enemy soon after Germany began building its High Seas Fleet in 1897. The Kiel Canal gave the fleet access to the Baltic from its main base at Wilhelmshaven on the North Sea coast of Schleswig-Holstein, making the port of Kiel an important naval centre.

3 I rejoice in the thought that within the next few years there will be 75 first-class battleships afloat, all manned by English-speaking sailors and constituting the most formidable argument or guarantee for universal peace that the world has ever seen.

Arthur Lee to President Theodore Roosevelt, 24 May 1905; David Burton *Theodore Roosevelt and his English Correspondents* (1973) p.34. Much as he admired Britain's imperial achievement, Roosevelt could not move the United States out of its own diplomatic isolation and join an Anglo-American alliance. This was wishful thinking on Lee's part, prompted by the sense that Britain now needed as many allies as it could find.

4 Germany is going to contest with us the Command of the Sea, and our commercial position … She must have an outlet for her teeming population, and vast acres where Germans can live and remain Germans. These acres only exist within the confines of our empire. Therefore, *l'Ennemi c'est l'Allemagne.*

Lord Esher, *Journal*, 3 Dec. 1907. German *Lebensraum* (living space) in fact lay in European Russia.

5 A policy aiming at the encirclement of Germany and seeking to form a ring of Powers in order to isolate and paralyse it would be disastrous to the peace of Europe. The forming of such a ring would not be possible without exerting some pressure. Pressure provokes counter-pressure. And out of pressure and counter-pressure finally explosions may arise.

German chancellor Bernhard von Bülow to the Reichstag, 14 Nov. 1906; Immanuel Geiss *German Foreign Policy 1871–1914* (1976) p.121. Encirclement (*Einkreisung*) was the accusation that Germany levelled at France and Russia, with Britain moving ever closer to them. Von Bülow, chancellor in 1900–9, was unable to prevent the Triple Entente.

6 They saw their armies and navies grow larger and more portentous; some of their ironclads at the last cost as much as their whole annual expenditure upon advanced education; they accumulated explosives and the machinery of destruction; they allowed their national traditions and jealousies to accumulate; they contemplated a steady enhancement of race hostility as the races drew closer without concern or understanding.

H.G. Wells *The War in the Air* (1908) p.246. Although a work of fiction, the novel reflected closely the tensions in the real world of a Europe divided into heavily armed camps and dangerously volatile.

ROAD TO CATASTROPHE, 1908-14

7 Please restrain Conrad … He must stop this warmongering. It would be tempting to strike down the Serbians … but what use are such cheap laurels when we might risk the impossible war on three fronts [against Serbia, Russia and France]? Then it would be the end of the song.

Austrian Archduke Franz Ferdinand, heir to the imperial throne, 1908; *History Today*, July 1963, p.483. In Oct. 1908 Austria-Hungary had annexed the protectorate of Bosnia-Herzegovina, provoking the fury of the Balkan kingdom of Serbia, which claimed a superior right to the territory. The Serbs looked to Russia for support, and though the crisis passed, the underlying causes remained unsettled. Franz Conrad von Hötzendorff, chief of staff of the Austrian army, was an ardent expansionist.

8 No war in Europe can bring us much. There would be nothing for us to gain in the conquest of fresh Slav or French territory … A war, lightly provoked, would have a bad effect on the country … Every great war is followed by a period of liberalism.

Bernhard von Bülow to Crown Prince Wilhelm, 1908; D.E. Kaiser *Journal of Modern History* Vol.55 (1983) pp.455–6.

1 When the moment comes the gates will be flung open, the drawbridges will be lowered, and hordes of enemies will pour into Germany over the Vosges, the Maas, the Königsau, the Niemen, the Bug and even over the Isonzo and the Tyrolean Alps, destroying and annihilating all in their path. The danger is gigantic.

Field Marshal Count von Schlieffen in *Deutsche Revue*, Jan. 1909. Von Schlieffen had drafted a war plan that envisaged the rapid defeat of France in the west before the main German effort was directed against Russia in the east. In this nightmare scenario he sees the Reich assaulted on three sides, not only from east and west but also from the south (where Italy was supposedly Germany's ally).

2 We want eight and we won't wait.

Slogan coined by George Wyndham, March 1909. In 1906 Britain had launched HMS *Dreadnought*, a revolutionary battleship that made all others obsolete overnight. Germany retaliated by starting to build its own, and in 1909 Britain countered by stepping up the naval arms race, putting no fewer than eight new battleships on the stocks.

3 The battle of Armageddon comes along in September 1914. That date suits the Germans, if ever they are going to fight. Both their Army and Fleet then mobilized, and the Kiel Canal finished, and their new building complete.

Admiral Sir John Fisher to Mrs Reginald McKenna, 5 Feb. 1911; Mackay (1973) p.434–5. A remarkably accurate forecast. Germany had begun widening the locks of the Kiel Canal to take its Dreadnoughts, and the work was due to be finished in the summer of 1914. Armageddon, according to the Book of Revelation 16:14–16, was the place where the kings of the earth were to be gathered together for 'the battle of that great day of God Almighty'.

4 If a situation were to be forced upon us where peace could only be preserved by the surrender of the great and beneficent position Britain has won by centuries of heroism and achievement, by allowing Britain to be treated, where her interests were vitally affected, as if she were of no account in the Cabinet of Nations, then I say emphatically that peace at that price would be a humiliation intolerable for a great country like ours to endure.

Chancellor of the exchequer David Lloyd George, 21 July 1911; Bentley B. Gilbert *David Lloyd George* (1987) p.450. This speech came at the height of a second crisis over Morocco, when Germany openly challenged the French position there by sending the gunboat *Panther* to Agadir on 1 July. The warning to Germany was issued by a man thought of as the least belligerent member of the cabinet, and it was all the more telling for that.

5 If we again slip away from this affair with our tail between our legs and if we cannot bring ourselves to put forward a determined claim which we are prepared to force through with the sword, I shall despair of the future of the German empire. I shall then resign. But before handing in my resignation I shall move to abolish the Army and to place ourselves under Japanese protectorate.

German army chief of staff Helmuth von Moltke (nephew of the victor of the wars of 1864–71), Aug. 1911; Volker Berghahn *Germany and the Approach of War in 1914* (1993 edn) p.109.

6 The tocsin will be sounded in Europe and sixteen to eighteen million men, the flower of different nations, will march against each other … What will be the result? After this war we shall have mass bankruptcy, mass misery, mass unemployment and great famine.

August Bebel at the time of the Agadir crisis, 1911; Mann (1974) p.480. All too true, but odd that the Marxist Bebel did not see socialism rising from the wreckage of the aftermath.

7 I have saved the German people their right to sea power and self-determination in arms matters, and I have shown the British that they bite into granite when they touch our armaments.

Wilhelm II, April 1912; Gerhard Ritter *The Sword and the Sceptre* Vol.2 (1972) p.188.

8 H.M. [the Kaiser] envisaged the following: Austria, must deal energetically with the foreign Slavs [Serbia] … If Russia supports the Serbs … war would be inevitable for us … The Fleet must naturally prepare itself for war with England … The Chief of the General Staff [Moltke] says: War the sooner the better, but he does not draw the logical conclusion from this, which is to present Russia or France or both with an ultimatum which would unleash the war with right on our side.

Admiral Georg Alexander von Müller, diary entry, 8 Dec. 1912, regarding a high-level strategy conference in Berlin that day; J.G.C. Röhl 'Admiral von Müller and the Approach of War' in *Historical Journal* Vol.12 (1969) pp.661 ff.

9 You may believe me, many dogs spell the death of the hare.

Helmuth von Moltke to Freiherr von Freytag-Loringhoven; Ritter (1972) p.116. Deep pessimism over German's fate should war come.

10 The [situation is] most fraught with threatening consequences for the general peace; it would bring forward, in its full historical development, the question of the struggle of Slavdom not only with Islam but also with Germanism. In this event one can scarcely set one's hopes on any palliative measures and must prepare for a great and decisive general European war.

A.P. Izvolsky to S.D. Sazonov, 23 Oct. 1912; D.C.B. Lieven *Russia and the Origins of the First World War* (1983) p.44. Izvolsky had been Sazonov's predecessor as Russian foreign minister. His comment is on the likely sequel of a victory by the Balkan states in their war with Turkey, which had broken out earlier in the month. In other words, their next target would be Austria's Balkan fiefs, and Russia would be drawn in to back them up.

1 The bankers will not find money for such a fight, the industries will not maintain it, the statesmen cannot … There will be no general war.

The American Starr Jordan, *The Independent*, 27 Feb. 1913. A rational view, which failed to take into account the wild irrationality of nationalist behaviour.

2 Since the Dreyfus affair, we have in France a militarist and nationalist party which will not brook a *rapprochement* with Germany at any price … The majority of Germans and Frenchmen want to live in peace, that cannot be denied. But a powerful minority in both countries dreams only [of] battles, conquests, or revenge. That is the danger beside which we must live as if next to a powder-barrel which the slightest imprudence might blow up.

Jules Cambon, French ambassador in Berlin, 20 Feb. 1914; John F.V. Keiger *France and the Origins of the First World War* (1983) p.134.

3 While it is only natural that one should be stricken with horror at the brutal and shocking assassination of Archduke Francis Ferdinand, it is impossible to deny that his disappearance from the scene is calculated to diminish the tenseness of the situation … The news of his death is almost calculated to create a feeling of universal relief.

F. Cunliffe-Owen, correspondent of the *New York Sun*, 29 June 1914. Surely one of the greatest misjudgements in the history of journalism. On 28 June Franz Ferdinand and his wife were shot dead by a Serb nationalist in the Bosnian city of Sarajevo. To avenge this outrage Austria went to war with Serbia on 28 July, supported by Germany. Russia stood by Serbia, and France mobilized on behalf of its ally Russia. Britain, in turn, came in with France and Russia on the grounds of its 1839 guarantee of a neutral Belgium, after German forces crossed the Belgian frontier in accordance with the Schlieffen Plan (see 705:1). Five weeks after Sarajevo World War I had begun.

4 'So they've killed Ferdinand,' said the charwoman to Mr Schweik … 'I expect the Turks did it,' [replied Schweik] … Oh, there's bound to be war. Serbia and Russia'll help us [and] the Germans 'll attack us, because the Germans and the Turks stand by each other … Still, we can join France, because they've had a grudge against Germany ever since '71.'

Jaroslav Hasek, from his hilarious novel *The Good Soldier Schweik* (1930) Bk 1, Ch.1. The Czech Schweik was a citizen of Austria. His prediction of the international line-up in July 1914 has a mad logic all of its own and aims no farther off the mark than Cunliffe-Owen's.

5 Dear friend,

Again I say a terrible storm cloud hangs over Russia. Disaster, grief, murky darkness and no light. A whole ocean of tears, there is no counting them, and so much blood … We all drown in blood. The disaster is great, the misery infinite.

Grigory Rasputin to Nicholas II, July 1914; Alex de Jonge *The Life and Times of Grigorii Rasputin* (1982) pp.239, 240. The Orthodox priest Rasputin had established an extraordinarily close relationship with the tsar and tsarina. Prone to apocalyptic visions, he spoke better than he knew in this one.

6 We are within measurable, or imaginable, distance of a real Armageddon, which would dwarf the Ulster and Nationalist Volunteers to their true proportion. Happily there seems to be no reason why we should be anything more than spectators. But it is a blood-curdling prospect – is it not?

British prime minister Herbert Asquith to his mistress Venetia Stanley, 24 July 1914; *H.H. Asquith Letters to Venetia Stanley* (1982) p.123. How anyone in Asquith's position could think that Britain could stand aside from the war beggars belief.

7 They have killed Jaurès.

Marguerite Poisson, witness to the assassination of Jean Jaurès, 31 July 1914. As a socialist, Jaurès was opposed to the war, and the conviction that the murder was the work of pro-war circles is lent credibility by Péguy's prediction: 'Just as soon as war is declared, the first thing we shall do is to shoot Jaurès.'

8 When war comes, parties will cease to exist. We are only German brothers.

Wilhelm II to the people of Berlin, 31 July 1914, on the eve of Germany's entry into war. Political divisions were, indeed, obliterated, and the Marxist Social Democrats, instead of opposing the war as their ideology demanded, voted in its favour.

9 When you march into France, let the man on the right brush the Channel with his sleeve.

Alfred von Schlieffen's injunction to the German army; Barbara Tuchman *The Guns of August* (1962) Ch.2.

1 The lamps are going out all over Europe; we shall not see them lit again in our lifetime.

British foreign secretary Sir Edward Grey, on the eve of Britain's entry into the war, 3 Aug. 1914, *Twenty-Five Years* (1925) Vol.2, Ch.18. Grey stood watching the evening lamps come on from his window in the Foreign Office.

2 Just for a word – 'neutrality', a word which in wartime has so often been disregarded, just for a scrap of paper – Great Britain is going to make war on a kindred nation who desires nothing better than to be friends with her.

German chancellor Theobald von Bethmann Hollweg to the British ambassador, Sir Edward Goschen, 4 Aug. 1914; *British Documents on the Origins of the War* Vol.11 (1926) p.351. Britain's formal justification for going to war with Germany was to make good its pledge of Belgian neutrality (given in 1839), but the real reason was to prevent Germany from dominating Europe. Note Bethmann Hollweg's regret at a war between two countries of the same Anglo-Saxon stock.

3 There's an east wind coming … such a wind as never blew on England yet. It will be cold and bitter, Watson, and a good many of us may wither before its blast. But it's God's own wind, none the less, and a cleaner, better, stronger land will lie in the sunshine when the storm has cleared.

Sir Arthur Conan Doyle 'His Last Bow' (1915). Sherlock Holmes speaks on the eve of war, words written before the full enormity of the war had made itself felt.

JUDGEMENT AND PROPHECY

4 The official documents afford ample proofs that during the July crisis [of 1914] the emperor, the German military leaders and the foreign ministry were pressing Austria-Hungary to strike against Serbia without delay, or alternatively agreed to the despatch of an ultimatum to Serbia couched in such sharp terms as to make war between the two countries more than probable, and that in doing so they deliberately took the risk of a continental war against Russia and France.

Fritz Fischer *Germany's Aims in the First World War* (1961) Ch.2. Fischer's thesis of a planned German 'lunge for world power' was decidedly unpopular in Germany when his book was published.

5 Nowhere was there conscious determination to provoke a war. Statesmen miscalculated. They used the instruments of bluff and threat which had proved effective on previous occasions. This time things went wrong. The deterrent on which they relied failed to deter; the statesmen became the prisoners of their own weapons. The great armies, accumulated to provide security and preserve peace, carried the nations to war by their own weight.

A.J.P. Taylor *The First World War* (1963) Ch.1. War by accident, rather than by design, as Fischer claimed.

6 Prussia-Germany can no longer fight any war but a world war; and a war of hitherto unknown dimensions and ferocity. Eight to ten million soldiers will swallow each other up and in doing so eat all Europe more bare than any swarm of locusts. The devastation of the Thirty Years War compressed into the space of three or four years and extending over the whole continent; famine, sickness, want, brutalizing the army and the mass of the population; irrevocable confusion of our artificial structure of trade, industry and credit, ending in general bankruptcy; collapse of the old states and their traditional statecraft, so that crowns will roll by dozens in the gutter and no one be found to pick them up. It is absolutely impossible to predict where it will end and who will emerge from the struggle as victor. Only *one* result is absolutely certain: general exhaustion and the establishment of conditions for the final victory of the working class.

Friedrich Engels, 1887; James Joll *The Second International* (1974) p.107. Words written when the death of the old Kaiser Wilhelm I was imminent. Engels feared that it would plunge Europe into general war, but his nightmare scenario did not materialize until 1914.

World War I, 1914–18

1914: FIRST BLOOD

1   Never such innocence,
     Never before or since,
     As changed itself to part
     Without a word – the men
     Leaving the gardens tidy,
     The thousands of marriages
     Lasting a little while longer:
     Never such innocence again.

Philip Larkin 'MCMXIV' (1964) last stanza.

2 The plunge of civilization into this abyss of blood
and darkness ... is a thing that so gives away the
whole long age during which we have supposed the
world to be with whatever abatement, gradually
bettering, that to have to take it all now for what the
treacherous years were all the while really making
for and *meaning* is too tragic for any words.

Henry James, 5 Aug. 1914; *The Letters of Henry James* Vol.2
(1920) p.384. The American writer, who had lived in England
since 1869, was intensely pro-British and became a British
citizen before he died in 1916.

3 The world of peace which has now collapsed with
such shattering thunder – did we not all of us have
enough of it? Was it not foul in all its comfort? Did
it not fester and stink with the decomposition of
civilization? Morally and psychologically I felt the
necessity of this catastrophe and that feeling of
cleansing, of elevation and liberation which filled
me, when what one had thought impossible really
happened.

The German writer Thomas Mann, 1914; George Clare *Last
Waltz in Vienna* (1982 edn) p.56.

4 I understand what Christ suffered in Gethsemane
as well as any man living.

Keir Hardie, 6 Aug. 1914; Ian McLean *Keir Hardie* (1975). The
socialist Hardie opposed Britain's entry into the war on 4 Aug.
and was howled down by a hostile mob at a meeting in
Aberdare. (For Christ's agony in the Garden of Gethsemane
on the eve of his execution see Matthew 26:36–75.)

5 And behind the diplomatists, dimly heard in the
official documents, stand vast forces of national
greed and national hatred – atavistic instincts, harmful to mankind at its present level, but transmitted
from savage and half-animal ancestors, concentrated and directed by governments and the press,
fostered by the upper class as a distraction from
social discontent, artificially nourished by the
sinister influence of the makers of armaments,
encouraged by a whole foul literature of 'glory', and
by every textbook of history with which the minds of
children are polluted.

Bertrand Russell, letter to *The Nation*, 15 Aug. 1914.

6 YOUR COUNTRY NEEDS YOU

Slogan on recruiting poster, designed by Alfred Leete, 1914,
featuring Field Marshal Lord Kitchener, British secretary of
state for war, glowering at potential cannon-fodder.

7 If not a great soldier, he is at least a great poster.

Margot Asquith, wife of the prime minister, Herbert Asquith,
1914; *More Memories* (1933) Ch.6.

8 Your duty cannot be done unless your health is
sound. So keep constantly on your guard against any
excesses. In this new experience you may find
temptations in both wine and women. You must
entirely resist both temptations, and, while treating
all women with perfect courtesy, you should avoid
any intimacy.

Lord Kitchener, message to the soldiers of the British
Expeditionary Force (BEF) embarking for action in France;
published in *The Times*, 19 Aug. 1914.

9   Mademoiselle from Armenteers, parley-voo.
     Mademoiselle from Armenteers, parley-voo.
     Mademoiselle from Armenteers,
     Hasn't been kissed for forty years,
     Inky, pinky, parley-voo.

Edward C. Rowland, song, attrib. The town of Armentières,
in northeast France, just inside the frontier with Belgium, was
used by the British army for rest and recreation. It is not
difficult to imagine the troops' adaptation of this verse.

10   On Sunday I walk out with a soldier
     On Monday I'm taken by a tar.
     On Tuesday I'm out
     With a baby Boy Scout,
     On Wednesday an Hussar.

Arthur Wimperis and Herman Finck (1914). The recruiting
song was performed in music-halls by popular songstresses all
over the country.

1 We don't want to lose you.
But we think you ought to go.
Paul Rubens 'Your King and Country Want You' (1914).

2 DADDY, WHAT DID *YOU* DO IN THE GREAT WAR?
Recruiting poster, showing a pensive father who had avoided military service being asked an unanswerable question by his small daughter.

3 If the British empire resolves to fight the battle cleanly, to look upon it as something more than an ordinary war, we shall one day realize that it has not been in vain, and we, the British empire, as the chosen leaders of the world, shall travel along the road of human destiny and progress, at the end of which we shall see the patient figure of the Prince of Peace pointing the star of Bethlehem which leads us on to God.
Horatio Bottomley, recruiting speech, 14 Sept. 1914; Alan Hyman *The Rise and Fall of Horatio Bottomley* (1972) Ch.12. The odious Bottomley had a good war as 'England's recruiting sergeant'.

4 I find war detestable, but even more detestable are those who praise war without participating in it.
The French writer Romain Rolland 'Inter Arma Caritas' in *Journal de Genève*, Sept. 1914.

5 Eighteen, by Jove! You've timed your lives wonderfully, my boys. To be eighteen in 1914 is to be the best thing in England … Eighteen years ago you were born for this day. Through the last eighteen years you've been educated for it. Your birth and breeding were given you that you might officer England's youth in this hour.
Ernest Raymond *Tell England* (1922); Peter Parker *The Old Lie* (1987) Ch.10.

6 They shall grow not old, as we that are left grow old:
Age shall not weary them, nor the years condemn.
At the going down of the sun and in the morning
We will remember them.
Laurence Binyon 'For the Fallen' (1914). Written, surprisingly, not after the huge slaughter on the Western Front but before it began.

7 The United States must be neutral in fact as well as in name … We must be impartial in thought as well as in action.

President Woodrow Wilson, message to the Senate, 18 Aug. 1914; *The Papers of Woodrow Wilson* Vol.30 (1979) p.394. The United States stayed out of the war as long as it seemed that Germany could not win it, but neutrality was easier said than done.

8 It is my Imperial and Royal Command that you should concentrate your energies for the immediate present upon one single purpose, that is, that you address all your skill and all the valour of my soldiers to exterminate first the treacherous English [and] walk over General French's contemptible little army.
Kaiser Wilhelm II, on the British Expeditionary Force (BEF), 19 Aug. 1914; Nigel Rees *Sayings of the Century* (1984) p.30, where it is said that the order was a British forgery, probably the work of General Sir Frederick Maurice and published in BEF Routine Orders for 24 Sept. 1914. It was on the strength of this alleged comment that the survivors of the BEF called themselves the Old Contemptibles. General Sir John French was commander of the BEF.

9 You will be home before the leaves have fallen from the trees.
Kaiser Wilhelm II to troops leaving for the front, Aug. 1914; Barbara Tuchman *The Guns of August* (1962) Ch.9.

10 I have misunderstood this Kaiser, I have thought him a waverer. He is a Jupiter, standing on the Olympus of his iron-studded might, the lightning-bolts in his grasp. At this moment he is God and master of the world.
Graf Hans von Pfeil, 25 Aug. 1914; John Röhl *The Kaiser and his Court* (1994) p.9. By the end of the war, opinion had changed (see 721:10).

11 Behind all this rose a tall chimney. It seemed a symbol of the gigantic area of German economic life … This area, full of thundering trains, of smoking chimneys, of blazing furnaces, of whizzing looms, an immeasurable domain of industrial life, spread itself before my thought. To us had been given the task of taking in our hands the whole of this agitated world, of making it serviceable for the purposes of war, of forcing upon it our uniform rule, and of awakening its titanic strength to the needs of our defence.
Walter Rathenau, Aug. 1914; Albrecht Mendelssohn Bartholdy *The War and German Society* (1937) Ch.13. Rathenau was director of the German war economy, assassinated as a Jew by right-wing elements in 1922 despite his enormous contribution to the war effort in gearing the resources of German heavy industry behind the armed forces.

12 If a way was found of entirely wiping out the whole of London it would be more humane to

employ it than to allow the blood of A SINGLE GERMAN SOLDIER to be shed on the battlefield.
Matthias Erzberger, German Catholic politician, *Der Tag* (The Day), 21 Oct. 1914.

1 One will probably have to count on a very increased sense of power on the part of the workers and labour unions, which will also find expression in increased demands on the employers and for legislation. It would therefore be advisable, in order to avoid internal difficulties, to distract the attention of the people and to give phantasies concerning the extension of German territory room to play.
Alfred Hugenberg, 7 Nov. 1914; Gerald Feldman *Army, Industry and Labor in Germany 1914–1918* (1966) p.136. Base ingratitude from the head of the ultra-conservative German National People's Party towards the Marxist Social Democrats, who had supported Germany's entry into the war instead of opposing it, as all good Marxists were supposed to do.

2 We have but one, one only hate.
We love as one, we hate as one.
We have one foe and one alone:
England!
Ernst Lissauer *Hassgesang gegen England* (The Hymn of Hate) (1914). Lissauer was declared unfit for military service in 1914 but nevertheless made his own personal contribution in this Anglophobic anthem.

3 There is being circulated everywhere a story that an immense force of Russian soldiers – little short of a million, it is said – have passed, or are still passing, through England on their way to France … It is said in confirmation that belated wayfarers at railway stations throughout the country saw long train after long train running through with blinds drawn, but still allowing glimpses of carriages packed with fierce-looking bearded fellows in fur hats.
Michael MacDonagh of *The Times*, 8 Sept. 1914; *In London during the Great War* (1935) pp.21–2. A vivid tribute to wishful thinking, the only missing detail being that the Russians 'had snow on their boots'. The Russian army, in fact, had its hands more than full holding the massive German offensive on the Eastern Front after a big defeat at Tannenberg late in Aug.

4 The angel of the Lord on the traditional white horse and clad all in white with flaming sword, faced the advancing Germans at Mons and forbade their further progress.
Brigadier John Charteris, letter, 5 Sept. 1914; *At G.H.Q.* (1931) pp.25–6. In the retreat from the Belgian city of Mons British troops claimed to have seen an angel in the sky. The Angel of Mons was just one of the legends generated in minds dazed with battle-weariness.

5 My centre is giving way, my right wing falling back. Situation excellent. I am going over to the attack.
General Ferdinand Foch, 8 Sept. 1914; Basil Liddell Hart *Foch: Man of Orleans* (1931) Ch.9. Words purportedly spoken during the First Battle of the Marne, as British and French forces repelled the Germans in an engagement dangerously close to Paris.

6 *Aux gares, citoyens!*
Montez dans les wagons!
(To the stations, citizens!/Get on board the trains!)
Parisian parody of 'La Marseillaise', improvised during the panic of the First Battle of the Marne, as the German army closed in on the French capital.

7 My friend, we shall not have time to make them. I shall tear up the Boches [Germans] within two months.
Fatuous optimism from the French general, Joseph Joffre, Nov. 1914, rejecting the notion that his troops needed steel helmets. French soldiers had gone to war without them and paid a high price for it.

8 *Union Sacrée* (Sacred Union)
French prime minister René Viviani, 22 Dec. 1914. National unity was the rallying cry of all the belligerents as the first shock of war hit them. It was to come under increasing strain the longer no end seemed to be in sight.

9 We shall never sheathe the sword, which we have not lightly drawn, until Belgium receives in full measure all and more that she has sacrificed, until France is adequately secured against the menace of aggression, until the rights of smaller nationalities of Europe are placed upon an unassailable foundation, and until the military might of Prussia is wholly and finally destroyed.
Prime minister Herbert Asquith, Nov. 1914; *Speeches of the Earl of Oxford and Asquith* (1927) p.224. The first statement of British war aims, making it clear to Germany that it was going to be a long war. Germany's breach of Belgian neutrality was the technical reason for Britain going to war.

10 Whatever feats of arms the German Navy may hereafter perform, the stigma of the baby-killers of Scarborough will brand its officers and men while sailors sail the seas.
Winston Churchill to the mayor of Scarborough, 20 Dec. 1914; Arthur Marder *From the Dreadnought to Scapa Flow* Vol.2 (1965) Ch.7. On 16 Dec. 1914 German battlecruisers bombarded the Hartlepools, Scarborough and Whitby to provoke a confrontation with the Royal Navy's Grand Fleet. Scarborough, with 18 dead, suffered much less than Hartlepool, where 118 people were killed, but because

Scarborough was an undefended harbour, the bombardment could be called an atrocity, and Churchill, as first lord of the Admiralty, took full advantage of the propaganda possibilities.

1 We who strike the enemy where his heart beats have been slandered as 'baby-killers' and 'murderers of women' … What we do is repugnant to us too, but necessary. Very necessary. Nowadays there is no such animal as a noncombatant: modern warfare is total warfare. A soldier cannot function at the front without the factory worker, the farmer, and all the other providers behind them … My men are brave and honourable. Their cause is holy, so how can they sin while doing their duty? If what we do is frightful, then may frightfulness be Germany's salvation.
Captain Peter Strasser, 1915; Aaron Norman *The Great Air War* (1968). Strasser commanded the German navy's airship programme.

2 Though you might not believe it, we had a truce for the day just along our bit of the line. Somehow or other we arranged with the Germans opposite to stop fighting till midnight on Christmas night; all Christmas we were walking about outside in front of our trenches. The Germans came out of theirs and we met halfway and talked and exchanged souvenirs, our own bullets for theirs.
Private Warwick Squire, early Jan. 1915; Malcolm Brown *The Imperial War Museum Book of the First World War* (1991) Pt 2. By the autumn of 1914 the war on the Western Front had become bogged down into trench warfare along a line stretching from the North Sea down to Switzerland. This truce was a brief respite from the carnage that accompanied this deadlock until the spring of 1918.

1915: STALEMATE AND SIDESHOW

3 [This war] disregards all the restrictions known as International Law, which in peacetime the states had bound themselves to observe; it ignores the pre-rogatives of the wounded and the medical service, the distinction between civil and military sections of the population, the claims of private property. It tramples in blind fury on all that comes in its way, as though there were to be no future and no peace among men after it is over.
The eminent Austrian psychiatrist Sigmund Freud 'Thoughts for the Times on War and Death', spring 1915; *Standard Edition of the Complete Psychological Works of Sigmund Freud* Vol.14 (1957).

4   Now God be thanked who has matched us with His hour,
    And caught our youth and wakened us from sleeping.
Rupert Brooke 'Peace' (1915). Brooke wrote this and the following two poems at the beginning of 1915 before embarking for service in the Mediterranean, where he died in April 1915.

5   If I should die, think only this of me:
    That there's some corner of a foreign field
    That is for ever England.
Rupert Brooke 'The Soldier' (1915).

6   Blow out, you bugles, over the rich Dead!
    There's none of these so lonely and poor of old,
    But dying, has made us rarer gifts than gold.
    These laid the world away; poured out the red
    Sweet wine of youth; gave up the years to be
    Of work and joy, and that unhoped serene
    That men call age; and those who would have been,
    Their sons they gave, their immortality.
Rupert Brooke 'The Dead' (1915).

7 As for the workmen who are said to get drunk now … Take and shoot two or three of them, and the 'drink habit' would cease, I feel sure … These sub-people don't care what the king or anyone else does – they mean to have their drink.
General Sir Douglas Haig to his wife, 10 May 1915; Robert Blake (ed.) *The Private Papers of Sir Douglas Haig 1914–1919*. Haig commanded the First Corps of the BEF and in Dec. 1915 became commander-in-chief of British forces in France. Drunkenness was indeed a problem, but the government tackled it in a less drastic way, by introducing licensing hours in public houses, an innovation that survived the war.

8 Mother and I declared support of our country. She declared that the military situation imperatively required the admission of women to munition factories … to liberate men for the front … Mr Lloyd George only too gladly said yes.
Christabel Pankhurst *Unshackled* (1959 edn) Ch.17. Mrs Pankhurst, pre-war champion of women's rights, rallied round the flag as soon as the war broke out, and women took up all kinds of jobs on the home front. Their reward (if they were over the age of 30) was the vote when the war ended. Lloyd George was minister of munitions in Asquith's coalition government.

9 Sometimes the trains were packed, so of course the porters knew that we were all munition kids, and they'd say, 'Go on, girl, hop in there,' and they would open first-class carriages. And there'd be officers sitting there and some of them used to look at us as if we were insects. And others used to mutter, 'Well, they're doing their bit.'

Caroline Rennies, munitions worker; Brown (1991) Pt 6.

1 Sir,

I am afraid that the theory of using 4-bores against Zeppelins will not hold water. Catch those white-livered curs, the Huns, descending to 2,000 or 3,000 feet! Nine thousand feet is about the lowest they ever come, and when picked out by searchlights they rise to 12,000 feet and over.

W.H. Bradish, letter to *The Shooting Times*, 1915; James Irvine Robertson (ed.) *Random Shots* (1990) p.138.

2 Our whole duty, for the present, at any rate, is summed up in the motto, 'America First'. Let us think of America before we think of Europe, in order that America may be fit to be Europe's friend when the day of tested friendship comes.

President Woodrow Wilson, 20 April 1915; *The Papers of Woodrow Wilson* Vol.33 (1980) p.38.

3 American Citizens:

UPHOLD THE HANDS OF THE PRESIDENT in his noble efforts to PRESERVE PEACE by urging that Congress empower him to STOP THE EXPORTATION OF ARMS AND AMMUNITION from the United States to Europe.

Poster of the Organization of American Women for Strict Neutrality; Lloyd C. Gardner *Imperial America* (1976) p.83. Britain and France came to rely heavily on imports of armaments from the United States, and US arms manufacturers prospered accordingly. When the Atlantic liner *Lusitania* was sunk by a German submarine on 7 May 1915, with considerable loss of American life, it was carrying a consignment of weapons for Britain. These were said by some to have been loaded deliberately in order to provoke the sinking and bring the USA into the war against Germany, precisely what American neutralists feared. The export of arms in US vessels was not banned until the passage of the Neutrality Acts of 1935–7 (see 823:1).

4 There is such a thing as a man being too proud to fight.

President Woodrow Wilson, 10 May 1915; *The Papers of Woodrow Wilson* Vol.33 (1980) p.149. Wilson was speaking soon after the sinking of the *Lusitania*. The incident came close to drawing the United States into the war in Europe, but Wilson was preoccupied by a simultaneous crisis with Japan over its expansionism in China (see 792:3) and could not afford a war on two fronts. Moreover, the European war had not yet reached the point where a German victory seemed

possible, and Wilson decided to remain neutral in the hope of Allied success.

5   Take up our quarrel with the foe:
        To you from failing hands we throw
        The torch; be yours to hold it high.
        If ye break faith with us who die
        We shall not sleep, though poppies grow
        In Flanders fields.

John McCrae 'In Flanders Fields' (May 1915). McCrae was a Canadian doctor, and this last stanza of his famous poem was an appeal to the United States to come into the war. The call went unheeded.

6 The war seems to be resolving itself largely into a question of killing Germans … If then two millions … more of Germans have to be killed, at least a corresponding number of Allied soldiers will have to be sacrificed to effect that object … I am anxious that we should realize the probable dimensions and provide for [them] before it is too late.

Cabinet minister Lord Curzon, 21 June 1915; R.J.Q. Adams and P.P. Poirier *The Conscription Controversy in Great Britain, 1904–1918* (1987) Ch.6. The British army was an entirely volunteer force, whereas the Continental armies were largely conscripted. Conscription in Britain was introduced in 1916, first for unmarried men and then for married men.

7 The effects of the successful gas attack were horrible. I am not pleased with the idea of poisoning men. Of course, the entire world will rage about it first and then imitate us. All the dead lie on their backs, with clenched fists; the whole field is yellow.

German cavalry officer Rudolf Binding, 24 April 1915; Guy Chapman (ed.) *Vain Glory* (1968) p.147. The first use of poison gas on the Western Front – in this case, mustard gas – took a dreadful toll.

8   If you could hear, at every jolt, the blood
        Come gargling from the froth-corrupted lungs,
        My friend, you would not tell with such high
            zest
        To children ardent for some desperate glory,
        The old Lie: Dulce et decorum est
        Pro patria mori.

Wilfred Owen 'Dulce et decorum est' (1917), poem written after a gas attack. See 77:3.

9   Well, as to that, the nastiest job I've had
        Was last year on this very front
        Taking the discs at night from men
        Who'd hung for six months on the wire
        Just over there.

The worst of all was
They fell to pieces at a touch.
Thank God we couldn't see their faces;
They had their gas masks on.
Richard Aldington 'Trench Idyll'.

1 *Ludendorff*: The English soldiers fight like lions.
   Hoffman: True. But don't we know that they are lions led by donkeys.
Alan Clark *The Donkeys* (1961). This exchange may have been a fabrication by Clark, and its authenticity was disputed soon after his book was published. Francisque Sarcey has the sentence *Vous êtes des lions conduits par des ânes!* (*Le Siège de Paris* (1871) p.57), but the phrase that gave Clark his book title does not appear in the memoirs of General Erich von Falkenhayn, where Clark claimed it came from.

2 They were never in better heart, and are longing for a fight. With the enthusiasm of ignorance they will tear their way through the German line.
General Sir Douglas Haig, diary entry, 12 Sept. 1915; David Milsted *Chronicle of the 20th Century in Quotations* (1996) p.18.

3   God heard the embattled nations sing and
        shout
        'Gott strafe England!' and 'God save the King!'
        God this, God that, and God the other thing.
        'Good God,' said God, 'I've got my work cut
        out!'
British writer J.C. Squire, 1914.

4 Well, if you knows of a better 'ole, go to it.
'Ol' Bill', the cartoon character of Bruce Bairnsfather, 1915. Men sheltered in shell-holes on the optimistic assumption that heavy artillery could not strike twice in the same place. 'Ol' Bill' was a British propaganda weapon aiming to show, no matter how implausibly, that the hell of the trenches had its funny side.

5 I realize that patriotism is not enough. I must have no hatred or bitterness towards anyone.
Edith Cavell, 11 Oct. 1915, the day before her execution; *The Times*, 23 Oct. 1915. Nurse Cavell, a British citizen, was shot by the Germans for aiding escapees from occupied Belgium. She became a national heroine, with a statue in central London and another close to Norwich Cathedral.

6 My God, all that these heroic soldiers want is to introduce Thy name to the French and English. Please accept this honourable desire of ours and make our bayonets sharper so that we may destroy our enemy! ... If God wills, the enemy will make a landing, and we will be taken [to the front], then the wedding ceremony will take place, won't it?

Turkish soldier Hasan Ethem to his mother, 17 April 1915; Tim Travers *Gallipoli 1915* (2001) p.229. On 25 April British and Anzac troops landed on the peninsula of Gallipoli between the Aegean Sea and the Sea of Marmara. The objective was Constantinople, in an attempt to open up a new front to knock Germany's ally, Turkey, out of the war. But the operation was a disaster and led to the evacuation of the survivors between 17 Dec. 1915 and 8 Jan. 1916.

7 There are poets and writers who see naught in war but carrion, filth, savagery and horror ... They refuse war the credit of being the only exercise in devotion on the large scale existing in this world. The superb moral victory over death leaves them cold. Each one to his taste. To me this is no valley of death – it is a valley brim full of life at its highest power.
General Sir Ian Hamilton, commander of the Anzac forces at Gallipoli, diary entry, 30 May 1915 (see 699:5).

8 Merely a lot of childish youths without strength to endure or brains to improve their conditions ... From what I saw of the Turk I am convinced he is ... a better man than those opposed to him ... Sedition is talked around every tin of bully beef on the peninsula ... I do not like to dictate this sentence, even for your eyes, but the fact is that after the first day at Suvla [one of the three invasion beaches] an order had to be issued to officers to shoot without mercy every soldier who lagged behind or loitered in an advance.
Australian journalist Keith Murdoch to the Australian prime minister, Aug. 1915; Alan Moorehead *Gallipoli* (1956) p.310. Murdoch (father of Rupert) visited the beachhead in 1915 and wrote a scathing report to the Australian premier, which was also passed on to the British prime minister, Asquith. It helped to bring about the eventual withdrawal.

9 My God, it would have been easier than I thought; we simply couldn't have failed ... and because we didn't try, another million lives were thrown away and the war went on for another three years.
Admiral Sir Roger Keyes, 1925, reflecting on the Royal Navy's failure to pass the Turkish forts in the prelude to the landing on 25 April 1915; Cecil Aspi nall-Oglander *Roger Keyes* (1951).

10 It is doubtful if even Great Britain could survive another world war and another Churchill.
Un-named US army staff officer's comment on Gallipoli, early 1920s; Moorehead (1956) Epilogue. The Gallipoli adventure was the brain-child of Winston Churchill, first lord of the Admiralty. It forced his resignation and dogged him for years to come.

1916: ATTRITION

1 The Germans will doubtless attack again. Let every man work and stay alert to achieve the same success as yesterday ... Courage! We will take them! (*On les aura!*)

General Philippe Pétain, during the Battle of Verdun, 16 April 1916. *On les aura!* became the inspiration for a famous French recruiting poster. The battle began on 21 Feb. and went on until mid-Dec. In the process, the French and German armies almost bled each other to death. Pétain was replaced by General Robert Nivelle three days after making this rousing summons.

2 We had to jump from corpse to corpse. If we stepped in the mud on either side, we'd get stuck. We had to use the dead face-down because if we stepped on their stomachs our feet would sink in. It was disgusting. It was terrible. We were surrounded by death.

Marcel Batreau, survivor of Verdun, interviewed for the BBC television programme *The People's Century* (1995).

3 *Ils ne passeront pas!* (They shall not pass!)

General Robert Nivelle, order of the day at Verdun, 23 June 1916; Alistair Horne *The Price of Glory: Verdun 1916* (1962) Ch.18. The words are often wrongly attributed to General Pétain.

4   Eyes full of uttermost sleep, the circlet of
        shadow around their brows, blue, waxen,
        decaying in the smoke of night
    Which sank down, threw shadows far, which
        spread its vault from hill to hill, over forest
        and rottenness, over brains full of dreams,
        over the hundred dead none carried away,
    Over the mass of fire, over laughter and
        madness, over crosses in fields, over pain
        and despair, over rubble and ash, over the
        river and the ruined town.

German writer Anton Schnack 'Nocturnal Landscape' (1920).

5 Breath of hope that seeps over the scorched fields, raging fever of impatience, of disappointment, of the most agonizing terror of death, insensate question: why? Why do they not make an end?

Erich Maria Remarque *Am Westfront, Nichts Neues* (All Quiet on the Western Front) (1929) pp.309–10. Germans, like British and French, were enduring, but desperate for a way out of their nightmare on the Western Front.

6 Chatfield, there seems to something wrong with our bloody ships today.

Admiral Sir David Beatty, 31 May 1916; Winston Churchill *The World Crisis* (1927) Ch.41. During the Battle of Jutland between the Royal Navy's Grand Fleet and the German High Seas Fleet the two British battlecruisers *Indefatigable* and *Queen Mary* blew up after receiving direct hits. They had been expected to survive enemy broadsides.

7 Jellicoe was the only man on either side who could lose the war in an afternoon.

Winston Churchill (1927) Pt 1, Ch.5. Admiral Sir John Jellicoe commanded the British Grand Fleet. If it had lost an engagement with the High Seas Fleet, the British Isles would have been open to a German seaborne invasion.

8 Providence is on the side of the British Empire after all.

Lord Northcliffe, 6 June 1916; A.J.P. Taylor *English History 1914–1945* (1965) p.58. The newspaper magnate Northcliffe was rejoicing at the news of the death of Lord Kitchener, drowned as he set out for Russia to urge greater efforts on the Eastern Front.

9 HE KEPT US OUT OF WAR!

Slogan coined after the speech by Governor Martin H. Glynn of New York nominating Woodrow Wilson as Democratic presidential candidate, 15 July 1916. Wilson was bidding for a second term, and there were no votes in interventionism.

10   I have a rendezvous with Death
        At some disputed barricade ...
        And I to my pledged word am true.
        I shall not fail that rendezvous.

Alan Seeger 'Rendezvous' in *Poems* (1917) p.144. A US citizen who did not keep out of the war, Seeger was killed on the Somme in 1916. The poem is thus a prophecy of his own death.

11 You will be able to go over the top with a walking stick, you will not need rifles. When you get to Thiepval you will find the Germans all dead, not even a rat will have survived.

Brigadier addressing the Newcastle Regiment, 1 July 1916; Milsted (1996) p.20. 1 July was the first day of the Battle of the Somme, designed to break through the German trench line, relieve the French at Verdun and end the deadlock on the Western Front. 'Over the top' meant over the trench parapet and into no man's land, advancing towards the enemy line.

12 At the first assault we over-ran the enemy's front line almost everywhere and in places are well within his territory.

The Times, 3 July 1916. Not so.

13 The first casualty when war comes is truth.

Senator Hiram Johnson, 1917; Philip Knightley *The First Casualty* (1982 edn) p.1.

1 They advanced in line after line, dressed as if on parade, and not a man shirked going through the extremely heavy barrage, or facing the machine-gun and rifle fire that finally wiped them out … Hardly a man of ours got to the German front line.
Brigadier Rees, commanding the 94th Infantry Brigade, July 1916; Tim Travers *The Killing Ground* (1987) p.158. Some 20,000 men died in the attack on 1 July 1916, the first day of the Battle of the Somme and the worst death-toll for a single day in the history of the British army.

2 See that little stream. We could walk to it in two minutes. It took the British a whole month to walk to it – a whole empire walking very slowly, dying in front and pushing forward behind. And another empire walked very slowly backwards a few inches a day, leaving the dead like a million bloody rugs.
F. Scott Fitzgerald *Tender is the Night* (1933) Bk 3, Ch.1. The main character, Dick Diver, visits a trench preserved at Beaumont-Hamel, close to Thiepval, on the Somme. Sir Edwin Lutyens's Memorial to the Missing of the Somme was built at Thiepval in 1927–32.

3 The Devonshires held this trench,
The Devonshires hold it still.
Plaque in the tiny Devonshire Cemetery at Mametz on the Somme, 4 miles east of Albert. The cemetery holds 163 men of the 8th and 9th battalions of the Devonshire Regiment, all of whom died in attacks on the first day of the Battle of the Somme. A mass grave was fashioned out of the support line trench from which the Devonshires went over the top.

4 War is a misfortune, but it is even more unfortunate that we must place it in the hands of the military.
French premier Aristide Briand, Aug. 1916; John Terraine *The Smoke and the Fire* (1980) p.63.

5 The word 'peace' is a sacrilege.
Aristide Briand, Sept. 1916; David Lloyd George *The War Memoirs of David Lloyd George* Vol.2 (1933) Ch.31.

6 They were enormously cheered by a new weapon which was to be tried with them for the first time … I have heard that one name for them is the 'Hush-Hush'. But their real name is Tanks … Yesterday the troops got out of their trenches laughing and shouting and cheering again because the Tanks had gone on ahead and were scaring the Germans dreadfully.
Philip Gibbs, *Daily Chronicle*, 18 Sept. 1916; Martin J. Farrar *News from the Front* (1999 edn) pp.131–2. Another piece of journalistic propaganda: tanks were not the miracle weapon here portrayed and a breakthrough remained elusive.

7 The Somme offensive had been a bloody and disastrous failure; he was not willing to remain in office, if it was to be repeated next year.
David Lloyd George, 1 Nov. 1916; as recorded by Sir Maurice Hankey in *The Supreme Command 1914–1918* Vol.2 (1961) p.556. Lloyd George was soon to be prime minister, when he ousted Asquith on 7 Dec. Hankey was soon to be secretary of his war cabinet. Lloyd George did *not* resign in 1917, when still more disastrous offensives were mounted on the Western Front.

8 We are surely but surely killing off the best of the male population of these islands … To many of us it seems as if the prospect of a 'knock-out' was, to say the least of it, remote … Can we afford to go on paying the same sort of price for the same sort of gains?
Lord Lansdowne, memorandum, 13 Nov. 1916; quoted in full in Lloyd George (1933) pp.862–72. Lansdowne's call for a negotiated peace got nowhere.

9 I have not seen any dead. I have done worse. In the dank air I have *perceived* it, and in the darkness, *felt* it … No Man's Land under snow is like the face of the moon: chaotic, crater-ridden, uninhabitable, awful, the abode of madness.
Wilfred Owen to his sister, 19 Jan. 1917, on the winter landscape of the Somme in the aftermath of the long, inconclusive battle; John Bell (ed.) *Wilfred Owen: Selected Letters* (1985) p.215.

10 So long as you have capitalism you will have war … If [our masters] want to fight, let the kings, emperors, presidents, tsars, financiers and manufacturers, let them fight it out among themselves. The workers have no cause to quarrel, the workers of all countries are brothers … They have one enemy only, that enemy is the parasite, scoundrelly capitalist gang who use them to further their own base and dishonourable ends.
Speaker in Finsbury Park, London, voicing the classic Marxist view of war. The internationalist solidarity of socialism, abandoned at the outbreak of war, was now resurfacing as the cost of fighting grew insupportable.

SONGS OF WAR

11 It's a long way to Tipperary,
It's a long way to go.
It's a long way to Tipperary
To the sweetest girl I know.
Goodbye, Piccadilly!

Farewell, Leicester Square!
It's a long, long way to Tipperary,
But my heart's right there!

Written before the war by Jack Judge, this became the marching song of the British army after it was made a popular hit by the music-hall artiste Florrie Forde in Christmas pantomime, 1914.

1   We are Fred Karno's army,
     The ragtime infantry;
     We cannot fight, we cannot shoot,
     What bloody good are we?

Song sung to the tune of the hymn 'The Church's one foundation/Is Jesus Christ Our Lord'. Fred Karno was a leading music-hall entertainer of the day, heading a troupe that specialized in organized chaos on the stage. Ragtime was the syncopated popular music coming out of black America and highly fashionable at the time of World War I.

2   Keep the home fires burning while your hearts
         are yearning.
     Though your lads are far away, they dream of
         home.
     There's silver lining through the dark cloud
         shining.
     Turn the dark cloud inside out, till the boys
         come home.

1914 song, music by Ivor Novello, who is also sometimes credited with the first line of the lyric, otherwise the work of the American Lena Guilbert Ford.

3   Pack up your troubles in your old kit bag
     And smile, smile, smile!
     While you've a lucifer to light your fag,
     Smile, boys, that's the style.
     What's the use of worrying?
     It never was worth while.
     So, pack up your troubles in your old kit bag
     And smile, smile, smile.

George Asaff 'Pack up your troubles in your old kit bag' (1915); music by Felix Powell.

4   Goodbyee, goodbyee.
     Wipe the tear, baby dear, from your eye-ee.
     Though it's hard to part, I know,
     I'll be tickled to death to go.

R.P. Weston and Bert Lee 'Good-by-ee' (1917).

5   Take me back to dear old Blighty,
     Put me on the train to London Town.

A.J. Mills, Fred Godfrey and Bennett Scott 'Take me back to dear old Blighty' (1916). Blighty was a corruption of the Hindi word for England; hence 'a Blighty one', a wound, sometimes self-inflicted, that could get a soldier sent home.

6   Oh the moon shines bright on Charlie Chaplin.
     His boots are crackin'
     For want of blackin'.
     And his poor pantaloons they need a-mendin'
     Before they send him
     To the Dardanelles.

Anon.

7   The bells of Hell go ting-a-ling-a-ling
     For you, but not for me.
     O Death, where is thy sting-a-ling-a-ling,
     Where, grave, thy victory?

Anon.

8   *Ah, Dieu! que la guerre est jolie.*
     Avec ses chants, ses longs loisirs.

(Ah God! What a pretty thing is war./With its songs, its long hours of leisure.)

Guillaume Apollinaire 'L'Adieu du cavalier' (The Cavalryman's Farewell) in *Calligrammes* (1918).

9   Oh, oh, oh, it's a lovely war!
     What do we want with eggs and ham,
     When we've got plum and apple jam?
     Form fours, right turn!
     How shall we spend the money we earn?
     Oh, oh, oh, it's a lovely war!

Title song of the musical *Oh, What a Lovely War!* devised by Joan Littlewood and Charles Chilton, which was first staged at the Theatre Royal, Stratford, and directed by Littlewood in March 1963.

10   When this lousy war is over,
     No more soldiering for me.
     When I get my civvy clothes on,
     Oh, how happy I shall be!
     No more church parades on Sunday,
     No more putting in for leave.
     I shall kiss the sergeant-major.
     How I'll miss him, how he'll grieve!

Song from *Oh, What a Lovely War!*, sung to the tune of the hymn 'What a friend we have in Jesus'.

1917: IN THE BALANCE

11 We intend to begin unrestricted submarine warfare from the first of February ... Nevertheless an attempt will be made to keep the United States neutral. In the event that this should not succeed we shall offer Mexico an alliance ... Please point out to [Mexico] that the ruthless employment of our

U-boats opens up the prospect of England being compelled to make peace within a few months.

Zimmermann Telegram from the German foreign ministry to the German ambassador in Mexico, 16 Jan. 1917; from the full text quoted in Barbara Tuchman *The Zimmermann Telegram* (1958) pp.201–2. Because the Royal Navy controlled the surface of the Atlantic, the German navy relied on its submarines to intercept supplies reaching Britain from the neutral United States. Up to this point German U-boats had not launched a full-scale offensive against US shipping, but now the decision was taken to do so, even though the move would almost certainly bring the USA into the war. This was a calculated risk: Germany believed it could win before the full power of the USA could be brought to bear. The German involvement of Mexico was like a red rag to the American bull, since the USA had been severely at odds with Mexico since the Mexican revolution of 1910 (see 618:12). When British intelligence decoded the telegram and disclosed it to Washington, the effect was explosive.

1 It must be a peace without victory ... Only a peace between equals can last ... I am proposing, as it were, that the nations should with one accord adopt the doctrine of President Monroe as the doctrine of the world: that no nation should seek to extend its polity over any other nation or people, but that every nation should be left free to determine its own policy, its own way of development, unhindered, unthreatened, unafraid, the little along with the great and the powerful.

President Woodrow Wilson, address to the Senate, 22 Jan. 1917; *The Papers of Woodrow Wilson* Vol.40 (1982) p.539. Wilson hoped that, unlike the American Civil War, the war would be ended by a compromise treaty. The reference to the Monroe Doctrine of 1823 is intriguing. Whatever its original purpose, this had become a prescription for US hegemony over the republics of Latin America (see 797:2). Did Wilson intend a similar hegemony over the world at large?

2 The Allies must not be beaten. It would mean the triumph of Autocracy over Democracy; the shattering of all our moral standards; and a real, though it may seem remote, peril to our independence and our institutions.

US secretary of state Robert Lansing, 28 Jan. 1917; Daniel M. Smith *Lansing and American Neutrality 1914–1917* (1958) p.154. Lansing was strongly Anglophile, all the more so after seeing the decrypt of the Zimmermann Telegram. Here he reveals the basic reason for US entry into the war: to secure a victory over Germany that Britain, France and Russia were no longer capable of achieving.

3 Once lead this people into war, and they'll forget there ever was such a thing as tolerance. To fight you must be brutal and ruthless, and the spirit of ruthless brutality will enter into the very fiber of our national life, infecting Congress, the courts, the policeman on the beat, the man on the street ... If there is any alternative, for God's sake, let's take it.

President Woodrow Wilson, 1 April 1917; Arthur Link *Woodrow Wilson and the Progressive Era* (1954) Ch.10. This was Wilson on the eve of America's entry into the war, as reported by the journalist Frank Cobb, but there is a suspicion that Cobb published what he wanted Wilson to say, not what he actually said. (See the article by Jerold S. Auerbach in *Journal of American History* Vol.54 (1968) pp.608–17.)

4 Our object ... is to vindicate the principles of peace and justice in the life of the world as against selfish and autocratic power and to set up amongst the really free and self-governed peoples of the world such a concert of purpose and action as will henceforth ensure the observance of those principles ... The world must be made safe for democracy. Its peace must be planted upon the tested foundations of political liberty ... It is a fearful thing to lead this great peaceful people into war, into the most terrible and disastrous of all wars, civilization itself seeming to be in the balance. But the right is more precious than peace, and we shall fight for the things which we have always carried nearest to our hearts.

President Woodrow Wilson, message to Congress calling for a declaration of war on Germany, 2 April 1917; *The Papers of Woodrow Wilson* Vol.41 (1983) pp.526–7.

5 America has at one bound become a world power.

David Lloyd George, 6 April 1917; Milsted (1996) p.23.

6 The Americans came in to pick up the dead men's caps.

Popular British saying, passed on to JM by his grandmother, whose son was killed in March 1918.

7 The whole perspective is changed today by the revolution in Russia and the intervention of America. The scale of values is transformed, for the democracies are unloosed.

American commentator Walter Lippmann, late April 1917; Ronald Steel *Walter Lippmann and the American Century* (1980) p.113.

8 Please God, let there be victory before the Americans arrive.

General Sir Douglas Haig, diary entry, 1917.

9   Over there! Over there!
    Send the word, send the word over there,
    That the Yanks are coming,
    The Yanks are coming ...

We'll be over, we're coming over,
And we won't come back
Till it's over over there.
George M. Cohan 'Over there!' (1917)

1 Lafayette, we are here!
Colonel Charles E. Stanton, 4 July 1917; Henry F. Woods *American Sayings* (1945). Stanton was speaking at the tomb of the Marquis de Lafayette in Paris, in tribute to the man who had fought alongside the Americans in the War of Independence (see 511:3).

2 All along the French lines the troops are tired and discontented. There were unpleasant signs of disintegration, and the patriotic officers fear decomposition of the armies as a result of German propaganda, war-weariness, inaction and weak administration ... After all the sacrifices made and the glory achieved it would be a sad ending if the Russian example was followed in France.
Lord Esher to Lord Derby, 26 June 1917; John Terraine *The Road to Passchendaele* (1977) Ch.3. The French spring offensive led by General Nivelle had rapidly come to grief, and several French regiments were on the verge of mutiny. The reference to Russia is to the Revolution of March, which had deposed the tsar and which had gravely undermined the fighting capacity of the Russian army (see 724:10).

3 *Adieu la vie,*
Adieu l'amour,
Adieu à toutes les femmes.
C'est bien fini,
C'est pour toujours,
De cette guerre infâme.
C'est à Craonne,
Sur le plateau,
Qu'ils ont laissé leur peau:
Car ils sont tous condamnés,
Ce sont les sacrifiés.
(Farewell to life,/Farewell to love,/Farewell to women all./It's come to the end,/It's for ever,/All through this cursèd war./It was at Craonne,/On the plateau,/Where they left their hides:/For they are all condemned men,/They are the sacrificial lambs.)
Anon. 'The Song of Craonne' (1917). The disastrous French spring offensive took place on the plateau of Craonne, midway between Rheims and Laon.

4 'Good morning! Good morning!' the General said
  When we met him last week on the way to the Line.
  Now the soldiers he smiled at are most of 'em dead,

And we're cursing his staff for incompetent swine.
  'He's a cheery old card,' grunted Harry to Jack
  As they slogged up to Arras with rifle and pack.
      . . . .
  But he did for them both by his plan of attack.
Siegfried Sassoon 'The General' (1917). The British spring offensive took the name of the Battle of Arras (April–May 1917).

5 One of our men was unfortunate enough to step out of line and fell into one of these mud-holes ... We ... managed to loop [a rope] securely under his armpits ... but it was useless. The poor fellow now knew he was beyond all aid and begged me to shoot him rather than leave him to die a miserable death by suffocation ... I am not afraid to say therefore that I shot this man at his own urgent request.
Private soldier; Bryan Cooper *The Ironclads of Cambrai* (1967). The Third Battle of Ypres, otherwise known as Passchendaele, began on 31 July and went on until Nov. The artillery barrage prefacing it destroyed the drainage system of the battlefield and turned it into a deadly swamp.

6 I died in Hell
  (They called it Passchendaele).
Siegfried Sassoon 'Memorial Tablet (Great War)' (1917).

7 What passing-bells for these who die as cattle?
  – Only the monstrous anger of the guns.
  Only the stuttering rifles' rapid rattle
  Can patter out their hasty orisons.
Wilfred Owen 'Anthem for Doomed Youth' (1917).

8 *Morire non basta.* (It is not enough to die.)
The Italian poet-patriot Gabriele D'Annunzio, late 1917; quoted in the novel by Ernest Hemingway *Across the River and Into the Trees* (1950) Ch.6. Hemingway, who served on the Italian front, recalls a florid harangue by D'Annunzio before an assembly of bemused Italian troops hard put to understand what he was talking about. Presumably the great man wanted them to die with style. Hemingway incorrectly renders the injunction as *Morire non a basta.*

9 Twelve volunteers were called for to carry picks and shovels ... but once on parade they realized that their job was to shoot poor 'A'. On his being brought out he broke away from the sergeant of the guard, and the firing party fired at him on the run, wounding him in the shoulder. They brought him back on a stretcher and the sergeant of the guard was ordered ... to finish him off as he lay wounded.

Anon. soldier, undated; William Moore *The Thin Yellow Line* (1974) Ch.6. Several British soldiers were executed for desertion or 'cowardice in the face of the enemy'.

1 I believe that this war, upon which I entered as a war of defence and liberation, has now become a war of aggression and conquest … I have seen and endured the sufferings of the troops, and I can no longer be a party to prolonging their sufferings for ends which I believe to be evil and unjust.

Siegfried Sassoon, 'Declaration' of 15 June 1917, published in *The Times*, 31 July 1917; *Siegfried Sassoon Diaries 1915–1918* (1983) pp.173–4.

2 I'd like to see a Tank come down the stalls,
  Lurching to rag-time tunes, or 'Home, Sweet
    Home',
  And there'd be no more jokes in Music-halls
  To mock the riddled corpses round Bapaume.

Siegfried Sassoon 'Blighters' (1917). Sassoon was disgusted at the apparent indifference of the British civilian population to the horrors of war on the Western Front. The French town of Bapaume was close to the front line on the Somme.

3 The day was one of memorable achievement. On a front of over six miles an advance had been made varying from three miles to four … The unregistered bombardment of the artillery had done all that was claimed for it. The tanks had enabled the assault to burst without warning through un-cut wire, to over-run trenches, and to crush well-sited strong points which linked up the whole powerful system of defence.

The day: 20 Nov. 1917 in the Battle of Cambrai, as described in *The Official History of the War, 1917* (1922) p.47. The truth was less comforting.

4 Coal has run out. The electric light is cut off in most houses … The trams are not running. Neither potatoes nor turnips are to be had – they were our last resource – there is no fish – and Germany has at last ceased to trumpet the fact that it can't be starved out.

British citizen Ethel Cooper, Leipzig, 4 Feb. 1917; *Behind the Lines* (1982) p.181. Since 1914 the Royal Navy had imposed a blockade on Germany, which was beginning to have a serious impact on food supplies.

5 My Tuesdays are meatless,
  My Wednesdays are wheatless,
  I'm getting more eatless each day.
  My coffee is sweetless,

  My bed it is sheetless,
  All sent to the YMCA.

Plaint from the land of abundance; Thomas A. Bailey *Voices of America* (1976) p.346. Even Americans had to tighten their belts, at the behest of the food administrator, Herbert Hoover.

6 Admiral Jellicoe took a paper out of his pocket and handed it to me. It was a record of tonnage losses for the last few months … 'Yes,' he said, as quietly as though he were discussing the weather and not the future of the British empire, 'it is impossible for us to go on with the war if losses like this continue'… 'Is there no solution for the problem?' I asked. 'Absolutely none that we can see now,' Jellicoe announced.

Admiral William Sims, US navy commander in Europe; Terraine (1977). Britain's Atlantic supply-line from the United States was close to being severed by U-boat warfare. The solution, which the Admiralty reluctantly adopted, was the convoy system.

7 We do … exhort and charge all heads of households
  TO REDUCE THEIR CONSUMPTION OF BREAD IN THEIR RESPECTIVE FAMILIES BY AT LEAST ONE-FOURTH OF THE QUANTITY CONSUMED IN ORDINARY TIMES.
  TO ABSTAIN FROM THE USE OF FLOUR IN PASTRY AND CAREFULLY TO RESTRICT THE USE THEREOF IN ALL OTHER ARTICLES THAN BREAD.

George V, proclamation, 2 May 1917; Brown (1991) Pt 7. Lloyd George had set up a Food Department in Dec. 1916 and went on to make an appeal for voluntary rationing. Here belt-tightening is urged on his subjects by a monarch who has nobly taken the pledge of total abstinence from alcohol for the duration of the war. Compulsory food rationing was introduced in Feb. 1918.

8 If God spares us to return home it must be our resolve to build a new England on the principles of righteousness, justice and brotherhood … Let those who want to see those things removed from our national life which have in the past brought dishonour on the fair name of England – social injustice, luxury on the one hand and grinding poverty on the other, bad housing, immorality, class hatred and the like – band themselves together and say 'These things need not be. These things shall not be.'

Rev. Victor Tanner, sermon during the Battle of Passchendaele, late 1917; Brown (1991) Pt 8. The hope that the rigours of war could point the way to a better post-war world was to be a growing theme in the final year of the conflict.

1918: FIGHT TO THE FINISH

1 I vow to thee, my country – all earthly things
   above –
   Entire and whole and perfect, the service of my
   love.

Cecil Spring Rice 'I Vow to Thee, My Country', Jan. 1918.
Spring Rice had been British ambassador to the United States.

2 In the workshop there were some decently
behaved people sitting down and working quietly ...
Then from the other door marched in singing 'The
Red Flag', a gang of these Conscientious Objectors
... As they went out they started shouting and
yelling, and so for the benefit of everyone concerned
I shouted to these men, 'You damned mutinous
swine, I have come down here to restore order, and
if you do not behave yourselves I will give you hell.'

Major George Blake, acting governor of Wandsworth Prison;
John Rae Conscience and Politics (1970) p.231. Conscientious
objectors were men who refused to perform military service
on grounds of conscience. These objectors were clearly
socialists and just as evidently branded as subversives by the
penal establishment.

3 Lytton Strachey ... preferred to appear before a
military tribunal as a conscientious objector ...
Asked by the chairman ... 'What would you do if
you saw a German soldier trying to violate your
sister?' he replied with an air of noble virtue: 'I
would try to get between them.'

Robert Graves Goodbye to All That (1929) Ch.23.

4 To secure for the producers by hand and brain the
full fruits of their industry, and the most equitable
distribution thereof that may be possible, upon the
basis of the common ownership of the means of
production and the best obtainable system of
popular administration and control of each industry
and service.

Clause 4 of the Labour Party Constitution, adopted in Feb.
1918; Labour Party Seventeenth Annual Report (1918) p.140.
During the war many industries had been taken under
government control, and here the Labour Party dedicated
itself to the post-war nationalization of industry. That
programme had to wait until after 1945 to be enacted.

5 I realize that, in speaking to you this afternoon,
there are certain limitations placed on the right of
free speech. I must be exceedingly careful, prudent,
as to what I say, and even more careful and prudent
as to how I say it. I may not be able to say all I think;

but I am not going to say anything that I do not
think.

Eugene V. Debs, leader of the American Socialist Party,
16 June 1918; Eugene V. Debs Speaks (1970) p.244. Debs
was given a ten-year jail sentence for sedition after publicly
denouncing the anti-sedition law of 1917. Even in a democracy
as devoted to the principle of free expression as the United
States, the war brought stringent curbs on it, bearing out the
fears attributed to Wilson on 1 April 1917 (see 717:3).

6 1. Open covenants of peace, openly arrived at,
after which there shall be no private international
understandings of any kind but diplomacy shall
proceed always frankly and in the public view.

2. Absolute freedom of navigation upon the seas,
outside territorial waters, alike in peace and in war,
except as the seas may be closed in whole or in part
in international action for the enforcement of
international covenants.

3. The removal, so far as possible, of all economic
barriers and the establishment of an equality of trade
conditions among all the nations consenting to the
peace and associating themselves for its maintenance.

4. Adequate guarantees given and taken that
national armaments will be reduced to the lowest
point consistent with national security.

5. A free, open-minded, and absolutely impartial
adjustment of all colonial claims, based upon a strict
observance of the principle that in determining all
such questions of sovereignty the interests of the
populations concerned must have equal weight with
the equitable claims of the government whose title is
to be determined.

6. The evacuation of all Russian territory ...

14. A general association of nations must be
formed under specific covenants for the purpose of
affording mutual guarantees of political
independence and territorial integrity to great and
small states alike.

President Woodrow Wilson, 'The Fourteen Points', 8 Jan.
1918; Foreign Relations of the United States 1918 Supplement 1
(1933) pp.12–17. This critically important policy statement
was made partly to set out US war aims, partly to rival the
foreign policy pronouncements of the new Bolshevik regime
in Russia. Points 1 to 5 and 14 were Wilson's personal
contribution. Point 1 stated his professed belief in open
diplomacy, as opposed to the secret wartime agreements
reached between the European powers. Point 2 was a demand
that oceanic trade should never again be disrupted either by
submarine warfare or by the surface restrictions imposed by
Britain (which strained Anglo-American relations severely in
1916). Point 3 looked to a world of free trade, with no
barriers to US exports. Point 4 was pious but meaningless.
Point 5 reflected America's long-standing anti-colonialism.

Point 6 guaranteed the survival of Bolshevism in Russia as soon as the German government accepted the Fourteen Points as the Allied condition for the Armistice of 11 Nov. 1918. Point 14 envisaged what became the League of Nations, the world body designed to secure post-war international peace and security (see 807:8–809:4).

1 Saturday was a remarkable day … We actually got down to work at half past ten and finished remaking the map of the world, as we would have it, at half past twelve o-clock.
Wilson's confidant Colonel Edward House, diary entry, 9 Jan. 1918; *The Papers of Woodrow Wilson* Vol.45 (1984) pp.550–51. House's comment is on the final drafting of the Fourteen Points (see 720:6) on 5 Jan. 1918.

2 The good Lord had only ten.
French premier Georges Clemenceau on the Fourteen Points, attrib.

3 My home policy? I wage war. My foreign policy? I wage war. Always, everywhere, I wage war … And I shall continue to wage war until the very last moment.
Georges Clemenceau, 8 March 1918; *Discours de guerre* (1968) p.172.

4 The great moment had come. The curtain of fire lifted from the front trenches. We stood up. We moved in step, irresistibly towards the enemy lines. I was boiling with a mad rage which had taken hold of me and all the others in an incomprehensible fashion. The overwhelming wish to kill gave wings to my feet. The monstrous desire for annihilation which hovered over the battlefield thickened the brains of men in a red fog.
Ernst Jünger *The Storm of Steel* (1929). Jünger was leader of an elite detachment of 'storm troops', the spearhead of the German spring offensive in the west, launched on 21 March 1918 and made possible by the recent peace treaty with Soviet Russia (see 729:4). It cut deep into the Allied line and came close to giving Germany victory on both fronts.

5 The incongruous picture came back to me of myself standing alone in a newly created circle of hell during the 'emergency' of March 22, 1918, and gazing, half-hypnotized, at the dishevelled beds, the stretchers on the floor, the scattered boots and piles of muddy khaki, the brown blankets turned back from smashed limbs bound to splints by filthy blood-stained bandages. Beneath each stinking wad of sodden wool and gauze, an obscene horror waited for me – and all the equipment that I had for attacking it … was one pair of forceps standing in a potted meat glass jar full of methylated spirits.

Vera Brittain *Testament of Youth* (1933) Ch.8. Brittain served as a nurse in France and here describes the chaos of a field hospital the day after the first German onslaught.

6 As soon as I got near the town [Albert] … strange figures, which looked very little like soldiers, and certainly showed no sign of advancing, were making their way back … Men carrying a bottle of wine under their arm and another one open in their hand … Men with top hats on their heads. Men staggering. Men who could hardly walk.
Rudolf Binding, 28 March 1918; *A Fatalist at War* (1929). German troops overran Allied supply depots during their advance, and after years of privation some succumbed to the delights of the cornucopia.

7 Come on, you sons of bitches! Do you want to live for ever?
US Marine sergeant Daniel Daly, attrib.; *American Heritage Dictionary of American Quotations* (1997) p.549. A war-cry during the Battle of Belleau Wood, 4 June 1918, although Frederick the Great may have first claim on it, shouting at his Guards on 18 June 1757 at the Battle of Kolin: 'You scum, would you live for ever?' (see 471:7).

8 Every position must be held to the last man: there must be no retirement. With our backs to the wall, and believing in the justice of our cause, each one of us must fight on to the end.
General Sir Douglas Haig, order of the day, 12 April 1918; Duff Cooper *Haig* Vol.2 (1936) Ch.23. The line was held, and in the summer of 1918 the German army began to collapse.

9 The war is not yet won. We will win it if the homeland no longer stabs the Army in the back.
Colonel Max Bauer to General Erich von Ludendorff, 12 July 1918; Feldman (1966) p.502. On 18 Nov. 1919 Paul von Hindenburg, Ludendorff's fellow commander, told a Reichstag committee of inquiry: 'As an English General has very truly said, "The German Army was stabbed in the back".' The English general in question was probably Sir Frederick Maurice. The so-called *Dolchstoss* (stab-in-the-back) theory explained away the German defeat in the west by blaming it on betrayal by socialist politicians in Germany – a powerful myth, which was assiduously and successfully exploited by Hitler.

10 What sins Germany has committed in the last three decades it must now pay for. It was politically paralysed through its blind faith in, [and] its slavish devotion to, the will of a puffed-up, vainglorious and self-over-estimating fool.
Admiral Albert Hohman, diary entry, 6 Oct. 1918; Röhl (1994) p.27. Kaiser Wilhelm II had been on the imperial throne for 30 years but was compelled to abdicate on 9 Nov. Come 1933, German devotion was to be switched to another supposedly invincible leader.

1 At two minutes to eleven, opposite the South African Brigade, at the easternmost point reached by the British armies, a German machine-gunner, after firing off a belt without a pause, was seen to stand up, take off his helmet, bow, and then walk slowly to the rear. There came a second of expectant silence, and then a curious rippling sound, which observers far behind the front likened to the noise of a light wind. It was the sound of men cheering from the Vosges to the sea.

John Buchan *The King's Grace* (1935) p.203. At 11 o'clock in the morning of 11 Nov. 1918 an armistice came into force along the Western Front; World War I was over. The Vosges mountains in Alsace stood at the southern end of the Front, stretching upwards to the North Sea.

2 Outside the Admiralty a crazy group of convalescent Tommies ... seized two of my companions and disappeared into the clamorous crowd, waving flags and shaking rattles. Wherever we went a burst of enthusiastic cheering greeted our Red Cross uniforms, and complete strangers adorned with wound stripes rushed up and shook me warmly by the hand. After the long blackness it seemed like a fairy tale to see the street lamps shining through the chill November gloom.

Vera Brittain, in London on Armistice Night (1933) Ch.9. Note the echo of Grey on 3 Aug. 1914 (see 707:1) as the lights went on again. British soldiers were known as Tommies, from Tommy Atkins, a late-Victorian nickname for the infantryman.

3   When the days of rejoicing are over,
     When the flags are stowed safely away,
     They will dream of another wild 'War to end
          Wars'
     And another wild Armistice day.
     But the boys who were killed in the trenches,
     Who fought with no rage and no rant,
     We left them stretched out on their pallets of
          mud
     Low down with the worm and the ant.

Robert Graves 'Armistice Day, 1918'. In 1914 the writer H.G. Wells published a book entitled *The War That Will End War*. He later said: 'I launched the phrase "The war to end war" – and that was not the least of my crimes.'

4   And pile them high at Gettysburg,
     And pile them high at Ypres and Verdun.
     Shovel them under and let me work.

Carl Sandburg 'Grass' (1918).

SUMMATION

5 In the stage of the wearing-out struggle losses will necessarily be heavy on both sides, for in it the price of victory is paid. If the opposing forces are approximately equal in numbers, in courage, in moral [*sic*] and in equipment, there is no way of avoiding payment or of eliminating this phase of the struggle.

General Sir Douglas Haig, despatch of 21 March 1919; *Sir Douglas Haig's Despatches* (1919) pp.320–21. To Haig there was no alternative to attrition.

6 In the wars of today, which comprise entire peoples, thought is enlisted; thought kills as well as cannon; it kills the soul; it kills beyond the seas; it kills across centuries; it is the heavy artillery which works at a distance.

Romain Rolland *Clérambault* (1920).

7 The war proved that socialism was not a Utopia because universal labour and capital, mobilized for four years for destruction, could be mobilized just as well in order to create. The war proved that class antagonism really is the law of contemporary society because ... it accentuated fortune and misery, [and] concentrated capitalism as well as the international proletariat.

French socialist Léon Blum, *L'Humanité*, 11 April 1919.

8 The statesmen were overwhelmed by the magnitude of events. The generals were overwhelmed also. Mass, they believed, was the secret of victory. The mass they invoked was beyond their control. All fumbled more or less helplessly. They were pilots without a chart, blown before the storm and not knowing where to seek harbour ... The Unknown Soldier was the hero of the First World War.

A.J.P. Taylor *The First World War* (1963) Preface. The body of one unidentifiable soldier was buried in Westminster Abbey, London, another beneath the Arc de Triomphe in Paris. Both 'Unknown Soldiers' represented the millions who died in the fighting: 947,000 from the British empire; 1,385,000 from France.

EPITAPHS

9 A Soldier of the Great War, known unto God.

Inscription on the graves of unidentified soldiers buried in war cemeteries.

1 Their Name Liveth For Evermore.

Bible, Apocrypha, Ecclesiasticus 44:14. Inscription on the Cenotaph, Whitehall, London, unveiled on 11 Nov. 1920. The word cenotaph means, literally, an empty tomb; a monument to those buried elsewhere. The phrase was chosen by the writer Rudyard Kipling, who lost his son in the war and who was actively involved in the Imperial War Graves Commission after the war.

2 *Sui memores alios fecere merendo.* (By the sacrifice they made they earned the remembrance of others.)

Inscription on the Memorial Building, Clare College, Cambridge. It is a quotation from Virgil *Aeneid* Bk 6, line 663.

3 They died to save their country and they only saved the world.

G.K. Chesterton 'The English Graves' (1922).

4 That's what you all are ... All of you young people who served in the war. You are all a *génération perdue* [a lost generation].

Anon. French garage owner to one of his mechanics, who failed to mend the car of the American writer Gertrude Stein; Ernest Hemingway *A Moveable Feast* (1964) Ch.3.

5 I saw Major Johnstone, who is here to lay the bases of an American History. We discussed the right name of the war. I said that we called it now *The War*, but that this could not last. The Napoleonic War was *The Great War*. To call it *The German War* was too much flattery for the Boche. I suggested *The World War* as a shade better title, and finally we mutually agreed to call it *The First World War* in order to prevent the millennium folk from forgetting that the history of the world was the history of war.

Lieutenant Colonel Charles A'Court Repington, diary entry, 10 Sept. 1919. Repington's book *The First World War 1914–1918* was published in 1920. In Britain the war was, in fact, most usually called 'The Great War' (as the first of the epitaphs above makes clear) or 'The Last War', meaning not the war just gone but the last of all wars. In choosing an alternative title Repington was tempting providence: a first is bound to imply a second (and a second, a third).

The Russian Revolution, 1914–24

TSARISM IN EXTREMIS, 1914–17

1 For us, the Russian Social Democrats, there cannot be the slightest doubt that from the standpoint of the working class and the labouring masses of all the nations of Russia the lesser evil would be the defeat of the tsarist monarchy, the most reactionary and barbarous of governments.

Lenin (Vladimir Ilyich Ulyanov) 'The War and Russian Social Democracy', Nov. 1914 (NS); *Collected Works* Vol.21 (1964) pp.32–3. At the outbreak of war Lenin was living in exile in Switzerland.

2 Threatening signs of growing demoralization are becoming more and more evident. Cases of desertion and of soldiers voluntarily giving themselves up to the enemy are becoming more frequent. It is difficult to expect selflessness and enthusiasm from men sent into battle without weapons and ordered to take rifles from their dead comrades.

General A.A. Polivanov, minister of war, report, 29 July 1915 (NS); *Archive of the Russian Revolution* Vol.18 (1925) p.15. After a year of hard fighting on the front with Germany, the war was not going well for the Russians.

3 Sometimes in our battles with the Russians we had to remove the mounds of enemy corpses from before our trenches in order to get a clear field of fire against fresh assaulting waves.

General Paul von Hindenburg; Alex De Jonge *The Life and Times of Grigorii Rasputin* (1982) p.252. Hindenburg, later president of the Weimar Republic (see 753:8), was German commander in the field on the Eastern Front.

4 If You, Sire, should take over the direct command of our glorious army – You, Sire, the last refuge of Your people – who will then pass judgement, in the event of failure or defeat? Is it not really obvious, Sire, that You will then have voluntarily surrendered Your inviolate person to the judgement of the people? – and that is fatal to Russia.

Mikhail Rodzianko, chairman of the duma (parliament) to Nicholas II, 12 Aug. 1915 (NS); Frank A. Golder (ed.) *Documents of Russian History, 1914–17* (1927) p.209. In Aug. 1915 the tsar took personal command of Russia's armed forces, a decision that sounded the death knell of the monarchy, given his complete unfitness for the responsibility.

5 'I came,' said Rasputin, 'to Tsarskoe, and walked in. Papa sat there looking glum. I stroked his head and said, "Why so sad?" He replied, "Scoundrels are about me! No boots, no guns. It is necessary to advance, but to advance it is impossible."'

Alexei Khvostov, minister of the interior; Golder (1927) p.215. 'Papa' was the tsar, and Tsarskoe was his summer residence outside the Russian capital.

6 You let the chauffeur keep the wheel. More than this, you try not to get in his way, even helping him with advice, directions and cooperation. You are quite right – this is necessary. But what will you endure at the thought that even your restraint will not carry you through, that even with your help the chauffeur cannot drive!

Vasily Maklakov, leading *Kadet* (liberal) politician, *Russkia Vedomosti*, 27 Sept. 1915 (NS). A sardonic comment on the tsar's leadership.

7 Life is *advancing*, through the defeat of Russia, towards a revolution in Russia and, through that revolution and in connection with it, towards a civil war in Europe.

Lenin, Sept. 1915 (NS); *Collected Works* Vol.21 (1964) p.382.

8 We regard civil wars, i.e. wars waged by an oppressed class against the oppressor class, by slaves against slave-holders, by serfs against landowners, and by wage-earners against the bourgeoisie, as fully legitimate, progressive and necessary.

Lenin 'Socialism and War' (1915); *Collected Works* Vol.21 (1964) p.299.

9 All over Falconet's statue [of Peter the Great] swarmed a crowd of little boys, hanging on to the tail, sitting on the serpent, smoking under the horse's belly. Total demoralization. Petersburg finis.

The poet Alexander Blok *Memoirs* (1921) p.11. The scene in Petrograd, Easter 1916. An ominous glimpse of the open contempt being displayed for the monarchy in the city that Tsar Peter had made its showplace two centuries earlier. By then the capital's name of St Petersburg had been dropped because of its German style in favour of the Russian Petrograd (City of Peter).

10 I hear whispers that the Russian infantry has lost heart and that anti-war propaganda is rife in the ranks. It is little wonder that they are downhearted after being driven to the slaughter over the same ground seven times in about a month, and every time taking trenches where their guns could not keep them.

General Sir Alfred Knox, diary entry, 28 Oct. 1916 (NS); *With the Russian Army, 1914–1917* p.488. Knox was military attaché at the British embassy in Russia.

1 Recently … the conviction has been expressed without exception, that 'we are on the eve of great events' in comparison with which '1905 was but a toy'.

Political police report on the situation in Oct. 1916 (NS); *Red Archive* Vol.5 (1926) pp.6–7. The reference to 1905 is to the abortive revolution of that year (see 678:2).

2 The industrial proletariat of the capital is on the verge of despair and … the smallest outbreak due to any pretext will lead to uncontrollable riots with thousands and tens of thousands of victims.

Political police report, Oct. 1916 (NS); Raymond Pearson *The Russian Moderates and the Crisis of Tsarism 1914–17* (1977) p.107.

3 Russia is a very large lunatic asylum. If you visit an asylum on an open day you may not realize you are in one. It looks normal enough but the inmates are all mad.

The writer Zinaidi Gippius, diary entry, Nov. 1916 (NS); *Memoirs* (1929) p.54.

4 I feel cruel worrying you, my sweet, patient Angel – but all my trust lies in our Friend, who only thinks of you, Baby & Russia – And guided by Him we shall get through this heavy time. It will be hard fighting, but a Man of God's is near to guide yr boat safely through the reef … Be Peter the Great, Ivan the Terrible, Emperor Paul – crush them all under you … be the Master, & all will bow down to you.

Tsarina Alexandra to Nicholas II, 31 Oct. 1916 (NS) and 14 Dec. 1916 (NS); *Letters of the Tsarina to the Tsar 1914–1916* (1924) pp.429, 455, 456. The letters were written in English. The 'Friend' is Rasputin; 'Baby' is Alexis, the haemophiliac tsarevich, their only son and heir to the throne.

5 The utter exceptional quality of the debauched peasant shot in the back at Yusupov's 'gramophone party' is to be perceived most of all in the fact that the bullet that killed him hit the very heart of the ruling dynasty.

Alexander Blok *Memoirs* (1921) p.10. On 29 Dec. 1916 (NS) Rasputin was assassinated (with difficulty) by a group of aristocrats led by Prince Felix Yusupov, at Yusupov's residence in Petrograd. The murderous soirée began to the tune of a gramophone playing 'Yankee Doodle'.

6 This is a *hooligan* movement, young people run and shout that there is no bread, simply to create excitement, along with the workers who prevent others from working. If the weather was very cold they would probably all stay at home. But all this will pass and become calm if only the Duma will behave itself.

Tsarina Alexandra, diary entry, 10 March 1917 (NS); Richard Pipes *The Russian Revolution 1899–1919* (1990) p.275. Delusion at the highest level as popular unrest came rapidly to a head.

7 Situation serious. In the capital anarchy. Government paralysed. Transport of food and fuel completely disorganized. Public disaffection growing. On the streets chaotic shooting. Army units fire at each other.

Mikhail Rodzianko, chairman of the duma, telegram shown to the tsar, 11 March 1917 (NS); N. Adveev *et al.* (eds) *Revolution 1917* Vol.1 (1923) p.37.

8 Now after two days of unimpeded movement on the streets, when revolutionary circles have raised the slogans 'Down with the war' and 'Down with the government', the people have become convinced that the revolution has begun.

Political police report, 11 March 1917 (NS); Pipes (1990) p.279.

9 The grudges of centuries were now being aired, we could find no common language – this was the accursed legacy of the old regime.

Anon. junior army officer, 11 March 1917 (NS); *Red Archive* Vols 50–51 (1932) p.200. Next day, 12 March, the tsarist order was swept away by the revolutionary upsurge.

PROVISIONAL GOVERNMENT, MARCH–NOVEMBER 1917

10 I remember the moment when the blackish-grey sediment, pressing at the doors like a never-ceasing flood, drowned the Duma … From the first moment of that inundation, repulsion filled my soul … I felt helpless. Something dangerous, terrifying and abominable had been unleashed which threatened us all alike.

Vasily Shulgin *Dni* (1925) pp.152–4. Shulgin, a Nationalist Party member, recalls the invasion of the parliament by insurgents on 12 March 1917 (NS).

11 I got up and saw two soldiers, their bayonets hooked into the canvas of Repin's portrait of

Nicholas II, rhythmically tugging it down from both sides. A minute later, over the chairman's seat in the White Hall of the Duma, there was an empty frame.
N. Sukhanov, an eyewitness account, 13 March 1917 (NS); *The Russian Revolution 1917* (1955).

1 The orders of the Military Commission of the State Duma are to be obeyed with the exception of those instances in which they contradict the orders and decrees of the Soviet of Workers' and Soldiers' Deputies.
Sect.4, Order no.1 of the Petrograd Soviet, *Izvestiya* (News), 15 March 1917 (NS). This order effectively set up the Soviet as a rival authority to the provisional government.

2 The women, who had suffered much from the war, replied, 'Stop fighting and come home. Work in the fields has stopped altogether here. We shall soon have to sell the last horse.'
V. Lysov, March 1917 (NS); I.V. Igritsky (ed.) *1917* (1929) p.287.

3 What's the use of turning up our toes in Galicia, when back at home they're going to divide up the land?
Russian soldier, spring 1917 (NS); Geoffrey Hosking *A History of the Soviet Union* (1985). Peasants began deserting in droves to seize land from the owners of the great estates, just as the French peasantry had done in 1789 (see 516:9).

4 What has happened in Russia reminds us of the earlier days of the French Revolution. We recall with what a glow of hope the fall of the Bastille was received by liberal-minded men throughout the world [but] it is too soon to say that all danger is over in Russia.
Andrew Bonar Law, British Conservative Party leader, 22 March 1917; *H.C. Deb.* Vol.91, Col.2085.

5 As I studied his face, I seemed to see behind his smile and charming eyes a stiff, proper mask of utter loneliness and desolation … When I began to know this living mask I understood why it had been so easy to overthrow his power. He did not wish to fight for it and it simply fell from his hands.
Alexander Kerensky on a visit to the fallen tsar, 3 April 1917 (NS); *The Catastrophe* (1927) pp.264–9. Kerensky was soon to become leader of the provisional government.

6 After 2 o'clock it cleared and thawed. Walked for a short time in the morning. Sorted my belongings and books and sorted the things I want to take with me in case I go to England.

Nicholas II, diary entry, 5 April 1917 (NS); *Diary* (1923). The former tsar was hoping to be given political asylum in Britain, and the British government agreed to this, but citing hostile public opinion as his reason, on 6 April King George V withdrew from any commitment to welcome the imperial family on to British soil.

7 The main thing is not to let ourselves get caught in stupid attempts at 'unity' with social patriots, or still more dangerous … with vacillators like Trotsky & Co.
Lenin to Alexandra Kollontai, 15 March 1917 (NS); *Collected Works* Vol.35 (1966), p.240. Trotsky was highly suspect to Lenin as a Menshevik. Kollontai was a high-born revolutionary lady, close to Lenin until she fell out of favour in 1921.

8 We must now unconditionally seek to create in Russia the greatest possible chaos … We should do all we can … to exacerbate the differences between the moderate and extremist parties, because we have the greatest interest in the latter gaining the upper hand, since the Revolution will then become unavoidable and assume forms that must shatter the stability of the Russian state.
Count Brockdorff-Rantzau to the German foreign office, 2 April 1917 (NS); W. Hahlweg *Lenin's Return* (1959) p.47. The count was German ambassador to Denmark, urging German promotion of Lenin's return from Switzerland to Russia. Lenin left under German sponsorship, in the famous sealed train, on 9 April.

9 Russia is a peasant country, one of the most backward of European countries. Socialism *cannot* triumph there *directly* and *immediately*.
Lenin, farewell letter to the workers of Switzerland, 8 April 1917 (NS); *Collected Works* Vol.23 (1964), p.372. Lenin here follows the orthodox Marxist line that a socialist revolution could take place only in an industrialized country. He was soon to say otherwise.

10 The specific feature of the present situation in Russia is that it represents a *transition* from the first stage of revolution which owing to the insufficient class-consciousness and organization of the proletariat, led to the assumption of power by the bourgeoisie – *to the second* stage which must place power in the hands of the proletariat and the poor strata of the peasantry.
Lenin *The April Theses*, April 1917 (NS); *Selected Works* Vol.6 (1935) p.22. Within hours of his arrival in Petrograd on 16 April, Lenin had discarded the belief that only when the bourgeois revolution of the provisional government had been consummated could a socialist revolution happen. To most of his audience, including many of his own Bolshevik Party, this was heresy bordering on madness.

1 Ought to stick our bayonets into a fellow like that. Must be a German.

Anon. soldier after Lenin's speech on returning to Petrograd, 16 April 1917 (NS); Sukhanov (1955) pp.270–77. Lenin's call for an end to the war short of a Russian victory was seen as treason by Russian nationalists. The surmise about Germany was all too true.

2 The throne is now occupied which has been empty for thirty years since the death of Bakunin. From this seat the banner of civil war has been unfurled in the midst of revolutionary democracy. Lenin's programme is sheer insurrectionism, which will lead us into the pit of anarchy. These are the tactics of the universal apostle of destruction.

I.P. Goldenberg, 17 April 1917 (NS); Robert Service *Lenin* (2000) p.267. Lenin seen as the successor to the anarchist Bakunin by a fearful socialist.

3 ALL POWER TO THE SOVIETS OF WORKERS, SOLDIERS AND PEASANTS! PEACE! BREAD! LAND!

Slogans developed by Lenin after his arrival in Petrograd on 16 April 1917 (NS). The Bolsheviks thus backed the rival authority to the provisional government, the Soviets (Councils), as well as promising an end to Russian involvement in the war with Germany and Austria-Hungary, economic security and the ownership of land by the peasantry. The last of these was a short-term, tactical concession by a revolutionary determined ultimately to place ownership of property in the hands of the state.

4 We have been referred to 1792 as an example of how we should carry out the Revolution of 1917. But how did the French Republic of 1792 end? It turned into a base imperialism which set back the progress of democracy for many a long year. Our duty is to prevent that very thing from happening so that our comrades who have just come back from exile in Siberia shall not have to go back there, and so that that comrade [Lenin] who has been living all this time in safety in Switzerland shall not have to fly back there.

Alexander Kerensky, June 1917 (NS); M. Phillips-Price *My Reminiscences of the Russian Revolution* (1921). In the Bolshevik paper *Pravda* (Truth) on 20 June 1917 (NS) Lenin had held up the Jacobins of the French Revolution as a model for Russia.

5 It is time to put an end to all this. It is time to hang the German agents and spies, with Lenin at their head, to dispel the Council of Workmen and Soldiers' Deputies and scatter them far and wide, so that they should never be able to come together again!

General Lavr Georgyevich Kornilov, 11 Aug. 1917 (NS); General A. Lukomsky *Memoirs of the Russian Revolution* (1922). Lukomsky was Kornilov's chief of staff. Four weeks later Kornilov attempted a coup d'état, prompted by an abortive Bolshevik rising against the provisional government in July. His right-wing bid for power likewise collapsed, but it weakened the government and helped to make possible the second Bolshevik insurgency in Nov.

6 All the objective conditions for a successful insurrection exist. We have the exceptional advantage of a situation in which *only* our victory in the insurrection can put an end to that most painful thing on earth, vacillation … The people … are tormented by the irresolution of the Socialist Revolutionaries and the Mensheviks; and … we are definitely breaking with those *parties* because they have destroyed the revolution.

Lenin to the Central Committee of the Bolshevik Party, 27 Sept. 1917 (NS); *Collected Works* Vol.26 (1964) p.27. Lenin's call for a coup d'état was sent from Finland where he had fled after the failure of the July uprising. The Socialist Revolutionaries were the party of the Russian peasantry.

7 There is no doubt that there occur such historical situations where the oppressed class has to recognize that it is better to go down to defeat than to surrender without a fight. Does the Russian working class now find itself in such a situation? *No, a thousand times no!!!*

Grigory Zinoviev and Lev Kamenev, statement, 24 Oct. 1917 (NS); Lenin *Collected Works* Vol.21 (1964) p.495. Two senior Bolsheviks reject Lenin's summons to revolution.

8 Seizure of power is the point of the uprising; its political task will be clarified after the seizure.

Lenin, letter, 6 Nov. 1917 (NS); James Bunyan and H.H. Fisher (eds) *The Bolshevik Revolution 1917–1918* (1934) p.96. In other words, shoot first and ask questions afterwards. On the eve of the projected coup, Lenin makes clear that his immediate objective is to control the Russian state; without that control, a Marxist revolution was no more than a theoretical possibility.

THE BOLSHEVIK COUP, NOVEMBER 1917

9 In such a country it was quite easy to start a revolution, as easy as lifting a feather.

Lenin, report to the 7th Congress of the Bolshevik Party, 7 March 1918 (NS); *Selected Works* Vol.2, Bk 1 (1946), p.429.

10 *Ten Days that Shook the World*

Title of book published in 1919 by the American journalist John Reed, a fervent admirer of Lenin. His ashes were placed in the wall of the Kremlin after his death in Moscow on 17 Oct. 1920 (NS). The ten days in question were the days following the Bolshevik coup d'état of 7 Nov. 1917. (A conscious echo of the title came in the book *Two Hours that Shook the World* by Fred Halliday, published in the aftermath of the terrorist attacks on New York and Washington on 11 Sept. 2001.)

1 You are pitiful isolated individuals; you are bankrupt; your role is played out. Go where you belong from now on – into the dustbin of history.
Leon Trotsky to the Menshevik leader, Julius Martov, 7 Nov. 1917 (NS); L. Trotsky *History of the Russian Revolution* (1933) Vol.3, Ch.10. Trotsky himself had been a Menshevik until the July rising, when he became a Bolshevik. He was right about his former confrères, whom Lenin put into the oubliette by the early 1920s, although Trotsky, too, was binned by Stalin after Lenin's death.

2 Private ownership of land shall be abolished for ever … All land … shall become the property of the whole people, and pass into the use of those who cultivate it.
Decree on Land, 8 Nov. 1917 (NS); Bunyan and Fisher (1934) pp.129–30. The first act of the new régime was to nationalize landed property, though in fact the Bolsheviks were not yet strong enough to take it from the peasants who had been dispossessing their landlords since the spring.

3 We shall offer peace for the peoples of all the belligerent countries upon the basis of the Soviet terms – no annexations, no indemnities, and the right of self-determination of peoples. At the same time, according to our promise, we shall publish and repudiate the secret treaties.
Lenin, 8 Nov. 1917 (NS); Bunyan and Fisher (1934) pp.125–8. The Decree on Peace looked forward to Russia's withdrawal from World War I in accordance with the idealistic programme proclaimed by the Soviets since the revolution in March. The secret treaties were the accords entered into by the provisional government, now to be exposed to public knowledge.

4 There has been no transfer of power to the Soviets, but a seizure of power by one party – the Bolsheviks.
Feodor Dan, *Izvestiya*, 8 Nov. 1917 (NS). Dan, a leading Menshevik, had been opposed to the Bolsheviks since the 1903 split in the Social Democrat Party. An accurate statement: despite the pledge of 'All power to the Soviets', the Bolsheviks had no intention of sharing power with the several left-wing groupings that made up the Soviets' membership.

5 We take the stand that it is necessary to form a Socialist government of all parties in the Soviet … The alternative is – a purely Bolshevik government which can maintain itself only by means of political terror.
Statement by Bolshevik ministerial dissidents, *Novaya Zhizn* (New Life), 18 Nov. 1917 (NS).

6 Lenin, Trotsky and their fellow travellers are already poisoned by the toxin of power, as demostrated by their shameful attitude to freedom of speech, freedom of the individual and all the rights for which the democracy struggled. These blind fanatics and unscrupulous adventurers are racing at breakneck speed towards something they call 'social evolution', but they are in fact on the path to anarchy, the ruin of the proletariat and the revolution.
Maxim Gorky, *Novaya Zhizn*, 20 Nov. 1917 (NS). The writer Gorky later became reconciled to Lenin (see 735:4), but his forebodings were soon borne out.

7 Stalin … produced – and not only on me – the impression of a grey blur, looming up now and then dimly and not leaving any trace.
N. Sukhanov (1955) p.230. Stalin's role in the 1917 Revolution was marginal.

8 If in a burst of enthusiasm the people has elected a very good parliament … then we ought to make it a long parliament, and if the elections have not proved a success, then we should seek to disperse parliament not after two years but, if possible, after two weeks.
Lenin, *Pravda*, 22 Dec. 1917 (NS); *Collected Works* Vol.35 (1966) pp.184–5. In the elections to the Constituent Assembly due to meet in Jan. 1918, the Bolsheviks took only 175 seats, well behind the 370 of the peasants' party, the Socialist Revolutionaries.

9 We … will put a bullet into anyone who deceived us. We don't care whether it is Kerensky, Lenin, or someone else! We are fed up living as we did … Now we are going to take everything into our own hands!
Anon. Russian sailor to a right-wing Socialist Revolutionary, 18 Jan. 1918 (NS); Oliver Radkey *The Sickle under the Hammer* (1953) p.182. The remark was made on the day the constituent assembly convened, far from a vote of confidence in parliamentary democracy.

10 THE HIRELINGS OF BANKERS, CAPITALISTS AND LANDLORDS … THE SLAVES OF THE AMERICAN DOLLAR, THE BACKSTABBERS … DEMAND IN THE CONSTITUENT ASSEMBLY ALL POWER FOR THEMSELVES AND THEIR MASTERS – ENEMIES OF THE PEOPLE.

Headlines in *Pravda*, 19 Jan. 1918 (NS). The assembly was dissolved on Lenin's instructions the same day, 24 hours after it met.

1 Freedom only for the supporters of the government, only for members of one party – however numerous they may be – that is no freedom at all. Freedom is always and exclusively freedom for the one who thinks differently.

The Polish Marxist Rosa Luxemburg in her tract *The Russian Revolution*, written in Breslau prison, summer 1918. Compare the English libertarian William Hazlitt: 'The love of liberty is the love of others; the love of power is the love of ourselves' (*Political Essays*; 1819).

RUSSIA LEAVES THE WAR, MARCH 1918

2 In refusing to sign the annexation peace Russia at the same time declares the war with Germany, Austria-Hungary, Bulgaria and Turkey at an end.

Trotsky, declaration to the peace conference at Brest-Litovsk, 10 Feb. 1918 (NS); Bunyan and Fisher (1934) p.510. The 'Neither War Nor Peace Formula' rejected by Germany and by Lenin.

3 Those who stand on the side of revolutionary war point out that by this very step we will be engaged in a civil war with German imperialism and that thereby we'll awaken revolution in Germany. But look! Germany is only pregnant with revolution, and a completely healthy baby has been born to us, the baby that is the socialist republic, which we shall be killing if we begin a war.

Lenin, 22 Jan. 1918 (NS); Service (2000) p.339.

4 It is impossible for a ruined peasant country to wage a modern war against advanced imperialism without an army and without the most serious economic preparation.

Lenin, 24 Feb. 1918 (NS); *Collected Works* Vol.27 (1965) p.59. The Bolshevik government signed a humiliating peace treaty with Germany on 3 March 1918, which deprived Russia of a huge percentage of its population and resources.

5 It is the absolute truth that without a German revolution we are doomed … under all conceived vicissitudes, if the German revolution does not come, we are doomed.

Lenin, report to the 7th Congress of the Bolshevik Party, 7 March 1918 (NS); *Collected Works* Vol.27 (1965) p.98. German Marxist revolutions were to take place in Berlin (Jan. 1919) and in Bavaria (April 1919), but they were soon repressed by right-wing forces. Bolshevik Russia survived

nonetheless, not least because of President Woodrow Wilson's insistence in his Fourteen Points address of 4 Jan. 1918 that Germany withdraw its armies from Russia (see 720:6). Germany's acceptance of this condition in Oct. 1918 thus effectively annulled the Treaty of Brest-Litovsk (see 729:4), and Russia formally abrogated it two days after the armistice that ended World War I on 11 Nov. The Bolshevik regime could then fight for its survival from an incomparably stronger base than it had held at the outbreak of civil war in Russia in March 1918.

DICTATORSHIP OF THE PROLETARIAT, 1918–20

6   They march with sovereign tread.
With a hungry cur yapping at their feet.
And Jesus Christ holds up the blood-red
      banner,
White roses on his head.

Alexander Blok 'The Twelve', Jan. 1918 (NS). The Bolshevik Revolution as the work of a messianic Christ and his disciples.

7 Power to the Soviets means the complete transfer of the country's administration and economic control into the hands of the workers and peasants.

Lenin, 27 Sept. 1917 (NS); *Collected Works* Vol.25 (1964) p.373.

8 The city leads the village. The village inevitably follows the city.

Lenin *The Year 1919*; *Collected Works* Vol.16 (1963) p.442. An unequivocal affirmation of the primacy of the urban over the agrarian revolution.

9 The Bolshevist Government, acting in our names, is not the authority of the proletariat and the peasants, but a dictatorship of the Bolshevik party, self-governing with the aid of the Cheka and the police.

Resolution passed by 10,000 workers of the Putilov factory in Petrograd, 10 March 1919 (NS); George Leggett *The Cheka* (1981) p.313. The Cheka, short for the Russian *Vecheka* (All-Russian Extraordinary Commission for Combating Counter-Revolution, Sabotage and Speculation), was founded on 20 Dec. 1917.

10 The Soviets … are … organs of government *for the working people* by the advanced section of the proletariat, but not *by the working people* as a whole.

Lenin, 19 March 1919 (NS); *Collected Works* Vol.29 (1965) p.183.

11 If we say that it is not the Party but the trade unions that put up the candidates and administrate, it may sound very democratic and might help us to catch a few votes, but not for long. It will be fatal for the dictatorship of the proletariat.

Lenin, 30 Dec. 1920 (NS); *Collected Works* Vol.32 (1965) pp.20–21.

1 As for 'personal dictatorship', excuse the expression, but it is utter nonsense. The apparatus has already become gigantic – in some places *excessively so* – and under such conditions a 'personal dictatorship' is entirely unrealizable and attempts to realize it would only be harmful.

Lenin to N.A. Rozhkov, 29 Jan. 1919 (NS); Richard Pipes *The Unknown Lenin* (1998) p.52, a collection of hitherto unpublished documents.

2 Soviet Socialist democracy does not in any way contradict one-man management and dictatorship; the will of the class is sometimes given effect by a dictator, who sometimes does more alone and often is more than necessary.

Lenin, 19 March 1919 (NS); *Collected Works* Vol.29 (1965) p.183.

3 All educational work in the Soviet Republic of workers and peasants, in the field of political education in general and in the field of art in particular, should be imbued with the spirit of the class struggle being waged by the proletariat for the successful achievement of the aims of its dictatorship.

Lenin, 8 Oct. 1920 (NS); *Collected Works* Vol.31 (1966) pp.316–17.

4 Does not our land resemble today's tramcars, which drag themselves along Moscow's dreary streets? … [Their passengers exude] mindless hatred for the tram driver – this expresses the feeling of this casual mass towards the government, the state, the organization. Indifference and irony towards those who crowd at the tram's entrance hoping to get in – this is their attitude towards the community, towards solidarity.

Isaac Steinberg, 1920; *Power and Terror in the Revolution* (1974) p.15.

5 'So you've been over to Russia?' said Bernard Baruch, and I answered very literally, 'I have been over into the future and it works.'

American journalist Lincoln Steffens, April 1919 (NS); *The Autobiography of Lincoln Steffens* (1931) Vol.2, p.79.

WAR COMMUNISM, 1918–20

6 All lands of the former landlords are now in the hands of the peasants … to take back the land from the peasants is impossible under any condition.

Statement by the Bolshevik commissar of agriculture, *Novaya Zhizn*, 13 Jan. 1918 (NS). Bolshevik control of the Russian economy was incomplete as long as the peasantry held on to the land it had seized in 1918.

7 They arrested me and my family … and left a guard with us with a warning not to go out of the house. They also placed armed guards around my farm and made threats to my labourers. Then they took away all my grain and seeds, except for 655 kilograms of rye, and locked up my barns.

Small landowner from the Samara district, on the peasantry's expropriation of his property, 27 Jan. 1918 (NS); Orlando Figes *Peasant Russia, Civil War* (1989) p.53. Compare France in the summer of 1789 (see 516:9).

8 Armed detachments of Red Guards and hired soldiers are roaming over villages and hamlets in quest of bread, making searches, laying traps with more or less success. Sometimes they return with bread; at other times they come back carrying the dead bodies of their comrades who fell in the fight with the peasants.

Novaya Zhizn, 19 April 1918 (NS). To feed the cities and the Bolshevik Red Army the government resorted to forced requisitions of foodstuffs.

9 The obstinacy of the greedy kulaks and wealthy peasants must be brought to an end … The reply to the violence of the grain holders upon the rural poor must be violence upon the bourgeoisie [and the government will] make use of armed troops in the case of resistance to requisition of grain and other foodstuffs.

Decree, *Pravda*, 15 May 1918 (NS). All grain surplus to minimum requirements was to be surrendered to the authorities; in effect, the decree signified a declaration of war on the richer peasantry and it was met with bitter resistance.

10 They were able to reduce piecemeal the backward masses of the distant villages. The corn began to come in. True, I had never tasted any of the fruits of the requisitions. I lived during these days almost exclusively on potato skins and dried fish. But those who were organized in trade unions and who were members of factory committees began to receive again their quarter of a pound of bread a day.

M. Phillips-Price *My Reminiscences of the Russian Revolution* (1921) p.311. Phillips-Price was Moscow correspondent of the *Manchester Guardian*; he draws a remarkably sympathetic picture of the campaign for grain requisition in the summer of 1918.

1 These spiders have grown fat at the expense of peasants … These leeches have drunk the blood of toilers, growing the richer the more the worker starved in the cities and factories. These vampires have gathered and continue to gather in their hands the lands of landlords, enslaving, time and time again, the poor peasants. Merciless war against these kulaks! Death to them!

Lenin, early Aug. 1918 (NS); *Collected Works* Vol.28 (1965) pp.56–7. A declaration of war on the richer peasants, foreshadowing Stalin's campaign under the first five-year plan (see 737:6).

2 Putting a gun to my chest, they demanded vodka from me, but since I had none and refused to buy any for them, they beat me and then beat my wife. I asked them to allow my five-year-old son, who was shaking with fear, to go, but they refused, at which my wife became so petrified that she defecated there and then.

Petition to the People's Commissariat of Internal Affairs (NKVD) by the peasant E. Doraev, against the behaviour of local Bolshevik party functionaries, May 1919 (NS); Figes (1989) p.358.

3 Let us … take the most concrete example of state capitalism … It is Germany. Here we have the 'last word' in modern, large-scale capitalist engineering and planned organization, *subordinated to Junker-bourgeois imperialism*. Cross out the words in italics and [substitute] a *Soviet* state, that is, a proletarian state, and you will have the *sum total* of the conditions necessary for socialism.

Lenin, March 1918 (NS); Pipes (1990) pp.677–8.

4 State capitalism under the dictatorship of the proletariat – this is an absurdity, soft-boiled boots. For state capital presupposes the dictatorship of finance capital; it is the transfer of production to the dictatorially organized imperialist state. State capitalism without capitalists is exactly the same sort of nonsense.

Nikolai Bukharin in *Kommunist* no.3 (1918). Bukharin was one of Lenin's most senior colleagues.

5 Along with sentencing by the courts it is necessary to retain administrative sentencing – namely, the concentration camps. Even today the labour of those under arrest is far from being utilized in public works, and so I recommend that we retain those concentration camps for the exploitation of labour of persons under arrest.

Felix Dzerzhinsky, 17 Feb. 1919 (NS); Pipes (1990) p.834. The camps were the nucleus of the so-called Gulag Archipelago. In 1922 they were renamed 'forced labour camps'. By the time of Lenin's death in 1924 there were 315 of them, with 70,000 inmates. Dzerzhinsky headed the Cheka, which operated the camps.

6 It is said that compulsory labour is unproductive. This means that the whole socialist economy is doomed to be scrapped, because there is no other way of attaining socialism except through the command allocation of the entire labour force by the economic centre.

Leon Trotsky, speech to the 3rd Congress of Trade Unions, April 1920 (NS); Pipes (1990) p.704.

7 Communism is Soviet power plus the electrification of the whole country.

Lenin, 20 Dec. 1920 (NS); *Collected Works* Vol.31 (1966) p.516.

TERROR, 1917–20

8 You wax indignant at the naked terror which we are applying against our class enemies, but let me tell you that in one month's time at the most it will assume more frightful forms, modelled on the Terror of the great French revolutionaries. Not the Fortress but the guillotine will await our enemies.

Leon Trotsky to the Soviet Executive, 29 Nov. 1917 (NS); Geoffrey Swain *The Origins of the Russian Civil War* (1996) p.257. The 'Fortress' was the Peter-Paul Fortress, the traditional repository for political prisoners – equivalent to the Paris Bastille.

9 Do not think that I seek forms of revolutionary justice; we are not now in need of justice. It is war now – face to face, a fight to the finish. Life or death!

Felix Dzerzhinsky, 20 Dec. 1917 (NS); Leggett (1981) p.17. The head of the brand-new political police proclaims his agenda.

10 In one place they will put into prison a dozen rich men, a dozen scoundrels, a half-dozen workers who shirk on the job … In another place they will set them to cleaning outside toilets. In a third they will give them yellow tickets after a term in prison … so that the entire people … will act as the overseers of them as harmful people. In a fourth they will shoot on the spot one out of every ten guilty of sloth.

Lenin, 9 Jan. 1918 (NS); *Collected Works* Vol.26 (1964) p.414.

11 The Marxists, prosaic, dry, and businesslike, are the bookkeepers and clerks of the revolution, the Socialist Revolutionaries its prophets, heroes, and poets.

P. Surmin 'The Poets of Revolution', 6 July 1918 (NS); Leggett (1981) p.70. The Socialist Revolutionaries, the party of the peasantry, although they greatly outnumbered the Bolsheviks, were incapable of outmanoeuvring them and soon vanished from the political scene.

1   *Belsatzar ward in selbiger Nacht*
     Von seinen Knechten umgebracht.
(That very night was Belshazzar/Butchered by his slaves.)

Graffiti on the wall of the cellar in Ekaterinburg, where the tsar and his family were said to have been murdered on 16 July 1918 (NS); Anthony Summers and Tom Mangold *The File on the Tsar* (1976) p.75. The quotation was adapted from a poem by the German writer Heinrich Heine, based on the Book of Daniel (Ch.5). The German 'Balsazar' has been modified to underscore the reference to the tsar. Who wrote it and when, we shall never know.

2 You must … *instantly* introduce mass terror, *shoot and transport* hundreds of prostitutes who get the soldiers drunk, ex-officers, etc. Not a minute to be wasted … You must act at full stretch: mass searches. Executions for possession of weapons. Mass deportations of Mensheviks and unreliable elements.

Lenin, telegram of 9 Aug. 1918 (NS); *Collected Works* Vol.28 (1965) p.142.

3 There is no sphere of life exempt from Vecheka coverage. The Vecheka must look after everything: the armed forces, food production, education and culture, all economic organizations, medical services, fire prevention, the communications systems, etc., etc.

Martyn Latsis, director of the Secret Operational Department of the Cheka, late 1920; Leggett (1981) p.349. Latsis was to be executed in Stalin's purge some time in 1938.

4 The terror of Tsarism was directed against the proletariat. The gendarmerie of Tsarism throttled the workers who were fighting for the Socialist order. Our Extraordinary Commissions [the Cheka] shoot landlords, capitalists, and generals who are striving to restore the capitalist order.

Leon Trotsky *Terrorism and Communism* (1920). Trotsky's rejoinder to the criticism of Bolshevik terror tactics by the German Marxist Karl Kautsky. In practice the terror destroyed not just the obvious embodiments of the *ancien régime*, but anyone it considered might conceivably pose a threat to Bolshevism, no matter how remote. So the foundations were laid for Stalin's purges in the 1930s, in which Trotsky himself became one of the most prominent victims (see 742:9).

CIVIL WAR, 1918–21

5 I saw a boundless hatred of ideas and of people, of everything that was socially or intellectually higher than the crowds, of everything which bore the slightest trace of abundance, even of inanimate objects, which were the symbols of some culture strange or inaccessible to the crowd.

General Anton Denikin *Memoirs* Vol.2 (1922) pp.147–8. Denikin was one of the most prominent White (reactionary) generals in the civil war, operating in the Kuban region east of the Black Sea.

6 The mounted platoon entered the village, met the Bolshevik committee, and put the members to death, after which they demanded the surrender of the murderers [of several White troops] … They were delivered to us and executed on the spot … After the execution, the houses of the culprits were burned and the whole male population under forty-five whipped soundly, the whipping being done by the old men.

White Colonel M. Drozdovsky, diary entry, 22 March 1918 (NS); *Dnevnik* (Diary) (1923).

7 Drinking parties frequently ended in shooting at fellow customers, at mirrors or in the air; the officers saw partisans, underground workers and Bolsheviks everywhere.

Ilya Ehrenburg *First Years of Revolution* (1962) p.94. White officers on the edge.

8 At the present time, the prisons of the socialist-communist state swallow up mainly the proletariat of town and country. A free people has no need of prisons, and where there are prisons, the people are not free. Prisons are an eternal menace to the toilers, an attempt to stifle their conscience and free will, and an index of their serfdom. This was the attitude to prisons, and the reason why the Makhnovists demolished them wherever they went.

P. Arshinov *History of the Makhno Movement* (1923) p.149. The Ukrainian peasant N.I. Makhno led an anarchist force during the civil war, at first allied to the Bolshevik Red Army but ultimately destroyed by it in Aug. 1921.

9 Undressing an officer naked, they tore bits of skin in the shape of epaulettes from his shoulders, and in place of the little stars hammered in nails; they cut strips of skin along the line of the trouser strips and sword belt – this they called 'dressing him up in uniform'. It took no little time and considerable art.

Maxim Gorky *O Russkom Krestyanstve* (On the Russian Peasantry) (1922). Gorky witnessed these and other Bolshevik atrocities.

1 Armed detachments would be put off the train as 'landing parties'. The appearance of a leather-coated detachment in a dangerous place invariably had an overwhelming effect. When they were aware of the train just a few kilometres behind the firing-line, even the most nervous units, their commanding officers especially, would summon up all their strength.
Leon Trotsky *My Life* (1930) pp.419–20. Trotsky directed military operations from his armoured train.

2 What is better? To ferret out, to imprison, sometimes even to shoot hundreds of traitors … who 'come out' … against the Soviet power, *in other words, in favour of Denikin*? Or to allow matters to reach a pass enabling Kolchak and Denikin to slaughter, shoot and flog to death tens of thousands of workers and peasants? The choice is not difficult to make.
Lenin to the Bolshevik Central Committee, July 1919 (NS); *Collected Works* Vol.29 (1965) pp.436 ff. Admiral Alexander Kolchak was another prominent White leader.

3 Though the masses may want new principles, and might for a moment submit to a reintroduction of very old principles in desperate hope of less hunger and less cold, no one but a lunatic would imagine that they would for very long willingly submit to them.
Arthur Ransome *Six Weeks in Russia in 1919* (1919) p.196. The English writer catches the intense war-weariness and resignation of the majority of Russian people, who preferred submission to Bolshevik control over the return to the past offered by the Whites or the endless turbulence of civil conflict.

4 The glorious emblem of the workers' state – the sickle and hammer – has in fact been replaced by the Communist authorities with the bayonet and barred window, for the sake of maintaining the calm and carefree life of the new bureaucracy of Communist commissars and functionaries.
'What We Are Fighting For', Kronstadt Temporary Revolutionary Committee, 8 March 1921 (NS); *The Truth about Kronstadt* (1921) pp.82–3. The last act of the civil war came in March 1921 with the revolt against Bolshevik authority by the naval garrison of the island fortress of Kronstadt, offshore from Petrograd. This insurgency by the Russian far left was suppressed within days at high cost to both sides.

5 This Kronstadt affair in itself is a petty incident. It no more threatens to break up the Soviet state than

the Irish disorders are threatening to break up the British Empire.
Lenin, 15 March 1921 (NS); *Collected Works* Vol.36 (1966) p.538.

6 17 March [NS] – Kronstadt has fallen today. Thousands of sailors and workers lie dead in the streets. Summary execution of prisoners and hostages continues. 18 March [NS] – the victors are celebrating the anniversary of the Commune of 1871. Trotsky and Zinoviev denounce Thiers and Gallifet for the slaughter of the Paris rebels.
Alexander Berkman; *The Bolshevik Myth: Diary 1920–1922* (1925) p.303. For the Paris Commune see 670:3–671:6.

7 While the state exists there is no freedom. When freedom exists there will be no state.
Lenin *The State and Revolution* (1917); *Collected Works* Vol.33 (1966) p.95.

LENIN'S FINAL YEARS, 1921–4

8 A peculiar war communism … was forced on us by extreme want, ruin and war … It was not, and could not be, a policy that corresponded to the economic tasks of the proletariat. It was a makeshift.
Lenin, 21 April 1921 (NS); *Collected Works* Vol.32 (1965) pp.342–3. Lenin coined the term 'War Communism' for the requisition programme adopted during the civil war. He justified it as an emergency measure that could now be replaced by a 'New Economic Policy' (NEP), which would leave the peasantry alone and give scope to private business activity.

9 The transition to the new economic policies represented the collapse of our illusions.
Nikolai Bukharin on the NEP, attrib.; not all Bolsheviks were enthusiasts for Lenin's U-turn.

10 They have coined a new word – *nepman* … symbol of degradation, object of scorn and contumely! Pariahs, social swine! Villain on the stage, villain in the motion pictures, villain in everyday life! *Nepman* – label, curse, anathema!
Maurice Hindus *Broken Earth* (1925).

11 The words of St Paul that were posted up everywhere, '*He that doth not work, neither shall he eat!*' became ironical, because if you wanted any food you really had to resort to the black market instead of working.
Victor Serge *Memoirs of a Revolutionary 1901–1941* (1967) p.115. The quotation from St Paul is in the Second Epistle to the Thessalonians 3:10.

1 All the time they grow thinner and thinner, and some of them die and the rest get ready to follow them. In their faces is absolute despair ... 'One of my children died yesterday,' says an old peasant, almost without looking up at me. 'Another died three days ago. We shall all die soon.'

C.E. Bechhofer *Through Starving Russia* (1921). The summer of 1921 saw famine sweep across the Volga region, killing hundreds of thousands of peasants.

2 It is now and only now, when in the regions afflicted by the famine there is cannibalism and the roads are littered with hundreds if not thousands of corpses that we can (and therefore must) pursue the acquisition of valuables with the most ferocious and merciless energy ... We must now give the most decisive and merciless battle to the Black Hundreds clergy and subdue their resistance with such brutality that they will not forget it for decades to come.

Lenin, 19 March 1922 (NS); Richard Pipes *Russia under the Bolshevik Regime 1919–1924* (1994) p.35. Lenin seizes on the aftermath of the famine as an opportunity to strike against the Orthodox Church. The Black Hundreds were the reactionary gangs formed to persecute Jews in the wake of the assassination of Tsar Alexander II in 1881 (see 677:1).

3 Get down to business, all of you. The capitalists will be beside you ... They will make a profit from you of several hundred per cent. They will profiteer all around you. Let them make a fortune, but learn from them how to run a business. Only then will you be able to build a communist republic.

Lenin, speech, 17 Oct. 1921 (NS); *Collected Works* Vol.33 (1966) pp.71–2. Paradoxical advice to a presumably bemused audience.

4 On the matter of deporting the Mensheviks, Popular Socialists, Kadets and the like from Russia. Several *hundred* such gentlemen ... must be deported without mercy. We will purge Russia for a long time to come.

Lenin to Joseph Stalin, 17 July 1922 (NS); Pipes (1998) pp.168–9. Despite his economic reversal, Lenin was still a political monopolist.

5 Comrade Stalin, having become Secretary General, has concentrated *unlimited authority* in his hands and I am not certain *whether he will always be capable of using that authority with sufficient caution* ... Stalin is too rude and this defect ... becomes intolerable in the post of Secretary General. That is why I suggest that comrades think of a way of removing Stalin from that post.

Lenin, 25 Dec. 1922 (NS) and 4 Jan. 1923 (NS); *Selected Works* (1968) pp.682–3. The words are part of Lenin's so-called 'Testament', in which he reviewed the performance of his possible successors. They were prompted by Stalin's insulting behaviour towards Lenin's wife, and on 5 March 1923 (NS) Lenin wrote to Stalin, threatening to sever relations with him. Four days later he suffered a massive stroke and died on 21 Jan. 1924 (NS).

LENIN'S ACHIEVEMENT

6 May I, before descending to the tomb, see the humiliation of the arrogant bourgeois democracies, today shamelessly triumphant.

Georges Sorel *Reflections on Violence* (1919 edn) App.3 'In defence of Lenin'. A paean from the father of Syndicalism (and admirer of Mussolini), written after the victory of the capitalist West in World War I.

7 Lenin is an artist who worked on humans as other artists work on marble or metal. But human beings are harder than granite and less malleable than iron. The artist has failed. The task has proven beyond his powers.

Benito Mussolini, July 1920 (NS); *Opera Omnia* Vol.15 (1954) p.93. A premature political obituary, the wishful thinking of a one-time socialist now the purveyor of a new brand of right-wing ideology, fascism.

8 Who whom?

Lenin, 17 Oct. 1921 (NS); *Collected Works* Vol.33 (1966) p.65. A famous ellipsis, to be understood as 'Who controls whom?' The question succinctly expresses Lenin's view of the world as a matter of power relationships, the view of a ruthless political warrior convinced that he was involved in life-or-death combat with equally merciless opponents. Self-revelation in just two words.

9 I cannot listen to music, it excites my nerves. I feel like talking nonsense and caressing people who, living in such a filthy hell, can create such beauty. Because today one must not caress anyone: they will bite off your hand. One must break heads, pitilessly break heads, even if, ideally, we are opposed to all violence.

Lenin to Gorky; Maxim Gorky *Vladimir Lenin* (1924). The doyen of revolutionaries resists the temptation to be a human being.

10 Life is organized with such devilish cunning that if one does not know how to hate, it is impossible truly to love. This in itself, this ambivalence in the soul, is what corrupts man to his very core, this law of love through the road of hate condemns life to destructiveness.

Maxim Gorky (1924); Bertram Wolfe *The Bridge and the Abyss* (1957) p.157. An ambiguous judgement on a leader progressing to a better world through a sea of blood.

1 Out of every hundred Bolsheviks 70 are fools and 29 rogues, and only one a real socialist.

Lenin, marginalia; Bertram Wolfe *Lenin and the Twentieth Century* (1984) p.190. No prizes for guessing who was in the minority of one.

2 The dead Lenin seems to have been reborn: there you have the solution of the riddle of the risen Christ. He has been resurrected for us again ... The real danger begins when the bureaucracy makes attitudes towards Lenin and his teaching a subject of automatic reverence.

Leon Trotsky 'On Unctuousness' (unpublished article, 1927). Written when the embalmed body of Lenin had been placed in the mausoleum in Red Square, Moscow, as a lasting reminder to the living world of his achievement.

3 The Germans turned upon Russia the most grisly of all weapons. They transported Lenin in a sealed truck like a plague bacillus from Switzerland to Russia ... He alone could have led Russia into the enchanted quagmire; he alone could have found the way back to the causeway. He saw; he turned; he perished ... The Russian people were left floundering in the bog. Their worst misfortune was his birth, their next worst – his death.

Winston Churchill *The World Crisis: The Aftermath* (1929) p.76.

4 The darkness of death only emphasizes the more strongly to the world his great importance – his importance ... as the leader of the working class of the world.... There is no force which can put out the torch which Lenin raised aloft in the stifling darkness of a mad world.

Maxim Gorky *V.I. Lenin* (1931) p.46. Deification, towards which Gorky had moved from the hostility of 1917 and the ambivalence of 1924 (see 728:6 and 734:10).

5 The great modesty of the genius of the revolution, Vladimir Ilyich Lenin, is known ... While ascribing

great importance to the role of leaders and organizers of the masses, Lenin at the same time mercilessly stigmatized every manifestation of the cult of the individual ... Lenin resolutely stood out against every attempt at belittling or weakening the directing role of the party in the structure of the Soviet State ... During Lenin's life the Central Committee of the party was a real expression of collective leadership of the party and of the nation.

Nikita Khrushchev, speech to the 20th Congress of the Communist Party of the Soviet Union, 25 Feb. 1956; *The Dethronement of Stalin* (1956) pp.3,4. While Stalin was toppled from his pedestal, Lenin's mystique was still unassailable.

6 From the earliest days socialist structures were replaced by state institutions. In part spontaneously, the Bolsheviks began using the vast arsenal assembled by the state: the unlimited power of the bureaucracy, strict centralization, undivided state power, regimentation of public life, and ideology as a substitute for religion. The imperial style of government was thus preserved by the Bolsheviks. Having destroyed first the tsarist and then the bourgeois dictatorship, Lenin replaced them by the dictatorship of his Party. Since the historical traditions which created the Bolsheviks were incapable of evolution, one form of oppression was replaced by another, both harsher and more repugnant.

Dmitri Volkogonov *Lenin* (1995 edn) p.480. The continuity between tsarism and Leninism underscored by a revisionist Russian historian of the post-Communist era.

7 His impact not just on Russia but on world history in the 20th century has been incalculable. In 1990 a poll in what was still, just, the Soviet Union, put him third among world figures for all ages, after Peter the Great and Christ. Like Christ, he became for his people a martyr and a saint, whose teachings could not be challenged. Like Peter his revolution was one of Westernization and modernization, often through barbaric methods.

Beryl Williams *Lenin* (2000) pp.205–6. Hagiolatry proof against history.

Stalinism and Maoism, 1924–40

RUSSIA: SUCCESSION STRUGGLE, 1924–28

1 To lead the Party otherwise than collectively is impossible. Now that Ilyich [Lenin] is not with us, it is silly to dream of such a thing.
Joseph Stalin, Dec. 1925; Robert Tucker *Stalin as Revolutionary* (1973) p.310. A triumvirate of Stalin, Zinoviev and Kamenev had already been formed before Lenin's death, designed to keep Trotsky from succeeding Lenin as supreme head of the Soviet Union.

2 He is needed by all of them – by the tired radicals, by the bureaucrats, by the *nepmen*, the kulaks, the upstarts, the sneaks, by all the worms that are crawling out of the upturned soil of the manured revolution.
Leon Trotsky on Stalin, 1924; *Stalin* (1940; 1967 edn) p.393. The antagonism between Trotsky and Stalin dated from the early days of the civil war in 1918.

3 Civilization has made the peasantry its pack animal. The bourgeoisie in the long run only changed the form of the pack.
Leon Trotsky *History of the Russian Revolution* (1933) Vol.3, Ch.1. For Trotsky the Russian peasantry was a decisive obstacle to the fulfilment of the revolution. Hence his belief that only the advent of Marxist Socialist regimes in the advanced industrial societies of Europe could guarantee success in Russia. Compare Lenin in 1918 (see 729:4).

4 The contradictions in the position of a workers' government in a backward country with an overwhelmingly peasant population could be solved only on an international scale, in the arena of the world proletarian revolution.
Leon Trotsky *The Year 1905* (1922) Preface. In spite of the failure to generate a revolution in Germany in 1919, Trotsky persisted in the orthodox internationalist view that revolution in Russia had to be buoyed up by a Marxist upsurge elsewhere if it were to survive.

5 The victory of socialism in one country, even if that country is less developed in the capitalist sense, while capitalism remains in other countries, even if those countries are more developed in the capitalist sense – is quite possible and probable.
Joseph Stalin, *On the Road to October*, 17 Dec. 1924, Preface; *Works* Vol.6 (1953) p.387. Stalin took this pragmatic line not least to outface Trotsky in the succession contest.

6 What is the party today? Nothing but a herd of sheep, not daring to have opinions but only trying to please, fearing any independent acts.
I.I. Litvinov, 1924; Vladimir Brovkin *Russia After Lenin* (1998) p.54.

7 My party – right or wrong … I know one cannot be right against the Party … for history has created no other way for the realization of what is right.
Leon Trotsky, May 1924; Leonard Schapiro *The Communist Party of the Soviet Union* (1970) p.381.

8 A true Bolshevik … would be ready to believe that black was white, and white was black, if the Party required it.
Grigory Pyatakov, 1928; Robert Conquest *The Great Terror* (1990) p.113. Pyatakov was purged and executed early in 1937.

9 If they say today, let us have democracy in the Party, tomorrow they will say, let us have democracy in the trade unions; the day after tomorrow, workers who do not belong to the Party may well say: give us democracy too … and surely then the myriad peasants could not be prevented from asking for democracy.
Lev Kamenev, 1924; Conquest (1990) pp.114–15.

10 So long as you don't have a union card, you'd better not give him any trouble. He is the working class. Like lava from a volcano he sweeps away everything in his path.
Vladimir Mayakovsky *The Bedbug* (1928) Sc.1. A comment on the main character in the play, Ivan Prisypkin, a man of the people, in a biting satire on NEP (New Economic Policy) Russia. Mayakovsky killed himself in 1930. In 1935 he was given Stalin's imprimatur for some unfathomable reason and became an official cult-figure.

11 On pay-days, some drunkard proletarians lay dead drunk on the side-walks and others reviled you as you passed. I was despised as a bespectacled intellectual.
Victor Serge *Memoirs of a Revolutionary* (1967) p.149. Serge was a colleague of Trotsky, writing here of Leningrad in 1925 under the New Economic Policy, when the writ of the Party evidently did not run far.

12 You, Red executioners, you'd better know that the steam engine of peasant patience is going to explode some day. You'd better know that the peasants curse you usurpers in their morning prayer. You are stealing the last cow, the last belongings … Why did you fool us with words such as freedom, land, peace, equality?

Peasant protest, March 1925; Vladimir Brovkin *Russia after Lenin* (1998) pp.74, 75. Remarkable evidence of agrarian discontent with the Bolshevik regime.

1 Our policy in relation to the countryside should develop in the direction of renewing, and in part abolishing, many restrictions which put the brake on the growth of the well-to-do and kulak farm. To the peasants we must say: 'Enrich yourselves, develop your farms, and do not fear that restrictions will be put upon you.'

Nikolai Bukharin, *Pravda* (Truth), 24 April 1925. Bukharin soon had to retract this echo of the exhortation of Guizot in the 1840s (see 533:2) in urging the appeasement of rural conservatism.

2 The First Secretary poses his candidature for the post of grave-digger of the Revolution.

Leon Trotsky to Stalin, 26 Oct. 1926; Isaac Deutscher *The Prophet Unarmed* (1959) pp.296–7. The ultimate insult, echoing as it did Karl Marx's verdict on Napoleon I and Napoleon III as terminators of the First and Second French Republics. Trotsky had just been deprived of his seat on the Politburo, the inner circle of Soviet government.

3 Another chapter opened in France when … the Thermidorians and the Bonapartists … began to exile and shoot the left Jacobins … Do you, Comrade Soly, see clearly, in which chapter you are preparing to shoot us? I fear … that you are about to do so in … the Thermidorian chapter.

Leon Trotsky, 24 July 1927; Deutscher (1959) p.344. Trotsky was contesting accusations by Stalin contrived to lead to his expulsion from the party. Soly, an old Bolshevik, now a confirmed Stalinist, had raised the analogy of the French Revolution. For Thermidor see 525:12.

4 Yes, I am rude, comrades, toward those who rudely and treacherously wreck and split the Party. I have never concealed this and do not do so now. It may be that a certain softness should be shown toward splitters. But it doesn't come off with me.

Joseph Stalin *Pravda*, 2 Nov. 1927. Speaking to the 15th Party Congress, Stalin was referring to Lenin's 'Testament' (see 734:5) in which Lenin had accused Stalin of abusive behaviour to his wife and other Party members. Here he adroitly turns an admission into a powerful self-justification. The terms of the Testament were made known to the Congress delegates in the strictest confidence. Trotsky, the target of these remarks, was expelled from the Party on 14 Nov.

5 What is no longer human, but something devilish, is that … he can't help revenging himself on people, on everybody, but especially those who are superior to him or better at something.

Nikolai Bukharin on Stalin, 1928; Joel Carmichael *Stalin's Masterpiece* (1976) p.116.

COLLECTIVIZATION, 1927–36

6 The way out is to unite the small and dwarf peasant farms gradually but surely, not by pressure but by example and persuasion, into large farms based on common, cooperative, collective cultivation of the land … There is no other way out.

Joseph Stalin, Dec. 1927; *Works* Vol.10 (1954) pp.312–13. Stalin had by this juncture decided to abandon the New Economic Policy of coexistence with private enterprise in agriculture and light industry and to go all-out for a command economy under the first of a series of five-year plans running from 1928 to 1933. The farms, which had been in the hands of the peasants since 1917, were now to be 'collectivized', that is, placed under the control of the Soviet state.

7 Now we are able to carry on a determined offensive against the kulaks, eliminate them as a class … It is ridiculous and foolish to discourse at length on dekulakization. When the head is off one does not mourn for the hair.

Joseph Stalin, 27 Dec. 1929; *Works* Vol.12 (1955) p.179. The kulaks, the richer peasants, were now seen as the enemy of the state and the most serious obstacle to socialization of the economy.

8 The 'kulak' child was loathsome, the young 'kulak' girl was lower than a louse. They looked on the so-called 'kulaks' as cattle, swine, loathsome, repulsive. They had no souls; they stank; they all had venereal diseases; they were enemies of the people and exploited the labour of others.

Vasily Grossman *Forever Flowing* (1972). Grossman, a Russian Jew, draws an implicit parallel between the Soviet treatment of the richer peasantry with subsequent Nazi treatment of the Jews of Europe.

9 You must assume your duties with a feeling of the strictest Party responsibility, without whimpering, without any rotten liberalism. Throw your bourgeois humanitarianism out of the window and act like Bolsheviks worthy of Comrade Stalin. Beat down the kulak agent wherever he raises his head. It's war – it's them or us! The last decayed

remnant of capitalist farming must be wiped out at any cost!
Victor Kravchenko *I Chose Freedom* (1946) pp.91–2. A Party functionary addresses the shock troops of collectivization.

1 They become dizzy with success, lose all sense of proportion, lose the faculty of understanding realities, reveal a tendency to overestimate their own strength and to underestimate the struggle of the enemy; reckless attempts are made to settle all the problems of socialist construction in 'two ticks'.
Joseph Stalin, *Pravda*, 2 March 1930. The leader professes to reprimand the apparatchiks for their over-zealousness in the collectivization drive.

2 Stock was slaughtered every night in Gromyachy. Hardly had dusk fallen when the muffled, short bleats of sheep, the death squeak of pigs, or the lowing of calves could be heard … 'Kill, it's not ours any more' … And they killed. They ate till they could eat no more … Everyone blinked like an owl, as if drunk from eating.
The novelist Mikhail Sholokhov *The Upturned Soil* (1934) p.152.

3 The peasant is adopting a new tactic. He refuses to reap the harvest. He wants the bread grain to die in order to choke the Soviet Government with the bony hand of famine. But the enemy miscalculates. We will show him what famine is.
S.P. Kossiov, first secretary of the Ukraine, summer 1930; Petro Grigorenko *Memoirs* (1933) p.36.

4   A Tsar rules the world,
    A Tsar without mercy,
    And his name is Hunger.
Trad. Russian saying.

5 For the Workers' State to survive, the kulaks and indeed the individualistic peasantry had to be destroyed … The famine issue is, in a sense, irrelevant.
Not Stalin, but the English historian A.J.P. Taylor, writing to the journalist Malcolm Muggeridge, 13 Feb. 1933; Kathleen Burk's biography of Taylor *Troublemaker* (2000) p.123. Muggeridge was an eyewitness of the famine (see 738:12); Taylor was not.

6 In the terrible spring of 1933 I saw people dying from hunger. I saw women and children with distended bellies, turning blue, still breathing but with vacant, lifeless eyes. And corpses – corpses in ragged sheepskin coats and cheap felt boots; corpses in peasant huts, in the melting snow of the old

Vologda, under the bridges of Kharkov … I saw all this and did not go out of my mind or commit suicide.
Lev Kopelev, a Party activist, *The Education of a True Believer* (1977) p.12.

7 Day and night it was guarded by militia keeping the starving peasants and their children away from the restaurant … In the dining room, at very low prices, white bread, meat, poultry, canned fruit and delicacies, wines and sweets were served to the district bosses … Around these oases famine and death were raging.
Hryhory Kostiuk *Stalinist Rule in the Ukraine* (1960) p.44.

8 It has to be this way, because then it will be easier to remake the peasants' smallholder psychology into the proletarian psychology that we need. And those who die of hunger, let them die. If they cannot defend themselves against death from starvation, it means that they are weak-willed, and what can they give to society.
Stefan Podlubny, diary entry, 14 Aug. 1933; Sheila Fitzpatrick (ed.) *Stalinism: New Directions* (2000) p.102. The words of a 19-year-old apprentice printer.

9 The 'famine' is mostly bunk.
Walter Duranty to H.R. Knickerbocker, 27 June 1933; S.J. Taylor *Stalin's Apologist* (1990) p.210. Duranty was Moscow correspondent of the *New York Times* and an uncritical admirer of Stalin.

10 It seems that you are a good storyteller, you've made up such a fable about famine, thinking to frighten us, but it won't work. Wouldn't it be better for you to leave [your] post … and join the Writers' Union? Then you can write your fables and fools will read them.
Joseph Stalin to Terekhov, first secretary of Kharkov, 1933; Robert Conquest *The Harvest of Sorrow* (1986) pp.324–5.

11 On the road to the village, former ikons with the face of Christ had been removed; but the crown of thorns had been allowed to remain – an appropriate symbol for what the village had experienced.
William Henry Chamberlin *Russia's Iron Age* (1934) p.368. The American writer Chamberlin lived in the Soviet Union from 1924 to 1934.

12 One particularly remarkable scene I stumbled on by chance at a railway station in the grey early morning; peasants with their hands tied behind them being loaded into cattle trucks at gun-point … all so silent and mysterious and horrible in the half-light, like some macabre ballet.

Malcolm Muggeridge, early 1933, *Chronicles of Wasted Time* Vol.I (1972) pp.257–8. Muggeridge, Moscow correspondent for the *Manchester Guardian*, witnessed the Ukraine famine.

I In our country there are no longer any landlords and kulaks, merchants and usurers who could exploit the peasants. Consequently our peasantry is a peasantry emancipated from exploitation.

Joseph Stalin, 25 Nov. 1936; *Leninism* (1940) p.566.

INDUSTRIALIZATION, 1927–35

2 Sixteen men in Moscow today are attempting one of the most audacious economic experiments in history ... One suspects that Henry Ford would quail before [it]. For lesser mortals a journey to the moon would seem about as possible.

The American economist Stuart Chase on the projected Soviet five-year plan, *New York Times*, 11 Dec. 1927.

3 Should we, perhaps, for the sake of greater caution, retard the development of heavy industry so as to make light industry, which produces chiefly for the peasant market, the basis of our industry? Not under any circumstances! That would be ... suicidal; it would mean ... transforming our country into an appendage of the world capitalist system of economy.

Joseph Stalin, 28 May 1928; Hiroaki Kuromiya *Stalin's Industrial Revolution* (1988) p.19.

4 The appearance of the streets is changing. Only two-three years ago they were crowded with signs of private merchants ... and show windows attracted shoppers. Now private traders are not seen ... The show windows have become empty ... There disappeared from the streets the expensive fur coats and the provocative, tasteless apparel by which NEP men were plainly distinguishable to the eye. The streets have turned grey.

Soviet government description in 1936 of the austerity of 1929; Kuromiya (1988) p.82.

5 If one wants to build a new house, one saves up money and cuts down consumption for a while. Otherwise the house would not be built. This is all the more true when it is a matter of building an entire new human society. We had to cut down consumption for a time, collect the necessary resources, and strain every nerve. This is precisely what we did and we built a socialist society.

Joseph Stalin, interview with Roy Howard, 1936; Kuromiya (1988) p.231.

6 We are advancing full steam ahead along the path of industrialization – to Socialism, leaving behind the age-long 'Russian' backwardness. We are becoming a country of metal, a country of automobiles, a country of tractors. And when we have put the USSR in an automobile, and the *muzhik* on a tractor, let the worthy capitalists who boast so loudly of their 'civilization', try to overtake us.

Joseph Stalin, *Pravda*, 7 Nov. 1929, an article published just two weeks after the beginning of the Wall Street Crash in the United States (see 764:12). *Muzhik* (peasant) means, literally, 'little man', as peasants had the legal status of minors.

7 She observed for a day how people worked with a machine, and then was assigned to this machine. So now, after having stayed in the plant for several months, she knows neither the names of the parts she makes with the machine nor what role the parts play in the tractor.

Young Komsomol worker at the Stalingrad Tractor Plant, 1930; Kuromiya (1988) p.217. Komsomol, the Young Communist League, was the youth wing of the Party.

8 One feature of the history of old Russia was the continual beatings she suffered for falling behind, for her backwardness ... That is why we must no longer lag behind ... We are fifty or a hundred years behind the advanced countries. We must make good this distance in ten years. Either we do it or they crush us.

Joseph Stalin, Feb. 1931; *Problems of Leninism* (1945) pp.445–6.

9 We must finish once and for all with the neutrality of chess. We must condemn once and for all the formula 'chess for the sake of chess', like the formula 'art for art's sake'. We must organize shock brigades of chess players, and begin immediate realization of a five-year plan for chess.

N.V. Krylenko, 1932; Boris Souvarine *Stalin* (1939) p.575. Planning reduced to absurdity by this senior apparatchik. His enthusiasm did not save him from victimization later in the 1930s.

10 To put it brutally – you can't make an omelette without breaking eggs, and the Bolshevik leaders are just as indifferent to the casualties that may be involved in their drive toward socialism as any General during the World War who ordered a costly attack in order to show his superiors that he and his division possessed the proper soldierly spirit. In fact, the Bolsheviki are more indifferent because they are animated by fanatical conviction.

Walter Duranty, *New York Times*, 31 March 1933.

1 The most outstanding and decisive of those changes [in the work-force] is the transformation of the basic masses of the workers into shock workers, into people who have acquired a new attitude toward labour, regarding it as a matter of honour. By his example, the shock worker kindles the enthusiasm of the backward workers, educates them and overcomes the non-proletarian, petty-bourgeois traditions brought into the proletarian environment from outside.

The Fulfilment of the First Five-Year Plan (1933) p.183. The military imagery is significant: industrialization was the prerequisite of national security against a hostile outside world.

2 During this period, the USSR has become radically transformed and has thrown off the oppressive weight of backwardness and medievalism. From an agrarian country it has become an industrial country ... How was it possible for these colossal changes to take place in a matter of three or four years on the territory of a vast state with a backward technique and a backward culture? ... Naturally, this enormous progress could take place only on the basis of the successful building of socialism.

Joseph Stalin, 26 Jan. 1934; *Collected Works* Vol.13 (1955) pp.312–15.

3 At the 'Red Dawn' plant, during a conversation about the Stakhanovite movement among the women workers of the winding department on 17 October [1935], one worker, Pavlova, announced that she was transferring from 12 bobbins to 15. After the break, worker Smirnova hung a dirty rag on Pavlova's machine and said: 'There's a prize for your activism in transferring to more intensive work!'

Sheila Fitzpatrick *Everyday Stalinism* (1999) p.105. A risky putdown. The miner Alexei Stakhanov (1905–77) cut 102 tons of coal in a single shift on 1 Sept. 1935. He was instantly made the hero of a national production drive and the word Stakhanovite became the synonym for a worker achieving record output.

4 Everybody now says that the material condition of the toilers has considerably improved, that life has become better, more cheerful.

Joseph Stalin, *Pravda*, 2 Dec. 1935. A celebrated affirmation of faith in the industrialization drive.

5 The *brigadir*-welder Vl. Baranov (28, the best Stakhanovite at Elektrozavod) glided across the floor in a slow tango with Shura Ovchinnikova (20, the best Stakhanovite at TsAGI). He was dressed in a black Boston suit that fully accentuated his solidly built figure; she was in a crepe de chine dress and black shoes with white trimming.

Two Stakhanovites celebrating the New Year, 1936; Lewis Fiegelbaum *Stakhanovism and the Politics of Productivity in the USSR, 1935–1941* (1988) p.230.

THE PURGE, 1934–40

6 *Za chto?* (What for?)

The question asked by the myriad Russians arrested in the purges carried out by Stalin in the 1930s. The accused repeated the question so often that fellow-prisoners described it as 'record number one' and told them to turn it off.

7 Writers are the engineers of human souls.

Joseph Stalin, attrib. 'That baleful murderer of the human spirit', as Jan Morris has described him, had a consuming ambition to be considered a great writer.

8 Years of friendship and fighting side by side in a common cause might as well never have been. He could wipe it all out at a stroke – and X would be doomed.

Stalin's daughter, Svetlana Alleluyeva *Twenty Letters to a Friend* (1967) p.86.

9 If he had offended someone, he would constantly excuse himself, if he thought that was necessary, but subsequently everyone of whom Stalin had asked forgiveness was executed or killed on his orders.

Lydia Nord *Marshal M.N. Tukashevsky* (1978).

10 That blending of grit, shrewdness, craftiness and cruelty which has been considered characteristic of the statesmen of Asia.

Veteran Bolshevik Leonid Krasin on Stalin's attributes; Trotsky (1940) p.1.

11 Capitalist encirclement is not simply a geographical expression. It means that around the USSR there are hostile class forces, ready to support our class enemies morally, materially, by means of financial blockade and, when the opportunity offers, by means of military intervention.

Joseph Stalin, July 1930; *Works* Vol.12 (1955). The siege mentality that gave such powerful reinforcement to the Stalinist terror.

1 We live, deaf to the land beneath us,
Ten steps away no one hears our speeches,
All we hear is the Kremlin mountaineer,
The murderer and peasant-slayer.
His fingers are fat as grubs
And the words, final as lead weights, fall from
    his lips,
His cockroach whiskers leer
And his boot tops gleam.
Around him a rabble of thin-necked leaders –
Fawning half-men for him to play with.
They whinny, purr or whine
As he prates and points a finger.
One by one forging his laws, to be flung
Like horseshoes at the head, the eye or the
    groin.
And every killing is a treat
For the broad-chested Ossete.

The poet Osip Mandelstam on Stalin, Nov. 1933. Mandelstam was arrested in May 1934 when the secret police found a copy of this poem. He died in a labour camp on 26 Dec. 1938. The word 'Ossete' means of Iranian blood, a thrust at Stalin's Georgian origin.

2 'Who killed him?' I ask, no answer comes, but I know what will happen now: after all, I've written about the burning of the Reichstag. And that night I had a dream but I don't dare tell it even to Boris [her husband]: they themselves killed Kirov so as to start a new terror.

Vera Panova, journalist in Rostov, in the wake of the assassination of the Leningrad Party chief Sergei Kirov on 1 Dec. 1934; Robert Tucker *Stalin in Power* (1990) p.301. Hitler used the burning of the Reichstag on 27 Feb. 1933 as a pretext to launch a campaign of terror against his political opponents (see 754:2). Panova's surmise was almost certainly correct.

3 When the woman I love presents me with a child the first word it shall utter will be: Stalin.

A.O. Aodienko, *Pravda*, 1 Feb. 1935.

4 The small hall echoed with stormy applause, rising to an ovation! ... However, who would dare to be the *first* to stop? ... After eleven minutes the director of the paper factory assumed a business-like expression and sat down in his seat ... That same night the factory director was arrested [and] his interrogator reminded him: 'Don't ever be the first to stop applauding!'

Alexander Solzhenitsyn *The Gulag Archipelago* (1999 edn) pp.27, 28. This sounds incredible, but it rings all too true.

5 I don't like the constant adulation of this 'great strategist', 'wise chief', and so on ... I personally do not feel this love or even great respect.

Mikhail Molochko, diary entry, 3 Feb. 1935; Roy Medvedev *Let History Judge* (1989) p.680. Amazingly, Molochko was not purged but died in action in the war with Finland in 1940.

6 They are no longer human beings ... They are really cogs in some terrible machine. There is taking place a real dehumanization of the people working in the Soviet apparatus, a process of transforming human power into an empire of the 'iron heel'.

Nikolai Bukharin, 1935, referring to Jack London's book *The Iron Heel* (1907), an indictment of Western capitalism; Carmichael (1976) p.109.

7 A complicated network of decorative deceit in words and action is a highly essential characteristic of Fascist regimes of all stamps and hues.

Nikolai Bukharin, *Izvestiya* (News), 6 July 1936. This was the last article to appear under Bukharin's name. One needs to read between the lines to appreciate that Bukharin was equating Stalinism with Fascism.

8 It's all 'lies' what they write in the draft of the new constitution, that each citizen can write in the press and speak out. Of course it isn't so, you try speaking up, tell how many people died of hunger in the USSR, and you'd get 10 years.

Anon. comment on the 1936 Constitution; Fitzpatrick (1999) p.180.

9 There you have one of the last sharp and easiest means that, before death, leaving this world, one can for the last time spit on the Party, betray the Party.

Joseph Stalin, Dec. 1936, on the suicide of a Moscow Party official who killed himself in protest at the arrest of a friend; Fitzpatrick (1999) p.175.

10 He sought to strike, not at the ideas of his opponent, but at his skull.

Leon Trotsky, 1936; Conquest (1990) p.418 (see 742:9).

11 If only someone would report all this to Stalin.

The poet Boris Pasternak, as reported by the novelist Ilya Ehrenburg in *Novy Mir* (New State) (1962) no.5, p.152.

12 I am leaving life. I am lowering my head not before the proletarian axe which must be merciless but also virginal. I feel my helplessness before a hellish machine, which, probably by the use of medieval methods, has acquired gigantic power, fabricates organized slander, acts boldly and confidently.

Nikolai Bukharin, early March 1937; Medvedev (1989) p.366. The opening words of a letter written shortly before Bukharin's arrest. After his wife had memorized it, it was burned. The text was published in the West in 1965 and in the Soviet Union in 1988 to coincide with Bukharin's posthumous rehabilitation, half a century after he was executed.

1 Our Party will mercilessly crush the band of traitors and betrayers, and wipe out all the Trotskyist Right dregs … We shall totally annihilate the enemies – to the last man – and scatter their ashes to the winds.

Nikita Khrushchev, 6 June 1937; Bruce Franklin *The Essential Stalin* (1973) p.29. In 1956 the same Nikita Khrushchev denounced Stalin for the purges that he had assisted in carrying through in the 1930s as a rising figure in the Party.

2 The GPU has uncovered a whole group of high-ranking secret agents, including Marshal Tukachevsky. The usual exceptions. A replay of the French Revolution. More suspicion than fact. They have learned from the French how to kill one's own.

Andrei Anghilovsky, diary entry, June 1937; Véronique Garros et al. (eds) *Intimacy and Terror: Soviet Diaries of the 1930s* (1995) p.162. The GPU (Main Political Administration) was the political police under another name, when the Cheka was re-titled in Feb. 1922.

3   A pack of lies! Shoot him. J. Stalin.
       Agreed. Blackguard! A dog's death for a dog.
         Beria.
       Maniac. Voroshilov.
       Swine! Kaganovich.

Comments on the letter from a Soviet general pleading for his life; R.W. Davies *Soviet History in the Gorbachev Revolution* (1989) p.67. Read to the Plenum of the Central Committee by Marshal Zhukov, June 1957, and published in 1988. Lavrenti Beria was head of the Secret Police, Kliment Voroshilov was minister of defence, and Lazar Kaganovich was Stalin's brother-in-law.

4 My wife was pregnant. She cried, and begged me to sign, but I couldn't. That day I examined the pros and cons of my own survival. I was convinced that I would be arrested – my turn had come. I was prepared for it. I abhorred all this blood and I couldn't stand it any longer. But nothing happened. I was told later that my colleagues had saved me – at least indirectly. Quite simply, no one dared to report to the hierarchy that I hadn't signed.

Boris Pasternak on his refusal to subscribe to a statement approving the execution of several Red Army generals, c.1937; *The Reporter*, 27 Nov. 1958.

5 It was essential to smile – if you didn't, it meant you were afraid or discontented … The mask was taken off only at home, and then not always – even from your children you had to conceal how horror-struck you were, otherwise, God save you, they might let something slip in school.

Nadezhda Mandelstam *Hope Against Hope* (1971) pp.304–5. The wife of the purged poet Osip Mandelstam.

6   You can pray *freely*,
       But just so God alone can hear.

Tanya Khodkevich was given a ten-year sentence for writing this verse; Solzhenitsyn (1999 edn) p.23.

7 Your future will depend on how the trial goes and on its results. If you begin to lie and to testify falsely, blame yourself. If you manage to endure it, you will save your head and we will feed and clothe you at the Government's expense until your death.

L.M. Zakhovsky, commissar for state security, to the old Bolshevik, Rozenblum, 1937; revealed by Nikita Khrushchev in the secret speech of 25 Feb. 1956 (*The Dethronement of Stalin*, p.16). After severe torture, Rozenblum is told that if he incriminates himself by subscribing to the government's falsehoods about him, he will live – presumably in a labour camp. Zakhovsky is once said to have boasted that he could persuade Karl Marx to admit to being an agent of Bismarck.

8 He lies like an eyewitness.

Old Russian saying.

9 If these vermin had fallen into our hands, any one of us would have torn them apart. But the old swine Trotsky is still alive. I think his time will come, too, and we will deal with him in the proper way.

Alexei Stakhanov, the hero of Soviet labour, *The Story of My Life* (1937) p.126. Trotsky was mortally wounded in Mexico on 20 Aug. 1940 by a Stalinist agent who drove an ice-axe into his head; he died next day.

10 Tsar Ivan hated the boyars, who lived in their patrimonies like little tsars and tried to limit his autocratic power. He began to banish and execute the rich and strong boyars … To fight the boyars he recruited from among the landowners a special force, several thousand strong. This force he called the *oprichniki*.

A.V. Shestakov *A Short History of the USSR* (1938) pp.49–50 (text personally approved by Stalin for the Russian edn published in 1937). The subject is the 16th-century Tsar Ivan IV, the Terrible (see 172:6), and the parallel with the purge of the late 1930s is clear. The boyars were the feudal nobility of Old Russia.

1 Better that ten innocent people should suffer than that one spy get away. When you cut down the forest, wood chips fly.

Nikolai Yezhov, head of the secret police 1936–8; Medvedev (1989) p.603.

2 The old generation with whom ... we once embarked upon the road of revolution ... has been swept off the stage. What Tsarist deportations, prisons, and *katorga* [hard labour], what the privations of life in exile, what civil war, and what illness had not done, Stalin, the worst scourge of the revolution, has accomplished in these last few years.

Leon Trotsky's obituary of one of his sons, 20 Feb. 1938; Isaac Deutscher *The Prophet Outcast* (1963) p.399. The son died on 16 Feb. 1938 after an appendicitis operation, his death possibly arranged by Stalin's secret police. Another son was executed in the purge on 29 Oct. 1937.

3 If my underlings have occupied all the crucial positions in the apparatus, how is it that Stalin is in the Kremlin and that I am in exile?

Leon Trotsky, 1938; Deutscher (1963) p.412.

4 At one moment during the trial a clumsily directed arc lamp clearly revealed to attentive members of the audience a drooping moustache and yellowish face peering out from behind the black glass of one of the private boxes that commanded a view of the courtroom.

Joseph Stalin observing the final stage of Bukharin's trial, March 1938; Fitzroy Maclean *Eastern Approaches* (1949; 1982 edn) pp.119–20.

5 Time will pass. The hateful traitors' graves will become overgrown with tall weeds and thistles, covered with the eternal scorn of the Soviet People, of the entire Soviet nation. While over us, over our happy country, the bright rays of our sun will continue to shine, just as radiantly and joyously as ever. We, our people, shall continue marching along the road, cleared of the last filth and abomination, with our beloved Leader and Teacher, Great Stalin, ahead of us, on and on towards Communism!

Andrei Vyshinsky, 11 March 1938; Arkady Vaksberg *The Prosecutor and the Prey* (1990) p.120. The close of the summing-up for the prosecution at the trial of Nikolai Bukharin and others.

6 Koba, why do you need me to die?

Nikolai Bukharin to Stalin, 13 March 1938; Robert Tucker *Stalin in Power* (1990) p.500. The opening words of a note written after Bukharin was sentenced to death; it was found in Stalin's desk drawer after his death in 1953. Koba was Stalin's first revolutionary pseudonym, taken from the name of a 19th-century fictional Georgian patriot.

7 When Stalin kissed me, he said in my ear, 'If you're a traitor, I'll kill you.'

Alexander Kosarev after a Kremlin banquet in the summer of 1938; Medvedev (1989) p.595.

8 How long I have waited for this!

Nikolai Yezhov, on his arrest, early April 1939; Medvedev (1989) p.460. Yezhov had replaced G.G. Yagoda as head of the secret police on 26 Sept. 1936. He, in turn, was replaced by Lavrenti Beria in Dec. 1938 and was executed in 1940.

9 Can't we arrange things so that people stay on in the camps? If not, we release them, they go back home and pick up again with their old ways. The atmosphere in the camp is different, there it's harder to go wrong. Anyway, we have the voluntary-compulsory [state loan]. So let's have voluntary-compulsory staying-on.

Joseph Stalin, 25 Aug. 1938; Dmitri Volkogonov *Stalin* (1991) p.188.

10 Labour is a matter of honour, valour and heroism.

Inscription over the gates of all labour camps in the Kolyma region. Compare the slogan *Arbeit Macht Frei* (Work Makes You Free) above the gate at the Nazi extermination camp at Auschwitz (see 837:1).

11 The Kolyma was the greatest and most famous island, the pole of ferocity of that amazing country of *Gulag* which, though scattered in an archipelago geographically, was, in the psychological sense, fused into a continent – an almost invisible, almost imperceptible country inhabited by the zek people. And this Archipelago crisscrossed and patterned that other country within which it was located, cutting into its cities, hovering over its streets. Yet there were many who did not even guess at its presence and many, many others who had heard something vague. And only those who had been there knew the whole truth.

Alexander Solzhenitsyn (1999 edn) pp.xv–xvi. Kolyma in northeastern Siberia fronts on to the Sea of Okhotsk. The word Gulag is an acronym for *Glavnoe Upravlenie Lagerei* (Main Camp Administration). Zek is an abbreviation of the Russian word for prisoner.

12   Kolyma, wonderful planet,
     Twelve months winter, the rest summer.

Labour camp rhyme.

1   I have learned how faces fall to bone,
How under the eyelids terror lurks,
How suffering inscribes on cheeks
The hard lines of its cuneiform texts.
How glossy black or ash-fair locks
Thin overnight to tarnished silver
How smiles fade on submissive lips,
And fear quavers in a dry titter.

Anna Akhmatova *The Requiem*, March 1940.

2 The policy of cutting off heads is fraught with major dangers for the Party ... It is a method of bloodletting ... dangerous and contagious; today you cut off one, tomorrow a second, and then a third. Who would remain in the Party?

Joseph Stalin, 1925; *Collected Works* Vol.5 (1953) p.246.

3 Of Christ's twelve Apostles, Judas alone proved to be traitor. But if he had acquired power, he would have represented the other eleven Apostles as traitors.

Leon Trotsky (1940) p.421.

WESTERN APPROACHES

4 It is easy by merely traveling through the country, seeing long lines of freight cars packed with prisoners and considerable numbers of men being marched off to work ... under armed guard, by talking with railroad workers and fellow passengers on trains, to find abundant confirmation of the general impression in Moscow: that Karelia [bordering Finland] has been used as a place of exile and forced labour on a gigantic scale.

William Henry Chamberlin, diary entry, March 1931; *Russia's Iron Age* (1935) p.365.

5 Lady Astor ... having no veneration for dictators nor any awe of eminent persons, frightened the wits out of the interpreters during an interview with Stalin by asking that cunning Caucasian why he had slaughtered so many Russians ... He took it very quietly, replying that ... the violent death of a large number of people was necessary before the Communist State could be firmly established. The reply was not unreasonable. Many Englishmen, including King Charles, had to be killed before Cromwell could be sure of his Commonwealth.

St John Ervine *Bernard Shaw* (1956) p.518. A meeting with Stalin on 27 July 1931.

6 Tomorrow I leave the land of hope and return to our Western countries of despair.

George Bernard Shaw, Moscow, July 1931; David Caute *The Fellow-Travellers* (1973) p.62. Shaw accompanied Lady Astor on a closely guided tour of the USSR. This was his entry in the visitor's book of the deluxe Metropole Hotel in Moscow.

7   I'm always thinking of Russia,
I can't keep her out of my head,
I don't give a damn for Uncle Sham,
I'm a left-wing radical Red.

H.H. Lewis *Thinking of Russia* (1932).

8 Soviet Russia represents a new civilization and a new culture with a new outlook on life, involving a new pattern of behaviour alike in personal conduct and in the relation of the individual to the community; all of which I believe is destined to spread, owing to its superior intellectual and ethical fitness, to many other countries in the course of the next hundred years.

Beatrice Webb, diary entry, 28 July 1932; *The Diary of Beatrice Webb* Vol.4 (1985) p.275. Webb and her husband, Sidney, went on to write a tome entitled *Soviet Communism: A New Civilization?* (1935). In the second edn, published in 1937, the question-mark was removed.

9 Russia proves that you can change human nature sufficiently in one generation ... these kids despise a business man ... Service for profit is a sham ... I believe they will make a race, the meanest of which will be as noble as the best men of our day.

The American 'muckraker' Lincoln Steffens *The Letters of Lincoln Steffens* Vol.2 (1938) pp.627–8.

10 In the abominable distress of the present world now Russia's Plans seem to me salvation ... the miserable arguments of its enemies, far from convincing me, make my blood boil.

André Gide, 23 April 1932; *Journals* Vol.2 (1949) p.232. The French writer, who saw the economic performance of the USSR in contrast with the Great Depression in the West, later became more critical of Stalinism.

11 Offered to us as a means of improving the economic situation, [Communism] is an insult to our intelligence. But offered as a means of making the economic situation *worse*, that is its subtle, its almost irresistible, attraction ... When Cambridge undergraduates take their inevitable trip to Bolshiedom, are they disillusioned when they find it all dreadfully uncomfortable? Of course not. That is what they are looking for.

John Maynard Keynes *New Statesman and Nation*, 10 Nov. 1934. The most prominent liberal economist of his generation appraises Soviet planning.

1 Basically I do not observe much difference between the general character of a trial in Russia and in this country.

Professor Harold Laski *Law and Justice in Soviet Russia* (1935) p.21.

2 For the first time in history we are witnessing a struggle, cold-blooded in purpose and mapped out to the least detail, between man and 'all that is called God'. Communism is by its nature anti-religious. It considers religion as 'the opiate of the people' because the principles of religion which speak of a life beyond the grave dissuade the proletariat from the dream of a soviet paradise which is of this world. [Communism] in Russia ... has been a contributing factor in rousing men and materials from the inertia of centuries ... Nevertheless ... it is terrorism that reigns today in Russia, where former comrades in revolution are exterminating each other.

Pope Pius XI *Divini Redemptoris*, 19 March 1937; Claudia Carlen (ed.) *The Papal Encyclicals 1903–1939* (1981) p.542.

3 His naïve belief that this and other penal settlements are now maintained ... deliberately for the purpose of making, out of this forced labour, a net pecuniary profit to add to the State revenue, will be incredible to anyone acquainted with the economic results of the chain-gang, or of prison labour, in any country in the world.

Sidney and Beatrice Webb *Soviet Communism: A New Civilization* (1937) p.585. The Webbs comment on the Russian scientist, Professor Tchernyavin, arrested on a charge of sabotage, who escaped from the USSR in 1931.

4 It is my opinion that so far as the political defendants are concerned, sufficient crimes under Soviet law, among those charged in the indictment, were established by the proof and beyond a reasonable doubt to justify the verdict of guilty of treason and the adjudication of the punishment provided by Soviet criminal statutes.

Joseph E. Davies, US ambassador to the Soviet Union, 13 March 1938; *Foreign Relations of the United States: The Soviet Union 1933–1939* (1952) p.532.

5 The accounts of the most widely read Moscow correspondents all emphasize that since the close scrutiny of every person in a responsible position,

following the trials a great many abuses have been discovered *and rectified* ... Habitual rectification can hardly do anything but give the ordinary citizen more courage to protest, loudly, whenever in future he finds himself being victimized by someone in the Party or someone in the Government. That sounds to me like democracy.

Owen Lattimore, June 1938; *Pacific Affairs* Vol.11, pp.371–2. Lattimore was making a rejoinder to Chamberlin's well-founded allegation that the purge trials of 1936–8 were a grisly farce.

6 The Soviet labour camp provided a freedom for its inmates not usual in our own prisons in this country.

British communist Pat Sloan *Russia Without Illusions* (1938) p.246.

7 Fear haunts workers in a capitalist land. Fear of dismissal, fear that a thousand workless men stand outside the gate eager to get his job, breaks the spirit of a man and breeds servility. Fear of unemployment, fear of slump, fear of trade depression, fear of sickness, fear of an impoverished old age lie with crushing weight on the mind of the worker ... Nothing strikes the visitor to the Soviet Union more forcibly than the absence of fear.

Rev. Hewlett Johnson *The Socialist Sixth of the World* (1939) p.225. Johnson, the Anglican 'Red Dean' of Canterbury, was a worshipper at Stalin's altar.

CHINESE REVOLUTION, 1922–40

8 If we do not join this party we shall remain isolated; we shall preach a communism which is certainly a great ideal but which the masses cannot follow. If we do join the party ... we can rally the masses around us and split the KMT.

Liu Jen-ching, Nov. 1922; A.S. Whiting *Soviet Policies in China 1917–21* (1953) p.95. The argument for communists to enter the Guomindang (Chinese Nationalist Party, Kuomintang, KMT) as a 'bloc within' and use their membership to serve their own political ends.

9 Dr Sun is of the opinion that, because of the non-existence of conditions favourable to their successful application in China, it is not possible to carry out either the Communist or even the Soviet system in China. M. Joffe agrees entirely with this view.

Joint manifesto of Sun Yat-sen (Sun Yixian) and Adolf Joffe, 26 Jan. 1923; *A Documentary History of Chinese Communism* (1952) p.70. Sun was leader of the Guomindang; Joffe was

Lenin's envoy in China. Their alliance was directed against the warlord regime in Beijing.

1 The peasants are widely scattered; therefore it is not easy to organize them into an effective force. Their cultural standards being low and needs being simple, their outlook is therefore conservative. China being a big country, making it easy for them to migrate, they therefore tend to stay away from difficulty and become complacent. Those are the three factors preventing them from participating in the revolution.

Chen Duxiu (Ch'en Tu-hsiu), secretary of the Chinese Communist Party, 1923; Jerome Ch'en *Mao and the Chinese Revolution* (1965) p.108. Chen, in line with the orthodox Marxist thinking of the Soviet Russian leadership, saw peasants as a counter-revolutionary force.

2 The National Government shall construct the Republic of China on the revolutionary basis of the Three Principles of the People.

The primary requisite of reconstruction lies in the people's livelihood ... the government should, in cooperation with the people, strive to develop agriculture to feed them, to develop the textile industry to meet their clothing requirements; to work out a larger scale housing project to furnish them with better living-quarters; to improve and construct roads and canals to facilitate their travels.

Second in importance is the people's sovereignty. The government should train and direct the people in their acquisition of political knowledge and ability, thereby enabling them to exercise the powers of suffrage, recall, initiative and referendum.

Third comes nationalism. The government should help and guide the racial minorities in the country towards self-determination and self-government. It should resist foreign aggression, and simultaneously revise foreign treaties in order to restore our equality and independence among the nations.

Sun Yat-sen *Fundamentals of National Reconstruction* (1924) pp.9–10. The Chinese Nationalist Party's equivalent of the Decalogue, although in practice nationalism came well ahead of political democracy and economic welfare.

3 Some of our own Chinese Communists who are in Russia always scold other people as slaves of America, of England and of Japan, never realizing that they themselves have already completely become slaves of Russia.

Chiang Kai-shek (Jiang Jieshi), March 1924; S.I. Hsiung *The Life of Chiang Kai-shek* (1948) p.212. Chiang, who became head of

the Nationalist Party after the death of Sun Yat-sen in 1925, was passionately anti-Soviet.

4 In a very short time ... several hundred million peasants will rise like a mighty storm, like a hurricane, a force so swift and violent that no power, however great, will be able to hold it back. They will smash all the trammels that bind them and rush forward along the road to liberation. They will sweep all the imperialists, warlords, corrupt officials, local tyrants and evil gentry into their graves.

Mao Zedong (Mao Tse-tung), 20 March 1927; *Selected Works* (1970 edn) p.10. After a survey of conditions in Hunan province, Mao drew the heretical conclusion that the Chinese peasantry had high revolutionary potential and that the main effort of the Communist Party should be put into the countryside rather than the cities.

5 A revolution is not a dinner-party, or writing an essay, or painting a picture, or doing embroidery; it cannot be so refined, so leisurely and gentle, so temperate, kind, courteous, restrained and magnanimous. A revolution is an insurrection, an act of violence by which one class overthrows another.

Mao Zedong, 20 March 1927; *Selected Works* (1970 edn) p.13.

6 The men of the Right ... have to be utilized to the utmost, squeezed like a lemon, and then thrown away.

Joseph Stalin, 5 April 1927; E.H. Carr *Foundations of a Planned Economy* Vol.3, Pt 3 (1978) p.759. One week later came the rightist coup in Shanghai.

7 Together or separately they attacked the headquarters of working-class organizations scattered throughout the city ... Their quarters were occupied, the pickets and their supporters were given short, brutal shrift. Their arms were seized and even their clothes and shoes ripped from them. Every man who resisted was shot down where he stood. The remainder were lashed together and marched out to be executed either in the streets or at Lunghua ... In the mêlée [at the General Labour Union headquarters] Ku Chen-chung and his vice-commander, a young man named Chou En-lai [Zhou Enlai], escaped.

Harold Isaacs *The Tragedy of the Chinese Revolution* (1938) pp.202–3, describing the coup in Shanghai on 12 April 1927, whereby Chiang Kai-shek moved against the Chinese Communist Party, which had until then been his ally. Zhou En Lai went on to become foreign minister of the Communist People's Republic founded by Mao in 1949.

1 Their purpose is rather obvious: they wish to use the Kuomintang [Guomindang] as their cover-up and to destroy it from within. To them the Kuomintang is like an egg-shell and they, like chickens in embryo, are hatched within; they only wait for the right moment to break the eggshell and emerge as fully-fledged chickens.

Wang Jingwei (Wang Ching-wei), autumn 1927; Dun J. Li (ed.) *The Road to Communism* (1969) p.105. Wang, leader of the left wing of the Nationalist Party, had been seen by the communists as a partner. After the Shanghai coup of April 1927 he joined forces with Chiang Kai-shek and here reveals his true feelings about the communists.

2 Two lots of 500 and 1,000 men each were taken out and machine-gunned. Realizing that this was a waste of ammunition, the soldiers loaded the victims on boats, took them down the river below the city, and pushed them overboard in lots of ten or twelve men tied together. The slaughter continued for four or five days.

Jay Calvin Huston, an American eyewitness of the suppression of the communist insurrection in Canton, Dec. 1927; Robert C. North *Moscow and Chinese Communists* (1953) p.120. On Stalin's orders the Chinese communists staged urban risings against the Nationalist government, which were mercilessly put down. In Canton the insurgents wore red neckerchiefs. Although they quickly threw them away, the red dye stayed on their skin and marked them out for seizure. The executions by drowning bring to mind the *noyades* at Nantes by French revolutionaries in Dec. 1793.

3 Without the big cities, productive areas, and especially a high tide of the strike movement ... there can be no victory of political power in one or several provinces. To think of 'encircling the city with the countryside' or of 'relying on the Red Army alone to win key cities' is illusory ... The villages are the limbs of the ruling class. The cities are their brains and heart. If we cut out their brains and heart, they cannot escape death; but if we simply cut off their appendages it will not necessarily kill them.

Li Li-san, 29 March and 5 April 1930; Richard C. Thornton *The Comintern and the Chinese Communists, 1928–1931* (1969) p.127 and Stuart Schram *Mao Tse-tung* (1967) p.142. In the aftermath of the massacres of communists in the cities during 1927, the Party leader Li-Li-san clung (with Stalin's approval) to the concept of urban insurrection, as opposed to Mao's faith in the rural revolution.

4 The enemy advances, we retreat; the enemy halts, we harass; the enemy tires, we attack; the enemy retreats, we pursue.

Mao Zedong, 5 Jan. 1930; *Selected Military Writings of Mao Tse-tung* (1966) p.72. The tactics of guerrilla struggle, making a virtue of the necessity for an inferior communist force to avoid positional warfare with a superior Nationalist enemy, either in open country or, as Li Li-san wished, in a frontal assault on urban centres. A further rising in Changsha was attempted in July 1930, but it was soon snuffed out. Li Li-san was then recalled to Moscow in disgrace and Mao became Communist Party leader, developing a distinctively Chinese version of Marxism, which challenged Moscow's claim to leadership of the world communist movement.

5   A million workers and peasants leap up joyfully
    And roll up Kiangsi like a mat.
    As we reach the rivers of Hunan and Hupei
    We sing the Internationale. It pierces us
    Like a whirlwind from the sky.

Mao Zedong, July 1930; *The Poems of Mao Tse-tung* (1972) p.49. Mao the poet celebrates the installation of his Soviet in Kiangsi province in southeast China. For the Internationale see 671:6.

6 The 'Red Peril' is real enough in China to-day, and it will continue to make life a burden and a terror to millions, until, in Heaven's good time, benevolent despotism in the hands of a strong ruler shall have restored China's ancient ways of stability. But the Red Peril with which the Kuomintang [Guomindang] propagandists would make our flesh creep, the vision of China's millions organized to Communism for Russia's purposes of world-revolution, may be dismissed as impossible.

J.O.P. Bland *China: The Pity of It* (1932) p.284. For Bland, not even the Nationalists, let alone the communists, could serve the true need of China: a traditionalist empire.

7 The New Life Movement is the basis upon which we as a nation can build a new life for ourselves. Its purpose is to incorporate some of our ancient virtues, such as propriety, righteousness, honesty, and shamefulness into the conduct of our daily lives. The process begins with the rectification of our outward conduct and ends with the reconstruction of our inner mind ... An individual who has succeeded in doing this will achieve a great deal in his life; a nation that can do likewise will definitely become wealthy, strong, and prosperous.

Chiang Kai-shek, 19 Feb. 1935, on the first anniversary of his New Life Movement; Li (1969) pp 130, 131. The values of the movement were based on the Confucian ideals of the suppressers of the Taiping Rebellion of 1850–64, which Chiang identified with communism.

1 It proclaims to the world that the Red Army is an army of heroes and that the imperialists and their jackals, Chiang Kai-shek and his like, are perfect nonentities … It declares to the approximately two hundred million people of eleven provinces that only the road of the Red Army leads to their liberation … It has sown many seeds in eleven provinces, which will sprout, grow leaves, blossom into flowers, bear fruit and yield a harvest in the future.

Mao Zedong on the Long March, 27 Dec. 1935; *Selected Works* Vol. 1 (1954) p.161. The March, from Oct. 1934 to Oct. 1935, was also a huge retreat from Kiangsi to Shensi province, which cost the lives of most of its participants, but it enabled communism to survive.

2 The Red Army is not afraid of hardship on the march, the long march.

Ten thousand waters and a thousand mountains are nothing …

The far snows of Minshan only make us happy And when the army pushes through, we all laugh.

Mao Zedong, Oct. 1935; *The Poems of Mao Tse-tung* (1972) p.65. Upbeat verse about an epic feat, which was also a nightmare of attrition.

3 Many people think it is impossible for the guerrilla to exist long in the enemy's realm. Such a belief reveals a lack of understanding of the relationship that should exist between the people and the troops. The former may be likened to water and the latter to the fish that swim in it.

Mao Zedong *On Guerrilla Warfare* (1937). The classic expression of Mao's belief in a symbiosis between communist forces and the pro-revolutionary peasantry.

4 1. The three principles of Dr Sun Yat-sen being what China needs today, our Party pledges itself to fight for their complete realization.

2. The Communist Party will discontinue completely its policy of insurrection aimed at overthrowing the Kuomintang [Guomindang] regime and its policy of forcible confiscation of the land of the landlords.

3. The present Red government will be reorganized as a Special Region of the Republic of China, established as a democracy based on universal suffrage.

4. The name of the Red Army will be abolished and its designation changed; it will be reorganized as the National Revolutionary Army and will be subject to the orders of the Military Council of the National Government.

Agreement between the Guomindang and the Chinese Communist Party for a revival of the United Front, 22 Sept. 1937; *Selected Works* Vol.4 (1956) p.143. The change of policy was brought about by the recent outbreak of full-scale war between Japan and China (see 793:1).

5 Every Communist must grasp the truth: 'Political power grows out of the barrel of a gun.' Our principle is that the Party commands the gun, and the gun will never be allowed to command the Party.

Mao Zedong, 6 Nov. 1938; *Selected Works* Vol.2 (1954) p.228. A famous maxim, which Mao was to follow unswervingly, both in and out of power.

6 The first stage of the Chinese revolution … is a bourgeois-democratic revolution of the new type. Although it is not a proletarian-socialist revolution of the newest type, certainly it already forms a part, an important part, of it and has been a great ally of it. The first stage of the revolution is certainly not meant to, and certainly cannot, build up a capitalist society under the dictatorship of the Chinese bourgeoisie, but is meant to set up a new democratic society of the joint dictatorship of all the revolutionary classes. After the first stage is accomplished, the development will be carried forward into the second stage, namely, the building up of Chinese socialist society.

Mao Zedong *On the New Democracy*, 19 Jan. 1940; *A Documentary History of Chinese Communism* (1952) p.266. Mao makes it clear that collaboration with Chiang Kai-shek and the Nationalists was only a transitional phase on the road to an unchallengeable Marxist government. The Nationalists too saw partnership with the communists as no more than an expedient, and the United Front against Japan was soon replaced by an undeclared civil war, flaring into full-blooded conflict after Japan's defeat in 1945.

Fascism and National Socialism, 1919–39

FASCISM IN ITALY, 1919–39

1 He is very ambitious. He is motivated by the conviction that he represents a significant force in the destiny of Italy, and he is determined to make this prevail. He is a man who does not resign himself to positions of secondary rank. He intends to rate first and to dominate.

Report of the inspector-general of public security on Benito Mussolini, 4 June 1919; Renzo de Felice *Mussolini* (1965) p.73. Mussolini had launched the fascist movement in Milan on 23 March 1919 and was an understandable target of police scrutiny.

2 You tremble with fear! You have there the most abject con-man ever brought to light in the history of the scum of the universe and you let him set his pig's trotter on your neck. Any other country – even Lapland – would have overthrown that man ... Is there nothing to hope for? What about your promises? At least prick that belly which weighs you down, let some of the air out.

Gabriele D'Annunzio to Mussolini, 16 Sept. 1919; John Woodhouse *Gabriele D'Annunzio* (1998) p.334. The flamboyant nationalist D'Annunzio had occupied the port of Fiume (Rijeka) in Yugoslavia and expected support, which was not forthcoming from the Italian prime minister, Francesco Nitti, nor, in the event, from Mussolini. See 802:1.

3 I believe that parliamentary institutions are destined to collapse. I also believe that the Italian political system is fated to go under unless it is renewed by the animating force of Italy's creative geniuses, and unless it rids itself of those two scourges of Italian society: lawyers and professors.

Filippo Marinetti, 1919; Jeffrey T. Schnapp *A Primer of Italian Fascism* (2000) pp.274–5. The doyen of Futurism was a fervent admirer of Mussolini.

4 What is Italian fascism? It is the insurrection of the lowest stratum of the Italian bourgeoisie, the stratum of the layabouts, of the ignorant, of the adventurers to whom war gave the illusion of being good for something and of necessarily counting for something, who have been carried forward by the state of political and moral decadence.

The communist Antonio Gramsci, *L'Ordine Nuovo*, 25 May 1921. Compare Karl Marx on the calibre of Louis-Napoleon's following (see 668:7).

5 Sympathizers follow the fascist movement with satisfaction, and if they do not approve of it, they at least justify its violence, for they feel that in no other way would a scant minority of hardy souls have been able to wear down the preponderance of socialists, anarchists and popolari who by virtue of government inaction would no doubt have driven Italy into a chaotic and Bolshevik state as in Russia.

Report by district attorney, Florence, 19 June 1921; Charles S. Maier *Recasting Bourgeois Europe* (1975) p.316. Italian conservatives quickly saw Mussolini's movement as their first line of defence against communism.

6 We permit ourselves the luxury of being aristocratic and democratic, conservative and progressive, reactionary and revolutionary, accepting the law and going beyond it, according to the circumstances of the time, place and environment, in a word, of the 'history' in which we must live and act.

Benito Mussolini's highly eclectic programme for the 1921 election; *Opera Omnia* Vol.16 (1955) p.212.

7 Terrorized by an unpunished fascist band using clubs, revolvers etc. Union organizers and municipal administrators forced to leave for fear of death. Workers forced to lock themselves at home because of continuous beatings and threats of beatings. Unions and socialist clubs ordered to dissolve themselves within 48 hours or face physical destruction.

Deputy Luigi Fabbri to prime minister Ivanoe Bonomi, 1 Oct. 1921; John Pollard *The Fascist Experience in Italy* (1998) p.31. Fascist squads were waging war on government institutions and the Socialist Party, creating a chaos that their leader would, they hoped, step in to bring to an end.

8 Let Rome do as it likes. We are in charge here. We will take care of Rome on the day we can fall on that nest of owls and clean it out. We have only one goal: to deprecate, to reveal the absurdity of the state that governs us ... We want to destroy it with all its venerable institutions.

Italo Balbo *Diario 1922* (1932) p.30. Balbo, the fascist boss of Ferrara, was a leading figure in the campaign of violence that was the prelude to Mussolini's take-over in Oct. 1922.

9 The Browning pistol. The only thing which a fascist loves with an almost carnal love. When nothing else is faithful to the fascist, the Browning pistol is his only and eternal security. And that's enough.

Fascist Party member, c.1922; Emilio Gentile *Storia del Partito Fascista 1919–1922* (1989) p.499. Compare Hermann Goering (see 756:8).

1 Lips made prominent, contemptuous, by an audacity, a pugnaciousness, which spits on everything which is vain, slow, cumbersome, useless. Massive head, but ultra-dynamic eyes which vie with the speed of cars racing across the plains of Lombardy ... The square head, a new type of shell or box full of powerful explosive, or simply the cubic will of the State, the head ready to charge into someone's chest like a bull.

Filippo Marinetti on the compelling physiognomy of the new leader, 1923; Roger Griffin (ed.) *Fascism* (1995) p.46.

2 Every day you proclaim you want to re-establish the authority of the State and the laws. Do it, if you still have time; otherwise you are really going to destroy the fundamental core of our political life, the moral sense of the nation. The only result of your policy will be to keep the country split between masters and servants, because you believe democracy breeds anarchy and revolt ... We deplore the idea that ... our people is the only one on earth incapable of self-control, which must be ruled by force.

Giacomo Matteotti, 30 May 1924; Stanislav Pugliese *Italian Fascism and Anti-Fascism* (2001) p.69. The socialist deputy Matteotti protests against Mussolini's rigging of the recent general election. Shortly afterwards he was abducted by fascist thugs and murdered, in a chilling demonstration of the fascist government's power to silence opponents.

3 If fascism has been nothing more than castor oil and the truncheon instead of being a proud passion of the best of Italian youth, then I am to blame. If fascism has been a criminal association, then I am the chief of this criminal association ... Italy wants peace, tranquillity, calm in which to work. We shall give her this tranquillity by loving means if possible but by force, if necessary.

Benito Mussolini to the Italian parliament, *Il Popolo d'Italia*, 3 Jan. 1925. 'Castor oil and the truncheon' was a reference to the fascist squads' methods of dealing with political opposition – copious doses of castor oil and beatings. This speech marked the point from which Mussolini became unchallengeable.

4 We want to insert the fascist revolution into the state. What does this mean? It means to legalize fascist illegality.

Roberto Farinacci, 22 Feb. 1925; *A Golden Age of the National Fascist Party* (1927) p.23. A candid admission of the basic purpose of the new regime from the party boss of Cremona. Farinacci stood on the radical wing of the movement, unwilling (unlike Mussolini) to come to terms with conservative forces in Italian life.

5 The first benefit of Benito Mussolini's direction in Italy begins to be felt when one crosses the Italian frontier and hears 'The train is arriving on time'.

Princess Eulalia of Spain *Courts and Countries after the War* (1925) Ch.13. Perhaps the origin of the repeated claim that whatever else Mussolini did or did not do, he 'made the trains run on time'.

6 All ... for the state, nothing outside the state and no one against the state.

Benito Mussolini, 28 Oct. 1925; *Opera Omnia* Vol.21 (1956) p.425.

7 Opposition is not necessary for the working of a healthy political regime. Opposition is senseless, superfluous in a totalitarian regime like the fascist regime ... So, let no one hope, after this speech, to see anti-fascist journalists appear – no. Or that the resurrection of anti-fascist organizations will be allowed: not that either.

Benito Mussolini, 26 May 1927; *Discorsi* (Speeches) (1935) p.126.

8 Italy has the singular privilege ... to be the only European nation which is the seat of a universal religion. This religion was born in Palestine but it became Catholic and universal in Rome. If it had stayed in Palestine it would probably have remained just another of the sects ... and very probably would have died out, leaving no trace.

Benito Mussolini, 13 May 1929; Pollard (1998) p.73. In Feb. 1929 Mussolini had signed a concordat with the papacy, supposedly ending the long antagonism between the Italian state and the Vatican, but Pius XI was outraged by the assertion that Italy was doing Catholicism a favour by allowing it to maintain its headquarters inside the nation's capital.

9 To monopolize completely the young ... for the exclusive advantage of a party and of a regime based on an ideology which clearly resolves itself into a true, a real pagan worship of the State ... is no less in conflict with the natural rights of the family than it is in contradiction with the supernatural rights of the Church.

Pope Pius XI *Non Abbiamo Bisogno* (We Have No Need), 29 June 1931; Claudia Carlen (ed.) *The Papal Encyclicals 1903–1939* (1981) p.453. A strong protest against the restrictions placed by Mussolini on the independent activity of Catholic organizations.

1 It is a hierarchical communism that denies both an egalitarian state and an anarchic individualism ... which resists private management and assigns a public value to the work performed by individuals ... All social life is rationalized. The economic world moves in the direction of unitary organization, which makes possible the realization of a dream: a planned economy that can overcome the chaos produced by liberal economics.

Ugo Spirito on the fascist corporate state, *Corporatism as Absolute Liberalism and Absolute Socialism* (1932). Corporatism was supposed to sweep away class conflict, with the government presiding over a partnership of employers and employed. In practice, business went into partnership with government at the expense of the workers.

2 I should be pleased, I suppose, that Hitler has carried out a revolution on our lines. But they are Germans. So they will end by ruining our idea.

Benito Mussolini, 1933; Christopher Hibbert *Benito Mussolini* (1963 edn) p.97.

3 1. Know that the fascist and in particular the soldier, must not believe in perpetual peace.

2. Days of imprisonment are always deserved.

3. The nation serves even as a sentinel over a can of petrol.

4. A companion must be a brother, first, because he lives with you, and secondly because he thinks like you.

5. The rifle and cartridge belt, and the rest, are confided to you not to rust in leisure, but to be preserved in war.

6. Do not ever say 'The government will pay' because it is *you* who pay; and the government is that which you willed to have, and for which you put on a uniform.

7. Discipline is the soul of armies; without it there are no soldiers, only confusion and defeat.

8. Mussolini is always right.

9. For a volunteer there are no extenuating circumstances when he is disobedient.

10. Only one thing must be dear to you above all: the life of the Duce [Mussolini].

Fascist Decalogue, 1934; Walter Oakeshott *The Social and Political Doctrines of Contemporary Europe* (1939) p.180.

4 Believe! Obey! Fight!

The Fascist creed is heroism; the Bourgeois creed is egoism.

Fascist slogans attrib. to Mussolini, painted on the walls of public buildings and recited by children in school. At best facile substitutions for thought, at worst recipes for disaster.

5   Hail, People of Heroes,
    Hail, Immortal Fatherland!
    Your children are born anew
    With faith in the ideal.
    The courage of your warriors,
    The strength of the pioneers,
    The vision of Alighieri,
    Shines today in every heart.

The fascist anthem, sung to the tune of the popular song *Giovinezza* (Youth). Dante Alighieri, the great medieval poet, was author of *La Divina Commedia* and a cult figure for Italian nationalists.

6 It will no longer be a question of moaning about the sceptical, mandolin-playing Italians, but rather of creating a new kind of man who is tough, strong-willed, a fighter, a latter-day legionary of Caesar for whom nothing is impossible.

Benito Mussolini in conversation with Emil Ludwig; *Colloqui con Mussolini* (Conversations with Mussolin) (1950) p.111. Italy re-invented, in epic style.

7 1. Human racial divisions are a fact of life.

2. There are master races and inferior races.

3. The concept of race is a purely biological concept.

4. The present population of Italy is Aryan in origin and its civilization is Aryan.

5. The addition of huge masses of people in the period since the Roman Empire is a legend.

6. A pure 'Italian race' now exists.

7. Now is the moment for Italians to declare themselves openly racist.

8. We must draw a clear distinction between the Mediterranean peoples of Europe (Westerners) on the one hand, and Levantines and Africans on the other.

9. The Jews do not belong to the Italian race.

10. The purely European physical and psychological characteristics of the Italians must not be changed in any way.

Manifesto of the racialist academics, *Il Giornale d'Italia*, 14 July 1938. This declaration, thought to have been written by Mussolini himself, was the basis of the anti-Semitic legislation introduced soon afterwards. Hitherto Italy had not copied the Nazi model.

8 Fifteen years of fascism had made everyone forget the problem of the South ... It is likely that the new institutions which come after fascism ... will perpetuate and aggravate, under new names and new labels, an eternal fascism. Without a peasant revolution, we shall never have a real Italian revolution, and vice versa.

Carlo Levi *Cristo si è fermato a Eboli* (Christ Stopped at Eboli) (1945) Ch.24. The oppositionist Levi was placed in domestic exile in the Lucania region of the Italian south, the most backward area of the country, both politically and economically. In his book, published after the fall of Mussolini, he relates his experience of the gulf between the peasantry and the Italian state.

NAZISM IN GERMANY: ADVENT, 1919–23

1 Such beings are incalculable, they come like fate without cause or reason, inconsiderately and without pretext. Suddenly they are here like lightning: too terrible, too sudden, too compelling and too 'difficult' even to be hated ... What moves them is the terrible egotism of the artist of the brazen glance, who knows himself to be justified for all eternity in his 'work' as the mother is justified in her child.

Friedrich Nietzsche *On the Genealogy of Morals* (1887) Sect.2. The philosopher Nietzsche, like the composer Richard Wagner, was one of the gods in Hitler's pantheon.

2   Things fall apart; the centre cannot hold;
     Mere anarchy is loosed upon the world,
     The blood-dimmed tide is loosed, and
        everywhere
     The ceremony of innocence is drowned;
     The best lack all conviction, while the worst
     Are full of passionate intensity.

William Butler Yeats 'The Second Coming' in *Michael Robartes and the Dancer* (1921).

3 Where he comes from, no one can say. From a prince's palace, perhaps, or a labourer's cottage. But everyone knows. He is the Führer. Everyone cheers him and he will one day announce himself, he for whom all of us are waiting, full of longing, who feel Germany's distress deep in our hearts, so that thousands and thousands of minds picture him, millions of voices call for him, one single German soul seeks him.

Kurt Hesse *Feldherr Psychologos* (General Psychology) (1922).

4 If necessity commands it, he does not shrink from shedding blood. Great questions are always decided by blood and iron ... He is concerned solely with

the attainment of his goal, even if that calls for trampling over closest friends.

Rudolf Hess, on leadership, 1922; Joachim Fest *Hitler* (1974) p.142. Hess was to become deputy leader of the party; here he quotes Bismarck (see 697:1).

5 This book is addressed to Germans of every party. Instead of government by party, I offer the ideal of the Third Reich. It is an old German concept and a great one. It arose when our First Reich fell; it was accelerated by the thought of a Thousand-Year Reich, but its underlying concept is the dawn of a German age, in which the German people would for the first time fulfil their destiny on earth. The Third Reich is a philosophical idea not for this but for the next world. Germany might perish because of the Third Reich dream.

Arthur Moeller van den Bruck *The Third Reich* (Jan. 1923) Preface. Hitler adopted the title for his Nazi state.

NAZISM IN GERMANY: FRINGE PARTY, 1922–31

6 His words were like a scourge. When he spoke of the disgrace of Germany, I felt ready to spring on any enemy. His appeal to German manhood was like a call to arms, the gospel he preached a sacred truth. He seemed another Luther.

Kurt Lüdecke, 1922; *I Knew Hitler* (1937) p.14. Lüdecke was converted to Nazism by this speech, a typical piece of electrifying oratory. He broke with Hitler in 1934 and survived. For Luther see 356:1.

7 What you stated there is the catechism of a new political creed coming to birth in the midst of a collapsing, secularized world ... 'To you a god has given the tongue with which to express our sufferings.'

Joseph Goebbels to Hitler, spring 1924, on Hitler's closing address at his trial after the failure of the Munich *Putsch* of 9 Nov. 1923; Fest (1974) p.200. Goebbels, who in 1933 became Nazi minister of propaganda, quotes from Goethe's play *Torquato Tasso* (1790), about the 16th-century Italian poet.

8 The great mass of the people ... will more easily fall victim to a big lie than to a small one.

Adolf Hitler *Mein Kampf* (1925) Bk 1, Ch.10. Given a short jail sentence after the collapse of the attempted coup d'état in Munich, Hitler spent his time writing a justification of his beliefs – *Mein Kampf* (My Struggle), which was to become the bible of National Socialism.

1 Friends, raise your right arm and cry out with me proudly, eager for the struggle, and loyal unto death, 'Heil Hitler!'

Gregor Strasser, 9 Jan. 1927; Jeremy Noakes and Geoffrey Pridham (eds) *Nazism 1919–1945* Vol.I (1983) p.55. Strasser, the Nazi radical executed in 1934, on the 'German greeting', which was to become a requirement for all subjects of the Third Reich after 1933.

2 Bourgeois nationalism has failed, and ... the concept of Marxist socialism has made life impossible in the long run. These old lines of action must be eradicated along with the old parties, because they are barring the nation's path into the future. We are eradicating them by releasing the two concepts of nationalism and socialism and harnessing them for a new goal, towards which we are working, full of hope, for the highest form of socialism is burning devotion to the nation.

Adolf Hitler, March 1928; Conan Fischer *The Rise of the Nazis* (1995) pp.138–9. Socialism had traditionally been an international movement. By coupling it with nationalism, the Nazis made a novel appeal to both radicals and conservatives.

3 One should not believe that parliamentarianism will be our Damascus ... We come as enemies! Like the wolf tearing into a flock of sheep, that is how we will come.

Joseph Goebbels *Der Angriff* (The Assault), April 1928. Goebbels on the coming election of 20 May 1928 in which the National Socialists gained only 12 seats. A candid affirmation of their contempt for democracy.

4 The feeling of unrest in Berlin went deeper than any crisis ... Berlin was the tension, the poverty, the anger, the prostitution, the hope and despair thrown out onto the streets. It was the blatant rich at the smart restaurants, the prostitutes in army top boots at corners, the grim, submerged-looking Communists in processions, and the violent youths who suddenly emerged from nowhere into the Wittenbergplatz and shouted 'Deutschland Erwache!'

Stephen Spender, on Berlin in 1930, *World within World* (1951). The young English poet captures the hectic atmosphere of the German capital in the early grip of depression. *Deutschland Erwache!* (Germany, wake up!) was the rallying cry of the Nazis.

5 The 'sense of world history' has spread out from the North over the entire world; a sense that was borne by a blue-eyed, blond race which, in several massive waves, has determined the spiritual contours of the world, while at the same time deciding which of them must perish ... And Germanic

Europe bequeathed to the world the radiant ideal of humanity ... in its paean to the grandest feature of the Nordic world – the ideal of freedom of conscience and of *honour* ... If, in the great struggle that is to come, this ideal is not victorious, all the West and its entire blood-line will die, as India and Greece once did, vanishing into eternity in chaos.

Alfred Rosenberg *Der Mythus des 20 Jahrhunderts* (The Paramount Idea of the 20th Century) (1930); Robert Pois (ed.) *Alfred Rosenberg: Selected Writings* (1970) pp.41, 83. Rosenberg was the high priest of Nazi racism, hanged in 1946 for his part in the Final Solution.

6 I aim to set up a thousand-year Reich and anyone who supports me in this battle is a fellow fighter for a unique spiritual – I would almost say divine – creation.

Adolf Hitler, June 1931; E. Calic *Unmasked: Two Interviews with Hitler in 1931* (1971) p.68.

NAZISM IN GERMANY: SEIZURE OF POWER, 1932–3

7 Millions Stand Behind Me.

Nazi election slogan, brilliantly subverted in the photomontage by John Heartfield. Entitled 'The Meaning of the Hitler Salute', it showed Hitler reaching up for a wad of banknotes held out by a huge anonymous figure behind him. The allegation was clear: Hitler was merely a pawn in the hands of German capitalism. That is, no doubt, how German industrialists saw him, but they were soon to have a brutal awakening.

8 That man for Chancellor? I'll make him a postmaster and he can lick the stamps with my head on them.

President Paul von Hindenburg on Hitler, 1932; John Wheeler Bennett *Hindenburg: The Wooden Titan* (1967). Despite the Nazis' strong performance in two elections in 1932, Hindenburg demurred at nominating Hitler as chancellor.

9 No danger at all. We've hired him for our act.

Franz von Papen, vice-chancellor of the Weimar Republic, on the choice of Hitler as chancellor, 30 Jan. 1933; Alan Bullock *Hitler and Stalin: Parallel Lives* (1993) p.283. The fatuous conviction that Hitler would be no more than a puppet manipulated by the forces of German conservatism.

10 Once we have power, we shall never again give it up, unless we are carried out as corpses from our offices.

Joseph Goebbels, diary entry, 6 Aug. 1932; *The Goebbels Diaries* (1948). The master of lies never spoke a truer word: his last ministerial act in May 1945 was to kill himself.

1 *In domestic policy.* Complete reversal of the present domestic political situation. No toleration of any activity which stands in the way of this aim (pacifism!). Those who don't agree must be broken. Elimination of Marxism lock, stock and barrel. Winning over young people and the whole nation to the belief that this fight alone can save us and every mind should be focused on this idea … Training the young generation and strengthening military preparedness by all possible means. The death penalty for high treason and the strongest authoritarian leadership of the state. Abolition of cancerous democracy!

Notes taken by Lieutenant General Liebmann, 3 Feb. 1933; *Questions on German History* (1989) p.330. A succinct résumé of the Nazi programme made by an admirer in the army, which also saw the Nazis as their creatures.

2 Restrictions on personal liberty, on the right of free expression, of opinion, including freedom of the press, on the right of association and assembly, and violations of the privacy of postal, telegraphic and telephonic communications and warrants for house-searches, orders for confiscations as well as restrictions on property rights, are permissible beyond the legal limits otherwise prescribed.

Decree for the protection of people and state, 28 Feb. 1933; Noakes and Pridham Vol.I (1983) p.142. The decree – drafted in advance – was issued immediately after the burning of the Reichstag, probably by a lone communist madman, Marinus van der Lubbe, but blamed on the communists as a whole and used to give the government dictatorial powers.

3 Today there is no point in being fussy about legal subtleties. What matters first is to let a strong, efficient government grow and then to support it wholeheartedly in order to suppress Bolshevism.

Karl Bachem of the Catholic Centre Party, spring 1933; Noakes and Pridham Vol.I (1983) p.165.

4 It is not enough for people to be more or less reconciled to our regime, to be persuaded to adopt a neutral attitude towards us; rather we want to work on people until they have capitulated to us, until they grasp ideologically that what is happening in Germany today not only *must* be accepted, but also *can* be accepted.

Joseph Goebbels, 15 March 1933; Noakes and Pridham Vol.2 (1984). Goebbels was Hitler's propaganda minister, with the mission of capturing the hearts and minds of the German public for the Nazi cause.

5 *Against* class struggle and materialism.
For the national community and an idealistic outlook.

Marx, Kautsky.
Against the falsification of our history and the denigration of its great figures.
For awe for our past.
Emil Ludwig, Werner Hegeman.
Against literary betrayal of the soldiers of the World War.
For the education of the nation in the spirit of military preparedness.
Erich Maria Remarque.

Incantations bellowed at the burning of books in Berlin, 10 May 1933; H. Brenner *The Cultural Policy of National Socialism* (1963) p.186. In each case the roar of the mob was followed by the dispatch of the condemned works into the flames. Ludwig was a Jew; Remarque was the author of *All Quiet on the Western Front*, published in 1929 and immediately turned into a Hollywood film (1930), a powerful protest against the carnage of World War I (see 714:5).

6 What progress we are making. In the Middle Ages they would have burned me. Now they are content with burning my books.

Sigmund Freud, May 1933, in the aftermath of the Berlin book burning of 10 May.

7 Wherever books are burned, men too are burned in the end.

Heinrich Heine *Almansor* (1823) line 2245.

8 Today, January 22nd, the Nazis held a demonstration on the Bülowplatz, in front of the Karl Liebknecht House … But the real masters of Berlin are not the Police, or the Army, and certainly not the Nazis. The masters of Berlin are the workers …

Today [May 1933] … the sun shines, and Hitler is master of this city. The sun shines, and dozens of my friends – my pupils at the Workers' School, the men and women I met at the I.A.H. – are in prison, possibly dead.

Christopher Isherwood 'A Berlin Diary (Winter 1932–3)' in *Goodbye to Berlin* (1939). Isherwood left Berlin in May 1933. Karl Liebknecht House was named after the Social Democrat leader executed on 15 Jan. 1919 after the failure of his attempted Soviet revolution. The I.A.H. (*Institut für Arbeiter Hilfe*, Institute for Workers' Aid) was a communist foundation set up to help the unemployed.

NAZISM IN GERMANY:
THE NIGHT OF THE LONG KNIVES, 1934

9 Are we revolutionaries or aren't we? If we are, then something new must surge up out of our movement,

like the mass armies of the French Revolution ...
You only get one chance to make something new
and big that'll help us lift the world off its hinges.

Ernst Röhm, head of the Nazi *Sturmabteilung* (Storm
Detachment, SA), early 1934; Geoff Layton *Germany: The Third
Reich 1933–45* (1992) pp.53–4. The SA leadership believed
that Hitler was betraying National Socialism through his
alliance with the army and business.

I   Here come the brown stormtroopers
     That keen-eyed squad of snoopers
     To check where each man stands
     Their job's to put the boot in
     Then hang around saluting
     With bloodstained empty hands.

Bertolt Brecht *Fear and Misery of the Third Reich* (1938),
Prelude to 'The Chalk Cross', set in Berlin in 1933. The brown
stormtroopers were the brown-shirted members of the SA.

2 They shouldn't imagine they will escape the night
of the long knives.

Ernst Röhm, May 1934; Noakes and Pridham Vol.1 (1983)
p.187. Famous penultimate words: Röhm and a host of others
were to be liquidated in the Night of the Long Knives, 30 June
1934.

3 The hammer will become once more the symbol
of the German worker and the sickle the sign of
the German peasant.

Adolf Hitler, 1 May 1934; Norman Baynes (ed.) *The Speeches
of Adolf Hitler 1922–1939* Vol.1 (1942) p.894. An odd
statement given the fact that these were the symbols of the
Nazis' arch-enemy, the Marxist Soviet Union. A sop to the
revolutionists of the SA on the day of the socialist festival,
now appropriated by National Socialism?

4 No nation can afford an eternal revolt from below
if that nation wishes to continue to exist as
an historical entity ... Permanent dynamism cannot
shape anything lasting. We must not let Germany
become a train tearing along to nowhere in
particular.

Franz von Papen, 17 June 1934; Fest (1974) p.459. A warning
shot from the conservative vice-chancellor, still confident that
he could steer Hitler in the right direction.

5 When the time was up, the two SS men re-entered
the cell, and found Röhm standing with his chest
bared. Immediately one of them ... shot him in the
throat, and Röhm collapsed on the floor. Since he
was still alive, he was killed with a shot point-blank
through the temple. The bullet not only penetrated
his skull, but also the ceiling of the cell below.

The execution of Ernst Röhm, 1 July 1934, as remembered by
the governor of the Stadelheim jail in Munich; Noakes and
Pridham Vol.1 (1983) p.180. Hitler got his retaliation in first,
not only against the SA but also against many other perceived
enemies.

6 Good chap, that Hitler! *He* showed how to deal
with political opponents.

Joseph Stalin, on the 1934 'Night of the Long Knives';
Christopher Andrew and Oleg Gordievsky *KGB: The Inside
Story* (1990). Congratulations from a connoisseur of purge,
soon to outdo his role-model (see 740:6–444:3).

7 They underestimate me. Because I come from
below, from the 'lower depths', because I have no
education, because my manners aren't what they
with their sparrow brains think is right ... They
could already see me thrashing in their nets. They
thought I'd become their tool ... I've taught them a
lesson they'll remember for a long time.

Adolf Hitler in the aftermath of the Röhm purge, on his
conservative sponsors; Fest (1974) pp.473, 474.

NAZISM IN GERMANY:
THE NEW ORDER, 1934–6

8 I swear by God this sacred oath: I will render
unconditional obedience to Adolf Hitler, the Führer
of the German nation and people, Supreme Commander of the Armed Forces, and will be ready as a
brave soldier to risk my life at any time for this oath.

Oath of 2 Aug. 1934; Noakes and Pridham Vol.1 (1983) p.186.
This oath was devised by the minister of defence, General
Werner von Blomberg, on the day of the death of President
Hindenburg and published on 20 Aug. Its consequences were
momentous in that it bound the army to Hitler personally
and not only to the German state.

9 I was a little shocked at the faces, especially those
of the women, when Hitler finally appeared on the
balcony for a moment. They reminded me of the
crazed expressions I saw once in the back country of
Louisiana on the faces of some Holy Rollers who
were about to hit the trail. They looked up at him as
if he were a Messiah, their faces transformed into
something positively inhuman.

William Shirer, 4 Sept. 1934; *Berlin Diary* (1941) p.24. The
American journalist Shirer at the Nuremberg Nazi Party rally,
filmed for posterity in Leni Riefenstahl's *Triumph of the Will*.

10 What the man gives in courage on the battlefield,
the woman gives in eternal self-sacrifice, in eternal

pain and suffering. Every child that a woman brings into the world is a battle, a battle waged for the existence of her people.

Adolf Hitler, *Frankfurter Zeitung*, 9 Sept. 1934. The Hitlerian reward for female adoration.

1 Everything which is useful for the nation is lawful; everything which harms it is unlawful.

Hans Frank *Journal of the Academy of German Law* (1934). The lawyer Frank later became ruler of German-occupied Poland.

2 Big cities, industrialism, intellectualism – these are all shadows that the age has cast upon my thoughts ... There are moments in which this tormented life falls away and nothing exists but the plains, expanses, seasons, soil, the simple word *Volk*.

The poet Gottfried Benn to the writer Klaus Mann; Fest (1974) p.428. One of the pillars of the Reich was the concept of the *Volk*, the racially pure people of Germanic stock, uncontaminated by alien blood.

3 Did he care about the fate of men whom he had earlier called his friends? He did not even know where they were to be found. Perhaps they were sitting at some café table in Prague, Zurich or Paris; perhaps they were being tortured in a concentration camp; perhaps they were hidden in a Berlin attic or cellar. Hendrik saw no reason to inform himself about these matters.

Klaus Mann *Mephisto* (1936) Ch.7. Hendrik Höfgen, the central figure in Mann's novel, is based on the actor Gustaf Gründgens, Mann's former brother-in-law. Gründgens, a one-time communist, was given the chance to play Mephistopheles in Goethe's *Faust* by Goering, founder of the Gestapo. Like Faust, he sold his soul to the devil and became the leader of theatrical life in the Reich. In 1981 the book was made into a film, starring Klaus-Maria Brandauer.

4 Why need we trouble to socialize banks and factories? We socialize human beings.

Adolf Hitler in conversation with Hermann Rauschning; *Hitler Speaks* (1939) Ch.14. So much for the idea that capitalism ran the Reich.

5 When I hear the word 'culture' I reach for my revolver.

Hermann Goering, attrib. Taken from the 1933 play by Hans Johst, *Schlageter* (Fighter): 'When I hear the word "culture" I take the safety catch off my Browning' (Act I, Sc.1).

6 I know there are some people in Germany who feel sick at the sight of this black uniform; we can understand their feelings and do not expect many people to love us. All those who have the interests of Germany at heart will and should respect us, and those who somehow, sometime have guilty consciences towards the Führer or the nation should fear us.

Heinrich Himmler, 12 Nov. 1935; Noakes and Pridham Vol.2 (1984) p.496. Himmler was head of the black-uniformed SS (*Schutzstaffel*) and of the Gestapo (*Geheimestaatspolizei*, the Secret State Police).

7 1. You are no longer to have a good, reliable friend or acquaintance with whom you can discuss your activity.

2. Therefore, do not tell anything to someone who might need to know; tell only the person who must know.

The first two orders in a long list of instructions for the communist underground, formulated to counteract Gestapo surveillance; Benjamin Sax and Dieter Kunz *Inside Hitler's Germany* (1992) p.477.

8 We have no butter ... but I ask you, would you rather have butter or guns? ... Preparedness makes us powerful. Butter merely makes us fat.

Hermann Goering, 17 Jan. 1936; Willi Frischauer *Goering* (1951) Ch.10. Goering was in charge of the four-year plan, launched in 1936 and predicated on war with Soviet Russia. To judge by his immense girth, Goering never went short of butter himself.

9 I go the way that Providence dictates, with the assurance of a sleepwalker.

Adolf Hitler, 15 March 1936. Spoken soon after the German re-militarization of the Rhineland, a move made by Hitler in the face of great hesitancy by his generals.

NAZISM IN GERMANY: RACISM

10 Anti-Semitism on purely emotional grounds will find its ultimate expression in the form of pogroms. The anti-Semitism of reason, however, must lead to the planned judicial opposition to and elimination of the privileges of the Jews ... Yet its ultimate goal must absolutely be the removal of the Jews altogether.

Adolf Hitler, 16 Sept. 1919; Fest (1974) p.115.

11 He is and remains the typical parasite, a sponger who, like a malign bacillus, spreads more and more as long as he will find some favourable feeding-ground. And the consequences of his existence, too, resemble those of the parasite: where he appears, the host nation will sooner or later die.

Adolf Hitler *Mein Kampf* (1925) on Jews.

1 Isn't the Jew a human being too? Of course he is; none of us ever doubted it. All we doubt is that he is a decent human being.

Joseph Goebbels *Der Angriff*, 30 July 1928.

2 One of the company, Emil, the optimist, tried to convince us: 'It'll all be over in a few days.' They don't understand my anger when I say: 'They should strike us dead instead. It would be more humane than the psychological death they have in mind.'

The Jewish woman doctor Herthar Nathorff, diary entry, 1 April 1933; Wolfgang Berry (ed.) *The Diary of Herthar Nathorff* (1987). Dr Nathorff was writing on the day of the official boycott of Jewish shops, surgeries and law offices throughout Germany.

3 Five of the Polish Jews arrested in Dresden were each compelled to drink one half litre [about 1 pint] of castor oil … Some of the Jewish men assaulted had to submit to the shaving of their beards or to the clipping of their hair in the shape of steps. One Polish Jew in Chemnitz had his hair torn out by the roots.

Report by the US consul in Leipzig, Ralph Busser, 5 April 1933; Noakes and Pridham Vol.2 (1984) p.523.

4 Anyone who has a hereditary illness can be rendered sterile by a surgical operation if, according to the judgement of medical science, there is a strong probability that his/her offspring will suffer from serious hereditary defects of a physical or mental nature.

Law of 14 July 1933; Noakes and Pridham Vol.2 (1984) p.457. Eugenics in action.

5 Remember that you are German.
If of sound stock, do not remain unwed.
Keep your body pure.
Keep spirit and soul pure.
As a German, choose someone of German or Nordic blood for your partner.
When choosing your spouse, look into their lineage.
Health is a precondition of external beauty.
Marry only out of love.
Seek not a playmate but a partner in marriage.
Wish for as many children as possible.

Handbook for the German Family; M. Mazower *The Dark Continent* (1998) p.77.

6 I Marriages between Jews and citizens of German or kindred blood are forbidden.

II Sexual relations outside marriage between Jews and nationals of German or kindred blood are forbidden.

III Jews will not be permitted to employ female citizens of German or kindred blood under 45 years of age as domestic servants.

Law for the Protection of German Blood and Honour, 15 Sept. 1935; Noakes and Pridham Vol.2 (1984) pp.535–6. One of the so-called Nuremberg Laws.

7 My cousin … sat down to play a piece of Mendelssohn he liked. While I was admiring his musicianship, an officious German rushed over to the musician and rapped loudly on the piano with his knuckles. 'Stop that!' he shouted. 'That is decadent Jewish music!'

The American Tom Derring, 1936; Martin Gilbert *A History of the Twentieth Century* Vol.2 (1998) p.106.

8 The blood principle which has always been embodied in the *Schutzstaffel* [SS] from the very beginning would be condemned to death if it were not inextinguishably bound up with the belief in the value and holiness of the soil.

Heinrich Himmler *Die Schutzstaffel als antibolschewistische Kampforganisation* (The SS as an Anti-Bolshevist Combat Organization) (1937) pp.27–31. The exaltation of *Blut und Boden* (Blood and Soil), the coupling of racism and the Nazi cult of the peasantry, was irreverently known (strictly in private) as *Blubo*.

9 We want for Germany an upper stratum, a new nobility continually selected over the centuries, which replenishes itself continually from the best sons and daughters of our nation, a nobility which never becomes senile, which taps tradition and the past in the darkest millennia whenever they are valuable and which eternally represents our nation's youth.

Heinrich Himmler, 8 Nov. 1937; B.F. Smith and A.E. Peterson *Heinrich Himmler* (1974) p.61. The SS as Germany's racial aristocracy.

10 Drive Carefully, Sharp Bend – Jews, 75 miles an hour!

Notice on the road outside Ludwigshaven, 1983; Martin Lowenthal *The Jews of Germany* (1938) p.411.

11 The synagogue had almost burned down and the firemen were looking on, taking care that the flames should not spread to other buildings … The same firemen … had visited [the toy shop] before me; dipping a brush in paint, they had written 'Jewish

Swine' obliquely across his window ... then ... they had kicked in the window with the heels of their boots ... One had drawn his dagger. He was cutting dolls open and he seemed disappointed each time that nothing but sawdust flowed from their limbs and bodies.

Günter Grass *The Tin Drum* (1959) Bk 1, 'Faith, Hope, Love'. The novel describes *Kristallnacht* in Danzig (Gdansk), 10–11 Nov. 1938. Death-camp guards referred to the corpses of their victims as *Puppen* (dolls). The Free City of Danzig, though not part of the Reich, housed a fiercely loyal Nazi movement. Fire brigades were under orders to save non-Jewish buildings from the flames.

1 I think it is imperative to give the Jews certain public parks, not the best ones, and tell them: 'You may sit on these benches.' These benches shall be marked 'For Jews only'. Besides that they have no business in German parks.

Joseph Goebbels, 12 Nov. 1938; Noakes and Pridham Vol.2 (1984) pp.559–60.

2 As for the question of isolation, I'd like to make a few proposals regarding police measures which are important also because of their psychological effect on public opinion. For example, anyone who is Jewish according to the Nuremberg Laws will have to wear a certain badge.

Reinhard Heydrich, 12 Nov. 1938; Noakes and Pridham Vol.2 (1984) p.566. Jews within Germany's jurisdiction were compelled to wear a yellow Star of David by a regulation of 1 Sept. 1941. Heydrich was second-in-command to Himmler and head of the SS *Sicherheitsdienst* (Security Service). The SS at this stage sought the expulsion of all German Jews from the Reich. The anti-Semitic Nuremberg Laws were enacted in 1935.

NAZISM IN GERMANY: THE CHURCHES

3 Neither of the denominations – Catholic or Protestant, they are both the same – has any future left ... That won't stop me tearing up Christianity in Germany, root and branch. One is either a Christian or a German. You can't be both.

Adolf Hitler, 1933; Layton (1992) p.100.

4 The German bishops have long ago said yes to the new State and have not only promised to recognize its authority ... but are serving the State with burning love and all our strength.

Bishop Berning, 21 Sept. 1933; M. Housden *Resistance and Conformity in the Third Reich* (1997) p.51. A minority of

Protestant bishops switched their allegiance to a Nazi-sponsored church organization.

5 He who would let blood, race and nationality take the place of God as the creator and master of political authority, undermines the state.

Appeal to the Protestant congregations of Prussia, 5 March 1935; Joachim Remak *The Nazi Years* (1969) p.100. Issued from the Berlin parish of Pastor Martin Niemöller, a prominent figure in German Christian resistance to Nazism (see 760:1).

6 *USA (Unser Selig Adolf)* ('Our Holy Adolf')

Nickname for Hitler used by the grandchildren of the composer Richard Wagner, whom Hitler venerated.

7   Adolf Hitler, you are our great leader.
        You have made our enemies shudder.
        May your Third Reich come,
        Your will alone be law on earth.
        Let us daily hear your voice,
        And command us through your leaders
        Whom we wish to obey even at the risk
        Of our own lives.
        We swear this.
        Heil Hitler!

D. Klinksiek *Women in the Nazi State* (1982) p.145. A parody of the Lord's Prayer.

8 Thirty to forty villagers got into the unlocked school on the night of 6 January 1937 to hang the crucifix back in its old place ... The accused ... hung the crucifix right up beside the picture of the Führer ... The court of Rhaunen, on 9 January 1937, ordered a custodial sentence.

Official report, 1937; Housden (1997) p.52.

9 Just as the Roman Catholic is convinced that the pope is infallible in all matters of religion and morals, so we National Socialists believe with the same inner conviction that for us the Führer is infallible in all political and other matters that concern the national and social interests of the people ... For we love Adolf Hitler, because we believe deeply and unalterably that he has been sent to us by God in order to save Germany.

Hermann Goering *Building a Nation* (1934) p.52.

10 Whoever exalts race, or the people, or the State ... and divinizes them to an idolatrous level, perverts an order of the world planned and created by God ... Should any man dare ... to place a mortal, were

he the greatest of all times, by the side of, or over, or against Christ, he would deserve to be called prophet of nothingness … To all those imprisoned in jail and concentration camps, the Father of the Christian world sends his words of gratitude and commendation … The day will come when the *Te Deum* of liberation will succeed to the premature hymns of the enemies of Christ.
Pope Pius XI *Mit Brennender Sorge* (With Burning Sorrow), 14 March 1937; Carlen (ed.) (1981) pp.527, 528, 533, 534. An impassioned denunciation of Nazism, stigmatizing it as fundamentally un-Christian, had little discernible impact on the majority of German Catholics.

1 The gods of our ancestors … were men, and had a weapon in their hand, symbolizing the attitude to life that is innate to our race – that of action, that of a man's responsibility for himself. How different the pale crucified one, expressing by his impassive attitude and by his decided look of suffering, humility and an extreme self-surrender, both qualities which contradict the basically heroic attitude of our race.
The SS paper *Das Schwarze Korps* (The Black Corps), 8 Jan. 1939. The black-uniformed SS worshipped the pagan gods of pre-Christian Germany. One focus of their cult was the cathedral at Quedlinburg in central Germany, deconsecrated for their devotions in 1938.

NAZISM IN GERMANY: THE FÜHRER STATE, 1936-9

2 He is as immune from criticism as a king in a monarchical country. He is something more. He is the George Washington of Germany – the man who won for his country independence from all her oppressors.
David Lloyd George on Hitler, *Daily Express*, 17 Sept. 1936. Lloyd George had a three-hour interview with Hitler at Berchtesgaden on 4 Sept. The current king, Edward VIII, was not, of course, immune from criticism as his determination to marry the American divorcée Mrs Wallis Simpson led to his abdication in Dec. 1936. Both he and his wife were admirers of Hitler.

3 This much was certain: he was no normal being. He was, rather, a morbid personality, a quasi-madman, a character out of the pages of Dostoyevsky, a man 'possessed'.
André François-Poncet, on Hitler, *The Fateful Years* (1949) p.291. François-Poncet, French ambassador in Berlin from 1931 to 1938, had a close-up view of the Führer.

4 A decadent by-product of Bolshevik Jewish corruption … We had Futurism, Expressionism, Realism, Cubism, even Dadaism. Could insanity go further? There were pictures with green skies and purple seas. There were paintings which could only be due to abnormal eyesight.
Adolf Hitler, 19 July 1937, opening the exhibition of 'Degenerate Art' in Munich. The Führer may not have known much about modern art, but he knew what he disliked.

5 [The nation] must be trained to absolute, pigheaded, unquestioning confident faith that in the end we will achieve everything that is necessary.
Adolf Hitler, late 1938, in the aftermath of the Munich Agreement; Fest (1974) p.569. Hitler was apparently fearful that German resolve was slackening.

6 These boys join our organization at the age of ten … and they will not be free again for the rest of their lives.
Adolf Hitler, 4 Dec. 1938; A. Klönne *Youth in the Third Reich* (1982) p.80. Boys spent four years in the first of the Nazi youth organizations before graduating to the Hitler Youth, after which they were absorbed into the SA, the SS or the armed forces.

7 For your information the Führer wishes to see an end to the use of waiters in all restaurants. The job of the waiter is, in the Führer's view, not the right sort of work for a man but rather appropriate for women and girls.
Martin Bormann to Robert Ley, 8 Feb. 1939; Noakes and Pridham Vol.2 (1984) p.245. Bormann was head of Hitler's Secretariat; Ley was director of the Labour Front.

8 The camera lingers lovingly on the Goebbels children, all clothed in white, who stand, curious but well behaved, next to Hitler, thus strengthening his reputation as a true lover of children – a special shot for the women in the audience.
Official account of the filming of the celebration of Hitler's 50th birthday on 20 April 1939; E.K. Bramstedt *Goebbels and National Socialist Propaganda 1925-1945* (1965) p.218.

9 Concentration camp is certainly, like any form of deprivation of liberty, a tough and strict measure. Hard, productive labour, a regular life, exceptional cleanliness in matters of daily life and personal hygiene, splendid food, strict but fair treatment, instruction in learning how to work again and how to learn the necessary crafts – these are the methods of education. The motto which stands above these camps reads: there is a path to freedom. Its

milestones are obedience, hard work, honesty, orderliness, cleanliness, sobriety, truthfulness, self-sacrifice and love of the Fatherland.
Heinrich Himmler, 21 Sept. 1939; Smith and Peterson (1974) p.111.

1 First they came for the Jews
And I did not speak out –
Because I was not a Jew.
Then they came for the Communists
And I did not speak out –
Because I was not a Communist.
Then they came for the trade unionists
And I did not speak out –
Because I was not a trade unionist.
Then they came for me –
And there was no one left
To speak out for me.
Martin Niemöller *Children of Light and Darkness* (1944) Foreword. Niemöller (see 758:5) was a Lutheran pastor who was first jailed, then imprisoned in concentration camps from 1937 to 1945. In 1941 he tried unsuccessfully to enlist in the submarine service, in which he had served in World War I.

America: Boom and Bust, 1919–39

THE ROARING TWENTIES

1 The era of wonderful nonsense.
The journalist Westbrook Pegler on the 1920s; *'Taint Right* (1936). The British war correspondent Philip Gibbs described the British army GHQ at the Château Beaurepaire, near Montreuil, as the 'City of Beautiful Nonsense' (*Realities of War* (1920) p.25).

2 America is the only nation in history which, by some miracle, has gone from barbarism to decadence without passing through the intermediate phase of civilization.
The French statesman Georges Clemenceau attrib., particularly apropos the 1920s.

RED SCARE, 1919–27

3 The trade union is to the American workers what the Council of Workmen and Soldiers is to Russia, Austria and Germany. The labor council is the central soviet.
Seattle Union Record, Feb. 1919. The strike movement that paralysed Seattle early in 1919 touched off a wave of stoppages and the so-called Red Scare.

4 This was a revolution, not a strike. Treat it as such. Do not in particular change working conditions, hours or wages. Let the men come back as though they had been on a vacation. Give them a chance to clean house in their organization, to kick out the red agitators, purge themselves of the I.W.W.-itch and put real Americans in control of the unions. Co-operate with the mass of loyal Americans in the union ranks. We'll tend to the other crowd.
Mayor Ole Hanson of Seattle, Feb. 1919; Walter V. Woehlke *Sunset* Vol.42 (April 1919) p.16. The IWW (Industrial Workers of the World) formed the militant wing of the American trade union movement.

5 Yesterday the enemy of liberty was Prussianism [imperial Germany]. Today it is radicalism … America is calling you. The steel strike will fail. Be a 100 per cent American. Stand by America.
Pittsburg Chronicle-Telegraph, 27 Sept. 1919.

6 These murderous wild beasts of our otherwise blessed republic should be given a bottle of water and a pint of meal and shoved out into the ocean on a raft, when the wind is blowing seaward.
Speaker in California, 1919, on the best way with dissenters; Nelson Van Valen *Pacific Historical Review* Vol.12 (1953) p.49. Another enthusiast for deportation would have had them placed 'in ships of stone with sails of lead, with the wrath of God for a breeze and hell for their first port' (William E. Leuchtenburg *The Perils of Prosperity 1914–1929* (1958) p.66).

7 If there be any doubt of the general character of the active leaders and agitators amongst these avowed revolutionists, a visit to the Department of Justice and an examination of their photographs there collected would dispel it. Out of the sly and crafty eyes of many of them leap stupidity, cruelty, insanity, and crime, from their lopsided faces, sloping brows, and misshapen features may be recognized the unmistakable criminal type.
US attorney-general A. Mitchell Palmer, 1920; House Committee on Rules *Hearings* (1920) p.27. Palmer masterminded the government's response to the Red Scare, breaching civil liberties to such a degree that he himself came under Congressional investigation.

8 By the Almighty I will fan the fire of discontent till I draw my last breath; until I see … a world full of joy and peace where there is no crime and no bloodshed, no sorrow and no outstretched hands of beggars, no parasites or robbers, no tyrants and no thrones, no gallows to throw their shadows of horror over a sick world. This is the world of the Industrial Workers of the World.
Elmer Smith, 1 May 1923; Tom Copeland *The Centralia Tragedy of 1919* (1993) pp.139–40. Smith acted as defence lawyer for the radical unionists of the IWW. In Centralia, Washington, on 11 Nov. 1919 four men were murdered by an anti-radical mob.

9 I am suffering because I am a radical and indeed I am a radical; I have suffered because I am an Italian, and indeed I am an Italian … but I am so convinced to be right that if you could execute me two times, and if I could be reborn two other times, I would live again to do what I have done already.
Bartolomeo Vanzetti at his trial, 1927; Francis Russell *Tragedy in Dedham* (1963). Vanzetti and his fellow anarchist, Nicola Sacco, were arrested for a double murder in May 1920 and executed on 23 Aug. 1928, in spite of multiple doubts over their guilt.

PROHIBITION, 1919–30

1 Section 1. After one year from the ratification of this article the manufacture, sale, or transportation of intoxicating liquors within, the importation thereof into, or the exportation thereof from the United States and all territory subject to the jurisdiction thereof for beverage purposes is hereby prohibited.
Opening section of the Eighteenth Amendment to the Constitution, making alcoholic drink illegal; ratified 16 Jan. 1919.

2 Oh, fatal Friday!
Monumental Dry Day!
Ah, dreadful Sixteenth Day of January
That expurgates the Nation's Commissary,
For all the years to come,
Of whisky, brandy, gin and beer and rum,
The sparkling flow of Veuve Cliquot and
Mumm
And all the wines – I cannot speak the worst;
Drought leaves me glum and dumb,
O Day accurst
Of Thirst!
Arthur Guiterman, lament over prohibition, which came into force on 16 Jan. 1920.

3 I make my money by supplying a public demand. If I break the law, my customers, who number hundreds of the best people in Chicago, are as guilty as I am. The only difference between us is that I sell and they buy. Everybody calls me a racketeer. I call myself a business man. When I sell liquor, it's bootlegging. When my patrons serve it on a silver tray on Lake Shore Drive, it's hospitality.
Al Capone, the notorious Chicago gang-leader; Andrew Sinclair *Prohibition* (1962) p.240.

4 You can get much farther with a kind word and a gun than you can with a kind word alone.
Al Capone, attrib.

5 The vast centres of population, where all the feeling for liberty that still persists in this country is kept alive, the great centres of tolerance and independence and thought and culture – the cities – all of them were wet before prohibition, and since.
The lawyer Clarence Darrow; *Debate on Prohibition* (1924) p.38. 'Wet' here means 'permissive' on alcohol.

6 Our country has deliberately undertaken a great social and economic experiment: noble in motive and far-reaching in purpose.

Herbert Hoover, 11 Aug. 1928; *The Memoirs of Herbert Hoover* Vol.2 (1952) p.201. Note the extremely careful choice of words, often misquoted as 'noble experiment'. Hoover's sibylline pronouncement reflected his wariness on the explosive prohibition issue in his acceptance speech as Republican candidate for the presidency.

7 Your drinking in Minneapolis, gentlemen, is done there in unspeakably vile dives that cater to the itinerant lumberman, to the harvest hands, and to the itinerant workers there – brothels, practically, most of them … A man will go there to get a drink, and there is a wink and the front door is locked and the curtains are pulled down, and something else besides drinking goes on.
Walter W. Liggett, 12 Feb. 1930; *Hearings on the Prohibition Amendment* (1930) p.12.

8 There is as much chance of repealing the Eighteenth Amendment as there is for a humming-bird to fly to the planet Mars with the Washington Monument tied to its tail.
Senator Morris Sheppard, resisting the call to end prohibition, 24 Sept. 1930. Repeal came, even so, in Dec. 1933.

FORWARD TO THE PAST, 1922–8

9 A hybrid race of people as worthless and futile as the good-for-nothing mongrels of Central America and Southeastern Europe.
Kenneth Roberts *Why Europe Leaves Home* (1922) p.22. Nativist view of a future United States if unrestricted immigration were allowed.

10 The truth is that the majority of non-Anglo-Saxon immigrants since the Revolution … have been, not the superior men of their native lands, but the botched and the unfit: Irishmen starving to death in Ireland, Germans unable to weather the *Sturm und Drang* [storm and stress] of the post-Napoleonic reorganization, Italians weed-grown on exhausted soil, Scandinavians run to all bone and no brain, Jews too incompetent to swindle even the barbarous peasants of Russia, Poland and Roumania.
H.L. Mencken 'On Being an American' (1922) in *Prejudices: A Selection* (1959) p.99. The iconoclast Mencken repeats the Know-Nothings' clichés of the mid-19th century (see 583:3).

11 On the one side is beer, bolshevism, unassimilating settlements and perhaps many flags – on the other side is constitutional government; one flag, stars and stripes.

Representative Tincher of Kansas in the debate on the National Origins Act of 1924; Leuchtenburg (1958) p.208. The act fixed immigration quotas on the basis of the 1890 census of the US population, thus aiming to guarantee in perpetuity the dominance of the White Anglo-Saxon Protestant (WASP) element. It remained in force until 1965.

1 We are marching backwards to the glorious age of the 16th century when bigots lighted faggots to burn men who dared to bring any intelligence and enlightenment and culture to the human mind.
Clarence Darrow, 13 July 1925; Edward J. Larson *Summer for the Gods* (1997) p.164. Darrow was defence counsel for the schoolteacher John T. Scopes, prosecuted by the state of Tennessee for teaching his pupils the theory of evolution and undermining their faith in biblical fundamentalism.

2 It is better to trust in the Rock of Ages than to know the age of rocks. It is better for one to know that he is close to the Heavenly Father than to know how far the stars in the heavens are apart.
William Jennings Bryan, *New York Times*, 22 July 1925. The veteran politician Bryan was chief witness for the prosecution in the Scopes trial (see 763:1). These words come from his final testimony, which he was not allowed to read to the court but which was published next day in the press. Although he was ridiculed under cross-examination by Darrow, Scopes was convicted. Bryan, however, died days later.

3 LAW AND ORDER MUST PREVAIL. COHABITATION BETWEEN WHITES AND BLACKS MUST STOP. BOOTLEGGERS, PIMPS, HANGERS-ON, GET RIGHT OR GET OUT. WIFE-BEATERS, FAMILY-DESERTERS, HOME-WRECKERS, WE HAVE NO ROOM FOR YOU. LAW VIOLATORS, WE ARE WATCHING YOU. BEWARE.
Sign carried by the Ku Klux Klan, articulating the anxieties of Redneck America. The 'Invisible Empire' of the Klan was resurrected in 1915, the year of the glorification of the original Klan in D.W. Griffith's film *Birth of a Nation*.

4   We rally round Old Glory in our robes of
            spotless white,
        While the Fiery Cross is burning in the silent,
            silv'ry night.
        Come and join our glorious army in the cause
            of God and Right.
        The Klan is marching on.
The Ku Klux Klan's version of the 'Battle Hymn of the Republic' (see 589:11). Potential victims – mostly blacks – were first intimidated by having a wooden cross set on fire outside their house. In 1981 the black custodian of the Panama Canal Zone archive told JM that this had happened to him when he came to live in a predominantly white area of the US-occupied Zone.

5   Alcohol Al for President,
        I stand for whiskey and bad government
        My platform is wet and I am too,
        And I get my votes from Catholic and Jew.
        The ignorant wop and the gangster too
        Are the trash I expect to carry me through.
Ku Klux Klan doggerel on Governor Al Smith of New York, Democratic candidate in the 1928 presidential election; Glenn Fieldman *Politics, Society, and the Klan in Alabama, 1915–1949* (1999) p.177.

6 No Governor can kiss the papal ring and get within gunshot of the White House.
Methodist Bishop Adna Leonard on Governor Smith; Leuchtenburg (1958) p.234. Smith's defeat marked the last electoral triumph for rural America over the urban values symbolized by New York. The Republican victor, Herbert Hoover, was at pains to stress his origins as a country boy.

BUSINESS ADMINISTRATION, 1920–32

7 America's present need is not heroics, but healing; not nostrums, but normalcy.
Senator Warren Harding of Ohio, 20 May 1920, tuning into the yearning for a quiet life after the upheaval of war and postwar tensions.

8 The convention will be deadlocked, and … some twelve or fifteen men, worn-out and bleary-eyed for lack of sleep, will sit down, about two o'clock in the morning, around a table in a smoke-filled room in some hotel, and decide the nomination.
Harry M. Daugherty, 20 Feb. 1920; *New York Times*, 21 Feb. 1920. Daugherty was campaign manager for Harding. His prediction was made four months before the deadlock in the Republican nominating convention was broken by the choice of Harding.

9 I must utter my belief in the divine inspiration of the founding fathers.
President Warren Harding, inaugural address, 4 March 1921. Harding first used the phrase on 22 Feb. 1918 (Washington's birthday): 'It is good to meet and drink at the fountains of wisdom inherited from the founding fathers of the Republic.'

10 My God, how the money rolls in.
Jesse Smith, close associate of President Harding in the so-called 'Ohio Gang', citing an all-too-appropriate popular song; Leuchtenburg (1958) p.92. The corruption of the Harding administration was legendary.

11 Harding was not a bad man. He was just a slob.
Alice Roosevelt Longworth *Crowded Hours* (1933). The daughter of President Theodore Roosevelt was a notoriously

mordant woman, though it is impossible to quarrel with her verdict on the 29th president, who died in office on 2 Aug. 1923.

1 He looks as though he had been weaned on a pickle.

Alice Roosevelt Longworth on Calvin Coolidge, Harding's successor as president, elected in his own right in 1924. The austere and taciturn Coolidge was the antithesis of the self-indulgent Harding.

2 The chief business of the American people is business.

President Calvin Coolidge, *New York Times*, 18 Jan. 1925.

3 The man who builds a factory builds a temple; the man who works there worships there.

President Calvin Coolidge; Leuchtenburg (1958) p.188.

4 He picked up twelve men from the bottom ranks of business and forged them into an organization that conquered the world.

Bruce Barton *The Man Nobody Knows: A Discovery of the Real Jesus* (1924) p.162. Christ as the Founding Father of American capitalism.

5 There is something sacred about big business. Anything which is economically right is morally right.

Henry Ford, doyen of the American automobile industry; Sinclair (1962) p.387.

6 Just as in Rome one goes to the Vatican and endeavours to get an audience with the Pope, so in Detroit one goes to the Ford Works and endeavours to see Henry Ford.

British visitor to the Ford plant; Leuchtenburg (1958) p.187.

7 A hard cruel city. No culture. Blasé, gaudy, noisy. No one talks to you except in dollars and mass production and the way they boss labour. A very undesirable place.

Ernest Bevin on Detroit, Oct. 1926; Alan Bullock *The Life and Times of Ernest Bevin* Vol.1 (1960) p.360.

8 The very simple principle of Least Government, with its companion principle of Least Taxation, seems to me pretty near all that this country needs, if put in practice, to make it entirely safe for democracy.

Charles N. Fay, vice-president of the National Association of Manufacturers, *Business in Politics* (1926) p.47. The voice of conservative Republicanism throughout the century, here quoting from Woodrow Wilson (see 717:4).

9 I do not choose to run for President in 1928.

President Calvin Coolidge, 2 Aug. 1928. A wise decision in view of the plight of his successor, Herbert Hoover, in the face of the Great Crash of 1929.

10 We were challenged with a peacetime choice between the American system of rugged individualism and a European philosophy of diametrically opposed doctrines – doctrines of paternalism and state socialism.

Herbert Hoover, 22 Oct. 1928; *The New Day* (1928) p.154. 'Rugged individualism' won Hoover the election in 1928 and lost it for him disastrously in 1932.

11 We in America today are nearer to the final triumph over poverty than ever before in the history of any land. The poorhouse is vanishing from among us.

Herbert Hoover, 11 Aug. 1928; (1928) p.16.

COLLAPSE, 1929-32

12 The future appears brilliant … We have the greatest and soundest prosperity, and the best material prospects of any country in the world.

Thomas J. Lamont to President Herbert Hoover, 22 Oct. 1929; Piers Brendon *The Dark Valley* (2000) p.63. Two days later the New York stock market collapsed.

13 By eleven o'clock the market had degenerated into a wild, mad scramble to sell. In the crowded boardrooms across the country the ticker told of a frightful collapse … By eleven thirty the market had surrendered to blind, relentless fear. This, indeed, was panic.

J.K. Galbraith *The Great Crash, 1929* (1963 edn) p.12. 'Black Thursday', 24 Oct. 1929, in the New York Stock Exchange, the beginning of the Great Depression.

14 Wall Street Lays An Egg.

Sime Silverman, headline in *Variety*, 30 Oct. 1929.

15 The staff saw their savings going down in chaos; since they were certainly operating on margin, they might at this moment already have been wiped out … while their employer, reputedly one of the shrewdest financiers in New York, was calmly sitting upstairs eating pompano and saddle of lamb.

Claud Cockburn *I, Claud* (1967) p.100. Cockburn describes the hysteria among the servants in the New York house of Sir Edgar Speyer at lunchtime on Black Thursday, 24 Oct. 1929.

1 On 24 October 1929 the American crisis burst out, and it came unexpectedly, like a bombshell. For us poor provincials of old Europe the catastrophe took us completely unawares. We were shaken and thunderstruck as the world was by the news of Napoleon's death. This because we had always been led to believe that this was the land of prosperity, limitless, total prosperity, without any possibility of eclipse or decline. Everyone was rich ... At a certain moment this scenario collapsed. There ensued a series of black days, extremely black days ... Following on from prosperity have come the lines of men waiting for soup and bread in the great cities of the USA.

Benito Mussolini, 18 Dec. 1930; *Speeches* (1935) p.262.

2 The situation varies from week to week, but on a certain day last month, less than one third of the outside shops on the ground floor were rented. Elevators had stopped running from the forty-second to the sixty-seventh floor. Many floors were not finished at all – merely big plastery spaces.

The humorist James Thurber in a deadly serious piece on the recently opened Empire State Building, New York, *Fortune*, Jan. 1932.

3   What of the skyscrapers?
    We observe them more coolly.
    What contemptible hovels skyscrapers are
        when they no longer yield rents!
    Rising so high, full of poverty? Touching the
        clouds, full of debt?

Bertolt Brecht 'Late Lamented Fame of the Giant City of New York' (1929–33) in *Poems 1913–1956* (1976).

4 What does prohibition amount to, if your neighbor's children are not eating? It's food, not drink, is our problem now. We were so afraid the poor people might drink, now we fixed it so they can't eat ... The working class didn't bring this on, it was the big boys that thought the financial drunk was going to last forever.

Will Rogers, 1931; *The Autobiography of Will Rogers* (1949) p.255. The comedian Will Rogers gave a satirical running commentary on American politics until his death in 1935.

5 There is not a garbage dump in Chicago which is not diligently haunted by the hungry. Last summer in the hot weather, when the smell was sickening and the flies were thick, there were a hundred people a day coming to one of the dumps, falling on the heap of refuse as soon as the truck had pulled out and digging in it with sticks and hands.

Edmund Wilson *New Republic*, 1 Feb. 1933, p.320.

6 We have been eating wild green ... such as Polk salad. Violet tops, wild onions, forget me not, wild lettuce and such weeds as cows eat as a cow wont eat a poison weeds ... Our family are in bad shake children need milk women need nourishments food shoes and dresses – that we cannot get and there at least 10,000 hungry people in Harlan County daily.

Letter from a miner in Harlan County, Kentucky, *The Nation*, 8 June 1932.

7 Prosperity is just around the corner.

President Herbert Hoover, attrib.

8   Hoover is my Shepherd, I am in want.
    He maketh me to lie down on park benches.
    He leadeth me by still factories.
    He restoreth my doubt in the Republican Party.
    He guideth me in the path of the unemployed
        for his party's sake.
    Yea, though I walk through the valley of soup
        kitchens,
    I am hungry.

E.J. Sullivan 'The 1932nd Psalm' (1932). *Mutatis mutandis*, the same dirge was to be sung about Roosevelt after 1933.

9 Such a little man could not have made so big a depression.

Norman Thomas, leader of the American Socialist Party, on Hoover; attrib.

10 At the cinema ... for three hours he rides the plains of Arizona, tastes the night life of Paris or New York, makes a safe excursion into the underworld, sails the seven seas or penetrates the African jungle. Famous comedians make him laugh and forget his difficulties and discouragements.

E.W. Babbe *The Unemployed Man* (1933) p.183. Escapism via the movies.

11   Once I built a railroad, now it's done.
    Brother, can you spare a dime?

E.Y. Harburg 'Brother, Can You Spare a Dime?' (1932). A classic Depression lament, contrasting the years of high achievement with the current slump.

12 If there are enough fellows with guts in this country to do like us, we will march eastward and we will cut the East off ... We have got the granaries; we have the hogs, the cattle, the corn; the East has nothing but mortgages on our places. We will show them what we can do.

Oklahoma farmer, as reported by the journalist Oscar Ameringer, 1932; House *Hearing on Unemployment* (1932) pp.100–101. A token of the plight of Western farmers, who had suffered throughout the 1920s as well as the 1930s.

1 That mob ... was a bad looking mob. It was animated by the essence of revolution ... Had [the president] let it go on another week I believe that the institutions of our government would have been very severely threatened.

Chief of staff General Douglas MacArthur, 28 July 1932; *The Memoirs of Herbert Hoover* Vol.3 (1953) p.228. The US army's dispersal of the 'Bonus Army' of unemployed war veterans marching on Washington drove a final nail into Hoover's coffin in the run-up to the election.

2 Democracy: A government of the masses. Authority derived through mass meeting or any other form of 'direct' expression. Results in mobocracy. Attitude toward property is Communistic – negating property rights. Attitude toward law is that the will of the majority shall regulate, whether it be based upon deliberation or governed by passion, prejudice and impulse, without restraint or regard for consequences. Results in demagogism, license, agitation, discontent, and anarchy.

US Army Training Manual 2000–25 (1932). The philosophy underlying the action of MacArthur, shared by all on the American right.

3 This is not an issue as to whether people shall go hungry or cold in the United States ... It is a question as to whether the American people, on one hand, will maintain the spirit of charity and mutual self-help through voluntary giving and the responsibility of local government as distinguished, on the other hand, from appropriations out of the Federal Treasury.

President Herbert Hoover, Feb. 1931; *The Memoirs of Herbert Hoover* Vol.3 (1953) p.55. After more than a year of economic disaster, Hoover still clung to the nostrums of the past.

4 The people of the United States are now confronted with an emergency more serious than war ... There must be power in the states and the nation to remold, through experimentation, our economic practices and institutions to meet changing social and economic needs ... This Court has the power to prevent an experiment ... But, in the exercise of this high power, we must be ever on our guard, lest we erect our prejudices into legal principles. If we

would guide by the light of reason, we must let our minds be bold.

Supreme Court Justice Louis Brandeis, 1932, in the case of New State Ice Company v. Liebmann; John Major (ed.) *The New Deal* (1968) pp.107, 108. Brandeis spoke for the liberal minority on the Court.

5 Has the prophecy of Henry Adams, that we are all on a machine which cannot go forward without disaster and cannot be stopped without ruin, come true?

William Dodd, 1932; Leuchtenburg (1958) p.268. The Boston Brahmin Adams was repelled by the capitalism that burgeoned in the post-Civil War generation (see 643:5).

ROOSEVELT AND THE PROMISE OF A NEW DEAL, 1932–3

6 Franklin D. Roosevelt is an amiable man with many philanthropic impulses, but he is not the dangerous enemy of anything ... He is a pleasant man who, without any important qualifications for the office, would very much like to be President.

The columnist Walter Lippmann on the governor of New York, 1932, *Interpretations 1931–1932* (1932) pp.251–2. A famous characterization, well off target, as the New Deal was to prove.

7 A second-class intellect, but a first-class temperament.

Oliver Wendell Holmes Jr on Roosevelt, 1933. In 1932 Justice Holmes said he would have voted for Hoover.

8 These unhappy times call for the building of plans ... that build from the bottom up and not from the top down, that put their faith once more in the forgotten man at the bottom of the economic pyramid.

Franklin D. Roosevelt, 7 April 1932; *Public Papers and Addresses of Franklin D. Roosevelt* Vol.1 (1938) p.625. See 644:9.

9 The country needs, and, unless I mistake its temper, the country demands bold, persistent experimentation. It is common sense to take a method and try it: if it fails, admit it frankly and try another. But above all, try something.

Franklin D. Roosevelt, 22 May 1932; *Public Papers* Vol.1 (1938) p.646.

10 I pledge you, I pledge myself, to a new deal for the American people.

Franklin D. Roosevelt, acceptance speech for the presidential nomination, 2 July 1932; *Public Papers* Vol.1 (1938) p.659. A card-game metaphor, with the president as the dealer, albeit a dealer biased no longer in favour of business.

I Happy days are here again!
The skies above are clear again!
Let us sing a song of cheer again!
Happy days are here again!

Roosevelt campaign song, 1932, though written in 1929.

2 Any government, like any family, can for a year spend a little more than it earns. But you and I know that a continuation of that habit means the poorhouse.

Franklin D. Roosevelt, 30 July 1932; *Public Papers* Vol.1 (1938) p.663. Both then and throughout the 1930s Roosevelt was reluctant to depart from the orthodoxy of a balanced budget.

3 The first theory is that if we make the rich richer, somehow they will let a part of their prosperity trickle down to the rest of us. The second theory … was the theory that if we make the average of mankind comfortable and secure, their prosperity will rise upward … through the ranks.

Franklin D. Roosevelt, 2 Oct. 1932; *Public Papers* Vol.1 (1938) p.772. See 646:4.

4 Say that civilization is a tree which, as it grows, continually produces rot and dead wood. The radical says: 'Cut it down.' The conservative says: 'Don't touch it.' The liberal compromises: 'Let's prune, so that we lose neither the old trunk nor the new branches.'

Franklin D. Roosevelt in the 1932 campaign; Arthur Schlesinger Jr *The Politics of Upheaval* (1960) pp.648–9. A classic expression of the liberal alternative to the extremes of reaction and revolution.

5 The people seem dreary, even apathetic. The Washington banks have closed, the banks throughout the country are closing; and, though the newspapers are trying to conceal the news that New York and Illinois have given up, there creeps over us, through all the activity and pomp, a numbness of life running out.

Edmund Wilson 'Washington: Inaugural Parade' in *The American Earthquake* (1958) p.478. An impression of the atmosphere on 4 March 1933 immediately before Franklin D. Roosevelt's inauguration as president of the United States.

6 First of all let me assert my firm belief that the only thing we have to fear is fear itself – nameless,

unreasoning, unjustified terror … I shall ask the Congress for the one remaining instrument to meet the crisis – broad Executive power to wage a war against the emergency as great as the power that would be given to me if we were in fact invaded by a foreign foe.

President Franklin D. Roosevelt, inaugural address, 4 March 1933; *Public Papers* Vol.2 (1938) pp.11, 15. Perhaps Roosevelt's greatest achievement was to restore a sense of confidence in a public shattered by the Depression.

NEW DEAL IN ACTION, 1933–4

7 The taxi-cab driver was tinged with 'Red' and had just said, 'To hell with all your politics. What we need is a Stalin.' The iceman said, 'Oh yeah? We got what we want. We want Roosevelt.' … Said the cripple … 'All we can do is pray for him, buddy, and let him have his hand.'

Beatrice B. Beecher to President Roosevelt's wife, Eleanor, 24 May 1933, reporting a conversation she had overheard; Frank Freidel *Franklin D. Roosevelt: Launching the New Deal* (1973) p.505.

8 Though a stubborn animal, the southern mule had been trained to work delicately between the cotton rows … pulling the cultivator over the weeds. Soon it was reported that farmers found it difficult to persuade the mules to forget their training. The animals balked at having to trample the cotton plants as they dragged behind them the plows turning up the rows.

Alger Hiss *Recollections of a Life* (1988) p.64. In 1933 Hiss was working for the Agricultural Adjustment Administration (AAA), whose job was to cut back agricultural production in an effort to raise farm prices. On the cotton plantations of the South this was easier said than done.

9 There is no choice presented to American business between intelligently planned and controlled individual operations and a return to the gold-plated anarchy that masqueraded as 'rugged individualism' … Unless industry is sufficiently socialized by its private owners and managers so that great essential industries are operated under public obligation appropriate to the public interest in them, the advance of political control over private industry is inevitable.

Donald Richberg, deputy head of the National Recovery Administration (NRA), 1933; Arthur Schlesinger Jr *The Coming of the New Deal* (1958) p.115. The NRA was a public-private partnership between government and business, in which big producers gradually came to have the upper hand, as they did under the AAA.

1 'Do nothing,' some business and financial leaders replied. They argued that a depression was the scientific operation of economic laws that were God-given and not man-made. They could not be interfered with. Depressions were phenomena like the one described in the biblical story of Joseph and the seven kine, fat and lean. The leaders said we were in the seven lean years that must inevitably follow the seven full years. And they further explained that we were in the lean years because we had been spend-thrifts and wastrels in the roaring twenties. We had wasted what we had earned instead of spending it.
Marriner Eccles *Beckoning Frontiers* (1951) p.75. Eccles was governor of the Federal Reserve Board, the central bank of the United States, and a firm believer in government intervention to counteract the Depression.

2 You have made yourself the trustee for those in every country who seek to mend the evils of our condition by reasoned experiment within the framework of the existing social system. If you fail, rational choice will be gravely prejudiced through-out the world, leaving orthodoxy and revolution to fight it out. But, if you succeed, new and bolder methods will be tried everywhere, and we may date the first chapter of a new economic era from your accession to office.
British economist John Maynard Keynes, open letter to President Roosevelt, *New York Times*, 31 Dec. 1933.

3 A promised land, bathed in golden sunlight, is rising out of the gray shadows of want and squalor and wretchedness down there in the Tennessee Valley these days. Ten thousand men are at work, building with timber and steel and concrete the New Deal's most magnificent project, creating an empire with potentialities so tremendous and so dazzling that they make one gasp.
Lorena Hickok to Harry L. Hopkins, 6 June 1934; *One Third of a Nation* (1981) p.269. Ms Hickok reported regularly to Hopkins, head of the Federal Emergency Relief Administration, on conditions across the United States from 1933 to 1936. The same day she wrote to Eleanor Roosevelt that the project to bring hydro-electric power to the area 'doesn't even make a dent' in Tennessee's rural poverty (p.272).

4 Dear President Pleas – give me a Job and I well Do my Best all I want is a Chance and I well Prove to the world that I can Come up the hill in Stead of goin Down.

Letter to the White House from a black woman in jail in North Carolina, 1 Feb. 1934; *Down and Out in the Great Depression* (1983) p.85.

5 To attempt a defense of democracy these days is a little like defending paganism in 313 or the divine right of kings in 1792. It is taken for granted that democracy is bad and that it is dying.
George Boas *Harper's Magazine*, Sept. 1934. By the Edict of Milan in 313 the Roman Emperor Constantine gave religious freedom to Christians; in 1792 the French Revolution deposed King Louis XVI.

6 His impulse is one which makes toward the fuller life of the masses of the people in every land and which, as it glows the brighter, may well eclipse both the lurid flames of German Nordic self-assertion and the baleful unnatural lights which are diffused from Soviet Russia.
Winston Churchill on Franklin Roosevelt, *Collier's Magazine*, 29 Dec. 1934.

NEW DEAL EMBATTLED, 1935–6

7 If the commerce clause were [so] construed … the federal authority would embrace practically all the activities of the people and the authority of the State over its domestic concerns would exist only by sufferance of the federal government … The authority of the federal government may not be pushed to such an extreme.
Supreme Court Chief Justice Charles Evans Hughes, 27 May 1935, in Schechter Poultry Corporation v. US; Major (1968) p.105. Article 1, Sect.8, Clause 3 of the Constitution gave Congress the power to regulate commerce 'among the several States', and Roosevelt used this as the basis of the National Industrial Recovery Act of 1933, a main pillar of the early New Deal, which the Court now struck down.

8 We have been relegated to the horse-and-buggy definition of interstate commerce.
President Franklin D. Roosevelt, 31 May 1935; *Public Papers* Vol.4 (1938) p.22. His reaction to the Supreme Court's invalidation of the National Industrial Recovery Act four days earlier.

9 Courts are not the only agency of government that must be assumed to have the capacity to govern … the power to tax and to spend includes the power to relieve a nationwide maladjustment by conditional gifts of money.
Supreme Court Justice Harlan Stone, 6 Jan. 1936, dissenting from the decision to declare the Agricultural Adjustment Act of 1933 unconstitutional; Major (1968) pp.109, 110.

1 Nothing could threaten the race as seriously as this. It is begging the unfit to be more unfit. Even such a measure as old-age insurance … removes one of the points of pressure which has kept many persons up to the strife and struggle of life.

George B. Cutten *Professors and the New Deal* (1936) p.15. A Darwinian critique of the social security legislation of 1935 from a member of the ultra-conservative American Liberty League. The Social Security Act gave the United States the rudiments of a welfare state, but, as Roosevelt himself acknowledged, this still left America a generation or more behind many European countries in this respect.

2 Employees shall have the right of self-organization, to form, join, or assist labor organizations, to bargain collectively through representatives of their own choosing, and to engage in concerted activities, for the purpose of collective bargaining or other mutual aid or protection.

National Labor Relations Act, Sect.7, 5 July 1935, the achievement of Senator Robert Wagner of New York; Major (1968) p.127. The act revived the collective bargaining provisions of the National Industrial Recovery Act, declared unconstitutional the previous May.

3 Yes, we are on our way back – not just by pure chance, not by a mere turn of a wheel in a cycle; we are coming back soundly because we planned it that way.

President Franklin D. Roosevelt, *New York Times*, 24 Oct. 1935. Economic recovery *was* taking place by this time, but to call it a planned recovery was taking too much political credit. Roosevelt's claim was made with a presidential election year ahead.

4 I have no political ambitions for myself or for my children.

Joseph P. Kennedy *I'm For Roosevelt* (1936) p.3. The multimillionaire Kennedy was head of Roosevelt's Securities and Exchange Commission, the watchdog of Wall Street. He did, in fact, have presidential aspirations in 1940 and thereafter saw his sons Joseph and John as potential Democratic candidates.

5 There is a mysterious cycle in human events. To some generations, much is given. Of other generations much is expected. This generation of Americans has a rendezvous with destiny.

President Franklin D. Roosevelt, 27 June 1936; *Public Papers* Vol.5 (1938) p.235.

6 There is now in California anger instead of fear. The stupidity of the large grower has changed terror into defensive fury … The large growers, who have been shown to be the only group making a considerable profit from agriculture, are devoting their money to tear gas and rifle ammunition. The men will organize and the large growers will meet organization with force.

John Steinbeck *The Nation*, 12 Sept. 1936, p.304. After making a survey of migrant labour in California, Steinbeck went on to write his novel *The Grapes of Wrath* (1939).

7 Never before in all our history have these forces been so united against one candidate as they stand today. They are unanimous in their hate for me – and I welcome their hatred.

President Franklin D. Roosevelt, 31 Oct. 1936, *Public Papers* Vol.5 (1938) pp.568–9. A powerful rejoinder to the criticism of himself in business circles, which by then had reached unprecedented heights.

8 I have known men who had been in German, Spanish, Russian concentration camps who could yet speak of Hitler, Franco, Stalin with far more self-control and objectivity than many rich Americans spoke or still speak of Roosevelt.

Denis Brogan *The Price of Revolution* (1951) p.234, note 1. Despite (or because of) this loathing, Roosevelt was re-elected by a huge margin in the 1936 election.

9 As Maine goes, so goes Vermont.

James A. Farley, Roosevelt's Postmaster General, on the morrow of the 1936 election. Until 1936 no candidate elected in the 'bell-wether' state of Maine had lost a presidential contest. In 1936 only Vermont followed Maine into the Republican camp. The other 46 states went for Roosevelt, in one of the most decisive victories in American political history.

DIMINUENDO, 1937–9

10 I see one-third of a nation ill-housed, ill-clad, ill-nourished.

President Franklin D. Roosevelt, second inaugural address, 20 Jan. 1937; *Public Papers* Vol.6 (1941) p.5. A candid admission that the New Deal still had much to accomplish.

11 The Courts … have cast doubts on the ability of the elected Congress to protect us against catastrophe by meeting squarely our modern social and economic conditions. We are at a crisis in our ability to proceed with that protection … In the last four years the sound rule of giving statutes the benefit of all reasonable doubt has been cast aside. The Court has been acting not as a judicial body, but as a policy-making body.

President Franklin D. Roosevelt, 9 March 1937; *Public Papers* Vol.6 (1941) p.124. In his anger at the Supreme Court's invalidation of so many New Deal enactments, Roosevelt proposed to retaliate by appointing up to six extra Justices. His plan caused a huge furore, with widespread accusations of presidential dictatorship.

1 The cardinal principle of statutory construction is to save and not to destroy. We have repeatedly held that as between two possible interpretations of a statute … our plain duty is to adopt that which will save the act.
Supreme Court Chief Justice Charles Evans Hughes, 12 April 1937, upholding the National Labor Relations Act of 1935 and reversing the court's attitude to New Deal legislation; Major (1968) p.110.

2 A switch in time saved nine.
An appropriate comment on the court's volte-face, which helped to defeat the Roosevelt plan, rejected by the Senate Judiciary Committee in June 1937.

3 Suddenly, without apparent warning, there is a terrific roar of pistol shots, and men in the front ranks of the marchers go down like grass before a scythe. The camera catches approximately a dozen falling simultaneously in a heap … Instantly the police charge on the marchers with riot sticks flying. At the same time tear gas grenades are seen sailing into the mass of demonstrators, and clouds of gas rise over them. Most of the crowd is now in flight.
St Louis Post Dispatch on the 'Memorial Day Massacre', 30 May 1937. In this clash outside the works of the Republic Steel Corporation in Chicago ten men were shot dead. It was filmed by Paramount News, but not exhibited publicly for fear of 'inciting riots'. The incident symbolized the conflict between big business and the New Deal as the sponsor of industrial unionism by the National Labor Relations Act of 1935, by which Roosevelt had forged a close alliance with the trade union movement.

4 I won't stay and knowingly and consciously have an unbalanced budget in order to correct the mistakes made by other people. We have come to a crossroad. The crossroad is when private business needed the money which the government has been taking up to this time and we are at that crossroad now.
Secretary of the treasury Henry Morgenthau Jr, 20 Oct. 1937; J.M. Blum From the Morgenthau Diaries Vol.1 (1959) pp.388–9. In Aug. 1937 the economy had gone into recession, partly because Roosevelt had cut back sharply on government spending after his re-election. Morgenthau backed him firmly, but Roosevelt was forced to return to deficit finance in April 1938.

5 We can no more spend ourselves rich than we can drink ourselves sober.

New York Times editorial; Randolph Paul Taxation for Prosperity (1947) p.84.

6 The enforcement of free competition is the least regulation business can expect … Once it is realized that business monopoly in America paralyzes the system of free enterprise on which it is grafted … action by the government to eliminate these artificial restraints will be welcomed by industry throughout the nation.
President Franklin D. Roosevelt, 29 April 1938; Public Papers Vol.7 (1941) p.320. A final thrust at Roosevelt's enemies in the business world, even though it was already evident that the American economy hinged on the success of the big corporations.

7 We shall tax and tax, and spend and spend, and elect and elect.
Harry L. Hopkins, attrib., on the mid-term election of Nov. 1938. In the event, the Republicans made significant gains at the expense of the Democrats.

8 He had the purity of St Francis of Assisi combined with the sharp shrewdness of a race-track tout.
Joseph E. Davies on Harry L. Hopkins, head of the New Deal relief programme. Davies was US ambassador in Moscow at this time.

9 Work is America's answer to the need of idle millions … Work, not charity … peaceful work, not regimentation to build the machines of war.
Inscription on the Works Projects Administration pavilion at the New York World's Fair, 1939. Yet it was World War II that ended the unemployment problem. In 1939 nearly 10 million people remained unemployed after six years of the New Deal.

JUDGEMENTS

10 Generally the prophecy can be made that the government will be taken over by some form of Liberals or by a species of Fascists. The seed of the right-wing Conservative is not disclosed in the womb of near time by any mental X-ray. He rests, sterile, with his theories and methods, in the grave of political history in America.
The columnist Arthur Krock; H.W. Baldwin and S. Stone We Saw it Happen (1938) p.349. Wrong on fascism, wrong on conservatism, which began a powerful renaissance at the expense of liberalism with the election of Richard Nixon in 1968.

11 I believe in the things that have been done. They helped but they did not solve the fundamental problems … I never believed the Federal government could solve the whole problem. It bought us time to think.

Eleanor Roosevelt, Feb. 1939, *Harper's Magazine*, Vol.180 (1939) p.136.

1 It seems politically impossible for a capitalistic democracy to organize expenditure on the scale necessary to make the grand experiment which would prove my case – except in war conditions [which would be] the stimulus, which neither the victory nor the defeat of the New Deal could give you, to greater individual consumption and a higher standard of life.

John Maynard Keynes *The New Republic*, 29 July 1940. American rearmament did indeed vanquish the Depression, as the New Deal had never fully managed to do.

2 How did the New Deal come into existence? It was because there was an awfully sick patient called the United States of America … And they sent for the doctor. And it was a long process – took several years before those ills, in particular that illness of ten years ago, were remedied. But after a while they were remedied … And when victory comes, the program of the past, of course, has got to be carried on … so that the conditions of 1932 and the beginning of 1933 won't come back again.

President Franklin D. Roosevelt, 28 Dec. 1943; *Public Papers* Vol.12 (1950) p.572. An optimistic retrospective from the White House, pointedly fixing the blame for the slump on his predecessor.

3 Although it has been said repeatedly that we need a new conception of the world to replace the ideology of self-help, free enterprise, competition, and beneficent cupidity upon which Americans have been nourished since the foundation of the Republic, no new conceptions of comparable strength have taken root and no statesman with a great mass following has arisen to propound them.

The political scientist Richard Hofstadter *The American Political Tradition* (1948) p.vii. A pessimistic conclusion: laissez-faire had not been supplanted in the USA, but it had been substantially moderated.

4 Flawed as a matter of political leadership, Roosevelt's Grand Experiment took the form of what can be called broker leadership … Such an approach had profound implications … It meant that he ignored the possibilities for the future of a voting alignment of great strength – one composed of less privileged farm groups, masses of unorganized or ill-organized industrial workers, consumers, Negroes, and other minority groups.

James MacGregor Burns *Roosevelt: the Lion and the Fox* (1956) p.198. Roosevelt did, in fact, put together just such a coalition, but its radicalism was always blunted by his dependence on the highly conservative Democrats of the South.

5 The conclusion seems inescapable that, traditional as the words may have been in which the New Deal expressed itself, in actuality it was a revolutionary response to a revolutionary situation … The searing ordeal of the Great Depression purged the American people of their belief in the limited powers of the federal government and convinced them of the necessity of the guarantor state. And as the Civil War constituted a watershed in American thought, so the depression and its New Deal marked the crossing of a divide from which, it would seem, there could be no turning back.

Carl N. Degler *Out of Our Past* (1959) p.416. The New Deal as the third American Revolution, after the War of Independence and the Civil War.

Britain between the Wars, 1918–39

STRIFE, 1918–25

1 What is our task? To make Britain a fit country for heroes to live in … Slums are not fit homes for the men who have won this war or for their children. They are not fit nurseries for the children who are to make an imperial race.

David Lloyd George, election speech, *The Times*, 25 Nov. 1918. The Liberal Lloyd George won the 1918 election as leader of a coalition that was overwhelmingly Conservative.

2 Unless the supplies of coal in this country were increased, it was not impossible that there might be a revolution. Even now the spirit of lawlessness was apparent, and no one could say what might happen if, for instance, there was no coal in the East End in December.

Cabinet minute, 25 Nov. 1918; Barry Supple *The History of the British Coal Industry* Vol.4 (1987) p.118. Fears of a post-war upsurge in the innermost sanctum of government. The East End was the working-class district of London.

3 In a short time we might have three-quarters of Europe converted to Bolshevism … He believed that Great Britain would hold out, but only if the people were given a sense of confidence – only if they were made to believe that things were being done for them.

David Lloyd George, cabinet minutes, 3 March 1919. The prime minister plays up the notion of a 'red menace' in an attempt to persuade his Conservative colleagues in the Coalition government to accept the need for social and economic reform.

4 The present system of ownership and working in the coal industry stands condemned and some other system must be substituted for it, either nationalization or a measure of unification by national purchase and/or by joint control.

Interim report of the Sankey Commission on the Coal Industry, 20 March 1919; Cmd.84. A surprising endorsement of Labour Party policy, not to be achieved until 1947.

5 Get on ta t'field. That's t'place.

Herbert Smith, 12 April 1921; A.J.P. Taylor *English History 1914–1945* (1965) p.146. The Yorkshireman Smith was president of the Miners' Federation of Great Britain. The projected General Strike by railwaymen, dockers and miners collapsed on Black Friday, 15 April 1921, but the miners stayed on the field of battle.

6 'Why should a miner earn six pounds a week? Leisure! They'd only spend it in a bar! Standard of life! You'll never teach them Greek, Or make them more contented than they are!' That's how my port-flushed friends discuss the Strike.

Siegfried Sassoon 'The Case for the Miners' (1921), written after the experience of Black Friday.

7 It is impossible to expect people to subsist upon the unemployment benefit … The King appeals to the government to meet this grave … difficulty with the same liberality as they displayed in dealing with the enormous daily cost of the war.

George V, late 1921; Harold Nicolson *King George the Fifth* (1952) p.342.

8 Every five hours round the clock a life was lost. Every 215,000 tons of coal raised was stained with the crimson of one man's blood. Every working day 850 men and boys were injured.

Herbert Smith, giving evidence to the Buckmaster Court of Inquiry on Wages, 1924; Supple (1987) p.426.

9 It would be possible to say without exaggeration that the miners' leaders were the stupidest men in England if we had not had frequent occasion to meet the owners.

The Conservative Lord Birkenhead, 1925; Charles Loch Mowat *Britain between the Wars* (1955) p.300. In the mining industry both sides were intransigent enemies.

10 I don't care a hang for any government, or army or navy. They can come along with their bayonets. Bayonets don't cut coal. We have already beaten, not only the employers, but the strongest government in modern times.

A.J. Cook, secretary of the Miners' Federation of Great Britain, Aug. 1925; W.H. Cook *The General Strike* (1930) p.295. Jubilation after Red Friday, when the government had averted a miners' strike by accepting a compromise over miners' pay and so bought time for the next big confrontation, which came with the General Strike of 1926.

11 The thing is not finished. The danger is not over. Sooner or later this question has got to be fought out by the people of the land. Is England to be governed by Parliament and by the Cabinet or by a handful of trade union leaders? If a Soviet is established here … a grave position will arise.

Sir William Joynson-Hicks, Conservative home secretary, *The Times*, 3 Aug. 1925.

LIBERALISM MARGINALIZED, 1919–29

1 The tendency will be to squeeze out the middle Party. It will be attacked by the Conservatives as half revolutionary, and at the same time blamed by the Labour Party for the delay of reforms.

Aneurin Williams, *The Contemporary Review*, Feb. 1919. An ominous prophecy for the Liberal Party, seen as liable to be crushed between the upper and nether millstones of conservatism and socialism.

2 Cleverness, ingenuity, adroitness! There has been nothing like it in human history. But, after all, character is more than cleverness. Sticking to a principle is more than adroitly shifting from one position to another. And, in the view of Liberals, Mr Lloyd George has shown himself a faithless trustee of their traditions and beliefs.

Sir John Simon, *Liberal Magazine*, Aug. 1921. Simon attacked Lloyd George for splitting the Liberal Party and presiding over the Conservative-dominated coalition. In 1931 he joined the Conservative-dominated coalition government of Ramsay MacDonald (see 778:1).

3　　Lloyd George, no doubt,
　　When his life ebbs out,
　　Will ride on a flaming chariot,
　　Seated in state
　　On a red-hot plate
　　'Twixt Satan and Judas Iscariot.

Trad. rhyme; Trevor Wilson *The Downfall of the Liberal Party 1914–1935* (1966) p.380. Testimony to the hatred of non-Coalition Liberals towards the apostate Lloyd George.

4 Our main object in the immediate future is the destruction of the Liberal Party and the absorption of as much of the carcass as we can secure. One of the three parties has to disappear and the one that is spiritually dead and has been so for thirty years or more is the natural victim.

Leo Amery, diary entry, 8 Dec. 1923; *The Leo Amery Diaries* Vol.1 (1980) p.361. The Conservative Amery was writing two days after his party's defeat in the general election, which left the Liberals holding the balance of power.

5 The Liberal Party has fallen between two stools … It represents itself as standing between the two

extremes of reaction on the one side and of revolution on the other side, and it appeals to all the timid people who are afraid of a move in any direction.

The Liberal MP Andrew MacCallum-Scott, diary entry, 12 Jan. 1925; Michael Bentley *The Liberal Mind 1914–1929* (1977) p.158. In the general election of Oct. 1924 the Liberals were reduced to a mere 40 seats in the House of Commons.

6 I am enough of a traditionalist to see with regret the end of power which goes back directly to 1832 and the great epoch of reform, and, indirectly, to the Revolution of 1688. The funerals of historical entities are melancholy events.

Professor Harold Laski to Justice Oliver Wendell Holmes, 30 May 1926; *Holmes–Laski Letters* Vol.2 (1953 edn) p.89. A socialist laments the decline of the Liberal Party.

7 At the moment, individual enterprise cannot restore the situation within a time for which we can wait. The state must therefore lend its aid and, by a deliberate policy of national development, help to set going at full speed the great machine of industry.

Liberal manifesto, *We Can Conquer Unemployment* (1929) p.9. A pre-election call for deficit spending, anathema to both Labour and Conservative leaderships.

8 The fact that many workpeople who are now unemployed would be receiving wages instead of unemployment pay would mean an increase in effective purchasing power which would give a general stimulus to trade. Moreover, the greater trade activity would make for further trade activity; for the forces of prosperity, like those of trade depression, work with cumulative effect.

John Maynard Keynes and Hubert Henderson *Can Lloyd George Do It?* (1929) p.25. In other words, the 'multiplier principle', generating prosperity by rippling consumerism. But though these economists put their faith in Lloyd George, the electorate did not.

9 An agreed programme would not save the situation if the socialists make a mess of the job … the consequence would be that the discredit would fall more hardly on the Liberals than on the socialists … On the other hand, if you can conceive of the possibility of the socialists doing the job well, the young men of our party would leave us and join the party which was carrying through a Liberal programme successfully. Either way the Liberal Party would be done for.

David Lloyd George to C.P. Scott, editor of the *Manchester Guardian*, 30 April 1929; Peter Rowland *Lloyd George* (1975) p.654. In the general election on 30 May, despite presenting the most constructive programme for economic change, the Liberals took only 59 seats. As Lloyd George foresaw, the Liberal Party was now in a no-win situation.

1 There can only be one result – very likely final for our life-time, namely a Lib-Lab block in some form or another and a Conservative Right hopelessly excluded from power.

Winston Churchill to Stanley Baldwin, 29 June 1929; Bentley (1977) p.140. Not so: Liberals tended to move right, not left, and the Conservatives were to dominate the 1930s. The prediction fits better with the politics of Britain post-1997.

GOING INTO LABOUR, 1924

2 Today, 23 years ago dear Grandmama died. I wonder what she would have thought of a Labour government.

George V, diary entry, 22 Jan. 1924; Kenneth Rose *King George the Fifth* (1983) p.326. The Conservative premier, Stanley Baldwin, resigned on this day, and the king sent for Ramsay MacDonald to form Britain's first Labour government.

3 What changes are taking place. A socialist govt. actually in power. But don't get uneasy about your investments or your antiques. Nothing will be removed or abstracted … They are all engaged in looking as respectable as lather and blather will make them.

David Lloyd George to his daughter, Megan, 4 Feb. 1924; K.O. Morgan (ed.) *Lloyd George Family Letters, 1885–1936* (1973) p.202. Even if it had wanted to be, the minority Labour government of Ramsay MacDonald was in no position to be socialist, dependent as it was on Liberal support.

4 We shall concentrate, not first of all on the relief of unemployment, but on the restoration of trade … The government have no intention of drawing off from the normal channels of trade large sums for extemporized measures which can only be palliatives.

Ramsay MacDonald, 12 Feb. 1924; *H.C. Deb.* Vol.169, Col.759. The new prime minister subscribes to economic orthodoxies as the antidote to depression.

5 It is no part of my job as Chancellor of the Exchequer to put before the House of Commons proposals for the expenditure of public money. The function of the Chancellor of the Exchequer, as I understand it, is to resist all demands for expenditure made by his colleagues and, when he can no longer resist, to limit the concession to the barest point of acceptance.

Philip Snowden, 30 July 1924; *H.C. Deb.* Vol.176, Cols 2091–2. Gladstone, high priest of retrenchment, would have been proud of him.

6 To every outworn shibboleth of 19th-century economics he clung with fanatic tenacity. Economy, Free Trade, Gold – these were the keynotes of his political philosophy, and deflation the path he trod with almost ghoulish enthusiasm.

Robert Boothby on Philip Snowden; Robert Rhodes James *Bob Boothby* (1991) p.102. Boothby, along with Harold Macmillan, was a moderate Conservative, seeking a way forward from the thought and practice of the older generation.

7 It would be desirable to have cells in all the units of the troops, particularly among those quartered in the large centres of the country, and also among factories working on munitions and at military store depots … In the event of the danger of war, with the aid of the latter and in contact with the transport workers, it is possible to paralyse all the military preparations of the bourgeoisie, and make a start in turning an imperialist war into a class war.

Extract from the Zinoviev letter of 15 Sept. 1924; *The Zinoviev Letter* (1967) pp.xii, xiii. The letter was supposedly from the president of the Communist International, Grigory Zinoviev, to the central committee of the British Communist Party. In reality a forgery, the letter cost the Labour Party the election of 29 Oct. 1924 and gave the Conservative Party a massive victory as saviours of the country from the 'red menace'.

8 Get up, you lazy devil! We're buggered!

J.H. Thomas to Philip Snowden, 25 Oct. 1924; Colin Cross *Philip Snowden* (1966) p.212. Thomas reacts to the publication of the Zinoviev letter. Thomas was noted for his colourful language and for his heavy drinking. After one serious bout he told the Conservative Lord Birkenhead, 'I've an 'ell of an 'eadache.' 'Take two aspirates,' was Birkenhead's advice.

BALDWIN AND CONSERVATISM, 1919–31

9 They are a lot of hard-faced men who look as if they had done very well out of the war.

J.M. Keynes 'The Economic Consequences of the Peace', Dec. 1919; *Collected Writings* Vol.2 (1971) p.91. Keynes quotes the comment of 'a Conservative friend' (in fact, Stanley Baldwin) on the House of Commons brought in by the election of Dec. 1918, more than half of whom were Conservatives. Keynes identified the man in question as Baldwin in a letter to Kingsley Martin, editor of the *New Statesman*, in Nov. 1941 (Kingsley Martin *Editor* (1968) p.307).

10 To me England is the country, and the country is England … The sounds of England, the tinkle of the

hammer on the anvil in the country smithy, the corn-crake on a dewy morning, the sound of the scythe against the whetstone, and the sight of a plough team coming over the brow of a hill.
Stanley Baldwin *On England* (1926) p.5. The prime minister of an overwhelmingly urban Britain proclaims his loyalty to rural England. Compare his successor, John Major (see 926:9).

1 Mr Baldwin paused perhaps a shade longer and then said with conviction: 'Rousseau argued that all human progress was from contract to status, but Maine made it clear once and for all that the real movement was from status to contract.' He paused again and this time for quite a while, and suddenly a look of dawning horror, but at the same time of immense humanity and confederacy stole across his face. 'Or was it,' he said, leaning just a little towards me, 'or was it the other way round?'
Frank Pakenham *Born to Believe* (1953) pp.71–2. Stanley Baldwin was no doctrinaire ideologue.

2 I have for myself come to the conclusion that owing to the conditions which exist in the world today, having regard to economic environment, having regard to the situation of our country, if we go pottering along as we are we shall have grave unemployment with us to the end of time, and I have come to the conclusion that the only way of fighting this subject is by protecting the home market.
Stanley Baldwin, 25 Oct. 1923; John Ramsden *The Age of Balfour and Baldwin 1902–40* (1978) p.178. Baldwin announces his conversion to protectionism, which cost the Conservatives the general election of Dec. 1923.

3 Free Trade is not a theory. It is a fact – the one supreme fact in our economic polity, eighty years old, still going strong, and capable of summoning defenders, if the truth were told, from the inner consciousness of multitudes of those who are proposing … to destroy … the system on which our trade rests and our unexcelled prestige has been erected.
Glasgow Herald, 9 Nov. 1923. The Liberal riposte to Baldwin's embrace of protectionism, still a step too far for most of the British electorate.

4 Our great enemies of the future are not going to be the Liberals, who are moribund, but Labour, which is very much alive. You are not going to beat Labour on a policy of tranquillity, negation or sitting still. There is a vitality in Labour at present in the

country, and unless we can share a vitality of that kind we shall be unable to conquer.
Stanley Baldwin, 11 Feb. 1924; Ramsden (1978) p.187. Pending this regeneration, Labour was to be conquered by the notorious Zinoviev letter (see 774:7).

5 A strong Conservative Party with an overwhelming majority and a moderate and even progressive leadership is a combination which has never been tested before. It might well be the fulfilment of all that Dizzy and my father aimed at in their political work.
Winston Churchill to his wife, Clementine, 8 March 1925; Ramsden (1978) p.187. In 1924 the Liberal Churchill rejoined the Conservative Party (which he had left in 1904), with his guiding stars as Benjamin Disraeli and his father, Lord Randolph Churchill.

6 What the proprietorship of these papers is aiming at is power, and power without responsibility – the prerogative of the harlot through the ages.
Stanley Baldwin, quoting his cousin, Rudyard Kipling, 17 March 1931; Keith Middlemas and John Barnes *Baldwin* (1969) p.600. For the past two years Baldwin had been under heavy attack by the *Daily Mail* and *Daily Express*. A party agent present in the hall is credited with the muttered comment: 'Bang goes the harlot vote!'

GENERAL STRIKE, 1926

7 Not a penny off the pay, not a minute on the day.
A.J. Cook, 3 April 1926, slogan for the striking miners, who were to join forces with unionists in other industries to bring the country to a standstill and compel the government to make concessions.

8 They are going to squash it. It won't last more than a few days. A few of those people [the strike leaders] will be shot, of course, more of them will get arrested … You see Walter, they have come to the conclusion they must fight.
J.H. Thomas to Walter Citrine, general secretary of the Trades Union Congress, late April 1926; Walter Citrine *Men and Work* (1964) p.157. Thomas's prediction of savage reprisals against the leadership of the General Strike, beginning on 3 May, was not borne out, but he was right about its durability: it lasted only nine days. The government won partly because of the deep divisions within the Labour movement and partly because it had prepared the ground carefully since its apparent retreat in Aug. 1925, basing its strategy on contingency plans developed by Lloyd George when faced with the prospect of a general stoppage in 1921.

1 The university fermented. Recruiting agencies opened all over the place, and undergraduates bicycled wildly from one to the next, offering their services for such glamorous pursuits as engine-driving, tram-driving, or the steel-helmeted special constabulary. I don't think there was any strong political feeling. Just Hurrah Patriotismus or fun.
Cambridge University undergraduate, May 1926; Julian Symons *The General Strike* (1957) p.74. The majority of Cambridge dons and students opposed the strike and rallied to the government.

2 After a few days I found much of my sympathy was with the men rather than with the employers or the government. For one thing I had never realized the appalling poverty which existed then … the squalor of those living conditions could not have been endured by anyone earning sufficient wages to get out of it.
Special constable, 1926; Symons (1957) p.111. The volunteer special constables were loathed by the strikers as willing collaborators of the Establishment.

3 I have never disguised that in a challenge to the Constitution, God help us unless the government won.
J.H. Thomas, 3 May 1926; *H.C. Deb.* Vol.195, Col.81.

4 The failure of the General Strike of 1926 will be one of the most significant landmarks in the history of the British working class. Future historians will, I think, regard it as the death-gasp of that pernicious doctrine of 'workers' control' of public affairs through the trade unions and by the method of direct action.
Beatrice Webb, diary entry, 4 May 1926; Margaret Cole (ed.) *Beatrice Webb's Diaries, 1924–1932* (1956) p.92. Fabians such as Mrs Webb had never seen eye to eye with syndicalism.

5 I am a man of peace. I am longing and working and praying for peace, but I will not surrender the safety and the security of the British constitution. You placed me in power eighteen months ago by the largest majority accorded to any party for many, many years. Have I done anything to forfeit that confidence? Cannot you trust me to ensure a square deal to secure even justice between man and man?
Prime minister Stanley Baldwin, 8 May 1926; Symons (1957) p.181. The first two sentences of the peroration of this radio broadcast for the BBC were written by John Reith, its director; the rest were by Baldwin himself. The talk was given from Reith's house in Westminster.

6 All ranks of the Armed Forces of the Crown are hereby notified that any action which they may find necessary to take in an honest endeavour to aid the Civil Power will receive … the full support of His Majesty's government.
British Gazette, 8 May 1926. King George V objected to this inflammatory bulletin, put out by the government newspaper edited by Winston Churchill.

7 He had heard I had been badly wounded in the war – 'In the head, wasn't it?' I said yes, but that my present attitude was not traceable thereto.
Conversation between Winston Churchill and John Reith, 9 May 1926; John Reith *Into the Wind* (1949) p.112. Reith was seriously wounded by a German sniper on 7 Oct. 1915. Reith's answer refers to his determination not to allow Churchill to commandeer the BBC, which he directed, as an appendage of the government during the General Strike.

8 Our old country can well be proud of itself, as during the last nine days there has been a strike in which 4 million people have been affected, not a shot has been fired and no one killed. It shows what a wonderful people we are.
George V, diary entry, 12 May 1926; Rose (1983) p.343.

9 We have committed suicide. Thousands of members will be victimized as a result of this day's work.
Ernest Bevin, 27 May 1926, on the situation after the TUC called off the General Strike on 12 May; Alan Bullock *The Life and Times of Ernest Bevin* Vol.1 (1960) p.337.

10 If any section of the country or any foolish person in the country thinks that after the events of last week and yesterday he can scrape the faces of trade unionists in the dust he is very much mistaken.
Ramsay MacDonald, 13 May 1926; *H.C. Deb.* Vol.195, Col.1044. Brave words to hearten the troops he never wanted to go over the top.

11 A strike which opens with a football match between the police and the strikers and ends in unconditional surrender after nine days with densely packed reconciliation services at all the chapels and churches of Great Britain, attended by the strikers and their families, will make the Continental socialists blaspheme.
Beatrice Webb, diary entry, 18 May 1926; *The Diary of Beatrice Webb* Vol.4 (1965) pp.81–2. A tribute, not a condemnation, from the mother of moderate socialism.

12 I decline utterly to be impartial as between the fire brigade and the fire.

Winston Churchill, 7 July 1926; *H.C. Deb.* Vol.197, Col.2216. The editor of the *British Gazette* justifies his militancy during the General Strike.

1 Towards the end of the strike things were awful. No coal, no clothes. We were in rags and a lot of us had no shoes. I remember going with my mother and my brother to a colliery tip about four miles away. The weather was getting very cold. It took us a day to pick two buckets of tiny bits of coal. The tip had been picked clean.

Kenneth Maper, Welsh miner; Nigel Gray *The Worst of Times* (1985) pp.29–30. The miners stayed out until 19 Nov., more than six months after the rest of the nation's workforce had gone back.

2 Section 1. It is hereby declared that any strike is illegal if it (i) has any object other than or in addition to the furtherance of a trade dispute. (ii) is a strike designed or calculated to coerce the government either directly or by inflicting hardship upon the community.

Section 4. It shall not be lawful to require any member of a trade union to make any contribution to the political fund of a trade union.

Trades Disputes Act, 1927; *The Public General Acts* (1927) pp.328, 332. The Conservative government's punitive legislation on the unions in the wake of the General Strike. Repealed by the Labour government in 1946.

LABOUR'S SECOND COMING, 1929–31

3 I confess I look with alarm on the spirit that the Labour Party is inculcating into the rising population that they need not rely on their own efforts, but can always rely on the State assisting them.

The banker R.H. Brand to the Liberal Lord Lothian, 5 Dec. 1929. A gross libel on a Labour government bending over backwards to be laissez-faire in its approach to the slump after Ramsay MacDonald formed his second government in June 1929.

4 To establish people in incomes which represent no effort to get out to work is the very antithesis of socialism. The State as Lady Bountiful may be a fatal extension of Toryism but is not the beginning of socialism.

Ramsay MacDonald, diary entry, 17 Dec. 1929.

5 This nation has to be mobilized and rallied for a tremendous effort, and who can do that except the government of the day? ... What a fantastic

assumption it is that a nation which within the lifetime of every one has put forth efforts of energy and vigour unequalled in the history of the world, should succumb before an economic situation such as the present.

Sir Oswald Mosley, resignation speech, 28 May 1930; *H.C. Deb.* Vol.239, Cols 1371–2. In Jan. 1930 Mosley had put forward a plan for economic recovery entailing bold government initiatives and expenditure. It was rejected by the Labour cabinet, and Mosley left office, going on to found his New Party in Feb. 1931.

6 As I see it the position of the government may be likened to that of the captain and officers of a great ship which has run aground on a falling tide; no human endeavour will get the ship afloat until in the course of nature the tide again begins to flow.

Sir John Anderson, 30 July 1930; David Marquand *Ramsay MacDonald* (1977) p.548. Fatalism as the answer, in the view of a Whitehall mandarin.

7 Alas! Alas! Balmoral is inevitable; but why the castles of the wealthiest, most aristocratic, most reactionary and by no means the most intellectual of the Conservative Party? ... He *ought* not to be more at home in the castles of the great than in the homes of his followers. It argues a perverted taste and a vanishing faith.

Beatrice Webb on Ramsay MacDonald, 5 Sept. 1930; Cole (ed.) (1956) p.249. Mrs Webb deeply mistrusted MacDonald's apparent preference for the company of the ruling class. Balmoral Castle, near Braemar, is the royal residence in Scotland, to which prime ministers are still ritually invited.

8 I have waited 50 years to see the boneless wonder sitting on the Treasury Bench.

Winston Churchill on Ramsay MacDonald, 28 Jan. 1931; *H.C. Deb.* Vol.247, Col.1022. Calling to mind a freak seen in a Victorian sideshow in his childhood. The Treasury bench is the seating reserved for government ministers in the chamber of the House of Commons.

9 An expenditure which may be easy and tolerable in prosperous times becomes intolerable in a time of grave industrial depression.

Philip Snowden, 11 Feb. 1931; *H.C. Deb.* Vol.248, Col.447. The orthodox response by MacDonald's chancellor of the exchequer to the call for deficit spending as a means of pulling the country out of the slump.

10 Laissez-faire, as understood before the War, can never be recreated. If for no other reason, the Russian Five-Year Plan cuts across the whole thing. Whilst it may be impossible to introduce a similar form in this country, to leave our industries languishing and our people to the tender mercies of a worn-out 19th-century system is an insane policy.

Ernest Bevin, 26 May 1931; Bullock Vol.1 (1960) p.434. In 1931 a voice in the wilderness. Bevin was general secretary of the mighty Transport and General Workers' Union and a key figure in the Labour movement.

1 The Right Honourable gentleman has sat for so long on the fence that the iron has entered his soul.

David Lloyd George, June 1931; Taylor (1965) p.54, note 1. The target of the Liberal leader was Sir John Simon, who defected from the Liberal Party to become foreign secretary in MacDonald's National government and leader of the National Liberals. Ten years earlier Simon had attacked Lloyd George for presiding over a similar Conservative-dominated coalition (see 773:2).

2 Luxury hotels and luxury flats, Bond Street shopping, racing and high living in all its forms is to go unchecked; but the babies are not to have milk and the very poor are not to have homes.

Beatrice Webb, diary entry, 4 Aug. 1931; Vol.4 (1985) p.249. Her comment on the report of the government's Economy Committee published on 31 July, which urged drastic cuts in government spending, including a 20% reduction in unemployment relief.

3 There is only one thing that will impress the people who know in this country and abroad, and that is a sight of an axe honestly laid at the upas-tree of colossal expenditure … New taxes are no substitute for a lessened burden.

The Times, 21 Aug. 1931. The upas tree of Java yielded a sap used as arrow poison and was believed lethal to anyone standing beneath its branches. Presumably 'the people who know' were the financiers of the City of London and the now ruined Wall Street.

4 All this sentimentality about workers is trash. Unemployed must sacrifice too.

Note of conversation between Ramsay MacDonald and J.H. Thomas, 23 Aug. 1931; Marquand (1977) pp.630–31. The memorandum was taken by MacDonald's daughter, Sheila.

5 A scheme which inflicted reductions and burdens in almost every other direction, but made no appreciable cut in unemployment insurance benefit, would alienate much support and lose the Party their moral prestige which was one of their greatest assets. In conclusion the prime minister said that it must be admitted that the proposals as a whole represented the negation of everything that the Labour Party stood for, and yet he was absolutely

satisfied that it was in the national interest to implement them if the country was to be secured.

Conclusions of cabinet meeting, 23 Aug. 1931; Marquand (1977) p.634. The second Labour government in its death throes. On 24 Aug. MacDonald resigned as Labour prime minister and on 25 Aug. took office once more as leader of a National government dominated by the Conservative Party.

NATIONAL CONSERVATISM, 1931–9

6 We, the loyal subjects of His Majesty the King, do hereby present to my Lords Commissioners of the Admiralty our representative, to implore them to amend the drastic cuts in pay which have been inflicted on the lowest paid men of the lower deck.

Manifesto of the Royal Navy ratings' mutiny at Invergordon, 15 Sept. 1931, in response to the National government's decision to impose a cut in basic daily pay of 25%; Stephen Roskill Naval Policy between the Wars Vol.2 (1976) p.132.

7 The Lords Commissioners of the Admiralty view with the gravest concern the injury which the prestige of the British Navy has suffered … The Board rely on the personnel of the fleet to do their utmost to restore the confidence of the country by their future behaviour.

Admiralty signal, 17 Sept. 1931; Roskill (1976) pp.113–14. No support from this quarter for the desperation of the lower deck.

8 I hope you have read the election programme of the Labour Party … This is not socialism. It is Bolshevism run mad.

Philip Snowden, 17 Oct. 1931; Cross (1966) p.319. In the 1890s Snowden began his political career on the left of the Labour movement; he had since travelled far.

9 'Labour' had to be thrashed, but it cannot be destroyed. We could not trust them with the Bank of England – just yet.

Thomas Jones to Gwendoline Davies, 28 Oct. 1931; A Diary with Letters (1954) p.20. Jones had been confidant to Lloyd George and Baldwin since 1916. In the general election of 27 Oct. Labour was almost annihilated.

10 Whether new leaders will spring up with sufficient faith, will-power and knowledge to break through the tough and massive defences of British profit-making capitalism with its press and its pulpits, its Royalties and House of Lords, its elaborate financial entanglements of credit and currency all designed to maintain ancient loyalties, and when necessary, promote panics in favour of the *status quo*, I cannot foresee.

Beatrice Webb on the future of Labour, 28 Oct. 1931; Cole (ed.) (1956) p.295.

1 People have thought that benefit was so certain and so much of a right that they built up their lives on the certainty of getting money from the Employment Exchange on Friday. Their family life has centred on that principle. We cannot allow that principle to go on.

Wilfred Eady, senior civil servant at the ministry of labour, to a conference of means test inspectors, 18 Dec. 1931; Alan Deacon and Jonathan Bradshaw *Reserved for the Poor* (1983) p.18. State benefit was given only if a family's income did not reach a certain level.

2 If he were to be so foolish as to try a fall with our organization, Ll.G's fate would be mild in comparison. If he starts to stick pins in the horse that carried him to the victory and is maintaining him in the front of the race, he may find that however patient a nag the Tory Party may be, if he does put its back up, it will kick him over the moon.

J.C.C. Davison, July 1932, *Memoirs of a Conservative* (1969) pp.379–80. A brutal judgement on Ramsay MacDonald, like Lloyd George a dispensable figurehead for an essentially Tory regime.

3 Nothing to do with time; nothing to spend; nothing to do tomorrow nor the day after; nothing to wear; can't get married. A living corpse; a unit of the spectral army of three million lost men.

Walter Greenwood *Love on the Dole* (1933) p.225. The most graphic novel of unemployment to come out of the 1930s.

4 Without underrating the hardships of our situation, the long tragedy of the unemployed, the grievous burden of taxation, the arduous and painful struggle of those engaged in trade and industry, at any rate we are free from that fear which besets so many less fortunately placed, the fear that things are going to get worse. We owe our freedom from that fear to the fact that we have balanced our budget.

Neville Chamberlain, chancellor of the exchequer, 25 April 1933; *H.C. Deb.* Vol.277, Cols 60–61. A confident rejection of the argument for deficit spending, just getting under way in the United States after Roosevelt's inauguration on 4 March and perhaps an oblique jibe at Roosevelt's assertion that Americans had nothing to fear but fear itself (see 767:6).

5 To get there we had to cross the derelict shipyard, which was a fantastic wilderness of decaying sheds, strange mounds and pits, rusted iron, old concrete and new grass ... Down the Tyne we could see the idle ships lying up ... fine big steamers rusting away in rows.

J.B. Priestley *English Journey* (1934) pp.315–16. The writer Priestley toured the country in 1933, here visiting its former shipbuilding powerhouse in the northeast.

6 I used to wait outside the same bakery every morning with a crowd of other blokes hoping someone would get the sack or would be too ill to crawl into work. One morning there was an accident at the top of my road. My mate who was a roundsman for the bakery was lying in a pool of blood. I didn't know whether to run down to tell his wife or run on and get his job. So I ran on.

Anon. unemployed man; Gray (1985) p.186.

7 The third England, I concluded, was the new postwar England ... America, I supposed, was its real birth-place. This is the England of arterial and bypass roads, of filling stations and factories that look like exhibition buildings, of giant cinemas and dance-halls and cafés, bungalows with tiny garages, cocktail bars, Woolworths, motor-coaches, wireless, hiking, factory girls looking like actresses, greyhound racing and dirt tracks, swimming pools and everything given away for cigarette coupons.

J.B. Priestley (1934) p.401. The beginning of the post-1945 affluence was already visible in parts of Britain, particularly southeastern England, in and around London. The first and second Englands were the countryside, and the industrial Midlands and North; by the end of the 20th century both had been dwarfed by this burgeoning third force.

8 Banking and credit, transport, water, coal, electricity, gas, agriculture, iron and steel, shipping, shipbuilding, engineering, textiles, chemicals, insurance – in all these the time has come for drastic reorganization, and for the most part nothing short of immediate public ownership and control will be effective.

Labour Party programme, *For Socialism and Peace* (1934) p.15. A full-blooded manifesto (though a careful caveat sits inside it) that laid the foundations for much of the Labour government's achievement between 1945 and 1951. Philip Snowden (*Daily Herald*, 15 Oct. 1928) had said he would like to see the word 'nationalization' banned from the socialist vocabulary! Clause 4 of the Labour Party constitution of 1918 (see 720:4) was rescinded by Labour Party leader Tony Blair on 29 April 1995.

9 The United States have not found unbalanced budgets and profligate public expenditure any remedy for unemployment: indeed, they are looking with growing envy at the results achieved here by less spectacular methods.

Sir Frederick Leith-Ross, 1935, in response to Lloyd George's call for a British New Deal. A tart put-down for the Americans, who, even so, found little to inspire them in the British government's remedies for depression. Leith-Ross was chief economic adviser to the National government.

1 True to our traditions, we have avoided all extremes. We have steered clear of fascism, communism, dictatorship, and we have shown the world that democratic government, constitutional methods and ordered liberty are not inconsistent with progress and prosperity.

Stanley Baldwin, Nov. 1935; Ramsden (1978) p.331. On 14 Nov. the Conservatives under Baldwin won a decisive victory in the general election. The Communist Party took only one seat in the Commons, the British Union of Fascists won none.

2 Some of the displays were absolutely bestial. Many of the faces of the women were lined with destitution; their eyes flared and gleamed with hate and passion; their hair was dishevelled; their language filthy with oaths and some obscenity; they filled one with loathing and fear just like the French Revolution studies. Night after night their misery was upon me. To this, the fact that I helped to save them has perversion brought both them and me.

Ramsay MacDonald, diary entry, 15 Nov. 1935. MacDonald lost his seat at Seaham in the 1935 general election by a humiliating margin, after a campaign marked by vicious recrimination for his policy since 1931 (when the same electorate gave him a comfortable majority).

3 I am going to help you. Something will be done for you.

Edward VIII, 18 Nov. 1936; Malcolm Muggeridge *The Thirties* (1940) p.281. Spoken during a tour of South Wales, a promise unfulfilled by a monarch who soon after abdicated. Often rendered as 'Something must be done'.

4 It is only because miners sweat their guts out that superior persons can remain superior. You and I and the editor of the *Times Lit. Supp.*, and the Nancy poets and the Archbishop of Canterbury and Comrade X, author of *Marxism for Infants* – all of us *really* owe the comparative decency of our lives to poor drudges underground, blackened to the eyes, with their throats full of coal dust, driving their shovels forward with arms and belly-muscles of steel.

George Orwell *The Road to Wigan Pier* (1937) p.35. Orwell's purpose in writing this book was to bring home to middle-class readers the appalling conditions of working-class life.

5 I have suffered hardships for years. Rain and cold and wind on the way will mean nothing to me after that. I have suffered all that a man may suffer. Nothing that can happen on the road between here and London can be worse.

Anon. 60-year-old man pleading to go on the march from Jarrow, Co. Durham, to London, which set off on 5 Oct. 1936; Ellen Wilkinson *The Town that Was Murdered: The Life-Story of Jarrow* (1939) p.200. Wilkinson, Labour MP for Jarrow, organized the march. The man quoted died before the marchers returned.

6 The policy of marches is, in my view, a revolutionary policy. It involves substituting for the provisions of the Constitution the methods of organized mob pressure.

Hensley Henson, bishop of Durham, *The Times*, 24 Oct. 1936. An episcopal view of the celebrated Jarrow March of the unemployed. Henson's diocese covered one of the most distressed areas in the country.

7 Twenty million people are underfed but literally everyone in England has access to a radio. Whole sections of the working-class who have been plundered of all they really need are being compensated, in part, by cheap luxuries which mitigate the surface of life … It is quite likely that fish and chips, art-silk stockings, tinned salmon, cut-price chocolate … the movies, the radio, strong tea and the Football Pools have between them averted revolution.

George Orwell (1937) pp.89–90.

8 Tory spokesmen are not talking sheer nonsense when they claim that the National government has pulled Great Britain through the greatest depression in history.

Professor G.D.H. Cole, Feb. 1938; Ramsden (1978) p.295. Quite an admission coming from an eminent socialist, though it neglects the part played by rearmament in economic revival.

9 His conclusion is that the major, if not the only remedy for chronic unemployment is lower wages … He admitted almost defiantly that he was not personally concerned with the condition of the common people … Possibly there might be an attraction in communism or in a socialist middle way; but, he repeated, there was, as yet, no proof of that, and he was not going to think about it.

Beatrice Webb, diary entry, 10 Aug. 1938; Vol.4 (1965). On a conversation she had with Sir William Beveridge, who, four years later, was to be hailed as the founder of the welfare state (see 859:4).

1 It is impossible to regard the real issue of today as being that of a struggle between the theories of free competition and planned production – between *laissez-faire* and State intervention … The two systems have in practice merged. Competition and planned production, State enterprise and private enterprise, exist side by side.

Harold Macmillan *The Middle Way* (1938) pp.173–4. The moderate Conservative Macmillan foreshadows the consensus policy that was adopted by the Conservative Party after 1945.

MOSLEY AND FASCISM, 1927–36

2 We have lost the good old British spirit. Instead we have American journalism and black-shirted buffoons making a cheap imitation of ice-cream sellers.

Sir Oswald Mosley, 1927; Martin (1968) p.45. Mosley was speaking after the break-up of his Labour Party meeting in Cambridge by pro-Fascist undergraduates, forerunners of his own fascist movement of the 1930s. Mosley's jibe was aimed at the Italians who had opened ice-cream parlours all over Britain during the past generation.

3 Tom Mosley is a cad and a wrong 'un and they will find it out.

Stanley Baldwin, 21 June 1929; Thomas Jones *Whitehall Diary* Vol.2 (1969) p.195. 'They' were the Labour Party, which had recently ousted the Conservatives.

4 He is too 'logical' and if he had his way would attempt presently to 'Russianize' … our government.

Thomas Jones, 22 May 1930; Vol.2 (1969) p.250. The subject was Mosley, though he was a totalitarian of the right, not the left.

5 I beg Tom [Mosley] not to get muddled up with the fascist crowd. I say that fascism is not suited to England. In Italy there was a long tradition of secret societies. In Germany there was a long tradition of militarism. Neither had a sense of humour. In England anything on those lines is doomed to failure and ridicule.

The associate of Mosley, Harold Nicolson, 24 Nov. 1931; *Diaries and Letters 1930–1939* (1966) p.97. Mosley's New Party had recently failed to win a single seat in the general election of 27 Oct. He then formed the British Union of

Fascists (BUF). Fascists had been in power in Italy since 1922, and Nazism was going from strength to strength in Germany.

6 Fascism is the greatest constructive and revolutionary creed in the world … The steel creed of an iron age, it cuts through the verbiage of illusion to the achievement of a new reality.

Sir Oswald Mosley *The Greater Britain* (1932) pp.150–51. After the failure of his New Party, Mosley plunged into the totalitarianism he embraced for the rest of his life.

7 When the spoilt body of Capitalism is put into the straitjacket of the Fascist state, these little by-products of the political system which Capitalism has made possible will of course be cleaned up too.

William Joyce, c.1934; Nicholas Mosley *Beyond the Pale: Sir Oswald Mosley and Family 1933–1980* (1983) p.95. Joyce, one of the most extreme of Mosley's adherents, was writing about the 'miserable pedantic intellectuals, who skulked in lecture rooms throughout the war'. He was expelled from the BUF in 1937 and spent World War II in Germany, where he broadcast radio propaganda to Britain, known to his audience as 'Lord Haw-Haw'. He was executed for treason in 1945.

8 I saw case after case of single interrupters being attacked by ten to twenty Fascists. Again and again, as five or six Fascists carried out an interrupter by arms and legs, other Blackshirts were engaged in hitting or kicking his body. I saw several respectable people who merely rose in their places and made no struggle, treated with unmerciful brutality. It was a deeply shocking scene for an Englishman to see.

Geoffrey Lloyd, parliamentary private secretary to Stanley Baldwin, 14 June 1934; *H.C. Deb.* Vol.290, Col.193. Lloyd was present at the huge rally of Mosley's BUF at the exhibition centre at Olympia, London, on 7 June. Mosley's men wore black shirts, copied from the *camicie nere* of Mussolini's Fascisti. Mosley at the rally described the ejection of the largely communist hecklers as a triumph for free speech – free, that is, for himself and his devotees.

9 *P.C.*: The prisoner used insulting words and behaviour.
    Magistrate: What did he say?
    P.C.: He said, 'Fascism means hunger and war.'

Dialogue in court case arising from the Olympia rally, as reported in the *New Statesman*, 23 June 1934.

10 For the first time I openly and publicly challenge the Jewish interest in this country, commanding commerce, commanding the press, commanding the cinema, dominating the City of London, killing industry with the sweatshops. Those great interests are not intimidating, and will not intimidate the Fascist movement of the modern age.

Sir Oswald Mosley, 14 April 1935, *Manchester Guardian*, 15 April 1935. Mosley regularly denied he was anti-Semitic, but the BUF tried to stage a provocative march through the Jewish quarter of London's East End on 12 Oct. 1936.

A VERY BRITISH COMMUNISM, 1925–39

1 Serve you bloody well right, you've no respect for private property.

Convicted burglar to the communist Harry Pollitt, Nov. 1925; John Mahon *Harry Pollitt* (1976) p.127. Pollitt served close on a year in Wandsworth jail as a political prisoner.

2 We Refuse to Starve in Silence.

Slogan of the National Unemployed Workers' Movement, whose communist organizer, Wal Hannington, promoted a succession of hunger marches and demonstrations in the inter-war years. The NUWM's initiative was eventually followed by Labour, most notably in Ellen Wilkinson's Jarrow March of 1936 (see 780:5), which gained far more publicity.

3 How long is London to be subjected to the indignity of having its police forces – regular and special – mobilized to deal with the communist HANNINGTON and his Marchers, but in reality with HANNINGTON and the revolutionary riffraff of London? Ninety per cent of the Marchers may well be dupes, pawns in a communist game directed by the master-intriguers of Moscow.

Daily Telegraph, 1 Nov. 1932.

4　　Now they've no work, like better men
　　Who sit at desks and take much pay.
　　They sleep long nights and rise at ten
　　To watch the hours that drain away.

Stephen Spender 'Unemployed'. The poet joined the Communist Party in Feb. 1937, in the face of communist criticism that he was no more than a conscience-stricken liberal.

5 Then dawns the day of ... the Mussolinis, the Churchills and the Hitlers. The 'liberal-minded statesmen', the 'enlightened intellectuals', the whole paraphernalia of constitutionalism, are bundled off the stage. It is at this point [that] the final struggle approaches ... And the struggle for communism can surely be won by the workers of Britain, unshakeably allied to the workers of all the world.

John Strachey *The Coming Struggle for Power* (1934 edn) pp.376, 396 (first pub. Nov. 1932). In 1931 Strachey was briefly a member of Mosley's New Party before becoming a communist.

6 I've always thought that the Holy Roman Church with its fanaticism, its Inquisition and its fundamental falsity, the most sinister organization in the history of mankind. Now it may be that we are in for a similar racket at the hands of the Third International and the S.P.U. [Social and Political Union]. Equally fanatical, equally cruel, equally false.

Robert Boothby to John Strachey, 7 Nov. 1932; Hugh Thomas *John Strachey* (1973) p.134. The Third International was the Communist International or Comintern, founded by Lenin in 1919 to direct the activities of communist parties throughout the world from Moscow.

7　　You above all who have come to the far end, victims
　　Of a run-down machine, who can bear it no longer ...
　　Need fight in the dark no more, you know your enemies.
　　You shall be leaders when zero hour is signalled,
　　Wielders of power and welders of a new world.

Cecil Day-Lewis *The Magnetic Mountain* (March 1933). This poem was hailed by the *Partisan Review* of New York as 'perhaps the most important revolutionary poem as yet written by an Englishman'. Day-Lewis was, in fact, Irish-born and at the time of writing not yet a member of the Communist Party, which he joined in 1936.

8 There is no one in politics today worth sixpence outside the ranks of liberals except the post-war generation of intellectual communists under thirty-five. Perhaps in their feelings and instincts they are the nearest thing we have to the typical nervous nonconformist English gentleman who went to the Crusades, made the Reformation, fought the Great Rebellion, won us our civil and religious liberties, and humanized the working classes during the last century.

John Maynard Keynes in conversation with Kingsley Martin, editor, *New Statesman and Nation*, 28 Jan. 1939.

9 Where before the dream of democracy was a counter-revolutionary opiate, today the fight for democratic rights against fascism has become a mass fight against the main attack of finance capital.

Palme Dutt, *Unsere Zeit* (Our Times), 24 April 1933. Dutt, leader of the British Communist Party, urges a united front with the Labour Party against Nazi Germany, just three months after Hitler's accession to power. This policy of cooperation was a drastic U-turn after years of outright hostility to Labour, but the Labour leadership did not respond.

1 The philosophy of the Red International cannot mix with our form of democracy.

Ernest Bevin, June 1935; Bullock Vol.1 (1960) p.559. Bevin was speaking against the call for a united front between the Labour movement and the Communist Party.

2 Guy put it to me that the best way to help anti-fascism … was to help him in his work with the Russians.

Anthony Blunt, 20 Nov. 1979; Andrew Boyle *The Climate of Treason* (1980 edn) p.72. Blunt was exposed as a Soviet spy by prime minister Margaret Thatcher in a statement to the House of Commons on 15 Nov. Guy Burgess, a spy for the Soviet Union, had recruited Blunt in about 1935. He and his fellow traitor Donald Maclean fled to Moscow on 25 May 1951.

3 Be Dead, or Red.

A.J.M. Smith 'The Face' in *New Verse* (Sept. 1936). A pre-echo of the famous slogan of the late 1950s.

4 Fortunately I was never asked either in public or in private, except on one occasion, whether I was a communist … The exception was Katharine, Duchess of Atholl … I had no choice but to answer 'No' out of a constricted throat; she said: 'your word is good enough for me' … I was lunching with Katharine Atholl in their house in Chelsea when the Duke, a tall figure bent by age, shambled into the room, wagged a finger at me, remarked, 'You naughty boy, you are leading Katharine into bad ways,' and shambled out again.

The Hungarian-born communist Arthur Koestler, moving in exalted social circles; *The Invisible Writing* (1969) pp.448–9. The 'Red Duchess', a Conservative by upbringing, was an enthusiastic supporter of left-wing causes.

5 If there were things to disagree with the communists about, what I felt at the time was that they were a lot nearer being a creative force in British politics than any other that I could see. Also they were a force that was small, poor and adventurous, and the distance between their thoughts and their actions appeared to me to be a lot shorter than it was when you came to the Labour people, the 'progressive intellectuals'.

Claud Cockburn *I, Claud* (1967 edn) p.153. The communist journalist Cockburn produced that lively cyclostyled periodical *The Week*, predecessor in many ways to *Private Eye*, an exhilarating cocktail of insider gossip on the contemporary scene.

6 [The Left Book Club's] success and scope, so far from being injured, is probably the greater because it is recognized by the public as an independent commercial enterprise on its own feet, and not the propaganda of a particular political organization.

The Comunist Party boss, Palme Dutt; Paul Laity (ed.) *Left Book Club Anthology* (2001) p.xv. The Left Book Club, founded by the fellow-travelling publisher Victor Gollancz in 1936, soon secured an impressive membership. Its output was highly valued by the Communist Party, whose ideas it generously propagated, since it was not generally regarded as a mouth-piece of the party line.

7   Dan, Dan, Dan
    The Communist Party Man
    Working underground all day
    In and out of meetings
    Bringing fraternal greetings
    Never seeing the light of day.

Ditty composed by Oxford University undergraduate communists; Francis Beckett *Enemy Within: The Rise and Fall of the British Communist Party* (1995) p.66. Oxford provided a touch of frivolity in its communism; Cambridge furnished the deadly serious quartet of spies – Blunt, Philby, Burgess and Maclean (see 783:2).

8 Communists were very sectarian, got drunk, wore beards and did not worry about their examinations. [Then] communists started shaving, tried to avoid being drunk in public, worked for first-class degrees and played down their Marxism-Leninism.

The future Labour cabinet minister Denis Healey, a Communist Party member in 1937; *The Time of My Life* (1989) p.35. Healey contrasts the lifestyle of CP members in the 'Class against Class' period of uncompromising rejection of democratic socialism with their demeanour under the party's United Front doctrine post-1934, once the fundamental challenge of Nazism had begun to make itself felt.

9 One of the most backward sections of the Comintern. It has not succeeded in breaking through to the main section of the British working class.

D. Manuilsky, apparatchik of the Communist International, on the disappointing performance of the British party; *Daily Worker*, 17 March 1939. After nearly 20 years of effort the CP had a membership of just under 18,000, and one lone MP in the House of Commons, the Scots miners' leader, Willie Gallacher. The Labour Party of Attlee and Bevin, which had adamantly set its face against collaboration, remained the only credible standard-bearer of the Red Flag.

Imperialism and Nationalism, 1914–45

HIGH TIDE AND AFTER

1 The Great War of 1914–18 was from the Asian point of view a civil war within the European community of nations. The direct participation of Asian countries … was at the invitation and by the encouragement of one of the parties, the Entente Powers, and was greatly resented by the Germans.
K.M. Panikkar *Asia and Western Dominance* (1953) Pt 5. Not all Asian combatants possessed this political awareness. German resentment sprang largely from the fact they had no Asian colonial auxiliaries to call on, although they were allied to the predominantly Asian state of Turkey. The Entente powers were Britain, France, Italy and Russia.

2 Imperialism is capitalism in that stage of development in which the domination of monopolies and finance capital has taken shape; in which the export of capital has acquired pronounced importance; in which the division of the world by the international trusts has begun, and in which the partition of all the territory of the earth by the greatest capitalist countries has been completed.
Lenin *Imperialism: The Highest Stage of Capitalism* (1916) Ch.7. This treatise was heavily influenced by J.A. Hobson's *Imperialism: A Study* (see 684:3), but the struggle for extra-European colonies was a side-show in the Great War, not the central issue that Lenin appears to have made it.

3 No peace can last, or ought to last, which does not recognize and accept the principle that governments derive all their just powers from the consent of the governed, and that no right anywhere exists to hand peoples about from sovereignty to sovereignty as if they were property.
President Woodrow Wilson, 22 Jan. 1917; Ruhl J. Bartlett (ed.) *The Record of American Diplomacy* (1964 edn) p.453. The doctrine of self-determination, first proclaimed on 25 May 1916 and intended to apply to the empires of all the belligerents in the war.

4 If the whole of the great semicircle which runs from Cape Town to Cairo, thence through Palestine, Mesopotamia and Persia to India and so through Singapore to Australia and New Zealand is either under British control or in the hands of small neutral countries like Portugal and Holland who cannot menace our security, then all the parts of the British Empire which lie on that semicircle will be in a position to render each other mutual support.
The Conservative politician Leo Amery to W.M. Hughes, 12 Oct. 1917; *The Leo Amery Diaries* Vol.1 (1980) p.173. A grandiose vision of empire, which failed to realize that this huge tract of the globe overstretched even Britain's resources, as World War II was to prove.

5 When they were alone Clemenceau said, 'Well, what are we to discuss?' 'Mesopotamia and Palestine,' replied Ll. G. 'Tell me what you want,' asked Clemenceau. 'I want Mosul,' said Ll. G. 'You shall have it,' said C., 'Anything else?' 'Yes, I want Jerusalem too,' continued Ll. G. 'You shall have it,' said Clemenceau, 'but Pichon [French foreign minister] will make difficulties about Mosul.'
Maurice Hankey, secretary to the British cabinet, reporting an exchange between the British and French premiers, Lloyd George and Clemenceau, 4 Dec. 1918; Stephen Roskill *Hankey: Man of Secrets* Vol.2 (1974) pp.28–9. Their dialogue is a classic instance of the diplomacy of imperialism as it had always been up to this point in history and would have borne out the worst suspicions of Lenin and Wilson. Mosul was an oil-producing region of Mesopotamia (present-day Iraq).

6 To those colonies and territories which as a consequence of the late war have ceased to be under the sovereignty of the States who formerly governed them and which are inhabited by peoples not yet able to stand by themselves under the strenuous conditions of the modern world, there should be applied the principle that the well-being and development of such peoples form a sacred trust of civilization and that securities for the performance of this trust should be embodied in this Covenant.
Article 22 of the Covenant of the League of Nations and of the Treaty of Versailles, signed on 28 June 1919; Bartlett (1964 edn) p.468. This article established the so-called Mandate System, whereby the colonies of the defeated powers, Germany and Turkey, were handed over to the victors under the above conditions. While the mandates seemed to promise a new era in the story of imperialism, they were intended in practice to reward the winners of World War I with fresh colonial possessions. One of the main architects of the system, General Smuts of South Africa (which acquired the former German Southwest Africa as a mandate), described it chiefly as a way of taking the sting out of imperial suzerainty – not the view of the leaderships of the mandated territories, who saw themselves on the road to independence.

7 May the Holy War of the Peoples of the East and the toilers of the whole world burn with unquenchable fire against Imperialist England.

Prayer of the Congress of Eastern Peoples, sponsored by the Communist Third International in Sept. 1920; A.S. Klieman *Foundations of British Policy in the Arab World* (1970) p.81. The Soviet Union under Lenin was an enthusiast for the forces of nationalism in the empires of the West, but not for the nationalist movements within its own boundaries.

1 It should be borne in mind that in addition to the right of nations to self-determination, there is also the right of the working class to consolidate its power, and the right of self-determination is subordinate to this latter right ... this must be said bluntly – the right of self-determination cannot and must not serve as an obstacle to the working class in exercising its right to dictatorship.

Excerpt from speeches by Stalin at the 12th Party Congress, 23 and 25 April 1923; X.J. Eudin and R.C. North *Soviet Russia and the East 1920–1927* (1957) pp.62–3. Stalin was at this time commissar for nationalities in the Soviet Union, and his chief preoccupation was to make certain that the various nationalist components of the USSR were denied the opportunity to break away as independent states. This they did not achieve until the disintegration of the Soviet Union in 1991 into 15 sovereignties. Many other communities, notably the Chechens, remained inside Russia, however.

2 The counter-offensive of native energy stirred up by European dynamism [is] a peril which is all the more to be feared since the whole economic structure of Europe has been built upon what might be termed the pile-work of the colonies. Its ominous murmurings may be heard among the colonized peoples ... Now that the active forces of Europe have, as a result of the War, been scattered, now that its monetary wealth has been destroyed and industrial power overthrown by world conflict, they have grown considerably bolder and stronger.

Albert Sarraut, French colonial minister, 1931; Christopher Thorne *The Limits of Foreign Policy* (1968) p.113. Sarraut was speaking of the weakening of Europe by its losses in World War I, by the economic depression that swamped it in 1929 and by the challenge of Japan in its recent conquest of Manchuria, which threatened the whole European position in China.

3 They [the president of the United States and the prime minister of the United Kingdom] respect the right of all peoples to choose the form of government under which they will live; and they wish to see sovereign rights and self-government restored to those who have been forcibly deprived of them.

Atlantic Charter, Article 3, 12 Aug. 1941; Bartlett (1964 edn) p.624. The terms of the Charter, signed by Roosevelt and Churchill, were hailed as a pledge of liberation by the inhabitants of colonial dependencies. In Churchill's view they were addressed only to Europeans living under German

occupation, but Roosevelt considered they also applied to the overseas empires.

4 I venture to think that the Allied declaration that [they] are fighting to make the world safe for freedom of the individual sounds hollow, so long as India, and for that matter, Africa, are exploited by Great Britain, and America has the Negro problem in her own home.

Mahatma Gandhi, 1942; *Foreign Relations of the United States 1942* Vol.I (1960) p.677.

5 We mean to hold our own. I have not become the King's First Minister in order to preside over the liquidation of the British empire.

Winston Churchill, speech in London, 10 Nov. 1942; *The End of the Beginning* (1943) p.215. Churchill was speaking in response to recent anti-colonial declarations in China by the American Wendell Willkie, Republican presidential candidate in 1940.

6 [I told him] that President Roosevelt had given him the British Empire which ... was lost up until the time we entered the war.

Patrick Hurley, US ambassador to China, to Churchill, April 1945; *Foreign Relations of the United States 1945* Vol.7 (1969) p.329. Condescending words from an ardent American anti-imperialist, determined not to restore the British empire in Asia but to remove it.

7 The basic objectives of the trusteeship system ... shall be ... to promote the political, economic, social, and educational advancement of the inhabitants of the trust territories, and their progressive development towards self-government or independence.

Article 76 of the United Nations Charter, signed on 26 June 1945; Bartlett (1964 edn) p.689. The UN trusteeship system continued the League of Nations mandate system and gave a sharp stimulus to decolonization in the post-war world.

THE ARAB WORLD AND BRITAIN

8 Two conclusions rule out the conception of an independent Jewish Palestine from practical politics. The first is that the province ... is not Jewish, and that neither Mohammedan nor Arab would accept Jewish authority; the second that the capital, Jerusalem, is equally sacred to three faiths, Jewish, Christian and Moslem, and should never, if it can be avoided, be put under the exclusive control of any one local faction.

The celebrated traveller Gertrude Bell, then assistant political officer in Baghdad, 23 June 1917; FO 371/3059/162432 'The

Turkish Provinces in Asia' (no.4) Syria. Important reasons why self-determination for Palestine was not included in the Balfour Declaration of Nov. 1917 (see 786:1).

I His Majesty's government view with favour the establishment in Palestine of a national home for the Jewish people, and will use their best endeavours to facilitate the achievement of this object, it being clearly understood that nothing shall be done which may prejudice the civil and religious rights of existing non-Jewish communities in Palestine, or the rights and political status enjoyed by Jews in any other country.

British foreign secretary Arthur Balfour to Lord Rothschild, 2 Nov. 1917; I. Friedman *The Question of Palestine 1914–18* (1973) pp.279–80. The ambiguous nature of this critically important statement, henceforth known as the Balfour Declaration, was the fatal flaw in the British mandate for Palestine. The Zionists interpreted the term 'Jewish national home' as meaning that Palestine would become an independent Jewish state. Balfour at the time apparently had in mind a Zionist enclave within Palestinian territory, alongside the majority Arab population.

2   I loved you, so I drew these tides of men into
      my hands and wrote my will across the sky in
      stars.
    To earn you freedom, the seven-pillared
      worthy house, that your eyes might be
      shining for me
    When we came.

T.E. Lawrence *The Seven Pillars of Wisdom* (1926) Dedication. 'Lawrence of Arabia' led the Arab revolt against the Ottoman Turkish empire in the Middle East from June 1916 on. In these words of high romantic bravura he appears to claim to have achieved Arab independence single-handed. The biblical allusion is to Proverbs 9:1: 'Wisdom hath builded her house, she hath hewn out her seven pillars.'

3 Do we have to ask a nation whether it wants independence? Ours is the oldest of civilizations. Our ancestors have handed down to us undisputed social virtues. Our civic sense is there for everyone to see. One can see it in our respect for the rule of law, our even temper and identity of outlook. To ask a nation like this whether it is agreed on independence is an affront to it.

Sa'ad Zaghlul, speech to Sir Reginald Wingate, London, 1919; J.M. Ahmed *The Intellectual Origins of Egyptian Nationalism* (1960) p.115. Zaghlul was elected as leader of the Wafd, an Egyptian nationalist organization set up in Nov. 1918, to present the case for Egyptian independence to the Paris Peace Conference. The British arrested Zaghlul to prevent him from going to Paris to petition President Wilson, the professed advocate of self-determination.

4 Zionism, be it right or wrong, good or bad, is rooted in age-long tradition, in present needs, in future hopes, of far profounder import than the desires and prejudices of the 700,000 Arabs who now inhabit the ancient land.

Arthur Balfour, 11 Aug. 1919; *Documents on British Foreign Policy 1919–1939* 1st Series, Vol.4, p.345. The man who gave his name to the Balfour Declaration reveals his real priorities for Palestine.

5 Personally, I am so convinced that Palestine will be a rankling thorn in the flesh of whoever is charged with its Mandate, that I would withdraw from this responsibility while we yet can.

Lord Curzon to Balfour, 20 Aug. 1919; Balfour Papers 49734/154–60.

6 The greatest of the real difficulties of Zionism is that it has to take place in Zion.

G.K. Chesterton, despatch written for the *Daily Telegraph*, spring 1920; M. Ffinch *G.K. Chesterton* (1986) p.260. In view of the marked anti-Semitic sentiments displayed in the despatch, the editor felt unable to publish it.

7 Unauthorized statements have been made to the effect that the purpose in view is to create a wholly Jewish Palestine. Phrases have been used such as that Palestine is to become 'as Jewish as England is English'. His Majesty's Government regard any such expectations as impracticable and have no such aim in view. Nor have they at any time contemplated, as appears to be feared by the Arab Delegation, the disappearance or the subordination of the Arabic population, language or culture in Palestine.

Winston Churchill, colonial secretary, June 1922; Walter Laqueur and Barry Rubin (eds) *The Israel-Arab Reader* (1976 edn) p.46.

8 [Palestine will be] for England a little loyal Jewish Ulster in a sea of potentially hostile Arabism.

Sir Ronald Storrs, British governor of Jerusalem, on the Palestine Mandate in the 1920s; *Guardian*, 8 Jan. 2003.

9 At the highest point we found a stone, on which the Jews had written in Hebrew, English and Arabic, 'Palestine is ours'. Our teacher translated it for us, but before he had finished we had read it in Arabic and scratched it out with our nails. We brought pieces of limestone and wrote, 'Palestine is Arab, it's for our people, not for the Jews'.

Recollections of a Palestinian teacher who as a boy in the 1930s had climbed with his classmates to the peak of Mount Jermaq; R. Sayigh, *Palestinians: From Peasants to Revolutionaries* (1979) p.46.

1 There's a picture stamped on my mind of all the people – men, women and children – gathered together on the threshing floor. Later when I asked about the incident, they told me that the British had collected all the people there and blown up the whole village … They said that some people working with the Revolution had taken shelter in the village … This was enough for the British to destroy all the houses. But the people went down to the city [Acre] to get help to rebuild.

A Palestinian recalling an incident during the Arab rebellion of 1936–9, when some 15,000 militants were involved in an organized anti-imperialist struggle; Sayigh (1979) p.43.

2 I was optimistic enough to hope that the importance of our role of guide, counsellor and friend would grow from year to year owing to the new order of things. The latent element of dictation being now removed we would be in a position of elder and younger brothers, of two partners in a firm; though by the nature of things our influence must be the greater in world affairs.

Sir Miles Lampson, British envoy to Egypt, 6 Nov. 1936; Hoda G.A. Nasser *Britain and the Egyptian Nationalist Movement 1936–1952* (1994) pp.27–8. Lampson was referring to the 1936 treaty with Egypt, whereby Britain renounced the right to intervene in Egypt's internal affairs (as the United States had renounced similar rights in Panama the same year). Six months earlier he had threatened Egyptian ministers with the termination of their political careers if they failed to abide by the treaty.

3 His Majesty's government believe that the framers of the Mandate in which the Balfour Declaration was embodied could not have intended that Palestine should be converted into a Jewish State against the will of the Arab population of the country.

White paper on Palestine, 17 May 1939; Charles D. Smith *Palestine and the Arab-Israeli Conflict* (1988) p.105. This effectively reversed the 1917 Balfour Declaration, in a desperate attempt to win the support of the Arab world as World War II loomed, by promising that Palestine would become a sovereign Arab state in ten years' time.

4 The Arabs are not a nation but a mole that grew in the wilderness of the eternal desert. They are nothing but murderers.

Avraham Stern, 1940; N. Masalha *Expulsion of the Palestinians* (1992) p.30. Stern was founder of the Stern Gang, a Zionist terrorist organization committed to the weapon of political assassination.

5 If our dreams for Zionism are to end in the smoke of assassins' pistols and our labours for its future to produce only a new set of gangsters worthy of Nazi Germany, many like myself will have to reconsider the position we have maintained so consistently in the past.

Winston Churchill, following the murder of his personal friend, the colonial secretary, Lord Moyne, by the Stern Gang in Cairo, 6 Nov. 1944; *H.C. Deb.* Vol.404, Col.2242. Churchill had been supportive of the Zionist cause, but this killing changed everything for him.

6 I do not think we should take the responsibility upon ourselves of managing this very difficult place while the Americans sit back and criticize … I am not aware of the slightest advantage which ever accrued to Great Britain from this painful and thankless task. Somebody else should have their turn now.

Winston Churchill, minute to colonial secretary and chiefs of staff, 6 July 1945; *Triumph and Tragedy* (1954) p.654. Many Americans were critical of British policy in Palestine, and in the Biltmore Declaration of 1942 pro-Zionists in the USA had demanded a Jewish state in Palestine.

THE ARAB WORLD AND FRANCE

7 Muslim students, while remaining Muslim, should become so French in their character that no Frenchman, however deeply racist or religiously prejudiced he might be … will any longer dare to deny them French fraternity.

Maurice Violette, governor general of Algeria, 1925; D.C. Gordon *The Passing of French Algeria* (1966) p.36. Violette was one of the more liberal French colonial administrators in advocating kinship between the Muslim majority and the French, but most of the French who had settled in Algeria since the mid-19th century (the *pieds noirs*) did not share his view.

8 As I write these lines, there is not a single Arab, a single Bedouin from the extreme south of Tunisia to the western confines of Morocco, who does not know of the great Russian Revolution, and who, when facing the Orient, does not beg his God to make the reign of justice triumph, together with the Republic of the Soviets, over the land of Islam and the world.

Vigné d'Octon *La Nouvelle Gloire du sabre* (1920) p.136. The French radical writer and journalist d'Octon devoted his life to denouncing the evils of colonialism, but he was blind to the position of the national minorities of the USSR.

9 It is to be foreseen – and indeed I regard it as a historic truth – that in the more or less distant future North Africa – modernized, civilized, living its own autonomous life – will detach itself from metropolitan France. When this occurs – and it must be our supreme political goal – the parting must occur without pain and the nations must be able to continue to view France without fear. The African peoples must not turn against her. For this reason, we must from today, as a starting point, make ourselves loved.

Marshal Louis Lyautey, 14 April 1925; E. Behr *The Algerian Problem* (1961) p.40. In the event, the parting was to be horrendously painful after the ferocity of the Algerian war of 1954–62 (see 871:1–871:8). The prospect of an independent Algeria was rendered even more problematic by the fact that Algeria was not a colony but administered as an extension of metropolitan France.

1 Islam is my religion, Arabic my tongue, Algeria is my country ... and independence is a natural right for all people on earth.

The proclamation of the Ulemas (religious teachers) Association, an Algeria-wide organization, founded in 1931; Behr (1961) p.41.

2 The Algerian people is conscious of its personality and no longer conceives the end of the problem of its liberation in a form other than the Algerian Fatherland ... Henceforth an Algerian Moslem will ask nothing else but to be an Algerian Moslem.

Manifeste du peuple algérien, signed by the leading nationalist Ferhat Abbas and 55 Moslem lawyers, doctors and teachers and professional politicians, 10 Feb. 1943, significantly, soon after the Allied invasion of Nov. 1942, led by the avowed champion of decolonization, the United States.

AFRICA

3 Instead of mixing up black and white in the old haphazard way, which, instead of lifting up the black, degraded the white, we are now trying to lay down a policy of keeping them apart as much as possible in our institutions. In land ownership, settlement and forms of government we are trying to keep them apart, and in that way laying down in outline a general policy which it may take a hundred years to work out, but which in the end may be the solution of our Native problem.

General Jan Christiaan Smuts, 22 May 1917; W.K. Hancock *Smuts: The Fields of Force 1919–1950* (1968) p.113. Apartheid foreshadowed by an Afrikaner moderate, the partner of Britain in the Union of South Africa that was established in 1910. 'Native' in the South African context denoted black Africans. See 874:5.

4 Power-crazy psychopaths are particularly numerous in the colonies – far more so, proportionately, than in France. They belong to the large class of unbalanced individuals who seek out colonial life; their psychic make-up is particularly attracted by the exotic. The life of the tropics attracts them like a lover. It satisfies all their psychic tendencies or passions: for novelty, mystery, authority, liberty, brilliant deeds, tours in the open air, aspirations towards unknown sexual experience, dreams of opium and hashish intoxication ... It gives reality to all the mirages of their spirits.

Dr Cazenove 'Memento de psychiatrie coloniale africaine' in *Bulletin du Comité d'Études historiques et scientifiques de l'Afrique occidentale française* 1927, no.1, p.40.

5 To dominate in order to serve. This is the sole excuse for colonial conquest; it is its full justification. To serve Africa means to civilize it ... not only to exploit and grow rich: but to make men better, happier, more humane.

Pierre Ryckmans *Dominer pour servir* (1931) p.5. Ryckmans, later governor general of the Belgian Congo, introduced the phrase *dominer pour servir* as most aptly expressing the Belgian approach to colonization.

6 At a signal from the 'farmer' [the trading company agent] the militiaman grabs hold of a poor devil who seems to have brought an insufficient quantity of latex. The balls of rubber are thrown on the ground while their owner is given some rough handling. After which, with a rope round his neck, he is sent to swell the ranks of the column of 'bad characters' who will spend that night in prison ready to be transferred to the Congo-Ocean railway line as 'volunteers'. It goes without saying that no register of committals to gaol bears any record of these arrests.

Marcel Homet *Congo, terre de souffrances* (1934) pp.65–6. Homet describes the system of forced labour used to extract rubber in the Middle Congo in the 1930s.

7 Imperialism is absolutely necessary to a people which desires spiritual as well as economic expansion ... It is Italy's mission to civilize Africa. Italy's position in the Mediterranean gives her this right and imposes the duty upon her.

Benito Mussolini, 1934; G.T. Garratt *Mussolini's Roman Empire* (1938) p.51.

8 Some were blinded. When others saw the burns spread upon their arms and legs and felt the increasing pain … they … broke and fled. From their easy perches in high heaven the Italians could see … with a feeling of rich treasure trove, an Ethiopian force jerked suddenly backward, horrified and scattered. Bombing had never shown such an aesthetic result. Total dispersion.

G.L. Steer *Caesar in Abyssinia* (1937) p.233. From an eyewitness account of Italy's first indiscriminate use of mustard gas, sprayed from aircraft on the lightly clothed Ethiopian soldiers and civilians, 22 Dec. 1935. Italy's war on Ethiopia destroyed one of the only two independent states south of the Sahara; the other was Liberia.

1 The general impression clearly left upon the chief and the state-elders in Akim-Abuakwa was that in policy and attitude the missionaries had proved antagonistic towards African ways and had not only condemned everything but had also been anxious to substitute for it what was European.

The Paramount Chief of the Akim Abuakwa State, Gold Coast (Ghana), sets out his grievances regarding the impact of missionary activities on the life of his people; L.H. Gann and P. Duignan *Colonialism in Africa* Vol.2 (1970) p.441.

2 We have assumed that it will be towards some form of representative parliamentary government that a united Nigeria will some day aspire. We may also assume that for a people so backward and so divided in religion and culture, and who never knew any unity but that imposed by Britain upon this arbitrary block of Africa, that day will be very distant.

Margery Perham *Native Administration in Nigeria* (1937) p.361.

3 Nigeria is not a nation. It is a mere political expression. There are no 'Nigerians' in the same sense that there are 'English', 'Welsh' or 'French'.

Obafemi Awolowo *Path to Nigerian Freedom* (1943) pp.47–8. A future political leader of an independent Nigeria warns the UK of the unwisdom of developing Nigeria into a unitary state in view of its huge ethnic diversity. Nigeria gained independence in 1960 but disintegrated with the secession of Biafra in the late 1960s and was reconstituted only by military force.

4 The senior commander whom I saw with a horsewhip placed on his desk, proud of sending for the boy to wipe up the blood which, with his own hand, he had caused to be spilled over the ground was quite convinced that he was doing a good day's work! He wittily called these crises of brutality 'kindness week'; and all this happened in the year of grace 1943.

Father Lelong *Ces Hommes qu'on appelle anthropophages* (These Men They Call Cannibals) (1946) p.164. Lelong reveals how French colonial administrators could become agents of exploitation and oppression.

5 But in French Africa, as in all other territories where men are living under our flag, there will be no real progress unless the inhabitants … rise, stage by stage, to the level where they will be capable of participating, within their own country, in the management of their own affairs. It is France's duty to make sure that this comes to pass.

Charles de Gaulle, speaking at the Brazzaville Conference, 1944; H. Michel and B. Mirkine-Guetzévitch (eds) *Les Idées politiques et sociales de la Résistance* (1954) p.339. De Gaulle's talk of encouraging indigenous peoples towards independence was an acknowledgement of the large contribution made by France's African colonies to his war effort. Later on in the same conference, however, de Gaulle made clear his loyalty to the concept of empire and his intention that it would be France alone that would determine how and when sovereignty would be granted.

INDIA

6 We have seen in our country some brand of tinned food advertised as entirely made and packed without being touched by hand. This description applies to the governing of India, which is as little touched by the human hand as possible. The governors need not know our language, need not come into personal touch with us except as officials … But we, who are governed, are not a mere abstraction. We on our side, are individuals with living sensibilities.

The Indian philosopher Rabindranath Tagore *Nationalism* (1917) pp.24–5.

7 The policy of His Majesty's government, with which the government of India are in complete accord, is that of the increasing association of Indians in every branch of the administration, and the gradual development of self-governing institutions, with a view to the progressive realization of responsible government in India as an integral part of the British empire.

Edwin Montagu, secretary of state for India, 20 Aug. 1917; K.K. Aziz *The Making of Pakistan* (1967) p.35. This announcement, made in response to joint Hindu and Moslem pressure, seemed to promise dominion status (independence) to India, on a par with Canada, Australia, New Zealand and South Africa. If fulfilled, it would have made India the first non-white dominion, but it was not, and Indian aspirations remained unsatisfied.

1 All the dwellers in Hindustan should raise their voices in thanksgiving to Almighty God, day and night, that he has placed them under the shadow of a strong and just King … Day and night I pray Almighty God to lengthen his days, to elevate the star of his greatness, and to give him victory over the tyrant enemy.

Raja Khan, Indian army, 11 Nov. 1917; David Omissi (ed.) *Indian Voices of the Great War* (1999) p.333. For some Indians, like this Lancer, loyalty to the imperial crown meant more than independence.

2 I fired and continued to fire till the crowd dispersed, and I considered that this was the least amount of firing which would produce the necessary moral and widespread effect … not only on those who were present, but more specially throughout the Punjab. There could be no question of undue severity.

Brigadier Reginald Dyer, report of 25 Aug. 1919; *The Amritsar Massacre: General Dyer in the Punjab 1919* (2000) p.64. On 13 April 1919 troops under Dyer's command killed nearly 400 Indian demonstrators and wounded more than 1,000 in the Punjabi city of Amritsar in northern India.

3 Is it any wonder that their vision grows dim when they look toward us, and that we should irritate them when we talk of democracy and liberty? These words were not coined for our use.

Jawaharlal Nehru, 1924; Dorothy Norman (ed.) *Nehru* Vol.1 (1965) p.346. Nehru, one of the founding fathers of an independent India, protests at the undemocratic 1919 Indian franchise, which placed India roughly where Britain had been under the Reform Act of 1832.

4 Until England is in difficulties we keep silent, but in the next European war – aha, aha! Then is our time … Clear out, you fellows, double quick, I say. We may hate one another, but we hate you most … If it's fifty-five hundred years we shall get rid of you, yes, we shall drive every blasted Englishman into the sea.

The Muslim Dr Aziz in E.M. Forster's novel *A Passage to India* (1924) Ch.37. 'We may hate one another' is a reference to Hindu–Moslem animosity, which was to lead to the partition of the subcontinent in 1947.

5 I never allowed anyone to shout 'Mahatma Gandhi' without giving him six on the bottom with a stick.

John Rivett-Carnac, Indian police officer, 1919–27; Charles Allen (ed.) *Plain Tales from the Raj* (1967 edn) p.247.

6 At the back of the jewel was the squalor, hunger, filth, disease, and beggary. Only when I came out of the army could I see what a terrible thing it was that a country had been allowed to exist like this. Such snobbery, so many riches, so much starvation.

Ed Brown, Indian army 1919–28; Allen (1967 edn) p.261.

7 It is alarming and nauseating to see Mr Gandhi, a seditious Middle Temple lawyer, now posing as a fakir of a type well-known in the East, striding half-naked up the steps of the vice-regal palace, while he is still organizing and conducting a campaign of civil disobedience, to parley on equal terms with the representative of the King-Emperor.

Winston Churchill, denouncing the meeting between Gandhi and the viceroy, Lord Irwin, 23 Feb. 1931; Martin Gilbert *Winston S. Churchill* Vol.5 (1976) p.390.

8 Non-violence for me is not a mere experiment. It is part of my life and the whole of the creed of Satyagraha, Non-cooperation, Civil Disobedience, and the like are necessary deductions from the fundamental proposition that Non-violence is the law of life for human beings. For me it is both a means and an end and I am more than ever convinced that in the complex situation that faces India, there is no other way of gaining real freedom.

Mahatma Gandhi to C.F. Andrews, 15 June 1933; Judith Brown *Gandhi and Civil Disobedience* (1970) p.342. Even though Gandhi had moderated his campaign of passive resistance to the British Raj, the government refused to negotiate with him and made him a political prisoner.

9 In anticipation she tasted the agreeable atmosphere of Clubs, with punkahs flapping and bare-footed white-turbaned boys reverently salaaming; and maidans where bronzed Englishmen with little clipped moustaches galloped to and fro, whacking polo balls. It was almost as nice as being really rich, the way people lived in India.

George Orwell's novel *Burmese Days* (1934) p.96. The white man's privileged Indian lifestyle. Punkahs were a type of air-conditioning, hand-operated by servants pulling on louvres. Maidans were open spaces used as sports or parade grounds.

10 The principle of European democracy cannot be applied to India without recognizing the facts of communal groups … The Muslim demand for the creation of a Muslim India is, therefore, perfectly justified … I would like to see the Punjab, North-western Frontier Province, Sind and Baluchistan amalgamated into a single state.

Muhammad Iqbal, 1930; A. Ahmad *Islamic Modernism in India and Pakistan 1857–1964* (1967) p.162. The poet, philosopher and political thinker Iqbal was the first to put forward the proposal for a separate Muslim state in India, yet he does not include East Bengal (present-day Bangladesh, which broke away from Pakistan in 1971). It was Chawdhari Rahmat Alî who coined the name Pakistan for the proposed new state. This was mnemonically constructed from the names of the Muslim-majority provinces of northwestern India: *P*unjab, *A*fghania, *K*ashmir, *S*ind and Baluchi*stan*.

1 Depart! We have had enough of your evasions and ambiguities … Make the country free now and we will defend it … The freedom of India will be at once the symbol and the beginning of the liberation of all other Asian peoples.

'Quit India' resolution issued by the All-India Congress on 8 Aug. 1942; Jan Romein *The Asian Century* (1962) p.298. This resolution was put out at a moment when the British Raj was in danger of invasion by Japan, then sweeping all before it in Southeast Asia.

2 I have become a queer mixture of the East and the West, out of place everywhere, at home nowhere. Perhaps my thought and approach to life are more akin to what is called Western than Eastern, but India clings to me, as she does to all her children … I am a stranger and alien in the West. I cannot be of it. But in my own country also sometimes, I have an exile's feelings.

Jawaharlal Nehru *Toward Freedom* (1941) pp.352–3. The angst of the *déraciné* Old Harrovian, who nevertheless managed to live down his guilty past to become one of the key figures in the Indian nationalist movement.

3 Not content with a civil disobedience campaign Indian people are now morally prepared to employ other means for achieving their liberation. The time has, therefore, come to pass on to the next stage of our campaign. All organizations whether inside India or outside must now transform themselves into a disciplined fighting organization under one leadership. The aim and purpose … should be to take up arms against British Imperialism.

Subhas Chandra Bose, 4 July 1943; *Netaji Subhas Chandra Bose: His Life and Work* (1946) p.313. Bose, a leading figure in the pre-war Indian Congress Party, came to reject Gandhi's passive resistance tactics in favour of guerrilla warfare against the British. Like his Chinese counterpart Wang Jingwei (Wang Ching-wei) (see 793:4), he joined forces with the Japanese and died fighting alongside them in 1945.

4 At some future date, I would like to talk with Marshal Stalin on the question of India … I feel that the best solution would be reform from the bottom, somewhat on the Soviet line.

President Franklin D. Roosevelt to Stalin, Dec. 1943; *Foreign Relations of the United States: The Conference at Cairo and Tehran 1943* (1961) p.482. Roosevelt tossed out this extraordinary idea at the Tehran Conference; it was not shared with Churchill, for understandable reasons. Stalin, interestingly, disagreed.

SOUTHEAST ASIA

5 What Burma wants to know is whether in fighting with many other countries for the freedom of the world, she is also fighting for her own freedom … The demand for complete self-government is an unanimous demand of the Burmese people, and it was made incessantly long before the Atlantic Charter.

The prime minister of Burma, U Saw, in a letter to *The Times*, Oct. 1941. Since 1937 Burma had enjoyed a limited autonomy. For the Atlantic Charter see 785:3.

6 I have never liked the Burmese, and you people must have had a terrible time with them for the last fifty years. Thank the Lord you have He-Saw, We-Saw, You-Saw under lock and key. I wish you could put the whole bunch of them into a frying pan with a wall around and let them stew in their own juice.

President Franklin D. Roosevelt to Winston Churchill, 16 April 1942; Christopher Thorne *Allies of a Kind* (1978) p.6. U Saw had recently made contact with the Japanese and was hanged in 1948.

7 Now how about our Land of Birth, Indonesia? Thick fog blankets the country. People live like cavemen, kept in the dark. Noble and holy character and love of country like that possessed by the Japanese, French, and Dutch are still below the surface here. If this description is accurate, can our people move ahead like other nations? … Of course, we can if there are leaders to enlighten our people.

The prominent Indonesian nationalist Raden Soetomo *A Garland of Flowers, No. VIII, Ready for Sacrifice* (1932) p.256. Indonesia was the nationalist name for the vast colony of the Dutch East Indies.

8 The history of Islam in recent times has been one of conflict with the evil machinations of England. Muslims all over the world should unite for a crusade to defeat the Americans and British who are the enemies of religion.

It is very fortunate, indeed, that Java lives under the protection of the Dai Nippon Army. Let us, therefore, set up a Muslim volunteer corps on Java, so that it may become the trailblazer in the effort to destroy America and England.

Letter from Javanese Muslims to the Japanese commander-in-chief, in the Japanese-sponsored periodical *Djawa Baroe*, 1 Oct. 1943. A pre-echo of the post-Sept. 2001 Holy War antagonism between Islamic fundamentalists and the Anglo-American anti-terrorist partnership.

1 This I know: we of Indonesia and the citizens of many countries of Asia and Africa have seen our dearest and best suffer and die, struggle and fail, and rise to struggle and fail again – and again be resurrected from the very earth, and finally achieve their goal. Something burned in them: something inspired them. They called it nationalism ... For us there is nothing ignoble in that word. On the contrary, it contains for us all that is best in mankind and all that is noblest.

The Indonesian nationalist leader Ahmed Sukarno, Sept. 1945; Louis L. Snyder *The Dynamics of Nationalism* (1964) p.336. On 17 Aug. 1945, two days after the Japanese surrender, Sukarno had confidently proclaimed the independence of the Republic of Indonesia.

2 Our maxim is the removal of our enemies one by one. It is a question of using others without being used ourselves ... We must keep the enemy out of breath with constant attacks ... Our aim is to set up zones under revolutionary government, and thus gradually form a unified state rule in the whole country.

The Vietnamese nationalist Ho Chi Minh, 6 Aug. 1944; F. Ansprenger *The Dissolution of the Colonial Empires* (1989) p.150. The blueprint for the guerrilla struggle, first against the French, then against the Americans, which finally led to the realization of Ho's vision in 1975.

CHINA AND JAPAN

3 Lord Grey held the view that if you are going to keep Japan out of North America, out of Canada, out of the United States, out of Australia, out of New Zealand, out of the islands south of the equator in the Pacific, you could not forbid her to expand in China. A nation of that sort must have a safety-valve somewhere.

Arthur Balfour, British foreign secretary, 1917; Ian Nish *Alliance in Decline* (1972) p.7. The view that Japan should be compensated for the refusal to allow Japanese immigrants into the areas listed by Western tolerance of its expansionism in China. In 1915 Japan had presented China with the Twenty-

One Demands, which, if accepted *in toto*, would have made China a Japanese colony. Only the United States, China's self-styled protector, had demurred. Britain in 1917 was Japan's ally by the treaty of 1902 and saw Japan as a guarantor of order in a politically chaotic China.

4 The ideals of President Wilson were defeated! The power politics of Clemenceau ... triumphed! Japan's demand for a free hand in Shantung was satisfied! These heavy blows were too much for the young people of China to bear ... They organized and led the heroic and patriotic movement which succeeded in defending their country's rights. Without the May 4th Movement, our delegates [at the Peace Conference] might have signed the Peace Treaty and these rights might have been lost.

The Chinese nationalist thinker Hu Shih, 1920; Jerome Ch'en *Mao and the Chinese Revolution* (1965) p.61. China had expected the reacquisition of the province of Shantung, taken by Japan from Germany in 1914, but at the Paris Peace Conference of 1919 Japan was allowed to keep the conquest. The nationalist May Fourth Movement acquired its name from the day the news of the Shantung concession reached China.

5 No dogs or Chinese allowed.

Sign said to have been erected in the public gardens of the Shanghai International Settlement some time before 1927. The Settlement was administered by Britain, France and the United States.

6 The Powers should yet recognize ... the essential justice of the Chinese claim for treaty revision ... H.M. government attach the greatest importance to the sanctity of treaties, but they believe that this principle may best be maintained by a sympathetic adjustment of treaty rights to the equitable claims of the Chinese.

British government statement, 25 Dec. 1926; Dorothy Borg *American Policy and the Chinese Revolution* (1947) p.231. A reaction to the Nationalist Party's demand for the revision of the 'unequal treaties' forced on China over the past century; in practice the adjustments made were marginal.

7 The Chinese National Revolution will eventually succeed and its triumph will mark the beginning of the true friendship and cooperation between China and Japan. [I] hope that our friends in Japan will understand this work for the victory of the [Chinese] National Revolution, and thereby lay the foundation of the cooperation of our two countries.

The Chinese Nationalist leader Chiang Kai-shek (Jiang Jieshi), 6 March 1928; Ch'en (1965) p.145. Chiang had recently reunified China, with the exception of Manchuria in northeastern China, which his government now planned to regain from its two overlords, the USSR and Japan. Neither was disposed to concede, and this same year the Japanese assassinated the Manchurian warlord Chang Tso-lin on suspicion that he was prepared to make a deal with Chiang. In 1931 Japan provoked a major international crisis by taking over the whole of Manchuria and making it the satellite state of Manzhuguo (Manchukuo). Both the Soviet Union and China were powerless to reverse the seizure.

1 *Saturday, December 18.* A day of complete anarchy. Several big fires raging today, started by the soldiers, and more are promised ... Some houses are entered from five to ten times in one day, and the poor people looted and robbed and the women raped. Several were killed in cold blood, for no apparent reason whatever.

Thursday, December 23. Seventy men were taken from our camp at the Rural Leaders' Training School and shot. No system – soldiers seize anyone they suspect. Callouses on hands are proof that the man was a soldier, a sure death warrant. Rickshaw coolies, carpenters and other laborers are frequently taken.

Dr M. Searle Bates, diary entries, Dec. 1937; Harold Timperley *What War Means* (1938) pp.25–9. Dr Bates was an American teacher at Nanjing (Nanking) University, an eyewitness to the Japanese 'Rape of Nanking', five months after the outbreak of full-scale war between Japan and China.

2 Japan [cannot] morally leave China permanently in the turmoil created by the Powers or ... let her continue in a feudal backwater as a semi-colony being systemically exploited ... The Asian peoples must turn their backs on the self-centred individual-istic materialism of Europe and devote themselves to lives rooted in Asia.

Kawai Tatsuo, Feb. 1938; Ian Nish *Japanese Foreign Policy 1869–1942* (1977) p.304. Kawai, head of the information bureau of Japan's foreign ministry, foreshadows the 'new order' in East Asia proclaimed in Nov. 1938. It professed the policy of Pan-Asianism, based on partnership between China and Japan, to which the Chinese nationalist leader Sun Yat-sen (Sun Yixian) had subscribed in the early years of the century. In reality the new order was to be an imperialism far more stringent than anything China had experienced under the West.

3 Whenever the word *Japan* is spoken in front of the Chinese people, they immediately think of soldiers of fortune who work for intelligence agencies, and criminals. We associate the term *Japanese* with those who engage in opium traffic, selling morphine, making cocaine, distributing heroin, establishing opium dens, monopolizing prostitution, secretly

dealing in arms, assisting bandits, and protecting undesirable elements.

Chiang Kai-shek, 26 Dec. 1938; James W. Morley (ed.) *The China Quagmire* (1938) p.386. The Chinese leadership's riposte to the Japanese new order.

4 The reason that I sullied my good name ... was because at a time of national emergency, we cannot preserve the life of our state unless we depend upon our wits. If we can take advantage of the enemy's lack of caution and restore territory and console the homeless people – if I could do that – I don't care how difficult the remainder of my life might be. Understanding people will feel sympathy for my difficulties and will not accuse my policies as being unjust.

Wang Jingwei (Wang Ching-wei), last testament, c.1944; John Hunter Boyle *China and Japan at War 1937–1945: The Politics of Collaboration* (1972) pp.351–2. Wang defected from the government of Chiang Kai-shek on 31 Dec. 1938 and in 1940 formed a puppet regime under Japanese auspices; he died in Japan in 1944. It is worth remembering that Wang could claim to be following in the footsteps of the founding father of Chinese nationalism, Sun Yat-sen, who had once declared: 'China is nothing without Japan; Japan is nothing without China.' See 793:2.

5 Write on my tomb, 'Here lies a black man, killed fighting a yellow man for the protection of a white man.'

Anon. pro-Japanese American Negro writing in 1942–3; Thorne (1978) p.9. A decidedly fringe view, though it reflected a wider American unease at fighting a Far Eastern war where victory would mean the rescue of European imperialism after the brief period of Japanese conquest.

6 Churchill is old. A new British government will give Hong Kong to China and next day China will make it a free port.

Vice-President Henry Wallace, June 1944, quoting President Roosevelt; *Foreign Relations of the United States 1944 China* (1967) p.231. Churchill had said 'never will we yield an inch of territory that is under the British flag'. Roosevelt did not press the point.

THE SOVIET UNION AND EASTERN EUROPE

7 In all this thinking and deciding upon the fight against Austria, there rang through the depths of my soul the questions ... Shall we make good, once for all, the disaster that overwhelmed us as a nation in the Battle of the White Mountain three centuries ago? Can we vanquish in ourselves the influence of Austria and of the centuries of subjection to her? Is the hour of the fulfilment of Comenius' Testament at hand: 'I too believe before God that, when the storms of wrath have passed, to thee shall return the rule over thine own things, O Czech people!'

Thomas Garrigue Masaryk *The Making of a State* (1927) pp.50–51. Masaryk (1850–1937) led the wartime campaign for independence from Austria-Hungary and became the first president of the new state of Czechoslovakia in 1918. The kingdom of Bohemia was conquered by Austria in the Battle of Mohács (1526), and the Czech attempt to restore it was defeated in the Battle of the White Mountain on 8 Nov. 1620. Comenius was Jan Amos Komensky, a 17th-century Czech patriot, who wrote his Testament at the close of the Thirty Years War (1618–48).

1 Muslims of Russia, Tatars of the Volga and the Crimea, Kirghiz and Sarts of Siberia and Turkestan, Turks and Tatars of Transcaucasia, Chechens and mountaineers of the Caucasus … Your beliefs and usages, your national and cultural institutions are henceforth free and inviolable. Organize your cultural life freely and without hindrance. You have a right to this.

Special appeal addressed to 'All Muslim toilers of Russia and the East', 20 Nov. 1917; Robert Conquest *Soviet Nationalities Policy in Practice* (1967) p.22. Every effort was made by the Bolsheviks to gain the support of the Muslim minorities, with the promise of national autonomy, but this liberalism was short lived.

2 Germany would gain one man, but I would lose a nation.

Josef Pilsudski, 1918; Norman Davies *Heart of Europe* (1984) p.141. The Polish nationalist leader refuses an offer from the German governor of Warsaw to rule Poland under German suzerainty.

3 The Baltic Sea has to become a 'Sea of Soviet Revolution', and the independent Baltic States standing in the way of Soviet Russia to Western Europe must be eliminated, if necessary by force.

Izvestiya (News), 25 Dec. 1918. Latvia, Lithuania and Estonia had seceded from Russia under German sponsorship in 1918, but Moscow was too weak to bring them back into the fold until 1940. They regained their independence in 1989.

4 The right freely to secede from the USSR is reserved to every Union Republic.

Soviet Constitution of 1936, Article 17. A purely nominal gesture to the constituent nationalities of the Soviet Union; Stalin would never have tolerated even the merest thought of secession.

5 The crowds were ragged, thin, and anaemic, with sunken … cheeks and great hollow eyes. Nothing could have seemed more gloomy and depressing than the picture they presented. Yet the enthusiasm of a people raised unexpectedly and almost miraculously like Lazarus from the dead … was such that it carried me, at last, away.

Sir Esmé Howard, Warsaw, Feb. 1919, *Theatre of Life* Vol.2 (1936) p.320. Howard witnessed the popular acclamation of the newly re-created Polish state after more a century of partition between Russia, Germany and Austria.

6 Poland, below me, was alone. As alone as it had been the day Germany attacked, six years before, I thought of the rage of the civilized world when Hitler demanded a corridor to Danzig and compared it to the complacency of the same world as a new dictatorial force, Russia, took not only Danzig or a corridor but half of the entire country … What, I asked myself, was the essential difference between Hitler and Stalin? I could find none.

Stanislaw Mikolajczyk *The Pattern of Soviet Domination* (1948) p.136. Mikolajczyk, prime minister of the Polish government-in-exile until 1945, refers to his flight over Poland soon after the end of World War II, which began with the destruction of the Polish republic by Nazi Germany and the Soviet Union. By this time Poland had been consigned to the USSR at the Yalta Conference of Feb. 1945.

IRELAND

7 The Defenders of this Realm have worked well in secret and in the open. They think that they have pacified Ireland. They think that they have purchased half of us and intimidated the other half. They think that they have foreseen everything, think that they have provided against everything; but the fools, the fools, the fools! … Ireland unfree shall never be at peace.

Padraic Pearse, oration at the graveside of the Irish nationalist, O'Donovan Rossa, 1 Aug. 1915, *Political Writings and Speeches* (1952) p.137.

8 In every generation the Irish people have asserted their right to national freedom and sovereignty; six times during the last three hundred years they have asserted it in arms. Standing on that fundamental right and again asserting it in arms in the face of the world, we hereby proclaim the Irish Republic as a Sovereign Independent State.

Part of the proclamation of the Provisional Government of the Irish Republic, Easter Monday, 24 April 1916; A.C. Hepburn

The Conflict of Nationality in Modern Ireland (1980) pp.94–5. All seven signatories, leaders of the Easter Rising, were subsequently executed by the British government. The term 'Provisional' echoes down the years, now through the Provisional IRA. It was formed in 1969 with the covert assistance of the Irish government in Dublin to counteract the Marxist take-over of the existing Irish Republican Army.

1 War is a terrible thing but war is not an evil thing. It is the things that make war necessary that are evil … Many people in Ireland dread war because they do not know it. Ireland has not known the exhilaration of war for over a hundred years. Yet who will say that she has known the blessings of peace? When war comes to Ireland, she must welcome it as she would welcome the Angel of God, and she will … We must not faint at the sight of blood. Winning through it, we (or those of us who survive) shall come unto great joy.

Padraic Pearse 'Peace and the Gael', Dec. 1915; (1952) pp.217–18.

2 He [Pearse] was a manic, mystic nationalist with a cult of blood sacrifice and a strong personal motivation towards death. A nation which takes a personality of that type as its mentor is headed towards disaster.

Conor Cruise O'Brien, Irish Times, 15 Nov.1979.

3 We are told that if Irishmen go by the thousand to die, not for Ireland, but for Flanders, for Belgium, for a patch of sand on the deserts of Mesopotamia, or a rocky trench on the heights of Gallipoli, they are winning self-government for Ireland. But if they dare to lay down their lives on their native soil, if they dare to dream even that freedom can be won, then they are traitors to their country.

Sir Roger Casement, 25 June 1916; Brian Inglis Roger Casement (1973) App.1. Casement had landed in Ireland from a German submarine on the eve of the Easter Rising of 1916 but was soon arrested. This is from his speech from the dock at his trial for high treason, where he was condemned to death.

4 I write it out in verse –
MacDonagh and MacBride
And Connolly and Pearse
Now and in time to be
Wherever green is worn,
Are changed, changed utterly:
A terrible beauty is born.

W.B. Yeats 'Easter 1916', written between May and Sept. 1916. Yeats's poem became the most celebrated invocation of the Easter Rising of 1916, when a tiny group of republicans led

by Padraic Pearse seized the centre of Dublin before being overwhelmed by the British army.

5 Now, men, Sinn Fein has had all the sport up to the present, and we are going to have the sport now … You may make mistakes occasionally, and innocent persons may be shot, but that cannot be helped, and you are bound to get the right parties sometime. The more you shoot, the better I will like you, and I assure you, no policeman will get into trouble for shooting any man.

Colonel Smyth, Royal Irish Constabulary divisional commander for Munster, 17 June 1920; Dorothy Macardle The Irish Republic (1951) p.360. After World War I the Irish Republican movement entered into an armed struggle against Britain, with no quarter given by either side.

6 It is not guerrilla warfare. It is the warfare of the red Indian, of the Apache. It is the warfare, which nearly a hundred years ago the government of India had to suppress, and which was known as 'Thuggee' – the manoeuvres of the thugs of that country … this is not freedom by fighting; this is rebellion by murder.

The British foreign secretary Lord Curzon, 20 Oct. 1920; Irish Political Documents 1916–1949 (1985) p.85.

7 If we have a British government terrorized, and a British government submitting to negotiations with a gang of murderers, what a vista is opened! A British government brought to heel here may be brought to heel elsewhere than in Ireland by methods of this kind. They are beginning in India. We hear of something in Egypt.

Colonel Gretton, 31 Oct. 1921; H.C. Deb. Vol.147, Cols 1393–4.

8 Think – what have I got for Ireland? Something which she has wanted these past seven hundred years. Will anyone be satisfied at the bargain? Will anyone? I tell you this – early this morning I signed my death warrant.

Michael Collins, letter written immediately after signing the treaty ending the war with Britain, 6 Dec. 1921; Leon Ó Broin Michael Collins (1980) p.113. The treaty recognized an Irish Free State, whose territory excluded six of the counties of Ulster and which nominally owed loyalty to the British crown. Extreme Irish Republicans consequently refused to accept the treaty, and a civil war ensued, in which Collins died in an ambush on 22 Aug. 1922.

9 It inflicts a grievous wound upon the dignity of this nation by thrusting the King of England upon us … It will be the duty of those who frame the Constitution … to relegate the King of England to the exterior darkness as far as they can.

George Gavan Duffy, 21 Dec. 1921; *Dáil Eireann Deb.* p.85. The treaty settlement denied Ireland a republic, retaining the king as titular head of state, a bitter pill for Irish nationalists to swallow. Duffy nonetheless voted to ratify the treaty.

1 If … our last cartridge had been fired, our last shilling had been spent, and our last man were lying on the ground and his enemies howling round him and their bayonets raised, ready to plunge them into his body, that man would say – true to the traditions handed down – if they said to him 'Now, will you come into our Empire?' – he should say, and he would say 'No! I will not.'

Cathal Brugha (né Charles Burgess) 7 Jan. 1922; *Dáil Eireann Deb.* p.330. A Republican Ultra denounces the Anglo-Irish Treaty of 1921.

2 What remains between this Treaty and the fullness of our rights? It gives to Ireland complete control over her internal affairs. It removes all English control or interference within the shores of Ireland. Ireland is liable to no taxation from England, and has the fullest fiscal freedom. She has the right to maintain an army and to defend her coasts. When England is at war, Ireland need not send one man nor contribute a penny.

Kevin O'Higgins, 19 Dec. 1921; *Dáil Eireann Deb.* p.45. Although citizens of the new Irish Free State were not liable to conscription into the British armed forces, many of them nevertheless fought for Britain in World War II.

3 I respectfully suggest that this conference [the final treaty negotiation] was called because England found it impossible to carry on her work in Ireland and to preserve and carry on her Empire; and having failed to force British sovereignty on the Irish nation for 750 years, she has done it now by diplomacy.

Harry Boland, 7 Jan. 1922; *Dáil Eireann Deb.* p.302. Boland, secretary to Eamon de Valera, leader of the anti-treaty movement, puts his finger on what was to be a key weakness in British imperialism, namely the inability to crush nationalism by military means, particularly in an empire that took in one-fifth of the world's population.

4 The whole map of Europe has been changed … The modes of thought of men, the whole outlook on affairs, the grouping of parties, all have encountered violent and tremendous changes in the deluge of the world war. But as the deluge subsides and the waters fall short, we see the dreary steeples of Fermanagh

and Tyrone emerging once again. The integrity of their quarrel is one of the few institutions that has been unaltered in the cataclysm which has swept the world.

Winston Churchill, 16 Feb. 1922; *H.C. Deb.* Vol.150, Col.1270. Fermanagh and Tyrone were two of the seven counties of Ulster which, with four of the others (Antrim, Londonderry, Armagh and Down), formed the territory of Northern Ireland.

5 Article 2. The National territory consists of the whole island of Ireland, its islands and the territorial seas.

From the revised Irish Constitution, issued by Eamon de Valera, 11 May 1937; Arthur Mitchell and Padraig O'Snodaigh *Irish Political Documents: 1916–1949* (1985) p.216. The Free State thereby laid formal claim to Northern Ireland, part of the United Kingdom under the treaty of 1921. It was a provocative gesture, ultimately rescinded as part of the Good Friday agreement of 1998 (see 931:9).

6 This was indeed a deadly moment in our life, and if it had not been for the loyalty and friendship of Northern Ireland we should have been forced to come to close quarters or perish for ever from the earth. However, with a restraint and poise to which, I say, history will find few parallels, His Majesty's Government never laid a violent hand upon them, though at times it would have been quite easy and quite natural, and we left the Dublin Government to frolic with the Germans and later with the Japanese representatives to their hearts' content.

Winston Churchill, 13 May 1945; Martin Gilbert *'Never Despair'* (1988) p.12. This radio broadcast produced the following riposte by the Irish prime minister, Eamon de Valera, on 16 May.

7 Mr Churchill is proud of Britain's stand alone, after France had fallen and before America joined the war. Could he not find in his heart the generosity to acknowledge that there is a small nation that stood alone not for one year or two, but for several hundred years against aggression; that endured spoliations, famines, massacres in endless succession … a small nation that could never be got to accept defeat and has never surrendered her soul.

Eamon de Valera, 16 May 1945; Maurice Moynihan (ed.) *Speeches and Statements by Eamon de Valera 1917–1973* (1980) pp.475–6. In fact, Ireland was something less than neutral, particularly after the United States came into the war in Dec. 1941, although it refused to allow Britain to use naval bases that would have been valuable assets in the Battle of the Atlantic.

1 This temperamental country needs quiet treatment and a patient, consistent policy. But how are you to control Ministerial incursions into your china shop? Phrases make history here.

The British ambassador to Dublin, commenting on the Churchill–de Valera exchange; Conor O'Clery *Phrases Make History Here* (1987 edn) p.1.

LATIN AMERICA

2 [The Monroe Doctrine] was founded upon a fact, namely, the superior power of the United States to compel submission to its will ... In its advocacy of the Monroe Doctrine, the United States considers its own interests. The integrity of other American nations is an incident, not an end.

US secretary of state Robert Lansing, Nov. 1915; Arthur Link (ed.) *The Papers of Woodrow Wilson* Vol.35 (1980) pp.249, 252. A candid expression of American hegemony over Latin America.

3 Right or wrong ... the extremist consequences seem upon us. But INTERVENTION (that is, the rearrangement and control of Mexico's domestic affairs by the U.S.) there shall not be now or at any time if I can prevent it.

President Woodrow Wilson to his confidant Colonel Edward House, 22 June 1916; P. Edward Haley *Revolution and Intervention* (1970) p.216. A large force of US army troops had crossed into Mexico on 15 March 1916 after the killing of American miners by the bandit leader Pancho Villa. The expedition, which failed to capture Villa, was withdrawn in Feb. 1917 as war with Germany loomed.

4 The people, as a rule, are untrustworthy, poorly educated, lazy and dirty ... They resent our marked superiority as to intelligence, ability, wealth, and, above all, our power; and the whole structure of ill feeling is based on the jealousy of a small, narrow minded and insignificant country for one which is greater in every way and which has lifted it to whatever slight degree of world's prominence it may have.

Captain Montgomery Taylor USN, 21 Oct. 1921, speaking of the American protectorate of Panama; John Major *Prize Possession: The United States and the Panama Canal 1903–1979* (1993) p.65.

5 I believe [we] had a moral duty to clean that place up and establish decency down there, because it did not exist. You have no idea of the conditions, if you have not been there, that did exist when we landed in Haiti. The Aegean [*sic*] stables were Paradise compared to it.

Colonel Eli K. Cole, US Marines, 1921; US Senate *Hearings on Haiti and Santo Domingo* (1921) Pt 1, p.392. The Marines occupied Haiti from 1915 to 1934. 'Aegean', which should read 'Augean', was a reference to the cleansing of the stables of King Augeus, one of the labours imposed on Hercules.

6 My administration will offer full guarantees to all businesses and enterprises which are worthy of the protection of the government, and there is no reason to fear that any disorder will occur because I have sufficient material force to stamp it out.

Cuban president-elect General Gerardo Machado, 1925; Louis A. Pérez Jr *Cuba and the United States: Ties of Singular Intimacy* (1990) pp.178–9. A speech at a lunch arranged by the National City Bank of New York to reassure his audience that Cuba would be made safe for US investment.

7 When you hit a rock with an egg, the egg breaks. Or when you hit an egg with a rock, the egg breaks. The United States is the rock. Panama is the egg. In either case, the egg breaks.

Anon. Panamanian diplomat on the power differential between Washington and its minuscule isthmian fiefdom; *New York Times*, 2 Oct. 1927.

8 What are we to do when government breaks down and American citizens are in danger of their lives? Are we to stand by and see them killed because ... a government cannot afford reasonable protection?

Secretary of state Charles Evans Hughes, 18 Feb. 1928; *New York Times*, 19 Feb. 1928. Hughes was defending US intervention in the affairs of Latin American states, against a storm of protest at Washington's policy during the Pan-American conference in Havana.

9 Dear Sir: I have the honour to inform you that on this date your mine has been reduced to ashes, by disposition of this command, to make more tangible our protest against the warlike invasion that your government has made in our territory, without any more right than that of brute force.

The Nicaraguan guerrilla leader Augusto Sandino to the manager of the US-owned La Luz Mine, 29 April 1928; Lester D. Langley *The Banana Wars* (1983) p.202.

10 So far as Latin America is concerned, the Doctrine is now, and always has been, not an instrument of violence and oppression, but an unbought, freely bestowed, and wholly effective guaranty of their freedom, independence, and territorial integrity against the imperialistic designs of Europe.

Under-secretary of state J. Reuben Clark, memorandum on the Monroe Doctrine, 17 Dec. 1928; Bartlett (1964 edn) p.549. This renounced the Roosevelt Corollary of 6 Dec.

1904 (see 618:8), in an attempt to assuage Latin American feelings, though it was not published until 1930.

1 Europe is the matrix of our culture and the well-spring from which we have drunk Graeco-Roman civilization, of which we are so justly proud. America – which is the continent of the future – cannot lose permanent contact with mother Europe without bastardizing its most noble traditions or disowning a glorious past.

Jésus María Yepes of Colombia, Dec. 1929. By 'America', Yepes means not the USA but Latin America. A plea for Hispanic America to reach out to Europe and not let itself be cut off from contact by a US insistence on closing the hemisphere to further European influences. Compare Simón Bolívar 545:4.

2 I spent 33 years ... being a high-class muscle man for Big Business, for Wall Street and the bankers. In short, I was a racketeer for capitalism ... I helped purify Nicaragua for the international banking house of Brown Brothers in 1909–1912. I helped make Mexico and especially Tampico safe for American oil interests in 1916. I brought light to the Dominican Republic for American sugar interests in 1916. I helped make Haiti and Cuba a decent place for the National City [Bank] boys to collect revenue. I helped in the rape of half a dozen Central American Republics for the benefit of Wall Street.

Major General Smedley D. Butler, US Marine Corps, Aug. 1931; Jules Archer The Plot to Seize the White House (1973)

p.118. An extraordinary revelation from a senior interventionist who became a political radical after he was passed over for commandant of the Marine Corps.

3 The essential qualities of a true Pan Americanism must be the same as those which constitute a good neighbor, namely, mutual understanding, and, through such understanding, a sympathetic appreciation of the other's point of view.

President Franklin D. Roosevelt, 12 April 1933, Public Papers 1933 (1938) pp.129–33. In his inaugural address on 4 March 1933 Roosevelt had dedicated the United States to the policy of the good neighbour in international relations. This he now applied to Latin America, apparently turning his back on the 'big stick' approach of Theodore Roosevelt.

4 He may be a son of a bitch, but he's our son of a bitch.

President Franklin D. Roosevelt, attrib., on the Nicaraguan dictator Anastasio Somoza. Somoza's forces succeeded in killing the rebel leader Sandino on 21 Feb. 1934. Shortly afterwards Somoza was given the honour of a state visit to Washington and was greeted at Union Station by Roosevelt himself.

5 That is a new approach that I am talking about to these South American things. Give them a share. They think they are just as good as we are, and many of them are.

President Franklin D. Roosevelt, 12 Jan. 1940; David Green The Containment of Latin America (1971) p.38. A backhanded compliment to Hispanic America by its colossal northerly good neighbour.

The Post-war Settlement and After, 1918–29

THE SHOCK OF PEACE, 1918–19

1   There died a myriad,
And of the best, among them,
For an old bitch gone in the teeth,
For a botched civilization.
Ezra Pound 'E.P. Ode pour l'élection de son sépulcre' in *Hugh Selwyn Mauberley* Pt 5 (1920).

2 The War of the Giants has ended; the wars of the pygmies begin.
Winston Churchill on the chaos of the post-war world; Norman Davies *Europe, A History* (1996) p.926.

3 No more wars for me at any price! Except against the French. If there's ever a war with them, I'll go like a shot.
The poet Edmund Blunden; Robert Graves *Goodbye to All That* (1929) p.240. Anti-French feeling was common among British troops who had fought on the Western Front.

4 The prime minister said he had never hoped for such a rapid solution nor envisaged such a complete collapse of German power.
Paul Cambon, French ambassador in London, citing Lloyd George's reaction to the previous day's armistice, 12 Nov. 1918; *Ministère des affaires étrangères* PA-AP 42, Paul Cambon Papers, Vol.68.

5 No man can dominate the world, it has been tried before, and now he has utterly ruined his Country and himself. I look upon him as the greatest criminal known for having plunged the world into this ghastly war.
George V, diary entry, referring to his cousin Kaiser Wilhelm II of Germany, now exiled in Holland, Nov. 1918; Kenneth Rose *King George V* (1985) p.229. In the vengeful mood of the time there were calls for the Kaiser to be hanged, but the Dutch would not hand him over to the Allies for trial, and he lived in the Netherlands until his death in 1941. French and British efforts to try leading German officers for war crimes came to nothing, in contrast with the war crimes trials held after 1945 (see 843:6).

6 Yes we have won the war and not without difficulty; but now we are going to have to win the peace, and that perhaps will be even more difficult.
French prime minister Georges Clemenceau to his aide General Henri Mordacq, Nov. 1918; Henri Mordacq *Le Ministère Clemenceau* Vol.3 (1931) p.5. In a speech at Verdun

on 20 July 1919 Clemenceau would voice the same sentiment in more epigrammatic form: *Il est plus facile de faire la guerre que la paix* (It is easier to make war than to make peace) (*Discours de paix* (1938) p.122).

7 In my poor country France, there are hundreds of villages into which no one has been able to return. Please understand: it is a desert, it is desolation, it is death.
French minister for the liberated areas of northeastern France, c.1919; P.M. Burnett *Reparation at the Paris Peace Conference from the Standpoint of the American Delegation* (1965) Vol.1, p.33. With close on 1,500,000 dead and 11 of her *départements* laid waste, France bore deep emotional as well as material scars.

8 We must not allow any sense of revenge, any spirit of greed, any grasping desire to overrule the fundamental principles of justice.
British prime minister David Lloyd George looks ahead to the peace conference, election speech, Nov. 1918; Peter Rowland *Lloyd George* (1975) p.463. Despite such pieties, the 'Welsh Wizard' successfully exploited the anti-German mood while campaigning for the UK general election (14 Dec.). His Conservative-dominated national coalition government romped to a massive victory.

9 The Germans, if this government is returned, are going to pay every penny; they are going to be squeezed as a lemon is squeezed – until the pips squeak. My only doubt is not whether we can squeeze hard enough, but whether there is enough juice.
Sir Eric Geddes, minister of transport in the coalition government, election speech to the Beaconsfield Club, Cambridge, 10 Dec. 1918; Nigel Rees *Cassell's Companion to Quotations* (1997) p.255.

10 Their troops had fought without arms or munitions; they had been outrageously betrayed by their Government, and it was little to be wondered at if, in their bitterness, the Russian people had rebelled against the alliance.
David Lloyd George, meeting in London with Clemenceau, Dec. 1918; David Lloyd George *The Truth About the Peace Treaties* (1938) Vol.1, p.321. Unlike Clemenceau and President Wilson, Lloyd George favoured inviting Russia to the peace conference.

11 A lot of impossible folk fighting among themselves. You cannot do business with them, so you shut them all up in a room and lock the door and tell them that when they have settled matters among themselves you will unlock the door and do business.

President Woodrow Wilson on Soviet Russia, autumn 1918; V.S. Mamatey *The United States and East Central Europe 1914–1918: A Study in Wilsonian Diplomacy and Propaganda* (1957) p.297. Russia would not be represented at the peace conference.

1 In the eyes of a Wilson, a Lloyd George, a Clemenceau, a Masaryk, a Beneš, a Venizelos, the flight of the Kaiser Wilhelm and the departure of the Emperor Charles completed the flight of Louis XVI … 1918 was a sort of European 1792.

Bertrand de Jouvenel *After the Defeat* (1941) p.7. A French political philosopher sees 1918 – a year in which multinational empires were succeeded by nation-states based on liberal democratic principles – as a bourgeois triumph. Tomáš Masaryk and Edvard Beneš were founding fathers of Czechoslovak nationalism; Masaryk was Czechoslovakia's first president and Beneš its first foreign minister and later president; Eleuthérios Venizelos was five times Greek prime minister; the Emperor Charles was Karl Franz Josef, last emperor of Austria-Hungary.

2 It was as if someone had picked up the world and shaken it into utter confusion. There were no permanent values. What were paper or diamonds, gold, houses or factories? A transient illusion, a fleeting gleam, a dissolving fantasy.

Polish-born, Jewish-American writer, Sholem Asch, on the post-war *Zeitgeist*; *The Calf of Paper* (1936) p.24.

REDRAWING THE MAP OF EUROPE: THE PARIS PEACE CONFERENCE, 1919

3 You hold in your hands the future of the world.

President Raymond Poincaré of France, 18 Jan. 1919, to delegates at the opening of the Paris Peace Conference; Margaret Macmillan *Peacemakers* (2001) p.71.

4 We were journeying to Paris, not merely to liquidate the war, but to found a new order in Europe. We were preparing not Peace only, but Eternal Peace. There was about us the halo of some divine mission. We must be alert, stern, righteous and ascetic. For we were bent on doing great, permanent and noble things.

Harold Nicolson *Peacemaking, 1919* (1964) pp.31–2. Nicolson, a British diplomat at the conference, remarked: 'How fallible one feels here! A map – a pencil – tracing paper. Yet my courage fails at the thought of the people whom our errant lines enclose or exclude, the happiness of several thousands of people' (Nicolson (1964) p.269).

5 Our unanimity was indeed remarkable. There – in what had been the *cabinets particuliers* [private dining rooms] of Maxim's – was elaborated an Anglo-American case covering the whole frontiers of Jugo-Slavia, Czecho-Slovakia, Rumania, Austria and Hungary. Only in regard to Greece, Albania, Bulgaria and Turkey in Europe did any divergence manifest itself. And even here the divergence was one of detail only, scarcely one of principle.

Harold Nicolson (1964) p.257. The unanimity did not extend to the French, however: Britain and France disagreed over the allocation of former Ottoman territory; France and the US were at odds over the terms for defeated Germany. By the end of Jan. 1919 Franco-US relations had degenerated to such an extent that President Wilson remarked to his doctor: 'the rank and file of the people of the United States had turned from being pro-French to being pro-British' (A.S. Link (ed.) *The Papers of Woodrow Wilson* Vol.56, pp.86–7).

6 He felt about France what Pericles felt of Athens – unique value in her, nothing else mattering; but his theory of politics was Bismarck's. He had one illusion – France; and one disillusion – mankind, including Frenchmen, and his colleagues not least.

John Maynard Keynes on Clemenceau; *The Economic Consequences of the Peace* (1919) Ch.3.

7 How can I convey to the reader any just impression of this extraordinary figure of our time, this syren, this goat-footed bard, this half-human visitor to our age from the hag-ridden magic and enchanted woods of Celtic antiquity.

John Maynard Keynes on Lloyd George; R.F. Harrod *The Life of John Maynard Keynes* (1951) p.257.

8 Like Odysseus, the President looked wiser when seated.

John Maynard Keynes on Wilson; Keynes (1919) Ch.3. Keynes's mythological allusion is to the ambassadorial visit of Odysseus and Menelaus to Troy to demand the peaceful return of Helen, a visit that was unable to prevent the Trojan War.

9 Why do the British have such sad faces and such cheerful bottoms?

Marshal Ferdinand Foch, after seeing dancing in the ballroom of the Hôtel Majestic, headquarters of the British empire delegation; E.J. Dillon *The Inside Story of the Peace Conference* (1920) p.31.

10 The moral atmosphere in Paris is not encouraging. All the small states out for more territory and France is not unnaturally in fear of a revived and vengeful Germany. My own view is that passion still runs too high to get a really enduring settlement now, but that if a Treaty *tel quel* is signed there will be an appeasement and by degrees readjustments and modifications can be introduced which will give Europe a prospect of stability.

The historian H.A.L. Fisher, who was in Paris during the conference, 1919; Martin Gilbert *The European Powers* (1965) p.92. An early use of the term 'appeasement', but used here in a non-pejorative sense (see 829:10). Fisher's was very much the British view; the French wanted the peace settlement enforced to the letter.

1 Germany ought to be deprived of all entrance and assembling grounds, that is of all sovereign territory on the left bank of the river [Rhine], that is, of all facilities for invading quickly, as in 1914, Belgium, Luxembourg, for reaching the coast of the North Sea and threatening the United Kingdom, for out-flanking the natural defences of France, the Rhine and the Meuse, conquering the Northern provinces and entering upon the Paris area.

Marshal Ferdinand Foch, memorandum to the conference, Jan. 1919; André Tardieu *The Truth about the Treaty* (1921) p.146.

2 The fact is the Germans are, and will continue to be, the dominant factor on the Continent of Europe, and no permanent peace is possible which is not based on that fact.

South Africa's prime minister General Jan Christiaan Smuts to Lloyd George, 17 March 1919; Sir Keith Hancock *Smuts: A Biography* Vol.1 (1962) pp.510–11. Smuts appears to accept German supremacy in Europe only months after victory in a war fought to destroy it.

3 I cannot conceive any greater cause of future war than that the German people, who have certainly proved themselves one of the most powerful and vigorous nations in the world, should be surrounded by a number of small states, many of them consist-ing of people who have never previously set up a stable government for themselves, but each of them containing large masses of Germans clamouring for reunion with their native land. The proposal of the Polish commission … must in my judgement, lead sooner or later to a new war in Eastern Europe.

David Lloyd George, memorandum to the Council of Four (the Conference's executive core: Lloyd George, Wilson, Clemenceau and the Italian premier, Vittorio Orlando), 25 March 1919; Gilbert (1965) p.225. The recommendations of the Polish commission included the transfer of the port of Danzig (Gdansk) to Poland, and a 'corridor' connecting Poland to the Baltic. At Lloyd George's insistence, Danzig – German-speaking but economically vital to the Poles – would become

a 'free city' under League of Nations supervision in the treaty. The fragmentation of the Austro-Hungarian empire created a power vacuum in central Europe, filled first by Hitler's Germany, then by Stalin's USSR.

4 You may strip Germany of her colonies, reduce her armaments to a mere police force and her navy to that of a fifth-rate power; all the same in the end if she feels that she has been unjustly treated in the peace of 1919 she will find means of exacting retribution from her conquerors.

David Lloyd George, from the 'Fontainebleau Memorandum' to the Council of Four, March 1919; Macmillan (2001) p.208. The memorandum, which proposed that Germany lose less territory than was demanded by the French – and in particular that Germany retain a demilitarized Rhineland – infuriated the French, who saw it as a volte-face.

5 What would be the outcome on the world if these French politicians were given a free hand and allowed to have their way and secure all that they claim France is entitled to? My opinion is that if they had their way the world would go to pieces in a very short while.

President Woodrow Wilson to Grayson, his doctor, April 1919; Link Vol.57 (1987) pp.50–51.

6 I obtained definitively the occupation of the Rhineland for fifteen years with a partial evacuation at five year intervals. Of course, in the case of Ger-many not observing the treaty, no partial evacuation, no final evacuation.

President Georges Clemenceau to Mordacq, 15 April 1919; Mordacq Vol.3 (1931) pp.220–21. France and the USA compromised on the Rhineland, agreeing to permanent demilitarization and temporary Allied occupation. The French cabinet approved the peace terms on 4 May. 'Observing the treaty' refers to the timely payment by Germany of war reparations (the financial indemnity the Allies would impose on Germany as part of the treaty; see 803:1), on which France's evacuation would depend.

7 We have now reached an impasse. The Italians say they won't sign the German Treaty unless they are promised Fiume and the whole Treaty of London. No one will give them Fiume and President Wilson won't give them Dalmatia, which he says would contravene the ethnical principle.

Maurice Hankey, British secretary to the Peace Conference, sums up the disagreement on the 'Adriatic question' that led to an Italian walkout in April 1919; *The Supreme Control at the Paris Peace Conference 1919* (1963) pp.115–16. The secret Treaty of London (April 1915) between Britain, France, Russia and Italy had promised Italy territorial gains in the Trentino, Istria and Dalmatia (at the expense of Austria) and Albania in return for Italy joining the Allies in World War I. The Italians now wanted the Istrian port of Fiume (Rijeka in Croatia) as well, but were denied this and other claims in Istria and Dalmatia by the Council of Four.

1 My God, my God! Italy or Yugoslavia? The blonde or the brunette?

President Georges Clemenceau to Orlando, 1919; V.E. Orlando *Memoirs 1915–1919* (1960) p.370. When (in Aug. 1919) Italy agreed that Fiume be given to Yugoslavia along with the whole of Dalmatia, a flamboyant Italian nationalist, Gabriele D'Annunzio, seized Fiume with a force of volunteers and established a maverick dictatorship (see 749:2). Italy and Yugoslavia settled their differences in the Treaty of Rapallo (Nov. 1920), which gave Istria to Italy and Dalmatia to Yugoslavia and made Fiume a free state. Italy forced D'Annunzio's surrender in Dec. 1920.

2 *Que voulez-vous que je fasse entre deux hommes dont un se croit Napoléon et l'autre Jésus Christ?* (What do you expect when I'm between two men of whom one thinks he is Napoleon and the other thinks he is Jesus Christ?)

President Georges Clemenceau to André Tardieu, referring, respectively, to Lloyd George and Woodrow Wilson, quoted in a letter from Nicolson to his wife, 20 May 1919; J. Lees-Milne *Harold Nicolson* (1980) Vol.1, Ch.7. Clemenceau was explaining why he gave in to Lloyd George at the peace conference.

THE TREATY OF VERSAILLES, 1919

3 The demand is made that we shall acknowledge that we alone are guilty of having caused the war. Such a confession in my mouth would be a lie.

Count Ulrich von Brockdorff-Rantzau, German foreign minister, inveighs against Article 231 of the treaty (see 803:1), 7 May 1919; Hajo Holborn 'Diplomats and Diplomacy in the Early Weimar Republic' in Gordon Craig and Felix Gilbert (eds) *The Diplomats 1919–1939* (1963) p.141. The German delegation had been summoned to the Trianon Palace Hotel in Versailles, where the principal peace terms were read to them by Clemenceau.

4 The worst act of world piracy ever committed under the flag of hypocrisy.

German banker Max Warburg on the treaty terms, May 1919; Macmillan (2001) p.475. The treaty was greeted with outrage in Germany. Wilson, once venerated, became an object of odium (when he died in 1924 the German embassy in Washington did not fly its flag at half-mast).

5 We do not deny the responsibility of those in power before and during the war, but we believe that all the great powers of Europe who were at war were guilty.

Max Weber and other German academics in response to the treaty terms, summer 1919; A. Luckau *The German Delegation at the Paris Peace Conference* (1971) p.47.

6 This is not peace. It is an armistice for twenty years.

Marshal Ferdinand Foch, May 1919; Alistair Horne *To Lose a Battle* (1990 edn) p.64. Foch, who boycotted the signing ceremony, told the *New York Times*: 'The next time, remember, the Germans will make no mistake. They will break through into northern France and seize the Channel ports as a base of operations against England' (P. Mantoux *The Deliberations of the Council of Four* Vol.2 (1992 trans.) p.473). See 829:8.

7 We came to Paris confident that the new order was about to be established; we left it convinced that the new order had merely fouled the old. We arrived as fervent apprentices in the school of President Wilson; we left as renegades.

Harold Nicolson (1964) p.187. There was soul-searching also in the American delegation, secretary of state Robert Lansing describing the terms as 'immeasurably harsh and humiliating' (Macmillan (2001) p.477). German counterproposals put forward on 29 May found some sympathy with Britain, but the sole concession to be wrung from the French was a plebiscite for Upper Silesia so that inhabitants could decide if they stayed with Germany or joined Poland.

8 '*Faites entrer les Allemands,*' says Clemenceau ... A hush follows.

Through the door ... appear two *huissiers* [ushers] with silver chains ... After them come four officers of France, Great Britain, America and Italy. And then, isolated and pitiable, come the two German delegates, Dr Müller, Dr Bell ... They are deathly pale. They do not appear as representatives of a brutal militarism. The one is thin and pink-eyelidded: the second fiddle in a Brunswick orchestra. The other is moon-faced and suffering: a *privat-dozent* [private tutor]. It is all most painful.

They are conducted to their chairs. Clemenceau at once breaks the silence. '*Messieurs,*' he rasps, '*la séance est ouverte.*' ... 'We are here to sign a Treaty of Peace.'

Harold Nicolson describes the moments before the signing of the Treaty of Versailles, 28 June 1919; J. Carey (ed.) *The Faber Book of Reportage* (1987) p.491. Hermann Müller was the new German foreign minister, Ulrich von Brockdorff-Rantzau having resigned as foreign minister and as head of the German delegation on 20 June.

9 ARTICLE 42: Germany is forbidden to maintain or construct any fortifications either on the left bank of the Rhine or on the right bank to the west of a line drawn 50 kilometres [30 miles] to the east of the Rhine …

ARTICLE 51: The territories which were ceded to Germany in accordance with the Preliminaries of Peace signed at Versailles on 26 February, 1871, and the Treaty of Frankfurt of 10 May, 1871 are restored to French sovereignty as from the date of the Armistice of 11 November, 1918. The provisions of the Treaties establishing the delimitation of the frontiers before 1871 shall be restored …

ARTICLE 81: Germany … recognizes the complete independence of the Czecho-Slovak State which will include the autonomous territory of the Ruthenians to the south of the Carpathians …

ARTICLE 87: Germany … recognizes the complete independence of Poland and renounces in her favour all rights and title over the territory bounded by the Baltic Sea, the eastern frontier of Germany as laid down in Article 27 of Part II (Boundaries of Germany) of the present Treaty.

Articles 42, 51, 81 and 87 of the Treaty of Versailles, relating to German territorial losses and Germany's relationship with the new nations of Central Europe; D. Sinclair *Hall of Mirrors* (2001) pp.432–5. In addition, Germany also lost small chunks of territory to Denmark and Belgium, while the Saarland was to be governed by an international commission for 15 years until a referendum was held to decide its future. Control of German colonies overseas passed to the Allies under the guise of mandates from the League of Nations (see 784:6).

1 ARTICLE 231: The Allied and Associated Governments affirm and Germany accepts the responsibility of Germany and her allies for causing all the loss and damage to which the Allied and Associated Governments and their nationals have been subjected as a consequence of the war imposed upon them by the aggression of Germany and her allies …

ARTICLE 235: In order to enable the Allied and Associated Powers to proceed at once to the restoration of their industrial and economic life, pending the full determination of their claims, Germany shall pay in such instalments and in such manner (whether in gold, commodities, ships, securities or otherwise) as the Reparation Commission may fix, during 1919, 1920, and the first four months of 1921, the equivalent of 20,000,000,000 gold marks.

Articles 231 and 235 of the Treaty of Versailles, dealing with war reparations; Sinclair (2001) pp.432–5. The 'full determination' of reparations would be fixed in 1921 at 132 billion marks (£6.6 billion). Article 231 is the notorious 'war guilt'

clause, a cause of profound anger and resentment in Germany. The wording of the clause was finalized by a young lawyer named John Foster Dulles, a future US secretary of state.

2 [Reparations] created resentment, suspicion and international hostility. More than anything else, they cleared the way for the Second World War.
A.J.P. Taylor *The Origins of the Second World War* (1961) p.71.

3 The military clauses of the Treaty … had to make do in place of the destruction of Bismarck's united Germany, and render it impossible for Germany to transform her overwhelming strength in people and industry into the equivalent in military might. These clauses suffered from a serious and dangerous drawback; they would not enforce themselves. On the contrary, the ability of the treaty to restrain German power depended entirely on the readiness of the victors to enforce it to the letter. Here was the difference between weakening a beast and chaining it down.
Correlli Barnett *The Collapse of British Power* (2002 edn) p.319. A modern historian's retrospective view of the treaty not as too severe but as insufficiently so.

4 Never has the substance of a treaty of peace so grossly betrayed the intentions which were said to have guided its construction as is the case with this Treaty.
Editorial of a left-wing Austrian newspaper, reacting to the terms of the treaty with Austria, June 1919; E. Howard *Theatre of Life: Life Seen from the Stalls 1905–1936* (1936) p.382. The Treaty of St Germain-en-Laye (Sept. 1919) gave the new Austrian state its present borders and an area one-eighth the size of the old Austria-Hungary. Many Austrians had hoped for *Anschluss* (Union) with Germany: they would get it in March 1938 (see 823:7).

5 ARTICLE 12: The Members of the League agree that, if there should arise between them any dispute likely to lead to a rupture they will submit the matter either to arbitration or judicial settlement or to enquiry by the Council, and they agree in no case to resort to war until three months after the award by the arbitrators or the judicial decision, or the report by the Council …

ARTICLE 16: Should any Member of the League resort to war in disregard of its covenants … it shall ipso facto be deemed to have committed an act of war against all other Members of the League, which hereby undertake immediately to subject it to the severance of all trade or financial relations, the prohibition of all intercourse between their nationals and the nationals of the covenant-breaking State, and the prevention of all financial, commercial or personal intercourse between the nationals of the covenant-breaking State and the nationals of any other State, whether a Member of the League or not.

It shall be the duty of the Council in such case to recommend to the several Governments concerned what effective military, naval or air force the Members of the League shall severally contribute to the armed forces to be used to protect the covenants of the League.

Articles 12 and 16 of the Treaty of Versailles; J.A.S. Grenville (ed.) *The Major International Treaties 1914–1973* (1974). At Wilson's urging, the Covenant of the League of Nations was made an integral part of the treaty. Created to preserve international peace and security, the League came into official being with 58 member-states on 10 Jan. 1920 but was weakened at the outset by the non-participation of the USA (see 808:4–809:2). It had successes in the arenas of social and economic affairs and international law (setting up the International Labour Organization and continuing the International Court of Justice, both of which function in a similar form today), but would fail in its primary political purpose of preventing future war. Its weapons, fatally for its avowed intentions, would be the blunt swords of sanctions and condemnation, rather than the sharp steel of threatened or actual military action.

1 Curious, I seem to hear a child weeping.

Caption to a cartoon by Will Dyson in the British *Daily Herald*, 29 June 1919; David Milsted *Chronicle of the 20th Century in Quotations* (1996) p.33. Clemenceau is the speaker. He stands outside the Palace of Versailles, and in the background is a child with a placard on which appear the words 'Class of 1940'.

2 One could not help feeling that in a moment all that has happened in the last fifty years was wiped away; the French soldiers were back again in the place where they used to be under the Monarchy and the Revolution; confident, quick, debonair, feeling themselves completely at home in their historical task of bringing a higher civilization to the Germans.

British military observer John Headlam-Morley records his thoughts on a visit to the occupied Rhineland, 1919; A. Headlam-Morley, R. Bryant and A. Cienciala (eds) *A Memoir of the Peace Conference 1919* (1972).

NEW NATIONS IN CENTRAL AND EASTERN EUROPE, 1919–23

3 If you ask me what is my native country, I answer: I was born in Fiume, grew up in Belgrade, Budapest, Pressburg [Bratislava in Slovakia], Vienna and Munich, and I have a Hungarian passport; but I have no fatherland. I am a very typical mix of old Austria-Hungary: at once Magyar, Croatian, German and Czech; my country is Hungary; my mother tongue is German.

The dramatist Odon von Horvath (1901–38); J. Rupnik *The Other Europe* (1988) p.41. The ethnic jigsaw of Eastern Europe, whose complexities were obscured behind the monolithic façades of multinational empires before World War I, risked becoming a tinderbox in the post-war context of newly independent ethnic-linguistic nation-states, each with their own competing territorial claims.

4 I am a Catholic of these parts.

Response by a peasant in an ethnically mixed region of what is now Belarus when asked by an outside investigator to state his nationality, c.1920; Norman Davies *White Eagle, Red Star, The Polish-Soviet War 1919–1920* (1972). An illustration of the difficulties of establishing identity on a basis of nationality in some parts of Central and Eastern Europe.

5 Who are the Slovaks? I can't seem to place them.

David Lloyd George, 1916; M.G. Fry *Lloyd George and Foreign Policy* Vol.1 (1977) p.255. By 1919 he had located them, and they had established the state of Czechoslovakia in combination with their fellow Slavs, the Czechs.

6 Filled now as ever with unchangeable love for my people I will no longer set my person as a barrier to their free development. I recognize in advance the decision which German-Austria will take on its future form of state. The people has now taken over the government through its representatives. I renounce any participation in the business of the state. Simultaneously, I relieve my government of office.

Emperor Charles I (Karl Franz Josef) of Austria-Hungary, last proclamation, 11 Nov. 1918; Gilbert (1965) p.197. Habsburg political power in Central Europe ends after six and a half centuries. An Austrian republic was declared the next day. The name German-Austria would be abandoned in the Treaty of St Germain-en-Laye (see 803:4), under whose terms Austria was forbidden to join with Germany.

7 I know your history. In your country you have oppressed those who are not Magyar. Now you have the Czechs, Slovaks, Rumanians, Yugoslavs as enemies; I hold these people in the hollow of my hand. I have only to make a sign and you will be destroyed.

General Louis Franchet d'Esperey, supreme commander of the Allied armies in the East, to Count Mihály Károlyi, head of the Hungarian government, in Belgrade, Nov. 1918; P. Azan *Franchet d'Esperey* (1949) pp.231–2. Károlyi handed over power in Jan. 1919 to Béla Kun's communist regime, which waged war on Czechoslovakia and Romania. The Romanians occupied Budapest from Aug. to Nov. 1919, after which the counterrevolutionary Admiral Horthy restored order and ruled as regent. By the Treaty of Trianon (June 1920) Hungary lost three-fifths of its former territory to Czechoslovakia, Romania and Yugoslavia, to become a 'Magyar rump' (Eric Hobsbawn *Age of Extremes* (1994) p.32). Hungary, co-ruler with Austria though the *Ausgleich* (Compromise) of 1867, had systematically persecuted its minorities. As the Hungarian prime minister said to his Austrian counterpart: 'You look after your Slavs, and we shall look after ours.'

1 It will be a turbulent nation as they are a turbulent people, and they ought not to have a navy to run amok with.
President Woodrow Wilson, arguing against allowing the new South Slav state (later known as Yugoslavia) its own navy, 1918; Link Vol.54 (from 1966) p.149. The Kingdom of Serbs, Croats and Slovenes, consisting of Serbia and the southern parts of the vanished Austria-Hungary, had been proclaimed by Prince Alexander of Serbia on 1 Dec. 1918. The USA recognized the new state in Feb. 1919; Britain and France did so in June.

2 We both took a ride on the same red tram, but while I got out at a stop marked *Polish Independence*, you wish to travel on to the station *Socialism*.
Josef Pilsudski, socialist-turned-Polish-nationalist, reacts to being greeted as 'Comrade' on his return to Warsaw after World War I; A. Zamoyski *Paderewski* (1982) p.178.

3 The Poles are developing an appetite like a freshly hatched sparrow.
H. Kessler, German emissary, Dec. 1919; *In the Twenties: The Diaries of Harry Kessler* (1971) p.23. After Pilsudski's Polish Legions had seized power from the German occupation forces, an independent Polish republic was declared on 11 Nov. 1918, with Pilsudski as head of state. Some Polish politicians used historical arguments to urge the re-creation of a greater Poland, embracing much of what is now Lithuania, Belarus and Ukraine. In April 1919 the Poles took advantage of the upheaval of the Russian Civil War to advance into Lithuania and Ukraine.

4 It fills me with despair the way in which I have seen small nations, before they have hardly leapt into the light of freedom, beginning to oppress other races than their own.
David Lloyd George, referring to the Poles' holding of eastern Galicia (a region of central Europe formerly belonging to Austria-Hungary) in the teeth of Ukrainian resistance, Dec. 1919; Macmillan (2001) p.236. The area was formally consigned to Poland in 1923.

5 How many members ever heard of Teschen? I do not mind saying that I have never heard of it.
David Lloyd George in the House of Commons, 1919; Nicolson (1964) p.25. Hostilities had broken out between Czechoslovakia and Poland over the status of Teschen (Cieszyn), a mineral-rich and ethnically mixed area of southern Silesia. The territory was divided between Poland and Czechoslovakia in July 1920. A plebiscite would divide Upper Silesia between Germany and Poland in 1921. Teschen was seized by Poland in the aftermath of Munich, Oct. 1938.

6 To the West! Over the corpse of White Poland lies the road to worldwide conflagration.
Marshal Mikhail Tukhachevsky, order to Bolshevik troops advancing on Warsaw, 4 July 1920; Norman Davies *God's Playground: A History of Poland* Vol.2 (1982) p.296. During 1919–20 Polish and Soviet armies fought a brutal war in the areas of Eastern Europe vacated by the German army. Tukhachevsky was to be a prominent victim of Stalin's purges in the 1930s (see 740:6–744:3).

7 If Charles Martel had not checked the Saracen conquest at the Battle of Tours, the interpretation of the Koran would now be taught at the schools of Oxford, and her pupils might demonstrate to a circumcised people the sanctity and truth of the revelation of Mahomet. Had Pilsudski and Weygand failed to arrest the triumphant advance of the Soviet Army at the Battle of Warsaw, not only would Christianity have experienced a dangerous reverse, but the very existence of Western civilization would have been imperilled. The Battle of Tours saved our ancestors from the yoke of the Koran: it is probable that the Battle of Warsaw saved Central, and parts of Western Europe from a more subversive danger – the fanatical tyranny of the Soviet.
Lord D'Abernon *The Eighteenth Decisive Battle of World History* (1931) p.49. D'Abernon was British ambassador in Berlin and a witness of the so-called 'miracle on the Vistula' of 15–16 Aug. 1920, in which Franco-Polish forces routed five invading Bolshevik armies. By Sept. 1920 Lenin was asking for peace. The Soviet–Polish Treaty of Riga (March 1921) fixed Poland's eastern border well beyond what the Allies would have wished. A.J.P. Taylor said of the Red Army's defeat: 'from that moment there was not the slightest prospect, during the next twenty years, that Communism would triumph anywhere in Europe beyond the Russian frontiers' (Taylor (1961) p.66). Maxime Weygand, Marshal Foch's chief of staff, was Pilsudski's military adviser; as chief of staff to the French army he would be the man responsible for the disastrous French strategy of 1940 (see 846:3).

8 If Poland had become Soviet, the Versailles treaty would have been shattered, and the entire international system built up by the victors would have been destroyed.
Lenin (Vladimir Ilyich Ulyanov), early 1920s; M.K. Dziewanowski *Joseph Pilsudski: A European Federalist*

1918–22 (1969) p.305. Like d'Abernon – if in language less florid – Lenin appreciates the wider significance of the Polish victory.

1 Our firmest guarantee against German aggression is that behind Germany, in an excellent strategic position, stand Czechoslovakia and Poland.
President Georges Clemenceau to the Council of Four, 1919; Taylor (1961) p.63. France made treaties with Poland (1921), Czechoslovakia (1924), Romania (1926) and Yugoslavia (1927) (the 'Little Entente') in an attempt to encircle post-war Germany, but the alliance was not formidable and Clemenceau's confidence was misplaced.

DISMANTLING THE OTTOMAN EMPIRE, 1919–27

2 The presence of the Turks in Europe has been a source of unmitigated evil to everybody concerned. I am not aware of a single interest, Turkish or otherwise, that during nearly 500 years has benefited by that presence. Indeed the record is one of misrule, oppression, intrigue and massacre, almost unparalleled in the history of the Eastern world.
Lord Curzon, minutes of a meeting of the British cabinet's Eastern Committee (of which Curzon was chairman), 23 Dec. 1918; *Curzon Papers*, India Office Library, F112/274. Compare Gladstone in 1876 (see 695:8).

3 Let it be a buffalo, let it be an ox, let it be any animal whatsoever; only let it come quickly.
Anon. inhabitant of Constantinople, praying for the swift creation of a successor state to the defeated Ottoman empire, c.1919; A. Ryan *The Last of the Dragomans* (1951) p.130.

4 The Turks are good workers, honest, in their relations, and a good people as subjects. But as rulers they are insupportable and a disgrace to civilization, as is proved by their having exterminated over a million Armenians and 300,000 Greeks during the last four years.
Eleuthérios Venizélos, Greek prime minister, to the Supreme Council of the Paris Peace Conference, Feb. 1919; *Papers Relating to the Foreign Relations of the United States: The Paris Peace Conference 1919* Vol.3, p.872. Venizelos proposed a greater Greece embracing southern Albania, two-thirds of the coast of western Anatolia, plus Greek-speaking Smyrna (Turkish Izmir, a seaport on the Aegean coast of Anatolia) and its hinterland. In the autumn of 1922, however, Turkey drove every Greek out of Anatolia (see 807:3). Its genocide of the Armenians took place in 1915.

5 President Wilson, M. Clemenceau and I decided today that you should occupy Smyrna.
David Lloyd George to Venizélos, 6 May 1919; M. Llewelyn Smith *Ionian Vision: Greece in Asia Minor, 1919–1922* (1973) p.79. The British military expert Sir Henry Wilson described the decision as 'mad and bad'; Curzon thought it was 'the greatest mistake that had been made in Paris' (J.A. Gidney *A Mandate for Armenia* (1967) p.113). The Greeks occupied Smyrna on 15 May.

6 We must pull on our peasant shoes, we must withdraw to the mountains, we must defend the country to the last rock. If it is the will of God that we be defeated, we must set fire to all our homes, to all our property; we must lay the country in ruins and leave it an empty desert.
Mustafa Kemal (later known as Kemal Atatürk) strikes a Churchillian note, June 1919; P.B. Kinross *Atatürk: A Biography of Mustafa Kemal, Father of Modern Turkey* (1964) p.671. While the Allies pondered how to carve up Asian Turkey, nationalists under Atatürk organized themselves politically and militarily. By the end of 1919 they controlled much of the Anatolian interior, and Atatürk had set up Ankara as a rival capital. The Treaty of Sèvres (Aug. 1920) between the Allies and the sultan's government, reduced Turkey's geographical area by concessions to Greece, the Kurds and the Armenians. Only Poincaré among the Allies alluded to the unfortunate connotations of signing a treaty in a Parisian suburb known for its exquisitely fragile porcelain. Atatürk's counterattack would smash Sèvres in pieces.

7 Our military intelligence had never been more thoroughly unintelligent.
David Lloyd George, referring to the surprise defeat by a Turkish nationalist army of a French force in southern Anatolia, 28 Feb. 1920; *Memoirs of the Peace Conference* Vol.2 (1939) p.830. Lloyd George had not known of the existence of Kemal's irregulars. British forces led an Allied occupation of Constantinople in mid-March.

8 Venizélos thinks his men will sweep the Turks into the mountains. I doubt it will be so.
Lord Curzon, now foreign secretary, to the British high commissioner in Constantinople, June 1920; M.L. Dockrill and J.D. Goold *Peace Without Promise: Britain and the Peace Conferences, 1919–1923* (1981) p.210. With Lloyd George's blessing, the Greeks had moved 250 miles inland from Smyrna by Aug.

9 It is perhaps no exaggeration to remark that a quarter of a million persons died of this monkey's bite.
Winston Churchill *The Aftermath: Being a Sequel to the World Crisis* (1941) p.386. On 25 Oct. 1920 the young Greek king, Alexander, died after being bitten by a monkey while walking in the grounds of his palace. Churchill's questionable, if memorably couched, contention was that had Alexander lived

and continued to rule Greece with Eleuthérios Venizélos (who was ousted in Greek elections the same year), the bloody outcome of the Greco-Turkish War of 1919–22 would have been averted.

1 Soldiers, your goal is the Mediterranean.

Kemal Atatürk, ordering a counterattack against the over-stretched Greeks, 26 Aug. 1922; Kinross (1964) p.354. When the Turks reached Smyrna on 10 Sept. they burned the city's Greek districts to the ground.

2 All day long I have been passing them, dirty, tired, unshaven, wind-bitten soldiers, hiking along the trails across the brown, rolling, barren Thrace countryside. No bands, no relief organizations, no leave areas, nothing but lice, dirty blankets, and mosquitoes at night. They are the last of the glory that was Greece. This is the end of their second siege of Troy.

Ernest Hemingway, reporting for the *Toronto Star*, describes the return to Europe of the defeated Greeks, Oct. 1922; Macmillan (2001) pp.462–3.

3 Hitherto we have dictated our peace treaties. Now we are negotiating one with the enemy who has an army in being while we have none, an unheard-of position.

Lord Curzon, on the signing of the Treaty of Lausanne between the Allies, Greece and Turkey, 24 July 1923; D. Gilmour *Curzon* (1994) p.556. Greece surrendered Smyrna and eastern Thrace, and the Greek population of Smyrna was exchanged for Turkish populations in Greece.

4 Gentleman, it was necessary to abolish the fez, which sat on the heads of our nation like a symbol of ignorance, negligence, fanaticism and hatred of progress and civilization, to accept in its place the hat, the headgear worn by the whole civilized world.

Kemal Atatürk to the Turkish assembly, Aug. 1927; Milsted (1996) p.41. Under Atatürk's dictatorship the new republic of Turkey, declared on 29 Oct. 1923, was forcibly and rigorously Westernized.

5 The greatest oil field in the world extends all the way up to and beyond Mosul, and even if it didn't we ought as a matter of safety to control sufficient ground in front of our vital oil-fields to avoid the risk of having them rushed at in the event of war.

Conservative politician Leo Amery, c.1919; J. Barnes and D. Nicholson (eds) *The Leo Amery Diaries* Vol.1 (1980) p.232. Mosul, part of Mesopotamia (Iraq), was occupied by British troops after World War I. France and Britain clashed over Mesopotamia's oil, just as they had clashed over Syria, but came to an agreement in Dec. 1919, with France accepting a share of the oil in return for allowing a pipeline to be built

from Mosul across Syria to the Mediterranean Sea. Mosul would be referred to the League of Nations by the Treaty of Lausanne (1923), which gave it to Iraq in 1925.

6 Oil, the blood of the earth, has become, in time of war, the blood of victory.

Henri Bérenger, French government minister responsible for energy, speaking at a conference on oil, 1918; Alan Furst *Blood of Victory* (2002).

7 The whole of it, and forever!

Following the French occupation of Damascus on 26 July 1920, the French premier Alexandre Millerand (who replaced Clemenceau in Jan.) proclaims that Syria will henceforth be French; D. Fromkin *A Peace to End All Peace* (1989) p.439. Faisal, the Arab prince who had assisted the Allies in their wartime Palestinian and Syrian campaigns and who had, with British blessing, been nominal ruler of Syria, was expelled and given Iraq in compensation. The French divided Syria into sub-units, one of which, called Greater Lebanon (proclaimed on 20 Aug. 1920 and including Beirut, Sidon, Tyre, Tripoli and the Bekaa Valley) was the predecessor of modern-day Lebanon.

THE LEAGUE OF NATIONS: CHAMPIONS AND CRITICS, 1916–29

8 Generally it appears to me that any such scheme is dangerous to us, because it will create a sense of security which is wholly fictitious … It [a league of nations] will only result in failure and the longer that failure is postponed the more certain it is that this country will have been lulled to sleep … in the course of time it will almost certainly result in this country being caught at a disadvantage.

Sir Maurice Hankey, British cabinet secretary, memorandum to Balfour, the foreign secretary, on the idea of a League of Nations, 1 May 1916; Barnett (2002 edn) p.245.

9 I do not myself believe that a European peace founded only on nationality, and without any other provisions, is likely to be desirable or even in all respects beneficial.

Lord Robert Cecil, c.1919; V.H. Rothwell *British War Aims and Peace Diplomacy 1914–1918* (1971) p.159. Minister of state at the Foreign Office and a rare British enthusiast for the League, Cecil helped to draft the League of Nations Covenant (see 803:5).

10 There must be a League of Nations and this must be virile, a reality, not a paper League.

President Woodrow Wilson, 1918; A. Willert *The Road to Safety: A Study in Anglo-German Relations* (1953) pp.152–3. The strength of Wilsonian rhetoric was not always matched by equivalent clarity of thinking on how the 'virility' of the League was to make itself felt.

1 When the President talks of 'self-determination' what unit has he in mind? Does he mean a race, a territorial area, or a community? … It will raise hopes which can never be realized. It will, I fear, cost thousands of lives. In the end it is bound to be discredited, to be called the dream of an idealist who failed to realize the danger until it was too late to check those who attempt to put the principle into force.

US secretary of state Robert Lansing *The Peace Negotiations: A Personal Narrative* (1921). Wilson would backtrack on the question of self-determination in a later speech to Congress: 'When I gave utterance to those words, I said them without the knowledge that nationalities existed, which are coming to us day after day' (H.W.V. Temperley (ed.) *A History of the Peace Conference of Paris* Vol.4 (1920–24) p.429).

2 While recognizing the right of national self-determination, we take care to explain to the masses its limited historic significance and we never put it above the interests of the proletarian revolution.

Leon Trotsky; Dziewanowski (1969) p.202. Internationalism Soviet-style: Russian imperialism in socialist guise.

3 I like the League, but I do not believe in it.

Georges Clemenceau on the League of Nations, *c.*1919; Lord Robert Cecil *A Great Experiment* (1941) p.59. French and British advocates of the League had differing views of its *raison d'être*: France regarded it as a bastion against future German aggression; for Britain it was a forum for the peaceful resolution of international disputes (or an innocuous talking shop).

4 I have loved but one flag and I cannot share that devotion and give affection to the mongrel banner invented for a league. Internationalism, illustrated by the Bolshevik and by the men to whom all countries are alike provided they can make money out of them, is to me repulsive. National I must remain, and in that way I like all other Americans can render the amplest service to the world. The United States is the world's best hope, but if you fetter her in the interests and quarrels of other nations, if you tangle her in the intrigues of Europe, you will destroy her power for good and endanger her very existence.

Senator Henry Cabot Lodge, speech to the US Senate, 12 Aug. 1919; *Congressional Record* Vol.58, pp.3778–84. Lodge, Republican chairman of the Senate Foreign Relations Committee, was the foremost opponent of US ratification of the League of Nations, and like other opponents he invoked George

Washington's warning that the United States should stand aloof from permanent alliances (see 662:7). Article 9, Sect.2 of the US Constitution gave the Senate power to approve or disapprove treaties entered into by the president.

5 At the front of this great Treaty is put the Covenant of the League of Nations. It will also be at the front of the Austrian treaty and the Hungarian treaty and the Bulgarian treaty and the treaty with Turkey. Unless you get the united, concerted purpose and power of the great Governments of the world behind this settlement, it will fall down like a house of cards. There is only one power to put behind the liberation of mankind, and that is the power of mankind. It is the power of the united moral forces of the world, and in the Covenant of the League of Nations the moral forces of the world are mobilized.

President Woodrow Wilson, speech at Pueblo, Colorado, 25 Sept. 1919; *The Papers of Woodrow Wilson* Vol.63 (1990) pp.502–3. Wilsonian idealism; Wilsonian rhetoric. Wilson insisted on the inclusion of the League of Nations Covenant in the individual peace treaties (see 803:5), only to see them for that very reason run into trouble with the US Senate. Already exhausted by his efforts in Paris, he embarked on a strenuous campaign to rally US opinion in their favour.

6 There seems to me to stand between us and the rejection or qualification of this treaty the serried ranks of those boys in khaki, not only these boys who came home, but those dear ghosts that still deploy upon the fields of France.

President Woodrow Wilson, 25 Sept. 1919; *The Papers of Woodrow Wilson* Vol.63 (1990) p.512. Wilson collapsed shortly after his Pueblo speech and later suffered a stroke that left him incapable of governing during the final year of his presidency.

7 If the League includes the affairs of the world, does it not include the affairs of all the world? … How shall you keep from meddling in the affairs of Europe or keep Europe from meddling in the affairs of America? … Mr President, there is another and even more commanding reason why I shall record my vote against this treaty. It imperils what I conceive to be the underlying, the very first principles of this Republic. It is in conflict with the right of our people to govern themselves free from all restraint, legal or moral, of foreign power.

Republican Senator William E. Borah (the 'Lion of Idaho'), 19 Nov. 1919; *Congressional Record*, Vol.58, pp.8781–4. Borah's impassioned cry, 'I cannot give my consent to exchange the doctrine of George Washington for the doctrine of Frederick the Great translated into mendacious phrases of peace,' struck a chord with many, and the Senate rejected the Treaty of Versailles and, with it, US entry into the League. Instead of joining the League, the United States reverted to its traditional isolationism (see 822:7–823:6).

1 The League exists as a foreign agency. We hope it will be helpful. But the United States sees no reason to limit its own freedom and independence by joining it.

President Calvin Coolidge, 6 Dec. 1923; Milsted (1996) p.36. After the nebulous idealism of Wilson, the terse pragmatism of 'Silent Cal'.

2 We had a perfect right to refuse to enter into the treaty … Nevertheless, President Wilson … was our negotiator; he was our agent; he was the only one to whom the nations of Europe could look to ascertain what would be satisfactory to the people of the United States. When the League was completed, when we refused to become a member of it, and Europe was left with an incomplete organization, left without the support of the most populous and richest and most potentially powerful nation whose name was written into the covenant; when Europe was left with that incomplete organization to deal with the world parties that were set loose by the adjustment of territory and of sovereignty under the Treaty of Versailles, what would we naturally have said, what would any gentleman have said to another who had been brought into such an untoward condition by his representative and agent?

Senator Elihu Root, speech, *New York Times*, 28 Dec. 1926. Root's speech went on to lament what he saw as American failure to support the League's undertakings: 'Has there ever been an exhibition by America of friendship or sympathy with the League and its work? … We, the great peace-loving people, what have we done to help in this wonderful new work? No sympathy, no moral support, no brotherhood.'

3 My offensive equipment being practically *nil*, it remains for me to fascinate him with the power of my eye.

Caption to a cartoon entitled 'Moral Suasion', lampooning the impotence of the League of Nations, *Punch*, July 1920; *The Guinness Encyclopedia of World History* (1992) p.183. The words are those of a frightened-looking rabbit representing the League, confronted by the snake of 'International Strife'. The League had no armed force of its own, but depended on concerted action by its most powerful member-states (Britain and France) to impose its authority – what became known as 'collective security'.

4 The League is not a military or economic unit and possesses no central executives. It is a society of

sovereign states … I doubt whether the League as a League could declare war or wage war. The force would have to be supplied by each state separately, of its own deliberate will … The question is whether … the various Parliaments and Governments will … have sufficient loyalty to the League … to be ready to face the prospect of war not in defence of their own frontiers or immediate national interests, but simply to defend the peace of the world.

Gilbert Murray *The Ordeal of this Generation: The War, the League and the Future* (1929) p.91. The distinguished scholar and pro-Leaguer identifies the impotence at the heart of the League.

INTERNATIONALISTS AND PRAGMATISTS: INTERNATIONAL RELATIONS, 1921–9

5 Britain: two million unemployed. France: excessive military costs and a decrease in the birth rate. Spain: troubles in Morocco and a vast deficit. Italy: border disputes and weak currency … The Balkans: political confusion … Turkey: depression from ten years of war. Poland: currency problems and internal conflicts. Russia: economic collapse, epidemic and hunger … And Germany? In the middle of it lies the carrier of the infection, Germany, which has been inoculated with the pestilential bacillus of Versailles. No one wishes to administer the necessary antidote, yet everyone wonders why they can hear a death rattle all over Europe.

From an article describing the 'illnesses of Europe' in *Berliner Illustrierte* (a German news magazine), 1923; J. Weitz *Hitler's Diplomat: Joachim von Ribbentrop* (1992) p.33.

6 The sword must be kept sharp.

General Hans von Seeckt, order of the day to the new *Reichswehr*, 1921; Barnett (2002 edn) p.277. The *Reichswehr*, the army of the Weimar Republic, was limited by the Versailles Treaty to 100,000 men, though retaining in its title the name of the imperial Reich. Von Seeckt's injunction reflects the enduring militarism of German traditionalists such as himself.

7 Our policy is frankly the re-establishment of Germany as a stable state in Europe … any idea of obliterating Germany from the comity of nations or treating her as an outcast is not only ridiculous but insane.

Lord Curzon, British foreign secretary, speaking at the Imperial Conference, 1921; *British Cabinet Papers* 32/2 Pt 1 E-4. Britain was anxious to enfold Weimar Germany in a diplomatic embrace; the French remained profoundly apprehensive of a German revival.

1 The German Reich and the Russian Socialist Federal Soviet Republic mutually agree to waive their claims for compensation for expenditure incurred on account of the war, and also for war damages, that is to say, any damages which may have been suffered by them and by their nationals in war zones on account of military measures.

From Article 1(a) of the Treaty of Rapallo, signed by Walther von Rathenau, German foreign minister, and People's Commissar Chichin of the USSR, 16 April 1922; J.A.S. Grenville (ed.) *The Major International Treaties 1914–1973* (1974). The 'outcasts' of Versailles mutually cancelled pre-war debts, renounced war claims and agreed to cooperate on economic matters. Rapallo also paved the way for secret agreements between the German high command and its Russian counterpart that enabled the *Reichswehr* to manufacture munitions and carry out training in violation of the Treaty of Versailles. It was an instance, like the later Nazi–Soviet Pact (see 828:3), of the partnership of two revisionists overriding ideological differences. The agreement would be reinforced by the Treaty of Berlin (April 1926).

2 Germany is a tramp – out of a job, hungry, poorly clothed and desperate. It is for us to decide whether he will become a citizen or an I.W.W.

Captain Eddie Rickenbacker, 4 Jan. 1923; Lloyd C. Gardner *Imperial America* (1976) p.109. The implied concern is that an economically devastated Germany will turn Bolshevik. For the IWW (Industrial Workers of the World) see 648:4.

3 The Boers were not treated as moral pariahs and outcasts. Decent human relationships were re-established and a spirit of mutual understanding grew up … South Africa today is perhaps the most outstanding witness in the realm of politics to the value of a policy of give and take, of moderation and generosity, of trust and friendship, applied to the affairs of men.

General Jan Christiaan Smuts, speech, Oct. 1923; Hancock (1962) p.135. Citing the supposedly benign effects of British magnanimity to the Boers as a precedent (see 693:2), South Africa's premier urges diplomatic generosity towards Germany.

4 Our attitude can only be the attitude of saying that anything done to disrupt the German Reich or the German state meets with our emphatic disapproval.

Lord Curzon, speaking at the Imperial Conference, 1923; in *British Cabinet Papers* 32/9 E-13. In 1923, when Germany defaulted on reparations payments, the French occupied the industrial Ruhr to forcibly extract the payments Germany had failed to make. The British, who did not join the Franco-

Belgian occupying forces, condemned the move. To add to its economic woes Weimar Germany was now shaken by communist and nationalist uprisings and, in the Rhineland, by separatist movements encouraged by the French, who were pressing for the dismemberment of Germany they had failed to achieve at Versailles.

5 I believe that the execution of the Dawes Plan is necessary … If it failed because American bankers would not aid, we should have, in my judgment, not only chaotic conditions abroad but a feeling of deep despair.

US secretary of state Charles Evans Hughes, 19 Sept. 1924; Herbert Feis *The Diplomacy of the Dollar* (1950) p.42. Devised by the US banker Charles G. Dawes, the Dawes Plan aimed to create a more realistic schedule for reparations payments by Germany – which had fallen into default – by providing loans to enable Germany to make its annual payments. The plan stabilized the German economy in the 1920s and was replaced in 1929 by the Young Plan, which radically reduced the total amount of reparations.

6 A restless and aggressive power, full of energy, and somewhat like the Germans in mentality … Japan is not at all an altruistic power.

Lord Curzon on Japan, 1921; Barnett (2002 edn) p.250. The notion of Japan as a 'yellow Prussia' had begun to spread in the West. Britain's alliance with Japan dated back to 1902.

7 The strategic position of Japan has been greatly strengthened as a result of the Naval Treaty.

Lord Curzon, speaking at the Imperial Conference, 1923; *British Cabinet Papers* 32/9. In the Washington Treaty (Feb. 1922) the ratio of tonnage of battleships and battlecruisers was laid down as 5:5:3 between the fleets of the USA, Britain and Japan. The Anglo-Japanese Alliance was abrogated and replaced by a four-power treaty concluded between Japan, Britain, France and the USA, aiming at the maintenance of the status quo in the Pacific. As part of the agreement, the signatories agreed not to fortify and construct new bases with the exception of Singapore. The Nine-Power Treaty (1922) multilateralized America's 'Open Door' policy towards China, the signatories agreeing to respect China's territorial integrity and independence and to maintain the principle of open and equal access for all nations to China's markets.

8 A war with Japan! But why should there be a war with Japan? I do not think there is the slightest chance of it in our lifetime.

Winston Churchill, letter, 15 Dec. 1924; K. Middlemass and J. Barnes *Baldwin: A Biography* (1969) p.327. The chancellor of the exchequer ridicules Admiralty fears of Japanese naval strength and British powerlessness in the Far East. The Conservative government had decided to build a naval base in Singapore in the autumn of 1923, but its construction would not be completed until 1938.

1 The least idealist nation in the world, and the most realist, watches, waits, plans, and despite all her dynastic catastrophes and changes of political form, remains after the war more identical with what she was before it than any other nation in Europe.
Brigadier General J.H. Morgan, 1924; A.C. Murray *Reflections on Some Aspects of British Foreign Policy Between the Wars* (1946) p.10. From 1920s Britain a rare note of caution about German power.

2 The draft of the constitution of a European family within the orbit of the League of Nations ... the beginning of a magnificent work, the renewal of Europe.
Aristide Briand, French prime minister, initials the Locarno Treaties, Switzerland, 16 Oct. 1925; M. Mazower *Dark Continent* (1998) p.111. The treaties, signed by Britain, France, Belgium, Italy and Germany, guaranteed Germany's frontiers with France, Belgium and Holland and were intended to remove the potential causes of a Franco-German war. They were followed by Germany's admittance to the League in 1926. Locarno did not address the question of Germany's other borders, with Austria, Czechoslovakia and Poland.

3 We have a peculiar interest because the true defence of our country, owing to scientific development, is now no longer the Channel ... but upon the Rhine.
Austen Chamberlain, British foreign secretary, speech to the Imperial Conference in the light of the Locarno Treaties, 1926; *British Cabinet Papers* 32/46 E-8. Note the focus on Western not Eastern Europe, where Britain had few interests. See Baldwin (816:11).

4 You can have no conception how profoundly pacific our people are now.
Austen Chamberlain to the British ambassador to China, 1926; *The Life and Letters of Sir Austen Chamberlain* (1939) p.367.

5 We do not wish to put ourselves in the power of the United States. We cannot tell what they might do if at some future date they were in a position to give us orders about our policy, say, in India, Egypt, or Canada, or on any other great matter behind which their electioneering forces were marshalled.
Winston Churchill, 20 July 1927; Martin Gilbert (ed.) *Companion Volume to the Years 1922–1939* p.1033. Written at the time of the Anglo-American row over naval disarmament at the Geneva conference of 1927.

6 The high contracting parties solemnly declare in the names of their respective peoples that they condemn recourse to war for the solution of international controversies, and renounce it as an instrument of national policy in their relations with one another.
Kellogg–Briand Pact, Article 1, signed in Paris, 27 Aug. 1928; J.A.S. Grenville (ed.) *The Major International Treaties 1914–1973* (1974) p.108. The pact, outlawing aggressive war, was signed by 64 countries, including Italy, Germany, Japan and the USSR. Frank B. Kellogg, US secretary of state (1925–9), was awarded the Nobel Peace Prize for his work on the pact, though it did nothing to prevent the descent into international anarchy in the 1930s. France had wanted a US guarantee of its frontier with Germany, but an isolationist America was not prepared to give it.

7 So sublime that it should be called transcendental.
Benito Mussolini, Italian Fascist dictator, speech to the Italian Chamber of Deputies mocking the Kellogg–Briand Pact, 1928; R.J.B. Bosworth *Mussolini* (2002) p.245.

8 I think that among peoples constituting geographical groups, like the peoples of Europe, there should be some kind of federal bond ... Obviously, this association will be primarily economic, for that is the most urgent aspect of the question ... Still, I am convinced that this federal link might also do useful work politically and socially, and without affecting the sovereignty of any of the nations belonging to the association.
Aristide Briand, speech to the Assembly of the League of Nations, 5 Sept. 1929; Davies (1996) p.951. France's idealist foreign minister proposes European union *avant la lettre* in a speech often seen as the moment of conception for what became the European Union.

9 [He] really was persuaded that 'our true nationality is mankind' ... he really did believe that men were naturally good, that they could be brought into line though they looked like horses at the starting gate for ever facing opposite ways and savaging each other ... In short and in his own words he held that we were eternally moving in a great surge towards righteousness.
Robert Vansittart on James Ramsay MacDonald, British prime minister in 1924 and from 1929 to 1935, *The Mist Procession* (1958) pp.373–4. Vansittart, permanent secretary at the British Foreign Office, was deeply anti-German and sceptical to a degree on the subject of internationalism.

10 I gave and gave and gave until my followers turned against me ... If they could have granted me just one concession, I would have won my people. But they gave nothing ... That is my tragedy and their crime.
Gustav Stresemann, foreign minister of Weimar Germany, 1929; Horne (1990 edn) p.65. Evidence of the continuing diplomatic gulf between Germany and France in the post-war

period, despite Stresemann's policy of *rapprochement*. The moderate Stresemann, negotiator of Germany's entry to the League of Nations and winner of the Nobel Peace Prize in 1926 with Aristide Briand for their work on the Locarno Treaties (see 811:2), died in 1929.

1 The most generous gesture in French history.

André Tardieu, French prime minister, June 1930, on what he hoped would be Germany's perception of the quitting of the Rhineland by French troops in 1930 (the Versailles Treaty had originally imposed a 15-year Allied occupation); R. Binion *Defeated Leaders* (1960) p.299.

2 The statesmen who dominated the international system in the 1920s shared a common set of assumptions which could be traced ... back to the world of imperialism and economic rivalry which they had been brought up in before 1914 ... The year 1918 had been a dividing-line of sorts, but not a decisive one. In many cases diplomacy was still dominated by ... small specialized elites ... They all shared the view that the international system was dominated by a small group of great powers, and that the desirable course was to establish, by agreement if possible, some sort of balance between them.

Richard Overy *The Origins of the Second World War* (1987) pp.5–6.

3 For much of the 1920s international affairs were conducted in a sort of vacuum. Britain and France achieved a predominance quite out of proportion to their real strengths because of the temporary unwillingness or inability of the other powers to intervene decisively in world politics. The great-power system was played with only two of the major states fully committed to maintaining it.

Richard Overy (1987) pp.7–8.

4 It turned out that the dollar *in the amounts in which it was made available and linked to an inadequate foreign policy*, could not counteract or control certain basic and historic forces. It could not, for example, change the low birth rate in France, which made that country yielding, or the high birth rate in Japan, which made that country crowded and restless. Nor could it wipe out that sense of frustration, envy, and hatred, which again turned Germany into an aggressor.

Herbert Feis *The Diplomacy of the Dollar* (1950) pp. 65–6. Feis is not dismissing US economic foreign policy in the 1920s, as he makes clear in the italicized section. He writes at the time of the Marshall Plan for Europe (see 811:2), when US government money (not private loans) was injected into Europe on a massive scale to stabilize it against the perceived threat of communist subversion. If government aid on that scale had been furnished in the 1920s, he believes, the chaos of the 1930s could have been prevented. As he writes: 'When the smash [of 1929] came it was heard round the world. The German Republic fell into the ruins and Hitler rose from them' (p.45).

The Road to War, 1929–39

NEW WEAPONS, NEW TACTICS

1 The tactic is brutally simple: spearhead tanks move forward ... smashing all obstacles, reducing houses to rubble: motorized infantry, supporting artillery follow them, taking advantage of the path they have carved out; the enemy forward lines, caught unawares, are soon broken and the fast armoured penetration dashes on to bring victory, just as the cavalry did in the past.
General Estienne, 1921. A French disciple of Liddell Hart (see 814:1) outlines some of the features of what would later be known as *Blitzkrieg* (lightning war). Pétain's policy (see 813:2), however, dominated French military thinking until the mid-1930s.

2 Tanks assist the advance of the infantry, by breaking static obstacles and active resistance put up by the enemy.
Marshal Philippe Pétain, 1921; Alistair Horne *To Lose a Battle* (1990 edn) p.79. A view of the tank as having a purely supportive role in warfare.

3 Cavalry will never be scuppered to make room for the tanks: in the course of time cavalry may be reduced as the supply of horses in this country diminishes. This depends greatly on the life of fox-hunting.
Journal of the RUSI (Royal United Services Institution), Feb. 1921.

4 A people who are bombed today as they were bombed yesterday, and who know that they will be bombed again tomorrow and see no end of their martyrdom, are bound to call for peace at length.
General Giulio Douhet *The Command of the Air* (1921). Douhet's theories persuaded Mussolini that air power was the key weapon of the future and would help swing the balance of power in the Mediterranean in Italy's favour.

5 [The] foundations of the Maginot Line were the war cemeteries of France.
Anon.; V. Rowe *The Great Wall of France: The Triumph of the Maginot Line* (1959) p.16. The Maginot Line was a system of fortifications built along France's industrialized border from Switzerland to Luxembourg between 1929 and 1936 under the direction of the French war minister, André Maginot. It cost an estimated 7 billion francs and was a dangerous delusion – some French officers jocularly dismissed it as the 'Imaginot Line'. It was not continued along the Belgian frontier

after 1936 because the Belgians withdrew from alliance with France on 6 March, the day before Hitler's troops marched into the Rhineland (see 818:8). Consequently, when the Germans attacked France in May 1940, their main thrust went past the northern end of the line. Though they did mount a ground attack on the line, it was not breached.

6 The number of our capital ships is now so reduced that should the protection of our interests render it necessary to move our ships to the East, insufficient vessels of this type would be left in Home Waters to ensure the security of our trade and territory in the event of any dispute arising with a European power.
Admiral of the Fleet Sir Frederick Field, April 1931; *British Cabinet Papers* 27/476. The effects of nearly ten years of the Washington Treaty (see 810:7). The London Naval Treaty (April 1930) had extended the moratorium on the building of new capital ships until 1936 and also applied it to cruisers.

7 For major military liabilities, such as might arise under the Covenant of the League of Nations or the Treaty of Locarno, we are but ill-prepared ... We alone among the Great Powers ... have neglected our defences to the point of taking serious risks.
British army chief of staff, annual review, 1932; *British Cabinet Papers* 53/22. British rearmament began in 1935.

8 I think it is well also for the man in the street to realize that there is no power on earth that can prevent him from being bombed. Whatever people may tell him, the bomber will always get through ... The only defence is in offence, which means that you have to kill more women and children more quickly than the enemy if you want to save yourselves.
British prime minister Stanley Baldwin, 10 Nov. 1932; *H.C. Deb.* Vol.270, Col.632. No doubt Baldwin knew his words would be published on Armistice Day.

9 Morale is more important in winning battles than weapons. Continuously repeated, concentrated air attacks, have the most effect on the morale of the enemy.
Colonel Wolfram von Richthofen; Piers Brendon *The Dark Valley* (2000) p.334. Von Richthofen was chief of staff of the German Condor Legion that fought on the Nationalist side in the Spanish Civil War (see 821:6).

10 *Achtung – Panzer!* (Beware – Tanks!)
The ominous title of Heinz Guderian's 1937 book on mobile warfare, which contained what amounts to a blueprint for the

Blitzkrieg campaign, led by Guderian himself as commander in chief of the Panzer divisions during the invasion of France in spring 1940. It was not translated into English before the outbreak of war.

1 It was principally the books and articles of the Englishmen, Fuller, Liddell Hart and Martel, that excited my interest and gave me food for thought. These far-sighted soldiers were even then trying to make of the tank something more than an infantry support weapon. They envisaged it in relation to the growing motorization of our age and thus they became pioneers of a new kind of warfare on a massive scale.
Heinz Guderian *Panzer Leader* (1952). Basil Liddell Hart, ignored by the British War Office in the early 1920s, became something of a cult figure in the late 1930s, when his preoccupation with the threat of air warfare, allied to his perception that land battles were best left to Britain's European allies, influenced British strategy.

LEBENSRAUM AND THE DRANG NACH OSTEN: THE SEEDS OF NAZI EXPANSIONISM, 1924–33

2 The foreign policy of a *völkisch* state must first of all bear in mind the obligation to secure the existence of the race incorporated in this State ... Only a sufficiently large space on this earth can ensure the independent existence of a nation.
Adolf Hitler outlines his belief in the need for *Lebensraum* (living space) in *Mein Kampf* (1925; 1969 trans.); Jeremy Noakes and Geoffrey Pridham (eds) *Nazism 1919–45* Vol.3 (2001 edn) p.6.

3 We National Socialists have intentionally drawn a line under the foreign policy of pre-war Germany. We are taking up where we left off six hundred years ago. We are putting an end to the perpetual German march towards the South and West of Europe and turning our eyes to the land in the East ... When we speak of new land in Europe today we must principally bear in mind Russia and the border states subject to her.
Adolf Hitler (1925; 1969 trans.); Noakes and Pridham Vol.3 (2001 edn) p.7. He envisages a German 'drive to the east' (*Drang nach Osten*) and the settling of ethnic Germans in Eastern Europe. In fact, there was continuity with the geo-politics of the empire; after the failure to smash France in 1914, the main German thrust was against Russia until Russia was forced out of the war in March 1918 (see 729:4).

4 England does not want Germany to be a world power, but France does not want Germany to exist at all ... England does not want a France whose military fist, unobstructed by the rest of Europe, can undertake a policy which one way or the other, must one day cut across English interests ... And Italy too cannot and will not want a further reinforcement of France's position of superior power in Europe. On the coldest and soberest reflection it is at the present time primarily these two states, England and Italy, whose most natural selfish interests are not, at any rate essentially, opposed to the German people's requirements for existence and are indeed to some extent identified with them.
Adolf Hitler (1925; 1969 trans.); Noakes and Pridham Vol.3 (2001 edn) p.8. Hitler's francophobia was at its height following French occupation of the Ruhr in 1923 (see 810:4). He went on advocating closer German ties with Italy and Britain: his first foreign-policy moves after taking power in 1933 were attempts to secure Germany's position by means of bilateral agreements with those two countries.

5 In any conflict involving Germany, regardless on what grounds, regardless for what reasons, France will always be our adversary.
Adolf Hitler, c.1928; T. Taylor (ed.) *Hitler's Secret Book* (1962) p.128. Hitler's so-called 'Second Book' restated the ideas of *Mein Kampf* but also expressed worries about France's system of strategic alliances in Eastern Europe (see 806:1). The destruction of this system became a key facet of Nazi foreign policy after 1933.

6 Overcoming Marxism and its consequences until they have been completely exterminated. The creation of a new unity of mind and will for our people.
Adolf Hitler to Colonel Walther von Reichenau, 4 Dec. 1932; Noakes and Pridham Vol.3 (2001 edn) p.8. The first of five 'tasks for the future' for Germany, listed by Hitler on the eve of taking power. Von Reichenau, a *Reichswehr* officer with Nazi sympathies, rose to high rank as one of the *Wehrmacht*'s senior commanders.

7 Academic ingenuity has discovered in these pronouncements the disciple of Nietzsche, the geopolitician, or the emulator of Attila. I hear in them only the generalizations of a powerful, but uninstructed intellect; dogmas which echo the conversation of any Austrian café or German beerhouse.
A.J.P. Taylor *The Origins of the Second World War* (1961) p.98. The British historian argues against the view of Hitler as systematic strategist; see 819:9.

THE SLUMP AND THE BREAKDOWN OF INTERNATIONAL DIPLOMACY, 1929–32

1 Then the field will be cleared for the appearance of a Mussolini, and it is almost certain that the army will rally to his support.

A far-sighted journalist in the *Japan Advertiser*, 17 Dec. 1927, on the likely effects of a future economic depression on Japan. US trade with Japan in the 1920s had promoted a prosperity that had damped down the Japanese expansionists seeking an empire in China. The crash of 1929 (see 764:12–767:6) shattered not only Japanese agriculture and industry but also Japanese liberalism. In Japan, as in Germany, the slump would bring to the fore radical nationalists who began to look for answers to domestic economic problems in expansionist foreign policies.

2 A virtual declaration of economic war on the rest of the world.

The historian Richard Hofstadter on the protectionist Smoot–Hawley tariff bill, signed by President Hoover on 17 June 1930, *The American Political Tradition* (1971 edn) p.302. The legislation, intended to help those hit by the Depression, increased import duties on agricultural produce and manufactured goods. European nations retaliated: France manipulated its currency in an attempt to remain competitive abroad, while Britain abandoned its commitment to free trade, introducing the protectionist system of 'imperial preference' in 1932. The isolationist and protectionist climate fuelled the growth of fascist movements that favoured economic independence on nationalist grounds.

3 [If] the world crisis of 1931 may be regarded as comparable to the World War of 1914, then the failure of the *Credit-Anstalt* at Vienna … may be taken as the analogue to the murder of the Archduke Ferdinand at Sarajevo.

Arnold Toynbee in A.J. Toynbee (ed.) *Survey of International Affairs 1931* (1932) p.58. The collapse of the Credit-Anstalt, Austria's largest bank, rocked Europe's financial system. The response of US President Herbert Hoover was to offer a year-long moratorium on the payment of war debts, but this offered only temporary relief.

4 It is a publicly acknowledged fact that our national situation has reached an impasse, that there is no way of solving the food, population and other important problems, and that the only path left open to us is the development of Manchuria and Mongolia.

Lieutenant Colonel Ishiwara Kanji, c.1931; P. Duus (ed.) *The Cambridge History of Japan* Vol.7 (1988) p.292. Ishiwara, a nationalist zealot in the Japanese army garrisoned in Kwantung, southern Manchuria, leased to Japan following the Russo-Japanese War of 1905, was one of the instigators of the 'Mukden Incident'.

5 The first blast in a war that would go on for nearly 15 years and culminate in the atomic holocausts of Hiroshima and Nagasaki.

Piers Brendon (2000) p.182. A modern historian describes the import of the 'Mukden Incident' of 18 Sept. 1931. Having engineered a confrontation with local Chinese forces via a deliberate act of sabotage on the South Manchuria Railway, the Kwantung army went on to occupy Manchuria on its own initiative. The League of Nations denounced the invasion and appointed a commission of enquiry under Lord Lytton, whose report (Oct. 1932) explored the setting up of a regime in Manchuria that safeguarded Japanese economic rights. But in Feb. 1932 Japan, which hereafter fell increasingly under the control of its military, proclaimed Manchuria as the puppet state of Manchukuo. The League failed to expel Japan, and Japan announced its withdrawal from the League in March 1933. The impotence of the League had been starkly underlined.

6 The very people … who have made us disarm … are urging us forward to take action. But where will action lead us to? If we withdraw ambassadors, that is the first step. What is the next, and the next? If you enforce an economic boycott you will have war declared by Japan and she will seize Hong Kong and Singapore and we cannot, as we are placed, stop her. You will get nothing out of Washington but words, big words, but only words.

Stanley Baldwin, lord president of the Council, letter, 27 Feb. 1932; Middlemass and Barnes (1969) p.729. Britain's stance was basically pro-Japanese: alarmed at the growth of Chinese nationalism, it saw its old ally Japan as a force for regional stability. See 823:3.

7 [France has] virtually attained the very thing that we have traditionally sought to avoid in Europe, hegemony, if not dictatorship, political and financial.

Sir Robert Vansittart, permanent secretary at the British Foreign Office, 1932; D. Reynolds *Britannia Overruled: British Policy and World Power in the Twentieth Century* (1991) p.118. Evidence of the coolness of Anglo-French relations, even on the eve of Hitler's coming to power. They would remain cool until well into the 1930s.

8 The more I study the face of a German cavalry officer, the more I admire his horse.

French prime minister Édouard Herriot to the British foreign secretary, Sir John Simon, at the Lausanne Conference, July 1932; J. Simon *Retrospect* (1952) p.188. Herriot is referring to Franz von Papen, the German chancellor, who negotiated a final reduction of Germany's war debts at the conference. By Jan. 1933 Germany's chancellor would be (in von Papen's words) a 'Bohemian corporal', who would be even less to Herriot's taste.

FACING THE DICTATORS, 1933–6

1 That this house refuses in any circumstances to fight for King and Country.
Motion for debate in the Oxford Union, 9 Feb. 1933; David Milsted *Chronicle of the 20th Century in Quotations* (1996) p.61. The motion was carried by 275 to 153.

2 Thank God for the French army.
Winston Churchill in the House of Commons, 23 March 1933; Horne (1990 edn) p.66. Hitler had proclaimed the Third Reich on 15 March 1933.

3 Fascism means war.
Left-wing writer and politician John Strachey, *The Menace of Fascism* (1933).

4 I fear War more than Fascism.
Vera Brittain *Diary of the Thirties 1932–1939: Chronicle of Friendship* (1986) p.256. Brittain, a socialist, campaigned against British rearmament, which began in 1935.

5 Herr Hitler is certainly not devoid of ideals … he undoubtedly desires to re-inculcate the old German virtues of loyalty, self-discipline and service to the State … Herr Hitler will win support which may be very valuable to him if he will genuinely devote himself to the moral and economic resurrection of his country.
The Times, July 1933; Martin Gilbert *The European Powers* (1965) p.192.

6 The idea started off as a boy; the English tried to turn it into a hermaphrodite; while, in the hands of the French, it would become nothing but a girl.
Benito Mussolini to the German ambassador, 1933, referring to his Four-Power Pact; R.J.B. Bosworth *Mussolini* (2002) p.274. The pact (between Italy, Germany, France and Britain) was signed on 15 July 1933 but never ratified. Mussolini's attempt to seize the diplomatic initiative with the new Germany was a blatant attempt to return to old-style 'Great Powers' diplomacy.

7 The German people and their government are deeply humiliated by the deliberate refusal of a real, moral and actual equality to Germany.
Adolf Hitler, withdrawing from disarmament talks in Geneva, 14 Oct. 1933; Milsted (1996) p.52. Britain and Italy had pressed for equality of armaments between the powers, while France had attempted to make equality of armaments dependent on a further period of German disarmament. Germany left the League of Nations at the same time.

8 After a silence, a brief moment of anguish, to the astonishment of the party and union leaders, this encounter triggered a delirious enthusiasm, an explosion of shouts of joy. Applause, chants, shouts of 'Unity, Unity' … the Popular Front had just been born before our eyes.
Anon. witness of the meeting of socialist and communist demonstrators during a one-day strike in Paris in protest against Nazism, 12 Feb. 1934; H.R. Lottman *The Left Bank* (1982) p.78. The term 'Popular Front' appeared for the first time in *L'Humanité* (the French communist newspaper) on 12 Oct. 1933. Hitherto, communists throughout Europe had been under orders from Stalin to wage political war on socialists. The advent of Hitler brought them together in the face of a common enemy.

9 France will henceforth assure her security by her own means.
Louis Barthou, French foreign minister, 17 April 1934; Taylor (1961) p.107. Taylor remarks acidly: 'The French had fired the starting pistol for the arms race. Characteristically they then failed to run it.'

10 It is my will, and the indomitable will of the German people, that Austria become an integral part of the Reich!
Adolf Hitler to Mussolini, 15 June 1934, during a meeting in which Mussolini insisted on continued independence for Austria; Milsted (1996) p.52. Konstantin von Neurath, the German foreign minister, describing the first meeting between Hitler and Mussolini, remarked, 'Their minds didn't meet; they didn't understand each other' (Noakes and Pridham Vol.3 (2001 edn) p.54), while Mussolini described Hitler as 'a mad little clown' (Milsted (1996) p.52). Following an abortive Austrian Nazi coup in Vienna in July 1934, in which the Austrian chancellor, Dollfuss, was assassinated, Mussolini ordered 40,000 Italian troops to the Austrian border.

11 The greatest crime to our own people is to be afraid to tell the truth … Since the day of the air, the old frontiers are gone. When you think about the defence of England you no longer think of the chalk cliffs of Dover; you think of the Rhine. That is where our frontier lies.
Stanley Baldwin, 30 July 1934; *H.C. Deb.* Vol.292, Col.2339. Compare Austen Chamberlain in 1926 (811:3).

12 In the years that are coming, there is more reason to fear for Germany than to fear Germany.
The Times, July 1934; Taylor (1961) p.106. Anti-communism was the mainspring of *The Times*'s sympathetic attitude to Germany and its territorial claims, an attitude that endured until the late 1930s.

13 I renounce war and never again will I support or sanction another.
The 'peace pledge' of the Rev. Dick Sheppard, pacifist and canon of St Paul's Cathedral, London; Milsted (1996) p.61. On

16 Oct. 1934 Sheppard published a letter in the *Manchester Guardian* inviting people to send him a postcard with the above undertaking. More than 100,000 Britons had done so by 1936.

1 How can we still believe in the offensive when we have spent thousands of millions to establish a fortified barrier? Would we be mad enough to advance beyond this barrier upon some doubtful adventure?

General Maurin, French minister of war, Chamber of Deputies, 15 March 1935; Horne (1990 edn) p.33. A telling revelation of France's defensive posture of the mid-1930s: Maurin was attacking proposals for the establishment of an armoured corps. Hitler would announce German rearmament, and the creation of a new peacetime German army of 36 divisions, the following day, having leaked the existence of the *Luftwaffe* to the British press on 10 March. The 'barrier' is the Maginot Line (see 813:5).

2 These feeble creatures can't give us any trouble. Perhaps the Abyssinians caught them young.

Benito Mussolini, describing the British delegation at the Stresa Conference (see 817:8), April 1935; L.S. Amery *My Political Life* Vol.3 (1955) p.166. The 'creatures' in question were Ramsay MacDonald and his appeasing foreign secretary Sir John Simon. The implication is that the British have, politically speaking, been castrated, as the Italians had literally been at Adowa in 1896 (see 692:6). MacDonald was seeking to use Italy as a counter to Nazi Germany and did not challenge Mussolini's increasingly bellicose attitude towards Abyssinia (Ethiopia).

3 I never saw a better dressed fool.

Benito Mussolini on the well-tailored Anthony Eden, British minister for League of Nations affairs, spring 1935; Brendon (2000) p.271. Eden had travelled to Rome in an abortive attempt to reach a territorial compromise with Mussolini on Abyssinia.

4 The Pope! How many divisions has he got?

Joseph Stalin to the French prime minister, Pierre Laval, 13 May 1935; Winston Churchill *The Second World War* Vol.1 (1949 edn) Ch.8, p.121. Laval had asked Stalin to make concessions to Russian Catholics.

5 It is utterly inconceivable that Christ could be the pilot of a bombing aeroplane.

Canon Charles Raven, pacifist clergyman, 1935; M. Ceadel *Pacifism in Britain 1914–1945: The Defining of a Faith* (1980) p.205.

6 An agreement must be reached between the two great Germanic peoples through the permanent elimination of naval rivalry. One will control the sea, the other will be the strongest power on land. A defensive and offensive alliance between the two will inaugurate a new era.

Adolf Hitler, directive to the negotiators who signed an Anglo-German naval agreement, 18 June 1935; A. Kuhn *Hitler's Foreign Policy Programme* (1970) p.168. The agreement, permitting Germany to build a navy up to 35% the size of Britain's as well as the same number of submarines, was signed by Britain without reference to its partners in the 'Stresa Front' (see 817:8). Hitler described the day of the agreement as 'the happiest day of my life' (*The Ribbentrop Memoirs* (1954) p.54).

7 It is a cardinal requirement of our national and Imperial security that our foreign policy should be so conducted as to avoid the possible development of a situation in which we might be confronted simultaneously with the hostility of Japan in the Far East, Germany in the West and any power on the main line of communications between the two.

Report of the British Defence Requirements Committee, 1935; Richard Overy *The Origins of the Second World War* (1987) p.18. The avoidance at all costs of simultaneous challenges in three main areas of strategic importance – Europe, the Mediterranean and India – was the essence of British strategy in the 1930s.

8 Stresa is dead.

Benito Mussolini to von Hassell, German ambassador in Rome, 27 Jan. 1936; Noakes and Pridham Vol.3 (2001 edn) p.61. The Stresa Conference of April 1935 between Britain, France and Italy had had the aim of forming a common front against Germany following Hitler's announcement in March 1935 that Germany would not be bound by the limitations imposed upon its armaments by the Treaty of Versailles (see 802:3–804:2).

ITALY IN ABYSSINIA, 1935–6

9 I think for Italy as the great Englishmen who have made the British Empire have thought for England.

Benito Mussolini, speech, July 1935; *The Times*, 1 Aug. 1935.

10 For 40 years, Italy has desired to conquer our country, but Abyssinia knows how to fight to the last man to preserve the country's independence. Italians, fortified though they may be by all modern weapons, will yet see how a poor but united people will defend their country and their emperor.

Abyssinian emperor Haile Selassie (the 'Lion of Judah'), speech to the Abyssinian parliament, 18 July 1935; Milsted (1996) p.62. Italian forces invaded Abyssinia from the Italian colony of Eritrea on 3 Oct. and soon destroyed the primitive capability of Abyssinia's resistance.

1 Cannot this eleventh hour be so used as to make it unnecessary to proceed further along the unattractive road of economic action against a fellow member, an old friend, and a former ally?

British foreign secretary Sir Samuel Hoare, speech in the House of Commons, 22 Oct. 1935; *H.C. Deb.* Vol.305, Col.32. Hoare opposed League of Nations proposals for economic sanctions against Italy for its invasion of Abyssinia. Some sanctions would be applied, but they omitted an oil embargo, which would have stopped Italy in its tracks.

2 I shall be but a short time to-night. I have seldom spoken with greater regret, for my lips are not yet unsealed. Were these troubles over I would make a case, and I guarantee that not a man would go into the Lobby against us.

Stanley Baldwin, 10 Dec. 1935; *H.C. Deb.* Vol.307, Col.856. On 18 Dec. Baldwin forced Hoare to resign for agreeing the Hoare–Laval Pact with the French premier Pierre Laval. The pact, which recognized Italy's right to keep its gains in Abyssinia, provoked outrage when it was made public. Hoare's supporters rightly protested that Hoare had adhered to government policy in agreeing to the pact and was sacked only when it proved unpopular.

3 I still have in mind the spectacle of a little group [of Ethiopian cavalry] … blooming like a rose when some of my fragmentation bombs fell in their midst. It was great fun and you could hit them easily.

Vittorio Mussolini, Italian air force pilot and son of the Duce, Feb. 1936; T.M. Coffey *Lion by the Tail* (1974) p.234. On 1 Jan. 1936 Haile Selassie remarked: 'Italy proceeds on her barbarous way with impunity' (Brendon (2000) p.277).

4 Do the peoples of the world not realize that by fighting on until the bitter end I am not only performing my sacred duty to my people, but standing guard in the last citadel of collective security.

Haile Selassie to *The Times* correspondent in Addis Ababa, spring 1936; A.J. Toynbee (ed.) *Survey of International Affairs 1935* Vol.2 (1936) p.356. A pertinent reference to the supposed basic purpose of the League of Nations, whose credibility was fatally undermined by the weakness of the European democracies in the face of Italian aggression. Selassie left his capital and went into exile on 2 May 1936.

5 Italy has her empire. It is a Fascist empire because it bears the indestructible sign of the will and power of Rome.

Benito Mussolini, speech in Rome, 9 May 1936; Milsted (1996) p.65. Italian forces had entered Addis Ababa a few days before. On a pavement in the centre of Rome one can still see the inscription *L'Italia ha finalmente il suo impero* (At last Italy has her empire). Mussolini had committed 650,000 troops to subduing Abyssinia.

6 It is us today. It will be you tomorrow.

Haile Selassie leaves the platform after addressing the League of Nations, Geneva, June 1936; L. Mosley *Haile Selassie: The Conquering Lion* (1964) p.241.

7 The League of Nations no longer condemns the fascist acts of aggression; the League 'notes', the League 'does this and this', the League 'deplores' – the League makes a hypocritical show of balancing between the criminal and his victim … Even more intolerable are the lies concealed in these formulae, and what can be read between the lines: the League's confession of impotence, its abject surrender, its acceptance of the *fait accompli*.

Léon Blum, French prime minister, *New York Times*, 2 July 1936. Mussolini agreed, saying 'the League is a farce' (Brendon (2000) p.282). Blum is transferring the guilt: the League was effectively its two most powerful Western members, Britain and France, and it was they who bore the responsibility for failing to stand up to Italy.

THE BERLIN–ROME AXIS AND THE ANTI-COMINTERN PACT, 1936

8 In accordance with the fundamental right of a nation to secure its frontiers … the German government has today restored the full and unrestricted sovereignty of Germany in the demilitarized zone of the Rhineland.

Adolf Hitler, 7 March 1936; Nuremberg Document 46-TC. Angered by the Franco-Soviet Pact of Feb. 1936 and claiming that Germany's borders were threatened by France, Hitler sent 22,000 German troops into the Rhineland on 7 March 1936, in defiance of Article 43 of the Treaty of Versailles. The force of 22,000 was small, German rearmament being in its infancy, and both Hitler and the *Wehrmacht* were nervous, though they had no need to be.

9 After all, they are only going into their own backgarden.

Lord Lothian (Philip Kerr), March 1936, on the German march into the Rhineland.

10 Well, there we are. I see there is nothing to be done.

Pierre-Etienne Flandin, French foreign minister, on the German re-militarization of the Rhineland, March 1936; P. Reynaud *In the Thick of the Fight* (1955) p.129. General Gamelin, the French army commander-in-chief, exaggerated the size of the German army and warned that French military action in response to the occupation would lead to general mobilization. Thus, in the words of a modern British historian, 'Hitler got away with his first and most desperate gamble' (Horne (1990 edn) p.84).

1 The Revolution in pearl-grey gloves.

Anon. description of the French socialist leader Léon Blum; J. Colton *Léon Blum: Humanist in Politics* (1974 edn) p.59. Blum formed a Popular Front ministry of centre and left-wing parties on 4 June 1936. Contemporary satirists mocked his dandified appearance, while anti-Semites in the French chamber of deputies told the Jewish Blum to 'go back to Jerusalem' (James Joll *Intellectuals in Politics* (1960) p.5).

2 Thanks for paid holidays.

Note said to have been found in the pocket of a suit sent to the cleaners by Léon Blum after his return to France from a German concentration camp in 1945; Gilbert (1965) p.164. In response to a wave of strikes in May and June 1936, Blum's Popular Front government had introduced a 40-hour working week and paid holidays, nationalized the Bank of France and introduced programmes of public works.

3 The majority of the National [Conservative and National Labour] Party are at heart anti-League and anti-Russian and what they would really like would be a firm agreement with Germany and possibly Italy by which we would purchase peace at the expense of the smaller states.

Harold Nicolson, diary entry, 16 July 1936; Nigel Nicolson (ed.) *Diaries and Letters* (1966) p.263.

4 Do you really think that I will allow myself to be photographed shaking hands with a negro?

Adolf Hitler, summer 1936; Duff Hart-Davis *Hitler's Olympics* (1988) p.38. The Führer was responding to a proposal by Hitler Youth leader Baldur von Schirach that he be photographed with Jesse Owens, the black American sprinter and winner of four gold medals at the Berlin Olympic Games.

5 Our German neighbours have ascribed to themselves a teutonic type that is fair, long-headed, tall and virile. Let us make a composite picture of a typical Teuton from the most prominent exponents of this view. Let him be as blond as Hitler, as dolichocephalic as Rosenberg, as tall as Goebbels, and as manly as Streicher. How much would this resemble the German ideal?

Julian Huxley and A.C. Haddon *We Europeans: A Survey of 'Racial' Problems* (1936) p.13. Hitler was dark-haired; Alfred Rosenberg did not possess the supposedly archetypal Teutonic head; the dwarfish Joseph Goebbels did not measure up to heroic Aryan proportions; while the brutish Julius Streicher had the reputation of a gross sexual deviant. Dolichocephalic means 'having a long or narrow head', perceived by some as a characteristic of the typical Anglo-Saxon.

6 This policy should aim resolutely at keeping us apart from the quarrels of our neighbours.

Leopold III, king of the Belgians, revokes the Franco-Belgian Treaty, 14 Oct. 1936, returning his country to neutral status.

France's Maginot Line defensive strategy begins to unravel, for France was now unable to enter neutral Belgium in the event of war or to build the line alongside the Belgian frontier.

7 Ribbentrop, bring me England into the Anti-Comintern Pact. That is my greatest wish! I have sent you as the best horse in my stable. See what you can do ... But if all efforts come to nothing, well then I'm prepared for war, though I'd regret it a lot, but if it has to be ... But I believe it would be a short war and I'd offer generous terms to England, an honourable, mutually acceptable peace. Then I'd still want England to join the Anti-Comintern Pact. Ribbentrop, you hold all the trumps. Play them well.

Adolf Hitler briefs Joachim von Ribbentrop, who was posted to London as German ambassador, Oct. 1936; J. Weitz *Hitler's Diplomat* (1992) p.111. Ribbentrop would court pro-Nazi, right-wing circles in British society in pursuit of Hitler's aim of an Anglo-German, anti-communist alignment. On 25 Nov. 1936 Germany and Japan signed the Anti-Comintern Pact, dedicated to 'to protect European culture and civilization and world peace from the Bolshevik menace' (Milsted (1996) p.64). Italy joined the pact a year later.

8 This vertical line between Rome and Berlin is not a partition, but rather an Axis around which all the European states animated by the will to collaboration and peace can also collaborate ... With the agreement of 11 July there disappeared any element of dissension between Berlin and Rome.

Benito Mussolini, speech at Milan, 1 Nov. 1936, referring for the first time to a Berlin–Rome 'Axis'; Royal Institute of International Affairs *Documents on International Affairs, 1936* (1937) pp.345–6. The 'agreement of 11 July' was an agreement between Germany and Austria, by which Austria agreed to pursue a pro-German foreign policy in return for German recognition of Austrian independence.

9 German policy had to reckon with two hate-inspired antagonists, Britain and France, to whom a German colossus ... was a thorn in the flesh.

Germany's problem could only be solved by means of force, and this was never without risk ... There still remain the questions of 'when' and 'how'. In this matter, there were three cases to be dealt with:

Case 1: the period 1943–5. After this date only a change for the worse, from our point of view, could be expected ... If the *Führer* was still living, it was his unalterable determination to resolve Germany's problem of space by 1943–5 at the latest.

Case 2: if internal strife in France should absorb the French completely, then the time for action against the Czechs had come.

Case 3: If France is so ambivalent in war that she cannot proceed against Germany … our first objective, if embroiled in war, must be to overthrow Czechoslovakia and Austria simultaneously.

Part of the Hossbach Memorandum, a minute of a strategy meeting attended by Hitler, Goering, and senior German ministers and military chiefs, 5 Nov. 1937, and written up by Colonel Friedrich Hossbach, Hitler's military adjutant; Noakes and Pridham Vol.3 (2001 edn) p.77. The memorandum, cited at the Nuremberg Tribunal as evidence of Hitler's having planned to wage offensive war, was famously dismissed as evidence of forward planning by A.J.P. Taylor: 'Hitler's exposition was in large part day-dreaming … he did not reveal his innermost thoughts. The memorandum tells us what we know already, that Hitler (like every other German statesman) intended to become the dominant Power in Europe. It also tells us that he speculated how this might happen. His speculations were mistaken' (Taylor (1961) pp.169–71).

'TOTAL AND RUTHLESS WAR': THE SPANISH CIVIL WAR, 1936–9

1 The fall of the monarchy gave me a greater shock than any fall from a pony.

Polo tutor of Alfonso XIII of Spain on his pupil's abdication, 14 April 1931; Raymond Carr The Spanish Tragedy (1977) p.28. After the collapse of the regime led since 1923 by Alfonso's ally, Miguel Primo de Rivera, the king left the country and a republican administration was set up under Niceto Alcala Zamora. The Spanish Second Republic (1931–9) saw increasing political disorder and polarization between left and right.

2 A vote for the conservative candidate is a vote for Christ.

Bishop of Barcelona, during the general election, Feb. 1936; J. Alvarez de Vayo Freedom's Battles (1940) p.13. The Popular Front of left-wing parties won the election, introducing agrarian and other reforms that aroused the opposition of the landlords and the Catholic church.

3 Spain is in anarchy, and we are today present at the funeral service of democracy.

José María Gil Robles, leader of the centre-right Catholic alliance, in the Cortés, June 1936; R. Fraser Blood of Spain: The Experience of the Civil War 1936–1939 (1979) p.90. The months following the Popular Front's victory saw an explosion of interfactional violence.

4 All over Spain the sky is cloudless.

General Emilio Mola, coded broadcast message signalling the start of the Nationalist uprising that began the civil war, 18 July 1936; Ivan Maisky Spanish Notebooks (1966) p.40. The uprising began with a military rebellion in Spanish Morocco, after which fighting spread to cities on the Spanish mainland. Maisky was Soviet ambassador to Britain at the time.

5 ¡No pasarán! (They shall not pass!)

Dolores Ibárruri (La Pasionaria), radio broadcast from Madrid, 19 July 1936, reacting to the Nationalist insurgency; Speeches and Articles 1936–38 (1938) p.7. Ibarurri, the Basque founder of the Spanish Communist Party who had helped establish the Popular Front government, was known as 'La Pasionaria' (the passion flower), a pen name under which she wrote for left-wing newspapers. Her words, echoing the French slogan used at Verdun in 1916 (see 714:3), swiftly entered revolutionary folklore.

6 It may be that the system of parliamentary Government which suits Great Britain suits few other countries besides. Recent Spanish governments have tried to conform to the parliamentary type of republican democracy, but with scant success.

The Times, 10 Aug. 1936. Slavish defence of British non-intervention in the Civil War, the British government having proposed a five-power declaration of neutrality on 4 Aug. British and French neutrality in the face of German and Italian military support for the insurgents meant that the USSR was the only power to give military aid to Republican Spain.

7 It is necessary to spread an atmosphere of terror. We have to create an impression of mastery.

General Emilio Mola, summer 1936; Anthony Beevor The Spanish Civil War (1982) p.77. Nationalist execution squads were particularly active in the early months of the war, and Republicans retaliated in kind.

8 I fired two bullets into his arse for being a queer.

Anon. Falangist executioner of the poet and dramatist Federico García Lorca, shot without trial in Granada on 19 Aug. 1936; Carr (1977) p.123.

9 Just a lot of bloody dagoes killing each other.

Randolph Churchill (son of Winston) describing what he claimed was the British view of the Civil War; A. Lunn Spanish Rehearsal (1937) p.43.

10 Il vaut mieux mourir debout, que vivre à genoux! (It is better to die on your feet than to live on your knees!)

Dolores Ibárruri, addressing a pro-Republican rally in Paris, L'Humanité (the French communist newspaper), 4 Sept. 1936. She also addressed the democracies: 'It is Spain today, but it may be your turn tomorrow' (Alexander Werth Destiny of France (1937) pp.383–4). Compare Haile Selassie 818:6.

11 ¡Viva la muerte! (Long Live Death!)

The motto of the Spanish Foreign Legion, coined by its founder General Millán Astray; Paul Preston Comrades! Portraits from the Spanish Civil War (1999) p.31. The cult of death appalled and fascinated the many writers and artists who travelled to Spain to fight for the Republic.

1 This is the temple of the intellect and I am its high priest. It is you who profane its sacred precincts. You will win [*vencereis*] but you will not convince [*no convencereis*]. You will win because you have more than enough brute force; but you will not convince, because to convince means to persuade. And to persuade you need something that you lack: reason and right in the struggle.

Basque philosopher Miguel de Unamuno, rector of the University of Salamanca, 12 Oct. 1936, speaking at a celebration of the anniversary of Columbus' 'discovery' of America; Preston (1999) p.30. The elderly Unamuno's words were directed at General Millán Astray, the henchman of Franco and a maimed and sinister veteran of Spain's colonial wars, with whom he became embroiled in an incendiary public altercation. Unamuno was probably only saved from lynching by Astray's toughs by the fact that Franco's wife was on the platform next to him.

2 Waiters and shop-walkers looked you in the eye and treated you as an equal. Servile and even ceremonial forms of speech had temporarily disappeared. Nobody said '*Señor*' or '*Don*' or even '*Usted*'; everyone called everyone else 'Comrade' and 'Thou', and said '*Salud!*' instead of '*Buenos días*' ... Practically everyone wore rough working-class clothes, or blue overalls or some variant of the militia uniform. All this was queer and moving. There was much in it that I did not understand, in some ways I did not even like it, but I recognized it immediately as a state of affairs worth fighting for.

George Orwell describes the revolutionary mood in Barcelona, late 1936; *Homage to Catalonia* (1938) pp.8–9. In some parts of Spain the right-wing insurgency triggered exactly the kind of social revolution it had been intended to prevent.

3 I will destroy Madrid rather than leave it to the Marxists.

Francisco Franco y Bahamonde, Oct. 1936; Beevor (1982) p.139. General Mola unwittingly coined a new phrase when he famously boasted that Nationalists were encircling Madrid with four columns and that he had a 'fifth column' of secret supporters working for him inside the city. In the bombing of Madrid, Nov. 1936, Franco's forces used Junkers and Savoia-Marchetti bombers supplied, respectively, by Nazi Germany and Fascist Italy.

4 The armies marching on Madrid, Barcelona and Valencia are also marching against London, Paris and Washington.

Republican radio broadcast during the Battle of Madrid, 1936; R. Colodny *Struggle for Madrid* (1958) p.145. Other Republican broadcasts described Madrid as 'the universal frontier that separates liberty and slavery' (Hugh Thomas *The Spanish Civil War* (1990 edn) p.481).

5 In a civil war, a systematic occupation of territory, accompanied by the necessary purges, is preferable to a rapid defeat of the enemy armies, which in the end leaves the country still infested with enemies.

Francisco Franco y Bahamonde to the Italian chief of staff following the Italian Fascists' failure to take Republican Guadalajara; J.F. Coverdale 'The Battle of Guadalajara, 8–22 March 1937' in *Journal of Contemporary History* Vol.9 (Jan. 1974) p.70.

6 Most of Guernica's streets began or ended at the Plaza. It was impossible to go down many of them, because they were walls of flame. Debris was piled high ... I moved round the back of the Plaza among survivors. They had the same story to tell: aeroplanes, bullets, bombs, fire.

Within twenty-four hours, when the grim story was told to the world, Franco was going to brand these shocked, homeless people as liars. So-called British experts were going to come to Guernica, when the smell of burnt human flesh had been replaced by petrol dumped here and there among the ruins by Mola's men, and deliver pompous judgements: 'Guernica was set on fire wilfully by the Reds.'

Noel Monks, 1937; J. Carey (ed.) *The Faber Book of Reportage* (1986) p.521. On 26 April 1937 the German Condor Legion, a *Luftwaffe* detachment of 150 aircraft under General Hugo Sperrle sent by Hitler to assist Franco, carpet-bombed the Basque town of Guernica for three hours, wreaking terrible destruction and killing more than a thousand people. World opinion, informed through *The Times* and the *New York Times* on 28 April, was horrified; democratic governments reacted pusillanimously; Hitler noted the success of the massed aerial bombardment; and Franco's GHQ claimed the town had been destroyed by its Republican defenders as they withdrew. It was only in 1999 that the Spanish government finally admitted that Franco had lied about Guernica.

7 No, *you* did.

Pablo Picasso's almost certainly apocryphal response to a Gestapo officer who, when visiting the artist's Paris studio in World War II, looked at the canvas of his painting *Guernica* and asked 'Did you do that?'; Ian Crofton *Brewer's Curious Titles* (2002) p.198. Picasso's stark and monochromatic depiction of the events of 26 April, now in Madrid, has since become an icon of modern art.

8 By a tragic coincidence this war, essentially Spanish, has 'caught on' abroad ... Spain is thus suffering vicariously the latent civil war which Europe is – so far – keeping in check.

The writer and diplomat Salvador de Madariaga, writing on the anniversary of the rebellion that began the Civil War, *The Times* 19 July 1937.

1 [I am] delighted that the Italians should be horrifying the world by their aggressiveness for a change, instead of charming it by their skill at playing the guitar.

Benito Mussolini, on the Italian bombing of Barcelona, March 1938, which caused international outrage; Malcolm Muggeridge (ed.) *Ciano's Diary 1937-1938* (1952) p.92. The Italian foreign minister Count Galeazzo Ciano commented: 'This will send up our stock in Germany ... where they love total and ruthless war' (Beevor (1982) p.227). By now the Nationalists had captured most of Catalonia and had cut Republican Spain in two.

2 The place stank of dead and decomposing bodies ... Shells screamed directly overhead as we lay against the rock wall of a terrace; some dropped ten, twenty metres away. As dark came, enemy began to use tracer bullets in rifles and machine-guns, and shelled the hillside methodically ... Bullets were always in the air; the reddish and pink tracer bullets seemed to move slowly and weirdly. Sounds of men screaming '*Socorro, socorro!*' ('Help, help!') and groaning '*Madre*', kept us up all night.

Anon. member of the International Brigades (the international volunteer force that fought on the Republican side), diary entry; Brendon (2000) p.345. He is describing the Nationalist bombardment near Gandesa during the Battle of the Ebro (July–Nov. 1938), an abortive Republican counter-offensive and the last and bloodiest operation of the civil war.

3 You can go with pride. You are history. You are legend. You are the heroic example of the solidarity and universality of democracy ... We shall not forget you, and, when the olive tree of peace puts forth its leaves, entwined with the laurels of the Spanish Republic's victory – come back!

Dolores Ibárruri says farewell to the International Brigades, Barcelona, 29 Oct. 1938; Preston (1999) p.304. The Spanish prime minister Juan Negrín had proposed the withdrawal of the Brigades in the hope that it might prompt British and French intervention on the side of the Republic. It did not.

4 Among the first soldiers in the history of the world who really knew what they were fighting for.

Alvah Bessie, an American who fought with the International Brigades; V. Brome *The International Brigades* (1965) p.34. In their ranks had fought French, Britons, Germans and Austrians, Poles, Ukrainians, Italians, Americans, Czechs, Yugoslavs, Hungarians, Scandinavians and Russians.

5 Spain's desired Catholic victory.

Pope Pius XII, message to Franco, April 1939, following the Nationalists' final victory; L.A. Fernsworth *Spain's Struggle for Freedom* (1957) p.236. It would be nearly 40 years before

Spain again enjoyed democratic rule, following General Franco's death in 1975.

6 A military state at war with its own people. This is not just a figure of speech: it is a terse definition of the legal basis of the present Spanish state.

Salvador de Madariaga on Franco's regime, 1939; Beevor (1982) p.266. Franco declared after his victory: 'The war is over, but the enemy is not dead.' It is estimated that between 1939 and 1943 as many as 200,000 Spaniards died by execution or politically motivated assassination.

AMERICA ISOLATED, 1933–7

7 This house sees more hope in Moscow than Detroit.

Motion for a debate in the Cambridge Union, 1932; M. Mazower *Dark Continent* (1998) p.106.

8 In the field of world policy, I would dedicate this Nation to the policy of the good neighbor – the neighbor who resolutely respects himself and, because he does so, respects the right of others – the neighbor who respects his obligations and respects the sanctity of his agreements in and with a world of neighbors.

President Franklin D. Roosevelt, inaugural address, 4 March 1933; *Public Papers* Vol.2 (1938) p.14. Noble rhetoric, but what did it mean in practice?

9 We are not isolationists except insofar as we seek to isolate ourselves completely from war. Yet we must remember that so long as war exists on earth there will be some danger that even the nation which most ardently desires peace may be drawn into war. I have seen war. I have seen war on land and sea. I have seen blood running from the wounded. I have seen men coughing out their gassed lungs. I have seen the dead in the mud. I have seen cities destroyed ... I have seen children starving. I have seen the agony of mothers and wives. I hate war.

President Franklin D. Roosevelt, speech at Chatauqua, New York State, 14 Aug. 1936; *Public Papers* Vol.5 (1938) p.289. As assistant secretary of the navy in World War I, Roosevelt had not expressed this revulsion, but as a presidential candidate in 1936 it certainly helped to re-elect him.

10 To Hell with Europe and with the rest of those nations.

Senator Thomas D. Schall, mid-1930s; Robert Dallek *Franklin D. Roosevelt and American Foreign Policy 1932–1945* (1979) p.95.

1 EXPORT OF ARMS, AMMUNITION, AND IMPLEMENTS OF WAR

Section 1(a) Whenever the President shall find that there exists a state of war between, or among, two or more foreign states, the President shall proclaim such fact, and it shall thereafter be unlawful to export, or attempt to export, or cause to be exported, arms, ammunition, or implements of war from any place in the United States to any belligerent state named in such proclamation, or to any neutral state for transshipment to, or for the use of, any such belligerent state.

Neutrality Act, 1 May 1937. The US Congress passed three neutrality acts between 1935 and 1937. US military aid to Britain would be given (at Roosevelt's insistence) from June 1940, and conscription began in Sept. 1940, all justified in the name of self-defence.

2 It seems to be unfortunately true that the epidemic of world lawlessness is spreading. And mark this well! When an epidemic of physical disease starts to spread, the community approves and joins in a quarantine of the patients in order to protect the health of the community against the spread of the disease. It is my determination to pursue a policy of peace. It is my determination to adopt every practicable measure to avoid involvement in war.

President Franklin D. Roosevelt, from his so-called 'Quarantine speech', Chicago, 5 Oct. 1937; *Public Papers 1937*. Full-scale war had broken out between China and Japan in July 1937 (see 793:1). America, China's self-styled protector under the 'Open Door' policy (see 810:7), was bound to support the Chinese but was not strong enough to challenge Japan in the Western Pacific, where the Philippines, her colony, was vulnerable. Nor could the Neutrality Acts help: Britain could buy and transport American weaponry across the Atlantic in its huge merchant fleet, but Japan, not China, controlled the sea-lanes of the Pacific.

3 It is always best and safest to count on nothing from the Americans but words.

Neville Chamberlain, Oct. 1937. Roosevelt's Quarantine speech (see 823:2) had appeared to be a move in the direction of sanctions but proved to be nothing of the kind. Chamberlain, who succeeded Baldwin as British prime minister in May 1937, was hoping for more tangible US support against Japanese pressure on British interests in China. Keith Feiling *The Life of Neville Chamberlain* (1946) p.325. See Baldwin 815:6.

4 *England Expects Every American To Do His Duty*.

Title of a book by the American isolationist Quincy Howe, published in 1938. An ironically punning twist on Admiral Lord Horatio Nelson's celebrated signal at Trafalgar, 1805 (see 533:8).

5 I will bet you an old hat … that … when he [Hitler] wakes up and finds out what has happened, there will be a great rejoicing in the Italian and German camps. I think we ought to introduce a bill for statues of [Senators] Austin, Vandenberg, Lodge … and … Taft to be erected in Berlin and put the swastika on them.

President Franklin D. Roosevelt to secretary of the treasury Henry Morgenthau, after the Senate Foreign Relations Committee's rejection on 11 July 1939 of his wish to repeal the US arms embargo; Dallek (1979) p.191.

6 Americans were misled by their own strength. They started from the correct assumption that Germany, after defeat, was no danger to themselves; they went on from this to the mistaken assumption that she could not be a danger to the countries of Europe.

A.J.P. Taylor (1961) p.57.

APPEASEMENT: FROM THE ANSCHLUSS TO THE MUNICH AGREEMENT, 1938

7 The whole history of Austria is just one uninterrupted act of high treason … I am going to solve the so-called Austrian problem one way or another … Perhaps you will wake up one morning in Vienna to find us there – just like a spring storm … such an action would mean blood … Don't think for a moment anybody is going to thwart my decisions … I give you once more and for the last time, the opportunity to come to terms … Think over it, Herr Schuschnigg, think it over well. I can only wait until this afternoon.

Adolf Hitler, accompanied by the forbidding trio of Sperrle, von Reichenau and Keitel, browbeats the Austrian chancellor Kurt von Schuschnigg, at Berchtesgaden, 12 Feb. 1938; K. von Schuschnigg *Austrian Requiem* (1947) pp.20–25. Pressure on Austria had increased following Italy's alliance with Germany in 1936 (see 819:8), and Hitler now demanded the release of Austrian Nazi prisoners, the appointment of Austrian Nazis to high government rank and Austro-German military and economic coordination. Von Schuschnigg announced a plebiscite on Austrian independence to take place on 13 March 1938, but Goering demanded that he abandon the plebiscite and resign in favour of the Nazi sympathizer, Arthur Seyss-Inquart. The *Wehrmacht* marched into Austria, supposedly to re-establish order, on 12 March.

8 The whole city behaved like an aroused woman, vibrating, writhing, moaning, and sighing lustfully for orgasm.

George Clare *Last Waltz in Vienna* (1982 edn) p.195. Clare witnessed Hitler's arrival in Vienna on 12 March 1938. The pro-German *Daily Mail* journalist Ward Price commented: 'If this was rape never have I seen a more willing victim.' Dissidents and Jews were less happy at the turn of events. The arrival of the *Wehrmacht* brought in its wake horrific attacks on Vienna's Jews, who by the beginning of April were beginning to be transported to the Dachau concentration camp.

1 Thank goodness Austria is out of the way.

Sir Alexander Cadogan, head of the British Foreign Office, to Sir Nevile Henderson, British ambassador to Germany, March 1938; David Dilks (ed.) *The Diaries of Sir Alexander Cadogan OM 1938–1945* (1971) p.70.

2 The advance of the Nazis was like a symphony: the Saar was the allegro, the Rhineland the andante, Austria the scherzo, there remained the finale to be played.

Action, 19 March 1938. *Action* was the main propaganda organ of Oswald Mosley's British Union of Fascists (BUF). The Saarland, detached from Germany by the Treaty of Versailles in 1919, was reabsorbed after a referendum on 13 Jan. 1935. The Rhineland, demilitarized by Versailles, was reoccupied by German troops on 7 March 1936 (see 818:8). Austria was incorporated into Germany by the *Anschluss* of 13 March 1938. Czechoslovakia followed piecemeal by the Munich Agreement of 1 October 1938 and the German invasion of 15 March 1939, but that was by no means the finale for the Nazis.

3 1. Restoration of complete equality of the German national group with the Czech people;

2. Recognition of the Sudeten German national group as a legal entity for the safeguarding of this position of equality within the state …

4. Building up of Sudeten German self-government in the Sudeten German settlement area in all branches of public life.

Konrad Henlein, leader of the Sudeten Germans of Czechoslovakia, demands made at the Sudeten German Party Congress at Carlsbad, Bohemia, 24 April 1938; *Documents on German Foreign Policy* (1949–83) Series D, Vol.2, p.198. Hitler had assured Henlein at a meeting in Berlin on 28 March: 'I will stand by you; from tomorrow you will be my viceroy [*Statthalter*]. I will not tolerate difficulties being made for you by any department whatsoever within the Reich.' The ethnically German Sudetenland lay inside Czechoslovakia's western borders. The Sudetens claimed they were persecuted by the Czechs and looked to Hitler as their liberator.

4 The clouds of mistrust and suspicion have been cleared away.

Neville Chamberlain, 2 May 1938, the day on which he signed the Anglo-Italian agreement; Milsted (1996) p.65. Chamberlain accepted Italian annexation of Abyssinia in exchange for Italian withdrawal from Spain. Chamberlain's 'conversations' with Mussolini led, in Feb., to the resignation as foreign secretary of Anthony Eden. Lord Halifax succeeded him.

5 It carries no approval of anything his regime may do.

Sir Nevile Henderson indicates to Sir Stanley Rous, secretary of the English Football Association, that the English football team should make a Nazi salute before their game against Germany in Berlin, 14 May 1938; David Downing *The Best of Enemies: England v Germany* (2000). According to Downing, during the match, won 3–6 by England, Henderson is said to have offered his binoculars to a tight-lipped Goering with the words: 'What wonderful goals. You really ought to get a closer look at them.'

6 In a year.

The response to Chamberlain by the head of the military Supply Board when the British prime minister asked how long it would be before British armaments reached approximate parity with Germany's, July 1938; Feiling (1946) p.35. British and French production of tanks and aircraft would overtake Germany's in the summer of 1939.

7 I am very much afraid that the senile ambition of Chamberlain to be the peacemaker of Europe will drive him to success at any price, and that will be possible only at our expense.

Jan Masaryk, Czech ambassador to London, Sept. 1938; V.S. Mamatey and R. Luza *A History of the Czechoslovak Republic 1918–1948* (1973) p.247.

8 I can only tell the representatives of the democracies that, if these tormented creatures cannot by their own exertions come to their rights, they will demand both their rights and assistance from us.

Adolf Hitler, 16 Sept. 1938, referring to the Sudeten Germans; Milsted (1996) p.66. Following a Nazi propaganda campaign alleging Czech atrocities against the Sudeten Germans, and urged by Britain and France to make concessions, the Czech government had conceded Sudeten autonomy on 4 Sept., but Hitler instructed Henlein to avoid a compromise solution.

9 *Es tut mir lied, aber das geht nicht mehr*. (I am sorry, but all that is no longer of any use.)

Adolf Hitler responding to Chamberlain's request for a discussion of a timetable for the orderly transfer of the Sudetenland from Czechoslovakia to Germany, Bad Godesberg, 22 Sept. 1938; Ivone Kirkpatrick *The Inner Circle* (1959) pp.114–18. Hitler demanded the evacuation of the Sudetenland by the Czechs by 1 Oct. The Czech government rejected the demand, and Britain promised to support the French, who began mobilization, should they go to war in defence of Czechoslovakia.

10 Before us stands the last problem that must be solved and will be solved. It is the last territorial claim that I have to make in Europe, but it is the claim from which I will not recede and which, God willing, I will make good … With regard to the problem of the Sudeten Germans, my patience is now at an end! I have made Mr Beneš an offer which is nothing more but the carrying out of what he himself has promised. The decision now lies in his hands. Peace or War! He will either accept this offer and now at last give to the Germans their freedom or we will go and fetch this freedom for ourselves.

Adolf Hitler, speaking at the Berlin Sportpalast, 26 Sept. 1938; M. Domarus (ed.) *Hitler: Speeches and Proclamations 1932–1945* (1962) p.932. Beneš was the Czech president.

1 Armed conflict between nations is a nightmare to me, but if I were convinced that any nation had made up its mind to dominate the world by fear of its force I should feel it should be resisted.

Neville Chamberlain, 26 Sept. 1938, the day he announced the mobilization of the British Fleet; Milsted (1996) p.66.

2 How horrible, fantastic, incredible it is that we should be digging trenches and trying on gas-masks here because of a quarrel in a far-away country between people of whom we know nothing.

Neville Chamberlain, speaking on BBC Radio, reported in *The Times*, 28 Sept. 1938. Two days later he flew to Munich to meet Hitler at a four-power conference chaired by Mussolini. Opponents of Chamberlain saw the digging of trenches and distribution of gas masks as scare tactics designed to influence public opinion in favour of his policy.

3 Praise be to God and Mr Chamberlain. I find no sacrilege, no bathos, in coupling those two names.

British columnist Godfrey Winn, *Sunday Express*, 28 Sept. 1938.

4 Good Man.

President Franklin D. Roosevelt, telegram to Chamberlain, 28 Sept. 1938; Dallek (1979) p.166.

5 When I come back I hope I may be able to say, as Hotspur says in *Henry IV*, 'out of this nettle, danger, we pluck this flower, safety'.

Neville Chamberlain to journalists at Heston Airport, London, morning of 29 Sept. 1938, before flying to Munich; Correlli Barnett *The Collapse of British Power* (2002 edn) p.546. The line comes from Act 2, Sc.3 of Shakespeare's *Henry IV, Pt I*.

6 As soon as Hitler sees that old man he will know he has won the battle. Chamberlain is not aware that to present himself to Hitler in the uniform of a bourgeois pacifist and British parliamentarian is the equivalent of giving a wild beast a taste of blood.

Benito Mussolini, Sept. 1938; Brendon (2000) p.488.

7 1. The evacuation shall begin on 1 October.

2. The United Kingdom, France and Italy agree that the evacuation of the territory shall be completed by 10 October, without destruction of any of the existing installations.

From the Munich Agreement, signed on 30 Sept. 1938; *Documents on German Foreign Policy* Series D, Vol.2 (1949–83) p.1014. Chamberlain and the French premier Édouard Daladier accepted the phased occupation of the Sudetenland and other industrial areas and fortifications by Germany by 10 Oct., but in the event German troops marched into the Sudetenland on 1 Oct. An annex to the agreement promised that Germany and Italy would guarantee Czechoslovakia once issues relating to national minorities in Czechoslovakia had been settled. There was no Anglo-French guarantee of Czechoslovakia's new borders. The agreement bore out Hitler's earlier prediction that Britain and France would make no attempt to prevent Eastern Europe from falling into German hands. Edvard Beneš resigned in disgust.

8 If ever that silly old man comes interfering here again with his umbrella, I'll kick him downstairs and jump on his stomach in front of the photographers.

Adolf Hitler on Chamberlain, after the Munich Agreement; Kirkpatrick (1959) pp.135. The remark was passed to a British diplomat by a source close to Hitler. Better known to posterity is a remark, attributed to Hitler, referring to the written pledge that Germany and Britain would never go to war again, triumphantly waved to the crowd at Heston by Chamberlain on his return from Munich: 'Well, he seemed such a nice old gentleman, I thought I would give him my autograph as a souvenir' (M.J. Cohen *The Penguin Thematic Dictionary of Quotations* (1998) p.24).

9 My good friends, this is the second time in our history that there has come back from Germany to Downing Street peace with honour. I believe it is peace for our time. We thank you from the bottom of our hearts. And now I recommend you to go home and sleep quietly in your beds.

Neville Chamberlain, speaking to cheering crowds from a first-floor window of 10 Downing Street after his return from Munich, 1 Oct. 1938, *The Times*. The sense of relief was shared in France, where a crowd of half a million turned out to welcome Daladier back from Germany. The phrase 'peace for our time' seems to be based on words in the Order of Morning Prayer in the Anglican liturgy: 'Give peace in our time, O Lord.' The phrase 'peace with honour' refers to Disraeli's claim after his return from the Congress of Berlin (see 696:4).

10 The prime minister has believed in addressing Herr Hitler through the language of sweet reasonableness. I have believed that he was more open to the language of the mailed fist … We have taken away the defences of Czechoslovakia at the same breath as we have guaranteed them, as though you were to deal a man a mortal blow and at the same time insure his life … I have given up the privilege of serving … a leader whom I still regard with the deepest admiration and affection. I have ruined, perhaps, my political career. But that is a little matter; I have retained something which is to me of great value. I can still walk about the world with my head erect.

Alfred Duff Cooper, first lord of the Admiralty, resignation speech to the House of Commons, 3 Oct. 1938; Martin Gilbert and Richard Gott *The Appeasers* (1963) p.183. Churchill sent a note of congratulations to Cooper: 'Your speech … was admirable in form, massive in argument, and shone with courage and public spirit.' A.J.P. Taylor wrote to him: 'If England is in future to have a history, your name will be mentioned with respect and admiration.' Josiah Wedgwood also sent a supportive letter, saying, 'I do dislike belonging to a race of clucking old hens and damned cowards' (A. Duff Cooper *Old Men Forget* (1953) p.249).

1 I do not begrudge our loyal, brave people … the natural, spontaneous outburst of joy and relief when they learned that the hard ordeal would no longer be required of them at the moment; but they should know the truth. They should know that there has been gross neglect and deficiency in our defences; they should know that we have sustained a defeat without a war, the consequences of which will travel far with us along our road; they should know that we have passed an awful milestone in our history, when the whole equilibrium of Europe has been deranged, and that the terrible words have for the time being been pronounced against the Western democracies: 'Thou art weighed in the balance and found wanting.'

Winston Churchill, House of Commons, 5 Oct. 1938; B. MacArthur (ed.) *The Penguin Book of Twentieth-Century Speeches* (1992) p.175. Churchill was speaking during the four-day debate on the Munich Agreement. Chamberlain won the vote, but 30 Conservative MPs abstained. Churchill quotes the Book of Daniel 5:25.

2 The League of Nations and collective security are dead. International relations are entering an era of the most violent savagery and brute force.

Ivan Maisky, Soviet ambassador in London, reacts to Munich; Brendon (2000) p.577. Fear of communism and a preparedness to countenance a Nazi-dominated Eastern Europe as a barrier against it meant that Britain and France were unwilling to draw the USSR into an anti-German front. Only when Germany invaded Russia in 1941 did such an alliance come into being.

3 Under pressure from the ruthless, the clueless combined with the spineless to achieve the worthless.

A modern historian, Norman Davies, enjoys himself verbally at Chamberlain's expense, *Europe, A History* (1996) p.990.

4 What has become of the assurance 'We don't want Czechs in the Reich'? What regard has been paid here to that principle of self-determination on which Herr Hitler argued with me so vehemently at Berchtesgaden when he was asking for the severance of Sudetenland from Czecho-slovakia and its inclusion in the German Reich?

Neville Chamberlain, speech to the Birmingham Conservative Association, 17 March 1939; MacArthur (1992) p.176. The German occupation of Prague on 15 March was accompanied by the secession of Slovakia from Czechoslovakia and an agreement – signed under duress by the ailing Czech president, Hacha – that the Czech heartlands of Bohemia and Moravia become a German protectorate. A British historian has remarked that after the German occupation of Czechoslovakia 'even those most stubborn in self-delusion … at last perceived, like flat-earthers converted to Copernican astronomy, that moralizing internationalism did not accord with the observable facts' (Barnett (2002 edn) p.557).

5 These men are not made of the same stuff as the Francis Drakes and the other magnificent adventurers who made the empire. They, after all, are the tired sons of a long line of rich men and they will lose their empire.

Benito Mussolini to Count Ciano, following a meeting with Chamberlain, diary entry by Count Ciano, 11 Jan. 1939; *Diary 1937-1943* (1947 trans.) p.176.

6 An earnest opinionated provincial was bound to err if he plunged into diplomacy.

Sir Robert Vansittart, on Chamberlain, *The Mist Procession* (1938) p.430. Vansittart, an anti-appeaser, had been demoted by Chamberlain to the non-job of chief diplomatic adviser to the foreign secretary.

7 *Monsieur J'aime Berlin* (Mr I-love-Berlin).

A punning French nickname for Chamberlain, late 1930s; Brendon (2000) p.511.

POLAND AND THE NAZI–SOVIET PACT, 1939

8 Danzig is German, will always remain German, and will sooner or later become part of Germany.

Adolf Hitler to the Polish foreign minister, Colonel Josef Beck, Jan. 1939; Noakes and Pridham Vol.3 (2001 edn) p.126. In the winter of 1938–9 Hitler attempted to make Poland a German satellite and was testing the water by seeing if the Poles would agree to relinquish German-speaking Danzig.

1 We are considering a situation in which we, allied to France, would be engaged in war with Germany and Italy simultaneously and when Japan would also be a potential enemy ... The British Empire and France would thus be threatened at home, in the Mediterranean and in the Far East at the same time, and it would be hard to choose a worse geographical combination of enemies.

British strategic memorandum put to the Anglo-French Staff conversations about joint strategy in the event of war, 20 March 1939; British Cabinet Papers 29/159.

2 If any action was taken which clearly threatened the independence of Poland so that Poland felt bound to resist with her national forces, His Majesty's government would at once lend them all the support in her power.

British guarantee to Poland, drafted by Chamberlain and passed to Colonel Beck by Lord Halifax, 31 March 1939; British Cabinet Papers 23/95. Beck famously accepted the assurance between 'two flicks of the ash off his cigarette' (Barnett (2002 edn) p.560). The wording of the assurance was agreed by the British cabinet following reports from Berlin that a German invasion of Poland was imminent.

3 The Third Reich and the Italian Empire are resolved to act side by side and with united forces to secure their living space.

From the German–Italian Pact of Steel, a ten-year pact of friendship and alliance signed in Berlin by Hitler and Mussolini on 22 May 1939; Milsted (1996) p.68. The pact, which held each party to help the other unconditionally in the event of war, was a rebuff to Anglo-French hopes of detaching Italy from Germany.

4 Any action, whatever its form, which would tend to modify the *status quo* in Danzig, and so provoke armed resistance by Poland, would bring the Franco-Polish agreement into play and oblige France to give immediate assistance to Poland.

French declaration on Danzig, sent by Georges Bonnet, the French foreign minister, to Ribbentrop, 1 July 1939; Gilbert and Gott (1963) p.251.

5 If only the Albanians had possessed a well-armed fire brigade, they could have pushed us back into the Adriatic.

Italian chief of staff Filippo Anfuso on his country's ineptly conducted invasion of Albania, 7 April 1939; B.J. Fischer *King Zog and the Struggle for Stability in Albania* (1984) p.279.

6 If for fear of making an alliance with Russia we drove that country into the German camp we should have made a mistake of vital and far-reaching importance.

Admiral Lord Chatfield, memorandum of the cabinet foreign policy committee, 11 April 1939; British Cabinet Papers 27/624. An ominous prediction that was soon to be fulfilled (see 828:3).

7 That bastard of the Versailles treaty.

Vyacheslav Molotov, Soviet foreign minister, refers to Poland, July 1939; Milsted (1996) p.68. Revisionist speaks to revisionist: both the USSR and Germany had an interest in destroying the 1919 settlement. Molotov was to be involved in the negotiations for the Nazi–Soviet Pact the following month (see 828:3).

8 Everything I undertake is directed against the Russians; if the West is too stupid and blind to grasp this, then I shall be compelled to come to an agreement with the Russians, beat the West, and then after their defeat turn against the Soviet Union with all my forces. I need the Ukraine so they can't starve us out like in the last war.

Adolf Hitler to Carl Burkhardt, League of Nations commissioner in Danzig, 11 Aug. 1939; C.J. Burkhardt *My Mission to Danzig 1937–39* (1962) p.272. Again, a prophecy fulfilled over the next two years.

9 What could England offer Russia? At best participation in a European war and the hostility of Germany, but not a single desirable end for Russia. What could we offer, on the other hand? Neutrality and staying out of a European war.

German official to Soviet chargé d'affaires, Georgi Astakhov, July 1939; Lewis Namier *Europe in Decay: A Study in Disintegration* (1950) p.246. Anglo-French military talks with the USSR in the summer of 1939 quickly foundered. Britain had guaranteed Poland within the frontiers of 1920 after Poland had acquired a wide belt of territory at the USSR's expense (see 805:7). This was unacceptable to the USSR in 1939, but Germany was prepared to see the territory revert to the USSR and set the Polish-Soviet border on the Curzon Line (the frontier fixed at Versailles in 1919) – for the time being.

10 I return to Rome completely disgusted with Germany, with its leaders, with their way of doing things. They have betrayed us and lied to us. Now they are dragging us into an adventure which we have not wanted and which might compromise the regime and the country as a whole. The Italian people will shudder in horror when they find out about the aggression against Poland and most probably will wish to fight the Germans ... The Duce's reactions are varied. At first he agrees with me. Then he says that honour compels him to march with Germany. Finally, he states that he wants his share of the spoils in Dalmatia and Croatia.

Count Ciano, Italian foreign minister, diary entry, 13 Aug. 1939; *Diary 1937–1943* (1947 trans.) p.258.

1 Will Poland accept the entry of Soviet troops in the Vilna corridor ... to make contact with the enemy; likewise will Poland give our troops access to Galicia; likewise allow them passage to get to Romania?

Marshal Kliment Voroshilov, chief Soviet representative in the Anglo-French-Soviet talks, to the French and British delegations, 14 Aug. 1939; A. Beaufre *The Fall of France* (1967) pp.109–10. On 23 Aug. the Poles eventually agreed not to rule out Polish–Soviet cooperation in the event of German military action, but by then Germany and the Soviet Union had signed the Molotov–Ribbentrop Pact (see 828:3).

2 Genghis Khan had millions of women and men killed by his own will and with a gay heart. History sees him only as a great state-builder ... I have sent my Death's Head units to the East with the order to kill without mercy men, women and children of the Polish race or language. Only in such a way will we win the *Lebensraum* that we need. Who, after all, speaks today of the annihilation of the Armenians?

Adolf Hitler, briefing his generals at Obersalzburg before the Nazi invasion of Poland, 22 Aug. 1939; Davies (1996) p.909.

3 In the event of a territorial and political transformation of the territories belonging to the Polish state, the spheres of interest of both Germany and the USSR shall be bounded approximately by the line of the rivers Narew, Vistula and San.

From a secret additional protocol to the Nazi–Soviet Non-Aggression Pact, 23 Aug. 1939; *Documents on German Foreign Policy* (1949–83) Series D, Vol.7, pp.245–7. Other parts of Eastern Europe, including the Baltic States, were similarly divided into Nazi and Soviet spheres. Germany beat the Western Powers to a deal with the Soviet Union by granting the Soviets a free hand in the areas they wished. After the signing of the agreement, Hitler fixed 26 Aug. as the date for the invasion of Poland.

4 Now Europe is mine. The others can have Asia.

Adolf Hitler, words reportedly spoken at Berchtesgaden on hearing of the Molotov–Ribbentrop Pact, 24 Aug. 1939; Donald Cameron Watt *How War Came* (1989) p.462. The normally teetotal Hitler sipped a little champagne in celebration.

5 'The scum of the earth, I believe?'

'The bloody assassin of the workers, I presume?'

Caption to a cartoon by David Low entitled 'Rendezvous', 24 Aug. 1939; illustrated in David Low *Low's Autobiography* (1956) p.319. The speakers are Hitler and Stalin.

6 I know what Hitler's up to. He thinks he has outsmarted me, but actually it is I who have outsmarted him.

Joseph Stalin to Nikita Khrushchev after the signing of the Molotov–Ribbentrop Pact; Richard Overy *Russia's War* (1997) p.50. Rash words: the USSR and Germany now stood on a common frontier, without Poland as a buffer for the USSR.

7 We would have preferred an agreement with the so-called democratic countries ... but Britain and France wanted to use us as hired men and not even pay us anything for it.

Joseph Stalin, 1 Sept. 1939; A. Yaklovlev *The Events of 1939: Looking Back after Fifty Years* (1989) p.8.

8 Your Excellency will have already heard of certain measures taken by His Majesty's Government ... These steps have ... been rendered necessary by military movements which have been reported from Germany and by the fact that apparently the announcement of a German–Soviet Agreement is taken in some quarters in Berlin to indicate that intervention by Great Britain on behalf of Poland is no longer a contingency that need be reckoned with. No greater mistake could be made. Whatever may prove to be the nature of the German–Soviet Agreement, it cannot alter Great Britain's obligation to Poland, which His Majesty's Government have stated in public repeatedly and plainly and which they are determined to fulfil.

Neville Chamberlain to Hitler, 23 Aug. 1939; Noakes and Pridham Vol.3 (2001 edn) p.137. Thirty German divisions moved towards the Polish border on the same day. The Anglo-Polish Treaty of Mutual Assistance was signed on 25 Aug. (it included a secret protocol pledging Britain to defend the *status quo* of Danzig). On hearing of the treaty, Hitler postponed his attack on Poland until 1 Sept.

9 The attack on Poland is to be carried out in accordance with the preparations made for 'Operation White' [*Fall Weiss*] ... Assignment of tasks and the operational objective remain unchanged.

　　Day of attack ...　1 September 1939
　　Time of attack ... 4.45 a.m.

Directive No.1 for the Conduct of the War, signed by Hitler at 12.30 p.m., 31 Aug. 1939; Noakes and Pridham Vol.3 (2001 edn) p.141. Using the justification of a fabricated attack on the German radio station at Gleiwitz, the Germans crossed Poland's western frontier at the appointed time on 1 Sept.

10 This morning the British Ambassador in Berlin handed the German Government a final note,

stating that, unless we heard from them by 11 o'clock that they were prepared at once to withdraw their troops from Poland, a state of war would exist between us. I have to tell you now that no such undertaking has been received and that consequently this country is at war with Germany.
Neville Chamberlain, broadcast from the Cabinet Room at 10 Downing Street; 3 Sept. 1939; Tom Hickman *What did you do in the War, Auntie? The BBC at War 1939–45* (1995) p.11. He concluded with the words: 'It is evil things that we will be fighting against – brute force, bad faith, injustice, oppression and persecution – and against them I am certain that the right will prevail.'

1 Mr L.S. Amery [Conservative MP for Sparkbrook in Birmingham], sitting very small near Anthony Eden, jumped up to shout at Greenwood – 'speak for England'. Others took up the cry. Chamberlain white and hunched. Margesson with sweat pouring down his face, Sir John Simon, [and] the Foreign Secretary [Lord Halifax], punctiliously looking holy.
Ralph Glyn, diary entry, 3 Sept. 1939; David Milsted *Brewer's Anthology of England and the English* (2001) pp.183–4.

2 In honouring our word we fight to defend our soil, our homes, our liberties.
Édouard Daladier announces to the Chamber of Deputies that France will be at war with Germany from 5.00 p.m. on 3 Sept. 1939; Ministère des affaires étrangères *The French Yellow Book* (1940).

3 The Führer has done nothing but remedy the most serious consequences which this most unreasonable of all dictates in history imposed upon a nation and, in fact, upon the whole of Europe, in other words repair the worst mistakes committed by … the statesmen of the Western democracies.
Joachim von Ribbentrop addresses German citizens of Danzig, Sept. 1939; US Department of State *The Treaty of Versailles and After* (1947) p.27. Ribbentrop characterizes Hitler's conquests as a forcible renegotiation of the Treaty of Versailles, often referred to in Germany as the *Diktat* ('dictated treaty').

4 Everything, underlying everything, a feeling of unfathomable horror.
Simone de Beauvoir on the mood in Paris on the eve on war; *The Prime of Life* (1962) p.303.

JUDGEMENTS

5   I sit in one of the dives
    on Fifty-second Street
    Uncertain and afraid

    As the clever hopes expire
    Of a low dishonest decade …
W.H. Auden 'September 1 1939'.

6 What a decade! A riot of appalling folly that suddenly becomes a nightmare, a scenic railway ending in a torture-chamber. It starts off in the hangover of the 'enlightened' post-war age, with Ramsay MacDonald soft-soaping into the microphone and the League of Nations flapping vague wings in the background, and it ends up with twenty thousand bombing planes darkening the sky and Himmler's masked executioner whacking women's heads off on a block borrowed from the Nuremberg museum. In between are the politics of the umbrella and the hand-grenade.
George Orwell, review of Malcolm Muggeridge's book *The Thirties* in New English Weekly, April 1940.

7 When one thinks of the lies and betrayals of those years, the cynical abandonment of one ally after another, the imbecile optimism of the Tory press, the flat refusal to believe that the dictators meant war, even when they shouted it from the house-tops, the inability of the moneyed class to see anything wrong whatever in concentration camps, ghettos, massacres and undeclared wars, one is driven to feel that moral decadence played its part as well as mere stupidity.
George Orwell 'Who are the War Criminals?' in *Tribune*, 22 Oct. 1943.

8 The decision which ultimately led to the Second World War was taken, from the highest and most sensible motives, a few days before the first [World] war ended. This was the decision to grant an armistice to the German government.
A.J.P. Taylor (1961) p.45, arguing that the Armistice and the Treaty of Versailles left 'the German problem' unsolved. See 802:6.

9 The British approach to diplomacy [in the 1930s] was … rather like their approach to sex, romantically remote from the distressing biological crudities.
Correlli Barnett (2002 edn) p.242.

10 [Appeasement] was more or less consistent with the main lines of British foreign policy going back into the nineteenth century. It was used to describe British policy towards Germany in the 1920s which was regarded then as sensible and statesmanlike … By appeasement was meant a policy of adjustment

and accommodation of conflicting interests broadly to conform with Britain's unique position in world affairs. It involved no preconceived plan of action, but rested on a number of political and moral assumptions about the virtue of compromise and peaceableness, which suited Britain's economic and imperial interests very well.

Richard Overy (1987) p.19. See 800:10.

1 Many Germans, women in particular, used to descant to me upon the radiance of his expression and his remarkable eyes. I must confess he never gave me any impression of greatness. He was a spellbinder for his own people. To the last, I continued to ask myself how he had risen to what he was and how he maintained his ascendance over the German people.

Sir Nevile Henderson declares himself baffled by the appeal of the Führer, *Failure of a Mission: Berlin 1937–1939* (1940) p.42.

2 In the end the war was Hitler's war. It was not, perhaps, the war he wanted. But it was the war he was prepared to risk, if he had to ... Always one returns to Hitler: Hitler exultant, Hitler vehement ... Hitler playing the great commander ... lecturing his Generals, hectoring his Army Commanders, threatening, cajoling, and appealing to German destiny. Above all, increasingly in a hurry, always raising the stakes ... steadily losing touch with reality, but never, as Paul Claudel once prophesied he would, going away ... Neither firmness nor appeasement, the piling up of more armaments or the demonstration of more determination would stop him.

Donald Cameron Watt (1989) p.613–24.

Crimes against Humanity, 1939–45

CATEGORIES

1 The term 'war crimes' … includes …

B. Violations of the laws or customs of war. Such violations shall include but not be limited to murder, ill-treatment or deportation to slave labor or for any other purpose of civilian population, of, or in, occupied territory, murder or ill-treatment of prisoners-of-war …

C. Murder, extermination, enslavement, deportation and other inhumane acts committed against any civilian population before or during the war.
US Department of State to the British ambassador in Washington, 18 Oct. 1945; R. John Pritchard and Sonia M. Zaide (eds) *The Tokyo War Crimes Trial* Vol.1 (1981) pp.xiv–xv.

2 The coloured triangles signify:
　　red – political prisoners
　　green – professional criminals
　　black – a-socials [who included gypsies]
　　pink – homosexuals
　　violet – Jehovah's Witnesses
The Jewish prisoners wear no triangle, but the Star of David.
Rudolf Vrba and Alfred Wetzler, extract from their report on Auschwitz, about 28 April 1944; Henry A. Zeiger (ed.) *The Case Against Adolf Eichmann* (1960) p.153. Vrba and Wetzler escaped from the Auschwitz death camp on 10 April. Their report, based on their own experience as prisoners, gave the outside world the first hard confirmation of conditions inside the camp. It was published in the United States on 2 Nov. 1944, the same day that the Nazi order was given to begin destroying the Auschwitz crematoria.

EUTHANASIA

3 Reichsleiter Bouhler and Dr Brandt are entrusted with the responsibility of extending the rights of specially designated physicians, such that patients who are judged incurable after the most thorough review of their condition which is possible, can be granted mercy killing.
Adolf Hitler, late Oct. 1939 (backdated to 1 Sept.); Benno Mueller-Hill *Murderous Science* (1988) p.40. Authorization for the euthanasia of mentally handicapped people. Philipp Bouhler was director of the Chancellery of the Führer; Karl Rudolf Brandt was doctor to Hitler's entourage.

4 These people went quietly into the room and showed no signs of being upset. Dr Wedmann operated the gas. I could see through the peephole that after a minute the people had collapsed or lay on the benches. There were no scenes and no disorder.
Dr August Becker on the first euthanasia gassing at the Brandenburg asylum on 4 Jan. 1940; Jeremy Noakes and Geoffrey Pridham (eds) *Nazism 1919–1945* Vol.3 (1988) pp.1019–20. Becker was a key functionary in T4, the organization named after the address of its head office, 4 Tiergartenstrasse, Berlin.

5 I hear that there is considerable disturbance about the hospital at Grafeneck. People recognize the grey buses of the SS and believe that they know what is going on when they see the chimney of the crematorium burning continuously.
Heinrich Himmler, Dec. 1940; J.S. Conway *The Nazi Persecution of the Churches 1933–45* (1968) p.271. High-level disquiet that the secret of the euthanasia programme was out.

6 If it is once accepted that people have the right to kill 'unproductive' fellow humans – then as a *matter of principle* murder is permitted for all unproductive people, in other words for the incurably sick, the people who have become invalids through labour and war, for us all when we become old, frail and therefore unproductive … Woe to mankind, woe to our German nation if God's holy commandment 'Thou shalt not kill' … is not only broken, but if this transgression is actually tolerated and permitted to go unpunished.
Bishop of Münster, Cardinal Count August von Galen, sermon, 3 Aug. 1941; Noakes and Pridham Vol.3 (1988) p.1038. Large-scale gassings were subsequently halted by Hitler on 24 Aug., but the euthanasia programme continued nonetheless.

7 I am quite sure that a man like the Bishop von Galen knows that after the war I shall exact retribution down to the last farthing. And, if he does not succeed in getting himself transferred, in the meanwhile, to the Collegium Germanicum in Rome, he may rest assured that in the balancing of our accounts no 'T' will remain uncrossed, no 'I' undotted!
Adolf Hitler, 4 July 1942; *Hitler's Table Talk 1941–1944* (1988 edn) p.555.

GYPSIES

1 The Gypsy question can only be considered solved when the main body of asocial and good-for-nothing mixed-blood Gypsies is collected together in large labour camps and kept working there, and when the further breeding of this population of mixed blood is stopped once and for all.

Dr Robert Ritter, 20 Jan. 1940; Mueller-Hill (1988) p.57. Ritter was director of the Research Institute for Racial Hygiene and Population Biology, set up in 1936 to provide a scientific basis for Nazi racist policy.

2 Gypsies who wander about in the countryside represent a twofold danger:
  1. as carriers of contagious diseases, especially typhus;
  2. as unreliable elements who neither obey the regulations issued by German authorities nor are willing to do useful work.

There exists well-founded suspicion that they provide intelligence to the enemy and thus damage the German cause. I therefore order that they are to be treated like the Jews.

Hinrich Lohse, Reichskommissar for the Baltic States, 4 Dec. 1941; Günter Lewy *The Nazi Persecution of the Gypsies* (2000) pp.123–4. Not all gypsies were to be treated like the Jews – that is, liquidated *en masse*. The supreme authority of the Final Solution, Heinrich Himmler, believed that pure-blooded gypsies were kin to the Aryan master-race worshipped by the Nazis and should, therefore, be spared. The theory was disputed by other high-ranking figures in the Reich, notably Hitler's secretary Martin Bormann, but Himmler had his way.

3 The shooting of the Jews is simpler than that of the Gypsies. One has to admit that the Jews go to their death composed – they stand very calmly whereas the Gypsies cry, scream and move constantly while they already stand at the place of the shooting. Several even jump into the ditch and pretend to be dead.

Junior officer Hans-Dietrich Walther, report of 4 Nov. 1941 on reprisal executions in Serbia; International Military Tribunal *Trial of the Major War Criminals* Vol.11 (1947) pp.1139–40.

4 Many men were arrested while on leave from the front, despite high decorations and several wounds, simply because their father or mother or grand-father had been a gypsy or a gypsy half-caste.

Rudolf Hoess *Commandant of Auschwitz* (1959) p.138. Hoess, commandant of Auschwitz, wrote this memoir early in 1947. On 26 Feb. 1943 the first large transport of gypsies arrived in Auschwitz, to be installed in a 'family camp'. Here Hoess gives

an instance of the mad logic whereby even loyalists could be condemned simply because of their racial background.

HOMOSEXUALS

5 We must exterminate these people root and branch. Just think how many people will never be born because of this, and how a people can be broken in nerve and spirit when such a plague gets hold of it. When someone in the Security Services, in the SS, or in the government has homosexual tendencies, he abandons the normal order of things for the perverted world of the homosexual. We can't permit such danger to the country; the homosexual must be entirely eliminated.

Heinrich Himmler to his doctor Felix Kersten; *The Kersten Memoirs* (1957) p.57. The homophobic Himmler saw the SS as a stud for the future Nordic thoroughbreds.

6 'You don't have to look so brainless, you arse fuckers,' said the officer. 'There you'll learn to do honest work with your hands and afterwards you'll sleep a healthy sleep. You are a biological mistake of the Creator. That's why you cannot be bent straight' … When I weighed not much more than six stones, one of the sergeants said to me one morning: 'Well, that's it. You want to go to the other side? It won't hurt. I'm a crack shot.'

Anon. homosexual survivor of Sachsenhausen concentration camp; Richard Plant *The Pink Triangle* (1987) p.174. Guards were paid 5 Reichsmarks for every prisoner 'shot while attempting to escape'.

7 The windows had a centimetre of ice on them. Anyone found with his underclothes on in bed, or his hands under his blanket – there were checks almost every night – was taken outside and had several bowls of water poured over him before being left standing for a good hour. Only a few people survived this treatment. The least result was bronchitis and it was rare for any gay person taken into the sick-bay to come out alive. We who wore the pink triangle were prioritized for medical experiments, and these generally ended in death.

Anon. Austrian homosexual on his experience in Sachsenhausen concentration camp; Heinz Heger *The Men with the Pink Triangle* (1980) pp.34–5. The punishment for suspected masturbation.

8 Most Jews refuse to see any similarity between their special situation and that of the same-sexers …

But there is no difference in the degree of hatred felt by the Christian majority for Christ-killers and Sodomites ... I was present when Christopher Isherwood tried to make this point to a young Jewish movie producer. 'After all,' said Isherwood, 'Hitler killed six hundred thousand homosexuals.' The young man was not impressed. 'But Hitler killed six *million* Jews,' he said sternly. 'What are you?' asked Isherwood. 'In real estate?'

Gore Vidal 'Pink Triangle and Yellow Star' in *The Nation*, 14 Nov. 1981.

JEHOVAH'S WITNESSES

1 The danger to the State from these Jehovah's Witnesses is not to be underestimated, since the members of this sect on the grounds of their unbelievably strong fanaticism are completely hostile to the law and order of the State. Not only do they refuse to use the German greeting [*Heil Hitler*], to participate in any National Socialist or State functions and to do military service, but they put out propaganda against joining the army, and attempt, despite prohibition, to distribute their publications.

Nazi comment on the Jehovah's Witnesses, about March 1933; Conway (1968) p.197.

2 A few days earlier they had witnessed the execution of some of their fellow believers and they could hardly be kept under control, so great was their desire to be shot with them. Their frenzy was painful to watch. They had to be taken back to their cells by force. When their time came, they almost ran to the place of execution. They wished on no account to be bound for they desired to be able to raise their hands to Jehovah.

Rudolf Hoess (1959) pp.88–9. Hoess describes the Jehovah's Witnesses in the Sachsenhausen concentration camp, where he served as adjutant from 1 Aug. 1938 until his transfer to Auschwitz on 1 May 1940.

POLES

3 We'll spare the little men, but the aristocrats, priests and Jews must be killed.

Reinhard Heydrich to General Carl-Heinz von Stulpnagel, 9 Sept. 1939; Callum MacDonald *The Killing of SS Obergruppenführer Reinhard Heydrich* (1989) p.38. SS policy on Poland was spelled out to the army soon after the outbreak of war.

4 In dealing with members of some Slav nationality, we must not endow those people with decent German thoughts and logical conclusions of which they are not capable, but we must take them as they really are ... I think it is our duty to take their children with us ... We either win over the good blood we can use for ourselves ... or else we destroy that blood.

Heinrich Himmler, Oct. 1939; Willi Frischauer *Himmler* (1953) pp.135–6. Polish children who corresponded to the blue-eyed, blond-haired Aryan ideal were taken to the Reich to be brought up as Germans. All other Poles were to be enslaved or exterminated.

5 The Führer told me that the leading groups in Polish society already in our hands are to be liquidated and whoever appears to replace them is to be detained and after an appropriate interval exterminated ... Gentlemen, we are not murderers. But as National Socialists, these times lay upon us all the duty to ensure that no further resistance emerges from the Polish people.

Governor general Hans Frank to a police conference in Krakow; Neil Ascherson *The Struggles for Poland* (1987) p.98.

6 The Orchestra very often played while the prisoners were at work. To the accompaniment of this music, the guards would call out prisoners whose work was especially feeble and shoot them there and then.

Polish miner deported to the Soviet labour camp at Maldiak, on the Kolyma peninsula in northeastern Siberia; Norman Davies *God's Playground* Vol.2 (1981) p.450. The comparison with the German death camps needs no emphasis (see 840:7).

7 The corpses had already been taken away, but blood was splashed all over the pavement, and bits of brain were sticking to the walls. People were kneeling all around, and in a few seconds the whole place was covered with red and white flowers and burning candles. Flowers were put in every bullet-hole in the wall.

General Tadeusz Bor-Komorowski *The Secret Army* (1984) p.156. The aftermath of a street execution in Warsaw described by the man who later commanded the Warsaw Rising of 1944. Red and white are the colours of the Polish flag.

PRISONERS-OF-WAR: SOVIET UNION

8 *Stalin*: Are there Poles still not released?
Polish ambassador: We have still not seen one

officer from the camp at Starobielsk which was dissolved in the spring of 1940.

Stalin: I shall go into that.

Dialogue in the Kremlin, 14 Nov. 1941; Stanislaw Kot *Conversations with the Kremlin and Despatches from Russia* (1963) p.112. Kot was the Polish ambassador. After the German invasion of the USSR on 22 June 1941 Polish prisoners-of-war taken by the Red Army in Sept. and Oct. 1939 were due to be released to fight on Russia's side. The Polish officers from the camp in question and from two others had, however, been executed by Stalin's secret police in April 1940, as Stalin no doubt well knew.

1 The hand of the Gestapo can easily be traced in this hideous frame-up ... The Polish prisoners were murdered by the Germans, and this wholesale murder took place recently; that is why the bodies had not decomposed.

Statement on Moscow Radio, 18 April 1943; *Keesing's Contemporary Archives* (1943) p.5731A. On 12 April 1943 the German government revealed that over 4,000 bodies of Polish army officers had been discovered in a mass grave in the forest of Katyn, near Smolensk. The Soviet counter-claim was that they had been killed by the Germans after the Nazi invasion, whereas the responsibility lay with Stalin and the soil conditions had mummified the corpses.

2 Alas, the German revelations are probably true. The Bolsheviks can be very cruel.

Winston Churchill to the Polish general, Wladislaw Sikorski, and the Polish ambassador, Count Raczynski, 15 April 1943; David Dilks (ed.) *The Diaries of Sir Alexander Cadogan* (1971) pp.520–21.

3 George, this is entirely German propaganda and a German plot. I am absolutely convinced the Russians did not do this ... I have noted with concern your plan to publish your unfavourable opinion of one of our allies ... I not only do not wish it, but I specifically forbid you to publish any information or opinion about an ally.

President Franklin D. Roosevelt to George H. Earle, March 1945; Louis Fitzgibbon *Katyn Massacre* (1977) p.179.

4 This forest scene is very dramatic. Ivan Susanin, an old Russian peasant, leads the Polish Army into a dense forest near Smolensk, into its very heart, from which there is no way out. He is killed, but the Polish army also remain there forever, frozen to death. After this scene my father used to leave.

Svetlana Alleluyeva *Only One Year* (1969) p.367. Stalin's daughter on her father's reaction to Mussorgsky's opera *Boris Godunov*.

5 The Soviet side, expressing profound regret over the Katyn tragedy, declares that this is one of the gravest crimes of Stalinism.

Soviet government statement, 13 April 1990. Exactly 50 years after the event, official acceptance of responsibility for the Katyn massacre. In March 1989 the communist government of Poland had broken its silence on the issue and accused the USSR of the crime, as had the Polish government-in-exile in April 1943. All told, some 15,000 Polish officers had been murdered, and the location of the graves of the missing 11,000 not executed at Katyn was disclosed in June 1990.

PRISONERS-OF-WAR: NAZI GERMANY

6 We must abandon the concept of soldierly comradeship. The communist is no comrade before and no comrade afterwards. What is involved is a struggle of annihilation.

Adolf Hitler to a gathering of senior army officers, 30 March 1941; Joachim Fest *Hitler* (1974) p.649, which cites the diary of General Franz Halder. The war against Stalin's Russia delineated.

7 Political commissars have initiated barbaric, Asiatic methods of warfare. Consequently they will be dealt with *immediately* and with maximum severity. As a matter of principle they will be shot at once whether captured *during operations or otherwise showing resistance*.

'Commissar order', 6 June 1941; Helmut Krausnick et al. *Anatomy of the SS State* (1968) p.532.

8 Bolshevism is the mortal enemy of National Socialist Germany. For the first time the German soldier faces not merely a military but also a political opponent. To fight against National Socialism is in his flesh and blood and he will do so with every means at his disposal: sabotage, insidious propaganda, arson and murder. The Bolshevist soldier has forfeited every claim to be treated as an honourable soldier and in keeping with the Geneva Convention.

Army order, 8 Sept. 1941; Krausnick (1968) p.524. The Geneva Convention of 27 July 1929 sought to guarantee the human rights of prisoners-of-war. Orders such as this removed this protection. The pretext was the Soviet Union's failure to subscribe to the Convention.

9 This criticism arises from the soldier's conception of a chivalrous war, whereas this is a matter of destroying a world ideology.

Field Marshal Wilhelm Keitel, comment on the doubts raised by Admiral Wilhelm Canaris on the order of 8 Sept. 1941; Krausnick (1968) p.526. Keitel, chief of the army high command, was notorious for his subservience to Hitler and amply earned the nickname 'Lakeitel' (*Lakai* meaning lackey).

1 Typhoid fever – Russian camp (20,000) doomed to die. Several German doctors fatally ill. In other camps in the area no typhoid but large numbers of prisoners dying daily through hunger. Makes a terrible impression but for the moment apparently nothing can be done.

General Franz Halder, diary entry, 14 Nov. 1941; Krausnick (1968) p.530, note 1. Nearly 50% of Red Army prisoners-of-war died in German captivity, compared with less than 10% of British, French and American prisoners. At least 3.3 million Russian POWs perished, 500,000 of them between Nov. 1941 and Jan. 1942.

2 It would be no exaggeration to state that mistakes in the treatment of prisoners-of-war have to a large extent been the cause of the increasing resistance of the Red Army and thus of the deaths of thousands of German soldiers ... An obvious consequence of this politically and militarily unwise treatment has been not only the weakening of the will to desert but a truly deadly fear of falling into German captivity.

Alfred Rosenberg to Field Marshal Wilhelm Keitel, 28 Feb. 1942; Alexander Dallin *German Rule in Russia, 1941–1945* (1957). Rosenberg, the doctrinaire of the 1930s, was minister in charge of the Occupied Eastern Territories.

3 After having eaten everything possible, including the soles of their boots, they have begun to eat each other, and, what is more serious, they have eaten a German sentry.

The jovial Reichsmarschall Hermann Goering, enjoying a joke with Count Galeazzo Ciano, the Italian foreign minister, late 1941; Malcolm Muggeridge (ed.) *Ciano's Diplomatic Papers* (1948) pp.464–5. Soviet prisoners-of-war, captured in millions during the first months of the German invasion, were left to starve in vast, makeshift camps and in their desperation resorted to cannibalism.

PRISONERS-OF-WAR: JAPAN

4 Biological warfare is inhumane and advocating such a method of warfare would defile the virtue and benevolence of the emperor.

Japanese General Ishii Shiro, 8 Feb. 1946; Sheldon Harris *Factories of Death* (1994) p.1. Ishii was in charge of biological warfare experiments in China from 1932 to 1945, carrying out his tests mostly on Chinese prisoners-of-war.

5 It is questionable whether in the case of a nation fighting for its honour such an idea of justice as propounded by the League of Nations will be upheld or not. In the case of a victorious enemy such a moral agreement might possibly be only a dead letter.

Lieutenant Colonel Hojo Enryo, lecture given in Berlin, Sept. 1941; Harris (1994) p.44. The reference is to the 1925 Convention outlawing bacteriological and chemical warfare.

6 One subject was exposed to a bomb burst containing buckshot mixed with 10mg bacilli and 10gm of clay ... Bomb burst 1 metre [about 3 feet] from the rear of the subject. He developed symptoms of typhoid fever with positive laboratory signs.

Interview with Dr Tabei Kanau, 24 Nov. 1947; Harris (1994) p.65. Dr Tabei worked on typhoid experiments from 1938 to 1943.

7 This information, particularly that which will finally be obtained from the Japanese with respect to the effect of BW [biological warfare] on humans, is of such importance to the security of this country that the risk of subsequent embarrassment should be taken.

US army Colonel R.M. Cheseldine, 26 Sept. 1947; Harris (1994) pp.219–20. The colonel was writing about the deal whereby General Ishii and others obtained immunity from prosecution for war crimes in exchange for providing the US government with detailed information about their experiments on human beings.

8 What he did, or was alleged to have committed in the line of duty as a medical officer and soldier in the Imperial Japanese Army, shall be denounced by any moral standards. Even so, one must not forget that it all happened under extremely abnormal circumstances. It was war.

The eldest daughter of General Ishii, *Japan Times*, 29 Aug. 1982.

9 You are not honourable prisoners-of-war. You are captives and you shall be treated as captives.

Japanese officer to American prisoners at Camp O'Donnell, the Philippines, 21 April 1942; Sidney Stewart *Give Us This Day* (1957) p.84. In the samurai code of bushido, soldiers who surrendered forfeited the right to be treated with respect.

10 I never can forget their groans and strangled breathing as they tried to get up. Some succeeded. Others lay lifelessly where they had fallen. I observed that the Jap guards paid no attention to these. I wondered why. The explanation wasn't long in coming. There was a sharp crackle of pistol and rifle fire behind us. Skulking along, a hundred yards behind our contingent, came a 'clean-up squad' of murdering Jap buzzards. Their helpless victims, sprawled darkly against the white of the road, were easy targets.

US pilot William E. Dyess, on the 'Death March' of the survivors of the surrendered Philippine fortress of Bataan, 11 April 1942; *Death March from Bataan* (1945) p.87.

1 The crime of which he was guilty was buying food through the fence. Some crime, I would say! Well, they took that boy to the graveyard, made him dig his own grave. During the time he was digging the grave, he up and hit one of the guards. For that he was stuck with bayonets many times. His body was left on the ground for all to look upon for seven days.

Merle Chandler on the execution of Private Donell K. Russell at Cabanatuan POW camp in the Philippines; Robert W. Levering *Horror Trek* (1948) pp.192–3.

PRISONERS-OF-WAR: UNITED STATES

2 It was freely admitted that some of our soldiers tortured Jap prisoners and were as cruel and barbaric at times as the Japs themselves. Our men think nothing of shooting a Japanese prisoner or a soldier attempting to surrender. They treat the Japs with less respect than they would give to an animal, and these acts are condoned by almost everyone.

Charles Lindbergh, diary entry, 13 July 1944; *The Wartime Journals of Charles A. Lindbergh* (1970). Lindbergh, the first man to fly the Atlantic alone, was attached as a civilian observer to US Marine Corps forces based in New Guinea.

3 We shot prisoners in cold blood, wiped out hospitals, strafed lifeboats, killed or mistreated enemy civilians, finished off the enemy wounded, tossed the dying into a hole with the dead, and in the Pacific boiled the flesh off enemy skulls to make table ornaments for sweethearts, or carved their bones into letter openers.

Edgar J. Jones, *Atlantic Monthly*, Feb. 1945, p.49. Jones was a war correspondent in the Pacific.

4 This Jap had been hit. One of my buddies was field-stripping him for souvenirs. I must admit it really bothered me, the guys dragging him around like a carcass. I was just horrified. This guy had been a human being. It didn't take me long to overcome that feeling.

Eugene B. Sledge, US Marine Corps; Studs Terkel *'The Good War'* (1984) Bk 1.

THE HOLOCAUST: PRELUDE TO GENOCIDE, 1925–40

5 If, at the beginning of the war and during the war, twelve or fifteen thousand of these Hebrew corrupters of the people had been held under poison gas, as happened to hundreds of thousands of our best German brothers in the field, the sacrifice of millions at the front would not have been in vain.

Adolf Hitler *Mein Kampf* (1925) Bk 2, Ch.15.

6 I want today to be a prophet again; if international finance Jewry inside and outside Europe should succeed in plunging the nations once more into a world war, the result will be not the Bolshevization of the earth, and thereby the victory of Jewry, but the annihilation of the Jewish race in Europe!

Adolf Hitler, 30 Jan. 1939; Ian Kershaw *Hitler 1936–45: Nemesis* (2000) p.153.

7 They take a Jew's life by throttling his livelihood, by 'legal' limitations, by cruel edicts, by such sadistic tortures that even a tyrant of the Middle Ages would have been ashamed to publicize them. It was part of the concept of that generation to burn a sinning soul, but it was not their habit to torture a man because he was born 'in sin', according to the hangman's ideas.

Chaim Kaplan, late 1939; *The Warsaw Diary of Chaim A. Kaplan* (1973) p.64. Kaplan, a Polish Jew, could not have conceived what lay ahead for his community as a result of the German defeat of Poland in Sept. and Oct. 1939.

8 The role of the armed forces, who are compelled impotently to watch this crime and whose reputation, particularly with the Polish population, suffers irreparable harm, need not be referred to again. But the worst damage which will accrue to the German nation from the present situation is the brutalization and moral debasement which, in a very short time, will spread like a plague among valuable German manpower. If high officials of the SS and police demand acts of violence and brutality and praise them publicly, then in a very short time we shall be faced with the rule of the thug.

General Johannes Blaskowitz, 6 Feb. 1940; Noakes and Pridham Vol.3 (1988) p.938. This protest against the systematic killing of both Jewish and non-Jewish Poles was to damage Blaskowitz's military career significantly.

1 *Arbeit Macht Frei* (Work Makes You Free)
Motto above the entrance gate to the first of the Auschwitz camps, opened in June 1940.

THE HOLOCAUST: WAR OF ANNIHILATION, 1941

2 Anyone who has ever looked at the face of a red commissar knows what the Bolsheviks are like. Here there is no need for theoretical expressions. We would be insulting the animals if we were to describe these men, who are mostly Jewish, as beasts. They are the embodiment of the Satanic and insane hatred against the whole of noble humanity. The shape of those commissars reveals to us the rebellion of the *Untermenschen* [subhumans] against noble blood.
Army newspaper article, 1941; Omer Bartov *The Eastern Front, 1941–45: German Troops and the Barbarization of Warfare.* For Hitler's 'Commissar order' of 6 June 1941 see 834:7.

3 I hereby charge you with making all necessary organizational, functional and material preparations for a complete solution of the Jewish question in the German sphere of influence in Europe.
Hermann Goering to Reinhard Heydrich, 31 July 1941; Raoul Hilberg (ed.) *Documents of Destruction* (1971) p.88. The official instruction to begin the programmed annihilation of European Jewry in specially built death camps.

4   The wild grasses rustle over Babi Yar.
    The trees look ominous,
    Like judges.
    Here all things scream silently,
    And, baring my head,
    Slowly I feel myself
    Turning grey.
    And I myself
    Am one massive, soundless scream
    Above the thousand thousand buried here.
Yevgeny Yevtushenko 'Babi Yar', 19 Sept. 1961; *The Poetry of Yevgeny Yevtushenko 1953 to 1965* (1966) p.149. More than 33,000 Jews were massacred in the ravine at Babi Yar, outside Kiev, over two days at the end of Sept. 1941.

5 The death we gave them was a nice quick death, compared with the hellish torment of thousands upon thousands in the dungeons of the GPU. Babies flew in a big arc through the air and we picked them

off in mid-flight before they landed in the pit or in the water.
Walter Mattner to his wife, 5 Oct. 1941; Guido Knopp *Hitler's Holocaust* (2000) p.52. The GPU was the Soviet secret police.

6 In the eastern sphere the soldier is not simply a fighter according to the rules of war, but the supporter of a ruthless racial ideology and the avenger of all the bestialities which have been inflicted on the German nation and those ethnic groups related to it. For this reason soldiers show full understanding for the necessity for the severe but just atonement being required of the Jewish subhumans.
Field Marshal Walther von Reichenau, 10 Oct. 1941; Noakes and Pridham Vol.3 (1988) p.1096. The invasion of Soviet Russia on 22 June had brought a sharp change of attitude in the army's high command compared with its feelings about the treatment of Poland in 1939–40 (see 827:9).

7 I have not heard that any criminal actions on the part of the armed forces were committed. I did hear rumours about very undesirable activities on the part of police forces in our rear areas.
General Heinz Guderian, 5 Nov. 1945; Richard Overy *Interrogations* (2001) p.183. The hero of tank warfare shifts responsibility for genocide.

8 We're not going to play at children's nurses; we're absolutely without obligations as far as these people are concerned. To struggle against the hovels, chase away the fleas, provide German teachers, bring out newspapers – very little of that for us ... For the rest, let them know just enough to understand our road signs, so that they won't get themselves run over by our vehicles.
Adolf Hitler, 17 Oct. 1941; *Hitler's Table Talk 1941–1944* (1988 edn) p.69.

9 At the place of execution there were snacks and schnapps. The police drank schnapps and had a snack in the intervals between shooting the groups of Jews and then got back to their bloody work in a state of intoxication.
David Ehof, organizer of the liquidation of the Borissov ghetto in Byelorussia, 19 Oct. 1941; Noakes and Pridham Vol.3 (1988) p.1099. Most of his police battalion were Latvians.

10 The Jews are to blame for this war. The treatment we give them does them no wrong. They have more than deserved it.
Joseph Goebbels 'The Jews are Guilty' in *Das Reich*, 16 Nov. 1941.

1 There are still about six million Jews living in Russia, and the problem can only be resolved by a biological elimination of the entire Jewish population of Europe ... It is self-evident that we should neither speak nor write about the setting of political goals. In the delicate situation in which Germany finds itself, it would be extremely harmful if the public got to know about these things.

Alfred Rosenberg, 18 Nov. 1941; Mueller-Hill (1988) p.47. Rosenberg was minister for the Occupied Eastern Territories.

THE HOLOCAUST:
THE FINAL SOLUTION, 1942

2 In lieu of emigration, the evacuation of the Jews to the east has emerged, after an appropriate prior authorization by the Fuhrer, as a further solution possibility ... Around 11 million Jews are involved in this final solution of the Jewish question ... In the course of the practical implementation of the final solution Europe will be combed from west to east.

Minutes of the Wannsee Conference, 20 Jan. 1942; Hilberg (1971) p.92. 'Evacuation' was code for extermination. Hitler's authorization was verbal, not written.

3 The discussion covered killing, eliminating and exterminating.

Adolf Eichmann on the Wannsee Conference of 20 Jan. 1942; Kershaw (2000) p.493. Eichmann kept the minutes of the conference, which did not spell out the fate of the Jews of Europe explicitly; this he did on 24 July 1961 during his trial in Jerusalem.

4 When I think about it, I realize that I'm extraordinarily humane. At the time of the rule of the Popes, the Jews were mistreated in Rome. Until 1830, eight Jews mounted on donkeys were led once a year through the streets of Rome. For my part, I restrict myself to telling them they must go away. If they break their pipes on the journey, I can't do anything about it. But if they refuse to go voluntarily, I see no other solution but extermination.

Adolf Hitler in conversation, 23 Jan. 1942; *Hitler's Table Talk 1941–1944* (1988 edn) p.235. The transcription was made by Heinrich Heim, an official in the Reich ministry of justice. The ultimate in cynicism, just three days after the Wannsee Conference.

5 Along with Bolshevism, Jewry is also about to experience its great disaster ... We must speed up this process coldly and ruthlessly, and we are doing mankind, tortured by Jewry for thousands of years, an inestimable service.

Joseph Goebbels, diary entry, 14 Feb. 1942; Louis P. Lochner (ed.) *The Goebbels Diaries* (1948) p.87. Private thoughts on a subject to which the minister of propaganda wished to give no publicity.

6 The discovery of the Jewish virus is one of the greatest revolutions that have taken place in the world. The battle in which we are engaged today is of the same sort as the battle waged during the last century, by Pasteur and Koch ... We shall regain our health only by eliminating the Jew.

Adolf Hitler, 22 Feb. 1942; *Hitler's Table Talk 1941–1944* (1988 edn) p.332. Louis Pasteur, the French founder of modern bacteriology, and the German scientist, Robert Koch, were benefactors of mankind in their war on disease. Hitler's claim to stand comparison with them is obscene.

7 A fairly barbaric practice will be used ... one that cannot be precisely described. Not many of the Jews will be left over. Roughly speaking, one can be sure that 60 per cent of them will have to be liquidated, while we will be able to put only 10 per cent into labour detachments.

Joseph Goebbels, diary entry, 27 March 1942; Gerald Fleming *Hitler and the Final Solution* (1985) p.62.

8 I am grateful for having been allowed to see this bastard race close up. If fate permits, I shall have something to tell my children. Syphilitics, cripples, idiots were typical of them ... They were not men but monkeys in human form.

Police sergeant Jacob, 21 June 1942; Noakes and Pridham Vol.3 (1988) p.1202.

9 The people were still standing like columns of stone, with no room to fall or lean. Even in death you could tell the families, all holding hands. It was difficult to separate them while emptying the room for the next batch. The bodies were tossed out, blue, wet with sweat and urine, the legs smeared with excrement and menstrual blood. Two dozen workers were busy checking mouths which they opened with iron hooks ... Dentists knocked out gold teeth, bridges and crowns with hammers.

SS officer Kurt Gerstein, witness of a gassing at Belzec death camp, 18 Aug. 1942, in a statement given on 6 May 1945; Martin Gilbert *The Holocaust* (1986) pp.427–8. Gerstein, a devout Christian, joined the SS in order to expose the evil of the Final Solution but was unable to convince his interrogators after his capture. He subsequently committed suicide.

1 2.IX.1942. This morning at three o'clock I attended a special action for the first time. Dante's hell seemed like a comedy in comparison. Not for nothing is Auschwitz called an extermination camp.

5.IX.1942. I was present this afternoon at a special action [gassing] applied to prisoners in the female camp, the worst I have ever seen. Dr Thilo was right this morning in telling me that we are in the *anus mundi* [arsehole of the world].

SS Dr Johann Kremer, 2 and 5 Sept. 1942, diary entries; Noakes and Pridham Vol.3 (1988) p.1204.

2 Because this war in our view is a Jewish war, the Jews are primarily bearing the brunt of it. In Russia, wherever there is a German soldier, the Jews are no more.

Karl Kretschmer to his wife, 27 Sept. 1942; Daniel Goldhagen *Hitler's Willing Executioners* (1996) p.404. An open admission that the army, as well as the SS, was committed to genocide.

3 My family, to be sure, were well provided for in Auschwitz. Every wish that my wife or children expressed was granted them. The children could live a free and untrammelled life. My wife's garden was a paradise of flowers. The prisoners never missed an opportunity for doing some little act of kindness to my wife or children, and thus attracting their attention. No former prisoner can say that he was in any way or at any time badly treated in our house.

Rudolf Hoess (1959) p.156. A touching portrayal of family life in a slaughterhouse. Hoess was executed in Auschwitz in 1947.

4 It was common practice to remove the skin from dead prisoners ... It was chemically treated and placed in the sun to dry. After that it was cut into shapes for use as saddles, riding breeches, gloves, house slippers and ladies' handbags. Tattooed skin was especially valued by SS men.

Czech Dr Franz Blaha, a prisoner in Dachau concentration camp, 9 Jan. 1946; Overy (2001) pp.194–5.

THE HOLOCAUST: INFERNO, 1943

5 Should we win the battle, no one will ask us afterwards how we did it. Should we lose, then we shall at the very least have hit decisively those subversives. Therefore, Himmler, I have after much deliberation decided to blot out once and for all the biological bases of Judaism, so that if the Aryan peoples emerge weakened from this conflict, at least

a crippling blow will have been dealt to those other forces.

SS officer Alfred Franke-Glicksch, account of conversation with Himmler, about Feb. 1943, relating to Himmler's meeting with Hitler at the time of the Stalingrad crisis, when Hitler appears to admit the possibility of losing the war; Fleming (1985) pp.149–50.

6 I will gladly atone in Heaven with my soul for what I have done here to the Jews.

Hans Rauter, 22 March 1943; Knopp (2000) p.126.

7 One should with renewed strength take measures against cruelty to animals and report it to the regiment. Special attention is to be devoted to the beef cattle, since through overcrowding in the railway cars great losses of the animals have occurred, and the food supply has thereby been severely damaged.

Commander of Police Regiment 25, 11 June 1943; Goldhagen (1996) p.269. Meanwhile, human beings were being stuffed into cattle trucks without any such solicitude.

8 I emphasized that I could not understand how Germans could quarrel over a few Jews. I said that people kept accusing me and my men of barbarism and sadism, while I was only doing my duty ... Kube replied that this way of carrying on was unworthy of a German or of the Germany of Kant and Goethe.

SS officer Eduard Strauch in conversation with Wilhelm Kube, 20 July 1943; Noakes and Pridham Vol.3 (1988) pp.1124, 1125.

9 We started with three and a half million Jews here. Of that number, only a few work companies remain. Everybody else has – let us say – emigrated.

Hans Frank, governor general of Poland, 2 Aug. 1943; Joachim Remak *The Nazi Years* (1969) p.158.

10 The twins were looked after by Mengele. He needed them, so he took great care of them ... He needed the twins alive, and they would receive white bread. When the rains came, he made sure that they worked in shelter, that is, in the washrooms. Every Saturday afternoon they would receive clean shirts.

Ernest Spiegel on Dr Josef Mengele; Gilbert (1986) p.756. Mengele worked in Auschwitz from 24 May 1943, performing experiments on the prisoners. His special interest was twins, many of whom he killed in the pursuit of his idea of medical science. After the war he fled to South America, where he later died.

11 Most of you will know what it means when a hundred corpses are lying side by side, or five hundred or a thousand are lying there. To have stuck it out and – apart from a few exceptions due to human weakness – to have remained decent, that is what has made us tough. This is a glorious page in our history and one that has never been written and can never be written.

Heinrich Himmler, speech to SS officers in Posen, 4 Oct. 1943; Noakes and Pridham Vol.3 (1988) p.1199.

THE HOLOCAUST: WAR LOST, WAR WON, 1944–5

1 *Hier ist kein warum.* (Here there is no 'why'.)
Primo Levi *If This is a Man* (1947; 2000 edn) p.45. The Italian scientist Levi was consigned to Auschwitz on 22 Feb. 1944. Here he describes his attempt to get water by breaking off an icicle outside the window of his hut. It was snatched away by a guard. 'Why?' asked Levi; this was the reply.

2 'When will all this extermination cease?' Dr Nyiszli asked Dr Mengele in Auschwitz. And Dr Mengele answered: 'My friend! It will go on, and on, and on.'
Benno Mueller-Hill (1988) p.104.

3 If you say: 'We can understand, as far as the men are concerned, but not about the children' … In my view, we as Germans, however deeply we may feel in our hearts, are not entitled to allow a generation of avengers filled with hatred to grow up with whom our children and grandchildren will have to deal because we, too weak and cowardly, left it to them.
Heinrich Himmler justifying child-murder in a speech of 5 May 1944; Noakes and Pridham Vol.3 (1988) p.1200.

4 If National Socialist Germany should collapse, then our enemies, those betrayers of our Greater Germanic aspirations who are now sitting in the concentration camps, shall not know the triumph of departing as victors. They shall not know that day; they shall go under with us!
Heinrich Himmler to his physician, Dr Felix Kersten, 5 March 1945; Fleming (1985) p.177.

5 I shall gladly jump into the pit, knowing that in the same pit there are five million enemies of the state.
Adolf Eichmann, 10 April 1945, at the Theresienstadt holding camp; cited on 7 July 1961 during his trial in Jerusalem; Gilbert (1986) p.792.

6 Nor have I left anyone in doubt that this time millions of European children of Aryan descent will

not starve to death, millions of grown men die in battle, and hundreds of thousands of women and children be burned and bombed to death in the cities, without the true culprits having to pay for their guilt, even if by more humane methods.
Adolf Hitler, Political Testament, 29 April 1945; Werner Maser (ed.) *Hitler's Letters and Notes* (1974) pp.350–51. Hitler dictated his final statement of belief the day before he committed suicide in his Berlin bunker.

THE HOLOCAUST: VICTIMS

7 *Cut to* the entire orchestra, rehearsing. Fania has hands poised over the keyboard; Alma, baton raised, starts the piece – an orchestral number of von Suppé. The sound is not quite horrible, but very nearly. The forty-odd players, apart from some of them being totally inadequate, are distressed by hunger and fear and never quite keep the music together.
Arthur Miller, screenplay for *Playing for Time* (1980); *Plays: Two* (1981) p.467. The film was based on the book by Fania Fénelon, who was transported to Auschwitz from France and was pianist in the camp orchestra.

8 In the first weeks of the camp's operation the orchestra played operetta melodies … in order to drown the cries of the victims in the gas chambers. Later, that was stopped.
Court judgement in the post-war trial of SS guards in the Treblinka death camp; Noakes and Pridham Vol.3 (1988) p.1205.

9 The father held the ten-year-old boy by the hand, speaking softly to him. The boy was struggling to hold back his tears. The father pointed a finger to the sky and stroked his head and seemed to be explaining something.
Hermann Graebe on a massacre in Russia, 5 Oct. 1942; Noakes and Pridham Vol.3 (1988) p.1101.

10 I'd like to go away alone
Where there are other, nicer people,
Somewhere into the far unknown,
There, where no one kills another.
Maybe more of us,
A thousand strong,
Will reach this goal
Before too long.
Alena Synkova, teenage prisoner in the Theresienstadt holding camp in Bohemia, c.1943; Hana Volavkova (ed.) *I Never Saw Another Butterfly* (1978) p.38. She survived the experience of captivity, unlike the vast majority of the Theresienstadt detainees.

1 On the streets children are crying in vain, children who are dying of hunger. They howl, beg, sing, moan, shiver with cold, without underwear, without clothing, without shoes, in rags, sacks, flannel … bound in strips round the emaciated skeletons, children swollen with hunger, disfigured, half-conscious, already completely grown-up at the age of five, gloomy and weary of life.

Stanislav Rozycki, a visitor to the Warsaw Ghetto; Noakes and Pridham Vol.3 (1988) p.1067. The ghetto was set up in Oct. 1940 and destroyed in Sept. 1943.

2 Amidst this destruction, the table in the centre of the room looked incongruous with glasses filled with wine, with the family seated around, the rabbi reading the Haggadah. His reading was punctuated by explosions and the rattling of machine-guns; the faces of the family around the table were lit by the red light from the burning buildings, nearby.

Tuvia Borzykowski on the first night of the Warsaw Ghetto rising, 19 April 1943; *Between Tumbling Walls* (1972) pp.57–8. The Jews of the ghetto rose in a desperate revolt. They were soon crushed, and the ghetto was razed to the ground, but the episode was to be a lasting inspiration for the Jews of Europe, both during and after the war. The reading of the Haggadah, a Hebrew text recited on the first two nights of Passover, was chosen as the moment for the rising to begin.

3 Sorting through ladies' underwear, I often found jewellery sewn into seams and corsets. Slit them open, and jewels and gold pieces would pour out. By the end of the session I often had a whole bucketful. Determined to hand in as little as possible, I buried some in the ground near the hut. Bank notes we never handed in: we used them as toilet paper.

Kitty Hart *Return to Auschwitz* (1981) pp.114–15. The author and her mother were prisoners in the Auschwitz death camp, here working in the unit that sorted out the belongings of murdered Jewish deportees.

4   You who live safe
     In your warm houses
     You who find, returning in the evening,
     Hot food and friendly faces:
     Consider if this is a man
     Who works in the mud
     Who does not know peace
     Who fights for a scrap of bread
     Who dies because of a yes or no.

Primo Levi (1947; 2000 edn) p.25.

5 Who has inflicted this upon us? Who has made us Jews different from all other people? Who has

allowed us to suffer so terribly up till now? It is God who has made us what we are, but it will be God, too, who will raise us up again. If we bear all this suffering and if there are still Jews left, when it is over, then Jews, instead of being doomed, will be held up as an example.

Anne Frank, diary entry, 11 April 1944; *Diary of a Young Girl* (1947). Anne Frank, her parents and her sister, together with four family friends, hid in Amsterdam from 6 July 1942 to 4 Aug. 1944, when they were betrayed and sent to Auschwitz. She died in Belsen concentration camp in the spring of 1945 after a forced march from Auschwitz. Over the two years in hiding Anne kept a diary, which survived to become one of the most extraordinary testaments of the Holocaust.

6 Dear finder, search everywhere, in every inch of soil. Tens of documents are buried under it, mine and those of other persons, which will throw light on everything that was happening here. Great quantities of teeth are also buried here. It was we, the Kommando workers, who have expressly strewn them all over the terrain, as many as we could, so that the world should find material traces of the millions of murdered people. We ourselves have lost hope of being able to live to see the moment of liberation.

Salmen Gradowski, Auschwitz, 6 Sept. 1944; Jadwiga Bezwinska and Danuta Czech *Amidst a Nightmare of Crime* (1973) pp.76–7. Gradowski was a member of the *Sonderkommando* whose job it was to take corpses from the gas chambers to the crematorium. Most of them were executed in their turn.

7 Hitler has lost every battle on every front except the battle against defenceless and unarmed men, women and children. He won the war against the Jews of Europe.

Zalman Grinberg, 27 May 1945; Gilbert (1986) p.811.

THE HOLOCAUST: ON THE OUTSIDE LOOKING IN

8 The Jews have done nothing but add to our difficulties by propaganda and deeds since the war began … The morally censorious attitude of the United States in general to other people's affairs has long attracted attention, but when it is coupled with unscrupulous Zionist 'sob-stuff' and misrepresentation, it is very hard to bear.

British Colonial Office mandarin J.T. Bennett, 18 April 1941; Bernard Wasserstein *Britain and the Jews of Europe 1939–1945* (1979) p.50.

1 I am to them the embodiment of a nemesis. They each and all believe every person, everywhere, has a RIGHT to come to the United States. I believe NOBODY anywhere has a RIGHT to enter the United States unless the United States desires.

US diplomat Breckinridge Long, diary entry, 4 Sept. 1941; Henry Feingold *The Politics of Rescue* (1970) p.136. Long forcefully resisted the entry of Jewish refugees.

2 RECEIVED ALARMING REPORT THAT IN FUHRER'S HEADQUARTERS PLAN DISCUSSED AND UNDER CONSIDERATION ACCORDING TO WHICH ALL JEWS IN COUNTRIES OCCUPIED OR CONTROLLED GERMANY NUMBER 3½–4 MILLION SHOULD AFTER DEPORTATION AND CONCENTRATION IN EAST BE AT ONE BLOW EXTERMINATED TO RESOLVE ONCE AND FOR ALL JEWISH QUESTION IN EUROPE STOP THE ACTION REPORTED PLANNED FOR AUTUMN METHODS UNDER DISCUSSION INCLUDING PRUSSIC ACID STOP.

Dr Gerhard Riegner, telegram to London and Washington, July 1942; Knopp (2000) photograph no.20. Riegner was the representative of the World Jewish Congress in Switzerland, his source an anonymous German industrialist. This was the first news received in the West of the gassing programme, already well under way by this time.

3 From all the occupied countries Jews are being transported in conditions of appalling horror and brutality to Eastern Europe. In Poland, which has been made the principal Nazi slaughterhouse, the ghettos established by the German invaders are being systematically emptied of all Jews except for a few highly skilled workers required for war industries. None of those taken away are ever heard of again.

Declaration by the Allied coalition against Germany, 17 Dec. 1942; Wasserstein (1979) p.173.

4 Humanity owes this vow [to turn back to God] to hundreds of thousands of people who, through no fault of their own and solely because of their nation or their race, have been condemned to death or progressive extinction.

Pope Pius XII, Christmas message, 1942; Saul Friedlander *Pius XII and the Third Reich* (1966) p.131. The pope came in for severe criticism for not making an explicit reference to the Jews in this address, not least from the president of the Polish government-in-exile in a letter to the pontiff on 2 Jan. 1943.

5 Those helpless unfortunates cannot be helped except by a landing in Europe, by a victory over German arms and a crushing of German might. There is no other way.

Adolf Berle, US assistant secretary of state, to a protest meeting in Boston, 2 May 1943; Knopp (2000) p.246.

6 What made the most impression on them was the extermination of the Jews. They had both witnessed atrocities. One of the Belgians saw truckloads of Jews carried off into a wood and the trucks returning a few hours later – empty. Bodies of Jewish children and women were left lying in ditches and along the railways. The Germans themselves, they added, boasted that they had constructed gas chambers where Jews were systematically killed and buried.

British embassy official, Stockholm, to Foreign Office, London, 18 May 1943; David Bankier *The Germans and the Final Solution* (1992) p.110. The Belgians were escapees from a camp close to the Belzec extermination centre, the destination of the transports in question.

7 One danger in it all is that their activities may lend color to the charges of Hitler that we are fighting this war on account of and at the instigation and direction of our Jewish citizens.

Breckinridge Long, diary entry, 20 April 1943; Fred L. Israel *The War Diary of Breckinridge Long* (1966) p.307. The reference is to the American Jewish organizations lobbying the US government to take action to rescue European Jewry.

8 In the name of God and of the German Reich, we here express the further plea that the responsible leadership of the Reich should abandon the persecution and destruction of many men and women who have been struck down while in German hands without legal conviction.

Bishop Theo Wurm, secretly circulated letter of protest, late 1943; Conway (1968) p.265.

9 They have not only failed to facilitate the obtaining of information concerning Hitler's plans to exterminate the Jews of Europe but in their official capacity have gone so far as to surreptitiously attempt to stop the obtaining of information concerning the murder of the Jewish population of Europe ... The matter of rescuing the Jews from extermination is a trust too great to remain in the hands of men who are indifferent, callous and perhaps even hostile.

US Treasury Department memorandum to President Roosevelt, 17 Jan. 1944; Walter Laqueur *The Terrible Secret* (1980) pp.223–3 and Feingold (1970) p.241. The memorandum was originally entitled 'Report to the Secretary [of the Treasury, Henry Morgenthau Jr] on the Acquiescence of this

Government in the Murder of the Jews'. Morgenthau – a Jew – was convinced that the State Department was obstructing proposals to bring Jews out of Nazi-occupied Europe. The chief target of his attack was Breckinridge Long.

1 We live in an age which is raging with mad ideas and demons, no less than the Middle Ages. Our allegedly 'enlightened' age, instead of indulging in an orgy of crazed witch-hunting, feasts in an orgy of maniacal Jew-hatred … Today, the blood of millions of slaughtered Jews, of men, women, and children, cries to heaven. The Church is not permitted to be silent.
Pastor Walter Hochstadter, summer 1944; Goldhagen (1996) p.431. This clandestine leaflet was distributed to German troops serving in the east, a rare and brave example of protest, which could easily have cost the author his life.

2 There is no doubt that this is probably the greatest and most horrible crime ever committed in the whole history of the world, and it has been done by scientific machinery by nominally civilized men in the name of a great State and one of the leading races of Europe.
Winston Churchill to foreign secretary Anthony Eden, 11 July 1944; Wasserstein (1979) p.259. Churchill was rejecting the proposal to bargain with Germany over the fate of the Jews of Hungary.

3 In my opinion a disproportionate amount of the time of the Office is wasted on dealing with these wailing Jews.
British Foreign Office official A.R. Dew, 1 Sept. 1944; Martin Gilbert Auschwitz and the Allies (1981) p.312.

4 I visited every nook and cranny of the camp because I felt it my duty to be in a position from then on to testify at first hand about those things in case there ever grew up at home the belief or assumption that the stories of Nazi brutality were just propaganda.
General of the Army Dwight D. Eisenhower on his visit to Buchenwald concentration camp, 13 April 1945; Crusade in Europe (1948) p.409.

5 Though we had heard and reported many stories of Nazi massacres of Jews and Slavs, we had never believed in the possibility of 'genocide' … Now we were to realize that our propaganda had fallen far behind the truth.
Richard Crossman Palestine Mission (1946) p.18.

6 *Robert Jackson*: You knew of the policy of the Nazi party and the policy of the government towards the Jews, did you not?

Albert Speer: I knew that the National Socialist Party was anti-Semitic, and I knew that the Jews were being evacuated from Germany.
Exchange at the Nuremberg war-crimes trial, 21 June 1946; Gitta Sereny Albert Speer and his Battle with the Truth (1995) pp.339, 707–8. Jackson was the chief US prosecuting counsel; Speer had been Hitler's armaments minister from 1942 to 1945. At Nuremberg he denied knowledge of the Final Solution but admitted his share of responsibility for Hitler's policy. Only in 1977 did he acknowledge that he had consciously looked the other way.

7 Under the guise of operating a Nazi labour factory first in Poland and then in the Sudetenland, Mr Schindler managed to take in as employees and protect Jewish men and women destined for death in Auschwitz and other infamous concentration camps.
M.W. Beckelmann, reference for Oskar Schindler, 1949; Thomas Keneally Schindler's Ark (1982) Epilogue. Schindler saved the Jews who worked for him by every means at his disposal, including bribery and forgery. The film Schindler's List (1993), based on Keneally's book, graphically told his story.

8 It was as though in those last minutes he was summing up the lesson that this long course in human wickedness had taught us – the lesson of the fearsome, word- and thought-defying *banality of evil*.
Hannah Arendt Eichmann in Jerusalem (1964 edn) p.252. Comment on Eichmann's last words before his execution in Israel on 31 May 1962 for crimes against the Jewish people, crimes against humanity and war crimes.

9 Not finding the Nazis guilty of real war crimes at all commensurate with the monstrous ones of the victors, they resorted to the only alternative open to hypocrites and liars, namely, to fabricate a mass atrocity. This they did with the legend of the six million Jews 'gassed' … This is a fabrication and swindle.
American Austin J. App A Straight Look at the Third Reich (1974) p.48. One of the earliest exponents of Holocaust denial, the proposition that the Nazi extermination of millions of European Jews never actually happened.

10 The following question must be deemed admissible, indeed necessary: Did the National Socialists carry out, did Hitler perhaps carry out an 'Asiatic' deed because they regarded themselves and their kind as the potential or real victims of an 'Asiatic' deed? Wasn't the 'Gulag Archipelago' more original than Auschwitz? Wasn't class murder on the part of the Bolsheviks logically and actually prior to race murder on the part of the Nazis?

The historian Ernst Nolte, *Frankfurter Allgemeine Zeitung*, 6 June 1986. Mitigation, if not exculpation, by relativist morality. The 'Asiatic deed' was mass slaughter on the pattern of Genghis Khan.

❙ I'm forming an association especially dedicated to all those liars, the ones who are trying to kid people that they were in these concentration camps. It's called 'The Auschwitz Survivors, Survivors of the Holocaust, and Other Liars' – 'A.S.S.H.O.L.E.S'.

Can't get more tasteless than that. But you've got to be tasteless because these people deserve all our contempt.

David Irving, speech in Canada, 5 Oct. 1991; Richard Evans *Lying About Hitler* (2001) pp.132–3. The British writer Irving, a determined counterfeiter of the history of Nazi Germany, brought a libel action against the American academic Deborah Lipstadt for her criticism of his work in her book *Denying the Holocaust* (1994). Whatever reputation he had as an historian was destroyed when he lost the case in April 2000. Professor Evans was the key defence witness.

World War II, 1939–45

PHONEY WAR, 1939–40

1 There is something phony about this war. You would think that they would do what they are going to do while Germany and Russia are still busy in the east, instead of waiting until they have cleaned up … there.
Senator William E. Borah, 17 Sept. 1939; Marian C. McKenna *Borah* (1961) p.365. Thus the phrase 'phoney war' was born. The reference to the east is to the Nazi–Soviet extinction of Poland, when British and French forces made no attack on Germany from the west.

2 Oh, you can't do that, that's private property: you'll be asking me to bomb the Ruhr next.
Sir Kingsley Wood, minister for air, to Leo Amery, 5 Sept. 1939; Edward Spears *Prelude to Dunkirk* (1954) pp.21–2. Amery had touched on the idea of setting the Black Forest on fire with incendiary bombs. The Ruhr was Germany's industrial heartland and the basis of its war machine.

3 *Une drôle de guerre.* (A funny kind of war.)
Édouard Daladier, French prime minister, 22 Dec. 1939. Not so funny for the Poles and then the Finns (at war with Russia).

4   There'll always be an England
     While there's a country lane;
     Wherever there's a cottage small
     Beside a field of grain.
Ross Parker and Hugh Charles 'There'll always be an England' (1939).

5   We'll meet again.
     Don't know where, don't know when.
     But I know we'll meet again some sunny day.
Ross Parker and Hugh Charles 'We'll meet again' (1939).

6   We're gonna hang out the washing on the
       Siegfried Line.
     Have you any dirty washing, mother dear?
Jimmy Kennedy and Michael Carr 'We're gonna hang out the washing on the Siegfried Line' (1939). The Siegfried Line was Germany's fortified line of defence along its western border, not pierced until 1945. The song typifies the vacuous British optimism of the opening months of the war. See 845:10.

7   Hitler has only got one ball.
     Goering has two but they're too small.
     Himmler has something sim'lar,
     But poor old Goebbels has no balls at all.
British army words, sung to the tune 'Colonel Bogey'. In 1945 Soviet pathologists examining the charred remains of what was said to be Hitler's body claimed it had only one testicle. The would-be starlets on the casting-couch at Goebbels' Berlin film studio would have denied the assertion in the last line.

8 The most dangerous aspect is the psychological one; a sense of false security is engendered, a feeling of sitting behind an impregnable iron fence; and should the fence perchance be broken, the French fighting spirit might well be brought crumbling with it.
General Alan Brooke on France's Maginot Line, diary entry, 6 Feb. 1940; Alistair Horne *To Lose a Battle* (1969) p.92. A prophecy realized in May, although the Maginot Line was not penetrated but by-passed at its northern end, since, after objections from neutral Belgium, it had not been completed along the Belgian frontier.

9 Whatever may be the reason … one thing is certain – he missed the bus.
Prime minister Neville Chamberlain on Hitler, *The Times*, 5 April 1940. Within a week, Hitler had successfully invaded Denmark and Norway; within just over five weeks Chamberlain had resigned.

THE BATTLE OF BRITAIN, 1940

10 NOW WE'RE AT THEIR THROATS!
Daily Express, front-page headline, 11 May 1940. A bellicose response to the German attack in the west, which began on 10 May 1940 and ended in outright German victory six weeks later.

11 I have nothing to offer but blood, toil, tears and sweat.
Winston Churchill, first speech as prime minister, 13 May 1940; *H.C. Deb.* Vol.360, Col.1502. Churchill replaced Chamberlain on 10 May.

12 We shall not flag or fail. We shall go on to the end. We shall fight in France, we shall fight on the seas and oceans, we shall fight with growing confidence and growing strength in the air, we shall defend our island, whatever the cost may be. We shall fight on the beaches, we shall fight on the landing grounds, we shall fight in the fields and in the streets, we shall fight in the hills; we shall never surrender.
Winston Churchill, 4 June 1940; *H.C. Deb.* Vol.361, Col.796. A speech made immediately after the evacuation from

Dunkirk of most of the British army. Substantial British detachments remained in France, and the idea of establishing a redoubt in Brittany was briefly entertained, but they, too, were brought out. A magnificent piece of defiant rhetoric, on hearing which Churchill's minister of war, Anthony Eden, is said to have muttered: 'Fight? What with? Broken bottles?' (The army had left all its tanks and artillery in France.)

1 Our great-grandchildren, when they learn how we began this War by snatching glory out of defeat, and then swept on to victory, may also learn how the little holiday steamers made an excursion to hell and came back glorious.

The writer J.B. Priestley, broadcast, 5 June 1940; Godfrey Smith (ed.) *How it was in the War* (1989) p.71. Praise for the part played by the 'little ships' in the rescue of the British Expeditionary Force from Dunkirk, 27 May to 3 June 1940. Most of the troops were taken on board vessels of the Royal Navy, but the role of the small ships was played up to boost national morale.

2 In three weeks Britain will have her neck wrung like a chicken.

General Maxime Weygand, June 1940, attrib. On 30 Dec. 1941 Churchill quoted this prediction and commented, 'Some chicken! Some neck!' (*Complete Speeches* Vol.6 (1974) p.6544).

3 What General Weygand called the Battle of France is over. I expect that the Battle of Britain is about to begin ... Upon this battle depends the survival of Christian civilization. Upon it depends our own British life and the long continuity of our institutions and our Empire. The whole fury and might of the enemy must very soon be turned on us. Hitler knows that he will have to break us in this island or lose the war. If we can stand up to him, all Europe may be free, and the life of the world may move forward into broad, sunlit uplands; but if we fail, then the whole world, including the United States, and all that we have known and cared for, will sink into the abyss of a new dark age made more sinister, and perhaps more protracted, by the lights of a perverted science ... Let us therefore brace ourselves to our duty, and so bear ourselves that, if the British Commonwealth and its Empire last for a thousand years, men will still say, 'This was their finest hour.'

Winston Churchill, 18 June 1940; *H.C. Deb.* Vol.362, Col.60. Speech made on Waterloo Day as the French government moved towards an armistice that would leave Britain isolated.

4 Take One With You.

Slogan, current in the summer of 1940, with a German invasion highly probable. The injunction to kill a German as

you yourself were killed was a counsel of despair at a time of supreme national crisis.

5 Went the day well?
  We died and never knew.
  But, well or ill,
  Freedom, we died for you.

Epigraph to the film *Went the Day Well?* (1942); Anthony Aldgate and Jeffrey Richards *Britain Can Take It* (1986) p.128. The film was based on a short story by Graham Greene, about a German attempt to take over an English village in 1940, first published in *Collier's Weekly*, 29 June 1940.

6 Mr Brown goes off to Town
  On the eight twenty-one.
  He comes back each evening,
  And he's ready with his gun.

Song celebrating the Home Guard, a volunteer force of men and youths too old or too young for military service. It was first proposed by Churchill in Oct. 1939 and formed in June 1940.

7 Never in the field of human conflict was so much owed by so many to so few.

Winston Churchill, 20 Aug. 1940; *H.C. Deb.* Vol.364, Col.1166. This tribute to RAF Fighter Command was first made privately to Churchill's chief of staff, General Hastings Ismay, on 16 Aug. (Martin Gilbert *Finest Hour* (1983) p.756).

8 These two great organizations of the English-speaking democracies, the British Empire and the United States, will have to be somewhat mixed up together in some of their affairs for mutual and general advantage ... I could not stop [this process] if I wished; no one can stop it. Like the Mississippi, it just keeps rolling along. Let it roll. Let it roll on full flood, inexorable, irresistible, benignant, to broader lands and better days.

Winston Churchill, 20 Aug. 1940; *H.C. Deb.* Vol.354, Col.1171. Said as Churchill was negotiating for the release of 50 American destroyers to the Royal Navy as the symbol of Anglo-American partnership against the enemy, in spite of US neutrality.

9 I shall say it again and again and again. Your boys are not going to be sent into any foreign wars.

President Franklin D. Roosevelt, 30 Oct. 1940; *Public Papers 1940* (1941) p.517. With a presidential election only days away, he could say nothing else, but preparations for an American entry into the war were already taking shape. That, of course, would be construed as entry into an American, not a foreign, war.

10 We must be the great arsenal of democracy.

President Franklin D. Roosevelt, 29 Dec. 1940; *Public Papers 1940* (1941) p.643. Safely re-elected, Roosevelt could afford to be bolder in his support for Britain in its war with Germany. This speech was the prelude to the Lend–Lease programme whereby America gave Britain huge quantities of food, raw materials and military supplies. It presupposed that the United States itself would be an auxiliary, not a combatant, but Roosevelt was readying the country to enter the war throughout 1941.

1 Give us the tools and we will finish the job.
Winston Churchill, 9 Feb. 1941; *Complete Speeches* Vol.6 (1974) p.6350. An appeal to the United States for the gift of military supplies, since Britain had reached the point where it could no longer pay for them. Nor, however, could it hope to win the war against Germany single-handed. American intervention was vital, particularly as the Soviet Union was not yet an ally.

THE BLITZ, 1940–41

2 'There is an air-raid warning on, sir,' said the stationmaster. 'Will you take cover?' 'Not at all,' said Churchill through his long cigar. 'It's only a red one, isn't it?'
US General Raymond E. Lee at Victoria Station, 28 Aug. 1940, witnessing Churchill's reaction to the news of German bombers over London; *The London Observer* (1972) pp.39–40. 'A red one' was a full-scale alert. General Lee was stationed in London throughout most of the Blitz and kept a diary of his experiences.

3 These people are exceedingly brave, tough and prudent. The East End, where disaster is always just around the corner, seems to take it better than the more fashionable districts in the West End.
American radio commentator Ed Murrow, 9 Sept. 1940; *This Is London* (1941) p.171. Murrow was the London-based European director of the Columbia Broadcasting Service (CBS). The first sustained bombing attack on the capital came on 7 Sept., and the raids went on until May 1941.

4 The press versions of people's smiling jollity and fun are gross exaggeration. On no previous investigation has so little humour, laughter or whistling been recorded.
Mass-Observation report on the East End, 10 Sept. 1940; Angus Calder *The Myth of the Blitz* (1991) p.133.

5 There'd been air raids in the other war, I know, but the only thing at all like those shelters that I could think of was the hold of a slave ship on its way from Africa to America, full of hundreds and hundreds of people who were having things done to them that they were quite powerless to resist.

Henry Moore; William Packer *Henry Moore* (1985) p.116. The sculptor made a celebrated collection of drawings of the Londoners who sheltered at night on the platforms of the stations of the Underground.

6 This story was told to me by a Chinese friend – otherwise I should not have dared to tell it. In a street of a certain character (as a certain kind of journalist would call it) an A.R.P. [air raid precautions] warden noticed an imperfect blackout. He said to a woman who answered his knock: 'There's a chink in that room up there.' 'No,' she said, 'it's not a Chink: it's a Japanese gentleman.'
Kingsley Martin, 28 Sept. 1940; *Critic's London Diary* (1960) p.93.

7 Some of the damage in London is pretty heartbreaking but what an effect it has had on the people! What courage! What determination! … Everybody absolutely determined: secretly delighted with the *privilege* of holding up Hitler. Certain of beating him; a certainty which no amount of bombing can weaken, only strengthen.
Film director Humphrey Jennings to his wife, 20 Oct. 1940; Mary-Lou Jennings (ed.) *Humphrey Jennings* (1982) p.25.

8 I feel quite exhausted after seeing and hearing so much sadness, sorrow, heroism and magnificent spirit. The destruction is so awful, and the people so *wonderful* – they *deserve* a better world.
Queen Elizabeth to Queen Mary, the Queen Mother, 19 Oct. 1940; Angus Calder *The People's War* (1969) p.524. Letter written after a tour of the blitzed East End. When Buckingham Palace was bombed, the queen famously remarked: 'Now I can look the East End in the face.'

9 I boast of being the only man in London who has been bombed off a lavatory seat while reading Jane Austen. She went into the bath; I went through the door.
Kingsley Martin, 26 Oct. 1940; *Critic's London Diary* (1960) p.94.

10 The first thing which the rescue squads and the firemen saw, as their torches poked through the gloom and the smoke and the bloody pit which had lately been the most chic cellar in London, was a frieze of other shadowy men, night-creatures who had scuttled within as soon as the echoes ceased, crouching over any dead or wounded woman, any *soignée* corpse they could find, and ripping off its necklaces, or earrings, or brooch: rifling its handbag, scooping up its loose change.
Nicholas Monsarrat *Breaking In, Breaking Out* (1971) p.288. The scene is the Café de Paris in London, which took a direct hit on 8 March 1941. A darker sidelight on the Blitz.

1 The most spectacular ruins in Hull are along the bank of the river Hull … particularly the east side. Here one sees the still smouldering remains of the tall flour mills and stores … Further east and north-east the industrial and working-class residential areas have suffered heavily … and a large power-station is almost unrecognizable. The gas-works looks almost untouched, but Hull was without gas for six weeks after the May raids.

Mass-Observation report on the aftermath of the German raids on the East Yorkshire city of Hull on 7 and 8 May 1941; Tom Harrisson *Living Through the Blitz* (1976) pp.267–8. Hull was the most heavily targeted provincial city in Britain.

FRANCE UNDER OCCUPATION, 1940–44

2 *La France a perdu une bataille! Mais la France n'a pas perdu la guerre!* (France has lost a battle! But France has not lost the war!)

Poster issued in the name of General Charles de Gaulle, late July 1940. The sentences do not appear in the BBC radio address made by de Gaulle in London on 18 June 1940, as many have supposed. On 28 May, Duff Cooper, minister of information, had said: 'Even if the Allies lost this battle, we should not have lost the war.'

3 *Travail, Famille, Patrie* (Work, Family, Country)

François de la Rocque, attrib. Motto on Vichy coinage, summarizing the values allegedly betrayed by the Third Republic. The puppet French state sanctioned by the Germans had its headquarters in the spa town of Vichy, in central France.

4 *Une jachère de nouveau emblavée.* (Fallow made wheatfield again.)

Motto on a commemorative plate issued in support of the Vichy regime, c.1941. It captures perfectly Vichy's argument that the soul of France lay in the simple, earthy values of the peasantry, neglected under the Third Republic but now triumphantly restored.

5   Before you, the saviour of France,
     We, your boys, swear to follow in your steps …
     For Pétain is France, France is Pétain.

André Montagnard 'Maréchal, Nous Voilà!' (Marshal, Here We Are!), composed in 1941 as part of the cult of the elderly Marshal Philippe Pétain as the supposed redeemer of defeated France and head of the Vichy regime.

6 If we collaborate with Germany … that is to say, if we work for her in our factories, if we give her certain facilities, we can save the French nation; reduce to a minimum our territorial losses in the colonies and on the mainland; play an honourable – if not important – role in the future of Europe.

Admiral François Darlan, 14 May 1941; Julian Jackson *France: The Dark Years 1940–1944* (2001) p.179. Darlan was deputy premier and Pétain's designated successor. He defected to the Allies after their invasion of northwest Africa in Nov. 1942 and was assassinated on 24 Dec. 1942.

7 To treat with yesterday's enemy is not cowardice, it is wisdom; the acceptance of the inevitable … What is the point of battering oneself against the bars of one's cage?

The writer André Gide *Journal 1939–1949* (1954) p.65.

8 Our worst defeat had the fortunate result of ridding us of democracy.

Charles Maurras, *Action française*, 15 Jan. 1942. Right-wing authoritarians such as Maurras came into their own under the occupation.

9 Official black Citroens cruised the streets of Nice and passengers attentively scrutinized passers-by. At any moment, a pedestrian would be asked to get into a car … The car went to a synagogue. There the victim was undressed. If he was circumcised, he automatically took his place in the next convoy to Drancy.

Leon Poliakov, a French Jew, on the German round-up of Jews in Nice, late 1943; S. Zuccotti *The Holocaust, the French and the Jews* (1993) p.181. Drancy was an internment camp on the edge of Paris, from which transports were sent to the Auschwitz death camp in occupied Poland.

10 If the Germans are beaten, General de Gaulle will return. He will be supported, and I have no illusions about this, by 80 or 90 per cent of the French people and I shall be hanged. So what? There are two men who can save our country at the present time, and if I weren't Laval, I would like to be General de Gaulle.

Collaborationist premier Pierre Laval, 17 Nov. 1943; Geoffrey Warner *Pierre Laval and the Eclipse of France* (1968) p.352. Laval was executed for treason in Oct. 1945.

11 *Il a fait ce qu'il a pu.* (He did what he could.)

A peasant's generous verdict on Laval, who claimed to have striven to mitigate German occupation policy from the inside.

12 Kill the German to purify our territory, kill him because he kills our people … Kill those who denounce, those who have aided the enemy … Kill the policeman who has in any way contributed to the arrest of patriots … Kill the *miliciens*, exterminate them … strike them down like mad dogs … destroy them as you would vermin.

Philippe Viannay 'The Duty to Kill' March 1944; Jackson (2001) p.479. With Germany falling increasingly on to the defensive, the resistance movements in France became more and more radical. The *miliciens* were paramilitaries dedicated to the occupation regime.

1 What I had not expected was the emotion which suddenly took hold of me, at the sight, under the gold braid of his képi gleaming in the sun … of Marshal Pétain … I was overcome, and although I did not go as far as to shout, I was filled with a feeling of love and gratitude.

Claude Mauriac on Pétain's visit to Paris, 26 April 1944; *La Terrasse de Malagar* pp.164–8. Pétain had come to Paris for a service in Notre Dame Cathedral to commemorate the hundreds of dead killed in an Allied bombing raid six days earlier. In this moment of grief he could still have powerful emotional appeal as a focus for French national feeling.

2   *Les sanglots longs*
       Des violins
       De l'automne
       Blessent mon coeur
       D'une langueur
       Monotone.

(The drawn-out sobs of the autumn violins grieve my heart with their monotonous languor.)

Paul Verlaine 'Song of Autumn' (1866). The poem was broadcast from London as the coded signal to the French Resistance that the D-Day invasion had begun on 6 June 1944.

3 In the front rank there is one man in uniform; he is a head taller than the rest. '*Vive de Gaulle! Vive de Gaulle!*' the crowd yells … Behind him, after two or three ranks of silent officials, a human herd prances, dances, sings, enjoys itself utterly; from it there stick out tank-turrets sprinkled with soldiers and with girls whose destiny does not seem likely to be a nunnery.

Adrian Dansette on Paris on 26 Aug. 1944, the day of the city's final liberation; *Histoire de la Libération de Paris* (1946) p.412.

4 We were never more free than under the German occupation.

The philosopher Jean-Paul Sartre *Lettres françaises*, 9 Sept. 1944. A paradox taken out of context by Sartre's anti-communist enemies. Sartre is claiming that the French were forced into commitment by the occupation, and the best of them achieved an intellectual liberty that was the truest form of resistance.

THE BATTLE OF THE ATLANTIC, 1941–3

5 The only thing that ever really frightened me during the war was the U-boat peril.

Winston Churchill *Their Finest Hour* (1949) p.529.

6 When you see a rattlesnake poised to strike, you do not wait until he has struck before you crush him.

President Franklin D. Roosevelt, 11 Sept. 1941; *Public Papers 1941* (1950) p.390. Justification of American anti-submarine activity in the Atlantic after a U-boat attack on USS *Greer* on 4 Sept.

7 Dec. 10th 1941. U Boat attack on convoy. Sinking three ships … Picked up fifty survivors. All but six Hindous (Lascars). Nightmare of a night. But exciting.

Diary entry of Donald Canham in HMS *Alisma*; Chris Howard Bailey *The Battle of the Atlantic* (1994) p.78.

8 Merchant shipping will be sunk without warning with the intention of killing as many of the crew as possible … U-boats are to surface after torpedoing and shoot up the lifeboats.

Adolf Hitler, 3 Jan. 1942; John Terraine *Business in Great Waters* (1989) p.467. A personal order to Admiral Karl Doenitz, head of the submarine command.

9 Sighted sub. Sank same.

Donald F. Mason, 28 Jan. 1942. A laconic situation report from an American aircraft over the Atlantic.

10 In my imagination I can see what it must be like inside the ship, the boiler room or engine room of a ship that's torpedoed, because as they go down the engines are still moving … and the crew inside the ship in the engine room. They wouldn't stand a chance whatsoever in any way.

Lieutenant Roy Dykes RNVR; Bailey (1994) pp.143–4.

11 If we lose the war at sea we lose the war.

Admiral of the Fleet Sir Dudley Pound, First Sea Lord, 5 March 1942; Correlli Barnett *Engage the Enemy More Closely* (1991) p.460. If the U-boat offensive succeeded, American troops and supplies could not be ferried across to Britain in readiness for an invasion of western Europe.

12 I was ushered with great solemnity into the shrine where stood a bronze-coloured column surmounted by a larger circular bronze-coloured face, like some eastern goddess who was destined to become the oracle of Bletchley, at least when she felt like it. She was an awesome piece of magic.

F.W. Winterbotham *The Ultra Secret* (1974). The 'Bombe', a computer that penetrated the mechanism of the German Enigma coding machine, producing invaluable decrypts for 'Station X', the government Code and Cypher School at Bletchley Park, north of London. This information was a critical asset in the anti-submarine war.

1 We sat helpless 265 metres [870 feet] below. Our nerves trembled. Our bodies were stiff from cold, stress and fear. The mind-searing agony of waiting made us lose any sense of time and any desire for food. The bilges were flooded with water, oil and urine. Our washrooms were under lock and key; to use them would have meant instant death, for the tremendous outside pressure would have over-whelmed the outflow.

First Officer Herbert Werner of *U230*; *Iron Coffins* (1969) p.119. Werner describes the situation inside the submarine on 12 May 1943 after more than ten hours of continual attack. On 24 May Admiral Doenitz withdrew all U-boats from the North Atlantic, admitting that they had lost the battle.

STRATEGIC AIR OFFENSIVE, 1942–5

2 We are free, if we will, to employ our rapidly increasing air strength in the proper manner. In such a manner as would avail to knock Germany out of the war in a matter of months, if we decide upon the right course. If we decide upon the wrong course, then our air power will now, and increasingly in the future, become inextricably implicated as a subsidiary weapon in the prosecution of vastly protracted and unavoidable land and sea campaigns … In the last analysis … the one way in which Germany can be defeated is by air attack.

Air Marshal Sir Arthur Harris, commander-in-chief Bomber Command, to Churchill, 17 June and 3 Sept. 1942; Dudley Saward *'Bomber' Harris* (1984) pp.160, 169.

3 The aim of the bomber offensive is the progressive destruction and dislocation of the enemy's war industrial and economic system and the undermining of his morale to a point where his capacity for armed resistance is fatally weakened.

British chiefs of staff review, 30 Oct. 1942; John Terraine *The Right of the Line* (1985) p.504. Harris hoped to achieve these objectives by 1 April 1944 but failed to do so.

4 In spite of all that happened at Hamburg, bombing proved a comparatively humane method. For one thing, it saved the flower of the youth of this country and of our allies from being mown down by the military in the field, as it was in Flanders in the war of 1914–1918.

Air Marshal Sir Arthur Harris *The Bomber Offensive* (1947) p.176. Hamburg was destroyed in a firestorm after incendiary bomb raids in July 1943, and many thousands of its citizens met appalling deaths.

5 I informed Hitler that armaments production was collapsing and threw in the further warning that a series of attacks of this sort, extended to six more major cities, would bring Germany's armaments production to a total halt.

Albert Speer on an interview with Hitler, 2 Aug. 1943, after the RAF's incendiary raids on Hamburg; *Inside the Third Reich* (1970) p.284. Speer was Hitler's minister for armaments production.

6 To bomb cities as cities, deliberately to attack civilians, quite irrespective of whether or not they are actively contributing to the war effort is a wrong deed, whether done by the Nazis or ourselves.

Bishop George Bell, Sept. 1943; Ronald Jasper *George Bell* (1967) p.276. Bell's opposition to the aerial bombing of German cities made him extremely unpopular in a Britain thirsting for retribution after the German air attacks it had suffered since 1940.

7 It is a maintainable proposition that it was Mrs Carrie [*sic*] Nation who sowed the seed which flowered abundantly in the Anglo-American bombing offensive in the present war … As she pelted the liquor industry with bricks, so their air power has pelted the war industry with bombs.

J.M. Spaight *Bombing Vindicated* (1944) p.141. Carry Nation, the militant prohibitionist, attacked American saloons in the 1890s, not with bricks but with a hatchet. She failed to close them down, just as the strategic bombing offensive failed to close down German industry, until the last months of the European war.

8 We were going after military targets. No point in slaughtering civilians for the mere sake of slaughter … The entire population got into the act and worked to make those airplanes or munitions of war … men, women, children. We knew we were going to kill a lot of women and children when we burned that town. Had to be done.

US Army Air Force General Curtis E. LeMay on the incendiary raid on Tokyo on 9 March 1945; *Mission with LeMay* (1965) p.384. This attack, planned by LeMay, killed an estimated 50,000 people.

9 What was criminal in Coventry, Rotterdam, Warsaw and London has now become heroic in Dresden and now in Tokyo.

The American Oswald Garrison Villard, 1945; Conrad C. Crane *Bombs, Cities and Civilians* (1993) p.120. Warsaw was bombed by the German Luftwaffe in 1939, Coventry and Rotterdam in 1940, and London in 1940–41. Dresden was bombed by the US Army Air Force and the Royal Air Force on 14 and 15 Feb. 1945, and Tokyo by the USAAF on 9 March 1945.

1 It seems to me that the moment has come when the question of bombing of German cities simply for the sake of increasing the terror, though under other pretexts, should be reviewed.

Winston Churchill in the aftermath of Dresden, 28 March 1945; Martin Gilbert *Road to Victory* (1986) p.1257. Churchill was persuaded to tone down this memorandum, but it was an indication of how sensitive a subject bombing had become as the war approached its end.

THE MEDITERRANEAN: NORTH AFRICA AND ITALY, 1940–44

2 Audience with King Farouk ... I told him, much to his amusement, that our troops in the Western Desert had captured a general with four ladies in a smart motor car. This thrilled him and he said he hoped I would let him know later what was done with the four ladies.

Sir Miles Lampson, British ambassador to Egypt, diary entry, 17 June 1940; *The Killearn Diaries 1934–1946* (1972) p.119. The general in question was Italian. Italy had declared war on Britain and France on 10 June, and its colony of Libya in the Western Desert adjoined Egypt The king had an inordinate appetite for women, as remembered in Eartha Kitt's rendition of the song 'Monotonous': 'King Farouk's on tenterhooks for me.'

3   Underneath the lantern by the barrack gate,
    Darling I remember the way you used to wait.
    'Twas there that you whispered tenderly
    That you loved me,
    You'd always be
    My Lilli of the lamplight,
    My own Lilli Marlene.

English version of the original German song '*Lilli Marlene*', taken up by the British 8th Army during its campaign in the Western Desert.

4 There exists a real danger that our friend Rommel is becoming a kind of magician or bogey-man to our troops, who are talking far too much about him. He is by no means a superman, although he is undoubtedly very energetic and able. Even if he were a superman, it would still be highly undesirable that our men should credit him with supernatural powers.

General Sir Claude Auchinleck to his senior commanders; Desmond Young *Rommel* (1950) Ch. 2. General Erwin Rommel was appointed commander of the German Afrika Korps on 15 Feb. 1941 to rescue the Italians from defeat and immediately proved himself a formidable exponent of tank warfare, so much so that he forced Auchinleck's removal in Aug. 1942.

5 At first it was impressive, but after half an hour deadly monotonous. It was like everything German – overdone.

Evelyn Waugh on a Luftwaffe dive-bomber attack in Crete, about 26 May 1941; *The Diary of Evelyn Waugh* (1976) p.502. Crete was abandoned to the Germans shortly afterwards.

6 The prime minister wins debate after debate and loses battle after battle. The country is beginning to say that he fights debates like a war and the war like a debate.

Aneurin Bevan, 2 July 1942; Gilbert (1986) p.138. The Labour MP Bevan was speaking in a debate on a motion of censure on Churchill's government after the surrender of the garrison at Tobruk, Libya, on 20 June. This followed the surrender of Singapore to the Japanese on 15 Feb. The motion was defeated by 475 votes to 25.

7 Let no man surrender so long as he is unwounded and can fight.

General Bernard Montgomery to the British 8th Army, 30 Oct. 1942, on the eve of the Battle of El Alamein. Montgomery had succeeded Auchinleck at a time when Rommel seemed poised to break through and take Britain's crucial passageway to India, the Suez Canal. Hence the urgency of this order of the day.

8 It has been a fine battle. There is no doubt of the result ... But we must not think that the party is over ... We must keep up the pressure. We intend to hit this chap for six out of North Africa.

General Bernard Montgomery, 5 Nov. 1942; Nigel Hamilton *Monty: Master of the Battlefield 1942–1944* (1983) pp.8, 9. Montgomery announces his victory in the Battle of El Alamein, in which the forces of Rommel's Afrika Korps were pushed back into a retreat that ended in capitulation six months later in Tunisia.

9 In defeat unbeatable: in victory unbearable.

Winston Churchill on General Montgomery; Edward Marsh *Ambrosia and Small Beer* (1964) Ch.5. No one had a higher opinion of Montgomery than Montgomery himself.

10 Now this is not the end. It is not the beginning of the end. But it is, perhaps, the end of the beginning.

Winston Churchill, 10 Nov. 1942; *The End of the Beginning* (1943) p.214. Speaking of the recent British victory at El Alamein.

11 At the same time we make this wide encircling movement in the Mediterranean, having for its primary object the recovery of the command of that vital sea, but also … the exposure of the under-belly of the Axis, especially Italy, to heavy attack.

Winston Churchill, 11 Nov. 1942; *H.C. Deb.* Vol.385, Col.28. The Anglo-American invasion of northwest Africa began on 8 Nov. 1942, promoted by Churchill in the teeth of an American preference for an assault on France. The usual, but erroneous, version of this phrase is 'soft under-belly'. The mountainous terrain of Italy was to prove anything but soft for the attacking Allied forces.

1 Some of you Britishers know the old story – we had a general called U.S. Grant. His name was Ulysses Simpson Grant, but in my and the Prime Minister's early days he was called 'Unconditional Surrender' Grant. The elimination of German, Japanese and Italian war power means the unconditional surrender by Germany, Italy and Japan.

President Franklin D. Roosevelt, 24 Jan. 1943; *Foreign Relations of the United States: The Conferences at Washington 1941–1942 and Casablanca 1943* (1968) p.729. For Grant and unconditional surrender see 590:2. This policy, announced at a press conference in Casablanca after the successful Anglo-American landings in northwest Africa, was highly controversial. Its critics claimed that it left the Axis powers nothing to lose by fighting to the bitter end, but it was applied to Germany and Japan. Italy, which surrendered on 2 Sept. 1943, was treated more leniently.

2   But she would weep to see today
      How on his skin the swart flies move;
      The dust upon the paper eye
      And the burst stomach like a cave.

Keith Douglas 'Vergissmeinnicht' (1943). The poem was written after Douglas saw the corpse of a German soldier in Tunisia. Douglas himself was killed in Normandy on 9 June 1944.

3 Suddenly, three ME109s roared at nought feet over O.P. Hill, we all panicked, ran in circles, crashed into each other. It was pointless to lie down. As they roared over, I came to attention and gave the Nazi salute. It saved our lives I tell you!

Spike Milligan, 25 Feb. 1943; *'Rommel?' 'Gunner Who?'* (1974) p.93. The comic genius Milligan was serving with the Royal Artillery in Tunisia. The O.P. (Observation Post) housed artillery spotters.

4 During battle, it is very important to visit frequently hospitals containing newly wounded men. Before starting such an inspection, the officer in charge of the hospital should inform the inspecting general which wards contain men whose conduct does not merit compliments.

General George S. Patton Jr *War as I Knew it* (1947). On 3 and 10 Aug. 1943, after the recent invasion of Italy, Patton slapped American soldiers, whom he considered cowards, in Sicilian hospitals. The incidents momentarily threatened his career, but his punishment was a reprimand and not dismissal.

5 We hoped to land a wild cat that would tear out the bowels of the Boche. Instead we have stranded a vast whale with its tail flopping about in the water.

Winston Churchill on the Anzio landing, 29 Feb. 1944; Gilbert (1986) p.667. Allied troops landed at Anzio on 22 Jan. but failed to move inland and take nearby Rome.

6 The Abbey at Monte Cassino was the creation of one of man's noblest dreams … but this morning the tired infantrymen, fighting for their lives near its slopes, were to cry for joy as bomb after bomb crumbled it into dust.

H.L. Bond *Return to Cassino* (1964) p.135. The Benedictine monastery of Monte Cassino, which dominated the road from Naples to Rome, was first assaulted on 24 Jan. 1944. It was bombed on 13 Feb. but not taken until 18 May after severe Allied losses.

7   Looking round the mountains, in the mud and
          rain,
      There's lots of little crosses, some which bear
          no name.
      Blood, sweat and tears and toil are gone,
      The boys beneath them slumber on.
      These are your D-Day dodgers, who'll stay in
          Italy.

Last verse of a soldiers' song inspired by the vicious allegation of Nancy, Lady Astor that the troops in Italy were sitting it out while the real fighting was going on in Normandy after the D-Day invasion of 6 June 1944.

8 There was only one catch and that was Catch-22, which specified that a concern for one's own safety in the face of dangers that were real and immediate was the process of a rational mind. Orr was crazy and could be grounded. All he had to do was ask; and as soon as he did, he would no longer be crazy and would have to fly more missions.

Joseph Heller *Catch-22* (1955) Ch. 5. Heller's novel is set on an American air base in Italy.

9 My friend, you do not consider sufficiently one great difficulty. In Italy, we were fighting our way not through a country, but through an art gallery and a museum. It was no longer the Art of War but the War of Art. How could we deploy our full strength? The fifteenth century? I could not attack

but had to make an outflanking movement. The sixteenth? Then I permitted myself a little machine-gun fire. The seventeenth? Ah! Now we could have artillery support. The eighteenth meant tanks and for the nineteenth, monsieur, I had no hesitation in calling in the air. If only Italy had all been built in the twentieth century we should be on the Alps by now!

French General Joseph de Monsabert, autumn 1944; Wynford Vaughan-Thomas *How I Liberated Burgundy* (1985) p.40.

SOVIET RUSSIA, 1941–5

1 We have only to kick in the door and the whole rotten structure will come crashing down.

Adolf Hitler shortly before the German invasion of the Soviet Union on 22 June 1941.

2 My people and I, Josef Vissarionovich Stalin, firmly remember your wise prediction: Hitler will not attack in 1941!

Lavrenti Beria to Stalin, 21 June 1941; Richard Overy *Russia's War* (1997) p.34. Stalin had been warned several times, by his own agents and by Churchill, that a German invasion was planned for the summer of 1941, but he ignored them all.

3 If Hitler invaded Hell, I would at least make a favourable reference to the Devil in the House of Commons.

Winston Churchill, 21 June 1941, the eve of the German invasion of the USSR; *The Grand Alliance* (1950) p.331.

4 It is hardly too much to say that the campaign against Russia has been won in fourteen days.

General Franz Halder, diary entry, 3 July 1941. Early German successes were staggering, and Halder's view was shared by many British and American military observers.

5 If we see that Germany is winning the war, we ought to help Russia, and if Russia is winning we ought to help Germany; and in that way let them kill as many as possible.

Senator Harry S Truman, *New York Times*, 24 July 1941.

6 There is no doubt that the absence of a second front in Europe considerably relieves the position of the German army.

Joseph Stalin, 6 Nov. 1941; *Vital Speeches of the Day*, 1 Dec. 1941, p.102. Precisely the same held true of the situation between Sept. 1939 and June 1941, thanks to the Non-Aggression Pact that Stalin signed with Nazi Germany on 23 Aug. 1939.

7 The mortuary itself is full. Not only are there too few trucks to go to the cemetery, but, more important, not enough gasoline to put in the trucks, and the main thing is – there is not enough strength left in the living to bury the dead.

Vera Inber, diary entry, 26 Dec. 1941; *Leningrad Diary* (1971). Leningrad was besieged from Sept. 1941 to Jan. 1943, and close on a million of its inhabitants died of starvation or enemy action in the winter of 1941–2.

8 Each position, each metre of Soviet territory must be stubbornly defended, to the last drop of blood. We must cling to every inch of Soviet soil and defend it to the end!

Joseph Stalin, Order 227, 'Not a Step Back!', 28 July 1942; Overy (1997) p.158. A desperate directive.

9 Surrender is forbidden. Sixth Army will hold their positions to the last man and the last round, and by their heroic endurance will make an unforgettable contribution to the establishment of a defensive front and the salvation of the western world.

Adolf Hitler to Field Marshal Friedrich von Paulus in Stalingrad, 3 Jan. 1943. Hitler promoted von Paulus to the rank of field marshal in the knowledge that no German field marshal had ever surrendered.

10 At the bottom of the trenches there lay frozen green Germans and frozen grey Russians and frozen fragments of human shapes, and there were helmets, Russian and German, lying among the thick debris … How anyone could have survived was hard to imagine. But now everything was silent in this fossilized shell, as though a raving lunatic had suddenly died of heart failure.

Alexander Werth *Russia at War, 1941–1945* (1964). The journalist Werth was in Stalingrad shortly after the German surrender on 31 Jan. 1943, a decisive turning point in the war.

11 I ask you: Do you want total war? Do you want it, if necessary, more total and more radical than we can even imagine it today?

Joseph Goebbels, speech to a hand-picked audience in the Berlin Sports Palace, 18 Feb. 1943; Jeremy Noakes and Geoffrey Pridham (eds) *Nazism 1919–1945* Vol.4 (1998) p.665. A question expecting the answer 'Yes'. By total war, Goebbels meant the complete mobilization of the German people behind the war effort after the surrender of Stalingrad.

12 You have, of course, read Dostoyevsky? Do you see what a complicated thing is a man's soul, man's psyche? Well then, imagine a man who has fought from Stalingrad to Belgrade – over thousands of kilometres of his own devastated land, across the dead bodies of his comrades and dearest ones. How can such a man react normally? And what is so awful in his having fun with a woman, after such horrors?

Milovan Djilas *Conversations with Stalin* (1962) pp.101–2. Stalin, justifying Red Army atrocities, on 11 April 1945.

1 This war is not as in the past: whoever occupies a territory also imposes on it his own social system.

Joseph Stalin to the Yugoslav Milovan Djilas, 11 April 1945; Djilas (1962) p.105. Stalin was, in fact, invoking a principle underlying the 1648 Treaty of Westphalia: *Cuius regio, eius religio* (Whoever rules the territory imposes his religion on it). He was referring to the post-war division of Europe envisaged by the Yalta Agreement of 11 Feb. 1945, between a Soviet east and an Anglo-American west.

2 When signing the instrument of capitulation [in Oct. 1939], the Polish general said: 'A wheel always turns.' He was to prove right in the end, though hardly – as far as the subsequent fate of his fatherland was concerned – in the sense his words had been meant to convey.

Field Marshal Erich von Manstein *Lost Victories* (1958). More than a touch of *Schadenfreude* here. The Pole was looking forward to Polish independence after German defeat. Instead, Poland was consigned to the victorious USSR.

3 On 30 April 1945 the Führer took his own life and thus it is that we who remain – having sworn him an oath of loyalty – are left alone. According to the Führer's order, you, German soldiers, were to fight on for Berlin, in spite of the fact that ammunition has run out and in spite of the general situation, which makes further resistance on our part senseless. My orders are: to cease resistance forthwith.

General Karl Weidling, to the German forces in Berlin under attack by the Red Army, 2 May 1945; John Erickson *The Road to Berlin* (1983) p.617. Hitler committed suicide in the bunker of the Reich Chancellery on 30 April. With his death, Weidling asserts, the troops were absolved from their oath to obey his orders. There is a clear implication, too, that in killing himself, Hitler deserted his followers.

LIBERATION IN WESTERN EUROPE, 1944–5

4 Our landings in the Cherbourg-Le Havre area have failed to gain a satisfactory foothold and I have withdrawn the troops. My decision to attack at this time and place was based on the best information available. The troops, the air and the navy did all

that bravery and devotion to duty could do. If any blame or fault attaches to the attempt, it is mine alone.

General Dwight D. Eisenhower, 5 June 1944; Geoffrey Perret *Eisenhower* (1999) p.282. Note written on the eve of D-Day, to be made public in case the invasion was thrown back. Eisenhower was Supreme Commander of the Allied Expeditionary Force.

5 Held a final meeting at 0415. This time the prophets [weather forecasters] came in smiling, conditions having shown a considerable improvement. It was therefore decided to let things be and proceed … I am under no delusions as to the risks involved in this most difficult of all operations … We shall require all the help that God can give us & I cannot believe that this will not be forthcoming.

Admiral Sir Bertram Ramsay, diary entry, 5 June 1944; *The Year of D-Day* (1994) p.83. Admiral Ramsay was naval commander of the invasion force due to land in Nazi-occupied France on 6 June. The landing was scheduled for 5 June but had to be postponed for 24 hours because of bad weather in the English Channel.

6 We sure liberated the hell out of this place.

American soldier, comment on the ruins of a village in Normandy.

7 An American … said, most aptly, that flying-bombs made him feel like the slot in a roulette table. The board goes round and then there is a tense pause and then – Bing; it's in your slot or someone else's.

Kingsley Martin, *New Statesman and Nation*, 15 July 1944. The first 'flying-bomb' or V1 (Vengeance weapon) landed in southeast England on 13 June. A pilotless plane, its engines cut out over the target, giving a few seconds of silence before it fell to earth and detonated. Both this missile and the supersonic V2 failed to swing the war in Germany's favour.

8 News filtered through of an attempt by army on Hitler's life which was unfortunately unsuccessful.

Admiral Sir Bertram Ramsay, diary entry, 20 July 1944; *The Year of D-Day* (1994) p.108. Officers in the Wehrmacht mounted an abortive coup against the Nazi regime, beginning with an assassination attempt at Hitler's headquarters in east Prussia.

9 I have … done what I could to ensure that this spirit [of Nazism] – with its excessive nationalism, persecution of other races, agnosticism, and materialism – is defeated.

Count Helmuth von Moltke to his sons, Oct. 1944; Joachim Fest *Plotting Hitler's Death* (1996) p.328. Von Moltke, a prominent figure in the German resistance to Hitler, was arrested in Jan. 1944 and executed a year later.

1 A very small clique of ambitious, wicked, and stupidly criminal officers forged a plot to eliminate me and, along with me, virtually the entire leadership of the Wehrmacht … We will settle accounts the way we National Socialists are accustomed to settling them.
Adolf Hitler, radio broadcast, midnight, 20 July 1944; Fest (1996) p.278. The purge that followed was bloody and prolonged, and the executions of the conspirators were filmed on Hitler's orders. 'I want them to be hanged, strung up like butchered cattle,' he told the trial judge, Roland Freisler.

2 Paris must either not fall into the hands of the enemy or the enemy must find it only a wasteland.
Adolf Hitler to the military commandant of Paris, General Dietrich von Choltitz, 23 Aug. 1944. Von Choltitz ignored the order, even after Hitler asked on 25 Aug.: 'Is Paris burning?'

3 Great news, *mon colonel*, we have found the weak point in the German defences. Every one is on a vineyard of inferior quality.
French army officer, Chalons-sur-Saône, Sept. 1944; Vaughan-Thomas (1985) p.153. The colonel's response: 'General de Monsabert must know of this at once, but he will give only one order, "J'attaque".'

4 I think we might be going a bridge too far.
General Sir Frederick Browning, attrib., 10 Sept. 1944. Comment on Field Marshal Montgomery's plan to drop paratroops to seize the bridge at Arnhem on the Rhine, beyond the first two objectives of Grave on the Maas and Nijmegen on the Waal. The operation was launched on 17 Sept., but the Arnhem bridge was not taken, and the project ended in costly failure.

5 Nuts! (Bollocks!)
General Anthony McAuliffe, 22 Dec. 1944. McAuliffe was US commander of the besieged garrison in Bastogne, Belgium, during the German midwinter attack in the Ardennes. This was his reply to the German demand for surrender.

6 As the photographers rushed up to secure good vantage points, he turned to them and said, 'This is one of the operations connected with this great war which must not be reproduced graphically' … I shall never forget the childish grin of intense satisfaction that spread all over his face as he looked down at the critical moment.
General Sir Alan Brooke on Churchill and his entourage urinating on the Siegfried Line, 3 March 1945; *War Diaries 1939–1945* (2001) pp.667–8. Churchill also peed into the Rhine on 26 March.

7 I picked my way over corpse after corpse in the gloom until I heard one voice that rose above the gentle, undulating moaning. I found a girl, she was a living skeleton, impossible to gauge her age for she had practically no hair left on her head and her face was a yellow parchment sheet with two holes in it for eyes. She was stretching out her stick of an arm and gasping something. It was 'English, English, medicine, medicine', and she was trying to cry but had not enough strength. And beyond her down the passage, there were convulsive movements of dying people too weak to raise themselves from the floor.
The BBC war correspondent Richard Dimbleby at Belsen concentration camp, 19 April 1945; Tom Hickman *What did you do in the War, Auntie? The BBC at War 1939–45* (1995) p.190. The camp at Belsen in north Germany was used as a dumping ground for prisoners marched in from all over Europe as the Germans retreated in the last months of the war. Tens of thousands died there, and it became an immediate symbol of German barbarity.

THE PACIFIC, CHINA AND BURMA, 1941–5

8 It is significant that despite the claims of air enthusiasts no battleship has yet been sunk by bombs.
Caption underneath a photograph of USS *Arizona*, 29 Nov. 1941. *Arizona* was sunk by Japanese aircraft in the Pearl Harbor attack eight days later.

9 Praise the Lord and pass the ammunition.
Attrib. to two US navy chaplains during the Pearl Harbor attack. Later set to music by Frank Loesser, when it became a highly popular song.

10 Whoever can surprise well must Conquer.
The American naval captain, John Paul Jones, 10 Feb. 1778.

11 We had won the war … Hitler's fate was sealed. Mussolini's fate was sealed. As for the Japanese, they would be ground to powder. All the rest was merely the proper application of overwhelming force.
Winston Churchill *The Grand Alliance* (1950) p.539. His reaction to the news of Pearl Harbor on 7 Dec. 1941.

12 Yesterday, December 7, 1941 – a date which will live in infamy – the United States of America was suddenly and deliberately attacked by naval and air forces of the Empire of Japan.
President Franklin D. Roosevelt, 8 Dec. 1941; *Public Papers 1941* (1950) p.514.

1 A military man can scarcely pride himself on having 'smitten a sleeping enemy'; in fact, to have it pointed out is more a matter of shame.
Admiral Yamamoto Isoroku, 9 Jan. 1942; Hirosuki Asawa *The Reluctant Admiral* (1979) p.286.

2 I feel all we have done is to awake a sleeping giant and fill him with a terrible resolve.
Admiral Yamamoto Isoroku, attrib. Authenticity doubtful, but given currency not least by its use in the film *Tora! Tora! Tora!* (1970).

3 If the army can't fight better than it is doing at the present we shall deserve to lose our empire!
General Sir Alan Brooke, diary entry, 18 Feb. 1942: *War Diaries 1939–1945* (2001) p.23. Written three days after the surrender of the island fortress of Singapore to a numerically inferior Japanese force.

4   We're the battling bastards of Bataan;
     No mama, no papa, no Uncle Sam;
     No aunts, no uncles, no cousins, no nieces;
     No pills, no planes, no artillery pieces.
     And nobody gives a damn.
Song of the besieged US army garrison in Bataan, the Philippines, early 1942; Thomas A. Bailey *Voices of America* (1976) p.423. Like the British forces in Burma during the war in the Far East, US troops in the Philippines thought of themselves as a 'forgotten army' in a conflict whose strategy was 'Europe first'.

5 There are no atheists in the foxholes.
Father William Cummings, US army chaplain, sermon in the besieged citadel of Bataan, early 1942; Sidney Stewart *Give Us This Day* (1957) p.85. Father Cummings died when the unmarked Japanese ship carrying prisoners-of-war was torpedoed by an American submarine on 15 Dec. 1944.

6 I came through and I shall return.
General Douglas MacArthur on arrival in Australia, 17 March 1942, after escaping from the Philippines; Geoffrey Perret *Old Soldiers Never Die* (1996) p.282.

7 1. Japan can be defeated in China. 2. It can be defeated by an air force so small that in other theaters it would be called ridiculous. 3. I am confident that, given real authority in command of such an air force, I can cause the collapse of Japan.
General Claire Lee Chennault to Wendell Willkie, 8 Oct. 1942; Anna Chennault *Chennault and the Flying Tigers* (1963) p.203. After the fall of Burma to Japan in the spring of 1942 Chennault, an aviator in the employ of the Chinese Nationalist government, believed that the road to victory lay in air power. This thesis was warmly approved by the Chinese Nationalist leader, Chiang Kai-shek (Jiang Jieshi), who wished to keep his troops out of a Burma campaign and conserve them for a

post-war showdown with the communist army of Mao Zedong (Mao Tse-tung).

8 Mark this day in red on the calendar of life. At long, at very long last, F.D.R. has finally spoken plain words, and plenty of them, with a firecracker in every sentence. 'Get busy or else.' A hot firecracker. I handed this bundle of paprika to the Peanut and then sank back with a sigh. The harpoon hit the little bugger right in the solar plexus, and went right through him. It was a clean hit, but beyond turning green and losing the power of speech, he did not bat an eye.
General Joseph Stilwell, diary entry, 19 Sept. 1944; *The Stilwell Papers* (1949) p.305. Stilwell was US military adviser to Chiang Kai-shek. He had long been working to persuade Chiang to play an active role in Burma with little success. In Sept. 1944 Roosevelt's patience with Chiang snapped, but when Chiang demanded Stilwell's dismissal in Oct., Roosevelt acquiesced. The Peanut was Generalissimo Chiang.

9   When you go home
     Tell them of us and say,
     For your tomorrow
     We gave our today.
Inscription on the British war memorial at Kohima on the Burma–India border, where a Japanese onslaught was halted in 1944. Reminiscent of the verse commemorating the Spartans of Thermopylae (see 55:5).

10 The seeming 'helplessness' of our cousins strikes me as amusing when it is not annoying. I am sure that what they wish in their hearts is that we would haul down the Stars and Stripes and hoist the White Ensign on all our ships.
US navy chief of naval operations, Admiral Ernest J. King, to Admiral Harold R. Stark, 5 Nov. 1943; Robert W. Love Jr (ed.) *The Chiefs of Naval Operations* (1980) p.175. The Anglophobe Admiral King saw the Pacific War as the exclusive responsibility of the US navy.

11 I told the President he could never justify releasing a bunch of Chinese in Formosa [Taiwan] and abandoning a lot of Filipinos in Luzon. We had been thrown out of Luzon at the point of a bayonet and we should regain our prestige by throwing the Japanese out at the point of a bayonet.
General Douglas MacArthur on his meeting in Hawaii with President Roosevelt, 27 July 1944; Jay Luvaas (ed.) *Dear Miss Em: General Eichelberger's War in the Pacific, 1942–1945* (1972) p.155. The US navy planned to by-pass the Philippines *en route* to Japan and take the island of Formosa instead. MacArthur, who had served as military adviser to the Philippine commonwealth from 1935 to 1941, persuaded Roosevelt to adopt his strategy. Luzon was lost in the spring of 1942.

1 The purity of youth will usher in the Divine Wind.
Vice-Admiral Onishi, 1944. The mantra of the kamikaze, young suicide pilots sent out to attack US navy ships on a one-way mission.

2 The Third Fleet's sunken and damaged ships have been salvaged and are retiring at high speed toward the enemy.
US Admiral William Halsey in response to the Japanese claim in Oct. 1944 that his fleet had been sunk; E.B. Potter *Bull Halsey* (1985).

3 The raising of that flag on Mount Suribachi means a Marine Corps for the next five hundred years.
Secretary of the navy James Forrestal. The reference is to the hoisting of the Stars and Stripes on the heights of the Japanese island Iwo Jima on 23 Feb. 1945, an event immortalized by photographer Joe Rosenthal.

THE ATOMIC BOMB, 1939–45

4 Some recent work by E. Fermi and L. Szilard … leads me to expect that the element uranium may be turned into a new and important source of energy in the near future … This new phenomenon would also lead to the construction of bombs … A single bomb of this type, carried by boat or exploded in a port, might very well destroy the whole port together with some of the surrounding territory.
Albert Einstein to President Roosevelt, 2 Aug. 1939; *Einstein on Peace* (1960) pp.294–5. The European nuclear physicists Enrico Fermi (Italian) and Leo Szilard (Hungarian) both moved to the United States in 1938 and pioneered the atomic bomb.

5 Jim, you'll be interested to know that the Italian navigator has just landed in the New World.
Arthur Compton to James Corant, 2 Dec. 1942; Richard S. Hewlett and Oscar E. Anderson Jr *The New World, 1939/1946* (1962) p.112. Coded telephone message to say that the first self-sustaining chain reaction, initiated by Enrico Fermi, had just taken place.

6 When a 'bomb' is finally available, it might perhaps, after mature consideration, be used against the Japanese, who should be warned that this bombardment will be repeated until they surrender.
Churchill–Roosevelt, secret agreement, 18 Sept. 1944; Gilbert (1986) p.970. The warning was issued in the Potsdam Declaration of 26 July 1945.

7   If the radiance of a thousand suns
    Were to burst into the sky
    That would be like

The splendour of the Mighty One …
I am become Death, the shatterer of worlds.
The Bhagavad Gita, Ch.11, Sects 12 and 32; quoted by J. Robert Oppenheimer, director of the atomic bomb project, on the occasion of the successful test of the first nuclear device on 16 July 1945.

8 Stimson, what was gunpowder? Trivial. What was electricity? Meaningless. This Atomic Bomb is the Second Coming in Wrath.
Winston Churchill to the US secretary of war, Henry Stimson, at the Potsdam Conference, July 1945; Herbert Feis *The Atomic Bomb and the End of World War II* (1966) p.87.

9 The morning was still, the place was cool and pleasant. Then a tremendous flash of light cut across the sky. Mr Tanimoto has a distant recollection that it travelled from east to west, from the city toward the hills. It seemed a sheet of sun.
John Hersey *Hiroshima* (1946) Ch.1, on the nuclear annihilation of the city on 6 Aug. 1945.

10 We have resolved to endure the unendurable and suffer what is insufferable.
Emperor Hirohito, radio broadcast, announcing the unconditional surrender of Japan on 14 Aug. 1945, after a second atomic bomb destroyed the city of Nagasaki on 9 Aug.

HOME FRONT USA, 1941–5

11 There shall be no discrimination in employment of workers in defense industries or government because of race, creed, color, or national origin.
Presidential executive order, 25 June 1941, issued to forestall a protest march on Washington by American blacks.

12 We shall not be moved.
Woody Guthrie, 7 Dec. 1941; Geoffrey Perret *Days of Sadness, Years of Triumph* (1973) p.205. Sung in response to a projected mob attack on a Los Angeles bar owned by a Japanese-American.

13 It is actually a penitentiary – armed guards … barbed wire, confinement at nine, lights out at ten. The guards are ordered to shoot anyone who approaches within twenty feet of the fence.
Japanese-American on the 'relocation camp' to which the ethnic Japanese of the West Coast were transported after Pearl Harbor; Perret (1973) p.224.

14 Who will do the cooking, the washing, the mending, the humble homely tasks to which every woman has devoted herself? Think of the humiliation! What has become of the manhood of America?

US senator in response to the bill introduced by Representative Edith Nourse Rogers to establish the Women's Auxiliary Army Corps (WAAC); Sheila Rowbotham *A Century of Women* (1997) p.254. The bill was defeated, but the WAAC came into being not long afterwards, and American women moved out of the kitchen into the armed forces and the munitions factories.

1 Never before had war demanded such techno-logical expertness and business organization ... The modern American genius, the genius of the country of Whitney, Morse, and Edison, precisely fitted such a war.

Historian Allan Nevins on the war's regeneration of US industry; Richard R. Lingeman *Don't You Know There's a War On?* (1979) p.133.

2 The house I live in
A plot of earth, a street,
The grocer and the butcher
And the people that I meet;
The children in the playground,
The faces that I see;
All races, all religions,
That's America to me.

Lewis Allen and Earl Robinson 'The house I live in' (1942). The US equivalent of 'There'll always be an England' (see 845:4).

3 Weren't you bragging just a little, Yamamoto? Your people are giving their lives in useless sacrifice. Ours are fighting for a glorious future of mass employ-ment, mass production and mass distribution and ownership.

Saturday Evening Post, 29 Aug. 1942.

4 Clark Gable shouldn't be allowed to be a soldier. War is too serious for us to be playing sentimental games. He has a duty and Hollywood has a duty and they should be made to stick to it.

Kyle Crichton *Collier's Magazine*, 9 Jan. 1943. The film star Clark Gable went into uniform in 1942. This writer believed he would have served the country better by making propaganda movies.

5 It is my conviction ... that the problem of race, intensified by economic conflict and war nerves ... will eventually ... occupy a dominant position as a national problem. It is becoming comparable to the issues of labor and relief which plagued the national government ten years ago.

Black spokeswoman Pauli Murray to President Roosevelt, 18 June 1943; John M. Blum *V was for Victory* (1976) p.218.

6 We have come to a clear realization of the fact that true individual freedom cannot exist without economic security and independence. Necessitous men are not free men. People who are hungry and out of a job are the stuff of which dictatorships are made. In our day those economic truths have become accepted as self-evident. We have accepted, so to speak, a second Bill of Rights under which a new basis of security and prosperity can be established for all – regardless of station, race or creed.

President Franklin D. Roosevelt, State of the Union message, 11 Jan. 1944; *Public Papers 1944–45* (1950) p.41. Two weeks earlier Roosevelt had declared that 'Dr New Deal' had stepped aside to make way for 'Dr Win the War', so this was a long-term vision.

7 The people in the States do not know how lucky they are. They have come out of this war very easy. The country is all in one piece, and they have clean homes to go to. Over here the people have nothing, the Japs took everything away from them.

James J. Fahey, diary entry, 17 May 1945; *Pacific War Diary 1942–1945* (1963).

HOME FRONT BRITAIN, 1939–45

8 This is the people's war. It is our war. We are the fighters. Fight it with all that is in us. And may God defend the right.

Jan Struther, *The Times*, Sept. 1939. Another famous coinage. This writer created the character of 'Mrs Miniver', a patriotic middle-class English housewife, later the heroine of a Holly-wood film (1942) starring Greer Garson and Walter Pidgeon.

9 Nothing is more certain than that this war will mark the transition from monopoly capitalism to socialism.

The Conservative Robert Boothby to David Lloyd George, 7 Nov. 1939; Paul Addison *The Road to 1945* (1994) p.72.

10 The Connollys were found at last and assembled. Doris had been in Barbara's bedroom trying on her make-up, Micky in the library tearing up a folio, Marlene grovelling under the pantry sink eating the remains of the dogs' dinners.

Evelyn Waugh *Put Out More Flags* (1942) Pt 2, Ch.1. This extract from his novel voices Waugh's revulsion at the barbarianism of working-class evacuees, early 1940. On the outbreak of war, children were evacuated from London and other cities to escape their expected devastation.

1 If we speak of democracy, we do not mean a democracy which maintains the right to vote but forgets the right to work and the right to live. If we speak of freedom, we do not mean a rugged individualism which excludes social organization and economic planning. If we speak of equality we do not mean a political equality nullified by social and economic privilege. If we speak of economic reconstruction, we think less of maximum production (though this too will be required) than of equitable distribution.

The Times, editorial, 1 July 1940; written by the historian E.H. Carr. A visionary leader at a time when the future could not have looked more bleak.

2 With regard to the post-war period, Lady Montgomery thinks it will be a much more difficult time for most of us than during the war years. One problem she could see was the finding of girls willing to enter domestic service after having been employed for so long in the Services, in the munitions, etc.

Anon.; Michael Bateman (ed.) This England (1969) p.55.

3 Many in this country have persuaded themselves that the cessation of hostilities will mark the opening of the Golden Age (many were persuaded last time also). However this may be, the time for declaring a dividend on the profits of the Golden Age is the time when those profits have been realized in fact, not merely in the imagination.

Sir Kingsley Wood, chancellor of the exchequer, 17 Nov. 1942, on the imminent Beveridge Report on social security; Correlli Barnett The Audit of War (1986) p.27. As keeper of the national treasury, Wood was aghast at the financial commitment entailed in Beveridge's proposals.

4 Most people want something new after the war … New Britain should be free, as free as humanly possible, of the five giant evils, of Want, of Disease, of Ignorance, of Squalor and of Idleness.

Sir William Beveridge, 6 Dec. 1942; The Pillars of Security and Other Wartime Essays and Addresses (1943). Beveridge was looking to a post-war Britain, which would guarantee a welfare state providing social security, a national health service, a complete system of state education, housing and full employment. Quite a change from the view he took in 1938 (see 780:9).

5 No excuse any more for unemployment and slums and under-feeding. Using even half the vision and energy and invention and pulling together we've done in this war, and what is there we cannot do?

Anon. young radical, Sept. 1944; J.L. Hodson The Sea and the Land (1945) p.238.

6 Supremely popular as he is today, this is closely connected with the idea of Winston the war leader, Bulldog of Battle, etc. Ordinary people widely assume that after the war he'll rest on his magnificent laurels. If he doesn't, many say they will withdraw support, believing him no man of peace, domestic policy, or human detail.

Tom Harrisson Political Quarterly (1944) Vol.15, p.23. Harrisson was director of Mass-Observation, a pioneering survey of British public opinion, which began work in the late 1930s. Here he predicts the result of the 1945 election, which few in 1944 expected.

7 I declare to you from the bottom of my heart, that no socialist system can be established without a political police … [The Labour Party leadership] would have to fall back on some form of Gestapo, no doubt very humanely directed in the first instance.

Winston Churchill, 4 June 1945; Martin Gilbert 'Never Despair' (1988) p.32. The prime minister's opinion of his erstwhile colleagues in the coalition government in a broadcast at the outset of the election campaign. In the result announced on 26 July the Conservative Party suffered a massive defeat.

HOPES FOR THE FUTURE, 1941–5

8   There'll be bluebirds over
        The white cliffs of Dover
        Tomorrow, just you wait and see.
        There'll be love and laughter
        And peace ever after
        Tomorrow, when the world is free.

US songwriter Nat Burton 'The White Cliffs of Dover' (1941).

9 In the future days, which we seek to make secure, we look forward to a world founded upon four essential human freedoms. The first is freedom of speech and expression – everywhere in the world. The second is freedom of every person to worship God in his own way – everywhere in the world. The third is freedom from want – which, translated into world terms, means economic understandings which will secure to every nation a healthy peace-time life for its inhabitants – everywhere in the world. The fourth is freedom from fear – which means a worldwide reduction of armaments to such a point and in such a thorough fashion that no nation will be in a position to commit an act of physical aggression against any neighbor.

President Franklin D. Roosevelt, 6 Jan. 1941; *Public Papers, 1940* (1941) p.672.

1 It now becomes our time to be the powerhouse from which the ideals spread throughout the world and do their mysterious work of lifting the life of mankind from the level of the beasts to what the Psalmist called a little lower than the angels ... It is in this spirit that all of us are called ... to create the first great American century.

Republican editor and publisher Henry Luce, *Life*, 17 Feb. 1941. An impassioned summons to the USA to enter into its own. The biblical reference is to Psalm 8:2.

2 Some have spoken of the 'American Century'. I say that the century on which we are entering – the century which will come out of this war – can and must be the century of the common man.

Democratic Vice-President Henry Wallace, 8 May 1942; Lord Russell (ed.) *Democracy Reborn* (1944) pp.191–6. A riposte to the conservative vision of Henry Luce by Roosevelt's radical running-mate, dropped from the Democrats' ticket in 1944 in favour of Harry S Truman.

3 America will believe it her duty to concern herself with the rest of the world, but she will not do this without being paid for it. The payment she will demand will not be material but moral. No country is more convinced than this one that she is right, or is more arrogant in her moral superiority. If she intervenes in the affairs of the world it will be to impose her ideas, and she will consider her intervention a blessing for lost and suffering humanity. The prospect is cheerless. Whether run by the American left or right, the world will in either case suffer a singular form of tyranny, at once biblical and materialistic.

French commentator Raoul de Roussy de Sales, 7 July 1942; *The Making of Tomorrow* (1943).

4 Resolved ... that the Congress hereby expresses itself as favoring the creation of appropriate international machinery with power adequate to establish and to maintain a just and lasting peace among the nations of the world, and as favoring participation by the United States therein through its constitutional processes.

Fulbright Resolution, passed by the House of Representatives, 21 Sept. 1943; Ruhl J. Bartlett (ed.) *The Record of American Diplomacy* (1964 edn) p.675. This resolution, sponsored by Congressman J. William Fulbright of Arkansas, looked

forward to American membership of a world body that became the United Nations Organization. It thus turned its back on the US Senate's repudiation of the League of Nations on 19 March 1920. The Senate passed its own form of the resolution on 5 Nov. 1943.

5 The peace of Europe is the cornerstone of world peace. Within a single generation Europe has now been the focal centre of two world conflicts which were due above all to the existence on this continent of thirty sovereign states. This anarchy must be remedied by the creation of a Federal Union between the European peoples ... The Federal Union must be based on a declaration of civil, political and economic rights which guarantees the free development of the human personality and the normal functioning of democratic institutions; moreover it must rest on a declaration of the rights of minorities to an autonomous existence compatible with the integrity of the nation states of which they form a part.

Draft Declaration of the European Resistance Movements, July 1944; Richard Vaughan (ed.) *Post-War Integration in Europe* (1976) p.18. The conception of what was to become the European Union.

6 We the peoples of the United Nations, determined to save succeeding generations from the scourge of war, which twice in our life-time has brought untold sorrow to mankind, and to reaffirm faith in fundamental human rights, in the dignity and worth of the human person, in the equal rights of men and women and of nations large and small, and to establish conditions under which justice and respect for the obligations arising from treaties and other sources of international law can be maintained, and to promote social progress and better standards of life in larger freedom, and for these ends to practise tolerance and live together in peace with one another as good neighbors, and to unite our strength to maintain international peace and security, and to ensure, by the acceptance of principles and the institution of methods, that armed force shall not be used, save in the common interest, and to employ international machinery for the promotion of the economic and social advancement of all peoples, have resolved to continue our efforts to accomplish those aims.

Archibald MacLeish, part author of Preamble to the Charter of the United Nations, adopted on 26 June 1945; Bartlett (1964 edn) p.676. The American poet MacLeish served as an assistant secretary of state during the framing of the charter in 1944 and 1945.

End of Empire, 1945–94

RECESSIONAL, 1945–64

1 Quite apart from the advent of the atomic bomb … the British Commonwealth and Empire is not a unit that can be defended by itself. It was the creation of sea power. With the advent of air warfare the conditions which made it possible to defend a string of possessions scattered over five continents by means of a Fleet based on island fortresses have gone.

Prime minister Clement Attlee, 1 Sept. 1945; Ronald Hyam (ed.) *The Labour Government and the End of Empire 1945–1951* Pt 3 (1992) p.207.

2 A straight issue would be reached with the Middle East and India. Either they would have to lend us the money for our troops there, or we should have to move our troops out.

R.W.B. Clarke to Sir David Waley, 15 Feb. 1946; *Anglo-American Economic Collaboration in War and Peace 1942–1949* (1982) p.147.

3 We must not for sentimental reasons based on the past give hostages to fortune. It may be we shall have to consider the British Isles as an easterly extension of a strategic area the centre of which is the American continent rather than as a power looking eastwards through the Mediterranean to India and the East.

Clement Attlee, 2 March 1946; Alan Bullock *The Life and Times of Ernest Bevin* Vol.3 (1983) p.242.

4 We place the independence of India in hostile and feeble hands, heedless of the dark carnage and confusion which will follow. We scuttle from Egypt which we twice successfully defended from foreign massacre and pillage.

Winston Churchill, 1 Aug. 1946; *H.C. Deb.* Vol.426, Cols 1256–7.

5 It is with deep grief that I watch the clattering down of the British Empire with all its glories and all the services it has rendered to mankind.

Winston Churchill, 6 March 1947; *H.C. Deb.* Vol.434, Col.678.

6 No territory can leave the British Empire when by so doing, it imperils Imperial strategy and Imperial communications. I do not see why we should have any diffidence whatsoever in enunciating that as a

principle. The Russians certainly have not … The Americans have held on to Panama … only on the grounds of their security. We who are very much more vulnerable than they are, need have no hesitation … in putting that limitation to any further grant of self-government.

Conservative MP David Hammans, 1949; *H.C. Deb.* Vol.467, Cols 616–7.

7 I have met the African native and I am fond of him. I realize that, if he is to get where we want him to get, he must be led properly, with firmness and kindness. I say to him that he must have patience, and then the slogan which he is so fond of displaying of 'Africa for the Africans' may well come about, but it will be an Africa for Africans of all colours.

South African-born Conservative MP Sir Ian Fraser, 20 July 1949; *H.C. Deb.* Vol.467, Cols 1465–6. Multi-racialism as the latest variant of colonialism.

8 At the end of the war Britain was faced with three possible courses of action: to maintain her political domination in South-East Asia by force; to abandon her entire position in the area; or to come to an amicable settlement whereby both national aspirations and British interests and influence were safeguarded. We chose the last of these courses, and our policy in India, Pakistan, Ceylon and Burma has, in the event, proved to have been one of the major factors in ensuring that the countries of South-East Asia, if not yet actual allies in the struggle against Soviet communism, are at least looking to the West for support, rather than to Russia. The French and the Dutch have been slower to appreciate the inevitable march of events in Asia.

Cabinet paper, Oct. 1949; A.J. Stockwell (ed.) *Malaya* Pt 2 (1995) pp.162–3. A self-congratulatory rationale of British decolonization.

9 I ended today extremely gloomy about British prospects everywhere. In Kenya: the Mau Mau. In Egypt and Persia: the Americans refusing to support us. Even Iceland in process of destroying our deep-sea fishing industry. I see no reason why there should be any end to the surrenders demanded of us. International law and the temper of international opinion is all set against things which made us a great nation, i.e. our activities outside our own territory.

Evelyn Shuckburgh, private secretary to the British foreign secretary, Anthony Eden, 7 Jan. 1953; *Descent to Suez: Diaries 1951–56* (1986) p.71.

1 He then went into a long homily about how the whole of Africa was embittered by British rule … [He is] someone in whom the term Colonial or Colonialism produces a pathological and not an intellectual reaction.

Colonial secretary Oliver Lyttelton, 11 June 1953; D. Goldsworthy (ed.) *The Conservative Government and the End of Empire 1951–1957* (1994) pp.331, 332. Note on an interview with the Indian prime minister, Jawaharlal Nehru. Nehru promoted the non-aligned bloc of Third World countries, distancing themselves from the Cold War and focusing on the issue of decolonization, notably in the Bandung Conference of April 1955. Their criticism was deeply resented in British government circles.

2 Any attempt to retard by artificial delays the progress of Colonial peoples towards independence would produce disastrous results. Among other consequences, when power had eventually been transferred, it would be handed over to a local leadership predisposed towards an anti-British policy.

British government report, 21 Jan. 1954; A.N. Porter and A.J. Stockwell *British Imperial Policy and Decolonization 1938–1964* Vol.2 (1989) p.284. The argument for compromise with nationalism.

3 We ourselves are the first colony in modern times to have won independence. We have a natural sympathy with those who would follow our example.

Secretary of state John Foster Dulles, *Department of State Bulletin*, 21 June 1954, p.336. Dulles's fellow feeling was guaranteed only insofar as the successor-states to European imperialism were well-disposed to the West and steered clear of flirtations with communism.

4 There are some people who believe – and many more who say – that we have lost our resolution. Great Empires in the past, they say, and, they add, it might be true of our Commonwealth, have always decayed from within when beset by weariness and the desire to give way in the struggle. If an individual or a people, it has been said, ceases to believe in itself, its aims and ideals, others with firmer aims and beliefs will climb into the saddle.

Alan Lennox-Boyd, colonial secretary, 22 Sept. 1956; Philip Murphy *Alan Lennox-Boyd* (1999) p.163. Gloom engendered by the Suez crisis (see 869:1–870:2).

5 The Tory Party must be cured of the British Empire, of the pitiful yearning to cling to the relics of a bygone system … The Tory Party has to find its patriotism again, and to find it, as of old, in this England.

Enoch Powell to Iain Macleod, 11 Feb. 1957; Philip Murphy *Party Politics and Decolonization* (1995) p.164. An extraordinary conclusion coming from a man who had entered politics in 1945 to retain India as the hub of the empire.

6 I impressed on him that we must get rid of this horrible word 'independence'. What we wanted was a word like 'home rule'. The thing to do was to think of the Arabic for 'home rule' and then work backwards from it.

Prime minister Harold Macmillan , 28 June 1958; Murphy (1999) p.193. Macmillan's response to a proposal from Lennox-Boyd for an independent federation of the Arab sheikdoms of the Persian Gulf. Better, in Macmillan's view, to have them as individual principalities and play one off against the other (Murphy (1999) p.192).

7 The Fourth Republic was born with the war in Indochina. It died with the war in Algeria. Amongst all the errors of the Republic, the most fatal was its failure to establish new relationships with the overseas territories.

Jacques Fauvet *La Quatrième République* (1959) p.12. The Fourth French Republic was founded in 1946 at the start of the war in Vietnam and collapsed in 1958, following a revolt by the settlers in Algeria after more than three years of war there (see 871:1–871:8).

8 The Soviet Union, faithful to the policy of peace and support for the struggle of oppressed peoples for their national independence, the policy proclaimed by Vladimir Ilyich Lenin, founder of the Soviet State, calls upon the United Nations to raise its voice in defence of the just liberation of the colonies and to take immediate steps toward the complete abolition of the colonial system of government.

Nikita Khrushchev at the UN General Assembly, 23 Sept. 1960; H. Hanak *Soviet Foreign Policy since the Death of Stalin* (1972) p.296. Under Stalin the USSR did little to support decolonization, but under his successor, Khrushchev, it threw itself strongly behind the independence movement.

9 National liberation, national rebirth, handing back the nation to the people, Commonwealth, whatever the rubrics brought into play or the new formulas introduced, decolonization is always a violent phenomenon.

Franz Fanon *Les Damnés de la terre* (The Wretched of the Earth) (1961) opening words. This book by the French West Indian Fanon had a great vogue in the 1960s as a manifesto of the newly emergent states brought into being by the disintegration of the old empires.

1 Great Britain has lost an Empire and has not yet found a role.

Dean Acheson, 5 Dec. 1962; Alistair Horne *Harold Macmillan* Vol.2 (1989) p.429. A famous pronouncement, often seen as a nudge towards British involvement in Europe, which Macmillan appears to have thought of as a substitute for the British empire.

2 No one can stop African countries marching forward to independence, but it would be absurd to deceive ourselves that those to whom we are handing over power are as civilized as we are, or think we are.

Gerald Sayers of the Conservative Research Department to the *Holsworthy Post*, 25 June 1962; Murphy (1995) p.130. Sayers was defending the Conservative MP for Tavistock, Sir Henry Studholme, accused of having suggested that cannibalism was still widely practised in Africa.

3 Were the countries [of Africa] ready for independence? Of course not. Nor was India, and the bloodshed that followed the grant of independence there was incomparably worse than anything that has happened since to any country. Yet the decision of the Attlee Government was the only realistic one. Equally we could not possibly have held by force to our territories in Africa. We could not, with an enormous force engaged, even continue to hold the small island of Cyprus. General de Gaulle could not contain Algeria. The march of men towards their freedom can be guided, but not halted. Of course there were risks in moving quickly. But the risks of moving slowly were far greater.

Iain Macleod, *The Spectator*, 13 Jan. 1964, p.127. Macleod was Conservative colonial secretary from 1959 to 1961 and, as such, a high-speed decolonizer.

4 I have long realized that the Colonial Office is nearing its end and had always hoped that it would have an honourable and dignified funeral. I must say I profoundly dislike the present trend of thinking which seems to me very like chucking a rotten carcass on the rubbish heap so that the vultures can peck its decaying flesh.

Sir Hilton Poynton, permanent under-secretary at the Colonial Office, to the head of the civil service, 28 Oct. 1964; D.J. Morgan (ed.) *The Official History of Colonial Development*

Vol.4 (1980) p.24. A Whitehall mandarin's lament for the end of an era.

INDIA, 1944–7

5 The future of India is the problem on which the British Commonwealth and the British reputation will stand or fall in the post-war period ... Our prestige and prospects in Burma, Malaya, China and the Far East generally are entirely subject to what happens in India. If we can secure India as a friendly partner in the British Commonwealth our predominant influence in these countries will, I think, be assured; with a lost and hostile India, we are likely to be reduced in the East to the position of commercial bag-men.

Field Marshal Lord Wavell, viceroy of India, to Winston Churchill, Oct. 1944; Penderel Moon (ed.) *Wavell: The Viceroy's Journal* (1973) pp.94–5.

6 I thought the interview with Gandhi, naked except for a dhoti [loincloth] and looking remarkably healthy, was rather a deplorable affair. S. of S. began with his usual sloppy benevolence to this malevolent old politician, who for all his sanctimonious talk has, I am sure, very little softness in his composition.

Field Marshal Lord Wavell, 3 April 1946; Moon (1973) p.236. Wavell greatly preferred Moslems to Hindus. The 'S. of S.' was Lord Pethick-Lawrence, secretary of state for India and one of a three-man British mission to India.

7 It is a Herculean task that faces me. I am being tested. Is the *satyagraha* of my conception a weapon of the weak or really that of the strong? I must realize the latter or lay down my life in the attempt to attain it.

Mohandas Gandhi, *Harijan*, 8 Dec. 1946; Judith M. Brown *Gandhi* (1989) p.361. Gandhi's ideal of *satyagraha* (non-violence) was to be tested to destruction in the appalling violence between Muslims, Hindus and Sikhs that accompanied the move to independence and that cost him his own life when he was assassinated by a fellow Hindu on 20 Jan. 1948.

8 The Prime Minister said that it was impossible to be confident that the main political parties in India had any real will to reach agreement between themselves ... The situation might so develop as to result in civil war ... One thing was quite certain, viz., that we could not put the clock back and introduce a period of firm British rule. Neither the military nor the administrative machine in India was any longer capable of this.

Cabinet conclusions, 10 Dec. 1946; Nicholas Mansergh (ed.) *Constitutional Relations between Britain and India: The Transfer of*

Power, 1942–1947 Vol.9 (1980) p.319. An admission by Clement Attlee that withdrawal from India was on the horizon, made public on 20 Feb. 1947, when the end of the Raj was scheduled for June 1948.

1 We want a separate state of our own. There we can live according to our own notions of life ... We should be free ... Is Britain going to stand with its bayonets and hand over authority to the Indian majority?
Mohammed Ali Jinnah, 14 Dec. 1946; Hector Bolitho *Jinnah: Creator of Modern Pakistan* (1954) p.173. Jinnah led the movement for a Muslim state of Pakistan that brought about the partition of the subcontinent.

2 Pakistan is, in fact, a thoroughly unsatisfactory solution of the Indian problem; and to give any support to it during the period of our evacuation would be to render that evacuation much more difficult, and the likelihood of civil war in India greater.
Field Marshal Lord Wavell, 14 Dec. 1946; R.J. Moore *Escape from Empire* (1983) p.199. Though basically pro-Muslim, Wavell hated the prospect of partition.

3 Once a line of division is drawn in the Punjab all Sikhs to the west of it and all Muslims to the east of it will have their [penises] chopped off.
Senior superintendent of police, Delhi, late March 1947; Penderel Moon *Divide and Quit* (1962) p.88. All too true in the massacres that followed the partition of the Punjab in northwest India.

4 We are on a ship which contains a large quantity of highly inflammable material. The ship is on fire, but the fire has not yet reached the magazines. We MUST put the fire out very soon, or at least check it. Thereafter we have to get up steam and sail the ship to port – a British port if possible.
General Sir Hastings Ismay, 18 July 1947; Moore (1983) p.238. Ismay was chief of staff to the new (and last) viceroy of India, Lord Louis Mountbatten, responsible for the negotiations that led to the partition of Aug. 1947.

5 Here, as I speak to you to-night in Delhi, we are celebrating ... India's Independence Day. In the Atlantic Charter, we, the British and Americans, dedicated ourselves to champion the self-determination of peoples and the independence of nations. Bitter experience has taught us that it is often easier to win a war than to achieve a war aim; so let us remember August 15th – V.J. Day – not only as the celebration of a victory, but also as the fulfilment of a pledge.

Lord Louis Mountbatten, 15 Aug. 1947; Alan Campbell-Johnson *Mission with Mountbatten* (1951) p.151. When Churchill drew up the Atlantic Charter with Roosevelt in Aug. 1941 he did not see it as applicable to the British empire, as Roosevelt did, and so here Mountbatten is following the American interpretation. V.J. Day (Victory over Japan Day) was the day of Japan's surrender in 1945.

6 Long years ago we made a tryst with destiny, and now the time comes when we shall redeem our pledge, not wholly or in full measure, but very substantially. At the stroke of the midnight hour, when the world sleeps, India will awake to life and freedom. A moment comes, which comes but rarely in history, when we step out from the old to the new, when an age ends, and when the soul of a nation long suppressed finds utterance.
Jawaharlal Nehru, 14 Aug. 1947; Sarvepalli Gopal *Jawaharlal Nehru* Vol.1 (1975) p.362. Eloquent oratory as India approached independence at midnight on 14 Aug., although, as Nehru notes, not as an entire subcontinent but partitioned between India and Pakistan.

7 India! The finest jewel in the British Crown it was called. It has now been cast like pearls before swine, and not because the Indians wanted it but because of a small minority who had been got at by communist influence.
Delegate at the Conservative Party conference, Oct. 1947; David Goldsworthy *Colonial Issues in British Politics 1945–1961* (1971) p.180, note 3.

FRANCE AND VIETNAM, 1945–7

8 All men are created equal; they are endowed by their creator with certain inalienable rights; among these are Life, Liberty and the pursuit of happiness. This immortal statement was made in the Declaration of Independence of the United States of America in 1776. In a broader sense, this means: All the peoples on the earth are equal from birth, all the peoples have a right to live, to be happy and free.
Ho Chi Minh, 2 Sept. 1945; Bernard Fall (ed.) *Ho Chi Minh on Revolution* (1967) p.141. The Vietnamese nationalist leader proclaiming independence on the American model, supposedly with advice from members of the US Office of Strategic Services; a ripe irony here.

9 The French are foreigners. They are weak. Colonialism is dying out. Nothing will be able to withstand world pressure for independence. They may stay for a while; but they will have to go because the white man is finished in Asia. But if the Chinese stay now, they will never leave. As for me, I prefer to smell French shit for five years, rather than Chinese shit for the rest of my life.

Ho Chi Minh, March 1946; US Department of Defense *The Pentagon Papers* Vol.1 (1971) pp.18–19. China and Vietnam had been enemies for centuries, and Chinese Nationalist forces had entered northern Vietnam after the Japanese surrender in 1945.

1 If the tiger ever stands still the elephant will crush him with his mighty tusks. But the tiger does not stand still. He lurks in the jungle by day and emerges by night. He will leap upon the back of the elephant, tearing huge chunks from his hide, and then he will leap back into the dark jungle. And slowly the elephant will bleed to death.

Ho Chi Minh; Jean Lacouture *Ho Chi Minh* (1968) p.138. The recipe for victory by the leader of the Vietnamese insurgency, which took the form of classic guerrilla warfare.

2 In our republican doctrine colonialism achieves its final objective and true justification only when it ends, i.e. when colonial peoples are sufficiently emancipated to govern themselves.

French prime minister Léon Blum, 23 Dec. 1946; R.E.M. Irving *The First Indochina War 1945–54* (1975) p.38. The high idealism of the veteran socialist was not shared by the French army, which saw Vietnam as the chance to redeem the reputation it had lost in the defeat of 1940 by smashing the Vietnamese challenge.

3 Unless events take a very unexpected turn for the better, we are about to see a French army reconquer the greater part of Indochina, only to make it impossible for any French merchant or planter to live there outside barbed-wire perimeters thereafter. Whatever may be the solution of the problems of colonial Asia, this is not it.

Singapore *Straits Times*, 30 Dec. 1946. War between France and the communist-led Vietminh had recently begun in Vietnam.

4 *Goût discutable* (Questionable taste)

The response of a French army officer to criticism by an American woman of French colonialism in Vietnam, c.1947; JM personal knowledge. For the climax of the war see 879:9.

INDONESIA, 1945–9

5 The Dutch are graciously permitting us entry into the basement while we have climbed all the way to the top floor and up to the attic.

Mohammed Hatta, 18 Oct. 1945; Robert J. McMahon *Colonialism and Cold War* (1981) p.96. The Dutch had offered their East Indies colony limited autonomy, well short of the independence its nationalists had recently declared.

6 An armed conflict between the Dutch and the Indonesians was … bound to disturb our own relations with native populations throughout South-East Asia.

Clement Attlee, 20 May 1947; McMahon (1981) p.155.

7 The big cities can be occupied by the Dutch forces, but the rural countryside cannot be captured … So the Republican government must and will continue to function outside the big cities.

Mohammed Natsu, Indonesian minister of information, 19 Dec. 1948; George Kahin *Nationalism and Revolution in Indonesia* (1952) p.394. Dutch forces had just captured the capital city of Jakarta, but Indonesian guerrillas controlled the rural hinterland. This strategic impasse had proved the prelude to Mao's victory in China, and most of the wars of decolonization followed the pattern.

8 Our friends in Western Europe … should try to realize how disastrous it would be to them, and to the cause of Western civilization, if ever it could be said that the Western Union for the defense of freedom in Europe was in Asia a syndicate for the preservation of decadent empires.

The influential columnist Walter Lippmann, *New York Herald Tribune*, 10 Jan. 1949. Washington threatened the Dutch with the withdrawal of Marshall Aid under the European Recovery Program if they refused to come to terms with the Indonesian nationalists. The Americans considered they were safe in doing so because the Indonesian leadership was not communist.

9 If Indonesia should come under communist influence, then Indo-China, Siam, Malaya and the Philippines will be subjected to communistic pressure from China on the North and Indonesia on the South. Under such pressure, it will be difficult to prevent these countries from falling under communist domination.

Standard Vacuum Oil Company memorandum, Sept. 1949; McMahon (1981) p.289. An early expression of the domino theory (see 880:8). US support for Indonesian nationalism was seen as the best guarantee against a communist take-over, and in 1965 General Suharto's murderous suppression of the Indonesian Communist Party was to have solid American backing.

MALAYA, 1948–52

10 The prospect of the rise of a strong independence movement in Malaya, at any rate within the next generation or so, appears to be exceedingly remote.

William Linehan, constitutional adviser to the Malayan Union, 2 March 1948; Stockwell (1995) p.1. An analysis based on the perceived apathy of the majority Malay population. An insurrection led by communists from the Chinese minority broke out three months later.

1 Is it really the discontented labourer who of his own accord proceeds to arson and sabotage and murder? Is it the hired thug, the petty gunman? No, it is not. Those are the people who are pushed by inflammatory speeches in the hope of reward into the front line. Behind, in the shadows, skulk the professional sedition-mongers. What do they represent, when they demonstrate under a foreign flag; their speeches and their pamphlets are one long incitement to violence and anarchy; their salutation is the clenched fist. They represent a tyranny as complete, as unscrupulous, as sinister as that of Nazi Germany.

A.W. Wallich, chairman of the Federation of Malay States Chamber of Commerce, late summer 1948; Anthony Short *Communist Insurrection in Malaya* (1975) pp.68–9.

2 The local village and *kampong* [hamlet] talk, more or less openly, goes like this: 'The government is getting weaker and weaker – Communism which is to liberate us all is triumphant in China and will shortly be the same in Siam and then here. Russia has the biggest and best bomb. This government is terrified and has recognized communism in China and will shortly hand over to communism here or will have power wrested from it by the liberating armies. Anyway they admit that they will be compelled to leave this country in a few years.' And it goes on: 'Do you want to be a man marked as a running dog, a helper of imperialism and if you do not want to be tortured and have your throat cut, you had better help the liberating army and the people's government now.'

British analysis of local opinion in Malaya, early 1950; Short (1975) pp.219–20.

3 The first [fact] was that the problem of clearing communist banditry from Malaya was similar to that of eradicating malaria from a country. Flit guns and mosquito nets, in the form of military and police, though giving some very local security if continuously maintained, effected no permanent cure. Such a permanent cure entailed the closing of all the breeding areas. In this case the breeding areas of communists were the isolated squatter areas, the unsupervised labour on estates, especially smallholders and Chinese estates without managers. Once these were concentrated there might be some chance of controlling the communist cells therein.

This showed clearly that a quick answer was not to be reckoned on.

General Sir Harold Briggs *Report on the Emergency in Malaya* (1950); Short (1975) p.242. General Briggs was author of the Briggs Plan, drafted in the spring of 1950. It failed to produce substantial results.

4 The foundations of the MCP's [Malayan Communist Party's] creed are solidly laid in international communism and Marxism-Leninism. No deviation is apparent. Since the outbreak of the armed revolt in Malaya the international aspect of communism has been stressed, however much anti-British or local material may also have been included. Pains have been taken to present the Malayan situation as part of a world liberation movement, which in South-east Asia erupts in force of arms in Indo-China, Burma, Indonesia, China and to some extent in India. The objective of the Malayan revolution is a liberation of the people and establishment of a 'Democratic People's Republic'. This can only be achieved through the annihilation of the 'British Imperialists'.

J.N. McHugh *Anatomy of Communist Propaganda, July 1948– December 1949* (1950); Short (1975) p.315.

5 Hateful as it is, the MCP is a powerful movement, selflessly served by determined men and women, and compared with it other political movements are pallid and ineffectual. In fact, with the communists in the jungle Malaya politically is an almost empty vessel, a vacuum waiting to be filled by the communists should they break through the lid that is the security forces. Only the troops and police stand in between, but they have created and perpetuated, with the Emergency regulations and the government's attitude, conditions that stifle the growth of any alternative system to communism. The few seeds and nuclei inside the vessel waste away in the rarefied atmosphere.

The Round Table Vol.42 (June 1952) p.235. A criticism of the policy of General Sir Gerald Templer, appointed to crush the insurgency early in 1952. His methods succeeded, but his critics thought he was turning Malaya into a military dictatorship.

CHINA, 1948–9

6 There is no sign of uneasiness among the British residents here. British businessmen mean to carry on unless physically forced to leave. They are confident that a communist government would find the cooperation of the British import merchants indispensable to keep up the standard of living among the Chinese population.

Ward Price, foreign correspondent of the *Daily Mail*, Shanghai, Christmas 1948; Noel Barber *The Fall of Shanghai* (1979) p.150. Gross self-delusion in the citadel of Western influence in China as Mao Zedong (Mao Tse-tung) and the People's Liberation Army took over the country.

1 Three Chinese boys in long white gowns served cocktails, followed by a meal consisting of roast beef and Yorkshire pudding and rhubarb pie. Not more than a hundred yards away a full orchestra of rifles and machine-guns was making so much noise that speech was frequently impossible.

David Middleditch, Shanghai, 25 May 1949; Barber (1979) p.150. The Brits keep up standards as the Chinese communists take over the city.

2 Have rejoined the Fleet. God save the King!

Lieutenant Commander John Kerans RN, 31 July 1949. Kerans brought the badly damaged frigate HMS *Amethyst* down the Yangtse past Chinese communist batteries in an exploit that was undoubtedly heroic but that signified the withdrawal of the British presence from China after more than a century of imperialist control.

THE MIDDLE EAST: EGYPT, PALESTINE, IRAN AND CYPRUS, 1946–55

3 What happens here [Egypt] will set the pace for us all over Africa and the Middle East.

Prime minister Winston Churchill to his foreign secretary, Anthony Eden, 15 Jan. 1953; Goldsworthy (1994) p.122.

4 Our oil interests in the Middle East were indeed important, but our ability to defend them could only be impaired if we insisted on remaining in Egypt against the will of the Egyptian people and so worsened our relations with the remainder of the Arab world.

Prime minister Clement Attlee, 7 June 1946; Hyam Pt I (1992) p.17.

5 If the Jews, with all their sufferings, want to get too much at the head of the queue, you have the danger of another anti-Semitic reaction through it all.

Ernest Bevin, 13 Nov. 1945; Bullock Vol.3 (1983) p.181. In the wake of the Holocaust Zionists understandably called for a wholesale exodus of the surviving Jews of Europe to Palestine. Bevin himself was accused of anti-Semitism after making these remarks, but his main concern was to keep the Arabs of the Middle East on side, given the importance of their oil

resources, and he therefore resisted a large influx of Jews, which could swamp the native Palestinian Arab population.

6 All our defence requirements in the Middle East … demand that an essential feature of our policy should be to retain the cooperation of the Arab States, and to ensure that the Arab world does not gravitate towards the Russians … We cannot stress too strongly the importance of Middle East oil resources to us both in peace and war.

British chiefs of staff memorandum, 10 July 1946; William Roger Louis 'British Imperialism and the End of the Palestine Mandate' in William Roger Louis and Robert W. Stookey (eds) *The End of the Palestine Mandate* (1986) pp.13–14. The argument for favouring Arabs against Jews in Palestine.

7 The very existence of an underground, which oppression, hanging, torture, and deportation fail to crush or weaken must, in the end, undermine the prestige of a colossal regime that lives by the legend of its omnipotence. Every attack which it fails to prevent is a blow to its standing. Even if the attack does not succeed it makes a dent in that prestige, and that dent widens into a crack which is extended with every succeeding attack.

Menachem Begin *The Revolt: The Story of the Irgun* (1951) p.52. Begin, leader of the Zionist terrorist organization Irgun Zvai Lumi, waged a ruthless guerrilla campaign against the British Mandate. He subsequently became prime minister of Israel.

8 Hitler was right.

British populist endorsement of the Final Solution, in reaction to Zionist terrorism in Palestine, notably the dynamiting of the King David Hotel in Jerusalem on 22 July 1946. The hotel was targeted because it housed the HQ of the Mandate.

9 Every time you blow up a British arsenal, or wreck a British jail, or send a British railroad train sky high, or rob a British bank, or let go with your guns and bombs at the British betrayers and invaders of your homeland, the Jews in America make a little holiday in their hearts.

American playwright Ben Hecht, *New York Herald Tribune*, 15 May 1947. Hecht was writing on behalf of the American League for a Free Palestine, a fervently pro-Zionist group. The atrocities they rejoiced in certainly pushed Britain into referring Palestine to the United Nations and then into terminating the Mandate on 15 May 1948.

10 Iraq will without hesitation cancel its oil concessions in the events of the implementation of a decision against the interests of the Arabs in Palestine.

Iraqi government statement to the Arab League Political Committee, 19 Sept. 1947; Walid Khalidi 'The Arab Perspective' in Louis and Stookey (1986) p.117. In Dec. 1947, however, Iraq made its threat conditional on parallel cancellation by Saudi Arabia and other Arab oil-producing states. A concerted oil embargo was not brought into play until Oct. 1973, in retaliation against America's support for Israel in the Yom Kippur War (see 934:6).

1 As long as America is a major power, and as long as she is free of major war, anyone taking on the Jews will indirectly be taking on America.

Hector McNeil, adviser to Ernest Bevin, on Palestine, 14 Jan. 1949; Louis and Stookey (1986) p.27. Support for Zionism from the United States, particularly from President Truman himself and his White House legal counsel, Clark Clifford, was a decisive factor in the conflict that developed over Palestine and heavily outweighed the State Department's preoccupation with the need to take Arab interests into consideration. See 932:2.

2 I thought the nationalization was a completely unilateral act and I said that if we didn't do anything about this within five years we should lose the Suez Canal, which proved to be right, almost to the day.

Sir Eric Drake, general manager of the Anglo-Iranian Oil Company, late summer 1951; Brian Lapping *End of Empire* (1985) p.209. The company was nationalized on 2 May 1951 by the government of Dr Muhammad Musaddiq (who had been appointed prime minister in April), triggering a huge international crisis.

3 The entire Iranian nation which is proud to live under the holy banner of Islam, expresses its hatred of any yielding or recourse to foreigners regardless of the bloc or group to which they belong.

Ayatollah Kashani, 13 July 1951; Ronald W. Ferrier 'The Anglo-Iranian Oil Dispute: A Triangular Relationship' in James A. Bill and William Roger Louis (eds) *Musaddiq, Iranian Nationalism and Oil* (1988) p.180. Islamic fundamentalism allied to anti-imperialist nationalism, not for the first nor for the last time.

4 [I am] authorized by the will of the nation to share in the movement launched to protect the independence of the country, to sever the grip of the foreigners and to re-establish the prestige, the glory and the honour of the Persia of ancient times ... the shattering of the chains of colonialism ... toppling the pillars of oppression.

Muhammad Musaddiq, 20 March 1953; Richard Cottam *Nationalism in Iran* (1979) p.284.

5 We were, perhaps, slow in realizing that he was essentially a rich, reactionary, feudal-minded Persian, inspired by a fanatical hatred of the British and a desire to expel them and all their works from the country, regardless of the cost ... This unique character truly sowed the wind and reaped the whirlwind.

Secretary of state Dean Acheson on Musaddiq; *Present at the Creation* (1971) p.504.

6 Not wishing to be accused of trying to use the Americans to pull British chestnuts out of the fire, I decided to emphasize the communist threat to Iran rather than the need to recover control of the oil industry. I argued that even if a settlement of the oil dispute could be negotiated with Musaddiq, which was doubtful, he was still incapable of resisting a coup by the Tudeh [Communist] Party, if it were backed by Soviet support. Therefore he must be removed.

C.M. Woodhouse, MI6 representative in Iran; *Something Ventured* (1982) p.117. Musaddiq was removed on 20 Aug. 1953 in a coup arranged by the American Central Intelligence Agency (CIA) in collaboration with British Intelligence (MI6). The short-term result was to restore Western oil interests; the long-term outcome was lasting Iranian resentment of the United States. In 1979 the chickens came home to roost when America's protégé, the Shah, was deposed and Iran thrown into a bitterly anti-Western Islamic revolution under the Ayatollah Khomeini (see 938:7).

7 If we go out of the Sudan and Egypt it will be another stage in the policy of scuttle which began in India and ended at Abadan. It will lead to the abandonment of our African colonies.

Evelyn Shuckburgh, diary entry, 30 Jan. 1953; *Descent to Suez* (1986). Abadan was the site of the Anglo-Iranian Oil Company's refinery.

8 It has always been understood that there are certain territories in the Commonwealth which, owing to their particular circumstances, can never expect to be fully independent ... The question of the abrogation of British sovereignty cannot arise.

Henry Hopkinson, minister of state at the Colonial Office, 28 July 1954; *H.C. Deb.* Vol.531, Col.511. The territory in question was Cyprus.

9 We have taken up the struggle to throw off the English yoke ... The warriors of Marathon, the warriors of Salamis ... are looking to us.

Colonel George Grivas, proclamation, 1 April 1955; Lapping (1985) p.324. Grivas led the EOKA movement, which had the object of integrating Cyprus with Greece (*enosis*). Although he failed in this, Cyprus became an independent state in 1960.

SUEZ, 1956

1 What is all this poppycock you have sent me about isolating and quarantining Nasser? Can't you understand that I want Nasser murdered?

Anthony Nutting, minister of state at the Foreign Office, March 1956, quoting Anthony Eden; Lapping (1985) p.262. In his book on Suez (*No End of a Lesson* (1967) p.34) Nutting did not use the word 'murdered' but instead the euphemism 'destroyed'; here he felt free to give an accurate recollection. Gamal Abdel Nasser was president of Egypt following the revolution of 26 July 1952 that toppled the Egyptian monarchy.

2 At this moment as I talk to you, some of your Egyptian brethren are proceeding to administer the canal company and to run its affairs. They are taking over the canal company at this very moment – the Egyptian canal company, not the foreign canal company.

President Nasser, 26 July 1956; *Documents on International Affairs 1956* (1959) p.113. Nasser made this speech in Alexandria on the fourth anniversary of the 1952 revolution. The nationalization of the Anglo-French Suez Canal Company was in retaliation to the American refusal to finance the Aswan Dam, a huge irrigation project on the upper Nile. The crisis that ensued marked a watershed in the process of decolonization.

3 You have only one course of action and that is to hit, hit now, and hit hard. Otherwise it will be too late. If [Nasser] is left alone, he will finish all of us.

Nuri es-Sa'id, prime minister of Iraq, to prime minister Anthony Eden, 26 July 1956; Hugh Thomas *The Suez Affair* (1966) p.38. Nuri and Faisal II, king of Iraq, were dining at 10 Downing Street when the news of Nasser's nationalization of the Suez Canal Company came through. Eden did hit, but not hard or fast enough. He was forced to resign in Jan. 1957, and the Iraqi monarchy was destroyed in the revolution of July 1958.

4 I said that I agreed that Nasser should not 'get away with it', but the question was how his course should be reversed and he could be brought to 'disgorge'.

Secretary of state John Foster Dulles, 1 Aug. 1956; W. Scott Lucas *Britain and Suez* (1996) p.52. Dulles had just met Eden in London.

5 This episode must be recognized as part of the struggle for the mastery of the Middle East … It is all very familiar. It is exactly the same that we encountered from Mussolini and Hitler in those years before the war.

Not Eden, but Hugh Gaitskell, leader of the Opposition, 2 Aug. 1956; *H.C. Deb.* Vol.557, Col.1613.

6 There is no doubt in our minds that Nasser, whether he likes it or not, is now effectively in Russian hands, just as Mussolini was in Hitler's. It would be as ineffective to show weakness to Nasser now in order to placate him as it was to show weakness to Mussolini.

Anthony Eden to President Eisenhower, 1 Oct. 1956; Lucas (1996) p.69. The appeal to American anti-communist instincts was ignored.

7 I hope that we shall always stand together in treaty relations covering the North Atlantic, [but] any areas encroaching in some form or other on the problem of so-called colonialism find the US playing a somewhat independent role.

Secretary of state John Foster Dulles, press conference, 2 Oct. 1956; Lucas (1996) pp.69–70. Anti-colonialism was to be the governing force in American policy, in spite of Dulles's sympathy with Britain in many respects (see 862:3).

8 It is nothing less than tragic, at this very time, when we are on the point of winning an immense and long-hoped-for victory over Soviet colonialism in Eastern Europe, [that] we should be forced to choose between following in the footsteps of Anglo-French colonialism in Asia and Africa or split our course away from theirs.

Secretary of state John Foster Dulles, 1 Nov. 1956; W. Scott Lucas *Divided We Stand* (1991) p.278. Dulles was speaking before the US National Security Council. The reference to Eastern Europe is to the anti-Soviet movements in Poland and Hungary (see 895:2 and 895:7). By this point Britain and France had begun an air attack on Egypt in collusion with Israel.

9 If we had allowed things to drift, everything would have gone from bad to worse. Nasser would have become a kind of Moslem Mussolini, and our friends in Iraq, Jordan, Saudi Arabia, and even Iran would gradually have been brought down. His efforts would have spread westwards, and Libya and North Africa would have been brought under his control.

Anthony Eden to Eisenhower, 5 Nov. 1956; Lucas (1996) p.101. A domino theory for the Middle East, announced as British and French ground forces invaded Egypt.

10 There are countries now which need not have sent a navy or air force to the coasts of Britain but could have used other means, such as rocket techniques … We are fully determined to crush the aggressors and restore peace in the East through the use of force. We hope at this critical moment you will display due prudence and draw the correct conclusions from this.

Soviet note to Britain, 5 Nov. 1956; Lucas (1991) p.290. This threat may not have carried as much weight as the American warning that the US would withdraw support from sterling if the invasion were not brought to a halt, yet the news that a nuclear-capable squadron of Ilyushin bombers had been dispatched to Syria made uncomfortable listening for the invasion fleet off Port Said on the afternoon of 5 Nov., as JM can personally testify.

1 During the past four weeks, I have felt sometimes that the Suez Canal was flowing through my drawing-room.

Lady Eden, Nov. 1956; David Milsted *The Guinness Chronicle of the Twentieth Century in Quotations* (1996) p.172.

2 Selwyn, why did you stop?

John Foster Dulles to the British foreign secretary, Selwyn Lloyd, 17 Nov. 1956; Selwyn Lloyd *Suez 1956* (1978) p.219. British and French forces halted within hours of landing on Egyptian soil, largely as a result of American pressure. The crisis thus ended in a triumph for Egyptian nationalism and in a decisive defeat for the Anglo-French attempt to reimpose colonialism in Egypt.

PANAMA, 1953–79

3 The status of Great Britain in certain British crown colonies demonstrates vividly the disastrous cumulative effect of small concessions granted seriatim over long periods of years.

US ambassador in Panama, John Wiley, to secretary of state John Foster Dulles, 20 March 1953; John Major *Prize Possession* (1993) p.243.

4 [The United States] must be exceedingly careful that the future years do not bring about for us, in Panama, the situation that Britain has to face in the Suez.

President Eisenhower to secretary of defense Charles Wilson, 25 July 1956; *Foreign Relations of the United States 1955–57* Vol.7 (1987) p.281.

5 The basic problem ... is the exercise of American control over a part of the territory of Panama in this age of intense nationalist and anti-colonialist feeling ... It seems to me entirely proper and necessary for the United States to take the initiative in proposing new arrangements that would redress some of Panama's grievances.

Senator William Fulbright *Old Myths and New Realities* (1964) pp.20, 21. Fulbright's book appeared in the same year that

violent protests took place in Panama over the American presence in the Canal Zone.

6 We bought it, we paid for it, it's ours, and we should tell Torrijos and company that we are going to keep it.

Ronald Reagan, 1976; Major (1993) p.344. The United States had not in fact bought the Panama Canal. General Omar Torrijos was the military ruler of Panama.

7 The future security and well-being of the United States are threatened by the administration's proposed abandonment of sovereignty over the Panama Canal and the Canal Zone ... A U.S. retreat from Panama would probably put the last nail in the coffin of the Monroe Doctrine.

New York Times defence correspondent Hanson Baldwin, *AEI Defense Review*, 1977. Baldwin was attacking Jimmy Carter's negotiation of a treaty to liquidate the Panama Canal Zone established in 1904 and to consign the canal to Panama in 1999. For the Monroe Doctrine see 614:7.

8 The past is dead. Teddy Roosevelt is in the ground.

US Canal Zone resident, *New York Times*, 1 Oct. 1979. Mourning for Theodore Roosevelt's achievement, the Canal Zone, which had just ceased to be.

9 [The 1977 treaties had shown] that we are sincere in our desire to relegate hemispheric paternalism and hegemony to the history books.

Gale McGee 'After Panama' in *South Atlantic Quarterly* Vol.78 (1979) p.7. In Dec. 1989 US forces invaded Panama to depose its military dictator General Manuel Noriega.

EAST OF SUEZ, 1967–8

10 He told me that when the British Empire finally sank beneath the waves of history it would leave behind only two monuments: one was the game of Association Football, the other was the expression 'Fuck Off'.

Governor of Aden Colony, Sir Richard Turnbull, c.1967; Denis Healey *The Time of my Life* (1989) p.283. Healey, Labour minister of defence at the time, was visiting Aden as part of the movement towards British withdrawal from the remaining dependencies east of Suez, marking the effective end of the British empire in Asia

11 'Be British, George, be British – how can you betray us?' [they said]. They had expressed nothing but horror and consternation ... The main American complaint was not about the withdrawal from the Far East but about the decision to leave the Persian Gulf.

Richard Crossman, 12 Jan. 1968; *Diaries of a Cabinet Minister* Vol.2 (1976) pp.646–7. The foreign secretary, George Brown, reports to the cabinet the US reaction to the British decision to withdraw its forces from the Far East and the Persian Gulf. The policy was highly unwelcome to an America deeply involved in Vietnam.

ALGERIA, 1945–62

1 The shock which I felt at the pitiless butchery that caused the deaths of thousands of Muslims, I have never forgotten. From that moment my nationalism took definite form.

Algerian poet Kateb Yacine, on the aftermath of the massacres in the town of Sétif, 8–12 May 1945; Alistair Horne *A Savage War of Peace* (1977) p.27. The atrocities were committed by Muslims and avenged with even greater ferocity by the Europeans of Algeria.

2 The only possible negotiation is war … Algeria is France. And who among you … would hesitate to employ every means to preserve France?

François Mitterrand, socialist minister of the interior, 5 and 12 Nov. 1954; Horne (1977) p.99. The Algerian nationalist insurrection broke out on 1 Nov. 1954.

3 What we are witnessing in Algeria is nothing short of the disintegration of the state; it is a gangrene which threatens France herself.

Robert Delavignette, 1957; Horne (1977) p.234. In the Algerian struggle abominable atrocities were committed by both sides, to the point where French democracy itself appeared under threat.

4 Either you consider *a priori* that every Arab, in the country, in the street, in a passing truck is *innocent* until he's proven the contrary … Or you will … consider that every Arab is a *suspect*, a possible *fellagha* [Algerian nationalist fighter] … because that, my dear sir, is the truth.

French army officer; Horne (1977) p.174. The French army was determined to win in Algeria in order to wipe out the recollection of its defeat in Vietnam.

5 *Je vous ai compris.* (I have understood you.)

General Charles de Gaulle, Algiers, 4 June 1958, speaking to the French settlers of Algeria; Jean Lacouture *De Gaulle* Vol.2 (1985) p.519. The settlers' revolt on 13 May had destroyed the Fourth Republic and returned de Gaulle to power. They therefore acclaimed his speech as an affirmation of his solidarity with them, but the utterance was delphic and

de Gaulle had by his own account already accepted that Algeria was destined for independence.

6 We shall go right to the end of the line, even with arms in our hands, to defend *Algérie française* … The determination of the French of Algeria will conquer the self-determination of de Gaulle. Algiers may become Budapest, but we shall remain … For us, henceforth, it's either the suitcase or the coffin!

Joseph Ortiz, leader of the French National Front, a neo-fascist organization founded on 1 Nov. 1958; Horne (1977) p.351. De Gaulle had promised Algeria self-determination on 16 Sept. 1959, a solution effectively conceding Algerian independence. Ortiz posed the alternatives of exile or death. The reference to Budapest is to the Hungarian insurrection of 1956, when the centre of the city became a bloody battle-ground (see 895:7).

7 *Françaises, Français!* Look where France risks going, in contrast to what she was about to become. *Françaises, Français! Aidez-moi!*

Charles de Gaulle, 23 April 1961; Horne (1977) p.455. In this national broadcast de Gaulle responded to an attempted coup d'état by a trio of rebellious generals, Jouhaud, Zeller and Challe. The coup collapsed when the nation rallied to de Gaulle.

8 This people has had to submit, since 1830, to the fact of colonialism. A European population has been created, heterogeneous in its origins, but soldered together by its integration within French nationality … It has benefited from exorbitant privileges … Independence is going to pose the problem of these Europeans. We wish to settle this in all equity, and we do not refuse to these people the right to unite themselves to the Algerian people and even to be merged into them.

Algerian nationalist Belkacem Krim, about May 1961; Horne (1977) p.471. Negotiations on Algerian independence between France and the Algerian *Front de Libération Nationale* (FLN) began on 20 May 1961. They resulted in the recognition of an independent Algeria on 3 July 1962. Most of the European community Krim refers to chose to leave Algeria and settle in France, taking the option of the suitcase rather than the coffin.

WEST AFRICA, 1946–60

9 France, together with the overseas peoples shall form a union founded upon equality of rights and duties, without distinction of race or religion … Faithful to her traditional mission, France proposes to guide the peoples for whom she has assumed responsibility into the freedom to administer themselves and to manage their own affairs democratically, rejecting any system of colonial rule based on arbitrary power.

Constitution of the French Fourth Republic, 1946, Preamble; John Chipman *French Power in Africa* (1989) p.95. The French Union set an African relationship with France that fell well short of independence.

1 What is wanted now is a vigorous policy of African local government which will progressively democratize the present forms and bring literates and illiterates together, in balanced and studied proportions, for the management of local finances and services. Failing this we shall find the masses apt to follow the leadership of demagogues who want to turn us right out very quickly.

Frederick Pedler, Colonial Office, 1 Nov. 1946; Hyam Pt 1 (1992) pp.117–18.

2 In the Gold Coast, the territory where Africans are most advanced politically, internal self-government is unlikely to be achieved in much less than a generation.

Sir Andrew Cohen, 22 May 1947; John Hargreaves *Decolonization in Africa* (1996 edn) p.107. The Fabian socialist Cohen was head of the Africa Division of the Colonial Office.

3 The large numbers of African soldiers returning from service with the Forces … by reason of their contacts with other peoples including Europeans had developed a political and national consciousness. [There was also] a feeling of political frustration among the educated Africans who saw no prospect of ever experiencing political power under existing conditions [as well as] a failure of the Government to realize that with the spread of liberal ideas, increasing literacy and a closer contact with political developments in other parts of the world, the star of rule through the Chiefs was on the wane. The achievement of self-rule in India, Burma and Ceylon had not passed unnoticed on the Gold Coast.

Report of the Commission of Inquiry into the Gold Coast riots of early 1948; R.C. Bridges *et al. Nations and Empire* (1969) p.312. This unrest provoked rapid constitutional advance in the Gold Coast, which, as Ghana, became the first black African colony to achieve full independence on 6 March 1957. 'Rule through the chiefs' was the policy of indirect rule via tribal chiefs, the representatives of African rural traditionalism, now under attack by the westernized urban nationalists of a new generation.

4 It is obvious to any critical student of history that, had the Tories been in power, neither India nor Ceylon nor Palestine nor Burma would have been free. We need not add the Gold Coast for obvious reasons. So it boils down to this fact: no colonial territory can ever hope to be free with a Tory government in power in Britain.

West African Pilot in *The West African Press Survey*, 6 Nov. 1951. In fact, no fewer than 17 colonies were moved to independence by the Conservative government between 1951 and 1964, the great majority of them in Africa.

5 There are those who will weep no tears if the Gold Coast comes a cropper and delude themselves with the idea that failure or breakdown in the Gold Coast will provide them with an excuse to slow down the rate of political advance in Africa. They forget that you cannot slow down a flood – the best you can hope to do is to keep the torrent within its proper channel.

Sir Charles Arden-Clarke, governor of the Gold Coast, c.1953; Lapping (1985) p.382.

6 We prefer poverty in liberty to riches in slavery.

Sékou Touré, leader of the French West African colony of Guinea, 1958; Patrick Manning *Francophone Sub-Saharan Africa 1880–1985* (1988) p.149. In 1958 de Gaulle created the French Community as the replacement for the French Union. Guinea alone chose not to join, and when they left the country French administrators were reported to have destroyed their office equipment in a final gesture of spiteful fury.

7 To continue to govern a discontented and possibly rebellious Nigeria would … present well-nigh insoluble administrative problems in view of the transfer of effective power that has already taken place in the domestic field. It might even need substantial military forces.

Alan Lennox-Boyd, colonial secretary, to prime minister Harold Macmillan, 25 Oct. 1958; Murphy (1999) p.190. Nigeria achieved independence in 1960 as one of the foremost states of black Africa.

EAST AFRICA, 1949–52

8 This is a British Colony for better or worse. The choice has been made, and this Kenya and its people are for ever British.

Sir Philip Mitchell, governor of Kenya, quoted by Archer Baldwin MP, 20 July 1949; *H.C. Deb.* Vol.467, Col.1463.

1 We scorn you like the drippings of a privy; rage, you English thieves, white swine, burst if you want … You English are liars, thieves, drunkards, idlers, who drain away the money of the black folk.
Semakula Mulumba (Uganda), telegram to prime minister Clement Attlee, about June 1950; Stephen Howe *Anti-Colonialism in British Politics* (1993) p.193.

2   I speak the truth and vow before God
     And before this movement,
     The movement of Unity,
     The Unity which is put to the test
     The Unity that is mocked with the name of
       'Mau Mau',
     That I shall go forward to fight for the land,
     The lands of Kirinyaga that we cultivated,
     The lands which were taken by the Europeans.
     And if I fail to do this
     May this oath kill me,
     May this seven kill me,
     May this goat kill me.
Josiah Mwangi Kariuki *Mau Mau Detainee* (1963) pp.25–33. The so-called 'Mau Mau' oath, administered to tribesmen fighting the British presence in Kenya. Rituals in the ceremony were repeated seven times, and participants bit into the flesh of a slaughtered goat.

3 Mau Mau is a movement which in its origins and development is wholly evil. It is the worst enemy of African progress in Kenya.
Father Trevor Huddleston, Dec. 1952; Lapping (1985) p.421. A serious charge, coming as it did from one of the leading supporters of the black cause in South Africa. The Mau Mau insurgency was eventually suppressed, and Kenya became independent in 1963 under the leadership of Jomo Kenyatta, who had been put on trial as a tacit supporter of Mau Mau.

THE BELGIAN CONGO, 1959–60

4 The danger lies not so much in the possibility that the Belgians will not compromise eventually with the force of nationalism, but that when they do they will find the Africans almost totally inexperienced in handling the responsibilities which they are certain to demand and eventually to get.
American commentator Chester Bowles, 1955; Colin Legum *Congo Disaster* (1972) p.47.

5 The object of our presence in the Dark Continent was thus defined by Leopold II: to open these backward countries to European civilization, to call their peoples to emancipation, liberty, and progress, after having saved them from slavery, disease, and poverty. In continuation of these noble aims, our firm resolve today is to lead, without fatal evasions but without imprudent haste, the Congolese peoples to independence in prosperity and peace.
Baudouin I, king of the Belgians, Jan. 1959; Legum (1972) p.59.

6 In a country where the white man is both judge and jury, it is human that the black man should begin to feel that he can get no justice because he is black.
Belgian parliamentary commission of inquiry into the Congo riots of Jan. 1959; Legum (1972) p.61.

7 After independence every Congolese who so wishes and who can afford it may buy a double-barrelled gun.
Election leaflet by the *Mouvement National Congolais*, 1960; René Lemarchand *Political Awakening in the Belgian Congo* (1964) p.219.

8 We have known ironies, insults, blows that we endured morning, noon and evening, because we are Negroes. Who will forget that to a black one said '*tu*', certainly not as to a friend, but because the more honourable '*vous*' was reserved for whites alone?
Patrice Lumumba, prime minister of the Belgian Congo, at the independence-day ceremony, 30 June 1960; Manning (1988) p.151.

9 The President expressed his wish that Lumumba would fall into a river full of crocodiles; Lord Home said regretfully that we have lost many of the techniques of old-fashioned diplomacy.
Memorandum of conversation by President Eisenhower's son John, 19 Sept. 1960; *Foreign Relations of the United States 1958–1960* Vol.14, p.495. Eisenhower and British foreign secretary Home were both fearful that Lumumba would bring the Russians into the Congo to back him in his bid to end the secession of the mineral-rich province of Katanga. The immunization of the Congo against communism was eventually achieved by introducing a United Nations peace-keeping force. Lumumba, meanwhile, was murdered, almost certainly with Belgian complicity, early in Feb. 1961.

CENTRAL AFRICA, 1960–64

10 I am opposed to domination by either black or white which is what most politicians want … Nevertheless we cannot afford to overlook the vital contribution which has been made and is still being made by the Europeans. 'Africa for the Africans' is a tragically impossible slogan.

Sir Roy Welensky, prime minister of the Central African Federation, 1960; *4000 Days* (1964) p.288. The Federation was created in 1953 by the combination of Nyasaland, Northern Rhodesia and Southern Rhodesia. It was supposedly an experiment in multi-racial government.

1 I myself can visualize that if we have them in the house here they will share the restaurant with us and they will share the bars with us. We will be living cheek by jowl with them and what sort of legislation can the people of this country expect when we our-selves are being conditioned to living cheek by jowl with Africans?

William Harper, leader of the Dominion Party in the Central African Federation, 23 Aug. 1960; James Barber *Rhodesia: The Road to Rebellion* (1967) p.46.

2 Your Federation is the last major British bastion in Africa. All attempts to disrupt and dismember it by sinister forces in Whitehall (and Washington) are a crime against the British Commonwealth and indeed, against white civilization itself. Two blacks do not make a white – you need at least six!

Conservative MP Henry Kerby, 29 Sept. 1960; Murphy (1995) p.83.

3 What these well-meaning people mean is that the quality and quantity of the crumbs on which the Africans feed today should be increased. What the normal and true African wants today is bread, not crumbs, and he wants to eat it at the table not under the table.

Nkomo Khumalo, 18 Sept. 1966; Barber (1967) p.59. An exposure of the reality underlying the Federation – that is, white supremacy masquerading as racial partnership.

4 A mere declaration of independence would have no constitutional effect. The only way Southern Rhodesia could become a sovereign independent state is by an Act of the British Parliament; a declaration of independence would be an open act of defiance and rebellion and it would be treasonable to give effect to it.

British government statement, 27 Oct. 1964; Elaine Windrich (ed.) *The Rhodesian Problem* (1975) p.208. Even so, Southern Rhodesia proclaimed its independence on 11 Nov. 1965, and Britain was unable to bring it to heel. The white-controlled government was eventually forced to give way after a prolonged African guerrilla war, and the country became independent in 1980 as Zimbabwe, on the basis of African majority rule.

SOUTH AFRICA, 1954–94

5 Apartheid comprises a whole multiplicity of phenomena. It comprises the political sphere; it is necessary in the social sphere; it is aimed at in Church matters; it is relevant to every sphere of life. Even within the economic sphere it is not just a question of numbers. What is of more importance there is whether one maintains the colour-bar or not.

Hendrik Verwoerd, South African minister of native affairs, 1954; T.R.H. Davenport *South Africa: A Modern History* (1977) p.270. Apartheid, the Afrikaans word for 'separate develop-ment', enforced strict segregation of whites and non-whites. Verwoerd was its arch-doctrinaire.

6 Call it paramountcy, *baaskap* [overlordship] or what you will, it is still domination ... Either the white man dominates or the black man takes over ... The only way the European can maintain supremacy is by domination ... And the only way they can maintain domination is by withholding the vote from non-Europeans. If it were not for that we would not be here in Parliament today.

Johannes Strijdom, South African prime minister, 20 April 1955; H.J. May *The South African Constitution* (1955) p.53.

7 *Naught for your Comfort*

Title of the book published in 1956 by the Anglican priest Father Trevor Huddleston, who had worked for years in the black African townships of Johannesburg. It is a quotation from G.K. Chesterton's *The Ballad of the White Horse* (1911; Bk 1, p.18): 'I tell you naught for your comfort.'

8 The wind of change is blowing through this continent, and, whether we like it or not, this growth of [African] national consciousness is a political fact.

Prime minister Harold Macmillan , Cape Town, 3 Feb. 1960; *Pointing the Way* (1972) p.475. Macmillan spoke to a largely unreceptive South African audience about the need to make some adjustment to the pressures of nationalism in sub-Saharan Africa.

9 [I am] concerned that when there are riots, whether on the part of whites or on the part of blacks, if it is necessary to shoot, only one person is shot dead.

Carel de Wet, 21 March 1960; *South African House of Assembly Debates* Vol.104, Col.3732. That same day police fired on a non-violent black protest at Sharpeville township, near Johannesburg, killing 67 people, a landmark event in the history of post-war South Africa. De Wet was minister for Bantu affairs.

1 South Africa has become the polecat of the world.
The nationalist *Die Burger* (The Citizen), soon after the Sharpeville massacre of 21 March 1960; Helen Suzman *In No Uncertain Terms* (1993) p.52.

2 We will stand like walls of granite.
Prime minister Hendrik Verwoerd, *Die Vaderland* (The Fatherland), 1 Dec. 1960. An adamantine rejoinder to the call for change in the face of internal unrest and external pressure. The Voortrekker monument to the Great Trek of 1834, unveiled in 1949, was a huge granite structure, reflecting the implacable obduracy of Afrikaner nationalists.

3 Southern Africa is the escarpment where the wind of change begins to veer.
Anon., early 1960s. A reference not just to South Africa, but to its satellite South West Africa, to the Portuguese colonies of Angola and Mozambique and to the Central African Federation of the Rhodesias and Nyasaland. All bar South Africa and South West Africa were in the hands of African nationalists by 1980.

4 *Guilty Land*
Title of book published in 1962 by the South African liberal activist Patrick van Rensburg, itself a quotation from the American abolitionist, John Brown (see 587:3).

5 I have fought against white domination, and I have fought against black domination. I have cherished the ideal of a democratic and free society in which all persons live together in harmony and with equal opportunities. It is an ideal which I hope to live for and to achieve. But if needs be it is an ideal for which I am prepared to die.
Nelson Mandela, 20 April 1964; *Long Walk to Freedom* (1994) p.354. Extemporized conclusion to his prepared statement from the dock at his trial for treason. Mandela was sentenced to life imprisonment and released on 11 Feb. 1990. He was inaugurated as president of South Africa on 10 May 1994.

6 Unless something drastic is done very soon, then bloodshed and violence are going to happen … almost inevitably … A people made desperate by despair and injustice and oppression will use desperate means.
Desmond Tutu, bishop of Johannesburg, to the South African prime minister, Balthazar Johannes Vorster, 23 May 1976; Frank Welsh *A History of South Africa* (2000 edn) p.474. Three weeks later South African police fired on a crowd of demonstrating black schoolchildren in the township of Soweto, killing more than 20. In the following nine months, over 500 more protesters were killed.

7 Black consciousness is in essence the realization by the black man of the need to rally together with his brothers around the cause of their subjection – the blackness of their skin – and to operate as a group in order to rid themselves of the shackles that bind them to perpetual servitude … Blacks no longer seek to reform the system … [They] are out to completely transform the system and to make of it what they wish.
Black activist Steve Biko *I Write What I Like* (1979) p.149. Biko died on 12 Sept. 1977 after a spell in police custody, immediately becoming a leading martyr of the black South African cause.

8 Together, hand in hand, with our boxes of matches and our necklaces, we shall liberate this country.
Winnie Mandela, *The Times*, 13 April 1986. A reckless speech by the wife of the imprisoned Nelson Mandela. Black South Africans suspected of collaborating with the Nationalist government were sometimes 'necklaced' – that is, roasted alive with a burning tyre around their necks.

9 Out of the experience of an extraordinary human disaster that lasted too long, must be born a society of which all humanity will be proud … Never, never, and never again shall it be that this beautiful land will again experience the oppression of one by another.
Nelson Mandela, presidential inaugural address, 10 May 1994; Leonard Thompson *A History of South Africa* (2001 edn) p.264.

The Cold War, 1945–89

OPENING MOVES, 1945–6

1 Ambassador Harriman said that in effect what we were faced with was a 'barbarian invasion of Europe', that Soviet control over any foreign country did not mean merely influence on their foreign relations but the extension of the Soviet system with secret police, extinction of freedom of speech, etc., and that we had to decide what should be our attitude in the face of these unpleasant facts.

Averell Harriman, US ambassador in Moscow, to the State Department, 20 April 1945; *Foreign Relations of the United States 1945* Vol.5 (1967) p.234. Harriman was advising a receptive President Truman to take a hard line with Stalin over conditions in the newly acquired Soviet satellite empire in East Europe, but Truman's power to influence Soviet policy was severely limited.

2 Unless Russia is faced with an iron fist and strong language, another war is in the making. Only one language do they understand – 'How many divisions have you?' … I'm tired of babying the Soviets.

President Harry S Truman, 5 Jan. 1946; Martin Walker *The Cold War* (1993) p.37. Truman was lecturing his secretary of state, James Byrnes, who was suspected of wanting to make a diplomatic deal with Stalin on the future of Europe.

3 Marxists have more than once pointed out that the capitalist world economic system contains in itself the seeds of a general crisis and of warlike clashes.

Joseph Stalin, 9 Feb. 1946; William O. McCagg Jr *Stalin Embattled 1943–1948* (1978) p.217. This speech, reviving the argument that conflict was inevitable between capitalism and communism, was described by Supreme Court Justice William O. Douglas as a 'declaration of World War III'.

4 Soviet leaders are driven … to put forward a dogma which pictures the outside world as evil, hostile and menacing, but as bearing within itself germs of a creeping disease and destined to be racked with growing internal convulsions until it is given final coup de grace by rising power of socialism and yields to new and better world.

George Kennan to the State Department, 22 Feb. 1946; *Memoirs 1925–1950* (1972) pp.549–51. Kennan, a senior diplomat in the US Moscow embassy, sends his famous 'long telegram', which was destined to shape the American reaction to the USSR profoundly in the early years of the Cold War.

5 From Stettin in the Baltic to Trieste in the Adriatic, an iron curtain has descended across the Continent.

Winston Churchill, 5 March 1946; *Winston Churchill: His Complete Speeches, 1897–1963* (1974) Vol.7, p.7290. See also Churchill's telegram to Truman of 12 May 1945: 'An iron curtain is drawn down upon their front. We do not know what is going on behind' (*The Second World War* Vol.6 (1953) pp.498–9). Note that the 1946 speech placed the Soviet zone of Germany outside the curtain.

6 It would appear that the natural frontier of Russia was from Danzig or perhaps Stettin to Trieste.

Friedrich Engels, *New York Daily Tribune*, 12 April 1853.

7 Communism … must be viewed not merely as a political creed but as a religious dogma and faith which can inspire such fanaticism and self-sacrifice as we associate with the early Christians and the rise of Islam.

Christopher Warner, British Foreign Office, 2 April 1946; Victor Rothwell *Britain and the Cold War 1941–1947* (1982) p.257. Written in the wake of the alarm touched off by Stalin's speech of 9 Feb. (see 876:3).

8 I am more than ever convinced that communism is on the march on a worldwide scale which only America can stop.

Senator Arthur H. Vandenberg to John Foster Dulles, 13 May 1946; David Green *The Containment of Latin America* (1971) pp.276–7. Vandenberg was soon to be chairman of the Senate Foreign Relations Committee (see 877:7), and his fellow Republican, Dulles, was secretary of state from 1953 to 1959.

9 We should recognize that we have no more business in the political affairs of Eastern Europe than Russia has in the political affairs of Latin America, western Europe and the United States … Whether we like it or not, the Russians will try to socialize their sphere of influence just as we try to democratize our sphere of influence.

Henry Wallace, 12 Sept. 1946; *Keesing's Contemporary Archives 1946–1948* (1948) p.8151. This public plea by the secretary of commerce for recognition of the *fait accompli* of the Soviet empire led to his immediate dismissal by President Truman.

10 Is it not clear that … unrestricted application of the principles of 'equal opportunity' would in practice mean the veritable economic enslavement of the small states and their subjugation to the rule and arbitrary will of strong and enriched foreign firms, banks, and industrial corporations.

Vyacheslav Molotov, Soviet foreign minister, Oct. 1946; Walker (1993) p.46. A remarkable public admission of the power of American capitalism in the post-war world and of the Soviet Union's inability to match it.

ICING UP, 1947-9

1 I believe that it must be the policy of the United States to support free peoples who are resisting attempted subjugation by armed minorities or by outside pressures.

Truman Doctrine, 12 March 1947; *Public Papers* 1947 (1963) pp.176–80. Truman's pledge applied specifically to Greece and Turkey but had global implications (although it was not applied in the case of the communist take-over of Czechoslovakia in Feb. 1948).

2 The patient is sinking while the doctors deliberate.

General George Marshall, US secretary of state, 28 April 1947; Forrest Pogue *George Marshall* Vol.3 (1987) p.200. Marshall had just returned from a fruitless foreign ministers' meeting in Moscow, held to discuss the future of post-war Europe.

3 Let us not be deceived – we are today in the midst of a cold war.

Bernard Baruch, 16 April 1947, in a speech written by Herbert Bayard Swope.

4 Our policy is directed not against any country or doctrine but against hunger, poverty, desperation and chaos. Its purpose should be the revival of a working economy in the world so as to permit the emergence of political and social conditions in which free institutions can exist.

General George Marshall, speaking at Harvard University, 5 June 1947; *A Decade of American Foreign Policy: Basic Documents* (1950) pp.1268–70. This speech launched the so-called Marshall Plan of aid to Europe. It was designed to rescue western Europe from communist subversion, although the aid was also offered to the Soviet Union and its East European satellites. Stalin saved Washington much embarrassment by returning a point-blank refusal and by ordering the East European regimes to follow suit. The governments of western Europe gratefully accepted.

5 It was like a life-line to a sinking man. It seemed to bring hope where there was none. The generosity of it was beyond our belief.

Ernest Bevin, on the Marshall Plan, 1 April 1949; Alan Bullock *Ernest Bevin* Vol.3 (1983) p.405.

6 The 'Marshall Plan' has been compared to a flying saucer – nobody knows what it looks like, how big it is, in what direction it is moving, or whether it really exists.

The American diplomat Ben T. Moore to Clair Wilcox, 28 July 1947; *Foreign Relations of the United States 1947* Vol.3 (1972) p.239.

7 To me 'bipartisan foreign policy' means ... that America speaks with maximum authority against those who would divide and conquer us and the free world ... it simply seeks national security ahead of partisan advantage.

Senator Arthur Vandenberg, 5 Jan. 1950; *The Private Papers of Senator Vandenberg* (1952) pp.552–3. Vandenberg, Republican chairman of the Senate Foreign Relations Committee, followed a policy of cooperation with the Democratic government of President Truman in respect of Europe but not on China, where the Nationalist regime of Chiang Kai-shek (Jiang Jieshi) demanded, but did not get, its own Marshall Aid programme.

8 The lines are drawn. The response is awaited. I do not need to point out ... the repercussions of a failure to meet the Soviet challenge, in terms not only of the control of Europe, but of the impact which such a failure would have on the Middle and Far East and throughout the whole world.

General Walter Bedell Smith, US ambassador in Moscow, 11 July 1947; *Foreign Relations of the United States 1947* Vol.3 (1972) p.327. His comment on Stalin's ban on Czechoslovak acceptance of Marshall Aid.

9 It is clear that the main element of any United States policy toward the Soviet Union must be that of a long-term, patient but firm and vigilant containment of Russian expansive tendencies.

George Kennan 'The Sources of Soviet Conduct' in *Foreign Affairs*, July 1947, Vol.25, p.57. Kennan thus articulated the American response to what was seen as Stalin's expansionism in the late 1940s.

10 It amounts to Soviet acceptance of the division of the world into two.

The British diplomat Frank Roberts, 6 Oct. 1947; Victor Rothwell *Britain and the Cold War 1941–1947* (1982) p.286. On the founding of the Cominform, the successor organization to the Comintern, dissolved by Stalin in 1943 as a conciliatory gesture to the West but now revived under a new title with the objective of promoting communist revolution.

11 He [Winston Churchill] believes that now is the time, promptly, to tell the Soviet Union that if they do not retire from Berlin and abandon eastern Germany, withdrawing to the Polish frontier, we will raze their cities … The only vocabulary they understand is the vocabulary of force.

Lewis Douglas, US ambassador to London, 17 April 1948; *Foreign Relations of the United States 1948* Vol.2 (1973) p.895. Churchill was reacting to the Soviet inception of a blockade of road and rail access to the British, French and American sectors of Berlin. The United States had a war plan, Operation Broiler, which envisaged the atomic destruction of the six largest cities of the USSR, but only after the outbreak of general war, not as a pre-war threat.

1 If we mean that we are to hold Europe against communism, we must not budge. I believe the future of democracy requires us to stay here until forced out.

General Lucius D. Clay, US military governor in Berlin, 24 June 1948. Clay had wished to force a road or rail convoy through to Berlin, but he was overruled for fear it would trigger a full-scale war with the Soviet Union. The alternative was an Anglo-American airlift of supplies into the beleaguered city, which succeeded against the odds.

2 I don't think he should have tucked tail and gone to the air.

Senator Strom Thurmond, Jan. 1984; recorded for a BBC Radio Four programme on the centenary of President Truman's birth. Thurmond, Truman's opponent in the presidential election of 1948, believed that resorting to the airlift was an act of cowardice, not reasonable caution.

3 I regret very much that we are in Berlin at all … From the military point of view it makes no sense whatever to have US forces in an enclave that could be chopped off with ease. From the political point of view, Berlin has become the important symbol it now is largely because we ourselves have made it so … Our present hysterical outburst of humanitarian feelings about the [Germans] keep reminding me that just 3½ years ago I would have been considered a hero if I had succeeded in exterminating those same Germans with bombs.

Ambassador Walter Bedell Smith, 28 Sept. 1948; *Foreign Relations of the United States 1948* Vol.2 (1973) p.1195. Smith's defeatism came at a moment when it had not yet been established that the airlift could supply Berlin through the coming winter. When it did, Stalin lifted the blockade in the spring of 1949.

4 Do you know what the basis of our policy is? It is fear. Fear of you, fear of your government, fear of your policy.

Paul-Henri Spaak, 28 Sept. 1948. The Belgian prime minister, addressing the United Nations General Assembly in Paris, was speaking of Stalinist Russia at a time when the fate of West Berlin still lay in the balance.

5 The parties agree that an armed attack against one or more of them in Europe or North America shall be considered an attack against them all.

Opening words of Article 5, North Atlantic Treaty, signed on 4 April 1949; Richard Vaughan *Post-War Integration in Europe* (1976) p.40. The Berlin blockade gave a decisive impetus to the formation of a western alliance, the North Atlantic Treaty Organization (NATO), which was set up to defend its members – Belgium, Canada, Denmark, France, Iceland, Italy, Luxembourg, The Netherlands, Norway, Portugal, the United Kingdom and the United States – against a potential attack by the Soviet Union.

GERMANY REARMED, 1949–54

6 The two European countries which could constitute serious threats to our strategic interests are a resurgent Germany and Russia … If Russia does become hostile, Germany is the only country whose geographical position, manpower and resources could provide the aid which might be essential to our preservation.

British military planning staff, July 1944; Saki Dockrill *Britain's Policy for West German Rearmament 1950–1955* (1991) p.6.

7 Not even if the Allies were to demand a German contribution as being indispensable for European security would the establishment of German armed forces be considered.

Konrad Adenauer, 16 Dec. 1949; Olav Riste (ed.) *Western Security: The Formative Years* (1985) p.170. The new West German chancellor, elected in Sept. 1949, was responding to the political unpopularity of rearmament in the Federal Republic, established in Sept. 1949.

8 Her rearmament seems essential if western defence is to be real … [It] might then be possible to defend the Elbe instead of the Rhine, with great effect upon the morale of the Low Countries and France [and] make available efficient manpower on a significant scale.

Kenneth Younger, minister of state at the Foreign Office, 6 July 1950; Riste (1985) pp.251–2. Younger was supporting the American call for a forward defence of western Europe.

9 If we need Germany's help and want Germany to form part of our western bloc, we must make her a full member of the club and reconcile ourselves to seeing her smoking a large cigar in a big chair in front of the fire in the smoking room.

Ivo Mallet, Foreign Office mandarin, 16 Nov. 1950; Dockrill (1991) p.46.

1 Since Turkey recovered twenty years ago France has taken her place as the sick man of Europe. She exploits her feebleness and the debt which others owe to her to secure palliatives from abroad.
Robert Scott of the Foreign Office, 25 Nov. 1952; Dockrill (1991) p.106. France, after three German invasions in 70 years, was understandably fearful of a rearmed Germany and had proposed a European Defence Community (EDC) within which Germany would be unable to use its military forces independently.

2 If ... the European Defense Community should not become effective; if France and Germany remain apart ... that would compel an agonizing reappraisal of basic United States policy.
US secretary of state John Foster Dulles, 14 Dec. 1953. French politicians were extremely reluctant to endorse the EDC, and if they vetoed the project Dulles was threatening to reconsider US military commitment to western Europe under NATO. In the event, when the French Assembly rejected the EDC in Aug. 1954, Germany was brought into the west European defence structure as a member of NATO.

THE FAR EAST, 1945–54

3 It is not the policy of this GOVT to assist the French to re-establish their control over Indochina by force and the willingness of the USA to see French control re-established assumed that French claim to have the support of the population of Indochina is borne out by future events.
US government statement, Oct. 1945; The Pentagon Papers Vol.I (1971) p.17. The leader of the Vietnamese nationalist movement, Ho Chi Minh, was a communist, but at this stage anti-colonialism prevailed over anti-communism as a determinant of US policy.

4 We are building in Japan a self-sufficient democracy, strong enough and stable enough to support itself and at the same time serve as a deterrent against any other totalitarian war threats which might hereafter arise in the Far East.
Kenneth Royall, US army secretary, 6 Jan. 1948; Walker (1993) p.66. Japan, like West Germany, was to be revived as an industrial power, but unlike Germany it was not recruited as a military ally of the United States. Japanese memories of the nuclear devastation of Hiroshima and Nagasaki in 1945 largely saw to that.

5 Question whether Ho as much nationalist as Commie is irrelevant. All Stalinists in colonial areas are nationalists.
US secretary of state Dean Acheson, May 1949; The Pentagon Papers Vol.I (1971) p.51. A sharp change of mind on

communist-led nationalism in Vietnam as a communist victory in Vietnam's northern neighbour, China, loomed on the horizon.

6 Not only in China but also in the world without exception, one either leans to the side of imperialism or to the side of socialism. Neutrality is mere camouflage and a third road does not exist.
Mao Zedong (Mao Tse-tung), 1 July 1949; A Documentary History of Chinese Communism (1952) pp.453–4. Mao, soon to be head of the communist People's Republic of China (see 748:6), was unequivocally taking the Soviet side in the Cold War.

7 Nothing that this country did or could have done within the reasonable limits of its capabilities could have changed that result; nothing that was left undone by this country has contributed to it.
US secretary of state Dean Acheson, 30 July 1949; letter of transmittal for the so-called China White Paper (1949) p.xvii. By the summer of 1949 it was clear that China would soon go communist. The white paper was issued in defence of the Truman government's policy of not being drawn into a major war on the Asian mainland as part of its general resistance to communist expansion. The front in Europe was considered immeasurably more important, and a second front in China was seen as dangerous over-extension of US resources.

8 This defensive perimeter runs along the Aleutians to Japan and then goes to the Ryukyus ... [and] from the Ryukyus to the Philippine Islands.
US secretary of state Dean Acheson, 12 Jan. 1950; Department of State Bulletin, 23 Jan. 1950, p.115. This perimeter excluded the Chinese Nationalist-held island of Taiwan (Formosa) as well as South Korea. Both were to be drawn inside it on the outbreak of war in Korea five months later. The Aleutians are the island chain off the coast of Alaska. The Ryukyus are the island group south of the Japanese home islands, centring on Okinawa, which were seized by the Americans at great cost in 1945 and were, in 1950, an important US base. Japan, still under American occupation, was another vital base area, as was the recently independent Philippines.

9 The French through their folly ... have left us with two ghastly courses of action:
    1. To wash our hands of the country [Vietnam] and allow the communists to overrun it.
    2. To continue to pour treasure (and perhaps eventually lives) into a hopeless cause.
Charlton Ogburn Jr to Dean Rusk, 18 Aug. 1950; Foreign Relations of the United States 1950 Vol.6 (1976) p.863. Simultaneously with his pledge to defend South Korea in June 1950, President Truman committed the United States to enhance its support for the French in their war with the communist-led nationalists in Vietnam. Option 2 was followed from 1950 to 1973; Option 1 in 1975.

1 We face an entirely new war.

General of the Army Douglas MacArthur, Nov. 1950; *Foreign Relations of the United States 1950* Vol.7 (1976) pp.1237–8. On 25 June 1950 North Korea invaded South Korea. After a severe initial setback, US troops commanded by General MacArthur were authorized in late Sept. to cross the 38th parallel dividing the two countries. The prompt result was Chinese communist intervention to prevent the US establishing a military presence on the Chinese frontier. By the end of Nov. the US army was in full retreat, and MacArthur's response was to widen the war beyond Korea, with a direct assault on China.

2 If we lose the war to communism in Asia the fall of Europe is inevitable … we must win. There is no substitute for victory.

General of the Army Douglas MacArthur to Representative Joseph Martin, 20 March 1951. MacArthur's strategy could well have brought in China's ally, the USSR, not only in Korea but in Europe, where the USA had nothing but nuclear weapons to hold the line. MacArthur was accordingly dismissed by President Truman on 10 April 1951.

3 I fired him because he wouldn't respect the authority of the President … I didn't fire him because he was a dumb son-of-a-bitch, although he was.

President Harry S Truman, a retrospective on his dismissal of MacArthur; Merle Miller *Plain Speaking* (1973) p.287.

4 If he'd been a real hero he'd have gone down with the ship.

Senator Harry S Truman to his daughter, Margaret, 1942, on General MacArthur after the surrender of the US garrison in the Philippines; Robert H. Ferrell *Harry S Truman and the American Presidency* (1983) p.126.

5 Like the old soldier in that ballad, I now close my military career and just fade away, an old soldier who tried to do his duty as God gave him the sight to see that duty.

General of the Army Douglas MacArthur to a joint session of Congress, 19 April 1951; Geoffrey Perret *Old Soldiers Never Die* (1996) p.571. MacArthur returned to the United States to a hero's welcome, but the Republican nomination for the presidency in 1952 went not to him but to his erstwhile subordinate, Dwight D. Eisenhower.

6 Red China is not the powerful nation seeking to dominate the world … This strategy would involve us in the wrong war, at the wrong place, at the wrong time, with the wrong enemy.

General of the Army Omar Bradley, 15 May 1951; *Military Situation in the Far East Hearings* Pt 2, p.732. A flat dismissal of the MacArthur strategy for the Far East by the chairman of the joint chiefs of staff. By the time Bradley spoke, the front in

Korea had been stabilized, and in July 1953 the war ended with a truce agreement.

7 There is the risk that, as in Korea, Red China might send its own army into Indo-China. The communist Chinese regime should realize that such a second aggression could not occur without grave consequences which might not be confined to Indo-China.

US secretary of state John Foster Dulles, 2 Sept. 1953; Melvin Gurtov *The First Vietnam Crisis* (1967) p.32. The parallel was inexact: China entered Korea because the North Koreans were losing the war. It did not need to enter the Vietnam war between the French colonial regime and the North Vietnamese because the North Vietnamese were by this stage winning.

8 You have a row of dominoes set up, you knock over the first one, and what will happen to the last one is the certainty that it will go over very quickly. So you could have a beginning of a disintegration that would have the most profound influences.

President Dwight D. Eisenhower, 7 April 1954; *Public Papers 1954* (1960) p.383. For all that, Eisenhower did not support those within his administration, including Vice-President Richard Nixon, who favoured direct US intervention in Vietnam to save the French. (The French minister-resident in Indochina first stated the domino theory on 26 April 1952.)

9 I would like to emphasize that … insofar as the free world is concerned, the French Union forces at Dien Bien Phu are fighting a modern Thermopylae.

US under-secretary of state Walter Bedell Smith, April 1954; *Department of State Bulletin*, 19 April 1954, p.3. The French garrison in the fortress of Dien Bien Phu was close to defeat at the hands of the North Vietnamese, and it fell on 7 May, just as the Spartans at Thermopylae also succumbed (see 55:2).

10 To jaw-jaw is better than to war-war.

Prime minister Winston Churchill, *New York Times*, 27 June 1954. Churchill had strongly opposed American military involvement in Vietnam, primarily because it could have left Europe wide open to a Soviet attack. The war was ended by a diplomatic settlement, dividing the country and bringing about a French withdrawal, although the North Vietnamese persisted in a struggle for reunification.

PEACEFUL COEXISTENCE, 1953–64

11 We firmly stand by the belief that there are no disputed or outstanding issues today which cannot be settled peacefully by mutual agreement between the parties concerned. This also relates to disputed issues between the United States of America and the

Soviet Union. We stand, as we have always stood, for the peaceful coexistence of the two systems.

Georgi Malenkov, 8 Aug. 1953; *Soviet News*, 15 Aug. 1953. A marked departure from the hostile stance taken by Stalin in his final years.

1 The detachment of any major European satellite from the Soviet bloc does not now appear feasible except by Soviet acquiescence or war.

National Security Council (NSC-62/2), 30 Oct. 1953; John Lewis Gaddis *Strategies of Containment* (1982) p.155. The fundamental reason why the so-called 'roll-back' of communism from East Europe was an impossibility until the USSR accepted it (as it eventually did in 1989; see 897:3).

2 If anyone believes that our smiles involve abandonment of the teaching of Marx, Engels and Lenin, he deceives himself poorly. Those who wait for that must wait until a shrimp learns to whistle.

Nikita Khrushchev, *New York Times*, 18 Sept. 1955.

3 The ability to get to the verge without getting into the war is the necessary art. If you cannot master it, you inevitably get into a war. If you try to run away from it, if you are scared to go to the brink, you are lost.

US secretary of state John Foster Dulles, *Life* magazine, 16 Jan. 1956, p.78. Dulles was no enthusiast for coexistence.

4 There are only two ways: either peaceful coexistence or the most destructive war in history. There is no third way.

Nikita Khrushchev, 25 Feb. 1956; Robert V. Daniels (ed.) *A Documentary History of Communism* Vol.2 (1985) p.225. A speech complementing the denunciation of Stalin at the 20th Party Congress (see 890:8).

5 Except under very exceptional circumstances ... an immoral and short-sighted conception.

US secretary of state John Foster Dulles, opining on neutralism, 9 June 1956; *Department of State Bulletin*, 18 June 1956. Neutralism was the policy adopted by a number of states – principally India, Egypt and Yugoslavia – which refused alliance with either side in the Cold War. Dulles (like Mao Zedong, see 879:6) believed in a black-and-white world with no shades of grey.

6 We base ourselves on the idea that we must peacefully coexist ... Whether you like it or not, history is on our side. We will bury you.

Nikita Khrushchev, *The Times*, 19 Nov. 1956. Spoken in the aftermath of the Suez crisis, in which Khrushchev had threatened Britain and France with Soviet missile attack unless they withdrew from Egypt; this remark was taken as a promise to bury the West under a mountain of nuclear rubble. In fact, it

meant that communism would attend the funeral of capitalism, as Khrushchev himself later explained (*New York Times*, 17 Sept. 1959).

7 The near future will bring the forces of peace and socialism new successes. The USSR will become the leading industrial power of the world. China will become a mighty industrial state ... In these conditions a real possibility will have arisen to exclude war from the life of society even before socialism achieves complete victory on earth, with capitalism still existing in a part of the world.

Communiqué of the Moscow Conference of Communist and Workers' Parties, Nov. 1960; John Gittings (ed.) *Survey of the Sino-Soviet Dispute* (1968) p.360. An unsuccessful Soviet attempt to associate China with the policy of coexistence.

8 If we cannot now end our differences, at least we can help make the world safe for diversity. For, in the final analysis, our most basic common link is that we all inhabit this small planet. We all breathe the same air. We all cherish our children's future. And we are all mortal.

President John F. Kennedy, 10 June 1963; *Public Papers 1963* (1964) p.462. A key speech, looking to coexistence, not confrontation, in the aftermath of the Cuban missile crisis, but Kennedy did not live to fulfil its promise.

9 A nuclear test-ban treaty does not mean the end of the arms race. You do not like our social system and we do not like yours. No treaties can overcome the concrete contradictions between the two social systems.

Nikita Khrushchev, 8 Aug. 1963. The Soviet leader was trying, perhaps, to win Chinese support for his policy of accommodation with Washington.

10 Two large powers – i.e., the United States and the Soviet Union – are trying to become friends and take over control of the whole world. How can we approve of such a development?

Mao Zedong, 10 July 1964; Dennis J. Doolin *Territorial Claims in the Sino-Soviet Conflict* (1965) p.43.

BERLIN, 1958–63

11 Berlin is the testicles of the West ... Every time I want to make the West scream, I squeeze on Berlin.

Nikita Khrushchev, Nov. 1958; Jeremy Isaacs and Taylor Downing *Cold War* (1998) p.171. The USSR was threatening to sign a treaty with East Germany giving it control of access to West Berlin, prompting a major international crisis.

1 The bone in my throat.

Nikita Khrushchev, on West Berlin; Michael Beschloss *The Crisis Years* (1991) p.223. West Berlin was a vulnerable Western asset, but it was also a dangerous Soviet liability, since discontented East Germans could leave the country by crossing from East to West Berlin and thence to West Germany. More and more were beginning to do so.

2 It's going to be a cold winter.

President John F. Kennedy to Khrushchev, 4 June 1961. The two leaders came together in Vienna, but there was no meeting of minds on Berlin – nor on any other issue.

3 No one has the intention of building a wall.

East German leader Walter Ulbricht, *Neues Deutschland*, 17 June 1961. A remarkable disclosure in the East German newspaper, publicizing the possibility that the only solution to the outflow from East Germany was a physical barrier between East and West Berlin.

4 If the present situation of open borders remains, collapse is inevitable.

Walter Ulbricht, sending a warning to Moscow, early July 1961; Vladislav Zubok and Constantine Pleshakov *Inside the Kremlin's Cold War* (1996) p.251.

5 It's not a very nice solution, but a wall is a hell of a lot better than a war.

President John F. Kennedy, reacting to the building of the Berlin Wall on 13 Aug. 1961; Kenneth P. O'Donnell and David F. Powers *Johnny We Hardly Knew Ye* (1972) p.350.

6 The tension escalated very rapidly for the one reason that this was Americans confronting Russians. It wasn't East Germans. There was live ammunition in both tanks of the Russians and the Americans.

US Colonel James Atwood, on the stand-off between the armour of the USA and the USSR at the Checkpoint Charlie crossing through the Berlin Wall, 27 Oct. 1961; Isaacs and Downing (1998) p.183. In fact, neither side had any intention of allowing the crisis to detonate a third world war, and no Western attempt was made to breach the Wall, which stood intact until 9 Nov. 1989.

7 All free men, wherever they may live, are citizens of Berlin. And therefore, as a free man, I take pride in the words *Ich bin ein Berliner* [I am a Berliner].

President John F. Kennedy, speaking in West Berlin, 26 June 1963; *Public Papers 1963* (1964) p.525. A promise of enduring American protection for West Berlin; and the cause of some merriment among Kennedy's Berlin audience, since a *Berliner* also means a jam doughnut.

THE BOMB, 1946–63

8 The atom bomb is a paper tiger which the US reactionaries use to scare people. It looks terrible, but in fact it is not. The outcome of a war is decided by the people, not by one or two new weapons.

Mao Zedong, in conversation with his American sympathizer Anna Louise Strong, Aug. 1946.

9 We have got to have this thing over here whatever it costs … We've got to have the bloody Union Jack flying on top of it.

British foreign secretary Ernest Bevin, on the atomic bomb, 26 Oct. 1946; Bullock Vol.3 (1983) p.352.

10 America can get what she wants if she insists upon it. After all, we've got it and they [the Soviet Union] haven't and won't have for a long time to come.

Bernard Baruch to David Lilienthal, Dec. 1946; Gregg Herken *The Winning Weapon* (1980) p.171. The millionaire financier Baruch was the Truman administration's spokesman on nuclear arms control; Lilienthal was chairman of the US Atomic Energy Commission. It is worth mentioning that the British, America's wartime partners in the development of the bomb, were excluded from access to American nuclear data by the Atomic Energy Act of 1946.

11 The physicists have known sin; and this is a knowledge which they cannot lose.

J. Robert Oppenheimer, 25 Nov. 1947. Oppenheimer had directed the construction of the atomic bomb at Los Alamos during World War II.

12 Oppenheimer when he went into Truman's office with Dean Acheson said to the latter, wringing his hands: 'I have blood on my hands.' Truman later said to Acheson: 'Never bring that fucking cretin in here again. He didn't drop the bomb. I did. That kind of weepiness makes me sick.'

Jean-Jacques Salomon *Science et Politique* (1970).

13 It is certain that Europe would have been communized and London would have been under bombardment some time ago, but for the deterrent of the atomic bomb in the hands of the United States.

Winston Churchill, 25 March 1949; Martin Gilbert *'Never Despair'* (1988) p.464.

14 Why, a President who didn't approve going ahead on the H-bomb all-out would be hanged from a lamp-post if the Russians should get it and we hadn't.

Senator Brien McMahon; David Lilienthal *The Journals of David E. Lilienthal* Vol.3 (1966) p.424. Senator McMahon was chairman of the Joint Committee on Atomic Energy. On 29 Aug. 1949 the Soviet Union exploded its first atomic device, touching off a clamour in the United States for the hydrogen bomb, 1,000 times more destructive than atomic weapons.

1 The assault on free institutions is worldwide now, and in the context of the present polarization of power a defeat of free institutions anywhere is a defeat everywhere … The United States, in cooperation with other free countries [should] launch a build-up of strength which will support a firm policy directed to the frustration of the Kremlin design.

National Security Council (NSC-68), 7 April 1950; *Foreign Relations of the United States 1950* Vol.I (1977) pp.240, 287. This policy paper from the National Security Council called for a massive American and European conventional rearmament programme to face an anticipated war with the USSR in 1954. It was to run in conjunction with the effort to produce a hydrogen bomb and was designed to move away from the current total dependence on nuclear weapons. The principal author was Paul Nitze, later adviser on nuclear arms control to President Reagan.

2 We may be likened to two scorpions in a bottle, each capable of killing the other, but only at the risk of his own life.

J. Robert Oppenheimer, on the East–West balance of terror; *Foreign Affairs* Vol.31 (July 1953) p.529.

3 You may reasonably expect a man to walk a tightrope safely for ten minutes; it would be unreasonable to do so without accident for two hundred years.

Bertrand Russell, the campaigner against nuclear weapons; D. Bagley *The Tightrope Men* (1973).

4 Atomic weapons have virtually achieved conventional status within our armed services.

President Dwight D. Eisenhower, 8 Dec. 1953; *Public Papers 1953* (1960) p.815. A terrifying declaration, given the awesome destructive power of the nuclear arsenal.

5 Local defenses must be reinforced by the further deterrent of massive retaliatory power … The basic decision was to depend primarily upon a great capacity to retaliate, instantly, by means and at places of our choosing.

US secretary of state John Foster Dulles, 12 Jan. 1954; *Department of State Bulletin*, 25 Jan. 1954, pp.107–8. In the aftermath of the Korean War, the US scaled down its conventional forces and placed its first reliance on nuclear strike capability.

6 It was an ironic fact that we had reached a stage where safety might well be the child of terror and life the twin of annihilation.

Prime minister Winston Churchill, 2 Feb. 1955, as recorded by the Canadian statesman Lester Pearson; *Memoirs* Vol.2 (1974) p.80. Churchill was speaking of the hydrogen bomb, now in the possession of both the United States and the Soviet Union. Compare 833:2.

7 The east wind is prevailing over the west wind … Let us imagine, how many people will die if war should break out? Out of the world's population of 2,700 million, one-third – or, if more, half – may be lost … I debated this question with a foreign statesman [Nehru]. He believed that if an atomic war was fought, the whole of mankind would be annihilated. I said that if the worst came to the worst and half of mankind died, the other half would remain while imperialism would be razed to the ground, and the whole world would become socialist.

Mao Zedong, 18 Nov. 1957; Gittings (1968) p.82. Chairman Mao looks on the bright side of life after the recent Soviet launch of the first space satellite, *Sputnik*, which appeared to give the USSR a decisive lead over the USA in missile technology.

8 Now, with the atomic bomb, the number of troops on each side makes practically no difference to … the outcome of a war. The more troops on a side, the more bomb fodder.

Nikita Khrushchev, in conversation with Mao, 31 Aug. 1958; Strobe Talbott (ed.) *Khrushchev Remembers* Vol.I (1971) pp.467–70. This strategic lesson was delivered during Khrushchev's visit to Beijing, but it fell on deaf ears.

9 He [Khrushchev] wants to improve relations with the United States? Good, we'll congratulate him with our guns … Let's get the United States involved, too. Maybe we can get the United States to drop an atom bomb on Fujian … Let's see what Khrushchev says then.

Mao Zedong, early Aug. 1958; Vladislav Zubok and Constantine Pleshakov *Inside the Kremlin's Cold War* (1996) p.221. Maoist brinkmanship over the Chinese Nationalist-held offshore islands of Quemoy and Matsu. Mao began a bombardment of the islands on 23 Aug., the 19th anniversary of the Nazi–Soviet Pact of 1939.

10 One does not need to be an extreme pessimist, and imagine a third world war to be the end of the world, to be none the less conscious of the fact that today a world war could not but be a war of mass annihilation … For the Chinese theoreticians it is sufficient to make the assertion that the result would be socialism.

Edvard Kardelj *Socialism and War* (1960) Ch.12. The book by the Yugoslav communist Kardelj was attacked by the Chinese as defeatist revisionism.

1 We will all go together when we go,
 All suffused with an incandescent glow ...
 When the air becomes uranious,
 We will all go simultaneous,
 Oh, we all will go together when we go.

Tom Lehrer's revivalist hymn for the thermonuclear era, 'We Will All Go Together When We Go' (1953).

2 Restraint? Why are you so concerned with saving their lives? The whole idea is to kill the bastards. At the end of the war if there are two Americans and one Russian left alive, we win.

US Air Force General Thomas Power, head of the Strategic Air Command, the American nuclear strike force; Walker (1993) p.167. The reply, from William Kaufmann, was: 'Then you had better make sure that they are a man and a woman.'

3 More Damage Per Dollar

Cost-effectiveness as a justification for nuclear warfare, early 1960s. The Soviet equivalent, one giggling Pentagonian suggested, might be: 'More Rubble Per Rouble.'

4 Limited nuclear capabilities, operating independently, are dangerous, expensive, prone to obsolescence and lacking in credibility as a deterrent.

Secretary of defense Robert S. McNamara, June 1962; Lawrence Freedman *The Evolution of Nuclear Strategy* (1989 edn) p.307. So much for the British 'independent deterrent' and the French *force de frappe*.

5 The central purpose of this treaty is, through a partial ban on nuclear tests, to prevent all the threatened peace-loving countries, including China, from increasing their defence capability, so that the United States may be more unbridled in threatening and blackmailing these countries.

Chinese government statement, 31 July 1963; Gittings (1968) p.188. A denunciation of the Test Ban Treaty initialled by the Soviet Union, the United Kingdom and the United States on 25 July. The treaty, which banned all but underground nuclear tests, was seen by the Chinese (and the French) as an attempt to preserve the signatories' monopoly of nuclear weapons.

CLOSED HEMISPHERE: LATIN AMERICA, 1947–87

6 Soviet policy in South America subjects the Monroe Doctrine to its severest test. There is a highly organized effort to extend to the South American countries the Soviet system of proletariat dictatorship.

John Foster Dulles, 1947; Green (1971) p.263. Soon after this pronouncement by the Republican secretary of state-in-waiting, the United States promoted the Rio Treaty, the first of its anti-communist alliance systems. For the Monroe Doctrine see 614:7.

7 I think there has always been a Marshall Plan in effect for the western hemisphere. The foreign policy of the United States in that direction has been set for one hundred years, known as the Monroe Doctrine.

President Harry S Truman, 14 Aug. 1947; *Public Papers 1947* (1963) pp.383–4. An interesting comment in the light of the US hegemony established over Latin America through the Monroe Doctrine. Latin America, like China, received no Marshall Aid. Since it was so dependent on Washington, it was thought to need no inducements for its loyalty, and Truman's statement reflects the complacency of the Colossus of the North towards its good neighbours of the South.

8 That the domination or control of the political institutions of any American state by the international communist movement, extending to this hemisphere the political system of an extra-continental power, would constitute a threat to the sovereignty and political independence of the American states, endangering the peace of America, and would call for appropriate action in accordance with existing treaties.

Part of the US draft resolution on Guatemala, placed before the conference of the Organization of American States, March 1954; Gordon Connell-Smith *The United States and Latin America* (1974) p.213. The resolution, proposed by secretary of state Dulles, was toned down to meet Latin American feeling that it gave a blank cheque for US intervention. It was used, however, to sanction an American-sponsored coup in June 1954, which overthrew the allegedly pro-communist government of Guatemala.

9 We consider that the Monroe Doctrine has outlived its time, has outlived itself, has died, so to say, a natural death. Now the remains of this doctrine should best be buried as every dead body is, so that it should not poison the air with its decay.

Nikita Khrushchev, *Soviet News*, 13 July 1960. A frontal challenge to US supremacy in Latin America, as the USSR ranged itself alongside the revolutionary Cuban regime of Fidel Castro, which came to power in Jan. 1959.

10 *The Perfect Failure*

The apt title of the 1987 book by Trumbull Higgins about the disastrous Bay of Pigs invasion of Cuba in April 1961, when anti-Castro forces landing in Cuba hardly got off the beach, thanks partly to inadequate American support but mainly to the Cuban population's loyalty to the Castro government.

1 This urgent transformation of Cuba into an important strategic base – by the presence of these large, long-range and clearly offensive weapons of sudden mass-destruction – constitutes an explicit threat to the peace and security of all the Americas.

President John F. Kennedy, 22 Oct. 1962; *Public Papers 1962* (1963) pp.806–9. In Oct. 1962 the United States detected the installation of Soviet nuclear missile sites in Cuba, less than 100 miles from the American mainland. This produced the gravest international crisis of the post-1945 era. Given the long-standing American proprietary attitude to Cuba, this was an extremely dangerous move for the USSR to make, and it brought the world close to nuclear war.

2 Less Profile, More Courage.

Slogan on banners carried by opponents of a moderate response to the Cuban missile crisis, 1962. A direct criticism of Kennedy, in a neat distortion of the title of his book *Profiles in Courage*.

3 We're eyeball to eyeball and I think the other fellow just blinked.

US secretary of state Dean Rusk, 24 Oct. 1962. When Washington imposed a naval blockade on Cuba, the Soviet Union backed down and the missiles were withdrawn in exchange for a secret American pledge never again to mount an invasion of Cuba.

4 This is the first time I ever heard it said that the crime is not the burglary, but the discovery of the burglary.

US ambassador to the United Nations, Adlai Stevenson, on the Soviet interpretation of the Cuban missile crisis, 25 Oct. 1962.

5 How can it be that we suffered defeat, when revolutionary Cuba exists and is growing stronger? Who really retreated and who won in this conflict?

Nikita Khrushchev, *Pravda* (Truth), 17 Jan. 1963. The Soviet leader tries to make a virtue of necessity, although throughout 1963 the Kennedy administration continued to work to overthrow Castro's regime.

6 In recklessly introducing the rockets into Cuba and then humiliatingly withdrawing them, the Soviet leaders moved from adventurism to capitulationism and brought disgrace to the Soviet people, the Cuban people, the people of the socialist camp and the people of the whole world.

Chinese government statement, 1 Sept. 1963; Gittings (1968) p.183. Damned when they did and damned when they didn't.

7 We don't propose to sit here in our rocking chair with our hands folded and let the communists set up any government in the western hemisphere.

President Lyndon B. Johnson, 3 May 1965, shortly after authorizing the invasion of the Dominican Republic to forestall a supposed communist take-over of the Dominican government.

8 The Organization of American States couldn't pour piss out of a boot if the instructions were written on the heel.

President Lyndon B. Johnson; Eric Goldman *The Tragedy of Lyndon Johnson* (1969). The invasion of the Dominican Republic was nominally a collective operation mounted by the Organization of American States. Johnson's partners from the OAS were mostly reluctant warriors, however, and he did not trouble to conceal his contempt for them.

9 How close we could look into a bright future should two, three or many Vietnams flourish throughout the world with their share of deaths and their immense tragedies, their everyday heroism and their repeated blows against imperialism, impelled to disperse its forces under the sudden attack and the increasing hatred of all peoples of the world.

Ernesto 'Che' Guevara, 16 April 1967; John Gerassi *Venceremos!* (1968) p.423. Guevara's attempt to provoke a second Vietnam in Bolivia ended with his death seven months later.

10 Not a nut or bolt will be allowed to reach Chile under Allende. Once Allende comes to power, we shall do all within our power to condemn Chile and the Chileans to utmost desperation and poverty, a policy designed for a long time to come to accentuate the hard features of a communist society in Chile.

US ambassador Edward Korry, *International Herald Tribune*, 22 Nov. 1975. The Marxist president of Chile, Salvador Allende, freely elected in 1970, was ousted and killed in 1973 in an American-sponsored coup, which led to the installation of the military dictator General Augusto Pinochet. Chile had been made safe for democracy.

11 How much did the President forget, and when did he forget it?

Anon. on the Iran-Contra scandal of 1986–7. The Reagan administration sold weapons to Iran to secure the release of an American hostage. The proceeds of the sale were then used to fund the right-wing 'Contra' guerrillas fighting the allegedly communist government of Nicaragua. President Reagan, a professional amnesiac when he chose to be, claimed to have had a lapse of memory over the deal. The question put here was an echo of the question asked about President Nixon's knowledge of the Watergate break-in and its cover-up (see 910:6).

I As a matter of fact, I was very definitely involved in the decisions about the support to the freedom fighters. It was my idea to begin with.
President Ronald Reagan, 5 May 1987. Reagan's spin-doctors soon rushed in to explain away this embarrassing truth.

VIETNAM

2 There is another type of warfare – new in its intensity, ancient in its origin – war by guerrillas, subversives, insurgents, assassins; war by ambush instead of by combat, by infiltration instead of by aggression, seeking victory by eroding and exhausting the enemy instead of engaging him. It is a form of warfare uniquely adapted to what have been strangely called 'wars of liberation', to undermine the efforts of new and poor countries to maintain the freedom they have finally achieved.
President John F. Kennedy, 6 June 1962; *Public Papers 1962* (1963) pp.453–4. Kennedy was seeking to move US strategy away from absolute reliance on the nuclear deterrent and to strengthen America's capacity to make a conventional response to a conventional threat. The classic instance of such a threat appeared to be the continuing bid by communist North Vietnam to incorporate South Vietnam (see 880:9). Thus began the counter-insurgency programme in Vietnam, first with a limited number of US military advisers and ultimately with a full-scale commitment to war after Kennedy's death in Nov. 1963.

3 All Vietnam is not worth the life of a single American boy.
Senator Ernest Gruening, 6 Aug. 1964. On 7 Aug. both Houses of Congress approved the Tonking Gulf Resolution, giving President Johnson plenary powers to act in defence of South Vietnam against communist attack. So began the disastrous US intervention, which was to cost America dearly and bring down Johnson himself. At the time it was made, Senator Gruening's comment was deeply unpopular, but it stated a truth that was to become the basis of a rising swell of protest against the Vietnam War.

4 We are not about to send American boys 9 or 10,000 miles away from home to do what Asian boys ought to be doing for themselves.
President Lyndon B. Johnson, 21 Oct. 1964; *Public Papers 1963–64* Bk 2, pp.1390–91. Johnson campaigned for election in 1964 as the candidate pledged to keep America out of war, as Wilson had in 1916 (see 714:9) and as Roosevelt had in 1940 (see 846:9).

5 I believed that the loss of China had played a large role in the rise of Joe McCarthy. And I knew that all these problems, taken together, were chickenshit

compared with what might happen if we lost Vietnam.
President Lyndon B. Johnson; Doris Kearns *Lyndon Johnson and the American Dream* (1976) p.253.

6 I sleep each night a little better, a little more confidently because Lyndon Johnson is my President. For I know he lives and thinks and works to make sure that for all America and indeed, the growing body of the free world, the morning shall always come.
Jack Valenti, a prominent member of the White House staff, 28 June 1965; *Congressional Record* Vol.111, App.A 3583.

7 My solution to the problem would be to tell them frankly that they've got to draw in their horns and stop their aggression, or we're going to bomb them back into the Stone Age.
General Curtis E. LeMay *Mission with LeMay: My Story* (1965) p.565. General LeMay had incinerated Tokyo in 1945 (see 850:8) and proposed to reduce North Vietnam to submission by the same application of strategic air power.

8 The greatest fear of US imperialism is that people's wars will be launched in different parts of the world.
Senior Chinese communist Lin Biao (Lin Piao), 2 Sept. 1965; Samuel B. Griffith *Peking and People's Wars* (1966) p.102. Fighting words, but China did not intervene directly in Vietnam, as it had done in Korea, largely because the United States wisely held back from a ground invasion of North Vietnam.

9 We cannot remain silent on Viet Nam. We should remember that whatever victory there may be possible, it will have a social stigma ... It will always be a case of a predominantly white power killing an Asian nation.
Eugene Carson Blake, *Washington Sunday Star*, 13 Feb. 1966.

10 Declare the United States the winner and begin de-escalation.
Senator George Aiken, 19 Oct. 1966.

11 I ain't got no quarrel with them Viet Congs. No Viet Cong ever called me nigger.
Muhammad Ali, 30 April 1967. When the world heavyweight boxing champion refused to be drafted for military service in Vietnam, he was convicted of draft evasion and stripped of his world title.

12 There may be a limit beyond which Americans and much of the world will not permit the United States to go. The picture of the world's greatest superpower killing or seriously injuring 1,000 non-combatants a week while trying to pound a tiny backward nation into submission is not a pretty one. It could conceivably produce a costly distortion in the American national consciousness and in the world image of the United States – especially if the damage to North Vietnam is complete enough to be 'successful'.

US secretary of defense Robert McNamara to President Johnson, 19 May 1967; full text in *Foreign Relations of the United States 1964–1968* Vol.5 (2002) pp.423–38.

1 There is aggression against Vietnam, Laos, Thailand and India, and in the next decades there will be one and a half billion Chinese armed with nuclear weapons. China has declared world revolution and is doing something about it.

US secretary of state Dean Rusk, *New York Times,* 13 Oct. 1967. The Yellow Peril was, in fact, more preoccupied with its Cultural Revolution (see 897:12) than with crusades abroad.

2 To save the town it became necessary to destroy it.

Anon. US army officer on the destruction of the township of Ben Tre, 8 Feb. 1968.

3 How come you ain't killed them yet? I want them dead.

Paul Meadlo, 24 Nov. 1969, quoting Lieutenant William Calley of the US army. On 15 March 1968 Calley ordered the killing of the inhabitants of the Vietnamese village of My Lai, which the US army attempted to conceal.

4 Hey, hey, LBJ, how many kids did you kill today?

Anti-war chant, 1968.

5 The issue is can we by military means keep the North Vietnamese off the South Vietnamese. I do not think we can.

Dean Acheson, 26 March 1968; Douglas Brinkley *Dean Acheson: The Cold War Years* (1992) p.261. The so-called Wise Old Men, including Acheson, were brought in as advisers in the aftermath of the Tet offensive by the North Vietnamese in Jan. 1968. The offensive was a military failure, but it demonstrated that an American victory in Vietnam was illusory and marked the beginning of an agonizingly slow process of disengagement.

6 The conventional army loses if it does not win. The guerrilla wins if he does not lose.

Henry Kissinger, Jan. 1969. Kissinger was national security adviser and later secretary of state for the newly elected president, Richard Nixon. This conviction underlay the negotiations with North Vietnam that eventually led to US withdrawal from the war in 1973.

7 Except for the threat of a major power, involving nuclear weapons … the United States is going to encourage and has a right to expect that this

problem will be increasingly handled by, and the responsibility for it taken by, the Asian nations themselves.

President Richard M. Nixon, 25 July 1969; *Public Papers 1969* (1971) p.549. The so-called Nixon Doctrine, reverting to the policy set by Eisenhower in 1954, when it was opposed by Nixon, who then argued for direct US intervention.

8 Let not historians record that when America was the most powerful nation in the world we passed on the other side of the road and allowed the last hopes for peace and freedom for millions of people to be suffocated by the forces of totalitarianism. And so tonight – to you, the great silent majority of my fellow Americans – I ask for your support.

President Richard M. Nixon, on Vietnam, 3 Nov. 1969; *Public Papers 1969* (1971) p.909. Despite his concern to pass responsibility for the war to South Vietnam, Nixon remained anxious to preserve Middle America's faith in his anti-communist credentials.

9 If, when the chips are down, the world's most powerful nation, the United States of America, acts like a pitiful, helpless giant, the forces of totalitarianism and anarchy will threaten free nations and free institutions throughout the world.

President Richard M. Nixon, 30 April 1970; *Public Papers 1970* (1971) p.409.

10 Television brought the brutality of war into the comfort of the living room. Vietnam was lost in the living rooms of America – not on the battlefields of Vietnam.

Marshall McLuhan, *Montreal Gazette,* 16 May 1975. McLuhan wrote soon after the fall of South Vietnam to the communist forces of the North in April 1975.

11 Give Saigon the Bomb.

'Little Old Lady in Tennis Shoes', April 1975. Remark made to JM as the best way of preventing the communist annexation of South Vietnam, in National Archives Reading Room, Washington, D.C. The advice was not taken by the US government.

DÉTENTE AND DÉNOUEMENT

12 We look at each country in terms of its own conduct rather than lumping them all together and saying that because they have this kind of philosophy they are all in utter darkness.

President Richard M. Nixon to the Chinese premier Zhou Enlai (Chou En-lai), Beijing, Feb. 1972; *Public Papers 1972* (1974) p.369. The essence of détente, the relaxation of tension between East and West.

1 We shall strive to shift this historically inevitable struggle on to a path free from the perils of war, of dangerous conflicts, and an uncontrolled arms race.

Leonid Brezhnev, 1972; Gaddis (1982) p.313. On 3 Oct. the US and the USSR signed a Strategic Arms Limitation Treaty, placing a ceiling on their missile armoury. What they retained was still enough to annihilate the planet.

2 Our method for preventing nuclear war rests on a form of warfare universally condemned since the Dark Ages – the mass killing of hostages.

Fred Iklé *Foreign Affairs* Vol.51 (Jan. 1973) p.14. An indictment of the policy of mutually assured destruction (known by the appropriate acronym MAD), whereby the lives of hundreds of millions on either side in the Cold War were the only guarantee against nuclear suicide.

3 The cold war ... however much politicians prattle of détente, has no more closed than the earth has stopped rotating.

M.R.D. Foot *Resistance* (1976) p.74.

4 There is no Soviet domination of Eastern Europe and there never will be under a Ford administration.

President Gerald Ford, 7 Oct. 1976. An own goal by Nixon's successor, in a presidential election debate with Jimmy Carter, the man who was to succeed him after he lost the election.

5 You may rest assured that the American people and our government will continue our firm commitment to promote respect for human rights not only in our own country but also abroad.

President Jimmy Carter to Andrei Sakharov, Feb. 1977; Joshua Muravchik *The Uncertain Crusade* (1988) p.27. Carter had made human rights one of his top priorities, and his reply to a letter from the doyen of Russian dissidents, Sakharov (see 893:4), caused a furore in Moscow.

6 An attempt by any outside force to gain control of the Persian Gulf region will be regarded as an assault on the vital interests of the United States of America, and such an assault will be repelled by any means necessary, including military force.

President Jimmy Carter, 23 Jan. 1980; *Public Papers 1980* Vol.1 (1981) p.197. A blunt warning to the Soviet Union after its intervention in nearby Afghanistan four weeks earlier and highly relevant a decade later when Iraq invaded Kuwait.

7 Like the sorry tapping of Neville Chamberlain's umbrella on the cobblestones of Munich.

Ronald Reagan on the foreign policy of Jimmy Carter, 1980. Reagan, the Republican contender in the 1980 presidential election, believed that no compromise with communism was possible (although the alternative to Chamberlain's appeasement of Hitler was war).

8 Let us be aware that while they preach the supremacy of the state, declare its omnipotence over individual man, and predict its eventual domination of all people on the Earth, they are the focus of evil in the modern world. I urge you [not] to ignore the facts of history and the aggressive impulses of an evil empire, to simply call the arms race a giant misunderstanding and thereby remove yourself from the struggle between right and wrong and good and evil.

President Ronald Reagan, 8 March 1983; *Public Papers 1983* Vol.1 (1984) p.365.

9 What if free people could live secure in the knowledge that if their security did not rest upon the threat of instant US retaliation to deter a Soviet attack, that we could intercept and destroy strategic ballistic missiles before they reached our soil or that of our allies?

President Ronald Reagan, 23 March 1983; *Public Papers 1983* Vol.1 (1984) p.442. The attempt to improve on the concept of mutual assured destruction and give the West absolute security by way of the Strategic Defense Initiative – 'Star Wars', as it became known – an anti-missile shield in space. The SDI was taken up again by President George W. Bush.

10 My fellow Americans, I'm pleased to tell you today that I've signed legislation that will outlaw the Soviet Union forever. We begin bombing in five minutes.

President Ronald Reagan, 11 Aug. 1984; David E. Kyvig (ed.) *Reagan and the World* (1990) p.1. The president tests a microphone, not knowing that his words are going out live.

11 Mr Gorbachev, open the gate! Mr Gorbachev, tear down this wall!

President Ronald Reagan at the Berlin Wall, 12 June 1987; *Public Papers 1987* Vol.1 (1989) p.635. Who, including Reagan, could possibly have believed that the Wall would come down in Nov. 1989? With its fall, the Cold War was effectively over, and Reagan could plausibly claim to have won it.

12 By the grace of God, America won the Cold War.

President George Bush, 28 Jan. 1992; *Public Papers 1992* Vol.1 (1993) p.157.

13 I do not regard the end of the Cold War as a victory for one side ... The end of the Cold War is our common victory.

Mikhail Gorbachev, Jan. 1992; Isaacs and Downing (1998) p.417.

The Communist World, 1945–2001

SOVIET UNION:
THE LAST YEARS OF STALIN, 1945–53

1 Guided by the method of socialist realism, studying conscientiously and attentively our reality, striving to penetrate more deeply into the processes of our development, the writer must educate the people and arm them ideologically.

Andrei Zhdanov, 21 Aug. 1946; George S. Counts and Nucia Lodge *The Country of the Blind: The Soviet System of Mind Control* (1949) p.96. Zhdanov, Stalin's right-hand man, led a ferocious campaign against 'bourgeois intellectual' influences.

2 It would be hard to say if she is a nun or a whore; better, perhaps, to say that she is a little of both; her lusts and her prayers intertwine.

Andrei Zhdanov, 21 Aug. 1946; Martin McCauley *The Soviet Union 1917–1991* (1993) p.193. His target was Anna Akhmatova, perhaps the greatest Russian poet of the 20th century. Publication of her work was banned in 1946 for being 'too remote from socialist reconstruction'.

3 When Ivan the Terrible had someone executed, he would spend a long time in repentance and prayer. God was a hindrance to him in this respect. He should have been more decisive.

Joseph Stalin to the film director Sergei Eisenstein, Feb. 1947; Orlando Figes *Natasha's Dance: A Cultural History of Russia* (2002) p.498. Stalin was not best pleased with Eisenstein's portrayal of Ivan in the second part of his epic on the tsar, *The Boyars' Plot*. He banned the film's release, and Eisenstein died in disgrace in 1948. See 742:10.

4 It is well known that Soviet penal policy is based on the principle of corrective labour. This is applied at all stages – in the shape of supervised work at one's own job for light offences, work in corrective labour settlements for sentences up to three years, employment on big public works (canals, railways, land improvement schemes etc), while living in corrective labour camps, for major offences. Tens of thousands of people have been reclaimed for society in this way; and the system has no practical bearing on Soviet economic planning, which depends entirely upon the informed initiative of free labour.

Andrew Rothstein *Man and Plan in the Soviet Economy* (1948) p.296 footnote. A paean of praise for the Gulag from a devoted Western Stalinist. The camps did, in fact, serve an important economic function, providing a ceaseless supply of expendable labour for projects in outlying areas where free labour would have been difficult to recruit.

5 Everything depended on what Stalin appeared to be thinking when he glanced in your direction. Sometimes he would glare at you and say, 'Why don't you look me in the eye today? Why are you averting your eyes from mine?' or some other such stupidity. Without warning he would turn on you with real viciousness.

Nikita Khrushchev *Khruschev Remembers* (1971) pp.257–8. By the late 1940s, after years of loyal service in the Ukraine, Khrushchev was a senior figure in the Soviet hierarchy.

6 I vacationed with him one year. I lived next door. I told my friends ... They said that if you're still alive after this vacation, say 'Thank God'. Why? Because I had to dine with him every day. It means I had to be drunk every day ... If you don't eat and drink with him you're his enemy.

Nikita Khrushchev on Stalin, 20 March 1956; Cold War International History Project *Bulletin*, March 1998, p.47.

7 You come to Stalin's table as a friend, but you never know if you'll go home by yourself or if you'll be given a ride – to prison!

Marshal Nikolai Bulganin; Khruschev (1971) p.258. Bulganin was a colleague of Khrushchev in the ruling circle, and after Stalin's death formed a duumvirate with Khrushchev until he was ousted in 1958.

8 I remember once Stalin made me dance the 'gopak' before some top party officials. I had to squat down on my haunches and kick out my heels, which frankly wasn't very easy for me. But I did it and tried to keep a pleasant expression on my face. As I later told Anastas Ivanovich Mikoyan, 'When Stalin says dance, a wise man dances.'

Nikita Khrushchev (1971) p.301. The Armenian Mikoyan made foreign trade his field of expertise.

9 One day Mikoyan and I were taking a walk around the grounds and Stalin came out on the porch of the house. He seemed not to notice Mikoyan and me. 'I'm finished,' he said to no one in particular. 'I trust no one, not even myself.'

Nikita Khrushchev (1971) pp.306–7.

1 Some time ago, the bodies of State Security uncovered a group of terrorist doctors who set themselves the task of cutting short the lives of prominent public figures in the Soviet Union by administering harmful treatments ... It has been established that all these killer doctors, these monsters who trod underfoot the holy banner of science and defiled the honour of men of science, were in the pay of foreign intelligence services.
Soviet government statement by the news agency Tass, 13 Jan. 1953; Yakov Rapoport *The Doctors' Plot* (1991) pp.74, 75. Russian Jewish doctors working in the Kremlin were accused of killing, among others, Zhdanov. This would have led to their show trial and execution, but Stalin died on 5 March and a month later they were released.

2 You are blind like young kittens; what will happen without me? The country will perish because you do not know how to recognize enemies.
Joseph Stalin to his entourage, as quoted by Khruschev in his speech to the 20th Party Congress on 25 Feb. 1956; *The Dethronement of Stalin* (1956) p.25. Stalin spoke at the time of the so-called Doctors' Plot in Jan. 1953.

3 At what seemed like the very last moment he suddenly opened his eyes and cast a glance over everyone in the room. It was a terrible glance, insane or perhaps angry and full of the fear of death and the unfamiliar faces of the doctors bent over him. The glance swept over everyone in a second. Then something incomprehensible and awesome happened ... He suddenly lifted his left hand as though he were pointing to something above or bringing down a curse on us all. The gesture was incomprehensible but full of menace, and no one could say to whom or at what it might be directed.
Stalin's daughter, Svetlana Alleluyeva *Twenty Letters to a Friend* (1967) p.10. An eyewitness account of Stalin's death throes, 5 March 1953.

4   Grimly clenching
His embalmed fists,
Just pretending to be dead,
He watched from inside ...
I fancy there's a telephone in that coffin.
Stalin instructs
Enver Hoxha.
From that coffin where else does the cable go?
While Stalin's heirs walk this earth,
Stalin still lurks in the mausoleum.
Yevgeny Yevtushenko 'The Heirs of Stalin' (1962). Stalin was entombed alongside Lenin in the mausoleum in Red Square, Moscow, but his body was later removed as a symbol of de-Stalinization. Enver Hoxha, dictator of Albania (1954–85), was an ultra Stalin loyalist.

5 When Stalin died in 1953, the Soviet Union was the greatest industrial, scientific and military power in the world, and showed clear signs of moving to overtake the US in all these areas. This was despite the devastating losses it suffered [in World War II]. The various peoples of the USSR were unified. Starvation and illiteracy were unknown throughout the country. Agriculture was completely collectivized and extremely productive. Preventive health care was the finest in the world, and medical treatment of exceptionally high quality was available free to all citizens. Education at all levels was free. More books were published in the USSR than in any other country. There was no unemployment.
Bruce Franklin (ed.) *The Essential Stalin* (1973) p.8. A panegyric by a fervent American Stalinist. Stalin himself could not have summarized his achievement better ... or more mendaciously.

6 Stalin, comrades, is such a figure that many historians will break their teeth trying to learn about him, and there will still be something left to learn.
Nikita Khrushchev, speech to Polish party leaders, 20 March 1956; Cold War International History Project *Bulletin*, March 1998, p.49.

SOVIET UNION: THE KHRUSHCHEV ERA, 1953–64

7 The method of collective leadership is the basic principle of party leadership, violation of which in party work cannot be viewed otherwise than as a manifestation of bureaucratic habits, which freeze the initiative and self-reliance of party organizations and party members.
Georgi Malenkov, *Pravda* (Truth), 16 April 1953. Just six weeks after Stalin's death came the first sign of a break with his personal dictatorship by his nominal successor. Malenkov resigned in Feb. 1955, by which time Khrushchev had become the undisputed leader of the Soviet Union as First Secretary of the Party. Compare Stalin's pledge to collective leadership in 1925 (see 736:1).

8 We are concerned with a question which has immense importance for the party now and for the future – with how the cult of the person of Stalin has been gradually growing, the cult which became at a certain specific stage the source of a whole series of grave perversions of party principles, of party democracy, of revolutionary legality.

Nikita Khrushchev, speech to the 20th Congress of the Communist Party of the Soviet Union, 25 Feb. 1956; *The Dethronement of Stalin* (1956) p.3. Khrushchev's denunciation of Stalin was supposedly for the ears of Congress delegates only, but it was quickly leaked to the West. It caused an enormous sensation in the USSR and beyond, revealing as it did the party leadership's commitment to 'de-Stalinization', which had already been in process for some time, notably with the release of many of the prisoners whom Stalin had put in the labour camps of the Gulag.

1 Previously all good was due to the superhuman qualities of one man; now all the evil is attributed to his equally exceptional and shocking defects ... The real problems are skipped over – how and why Soviet society ... could and did depart from the self-chosen path of democracy and legality to the point of degeneration.

Palmiro Togliatti, 16 June 1956; Mark Frankland *Khrushchev* (1966) p.124. Togliatti, leader of the Italian Communist Party, asks a fundamental question not raised by Khrushchev in his speech of 25 Feb.

2 We were scared – really scared. We were afraid the thaw might unleash a flood, which we wouldn't be able to control and which could drown us. How could it drown us? It could have overflowed the banks of the Soviet riverbed and formed a tidal wave which would have washed away all the barriers and retaining walls of our society.

Nikita Khrushchev *Khrushchev Remembers: The Last Testament* (1974) p.79.

3 A pig ... never shits where it eats, it never shits where it sleeps ... But Pasternak, who counts himself one of the leading members of our society, has done this. He shat where he ate, he shat on those by whose labours he lives and breathes.

Vladimir Semichastnyi, head of the Komsomol (Communist Youth League), on the publication in the West in 1957 of Boris Pasternak's novel of early 20th-century revolutionary Russia, *Dr Zhivago*; William J. Thompson *Khrushchev* (1997 edn) p.197. The departure from Stalinist norms clearly had its limits.

4 They were and still are shackled by old notions and methods ... they have become divorced from the life of the party and country ... They take a conservative attitude and cling stubbornly to obsolete forms and methods of work that are no longer in keeping with the interests of the movement toward communism.

Decree anathematizing the so-called Anti-party Group, 29 June 1957; Mervyn Matthews (ed.) *Soviet Government* (1974) p.185. Khrushchev's three main opponents – Malenkov, Kaganovich and Molotov – were thus decisively demoted. They kept their lives, which would certainly have been lost under Stalin.

5 In the current decade (1961–70) the Soviet Union, in creating the material and technical basis of communism, will surpass the strongest and richest capitalist country, the USA, in production per head of population; the people's standard of living and their cultural and technical standards will improve substantially; everyone will live in easy circumstances; all collective and state farms will become highly productive and profitable enterprises; the demand of the Soviet people for well-appointed housing will, in the main, be satisfied; hard physical work will disappear; the USSR will have the shortest working day.

Programme of the Communist Party of the Soviet Union, adopted by the 22nd Party Congress, 31 Oct. 1961; *New Times*, 29 Nov. 1961. A utopian dream, never realized under communism.

6 We should take your pants down and set you down in a clump of nettles until you understand your mistakes ... Are you a pederast or a normal man? Do you want to live abroad? Go on, then; we'll take you free as far as the border. Live out there in the 'free world'. Study in the school of capitalism ... But we aren't going to spend a kopeck on this dog shit.

Nikita Khrushchev to the painter Zheltovsky; 1 Dec. 1962; P. Johnson, *Khrushchev and the Arts* (1965) pp.103–4. Like Hitler (see 759:4), Khrushchev had fixed views on modern art.

7 Who will de-Stalinize the de-Stalinizers?

Jean-Paul Sartre, the French Marxist philosopher, attrib. A play on the well-known question *Quis custodes ipsos custodiet?* (Who will guard the guards?)

8 Impulsive, sensitive of his own dignity and insensitive to anyone else's feelings; quick in argument, never missing or overlooking a point; with an extraordinary memory and encyclopedic information at his command; vulgar, and yet capable of a certain dignity when he is simple and forgets to 'show off'. Ruthless but sentimental – Khrushchev is a sort of mixture between Peter the Great and Lord Beaverbrook.

Harold Macmillan, early March 1959; Alistair Horne *Harold Macmillan* Vol.2 (1989) p.128. The British prime minister saw

Khrushchev at close quarters during his visit to the USSR in Feb. 1959. Peter the Great was the tsar who wrenched Old Russia out of the Middle Ages in the early 18th century (see 442:2–446:5); Lord Beaverbrook was the tabloid newspaper magnate who crusaded energetically but unsuccessfully for his idiosyncratic brand of conservatism.

1 He who thinks he can charm the workers with nice revolutionary phrases is mistaken … If one does not show concern for the growth of material and spiritual wealth, then people will listen today, they will listen tomorrow, and then they will say: 'Why do you always promise us everything in the future, talking, so to speak, about life beyond the grave. The priest has already talked to us about that.'

Nikita Khrushchev, *Pravda*, 22 Sept. 1964. Khrushchev was well aware of the need to provide jam today, but within the month he was removed from power.

2 Could we have called him to order sooner? The members of the Praesidium did this, warned him, but except for coarse rebuffs and insults they heard nothing from him, although he did not employ repression in relation to members of the Praesidium. It is harder to struggle with a living cult than with a dead one. If Stalin destroyed people physically, Khrushchev destroyed them morally. The removal of Khrushchev from power is a sign not of the weakness but of the strength of the party, and this should be a lesson.

Mikhail Suslov, report on the ousting of Khrushchev, Oct. 1964; *Politichesky Dnevnik* (Political Diary) (1965) p.6. The deposition of Khrushchev marked a partial reversion to Stalinism under his successor Leonid Brezhnev. Suslov, the arch-doctrinaire, has rightly been described as the 'guardian of ideological rectitude' (McCauley (1993) p.340).

3 You stuck listening devices all over the dacha. Even in the bathroom – you spend the people's money to eavesdrop on my farts.

Nikita Khrushchev, post-1964; Sergei Khrushchev *Khrushchev on Khrushchev* (1990) p.247. Even out of power Khrushchev was under surveillance.

SOVIET UNION:
THE BREZHNEV YEARS, 1964–82

4 These are not merely moral monsters but active henchmen of those who stoke the furnace of international tension, who wish to turn the cold war into a hot one, who have not abandoned the mad dream of raising their hand against the Soviet

Union. No mercy can be shown to such henchmen … Time will pass and no one will even remember them. The pages steeped in bile will rot in the dump. After all, history has time and again confirmed that slander, however thick and venomous it be, inevitably evaporates under the warm breath of truth.

D. Yeremin, *Isvestiya*, 13 Jan. 1966, on the writers Andrei Sinyavsky and Yuli Daniel, tried and condemned for anti-Soviet activity. Reminiscent of Andrei Vyshinsky at his worst (see 743:5).

5 I do not regard myself as an enemy; I am a Soviet man, and my works are not hostile works. In this fantastic, electrified atmosphere anybody who is 'different' may be regarded as an enemy, but this is not an objective way of arriving at the truth. Most of all, however, I do not see why enemies have to be invented, why monsters have to be piled on monsters by means of a literal-minded interpretation of literary images.

Andrei Sinyavsky, 12 Feb. 1966; Mary Hayward (ed.) *On Trial* (1966) pp.147–8. The writers Sinyavsky and Yuli Daniel were charged with producing 'slanderous inventions defamatory to the Soviet political and social system'. Sinyavsky was sentenced to seven years' imprisonment, Daniel to five. Their trial was one of the first signs that the USSR under Brezhnev had started to veer back towards Stalinism.

6 [In the mid-1960s] a new force emerged from within the Cultural Opposition, a force which stood not only against official culture but also against many aspects of the ideology and practice of the regime. It emerged as the result of the collision of two opposing trends: the striving of society to obtain greater information about politics and society, and the efforts of the regime to control even more completely every aspect of the information given to the public. This force came to be known as *samizdat*.

Andrei Amalrik *Will the Soviet Union Survive until 1984?* (1970) (English trans. of the original Russian, pub. in 1969 in Amsterdam). *Samizdat* means self-publishing – that is, clandestine literature, produced on underground presses or published abroad. Amalrik was a liberal historian. The Cultural Opposition were the dissidents of the literary and artistic world.

7   In the mad house
    Wring your hands,
    Press your white forehead
    Against the wall
    Like a face into a snowdrift.

Natalia Gorbanevskaya, 1966; Abraham Rothberg *The Heirs of Stalin* (1972) p.293. The poem was written after the writer

Yury Galanskov was committed to a mental hospital and dosed with tranquillizers. The poet herself was (when pregnant) placed in a psychiatric ward after protesting against the Soviet invasion of Czechoslovakia in 1968 (see 896:3). Brezhnev's treatment of dissidents, it was sometimes said, marked an improvement on Stalin's handling of his opposition: an injection in the buttocks replaced a bullet in the back of the head.

1 It is time to think clearly: the incarceration of free-thinking healthy people in madhouses is *spiritual murder*, it is a variation of the *gas chamber*, but even more cruel: the torture of the people being killed is more malicious and more prolonged. Like the gas chambers these crimes will *never* be forgotten, and all those involved in them will be condemned for all time, during their life and after their death.

Alexander Solzhenitsyn, June 1970; Leopold Labedz (ed.) *Solzhenitsyn* (1973) Ch.17. An open comparison with the Nazi Holocaust of World War II from one of the most outspoken critics of the Brezhnev regime, by then a marked man.

2 A new, soundless command has been given: cloak the past in the mist. The reader who has not caught the sound of the command will not understand why neither *Cancer Ward* nor *The First Circle* have been published to this day. Why the author's archive was confiscated from him two years ago and has still not been returned. Why libraries have stopped issuing *One Day in the Life of Ivan Denisovich* ... Why, year after year, on special instructions, malicious lies are circulated about Solzhenitsyn: that he cooperated with the Germans! He was a prisoner of war! A criminal and a thief! A schizophrenic! You see, they have to invent a way of dealing with a writer who carries on exposing Stalinism *after* the command has been given to forget about it.

Lydia Chukovskaya, July 1968; Peter Reddaway (ed.) *Uncensored Russia* (1972) p.335. The writer Alexander Solzhenitsyn was expelled from the Union of Writers in 1969 and deported from the Soviet Union in 1974. His first novel, *One Day in the Life of Ivan Denisovich*, about life in one of Stalin's labour camps, was published in the USSR in 1962; thereafter he was forced to publish abroad.

3 If you think that we ever will allow anybody to speak and write anything that comes into his head, then this will never be.

V.A. Medvedev, secretary for ideology of the Leningrad party committee, to the mathematician Revolt Pimenov, July 1970; Rothberg (1972) p.339.

4 Our society is infected by apathy, hypocrisy, petit bourgeois egoism, and hidden cruelty. The majority

of representatives of its upper stratum – the party apparatus of government and the highest, most successful layers of the intelligentsia – cling tenaciously to their open and secret privileges and are profoundly indifferent to the infringement of human rights, the interests of progress, security, and the future of mankind.

Andrei Sakharov, memorandum to Brezhnev, 5 March 1971; *Sakharov Speaks* (1974) pp.153–4. The nuclear physicist Sakharov became the leading spokesman for human rights in the 1970s. He knew too much about atomic weapons to be deported like Solzhenitsyn, and was instead placed in exile from Moscow.

5 We have ways of making you walk.

Caption on the front page of the British satirical fortnightly *Private Eye*, accompanying a photograph of the West German chancellor, Helmut Schmidt, helping Brezhnev to his feet at the Helsinki Conference on Security and Cooperation in Europe, Aug. 1975. Brezhnev was by then an ailing man, and for the next decade the USSR was in the hands of a geronto-cracy – Brezhnev and his successors, Yuri Andropov, who died in 1984, and Constantin Chernenko, who died in 1985 after only 13 months as general secretary.

SOVIET UNION: GORBACHEV, 1984–91

6 An inalienable component of socialist democracy is *glasnost*. Broad, timely and frank information is testimony of faith in people, of respect for their minds and feelings and for their capacity to work things out themselves in one situation or another.

Mikhail Gorbachev, 10 Dec. 1984; Archie Brown *The Gorbachev Factor* (1996) p.125. *Glasnost*, most often translated as 'open-ness', was the very reverse of the secretiveness that had characterized both the tsarist and communist regimes in Russia for generations. In the reign of Tsar Alexander II it was described by the radical Nikolai Chernyshevksy as 'a bureau-cratic expression, a substitute for freedom of speech' (Brown (1996) p.125), but in Gorbachev's brief time in power it was taken seriously, and the exposures it produced helped to bring down communism in the USSR.

7 An acceleration of scientific and technological progress insistently demands a profound *perestroika* of the system of planning and administration of the entire economic mechanism. Without all of that, what we are talking about today may remain only pious wishes.

Mikhail Gorbachev, June 1985; Brown (1996) p.123. *Perestroika* (restructuring) was, like *glasnost*, the watchword of the Gorbachev regime after he took office in March 1985 as leader of the Soviet Union.

1 1. Democracy is the wholesome and pure air without which a socialist public organization cannot live a full-blooded life.

2. No party has a monopoly over what is right.
Mikhail Gorbachev, 27 Feb. 1986. Two statements running diametrically counter to everything the Soviet government had stood for since 1917.

2 Levels of pollution exceed the permitted norms by a small amount, but not to an extent that calls for special measures to protect the population.
Soviet government statement on the reactor explosion at the Chernobyl nuclear power station, 26 April 1986; Dmitri Volkogonov *The Rise and Fall of the Soviet Empire* (1999 edn) p.479. This was a grossly misleading announcement. Chernobyl was a disaster of vast proportions, and it exposed many of the flaws in the Soviet system.

3 An event has occurred that surpasses everything that has happened before in terms of its political consequences … We are talking about the people's loss of faith in our army, for whose sake the people have made many sacrifices. And for a long time. A blow has also been struck against the political leadership of the country, against its authority.
Mikhail Gorbachev, 29 May 1987; Volkogonov (1999 edn) pp.521–2. On that day, a 19-year-old West German, Matthias Rust, flew across the USSR to land his light aircraft in Red Square, in the heart of Moscow. The incident was a humiliation for the Soviet regime and led to the immediate dismissal of the relevant high commanders.

4   Sausage prices twice as high.
   Where's the vodka for us to buy?
   All we do is sit at home
   Watching Gorby drone and drone.
Popular ditty of the late 1980s; Martin McCauley *Gorbachev* (1998) p.118. Gorbachev was never as popular in the Soviet Union as he was in the West, and he bore the blame for continuing shortages, sharpened by his campaign against alcoholism.

5 The president [Gorbachev] and the Supreme Soviet are attempting to marketize and democratize the Soviet Union, a state that no longer exists. The final collapse of the political centre means that there is little prospect of any reform programme being implemented by it … What is falling apart is not just the empire, but the ideology which held it together.
Andrankik Migranyan, *Isvestiya*, 20 Sept. 1990. An acid comment on the terminal decline of the USSR, now beyond help and, thanks to *glasnost*, published in government media!

6 Tell President Bush I am touched. Thank him for his concern. He has done what a friend should do. But tell him not to worry. I have everything in hand.
Mikhail Gorbachev, 20 June 1991; McCauley (1998) p.216. The mayor of Moscow, Gavriil Popov, had told the US ambassador that a coup against Gorbachev was in the making. It came, not then but on 18 Aug.

7 Society now has liberty, it has been emancipated politically and spiritually. And that is the main achievement that we have not fully comprehended because we have not yet learned how to use that liberty.
Mikhail Gorbachev, farewell address, 25 Dec. 1991; Volkogonov (1999 edn) p.529. Gorbachev was the object of an abortive coup d'état in Aug. 1991. He survived it, but it left him mortally wounded politically and he was compelled to resign four months later. With him went 74 years of communism and the Soviet Union itself.

8 Gorbachev was the best thing the Communist Party had to offer. He played the central role in a remarkable chapter of world history but was forced in the end to go, because in the historical play there was no longer any room for a man who still wanted to be a communist.
Wall Street Journal, 27 Dec. 1991. Gorbachev, unlike his successor Boris Yeltsin, never abjured his communism.

EASTERN EUROPE, 1945–89

9 When God created man, he gave him three qualities: to be honest, to be clever, and to be communist. Then came the devil who decided that this was too much. A man should have only two of the three qualities, in any combination – a man can be either honest and communist, but then he is not clever; or clever and communist, but then he is not honest; or clever and honest, but then he is not a communist.
East European political joke, also made about the Nazis by their German opposition. *Mutatis mutandis.*

10 I will shake my little finger – and there will be no more Tito.
Joseph Stalin as reported by Khrushchev in his speech to the 20th Party Congress of the CPSU, 25 Feb. 1956; *The Dethronement of Stalin* (1956) p.25. In 1948 Stalin sought to crush Tito, the head of the Yugoslavian Communist Party, for refusing to accept his leadership but could not bring Tito to heel.

11 The information bureau unanimously resolves that … the leaders of the Communist Party of

Yugoslavia have taken the path of seceding from the united socialist front against imperialism, have taken the path of betraying the cause of international solidarity of the working people, and have taken up a position of nationalism.

Resolution of the Communist Information Bureau, 28 June 1948; *The Soviet-Yugoslav Dispute* (1984) p.68. Yugoslavia was expelled from the Cominform as a deviant state, but Tito survived, unlike many other communist leaders in East Europe.

1 The completion and reconstruction of the government was carried out *in a strictly constitutional, democratic and parliamentary manner* ... I have said that the reconstructed government is an expression of the *regenerated* National Front. To this, I must expressly add that the component parts of the regenerated National Front can only be *regenerated* political parties and non-party organizations. The agents of reaction must be *unconditionally* removed from these parties and organizations ... The purge of our public life is now going on.

Klement Gottwald, 10 March 1948; *Selected Speeches and Articles, 1929–53* (1954) pp.171–3. The Czech communist leader justifies the coup d'état of 25 Feb. 1948, which gave communism control of Czechoslovakia.

2 I understand that the tendencies towards separating our Polish road from the Soviet experience and practice are completely false ... Nowhere in the world outside the Soviet Union has socialism been built, and nowhere in the world has any party had, nor can it have, such practice and such experience as the CPSU. Therefore it would be entirely false even to think that there is some wholly different conception, some other means of solving ... the problems of building socialism.

Wladislaw Gomulka, Sept. 1948; Robert V. Daniels (ed.) *A Documentary History of Communism* Vol.2 (1985) pp.163–4. The Polish communist leader Gomulka was deposed for alleged revisionism, to which he here confessed.

3 Laszlo Rajk, as cabinet minister and member of the national assembly, that is, as a public servant, grossly abusing his official position, gave secrets to foreign powers which seriously endangered the interests of the Hungarian state; by doing so he committed the crimes of espionage and sedition.

Indictment of Laszlo Rajk, Sept. 1949; *Documents on International Affairs 1949–50* (1953) p.391. The Hungarian communist leader Rajk was purged by Stalin, along with senior figures in several other East European states.

4   After the rising of the 17th June
The Secretary of the Writers' Union
Had leaflets distributed in the Stalinallee
Stating that the people
Had forfeited the confidence of the
    government
And could win it back only
By redoubled efforts. Would it not be easier
To dissolve the people
And elect another?

Bertolt Brecht 'The Solution' (1953). On 17 June 1953 anti-communist riots in East Berlin were rapidly suppressed. The writer Brecht, a lifelong Marxist, gives a surprising reaction. Stalinallee was the grandiose boulevard running through the city centre, later re-named Karl Marx Allee after Stalin's fall from grace.

5 The whole system becomes polycentric, and even in the communist movement itself we cannot speak of a single guide but rather of a progress which is achieved by following paths which are often different.

Palmiro Togliatti, 16 June 1956; *The Anti-Stalin Campaign* (1956) pp.138–9. The Italian communist leader saw an end to the Soviet doctrinal monopoly in the wake of de-Stalinization, but it was not to be.

6 What is immutable in socialism can be reduced to the abolition of the exploitation of man by man. The roads of achieving the goal can be and are different. They are determined by various conditions of time and place. The model of socialism can also vary. It can be such as that created in the Soviet Union; it can be shaped in a manner as we see it in Yugoslavia; it can be different still.

Wladislaw Gomulka, 20 Oct. 1956; Paul Zinner (ed.) *National Communism and Popular Revolt in Eastern Europe* (1956). A notable change from his 1948 statement (see 895:2). Gomulka returned to office after years in the wilderness, when Poland achieved a small measure of autonomy within the Soviet bloc.

7 The Soviet troops are assisting the Hungarian people to retain their independence from imperialism.

London *Daily Worker*, 7 Nov. 1956. In late Oct. 1956 a widespread anti-Soviet rising took place in Hungary, leading quickly to the installation of a government under the communist Imre Nagy. When Nagy proclaimed Hungary a multi-party state and its withdrawal from the Soviet alliance system, Khrushchev sent in the Red Army to suppress the rebellion. Here the British Communist Party newspaper hews to the party line that the purpose of the Soviet intervention was to protect Hungary against counter-revolution. From Moscow's point of view the intervention was essential to deter the rest of its East European satellites from following Hungary's example, as they did in 1989.

1 May God spare me the punishment of being rehabilitated by my own murderers.

Imre Nagy, 1958. At his treason trial Nagy refused to make a plea for clemency. There is doubt as to whether he said this, but even if he did not, the words stand as his epitaph. Nagy was put to death but was posthumously rehabilitated and buried in Budapest with full honours on 16 June 1989.

2 In the service of the people we followed such a policy that socialism would not lose its human face.

Alexander Dubček, *Rudé Pravo*, 19 June 1968. A famous statement by the communist head of the Czechoslovak government. As in Hungary in 1956, the Czech party appeared dangerously ready to give up its monopoly of power and join forces with anti-Soviet nationalism.

3 The peoples of the socialist countries and communist parties certainly do have and should have freedom for determining the ways of advance of their respective countries. However, none of their decisions should damage either socialism in their country or the fundamental interests of other socialist countries ... Discharging their internationalist duty toward the fraternal peoples of Czechoslovakia and defending their own socialist gains, the USSR and the other socialist states had to act decisively and they did act against the antisocialist forces in Czechoslovakia.

S. Kovalev, *Pravda*, 25 Sept. 1968; an exposition of the so-called Brezhnev Doctrine, justifying intervention to nip another potential breakaway in the bud. Dubček, like Nagy, was deposed; unlike Nagy, he was not executed.

4 They need not accept the lie. It is enough for them to have accepted their life with it and in it. For by this very fact, individuals confirm the system, fulfil the system, make the system, *are* the system.

Vaclav Havel; Timothy Garton Ash *The Uses of Adversity* (1991 edn) p.173. The dissident Czech writer Havel describes the corrosion of the spirit under totalitarianism.

5 My friends! We return to work on 1 September. We all know what that day reminds us of, of what we think ... of the fatherland ... of the family which is called Poland ... We got all we could in the present situation. And we will achieve the rest, because we now have the most important thing: our INDEPENDENT SELF-GOVERNING TRADES UNIONS. That is our guarantee for the future ... I declare the strike ended.

Lech Walesa, 31 Aug. 1980; Timothy Garton Ash *The Polish Revolution: Solidarity* (1999 edn) p.71. Walesa led the strike in the Gdansk shipyard that forced the communist government of Poland to recognize the trade union Solidarity. 1 Sept. was the day of the outbreak of World War II in 1939, when Nazi Germany began its attack on Poland with a naval bombardment of Gdansk (Danzig).

6 The winter is yours – the spring will be ours.

Graffito in Warsaw, Dec. 1981, soon after the disbanding of the Solidarity trade union movement by the Polish communist government. Brave words at a moment of deep despair.

7 It's the Poles who have showed the world that *something like this* [the achievement of Solidarity] is possible. Sooner or later these deeds will be seen to have set an example. When other nations begin to follow this example, the Soviet order will be faced with its most serious threat.

The Polish dissident Adam Michnik; Garton Ash (1991 edn) pp.183–4. Words written in the aftermath of the repression of Solidarity by the Polish government in Dec. 1981. Wishful thinking then but borne out before the close of the decade.

8 We pretend to work and they pretend to pay us.

Anon. Polish saying from the 1980s.

9 Before the Mother of Jasna Góra I want to give thanks for all the proofs of this solidarity which have been given by my compatriots, including Polish youth, in the difficult period of not many months ago. It would be difficult for me to enumerate all the forms of this solicitude which surrounded those who were interned, imprisoned, dismissed from work, and also their families. You know this better than I.

Pope John Paul II, 18 June 1983; Brian MacArthur (ed.) *The Penguin Book of Twentieth-Century Speeches* (1992) p.111. The pope was addressing a large crowd at the Czestechowa Monastery at a time when the Solidarity union had been dissolved by the communist government and when the prospects for change appeared non-existent.

10 We found ourselves in a territory ruled by an absolutist and much-feared, half-demented warden ... He was a genuinely dangerous person, and quite unpredictable ... Once, in our presence, he sighed and said in a genuine way, 'Hitler did things differently – he gassed vermin like you right away!' Once he shouted at me how much he'd love to put me up against the wall and shoot me.

Vaclav Havel on his time in prison, 1979–83; *Disturbing the Peace* (1990) pp.148–9. Havel became his country's head of state after the collapse of communism in 1989, stepping down in 2003.

1 We have had twenty years of economic stagnation, sterility and incalculable moral loss.
Alexander Dubček, 13 Nov. 1988, on accepting the Nobel Peace Prize.

2 When your neighbour starts changing his wallpaper, you don't necessarily feel obliged to do the same.
East German ideological spokesman Kurt Hager, West German magazine *Stern* (Star), 9 April 1987. A public expression of alarm at the disturbing influence of Gorbachev's reform programme in the USSR.

3 We must heed the impulses of the times. Those who delay are punished by life itself.
Mikhail Gorbachev, 8 Oct. 1989. Gorbachev visited East Berlin as part of the celebrations of the fortieth anniversary of the German Democratic Republic, but this was his thinly veiled warning to the East German regime, soon to be overthrown after the Berlin Wall was breached on 9 Nov.

4 *Tschüs, Egon*! (Bye-bye, Egon!)
Taunt thrown at Egon Krenz, the successor to Erich Honecker, who had been forced to resign as head of the East German government on 18 Oct. 1989.

5 We're not kids! We're not kids!
Crowd responding to a Czech communist minister's accusation that only students were rebelling against the regime, Nov. 1989.

6 There are Soviet troops in Czechoslovakia, but that does not mean they are there to solve the country's internal problems.
Dmitri Yazov, Soviet defence minister, 23 Nov. 1989. A notification that the USSR would do nothing to help the tottering Czechoslovak communist government.

7 We are witnessing sad things in other socialist countries.
Cuban leader Fidel Castro, *Independent*, 11 Nov. 1989. A comment following the fall of the Berlin Wall on 9 Nov. Castro must have wondered how much support he could now count on from Soviet Russia.

CHINA: MAO IN POWER, 1949–76

8 To bring prosperous development to literature, the arts and scientific work, it is necessary to adopt the policy of 'letting all the flowers bloom together and all schools contend in airing their views'.

Lu Ting-yi, 26 May 1956, *Current Background*, 15 Aug. 1956, pp.3–4. Lu was head of the Chinese Communist Party's propaganda department. This was a first reaction to Soviet de-Stalinization, later endorsed by Mao himself on 27 Feb. 1957, but the encouragement of criticism was short lived.

9 The spring of 1958 witnessed the beginning of a leap forward on every front in our socialist construction. Industry, agriculture and all other fields of activity are registering greater and more rapid growth.
Liu Shaoqi (Liu Shao-ch'i), 5 May 1958; *Current Background*, 2 June 1958, p.7. In fact, the 'Great Leap Forward' proved to be a monumental disaster, as even Mao himself had to admit to some degree. Liu was head of state of the People's Republic in 1959–68 (see 898:3).

10 The chaos caused was on a grand scale and I take responsibility. Comrades, you must all analyse your own responsibility. If you have to shit, shit! If you have to fart, fart! You will feel much better for it.
Mao Zedong (Mao Tse-tung), 23 July 1959; Stuart Schram (ed.) *Mao Tse-tung Unrehearsed* (1974) p.146. A public admission that the Great Leap Forward had fallen well short of the expectations built up around it.

11 The propaganda department of the Central Committee is the palace of the King of Hell. We must overthrow the palace of the King of Hell and set the little devils free. I have always advocated that whenever the central organs do bad things, it is necessary to call upon the localities to rebel, and to attack the centre.
Mao Zedong, March 1966; Stuart Schram *The Thoughts of Mao Tse-tung* (1989) p.172. The philosophy of the Cultural Revolution, Mao's assault on the alleged revisionists at the heart of the Chinese Communist Party. This was to prove an even worse catastrophe than the so-called Great Leap Forward.

12 The great proletarian Cultural Revolution now unfolding is a great revolution that touches people to their very souls … Our objective is to struggle against and crush those persons in authority who are taking the capitalist road, to criticize and repudiate the reactionary bourgeois academic 'authorities' and the ideology of the bourgeoisie and all other exploiting classes and to transform education, literature and art and all other parts of the superstructure that do not correspond to the socialist economic base, so as to facilitate the consolidation and development of the socialist system.
Decision of the Central Committee of the Chinese Communist Party, 8 Aug. 1966, *Peking Review*, 12 Aug. 1966.

1 Imperialism is moribund, capitalism parasitic and rotten. Modern revisionism is a product of imperialist policies and a variant of capitalism. They cannot produce any works that are good. Capitalism has a history of several centuries, but it has only a pitiful number of classics ... On the other hand, there are some things that really flood the market, such as rock-and-roll, jazz, strip-tease, impressionism, symbolism, abstractionism, Fauvism, modernism – there's no end to them ... In a word, there is decadence and obscenity to poison and corrupt the minds of the people.

Jiang Qing (Chiang Ch'ing), Mao's wife, 26 Nov. 1966; Dick Wilson *Mao* (1979) pp.405–6. Madame Mao was a zealot wife, here voicing the xenophobia at the heart of China for generations.

2 Have no fear of chaos. The more chaos you dish up and the longer it goes on, the better. Disorder and chaos are always a good thing. They clarify things ... But never use weapons.

Mao Zedong, addressing his Red Guards, 6 April 1967; Wilson (1979) p.412.

3 When I moved closer for a better look, someone held his arms behind his back while others tried to force him to bend forward from the waist in the position known as 'doing the airplane'. Finally, they forced him down and pushed his face toward the ground until it was really touching the dirt, kicking him and slapping him in the face.

Li Zhisui, 18 July 1967; *The Private Life of Chairman Mao* (1994) p.489. Dr Li was Mao Zedong's personal physician. The man being maltreated was Liu Shaoqi, Chinese head of state.

4 Pufang's back had been severely injured when Red Guards forced him out of an upper storey window at Peking University during the Cultural Revolution. [He] was paralysed from the waist down. He could not move and lay in bed at a social relief hospital. But he had to earn his living by weaving waste-paper baskets with iron wire.

Xinhua News Agency dispatch, 26 Feb. 1980; David Bonavia *Deng* (1989) p.126. Deng Pufang was the eldest son of Deng Xiaoping, one of China's most senior communists and future head of the Chinese government.

5 When Lin Biao called for everything that represented the old culture to be destroyed, some pupils in my school started to smash things up. Being more than 2,000 years old, the school had a lot of antiques and was therefore a prime site for action.

The school gateway had an old tiled roof with carved leaves. They were hammered to pieces ... The pair of giant bronze incense-burners in front of the temple were toppled, and some boys urinated into them.

Jung Chang *Wild Swans* (1991) pp.291–2. Vandalism became an expression of militant Maoism in the Cultural Revolution. Lin Biao (Lin Piao) was the arch-priest of the Cultural Revolution movement and Mao's heir-apparent. He died in mysterious circumstances in 1971, allegedly after a failed coup attempt.

6 A proletarian party must ... get rid of the stale and take in the fresh air, for only thus can it be full of vitality. Without eliminating waste matter and absorbing fresh blood, the party has no vigour.

Mao Zedong, Aug. 1968; Wilson (1979) p.421.

7 The conception which underlies the Cultural Revolution is that the reconciliation of democracy with good order can be made by imbuing the whole nation with the ideology expressed in the phrase 'serve the people' ... None of the great religions has succeeded in producing a satisfactory society. The purpose of the Thought of Mao Tse-tung [Mao Zedong] is to create a setting in which the claims of the ideal are not at variance with the necessities of daily life.

Joan Robinson *The Cultural Revolution in China* (1969) Introduction. Veneration from a Western academic, reminiscent of the tributes laid at Stalin's feet by the fellow travellers of the 1930s (see 744:5–745:7).

CHINA AND THE SOVIET UNION: THE SINO-SOVIET DISPUTE, 1949–69

8 The Communist Party of the USSR is our best teacher from whom we must learn.

Mao Zedong 'On the People's Democratic Dictatorship', July 1949; Daniels Vol.2 (1985) p.183.

9 Stalin wanted to prevent China from making revolution, saying that we should not have a civil war and should cooperate with Chiang Kai-shek, otherwise the Chinese nation would perish.

Mao Zedong, 24 Sept. 1962; Schram (1974) p.191. Stalin continued to recognize the government of Chiang, even when he was on the verge of defeat by Mao in 1949.

10 Buddhas are made several times lifesize in order to frighten the people ... Stalin was that kind of a person ... When Chinese artists painted pictures of me together with Stalin, they always made me a little bit shorter.

Mao Zedong, 10 March 1958; Schram (1974) p.99. By then, however, Mao had grown to equally Stalinist proportions.

1 Khrushchev has said that we have one pair of trousers for every five people in China, and sit around eating out of the same bowl of watery cabbage soup.
Mao Zedong, Jan. 1964; Anna Louise Strong *China Quarterly* Vol.103 (1985) p.504.

2 The Soviet revisionist leading clique has given the green light to decadent fiction and to photographs of nude women, all of which come from the West; and it publishes fashion and hair-style magazines, to corrupt the Soviet people, particularly the youth.
Chinese student at Beijing rally to welcome students returned from Moscow, 5 Nov. 1966; John Gittings (ed.) *Survey of the Sino-Soviet Dispute* (1968) p.277.

3 You new tsars in the Kremlin, listen: 'The great Soviet people will one day rebel against you, and overthrow you – you handful of arch criminals who are trying to undermine the friendship between the people of China and the Soviet Union.'
People's Daily 14 Feb. 1967; Gittings (1968) p.52.

4 Lies cannot cover up the wolf's murderous claws!
Chinese comment on the outbreak of fighting on the Sino-Soviet border in Manchuria, March 1969, moving the dispute between the two communist powers from a war of words into a bloody conflict.

CHINA: DE-MAOIZATION, 1976–89

5 He felt that the dogmas that Mao proposed in his old age were simply a cover for feudalism. Since China lacked a mature working class, the Communist Party developed as a peasant party led by revolutionary intellectuals, and the revolution it carried out was not proletarian-socialist but peasant, with a strong feudal tinge. After the revolution Chinese society therefore gradually evolved into a new form of oriental despotism.
The dissident Fa Shengi on his colleague Wang Shenyou, executed on 21 April 1977; John Gittings *China Changes Face* (1989) p.159.

6 We are now carrying out the modernizations of industry, agriculture, national defence, and science and technology. However, the adjective 'socialist' should be prefixed to these four modernizations. We call them the 'socialist four modernizations'.
Deng Xiaoping, 1978; Bonavia (1989) p.182. Deng, a victim of the Cultural Revolution (see 898:4), was now Chinese head of government.

7 We want to be masters of our own destiny. We need no gods or emperors. We do not believe in the existence of any saviour. We want to be masters of the world and not instruments used by autocrats to carry out their wild ambitions. We want a modern lifestyle and democracy for the people. Freedom and happiness are our sole objectives in accomplishing modernization. Without this fifth modernization all others are merely another promise.
Wei Jingsheng, Jan. 1979; James D. Seymour *The Fifth Modernization: China's Human Rights Movement 1978–1979* (1980) p.50. Wei demanded this fifth modernization in a poster mounted on the so-called Democracy Wall in Beijing in Dec. 1978. For this he was jailed for 15 years.

8 They are impatient and tired of waiting. They feel they have been waiting thirty years and now have to wait another thirty years ... They say: Your cadres have already been rewarded for your suffering. Why must we the people go on suffering without end?
Chen Yün, spring 1979; Gittings (1989) p.108. A senior communist voices popular discontent with the standard of living in the People's Republic.

9 Communist society will not flourish in a courtyard behind locked doors. Opening the country to the outside world is not an expedient measure but a fundamental principle for building a socialist society, as well as the only road to a communist society.
Li Honglin *People's Daily*, 15 Oct. 1984; Gittings (1989) p.239.

10 The main task of socialism is to develop the productive forces, steadily improve the life of the people, and keep increasing the material wealth of the society. Therefore, there can be no communism with pauperism, or socialism with pauperism. So to get rich is no sin.
Deng Xiaoping, 2 Sept. 1986; Gittings (1989) p.109. Compare Guizot (see 553:2).

11 Faced with the reality of poverty and dictatorship, we can endure it. But we cannot allow our descendants to grow up in the stranglehold of lack of freedom, democracy and people's rights.
Student manifesto, Dec. 1986; Gittings (1989) p.173.

12 Armoured personnel carriers formed the spearhead while soldiers on foot shot to kill from both sides. Meanwhile, the first of the night's armoured cars and tanks smashed its way through the citizens' barricades to the east. It showed all the ruthlessness which must be contained in the army's orders to smash the 'turmoil' allegedly created by the mass movement. Several cyclists who could not get out of the way in time were crushed or tossed aside.

John Gittings, eyewitness of the start of the Tiananmen Square massacre, 4 June 1989; *China through the Sliding Door* (1999) p.148. Pro-democracy demonstrators in Beijing were savagely suppressed by the government of the People's Republic.

1 Truthfulness means precisely upholding the party's ideological line.

Jiang Zemin, June 1989, after the Tiananmen massacre of 4 June. Jiang was one of the most senior figures in the hierarchy of the People's Republic and the successor to Deng Xiaoping after Deng's death in 1997. Although Jiang was, like Deng, an economic reformer, he drew the line at the political democracy demanded by the demonstrators in Tiananmen Square. Gorbachev's full-blooded *perestroika* was too risky an example to be followed.

YUGOSLAVIA: FROM COMMUNISM TO BLOOD FEUD, 1989–2001

2 We communists were the last empire.

Milovan Djilas, 1992; Michael Ignatieff *Blood and Belonging* (1993) p.37. Under the communist regime of President Josef Broz Tito, Yugoslavia's multinational state held together successfully. With the collapse of communism in Eastern Europe in 1989, however, fissures began to appear, which soon led to civil war. Djilas, then 82 years old, had been first a close aide and then a sharp critic of Tito, for which he served 13 years in jail.

3 The Battle of Kosovo contains within itself one great symbol. That is the symbol of heroism. It is commemorated in our songs, dances, literature and history. Six centuries later we are again involved in battles, and facing battles. They are not battles with arms, but these battles cannot be excluded.

Serbian leader Slobodan Milosevic, 28 June 1989; Adam LeBor *Milosevic* (2002) p.122. Milosevic was commemorating the Battle of Kosovo, 28 June 1389, when the Serbs were defeated by the Turks. The province of Kosovo was to the Serbs their ancestral heartland, though by then it was inhabited by an overwhelming majority of ethnic Albanians, who had begun to demand a large measure of autonomy, thus threatening Serb hegemony over Yugoslavia as a whole and providing a dangerous precedent for the other ethnic and

religious groups in the country to break away from Serb control.

4 The region is undergoing ethnic cleansing.

The Times, 21 May 1992, reporting a statement by the Serb government. In April and May 1992 Serb paramilitaries, led by the man known as Arkan (Zeljko Raznatovic), conducted a reign of terror in Bosnia-Herzegovina after the province opted for independence on 1 March. Muslim populations were forcibly expelled from their homes in a systematic programme of rape, mutilation and murder, first developed by Arkan's forces in Croatia during late 1991. So a new term passed into the world's political vocabulary.

5 Why target that mosque, that bridge? That bridge has survived attacks from the Venetians. And the mosque – what have they done to the mosque! It is 500 years old. It survived two world wars, and now it is a pile of bricks. It took this kind of hatred to bring it to the ground.

The Muslim civil engineer Nerkez Mackiz; Janine Di Giovanni *The Quick and the Dead: Under Siege in Sarajevo* (1994) p.101. Mackiz was speaking of the destruction by Croatian artillery of the beautiful bridge at Mostar in southwest Bosnia on 9 Nov. 1993. The bridge was built by the Ottoman Turks in 1567, and its annihilation was a graphic token of the vicious spite running throughout what had been Yugoslavia.

6 There are so many. It is going to be a meze. There will be blood up to your knees … Beautiful. Keep the good ones over there. Enjoy them.

General Ratko Mladic at Srebrenica, mid-July 1995; *Newsday*, 8 Aug. 1995. General Mladic, head of the Bosnian Serb forces, presided over an orgy of rape and the massacre of up to 8,000 men and boys in the Muslim town of Srebrenica. The episode was the worst of its kind in Europe since the end of World War II and determined the West to intervene militarily to bring the war in Bosnia to an end. Mladic and his 'president', Radovan Karadzic, were indicted for genocide and eight years later were still being hunted down. Meze is Turkish for a long feast of many small dishes.

7 They came into the house, and said either we arrest you and take you with us, or we will kill everyone. So what else could he do, just sit in the car. He did not blink an eye, and said of course I will go and he left.

Mira Markovic, wife of Slobodan Milosevic, on his arrest by the Serbian government on 1 April 2001; LeBor (2002) p.316. Milosevic was indicted for crimes against humanity and genocide and extradited to The Hague for trial on 28 June 2001, the anniversary of the Battle of Kosovo.

The United States since 1945

HAIL TO THE CHIEFS!

1 The Buck Stops Here.

Slogan displayed on the desk of President Harry S Truman, meaning that here sat the man with ultimate responsibility. Doubly apt, since the buck is a counter placed before the dealer in poker and Truman was an enthusiastic poker player.

2 Eisenhower was a subtle man, and no fool, though in pursuit of his objectives he did not like to be thought of as brilliant; people of brilliance, he thought, were distrusted.

David Halberstam *The Best and the Brightest* (1969). Eisenhower tended to be underestimated during his presidency, but thereafter his political reputation rose considerably.

3 There is something very eighteenth-century about this young man. He is always on his toes during our discussions. But in the evening there will be music and wine and pretty women.

Harold Macmillan on John F. Kennedy, *New York Journal-American*, 21 Jan. 1962. A revealing insight into the two sides of Kennedy's persona.

4 Johnson's instinct for power is as primordial as a salmon's going upstream to spawn.

Theodore H. White on Lyndon Johnson *The Making of the President 1964* (1965). A comment inspired by Johnson's masterly take-over after Kennedy's assassination.

5 Would you buy a used car from this man?

The American comedian Mort Sahl questions the integrity of the 1960 Republican candidate for the presidency, Richard Nixon. Nixon's conduct as president between 1969 and 1974 answered the question.

6 Gerry Ford is so dumb that he can't fart and chew gum at the same time.

Lyndon Johnson on Gerald Ford, attrib. One of his more repeatable jibes.

7 A simple and proper function of government is just to make it easy for us to do good and difficult for us to do wrong.

Jimmy Carter, 15 July 1976, accepting the presidential nomination of the Democratic Party. As a practising Christian, Carter brought a rare (though ineffectual) moral presence to US politics.

8 The acting president of the United States.

The writer Gore Vidal on Ronald Reagan, c.1981. Matchless as head of state, this product of the Hollywood dream factory was seriously defective as head of government.

9 Let others have the charisma. I've got the class.

George Bush, *Guardian*, 3 Dec. 1988. President Bush had none of Reagan's affable charm, but he was a graduate of Yale, born into the East Coast establishment.

10 He is smart. But he is a Bubba. He loves Elvis, but he reads philosophy and theology.

Mandy Grunwald on William Jefferson Clinton, c.1992; Kate Marton *Hidden Power* (2001) p.314. Capturing the dichotomy in Clinton: a Rhodes Scholar and yet a 'bubba' or 'redneck' with all the tastes of a poor white Southerner.

11 It's amazing I won. I was running against peace, prosperity and incumbency.

President George W. Bush, 14 June 2001; Michael Moore *Stupid White Men* (2002 edn) p.vii. Bush became president after the most tightly contested election in American history. His Democratic opponent, Vice-President Al Gore, was ultimately denied the prize through a decision by Bush's conservative sympathizers on the US Supreme Court, validating the controversial vote in the key state of Florida, where Bush's brother, Jeb, was governor.

NATIONAL INSECURITY, 1947–57

12 When I see a bird that walks like a duck and swims like a duck and quacks like a duck, I call it a duck.

Labour leader Walter Reuther, attrib. Reuther had no difficulty in spotting a communist.

13 In effect it makes service in the Government subject to the risk that some malevolent or crazy person may accuse you of being leftist … In practical effect, the usual rule that men are presumed innocent until proved guilty is in reverse.

David Lilienthal, 23 March 1947; *The Journals of David E. Lilienthal* Vol.2 (1964) p.163. Lilienthal, the head of the US Atomic Energy Commission, was commenting on President Truman's 'Loyalty Order' of 21 March 1947, which refused Federal employment if there were 'reasonable grounds for belief that the person involved was disloyal to the Government of the United States'.

1 You have produced a capital city on the eve of its Reichstag fire. This is the beginning of concentration camps in America!

The screenwriter Dalton Trumbo, Oct. 1947; David Caute *The Great Fear* (1978) p.494. Trumbo was appearing before the House Committee on Un-American Activities (HUAC), which was then investigating alleged communist subversion in Hollywood. For the Reichstag fire see 754:2. Concentration camps had already been introduced when Japanese-Americans were interned in the aftermath of Pearl Harbor (see 857:13).

2 My brothers and I will be happy to subscribe generously to a pest removal fund. We are willing to establish such a fund to ship to Russia the people who don't like our American system of government and prefer the communistic system to ours.

Jack Warner of Warner Bros., a friendly witness before the HUAC, Oct. 1947; Stefan Kanfer *A Journal of the Plague Years* (1973) p.42. One of the great Hollywood moguls lends his aid to the purge.

3 Communists can hang out all the iron curtains they like, but they'll never be able to shut out the story of a land where free men walk without fear and live with abundance.

Eric Johnston, president of the Motion Picture Association, Oct. 1947; Kanfer (1973) p.65. Johnston had earlier denied he supported a blacklist of targeted Hollywood actors and writers, but this was his position before the HUAC.

4 Have you ever heard of Rip Van Winkle? If some people in the United States don't wake up and get out of the long sleep, we will find some of the difficulties here that they have encountered in France and Italy and Yugoslavia and Poland and Finland, and some of these South American countries.

Representative J. Parnell Thomas of the HUAC, Oct. 1947; Kanfer (1973) p.69. Rip Van Winkle was the central character in Washington Irving's 1820 short story of a man who fell asleep in colonial America and woke up years later in the United States.

5 In this century, within the next decades, will be decided for generations whether all mankind is to become communist, whether the whole world is to be become free, or whether, in the struggle, civilization is to be completely destroyed or completely changed. It is our fate to live upon that turning-point in history ... It is popular to call it a social crisis. It is in fact a total crisis – religious, moral, intellectual, social, political, economic.

Whittaker Chambers *Witness* (1953) p.7. In Aug. 1948 the former communist Chambers accused Alger Hiss, until

recently a senior member of the State Department, of giving secret documents to him in the late 1930s when he acted as a communist agent of the Soviet Union. In Jan. 1950 Hiss was convicted of perjury after denying the allegation, and his case became a Cold War *cause célèbre*.

6 This charge goes beyond the personal. Attempts will be made to use it, and the resulting publicity, to discredit great achievements of this country in which I was privileged to participate.

Alger Hiss to the chairman of the HUAC, 24 Aug. 1948; *In the Court of Public Opinion* (1957) p.102. Hiss asserted that his arraignment was a political attack on the New Deal and the United Nations. He had served in the Agricultural Adjustment Administration and played a key role in drafting the United Nations Charter. President Truman shared this view, describing the attack on Hiss as a 'red herring', designed to damage the Democrats in the forthcoming presidential election.

7 We'll name them as they jump out of windows.

Karl Mundt of the HUAC, 20 Dec. 1948; Walter Goodman *The Committee* (1969 edn) p.267. Hours earlier, a former State Department official, Laurence Duggan, had died after falling from a high window in midtown Manhattan. Two weeks earlier the Committee had been told that Duggan was a member of a six-man communist cell, and this was Mundt's reply when asked if he would release the other five names.

8 Revolution, which was once a word spoken with pride by every American who had the right to claim it, has become a word spoken with timidity and doubt and even loathing.

Archibald MacLeish, former Librarian of Congress, *Atlantic Monthly*, Aug. 1949.

9 I should like to make it clear to you that whatever the outcome of any appeal which Mr Hiss or his lawyers may take in this case I do not intend to turn my back on Alger Hiss.

Secretary of state Dean Acheson, 25 Jan. 1950; *Present at the Creation* (1969) p.360. On 21 Jan. Hiss had been found guilty of the charges against him. Acheson's statement was an act of friendship, not a reflection on the verdict.

10 I have here in my hand a list of 205 – a list of names that were made known to the Secretary of State as being members of the Communist Party and who nevertheless are still working and shaping policy in the State Department ... There the bright young men who were born with silver spoons in their mouth are the ones who have been the worst.

Senator Joseph McCarthy launching his anti-communist crusade at Wheeling, West Virginia, on 9 Feb. 1950; Thomas C. Reeves *The Life and Times of Joe McCarthy* (1982) p.224 and Michael W. Miles *The Odyssey of the American Right* (1980) p.143.

1 [Part of] a conspiracy on a scale so immense as to dwarf any previous such venture, in the history of man ... always and invariably serving the world policy of the Kremlin.

Senator Joseph McCarthy on General of the Army George Marshall, 14 June 1951; see *Congressional Record, Senate* pp.6556–6603 for full text. On 3 Oct. 1952 Marshall's wartime colleague, General of the Army Dwight Eisenhower, Republican candidate in the presidential election, planned to make a public defence of General Marshall in a speech attended by Senator McCarthy but was persuaded to omit the passage for fear of the political consequences (see Reeves (1982) pp.437–9).

2 The issue between Republicans and Democrats is clearly drawn ... by those that have been in charge of twenty years of treason.

Senator Joseph McCarthy at the Republican National Convention, 9 July 1952; Lawrence Wittner *Cold War America* (1978) p.86.

3 McCarthyism is Americanism with its sleeves rolled.

Senator Joseph McCarthy, attrib. McCarthy was the self-styled champion of blue-collar America versus the East Coast élite.

4 I do not like subversion or disloyalty in any form and if I had ever seen any I would have considered it my duty to have reported it to the proper authorities. But to hurt innocent people whom I knew many years ago in order to save myself is, to me, inhuman and indecent and dishonorable. I cannot and will not cut my conscience to fit this year's fashions.

Lillian Hellman to the chairman of the HUAC, 19 May 1952; *Scoundrel Time* (1976) p.81. Hellman was refusing to testify against alleged communist associates; instead she took the Fifth Amendment to the Constitution, which protected her right to keep silent.

5 1. Between 1929 and mid-1942, more probably than not, J. Robert Oppenheimer was a sufficiently hardened communist that he either volunteered espionage information to the Soviets or complied with a request for such information. 2. More probably than not, he has since been functioning as an espionage agent; and 3. More probably than not, he has since acted under a Soviet directive in influencing United States military, atomic energy, intelligence, and diplomatic policy.

William L. Borden to J. Edgar Hoover, 7 Nov. 1953; John Major *The Oppenheimer Hearing* (1971) p.32. Borden, a former official in the US Atomic Energy Commission, triggered an investigation into the director of the wartime atomic bomb

project. Oppenheimer subsequently lost his post as adviser to the Commission, along with his security clearance.

6 When public men indulge themselves in abuse, when they deny others a fair trial, when they resort to innuendo and insinuation, to libel, scandal and suspicion, then our democratic society is outraged, and democracy is baffled. It has no apparatus to deal with the boor, the liar, the lout, and the antidemocrat in general.

Senator William Fulbright, 2 Feb. 1954; *Congressional Records* Vol.100, p.1105. Fulbright was the only senator to vote against the appropriation for McCarthy's investigative subcommittee.

7 Upon what meat does Senator McCarthy feed? Two of the staples of his diet are the investigations (protected by immunity) and the half truth.

The broadcaster Edward R. Murrow, 9 March 1954; Reeves (1982) p.564. Murrow was presenting a television programme that marked the beginning of a backlash against McCarthy, strengthened by McCarthy's attack on the US army in televised hearings that opened on 18 Feb.

8 Until this moment, Senator, I think I never really gauged your cruelty or your recklessness.

US army counsel Joseph Welch to Senator Joseph McCarthy during the army–McCarthy hearings, 9 June 1954; Reeves (1982) pp.630–31. The remark was carefully planned and not the spontaneous burst of outrage it seemed at the time. It pricked McCarthy's balloon, and on 2 Dec. 1954 he was condemned by the Senate for his conduct. He died of alcoholic poisoning on 2 May 1957.

9 When his day of destiny came, he looked around, innocently, saw the gargoyles of Anti-Christ staring and sneering at him from everywhere, and innocently he reached out to crush them ... We, too, are reaching out to crush them. We mean it. We are McCarthyites.

William S. Schlamm 'Across McCarthy's Grave' in *National Review*, 18 May 1957.

10 MCCARTHY WAS MURDERED BY THE COMMUNISTS BECAUSE HE WAS EXPOSING THEM.

William Loeb, editor of the *Manchester Union Leader*, May 1957; Reeves (1982) p.672.

BLACK AMERICA, 1948–93

11 It is hereby declared to be the policy of the President that there shall be equality of treatment and opportunity for all persons in the armed services without regard to race, color, religion or national origin.

President Harry S Truman, Executive Order 9981, 26 July 1948; E. David Cronon *Twentieth Century America* Vol.2 (1966) p.449. Up to this point the US armed forces had been racially segregated. This was a high-risk initiative in an election year when racist Southern Democrats had hived off to form the States' Rights Party, led by Governor Strom Thurmond of South Carolina.

1 We conclude that in the field of public education the doctrine of 'separate but equal' has no place. Separate educational facilities are inherently unequal.

Chief Justice of the US Supreme Court Earl Warren, judgement in Brown v. Board of Education of Topeka, 17 May 1954; H.S. Commager *Documents of American History* (1973 edn) p.604. This landmark judgement nullified the Court's decision of 1896 on segregated public facilities for whites and blacks (see 642:2).

2 Take such proceedings ... as are necessary and proper to admit to public schools on a national non-discriminatory basis with all deliberate speed the parties to these cases.

Chief Justice Earl Warren, 31 May 1955; Cronon Vol.2 (1966) p.456. This pronouncement implemented the decision of 17 May 1954. It referred back to the 1911 opinion of Justice Oliver Wendell Holmes Jr: 'A state cannot be expected to move with the celerity of a private business man; it is enough if it proceeds, in the language of the English Chancery, with all deliberate speed.' It remained to be seen whether America's black community would be content with that rate of progress.

3 It is destroying the amicable relations between the white and Negro races that have been created through 90 years of patient effort by the good people of both races. It has planted hatred and suspicion where there has been heretofore friendship and understanding.

Southern Manifesto, 12 March 1956; *Congressional Record* Vol.102, pp.4515–16. An attack on the Supreme Court decision by 19 senators and 8 representatives from the South. The future president, Lyndon Johnson, was one of the three southern senators who refused to sign.

4 Don't you realize that the whites will soon be outnumbered in the South? We have to preserve ourselves – there's a morality in self-preservation. Anyway, the nigrahs can never run the place – they're congenitally incapable of it. They've never produced a single genius.

James Morris *Coast to Coast* (1956) Ch.9. White opinion in Charleston, South Carolina, in the mid-1950s.

5 *We have discovered a new and powerful weapon – non-violent resistance.* Although law is an important factor in bringing about social change, there are certain conditions in which the very effort to adhere to new legal decisions creates tension and provokes violence. We had hoped to see demonstrated a method that would enable us to continue our struggle while coping with the violence it aroused. Now we see the answer: face violence if necessary, but refuse to return violence.

Martin Luther King Jr *Our Struggle: The Story of Montgomery* (1957) p.6. In 1955 black people in Montgomery, Alabama, began a boycott of the town's buses after the arrest of Rosa Parks on 5 Dec. for refusing to move to the rear of a bus (the section designated for blacks). Rev. King then developed a protest movement based on the Gandhian principle of passive resistance (see 863:7).

6 It seemed a long way from 143rd Street. Shaking hands with the Queen of England was a long way from being forced to sit in the colored section of the bus going into downtown Wilmington, North Carolina.

Althea Gibson after winning the women's tennis singles title at Wimbledon, 1957; *Women-Sports* magazine, March 1976.

7 If they don't want us to mix with them in their equality, give us a place in America. Set it aside ... Give us three, four or more states. We have well earned whatever they give us; if they give us twenty-five states, we have well earned them. Give us a territory. Give us the same instrument that they had to start a civilization in that territory.

Elijah Mohammed, leader of the Nation of Islam, 31 May 1959; E.U. Essien-Udom *Black Nationalism* (1962) p.260. An impossible aspiration, but the Black Muslims secured a large following, based on deep disillusion with white liberal reform. Their most famous convert was the world heavyweight boxing champion Cassius Clay, who announced on 26 Feb. 1964 that henceforth he would be known as Muhammad Ali.

8 I didn't know that a Negro could register and vote ... When they asked for those to raise their hands who'd go down to the courthouse the next day, I raised mine. Had it up as high as I could get it. I guess if I'd had any sense I'd a-been a little scared, but what was the point of being scared? The only thing they could do to me was kill me and it seemed like they'd been trying to do that a little bit at a time ever since I could remember.

Fannie Lou Hamer, 1962; *To Praise Our Bridges* (1967).

1 If we do not now dare everything, the fulfilment of that prophecy, recreated from the Bible in a song by a slave, is upon us:

God gave Noah the rainbow sign,
No more water, the fire next time!

The black writer James Baldwin 'Down at the Cross' in the *New Yorker*, 1962, closing words.

2 I draw the line in the dust and toss the gauntlet before the feet of tyranny, and I say, Segregation now! Segregation tomorrow! Segregation forever!

George Wallace, 21 May 1963; Harvard Sitkoff *The Struggle for Black Equality 1954–1980* (1981) p.156. Wallace, governor of Alabama, was defying the Kennedy administration's efforts to implement civil rights for blacks in the South, specifically by enabling them to enrol as students at the University of Alabama.

3 It ought to be possible for American consumers of any color to receive equal service in places of public accommodation, such as hotels and restaurants and theaters and retail stores, without being forced to resort to demonstrations in the street, and it ought to be possible for American citizens of any color to register and to vote in a free election without interference or fear of reprisal … In short, every American ought to have the right to be treated as he would wish to be treated, as one would wish his children to be treated. But this is not the case.

President John F. Kennedy, televised address to the nation, 10 June 1963; Sitkoff (1981) p.157. Hours later, Medgar Evers, a representative of the National Association for the Advancement of Colored People (NAACP), was murdered by a sniper in Mississippi. The legislation to implement these rights was put through after Kennedy's death by his successor, Lyndon Johnson, in 1964 and 1965.

4 I have a dream that one day this nation will live out the true meaning of its creed: 'We hold these truths to be self-evident; that all men are created equal.' When we let freedom ring, when we let it ring for every village and every hamlet, for every state and every city, we will be able to speed up that day when all of God's children, black men and white men, Jews and Gentiles, Protestants and Catholics, will be able to join hands and sing in the words of the old Negro spiritual, 'Free at last! Free at last! Thank God Almighty, we are free at last!'

Rev. Martin Luther King Jr, 28 Aug. 1963; *Congressional Record*, 18 April 1968, Vol.114, p.9165. Perhaps the most eloquent expression of the campaign for civil rights, at the climax of the march on Washington, which ended at the Lincoln Memorial.

5 Revolutions are never fought by turning the other cheek. Revolutions are never based upon love-your-enemy and pray-for-those-who [de]spitefully-use-you. And revolutions are never waged singing 'We Shall Overcome'. Revolutions are based upon bloodshed.

Black Muslim militant Malcolm X, 8 April 1964; George Breitman (ed.) *Malcolm X Speaks* (1965) p.50. A wholesale rejection of the non-violent resistance philosophy of Martin Luther King Jr.

6 You show me a black man who isn't an extremist and I'll show you one who needs psychiatric attention.

Malcolm X *The Autobiography of Malcolm X* (1966) p.394.

7 Be peaceful, be courteous, obey the law, respect everyone; but if someone puts his hand on you, send him to the cemetery.

Malcolm X, c.1964; Breitman (1965). Malcolm X was shot dead by the rival Black Muslims on 21 Feb. 1965.

8 At times history and fate meet at a single time at a single place to shape a turning-point in man's unending search for freedom. So it was at Lexington and Concord. So it was a century ago at Appomattox. So it was last week in Selma, Alabama … The Constitution says that no person shall be kept from voting because of his race or his color. We have all sworn an oath before God to support and to defend that Constitution. We must now act in obedience to that oath … A century has passed – more than one hundred years – since equality was promised. And yet the Negro is not equal. A century has passed since that day of promise. And the promise is unkept. The time of justice has now come. And I tell you that I believe sincerely that no force can hold it back.

President Lyndon Johnson, 15 March 1965; *Public Papers 1965* Vol.1 (1966) pp.281, 284. Johnson spoke against the background of white racist attacks on a civil rights march from Selma to Montgomery, Alabama, led by Martin Luther King. He refers back to Lincoln's Emancipation Proclamation of 22 Sept. 1862 (see 590:8). The skirmishes at Lexington and Concord marked the outbreak of the American Revolution on 19 April 1775. The Civil War ended with the surrender of the South at Appomattox courthouse on 9 April 1865.

9 Our life must be purposed to implement human rights … To demand those God-given rights is to seek black power – the power to build black institutions of splendid achievement.

Rev. Adam Clayton Powell, 29 May 1966. The New York congressman voices the new words in the civil rights vocabulary: black power.

1 The single black student in the Southern university, the promoted porter in Marietta, Georgia – all ease the liberals' conscience like a benevolent but highly addictive drug. And, for them, 'moderation' is a kind of religious catch phrase.

Le Roi Jones 'Tokenism: 300 years for five cents' in *Home* (1966).

2 I say violence is necessary. It is as American as cherry pie.

H. Rap Brown, *Washington Evening Star*, 27 July 1967. Brown was a militant figure in the Southern Negro Christian Conference (SNCC).

3 Our people are a colony within the United States; you are colonies outside the United States ... In [the] cities we do not control our resources. We do not control the land, the houses or the stores. These are owned by whites who live outside the community. These are very real colonies, as their capital and cheap labor are exploited by those who live outside the cities. White power makes the laws and enforces those laws with guns and nightsticks in the hands of white racist policemen and black mercenaries.

The black activist Stokeley Carmichael, speaking in Cuba, 1967; Robert L. Allen *A Guide to Black Power in America* (1969) p.6. The black predicament in the United States as a parallel of the Third World.

4   If you're white,
    You're all right.
    If you're brown,
    Stick around.
    But if you're black,
    Get back, get back.

Black children's rhyme, 1950s; H. Rap Brown *Die Nigger Die!* (1969) p.2.

5 Like anybody, I would like to live a long life. Longevity has its place. But I'm not concerned about that now. I just want to do God's will. And He's allowed me to go up to the mountain. And I've looked over, and I've seen the promised land. I may not get there with you, but I want you to know tonight that we as a people will get to the promised land.

Martin Luther King Jr, 3 April 1968, the day before his assassination in Memphis, Tennessee.

6 He stood in that line of saints which goes back from Gandhi to Jesus; his violent end, like theirs, reflects the hostility of mankind to those who annoy

it by trying hard to pull it one more painful step up the ladder from ape to angel.

I.F. Stone on Martin Luther King Jr, 'The fire has only just begun' (1968).

7 America's a bitch. Being Black in this country is like somebody asking you to play white Russian roulette and giving you a gun with bullets in all the chambers.

H. Rap Brown; Brown (1969) p.19.

8 The time may have come when the issue of race could benefit from a period of 'benign neglect'.

Daniel Patrick Moynihan, memorandum to President Richard Nixon, *Washington Evening Star*, 2 March 1970. In the mid-1960s the Democrat Moynihan had been a key adviser to President Johnson on civil rights legislation. Now serving a Republican president, he urges a go-slow on further reform.

9 I do not believe we are any nearer a solution to the black-white controversy than we were in 1870 ... Furthermore, I do not believe it is possible for a black to ever be fully accepted, without any reservation, into the power structure of this country, or even accepted generally as a complete man.

E. Frederic Morrow *Way Down South Up North* (1973) p.120. The grandson of a slave, Morrow had worked with the Eisenhower administration in the field of civil rights during the 1950s.

10 Loose shoes, a tight pussy, and a warm place to shit.

Earl Butz on the aspirations of black Americans, late 1970s. Butz, a member of the Carter administration, was instantly dismissed for this remark.

11 Our flag is red, white and blue, but our nation is a rainbow – red, yellow, brown, black, and white – and we're all precious in God's sight.

The black minister Rev. Jesse Jackson, 17 July 1984, at the Democratic National Convention.

12 Now if you're average and *white*, honey, you can go far. Just look at Dan Quayle. If that boy was colored, he'd be washing dishes somewhere.

Annie Elizabeth Delang *Having Our Say* (1992) Ch.17. Quayle, George Bush's vice-president, was not noted for his intellectual prowess.

13 I'm going to make her cry. I'm going to sing 'Dixie' until she cries!

Carol Moseley-Braun, reporting the words of the senator for North Carolina, Jesse Helms, *Newsweek*, 16 Aug. 1993. The racist Helms taunts a black congresswoman with the battle-hymn of the Confederacy (see 588:9).

WOMEN'S LIBERATION, 1960-92

1 A woman without a man is like a fish without a bicycle.
Gloria Steinem, attrib. (and attribution doubtful). Steinem was the doyenne of the women's movement in the United States.

2 A liberated woman is one who has sex before marriage and a job after.
Gloria Steinem, *Newsweek*, 28 March 1960.

3 The Committee's aim was simple enough: their sleuths studying an organization known as Women Strike for Peace had learned that some of the strikers seemed to have past associations with the Communist Party or its front groups. Presumably if these were exposed, right-thinking housewives would give up peace agitation and go back to the kitchen.
The columnist Russell Baker, *Detroit Free Press*, 16 Dec. 1962. Sixteen members of the WSP were given subpoenas to appear before the HUAC. Their testimony helped put the women's cause on the map, as well as bringing ridicule on the Committee.

4 If I am right, the problem that has no name stirring in the minds of so many American women today is not a matter of loss of femininity or too much education, or the demands of domesticity. It is far more important than anyone recognizes. It is the key to these other old and new problems which have been torturing women and their husbands and children, and puzzling their doctors and educators for years. It may well be the key to our future as a nation and a culture. We can no longer ignore that voice within women that says: 'I want something more than my husband and my children and my home.'
Betty Friedan *The Feminine Mystique* (1963) p.27.

5 We're half the people; we should be half the Congress.
Jeanette Rankin, *Newsweek*, 14 Feb. 1966.

6 We, men and women who hereby constitute ourselves as the National Organization for Women, believe that the time has come for a new movement toward true equality for all women in America, and toward a fully equal partnership of the sexes, as part of the world-wide revolution of human rights now taking place within and beyond our national borders.
NOW statement of purpose, 1966; Mary Beth Norton and Ruth M. Alexander (eds) *Major Problems in American Women's History* (1996 edn) p.445.

7 Many women do not recognize themselves as discriminated against; no better proof could be found of the totality of their conditioning.
Kate Millett *Sexual Politics* (1969).

8 Let it all hang out. Let it seem bitchy, catty, dykey, frustrated, crazy, nutty, frigid, ridiculous, bitter, embarrassing, man-hating, libelous, pure, unfair, envious, intuitive, low-down, stupid, petty, liberating. *We are the women that men have warned us about.*
Robin Morgan *Goodbye to All That* (1970).

9 Section 1. Equality of rights under the law shall not be denied or abridged by the United States or by any State on account of sex.
Equal Rights Amendment (ERA) to the Constitution, approved by the United States Senate on 22 March 1972; Norton and Alexander (1996 edn) p.483. The amendment was never ratified by the requisite majority of 38 states.

10 It's like pushing marbles through a sieve. It means the sieve will never be the same again.
Nora Ephron *Crazy Salad* (1972) Ch.6. Ephron, a delegate to the 1972 Democratic National Convention, reflects on the struggle to ratify the Equal Rights Amendment.

11 Anti-family, anti-children, and pro-abortion. It is a series of sharp-tongued, high-pitched, whining complaints by unmarried women. They view the home as a prison, and the wife and mother as a slave. To these women's libbers, marriage means dirty dishes and dirty laundry ... Women's lib is a total assault on the role of the American woman as wife and mother, and on the family as the basic unit of society.
Phyllis Schlafly on *Ms* magazine, Feb. 1972; *Phyllis Schlafly Report 5*. Mrs Schlafly led the anti-feminist charge on behalf of conservative women throughout the United States.

12 A state criminal abortion statute of the current Texas type, that excepts from criminality only a *life-saving* procedure on behalf of the mother, without regard to pregnancy stage and without recognition of the other interests involved is violative of the Due Process Clause of the Fourteenth Amendment.
United States Supreme Court decision in the case of Roe v. Wade, 1973; Norton and Alexander (1996 edn) p.486.

A highly controversial decision restricting the authority of states such as Texas to pass laws prohibiting abortion. The due process clause of Section 1 of the 1868 amendment reads: 'nor shall any State deprive any person of life, liberty, or property, without due process of law'.

1 If men could get pregnant, abortion would be a sacrament.

Florynce Kennedy, *Ms* magazine, March 1973.

2 In commercial law, the person duped was too often a woman. In a section on land tenure, one 1968 textbook explains that 'land, like women, was meant to be possessed'.

Ruth Ginsburg, *Ms* magazine, April 1974. Ginsburg later became a Supreme Court Justice after nomination by President Clinton.

3 In politics women ... type the letters, lick the stamps, distribute the pamphlets and get out the vote. Men get elected.

Claire Boothe Luce, *Saturday Review*, 15 Sept. 1974.

4 I am working for the time when unqualified blacks, browns and women join the unqualified men in running our government.

Sissy Farenthold, *Los Angeles Times*, 18 Sept. 1974.

5 So few grown women like their lives.

Publisher of the *Washington Post*, Katharine Graham, *Ms* magazine, Oct. 1974.

6 A Positive Woman cannot defeat a man in a wrestling or boxing match, but she can motivate him, inspire him, encourage him, teach him, restrain him, reward him, and have power over him that he can never achieve over her with all his muscle.

Phyllis Schlafly *The Power of the Positive Woman* (1977). The title of Mrs Schlafly's book may have been inspired by Norman Vincent Peale's *The Power of Positive Thinking* (1952). This was also adapted by a burlesque artiste who gave herself the name of Norma Vincent Peel; she called her act 'The Power of Positive Stripping'.

7 White women ... say things like they don't want men opening doors for them anymore, and they don't want men lighting their cigarettes for them anymore. Big deal ... Black women don't quibble about things that are not important.

Wilma Rudolph *Wilma* (1977) Ch.14.

8 Betty Ford will be remembered as the unelected First Lady who pressured second-rate manhood on American women.

Anti-Equal Rights Amendment advertisement on the wife of President Gerald Ford, who campaigned energetically for the ERA.

9 Many women have never accepted their God-given roles. They live in disobedience to God's laws and have promoted their godless philosophy throughout our society ... ERA is not merely a political issue, but a moral issue as well. A definite violation of holy Scripture, ERA defies the mandate that 'the husband is the head of the wife, even as Christ is the head of the Church' (Ephesians 5:23).

Rev. Jerry Falwell *Listen, America* (1980) pp.150–51. Falwell, founder of the Moral Majority organization in 1979, was one of an influential cohort of 'prime-time preachers', commanding a television audience of millions.

10 Under the proposed Equal Rights Amendment, wherever males are accustomed to appear in public, nude above the waist, equal rights are absolutely guaranteed to females. Such places would most certainly include swimming pools, tennis courts and drive-in theaters.

Nebraskan insurance executive; Jane J. Mansbridge *Why We Lost the ERA* (1986) p.144. The amendment was lost in 1982, after ten years of debate, when it had been ratified by only 35 of the necessary 38 States of the Union.

11 Women's liberationists operate as Typhoid Marys carrying a germ called lost identity. They try to persuade wives that they have missed something in life because they are known by their husband's name and play second fiddle to his career ... As a homewrecker, women's liberation is far in the lead over 'the other man', 'the other woman', or 'incompatibility'.

Phyllis Schlafly; Rebecca Clutch *Women of the New Right* (1987). 'Typhoid Mary' was an Irish-American cook who infected several of the kitchens of the American ruling class in the era of Theodore Roosevelt until placed in an isolation hospital in New York harbour.

12 My working relationship became even more strained when Judge Thomas began to use work situations to discuss sex ... His conversations were very vivid. [In late 1982] I began to feel severe stress on the job. I began to be concerned that Clarence Thomas might take out his anger with me by degrading me or not giving me important assignments. I also thought that he might find an excuse for dismissing me.

Anita Hill, 1991; Norton and Alexander (1996 edn) pp.499, 500, 501. Hill was testifying to the Senate Judiciary Committee on the nomination of Thomas as a Justice of the US Supreme Court. Her testimony did not deny him the appointment. Thomas was confirmed in the Senate by 52 votes to 48.

1 I think it's about time we voted for senators with breasts. After all, we've been voting for boobs long enough.

Claire Sargent, senatorial candidate, *Newsweek*, 5 Oct. 1992.

DALLAS, 22 NOVEMBER 1963

2 Higher Authority [President Kennedy] asked how soon we could get into action with the external sabotage program.

Memorandum of meeting on 19 June 1963, held to discuss covert action by the United States against Cuba; Mark J. White (ed.) *The Kennedys and Cuba* (1999) p.331. It has been suggested that this programme prompted Cuban counter-action against Kennedy through the medium of Lee Harvey Oswald, the alleged lone assassin.

3 Dallas is a very dangerous place. I wouldn't go there. Don't you go.

Senator William Fulbright to President Kennedy, 3 Oct. 1963; Gus Russo *Live by the Sword* (1998) p.273. Ambassador Adlai Stevenson was assaulted in Dallas during a visit there on 24 Oct.

4 We're nothing but sitting ducks in a shooting gallery.

Jacqueline Kennedy to a member of the Secret Service, 22 Nov. 1963; C. David Heymann *A Woman Named Jackie* (1989) p.256.

5 Jackie, if somebody wants to shoot me from a window with a rifle, nobody can stop it, so why worry about it?

President John F. Kennedy to his wife, 8 a.m., 22 Nov. 1963; Edward Klein *All Too Human* (1996) p.343.

6 You sure can't say Dallas doesn't love you, Mr. President.

Nellie Connally, wife of the governor of Texas, John Connally, seconds before the assassination; Russo (1998) p.293.

7 What I saw made my blood run cold. Poised in the corner window of the sixth floor was the same young man I had noticed several times before the motor-cade arrived. There was one difference – this time he held a rifle in his hands, pointing towards the presidential car.

Howard Brennan, witness to the shooting, looking up to the windows of the Texas Book Depository, where Oswald sat waiting; *Eyewitness to History* (1987).

8 You killed my President, you son of a bitch!

Jack Ruby as he shot Oswald dead, 24 Nov. 1963; John Kaplan and Jon Waltz *The Trial of Jack Ruby* (1966) p.150.

9 I personally believe Oswald was the assassin … As to whether he was the only man gives me great concern; we have several letters … written to him from Cuba referring to the job he was going to do, his good marksmanship, and stating when it was all over, he would be brought back to Cuba and presented to the chief. We do not know if the chief was Castro.

J. Edgar Hoover, director of the FBI, 12 Dec. 1963; *Associated Press*, 8 Dec. 1977.

10 It's incredible! … They have a man that was … instructed by the CIA and the Attorney General [Robert Kennedy] to assassinate Castro after the Bay of Pigs … so he [Castro] tortured [them] and they told him all about it. [Castro] called Oswald and a group in and told them … Go … get the job done.

President Lyndon Johnson, telephone call to the attorney-general, Ramsey Clark, 1967; Russo (1998) p.395.

11 You can imagine what the reaction of the country would have been if this information [about Cuban involvement] came out. I was afraid of war.

President Johnson to the columnist Drew Pearson, *Washington Post*, 14 Nov. 1993.

12 I never believed that Oswald acted alone.

Lyndon Johnson, 1969; *Atlantic Monthly*, July 1973.

WATERGATE

13 You open that scab there's a hell of a lot of things and we just feel that it would be very detrimental to have this thing go any further … Play it rough. That's the way they play it and that's the way we are going to play it.

President Richard Nixon to his White House chief of staff, H.R. Haldeman, 23 June 1972; *Watergate and the White House* Vol.3 (1974) p.229. The famous 'smoking gun', the revelation that Nixon had from the outset directed a cover-up of the break-in at the Democratic National Committee HQ in the Watergate apartment building in Washington, D.C., on 17 June.

1 Katie Graham is gonna get her tit caught in a big fat wringer.

John Mitchell, US attorney-general, to Carl Bernstein of the *Washington Post*, 29 Sept. 1972; Harold Evans *The American Century* (1998) p.576. Katharine Graham was publisher of the *Washington Post*, which exposed the Watergate break-in.

2 I think we ought to let him hang there, let him twist slowly, slowly in the wind.

John Ehrlichman, telephone conversation with John Dean, 7 March 1973; Fred Emery *Watergate* (1994) p.247. Ehrlichman was Nixon's domestic policy adviser, Dean the president's counsel. The subject was the acting director of the FBI, L. Patrick Gray, then facing hearings on the confirmation of his appointment, stalled because Gray did not provide answers to senators' questions about Watergate.

3 We have a cancer within, close to the presidency, that is growing. It is growing daily.

John Dean, in conversation with President Nixon, 21 March 1973; White House tape.

4 I don't give a shit what happens. I want you all to stonewall, let them plead the Fifth Amendment, cover up or anything else, if it'll save it, save the plan. That's the whole point.

President Nixon, in conversation with John Dean, 22 March 1973; Emery (1994) p.278. A beleaguered president fulminates in private, not all his expletives deleted.

5 There can be no whitewash at the White House.

President Nixon, 30 April 1973; *Public Papers 1973* (1975) p.332. A televised broadcast to the nation after Nixon had sacrificed Ehrlichman and his chief of staff, Haldeman, in a bid to distance himself from the scandal.

6 The central question is simply put: What did the President know and when did he know it?

Senator Howard Baker, 25 June 1973; Emery (1994) p.363. Although a Republican, Baker was not one of those who believed 'My President, right or wrong'.

7 I made my mistakes, but in all my years of public life, I have never, *never* profited from public service … I welcome this kind of examination because people have got to know whether or not their president is a crook. Well, I'm not a crook.

President Nixon, press conference at Disney World, *New York Times*, 12 Nov. 1973.

8 I have never been a quitter. To leave office before my term is completed is abhorrent to every instinct in my body.

President Nixon, 8 Aug. 1974, announcing his resignation in a national televised broadcast.

9 The country needs good farmers, good businessmen, good plumbers, good carpenters.

President Nixon, 9 Aug. 1974, on leaving the White House after resigning the presidency; *Public Papers 1974* (1975) p.631. A Freudian slip by the ex-president? 'The Plumbers' was the sobriquet given to the men who burgled the offices of the Democratic National Committee in the Watergate complex in June 1972 and triggered the scandal that brought Nixon down.

10 Our long national nightmare is over. Our Constitution works.

President Gerald Ford, *New York Times*, 10 Aug. 1974.

11 I brought myself down. I gave them a sword. And they stuck it in, and they twisted it with relish. And I guess if I had been in their position, I'd have done the same thing.

Richard Nixon, television interview with David Frost, 4 May 1977. Nixon was doomed when the Supreme Court ordered him to release all the tapes of his secret White House conversations on 24 July 1974. He had given out a carefully edited selection on 30 April, omitting the worst details of his involvement.

BEYOND THE NEW DEAL: ONE STEP FORWARD, TWO STEPS BACK

12 It made a pang go through me to realize what a difference it made that *he could walk* and move about, and how little of the magnificence that President Roosevelt had he has. Not even in the President's office. To succeed a man who had acquired such an aura is a tough break for anyone.

David Lilienthal, on Roosevelt's apparently insignificant successor, Harry S Truman, late April 1945; *The Journals of David E. Lilienthal* Vol.1 (1964) p.697. Lilienthal was chairman of the Tennessee Valley Authority. Roosevelt could not walk because he was paralysed from the waist down by poliomyelitis.

13 The objectives for our domestic economy which we seek in our long-range plans were summarized by the late President Franklin D. Roosevelt over a year and a half ago in the form of an economic bill of rights. Let us make the attainment of those rights the essence of postwar American economic life.

President Harry S Truman, 6 Sept. 1945; *Public Papers 1945* (1961) p.279. Truman proclaims his determination to complete his predecessor's unfinished work.

14 No professional liberal is intellectually honest. That's a real indictment – but true as the Ten Commandments. Professional liberals aren't familiar with the Ten Commandments or the Sermon on the Mount.

President Harry S Truman, 1948; Margaret Truman *Harry S. Truman* (1973) p.8. At heart, Truman was a Midwestern populist with an inveterate mistrust of East Coast liberals.

1 I never did give anybody hell. I just told the truth, and they thought it was hell.

President Harry S Truman, 1948. Truman became known as 'Give 'Em Hell Harry' during his barn-storming, whistle-stop tour in the 1948 election campaign.

2 You can't make a soufflé rise twice.

Alice Roosevelt Longworth on the defeat of Republican candidate, Thomas E. Dewey, in the 1948 election. Dewey was a two-time loser, having already gone down to Franklin Roosevelt in 1944. Mrs Longworth was the daughter of President Theodore Roosevelt and a personality with an acid tongue.

3 DEWEY BEATS TRUMAN

Chicago Daily Tribune, 3 Nov. 1948. Truman was widely expected to lose the 1948 election to Dewey, but won a surprising victory. The margin was the narrowest since 1916, when the Republican Charles Evans Hughes just failed to defeat President Woodrow Wilson (and went to bed on election night confident of the presidency).

4 Where Roosevelt consciously intended his measures to alter the pattern of American society, Truman does not really want to change anything at all.

Joseph and Stewart Alsop *Saturday Evening Post*, 31 Dec. 1949. A harsh verdict on a president who was hugely preoccupied with the Cold War and marking an abiding distaste for his political style.

5 We are following not in the footsteps of Russia, but in the footsteps of England. We are being drawn into socialism on the British gradualist model. We are well on the road – much further along than our people suspect.

John T. Flynn *The Road Ahead* (1949) p.10. Truman's creeping Fabianism as seen by an ultra-right-wing commentator.

6 I am completely satisfied that General Eisenhower will give the country an Administration inspired by the Republican principles of continued and expanding liberty for all as against the continued growth of New Deal socialism.

Senator Robert Alonzo Taft, 1952; William S. White *The Taft Story* (1954) pp.189–91. Taft, an unreconstructed Republican, lost the 1952 presidential nomination to General Eisenhower, but secured a pledge that Eisenhower would follow a strictly conservative line.

7 For years I thought what was good for our country was good for General Motors, and vice versa.

Charles E. Wilson, former president of General Motors, 15 Jan. 1953, in nomination hearings as Eisenhower's secretary of defense; Robert Donovan *Eisenhower* (1956) p.25.

8 I believe that for the past twenty years there has been a creeping socialism spreading in the United States.

President Eisenhower, 11 June 1953; Donovan (1956) p.335.

9 [The Democrat victories] were all achieved under a doctrine of 'spend and spend, and elect and elect'. It seemed to me that this had to be stopped … We were coming to the point where we looked toward a paternalistic state to guide our steps from cradle to grave.

President Eisenhower, 28 Nov. 1959; Robert Ferrell (ed.) *The Eisenhower Diaries* (1981) p.374. In fact, Eisenhower did little to dismantle the Federal apparatus constructed to restabilize the American economy, and his brand of Republicanism was relatively willing to accommodate to the New Deal achievement.

10 In a community where public services have failed to keep abreast of private consumption things are very different. Here, in an atmosphere of private opulence and public squalor, the private goods have full sway.

John K. Galbraith *The Affluent Society* (1958) Ch.18. A famous characterization of the America of the 1950s.

11 We stand today on the edge of a new frontier – the frontier of the 1960s – a frontier of unknown opportunities and perils – a frontier of unfulfilled hopes and threats.

John F. Kennedy, accepting the Democratic party's nomination as presidential candidate, *New York Times*, 16 July 1960.

12 He is a different type of liberal from any we have known. He is in love not with lost causes, not with passionate evocations, not with insuperable difficulties; he is in love with political effectiveness.

James MacGregor Burns, *New Republic*, 31 Oct. 1960. During his brief time in power, however, Kennedy did not prove to be especially effective in getting much of his legislation through Congress.

13 [The] conjunction of an immense military establishment and a large arms industry is new in the American experience … We recognize the imperative need for this development. Yet we must not fail to comprehend its grave implications … In the councils of government, we must guard against the acquisition of unwarranted influence, whether sought or unsought, by the military–industrial complex. The potential for the disastrous rise of misplaced power exists and will persist.

President Dwight D. Eisenhower, farewell address, 17 Jan. 1961; *Public Papers 1960–1961* (1961) pp.657–8. An extraordinary pronouncement coming from a general of the army, but a sombre indication of the shadow thrown by the Cold War over the American democratic system.

1 Let the word go forth from this time and place, to friend and foe alike, that the torch has been passed to a new generation of Americans.

President John F. Kennedy, 20 Jan. 1961, inaugural address; see *Public Papers 1961* (1962) pp.1–3 for full text.

2 He no longer collects from his patients for his services, he submits his bills (in triplicate or quadruplicate) to the government for payment. And the government, because it must inevitably control what it subsidizes, will eventually tell him how to practise, how many patients he can see, how much money he can make – and in effect dictate what his home life shall be.

E.V. Askey, president of the American Medical Association, 'If your husband's practice were socialized' in *The Doctor's Wife* (March-April 1961) p.20. Representative of the abiding conservatism in the United States, which Kennedy had vowed to reverse.

3 Just think how much you're going to be missing. You won't have Dick Nixon to kick around anymore.

Richard Nixon, *New York Times*, 3 Nov. 1962. Nixon had just been defeated in the California gubernatorial election and seemed to have no political future.

4 If you looked at my record, you would know that I am a Roosevelt New Dealer. As a matter of fact, to tell the truth, John F. Kennedy was a little too conservative to suit my taste.

President Lyndon Johnson, 23 Nov. 1963; William E. Leuchtenburg *In the Shadow of FDR* (1993 edn) p.137. A surprising comment on Kennedy just 24 hours after his death, though it was certainly true that Johnson aimed to augment the New Deal.

5 Now Washington, the god-like, and Lincoln, the saintly, have been joined by Kennedy, the Young Chevalier. Historians may protest, logicians may rave, but they cannot alter the fact that any kind of man, once touched by romance, is removed from

all categories and is comparable only with the legendary.

Gerald W. Johnson, *New Republic*, 7 Dec. 1963. The Camelot myth of a knight in shining armour, struck down before his time.

6 That his most admirable qualities were not invested in his handling either of politics or power hardly occurs to those admirable elegists who now bemoan the death of a hero.

Alistair Cooke on Kennedy, *Esquire* magazine, 1964; Nick Clarke *Alistair Cooke* (1999) p.371.

7 We have never lost sight of our goal – an America in which every citizen shares all the opportunities of his society, in which every man has a chance to advance his welfare to the limit of his capacities. We have come a long way toward this goal. We still have a long way to go. The distance which remains is the measure of the great unfinished work of our society. To finish that work I have called for a national war on poverty … Today we are asked to declare war on a domestic enemy which threatens the strength of our nation and the welfare of our people.

President Lyndon Johnson, 16 March 1964; *Public Papers 1963–64* Vol.1 (1965) pp.376, 380. Within months, Johnson's war on the home front was to be eclipsed by his war in Vietnam.

8 The Great Society rests on abundance and liberty for all. It demands an end to poverty and racial injustice. It is a place where the city of man serves not only the needs of the body and the demands of commerce but the desire for beauty and the hunger for community.

President Lyndon Johnson, 22 May 1964; *Public Papers 1963–64* Vol.1 (1965) p.704. Johnson, a Roosevelt protégé, looked to consummate the New Deal.

9 I would remind you that extremism in the defense of liberty is no vice. And let me remind you also that moderation in the pursuit of justice is no virtue.

Senator Barry Goldwater, 16 July 1964; Theodore H. White (1965) p.217. Goldwater stood for deeply conservative Republicanism in the 1964 election. This celebrated quotation is from his acceptance speech at the Republican National Convention.

10 In your heart you know he's right.

Goldwater slogan in the 1964 election. An appeal to the subliminal preferences of the average voter. In the 1976 election, when Jimmy Carter confessed in *Playboy* magazine to having lustful thoughts about other women, this was adroitly transposed into: 'In his heart he knows your wife.'

1 The breakthroughs of the Eighty-ninth Congress – in education, in medical care, in civil rights, in housing – exceeded the New Deal achievements in their impact on American society.

Lawrence O'Brien *No Final Victories* (1974) p.195. A partisan verdict from a zealous Democrat on the legislation of 1965–6 which in retrospect appears as the last big liberal achievement in 20th-century America.

2 We have a responsibility to the victims of crime and violence … It is a responsibility to put away childish things – to make the possession and use of firearms a matter undertaken only by serious people who will use them with the restraint and maturity that their dangerous nature deserves – and demands.

Robert F. Kennedy, 11 July 1967; National Commission on the Causes and Prevention of Violence *Firearms and Violence in American Life* (1970) p.v. Kennedy was shot and mortally wounded on 5 June 1968 while campaigning for the presidency.

3 One of those goals was summed up in a theme we developed during the campaign: to break the pattern of the century's middle third at the start of its final third.

Raymond Price *With Nixon* (1977) p.45. On the Republican strategy in the 1968 election to make a decisive break with New Deal liberalism, dominant since 1933.

4 A new Establishment – the media, universities, conglomerate corporations, research and development corporations – has achieved much of the power of the industrial and financial establishment dethroned politically by the New Deal. This new Establishment thrives on a government vastly more powerful than that deplored by the business titans of the Nineteen-Thirties.

Kevin Phillips *The Emerging Republican Majority* (1969) p.37. Nixon's Republicans saw their task as the dethronement of that liberal establishment, much as Margaret Thatcher was determined to overturn the post-war consensus in Britain a decade later.

5 That's one small step for a man, one giant leap for mankind.

Neil Armstrong, 20 July 1969. Spoken as he became the first man to set foot on the moon. The word 'a' was lost in transmission, ruining the pointed antithesis. Not everyone saw the achievement like this, notably the black Florida doctor, Henry Jenkins, who's priority was to 'treat malnourished children with prominent ribs and pot bellies.'

6 In the United States today, we have more than our share of the nattering nabobs of negativism.

Vice-President Spiro T. Agnew, 11 Sept. 1970. Agnew was Nixon's running-mate (known irreverently as 'Zorba the Veep') until his enforced resignation on 10 Oct. 1973 after pleading guilty to charges of tax evasion.

7 Let each of us ask – not just what government can do for me but what can I do for myself?

President Richard Nixon, 20 Jan. 1973; *Public Papers 1973* (1975) p.14. A direct rebuttal of Kennedy's inaugural injunction: 'Ask not what your country can do for you. Ask what you can do for your country.' Samuel Smiles would have been proud of Nixon.

8 This administration is not sympathetic to corporations; it is indentured to corporations.

Ralph Nader, on the Nixon government, *Washington Post*, 4 Oct. 1972. In 1965 the radical Nader had written a devastating exposé of the US automobile industry; in 2000 he stood as a third-party candidate in the presidential election.

9 He promised only to manage our affairs sensibly and with a degree of charity. We in turn responded, and so elected the country's first national city manager.

Washington Post, 24 Dec. 1978, on Carter's first two uninspiring years.

10 Government cannot solve our problems. It cannot define our vision. Government cannot eliminate poverty, or provide a bountiful economy, or reduce inflation, or save our cities, or cure illiteracy, or provide energy.

President Jimmy Carter, 1980. A Democrat in retreat from the traditional prescriptions of liberalism, his words quoted by a disgusted son of the New Deal, Arthur Schlesinger Jr, in *New Republic*, 12 April 1980.

11 Jimmy Carter will never escape the verdict of being the first Democratic president to violate the spirit and substance of New Deal liberalism.

Frank Annunziata, *USA Today*, Nov. 1980.

12 No, *no!* *Jimmy Stewart* for Governor – Reagan for best friend.

Hollywood studio boss, Jack Warner, attrib.; Max Wilk *The Wit and Wisdom of Hollywood* (1972). Supposedly said when he heard that Reagan was planning to enter the campaign for the governorship of California (which he won).

13 Government is like a big baby – an alimentary canal with a big appetite at one end and no responsibility at the other.

The future president Ronald Reagan, when running for governor in California, 1966.

1 With our eyes fixed on the future, but recognizing the realities of today ... we will achieve our destiny to be as a shining city on a hill for all mankind to see.

Ronald Reagan, 17 March 1978. Reagan quotes from John Winthrop, first governor of Massachusetts Bay Colony, who sailed to America in March 1630. In his *A Model of Christian Charity* (1630) Winthrop wrote: 'We must consider that we shall be as a City upon a hill. The eyes of all people are upon us.' See 432:3.

2 Reagan's arrival in Washington coincided with the arrival of the insight we now know as supply-side economics. He believed that the encumbrances on government were the cause of the sclerosis of the 1970s.

The conservative commentator William Buckley, 16 May 1989; Lou Cannon *President Reagan: The Role of a Lifetime* (1991) p.90. Supply-side economics, relying on tax reduction as a stimulus to investment, was the reverse of the so-called 'tax and spend' philosophy of Democratic administrations since the New Deal.

3 Honey, I forgot to duck.

President Reagan to his wife Nancy, 30 March 1981; Evans (1998) p.627. Reagan was shot as he left an hotel in Washington, D.C. He was quoting the words of the boxer Jack Dempsey after he lost his heavyweight title to Gene Tunney on 23 Sept. 1926.

4 An amiable dunce.

Clark Clifford, *Wall Street Journal*, 8 Oct. 1981. The verdict of a lifelong Democrat on Ronald Reagan. Reagan was somewhat less than both, in fact.

5 History buffs probably noted the reunion at a Washington party a few weeks ago of three ex-presidents, Carter, Ford and Nixon: See No Evil, Hear No Evil and Evil.

Senator Robert Dole, 26 March 1983.

6 I was cooking breakfast this morning for my kids, and I thought, 'He's just like a Teflon frying pan. Nothing sticks to him.'

Michael Kenney, *Boston Globe*, 24 Oct. 1984. Whatever his defects as a head of government (and there were plenty), Reagan came out unscathed.

7 For seven years he has lived in the White House and run the country like some kind of cheap imitation of an old John Wayne movie.

Hunter S. Thompson, late 1987; *Generation of Swine* (1988) p.299.

8 Greed is all right. Greed is healthy. You can be greedy and still feel good about yourself.

Ivan Boesky, commencement address, School of Business Administration, University of California, Berkeley, 18 May 1986. Boesky, a Wall Street arbitrageur and an epitome of the 1980s, was jailed for large-scale fraud.

9 The free enterprise system is clearly outlined in the Book of Proverbs in the Bible. Jesus Christ made it clear that the work ethic was a part of His plan for man. Ownership of property is biblical. Competition in business is biblical. Ambitious and successful business management is clearly outlined as a part of God's plan for His people.

Rev. Jerry Falwell *Listen, America* (1981) p.12. President Reagan was close to religious fundamentalists such as Falwell, whose Moral Majority harked back passionately to the 1920s cult of business activity (see 764:5).

10 The masquerade is over, it's time to ... use the dreaded L-word; to say the policies of our opposition ... are liberal, liberal, liberal.

Ronald Reagan, *New York Times*, 16 Aug. 1988. Liberalism replaces socialism and communism as one of the dirtiest words in the American political vocabulary.

11 Much happened in the way of silent rot as we mortgaged much of our future vitality.

The columnist George F. Will, *Newsweek*, 9 Jan. 1989. Not the onslaught of a political opponent but the sad conclusion of a political friend at the end of Reagan's incumbency. Will refers to the astronomical increase of the US national debt and its trade and budget deficits. The last of these was brought about by the decision to forego government revenue by cutting taxes, while at the same time retaining most Federal welfare programmes and massively increasing defence expenditure.

12 Americans are conservative. What they want to conserve is the New Deal.

George F. Will; Cannon (1991) p.21. A political truth recognized by Reagan, who, in spite of his rhetoric, did little to touch the welfare spending that had been inaugurated by Roosevelt in 1933.

13 The Congress will push me to raise taxes and I'll say no, and they'll push, and I'll say no, and they'll push me again. And I'll say to them: 'Read my lips: no new taxes.'

George Bush, 19 Aug. 1988; Herbert S. Parmet *George Bush* (2001 edn) p.348. From his acceptance speech as Republican presidential candidate.

14 I will keep America moving forward ... for a better America, for an endless enduring dream and a thousand points of light.

George Bush, 19 Aug. 1988; Parmet (2001 edn) p.348.

1 There are some striking similarities between the two Republican presidents, Herbert Hoover and George Bush, and their times. The two periods of widest income differential between the rich and the middle class were then and now … The obscene, multi-million-dollar salaries taken today by executives of even poorly performing companies have never been more lightly taxed, except in the Hoover years.

Brandt Ayers, *Anniston Star*, 25 Oct. 1992; Leuchtenburg (1993) p.269.

2 It's the economy, stupid!

James Carville, 1992; *American Heritage Dictionary of American Quotations* (1997) p.389. Carville was campaign manager to Bill Clinton in the 1992 election, where the key to victory was the country's economic performance. Clinton was extremely lucky in that while he could blame the sluggish rate of growth on his opponent, George Bush, throughout most of his time in the White House, from 1993 to 2001, he could claim credit for the revival that came soon after his first inauguration.

3 A joyous, optimistic practitioner of the art of politics and an assiduous student of public policy; a man with a lifelong fondness for power and a clear understanding of how to get it, a warm and passionate man, with an intelligent, patient and forgiving wife, a man who is capable of both courage and infidelity.

Brandt Ayers on Bill Clinton; Leuchtenburg (1993) p.263. An interesting assessment, especially if read between the lines. Clinton had many of the attributes that could have made him an outstanding president, but they were cancelled out by his cavalier abuse of his office.

4 The bottom line is we don't like Clinton. He steals our money, he steals our guns, and sends Americans overseas to die.

Grover Norquist, mid-1990s; James D. Retter *Anatomy of a Scandal* (1998). This right-wing activist detested Clinton for failing to bring in further tax cuts, for supporting gun control and for allowing American forces to be used in peace-keeping operations in such trouble spots as Somalia and the former Yugoslavia. He was particularly incensed by Clinton's attempt in 1993 to reform US health-care provision, a bid spearheaded by Clinton's wife, Hillary, but stopped in its tracks the following year by conservative opposition in Congress.

5 I want to say one thing to the American people. I want you to listen to me … I did not have sexual relations with that woman, Miss Lewinsky: I never told anybody to lie, not a single time, never. These allegations are false.

President Bill Clinton, 21 Jan. 1998; *Keesing's Record of World Events*, Jan. 1998, p.41996. Clinton's sexual encounters with the White House intern Monica Lewinsky led him into perjury and obstruction of justice, crimes for which he was impeached by the House of Representatives and put on trial by the Senate. This denial itself was a lie, and Clinton hung on stubbornly for months in a refusal to state the truth.

6 I did have a relationship with Ms Lewinsky that was not appropriate. In fact it was wrong. It constitutes a critical lapse in judgment and a personal failure on my part for which I am solely and completely responsible.

President Clinton, 17 Aug. 1998; *Keesing's Record of World Events*, Aug. 1998, p.42433. Clinton was eventually acquitted by the Senate on 12 Feb. 1999, but the Lewinsky affair cast a baleful shadow over his second term.

7 And to the C students, I say you, too, can be President of the United States.

President George W. Bush, commencement address at Yale University, 21 May 2001. Bush took a third-class degree at Yale. His words of encouragement to the academic also-rans of his alma mater reportedly met with a stony silence.

8 A dictatorship would be a heck of a lot easier, there's no question about it.

President George W. Bush, 27 July 2001. Anguished words from a Republican president whose party had recently lost control of the Senate thanks to one of their own crossing the floor and joining the Democrats. Bush's difficulties with Congress were soon to be removed by his dizzying elevation in stature after the catastrophe of 9/11 (see 941:9). Come the mid-term elections of 2002, Bush's frustration over the requirements of democracy fell away when the Republicans regained their majority.

9 You know, I had a drinking problem. Right now I should be in a bar in Texas, not the Oval Office. There is only one reason why I am in the Oval Office and not in a bar. I found faith. I found God. I am here because of the power of prayer.

President George W. Bush to an assemblage of religious leaders, Christian, Jewish and Muslim, Sept. 2002; David Frum *The Right Man* (2003) p.283. The one-time alcoholic, now born again, ascribes his installation in the White House to a higher authority than the US Supreme Court or his brother, the governor of Florida (see 901:11). Frum was one of Bush's speech-writers.

10 I think the American people – I hope the American – I don't think, let me – I hope the American people trust me.

President George W. Bush, 18 Dec. 2002. Bush was legendary for his inarticulateness, but this was no political handicap in the United States at the dawn of the 21st century.

Britain since 1945

LABOUR REVOLUTION, 1945–51

1 By noon it was clear the Socialists would have a majority. At luncheon, my wife said to me, 'It may well be a blessing in disguise.' I replied, 'At the moment it seems quite effectively disguised.'
Winston Churchill on the Labour landslide in the 1945 general election; *The Second World War* Vol.6 (1954) p.583.

2 It seems ... that there are three essential conditions without which we have not a hope of escaping what might be described, without exaggeration and without implying that we should not eventually recover from it, as a financial Dunkirk. These conditions are (a) an intense concentration on the expansion of exports, (b) drastic and immediate economies in our overseas expenditure, and (c) substantial aid from the United States on terms which we can expect. They can only be fulfilled by a combination of the greatest enterprise, ruthlessness and tact.
The economist John Maynard Keynes, 13 Aug. 1945; *The Collected Writings of John Maynard Keynes* Vol.24 (1979) p.410. Keynes sets out the grim economic backdrop for a government elected to bring in a wide array of reforms, including the maintenance of full employment, wholesale nationalization of public utilities and the setting up of a comprehensive health service. Since Lend–Lease from the USA was terminated at precisely this moment, Britain was to depend on a huge loan from the United States, negotiated with difficulty and loaded with several unfavourable conditions.

3 We are the masters at the moment – and, not only for the moment, but for a very long time to come.
Sir Hartley Shawcross, attorney-general in the post-war Labour government, 2 April 1946; *H.C. Deb.* Vol.421, Col.1213. Shawcross made this triumphalist comment in the debate on the third reading of the Trade Disputes and Trade Unions Bill, which rescinded the anti-union legislation consequent on the General Strike of 1926 (see 775:7–777:2). It underlines the often bitter nature of political discourse following the election of Attlee's radical government and is usually misquoted as 'we are the masters now'.

4 We know that the organized workers of this country are our friends. As for the rest, they don't matter a tinker's cuss.
Emanuel Shinwell, minister of fuel and power, speaking to the Electrical Trades Union conference at Margate, 7 May 1947; *Conflict Without Malice: An Autobiography* (1955) p.185. Shinwell was chairman of the committee that drafted the manifesto *Let Us Face the Future* on which the party won its massive victory

in 1945. He had begun his political life as one of 'the wild men of Clydeside', and this comment reflects the dedication to working-class interests that had so far been the hallmark of his politics.

5 The French called the occupying Germans 'the grey lice'. That is precisely how I regard the occupying army of English socialist governments.
Evelyn Waugh, diary entry, 23 Nov. 1946; Michael Davie (ed.) *The Diaries of Evelyn Waugh* (1978) p.663. Waugh, novelist, Roman Catholic and high Tory, voices the shock and loathing felt by many Conservatives for Attlee's administration.

6 That is why no amount of cajolery can eradicate from my heart a deep burning hatred for the Tory Party that inflicted these experiences on me. So far as I am concerned they are lower than vermin.
Aneurin Bevan, minister for health in Attlee's government, speaking at a Labour Party rally, Belle Vue, Manchester, 5 July 1948 (the day the National Health Service was launched); Michael Foot *Aneurin Bevan: A Biography* Vol.2 (1973) p.238. *The Times* fastened on the term 'vermin', and a storm ensued, with retired colonels and others forming 'vermin clubs'. Addressing a meeting in Leicester in 1950, Attlee was met with upper-class cries of 'What about the vermin?' (see Robert Blake *The Conservative Party from Peel to Churchill* (1970) p.263).

7 Conservatives do not believe that political struggle is the most important thing in life ... The simplest among them prefer fox-hunting – the wisest religion.
Quintin Hogg (later Viscount Hailsham) *The Case for Conservatism* (1947) p.10. In the wake of the devastating election defeat in 1945 the Conservatives had to re-evaluate and restate their philosophy. This famous line encapsulates what Hogg saw as a key ideological difference between conservatism and socialism – the role and status of politics. Enoch Powell said something very similar: 'No one is forced to be a politician. It can only compare with fox-hunting and writing poetry. These are two things that men do for sheer enjoyment too' (attrib., 1973).

8 It would have been impossible for the Conservative Party, after its defeat in 1945, to reform and reorganize itself if it had contemptuously said that the electors had chosen wrongly. Instead, we started from the assumption that it was we, the Conservative Party, who were at fault and not the people of this country.
Iain Macleod MP, speaking of the party's 1945 policy review at the annual conference, 1962; I.R. Ramsden 'From Churchill to Heath' in R. Butler (ed.) *The Conservatives: A History from their*

Origins to 1965 (1977) p.425. The policy review laid the foundations for the eventual Conservative recovery after the traumatic election defeat in 1945 and their acceptance of the 'post-war consensus'. Major changes of policy with respect to public ownership, the welfare state and Keynesian demand management were promoted, just short of precipitating party splits. The parallels with the Conservatives' position post-1997 are obvious, although the latter has the additional complication of 'Europe'.

1 I stuffed their mouths with gold.

Aneurin Bevan, minister for health in the post-war Labour government; Brian Abel-Smith *The Hospitals 1800–1948* (1964) p.480. Bevan is referring to his method for getting hospital consultants 'on side' over his proposals to nationalize this branch of the service. They were to be paid handsomely for their NHS work, as well as retaining the right to private practice.

2 I know now that the right kind of leader is a desiccated calculating machine who must not allow himself in any way to be swayed by emotion. If he sees injustice and suffering he must not let it move him.

Aneurin Bevan, speaking at the Labour Party conference, 1954; Kenneth Harris *Attlee* (1982) p.522. The quote is often taken as referring to the shadow chancellor, Hugh Gaitskell, but Bevan had Attlee in his sights. The previous day, a Bevanite amendment opposing German rearmament had been narrowly defeated. Attlee had told the conference that 'foreign affairs lend themselves to emotionalism, which is a bad guide in foreign affairs'. Bevan, the passionate socialist and rebel, is mocking Attlee's clinical approach to the subject.

3 Unless the right honourable gentleman changes his policy and methods and moves without the slightest delay, he will be as great a curse to this country in peace as he was a squalid nuisance in time of war.

Winston Churchill, leader of the Conservative Opposition, 6 Dec. 1945; *H.C. Deb.* Vol.416, Col.2544. Churchill is referring to Bevan, who in 1942 had supported a motion of censure on his government after the fall of Tobruk (see 851:6).

4 A sheep in sheep's clothing.

Winston Churchill, referring to Clement Attlee; Alec Douglas-Home (Lord Home of the Hirsel) *The Way the Wind Blows* (1976) p.98. Attlee was an enigma to many, a self-effacing man who nevertheless came to dominate the Labour Party. Opponents, like Churchill, chose to emphasize the apparently colourless aspects of his character.

5 He is a modest little man with much to be modest about.

Another of Winston Churchill's assessments of Attlee, then leader of the Labour Opposition; reported in the *Chicago Herald Tribune* 'Magazine of Books', 27 June 1954.

6 An empty taxi arrived at 10 Downing Street, and when the door was opened, Attlee got out.

Another comment on Attlee's apparent lack of personality; A. Wilson *The Wrong Set* (1949) p.89. This jibe is often incorrectly attributed to Churchill (who repudiated it), but it first appeared in Wilson's book.

7 If you feed a grub on royal jelly, it may turn into a queen bee.

Winston Churchill offers his own explanation of Attlee's success, despite his apparent diffidence and self-effacement; T. Burridge *Clement Attlee* (1985) p.3. Attlee undoubtedly grew in stature as prime minister.

8   Few thought he was ever a starter –
      There were many who thought themselves
         smarter –
      But he ended PM,
      CH and OM,
      An Earl and a Knight of the Garter.

Clement Attlee on himself, 1956; Harris (1982) p.545. PM stands for prime minister, CH for Companion of Honour, and OM for Order of Merit. Retiring prime ministers traditionally had an earldom conferred on them. The Order of the Garter is the highest order of chivalry in Britain.

CONSERVATIVISM PARAMOUNT, 1951–64

9 We are seeking to build a lighthouse rather than dress a shop window.

Winston Churchill, leader of the Conservative Opposition, in the run-up to the 1951 general election; Paul Addison *Churchill on the Home Front: 1900–1955* (1992) p.405. The comment embodies Churchill's Tory belief that policy springs from the exercise of power in circumstances that cannot be predicted; broad statements of principle with minimum detail are what should be offered to the electorate. The imagery also appears in the Conservatives' policy document, *Leadership with a Purpose: A Better Society*, launched at the annual conference in Oct. 2002, which reads: 'We will act in opposition as a lighthouse, rather than a shop window. One year into our policy renewal programme, this document shows clearly the direction of the lighthouse's beam, trusting people, not politicians' (*The Times*, 11 Oct. 2002).

10 I said that, when I first went to Bishop Auckland in 1928, and met leading members of the party, they were nearly all unemployed miners, shabby and hungry. Last month they were in evening dress (not optional), yes, including some miners, at civic dinner of Labour-controlled Council.

Hugh Dalton, diary entry, 24 March 1955; Ben Pimlott (ed.) *The Political Diary of Hugh Dalton 1945–60* (1986) pp.620–21. Dalton, who was one-time chancellor in Attlee's post-war administration, reflects on the changes noted on a visit to Bishop Auckland, which in the 1920s and 1930s was mired in economic and social distress. The entry pinpoints the embourgeoisement of the working class in one of Labour's heartland areas, Co. Durham, something that was beginning to cost Labour dear. Two subsequent electoral defeats were to promote Labour revisionism, just as the Conservatives had had to move on to the centre ground after 1945.

1 Waiting for the Smack of Firm Government.

Heading of a *Sunday Telegraph* editorial written by Donald McLachlan, 3 Jan. 1956. McLachlan was taking the prime minister, Anthony Eden, to task for alleged timidity and indecisiveness. He observed that: 'There is a favourite gesture of the Prime Minister which is sometimes recalled to illustrate this sense of disappointment. To emphasize a point, he will clench one fist to smack the open palm of the other – but the smack is seldom heard. Most Conservatives, and almost certainly some of the wiser Trade Union leaders, are waiting to feel the smack of firm government' (D. Dutton *Anthony Eden: A Life and Reputation* (1997) p.378).

2 The Establishment.

Henry Fairlie, journalist, *The Spectator*, 23 Sept. 1955. This term has entered the language as a synonym for the network of governing power, both political and social. Fairlie says: 'By the "Establishment", I do not mean only the centres of official power – though they are certainly part of it – but rather the whole matrix of official and social relations within which power is exercised. The exercise of power in Britain (more specifically, in England) cannot be understood unless it is recognized that it is exercised socially.' Hugh Thomas claims to have used the term a year earlier, and it appears in the title of his later edited work, *The Establishment: A Symposium* (1959). Thomas defines it as: 'the English constitution, and the groups of institutions and outlying agencies built round it to assist in its protection; it naturally includes all those who stand around it like commissionaires before these protective institutions to protect them' (Thomas (1959) p.14). Anthony Sampson's *Anatomy of Britain* (1962) was the definitive study of the Establishment in the Macmillan era. The term gave its name (very appropriately) to the satire club, The Establishment, set up by Peter Cook in 1961.

3 Yes.

R.A. Butler speaking of the prime minister, Anthony Eden, Dec. 1955; R. James *Anthony Eden* (1986) p.426. Before departing on holiday from London airport, Butler was asked by a journalist: 'Is Mr Eden the best Prime Minister we have got.' He naturally replied 'Yes' – an apparently feline remark, which was instantly widely reported. Butler later commented: 'I do not think it did Anthony any good. It did not do me any good either.'

4 Anthony's father was a mad baronet and his mother a very beautiful woman. That's Anthony – half mad baronet, half beautiful woman.

R.A. Butler on Anthony Eden; Patrick Cosgrave *R.A. Butler* (1981) p.12.

5 Let us be frank about it: most of our people have never had it so good. Go around the country, go to the industrial towns, go to the farms, and you'll see a state of prosperity such as we have never had in my lifetime – nor indeed ever in the history of this country. What is beginning to worry some of us is 'Is it too good to be true?' or perhaps I should say 'Is it too good to last?'

Prime minister Harold Macmillan, speaking at Bedford, *The Times*, 22 July 1957. The phrase 'you have never had it so good' had been employed by President Truman in the 1948 presidential campaign. In the eyes of political opponents it epitomized what they saw as a selfish appeal to materialism.

6 I thought the best thing to do was to settle up these little local difficulties, and then turn to the wider vision of the Commonwealth.

Prime minister Harold Macmillan, *The Times*, 8 Jan. 1958. Macmillan made this remark before leaving on a tour of the Commonwealth. The 'little local difficulties' referred to the resignations of the chancellor, Peter Thorneycroft, and his two lieutenants in the Treasury, Enoch Powell and Nigel Birch. As Thorneycroft made clear in his letter of resignation, the trio regarded the limitation of public expenditure as 'a prerequisite to the stability of the pound, the stabilization of prices and the prestige and standing of our country in the world', an early statement of classic monetarist doctrine.

7 And all these financiers, all the little gnomes of Zurich and the other financial centres about whom we keep on hearing started to make their dispositions in regard to sterling.

Harold Wilson, principal Opposition spokesman on economic affairs, 12 Nov. 1956; *H.C. Deb.* Vol.560, Col.579. Wilson accuses the Conservative government of economic misman-agement, weakening sterling and encouraging speculation by the bankers of Switzerland.

8 There has been an important transfer from property-incomes to wages since 1939; and the distribution of wealth is now much more egalitarian. Certainly, much remains to be done; but fiscal policies offer a simpler and quicker way of doing it than wholesale collectivization. This does not mean that nationalization may not be justified on other grounds, nor that over the long period it has no influence of any kind on income-distribution, nor that the egalitarian objective to which it was directed has lost its relevance. It simply means that the ownership of the means of production … is no longer the essential determinant of the distribution of incomes; private ownership is compatible with a high degree of equality, while state ownership, as the

Russian experience has demonstrated, may be used to support a high degree of inequality.

Anthony Crosland *The Future of Socialism* (1956) p.89. Crosland's arguments were designed to support Gaitskell's attempts to develop the Labour Party's social democratic tradition and to 'modernize' the party by moving it away from its identification solely with working-class interests. Crosland's work was to be the guiding star of a new generation of modernizing social democrats seeking a response to Conservative electoral dominance. The Conservatives had been in the same position after 1945 when they had been forced to adapt to Labour's post-1945 hegemony.

1 As I have already said, I am against starting on a new election programme now. But I do think we should clear our minds on these fundamental issues and then try to express in the most simple and fundamental fashion what we stand for in the world today. The only official document which embodies such an attempt is the party Constitution, written over forty years ago, It seems to me that this ought to be brought up to date. For instance, can we really be satisfied today with a statement of fundamentals which makes no mention at all of colonial freedom, race relations, disarmament, full employment or planning? The only specific reference to our objectives at home is the well-known phrase: 'To secure for the workers by hand or brain the full fruits of their industry and the most equitable distribution thereof that may be possible, upon the basis of the common ownership of the means of production, distribution and exchange.' Standing on its own, this cannot possibly be regarded as adequate. It lays us open to continual misrepresentation.

Hugh Gaitskell, leader of the Labour Party, speaking at the 1959 party conference a few weeks after Labour's third successive general election defeat; *Report of the Fifty-Eighth Annual Conference of the Labour Party* (1959) pp.107–9. Clause 4 (printed on the back of party membership cards) committed the party, at least formally, to extensive public ownership. Deep suspicion among trade unionists and other rank-and-file members, combined with lack of support on the National Executive Committee (NEC), defeated Gaitskell's proposed innovation. It had to await another modernizing generation facing a similar electoral dilemma. A special conference called by Tony Blair, leader of the Labour Party, dropped Clause 4 in 1995.

2 With background and education you naturally go to the top. I take my hat off to the Conservatives. I recognize them as gentlemen. The Labour Party are only men.

Mark Abrams and Richard Rose (with Rita Hinden) *Must Labour Lose?* (1960) p.88. Evidence for continuing working-class deference among 'natural' Labour supporters.

3 We know what happens to people who stay in the middle of the road. They get run over.

Aneurin Bevan makes a brutal contribution to the debate over Labour's future direction following its defeat in 1951, *Observer*, 9 Dec. 1953.

4 There are some of us, Mr Chairman, who will fight and fight and fight again to save the party we love.

Hugh Gaitskell, Labour Party leader, speaking at the party conference, Oct. 1960; Barbara Castle *Fighting All the Way* (1993) p.325. Defeated in his attempts to remove Clause 4, Gaitskell opened another front in the battle to modernize the party, taking on the Left in a struggle over unilateral nuclear disarmament.

5 Greater love hath no man than this – that he lay down his friends for his life.

Jeremy Thorpe, Liberal MP, commenting on Macmillan's 'Night of the Long Knives' in which seven senior ministers (one-third of the cabinet) were 'required to resign' at an hour's notice on Friday, 13 July 1962; A. Horne *Macmillan 1957–1986* (1989) p.347. Thorpe later (1967) went on to become the leader of the Liberal Party. The chief casualty of Macmillan's 'restructuring' was Selwyn Lloyd, chancellor of the exchequer. David Eccles, minister of education, commented bitterly that he was 'sacked with less notice than a housemaid' (Horne (1989) p.347).

6 I was determined that no British government should be brought down by the action of two tarts.

Harold Macmillan; Anthony Sampson *Macmillan: A Study in Ambiguity* (1967) p.243. Macmillan is referring to Christine Keeler and Mandy Rice-Davies, the two women at the heart of the Profumo scandal in 1963. Keeler was sleeping with the Soviet military attaché, Yevgeny Ivanov, in the same period that she was consorting with John Profumo, Conservative minister of war, who denied the relationship in a statement to the House of Commons.

7 A great party is not to be brought down because of a scandal by a woman of easy virtue and a proved liar.

Lord Hailsham, speaking of the Profumo scandal, June 1963; Sampson (1967) p.243. The 'woman of easy virtue' was the call-girl Christine Keeler; the 'proved liar' was John Profumo, the minister at the heart of the affair who had just resigned. Lord Hailsham's comment was made in an emotional but possibly well-rehearsed outburst on television.

8 He would say that, wouldn't he?

Mandy Rice-Davies, *Guardian*, 1 July 1963. The call-girl in the Profumo scandal was speaking on 29 June 1963, during the trial of Stephen Ward, on being told in court that Lord Astor claimed that allegations concerning himself and his house parties at Cliveden were untrue.

1 'Rab' [Butler] wasn't her cup of tea. When she got the advice to call Alec, she thought 'Thank God'. She loved Alec – he was an old friend. They talked about dogs and shooting together. They were both Scottish landowners, the same sort of people, like old school friends.

Lord Charteris, private secretary to the queen; Ben Pimlott *The Queen: A Biography of Elizabeth II* (1996) p.332. Charteris is speaking of Macmillan's surprise decision to recommend the Earl of Home to the queen as his successor, even though to most observers the obvious heir-apparent was Butler. Home renounced his title, won a by-election and took his seat in the House of Commons as prime minister and leader of the Conservative Party.

2 As far as the fourteenth earl is concerned, I suppose Mr Wilson, when you come to think of it, is the fourteenth Mr Wilson.

Alec Douglas-Home, riposte to Harold Wilson's jibe that, with his succession to Harold Macmillan as leader of the Conservative Party, 'the whole [democratic] process has ground to a halt with a fourteenth earl'; Edward Heath *The Course of My Life* (1988) p.266. After his riposte, Douglas-Home commented that 'I heard no more of that particular line of inverted snobbery' (Home (1976) p.186).

3 In bygone days, commanders were taught that when in doubt, they should march their troops towards the sound of gunfire. I intend to march my troops towards the sound of gunfire.

Jo Grimond, leader of the Liberal Party, speech to the party assembly; *The Times*, 15 Sept. 1963. In the 1964 general election only nine Liberals survived the bombardment to become MPs. Compare David Steel (see 925:2).

4 The Britain that is going to be forged in the white heat of this revolution will be no place for restrictive practices or for outdated methods on either side of industry ... so we are going to need a new attitude. In some industries we shall have to get right away from the idea of apprenticeship to a single firm. There will have to be apprenticeship with the industry as a whole, and the industry will have to be responsible for it. Indeed, if we are going to end demarcation and snobbery in our training for skill and for science why should not these apprenticeship contracts be signed with the State itself? Then again, in the Cabinet room and the board room alike those charged with the control of our affairs must be ready to think and speak in the language of our scientific age.

Harold Wilson *Purpose in Politics* (1964) pp.27–8. This passage – usually paraphrased as 'the white heat of technological revolution' – comes from a speech to the Labour Party annual conference, Oct. 1963. Wilson sought to link technological and skill development to prosperity in a changing and competitive world, thereby hoping to appeal to middle-class and affluent working-class voters. This espousal of 'science' contributed to Labour's narrow election victory the next year.

5 Thirteen Years of Tory Misrule.

Labour slogan in the general election of Oct. 1964. The Labour manifesto talks of the 'wasted years of Conservative rule'. Usually conflated and quoted as 'thirteen wasted years'.

LABOUR RETURNED, 1964–70

6 You must understand that I am running a Bolshevik Revolution with a Tsarist Shadow Cabinet.

Harold Wilson, speaking of the shadow cabinet colleagues he had 'inherited' from Hugh Gaitskell, following his untimely death in Jan. 1963; Janet Morgan (ed.) *The Backbench Diaries of Richard Crossman* (1981) p.987. Although he was to lead the party to a narrow general election victory in 1964, Wilson was generally detested by Gaitskell's entourage for being a left-wing Bevanite (Wilson had resigned in 1951 along with Bevan) and for opposing Gaitskell's revisionism in 1960. Wilson was to prove repeatedly that he was no Lenin, but this early sense of isolation later fed a continuing paranoia that cabinet colleagues were plotting against him.

7 I'm under no illusions that Donovan may be the political end of me with our own people. I'm taking a terrific gamble and there is absolutely no certainty that it will pay off. My only comfort is that I am proposing something I believe in. I see no objection in principle to asking the trade union movement to adapt itself to changing circumstances and my one aim is to strengthen it. One doesn't do that by clinging to things as they are.

Barbara Castle *The Castle Diaries, 1964–76* p.296. As the minister responsible for industrial relations, Castle sought to develop ideas in the recently published Donovan Report. These were embodied in a white paper, *In Place of Strife*, which sought to extend unions' workplace rights in return for a limitation on unofficial 'wildcat' strikes. The proposal was bitterly resisted by the unions, and she was forced to withdraw the proposal. She felt badly let down by her colleagues, both left and right, within government.

8 *Hugh Scanlon*: Prime Minister, we don't want you to become another Ramsay MacDonald.

Harold Wilson: I have no intention of becoming another Ramsay MacDonald. Nor do I intend to be another Dubček. Get your tanks off my lawn, Hughie.

Exchange between Harold Wilson, prime minister, and Hugh Scanlon, trade union leader, at Chequers, June 1969; P. Jenkins *The Battle of Downing Street* (1970) p.140. The labour government and the trade union movement were locked in combat over *In Place of Strife*. The trade unions insisted on voluntary self-regulation, which was eventually accepted. Ramsay MacDonald had dealt with the financial crisis of 1931 by forming a predominantly Conservative 'National' government, thereby splitting the Labour Party (see 780:2). Alexander Dubček was first secretary of the Czechoslovak Communist Party who proposed sweeping reforms, which led to the Soviet occupation of his country in Aug. 1968 (see 896:3).

1 From now the pound abroad is worth 14 per cent or so less in terms of other currencies. It does not mean, of course, that the pound here in Britain, in your pocket or purse or bank, has been devalued.
Harold Wilson, prime ministerial broadcast, 19 Nov 1967; Ben Pimlott *Harold Wilson* (1993) p.483. Another balance-of-payments crisis had led to a devaluation of the pound. These innocent (and accurate) comments came to haunt the Labour government when the public saw them as 'spin' designed to make light of national humiliation. Curiously, Wilson seemed to have had little appreciation of the impact of devaluation on public opinion, saying: 'Don't you see, devaluation has made me the most powerful Prime Minister since Walpole?'

2 A week is a long time in politics.
Harold Wilson; Nigel Rees *Sayings of the Century* (1984) p.149. When asked by Rees in 1977, Wilson was unable to remember when or even if he had uttered this dictum, always associated with him. Rees suggests the words were probably said at a lobby briefing at the time of the 1964 sterling crisis, shortly after Wilson became prime minister. A journalist recalled Wilson saying 'Forty-eight hours is a long time in politics' at a party conference in 1960. On 22 March 1886 Joseph Chamberlain said to Arthur Balfour: 'In politics there is no use looking beyond the next fortnight' (Robert Stewart (ed.) *A Dictionary of Political Quotations* (1984) p.32).

3 Those whom the gods wish to destroy, they first make mad. We must be mad, literally mad, as a nation to be permitting the annual inflow of some 50,000 dependants, who are for the most part the material of the future growth of the immigrant-descended population. It is like watching a nation busily engaged in heaping up its own funeral pyre. So insane are we that we actually permit unmarried persons to immigrate for the purpose of founding a family with spouses and fiancées whom they have never seen.
Enoch Powell, MP for Wolverhampton, speaking to a meeting of the Conservative Political Centre, Birmingham, 20 April 1968; Simon Heffer *Like the Roman: The Life of Enoch Powell* (1998) p.451. The speech caused uproar, and Powell was deified and vilified in equal measure. He was sacked from the shadow cabinet by Edward Heath, and the speech effectively ended his political career. The passage is usually remembered as his 'Rivers of Blood' speech from the peroration in which Powell said: 'As I look ahead, I am filled with foreboding. Like the Roman, I seem to see the River Tiber foaming with much blood' (Heffer (1998) p.454). The peroration refers to the Sybil's prophecy in Bk 4 of the *Aeneid*.

4 Selsdon Man is designing a system of society for the ruthless and the pushing, the uncaring ... His message to the rest is: you're out on your own.
Harold Wilson, 21 Feb. 1970; Hugo Young *One of Us* (1989) p.59. In Jan. 1970 the Conservative shadow cabinet met at the Selsdon Park Hotel outside London to develop policies for the expected general election. The resulting communiqué, with its emphasis on tax cuts, more selectivity in social services and law and order, enabled Wilson to identify 'Selsdon Man' as a primitive Neanderthal, bent on destroying the hard-won fruits of socialism.

THE HEATH GOVERNMENT, 1970–74

5 This would, at a stroke, reduce the rise in prices, increase productivity and reduce unemployment.
Edward Heath, attrib. in the general election campaign of 1970 but actually from a press release by Conservative Central Office; *Daily Telegraph*, 17 June 1970. Heath had been under pressure to announce that the Conservatives would be able to curb price rises but had been understandably reluctant to make this claim. However, the previous day, the Labour government had had to announce a trade deficit of £31 million, and canvassing was showing that prices were a major issue among working-class women voters. Central Office asserted that a combination of tax cuts and price restraint would have an immediate impact.

6 He [Harold Wilson] is going around stirring up apathy.
William Whitelaw, Conservative shadow cabinet minister, on the tactics of the Labour Party in the 1970 election campaign. It has been claimed that this is a mis-quotation and that Whitelaw actually said: 'The Labour Party is going around stirring up complacency' (see Simon Hoggart *On the House* (1982) p.38). The effect is the same.

7 The alternative to expansion is not, as some occasionally seem to suppose, an England of quiet market towns linked only by trains puffing slowly and peacefully through green meadows. The alternative is slums, dangerous roads, old factories, cramped schools, stunted lives.
Prime minister Edward Heath, pre-conference message to Conservative Party workers, 30 Sept. 1973; M. Weiner *English Culture and the Decline of the Industrial Spirit 1850–1980* (1981) p.162. For some, Heath's policies represent the first glimmerings of Thatcherism and the harbinger of the end of

the post-war consensus. For others, Heath was a technocrat *par excellence*, seeking to modernize and reinvigorate that consensus.

1 It was a pleasant evening, with Heath talking of his yacht and musical interests. At one stage he showed us a new piano he had bought and at our invitation played one or two short pieces. Then Vic Feather called out, 'Play the Red Flag for Jack' and the leader of the Tory Party cheerfully played Labour's national anthem.

Jack Jones *Union Man* (1986) p.70. Heath had invited a group of leading trade unionists to his Albany flat shortly before the 1970 general election. Jack Jones was leader of the Transport and General Workers Union; Vic Feather was general secretary of the Trades Union Congress (TUC). The TUC were soon to be locked in combat with Heath's government over the Conservatives' Industrial Relations Bill.

2 This is no time to be mealy-mouthed. Since the end of the Second World War we have had altogether too much socialism. There is no point in my trying to evade what everybody knows. For half of those thirty years Conservative Governments, for understandable reasons, did not consider it practicable to reverse the vast bulk of the accumulated detritus of socialism which on each occasion they found when they returned to office. So we tried to build on its uncertain foundations instead … I must take my share of the blame for following too many of its fashions.

Sir Keith Joseph, member of Heath's shadow cabinet (with a roving responsibility for developing private-sector policies), speech at Upminster, 21 June 1974; Andrew Denham and Mark Garnett *Keith Joseph* (2001) p.247. The Upminster speech has passed into right-wing legend. Sir Keith, labelled the 'Mad Monk' because of his passionate intensity and messianic zeal for neo-liberalism, argued that by clinging to Keynesian interventionist policies both parties were responsible for Britain's relative decline and that until he realized this fact he hadn't been a 'real Conservative'. In fact, he had always promoted free-market policies but had been frustrated at his inability to influence government policy. He was instrumental in setting up the Centre for Policy Studies to promote his views. His decision not to contest the leadership election in 1975 led to Margaret Thatcher's candidature.

3 It is the unpleasant and unacceptable face of capitalism, but we should not suggest that the whole of British industry consists of practices of this kind.

Prime minister Edward Heath, speaking on Lonrho, 15 May 1973; *H.C. Deb.* Vol.856, Col.1243. The Lonrho company was undergoing a boardroom battle, during which it emerged that $100,000 had been lodged in the Cayman Islands for the chairman, a former Conservative minister, Duncan Sandys.

This was regarded as particularly provocative at a time when workers were being asked to moderate pay claims.

4 People can clean their teeth in the dark, use the top of the stove instead of the oven, all sorts of things, but they must use less electricity.

Conservative minister Patrick Jenkin, radio broadcast, 15 Jan. 1974; *The Times*, 16 Jan. 1974. A miners' strike brought on a fuel crisis, and Heath lost the election he called in response.

THE LAST OF OLD LABOUR, 1974–9

5 If Labour is the answer, it must have been a bloody silly question.

Graffito, reported in *Daily Telegraph*, 25 Jan. 1979.

6 She is so clearly the best man among them and she will, in my view have an enormous advantage in being a woman too. I can't help feeling a thrill, even though I believe her election will make things more difficult for us.

Barbara Castle *The Castle Diaries 1974–76* (1980) p.309. A surprising reaction from a long-standing Labour politician to the election of Margaret Thatcher as leader of the Conservative Party in Feb. 1975, when she ousted Heath, twice defeated in the 1974 general elections of Feb. and Oct.

7 I stand before you tonight in my *Red Star* chiffon evening gown, my face softly made up, my fair hair gently waved – the Iron Lady of the Western world. Me?

Margaret Thatcher, 31 Jan. 1976; 'Maggie: The First Lady' Pt 2, 13 March 2003 (shown on ITV1). Thatcher's response to criticism in the Soviet journal *Red Star*.

8 All political lives, unless they are cut off in midstream at a happy juncture, end in failure, because that is the nature of politics and of human affairs.

Enoch Powell, *Sunday Times*, 6 Nov. 1977. On the eve of the Thatcher imperium, Powell's comment is a sceptical Tory's reminder of the transitory nature of political success.

9 That part of his speech was rather like being savaged by a dead sheep.

Denis Healey, chancellor of the exchequer, 14 June 1978; *H.C. Deb.* Vol.952, Col.1027. On the contribution of the shadow chancellor, Sir Geoffrey Howe, to a debate on the economy.

10 CRISIS? WHAT CRISIS?

Sun headline, 10 Jan. 1979, referring to the 'Winter of Discontent' with its multiplying strikes and inflationary wage claims. These three words helped to bring down the Labour government in 1979. Often attrib. to the prime minister, James Callaghan, they were, in fact, a journalistic gloss on

Callaghan's actual words on his return (looking tanned and relaxed) from an economic conference in Guadaloupe. He said: 'I don't think other people in the world would share the view there is mounting chaos.'

1 I've got to have togetherness. There must be a dedication to a purpose, agreement about direction. As a leader I have a duty to try and inspire that. If you ... choose a team in which you encounter a basic disagreement, you will not be able to carry out a programme, you won't be able to govern ... it must be a Cabinet that works on something much more than pragmatism or consensus. It must be a conviction government ... As prime minister I could not waste time having any internal arguments.

Margaret Thatcher, leader of the Conservative Opposition, interview with Kenneth Harris, *Observer*, 25 Feb. 1979. Although her first cabinet represented different strands within the Conservative Party, this statement, made while she was still leader of the Opposition, encapsulates her determined belief in 'conviction politics'. As events were to show, this entailed removing all those who disagreed with her.

2 Mainly by intuition I came to believe in what we would now call capitalist non-interventionist economic theories and to discard completely the fashionable paternalistic and socialist doctrines of the mid-1940s. So even at fourteen years of age I had conceived a distrust of socialism and a sympathy with the liberal free-market views which, unknown to me, Professor Hayek was expressing in the *Road to Serfdom* – a book I was not to read for almost forty years.

Norman Tebbit *Upwardly Mobile* (1988) p.10. An idea whose time had come clearly resonated with many like Tebbit, who had instinctively rejected the prevailing orthodoxy even at the time of its greatest influence.

3 Labour Isn't Working.

Saatchi and Saatchi, poster for the Conservatives, 1979 general election campaign.

THE THATCHER EARTHQUAKE, 1979–90

4 There are times, perhaps once every thirty years, when there is a sea-change in politics. It then does not matter what you say or what you do. There is a shift in what the public wants and what it approves of. I suspect there is now such a sea-change and it is for Mrs Thatcher.

James Callaghan, Labour prime minister, reflects on the nature of Margaret Thatcher's general election triumph in 1979;

Kenneth O. Morgan *Callaghan: A Life* (1997) p.697. Callaghan never expected to win the election.

5 The prime ministers who are remembered are those who think and teach, and not many do. Mrs Thatcher ... influenced the thinking of a generation.

Tony Benn MP, senior left-wing Labour politician; Peter Hennessy *The Prime Minister: The Office and its Holders Since 1945* (2000) p.398.

6 Any woman who understands the problems of running a home, will be able to understand the problems of running a country.

Margaret Thatcher, speaking during the general election campaign that propelled her to victory, *Observer*, 8 May 1979.

7 Where there is discord, may we bring harmony. Where there is error may we bring truth. Where there is doubt may we bring faith. Where there is despair may we bring hope.

Margaret Thatcher utters the prayer of St Francis of Assisi on the steps of 10 Downing Street after her first election victory, 4 May 1979; Young (1989) pp.136–7. To many, the promise of harmony sat uneasily with her combative and confrontational style.

8 We are a cavalry regiment headed by a corporal in the Women's Royal Army Corps.

The Conservative grandees' view of Margaret Thatcher's first cabinet, May 1979; 'Maggie: The First Lady' Pt 3, 20 March 2003 (shown on ITV1). The Junkers of Germany felt much the same way about Adolf Hitler in Jan. 1933. Both they and the Tory establishment were soon to feel very differently – in the Tories' case when the estate owners were supplanted by the estate agents, as Denis Healey so sardonically put it.

9 To those waiting with bated breath for that favourite media catch-phrase, the U-turn, I have only this to say: 'You turn if you want to. The lady's not for turning.'

Prime minister Margaret Thatcher, speaking at the Conservative Party conference, *Daily Telegraph*, 11 Oct. 1980. The line was designed to recall Heath's abandonment in office of right-wing manifesto pledges on tax, social security and law and order and to signal her determination not to 'trim'. The phrase, coined by the playwright Ronald Millar (later knighted for his services) is a pun on the title of the play by Christopher Fry, *The Lady's not for Burning*.

10 She cannot see an institution without hitting it with her handbag.

Sir Julian Critchley, backbench Conservative MP, *The Times*, 21 June 1982. From this point on, the flailing handbag became a symbol of the 'Thatcher style'. Her radical, frontal assault on institutions offended many traditional Tories for whom institutions were not mere obstacles to be bulldozed but repositories of accumulated, corporate wisdom.

1 A Tory is someone who thinks institutions are wiser than those who operate them.

Enoch Powell, *Daily Telegraph*, 31 March 1986. Powell's brand of Toryism, which stressed the authority immanent in institutions, made him wary of Thatcher's institutional iconoclasm, despite the fact that, like Powell, she was an ardent free-marketeer.

2 Just rejoice at that news and congratulate our forces and the Marines. Rejoice!

Margaret Thatcher speaking in Downing Street on the retaking of South Georgia from the Argentines, *Daily Telegraph*, 26 April 1982. The island of South Georgia was seized by Argentina at the same time as it invaded the Falkland Islands on 2 April 1982. The British recapture of the Falklands paved the way for the Conservatives' re-election in 1983.

3 The longest suicide note in history.

Gerald Kaufman Labour MP, 1983; Denis Healey *The Time of My Life* (1983) p.500. Kaufman is referring to the Labour Party's *New Hope for Britain* general election manifesto. The biggest customer for the manifesto was the Conservative Party, which distributed it to 'opinion formers' around the country. Labour, led by Michael Foot, suffered a comprehensive defeat in the general election of that year.

4 The general election of 1983 has produced one important result that has passed virtually without comment in the media. It is that, for the first time since 1945, a political party with an openly socialist policy has received the support of over eight and a half million people. This is a remarkable development by any standards and its deserves some analysis ... the 1983 Labour manifesto commanded the loyalty of millions of voters and a democratic socialist bridge-head has been established from which further advances in public understanding and support can be made.

Tony Benn, *Guardian*, 20 June 1983. Benn lost his seat in the débâcle that saw Labour plunge almost to third place behind the Social Democratic Party–Liberal Alliance. Contrary to other colleagues, Benn saw cause to hail this performance as a welcome development and a testament to ideological purity. The Labour Party went on to lose the next two general elections, even though they jettisoned their radicalism.

5 I don't know whether it [monetarism] will work or not. Why is there no critique of it? Because no one has any alternative. There is nothing else to try. There is no easy popularity ... I believe that people accept that there is no alternative.

Norman St John Stevas, Leader of the House; Eric J. Evans *Thatcher and Thatcherism* (1997) p.45. 'There is no alternative' (TINA) entered the political lexicon and became a propaganda rallying-cry for the monetarists. Despite being a thorough Thatcher loyalist, St John Stevas was the first 'wet' to be sacked in Jan. 1981 as Thatcher put together a more congenial cabinet. By a process of transference, Thatcher herself came to be known as 'TINA'.

6 Ted was a very good No. 2 (pause). Not a leader (pause). Now you have a real leader (long pause). Whether she is leading you in the right direction ...

An aged Harold Macmillan (Lord Stockton) reflects on the leadership qualities of Edward Heath and Margaret Thatcher; N. Fisher *Harold Macmillan* (1982) p.362.

7 There are three bodies no sensible man directly challenges: the Roman Catholic Church, the Brigade of Guards and the National Union of Mineworkers.

Harold Macmillan, speaking on Mrs Thatcher's first confrontation with Arthur Scargill and the National Union of Mineworkers (NUM), *Observer*, 22 Feb. 1981. The comment echoes Baldwin's observation much earlier in the century: 'Do not run up your nose against the Pope or the NUM' (R.A. Butler *The Art of Memory* (1982) p.110). Thatcher was prepared to discount this core piece of received party wisdom and to destroy 'the enemy within' in the strike of 1984–5, when the NUM suffered a devastating defeat.

8 He didn't riot. He got on his bike and looked for work.

Norman Tebbit MP, speech to the Conservative Party conference, Blackpool, *Daily Telegraph*, 16 Oct. 1981. Then employment secretary in Thatcher's government, Tebbit is referring to his unemployed father during the Depression and contrasting his father's self-help response to adversity with the attitude of rioters in Britain during the previous summer. The speech was received with a rousing ovation at the conference but provoked widespread controversy in the country at a time when unemployment stood at three million.

9 The word 'conservative' is used by the BBC as a portmanteau word of abuse for anyone whose views differ from the insufferable, smug, sanctimonious, naïve, guilt-ridden, wet, pink orthodoxy of that sunset home of the third-rate minds of that third-rate decade, the nineteen-sixties.

Norman Tebbit, *Independent*, 24 Feb. 1990. This robust statement voices a deep Tory suspicion of the allegedly left-leaning BBC and also a distaste for the 1960s, seen as a time when 'permissiveness' (under a Labour home secretary, Roy Jenkins) added social and moral decay to the economic failure of the post-war consensus.

10 [Soon after Mrs Thatcher's second election victory in 1983] a senior Department of Education

official warned in a secret report that legislative powers might be necessary to 'rationalize' the schools' curricula. 'We are in a period of considerable social change,' he wrote. 'There may be social unrest, but we can cope with the Toxteths ... but if we have a highly educated and idle population we may possibly anticipate more serious conflict. People must be educated once more to know their place.'
Marxist journalist John Pilger *Distant Voices* (1992) p.29. The report, which came in the wake of the inner-city riots of 1983, was ammunition to support the claim that Thatcher was nothing but an authoritarian saviour of capitalism, creating, through recession, a compliant 'reserve army of labour' and that the purpose of education was to ensure its deference and compliance. Compare the Liberal Robert Lowe in 1867 (see 650:4).

1 Those were the values when our country became great. But not only did our country become great internationally, also much advance was made in this country – through voluntary rather than state action.
Margaret Thatcher on 'Victorian values', television interview with Brian Walden (who introduced the phrase), 17 Jan. 1983.

2 I have the good fortune to be the first Liberal leader for over half a century who is able to say to you at the end of our annual assembly: 'Go back to your constituencies, and prepare for government.'
David Steel, Liberal Party leader, *The Times*, 19 Sept. 1985. In the 1987 general election only 22 candidates from the Liberal-Social Democratic Party Alliance came top of the poll.

3 Because you are from the people, because you are of the people, because you live with the same realities as everybody else lives with, implausible promises don't win victories. I'll tell you what happens with impossible promises. You start with far-fetched resolutions. They are then pickled into a rigid dogma, a code, and you go through the years sticking to that, out-dated, misplaced, irrelevant to the real needs and you end up in the grotesque chaos of a Labour Council – a *Labour* Council – hiring taxis to scuttle round a city handing out redundancy notices to its own workers.
Neil Kinnock, leader of the Opposition, speaking at the Labour Party annual conference, Oct. 1985; *Report of the Annual Conference of the Labour Party* (1985) pp.127–8. Kinnock is referring to Liverpool, which was controlled by the Militant Tendency, led by Derek Hatton, whose mismanagement had reduced the city to a parlous state. More generally, the speech is an attack on all forms of the 'Loony Left' from which the Labour Party had to disassociate itself if it were to hope to win power again.

4 You all know as well as I do that John Biffen is that well-known semi-detached member of the Cabinet.
Bernard Ingham, Thatcher's press secretary, May 1986; B. Ingham *Kill the Messenger* (1991) p.327. The urbane John Biffen MP had offended the prime minister by suggesting in a television interview in May 1986 that the next election should be fought on a more 'balanced ticket' – that is, that different sections of the party should be represented in cabinet. Although in ideological terms Biffen was a Thatcherite, he always displayed an independent cast of mind. He was dismissed soon afterwards for this piece of public dissension.

5 He is not the sewage, only the sewer.
John Biffen on Bernard Ingham; Ingham (1991) p.361. Biffen is rightly suggesting that Ingham is 'the monkey and not the organ grinder' and that responsibility for 'spin' and negative briefings lay at the very top.

6 GOTCHA!
Triumphalist *Sun* headline on the sinking of the Argentinian cruiser *General Belgrano*, 4 May 1982, with the loss of 323 lives. At the time of the sinking, the *General Belgrano* was 30 miles outside the exclusion zone set up by the British, and the legality of the act was therefore questioned. Relatives of those lost in the incident are currently suing the British government at the European Court of Human Rights for contravening the rules of war as embodied in the 1907 Hague Convention.

7 There is no such thing as society. There are individual men and women, and there are families.
Margaret Thatcher, *Woman's Own*, 31 Oct. 1987. The comment was interpreted by her opponents as further evidence of her rejection of social responsibility in favour of ruthless individualism.

8 First of all the Georgian silver goes, then all that nice furniture that used to be in the saloon. Then the Canalettos go.
Ex-prime minister Harold Macmillan, commenting on the Conservative government's privatization programme in a speech to the Tory Reform Group, *The Times*, 9 Nov. 1985. Usually shortened to 'selling off the family silver'. By this time privatization, barely hinted at in the Conservative's election manifesto in 1979, was in full swing. As a patrician, a 'One-Nation Conservative' and a founder-member of the post-war consensus, Macmillan and other 'wets' were seen by Mrs Thatcher as limply conspiring in Britain's decline.

9 Every Prime Minister needs a Willie.
Prime minister Margaret Thatcher, speaking at the farewell dinner in honour of William Whitelaw, her trusted confidant and adviser, *Guardian*, 7 Aug. 1990. Mrs Thatcher was apparently unconscious of the *double entendre*.

10 When she goes she will go very fast. Our wives will have soaped the stairs for her.
Anon. cabinet minister, 1980; Hennessy (2000) p.433. When it finally came a decade later, her fall was indeed rapid, brought about by a succession of crises, all of which involved both

Europe and the proper conduct of cabinet government. A key moment in this process was the resignation speech of Sir Geoffrey Howe, former foreign secretary, deputy leader of the Conservative Party and Leader of the House of Commons. Many thought the speech had been written by the formidable Elspeth, Lady Howe: 'From the moment he rose to his feet Geoffrey got into it. He was personally wounding – to a far greater extent than mere policy differences would justify. Elspeth's hand in every line' (diary entry, 13 Nov. 1990; Alan Clark *Diaries* (1993) p.347).

1 It is rather like sending your opening batsman to the crease only for them to find, the moment the first balls are bowled that their bats have been broken before the game by the team captain.

Geoffrey Howe, 13 Nov. 1990; *H.C. Deb.* Vol.180, Col.464. In his resignation statement, Howe accused Thatcher (the 'team captain') of systematically undermining any attempt to forge a moderate, 'middle-of-the-road' position on Europe. The speech was designed to rally all those within the Conservative Party who nursed resentments against the prime minister, and it succeeded in bringing about her rapid fall from power.

2 Shortly after Mrs Thatcher's defenestration in November 1990, I ran into Heath in a Westminster corridor. I quoted a Spanish proverb: If you wait by the river long enough, the body of your enemy will float by. Heath broke into a broad grin: 'Rejoice, rejoice,' was his reply.

Conservative MP Sir Julian Critchley, *Observer*, 27 June 1993. For Thatcher's 1982 exhortation to rejoice see 924:2; for defenestration see 451:5. Heath, ousted by Thatcher as party leader in 1975, was at daggers drawn with her ever since.

3 I want her isolated. I want her destroyed.

Prime minister John Major on his predecessor, diary entry, June 1991; *Sunday Telegraph*, 19 Sept. 1999. Thatcher enraged Major with her constant interference. The diaries record that he called her 'mad', 'loopy' and 'emotional' as well as indicating that, in spite of signing her nomination papers for the 1990 leadership contest, Major apparently conspired to see her removed.

4 The liberty of individuals and of societies is an absolute value to democratic socialists. But, too often, socialism has been associated with the very opposite – parodied by its association with an uncaring bureaucracy. At times we seem to have permitted a set of beliefs that begin from this practical desire to foster the political and economic liberty of all people to look like a dogma that regarded liberty as a tedious bourgeois fad … we need to convey … that there is no essential contradiction between collective provision and individual freedom since the one reinforces and makes possible the other.

Neil Kinnock, leader of the Labour Party, *The Future of Socialism*, Fabian Tract no.509 (1985) pp.3–5. Following Labour's second general election defeat, Kinnock and others begin a painful review of the party's purposes and aims, akin to that which had been undertaken in the 1950s. The role of 'liberty' became particularly prominent in the face of Conservative success with libertarian policies.

PLUS ÇA CHANGE, 1990–2002

5 LABOUR'S DOUBLE WHAMMY!

Conservative general election poster, 1992. The 'double whammy' the electorate were told to expect was an increase in both taxation and inflation. Against all expectations, old fears about Labour 'tax and spend' policies gave John Major a narrow victory.

6 IF KINNOCK WINS TODAY, WILL THE LAST PERSON IN BRITAIN PLEASE TURN OUT THE LIGHTS?

Sun headline, 8 April 1992, election day. This was the culmination of a ferocious tabloid campaign directed at the Labour Party in general and its leader, Neil Kinnock, in particular. By the time of the 1997 general election, the Murdoch press, of which the *Sun* formed part, had swung behind Tony Blair's New Labour.

7 IT'S THE SUN WOT WON IT!

Sun headline, 9 April 1992. On the day after the Conservatives' re-election, the *Sun* takes credit for the result.

8 I want to see us build a country that is at ease with itself, a country that is confident, and a country that is prepared and willing to make the changes necessary to provide a better quality of life for all its citizens.

Prime minister John Major, words on the doorstep of 10 Downing Street after kissing hands at Buckingham Palace, *The Times*, 29 Nov. 1990. Once elected in his own right in 1992, he sought to moderate the abrasive tone of Thatcherism and provide what his chancellor, Kenneth Clarke, was to describe as 'Thatcherism with a human face' (an echo of Alexander Dubček in 1968, see 896:2).

9 Fifty years from now, Britain will still be the country of long shadows on county [cricket] grounds, warm beer, invincible green suburbs, dog lovers and – as George Orwell said – old maids bicycling to Holy Communion through the morning mist.

Prime minister John Major, speech to the Conservative Group for Europe, 22 April 1993; Jeremy Paxman *The English* (1998) p.142. The speech recalls one of Baldwin's 'fireside chats' made in 1924, which paints a similar idyllic picture of an enduring England over which can be heard 'the corncrake on a dewy morning' (Paxman (1998) p.143). Major was selective in his choice of imagery. Orwell actually wrote: 'The clatter of clogs in the Lancashire mill towns, the to-and-fro of the lorries on the Great North Road, the queues outside the Labour Exchanges, the rattle of pin tables in the Soho pubs, old maids biking to Holy Communion through the mists of the autumn mornings, these are not only fragments, but characteristic fragments, of the English scene' (*The Lion and the Unicorn: Socialism and the English Genius* (1941) p.10).

1 It is time to return to those old core values. Time to get back to basics.

Prime minister John Major, speaking at the Conservative Party conference, Oct. 1993; Hennessy (2000) p.468. This ill-thought out initiative came to haunt Major as 'sleaze' allegations of both a pecuniary and a sexual nature against Conservative MPs mounted.

2 A decent, honourable man who screwed up, frankly, by not being up to the job.

Anon. cabinet colleague sums up John Major; Hennessy (2000) p.475.

3 We have to make it clear to working people that we understand their aspirations and that we want to make them better off, that we are against taxation for its own sake; that we are tough on crime; that we stress individual responsibility. A new Labour Party: we must at some appropriate point say to the public – and to the party – that we are a new Labour Party. Radical in intent, driven by change, underpinned by conviction, confident in our beliefs and ready to sweep the Conservatives away.

Brian Gould *Strategy for the Leadership Election and Beyond* (internal Labour Party memorandum) 17 May 1994; *The Unfinished Revolution* (1998) p.201. Gould, an influential figure in Labour circles from 1985, became a senior adviser to Tony Blair. He was one of the principal architects of Labour's modernization programme, and his memorandum, written in the immediate aftermath of the death of the party leader, John Smith, encapsulates its language, priorities and general themes. Under Blair's leadership after 1994, it yielded huge electoral dividends, principally by taking much of the 'Thatcher revolution' on board.

4 Labour's coming home! (Applause). Seventeen years of hurt never stopped us dreaming. Labour's coming home! (Applause) As we did in 1945 and 1964, I know that was then, but it could be again – Labour's coming home! (Applause). Labour's coming home!

Tony Blair, leader of the Labour Party, speech to the Labour Party conference, Oct. 1996; *Labour Party Conference Verbatim Report* (1996) p.87. The refrain, 'Labour's coming home' was a play on the Euro '96 slogan 'Football's Coming Home!', recruiting sporting enthusiasm behind the political drive to power.

5 Ask me my three priorities for government and I tell you: education, education and education.

Tony Blair, speech to the Labour Party conference, Oct. 1996; *Labour Party Conference Verbatim Report* (1996) p.83. Blair argued that though the Tories talked about enterprise and initiative, only Labour could give the people the educational opportunities that would make these things a reality – another interesting attempt to harness Thatcherite themes to Labour values in a New Labour synthesis. The phrase 'education, education, education' was originally coined by the 19th-century French historian, Jules Michelet.

6 I met a man polishing his Ford Sierra, self-employed electrician, Dad always voted Labour. He used to vote Labour, he said, but he bought his own home, he had set up his own business, he was doing quite nicely, so he said I've become a Tory. He was not rich but he was doing better than he did, and as far as he was concerned, being better off meant being Tory too.

Tony Blair, speech to the Labour Party conference, Oct. 1996; *Labour Party Conference Verbatim Report* (1996) p.81. Usually quoted as 'Sierra Man'. Labour's task was to 'connect' with the swathes of lower-middle class and blue-collar workers who had been drawn into the Thatcherite fold.

7 Things Can Only Get Better.

Labour election slogan, 1997, derived from a song by D:ream.

8 They share the view that the Conservative Party needs a confrontation between traditionalists (nasties) and modernizers (nice), akin to Labour's Clause 4 battle.

Lord Tebbit, *Daily Telegraph*, 11 Oct. 2002. Tebbit claimed that a group of Conservatives called 'The Movement', led by supporters of Iain Duncan Smith's defeated leadership rivals, Kenneth Clarke and Michael Portillo, were seeking to engineer his expulsion from the party as a way of underscoring its commitment to change (and eroding Duncan Smith's position).

BRITAIN AND EUROPE, 1946-92

9 We are with Europe but not of it. We are linked but not comprised. We are interested and associated but not absorbed.

Winston Churchill, speech in Zurich, 19 Sept. 1946; W. Lipgens *A History of European Integration 1945–1947: The Formation of the European Unity Movement* (1982) p. 318. This became the theme of Margaret Thatcher's Bruges speech and epitomizes later Conservative Eurosceptic attitudes.

10 I love France and Belgium, but we must not allow ourselves to be pulled down to that level.

Private comment from Winston Churchill to his doctor, 1953; Alfred Grosser *The Western Alliance: European–American*

Relations since 1945 p.121. The remark was made in the wake of the 1951 Treaty of Paris, which established the European Coal and Steel Community (ECSC), the first supranational organization in post-war Europe and an important stepping stone to the European Economic Community (EEC). Attlee's government had declined membership of the ECSC, and Churchill's comment echoes British indifference to European integrationist initiatives at this time.

1 Once you open that Pandora's box, you'll find it full of Trojan horses.

A gloriously mixed metaphor from Labour's foreign secretary, Ernest Bevin; N. Nugent *The Government and Politics of the European Union* (1999) p.13. Bevin was referring to the 1948 Hague Conference, the avowed aim of which was to promote West European political and economic union. Politicians of both main parties in the UK were opposed to membership of any post-war European organization with supranational aspirations and intentions. Only the tiny Liberal Party was Europeanist.

2 It's no damn good – the Durham miners won't wear it.

Herbert Morrison, Leader of the Commons (and foreign secretary for seven months in 1951) in Attlee's post-war Labour administration; Kenneth O. Morgan *Labour in Power: 1945–1951* (1984) p.420. Morrison rejects any possibility that the Labour Party could consider handing over the recently nationalized coal industry to the proposed supranational European Coal and Steel Community.

3 Between the mainland and the high seas, we shall always choose the high seas.

Winston Churchill on the choice between Europe and the wider world; F. Giordano and S. Persaud *The Political Economy of Monetary Union: Towards the Euro* (1998) p.159. On 5 June 1944, the eve of D-Day, Churchill had described to de Gaulle his concept of the 'three circles' of British foreign policy – that is, the Empire, the United States and Europe. In this scheme of things, Europe came a poor third.

4 For centuries we have looked towards the open sea and the world beyond and we will continue to do so.

James Callaghan, Labour MP and future home secretary and prime minister makes a very similar observation to Churchill's; Kenneth O. Morgan *Callaghan: A Life* (1997) p.396. Writing at the time of Heath's application to join the European Economic Community, Callaghan believed the EEC to be inward-looking, parochial, protectionist and anti-socialist.

5 The Common Market is the Continental System all over again. Britain cannot accept it. I beg you to give it up. Otherwise, we shall be embarking on a war which will doubtless be economic at first but which runs the risk of gradually spreading into other fields.

Prime minister Harold Macmillan, plea to General de Gaulle to join with his projected European Free Trade Area (EFTA) in a wider free trade grouping, June 1958; Fisher (1982) p.310. The Continental System refers to the economic structure set up by Napoleon in 1806 and 1807 to combat the British naval blockade of continental Europe. Britain took the lead in establishing EFTA in Nov. 1959 as a non-supranational counterweight to the EEC, with Britain, Sweden, Norway, Denmark, Austria, Switzerland and Portugal as its members.

6 One thing above all they assuredly would not forget, Lancastrian or Yorkist, squire or lord, priest or layman; they would point to the kingship of England, and its emblems everywhere visible … the kingship would have seemed to them, as it seems to us, to embrace and express the qualities that are peculiarly England's; the unity of the Crown in Parliament, so natural as not to be aware of it; the homogeneity of England, so profound and embracing that the counties and regions make it a hobby to discover their differences and assert their peculiarities; the continuity of England, which has brought this homogeneity about by the slow alchemy of centuries.

Enoch Powell; Heffer (1998) p339. The roots of Powell's profound antipathy to membership of the European Economic Community can be found in statements such as this. Powell accepted the loss of empire but saw its substitution by the EEC as a false and dangerous alternative in the search for post-imperial national identity.

7 It does mean, if this is the idea, the end of Britain as an independent European state. I make no apology for repeating it. It means the end of a thousand years of history.

Hugh Gaitskell, leader of the Labour Party speaking to the Labour Party conference in Brighton, Oct. 1962; *Britain and the Common Market: Text of Speeches Made at the 1962 Labour Party Conference, October 1962* (1962) p.12. Gaitskell's oft-quoted speech was made in the context of the Conservative government's application to join the European Economic Community. Labour's suspicion of the Community as essentially a business-orientated 'rich man's club' lasted until the mid-1980s.

8 It might have been thought that our English friends, in proposing their entry, had agreed to transform themselves to the point where they could apply all the required conditions. The question today is whether they can accept coming inside a single tariff wall, removing all preferences for the Commonwealth, abandoning any privileges for their own farmers, and repudiating the pledges they made to their EFTA partners. This is the real question. It cannot be said at the present time, Britain is ready to do these things. Will she ever be? To that question only Britain can reply.

President Charles de Gaulle, vetoing the UK's first application to join the European Economic Community, 14 Jan. 1963; Sampson (1967) p.221. While de Gaulle based his rejection on the alleged British lack of commitment to the principles of the EEC, it sprang fundamentally from his determination to maintain French leadership of Europe. French objections were overcome only when Georges Pompidou succeeded de Gaulle as president. Britain entered the EEC in 1973.

1 On 28 October 1971 the House of Commons voted, by 356 to 244, in favour of the United Kingdom joining the European Community. It was my greatest success as Prime Minister. I had been conscious of a great weight of responsibility as I stood at the despatch box. No Prime Minister in time of peace has ever asked the House to take such a positive and historic decision as I was asking it to do that night ... I then returned to my private sitting room at No. 10, and I played the First Prelude from Book 1 of Bach's 'Well-Tempered Clavier' on my clavichord.

Edward Heath (1988) pp.380–81. Heath, an ardent Europeanist, told the House on that night: 'I want Britain as a member of a Europe which is united politically, and which will enjoy lasting peace and the greater security which would ensue' (Heath (1988) p.380).

2 The Conservative 'Yes' campaign was launched by Mrs Thatcher on 16 April at St Ermin's Hotel ... She quoted Disraeli, Churchill and Macmillan to demonstrate the Conservatives were the pro-European party, adding: 'It is a fact there has been peace in Europe for the past quarter of a century, and for that alone I am grateful ... It is a myth that our membership will suffocate national tradition and culture. Are the Germans any less German for being in the Community, or the French any less French? Of course they are not.'

Edward Heath (1988) p.544. Harold Wilson's Labour government renegotiated the terms of British entry to the European Economic Community, and these were put to the British people in a referendum on 5 June 1975. As Heath indicates, Margaret Thatcher – later so hostile to the European idea – was prominent in the 'Yes' campaign, which won over 60% of the vote.

3 She is an agnostic who continues to go to church. She won't become an atheist, but on the other hand she certainly won't become a true believer.

Christopher Soames, Churchill's son-in-law, reflects on Thatcher's attitude to Europe in the first year of her

premiership, 1979; Young (1989) p.185. Her robust attitude towards the European Union first manifested itself in a quest to reduce (and to obtain a rebate on) the UK's contribution to the EU's budget. Her attitude towards the EU contrasted sharply with what she and her supporters saw as the dreamy and idealistic internationalism of Heath.

4 We have not successfully rolled back the frontiers of the state in Britain, only to see them re-imposed at a European level, with a European super-state exercising a new dominance.

Prime minister Margaret Thatcher, speech in Bruges, 20 Sept. 1988; We the Nation: The Conservative Party and the Pursuit of Power (1995) p.367. The speech, which trumpeted an anti-federalist, Gaullist vision of a 'Europe of Nations', became holy writ for Conservative Eurosceptics.

5 This is all a German racket designed to take over the whole of Europe.

Nicholas Ridley, Conservative trade and industry secretary, interview on European Monetary Union with Dominic Lawson, The Spectator, 10 March 1990. In the ensuing furore, Ridley was forced to resign.

6 The president of the Commission, Mr Delors, said at a press conference the other day that he wanted the European Parliament to be the democratic body of the Community, he wanted the Commission to be the Executive, and he wanted the Council of Ministers to be the Senate. No. No. No.

Margaret Thatcher, 30 Oct. 1990; H.C. Deb. Vol.178, Col.873. With this triple negative she sealed her fate (see 925:10).

7 UP YOURS, DELORS!

Sun headline, 1 Nov. 1990. The Sun's reaction to Mrs Thatcher's outburst of 30 Oct. and to the publication of the Delors Report, which anticipated a European Union with a single currency issued by a European Central Bank. The Murdoch press has maintained its hostility to British adoption of the single currency. On 8 Jan. 2002 the Sun greeted the launch of the Euro with: 'The Euro is born. And thank goodness, Britain is not part of it.'

8 So what are we Little Englanders seeking to protect from European contamination? The Monarchy, Parliament, the Church of England, the English language, the island race? It is far too late. The damage has already been done – largely by our own hands. Compared to the damage already done by, say, Rupert Murdoch and Andrew Neil, that done by Mr Delors is not serious at all. Indigenous populism, philistinism and cultural vandalism are a much deeper threat than anything emanating from Brussels. When Mr Delors used to appear on our television screens, he showed the greatest possible

respect for the English language. Not so most BBC broadcasters. Indeed, it was not some Brussels bureaucrat but the Controller of BBC Radio who insisted on having more Brummy accents on the air.
Sir Peregrine Worsthorne, columnist, *Sunday Telegraph*, 1 Jan. 1995. Going against prevailing Conservative Party Euro-scepticism, Worsthorne argues the High Tory case for greater European integration, based on a distaste for mass culture.

1 The tragedy is – and it is for me personally, for my party, for our whole people and for my right hon. friend herself, a very real tragedy – that the Prime Minister's perceived attitude towards Europe is running increasingly serious risks for the future of our nation. It risks minimizing our influence and maximizing our chances of once again being shut out. We have paid heavily in the past for late starts and squandered opportunities in Europe. We dare not let that happen again. If we detach ourselves completely as a party or as a nation, from the middle ground of Europe, the effect will be incalculable and very hard to correct.
Foreign secretary Sir Geoffrey Howe, resignation speech to the House of Commons, 13 Nov. 1990; *H.C. Deb.* Vol.180, Col.465. Howe accused the prime minister of making constructive engagement with Europe impossible and his speech triggered Thatcher's fall from power (see 926:1).

2 There's no point in having a future if I don't have a country.
Iain Duncan Smith MP, *Daily Telegraph*, 9 Oct. 2002. This was Duncan Smith's attributed response to the whips attempting to put pressure on him to 'toe the party line' over the Treaty on European Union (TEU) (otherwise known as the Maastricht Treaty) in 1992. The treaty set a timetable for monetary union, and although the UK obtained an opt-out, Conservative Eurosceptics saw it as another stage in the seemingly inexorable march towards European integration. Duncan Smith won the leadership of the Conservative Party in 2001 against 'big hitters' like Kenneth Clarke and Michael Portillo not least because of his Eurosceptic credentials.

NORTHERN IRELAND, 1969–98

3 The people of Ulster will not surrender their Parliament without a fight. What we see today on the streets of our Province – the disorders – will look like a Sunday school picnic if Westminster tries to take our Parliament away.
Ulster Unionist William Craig, 24 April 1969; *Northern Ireland, 1968–1973: A Chronology of Events* Vol.1 (1973) p.25. The settlement of 1921 gave Northern Ireland its own legislature,

dominated by the Ulster Unionist Protestant majority, which discriminated severely against the Roman Catholic minority in the province. The early months of 1969 saw Catholic protests in the shape of a civil rights movement modelled on the black civil rights movement of the 1960s in the American South (see 905:4). This was met with extreme violence by the Protestants, who feared, like Craig, that the British government in London would react by ending their autonomy (as it did in 1972).

4 For half a century it [the Unionist government] has misgoverned us, but it is on the way out. Now we are witnessing its dying convulsions. And with traditional Irish mercy, when we've got it down, we will kick it into the ground.
Bernadette Devlin MP, 20 Nov. 1969; *The Price of my Soul* (1969) p.206. Ms Devlin, the militant Catholic dissenter, once described as 'Fidel Castro in a mini-skirt', was elected to the House of Commons on 17 April, taking a former Unionist seat when she was 21 years old.

5 For God's sake bring me a large Scotch. What a bloody awful country.
Reginald Maudling, Conservative home secretary, after a visit to Northern Ireland, 1 July 1970; *Sunday Times* Insight Team *Ulster* (1972) p.213. Britain had sent troops into the province on 14 Aug. 1969 after the outbreak of serious clashes between the Protestant and Catholic communities.

6 The rifles had been moved very quickly because of the decision that it would be better to have them nearer the border than Dublin if it was necessary for them to be distributed to civilians in Northern Ireland.
Colonel Michael Hefferon, the Republic of Ireland's director of intelligence; Tony Geraghty *The Irish War* (1998). Alarmed at the Marxism of the Irish Republican Army in Northern Ireland, several figures in the Irish government mounted a clandestine operation to arm and fund what became the Provisional IRA, although the move was halted by the Irish prime minister, Jack Lynch.

7 It strikes me that the [British] Army ran amok that day and shot without thinking what they were doing … I would say without hesitation that it was sheer unadulterated murder. It was murder.
Major Hubert O'Neill, Derry City coroner, on the 'Bloody Sunday' shootings, 30 Jan. 1972; *Irish Times*, 22 Aug. 1973. British troops fired on a Catholic march, killing 13 people. Their claim was that they were acting in self-defence and responding to an armed threat. An inquiry into the episode continues over 30 years later.

8 The Irish Government fully accepted and solemnly declared that there could be no change in the status of Northern Ireland until a majority of the people of Northern Ireland desired a change in that status.

The British Government solemnly declared that … if in the future, the majority of the people of Northern Ireland should indicate a wish to become part of a united Ireland, the British Government would support that wish.

Sunningdale Declaration, *Irish Times*, 10 Dec. 1973. A solution that gave the Protestant majority in Northern Ireland a veto on unification as long as they remained the majority.

1 That scheme [what became Sunningdale] will fail for the Unionist people are determined that they will never submit their necks to the heel of a Southern Parliament.

Rev. Ian Paisley, *Irish Times*, 23 Nov. 1973. Paisley represented the extremist political wing of Ulster unionism, seeing unification with the Republic as a capitulation to Roman Catholicism.

2 The people on this side of the water … see property destroyed by evil violence and are asked to pick up the bill for rebuilding it. Yet people who benefit from all this now viciously defy Westminster, purporting to act as though they were an elected government; people who spend their lives sponging on Westminster and British democracy and then systemically assault democratic methods. Who do these people think they are?

Prime minister Harold Wilson, *Irish Times*, 27 May 1974. The British response to a strike by Protestant Unionists that destroyed the Sunningdale agreement, underlining London's powerlessness to direct the course of events in the province.

3 If you wash your hands of Northern Ireland, you wash them in blood.

Margaret Thatcher, speaking to the Conservative Party conference, *Irish Times*, 14 Oct. 1978. For decades the party had officially styled itself the Conservative and Unionist Party. Here is its leader's response to the call for British withdrawal from Northern Ireland.

4 Who here really believes that we can win the war through the ballot box? But will anyone here object if, with a ballot paper in this hand, and an armalite in this hand, we take power in Ireland?

Danny Morrison, director of publicity for Provisional Sinn Féin (the political voice of the Provisional IRA), *Irish Times*, 2 Nov. 1981. The armalite was the IRA's rifle.

5 Today we were lucky, but remember, we only have to be lucky once – you will have to be lucky always.

Provisional IRA, statement addressed to Mrs Thatcher, after its bombing of the Grand Hotel, Brighton, *Irish Times*, 13 Oct. 1984. The members of the British cabinet were staying in the hotel for the party conference when an IRA bomb blew it up. Mrs Thatcher escaped unhurt, but five people were killed and more than 30 others injured in the blast.

6 We must try to find ways to starve the terrorist and the hijacker of the oxygen of publicity on which they depend.

Margaret Thatcher, speech to the American Bar Association, London, 15 July 1985; *The Times*, 16 July 1985. The Thatcher government imposed a media ban on the voices of senior figures in Sinn Féin – they could be filmed, but their voices had to be overdubbed by actors. The ban was not lifted until 1994.

7 [The British government] have no selfish strategic or economic interest in Northern Ireland. Their primary interest is to see peace, stability and reconciliation established by agreement among all the people who inhabit the island, and they will work together with the Irish government to achieve such an agreement, which will embrace the totality of relationships.

Paragraph 4, Downing Street Declaration, Dec. 1993; Paul Bew *et al. Northern Ireland: Between War and Peace* (1997) p.208. Yet another attempt to secure an Anglo-Irish solution of the Northern Ireland problem.

8 ADAMS – REMEMBER COLLINS 1922

A warning graffito from Nationalist ultras to the head of Provisional Sinn Féin, Gerry Adams, during the first Provisional IRA cease-fire. Michael Collins, who signed the 1921 treaty, was killed in an ambush on 22 Aug. 1922 (see 795:8).

9 All participants … reaffirm their commitment to the total disarmament of all paramilitary organizations. They also confirm their intention to continue to work constructively and in good faith with the Independent Commission, and to use any influence they may have, to achieve the decommissioning of all paramilitary arms within two years.

Part of Good Friday Agreement, 10 April 1998; Michael Cunningham *British Government Policy in Northern Ireland 1969–2000* (2001) p.121. The agreement, apart from setting up a disarmament framework in the shape of an independent inspection body, restored a Northern Ireland parliament, in suspense since 1972, now with the full participation of Sinn Féin. Five years on, disarmament had not begun in any meaningful sense, and the parliament at Stormont was closed down following a loss of confidence in Sinn Féin's intentions. Northern Ireland remained as intractable as ever.

Middle East Vortex, 1948–2003

ISRAEL: FOUNDATION YEARS, 1948–56

1 The Jews ordered all my family to line up against a wall and they started shooting us. I was hit in the side, but most of us children were saved because we hid behind our parents. The bullets hit my sister Kadri (four) in the head, my sister Sameh (eight) in the cheek, my brother Mohammed (seven) in the chest. But all the others with us against the wall were killed: my father, my mother, my grandfather and grandmother, my uncles and aunts and some of their children.

Fahimi Zidan, a 12-year-old Palestinian Arab boy, describes the massacre by a combined force of Irgun and Stern Gang of 254 inhabitants of the village of Deir Yassin in Palestine on 4 April 1948; David Hirst *The Gun and the Olive Branch: The Roots of Violence in the Middle East* (1977) p.125. The massacre was perpetrated to stampede Arabs out of Palestine in order to clear the ground for Israeli settlement. It succeeded beyond expectation: at the close of the Arab–Israeli war in 1949 some four-fifths of the Arab population of Palestine had fled the territory to become refugees in neighbouring Arab states. The name Deir Yassin has since been branded on Palestinian minds.

2 The counsel offered by Mr Clifford was based on domestic political considerations, while the problem which confronts us was international. I said bluntly that if the President were to follow Mr Clifford's advice and if in the elections I were to vote, I would vote against the President.

US secretary of state George Marshall, 12 May 1948; *Foreign Relations of the United States 1948* Vol.5 (1976) p.975. President Truman's legal counsel, Clark Clifford, had argued for diplomatic recognition of the state of Israel as soon as it proclaimed its independence when the British mandate over Palestine ended on 15 May 1948 (see 867:9). Marshall opposed this view in the knowledge that this would antagonize the Arab states of the Middle East, whose oil resources were of growing importance to the United States. He believed that Clifford was responding to pressure from the Zionist lobby in Washington in a bid to secure the Jewish vote in the forthcoming presidential election.

3 The Government has been informed that a Jewish state has been proclaimed in Palestine, and recognition has been requested by the provisional government thereof. The United States recognizes the provisional government of the *de facto* authority of the new state of Israel.

President Truman, statement, 6.11 p.m. Washington time, 14 May 1948; *Foreign Relations of the United States 1948* Vol.5 (1976) p.992. Recognition was accorded 11 minutes after the proclamation of the state of Israel, and Israel thereafter became the protectorate of the United States in the heart of the Arab world.

4 We are embarking on a course that will greatly endanger any hope of a peaceful alliance with forces who could be our allies in the Middle East. Hundreds of thousands of Arabs who will be evicted from Palestine, even if they are to blame, and left hanging in mid-air, will grow to hate us.

Aharon Zisling, Israeli agriculture minister, 16 June 1948; Simha Flapan *The Birth of Israel* (1987) p.110. The majority of Palestinian Arabs were systemically expelled from their homeland by Israeli forces so that Israelis could outnumber Palestinians in the new state they created during the war of 1948–9. At its end Israel controlled all of Palestine except for the Gaza Strip, which was occupied by Egypt, and the West Bank of the River Jordan, which was held by the Kingdom of Jordan. What Zisling said was all too true, but he represented a minority of Israeli opinion.

5 Their enjoyment is nervous excitement, animal merriment. One gets the image that they are constantly running from ghosts that are pursuing them. They are as machines that move with madness, speed and convulsion that does not cease. Many times I thought it was as though the people were in a grinding machine that does not stop day or night, morning or evening. It grinds them and they are devoured without a moment's rest. They have no faith in themselves or in life around them.

The Arab thinker Sayyid Qutb on his life in the United States from 1949 to 1951; Yvonne Y. Haddad *Contemporary Islam and the Challenge of History* (1982) p.90. The Egyptian Qutb, one of the main influences behind present-day Islamic fundamentalism, expresses his distaste for the materialism of the American lifestyle.

6 [Israel] may, no – it *must* ... invent dangers, and to do this it must adopt the method of provocation-and-revenge ... And above all – let us hope for a new war with the Arab countries, so that we may finally get rid of our troubles and acquire our space. (Such a slip of the tongue: Ben-Gurion himself said that it would be worth while to pay an Arab a million pounds to start a war.)

Moshe Sharett, Israeli foreign minister, 26 May 1955; Livia Rokach *Israel's Sacred Terrorism* (1980) p.44. Sharett sought an accommodation with the Palestinians, whereas the prime minister, David Ben-Gurion, Israel's founding father, thrived on confrontation and dropped Sharett as an appeaser.

1 Surrounded by hostile armies on all its land frontiers, subjected to savage and relentless hostility, exposed to penetration raids and assaults by day and by night, suffering constant toll of life among its citizens, bombarded by threats of neighbouring governments to accomplish its extinction by armed force ... embattled, blockaded, besieged, Israel alone among the nations faces a battle for its security anew with every approaching nightfall and every rising dawn.

Abba Eban, Israeli ambassador to the United Nations, 1 Nov. 1956; Conor Cruise O'Brien *The Siege* (1988 edn) p.391. Eban, who was speaking at the height of the Suez crisis, when Israel attacked Egypt in conjunction with Britain and France (see 869:1–870:2), was eloquently voicing the notion of Israel as a potential victim encircled by Arab enemies.

2 The danger lies in Islamic psychology, which cannot integrate itself into the world of efficiency and progress, that lives in a world of illusion, perturbed by attacks of inferiority complexes and megalomania, lost in dreams of the holy sword. The danger stems from the totalitarian conception of the world, the passion for murder deeply rooted in their blood, from the lack of logic, the easily inflamed brains, the boasting, and above all: the blasphemous disregard for all that is sacred to the civilized world ... their reactions – to anything – have nothing to do with good sense. They are all emotional, unbalanced, instantaneous, senseless. It is always the lunatic that speaks from their throat.

Dr A. Carlebach, *Ma'ariv*, 7 Oct. 1955. An Israeli view of the Palestinian mentality.

COLD WAR ARENA, 1957–70

3 The President is authorized to undertake in the general area of the Middle East, military assistance programs with any nation or group of nations of that area desiring such assistance. Furthermore, the United States regards as vital to the national interest and world peace the preservation of the independence and integrity of the nations of the Middle East. To this end, if the President determines the necessity thereof, the United States is prepared to use armed forces to assist any such nation or group of nations requesting assistance against armed aggression from any country controlled by international communism.

Joint resolution of Congress, 5 March 1957; Ruhl J. Bartlett *The Record of American Diplomacy* (1964 edn) p.845. Legislative approval of the 'Eisenhower Doctrine', whereby the United States aimed to prevent the Soviet Union from filling the power vacuum created by the recent Anglo-French defeat over Suez (see 869:10). Washington had already tried to create an anti-communist alliance system for the Middle East in 1955 – the Baghdad Pact – but Iraq was the only Arab state to join it. When Iraq succumbed to a republican revolution in July 1958, the doctrine was invoked to send in British and American forces to protect Jordan and Lebanon against a similar upheaval.

4 The Near East, according to some scholars, has been in a state of political and cultural disequilibrium since the arrival of Napoleon in Egypt in 1798. The area's institutions and religions have steadily declined in vigor, as a result of the impact of Western culture, and native resistance to communism per se has therefore been disappointing.

US State Department staff study, 30 Oct. 1957; *Foreign Relations of the United States 1955–1957* Vol.12 (1988) p.622. Not only a serious underestimate of Islamic hostility to communism but also a failure to appreciate the depth of resentment against the West among Islamic traditionalists.

5 The rising tide of Soviet penetration, and the trends in Arab politics which that penetration encouraged and fortified, threatened major American and allied interests in the region ... and ... a continuation of the process, which could involve the Nasserization of Jordan, the Lebanon, Libya, Tunisia, Morocco, Saudi Arabia and the Persian Gulf, would present ... a security crisis of major, and potentially catastrophic proportions.

US State Department policy study, 1967; Eugene Rostow, *International Affairs*, April 1971, p.280. A domino theory for the Middle East, equating Nasser's regime with communism; in fact, Nasser had put leading Egyptian communists in jail.

6 The Security Council ... [affirms] that the fulfilment of Charter principles requires the establishment of a just and lasting peace in the Middle East which should include the application of the following principles:

1. Withdrawal of Israeli armed forces from territories occupied in the recent conflict.

2. Termination of all claims or states of belligerency and respect for and acknowledgement of the sovereignty, territorial integrity and political

independence of every State in the area and their right to live in peace within secure and recognized boundaries free from threats or acts of force.

United Nations Security Council Resolution 242, 22 Nov. 1967; Robert Ferrell (ed.) *America in a Divided World* (1975) p.190. In June 1967 Israel secured all of Palestine by conquering the Gaza Strip and the West Bank in the lightning Six-Day War against the surrounding Arab states. This resolution sought the quid pro quo of Israeli withdrawal from the occupied territories in exchange for Arab recognition of Israel's statehood. Although both Egypt and Jordan eventually gave their recognition to Israel under American persuasion, the United States made no serious effort to bring about an Israeli withdrawal from the West Bank and Gaza, and 36 years on Israel remains in full occupation. The only reference to the Palestinians in the resolution was to the necessity of achieving 'a just settlement of the refugee problem'.

1 Israel has swallowed a serpent.

Palestinian saying about the conquest of the West Bank and the Gaza Strip.

2 Fatah is the armed humanitarian movement whose goal is the freeing of the Jews from their nationalistic and Nazi enslavement and the finding of a final solution for the Jewish problem.

Fatah pamphlet, Oct. 1968; Ze'ev Schiff and Raphael Rothstein *Fedayeen* (1972) p.127. The organization of Fatah (Conquest) was founded in 1959 by Yasser Arafat and became the leading political voice of the Palestinian community. The phrase 'final solution' is a chilling echo of the objective of the Holocaust (see 838:2–839:4).

3 It is not as though there was a Palestinian people in Palestine considering itself as a Palestinian people, and we came and threw them out and took their country away from them. They did not exist.

Israeli prime minister Golda Meir, *The Sunday Times*, 15 June 1969. A notorious example of the Israeli refusal to countenance the Palestinians as a political reality.

4 I think the Middle East now is terribly dangerous. It is like the Balkans before World War I – where the two superpowers, the United States and the Soviet Union, could be drawn into a confrontation that neither of them wants because of the differences there.

President Richard Nixon, 1 July 1970; *Public Papers 1970* (1971) p.557.

5 We could not allow Hussein to be overthrown by a Soviet-inspired insurrection. If it succeeded, the entire Middle East might erupt in war ... the possibility of a direct U.S.–Soviet confrontation was

uncomfortably high. It was like a ghastly game of dominoes, with a nuclear war waiting at the end.

President Richard Nixon, 20 Sept. 1970; *RN: The Memoirs of Richard Nixon* (1978) p.483. Nixon was speaking of the 'Black September' conflict in Jordan between the Jordanians and Arafat's Palestinian movement, which had fled to Jordan after the 1967 war. Syria, with Moscow's blessing, had sent a force into Jordan to support the Palestinians, who were eventually expelled and decanted into the Lebanon.

THE OIL SHOCK, 1973

6 In view of the increase of American military aid to Israel, the Kingdom of Saudi Arabia has decided to halt all oil exports to the United States of America for taking such a position.

Statement by Saudi Arabia, 20 Oct. 1973; Abdulaziz al-Sowayegh *Arab Petro-Politics* (1984) p.132. On 6 Oct. 1973 Egypt and Syria attacked Israel in the so-called Yom Kippur/ Ramadan War. When on 19 Oct. Washington announced a $2.2 million programme of military aid to Israel, the Arab oil-producing states placed an embargo on petroleum exports to the US. The deeply conservative Saudi Arabia had hitherto been a loyal American ally, making this pronouncement nothing less than revolutionary.

7 We possess – each of us – nuclear arsenals capable of annihilating humanity. We – both of us – have a special duty to see to it that confrontations are kept within bounds that do not threaten civilized life. Both of us, sooner or later, will have to come to realize that the issues that divide the world today, and foreseeable issues, do not justify the unparalleled catastrophe that a nuclear war would represent.

US secretary of state Henry Kissinger, press conference statement, 25 Oct. 1973; *Years of Upheaval* (1982) p.594. The United States had just gone on to a heightened state of military alert in response to a Soviet proposal that Washington and Moscow should send a joint peace-keeping force to Egypt. In the American view this could have led to a general war.

8 The Arab man who stormed the enemy's fortress in the Canal, Sinai and Golan ... when he bore arms in the Ramadan War, then turned off the petrol taps, challenged the enemies, all his enemies ... has defined his immediate objective as one of complete liberation and the rejection of tutelage ... The feelings of tragedy, misfortune, perplexity, failure, scorn and the deadening weight which oppressed our society ... before the Ramadan War have now been relegated to oblivion ... and with them the White Tyrant.

Zuheir Mardini, *Al-Jadid*, 21 Dec. 1973. Arab exaltation at the apparent humbling of Israel after the successive Arab humiliations of the wars of 1948–9, 1956 and 1967, when Israel had advanced to the east bank of the Suez Canal, and taken the Sinai Peninsula from Egypt and the strategic Golan Heights from Syria. The 'White Tyrant' was the United States.

1 The greatest shock, the most potent sense of a new era, of any event of recent years … change, drastic not only by recent standards but even in some respects by those of the two centuries since the Industrial Revolution … This was the first time that major industrial states had to bow to pressure from pre-industrial ones.

International Institute for Strategic Studies *Strategic Survey 1973* (1974) p.1. An apocalyptic contemporary verdict on what seemed like a political earthquake. In the event, the embargo was lifted after only five months when the oil producers realized how much they had to lose from it. The map of Israel remained unchanged.

2 You can conjure up a situation where there is another oil embargo and people in this country are not only inconvenienced and uncomfortable, but suffer and they get tough-minded enough to set down the Jewish influence in this country and break that lobby. It's so strong you wouldn't believe now … They own, you know, the banks in this country, the newspapers … you just look at where the Jewish money is in this country.

General George Brown, chairman of the joint chiefs of staff, Oct. 1974; *Washington Post*, 13 Nov. 1974. A retraction was published in the *Post* the following day.

3 The Palestine cause is alive in the world today because of oil. If it had not been for oil then the world would not give a thought to Palestine.

Saudi oil minister Sheikh Ahmed Zaki Yamani, *Middle East Economic Survey*, 17 Jan. 1977.

TO CAMP DAVID, 1977–8

4 We were granted our right to exist by the God of our fathers at the glimmer of the dawn of human civilization nearly four thousand years ago. For that right, which has been sanctified in Jewish blood from generation to generation, we have paid a price unexampled in the annals of the nations.

Menachem Begin, prime minister of Israel, 20 June 1977; O'Brien (1988 edn) p.560. Begin, former Irgun terrorist, took office the following day as leader of the right-wing Likud Party, breaking the dominance of the left-of-centre Mapai.

5 There is no argument in Israel about our historic rights in the land of Israel. The past is immutable and the Bible is the decisive document in determining the fate of our land.

Bipartisanship on the provenance of the Israeli claim to Palestine from the Mapai leader Shimon Peres, *New York Times*, 6 Aug. 1978.

6 In our view the future of the West Bank and Gaza lies in close association with Jordan and … an independent Palestinian state harboring irredentist feeling in this truncated territory would not be a realistic or durable solution.

Assistant secretary of state Harold H. Saunders, 12 June 1978; Edward W. Said *The Question of Palestine* (1980) p.189. In the Camp David Agreement of 17 Sept. 1978, between Israel and Egypt and brokered by President Jimmy Carter, provision was made for Palestinian autonomy in the occupied territories, but this was effectively nullified soon afterwards when Israel stepped up the expansion of its settlements in both areas.

7 It meant continuing to align U.S. interests with isolated and repressive regimes whose major virtues, in the cases of Israel and Egypt, were that they were willing recipients of U.S. arms, loan services, technical expertise of the kind that would further transistorize and render politically illiterate the vast majority of the people, whose interests could never be served by imports of Kentucky Fried Chicken franchises, Coca-Cola, Detroit automobiles, and Marriott hotels.

Edward W. Said on the significance of the Camp David Agreement; Said (1980) p.190.

ISRAEL IN LEBANON, 1982: ANOTHER BLACK SEPTEMBER

8 In my childhood I have suffered fear, hunger and humiliation when I passed from the Warsaw Ghetto, through labour camps, to Buchenwald … I hear too many familiar sounds today, sounds which are being amplified by the war. I hear 'dirty Arabs' and I remember 'dirty Jews'. I hear about 'closed areas' and I remember ghettos and camps. I hear 'two-legged beasts' and I remember 'Untermenschen'.

Shlomo Shmelzman, *Haaretz*, 11 Aug. 1982. The Warsaw Ghetto was instituted in 1940 by the Nazis as a pen for the Jews of the city, and destroyed after the Ghetto Rising of 1943. Buchenwald was a notorious Nazi concentration camp. Begin had referred to the Palestinian Arabs as 'two-legged beasts' in a recent speech. The war was the Israeli invasion of Lebanon on 5 June 1982, designed to smash the Lebanese headquarters of Arafat's Palestine Liberation Organization (PLO).

1 The Arab towns and villages are to become like ghettos … surrounded by large Jewish dormitory suburbs, settlements, military camps – all served, linked and carved up by fast access highways.

Meron Benvenisti, former deputy mayor of Jerusalem and a critic of the policy of planting Jewish settlements in the occupied territories, *Jerusalem Post*, 10 Sept. 1982.

2 *Goyim* kill *goyim*, and they immediately come to hang the Jews.

Menachem Begin, *New York Times*, 26 Sept. 1982. Begin was commenting on the massacre of Palestinians on 16 Sept. in the two Lebanese refugee camps of Sabra and Chatila. The massacre was carried out by the Lebanese Christian Phalange but with Israeli complicity, denied by Begin as a classic instance of scapegoating. *Goy* is an offensive Hebrew word for a non-Jew.

3 Even though we're at this moment urging Israel to move, that doesn't mean that we've moved one step away from our moral obligation to the preservation of Israel as a sovereign state.

President Ronald Reagan, 17 Sept. 1982; *Public Papers 1982* Vol.2 (1983) p.1177. The day after the Sabra and Chatila massacres, the United States stands firm behind its protégé.

4 A man who puts a snake into a child's bed and says: 'I'm sorry. I told the snake not to bite, I didn't know snakes were so dangerous.' It's impossible to understand. This man's a war criminal.

Israeli writer Amos Elon, *New York Times*, 27 Sept. 1982. The subject is the Israeli defence minister, Ariel Sharon, who condoned the massacres of 16 Sept.

5 He can best be described as a Patton-like, swashbuckling general who rose in the ranks of the Israeli Defence Forces, proved himself to have an uncanny feel for battle, but at the same time to be a most difficult person to command. Few, if any, of his superior officers over the years had a good word to say for him as far as human relations and integrity were concerned, although none would deny his innate ability as a field soldier.

President of Israel, Chaim Herzog, on Ariel Sharon, *The Arab–Israeli Wars* (1982) p.120.

6 The Israeli invasion of Lebanon … was designed to destroy once and for all any hope among the people of the West Bank and Gaza that the process of shaping the Palestinian people into a nation could succeed.

Harold H. Saunders, *Foreign Affairs* Vol.61 (Fall 1982) p.110. Saunders had served as assistant secretary of state for Near Eastern and South Asian Affairs in the Carter administration.

7 It is our view that responsibility is to be imputed to the Minister of Defence for having disregarded the danger of acts of vengeance and bloodshed by the Phalangists against the population of the refugee camps and having failed to take this danger into account when he decided to have the Phalangists enter the camp.

Inquiry report on the Sabra and Chatila massacres, 8 Feb. 1983; *Keesing's Record of World Events* 1983, p.32044. Ariel Sharon resigned on 11 Feb. 1983, but his political career was not over.

VIA DOLOROSA: A ROAD TO PEACE?

8 When we have settled the land, all the Arabs will be able to do about it will be to scuttle around like drugged roaches in a bottle.

General Rafael Eitan, chief of staff of the Israeli defence forces, on the settlement programme in the occupied territories, *New York Times*, 14 April 1983.

9 The Arabs are cancer, cancer in the midst of us … There is only one solution, no other, no partial solution: the Arabs out! Out! … Do not ask me how … Let me become defense minister for two months and you will not have a single cockroach around here! I promise you a *clean* Eretz Israel [Land of Israel]! Give me the power to take care of them!

Rabbi Meir Kahane, 1980s; Ehud Sprinzak *The Ascendance of Israel's Radical Right* (1991) p.23. Kahane, who emigrated to Israel from New York, was assassinated in 1990.

10 We've got to find a settlement there. You, know, I turn back to your ancient prophets in the Old Testament, and the signs foretelling Armageddon, and I find myself wondering if – if we're the generation that's going to see that come about. I don't know if you've noted any of the prophecies lately, but, believe me, they certainly describe the time we're going through.

President Ronald Reagan, *New York Times Magazine*, 27 Nov. 1983, p.64. Reagan was speaking to the head of the American Israel Public Affairs Committee, a key component of the Zionist lobby in the United States. The context was the killing by an Arab suicide bomber of some 300 American and French peace-keeping troops in their Lebanon barracks on 23 Oct. 1983. The force was withdrawn early in 1984.

1 There is a tendency in Washington to refer to the Libyan dictator, Muhammad Gaddafi, as a crazy man. Armchair psychologists justify the glib label by pointing to his fanatic extremism, his failure to put realistic limits on boastful pronouncements and his periodic fits of deep depression when he retreats to the desert and broods in his tent.

American columnist Jack Anderson, March 1982; Mary Kaldor and Paul Anderson (eds) *Mad Dogs* (1986) p.63. On 5 April 1986 two American servicemen were killed when a bomb exploded in a discotheque in West Berlin; Libyan involvement was suspected. On 15 April a large-scale retaliatory US air raid was launched on Libya, aimed principally at Colonel Gaddafi, who escaped with his life.

2 We don't have to be historians to 'know' inside ourselves that there are right and wrong ways to act, even in the struggle to act, even in the struggle against evil; assassination is wrong, yet military action can be right.

American professor, James Turner Thompson, 1986; Kaldor and Anderson (1986) p.63.

3 Article 6. The Islamic Resistance Movement is a distinct Palestinian Movement which owes its loyalty to Allah, derives from Islam its way of life and strives to raise the banner of Allah over every inch of Palestine …

Article 11. The Islamic Resistance Movement believes that the land of Palestine has been an Islamic Waqf [religious endowment] throughout the generations and until the Day of Resurrection, no one can renounce it or part of it, or abandon it or part of it.

Charter of Hamas, 18 Aug. 1988. Kirsten E. Schulze (ed.) *The Arab–Israeli Conflict* (1999) p.116. An absolutist Palestinian rejoinder to the equally unconditional Zionist claim to the territory, issued in the wake of the outbreak of the Palestinian Intifada (Uprising) of Oct. 1987. The Hamas organization was committed to terrorism as an essential weapon in the struggle with Israel.

4 I repeat for the record that we renounce, totally and absolutely, all forms of terrorism, including individual, group and state terrorism.

Yasser Arafat, head of the Palestine Liberation Organization, the mainstream body representing Palestinian nationalism, 14 Dec. 1988; Avi Shlaim *The Iron Wall* (2000) p.466. These words were designed to reassure Israel, whose right to exist as a sovereign state Arafat had recently recognized, but over the next 15 years he continually failed to impose his will on dissident terrorist factions, such as Hamas, Hezbollah and Islamic Jihad.

5 The men who kept us were far from the cliché image of the terrorist. They were a composite of different needs and motivations. Imagine a man aged twenty to thirty, but with the maturity and intelligence of a thirteen-year-old, a mind steeped in fundamentalist and medieval suspicion, a mind propagandized into a set of beliefs and values which it was not informed enough to understand, but weak and fearful enough to accept unquestioningly. The natural and healthy instincts of youth are twisted and repressed by a religious and moral code that belongs more to the days of the Inquisition. Then, imagine the final absurdity. Into the hands of such a person someone places a machine gun and tells him to take his freedom. This was the kind of person to whom we were subject and the contemplation of it was disturbing.

Brian Keenan *An Evil Cradling* (1992) pp.137–8. The Belfast man Keenan was kidnapped in Beirut in 1986 and held prisoner by Shi'ia militants for four-and-a-half years until his release in 1990. He and other detainees, such as John McCarthy, Terry Waite and Terry Anderson, were thus all sucked into the tornado of the Middle East.

6 The Bible Belt is Israel's safety belt.

Rev. Jerry Folwell, 1980s. Quite apart from the influential Jewish lobby in the United States, Israel had behind it the many Christian fundamentalists of the American South, who formed an important part of the constituency of President Ronald Reagan and the Republican Party. Together they ensured that no US administration would stray far from Washington's commitment to guarantee Israel's future.

7 Do you see my left shoe, that is Yitzhak Rabin. Do you see my right shoe, that is Yitzhak Shamir. Two Yitzhaks, two shoes, so what's the difference?

Anon. Arab janitor in Jerusalem reacts to the electoral victory of Rabin's Labour Party on 23 June 1992; Shlaim (2000) p.502. Rabin had been every bit as hawkish as Shamir, leader of the right-wing Likud, ordering, for example, as head of the Israeli Defence Forces, that captured Palestinian militants should have their arms broken. Immediately after the election, however, he entered into secret talks with Arafat's representatives, which resulted in the Oslo Agreement of Aug. 1993. There *was*, therefore, a difference between Rabin and Shamir, and Rabin paid for it with his life (see 938:3).

8 The Government of the State of Israel and the Palestinian team representing the Palestinian people agree that it is time to put an end to the decades of confrontation and conflict, recognize their mutual legitimate and political rights, and strive to live in peaceful coexistence and mutual dignity and achieve a just, lasting and comprehensive peace settlement through the agreed political process.

Oslo Agreement, 19 Aug. 1993, brokered by the United States and facilitated by the government of Norway; *Keesing's Record of World Events*, Sept. 1993, p.39659. The Agreement, which established an autonomous Palestinian authority in the West Bank and Gaza Strip, was sealed by a famous handshake between Rabin and Arafat on the south lawn of the White House at the instance of President Bill Clinton.

1 You are even worse than Chamberlain. He imperilled the safety of another people, but you are doing it to your own people.

Binyamin Netanyahu, leader of Likud, to foreign minister, Shimon Peres, Sept. 1993; Shlaim (2000) p.521. Munich (see 825:9) invoked yet again as the eternal symbol of betrayal.

2 I shall, God willing, shortly after saying these words, be meeting my God with pride, dignity and having avenged my religion and all the martyrs who precede me on this route ... Let us continue until we achieve our desired target and the Godly gratification and thus arrive at our Godly promise. We belong to God and to God we shall return.

Salah Ghandour, 25 May 1995; Hala Jaber *Hezbollah: Born with a Vengeance* (1997) p.86. The last testament of a suicide bomber who died killing 12 Israeli soldiers in southern Lebanon. Hezbollah (Party of God) is a Shi'ia Palestinian terrorist group formed under Iranian auspices after the Israeli invasion of Lebanon in 1982.

3 As Israeli as hummus pie. He was trained by his rabbis, and as far as I am concerned, he pulled the trigger for them.

Israeli author Ze'ev Chafetz on Yigal Amir, the Israeli law student who assassinated Rabin at a peace rally in Tel-Aviv on 4 Nov. 1995; Amos Elon *A Blood-Dimmed Tide* (2000 edn) p.319. 'When I shot Rabin,' Amir later said, 'I felt as if I was shooting a terrorist' (Shlaim (2000) p.549).

4 A two-state solution to the Israeli–Palestinian conflict will only be achieved through an end to violence and terrorism, when the Palestinian people have a leadership acting decisively against terror and willing and able to build a practising democracy based on tolerance and liberty, and through Israel's readiness to do what is necessary for a democratic Palestinian state to be established, and a clear, unambiguous acceptance by both parties of the goal of a negotiated settlement ... The settlement will resolve the Israeli–Palestinian conflict, and end the occupation that began in 1967.

Road Map to a permanent solution to the Israeli–Palestinian conflict, drafted by the United States, the United Nations, the

European Union and Russia, and presented to Ariel Sharon, prime minister of Israel, and to Mahmoud Abbas (Abu Mazen), prime minister of the Palestinian Authority, 30 April 2003. As part of the proposed agreement, Israel was to halt all settlement activity in the West Bank and the Gaza Strip, and to withdraw from the Palestinian areas occupied since 28 Sept. 2000. This was the day when the Likud leader, Ariel Sharon, single-handedly wrecked the existing peace process and provoked a second Intifada by his visit to the Temple Mount in Jerusalem, site of the Dome of the Rock, one of the most sacred sites in the Islamic world. The visit came immediately after the Israeli prime minister, Ehud Barak, had indicated a readiness to compromise with the Palestinians on the status of Jerusalem. Whether Sharon and the Palestinian militants would also now be ready to reach an accommodation and this initiative succeed where so many others had failed remained an open question.

REVOLUTION IN IRAN

5 Such stability as now obtains in the Middle East is, in my view, largely the result of the strength and Western orientation of Israel on the Mediterranean and Iran on the Persian Gulf. These two countries, reliable friends of the United States, together with Saudi Arabia, have served to inhibit and contain those irresponsible and radical elements in certain Arab states – such as Syria, Libya, Lebanon and Iraq – who, were they free to do so, would pose a grave threat indeed to our principal sources of petroleum in the Persian Gulf.

Senator Henry Jackson, 21 May 1973; *Congressional Record*, p.S.9446.

6 Iran under the great leadership of the Shah is an island of stability in one of the most troubled areas of the world. This is a great tribute to you, Your Majesty, and to your leadership, and to the respect, admiration and love which your people give to you.

President Jimmy Carter toasts the Shah of Iran, 31 Dec. 1977; *Public Papers 1977* Vol.2 (1978) p.2221.

7 Are we to be trampled under foot by the boots of America simply because we are a weak nation and have no dollars? ... Let the American President know that in the eyes of the Iranian people he is the most repulsive member of the human race today because of the injustice he has imposed on our Moslem nation. Today the Koran has become his enemy, the Iranian nation has become his enemy. Let the American government known that its name has been ruined and disgraced in Iran ... All of our troubles today are caused by America and Israel.

Israel itself derives from America; these deputies and ministers that have been imposed upon us derive from America – they are all agents of America, for if they were not, they would rise up in protest.

Ayatollah Khomeini, 27 Oct. 1964; Imam Khomeini *Islam and Revolution* (1985 edn) pp.185–6, 187. The Shi'ia fundamentalist Iranian religious leader Khomeini was exiled from Iran after making this inflammatory speech. His return in 1978 sparked the revolution that forced out the Shah in Jan. 1979 and put American interests under immediate threat.

1 America, Superdevil of the twentieth century, has for so many years exerted intense effort to expand its hegemony and impose its policies worldwide. Pigheadedly, she continues her seditious campaigns to exploit, tyrannize, intimidate, spy, assassinate.

Introduction to a selection of American documents seized after the occupation of the US embassy in Tehran on 4 Nov. 1979; John Simpson *Behind Iranian Lines* (1988) p.145. The staff of the embassy were to be held hostage until the day Carter left office, an enormously damaging blow to American prestige, which cost Carter the 1980 presidential election. A rescue attempt on 25 April 1980 failed completely.

2 What happened in Tehran was the diplomatic equivalent of Pearl Harbor. It was bad. We totally missed the significance of the Revolution. We supported the Shah much too long. We couldn't cut loose from him … It was laziness, sheer intellectual laziness.

Moorhead Kennedy, American diplomat and hostage; Simpson (1988) p.158.

3 For a millennium, the struggle for mankind's destiny was between Christianity and Islam; in the twenty-first century, it may be so again. For, as the Shi'ites humiliate us, their co-religionists are filling up the countries of the West.

Patrick Buchanan, 1980; John L. Esposito *The Islamic Threat: Myth or Reality?* (1992) p.175. The ultra-conservative Buchanan responds to the hostage crisis and to Moslem immigration into western Europe and North America. Iran subscribed to the Shi'ite wing of Islam.

4 You shouldn't worry about what is going on in Iran. Instead, you should look at everything that is going on in America! Why didn't you get upset [in 1967] when Jerusalem was conquered by the Jews? That would have been the time to open your mouth. When the Jews made themselves into the enemies of all religions, the Pope kept his mouth shut! The Pope kept quiet because the Americans wanted him to. America has spoiled everyone … The rulers of the world are America's serfs – the Pope too!

Ayatollah Khomeini responds to the pope's concern over events in Tehran during 1980; John K. Cooley *Payback* (1991) p.26.

5 The author of *The Satanic Verses* book, which opposes Islam, the Prophet, and the Koran, and all those involved in its publication who were aware of its content, are sentenced to death. I call on faithful Muslims to promptly execute them wherever they find them, to that no one else will dare to blaspheme Muslim sanctities.

Fatwa issued by Ayatollah Khomeini, 14 Feb. 1989; Cooley (1991) p.174. *The Satanic Verses*, written by Salman Rushdie, earned him this death sentence for slurring the divinity of the Prophet Muhammad and forced him into hiding under police protection. The Ayatollah himself died in June 1989, and the Iranian revolution then moderated, but the shock it generated to American interests was lasting.

IRAQ AND KUWAIT

6 We can envisage an Iraqi scenario in which religious unrest among the Shi'ites and trouble with the Kurds lead to the downfall of the present regime. Then a group of dedicated communists seizes power and calls for Soviet support. The next thing we know, Soviet troops will be landing in Baghdad.

Saudi chief of intelligence, Prince Turki, *Fortune* magazine, March 1980, p.55. This assessment was made in the wake of the recent Soviet occupation of Afghanistan. The regime in question was that of Saddam Hussein in Iraq, which represented the Sunni Muslim minority and which suppressed the majority Shi'ites and the Kurds in the north of the country. In the event, the USSR had its hands more than full in Afghanistan and the predicted invasion came not from that quarter but from the United States.

7 While a people are gassed, the world is largely silent. There are reasons for this. Iraq's great oil wealth, its military strength, a desire not to upset the delicate negotiations seeking an end to the Iran–Iraq war. Silence, however, is complicity. A half century ago, the world was silent as Hitler began a campaign that culminated in the near extermination of Europe's Jews. We cannot be silent to genocide again.

Senator Claiborne Pell, 1988; John Bulloch and Harvey Morris *The Gulf War* (1989) p.264. Senator Pell was speaking of the massacre by Saddam Hussein's dictatorship of some 5,000 Kurdish civilians in the township of Halabja in northern Iraq in March 1988 by means of chemicals sprayed from aircraft. His Prevention of Genocide Act was termed 'premature' and 'counter-productive' by a Reagan White House, which had backed Iraq against Iran in the war between them that raged throughout most of the 1980s.

1 A line has been drawn in the sand.
President George Bush, 8 Aug. 1990; *Public Papers 1990* Vol.2 (1991) p.1114. On 2 Aug. 1990 Iraqi forces invaded the tiny neighbouring state of Kuwait. The Iraqi leader, Saddam Hussein, claimed that shortly beforehand the US ambassador to Iraq, April Glaspie, had indicated that Washington had no interest in Iraq's dispute with Kuwait over its behaviour during Iraq's war with Iran. The United States, he consequently appeared to believe, would stand aside when Iraq took matters into its own hands. He was mistaken, as President Bush soon demonstrated.

2 Iraq controls some 10 per cent of the world's proven oil reserves. Iraq plus Kuwait controls twice that. An Iraq permitted to swallow Kuwait would have the economic and military power, as well as the arrogance, to intimidate and coerce its neighbors – neighbors who control the lion's share of the world's remaining oil reserves. We cannot permit a resource so vital to be dominated by one so ruthless. And we won't.
President George Bush, 11 Sept. 1990; *Public Papers 1990* Vol.2 (1991) p.1219.

3 It should by now be clear that we are facing a mood and a movement far transcending the level of issues and policies and the governments that pursue them. This is no less than a clash of civilizations – the perhaps irrational but surely historic reaction of an ancient rival against our Judaeo-Christian heritage, our secular present, and the worldwide expansion of both. It is crucially important that we on our side should not be pushed into an equally historic but also equally irrational reaction against that rival.
Professor Bernard Lewis 'The Roots of Muslim Rage' in *Atlantic Monthly* Vol.266 (Sept. 1990) p.60.

4 Given the magnitude of the U.S. military buildup in the Gulf and its past records of invasions of and interference in Third World countries, it is likely that the situation in the Gulf will lead to full-scale war ... It is indeed hypocritical for the U.S. to come to the aid of Kuwait while it remains silent about Israel's invasion and occupation of the West Bank, Gaza Strip, Golan Heights, Lebanon and its bombing of Tyre, Sidon and West Beirut, which wounded and killed hundreds of civilians.
The Malaysian journal *Aliran* Vol.10 (1990) p.38. A Muslim reaction to America's stance on Kuwait.

5 Saddam is a one-man show ... If and when we choose violence he ought to be the focus of our efforts. I don't see us making a big invasion. To try and beat Iraq on the ground risks destroying Kuwait in order to save it.
US Air Force chief of staff General Michael Dugan, dismissed on 17 Sept. 1990 for making this disclosure to journalists; *Keesing's Record of World Events*, Sept. 1990, p.37696. General Dugan was speaking of the aim to 'decapitate' the Iraqi leadership through the assassination of Saddam Hussein by means of air power, akin to the strike against Gaddafi in 1986 (see 937:1).

6 [This will be] the Mother of Battles.
Saddam Hussein, *The Times*, 7 Jan. 1991.

7 Our strategy for going after this army is very, very simple. First we are going to cut if off, and then we are going to *kill* it.
US Army chief of staff Colin Powell, 23 Jan. 1991; *U.S. News and World Report*, 4 Feb. 1991.

8 Since the demise of the Soviet 'Evil Empire' there has been a hunger among Americans for a moral clarity to justify and shape their foreign policy, and Mr Hussein provided it in spades.
Editorial, *New York Times*, 24 Feb. 1991. Following a long campaign of bombing in Iraq, American and allied ground forces drove the Iraqi army out of Kuwait in a matter of days. At that they stopped short, since the United Nations resolution authorizing the liberation of Kuwait did not extend to the invasion of Iraq and the elimination of Saddam Hussein's regime, which therefore survived the war.

AL-QAEDA, 9/11 AND OPERATION IRAQI FREEDOM

9 For more than seven years the US has been occupying the lands of Islam in the holiest of places, the Arabian peninsula, plundering its riches, dictating to its rulers, humiliating its people, terrorizing its neighbours, and turning its bases in the peninsula into a spearhead through which to fight the neighbouring Muslim peoples ... The ruling to kill the Americans and their allies – civilian and military – is an individual duty for every Muslim who can do it in any country in which it is possible to.
Manifesto and *fatwa* issued by al-Qaeda, 23 Feb. 1998; Ahmed Rashid *Taliban* (2001 edn) p.134. The fundamentalist Saudi leader of al-Qaeda (The Base), Osama bin Laden, made his headquarters in Afghanistan after its seizure in 1996 by the ultra-orthodox Taliban (Students of Islam). Like the

revolutionaries of Iran, he saw the United States as the 'Great Satan' of the world, even though both he and the Americans had been on the same side in the resistance to the Soviet occupation of Afghanistan during the 1980s.

1 Be patient.

Osama bin Laden, 11 Sept. 2001; *Keesing's Record of World Events*, Dec. 2001, p.44496. Bin Laden was the mastermind behind an attack on two buildings symbolic of American capitalism, the twin towers of the World Trade Center in New York. His followers had already planted a bomb in the basement of the Center in 1993, but this time the assault was altogether more ambitious. Two hijacked airliners flew into the towers on the morning of 11 Sept. 2001, while a third dived into the Pentagon, the US Defense Department in Washington. A fourth, purportedly aiming for the Capitol or the White House, crashed in Pennsylvania. Altogether, close on 3,000 people died that day as a result. Bin Laden's words come from the video of a meeting in Oct. 2001, when he recalled speaking by telephone to a supporter soon after the first plane struck the north tower of the Center, knowing that a second was on its way to hit the south tower.

2 To say it looks like a war zone and to tell you about bodies and blood in the street would not begin to describe what it's like. It is unimaginable, devastating, unspeakable carnage.

Firefighter Scott O'Grady of the Fire Department of New York, 11 Sept. 2001, on the scene after the collapse of both towers in the aftermath of the air strikes. 343 firemen died in the effort to evacuate the towers.

3 Let's roll.

Todd Beamer, passenger on United Airlines Flight 93; *Evening Standard*, 11 Sept. 2002. This flight was brought down in Pennsylvania, short of its intended target in Washington, after a death struggle between passengers and hijackers. Beamer spoke these words over his mobile phone; they are inscribed on the monument in the field where Flight 93 came down.

4 United We Stand.

Slogan displayed throughout the United States after the atrocity of 9/11. It invokes a rallying-cry of the American Revolution, inspired by John Dickinson's 'Liberty Song' of 1768: 'Then join hand in hand, brave Americans all./By uniting we stand, by dividing we fall.'

5 Have faith in God, but nuke 'em just the same.

Graffito in New York following 11 Sept.

6 Not in my son's name, you don't. I don't want my son used as a pawn to justify the killing of others.

Professor Orlando Rodriguez, whose son Gregory died on 11 Sept., answers calls for massive retaliation.

7 The Americans love Pepsi Cola, but we love death.

Placard waved by an Afghan in Pakistan, Sept. 2001.

8 It's now a very good day to get out anything we want to bury. Councillors' expenses?

Jo Moore, personal assistant to British government minister, Stephen Byers, e-mail, 11 Sept. 2001; *The Times*, 9 Oct. 2001. A piece of advice that plumbed new depths of political cynicism, for which Ms Moore was eventually (but not immediately) compelled to resign.

9 These acts shatter steel, but they cannot dent the steel of American resolve. America was targeted for attack because we're the brightest beacon for freedom and opportunity in the world. And no one will keep that light from shining. Today our nation saw evil, and we responded with the best of America.

President George W. Bush, *The Times*, 12 Sept. 2001.

10 A brilliantly orchestrated feat of planning, coordination and execution backed by formidable religious convictions, the attack on New York and Washington exemplifies something that has come to characterize the modern world: the union of the symbolic with the actual, the mythical with the material, in a single act of destruction shown live on television. It is a perfect example of what extremists of an earlier period termed the 'propaganda of the deed'. Faced with such fiendish efficiency, liberal democracy is wrong-footed. The crucial evidence that would persuade the whole world of bin Laden's complicity is withheld on security grounds. The language, and exigencies of war replace those of justice, confirming the Islamic argument that Western justice is a godless sham.

Jonathan Freedland, *Guardian*, 10 Oct. 2001.

11 If inciting people to do that is terrorism, and if killing those who kill our sons is terrorism, then let history be witness that we are terrorists.

Osama bin Laden, Oct. 2001; *Keesing's Record of World Events*, Jan. 2002, p.44546.

12 States like these, and their terrorist allies, constitute an axis of evil, arming to threaten the peace of the world. By seeking weapons of mass destruction, these regimes pose a grave and growing danger. They could provide these arms to terrorists, giving them the means to match their hatred. They could attack our allies or attempt to blackmail the United States. In any of these cases, the price of indifference could be catastrophic.

President George W. Bush, State of the Union address, 29 Jan. 2002; *Keesing's Record of World Events*, Jan. 2002, pp.44591–2. Bush was referring to Iraq, Iran and North Korea as the trio of the 'axis of evil', now in America's sights in the wake of 11 Sept. By this time the United States had purged Afghanistan of the Islamic fundamentalist regime of the Taliban, which had provided bin Laden and his al-Qaeda organization with its base of operations. Now it looked elsewhere in its war on terror.

1 God's Punishment.

Headline, Iraq's state-owned newspaper *Al-Iktisadi*, 11 Sept. 2002. Compare the comment of Tsar Nicholas I on the fire that destroyed the British Houses of Parliament in 1834: 'God's judgement on the Reform Bill.'

2 All the world now faces a test, and the United Nations a difficult and defining moment. Are Security Council resolutions to be honored and enforced, or cast aside without consequence? Will the United Nations serve the purpose of its founders or will it be irrelevant?

President George W. Bush before the UN General Assembly, 12 Sept. 2002; *Keesing's Record of World Events*, Sept. 2002, p.45007. Bush was making the point that Iraq had failed to respond adequately to every UN resolution passed in the 1990s. The United Nations now had the chance to enforce its will on Saddam Hussein; if it did not do so, he declared that the United States and its associates would take unilateral military action against Iraq.

3 The Security Council ...

1. Decides that Iraq has been and remains in material breach of its obligations under relevant resolutions ...

9. Demands ... that Iraq cooperate immediately, unconditionally, and actively with UNMOVIC and the IAEA [the United Nations Monitoring, Verification and Inspection Commission and the International Atomic Energy Agency] ...

13. Recalls ... that the Council has repeatedly warned Iraq that it will face serious consequences as a result of its continued violation of its obligations.

United Nations Security Council Resolution 1441, 8 Nov. 2002; *Keesing's Record of World Events*, Nov. 2002, pp.44115–6. The resolution was passed unanimously by all 15 members of the Security Council, including Iraq's Arab neighbour, Syria.

4 'I'll come and see you in the morning. I'm worried you all have something left.'

'We evacuated everything. We don't have anything left.'

Telephone dialogue between two Iraqi commanders, 26 Nov. 2002, as presented to the United Nations on 5 Feb. 2003 by the US secretary of state, Colin Powell; *The Economist*, 8 Feb. 2003, p.25. Set out as evidence that Iraq was concealing its weapons of mass destruction and was consequently in material breach of its obligations under Resolution 1441.

5 You're thinking of Europe as Germany and France. I don't. I think that's Old Europe. If you look at the entire NATO, Europe today, the centre of gravity is shifting to the East, and there are a lot of new members.

US secretary of defense Donald Rumsfeld, *New York Times*, 24 Jan. 2003. His answer to a question on European opposition to a war with Iraq, notably by France and Germany. The new East European members of NATO were strongly behind the United States in its determination to go to war, regardless of the United Nations if need be. These remarks were bitterly resented by France and Germany.

6 France is an old country that does not forget and knows everything it owes to the freedom fighters who came from America and elsewhere.

French foreign minister Dominique de Villepin, *The Times*, 15 Feb. 2003. A pointed reference to the Americans who had fought and died in France in two world wars.

7 We SHELL not EXXONerate Saddam Hussein for his actions. We will MOBILize to meet this threat in the Persian GULF until an AMOCOble solution is reached. Our plan is to BPrepared. Failing that, we ARCOming to kick his ass.

Words put in the mouth of President Bush in a poster issued by DemocracyMeansYou.com, one of the groups protesting against a war with Iraq, Feb. 2003. For them, oil was obviously the sole *raison d'être* of American policy towards Iraq.

8 I don't think the next step should be let's send in more inspectors to get stiffed.

US secretary of state Colin Powell, *The Times*, 2 Feb. 2003. The answer to the French argument that the UN inspection team, headed by Hans Blix, would secure Iraq's disarmament without the need for war.

9 People are used to a different century. People are used to Pearl Harbor. They are used to being attacked and then responding.

Donald Rumsfeld, *The Times*, 10 Feb. 2003. The view, already expressed by President Bush, that the world would be a safer place if the United States did not wait to retaliate against the terrorism of the 'axis of evil' but took the initiative itself in a policy of 'first strike'. At Pearl Harbor on 7 Dec. 1941, as in New York and Washington on 11 Sept. 2001, America had taken huge punishment; now others were to be on the receiving end.

10 Yes, the American troops have advanced further. This will only make it easier for us to defeat them.

Iraqi information minister Muhammad Said al-Sharif, *The Times*, 22 April 2003. After the United States and Britain opened hostilities on 18 March, British troops encircled Basra while American armour drove towards Baghdad. The minister strove daily to make the best of a dire Iraqi situation. He was known to the coalition forces as 'Comical Ali' (the general responsible for the Halabja massacre of 1988 having been given the grim sobriquet of 'Chemical Ali').

1 Baghdad, its people and leadership, is determined to force the Mongols of our age to commit suicide at its gates.

Saddam Hussein, *The Times*, 22 April 2003. In 1258 the Mongols sacked Baghdad and terminated the Abbasid caliphate; in 2003 Saddam hoped against hope for a different outcome.

2 When we talk about Arab civilization, we talk about Baghdad, because it was there that the Arab enlightenment started. It makes us sad to see Baghdad under occupation, because it reminds us of the time that the Mongols burned all the manuscripts and threw them into the Tigris.

The Jordanian Adnan Abu-Odeh, *New York Times*, 10 April 2003. By 9 April American forces had moved into the heart of the Iraqi capital and ended the Saddam Hussein regime. It was Iraqis, not Americans, who behaved like the Mongols in destroying and looting the priceless contents of the National Museum, though American forces were slow to enter it. In 1258 it is said the River Tigris was first red with the blood of the defenders of the city, then black with the ink from the texts the Mongols flung into it.

3 With those attacks [of 11 Sept. 2001], the terrorists and their supporters declared war on the United States. And war is what they got … Our commitment to liberty is in America's tradition, declared at our founding, affirmed in Franklin Roosevelt's Four Freedoms, asserted in the Truman Doctrine and in Ronald Reagan's challenge to an evil empire. We are committed to freedom in Afghanistan, in Iraq and in a peaceful Palestine. The advance of freedom is the surest strategy to undermine the appeal of terror in the world … You all can know, friend and foe alike, that our nation has a mission. We will answer threats to our security and we will defend the peace … The war on terror is not over, yet it is not endless. We do not know the day of final victory, but we have seen the turning of the tide.

President George W. Bush, *New York Times*, 2 May 2003. Speaking on the deck of the aircraft carrier *Abraham Lincoln*, the president declared the war with Iraq at an end. Yet, as he was at pains to emphasize, this marked only the closure of one phase in the American struggle with terrorism, which stretched far into the foreseeable future. For the Four Freedoms, the Truman Doctrine and the 'evil empire' see 859:9, 877:1 and 888:8.

Globalization

GLOBALIZATION:
THE WAY WE LIVE NOW

1 'Globalization' is on everybody's lips; a fad word fast turning into a shibboleth, a magic incantation, a pass-key meant to unlock the gates to all present and future mysteries. For some, 'globalization' is what we are bound to do if we wish to be happy; for others, 'globalization' is the cause of our unhappiness. For everybody, though, 'globalization' is the intractable fate of the world, an irreversible process.
Zygmunt Bauman *Globalization: The Human Consequences* (1998) p.1.

2 I believe that if you want to understand the post-Cold War world you have to start by understanding that a new international system has succeeded it – globalization. This is 'The One Big Thing' people should focus on. Globalization is not the only thing influencing events in the world today, but to the extent that there is a North Star and a worldwide shaping force, it is this system. What is new is the system. What is old is power politics, chaos, clashing civilizations and liberalism. And what is the drama of the post-Cold War world is the interaction between this new system and these old passions.
Thomas L. Friedman *The Lexus and the Olive Tree* (1999) p.xviii.

3 Never in 2,000 years has the doctrine of the free market spread so widely across the globe. Communism has been buried, socialism is in deep retreat, and even the hardiest proponents of social democracy are beset by doubt. Adam Smith has vanquished Marx, immobilized Keynes, and turned many thoughts away from Jesus ... Just as religion is on the defensive, so also democracy and political pluralism, two important doctrines associated with capitalism, are being taken up with less enthusiasm, and in fewer countries, than the system of wealth creation that is now everywhere regarded as the most effective that humanity has yet devised.
Financial Times, editorial, 'Capitalism at Christmas', 24 Dec. 1993. In 1776 Adam Smith published the bible of free-market capitalism, *The Wealth of Nations*. In 1867, the revolutionary socialist Karl Marx issued his counterblast, *Das Kapital*. The economist John Maynard Keynes argued successfully for a middle way between these two extremes. Both now seemed to have been eclipsed, along with Christian altruism.

GLOBAL VILLAGE:
THE VIRTUAL COMMUNITY

4 We can now live, not just amphibiously, in divided and distinguished worlds, but pluralistically in many worlds and cultures simultaneously ... The electro-magnetic discoveries have recreated the simultaneous 'field' in all human affairs so that the human family now exists under conditions of a 'global village'.
Canadian sociologist Marshall McLuhan *The Gutenberg Galaxy* (1962) p.31. McLuhan, writing well before the telecommunications revolution of the 1980s, coined the term 'global village'.

5 There is no such thing as a global village. Most media are rooted in their national and local cultures.
Media magnate Rupert Murdoch, *Business Review Weekly*, 17 Nov. 1989. In the eyes of Murdoch's critics, his ever-expanding multi-media empire, far from recognizing cultural diversity, is driving towards worldwide cultural monopoly.

6 The defensive battle of the Chinese regime against faxes, e-mail and TV broadcasts from the capitalist world serves not only to keep it in power but also to keep at bay a different concept of society. Where television pictures from the world of universal commodities are still frowned upon, as in North Korea and some Islamic countries, photographs and detailed reports do the rounds instead. Even in Iran, where American heavy metal is the most popular music among middle-class teenagers, the Ayatollahs no longer have their sovereign air space under firm control.
New Perspectives Quarterly, Fall 1995, p.3. Media images of western lifestyles played a significant role in the collapse of communism in Eastern Europe.

7 American entertainment offers a great variety of individual options, individual choice and individual expression. That is what people want everywhere ... As a result of its unrestricted creative freedom, the US entertainment industry produces originality that cannot be found anywhere else in the world.
Michael Eisner, president and chairman of the Walt Disney Corporation, *New Perspectives Quarterly*, Fall 1995, p.9. Disney is a global giant, not merely in terms of film production and distribution but through its many associated commercial enterprises. The US is the biggest exporter of films and television programmes to the rest of the world, and the smallest importer.

1 As the peasant sits in the evening with his family to watch the TV that his son has purchased from the fruits of his labour in Saudi Arabia, the intrigues of J.R. Ewing and Sue Ellen in *Dallas* strip him of what is left of his legitimacy as a cultural bearer in his own culture. Between programmes, he is told in English that he should be drinking Schweppes or in dubbed Arabic that he should use deodorant, and that all his problems are caused by having too many children – a total package of imported ideas.

The Egyptian commentator F. El Guindi *Middle East Insight* Vol.2 (1982) p.21. Advertising, as the essential partner of commercial television, has probably had a greater influence in promoting Western material aspirations than the programmes themselves.

2 Many of us change places – moving homes and travelling to and from places which are not our homes. Some of us do not need to go out and travel: we can dash or scurry or flit through the Web, netting and mixing on the computer screen messages born in opposite corners of the globe. But most of us are on the move even if physically, bodily, we stay put. When, as is our habit, we are glued to our chairs and zap the cable or satellite channels on and off the TV screen – jumping in and out of foreign spaces with a speed much beyond the capacity of supersonic jets and cosmic rockets, but nowhere staying long enough to be more than visitors, to feel *chez soi* [at home].

Zygmunt Bauman (1998) p.77. The first satellite was launched in 1969. Now several hundred circle the earth, giving television access to billions of people, even those without electricity, but with solar panels instead.

3 With the information technologies already available, I can sit on the beach of my Florida home with a lap-top computer and a cellular phone and monitor the video images installed throughout my manufacturing company in Ohio to insure that my people are on the job and doing their work properly.

US company owner interviewed on US National Public Radio, 31 Aug. 1994; David C. Korten *When Corporations Rule the World* (1995) p.103.

4 It's what I've always wanted – to be in touch with a community of ideas like this … There's something thrilling about the Internet … It almost doesn't matter what anyone says. It's more the thrill of knowing you're in touch with people laterally, rather than through a filter of some kind.

Brian Eno, British rock musician, interviewed in *i-D*, Oct. 1993.

5 It's a bit like a neighbourhood pub or coffee shop. It's a little like a salon where I can participate in a hundred ongoing conversations with people who don't care what I look like or sound like, but who do care how I think and communicate. There are seminars and word fights in different corners.

The computer enthusiast Howard Rheingold *Virtual Community: Homesteading on the Electronic Frontier* (1993) p.66. Following around 20 years of experiments in the UK and US into computer message interchanges, the Internet was launched in 1983. Collaboration between the US and EU resulted in the creation of the World Wide Web in 1996.

6 Enthusiasm for a medium that keeps you away from human beings strikes me as worrying. That you would rather live in an unreal time and space, with unreal people who don't even give their names – you can say whatever you like, you can be whoever you like – means that people aren't anyone, they become more and more unreal.

British satirical journalist Ian Hislop, speaking on Channel Four TV, 19 March 1996.

7 Cyberspace is where a long-distance phone call takes place. Cyberspace is where the bank keeps your money. Where your medical records are stored. All of this stuff is out there somewhere. There is really no point in thinking about its geographical location. Information is extra-geographical.

American science-fiction writer William Gibson, interviewed in Simon Dwyer (ed.) *Rapid Eye 3* (1995). The coinage 'cyberspace' originated in Gibson's science-fiction book *Neuromancer* (1984) to describe conceptual space where words, data, human relationships and power are all manifested.

8 All over the world, people switched on their computers to find messages waiting for them purporting to come from people they know, labelled 'I Love You'. Hearts thumping, overweight Senators in the American Mid-West, sharp-faced bankers in Zurich, Ministers of the Crown at Westminster, acne-ridden boys and girls in the suburbs of Sydney, all eagerly clicked open the file and then read its personal attachment, desperate to read more, so that within a matter of hours the 'love-bug' had spread to the four corners of the globe, eating up files and bringing cyber commerce to a standstill.

Daily Telegraph, editorial on the bizarre 'love-bug' incident. Just after midnight on 4 May 2000 the virus control centre of Message Labs in Cirencester, England, intercepted a copy of this e-mail. By the following midday tens of millions of computers worldwide had been disabled, including those in the Houses of Parliament, the US Congress and the White

House. Clean-up costs were estimated in billions of dollars. The culprit was thought to be a young Filipino computer buff in Manila. The episode is a classic example of what damage can be caused to the global communications system by a dedicated wrecker.

1 Fundamentalism is a child of globalization, which it both responds to and utilizes. Fundamentalist groups almost everywhere have made extensive use of new communications technologies.

Anthony Giddens *Runaway World* (2002) pp.49–50. The mobile phone, recorded television broadcasts, training videos, Internet messages and electronic money transfers have all played a vital role in spreading the word and organizing terrorist action by religious fundamentalists.

MONEY MAKES THE WORLD GO ROUND

2 An organized money market has many advantages. But it is not a school of social ethics or of political responsibility.

R.H. Tawney *Religion and the Rise of Capitalism* (1926) p.177.

3 The daily turnover of foreign exchange transactions is of the order of $1 trillion [one million million] a day, of which only 15 per cent corresponds to actual commodity trade and capital flows. Within this global financial web, money transits at high speed from one banking haven to the next, in the intangible form of electronic transfers. 'Legal' and 'illegal' business activities have become increasingly intertwined and vast amounts of unreported private wealth have been accumulated.

Michael Chossudovsky *The Globalization of Poverty* (1998) p.20. Chossudovsky uses an estimate from *The Economist*, 15 Aug. 1992, p.61.

4 In matters of finance and politics, if not culture, we are becoming the world and much of the world wants to become us.

Richard Grasco, chairman of the New York Stock Exchange, 1997; Leonard Seabrooke *U.S. Power in International Finance* (2001).

5 The international financial system has been shaped to extend US financial and political power, not to promote the world public good. And that is what it has done.

Will Hutton *The World We're In* (2000) pp.199–200. Hutton claims that since 1974, when American capital controls were lifted, the drive to integrate the world's markets around the dollar has resulted in such overall dominance in banking and

financial services that the rest of the world 'becomes enslaved to the prevalent US financial and economic ideology'.

6 'Turbo-capitalism' is a bad joke. What Marxists argued a hundred years ago, and was then absolutely wrong, is today a reality. The capitalists are becoming richer and richer, while the working class is becoming impoverished.

The conservative American economist Edward Luttwak, *Die Weltwoche* (The Weekly World), 31 Aug. 1995. Luttwak coined the term 'turbo-capitalism' to denote high-powered capitalist dynamism. Starting as a devotee of the phenomenon, he became one of its sharpest critics.

7 I used to think if there was reincarnation, I wanted to come back as the President or the Pope or a .400 baseball-hitter, but now I want to come back as the bond market. You can intimidate everybody.

Bill Clinton's campaign manager, James Carville, 1993; Walter Dean Burnham 'Realignment Lives: The 1994 Earthquake and its Implications' in Colin Campbell and Bert A. Rockman (eds) *The Clinton Presidency* (1996) p.381. Carville was expressing his frustration at the Clinton administration's inability to put through reforms in health and education because federal bonds began to fall in value as investment bankers forged a united front against fresh government spending.

8 [Financial globalization] which has induced such dramatic increases in private capital flows has also exhibited significantly improved capacities to transmit ill-advised investments … One can scarcely imagine the size of losses ($1 billion) of a single trader employing modern techniques that contributed to the demise of Baring's in 1995 being accomplished in the paper-trade environment of earlier decades. Clearly our productivity to create losses has improved measurably in recent years.

Alan Greenspan, chairman of the US Federal Reserve; Friedman (1999) pp.109–10. Baring's Bank, Britain's oldest merchant banking group, collapsed on 26 Feb. 1995 after the discovery that its 28-year-old trader in Singapore, Nick Leeson, had run up huge debts through financial derivative contracts. He received a prison sentence in Singapore for illegal trading.

9 Rarely has the world witnessed such capricious and vacuous venality dressed up as 'enterprise'; rarely have so many been gulled by such duplicity.

Will Hutton (2000) p.356. He refers to the series of investment fiascos, particularly in telecom share trading, running into the loss of trillions of dollars, during the late 1990s.

10 As an anonymous participant in financial markets, I never had to weigh the social consequences of my actions … I felt justified in ignoring them on the grounds that I was playing by the rules.

George Soros, the Hungarian-born US investor, *The Crisis of Global Capitalism* (1998) p.196. As a currency speculator Soros made a huge fortune out of the sterling crisis resulting from Britain's withdrawal from the Exchange Rate Mechanism in Sept. 1992.

1 There are spooks in the anarchic global financial forest, a forest that has been carelessly if deliberately cultivated, deregulated and then allowed to run riot by respected central bankers like Hans Tietmayer, Eddie George and Alan Greenspan. The spooks attack like bolts of lightning, unexpectedly and out of the blue. No one, except perhaps for one or two very brave economists, predicted Japan's descent into an economic morass. Nobody predicted the South East Asian crisis. And no one – least of all the Nobel Prize economists running the Long-term Capital Management Fund – predicted Russia's default in 1998.

Ann Pettifor, programme coordinator at the London-based New Economics Foundation, 'Debt' in Emma Bircham and John Charlton (eds) *Anti-Capitalism* (2001) p.46. Tietmayer, George and Greenspan were heads of the German, British and American central banks respectively. In the latter half of 1997 unpredicted serious speculative damage hit most of the 'tiger economies' of Southeast Asia. On 17 Aug. 1998 the Russian government froze its foreign debt repayments and devalued the rouble by a third without warning. Japan's over-borrowing and over-consumption in the 1980s led to debts that could not be repaid, bankruptcy and unemployment. Japan then entered a decade-long struggle with domestic recession following devaluation of the yen.

2 The World Is Ten Years Old.

It was born when the Wall fell in 1989. It's no surprise that the world's youngest economy – the global economy – is still finding its bearings … Many world markets are only recently freed, governed for the first time by the emotions of the people rather than the fists of the state … The spread of free markets and democracy around the world is permitting more people everywhere to turn their aspirations into achievements. And technology, properly harnessed and liberally distributed, has the power to erase not just geographical borders but also human ones. It seems to us that, for a 10-year-old, the world continues to hold great promise. In the meantime, no one ever said growing up was easy.

The major US investment bank Merrill Lynch, full-page advertisement, 11 Oct. 1998, seeking to shore up the confidence of the American public at the height of the global economic crisis; Friedman (1999) p.xiv.

BORDERLESS BUSINESS

3 Before national identity, before local affiliation, before German ego or Italian ego or Japanese ego – before any of this comes the commitment to a single unified global mission.

Japanese business strategist Kenichi Ohmae *The Borderless World: Power and Strategy in the Interlinked Economy* (1990) p.94. Through mergers and take-overs, often at international level, large corporations have transformed themselves into highly organized global networks of production and distribution that are historically unique. It is estimated that the major 500 multinational corporations (MNCs) account for two-thirds of world trade.

4 Corporate executives dream of a global market made up of people with homogenized tastes and needs … Logos on bottles, boxes, and labels are global banners, instantly recognizable by millions who could not tell you the color of the UN flag.

Richard J. Barnet and John Cavanagh 'The Sound of Money' in *Sojourners*, Jan. 1994, p.12.

5 The issue [of consumerism] is deeper than greed and selfishness. Material consumption – buying and possessing things – has become the primary way of belonging in America and around the world. If we can't buy, we can't belong.

Jim Wallis *The Soul of Politics: A Practical and Prophetic Vision* (1994) Ch.7. The plentiful supply of cheap and varied goods to the developed world has created a symbiotic relationship between supplier and consumer.

6 Transnational corporations are the economic giants that roam the earth in search of profit. These huge companies are the main 'players' in the globalization game, intent on dominating the world economy.

Steve Tibbett, spokesman for War on Want, 'Borderless Business' in Craig Donnellan (ed.) *Globalization* Vol.55 of *Issues* (2002) p.18. MNCs tend to concentrate production where labour cost are lower than in the West, especially in Southeast Asia, and their critics accuse them of readily moving their factories to new locations to make even greater profit. Their defenders, however, argue that these claims are exaggerated and that setting up new production and distribution systems is too complex to be undertaken lightly.

THE BIG LENDERS

7 The trouble was that since the 1970s, the World Bank and the International Monetary Fund, politically backed by the USA, had pursued a policy systematically favouring free-market orthodoxy, private enterprise and global free trade, which suited the late twentieth-century US economy as well as it had the mid-nineteenth-century British one, but not necessarily the world.

Eric Hobsbawm *Age of Extremes: The Short Twentieth Century* (1994) p.578. The IMF and the World Bank were set up as a result of the Bretton Woods Conference of 1944 . The IMF's role was to promote international financial stability by providing short-term loans to governments. Much of its funding has gone to countries with serious balance-of-payment deficits. For instance, in 1976 the UK received a loan of $3.9 billion, and public spending had to be cut by £2.5 billion in accordance with the terms of the loan.

1 In a globalized world, one can no longer afford not to adapt ... The world is in the hands of these guys.

Michael Camdessus, head of the IMF in Washington, 5 Feb. 1996; Hans-Peter Martin and Harald Schumann *The Global Trap* (1997 edn) p.189. 'These guys' being the Wall Street fund managers. In Jan. 1995 Camdessus authorized a loan of $17.5 billion to Mexico, subsidizing a US government loan, to rescue Mexico from bankruptcy. Operation 'Peso Shield' was in response to panic among foreign investors, who had been promised high returns on government bonds, as they viewed the prospect of losses of billions of dollars when the Mexican economy faltered and the peso went into free fall. Critics accused Camdessus of using public money to bail out private shareholders. The Clinton administration, however, wanted to ensure the survival of the Mexican economy to avoid even greater numbers of 'wet backs' (illegal immigrants) fleeing Mexico for the US.

2 To address poverty, economic growth is not an option: it is a necessity.

Mahbub ul Haq, former vice-president of the World Bank, April 1994; Korten (1995) p.37. The World Bank makes longer term loans for specific projects to promote modernization in developing countries. There are 183 member-states, which must, first, be members of the IMF. In 2000 the Bank lent almost £12 billion. Funds are built up from member-countries' contributions, from bonds floated on the world's financial markets and from earnings from the Bank's assets.

3 The pressure to lend ... is both internal and external: it comes from the Bank's member-countries, and is strongly reinforced by the institution's natural proclivity toward bureaucratic self-aggrandizement ... But the Bank's haste to lend has meant that the quality of the projects it finances has been declining for years. We've seen that even in purely conventional economic terms an alarming number of these projects have been failures, not to speak of the enormous ecological and social damage they have inflicted. It would be only just if the Bank were to forgive the debts owed by many nations with

net negative transfer problems, especially since many of these countries – such as Brazil – have also been the sites of some of the worst Bank-financed fiascos.

Bruce Rich *The World Bank, Economic Impoverishment and the Crisis of Development* (1994) p.309. In the 1980s the Brazilian economy nose-dived into chaos, with an average annual inflation rate between 1985 and 1992 of 730%. In 1992 it headed the world league-table of debtors, with liabilities of $121 billion. The conditions attached to successive rescue loans from the Bank and the IMF were ignored, but the loans kept on being made all the same.

4 The ideal solution would be to abolish the Fund and the Bank – wind them up and disperse their expertise to other activities. The Bank and the Fund were the progeny of a generation that regarded government management of banking and finance as being the only way forward. Yet in the intervening years, we have become increasingly aware of the advantages of getting government and politics out of monetary policy and finance.

Sir Alan Walters *Do We Need the IMF and the World Bank?* (1994) p.22. Walters was Margaret Thatcher's financial policy adviser. He claims that much of the money lent to developing countries is wasted through incompetence and corruption and that loans made on an entirely commercial footing through the private sector would be better used.

5 Adjustment is the necessary first step on the road to sustainable, poverty-reducing growth. But adjustment programs in Sub-Saharan Africa have been burdened with unrealistically high hopes ... Some proponents of adjustment thought it could quickly put African countries onto a much higher growth path than before. Too often there has been little effort to determine whether Africa's disappointing performance in the aggregate represents a failure to adjust or a failure of adjustment ... pessimism is unwarranted, for there has been progress. The turnaround in growth shows that adjustment – even incomplete adjustment – can put African countries back on the road to development.

International Bank for Reconstruction and Development (World Bank) *Adjustment in Africa* (1994) pp.15–16. Structural adjustment requirements, a condition of obtaining loans from the Bank, include movement towards privatization of production and services, prioritizing the export market, scaling down the civil service and other public cost-saving measures, as well as giving encouragement to foreign companies.

6 Africa does need development assistance, just as it needs debt relief from its crushing international debt burden. But aid and debt relief can only go so far. We are asking for the opportunity to compete, to sell our goods in western markets. In short, we want to trade our way out of poverty.

President Yoweri Museveni of Uganda; Stephen Byers 'The IMF and World Bank Orthodoxy is Increasing Global Poverty' in the *Guardian*, 19 May 2003. Byers, ministerial head of the UK delegation to the World Trade Organization (WTO) conference in Seattle (see 950:4), claims that an increase of just 1% of Africa's share of world exports would generate around £43 million – five times the amount of aid Africa receives.

1 Zimbabwe (once considered the 'bread basket' of Southern Africa) was severely affected by the famine and drought which swept Southern Africa in 1992. The country experienced a drop of 90 per cent in its maize crop, located largely in less productive lands. Yet ironically at the height of the drought, tobacco for export (supported by modern irrigation, credit, research, etc.) registered a bumper harvest. While 'the famine forces the population to eat termites', much of the export earnings from Zimbabwe's tobacco harvest were used to service the external debt.

Michael Chossudovsky (1998) p.106.

2 Debt is a direct expression of the unjust global economic order which is the result of a long history of slavery, exploitation and terms of trade which are detrimental to the poor.

Jubilee 2000 *Latin America/Caribbean Platform Declaration* (1999). In conjunction with organizations such as the Red Cross, the Jubilee movement has pushed for debt reduction for the poorest countries. By the end of 2000, as a result of international pressure, 24 countries were included in the debt-relief programme. However, the IMF was given enhanced powers to approve the debtor countries' economic policies before granting debt relief.

3 The US Treasury recognizes, quite correctly, that the combination of debt plus structural adjustment plus massive privatization is a far more efficient instrument than colonization ever was for keeping countries in line.

Susan George 'Corporate Globalization' in Bircham and Charlton (2001) p.15.

4 All too often the dogma of liberalization became an end in itself, not a means to achieving a better financial system.

Joseph Stiglitz, 19 Jan. 2000, reported on the Internet service Business Line; Hutton (2000). Stiglitz said this soon after leaving his post as chief economist of the World Bank. In his three years at the Bank he had become increasingly frustrated by the rigid application by both the Bank and the IMF of the so-called 'Washington Consensus' neo-liberal economic policies. He had fought against the IMF's austerity programme in Asia on the grounds that it would lead to what he called 'a synchronized recession', but to no avail.

FREE-TRADE WINDS

5 We don't need to build up walls, we need to build bridges. We don't need protection, we need opportunity. But in a world of stiff competition we also need more than free trade. We need fair trade with fair rules ... As a result of our efforts to create a new global trading system, the world isn't just a better place for Americans to do business, make money, and create jobs, it's also a safer place. The fact is that fair trade among free markets does much more than simply enrich America, it enriches all partners to each transaction ... That's why we have worked so hard to help build free-market institutions in Eastern Europe, Russia, and the former Soviet republics. That's why we have supported commercial liberalization in China – the world's fastest-growing market. Just as democracy helps make the world safe for commerce, commerce helps make the world safe for democracy. It's a two-way street.

US President Bill Clinton *Between Hope and History* (1996) p.34. The president's critics accused him of being unrealistic about the likelihood of achieving his goals on human rights and nuclear proliferation control through increased international trade.

6 The WTO is a friend of the poor. Its rules protect the weak in a world of unequal power ... Of course, the WTO is not perfect. But it is better than the law of the jungle, where might equals right.

Philippe Legrain 'Dump those Prejudices' in Donnellan (2002) pp.11, 12. Legrain has been a special adviser to the WTO, which was created in 1995. Its membership is based largely on that of its predecessor, GATT (the 1947 General Agreement on Tariffs and Trade). Its stated aim is to work towards a fairer, more equitable system, giving greater help to poorer members. However, the richer members continue to exert their strength to their own advantage in negotiations over trading laws.

7 If we want to fight global inequality, we should lower these [trade] barriers, and allow agriculture to do for Africa what textiles and micro-chips have done for Asia.

British foreign secretary Jack Straw 'Globalization is Good for Us' in Donnellan (2002) p.17. Straw is referring to trade barriers still in place, erected by the US and the European Union to protect their own agriculture from cheaper competition, despite WTO agreements.

1 The South's weakness also stems from its lack of bargaining power and negotiating strength in international relations. Being heavily indebted and dependent on bilateral aid donors and multilateral loan organizations, developing countries have been drained of their capacity to negotiate (even on the terms of loan conditionalities). The powers of the United Nations, in which the South is in a more favourable position, have been diminished, whereas the mandate and powers of the institutions under the control of developed countries (the IMF, the World Bank and WTO) have been increased tremendously. The North has leverage in the Bretton Woods institutions and the WTO to shape the content of globalization to serve their needs, and to formulate policies which the developing countries have to take on.

Martin Khor *Globalization and the South: Some Critical Issues* (United Nations Conference on Trade, Aid and Development) April 2000.

2 Ghana's government used to help small-scale farmers like Lydia by subsidizing the prices of things like seeds, tools, and fertilizers. Ghana's no longer allowed to do this, according to the rules set by international organizations like the World Bank, the IMF and the WTO. They're forcing Ghana to liberalize its economy. This means the government has to spend money on making things to sell to other countries, instead of spending money to help farmers like Lydia. The government is also forced to make it easier for other countries and companies to trade in Ghana.

Christian Aid *Trade for Life* in Donnellan (2002) p.25.

3 We oppose the profit-orientated New Economic Policy with its attendant liberalization, privatization and globalization because it marginalizes and even excludes a majority of people and exhausts the resources of the nation for the sake of the accumulation of profit. We, therefore, propose that India quits the WTO. We propose that India refuses to submit to any conditionalities and structural adjustment programmes imposed by the World Bank, IMF and similar international institutions.

Founding statement of the National Alliance of Peoples' Movements, 1993.

4 The battle lines are drawn. In the next few days tens of thousands of protesters will descend on Seattle in a bid to stop a new round of trade negotiations by the World Trade Organization. They see themselves as Luke Skywalkers to the WTO's Darth Vader, fighting to save the world from the threat of increased poverty and environmental destruction ... On the other side of the barricades will be a small army of corporate lobbyists, many of them linked to Western governments. They see themselves – and the WTO – as defenders of a global free-trade system that enshrines the principles of multilateralism and promises unprecedented prosperity. Both sets of protagonists pose a profound threat to a constituency that will not be well represented in Seattle – namely, the world's poor.

Independent, editorial, 'Senseless in Seattle', 28 Nov. 1999. The hero of the 1977 film *Star Wars* was Luke Skywalker, its villain Darth Vader. The Seattle conference of the WTO was the scene of massive protests over its alleged bias against the poor of the Third World.

5 When the Death Star of the WTO exploded with the protests in Seattle, GATS was the hatch pod in which Darth Vader made his escape.

Rob Newman, comedian, *Guardian*, Dec. 1999; Bircham and Charlton (2001) p.32. Despite the disruptions at Seattle, the General Agreement on Trade in Services (GATS) gave major new rights to MNCs while removing discretionary governmental powers regarding the provision of public services such as health, education and social services. Article XVI:2(a) prohibits any limitation on the number of service suppliers and thereby opens the door to private competition.

6 Our young people have things to say about the world they will inherit ... It's time we listened. Why am I writing this? To try to make Canadians realize what a truly apathetic bunch we've become – and ask if this is really what we want our country to be? Something is amiss in our society and our government: do we care?

The Canadian Beverley Young, *Macleans's Magazine*, 1 July 2000, p.18. Her 22-year-old son was arrested in June 2000 in the protests in Windsor, Ontario, against the proposed Free Trade Area of the Americas.

EARTH IN THE BALANCE

7 The history of life on earth has been a history of interaction between living things and their surroundings ... Only within the moment of time represented by the present century has one species

acquired significant power to alter the nature of the world.

Rachel Carson *Silent Spring* (1962) p.2. Carson's book drew the general public's attention for the first time to the issue of environmental degradation.

1 Even the most ardent environmentalist doesn't really want to stop pollution. If he thinks about it, and doesn't just talk about it, he wants to have the *right amount* of pollution. We can't really *afford* to eliminate it – not without abandoning all the benefits of technology that we not only enjoy but on which we depend.

The conservative American economist, Milton Friedman *There's No Such Thing as a Free Lunch* (1975) Introduction.

2 Approximately 80 per cent of our air pollution stems from hydrocarbons released by vegetation, so let's not go overboard in setting and enforcing tough emission standards from man-made sources.

Ronald Reagan, *Sierra*, 10 Sept. 1980; 'Killer Trees' in Mark Green and Gail MacColl (eds) *Reagan's Reign of Error* (1987). Reagan was elected president of the US soon afterwards.

3 For generations, we have assumed that the efforts of mankind would leave the fundamental equilibrium of the world's systems and atmosphere stable. But it is possible that with all these enormous changes (population, agriculture, use of fossil fuels) concentrated into such a short period of time, we have unwittingly begun a massive experiment with the systems of this planet itself.

UK prime minister Margaret Thatcher, speech to the Royal Society, Sept. 1988; *The Downing Street Years* (1993) pp.640–41. Thatcher was slow to accept even the possibility that modern industrial activity was producing climate change. The continuance of nuclear power, she claimed, was still valid since, unlike fossil fuels, it did not produce carbon dioxide or acid rain. 'However, this did not attract the environmental lobby towards it: instead they used the concern about global warming to attack capitalism, growth and industry.'

4 The global environment crisis is, as we say in Tennessee, real as rain, and I cannot stand the thought of leaving my children with a degraded earth and a diminished future.

Al Gore *Earth in the Balance* (1992) p.16. His book was written after extensive study, including visits to the polar ice-cap. The Democrat Gore was elected vice-president of the United States in 1992, as running-mate to Bill Clinton. In 1993, to address global warming, he tried to introduce a comprehensive energy tax on oil, coal and natural gas, but Congressional pressure reduced this to nothing more than a tax of 4.3 cents per gallon on petrol.

5 I have seen the future of much of the Pacific Rim, and I am scared out of my mind. One quarter of the population of the planet, certainly about 1.2 billion Chinese, are about to transform their standard of living, and in the process, wreck a large proportion of the globe.

British architect John Sergeant, *Newsweek*, 9 May 1994, after an extensive tour of the Far East.

6 We must learn to think and act from our hearts, to recognize the interconnectedness of all living creatures, and to respect the value of each thread in the vast web of life. This is a spiritual perspective, and it is the foundation of all Green politics.

German environmentalist Petra Kelly *Thinking Green* (1994) p.37. Kelly, a leading figure in the Green Party, campaigned from the vantage-point of her seat in the Bundestag. As a result of her party's pressure Germany made some headway on Green issues, such as the recycling of household waste.

7 Worrying about starving future generations won't feed them. Food biotechnology will.

Advertisement by the Monsanto corporation; John Baxter 'GM Foods' in Bircham and Charlton (2001) p.115. The company has developed genetically modified strains of food crops, which, it claims, will produce much higher yields than traditional varieties and avoid the use of insecticides and chemical fertilizers. Public concern about the long-term effects on existing plant life and human health has caused serious resistance to Monsanto, including a five-year ban on its commercial imports into the European Union. In Feb. 2003 Representative Bill Thomas, chairman of the House Ways and Means Committee, declared that if the EU did not lift the ban there would be strong support in Congress for the US to leave the WTO in 2005.

8 The genetic manipulation of a plant or animal species enables companies, by enforcing industrial patents, to become owners of all the modified plants and animals subsequently produced. By buying up rival seeds and patents, or removing competitors from the market, a firm can become the owner of an entire species. It's the logic of industry, applied to life. Genetic manipulation is a way of being paid royalties for life itself.

José Bové, French activist; Bircham and Charlton (2001) p.110. Bové, a prominent member of the *Confedération Paysanne*, represented small farmers protesting against global agribusiness. He was put on trial for attacking the McDonald's restaurant in the small town of Millau, in southwest France, in July 2000.

9 We try to make a difference to the people and places that produce coffee, to the countries we visit and the families we touch. Through our purchasing of organic, shade-grown and fair-trade coffees, and through our partnerships with organizations such as Conservation International and CARE, we contribute to social, economic and environmental sustainability. To improve the lives of families in coffee-farming communities, we make long-term investments, such as building schools, health clinics and coffee processing facilities.

Starbucks Coffee Company leaflet, 'Our Place in the World', 2002. Starbucks, along with McDonald's and Nike, had been one of the main targets of anti-globalization protest in the 1990s. Here it bids to improve its image.

WORKERS OF THE WORLD

1 Most people think it's great that the world can now work together to produce a massive amount of choice in what we can buy in our superstores, but what if the world isn't working together at all? What if the system is working in such a way that the rich keep getting richer and the poor keep getting poorer?

Christian Aid 'Trade: The Good, the Bad and the Decidedly Ugly' in Donnellan (2002) p.25. It is estimated that 1.3 billion people still have to survive on less than $1.00 a day. Between 1975 and 1997, as global trade expanded, average wealth in the world's richest 31 countries increased, while that in the poorest 31 declined.

2 The recent quantum leap in the ability of transnational corporations to relocate their facilities around the world in effect makes all workers, communities and countries, competitors for these corporations' favor. The consequence is a 'race to the bottom' in which wages and social conditions tend to fall to the level of the most desperate.

Jeremy Brecher 'Global Village or Global Pillage?' in The Nation, 6 Dec. 1993, pp.685–8.

3 About two-thirds of the world's population have gained little or no substantial advantage from rapid growth. In the developing world, the lowest quartile of income earners have witnessed trickle-up rather than trickle-down.

Financial Times, editorial, 24 Dec. 1993. The 'trickle-down' theory supposes that prosperity at the top of society percolates down through social strata, eventually benefiting the poorest. Through 'trickle-up', the reverse process makes the rich richer at the expense of the poorest.

4 First, rich landowners came in and offered people 50,000 rupees an acre to sell their paddy fields.

Usually our land would sell for 1,000 rupees an acre. It was hard for people to resist that much money. Then bulldozers came in and knocked down all the trees and ploughed up all the fields. Afterwards, they built huge concrete jetties out to the sea and pumped seawater into the ponds they had created. Within a year our wells were full of salt and we had swarms of mosquitoes in our village. We are caught between the large fishing trawlers that have taken away our ability to fish and the large aquaculture farms that have taken away our ability to farm. We have nothing left to do except stay and fight.

Govinda Ma, villager in Andhra Pradesh, India; Bircham and Charlton (2001) p.238.

5 Indonesia is rich in raw materials yet the people live in misery. The people can no longer afford to eat or buy medicine. This is all the fault of the system – this is what we have to smash.

Cecep Daryus, Indonesian student leader, 1998; Clare Fermont in International Socialism Vol.80 (1998) p.4.

6 The Special Economic Zones were presented as China's 'window to the world'. But the reality is sweatshops, over-exploitation, untold misery. Peasants are forced to migrate to the zones and the cities, where they are plunged into conditions of indescribable squalor … These are the abominable conditions of exploitation foisted upon us by the multinational corporations through their 'free trade' agreements.

Cai Chongguo, China Labour Bulletin (1999).

7 You're running because you want that raise, to be all you can be. But it's not easy when you work sixty hours a week making sneakers in an Indonesian factory and your friends disappear when they ask for a raise. So think globally before you decide it's so cool to wear Nike.

Poster by the Canadian group Adbusters, undated; Sustainable Human Development (2002) p.29. Adbusters attempts to challenge attitudes to consumption by what they call 'subvertising' – subversive advertising. North American TV stations have refused to run their ads because they fear that the big companies will withdraw their own commercials in retaliation.

8 However awful conditions in a Nike factory may be, they are usually worse in a local sweatshop.

Philippe Legrain 'Dump those Prejudices' in Donnellan (2002) p.11. The Nike sportswear corporation manufactures trainers, sweatshirts and baseball caps for the world market, with enormous success.

1 The 'transition' in most of the countries of the former Soviet bloc in Central and Eastern Europe and the CIS [Commonwealth of Independent States] is a euphemistic term for what in reality has been a Great Depression. The extent of the collapse in output and the skyrocketing nature of inflation has been historically unprecedented. The consequences for human security have been calamitous. By conservative estimates, over 100 million people have been thrown into poverty and considerably more hover precariously just above subsistence.

United Nations Development Programme *Regional Transition 1999: The Human Cost of Transition.* 'Transition' is the term for the socio-economic movement from communism to capitalism.

2 Will the whole world turn into one big Brazil, into countries with complete inequality and ghettos for the rich élite? With this question you take the bull by the horns. Of course even Russia is becoming Brazil.

Former Soviet President Mikhail Gorbachev, 29 Sept. 1995; Martin and Schumann (1997 edn) p.163. The last leader of the Soviet Union until its collapse in 1991, Gorbachev presided over the death throes of Marxist socialism in Russia, which then, in his view, plunged into a no-holds-barred capitalism, red in tooth and claw.

3 The market is not a panacea for all problems.

Russian president Boris Yeltsin, speech to the Russian parliament, *The Times,* 25 Sept. 1997. Yeltsin, Gorbachev's successor, found himself grappling with an economic crisis to which capitalism did not seem to have all the answers.

4 What an astounding thing it is to watch a civilization destroy itself because it is unable to re-examine the validity, under totally new circumstances, of an economic ideology … I believe that free markets are absolutely necessary to improve efficiency, control prices, enforce innovation and encourage choice. But free markets must be composed of nations with economies that are reasonably homogeneous and which are willing to accept some financial disciplines. Otherwise the 'levelling of wages will be overwhelmingly downward' and the free market will be corrupted by competitive devaluation. We need regional not global trade. What an irony that just as socialism has been discredited, the misinterpretation and misapplication of liberal ideas will create a new class war.

Sir James Goldsmith, *The Times,* 5 March 1994. Goldsmith, founder of the UK Independence Party, although fiercely opposed to further British integration with the EU, saw Europe as an appropriate trading group for the free movement of goods and capital. Bilateral trading agreements with other regions of the world should be entered into only if they were beneficial to the fundamental national economy and not merely the corporate economy.

5 The global economy is leaving millions of disaffected workers in its train. Inequality, unemployment, and endemic poverty have become its handmaidens. Rapid technological change and heightening international competition are fraying the job markets of the major industrial countries. At the same time systematic pressures are curtailing every government's ability to respond with new spending. Just when working people most need the nation-state as a buffer from the world economy, it is abandoning them.

Ethan B. Kapstein 'Workers and the World Economy' in *Foreign Affairs* Vol.75, May/June 1996. Kapstein's concern is for workers in the developed world who face unemployment when production centres move abroad. He calls for government retraining schemes and job creation in spite of public-sector spending constraints.

6 We have failed to grasp the idea that all of us – workers, environmentalists, opponents of privatization, defenders of local amenities, human rights and social justice campaigners – are threatened by the same global forces. We have been divided by our ideological differences and suspicions of each other's tactics. Above all, we have failed to understand how powerful we can be if we work together.

The campaigner for global democracy, George Monbiot; Bircham and Charlton (2001) p.5. He argues that the protests at the WTO meeting in Seattle began a process of cooperation and mutual support between various movements confronting neo-liberalism. While recognizing the challenge of holding such a disparate coalition together, he hopes that eventually 'the world will belong to its people once again'.

NATIONS AND MULTINATIONALS

7 To found a great empire for the sole purpose of raising up a people of customers, may at first sight appear a project fit only for a nation of shopkeepers. It is, however, a project altogether unfit for a nation of shopkeepers; but extremely fit for a nation whose government is influenced by shopkeepers.

Adam Smith, Scottish philosopher and economist, *The Wealth of Nations* (1776) Bk 4, Ch.7, Pt 3. Smith could hardly have imagined the extent of the influence exerted by the 21st-century commercial lobbyist.

1 In this new market … billions can flow in or out of an economy in seconds. So powerful has this force of money become that some observers now see the hot-money set becoming a short of shadow world government – one that is irretrievably eroding the concept of the sovereign powers of a nation-state.
Business Week, 20 March 1995, p.46.

2 Multilateral companies are truly the servants of demanding consumers around the world … When governments are slow to grasp the fact that their role has changed from protecting their people and their national resource base from outside threats to ensuring that their people have the widest range of choice amongst the best and cheapest goods and services from around the world … they discourage investment and impoverish their people.
Kenichi Ohmae, director of the Japanese office of the American management consultancy McKinsey, *The Borderless World* (1990) pp.x–xi. In terms of financial power MNCs can rival entire nations. General Motors, the American auto-mobile giant, has financial assets greater than those of Denmark.

3 In so many spheres, the political leaders no longer have real sovereignty of decision-making. But they have the idea that they themselves can still resolve the central questions. I mean, they have only the fancy, only the illusion that this is so.
Boutros Boutros-Ghali, retiring secretary-general of the United Nations, interview, 22 July 1996; Martin and Schumann (1997 edn) p.185.

4 In the cabaret of globalization, the state goes through a strip-tease and by the end of the performance it is left with the bare necessities only: its powers of repression. With its material basis destroyed, its sovereignty and independence annulled, its political class effaced, the nation-state becomes a simple security service for the mega-companies.
Sous-Commandant Marcos 'Sept pièces du puzzle néo-libéral; la quatrième guerre mondiale a commencé' (Seven Pieces of the Neo-liberal Jigsaw: The Fourth World War has Begun) in *Le Monde diplomatique* Aug. 1997, pp.4–5. Statement by a guerrilla leader from the Mexican province of Chiapas.

5 GATS [General Agreement on Trade in Services] locks countries into a system of rules that means it is effectively impossible for governments to change policy or for voters to elect a new government that has different policies.

Barry Coates, director of the World Development Movement, 'GATS' in Bircham and Charlton (2001) p.29. At the same time that 75% of countries have now achieved at least nominal democracy through competitive election systems, frustration and disenchantment with politicians has set in among many electorates around the world.

6 Governments face their first great challenge of the post-Cold War era. If the global economy stumbles, then we will face a series of difficult choices. We could take the advice of the Stop the World campaigners, retreat into our national economies and close our markets. But this would put at risk the real benefits that globalization, and global capitalism, have brought to millions.
British foreign secretary Jack Straw 'Globalization is Good for Us' in Donnellan (2002) p.17.

7 Certainly, state-dominated development has failed. But so has stateless development … History has repeatedly shown that good government is not a luxury but a vital necessity. Without an effective state, sustainable development, both economic and social, is impossible.
International Bank for Reconstruction and Development (World Bank) *The State in a Changing World* (1997) p.ii.

8 There is a widespread belief that markets are self-correcting and a global economy can flourish without any need for a global society … This idea was called laissez-faire in the nineteenth century … I have found a better name for it: market fundamentalism … Market fundamentalism undermines the democratic political process and the inefficiency of the political process is a powerful argument in favour of market fundamentalism. The institutions of representative democracy that for so long have functioned well in the United States and much of Europe, and elsewhere, have become endangered, and civic virtue, once lost, is difficult to recapture.
George Soros (1998) p.xx. The arch-speculator of the early 1990s has started to use his fortune to raise democratic consciousness in a world dominated by market forces, through his Soros Foundation. His more philanthropic activities in recent years have gained him the title of 'St George'.

9 A nation's economic might is concentrated and manifested in the economic power and inter-national competitiveness of its largest enterprises and groups … The State will encourage big state-owned business to become international com-petitive corporations … The country will develop thirty to fifty large state-owned enterprises over the next five years.

Bai Rongchun, director general of China's Industrial Planning Department, July 2001. China, as the world's largest nation, is developing its own nationally run enterprise system, resisting the worldwide drive to industrial privatization, while rapidly increasing its share of global markets.

1 Japanese capitalism depends for its political legitimacy on the renewal of the social contract which underwrites its full employment culture. Yet Japanese employment practices are under siege from transnational organizations as policies of concealed protectionism. Germany's economic dilemma has some similar features. High levels of social protection are an integral part of Germany's post-war consensus capitalism. The German state cannot relinquish its role as final guarantor of full employment, nor can it hope to achieve that objective primarily by enforcing American-style labour flexibility. Yet international economic orthodoxy continues to demand that Germany adopts the hire-and-fire practices of the Anglo-Saxon free market.

John Gray *False Dawn: The Delusions of Global Capitalism* (1998) p.203.

2 I am a disciple of Ludwig Erhard. This party will never follow a policy geared only to the market; social conditions are also a part of it, and so there is not going to be any social dismantling.

Chancellor of Germany, Helmut Kohl, *Frankfurter Allgemeine Zeitung*, 12 April 1996. Two months later in Bonn, following the largest trade union demonstration since World War II, protesting against the erosion of social provision, wage cuts and rising unemployment, he accused the head of the German Trade Union Federation, Dieter Schulte, of trying to protect labour's vested interests and gambling away Germany's future in the global economy. Erhard was the architect of the West German post-war *Wirtschaftswunder* (economic miracle) and founder of the social market economy, in which a fundamentally capitalist economic order is supported by substantial government provision of social welfare. The philosophy could be said to have been established by Bismarck in the 1880s (see 674:5).

GLOBAL GOVERNANCE

3 The emergence of a global economy and global society demands that we strengthen global governance.

British foreign secretary Jack Straw 'Globalization is Good for Us' in Donnellan (2002) p.17.

4 As the twenty-first century approaches, the planet is in the grip of two vast opposing forces: globalization and fragmentation ... The United Nations can help deal with the challenges that globalization and fragmentation pose now and in the future, but it lacks political, military, material and financial resources to accomplish these tasks ... Finding the right formula which will enable funds to flow automatically while keeping expenditures under control is a project the secretary-general must bring to fruition in the next century.

UN secretary-general Boutros Boutros-Ghali in *Foreign Affairs* Vol.75, March–April 1996. In 1996, in response to a clamour that the UN was overreaching itself, the Clinton administration demanded the replacement of the Egyptian Boutros Boutros-Ghali as secretary-general. The usual extension to his term of office was vetoed by the US, and he was replaced by Kofi Annan from Ghana.

5 Global democracy is meaningless unless ultimate power resides in a directly elected assembly. This means, of course, that a resident of Kensington would have no greater influence than a resident of Kinshasa ... To preserve local democracy, its scope must be limited by subsidiarity. It could not interfere in strictly national decision-making, in other words, but would seek to do only what existing global bodies are attempting – and failing – to do today: resolving disputes, tackling global poverty, defending people from oppression and protecting the world's resources.

George Monbiot 'How to Rule the World: Rich Nations Should Stop Running the Planet and Give Way to Global Democracy' in Donnellan (2002) pp.23, 24.

6 At the global level, as at that of the nation-state, the free market does not promote stability or democracy. Global democratic capitalism is as unrealizable a condition as worldwide communism.

John Gray (1998) p.21. Gray sees global laissez-faire leading to a world of anarchic market forces, shrinking natural resources and inter-state conflict.

7 The central challenge we face today is to ensure that globalization becomes a positive force for all the world's people, instead of leaving billions behind in squalor.

UN secretary-general Kofi Annan, April 2000, in Donnellan (2000) p.20.

8 The powerlessness we feel is not a sign of personal failings, but reflects the incapacities of our institutions. We need to reconstruct those we have, or create new ones. For globalization is not incidental to our lives today. It is a shift in our very life circumstances. It is the way we live now.

Anthony Giddens (2002) p.19. Professor Giddens, of the London School of Economics, points to an average annual growth rate of 5% in those countries that have opened up to external markets but accepts that this has also brought increasing economic inequalities within them. A 'transformationalist' regarding globalization, he sees the absolute need for accompanying social reforms to mitigate these effects. He regards the UN aim to halve world poverty by 2015 as difficult, but not impossible, to achieve.

1 There is little reason to take seriously the idea that supra-national institutions will be more powerful in the twenty-first century than they were in the twentieth. In purely financial terms, institutions like the United Nations and the International Monetary Fund are in no stronger position than their inter-war precursors.

Niall Ferguson *The Cash Nexus* (2001) p.421.

FUTURE INDEFINITE

2 What struck me both last night and again today is this real sense of confidence and optimism. You just want to bottle it and keep it.

UK prime minister Tony Blair hails the birth of the 3rd millennium; *Observer*, 2 Jan. 2000.

3 The issue is not how to stop globalization. The issue is how we use the power of community to combine it with justice. If globalization works only for the benefit of the few, then it will fail and will deserve to fail. But if we follow the principles that have served us so well at home – that power, wealth and opportunity must be in the hands of the many, not the few – if we make that our guiding light for the global economy, then it will be a force for good and an international movement that we should take pride in leading. Because the alternative to globalization is isolation.

UK prime minister Tony Blair, speaking at the Labour Party Conference, *The Times*, 3 Oct. 2001.

4 In the less than 13 years since the Berlin Wall fell, globalization has replaced the Cold War as the defining dynamic of the era. People mean different things by it – capitalist triumphalism, corporate imperialism, a benign communications revolution or the export of world music. Tony Blair's notion of

growing interdependence, however, is a useful tool here. We travel everywhere on the globe, we can communicate with anyone, peoples displaced by faraway tyrannies or economic disasters end up in our ports and cities, fanatics animated by antique, distant disputes blow up our night-clubs. And we can see, if our eye is turned that way, the horrors of the world. We are, perhaps for the first time, morally interdependent.

David Aaronovitch, *Observer*, 23 March 2003. Aaronovitch is looking for a more equal working partnership between the US and the EU.

5 Some suggest that the UN's irrelevance is beyond dispute, and it only remains to be seen whether we will confirm our irrelevance by obliging the United States or ensure our irrelevance by failing to oblige the United States ... I am reminded of an old story about Adam and Eve in the Garden of Eden. Adam finds Eve is becoming a bit indifferent to him. So he asks her: 'Eve, is there some one else?' One could well ask the same question about the United Nations. Is there any other institution that brings all the countries of the world together to pursue collectively the security and welfare so essential to our common humanity?

Shashi Taroor, UN under-secretary-general for communications and public information; *Independent on Sunday*, 9 March 2003. Taroor is responding to President George W. Bush's speech before the UN on 12 Sept. 2002, in which he asked: 'Will the United Nations serve the purpose of its founders or will it be irrelevant?' Taroor insists that the 'i' word should instead be 'indispensable'.

6 In spite of President Bush's apparent turn towards unilateralism, there is little the United States can do in most contexts without the collaboration of other nations. Geopolitically, the world is becoming more polycentric. The EU [European Union] has nothing like the military muscle of the United States, but nevertheless is becoming more and more an independent player in world affairs. Russia retains its potential as a major power. Japan, South Korea and China continue to develop their geopolitical clout, and India is certain to assume a more powerful influence in world affairs than it has hitherto.

Anthony Giddens (2002) p.xxiii. The reference to Bush is to his decision in March 2001 to withdraw from the Kyoto Protocol on climate change of 11 Dec. 1997, framed to tackle the crisis of global warming. In the light of America's resolve to go to war with Iraq in 2003 regardless of the United

Nations (see 942:5), polycentrism seems an unlikely force for the immediate future.

1 The lesson for the twenty-first century is that the fight for security, prosperity and justice can no longer be won on any one nation's ground. It is international. It requires agreement on values. It is predicated on an acknowledgement of interdependence. It requires a political narrative. It requires courage and leadership. America, for the moment, has disqualified itself from the task. It falls to Europe to undertake it.

Will Hutton (2000) p.370. Hutton saw the European Union as the model for any future world government organization.

2 Sure, it may seem unfair that America assumes a disproportionate burden for sustaining globalization. It means there are a lot of free riders, many of whom, like the French, will piggyback on us while criticizing us all along the way. It comes with the job … The very reason we need to support the UN and the IMF, the World Bank and the various world development banks is that they make it possible for the U.S. to advance its interests without putting American lives or treasure on the line everywhere, all the time … The global system cannot hold together without an activist and generous American foreign policy. Attention, K-mart shoppers: Without America on duty, there will be no America Online.

Thomas L. Friedman (1999) pp.374, 376. Friedman castigates the Republicans in Congress for being 'mean-spirited' over funding for international aid in the expectation that global free trade alone will solve everything.

3 The WTO in the twenty-first century will continue to play a vital role in the maintenance of international peace and prosperity. In short order, the WTO will become a universal economic organization, embracing virtually every country in the world. The scope of the WTO has expanded vastly, as well; it will cover virtually every aspect of international trade and investment, exceeding the vision of its post-World War II founders. Yet, the WTO faces unprecedented new challenges: helping with other IGOs [Inter-Governmental Organizations] to manage the process of globalization with its attendant social dislocations, as well as helping to ameliorate poverty in the developing world and ending the North–South divide.

Mitsuo Matsushita, Thomas J. Schoenbaum and Petros C. Mavroidis *The World Trade Organization: Law, Practice and Policy* (2003) p.612. Analysts of the heavily criticized WTO stake a

far-reaching claim for its global role in the 21st century – perhaps even rivalling the UN.

4 More and more people who are bypassed by the new world order are crafting their own strategies for survival and development, and in the process are spinning their own transnational web to embrace and connect people across the world. On dreams of a global civilization that respects human diversity and values people one by one, a global civil society is beginning to take shape – mostly off camera. It is the only force we can see that can break the gridlock. The great question of our age is whether people, acting with the spirit, energy and urgency our collective crisis requires, can develop a democratic global consciousness rooted in authentic local communities.

Richard J. Barnet and John Cavanagh *Global Dreams: Imperial Corporations and the New World Order* (1994) pp.429–30. An alternative view of globalization that emphasizes the way in which the cross-fertilization of ideas at a cultural level and the sharing of experiences may lead to a less materialistic world community.

5 I believe that the world has moved closer to oneness and more people see each other as one with the other … It is possible to have new thoughts and new common values for human and all other forms of life.

Wangam Maathai, coordinator of the Kenya Green Belt Movement, 'All We Need is Will' in *Can the Environment be Saved without a Radical New Approach to World Development?* (1992) p.27.

6 Islam is for us not just a religion but a way of life. We Saudis want to modernize, but not necessarily Westernize.

Bandar bin Sultan, *New York Times*, 10 July 1994. He acknowledges the attraction of high-tech imports but claims that the importation of Western social and political institutions can be deadly: 'Look at the Shah of Iran' (who was deposed in 1979; see 938:7).

7 The West is overwhelmingly dominant now and will remain number one in terms of power and influence well into the twenty-first century. Gradual, inexorable, and fundamental changes, however, are also occurring in the balances of power among civilizations, and the power of the West relative to that of other civilizations will continue to decline … The most significant increases in power are accruing and will continue to accrue to Asian civilizations, with China gradually emerging as the society most likely to challenge the West for global influence. These shifts in power among civilizations are leading and will lead to the revival and increased cultural assertiveness of non-Western societies and to their increasing rejection of Western culture.

Samuel P. Huntington *Clash of Civilizations* (1996) pp.82, 83. A leading American sceptic questions the durability of Western capitalist power.

1 To me, the attraction of that region [the Far East] is demographic. You have a much larger proportion of working age, or younger than working age, people than in the West. And all things being equal, that means that their GDP [Gross Domestic Product] has to be greater in the long run, which should filter into profit. I don't think SARS will change that. In my view it's an acute problem, not a chronic one. I'm more concerned by the level of HIV/AIDS in the region, which could be being covered up. That's more likely to affect the economics of the region in the long term.

John Hainsworth of Rickman Tooze, *Independent on Sunday*, 27 April 2003. SARS (Severe Acute Respiratory Syndrome), the recently discovered Chinese malady, began to strike the world at large in Feb. 2003. HIV (Human Immunodeficiency Virus), which breaks down the body's immune system, originated in Central Africa and spread throughout the world from the 1980s on, most often sexually transmitted. Without adequate treatment, AIDS (Acquired Immune Deficiency Syndrome), the end result of HIV infection, almost always results in death. Worldwide, as of mid-May 2003, fewer than 1,000 people were officially reported to have died from SARS, whereas millions are known to have died from AIDS, and the figure is rapidly rising in Africa and Asia.

2 If I am compelled to guess the future, I would estimate that the global system will, indeed, probably experience a series of terrible events – wrenching calamities that are economic or social or environmental in nature – before common sense can prevail. It would be pleasing to believe otherwise, but the global system so dominates and intimidates present thinking that I expect societies will be taught still more painful lessons before they find the will to act.

William Greider *One World, Ready Or Not; The Manic Logic of Global Capitalism* (1997) p.473.

3 Were SARS happening in isolation, it might not matter so much. But it comes on top of quite a serious global turndown and great social tension after the 11 September terrorist attacks. Already the flow of FDI [Foreign Direct Investment] funds has started to fall. To invest abroad is to lay oneself open to attack from non-governmental organizations and local groups that happen, for whatever reason, to dislike multinationals. Why bother? Indeed, it is possible – I very much hope this is wrong – that we have already passed the high point of globalization.

Hamish McRae 'Goodbye, Small World' in the *Independent on Sunday*, 27 April 2003.

4 The capitalist system can be compared to an empire that is more global in its coverage than any previous empire. It rules an entire civilization and, as in other empires, those who are outside its walls are considered barbarians … Far from seeking equilibrium, it is hell-bent on expansion. It cannot rest as long as there are markets or resources that remain unincorporated. In this respect, it is little different from Alexander the Great or Attila the Hun, and its expansionary tendencies may well prove its undoing.

George Soros (1998) pp.103, 104.

5 Today, the system of capitalism is at a crossroads just as it was during the Great Depression. In the 1930s, capitalism was saved by Keynes, who thought of policies to create jobs and rescue those suffering from the collapse of the global economy. Now, millions of people around the world are waiting to see whether globalization can be reformed so that its benefits can be more widely shared … If we are to make globalization with a human face succeed, then our voices must be raised. We cannot, we should not, stand idly by.

Joseph Stiglitz *Globalization and its Discontents* (2003 edn) pp.249–50, 252.

Index

References in **bold** face within this index indicate a quotation by, or attributed to, the relevant speaker or source. References in light face indicate that the person or topic is referred to in either the quotation or the gloss. Spans of references – 740:6–744:3, for example – are to subsections within chapters or, sometimes, to entire chapters. Quotations have been numbered consecutively from the first quotation to start on each page. Although quotations in the 'Quotations and History' section are identified by roman page numerals, they, too, are numbered page by page.

The index is arranged on a letter-by-letter basis. Sources with the same name are organized in the order saints, popes and heads of state. Monarchs and rulers with the same first name are given alphabetically according to country: thus rulers of France precede those of Russia and Spain. For reasons of space secondary sources have not been indexed.

Wherever possible, a speaker's title at the date of the relevant quotation has been given in the gloss. In the index, however, the title given is the one by which the speaker was known at the date of the last quotation by that person to be included in this book. The Duke of Wellington, for example, is indexed under Wellington, even though quotations by him that date from before 1809 appear in the glosses as being by Sir Arthur Wellesley. Where necessary, subsequent or better known titles have been included in glosses as an aid to identification.